WINE ENTHUSIAST
MAGAZINE

Essential BUYING GUIDE 2007

RUNNING PRESS
PHILADELPHIA • LONDON

Printed in the United States

9 8 7 6 5 4 3 2
Digit on the right indicates the number of this printing

Library of Congress Control Number: 2006900801

ISBN-13: 978-0-7624-2749-9
ISBN-10: 0-7624-2749-3

Cover design by Bill Jones
Interior design by Jan Greenberg and Bill Jones
Edited by Sarah O'Brien and Jennifer Leczkowski
Typography: Garamond and Helvetica Neueland Condensed

This book may be ordered by mail from the publisher.
Please include $2.50 for postage and handling.
But try your bookstore first!

Running Press Book Publishers
2300 Chestnut Street Suite 200
Philadelphia, PA 19103-4371

Visit us on the web!
www.runningpresscooks.com
www.winemag.com

PHOTOGRAPHY CREDITS

Cover photo: Courtesy of *Wine Enthusiast Magazine*
p. 1: © Susie M. Eising Food Photography/Stockfood America
p. 3 top: © Ted Stefanski/Cephas, bottom: © Kevin Judd/Cephas
p. 4: © Nigel Blythe/Cephas
p. 5: Courtesy of *Wine Enthusiast Magazine*
p. 7: © Mick Rock/Cephas
p. 8: © Mick Rock/Cephas
p 10-11 all: Courtesy of *Wine Enthusiast Magazine*
p. 12: © Louis de Rohan/Cephas
p. 32: © Kevin Judd/Cephas
p. 96: © Walter Geiersperger/Cephas
p. 107: © Steven Morris/Cephas
p. 139: © Mick Rock/Cephas
p. 213: © Mick Rock/Cephas
p. 231: © Mike Newton/Cephas
p. 305: © Kevin Judd/Cephas
p. 326: © Mick Rock/Cephas
p. 345: © Juan Espi/Cephas
p. 363: © Mick Rock/Cephas
p. 417: © Ted Stefanski/Cephas
p. 419: © Mick Rock/Cephas
p. 420: © Clay McLachlan/Cephas

Contents

SAUTERNES
FOND DE CAVE
FOND DE CAVE
SAUTERNES
SAUTERNES

Foreword

It sounds like a dream come true for many wine enthusiasts: making a living by sipping and evaluating the greatest wines from all over the world. Yes, it's true that members of our tasting panel sample thousands of wines every year. But of course, there is a great deal of work involved in actually tasting wine for review purposes (see How We Taste and Rate on page 8). But even given all the procedures and pressures, there is sublime pleasure to be had in trying new wines, whether the wine is a new grape variety, was produced in an unfamiliar region, or is just a new vintage of an old favorite. Every time we uncork, there is a new experience to be had. It's almost always pleasurable at some level; sometimes, it's simply sublime. And that brings us to this book.

The *Wine Enthusiast Essential Buying Guide 2007* includes approximately 25,000 reviews of wines, the best that our tasting panel has sampled since we established the tasting and review program in 1999. We've arranged the reviews so that the book is as easy to use as possible—divided according to countries and alphabetized by producer name. Three other crucial bits of information are presented as prominently as possible: the quality score (based on the *Wine Enthusiast* 100-point scale), the vintage, and the grape variety, wherever possible. Experienced wine enthusiasts can go straight to the producing countries and producers whose wines they've enjoyed in the past or have currently cellared to check scores. Novices will find this guide an indispensable tool to peruse before treks to the retail store. The *Wine Enthusiast Essential Buying Guide 2007* makes it easy to find values, track the performance of certain producers' wines over time, and get an idea of the general characteristics of wines from a certain region.

It's all about enjoyment: drinking what you like while continuing to experiment, trying some new wines, and taking advantage of the charm and power of wine. It's mind-boggling, the diversity that variables of grape variety, climate, soil, vineyard technique, and winemaking skill can produce.

We also encourage you to check us out online at www.winemag.com for our continually updated wine database, as well as the world's best vintage chart. It is the ideal companion to this book, providing you with everything you need to make wise buying decisions when at the retail store or restaurant.

Cheers,

Adam Strum
Publisher and Editor-in-Chief
Wine Enthusiast Magazine

Wine-Buying Strategies

SMART WINE BUYING TAKES PLANNING

In America, most wine is consumed the night it is bought. Whether it is a bottle of Opus One for a dinner party or a box of Franzia White Zin to improve Tuesday-night leftovers, it's often opened immediately with little thought.

Unfortunately, buying wine that way sacrifices a great deal of the pleasure of wine, and rarely provides the best deal. Pretentious though it may seem, it's worthwhile to develop a strategy for acquiring wine. It's both fun and rewarding.

There are a number of reasons for planning your purchases, but they almost all lead to having a supply on hand, ideally in a wine cellar or refrigerated storage cabinet. The most obvious advantage is that some wines improve with age, and even if you can afford to buy properly aged vintages, they may be very difficult to find. Buying young saves money, but also means that you'll be able to enjoy the wine when it's at its peak.

Of course, most wine doesn't improve with age, but if you're reading this, you most likely appreciate the wine that does. Most better reds certainly improve with a few years, and though many of today's wines are made to reach their peaks within a decade, most are released when they're only two or three years old. Hold them for even three or four years and they will improve tremendously. But if you buy wines at that peak stage, you will have to pay a premium.

Serious collectors, of course, often see wine as an investment that can be sold at an appreciated value in the future. Others see the real value in having far better wines to drink themselves.

Of course, some wines just keep on improving for decades: top Bordeaux, Burgundies, Napa Cabs, Barolos, and many Spanish wines fall in this category. It's not wise to drink them when they're only a few years old; if you do, they probably won't be much better than ordinary wines. Some people even develop a taste for old wines that many would consider past their prime, while others enjoy learning what happens to wines as they age.

You can obviously save a great deal when you cellar wines yourself, but even cursory planning can also save a lot of money. Buying wine on sale can be very rewarding. Almost every retailer offers at least 10 percent off for full cases, sometimes mixed cases, and that's like getting more than a bottle free with each case.

Some wines are even sold as futures. This primarily applies to top labels, but even some relatively modest wineries sell wine this way if it's in short supply. For example, after disastrous fires and earthquakes in wine warehouses, some producers in California offered attractive futures for their wines to maintain cash flow.

When all is said and done, however, perhaps the best reason for planning ahead is to have the right wine on hand when you want it. It's awful nice to be able to go into your cellar and grab a perfectly aged bottle that's the perfect match for dinner, or to take a special treat to a celebration without a trip to the wine store. In many areas, finding a special bottle could require ordering ahead, or a long drive to a state-controlled liquor store that is open during limited hours.

The only downside to having good wines on hand is a mixed one: You're more likely to enjoy it!

WHAT DO YOU LIKE?

Of course, it doesn't make much sense to have a cellar full of wine you don't like. Wine-buying guides provide good reference points for wines you've never tasted, but you'll probably want to buy only one bottle of a wine you haven't tasted instead of many, even if the producer has a good reputation or a well-known reviewer has awarded it a high score. Reputation and wine scores should be starting points, since people's tastes differ widely. Fortunately, there are a lot of ways to help guide your purchases.

One way to improve your odds is to learn which reviewers have tastes that mirror yours. For example, if you love massive Cabernets, which are extremely full bodied and high in alcohol, find which critics rave over them. Also learn which reviewers prefer more restrained wines that might be more suitable for enjoying with food.

All that said, the best way to learn what you like is by tasting wine. Take wine-tasting classes at wine stores or local colleges and adult schools. Attend wine events where you can taste a wide variety of wines. Try wines by the glass when available at restaurants and bars. Wine clubs and tasting parties with friends can be both great fun and very informative. Take recommendations from friends, but be sure to consider whether their tastes are similar to yours. Whatever you do, pay attention and take notes. And don't forget to spit (when you're at a tasting, not at a restaurant!)—otherwise, all the wine will taste great!

You'll almost always find some surprises, particularly with some inexpensive wines. Most important, accept your own tastes. Drinking wine isn't about forcing yourself to learn to like wines that don't suit you. Remember, above all of the terminology and technicality, the most important thing about wine should be the ability to get the most out of every glass, so that you actually enjoy what you're drinking. Drink—and buy—what you like and don't apologize or try to impress others.

MAKING THE PURCHASE

Once you've decided what wine you like, buy more of it. Although wine choices were once very limited, and still are in some states, in most areas, choices have multiplied, and expand daily as restrictive laws fall to lawsuits or change to reflect today's attitudes and to increase tax revenues.

The old-time wine store—and its modern counterpart—remains one of the best places to buy wines. Clerks in these stores tend to be knowledgeable about wine, and if you become a regular, they can learn more about your tastes and steer you toward wines you'll likely enjoy. Many shops now offer classes, wine tastings, and other events, and some will even order special wines and ship or deliver them to your home.

In many states, you can buy wine in supermarkets, giant discounters, club stores, discount wine and liquor outlets, and even convenience stores. And they're not just selling basic wine, either. Costco has emerged as one of the nation's largest retailers of fine wines including some that cost hundreds of dollars a bottle.

With barriers to interstate shipping of wine falling, direct purchases from wineries are making more and more sense. While it hardly pays to buy widely distributed wines direct from the wineries and pay shipping when you can buy the same wine at a neighborhood store many times for less, often the only place to get some wines is from the winery. This includes special bottles from big producers, including limited production bottlings and library wines.

For these wines, the most fun of all is to visit the winery, where you can taste before buying. As wineries spring up all over the country, that may not require a trip to Napa Valley. Many wineries also sell directly over the Internet, by brochure or mail, or by phone, and many independent firms sell wines from many producers as well.

If you're especially fond of certain wineries' wines, it can be fun to sign up for their wine clubs. They typically send a few bottles to members a few times a year, generally at a discount, often including wines not available except to club members or at the winery. Most wine clubs have special events, too, often at the wineries but some in other locations.

Whatever you do, don't forget the wine once it's in your cellar. While some wines improve with age, most don't.

How We Taste and Rate

Although *Wine Enthusiast* was first published in 1988, the magazine didn't regularly publish its own wine reviews until 1999. Beginning that year, the magazine's *Buying Guide* began to include the reviews of its own editors and other qualified tasters. The *Wine Enthusiast Essential Buying Guide 2007* focuses on new releases and selected older wines.

Today, approximately 500 wine reviews are included in each issue of *Wine Enthusiast Magazine.* Each review contains a score on the 100-point scale, the full name of the wine, its suggested national retail price, and a tasting note. If a price cannot be confirmed, $NA (not available) will be printed. Prices are for 750 ml bottles unless otherwise indicated.

This compilation contains all of the wines formally reviewed by the *Wine Enthusiast* tasting panel from its inception through the final issue of 2005. Because of the limitations of print, full reviews are only included for wines tasted within the past two years. For the full text of earlier reviews, please log onto the magazine's Web site at www.winemag.com.

Regular contributors to our Buying Guide include Tasting Director/Senior Editor Joe Czerwinski, Senior Editor Daryna Tobey, and Contributing Editor Michael Schachner in New York; European Editor Roger Voss in Bordeaux; Italian Editor Monica Larner in Rome; West Coast Editor Steve Heimoff in California; and Contributing Editor Paul Gregutt in Seattle. Past contributors whose initials may appear in this guide include former Tasting Directors Mark Mazur and Chuck Simeone, former Tasting Coordinator Kristen Fogg, Contributing Editor Jeff Morgan, and former contributing tasters Martin Neschis and Larry Walker.

If a wine was evaluated by a single reviewer, that taster's initials appear following the note. When no initials appear, the wine was evaluated by two or more reviewers and the score and tasting note reflect the input of all tasters.

TASTING METHODOLOGY AND GOALS

Tastings are conducted individually or in a group setting and performed blind or in accordance with accepted industry practices (it is not possible to taste the wines blind when visiting producers, for example). When wines are tasted in our offices or for specific tasting features, they are tasted blind, in flights defined by grape variety, place of origin, and vintage.

We assess quality by examining five distinct characteristics: appearance, bouquet, flavor, mouthfeel, and finish. Above all, our tasters are looking for balance and harmony, with additional consideration given for ability to improve with age. Price is not a factor in assigning scores to wines. When possible, wines considered flawed or uncustomary are retasted.

ABOUT THE SCORES

Ratings reflect what our editors felt about a particular wine. Beyond the rating, we encourage you to read the accompanying tasting note to learn about a wine's special characteristics.

Classic 98–100:	The pinnacle of quality.
Superb 94–97:	A great achievement.
Excellent 90–93:	Highly recommended.
Very Good 87–89:	Often good value; well recommended.
Good 83–86:	Suitable for everyday consumption; often good value.
Acceptable 80–82:	Can be employed in casual, less-critical circumstances.

Wines receiving a rating below 80 are not reviewed.

SPECIAL DESIGNATIONS

Best Buys are wines that offer a high level of quality in relation to price. There are no specific guidelines or formulae for determining Best Buys, but they are generally priced below $15.

Editors' Choice wines are those that offer excellent quality at a price above our Best Buy range, or a wine at any price with unique qualities that merit special attention.

Cellar Selections are wines deemed highly collectible and/or requiring time in a temperature-controlled wine cellar to reach their maximum potential. A Cellar Selection designation does not mean that a wine must be stored to be enjoyed, but that cellaring will probably result in a more enjoyable bottle. In general, an optimum time for cellaring will be indicated.

Contributors

Tasting Director and Senior Editor Joe Czerwinski joined *Wine Enthusiast Magazine* in 1999 as an associate editor. In addition to managing the entire tasting and review program, he reviews wines from France, Germany, Italy, New Zealand, Portugal, and the Eastern United States.

West Coast Editor Steve Heimoff was born in New York City and moved to California to attend grad school. He quickly discovered wine, which became his passion. He has been with *Wine Enthusiast Magazine* for 13 years and reviews virtually all of the California wines. His book, *A Wine Journey along the Russian River*, was published in 2005 by University of California Press.

Senior Editor Daryna Tobey has been with *Wine Enthusiast Magazine* since 2001. As the magazine's Australian wine reviewer, she has written feature-length articles on the Barossa and Clare Valleys, McLaren Vale, and the Adelaide Hills based on her Australian travels.

European Editor Roger Voss is a wine and food author and journalist. He has been writing on wine and food for the past 25 years. His books include *France: A Feast of Food and Wine*; *The Wines of the Loire*; *Pocket Guide to the Wines of the Loire, Alsace, and the Rhône;* and *Fortified Wines*. He is based in Bordeaux, France, from where he reviews the wines of Austria, France, and Portugal.

Monica Larner has lived in Italy on and off for the past 15 years and is *Wine Enthusiast Magazine*'s Italian Editor. Based in Rome, she is a member of the Italian Association of Sommeliers and has published three books on her adopted home. When not in Europe, she can be found with pruning shears in hand on the family-run Larner Vineyard in Santa Barbara Country, California.

In addition to reviewing Pacific Northwest wines for *Wine Enthusiast Magazine*, Seattle-based **Contributing Editor Paul Gregutt** writes on wine for the *Seattle Times*, the *Yakima Herald-Republic*, the *Walla Walla Union-Bulletin*, and *Pacific Northwest* magazine. He has written two editions of Northwest Wines, and his next book on Washington wines will be published by the University of California Press in the spring of 2007.

Michael Schachner is a New York-based journalist specializing in wine, food, and travel. His articles appear regularly in *Wine Enthusiast Magazine,* for which he is a contributing editor and a member of the magazine's tasting panel. In addition, he is a wine consultant and professional speaker. His areas of wine expertise include Spain, Italy, and South America.

Argentina

Argentina features a vaunted winemaking history that began some five hundred years ago when Spanish missionaries first arrived and planted vines. But it wasn't until about two hundred years ago that Argentina developed a commercial wine industry, largely centered in the province of Mendoza, located about four hundred miles directly west of Buenos Aires.

For all intents and purposes, Argentina's wine industry was until fairly recently geared toward domestic consumption. Nineteenth and early twentieth- century immigrants from Spain and Italy had a huge thirst for wine, and the vineyards that they planted along the western edge of the country, where the climate is dry, the temperatures are warm, and there's plenty of water available from the mighty Andes, produced copious amounts of varietal and blended reds that the Argentine population drank with nary a complaint.

Harvesting grapes in a vineyard of Peñaflor, Mendoza, Argentina.

To a large extent, that's still the case. Argentineans remain the primary consumers of their own wines. But as the global wine market began to take shape in the latter half of the twentieth century, Argentina refocused its winemaking and marketing efforts to highlight exports. Today, there are approximately one hundred wineries throughout Argentina that are sending their wines overseas. Mendoza, with its numerous subzones, remains front and center among wine regions, with areas like San Rafael, La Rioja, San Juan, Salta, and Cafayate vying for second chair.

Due to a pervasive hot, dry climate, it's safe to say that red wines outperform white wines in almost all parts of Argentina; although the higher one goes into the Andes, the cooler it gets and the crisper the white wines become. And with such deep Italian and Spanish roots running through the country's people, that makes sense.

Malbec, which was brought to Argentina from France some 150 years ago, has emerged as Argentina's signature grape. It is grown throughout the country, and while it varies in style, one can safely call it fruity, aromatic, and lush. In flatter, warmer vineyards, Malbec can be soft and simple, an easy wine for everyday drinking and blending. But if taken into the foothills of the mountains or grown in old vineyards, it can be a wine of immense character.

Joining Malbec on the red roster is Cabernet Sauvignon, which is flavorful and serious when coming from top wineries like Terrazas de Los Andes, Catena Zapata, Norton, Cobos, or Chakana, to name several. Picked ripe, like in California and aged mostly in French oak barrels, Argentinean Cabernet has what it takes.

Other red grapes one frequently encounters are Bonarda and Sangiovese, both of which were brought over from Italy, as well as Merlot, Syrah, Tempranillo, and even some Pinot Noir.

Among white wines, one of Argentina's best and most distinctive offerings is Torrontés, an import from Galicia in Spain. Floral and occasionally exotic in scent and taste, Torrontés seems to do best in the more northern Salta region, where there's higher humidity and more rain than in Mendoza.

And as stated before, the Andean foothills are proving to be the prime spot for Chardonnay. At elevations of more than 3,000 feet above sea level, warm days and cool nights yield naturally fresh and properly acidic wines. Flavors of pineapple, green banana, and other tropical fruits are common among Argentina's modern-day Chardonnays.

ACHÁVAL-FERRER

Achával-Ferrer 2002 Finca Altamira Malbec (Mendoza) $85. The nose is all bacon, game, and leather along with graphite and berry fruit. Surprisingly firm and juicy on the palate; the acidity is rather sharp, which manufactures a racy, hard mouthfeel. No complaints with the exotic flavors coming from this old-vines wine. But the feel is astringent and the finish has some heat. Unconventional. **88** —*M.S. (7/1/2005)*

Achával-Ferrer 2001 Quimera Red Blend (Mendoza) $55. **85** —*M.S. (5/1/2003)*

ALAMOS

Alamos 2002 Cabernet Sauvignon (Mendoza) $10. Leathery and light, and not strong in the area of true Cabernet character. There isn't much richness or weight, and the berry fruit is bland. Okay, but lacks punch. **84** —*M.S. (7/1/2004)*

Alamos 1999 Cabernet Sauvignon (Mendoza) $13. **84** —*M.S. (11/1/2002)*

Alamos 2003 Chardonnay (Mendoza) $10. Despite spending just five months on oak staves, the nose is toasty. There's also good pear and banana notes as well as some vanilla. Tasted shortly after bottling; it should round out by the time you're reading this review. The balance seems to be right on the spot. **87** —*M.S. (7/1/2004)*

Alamos 2001 Chardonnay (Mendoza) $13. **83** —*M.S. (7/1/2002)*

Alamos 2003 Malbec (Mendoza) $10. Saturated and extracted, with an incredibly deep purple tint paving the way for manly aromas of espresso, campfire, and toasted coconut. The palate, meanwhile, runs a bit sweet, with boysenberry and plum. Soft on the back end, but with enough spine to see it through. For fans of bold reds. **88 Best Buy** —*M.S. (3/1/2005)*

Alamos 2001 Malbec (Mendoza) $11. **86** —*M.S. (5/1/2003)*

Alamos 2002 Pinot Noir (Mendoza) $10. Comes from the cooler Tupungato area, and shows a rooty, spicy, berry nose along with good color. The palate offers some true Pinot character, a bit of pepper and some leather before turning thin. Finishes light, with a hint of chocolate. **85** —*M.S. (7/1/2004)*

Alamos 2000 Bonarda (Mendoza) $13. **84** —*M.S. (11/1/2002)*

Alamos 2003 Viognier (Mendoza) $10. Hailing from the high-altitude, rugged Tupungato subregion, this Viognier is purely Argentine in style. Yes, it has true honeysuckle aromas and pure honey flavors, but it's also rather lemony and lean, with a thin midpalate and a tight, light finish. **86** —*M.S. (7/1/2004)*

ALBERTI

Alberti 154 2002 Cabernet Sauvignon (Mendoza) $10. Cherry and earth aromas have a hint of leather, which adds rusticity to the wine. Can't-miss notes of clove and nutmeg seriously bolster flavors of cherry and plum, and by the time the finish rolls around, that clove quality is magnified. Ultimately this is a spicy, leaner Cab, but good acids and tannins keep it upright. **86 Best Buy** —*M.S. (7/1/2004)*

Alberti 154 2002 Merlot (Mendoza) $10. Short on freshness and focus; the wine starts out a touch musty, and in the mouth, flavors of cotton candy, strawberry, and red licorice seem confectionary. Caramel on the finish and a chewy ending texture are the lasting impressions. **83** —*M.S. (7/1/2004)*

ALFREDO ROCA

Alfredo Roca 2004 Chardonnay (San Rafael) $12. Waxy and oily, with flavors of orange and other citrus fruits. The feel is kind of flat and heavy, with chunky melon on the finish. Imported by Hand Picked Selections. **82** —*M.S. (11/15/2005)*

Alfredo Roca 2004 Tocai Friulano (San Rafael) $12. Heavy on the nose, with a strong scent of mineral and vitamins. Soft in the mouth, with a round texture but little flavor backing it up. Registers more vapid than anything. Imported by Hand Picked Selections. **81** —*M.S. (12/31/2005)*

ALTA VISTA

Alta Vista 2002 Premium Chardonnay (Mendoza) $10. **84** —*M.S. (5/1/2003)*

Alta Vista 1999 Malbec (Mendoza) $12. **82** —*M.S. (11/1/2002)*

Alta Vista 1998 Alto Malbec (Mendoza) $60. **84** —*M.S. (11/1/2002)*

Alta Vista 2002 Grande Reserve Malbec (Mendoza) $20. Almost floral, but with aromas of crushed minerals and tar. Airing reveals some coconut, but swirling unleashes an onslaught of balancing snappy red fruit. Definitely an oaky Malbec, with powerful finishing flavors of coffee, bitter chocolate, and vanilla. **89** —*M.S. (7/1/2005)*

Alta Vista 2001 Premium Malbec (Mendoza) $10. Though not off-putting, there's nothing particularly premium about this sweet, woody wine. Cloying mocha aromas and flavors mask indistinct red fruit and create a wine that's much like a milk chocolate bar. A very easy mouthfeel, but nothing complex. **83** —*M.S. (1/1/2004)*

Alta Vista 2000 Red Blend (Mendoza) $8. **82** —*M.S. (5/1/2003)*

Alta Vista 2002 Malbec-Tempranillo (Mendoza) $8. Light on the nose, with shy strawberry and cherry aromas. Quite skinny on the palate, with inconsistent cherry cola and oak flavors. Very light on the finish, but buttery. Shows questionable barrel notes. **82** —*M.S. (10/1/2004)*

Alta Vista 2002 Premium Torrontés (Mendoza) $10. **83** —*M.S. (5/1/2003)*

Alta Vista 2000 Cosecha White Blend (Mendoza) $8. **80** —*M.S. (5/1/2003)*

ALTAS CUMBRES

Altas Cumbres 2002 Cabernet Sauvignon-Malbec (Mendoza) $9. Quite flowery and round, with pure grape, cherry, and berry aromas and flavors. Very fresh and spunky, and well made. Finishes with lots of fruit, integrated oak, and hints of coffee and chocolate. **88 Best Buy** *—M.S. (11/15/2004)*

Altas Cumbres 2003 Viognier (Mendoza) $9. A bit of celery interferes with the otherwise clean fruit on the bouquet. Flavors of apple, lemon, and lime are sweet and satisfactory. Finishes full, with a grabby feel. **84** *—M.S. (11/15/2004)*

ALTOCEDRO

Altocedro 2001 Reserva Malbec (Mendoza) $17. Fresh-cut oak sits front and center, and behind it there's textbook plum and berry fruit. Racy and tannic, but solid and fruity. Almost exactly as expected, although a bit thin as it gets more air. **85** *—M.S. (11/15/2005)*

ALTOS LAS HORMIGAS

Altos Las Hormigas 2003 Malbec (Mendoza) $12. Starts full and oaky, but not sappy or overly creamy. Settles to offer aromas of campfire, lavender, black peppercorn, and plenty of snappy berry fruit. Fine texture and depth of flavor, with cherry, plum, and vanilla. A complete wine with an intense spice element. **89 Best Buy** *—M.S. (7/1/2005)*

Altos Las Hormigas 2004 Reserva Viña Hormigas Malbec (Mendoza) $23. Potent and piercing right off the bat. The color says a lot, and the nose is confirmation that with this Malbec you're not playing around. The berry level is up there, and the flavors of blackberry, cassis, and plum are deep and satisfying. A nice layer of roasted fruit and oak carry the finish, and overall this wine offers a lot of juice per sip. **91** *—M.S. (12/31/2005)*

ALTOSUR

Altosur 2002 Estate Bottled Cabernet Sauvignon (Mendoza) $10. Tobacco, sugar beet, and cough drop aromas don't offer much, while blatant wood resin on the palate is wrapped tightly around blowsy blackberry fruit. Tough and tannic. **81** *—M.S. (7/1/2005)*

Altosur 2002 Merlot (Mendoza) $10. Quite jumbled and big at 14.2% alcohol. This wine is cast in stone, it's so hard and tannic, even for Merlot. But under the bombarding tannic wall there's racy, dark berry fruit. Ripped and hard, it badly needs meat to ease the tannins. By itself, it's no joy ride. **85 Best Buy** *—M.S. (7/1/2005)*

AMOR DE LOS ANDES

Amor de los Andes 2002 Malbec (Mendoza) $15. Jammy, sweet aromas conjure notes of a rose garden in bloom, but the palate is more scattered. On offer is basic cherry, raisin, and cotton candy. Sweet on the finish, yet good in a simple way. **84** *—M.S. (3/1/2005)*

Amor de los Andes 2002 Tempranillo (Mendoza) $15. Fairly overripe, with jammy aromas touched by raspberry and mocha. Somewhat lactic on the palate, with strawberry and other berry notes. Finishes flat although it never offends. **83** *—M.S. (3/1/2005)*

ANDALHUE

Andalhue 2004 Organico Malbec (Mendoza) $12. Good in color, with modest black-fruit aromas. Sports some tartness along with typical cherry and chocolate flavors. Fine in terms of size, but with an electric streak of acidity running through the center. Finishes chocolaty. **84** *—M.S. (11/15/2005)*

ANDES GRAPES

Andes Grapes 2002 Maia Malbec (Mendoza) $8. Light from the beginning, with simple cherry, raisin, and spice aromas. Somewhat hollow in the midpalate, with cherry and raspberry flavors. Finishes light; good enough but lacking body. **84** *—M.S. (10/1/2004)*

Andes Grapes 2002 Maia Syrah (Mendoza) $8. Smells of Sherry and caramel, while the fruit is just okay at the core and weak around the edges. Finishes flat. **81** *—M.S. (10/1/2004)*

ANGARO

Angaro 2002 Finca la Celia Cabernet Sauvignon-Tempranillo (Uco Valley) $6. **83** *—M.S. (5/1/2003)*

Angaro 2002 Finca la Celia Chardonnay (Uco Valley) $6. **83** *—M.S. (5/1/2003)*

Angaro 2002 Finca la Celia Red Blend (Uco Valley) $6. **81** *—M.S. (5/1/2003)*

Angaro 2002 Finca la Celia Sauvignon Blanc (Uco Valley) $6. **82** *—M.S. (5/1/2003)*

ANTONIO NERVIANI

Antonio Nerviani 2001 Reserve Malbec (Mendoza) $16. Green and funky at first, but it changes rapidly. There's also candy and raisin on the nose. The mouth is sort of lean and herky-jerky, with sugar beet and spice. Finishes heavy and syrupy, with a hint of sour weediness. **81** *—M.S. (11/15/2005)*

ARGENTINE BEEF

Argentine Beef 2003 Cabernet Sauvignon (Cafayate) $10. Fairly vegetal, with olive and bell pepper aromas. Light and green, without much fruit besides strawberry and plum. Acceptable mouthfeel with medium tannins. Less than rosy and ripe. **81** *—M.S. (12/31/2005)*

BALBI

Balbi 2002 Malbec (Mendoza) $8. **83** *—M.S. (12/1/2003)*

Balbi 1998 Malbec (Mendoza) $8. 80 *—M.S. (11/15/2001)*

Balbi 2002 Syrah (Mendoza) $8. Lean and short, with aromas of mustard and cured meats. The palate is modest at best, with sour raspberry and pie-cherry flavors. An herbal, sharp finish leaves a pickled lasting note. **81** *—M.S. (2/1/2004)*

Balbi 1998 Syrah (Mendoza) $8. 86 Best Buy *(10/1/2001)*

Balbi 1997 White Blend (Mendoza) $7. 83 *—S.H. (8/1/2000)*

BENMARCO

BenMarco 2002 Malbec (Mendoza) $20. 90 *—M.S. (12/1/2003)*

BIG DADDY VINEYARDS

Big Daddy Vineyards 2002 Bodega Polo Cabernet Sauvignon (La Consulta) $8. 82 *—M.S. (5/1/2003)*

Big Daddy Vineyards 2003 Bodega Polo Chardonnay (San Martin) $8. Strange aromas of campfire and grilled hot dogs barely resemble Chardonnay. In the mouth, coconut, vanilla, and wood resin are odd and overwhelming. Is that the flavor of oak dust on the finish? **80** *—M.S. (2/1/2004)*

Big Daddy Vineyards 2002 Bodega Polo Malbec (San Martin) $8. 85 *—M.S. (5/1/2003)*

Big Daddy Vineyards 2002 Sanes SA Malbec (Mendoza) $8. 86 Best Buy *—M.S. (5/1/2003)*

Big Daddy Vineyards 2003 Bodega Polo Merlot (Carodilla) $8. Sweet to the nose, with caramel and green bean aromas vying with the fruit notes. More green interjects itself into the flavor profile, while some okay caramel pops up on the warm, clinging finish. Good texture and feel, but not quite right in terms of flavor. **83** *—M.S. (7/1/2004)*

Big Daddy Vineyards 2002 Bodega Polo Merlot (Uco Valley) $8. 87 Best Buy *—M.S. (5/1/2003)*

Big Daddy Vineyards 2002 Sanes SA Red Blend (Mendoza) $8. 83 *—M.S. (5/1/2003)*

Big Daddy Vineyards 2002 Sanes SA Syrah (Mendoza) $8. 86 Best Buy *—M.S. (5/1/2003)*

Big Daddy Vineyards 2002 Sanes SA Tempranillo (Mendoza) $8. 84 *—M.S. (5/1/2003)*

BODEGA CATENA ZAPATA

Bodega Catena Zapata 1999 Nicolas Catena Zapata Cabernet Blend (Mendoza) $90. 92 Cellar Selection *—M.S. (5/1/2003)*

Bodega Catena Zapata 2001 Agrelo Vineyard Cabernet Sauvignon (Mendoza) $23. 84 *—M.S. (5/1/2003)*

Bodega Catena Zapata 2002 Chardonnay (Mendoza) $30. This barrel fermented, full-bodied wine delivers lots of depth, clean apple and pear fruit, and big, yummy toast and spice notes. It's a round, well-balanced Chardonnay that screams of the terroir of Mendoza —which means there's size, acidity, and power. **89** *—M.S. (7/1/2004)*

Bodega Catena Zapata 2000 Catena Alta-Agelica Vineyard Malbec (Mendoza) $55. 90 *—M.S. (5/1/2003)*

BODEGA ELVIRA CALLE

Bodega Elvira Calle 2003 Alberti 154 Malbec (Mendoza) $10. Big and bulky, with aromatic hints of cheddar cheese, tobacco, licorice, and espresso. The palate is sweet and chewy, while the finish delivers a wave of black pepper and mushroom. **84** *—M.S. (11/15/2004)*

BODEGA FAMILIA BARBERIS

Bodega Familia Barberis 2003 Cava Negra Malbec (Mendoza) $8. Jammy, with bubble gum aromas. Along the way there's some talcum powder and mint scents. Fairly fruity and modestly smooth, with fresh, friendly flavors but also a touch of grassy green at the center. **84 Best Buy** *—M.S. (11/15/2005)*

Bodega Familia Barberis 2002 Blason Tempranillo (Mendoza) $10. 81 *—M.S. (5/1/2003)*

BODEGA LA RURAL

Bodega La Rural 2000 Felipe Rutini Chardonnay (Tupungato) $17. 82 *—M.S. (5/1/2003)*

BODEGA LOPEZ

Bodega Lopez 2002 Malbec Xero Malbec (Mendoza) $9. Light to the eye, with lean strawberry and alfalfa aromas. The fruit is basic, with light pepper and spice nuances to the finish. Some broad-brushed oak adds sweetness and vanilla to the flavor profile. **84** *—M.S. (11/15/2004)*

BODEGA LURTON

Bodega Lurton 2003 Cabernet Sauvignon (Uco Valley) $9. The nose features a mish-mash of rubber, cinnamon, and red fruit, and then turns toward tomato upon airing. Cherry and raspberry flavors are best called "fresh," while the finish is light and modestly tannic. **84** *—M.S. (11/15/2004)*

Bodega Lurton 2003 Malbec (Uco Valley) $9. Moderately perfumed, with a mostly smooth, likable bouquet. It runs fairly sweet, with a good mix of fruit and oak. Finishes in a clean, wavy ride. Notes of chocolate and blueberry accent the flavor profile. **86 Best Buy** *—M.S. (11/15/2004)*

Bodega Lurton 2003 Torrontés (Mendoza) $7. What a score! Torrontés, a little-known Spanish white winegrape, turns out to be a superstar in Mendoza. Packed tight with bright, vivid, penetrating fruit, this strikingly flavorful wine begins with lovely scents of citrus, orange peel, and tangerine and takes off from there. It moves into still more complexity, with traces of diesel, talc, and flower petal. Think Viognier, Gewürztraminer and Riesling, blended and punched up with a full-bodied, lingering finish. **90 Best Buy** *—P.G. (11/15/2004)*

BODEGA NANNI

Bodega Nanni 2001 Single Estate Vineyard Malbec (Cafayate) $11. **84** *—M.S. (12/1/2003)*

BODEGA NOEMÍA DE PATAGONIA

Bodega Noemía de Patagonia 2002 Malbec (Rio Negro Valley) $140. Exotic and refined, with a stately bouquet of violets, mineral, and cassis. Sensational quality for a wine from rugged Patagonia. It bursts with black raspberry propelled by firm acids. Then it folds back into a darker space, where fudge and pepper notes make for a warming, spicy finish. Shows off the skill of Danish winemaker Hans Vinding-Diers. **92** *—M.S. (7/1/2005)*

BODEGA NORTON

Bodega Norton 1999 Chardonnay (Mendoza) $8. **80** *—M.S. (7/1/2002)*

Bodega Norton 2003 Reserve Malbec (Mendoza) $21. Ripe and dense, with aromas of balsamic reduction, berry fruit, and bread dough. The palate runs exceptionally sweet and rich, but it's not cloying or syrupy. Totally holes-free, with can't-miss flavors and solid tannins. Drink now or hold through 2007. **89** *—M.S. (11/15/2005)*

Bodega Norton 1999 Merlot (Mendoza) $8. **85 Best Buy** *—M.S. (11/1/2002)*

Bodega Norton 2002 Sauvignon Blanc (Mendoza) $8. **85** *—M.S. (5/1/2003)*

BODEGA PRIVADA

Bodega Privada 2003 Chardonnay (Mendoza) $8. Sweet at the core, with a bouquet that's rimmed by applesauce and canned-pear aromas. Flavors of lettuce greens, apple, and pear create a light mix, while the finish is simple and largely clean. From Lucas Lucchini. **84** *—M.S. (7/1/2004)*

Bodega Privada 2002 Merlot (Mendoza) $8. A touch rusty and thin to the eye, but mostly lean and clean on the nose, despite some leafiness. Modest tannins support flavors of dried cherry, raisin, and spice, and while it's not multidimensional by any stretch, it's not hard to drink, either. **84** *—M.S. (7/1/2004)*

Bodega Privada 2002 Syrah (Mendoza) $8. Chewy and meaty, with chunky black fruit on the nose and jammy cherry and raspberry notes on the palate. Finishes smooth and solid for the most part, with a pretty good mouthfeel. A good everyday wine. **85 Best Buy** *—M.S. (7/1/2004)*

BODEGA Y CAVAS DE WEINERT

Bodega y Cavas de Weinert 2000 Gran Viño Bordeaux Blend (Luján de Cuyo) $26. Sharp, spiky, and raw to start, with sassy fruit and aromas of smoked meat and polished leather. In the mouth, more identifiable flavors of plum, raspberry, and beet take over, and time allows for it to unfold. Finishes sturdy, with perfect tannins and perky acids. Match this with grilled beef and you're on your way. Sophisticated yet antique. How nice to see an individual wine like this. **90 Editors' Choice** *—M.S. (7/1/2005)*

BODEGAS ESCORIHUELA

Bodegas Escorihuela 2003 High Altitude Cabernet Sauvignon-Malbec (Agrelo) $10. Purple in color, with potent berry aromas. The blend is 65% in favor of Malbec, and the wine boasts black raspberry and plum flavors. Finishes hefty and warm, with notes of cola. **86 Best Buy** *—M.S. (11/15/2004)*

Bodegas Escorihuela 2002 High Altitude Cabernet Sauvignon-Malbec (Mendoza) $10. Good as it is on its own, Malbec only gets better when blended with Cabernet, as it is here, in a 2:1 proportion. This wine explodes with spice and tight, tart fruit. Berries, currants, and cherries highlight the full, round mid-palate, leading confidently into a finish folded in cocoa and toast. Clean, elegant, and stylish, it carries none of the mushroom or funk flavors that often come with inexpensive Argentine reds. **90 Best Buy** *—P.G. (11/15/2004)*

Bodegas Escorihuela 2002 High Altitude White Blend (Mendoza) $10. This made-for-export line features sleek packaging picturing Argentinean wildlife, and in the bottle what's coming out seems good. This white blend is ripe, with loads of apple and lemon on the nose, and lemon meringue on the palate. It's unwooded, yet naturally spicy. **86** *—M.S. (7/1/2004)*

BODEGAS Y VIÑEDOS SANTA SOFIA

Bodegas y Viñedos Santa Sofia 2002 Urban Oak Red Blend (Uco Valley) $9. Smooth and burly, with meaty, berry aromas preceding a friendly, hefty palate that's chock full of black plum, chocolate, and vanilla. With its open-knit finish, this has most of what the average wine lover seeks. This Tempranillo-Malbec blend is solid. **88 Best Buy** *—M.S. (2/1/2004)*

BROQUEL

Broquel 2000 Cabernet Sauvignon (Mendoza) $15. **87** *—M.S. (5/1/2003)*

Broquel 2002 Chardonnay (Mendoza) $15. Trapiche's high-end Chardonnay scores points for its heft, power, and all-important balance. The nose features baked apple, popcorn, and some wood, but it's not over the top. Flavors of apple, pineapple, and butterscotch are smooth and soft, while a bracing shot of acidity keeps everything in line. **88** *—M.S. (7/1/2004)*

Broquel 2002 Malbec (Argentina) $15. This upper middle-class Trapiche brand seems to be here to stay, and the Malbec offers round, chunky aromas of sweet berries and vanilla, followed by a juicy palate loaded with plum and cherry. Some dark campfire notes to the finish let you know this is real wine. **89** *—M.S. (10/1/2004)*

Broquel 2000 Malbec (Mendoza) $15. **88** *—M.S. (5/1/2003)*

BYBLOS

Byblos 2004 Semi-Sweet Bonarda (Mendoza) $8. A sugary kosher brother to the dry Bonarda; this is basically a replacement for sweet Concord-based wines. It offers cotton candy and cherry flavors, and a sticky yet not too heavy mouthfeel. **82** *—M.S. (11/15/2005)*

CABRINI

Cabrini 2000 Malbec (Mendoza) $11. **86 Best Buy** *—M.S. (11/1/2002)*

CARLOS BASSO

Carlos Basso 2000 Malbec (Mendoza) $12. **83** *—M.S. (11/1/2002)*

CARMELO PATTI

Carmelo Patti 2002 Extra Brut (Mendoza) $19. More of an artisan bubbly from a small producer in Argentina. Gold-amber in color, with mild toast and cornflake aromas. A bit heavy on the tongue, with apple as the main course. Turns almondy and rounder on the finish. Definitely shows some Champagne personality. **87** *—M.S. (12/31/2004)*

CASA BOHER

Casa Boher 2003 Malbec (Mendoza) $11. Smooth and full of berry, marzipan, and Christmas spice aromas. Comes on strong as it opens, revealing blueberry and black cherry flavors. Quite fresh and snappy, but with ample heft. A fine everyday red with guts. **87 Best Buy** *—M.S. (7/1/2005)*

Casa Boher 2003 Sauvignon Blanc (Mendoza) $11. Blunt and clumsy, with a slight vegetal streak to the chunky nose. The flavor profile is sweet and candied, while the finish hits with a wave of applesauce and peach flavors. Hangs rather heavily on the palate. **83** *—M.S. (7/1/2005)*

CASATERRA

Casaterra 2002 Cabernet Sauvignon (Mendoza) $7. Not on a par with the brand's more impressive Chardonnay; this Cabernet is aggressive and unbalanced. The palate is sweet. **80** *—M.S. (7/1/2004)*

Casaterra 2002 Malbec (Mendoza) $8. Run-of-the-mill berry and earth on the nose, followed by adequate blackberry and cherry flavors. A leathery mouthfeel created by stiff tannins pushes life into the finish. Doesn't stand up to intense airing and swirling. **84** *—M.S. (10/1/2004)*

CASTLE VIEW

Castle View 2004 Cabernet Sauvignon (Mendoza) $6. Limited red-fruit aromas mix with violets on the nose, while the mouth is tight, linear and flat, with basic red fruits. Not bad, but not complex, with a touch of artificiality on the finish. **83 Best Buy** *—M.S. (11/15/2005)*

Castle View 2004 Malbec (Mendoza) $6. Soft red fruit on the nose is followed by a creamy, almost lactic strawberry flavor. Seems kind of empty and rough, with candied heat and milk chocolate on the finish. **82** *—M.S. (12/31/2005)*

CATENA

Catena 2002 Cabernet Sauvignon (Mendoza) $20. Snappy and polished, with more around the edges than in the middle. Nonetheless, it's got nice black fruit, some tar and rubber, and ample vanilla. Well oaked but not "woody," with raspberry, red currant, and vanilla on the palate. Easy on the finish, if simple. Imported by Billington Imports. **87** *—M.S. (11/15/2005)*

Catena 2003 Chardonnay (Mendoza) $18. Very good and fresh; one of the better examples of a balanced Argentine Chardonnay that you'll encounter. Aromas of pear, vanilla, and oak are solid and well blended, while the peach and pear flavors are exact. Some citrus, mineral, and baking spice on the finish create a fine ending. **90 Editors' Choice** *—M.S. (3/1/2005)*

Catena 2000 Agrelo Vineyards Chardonnay (Mendoza) $15. **85** *—M.S. (7/1/2002)*

Catena 2002 Alta Chardonnay (Mendoza) $30. Made from Catena's Adrianna Vineyard, this bulky reserve-level wine deals mature aromas of corn, wheat, and melon more than anything zingy or zesty. The full-bodied palate is ripe and meaty, with chunky cantaloupe and peach flavors. Warm and oaky on the back end, if maybe a little too heavy. Drink now. **88** *—M.S. (3/1/2005)*

Catena 2002 Malbec (Mendoza) $22. Full and toasty, with an overt, burnt, almost charred nose. Mineral, charcoal, and red plum carry the zesty palate to an open, tasty, long finish. Closing notes of espresso, tree bark, and bitter chocolate are obvious and appropriate. **88** *—M.S. (3/1/2005)*

Catena 2001 Bodega Catena Zapata Malbec (Mendoza) $50. **90** *—M.S. (12/1/2003)*

CATENA ALTA

Catena Alta 2000 Chardonnay (Mendoza) $32. **84** *—M.S. (5/1/2003)*

Catena Alta 2000 Angelica Vineyard Malbec (Mendoza) $55. **90** *—M.S. (5/1/2003)*

CAVAS DE SANTOS

Cavas de Santos 2002 Cabernet Sauvignon (Mendoza) $11. Light and brushy, with aromas of red cherry, citrus peel, and leather. Decent cherry and chocolate flavors take care of the palate, which is limited but not bad. Scratchy on the finish, with an initial push that does better than the lasting notes. **83** *—M.S. (11/15/2005)*

CAVAS DEL CONDE

Cavas del Conde 2002 Cabernet Sauvignon (Mendoza) $9. The bouquet is all about stewed, raisiny fruit. Heavy as lead, with sticky raisin and prune flavors. Finishes ponderous, with zero agility. **80** *—M.S. (11/15/2005)*

CAVAS DEL VALLE

Cavas del Valle 2000 Malbec (Tupungato) $15. **85** *—M.S. (11/1/2002)*

CHAKANA

Chakana 2004 Cabernet Sauvignon (Mendoza) $12. The spice-to-fruit ratio on the bouquet is solid if not out of the ordinary. Tight cherry, plum, and raspberry flavors carry the palate, while the finish is largely on the money. A deep and chewy, full-bodied Cabernet. **87 Best Buy** *—M.S. (11/15/2005)*

Chakana 2004 Malbec (Mendoza) $12. Serious stuff that requires at least 10 minutes of airing to shed its rusticity and reveal its charms and qualities, among which are smoky plum aromas and flavors that bring spice and chocolate along for the ride. Layered and warm on the finish, with plumpness and hard spice. **88 Best Buy** *—M.S. (11/15/2005)*

Chakana 2003 Reserve Malbec (Mendoza) $23. Attractive lavender and violet notes accent typical black-fruit aromas, and the result is a mix of syrup and fresh summer plums. The palate is exceedingly ripe as it bursts with blackberry flavors and a heavy underblast of chocolate. Tight on the finish, but only at first. Soon it expands to reveal toasty, burly flavors and tannins. Delicious and sporty. **90** *—M.S. (11/15/2005)*

CHANDON

Chandon NV Fresco Brut (Mendoza) $11. **85 Best Buy** *—D.T. (11/15/2002)*

CINCO TIERRAS

Cinco Tierras 2003 Malbec (Mendoza) $10. Ripe and smoky, with attractive nuances to the forward bouquet. This is a nice wine with spunky plum flavors balanced by adequate but not overpowering oak. Cola, wood grain, and toast notes help the finish along. Medium in weight and pure; mildly tannic. **85 Best Buy** *—M.S. (12/31/2005)*

CLOS DE LOS SIETE

Clos de los Siete 2003 Malbec (Mendoza) $16. Pure and inky. The nose offers graphite, earth, and a huge amount of blackberry. The ripe palate is deep and defined, with a layer or two of complexity. Finishes with oak shadings, a splash of mint, and chocolate. Because the vineyards that yield this wine are still young, expect only better things in the future. Congratulations to Clos leader Michel Rolland and his gang of seven. **91 Editors' Choice** *—M.S. (7/1/2005)*

CONCHA Y TORO

Concha y Toro 2002 Xplorador Malbec (Mendoza) $7. Lots of black fruit with a touch of earth and an herbal undercurrent. Forward and jammy, with solid black cherry, plum, and pepper. Finishes a bit spicy, with chocolate to sweeten it up. Nothing to take issue with here; quite good value. **86 Best Buy** *—M.S. (11/15/2005)*

Concha y Toro 2000 Xplorador Malbec (Mendoza) $8. **85 Best Buy** *—M.S. (11/1/2002)*

CRISTOBAL 1492

Cristobal 1492 2003 Bonarda (Mendoza) $10. Violet and rich to the eye, with full-force boysenberry aromas. Aggressive and full-bodied, with rubbery tannins and massive flavors of bacon, molasses, and black fruits. Very good Bonarda, a grape that usually fails to impress. And for the price it's well worth a try. **87 Best Buy** *—M.S. (11/15/2005)*

Cristobal 1492 2003 Malbec (Mendoza) $10. Bubble gum and spice aromas, with chunky, off-centered fruit. Smells as if it might have gone through carbonic maceration, meaning it's candied and rubbery, with bright, gummy fruit flavors. **80** *—M.S. (12/31/2005)*

Cristobal 1492 2003 Oak Reserve Shiraz (Mendoza) $19. The oak here has resulted in bacon and wet-dog aromas, and the bouquet stays funky. Bold berry, carob, and pepper on the palate set the stage for a warm, almost lactic finish. Has merits but doesn't sing. **83** *—M.S. (11/15/2005)*

CROTTA

Crotta 2001 Tempranillo (Mendoza) $8. **84** *—M.S. (5/1/2003)*

DAVIS FAMILY

Davis Family 2000 Gusto Vita Malbec (Mendoza) $30. **90** *—M.S. (5/1/2003)*

DIABLO DE UCO

Diablo de Uco 2003 Malbec (Mendoza) $13. Solid up front, with earth, root beer, and black-fruit aromas. The feel, however, is quite zippy, with sharp acidity pushing the plum and black cherry flavors toward the realm of tangy. It's no surprise that it finishes kind of rowdy and jumpy. Still, it tastes good and clean. **85** *—M.S. (12/31/2005)*

Diablo de Uco 2002 Merlot (Mendoza) $13. Murky aromas of earth and coal turn bland before veering toward cheesy. Flavors of red raspberry and pie-cherry are tart, while the mouthfeel is scouring due to high acidity. Ultra tart and fresh, but ultimately sour and short. **82** *—M.S. (11/15/2004)*

DOMAINE JEAN BOUSQUET

Domaine Jean Bousquet 2004 Chardonnay (Tupungato) $11. Full-bodied and ripe, starting with the butterscotch and toast aromas and continuing on to the sweet-styled palate that offers pear, apple butter, and walnut flavors. Thick more than lean, with one of the roundest and creamiest mouthfeels going. **86 Best Buy** *—M.S. (7/1/2005)*

Domaine Jean Bousquet 2004 Merlot (Mendoza) $11. This Merlot from Tupungato has clean, proper aromas and a fair amount of zesty cherry and raspberry flavors. Tangy on the finish, if a bit lean. Still, there's enough purity and power to elevate it to the quality level. Young and ready to go; a BBQ wine of the first order. **86 Best Buy** *—M.S. (11/15/2005)*

DOMINGO HERMANOS

Domingo Hermanos 2001 Palo Domingo Red Blend (Salta) $49. This small-production tribute wine hails from Salta. It's a firm, thick wine with full-force plum, berry, and caramel aromas and flavors. The finish is rich and saturated, and overall it's a good, brooding wine with some class and style. Just 116 cases produced. **87** *—M.S. (7/1/2004)*

DON MIGUEL GASCÓN

Don Miguel Gascón 2004 Malbec (Mendoza) $13. Bright purple in color, with heavy smoke and rubber aromas that together come across as bacon and bitter chocolate. Cassis, plum, and tobacco rest comfortably on the palate, while the finish is grapy, extracted, and toasty. In recent years this wine has carved out its own style, and this vintage fits the model. **87** *—M.S. (11/15/2005)*

Don Miguel Gascón 2002 Malbec (Mendoza) $12. 87 *—M.S. (12/1/2003)*

Don Miguel Gascón 2000 President's Blend Malbec (Mendoza) $20. 86 *—M.S. (11/1/2002)*

Don Miguel Gascón 2002 Syrah (Mendoza) $12. Inky purple in color, with a dense bouquet of bacon, coffee grinds, and plum. The palate is grapey at first, while a textured but mildly tangy finish comes next. Fairly high-voltage and powerful, but not very elegant. Best for fans of thick, extracted reds. **84** *—M.S. (2/1/2004)*

Don Miguel Gascón 2004 Viognier (Mendoza) $12. Lively, with young legs. The bouquet blasts forth with lemon curd and ripe apple aromas, which are followed by a plump yet racy palate full of spicy apple, pear and mild mineral notes. Not meant for the long haul. **86** *—M.S. (11/15/2004)*

Don Miguel Gascón 2002 Viognier (Mendoza) $12. A meaty, bold wine, with peach, custard and crushed vitamin comprising the nose. Tastes sweet and cloying, with sugary citrus flavors. A sticky, heavy finish is saturated with tropical fruit and sweet almond candy. The feeling here is that this is too ponderous. **83** *—M.S. (2/1/2004)*

DOÑA PAULA

Doña Paula 2003 Estate Cabernet Sauvignon (Luján de Cuyo) $15. Good value in Cabernet, blending ripe cassis with just enough weedy, tobaccoey complexities. Medium-weight, folding in hints of cedar on the midpalate. Simultaneously mouthwatering and chewy on the finish. Drink now with burgers or hold another 2–3 years and serve with roast beef. **89** *(12/31/2004)*

Doña Paula 2003 Estate Chardonnay (Luján de Cuyo) $15. Toasty and nutty on the nose, this is a big, woody wine that's barrel-fermented in 80% new French oak. Peach and pear notes support the wood on the palate, and the wine finishes crisp, with a hint of grapefruit. **86** *(12/31/2004)*

Doña Paula 2002 Sélección de Bodega Single Vineyard Chardonnay (Luján de Cuyo) $29. The richest and most concentrated on Doña Paula's Chards, this one has enough fruit intensity to support the oak treatment. Melon and citrus aromas lead the way, accented by light toasted-oat scents. Melon and white peach flavors flow easily across the palate, riding a rich, viscous mouthfeel. Smooth finish, nicely integrating fruit and oak. **89** *(12/31/2004)*

Doña Paula 2003 Estate Malbec (Luján de Cuyo) $15. Nicely done, with bright raspberry aromas that leap from the glass. Mixed berries and vanilla on the palate, a fleshy, creamy mouthfeel and a supple finish make this deceptively easy to drink. **87** *(12/31/2004)*

Doña Paula 1999 Selección de Bodega Single Vineyard Malbec (Luján de Cuyo) $12. 84 *—M.S. (12/1/2003)*

Doña Paula 2002 Estate Merlot (Tupungato) $15. Crisp and tight, with firm tannins and acids. Also a bit vegetal, but not overly. Flavors of black fruit and licorice are standard fare. A pedestrian, drinkable Merlot with some style. **85** *—M.S. (10/1/2004)*

Doña Paula 2003 Estate Shiraz-Malbec (Luján de Cuyo) $15. Boasts an extra measure of complexity over the unblended Malbec, adding smoke, spice, and herb notes to the lush, fruity base. Peppery and briary on the finish. **88** *(12/31/2004)*

ECOS

Ecos 2002 Malbec (Mendoza) $12. Violet and pretty, with a forceful bouquet that starts out rustic before finding its stride. The palate is flush with fruit, primarily black currant and boysenberry. The finish, however, is not too long and loses clarity quickly. **85** *—M.S. (10/1/2004)*

EL NIÑO

El Niño 2003 Malbec (Mendoza) $19. Cranberry and sweet beet aromas are gritty but pure, while the palate pushes high-octane black fruit along with chocolate and raisin flavors. Lively in terms of feel, with very nice acidity providing balance. Finishes long and smoky, with pop. **88** *—M.S. (7/1/2005)*

ELSA

Elsa 2001 Chardonnay (San Rafael) $11. 80 *—M.S. (7/1/2002)*

Elsa 2002 Sémillon-Chardonnay (San Rafael) $8. 83 *—M.S. (5/1/2003)*

ENRIQUE FOSTER

Enrique Foster 2002 Limited Edition Malbec (Luján de Cuyo) $36. Starts a little sour, pickled and funky, but airing lets it find its legs and shine. Plum and snappy berry fruit is a touch tart, but not too much so. With time, it fattens up, displaying charcoal, coffee, and chocolate on the finish. **87** *—M.S. (11/15/2004)*

ESCALERA AL SOL

Escalera al Sol 1999 Syrah (Mendoza) $6. 83 *(10/1/2001)*

ETCHART

Etchart 1999 Chardonnay (Cafayate) $NA. 83 *—M.S. (9/1/2001)*

Etchart 1999 Torrontés (Cafayate) $NA. 84 *—M.S. (9/1/2001)*

FABRE MONTMAYOU

Fabre Montmayou 2002 Gran Reserva Malbec (Mendoza) $15. This you just have to love, especially for the price. Starts with graham cracker, kirsch, and black cherry aromas before transitioning to chocolate, vanilla, and coffee. Shows subtle touches but a lot of Argentinean power and pizzazz. Restrained but ripe; robust yet suave. **90 Best Buy** *—M.S. (7/1/2005)*

FALLING STAR

Falling Star 2002 Cabernet Sauvignon (Mendoza) $6. Trapiche is behind this fruity, somewhat sweet Cabernet that should have mass appeal. The bouquet is packed with rubber, smoked meat, and plum, while the palate runs sweet, with raspberry and beet flavors. Some milk chocolate on the finish leaves a chewy, sweet impression. **84 Best Buy** *—M.S. (2/1/2004)*

Falling Star 2002 Chardonnay (Mendoza) $5. Aromas of gumdrop, lemon juice, and anise create a stylish impression, however, the wine turns more zesty and tangy in the mouth. Flavors of grapefruit, lemon, and apple are open yet ultimately rather simple. **84 Best Buy** *—M.S. (2/1/2004)*

Falling Star 2000 Chardonnay (Mendoza) $5. 80 *—M.S. (11/15/2001)*

Falling Star 2001 Merlot-Malbec (Mendoza) $6. 80 *—M.S. (5/1/2003)*

FAMILIA CASSONE

Familia Cassone 2001 Malbec (Luján de Cuyo) $9. 84 *—M.S. (12/1/2003)*

FAMILIA LLAVER ORO

Familia Llaver Oro 2001 Sauvignon Blanc (Mendoza) $16. Gold in color, with a mute nose that doesn't offer much in the way of typical SB character. The palate deals apple and pear, and while that's not usual, neither is the mouthfeel, which is plump and flat. **82** *—M.S. (2/1/2004)*

FAMILIA ZUCCARDI

Familia Zuccardi 2000 Q Cabernet Sauvignon (Mendoza) $20. Ample leather and dark-fruit aromas yield to tobacco and oak on the nose. Flavors of sweet plums and chocolate create a masculine palate, and the finish is deeply charred and toasty. The extraction is big and the tannins full. **87** *—M.S. (2/1/2004)*

Familia Zuccardi 2000 Q Chardonnay (Mendoza) $20. Brownish gold and losing speed with each passing moment. The oxidized, buttery nose is overdone and waxy, while the palate yields cider and cinnamon, seemingly the leftovers from the oaking it went through. The mouthfeel is flat, and overall it's much like apricot juice. **81** *—M.S. (2/1/2004)*

Familia Zuccardi 2000 Q Malbec (Mendoza) $20. 88 *—M.S. (12/1/2003)*

Familia Zuccardi 1998 Q Malbec (Mendoza) $22. 84 *—M.S. (11/15/2001)*

Familia Zuccardi 1999 Q Merlot (Mendoza) $22. 90 *—C.S. (5/1/2002)*

Familia Zuccardi 2000 Q Tempranillo (Mendoza) $20. The nose is heavily barrel dominated; aromas of barbecue sauce and sawdust overwhelm any piquant red fruit that might be hanging around. Flavors of light cherry, molasses, and red chilies turn lemony as the oak takes over the palate. This wine really pushes the oak, so much so that it falters. **82** *—M.S. (2/1/2004)*

FANTELLI

Fantelli 2003 Chardonnay (Mendoza) $8. Gold in color, with apricot and peach aromas. It's heavy and ripe, with baked apple and orange flavors. Soft on the palate, without much force or acidity. Drink now to enjoy the chunky body and caramel-laden finish. **84** *—M.S. (10/1/2004)*

Fantelli 2000 Chardonnay (Mendoza) $9. 82 *—M.S. (7/1/2002)*

Fantelli 2001 Malbec (Mendoza) $9. 84 *—M.S. (12/1/2003)*

Fantelli 2002 Merlot (Mendoza) $8. Sweet cherry and cotton candy aromas emanate from the nose, while dark berry fruit and earth notes carry the palate. A touch prickly and acidic for Merlot, but not bad. Finishes with above-average fruit and mild tannins. **86 Best Buy** *—M.S. (10/1/2004)*

Fantelli 1999 Sangiovese (Mendoza) $10. **84** *—C.S. (5/1/2002)*

Fantelli 2001 Syrah (Mendoza) $9. Basic plum and berry fruit aromas have a note of rubber that gets more aggressive with time. Simple, with open raspberry, plum, and mild vanilla flavors. A light, buttery, chocolaty finish leaves a round, friendly impression. **85** *—M.S. (2/1/2004)*

Fantelli 2003 Torrontés (Mendoza) $8. Very light in color, with matching lightweight aromas of hay, licorice gumdrop, and papaya. Not terribly complex, but light and easy, with honeydew and tropical fruit flavors. Critics could equate it to water while admirers will laud its freshness. **85 Best Buy** *—M.S. (10/1/2004)*

FELIPE RUTINI

Felipe Rutini 1999 Reserve Chardonnay (Mendoza) $19. **83** *—M.S. (7/1/2002)*

Felipe Rutini 2001 Malbec (Mendoza) $20. **89** *—M.S. (12/1/2003)*

Felipe Rutini 2002 Merlot (Mendoza) $20. This is La Rural's top line, and before we've been a fan of the Malbec. But this wine has serious balance issues; it's acidic and sour at the core, with heavy oak and not enough flesh. Hails from the cooler Tupungato region, something that's evident in the wine's thin structure. **82** *—M.S. (3/1/2005)*

Felipe Rutini 2000 Merlot (Tupungato) $18. **86** *—M.S. (5/1/2003)*

FILLIPO FIGAR

Fillipo Figar 2000 Anastasia Cabernet Sauvignon (Mendoza) $10. **84** *—M.S. (11/1/2002)*

FILUS

Filus 2003 Reserve Malbec (Mendoza) $16. Sweet and woody from start to finish. In between the powerful oak waves you'll find smoked meat and leather. Ripe in the mouth, with blueberry and blackberry flavors, then tannic and very woody on the finish. In fact, oak takes over as the dominant characteristic about halfway through. **85** *—M.S. (12/31/2005)*

FINCA DE DOMINGO

Finca de Domingo 2003 Torrontés (Argentina) $8. Sharp on the nose, with aromas of lemon-lime. Basic apple and spice flavors control the lean, subdued palate. Finishes heavy and fairly bland. **82** *—M.S. (7/1/2004)*

FINCA DEL VALLE

Finca del Valle 2001 Cabernet Sauvignon (Mendoza) $8. Lean and clean, but very thin. Aromas of cherry and raisins lead into a strawberry-raspberry palate that packs little punch. The midpalate is tangy, while the finish fails to register much beyond tart fruit and dry earth. **83** *—M.S. (2/1/2004)*

Finca del Valle 2001 Chardonnay (Mendoza) $7. Bland and indifferent, with butterscotch and chemical aromas. Some apple and citrus carry the palate into a forward but midland finish. Thick and sweet mango and banana flavors are what's left behind. **81** *—M.S. (2/1/2004)*

Finca del Valle 2001 Merlot (Mendoza) $7. Starts off with cola and rooty aromas, but turns stewed rather quickly. A bit syrupy and green in the mouth, with a fairly strong oak veneer. Some drying wood and a touch of cough drop define the finish. **82** *—M.S. (2/1/2004)*

Finca del Valle 2002 Trinomium Red Blend (Mendoza) $10. Light, with raspberry and citrus-rind aromas. Flavors of cherry, cola, and burnt meat lead into a creamy, oaky finish. Fairly low-acid, with a soft feel. The mix is Malbec (70%) along with Cab and Merlot. **86 Best Buy** *—M.S. (2/1/2004)*

FINCA EL PORTILLO

Finca El Portillo 2004 Chardonnay (Mendoza) $9. Chunky and forward, with nectarine and pineapple flavors. Zesty and fairly intense, with a simple, forward finish. Fruity for sure, with balance and an easy personality. **85 Best Buy** *—M.S. (11/15/2005)*

Finca El Portillo 2004 Merlot (Alto Valle de Uco) $9. Fairly charred and leathery for what's here, meaning the fruit isn't really up to the oak. The palate is tangy and slightly candied, with berry flavors covered by a burnt overlay. The finish is acidic and a touch raw. Imported by The San Francisco Wine Exchange. **83** *—M.S. (12/31/2005)*

FINCA FLICHMAN

Finca Flichman 1999 Syrah (Mendoza) $10. **83** *—M.S. (11/15/2001)*

Finca Flichman 1999 Syrah (Mendoza) $NA. **83** *—M.S. (9/1/2001)*

FINCA KOCH

Finca Koch 2001 Cabernet Sauvignon (Tupungato) $17. **88** *—M.S. (5/1/2003)*

FINCA LA DANIELA

Finca La Daniela 2002 Malbec (Mendoza) $11. Earthy yet fresh, with red fruit aromas that flow directly onto the sweet, oozing palate. Quite simple, but ready to drink. It's got chocolate and fruit syrup on the finish along with integrated tannins and acidity. Textbook fashion. **86 Best Buy** *—M.S. (5/1/2005)*

FINCA SOPHENIA

Finca Sophenia 2003 Estate Cabernet Sauvignon (Tupungato) $18. If you like a dark, saturated wine with a ton of ripeness and richness, then this is it. The color is opaque, the bouquet full of rubber, blackberry, and chocolate. It's intense stuff, with black cherry and cassis flavors preceding a finish dense with bitter notes, licorice, and vanilla. Solid to the core. **90 Editors' Choice** *—M.S. (11/15/2005)*

Finca Sophenia 2003 Malbec (Mendoza) $17. Purple to the eye, with intense aromas of mint, licorice, and saturated black fruit. The mouth is like blueberry-blackberry compote, while the oak seems heavy given the wine's higher acids and limited depth. Has plenty of positives but sings just one note. **87** *—M.S. (3/1/2005)*

Finca Sophenia 2002 Merlot (Mendoza) $17. Somewhat heavy and overripe, with plum and earth aromas. The palate carries a heavy, weighty feel, with rather murky flavors. Rubbery tannins create a stick-to-the-cheeks sensation. Seems like the winemaking effort was here but maybe not the grapes. **84** *—M.S. (3/1/2005)*

Finca Sophenia 2004 Altosur Sauvignon Blanc (Mendoza) $10. This snappy, high-altitude version from Finca Sophenia scores points for its attractive nose of citrus and wet stones, and the palate holds form. Flavors of grapefruit, tangerine, and cantaloupe aren't fancy but they are nice and fresh. Cleansing acidity and crispness help it along. **86 Best Buy** *—M.S. (11/15/2005)*

FINCA URQUIZA

Finca Urquiza 2001 Malbec (Mendoza) $12. Fruity and floral on the nose, which is by far the wine's high point. The palate, however, is too acidic to handle the weight of the fruit, which isn't much. In the end, the wine's racy and intense, offering more on the nose than in the mouth. **83** *—M.S. (3/1/2005)*

FUNDACION DE MENDOZA

Fundacion de Mendoza 1999 Prestigio Cabernet Blend (Mendoza) $15. **83** *—M.S. (11/1/2002)*

FUNKY LLAMA

Funky Llama 2003 Chardonnay (Mendoza) $6. A little oily and heavy, but the buttercup and candle wax aromas seem more real than artificial. The palate is plump, a bit sugary, but the apple and orange notes are clear. Finishes juicy enough and not overly cloying. **84 Best Buy** *—M.S. (3/1/2005)*

Funky Llama 2003 Tempranillo (Mendoza) $6. Generally gimmicky names draw no applause from these parts, but here we like this wine's raspberry, graham cracker, and orange-peel nose along with its crystallized raspberry and strawberry flavors. It's slightly gritty and sugary, but overall it's still fresh enough to handle the sweetness. **84 Best Buy** *—M.S. (3/1/2005)*

GENTILE COLLINS

Gentile Collins 2001 Malbec (Mendoza) $8. **86** *—M.S. (5/1/2003)*

GOUGENHEIM WINERY

Gougenheim Winery 2003 Otoño Malbec (Mendoza) $10. Sweet and extracted, with medicinal aromas of kirsch meeting chocolate bonbons. Carob, malted milk, and raspberry liqueur are the dominant flavors, while the finish is spirited, i.e. grabby and aggressive. Best if you like yours saturated and big-boned. **86 Best Buy** *—M.S. (7/1/2005)*

Gougenheim Winery 1999 Silvestre Red Blend (Tupungato) $15. Seems like time forgot this Cabernet-Merlot-Malbec trio, and now it's unstable. The nose is pure barnyard, with hints of peanut and saddle. The palate is cooked and tired. Not horrible but still best to skip. **80** *—M.S. (3/1/2005)*

GRAFFIGNA

Graffigna 1999 Selection Especial Cabernet Sauvignon (Tulum Valley) $10. **82** *—C.S. (5/1/2002)*

Graffigna 2001 Don Santiago Malbec (San Juan) $20. Violet in color, with pickled aromas marring black plum. Flavors of red cabbage and plum are tart, and the mouthfeel is that of a citrus-based juice. From the more eastern district of San Juan. **81** *—M.S. (3/1/2005)*

Graffigna 2003 G Malbec (Pedernal Valley) $18. Cola, mint, vanilla, and black fruit control the bouquet, with acid-propelled cherry and red plum flavors coming next. Freshness and clarity are attributes, although some might say it's too much of a tart, straight-shooter. Alive and snappy for sure. **85** *—M.S. (12/31/2005)*

Graffigna 1999 Selection Especial Malbec (Tulum Valley) $10. **85 Best Buy** *—C.S. (5/1/2002)*

Graffigna 1999 Syrah (Tulum Valley) $18. **81** *— (1/1/2004)*

Graffigna 2000 Don Santiago Syrah (Tulum Valley) $18. Strange aromas lead you to a palate of canned fruit and sugar. This is a weird wine with no balance and too much radical sweetness. Definitely not ready for the big leagues. **80** *—M.S. (2/1/2004)*

Graffigna 2001 Selección Especial Syrah-Cabernet (Tulum Valley) $10. Sharp at first, with funky, sulfuric aromas. The palate is heavily pickled and out of whack. A medicinal finish with a note of sugar beet won't win many fans. **80** *—M.S. (2/1/2004)*

HENRY LAGARDE

Henry Lagarde 2000 Malbec (Luján de Cuyo) $12. **86** *—M.S. (12/1/2003)*

Henry Lagarde 2000 Merlot (Luján de Cuyo) $10. **87** *—M.S. (5/1/2003)*

HUMBERTO BARBERIS

Humberto Barberis 1999 Malbec (Mendoza) $13. **83** *—M.S. (5/1/2003)*

INCA

Inca 2002 Cabernet Sauvignon-Malbec (Salta) $NA. Sweet at first, then it turns toward beet juice and bell pepper. The flavor profile is defined by cola, licorice, and green pepper, while the spicy finish is marinade-like. **81** *—M.S. (7/1/2004)*

Inca 2003 Torrontés (Salta) $NA. From high-altitude vineyards in the northern Salta region comes this well-made, zippy white blend. On the nose, tarragon combines with citrus, peach, and nectarine, while in the mouth, things are solid and even a touch creamy. Finishing flavors of banana, melon, and lychee are typical of Torrontés. **86** *—M.S. (7/1/2004)*

J. & F. LURTON

J. & F. Lurton 2002 Gran Lurton Cabernet Sauvignon (Mendoza) $18. Starts out showing red-fruit aromas of currant, plum, and raspberry. The palate stays the course, offering raspberry and strawberry flavors. Shows plenty of ripeness, moderate tannins, and some buttery, vanilla-based oak. Fresh but simple. Drink now. **87** *—M.S. (7/1/2005)*

J. & F. Lurton 2002 Chacayes Malbec (Mendoza) $75. This is what full-force, high-elevation Malbec is all about. The color is opaque, the nose a potent brew of herbal mint, blackberry, and earth. With layers of warmth and depth on the finish, this wine represents the bigger is better school of thought. **92** *—M.S. (11/15/2004)*

J. & F. Lurton 2002 Reserva Malbec (Mendoza) $13. The bouquet springs with red licorice, black cherry, and blueberry, but also a hint of minty green. Not sharp but piquant on the tongue, with hints of cherry candy and grainy oak. Good on the surface but there's not a whole lot underneath. A solid quaff to match with burgers or pizza. **86** *—M.S. (7/1/2005)*

J. & F. Lurton 2003 Tierra del Fuego Red Blend (Mendoza) $6. Lighter framed than your average Argentinean red, but good in its red-fruit base. The nose shows red berry, vanilla, and adequate depth, while the palate is dry and lean, with cherry as the dominant fruit. **85 Best Buy** *—M.S. (11/15/2004)*

KAIKEN

Kaiken 2003 Cabernet Sauvignon (Mendoza) $13. Starts out heavily smoked, almost woodsy. Stays oaky throughout, while showing an overt candied, sweet, medicinal core. Not very edgy, with a lot of marshmallow, vanilla, and syrup. Made at twice the production level as the inaugural 2002, and with a new premium wine competing for top fruit; still good but not special like the '02. **86** *—M.S. (7/1/2005)*

Kaiken 2003 Ultra Cabernet Sauvignon (Mendoza) $23. Clumsy at first, but admittedly tasted a month prior to release. Time frees up deep, sturdy fruit overlayed with a sheet of creamy oak that yields vanilla, resin, and subtle spice flavors. Chunky and ripe; the berry fruit is 100% mature. Will knit together with more time in bottle. Better in 2006. **90 Editors' Choice** *—M.S. (7/1/2005)*

Kaiken 2002 Malbec (Mendoza) $13. This new brand from Montes in Chile scored big with its inaugural Cabernet and the Malbec is just as good, if not better. The tint is a purple haze, while the nose is dark, masculine, and full of ultraripe black fruit. Deep and rich throughout—and totally delicious—it's what good South American reds are all about: bursting fruit, body, and value. **91 Best Buy** *—M.S. (3/1/2005)*

LA YUNTA

La Yunta 2002 Torrontés (Famatina Valley) $9. From the La Rioja region, this colorless white offers virtually nothing in terms of aromas and then barely a smack of candied fruit flavor. It's overly thin, with microscopic amounts of citrus. **80** *—M.S. (7/1/2004)*

LAS MORAS

Las Moras 2004 Bonarda (San Juan) $8. Broad and clean, with solid berry and cherry aromas along with some citrus zest. The palate offers bright berry flavors, while the finish is full, leathery, and tight. Commendable for its forward fruit and quality mouthfeel. A good introduction to Bonarda. Imported by 57 Main Street Wine Co. **85 Best Buy** *—M.S. (11/15/2005)*

Las Moras 2004 Shiraz (San Juan) $8. Sturdy and solid, with some leather and spice to the nose. Loud and racy on the palate, with some heat and spice on the back side. This is yet another solid, forward wine from Argentina, and for the money, you can't really go wrong. **87 Best Buy** *—M.S. (10/1/2005)*

LAUREL GLEN

Laurel Glen 2003 Terra Rosa Malbec (Mendoza) $14. Pure and linear, without a spot of funk or wayward oak. The nose is beefed up with aromas of tar, smoke, leather, and blackberry, yet the palate is a bit candied. Easygoing enough to rank as a very good everyday wine. And you'll never say corchado after opening it; it's sealed with a screw cap. **87** *—M.S. (7/1/2005)*

Laurel Glen 2001 Vale La Pena Malbec (Mendoza) $30. **91** *—M.S. (12/1/2003)*

LOS CARDOS

Los Cardos 2002 Cabernet Sauvignon (Luján de Cuyo) $8. The nose deals earth, soy sauce, game, and a distant note of green pepper. There's good extract and color throughout, with some syrupy sweetness to offset the mildest note of green bean. Pepper and other spices on the finish create interest. **85 Best Buy** *—M.S. (2/1/2004)*

Los Cardos 2004 Chardonnay (Luján de Cuyo) $9. A soft, fruity, medium-weight Chardonnay, with obvious flavors of peach and vanilla. Finishes with a touch of grapefruit. **85** *(12/31/2004)*

Los Cardos 2002 Chardonnay (Luján de Cuyo) $8. With its soft pear and banana aromas, the bouquet is welcoming. Flavors of mango and lychee are sweet, while a note of white pepper adds spice. Licorice and nutmeg provide depth to the lemony finish. Nice and drinkable. **85 Best Buy** *—M.S. (2/1/2004)*

Los Cardos 2003 Merlot (Tupungato) $10. Boisterous and overcooked, with heavily roasted aromas and flavors. Not a polished, prime-time wine. **80** *—M.S. (10/1/2004)*

Los Cardos 2004 Sauvignon Blanc (Tupungato) $9. The must for this wine spends up to two weeks refrigerated on its gross lees prior to fermentation, according to winemaker Gandolini. The result is a grapefruity, slightly grassy wine that's rounder and softer on the midpalate, filling in with flavors of melon and fig. Tart on the finish. **85 Best Buy** *(12/31/2004)*

Los Cardos 2002 Syrah (Luján de Cuyo) $8. Some funky leather, barnyard, and charred beef get it going, followed by ripe flavors of berry and sweet chocolate. A finish with sweetness, vanilla, and carob is borderline cloying, but not quite. **85 Best Buy** *—M.S. (2/1/2004)*

LUCA

Luca 2000 Malbec (Altos de Mendoza) $37. **90** *—M.S. (12/1/2003)*

LUIGI BOSCA

Luigi Bosca 2002 Finca La Linda Cabernet Sauvignon (Mendoza) $10. Somewhat complex, as it begins with heavy bacon and tire rubber aromas that ultimately give way to more floral notes. Fairly thick on the palate, with sweet red fruits, glycerol, and tannins. Finishes a touch flat and sugary, with some Port-like heat. A hard one to peg. **86 Best Buy** *—M.S. (3/1/2005)*

Luigi Bosca 2004 Reserva Chardonnay (Mendoza) $15. Quite full and plump, with oily aromas along with hints of wood resin and nectarine. More citrus than expected on the tongue, primarily overripe white grapefruit. Somewhat low-acid on the finish, but good overall. **86** *—M.S. (3/1/2005)*

Luigi Bosca 2002 Finca La Linda Malbec (Mendoza) $10. Intriguingly herbal, with spice, leather, and oregano aromas as opposed to Malbec's more common jammy blueberry and blackberry characteristics. The palate is moderately juicy, with hints of pepper, baking spices, and earth. Different than the pack, which is admirable. **87 Best Buy** *—M.S. (3/1/2005)*

Luigi Bosca 2001 Reserva Merlot (Mendoza) $16. Rusty in color, with country aromas of sweaty leather, horsehide, and hay. Ponderous on the palate, with sour plum and murky baked fruit. Surely not a disaster but brings with it some heavy overriding characteristics. **82** *—M.S. (3/1/2005)*

Luigi Bosca 1997 Finca Los Nobles Malbec-Verdot (Mendoza) $58. This is a stylish throwback, like the new Knicks putting on vintage Frazier jerseys. The nose is spicy and slightly herbal, with fresh basil, cinnamon, and leather mixing with dried black fruits. Still vital and kicking on the palate, with juicy plum, blueberry, coffee, and chocolate flavors. Toasty and spicy on the finish; drink or continue to hold. **91** *—M.S. (7/1/2005)*

Luigi Bosca 2004 Reserva Sauvignon Blanc (Maipú) $15. Dull passion fruit is about the best you get from the bouquet, while the palate is weak and watery, with light tropical fruit flavors. Finishes with banana notes. **81** *—M.S. (7/1/2005)*

Luigi Bosca 2003 Finca La Linda Tempranillo (Mendoza) $10. Perfect color combined with one of the more atypical but interesting bouquets you'll find stirs intrigue. Aromas of mint, berry syrup, and most of all, clove, are intense, while the black licorice and espresso accents on the palate work. Not Spanish in style nor is it reserved. This is a bruising wine with a unique Mendoza identity. **87 Best Buy** *—M.S. (3/1/2005)*

LUIS CORREAS

Luis Correas 1997 Malbec (Mendoza) $9. **82** *—C.S. (5/1/2002)*

MARTINO

Martino 2002 Malbec (Luján de Cuyo) $19. Herbal and spicy, with lactic notes and ripe blueberry aromas. Quite fruity and sprawling, with big plum and berry flavors. Thick in the mouth and large on the finish, with syrup and just enough acid to keep it balanced. **87** *—M.S. (12/31/2005)*

MAYOL

Mayol 2003 Pircas Vineyard Bonarda (Mendoza) $15. Dense and dark, with a color akin to purple ink. Catchy, well-made, the fruit is ripe and abnormally friendly, while the structure is solid. What makes this an above-average wine in its class is that the acidity is mellow, not shrill as is often the case. **87** *—M.S. (11/15/2004)*

Mayol 2003 Sebastian Vineyard Cabernet Sauvignon (Tupungato) $15. Basic and juicy, with olive on the nose along with black fruit. Ripe and tannic, with berry and plum flavors and a robust, somewhat tannic mouthfeel. Pushes cherry and blackberry late; good but standard. **84** *—M.S. (12/31/2005)*

Mayol 2002 Montuiri Vineyard Malbec (Luján de Cuyo) $15. A single-vineyard heavyweight with sweet aromas of oak, caramel, and berry syrup. The palate is stewy and dark, with blackberry and pepper notes. The feel across the tongue is stand-up, with chocolate and coffee notes coming on late. **88** *—M.S. (7/1/2004)*

MAYU

Mayu 2003 Malbec (San Juan) $11. Dark and jammy on the nose, with a spot of vinegar and sharp leather. Tangy plum and cherry flavors on the palate, with sharp-edged tannins. The puckery finish shows coffee and mocha shadings. Imported by Table 31 Imports. **82** *—M.S. (11/15/2005)*

MEDRANO

Medrano 2001 Cabernet Sauvignon (Maipú) $9. This American-owned label provides just enough quality and true flavor to merit a look. The nose is syrupy and a touch cooked, but the plum and berry flavors are solid. Some coffee and chocolate notes on the finish make up for the wine's specious balance. **84** *—M.S. (7/1/2004)*

Medrano 2001 Malbec (Luján de Cuyo) $9. Raspberry and pie cherry aromas are at first sharp but turn earthy in time. In the mouth, it has a proper feel and expressive cherry and blackberry flavors. The finish is round, with grip and bitter chocolate notes. It goes down easy, with a dab of toasty oak flavor. **86** *—M.S. (2/1/2004)*

Medrano 2001 Syrah (Mendoza) $9. Standard black fruit and unwelcome green notes carry the nose, while an odd mix of oak and indistinct berry fruit man the palate. This wine offers body and grabby tannins, but also some pickled flavors and an unfocused structure. **84** *—M.S. (7/1/2004)*

MELIPAL

Melipal 2003 Reserve Malbec (Mendoza) $40. Driving and powerful. The nose offers balsamic notes along with piercing hints of road tar, crude oil, crushed lavender and leather. The palate is packed full of tobacco, citrus, and bright berry fruit. Not the least bit soft, with a zesty mouthfeel that toes the line between balanced and overt. Will show its best in 2006–07. **91** *—M.S. (11/15/2005)*

MICHEL TORINO

Michel Torino 2001 Cabernet Sauvignon (Cafayate) $14. Slightly weedy and green, with sour cherry and weak raspberry flavors. Finishes tight and solid, but without much flavor to back things up. **82** *—M.S. (7/1/2004)*

Michel Torino 1999 Don David Cabernet Sauvignon (Cafayate) $14. **83** *— (5/1/2002)*

Michel Torino 2000 Malbec (Cafayate) $10. **81** *—D.T. (5/1/2002)*

Michel Torino 2002 Don David Malbec (Cafayate) $14. Compact, potent, and saturated, with plenty of leather and licorice aromas along with leather. Fairly fruity, with blackberry and cherry, a hint of bitter chocolate, and buttery oak. A big red, but tasty and made for grilled meats. **87** *—M.S. (10/1/2004)*

Michel Torino 2001 Don David Malbec (Cafayate) $14. Aromas of tomato, molasses, and plum jam are bulked up by oak and earth, and the end result is a bit scrambled. In the mouth, things don't really get better; the flavors are of raspberry and sour cherry, while the finish is astringent and acidic. **83** *—M.S. (7/1/2004)*

Michel Torino 2003 Don David Torrontés (Cafayate) $14. Attractive aromas of flowers and lemon-lime kick it off, followed by cinnamon-baked apple, star anise, tarragon, and white pepper. The attitude is forward and bold, and the finish dry and long. A good Torrontés that pops on the palate. **86** *—M.S. (10/1/2004)*

Michel Torino 2000 Don David Torrontés (Cafayate) $14. **84** *—M.S. (5/1/2003)*

MIL PIEDRAS

Mil Piedras 2003 Malbec (Mendoza) $12. Raisiny, with a texture that's flat as Kansas. Finishes hard, with dull flavors. Imported by Epic Wines. **80** *—M.S. (11/15/2005)*

MJ GALLIARD

MJ Galliard 2003 Malbec (Mendoza) $20. At 14.5% alcohol, this wine is too big to have the flaws that it does. The nose is muddy, dark, and heavy, while the palate is short and bitter, with strange rubbery flavors peeking through the heavy tannins. **82** *—M.S. (7/1/2004)*

MJ Galliard 2003 Sauvignon Blanc (Mendoza) $20. Bland, with oak-driven aromas of butter and roast corn. In the mouth, there's banana, pineapple, and other sweet, ripe fruits, but to say it's traditional Sauvignon Blanc would be a stretch of great magnitude. And the alcohol, which clocks in at 14.2%, seems high. **83** *—M.S. (7/1/2004)*

ÑANDÚ

Ñandú 2004 Malbec (Mendoza) $12. Smells of coffee syrup and green beans, with fudge and gamy fruit in support. Rather cloying on the palate, with a bitter, black-pepper finish. Very hard and bordering on too tough to drink. **81** *—M.S. (11/15/2005)*

NATIVO

Nativo 2002 El Felino Malbec (Mendoza) $16. **88** *—M.S. (12/1/2003)*

NAVARRO CORREAS

Navarro Correas 2002 Colección Privada Cabernet Sauvignon (Mendoza) $11. A touch of rubber mixes with aromas of cassis and blackberry to set the stage for a juicy, fresh palate loaded with cherry and plum flavors. Nothing crazy here, just solid red wine that makes the grade at all check points. **87 Best Buy** *—M.S. (11/15/2005)*

Navarro Correas 2002 Gran Reserva Cabernet Sauvignon (Mendoza) $19. Moderately powerful, with red plum, tomato, and spicy wood to the nose. The palate registers as nondescript, with standard fruit and oak. Grabby tannins, butter, and vanilla dominate the finish. Seems more acidic and hard than ideal. **84** *—M.S. (11/15/2005)*

Navarro Correas 2001 Colección Privada Chardonnay (Mendoza) $16. **84** *—M.S. (11/1/2002)*

Navarro Correas 2003 Colección Privada Malbec (Mendoza) $10. Jammy and fresh, with hints of raspberry and rhubarb. In the mouth, it's fairly rich, with black plum and chocolate. It successfully plays both sides of the fence: It's medium-weight and not overdone, yet it packs punch and offers layers of creamy fruit. A high-water mark for this winery. **89 Best Buy** *—M.S. (3/1/2005)*

Navarro Correas 2001 Gran Reserva Altos del Rio Malbec (Mendoza) $23. **89** *—M.S. (12/1/2003)*

Navarro Correas 2000 Colección Privada Merlot (Mendoza) $16. 86 *—M.S. (11/1/2002)*

NIETO SENETINER

Nieto Senetiner 2002 Limited Edition Bonarda (Luján de Cuyo) $30. Strong and bulky, with leather, oak, and dark-fruit aromas. Starts better than it finishes. Along the way are moderately rich plum and berry fruit. A heavy whack of wood late brings it down a notch. **84** *—M.S. (10/1/2004)*

Nieto Senetiner 2000 Cadus Cabernet Sauvignon (Luján de Cuyo) $40. Saucy and woody, with nondescript yet powerful black-fruit aromas. Like the Cadus Malbec, this wine has fierce tannins that form a barrier around the body. Inside is the fruit and good stuff; outside are the tannins and a lot of nonintegrated French oak. **85** *—M.S. (10/1/2004)*

Nieto Senetiner 2004 Reserva Chardonnay (Mendoza) $10. If it seems dilute and distant up front, the palate packs more punch. There's melon, pear, and citrus rolled into an amorphous mish-mash, while the finish delivers mostly ripe melon. Runs a touch watery at the core, but with freshening acidity. **86 Best Buy** *—M.S. (7/1/2005)*

Nieto Senetiner 2001 Cadus Malbec (Mendoza) $37. Opaque purple in color, with harsh aromas of cigar ash, green beans, and pencil lead. Flavors of carob and beet are not that friendly, while the mouthfeel is rock hard; the tannins are piercing and the feel is scouring. **81** *—M.S. (11/15/2005)*

Nieto Senetiner 2000 Cadus Estiba 39 Malbec (Mendoza) $60. Inky as night, with lush, ripe aromas of berries, tree bark, cola, and all sorts of other herb-infused elixirs. The palate is totally seductive, with cherry and blackberry overflowing. Chewy and round on the finish, with lemony oak kicking in. This is a block wine from a single vineyard and it's all the way strong. **92 Editors' Choice** *—M.S. (12/31/2005)*

Nieto Senetiner 2002 Reserva Nieto Malbec (Luján de Cuyo) $10. A bit quiet on the nose, but clean and properly fruity. Black cherry, blackberry, and chocolate flavors make for a sweet, lively mouthful. Finishes both sugary and dark, almost like a dessert. **88 Best Buy** *—M.S. (10/1/2004)*

Nieto Senetiner 2002 Cadus Syrah (Mendoza) $37. Saturated, with aromas of moist earth, prune, tightly woven oak, and leather. It's not a funky, animal-driven style of Syrah; just the opposite, it's creamy and rich, with waves of chocolate and vanilla crashing alongside chunky black fruit. Seems apparent that the Nieto Senetiner winery found its stride in 2002; all its top wines are excellent. **91 Editors' Choice** *—M.S. (12/31/2005)*

NORTON

Norton 2002 Cabernet Sauvignon (Mendoza) $8. A bit light, but it shows snap and spice. Has a mild streak of vegetal green, yet the feel is rich enough and the balance good enough to help it hold its own. **84** *—M.S. (7/1/2004)*

Norton 2002 Malbec (Mendoza) $8. Blackberry and raisins on the nose, and then a round, sweet palate that's nice and slightly smoky. Pretty good Malbec, especially for the price, and rather tasty. **86** *—M.S. (7/1/2004)*

Norton 2002 Reserve Malbec (Mendoza) $16. Norton has hit a home run with this Malbec, one of the best wines we've ever tried from the bodega. Aged in all new French oak, the wine is pure, deep, and sweet, with ample spice and chocolate rounding out the body. A big wine with balance and pizzazz. **90** *—M.S. (7/1/2004)*

Norton 2002 La Privada Red Blend (Mendoza) $20. Norton's proprietary house blend features a sensuous mix of Cabernet, Merlot, and Malbec, all from the scintillating '02 harvest. This is one of the best wines Norton has made in ages, if not in its history. Tobacco, tar, and chocolate aromas accent the deep, saturated bouquet. And the flavors and feel are pure New World in that ripeness and drinkability take precedence over complexity. **91 Editors' Choice** *—M.S. (7/1/2004)*

Norton 2002 Sangiovese (Mendoza) $8. Expunge all ideas of conventional Chianti and then you can get after the sweet cherry fruit and the soft, chewy palate that come with this Argentine Sangiovese. Totally New World, with moderate depth and a weak finish. **85** *—M.S. (7/1/2004)*

Norton 2003 Sauvignon Blanc (Mendoza) $8. Grapefruit aromas precede a surprisingly plump, full body and then an avalanche of tropical fruit flavors. Shows enough true SB character to earn a recommendation, but it's a bit chunkier than most in this range. **85** *—M.S. (7/1/2004)*

Norton 2003 Torrontés (Mendoza) $8. Smells like it should, with light, exotic lychee aromas as well as notes of wildflower. In the mouth, it's a bit more meaty and a touch less zesty than ideal, and it finishes soft. But along the way it's tasty and would match well with take-out Chinese food. **85** *—M.S. (7/1/2004)*

O. FOURNIER

O. Fournier 2002 B Crux Red Blend (Mendoza) $21. Intense and saucy, with strong aromatic hints of barbecued meat, marinade, and crushed red pepper. Deeper down there's cherry and baked plum flavors. Smooth but just racy enough, with excellent acid-tannin balance. Finishes with vanilla, pepper, and fresh tomato. It's 60% Tempranillo, 20% Malbec, and 20% Merlot. **89** *—M.S. (7/1/2005)*

PASCUAL TOSO

Pascual Toso 2002 Reserve Malbec (Mendoza) $18. Fairly round and inviting, but with a leafiness that brings total ripeness into question. Flavors of blueberry and plums are textbook Malbec, while the lasting, fruity finish is deep and features a hint or two of spice and chocolate. **86** *—M.S. (7/1/2004)*

PIATTELLI

Piattelli 2001 Cabernet Sauvignon (Mendoza) $15. Despite the cheesy note to the nose, the rest of this wine is rock solid. The bouquet features solid oak cloaking berry fruit, while on the palate you'll find cherry, cassis, and licorice. With its soft, simple finish along with bits of chocolate and vanilla, it's a nice Cabernet. From the Tupungato subregion. **87** *—M.S. (7/1/2004)*

PRELUDIO

Preludio 2003 Tempranillo (Mendoza) $14. Rustic and bulky, but not without its merits. The bouquet begins with sweet maple syrup aromas that set the stage for cassis and black plum flavors. It's a touch stewy and chocolaty, but the earthy tannins manage to add edge and teeth. **85** *—M.S. (11/15/2005)*

PULMARY

Pulmary 2004 Donaria Malbec (Mendoza) $20. A touch lean and green, with hints of rhubarb and burning brush. Raspberry and strawberry flavors are dominant, but there's a hole in the middle of the palate that renders the mouthfeel somewhat hollow. Finishes top-heavy, with a sweet superficiality. **83** *—M.S. (12/31/2005)*

QUARA

Quara 2004 Malbec (Cafayate) $9. Damp and murky, with aromas of burnt toast and flavors of beets and raspberry. The feel is round and lactic, with unfocused grapy fruit. **82** *—M.S. (11/15/2005)*

Quara 2004 Torrontés (Cafayate) $9. Floral and fresh, with some blossom and honey aromas. Rather plump and soft, but with enough acidity to keep the feel solid. Flavors of banana, papaya, citrus, and stone fruit are fresh and tasty. Proves that Cafayate is the prime region for Torrontés. **85 Best Buy** *—M.S. (12/31/2005)*

RICARDO SANTOS

Ricardo Santos 2003 La Madras Vineyard Malbec (Mendoza) $18. Far more lean and raw than expected, with an overriding green tobacco note to the nose. Grassy on the palate, with raspberry and a bit of rhubarb. Finishes sweety and jammy, with some protruding tannins. Not a bad wine but disappointing compared to the previous vintage. **84** *—M.S. (12/31/2005)*

RINCON PRIVADO

Rincon Privado 1996 Special Reserve Cabernet Sauvignon (San Rafael) $20. **83** *—M.S. (5/1/2003)*

Rincon Privado 1999 Merlot (San Rafael) $11. **84** *—M.S. (5/1/2003)*

ROMANCE

Romance 2002 Red Blend (Mendoza) $8. A concept wine aimed at capitalizing on Argentina's reputation as a romantic, tango-loving country. The blend of Bonarda, Malbec, and Cabernet is out of the ordinary, with strange, ultrasweet flavors that turn sour upon deeper inspection. **82** *—M.S. (7/1/2004)*

ROSELL BOHER

Rosell Boher 1999 Grande Cuvée Millésimée (Argentina) $40. A little bit amber as it shows off nice Pinot Noir color. Quite yeasty, toasty, and stylish. A pleasant surprise from Argentina; this bubbly shows style and polish. The palate is bodied, with spicy peach and light berry flavors. Peppery and long, with a plump, laudable mouthfeel. **89 Editors' Choice** *—M.S. (12/31/2004)*

SALENTEIN

Salentein 2001 Cabernet Sauvignon (Mendoza) $18. **91** *—S.H. (1/1/2002)*

Salentein 2003 El Portillo Chardonnay (Mendoza) $9. Creamy yet dry on the nose, with a dusty overall bouquet and not too much fruit. The fruit on the palate is sweet but nondescript. Possibly too acidic as well. **84** *—M.S. (7/1/2004)*

Salentein 2002 Malbec (Mendoza) $18. Better than the '01, but still acidic and tannic. That said, it does offer attractive coffee and coconut aromas, and also interplay between cocoa and plum. The flavor mix is mostly complete, and there's some nice spice to the finish. **86** *—M.S. (7/1/2004)*

Salentein 2001 Malbec (Mendoza) $18. **91** *—S.H. (1/1/2002)*

Salentein 2001 Finca el Portillo Malbec (Uco Valley) $9. **87 Best Buy** *—M.S. (12/1/2003)*

Salentein 2001 Merlot (Mendoza) $19. Quite nice, with heavy, masculine aromas of leather and charcoal spicing up the dark berry fruit that's on display. Round in the mouth, with cherry and raspberry flavors preceding a chewy, chocolaty finish. Spreads out nicely from front to back. **88** *—M.S. (7/1/2004)*

Salentein 2003 Finca el Portillo Sauvignon Blanc (Mendoza) $9. The nose is slightly more vegetal than ideal, but in the mouth there is both good acids and body. Flavors of baked apples and dried mangoes seem sweet, and that's because residual sugar is present. **85** *—M.S. (7/1/2004)*

Salentein 2002 Syrah (Mendoza) $18. Jammy and saturated, with ripe plum, berry, and tar aromas. It's fairly sweet and hedonistic in the mouth, but with enough pulsing acidity to keep things in balance. Smoky, racy, and juicy on the back palate; this is one of the better Salentein wines we've tried lately. **88** *—M.S. (3/1/2005)*

SAN HUBERTO

San Huberto 2002 Bonarda (Aminga Valley) $7. Open and light, with raspberry and foresty aromas. Very lean on the palate. Shows red raspberry and pepper flavors in front of an innocuous, flyweight finish. A thin wine that manages to taste decent. **82** *—M.S. (10/1/2004)*

San Huberto 2002 Chardonnay (Aminga Valley) $8. Light pear, pineapple, and honey aromas don't hold up to much airing or swirling. In the mouth, it's all citrus, largely lemon and orange. Finishes perky and zesty, but without much focus. Hails from La Rioja. **83** *—M.S. (10/1/2004)*

San Huberto 1997 Malbec (Argentina) $9. 82 *—J.C. (5/1/2002)*

San Huberto 2002 Torrontés (Aminga Valley) $7. Pungent, with aromas of green herbs, litchi fruit, and green melon. Starts better than it finishes, and along the way you'll find moderate peach and melon flavors riding on a competent palate. **84** *—M.S. (10/1/2004)*

SAN POLO

San Polo 2004 Auka Merlot (San Carlos) $15. Simple red-fruit aromas are okay but fail to register above that. The palate is tasty enough, with sweet plum and blackberry flavors. Creamy on the finish, yet a bit candied and cloying. Improves with airing. **84** *—M.S. (12/31/2005)*

SAN TELMO

San Telmo 2000 Cabernet Sauvignon (Mendoza) $10. 82 *—C.S. (5/1/2002)*

San Telmo 2000 Chardonnay (Mendoza) $10. 82 *—M.S. (11/15/2001)*

San Telmo 2003 Malbec (Mendoza) $7. Jammy, sweet, and leathery on the nose, with a kick of sourness. The palate is common, with medium red fruit that's strawberry-raspberry in style. Adequate on the palate, and generally satisfying. **84 Best Buy** *—M.S. (3/1/2005)*

San Telmo 2003 Shiraz (Mendoza) $7. A bit rubbery and raw, but with a hearty backbone. The nose deals plum and black cherry along with some smoky wet leather, while the palate is grapey with a touch of blueberry. Finishes clean and simple. **86 Best Buy** *—M.S. (3/1/2005)*

SANTA JULIA

Santa Julia 2001 Cabernet Sauvignon (Mendoza) $8. 84 *—M.S. (5/1/2003)*

Santa Julia 1996 Oak Reserva Malbec Cabernet Sauvignon (Mendoza) $10. 87 Best Buy *—M.S. (5/1/2000)*

Santa Julia 2000 Reserva Cabernet Sauvignon (Mendoza) $11. 86 *(12/15/2001)*

Santa Julia 2002 Chardonnay (Mendoza) $9. Creamy and sweet up front, with some butterscotch on the nose. Pear and papaya flavors are tropical and sweet, and the melony finish is warm and satisfying. Quite fruity and fun to drink. **85** *—M.S. (2/1/2004)*

Santa Julia 2000 Chardonnay (Mendoza) $7. 84 Best Buy *—M.S. (11/15/2001)*

Santa Julia 2000 Reserva Chardonnay (Mendoza) $9. 85 *(12/15/2001)*

Santa Julia 2001 Malbec (Mendoza) $9. 87 Best Buy *—M.S. (5/1/2003)*

Santa Julia 2002 Reserva Malbec (Mendoza) $10. 86 *—M.S. (12/1/2003)*

Santa Julia 1999 Reserva Malbec (Mendoza) $10. 84 *—M.S. (11/15/2001)*

Santa Julia 2001 Santa Julia Merlot (Mendoza) $8. 85 *—M.S. (5/1/2003)*

Santa Julia 2001 Santa Julia Red Blend (Mendoza) $9. 83 *—M.S. (5/1/2003)*

Santa Julia 2002 Torrontés (Argentina) $8. 85 *—M.S. (11/15/2003)*

Santa Julia 2000 Torrontés (Mendoza) $7. 87 Best Buy *(12/15/2001)*

Santa Julia 2000 Tardio Torrontés (Mendoza) $10. 85 Best Buy *—M.S. (11/15/2001)*

Santa Julia 2002 Viognier (Mendoza) $8. 85 *—M.S. (5/1/2003)*

SEPTIMA

Septima 2003 Cabernet Sauvignon (Mendoza) $8. Funky on the nose, with aromas of cream cheese, green bean, and red fruit. Beets and cherries carry the palate to a cloying, immensely sugary palate. Struggles as Cabernet. **81** *—M.S. (3/1/2005)*

Septima 2002 Reserva Cabernet Sauvignon-Malbec (Mendoza) $14. This Cab-Malbec mix starts with sweet, syrupy aromas that grow more masculine with airing, with violet and rose petal scents along with some oak-driven caramel. The palate is round and sizable, with chocolate and plum flavors. Finishes meaty and chunky. From a newer winery owned by Codorníu of Spain. **88** *—M.S. (11/15/2004)*

Septima 2002 Malbec (Mendoza) $9. 88 Best Buy *—M.S. (12/1/2003)*

SORBUS

Sorbus 2004 Malbec (Mendoza) $8. Clean and in your face, with touches of mint and leather to the cherry-dominate bouquet. Good in the mouth, with a nice feel, moderate but noticeable tannins and fresh plum, berry and integrated oak flavors. Competent and lengthy on the finish. **86 Best Buy** *—M.S. (12/31/2005)*

SUSANA BALBO

Susana Balbo 2001 Malbec (Mendoza) $27. 89 *—M.S. (12/1/2003)*

TANGO

Tango 2002 Cabernet Sauvignon (Mendoza) $9. Rubbery on the nose, with bold lactic aromas along with spice and red fruit. The sketchy palate reveals cherry and chocolate, and those flavors come with a kick. Fairly aggressive given the depth of fruit and polish. **84** *—M.S. (11/15/2004)*

Tango 2002 Chardonnay (Mendoza) $9. A little old by now, but the smooth, light aromas convey additional life and freshness. The palate mixes citrus and apple, while there's some white-pepper spice on the finish. Fairly full, but low-acid. **84** *—M.S. (3/1/2005)*

Tango 2001 Malbec (Mendoza) $10. **83** *—M.S. (12/1/2003)*

Tango 2002 Merlot (Mendoza) $9. Quite funky at first, with initial cotton-candy aromas that mix in hints of leather and light red fruit. Things find a more even keel aided by time in the glass, and finally it ends softly. Not much stuffing, but not bad. **85 Best Buy** *—M.S. (11/15/2004)*

TANGO SUR

Tango Sur 2003 Cabernet Sauvignon (Mendoza) $8. Raisiny and fat, not exactly the most welcoming notes. Tastes overripe and sugary, with a finish too much like sherry. **80** *—M.S. (3/1/2005)*

Tango Sur 2003 Malbec (Mendoza) $8. Ripe and heavy on the nose, with hints of stewed plum, berries, and chocolate. More chunky prune and plum follows in the mouth. Entirely drinkable but not refined. **83** *—M.S. (3/1/2005)*

Tango Sur 2003 Tempranillo (Mendoza) $8. Clean and medium weight, with simple red-fruit and cherry-cola aromas. Forward plum and berry carry the palate, which spreads out with no frills over the finish. Somewhat smoky and burnt on the aftertaste, but still pretty good mainstream stuff. **85 Best Buy** *—M.S. (3/1/2005)*

TAPIZ

Tapiz 1999 Cabernet Sauvignon (Mendoza) $8. **85 Best Buy** *—M.S. (11/15/2001)*

Tapiz 2000 Chardonnay (Mendoza) $8. **84** *—S.H. (7/1/2002)*

Tapiz 2002 Malbec (Mendoza) $8. Deep purple in hue, with saturated dark-fruit aromas along with pinches of cola and creamy oak. Fairly concentrated for a wine of this stature; for less than $10 you get vanilla and chocolate accents atop youthful, bouncy blackberry. The mouthfeel is plump, and there's a toasted coconut flavor on the finish. **87 Best Buy** *—M.S. (2/1/2004)*

Tapiz 2000 Malbec (Mendoza) $8. **85** *—M.S. (11/1/2002)*

Tapiz 2001 Merlot (Mendoza) $8. **84** *—S.H. (1/1/2002)*

TEKIAH

Tekiah 2003 Syrah (Argentina) $11. Scents of dull plum give way to brighter, more candied fruit and a dose of caramel. Medium in body, finishing on a note of slightly bitter dark chocolate. **84** *—J.C. (4/1/2005)*

TERRA ROSA

Terra Rosa 2002 Cabernet Sauvignon (Mendoza) $10. Hard on the nose, with cracked pepper and rubber. Once it opens, you get spicy plum, cherry, and meaty tannins. Finishes with overt wood notes and some sweet and sour. Spicy and unconventional, but not bad. **85** *—M.S. (10/1/2004)*

TERRAZAS DE LOS ANDES

Terrazas de Los Andes 2004 Cabernet Sauvignon (Mendoza) $12. Dark and chewy, with cassis, blackberry, and a slight hint of green to the nose. A solid red made for early consumption, this Cab has soft tannins, lots of oak-based vanilla and an easygoing personality. **86** *(5/1/2005)*

Terrazas de Los Andes 2002 Alto Cabernet Sauvignon (Mendoza) $9. Rubbery, smoky aromas to the cranberry and blueberry fruit. Tastes sweet and ripe, with ample cherry and blackberry notes. A tight finish with coffee notes and big tannins render it substantive. **85** *—M.S. (2/1/2004)*

Terrazas de Los Andes 2003 Reserva Cabernet Sauvignon (Mendoza) $16. Big and sassy, with smoky aromas of barbecued meat, baked dark fruits, eucalyptus, and leather. In the mouth, it's more sweet than subdued, with cassis, blackberry and hints of chocolate. Very much in the modern style, with a plush feel and the aftertaste of coffee meeting cola. **90** *(5/1/2005)*

Terrazas de Los Andes 2001 Reserva Cabernet Sauvignon (Mendoza) $15. Somewhat restrained and dark to the nose, but within there's buried sweet fruit, leather, and pepper. The mouthfeel is round, with only modest tannins making themselves felt. Finishes roasty and spicy, with proper balance and overall integration. **87** *—M.S. (7/1/2004)*

Terrazas de Los Andes 1999 Reserva Cabernet Sauvignon (Mendoza) $17. **87** *—C.S. (5/1/2002)*

Terrazas de Los Andes 2004 Chardonnay (Mendoza) $12. Lemon, cream and toasty aromas are backed by flavors of melon, pineapple, and banana. A typical but simple New World Chard: meaning it's a blend of sweet fruit, light oak, and modest acidity. **85** *(5/1/2005)*

Terrazas de Los Andes 2000 Alto Chardonnay (Mendoza) $8. **83** *—M.S. (7/1/2002)*

Terrazas de Los Andes 2002 Reserva Chardonnay (Mendoza) $15. From Tupungato, this is a very good Chardonnay that offers aromas of pear, vanilla, and toasted bread. It's almost Burgundian in style, with almond and white pepper accenting apple and mild citrus. Would be a good choice with fish or fowl. **89** *—M.S. (7/1/2004)*

Terrazas de Los Andes 2004 Malbec (Mendoza) $12. Aggressive and a tad bit rough, but it's still young. Time should soften it up, and what will then be waiting is a ton of rugged black fruit, some creamy oak, and a whole lot of vanilla and carob. Made for the masses; loaded with power. **86** *(5/1/2005)*

Terrazas de Los Andes 2002 Alto Malbec (Mendoza) $8. **85 Best Buy** *—M.S. (12/1/2003)*

Terrazas de Los Andes 2003 Reserva Malbec (Mendoza) $16. Lots of color and intensity. The bouquet blasts with heavy-metal blackberry and blueberry aromas, while the palate is rich and soft, yet structured enough to avoid mushiness. That said, this is a ripe, beefy red, exactly the type of jammy, fruity Malbec that has helped solidify Argentina's name. **89** *(5/1/2005)*

ARGENTINA

Terrazas de Los Andes 2000 Reserva Malbec (Mendoza) $17. 87 —*M.S. (5/1/2003)*

TRAPICHE

Trapiche 2003 Cabernet Sauvignon (Mendoza) $7. Dense and heavy, with dull black fruit that falls apart with time. Basic raspberry and vanilla flavors lead the way to a thick, creamy finish that shows little life. Flat and lacking complexity, with a strange aftertaste. **82** —*M.S. (7/1/2004)*

Trapiche 2003 Medalla Cabernet Sauvignon (Mendoza) $25. Sawdust and mint smother the oaky nose, while the palate pushes dark fruit and even more resiny wood. Clearly the intent was to offer a barrique-style wine, but the result, while not bad, doesn't really click. What you get is coffee, vanilla and resin but not a lot of fruit. **84** —*M.S. (12/31/2005)*

Trapiche 2003 Oak Cask Cabernet Sauvignon (Mendoza) $10. Lightly but properly oaked, with strong, likable hints of mocha, coffee, and mint. It's a textbook New World, bargain-priced Cab, with plum and cassis flavors that are fresh and easy. Shows good structure, tannin and ripeness, with yet more finishing oak. A quintessential by-the-glass pour. **86 Best Buy** —*M.S. (12/31/2005)*

Trapiche 2000 Oak Cask Cabernet Sauvignon (Mendoza) $9. 87 Best Buy —*M.S. (5/1/2003)*

Trapiche 2001 Oak Cask Chardonnay (Mendoza) $9. 84 —*M.S. (5/1/2003)*

Trapiche 1999 Malbec (Mendoza) $10. 83 —*D.T. (5/1/2002)*

Trapiche 2001 Oak Cask Malbec (Mendoza) $10. 87 —*M.S. (12/1/2003)*

Trapiche 2002 Merlot (Mendoza) $7. 84 —*M.S. (5/1/2003)*

Trapiche 1999 Iscay Red Blend (Mendoza) $50. 87 —*C.S. (5/1/2002)*

TRIVENTO

Trivento 2002 Golden Reserve Malbec (Mendoza) $20. Concha y Toro's Argentinean branch makes this heavyweight wine, which goes heavy on the oak, toast and horseradish. It's opaque in color, with monster tannins backing plum and blackberry fruit. Finishes hot, peppery and short, but with a lot of texture. **87** —*M.S. (3/1/2005)*

TRUMPETER

Trumpeter 2002 Cabernet Sauvignon (Mendoza) $9. More oak than balance, and the fruit seems tart. Grippy tannins and racy acids create a tougher than usual mouthfeel, and overall the flavors just aren't that exciting. Good enough, but better to stick with the Malbec. **84** —*M.S. (7/1/2004)*

Trumpeter 2002 Chardonnay (Mendoza) $9. Fresh and forward, with full tropical fruit aromas accented by some oak. Flavors of pineapple, mango, and vanilla work because there's some crisp acidity pushing it all while not allowing it to feel heavy. **85** —*M.S. (7/1/2004)*

Trumpeter 2000 Tupungato Chardonnay (Argentina) $12. 85 —*M.S. (7/1/2002)*

Trumpeter 2002 Malbec (Mendoza) $9. Deep berry fruit, sweet perfume, and beyond average complexity. From an excellent vintage, it offers violets on the nose and a sweet, rich body. A no-brainer among under-$10 reds. **87 Best Buy** —*M.S. (7/1/2004)*

Trumpeter 2003 Malbec-Syrah (Mendoza) $9. From cooler Tupungato, this blend seems marinated on the nose, with rubbery accents to the dark fruit. The bulky palate spills over with raspberry and plum, while the finish is mildly acidic. Nonetheless it's a full-force red with plenty of fuel in the tank. **85 Best Buy** —*M.S. (3/1/2005)*

Trumpeter 2003 Merlot (Mendoza) $9. The bouquet is downright saucy, with molasses, brown sugar, and leather aromas. Standard plum and berry make for an average palate, while modest coffee and spice carry the finish. Generally good, but fails to make an impression. **84** —*M.S. (3/1/2005)*

Trumpeter 2000 Merlot (Tupungato) $12. 86 Best Buy —*M.S. (11/1/2002)*

Trumpeter 2000 Syrah (Luján de Cuyo) $12. 85 —*M.S. (11/1/2002)*

VALENTIN BIANCHI

Valentin Bianchi 2001 Elsa Barbera (San Rafael) $8. 82 —*M.S. (5/1/2003)*

Valentin Bianchi 2002 Cabernet Sauvignon (San Rafael) $18. Shows full plum and blackberry aromas, but not necessarily textbook Cabernet aromas. It's pretty soft and chunky across the tongue, leaving a creamy sensation. Has some oak, but it's not a huge factor. Finishes blunt. **87** —*M.S. (7/1/2004)*

Valentin Bianchi 1999 Cabernet Sauvignon (Mendoza) $14. 87 —*M.S. (11/1/2002)*

Valentin Bianchi 2000 Enzo Bianchi Gran Cru Cabernet Sauvignon (San Rafael) $53. It's 86% Cabernet with some Malbec and Merlot, and the fruit is of the masculine, sturdy stock. The nose offers dusty red fruit, oak, leather, and earth. In the mouth, a core of cherry and cassis is surrounded by spice. It's almost elegant but not quite; it's bigger than that, but neither heavy nor overripe. **89** —*M.S. (7/1/2004)*

Valentin Bianchi 2002 Famiglia Bianchi Cabernet Sauvignon (San Rafael) $18. Shows a touch of heat to the fully ripe flavors of plum and blackberry, but otherwise shines, with the emphasis on fruit rather than oak. Picks up some leafy notes on the finish. **88** *(10/1/2004)*

Valentin Bianchi 1997 Particular Proprietor's Reserve Cabernet Sauvignon (San Rafael) $28. 84 —*M.S. (5/1/2003)*

Valentin Bianchi 2000 Chardonnay (San Rafael) $15. 87 —*M.S. (7/1/2002)*

Valentin Bianchi 2003 Famiglia Bianchi Chardonnay (San Rafael) $18. 85 *(10/1/2004)*

Valentin Bianchi 2002 Malbec (San Rafael) $18. Clean and a tad bit earthy, but sort of thin and simple. Among grapey reds that are quaffable and not offensive, this can lead the list. **84** —*M.S. (7/1/2004)*

Valentin Bianchi 1999 Malbec (Mendoza) $13. 89 Best Buy —*M.S. (11/1/2002)*

Valentin Bianchi 2003 Elsa Malbec (San Rafael) $9. A bit soft and simple, but fine as an everyday quaffer. Plum and blackberry fruit is front and center, accented by hints of chocolate, leather, and spice. **84** *(10/1/2004)*

Valentin Bianchi 2003 Famiglia Bianchi Malbec (San Rafael) $18. A lot of funk on the nose, with strong but passing aromas of clam shell and cleanser. Better in the mouth, where grapy fruit takes over. Very extracted, with coffee and vanilla on the full-weight finish. **83** —*M.S. (11/15/2005)*

Valentin Bianchi 2003 Particular Malbec (San Rafael) $30. A big, ripe, saturated offering, the type of wine most red-wine enthusiasts want, and also the type of wine that has earned Argentina its reputation for making serious Malbec. The color is purple, the bouquet rubbery and smoky. The palate is dynamite; the black-fruit flavors are superb and the coffee and dark chocolate nuances just right. A stud of a wine that could use about a year in bottle to reach its peak. **91 Editors' Choice** —*M.S. (7/1/2005)*

Valentin Bianchi 2003 Particular Merlot (Mendoza) $30. Potent and layered, as it begins with sharp, spicy aromas before opening to show deeper black fruit. Saturated plum and blackberry flavors are touched up by a certain saucy spiciness, while the resonating mouthfeel is beefy and rich. This is serious Argentinean Merlot, yet it doesn't quite register as great. **88** —*M.S. (11/15/2005)*

Valentin Bianchi 2003 Sauvignon Blanc (San Rafael) $18. Light in color, with equally light pear and cream notes to the nose. Californian Bob Pepi consults on this wine, which shows flavors of fresh lettuce, honey, citrus, and stones. Not bad, but a tad sour. **85** —*M.S. (7/1/2004)*

Valentin Bianchi 2004 Famiglia Bianchi Sauvignon Blanc (San Rafael) $15. Nice as a total package, with pear, citrus and mineral aromas. Tangy and fresh on the palate, with grab and medium-strength citrus and melon flavors. Zesty and long, yet ultimately it settles at fresh and simple. **84** —*M.S. (11/15/2005)*

Valentin Bianchi 2003 Elsa White Blend (San Rafael) $9. Totally fresh and likable, with apple aromas and flavors as well as an easygoing attitude. Fairly neutral as whites go, but good for salads and Asian foods. **83** —*M.S. (7/1/2004)*

VIÑA COBOS

Vina Cobos 1999 Malbec (Mendoza) $65. 92 Cellar Selection —*M.S. (11/1/2002)*

Viña Cobos 2002 Cobos Malbec (Mendoza) $60. This ultra extracted, inky Malbec comes from a partnership that includes Paul Hobbs, and while you cannot argue with the wine's density, purity, and power, it probably isn't for everyone. With 14.8% alcohol, a ton of color, and loads of clove-packed oak, it's giant. Perhaps you wish it less aggressive and more approachable. Or maybe you outright love it, like we did. Regardless, it needs three years of bottle age, that or several hours of air if you plan to drink it now. **93 Editors' Choice** —M.S. (3/1/2005)

Viña Cornejo Costas 2003 Don Rodolfo Malbec (Cafayate) $10. Pickle and sauerkraut notes mix with raisins and leather on the nose. It maintains that funky, pickled flavor throughout. Along the way there's red-berry fruit and some heat-bearing spice. Unconventional and strange, but acceptable. **82** —*M.S. (11/15/2004)*

Viña Cornejo Costas 2002 Don Rodolfo Tannat (Cafayate) $10. Candied and sweet on the nose, but sour on the tongue. Simply put, it's astringent, lean, and acidic, all common traits of this hard-to-master grape more frequently found in Uruguay. **81** —*M.S. (3/1/2005)*

VINITERRA

Viniterra 1999 Luján de Cuyo Malbec (Mendoza) $15. 90 Best Buy —*M.S. (5/1/2003)*

WEINERT

Weinert 2002 Weinert Carrascal Bordeaux Blend (Mendoza) $13. Leathery and reserved, with aromas of wet earth, black pepper, jalapeños, and bell pepper. And while that may sound unripe to you, in the mouth, the wine deals snappy red fruit and bona fide ripeness. Yes, it's a touch tight in terms of feel, but for a real taste of old-style South American wine, this is it. **87** —*M.S. (7/1/2005)*

XUMEK

Xumek 2003 Sol Huarpe Malbec (San Juan) $18. Dark in color and rich on the nose, with marzipan, blackberry, and a touch of leather. This is a powerful, modern-style Malbec with exciting, deep fruit and several layers of depth. Mildly syrupy in the middle, but not the least bit out of whack. Hails from the warm, somewhat northern San Juan zone. **90 Editors' Choice** —*M.S. (12/31/2005)*

YACOCHUYA

Yacochuya 2000 Malbec (Cafayate) $48. 93 —*M.S. (12/1/2003)*

ZOLO

Zolo 2003 Chardonnay (Mendoza) $14. Heavy and flat, with bulky butterscotch and ultraripe peach aromas. Starts better than it finishes; the initial citrus and melon flavors show some pop, but airing turns it mealy. **82** —*M.S. (11/15/2005)*

Zolo 2003 Merlot (Mendoza) $14. Fresh and alert, with snappy red raspberry and pie cherry flavors. Seems almost citrusy due to perky acids, while outsized tannins make sure there's length to the finish. **84** —*M.S. (11/15/2005)*

Australia

Although Philip Schaffer was the first to plant a successful vineyard in Australia in 1791, it was not until the mid-nineteenth century that grape growing and viticulture was more widespread throughout South Australia, Victoria, and New South Wales. In the 1880s, however, phylloxera (see Glossary) spread through Victoria and New South Wales. South Australia's very stringent (and still existent) quarantine policy spared its vines from the louse and, to this day, the state is the seat of Australia's wine production.

Zinfandel vines of Cape Mentelle, Margaret River, Western Australia.

It's only been during the past twenty or so years that Australia has become known on the world stage as a premium wine-producing nation. It is now home to about 1,800 wineries and is the fourth-largest wine-exporting country (behind France, Italy, and Spain), with export sales topping $2.7 billion in 2004. The country's biggest export markets are the United States and the United Kingdom, though Australian wine is exported to over one hundred countries.

Australia is vast; at over 7.6 million square kilometers, it is roughly the size of the continental United States, but is home to only about 15 percent of America's population. In spite of its size, many wine drinkers outside Australia have it in their heads that Oz wines all taste the same. To characterize them all as broad-shouldered, plum- and berry-flavored, well-oaked wines that are high in alcohol is as short-sighted as saying that all Americans—from the Bronx to Alabama—have the same accent. With that in mind, here's a broad overview of some of the country's best-known winemaking regions, or Geographical Indications (GIs), and the wines for which each region is best known.

The general area around Perth, in the southwestern corner of Western Australia, is home to some of the country's most coveted, premium-quality wines. The Margaret River GI is the most renowned of the GIs in Western Australia. The region's maritime climate yields structured, age-worthy Cabernet Sauvignons, and some of the country's best Chardonnays. Semillon and Sauvignon Blanc blends are successful here, too.

In South Australia, where most of Australia's wine is produced, most GIs are located within a drive of the port city of Adelaide. It is in this state that Shiraz flourishes—just about every winery makes one.

Clare Valley, home of Australia's best Riesling (all of which is sealed with a screwcap), is located about eighty-five miles north of Adelaide. It has an altitude of 400 to 500 meters above sea level, and benefits from cool evening breezes and warm summers. Barossa Valley, just southwest of Clare, is hot, dry, and flat, with summertime temperatures that can top 100 degrees Fahrenheit. Most of Australia's flagship Shirazes come from Barossa Valley. The wines are generally big and broad, with luscious, extracted plum and berry fruit. Grenache and Cabernet Sauvignon, too, are very good here. Eden Valley, just south of Barossa, succeeds with both reds and whites, but you'll find that its Rieslings, Chardonnays, and Viogniers are among the country's best.

Directly south of Adelaide are McLaren Vale and, to its east, the Adelaide Hills. Like Barossa Valley, McLaren Vale also specializes in Shiraz and Grenache (and to a lesser degree, Cabernet). The Vale's microclimates are varied—some areas are flat and hot, others cooler, yielding wines from one GI that can taste very different. Most McLaren Vale reds, though, are lush in the mid-palate, often with a silky, chalky feel. The Adelaide Hills, at an altitude of about 400 meters above sea level, specializes in wines that thrive in cooler climates: Sauvignon Blanc, Chardonnay, Pinot Noir, Riesling, and other aromatic whites. Other reds can thrive in the region's warmest sites. Coonawarra, even farther south from Adelaide, is famed for its terra rossa soils, from which yield long-lived Cabernet Sauvignon.

Though there are a number of winegrowing regions in the state of Victoria, the best known is the Yarra Valley, from whence come some very good Chardonnays and Pinot Noirs. Wines from this region are often delicate and understated, rather than powerful, which again proves just how broad the spectrum is on Australia's wine styles. Rutherglen, in northeastern Victoria, is home to the country's (and really, some of the world's) most renowned fortified Muscats. Tasmania, the island just south of Victoria, is home to some of Australia's coolest grape-growing sites. As such, Riesling, Chardonnay, and Pinot Noir thrive here; production of sparkling wines containing the latter two grapes is also a specialty.

Just north of Sydney in New South Wales lies the Hunter Valley, an area with hot temperatures moderated by mild maritime breezes, and rain in the months leading up to harvest. This is Semillon country; the region's famed white wine is known for its long aging potential. Shiraz and Chardonnay are also very good here.

3 HILLS HIGH

3 Hills High 2001 Cabernet Sauvignon (South Australia) $20. Right out of the gate, this Cab is very fragrant, like blackberries and cinnamon, and turns nutty, almost Porty, the longer it sits in the glass. The palate, on the other hand, takes a while to come around. Straightaway, the palate is a little dumb, but with time it opens nicely, turning out fine plum flavors framed in oak and nutshells. Wooly tannins come through on the finish. **87** *—D.T. (12/31/2005)*

3 Hills High 2004 Sauvignon Blanc (Adelaide Hills) $18. A Sauvignon with a lot of heart, if not a lot of complexity. Offers citrus and tropical fruit edged with minerals; a good, everyday wine. **86** *—D.T. (12/1/2005)*

ABBEY ROCK

Abbey Rock 2000 Cabernet Sauvignon-Merlot (South Eastern Australia) $10. 86 Best Buy *—M.S. (12/15/2002)*

Abbey Rock 2001 Shiraz (South Eastern Australia) $10. 85 *—K.F. (3/1/2003)*

ABBEY VALE

Abbey Vale 2004 Vat 351 Chardonnay (Margaret River) $9. So light in color, it's almost clear. Talc-powder aromas waft from the nose; on the palate, delicate yellow fruit is accented by floral notes. It's very unusual to find Margaret River wines at this price, so grab it up. **87 Best Buy** *—D.T. (5/1/2005)*

Abbey Vale 2000 Verdelho (Margaret River) $14. 83 *—D.T. (9/1/2001)*

ALDINGA BAY

Aldinga Bay 2001 Sangiovese (McLaren Vale) $19. Brown sugar and molasses coat generic red fruit on the palate—you'd never peg this as Sangiovese (but then, who would ever guess Australian Sangiovese?). Starts off with marshmallow on the nose, and finishes with juicy, lipsmacking fruit. **85** *—D.T. (5/1/2004)*

ALICE WHITE

Alice White 2001 Cabernet Sauvignon (South Eastern Australia) $8. 84 *—C.S. (6/1/2002)*

Alice White 1999 Cabernet Sauvignon (South Eastern Australia) $7. 84 *(6/1/2001)*

Alice White 2000 Cabernet Sauvignon-Shiraz (South Eastern Australia) $7. 87 Best Buy *—M.N. (6/1/2001)*

Alice White 2002 Chardonnay (South Eastern Australia) $8. 86 Best Buy *—D.T. (8/1/2003)*

Alice White 2003 Merlot (South Eastern Australia) $7. Big, big fruit, a total blast of blackberry jam and subtler layerings of cherries, briary berries, and milk chocolate. It's a lip-smackingly tasty wine, quite dry, with a bright burst of acidity, and a great value from Down Under. **85** *—S.H. (9/1/2004)*

Alice White 2004 Semillon-Chardonnay (South Eastern Australia) $7. This white's aromas are quite nice and feminine, but the palate disappoints. Vague yellow fruit and chalk flavors are dilute and over before it starts. If the flavors showed the promise that the nose showed, it would have been a much better wine. **82** *—D.T. (3/1/2005)*

Alice White 2001 Shiraz (South Eastern Australia) $8. 86 Best Buy *—K.F. (3/1/2003)*

Alice White 1999 Shiraz (South Eastern Australia) $8. 83 *—M.N. (6/1/2001)*

ALKOOMI

Alkoomi 2000 Southlands Red Blend (Western Australia) $11. 84 *(9/1/2001)*

Alkoomi 2004 Sauvignon Blanc (Frankland River) $20. Crisp and minerally on the nose, but with a backing of passion fruit, fresh-cut grass and citrus. Quite zesty and acidic, with lean, stylish grapefruit flavors. Long and pure, with mild spritz and a cleansing quality to it. **88** *(7/1/2005)*

Alkoomi 2001 Sauvignon Blanc (Frankland River) $17. 87 *(8/1/2002)*

Alkoomi 2001 Shiraz (Frankland River) $22. Shows rustic flavors like hay and earth over its red plum fruit. In spite of its earthiness, this feels like a wiry, bright wine, probably thanks to its undercurrent of eucalyptus. On the nose, you'll find grape, plum, chalk and earth flavors. Another very good wine from this always dependable Oz winery. **88** *—D.T. (5/1/2004)*

Alkoomi 2000 Southlands White Blend (Western Australia) $11. 86 Best Buy *—D.T. (9/1/2001)*

ALL SAINTS

All Saints 1999 Cabernet Sauvignon (Rutherglen) $30. 92 *—S.H. (1/1/2002)*

All Saints 1999 Carlyle Reserve Shiraz (Rutherglen) $40. 90 Cellar Selection *—M.S. (3/1/2003)*

ALLANDALE

Allandale 2002 Chardonnay (Hunter Valley) $18. On the nose, smoke and pineapple take on a milky quality. Yellow peach fruit is sturdy, rather than fleshy and juicy, in the mouth, and is dressed in a buttery-creamy cloak. Medium-weight, with a long, tangy finish. **86** *(7/2/2004)*

AMBERLEY

Amberley 1997 Reserve Cabernet Sauvignon (Margaret River) $45. 1997 is the current vintage on this reserve wine, but it already feels tired. Brown-red in color; monotone and lean on the palate. **82** *—D.T. (8/1/2005)*

Amberley 2002 Charlotte Street Chardonnay (Western Australia) $11. A pleasant wine, and one in which pineapple is the principal note. The nose also shows citrus and white pepper, and the palate, a slick, soft creamsicle flavor and feel. Straightforward, and a good bet for wine novices. **84** *(7/2/2004)*

Amberley 2003 Proprietary Chenin Blanc (Margaret River) $13. Chenin from Australia isn't something we see often in these parts. This version is round and soft in the mouth, with medium body and loads of peach flavors and aromas. The fruit is a little sweet, but it's an easy, enjoyable choice. **86** *—D.T. (11/15/2004)*

Amberley 2001 Proprietary Semillon-Sauvignon Blanc (Margaret River) $15. 83 *—D.T. (5/1/2004)*

ANDREW GARRETT ESTATES

Andrew Garrett Estates 2002 Kelly's Promise Chardonnay (South Eastern Australia) $9. Like white shoes—so fresh and summery that it would almost be a sin to drink after Labor Day, when you're spending time indoors. This is bright, sunny, and just the thing to gulp down on the porch. Tropcial and citrus fruit through and through, with a smokiness accenting the fruit on the nose. **86** *(7/1/2004)*

ANDREW HARRIS

Andrew Harris 2000 Reserve Chardonnay (Mudgee) $23. 89 *—J.C. (7/1/2002)*

ANDREW PEACE

Andrew Peace 2002 Chardonnay (South Eastern Australia) $8. Has smoky, buttery scents, along with some peach and corn. Its body is fairly full, with flavors that turn odd just after palate entry–sour, vegetal, steely. Short and dilute on the finish. A surprising finish, considering Peace's red wines have performed much better. **80** *(7/2/2004)*

Andrew Peace 2002 Red Blend (South Eastern Australia) $8. Juicy and fruit-driven, this wine's a simple solution for large gatherings. Bouncy and Beaujolais-weight, there's cherry fruit with some earth and brown sugar in the background. Finishes toasty. A blend of Shiraz, Cabernet Sauvignon, Grenache, and Mataro. **86 Best Buy** *—D.T. (5/1/2004)*

Andrew Peace 2002 Shiraz (South Eastern Australia) $8. 85 *—D.T. (12/31/2003)*

ANGOVE'S

Angove's 1999 Classic Reserve Cabernet Sauvignon (South Eastern Australia) $10. 86 Best Buy *(9/1/2001)*

Angove's 2002 Long Row Cabernet Sauvignon (South Australia) $10. A sturdy, good choice for a $10 wine. Flavors and aromas are light and red (think plum and watermelon). The soft red-pencil-eraser finish comes to a gentle close. **84** *—D.T. (11/15/2004)*

Angove's 2003 Vineyard Select Cabernet Sauvignon (Coonawarra) $20. This is a pretty solid Cab, crisp and smooth on the palate, with black cherry fruit at the fore. On the nose, it offers more black cherry, plus unusual rice-cracker and marinade aromas. **87** *—D.T. (12/31/2005)*

Angove's 2002 Bear Crossing Cabernet Sauvignon-Merlot (South Australia) $7. 84 *—D.T. (6/1/2003)*

Angove's 2003 Bear Crossing Chardonnay (South Australia) $7. Nose doesn't reveal much more than butter, or light coconut aromas. In the mouth, there's an odd filminess to the texture, and flavors of gold apple that are punctuated by bright herb (and maybe some alcohol) on the finish. **82** *—D.T. (11/15/2004)*

Angove's 2001 Bear Crossing Chardonnay (South Australia) $7. 85 Best Buy *—J.C. (7/1/2002)*

Angove's 2000 Classic Reserve Chardonnay (South Australia) $9. 86 *—M.N. (6/1/2001)*

Angove's 2003 Long Row Chardonnay (South Australia) $10. Creamy, buttery aromas hint at what's to come in the mouth: yellow fruit gussied up with some cream and toast, with a heavyish, clumsy mouthfeel. Good, but pretty straightforward. **84** *—D.T. (12/31/2004)*

Angove's 2005 Nine Vines Rosé (South Australia) $10. Dark red-garnet in color, with aromas of meat, mineral, and plum. I like this rosé for its full body and dark berry-and-chalk flavor profile. It's 70% Grenache and 30% Shiraz, a grownup (read: dry and full) version of rosé at an affordable price. Its modern, sleek packaging, too, belies its cost. **86 Best Buy** *—D.T. (11/15/2005)*

Angove's 2001 Classic Reserve Pinot Noir (South Australia) $10. 84 *—D.T. (6/1/2003)*

Angove's 2001 Classic Reserve Sauvignon Blanc (South Australia) $10. Waxy canned pineapple aromas lead the way into a palate that's entirely lemon, lime, and grapefruit. It's sharp and light, which means that well-chilled it will come across as being refreshing. On the negative side of things, there's a strong candied quality to the wine that can't be ignored. **84** *(1/1/2004)*

Angove's 2004 Vineyard Select Sauvignon Blanc (Adelaide Hills) $19. A spare, austere, lemony sort of Sauvignon. It is almost unforgiving at first, but after a few sips, you get used to the style and begin to appreciate the minerally, chalky feel. A natural with white fish, or any rich sauces that beg to be cut with a laser-edged white. Imported by Empson (USA) Ltd. **87** *—D.T. (12/1/2005)*

Angove's 2002 Bear Crossing Shiraz (South Australia) $7. 86 Best Buy *—D.T. (11/15/2003)*

Angove's 1999 Classic Reserve Shiraz (South Australia) $9. 83 *(10/1/2001)*

Angove's 2002 Sarnia Farm Shiraz (Padthaway) $14. A conservative, buttoned-up wine: It has a rigid core of black fruit, with graham cracker and oak accents. It has a nice fatness in midpalate, and smooths out into a juicy finish. A very good wine, and one that won't break the bank. **88** *—D.T. (12/31/2004)*

Angove's 2002 Vineyard Select Shiraz (McLaren Vale) $20. Smooth, chewy tannins on the palate with ripe red fruit flavors (plum, cherry, raspberry) are a tasty, winning combination. The sweet accents on the nose (caramel, sweet tart, toffee) may appeal more to others than they did me—still, the quibble is a minor one. **89** *—D.T. (3/1/2005)*

AUSTRALIA

ANNIE'S LANE

Annie's Lane 2003 Chardonnay (Clare Valley) $NA. 86 *—D.T. (1/1/2002)*

Annie's Lane 2002 Chardonnay (Clare Valley) $13. 88 *—D.T. (8/1/2003)*

Annie's Lane 2003 Riesling (Clare Valley) $14. Nose is a nice mix of lime, gooseberry, and jasmine, and the mouthfeel is a mix of chalky smoothness and a dash of viscosity. Peach, pear, and lime peel flavors fade into a medium-length finish. **88 Best Buy** *—D.T. (5/1/2004)*

Annie's Lane 2004 Coppertrail Riesling (Clare Valley) $14. Some Rieslings bowl you over with flavor and acid, but this isn't one of them. You know all that talk you hear about the grape's versatility with food? They could have been talking about this wine, and its wet-stone texture, and lemon and pear flavors. **87** *—D.T. (10/1/2005)*

Annie's Lane 1999 Copper Trail Shiraz (Clare Valley) $32. 86 *—D.T. (12/31/2003)*

ANNVERS

Annvers 2001 Cabernet Sauvignon (Langhorne Creek) $28. A very good wine, but not an opulent, fleshy wine. It's medium-weight, with plum skin and tea accents on the palate, and a nose that takes a little while to open. There's a fair amount of oak here as well—if that bothers you, look elsewhere. **87** *—D.T. (5/1/2004)*

ANTIPODEAN

Antipodean 1999 Chardonnay (Eden Valley) $NA. 83 *—D.T. (8/1/2003)*

AQUILA

Aquila 2000 Cabernet Sauvignon (Margaret River) $15. 84 *—D.T. (10/1/2003)*

ARMSTRONG

Armstrong 1999 Shiraz (Victoria) $54. 88 *(11/1/2001)*

ARTHUR'S CREEK

Arthur's Creek 1995 Estate Cabernet Sauvignon (Yarra Valley) $40. 84 *(9/1/2001)*

ARUNDA

Arunda 1999 Cabernet Sauvignon-Merlot (South Eastern Australia) $9. 85 *—S.H. (6/1/2002)*

Arunda 2001 Shiraz-Cabernet (South Eastern Australia) $9. 86 *—S.H. (1/1/2002)*

AUSVETIA

AusVetia 1997 Shiraz (South Australia) $60. 89 *(11/1/2001)*

BALGOWNIE ESTATE

Balgownie Estate 2002 Shiraz (Bendigo) $30. Right out of the bottle, this wine brims with blackberry and cassis aromas and flavors, but with air, it takes on more earthy, briary—even nutty, as is the case with the nose—notes. Has a chalky feel and medium body; restrained and food friendly. Imported by Old Bridge Cellars. **89** *—D.T. (10/1/2005)*

BALLANDEAN

Ballandean 2002 Cabernet Sauvignon (Granite Belt) $13. This wine is fragrant and concentrated, but its flavors are sour enough to make it almost difficult to drink. Has musky, men's cologne aromas, and sour plum plus stalky greenness on the palate. Tannins are thick and sawdusty. **82** *—D.T. (12/31/2005)*

Ballandean 2002 Shiraz (Granite Belt) $13. One of the few Queensland offerings we see stateside; this one has cool plum and coconut-candy bar aromas, with plum flavors persisting through. Its pulpy, newsprint-y texture is a detraction. 1,200 cases produced. **83** *—D.T. (12/1/2005)*

BALNAVES OF COONAWARRA

Balnaves of Coonawarra 1998 The Blend Bordeaux Blend (Coonawarra) $15. 85 *—M.S. (12/15/2002)*

Balnaves of Coonawarra 1998 Cabernet Sauvignon (Coonawarra) $30. 85 *—M.S. (12/15/2002)*

Balnaves of Coonawarra 1998 The Tally Reserve Cabernet Sauvignon (Coonawarra) $75. 87 *—D.T. (12/31/2003)*

Balnaves of Coonawarra 1997 Cabernet Sauvignon-Merlot (Coonawarra) $30. 89 *—J.F. (9/1/2001)*

Balnaves of Coonawarra 1998 Shiraz (Coonawarra) $30. 88 *—K.F. (3/1/2003)*

BANNOCKBURN VINEYARDS

Bannockburn Vineyards 2001 Chardonnay (Geelong) $38. 87 *(7/2/2004)*

BANROCK STATION

Banrock Station 2004 Cabernet Sauvignon (South Eastern Australia) $7. Smells like beef bouillon and some mushroom, and tastes of plums and berries coated in an oaky veneer. A darkly flavored wine, but a hollow one. **82** *—D.T. (12/31/2005)*

Banrock Station 2003 Chardonnay (South Eastern Australia) $7. Just what you want in a chilled, porch-sippin', beach-lyin' wine. It's a straightforward, uncomplicated Chard, but one with fleshy white peach and Granny Smith apple flavors. Aromas are on the sweet side, though, with pineapple syrup and flowers taking the lead. **84** *(7/2/2004)*

Banrock Station 2001 Merlot (South Eastern Australia) $6. 82 *—C.S. (6/1/2002)*

Banrock Station 2004 Riesling (South Eastern Australia) $7. Finally, a Riesling at a truly introductory price. Green apple and pear aromas introduce a soft, sweetish, plump palate. It's a fresh and quaffable white, a simple rendition of the variety. **84 Best Buy** *—D.T. (10/1/2005)*

Banrock Station 2000 Semillon-Chardonnay (South Eastern Australia) $6. 88 Best Buy *—D.T. (9/1/2001)*

Banrock Station 2000 Shiraz (South Eastern Australia) $8. 87 Best Buy *(10/1/2001)*

Banrock Station 2003 Shiraz-Cabernet (South Eastern Australia) $6. Easy-drinking and pleasing. Vanilla bean, cream, and musky aromas usher in red fruit (plum, cherry, you name it), a judicious amount of wood, and a streak of anise. 43,000 cases produced. **86 Best Buy** *—D.T. (8/1/2005)*

BARNADOWN RUN

Barnadown Run 1999 Heathcote Cabernet Sauvignon (Victoria) $28. 87 *—J.C. (6/1/2002)*

Barnadown Run 2000 Heathcote/Bendigo Winery Shiraz (Victoria) $30. 84 *—D.T. (1/28/2003)*

BAROSSA VALLEY ESTATE

Barossa Valley Estate 1999 Chardonnay (Barossa Valley) $10. 87 Best Buy *—M.M. (10/1/2000)*

Barossa Valley Estate 2004 Spires Chardonnay (Barossa Valley) $12. Smells very nice. The wine deals vanilla bean, nutmeg, musk, and floral notes. This isn't a Chardonnay for the tropically inclined. There's fruit here, but it's taut (think unripe pear, sour apple, peach pit, that sort of thing). Sparse on the fluff overall. **86** *—D.T. (12/1/2005)*

Barossa Valley Estate 2003 Spires Chardonnay (Barossa Valley) $12. Smells and tastes appley, with a backbone of citrus. Light in body, the fruit doesn't sing loudly—we could only wish there were more of it. Finishes with tart citrus. **83** *(7/2/2004)*

Barossa Valley Estate 1998 Shiraz (Barossa Valley) $10. 89 Best Buy *(10/1/2000)*

Barossa Valley Estate 1999 Black Pepper Sparkling Shiraz (Barossa Valley) $NA. There's not much of this sparkler made, because the winery has to make the difficult decision of parting with E&E-quality grapes to do it. Has spicy, fireplace-smoke and plum aromas, with meaty, plummy flavors. On the palate, it offers good mousse and steady bead. Not currently available in the U.S. **90** *(3/1/2005)*

Barossa Valley Estate 2000 E&E Black Pepper Shiraz (Barossa Valley) $NA. Now showing unusual aromas of eucalyptus, roasted fruit, and pickle barrel. It's supple in the mouth, with over-the-top stone fruit flavors and fresh herb accents. Finishes on a bitter-chocolate note. Drinking well now. **90** *(3/1/2005)*

Barossa Valley Estate 1999 E&E Black Pepper Shiraz (Barossa Valley) $85. 92 *—D.T. (3/1/2003)*

Barossa Valley Estate 1998 E&E Black Pepper Shiraz (Barossa Valley) $80. 95 Editors' Choice *(11/1/2001)*

Barossa Valley Estate 1997 E&E Black Pepper Shiraz (Barossa Valley) $65. 90 *(10/1/2000)*

Barossa Valley Estate 1996 E&E Black Pepper Shiraz (Barossa Valley) $65. 91 *(4/1/2000)*

Barossa Valley Estate 1991 E&E Black Pepper Shiraz (Barossa Valley) $NA. One panelist thought this vintage was the best of the bunch, but all agreed that the wine is at its prime now. It's rich and very supple on the palate, with notes of milk chocolate, nut, cola, and earth. Finishes long and focused; just hot stuff. **93** *(3/1/2005)*

Barossa Valley Estate 2001 Ebenezer Shiraz (Barossa Valley) $30. With such rich blackberry and clove aromas, the wine's powerful berry and plum flavors should come as no surprise. There's spice on the palate, too, which is medium-sized, elegant—and maybe even a little lighter than you'd expect. **88** *(3/1/2005)*

Barossa Valley Estate 1999 Ebenezer Shiraz (Barossa Valley) $30. 90 *—D.T. (3/1/2003)*

Barossa Valley Estate 1997 Ebenezer Shiraz (Barossa Valley) $29. 90 *(10/1/2000)*

Barossa Valley Estate 2003 Spires Shiraz (Barossa Valley) $12. 85 *—D.T. (12/1/2005)*

Barossa Valley Estate 2001 Spires Shiraz (Barossa Valley) $10. 84 *—D.T. (12/31/2003)*

BARRATT

Barratt 2001 The Reserve Pinot Noir (Piccadilly Valley) $50. 84 *—D.T. (12/31/2003)*

BARWANG

Barwang 1997 Vintage Select Cabernet Sauvignon (South Eastern Australia) $10. 86 *(12/1/1999)*

Barwang 1998 Regional Selection Chardonnay (Yarra Valley) $14. 84 *—S.H. (9/1/2001)*

Barwang 1997 Vintage Select Chardonnay (South Eastern Australia) $10. 87 *(12/1/1999)*

Barwang 1998 Regional Selection Merlot (Coonawarra) $14. 87 *—J.F. (9/1/2001)*

Barwang 1999 Shiraz (South Eastern Australia) $9. 83 *(10/1/2001)*

Barwang 1997 Regional Selection Shiraz (Coonawarra) $18. 90 *(12/1/1999)*

Barwang 1997 Winemaker's Reserve Shiraz (Coonawarra) $20. 88 *—S.H. (10/1/2000)*

Barwang 1996 Winemaker's Reserve Shiraz (New South Wales) $25. 91 *(12/1/1999)*

BASEDOW

Basedow 1998 Shiraz (Barossa Valley) $20. 85 *(10/1/2001)*

BATTLE OF BOSWORTH

Battle of Bosworth 2002 Cabernet Sauvignon (McLaren Vale) $28. Ballsy one moment and then suave the next, Joch Bosworth's Cabernet is an interesting wine for a number of reasons: his vineyards are organic, and a small percentage (which varies between 2 and 7%) of the fruit for this bottling is cordon cut on the vines and left to dry, Amarone-style. Plus, this Cab just flat-out tastes good: it's brawny and plummy, with the cordon-cut fruit adding extra richness. Finishes with chocolate-mocha flavors. Drink after 2006, as the nose is still pretty closed and the tannins still substantial. **90** *—D.T. (3/1/2005)*

BECKETT'S FLAT

Beckett's Flat 2002 Reserve Chardonnay (Margaret River) $22. 87 *—D.T. (10/1/2003)*

Beckett's Flat 2002 Sauvignon Blanc-Semillon (Margaret River) $20. Quite herbal in the nose, with hints of hay, grass, and herbs. That theme continues throughout, with a tart lemon edge on the finish. Kosher. **80** *—J.M. (4/3/2004)*

Beckett's Flat 2001 Semillon-Sauvignon Blanc (Margaret River) $15. 84 *—D.T. (10/1/2003)*

Beckett's Flat 2001 Shiraz (Margaret River) $18. 87 *—M.S. (3/1/2003)*

BELLARINE ESTATE

Bellarine Estate 2000 James Paddock Chardonnay (South Eastern Australia) $15. 88 *—J.C. (7/1/2002)*

Bellarine Estate 1999 Shiraz (Bellarine Peninsula) $15. 81 *(10/1/2001)*

BENJAMIN NV MUSEUM RESERVE

Benjamin NV Museum Reserve Muscat (Victoria) $16. 95 *—S.H. (9/1/2002)*

Benjamin NV Museum Reserve Tokay (Victoria) $16. 92 *—L.W. (3/1/2000)*

BETHANY

Bethany 2002 Shiraz (Barossa) $37. This Shriaz offers pickling spice and wood aromas. On the palate, it's more of the same—dull wood, and some roasted fruit. Simple and flat. **81** *—D.T. (10/1/2005)*

BILLABONG

Billabong 1999 Shiraz (South Eastern Australia) $8. 85 Best Buy *(10/1/2001)*

BIMBADGEN

Bimbadgen 2001 Proprietary Grand Ridge Chardonnay (Hunter Valley) $10. The Grand Ridge is soft and round in the mouth, and shows honey, peach, and lactic-cream flavors. Interesting aromas—resin, golden raisin, and peach. Toasty-orange flavors on the finish. **85** *(7/2/2004)*

BIRD IN HAND

Bird in Hand 2001 Cabernet Sauvignon (Adelaide Hills) $28. A rustic-feeling wine with black cherries and plums at the fore; gummy, chewy tannins in the mouth and juicy plum and blackberry aromas complete the package. A very nice wine, and a good introduction to how nice Adelaide Hills reds can be. **88** *—D.T. (5/1/2004)*

Bird in Hand 2001 Merlot (Adelaide Hills) $28. **83** *—D.T. (1/1/2002)*

Bird in Hand NV Joy Pinot Noir (Adelaide Hills) $70. Aromas are of cherry and ginger; salmon-copper in color. What you get on the palate follows suit: light cherry and peach flavors, packaged in a medium-bodied sparkler that is soft on palate entry and grows crisper and more tangy toward the finish. Pleasantly perplexing in that it manages to feel both fragile and forceful. **88** *—D.T. (12/31/2004)*

Bird in Hand NV Sparkling Pinot Noir (Adelaide Hills) $25. What your preteen daughters would drink if they could: it's a light pink wine, ultrafeminine, with a frothy, moussey mouthfeel that will bring to mind stuffed animals and baby dolls—everything blush-colored and innocent. Cherry flavors and aromas through and through. Firms up on the finish. **84** *—D.T. (12/31/2004)*

BLACK CREEK

Black Creek 1998 Verdelho (Hunter Valley) $10. **82** *—M.M. (10/1/2000)*

BLACK OPAL

Black Opal 1999 Cabernet Sauvignon (South Eastern Australia) $11. **84** *—R.V. (11/15/2001)*

Black Opal 2000 Cabernet Sauvignon-Merlot (South Eastern Australia) $11. **84** *—D.T. (6/1/2003)*

Black Opal 2004 Chardonnay (South Eastern Australia) $10. Shows a dry, citrusy verve on the nose. Acids are in full force on the palate, which, with its citrus and gooseberry flavors, reminded me more of Sauvignon than of Chardonnay. Fattens up on the finish; a good, bargain-priced quaff. **85 Best Buy** *—D.T. (5/1/2005)*

Black Opal 2002 Chardonnay (South Eastern Australia) $14. This medium-weight wine has sweet cream and toast aromas, with a hint of tar; in the mouth, toasty, almost charred wood prevails. Finish is to the point, with talc and herb flavors. **83** *(7/2/2004)*

Black Opal 1998 Chardonnay (South Australia) $11. **83** *—L.W. (12/31/1999)*

Black Opal 2001 Shiraz (South Eastern Australia) $12. **84** *—D.T. (12/31/2003)*

Black Opal 1999 Shiraz (South Eastern Australia) $11. **83** *(10/1/2001)*

Black Opal 2001 Shiraz-Cabernet (South Eastern Australia) $12. **82** *—D.T. (1/1/2002)*

BLACK SWAN

Black Swan 2003 Chardonnay (South Eastern Australia) $8. Aromas are of buttered toast and pear; in the mouth, the pear, melon, and peach flavors are halfhearted, or not all that concentrated. A good pour if you need an inexpensive, cold quaff. **84** *(7/2/2004)*

Black Swan 2002 Chardonnay (South Eastern Australia) $8. **85** *—D.T. (8/1/2003)*

Black Swan 2004 Shiraz-Merlot Red Blend (South Eastern Australia) $9. Has a nice graham-crackery aroma, with a pulpy, woody feel and sour plum skin and rubber flavors. 155,000 cases produced. **82** *—D.T. (10/1/2005)*

Black Swan 2004 Shiraz-Cabernet (South Eastern Australia) $9. Smells like bread flour and tastes like black cherries. One-dimensional and simple; two-thirds Shiraz, and one-third Cab. 125,000 cases. **83** *—D.T. (10/1/2005)*

BLEASDALE

Bleasdale 2000 Mulberry Tree Cabernet Sauvignon (Langhorne Creek) $16. **87** *—J.C. (6/1/2002)*

Bleasdale 1999 Bremerview Shiraz (Langhorne Creek) $15. **89 Best Buy** *(10/1/2001)*

BLUE PYRENEES

Blue Pyrenees 1999 Cabernet Sauvignon (Victoria) $15. **82** *—M.S. (12/15/2002)*

Blue Pyrenees 1999 Estate Reserve Chardonnay (Victoria) $20. **87** *—J.C. (7/1/2002)*

Blue Pyrenees 1999 Estate Reserve Shiraz (Victoria) $20. **85** *—J.C. (9/1/2002)*

BLUE TONGUE

Blue Tongue 2002 Shiraz (South Eastern Australia) $7. **83** *—D.T. (1/1/2002)*

BOOKPURNONG HILL

Bookpurnong Hill 1999 Petite Verdot (South Eastern Australia) $40. **85** *—D.T. (9/1/2001)*

Bookpurnong Hill 1999 Shiraz (Riverland) $43. **87** *(11/1/2001)*

BOUTIQUE WINES

Boutique Wines 1998 The Region Chardonnay (Adelaide Hills) $22. **88** *(6/1/2001)*

BOX STALLION

Box Stallion 2001 The Enclosure Chardonnay (Mornington Peninsula) $30. This Chardonnay is a glowing-gold color, and its further impressions live up to the expectation that you get from its appearance buttery/nutty aromas, and a buttery texture. Structure and concentration are also not strengths here. Very expensive for what's in the bottle. 2,000 cases produced. **82** *—D.T. (5/1/2005)*

BRANSON COACH HOUSE

Branson Coach House 2002 Single Vineyard Greenock Block Shiraz (Barossa Valley) $45. Has meaty, bacon aromas with creamy, peppery highlights. In the mouth, it's brawn in a glass—not a dumb jock, mind you, but the amiable linebacker who also wins "Mr. Congeniality." It has a rich, creamy feel on the front palate, good meaty heft in the middle, and zips up with a juicy plum and anise conclusion. Muscular, mobile, and piquant, not fat and inert. **91** *—D.T. (12/31/2004)*

BREMERTON

Bremerton 2000 Sauvignon Blanc (Langhorne Creek) $17. **81** *—J.F. (9/1/2001)*

Bremerton 1999 Young Vine Shiraz (Langhorne Creek) $20. **86** *(10/1/2001)*

BROKENWOOD

Brokenwood 2004 Semillon (Hunter Valley) $22. The heart of this Semillon is bony and minerally; barely ripe peach flavors and a green-apple finish completes the flavor profile. Lightly petillant in the mouth, with a burst of Sweet Tart on palate entry. It's a pleasing, refreshing white. **87** *—D.T. (8/1/2005)*

Brokenwood 2002 Graveyard Vineyard Shiraz (Hunter Valley) $100. A gorgeous wine that defies the modern idea that wines have to be big and brash to be excellent. This one feels simultaneously fresh and old as the hills, with a meaty, merdy appeal. Red fruit aromas and flavors are concentrated and sprinkled in black pepper; the tannins are manageable now, but still substantial enough to age. A modest 13.5% alcohol, and, bless 'em, sealed with a screwcap. Tastes good now, but probably even better around 2009. **95** *—D.T. (8/1/2005)*

Brokenwood 2002 Rayner Vineyard Shiraz (McLaren Vale) $70. A spitfire of a Shiraz. High-toned blackberry and black cherry flavors have undertones of coffee and mocha. As nice as the flavors and aromas of fresh earth and cola are, the acids stick out some, giving the palate a prickly feel. Would easily have reached the next decile otherwise. **88** *—D.T. (10/1/2005)*

Brokenwood 2001 Wade Block 2 Vineyard Selection Shiraz (McLaren Vale) $37. Obviously well-pedigreed, but this wine is soft, and wants a little more acid. Its black fruit is just this side of sweet, backed up by mocha and marshmallow flavors. Medium-bodied and fruity, an easy-to-drink wine, but probably not much of an ager. Tasted twice. **86** *—D.T. (5/1/2004)*

BROOKLAND VALLEY

Brookland Valley 2000 Estate Cabernet Sauvignon-Merlot (Margaret River) $33. Says Cabernet-Merlot on the label, but Merlot makes up a whopping 5% of the blend. This wine is excellent, but its cool-climate profile isn't for everyone. This reviewer found a lot to like about the sweet-and-tart black fruit and eucalyptus aromas; cool, red fruit on the palate and lovely, clay-chalk finish. But the wine is taut, and the eucalyptus persistent. **90** *—D.T. (9/1/2004)*

Brookland Valley 2002 Chardonnay (Margaret River) $27. Smells toasty and musky, like roasted meat even. On the palate, soft yellow fruit gives way to a buttery finish. Good, but straightforward. **86** *—D.T. (5/1/2005)*

Brookland Valley 2002 Verse 1 Chardonnay (Margaret River) $16. Straightforward, with bright yellow fruit and some mustard seed flavors in the mouth. Finishes with oak and nut flavors. **84** *(1/1/2004)*

Brookland Valley 2004 Verse 1 Semillon-Sauvignon Blanc (Margaret River) $16. This is a lively Sem-Sauv in which the Sauvignon seems to steal the show. Semillon lends a hay-like aroma, but apart from that, zesty lime and grass flavors dominate. Tastes just as it smells, with a dry feel. Very nice. **88** *—D.T. (10/1/2005)*

Brookland Valley 2001 Verse 1 Shiraz (Margaret River) $18. **87** *—M.S. (3/1/2003)*

BROWN BROTHERS

Brown Brothers 2000 Patricia Reserve Cabernet Sauvignon (Victoria) $30. Black as black in color, which may or may not have anything to do with the 7% Petit Verdot inside. It's a straight-up plum-and-oak combo, dense in the mouth with tealike tannins that linger on the finish. **88** *(8/1/2004)*

Brown Brothers 2001 Estate Bottled Chardonnay (Victoria) $11. **84** *—D.T. (12/31/2003)*

Brown Brothers 2000 Patricia Reserve Merlot (Victoria) $30. Dust, dried herb, and pure black cherry aromas segue into black cherry, vanilla, and tree bark flavors on the palate. On the lighter side, as far as Merlot goes. Finishes with a bite of herb and coffee. **87** *(8/1/2004)*

Brown Brothers 2000 Patricia Reserve Shiraz (Victoria) $33. Opens with peppery-smoky aromas. This is a supple, elegant Shiraz, easy to drink, with blackberry, vanilla, and dill flavors that fade into a smooth finish. **88** *(8/1/2004)*

BRUMBY CANYON

Brumby Canyon 2002 Jillaroo Red Red Blend (South Australia) $14. The name requires another Australian-to-American English translation:

A "brumby" is a wild Australian horse; a "jillaroo," a farm worker. Thankfully, this wine doesn't taste like anything you'd find in a stable: it offers very ripe black cherry flavors, with some black soil joining in on the finish. Beaujolais-sized in body, this Shiraz (60%), Grenache (33%), Mataro (7%) blend is an inexpensive, easy quaffer. **87** —*D.T. (12/31/2004)*

BUCKELEY'S

Buckeley's 1999 Chardonnay (South Australia) $10. **84** —*M.S. (10/1/2000)*

Buckeley's 2001 Chardonnay (South Australia) $10. **85** —*J.C. (7/1/2002)*

Buckeley's 2002 Merlot (South Australia) $10. **85** —*S.H. (10/1/2003)*

Buckeley's 2001 Shiraz (South Australia) $12. **85** —*S.H. (10/1/2003)*

BULLETIN PLACE

Bulletin Place 1999 Cabernet Sauvignon (South Eastern Australia) $10. **83** —*C.S. (6/1/2002)*

Bulletin Place 2001 Chardonnay (South Eastern Australia) $8. **85** —*D.T. (11/15/2003)*

Bulletin Place 2002 Merlot (South Eastern Australia) $10. **83** —*D.T. (1/1/2002)*

Bulletin Place 2003 Shiraz (South Eastern Australia) $8. Though this Shiraz smells somewhat sweet, you thankfully don't get the same impression on the palate. Instead, there is red berry and plum fruit, with lemony-oak accents. It's simple, but still a steal. **84 Best Buy** —*D.T. (5/1/2005)*

Bulletin Place 1999 Shiraz (South Eastern Australia) $10. **84** —*M.N. (10/1/2001)*

BURTON

Burton 1999 Cabernet Sauvignon (Coonawarra) $27. **85** —*D.T. (6/1/2003)*

Burton 2000 Cabernet Sauvignon-Merlot (South Eastern Australia) $16. **88** —*D.T. (8/1/2003)*

BUSH BIKE

Bush Bike 2004 Riesling (Western Australia) $14. Offers fresh green produce and herb aromas. On the palate, the rocky-minerally feel is nice, but the weak lemon flavors don't quite live up to it. **83** —*D.T. (12/1/2005)*

CA'NA

Ca'Na 2000 Cabernet Sauvignon (Coonawarra) $24. **84** —*S.H. (1/1/2002)*

CALEDONIA AUSTRALIS

Caledonia Australis 2003 Mount Macleod Chardonnay (Gippsland) $17. This is a pretty Chard, with a medium-long, dry finish. Rounded on the palate, with stone fruit and light toast flavors, it zips up tight, tall and dry on the back end. **88** —*D.T. (8/1/2005)*

Caledonia Australis 2003 Mount Macleod Pinot Noir (Gippsland) $17. Not a please-everyone style of Pinot—we found that out the hard way in the tasting room. I enjoyed this wine quite a bit: it's tight, sour, and leathery, both intense and delicate at the same time. The finish is long and juicy, and the nose shows cherry, earth, and tree-bark notes. Another taster found it just too wiry, even thin. If you're tired of Pinots that taste like Shirazes, this is a good place to start. **89 Editors' Choice** —*D.T. (12/31/2005)*

CALLAHAN HILL

Callahan Hill 2000 Shiraz (South Eastern Australia) $9. **87 Best Buy** *(10/1/2001)*

CAMPBELLS

Campbells 1995 The Barkly Durif (Rutherglen) $30. **86** —*D.T. (6/1/2003)*

Campbells NV Muscat (Rutherglen) $17. Smells alcoholic at first, but after a few minutes in the glass, the aromas are of charred wood. Feels somewhat rough, or rustic, in the mouth—not the smooth unctuousness that other Oz dessert wines have—with burnt sugar/caramel and stewed fruit flavors. Smooths out on the finish. **87** —*D.T. (12/31/2004)*

Campbells 1998 Bobbie Burns Shiraz (Rutherglen) $20. **83** —*J.C. (9/1/2002)*

CANONBAH BRIDGE

Canonbah Bridge 1999 Vintage Reserve Champagne Blend (Victoria) $20. Pale copper-salmon in color, with bacon aromas and blackberry and cherry flavors. Cream aromas and flavors are present from the start through the brief finish. In the mouth, the mousse is soft but the cherry tautness gives it some spine. 52% Chardonnay, 24% Pinot Noir, 24% Pinot Meunier. **85** —*D.T. (12/31/2004)*

Canonbah Bridge 2002 Ram's Leap Merlot (Western Plains) $12. Has eucalyptus, earth, and red plum aromas. This is a straightforward wine, but one that has surprising finesse, particularly given its reasonable price. It shows firm, ripe red plum fruit on the palate, and takes on a little coffee with air. Medium-bodied, it finishes with a gummy, pencil-eraser feel. **86** —*D.T. (9/1/2004)*

Canonbah Bridge 2000 Ram's Leap Shiraz (New South Wales) $10. 84 *—D.T. (12/31/2003)*

CAPE CLAIRAULT

Cape Clairault 1996 The Clairault Reserve Red Bordeaux Blend (Margaret River) $35. 92 *—M.S. (10/1/2000)*

CAPE MENTELLE

Cape Mentelle 1999 Cabernet Sauvignon (Margaret River) $42. 88 *—D.T. (10/1/2003)*

Cape Mentelle 2002 Cabernet Sauvignon-Merlot (Margaret River) $19. Heavy Bourbon-barrel, toasty flavors distract from otherwise very pleasant mixed berry fruit on the palate, and sweet-fruit aromas also take on hints of green pepper. It's a well-built wine, but one that's not showing as well as it has in the past. **86** *—D.T. (12/31/2004)*

Cape Mentelle 2001 Trinders Cabernet Sauvignon-Merlot (Margaret River) $18. 90 Editors' Choice *—D.T. (10/1/2003)*

Cape Mentelle 2002 Chardonnay (Margaret River) $25. Certainly a buttery, toasty wine, but there's enough peach fruit here to back it up. It's medium-full in the mouth, with a resinous feel; finishes with good length. Oaky, but enjoyable. **87** *(7/2/2004)*

Cape Mentelle 2005 Sauvignon Blanc-Semillon (Margaret River) $13. Pungently grassy and herbal, with hints of passion fruit and grapefruit on the nose. In the mouth, the lush fruit flavors are considerably tamer, finishing long, and balanced by crisp acids. **88 Best Buy** *(12/15/2005)*

Cape Mentelle 2003 Shiraz (Western Australia) $23. Earthy and meaty, balanced by lifted hints of violets and peppery spice. Black plum and dark chocolate flavors evenly coat the palate, ending on a firm note that provides a sense of elegance. **90 Editors' Choice** *(12/15/2005)*

Cape Mentelle 2001 Shiraz (Margaret River) $19. 88 *—D.T. (10/1/2003)*

CARLEI

Carlei 2002 Green Vineyards Shiraz (Heathcote) $31. Has pleasing aromas of dust, earth, and black pepper, and a very nice surge of black berries and cherries on the palate. Wants a little more stuffing on the palate, and a little more length on the back, to catapult it into the next decile. Still, this is a very good wine with plenty to recommend it. Imported by USA Wine West. **87** *—D.T. (12/31/2005)*

CARRAMAR ESTATE

Carramar Estate 1999 Merlot (South Eastern Australia) $9. 83 *—D.T. (6/1/2002)*

CASCABEL

Cascabel 1999 Shiraz (Fleurieu Peninsula) $19. 84 *(10/1/2001)*

CHAIN OF PONDS

Chain of Ponds 1998 Ledge Shiraz (Adelaide Hills) $36. 88 *(11/1/2001)*

CHALICE BRIDGE

Chalice Bridge 2003 Cabernet Sauvignon-Shiraz (Margaret River) $16. Taut and twangy, this 65-35 Shiraz-Cab blend has black pepper in abundance, nose to finish, plus gumtree and black cherry flavors. Would have merited an even higher score had the alcohol (listed on the label at a modest 14%) not felt so evident. Imported by Low Country Imports. **87** *—D.T. (8/1/2005)*

Chalice Bridge 2001 Chardonnay (Western Australia) $16. 85 *—D.T. (8/1/2003)*

CHAPEL HILL

Chapel Hill 2002 Unwooded Chardonnay (South Australia) $15. Has down-the-line, straightforward yellow fruit flavors on the palate, with a minerally, dry feel that makes this wine a good choice to go with seafood, or rich, butter-based sauces. Aromas are light—think hay, wheat, and a little anise. **85** *(7/2/2004)*

CHARLES CIMICKY

Charles Cimicky 1999 Daylight Chamber Shiraz (Barossa Valley) $19. 88 *(10/1/2001)*

Charles Cimicky 1998 Signature Shiraz (Barossa Valley) $30. 89 *(11/1/2001)*

CHARLES MELTON

Charles Melton 2001 Cabernet Sauvignon (Barossa Valley) $44. The hints of toast and crème brûlée that accent mixed plum on the palate come through with more force on the finish. Black and red plum fruit on the palate is solid and pure. A really smart package. **91** *—D.T. (2/1/2004)*

Charles Melton 2000 Grenache (Barossa Valley) $37. This is a very good Grenache, with vivid violet and cherry aromas. "Vivid" is an appropriate word for what you get in the mouth, too—the wine's alcohol is noticeable, and its fruit fairly high toned. Cherry, earth, and red plum flavors meld on the palate and fade into an herb-tinged finish. **87** *—D.T. (9/1/2004)*

Charles Melton 2001 Nine Popes Red Blend (Barossa Valley) $39. Mint and bread flour on the nose, with raspberry and red plum flavors on the palate. Its smooth, oaky tannins continue through to the finish, where there's bread-flour and graham-cracker flavors. A terrific GSM. **90** *—D.T. (2/1/2004)*

Charles Melton 2004 Rosé (Barossa Valley) $16. Stop and smell the rosé and you'll get what I think a good rosé should smell like: a red wine with a slight chill. Deep plum, blackberry, and raspberry aromas are edged in flint, with like flavors on the palate and a finish where the flinty dryness is reprised. Deep pink-magenta in color—not shy. A curious blend of Shiraz, Grenache, Cab, and Pinot Meunier. **89** *—D.T. (12/31/2004)*

Charles Melton 2003 Rose of Virginia Rosé Blend (Barossa Valley) $15. Melton says Rose, we say rosé—a Grenache, Shiraz, Cabernet, and Petit Verdot rosé, to be precise. Though the nose is all cherry and raspberry, the main palate impression is a floral one, with some raspberries hiding in the background and on through the finish. A very nice wine, and fairly dry as well. **88** *—D.T. (2/1/2004)*

Charles Melton 2000 Shiraz (Barossa Valley) $39. Has eucalyptus and black fruit on the nose, but takes on hints of caramel with air; plum and berry fruit reads a little redder on the palate. A yummy, fiesty wine—energetic, yet cunning enough to act like a grownup, serious Shiraz when it needs to. **91** *—D.T. (2/1/2004)*

CHATEAU REYNELLA

Chateau Reynella 2002 Cabernet Sauvignon (McLaren Vale) $NA. This Cabernet is drinkable now, and showing soft red fruit with coffee-mocha notes on both the nose and the palate. Very juicy on the finish. Enjoy through 2008. **88** *—D.T. (3/1/2005)*

Chateau Reynella 2002 Chardonnay (McLaren Vale) $14. Aromas are of apple turnover and minerals. Slim bodied and a little soft, but don't dismiss this Chard right off as simple: It has a tight, sour core with peach and oak flavors rounding it out in the mouth. **87** *—D.T. (12/1/2005)*

Chateau Reynella 1999 Chardonnay (McLaren Vale) $11. **90 Best Buy** *—M.N. (6/1/2001)*

Chateau Reynella 2002 Basket Pressed Grenache (McLaren Vale) $24. Dark, smoky aromas have high-toned black cherry fruit underneath. On the palate, the smoke and black cherry continue, on a rather slight, feminine frame. A wine that will complement, not overpower, food. **87** *—D.T. (3/1/2005)*

Chateau Reynella 2000 Basket Pressed Shiraz (McLaren Vale) $28. **87** *—C.S. (3/1/2003)*

Chateau Reynella 1996 Basket Pressed Shiraz (McLaren Vale) $24. **90** *—M.S. (4/1/2000)*

CHEVIOT BRIDGE

Cheviot Bridge 1999 Cabernet Sauvignon-Merlot (Yea Valley) $16. **87** *—M.M. (12/15/2002)*

Cheviot Bridge 2000 Chardonnay (Victoria) $16. **90** *—J.C. (7/1/2002)*

Cheviot Bridge 2001 Pinot Noir (Yea Valley) $17. **87** *—D.T. (10/1/2003)*

CLARENDON HILLS

Clarendon Hills 2003 Brookman Cabernet Sauvignon (Clarendon) $75. This isn't an oversized Cab, but that's its appeal. It's excellent, with flavors of black cherry, cassis, and black grape that surge on the palate, and just don't let go. It's all swaddled tightly in young, smooth tannins, and gumtree and beef stock accents on the nose. Drink 2007 and beyond. **92** *—D.T. (8/1/2005)*

Clarendon Hills 2003 Sandown Cabernet Sauvignon (Clarendon) $70. This wine's flavors have a cooler-climate profile to them—think red and black cherry, rather than cassis or plum fruit. Blueberry and bread flour steps in midpalate, and march on through the long finish. Lifted, tight, and very pretty. **91** *—D.T. (8/1/2005)*

Clarendon Hills 2003 Clarendon Grenache (Clarendon) $73. What a ride. On the palate, it comes and goes in waves, with cassis surging one moment, and violets and black pepper the next. Tannins are manageable but textured, and the finish brings a nutty, earthy flavor and another burst of berry fruit. Delicious now, and should age well through the decade. **93** *—D.T. (8/1/2005)*

Clarendon Hills 2003 Kangarilla (Clarendon) Grenache (McLaren Vale) $80. Smells peppery and spicy, with meat, brown sugar, and red pencil eraser to boot. Very pretty, chewy red fruit on the midpalate, though it's still not at its peak. Finishes long, with chalky-woody tannins. Try after 2008. **92** *—D.T. (3/1/2005)*

Clarendon Hills 2003 Brookman (Clarendon) Merlot (McLaren Vale) $65. This is probably the best Merlot that I've had from the region. Aromas are fruit-sweet, with wide plum fruit and light caramel at the fore. There are green notes on the nose—fresh produce, and maybe some lima bean—but they are strangely appealing, and the wine boasts tremendous grip at midpalate. Finishes with dry wood and tealike tannins. **90** *—D.T. (3/1/2005)*

Clarendon Hills 2003 Astralis (Clarendon) Syrah (McLaren Vale) $375. A fantastic wine, but so young that it would qualify better as "fetus" than as "infant." Still very closed on the nose, showing cassis and black cherry aromas after much airing. Its color is a powerful, almost glowing, purple and its flavors—a vibrant surge of pure black and blueberries—are just as intense. Very concentrated and tight, with a linear, minerally frame underneath its monstrous tannins. Winemaker Roman Bratasiuk recommends aging for a mimum of 6 years before drinking; if you are as foolish as I and insist on opening a bottle today, decant for a minimum of 6–8 hours. Rating may look stingy by the time Bush finishes his second term. **95 Cellar Selection** *—D.T. (3/1/2005)*

Clarendon Hills 2003 Brookman Syrah (Clarendon) $75. Smells indescribably good, but it's hard to pick out specific scents—think instead of a farmers' market of the freshest fruit. It's no slouch on the palate, either, where the impression is similarly seamless: In the mix you might discern a rainbow of just-ripe fruit, earth, and wheat toast, for starters. It's balanced, restrained and pretty, and should stay that way through at least 2010. **95 Cellar Selection** *—D.T. (8/1/2005)*

Clarendon Hills 2003 Liandra Syrah (Clarendon) $90. This Syrah is sexy and compelling, but in the company of Roman Bratasiuk's other wines, feels softer and not quite as intense. It packs bright red raspberry and blackberry fruit on the palate, and richly fruity aromas on the nose. Drink over the next 3–4 years. **90** *—D.T. (8/1/2005)*

Clarendon Hills 2003 Piggott Range Syrah (Clarendon) $175. Thick and textured—almost wooly—on the palate. A sip brings big blackberry and smoke on the front palate, which tightens up to blueberry by the finish. The nose is very pretty, too, showing bread flour, blueberry, fresh herb and even some lavender. **92** *—D.T. (8/1/2005)*

CLASSIC MCLAREN

Classic McLaren 2000 Cabernet Sauvignon-Merlot (McLaren Vale) $19. 86 *—D.T. (12/31/2003)*

Classic McLaren 2000 La Testa Shiraz (McLaren Vale) $78. 89 *—D.T. (6/1/2003)*

CLONAKILLA

Clonakilla 2003 Hilltops Shiraz (New South Wales) $25. Though the aromas and flavors are really nice, this wine's flat, woody feel keeps it from being as excellent as it could be. It starts off with black olive and eucalyptus on the nose, and brings black cherry, plum, herb, and eucalyptus on the palate. Good acids; an even, balanced wine. **88** *—D.T. (12/1/2005)*

COCKATOO RIDGE

Cockatoo Ridge 2002 Cabernet Sauvignon-Merlot (South Australia) $7. An 80%–20% blend in favor of Cabernet, this is a simple, one-track wine with sweet fruit aromas and flavors. There's an underlying note of tartness—seeped tea, or herb—that is a out of joint with everything else, but it's still a good wine at a good price. **83** *—D.T. (9/1/2004)*

Cockatoo Ridge 2000 The Real Taste of Australia Cabernet Sauvignon-Merlot (South Australia) $7. 84 *—M.S. (12/15/2002)*

Cockatoo Ridge NV Brut (South Eastern Australia) $7. In this price category, you're lucky to find a sparkler that won't give you a killer headache the morning after revelry—so it's just gravy that this wine tastes good, too. Slight coppery hue, with dusty cherry aromas and flavors. It's soft, foamy, and goes down easy. **85 Best Buy** *—D.T. (12/31/2004)*

Cockatoo Ridge 2001 Chardonnay (South Australia) $7. 83 *—D.T. (8/1/2003)*

Cockatoo Ridge 2004 Sauvignon Blanc (South Eastern Australia) $7. A very dry, lean, spare style of Sauvignon. Smells fresh—like fresh green pea—and a green herbaceousness continues on the palate. It's just the thing for an outdoor party or wedding, but its wiry profile won't appeal to everyone. **84 Best Buy** *—D.T. (12/1/2005)*

Cockatoo Ridge 2000 Shiraz (South Australia) $7. 86 Best Buy *—K.F. (3/1/2003)*

COCKFIGHTER'S GHOST

Cockfighter's Ghost 1998 Premium Reserve Cabernet Sauvignon (Coonawarra) $35. 84 *—D.T. (6/1/2002)*

Cockfighter's Ghost 2001 Shiraz (McLaren Vale) $23. Straight out of the bottle, the wine tastes and smells quite a bit sweeter than it does after a few minutes in the glass. With air, the caramelly aromas and sweet fruit flavors settle nicely into an enjoyable, easy-drinking wine gussied up with a stony-chalky feel. Straightforward, but evolves nicely. **87** *—D.T. (9/1/2004)*

COLDSTREAM HILLS

Coldstream Hills 2000 Chardonnay (Yarra Valley) $18. 81 *—J.C. (9/10/2002)*

Coldstream Hills 2002 Pinot Noir (Yarra Valley) $18. 87 *—D.T. (10/1/2003)*

Coldstream Hills 2002 Sauvignon Blanc (Victoria) $18. Has youthful grapefruit, yellow peach, and hay aromas. Sweet fruit nectar—like yellow peach—greets you at palate entry. The wine is round in the mouth but finishes with an odd metallic note. Bring it to the beach, or to your next picnic. **86** *—D.T. (5/1/2004)*

COOKOOTHAMA

Cookoothama 2001 Chardonnay (South Eastern Australia) $11. Starts off with warm, inviting aromas of peach and ripe pear, blending in some nutmeg and clove. But the palate doesn't deliver on the early promise, lacking flavor and finishing spicy but short. **83** *—J.C. (1/1/2004)*

Cookoothama 2002 Sauvignon Blanc (King Valley) $10. 84 *—D.T. (1/1/2002)*

CORIOLE

Coriole 2004 Cabernet Sauvignon (McLaren Vale) $30. Smells of sweet blueberry and cumin and, with air, toasted marshmallows. The palate has lifted flavors of black cherry and blueberry, with a soft feel and a good helping of vanilla to round it out. On the sweet side, but an edge of oak saves it from being too lollied. **86** *—D.T. (12/31/2005)*

Coriole 2001 Mary Kathleen Reserve Cabernet Sauvignon-Merlot (McLaren Vale) $45. Aromas are of dark fruit and stable tack. Smooth tannins on the palate cushion fresh black cherry and plum flavors, tinged with a thread of fresh herb. Pretty now, but could go another five years easily. **89** *—D.T. (3/1/2005)*

Coriole 2003 Chenin Blanc (McLaren Vale) $15. This is a casual, porch-sippin' wine, lively and zippy, with prominent yellow peach flavors.

Clean on the close, with dust or mineral flavors and feel. Bright, grassy, and floral on the nose. **86** *—D.T. (5/1/2004)*

Coriole 2003 Sangiovese (McLaren Vale) $NA. From vines planted in 1982 comes this sturdy red, which features cherry and plum flavors, smooth tannins, and an herb-anise finish. Fresh red fruit aromas are a nice beginning. **87** *—D.T. (3/1/2005)*

Coriole 2004 (McLaren Vale-Adelaide Hills) Semillon-Sauvignon Blanc (McLaren Vale) $16. Coriole's varietal Semillon is now only distributed at cellar door. Their American Sem fans will have to instead enjoy this blend, which has dusty attic and pear aromas, and an unusual but fresh palate full of stone and fresh greens. Clean and quaffable. **86** *—D.T. (3/1/2005)*

Coriole 2001 Lloyd Reserve Shiraz (McLaren Vale) $65. Estate-grown; Coriole's flagship wine is the only one of their line to go through malolactic fermentation in barrels, rather than in open fermenters. Dark and meaty on the nose, this quietly powerful, sexy Shiraz has plum fruit at its core; the same plummy chord resonates on the finish. **91** *—D.T. (3/1/2005)*

Coriole 2001 Redstone Shiraz-Cabernet (McLaren Vale) $20. Peppery oak and mixed plum aromas preface classy black-plum fruit in the mouth. It's a medium-sized wine, with a pleasing, chalky feel; on the finish, the chalk is punctuated by a green note. Still, it's very good overall, with a size and feel appropriate for pairing with food. 80% Shiraz; 20% Cabernet. 2,000 cases produced. **87** *—D.T. (9/1/2004)*

CRAGG'S CREEK

Cragg's Creek 2003 Unwooded Chardonnay (Riverland) $15. The bottle may say Chardonnay, but blind, it smells more like Muscat. Orange blossoms and honey aromas and flavors reign here, as does a soft, oily texture. **80** *—D.T. (10/1/2005)*

CRANEFORD

Craneford 2000 Chardonnay (Barossa Valley) $12. **85** *—J.C. (7/1/2002)*

Craneford 2000 Quartet Red Blend (Barossa Valley) $24. **87** *—J.C. (9/1/2002)*

Craneford 2000 Semillon (Barossa Valley) $12. **90 Best Buy** *—J.C. (2/1/2002)*

Craneford 2004 Viognier (Adelaide Hills) $17. Smells like fresh whipping cream and melon, and the flavors are similar, but edged in some white pepper. This is a lithe Viognier, not a fat, alcoholic one, with a bony, dusty spine that stays the fresh-and-balanced course through the finish. **88** *—D.T. (12/31/2005)*

CULLEN

Cullen 2003 Mangan Bordeaux Blend (Margaret River) $40. A blend of Malbec, Petit Verdot and Merlot, dense and dark in color. There are ripe, juicy fruit aromas, with a light smokiness. Ripe, vibrant black fruits dominate with wood flavors in the background. This blend brings out the juiciness of the Merlot and balances it with the tannins of Malbec. **88** *(4/1/2005)*

Cullen 2002 Chardonnay (Margaret River) $55. From the low-yielding 2002 vintage, this wood-aged Chardonnay has finely knit tropical fruits with creamy wood and ripe green plums. It is ripe and rich, with a light touch of pepper hinting at the 14% alcohol. **89** *(4/1/2005)*

Cullen 2001 Ephraim Clarke Semillon-Sauvignon Blanc (Margaret River) $30. **89** *—D.T. (10/1/2003)*

CURRENCY CREEK ESTATE

Currency Creek Estate 2003 The Black Swamp Cabernet Sauvignon (Currency Creek) $17. Smells like demiglace, earth, and tree. On the palate, it's twangy, and not very well integrated: A filmy layer of oak hovers over cursory plum fruit. Simple, one-dimensional. **83** *—D.T. (12/31/2005)*

Currency Creek Estate 2003 Ostrich Hill Shiraz (Currency Creek) $17. A lighter-sized Shiraz, this one features red berry and cherry in abundance on the palate, but flattens out to a dusty, woody finish. Aromas run the gamut from black pepper and sweet raspberry to floral notes, then rhubarb and tomato. **86** *—D.T. (12/31/2005)*

CUTTAWAY HILL ESTATE

Cuttaway Hill Estate 2004 Southern Highlands Pinot Gris (Australia) $16. A thick, fat Gris. This version offers abundant peaches and apricots, spiced with some ginger, on both the nose and the palate. Pleasing and sunny; a good, food-friendly choice. **86** *—D.T. (12/1/2005)*

D'ARENBERG

D'Arenberg 2001 The Galvo Garage Bordeaux Blend (South Australia) $35. **87** *—D.T. (12/31/2003)*

D'Arenberg 1999 The Coppermine Road Cabernet Sauvignon (McLaren Vale) $65. **90** *—M.S. (12/15/2002)*

D'Arenberg 2001 The High Trellis Cabernet Sauvignon (McLaren Vale) $18. Fruit on the nose is very stewy, and doused in licorice. Mixed plum fruit flavors on the palate take on an iced-tea flavor; the finish shows more of the same plus a little green herb. This is a low-acid wine, in need of more structure. **85** *—D.T. (5/1/2004)*

D'Arenberg 2003 The Olive Grove Chardonnay (McLaren Vale) $16. Hints of vanilla, or whipping cream, dress up clear, pretty aromas of pear, peach and apple. On the palate, it's not a fat wine, nor is it wiry—it's somewhere in the middle, with a dry feel and pear, and mineral flavors. Has a flat woodiness on the finish, but overall it's a very nice Chardonnay. 2,000 cases produced. **89** *—D.T. (3/1/2005)*

D'Arenberg 2001 The Olive Grove Chardonnay (McLaren Vale) $15. **83** *—J.C. (7/1/2002)*

D'Arenberg 1999 The Custodian Grenache (McLaren Vale) $23. **85** *—D.T. (12/31/2003)*

D'Arenberg 2002 The Twentyeight Road Mourvèdre (McLaren Vale) $35. Classy, not sassy or brassy—think gallant older gentleman in a bowtie, not a shirtless, greased-up meathead. Aromas are of sturdy red fruit and get sweeter, like meat marinade, with air. Bramble, oak, and fresh herb nuances dress up the plum fruit on the palate; has some hold here on the tongue, and a chalk-claylike feel. **90** *—D.T. (3/1/2005)*

D'Arenberg 2001 D'Arry's Original Shiraz Grenache Red Blend (McLaren Vale) $18. D'Arry's original shows the best of both varieties–it's fresh, fun, and middleweight, with meaty, plummy flavors more associated with Shiraz. An enjoyable, drink-now wine. **88** *—D.T. (5/1/2004)*

D'Arenberg 2002 The Ironstone Pressings Red Blend (McLaren Vale) $65. Named for the ironstone deposits cleared from area vineyards, which—perhaps by power of suggestion—you can taste in the wine. What at first feels like a fistful of oak on the palate, smooths out to an earthy, minerally impression with air. The texture is also quite nice; chewy tannins rule the roost here. Fans of forward, fruity wines should keep shopping. **89** *—D.T. (3/1/2005)*

D'Arenberg 2003 The Laughing Magpie Shiraz Viognier Red Blend (McLaren Vale) $35. Meaty, peppery aromas give way to ones of cherry pie filling after airing. Rhone-styled, perhaps, on the palate, with a cracked-pepper quality accenting the black fruit; there's a lifted quality—the Viognier's floral notes—to the black cherry fruit, that feels overdone. This is a tasty wine, to be sure, but one whose 6% Viognier is about 3% too much. **88** *—D.T. (3/1/2005)*

D'Arenberg 2003 The Stump Jump Red Blend (McLaren Vale) $10. Smells of sweet berries, apples, and grapes. On the palate, it's a food-sized wine, but it's not very distinctive varietally (cut it some slack, it's a blended wine). Just the kind of no-brainer you want for pizza night. Grenache, Shiraz, and Mourvedre. 15,000 cases produced. **85 Best Buy** *—D.T. (3/1/2005)*

D'Arenberg 2003 The Cadenzia Rhône Red Blend (McLaren Vale) $NA. **89** *—D.T. (8/1/2005)*

D'Arenberg 2001 The Broken Fishplate Sauvignon Blanc (Adelaide Hills) $15. **82** *(8/1/2002)*

D'Arenberg 2000 The Dead Arm Shiraz (McLaren Vale) $65. **90** *—C.S. (3/1/2003)*

D'Arenberg 2002 The Footbolt Shiraz (McLaren Vale) $19. Smells like a blended fruit-box juice, and gives a similar impression on the palate. Distinct red raspberry, plum, apple, and grape flavors ride some rough wood on the palate. A straightforward Shiraz, but one that has not smoothed out yet. Give it six months or a year; maybe the wood will settle down. **86** *—D.T. (3/1/2005)*

D'Arenberg 1999 The Footbolt Shiraz (McLaren Vale) $17. **85** *(10/1/2001)*

D'Arenberg 2002 The Laughing Magpie Shiraz (McLaren Vale) $35. The wine's scant 7% Viognier is really noticeable, particularly on the nose, where feminine, floral aromas pretty up black-as-night oak and plum; this reviewer found violets among the wine's similarly dark flavors. The feel is chewy and substantial at midpalate, though a little too woody on the finish. **88** *—D.T. (5/1/2004)*

D'Arenberg 2002 The Hermit Crab White Blend (McLaren Vale) $15. Starts off with a kick of white pepper on the palate, which segues into fleshy stone fruit and a citrus-like tang. It's round in the mouth and moderately zesty, finishing a little less so. **85** *—D.T. (5/1/2004)*

D'Arenberg 2002 The Stump Jump White Blend (McLaren Vale) $10. **87** *—D.T. (11/15/2003)*

DALWHINNIE

Dalwhinnie 2001 Pyrenees Chardonnay (Australia) $40. This Chardonnay opens with fluffy, vanilla-like aromas that thicken to a custard-like density after a few minutes in the glass. As you'd expect, buttery, oaky accents are present on the palate, too, but its core is bright and citrusy. Folks who like a Chard with plenty of creamy fluff on its bones may find this score stingy. **87** *—D.T. (5/1/2005)*

DAVID FRANZ

David Franz 1999 Georgie's Walk Cabernet Sauvignon-Shiraz (Barossa-Langhorne Creek) $NA. The packaging is great: a heavy bottle, with all the wine's details handwritten in what looks like White-Out on an otherwise unlabeled bottle. But for all that style, what's in the bottle is good, but not quite as exciting as the outside package: there's stewy plum fruit, a heavy helping of wood, and caramel-and-cream aromas. **86** *—D.T. (11/15/2004)*

DAVID TRAEGER

David Traeger 1998 Shiraz (Victoria) $24. **83** *(11/1/2001)*

DAVID WYNN

David Wynn 1999 Chardonnay (Barossa Valley) $11. **82** *—M.N. (6/1/2001)*

DE BORTOLI

De Bortoli 2001 Cabernet Sauvignon (Yarra Valley) $35. This lighter-style Cab smells like a basket of plums with a few dates thrown in. On the palate, the wine has a sweet grape flavor and smooth tannins. Finishes with pulpy wood. **85** *—D.T. (10/1/2005)*

De Bortoli 1999 Melba Reserve Cabernet Sauvignon (Yarra Valley) $59. Though the wine contains fruit from the winery's oldest blocks, with only 1.5 tons harvested per acre, we didn't find it quite up to the quality of other De Bortoli wines. Nose shows hints of stewed fruit, molasses, and a leafy quality. In the mouth, it tastes similarly past its prime—dusty, slightly baked-tasting fruit. A bit of a disappointment, considering the wine's reputation. **84** *(11/1/2004)*

De Bortoli 2003 Chardonnay (Yarra Valley) $27. Pleasant tropical-summery aromas have nut and toast accents. The wine is round and medium-bodied in the mouth, with understated yellow fruit flavors. Finishes soft, with a lingering leesy note. **87** *(11/1/2004)*

De Bortoli 2003 dB Chardonnay (Big Rivers) $9. This Chard is a good wine, but it's not the best De Bortoli can do. Aromas are of cream and petrol, and the yellow-fruit flavors are light and straightforward. Lean in the mouth; fine for big groups or casual outings. **83** *—D.T. (12/31/2004)*

De Bortoli 2001 Deen Vat 7 Chardonnay (South Eastern Australia) $10. 84 *—D.T. (12/31/2003)*

De Bortoli 2003 Hunter Valley Chardonnay (Hunter Valley) $20. Very light yellow in the glass, with light floral/fresh meadow aromas to match. White meat and pear fruit is weighty on the front palate, and fades into a bright herbal-steeliness on the finish. Not hugely fat or mouthcoating. It's just the right size, and rather interesting at that. **87** *—D.T. (11/15/2004)*

De Bortoli 2003 dB Selection Petite Sirah (Big Rivers) $8. 85 Best Buy *—D.T. (11/15/2005)*

De Bortoli 2002 Pinot Noir (Yarra Valley) $34. Medium-lean in body, with a spicy-herb nose that also has medicinal, red-catsup hints. Tastes like a mix of fruits—plum and cranberry, surely, but also apple and even apricot. Taut cranberry flavors wind up the finish, where there's also chocolate, and some tea-like tannins. **86** *(11/1/2004)*

De Bortoli 2003 Windy Peak Pinot Noir (Victoria) $15. Not a fat wine—on the contrary, one whose cherry, orange tea, and earth flavors make it feel slim and dry. Offers similar aromas (oak, plum, cherry) that grow sweeter with air. A good introduction to Pinot at a fair price; 800 cases produced. **85** *—D.T. (12/31/2004)*

De Bortoli 2003 Windy Peak Cabernet Rosé Blend (Yarra Valley) $15. A vibrant wine, but one whose flavors and aromas err on the side of strawberry shortcake, whipped cream, and cheese. Dessert in a glass. **82** *—D.T. (10/1/2005)*

De Bortoli 2004 Deen Vat 2 Sauvignon Blanc (South Eastern Australia) $11. It smells like lemondrops, and has plenty of zesty acidity on palate entry. By midpalate, this high-strung Sauvignon settles down a bit, revealing melon in addition to the earlier citrus. It's less intense on the finish, but still a good buy. **86 Best Buy** *—D.T. (10/1/2005)*

De Bortoli 2002 Shiraz (Yarra Valley) $34. Smells of leather, black olives, and dusty spice. On the palate, the wine has a dry, dusty, chalky feel, medium body, and flavors of wheat cracker and plum. Finishes with good structure, and a dusty-peppery flavor. **87** *(11/1/2004)*

De Bortoli 1999 GS Reserve Shiraz (Yarra Valley) $59. Though there are pleasant aromas of meat and Port-like fruit, this wine seems rustic, even mature, at this stage of the game. Broad in the mouth, it has meaty, savory flavors and a finish laden with wooly, tea-like tannins. **84** *(11/1/2004)*

De Bortoli 2002 Gulf Station Shiraz (Yarra Valley) $20. 85 *(11/1/2004)*

De Bortoli 2004 Willowglen Shiraz-Cabernet (South Eastern Australia) $9. The aromas give a distinctly dessert-like impression: Think blackberry pie filling, cherry sorbet. Confected raspberry and black cherry flavors follow on the palate. With air, takes on a hint of weediness on both nose and palate. **82** *—D.T. (10/1/2005)*

DE IULIIS

De Iuliis 1999 Show Reserve Verdelho (Hunter Valley) $9. 83 *—J.C. (2/1/2002)*

DEAKIN ESTATE

Deakin Estate 2004 Chardonnay (Victoria) $9. A good quaffing wine, this Chardonnay is showing yellow fruit aromas, accented by white pepper and a little vanilla. The palate has citrus flavors and a smooth, if a little bulky, body. **85 Best Buy** *—D.T. (5/1/2005)*

Deakin Estate 2002 Chardonnay (Victoria) $8. Has smoke and pear aromas, with pear and anise following through on the palate. Its feel is lean and wiry; finishes with a bright herb or mint accent. **85 Best Buy** *(7/2/2004)*

Deakin Estate 2002 Shiraz (Victoria) $9. Smells like wheat biscuit and grape jelly, with purple fruit and toasty wood following up on the palate. Good but straightforward. **84** *—D.T. (5/1/2005)*

Deakin Estate 1998 Shiraz (Victoria) $12. 89 *(11/15/1999)*

DEEN DE BORTOLI

Deen De Bortoli 1999 Vat 8 Shiraz (South Eastern Australia) $10. 86 *(10/1/2001)*

DELATITE

Delatite 1999 Mansfield Chardonnay (Victoria) $16. 83 *—D.T. (8/1/2003)*

Delatite 2004 Sauvignon Blanc (Victoria) $19. Briny and odd, with flavors akin to watermelon rind mixed with ginger ale. If that sounds strange, join the club. One of our tasters commented that it "hardly seems like wine." **82** *—D.T. (8/1/2005)*

DEVIL'S LAIR

Devil's Lair 2001 Bordeaux Blend (Margaret River) $23. The best feature of this Bordeaux blend (nearly three-quarters Cabernet Sauvignon) is its cottony, furry tannins. Tobacco, wheat toast, and nutmeg flavors and aromas are compelling, if fading a little already, but they also cover up the wine's tart, plummy core. An Old World-styled wine, not a bruising fruit bomb. **87** *—D.T. (10/1/2005)*

Devil's Lair 1999 Fifth Leg Cabernet Sauvignon-Merlot (Margaret River) $22. 86 *—M.S. (12/15/2002)*

Devil's Lair 2002 Chardonnay (Margaret River) $23. This balanced Chard has fresh stone fruit, vanilla, and pineapple flavors, and light talc, citrus, and floral aromas. Seems to unfold on the finish—it's fatter and rounder on the back half than it is on the front. Straightforward and satisfying. **87** *(7/2/2004)*

Devil's Lair 2003 Fifth Leg Red Blend (Western Australia) $12. Rich cassis aromas are tinged with a ribbon of green. The berry and plum fruit flavors are flat, rather than ripe and textured. Fine for casual gatherings. A blend of Cab, Merlot, Shiraz, and Cab Franc. **83** *—D.T. (8/1/2005)*

Devil's Lair 2004 Fifth Leg White Blend (Western Australia) $12. A refreshing, utlitarian white, just right for apéritifs on the deck and summer weddings. Dust and lemondrop aromas; lemondrop and white peach flavors are couched in a soft, dry mouthfeel. Has acids manageable enough for wine newcomers, and enough quaffing enjoyment for anyone. 57% Sauvignon, 26% Semillon, 17% Chardonnay. **86** *—D.T. (8/1/2005)*

Devil's Lair 1999 Fifth Leg White White Blend (Margaret River) $11. 87 Best Buy *—D.T. (10/1/2003)*

DI GIORGIO FAMILY WINES

Di Giorgio Family Wines 2001 Lucindale Merlot (Limestone Coast) $22. 86 *—D.T. (12/31/2003)*

DIAMOND RIDGE

Diamond Ridge 2000 Shiraz (South Eastern Australia) $8. 81 *—J.C. (9/1/2002)*

DOMINIQUE PORTET

Dominique Portet 2002 Cabernet Sauvignon (Heathcote) $35. Smells fairly intense, like blackberry and meat, but tastes cool and crisp. It's not a rich deep wine; some might even call it light-bodied. Me? I think the cherry/black cherry characteristics on the palate will strike some as medicinal, but I liked them just fine. **87** *—D.T. (10/1/2005)*

Dominique Portet 2004 Fontaine Rosé Blend (Yarra Valley) $18. The wine's lactic/cheese aroma right out of the bottle was a turn off, but it blew with time to reveal rosy, raspberry prettiness on the nose. The same notes continue on the palate, where there's also black cherry in a supporting role, and a mineral-smooth feel. 41% Cab, 34% Shiraz, 25% Merlot. **87** *—D.T. (12/31/2005)*

Dominique Portet 2004 Handpicked Sauvignon Blanc (South Eastern Australia) $13. Aromas and flavors of almond and peanut shells dominate through the midpalate, at which point bright lemon notes rush in. Another reviewer found the wine a bit green, with asparagus or green bean accents. **84** *—D.T. (10/1/2005)*

DONNELLY RIVER

Donnelly River 1997 Shiraz (Currency Creek) $16. 87 *(10/1/2001)*

EDEN SPRINGS

Eden Springs 1999 High-Eden Shiraz (Eden Valley) $25. 87 *(11/1/2001)*

ELDERTON

Elderton 1999 Ashmead Single Vineyard Cabernet Sauvignon (Barossa Valley) $33. Elderton's single-vineyard Cab is much different from its regular bottling—this one has red fruit on the palate and the finish, but is a little low in acid. Smells of plums and maple syrup, and finishes with wood and an acidic bite. **86** *—D.T. (5/1/2004)*

Elderton 2004 Unwooded Chardonnay (South Australia) $14. A decent Chardonnay, but one that just isn't all that harmonious. There's burnt-matchstick on the nose, and twangy yellow flavors (mustard seed, citrus) lending tart flavors to the palate. 140 cases produced. **83** *—D.T. (10/1/2005)*

Elderton 2002 Riverina Botrytis Semillon (Barossa Valley) $17. The nose offers a pungent yet strangely alluring combination of petrol and honeysuckle. Butterscotch candy and apricot flavors dominate the palate, but the feel is thick. This is a good wine but one that wants grace, and a little more acidity. **86** *—D.T. (9/1/2004)*

Elderton 2003 The Ashmead Family Shiraz (Barossa) $30. Smells smoky sweet—like fruitcake, nut, and barbecue smoke. On the palate, the wine is narrow, rather than round and mouthfilling, with fresh herb, plum and blackberry flavors dominating. It's a very good wine, but falls short of anything more. **87** *—D.T. (12/1/2005)*

ELDREDGE VINEYARDS

Eldredge Vineyards 2002 Semillon-Sauvignon Blanc (Clare Valley) $14. 88 *—D.T. (12/31/2003)*

ELEMENT

Element 2001 Shiraz-Cabernet (Western Australia) $14. 88 *(7/1/2002)*

AUSTRALIA

ELLEN LANDING

Ellen Landing 1999 Cabernet Sauvignon (Riverland) $19. **86** *—D.T. (9/1/2001)*

Ellen Landing 2000 Shiraz (Riverland) $19. **85** *(3/1/2003)*

ELYSIAN FIELDS

Elysian Fields 2000 Chardonnay (Adelaide Hills) $23. **84** *—D.T. (8/1/2003)*

EPPALOCK RIDGE

Eppalock Ridge 2000 Shiraz (Victoria) $25. **88** *(11/1/2001)*

EPSILON

Epsilon 2004 Coalsack Shiraz (Barossa Valley) $23. This is a wine that hovers on the surface rather than getting too profound. Its fruit is lifted and sweet, accented by violet/floral notes. Finishes with black pepper. **85** *—D.T. (12/1/2005)*

EVANS & TATE

Evans & Tate 2002 Gnangara Cabernet Sauvignon (Western Australia) $11. Has tannins the texture of bread flour or chalk, and flavors of wheat, soil, and vibrant black plum. The nose smells like a forest (tree bark, earth, leaf) with a little eucalyptus and pepper thrown in. A very good value; Western Australian wines don't come cheap. **88 Best Buy** *—D.T. (5/1/2004)*

Evans & Tate 1999 Redbrook Cabernet Sauvignon (Margaret River) $49. **91** *(12/15/2002)*

Evans & Tate 2004 Chardonnay (Margaret River) $16. Offers sun-warmed, fresh golden apple and caramel aromas. Apple flavors come through as well but the texture is odd, like sawdust and mineral. I didn't enjoy this bottling quite as much as E&T's unwooded Chardonnay, but those who prefer caramel to fresh fruit and acidity will feel differently. **85** *—D.T. (12/1/2005)*

Evans & Tate 2001 Chardonnay (Margaret River) $15. **86** *(12/15/2002)*

Evans & Tate 2002 Gnangara Unwooded Chardonnay (Western Australia) $11. **85** *(12/15/2002)*

Evans & Tate 2000 Redbrook Chardonnay (Margaret River) $39. **87** *(12/15/2002)*

Evans & Tate 2003 Classic Red (Margaret River) $15. This blend of Shiraz (66%), Cab (28%), and Merlot (5%) has pleasing aromas and flavors of plum, with Band Aid and oak in supporting roles. Acids are lively. Not a big, rich wine for the cellar but it certainly is a good, everyday bottle. **86** *—D.T. (10/1/2005)*

Evans & Tate 2005 Underground Series Sauvignon Blanc (Western Australia) $11. This is a pretty interesting Sauvignon Blanc. White stone fruit aromas lead into a brisk, lemon-and-hay-flavored palate. Shows some anise and wax on the finish. **86 Best Buy** *—D.T. (11/15/2005)*

Evans & Tate 2001 Shiraz (Margaret River) $18. **89** *(12/15/2002)*

Evans & Tate 2004 Underground Series Shiraz (Western Australia) $11. Smells of earth and ink, with sweet berry fruit on the palate. Has a metallic note on the palate. **83** *—D.T. (12/31/2005)*

EVANS FAMILY

Evans Family 1998 Howard Shiraz (Hunter Valley) $20. **83** *(10/1/2001)*

FAT CROC

Fat Croc 2002 Chardonnay (South Eastern Australia) $8. "Won't cost you an arm and a leg" is Fat Croc's motto. Made in the unoaked, ripe and juicy Australian style, this nicely combines deliciously juicy, tropical fruit flavors with plenty of bracing acid. It avoids the hot, flabby, fake oak flavors that plague most cheap Chardonnays, and gives you a wine that will work better with many foods than a lot of the pricey stuff. **88 Best Buy** *—P.G. (11/15/2004)*

FEATHERTOP

Feathertop 2004 Sauvignon Blanc (Alpine Valleys) $16. A wiry, acidic Sauvignon that's just round enough not to be bracing. Offers vibrant aromas and flavors of lime and white peach. It's pleasingly tart, and plumps up toward the medium-long finish. **90** *—D.T. (8/1/2005)*

FIDDLERS CREEK

Fiddlers Creek 1999 Cabernet Sauvignon-Merlot (South Eastern Australia) $10. **84** *—M.S. (12/15/2002)*

FIRE BLOCK

Fire Block 2002 Old Vine Grenache (Clare Valley) $19. From vines planted in 1926. Though the wine's cherry flavors are a little sweet at first—imagine black cherry soda—it takes on deeper earthy notes with air. Aromas are a little too funky at first, but eventually go the way of black pepper. The message here? Give it some time in the glass to come around. **87** *—D.T. (10/1/2005)*

FIRE GULLY

Fire Gully 1999 Cabernet Sauvignon-Merlot (Margaret River) $23. **89** *(10/1/2003)*

Fire Gully 2002 White Blend (Margaret River) $19. Shows sweet, citrus flavors on the palate (think lemondrops) and a simple, sort of flat feel in the mouth. Finishes short. **82** *—D.T. (5/1/2004)*

FLINDER'S BAY

Flinder's Bay 1999 Shiraz (Margaret River) $18. 86 *(10/1/2001)*

FONTHILL

Fonthill 2001 Silk Shiraz (McLaren Vale) $32. Big fruit and wide-reaching eucalyptus aromas waft from the nose, while on the palate, blackberry and plum fruit flavors take on accents of bramble or fireplace. Dark but elegant; approachable now through 2008. **90** *—D.T. (5/1/2004)*

FOREFATHERS

Forefathers 2001 Shiraz (McLaren Vale) $18. 89 *—J.M. (1/1/2003)*

FOUR EMUS

Four Emus 2005 Sauvignon Blanc-Semillon (Western Australia) $11. A 50-50 blend, with aromas and flavors of green pea, mineral, and citrus. It's a fresh, crisp wine, but don't let the Sauvignon component bring visions of puckery, zesty New Zealand editions to mind. Nope. The Sem is an equal partner, adding both heft and a musky, haylike accent. It's nice to see value-priced wines from somewhere other than South Eastern Australia, too. **86 Best Buy** *—D.T. (11/15/2005)*

FOUR SISTERS

Four Sisters 2002 Trevor Mast 2002 Four Sisters Shiraz (South Eastern Australia) $12. Black plum fruit on the palate shares the spotlight with a meaty, stably flavor—the same note that I found on the nose. It's a straightforward wine, but a much different sort from other lollipop-styled ones that you'll find at this price point. **84** *—D.T. (5/1/2005)*

FOX CREEK

Fox Creek 2001 Duet Cabernet Sauvignon-Merlot (McLaren Vale) $22. 89 *—D.T. (12/31/2003)*

Fox Creek 2004 Chardonnay (McLaren Vale) $13. Light green pea and yellow fruit aromas; palate has peach and pear flavors, with just a hint of vanilla. This vintage, this Chard was barrel fermented for 3–4 weeks in what winemaker Chris Dix calls an "almost unwooded style." Future vintages, he says, will get more oak. **87** *—D.T. (3/1/2005)*

Fox Creek 2002 Chardonnay (South Australia) $15. 87 *—D.T. (8/1/2003)*

Fox Creek 2001 Red Blend (McLaren Vale) $20. 87 *—D.T. (12/31/2003)*

Fox Creek NV Vixen Red Blend (McLaren Vale) $15. 86 *—C.S. (12/1/2002)*

Fox Creek 2004 Sauvignon Blanc (South Australia) $13. The fruit is all McLaren Vale fruit, though the label says South Australia. Mineral and citrus aromas. On the palate, fresh-cut grass envelopes a citrus-rind spine; floral notes surface on the finish. Fresh, zingy and enjoyable. **87** *—D.T. (3/1/2005)*

Fox Creek 2001 Sauvignon Blanc (South Australia) $15. 86 *(8/1/2002)*

Fox Creek 2002 Reserve Shiraz (McLaren Vale) $74. Meaty, burnt sugary aromas are deep. On the palate, tannins are chewy and red fruit is dressed up with coffee and mocha; coffee continues through the long finish. Bears some resemblance to the 1994 Reserve Shiraz, which is still going strong. Drink through 2012. **91** *—D.T. (3/1/2005)*

Fox Creek 2001 Short Row Shiraz (McLaren Vale) $30. 89 *—D.T. (6/1/2003)*

Fox Creek 2001 JSM Shiraz-Cabernet (McLaren Vale) $19. This wine is 70% Shiraz, with Cabernets Franc and Sauvignon filling out the rest of the blend. The JSM isn't quite as good this vintage as it has been in the past, owing largely to its stewy fruit flavors. But it does have its high points. The wine's smooth tannins and sturdy frame are admirable, as are its clay, sand and mocha accents. **87** *—D.T. (11/15/2004)*

Fox Creek 2001 Shiraz-Grenache (McLaren Vale) $17. I like this wine's chewy grip on the palate, and its red plum, berry, and wheat-flour flavors. Well-made, it's just the ticket for a potluck dinner with friends—it would probably stand up equally well to spicy sauces and roasted fowl or meats. **88** *—D.T. (12/31/2004)*

Fox Creek 2002 Verdelho (South Australia) $15. 88 Editors' Choice *—D.T. (12/31/2003)*

FRANKLAND ESTATE

Frankland Estate 2001 Isolation Ridge Vineyard Chardonnay (Western Australia) $20. Has woodsy, hickory aromas, and yellow peach on the palate that tastes just shy of ripe. Wood flavors are also prominent; a good wine, but not as impressive as Frankland's Riesling from this same vineyard. **84** *(7/2/2004)*

Frankland Estate 2000 Olmo's Reward Red Blend (Western Australia) $26. Named for Dr. Harold Olmo, a UC Davis viticulturalist, this red is 42% Cabernet Franc, with Merlot, Cab Sauvignon, Malbec, and Petit Verdot making up the balance. With such a makeup, its core of very taut red plum shouldn't come as a surprise. Also has top-to-bottom herbal accents and a tangy-oak finish—all told, a good, but rather tough, unfamiliar style of wine for most. **86** *—D.T. (9/1/2004)*

Frankland Estate 2004 Isolation Ridge Vineyard Riesling (Frankland River) $20. Dry, stone, and hay notes on the nose are also present on the palate. The main flavor here is peach skin—it's almost sour, but pleasantly so. A little bulky, but has good length on the finish. **88** *—D.T. (10/1/2005)*

Frankland Estate 2002 Poison Hill Vineyard Riesling (Western Australia) $18. 85 *—D.T. (8/1/2003)*

FROG ROCK

Frog Rock 1999 Chardonnay (Mudgee) $20. 86 *—M.S. (3/1/2003)*

Frog Rock 1998 Shiraz (Mudgee) $25. 91 *(11/1/2001)*

GEMTREE

Gemtree 2003 Citrine Chardonnay (McLaren Vale) $15. This Chardonnay only gets three months in French oak, and it's no surprise—it's a fresh, clean rendition of the variety, with dust and melon flavors on the palate. Finishes fresh and minerally. **88** *—D.T. (3/1/2005)*

Gemtree 2003 Tatty Road CS-PV-MER Red Blend (McLaren Vale) $25. Roughly three quarters Cab Sauvignon and one quarter Petit Verdot, with a smidge of Merlot for good measure. Plums, cherries, and spices on the nose hint at what's under inside the palate's thick, tannic shell. Finishes with smooth tannins. **87** *—D.T. (3/1/2005)*

Gemtree 2003 Uncut Shiraz (McLaren Vale) $28. Gemtree's "regular" Shiraz bottling is just as good as its flagship, the Obsidian, though the latter is probably going to last longer in your cellar. This bottling has light fireplace-smoke aromas, and good intensity of fruit on the palate. Plum and black cherry flavors are the focus until black, smoky flavors pop up again midpalate. Medium-sized; appropriate with food. **89** *—D.T. (3/1/2005)*

GEOFF MERRILL

Geoff Merrill 1990 Cabernet Sauvignon (South Australia) $50. 89 *(2/1/2002)*

Geoff Merrill 1980 Cabernet Sauvignon (South Australia) $55. 89 (2/1/2002)

Geoff Merrill 1997 Reserve Cabernet Sauvignon (South Australia) $30. 82 *—S.H. (1/1/2002)*

Geoff Merrill 1995 Reserve Cabernet Sauvignon (South Australia) $35. 91 Cellar Selection *(2/1/2002)*

Geoff Merrill 2000 Pimpala Vineyard Estate Grown Cabernet Sauvignon-Merlot (McLaren Vale) $33. My favorite of the Geoff Merrill wines, and the only one with estate-grown fruit. A singular fresh-eucalyptus note pervades the wine; supplying its weighty core is mixed plum fruit. The eucalyptus note won't appeal to everyone, but it does me. It has its own character, like it or not, as a single-vineyard wine should. **91** *—D.T. (3/1/2005)*

Geoff Merrill 2002 Chardonnay (McLaren Vale) $20. This Chardonnay is round and toasty, with green apple and melon notes dominating. A nice size and not overdone on the oak, but there's a slight metallic hint on the back end. **86** *—D.T. (3/1/2005)*

Geoff Merrill 1996 Reserve Chardonnay (South Eastern Australia) $25. 90 Editors' Choice *(2/1/2002)*

Geoff Merrill 2004 Grenache Rosé (McLaren Vale) $15. A bright, cheerful shade of pink, with aromas of fresh berries. It's round on the palate, with a dry, minerally feel, and berry and cream flavors. A fairly priced but serious rose—not overtly sweet or forward, and a good companion for the table. **88** *—D.T. (3/1/2005)*

Geoff Merrill 2003 Liquid Asset (McLaren Vale) $19. One of Geoff Merrill's newest wines, the Liquid Asset's label is designed to look like a bank check. It's a pretty sophisticated blend for its intended, entry-level market, with black cherry notes dominating. It's an easy, enjoyable quaff and a red that I could even (gasp!) imagine chilling. 80% Shiraz, 15% Grenache, 5% Viognier. **86** *—D.T. (3/1/2005)*

Geoff Merrill 2004 Sauvignon Blanc (McLaren Vale) $20. Light citrus and stone aromas; has less freshness and verve than the Sem-Sauv blend. Still, it's a good, reliable white with mineral and citrus notes at the fore. **86** *—D.T. (3/1/2005)*

Geoff Merrill 2001 Shiraz (McLaren Vale) $23. Shows acorn/nut and mint aromas, and flavors of red plum and chalk that are still somewhat closed. Finishes with juicy plums. Still not at its peak; try in a year or two. **90** *—D.T. (3/1/2005)*

Geoff Merrill 1996 Henley Shiraz (Australia) $100. 93 Cellar Selection *(2/1/2002)*

Geoff Merrill 1998 Reserve Shiraz (McLaren Vale) $30. 89 *—S.H. (1/1/2002)*

Geoff Merrill 1996 Reserve Shiraz (McLaren Vale) $32. 90 *(11/1/2001)*

Geoff Merrill 1994 Reserve Shiraz (South Eastern Australia) $40. 90 Editors' Choice *(2/1/2002)*

GHOST GUM

Ghost Gum 2000 Chardonnay (South Eastern Australia) $9. 84 *—J.C. (7/1/2002)*

Ghost Gum 1998 Shiraz (South Eastern Australia) $9. 87 Best Buy *(10/1/2001)*

GIACONDA

Giaconda 2000 Chardonnay (Victoria) $80. 92 *(6/1/2003)*

Giaconda 2001 Aeolia Roussanne (Victoria) $75. 93 *(6/1/2003)*

Giaconda 2001 Nantua Les Deux White Blend (Victoria) $45. 90 *(6/1/2003)*

GIANT STEPS

Giant Steps 2002 Merlot (Yarra Valley) $35. This is a good red wine, with aromas of bacon bits and vanilla bean, but it is not very interesting or varietally distinct. It has red-plum flavors and a medium body, and closes with smooth, woody tannins. **86** *—D.T. (5/1/2005)*

GIBSON'S BAROSSAVALE

Gibson's BarossaVale 1999 Merlot (South Australia) $28. **83** *—C.S. (6/1/2002)*

Gibson's BarossaVale 2000 Shiraz (South Australia) $40. **89** *—K.F. (3/1/2003)*

Gibson's BarossaVale 2000 Australian Old Vine Collection Shiraz (Barossa Valley) $75. **87** *—K.F. (3/1/2003)*

GLEN ELDON

Glen Eldon 2001 Dry Bore Shiraz (Barossa Valley) $25. The Dry Bore has an earthy, dusty-cocoa overlay, nose to tail, like it's just taken a tumble through the desert. A dry, earthy-woodsy feel keeps the impression going, but the juicy, fat fruit on the front palate brings technicolor to the wine's initial sepia-toned impression. **89** *—D.T. (12/31/2004)*

GOLDING

Golding 2004 Sauvignon Blanc (Adelaide Hills) $15. Aromas are of fresh green peas, and flavors are of grass and limes. Medium-weight and just tart enough; a textbook, very good Sauvignon. **88** *—D.T. (8/1/2005)*

GORGE

Gorge 2004 Pinot Grigio (Hunter Valley) $15. Smells of clarified butter. On the palate, it offers hints of citrus and white peach, and a medium body. Dry on the finish, with more citrus. **85** *—D.T. (12/1/2005)*

GOUNDREY

Goundrey 2002 Offspring Cabernet Sauvignon (Western Australia) $15. Has rich coffee or capuccino notes on the nose, and reined-in mixed-berry fruit flavors that are juicy but blessedly not too sweet. Slim in body, this is the kind of Cab that will show best at the dinner table, with gravied meats and spaghetti alike. **88** *—D.T. (12/31/2004)*

Goundrey 2002 Offspring Chardonnay (Western Australia) $15. It's difficult to find many Western Australian wines at this price, and this Chard is a good introduction to how good the wines out there can be. White peach, citrus, and soy aromas preface peach and oak flavors on the palate. An easy-drinking wine, and one that's made to please everyone. **85** *—D.T. (12/31/2004)*

Goundrey 2002 Offspring Shiraz (Western Australia) $15. Blackberries and blueberries star on the palate; the nose, on the other hand, is all about black pepper. A slimmer-sized Shiraz rather than a huge, jammy one. **87** *—D.T. (5/1/2005)*

GRANT BURGE

Grant Burge 2001 Cameron Vale Cabernet Sauvignon (Barossa Valley) $20. Fruit on the nose has a stewed quality, plus a hint of leafiness. On the palate, blackberry and plum fruit wears a cloak of woody tannins. Juicy, and an easy drinker. **87** *—D.T. (2/1/2004)*

Grant Burge 2002 Barossa Vines Cabernet Sauvignon-Merlot (Barossa Valley) $12. Smells like toast and plush plums. The palate has a cool-vintage tanginess offsetting, perhaps overshadowing, its berry fruit. Dry; finishes with tangy oak. **85** *—D.T. (12/1/2005)*

Grant Burge 2002 Barossa Vines Chardonnay (Barossa Valley) $11. An unwooded Chard, one in which there's nothing to distract you from the bouncy, tropical yellow fruit on the palate. Smells nice, like fresh hay. A fun, easy-drinking white. **86** *—D.T. (2/1/2004)*

Grant Burge 2003 Barossa Vines Unwooded Chardonnay (Barossa Valley) $11. This Barossa Chard has lime, floral and butter notes on the nose. On the palate, there are yellow fruit flavors—think apples and bananas—and a mealy, weighty texture. Finishes with a little alcoholic warmth. Chill it and enjoy on the patio. **83** *(5/1/2004)*

Grant Burge 2002 Summers Chardonnay (Eden Valley) $17. Crisp and flavorful, with medium body and honey, pineapple, and toast aromatics. Its pineapple and nut flavors fade into a bright, citrus-pineapple finish. A very good wine, aptly named for the season in which it should be drunk. **87** *(7/2/2004)*

Grant Burge 2003 Summers Eden Valley Chardonnay (Barossa Valley) $18. Aged in 40% new French oak, and most all is barrel fermented. The oak shows most on the nose, which has a little vanilla, and on the very back palate. Otherwise, the wine is crisp and minerally in the mouth, with pear and citrus fruit. **87** *—D.T. (2/1/2004)*

Grant Burge 2001 Holy Trinity Rhône Red Blend (Barossa Valley) $33. Has a really fragrant, ripe berry bouquet. Feels quite thick on palate entry, full of red plum and black cherry flavors, but it lets up on the palate and finish, which are marked by smooth, soft tannins. **88** *—D.T. (5/1/2004)*

Grant Burge 1998 The Holy Trinity Rhône Red Blend (Barossa Valley) $35. **89** *—J.C. (9/1/2002)*

Grant Burge 2002 Thorn Riesling (Eden Valley) $19. This excellent Riesling puts your salivary glands into overdrive: In the mouth it's refreshing, dry, and puckery, with vibrant grapefruit, lemon, and melon notes. Finishes long and mouthwatering, and smells much the way it tastes: sweet and sour citrus, with some mineral or dust. **90** *—D.T. (8/1/2005)*

Grant Burge 2003 Kraft Sauvignon Blanc (Barossa Valley) $16. Clean and fresh in the mouth, with a taut, pear-fruit core that sticks it out through the finish. On the nose, there's green grass and fresh sweet peas. **87** *—D.T. (2/1/2004)*

Grant Burge 2003 Barossa Vines Shiraz (Barossa) $15. Bright red, bouncy berry aromas are buried underneath nut and vanilla on the nose. It tastes much the same—soft and approachable, with bright raspberry fruit. A good midweek wine. **86** *—D.T. (10/1/2005)*

Grant Burge 2000 Barossa Vines Shiraz (Barossa Valley) $11. **85** *—J.C. (9/1/2002)*

Grant Burge 2002 Filsell Shiraz (Barossa Valley) $30. So well done, from beginning to end. The nose offers a good balance of beef, cherry, plum, and black pepper notes. On the palate, it's mouthwatering, medium-sized, and moderately oaked—that is, there's no caramel or toast in sight. Focused; flavors of black cherry, blackberry, eucalyptus, and black pepper are mouthwatering, and the tannins smooth. **91** *—D.T. (10/1/2005)*

Grant Burge 1998 Filsell Shiraz (Barossa Valley) $25. **87** *—M.M. (6/1/2001)*

Grant Burge 2000 Meshach Shiraz (Barossa Valley) $82. Right out of the gate, this Shiraz may not push your buttons. Give it a few minutes to open up, though, and it offers attractive but restrained plum, cherry, and iron-ore aromas and flavors. Smooth tannins have a firm grip on the midpalate, and follow through to a juicy, lasting finish. Drink now–2013. **91** *—D.T. (8/1/2005)*

Grant Burge 2002 Miamba Shiraz (Barossa Valley) $15. Medium-bodied, with very bright plum, raspberry, and blackberry fruit. Gets more dense toward the finish, with gummy, chunky tannins. Coffee, eucalyptus, and mocha aromas on the nose. **88** *—D.T. (5/1/2004)*

Grant Burge 2000 Miamba Shiraz (Barossa Valley) $15. **89** *—S.H. (1/1/2002)*

Grant Burge 2002 Filsell Shiraz-Cabernet (Barossa Valley) $25. Has great weight in the midpalate, with chewy tannins and bright berry fruit that's tempered by a layer of chalk or talc. On the nose, berry fruit is buried under deep coffee, mocha, and mint aromas. Powerful, but has personality. **90** *—D.T. (5/1/2004)*

Grant Burge 2002 Balthasar Shiraz-Viognier (Barossa Valley) $32. Apart from a slight floral character on the nose, the 7% Viognier doesn't seem to add much to this wine. But that doesn't mean it's not a very good one: It has sweetish plum and cherry aromas, with oak in a supporting role, and tastes just as the nose would lead you to believe. Soft tannins; drink now. **88** *—D.T. (10/1/2005)*

GREEN POINT

Green Point 2002 Chardonnay (Yarra Valley) $16. Shows light stone fruit, and citrus flavors and aromas. It's zesty and lively on the palate, perhaps a little lean for some, but plumps up on the finish. A pre-dinner-or-raw bar sort of Chard. **86** *—D.T. (12/31/2004)*

Green Point 2002 Reseve Chardonnay (Yarra Valley) $25. There's some loud and proud fruit in this Yarra Chard. The wine is very light—almost clear—in color, with intense citrus and stone fruit flavors on the palate. Finishes medium-long with fresh herb and sweet talc powder. A classy, feminine, slinky wine. You want a plump, tropical model? Look elsewhere. **90** *—D.T. (12/31/2004)*

Green Point 2002 Shiraz (Victoria) $18. Big black and red fruit aromas have a barbecued smokiness. On the palate, mixed plums rest on a pillow of bread flour. Unfolds to juicy, ripe fruit on the finish, the floury texture holding on until the end. Very nice. **89** *—D.T. (12/31/2004)*

Green Point 2002 Reserve Shiraz (Yarra Valley) $25. On the nose, this Yarra Shiraz has smoldering, dried spice and barbecue-smoke notes that follow through to the palate, giving more pizzazz to its red plum and berry flavors. Has decent grip on the midpalate. This reserve is very good, but no better than the winery's regular Shiraz. **88** *—D.T. (5/1/2005)*

AUSTRALIA

GREG NORMAN ESTATES

Greg Norman Estates NV Sparkling Blend (Australia) $19. **91** *—K.F. (12/1/2002)*

Greg Norman Estates 2004 Chardonnay (Victoria) $14. A fine, food-friendly, medium-sized Chard whose nose and finish both show a fair amount of wood. Fruit in the center is not very demonstrative, some peach skin holding down the fort. **85** *—D.T. (12/1/2005)*

Greg Norman Estates 2002 Chardonnay (Victoria) $14. A solid wine with presence, not too big or overblown. The nose isn't all that expressive—we found subtle nut and chalk notes—but the palate offers up plenty of sturdy pear fruit, with shakes of nutmeg and chalk. Lingers on the close, with more nut flavors. **88** *(7/2/2004)*

Greg Norman Estates 2000 Chardonnay (Yarra Valley) $17. **84** *—J.C. (7/1/2002)*

Greg Norman Estates 1999 Shiraz (Limestone Coast) $17. **83** *—J.C. (9/1/2002)*

Greg Norman Estates 2000 Padthaway Reserve Shiraz (South Australia) $40. An okay vintage of a typically better wine. The wine is dominated by a nutty, amaretto or liqueurish note, with tangy oak on the finish. There's firm plum fruit and a piquant sweet-tartness that grabs on midpalate, though, that's quite nice. **88** *—D.T. (12/1/2005)*

Greg Norman Estates 1998 Reserve Shiraz (McLaren Vale) $40. **92** *(10/1/2003)*

Greg Norman Estates NV Sparkling Blend (South Eastern Australia) $16. A perennial favorite in the Australian sparklers arena, this wine balances pretty bread-flour and golden apple aromas and flavors with a crisp citrus cleanness. Blessedly dry on the palate; citrus, pear, and biscuit flavors bring it to a clean close. **88** *—D.T. (12/31/2004)*

Greg Norman Estates NV Sparkling Blend (Australia) $19. 85 *—D.T. (12/31/2003)*

GROOM

Groom 2003 Sauvignon Blanc (Adelaide Hills) $16. A sunny, lovely wine, the Groom smells of yellow fruit and vanilla bean (the latter note is strange, considering the wine's unoaked). On the palate, it's lively and crisp, with bright pineapple, citrus, and green grape flavors. Juicy and crisp on the finish, with chalk drawing the wine to its close. Delicious, and affordable to boot. **90 Editors' Choice** *—D.T. (5/1/2004)*

Groom 2001 Shiraz (Barossa Valley) $40. 94 *—J.M. (6/1/2003)*

GROSSET

Grosset 2002 Piccadilly Chardonnay (Clare Valley) $39. Aromas are super, like vanilla bean and fresh cream. The palate strikes a great balance of cream and clean, crisp citrus and stone fruit. The finish is long and zesty, and tastes of lime. Excellent overall. With only 90 cases imported to the U.S., you're more likely to find it on a restaurant list than on your retailer's shelf. **93** *—D.T. (9/1/2004)*

Grosset 2000 Piccadilly Chardonnay (Adelaide Hills) $31. 91 *—J.C. (7/1/2002)*

Grosset 2003 Polish Hill Riesling (Clare Valley) $29. Has beautiful yellow stone fruit aromas and flavors. The mouthfeel is fairly full, but a thread of citrus fruit keeps it zesty and nimble on the tongue. **91** *—D.T. (2/1/2004)*

Grosset 2001 Polish Hill Riesling (Clare Valley) $29. 92 *—J.C. (2/1/2002)*

Grosset 2002 Watervale Riesling (Clare Valley) $25. 87 *—D.T. (8/1/2003)*

GULLIN LANDSCAPE

Gullin Landscape 2000 Chardonnay (South Eastern Australia) $8. 83 *—D.T. (8/1/2003)*

HAAN

Haan 2002 Hanenhof Bordeaux Blend (Barossa Valley) $20. This is one pretty wine, with powdery tannins and a medium-sized body. The nose offers vanilla and blueberry-blackberry aromas. On the palate, there's a baseline of coffee, or cappuccino, with a fan of berry flavors. However sweet or cloying these descriptors make this wine sound, it really isn't. A blend of 78% Cabernet Sauvignon, 12% Merlot, and 10% Cabernet Franc. **90** *—D.T. (5/1/2005)*

HAMELIN BAY

Hamelin Bay 1999 Cabernet Sauvignon (Margaret River) $29. 88 *—C.S. (6/1/2002)*

Hamelin Bay 2000 Chardonnay (Margaret River) $28. 84 *—J.C. (7/1/2002)*

Hamelin Bay 2000 Sauvignon Blanc (Margaret River) $22. 82 *—J.C. (2/1/2002)*

Hamelin Bay 2004 Five Ashes Vineyard Semillon-Sauvignon Blanc (Margaret River) $19. Smells of hay, beeswax and citrus peel. On the palate, almond, hay and citrus flavors are pleasing, but the wine lacks stuffing. It is dry and clean, but would be even nicer if there were more here to appreciate. **85** *—D.T. (10/1/2005)*

HAMILTON'S EWELL VINEYARD

Hamilton's Ewell Vineyard 2000 Ewell Vineyard Cabernet Sauvignon (Barossa Valley) $18. 90 Editors' Choice *—M.S. (12/15/2002)*

Hamilton's Ewell Vineyard 2000 Railway Chardonnay (Barossa Valley) $13. 83 *—J.C. (7/1/2002)*

Hamilton's Ewell Vineyard 1999 Fuller's Barn Shiraz (Barossa Valley) $30. 88 *—K.F. (3/1/2003)*

HANDPICKED

Handpicked 2004 Chardonnay (South Eastern Australia) $13. This Chardonnay follows the same profile that many other please-everyone Chardonnays do: citrus and yellow stone fruit aromas and flavors, a dry mouthfeel, and a medium-sized body. It's a good wine, but it will be nothing new to regular Oz Chard drinkers. **84** *—D.T. (5/1/2005)*

HARDYS

Hardys 2001 Stamp of Australia Cabernet Sauvignon (South Eastern Australia) $6. 82 *—D.T. (1/1/2002)*

Hardys 1999 Tintara Cabernet Sauvignon (South Australia) $18. 83 *—J.C. (6/1/2002)*

Hardys 2000 Nottage Hill Cabernet Sauvignon-Shiraz (South Eastern Australia) $8. 84 *—M.S. (12/15/2002)*

Hardys 2003 Nottage Hill Chardonnay (South Eastern Australia) $8. Hardys Nottage Hill line is almost always a good buy, and this Chard fits the bill quite right. It smells of roasted peanuts and stone fruit, and maybe a little pineapple. Plump and easy in the mouth, there's melon and toast flavors, with a little sorghum sweetness. **85 Best Buy** *(7/2/2004)*

Hardys 2001 Nottage Hill Chardonnay (South Eastern Australia) $7. 85 Best Buy *—J.C. (7/1/2002)*

Hardys 2002 Stamp of Australia Chardonnay (South Eastern Australia) $6. **85** —*D.T. (8/1/2003)*

Hardys 2000 Tintara Chardonnay (South Australia) $15. **87** —*J.C. (7/1/2002)*

Hardys 2000 Nottage Hill Merlot (South Eastern Australia) $7. **84** —*D.T. (6/1/2002)*

Hardys 2000 Eileen Hardy Shiraz (South Australia) $90. On the nose, the sweet plum fruit is just this side of stewy; dark black and blueberry fruit on the palate is edged by caramel, toast, and maybe a little rubber. Medium-weight, with woodsy tannins on the finish. A solid, dark wine. **88** —*D.T. (5/1/2004)*

Hardys 1998 Eileen Hardy Shiraz (McLaren Vale & Padthaway) $70. **89** *(11/1/2001)*

Hardys 2001 Nottage Hill Shiraz (South Eastern Australia) $8. A smooth, straightforward wine, medium-bodied in the mouth, with mixed plum and caramel flavors. Smells of oak and meat; a no-brainer for Tuesday nights or backyard barbecues. **86 Best Buy** —*D.T. (5/1/2004)*

Hardys 2001 Oomoo Shiraz (McLaren Vale) $12. A down-the-line, straight-forward Shiraz, not superlayered or nuanced, but enjoyable. Fresh plum fruit is forward, and takes on sweet-spice accents of clove and cinnamon on the nose. **86** —*D.T. (12/31/2005)*

Hardys 2004 Stamp of Australia Shiraz (South Eastern Australia) $6. A good wine for wine newbies, featuring bouncy, fruit-ripe flavors and raspberry and smoke aromas. Has a Sweet-Tart flavor and feel, and a graham-cracker finish. **84 Best Buy** —*D.T. (12/31/2005)*

Hardys 2001 Stamp of Australia Shiraz (South Eastern Australia) $6. **83** —*D.T. (1/1/2002)*

HARTZ BARN WINES

Hartz Barn Wines 2001 Mail Box Merlot (Barossa Valley) $30. **83** —*D.T. (1/1/2002)*

HASTWELL & LIGHTFOOT

Hastwell & Lightfoot 2000 Shiraz (McLaren Vale) $28. This Shiraz's aromas change from caramel and stewed fruit to mineral and back to caramel; the palate offers up plenty of red plum and cherry, and a minerally feel. It's slight-bodied—not lean, but not a big wine, by any means—with caramel and gravelly-mineral on the finish. **87** —*D.T. (9/1/2004)*

HAWKERS GATE

Hawkers Gate 2000 Shiraz (McLaren Vale) $21. The nose offers stewy, jammy fruit and pickling-spice aromas. This is a lighter-sized wine that wants to be a heavyweight, with such dark oak, caramel, and black cherry flavors. Finishes with similar flavors. **85** —*D.T. (5/1/2004)*

HEARTLAND

Heartland 2004 Stickleback White Blend (South Australia) $11. Here, 25% Verdelho is an unexpected component to a typical Sem-Chard blend, and the overall result is a very pleasing one. This is a fresh, clean white, with pear and Granny Smith apple flavors and a flinty-chalky feel. Great for the outdoors, and priced reasonably enough to keep a few extras around the house. **88 Best Buy** —*D.T. (8/1/2005)*

HEATH WINES

Heath Wines 2002 Southern Roo Cabernet Sauvignon-Shiraz (South Australia) $14. Has aromas of anise gumdrop, chocolate, and coconut. On the palate, black plum and blackberry fruit tastes slightly underripe. Not a fleshy, generous red. 85% Cab, 15% Shiraz. **83** —*D.T. (5/1/2005)*

HEATHFIELD RIDGE

Heathfield Ridge 1999 Cabernet Sauvignon (Limestone Coast) $16. **84** —*M.S. (12/15/2002)*

Heathfield Ridge 2000 Reserve Chardonnay (Limestone Coast) $16. **83** —*D.T. (8/1/2003)*

Heathfield Ridge 1999 Shiraz (Limestone Coast) $16. **84** —*M.S. (1/28/2003)*

HEAVEN'S GATE

Heaven's Gate 2001 Shiraz (Barossa Valley) $15. **86** —*D.T. (12/31/2003)*

HEGGIE'S VINEYARD

Heggie's Vineyard 1996 Merlot (Eden Valley) $22. **82** —*M.M. (9/1/2001)*

Heggie's Vineyard 1999 Viognier (Eden Valley) $22. **85 Best Buy** —*D.T. (2/1/2002)*

Heggies Vineyard 2001 Chardonnay (Eden Valley) $20. **92** —*S.H. (1/1/2002)*

Heggies Vineyard 1998 Merlot (Eden Valley) $22. **84** —*S.H. (12/15/2002)*

HENSCHKE

Henschke 2000 Cyril Henschke Cabernet Sauvignon-Merlot-Cabernet Franc (Eden Valley) $100. A tribute to Stephen Henschke's father, this excellent Bordeaux-style blend is approachable even now, but could age through 2010, and maybe even beyond. The nose is just amazing, with mint, pepper, caraway seed, and cream, all over lush plum fruit. Plum fruit is juicy and ripe on the palate, swathed in smooth, chalky tannins that linger on the finish. **92** *—D.T. (5/1/2004)*

Henschke 2002 Lenswood Abbotts Prayer (Adelaide Hills) $70. This is an enjoyable wine, one with coffee and caramel accents on the nose, and plum, berry, and oak flavors. It's hard not to like, but at this price, shouldn't it be love at first sight? Merlot, with some Cab Sauvignon and Cab Franc. **87** *—D.T. (8/1/2005)*

Henschke 2002 Cranes Chardonnay (Eden Valley) $38. This is a very good Chardonnay, but one with oak around every turn. Has aromas of caramel, brown sugar, and nut, plus baked apple, and caramel flavors. Obviously well-made with quality fruit—we'd just like to see a little less wood next vintage. **87** *(7/2/2004)*

Henschke 2003 Lenswood Croft Chardonnay (Adelaide Hills) $45. An elegant style and size for Chardonnay, the Croft pleases again this vintage. Smells and tastes lightly nutty, like almonds and walnuts. Fuzzy peach flavors and feel complete the picture. **89** *—D.T. (8/1/2005)*

Henschke 1998 Lenswood Croft Chardonnay (Adelaide Hills) $40. 88 *(3/1/2000)*

Henschke 2003 Little Hampton Innes Vineyard Pinot Gris (Adelaide Hills) $30. 87 *—D.T. (8/1/2005)*

Henschke 2004 Little Hamptons Innes Vineyard Pinot Gris (Adelaide Hills) $30. Smells pretty and feminine—yellow peach, pencil eraser, and a definitive floral quality you might first attribute to Viognier. On the palate, it's delicate and elegant, with yellow peach, honey, and straw flavors. Feels dry and stony, yet smooth. **89** *—D.T. (8/1/2005)*

Henschke 2002 Henry's Seven (Barossa Valley) $30. A blend of 60% Shiraz, 35% Grenache, and 5% Viognier; I enjoyed this year's vintage much more than last year's. It's forward and approachable, with black and red cherry fruit wrapped in a black-earth blanket. **89** *—D.T. (5/1/2004)*

Henschke 2002 Johann's Garden Rhône Red Blend (Eden Valley) $30. This medium-bodied wine features taut plum fruit on the palate, and lots of eucalyptus on the nose and the finish. A strange but very good wine; I picked up a bananalike flavor among the plums on the palate. **87** *—D.T. (5/1/2004)*

Henschke 2001 Julius Riesling (Eden Valley) $25. 89 *—D.T. (8/1/2003)*

Henschke 2004 Lenswood Coralinga Sauvignon Blanc (Adelaide Hills) $27. Quite minerally on the nose, with flint and some pickled vegetable to boot. Grapefruit, green apple, and lemon-lime flavors carry the palate to a finish that is tart and tight. Seems to pick up speed along the way, thus it finishes better than it starts. **85** *(7/1/2005)*

Henschke 2002 Louis Semillon (Eden Valley) $25. Smells like a meadow, with fresh grass and flowers at the fore. Apricots and other yellow fruits flavor the palate. Has good grip in the mouth; a gummy, resinous feel lingers on the tongue and through the finish. A fine wine. **89** *—D.T. (2/1/2004)*

Henschke 1998 Hill of Grace Shiraz (Eden Valley) $300. "Hill of Grace has a smell that reminds me of my grandmother's handbag—cloth, with a wooden handle," says Stephen Henschke. Strange but understandable. I thought it smelled like an odd but nice mix of green olive, eucalyptus, and eggroll wrapper. It's a beautiful wine, with a base of red plums on the palate, dusted with mulling spices. Finishes with a flourish of clay and chalk. As excellent as this wine is, the '99 is even better. **94 Cellar Selection** *—D.T. (2/1/2004)*

Henschke 2003 Tilly's Vineyard White Blend (Eden Valley) $NA. 87 *—D.T. (1/1/2002)*

HERITAGE ROAD

Heritage Road 1999 Bethany Creek Vineyard Limited Reserve Cabernet Sauvignon (Barossa Valley) $30. 93 *—S.H. (6/1/2002)*

Heritage Road 1998 Reserve Cabernet Sauvignon (Limestone Coast) $16. 89 *(12/1/2000)*

Heritage Road 1999 Chardonnay (Hunter Valley) $13. 87 *—S.H. (6/1/2001)*

Heritage Road 2001 Sandy Hollow Vineyard Chardonnay (Hunter Valley) $12. 88 *—S.H. (1/1/2002)*

Heritage Road 2001 Shiraz (South Australia) $12. 85 *—S.H. (12/15/2002)*

Heritage Road 1998 Shiraz (South Australia) $10. 88 Best Buy *(12/1/2000)*

Heritage Road 1998 Reserve Shiraz (Limestone Coast) $16. 91 *(12/1/2000)*

HERMITAGE ROAD

Hermitage Road 1998 Chardonnay (Hunter Valley) $9. 85 *—M.M. (10/1/1999)*

HEWITSON

Hewitson 2001 L'Oizeau Shiraz (McLaren Vale) $27. Medium-bodied, with a soft mouthfeel, this wine is all about black cherry and eucalyptus, top to bottom. It's quite a nice wine, if one that doesn't have too many tricks up its sleeve. **87** *—D.T. (9/1/2004)*

HILL OF CONTENT

Hill of Content 2001 Grenache-Shiraz (Clare-McClaren Vale) $13. Has pretty aromas of cherry and mocha, and a chewy mouthfeel. Its plum and cherry fruit is bright, but tempered well by darker earth and oak notes. Finishes with tangy tea-oak flavors. The fruit is from Clare Valley (83%) and McLaren Vale (17%). **89** *—D.T. (9/1/2004)*

Hill of Content 2004 Benjamin's Blend (Western Australia) $14. This is an unwooded blend of Chardonnay, Semillon, and Sauvignon. Nose offers fresh green bean and grass aromas. Bulky in the mouth, with sour citrus and mineral flavors. **82** *—D.T. (10/1/2005)*

HILLSVIEW VINEYARDS

Hillsview Vineyards 1999 Blewitt Springs Cabernet Sauvignon (Fleurieu Peninsula) $15. 88 *—D.T. (6/1/2003)*

HOLLICK

Hollick 1998 Cabernet Sauvignon-Merlot (Coonawarra) $20. 83 *—J.C. (6/1/2002)*

Hollick 1999 Chardonnay (Coonawarra) $17. 83 *—J.C. (7/1/2002)*

Hollick 1998 Wilgha Shiraz (Coonawarra) $34. 87 *—J.C. (9/1/2002)*

HOPE ESTATE

Hope Estate 1999 Cabernet Sauvignon (Hunter Valley) $13. 86 *(7/1/2001)*

Hope Estate 2003 Chardonnay (Hunter Valley) $11. Smells like Brazil nuts and talc powder. On the palate, this minerally, dry wine has lingering peach-fuzz flavors. This bottling is not quite as good as last year's, but it's still a great value. 6,000 cases produced. **86 Best Buy** *—D.T. (5/1/2005)*

Hope Estate 2000 Chardonnay (Hunter Valley) $10. 87 *—J.C. (7/1/2002)*

Hope Estate 1999 Merlot (Hunter Valley) $13. 85 *(7/1/2001)*

Hope Estate 1998 Shiraz (Hunter Valley) $13. 83 *(4/1/2000)*

Hope Estate 1999 Shiraz (Hunter Valley) $13. 89 Best Buy *(7/1/2001)*

Hope Estate 2002 Verdelho (Hunter Valley) $8. 84 *—D.T. (12/31/2003)*

Hope Estate 1998 Verdelho (Hunter Valley) $9. 87 Best Buy *(7/1/2001)*

HOWARD PARK

Howard Park 2001 Mad Fish Bordeaux Blend (Western Australia) $16. This Bordeaux-style blend doesn't show much on the nose at first, but with air, you'll see very pretty red fruit and some dried spice. On the palate, the plum fruit is pure—not sweet, but nicely ripe. Medium in body with tealike tannins, it closes darker than it begins, with tea and oak flavors. A lovely wine. **89** *—D.T. (9/1/2004)*

Howard Park 2002 Leston Cabernet Sauvignon (Margaret River) $21. The Leston Cab is excellent again this year, with juicy, ripe black- and blueberries from start to finish. Has a smooth feel—like washed river rocks—and earthy, iron-ore nuances on the nose. Drinkable now, but will hold 3–5 years. **90** *—D.T. (12/1/2005)*

Howard Park 2002 Scotsdale Cabernet Sauvignon (Great Southern) $21. Has a green asparagus or pepper streak on the nose, plus a dominant acorn note that continues through to the palate, where there's also some just-ripe plum buried under mounds of dust. Winemaker Mike Kerrigan thinks that this is the style of wine that shines better with food, rather than in a wine-by-wine lineup. He's probably right. **86** *—D.T. (10/1/2005)*

Howard Park 1999 Cabernet Sauvignon-Merlot (Western Australia) $48. 88 *(10/1/2003)*

Howard Park 2003 Mad Fish Chardonnay (Western Australia) $18. An unwooded Chardonnay, with a peach-and-citrus profile. Soft and smooth in the mouth, the wine finishes with pear. Enjoyable, and easy to drink. **88** *(7/2/2004)*

Howard Park 2002 Leston Shiraz (Margaret River) $21. Such a juicy wine. Well-ripened plums, blackberries, and raspberries dominate the palate, though here and on the nose there are tea and earth accents, too. Takes on hints of anise with air. Drinking well now. **89** *—D.T. (10/1/2005)*

Howard Park 2000 Leston Shiraz (Margaret River) $30. 89 *(10/1/2003)*

Howard Park 2001 Mad Fish Shiraz (Western Australia) $16. 85 *—D.T. (10/1/2003)*

Howard Park 2001 Scotsdale Shiraz (Margaret River) $30. I somehow always prefer HP's Leston Shiraz to the Scotsdale, but at least the two bottlings do have their own personalities. This wine has woodsy tannins, and a slight greenness mixed in with its black grape and plum fruit. Finishes woody and wooly, with that leaf-stem flavor again. The note that is offputting to this reviewer stems from terroir, not flawed winemaking; the wine may be more attractive to others. **86** *—D.T. (11/15/2004)*

HUGH HAMILTON

Hugh Hamilton 1998 Shiraz (McLaren Vale) $16. 86 *(10/1/2001)*

INDIS

Indis 2004 Chardonnay (Western Australia) $15. Smells spicy and tropical, like something that you would want to drink on a beach vacation. The palate deals pineapple and coconut flavors, and good acidity. (Disclaimer: This review makes this wine sound sweeter and simpler than it actually is, but that's because I can't play steel-drum music in the background, and throw some sand between your toes.) **87** —*D.T. (12/1/2005)*

INNOCENT BYSTANDER

Innocent Bystander 2004 Rosé Pinot Noir (Yarra Valley) $16. I like this wine, though it is a little odd. The wine's cherry fruit also takes on an interesting orange character, through and through, plus accents of lavender. Closes taut, with sour cherries and citrus. Give it a go. 300 cases produced. **87** —*D.T. (10/1/2005)*

IRONWOOD

Ironwood 2003 Chardonnay (South Eastern Australia) $6. A straightforward South Eastern Australian offering that won't ruffle any feathers. Aromas are of golden apples and toast, and it tastes as it smells. Citrus accents bring it to a dry close. **85 Best Buy** —*D.T. (12/31/2004)*

IRVINE

Irvine 2002 Unoaked Chardonnay (Eden Valley) $16. Unoaked though it may be, we picked up a lot of nut, plus dusty yellow fruit, on the nose. Tastes perfumey and talcy, like a lady's dressing room, with spicedrops, pear, and melon in the background. Finish is tangy. **84** *(7/2/2004)*

JACKAROO

Jackaroo 2001 Big Red Red Blend (South Eastern Australia) $7. A blend of Cabernet Sauvignon, Shiraz, and Merlot. Carmel, red fruit, and herb aromas lead to a middle-weight palate that offers up plum and cherry fruit. Mouthfeel is soft; finishes with earth, plum, and orange-pekoe tea. An easy drinking wine, and a good choice if you're trying to sidestep the overly sweet and candied wines that are sometimes offered at this price point. **86 Best Buy** —*D.T. (12/31/2004)*

JACOB'S CREEK

Jacob's Creek 2003 Cabernet Sauvignon (South Eastern Australia) $9. Straightforward and lacking stuffing, this Cab has some berry fruit tucked under a veneer of oak. Aromas of soy sauce, plum and putty complete the picture. **83** —*D.T. (12/31/2005)*

Jacob's Creek 2001 Cabernet Sauvignon (South Eastern Australia) $10. 84 —*D.T. (6/1/2003)*

Jacob's Creek 2002 Reserve Cabernet Sauvignon (South Australia) $13. Very dark in color. This wine's aromas are pretty straightforward, just red berry and wood. On the palate, there's red fruit and earth. The highlight here is the wine's velvety, wooly texture. It's mainstream, yes, but it's food-friendly and tasty. **88 Best Buy** —*D.T. (12/31/2005)*

Jacob's Creek 2003 Cabernet Sauvignon-Merlot (South Eastern Australia) $9. Smells okay, but overdone and syrupy. Has a metallic note on the palate, plus sour berry and plum fruit. Tasted twice. **82** —*D.T. (8/1/2005)*

Jacob's Creek NV Brut Cuvée (South Eastern Australia) $12. Chief Winemaker Philip Laffer says that he wanted this wine to be of an "aperitif style—that once you count to five, it should all disappear." In both respects, the wine succeeds. It's 20% Pinot Noir, with very light stone fruit flavors and wide foamy mousse on the palate. Chalk and stone fruit flash on the finish. Only 3 or 4,000 cases on the U.S. market now, but many more are sure to follow. **85 Best Buy** —*D.T. (2/1/2004)*

Jacob's Creek 2003 Chardonnay (South Eastern Australia) $8. Has feminine, talc, and floral aromas, and sour, citrusy yellow fruit flavors. Mouthfeel is wide and somewhat viscous. It grows leaner on the finish, with citrus peel and fresh green-produce flavors. **84** *(7/2/2004)*

Jacob's Creek 2001 Chardonnay (South Eastern Australia) $8. 84 —*J.C. (7/1/2002)*

Jacob's Creek 1999 Chardonnay (South Eastern Australia) $9. 85 *(5/1/2000)*

Jacob's Creek 2000 Limited Release Chardonnay (Padthaway) $33. 89 *(6/1/2003)*

Jacob's Creek 2003 Reserve Chardonnay (South Eastern Australia) $13. Peach, butter and oak aromas and flavors make for a please-everyone style of wine. It's a medium-sized, food-friendly, reliably good Chardonnay. 444,000 cases produced. **86** —*D.T. (10/1/2005)*

Jacob's Creek 2001 Reserve Chardonnay (South Australia) $13. 84 —*D.T. (6/1/2003)*

Jacob's Creek 1999 Reserve Chardonnay (Barossa Valley) $16. 88 *(2/1/2001)*

Jacob's Creek 1997 Reserve Chardonnay (Padthaway) $14. 85 —*J.C. (10/1/1999)*

Jacob's Creek 2003 Merlot (South Eastern Australia) $9. Has a nice gum-eraser aroma and texure that you don't typically get in wines at this price. There's also hints of nail polish remover in the mid-palate. Finishes short. **83** —*D.T. (3/1/2005)*

Jacob's Creek 2001 Merlot (South Eastern Australia) $10. 84 —*D.T. (6/1/2003)*

Jacob's Creek 1998 Merlot (South Eastern Australia) $10. 84 *(5/1/2000)*

Jacob's Creek 2004 Riesling (South Eastern Australia) $9. Smells like dusty peaches. On the palate, it offers yellow-gumdrop flavors that start off fairly flavorfully, but quickly go dilute, then flavorless, by the finish. **82** —*D.T. (12/1/2005)*

Jacob's Creek 2003 Reserve Riesling (Clare Valley) $13. A pleasing powder puff of a wine, one that feels round and airy in the mouth, with a chalky flavor throughout. Finishes with fluffy lemon meringue. **88 Best Buy** *—D.T. (2/1/2004)*

Jacob's Creek 2003 Semillon-Chardonnay (South Eastern Australia) $8. Fragrances of talc, white stone fruit, and Silly Putty make for an interesting, eye-opening nose. On the palate, the wine feels round and minerally, but is not very demonstrative in terms of flavor, beyond some fresh citrus and herb notes. Easy-drinking and straightforward. **84 Best Buy** *—D.T. (11/15/2004)*

Jacob's Creek 1998 Shiraz (South Eastern Australia) $10. **88 Best Buy** *(5/1/2000)*

Jacob's Creek 1999 Shiraz (South Eastern Australia) $11. **84** *—J.C. (9/1/2002)*

Jacob's Creek 2001 Reserve Shiraz (South Australia) $13. Offers juicy, attractive plum fruit at a good price, and finishes with red clay flavors. It's forward and accessible, not complicated but still very good. **88 Best Buy** *—D.T. (2/1/2004)*

Jacob's Creek 1998 Reserve Shiraz (Barossa Valley) $18. **91** *(2/1/2001)*

Jacob's Creek 2002 Shiraz-Cabernet (South Eastern Australia) $8. Aromas are of sweet, dark fruit, roasted meat, and oak. Mouthfeel is somewhat dusty, with pedestrian red and black fruit, bolstered by just enough oak. **84 Best Buy** *—D.T. (12/31/2004)*

Jacob's Creek 2000 Shiraz-Cabernet (South Eastern Australia) $10. **83** *—J.C. (9/1/2002)*

Jacob's Creek 1999 Limited Release Shiraz-Cabernet (South Eastern Australia) $50. Shiraz from this well-tempered, pretty wine is from Barossa, and the Cab from Coonawarra. Aromas are crisp and racy—think black cherry and eucalyptus, plus some cinnamon or spice—and the same elements play out on the palate. Mouthfeel is dry and dusty, all the way through the medium-long finish. **89** *—D.T. (12/31/2004)*

Jacob's Creek 1997 Limited Release Shiraz-Cabernet (South Australia) $50. **90** *—D.T. (12/15/2002)*

Jacob's Creek 2003 Syrah-Grenache (South Eastern Australia) $8. Sweet, light, and fruity from top to bottom: Coconut, cherry, and chocolate aromas kick it off, and segue to cherry and raspberry flavors on the palate. A simple, easy quaffer. **83** *—D.T. (9/1/2004)*

JAMES ESTATE

James Estate 2000 Cabernet Sauvignon (McLaren Vale) $13. **86 Best Buy** *(11/1/2002)*

James Estate 2001 Sundara Cabernet Sauvignon-Merlot (South Eastern Australia) $9. **82** *(11/1/2002)*

James Estate 2000 Compass Chardonnay (Hunter Valley) $13. **90 Best Buy** *—S.H. (6/1/2002)*

James Estate 2001 Sundara Chardonnay (South Eastern Australia) $9. **84** *(11/1/2002)*

James Estate 2000 Reserve Merlot (Hunter Valley) $20. **87** *(11/1/2002)*

James Estate 2000 Sundara Semillon-Chardonnay (Hunter Valley) $9. **88 Best Buy** *—S.H. (6/1/2002)*

James Estate 1999 Shiraz (Hunter Valley) $13. **84** *—S.H. (6/1/2002)*

James Estate 2000 Reserve Shiraz (McLaren Vale & Langhorne Creek) $20. **88** *(11/1/2002)*

James Estate 2001 Verdelho (Hunter Valley) $13. **85** *(11/1/2002)*

JCP MALTUS

JCP Maltus 2003 The Colonial Estate L'Étranger Cabernet Sauvignon (Barossa Valley) $27. L'Étranger is the most appropriately named wine I've come across in a while. This bottling offers raisiny, bready aromas (think cinnamon-raisin bagel), and earthy, sweet-and-sour notes on the palate (think Sweet-Tart, tree, and raisin). A strange one, indeed. **84** *—D.T. (8/1/2005)*

JIM BARRY

Jim Barry 1997 McCrae Wood Bordeaux Blend (Clare & Eden Valleys) $30. **82** *—D.T. (9/1/2001)*

Jim Barry 2003 The Cover Drive Cabernet Sauvignon (South Australia) $17. Tastes a little more mainstream and crowd-pleasing than usual, the jaunty, pick-it-out-of-a-crowd eucalyptus character of vintages past toned down considerably. Still, there are very nice bitter chocolate and anise accents to the fruit on the palate, and tree bark or acorn notes on the nose. **88** *—D.T. (12/31/2005)*

Jim Barry 2002 The Cover Drive Cabernet Sauvignon (Clare Valley-Coonawarra) $15. I very much like and admire this wine for many reasons, but primarily because it doesn't taste like any other wine. There's black cherry fruit at the center, with currant, olive, and earthy flavors. It's a sizeable, though not overdone, wine with a nice chalk-clay texture, and aromas of eucalyptus, earth, and cool-climate fruit. Only in its second vintage but already consistently good. **90 Editors' Choice** *—D.T. (11/15/2004)*

Jim Barry 2004 The Lodge Hill Riesling (Clare Valley) $17. Oysters, porches, weddings—the Lodge Hill is just this type of wine. Citrus peel on the nose ushers in gooseberry and chalk flavors on the palate. It's clean and refreshing, with a medium-length finish. **85** *—D.T. (10/1/2005)*

Jim Barry 2001 Armagh Shiraz (Clare Valley) $100. A warming, lusty wine, with tannins that are soft and supple enough that the wine can be drunk now. Tastes like plum, caramel, and coffee; smells like pure red grapes, plus walnuts and roasted meat. Will cure whatever ails you. Drink now–2010. **92** *—D.T. (5/1/2004)*

Jim Barry 1996 Armagh Shiraz (Clare Valley) $75. **97** *(11/15/1999)*

Jim Barry 1999 Armagh Shiraz (Clare Valley) $100. 95 Cellar Selection *—S.H. (12/15/2002)*

Jim Barry 2002 McRae Wood Shiraz (Clare Valley) $35. 92 *—D.T. (1/1/2002)*

Jim Barry 2000 McRae Wood Shiraz (Clare Valley) $35. 89 *(12/1/2003)*

Jim Barry 2003 The Lodge Hill Shiraz (Clare Valley) $17. Creamier and fuller than other Clare Shirazes at its price point, this bottling offers spice, plum, and Sweet-Tart flavors. The drawback for me is a creamy-sweet lactic aroma—like a nose full of cheesecake—but that might be a turn-on for others. **85** *—D.T. (12/1/2005)*

Jim Barry 1999 The Mcrae Wood Shiraz (Clare Valley) $35. 92 Editors' Choice *—S.H. (12/15/2002)*

JINKS CREEK

Jinks Creek 2002 Pinot Noir (Gippsland) $30. This Pinot's fruit hails from Gippsland, in Victoria—plum fruit is red and softer than you'll get on many other Pinots, with anise, spice, and pepper accents. Has a nice, chalky mouthfeel; finishes with more red plum fruit. Enjoyable and very good, and very New World in style. **88** *—D.T. (9/1/2004)*

Jinks Creek 2002 Sauvignon Blanc (Gippsland) $20. More White Wine than Sauvignon, there's lightweight yellow fruit at its core, dressed up with confectioners' sugar and flour. Couple that with pineapple and passion fruit aromas on the nose, and meat-and-sugar flavors on the close, and you've just got a good but confused, varietally vague wine. **84** *—D.T. (5/1/2004)*

JOHN DUVAL WINES

John Duval Wines 2003 Plexus (Barossa Valley) $35. The first solo endeavor from former Penfolds head winemaker John Duval is an admirable one, containing 46% Shiraz, 32% Grenache, and 22% Mourvèdre. Blackberries and plums take on a hearty helping of spice and black pepper, nose to finish. Chewy tannins and charred meats linger on the midpalate as well. **90** *—D.T. (8/1/2005)*

KAESLER

Kaesler 2001 Cabernet Sauvignon (Barossa Valley) $22. The smooth tannins on this wine are just stupendous; the black plum and white pepper flavors are also excellent, but definitely secondary to the wine's silky texture. Burnt brown sugar comes through on the nose, perhaps an indication of the 50% new French oak treatment. **92 Editors' Choice** *—D.T. (2/1/2004)*

Kaesler 2002 Avignon Red Blend (Barossa Valley) $24. A GSM with a great, soft, milky-chalky mouthfeel, the Avignon has rich plum fruit layered with soil, and a shot of raspberry running through it. Keep this one in mind for next year's Thanksgiving—it would stand up superbly to turkey and roasted yams. **90** *—D.T. (2/1/2004)*

Kaesler 2002 Stonehorse Red Blend (Barossa Valley) $18. The cherry notes typical of Grenache are prevalent on the nose and on the palate, with Shiraz's darker plum fruit coming up quick behind. Lively in the mouth, with very bright fruit flavors. 2,000 cases produced. **86** *—D.T. (2/1/2004)*

Kaesler 2001 Old Bastard Shiraz (Barossa Valley) $110. Gets 100% new French oak for two years, and it shows. This is a big wine, with jammy berry and plum fruit that's doused in toasty, smoky flavors. Similar caramel-vanilla notes ring true on the nose. Finishes in a crescendo of caramel, and black plum and berry flavors. Excellent, to be sure, but also just massive. Don't try to drink this with anything other than a date and a bearskin rug—it's just not going to go with dinner. About 300 cases produced. **92** *—D.T. (2/1/2004)*

Kaesler 2000 Old Vine Shiraz (Barossa Valley) $NA. Gives an elegant but straightforward overall impression, with forward plum fruit and a subtle, claylike mouthfeel that overshadows all else. Wide bready, spicy aromas unfold on the nose. **89** *—D.T. (2/1/2004)*

KANGARILLA ROAD

Kangarilla Road 1997 Bordeaux Blend (McLaren Vale) $20. 86 *—M.S. (12/15/2002)*

Kangarilla Road 2000 Cabernet Sauvignon (McLaren Vale) $23. 82 *—D.T. (6/1/2002)*

Kangarilla Road 2002 Shiraz (McLaren Vale) $21. An unusual, enjoyable Shiraz. A mint-and-chocolate peppermint-patty quality pervades the wine, nose to tail, but the quality is an attractive one. Feels steely and linear on the palate, as though oak contributes to the wine's flavor, but not to its texture. Red and black plums, and some toasted oak flavors, persist through the finish. **89** *—D.T. (3/1/2005)*

Kangarilla Road 2000 Shiraz (McLaren Vale) $21. 87 *—J.C. (9/1/2002)*

Kangarilla Road 2003 Shiraz-Viognier (McLaren Vale) $21. The Viognier contributes beautiful floral aromatics to this wine, and the Shiraz, plenty of black pepper. The palate surges with berries and cherries—taut, fresh, and pure. Smooth and firm on the finish. Nicely done. **90** *—D.T. (3/1/2005)*

Kangarilla Road 2001 Zinfandel (McLaren Vale) $33. 85 *—S.H. (12/31/2003)*

KANGAROO RIDGE

Kangaroo Ridge 2002 Chardonnay (South Eastern Australia) $8. A Beringer Blass partner, and quite a success. Medium-soft in the mouth, with pineapple, pear, and apple aromas and flavors. It has good length on the finish, where it picks up some toast nuances. In spite of its fruit-driven profile, this isn't a sweet, insipid wine. Better than many wines we sampled that were twice the price. **87 Best Buy** *(7/2/2004)*

Kangaroo Ridge 2002 Shiraz (South Eastern Australia) $8. This brand's Chardonnay was a Best Buy, but its Merlot wasn't quite as enjoyable. Though the Merlot's style will surely have its fans, this reviewer found its flavors (chocolate-covered raisins or cookies?) a little too sweet. Aromas are of scone dough and dried fruit. **83** *—D.T. (9/1/2004)*

KATNOOK ESTATE

Katnook Estate 2000 Cabernet Sauvignon (Coonawarra) $22. This wine's a testament to how pretty, ripe New World fruit doesn't need to be overdone with toasty oak to be excellent. Nose is deep and earthy, and the earthy-dustiness carries over to the palate, where there's a surge of fruit-sweet, chewy plum, and berry fruit. Blackberry, plum, and clay linger on the finish. **90** *—D.T. (12/31/2004)*

Katnook Estate 2000 Odyssey Cabernet Sauvignon (Coonawarra) $50. Aromas are of roasted meat and tobacco. It's just an excellent wine, the oak overlay giving just enough flavor and patina to deep, liqueurish blackberry flavors. "Cigar box" is a descriptor I don't get to use often when talking about Oz wine, but it's appropriate here. Finishes long. Give the wood a little more time to integrate, then enjoy. Drink 2007–2013. **91 Cellar Selection** *—D.T. (10/1/2005)*

Katnook Estate 2001 Chardonnay (Coonawarra) $20. Cologne, butter, and brioche aromas are vibrant, and are backed up by overt caramel and cinnamon-bun flavors. Soft and plump in the mouth, and goes down easy. **85** *(7/2/2004)*

Katnook Estate 1999 Merlot (Coonawarra) $22. **83** *—D.T. (1/1/2002)*

Katnook Estate 2002 Shiraz (Coonawarra) $22. I've come to like Katnook's wines quite a lot, but this one is a disappointment. Though the wine has cool cherry fruit and black pepper aromas, it feels tired and weak on the palate. The berry fruit starts showing through on the finish, but its cameo appearance just isn't enough. **85** *—D.T. (12/1/2005)*

Katnook Estate 1999 Prodigy Shiraz (Coonawarra) $50. **90** *—K.F. (3/1/2003)*

KELLY'S PROMISE

Kelly's Promise 2000 Cabernet Sauvignon-Merlot (South Eastern Australia) $9. **87 Best Buy** *—M.S. (12/15/2002)*

Kelly's Promise 2002 Shiraz (South Eastern Australia) $8. Plum and cherry aromas and flavors, with cream and cheese on the nose and the finish. Straightfoward and simple. **83** *—D.T. (11/15/2004)*

KELLY'S REVENGE

Kelly's Revenge 2003 Shiraz (South Eastern Australia) $6. Aromas are somewhat meaty, and the palate delivers generic red fruit flavors and a thin feel. A simple quaffer. **83 Best Buy** *—D.T. (12/31/2005)*

KILLERBY

Killerby 1999 Cabernet Sauvignon (Western Australia) $30. **88** *(6/1/2001)*

Killerby 2002 Sauvignon Blanc (Margaret River) $15. Shows pleasing bright aromatics of citrus and fresh grass; on the palate, however, the yellow fruit is fairly dilute, and the mouthfeel a little heavy. **83** *—D.T. (5/1/2004)*

Killerby 1999 Shiraz (Western Australia) $30. **87** *(11/1/2001)*

KISSING BRIDGE

Kissing Bridge 2001 Chardonnay (South Eastern Australia) $8. **83** *—D.T. (6/1/2003)*

Kissing Bridge 2001 Shiraz (South Eastern Australia) $6. A dark, dark Shiraz: The nose shows dark earth, blackberry, and eucalyptus aromas; the palate has plum, blackberry, and toast. An easy, straightforward wine. **84** *—D.T. (9/1/2004)*

KNAPPSTEIN LENSWOOD VINEYARDS

Knappstein Lenswood Vineyards 2002 Lenswood Sauvignon Blanc (Adelaide Hills) $NA. Tastes of stone fruit and melon rind, but the stranger thing about this wine is its texture, which is powdery—almost like a dissolving Sweet-Tart. The nose shows meat and a pronounced petrol note. **84** *—D.T. (5/1/2004)*

KOONOWLA

Koonowla 2000 Shiraz (Clare Valley) $20. **87** *—D.T. (3/1/2003)*

KOOYONG

Kooyong 2001 Estate Pinot Noir (Mornington Peninsula) $31. What a nice wine. Garnet-colored; perfumed with violet, meat, black pepper and cherry aromas. Tannins are wooly and textured, and the palate offers up a sturdy black cherry shell with molten bittersweet chocolate inside. Dry and woody on the finish. **90** *—D.T. (10/1/2005)*

KOPPAMURRA

Koppamurra 1999 Red Blend (Limestone Coast) $20. **85** *—M.S. (12/15/2002)*

KURTZ FAMILY

Kurtz Family 2000 Boundary Row Grenache (Barossa Valley) $18. **88** *—J.C. (9/1/2002)*

LABYRINTH

Labyrinth 2003 Valley Farm Vineyard Pinot Noir (Yarra Valley) $35. Loved it last vintage, so what happened here? Aromas are funky, horsey, almost saline. In the mouth, there's a smooth, minerally feel that falls off toward the back end, but it doesn't have the verve it has had. Black cherry flavors; lightly lollied on the finish. **85** *—D.T. (12/1/2005)*

Labyrinth 2003 Viggers Vineyard Pinot Noir (Yarra Valley) $42. This Pinot is texturally very interesting, its robust, wooly tannins well obscuring the cherry and cola flavors underneath. That will change in the short term, I expect; a more integrated wine would lead to an even more favorable review. 283 cases produced. **89** *—D.T. (12/1/2005)*

LANGHORNE CROSSING

Langhorne Crossing 2003 Red Blend (Langhorne Creek) $11. Aromas are of sweet fruit, with tangy tea and oak accents. On the palate, it's a case of now you see it, now you don't: The black pepper, Sweet-Tart and red berry flavors that this wine offers are fleeting, but were fine while they lasted. **82** *—D.T. (12/1/2005)*

LANGMEIL

Langmeil 1985 Liqueur Shiraz Tawny Shiraz (Barossa Valley) $56. This tawny Shiraz has a good backbone but positively melts in the mouth. It's warming and seductive on the palate, with hazelnut and honey flavors joining more expected plum and blackberry characters of Shiraz. Gorgeous. **92** *—D.T. (3/1/2005)*

Langmeil 2002 Valley Floor Shiraz (Barossa Valley) $23. Meaty, white peppery aromas bring you around to red plum, berry, and toast on the palate. Feels very firm on the palate, with dusty-clay tannins and cocoa on the finish. Very nice! Drink now–2009. **90** *—D.T. (12/31/2004)*

LARK HILL

Lark Hill 1999 Canberra-Yass Valley Cabernet Sauvignon-Merlot (New South Wales) $35. A simple, sweetish wine overall. Caramel and marshmallow aromas give way to bright plum and raspberry fruit on the nose and the palate. A seeped-tea flavor, and a twinge of unsweetened chocolate keep the wine from tasting too confected. **83** *—D.T. (9/1/2004)*

LARRIKIN

Larrikin 2002 Shiraz (Barossa Valley) $28. This Shiraz is slender and feminine, its currant and black cherry fruit taking center stage. With air, bright eucalyptus, and aloe aromas show through; black pepper seeps into the palate. Very enjoyable. 1,800 cases produced. **89** *—D.T. (12/31/2004)*

LEASINGHAM

Leasingham 1997 Classic Clare Cabernet Sauvignon (Clare Valley) $35. 90 *—D.T. (9/1/2001)*

Leasingham 2001 Bin 56 Cabernet Sauvignon-Malbec (Clare Valley) $19. Not a burly wine, despite its components. There's juicy red fruit on the palate, though it's taut; cola, mocha, root beer, and big red fruit echo on nose and finish. Only 12% Malbec; only small amounts are exported to the U.S. **88** *—D.T. (2/1/2004)*

Leasingham 1999 Bin 56 Cabernet Sauvignon (Clare Valley) $19. 88 *—D.T. (6/1/2003)*

Leasingham 2003 Bin 7 Riesling (Clare Valley) $16. Though the wine wasn't aged within sight of a barrel, the warm vintage lends it vanilla-cream aromas and flavors. Granny Smith apple makes up the rest of the flavor profile. Has lively acids and a hint of spritz on the finish. **89** *—D.T. (2/1/2004)*

Leasingham 2001 Bin 7 Riesling (Clare Valley) $9. 87 Best Buy *—M.M. (2/1/2002)*

Leasingham 2003 Classic Clare Riesling (Clare Valley) $NA. A museum release that won't be on the market, probably, until late 2004, but is worth the wait. It's elegant, with subdued slate, citrus, and bread flour notes; however nice the flavors, the finessed mouthfeel is even more impressive. Juicy lime and crisp acids show through on the finish. **92** *—D.T. (2/1/2004)*

Leasingham 2003 Magnus Riesling (Clare Valley) $12. This reasonably priced Riesling shows trading-card bubblegum powder and white peach aromas. Firm white peach and citrus flavors are couched in a round, amply sized feel. A very good wine, from an always reliable producer. **87 Best Buy** *—D.T. (11/15/2004)*

Leasingham 2000 Bin 61 Shiraz (Clare Valley) $21. 83 *—D.T. (2/1/2003)*

Leasingham 1998 Bin 61 Shiraz (Clare Valley) $17. 85 *(10/1/2001)*

Leasingham 2001 Classic Clare Shiraz (Clare Valley) $45. Excellent. Flavors and aromas are taut and lifted: Raspberry and black cherry, mainly, wrapped around a core of iron ore and charred meats. Tightly wound, powerful, and delicious. 4,000 cases produced. **92** *—D.T. (8/1/2005)*

Leasingham 1998 Classic Clare Shiraz (Clare Valley) $35. 88 *(11/1/2001)*

Leasingham 1994 Classic Clare Shiraz (Clare Valley) $NA. A new release, despite the vintage, but not available in the U.S. Another Leasingham with a deep, penetrating nose; here, it's eucalyptus and black pepper. There's big berry and plum fruit on the front palate, and tobacco and oak on the back. Soft and lush, drinkable now. Quite good. **91** *—D.T. (2/1/2004)*

Leasingham 1994 Sparkling Shiraz (Clare Valley) $NA. Made in the methode champenoise style, of the same grapes that go into Classic Clare. Smells like Shiraz (which isn't always true of sparkling Shiraz), with full red plums that reappear on the palate. It's soft in the mouth, with fine mousse and bouncy red fruit. Finishes with steely-mineral drynesss. Winemaker Kerri Thompson suggests that you drink it like the Aussies do, as an apéritif before the Thanksgiving turkey. **89** *—D.T. (2/1/2004)*

Leasingham 2001 Magnus Shiraz-Cabernet (Clare Valley) $10. 85 *(12/31/2003)*

LEEUWIN ESTATE

Leeuwin Estate 1998 Art Series Cabernet Sauvignon (Margaret River) $NA. 92 *(10/1/2002)*

Leeuwin Estate 1996 Art Series Cabernet Sauvignon (Margaret River) $NA. 89 *(10/1/2002)*

Leeuwin Estate 1994 Art Series Cabernet Sauvignon (Margaret River) $NA. 88 *(10/1/2002)*

Leeuwin Estate 1999 Prelude Cabernet Sauvignon-Merlot (Margaret River) $29. 85 *—D.T. (10/1/2003)*

Leeuwin Estate 2001 Art Series Chardonnay (Margaret River) $65. Gingerbread and vanilla aromas are light, as are the vanilla accents on the palate. This wine's citrus core and soft, powdery feel are very nice. But it's still a lightweight, and somewhat of a disappointment, given its lofty reputation and past performance. **87** *—D.T. (5/1/2005)*

Leeuwin Estate 1999 Art Series Chardonnay (Margaret River) $65. 90 Cellar Selection *(10/1/2002)*

Leeuwin Estate 2001 Prelude Vineyards Chardonnay (Margaret River) $29. A zesty, crisp wine with verve—you'll need to have a few sips before the round, medium-full mouthfeel becomes apparent. Pear, pineapple—even orange—fluffs up a minerally spine. Light, pure yellow peach and nectarine notes are echoed on the medium-length finish. Smooth, harmonious, yummy. 1,000 cases produced. **89** *(7/2/2004)*

Leeuwin Estate 1999 Prelude Vineyards Chardonnay (Margaret River) $29. 89 *—J.C. (9/10/2002)*

Leeuwin Estate 2002 Art Series Riesling (Margaret River) $22. 88 *—D.T. (8/1/2003)*

Leeuwin Estate 2001 Siblings Semillon-Sauvignon Blanc (Western Australia) $20. 86 *(10/1/2002)*

Leeuwin Estate 1999 Art Series Shiraz (Margaret River) $NA. 89 *(10/1/2002)*

LEN EVANS

Len Evans 1999 Shiraz (McLaren Vale) $30. 89 *(11/1/2001)*

LIMB

Limb 2001 Patterson Hill Cabernet Sauvignon (Barossa Valley) $40. With such abyss-deep black aromas (steak, pepper, licorice) the palate, by not knocking you out with giant tannins and lots of charred oak, feels slender in comparison. This is a pleasing balance of smooth tannins, and pretty black plum and blueberry flavors. **87** *—D.T. (11/15/2004)*

Limb 2001 Three Pillars Red Blend (Barossa Valley) $20. A good wine; an unusual blend of Mourvèdre (50%), Cabernet Sauvignon (27%), and Shiraz (23%). Has a nice dusty texture, and an approachable, medium-weight size, but the plum fruit plays second fiddle to oak, dust, Sweet-Tart, earth, and other flavors. I'd love to see the fruit show its stuff more next vintage. **86** *—D.T. (12/31/2004)*

LIMELIGHT

Limelight 1999 Syrah (McLaren Vale) $50. 90 *(11/1/2001)*

LINDEMANS

Lindemans 1998 Pyrus Cabernet Blend (Coonawarra) $27. 90 *—M.S. (12/15/2002)*

Lindemans 2002 Bin 45 Cabernet Sauvignon (South Eastern Australia) $8. 85 *—D.T. (12/31/2003)*

Lindemans 2000 St. George Cabernet Sauvignon (Coonawarra) $30. Chalk dust, bubblegum powder, and juicy, fleshy berry fruit is a lovely aromatic combination, and the mix expresses itself just as nicely on the palate. The feel is velvety, and the oak noticeable, but still works well in terms of the the big picture. Very nice, and shows the best of what Lindemans can do. **90** *—D.T. (11/15/2004)*

Lindemans 1998 Cabernet Sauvignon-Merlot (Padthaway) $15. 88 Best Buy *—M.S. (12/15/2002)*

Lindemans 2001 Chardonnay (Padthaway) $13. 84 *—J.C. (7/1/2002)*

Lindemans 1997 Chardonnay (Padthaway) $13. 87 *(11/15/1999)*

Lindemans 2002 Bin 65 Chardonnay (South Eastern Australia) $8. 87 Best Buy *—D.T. (11/15/2003)*

Lindemans 1999 Bin 65 Chardonnay (South Australia) $10. 86 *(10/1/2000)*

Lindemans 2002 Reserve Chardonnay (South Australia) $10. 83 *—D.T. (8/1/2003)*

Lindemans 2002 Reserve Merlot (South Australia) $10. This is a slimmer-sized Merlot that features accents of seeped tea and mocha on the palate, with fruit playing second fiddle. Aromas are of baked fruit and cream. Good for casual gatherings. **84** *—D.T. (8/1/2005)*

Lindemans 2001 Bin 99 Pinot Noir (South Australia) $9. 84 *—J.C. (9/1/2002)*

Lindemans 2003 Bin 75 Riesling (South Eastern Australia) $8. On the nose, has a confected, lemon soda-poppy aroma. Heavy on the palate, with a zip of citrus on the finish. **83** *—D.T. (12/1/2005)*

Lindemans 2003 Bin 95 Sauvignon Blanc (South Eastern Australia) $8. Aromas are light—citrus pith and peach skin. In the mouth, it's a fresh, springtime wine; clean but not too lean, and soft around the edges. Flavors run the gamut of citrus fruits. Finishes round and clean. **86 Best Buy** —*D.T. (11/15/2004)*

Lindemans 2000 Bin 95 Sauvignon Blanc (South Australia) $9. 84 —*J.C. (2/1/2002)*

Lindemans 2002 Bin 77 Semillon-Chardonnay (South Eastern Australia) $8. 82 —*D.T. (1/1/2002)*

Lindemans 2000 Cawarra Semillon-Chardonnay (South Eastern Australia) $NA. 84 —*D.T. (2/1/2002)*

Lindemans 2001 Bin 50 Shiraz (South Eastern Australia) $9. 84 —*J.C. (9/1/2002)*

Lindemans 2002 Reserve Shiraz (South Australia) $10. This is a good-value wine with broad appeal, and a pretty sophisticated, chalky texture for the price. Its blackberry-oak-amaretto profile has an interloping strawberry note that wasn't a high point for me, but adds an approachable streak of red to an otherwise dark Shiraz. **86 Best Buy** —*D.T. (5/1/2005)*

Lindemans 2000 Cawarra Shiraz-Cabernet (South Eastern Australia) $6. 83 —*M.S. (12/15/2002)*

Lindemans 2004 Bin 70 White Blend (South Eastern Australia) $8. Not a blend that you see often, that's for sure—it's 70% Chardonnay, 30% Riesling. The wine offers light peach aromas and flavors, with moderate vanilla and cream to round it out. It's a broad-shouldered wine, particularly for one that contains Riesling. Good and inexpensive quaff. 5,400 cases produced. **84 Best Buy** —*D.T. (12/1/2005)*

LITTLE BOOMEY

Little Boomey 2004 Shiraz (South Australia) $7. Offers sweet black and raspberry aromas and flavors, with some earth accents. Gets simpler and softer with air. A quaffer. 82,800 cases produced. **83** —*D.T. (10/1/2005)*

LITTLE PENGUIN

Little Penguin 2003 Cabernet Sauvignon (South Eastern Australia) $7. The dominant aroma here is raspberry, which is followed up on the palate by some sweet, concentrated berry fruit. A good casual quaffer. **82** —*D.T. (11/15/2004)*

Little Penguin 2003 Chardonnay (South Eastern Australia) $7. The first edition of Southcorp's new brand yields is a nice, easily likeable Chard. Aromas are light, like talc powder or baking flour, mixed with a few golden apples. The feel is soft and fresh, with soft peach and apple flavors and a juicy finish. **85 Best Buy** —*D.T. (11/15/2004)*

Little Penguin 2003 Merlot (South Eastern Australia) $7. Smells and tastes like a confection: aromas are sweet and marshmallowy, and fruit on the palate is soft, sweet, and candied. Will please wine newbies, but may be too simple for others. **82** —*D.T. (3/1/2005)*

Little Penguin 2005 White Shiraz (South Eastern Australia) $8. Smells as rosy and pink as it looks. Just slightly off dry, this Shiraz tastes like flowers and peaches. Drink this quaff on the patio. **84 Best Buy** —*D.T. (12/1/2005)*

LOGAN AUSTRALIA

Logan Australia 1999 Chardonnay (Orange) $17. 84 —*J.C. (7/1/2002)*

Logan Australia 2000 Ripe Chardonnay (Hunter Valley) $10. 82 —*D.T. (8/1/2003)*

Logan Australia 2001 Logan Sauvignon Blanc (Orange) $13. Has a dryish, spritzy mouthfeel and flavors of unripe melon and stone fruits that vanish more quickly than we'd like. The nose has both light, feminine notes (apricot, honey) and more masculine scents of beef and musk. This Sauvignon was reviewed by two editors, with consistent notes. **84** *(5/1/2004)*

LONG FLAT

Long Flat 2004 Chardonnay (Yarra Valley) $14. This fruit comes from Cheviot Bridge shareholders, with the wine made at Yering Station. Lightly toasty, with hints of vanilla and sweet corn to the Golden Delicious apple flavors. Turns citrusy on the finish. **86** *(12/1/2005)*

Long Flat 2002 Merlot (South Eastern Australia) $8. Soft and fruity in the mouth, the Long Flat has plum and coffee flavors, and a nose that sports black pepper, toast, and an orange-liqueur note. Finishes with a sour herb, or metallic note, but it's fleeting. 5,000 cases imported to U.S. **84** —*D.T. (9/1/2004)*

Long Flat 2002 Cabernet-Shiraz-Malbec (South Eastern Australia) $8. Don't come looking for varietal character in this value-priced red—it's a blend of three varieties (55% Cab, 30% Shiraz, and 15% Malbec). What this wine delivers is red and black berry fruit with moderate oak and vanilla shadings. Tightens up on the finish, with a crisp blast of mint. **84** —*D.T. (11/15/2005)*

Long Flat 2004 Sauvignon Blanc (Adelaide Hills) $14. Quite tropical and fruity, with estery notes of banana on the nose before passion fruit and herbal-grassy flavors take firmer hold. Plump on the mid-palate, but turns hard and citrusy on the finish. **85** *(12/1/2005)*

Long Flat 2002 Semillon-Sauvignon Blanc (South Eastern Australia) $7. An 80-20 Semillon-Sauvignon blend, the wine's yellow fruit flavors are a little dilute, but its aromas of sweet yellow and citrus fruit are quite pleasant. Finishes with a mealy bananalike texture. **84** —*D.T. (5/1/2004)*

LONGVIEW

Longview 2003 Devil's Elbow Cabernet Sauvignon (Adelaide Hills) $19. Has aromas of plum, berry, and spice. On the palate, surging, mouthwatering flavors of tart plums and eucalyptus follow, couched in furry, dusty tannins. Lively acidity completes a lovely package. 400 cases produced. **90 Editors' Choice** *—D.T. (8/1/2005)*

Longview 2003 Black Crow Nebbiolo (Adelaide Hills) $20. Has welcoming, plummy aromas, with hints of lemony oak. The palate has a sturdy nutty-oaky shell that is the wine's focus, and some creaminess to the feel, but not quite enough plum stuffing to fill it out. Still a good wine. **86** *—D.T. (8/1/2005)*

Longview 2003 Yakka Shiraz-Viognier (Adelaide Hills) $19. Many will appreciate this restrained, pretty Shiraz; it is a food-friendly style and size, showing chalky-smooth tannins and flavors of cola and blackberry. This is evidence of how the Hills is having success with reds as well as its whites. **90** *—D.T. (8/1/2005)*

LONGWOOD

Longwood 1999 Shiraz (McLaren Vale) $28. **89** *—M.M. (6/1/2001)*

LONSDALE RIDGE

Lonsdale Ridge 2002 Merlot (Victoria) $8. This Merlot has some unusual characteristics, but it's still a compelling, value-priced offering. Both the aromas and flavors carry spice, bacon, straight-off-the-barbecue, rustic notes. There's mixed plums underneath it all, all of which is framed in a soft, easily accessible feel. **85 Best Buy** *—D.T. (9/1/2004)*

LORIKEET

Lorikeet NV Brut (South Eastern Australia) $10. Overall, the brut is pretty similar to Lorikeet's Extra Dry sparkler. Honeyed, tropical fruit, a medium body and light toasty aromas make for an easy, enjoyable value-priced bubbly. **86 Best Buy** *—D.T. (12/31/2005)*

Lorikeet NV Sparkling Shiraz (South Eastern Australia) $9. Raspeberry, blackberry, and plum flavors and aromas rule the roost here, with oak and cream in supporting roles. It wants some length on the finish, but overall, it's a fine introduction to sparkling Shiraz, and one of the least expensive on the U.S. market. **84 Best Buy** *—D.T. (12/31/2004)*

Lorikeet NV Brut (South Eastern Australia) $9. Smells pretty yeasty—caramelly, even—and the palate's toasty graham-cracker quality follows suit. Cherry flavors pick up midpalate, and drive the wine through the finish. Will have wide appeal, particularly for those who like their still Chards and Pinots fat and toasty. **85 Best Buy** *—D.T. (12/31/2004)*

LOWE

Lowe 1997 Ashbourne Vineyard Chardonnay (Hunter Valley) $18. **81** *—J.C. (9/10/2002)*

M. CHAPOUTIER AUSTRALIA

M. Chapoutier Australia 1999 Mount Benson Shiraz (Australia) $30. **88** *(11/1/2001)*

MACAW CREEK

Macaw Creek 2003 Grenache-Shiraz (South Australia) $17. Though this Grenache-Shiraz also contains some Cabernet Sauvignon and Petit Verdot, it still feels like a lightweight. The nose is pleasing, with fleshy plum and berry fruit, but the palate is sort of tart—think cranberry, veiled with a few ripe plums. 1,000 cases produced. **86** *—D.T. (5/1/2005)*

MACQUARIEDALE

Macquariedale 1999 Old Vine Semillon (Hunter Valley) $18. **87** *—J.C. (2/1/2002)*

MAD FISH

Mad Fish 2003 Cabernet Sauvignon-Shiraz (Western Australia) $15. It's not often that you find interesting wines, wines that have their own individual character, at this price. This red blend offers cool eucalyptus, earth, and nutmeg aromas, and a palate rife with mixed berries. It's dry (if you want sweet fruit, look elsewhere) and has soft, easy tannins—a wine suited for easy quaffing as it is to some contemplation. **87** *—D.T. (12/1/2005)*

Mad Fish 2004 Sauvignon Blanc (Western Australia) $15. Has a little candle wax and citrus on the nose. The mouthfeel has a citrusy kick, but relies on its smooth, minerally feel. Offers lemon and lime flavors, but its understated, for sure. **87** *—D.T. (12/1/2005)*

MAK

Mak 2001 Chardonnay (Adelaide Hills) $16. **87** *—J.C. (7/1/2002)*

MARCUS JAMES

Marcus James 2000 Shiraz (South Eastern Australia) $6. **84** *(10/1/2001)*

MARGAN

Margan 2000 Chardonnay (Hunter Valley) $12. **87** *—J.C. (7/1/2002)*

Margan 1999 Semillon (Hunter Valley) $13. **81** *—J.C. (9/1/2001)*

Margan 2001 Verdelho (Hunter Valley) $13. **89** *(2/1/2002)*

MARIENBERG

Marienberg 1997 Reserve Shiraz (South Australia) $20. **86** *(10/1/2001)*

MARINDA PARK

Marinda Park 2001 Pinot Noir (Mornington Peninsula) $26. 85 *—D.T. (10/1/2003)*

MARKTREE

Marktree 1999 Soldier's Block Vineyard Shiraz (New South Wales) $9. 85 *(10/1/2001)*

MARQUEE

Marquee 2004 Artisan Wines Classic Cabernet Sauvignon-Merlot (Victoria) $10. Smells almost cloying, like raspberries and strawberry preserves, with the barest hints of herb and earth. The same sweet fruit flavors appear on the palate, along with some Sweet-Tart. **83** *—D.T. (12/31/2005)*

Marquee 2002 Chardonnay (South Eastern Australia) $12. Marquee's lowest-priced offering performed best in our tastings. This bottling is vibrant and tasty, medium weight, with pure peach fruit, and accents of vanilla, tropical fruit, and grilled nuts. How's the bouquet? Just as nice as the palate. **88 Best Buy** *(7/2/2004)*

Marquee 2004 Artisan Wines Classic Chardonnay (Victoria) $10. Smells of peach and creamy vanilla, and unfolds to reveal forward apple, pear, and oak flavors on the palate. Crisp in the mouth; enjoyable and uncomplicated overall. **85 Best Buy** *—D.T. (12/1/2005)*

Marquee 2001 Macedon Ranges Chardonnay (Victoria) $27. From Cleveland Winery in Victoria, this Chard shows butter and burnt sugar aromas. On the palate, there is light butter and talc flavors, and a powdery textured finish. Wants more stuffing in the middle. **83** *(7/2/2004)*

Marquee NV Tawny Port (Rutherglen) $25. There's a lot to like about this wine, including biscuit, earth, and fresh herb aromas and orange, biscuit, stone fruit, and meat flavors. Has a sturdy shell, but a little hollowness in the midpalate. Doesn't have the unctuousness, or stickiness, that you typically get from fortified wines—for this reviewer, something was missing from this very good wine. For others, this characteristic might be a boon. **87** *—D.T. (12/31/2004)*

Marquee 2002 Hunter Valley Semillon-Chardonnay (New South Wales) $17. This is a wine of many personalities: The nose has nutty, cedary notes, but also some brininess. Fruit on the palate is just this side of ripe. A nice effort, but doesn't quite hit its stride. **83** *—D.T. (11/15/2004)*

Marquee 2001 Cabernet Sauvignon (Adelaide Hills) $28. If you're expecting big and overblown, just keep walking. Made at Chain of Ponds, this Cab offers pretty taut, borderline tart, flavors with a heap of outdoorsy, rustic elements. Briary, tree-bark aromas on the nose preface taut red plum and cherry fruit, and the texture on the finish is really nice and velvety. The near-tart element is the only thing that's keeping me from launching this into the next decile. **89** *—D.T. (12/31/2004)*

Marquee 2000 Saddler's Creek Cabernet Sauvignon (South Eastern Australia) $20. Taste this blind with friends, and place big bets: This wine's not likely to be identified as Australian, or New World at all, for that matter. Smells earthy, with iron accents that reminded me of mature Chianti. Ditto for the flavors: Stout cherry fruit, brown earth and some rustic oak. Very good, but not at all what you're expecting. 1,500 cases produced. **87** *—D.T. (12/31/2004)*

Marquee 1999 Pfeiffer Wines Marsanne (Victoria) $15. Medium-weight with honeyed Jolly Rancher and fresh green pea aromas. It's flat on the palate, and light on flavor, offering only light honey and butter notes. **83** *—D.T. (12/31/2004)*

Marquee NV Classic Muscat (Rutherglen) $25. Butterscotch and some noticeable alcohol on the nose; the palate has butterscotch, then a flash of peach and citrus, then chocolate-cherry candy. Smooth and unctuous, but not super-rich. A nice-sized wine for folks who are afraid of big stickies. **89** *—D.T. (12/31/2004)*

Marquee 2001 Port Phillip Estate Pinot Noir (Mornington Peninsula) $27. Round, overt aromas of plum fruit, cedar, and putty prepare you for a wine that's more brash than this one is. It's a slimmer-sized Pinot, the cedar and plum notes still present on the palate but taking second billing to a nice, rocky-minerally feel that lasts on the finish. **89** *—D.T. (8/1/2005)*

Marquee 2001 Chain of Ponds Shiraz (McLaren Vale) $25. Wheat bread and black-olive aromas segue to a medium-weight wine on the palate. Shows a Rhonish, fresh herb-and-black pepper brightness, framing chewy plum fruit. Finish shows some wood, and is not as vibrant as the palate. **87** *—D.T. (3/1/2005)*

Marquee Selections NV Classic Tokay (Rutherglen) $25. Sticky, syrupy, and full-bodied, but still not cloying, by any means. Smells of orange peel, cardamom, and caraway seeds, and has more orange, plus honey, hay, and meat flavors on the palate. As busy as it sounds, it has some delicacy, too, with shortcake flavors taking over midpalate and running hand-in-hand with honey through the finish. **90** *—D.T. (12/31/2004)*

MARQUIS PHILIPS

Marquis Philips 2000 Cabernet Sauvignon (South Eastern Australia) $15. 92 *—S.H. (6/1/2002)*

Marquis Philips 2000 Sarah's Blend (South Eastern Australia) $15. 93 Best Buy *—S.H. (6/1/2002)*

MATILDA PLAINS

Matilda Plains 2001 Red Blend (Langhorne Creek) $12. This 58% Cab, 28% Shiraz, 14% Merlot has an easy, simple feel and a palate chock-full of red plum, tomato, and tomato stem flavors. Fruit on the palate is sweet and stewy; all around, just an odd combination. **82** *—D.T. (9/1/2004)*

MCGUIGAN

McGuigan 2001 Bin 7000 Chardonnay (Hunter Valley) $10. 88 Best Buy *—J.C. (7/1/2002)*

McGuigan 2000 Genus 4 Chardonnay (Hunter Valley) $20. 86 *—D.T. (8/1/2003)*

McGuigan 1998 Bin 3000 Merlot (South Eastern Australia) $9. 89 Best Buy *(11/15/1999)*

McGuigan 2000 Bin 2000 Shiraz (Murray River Valley) $10. 86 *—P.G. (10/1/2001)*

McGuigan 2000 Black Label Shiraz (South Eastern Australia) $8. 86 Best Buy *—C.S. (3/1/2003)*

McGuigan 2001 Black Label Shiraz (South Eastern Australia) $10. 86 *—M.S. (6/1/2003)*

MCLAREN VALE PREMIUM WINES

McLaren Vale Premium Wines 2000 III Associates The Third Degree (McLaren Vale) $17. A compelling wine from a marketing perspective: The label says that the Associates won't tell you what's in it, but fully expect "the third degree by our refusal to comment," hence the wine's name. From a taste perspective, though, this is an odd wine: It has both meaty, green pepper flavors and ripe, juicy plum fruit, with stewy, grapy aromas on the nose. **85** *—D.T. (5/1/2004)*

MCPHERSON

McPherson 2001 Cabernet Sauvignon (Murray-Darling) $8. 85 *—D.T. (10/1/2003)*

McPherson 1999 Cabernet Sauvignon (South Eastern Australia) $8. 83 *—M.N. (6/1/2001)*

McPherson 2002 Chardonnay (Australia) $8. The bouquet is like a puffy cloud of confectioner sugar, laced with a ribbon of tight citrus. Tropical, buttery fruit shows in the mouth, with an impression of residual powdered sugar that lingers from the nose. Well-balanced, if a little sweet for the panel's taste. **85 Best Buy** *(7/2/2004)*

McPherson 1999 Chardonnay (South Eastern Australia) $7. 85 *—S.H. (10/1/2000)*

McPherson 2001 Merlot (South Eastern Australia) $8. 85 *—D.T. (11/15/2003)*

McPherson 2002 Shiraz (Australia) $8. This dry wine has seeped tea and oak flavors riding in the front seat. Still, there's a nice core of taut red fruit, and dusty red fruit on the nose, that make it worth a look. **84** *—D.T. (9/1/2004)*

McPherson 2000 Shiraz (South Eastern Australia) $8. 88 Best Buy *(10/1/2001)*

McPherson 2000 Reserve Shiraz (Goulburn Valley) $19. 89 *—M.S. (3/1/2003)*

MCWILLIAM'S HANWOOD ESTATE

McWilliam's Hanwood Estate 2004 Cabernet Sauvignon (South Eastern Australia) $12. Has aromas and flavors of raspberries and Sweet-Tart. The palate is accented with some oat and coconut flavors, too. Juicy, forward, and made to drink now. **86** *—D.T. (12/31/2005)*

McWilliam's Hanwood Estate 2002 Cabernet Sauvignon (South Eastern Australia) $12. 87 Best Buy *(10/1/2003)*

McWilliam's Hanwood Estate 2004 Chardonnay (South Eastern Australia) $12. A please-everyone style of wine, this Chardonnay is upbeat, easy to drink, and uncomplicated, and offers bright stone fruit and floral aromas. Maybe a wee bit soft, winding up with pineapple, peach, and lemon flavors. **87 Best Buy** *—D.T. (12/1/2005)*

McWilliam's Hanwood Estate 2001 Chardonnay (South Eastern Australia) $11. 82 *—D.T. (1/1/2002)*

McWilliam's Hanwood Estate 2003 Merlot (South Eastern Australia) $12. Though the aromas of Silly Putty, blackberry, vanilla, and dust are nice, what you get on the palate is pretty pedestrian: fresh berry flavors, and a lightish body. Straightforward but good. **84** *—D.T. (5/1/2005)*

McWilliam's Hanwood Estate 2002 Shiraz (South Eastern Australia) $12. 86 *(10/1/2003)*

MCWILLIAM'S OF COONAWARRA

McWilliam's of Coonawarra 2000 Cabernet Sauvignon (Coonawarra) $25. Fruit on the nose has a pretty black-peppery finish, with just a hint of herbal brightness. Mocha, chocolate, and eucalyptus are accents on the palate, which fades into sweet red berries, white pepper, and oak on the finish. **88** *—D.T. (11/15/2004)*

McWilliam's of Coonawarra 2000 Shiraz (Coonawarra) $25. This is a masculine, big-boned Shiraz, one with a black cherry-and-plum core. You want sweet and toasty? Look elsewhere. This wine's dry, chewy tannins and earth-and-oak finish recommend it well for a grilled steak, and/or a couple years in the cellar. **88** *—D.T. (9/1/2004)*

McWilliam's of Coonawarra 1999 Laira Vineyard Shiraz (Coonawarra) $25. 89 *(10/1/2003)*

MEEREA PARK

Meerea Park 1999 Alexander Munro Shiraz (Hunter Valley) $38. 89 *—M.S. (3/1/2003)*

Meerea Park 2000 The Aunts Shiraz (Hunter Valley) $24. 88 *—M.S. (3/1/2003)*

MESH

Mesh 2004 Riesling (Eden Valley) $25. This Hill Smith-Grosset joint venture is a very good wine, but not quite up to the snuff of past vintages. It smells like whipping cream and citrus (and goes the way of petrol with a little time in the glass), and unfolds to a bracing, minerally, sourish wine on the palate. Not overtly flavorful, but still enjoyable. **87** *—D.T. (10/1/2005)*

MITCHELL

Mitchell 2001 Sevenhill Vineyard Cabernet Sauvignon (Clare Valley) $25. Another Mitchell red that's drinkable even in its infancy, this Cab has soft but approachable tannins, and a great bouquet of pure plum and grape fruit. The palate shows black currant, mostly, dusted with pastry flour. Yum. **90** *—D.T. (2/1/2004)*

Mitchell 2001 Grenache (Clare Valley) $18. No longer called "The Growers," as it was in the past, because Mitchell's own fruit goes into this wine. Smells like cherries and cologne, with raspberry the most prevalent note on the palate. Soft in the mouth, it finishes with anise, herb, and more red fruit. 7% Mataro. **88** —D.T. (2/1/2004)

Mitchell 2002 Watervale Riesling (Clare Valley) $NA. **91** *—D.T. (2/1/2004)*

Mitchell 2000 Watervale Riesling (Clare Valley) $NA. **89** *—D.T. (2/1/2004)*

Mitchell 2002 Semillon (Clare Valley) $18. Though there's a base of sweet, rich yellow fruit at this wine's heart, what's more prevalent here are garden-fresh grass, or pea shoot notes, from nose through to the palate. Medium-weight, with a viscous mouthfeel. **89** *—D.T. (2/1/2004)*

Mitchell 2002 Peppertree Vineyard Shiraz (Clare Valley) $26. A soft, ripe, excellent Shiraz, and drinkable even at this early age. Licorice stands out on the palate, under which mixed plums forge a solid foundation. Finishes, appropriately enough, with black pepper. **91** *—D.T. (2/1/2004)*

Mitchell 2000 Peppertree Vineyard Shiraz (Clare Valley) $26. **82** *—D.T. (1/28/2003)*

Mitchell 1998 Peppertree Vineyard Shiraz (Clare Valley) $NA. **89** *—D.T. (2/1/2004)*

MITCHELTON

Mitchelton 1998 Marsanne (Goulburn Valley) $18. **90** *—S.H. (10/1/2000)*

Mitchelton 2000 Airstrip Rhône White Blend (Central Victoria) $20. **91 Editors' Choice** *(2/1/2002)*

Mitchelton 1996 Print Shiraz (Victoria) $45. **92** *(10/1/2000)*

Mitchelton 1999 Thomas Mitchell Shiraz (Victoria) $11. **83** *(10/1/2001)*

AUSTRALIA

MONDAVI/ROSEMOUNT

Mondavi/Rosemount 2002 Kirralaa Cabernet Sauvignon (South Eastern Australia) $15. A very, very dark Cab, and not fluffed up by vanilla or cream. Blackberry aromas; sturdy black fruit feels even darker with drying tealike tannins that start midpalate and don't let up through the medium-long finish. A big slab of beef is the knee-jerk solution to making it more approachable; cellaring a year or two may also help. **88** *—D.T. (12/31/2004)*

Mondavi/Rosemount 2003 Kirralaa Chardonnay (South Eastern Australia) $14. Nose is at once smoky and herbal, with a twist of lime. Feels lean and wiry in the mouth, its fruit flavors veering more toward peach fuzz and citrus peel than juicy fruit flesh. Finishes tangy and fresh, with a hint of butter. **86** *(7/2/2004)*

Mondavi/Rosemount 2001 Kirralaa Merlot (South Eastern Australia) $15. **87** *—D.T. (10/1/2003)*

Mondavi/Rosemount 2001 Kirralaa Bushvine Shiraz (South Eastern Australia) $15. **86** *—D.T. (10/1/2003)*

MOONDARRA

Moondarra 2001 Conception-Unfiltered Pinot Noir (Victoria) $50. **91** *—D.T. (10/1/2003)*

MORGAN SIMPSON

Morgan Simpson 2002 Row 42 Cabernet Sauvignon (McLaren Vale) $25. This wine gets full credit for its smooth, eraser-like tannins—the feel is just lovely, as are eucalyptus and black pepper aromas. All of these signs point to excellence, but the palate is a little disappointing, with sourish fruit and a strange watermelon note continuing through the finish. Still very good, with great potential. **87** *—D.T. (5/1/2005)*

Morgan Simpson 2002 Shiraz (McLaren Vale) $25. Steady and sturdy wins the race for this Shiraz. The dusty-clay-chalk aromas preface a surge of blackberries on the palate, which are joined immediately with more rocks and dust. Shows class and restraint, with nary a lick of obvious toast. **89** *—D.T. (12/31/2005)*

MOSS WOOD

Moss Wood 2001 Cabernet Sauvignon (Margaret River) $60. Deep black fruit notes on the nose go a little raisiny with air, but there are enough pleasant tree/earth aromas to distract you. On the palate, hickory smoke flavors mesh nicely with sweet fruit; tannins are soft and plush. Finishes medium-long, with juicy berry and cherry flavors. **90** *—D.T. (12/31/2004)*

Moss Wood 2003 The Amy's Blend Cabernet Sauvignon (Margaret River) $26. The "blend" in the wine's name refers to the fact that the grapes come from two vineyards: Glenmore (66%) and Montgomery Brothers (34%). Fruit on the nose is very concentrated, borderline syrupy or pruny. Moderate in size; the palate offers black plum and blackberry flavors. Very good, though you'd more likely guess South Australia than Margaret River if you taste it blind. **89** *—D.T. (5/1/2005)*

Moss Wood 2003 Chardonnay (Margaret River) $40. The palate announced loud and clear what this wine's color and aromas also suggest: There's just too much wood here. This is obviously a well-made wine, one with dry citrus and mineral components, and a surge of citrus on the medium-long finish. The toasty overlay, however, is overdone—without it, this wine would climb easily into the next decile. **87** *—D.T. (3/1/2005)*

Moss Wood 2001 Chardonnay (Margaret River) $45. **87** *—D.T. (10/1/2003)*

Moss Wood 1999 Pinot Noir (Margaret River) $36. **87** *—D.T. (10/1/2003)*

Moss Wood 2000 Semillon (Margaret River) $20. **89** *(10/1/2003)*

MOUNT HORROCKS

Mount Horrocks 2002 Riesling (Clare Valley) $21. **88** *—D.T. (8/1/2003)*

Mount Horrocks 2001 Cordon Cut Riesling (Clare Valley) $27. A tremendous, sweet Riesling, unctuous but not cloying. Smells like ripe green apples; tastes like petrol at palate entry, but melts seamlessly into honey, floral, and sweet chalk flavors. Winemaker Stephanie Toole says that it "actually goes with desserts—it doesn't fight with them." Amen, sister. **92** *—D.T. (2/1/2004)*

Mount Horrocks 1999 Shiraz (Clare Valley) $28. Wide black plum fruit sprawls out on the palate; Clare's signature chalky-limestoney mouthfeel is in full effect here. There's a ribbon of rusticity–tobacco, peanut shells, or something–running throughout. Nose is an unusual mix of granola, blueberry, and blackberry. As lush as it sounds, don't forget, it's from Clare, and bears scant resemblance to a Barossa bruiser. **89** *—D.T. (5/1/2004)*

MOUNT LANGI GHIRAN

Mount Langi Ghiran 2004 Riesling (Victoria) $18. Citrus, chalk dust and pear are this Riesling's main components, on both the nose and the palate. It's a very compelling wine, though spare and delicate in style. Finishes with a dusty-gumdrop note. Nicely done. **89** *—D.T. (10/1/2005)*

Mount Langi Ghiran 1999 Shiraz (Victoria) $36. A puzzling but still very good wine, because Oz Shiraz isn't supposed to taste like it's from the Rhône. There's a lot of black pepper and herbaceousness in this slim-bodied wine. Taut red plum and cherry is at its core, with all the pepper and fresh herb you could hope for. Bag it, and blind-taste it with some friends—not many will guess Australia. **88** *—D.T. (9/1/2004)*

MOUNT MARY

Mount Mary 2001 Quintet Bordeaux Blend (Yarra Valley) $120. A very delicate wine. On the nose, it has focused berry fruit and a stably undercurrent that follows through on the palate. It's smooth in the mouth, subtle in that it shines with the impression of bright berry fruit, but its size doesn't knock you over. Pretty, feminine and best of all, different. Imported by Old Bridge Cellars. **90** *(8/1/2005)*

MOUNTADAM

Mountadam 1997 Chardonnay (Eden Valley) $15. **89** *—M.M. (10/1/1999)*

MT. BILLY

Mt. Billy 2002 Harmony Rhône Red Blend (Barossa Valley) $36. This Rhône blend (half Shiraz, with Mataro and Grenache evenly split in the remainder) really does taste French, rather than Australian. This is a very good wine, one that offers sour but plump black plum fruit with a tobaccoey, herbaceous edge. It almost needs a "If you don't like Crozes-Hermitage, keep shopping" warning label—suits me just fine. Imported by Australian Wine Connection. **88** *—D.T. (12/31/2005)*

Mt. Billy 2002 Liqueur Shiraz (Barossa Valley) $26. So thick and so delicious. It is a deep, almost glowing, red-garnet color, and smells like fresh whipping cream and black pepper. Despite its almost 18% alcohol, this fortified Shiraz is very well-balanced. It floods the palate with sweet cassis and vanilla, then settles down to reveal smoky, charred wood flavors, smooth, gripping tannins, and a nutty, long finish. Torbreck winemaker Dave Powell is behind this sexy, must-try "late-night" dessert wine. Imported by Australian Wine Connection. **94** *—D.T. (12/31/2005)*

MT. JAGGED

Mt. Jagged 2001 Lightly Wooded Chardonnay (Southern Fleurieu) $18. **82** *—D.T. (8/1/2003)*

Mt. Jagged NV Sparkling Red Red Blend (South Australia) $18. Porty, blackberry aromas lead to off-dry flavors of cassis and blackberry. A soft-bodied, frothy wine for post-dinner, rather than during-dinner, enjoyment—cheese course, anyone? **86** *—D.T. (12/31/2005)*

MURDOCK

Murdock 2003 Riesling (Coonawarra) $22. This wine's a tough mistress. Though there are some piquant yellow-fruit aromas under a hefty dose of chalk dust, there's something very reserved and cool about the palate's offerings. Dust and chalk coat firm, white stone fruit flavors that taste a day short of ripe. The flavors aren't green or unpleasant by any means—they just indicate a very good, firm, not tropical, not overdone Riesling. **87** *—D.T. (12/31/2004)*

NARDONE BAKER

Nardone Baker 2001 Cabernet Sauvignon-Merlot (South Eastern Australia) $10. **86** *—M.S. (12/15/2002)*

NEIGHBOURS

Neighbours 1999 Shiraz (McLaren Vale) $20. **87** *—D.T. (3/1/2003)*

NEPENTHE

Nepenthe 2003 Tryst Cabernet Blend (Adelaide Hills) $14. What's not to like about this wine's red and purple plum flavors, smooth tannins, and easy mouthfeel? It's an enjoyable, straightforward quaffer; one to drink now. A blend of 60% Cab, 25% Zinfandel, and 15% Tempranillo. **86** —*D.T. (8/1/2005)*

Nepenthe 2001 The Fugue Cabernet Sauvignon-Merlot (Adelaide Hills) $20. Winemaker Peter Leske's 70-30 Cab-Merlot has good spine, with black cherry and red plum fruit at the fore. Cool menthol and black cherry aromas are exhilarating; finishes medium-long and earthy. A classy, fly-under-the-radar-but-impress-the-heck-outta-you wine. **91 Editors' Choice** —*D.T. (8/1/2005)*

Nepenthe 1999 Pinot Noir (South Australia) $25. **85** —*J.C. (9/1/2002)*

Nepenthe 2002 Tryst Red Blend (Adelaide Hills) $14. A blend of Cabernet, Tempranillo, and Zinfandel; you've got to hand it to Nepenthe for experimenting with new varieties. Smells cool-climate, with nuances of eucalyptus/fresh herb, and taut, cherry fruit. Soft and dry in the mouth, where red plum and tangy oak flavors are the key players. It's a nice red wine, but one that just hasn't hit its stride yet. **86** —*D.T. (12/31/2004)*

Nepenthe 2001 Sauvignon Blanc (Adelaide Hills) $17. **86** —*J.C. (2/1/2002)*

Nepenthe 1999 Zinfandel (South Australia) $36. **87** —*D.T. (6/1/2003)*

NINE STONES

Nine Stones 2003 Shiraz (Barossa) $12. A rustic-style, good-value Shiraz. Oak lends it a woodsy, dusty mouthfeel and aromas of coffee, oak, and black pepper. Purple and red plum and berry fruit on the palate is straightforward, yet tasty. **86** —*D.T. (5/1/2005)*

NINTH ISLAND

Ninth Island 2001 Riesling (Tasmania) $16. **87** —*D.T. (8/1/2003)*

NOON

Noon 2003 Reserve Cabernet Sauvignon (McLaren Vale) $55. Alluring aromas of black pepper, vanilla, chalk, and a streak of eucalyptus kick off this excellent wine. Tannins on the palate are still young and dominant, but the wine's attractive black plum and soil flavors will show through in a few years' time. Finishes long and smooth. Drink 2007+. **92** —*D.T. (3/1/2005)*

Noon 2003 Eclipse Grenache (McLaren Vale) $55. This Grenache has some dark, smoldering character but it's still a manageable size. Deep black cherry lurks beneath smoke, ash, and cream aromas and flavors. Finishes with fine, chalky tannins. Open a few hours before drinking. **91** —*D.T. (3/1/2005)*

Noon 2003 Reserve Shiraz (McLaren Vale) $55. Spice and black pepper is the name of the game on the nose, while youthful plum fruit on the palate is jazzed up with herb and earth. Finishes smooth and minerally; still closed overall, and probably not at its best until around 2008. **91** —*D.T. (3/1/2005)*

NORMAN WINES, LTD.

Norman Wines, Ltd. 2001 Teal Lake Cabernet Sauvignon-Merlot (South Eastern Australia) $13. **86 Best Buy** —*M.S. (12/15/2002)*

Norman Wines, Ltd. 2001 Teal Lake Pinot Noir (South Eastern Australia) $16. **82** —*D.T. (6/1/2003)*

NORMANS

Normans 1999 Chais Clarendon Cabernet Sauvignon (Adelaide Hills) $30. Call it what you want—big-boned, broad-chested, varón—but this is a manly, sizeable wine, and laudable because it doesn't have some of the cloying, messy richness that big Cabs can sometimes have. Smells of black pepper, and cola or root beer. There's mixed plum fruit, lively acids, and gripping tannins on the palate and the finish. Does let up with air, but still probably best after 2007. **92** —*D.T. (12/31/2004)*

Normans 2002 Old Vine Cabernet Sauvignon (South Australia) $15. Opens with meaty, molassey aromas that turn to tomato with air. On the palate, plum and oak are accented by minty flavors that come through in full force on the finish, along with some cherry cordial. Feminine-sized, with smooth tannins. **86** —*D.T. (12/31/2005)*

Normans 2002 Old Vine Grenache (McLaren Vale) $15. Vanilla and pepper aromas lead to sexy, vanilla and black cherry flavors on the palate and finish. A very good effort and an enjoyable wine, though a little heavy on the vanilla. **87** —*D.T. (3/1/2005)*

Normans 2001 Encounter Bay Shiraz (South Australia) $10. A sweeter, more forward style of Shiraz, with jammy berry and peanut aromas, and ripe plum and cherries on the palate. Soft on the palate; finishes with a light grip of tannins. **86 Best Buy** —*D.T. (3/1/2005)*

NUGAN FAMILY ESTATES

Nugan Family Estates 2002 3rd Generation Chardonnay (South Eastern Australia) $12. Shows pineapple, peach, and toast on the nose. On the palate, there's yellow stone fruit and clove at its core but wood and alcohol stand out a bit more. Finish is brief, with bright herb and wood notes. **82** *(7/2/2004)*

Nugan Family Estates 2001 Third Generation Chardonnay (South Eastern Australia) $11. **82** —*J.C. (7/1/2002)*

Nugan Family Estates 2002 KLN Vineyard Botrytis Semillon (Riverina) $22. The bouquet has a pleasing floral component, and the palate, an oily, though not clumsy, feel. Yellow peach fruit dominates in the mouth. It's a good wine, but not a vibrant, deep one. **84** —*D.T. (9/1/2004)*

O'LEARY WALKER

O'Leary Walker 2002 Cabernet Sauvignon-Merlot (Clare-Adelaide Hills) $15. This is a cool-climate red, which means it's no fruit bomb. Plum fruit is taut in the mouth, with fern, earth, and tree-bark aromas. Soft in the mouth, and drinkable now. **87** *—D.T. (2/1/2004)*

O'Leary Walker 2003 Watervale Riesling (Clare Valley) $15. Fragrant, with lovely honeysuckle aromas. Despite the vintage, still manages a lean, lithe mouthfeel and upbeat, citrus flavors. **87** *—D.T. (2/1/2004)*

O'Leary Walker 2002 Shiraz (Clare-McClaren Vale) $15. Sweet blackberry and plum fruit is bouncy and fresh, though goes a little green on the finish. Approachable now. **86** *—D.T. (2/1/2004)*

OAKRIDGE

Oakridge 2003 Pinot Noir (Yarra Valley) $21. An approachable Pinot: its feel is soft and round, and its cherry fruit falls squarely in the cherry cola camp, rather than the tart and rigid one. Starts to get serious on the finish, where firm tannins take hold. **86** *—D.T. (12/1/2005)*

OLIVERHILL

Oliverhill 2000 Bradey Block Grenache (McLaren Vale) $20. **87** *—J.C. (9/1/2002)*

Oliverhill 2000 Jimmy Section Shiraz (McLaren Vale) $33. **92 Editors' Choice** *(11/1/2001)*

ORIGIN

Origin 2002 Reserve Series Shiraz (Barossa Valley) $19. A Pinot-weight Shiraz with pleasing flavors of black cherry, earth and eucalyptus. Cooler notes prevail on the nose. Ends with seeped-tea flavors. **87** *—D.T. (10/1/2005)*

OUTBACK CHASE

Outback Chase 2003 Chardonnay (South Eastern Australia) $7. Tropical/yellow fruit on the palate, with decent concentration. It finishes with a generous dose of pulpy wood, but it is still a good, inexpensive quaffer. **84 Best Buy** *—D.T. (5/1/2005)*

OWEN'S ESTATE

Owen's Estate 1999 Cabernet Sauvignon-Shiraz (South Eastern Australia) $13. **86** *—S.H. (9/1/2001)*

Owen's Estate 1999 Merlot (South Eastern Australia) $15. **84** *—S.H. (9/1/2001)*

Owen's Estate 1998 Shiraz (South Australia) $15. **85** *(4/1/2000)*

OXFORD LANDING

Oxford Landing 1999 Limited Release Cabernet Sauvignon (South Australia) $10. **84** *—D.T. (9/1/2001)*

Oxford Landing 2004 Chardonnay (South Australia) $9. Smells like it tastes—full of toast, pear, and peach notes, accented by a piquant yellow flavor. Tasty and easy to drink. Imported by Negociants USA, Inc. **86 Best Buy** *—D.T. (8/1/2005)*

Oxford Landing 2000 Chardonnay (South Australia) $8. **83** *—D.T. (9/1/2001)*

Oxford Landing 2003 Merlot (South Australia) $9. Just the right size to enjoy with a meal. This is one juicy Merlot, with a parade of plum, blackberry, and raspberry flavors and aromas. Feels smooth, with oak adding an acorn-like accent through the finish. Imported by Negociants USA, Inc. **86 Best Buy** *—D.T. (5/1/2005)*

Oxford Landing 2002 Shiraz (South Australia) $9. Flavors and aromas are red and a little tart—not cherry, exactly, maybe more along the lines of persimmon? A fair amount of oak joins the fruit on the palate, and hangs on for a drying, oaky finish. **83** *—D.T. (5/1/2005)*

Oxford Landing 2004 Viognier (South Australia) $9. Typical with its floral and honey aromas. Medium-weight, with pear, melon, and floral notes. Its 14.5% alcohol is noticeable, but it's still a good wine at a good price. **86 Best Buy** *—D.T. (8/1/2005)*

OZ ROZ

Oz Roz 2004 Rosé of Shiraz (South Eastern Australia) $7. Smells like strawberry, oak, herb, and plum. Tastes, however, like a strawberry shortcake. Simple, and a little sweet. **83** *—D.T. (12/1/2005)*

PAIKO

Paiko 2002 Merlot (Murray-Darling) $10. Solid, offering rustic bark-leaf-smoke-nut nuances top to bottom, with blackberry and plum flavors underneath. A Band-aid note on the nose resurfaces on the finish. **86 Best Buy** *—D.T. (8/1/2005)*

Paiko 2004 Viognier (Murray-Darling) $10. This is a good, medium-sized white wine, but apart from a little viscosity on the finish, doesn't really show much of what Viognier is capable of. Smells like heavy yellow stone fruit, and offers honey and butterscotch Lifesaver flavors. **84** *—D.T. (12/1/2005)*

PALANDRI

Palandri 2001 Cabernet Sauvignon (Western Australia) $16. **87** *(8/1/2003)*

Palandri 2001 Cabernet Sauvignon-Merlot (Western Australia) $16. **87** *(8/1/2003)*

Palandri 2002 Merlot (Western Australia) $15. Aromas are dark and interesting, including black pepper and tree bark notes. Red-fruit flavors are tangy but tempered by a sandy, earthy component and lively acids. Wooly tannins complete the picture. 4,000 cases produced. **87** *—D.T. (8/1/2005)*

Palandri 2004 Boundary Road Sauvignon Blanc (Western Australia) $11. Will appeal to fans of grassy, green New Zealand Sauvignons. This Western Australian version has intense grass and green pea aromas that are repeated, though with less pizzazz, on the palate. Finishes flat. **84** *—D.T. (10/1/2005)*

PARACOMBE

Paracombe 2002 Cabernet Franc (Adelaide Hills) $30. This wine's pretty green. There's celery seed and weed on the nose; red, tomato-y fruit on the palate gets a dose of green bean toward the finish. **83** *—D.T. (8/1/2005)*

Paracombe 2002 The Reuben Red Blend (Adelaide Hills) $30. Aromas are of meat and tree bark; fruit flavors are more like plum skin than flesh. Not very giving. Tasted twice. **85** *—D.T. (8/1/2005)*

Paracombe 2004 Sauvignon Blanc (Adelaide Hills) $23. Fresh and lively bouquet, with aromas of grapefruit and green veggies, i.e. peas and beans. Pours on the citrus flavors, with accents of passion fruit and ginger. Spritzy feeling, with zesty acidity. Turns a bit lemony toward the back end. **87** *(7/1/2005)*

Paracombe 1999 Shiraz (Adelaide Hills) $28. 86 *—K.F. (3/1/2003)*

Paracombe 2001 Somerville Shiraz (Adelaide Hills) $80. A Shiraz with a Type A personality: Big and brash on the nose, with enthusiastic, forward flavors on the palate. Up front, it smells like marzipan, toast, raspberry, and blackberry, and similar notes ring true in the mouth. Finishes pretty long, with a biscuit or cracker-like flavor. Very tasty. **90** *—D.T. (8/1/2005)*

PARINGA

Paringa 2001 Individual Vineyard Shiraz (South Australia) $10. 90 Best Buy *—J.C. (11/15/2002)*

PARKER

Parker 2001 Terra Rosa Cabernet Sauvignon (Coonawarra) $30. Though its aromas are a little rich (think cola, amaretto, vanilla), this wine's a workhorse, not a show pony. It feels admirably sturdy to the core, with hearty red plum and cherry fruit and a rustic, earthy impression overall. An apt tribute to a wine bearing a "terra rossa" name. Drink through 2011. **90** *—D.T. (12/31/2004)*

PASSING CLOUDS

Passing Clouds 1998 Shiraz (Bendigo) $25. 85 *(11/1/2001)*

Passing Clouds 1998 Graeme's Blend Shiraz-Cabernet (Bendigo) $25. 86 *—J.C. (9/1/2002)*

PEARSON VINEYARDS

Pearson Vineyards 1999 Cabernet Franc (Clare Valley) $30. Smells spicy, like Mexican cinnamon; plum fruit on the palate is austere, with oak, herb, and tobacco accents. A very good wine, but it might benefit from a less wood. **87** *—D.T. (2/1/2004)*

Pearson Vineyards 1999 Cabernet Sauvignon (Clare Valley) $39. Though it spends three years in oak, it doesn't scream "wood" at all. There's dark black plum and berry fruit on the palate, but the dominating note here is one of deep, moist clay soil. That lovely clay shows on the nose, too, where there's also some licorice. A very good example of Clare Cab, with nice texture. **88** *—D.T. (2/1/2004)*

PENFOLDS

Penfolds 1998 Bin 389 Cabernet Sauvignon (Australia) $19. 89 *(3/1/2001)*

Penfolds 2001 Bin 407 Cabernet Sauvignon (South Eastern Australia) $26. Shows deep plum aromas on the nose, with juicy, judiciously oaked fruit on the palate. Medium in body, and finishes with toasty oak. A very good wine, and unmistakably Cabernet. **89** *—D.T. (5/1/2004)*

Penfolds 1996 Bin 407 Cabernet Sauvignon (South Australia) $25. 86 *—L.W. (12/31/1999)*

Penfolds 2001 Bin 707 Cabernet Sauvignon (South Australia) $80. Soft and supple in the mouth, with plum and oak the key flavor components. There are hints of sweetness here, from the brown-sugary aromas that appear with time in the glass, to the ripe, ripe fruit on the palate. Still, it's an excellent, delicious wine. Drink now–2008. **90** *—D.T. (11/15/2004)*

Penfolds 1998 Bin 707 Cabernet Sauvignon (South Australia) $90. 93 *(3/1/2001)*

Penfolds 2001 Thomas Hyland Cabernet Sauvignon (South Australia) $15. 87 *—D.T. (12/31/2003)*

Penfolds 2001 Koonunga Hill Cabernet Sauvignon-Merlot (South Eastern Australia) $9. 88 Best Buy *—M.S. (12/15/2002)*

Penfolds 1999 Bin 389 Cabernet Sauvignon-Shiraz (South Australia) $26. 87 *—M.S. (12/15/2002)*

Penfolds 1996 Bin 389 Cabernet Sauvignon-Shiraz (South Australia) $25. 88 *—L.W. (12/31/1999)*

Penfolds 2003 Koonunga Hill Chardonnay (South Eastern Australia) $11. Soft, easy, tropical, and sweet from beginning to end. This is just the no-brainer that people who want an inexpensive Aussie Chard are looking for. A good quaff. **83** *—D.T. (12/1/2005)*

Penfolds 2001 Koonunga Hill Chardonnay (South Eastern Australia) $10. 82 *—J.C. (7/1/2002)*

Penfolds 2003 Rawson's Retreat Chardonnay (South Eastern Australia) $9. This value-priced Chard is on the lean side, with pear, melon, and peach flavors that are just this side of ripe and juicy. Pear, melon, and anise aromas complete the picture. Most appropriate as an apéritif. **83** *(7/2/2004)*

Penfolds 2001 Rawson's Retreat Chardonnay (South Eastern Australia) $11. 83 *—J.C. (7/1/2002)*

Penfolds 2003 Thomas Hyland Chardonnay (South Australia) $14. Tastes and feels just shy of juiciness and roundness, but that isn't a bad thing. There's minerality at its core, wrapped in unyielding flavors of apple peel and unripe peach. It's an austere, spry wine, but a clean, correct one as well. **85** *(7/2/2004)*

Penfolds 2001 Thomas Hyland Chardonnay (Adelaide Hills) $18. 87 *—J.C. (7/1/2002)*

Penfolds 2000 Yattarna Chardonnay (Adelaide Hills) $65. 89 *—D.T. (10/1/2003)*

Penfolds 1998 Yattarna Chardonnay (South Eastern Australia) $65. 92 Cellar Selection *(3/1/2001)*

Penfolds 2002 Cellar Reserve Pinot Noir (Adelaide Hills) $35. One of Penfolds' few Adelaide Hills-designated wines, and the only one available in the States at the moment. This Pinot is very good, with lifted, tangy cherry and plum fruit at the fore, and admirable intensity and length. But it's not as good as I've seen it in past vintages; this one has a pervading pickling-spice or barrel note that was a detraction for me. **88** *—D.T. (8/1/2005)*

Penfolds 2000 Bin 2 Shiraz-Mourvedre (South Eastern Australia) $11. 90 *—J.C. (9/1/2002)*

Penfolds 2002 Reserve Bin Riesling (Eden Valley) $19. 87 *—D.T. (8/1/2003)*

Penfolds 1999 Reserve Riesling (Eden Valley) $15. 87 *—M.M. (2/1/2002)*

Penfolds 1997 Adelaide Hills Semillon (Adelaide Hills) $27. 89 *—M.S. (4/1/2000)*

Penfolds 2001 Koonunga Hill Semillon-Chardonnay (South Australia) $9. 82 *—D.T. (2/1/2002)*

Penfolds 2001 Bin 128 Shiraz (Coonawarra) $24. This is a medium-sized, drink-now Shiraz that's easy to like and hard to put down. Red and black plum fruit is dressed up with oak, toffee, and a hint of Grand Marnier. Finishes with smooth, chalky tannins. **87** *—D.T. (11/15/2004)*

Penfolds 1999 Bin 128 Shiraz (Coonawarra) $24. 88 *—J.C. (9/1/2002)*

Penfolds 1996 Bin 128 Shiraz (Coonawarra) $22. 89 *—S.H. (10/1/1999)*

Penfolds 1999 Bin 28 Kalimna Shiraz (South Australia) $24. 89 *—J.C. (9/1/2002)*

Penfolds 1999 Grange (South Australia) $225. An excellent wine as it always is, but this vintage of Grange is one that isn't just built for aging, it requires it. Its flavors and aromas require a good 20 minutes in the glass to show themselves, but with time, pretty eucalyptus/mint and anise aromas come through. In the mouth, this vintage feels more feminine than other recent vintages. It's very tightly wound, with tea, biscuit, and plum notes peeking through; its tannins are powdery and pretty, and its finish long and juicy. Drink 2012+. **93 Cellar Selection** *—D.T. (11/15/2004)*

Penfolds 1998 Grange (South Australia) $205. 95 *—D.T. (10/1/2003)*

Penfolds 1996 Grange (South Australia) $185. 96 Cellar Selection *(3/1/2001)*

Penfolds 2001 Kalimna Bin 28 Shiraz (South Eastern Australia) $24. Smooth and nicely balanced, this wine is all about its lovely fruit. The palate's plum fruit are dense and mouthfilling, and go the distance through the finish. Nose is deep with concentrated fruit, soil, and eucalyptus notes. Drink after 2006. **89** *—D.T. (11/15/2004)*

Penfolds 1996 Kalimna Bin 285 Shiraz (South Australia) $25. 86 *—L.W. (12/31/1999)*

Penfolds 1999 Magill Estate Shiraz (South Australia) $50. 91 *(9/1/2002)*

Penfolds 2001 Magill Estate Shiraz (South Australia) $50. Round, plush, and hedonistic, the Magill barely falls on the conservative side of "over the top" this year. Deep aromas of vanilla bean and meat segue to a blackberry-and-vanilla ride on the palate. Long and luscious on the finish; really quite sexy overall. **91** *—D.T. (11/15/2004)*

Penfolds 2001 RWT Shiraz (Barossa Valley) $80. This year, the RWT is tightly wound, masculine, and stately, but all in all, a pleasant walk in the dark. Smells like soil, meat, and char/smoke and tastes likewise, with those flavors enveloping black plum fruit on the palate. Juicy but taut on the finish, like there's some blueberries thrown in for good measure. Drink after 2008. **91 Cellar Selection** *—D.T. (11/15/2004)*

Penfolds 1999 RWT Shiraz (Barossa Valley) $70. 93 *(9/1/2002)*

Penfolds 2001 St. Henri Shiraz (South Australia) $40. Grape and blackberry flavors hold the fort down on the palate, and cassis is the main player on the nose. Although it is a very good wine, the feel here is dry, thick and woodsy—a curious thing considering that St. Henri is traditionally matured in old oak vats. Alcohol is also evident on both nose and palate. I love St. Henri in general, but this young one is looking a little awkward. **87** *—D.T. (10/1/2005)*

Penfolds 1999 St. Henri Shiraz (South Australia) $39. 91 *—D.T. (10/1/2003)*

Penfolds 2003 Thomas Hyland Shiraz (South Australia) $15. A dark but not very mouthfilling wine. This Shiraz offers cherry and rhubarb aromas, and a sour plum-and-tree bark profile to the palate. With air, the fruit seems riper, and the wood nuances more noticeable. **84** *—D.T. (12/31/2005)*

Penfolds 2002 Koonunga Hill Shiraz-Cabernet (South Eastern Australia) $12. This is an approachable wine with plum and tobacco aromas and flavors. Soft and somewhat hollow in the mouth, but still a fine everyday wine. 84,000 cases produced. **84** *—D.T. (10/1/2005)*

Penfolds 1999 Koonunga Hill Shiraz-Cabernet (South Eastern Australia) $15. **87** *(3/1/2001)*

Penfolds 1998 Koonunga Hill White Blend (South Australia) $8. **85** *—L.W. (12/31/1999)*

PENLEY ESTATE

Penley Estate 2001 Phoenix Cabernet Sauvignon (Coonawarra) $25. Smells of red fruit, caramel, ginger, and allspice, with black plum fruit and leafy flavors on the palate. Its alcohol is quite noticeable, though. Finishes dense and black. **86** *—D.T. (5/1/2004)*

Penley Estate 1999 Reserve Cabernet Sauvignon (Coonawarra) $58. **88** *—D.T. (6/1/2003)*

Penley Estate 1994 Pinot Noir-Chardonnay Sparkling Wine (Coonawarra) $30. Bananas, mineral, and cheese make for a less-than-appealing nose. The tart apple and citrus flavors on the palate are just acceptable as they lead into an adequately smooth finish that could be the wine's saving grace. Thin and lacking as a whole, but not offensive or poor. From Australia with age. **82** *—M.S. (1/1/2004)*

Penley Estate 2002 Hyland Shiraz (Coonawarra) $25. This Coonawarra Shiraz has meaty, stably aromas. On the palate, red plum fruit is pure and fairly unadorned, with slight earth and oak nuances. Tannins are velvety, almost furry. Very enjoyable; 1,000 cases produced. **90** *—D.T. (10/1/2005)*

Penley Estate 1999 Hyland Shiraz (Coonawarra) $25. **91 Editors' Choice** *—K.F. (3/1/2003)*

Penley Estate 2000 Special Select Shiraz (Coonawarra) $65. This wine has lots of nice flavors and aromas—cherry, raspberry, and graham cracker, among them—but feels disjointed and a little tart at this stage. A couple of years in the dark may do it some good; try after 2007. **88** *—D.T. (10/1/2005)*

PENMARA

Penmara 2000 Reserve Chardonnay (New South Wales) $13. **88** *—J.C. (7/1/2002)*

PENNA LANE

Penna Lane 2001 Cabernet Sauvignon (Clare Valley) $25. Smells like figs and dates rolled in bread flour. Fruit on the palate has the same stewy quality—more a sign of vintage conditions than anything, I guess. Easy on the palate, it finishes with molasses. **86** *—D.T. (2/1/2004)*

Penna Lane 2001 Shiraz (Clare Valley) $25. Has penetrating black pepper aromas, and soft red plum fruit on the palate. Goes down easy; drink now. **86** *—D.T. (2/1/2004)*

PENNY'S HILL

Penny's Hill 2002 Chardonnay (McLaren Vale) $18. Aromas are of sweet-smelling nectarines and melon. The panel was unanimous in describing this wine as harmonious—medium in body, but soft in demeanor, with all the parts in order. Flavors are of nectarine and mango, with toast and vanilla accents, and continue on through the finish. **87** *(7/2/2004)*

Penny's Hill 2003 Cadenzia Grenache (McLaren Vale) $30. Bright red fruit on the nose. The palate is smooth, though the wood isn't shy; overlaid with briary, tobaccoey notes. A very good wine, though the lifted cherry-eucalyptus flavor combination may not be for everyone. **88** *—D.T. (8/1/2005)*

Penny's Hill 1999 Shiraz (McLaren Vale) $33. **89** *(11/1/2001)*

PENNYFIELD WINES

Pennyfield Wines 2002 Basket Pressed Shiraz (Riverland) $22. Though this feminine-sized wine has a nice, dusty feel, its overall impression is a purple one. Smells sweet on the nose (think grape jam with some molasses), with grapy flavors returning on the palate. **86** *—D.T. (10/1/2005)*

PETALUMA

Petaluma 2001 Cabernet Sauvignon-Merlot (Coonawarra) $35. Medium-bodied with chewy tannins, this 50-50 Cab-Merlot blend offers a sturdy foundation of plum and black cherry fruit. Anise, tree bark, and spearmint accent the palate; spice, caramel, and grilled meat aromas play on the nose. Excellent and very enjoyable. **90** *—D.T. (8/1/2005)*

Petaluma 2001 Chardonnay (Piccadilly Valley) $28. One of this tasting's top performers—Adelaide Hills shines again. This is an elegant, harmonious Chardonnay, with white stone fruit at the core, and hazelnuts, vanilla, and talc flavors that accent rather than overwhelm the fruit. In the mouth it's round and pillowy; a hint of nut on the long finish is a satisfying close, just the mint on the pillow at turndown. **90 Editors' Choice** *(7/2/2004)*

Petaluma 2001 Tiers Chardonnay (Piccadilly Valley) $64. From a famed Adelaide Hills vineyard. Panelists agree that fruit gets shortshrift here—the focus is chalk, stone, or mineral. Pear and peach are most present on the finish. Austere in style; a wine that will shine more with food. **85** *(7/2/2004)*

Petaluma 2000 Riesling (Australia) $14. **88** *(2/1/2002)*

Petaluma 2002 Shiraz (Adelaide Hills) $30. Pretty brick/purple in color. Mixed plum aromas are accented with anise and cola notes. This is one nice Shiraz, of manageable size—just right for the dinner table.

There's a base of red plum fruit with smoky, meaty nuances that roll straight through the finish. **89** *—D.T. (3/1/2005)*

Petaluma 1999 Bridgewater Mill Shiraz (Australia) $15. **88** *—J.C. (9/1/2002)*

PETER LEHMANN

Peter Lehmann 2002 Cabernet Sauvignon (Barossa) $16. This wine is full of dark, earthy, stably, black olive-y aromas and flavors. Their predominance makes for an interesting wine, but also a wine that tastes mature beyond its years. Finishes with tree bark and leaf notes. Drink up. **86** *—D.T. (12/31/2005)*

Peter Lehmann 2002 Chardonnay (Barossa Valley) $12. Shows clarified butter and a zing of lime or lemon peel on the nose. A fatter-style Chard, this Barossa offering successfully follows the straightahead, stone-fruit-and-oak recipe. A good wine, but a pretty run-of-the-mill one. **85** *—D.T. (12/31/2004)*

Peter Lehmann 1998 Mentor Red Blend (Barossa Valley) $50. Has lifted aromas of rasberry and blueberry that turn almost pruny with air. Tree and earth flavors dominate the palate, which tastes a little sour and past its prime. This wine has been much better in other vintages. Tasted twice, with consistent results—could it be two bad bottles? **84** *—D.T. (8/1/2005)*

Peter Lehmann 2003 Riesling (Eden Valley) $16. This Riesling stays the citrus track, with zesty lemon and lime flavors and aromas rising even above those of white peach. A slick, olive-oily feel tempers the zesty citrus acidity well, making for a whole whose parts work together quite nicely. **88** *—D.T. (12/31/2004)*

Peter Lehmann 2003 Semillon (Barossa Valley) $11. This enjoyable white has all the right elements: It's mouthwatering and juicy, crisp and clean, offering dust and lemondrop aromas, with intense flavors of grapefruit and green apple. At this price, you can afford to keep a few bottles around the house, too. 70,000 cases produced. **89 Best Buy** *—D.T. (8/1/2005)*

Peter Lehmann 1999 Eight Songs Shiraz (Barossa Valley) $45. Delicious Barossa, through and though: Chewy tannins, rich plum and cassis flavors, and threads of soil, beef stock, and even some amaretto. Finishes long and rich; drinking well now. 600 cases produced. **90** *—D.T. (8/1/2005)*

Peter Lehmann 1998 Stonewell Shiraz (Barossa Valley) $75. Sturdy, masculine, and sexy. This excellent Shiraz's fruit core glows bright red (plum, cherry) but all of its bells and whistles—among them soil, black olive, blackberry—are dark as night. Unfolds with air to reveal streaks of cassis and mint as well. Medium-long and juicy on the finish. Drink through 2010. **91** *—D.T. (8/1/2005)*

Peter Lehmann 1997 The Barossa Shiraz (Barossa Valley) $15. **89** *(11/15/1999)*

PETERSONS

Petersons 1999 Shiraz (Mudgee) $20. **84** *(10/1/2001)*

PETTAVEL

Pettavel 2003 Evening Star Chardonnay (Geelong) $17. This Chard has spice and white pepper aromas, and a warm but comfortable tropical fruit, nut, and spice profile on the palate. Drink now. **87** *—D.T. (8/1/2005)*

Pettavel 2004 Evening Star Riesling (Geelong) $17. Though the style of this Riesling is juicier, more overtly fruity and somewhat heavier than is typical, the unusual combination still works here. Its medium weight is tempered by good acidity, and the palate's peach, tangerine, and honeyed flavors are balanced nicely by lemon and orange peel. 200 cases produced. **88** *—D.T. (8/1/2005)*

PEWSEY VALE

Pewsey Vale 2003 Riesling (Eden Valley) $15. Lovely acidity is this Riesling's hallmark; it's round but crisp in the mouth. Offers lovely lemon, lime and white pepper flavors in the mouth, and smells just as it tastes. Finishes with some length, and a chalky feel. **90 Best Buy** *—D.T. (2/1/2004)*

PIERRO

Pierro 2000 Red Table Wine (Margaret River) $45. **88** *—D.T. (10/1/2003)*

Pierro 2001 Semillon-Sauvignon Blanc (Margaret River) $25. **86** *—D.T. (10/1/2003)*

PIKE & JOYCE

Pike & Joyce 2004 Lenswood Pinot Gris (Adelaide Hills) $21. A lively wine, this wine is full of subtle red apple and pear flavors. The feel is dry; out of the bottle it's quite crisp but softens with air. At 180 cases made, might be hard to come by. **87** *—D.T. (8/1/2005)*

Pike & Joyce 2002 Sauvignon Blanc (Adelaide Hills) $20. This SB has fresh green pea and yellow fruit aromas, and trading-card powder and yellow fruit flavors. The texture is a little coarse, and the body bolder than many other SBs, but it's still a refreshing, food-friendly alternative to Chardonnay. **87** *—D.T. (5/1/2004)*

PIKES

Pikes 2000 Shiraz-Grenache-Mourvedre Red Blend (Clare Valley) $20. Here's proof that Pikes can make more than just a good Riesling. This red is over half Shiraz, with equal parts Grenache and Mourvèdre. The cool-climate fruit has cherry and mint nuances; the body is feminine but sinewy, and quite classy, reserved but still flavorful. **90** *—D.T. (5/1/2004)*

Pikes 2002 Riesling (Clare Valley) $18. **89** *—D.T. (8/1/2003)*

Pikes 2001 Reserve Riesling (Clare Valley) $23. 88 *—D.T. (8/1/2003)*

Pikes 1998 Reserve Shiraz (Clare Valley) $48. 89 *(11/1/2001)*

PINK KNOT

Pink Knot 2005 Rosé Blend (McLaren Vale) $12. This rosé is a blend of Shiraz, Cabernet, and Sangiovese. It tastes like tangerine and peach, but suffers from a strange, mushroomy-meaty aroma. 10,000 cases produced. 83 *—D.T. (12/1/2005)*

PIPING SHRIKE

Piping Shrike 2004 Shiraz (Barossa Valley) $14. Black cherry is the main component here, accented by plum flavors and earthy aromas. Down-the-line, basic, good Shiraz. 84 *—D.T. (10/1/2005)*

PIRRAMIMMA

Pirramimma 1998 Shiraz (McLaren Vale) $20. 87 *(10/1/2001)*

PLANTAGENET

Plantagenet 2003 Omrah Unoaked Chardonnay (Western Australia) $15. Both the nose and the palate of this Chardonnay focus on peach, apple, and citrus notes; we also found some floral and citrus accents. Medium-weight and soft in the mouth, it's a good quaffing wine, and will show even better with a little chill on it. 85 *(7/2/2004)*

Plantagenet 2001 Estate Shiraz (Mount Barker) $25. Not as good as the winery's less expensive bottling. The plum fruit in this Shiraz tastes a little sour, and finishes pretty woody. Fruit on the nose is high toned, with interesting ginger, soil, and plum accents. 85 *—D.T. (5/1/2004)*

Plantagenet 2001 Omrah Shiraz (Western Australia) $15. Nose is an outdoorsy mix of wood, earth, and leather aromas. On the palate, red plum fruit is angular, and almost liqueurish. Tannins are chewy, on the midpalate, and fade into a woody finish. 87 *—D.T. (5/1/2004)*

Plantagenet 1998 Omrah Shiraz (Western Australia) $18. 88 *—M.S. (10/1/2000)*

POOLES ROCK WINES

Pooles Rock Wines 2001 Chardonnay (Hunter Valley) $24. 87 *—D.T. (8/1/2003)*

PREECE

Preece 1998 Sauvignon Blanc (Victoria) $15. 87 *—S.H. (10/1/2000)*

PRIMO ESTATE

Primo Estate 2003 La Biondina White Blend (Adelaide Hills) $NA. "The little blonde," as its name translates, is made of Colombard. It's thick and round in the mouth, with peach, apricot, and grapefruit flavors that persist through the finish. A good choice if crispness isn't high on your list of priorities. 85 *—D.T. (5/1/2004)*

PUNTERS CORNER

Punters Corner 1999 Cabernet Sauvignon (Coonawarra) $25. 88 *—M.S. (12/15/2002)*

Punters Corner 1999 Cabernet Sauvignon-Merlot (Coonawarra) $27. 89 *(9/1/2001)*

Punters Corner 2002 Triple Crown Red Blend (Coonawarra) $20. A blend of 56% Cab, 30% Merlot, and 14% Shiraz. This is an odd, disjointed wine. An impression of cotton-candy sweetness competes with a weedy, green streak on both the nose and the palate. Underneath it all is pleasant red plum fruit and anise flavors, and a fine feel, all caught in the crossfire. 84 *—D.T. (5/1/2005)*

Punters Corner 2002 Shiraz (Coonawarra) $28. This wine feels well built and sturdy in the mouth, with smooth, integrated tannins. Its flavors and aromas, though, run the gamut from rhubarb to sour stone fruit to slight briary, stemmy notes. Tealike tannins on the finish have a shrill edge. 86 *—D.T. (10/1/2005)*

Punters Corner 2000 Spartacus Reserve Shiraz (Coonawarra) $62. Disappointing, considering its price and the performance of some past vintages. Though the nose offers pleasing pastry crust and plum fruit aromas, fruit on the palate tastes flat, with a slight green-bean note. Finishes dry, with sour plum fruit. Tasted twice. 84 *—D.T. (9/1/2004)*

Punters Corner 1998 Spartacus Reserve Shiraz (Coonawarra) $46. 85 *(11/1/2001)*

RANFURLYS WAY

Ranfurlys Way 2004 Chardonnay (Adelaide Hills) $25. This Chardonnay deals a tangy combo of golden apple and bright citrus against a toasty, lactic backdrop that was a detraction for me. Medium-full in the mouth, it shows more toast and apple notes on the nose. 85 *—D.T. (12/1/2005)*

Ranfurlys Way 2001 Shiraz (Clare Valley) $29. This wine follows the "give the people what they want" formula to a T, and does it very well. It smells like blackberry jam and is moderate in size, with a core of plums and berries. Nut and toast nuances on the finish are the bow on the package. 88 *—D.T. (12/31/2005)*

RED HILL ESTATE

Red Hill Estate 2001 Penguin's Kiss Chardonnay (Mornington Peninsula) $10. 83 *—D.T. (8/1/2003)*

RED KNOT

Red Knot 2004 Shiraz (McLaren Vale) $12. Smells syrupy-sweet, with toast and tea accents. On the palate, there's some nice black plum and cherry fruit. The finish reprises the tea and oak notes. Straightforward, but good. **86** *—D.T. (10/1/2005)*

REDBANK

Redbank 2002 The Fugitive Cabernet Sauvignon (Victoria) $15. This surely is a good-quality wine, but it follows a tried-and-true recipe. It offers dusty blackberry aromas, and blackberry and red plum flavors. It's just the right size on the palate, with smooth tannins and a gummy hold on the midpalate. At this price, you can afford to keep a few on your drink-now rack. **89** *—D.T. (5/1/2005)*

Redbank 1999 Percydale Cabernet Sauvignon-Merlot (King Valley) $15. **84** *—D.T. (9/1/2001)*

Redbank 1998 The Long Paddock Chardonnay (Victoria) $11. **85** *—M.M. (10/1/2000)*

Redbank 2002 The Long Paddock Chardonnay (Victoria) $10. **87** *—D.T. (8/1/2003)*

Redbank 2003 The Long Paddock Merlot (Victoria) $10. This is a nice, value-priced Merlot whose black peppery aromas and leathery, rustic flavors are welcome changes from the sweeter styled Merlots at this price point. Just the right addition to a family-style spaghetti dinner. **86 Best Buy** *—D.T. (10/1/2005)*

Redbank 2001 Sunday Morning Pinot Gris (King Valley) $16. **87** *—S.H. (1/1/2002)*

Redbank 2002 The Long Paddock Sauvignon Blanc (Victoria) $10. **85** *—D.T. (12/31/2003)*

Redbank 2001 The Anvil Shiraz (Heathcote) $50. Almost impenetrable at first, but with 15 minutes of air, coffee, plum skin, and eucalyptus/mint aromas begin to unfold. On the palate, it's a very textured wine; it has a thick veil of clay-chalky tannins, yet stays on the conservative side of richness and fullness. Its flavors reprise the aromas, for the most part, with an added accent of sea-breeze salinity that lasts through the finish. Will be at its best after 2007. **91** *—D.T. (8/1/2005)*

Redbank 2000 The Long Paddock Shiraz-Cabernet (Victoria) $10. **90 Best Buy** *—S.H. (12/15/2002)*

REDHOUSE

Redhouse 2001 Shiraz-Grenache (McLaren Vale) $15. This 50-50 Shiraz-Grenache blend has pretty powerful cherry and earth flavors on the front of the palate, but it lightens up some on the latter half. The wine's moderate size won't bowl you over, but the flavor explosion just might. **87** *—D.T. (12/31/2004)*

REILLY'S

Reilly's 2004 Barking Mad Riesling (Clare Valley) $13. Like Reilly's Watervale bottling, this will certainly inspire debate. The nose offers pineapple, resin, and waxy melon, and the palate deals a similar waxy, tart, Pixie-Stix kind of profile. I admire its tanginess and intensity—less enamored with the bulky feel—but its flavors are certainly atypical. **84** *—D.T. (10/1/2005)*

Reilly's 1999 Watervale Riesling (Clare Valley) $12. **87** *—M.M. (2/1/2002)*

Reilly's 1999 Dry Land Shiraz (Clare Valley) $25. **90** *(11/1/2001)*

RESCHKE

Reschke 2002 Bos Cabernet Sauvignon (Coonawarra) $30. This is a very good Cab, but one that doesn't really show the hallmarks that typically say "Coonawarra." Black fruit, coffee, and vanilla bean aromas and flavors take on black-peppery accents on the palate. Underneath it all is a sturdy base of smooth wood. **88** *—D.T. (5/1/2005)*

Reschke 2002 Vitulus Cabernet Sauvignon (Coonawarra) $26. Little brother to Reschke's "Bos" hence the name "Vitulus," which means "bull calf." This one's appropriately more jaunty and youthful, but unfolds nicely on the finish. Aromas are deep, mostly black cherry; flavors are of black cherry and mocha. **89** *—D.T. (5/1/2004)*

REYNOLDS

Reynolds 2001 Cabernet Sauvignon (New South Wales) $10. **83** *—S.H. (12/15/2002)*

Reynolds 2002 Chardonnay (New South Wales) $10. **86** *—D.T. (12/31/2003)*

Reynolds 2002 Reserve Chardonnay (Orange) $15. **87** *(9/1/2003)*

Reynolds 2001 Reserve Merlot (Orange) $15. **85** *(9/1/2003)*

Reynolds 2002 Reserve Sauvignon Blanc (Orange) $15. **84** *(9/1/2003)*

Reynolds 2001 Reserve Shiraz (Orange) $15. **87** *(9/1/2003)*

RIDDOCH ESTATE

Riddoch Estate 2002 Katnook Estate Cabernet Sauvignon-Merlot (Coonawarra) $11. It's a great thing to find a Coonawarra wine that's good and inexpensive. Its smooth texture is an asset. It tastes nothing like most other $10-ish Oz Cabs: Its plum fruit is fairly taut, and has gumtree-earthy accents, rather than sweetish, caramelly ones. Though I detected greenness on the nose right out of the bottle, it dissipates with time in the glass. **88 Best Buy** *—D.T. (5/1/2005)*

Riddoch Estate 2001 Cabernet Sauvignon-Shiraz (Coonawarra) $11. This 60-40 Cab-Shiraz blend has aromas of black olive and eucalyptus and taut plum and black cherry flavors. Its chalky, claylike mouthfeel is Coonawarra, all the way. I'm glad this wine is as affordable as it is—it will help value seekers appreciate regional differences among Australian wines. **87 Best Buy** *—D.T. (12/31/2004)*

Riddoch Estate 1996 Shiraz (Coonawarra) $18. **88** *(10/1/2000)*

RINGBOLT

Ringbolt 2001 Cabernet Sauvignon (Margaret River) $15. **88** *—D.T. (10/1/2003)*

RIPE

Ripe 1999 Chardonnay (Hunter Valley) $10. **85** *—J.C. (7/1/2002)*

RIVERINA ESTATES

Riverina Estates 2002 Bushman's Gully Chardonnay (South Eastern Australia) $7. A soft wine, with flavors of peach, and banana flavors on the finish. Smells sweet, with more peach and a douse of confectioners' sugar. **83** *(7/2/2004)*

Riverina Estates 2001 Lombard Station-Premium Selection Chardonnay (South Eastern Australia) $10. As the '70s song went, "if you like piña coladas," this wine is for you. Has nice jasmine-talc perfume and a cream-and-tropical fruit flavor profile. A good introduction to Chardonnay. **84** *(7/2/2004)*

Riverina Estates 2001 Lombard Station-Premium Selection Merlot (South Eastern Australia) $9. **85** *—D.T. (10/1/2003)*

Riverina Estates 2001 Warburn Semillon (South Eastern Australia) $10. **83** *—D.T. (9/1/2004)*

Riverina Estates 2001 Lombard Station-Premium Selection Semillon-Chardonnay (South Eastern Australia) $9. **85** *—D.T. (11/15/2003)*

Riverina Estates 1998 1164 Family Reserve Shiraz (Riverina) $29. **88** *—M.S. (3/1/2003)*

Riverina Estates 2002 Kanga's Leap Shiraz (South Eastern Australia) $7. This is a pretty straightforward Shiraz, with simple, sweet berries and plums on the nose, and bright cherry and raspberry fruit on the palate. **83** *—D.T. (9/1/2004)*

Riverina Estates 2000 Warburn Show Reserve Shiraz (Riverina) $15. **81** *—D.T. (1/28/2003)*

ROBINVALE

Robinvale 2003 Shiraz-Cabernet Sauvignon-Merlot Red Blend (Victoria) $20. A Demeter-certified wine, made with biodynamic grapes. Has fragrant aromas of ginger and cola going for it, though it's less of a powerhouse in terms of flavor. Smooth papery tannins give the wine structure, but the fruit on the palate is pretty pedestrian. **85** *—D.T. (12/31/2005)*

ROCKBARE

Rockbare 2002 Chardonnay (McLaren Vale) $12. **85** *—S.H. (10/1/2003)*

Rockbare 2002 Shiraz (McLaren Vale) $15. **85** *—S.H. (10/1/2003)*

ROCKFORD

Rockford 2001 Rod & Spur Cabernet Blend (Barossa Valley) $NA. A blend of two-thirds Cabernet and a third Shiraz, this is a wine with awesome balance and beautiful, pure plum fruit on the palate. Bouquet shows soft red plum and pine needles. **93** *—D.T. (2/1/2004)*

Rockford 2002 Rifle Range Cabernet Sauvignon (Barossa Valley) $53. This Cabernet is a youthful wine, with tannins that are still grabby. There's a lot to like here—briary, earthy aromas; taut, tightly wound fruit and a fresh eucalyptus bite on the finish. Best to wait a couple of years to see it at its best. **93** *—D.T. (8/1/2005)*

Rockford 1999 Moppa Springs Red Blend (Barossa Valley) $30. A GSM with fireplace, foresty, wheaty aromas that echo on the palate, where the prime flavors are pine, earth, and red plum. A terrific wine, this wine shows the best of what Grenache can do. **92** *—D.T. (2/1/2004)*

Rockford 2000 Semillon (Barossa Valley) $25. An excellent wine, with smooth, chalky tannins in the mouth followed by a long finish. Resin and lanolin aromas come through on the nose; flavors on the palate are more of the white-peach kind. Just lovely. **90** *—D.T. (2/1/2004)*

Rockford NV Black Shiraz (Barossa Valley) $NA. A hard-to-find wine outside of Rockford's mailing list and tasting room (only about 600 cases produced, and they go quickly), but certainly the standard-bearer as far as sparkling Shiraz goes. The average age of Rockford's nonvintage sparkling is 7 years; though it has 23 grams of residual sugar, it tastes just as I'd always envisioned a good sparking Shiraz would: like the still wine, but cold and with bubbles. Plums and juicy berries on the palate, with grape and violet aromas on the nose. Good luck finding it, but certainly grab it if you do. **92** *—D.T. (2/1/2004)*

ROCKY GULLY

Rocky Gully 2004 Shiraz (Frankland River) $14. Made by the folks at Frankland Estate, this Shiraz contains 5% Viognier, which didn't add the nuances that it typically does. Starts off on the nose with black and green pepper, which turns to toast and ink with some time in the glass. Inky on the palate, yes, but also a touch shrill. **85** *—D.T. (12/1/2005)*

ROSEMOUNT

Rosemount 2001 Traditional Cabernet Blend (McLaren Vale & Langhorne Creek) $30. Although this is a blend of Cabernet, Merlot, and Petit Verdot, the fruit tastes more red than black. Smells like soft, ripe red fruit and trading-card bubblegum powder, and tastes quite the same. Fruit is juicy on the palate, with a chalky feel that continues through the finish. A feminine, juicy wine to be enjoyed through 2007. **89** *—D.T. (5/1/2004)*

Rosemount 2002 Cabernet Sauvignon (South Eastern Australia) $12. Blackberry and bramble aromas on the nose; similar black fruit and oak flavors on the palate. Tealike tannins on the finish. A good, gets-the-job-done Cab. **84** *—D.T. (3/1/2005)*

Rosemount 2001 Diamond Label Cabernet Sauvignon (South Eastern Australia) $11. 86 *—D.T. (12/31/2003)*

Rosemount 2000 Hill of Gold Cabernet Sauvignon (Mudgee) $19. 89 *—M.S. (12/15/2002)*

Rosemount 1999 Orange Vineyard Cabernet Sauvignon (McLaren Vale & Langhorne Creek) $30. 82 *—M.S. (12/15/2002)*

Rosemount 2001 Show Reserve Cabernet Sauvignon (Coonawarra) $24. Smells of black pepper, smoke, and pastry crust. On the palate, yes, it's woody—smoky rather than caramel-sweet, though—with tight plum and briary earth underneath. This score reflects my expectation that more of the fruit will come to the fore in a couple of years; try again in 2006. **90** *—D.T. (8/1/2005)*

Rosemount 1998 Show Reserve Cabernet Sauvignon (Coonawarra) $24. 90 *—S.H. (6/1/2001)*

Rosemount 2001 Estate Bottled Cabernet Sauvignon-Merlot (South Eastern Australia) $9. 86 Best Buy *—M.S. (12/15/2002)*

Rosemount 1999 Chardonnay (South Eastern Australia) $12. 85 *—M.M. (10/1/2000)*

Rosemount 2004 Diamond Label Chardonnay (South Eastern Australia) $10. Though the nose doesn't show much—just a little hay—the palate doles out plenty of soft peach-fuzz flavors, plus some anise. 150,000 cases produced. **84** *—D.T. (10/1/2005)*

Rosemount 2002 Diamond Label Chardonnay (South Eastern Australia) $10. 86 *—D.T. (8/1/2003)*

Rosemount 2000 Estate Bottled Chardonnay (South Eastern Australia) $10. 86 *—M.M. (6/1/2001)*

Rosemount 2002 Giants Creek Chardonnay (Hunter Valley) $17. This is a medium-bodied wine, with not a lot of stuffing but some interesting flavors. Smolders with butterscotch, cinnamon and woodsmoke on the nose, against a backdrop of Golden Delicious apples. Palate flavors are similar, but not quite as pronounced—dried spices, honey, peach skin. Tasted twice. **85** *(7/2/2004)*

Rosemount 1999 Giants Creek Chardonnay (Hunter Valley) $17. 84 *—J.C. (7/1/2002)*

Rosemount 2001 Hill of Gold Chardonnay (Mudgee) $17. 85 *—J.C. (7/1/2002)*

Rosemount 2002 Orange Vineyard Chardonnay (Orange) $23. Has toasty, bready aromas backed up by green apple and pear. It's medium-weight, and not a very expressive wine, with some peach and buttered toast flavors peeking out on the palate. Finishes slightly herbal. **85** *(7/2/2004)*

Rosemount 1998 Orange Vyd Chardonnay (Hunter Valley) $22. 91 *(11/15/1999)*

Rosemount 2001 Roxburgh Chardonnay (Hunter Valley) $30. 89 *(2/1/2003)*

Rosemount 2003 Show Reserve Chardonnay (Hunter Valley) $20. This is a very good Chard, featuring toast, citrus, and tropical fruit aromas, and yellow stone fruit and toast flavors. Its recipe may be predictable, but the wine follows it well. **87** *—D.T. (10/1/2005)*

Rosemount 2001 Show Reserve Chardonnay (Hunter Valley) $18. 86 *(2/1/2003)*

Rosemount 2001 Chardonnay-Sémillon (South Eastern Australia) $8. 85 Best Buy *—D.T. (2/1/2002)*

Rosemount 2002 Diamond Label Chardonnay-Semillon (South Eastern Australia) $9. 86 *—D.T. (10/1/2003)*

Rosemount 2002 Merlot (South Eastern Australia) $12. Cola aromas preface mixed berry fruit on the palate. A fine red quaffing wine at a good price; not very varietally distinct. **84** *—D.T. (3/1/2005)*

Rosemount 2000 Diamond Label Merlot (South Eastern Australia) $11. 86 *—D.T. (6/1/2003)*

Rosemount 1999 Orange Vineyard Merlot (Orange) $26. 86 *—D.T. (6/1/2003)*

Rosemount 2004 Pinot Noir (South Eastern Australia) $12. Tastes like it smells: like soft, sweetish plums and raspberries, touched up by toast and vanilla. It's not a powerhouse Pinot, but is a fine intro to the variety at a decent price. 23,500 cases produced. **84** *—D.T. (12/1/2005)*

Rosemount 2001 Diamond Label Pinot Noir (South Eastern Australia) $12. 83 *—J.C. (9/1/2002)*

Rosemount 2001 Grenache-Shiraz (Australia) $9. 83 *—J.C. (9/1/2002)*

Rosemount 2001 GSM Rhône Red Blend (McLaren Vale & Langhorne Creek) $30. Aromas are lovely, of cherries, berries, and pastry crust. Fruit on the palate is red and juicy, yet taut, though there's just a hint of cherry or rhubarb. A food-friendly wine, one that would work well with any number of dishes. **89** *—D.T. (5/1/2004)*

Rosemount 2000 GSM Grenache Syrah Mouvedre (Barossa Valley) $30. 89 *(2/1/2003)*

Rosemount 2004 Diamond Label Riesling (South Eastern Australia) $10. This is a good cocktail-party Riesling, medium-sized (maybe a little heavy?), without the bracing acidity that enthusiasts either love or don't about the variety. This bottling deals fresh cream aromas, with lemon and peach skin flavors. 14,000 cases produced. **85 Best Buy** *—D.T. (12/1/2005)*

Rosemount 2002 Sauvignon Blanc (South Eastern Australia) $10. 85 *—D.T. (10/1/2003)*

Rosemount 2000 Estate Bottled Sauvignon Blanc (South Eastern Australia) $10. 85 *—J.F. (9/1/2001)*

Rosemount 2000 Semillon (South Eastern Australia) $NA. 82 *—D.T. (2/1/2002)*

Rosemount 2002 Semillon-Chardonnay (South Eastern Australia) $8. 86 Best Buy *—D.T. (10/1/2003)*

Rosemount 2002 Diamond Label Shiraz (South Eastern Australia) $12. 85 *—D.T. (10/1/2003)*

Rosemount 1999 Diamond Label Shiraz (South Eastern Australia) $11. 87 Best Buy *—M.S. (10/1/2000)*

Rosemount 2003 Hill of Gold Shiraz (Mudgee) $17. Earthier, oakier notes prevail in this wine, with sour plums buried deep beneath. Aromas are of tea, bramble, and plum. A straightforward wine, not too nuanced. 85 *—D.T. (10/1/2005)*

Rosemount 2000 Hill of Gold Shiraz (Mudgee) $19. 86 *(2/1/2003)*

Rosemount 1999 Orange Vineyard Shiraz (Orange) $26. 87 *—J.M. (12/15/2002)*

Rosemount 2000 Show Reserve Shiraz (McLaren Vale & Langhorne Creek) $24. 88 *—D.T. (6/1/2003)*

Rosemount 2001 Estate Bottled Shiraz-Cabernet (South Australia/Victoria) $8. 87 Best Buy *—S.H. (11/15/2002)*

Rosemount 2000 Balmoral Syrah (McLaren Vale) $50. 90 *—D.T. (12/31/2003)*

Rosemount 1998 Balmoral Syrah (McLaren Vale) $50. 90 *(11/1/2001)*

Rosemount 2002 Estate Bottled Traminer-Riesling (South Eastern Australia) $9. 83 *—D.T. (10/1/2003)*

ROSENBLUM

Rosenblum 2001 Feather Foot Man Jingalu Special Artist Series Shiraz (McLaren Vale) $31. 90 *—S.H. (1/1/2002)*

ROSS ESTATE

Ross Estate 1999 Cabernet Sauvignon (Barossa Valley) $20. 89 *—C.S. (6/1/2002)*

Ross Estate 1999 Old Vine Grenache (Barossa Valley) $18. 89 *—J.C. (9/1/2002)*

Ross Estate 2000 Shiraz (Barossa Valley) $20. 87 *—D.T. (3/1/2003)*

Rothbury Estate 2002 Chardonnay (South Eastern Australia) $8. 85 *—D.T. (8/1/2003)*

ROTHBURY ESTATE

Rothbury Estate 1998 Chardonnay (South Eastern Australia) $8. 86 Best Buy *—M.S. (10/1/2000)*

Rothbury Estate 2001 Brokenback Chardonnay (Hunter Valley) $30. This Hunter wine shows light peach and citrus aromas and flavors. Its feel, though, is crystalline, unyielding and hard to warm up to. Finishes lemony and hard, with a little toasted wood. 84 *(7/2/2004)*

Rothbury Estate 1999 Brokenback Shiraz (Hunter Valley) $34. 89 *—D.T. (12/31/2003)*

RUMBALL

Rumball NV SB16 Coonawarra Cuvee Shiraz (Coonawarra) $26. One of the best-known sparkling Shiraz makers in Australia, Peter Rumball's Coonawarra version offers some stewy fruit aromas and flavors, and caramel accents on the palate. However dark its flavors sound, it's still feels fresh on the palate. Finishes short. 84 *—D.T. (12/31/2004)*

RYMILL

Rymill 1996 Shiraz (Coonawarra) $17. 90 *(4/1/2000)*

SALENA ESTATE

Salena Estate 2001 Cabernet Sauvignon Cabernet Blend (South Australia) $10. Simple and fruity, with soft, cassis flavors. Alcohol shows through a bit on the finish. 84 *(9/2/2004)*

Salena Estate 1999 Ellen Landing Cabernet Sauvignon (South Eastern Australia) $18. 84 *—D.T. (6/1/2002)*

Salena Estate 2001 Chardonnay (Riverland) $11. 85 *—J.C. (7/1/2002)*

Salena Estate 2000 Merlot (Riverland) $11. 86 *—C.S. (6/1/2002)*

Salena Estate 2001 Shiraz (South Australia) $10. Medium-weight Shiraz, with smoky leathery notes that play off against dark, pruny fruit. A solid farmhouse-style red for rustic dishes. 85 *(9/2/2004)*

SALISBURY

Salisbury 1999 Shiraz (South Eastern Australia) $8. 87 Best Buy *(10/1/2001)*

SANDALFORD

Sandalford 1998 Cabernet Sauvignon (Western Australia) $24. 88 *(1/1/2004)*

Sandalford 2000 Merlot (Western Australia) $24. 86 *(7/1/2002)*

Sandalford 2001 Semillon-Sauvignon Blanc (Western Australia) $16. 85 *(7/1/2002)*

Sandalford 1998 Shiraz (Western Australia) $24. **90** *(7/1/2002)*

SCHILD ESTATE

Schild Estate 2002 Cabernet Sauvignon (Barossa Valley) $24. Though other tasting panelists liked it better, I can't get on board with the raisin-bran element that pervades this wine, nose to finish. Blackberry and oak flavors underneath are a little sweet, too; the whole package is good, though for the price, GI and vintage, I had hoped for more. Tasted twice, with consistent results. **84** *—D.T. (5/1/2005)*

Schild Estate 2003 Riesling (Barossa Valley) $15. Honeysuckle and white peach aromas; the palate shows some citrusy verve. The flavors are light and the mouthfeel and finish quite dry. Just the thing for an apéritif, or to be drunk outdoors. **86** *—D.T. (12/31/2004)*

Schild Estate 2002 Shiraz (Barossa) $24. Medium-sized, with deep, fruitcake and stewed berry aromas. The same notes follow through on the palate, which is dominated by cassis but puckers up with tight plum fruit on the finish. **88** *—D.T. (12/1/2005)*

SEAVIEW

Seaview 1997 Champagne Blend (South Eastern Australia) $10. **87** *—E.M. (11/15/1999)*

Seaview 1999 Brut Champagne Blend (South Eastern Australia) $10. **88 Best Buy** *(12/1/2001)*

Seaview NV Brut (South Eastern Australia) $10. It's hard to quibble with the fact that this wine almost always overdelivers for the price: It's fairly widely available and is good alone, or in sparkling cocktails. This year's edition shows wheat flour, ginger, and a banana note—unexpected, maybe, but still gets the job done. **84** *—D.T. (12/31/2004)*

SEXTON

Sexton 2003 Giant Steps Vineyard, Bernard Clones Chardonnay (Yarra Valley) $40. For the number of times I wrote descriptors of butter, butterscotch, and vanilla for this wine, I normally wouldn't like it as much as I did. It works here, because the aforementioned notes are light on the citrus spine. Finishes with—guess what?—butterscotch. **87** *—D.T. (5/1/2005)*

SHALLOW CREEK

Shallow Creek 2002 Shiraz (Victoria) $24. Has nice black plum fruit at its core, but it's obscured by strange, rubbery notes. The nose has even more unusual notes–catsup? Maybe aioli? A curiosity, from beginning to end. **84** *—D.T. (5/1/2004)*

SHAW AND SMITH

Shaw and Smith 2004 Sauvignon Blanc (Adelaide Hills) $19. This Sauvignon is as crisp and zesty as the Marlborough Sauvignons that are so in vogue right now, minus the lime-green flavors. Fresh-cut grass aromas usher in a bright, lemon-centric palate. As dry as they come; very appealing, and very intense. Just delicious. **90 Editors' Choice** *—D.T. (8/1/2005)*

SHEEP'S BACK

Sheep's Back 2001 Old Vine Shiraz (Barossa Valley) $23. Has deep, pleasing aromas of eucalyptus, earth, and cream. It's a big wine in the mouth, not blowsy but pretty enthusiastic with oak—red cherry and raspberry flavors are trimmed with caramel and oak flavors that widen to a creamy-vanilla close. **88** *—D.T. (12/31/2004)*

SHINGLEBACK

Shingleback 2002 Cabernet Sauvignon (McLaren Vale) $19. This Cab feels tall: not round, not muscular, but lanky and vertical. It's a textured wine, though, with sandy-floury tannins and a plum-and-cherry core. Aromas of stewy, dusty fruit, and powdery tannins on the finish, complete the pretty picture. **89** *—D.T. (12/31/2004)*

Shingleback 2002 Shiraz (McLaren Vale) $19. Smoke, pepper, red fruit, and vanilla aromas. Tastes dark and earthy, with powerful accents of earth, oak, and mushroom atop the plum fruit. Smooth, fine tannins on the palate; pure, taut plum fruit at the close. **89** *(11/15/2004)*

Shingleback 2002 D Block Reserve Shiraz (McLaren Vale) $50. Shingleback's signature Shiraz is heavy on the mocha, dried fruit, and liqueur aromas—really, it smells like fruitcake in a glass. Its flavors are similar: dried fruit, wheat, and nut, but more subdued than it is on the nose. Sweetish and forward; drink this one if it's just you, a partner, and the fireplace, and go for the regular Shingleback Shiraz if there's food on the table. **88** *—D.T. (10/1/2005)*

SHOTTESBROOKE

Shottesbrooke 2000 Shiraz (South Australia) $17. **88** *—C.S. (3/1/2003)*

Shottesbrooke 2000 Eliza Reserve Shiraz (McLaren Vale) $30. **91** *—C.S. (3/1/2003)*

SIMON GILBERT

Simon Gilbert 1999 Shiraz (Mudgee) $10. **83** *(10/1/2001)*

SIMON HACKETT

Simon Hackett 2000 Cabernet Sauvignon (McLaren Vale) $18. **89** *—M.S. (12/15/2002)*

Simon Hackett 1997 Foggo Road Cabernet Sauvignon (McLaren Vale) $38. **92** *(6/1/2001)*

Simon Hackett 2001 Chardonnay (Barossa Valley) $18. **85** *—D.T. (8/1/2003)*

Simon Hackett 2004 Brightview Chardonnay (Barossa Valley) $15. An easy-drinking, overt wine, but an enjoyable one. Aromas are vibrant and springy—flowers, lemon-lime, mineral. The palate offers up fleshy yellow fruit and stony-mineral accents that carry through the finish. **87** *—D.T. (3/1/2005)*

Simon Hackett 2002 Old Vine Grenache (McLaren Vale) $18. Bright, bouncy cherry and plum aromas; wood and earth are interspersed with mixed cherries on the palate. A straighforward, enjoyable Grenache. **87** *—D.T. (3/1/2005)*

Simon Hackett 2000 Old Vine Grenache (McLaren Vale) $18. 84 *—J.C. (9/1/2002)*

Simon Hackett 2000 Brightview Semillon (Barossa Valley) $15. 90 *—J.C. (2/1/2002)*

Simon Hackett 2001 Shiraz (McLaren Vale) $18. 85 *—D.T. (3/1/2003)*

Simon Hackett 1999 Shiraz (McLaren Vale) $18. 89 *(6/1/2001)*

SKILLOGALEE

Skillogalee 2003 Riesling (Clare Valley) $18. Smells big and oily, with some honeysuckle. In the mouth, it's smooth, with lemon and herb flavors. Clean on the back, with more citrus. **85** *—D.T. (5/1/2004)*

SMITH & HOOPER

Smith & Hooper 2000 Wrattonbully Limited Edition Merlot (South Australia) $30. 87 *—D.T. (6/1/2003)*

SONS OF EDEN

Sons of Eden 2003 Kennedy GSM Rhône Red Blend (Barossa Valley) $23. An enjoyable wine, but one that tastes more built for the masses than for wine sophisticates. Fruit on the palate is juicy and bright, like purple fruit and raspberries; the nose is awash with vanilla bean and cream. **86** *—D.T. (5/1/2005)*

SOUTHERN TRACKS

Southern Tracks 2001 Chardonnay (South Eastern Australia) $10. 84 *—D.T. (6/1/2003)*

SPRINGWOOD PARK

Springwood Park 1998 Nicholas Shiraz (McLaren Vale) $35. 89 *—D.T. (12/31/2003)*

ST. MARYS

St. Marys 1999 Shiraz (Coonawarra) $19. 87 *(10/1/2001)*

ST. ANDREWS ESTATE

St. Andrews Estate 2000 Adelaide Plains Shiraz (Adelaide Hills) $22. 89 *(11/1/2001)*

ST. HALLETT

St. Hallett 1999 Cabernet Sauvignon (Barossa Valley) $21. 85 *—D.T. (6/1/2002)*

St. Hallett 1999 Gamekeeper's Reserve Rhône Red Blend (Barossa Valley) $10. 88 *—M.M. (10/1/2000)*

St. Hallett 2001 Blackwell Shiraz (Barossa Valley) $30. Fruit is black and big, as it typically is, framed in spicy oak and claylike, chewy tannins. This vintage is elegant compared to the more unrestrained 2000 vintage. A bull, to be sure, but one that's more likely to buy something in the china shop than to break something. Drink 2006+. **90** *—D.T. (2/1/2004)*

St. Hallett 1997 Blackwell Shiraz (Barossa Valley) $25. 90 Cellar Selection *—J.C. (9/1/2002)*

St. Hallett 2002 Faith Shiraz (Barossa Valley) $20. St. Hallett's entry-level Shiraz is made from young-vine fruit. It's satisfying but simple, as it's meant to be, with plum and cherry flavors, and just a little burned sugar, on the palate. On the finish, black plum and cherry surfaces, with hints of eucalyptus and black pepper that are more pronounced in the winery's top bottlings. **88** *—D.T. (2/1/2004)*

St. Hallett 1999 Faith Shiraz (Barossa Valley) $18. 88 *(10/1/2001)*

St. Hallett 2001 Gamekeepers Reserve Shiraz (Barossa Valley) $NA. A blend of Shiraz, Grenache, Touriga, Malbec, Cabernet Franc and Mourvèdre; winemaker Stuart Blackwell says that the biggest export market for this wine in the U.S. is Houston, of all places, but taste the earth, graham cracker, and spice that coats the cherry fruit, and Texas barbecue sounds like a darned good idea (though the wine's back label says to drink it with "vegetarian lunches and Friday pizza"). Hey, either way, y'all. **88** *—D.T. (2/1/2004)*

St. Hallett 2000 Old Block Shiraz (Barossa Valley) $54. Nose has beautiful, permeating pine-needle, mocha and meaty aromas. In the mouth it boasts chewy tannins, cassis fruit, and slatelike accents. Finishes long; a sexy wine overall, with a beautiful, mouthcoating feel. **93** *—D.T. (5/1/2004)*

St. Hallett 1998 Old Block Shiraz (Barossa Valley) $40. 95 Editors' Choice *—S.H. (12/15/2002)*

St. Hallett 2001 Poachers White Blend (South Australia) $10. 88 *—S.H. (1/1/2002)*

STANLEY BROTHERS

Stanley Brothers 1998 Thoroughbred Cabernet Sauvignon (Barossa Valley) $22. 87 *—C.S. (6/1/2002)*

Stanley Brothers 1998 Pristine Chardonnay (Barossa Valley) $15. 86 *—M.M. (10/1/2000)*

Stanley Brothers 1998 Black Sheep Red Blend (Barossa Valley) $16. 86 *—M.S. (10/1/2000)*

STARVEDOG LANE

Starvedog Lane 1999 Cabernet Sauvignon (Adelaide Hills) $23. 84 *—D.T. (6/1/2003)*

Starvedog Lane 2000 Chardonnay (Adelaide Hills) $19. 84 *—D.T. (8/1/2003)*

Starvedog Lane 2003 Shiraz-Viognier (Adelaide Hills) $15. Has all the working parts that a good Oz red needs: fleshy plum fruit, judicious oak, and a please-all medium size. Smells earthy, and finishes with a taut smack of plum skin. Contains 6% Viognier, but its telltale floral qualities aren't so obvious here. **86** *—D.T. (8/1/2005)*

Starvedog Lane 2003 Sauvignon Blanc (Adelaide Hills) $15. Tropical yellow fruit and fresh garden greens on the nose let you know exactly what you're in for: A crisp, zesty, summery wine. Tangy grapefruit, peach, and grassy flavors follow through on the clean finish. **87** *—D.T. (9/1/2004)*

STEFANO LUBIANA

Stefano Lubiana NV Brut (Tasmania) $34. 84 *—M.M. (12/1/2001)*

Stefano Lubiana 1999 Riesling (Tasmania) $27. 84 *—M.M. (2/1/2002)*

STEVE HOFF

Steve Hoff 1999 Cabernet Sauvignon (Barossa Valley) $18. 83 *—J.C. (6/1/2002)*

Steve Hoff 2002 Rossco's Shiraz (Barossa) $40. Though this wine has the same cherry and plum fruit that many others in Barossa do this vintage, it is bolstered by mocha and toasty accents. A solid, food-weight wine, and one that would suit a burger or roast beef very well. **87** *—D.T. (10/1/2005)*

STICKS

Sticks 2003 Chardonnay (Yarra Valley) $16. Aromas are subtle; we detected some floral, citrus, and green apple aromas. Medium-weight with pear and melon flavors on the palate, it closes with a tart snap of lime. **85** *(7/2/2004)*

Sticks 2002 Pinot Noir (Yarra Valley) $15. 86 *—S.H. (10/1/2003)*

STONEHAVEN

Stonehaven 1997 Cabernet Sauvignon (Limestone Coast) $18. 88 *(11/1/2000)*

Stonehaven 1996 Reserve Cabernet Sauvignon (McLaren Vale) $40. 88 *(11/1/2000)*

Stonehaven 2001 Chardonnay (Limestone Coast) $13. 83 *(7/2/2004)*

Stonehaven 2000 Chardonnay (Limestone Coast) $16. 87 *—J.C. (7/1/2002)*

Stonehaven 1999 Chardonnay (South Eastern Australia) $9. 86 *(11/1/2000)*

Stonehaven 1999 Reserve Chardonnay (Padthaway) $29. 87 *—J.C. (7/1/2002)*

Stonehaven 2004 Winemaker's Selection Chardonnay (South Australia) $12. A bit nutty (almonds) at first, married nicely to pineapple and citrus aromas. Plump in texture, with broad, mouthfilling flavors, but finishes a touch rustic, with some unintegrated wood. **85** *(11/1/2005)*

Stonehaven 2000 Merlot (Padthaway) $9. 85 *—D.T. (6/1/2002)*

Stonehaven 2004 Winemaker's Selection Riesling (South Australia) $12. Produced exclusively from estate grown fruit, this was our favorite of Stonehaven's new line. Soft, round, and honeyed in the mouth yet mostly dry, with piquant flavors of apples and pears. Mouthwatering on the finish. Good value. **86** *(11/1/2005)*

Stonehaven 1999 Shiraz (South Eastern Australia) $9. 83 *(10/1/2001)*

Stonehaven 1998 Shiraz (Limestone Coast) $17. 87 *(11/1/2000)*

Stonehaven 1997 Reserve Shiraz (Padthaway) $46. 86 *(11/1/2001)*

Stonehaven 2003 Winemaker's Selection Shiraz (South Australia) $12. Shows some roasted fruit character, with predominantly earthy flavors and notes of cooked meat, coffee, cinnamon, and brown sugar. Low acidity and decent concentration give it a fat mouthfeel. **85** *(11/1/2005)*

STONEY RISE

Stoney Rise 2002 Shiraz (Limestone Coast) $19. This is one dry Shiraz now, with tree bark, black pepper, and high-toned black fruit aromas and flavors, and tealike tannins firmly gripping the palate. Give it a year or two to settle down and smooth out. **87** *—D.T. (12/31/2004)*

STRINGY BRAE

Stringy Brae 1999 Shiraz (Clare Valley) $30. 83 *—D.T. (1/28/2003)*

SYLVAN SPRINGS

Sylvan Springs 2000 Shiraz (McLaren Vale) $20. 84 *—D.T. (1/28/2003)*

AUSTRALIA

T'GALLANT

T'Gallant 2000 Imogen Pinot Gris (Mornington Peninsula) $18. 86 *—M.M. (2/1/2002)*

T'Gallant 2000 Pinot Noir (Mornington Peninsula) $25. 85 *—J.C. (9/1/2002)*

TAHBILK

Tahbilk 1999 Cabernet Sauvignon (Nagambie Lakes) $20. This Cab is already turning somewhat brick in color. Its flavors and aromas are of red fruit, but they are less fleshy than they are like skin and seeds. The wine's pleasing, smooth mouthfeel is its best feature. **84** *—D.T. (5/1/2005)*

Tahbilk 1994 Reserve Cabernet Sauvignon (Goulburn Valley) $35. 93 *(6/1/2001)*

Tahbilk 1998 Shiraz (Victoria) $18. 85 *(10/1/2001)*

Tahbilk 1996 1860 Vines Shiraz (Nagambie Lakes) $125. This is a wine that feels old-fashioned but still not ready to drink. It smells nutty and dusty, with black pepper and anise accents. Its plum fruit core is wound very tightly, and encased in a fair amount of good-quality oak. Tannins are thick and wooly, so much so that I'd forget that I even had this in the cellar until Bush is out of office, then drink through 2014 or so. **92 Cellar Selection** *—D.T. (8/1/2005)*

TAIT WINES

Tait Wines 2002 Basket Pressed Cabernet Sauvignon (Barossa Valley) $30. Anise and oak on the nose; winemaker Bruno Tait says, "Believe it or not, it's 15.5% alcohol," but I don't see why we're supposed to be so surprised. It's a sizeable wine, with woody tannins that linger on the palate, and mixed plum fruit underneath. A very nice wine, concentrated and intimidating. **91** *—D.T. (2/1/2004)*

Tait Wines 2000 Basket Press Shiraz (Barossa Valley) $25. 84 *—D.T. (1/28/2003)*

TALAGANDRA

Talagandra 2001 Chardonnay (Australia) $17. 85 *—J.C. (9/10/2002)*

TALTARNI

Taltarni 1995 Cabernet Sauvignon (Victoria) $16. 88 *—L.W. (12/31/1999)*

Taltarni 2000 Clover Hill Champagne Blend (Tasmania) $30. Dust, apple, mushroom, and toast aromas start things off, and reveal some stone fruit and talc on the palate. Its texture—moussey and frothy, rather than dry and crisp—reminds me of Cremant or Prosecco. 53% Chardonnay, 35% Pinot Noir, 12% Pinot Meunier. **87** *—D.T. (12/31/2005)*

Taltarni 2000 Sauvignon Blanc (Victoria) $13. 82 *—J.F. (9/1/2001)*

Taltarni 1997 Estate Grown Shiraz (Victoria) $16. 89 *—L.W. (12/31/1999)*

Taltarni NV Brut Tache Sparkling Blend (Victoria) $20. Light pink in color, with aromas of dust, earth, and cherry. It's medium-full in the mouth, cherry notes once again at the fore, but bolstered by earth, toast, and a racy, grape-fruit edge through the finish. Very enjoyable; 1,600 cases produced. **89** *—D.T. (12/31/2005)*

Taltarni 1998 Clover Hill Sparkling Blend (Tasmania) $29. 85 *—D.T. (12/31/2003)*

TAPESTRY

Tapestry 2002 Cabernet Sauvignon (McLaren Vale) $21. This Cab has a smooth, milky texture. Its core is cherry, verging on rhubarb, and black pepper is the main player on the nose. Light in size for a Cab. **86** *—D.T. (10/1/2005)*

Tapestry 1999 Bin 388 Cabernet Sauvignon (McLaren Vale) $25. 83 *—D.T. (6/1/2002)*

Tapestry 2002 Chardonnay (McLaren Vale) $15. A racy wine, with a tart streak: Aromas are of pear, green apple, and grapefruit. Feels clean in the mouth with citrus and peach fruit, and a hint of herb. Finishes with a peppery sourness. Bring a bottle to the raw bar. **85** *(7/2/2004)*

Tapestry 1999 Bin 338 Shiraz (McLaren Vale) $25. 87 *(11/1/2001)*

Tapestry 2001 The Vincent Shiraz (McLaren Vale) $36. From vines with a minimum age of 30 years, this is a pretty accessible style of Shiraz. The nose offers jammy, bright fruit with judicious oak accents, which deepen into nice hazelnut notes. In the mouth, smooth oak overlays mixed plum fruits. A feminine wine, rather than an overstuffed, burly one. **88** *—D.T. (11/15/2004)*

TATACHILLA

Tatachilla 1999 Cabernet Sauvignon (Padthaway) $20. 81 *—D.T. (6/1/2002)*

Tatachilla 2000 Breakneck Creek Cabernet Sauvignon (South Australia) $12. 83 *—J.C. (6/1/2002)*

Tatachilla 2000 Chardonnay (Padthaway) $15. 84 *—J.C. (7/1/2002)*

Tatachilla 2000 Chardonnay (Adelaide Hills) $25. 83 *—D.T. (8/1/2003)*

Tatachilla 1999 Chardonnay (McLaren Vale) $14. 80 *—J.C. (9/10/2002)*

Tatachilla 2001 Breakneck Creek Chardonnay (South Australia) $9. Toasty and thick in the mouth, it smells syrupy, like peach jelly and honey. The palate flavors reminded the panelists more of Gewürztraminer than Chardonnay. A puzzling wine. **82** *(7/2/2004)*

Tatachilla 1998 Grenache-Shiraz (McLaren Vale) $14. 84 *—J.C. (9/1/2001)*

Tatachilla 1999 Clarendon Vineyards Merlot (McLaren Vale) $35. 87 *—J.C. (6/1/2002)*

Tatachilla 1999 Wattle Park Merlot (South Australia) $10. 87 Best Buy *—M.M. (9/1/2001)*

Tatachilla 2000 Shiraz (McLaren Vale) $20. Shows eucalyptus, cola and thick black plum flavors on the nose. Black cherry, red plum and clove flavors hit you at palate entry; by midpalate, a pleasing chalk-clay feel steps in. A very good red wine, but not one you'd immediately recognize as Shiraz. **87** *—D.T. (5/1/2004)*

Tatachilla 2002 Breakneck Creek Shiraz (South Australia) $9. Smells and tastes of light brown sugar and soft red fruit. It's a simple, easy-drinking, accessible wine, and priced accordingly. **85** *—D.T. (9/1/2004)*

Tatachilla 1998 Foundation Shiraz (McLaren Vale) $45. 88 *—D.T. (3/1/2003)*

Tatachilla 2000 Chenin Blanc-Semillon-Sauvignon Blanc (South Australia) $9. 80 *—D.T. (2/1/2002)*

TATIARRA

Tatiarra 2003 Cambrian Shiraz (Heathcote) $58. This Shiraz has a remarkable texture—like smooth river stones—and offers a berry-basket full of juicy flavors. On the nose, aromas of coconut, toast, and chocolate (no, it's not at all candied, as it may sound) mingle with fresh raspberries. **90** *—D.T. (12/1/2005)*

TEAL LAKE

Teal Lake 2002 Cabernet Sauvignon-Merlot (South Eastern Australia) $13. Boasts tobacco and dried-spice aromas, then turns a bit tart and cranberryish on the palate. Lean and herbal on the finish. **83** *—J.C. (4/1/2005)*

Teal Lake 1999 Herzog Selection Chardonnay (South Eastern Australia) $12. 85 *(4/1/2001)*

Teal Lake 2001 Shiraz (South Eastern Australia) $13. 87 *—K.F. (3/1/2003)*

Teal Lake 2002 Shiraz-Cabernet (South Eastern Australia) $12. Simple leather and plum aromas and flavors; a medium-weight wine that turns a little tart on the finish. **84** *—J.C. (4/1/2005)*

TEMPLE BRUER

Temple Bruer 2001 Reserve (Langhorne Creek) $22. This is an interesting, pleasing blend of 81% Cabernet Sauvignon and 19% Petit Verdot, organically grown in Langhorne Creek. I like how unusual its characteristics are—aromas of menthol and blackberry, and flavors of clove, cinnamon and black plums. Altogether it is a harmonious, medium-bodied wine worth a look. **89** *—D.T. (5/1/2005)*

Temple Bruer 2001 Cabernet Sauvignon-Merlot (McLaren Vale & Langhorne Creek) $16. 88 *—D.T. (12/31/2003)*

Temple Bruer 2003 Chenin Blanc (Langhorne Creek) $15. If peach aromatherapy exists—that is, the purest, most concentrated smell of peach in a bottle—this nose is it. After a while, though, an acrylic-like aroma starts emerging, and the palate shows evidence of both acrylic and peach. Still, it's a worthwhile wine, but would have been better with the focus on the fruit. **84** *—D.T. (5/1/2005)*

Temple Bruer 1998 Reserve Merlot (Langhorne Creek) $20. 84 *—D.T. (6/1/2002)*

THE BLACK CHOOK

The Black Chook 2004 Shiraz-Viognier (South Australia) $18. This wine inspired some debate in the tasting room, others appreciating it more than I did. Made by Ben Riggs, a winemaker who certainly knows his way around Shiraz-Viogniers. The aromas are very sweet, with raspberry and blueberry holding court. The flavor? Blueberry jam. Tastes low in acid, but its 15% alcohol is no surprise. **84** *—D.T. (12/31/2005)*

THE EDGE

The Edge 2002 Sauvignon Blanc (King Valley) $16. The primary flavors are of lemon/lime pith and white peach, which hang on a clean frame. Fresh green accents are pleasant, but not for everyone. **86** *—D.T. (11/15/2004)*

THE GATE

The Gate 2003 Shiraz (McLaren Vale) $32. Another label from Shingleback winemaker John Davey, this vintage of The Gate delivers a well-structured, tasty wine full of black and white pepper, plum, and blackberry flavors. The nose shows milk chocolate, black berry, and cherry aromas. Very enjoyable; one to drink over the next 3 years. **89** *—D.T. (12/31/2005)*

THE GREEN VINEYARDS

The Green Vineyards 1999 The Forties Old Block Shiraz (Victoria) $30. 86 *(11/1/2001)*

THE LANE

The Lane 2002 Beginning Chardonnay (Adelaide Hills) $38. A new premium brand from the Starvedog Lane folks, this wine opens with pleasing mineral, chalk, and peach aromas. Close your eyes and you're drinking fruit nectar—the mango and peach flavors are that pure, and that ripe. A bright, sunny wine but also a firm one with good viscosity. Finish is medium-long and juicy. **89** *(7/2/2004)*

The Lane 2001 Reunion Shiraz (Adelaide Hills) $44. The nose offers permeating black-pepper aromas, and some maple sweetness. Black plum and cherry fruit on the palate is encased in a fairly dry, leathery mouthfeel; the finish brings more black cherry, leather and oak flavors. It's very good, mouthcoating and big in size, but a little less so in richness. **87** —*D.T. (9/1/2004)*

THE WINNER'S TANK

The Winner's Tank 2004 Shiraz (Langhorne Creek) $16. A wine that was a contest entry, hence its name. It's rich, but a little hollow; as one taster says, it tries too hard. Aromas are of grape jelly, nutmeg and wheat bread. In the mouth, it has similar flavors. **86** —*D.T. (12/1/2005)*

THIRSTY LIZARD

Thirsty Lizard 2002 Chardonnay (South Eastern Australia) $8. 83 —*D.T. (1/1/2002)*

Thirsty Lizard 2000 Shiraz (South Eastern Australia) $8. 81 —*D.T. (12/31/2003)*

THOMAS MITCHELL

Thomas Mitchell 1998 Marsanne (South Eastern Australia) $14. 86 Best Buy —*S.H. (10/1/2000)*

THREE BRIDGES

Three Bridges 1999 Golden Mist-Boytrytis Semillon (Riverina) $18. 91 —*J.M. (12/1/2002)*

TIM ADAMS

Tim Adams 2000 Cabernet Sauvignon (Clare Valley) $23. 89 —*D.T. (12/31/2003)*

Tim Adams 2003 Riesling (Clare Valley) $15. It's unfortunate that it's not available in the U.S., because this is a very refreshing Riesling, with steel-mineral and citrus flavors. Finishes crisp, like running river water. **87** —*D.T. (2/1/2004)*

Tim Adams 1994 Botrytis Riesling (Clare Valley) $NA. Fresh-sliced melon, mustard seed, and honey on the nose. Ripe peach, melon, hone,y and hay flavors are dry rather than cloyingly sweet. Finishes clean, with a dry, slatelike feel. **90** —*D.T. (2/1/2004)*

Tim Adams 2002 Shiraz (Clare Valley) $21. Yum. An excellent expression of Shiraz, with all its parts behaving as they should: Chalky tannins and good grip on the palate, and fresh herb and plum on the finish. Has a bright clay-epoxy note, plus brown sugar and beef, on the nose. Drink 2007–2010. **90 Editors' Choice** —*D.T. (2/1/2004)*

TIM GRAMP

Tim Gramp 2001 Proprietary Grenache (Clare Valley) $17. Aromas are of coffee and oak; palate flavors are of taut plum and tea. The feel is smooth, with good, chunky weight in the midpalate. Red fruit persists on the finish. **88** —*D.T. (9/1/2004)*

Tim Gramp 2000 Proprietary Shiraz (Clare Valley) $29. The nose offers dried spice, cigar box, and eucalyptus aromas, and the palate yields cool, taut red fruit, including a hint of tomato. Has a nice, gummy texture and lithe size; finishes with more red fruit and eucalyptus. **87** —*D.T. (9/1/2004)*

TIN COWS

Tin Cows 2000 Merlot (Yarra Valley) $13. 90 —*S.H. (1/1/2002)*

Tin Cows 2001 Shiraz (Yarra Valley) $13. 90 —*S.H. (1/1/2002)*

TINTARA

Tintara 2003 Reserve Grenache (McLaren Vale) $49. This is Tintara's first varietal Grenache to be released in the U.S., and what a splash it'll make. Lifted cherry and violet aromas have a light wheat-biscuit accent. The palate follows suit with the same violet and black cherry notes. It's fresh and vibrant, with a chalky-mineral finish. "It's really hard to get people to notice it," laments winemaker Rob Mann of the variety. With this wine, Rob, your troubles are over. **90** —*D.T. (3/1/2005)*

Tintara 2002 Reserve Shiraz (McLaren Vale) $49. Chewy on the palate, with vibrant plum, blueberry, and blackberry flavors that persist through the finish. Its aromas are similarly juicy and flavorful: plum and blackberry, and a dusting of bread flour. A pretty, concentrated, feminine-style Shiraz. 900 cases made, with 300 coming to the U.S. **90** —*D.T. (3/1/2005)*

TORBRECK

Torbreck 2002 Juveniles Red Blend (Barossa Valley) $25. Named for a wine bar in Paris for which this wine was formulated, this is a GSM with 60% Grenache, and equal parts Shiraz and Mourvèdre. In past vintages, I've found it lean and herbal, but this vintage brings flavors of ripe plum and cherry fruit, and earth, in equal measure. Light- to medium-bodied in the mouth, it's 100% tank fermented, with bread flour and eucalyptus aromas. **90 Editors' Choice** —*D.T. (2/1/2004)*

Torbreck 2002 Woodcutter's Red Blend (Barossa Valley) $20. Made from all young-vine fruit, Woodcutter's is aptly named in that the palate has earth and tree bark flavors that give black cherry fruit an even darker foil. Stewed fruit and pine needle aromas on the nose come back to clean up the finish. A fun, good, weeknight pizza wine. **88** —*D.T. (2/1/2004)*

Torbreck 2001 The Descendant Shiraz (Barossa Valley) $85. A junior Run Rig, in more ways than one: The Descendant's grapes come from a single vineyard made from Run Rig cuttings. The wine is aged in two-year-old Run Rig barrels, and, like its big brother, contains a small percentage of Viognier. The Viognier lends floral aromas to the nose; it's big and syrupy in the mouth at first, but smooth, silky tannins step in thereafter. Fruit is a little stewy, but that's the vintage conditions talking. 800 cases produced. **90** *—D.T. (2/1/2004)*

Torbreck 2001 The Struie Shiraz (Barossa Valley) $50. A textbook Shiraz, with all its components in the right places: There's big plum fruit on the palate backed by oak and earth; aromas are of pine and wheat. Aged in 30% new French oak. **89** *—D.T. (2/1/2004)*

Torbreck 2002 Woodcutter's White (Barossa Valley) $16. A 100% Semillon, with banana-cream aromas and honeysuckle and jasmine flavors. Light and fresh, with snappy white-pepper flavors on the finish. **85** *—D.T. (2/1/2004)*

TRENTHAM

Trentham 2000 Big Rivers Shiraz (Australia) $11. **88 Best Buy** *—D.T. (12/31/2003)*

TREVOR MAST

Trevor Mast 2001 Four Sisters Merlot (South Eastern Australia) $12. **83** *—D.T. (1/1/2002)*

TURKEY FLAT

Turkey Flat 2001 Cabernet Sauvignon (Barossa Valley) $36. A very good, pleasing Cabernet with bouncy plum and black berry fruit that verges on sweet. Nose has plum, eucalyptus, and mocha aromas; finishes a little woody, with more vivid plum. A straightahead, enjoyable wine. **87** *—D.T. (2/1/2004)*

Turkey Flat 2002 Marsanne-Semillon (Barossa Valley) $17. Fruit-driven and fresh, yellow fruit on the palate takes on honey accents as well. Dressed up with bright citrus notes. 10% barrel fermented in new French oak. **87** *—D.T. (2/1/2004)*

Turkey Flat 2001 Butchers Block Rhône Red Blend (Barossa Valley) $25. Tastes as its bouquet suggests, with soft, red plum and cherry fruit from beginning to end. Obvious and straightforward, but tasty. **87** *—D.T. (2/1/2004)*

Turkey Flat 2001 Shiraz (Barossa Valley) $36. Juicy and pleasurable on the palate—a great mix of berries and plums, caramel, and smooth tannins. The nose was a little closed when the wine was reviewed; aeration is probably in order if it's drunk now. **90** *—D.T. (2/1/2004)*

TWELVE STAVES

Twelve Staves 2000 Grenache (McLaren Vale) $18. **86** *—J.C. (9/1/2002)*

TWIN BEAKS

Twin Beaks 2002 Chardonnay (South Eastern Australia) $10. David Lynch fans aren't the only folks who will appreciate this Chard—those who like oak and all of its related flavors should queue up. It's golden in color, smells of nut and white pepper, and has flavors of cream, nuts, and peach fuzz. Smooth in the mouth and a little oily on the finish. A good wine, particularly for the price. **85 Best Buy** *—D.T. (12/31/2004)*

TWO HANDS

Two Hands 2002 Brave Faces Red Blend (Barossa Valley) $27. **86** *—D.T. (12/31/2003)*

Two Hands 2003 The Wolf Riesling (Clare Valley) $19. Stone fruit (particularly an alluring apricot-nectarine combination) dominates this viscous, fairly full Riesling, which has nice acidity and a finish that tastes like lemon drops. Breathe deeply enough and you're sure to find almonds. **90 Editors' Choice** *—D.T. (2/1/2004)*

Two Hands 2003 Lily's Garden Shiraz (McLaren Vale) $60. The nose is fairly closed now, showing just herb and ink aromas, but gives the impression that it's a blackberry volcano about to erupt. With such menace and potential on the nose, the fact that the palate flavors don't knock me on the floor is almost a disappointment. This is still an excellent, flavorful wine, with reined-in plum, blackberry, raspberry, and red pencil eraser notes. **90** *—D.T. (3/1/2005)*

TYRRELL'S

Tyrrell's 2002 Old Winery Cabernet Sauvignon-Merlot (New South Wales) $10. **88 Best Buy** *—D.T. (12/31/2003)*

Tyrrell's 2000 Old Winery Cabernet Sauvignon-Merlot (South Australia) $11. **84** *—D.T. (6/1/2003)*

Tyrrell's 1999 Moon Mountain Chardonnay (Hunter Valley) $21. **88** *—J.C. (7/1/2002)*

Tyrrell's 2003 Old Winery Chardonnay (Hunter Valley & McLaren Vale) $11. Round and mouthcoating, the Old Winery Chard pleases again this year. Offers up pretty floral aromas, followed by yellow peach and muted olive-oil flavors. Smolders on the end with a little hickory, or smoked meat. **86 Best Buy** *—D.T. (12/31/2004)*

Tyrrell's 2001 Old Winery-Hunter Valley/McLaren Vale Chardonnay (Hunter Valley) $14. **87** *—J.C. (7/1/2002)*

Tyrrell's 2000 Reserve Chardonnay (Hunter Valley) $37. **88** *—M.M. (6/1/2001)*

Tyrrell's 2000 Vat 47 Chardonnay (Hunter Valley) $50. **89** *(8/1/2003)*

Tyrrell's 2003 Lost Block Pinot Noir (South Eastern Australia) $14. Plots the course of many more expensive European renditions: Stable meets plum and cherry on the nose, with the same red fruit taking a tart, sour-cherry turn on the palate. That tartness is not a bad thing. Soft in the mouth, with lemony oak on the finish. **85** *—D.T. (11/15/2005)*

Tyrrell's 2000 Vat 6 Pinot Noir (Hunter Valley) $40. As good as this wine usually is, this bottling was a disappointment. It is already browning in color, and its fruit already starting to fade (though it's easy to see how the cherry and earth flavors were pretty and vibrant once upon a time). 2000 is the current vintage, though most other Oz Pinots are a year or two newer. **85** *—D.T. (10/1/2005)*

Tyrrell's 2003 Lost Block Semillon (Hunter Valley) $18. Light on both flavors and aromas, this is just the style of wine you'll want as an apéritif or with seafood. Light citrus aromas are followed up by firm white stone fruit flavors and a crisp, lean mouthfeel. Plumps up a bit on the finish. **86** *—D.T. (9/1/2004)*

Tyrrell's 2004 Moore's Creek Semillon-Sauvignon Blanc (South Eastern Australia) $9. Melon, citrus, and mineral fragrances are feminine and pretty; the palate, on the other hand, is a zesty, wake-me-up of a white. It's dry in the mouth, with citrus and mineral flavors. A lively, economical choice for brunch, lunch, or outdoor sipping. 1,500 cases produced. **86 Best Buy** *—D.T. (3/1/2005)*

Tyrrell's 2002 Moore's Creek Semillon-Sauvignon Blanc (Hunter Valley) $9. **85** *—D.T. (11/15/2003)*

Tyrrell's 2002 The Long Flat Semillon-Sauvignon Blanc (South Eastern Australia) $7. An 80-20 Semillon-Sauvignon blend, the wine's yellow fruit flavors are a little dilute, but its aromas of sweet yellow and citrus fruit are quite pleasant. Finishes with a mealy banana-like texture. **84 Best Buy** *—D.T. (5/1/2004)*

Tyrrell's 2001 Moore's Creek Shiraz (South Eastern Australia) $9. **86 Best Buy** *—K.F. (3/1/2003)*

Tyrrell's 2001 Reserve Shiraz (McLaren Vale) $12. Aromas are of black fruit and bread flour. On the palate, the alcohol is a little noticeable, but the plum and oak flavors are harmonious and tasty. A nice value. **87 Best Buy** *—D.T. (11/15/2004)*

Tyrrell's 2002 Rufus Stone Shiraz (McLaren Vale) $30. This Shiraz is medium-bodied and full of black cherry aromas and flavors. Dry, tealike tannins complete the picture. An enjoyable pizza or pasta accompaniment, though its price may prohibit casual, everyday consumption. **87** *—D.T. (3/1/2005)*

Tyrrell's 1998 Vat 9 Shiraz (Hunter Valley) $50. **88** *(12/31/2003)*

UBET

UBET 2001 Shiraz (South Eastern Australia) $10. **86** *—M.S. (3/1/2003)*

VASSE FELIX

Vasse Felix 2001 Cabernet Sauvignon (Margaret River) $30. **90** *—D.T. (10/1/2003)*

Vasse Felix 2000 Cabernet Sauvignon (Margaret River) $30. **92** *—S.H. (1/1/2002)*

Vasse Felix 1999 Cabernet Sauvignon (Western Australia) $30. **84** *—D.T. (9/1/2001)*

Vasse Felix 2001 Cabernet Sauvignon-Merlot (Margaret River) $20. **88** *—D.T. (10/1/2003)*

Vasse Felix 2003 Adams Road Cabernet Sauvignon-Merlot (Margaret River) $15. Tastes and smells like sweet berry and plum fruit, with oak flavors rearing up toward the finish. A good, pedestrian red wine. **84** *—D.T. (12/31/2005)*

Vasse Felix 2001 Chardonnay (Margaret River) $24. **88** *—D.T. (10/1/2003)*

Vasse Felix 2004 Adams Road Chardonnay (Margaret River) $15. The nose offers manageable amounts of toast and vanilla, which segue into tangy peach and citrus flavors on the palate. Dry in the mouth, and not too long on the finish, this is a simple, easy-to-like Chard. 900 cases imported. **86** *—D.T. (10/1/2005)*

Vasse Felix 2001 Heytesbury Chardonnay (Western Australia) $30. Full bodied and creamy on the palate, this iconic Margaret River Chard has sturdy, ripe peach and nectarine fruit, and nut and toast accents. Petrol and nut aromas, and a pear-apple finish, frame the wine nicely. **88** *(7/2/2004)*

Vasse Felix 2000 Heytesbury Chardonnay (Western Australia) $30. **87** *—J.C. (7/1/2002)*

Vasse Felix 1999 Heytesbury Red Blend (Western Australia) $40. **93 Editors' Choice** *—S.H. (12/15/2002)*

Vasse Felix 2001 Shiraz (Margaret River) $30. **91** *—S.H. (10/1/2003)*

Vasse Felix 1999 Shiraz (Margaret River) $30. **89** *(11/1/2001)*

Vasse Felix 2002 Adam's Road Shiraz (Margaret River) $15. A new lower-priced offering from Vasse Felix, and bargain as far as Margaret River offerings go. Don't pass judgment on this wine until it's been in the glass a few minutes—this one changes considerably with air. With patience, you'll see blackberry and black plum aromas, and ripbe blackberries (and a hint of blueberry) on the palate. Tannins are smooth, and run through the finish, where oak and eucalyptus wrap it up. **89 Editors' Choice** *—D.T. (5/1/2004)*

VIRGIN HILLS

Virgin Hills 1998 Red Blend (Victoria) $30. **86** *—J.C. (9/1/2002)*

VOYAGER ESTATE

Voyager Estate 1999 Shiraz (Margaret River) $19. **85** *(10/1/2001)*

WAKEFIELD ESTATE

Wakefield Estate 2001 Cabernet Sauvignon (Clare Valley) $15. A very good, straightforward, drink-now Cab, with wide-reaching toffee and caramel aromas. It's just right size—medium-boned, with a pleasing, easy texture. Plum and maybe even some blueberry on the palate are oaked judiciously, and both the wood and the juicy fruit persist through the finish. **87** *—D.T. (5/1/2004)*

Wakefield Estate 2002 Promised Land Cabernet Sauvignon-Merlot (South Australia) $13. **87** *—D.T. (11/15/2003)*

Wakefield Estate 2003 Promised Land Chardonnay (South Australia) $13. Sunny, lively, and unique in that it's floral on both the nose and the palate, where the fruit is bright and tropical. A good white wine, though the floral bits may throw you off from guessing that it is Chardonnay. **85** *(7/2/2004)*

Wakefield Estate 2000 St. Andrews Chardonnay (Clare Valley) $17. A thick, gooey wine, a triumph for fans of the butter-toast-candied fruit style. Aromas are of butterscotch, cocoa, and toasted coconut. Peach is at the core, but it's buried deep. **84** *(7/2/2004)*

Wakefield Estate 1999 St. Andrews Shiraz (Clare Valley) $60. Tastes like what we Americans expect a premium Australian Shiraz to taste like (and there's nothing wrong with that): Three parts ripe plum fruit, one part each oak and caramel. Fruit is sweet on the nose, and coupled with smoky grilled meats. It was "created to take on Grange," explained winemaker Adam Eggins. The wine is on its way, but still has a little farther to go. **90** *—D.T. (2/1/2004)*

WALLABY CREEK

Wallaby Creek 2000 Chardonnay (South Eastern Australia) $7. **82** *—D.T. (1/1/2002)*

Wallaby Creek 2000 Shiraz (South Eastern Australia) $7. **82** *—M.S. (1/28/2003)*

WANDIN VALLEY

Wandin Valley 2002 Chardonnay (Hunter Valley) $13. Apple pastry in a glass, with bready, baked-apple aromas, and clove and mealy apple flavors. Soft and middleweight on the palate, it finishes a little dilute. 500 cases produced. **85** *(7/2/2004)*

Wandin Valley 2002 Verdelho (Hunter Valley) $13. Pear and resin aromas are light. This wine's palate entry is really neat: you slide effortlessly into green-apple flavors and a nice, viscous texture, which clings through the dusty finish. Nice, unusual, and hey, what a bargain. **87** *—D.T. (11/15/2004)*

WARBURN

Warburn 2000 Show Reserve Durif (Riverina) $15. **88** *—D.T. (6/1/2003)*

WARRABILLA

Warrabilla 2000 Petite Sirah (Rutherglen) $27. **88** *—J.C. (9/1/2002)*

Warrabilla 2000 Shiraz (Rutherglen) $27. **87** *—J.C. (9/1/2002)*

WARRENMANG

Warrenmang 1999 Estate Shiraz (Victoria) $45. Offers powerful brown sugar aromas that are overcome by black pepper with air; black pepper accents plum and black cherry fruit flavors as well. Has some hold on the palate. It's not going to get any better than it is now. **89** *—D.T. (8/1/2005)*

WATER WHEEL

Water Wheel 2000 Chardonnay (Bendigo) $12. **84** *—D.T. (6/1/2003)*

WHITSEND ESTATE

Whitsend Estate 2002 Cabernet Sauvignon (Yarra Valley) $20. A well-made wine, one with a dryish mouthfeel and a Cab-typical flavor profile. Aromas are of dusty black fruit, pencil eraser, and orange, of all things. Black plums and earth flavors; a good, sturdy red overall. **87** *—D.T. (12/31/2004)*

WILLOW BRIDGE

Willow Bridge 2001 Winemaker's Reserve Cabernet Sauvignon-Merlot (Western Australia) $13. Yes, the wine is wooly, wild and woody—it's dry in the mouth, with woody tannins and earthy, bark flavors framing its focused plum fruit. What's nice about it, though, is that the wood is present more in texture than in flavor. Aromas continue with the rustic theme: dried spice, fireplace, acorn. **87** *—D.T. (9/1/2004)*

WILLOW CREEK

Willow Creek 1999 Tulum Reserve Chardonnay (Mornington Peninsula) $26. **86** *—S.H. (9/1/2001)*

Willow Creek 2000 Unoaked Chardonnay (Mornington Peninsula) $18. **85** *—S.H. (9/1/2001)*

WILLOWGLEN

Willowglen 2001 Shiraz (South Eastern Australia) $6. **84 Best Buy** *—D.T. (12/31/2003)*

WILSON VINEYARD

Wilson Vineyard (AUS) 2000 Gallery Series Cabernet Sauvignon (Clare Valley) $22. Just the right weight, with the feel (and the flavor) of clay running throughout. The nose offers earth, bark, and curry spice aromas. The palate has red plum fruit that segues into leather and earth on the finish. Quite enjoyable. **89** *—D.T. (5/1/2004)*

AUSTRALIA

WINDSHAKER RIDGE

Windshaker Ridge 2003 Carnelian (Western Australia) $13. An interesting, simple but pleasing wine. Aromas are of blackberry and violet, and the palate offers up a mixed berry basket full of flavor. Has papery-smooth tannins, and softens with air. A good quaff. 25,000 cases produced. **86** —*D.T. (8/1/2005)*

Windshaker Ridge 2003 Shiraz (Western Australia) $13. Tastes cool and crisp, just as it smells: think dried cherry fruit, with a minty streak. Feels thin at first, but give it some time in the glass to come around. 25,000 cases produced. **86** —*D.T. (12/1/2005)*

WINDY PEAK

Windy Peak 2002 Chardonnay (Victoria) $13. Aromas are deep and unusual—like a mix of petrol, olive oil, and smoke. It's a medium-bodied, sunny wine, with melon and pear flavors that pick up some toast toward the finish. **86** *(7/2/2004)*

Windy Peak 2000 Shiraz (Victoria) $13. 81 *(10/1/2001)*

WIRRA WIRRA

Wirra Wirra 2003 Scrubby Rise Chardonnay (McLaren Vale) $11. Medium-bodied, with light aromas and flavors of vanilla, cream, and stone fruit. Somewhat flabby; good, but not much different from many other Chardonnays at its price point. **84** —*D.T. (3/1/2005)*

Wirra Wirra 2004 Sexton's Acre Unwooded Chardonnay (McLaren Vale) $NA. Features talc, perfume, and citrus aromas and flavors. Simple and enjoyable. **84** —*D.T. (3/1/2005)*

Wirra Wirra 2002 Church Block Red Blend (McLaren Vale) $17. Aromatic, with smoke, earth, and barbecue on the nose. Dry tannins in the mouth; black plum and oak are the principal flavors here. Would pair well with a broad range of foods, from pizzas to pastas and burgers. A blend of Cabernet Sauvignon, Shiraz, and Merlot. 4,000 cases imported. **88** —*D.T. (3/1/2005)*

Wirra Wirra 2000 Scrubby Rise Red Blend (Fleurieu Peninsula) $10. 87 Best Buy —*J.C. (9/1/2002)*

Wirra Wirra 2001 Hand Picked Riesling (Fleurieu Peninsula) $13. 86 —*M.M. (2/1/2002)*

Wirra Wirra 2002 Shiraz (McLaren Vale) $27. A nice combination of earth, pencil eraser, and dried spice on the nose ushers in raspberry and black cherry flavors. It's a mid-sized Shiraz, accessible even now, with tannins that grip the midpalate and don't let up through the finish. 5,000 cases produced. **89** —*D.T. (3/1/2005)*

Wirra Wirra 1999 Shiraz (McLaren Vale) $28. 86 —*J.C. (9/1/2002)*

Wirra Wirra 2002 RSW Shiraz (McLaren Vale) $54. The nose is still fairly closed but shows some plum and bacon aromas. The palate is likewise not expressing much flavor, but the wine's formidable size, chewy tannins, and medium-long finish promise good things to come down the road. Drink 2007+. **91 Cellar Selection** —*D.T. (3/1/2005)*

Wirra Wirra 1998 RSW Shiraz (McLaren Vale) $67. 92 —*D.T. (12/31/2003)*

Wirra Wirra 2002 Scrubby Rise Shiraz (South Australia) $10. Blackberry and plum fruit is taut, accented by some exotic spice, and feels more dense on the front palate than on the toasty-oak finish. Still, it's a pleasing, easy-to-drink wine that's a safe bet for parties—particularly barbecues, as this seems just the ticket for a burger, or grilled meat. **86** —*D.T. (9/1/2004)*

Wirra Wirra 2000 Scrubby Rise White Blend (McLaren Vale) $13. 82 —*D.T. (1/1/2002)*

WISE

Wise 1999 Aquercus Unwooded Chardonnay (Margaret River) $10. 85 *(10/1/2000)*

Wise 2003 Single Vineyard Chardonnay (Western Australia) $25. Very toasty on the nose—with air, some fresh produce shows through. Wood dominates the palate, too, obscuring peach fruit underneath. **84** —*D.T. (12/1/2005)*

Wise 2001 Unwooded Chardonnay (Western Australia) $13. 83 —*J.C. (7/1/2002)*

Wise 2002 Eagle Bay Shiraz (Margaret River) $28. Tight, cool, and feminine, this Shiraz shows some of its region's best hallmarks: eucalyptus, black pepper, and solid plum and blackberry fruit. Smooth and minerally on the palate, with a black-peppery finish. **88** —*D.T. (12/1/2005)*

WIT'S END

Wit's End 2002 Shiraz (McLaren Vale) $NA. 88 —*D.T. (5/1/2005)*

WOLF BLASS

Wolf Blass 2002 Gold Label Cabernet Sauvignon (Coonawarra) $24. Even tasted blind, this excellent Cab's smooth, velvety-clay feel says "Coonawarra." It's a restrained, balanced wine with pencil eraser and red plum fruit flavors, and cherry brightening the finish; even still, it's the texture you'll remember. **90** —*D.T. (12/31/2004)*

Wolf Blass 2002 Grey Label Cabernet Sauvignon (Langhorne Creek) $32. Tasty, sexy, well built, and smooth. Not at all fat or flabby, the wine smells like mint and sweet fruit, but is, perhaps, a little nutty. Flavors are of beef, plum, and ripe raspberry, with little chips of coconut and toffee candy bar. **90** —*D.T. (11/15/2004)*

Wolf Blass 1998 Platinum Label Cabernet Sauvignon (Barossa Valley) $34. 90 —*D.T. (12/31/2003)*

Wolf Blass 2000 Presidents Selection Cabernet Sauvignon (South Australia) $20. 87 —*D.T. (6/1/2003)*

Wolf Blass 2001 Yellow Label Cabernet Sauvignon (South Australia) $14. 87 *—D.T. (12/31/2003)*

Wolf Blass 1999 Yellow Label Cabernet Sauvignon (South Australia) $12. 86 *(6/1/2001)*

Wolf Blass 2000 Black Label Cabernet Sauvignon-Shiraz (Barossa-Langhorne Creek) $60. Wolf Blass's top-level blended wine, this is 51% Cabernet and 49% Shiraz with straight-shooting cassis and black plum fruit on the palate. Finishes with flair-with chocolate, liqueur, and coffee, like a savory after-dinner drink. **89** *—D.T. (5/1/2004)*

Wolf Blass 1999 Chardonnay (South Australia) $12. 86 *—L.W. (3/1/2000)*

Wolf Blass 2004 Gold Label Chardonnay (Adelaide Hills) $21. A buttoned up, classy wine offering peach and fresh corn aromas and flavors. Medium-weight, the palate also has floral hints. 3,000 cases produced. **88** *—D.T. (8/1/2005)*

Wolf Blass 2003 Presidents Selection Chardonnay (South Australia) $14. Nice on the nose, with fresh herb, white plum flesh, and white pepper aromas. It's less striking on the palate, where a heavier feel and stony, woody flavors are at the fore, with yellow fruit in the background. **84** *(7/2/2004)*

Wolf Blass 2001 Presidents Selection Chardonnay (South Australia) $15. 84 *—D.T. (6/1/2003)*

Wolf Blass 2003 Yellow Label Chardonnay (South Australia) $12. A good, straightforward wine, with mealy aromas and flavors of apple and pear. Finishes somewhat lackluster, wtih some oak and apple skin. **84** *—D.T. (11/15/2004)*

Wolf Blass 2003 Yellow Label Merlot (South Australia) $12. Oak is this Merlot's star—on the palate it outshines the cherry and plum fruit. Aromas are of tea and mocha. Good, but pretty basic. **84** *—D.T. (10/1/2005)*

Wolf Blass 2001 Gold Label Riesling (Eden Valley) $12. 89 *—M.M. (2/1/2002)*

Wolf Blass 1999 Gold Label Riesling (South Australia) $12. 86 *—M.S. (10/1/2000)*

Wolf Blass 2000 Shiraz (South Australia) $12. 85 *—M.S. (3/1/2003)*

Wolf Blass 2002 Gold Label Shiraz-Viognier Shiraz (Barossa Valley) $NA. Only 6% Viognier, and only 1,000 cases produced, this wine won numerous trophies at Australian wine shows at the end of last year. An excellent wine, one in which black pepper flavors and aromas are so prevalent that drinking it with anything other than steak au poivre seems criminal. Smooth on palate entry; plum fruit and eucalyptus prevail through the finish. **90 Editors' Choice** *—D.T. (5/1/2004)*

Wolf Blass 1999 Platinum Label Shiraz (Barossa Valley) $72. Starts off with scents of caramel popcorn and oak; it feels mouthfilling, but its size is more about sweet fruit than it is about structure or tannins. Black plum fruit on the palate is just a little too sweet and syrupy for this reviewer's taste; others may think this rating too conservative. Past vintages have fared better. **87** *—D.T. (5/1/2004)*

Wolf Blass 2000 Presidents Selection Shiraz (South Australia) $20. 87 *—M.S. (3/1/2003)*

Wolf Blass 2002 Yellow Label Shiraz (South Australia) $12. Oak lends nutty, caroby aromas and big, woodsy tannins to this well-priced red; fleshy red plum and berry fruit makes up the balance. Has pretty good length on the finish, too. Well made, and, with 17,000 cases produced, should be relatively easy to find. **87 Best Buy** *—D.T. (5/1/2005)*

Wolf Blass 2001 Red Label Shiraz-Cabernet (South Australia) $12. 87 *—D.T. (12/31/2003)*

Wolf Blass 1999 Red Label Shiraz-Cabernet (South Australia) $12. 87 *—D.T. (9/1/2001)*

Wolf Blass NV Traditional Method Brut (South Australia) $11. 86 Best Buy *—D.T. (12/31/2003)*

WOMBAT GULLY

Wombat Gully 2001 Shiraz (South Eastern Australia) $10. 84 *—M.S. (1/28/2003)*

WOOD PARK

Wood Park 1998 Cabernet Sauvignon-Shiraz (King Valley) $22. 84 *—D.T. (9/1/2001)*

WOOP WOOP

Woop Woop 2004 Chardonnay (South Eastern Australia) $11. This dusty, pineapple-and-peach wine has a common flavor profile, but its round mouthfeel, lively acids, and crisp finish give it a leg up on other value-priced offerings. (Though its name may sound like an indigenous, endangered Oz animal, "Woop Woop" is actually another term for "way the hell out in the middle of nowhere.") **87 Best Buy** *—D.T. (12/31/2004)*

WYNDHAM ESTATE

Wyndham Estate 2001 Bin 444 Cabernet Sauvignon (South Eastern Australia) $10. 85 *—D.T. (10/1/2003)*

Wyndham Estate 1998 Bin 444 Cabernet Sauvignon (South Eastern Australia) $12. 84 *(9/1/2001)*

Wyndham Estate 2002 Bin 888 Cabernet Sauvignon-Merlot (South Eastern Australia) $10. Dusty black cherry aromas preface a similar profile on the palate: Dark plums, black cherry, wheat bread, and an earthy/leafy hint. It's a nice, medium-full weight, not so rich or mouthfilling that drinking it with dinner is out of the question. Finishes smooth. **87 Best Buy** *—D.T. (11/15/2004)*

Wyndham Estate 1999 Bin 888 Cabernet Sauvignon-Merlot (South Eastern Australia) $10. 86 Best Buy *—J.C. (6/1/2002)*

Wyndham Estate 2004 Bin 222 Chardonnay (South Eastern Australia) $9. Has lively acidity at the center and dominant citrus-pith flavors. Smells and tastes like it's been through a woodchipper, and finishes on a sweet note. **83** *—D.T. (12/1/2005)*

Wyndham Estate 2002 Bin 222 Chardonnay (South Eastern Australia) $9. 83 *—D.T. (6/1/2003)*

Wyndham Estate 2001 Show Reserve Chardonnay (South Eastern Australia) $19. Smells of sweet gumdrops, smoke and earth. In the mouth, it's similarly smoldering, with toast rounding out peach and pear flavors. A pretty straightforward, good wine. **85** *(7/2/2004)*

Wyndham Estate 2001 Bin 999 Merlot (South Eastern Australia) $10. 85 *—D.T. (6/1/2003)*

Wyndham Estate 2004 Bin 333 Pinot Noir (South Eastern Australia) $10. Has aromas of cherries and caraway seeds, which are followed up by straightforward cherry fruit flavors. Soft in the mouth; not much verve here. **83** *—D.T. (12/1/2005)*

Wyndham Estate 2004 Bin 777 Semillon-Sauvignon Blanc (South Eastern Australia) $9. A very dry wine that doesn't have much flavor to offset its minerally feel. Piquant green-herb aromas preface some dilute lemony flavors. 220,000 cases produced. Imported by Pernod Ricard. **82** *—D.T. (12/1/2005)*

Wyndham Estate 2002 Bin 777 Semillon (South Eastern Australia) $9. 84 *—D.T. (12/31/2003)*

Wyndham Estate 2001 Bin 555 Shiraz (South Eastern Australia) $10. 84 *—D.T. (10/1/2003)*

Wyndham Estate 1998 Bin 555 Shiraz (South Eastern Australia) $12. 88 *—M.M. (6/1/2001)*

WYNNS COONAWARRA ESTATE

Wynns Coonawarra Estate 2000 Cabernet Blend (Coonawarra) $13. 85 *—D.T. (12/31/2003)*

Wynns Coonawarra Estate 1998 Cabernet Blend (Coonawarra) $13. 87 *(11/1/2001)*

Wynns Coonawarra Estate 2001 Cabernet Sauvignon (Coonawarra) $11. Has cool, deep cherry on the nose, bolstered by olive and chalk dust. This is a dry, firm Cab with taut plum fruit at the center, plus some coconut/toffee accents. Reliably very good, and a very good value. **87 Best Buy** *—D.T. (11/15/2004)*

Wynns Coonawarra Estate 1999 Cabernet Sauvignon (Coonawarra) $14. 88 *—J.M. (12/15/2002)*

Wynns Coonawarra Estate 1998 Cabernet Sauvignon (Coonawarra) $15. 91 Best Buy *(11/1/2001)*

Wynns Coonawarra Estate 1991 Cabernet Sauvignon (Coonawarra) $NA. 91 *(11/1/2001)*

Wynns Coonawarra Estate 1990 Cabernet Sauvignon (Coonawarra) $NA. Acids are lively, and tannins hold on through the finish. Nose still isn't revealing its all, but the palate is full of plums and cherries, which wear a pleasing, brambly overlay. **90** *—D.T. (2/1/2005)*

Wynns Coonawarra Estate 1986 Cabernet Sauvignon (Coonawarra) $NA. Still kicking almost 20 years later, with good grip and fine tannins on the palate. Flavors are of black plum and earth; could still go another 5–10 years. **91** *—D.T. (2/1/2005)*

Wynns Coonawarra Estate 1962 Cabernet Sauvignon (Coonawarra) $NA. With air, shows cassis, meaty aromas. Smooth and medium-full on palate, with chewy tannins on the finish. **89** *—D.T. (2/1/2005)*

Wynns Coonawarra Estate 1990 John Riddoch Cabernet Sauvignon (Coonawarra) $NA. 92 *(11/1/2001)*

Wynns Coonawarra Estate 1998 John Riddoch, Limited Release Cabernet Sauvignon (Coonawarra) $35. 90 *—J.M. (12/15/2002)*

Wynns Coonawarra Estate 2002 Chardonnay (Coonawarra) $13. 88 *—D.T. (8/1/2003)*

Wynns Coonawarra Estate 2000 Chardonnay (Coonawarra) $13. 88 *(11/1/2001)*

Wynns Coonawarra Estate 2002 Red Blend (Coonawarra) $11. There's a lot to like about this wine: It's a medium, food-friendly size; its plum base has compelling accents of bramble and herb; it isn't at all sweet and hey, look at the price. The wine will probably taste even better to you once you see what else $11 buys you. Nicely done. **87 Best Buy** *—D.T. (10/1/2005)*

Wynns Coonawarra Estate 2002 Riesling (Coonawarra) $12. 90 Best Buy *—D.T. (11/15/2003)*

Wynns Coonawarra Estate 2001 Shiraz (Coonawarra) $14. 86 *—D.T. (12/31/2003)*

Wynns Coonawarra Estate 1999 Shiraz (Coonawarra) $15. 85 *(10/1/2001)*

Wynns Coonawarra Estate 1997 Michael Shiraz (Coonawarra) $49. 91 Cellar Selection *(11/1/2001)*

XANADU

Xanadu 1998 Lagan Estate Reserve Cabernet Sauvignon (Margaret River) $32. 89 *(10/1/2003)*

Xanadu 2000 Chardonnay (Margaret River) $15. 90 Best Buy *—J.C. (7/1/2002)*

Xanadu 2000 Merlot (Margaret River) $22. 88 *—C.S. (6/1/2002)*

Xanadu 2001 Shiraz (Frankland River) $18. 85 *(10/1/2003)*

Xanadu 2002 Shiraz-Cabernet (Frankland River) $10. **86 Best Buy** *(10/1/2003)*

YACCA PADDOCK

Yacca Paddock 2003 Shiraz-Tannat (Adelaide Hills) $65. This is an excellent red, and further evidence of the Hills' success with unusual grape varieties. Tannat (20%) gives this Shiraz more grip on the midpalate than most other regional Shirazes have. Good acids, plum and blackberry fruit, and black pepper nuances make this classy wine a winner, however difficult it might be to rationalize paying this much for such an odd blend. 250 cases produced. **90** *—D. T. (8/1/2005)*

YALUMBA

Yalumba 1999 Cabernet Sauvignon (Barossa Valley) $17. **87** *—J.C. (6/1/2002)*

Yalumba 2000 The Menzies Cabernet Sauvignon (Coonawarra) $45. Big, dark, and cool is the name of the game here. The fine fruit, all the way through, is blackberry and boysenberry, with a minerally-earthy overlay. This excellent Cab has wooly, textured tannins that will last at least through the end of the decade. **90** *—D. T. (5/1/2005)*

Yalumba 1997 The Menzies Cabernet Sauvignon (Coonawarra) $30. **83** *—D. T. (9/1/2001)*

Yalumba 2001 Y Series Cabernet Sauvignon (South Australia) $10. **84** *—D. T. (6/1/2003)*

Yalumba 2000 The Signature Cabernet Sauvignon-Shiraz (Barossa Valley) $45. The nose is interesting—dusty but also piquant, similar to mustard seed. This red's flavors are of dusty stone fruit, accompanied by pleasing, chewy tannins. It's not an overly ripe, sweet wine, which is why it would be a welcome presence at the dinner table. **87** *—D. T. (5/1/2005)*

Yalumba 1997 The Signature Cabernet Sauvignon-Shiraz (Barossa Valley) $44. **88** *—D. T. (12/15/2002)*

Yalumba 2002 Chardonnay (Barossa Valley) $15. Nectarine and grapefruit aromas are bright and focused; yellow stone fruit is the palate focus. Medium in body, but leans up by the close, with citrus pith and peach skin flavors. A good wine. **85** *(7/2/2004)*

Yalumba 2002 Heggies Vineyard Chardonnay (Eden Valley) $20. Round and more rustic than most Eden Valley Chards, it opens with mallowy, woody aromas that segue into vanilla, toast, and light yellow fruit on the palate. Finishes with a woody, wooly feel. **85** *(7/2/2004)*

Yalumba 2003 Wild Ferment Chardonnay (Eden Valley) $17. Whether due to the wild ferment, this is one of the more singular-tasting Chards we sampled. Aromas are of almond, banana cream pie, and green grapes. Green fruit—more green grapes, but also Granny Smith apples—reappear on the palate, and are refreshing. That's not to say that vanilla and oak aren't present—they are, but there's enough else going on. An interesting, very good wine. **87** *(7/2/2004)*

Yalumba 2003 Y series-Unwooded Chardonnay (Eden Valley) $9. A good wine at a good price: This unwooded Chard has fragrant floral, peach, pear, and pineapple aromas. Fruit-cocktail flavors on the palate are bold and assertive. A straightforward, fruity wine, and one that everyone in the room will enjoy. **86 Best Buy** *(7/2/2004)*

Yalumba 2001 Bush Vine Grenache (Barossa Valley) $15. **84** *(5/1/2003)*

Yalumba 2001 Tricentenary Grenache (Barossa Valley) $15. **87** *—D. T. (12/31/2003)*

Yalumba 2003 Tricentenary Vines Grenache (Barossa Valley) $32. Offers rich, pretty aromas of molasses, tea, mixed cherries and anise. On the palate, it has a Cotes-du-Rhônish style and weight, with plum, herb and pepper flavors. A very good wine in the grand scheme of things but perhaps a disappointment for this particular bottling, considering what these old vines are usually capable of. Tasted twice. **87** *—D. T. (3/1/2005)*

Yalumba 2000 Y Series Merlot (South Australia) $10. **82** *—S.H. (6/1/2002)*

Yalumba NV Antique Tawny Port (Barossa Valley) $17. **89** *(5/1/2003)*

Yalumba 2000 Mawsons Red Blend (Limestone Coast) $20. The nose is foresty and reminded me a little of Carmenère. In the mouth, there's mixed plum fruit, but seeped tea and tangy wood flavors are in the driver's seat. Finishes with tea and earth and smooth, chalky tannins; a blend of Cabernet, Shiraz, and Merlot. **87** *—D. T. (5/1/2004)*

Yalumba 2002 Rhône Red Blend (Barossa Valley) $30. Sixty percent Mourvèdre, with Grenache and Shiraz getting 30% and 10%, respectively. The texture's great—a little rough around the edges, but that's part of its charm. Juicy mixed plums on the palate get a strong kick of black pepper, which you'll also pick up on the nose. I see plenty of food-pairing potential here (lamb or rabbit, for starters), though winemaker Jane Ferrari says that cheese is the way to go. **91 Editors' Choice** *—D. T. (2/1/2004)*

Yalumba 2002 Mesh Riesling (Eden Valley) $25. **89** *(8/1/2003)*

Yalumba 2002 Y Series Riesling (South Australia) $10. **85** *(5/1/2003)*

Yalumba 2001 Shiraz (Barossa Valley) $17. From 20-year-old vines, and containing 5% Viognier, this is a simple, entry-level Shiraz with fresh berry-cherry-plum flavors. **85** *—D. T. (2/1/2004)*

Yalumba 1999 Shiraz (Barossa Valley) $16. **87** *(10/1/2001)*

Yalumba 2000 The Octavius Shiraz (Barossa Valley) $85. The nose brings licorice in abundance, and the palate, a first-class package of blackberries and chocolate, delivered in a smoky-oak envelope. Drink through 2015. **91** *—D. T. (8/1/2005)*

Yalumba 1995 The Octavius Shiraz (Barossa Valley) $80. **88** *(4/1/2000)*

Yalumba 2001 Y Series Shiraz (South Australia) $10. **82** *—D. T. (1/28/2003)*

Yalumba 2001 Shiraz-Viognier (Barossa Valley) $30. It's always interesting to see why some wineries will acknowledge small percentages of Viognier on the label and some won't—in this case, maybe it's because the Viognier clocks in at a whopping 9% of the wine's volume. In any case, it's just excellent, with sweet chalk or trading-gum powder on the nose, and dry tannins in the mouth. Plum fruit is beautiful, and framed by dry earth. Quite a classy wine. **90** *—D.T. (2/1/2004)*

Yalumba 2003 Viognier (Eden Valley) $17. Though aged in mature French barriques, this wine's toasty, leesy are in line with Yalumba's liberal use of oak. On the palate, it's lively and enjoyable, wtih light floral and honey notes atop white stone fruit. Medium-bodied; finishes with some fresh herb and a slick hard-candy feel. **87** *—D.T. (12/31/2004)*

Yalumba 2000 Viognier (Eden Valley) $17. 88 *—R.V. (11/15/2001)*

Yalumba 2002 Heggies Vineyard Viognier (Eden Valley) $20. Floral on the nose, with jasmine, clover, and the whole nine yards. On the palate the floral sweetness is reprised, and couched in waxy yellow fruit and olive oil flavors. A very good wine, and one that brings the out-of-doors inside. **87** *—D.T. (5/1/2004)*

Yalumba 2003 The Virgilius Viognier (Eden Valley) $40. Opens with aromas of pastry flour, olive oil, and honey. This is one beautifully textured wine; yellow fruit, floral and olive oil flavors ride the wave of unctuousness, rather than outshine it. Finishes long. **92** *—D.T. (3/1/2005)*

Yalumba 2001 The Virgilius Viognier (Barossa Valley) $36. 90 *(5/1/2003)*

Yalumba 2002 Y Series Viognier (South Australia) $10. 84 *—D.T. (12/31/2003)*

Yalumba 2000 Y Series Viognier (South Australia) $10. 84 *—S.H. (9/1/2002)*

YANGARRA ESTATE VINEYARD

Yangarra Estate Vineyard 2002 Old Vine Grenache (McLaren Vale) $20. The old-vine designation will make more sense when you see how black and extracted the wine appears in the glass. Aromas are abyss-deep, with dust and black soil over dark fruit. The palate holds nothing but the purest blackberry, dressed up with some toast. Finishes with taut cherry. A solid, masculine wine. **89 Editors' Choice** *—D.T. (9/1/2004)*

Yangarra Estate Vineyard 2003 GSM Rhône Red Blend (McLaren Vale) $20. An abyss of black pepper on the nose, with some whiffs of white cotton. Imagine strapping an eight-cylinder engine to a basket full of berries and black peppercorns and watching it go: That's what this wine tastes like. It's full-throttle and fruit-ripe, with lifted fruit, spice and black pepper on the finish. **92** *—D.T. (3/1/2005)*

Yangarra Estate Vineyard 2002 Shiraz (McLaren Vale) $20. Yangarra is becoming synonymous with excellent wines at fair prices. Nose is a little hot at first, but later reveals pastry flour and black pepper aromas. Ripe red plums and vanilla accents unfold in the mouth. Not a huge, rich wine, but certainly a classy one. **90 Editors' Choice** *(11/15/2004)*

YANGARRA PARK

Yangarra Park 2000 Cabernet Sauvignon (South Eastern Australia) $10. 84 *—D.T. (6/1/2002)*

Yangarra Park 2001 Chardonnay (South Eastern Australia) $10. 87 Best Buy *—S.H. (7/1/2002)*

Yangarra Park 2001 Merlot (South Eastern Australia) $10. 87 Best Buy *—S.H. (6/1/2002)*

Yangarra Park 2001 Shiraz (South Eastern Australia) $10. 87 Best Buy *—S.H. (9/1/2002)*

YARRA BURN

Yarra Burn 2000 Cabernet Sauvignon (Yarra Valley) $21. 89 *—D.T. (6/1/2003)*

Yarra Burn 2002 Chardonnay (Yarra Valley) $15. This Yarra Valley mainstay has aromas of olive oil and herb framing tropical fruit. Its fruit-cocktail flavor profile is refreshing and clean, but, as one reviewer points out, finishes with a heavy dose of charred wood. **86** *(7/2/2004)*

Yarra Burn 1997 Bastard Hill Chardonnay (Yarra Valley) $27. 86 *(6/1/2003)*

Yarra Burn 2000 Pinot Noir (Yarra Valley) $19. Stably, rhubarb aromas may remind you of a villages-level Burgundy, but that's where the similarity ends. In the mouth, it's thin, with weak cherry fruit, and an herbaceousness that lingers on the finish. Could use more concentration. **82** *(1/1/2004)*

YARRABANK

Yarrabank 1996 Cuvée Brut Champagne Blend (Australia) $32. 90 *—M.M. (12/1/2001)*

YELLOW TAIL

Yellow Tail 2003 Cabernet Sauvignon (South Eastern Australia) $7. Smells like trail mix, barbecued over an open fire. On the palate, it's butterscotch central. Caramel and oak try to steal the spotlight from the chocolate-covered cherry core, and only narrowly miss. Its low-acid, sweet style has millions of fans, but it's too much for this reviewer to handle. **82** *—D.T. (11/15/2004)*

Yellow Tail 2003 Cabernet Sauvignon-Shiraz (South Eastern Australia) $7. Straight out of the bottle, without air, the Tail shows some restraint. After a few minutes, sweet cotton candy and caramel aromas emerge. In the mouth, the wine starts out tasting like juicy berries and cinnamon, but morphs rather rapidly into cherry Slurpee. **83** *—D.T. (12/31/2004)*

Yellow Tail 2002 Chardonnay (South Eastern Australia) $7. 84 *—D.T. (6/1/2003)*

Yellow Tail 2003 Merlot (South Eastern Australia) $7. Nutty-brambly aromas and red fruit on the nose lead to plum and black raspberry fruit on the palate. There's some caramel flavor here, but it's not as prevalent as it has been in other wines by this brand. Flavors are a little bright overall, but it's still a good value. **84 Best Buy** *—D.T. (12/31/2004)*

Yellow Tail 2002 Shiraz (South Eastern Australia) $7. 86 Best Buy *—K.F. (3/1/2003)*

Yellow Tail 2000 Shiraz (South Eastern Australia) $7. 85 Best Buy *—M.N. (6/1/2001)*

YERING STATION

Yering Station 2000 Cabernet Sauvignon (Yarra Valley) $17. The nose is this wine's strongest suit. It evolves nicely, first showing eucalyptus and earth, and then mocha, anise and dense, sweet fruit. The wine's feel and flavors are also very good—it's feminine in size, focused on plum fruit. Finishes a little flat, but still very good overall. **88** *—D.T. (12/31/2004)*

Yering Station 2003 Chardonnay (Yarra Valley) $17. A pretty, talc-mineral note pervades from nose to palate, bolstered by tangy peach and pear fruit. It's a lighter style of Chard, not an explosion of flavors; finishes with a buttery-lactic note. Imported by Epic Wines. **86** *—D.T. (12/1/2005)*

Yering Station 2001 Chardonnay (Yarra Valley) $20. Medium-weight, with nuances of pear on the palate; the fruit is fairly overwhelmed by nutty, smoky notes, which persist through the finish. The nose likewise offers a similar toast-and-oak tag team. A good wine, but one in which the pretty fruit doesn't get its moment in the spotlight. **85** *(7/2/2004)*

Yering Station 1999 Chardonnay (Yarra Valley) $20. 90 *—S.H. (6/1/2001)*

Yering Station 2001 Pinot Noir (Yarra Valley) $17. Shows a nice synthesis of juicy red plum, earth, and leather on the palate. A medium-sized wine, but feels pretty sizable for a Yarra Pinot; has a nice tannic grip in midpalate, and smooth tannins on the medium-length finish. **89** *—D.T. (12/31/2004)*

Yering Station 1999 Pinot Noir (Yarra Valley) $22. 88 *(6/1/2001)*

Yering Station 2003 Reserve Pinot Noir (Yarra Valley) $36. This is not a Pinot you'd ever mistake for an Old World version—its palate is brimming with plums, berries, and noticeable wood, but it still retains some recognizable varietal character. Soft, dusty tannins give it a good feel. The nose, though, is trail-mix central: granola, dried fruit, dates. **88** *—D.T. (12/1/2005)*

Yering Station 2000 Reserve Pinot Noir (Yarra Valley) $36. 86 *(6/1/2003)*

Yering Station 2001 Shiraz (Yarra Valley) $17. Starts off with nutmeg and cinammon aromas, which grow sweeter and more grapy with air. Straightforward plum fruit on the palate, with a decent, medium-sized feel. A good wine, but a pretty ordinary one. **85** *—D.T. (12/31/2004)*

Yering Station 2001 Reserve Shiraz (Yarra Valley) $36. Violet in both color and aroma, this is a huge but elegant, mouthfilling wine, and one built for the long haul. Tannins are lush but taut, and the finish is long, with chalk, mint and smooth tannins. Drink 2006+. **91** *—D.T. (9/1/2004)*

Yering Station 2002 Shiraz-Viognier (Yarra Valley) $17. Not as good as Yering's Shiraz-Viogniers have been, but still a good wine. This vintage offers a nose full of amaretto, green herb—and, with some time, black and green pepper. On the palate the wine is on the thin side, with high-toned cherry and herb flavors. The soily-smooth texture is its high point. **85** *—D.T. (12/1/2005)*

Yering Station 2003 M.V.R. White Blend (Yarra Valley) $17. The idea of this wine really intrigues me—a Rhône blend from Yarra, comprised of nearly three-quarters Marsanne, 5% Roussanne, and the balance Viognier. It's floral and aromatic on the nose, with whiffs even of dime-store bubble gum. The palate has a slight viscous oiliness, but the flavors—some floral notes, maybe some green grapes—are light and innocuous. If the flavors were as titillating as the aromas, and the whole package amped up a notch in intensity, I wouldn't be able to put this wine down. **86** *—D.T. (12/31/2004)*

YUNBAR

Yunbar 2000 Craig's Cabernet Sauvignon (Barossa Valley) $23. 89 *—C.S. (6/1/2002)*

Yunbar 2000 Miracle Merlot (Barossa Valley) $23. 86 *—C.S. (6/1/2002)*

Yunbar 2000 Sinner's Shiraz (Barossa Valley) $23. 82 *—J.C. (9/1/2002)*

ZILZIE

Zilzie 2002 Selection 23 Chardonnay (Victoria) $10. A workhorse of a wine, one that will get the job done with ease but may not win any beauty contests. It's big and a little bulky in the mouth, with melon, pear, and danish pastry flavors and sour pear, matchstick, and lemon aromas. **85** *(7/2/2004)*

ZONTE'S FOOTSTEP

Zonte's Footstep 2003 Cabernet Sauvignon-Malbec (Langhorne Creek) $15. Sweet, plummy fruit wears heavy, lemon-tinged oak aromas. Tastes like wines half its price: simple plum and berry fruit, with a metallic edge. Finishes short. **82** *—D.T. (5/1/2005)*

Austria

Thanks to two grapes, and two wine styles, Austrian wine has an important presence on the international wine-making stage. One of these grapes is Riesling, of which Austrian wine producers are some of the greatest exponents. The other is Grüner Veltliner, of which Austrian wine producers have a virtual monopoly, but one they exploit with panache and stunning results.

The wine styles are both white, but otherwise completely different. There are beautifully crisp, balanced, dry whites; and there are some of the most impressive sweet, botrytis wines, rich, unctuous, and intense.

These are the traditional Austrian wine styles. In recent years, red wines have become increasingly important and of better quality. Using local as well as international grape varieties, Austrian reds now cover one third of the country's vineyards.

Austrian vineyards at Retz, Niederösterreich.

Austria's wine-making history goes back to ancient Roman days, with some of today's best vineyards planted at that time, Grape varieties—red and white—are found on Austrian labels, along with the geographic origin. Today's Austrian vineyards are found in the east of country, whereas classic areas are along the Danube Valley, north-west of Vienna, and in the far east in the province of Burgenland.

The Danube Valley offers superlatives, both in wine and in wine country. The beautiful Wachau vineyards, best known but also one of the smallest wine regions, are caught between steep mountain slopes and the wide Danube River. The purest, most elegant Rieslings and Grüner Veltliners are made by a succession of some of the best producers in Austria. Quality levels are specific to the region: the lightest style is Steinfeder, next is Federspiel, and the richest style is Smaragd.

Other Danube districts include the Kremstal and Kamptal. Both make great white wines: the Kamptal produces some of the most characteristic Grüner Veltliner, crisp, dry, and peppery, from vineyards that are generally cooler than those of Kremstal. One of Austria's most famed vineyard sites, Heiligenstein (rock of saints), is in Kremstal.

North of the Danube, stretching away to the north-east corner of the country, is the Weinviertel, the largest Austrian wine area. Great value wines come from here, mainly made with Grüner Veltliner. A new wine designation is DAC, modeled on the French AC or the Italian DOC: stressing geographic origin rather than grape variety, DAC wines are some of the best everyday dry white wines coming out of Austria.

The Burgenland is where the great dessert wines, and—increasingly—red wines come from. This is the hottest region of Austria, dominated by the marshy, shallow Neusiedlersee lake. Great sweet wines come from the villages all around the lake, while reds come from here as well as hillier vineyards further south.

Wines from Styria, a smaller area in the south east, are worth seeking out. The region has astonished the world with the quality of its Sauvignon Blanc and Chardonnay, and some great white wine makers are based there, as well.

ADOLF & HEINRICH FUCHS

Adolf & Heinrich Fuchs 2001 Classik Trocken Chardonnay (Südosteiermark) $13. **86** —*R.V. (11/1/2002)*

Adolf & Heinrich Fuchs 2003 Classic Halbtrocken Gewürztraminer (Burgenland) $NA. The term "Halbtrocken" means that the wine is semi-sweet. This increases the spicy character of the Gewürztraminer, but along the way some of the intensity is lost. Flavors of lychees make it powerful, but the sweetness makes this a simple wine. **84** —*R.V. (5/1/2005)*

Adolf & Heinrich Fuchs 2003 Classic Grüner Veltliner (Neusiedlersee) $NA. This is full bodied, much bigger than the Grüner Veltliner of the Weinviertel in northern Austria. From the hot Burgenland, this is rich, with pepper and white fruit flavors, but only a slight touch of acidity. The aftertaste has hints of caramel. **83** —*R.V. (5/1/2005)*

Adolf & Heinrich Fuchs 2003 Reserve Grüner Veltliner (Burgenland) $NA. This is something of a curiosity, a Grüner Veltliner which has been matured in wood. It gives the wine extra spiciness and intensity of flavor, although some of the pepper character of the grape is lost in the process. This wine is big, ripe, and full. **86** —*R.V. (5/1/2005)*

Adolf & Heinrich Fuchs 2003 Sauvignon Blanc (South Styria) $20. Smells much like a bowl of freshly made fruit cocktail: there's apple, pear, citrus, and kiwi. Spicy melon with hints of green herbs control the palate, while the mouthfeel is rich and chewy. Quite heavy and sweet, but good if you aren't looking for a lot of zest. **87** *(7/1/2005)*

Adolf & Heinrich Fuchs 2003 Classic Weissburgunder (Südosteiermark) $NA. From the southern Austrian region of Styria, this wine is marked by a touch of spice, and flavors of almonds and white fruits. It is clean, but quite fat, a sign of the warm vintage. **83** —*R.V. (5/1/2005)*

ALLRAM 2003 GAISBERG

Allram 2003 Gaisberg Grüner Veltliner (Kamptal) $25. Like many of the wines from Austria's hot 2003 vintage, this is really ripe. Weighty and slightly viscous on the palate, with scents of nectarine that merge easily into flavors of stone fruits, mineral oil, and a hint of white pepper. So rich on the finish it seems almost off dry. **90** —*J.C. (5/1/2005)*

ANTON BAUER

Anton Bauer 2001 Wagram Reserve (Donauland) $28. Starts with clove, coffee, and plum on the nose, while the flavors follow in a similar vein: plum, coffee, and dried spices. Medium-weight, with a tangy finish filled with soft tannins. Ready to drink. A blend of Cabernet Sauvignon, Blaüfrankisch, and Zweigelt, with tiny amounts of Syrah and Merlot. **84** —*J.C. (5/1/2005)*

BOCKFLIESS

Bockfliess 1999 Pinot Blanc (Weinviertel) $14. **86** —*J.C. (3/1/2002)*

BRAUNSTEIN

Braunstein 2002 Oxhoft Chardonnay (Burgenland) $18. Starts off with hints of honey and ripe melony scents, then adds toast and caramel accents to the melon and citrus fruit on the palate. Medium-bodied and balanced, with just a hint of burnt toast on the finish. **85** —*J.C. (11/15/2005)*

BRUNDLMAYER

Brundlmayer 2003 Langenloiser Kamptaler Terrassen Riesling (Kamptal) $25. A softer style than Bründlmayer's famed Heiligenstein wines, it has an immediate warmth and richness that goes with the ripe flavors of white currants and green fruits. There is freshness as well, which gives a great lift to the aftertaste. **89** —*R.V. (8/1/2005)*

Brundlmayer 2000 Langenloiser Steinmassel Riesling (Kamptal) $25. **90** —*J.C. (3/1/2002)*

Brundlmayer 2001 Lyra Zöbinger Heiligenstein Riesling (Kamptal) $48. **93** —*R.V. (8/1/2003)*

Brundlmayer 2001 Zöbinger Heiligenstein Alte Reben Riesling (Kamptal) $49. The nose is both deceptive and enticing, with its sweet fruit and honey aromas. But they lead to a stunningly rich wine from the great Heiligenstein vineyard, one that is dry with a fine mineral character. It has flavors of pink grapefruit, hedgerow fruit, white currants, and a layer of tannin to give structure. This great wine will age for a long time—10 to 15 years at least. **95 Cellar Selection** —*R.V. (8/1/2005)*

Bründlmayer 2000 Kamptaler Terrasssen Grüner Veltliner (Kamptal) $18. **87** —*J.C. (3/1/2002)*

DOMAINE WACHAU

Domaine Wachau 2002 Federspiel Terrassen Grüner Veltliner (Wachau) $13. Grüner Veltliner is Austria's own special white—it's fresh, but peppery, aromatic, spicy, and flowery. This example has all those flavors, and is a bargain, too. It comes from one of the world's great cooperatives. The fruit comes from the terraced vineyards of the Wachau region in the Danube Valley. The term "Federspiel" is used in the Wachau to denote a good everyday wine, and this is exactly that. **87 Best Buy** —R.V. (11/15/2004)

Domaine Wachau 2003 Dürnsteiner Kellerberg Smaragd Riesling (Wachau) $30. A classic Riesling from the Wachau, which combines intense, aromatic fruit with full flavors of white peaches and floral aromas. This is not as dry as most Wachau wines—it has a definite sweet aftertaste—but the whole wine is so well balanced that this sweeter character never dominates. **90** —*R.V. (5/1/2005)*

SCHLUMBERGER

Schlumberger NV Cuvée Klimt Brut (Osterreichischer Sekt) $20. 85 —*J.C. (12/31/2003)*

E. & M. BERGER

E. & M. Berger 2002 Grüner Veltliner (Kremstal) $11. 85 —*M.S. (11/15/2003)*

EICHINGER

Eichinger 2002 Strasser Gaisberg Grüner Veltliner (Kamptal) $25. A bit dark in color—polished brass—but shows lovely aromas of white peaches, corn oil, and green peppercorns. Oily and viscous in the mouth, with flavors of peppered peaches. Pronounced pepperiness on the finish, along with a hint of alcohol. Drink now. **89** —*J.C. (5/1/2005)*

ELFENHOF

Elfenhof 1999 Chardonnay Beerenauslese (Burgenland) $NA. Pale gold in color, this wine shows great, concentrated fruit, some of the botrytis dryness and flavors of toffee. Lacking acidity, it is ready to drink now. **87** —*R.V. (5/1/2004)*

Elfenhof 1999 Nebbiolo Eiswein (Neusiedlersee-Hügelland) $NA. A fresh, delicate wine intense sweetness, this has flavors of crisp summer fruits along with a touch of honey and citrus acidity. It's beautifully balanced and light. **89 Editors' Choice** —*R.V. (5/1/2004)*

EMMERICH KNOLL

Emmerich Knoll 2002 Ried Kreutles Grüner Veltliner Smaragd (Wachau) $33. A lovely, complex wine that starts with tangerines and dried spices, then opens up slowly to reveal layers of honey, citrus, and spice complexities. It's round in the mouth without being soft, finishing with good length. **90** —*J.C. (5/1/2005)*

ERIC & WALTER POLZ

Eric & Walter Polz 2000 Steirische Klassik Sauvignon Blanc (Südosteiermark) $27. 85 —*J.C. (3/1/2002)*

ERNST TRIEBAUMER

Ernst Triebaumer 2001 Sauvignon Blanc (Burgenland) $10. Stunningly rich and good, with the brilliantly pure and strong intensity of a Marlborough wine. Packed with lime, gooseberry, sweet nettle, and vanilla honey flavors that drink bone dry, with mouthwatering acidity. Outstanding and compelling and a world class value. **90** —*S.H. (10/1/2004)*

Ernst Triebaumer 2001 Traminer Beerenauslese (Burgenland) $32. This is a finely balanced wine, not hugely sweet, but with structure as well as opulent fruit. The Traminer lends a touch of spice, but it is well restrained. This is a style that could certainly partner savory foods as well as desserts. **87** —*R.V. (5/1/2004)*

Ernst Triebaumer 1999 Ausbruch Essenz (Burgenland) $135. This blend of Welschriesling and Chardonnay, hugely sweet, but with balanced, intense acidity, was produced in tiny quantities. Flavors of intense crystallized orange peel dominate, balanced with full, rich opulent fruit make this a wine to savor. **91** —*R.V. (5/1/2004)*

ERWIN SABATHI

Erwin Sabathi 2003 Klassik Sauvignon Blanc (Styria) $15. Modest apple, lime, and melon flavors in this light, quaffable Sauvignon. Finishes with a blast of zippy lime flavors, but lacks intensity otherwise. **84** —*J.C. (12/15/2004)*

Erwin Sabathi 2003 Poharnig Sauvignon Blanc (Styria) $30. Certainly it's minerally, but beyond that the bouquet runs a touch mute. Clean on the palate, with green apple, lemon-lime and that same minerality found on the nose. Light to medium in body, and easy to drink. **87** *(7/1/2005)*

F X PICHLER

F X Pichler 2001 Dürnsteiner Kellerberg Smaragd Grüner Veltliner (Wachau) $NA. F.X. Pichler, one of the icons of Austrian wine, never shies away from power in his wines. This wine is seriously packed with concentration of fruit, rich spices and pepper, flavors of ripe apricots. But there is acidity there, along with a creamy vanilla character, which bring the wine to a harmonious finish. **92** —*R.V. (5/1/2005)*

FEILER-ARTINGER

Feiler-Artinger 2000 Umriss Blaufränkisch (Burgenland) $25. 85 —*R.V. (11/1/2002)*

Feiler-Artinger 2000 1006 Cabernet Sauvignon-Merlot (Burgenland) $60. **90** —*R.V. (11/1/2002)*

Feiler-Artinger 2002 Beerenauslese Traminer (Burgenland) $NA. Aromas of lychees and spice follow through on the palate with ripe, spicy fruit, layering dry botrytis with richness. Light amounts of acidity suggest this is a wine which will age quickly. **88** —*R.V. (5/1/2004)*

Feiler-Artinger 1998 Ruster Ausbruch Welschriesling (Burgenland) $50. **93 Editors' Choice** —*R.V. (11/1/2002)*

Feiler-Artinger 2001 Ausbruch (Burgenland) $40. A rich, luxuriant wine, with smooth, ripe fruit balancing sweet honey, dry botrytis and poised, fresh acidity. A toasty, vanilla flavor gives an exotic feel to this wine, which should last for many years. Cellar Selection. **93 Cellar Selection** —*R.V. (5/1/2004)*

Feiler-Artinger 2002 Beerenauslese (Burgenland) $27. A blend of Welschriesling, Weissburgunder, and Chardonnay, in a fresh style, with crisp but ripe fruits, flavors of apricots and underlying honeyed botrytis. A deliciously fresh, lively wine. **89** *—R.V. (5/1/2004)*

Feiler-Artinger 1998 Ruster Ausbruch Pinot Cuvée (Burgenland) $60. **92** *—R.V. (11/1/2002)*

FELSNER

Felsner 2004 Gedersdorfer Vordernberg Grüner Veltliner (Kremstal) $19. Smells and tastes like a combination of sun-warmed stones and white peaches. It's round and ripe, showing just a touch of alcoholic warmth on the finish. **86** *—J.C. (11/15/2005)*

Felsner 2002 Gedersdorfer Weitgasse Zweigelt (Kremstal) $19. Opens with complex aromas of cranberry and cherry, but also dark chocolate, molasses, and barbecue sauce. A bit leaner in body than some of the other Zweigelts tasted for this issue, but also more interesting. Finishes with hints of game and citrus. **88** *—J.C. (5/1/2005)*

FORSTREITER

Forstreiter 2003 Kremser Kogl Bergwein Grüner Veltliner (Kremstal) $11. Fine, crisp, fresh fruit from a sand and loam vineyard close to the Danube, opposite Krems. It has is an attractive green streak, which gives the wine a lift and acidity. **89** *—R.V. (5/1/2005)*

FRANZ HIRTZBERGER

Franz Hirtzberger 1997 Grauburgunder (Austria) $37. **84** *(5/1/2004)*

Franz Hirtzberger 2003 Rotes Tor Grüner Veltliner Federspiel (Wachau) $25. Classically proportioned GV, with good balance and a plump mouthfeel that fills out the wine's celery leaf, mineral, and apple flavors. Long and stony on the finish. **87** *—J.C. (11/15/2005)*

Franz Hirtzberger 2001 Steinterrassen Federspiel Riesling (Wachau) $24. **93** *—R.V. (8/1/2003)*

FRANZ MITTELBACH

Franz Mittelbach 2002 Tegernseerhof Bergdistel Dürnsteiner Grüner Veltliner (Wachau) $24. Solid Grüner, with hints of peach and pear fruit alongside notes of smoke and minerals. Soft, round mouthfeel, hints of fresh green fruits and only a hint of pepper make this immediately approachable. **86** *—J.C. (12/15/2004)*

FREIE WEINGÄRTNER WACHAU

Freie Weingärtner Wachau 2001 Terrassen Grüner Veltliner Federspiel (Wachau) $11. **86** *— (11/1/2002)*

Freie Weingärtner Wachau 1995 Exceptional Reserve Riesling (Wachau) $35. **86** *—M.S. (5/1/2000)*

GRITSCH MAURITIUSHOF

Gritsch Mauritiushof 2003 1000 Eimerberg Select Neuburger (Wachau) $19. Neuburger is the grape variety, a cross between Weissburgunder (Pinot Blanc) and Sylvaner. The result is a richly textured white with lovely floral notes on the nose and flavors of honey, ripe peaches and citrus. Finishes soft, with hints of dried spices. **88** *—J.C. (11/15/2005)*

GROSS

Gross 1997 Grauburgunder (Austria) $20. **84** *(5/1/2004)*

GSELLMANN & GSELLMANN

Gsellmann & Gsellmann 2000 Gelber Muskateller Trockenbeerenauslese (Burgenland) $35. Dried apricot and ripe pear aromas carry just a hint of volatile acidity, but once past that it reveals dusty, earthy flavors alongside orange marmalade and dried apricots. Sweet and viscous, it finishes with lingering spice notes. **87** *—J.C. (12/15/2004)*

Gsellmann & Gsellmann 2001 Pannobile (Burgenland) $20. The unique combination of chocolate and spice in the aromas of this wine calls to mind chocolate Teddy Grahams, but its by no means a kiddie wine. It's full-bodied and soft, with flavors of tobacco, earth, and spice, and a smoky, coffee-like note on the finish. A blend of Zweigelt, Blaüfrankisch, and Merlot. **86** *—J.C. (5/1/2005)*

Gsellmann & Gsellmann 1998 Vom Goldberg Chardonnay-Weissburgunder Trockenbeerenauslese (Burgenland) $25/375 ml. Orange in color, with scents of toffee and burnt coffee, this is an oddly overdone TBA. Flavors of overcooked caramel deliver sweetness, lemony notes add a tart edge to the finish. **85** *—J.C. (12/15/2004)*

HANS IGLER

Hans Igler 2003 Pinot Blanc (Burgenland) $15. Scents of honey and underripe melon are bolstered by sturdy pear and citrus flavors. Finishes clean and citrusy; refreshing. **85** *—J.C. (11/15/2005)*

HEIDI SCHROCK

Heidi Schrock 1999 Ausbruch Pinot Blanc (Burgenland) $78. A hugely sweet wine, almost the essence of botrytis, made from 100% Pinot Blanc, with marmalade and orange peel flavors. There is a high level of acidity under all this sweetness, giving balance and complexity. This is as rich and concentrated as many TBAs. **91 Cellar Selection** *—R.V. (5/1/2004)*

Heidi Schrock 2001 Ruster Ausbruch (Burgenland) $67. A rare blend of Sauvignon Blanc and Furmint, the grape used in Tokaji in Hungary, this is a concentrated, elegant wine, almost delicate yet giving great sweetness and balancing acidity. This is a sweet wine that demands rich food, like blue cheeses, smoked meats, fruit desserts. **90** *—R.V. (5/1/2004)*

HEINRICH

Heinrich 1997 Red (Burgenland) $16. **82** —*J.C. (5/1/2000)*

HEISS

Heiss 1999 Riesling Trockenbeerenauslese (Burgenland) $50. There's a bit of VA to this wine, but also honeyed pear and pineapple fruit sweet enough to satisfy ardent sweet tooths. **86** —*J.C. (12/15/2004)*

Heiss 2001 Eiswein Traminer (Neusiedlersee) $45/ 375 ml. This is really sweet stuff, but it features some lovely dried spice notes that add complexity and balance out some of the residual sugar. Pears and honey on the nose, a slightly viscous mouthfeel and a long, honeyed finish. **91** —*J.C. (12/15/2004)*

HELMUT LANG

Helmut Lang 1999 Chardonnay TBA (Neusiedlersee) $35. **89** —*R.V. (11/1/2002)*

Helmut Lang 1999 Gewürztraminer Beerenauslese (Neusiedlersee) $35. **90** —*R.V. (11/1/2002)*

Helmut Lang 2000 Sauvignon Blanc Beerenauslese (Neusiedlersee) $NA. **83** —*R.V. (11/1/2002)*

Helmut Lang 1997 Eiswein Cuvée (Neusiedlersee) $38. **81** —*R.V. (11/1/2002)*

AUSTRIA

HIEDLER

Hiedler 2003 Heiligenstein Riesling (Kamptal) $49. Ludwig Hiedler owns 2.5 acres in the Heiligenstein vineyard, planted to Riesling. This wine is typical of the vineyard, full of minerality as well as intense flavors of apricots and a touch of citrus. It is powerful and should age slowly over the next 10 years. **91** —*R.V. (8/1/2005)*

Hiedler 2003 Steinhaus Riesling (Kamptal) $34. A soft, full wine with attractive acidity and good green flavors. Still young, it has some intensity, but will develop early, giving a delicious flowery wine with tropical fruit flavors. **87** —*R.V. (8/1/2005)*

HILLINGER

Hillinger 2003 Zweigelt Trocken (Burgenland) $17. Gets off to a bit of a rough start, overwhelmed by charred, burnt coffee aromas—but don't give up on it. The flavors are much fruitier, featuring liqueur-like black-cherry notes. The silky finish picks up hints of chocolate, but keeps pumping out the fruit. **87** —*J.C. (5/1/2005)*

HOGL

Hogl 2003 Ried Schon Grüner Veltliner Smaragd (Wachau) $22. Nicely balanced for such a big, full-bodied wine, with enough peppery spice, minerally intensity and pink grapefruit to keep the bulk in check. Does have some baked-apple notes suggestive of a warm vintage, but also a long, peppery finish. Drink now. **91 Editors' Choice** —*J.C. (5/1/2005)*

Hogl 2003 Loibner Vision Riesling Smaragd (Wachau) $25. Starts with scents reminiscent of honey, ripe apples, and pears and even hints of peach, then gains complexity on the palate, picking up additional notes of spice and mineral. Verges on full-bodied, with the weight carrying over onto the long, slightly oily finish. **88** —*J.C. (11/15/2005)*

ILSE MAZZA

Ilse Mazza 2002 Achleiten Riesling Smaragd (Wachau) $40. Bears a passing resemblance to Grüner Veltliner in its slightly leafy, peppery notes, but also shows apple and citrus flavors that are distinctively Riesling. Long and minerally on the finish. **87** —*J.C. (5/1/2005)*

JAUNEGG

Jaunegg 2004 Klassik Sauvignon Blanc (Styria) $15. A bit musky and earthy, with hints of stone fruit and grapefruit that enliven the aromas. Honeyed peaches shine on the ripe, weighty palate, but the flavors fade a bit quickly on the finish. **86** —*J.C. (11/15/2005)*

Jaunegg 2003 Knily Sauvignon Blanc (Styria) $25. Fairly pungent and different; this is no walk in the flower garden. The nose is green and carries a strong whiff of grass and/or alfalfa. In the mouth, it offers solid melon, nectarine, and mango. Better in the mouth than on the nose; it has a pleasantness and open-fruit quality that scores it some points. **87** *(7/1/2005)*

JOHANN DONABAUM

Johann Donabaum 2002 Spitzer Point Grüner Veltliner (Wachau) $22. As varietally true a GV as you'll find, with very peppery aromas alongside scents of celery leaf. On the palate, there's a blast of pepper, then some plump, slightly vegetal fruit. Not surprisingly, it's peppery on the finish. **87** —*J.C. (12/15/2004)*

Johann Donabaum 2003 Bergterrassen Riesling Smaragd (Wachau) $25. This richly textured yet impeccably balanced Riesling features aromas that are just enough off the beaten path to intrigue: cinnamon, brown sugar, red berries, and fresh greens, all wrapped around a solid core of ripe apple and pear fruit. The long, fruit-driven finish fades away elegantly, putting an exclamation point on this wine's quality. **91 Editors' Choice** —*J.C. (11/15/2005)*

JOSEF EHMOSER

Josef Ehmoser 2004 Hohenberg Grüner Veltliner (Donauland) $22. Slightly nutty and a bit reductive at first, but it opens up to reveal flavors of citrus, peach, and mineral and a soft, tender mouthfeel. Ends on an orangey note. **86** —*J.C. (11/15/2005)*

Josef Ehmoser 2003 Hohenberg Grüner Veltliner (Donauland) $22. This medium-weight GV carries plenty of almost fat, ripe peach flavors, but also a hard stony edge that sets it apart. Faint peppery notes chime in on the nose and palate, while the finish is long and minerally. **88** *—J.C. (12/15/2004)*

Josef Ehmoser 2003 Pinot Blanc (Donauland) $20. Plump and fruity, with pear, melon, and citrus flavors that satisfy without inspiring. Tart and citrusy on the finish, so worth trying with seafood appetizers. **86** *—J.C. (5/1/2005)*

JOSEF HIRSCH

Josef Hirsch 2003 Gaisberg Zöbing Riesling (Kamptal) $45. A fresh, delicate style, with light acidity and flavors of white currants. The wine is round, with some good green flavors, but is also gentle and easy. Ready to drink now. Bottled with a screwcap. **87** *—R.V. (8/1/2005)*

JOSEF JAMEK

Josef Jamek 2003 Ried Klaus Riesling Smaragd (Wachau) $70. This austere style of Riesling accurately reflects the mineral character that comes from the soil of the Ried Klaus vineyard. Lemon zest, white peach, and spice flavors combine with a steely streak that suggests this wine will age well. **88** *—R.V. (5/1/2005)*

JOSEF SCHMID

Josef Schmid 2002 Urgestein Bergterrassen Riesling (Kremstal) $23. This medium-weight Riesling is fruit-driven, but also boasts notable mineral and spice elements. Has ripe apples and dried spices on the nose, picking up oily, minerally notes on the palate. Finishes with lingering lime flavors. Drink now and over the next 10 years. **90 Editors' Choice** *—J.C. (5/1/2005)*

JURIS 2000 RESERVE CHARDONNAY

Juris 2000 Reserve Chardonnay (Burgenland) $25. This is the bells and whistles Chard. It opens with a strong aroma of buttered popcorn, and is very soft and oaky in the mouth. The chief flavor is a lemony, peachy custard, almost honey sweet, although the wine is totally dry. A bit over the top in terms of the winemaker interventions. **85** *—S.H. (10/1/2004)*

Juris 2001 Welschriesling TBA (Burgenland) $45. An enormously sweet wine, very intense, but manages to retain a feeling of structure and shape. Like drinking syrup, it has flavors of sweet apricots and still is able to bring acidity into the balance. **92** *—R.V. (5/1/2004)*

JURTSCHITSCH SONNHOF

Jurtschitsch Sonnhof 2001 Langenlois Schenkenbichl Grüner Veltliner (Kamptal) $21. **90** *—R.V. (11/1/2002)*

Jurtschitsch Sonnhof 2001 Langenlois Steinhaus Grüner Veltliner (Kamptal) $21. **89** *—R.V. (11/1/2002)*

Jurtschitsch Sonnhof 2000 Rotspon Red Blend (Kamptal) $28. **86** *—R.V. (11/1/2002)*

KOLLWENTZ

Kollwentz 2002 Sauvignon Blanc Beerenauslese (Burgenland) $74. A stunning blend of the crispness of Sauvignon Blanc with smooth, honeyed fruit flavors. Aromas of ripe pears are balanced on the palate with some structure layers of dryness from the botrytis. With its acidity, this wine should hold up well over the next 10 years. **92** *—R.V. (5/1/2004)*

Kollwentz 2002 Scheurebe TBA (Burgenland) $121. The advantage of this fat, ultrasweet wine is the streak of acidity which runs through it. The downside is the curious foxy aroma that is sometimes a character of this rare grape variety. **86** *—R.V. (5/1/2004)*

Kollwentz 1999 Welschriesling TBA (Burgenland) $121. A luxurious, opulent wine, deep gold in color, with ripe, luscious fruit. The wine has acidity, a fine sweet/dry botrytis structure and great deep layers of apricots, figs, and almonds. It should last for 20 years or more. **92 Cellar Selection** *—R.V. (5/1/2004)*

KRACHER

Kracher 2001 Nummer 7, Chardonnay TBA (Burgenland) $84. This is the more successful of Kracher's two Chardonnays. It is both hugely rich and elegant, combining some toast flavors well with the smooth concentrated fruit. To finish, there is a hint of orange marmalade and a fine, delicate balancing acidity. **94** *—R.V. (5/2/2004)*

Kracher 2003 Pinot Gris (Burgenland) $16. Best known for his numbered series of *trockenbeerenauslesen*, Kracher also shows a deft hand with dry wines, as evidenced by this tasty Pinot Gris. Opens with pineapple scents, then gives up plump, mouthfilling tropical and citrus flavors. Finishes in a rush of melon and orange. Yummy. **88** *—J.C. (5/1/2005)*

Kracher 2001 Nummer 9, Scheurebe TBA (Burgenland) $91. The most concentrated of the range of TBAs made by Kracher in 2001, this is almost too sweet, almost too concentrated. It is hugely liquorous, with very low alcohol because the sweetness of the grapes was too much for the yeasts, which gives it a character almost of intensely sweet, very pure grape juice. **91** *—R.V. (5/2/2004)*

Kracher 2001 Nummer 5, Welschriesling TBA (Burgenland) $74. A beautiful wine, structured, spicy, powered with flavors of apricots, intense layers of botrytis, and huge concentration. There is a hint of minerality typical of the grape which just counterpoints the richness and power of the wine. **94 Editors' Choice** *—R.V. (5/2/2004)*

Kracher 2001 Nummer 6 Grande Cuvée TBA (Burgenland) $81. The Grande Cuvée in Kracher's range is the blend that best typifies the vintage—in this case Welschriesling and Chardonnay. New oak aromas vie with toffee, while to taste the rich flavors of peaches and caramelised apples give the wine great intensity while still preserving some fresh acidity. **93 Editors' Choice** *—R.V. (5/2/2004)*

LEOPLOLD & SILVANE SOMMER

Leoplold & Silvane Sommer 2003 Spätlese Gewürztraminer (Neusiedlersee-Hügelland) $15. This is a sweet style of Gewürztraminer, with a fine spice and lychee character that gives a heady accent to the sweetness. This is a good full-bodied wine, but without too high alcohol. When to drink it is a difficult call—the only probable answer is by itself. **88** *—R.V. (5/1/2005)*

Leoplold & Silvane Sommer 2003 M Grüner Veltliner (Neusiedlersee-Hügelland) $15. A rich, spicy wine from a family winery near the Neusiedlersee, which has been in the wine biz since 1698. It's much richer than Grüner Veltliner usually is, but it has its own personality: it's spicy, with good acidity and plenty of varietal character. **87** *—R.V. (5/1/2005)*

Leoplold & Silvane Sommer 2001 Premium Reserve Grüner Veltliner Trocken (Neusiedlersee) $18. 88 *—R.V. (11/1/2002)*

LOIMER

Loimer 2003 Käferberg Grüner Veltliner (Kamptal) $25. This plump, medium-weight Grüner doesn't have the weight and richness of many 2003s, but makes up for it with its juicy, fresh, lipsmacking finish. Apple, citrus, and mineral notes don't show a lot of typical spice, but still satisfy. **88** *—J.C. (5/1/2005)*

Loimer 2003 Riesling (Langenlois) $17. A nice package, but one that lacks intensity. Begins with hints of apple, pear, and honey, then delivers understated lime and mineral flavors. Tart and mouthwatering on the finish. **84** *—J.C. (8/1/2005)*

Loimer 2003 Steinmassl Riesling (Kamptal) $40. Starts off with hints of machine oil and grassy-herbal notes, then eases into melon and mineral flavors that finish clean and fresh. **88** *—J.C. (8/1/2005)*

AUSTRIA

MALAT

Malat 2003 Dreigarten Grüner Veltliner (Kremstal) $29. Gerald Malat is a seminal figure in winemaking in Krems, the first to match grape variety to soil type in a region previously dominated by small holdings and tiny vineyards. So it's fitting that this Grüner Veltliner should power through with ripe, peppery fruit, and flavors of apples, pears, and spice. It needs a year or two to age. **90** *—R.V. (5/1/2005)*

Malat 2003 Silberbühel Riesling (Kremstal) $36. A youthful Riesling, still bursting with energy and vitality but nowhere near ready to drink. It has flavors of white peach, currants, and minerality. It is full, but the acidity shows through, giving a deliciously crisp, fresh aftertaste. **89** *—R.V. (5/1/2005)*

Malat 2004 Reserve Sauvignon Blanc (Austria) $36. Unconventional, with some briny notes to the musky nose that also brings with it honey and lychee. Pretty solid across the palate, where tangerine and melon flavors are sweetened by a shot of guava. Not the easiest wine to wrap yourself around, but not without its virtues. **86** *(7/1/2005)*

MANTLERHOF

Mantlerhof 2003 Wieland Riesling (Kremstal) $45. A soft style of wine that has green acidity and flavors of pink grapefruit. This is a wine that shows its background richness slowly, and will need some years to develop. **87** *—R.V. (8/1/2005)*

Mantlerhof 2004 Zehetnerin Riesling (Kremstal) $25. While the 2003 Zehetnerin is big and opulent, 2004 is crisp, green, clean and packed with green apple flavors. There is a steely intensity to this wine that shows it will age for many years. **90** *—R.V. (8/1/2005)*

Mantlerhof 2000 Roter Veltliner (Kremser) $18. 87 *—J.C. (3/1/2002)*

MARTIN PASLER

Martin Pasler 2001 Muskat Ottonel Trockenbeerenauslese (Burgenland) $30/375 ml. Muskat Ottonel seems to have an affinity for being made into unctuous late-harvest dessert wines that retain enough acidity to offset their enormous sweetness. This one has dried apricot, orange marmalade, and ripe melon flavors all balanced by mouthwatering acids on the long finish. **93 Editors' Choice** *—J.C. (12/15/2004)*

MELITTA & MATTHIAS LEITNER

Melitta & Matthias Leitner 2000 Riesling TBA (Neusiedlersee) $39. The Rhine Riesling, better known in the Danube vineyards further west, makes a rare appearance in the Burgenland with this sweet, ripe, spicy wine, which layers dryness within its honeyed flavors. **87** *—R.V. (5/1/2004)*

Melitta & Matthias Leitner 2000 Eiswein (Neusiedlersee) $NA. For an eiswein, this is impressively rich. A blend of Muskat Ottonel and Welschriesling, its opulence is tempered by a piercing layer of acidity. The grapes were picked on Christmas Eve 2000 by 24 members of the Leitner family. **90** *—R.V. (5/1/2004)*

NEUMEISTER WINERY

Neumeister Winery 2003 Moarfeitl Sauvignon Blanc (Styria) $37. Ripe and tropical, yet a bit over the top. This wine seems reflective of the hot 2003 vintage. It's sweet from start to finish, with a thick body that one reviewer labeled "cloying." If you like richness and size more than citrus and verve, this fits the bill. **86** *(7/1/2005)*

NIGL

Nigl 2002 Privat Grüner Veltliner (Kremstal) $50. From his tiny valley above Krems, Martin Nigl seems to produce effortless wines with all the right intensity of flavor and richness. This Privat (which, for him, is the equivalent of a reserve wine), is intense, concentrated, and packed with spice, pepper, and yellow apples. **91** *—R.V. (5/1/2005)*

Nigl 2001 Privat Grüner Veltliner (Kremstal) $39. 90 *—R.V. (11/1/2002)*

Nigl 2003 Privat Riesling (Kremstal) $71. Rich and concentrated, this wine comes from Martin Nigl's selection from old vines, which he bottles as his premium wines. It has denseness and concentration, but is still open and generous. There are flavors of green plums, lychees, other tropical fruit, and herbs. A great open-hearted wine, it should age well over 5–10 years. **91** —*R.V. (8/1/2005)*

NIKOLAIHOF

Nikolaihof 1990 Grüner Veltliner Smaragd (Wachau) $NA. As Grüner Veltliner ages, it becomes more and more like mature Riesling. This wine has petrol flavors, along with light acidity, and a taste of vanilla and toast. Still lively, this has a bone dry aftertaste. It could certainly age longer. **89** —*R.V. (4/1/2005)*

Nikolaihof 2000 Steiner Hund Riesling (Wachau) $51. Nikolaihof has been farmed biodynamically since 1971, and the benefits show in a wine like this, whose fresh, hedgerow aromas just sing from the glass. The fruit is fresh and intensely flavored, with currants and sweet pears alongside crafted acidity and just a touch of softness to finish. Not complex, but so drinkable. **90** —*R.V. (4/1/2005)*

NITTNAUS

Nittnaus 1999 Cabernet Sauvignon (Burgenland) $29. 83 —*J.C. (3/1/2002)*

Nittnaus 1999 Selection St. Laurent (Burgenland) $25. 84 —*J.C. (3/1/2002)*

Nittnaus 2000 Traminer (Burgenland) $NA. Harvested on December 24, 2000, this spicy wine has the classic eiswein freshness and acidity floating over the sweetness. There are aromas of fresh-cut flowers, flavors of fresh apricots, finishing with a touch of lychee. **89** —*R.V. (5/1/2004)*

OCHS

Ochs 1998 Ungerberg & Zeiselberg & Satz Welschriesling (Weiden am See) $29. 86 —*J.C. (3/1/2002)*

PITNAUER

Pitnauer 2002 Hagelsberg Ernte Pinot Blanc (Carnuntum) $20. This medium-weight white would be a fine accompaniment to almost any fish preparation. Its crisp apple and pear flavors carry a hint of liquid minerality that will enliven the dish's flavors without overwhelming them. **87** —*J.C. (12/15/2004)*

PLODER-ROSENBERG

Ploder-Rosenberg 2003 Sauvignon Blanc (Styria) $8. The bouquet shows some hints of peach, but the aromas and flavors are largely dominated by stony, minerally notes. Relatively light in body, it fades quickly on the finish. Refreshing. **84 Best Buy** —*J.C. (11/15/2005)*

PÖCKL

Pöckl 2003 Zweigelt (Burgenland) $15. There are modest sour-cherry scents on the nose alongside mushroom and clean earth aromas. Cherry and marshmallow flavors are a bit candied, leading into a finish that lingers. **84** —*J.C. (5/1/2005)*

PRAGER

Prager 2003 Durnstein Kaiserberg Riesling Smaragd (Wachau) $42. Can a wine be too minerally? This one's a candidate, with stony, minerally flavors that offer the merest hints of fresh greens or mint and crisp apple. It's a real mineral bath of flavor, backed by fresh limes; a tightly wound wine that needs a few years of age to open up. **89** —*J.C. (11/15/2005)*

Prager 2003 Steinriegl Riesling Smaragd (Wachau) $56. Great Rieslings like this are world-class wines. In the hands of Prager's owner, Toni Bodenstein, the grape comes through with beautiful, rich fruit, flavors of white currants and perfumes of hedgerow flowers. There is also a fine sense of the terroir, with a cool slate texture. **92** —*R.V. (5/1/2005)*

Prager 2003 Weissenkirchen Wachstum Bodenstein Riesling Smaragd (Wachau) $47. Exotically perfumed, boasting scents of tangerines, grapefruit, honey, and apple blossoms—a real cornucopia of aromas. Flavors are more restrained at this stage of its evolution, focused on honey and apple, but this medium-weight Riesling should evolve effortlessly for 10–15 years at least. The long, mouthcoating, minerally finish is ample testament to that. **91** —*J.C. (5/1/2005)*

R&A PFAFFL

R&A Pfaffl 2000 Exklusiv Chardonnay Trocken (Weinviertel) $18. 87 —*R.V. (11/1/2002)*

R&A Pfaffl 2001 Goldjoch Grüner Veltliner (Weinviertel) $18. 93 —*R.V. (11/1/2002)*

R&A Pfaffl 2001 Hundsleien Sandtal Trocken Grüner Veltliner (Weinviertel) $18. 90 —*R.V. (11/1/2002)*

R&A Pfaffl 2000 Hundsleiten Sandtal Grüner Veltliner (Weinviertel) $18. 92 —*R.V. (11/1/2002)*

R&A Pfaffl 2001 Terrasen Sonnleiten Riesling (Weinviertel) $18. 94 **Editors' Choice** —*R.V. (11/1/2002)*

RAINER WESS

Rainer Wess 2003 Riesling Trocken (Wachau) $26. Starts with lime and green-apple aromas, then delivers flavors of pineapple and minerals so intense they're like molten rock. Slightly oily-textured, and long on the finish. Fully dry. **89** —*J.C. (5/1/2005)*

REPOLUSK

Repolusk 2000 Gelber Muskateller (Austria) $23. **86** —*S.H. (9/1/2002)*

Repolusk 1999 Sweigelt Red Blend (Austria) $24. **86** —*S.H. (9/1/2002)*

Repolusk 2000 Roter Traminer Spätlese (Austria) $28. **86** —*S.H. (9/1/2002)*

Repolusk 2000 Weissburgunder (Austria) $23. **83** —*S.H. (9/1/2002)*

RUDI PICHLER

Rudi Pichler 2003 Hochrain Grüner Veltliner Smaragd (Wachau) $57. Wines like this rich wine from Rudi Pichler are the best expression of the granite and slate soil of the Wachau. The wine has just the right peppery character of Grüner Veltliner combined with the crisp acidity of the region. This is an excellent food wine. **88** —*R.V. (5/1/2005)*

Rudi Pichler 2003 Weissenkirchner Achleiten Riesling Smaragd (Wachau) $63. Fantastic stuff, even though it seems a bit closed at the moment. Nectarine and melon fruit on the nose; hints of greens as well. Full-bodied flavors are of ultraripe stone fruit and minerally diesel fuel, with peppery nasturtium blossoms on the finish. Approachable now. It may not be a 20-year wine, but should still hold easily through 2015. **93** —*J.C. (5/1/2005)*

SALOMON-UNDHOF

Salomon-Undhof 2001 Kremser Koegl Riesling (Kremstal) $23. **90** —*R.V. (11/1/2002)*

Salomon-Undhof 2003 Pfaffenberg Riesling (Kremstal) $27. This is a single-vineyard wine from the rocky slopes above Krems. It is finely crafted, aiming at elegance rather than power. At this stage, it is lean, showing high mineral character. It has good primary green fruits and acidity that will soften out over the next few years. **89** —*R.V. (8/1/2005)*

Salomon-Undhof 2003 Steinterrassen Riesling (Kremstal) $18. Leaner than the 2004 version of this wine, this 2003 has soft, fresh acidity, flavors of white peaches and a touch of crispness. It is ready to drink now, and makes a great summer apéritif wine. **86** —*R.V. (8/1/2005)*

Salomon-Undhof 2003 Undhof Kögl Reserve Riesling (Kremstal) $42. This is a great single-vineyard wine from the Kögl vineyard on the hill behind the streets of Krems. This wine is meant to be aged over many years, with its dense powerful character, its ripeness, and its big flavors of green plums, and long-lasting acidity. A great Riesling. **93 Cellar Selection** —*R.V. (8/1/2005)*

SCHLOSS GOBELSBURG

Schloss Gobelsburg 2001 Altheiligenstiftung Grüner Veltliner (Kamptal) $17. **88** —*R.V. (11/1/2002)*

SCHLOSSWEINGUT GRAF HARDEGG

Schlossweingut Graf Hardegg 2003 Tethys Austrian White Blend (Weinviertel) $25. This is an innovative and unusual blend of Chardonnay, Pinot Blanc, and Grüner Veltliner that has been barrel fermented and aged. It is ripe, packed with vanilla flavors and intense fruit. The Grüner Veltliner is hardly noticeable except by the fresh lift to finish. **90** —*R.V. (5/1/2005)*

Schlossweingut Graf Hardegg 2003 Veltlinsky Grüner Veltliner (Weinviertel) $11. Maximilian Hardegg's branded Grüner Veltliner is a hit with the smart set in Vienna. It is an easy-drinking wine, full of soft fruit and freshness. A touch of soft sweetness at the end adds to its mainstream appeal. **84** —*R.V. (5/1/2005)*

SEPP MOSER

Sepp Moser 2002 Gebling Riesling (Kremstal) $30. Deliciously fresh, perfumed fruit, with layers of hedgerow fruits and soft, ripe acidity. Sepp Moser, son of the famed Lenz Moser, handed over control of the winemaking to his son, Nikolaus, who has crafted a smooth, polished wine. **89** —*R.V. (8/1/2005)*

SONNHOF

Sonnhof 2000 Grüve Grüner Veltliner (Kamptal) $15. **83** —*J.C. (3/1/2002)*

Sonnhof 2000 Steinhaus Grüner Veltliner Trocken (Kamptal) $19. **86** —*J.C. (3/1/2002)*

STADT KREMS

Stadt Krems 2003 Grillenparz Riesling (Kremstal) $27. Melon and herb notes on the nose give way to citrus-tinged fruit on the palate. As one might expect from the heat of the vintage, it's a plump rather than racy Riesling, but has a long, mineral-laden finish. **89** —*J.C. (8/1/2005)*

STEFAN HOFFMAN

Stefan Hoffman 2001 Ausbruch Traminer (Neusiedlersee) $28. **90** —*R.V. (11/1/2002)*

STEININGER

Steininger 2003 Riesling Kabinett (Kamptal) $NA. A finely layered Riesling, crisp, dry and with fresh acidity. It has great lightness, poise and elegance without huge intensity. Delicious summer drinking. Karl Steininger's winery now forms part of the impressive Loisium wine museum at Langenlois. **85** —*R.V. (8/1/2005)*

STIFT KLOSTERNEUBURG

Stift Klosterneuburg 2000 Ried Stiftsbreite, Ausstich St. Laurent (Thermenregion) $NA. 86 *—R.V. (11/1/2002)*

Stift Klosterneuburg 2000 Ried Stiftsbreite Ausstich Riesling (Thermenregion) $NA. 86 *—R.V. (11/1/2002)*

TERRA GOMELIZ

Terra Gomeliz 2003 Sauvignon Blanc (Südosteiermark) $17. A classic Styrian Sauvignon Blanc, with catty aromas, good flavors of acidity, and flavors of hedgerow fruits and minerals. This is a great food wine with river fish, such as trout. **87** *—R.V. (5/1/2005)*

TSCHEPPE

Tscheppe 2002 Czamillonberg Chardonnay (Styria) $22. A balanced and appealing Chardonnay with a slight floral cast to its aromas and a custardy texture. Pear, mineral, and citrus flavors round out the package. **86** *—J.C. (12/15/2004)*

Tscheppe 2001 Possnitzberg Reserve Pinot Gris (Styria) $33. Oakier than Tscheppe's regular bottling but ultimately not any more pleasurable. Toasty, mealy scents mask peach and melon flavors; the mouthfeel is thick and rich. Finishes with a hint of alcohol and a strong taste of nutty oak. **87** *—J.C. (5/1/2005)*

TSCHERMONEGG

Tschermonegg 2002 Grauburgunder (Styria) $15. Honeyed citrus fruits on the nose, followed by a plump, medium-weight wine with flavors of peach and tangerine. Finishes clean. A nice rendition of Pinot Gris. **87** *—J.C. (11/15/2005)*

Tschermonegg 2003 Weissburgunder (Styria) $10. An easy quaffer, this Pinot Blanc boasts citrus and slate aromas backed by simple tangerine flavors that turn a little soft on the finish. **84** *—J.C. (11/15/2005)*

VELICH

Velich 2001 Darscho Chardonnay (Burgenland) $25. Decent enough Chardonnay, but vaguely anonymous, with plump apple and pear fruit covered by smoky, leesy notes, toasted marshmallow and charred oak. **85** *—J.C. (12/15/2004)*

Velich 2001 Tiglat Chardonnay (Burgenland) $55. Top-notch Austrian Chardonnay, with lovely aromas of citrus and honey-nut Cheerios matched by lemon custard and toasted whole-grain flavors. Layered and rich, yet balanced by zesty acidity. **89** *—J.C. (11/15/2005)*

Velich 1999 Welschriesling Trockenbeerenauslese (Burgenland) $75/375 ml. A golden-orange color with flecks of brown gives the (correct) impression of great ripeness. This is an unctuously sweet TBA, filled with layers of brown sugar, honey, caramel, and figs, accented by dried spices. Long and honeyed on the finish. **92** *—J.C. (12/15/2004)*

WALTER GLATZER

Walter Glatzer 2000 Grüner Veltliner Kabinett (Carnuntum) $11. 82 *—J.C. (3/1/2002)*

WEINBERGHOF FRITSCH

Weinberghof Fritsch 2003 Steinberg Grüner Veltliner (Donauland) $17. While the Steinberg does produce delicate wines, this is an exception. Powered and peppery, it is rich, ripe and full-bodied. Karl Fritsch has developed almost an international style, emphasizing fruit intensity, but he has not lost all the fine balance of an Austrian Grüner Veltliner. **90** *—R.V. (5/1/2005)*

WEINKELLEREI TIEDL

Weinkellerei Tiedl 1999 Barrique Blaufränkisch (Neusiedlersee) $15. 88 *—R.V. (11/1/2002)*

Weinkellerei Tiedl 2000 Blauer Zweigelt (Neusiedlersee) $15. 85 *—R.V. (11/1/2002)*

WEINRIEDER

Weinrieder 2003 Schneidersberg DAC Grüner Veltliner (Weinviertel) $12. The DAC (Districtus Austriae Controllatus) wines, designed for easy drinking but with a good character of terroir and character, have found just the right expression in this wine. It is made from old vines which give it beautiful integration, concentration and depth of fruit. **89 Best Buy** *—R.V. (5/1/2005)*

WENZEL

Wenzel 2001 Bandkraften Blaufränkisch (Burgenland) $25. This Burgenland producer has been a real discovery for us over the past year or so, excelling with sweet wines, dry whites, and reds. This spice-driven red relies on clove, cracked pepper, and tea notes for interest, layered against a backdrop of cherry-berry and plum fruit. Supple enough to drink now. **88** *—J.C. (5/1/2005)*

Wenzel 2002 Riesling Beerenauslese (Burgenland) $40/375 ml. Smells like essence of superripe peach, blended with honey and dried apricots. Peach, apricot, and bergamot flavors in the mouth are sweet but not overly heavy; this wine finishes on a fresh, clean note, not a sticky-sweet one. **91 Editors' Choice** *—J.C. (12/15/2004)*

Wenzel 2001 Saz Ruster Ausbruch (Burgenland) $120/375 ml. Apricot and orange marmalade scents presage this wine's viscous sweetness, but the wine also boasts incredible precision and clarity to its flavors. Dried apricots, honey, and citrus all come together in a complex swirl that never seems too heavy or cloying. Finishes with a hint of bergamots (the flavoring in Earl Grey tea). A blend of Furmint and Gelber Muskateller. **95** *—J.C. (12/15/2004)*

WERNER DUSCHANEK

Werner Duschanek 2000 Pinot Noir Spätlese (Mittelburgenland) $NA. **86** *—R.V. (11/1/2002)*

WIENINGER

Wieninger 2003 Herrenholz Grüner Veltliner (Vienna) $17. Shows good acidity for a 2003, with a crispness on the finish that belies the vintage. Peppery and a bit green-herbal-vegetal on the nose—classic GV. Then it delivers peach and mineral oil flavors on the palate and finish. Good value. **90 Editors' Choice** *—J.C. (5/1/2005)*

Wieninger 2003 Riedencuvee Riesling (Vienna) $15. A good value in Austrian Riesling, this wine delivers bright green-apple aromas, then pear and citrus flavors in a medium-bodied format. Finishes clean and fresh, with a tactile quality suggestive of talc. **89** *—J.C. (5/1/2005)*

Wieninger 2001 Nussberg Alte Reben White Blend (Vienna) $26. From a small parcel of mixed old vines (alte reben) in the Nussberg vineyard, this wine combines ripe pear and melon flavors with an intense stony minerality. The mouthfeel is slightly oily without being overly weighty or rich; the finish is long, long, long. **90 Editors' Choice** *—J.C. (12/15/2004)*

WILLI OPITZ

Willi Opitz 2001 White Blend (Neusiedlersee) $18. An extravagantly perfumed wine, with acidity and flavors of lychees and melons. Fresh, crisp, and exotic. **88** *—R.V. (5/1/2004)*

Willi Opitz 2001 Schilfwein Zweigelt (Neusiedlersee) $46. The Zweigelt is a red grape, and this wine, made from pressing dried grapes, has an attractive red/gold color. To taste, it has flavors of honey and marmalade, and lilting acidity. It's an unusual style, but very attractive. **87** *—R.V. (5/1/2004)*

WINZER KREMS

Winzer Krems 2003 Kellermeister Privat Kremser Kremsleiten Riesling (Kremstal) $15. A generous, rich, open style of Riesling from the excellent Krems cooperative. The wine is soft, full of fresh acidity and lively green fruit flavors. Well-balanced, and should be ready to drink within a year. **88** *—R.V. (8/1/2005)*

Winzer Krems 2004 Riesling von den Terrassen Riesling (Kremstal) $10. An initially gentle, easy wine opens out to give richness and generosity. It may not be complex, but it has great acidity, and good grapefruit flavors. The aftertaste is crisp and fresh. **86** *—R.V. (8/1/2005)*

WOHLMUTH

Wohlmuth 2001 Summus Chardonnay (Südosteiermark) $18. **87** *—R.V. (11/1/2002)*

Wohlmuth 2000 Summus Muskateller (South Styria) $16. **84** *—J.C. (3/1/2002)*

Wohlmuth 2000 Summus Pinot Gris (South Styria) $16. **84** *—J.C. (3/1/2002)*

Wohlmuth 2001 Summus Sauvignon Blanc (Südosteiermark) $20. **88** *—R.V. (11/1/2002)*

ZANTHO

Zantho 2002 St. Laurent (Burgenland) $13. Subtle spice and candied cherries on the nose give way to pure intense black cherries on the palate. Medium- to full-bodied, it does pick up a hint of heat on the finish, but also a spicy, cedary nuance. Drink now. **87** *—J.C. (5/1/2005)*

ZULL

Zull 2000 Odfeld Grüner Veltliner (Weinviertel) $17. **90** *—J.C. (3/1/2002)*

Chile

Chile saw its original grapevines arrive with sixteenth-century Spanish missionaries, but the first semblance of a modern winemaking industry dates back to the early part of the nineteenth century, when a naturalist by the name of Claudio Gay imported about sixty varieties of grapes from France. In turn, some of these grapes were planted in the Maipo Valley, which encompasses the city of Santiago, and by the 1850s commercial wine existed.

Wine barrels in the cellars of Viña Luis Felipe Edwards, Chile.

From an American's perspective, Chilean wine started to make its mark in the 1970s, when protectionist restrictions were lifted by the military dictatorship headed by Augusto Pinochet. Almost immediately, exports spiked, with value-priced wines pouring into America as well as other countries. Some thirty years later, Chile is one of the world's most aggressive exporters; its wines make it to nearly one hundred countries around the globe, with shipments to the United States leading the way.

In many ways, the climate, geology, and geography of Chile are like that of western North America, but turned upside-down. Chile's north is a bone-dry desert, roughly equal to Baja California, only drier. The middle of the country is verdant and river-fed, with soils perfect for all sorts of agriculture, not the least of which is grapes. So in that sense it's like California, Oregon, and Washington. And as one goes south it quickly gets colder and more rugged, not unlike British Columbia and eventually Alaska.

In the midsection of this 4,000-mile-long sliver of a country, there's a 500-mile chunk called the Central Valley, and within this valley there are a number of prime wine-growing regions. The most historic is Maipo, in which just about all grapes are grown. But it's Cabernet Sauvignon that has always been king in Maipo. Whether it's a simple everyday Maipo Cabernet like Cousiño-Macul's Antiguas Reservas or one of the country's best premium offerings like Concha y Toro's Don Melchor, a Maipo Cabernet is well worth hailing.

Other prominent wine regions include Aconcagua and Limari, the two northern frontiers of premium grape growing. There aren't many wineries there, but the wines are solid and true. Bordering Maipo to the west is the Casablanca Valley, first planted by Pablo Morandé and his family in the early 1990s. Cool and coastal, Casablanca and neighboring Leyda and San Antonio are prime spots for Chardonnay and Sauvignon Blanc but have trouble when it comes to producing ripe red wines.

South of Maipo is Rapel and its two parallel valleys: Cachapoal and Colchagua. Here the weather is warm, and the majority of grapes are red. Colchagua is arguably the leading region in Chile for red wines, and there's a plethora of big, burly wines based on Syrah, Cabernet Sauvignon, Merlot, Malbec, and Carmenère coming from Colchagua wineries including Montes, Casa Lapostolle, Viu Manent, MontGras, and Los Vascos.

Further south are the regions of Curicó and Maule. It was in Curicó that Miguel Torres of Spain set up shop in 1979 and introduced the then-revolutionary concept of steel-tank fermentation to Chile. To borrow a well-used phrase and apply it to how wine is now being made throughout the country: the rest is history.

AGUSTINOS

Agustinos 2000 Reserve Cabernet Sauvignon (Cachapoal Valley) $13. 85 *—D.T. (7/1/2002)*

Agustinos 2000 Reserve Carmenère (Maipo Valley) $13. 83 *—D.T. (7/1/2002)*

Agustinos 2000 Estate Chardonnay (Cachapoal Valley) $8. 84 *—M.S. (7/1/2002)*

Agustinos 2000 Reserve Merlot (Cachapoal Valley) $13. 85 *—C.S. (12/1/2002)*

ALFASI

Alfasi 1998 Cabernet Sauvignon (Maule Valley) $8. 82 *—J.C. (2/1/2001)*

Alfasi 1998 Reserve Cabernet Sauvignon (Maule Valley) $8. 80 *—M.S. (7/1/2003)*

Alfasi 2002 Reserve Chardonnay-Sauvignon (Maule Valley) $8. This 50-50 blend yields hints of diesel or kerosene on the nose, then adds honey and pear flavors. A bit rough and phenolic on the finish. **82** *—J.C. (4/1/2005)*

Alfasi 1998 Merlot (Maule Valley) $7. 85 *(4/1/2001)*

Alfasi 2001 Reserve Merlot (Maule Valley) $10. Strong tobacco and olive scents emerge from the glass, followed by modest cherry flavors with an intensely herbaceous edge. Lean. **82** *—J.C. (4/1/2005)*

Alfasi 1998 Flora Semi Dry Red Blend (Maule Valley) $10. 82 *—D.T. (7/1/2002)*

Alfasi 2001 Late Harvest Sauvignon Blanc (Maule Valley) $15. Simple and sweet, with aromas and flavors of apricot jam. Medium-weight and low in acidity. **82** *—J.C. (4/1/2005)*

CHILE

ALTAÏR

Altaïr 2002 Cabernet Sauvignon (Cachapoal Valley) $55. Powerful and cranked up to another level, with a lot of natural purity. Gigantic on the palate, with berry syrup, earth, and extremely powerful tannins. Tight and built like a fort; not an easy wine to just pop and quaff. The jackhammer tannins see to that. **88** *—M.S. (11/1/2005)*

Altaïr 2003 Sideral Red Blend (Rapel Valley) $29. Finely oaked, with lovely cedar scents accenting robust but smooth black cherry and dark plum aromas. Sings a pretty tune in the mouth, with ripe berry fruit, tobacco, toast, and a long finish. A significant step up from the first vintage. **91** *—M.S. (11/1/2005)*

ANTIYAL

Antiyal 1999 Red Blend (Maipo Valley) $30. 89 *—S.H. (12/1/2002)*

APALTAGUA

Apaltagua 2003 Cabernet Sauvignon (Colchagua Valley) $10. A bit rubbery and green, but still more solid than problematic. The red fruit on the palate is spunky, as it's driven by firm, grabby tannins and a lot of acid. Finishes with some buttery wood notes, but it weighs in more racy than heavy. **85 Best Buy** *—M.S. (11/1/2005)*

Apaltagua 2003 Carmenère (Colchagua Valley) $10. Straight-ahead in style, with red cherry on the nose along with some saucy, marinated aromas. Runs a bit lemony and lean on the palate, but at the surface level it's solid. Peppery and upright on the finish, with a little bitterness. For the most part, it's spicy and right. **85 Best Buy** *—M.S. (11/1/2005)*

Apaltagua 2003 Envero Carmenère (Colchagua Valley) $15. A Carmenère-based wine with dark blackberry aromas and a touch of cherry cough drop to the bouquet. This one veers toward juicy, with prime acidity pushing black plum and boysenberry flavors. Fairly long and moderately complex on the finish. With 15% Cabernet. **88** *—M.S. (11/1/2005)*

Apaltagua 2000 Envero Carmenère (Colchagua Valley) $15. **91 Best Buy** *—S.H. (12/1/2002)*

Apaltagua 2002 Grial Carmenère (Colchagua Valley) $40. Rock solid, with fully developed berry, plum, cola and fine-oak aromas. Rich and fancy, with all the best attributes Carmenère has to offer, including red plum fruit, earth, herbs, and chocolate. Big on the finish, but kept afloat by healthy acidity. A model for extracted New World Carmenère. **91 Editors' Choice** *—M.S. (2/1/2005)*

ARAUCANO

Araucano 2003 Carmenère (Colchagua Valley) $10. Deeper and more syrupy than many, but still nice. Tar, blackberry and warm earth aromas emanate from the bouquet, followed by a sweet, thick palate that feels heavy due to relatively low acidity. Fully ripe with a fine mouthfeel. Not vegetal in the least. **87 Best Buy** *—M.S. (12/1/2004)*

Araucano 2002 Alka Carmenère (Colchagua Valley) $55. Nice on the nose, with subtle lavender, plum, chocolate, and green-pepper notes. Extremely rich and creamy, maybe too much so; the palate is a heavyweight, with black plum, fudge, and vanilla. Very soft and low-acid, almost like dessert. Has its qualities and faults. **87** *—M.S. (2/1/2005)*

Araucano 2004 Sauvignon Blanc (Valle Central) $9. Falls firmly into the herbaceous, grassy style that emphasizes pickle barrel, jalapeño, and asparagus. But underneath you'll also find apple, melon, and a smidge of alfalfa. Good feel throughout, and consistent. **85 Best Buy** *—M.S. (7/1/2005)*

ARBOLEDA

Arboleda 2001 Cabernet Sauvignon (Maipo Valley) $15. Big enough and herbal, with cassis and cherry to the nose. More currant and plum carry the palate, and things seem to be on a clear path until the finish goes medicinal and syrupy, leaving a touch too much cough medicine on the finish. **86** *—M.S. (7/1/2005)*

Arboleda 1998 Cabernet Sauvignon (Maipo Valley) $20. **88** *(10/1/2001)*

Arboleda 2002 Carmenère (Colchagua Valley) $15. Dull and herbal, with a lot of the bell pepper and rhubarb character that Carmenère is well known for. While it has decent body and seems balanced, the aromatic and flavor profiles are decidedly vegetal. **82** *—M.S. (7/1/2005)*

Arboleda 1999 Carmenère (Maipo Valley) $20. **88** *—M.S. (3/1/2002)*

Arboleda 2000 Chardonnay (Central Valley) $8. **86** *—M.S. (3/1/2002)*

Arboleda 2000 Merlot (Colchagua Valley) $20. **88** *—M.S. (3/1/2002)*

Arboleda 1999 Merlot (Colchagua Valley) $20. **84** *—S.H. (5/1/2001)*

Arboleda 2002 Syrah (Colchagua Valley) $15. Dark and tight, with sturdy plum and berry aromas along with some minty oak in support. Plump and chunky on the palate, but stand up, with a finish that runs peppery. A touch raw and oaky, but still better than most Chilean Syrah. **86** *—M.S. (2/1/2005)*

Arboleda 2000 Syrah (Colchagua Valley) $20. **84** *—S.H. (12/1/2002)*

Arboleda 1999 Syrah (Colchagua Valley) $20. **83** *—S.H. (2/1/2003)*

ARESTI

Aresti 2003 Cabernet Sauvignon (Chile) $8. Rubbery and green, with heavy, weedy flavors and some heat. Turns toward barnyard as it opens up. Lacks pizzazz and probably won't inspire. **80** *—M.S. (7/1/2005)*

Aresti 1999 Family Collection Cabernet Sauvignon (Rio Claro) $26. **88** *—M.S. (3/1/2002)*

Aresti 2001 Montemar Cabernet Sauvignon (Curicó Valley) $8. **85 Best Buy** *—M.S. (7/1/2003)*

Aresti 1999 Reserva Cabernet Sauvignon (Rio Claro) $11. **89 Best Buy** *(9/1/2000)*

Aresti 2003 Carmenère (Curicó Valley) $8. Meaty up front, with soy and earth aromas. Rounds into better form on the palate, where cherry and blackberry flavors are modest but real. Round and chocolaty on the finish, with acidity that keeps it moving forward. **83** *—M.S. (11/1/2005)*

Aresti 2004 Chardonnay (Curicó Valley) $8. Smells like crushed vitamins, while the palate is crisp and lemony, with hints of green apple and spice. Not a bad wine in that it holds form all the way through. Seems just a bit resiny and grabby on the tongue. **84 Best Buy** *—M.S. (11/1/2005)*

Aresti 2002 Montemar Gewürztraminer (Curicó Valley) $8. **82** *—M.S. (7/1/2003)*

Aresti 2000 Montemar Merlot (Curicó Valley) $8. **81** *—D.T. (7/1/2002)*

Aresti 2000 Reserve Merlot (Rio Claro) $11. **86** *—M.S. (3/1/2002)*

Aresti 1999 Reserve Merlot (Rio Claro) $11. **87** *(9/1/2000)*

Aresti 2002 Montemar Sauvignon Blanc (Curicó Valley) $8. **83** *—M.S. (7/1/2003)*

Aresti 1999 Reserva Sauvignon Blanc (Rio Claro) $11. **87** *(9/1/2000)*

BALDUZZI

Balduzzi 1999 Reserva Cabernet Sauvignon (Maule Valley) $11. **81** *—M.S. (7/1/2003)*

BARON PHILIPPE DE ROTHSCHILD

Baron Philippe de Rothschild 2000 Reserva Cabernet Sauvignon (Maipo Valley) $10. **85** *—P.G. (12/1/2002)*

Baron Philippe de Rothschild 2001 Reserva Chardonnay (Casablanca Valley) $10. **85** *—P.G. (12/1/2002)*

Baron Philippe de Rothschild 2000 Escudo Rojo Red Blend (Chile) $15. **88 Best Buy** *—D.T. (7/1/2002)*

Baron Philippe de Rothschild 1999 Escudo Rojo Red Blend (Maipo Valley) $15. **81** *—S.H. (11/20/2002)*

BOTALCURA

Botalcura 2002 La Porfia Grand Reserve Carmenère (Central Valley) $18. Muddled and chunky, with raspberry and leather on the nose. Not entirely fresh or forward; instead it sits on the palate in bland, heavy fashion. Shows pepper and red fruit flavors, but not much texture or variety. **83** *—M.S. (7/1/2005)*

CALAMA

Calama 2001 Cabernet Sauvignon (Central Valley) $6. **83** *—M.S. (7/1/2003)*

Calama 2001 Merlot (Casablanca Valley) $9. **83** *—M.S. (7/1/2003)*

CALIBORO ESTATE

Caliboro Estate 2001 Erasmo Bordeaux Blend (Maule Valley) $30. Caliboro's first-ever release sports excellent aromatics. But like any serious red made from young grapes, it's not terribly concentrated.

The mouthfeel is light, while the depth and texture are modest. Still, it offers a glimpse of what's to come, and the future looks bright. A blend of 60% Cabernet Sauvignon, 30% Merlot, and 10% Cabernet Franc. **88** *—M.S. (11/1/2005)*

CALINA

Calina 2000 Reserve Cabernet Sauvignon-Carmenère (Maule Valley) $13. 86 *—D.T. (7/1/2002)*

Calina 2000 Reserve Cabernet Sauvignon (Colchagua Valley) $8. 84 *—S.H. (6/1/2001)*

Calina 2002 Reserve Carmenère (Maule Valley) $8. Made when Kendall-Jackson still owned this label, and it's a pretty decent legacy in terms of value-priced Carmenère. The bouquet features leather, cherry, caramel, and some foresty nuance, while the round palate is loaded with plum and dark berry. Some light oak and vanilla on the finish softens the back end. **85 Best Buy** *—M.S. (6/1/2004)*

Calina 2000 Reserve Carmenère (Maule Valley) $8. 90 *—S.H. (11/15/2001)*

Calina 2002 Reserve Chardonnay (Casablanca Valley) $8. This former Kendall-Jackson label produced a good, pedestrian Chard in 2002. It's fat, sweet, and goes heavy on the pear and apple. Finishes plump, lean, and clean. A simple yet confectionary white. **85 Best Buy** *—M.S. (8/1/2004)*

Calina 1996 Merlot (Maule Valley) $16. 90 *(11/15/1999)*

Calina 2001 Reserve Merlot (Maule Valley) $8. 86 *—M.S. (7/1/2003)*

CALITERRA

Caliterra 1998 Cabernet Sauvignon (Valle Central) $8. 84 *—M.S. (12/1/1999)*

Caliterra 2000 Cabernet Sauvignon (Colchagua Valley) $9. 87 *—M.S. (3/1/2002)*

Caliterra 1997 Reserve Cabernet Sauvignon (Maipo Valley) $13. 88 *—M.S. (12/1/1999)*

Caliterra 2001 Chardonnay (Valle Central) $8. 88 Best Buy *—S.H. (12/1/2002)*

Caliterra 1999 Chardonnay (Valle Central) $8. 86 *—S.H. (2/1/2001)*

Caliterra 2003 Merlot (Rapel Valley) $7. Strawberry preserves, leather, and some funk create an adequate nose, while the palate offers cherry, plum, and black olive. Seems salty and/or pickled on the finish. **83** *—M.S. (7/1/2005)*

Caliterra 2001 Merlot (Valle Central) $8. 83 *—D.T. (7/1/2002)*

Caliterra 1999 Merlot (Valle Central) $10. 85 *(10/1/2001)*

Caliterra 2003 Sauvignon Blanc (Valle Central) $8. Open on the bouquet, and very citrusy. This is one clean, lean wine. It's got forward lemon, lime, and orange flavors that ride nicely on the zippy, crisp palate. Good acids and modest depth make it a good bet for summer. **85 Best Buy** *—M.S. (6/1/2004)*

Caliterra 2000 Sauvignon Blanc (Valle Central) $9. 86 Best Buy *(10/1/2001)*

Caliterra 2001 Syrah (Valle Central) $NA. Scattered and gaseous at first, and only later does it show any true berry aromas. The palate offers mostly sour cherry and rhubarb, while the finish is raw and grippy. Not offputting, but could use more charm. **83** *—M.S. (6/1/2004)*

CANEPA

Canepa 1998 Chardonnay (Rancagua) $10. 80 *—M.S. (11/15/1999)*

CARMEN

Carmen 1999 Reserve Cabernet Blend (Maipo Valley) $15. 89 Best Buy *—S.H. (12/1/2002)*

Carmen 1999 Cabernet Sauvignon (Valle Central) $8. 84 *—D.T. (8/1/2001)*

Carmen 2003 Classic Cabernet Sauvignon (Maipo Valley) $7. Solid Chilean Cab, with herbal notes and chewy cassis and chocolate flavors. Fine with burgers and the like. **84** *(12/15/2004)*

Carmen 2001 Gold Reserve Cabernet Sauvignon (Maipo Valley) $70. With some rubber, prune, and earth, the nose is well put together. A second act of blackberry, cassis, and tobacco flavors is endearing, while the dark, woodsy finish is masculine, leaving a leftover espresso character. A touch heavy and awkward, but packs power. **88** *—M.S. (7/1/2005)*

Carmen 1999 Gold Reserve-Estate Bottled-Single Vineyard Cabernet Sauvignon (Maipo Valley) $65. 88 *—C.S. (12/1/2002)*

Carmen 2002 Nativa Cabernet Sauvignon (Maipo Valley) $16. Aggressive all the way, with a heartily toasted nose that conceals leather and stable aromas. Quite tannic and bitter on the palate, but also loaded with coffee and background notes of coconut. **86** *—M.S. (7/1/2005)*

Carmen 1999 Nativa Cabernet Sauvignon (Maipo Valley) $15. 85 *—M.S. (3/1/2002)*

Carmen 2002 Reserve Cabernet Sauvignon (Maipo Valley) $14. Lots of wood influence (14 months; one-third new) gives this wine a cedary, vanilla-laden sheen layered atop a base of cassis-flavored fruit. Creamy and supple, with some drying tannis showing up on the finish. **87** *(12/15/2004)*

Carmen 1999 Reserve Cabernet Sauvignon (Maipo Valley) $15. 87 *—M.S. (3/1/2002)*

Carmen 2003 Carmenère (Rapel Valley) $7. Spicy and grassy, from nose to palate to finish. The feel is snappy and charged up, with jumpy acids and pie cherry flavors. Finishes tangy and saucy. **82** *—M.S. (11/1/2005)*

Carmen 2002 Reserve Carmenère-Cabernet Sauvignon (Maipo Valley) $16. Quite leafy, with green olive but also some currant on the nose. Just when you think it might be too green, the Cab element rises up and to the fore come cassis, cherry, and herb flavors. Spicy and broad on the finish, with hints of spice and chocolate. **86** *—M.S. (11/1/2005)*

Carmen 2001 Chardonnay (Central Valley) $8. 85 *—M.S. (3/1/2002)*

Carmen 2002 Classic Chardonnay (Central Valley) $8. 85 *—M.S. (7/1/2003)*

Carmen 2000 Nativa Chardonnay (Maipo Valley) $13. 87 *—M.S. (3/1/2002)*

Carmen 1997 Reserva Chardonnay (Maipo Valley) $11. 85 *—M.N. (2/1/2001)*

Carmen 2001 Reserve Chardonnay (Maipo Valley) $13. 87 *—M.S. (3/1/2002)*

Carmen 2002 Winemaker's Reserve Chardonnay (Casablanca Valley) $45. Gold in color, and heavily oaked. The nose offers distant toast as well as oak and apple flavors. Quite chunky and soft, with a chalky, dry, rather flavor-free finish. Aging fast, with little zest. **83** *—M.S. (7/1/2005)*

Carmen 1997 Winemaker's Reserve Chardonnay (Casablanca Valley) $25. Handsomely constructed, this well-balanced Chardonnay is evidence of Chile's moving up in quality . . . and price. Attractive apple and tropical fruit aromas and flavors are supported by present, not overwhelming oak. The mouthfeel is round, the acidity adequate and the finish nicely spicy. A solid Chilean competitor in this price range. **89** *—M.M. (1/1/2004)*

Carmen 2003 Classic Merlot (Rapel Valley) $7. Slightly weedy and herbal, but it also boasts ripe plums and black cherries alongside mocha and caramel notes that make it easy to drink. **85 Best Buy** *(12/15/2004)*

Carmen 2002 Reserve Merlot (Rapel Valley) $14. After a year in a combination of French and American oak, this medium-weight Merlot has acquired pleasant smoke and dried spice notes that accent its tobacco and black cherry flavors. Supple tannins, crisp acids on the finish. **87** *(12/15/2004)*

Carmen 2000 Reserve Merlot (Rapel Valley) $15. 85 *—S.H. (12/1/2002)*

Carmen 1999 Reserve Merlot (Rapel Valley) $15. 85 *—J.C. (3/1/2002)*

Carmen 1999 Reserve Pinot Noir (Maipo Valley) $17. 83 *—J.C. (3/1/2002)*

Carmen 2000 Winemaker's Reserve Red Blend (Maipo Valley) $40. An excellent Bordeaux-style blend. The nose is deep and smoky, with a readiness that's exemplary. Rich, clean, and integrated on the palate, with layering and style. Sure, it's powerful and fruity, but there's also some mature subtlety to it. Really hits the spot. One of Carmen's best wines in years. **91 Editors' Choice** *—M.S. (11/1/2005)*

Carmen 1999 Winemaker's Reserve Red Blend (Maipo Valley) $40. 90 Editors' Choice *—C.S. (12/1/2002)*

Carmen 2002 Classic Sauvignon Blanc (Valle Central) $7. 85 Best Buy *—M.S. (7/1/2003)*

Carmen 2003 Reserve Sauvignon Blanc (Casablanca Valley) $14. Smoky and a bit flinty, this wine does reveal a mineral aspect of Chilean Sauvignon Blanc. It's also very citrusy, with flavors that run toward grapefruit and lime. **84** *(12/15/2004)*

Carmen 2001 Reserve Sauvignon Blanc (Casablanca Valley) $13. 86 *—M.S. (3/1/2002)*

Carmen 2002 Reserve Shiraz (Maipo Valley) $17. Dark and pruny, with molasses, chocolate, and beet juice on the nose. Semisweet raspberry and strawberry flavors set up a racy finish that carries live acidity and some serious tannins. **85** *—M.S. (2/1/2005)*

CARTA VIEJA

Carta Vieja 2003 Chardonnay (Maule Valley) $8. Funky and lactic, with sweet, heavy fruit that falls into the canned pear and apple class. Heavy on the finish, with some green bean and asparagus poking through the mix. **81** *—M.S. (7/1/2005)*

Carta Vieja 2003 Sauvignon Blanc (Maule Valley) $8. Melon and crushed children's vitamins comprise the nose, while spiked tangerine and pineapple flavors carry the palate. Fairly solid, with an almost jazzy mouthfeel. **83** *—M.S. (7/1/2005)*

CASA JULIA

Casa Julia 2000 Cabernet Sauvignon (Maipo Valley) $9. 82 *(7/1/2002)*

Casa Julia 2001 Reserve Cabernet Sauvignon (Maipo Valley) $12. 88 Best Buy *—M.S. (7/1/2003)*

Casa Julia 2002 Merlot (Rapel Valley) $8. 85 Best Buy *—M.S. (7/1/2003)*

Casa Julia 2000 Merlot (Rapel Valley) $9. 85 *—D.T. (7/1/2002)*

Casa Julia 2003 Sauvignon Blanc (Maule Valley) $10. Light peach, melon, and orange aromas sit in front of mildly sour tangerine and grapefruit flavors. Acidic, with a sharp finish, but ultimately it's clean. **82** *—M.S. (7/1/2005)*

Casa Julia 2001 Syrah (Maipo Valley) $8. 84 *—M.S. (7/1/2003)*

CASA LAPOSTOLLE

Casa Lapostolle 2003 Cabernet Sauvignon (Rapel Valley) $10. Intense and saturated, with dark aromas of pencil lead, tree bark, cola, and black fruits. In the mouth, it's full-force Cabernet. The blackberry and black cherry flavors are pure and satisfying, while the finish offers smoke, chocolate, and coffee. This wine features ripeness and an overall quality rarely achieved by others in the price range. **90 Best Buy** *—M.S. (11/1/2005)*

Casa Lapostolle 1999 Cabernet Sauvignon (Rapel Valley) $10. 81 *—J.C. (3/1/2002)*

Casa Lapostolle 2001 Cuvée Alexandre Apalta Vineyard Cabernet Sauvignon (Colchagua Valley) $22. Excellent Cabernet at any price, and one of the best Lapostolle wines we've tasted. Pitch dark and layered, with pulsating berry, tobacco, earth, and charcoal aromas. Luscious on the palate, where plum, cherry, and cassis flow toward a classic finish of soft tannins and chocolate. Immensely ripe and tasty. **92 Editors' Choice** *(3/1/2005)*

Casa Lapostolle 1998 Cuvée Alexandre Cabernet Sauvignon (Colchagua Valley) $25. 85 *—D.T. (8/1/2001)*

Casa Lapostolle 2003 Chardonnay (Casablanca Valley) $10. A touch creamy and fat on the bouquet, but backed by peach and tangerine flavors that sing of ripeness. Finishes scouring and tangy, but incredibly fresh. **87 Best Buy** *(3/1/2005)*

Casa Lapostolle 2001 Chardonnay (Casablanca Valley) $10. 88 Best Buy *—M.S. (11/15/2003)*

Casa Lapostolle 2003 Cuvée Alexandre Atalayas Vineyard Chardonnay (Casablanca Valley) $18. Surely one of the finest Chardonnays in Chile. The balance, level of toast, and depth make it world class. Peach, buttered toast, and nuts make for a fine palate, while the finish is warm and dotted with the flavor of toasted almonds and walnuts. Pretty and defined. **90 Editors' Choice** *(3/1/2005)*

Casa Lapostolle 2002 Cuvée Alexandre Chardonnay (Casablanca Valley) $17. A whiff of popcorn adds character to the nose, which is dominated by white stone fruits and apple. The palate offers pear, apple, and melon flavors, and then more popcorn-tinged oak. Even the finish is long and woody. If you like a ripe, well-crafted Chard with ample oak, this is for you. Fans of stripped down, natural Chards may find it too bolstered. **89** *—M.S. (6/1/2004)*

Casa Lapostolle 2000 Merlot (Rapel Valley) $11. 81 *—J.C. (3/1/2002)*

Casa Lapostolle 2002 Cuvée Alexandre Apalta Vineyard Merlot (Colchagua Valley) $19. Black cherry and mocha kick it off, while deep sniffers may uncover some eucalyptus and basil. Very supple and creamy, with seemingly edible plum and chocolate flavors gracing the full-bodied palate. Substantially complex for a wine this big and easy. **91 Editors' Choice** *(3/1/2005)*

Casa Lapostolle 2001 Cuvée Alexandre Merlot (Colchagua Valley) $20. A meaty, smoky, leathery current flows through the ripe bouquet, followed by tons of blackberry, chocolate, and clove flavors. Finishing touches of coffee and burnt toast mostly mask the mild green note one detects on the back palate. **88** *—M.S. (6/1/2004)*

Casa Lapostolle 1998 Cuvée Alexandre Merlot (Rapel Valley) $22. 85 *—J.F. (8/1/2001)*

Casa Lapostolle 2001 Apalta Red Blend (Colchagua Valley) $55. Full and forceful, with aromas of green herbs piercing the cassis and cherry aromas that carry the bouquet. With molasses, cassis, and black-plum flavors, it seems to have all that the wine is known for; however, there's also a green, tomato-like presence that may stem from the higher level of Carmenère that's going into the wine. **88** *—M.S. (6/1/2004)*

Casa Lapostolle 1999 Clos Apalta Red Blend (Chile) $60. 94 Editors' Choice *—M.S. (3/1/2002)*

Casa Lapostolle 2001 Sauvignon Blanc (Casablanca Valley) $8. 85 *—M.S. (3/1/2002)*

Casa Lapostolle 2003 Estate Bottled Sauvignon Blanc (Rapel Valley) $9. Aromatic but slightly bland. This is a textbook "starter" Sauvignon that will go down well. The plain palate is round, with notes of bitter herbs, apple, banana, and black pepper. The lasting mouthfeel is moderately thick and resiny. **85** *—M.S. (6/1/2004)*

Casa Lapostolle 2001 Cuvée Alexandre Syrah (Rapel Valley) $20. 88 *—M.S. (7/1/2003)*

CASA RIVAS

Casa Rivas 2001 Reserva Estate Bottled Cabernet Sauvignon (Maipo Valley) $10. 84 *—M.S. (12/1/2002)*

Casa Rivas 2002 Carmenère (Maipo Valley) $7. Quite herbal on the nose, with aromas of tomato and green peppers. In a word, it's basic Carmenère, with a fair amount of vegetal character. Under that, however, are pie cherry and raspberry flavors as well as piercing, razor-like acids. As a result, it's tangy and sharp. **83** *—M.S. (6/1/2004)*

Casa Rivas 2002 Gran Reserva Carmenère (Maipo Valley) $22. Herbal and cool on the bouquet, with a dark, masculine color. The palate is sweet and plummy, with berry nuances. Tannins come up on the finish, which is ripe and pulsing. Overall, it's integrated and original, a decent bet within the Carmenère category. **86** *—M.S. (6/1/2004)*

Casa Rivas 2002 Estate Bottled Chardonnay (Maipo Valley) $6. 84 *—M.S. (7/1/2003)*

Casa Rivas 2003 Merlot (Maipo Valley) $7. Quite green and minty, and that unripe, herbal streak continues onto the palate, where bell pepper takes over. Lean and clean on the finish, however, to such a point that it simply disappears. **82** *—M.S. (7/1/2005)*

Casa Rivas 2001 Estate Bottled Merlot (Maipo Valley) $6. **86** *—K.F. (12/1/2002)*

Casa Rivas 2003 Sauvignon Blanc (Maipo Valley) $7. Fresh and clean, as it should be. Round and full across the palate, with a forceful, direct orange flavor and little else getting in the way. Some lemon zest on the finish brings this easy drinker home. Not complex, but a nice quaff if properly chilled. **86 Best Buy** *—M.S. (6/1/2004)*

CASA SILVA

Casa Silva 2000 Quinta Generacion Cabernet Blend (Colchagua Valley) $25. **88** *—M.S. (7/1/2003)*

Casa Silva 2000 Classic Carmenère (Colchagua Valley) $10. **88 Best Buy** *—M.S. (3/1/2002)*

Casa Silva 2001 Reserve Estate Bottled Carmenère (Colchagua Valley) $15. **88** *—M.S. (7/1/2003)*

Casa Silva 2000 Reserve Merlot (Colchagua Valley) $15. **88** *—M.S. (3/1/2002)*

Casa Silva 2000 Quinta Generacion White Blend (Colchagua Valley) $20. **86** *—M.S. (3/1/2002)*

CHÂTEAU LA JOYA

Château La Joya 1998 Gran Reserva Cabernet Sauvignon (Colchagua Valley) $15. **87** *(6/1/2001)*

Château La Joya 1999 Reserva Cabernet Sauvignon (Colchagua Valley) $10. **87 Best Buy** *(6/1/2001)*

Château La Joya 2000 Gran Reserva Carmenère (Colchagua Valley) $20. **88** *—M.S. (3/1/2002)*

Château La Joya 1999 Gran Reserva Chardonnay (Colchagua Valley) $10. **86** *(6/1/2001)*

Château La Joya 2000 Reserva Chardonnay (Colchagua Valley) $10. **84** *(6/1/2001)*

Château La Joya 2001 Estate Bottled Reserve Malbec (Colchagua Valley) $12. **84** *—M.S. (7/1/2003)*

Château La Joya 2000 Gran Reserva Merlot (Colchagua Valley) $16. **87** *—M.S. (3/1/2002)*

Château La Joya 1999 Estate Bottled Gran Reserve Merlot (Colchagua Valley) $15. **87** *—C.S. (2/1/2003)*

Château La Joya 1999 Reserva Merlot (Colchagua Valley) $10. **84** *(6/1/2001)*

CHÂTEAU LOS BOLDOS

Château Los Boldos 1998 Grand Cru Cabernet Sauvignon (Requinoa) $45. **89** *—C.S. (12/1/2002)*

Château Los Boldos 1997 Grand Cru Cabernet Sauvignon-Merlot (Requinoa) $40. **87** *—D.T. (7/1/2002)*

Château Los Boldos 2001 Vielles Vignes Chardonnay (Requinoa) $16. **86** *—M.S. (7/1/2003)*

CONCHA Y TORO

Concha y Toro 2000 Almaviva Cabernet Blend (Puente Alto) $91. **92 Cellar Selection** *—M.S. (12/1/2002)*

Concha y Toro 2003 Casillero del Diablo Cabernet Sauvignon (Central Valley) $9. Dark in the glass, with dense fruitcake aromas along with notes of molasses and dried cherry. The palate is round and big, and the finish deals a heavy blast of grilled beef and coffee. Almost at the next level, but still a little awkward and bulky. **86 Best Buy** *—M.S. (8/1/2004)*

Concha y Toro 2000 Casillero del Diablo Cabernet Sauvignon (Maipo Valley) $10. **85** *(12/31/2001)*

Concha y Toro 1998 Casillero del Diablo Cabernet Sauvignon (Maipo Valley) $10. **85** *—M.S. (12/1/1999)*

Concha y Toro 1998 Don Melchor Cabernet Sauvignon (Maipo Valley) $40. **87** *—M.S. (3/1/2002)*

Concha y Toro 2001 Marqués de Casa Concha Cabernet Sauvignon (Rapel Valley) $16. This sensational value has a range of flavors, structure and other important characteristics that some wines costing five times more can't match. The nose is full of plum, black fruit, and coffee, while the palate is pure dynamite; it's a textbook modern Cabernet that hits the target squarely in the center. **91 Editors' Choice** *—M.S. (3/1/2004)*

Concha y Toro 1999 Marqués de Casa Concha Cabernet Sauvignon (Puente Alto) $15. **87** *(12/31/2001)*

Concha y Toro 1997 Private Reserve Don Melchor Cabernet Sauvignon (Maipo Valley) $40. **88** *—M.S. (2/1/2001)*

Concha y Toro 2001 Terrunyo Cabernet Sauvignon (Maipo Valley) $29. This luscious Cabernet makes you think that the Stags Leap District came to the Maipo Valley and dropped off a few secrets before heading home. Gorgeous leather and black fruit mix on the burly nose, which is backed up by lead pencil, tobacco and cassis. **92 Cellar Selection** *—M.S. (3/1/2004)*

Concha y Toro 1997 Terrunyo Cabernet Sauvignon (Maipo Valley) $29. **87** *—J.C. (2/1/2001)*

Concha y Toro 2004 Xplorador Cabernet Sauvignon (Central Valley) $7. Kicks off with some balsamic and olive aromas, while the palate is full of black cherry and berry fruit. Round and clean, with a soft feel despite having real tannic backbone. Likable in a mainstream way. **86 Best Buy** *—M.S. (11/1/2005)*

Concha y Toro 2001 Xplorador Cabernet Sauvignon (Maipo Valley) $8. 85 Best Buy *—M.S. (7/1/2003)*

Concha y Toro 2003 Casillero del Diablo Carmenère (Rapel Valley) $10. Exuberant on the nose, with rich blackberry, rubber, and bacon. Generous and bright on the palate, where cherry and blackberry flavors start vividly and then are softened by creamy, chocolaty oak. Best of all, there's nothing vegetal about it. **87 Best Buy** *—M.S. (5/30/2005)*

Concha y Toro 2003 Frontera Carmenère (Valle Central) $11. It may have been abandoned in its Bordeaux home, but Carmenère has found a home and a new life in Chile. It makes red wines with good juicy fruit, freshness, flavors of ripe plums. This example, blended with 10% Cabernet Sauvignon and 5% Syrah, is a great wine just to drink, full of fruit, with a touch of toast, vanilla, and smooth tannins. **84 Best Buy** *—R.V. (11/15/2004)*

Concha y Toro 2001 Terrunyo Carmenère (Cachapoal Valley) $28. Saturated and dark, with intoxicating aromas of mint, cola, mushroom, herbs, and black fruit. Very rich and smooth, with a meaty, chewy texture. Fruity throughout, with an espresso-like bitterness to the finish. This is Carmenère made in a forward, modern style, with no vegetal flavors. **89** *—M.S. (8/1/2004)*

Concha y Toro 1999 Terrunyo Carmenère (Peumo) $29. 91 *—M.S. (3/1/2002)*

Concha y Toro 2002 Amelia Chardonnay (Casablanca Valley) $33. The winemakers at CyT intentionally lowered the oak level on this wine, and now it's a much better Amelia than what we tasted in the past. It's still a figgy, round wine with papaya, pear, and banana, but the transition from palate to finish is seamless. And without all that wood, you really taste the purity of the Casablanca fruit. **90** *—M.S. (3/1/2004)*

Concha y Toro 2001 Amelia Limited Release Chardonnay (Casablanca Valley) $33. 88 *—M.S. (7/1/2003)*

Concha y Toro 2004 Casillero del Diablo Chardonnay (Central Valley) $9. Nice and clean, with ample stone fruit and apple aromas. No, not a lot of nuance on display. But plenty of ripe, pure apple and melon flavors followed by some length on the mildly creamy finish. Solid, with mass-market appeal. **87 Best Buy** *—M.S. (11/1/2005)*

Concha y Toro 2001 Casillero del Diablo Chardonnay (Casablanca Valley) $10. 86 *—M.S. (7/1/2003)*

Concha y Toro 1998 Casillero del Diablo Chardonnay (Casablanca Valley) $10. 85 *—M.S. (12/1/1999)*

CHILE

Concha y Toro 2000 Marqués de Casa Concha Chardonnay (Pirque) $15. 90 Editors' Choice *(12/31/2001)*

Concha y Toro 2002 Terrunyo Chardonnay (Casablanca Valley) $25. Smooth, with more integrated oak than the other Chardonnays. Flavors of green apple, fresh pear and vanilla are tasty and supported by a touch of wood. Fine acids stop short of being harsh, creating lasting melon and nectarine notes. **89** *—M.S. (3/1/2004)*

Concha y Toro 1998 Trio Chardonnay (Casablanca Valley) $9. 84 *—M.S. (12/1/1999)*

Concha y Toro 2003 Xplorador Chardonnay (Central Valley) $7. Given the price range at which this wine competes, it's something. The aromas are clean and pure: there's attractive honey, pineapple, and citrus. Cuddly flavors of orange, melon, and pear are harmonious, while the finish is clean and pure, albeit short. Medium-bodied and satisfying. **86 Best Buy** *—M.S. (6/1/2004)*

Concha y Toro 2001 Xplorador Chardonnay (Casablanca Valley) $7. 86 *—M.S. (7/1/2003)*

Concha y Toro 1999 Xplorador Chardonnay (Casablanca Valley) $8. 84 *—J.C. (2/1/2001)*

Concha y Toro 2003 Casillero del Diablo Merlot (Valle Central) $10. Huge and colorful, and very youthful. For density and lushness on what can best be described as basic Merlot, you're not going to find it much better than this. It's all blackberry, chocolate, and berries, but somehow they've squeezed some earth and spice in there as well. **88 Best Buy** *—M.S. (3/1/2004)*

Concha y Toro 2000 Casillero del Diablo Merlot (Rapel Valley) $10. 86 *(12/31/2001)*

Concha y Toro 2001 Marqués de Casa Concha Merlot (Peumo) $14. 87 *—M.S. (7/1/2003)*

Concha y Toro 1999 Marqués de Casa Concha Merlot (Peumo) $15. 88 *—J.C. (12/31/2001)*

Concha y Toro 2003 Marqués de Casa Concha Merlot (Peumo) $14. A wine the band Deep Purple could get into, because it's just that color and it rocks. The bouquet is dusty and loaded with dark chocolate and ripe blackberry. In the mouth, there's nothing miserly about it: lush plum, blackberry, and licorice flavors are full and forward. Highly enjoyable, especially at this price. **89 Best Buy** *—M.S. (11/1/2005)*

Concha y Toro 2004 Xplorador Merlot (Central Valley) $7. A bit hot and burnt, with wiry, raw fruit. But for the money it's a sturdy, drinkable red wine. Shows sticky black fruit and a bulky finish. Fits the bill at its price point. **83** *—M.S. (11/1/2005)*

Concha y Toro 2002 Xplorador Merlot (Rapel Valley) $7. 87 Best Buy *—M.S. (7/1/2003)*

Concha y Toro 1999 Xplorador Merlot (Rapel Valley) $8. 85 *—J.C. (2/1/2001)*

Concha y Toro 2002 Block 30 Terrunyo Sauvignon Blanc (Casablanca Valley) $20. 89 *—M.S. (7/1/2003)*

Concha y Toro 2003 Casillero del Diablo Sauvignon Blanc (Valle Central) $10. One sniff reveals solid grapefruit and other textbook aromas. Then a sip delivers pink grapefruit and a consistent, acid-propped attack. Some tangerine appears on the finish before it slips away quietly. **86 Best Buy** *—M.S. (3/1/2004)*

Concha y Toro 1999 Late Harvest Sauvignon Blanc (Maule Valley) $15. 89 *—J.M. (12/1/2002)*

Concha y Toro 2003 Terrunyo Sauvignon Blanc (Casablanca Valley) $20. This reserve-level bottling continues to set the bar for Chilean Sauvignon Blanc, and the credit goes to Ignacio Recabarren, the maestro behind CyT's Terrunyo line. It features intense nectarine, snap pea, and cucumber aromas followed by a sensational mouthful of citrus and minerals. **90** *—M.S. (3/1/2004)*

Concha y Toro 1999 Terrunyo Sauvignon Blanc (Casablanca Valley) $29. 88 *—J.C. (2/1/2001)*

CONDE DE VELÁZQUEZ

Conde de Velázquez 2001 El Conde Gran Reserva Cabernet Sauvignon (Aconcagua Valley) $10. Basic red plum, currant, and cough syrup are more than adequate aromas, while the palate offers tasty cherry and cassis. Very candied and won't be confused for a great wine, but serviceable. **84** *—M.S. (7/1/2005)*

Conde de Velázquez 2001 Reserva Cabernet Sauvignon (Aconcagua Valley) $7. Rubbery, with harsh aromas that seem weedy. Better on the palate, where strawberry and raspberry flavors rise up. Finishes grassy and leathery. **81** *—M.S. (7/1/2005)*

Conde de Velázquez 2003 El Conde Gran Reserva Chardonnay (Aconcagua Valley) $11. Yellow in color, and rather oaky. Spice and vanilla are the lead aromas and flavors, with peach, melon, and toast in the background. On the finish, the wood really rises up, creating cured ham and smoke aftertastes. Unusual for Chile. **84** *—M.S. (11/1/2005)*

Conde de Velázquez 2003 Sauvignon Blanc (Aconcagua Valley) $7. Tight and lemony, with sharp citrus aromas along with flavors of orange and other citrus fruits. Offers some texture and body, with freshness. **84 Best Buy** *—M.S. (2/1/2005)*

Conde de Velázquez 2002 Reserva Syrah (Aconcagua Valley) $7. Candied up front, with unfocused, murky aromas. The palate is lean and hot, with thin fruit and not much feel. Nothing horrible but nothing to get excited about. **81** *—M.S. (2/1/2005)*

CONO SUR

Cono Sur 2001 Reserve Merlot (Rapel Valley) $12. 85 *—M.S. (7/1/2003)*

Cono Sur 2001 Reserve Pinot Noir (Casablanca Valley) $12. 82 *—M.S. (7/1/2003)*

COUSIÑO-MACUL

Cousiño-Macul 2002 Antiguas Reservas Cabernet Sauvignon (Maipo Valley) $13. Starts out emitting the essence of tire rubber before settling down to show cooked fruit and tree bark. Remains stewy and deep throughout, with some grittiness to the mouthfeel. Not focused and fresh enough to rate higher. **83** *—M.S. (7/1/2005)*

Cousiño-Macul 1997 Antiguas Reservas Cabernet Sauvignon (Maipo Valley) $13. 83 *(2/1/2001)*

Cousiño-Macul 2002 Finis Terrae Cabernet Sauvignon-Merlot (Maipo Valley) $30. It is 55% Cabernet and 45% Merlot, mostly from the winery's new Buin vineyards, and it features a heavily toasted, oaky nose but also some solid fruit. The fruit is riper and richer than anything the winery did at Macul, as proven by its dark chocolate and blackberry qualities. Some spice and a nip of green pepper carry the finish. **88** *—M.S. (3/1/2004)*

Cousiño-Macul 2004 Chardonnay (Maipo Valley) $9. Too much scrambled egg and burnt, gaseous notes on the nose. Spritzy on the palate, with oak and banana flavors. Barely acceptable. **80** *—M.S. (7/1/2005)*

Cousiño-Macul 2003 Antiguas Reservas Chardonnay (Maipo Valley) $13. The opening aromas entail peach, pear, and some light oak—just what you'd hope for from a Chilean Chardonnay. Since only part of the wine was barrel aged, the body holds onto some snap and clarity. Still, some vanilla and lees character create richness and ultimately a good wine. **87** *—M.S. (3/1/2004)*

Cousiño-Macul 2001 Merlot (Maipo Valley) $9. 84 *—M.S. (7/1/2003)*

Cousiño-Macul 1998 Reserva Merlot (Maipo Valley) $15. 86 *(2/1/2001)*

Cousiño-Macul 2003 Doña Isadora Riesling (Maipo Valley) $9. Lately, this rather unique Riesling seems to have found its calling. It's big and chewy, and very un-German. The bouquet deals melon, honey, and floral notes, which are capped by dry, minerally stone-fruit flavors that spread onto the long finish. A pleasant surprise. **88 Best Buy** *—M.S. (3/1/2004)*

Cousiño-Macul 1999 Doña Isidora Riesling (Maipo Valley) $14. 82 *(2/1/2001)*

D. BOSLER

D. Bosler 2002 Birdsnest Pinot Noir (Casablanca Valley) $10. From Casa Julia, this is one of the better, more varietally correct Pinot Noirs

Chile is making. The nose is dry, leathery, and earthy, with a punch of cherry. The dried red fruit on the palate is intense and gritty, with racy acidity ensuring a brisk feel. **87 Best Buy** *—M.S. (7/1/2005)*

DALLAS CONTÉ

Dallas Conté 2000 Cabernet Sauvignon (Rapel Valley) $10. 85 *—M.S. (7/1/2003)*

Dallas Conté 1997 Cabernet Sauvignon (Colchagua Valley) $10. 88 *—M.S. (8/1/2000)*

Dallas Conté 2002 Chardonnay (Casablanca Valley) $10. 84 *—M.S. (7/1/2003)*

Dallas Conté 2001 Merlot (Rapel Valley) $10. Heavily oaked, with a strong essence of lemon on the nose and throughout. Flavors of tart cherry and bitter chocolate create a tangy, dark whole, while the overall feel is edgy and sharp. **84** *—M.S. (8/1/2004)*

Dallas Conté 1997 Merlot (Colchagua Valley) $10. 87 *—M.S. (5/1/2000)*

DE MARTINO

De Martino 1999 Estate Bottled Prima Reserva Cabernet Sauvignon (Maipo Valley) $13. 84 *—M.S. (12/1/2002)*

De Martino 1997 Reserva de Familia Cabernet Sauvignon (Maipo Valley) $35. 85 *—D.T. (8/1/2001)*

De Martino 1999 Prima Reserva Carmenère (Maipo Valley) $12. 89 *—M.S. (7/1/2003)*

De Martino 1999 Estate Bottled Chardonnay (Maipo Valley) $10. 81 *(2/1/2001)*

De Martino 1999 Prima Reserva Chardonnay (Maipo Valley) $13. 82 *(2/1/2001)*

De Martino 2000 Estate Bottled Prima Reserva Merlot (Maipo Valley) $13. 90 Editors' Choice *—M.S. (12/1/2002)*

De Martino 1998 Reserva de Familia Red Blend (Maipo Valley) $35. 85 *—J.C. (8/1/2001)*

De Martino 2004 Legado Reserva Sauvignon Blanc (Maipo Valley) $15. Grassy and fresh, with hints of cucumber, pickle and citrus. From start to finish the wine is pure S.B. The mouth offers tangerine, orange and lemon on an herbal base, and the feel is zesty, clean, and fresh. **87** *—M.S. (7/1/2005)*

DOMAINES BARONS DE ROTHSCHILD

Domaines Barons de Rothschild (Lafite) 2000 Le Dix de Los Vascos Cabernet Sauvignon (Colchagua Valley) $40. Very Bordeaux-like up front, with minty, herbal aromas that lead into a palate defined by cherry, cola, and chocolate. The finish mixes good fruit with sweet, oaky undertones. **89** *—M.S. (3/1/2004)*

Domaines Barons de Rothschild (Lafite) 2002 Los Vascos Cabernet Sauvignon (Colchagua Valley) $10. Soft, thick, and chewy. Red plums and raspberries define the palate, which is backed by a modest, oaky finish. A bit lactic and plump, but tasty. **86** *—M.S. (3/1/2004)*

Domaines Barons de Rothschild (Lafite) 2003 Los Vascos Chardonnay (Colchagua Valley) $10. This wine sees no oak, offering stony white peach and melon aromas as well as a whiff of celery. The acidity tends to play up the apple in the flavor profile, but there's also some banana. **86 Best Buy** *—M.S. (3/1/2004)*

Domaines Barons de Rothschild (Lafite) 2003 Los Vascos Sauvignon Blanc (Colchagua Valley) $10. Nearly translucent in color, with crisp aromas of passion fruit and orange. It's fresh, with lemon, lime and grapefruit flavors. Sharp, but good if you enjoy the razor-like style. **87 Best Buy** *—M.S. (3/1/2004)*

DOMUS AUREA

Domus Aurea 1999 Cabernet Sauvignon (Maipo Valley) $42. Seems a touch weedy at first, without much fruit. But that's more a reflection of the wine's age than any inherent underripeness. Still, it's starting to fade, and quickly. There's not a lot of zest left, and the finish seems chocolaty and syrupy. Was better a couple of years ago; now it's on the slide. **85** *—M.S. (11/1/2005)*

DON RECA

Don Reca 2003 Chardonnay (Cachapoal Valley) $30. The nose yields banana and floral aromas, while in the mouth it's chunky and round, with apple, pear, and some wood spice. Decent but subdued given that it's the winery's top Chardonnay. **85** *—M.S. (3/1/2004)*

Don Reca 2002 Merlot-Cabernet Sauvignon (Cachapoal Valley) $30. After spending 12 months in French oak, there doesn't seem to be as much fruit present as wood. Still, the wine manages to come together in the middle to create a good final impression. **85** *—M.S. (3/1/2004)*

ECHEVERRÍA

Echeverría 1999 Family Reserve Cabernet Sauvignon (Molina) $29. Mature, with notes of raisin, leather, and tree bark. For an aged reserve-level Chilean Cab, it impresses. The palate still holds some cedary notes, but there's depth and nuance and fruit as well. A serious wine with warmth, structure and just enough sly fruit to earn its mark. **90** *—M.S. (2/1/2005)*

Echeverría 2001 Reserva Cabernet Sauvignon-Merlot (Curicó Valley) $18. Sweet, condensed, and loaded with berry jam and lots of oak. The palate pitches the full assortment of dark fruits: plum, black cherry, and their buddies are all here. Finishes solid. The wine is 70% Cab and the rest Merlot. **88** *—M.S. (12/1/2004)*

Echeverría 2003 Unwooded Chardonnay (Molina) $9. Aromas of fresh-squeezed orange juice and chewable children's vitamins attest to the fact there's no oak to be found. Along the way are soft citrus and melon flavors, and a chalky but thin finish. **82** —*M.S. (2/1/2005)*

Echeverría 1999 Reserva Merlot (Chile) $16. 84 —*D.T. (7/1/2002)*

EL GRANO

El Grano 2001 Carmenère (Rapel Valley) $10. 87 —*M.S. (11/15/2003)*

EL HUIQUE

El Huique 2002 Reserva Carmenère (Colchagua Valley) $12. Heavy on the nose, with aromas of leather, vegetables, and cheese. Better with air, displaying simple berry and plum before a light, easy finish. Straightforward in every sense. **83** —*M.S. (2/1/2005)*

ENCIERRA

Encierra 2002 Vineyard Reserve Red Blend (Colchagua Valley) $25. Nice and meaty, with raisin, leather, and crystallized candy on the beefy bouquet. Blackberry and licorice dominate the palate on this blend of Cabernet, Syrah, Carmenère, and Merlot. With nice tannins and extract, you get a mouthful. It's also a little obtuse and oaky. **87** —*M.S. (12/1/2004)*

ERRAZURIZ

Errazuriz 2001 Cabernet Sauvignon (Aconcagua Valley) $12. 87 Best Buy —*M.S. (7/1/2003)*

Errazuriz 2000 Don Maximiano Founder's Reserve Cabernet Sauvignon (Aconcagua Valley) $60. One of Chile's old-school, top-shelf Cabernets seems challenged in this vintage. The nose is herbal and mildly green, but underneath there's a sweet, meaty quality that serves it well. Black fruit and some creamy, chocolaty oak bring it around the bend; Bordeaux-like in its style. **88** —*M.S. (3/1/2004)*

Errazuriz 1997 El Ceibo Estate Cabernet Sauvignon (Aconcagua Valley) $8. 88 *(11/15/1999)*

Errazuriz 1999 El Ceibo Estate Cabernet Sauvignon (Aconcagua Valley) $10. 85 —*S.H. (6/1/2001)*

Errazuriz 2002 Estate Cabernet Sauvignon (Aconcagua Valley) $10. Broad and deep, with some rich, ripe aromatics some might called stewy. But the wine itself is balanced and healthy, with cassis, cherry, and tobacco flavors. The finish sports a liqueur-like sweetness, and the tannins are just right. **88 Best Buy** —*M.S. (6/1/2004)*

Errazuriz 2002 Max Reserva Cabernet Sauvignon (Aconcagua Valley) $19. Unconventional on the nose, with hints of leather, raisin and corn chips. Mostly smooth from palate to finish, with flavors of berries, cherry, and chocolate. Holds form on the finish, which is solid, chewy, and fruity. **85** —*M.S. (7/1/2005)*

Errazuriz 1999 Reserva Cabernet Sauvignon (Aconcagua Valley) $25. 87 —*S.H. (12/1/2002)*

Errazuriz 2000 Viñedo Chadwick Cabernet Sauvignon (Maipo Valley) $70. Intense and dense, with campfire to the nose along with black fruit and tar. The palate is equally dark, with flavors of charcoal-studded cassis and plum. Bitter chocolate and espresso is what defines the powerful finish. A manly wine made entirely from the Chadwick family's home vineyard in Puente Alto. **91** —*M.S. (3/1/2004)*

Errazuriz 2003 Don Maximiano Estate Single Vineyard Carmenère (Aconcagua Valley) $25. A throwback wine to the days when nobody knew much about Carmenère. Why? Because it's natural and terroir-based. The result of which is raw bell pepper and herbal flavors along with zingy red plum and raspberry. At one moment it's green and leafy; at the next you taste Bordeaux and revel in its earthiness. **85** —*M.S. (11/1/2005)*

Errazuriz 2004 Estate Chardonnay (Casablanca Valley) $11. Opens with peach, nectarine, and cinnamon notes. In the mouth, there are plump melon, apple, and banana flavors. Finishes a bit flat and flabby, but still wet enough to remain likable. Short on stuffing but better around the edges. **85** —*M.S. (7/1/2005)*

Errazuriz 2000 Estate Chardonnay (Casablanca Valley) $10. 84 —*M.S. (7/1/2002)*

Errazuriz 2000 La Escultura Estate Reserva Chardonnay (Casablanca Valley) $10. 86 Best Buy —*M.S. (7/1/2002)*

Errazuriz 2001 Wild Ferment Chardonnay (Casablanca Valley) $NA. A bit of popcorn and baked apple spice up the largely bland nose, while the palate deals lean apple and lemon flavors. All in all, it's a cleansing, easygoing wine, one with sharp, lemony notes and plenty of pure-acid zing. **85** —*M.S. (6/1/2004)*

Errazuriz 2000 Fumé Blanc (Casablanca Valley) $10. 85 —*S.H. (5/1/2001)*

Errazuriz 1999 Don Maximiano Estate Reserva Merlot (Aconcagua Valley) $25. 82 —*D.T. (7/1/2002)*

Errazuriz 2004 Estate Merlot (Curicó Valley) $11. A fair amount of coffee and mocha are present on the chunky nose, while the palate deals red plum fruit and only the mildest touch of green peppers. Snappy yet savory enough, with chocolate on the textured finish. **86 Best Buy** —*M.S. (11/1/2005)*

Errazuriz 2000 Max Reserva Merlot (Aconcagua Valley) $25. The early impression is that this wine is funky and a touch vegetal. The nose deals mostly pepper and leather, but not much ripe fruit. And while it never gets very rich or fruity, the mouthfeel is okay and it fans out and broadens on the slightly green finish. **83** —*M.N. (3/1/2004)*

Errazuriz 2004 Estate Sauvignon Blanc (Casablanca Valley) $11. Simple, fresh, and mainstream, with warm tropical fruit on the nose and palate. Full melon, citrus, and mineral flavors are integrated and satisfying. Finishes zesty and lively, with proper weight and texture. **87 Best Buy** *—M.S. (2/1/2005)*

Errazuriz 1999 La Escultura Sauvignon Blanc (Casablanca Valley) $10. **87** *—S.H. (2/1/2001)*

Errazuriz 2003 La Cumbre Shiraz (Aconcagua Valley) $39. Heavily toasted on the nose, with tobacco, leather, and vanilla along with powerful dark fruit. Sweet and plump in the mouth, with a solid mouthfeel that doesn't falter. Tasty and long on the tail, with the essence of coffee and an inkling of popcorn. Oaky and expensive, but still very good. **88** *—M.S. (11/1/2005)*

Errazuriz 1999 Don Maximiano Estate Reserva Syrah (Aconcagua Valley) $25. **86** *—D.T. (7/1/2002)*

FRANCISCO GILLMORE

Francisco Gillmore 1998 Cabernet Franc (Maule Valley) $27. **83** *—D.T. (7/1/2002)*

Francisco Gillmore 1998 Concepcion Gran Reserva Cabernet Sauvignon (Maule Valley) $11. **86** *—C.S. (2/1/2003)*

Francisco Gillmore 2001 Concepcion Chardonnay (Maule Valley) $7. **83** *—M.S. (7/1/2003)*

Francisco Gillmore 1999 Concepcion Reserva Chardonnay (Maule Valley) $11. **83** *—M.S. (7/1/2003)*

Francisco Gillmore 1999 Concepcion Reserva Merlot (Maule Valley) $11. **80** *—M.S. (7/1/2003)*

GRAN ARAUCANO

Gran Araucano 2003 Chardonnay (Colchagua Valley) $19. A reserve-level Chardonnay that's soft, yeasty, and smooth, but carries enough zip and structure to avoid being flabby. The toasty palate offers fine apple and lemon notes, but the main thing here is the wavy body the coddles plenty of oak, vanilla, and buttered toast. **89** *—M.S. (2/1/2005)*

Gran Araucano 2004 Sauvignon Blanc (Casablanca Valley) $19. Heavy grapefruit and asparagus aromas create that grassy, herbaceous nose that some love and others dislike. In the mouth, there's additional apple and citrus but still a lot of pickle and grass. Zesty on the tongue, but too herbaceous for these taste buds. **85** *—M.S. (7/1/2005)*

GRAN DOMINIO

Gran Dominio 1999 San Cayetano Vineyards Gran Reserva Cabernet Franc (Maule Valley) $19. **85** *—S.H. (1/1/2002)*

Gran Dominio 1999 Nueva Aldea Vineyard Chardonnay (Iata Valley) $14. **85** *—S.H. (1/1/2002)*

GRAN ROBLE

Gran Roble 2003 Carmenère (Curicó Valley) $11. Chunky, ripe, and meaty, with aromas of black cherry, raisin, cinnamon, and earth. One of this label's best offerings to date; the palate deals monotone but healthy plum flavors before a dark, espresso-tinged finish. No real depth or complexity, but good. **84** *—M.S. (11/1/2005)*

GUELBENZU

Guelbenzu 2002 Jardin Cabernet Blend (Colchagua Valley) $9. **85** *—M.S. (7/1/2003)*

HARAS

Haras 2003 Chardonnay (Maipo Valley) $11. Haras de Pirque's basic Chard works because it doesn't try to do too much. Basic peach, pear and pineapple aromas pave the way toward apple, coconut, and banana flavors. Good texture; solid at its core. **86 Best Buy** *—M.S. (2/1/2005)*

HARAS DE PIRQUE

Haras de Pirque 2001 Elegance Cabernet Sauvignon (Maipo Valley) $40. Soft yet firm, and sweet yet stylish. The nose is dark and loaded with coffee and mocha, while in the mouth the blackberry and cassis really flow forth. With length and size compounded by firm, integrated tannins, this is a very solid signature wine for this new winery. **91** *—M.S. (3/1/2004)*

Haras de Pirque 2002 Estate Carmenère (Maipo Valley) $11. Spicy and alive in the nose, with a touch of herbal green but also plenty of deeper berry fruit. This one tastes good; the palate is long and substantial, with chocolate and pepper notes jazzing it up. **87** *—M.S. (3/1/2004)*

Haras de Pirque 2003 Elegance Chardonnay (Maipo Valley) $25. Fairly smoky, with aromas of campfire and roasted corn. Woody on the palate, but also plenty of citrus in the form of lemon and orange. Consistent throughout, meaning the wood resin influence is primary. **85** *—M.S. (2/1/2005)*

Haras de Pirque 2002 Estate Chardonnay (Maipo Valley) $11. Zesty and driving, but with a true barrel-fermented personality. Flavors veer toward the tropical side of things, so look for mango, pineapple, and citrus. Some citrus pith and bitterness appear on the finish. **86** *—M.S. (3/1/2004)*

Haras de Pirque 2002 Estate Sauvignon Blanc (Maipo Valley) $11. Citrus, lemon, and honey aromas are big and clumsy, while overall the wine runs very thick and mouthfilling for Sauvignon Blanc. Maybe that's because 10% was aged in oak. As for flavors, look primarily for orange and grapefruit. **85** *—M.S. (3/1/2004)*

KINGSTON FAMILY

Kingston Family 2004 Alazan Pinot Noir (Casablanca Valley) $28. Hillside fruit yields a seductive wine with flowery aromas offset by black cherry. Settles on the meaty, earthy, brawny style, with vigorous bitter chocolate, caramel, and vanilla flavors stemming from the new oak. The real deal in Chilean Pinot Noir. **89** *—M.S. (11/1/2005)*

Kingston Family 2004 Cariblanco Sauvignon Blanc (Casablanca Valley) $15. The bouquet deals a fine mix of citrus, melon, bell pepper, and asparagus, yet it's not vegetal. Shows weight and sweetness on the palate, thus it will offset Asian foods like magic. Interestingly, it's fermented in stainless steel barrels, not tanks, and with natural yeasts. **90** *—M.S. (11/1/2005)*

KUYEN

Kuyen 2002 Red Wine (Maipo Valley) $22. Alvaro Espinoza, owner of this label, has thrown a lot of hot, spicy oak at this tannic heavyweight, and it may need a few years to show its true identity. For now, it's dark and brooding, with black plum, blackberry, and bitter chocolate flavors. Finishes rather hard and acidic, which time may tame. Needs food to match the vise-grip tannins. It's 70% Syrah and 30% Cabernet. **88** *—M.S. (2/1/2005)*

LA CAPITANA

La Capitana 2002 Carmenère (Cachapoal Valley) $12. Clean and fruity, with a meaty character that conveys ripeness. More spicy and interesting than some of the other wines from La Rosa, with most of what you want: spice, size, and fruit. **87** *—M.S. (3/1/2004)*

LA PALMA

La Palma 2003 Cabernet Sauvignon (Cachapoal Valley) $7. More deep and grapey than the Cab-Merlot blend, but ultimately it falls into the same general range of acceptability. Flavors of bubble gum seem less than pure. **83** *—M.S. (3/1/2004)*

La Palma 2001 Cabernet Sauvignon (Rapel Valley) $10. 87 Best Buy *—D.T. (7/1/2002)*

La Palma 1999 Reserve Cabernet Sauvignon (Rapel Valley) $10. 89 Best Buy *—J.C. (3/1/2002)*

La Palma 2001 Cabernet Sauvignon-Merlot (Rapel Valley) $10. 83 *—D.T. (7/1/2002)*

La Palma 1999 Reserve Cabernet Sauvignon-Merlot (Rapel Valley) $10. 85 *—D.T. (7/1/2002)*

La Palma 2003 Chardonnay (Cachapoal Valley) $8. Fruity, with floral aromas that are ripe and clean. Flavors of pineapple and the local cherimoya are thin but nice. If properly chilled down, this one has "quaffable" written all over it. **86 Best Buy** *—M.S. (3/1/2004)*

La Palma 2002 Chardonnay (Cachapoal Valley) $8. 83 *—M.S. (7/1/2003)*

La Palma 2000 Chardonnay (Rapel Valley) $6. 82 *—J.C. (3/1/2002)*

La Palma 1999 Reserve Chardonnay (Rapel Valley) $10. 85 *—J.F. (8/1/2001)*

La Palma 2002 Merlot (Cachapoal Valley) $7. 84 *—M.S. (7/1/2003)*

La Palma 2000 Merlot (Rapel Valley) $6. 84 Best Buy *—J.C. (3/1/2002)*

La Palma 2000 Reserve Merlot (Rapel Valley) $12. 83 *—D.T. (7/1/2002)*

La Palma 2003 Sauvignon Blanc (Rapel Valley) $8. Clean and pure, with aromas of green grass, mint, and passion fruit. Crisp on the palate, and lean on the finish. It's snappy and tight, with a welcome lightness. **85** *—M.S. (3/1/2004)*

LA PLAYA

La Playa 1994 Maxima Claret Bordeaux Blend (Maipo Valley) $21. 85 *(2/1/2001)*

La Playa 2003 Block Selection Cabernet Sauvignon (Colchagua Valley) $11. With hickory, coal, and spice to the dark nose, this ranks as a masculine Cab with nary a flaw. The palate is chunky and ripe, with sweet dark-fruit flavors. And the finish is spicy and full, with meaty but suave tannins. A high-water mark for the La Playa label. **88 Best Buy** *—M.S. (11/1/2005)*

La Playa 2000 Estate Bottled Chardonnay (Maipo Valley) $7. The ripe pineapple and orange aromas and flavors here have appeal and there's a barely perceptible fizziness—or is it bright acidity—on the palate. All in all, the wine pleases and the fairly sweet fruit flavors are nicely balanced and checked by a slight dry chalkiness on the finish. **85** *—M.M. (1/1/2004)*

La Playa 1999 Estate Reserve Chardonnay (Maipo Valley) $11. 84 *—J.F. (8/1/2001)*

La Playa 2004 Merlot (Colchagua Valley) $8. Firm and a bit toasty, with some rubber and dark fruit on the nose. Offers sweet berry fruit and kirsch flavors and manages to stay on form through the finish. Likable and on the money. **85 Best Buy** *—M.S. (11/1/2005)*

La Playa 1999 Estate Reserve Merlot (Colchagua Valley) $10. 87 Best Buy *—M.S. (7/1/2003)*

La Playa 2003 Estate Sauvignon Blanc (Colchagua Valley) $7. Flat and heavy smelling, with sugary apple and mango flavors, which are strange for S.B. Nonetheless, it's adequately fresh, with some lemon and pineapple thrown in to stir interest. On the negative side, it's overly sweet. **82** *—M.S. (8/1/2004)*

LAURA HARTWIG

Laura Hartwig 1999 Gran Reserva Cabernet Blend (Colchagua Valley) $23. 90 *—M.S. (3/1/2002)*

Laura Hartwig 2002 Carmenère (Colchagua Valley) $12. Dense and ripe, with aromas of licorice, tar, and cola. The mouthfeel is starchy, with grippy tannins propping up black cherry, plum, coffee, and brown sugar flavors. Fairly tight and firm on the finish, with a burnt closing note. 86 *—M.S. (6/1/2004)*

Laura Hartwig 2000 Chardonnay (Colchagua Valley) $11. 87 Best Buy *—M.S. (2/1/2002)*

Laura Hartwig 2000 Gran Reserva Red Blend (Colchagua Valley) $20. Jammy, with strawberry aromas dominating the soft, meaty nose. In the mouth, you'll find round, mature fruit defined by red plum, cassis, and pepper. It ends with rich, ripe, saturated notes, but not much acidity and only modest tannins. 87 *—M.S. (6/1/2004)*

LAUREL GLEN

Laurel Glen 2000 Terra Rosa Cabernet Sauvignon (Valle Central) $10. 86 *—S.H. (2/1/2003)*

LEYDA

Leyda 2003 Estación Reserve Carmenère (Colchagua Valley) $12. Shows good depth of fruit, with leather and other earthy characteristics. The fruit is a touch hot and spicy, but it's sweet at the core and the vegetal character common to the variety is largely missing. Chocolate and pepper mix with oak notes on the finish. 86 *—M.S. (12/1/2004)*

LOICA

Loica 2004 Sauvignon Blanc (Maule Valley) $12. Mouthfilling, with plump citrus flavors. The body is sort of oily and round, but there isn't much cutting edge to speak of. Finishes a bit melony and soft. 82 *—M.S. (12/15/2005)*

LOS VASCOS

Los Vascos 2000 Cabernet Sauvignon (Colchagua Valley) $10. 84 *—J.C. (3/1/2002)*

Los Vascos 1999 Le Dix Cabernet Sauvignon (Colchagua Valley) $40. 88 *—M.S. (7/1/2003)*

Los Vascos 2000 Reserve Cabernet Sauvignon (Colchagua Valley) $18. 80 *—M.S. (12/1/2002)*

Los Vascos 1998 Reserve Cabernet Sauvignon (Colchagua Valley) $18. 87 *(2/1/2001)*

Los Vascos 2004 Chardonnay (Colchagua Valley) $10. Extra light and lean, with candied aromas that ultimately settle on passion fruit. Some sugary melon mixes with asparagus on the palate, while the finish is thin and sweet. 82 *—M.S. (2/1/2005)*

Los Vascos 2000 Chardonnay (Colchagua Valley) $11. 86 *(2/1/2001)*

Los Vascos 1996 Le Dix de Los Vascos Red Blend (Colchagua Valley) $40. 91 *—M.S. (5/1/2000)*

LUIS FELIPE EDWARDS

Luis Felipe Edwards 2001 Doña Bernarda Cabernet Sauvignon (Colchagua Valley) $24. Coconut, charcoal, plum, and cassis greet you, followed by somewhat raw plum and apple-skin flavors. Ends leathery, with a foreign briny flavor. Attacks well, but sharp acids hamper the balance. 85 *—M.S. (7/1/2005)*

Luis Felipe Edwards 2000 Estate Bottled Cabernet Sauvignon (Colchagua Valley) $8. 84 *—M.S. (12/1/2002)*

Luis Felipe Edwards 2001 Gran Reserva Cabernet Sauvignon (Colchagua Valley) $13. Sweet and complete, with a nice aromatic mix of dark plum, chocolate, and Bordeaux-like herbs. The mouth offers a racy blend of cherry and raspberry, which is followed by chocolate and vanilla. Somewhat simple, but with such good acid-tannin balance, it's more than acceptable. 87 *—M.S. (8/1/2004)*

Luis Felipe Edwards 2003 Pupilla Cabernet Sauvignon (Colchagua Valley) $8. Simple and lean, with light red fruit and no detectable oak to speak of. Flavors of sweet cherry and raspberry sherbet leave a gritty, lean finish. Not artisan but good. 83 *—M.S. (8/1/2004)*

Luis Felipe Edwards 1999 Reserva Cabernet Sauvignon (Colchagua Valley) $12. 85 *—M.S. (3/1/2002)*

Luis Felipe Edwards 2001 Carmenère (Colchagua Valley) $8. Some overt wood and lemon peel accent red fruit on the nose, while raspberry and cherry flavors are carried on a peppy, lean frame. A bit scouring on the back end, but with enough fruit and balance to pull it off. 86 *—M.S. (8/1/2004)*

Luis Felipe Edwards 1999 Estate Bottled Carmenère (Colchagua Valley) $11. 84 *—J.C. (8/1/2001)*

Luis Felipe Edwards 1999 Chardonnay (Colchagua Valley) $10. 88 Best Buy *—M.S. (11/15/1999)*

Luis Felipe Edwards 2003 Chardonnay (Colchagua Valley) $8. Soft and simple, but clean and fresh, with pear and apple aromas prior to papaya and yet more apple flavor. It's dry, lean, and a bit spicy on the finish, and overall it's a solid offering with a round, expansive mouthfeel. 85 Best Buy *—M.S. (6/1/2004)*

Luis Felipe Edwards 2002 Malbec (Colchagua Valley) $8. 86 Best Buy *—M.S. (12/1/2003)*

Luis Felipe Edwards 2001 Gran Reserva Malbec (Colchagua Valley) $13. 86 *—M.S. (12/1/2003)*

Luis Felipe Edwards 2001 Merlot (Colchagua Valley) $8. 85 Best Buy *—C.S. (12/1/2002)*

Luis Felipe Edwards 2001 Gran Reserva Merlot (Colchagua Valley) $13. This one veers a little toward the light side, but it's solid and well crafted, with clear red-fruit aromas, flavors of dried cherries and plums, and a fresh, acidic finish that supports the wine's simple structure. Some dark chocolate on the back end adds weight and masculinity. **86** *—M.S. (3/1/2004)*

Luis Felipe Edwards 2002 Shiraz (Colchagua Valley) $7. Initial aromas of wet dog and swimming pool blow off to reveal plum, cherry, and generic spice. Lasting notes of raisin and pepper are good, while a shortage of depth and grip renders it middle of the road but drinkable. **84** *—M.S. (8/1/2004)*

MANTA

Manta 2003 Sauvignon Blanc (Central Valley) $6. Appealing, with pure pineapple and stone-fruit aromas followed by a pithy, peppery palate defined by apple and citrus. Some plumpness on the finish, however, overall it's fairly clean and of proper weight and balance. From Casa Julia. **86 Best Buy** *—M.S. (2/1/2005)*

MATETIC

Matetic 2003 EQ Pinot Noir (San Antonio) $25. Not your average Pinot Noir; it's inky, with a nose of sugar beet, black-fruit liqueur, and a touch of alfalfa. Further nosing reveals mineral and black currants, characteristics more akin to a Mediterranean red than textbook Pinot. In the mouth, it's a hulk, with berry and kirsch, pepper and ultimately some heat. **86** *—M.S. (11/1/2005)*

Matetic 2003 EQ Syrah (San Antonio) $25. Opaque in color and dense throughout. Starts with a smoky, baked-plum personality before showing its true colors, which include a silky texture, soft tannins and masculine coffee, mocha, and pepper qualities. Great mouthfeel and a lot of richness. **90** *—M.S. (11/1/2005)*

MCMANIS

McManis 2002 River Junction Pinot Grigio (Central Valley) $10. 86 *—S.H. (1/1/2002)*

MELANIA

Melania 2004 Colección Éspecial Merlot (Maule Valley) $11. Nice color, with candied, sweet-as-sugar aromas. Black cherry and chocolate carry the reduced palate. Finishes slightly weedy. **83** *—M.S. (11/1/2005)*

MICHEL LAROCHE/JORGE CODERCH

Michel Laroche/Jorge Coderch 2002 Piedra Feliz Pinot Noir (Casablanca Valley) $NA. The first crop off young vines and not available yet in the U.S., Laroche's Chilean Pinot shows potential in its complex, slightly vegetal aromas but lacks stuffing and flavor intensity. **83** *(2/1/2004)*

MIGUEL TORRES

Miguel Torres 2000 Manso de Velasco Cabernet Sauvignon (Curicó Valley) $35. 90 *—M.S. (7/1/2003)*

Miguel Torres 2003 Santa Digna Cabernet Sauvignon (Curicó Valley) $12. Violet in color, and smells funky at first. Airing releases plum, blackberry, and licorice flavors. A bit medicinal on the finish, but that combination of warm, sweet and sticky works in this case. Bottom line: this is a ripe, fruity wine that requires some patience. Imported by Dreyfus, Ashby & Co. **86** *—M.S. (11/1/2005)*

Miguel Torres 2000 Santa Digna Cabernet Sauvignon (Curicó Valley) $13. 86 *—M.S. (3/1/2002)*

Miguel Torres 2003 Santa Digna Rosé Cabernet Sauvignon (Curicó Valley) $9. Very sweet, with more sugar than most folks will want. The color is attractive, as is the concept of a Cab-based rosé. But one must wonder what the market is for a sweet-style wine like this from South America. As for specific flavors, it's hard to pinpoint anything beyond generic berry and sucking candy. **84** *—M.S. (8/1/2004)*

Miguel Torres 2002 Santa Digna Carmenère-Cabernet Sauvignon (Curicó Valley) $25. Big and brooding, with bacon, blackberry, and butter aromas in addition to notes of lavender and violets. The thick palate offers blueberry fruit mixed with chocolate and sage. The finish is three-star large. Turns slightly herbal at the end. **88** *—M.S. (12/1/2004)*

Miguel Torres 2002 Maquehua Chardonnay (Curicó Valley) $19. 88 *—M.S. (7/1/2003)*

Miguel Torres 1999 Maquehua Chardonnay (Curicó Valley) $19. 90 Editors' Choice *—J.C. (2/1/2001)*

Miguel Torres 2000 Don Miguel Gewürztraminer-Riesling (Curicó Valley) $11. 88 Best Buy *—J.C. (2/1/2001)*

Miguel Torres 2003 Santa Digna Merlot (Curicó Valley) $10. Deep violet in color, almost to the point of oversaturation. The nose is chunky and youthful, with black fruit and iodine. More heavy black fruit follows on the sweet palate. Forward, but lacks detail and elegance. **83** *—M.S. (2/1/2005)*

Miguel Torres 2000 Conde de Superunda Red Blend (Curicó Valley) $70. A new blend of Cabernet Sauvignon, Carmenère, Monastrell, and Tempranillo, which alone makes it unique for Chile. The nose delivers a blast of menthol and the color is downright huge. Very plump and fruity, with a softness that serves it well. A real mouthful that's not overpowering but still packs punch. **90** *(11/15/2005)*

Miguel Torres 2000 Cordillera Red Blend (Curicó Valley) $26. 90 *—M.S. (3/1/2002)*

Miguel Torres 2000 Rosé Blend (Curicó Valley) $8. 82 *—J.C. (2/1/2001)*

Miguel Torres 2003 Santa Digna Sauvignon Blanc (Curicó Valley) $10. Harsh and weedy at first, and only later giving way to muddled fruit. Tart apple and citrus on the palate, and lemony late. Whets the whistle with piercing acids. **81** *—M.S. (2/1/2005)*

MILLAMAN

Millaman 2000 Cabernet Sauvignon (Curicó Valley) $8. 86 Best Buy *—M.S. (12/1/2002)*

Millaman 2000 Chardonnay (Curicó Valley) $8. 80 *—M.S. (7/1/2002)*

Millaman 2000 Sauvignon Blanc (Curicó Valley) $8. 85 *—M.S. (7/1/2003)*

MONTES

Montes 2000 Montes Alpha M Bordeaux Blend (Colchagua Valley) $72. The oak on this Cabernet-dominated wine is a bit lemony, while the palate is spicy and racy, not plump like it has been in the past. The flavors are dotted by wood resin and pepper, while the fruit is slightly shy. It's more reticent than the excellent 1999 version. **89** *—M.S. (3/1/2004)*

Montes 1996 Cabernet Sauvignon (Curicó Valley) $7. 89 *(11/15/1999)*

Montes 2001 Alpha Cabernet Sauvignon (Curicó Valley) $20. Tight and oaky at first, with aromas of lemon rind, maple, and leather. Next up, cassis and black cherry appear in the mouth, which precedes a tight, chocolaty finish that features good length and manly tannins. Very tightly wound, and powerful. **88** *—M.S. (3/1/2004)*

Montes 2000 Montes Alpha Cabernet Sauvignon (Curicó Valley) $20. 86 *—M.S. (7/1/2003)*

Montes 2004 Reserve Cabernet Sauvignon (Colchagua Valley) $10. Ripe and ready, with a rich, syrupy nose. Just right on the palate, where bold dark-fruit flavors are supported by lively tannins and just enough acid. Spice and coffee on the finish, with ample oak. **87 Best Buy** *—M.S. (11/1/2005)*

Montes 2001 Reserve Cabernet Sauvignon (Curicó Valley) $10. 86 Best Buy *—M.S. (7/1/2003)*

Montes 2000 Reserve Oak Aged Cabernet Sauvignon (Colchagua Valley) $10. 84 *—M.S. (7/1/2003)*

Montes 2004 Limited Selection Cabernet Sauvignon-Carmenère (Leyda Valley) $16. Big and oaky, with aromas of coconut, bacon, and wood resin. Very sweet and borderline syrupy on the tongue, where cocoa and clove flavors accent chewy, dark-fruit flavors. A touch green and minty in the middle, or is that the Carmenère? **86** *—M.S. (11/1/2005)*

Montes 2003 Purple Angel Carmenère (Colchagua Valley) $48. Big, bold and saturated, with dense aromas of baked fruit, spice, and licorice. This brand-new wine ranks as Chile's most pricey Carmenère, but it's surely one of the country's very best. It's ripe, packed with black fruit, and textured beyond ordinary. With oak, heft, and style, it's a winner. With 8% Petit Verdot. **90** *—M.S. (11/1/2005)*

Montes 2003 Alpha Chardonnay (Casablanca Valley) $23. A little oaky at first, resulting in some slight varnish-like aromas. But airing tones it down, and then you get popcorn, baked apple, and fresh pear notes. Ample and quite pleasurable throughout, with apple and banana flavors in front of a big, round finish. **89** *—M.S. (11/1/2005)*

Montes 2001 Alpha Chardonnay (Casablanca Valley) $20. 90 Editors' Choice *—M.S. (7/1/2003)*

Montes 2000 Montes Alpha Chardonnay (Curicó Valley) $20. 90 *—M.S. (2/1/2002)*

Montes 2003 Reserve Chardonnay (Curicó Valley) $10. Round and sugary, with simple but welcome notes of lemon verbena, apple, and vanilla. Sweet like candy corn, but with texture. A floral component adds complexity to what is otherwise as standard a Chard as you'll find. **86 Best Buy** *—M.S. (2/1/2005)*

Montes 1999 Reserve Chardonnay (Curicó Valley) $NA. A ripe, almost sweet wine with loads of pineapple and pear aromas and flavors. The mouthfeel is full and easy but a slight tang keeps it from getting too mushy. This veritable pineapple bomb wraps up with tangy, spicy oak notes. Simple, but fun. **84** *(1/1/2004)*

Montes 2002 Fumé Blanc (Curicó Valley) $10. 87 *—M.S. (11/15/2003)*

Montes 2000 Malbec (Colchagua Valley) $10. 89 Best Buy *—M.S. (3/1/2002)*

Montes 2004 Reserve Malbec (Colchagua Valley) $10. Round and open knit, with welcoming aromas. Very well shaped and solid, with cassis and blackberry flavors sitting comfortably in front of a spicy, chocolate-loaded finish. No flab or superficiality; this is a fine wine for the price. **88 Best Buy** *—M.S. (11/1/2005)*

Montes 2002 Reserve Oak Aged Malbec (Colchagua Valley) $10. 83 *—M.S. (12/1/2003)*

Montes 1999 Montes Alpha Apalta Vineyard Merlot (Colchagua Valley) $22. 85 *—D.T. (7/1/2002)*

Montes 2003 Reserve Merlot (Colchagua Valley) $10. Ignore the "reserve" qualifier because that's what Montes calls all of its basic varietals. This one starts with strange horseradish and pickled-oak aromas, but time unveils better and cleaner cherry and plum fruit prior to a warm finish. Improves with time, but green throughout. **83** *—M.S. (2/1/2005)*

Montes 2002 Reserve Special Cuvée Merlot (Colchagua Valley) $10. A bit earthy in color; it's not your average bright ruby. The nose is more refined and condensed than one might expect, with subdued scents of raspberry, plum, and cola. Suave in terms of texture, and long on the finish. **86** *—M.S. (3/1/2004)*

Montes 2002 Montes Alpha Merlot-Cabernet Franc (Colchagua Valley) $20. Big and forward, with spicy, pungent aromas and also a softening hint of bread dough. The palate features snappy red fruit with drying oak in support. The tannic structure holds its own but doesn't rise up too much. A weighty, driving wine. **88** *—M.S. (3/1/2004)*

Montes 2003 Limited Selection Pinot Noir (Casablanca Valley) $16. Not unattractive, with nice cinnamon, leafiness, and leather to the overriding strawberry nose. Fairly soft and meaty on the palate, and sweet at the core. Finishes creamy and thick, almost on the border of syrupy. **85** *—M.S. (7/1/2005)*

Montes 2002 Oak Aged Limited Selection Pinot Noir (Casablanca Valley) $16. Lightweight raspberry and strawberry aromas waft upward, setting you up for a palate of candied cherry. The finish, like the front palate, is sweet, with raisin touches. The feel is a bit gritty, and while it tastes clean and racy, the flavor is unusual for Pinot Noir. **85** *—M.S. (8/1/2004)*

Montes 2003 Reserve Sauvignon Blanc (Casablanca Valley) $10. Every year this Sauvignon Blanc manages to deliver fresh citrus aromas and flavors, a full blast of zest, and all the food-matching capabilities one could ask for. On the nose, it's mostly passion fruit, while flavors include green apple and kiwi. **88** *—M.S. (3/1/2004)*

Montes 2001Reserva Sauvignon Blanc (Curicó Valley) $10. 89 Best Buy *—M.S. (3/1/2002)*

Montes 2003 Montes Alpha Syrah (Colchagua Valley) $23. Rock solid and impressive in a very New World way. Prime aromas of earth, dark fruit, smoke, and more stir intrigue, and the palate delivers what it should: plump berry fruit, a good amount of oak, spice and full but manageable tannins. The finish of toast and pepper is textured and full. A high-octane wine that hits you with the kitchen sink. **91 Editors' Choice** *—M.S. (11/1/2005)*

Montes 2002 Montes Alpha Syrah (Colchagua Valley) $22. Smells exotic, with piquant notes of cinnamon, tree bark, and citrus peel. The body, however, runs a bit rough and raw. There's a lot of spice and chunky plum, but not much of that funky Syrah essence that fans are likely seeking. **86** *—M.S. (3/1/2004)*

Montes 2000 Montes Alpha Viñedo Apalta Syrah (Colchagua Valley) $22. 87 *(11/1/2001)*

Montes 2000 Late Harvest White Blend (Curicó Valley) $18. Gold in color, this blend of 50% Riesling and 50% Gewürztraminer is packed with apricot, peach, and honey notes along with walnut and peanut hints. It's rich and fruity, with marzipan and other sugary flavors. Modest acidity suggests it should be consumed soon. **88** *—M.S. (3/1/2004)*

MONTGRAS

MontGras 2000 Ninquén Mountain Vineyard Cabernet Sauvignon (Colchagua Valley) $30. 90 *(3/1/2003)*

MontGras 2001 Reserva Cabernet Sauvignon (Colchagua Valley) $10. Excellent red fruit is on display from start to finish. The bouquet is a sweet and sly mix of chocolate, toast, earth, and caramel, and once you taste it, well, it's your basic berry cornucopia. Very good in terms of feel and balance, with some complexity to boot. **90 Best Buy** *—M.S. (6/1/2004)*

MontGras 2003 Reserva Cabernet Sauvignon-Syrah (Colchagua Valley) $12. For those who like fruit over oak, this 50/50 blend, a marriage you don't see very often, is just what the doctor ordered. The Cab component sees a year in barrel; the Syrah no wood at all. The end result is a juicy, pure wine that sports blueberry and cassis as well as a touch of savory spice. Perfect for pizza or a barbecue. **88 Best Buy** *—M.S. (12/15/2005)*

MontGras 2000 Reserva Estate Bottled Carmenère (Colchagua Valley) $10. 84 *(3/1/2003)*

MontGras 2000 Reserve Chardonnay (Colchagua Valley) $9. 86 *—M.S. (3/1/2002)*

MontGras 2003 Reserva Merlot (Colchagua Valley) $11. Not all that "reserve" in its style, but perfectly likable. Cherry, cola, rubber, and leather carry the nose toward a palate defined by tangy cherry. Close to full-force on the finish, which is flush and packed. Tannic and full; a winner in its class. **87 Best Buy** *—M.S. (11/1/2005)*

MontGras 1999 Ninquén Red Blend (Colchagua Valley) $30. 89 *—M.S. (3/1/2002)*

MontGras 2003 Quatro Reserva Red Blend (Colchagua Valley) $16. This four-grape blend, hence the name, always manages to get it more right than wrong. The bouquet of plum, vanilla, and licorice is perfectly nice, while the black cherry and cassis flavors should draw fans. Tight, structured and flavorful, with ripe, mouthfilling tannins. **88** *—M.S. (11/1/2005)*

MontGras 2001 Sauvignon Blanc (Colchagua Valley) $6. 86 Best Buy *—M.S. (3/1/2002)*

MontGras 2002 Reserve Sauvignon Blanc (Casablanca Valley) $10. 86 *(3/1/2003)*

MontGras 2002 Limited Edition Syrah (Colchagua Valley) $16. Candied aromas kick start this meaty, plum-and-berry filled wine. After that, you draw some alfalfa and hay notes off the nose. The palate is sticky and big, with syrupy berry flavors preceding hot and spicy finishing notes. Unlike the average Syrah, but it has its merits. **86** *—M.S. (6/1/2004)*

MORANDÉ

Morandé 2001 Edicion Limitada-66 Barricas Cabernet Franc (Maipo Valley) $NA. 87 *—M.S. (7/1/2003)*

Morandé 2002 Cabernet Sauvignon (Valle Central) $7. 87 Best Buy *—M.S. (7/1/2003)*

Morandé 2001 Grand Reserve Vitisterra Cabernet Sauvignon (Maipo Valley) $13. 88 Best Buy *—M.S. (7/1/2003)*

Morandé 2000 House of Morande Cabernet Sauvignon (Maipo Valley) $30. 84 *—M.S. (7/1/2003)*

Morande 2000 Pionero Cabernet Sauvignon (Central Valley) $7. 85 Best Buy *—M.S. (12/1/2002)*

Morandé 2002 Reserve Terrarum Cabernet Sauvignon (Maipo Valley) $10. 86 Best Buy *—M.S. (7/1/2003)*

Morandé 2002 Vitisterra Grand Reserve Cabernet Sauvignon (Maipo Valley) $15. In the global Cabernet market, this stylish wine scores well. Aromas of coffee, mocha, and oak support plum and cassis. Additional currant flavors are thorough, although the finish is a touch gritty due to hard-packed tannins. Serious stuff, with depth and saturation. **88** *—M.S. (2/1/2005)*

Morandé 2001 Golden Reserve Carignane (Loncomilla Valley) $25. This is more of an experimental wine than a mainstream product. The blend is Carignan, Cab Franc, and Merlot, from one of Pablo Morandé's family vineyards. It smells of coconut and cotton candy: think Malibu rum and blackberry jam. The flavors are equally big and so is the acidity. It's a wine from another zone. **82** *—M.S. (3/1/2004)*

Morandé 2001 Terrarum Carmenère (Maipo Valley) $9. 87 Best Buy *(8/1/2002)*

Morandé 2003 Chardonnay (Maipo Valley) $8. Opens with simple apple and pear aromas, while the mouth is full and chunky. Overall the flavor is lasting, courtesy of heady residual sugar that tilts the wine toward candied. Will appeal mostly to those fancying sweeter Chardonnays. **84** *—M.S. (3/1/2004)*

Morandé 2001 Morandé Pionero Chardonnay (Central Valley) $7. 84 *—M.S. (7/1/2003)*

Morandé 2001 Terrarum Chardonnay (Maipo Valley) $10. 84 *(8/1/2002)*

Morandé 2001 Visiterra Chardonnay (Casablanca Valley) $15. 86 *(8/1/2002)*

Morandé 2002 Edición Limitada 88 Barricas Malbec (Maipo Valley) $17. 84 *—M.S. (12/1/2003)*

Morandé 2003 Merlot (Central Valley) $8. Chunky and meaty, with a strong streak of green pepper running through the middle of the bouquet. Flavors lean toward berry syrup, with notes of sweet and sour. The finish is dry and a bit weak, while the mouthfeel is just okay. **83** *—M.S. (8/1/2004)*

Morandé 2001 Grand Reserve Vitisterra Merlot (Maipo Valley) $13. 85 *—M.S. (7/1/2003)*

Morandé 2003 Terrarum Reserva Merlot (Maipo Valley) $11. The nose is mildly grassy, with a hint of citrus peel. The mouth is fuller, with a creamy feel along with plum and berry flavors. Fairly smooth on the finish, with chocolate/carob notes and a blast of spice. **85** *—M.S. (3/1/2004)*

Morandé 2002 Pinot Noir (Casablanca Valley) $7. 81 *—M.S. (7/1/2003)*

Morandé 2001 Edición Limitada Rosé de Pinot Noir (Casablanca Valley) $13. 85 *(8/1/2002)*

Morandé 2003 Reserva Organico Pinot Noir (Casablanca Valley) $11. This is a large, odd Pinot. It seems almost textbook at first, but then loses its focus upon extended airing. At 15.2% it has size on its side; flavors, meanwhile, include root beer, raspberry, chocolate, and tea. Finishes heavy, with coffee notes. **85** *—M.S. (3/1/2004)*

Morande 2001 Edicion Limitada Golden Reserve Red Blend (Loncomilla Valley) $80. Aged in new American oak for 20 months, this wine has intense aromas of vanilla and toast, but that's backed by ample blackberry, black cherry, and raspberry scents. It's a juicy, medium-weight wine, not overly rich, but packed with raspberries, dried herbs and brown sugar. Finishes long and toasty—and might be more reminiscent of some Riojas than most Chilean wines. A blend of Carignan, Merlot, and Cabernet Franc. **90** *(11/1/2005)*

Morandé 2000 Late Harvest Riesling (Casablanca Valley) $13. Made from Riesling, this wine was mildly affected by botrytis, yet it's still lively and zippy. Honey, butterscotch, and banana notes on the nose play opening act to papaya and mango flavors. Full and flavorful, and fairly well balanced for the style. **87** *—M.S. (3/1/2004)*

Morandé 2003 Sauvignon Blanc (Valle Central) $20. Clean but bland, with flavors that run sweet and candied; you get dried and sugared citrus rind and also some carrot. The finish, meanwhile, is borderline medicinal. **84** *—M.S. (3/1/2004)*

Morandé 2001 Sauvignon Blanc (Casablanca Valley) $11. 87 *(8/1/2002)*

Morandé 2000 Pionero Sauvignon Blanc (Central Valley) $7. 83 *—M.S. (7/1/2003)*

Morandé 2003 Syrah (Maipo Valley) $8. Fat and funky aromas yield some spice and floral notes. Beneath is leathery, meaty fruit and a wine with a chewy mouthfeel. Seekers may find black cherry, black plum, and licorice prior to a smoky, mildly awkward finish. **84** *—M.S. (3/1/2004)*

Morandé 2002 Grand Reserve Vitisterra Syrah (Maipo Valley) $15. Opaque and thick, yet despite its mammoth proportions the wine is lacking. It smells sweaty, while the flavor profile is sour at the core, with only modest surrounding fruit. Finishes starchy. **82** *—M.S. (8/1/2004)*

Morandé 2001 Vitisterra Grand Reserve Syrah (Maipo Valley) $15. **86** *—M.S. (7/1/2003)*

Morandé 1999 Edición Limitada Syrah-Cabernet (Maipo Valley) $18. **88** *(8/1/2002)*

Morandé 2002 Edición Limitada Carmenère (Maipo Valley) $20. The nose is almost salsa-like, with the pepper and tomato aromas that come up from the glass. But if you can get past the herbal gatekeeper, there's a nice mouthfeel and spicy fruit. A different path in Carmenère, one that requires a second, maybe a third taste to appreciate. **85** *—M.S. (3/1/2004)*

NIDO DE AGUILA

Nido de Aguila 2002 Armonía Bordeaux Blend (Maipo Valley) $20. An excellent Bordeaux-style blend of Cabernet, Merlot, and Cab Franc that sings a pretty tune. Concentrated but pleasantly fruity, with cherry, raspberry, and chocolate aromas and flavors. A long, developed finish with a core of spice and smoke cements this wine's position as a winner and a fine bargain. From a 10,000-case, family-owned Maipo operation that's worth watching. **91 Editors' Choice** *—M.S. (2/1/2005)*

Nido de Aguila 2003 Reserva Merlot (Maipo Valley) $15. Rusty in color, with tomato and light red fruit on the nose. Shows mostly roasted fruit flavors and leafiness. Not a lot of depth, but not offensive. **81** *—M.S. (12/15/2005)*

NUEVOMUNDO

Nuevomundo 2004 Cabernet Sauvignon-Malbec (Maipo Valley) $15. DeMartino's organic wine is dark and loaded with blackberry and other dark fruits, but with these flavors come some really hard tannins. Thus, the mouthfeel is like nails. That said, the hope and belief here is that it will soften over the next six months and will be ready to drink by late spring 2006. If not, then I've overrated it. **87** *—M.S. (12/15/2005)*

ODFJELL

Odfjell 2003 Armador Cabernet Sauvignon (Maipo Valley) $12. Earth, leather and bell-pepper aromas tangle with some fresher cherry and berry notes. Juicy and full in the mouth, with a red-fruit core followed by chocolate and mint on the finish. Good texture, but overall it's a touch green and medicinal. **85** *—M.S. (11/1/2005)*

Odfjell 2003 Orzada Cabernet Sauvignon (Colchagua Valley) $18. Deep in color with mint, tobacco, licorice, and coconut shadings to the deeply fruited nose. Very well tuned, with lush blackberry and cassis flavors in front of a moderately tannic, no-bull finish. **89** *—M.S. (11/1/2005)*

Odfjell 2003 Orzada Carignan (Maule Valley) $18. Colorful, with hints of mushroom to the cherry and raspberry nose. A very nice wine that is ripe but monotone. It's juicy and fruity, but ultimately simple. Chocolate and vanilla notes soften the finish. **87** *—M.S. (11/1/2005)*

Odfjell 2003 Armador Carmenère (Maule Valley) $12. The Odfjell family, originally from Norway, understands the shipping business and they also understand how to make wines with deep flavors and smooth textures. And whereas Carmenère frequently tastes of bell peppers or worse, this has to be one of the best, most full versions we've come across. Black olive, herbs, and dried fruits carry the nose. Lush in the mouth; truly delicious. **90 Best Buy** *—M.S. (11/15/2005)*

Odfjell 2003 Orzada Carmenère (Central Valley) $18. Black as night, with cola, mint, and very little herbaceousness. In fact, the whole package offers only the slightest note of Carmenère's notorious herbal character. Without that identity, it's pure and delivers unabridged ripeness. Finishes with bitter chocolate and vanilla. **90** *—M.S. (11/1/2005)*

Odfjell 2003 Armador Merlot (Maipo Valley) $12. Ripe as fresh-picked fruit, but with a creamy mouthfeel and a lot of natural warmth. Unlike so many murky, insipid Chilean Merlots, this wine has spine and spunk. **87 Best Buy** *—M.S. (11/1/2005)*

Odfjell 2002 Aliara Red Blend (Chile) $26. Hard and rubbery, with burnt coffee and mineral aromas. Very hard and tannic, with a borderline weedy, herbal note to the finish. Has its merits, but the feel is too hard and the love has gone on hiatus. **84** *—M.S. (11/1/2005)*

Odfjell 2003 Armador Syrah (Maipo Valley) $12. Rather gamy and savory, with aromas of black olive and cured meat followed by a creamy, baked-fruit palate that is simultaneously candied yet earthy. Don't judge it too quickly, it unleashes hidden pizzazz if given time. **86** *—M.S. (11/1/2005)*

PASO DEL SOL

Paso del Sol 2001 Cabernet Sauvignon (Central Valley) $6. **85 Best Buy** *—M.S. (12/1/2002)*

Paso del Sol 2004 Chardonnay (Central Valley) $6. Flat as a board, with vanilla, custard, and pear aromas. Nondescript white fruit carries everything to a sweet, bland finish. Mass market wine, no more no less. **81** *—M.S. (2/1/2005)*

Paso del Sol 2003 Merlot (Central Valley) $6. Jammy but dilute, with plum and red licorice flavors. A bit of caramel and toffee come on late, but that only works to create a thick, fudge-like mouthfeel. **82** *—M.S. (7/1/2005)*

PEÑALOLEN

Peñalolen 2003 Cabernet Sauvignon (Maipo Valley) $18. Begins with roasted, smoky aromas that morph straight to deep black fruit. Cassis and black cherry form a solid flavor core, and there's plenty of tannin and toast on the finish. Very solid and one of the best efforts yet from this label. **88** *—M.S. (12/15/2005)*

Peñalolen 2001 Cabernet Sauvignon (Maipo Valley) $16. Opens with a blast of white pepper in the aroma and flavor, and the blackberry fruit struggles to rise above that spicy power. Still, the wine is distinctive, and feels polished and complex on the palate. **86** *—S.H. (11/1/2004)*

Peñalolen 2000 Cabernet Sauvignon (Maipo Valley) $15. Seemingly stewed and a touch burnt, this heavy wine manages to shed some of its girth as it opens, but even then it remains rather bulky. Thick, ripe, chewy fruit and oak precede a grippy, spicy finish. Seems overripe and a bit weedy. **84** *—M.S. (11/1/2005)*

Peñalolen 2004 Sauvignon Blanc (Limarí Valley) $12. A little sweet to the nose but overall it's more crisp and minerally than fruity. Green apple and lemon-lime are the key flavor components, while the finish is light and crisp, with melon and citrus. Good basic white wine; nothing out of place. **85** *—M.S. (11/1/2005)*

Peñalolen 2002 Sauvignon Blanc (Casablanca Valley) $12. Terrific stuff, really a dynamic mouthful. True, it's simple in structure. But the grassy, lemon-and-lime flavors are extra rich, with fig and peach flavors that are so powerful, they last well into the finish of this bone dry, crisp wine. **87** *—S.H. (8/1/2004)*

PENGWINE

Pengwine 2003 Humboldt Reserve Cabernet Sauvignon (Maipo Valley) $16. Herbal and spicy, with leafy, red-fruit aromas. The palate is weighty, with vanilla and brown sugar flavors along with ample oak. Shows good snap and pop once it opens. **84** *—M.S. (11/1/2005)*

PORTA

Porta 2000 Estates Cabernet Sauvignon (Aconcagua Valley) $10. 86 Best Buy *—M.S. (12/1/2002)*

Porta 1999 Reserve Cabernet Sauvignon (Aconcagua Valley) $14. 83 *—M.S. (12/1/2002)*

Porta 2000 Chardonnay (Cachapoal Valley) $9. 86 *—M.S. (7/1/2002)*

Porta 2000 Reserve Chardonnay (Cachapoal Valley) $13. 83 *—M.S. (7/1/2002)*

Porta 2000 Estates Merlot (Aconcagua Valley) $9. 86 Best Buy *—M.S. (12/1/2002)*

Porta 1999 Grand Reserve Pinot Noir (Bío Bío Valley) $22. 85 *(8/1/2001)*

CHILE

PORTAL DEL ALTO

Portal Del Alto 1999 Gran Reserva Cabernet Sauvignon (Maipo Valley) $12. 87 Best Buy *—C.S. (12/1/2002)*

Portal Del Alto 2000 Hand Picked Selection Cabernet Sauvignon (Central Valley) $7. 86 Best Buy *—M.S. (12/1/2002)*

Portal Del Alto 1998 Reserva Cabernet Sauvignon (Maipo Valley) $12. 85 *—M.N. (2/1/2001)*

Portal Del Alto 2000 Chardonnay (Maule Valley) $7. 87 Best Buy *—M.M. (2/1/2001)*

Portal Del Alto 1999 Reserva Chardonnay (Valle Central) $12. 87 *—M.N. (2/1/2001)*

SAN NICOLAS

San Nicolas 2003 Cabernet Sauvignon (Curicó Valley) $8. Perfectly nice, with black cherry, leather, and some snap. Ripe and generally clean on the palate, with cola, black fruit, and easygoing tannins. Stays the course; quintessential basic Chilean Cabernet. **85 Best Buy** *—M.S. (11/1/2005)*

San Nicolas 2004 Chardonnay (Curicó Valley) $8. Sort of sweet on the bouquet, with hints of lemon-lime and candy. Natural tasting, and veering toward tropical. Moderate girth in terms of body, with a finish accented by toast and vanilla. **84 Best Buy** *—M.S. (11/1/2005)*

San Nicolas 2004 Sabrina Reserve Chardonnay (Curicó Valley) $11. Warm and a bit oaky, with aromas of vanilla and baked bread along with more standard apple and pear. Falls on the leesy side of the fence, with creamy, toasty flavors of butter, baked pear, and cream. From Santa Julia. **86 Best Buy** *—M.S. (11/1/2005)*

SAN PEDRO

San Pedro 2001 1865 Reserva Cabernet Sauvignon (Maipo Valley) $19. Winemaker Irene Paiva describes Maipo Cabernets as often having a minty or eucalyptus character, and that's certainly evident in this wine, alongside plump, ripe berry notes. Long and finely textured on the finish. **87** *(11/1/2005)*

San Pedro 2001 Cabo de Hornos Cabernet Sauvignon (Lontué Valley) $35. Smells lovely, with cedar, tea and cassis mingling effortlessly on the nose. In the mouth, it's bigger and fleshier than the '99 or '00, with a long finish filled with sweet fruit. **91 Editors' Choice** *(11/1/2005)*

San Pedro 1999 Cabo de Hornos Cabernet Sauvignon (Lontué Valley) $35. Harvested from dry-farmed vines 50 years old or more, rigorously selected on the sorting table, fermented after a short cold maceration, then put into French oak for 18 months and aged in bottle for a year before release, this wine gets coddled from start to finish. The results speak for themselves: floral, leather, and dried fruit aromas; flavors of cedar, cassis, and molasses; soft, supple tannins and a long, elegant finish. **91 Editors' Choice** *(11/1/2005)*

San Pedro 2004 Castillo de Molina Reserva Cabernet Sauvignon (Lontué Valley) $11. From a region winemaker Irene Paiva describes as cooler than Chile's other Cabernet growing regions, this wine shows some herbal notes on the nose, but also a wonderfully supple texture and finely wrought flavors of cherries, tobacco, and chocolate. **86 Best Buy** *(11/1/2005)*

San Pedro 2002 Castillo De Molina Reserva Cabernet Sauvignon (Lontué Valley) $10. Lots of tobacco, green bean, and berry fruit work the nose, followed by syrupy but standard red-fruit flavors on the tongue. Plum, fudge, and astringent tannins make for a mouthfeel that's at once soft but also hard. **84** *—M.S. (2/1/2005)*

San Pedro 2005 Gato Negro Cabernet Sauvignon (Central Valley) $5. Bright day-glo purple in color, this is a fresh, fruity, lightweight wine that delivers Cabernet flavors of cassis and chocolate without real weight or structure behind it. Serve it as you would a Beaujolais or light-bodied Côtes-du-Rhône. **83 Best Buy** *(11/1/2005)*

San Pedro 2000 1865 Reserva Cabernet Sauvignon (Maipo Valley) $20. 85 *—M.S. (7/1/2003)*

San Pedro 1865 2002 Reserva Carmenère (Maule Valley) $19. Smoky and herbal on the nose; like the rest of the Viña San Pedro offerings, this one is typical of its variety. Sappy, resiny, green notes alongside riper black cherry flavors end on a coffee-like note. **85** *(11/1/2005)*

San Pedro 2004 Castillo de Molina Reserva Chardonnay (Casablanca Valley) $11. Toasty and buttery smelling, but blends in enough pear, citrus, and anise flavor to retain interest. Crisp on the finish, where the oak become a bit aggressive. **84** *(11/1/2005)*

San Pedro 2002 Castillo de Molina Reserva Chardonnay (Lontué Valley) $11. 87 *—M.S. (7/1/2003)*

San Pedro 2002 San Andrés Chardonnay (Lontué Valley) $NA. 84 *—M.S. (7/1/2003)*

San Pedro 2002 35 South Land of Passion and Fantasy Merlot (Lontué Valley) $8. 84 *—M.S. (7/1/2003)*

San Pedro 2002 Gato Negro Merlot (Lontué Valley) $5. 82 *—M.S. (7/1/2003)*

San Pedro 2003 Gato Blanco Sauvignon Blanc (Valle Central) $5. Soft and creamy, with lactic pear and vanilla aromas. Mild peach and nectarine flavors, with a dilute finish. **82** *—M.S. (2/1/2005)*

San Pedro 2002 San Andrés Sauvignon Blanc (Lontué Valley) $NA. 85 *—M.S. (7/1/2003)*

San Pedro 2003 Castillo de Molina Reserva Shiraz (Lontué Valley) $11. Bold and fruity, with a dark nose full of rubber and coffee. The fruit on the palate is sweet if a bit baked, while the mouthfeel scores via ripe tannins and chocolaty warmth. For the money this is good South American Shiraz. **86 Best Buy** *—M.S. (11/1/2005)*

SANTA ALICIA

Santa Alicia 1998 Gran Reserva Cabernet Sauvignon (Maipo Valley) $14. 82 *—D.T. (7/1/2002)*

Santa Alicia 2001 Estate Bottled Reserve Carmenère (Maipo Valley) $8. 85 Best Buy *—M.S. (7/1/2003)*

Santa Alicia 2001 Estate Chardonnay (Maipo Valley) $6. 80 *—M.S. (7/1/2002)*

Santa Alicia 2001 Reserve Malbec (Maipo Valley) $8. Ripe and round, with a full blast of oak on the nose. For Malbec, it's rather light in weight, with cherry, raspberry, and plum flavors wrapped in a nicely textured package. Maybe not too much character, but what's here is just fine. **86** *—M.S. (8/1/2004)*

Santa Alicia 2000 Estate Bottled Reserve Merlot (Maipo Valley) $6. 88 Best Buy *—M.S. (12/1/2002)*

Santa Alicia 1999 Gran Reserva Merlot (Maipo Valley) $14. 84 *—D.T. (7/1/2002)*

Santa Alicia 2003 Reserve Sauvignon Blanc (Maipo Valley) $8. Grapefruit and other citrus aromas lead into a palate of yet more grapefruit and passion fruit. The zesty finish is long-lasting. **85 Best Buy** *—M.S. (3/1/2004)*

Santa Alicia 2001 Reserve Syrah (Maipo Valley) $8. Meaty and large, with aromas of bacon and leather. Starts off more confidently than it finishes, with early plum, butter, and cashew notes. Fairly bland on the finish, but still a nice wine with an easygoing personality and simple, clean flavor notes. **86 Best Buy** *—M.S. (8/1/2004)*

SANTA CAROLINA

Santa Carolina 2001 VSC Bordeaux Blend (Maipo Valley) $35. Red fruit and milk chocolate aromas do battle with green pepper, and while there's no clear winner, each makes its mark. The fruit seems solid and healthy, with the palate showing good tannins and acidity. But those bell pepper aromas and flavors are heavy and refuse to cease. **85** *—M.S. (11/1/2005)*

Santa Carolina 2001 Barrica Selection Cabernet Sauvignon (Maipo Valley) $13. 84 *(11/15/2003)*

Santa Carolina 1999 Reserva Cabernet Sauvignon (Colchagua Valley) $9. 84 *—D.T. (7/1/2002)*

Santa Carolina 1997 Reserva Cabernet Sauvignon (Maipo Valley) $9. 82 *—M.S. (11/15/1999)*

Santa Carolina 2003 Barrica Selection Carmenère (Rapel Valley) $13. Slightly green, but overall its better qualities outweigh the weaker ones. Almond paste and sweet black-fruit flavors carry the palate, backed by a finish of spice and herbs. **84** *—M.S. (12/15/2005)*

Santa Carolina 2003 Barrica Selection Chardonnay (Maipo Valley) $13. Light up front, with canned peach and pear aromas. Not that vibrant but clean, with sweet apricot and peach flavors. Good enough in the mouth, with a hint of banana and citrus on the finish. Not that oaky despite its "barrica" classification. Imported by Canandaigua Wine Co. **84** *—M.S. (12/15/2005)*

Santa Carolina 1998 Reserva de la Familia Chardonnay (Maipo Valley) $15. 90 Best Buy —*M.N. (2/1/2001)*

Santa Carolina 2002 Coleccion Especial Merlot (Rapel Valley) $7. 84 *(11/15/2003)*

Santa Carolina 2002 Coleccion Especial Sauvignon Blanc (Rapel Valley) $7. 84 *(11/15/2003)*

Santa Carolina 2002 Barrica Selection Syrah (Maule Valley) $13. 84 *(11/15/2003)*

SANTA EMA

Santa Ema 2000 Estate Bottled Cabernet Sauvignon (Maipo Valley) $9. 85 —*M.S. (7/1/2003)*

Santa Ema 2002 Reserve Cabernet Sauvignon (Maipo Valley) $14. On the heavier, stewed side, but still balanced enough to score points. The nose is earthy and dark, while the palate deals cooked plum and blackberry along with a touch of soy sauce. Round and surprisingly airy on the finish. It doesn't end as densely as it begins. **87** —*M.S. (7/1/2005)*

Santa Ema 1999 Reserve Cabernet Sauvignon (Maipo Valley) $14. 86 —*M.S. (12/1/2002)*

Santa Ema 2002 60/40 Barrel Select Cabernet Sauvignon-Merlot (Maipo Valley) $10. A blend of Cabernet Sauvignon and Merlot that's outright fruity, with earthy aromas of leather, forest floor, and barnyard. The palate, however, runs light, with red fruit and a hint of tomato. Healthy but lightweight on the finish. Laudable for its fresh qualities and undeniable brightness. **86 Best Buy** —*M.S. (2/1/2005)*

Santa Ema 1999 Barrel Select Cabernet Sauvignon-Merlot (Maipo Valley) $10. 87 —*D.T. (7/1/2002)*

Santa Ema 2001 Carmenère (Rapel Valley) $10. Open-knit and herbal, and mostly pleasant if entirely underwhelming. There's nothing offensive here; just your basics as far as cherry fruit, modest tannins, and a hint of the veggies. **83** —*M.S. (3/1/2004)*

Santa Ema 2002 Gran Reserva Carmenère (Cachapoal Valley) $17. Plenty of oak, which must be why it's called "Gran Reserva." Along with the lumber you'll find chocolate, marinade, and pickle. Fat on the palate, with bulky black plum and blackberry flavors. Licorice, coffee and green bean notes define the finish. **85** —*M.S. (2/1/2005)*

Santa Ema 2000 Reserve Carmenère (Rapel Valley) $16. 86 —*D.T. (7/1/2002)*

Santa Ema 2003 Chardonnay (Casablanca Valley) $9. Soft pear and apple aromas are clean if unspectacular. The flavor profile is mostly sugary apple and pear, while good Casablanca acidity ensures that the wine feels right on the palate. **84** —*M.S. (6/1/2004)*

Santa Ema 2003 Reserve Chardonnay (Casablanca Valley) $14. Fairly woody, but there's enough quality fruit supporting the oak to make it work. Butterscotch and apple aromas lead into a fruity, satisfying palate of melon, papaya, and apple. The persistent barrel influence yields vanilla and anisette on the chunky, creamy finish. **86** —*M.S. (2/1/2005)*

Santa Ema 2003 Merlot (Cachapoal Valley) $9. Sweet and grapey, but with enough darkness and structure to rank. Blueberry and cherry aromas precede snappy cherry and raspberry fruit. Rock solid and ripe at the core, with no funk or green. What a bargain Chilean Merlot is supposed to be. **86 Best Buy** —*M.S. (2/1/2005)*

Santa Ema 1998 Merlot (Maipo Valley) $9. 83 —*J.C. (2/1/2001)*

Santa Ema 1999 Reserve Merlot (Maipo Valley) $14. 82 —*D.T. (7/1/2002)*

Santa Ema 2001 Catalina Red Blend (Rapel Valley) $28. Fruity and secure, with ripe, roasted aromas of coffee, black fruit, and leather. Some cherry-cola and apple skin make for a lively, fresh palate, while the finish is smooth, warm and full. Good acidity and body. A Cabernet-Cab Franc blend that ranks among Santa Ema's best wines to date. **90** —*M.S. (2/1/2005)*

Santa Ema 2004 Sauvignon Blanc (Maipo Valley) $8. Seems a bit overripe. The nose is soft, unctuous and overtly fruity, with a heavy melon-meets-citrus smell. Equally soft and melony on the palate, with a thick finish. Perfectly acceptable but not as precise as it should be. **84 Best Buy** —*M.S. (7/1/2005)*

SANTA EMILIANA

Santa Emiliana 2002 Sincerity Merlot-Cabernet Sauvignon (Rapel Valley) $15. Alvaro Espinoza produced this wine from organically grown grapes in the vineyards of the giant Santa Emiliana winery. The plan is for the vineyard to become biodynamic. It is dark in color, almost black, very intense, with bitter chocolate and tarry fruit flavors. This is full of sweet tannins and fruit, ready to drink now. **88** —*R.V. (4/1/2005)*

SANTA HELENA

Santa Helena 2001 Selección del Directorio Reserva Cabernet Sauvignon (Central Valley) $11. Clean and rich, with a bouquet of ripe berry notes accented by soft oak. Flavors of plum and cherry are defined and rich, while the finish is of proper weight and style; it's chewy yet racy enough. As reds go, it's round and robust, and very satisfying. It's what Chilean Cabernet should be. **89** —*M.S. (8/1/2004)*

Santa Helena 2002 Vernus Cabernet Sauvignon (Colchagua Valley) $18. Way beyond satisfactory, with smoky leather to go with the red fruit and oak aromas. Typical cassis and plum carry the lively palate, which is tight and tannic but tasty and full of excitement. Not complex, but ripe and forward. Good Cab in the under-$20 category. **88** —*M.S. (2/1/2005)*

Santa Helena 2002 Siglo de Oro Carmenère (Central Valley) $9. Sour cherry notes on the nose are followed by mildly weedy flavors of plum and raspberry. Some oak flavor pumps up the bland finish. Lacking in complexity but serviceable. **83** *—M.S. (8/1/2004)*

Santa Helena 2002 Selección del Directorio Reserva Chardonnay (Casablanca Valley) $11. Overtly oaky, but in an artificial, overdone way. It's thick and woody, with bland fruit and resiny, fat flavor notes. **81** *—M.S. (8/1/2004)*

Santa Helena 2001 Selección del Directorio Reserva Merlot (Central Valley) $11. Modest aromas of cola, mint, and lemon peel are clean but hardly stellar. Flavors of cherry, plum, and blackberry carry some spice and oak, while the finish is equally oaky and lasting. A touch acidic, but that helps propel the flavors. **86** *—M.S. (8/1/2004)*

Santa Helena 2001 Late Harvest Riesling (Curicó Valley) $11. Pungent and forward, with can't-miss aromas of dried apricot and sweat. Flavors of white raisins and dried mango are super sweet, while the finish is thick and mouthcoating. **83** *—M.S. (8/1/2004)*

Santa Helena 2003 Siglo de Oro Sauvignon Blanc (Curicó Valley) $9. Fairly crisp and defined, with true passion fruit, grapefruit, and stone-fruit aromas. Flavors of oranges and mango are a bit sweet, but the finish offers just enough of a dry edge to keep the wine pushing forward. **85** *—M.S. (8/1/2004)*

SANTA INES

Santa Ines 2001 Estate Bottled Cabernet Sauvignon (Maipo Valley) $11. **85** *—M.S. (12/1/2002)*

Santa Ines 1999 Enigma Reserva Chardonnay (Maipo Valley) $15. **85** *—M.S. (7/1/2003)*

Santa Ines 2001 Estate Bottled Merlot (Maipo Valley) $8. **86** *—K.F. (12/1/2002)*

Santa Ines 2001 Legado de Armida Reserva Sauvignon Blanc (Maipo Valley) $10. **87** *—M.S. (7/1/2003)*

SANTA MARVISTA

Santa Marvista 2003 Reserva Merlot (Central Valley) $6. A touch dilute and broken up in the nose, but not bad or off. In the mouth, tangy strawberry and raspberry fruit leads into an easygoing finish. Despite a few signs of artificiality and manipulation, this is not a bummer of a wine. **83** *—M.S. (3/1/2004)*

SANTA RITA

Santa Rita 2000 Cabernet Sauvignon (Rapel Valley) $7. **83** *—D.T. (7/1/2002)*

Santa Rita 2001 120 Cabernet Sauvignon (Rapel Valley) $8. **84** *(8/1/2003)*

Santa Rita 2001 Casa Real Cabernet Sauvignon (Maipo Valley) $65. Made from 30-year-old vines, this wine represents the pinnacle of Santa Rita's production. It's lush and rich, with vanilla, cedar, tobacco, and cassis aromas. The palate is layered and textured, displaying the perfect mix of concentration and softness. Finishes supple, with smooth tannins and some chocolate and marshmallow. One of Chile's best. **93 Editors' Choice** *—M.S. (11/15/2004)*

Santa Rita 1997 Casa Real Cabernet Sauvignon (Maipo Valley) $40. **92** *—M.S. (5/1/2000)*

Santa Rita 1999 Floresta Apalta Estate Cabernet Sauvignon (Colchagua Valley) $30. **91 Editors' Choice** *(8/1/2003)*

Santa Rita 2000 Medalla Real Cabernet Sauvignon (Maipo Valley) $18. **88** *(8/1/2003)*

Santa Rita 2002 Medalla Real Special Reserve Cabernet Sauvignon (Maipo Valley) $18. Pretty much on the money, with verve, sass, and class. Plenty of black fruit, coffee, earth, and leather on the nose, followed by red plum, cassis, and vanilla-infused tobacco on the palate. Nice and tasty, with fine richness and a good mouthfeel. **88** *—M.S. (11/15/2004)*

Santa Rita 1998 Medalla Real Special Reserve Cabernet Sauvignon (Maipo Valley) $15. **82** *—M.N. (2/1/2001)*

Santa Rita 2001 Reserva Cabernet Sauvignon (Maipo Valley) $12. **87** *(8/1/2003)*

Santa Rita 1999 Reserva Cabernet Sauvignon (Maipo Valley) $11. **82** *—D.T. (8/1/2001)*

Santa Rita 2002 120 Carmenère (Colchagua Valley) $8. **86 Best Buy** *(8/1/2003)*

Santa Rita 1999 Reserva Carmenère (Rapel Valley) $11. **83** *—J.C. (8/1/2001)*

Santa Rita 2002 120 Chardonnay (Maipo Valley) $8. **85 Best Buy** *(8/1/2003)*

Santa Rita 2000 120 Chardonnay (Lontué Valley) $7. **84** *(2/1/2001)*

Santa Rita 1999 Medalla Real Special Reserve Chardonnay (Casablanca Valley) $13. **81** *—M.M. (8/1/2001)*

Santa Rita 2002 Reserva Chardonnay (Casablanca Valley) $12. **87** *(8/1/2003)*

Santa Rita 2000 Reserva Chardonnay (Casablanca Valley) $11. **85** *—M.M. (8/1/2001)*

Santa Rita 2002 120 Merlot (Rapel Valley) $8. The nose doesn't show much, especially at first, when you get light whiffs of dill and toasted corn. However, more fruit is apparent on the palate, primarily cherry and raspberry. Finally, some peppery notes seal the finish. **84** *—M.S. (3/1/2004)*

Santa Rita 2000 120 Merlot (Lontué Valley) $7. 86 Best Buy *—J.C. (3/1/2002)*

Santa Rita 2002 Reserva Merlot (Maipo Valley) $12. Round and fat, with a deep color and some earthy, mushroom notes to the nose. Flavors of blackberry and plum dominate, and the finish has some smoky character and a touch of natural, espresso-like bitterness. **86** *—M.S. (3/1/2004)*

Santa Rita 2000 Floresta Red Blend (Maipo Valley) $30. Dense and bold, with heavy oak, dark fruit, and brazen cedar and lemon notes. This is your prototype muscle wine; it has huge coffee, clove, and anise accents riding side by side with plum and berry fruit. It's a bit ponderous and chocolaty, but if you like yours sweet and saturated, you're in luck. **89** *—M.S. (12/1/2004)*

Santa Rita 1999 Floresta Apalta Estate Red Blend (Colchagua Valley) $30. 92 Editors' Choice *—M.S. (3/1/2002)*

Santa Rita 2003 120 Sauvignon Blanc (Lontué Valley) $8. Clean and nice, with an open yet crisp personality. The wine shows more than adequate lemon, green apple, and passion fruit notes, while the finish is surprisingly long. A winner in its class, with zest and pop. **85 Best Buy** *—M.S. (6/1/2004)*

Santa Rita 2001 Medalla Real Sauvignon Blanc (Rapel Valley) $18. 85 *—M.S. (3/1/2002)*

Santa Rita 2003 Reserva Sauvignon Blanc (Casablanca Valley) $12. The nose features pungent grapefruit, but it stops there. Flavors of cucumber, lime, and grapefruit make for a bold and forward palate. Overall, however, things seem sharp and oversized. **83** *—M.S. (3/1/2004)*

Santa Rita 2003 120 Shiraz (Maipo Valley) $8. Fermented in stainless steel but aged briefly on heavily toasted oak staves; this is one big, fruity red. The nose is roasted, offering coffee and charbroiled beef. The palate is young but smooth, with pounds of berry fruit. It's heavily oaked, but the fruit can handle it. **85 Best Buy** *—M.S. (11/15/2004)*

CHILE

SEÑA

Seña 2001 Bordeaux Blend (Aconcagua Valley) $70. Big and woody on first blush, but relaxes to show clove, cinnamon, and dry plum-like fruit. More spice and clove on the cedary palate, with a chewy, real-deal mouthfeel. Firm tannins and plenty of oak say lay this down for another couple of years. Not a monster fruit ball, but ample. **91** *—M.S. (2/1/2005)*

Seña 1998 Bordeaux Blend (Aconcagua Valley) $66. 89 *(10/1/2001)*

Seña 1997 Bordeaux Blend (Aconcagua Valley) $60. 92 *—S.H. (2/1/2001)*

SIEGEL

Siegel 2000 El Crucero Reserva Cabernet Sauvignon (Colchagua Valley) $13. 89 *—M.S. (12/1/2002)*

SINCERITY

Sincerity 2003 Merlot-Cabernet Sauvignon (Colchagua Valley) $17. Lavishly oaked, and that's just fine given that this wine shows more than adequate depth of fruit and lushness. Coffee, popcorn, and chocolate appear throughout its creamy, rich profile. Along the way berry and cassis flavors thrive. Quite lively and free of holes. It shows 21st-century Chile (and organic farming) in a positive light. **90** *—M.S. (12/15/2005)*

Sincerity 2002 Organically Grown Merlot-Cabernet Sauvignon (Colchagua Valley) $15. Consultant supreme Alvaro Espinoza has made a winner in this organic blend of 75% Merlot and 25% Cabernet. The nose is nicely roasted, with big, creamy fruit and strong chocolate notes. The palate is thick and balanced, with smooth flavors of black fruit and milk chocolate. All told, it's meaty and huge, but not overdone. And the tannins are pure velvet. **91 Editors' Choice** *—M.S. (8/1/2004)*

TARAPACA

Tarapaca 1997 Zavala Bordeaux Blend (Maipo Valley) $25. 87 *(8/1/2000)*

Tarapaca 1999 Gran Reserva Cabernet Sauvignon (Maipo Valley) $15. It's strange to encounter a current-release 1999 wine, and this offering is uneven. Some wet dog and pickle-barrel aromas wrestle on the spicy, lightly fruited nose. The palate is more than a touch green, while the finish is chewy and creamy, with ponderous, spicy oak. **82** *—M.S. (3/1/2004)*

Tarapaca 2003 Chardonnay (Maipo Valley) $8. Waxy oak, citrus, and apple kick it off, followed by almond, coconut, and apple flavors. A sharp beam of acidity makes it lively, but the flavors never really rise above basic. **83** *—M.S. (2/1/2005)*

Tarapaca 2001 Reserva Chardonnay (Casablanca Valley) $11. Very oaky and standard, with low-level acids that cause the wine to come across heavy and flat. From a taste perspective, it's woody and drying, with modest apple and pear flavors. The heavy finish cements this wine as a modern effort that got lost along the way. **84** *—M.S. (6/1/2004)*

Tarapaca 2002 Estate Bottled Merlot (Maipo Valley) $8. Aromas of earth, warm leather, and light red fruit are not what you'd call luscious, but overall the sweet berry fruit, modest spice, and forward personality make this a decent mid-level red. **84** *—M.S. (8/1/2004)*

Tarapaca 1999 Reserva Merlot (Maipo Valley) $12. 82 *—D.T. (7/1/2002)*

Tarapaca 2000 La Isla Vineyard Sauvignon Blanc (Maipo Valley) $14. **86** *—M.S. (7/1/2003)*

TERRA ANDINA

Terra Andina 2002 Cabernet Sauvignon (Valle Central) $8. Even if the nose is fat and murky, this wine still delivers a lot for under $10. The palate is both spicy and sweet, as is the finish, which starts out candy-like and then offers additional spice and substance. Weighty and extracted. **85 Best Buy** *—M.S. (12/1/2004)*

Terra Andina 2003 Carmenère (Central Valley) $8. Exhibits ripe black-fruit aromas of plum and blackberry, with pleasant shadings of vanilla and marzipan. Raspberry and plum make for a ripe and fruity palate that's devoid of any herbal, underripe flavors. Textbook stuff, with a couple of layers of fruit and tannins. **88 Best Buy** *—M.S. (11/1/2005)*

Terra Andina 2004 Chardonnay (Central Valley) $8. Oddly oily, with aromas of cotton candy. Heavy citrus and pineapple makes up the flavor profile, and the finish lacks intensity. Bland overall, and loses focus rapidly. **82** *—M.S. (11/1/2005)*

Terra Andina 2002 Reserve Chardonnay (Casablanca Valley) $13. Waxy and honeyed in the nose, with an aftershock of butterscotch. Pear, apple, and coconut dominate the sweet, simple palate. Finishes heavy and round, as do so many Chilean Chardonnays. **85** *—M.S. (8/1/2004)*

Terra Andina 2003 Merlot (Central Valley) $8. Spearmint, blackberry, and plum unfold on the juicy, easy nose. The palate spreads out with raspberry, red plum, and licorice flavors. Lengthy and textured on the finish, with a dose of spice. Easy to drink. **86 Best Buy** *—M.S. (2/1/2005)*

Terra Andina 2003 Sauvignon Blanc (Valle Central) $8. Clean but bland on the nose, with distant aromatics of pineapple, green apple, and cantaloupe. Tasty enough, with notes of kiwi, passion fruit, and pineapple. Not too racy or bracing, but pretty good along the way. **85 Best Buy** *—M.S. (8/1/2004)*

Terra Andina 2002 Shiraz (Central Valley) $8. Soft and flabby on the nose, with heavy berry syrup aromas. The palate is more red-fruit dominant, with plum and raspberry. Good zip and acidity, with a hint of buttery oak on the finish. **84 Best Buy** *—M.S. (2/1/2005)*

TERRA NOVA

Terra Nova 2003 Chardonnay (Curicó Valley) $7. Light and easy, with vanilla and a hint of spice. Peach and apple flavors lead to a fresh, short finish. Watery in the center. **83** *—M.S. (7/1/2005)*

TERRAMATER

TerraMater 2001 Altum Reserve Cabernet Sauvignon (Curicó Valley) $17. Dark and minty, with licorice and cassis aromas that are positive. In the mouth, it's got Cab's typical plum and cassis character, and the finish is round and spicy, with a little heat. If only the mouthfeel were less jumpy and more lush, this would be even better. **87** *—M.S. (7/1/2005)*

TerraMater 2001 Single Vineyard Cabernet Sauvignon (Maipo Valley) $8. **85** *—M.S. (12/1/2002)*

TerraMater 1999 Altum Reserve Single Vineyard Merlot (Maipo Valley) $20. Unusual and sweet in the nose, with something similar to cinnamon or all-spice aromas. There is quite a woody undertone here; you get it in the nose and again on the palate. This wine is the proverbial hare, not the tortoise. It starts fast, making a good impression, but it fades before the finish line. **83** *—M.S. (1/28/2004)*

TerraMater 2003 Reserva Merlot (Central Valley) $12. Nice and satisfying, but softer and less dynamic than the basic varietal bottling. Nonetheless, it packs spice, mocha, and earth aromas, all backed by ripe blackberry and plum. A blast of cough medicine and licorice on the finish is a sweet, almost cloying, touch. **87 Best Buy** *—M.S. (7/1/2005)*

TerraMater 2001 Unusual Cabernet-Zinfandel-Shiraz (Maipo Valley) $22. Unusual indeed. The blend is Cabernet, Zinfandel, and Shiraz, and frankly it's a mish-mash of oak, espresso, and sour fruit. Extremely lemony, with a fair amount of green. In no way does the fruit stand up to the huge pounding of oak it takes. Out of whack. **81** *—M.S. (2/1/2005)*

TerraMater 2004 Sauvignon Blanc (Maipo Valley) $9. Not a lot on the nose besides distant melon and honey, but the palate is brighter. On offer is a peach, melon, and orange flavor profile sitting in front of a round, chunky finish. Ripe but a bit soft-edged. **86 Best Buy** *—M.S. (7/1/2005)*

TERRANOBLE

TerraNoble 2001 Gran Reserva Cabernet Sauvignon (Maule Valley) $20. Clearly the producer is shooting for a rich, lavish style of Cab, and for the most part that's what you get. The bouquet is dense and full of bacon, mushroom, and black fruit, while the palate is thick with plum, raisin, and smoky, tangy, saucy notes. A firm, oaky, lengthy finish renders it consequential. **88** *—M.S. (3/1/2004)*

TerraNoble 2003 Reserva Cabernet Sauvignon (Colchagua Valley) $11. Raw and salty at first, with some baked aromas and wet leather. More snappy than fat on the tongue, where plum and berry flavors are supported by stern tannins. A tiny bit green in the middle as well as on the finish. Imported by Winebow. **85** *—M.S. (12/15/2005)*

TerraNoble 1999 Gran Reserva Carmenère (Maule Valley) $24. **86** *—J.C. (8/1/2001)*

TerraNoble 2001 Reserva Carmenère (Chile) $12. Nice, fresh and on the money. This is Carmenère in its ripest, most balanced state, and it is a fine red wine with a lot of spunk and natural flavor. The bouquet is perfumed and meaty, while the palate deals bacon, cassis, and black cherry. A smoky, mildly charred finish really helps it along. **89 Best Buy** *—M.S. (3/1/2004)*

TerraNoble 2003 Chardonnay (Casablanca Valley) $8. Light pear and apple aromas are clean and appealing. Look for a zesty palate with citrus and banana flavors, and then vanilla and spice on the finish. It's sweetly persistent and well proportioned. **86 Best Buy** *—M.S. (3/1/2004)*

TerraNoble 2000 Merlot (Maule Valley) $9. 81 *(8/1/2001)*

TerraNoble 2002 Gran Reserva Merlot (Maule Valley) $14. Very little difference exists between this and the so-called "reserva." This wine is oakier, with more powerful pickle and barrel notes. Otherwise it shows the same red-fruit flavors along with lively tannins and acids. **83** *—M.S. (7/1/2005)*

TRINCAO

Trincao 2001 Reserva Carmenère (Maipo Valley) $11. Leathery and rough at first, with a green element to the nose. Time opens it up, freeing milk chocolate, carob, and black pepper, all telltale flavors common to this grape variety. A medicinal edge to the flavor profile holds it back. **85** *—M.S. (8/1/2004)*

TWO BROTHERS

Two Brothers 2001 Big Tattoo Red Blend (Colchagua Valley) $9. 87 Best Buy *—M.S. (7/1/2003)*

Two Brothers 2003 Big Tattoo Syrah (Colchagua Valley) $9. A strong whiff of olive and leather carries the nose, which simply isn't that fruity. Berry fruit and some green notes on the palate. Oaky and drying late. **82** *—M.S. (11/1/2005)*

UNDURRAGA

Undurraga 2000 Cabernet Sauvignon (Colchagua Valley) $7. 85 Best Buy *—M.M. (2/1/2001)*

Undurraga 1999 Founder's Collection Cabernet Sauvignon (Maipo Valley) $25. 86 *—M.S. (7/1/2003)*

Undurraga 2001 Reserva Cabernet Sauvignon (Maipo Valley) $14. Crisp and smooth in the mouth, with clean, unblemished flavors of chocolate and cassis wrapped around a core of firm acidity. Lacks the herbal notes that seem to abound in Chilean Cabernet. **87** *(2/1/2004)*

Undurraga 2003 Reserva Carmenère (Colchagua Valley) $11. Starts with a spicy, baked quality as well as cola and leafy notes. Medium in body, with a slick flavor profile that's one part cherry and berry and one part herbal. Turns a bit more herbaceous with airing, bordering on vegetal. But still it's good Carmenère. **85** *—M.S. (12/15/2005)*

Undurraga 2001 Reserva Carmenère (Colchagua Valley) $11. 87 *—M.S. (7/1/2003)*

Undurraga 1999 Reserve Carmenère (Colchagua Valley) $11. 84 *—M.S. (3/1/2002)*

Undurraga 2000 Chardonnay (Maipo Valley) $7. An easy wine that opens with bright pineapple and citrus notes. Mild apple and pear flavors follow, and if the mouthfeel is a bit ethereal, it is a lively lightness. The dry subtly spicy finish has an interesting chalky note. **85** *—M.M. (1/1/2004)*

Undurraga 2001 Reserva Chardonnay (Maipo Valley) $12. 85 *—M.S. (7/1/2003)*

Undurraga 2002 Gewürztraminer (Maipo Valley) $9. 84 *—M.S. (7/1/2003)*

Undurraga 2001 Reserva Merlot (Maipo Valley) $12. 87 *—M.S. (7/1/2003)*

Undurraga 2001 Pinot Noir (Maipo Valley) $7. 86 Best Buy *—M.S. (3/1/2002)*

Undurraga 2002 Reserva Pinot Noir (Maipo Valley) $14. Shows a slightly sour, herbal twang that upstages the chunky black cherry and cola flavors. **84** *(2/1/2004)*

Undurraga 1999 Reserva Pinot Noir (Maipo Valley) $12. 84 *—M.M. (2/1/2001)*

Undurraga 2003 Sauvignon Blanc (Lontué Valley) $10. 85 *(12/31/2003)*

VALDIVIESO

Valdivieso 2001 Single Vineyard Reserve Cabernet Franc (Lontué Valley) $17. No issues of underripeness or herbaceousness here; this a meaty, sweet rendition of Cab Franc, one with sweet cherry and raspberry in spades. If you seek Loire-style leafiness or Bordeaux complexity, go elsewhere. This version is chewy, rich, ripe, and fleshy. **89** *—M.S. (8/1/2004)*

Valdivieso 2001 Cabernet Sauvignon (Central Valley) $8. 85 Best Buy *—M.S. (7/1/2003)*

Valdivieso 2000 Reserve Cabernet Sauvignon (Central Valley) $13. Ultra ripe but balanced, with beams of black plum and cherry driving through the bouquet. Totally mature berry fruit on the palate, and loud. Juicy and racy across the tongue. Good with a steak. **88** *—M.S. (2/1/2005)*

Valdivieso 1998 Reserve Cabernet Sauvignon (Central Valley) $20. 87 *—J.C. (3/1/2002)*

Valdivieso 2003 Chardonnay (Central Valley) $7. What a good, affordable Chard should be. It's soft and stable, with melon, apple, and cinnamon notes to the rich but balanced palate. The finish is soft and spreads out broadly, with just hint of acidic sharpness. Mouthfilling although not particularly complex. **87 Best Buy** *—M.S. (6/1/2004)*

Valdivieso 2003 Reserve Chardonnay (Casablanca Valley) $13. Heavy gold in color; a butterball of the first order. The nose is full of oak along with pear and apple. That's backed by a palate of sweet corn, mango, banana, and apple. Toasty on the finish, with a splinter of pithy bitterness. Good Casablanca acidity ensures pop on the tongue. **86** *—M.S. (12/15/2005)*

Valdivieso 2001 Reserve Chardonnay (Casablanca Valley) $13. Yellow in color, with a murky nose full of overripe fruit and corn. Heavy, with chunky melon and apple flavors. **81** *—M.S. (2/1/2005)*

Valdivieso 2003 Malbec (Rapel Valley) $7. Full-bodied and loaded with sweet aromas of violets and graham cracker. Flavors of blueberry, plum, and sugar beets lead into an oozing, rich finish. Round and thick, with plenty of extract. **87 Best Buy** *—M.S. (12/1/2004)*

Valdivieso 2000 Single Vineyard Reserve Malbec (Maule Valley) $17. The nose deals a lemony, oak-driven covering atop berry fruit. Flavors of plum and berry start fast but fade a bit as the oaky character of the wine takes over. Healthy and acidic, with length. Maybe too old, and from an average vintage. Drink now. **87** *—M.S. (12/1/2004)*

Valdivieso 1999 Single Vineyard Reserve Malbec (Curicó Valley) $23. 88 *—M.S. (3/1/2002)*

Valdivieso 2002 Merlot (Central Valley) $7. Clean and fruity, with a hint of smoke to the nose. Flavors of raspberry and cherry lead into a creamy, oaky finish that's firm. Textbook and tasty. **86** *—M.S. (3/1/2004)*

Valdivieso 2000 Single Vineyard Reserve Merlot (Lontué Valley) $17. Ripe and ready, with a forward personality. Pungent and full on the nose, with in-your-face but scratchy cherry and raspberry fruit controlling the palate. Not complex, but fruity and structured. Clamps down late with tannins. Good for burgers and simple grills. **87** *—M.S. (7/1/2005)*

Valdivieso 2002 Reserve Pinot Noir (Lontué Valley) $13. Clean, pure and sweet on the nose, yet shrill once it hits the palate. Look for juiced-up cherry and berry flavors followed by a scorching finish in which the acids rear up. Oddly, there seems to be a peanut note to the flavor profile. **86** *—M.S. (8/1/2004)*

Valdivieso NV Caballo Loco No. 5 Red Blend (Lontué Valley) $40. Few table wines are made in the solera style, whereby vintages are blended together to create a more harmonious whole. Here is that rare solera red, the fifth shot this winery has taken at the Crazy Horse. And it's a fine effort that features spicy and sweet aromas, ripe strawberry fruit, and lots of toasty, charred oak. Warning: Airing helps tame the overt oak, especially on the finish. **91** *—M.S. (1/1/2004)*

Valdivieso NV Caballo Loco No. 4 Red Blend (Lontué Valley) $35. 91 *—M.S. (3/1/2002)*

Valdivieso 2002 Sauvignon Blanc (Central Valley) $8. 84 *—M.S. (7/1/2003)*

Valdivieso 2000 Barrel Selection Reserve Syrah (Central Valley) $12. 84 *(10/1/2001)*

VALLETE FONTAINE

Vallete Fontaine 1999 Memorias Cabernet Sauvignon (Maipo Valley) $NA. 81 *—D.T. (11/15/2002)*

VERAMONTE

Veramonte 2002 Cabernet Sauvignon (Maipo Valley) $10. Plump and soft, this easygoing Cab delivers slightly weedy, cassis-laden fruit in an accessible format. Finishes with some plum notes but also black tea leaves. A nice weekday wine that will pair perfectly with burgers or steak. **86 Best Buy** *(2/1/2005)*

Veramonte 2002 Single Vineyard Cabernet Sauvignon (Maipo Valley) $35. Dense and chocolaty, with lots of cassis fruit flavors to back it up. The mouthfeel isn't quite as rich as the Merlot's, but it boasts the same soft tannins and crisp acidity on the finish. **89** *(2/1/2005)*

Veramonte 2000 Chardonnay (Casablanca Valley) $10. 85 *—J.M. (11/15/2001)*

Veramonte 2002 Merlot (Casablanca Valley) $10. A bit herbal, and doesn't show the same level of flavor intensity or mouthfeel that the Cabernet does. It still delivers varietal black cherry and mocha flavors, but finishes with tart flavors and lots of fresh herbs. **84** *(2/1/2005)*

Veramonte 2000 Merlot (Maipo Valley) $10. 90 Best Buy *—S.H. (12/1/2002)*

Veramonte 2002 Single Vineyard Merlot (Casablanca Valley) $35. Even after 14 months in French oak, this wine shows a lot of fruit. Black cherries abound on the nose and palate, accented by mocha, dried spices and a just a hint of herbaceousness. The plush mouthfeel ends in a velvety, herbally complex finish. **90** *(2/1/2005)*

Veramonte 2001 Primus Red Blend (Casablanca Valley) $20. Deep, with a zesty nose that's a bit sharp. Flavors of cherry, cassis, and toast are round and ripe, as are the tannins and finish. For a Casablanca red, one that mixes Carmenère with Merlot and Cabernet, it's on the spot. Best Primus to date? **89** *—M.S. (3/1/2004)*

Veramonte 1999 Primus Red Blend (Casablanca Valley) $20. 86 *—D.T. (7/1/2002)*

Veramonte 2004 Sauvignon Blanc (Casablanca Valley) $10. Highly aromatic, this explodes with bright passion fruit scents and herbal pungency. Lots of pink grapefruit flavor and a zesty, crisp finish make this eminently drinkable. Drink now, as an apéritif or with light appetizers. **88 Best Buy** *(2/1/2005)*

Veramonte 2001 Sauvignon Blanc (Casablanca Valley) $10. 85 *—S.H. (12/1/2002)*

VERANDA

Veranda 2002 Founder's Reserve Red Blend (Aconcagua Valley) $50. Boisset, a Burgundian négociant, is involved in this Franco-Chilean joint venture, and this blend is smooth and clean, with driving berry fruit. In the mouth, cherry and raspberry notes come across as high-voltage, especially in the midpalate, but with ample spice there's more than enough to latch on to. **87** *—M.S. (3/1/2004)*

VIÑA AQUITANIA

Viña Aquitania 2002 Agapanto Cabernet Sauvignon (Maipo Valley) $10. The nose offers leather, briar patch and smoky cherry fruit, while the leafy palate has good berry flavors along with touches of earth and herbs. It's 85% Cab and the rest Carmenère and Merlot. **87 Best Buy** *—M.S. (3/1/2004)*

Viña Aquitania 2002 Sol de Sol Chardonnay (Malleco) $32. From deep in the south of Chile comes this small-lot Chardonnay, surely one of the country's most interesting white wines. Felipe de Solminihac gets fruit from his in-laws' vineyard to make this snappy, lemon-tinged wine, which also delivers apple, melon, and citrus. Balanced and unique. **89** *—M.S. (3/1/2004)*

VIÑA BISQUERTT

Viña Bisquertt 2003 Casa La Joya Reserve Cabernet Sauvignon (Colchagua Valley) $9. Smoky and saturated, with jammy, smooth aromas of plum and cassis. Lots of tannin and depth, and thus it spreads out all over your palate in mouthfilling fashion. Features loads of plum and chocolate, with a likable chewiness. **87 Best Buy** *—M.S. (12/15/2005)*

Viña Bisquertt 2003 Casa La Joya Gran Reserve Chardonnay (Colchagua Valley) $13. Light melon and wax bean aromas are pretty solid, as is the melon and pear palate. It's a fairly plump, round wine with vanilla notes and a nice texture. Finishes a bit sweet, with a blast of banana. **85** *—M.S. (12/15/2005)*

Viña Bisquertt 2003 Casa La Joya Reserve Shiraz (Colchagua Valley) $9. Slightly herbal, with hints of tree bark and chewing gum. Runs a touch hard and tannic, with cherry and little more carrying the flavor profile. Firm, even hard, in the mouth. **82** *—M.S. (12/15/2005)*

VIÑA CASA TAMAYA

Viña Casa Tamaya 2001 Estate Bottled Reserve Red Blend (Limarì Valley) $15. A mix of three standard grapes with a pickled, marinated quality and a noticeable vegetal character. Light and simple, with tomato on the palate and bell pepper on the finish. **82** *—M.S. (8/1/2004)*

VIÑA CASAS DEL BOSQUE

Viña Casas del Bosque 2001 Cabernet Sauvignon (Rapel Valley) $11. 84 *—M.S. (7/1/2003)*

Viña Casas del Bosque 2000 Gran Bosque Cabernet Sauvignon (Rapel Valley) $17. More concentrated than the winery's other reds, with root beer, cassis, and toasty wood on the bouquet. Yet it's still a lightweight in the world of Cabernets. It's snappy and tea-like on the palate, with a clean finish. **86** *—M.S. (3/1/2004)*

Viña Casas del Bosque 2002 Reserve Cabernet Sauvignon (Rapel Valley) $12. Pretty light, with tea and licorice aromas in front of lean raspberry and cherry fruit. Since it doesn't deal the force of your average Cabernet, it's more like Cab Light. **84** *—M.S. (3/1/2004)*

Viña Casas del Bosque 2000 Reserve Cabernet Sauvignon (Rapel Valley) $17. 88 *—C.S. (12/1/2002)*

Viña Casas del Bosque 2000 Chardonnay (Rapel Valley) $9. 82 *—J.C. (7/1/2002)*

Viña Casas del Bosque 2001 Reserve Chardonnay (Casablanca Valley) $15. 82 *—M.S. (7/1/2003)*

Viña Casas del Bosque 2003 Reserva Merlot (Casablanca Valley) $12. Heavily toasted, with lemon and burnt-toast aromas. The palate is extremely lemony and short of any lushness normally associated with Merlot. Has color but no ripeness. Proof that Casablanca is not great for Bordeaux varieties. **80** *—M.S. (11/1/2005)*

Viña Casas del Bosque 2002 Reserve Merlot (Casablanca Valley) $12. Fairly herbal at first, with sharp currant and cherry aromas. Airing, however, exposes hidden qualities and more flesh; after about 10 minutes you get full plum and raspberry notes along with soft tannins. **85** *—M.S. (3/1/2004)*

Viña Casas del Bosque 2002 Reserve Pinot Noir (Casablanca Valley) $12. Brick red in color, with leathery aromas surrounding cherry and mint. The palate is lean and dry, with smoky flavors to the berry notes. With pulsing acidity, it's fresh and ripe on the finish. **85** *—M.S. (3/1/2004)*

Viña Casas del Bosque 2004 Sauvignon Blanc (Casablanca Valley) $10. Passion fruit and citrus aromas carry the nose, but they run alongside some strong vegetal aromas. Flavorwise, we're talking green apple and celery, while the finish is crisp. Has its strong points but also a bold vegetal underbelly. Multiple U.S. importers. **83** *—M.S. (11/1/2005)*

Viña Casas del Bosque 2002 Sauvignon Blanc (Casablanca Valley) $10. 85 *—M.S. (7/1/2003)*

Viña Casas del Bosque 2003 Casa Viva Sauvignon Blanc (Casablanca Valley) $7. Pale in color, with light straw aromas and powerful scents of cucumber and grapefruit. Not too aggressive in the mouth, with a softer, lower-acid profile. Flavors of banana and pineapple suggest very ripe fruit. **85 Best Buy** *—M.S. (3/1/2004)*

Viña Casas del Bosque 2002 Reserve Sauvignon Blanc (Casablanca Valley) $15. **83** *—M.S. (7/1/2003)*

Viña Casas del Bosque 2003 Reserva Syrah (Casablanca Valley) $12. Good color, but mossy and rooty, with lemon-cola aromas. Shrill and tangy, with heat. Fails to turn the corner toward ripeness. **80 Best Buy** *—M.S. (11/1/2005)*

VIÑA EL AROMO

Viña el Aromo 2001 Private Reserve Cabernet Sauvignon (Maule Valley) $10. Nice and open-knit, with touches of coffee, eucalyptus, and earth on the nose, and lots of textbook cassis, cherry, and raspberry on the palate. Powerful and flavorful, with a slight herbal streak through the center. **87** *—M.S. (6/1/2004)*

Viña el Aromo 2003 Chardonnay (Maule Valley) $10. A big enough Chard, with pear, apple, and citrus blossom aromas on the nose. The hefty palate gives sweet white fruit, while the finish is basic and sugary, and borderline cloying. **83** *—M.S. (6/1/2004)*

VIÑA LA ROSA

Viña La Rosa 2003 La Capitana Carmenère (Cachapoal Valley) $12. Quite deep and dark, with integrated scents of oak, bacon, cinnamon, and earth. Admirable and rich, with lush plum and sugar beet flavors in front of a warm, full-bodied finish. Shows a tiny touch of green, but generally it's a positive take on the grape. **87 Best Buy** *—M.S. (2/1/2005)*

Viña La Rosa 2004 La Capitana Chardonnay (Cachapoal Valley) $15. Crisp and refreshing, with little to no oak character. By no means is it overpowering, but instead it features light citrus and flower aromas followed by apple, fresh scallion, and spice. A touch tangy, but smooth enough. Zesty. **85** *—M.S. (11/1/2005)*

Viña La Rosa 2003 La Capitana Merlot (Cachapoal Valley) $12. Great color but a bit green on the nose. Amid the timid bell pepper and green bean accents—and they're just that, accents—there's dark fruit and espresso. Very good in terms of mouthfeel, with structure and balance. Lots of positives here; but alas, some of the veggies as well. **85** *—M.S. (11/1/2005)*

Viña La Rosa 2003 La Palma Merlot (Cachapoal Valley) $7. Spunky and spicy, but vegetal. In the mouth, green bean, and bell pepper gang up on the fat berry fruit, creating a mixed palate that doesn't register on the ripeness meter. Finishes big, with the taste of carob. **83** *—M.S. (2/1/2005)*

Viña La Rosa 2004 La Palma Sauvignon Blanc (Cachapoal Valley) $7. Quite nice, and decidedly full of fruit. Plump apple and peach flavors carry some mineral and adequate cleansing acids. Feels right on the tongue, with clean, fresh, simple flavors. **86 Best Buy** *—M.S. (2/1/2005)*

VIÑA LEYDA

Viña Leyda 2002 Estación Cabernet Sauvignon (Maipo Valley) $NA. Fairly green and lacking in expression. A bit sharp and tart, too. Amid a sea of Cabernet, your best bet is to keep on fishing. **83** *—M.S. (3/1/2004)*

Viña Leyda 2002 Reserve Carmenère (Colchagua Valley) $18. Starts out with plum, cherry, and red cabbage aromas, which lead to a palate of light red fruit and mild vegetal flavors. Broad and starchy on the finish, with some thickness. Has its moments but doesn't really strike up the band. **83** *—M.S. (11/1/2005)*

Viña Leyda 2003 Estación Chardonnay (Chile) $NA. Slight melon and peach aromas create a soft, mild nose. Basic apple and melon flavors follow, and the finish is bumped forward by some driving acidity. Almost Sauvignon Blanc-like due to some unusual grassy notes. **85** *—M.S. (3/1/2004)*

Viña Leyda 2001 Falaris Hill Vineyard Reserve Chardonnay (Leyda Valley) $17. This is one of the first Leyda wines in the United States. It's well toasted, with crystallized mango and pineapple fruit. The finish is long, yet rather sugary. The wine shows bold flavors, but it needs more stuffing. **85** *—M.S. (3/1/2004)*

Viña Leyda 2003 Cahuil Vineyard Reserve Pinot Noir (Leyda Valley) $22. Plenty of kick to this wine, but not necessarily in the best spots. The nose deals leather, horseradish, and dark fruits, while the palate sends up beet and pepper flavors with an almost nutty aftertaste. Gets better with airing, but still a touch funky. **84** *—M.S. (11/1/2005)*

Viña Leyda 2002 Las Brisas Vineyard Reserve Pinot Noir (Chile) $NA. The Leyda Valley, with its resemblance to the Sonoma Coast, could someday become Pinot country for Chile. This youngster gives an inkling of what might be the future via its ripe, rooty nose along with black cherry and cola flavors. Seems very Leyda, for what that's worth at this early point in the game. **87** *—M.S. (3/1/2004)*

Viña Leyda 2003 Lot 21 Pinot Noir (Leyda Valley) $32. Cranberry and spice on the nose, with a hint of herbal mint. The mouth is a bit jumpy and shrill, which yields a fresh feel. In the glass, there's candied cherry and raspberry flavors and then finishing notes of tomato and carob. **86** *—M.S. (11/1/2005)*

Viña Leyda 2002 Vintage Selection Red Blend (Central Valley) $22. Aromas are of leather, tomato, and stewed berry, followed by a hard, almost nutty palate. Tight and tannic, with a rubbery mouthfeel. **83** *—M.S. (11/1/2005)*

Viña Leyda 2004 Estación Reserve Sauvignon Blanc (Leyda Valley) $12. Ocean fresh, with melon and tropical aromas. Fairly full and rich in the mouth, where melon and pineapple flavors dominate. Delivers enough zest and power to please. Shows what this emerging coastal region can do with Sauvignon Blanc. **86** *—M.S. (11/1/2005)*

VIÑA REQUINGUA

Viña Requingua 2001 Potro de Piedra Family Reserve Cabernet Blend (Curicó Valley) $18. This Cabernet Sauvignon/Cab Franc blend is potent and deep, with syrupy berry aromas touched up by hints of mint, green herbs, and coffee. The palate is rich and rewarding, with sweet plum, berry, and brown sugar flavors. It finishes plump and big, with chewy extract and meaty tannins. **88** *—M.S. (6/1/2004)*

Viña Requingua 2003 Toro de Piedra Reserva Cabernet Sauvignon (Curicó Valley) $14. Warm and spicy, with plenty of ripe black fruit backing things up. Along the path you'll find tree bark and fresh-turned earth. By no means a lightweight, as it offers plum, blackberry, clove, and the works. Concentrated and tight; a brawny, firm Cabernet. **88** *—M.S. (11/1/2005)*

Viña Requingua 2003 Puerto Viejo Carmenère (Curicó Valley) $9. Overloaded with Middle Eastern spice aromas and a chewy, meaty quality that submerges any fruit that might be present. A total oddball with hefty oak; it tastes like cumin-infused syrup. **81** *—M.S. (11/1/2005)*

Viña Requingua 2003 Puerto Viejo Chardonnay (Curicó Valley) $10. A touch oaky on the nose, with nuances of cream, banana, and coconut. Flavors of apple and pear are supported by nutmeg and other sweet spices. Quite soft and round on the tongue, with finishing notes of vanilla and white pepper, both courtesy of the forceful oaking. **86 Best Buy** *—M.S. (6/1/2004)*

Viña Requingua 2002 Puerto Viejo Merlot (Curicó Valley) $10. Ripe and chunky, with pickled aromas to the plum and berry nose. In the mouth, look for dried cherry, herb, and carob flavors, then milk chocolate on the finish. Not boring, but strange. **84** *—M.S. (6/1/2004)*

VIÑA SAN ESTEBAN

Viña San Esteban 2002 Reserva Carmenère (Aconcagua Valley) $8. Quite pickled, with rough vegetal notes making for a difficult bouquet. Flavors of beets, pepper, and clove lead into a lean finish that's both sugary and spicy, much like sweet-and-sour sauce. On the plus side, the mouthfeel is pretty good. **82** *—M.S. (6/1/2004)*

Viña San Esteban 2001 Reserva Merlot (Aconcagua Valley) $8. Aromas of chili powder, cherry, and wild berries create a pleasant-smelling bouquet. Flavors of berries and cream lead into a lengthy, solid finish that's both soft and easy due to fine-grained tannins. **85 Best Buy** *—M.S. (3/1/2004)*

VIÑA SANTA MONICA

Viña Santa Monica 1999 Cabernet Sauvignon (Rapel Valley) $8. **83** *—M.S. (7/1/2003)*

Viña Santa Monica 2001 Riesling (Rapel Valley) $8. **84** *—M.S. (8/1/2003)*

VIÑEDOS DE CANATA

Viñedos de Canata 2001 Paso Hondo Reserva Cabernet Sauvignon (Bio Bìo Valley) $12. Murky and damp smelling, with buttery strawberry flavors. Peppery and dry, with a raw, thin mouthfeel. Acceptable at a base level. **80** *—M.S. (11/1/2005)*

Viñedos de Canata 2003 Paso Hondo Reserva Chardonnay (Bìo Bìo Valley) $12. Strikes a pleasing opening chord with its pear and vanilla aromas along with a splinter of oak. The palate is a bit toasty, with smooth apple and pineapple flavors. Becomes more lemony as it opens, with woody, resiny notes peeking through. **86** *—M.S. (11/1/2005)*

Viñedos de Canata 2003 Merlot (Curicó Valley) $9. Vinegar and horseradish mar the plum notes on the nose, while the palate is exceedingly lean and snappy. Raspberry flavors fade as fast they arrive, and overall it's devoid of richness. **81** *—M.S. (11/1/2005)*

Viñedos de Canata 2003 Paso Hondo Alta Seleccion Winemaker's Cuvée Red Blend (Bìo Bìo Valley) $16. Takes off a bit dirty, with a lot of earth and green tobacco. Finds its stride later on, as it displays red fruit but also some clamping tannins. Sort of herbal in character as it struggles for adequate ripeness. **83** *—M.S. (11/1/2005)*

VIÑEDOS TORREÓN

Viñedos Torreón 2003 Torreón de Paredes Sauvignon Blanc (Chile) $11. Not too much fruit comes off the nose, and the palate seems dilute and mildly watery. In between, there's some citrus, particularly lemon. Still, it is rather bland in the final analysis. **83** *—M.S. (6/1/2004)*

VINO DE EYZAGUIRRE

Vino de Eyzaguirre 2001 San Francisco de Mostazal Reserva Especial Merlot (Colchagua Valley) $8. Burnt and smoky on the nose, with a meaty, earthy undercurrent. Flavors of plum and berry are best at first but lose clarity with each passing minute. Fairly plump but unfocused, thus not even the catchy blue burlap bag the bottle comes in is of much help. **84** *—M.S. (8/1/2004)*

Vino de Eyzaguirre 2001 San Francisco de Mostazal Reserva Especial Syrah (Colchagua Valley) $8. **82** *—M.S. (7/1/2003)*

VIU MANENT

Viu Manent 2003 Estate Bottled Cabernet Sauvignon (Colchagua Valley) $8. Brawny and colorful, with big black-fruit aromas along with scents of olive and green bean. Not vegetal, but the wine does show a green streak in addition to fine black cherry and cassis flavors. Powerful and full-bodied. Easy to enjoy. **87 Best Buy** *—M.S. (11/1/2005)*

Viu Manent 2002 Reserve Cabernet Sauvignon (Colchagua Valley) $12. Lean and spicy, with some green in the middle of the nose that's similar to celery. Additional bell pepper hangs heavily on the palate, but there's just enough berry to offset it. Tight in terms of feel, with well-integrated tannins. Feels nice; tastes more herbal than ideal. **85** *—M.S. (2/1/2005)*

Viu Manent 2001 Special Selection La Capilla Vineyard Cabernet Sauvignon (Colchagua Valley) $20. Good and tight, especially at first. Some airing and swirling reveals finely scripted black plum and a good deal of oak-driven coffee and chocolate. Neither heavy nor light; it toes the line of balance. If there's anything to take issue with, it's that the acidity seems on the high side. **89** *—M.S. (7/1/2005)*

Viu Manent 2000 Special Selection Cabernet Sauvignon (Colchagua Valley) $20. This single-vineyard Cab has slight vegetal aromas and a flat mouthfeel. The nose is largely balanced, with just a hint of green bean and lemon. The palate is chunky and dark, with candied fruit, chocolate, and soft tannins. Not likely to improve; drink now or wait for the 2001. **85** *—M.S. (3/1/2004)*

Viu Manent 2003 Estate Bottled Carmenère (Colchagua Valley) $8. Sweet and saucy, as if it had been marinated. The fruit tastes ultra sweet at first, but then it veers quickly toward vegetal. More grabby and sticky on the finish than desirable. **82** *—M.S. (2/1/2005)*

Viu Manent 2002 Oak Aged Reserve Carmenère (Colchagua Valley) $12. Well-oaked and generous, with aromas of root beer, tree bark, licorice, and black cherry. A flavorful mix of plum, blackberry, and cherry defines the palate, which is sleek and juicy, with spice and size. A very drinkable, clearly defined red. **88 Best Buy** *—M.S. (6/1/2004)*

Viu Manent 2003 Barrel Fermented Reserve Chardonnay (Colchagua Valley) $12. A lively barrel-fermented wine with vanilla, pear, and apple aromas. Hefty but balanced, with a palate full of pear, buttered toast, and proper acidity. An very good wine in the South American mode. **88 Best Buy** *—M.S. (2/1/2005)*

Viu Manent 1999 Reserve Chardonnay (Colchagua Valley) $12. **83** *—M.S. (7/1/2003)*

Viu Manent 2002 Malbec (Colchagua Valley) $8. **85 Best Buy** *—M.S. (12/1/2003)*

Viu Manent 2003 Los Carlos Estate Single Vineyard Malbec (Colchagua Valley) $18. Exemplary Chilean Malbec from the winery that does it better than the rest. This is a purple fury of inky, rich quality. The nose is harmonious and the palate both juicy and big, with snappy black cherry and tons of chocolate. Tight and secure all the way through. Hits the spot. **91 Editors' Choice** *—M.S. (11/1/2005)*

Viu Manent 2001 Oak Aged Reserve Malbec (Colchagua Valley) $12. **84** *—P.G. (12/1/2003)*

Viu Manent 2001 Special Selection Malbec (Colchagua Valley) $16. **88** *—M.S. (12/1/2003)*

Viu Manent 2001 Viu 1 Malbec (Colchagua Valley) $50. **92** *—M.S. (12/1/2003)*

Viu Manent 2004 Merlot (Colchagua Valley) $8. Green bean and bell pepper aromas, then red pepper and more green pepper to the palate, which does offer some plum and berry. Finishes with red pepper flake. Not impressive. **80** *—M.S. (11/1/2005)*

Viu Manent 1999 Merlot (Colchagua Valley) $8. **83** *—D.T. (7/1/2002)*

Viu Manent 2003 Oak Aged Reserve Merlot (Colchagua Valley) $12. Blends raspberry aromas with horseradish, and after that there are flavors of cherry, toast, coffee, and lingering oak. Turns lemony upon airing, with coffee and spiky tannins on the finish. **83** *—M.S. (12/15/2005)*

Viu Manent 1999 Reserve Merlot (Colchagua Valley) $13. **83** *—D.T. (7/1/2002)*

Viu Manent 2001 Sauvignon Blanc (Colchagua Valley) $8. **87** *—M.S. (3/1/2002)*

Viu Manent 2004 Reserve Sauvignon Blanc (Colchagua Valley) $12. Easy and fruity, with sweet aromas preceding tangy orange on the palate. Finishes solid, with citrus all the way. Medium in weight, with a slight salty edge. **86** *—M.S. (2/1/2005)*

Viu Manent 2003 Secreto Sauvignon Blanc (Colchagua Valley) $12. Tropical fruit mixes with tarragon and pickle on the nose, a clear take on the so-called New Zealand style. Flavors of lemon and orange are tangy and sharp, while the body holds onto some welcome roundness. A good one for sushi and pre-meal salads. **87 Best Buy** *—M.S. (7/1/2005)*

Viu Manent 2004 Secreto Syrah (Colchagua Valley) $12. With spiced meat, earth, and bright fruit on the nose, this shouldn't remain a secret forever. The wine is super easy to drink because the tannins are reserved. As for flavor, it features lively dark fruits and enough chocolate to satisfy a cocoa hound. Fine texture and balance are the finishing touches. **88 Best Buy** *—M.S. (11/1/2005)*

WALNUT CREST

Walnut Crest 2003 Cabernet Sauvignon (Rapel Valley) $5. It's hard to imagine getting a better red wine for five bucks, which makes this one of the best Best Buys out there. On the mark at all check points, with ripe cherry and plum flavors and a clean, smooth finish. Surprisingly solid. **86 Best Buy** *—M.S. (11/1/2005)*

Walnut Crest 2003 Chardonnay (Casablanca Valley) $5. Fruity and ripe, with the full blast of banana, melon, and peach aromas. In the mouth, ripe melon and candied apple get a boost from modest acids. Finishes mild and adequately smooth. **84 Best Buy** *—M.S. (6/1/2004)*

Walnut Crest 2003 Merlot (Rapel Valley) $5. Jammy and funky on the nose, with aromas of raspberry candy and some vinegar. Flavors of apple skin and grape juice are acceptable but not developed. Finishes with a starchy mouthfeel and notes of burnt espresso. **83** *—M.S. (8/1/2004)*

Walnut Crest 2001 Shiraz (Rapel Valley) $6. **83** *—M.S. (7/1/2003)*

YALI

Yali 2002 Chardonnay (Rapel Valley) $6. Soft honeysuckle, pear, and apple aromas are nice enough, an.. the mouth is fairly full, with zesty fruit supported by oak that turns a bit coconutty. Tasty and fleshy. **85 Best Buy** *—M.S. (3/1/2004)*

Yali 2001 Syrah (Maipo Valley) $6. The strawberry notes on the nose are sweet and candied more so than refined or classy. Flavors of plum and cassis are good enough, while the finish is heavy and round. It falls off at the end, however, failing to hold its grip. **84** *—M.S. (8/1/2004)*

France

France is the source of some of the greatest wines in the world, but has also been the source of some of the worst. Despite a labeling system that is often confusing to many outside of France, French wine still gives the greatest pleasure of any wine-producing region. The style of French wine echoes that of the French themselves—elegant, well-dressed, showing an appreciation for the good things of life but never to excess. French wines go best with food, never overpowering either in flavor or in alcohol, always well-mannered, often beautiful.

Cabernet Sauvignon grapes in a vineyard at Château Pichon-Longueville-Baron, Pauillac, Gironde, France.

The fact that, today, the quality of even the least-expensive French wine has improved impressively, means that there is a whole new range of wines open to wine drinkers.

All these qualities make it worthwhile to spend some time to get to know French wine and to appreciate its many facets. The country produces all styles of wine, from the cool wines of the Loire Valley, to the stylish whites of Alsace, through the classics of Bordeaux and Burgundy, to the more powerful, muscular offerings of the Rhône, to the warm wines of Languedoc and Roussillon, suffused with sun. And, of course, there are the great Champagnes.

In a world of international brands, where origin doesn't matter, France offers an alternative ethos. There is much talk of terroir, of the place and the culture from which a wine comes. It makes every wine different, makes many of them special. There is no homogeneity here.

France is an ordered country, and despite the seeming chaos of French wine, there is order in the system. Wines come from places, and these places are designated appellations. An appellation—*appellation contrôlée* on a wine label—is not a guarantee of quality. It is a guarantee of origin, and a guarantee that the wine has been made following certain rules specifying grape varieties, soil, planting, yields, and winemaking. The wine has also passed a sensory test which approves its style and its typicity for the appellation.

There are nearly 280 appellations in France, ranging from the huge—Bordeaux appellation, or Champagne—to the tiny, single-vineyard appellations of Coulée de Serrant in the Loire Valley and Romanée-Conti in Burgundy. There are regional appellations, there are district appellations, and there are appellations which cover only one commune.

A good example of this hierarchy is in Burgundy. The main appellation of the region is plain and simple: red and white, Bourgogne Rouge or Bourgogne Blanc. Climbing up the hierarchy are district appellations such as Chablis, for white wines, Mâcon for white and red wines, Côte de Beaune for reds, and so on.

Rising again in quality while the area of the appellation gets smaller are village appellations: Vougeot, Auxey-Duresse, Pommard, Nuits-St-Georges. In these villages, certain superior vineyards are designated premier cru—and you will find the name of the vineyard on the label. At the top of the quality heap are the single-vineyard appellations, the Grand Cru: Clos de Vougeot being perhaps the most famous.

There is one other category of wine which is in some ways the most interesting and exciting: Vin de Pays. These are everyday, ready-to-drink wines that offer some of the best values in the world. The labels, unlike appellation wines, will show grape varieties. Coming generally from the warm south of France, the wines will be warm, ripe, and fruity. The best-known example is Vin de Pays d'Oc.

Having established some of the ground rules for French wine, let's examine the fascinations of the different regions in more detail.

By far the largest, the most important, and one of the best regions, both for great wines and for bargains, is Bordeaux. Great reds from the great chateaus are what make the headlines, but Bordeaux is so big, that there is plenty of choice. Appellations with the name Côtes in the title are always worth seeking out, as are the white wines (yes, Bordeaux makes whites, both dry and sweet). And the general level of quality has improved dramatically. The reds are fruity, but never over-alcoholic, always with a layer of tannin that makes them great food wines. The whites are fresh, the best with wood flavors to give complexity. They may all be called "chateau this," "chateau that," but that's simply a way of saying that many Bordeaux wines come from one individual property.

Cabernet Sauvignon, Merlot, and Cabernet Franc are the main red grapes; Sauvignon Blanc and Sémillon are the main whites. But most Bordeaux is not a single varietal wine—it is more often a blend, which makes these wines more than the sum of their individual parts.

Burgundy is the other big French wine. It is a fifth the size of the Bordeaux region, and produces correspondingly more expensive wines, with fewer bargains, and more disappointments. The best way to buy Burgundy is to follow the best producers, and reliable reviews from buying guides or wine magazines. If you take that advice, the most seductive wines (red from Pinot Noir, white from Chardonnay, always 100 percent) are in your glass. It's not just chance that the Burgundy bottle has rounded sides, the Bordeaux bottle has straight: Burgundy appeals to the senses, Bordeaux to the intellect.

Much larger in scale than Burgundy is the Rhône valley. From the alcoholic and powerful highs of Châteauneuf-du-Pape, through the dense elegance of the Syrah wines of appellations like Côte-Rôtie and Hermitage, this is red wine country. Rich and generous, these wines appeal to wine drinkers used to California reds. And, just like Bordeaux, there is also great value to be found in this region: wines labeled Côtes du Rhône. If they have a village name attached (Rasteau and Seguret are among the best), they will be that much better, even if more expensive.

Bordeaux, Burgundy, and the Rhône are the best-known wine regions of France except for Champagne. This sparkling wine from the chalk slopes east of Paris is France's best answer to a global brand. It is the drink of celebration, of success, and the best way to drown sorrows. And, unlike the still French wines, which have been successfully copied around the world, Champagne remains inimitable, despite thousands of attempts. The combination of cool climate, chalk soil and—there's no other word for it—terroir are just so special.

As a complete contrast, there are the hot, sun-drenched vineyards of the south. Languedoc and Roussillon don't just produce tanker loads of inexpensive wine. Some areas such as Corbières, Minervois, Coteaux du Languedoc, and Côtes de Roussillon offer a magic mix of great value, history, and some fascinating herbal and fruity flavors.

After these greats, come the Loire and Alsace regions, which produce some of the greatest and most fascinating wines in France. Bordeaux and the Rhône are known for reds, Burgundy for reds and whites. The two cool-climate areas of Loire and Alsace are where the whites shine.

Alsace is unique in France in that producers are allowed to put the grape variety on the label of an appellation wine. It is also unique in that the grapes are a mix of German and French: Riesling and Gewürztraminer, Muscat and Pinot Gris. These are not light wines, but they have a fruitiness and a richness that is quite different from the German models just across the Rhine river. At the top of this list are the Alsace Grand Cru vineyards, single vineyards that can produce astonishing quality and longevity.

The Loire Valley is a complete mix. Every style of wine can be found along its six-hundred-mile length. The greatest styles are the Sauvignon Blanc of Sancerre and Pouilly-Fumé, the models for Sauvignon Blanc around the world. And the Chenin Blancs of the central Loire—the sweet wines of Vouvray and Anjou—have a poise and acidity which allows them to age for decades, yet be fresh when young. The dry Chenins of Savennières are the purest expression of their granite soil to be found. Finally, to complete the mix are the reds of Chinon and Bourgueil and the fresh, easy whites of Muscadet.

It's obvious from this brief list that France has variety, in profusion perhaps, but it does mean that there is never a dull moment when reaching for a bottle of French wine. If your wish is to have the same, safe bottle of wine every day, then non-European brands are the better option.

A. SOUTIRAN

A. Soutiran NV Grande Cru Blanc de Blancs (Champagne) $45. 91 *—P.G. (12/1/2000)*

A. Soutiran NV Grande Cru Brut (Champagne) $40. 88 *—P.G. (12/15/2000)*

ABARBANEL

Abarbanel NV Cremant d'Alsace (Alsace) $18. 86 *(12/31/2000)*

Abarbanel 2000 Gewürztraminer (Alsace) $21. Kicks off with enticing aromas redolent of lychee and peach. On the palate if falters a bit, however, with a sugary quality that masks the fruit. The finish serves up pretty spice notes. Kosher. 81 *—J.M. (4/3/2004)*

Abarbanel 2002 Château de La Salle Old Vines (Beaujolais-Villages) $12. Fruity and fun, with plum, cherry, raspberry, and herb flavors that go down easily. Soft, supple and light textured, the wine shows its terroir well, finishing with a bright edge. Kosher. 87 *—J.M. (4/3/2004)*

Abarbanel 2002 Riesling (Alsace) $21. Kind of candy-like on the nose. On the palate, it serves up a bright, lemony edge, though it lacks the depth of finer Riesling. Clean, bright and dry on the finish. Kosher. 82 *—J.M. (4/3/2004)*

Abarbanel 2000 Syrah (Vin de Pays d'Oc) $11. 81 *(10/1/2001)*

Abarbanel 1999 Syrah (Vin de Pays d'Oc) $11. 83 *(4/1/2001)*

Abarbanel 1998 Syrah (Vin de Pays d'Oc) $10. 84 *—M.S. (5/1/2000)*

ABBOTTS

Abbotts 1998 Boreas Rhône Red Blend (Languedoc) $19. 88 *—M.M. (11/1/2000)*

Abbotts 1998 Cumulo Nimbus Shiraz (Minervois) $35. 91 *—M.M. (11/1/2000)*

Abbotts 2000 Cumulus Syrah (Minervois) $17. After the complex, varietally true bouquet of smoked meat, plum, and herbal-floral notes, this wine doesn't deliver quite the same wealth of flavor. Lean and high in acidity, it finishes with tea-like tannins. Pretty on the nose, but lacks charm on the palate. 85 *—J.C. (11/15/2005)*

AGRAPART & FILS

Agrapart & Fils 1996 Blanc de Blancs (Champagne) $37. 89 *—R.V. (12/1/2002)*

Agrapart & Fils NV Réserve Blanc de Blancs Brut (Champagne) $23. 90 *—R.V. (12/1/2002)*

ALAIN GRAILLOT

Alain Graillot 1999 La Guiraude (Crozes-Hermitage) $NA. 92 *—R.V. (6/1/2002)*

ALAIN GRAS

Alain Gras 1998 St.-Romain $22. 88 *—M.S. (11/1/2000)*

ALAIN POULET

Alain Poulet NV Tradition (Clairette de Die) $12. 84 *—S.H. (12/15/2000)*

ALBERT BICHOT

Albert Bichot 2002 (Criots-Bâtard-Montrachet) $250. A beautifully proportioned wine, which is full of ethereal flowery aromas, crisp, fresh fruit and just a touch of toast. It is so delicious to drink now that it is easy to forget it could age well over 7 years or more. 92 *—R.V. (9/1/2004)*

Albert Bichot 2003 Domaine du Pavillon Les Charmes Premier Cru (Meursault) $76. A blockbuster of a wine, with plenty of toast and flavors of sweet green plums. There is lively acidity at the end, which leaves a crisp, green aftertaste. 92 *—R.V. (9/1/2005)*

Albert Bichot 2003 Domaine du Clos Frantin (Grands-Echézeaux) $190. A big, structured but juicy wine that exudes perfumed Pinot Noir. Almost Californian in its richness, it has layers of dry tannins that make its pedigree clear. There is also impressive freshness and acidity to give the whole wine a lift. 91 *—R.V. (9/1/2005)*

Albert Bichot 2002 Domaine du Clos Frantin (Chambertin) $173. Dark tannins and aromas of sweet strawberries give this wine an immediate attraction. The fruit is dominant, as are new wood and heavy tannins on the finish. 89 *—R.V. (9/1/2004)*

Albert Bichot 2003 Domaine du Clos Frantin Les Malconsorts Premier Cru (Vosne-Romanée) $110. The elegance of the vineyard overcomes the richness of the vintage to yield a classic Vosne. While there is a new wood element, it is not too dominant, but supports the fruit tannins, the sweet red fruit and the long, dry but fresh finish. 91 *—R.V. (9/1/2005)*

Albert Bichot 2003 Domaine du Pavillon Clos de Ursulines (Pommard) $50. While this single vineyard, entirely owned by Bichot, is only a village wine, not a premier cru, it behaves like a premier cru, giving richness, structure, generosity and lively acidity. This is pure fruit, pure Pinot and purely delicious. 90 *—R.V. (9/1/2005)*

Albert Bichot 2003 Domaine du Pavillon Les Rugiens Premier Cru (Pommard) $90. A beautifully structured wine, with red fruit flavors that are immediately attractive. Yet there are enough tannins here to age it over 5 years or more. **90** *—R.V. (9/1/2005)*

Albert Bichot 1996 Millennium Cuvée (Gevrey-Chambertin) $29. 93 *(11/15/1999)*

ALBERT PIC

Albert Pic 1997 Montmains Premier Cru (Chablis) $33. 87 *—M.S. (10/1/1999)*

ALFRED GRATIEN

Alfred Gratien NV Brut (Champagne) $50. A very lean, dry style that focuses on its acidity and green fruits. This makes it a style that needs good bottle aging—the sample tasted was too young. But for those who like dry, crisp Champagnes, this is beautifully made. **88** *—R.V. (12/1/2005)*

Alfred Gratien NV Cuvée Paradis Rosé Brut (Champagne) $110. Onion-skin color leads to a wine that is packed with deep fruit flavors. Considerably dry but a great food wine, with good acidity and ability to age well in bottle. The sample tasted was too young, and needed at least a year's aging. **90 Cellar Selection** *—R.V. (12/1/2005)*

ANTONIN RODET

Antonin Rodet 2001 Chardonnay (Bourgogne) $11. 84 *—J.C. (10/1/2003)*

Antonin Rodet 1999 Chablis $15. 86 *(12/31/2001)*

Antonin Rodet 1999 Gevrey-Chambertin $34. 89 *(1/1/2004)*

Antonin Rodet 1999 Pommard $40. 88 *(12/31/2001)*

Antonin Rodet 1998 Nuits-St.-Georges $37. 88 *—P.G. (11/1/2002)*

Antonin Rodet 2002 Les Porêts (Nuits-St.-Georges) $44. A modern, spicy style of wine, which has toast and new wood aromas. It is dark and smoky, with new wood and ripe black fruit on the palate. **89** *—R.V. (9/1/2004)*

Antonin Rodet 2002 Rue de Chaux Premier Cru (Nuits-St.-Georges) $57. Powerful and dark, this wine has toasty, woody flavors as well as fine, ripe tannins. It's a powerful, smooth, well-structured wine. **88** *—R.V. (9/1/2004)*

ARTHUR METZ

Arthur Metz 2003 Cuvée Anne-Laure Gewürztraminer (Alsace) $11. Drier and crisper than many Gewürzes, with grapefruit and citrus blossom aromatics that flow easily into apple and pear flavors. Clean and citrusy on the finish, picking up hints of chalk dust. **86 Best Buy** *—J.C. (11/1/2005)*

AUGUSTIN FLORENT

Augustin Florent NV Syrah (Vin de Pays d'Oc) $9. 82 *(10/1/2001)*

BARON GASSIER

Baron Gassier 2003 Rosé Blend (Côtes de Provence) $9. A decent quaffing rosé, with a bright strawberry hue and aromas and flavors of bubblegum, cherries, and red plums. Turns herbal and slightly drying on the finish. **84** *—J.C. (12/1/2004)*

BARON PHILIPPE DE ROTHSCHILD

Baron Philippe de Rothschild 2000 Baron'Arques (Vin de Pays de L'Aude) $40. Very modern, with overt maple notes and plenty of black-fruit aromas. The toasty, tight bouquet oozes bitter chocolate and cassis, while the firm palate yields nothing but oak-enveloped plum and cherry. Needs two years to soften. From Baron Philippe de Rothschild and several Limoux-area growers known as the Vignerons du Sieur d'Arques. **89** *—M.S. (1/1/2004)*

Baron Philippe de Rothschild 1998 Baron'Arques (Vin de Pays d'Oc) $45. 88 *—M.M. (2/1/2002)*

Baron Philippe de Rothschild 2002 Mouton Cadet Rouge (Bordeaux) $8. Branded Bordeaux has a deservedly spotty reputation, but this year's Mouton Cadet aims to start turning that around. Cherries and chocolate on the nose, followed by smoky, earthy tobacco and black-cherry flavors. A silky texture makes it ready to drink now. **86 Best Buy** *—J.C. (6/1/2005)*

Baron Philippe de Rothschild 2003 Mouton Cadet Blanc (Bordeaux) $8. Yes—*that* Mouton Cadet—has been transformed into a clean fresh wine featuring notes of apple and citrus and touches of earth and herb. A blend of 50% Sémillon, 40% Sauvignon Blanc and 10% Muscadelle. **84 Best Buy** *—J.C. (6/1/2005)*

Baron Philippe de Rothschild 1999 Mouton Cadet Blanc (Bordeaux) $11. 81 *—J.C. (3/1/2001)*

Baron Philippe de Rothschild 1999 Merlot (Vin de Pays d'Oc) $10. 85 *—D.T. (2/1/2002)*

Baron Philippe de Rothschild 2000 Viognier (Vin de Pays d'Oc) $10. 85 *—S.H. (10/1/2001)*

BARONS EDMUND BENJAMIN DE ROTHSCHILD

Barons Edmund Benjamin de Rothschild 1998 Haut-Médoc $27. 88 *—J.C. (4/1/2001)*

BARTON & GUESTIER

Barton & Guestier 2000 Magnol (Médoc) $10. From the great 2000 vintage, this is suitably deep, impressive wine. Wood and vanilla aromas show through to taste with sweet blackcurrants, some sweet jelly flavors, balanced with a big, long-term aging structure. Magnol is a property in the southern Médoc, owned by Barton & Guestier. **87** —*R.V. (12/1/2004)*

Barton & Guestier 2002 Cabernet Sauvignon (Vin de Pays d'Oc) $6. This is a well-structured juicy, fruity wine. Aromas of red currants, and flavors of fresh black fruits, are balanced by firm, dry tannins and some acidity. **83** —*R.V. (12/1/2004)*

Barton & Guestier 2000 French Tom Private Collection Cabernet Sauvignon (Vin de Pays d'Oc) $14. 85 —*S.H. (1/1/2002)*

Barton & Guestier 2002 Chardonnay (Vin de Pays d'Oc) $6. There are sweet vanilla aromas, along with aromas of green plums. This is a soft, creamy wine, with just a touch of greeness, and a full, creamy texture. **82** —*R.V. (12/1/2004)*

Barton & Guestier 2002 Chardonnay (Mâcon-Villages) $9. A fresh, but full-bodied wine, which has aromas of citrus and sawn wood. It is ripe, smooth, with vanilla layers sandwiched between green fruits and white currants. This makes an attractive food wine for fish and white meat dishes. **84** —*R.V. (12/1/2004)*

Barton & Guestier 2000 Chardonnay Saint-Louis Tradition 2000 Chardonnay (Mâcon-Villages) $13. 86 —*S.H. (1/1/2002)*

Barton & Guestier 1998 Reserve Chardonnay (Vin de Pays d'Oc) $10. 86 Best Buy *(5/1/2000)*

Barton & Guestier 2001 Tradition (Pouilly-Fuissé) $9. This is a good price for a wine from this appellation. It's drier and earthier than the typical New World Chard, with peach flavors and crisp acidity. **85 Best Buy** —*S.H. (12/1/2004)*

Barton & Guestier 1998 Tradition Pouilly-Fuissé $17. 86 *(5/1/2000)*

Barton & Guestier 1999 Tradition Saint-Louis Chardonnay (Mâcon-Villages) $8. 82 —*D.T. (2/1/2002)*

Barton & Guestier 2001 Tradition (Vouvray) $NA. 84 *(11/15/2002)*

Barton & Guestier 2001 Tradition (Beaujolais-Villages) $8. 83 —*J.C. (11/15/2003)*

Barton & Guestier 2002 (Beaujolais) $9. Aromas of sweet strawberries make this an immediately attractive wine. It is lightly colored, with flavors of fresh fruit and just a hint of dryness. Soft and easy, it is almost like alcoholic strawberry juice. **82** —*R.V. (12/1/2004)*

Barton & Guestier 2000 Tradition Saint-Louis (Beaujolais) $13. 84 —*S.H. (1/1/2002)*

Barton & Guestier 2002 Muscadet Sevre Et Maine $9. Typical crisp, appley aromas set the scene for a wine with fresh, light, lively fruit and crisp acidity. **81** —*R.V. (12/1/2004)*

Barton & Guestier 2002 Merlot (Vin de Pays d'Oc) $7. Smells a bit funky and meaty, and turns watery in the mouth, with thin flavors of cherries. **82** —*S.H. (9/1/2004)*

Barton & Guestier 1999 Merlot (Vin de Pays d'Oc) $7. 82 —*D.T. (2/1/2002)*

Barton & Guestier 2000 French Tom Private Collection Merlot (Vin de Pays d'Oc) $14. 83 —*S.H. (1/1/2002)*

Barton & Guestier 1998 Reserve Merlot (Vin de Pays d'Oc) $10. 86 *(5/1/2000)*

Barton & Guestier 2001 Côtes-du-Rhône $9. This is an earthy, perfumed style of wine, full of sweet, juicy fruit and layers of dry tannins. For a basic Côtes du Rhône, this is a full-bodied rich wine. **84** —*R.V. (12/1/2004)*

Barton & Guestier 2000 Tradition (Côtes-du-Rhône) $NA. 85 *(11/15/2002)*

Barton & Guestier 2001 Tradition Châteauneuf-du-Pape $9. Attractive, lightewight wine with flavors of red plums and damsons. The tannins are soft, easy and the wine is ready to drink. **83** —*R.V. (3/1/2004)*

Barton & Guestier 2001 Founder's Collection Sauvignon Blanc (Bordeaux) $10. 84 *(11/15/2002)*

Barton & Guestier 2002 Shiraz (Vin de Pays d'Oc) $6. A deep purple colored wine, with violet and lavender perfumes. There are firm tannins, and flavors of sweet, black fruits, balanced with acidity. The wine is just spoilt by a touch of leaness to finish. **82** —*R.V. (12/1/2004)*

Barton & Guestier 2001 Syrah (Vin de Pays d'Oc) $7. 83 *(11/15/2002)*

BAUCHET PÈRE ET FILS

Bauchet Père et Fils 1998 Cuvée Saint Nicaise Premier Cru Blanc de Blancs Brut (Champagne) $44. Dusty and mushroomy, but also lively and lemony. The flavors are of clean earth and cultivated button mushrooms, chalk dust, and citrus. It's a relatively light-bodied Champagne that would serve well as an apéritif. **90** —*J.C. (12/1/2004)*

Bauchet Père et Fils NV Premier Cru Sélection Brut (Champagne) $35. 89 —*M.S. (12/15/2003)*

Bauchet Père et Fils NV Sélection Brut (Champagne) $NA. 81 —*M.S. (12/15/2003)*

Bauchet Père et Fils NV Sélection Roland Bouchet (Champagne) $33. Candied aromas call to mind confectioners' sugar, tart strawberries, and bubble gum. Light and frothy in the mouth, picking up chalky, orangey notes on the finish. **84** —*J.C. (12/1/2004)*

BEAUMONT DES CRAYÈRES

Beaumont des Crayères 1996 Nostalgie (Champagne) $60. The 200 growers who are members of the Beaumont des Crayères cooperative are all based in and around Epernay have the choice of great Chardonnay, which makes up 60% of this prestige cuvée. Full-bodied, toasty and now mature, it is is full of vanilla and honey flavors. This is a fine food wine, with its weight, its richness, and its finishing acidity. **91** *—R.V. (12/1/2004)*

BELLEFONTAINE

Bellefontaine 1999 Merlot (Vin de Pays d'Oc) $7. 83 *—D.T. (2/1/2002)*

BESSERAT DE BELLEFON

Besserat de Bellefon NV Cuvée des Moines Blanc de Blancs (Champagne) $NA. 83 *(1/1/2004)*

Besserat de Bellefon NV Cuvée des Moines Brut (Champagne) $35. 85 *—M.S. (12/15/2003)*

Besserat de Bellefon NV Cuvée des Moines Brut Rose (Champagne) $45. 84 *(1/1/2004)*

BILLECART-SALMON

Billecart-Salmon NV Brut Rosé (Champagne) $68. A bone-dry but delicious wine, with red fruits and a beautiful onion-skin color that just hints at rosé. Lovely acidity completes the serious and highly enjoyable wine. **92 Editors' Choice** *—R.V. (12/1/2005)*

Billecart-Salmon NV Blanc de Blancs Brut Grand Cru (Champagne) $65. From five grand cru vineyards in the Côte des Blancs, this 100% Chardonnay is a great wine, with some toast and almond flavors showing good bottle age, along with freshness, finesse, ripe white fruits, and a structured, lingering aftertaste. **94** *—R.V. (12/1/2005)*

BLANC DE LYNCH-BAGES

Blanc de Lynch-Bages 2002 White Blend (Bordeaux) $38. Another novelty white wine from a property better known for its Pauillac, the blend here is 40% Sémillon, 40% Sauvignon Blanc and 20% Muscadelle. It's light in body, offering up grassy notes of apple, mineral, and just hints of buttered toast. The mouthwatering finish is its best feature, picking up subtle wood tones. **86** *—J.C. (6/1/2005)*

BOLLINGER

Bollinger 1996 Grande Année Brut (Champagne) $90. Blockbuster aromas of honey and toast, ripe apples, and citrus are complex from the first pour and develop even more complexity with air, turning meatier and more savory. Creamy and smooth in the mouth, with cascading flavors of buttered nuts and lush fruit, all balanced by great acidity and length. Drink now or hold another 5 years. **94 Cellar Selection** *—J.C. (12/1/2004)*

Bollinger 1995 Grande Année Brut (Champagne) $90. **95 Cellar Selection** *—P.G. (12/15/2002)*

Bollinger 1992 Grande Année Brut (Champagne) $90. 89 *(12/15/2001)*

Bollinger 1988 R.D. Brut (Champagne) $150. 89 *(12/15/2001)*

Bollinger 1988 R.D. Extra Brut (Champagne) $150. 88 *(12/15/2001)*

Bollinger NV Special Cuvée Brut (Champagne) $50. The Bollinger style is always rich, food friendly, and impressive. This wine is all of those things, with power and intensity of flavor along with ripe fruit, a layer of toastiness and a dry aftertaste. This is a style of wine that can take even more bottle aging. **94 Editors' Choice** *—R.V. (12/1/2005)*

Bollinger NV Special Cuvée Brut (Champagne) $45. **92 Editors' Choice** *—P.G. (12/15/2002)*

Bollinger NV Special Cuvée Brut (Champagne) $45. 89 *(12/1/2000)*

BONNAIRE

Bonnaire NV Blanc de Blancs Brut (Champagne) $37. 90 *—R.V. (12/1/2002)*

BONNY DOON

Bonny Doon 2001 Heart of Darkness (Madiran) $18. Dark indeed, of color and soul. This brooding, sensual wine has cherries, plums, black pepper, and Provencal herbs flowing through its veins. To say it's fruity, tannic, and dry misses the point, which is Latin complexity. This Mediterranean red runs deep. **91** *—S.H. (2/1/2004)*

BOSQUET DES PAPES

Bosquet des Papes 2003 A La Gloire de Mon Grand-Père (Châteauneuf-du-Pape) $37. Made from vines planted by grandpa Joseph Boiron, this wine, created by Nicolas, is 98% Grenache. It is solid, not huge, with some jammy, sweet fruit, some licorice, herbs and a welcoming southern warmth. **88** *—R.V. (12/31/2005)*

Bosquet des Papes 2003 Cuvée Tradition (Châteauneuf-du-Pape) $30. This Cuvée Tradition is made from 50-year-old vines on the Boiron family estate. With aromas of lavender and southern perfumes, it is layered with dry fruits and herbal flavors, with firm tannins in the background. This is a classic Châteauneuf-du-Pape, not as alcoholic as many 2003s. **87** *—R.V. (12/31/2005)*

BOUCHARD AÎNÉ & FILS

Bouchard Aîné & Fils 2001 Chardonnay (Mâcon-Villages) $8. 83 *—J.C. (10/1/2003)*

Bouchard Aîné & Fils 2000 (Puligny-Montrachet) $50. 87 *—J.C. (10/1/2003)*

Bouchard Aîné & Fils 1999 Chardonnay (Bourgogne) $11. 85 *(11/15/2001)*

Bouchard Aîné & Fils 2000 Pinot Noir (Bourgogne) $11. 80 *—J.C. (10/1/2003)*

Bouchard Aîné & Fils 2000 (Pommard) $35. 87 *—J.C. (10/1/2003)*

Bouchard Aîné & Fils 1999 (Pommard) $NA. 86 *—P.G. (11/1/2002)*

Bouchard Aîné & Fils 1999 Clos du Roi (Beaune) $30. 91 Editors' Choice *(11/15/2001)*

Bouchard Aîné & Fils 2000 Cuvée Signature (Volnay) $34. 83 *—J.C. (10/1/2003)*

Bouchard Aîné & Fils 2000 Cuvée Signature Le Meix Bataille Premier Cru (Monthelie) $29. 87 *—J.C. (10/1/2003)*

BOUCHARD PÈRE & FILS

Bouchard Père & Fils 1998 Chardonnay (Chassagne-Montrachet) $39. 87 *—P.G. (7/1/2000)*

Bouchard Père & Fils 1997 Chardonnay (Puligny-Montrachet) $48. 90 *—P.G. (7/1/2000)*

Bouchard Père & Fils 2003 Beaune du Château Premier Cru (Beaune) $75. A blend of premier cru vineyards, this wine is fresh, with plenty of lively white fruit flavors. But there's enough richness there to balance the green flavors. 88 *—R.V. (9/1/2005)*

Bouchard Père & Fils 2003 (Chevalier-Montrachet) $230. Bouchard is in the fortunate position of having vines at all heights on the slope of this great vineyard. That gives a complete picture of the richness of the wines, the open fruitiness of this grand cru. Yellow-fruit flavors are accented by wood and spice. The wine also has good acidity, and fine structure for aging. 93 *—R.V. (9/1/2005)*

Bouchard Père & Fils 1998 Clos St.-Landry (Beaune) $50. 90 *—P.G. (7/1/2000)*

Bouchard Père & Fils 1998 La Vignée Chardonnay (Bourgogne) $10. 86 *—P.G. (7/1/2000)*

Bouchard Père & Fils 2003 Meursault Genevrières Premier Cru (Meursault) $75. It's the citrus character that is the most immediately obvious in this wine. But there is much more to it than just that: wood, ripe peaches, and quinces, and a layer of fresh acidity that more than balances the ripeness of the fruit. This is charming already, but should develop over the next few years. 92 *—R.V. (9/1/2005)*

Bouchard Père & Fils 2000 (Bonnes-Mares) $120. 96 Editors' Choice *—R.V. (11/1/2002)*

Bouchard Père & Fils 1998 (Pommard) $45. 87 *—P.G. (7/1/2000)*

Bouchard Père & Fils 2003 Beaune du Château Premier Cru (Beaune) $35. Bouchard makes a blend of premier crus for this proprietary wine. It's a juicy wine packed with sweet flavors. It's very generous, ripe, and rich. 89 *—R.V. (9/1/2005)*

Bouchard Père & Fils 2003 Beaune Marconnets Premier Cru (Beaune) $50. This is a big wine, powered by dusty, ripe tannins, and dense black fruit flavors. The power doesn't take away from the wine's freshness and its rich perfumes. 91 *—R.V. (9/1/2005)*

Bouchard Père & Fils 2003 Caillerets Ancienne Cuvée Carnot Premier Cru (Volnay) $70. A big-hearted, big-fruited wine, which has hints of vanilla. It is hugely ripe, jammy, and powerful, but still preserves a touch of freshness. 91 *—R.V. (9/1/2005)*

Bouchard Père & Fils 2003 Clos des Chínes Premier Cru (Volnay) $70. A wine from one of the best vineyards in Volnay, it offers great definition, solid tannins and dense fruit. It is both structured and fresh, fleshed out with juicy Pinot Noir flavors. Give it time; this is going to be one delicious wine. 93 *—R.V. (9/1/2005)*

Bouchard Père & Fils 2002Echézeaux $115. A powerful wine, filled with rich, solid fruit, high tannins, and shot through with dark plums, flavors of toast and a layer of acidity. 94 *—R.V. (9/1/2004)*

Bouchard Père & Fils 1998 La Vignée Pinot Noir (Bourgogne) $10. 86 *—P.G. (7/1/2000)*

Bouchard Père & Fils 2002 Le Corton (Corton) $67. Solid, rich wine, which is piled with tannins and beautifully crafted black fruits, acidity and firm tannins. 94 *—R.V. (9/1/2004)*

Bouchard Père & Fils 2002 Les Cailles Premier Cru (Nuits-St.-Georges) $60. A very good, elegant wine, this premier cru has beautifully ripe plum fruit accented with spice. Firm tannins suggest midterm aging. 88 *—R.V. (9/1/2004)*

Bouchard Père & Fils 2002 Rugiens Premier Cru (Pommard) $58. Huge, solid tannins give this wine great power. Concentrated ripe fruit and acidity drive through the tannins. A firm, solid wine. 90 *—R.V. (9/1/2004)*

Bouchard Père & Fils 2002 Volnay Clos des Chènes (Volnay) $46. Big, firm tannins dominate this wine, which has powerful fruit and wood flavors. This is a wine that will age well—give it at least 10 years for maturity. 91 *—R.V. (9/1/2004)*

BOUVET-LADUBAY

Bouvet-Ladubay NV Brut (Loire) $12. **86** *(11/15/1999)*

Bouvet-Ladubay 1998 Saphir Brut (Saumur) $16. **89** *—P.G. (12/15/2002)*

Bouvet-Ladubay 1998 Saphir Brut Vintage (Saumur) $85. **87** *—M.S. (12/15/2003)*

BROTTE

Brotte 2003 Château de Bord Laudun (Côtes-du-Rhône Villages) $16. Youthfully exuberant and fille with fruit, but also a bit tannic and drying on the finish. Leathery fruit seems a bit overdone, and there's a hint of volatility as well; tough call, and this may well settle down and be better than it is now given a couple of years in the cellar. **84** *—J.C. (2/1/2005)*

Brotte 2003 Domaine Bouvencourt (Vacqueyras) $25. A nice, easy-drinking Côtes-du-Rhône, with dark plum and blackberry aromas and flavors and hints of smoke and anise. It's neither too big nor too light—if Goldilocks were a wine-drinker, she'd say the weight on the palate is just right. **86** *—J.C. (2/1/2005)*

Brotte 2003 Domaine du Versant Doré (Condrieu) $48. Odd stuff, with vegetal notes appearing in place of the ripe floral aromas expected of Viognier. Corn, lime, and green tomatoes all show up on the nose or in the mouth, along with a slightly oily mouthfeel. **82** *—J.C. (2/1/2005)*

Brotte 2003 Les Brottiers (Côtes-du-Rhône) $10. This full-bodied white boasts layers of mouthfilling pears, melons, and dried spices, and it finishes long. With its richness it would be a fine accompaniment to cream-sauced fish or chicken dishes. **89** *—J.C. (2/1/2005)*

BRUNO PAILLARD

Bruno Paillard 1989 Brut (Champagne) $85. **91** *(12/1/2001)*

Bruno Paillard NV Première Cuvée Brut Rosé (Champagne) $55. With a touch of caramel aromas, this appears initially soft. But the palate is very dry and light, balanced with flavors of lychees and red fruits. Finishes with clean acidity. **90** *—R.V. (12/1/2005)*

Bruno Paillard NV Première Cuvée Brut Rosé (Champagne) $50. **90** *(12/1/2001)*

Bruno Paillard 1990 N.P.U. (Champagne) $185. **95 Cellar Selection** *(12/1/2001)*

Bruno Paillard NV Réserve Privée Brut (Champagne) $60. **91 Editors' Choice** *(12/1/2001)*

BRUT DARGENT

Brut Dargent NV Blanc de Blancs Brut (Jura) $11. Light apple and powdered sugar make for a less than powerful nose, while the palate offers fresh orange. Quite light and simple, but generally speaking it's clean and easy. Finishes slightly sweet. **84** *—M.S. (12/31/2005)*

CALVET

Calvet 1998 Bordeaux $7. **84** *(12/1/2000)*

Calvet 2002 Calvet Réserve (Bordeaux) $15. Turns citrusy and tart on the finish, but this is a decent little claret nonetheless. Smells just right, with cedar, vanilla, and cherries combining on the nose, then delivers a light, satiny-smooth mouthful of tart berries and vanilla flavor. **84** *—J.C. (6/1/2005)*

Calvet 1996 Réserve (Bordeaux) $10. **87** *(12/1/2000)*

Calvet 1998 Cabernet Sauvignon (Vin de Pays d'Oc) $7. **85** *(12/1/2000)*

Calvet 1998 Calvet Premiere Chardonnay (Bourgogne) $17. **89** *(12/1/2000)*

Calvet 1999 Pinot Noir (Bourgogne) $39. **83** *—P.G. (11/1/2002)*

Calvet 1999 Nuits-St.-Georges $39. **84** *—P.G. (11/1/2002)*

Calvet 1998 Calvet Première Pinot Noir (Bourgogne) $17. **85** *(12/1/2000)*

Calvet 2004 Extra Fruit XF (Bordeaux) $10. Middle of the road white wine, with a nose dictated by pink grapefruit, peach, and pear. Not the most exciting painting in the museum, but nothing wrong either. Good but sort of flat. **85 Best Buy** *(7/1/2005)*

Calvet 1998 Réserve (Bordeaux) $10. **88 Best Buy** *(12/1/2000)*

CAMILLE GIROUD

Camille Giroud 2003 Beaune Premier Cru Les Avaux (Beaune) $51. A ripe, juicy wine, one that has a good balance between new wood, acidity, and fresh red fruit flavors. Its dry tannins suggest aging potential. It's a good, solid wine, already delicious but will develop well. **89** *—R.V. (9/1/2005)*

CASTEL MONTPLAISIR

Castel Montplaisir 1997 Cahors $11. **84** *—J.C. (3/1/2001)*

CASTEL ROUBINE

Castel Roubine 1996 Cru Classe (Côtes de Provence) $12. **82** *—J.C. (3/1/2001)*

CATHERINE DE SAINT-JUERY

Catherine de Saint-Juery 1998 Coteaux du Languedoc $8. **84** *(10/1/2001)*

CATTIER

Cattier 1998 Cuvée Renaissance (Champagne) $NA. This is Cattier's best wine, a fine blend of 60% red grapes and 40% Chardonnay, very refined, sophisticated. It has an element of toast, ripe fruits, with green fruit flavors and almonds. It could well age over the next 5 years, but at this stage it is already well integrated, and delicious as a food wine. **89** *—R.V. (12/1/2004)*

CAVE DE LUGNY

Cave De Lugny 2001 Les Charmes Chardonnay (Mâcon-Lugny) $9. **82** *—S.H. (1/1/2002)*

CAVE DE SARRAS

Cave de Sarras 1998 Cuvée Champtenaud Syrah (St.-Joseph) $19. **87** *—M.S. (9/1/2003)*

CAVE DE TAIN L'HERMITAGE

Cave de Tain L'Hermitage 1999 Nobles Rives (Hermitage) $NA. **90** *—R.V. (6/1/2002)*

Cave de Tain L'Hermitage 2003 Crozes-Hermitage $13. Fresh and crisp, this is a wine which has fine acidity. It has an earthy, barnyard element which gives it weight and fatness. **84** *—R.V. (2/1/2005)*

Cave de Tain IL'Hermitage 2001 Hermitage $35. A ripe, spicy wood flavored wine, with tastes of fresh peaches and apricots. It is rich, with a balance that has come together well. This is 100 percent Marsanne, and that shows in the wine's full-body and dried fruit and spice. A great performance from the Tain cooperative. **90 Editors' Choice** *—R.V. (2/1/2005)*

Cave de Tain L'Hermitage 2001 Cornas $25. For lovers of Syrah, Cornas is the purest expression, with its dark, brooding tannins and heady fruit. This wine, from the Tain cooperative, is a classic Cornas, which just misses the intensity of some examples, but still has fine, dry tannins and long-lasting acidity. **88** *—R.V. (2/1/2005)*

Cave de Tain L'Hermitage 2002 Esprit de Granit (Saint-Joseph) $18. There is perfumed fruit, with aromas of red currants. This wine, named after the granite soil which forms the base of Saint-Joseph, is earthy, ripe, and firmly tannic, but with plenty of red fruit flavors. It should develop quickly, over the next 2-3 years. **87** *—R.V. (2/1/2005)*

Cave de Tain L'Hermitage 2001 Les Hauts du Fief (Crozes-Hermitage) $11. A fresh, lightly tannic wine, with acidity, flavors of red fruits. The dry tannins are ripe and easy, with good wood flavors. It is approachable, without great complexity—a great example of this inexpensive appellation. **86 Best Buy** *—R.V. (2/1/2005)*

CAVE DES VIGNERONS DE BUXY

Cave des Vignerons de Buxy 2000 Bourgogne Chardonnay (Côte Chalonnaise) $11. **85 Best Buy** *—D.T. (11/15/2002)*

CAVES DES PAPES

Caves des Papes 2001 Les Closiers (Châteauneuf-du-Pape) $24. Shows slight browning at the rim and seems to be drying out a bit on the palate, yet still retains some charm. Dried cherries and apricots sport a leathery overlay and a dusting of dried spices. Drink up. **83** *—J.C. (3/1/2004)*

Caves des Papes 2000 Réserve des Fustiers (Gigondas) $18. Crisply acidic, with scents of leather, dark chocolate, and cranberry. **83** *—J.C. (3/1/2004)*

Caves des Papes 2002 Les Caprices d'Antoine (Côtes-du-Rhône) $9. Seems soft and mature, but it's still drinkable—a noteworthy achievement in the deluge that was the 2002 vintage. Leather and cherry scents are followed by juicy cherry-berry fruit and hints of vanilla and spice. Drink up. **84** *—J.C. (11/15/2005)*

Caves des Papes 2003 Héritage Blanc (Côtes-du-Rhône) $11. This Côtes-du-Rhône blanc features pear and honeydew melon aromas that lead into similar flavors, with a touch of apple thrown into the mix. It's full-bodied but balanced by fresh acidity, finishing with hints of citrus and minerals. **87 Best Buy** *—J.C. (2/1/2005)*

CELLIER DES DAUPHINS

Cellier des Dauphins 2003 Prestige Rouge (Côtes-du-Rhône) $8. A solid burger red, with just enough tannin on the finish to stand up to grilled ground beef. Flavors are straightforward and pleasing, with touches of black cherries and white pepper. Drink now–2007. **85 Best Buy** *—J.C. (2/1/2005)*

Cellier des Dauphins 2003 Tradition (Côtes-du-Rhône Villages) $10. No doubt the sun-drenched 2003 vintage propelled this wine to reach greater heights than usual, with baked fruit scents accented by dried herbs and richer chocolate notes. Often a bit rustic and underripe, this wine is silky smooth and easy to drink this year, making it a solid value. **85 Best Buy** *—J.C. (11/15/2005)*

Cellier des Dauphins 2001 Réserve Les Dorinnes Blanc (Côtes-du-Rhône) $14. This blend of 50% Grenache blanc, 40% Viognier, and 10% Marsanne reveals an interesting blend of fruit and wood. Toasty, mealy notes on the nose fight a little with floral, anise scents, while the flavors combine lemon and clove. Medium-weight, with crisp acids and a citrusy finish. **85** *—J.C. (2/1/2005)*

CHANSON PÈRE ET FILS

Chanson Père et Fils 2000 Clos des Mouches (Beaune) $NA. 91 *—R.V. (11/1/2001)*

Chanson Père et Fils 2003 Vergennes (Corton) $136. Aromas of wood and fresh apples give a great lift to this wine. It's rich and creamy, piling toast and ripe white stone fruit on top of acidity and good green flavors. It is fresh at the moment, but will soon develop into a great wine. **91** *—R.V. (9/1/2005)*

Chanson Père et Fils 2003 Les Caradeux Premier Cru (Pernand-Vergelesses) $34. Lightly toasted new wood dominates the nose of this rich, complex wine. It tastes toasty, too, but also has plenty of rich, soft fruit flavors. The tannins are there, though, to add a dimension. What is missing it is the acidity. **88** *—R.V. (9/1/2005)*

Chanson Père et Fils 2000 Chambolle-Musigny $42. 87 *—R.V. (11/1/2002)*

Chanson Père et Fils 2002 Clos de Vougeot $90. Modern toasty wood dominates the wine, with concentrated black fruits and big tannins. This needs time to blend the wood and the black fruits, but should be great. **92** *—R.V. (9/1/2004)*

Chanson Père et Fils 2002 Clos des Mouches Premier Cru (Beaune) $48. This pretty, seductive wine has firm tannins, ripe, generous fruit and flavors of pure raspberries and cranberries. **89** *—R.V. (9/1/2004)*

Chanson Père et Fils 2002 Les Suchots Premier Cru (Vosne-Romanée) $89. A rich, concentrated wine that shows rich, red fruit and sweet tannins. It is in a modern, wood-dominated style but will develop well. **90** *—R.V. (9/1/2004)*

Chanson Père et Fils 2002 Les Vergelesses Premier Cru (Pernand-Vergelesses) $39. This is a fine, spicy wine, with serious concentration and intense, dark fruit flavors. Big, rich and concentrated, its solid tannins give it great structure. **89** *—R.V. (9/1/2004)*

Chanson Père et Fils 2003 Savigny-Dominode Premier Cru (Savigny-lès-Beaune) $36. An intensely perfumed wine, with layers of new wood adding complexity to the rich, black fruit flavors. This is dense and packed with dry tannins and rich, juicy fruit. **89** *—R.V. (9/1/2005)*

CHARLES DE CAZANOVE

Charles de Cazanove NV Brut Classique (Champagne) $26. 87 *—M.S. (6/1/2003)*

CHARLES DE FERE

Charles de Fere NV Reserve Blanc de Blancs Brut (France) $9. 84 *—P.G. (12/15/2002)*

Charles de Fere NV Tradition Brut Chardonnay (France) $10. 87 Best Buy *—P.G. (12/15/2002)*

Charles de Fere NV Blanc de Blancs Réserve Brut (France) $11. Yeasty, smooth, and round, with tropical-fruit aromas. Melon, apple, and nutmeg/cinnamon aromas are pretty nice while the finish is solid, warm, and round. A nice quaffer with just enough nuance and style to rise above the masses. **86 Best Buy** *—M.S. (12/31/2005)*

Charles de Fere NV Jean-Louis Cuvée Blanc de Blancs Brut (France) $10. Spry and alert, with crisp apple aromas and some baking spice for good measure. Equally crisp on the palate, where lime, green apple, and pepper run the show. Moderate but extended in terms of feel and finish; tasty and snappy overall. **87 Best Buy** *—M.S. (12/31/2005)*

CHARLES HEIDSIECK

Charles Heidsieck 1982 Blanc de Blancs des Chardonnay (Champagne) $185. 91 *(12/15/2003)*

Charles Heidsieck 1983 Blanc des Millénaires (Champagne) $170. 91 *(12/15/2003)*

Charles Heidsieck 1995 Blanc des Millénaires (Champagne) $95. This is an intensely floral wine, ripe, with structure and fragrant, creamy fruit. At first it seems soft, but that's because the richness of the fruit covers the firmness and comparatve youth of this fine wine. Great for apéritifs, it should age well over the next decade or so. **91** *—R.V. (12/1/2004)*

Charles Heidsieck 1995 Brut (Champagne) $65. A lighter style, with a creamy texture and a crisp, youthful feel. Lemon and toast dominate, but there's a deep apple and mineral core lurking below. **90** *—J.C. (12/1/2005)*

Charles Heidsieck NV Brut Réserve (Champagne) $40. This four-year-old bottling (indicated on the back label) is a rich Champagne, with some toasty maturity but also flavors of almonds, white currants and citrus peel. It is an intense, full-bodied food wine. **89** *—R.V. (12/1/2005)*

Charles Heidsieck NV Brut Réserve (Champagne) $35. 89 *(12/15/2003)*

Charles Heidsieck 1996 Brut Rosé (Champagne) $80. Creamy and loaded with orange, vanilla, and baked white bread. Lovely in the mouth, with the nicest blend of snappy tangerine, sweet melon, and yeast. Crisp on the edges, smooth in the middle, and complete as they come. **93** *—M.S. (12/15/2005)*

Charles Heidsieck 1981 Champagne Charlie (Champagne) $150. 92 *(12/15/2003)*

CHARLES HOURS

Charles Hours 2001 Cuvée Marie (Jurançon Sec) $18. 88 *(10/1/2003)*

CHARLES LAFITTE

Charles Lafitte 1989 Brut Orgueil de France (Champagne) $100. Rich and aged, but still fairly fresh. Smells like scrambled egg, vanilla, and pear, setting up flavors of citrus and apple. Plenty of zesty acidity keeps this wine kicking, and the butterscotch and dust on the finish are nice and add depth. **91** *—M.S. (12/31/2005)*

Charles Lafitte NV Cuvée Spéciale Brut (Champagne) $32. A simple, fresh style of wine, with attractive white currant flavors and good acidity. This Charles Lafitte brand describes itself as the successor to the George Goulet label, whose wines are now made elsewhere. **86** *—R.V. (12/1/2005)*

Charles Lafitte NV Grand Cuvée Brut Rosé (Champagne) $32. **89** *—M.S. (12/15/2003)*

Charles Lafitte NV Grande Cuvée Brut (Champagne) $27. **87** *—P.G. (12/1/2000)*

CHARLES VIENOT

Charles Vienot 1997 Pommard $25. Tart and not very generous, this is not a good example of a Pommard. Flavors tend to the sour end of the Pinot Noir range with tomato and cranberry predominating. Has fairly sharp acidity and a short finish, too. Wine like this should be declassified and sold as Bourgogne Pinot Noir, at best. **81** *(1/1/2004)*

CHARTOGNE-TAILLET

Chartogne-Taillet NV Cuvée Saint-Anne Blanc de Blancs Brut (Champagne) $41. **90** *—R.V. (12/1/2002)*

Chartogne-Taillet NV Cuvée Sainte-Anne Brut (Champagne) $33. **87** *—R.V. (12/1/2002)*

CHARTRON ET TRÉBUCHET

Chartron et Trébuchet 2004 Chardonnay (Mâcon-Villages) $11. Pleasantly floral on the nose, with hints of clover blossom and honey followed by plump, medium-bodied flavors of apples and pears, spiced with a bit of clove. **86 Best Buy** *—J.C. (11/15/2005)*

Chartron et Trébuchet 2003 Meursault $38. **87** *—J.C. (11/15/2005)*

Chartron et Trébuchet 2001Mâcon-Villages $11. **86** *—R.V. (11/15/2003)*

CHÂTEAU DE PARAZA

Château de Paraza 2002 Red Blend (Minervois) $9. This flagship wine from the Minervois is disappointing. It is lightweight, dominated by acidity. Maybe the vintage did not help, but this is has an undernourished feel to it which demands more in the way of richness. **83** *—R.V. (12/1/2004)*

CHÂTEAU PHÉLAN-SÈGUR

Château Phélan-Sègur 2000 Bordeaux Blend (Saint-Estèphe) $35. **92** *—R.V. (6/1/2003)*

CHÂTEAU PICHON LONGUEVILLE

Château Pichon Longueville 2000 Bordeaux Blend (Pauillac) $100. **92** *—R.V. (6/1/2003)*

CHÂTEAU AU GRAND PARIS

Château Au Grand Paris 2000 Bordeaux Blend (Bordeaux Supérieur) $10. **89 Best Buy** *—J.C. (11/15/2002)*

CHÂTEAU BEAUSÉJOUR-BECOT

Château Beauséjour-Becot 2000 Bordeaux Blend (Saint-Emilion) $65. **92** *—R.V. (6/1/2003)*

CHÂTEAU BEL AIR

Château Bel Air 2000 Perponcher Blanc (Bordeaux) $13. **89** *—R.V. (12/1/2002)*

CHATEAU BELON

Château Belon 2002 Bordeaux White Blend (Graves) $12. Zesty and clean, with scents of green apple and fresh straw that give way to flavors of grapefruit and herbs. Citrusy and fresh on the finish, but ultimately a little simple. Try with oysters or other simple seafood items. **84** *—J.C. (6/1/2005)*

CHÂTEAU BERTINERIE

Château Bertinerie 2004 Bordeaux White Blend (Premieres Côtes de Blaye) $12. A crisp, grassy, pure Sauvignon Blanc, which is fresh, acidic, and offers great grapefruit flavors. There's a lightness that balances the fine depth of flavor from this leading Blaye property. **88** *—R.V. (6/1/2005)*

CHÂTEAU BONNET

Château Bonnet 2001 Bordeaux Blend (Entre-Deux-Mers) $10. **89** *—R.V. (12/1/2002)*

Château Bonnet 1999 Reserve Bordeaux Blend (Bordeaux) $14. **86** *—R.V. (12/1/2002)*

Château Bonnet 2002 Bordeaux White Blend (Entre-Deux-Mers) $11. Why does nobody think about dry white Bordeaux? Blended from Sauvignon Blanc and Sémillon, it is a delicious white wine bargain. And Château Bonnet is one of the best examples. Made in the Entre-deux-Mers region by André Lurton, whose family seems to own or manage half of Bordeaux, it is full of flavors of orange and apricot with a touch of grapefruit to provide the freshness. There is a light toast character to round it off. **86 Best Buy** —*R.V. (11/15/2004)*

CHÂTEAU BOUSQUETTE

Château Bousquette 2001 Red Blend (Saint-Chinian) $15. The standard cuvée from Château Bousquette has light, fresh simple fruit, with good flavors of red plums and fruit tannins. It is finished with balancing acidity, and is certainly ready to drink now. **85** —*R.V. (12/1/2004)*

CHÂTEAU BRANE-CANTENAC

Château Brane-Cantenac 2001 Bordeaux Blend (Margaux) $40. A great, rich wine from what owner Henri Lurton calls a classic year. There are huge, sweet tannins, solid black fruit flavors and ripeness, without losing sight of balance between richness, dryness and acidity. This is a wine that will age over many years. **92** —*R.V. (6/1/2005)*

CHÂTEAU BROWN

Château Brown 2003 Bordeaux White Blend (Pessac-Léognan) $50. A fine, elegant white wine, rich with wood and toast flavors overlying the white peaches and pink grapefruit. **89** —*R.V. (6/1/2005)*

CHÂTEAU CAMPLAZENS

Château Camplazens 1999 La Garrigue La Clape Controlle (Coteaux du Languedoc) $13. **82** —*M.S. (9/1/2003)*

Château Camplazens 2000 La Reserve La Clape MM (Coteaux du Languedoc) $19. This special millennium bottling should be drunk up. There are some nice dried-spice and peppery aromas, and the wine is light and elegant despite lacking a great deal of ripeness. Turns herbal and tea-like on the finish. **84** —*J.C. (11/15/2005)*

CHÂTEAU CANON

Château Canon 2000 Bordeaux Blend (Saint-Emilion) $60. **96** —*R.V. (6/1/2003)*

CHÂTEAU CANON LA GAFFELIÈRE

Château Canon La Gaffelière 2000 Bordeaux Blend (Saint-Emilion) $50. **93** —*R.V. (6/1/2003)*

CHÂTEAU CANTENAC-BROWN

Château Cantenac-Brown 2000 Bordeaux Blend (Margaux) $30. **91** —*R.V. (6/1/2003)*

CHÂTEAU CAP DE FAUGÈRES

Château Cap de Faugères 2002 Bordeaux Blend (Côtes de Castillon) $20. This is the Castillon wine from the Émilion estate of Faugères, which is split in half by commune boundaries. The same care goes into this great value wine as into the Émilion, and this is a fine wine, full of superripe fruit and blackberry flavors. **89** —*R.V. (6/1/2005)*

CHÂTEAU CARBONNIEUX

Château Carbonnieux 2002 Bordeaux White Blend (Pessac-Léognan) $33. Toasty and nutty at first, but with aeration the fruit emerges—first as pungent passion fruit, then more elegantly as nectarine and limes. Finishes long, fresh and clean—a wine that can be drunk now and over the next five years, possibly longer. **90 Editors' Choice** —*J.C. (6/1/2005)*

CHÂTEAU CHASSE-SPLEEN

Château Chasse-Spleen 2000 Bordeaux Blend (Moulis) $35. **91** —*R.V. (6/1/2003)*

CHÂTEAU CITRAN

Château Citran 2002 Bordeaux Blend (Haut-Médoc) $NA. The beautiful Château at Citran has been renovated, as has the vineyard. As a result, the wines are worth looking out for, even in a lesser vintage. The wine has tannins, but the fruit is also fresh, with red fruit flavors. This is not a heavyweight, but will be attractive in 3–5 years. **87** —*R.V. (6/1/2005)*

CHÂTEAU CLERC-MILON

Château Clerc-Milon 2000 Bordeaux Blend (Pauillac) $60. **89** —*R.V. (6/1/2003)*

CHÂTEAU COS D'ESTOURNEL

Château Cos d'Estournel 2000 Bordeaux Blend (Saint-Estèphe) $130. **94** —*R.V. (6/1/2003)*

CHÂTEAU COURONNEAU

Château Couronneau 2001 Bordeaux Blend (Bordeaux Supérieur) $13. **84** —*J.C. (11/15/2005)*

CHÂTEAU D'OR ET DE GUEULES

Château d'Or et de Gueules 1998 Costières de Nimes $8. **84** —*J.C. (3/1/2001)*

CHÂTEAU D'ANGLUDET

Château d'Angludet 2001 Bordeaux Blend (Margaux) $25. Angludet is the story of an estate that has been built up painstakingly over several decades. The Sichels, whose family home this is, make very satisfying wines, which are always good values. The 2001, with its good structure, its black fruits and its sympathetic use of wood, has balance and elegance. Ripe fruits with tobacco aromas complete the package. **89** —*R.V. (6/1/2005)*

Château d'Angludet 2000 Bordeaux Blend (Margaux) $16. **89** —*R.V. (6/1/2003)*

CHÂTEAU D'ISSAN

Château d'Issan 2001 Bordeaux Blend (Margaux) $29. The moated castle of Issan belongs to the Cruse family, one of Bordeaux's most famous. Under the direction of Emmanuel Cruse, and with consultant Jacques Boissenot, the estate is enjoying something of a renaissance. With its great, generous, rich, and sweet fruit, its ripe tannins and its black jelly flavors, it makes a powerful statement. Wood is there, but doesn't dominate. The wine will develop over the next 5–10 years. **91 Editors' Choice** —*R.V. (6/1/2005)*

CHÂTEAU DE BASTET

Château de Bastet 2003 Cuvée Speciale (Côtes-du-Rhône) $18. A fresh, fruity wine, with red fruit flavors and soft, juicy tannins. It has a youthfulness at this stage that suggests it will age well over the next 4–5 years. The large 138-acre vineyard is surrounded by open land protecting it from chemicals from neighboring properties. Imported by Organic Vintners. **88** —*R.V. (4/1/2005)*

CHÂTEAU DE BEAUCASTEL

Château de Beaucastel 1998 Cuvée Hommage à Jacques Perrin (Châteauneuf-du-Pape) $240. **98** *(12/31/2001)*

Château de Beaucastel 1998 Châteauneuf-du-Pape $62. **96** *(12/31/2001)*

CHÂTEAU DE CAMARSAC

Château de Camarsac 2000 Bordeaux Blend (Bordeaux Supérieur) $8. **86** —*R.V. (12/1/2002)*

CHÂTEAU DE CAMPUGET

Château de Campuget 1998 Cuvée Prestige (Costières de Nimes) $14. **87** —*J.C. (3/1/2001)*

CHÂTEAU DE CHAMIREY

Château de Chamirey 2001 Chardonnay Mercurey $24. **88** —*J.C. (10/1/2003)*

Château de Chamirey 1999 Pinot Noir (Mercurey) $25. **87** —*P.G. (11/1/2002)*

CHÂTEAU DE CRUZEAU

Château de Cruzeau 2000 Bordeaux White Blend (Pessac-Léognan) $17. One of the many Pessac-Léognan properties owned by Andre Lurton, Cruzeau has a long history dating back to the 18th century. This 2000 vintage, now totally mature, has great vanilla flavors that balance well with the intense grapefruit flavors and toasty aromas. **90** —*R.V. (6/1/2005)*

CHÂTEAU DE FESLES

Château de Fesles 1999 Cabernet Franc (Anjou) $12. **86** —*M.M. (1/1/2004)*

CHÂTEAU DE FONSALETTE

Château de Fonsalette 1998 Réserve Syrah (Côtes-du-Rhône) $50. **85** *(11/1/2001)*

CHÂTEAU DE JAU

Château de Jau 2002 Jaja de Jau (Vin de Pays d'Oc) $9. **82** —*M.S. (9/1/2003)*

Château de Jau 2001 Talon Rouge (Côtes du Roussillon) $20. Young and boisterous, with a bright purple tint. This is sweet, jammy and grapy stuff, but firm tannins and lively acids keep it largely in balance. The palate is huge, with tarry, smoky edges surrounding rich plum fruit. A strapping middleweight for near-term drinking. **88** —*M.S. (1/1/2004)*

CHÂTEAU DE LA CHAIZE

Château de La Chaize 2001 Gamay (Brouilly) $12. **85** —*J.C. (11/15/2003)*

CHÂTEAU DE LA GARDINE

Château de La Gardine 2003 Cuvée Tradition (Châteauneuf-du-Pape) $40. This large, 132-acre estate is making great wines today. This 2003 is up with the best, full of flavor, fruit, richness, and layers of sweet licorice, black plums, and wood. Spice, coffee, and chocolate flavors complete a complex blend. With its dense, dusty tannins, it is certainly ageworthy. **93 Cellar Selection** —*R.V. (12/31/2005)*

Château de La Gardine 2001 Châteauneuf-du-Pape $40. Made with a not-so-subtle whack of wood, this Châteauneuf features aromas of toasted marshmallows to go along with ripe cherry flavors. Crisp and medium-bodied, with flavors of vanilla, toffee, or caramel and the recurring cherries. Doesn't seem like a long ager, but worth holding a few years to see if additional complexities develop. **87** —*J.C. (11/15/2005)*

CHÂTEAU DE LA ROCHE-AUX-MOINES

Château de La Roche-Aux-Moines 2002 Clos de La Bergerie (Savennières-Roche-Aux-Moines) $29. A ripe, full, intense wine with flavors of white currants, almonds, and toast. Sings purity of fruit, with a light touch of softness at the end, balanced with intense acidity. **92** *—R.V. (4/1/2005)*

Château de La Roche-Aux-Moines 2002 Les Clos Sacrés (Savennières) $45. This may be the least complex wine in Nicolas Joly's range of wines, but it is still full of complex flavors. Sweet currants mingle with tannins, pure layers of acidity and nut notes. A great expression of Chenin Blanc. **89** *—R.V. (4/1/2005)*

CHÂTEAU DE LA TERRIERE

Château de La Terriere 2001 Cuvée Jules du Souzy (Brouilly) $20. **84** *—J.C. (11/15/2003)*

CHÂTEAU DE LASCAUX

Château de Lascaux NV Red Blend (Coteaux du Languedoc) $10. **90 Best Buy** *—L.W. (10/1/1999)*

CHÂTEAU DE MARSANNAY

Château de Marsannay 2003 Chardonnay (Marsannay) $20. Big and rich, this wine just oozes rich, creamy caramel flavors. The fruit is superripe but still with good acidity and tastes of white peaches, toast, and cinnamon. Give this wine another year and it will be delicious. **90** *—R.V. (9/1/2005)*

Château de Marsannay 2003 Pinot Noir (Marsannay) $20. The wine is packed with jammy red fruits that give it juiciness and softness. Tannins are subdued, giving just enough structure to an otherwise forward wine. **88** *—R.V. (9/1/2005)*

CHÂTEAU DE MAUVANNE

Château de Mauvanne 1999 Cuvée 1 (Côtes de Provence) $14. Dried fruit and a light leafiness define the fresh, earthy nose that truly rings of the region. This tasty, balanced blend of Grenache, Syrah, and Carignan is crisp and loaded with cherry character and flavor. It's smooth but just rugged enough to excite. A sure thing with grilled steak or chops. **87** *—M.S. (1/1/2004)*

CHÂTEAU DE MEURSAULT

Château de Meursault 2003 (Meursault) $42. A rich and ripe, but very soft wine. For lovers of ripe New World Chardonnay, this is a treat. Lovers of white Burgundy, though, may feel that there is something missing. **87** *—R.V. (9/1/2005)*

Château de Meursault 2003 Clos du Château Chardonnay (Bourgogne) $21. This wine comes from the walled vineyard in front of Patriarche's Château de Meursault. Although it is simply Bourgogne Blanc, it is treated as a showpiece vineyard. That explains the richness, the weight, and the layers of well-judged new wood. This is as ripe as many Meursaults but will develop more quickly. **89** *—R.V. (9/1/2005)*

Château de Meursault 2002 Clos du Château Chardonnay (Bourgogne) $19. **86** *—J.C. (11/15/2005)*

Château de Meursault 1999 Premier Cru (Meursault) $50. **89** *(4/1/2003)*

Château de Meursault 2003 Pinot Noir (Beaune) $26. A soft, lightweight wine that is fresh and easy, but misses depth of flavor. It has jammy raspberry flavors and a fruity, acidic finish. **85** *—R.V. (9/1/2005)*

Château de Meursault 2003 Beaune-Cent-Vignes Premier Cru (Beaune) $33. Packed tannins support layers of dark, ripe fruit in this powerfully dry wine. With its dense fruit and herbal flavor this is a fine, solid wine that should age well. The Cent Vignes "Hundred Vines" vineyard is reputed for its heady wines, and this is no exception. **90** *—R.V. (9/1/2005)*

Château de Meursault 1999 Clos de Chênes Premier Cru (Volnay) $37. **86** *(4/1/2003)*

Château de Meursault 2003 Clos des Chênes Premier Cru (Volnay) $48. This wine has fruit buried beneath a dry, earthy, mushroomy character that should not be so prevalent in a wine so young. **82** *—R.V. (9/1/2005)*

Château de Meursault 2003 Clos des Epenots Premier Cru (Pommard) $48. A dry wine overall with firm fruit underlying the tannins. It has a sense of power but the dry feel, at this stage, is overwhelming. **86** *—R.V. (9/1/2005)*

Château de Meursault 1999 Grèves Premier Cru (Beaune) $31. **87** *(4/1/2003)*

Château de Meursault 2000 Premier Cru (Beaune) $27. **84** *(4/1/2003)*

CHÂTEAU DE PENNAUTIER

Château de Pennautier 2000 Cabernet Sauvignon (Vin de Pays d'Oc) $9. **86 Best Buy** *—M.S. (2/1/2003)*

Château de Pennautier 2000 L'Orangerie (Languedoc) $9. **85** *—M.S. (2/1/2003)*

Château de Pennautier 2001 Syrah (Vin de Pays d'Oc) $8. This is like a well-fed youngster. It's purple and offers mineral, lavender, and peppery black-fruit aromas. But things go a bit south on the palate. The fruit is supercharged by piercing acidity. And there's also a jolting bolt of sugar on the back palate. Ripe, modern, but clumsy, without the balance and harmony to score better. **82** *—M.S. (1/1/2004)*

CHÂTEAU DE PEZ

Château de Pez 1995 Bordeaux Blend (Saint-Estèphe) $30. 87 *(5/1/2000)*

CHÂTEAU DE PIZAY

Château de Pizay 2001 (Morgon) $NA. 86 *—J.C. (11/15/2003)*

CHÂTEAU DE ROCHEMORIN

Château de Rochemorin 2000 White Bordeaux Blend (Bordeaux) $15. 84 *(8/1/2002)*

CHÂTEAU DE RULLY

Château de Rully 2003 Pinot Noir (Rully) $NA. Vinified and bottled by Antonin Rodet, this wine comes from a vineyard owned by the counts de Ternay. It is a fresh, simple, juicy wine with pleasant, light red-raspberry flavors. It should develop quickly. 85 *—R.V. (9/1/2005)*

CHÂTEAU DE SÉGRIÈS

Château de Ségriès 1999 (Côtes-du-Rhône) $10. 85 *—J.C. (12/31/2000)*

CHÂTEAU DE SEGUIN

Château de Seguin 1999 Bordeaux Blend (Bordeaux Supérieur) $12. 85 *—R.V. (12/1/2002)*

Château de Seguin 2001 Cuvée Prestige 2000 White Blend (Bordeaux) $38. 85 *—R.V. (12/1/2002)*

CHÂTEAU DE SOURS

Château de Sours 2000 Bordeaux Blend (Bordeaux) $NA. 87 *—R.V. (11/15/2002)*

CHÂTEAU DE TRACY

Château de Tracy 2002 Pouilly-Fumé $30. Just enough chalk and mineral is present on the bouquet to complement the melon, citrus, and green herb notes. Very much of a streamlined, tight wine on the palate, where melon, lemon, and citrus pith come together. Refreshing, dry and firm; the perfect shellfish accompaniment. 89 *(7/1/2005)*

Château de Tracy 1999 Pouilly-Fumé $32. 88 *(8/1/2002)*

CHÂTEAU DE VALFLAUNÈS

Château de Valflaunès 1999 Espérance Pic Saint-Loup (Coteaux du Languedoc) $15. 80 *(10/1/2001)*

CHÂTEAU DES ALBIÈRES

Château des Albières 2001 Cuvée Georges Dardé (Saint-Chinian) $NA. Named after the founder of the local cooperative, this wine has fine, ripe juicy flavors and a layer of wood. This is a wine for early drinking, great with barbecues, and offering easy pleasure. 84 *—R.V. (12/1/2004)*

CHÂTEAU DES MILLE ANGES

Château des Mille Anges 1996 Bordeaux Blend (Premieres Côtes de Bordeaux) $13. 80 *—M.S. (7/1/2000)*

CHÂTEAU DES SARRINS

Château des Sarrins 1997 (Côtes de Provence) $20. 84 *—J.C. (3/1/2001)*

CHÂTEAU DESMIRAIL

Château Desmirail 2001 Bordeaux Blend (Margaux) $43. One of the many Margaux estates under the control of the Lurton family, this is a classic wine, with dry wood and dark tannins, flavors of black currants, and light acidity. There is no mistaking this as Bordeaux, with its serious, ageworthy fruits and tannins. 89 *—R.V. (6/1/2005)*

CHÂTEAU DOISY-DAËNE

Château Doisy-Daëne 2003 Bordeaux White Blend (Bordeaux) $34. This great Barsac Château also produces small quantities of dry white wine in most years. It is rich and creamy, with apricots as well as white peaches over the layer of spicy wood. 90 *—R.V. (6/1/2005)*

CHÂTEAU DU CRAY

Château du Cray 1998 Bourgogne Pinot Noir (Côte Chalonnaise) $13. 87 Best Buy *—D.T. (11/15/2002)*

CHÂTEAU DU TERTRE

Château du Tertre 2001 Bordeaux Blend (Margaux) $31. Under the same ownership as Giscours, and benefiting from big investment in recent years, this is an estate at the top of its form. The wine has aromas of sweet, new wood, while the palate is packed with tarry fruits and spicy wood and herbs. Flavors of ripe black currants give a rich, satisfying feel. This is a wine that is well structured, dense and, given another five years, will be delicious. 92 *—R.V. (6/1/2005)*

CHÂTEAU DUCLA

Château Ducla 2002 Bordeaux Blend (Bordeaux Supérieur) $13. 81 *—J.C. (6/1/2005)*

Château Ducla 1998 Bordeaux Blend (Bordeaux) $10. 82 *—J.C. (3/1/2001)*

CHÂTEAU DURFORT-VIVENS

Château Durfort-Vivens 2001 Bordeaux Blend (Margaux) $26. Gonzague Lurton, current president of the Margaux producers, has invested considerably in pushing this estate forward. The wine has rich, open, generous fruit, with soft but firmly present tannins and juicy flavors. Combined with a subtle used of new wood, this shows well, and will develop well over many years. **90 Editors' Choice** *—R.V. (6/1/2005)*

CHÂTEAU FAUGERES

Château Faugeres 2000 Bordeaux Blend (Saint-Emilion) $40. 90 *—R.V. (6/1/2003)*

CHÂTEAU FERRIÈRE

Château Ferrière 2001 Bordeaux Blend (Margaux) $27. Once the sole claim to fame of this estate was that it was the smallest, as well as one of the most obscure, of the classed growths. Now, its fame come from the quality of its wines. Winemaker Claire Villars-Lurton has crafted a wine that is dark and brooding, with big, powerful, intense fruit, dark flavors, and solid tannins. Bordeaux in style, but has a great, polished, ripe feel too. **93 Editors' Choice** *—R.V. (6/1/2005)*

CHÂTEAU FIGEAC

Château Figeac 2000 Bordeaux Blend (Saint-Emilion) $85. 86 *—R.V. (6/1/2003)*

CHÂTEAU FLAUGERGUES

Château Flaugergues 2003 Rosé Blend (Coteaux du Languedoc) $12. Soft flavors along with a burst of alcohol make this a powerful wine. It is peppery and full-bodied and not for the faint-hearted. **83** *—R.V. (12/1/2004)*

CHÂTEAU FOMBRAUGE

Château Fombrauge 2002 Bordeaux Blend (Saint-Emilion Grand Cru) $NA. Under the control of Bernard Magrez, this has become the largest of the Saint-Emilion grand cru vineyards. The wines are in a modern, dense style, with power-packed fruit, high extract, and huge, solid tannins. For a 2002, this is a big wine. **88** *—R.V. (6/1/2005)*

CHÂTEAU FONBADET

Château Fonbadet 2000 Bordeaux Blend (Pauillac) $50. This wine has a distinctly herbal aroma and flavor. Sage, thyme, and broccoli come to mind. The tannins are firm and frame secondary flavors, redolent of coffee, plum, and charry toast. Finishes with moderate length. Kosher. **89** *—J.M. (4/3/2004)*

CHÂTEAU FONRÉAUD

Château Fonréaud 1999 Red Blend (Listrac) $17. 88 *—R.V. (11/15/2003)*

CHÂTEAU FOURCAS-HOSTEN

Château Fourcas-Hosten 2002 Bordeaux Blend (Listrac-Médoc) $NA. This estate, long a positive bastion of traditional Bordeaux, has undergone quite a change with this wine. Packed with dark tannins, new wood flavors, and fresh, polished fruit. **88** *—R.V. (6/1/2005)*

CHÂTEAU FRANC-PÉRAT

Château Franc-Pérat 2004 Bordeaux White Blend (Bordeaux) $13. This is a big, rich wine, but with the fresh acidity that seems to be a hallmark of the 2004 whites. There are flavors of lime and grapefruit, and a layer of tannin to give this delicious wine good structure. **88** *—R.V. (6/1/2005)*

CHÂTEAU FUISSÉ

Château Fuissé 2002 Pouilly-Fuissé $35. More classic than the honeyed, unctuous 2003, with more obvious smoke and mineral shadings to complement its fresh apple and pear flavors. Long and pineappley on the finish. Drink now–2010. **88** *—J.C. (11/15/2005)*

Château Fuissé 2002 Les Brulés (Pouilly-Fuissé) $35. A bit obviously oaky, with caramel-toast notes atop baked apples and pears. Seems like ordinary oaky Chardonnay, right up until the strongly minerally finish, which gives it an extra dimension. **88** *—J.C. (11/15/2005)*

Château Fuissé 2002 Les Clos (Pouilly-Fuissé) $45. Just as good, but different in style from the flamboyant 2003, the 2002 Les Clos is more classic, with upfront aromas of smoke and mineral that enfold honey, baked apple, and citrus flavors. Finishes long, with a chalky, almost tactile quality. Drink now–2012. **90** *—J.C. (11/15/2005)*

Château Fuissé 2002 Les Combettes (Pouilly-Fuissé) $37. Smoke and mineral notes dominate the nose, but the rich flavors of baked apple come through strong on the palate. Finishes with healthy doses of spice, honey, and cleansing acidity. Drink now–2010. **89** *—J.C. (11/15/2005)*

Château Fuissé 2002 Vieilles Vignes (Pouilly-Fuissé) $50. A bit closed right now, but the concentration and elegance is still evident. You get glimpses of pear, apple, and citrus flavors and a long, anise-tinged finish, but hold another few years to let it blossom. Drink 2008–2015. **90 Cellar Selection** *—J.C. (11/15/2005)*

CHÂTEAU GÉNOT-BOULANGER

Château Génot-Boulanger 1999 Chambolle-Musigny $NA. 89 *—R. V. (11/1/2002)*

Château Génot-Boulanger 2002 Grèves Premier Cru (Beaune) $23. This wine has firm, dry tannins, excellent balance and delicious ripe fruit. Some wood there, but the tannins are more present. 90 *—R. V. (9/1/2004)*

Château Génot-Boulanger 2002 Les Combes (Corton) $NA. This rich, tannic wine has piles of black cherry fruit, framed nicely in wood and nutmeg flavors. 89 *—R. V. (9/1/2004)*

CHÂTEAU GISCOURS

Château Giscours 2000 Bordeaux Blend (Margaux) $45. 92 *—R. V. (6/1/2003)*

CHÂTEAU GLORIA

Château Gloria 2000 Bordeaux Blend (Saint-Julien) $30. 87 *—R. V. (6/1/2003)*

CHÂTEAU GRAND CORBIN-DESPAGNE

Château Grand Corbin-Despagne 2000 Bordeaux Blend (Saint-Emilion) $25. 90 *—R. V. (6/1/2003)*

CHÂTEAU GRAND MAYNE

Château Grand Mayne 2000 Bordeaux Blend (Saint-Emilion) $59. 91 *—R. V. (6/1/2003)*

CHÂTEAU GRANDE CASSAGNE

Château Grande Cassagne 2001 Les Rameaux Syrah (Costières de Nimes) $10. 90 Best Buy *—J.C. (11/15/2002)*

CHÂTEAU GREYSAC

Château Greysac 1998 Bordeaux Blend (Médoc) $NA. 84 *—S.H. (1/1/2002)*

CHÂTEAU HAUT BAILLY

Château Haut Bailly 2000 Bordeaux Blend Pessac-Léognan $40. 92 *—R. V. (6/1/2003)*

CHÂTEAU HAUT BERTINERIE

Château Haut Bertinerie 2002 Bordeaux White Blend (Premieres Côtes de Blaye) $20. Wood gives complexity to the wine's rich, soft fruit. Flavors of quince, honey, and grapefruit blend well with the vanilla of the wood. This is the top white cuvée from Bertinerie, produced from old vines. **90 Editors' Choice** *—R. V. (6/1/2005)*

CHÂTEAU HAUT BRETON LARIGAUDIERE

Château Haut Breton Larigaudiere 1999 Bordeaux Blend (Margaux) $45. A soft, ready-to-drink Margaux, with scents of damp clay and leather followed by black cherry and vanilla flavors. Boasts a pleasant creaminess on the palate and complicating hints of leather and earth on the finish. 86 *—J.C. (6/1/2005)*

CHÂTEAU HAUT-BEAUSEJOUR

Château Haut-Beausejour 1997 Bordeaux Blend (Saint-Estèphe) $23. 85 *(5/1/2000)*

CHÂTEAU HAUT-BRION

Château Haut-Brion 2000 Bordeaux Blend (Pessac-Léognan) $400. 96 *—R. V. (6/1/2003)*

CHÂTEAU HAUT-MARBUZET

Château Haut-Marbuzet 2002 Bordeaux Blend (Saint-Estèphe) $NA. Always a star turn, Haut-Marbuzet hasn't failed in 2002. It is a modern style of wine, dominated by toast and wood tannins. But there is plenty of rich, black fruit to balance, and the spices and vanilla flavors are already blending well together. 91 *—R. V. (6/1/2005)*

CHÂTEAU HOSANNA

Château Hosanna 2000 Bordeaux Blend (Pomerol) $179. 94 *—R. V. (6/1/2003)*

CHÂTEAU KIRWAN

Château Kirwan 2000 Bordeaux Blend (Margaux) $55. 94 *—R. V. (6/1/2003)*

CHÂTEAU L'HOSTE-BLANC

Château L'Hoste-Blanc 1999 Bordeaux Blend (Bordeaux Supérieur) $15. 91 *—R. V. (11/15/2002)*

CHÂTEAU LA BESSANE

Château La Bessane 2001 Bordeaux Blend (Margaux) $NA. Under the same ownership as Château La Paloumey in the Haut-Médoc, this is rich, with well-integrated flavors of blackberry and figs. There are fruit tannins that lie easily over the wood and the acidity. 87 *—R. V. (6/1/2005)*

CHÂTEAU LA BOUTIGNANE

Château La Boutignane 2001 Grande Réserve Blanc (Corbières) $13. **90 Best Buy** —*S.H. (12/31/2002)*

Château La Boutignane 1998 Grande Réserve Rouge (Corbières) $18. **94 Editors' Choice** —*S.H. (12/31/2002)*

Château La Boutignane 2002 Rosé de Saignee (Corbières) $10. **85** —*S.H. (1/1/2002)*

CHÂTEAU LA CANORGUE

Château La Canorgue 2001 Rhône Red Blend (Côtes du Luberon) $15. Nice clean nose, with scents of cherries and white pepper. But what are the green, stemmy flavors doing on the palate? Modest cherry fruit, but this medium-bodied wine finishes herbal and astringent. **83** —*J.C. (2/1/2005)*

CHÂTEAU LA CONSEILLANTE

Château La Conseillante 1998 Bordeaux Blend (Pomerol) $135. **95** —*R.V. (12/31/2001)*

CHÂTEAU LA CROIX MARTELLE

Château La Croix Martelle 2001 La Réserve du Sirus Red Blend (Minervois) $16. Produced from biodynamically grown grapes, this wine certainly has pure fruit. It also has fine tannins and a subtle mix of red fruit flavors, and juicy acidity.The tannins dominate the aftertaste. **87** —*R.V. (12/1/2004)*

CHÂTEAU LA FLEUR PÉTRUS

Château La Fleur Pétrus 2000 Bordeaux Blend (Pomerol) $75. **94** —*R.V. (6/1/2003)*

CHÂTEAU LA GAFFELIÈRE

Château La Gaffelière 2000 Bordeaux Blend (Saint-Emilion) $120. **94** —*R.V. (6/1/2003)*

CHÂTEAU LA GRAVE À POMEROL

Château La Grave à Pomerol 2000 Bordeaux Blend (Pomerol) $46. **89** —*R.V. (6/1/2003)*

CHÂTEAU LA LOUVIÈRE

Château La Louvière 2002 Bordeaux White Blend (Pessac-Léognan) $34. One of the great estates of the Graves, This vintage of La Louvière certainly fits into the classic whites of Bordeaux, packing impressive complexity into a wine dominated by Sauvignon Blanc. Intensity has been increased by the use of lees stirring following the Burgundy methods introduced by Denis Dubordieu. **93 Cellar Selection** —*R.V. (6/1/2005)*

CHÂTEAU LA NERTHE

Château La Nerthe 2000 Cuvée des Cadettes (Châteauneuf-du-Pape) $89. Right now, this wine tastes like a somewhat generic red wine—albeit one with excellent balance, fine oaking, and impressive concentration and length. Cedary, vanilla notes from new oak barrels need some time to integrate with the rich black cherry fruit and allow the true flavors of Châteauneuf to shine. Drink 2008–2015. **91** —*J.C. (2/1/2005)*

Château La Nerthe 2001 Blanc (Châteauneuf-du-Pape) $38. **90** —*M.S. (9/1/2003)*

CHATEAU LA ROSE BELLEVUE

Chateau La Rose Bellevue 2002 Cuvée Prestige Blanc (Premieres Côtes de Blaye) $12. Enticing aromas of green plums lead to a rich, ripe and intense wine packed with wood and fruit flavors. This wine, a blend of Sauvignon Blanc and the more aromatic Muscadelle, is a fine wine full of fresh fruits and spice. **88 Best Buy** —*R.V. (4/1/2005)*

Chateau La Rose Bellevue 2000 Cuvée Prestige Rouge (Premieres Côtes de Blaye) $13. This has pure, black currant fruit aromas and flavors, and wood and acidity on the palate. It is packed with fresh, vibrant fruit. **87** —*R.V. (4/1/2005)*

CHÂTEAU LA TOUR FIGEAC

Château La Tour Figeac 2000 Bordeaux Blend (Saint-Emilion) $40. **91** —*R.V. (6/1/2003)*

Château La Tour Figeac 2001 Bordeaux Blend (Saint-Emilion Grand Cru) $NA. A deep, intense color leads to aromas of black fruits, sweet tannins and spices. Flavors of cranberries, black plums, and dark cherries combine with layers of dry wood tannins into a wine that is still just emerging from its chrysalis. It has great, ripe, jammy Merlot flavors alongside the spice of the Cabernet Franc. Give this wine 10 years. **92** —*R.V. (4/1/2005)*

CHÂTEAU LA TOUR HAUT-BRION

Château La Tour Haut-Brion 2000 Bordeaux Blend (Pessac-Léognan) $60. **89** —*R.V. (6/1/2003)*

CHÂTEAU LABEGORCE MARGAUX

Château Labegorce Margaux 2001 Bordeaux Blend (Margaux) $50. Huge investment is paying off at Labegorce. And it has not resulted in a wine that is simply modern in style. For here the new wood is well integrated, the fruit is structured, and never too extracted, and the ripeness also has layers of Bordeaux dryness. **89** —*R.V. (6/1/2005)*

CHÂTEAU LABEGORCE ZÉDÉ

Château Labegorce Zédé 2001 Bordeaux Blend (Margaux) $NA. Owner Luc Thienpont, whose family also owns Vieux Château Certan and Le Pin in Pomerol, has crafted a classic Margaux with a modern face. Its solid tannins, dry flavors, and spice combine with some sweetness, fresh fruits, and great balance to give a hugely satisfying, and very food-friendly wine. **90** *—R.V. (6/1/2005)*

CHÂTEAU LAFLEUR-GAZIN

Château Lafleur-Gazin 2000 Bordeaux Blend (Pomerol) $45. **88** *—R.V. (6/1/2003)*

CHÂTEAU LAGRANGE

Château Lagrange 2002 Les Arums de Lagrange Bordeaux White Blend (Bordeaux) $21. Lagrange, now well at the top among the estates of Saint-Julien, started making a white wine in 1997 again after a break of 25 years. This 2002, from an 8-acre parcel, spent 11 months in wood, and is therefore layered in vanilla flavors. But it is the rich fruit and the balancing acidity that has the last word. **92** *—R.V. (6/1/2005)*

CHÂTEAU LAGREZETTE

Château Lagrezette 1997 Red Blend (Cahors) $20. **87** *—J.C. (3/1/2001)*

Château Lagrezette 2000 Tête de Cuvée Red Blend (Cahors) $20. All the Michel Rolland touches are present and accounted for: the color is bright, the texture soft, and the fruit is ripe and expressive. Aromas of mint, clove, and blackberries are intriguing, like a lure in front of a fish. And the finish is dark and luscious. It's an old-world Malbec wrapped in new clothes, clearly a wine for the new generation. **91** *—M.S. (1/1/2004)*

CHÂTEAU LANGOA-BARTON

Château Langoa-Barton 2000 Bordeaux Blend (Saint-Julien) $NA. **90** *—R.V. (6/1/2003)*

CHÂTEAU LARCIS-DUCASSE

Château Larcis-Ducasse 2000 Bordeaux Blend (Saint-Emilion) $NA. **88** *—R.V. (6/1/2003)*

CHATEAU LAROQUE

Château Laroque 2000 Bordeaux Blend (Saint-Emilion Grand Cru) $45. Gems like this from the stellar 2000 vintage are still available to consumers willing to explore lesser-known châteaus. Concentrated scents of black cherries and cassis emerge from the glass, followed by admirably pure flavors of black cherries and vanilla. It's supple enough to drink now, but appears to have the stuffing to go another 5–10 years. A long, berry-filled finish caps off this find. **90** *—J.C. (6/1/2005)*

CHÂTEAU LASCOMBES

Château Lascombes 2001 Bordeaux Blend (Margaux) $59. A fresh, fruity wine, with cigar and wood aromas, spice, and light black fruits. This wine comes from before the renaissance that is taking place at Lascombes, and shows the lightness of the wines produced under the old ownership. It is balanced and fresh, with a good, dry aftertaste. **88** *—R.V. (6/1/2005)*

CHÂTEAU LATOUR À POMEROL

Château Latour à Pomerol 2000 Bordeaux Blend (Pomerol) $75. **93** *—R.V. (6/1/2003)*

CHÂTEAU LAVILLE HAUT-BRION

Château Laville Haut-Brion 2002 Bordeaux White Blend (Pessac-Léognan) $135. This small estate, dedicated to white wines only, is part of the same stable as Château Haut-Brion itself. This superb wine is packed with ripe, sweet fruit, but equally importantly, shows intensity, layers of wood, a great citrus character, and the acidity so typical of 2002. This is a long-term wine: drink in 10–15 years. **93** *—R.V. (6/1/2005)*

CHÂTEAU LE DROT

Château Le Drot 1998 Bordeaux Blend (Bordeaux) $6. **85 Best Buy** *—D.T. (11/15/2002)*

CHÂTEAU LÉOVILLE POYFERRE

Château Léoville Poyferré 2000 Bordeaux Blend (Saint-Julien) $150. A solid wine, well structured, with soft but supple tannins that frame a core of blackberry, cassis, toast, coffee, anise, and herb notes. The finish has a hint of sage and thyme, ending with moderate length. Good Bordeaux from a good year. Kosher. **89** *—J.M. (4/3/2004)*

CHÂTEAU LES BARRAILLOTS

Château Les Barraillots 2001 Bordeaux Blend (Margaux) $27. A well-made, fresh, fruity wine, straightforward but ready to drink. Light, forward fruits and sweet spice layer over dusty, woody tannins. The wine is ripe and developing well. **86** *—R.V. (6/1/2005)*

CHÂTEAU LES ORMES DE PEZ

Château Les Ormes de Pez 2000 Bordeaux Blend (Saint-Estèphe) $30. **89** *—R.V. (6/1/2003)*

CHÂTEAU LESTRILLE CAPMARTIN

Château Lestrille Capmartin 2000 Prestige Bordeaux Blend (Bordeaux) $17. **84** —*R.V. (12/1/2002)*

CHÂTEAU LYNCH-BAGES

Château Lynch-Bages 2000 Bordeaux Blend (Pauillac) $100. **95** —*R.V. (6/1/2003)*

CHÂTEAU MAINE-GAZIN

Château Maine-Gazin 1997 Bordeaux Blend (Bordeaux) $17. **81** —*J.C. (4/1/2001)*

CHÂTEAU MALARTIC-LAGRAVIERE

Château Malartic-Lagraviere 2000 Bordeaux Blend (Pessac-Léognan) $35. **91** —*R.V. (6/1/2003)*

CHÂTEAU MARGAUX

Château Margaux 2001 Bordeaux Blend (Margaux) $300. "For me, this vintage is what makes Margaux special," says Margaux winemaker Paul Pontallier. He is right: With its denseness, spice, flavors of black currants layered with dryness and fresh acidity, this is a huge and impressive wine that never forgets that it is Margaux. It is still young, and the dry tannic aftertaste, which lasts for many minutes, shows this. **97** —*R.V. (6/1/2005)*

CHÂTEAU MARIS

Château Maris 1999 Red Blend (Minervois La Liviniere) $16. **86** —*M.M. (2/1/2002)*

CHÂTEAU MAROUÔNE

Château Marouône 1999 Red Blend (Côtes de Provence) $12. **83** —*M.M. (2/1/2002)*

CHÂTEAU MARTINENS

Château Martinens 2001 Bordeaux Blend (Margaux) $NA. A good example of the modern winemaking in Margaux, Martinens has spicy new wood aromas, sweet black fruit tastes, and freshness. The wood is integrated, the flavors are of red fruits, plums with some herbal character. This is confident, competent winemaking. **88** —*R.V. (6/1/2005)*

CHÂTEAU MAS NEUF

Château Mas Neuf 1998 Prestige des Gibelins Rhône Red Blend (Costières de Nimes) $15. **88** —*J.C. (12/31/2000)*

CHÂTEAU MAUCOIL

Château Maucoil 2003 Rhône Red Blend Châteauneuf-du-Pape $NA. A soft style of wine that has earthy characters. There are layers of dryness, but the plum-flavored fruit shows every sign of maturing quickly over 2–3 years. **85** —*R.V. (12/31/2005)*

CHÂTEAU MAZEYRES

Château Mazeyres 2002 Bordeaux Blend (Pomerol) $33. A ripe wine that is polished almost as bright as a diamond. Big, chocolaty flavors are balanced by some acidity and soft tannins. This is a seductive wine that belies the quality of the vintage, showing concentration and sweet, dense fruit. **90** —*R.V. (6/1/2005)*

CHÂTEAU MEYRE

Château Meyre 2001 L'Enclos Gallen Bordeaux Blend (Margaux) $NA. A special cuvée from the Avensan estate of Château Meyre, this is a modern style of wine, with big, extracted flavors, and ripe tannins. Powerful, intense, packed with dark fruit, it is almost like a Napa Cabernet in its richness. **88** —*R.V. (6/1/2005)*

CHÂTEAU MICHEL DE VERT

Château Michel de Vert 2003 Bordeaux Blend (Lussac Saint-Emilion) $9. Lussac is one of the so-called satellites of Saint-Emilion (villages that attach the magic Saint-Emilion name to their own). But it does have many attractive wines that emulate Saint-Emilion in every way except the high price. This wine, a blend of 80% Merlot and 20% Cabernet Franc, with a combination of dry austere blackcurrant fruit and sweet tannins, has that evocative cigar box, tobacco flavor that marks out a good Saint-Emilion. It finishes dry, tannic, and demanding either decanting or a few years' aging, but also ready to drink with food this holiday season. **89** —*R.V. (11/15/2005)*

CHÂTEAU MONBRISON

Château Monbrison 2001 Bordeaux Blend (Margaux) $45. One of the stars of Margaux, Monbrison 2001 is packed with rich, powerful black fruits, with open, generous fruit flavors and great new-wood flavors. This is an impressive, modern wine, powered with dense fruit, as well as some elegance and style. **91** —*R.V. (6/1/2005)*

CHÂTEAU MONGRAVEY

Château Mongravey 2001 Bordeaux Blend (Margaux) $30. This wine has pleasant, fresh fruit, some good tannins and ripe fruit. It is soft, with forward fruits, and a simplicity that makes it ready to drink now. **86** —*R.V. (6/1/2005)*

CHÂTEAU MONT-REDON

Château Mont-Redon 2003 Rhône Red Blend (Châteauneuf-du-Pape) $45. Famed for its use of all 13 Châteauneuf grape varieties,

Mont-Redon is also one of the great estates of the region. This 2003 captures the essence of Châteauneuf, with its herbal and warm, southern fruits, along with a power of black fruits and dark, brooding tannins. This will age magnificently. **92** *—R.V. (12/31/2005)*

CHÂTEAU MONTNER

Château Montner 2000 Rhône Red Blend (Côtes du Roussillon) $8. **87 Best Buy** *—M.S. (2/1/2003)*

CHÂTEAU MOULIN-À-VENT

Château Moulin-à-Vent 2002 Bordeaux Blend (Moulis-en-Médoc) $NA. A wine that has obviously suffered from the lightness of the 2002 vintage. The fruit is fresh and has easy red flavors, but the tannins are dry and dark, and are too austere for the fruit. **85** *—R.V. (6/1/2005)*

CHÂTEAU MOUTON ROTHSCHILD

Château Mouton Rothschild 2000 Bordeaux Blend (Pauillac) $450. **97** *—R.V. (6/1/2003)*

Château Mouton Rothschild 2002 Aile d'Argent Bordeaux White Blend (Bordeaux) $60. Château Mouton Rothschild's white wine fits easily into the rich, modern style favored for the Château's reds. There are layers of vanilla and wood, with a ripe, round creaminess. Could age, due to good depth of flavor and some complexity from the acidity. **90** *—R.V. (6/1/2005)*

CHÂTEAU OLIVIER

Château Olivier 2002 Bordeaux White Blend (Pessac-Léognan) $NA. A rich, smooth wine, with flavors of grapefruit and toast, and grassy, herbaceous aromas. Attractive and fresh on the finish. **87** *—R.V. (6/1/2005)*

CHÂTEAU PALMER

Château Palmer 2000 Bordeaux Blend (Margaux) $120. **94** *—R.V. (6/1/2003)*

CHÂTEAU PAPE-CLEMENT

Château Pape-Clement 2002 Bordeaux White Blend (Pessac-Léognan) $NA. A hugely toasty wine, one that tastes more like a California Chardonnay than a blend of Sauvignon, Sémillon, and Muscadelle. It works, because it is a great, rich wine, with balanced, ripe fruit, acidity and crisp fruit flavors. **92** *—R.V. (6/1/2005)*

CHÂTEAU PAVEIL DE LUZE

Château Paveil de Luze 2001 Bordeaux Blend (Margaux) $30. A well-flavored, well-structured wine, which emphasizes Margaux elegance. Flavors of black currant, Mediterranean herbs, and spices are all harmonious. It may not be a big wine, but it has richness, light tannins and good intensity. **87** *—R.V. (6/1/2005)*

CHÂTEAU PAVIE-DECESSE

Château Pavie-Decesse 2000 Bordeaux Blend (Saint-Emilion) $NA. **90** *—R.V. (6/1/2003)*

CHÂTEAU PECH-REDON

Château Pech-Redon 2001 La Centaurée Red Blend (Coteaux du Languedoc) $NA. A hugely powerful wine which wears its high alcohol (14%) lightly.That's because the fruit is tempered with fine acidity and dark black, wood flavored fruits. This is a wine that needs aging, with its power-packed tar and tannins. **91** *—R.V. (12/1/2004)*

CHÂTEAU PÉTRUS

Château Pétrus 2000 Bordeaux Blend (Pomerol) $150. **98** *—R.V. (6/1/2003)*

CHÂTEAU PHÉLAN-SÉGUR

Château Phélan-Ségur 2002 Bordeaux Blend (Saint-Estèphe) $21. A powerful, spicy wine that is dominated by wood and toast. The fruit is black but relatively lightweight, and is suffering at this stage from the strong wood flavors. **89** *—R.V. (6/1/2005)*

CHÂTEAU PIQUE-CAILLOU

Château Pique-Caillou 2002 Bordeaux Blend (Pessac-Léognan) $28. A well-balanced wine with dry fruits, flavors of black currants, and fine, fresh fruit. It is not a big wine, but benefits from elegance and freshness. It is ready to drink now. **87** *—R.V. (6/1/2005)*

CHÂTEAU PONTET-CANET

Château Pontet-Canet 2000 Bordeaux Blend (Pauillac) $70. **90** *—R.V. (6/1/2003)*

CHÂTEAU POUJEAUX

Château Poujeaux 2000 Bordeaux Blend (Moulis) $34. **87** *—R.V. (6/1/2003)*

CHÂTEAU PRIEURÉ-LES-TOURS

Château Prieuré-Les-Tours 2000 Cuveé Clara Bordeaux White Blend (Graves) $16. A finely balanced Graves that shows wood, rich spice, and toast as well as honey and smooth fruit flavors. It's an elegant, food-friendly wine. The release of this nearly 5-year-old wine shows just how well Graves wines can age. **88** *—R.V. (6/1/2005)*

CHÂTEAU PRIEURÉ-LICHINE

Château Prieuré-Lichine 2000 Bordeaux Blend (Margaux) $35. 91 *—R.V. (6/1/2003)*

CHÂTEAU PUECH-HAUT

Château Puech-Haut 2000 Clos du Pic Red Blend (Coteaux du Languedoc) $NA. An old vine cuvee of Syrah and Carignan, this great wine, bottled unfiltered, is packed with dense tannins. Flavors of new wood give style and structure. Powered by dense herbal fruits and ripe flavors, this is big, yet retains an essential food-friendly element. **92** *—R.V. (12/1/2004)*

Château Puech-Haut 2002 Téle de Cuvée Rhône White Blend (Coteaux du Languedoc) $NA. There is great intensity of flavor in this wine from its whole bunch maceration and its 8 month wood aging. This is serious, ripe wine with delicious exotic flavors from the blend of Roussanne, Marsanne, and Grenache Blanc. **91** *—R.V. (12/1/2004)*

CHÂTEAU RAUZAN DESPAGNE

Château Rauzan Despagne 2004 Cuvée de Landereau Bordeaux White Blend (Bordeaux) $12. A crisp, fresh wine, ready to drink now, with no wood aging, but with great ripe white-fruit flavors, and mouth-watering acidity. A great apéritif wine for the summer. **87** *—R.V. (6/1/2005)*

CHÂTEAU RAUZAN-SÉGLA

Château Rauzan-Ségla 2001 Bordeaux Blend (Margaux) $57. A huge, powerful, dense wine, which layers pure black fruits over dusty tannins. This is an impressive wine, proof of Rauzan-Ségla's improvements since Chanel took over ownership. It is packed with fruits, like an intense jelly, but also has dryness, acidity, and good aging potential. **94** *—R.V. (6/1/2005)*

CHÂTEAU RÉAL MARTIN

Château Réal Martin 2004 Rhône Red Blend (Côtes de Provence) $10. Comes out of the chute a little stinky and reductive, so give it a good decanting before serving. Once it comes around, the flavors are bold and fresh: watermelon and strawberry held together by a crisp, citrusy backbone. **85 Best Buy** *—J.C. (11/15/2005)*

Château Réal Martin 2001 Syrah-Grenache (Côtes de Provence) $13. A 50-50 blend of Syrah and Grenache that's marred by sulfury notes on the nose that come across as garlicky on the palate. Seems to have decent weight and texture, so may be worth a try if you are less sensitive to these compounds. **81** *—J.C. (11/15/2005)*

CHÂTEAU REYNON

Château Reynon 2003 Vieilles Vignes Bordeaux White Blend (Bordeaux) $17. This 2003, fat and full, shows skilled winemaking, extracting intensity of flavor and a fine balance from a hot, superripe year. Toast and cream flavors at the fore, along with a light touch of acidity. **88** *—R.V. (6/1/2005)*

CHÂTEAU ROLLAN DE BY

Château Rollan de By 2002 Bordeaux Blend (Médoc) $32. A fine effort from this reliable cru bourgeois, the 2002 Rollan de By boasts hints of toast and vanilla in its bouquet, but mostly offers up solid cassis fruit, with just a whiff of dried herbs. A velvety, supple texture and lush tannins suggest early drinkability. Try now–2010. **88** *—J.C. (6/1/2005)*

CHÂTEAU ROUBAUD

Château Roubaud 1998 Cuvée Prestige Red Blend (Costières de Nimes) $12. 87 *—M.M. (11/1/2000)*

Château Roubaud 2003 Cuvée Prestige Rosé Blend (Costières de Nimes) $12. This is a delicious, full-bodied rosé from the mouth of the Rhône in southern France. It is full of ripe strawberry fruit flavors. This is what fresh, fruity rosé is all about. It may not be summer for another six months, but this makes a great apéritif wine. You could even drink it with the Thanksgiving turkey. **88 Best Buy** *—R.V. (11/15/2004)*

CHÂTEAU ROUBINE

Château Roubine 1998 Cru Classe Red Blend (Côtes de Provence) $12. 83 *—D.T. (2/1/2002)*

Château Roubine 2000 Cru Classe White Blend (Côtes de Provence) $12. 86 *—M.M. (2/1/2002)*

CHÂTEAU ROUTAS

Château Routas 1999 Rouviere Rosé Blend (Coteaux Varois) $9. 88 Best Buy *(8/1/2000)*

Château Routas 2000 Coquelicot White Blend (Vin de Pays Var) $16. 87 *—M.M. (2/1/2002)*

CHÂTEAU RUSSOL GARDEY

Château Russol Gardey 1999 Grande Réserve Syrah (Minervois) $20. 87 *(10/1/2001)*

CHÂTEAU SAINT-COSMÉ

Château Saint-Cosmé 2001 Cuvée Classique Rhône Red Blend (Côtes-du-Rhône) $33. Has great, juicy fruit with flavors of sweet raspberries and strawberries; its more serious side shows layers of austere tannins. It should age well, at least over five to 10 years. **92** *—R.V. (3/1/2004)*

CHÂTEAU SAINT-GERMAIN

Château Saint-Germain 2000 Red Blend (Coteaux du Languedoc) $9. **87** —*R.V. (11/15/2003)*

CHÂTEAU SAINT-ROBERT

Château Saint-Robert 2002 Bordeaux White Blend (Graves) $17. A complex, ripe wine from one of the high achievers in the Graves. It has intense, flowery aromas, with a touch of vanilla and fresh, grassy character. Has grapefruit flavors; could age over five years. **88** —*R.V. (6/1/2005)*

CHÂTEAU SÉNÉJAC

Château Sénéjac 2002 Bordeaux Blend (Haut-Médoc) $NA. At the southern end of the Médoc, this estate is run by Thierry Rustman of Château Talbot in Saint-Julien. With its dense fruit, sweet tannins, and well-balanced acidity and dryness, this 2002 is a great success, still young but likely to develop well over 5 years. **91** —*R.V. (6/1/2005)*

CHÂTEAU SIGNAC

Château Signac 2000 Chusclan Cuvée Terra Amata Rhône Red Blend (Côtes-du-Rhône Villages) $20. Cleanly made in the modern style, with toast and vanilla cradling supple, low-acid black-cherry fruit. Soft, creamy, and easily accessible, yet with enough interest to inspire more than a single sip. **89** —*J.C. (3/1/2004)*

CHÂTEAU SIRAN

Château Siran 2000 Bordeaux Blend (Margaux) $40. **89** —*R.V. (6/1/2003)*

CHÂTEAU SMITH HAUT-LAFITTE

Château Smith Haut-Lafitte 2002 Blanc Bordeaux White Blend (Pessac-Léognan) $48. Undoubtedly the real deal in terms of size. The nose is rich, oily, and pungent, but it's hard to extract any true fruit aromas from it. The mouthfeel is similarly full, with melon, vanilla, and citrus. Essences of peach, orange pith, and white pepper work well on the finish. **88** *(7/1/2005)*

CHÂTEAU ST. ESTEVE D'UCHAUX

Château St. Esteve d'Uchaux 2000 Côtes du Rhône Village Red Blend (Côtes-du-Rhône) $14. **89 Best Buy** *(10/1/2003)*

CHÂTEAU TALBOT

Château Talbot 2000 Caillou Blanc Bordeaux White Blend (Bordeaux) $24. Oily and unexpressive, with aromas of wax beans and butterscotch. Underripe nectarine flavors carry the dull palate to an equally boring finish. Tasted twice. **80** *(7/1/2005)*

CHÂTEAU TAYAC-PLAISANCE

Château Tayac-Plaisance 2001 Bordeaux Blend (Margaux) $NA. A well-crafted, very drinkable wine that exhibits all the best in good, straightforward Bordeaux. Good ripe tannins and fine, classic fruits, with dryness and style rather than power. **86** —*R.V. (6/1/2005)*

CHÂTEAU THIEULEY

Château Thieuley 2003 Bordeaux White Blend (Bordeaux) $13. One of the top producers in the Entre-Deux-Mers, Francis Courselle's white has a freshness, lift and crispness that is not always apparent in 2003 whites. But there are also wood flavors to add complexity, and to produce a beautifully balanced wine. **91 Best Buy** —*R.V. (6/1/2005)*

Château Thieuly 2001 Bordeaux White Blend (Bordeaux) $6. **87** —*R.V. (12/1/2002)*

Château Thieuly 2000 Bordeaux Blend (Bordeaux) $76. **88** —*R.V. (12/1/2002)*

CHÂTEAU TOUR DE MIRAMBEAU

Château Tour de Mirambeau 2000 Cuvée Passion Bordeaux Blend (Bordeaux) $19. **91** —*R.V. (12/1/2002)*

Château Tour de Mirambeau 2002 Cuvée Passion Bordeaux White Blend (Bordeaux) $19. Old vines, low yields, and fermentation in wood give great complexity to this top cuvée from the Despagne family. There is a touch of wood flavor to this wine, but the main impression is of delicious, fresh fruit that has gained maturity from bottle age. It is in balance, with good acidity to give it a final lift. **90 Editors' Choice** —*R.V. (6/1/2005)*

CHÂTEAU TOUR LÉOGNAN

Château Tour Léognan 2003 Bordeaux White Blend (Pessac-Léognan) $NA. This is the second-label white wine from Château Carbonnieux. It's a fresh, uncomplicated wine, which is given richness from the wood flavors and softness from the superripe year. **87** —*R.V. (6/1/2005)*

CHÂTEAU TOUR SIMARD

Château Tour Simard 1999 Bordeaux Blend (Saint-Emilion Grand Cru) $40. Already showing some bricking at the rim, this St.-Emilion from the owner of Château Pavie is altogether different from that storied wine. Starts with scents of raisins, smoke, and leather, and continues in that vein on the palate, where the flavors run toward dried fruit and vanilla. Supple, soft tannins on the finish suggest early drinkability. **86** —*J.C. (6/1/2005)*

CHÂTEAU TRIMOULET

Château Trimoulet 1996 Bordeaux Blend (Saint-Emilion) $35. 86 *—J.C. (3/1/2001)*

CHÂTEAU TROPLONG-MONDOT

Château Troplong-Mondot 2000 Bordeaux Blend (Saint-Emilion) $85. 92 *—R.V. (6/1/2003)*

CHÂTEAU VAL JOANIS

Château Val Joanis 1999 Cuvée Réserve Les Griottes Red Blend (Côtes du Luberon) $20. 89 *—M.S. (9/1/2003)*

Château Val Joanis 2001 Red Blend (Côtes du Luberon) $13. Hints of cinnamon and clove reflect a small amount of new oak aging, but the dominant flavors are of plum and dusty earth. Not a powerhouse, it's a balanced, food-friendly wine at a reasonable price: the kind of wine that wins friends, not ratings competitions. **85** *—J.C. (2/1/2005)*

Château Val Joanis 2001 Vigne du Chanoine Trouillet Red Blend (Côtes du Luberon) $30. Scents of buttered popcorn lead the way, followed by waves of oak-derived flavors: cedar, vanilla, and chocolate, backed up by some black cherry notes. The mouthfeel is supple and creamy, the finish moderately tannic. Drink this lavishly oaked wine from 2007–2015, once the wood has integrated a little better with its fruit substrate. **88** *—J.C. (2/1/2005)*

Château Val Joanis 1998 Estate Bottled Rhône Red Blend (Côtes du Luberon) $10. 87 *—J.C. (3/1/2001)*

Château Val Joanis 2003 Réserve Les Merises Rosé Blend (Côtes du Luberon) $18. A passable attempt at a prestige rosé, with toasty, vanilla notes that supplant rather than support the watermelon, strawberry, and apple flavors. Imported by Chancel Père & Fils. **82** *—J.C. (11/15/2005)*

Château Val Joanis 2002 White Blend (Côtes du Luberon) $13. A fruit-salad white, with aromas and flavors that run the gamut from Asian pear to ripe apples and Hawaiian pineapple. Plump and medium-weight, picks up hints of honey and citrus on the lingering finish. **86** *—J.C. (3/1/2004)*

CHÂTEAU VERONIQUE

Château Veronique 2001 Red Blend (Coteaux du Languedoc) $13. Great ripe tarry fruit, tempered with structured wood bring out the character of this wood-aged wine dominated by Carignan and Grenache. This has solid, dark black fruits and great ripe flavors. It's big and powerful. **87** *—R.V. (12/1/2004)*

CHÂTEAU YON FIGEAC

Château Yon Figeac 1995 Bordeaux Blend (Saint-Emilion) $40. 91 **Editors' Choice** *(4/1/2001)*

CHEVALIER DE GRUAUD

Chevalier de Gruaud 1999 Bordeaux Blend (Saint-Julien) $45. A subsidiary label of Château Gruaud Larose, obviously destined for earlier drinking than the grand vin. Supple tannins frame cedar, tobacco, and earth notes, while the light frame holds just enough flesh to avoid leanness. **84** *—J.C. (6/1/2005)*

CHRISTIAN MOREAU PÈRE ET FILS

Christian Moreau Père et Fils 2001 Chablis $18. 84 *—J.C. (10/1/2003)*

CIRCUS BY L'OSTAL CAZES

Circus by L'Ostal Cazes 2004 Viognier (Vin de Pays d'Oc) $13. Mint and mineral notes are layered delicately over honeyed baked apple aromas in this full-bodied Viognier. Flavors of anise and honeyed stones show a touch of alcohol on the finish, but this is a solid first effort. **86** *—J.C. (11/15/2005)*

CLAUDE CHEVALIER

Claude Chevalier 2003 Les Gréchons Premier Cru (Ladoix) $45. A light, fresh wine with crisp green apple flavors. It is clean, and rounded out, with a touch of vanilla. Finishes with lively acidity. **86** *—R.V. (9/1/2005)*

CLOS DE L'ORATOIRE DES PAPES

Clos de L'Oratoire des Papes 2000 Les Choregies Rhône Red Blend (Châteauneuf-du-Pape) $75. More extracted and oakier than Clos de L'Oratoire's regular cuvée, this is a chunky, corpulent wine that displays plenty of cedary oak layered over prunes and black cherries. Moderately tannic, and worth holding to a few years to see if I've underestimated its potential. **87** *—J.C. (3/1/2004)*

Clos de L'Oratoire des Papes 2001 Rhône Red Blend (Châteauneuf-du-Pape) $34. Starts with smoky, leathery aromas, then moves on to scents of sun-baked stones. Mouthfilling dark, brandied cherries follow, finishing with a spike of acidity and firm tannins. Drink this full-bodied wine from 2007–2015. **88** *—J.C. (2/1/2005)*

CLOS DES BRUSQUIÈRES

Clos des Brusquières 2003 Rhône Red Blend (Châteauneuf-du-Pape) $32. This is a solid performance. The wine is dense, with dark, dry tannins, but overlying this is very direct, juicy fruit, with flavors of raspberries and dark cherries. It is not initially as generous as some 2003s, but the tannins and acidity suggest it is ageworthy. **91** *—R.V. (12/31/2005)*

CLOS FOURTET

Clos Fourtet 2000 Bordeaux Blend (Saint-Emilion) $51. 90 *—R.V. (6/1/2003)*

CLOS NARDIAN

Clos Nardian 2003 Bordeaux White Blend (Bordeaux) $100. Produced by Jonathan Maltus, who also makes the superstar Saint-Emilion wine, Le Dôme, this is a beautifully crafted wine that brings together tropical fruits, flavors of quince, and creamy vanilla. There is some good acidity, despite the hot year, which brings everything into balance. **91** *—R.V. (6/1/2005)*

COMTE CATHARE

Comte Cathare 1999 Syrache Rhône Red Blend (Vin de Pays d'Oc) $13. **85** *—M.M. (2/1/2002)*

Comte Cathare 1999 Syraz Syrah (Vin de Pays d'Oc) $15. **85** *—M.M. (2/1/2002)*

COMTE DE LANTAGE

Comte de Lantage 1995 Premier Cru Blanc de Blancs Brut (Champagne) $40. **84** *—M.S. (6/1/2003)*

COMTE LAFOND

Comte LaFond 2000 Sancerre $27. **88** *—S.H. (1/1/2002)*

COTE TARIQUET

Cote Tariquet 2001 White Blend (Vin de Pays des Cotes de Gascogne) $14. **83** *—M.S. (9/1/2003)*

COUDOULET DE BEAUCASTEL

Coudoulet de Beaucastel 2000 White Blend (Côtes-du-Rhône) $30. **87** *—M.S. (9/1/2003)*

DANIEL CHOTARD

Daniel Chotard 2003 Sancerre $22. Veers into the mineral, spiced-apple realm before displaying citrus in the form of grapefruit, melon, and peach. Quite minerally and dry, with a citrus and melon influence to the finish. Mainstream and healthy; perfect restaurant Sancerre. **89** *(7/1/2005)*

DANIEL RION

Daniel Rion 1999 Les Beaux-Monts (Vosne-Romanée) $52. **92** *—P.G. (1/7/2001)*

DE LADOUCETTE

De Ladoucette 2002 Pouilly-Fumé $39. Ultra flinty and tight, with crisp, almost lean lemon and pineapple flavors. This is one tight ball of citrus, and it doesn't have a whole lot of texture to it. Probably best with shellfish. **84** *(7/1/2005)*

DE SAINT GALL

De Saint Gall NV Bouzy Brut (Champagne) $32. **86** *—M.S. (12/1/2000)*

De Saint Gall NV Blanc de Blancs Premier Cru (Champagne) $35. **88** *—M.S. (12/15/2003)*

De Saint Gall 1990 Cuvée Orpale (Champagne) $99. **92 Editors' Choice** *—M.M. (12/15/2001)*

De Saint Gall NV Extra Brut (Champagne) $55. **89** *—M.S. (12/15/2003)*

De Saint Gall 1998 Blanc de Blancs Premier Cru (Champagne) $49. **90** *—M.S. (12/15/2003)*

De Saint Gall 1995 Premier Cru Blanc de Blancs (Champagne) $48. **92** *—J.C. (12/15/2001)*

DE SOUSA & FILS

De Sousa & Fils NV Cuvée de Caudalies Blanc de Blancs Vielles Vignes Brut (Champagne) $60. **87** *—R.V. (12/1/2002)*

DE VENOGE

De Venoge 1995 Brut Millesimé (Champagne) $NA. A ripe, balanced wine which is showing some good, toasty bottle age. De Venoge Vintage has a Pinot-dominated blend which ages the wine, but also gives elegance. The wine has flavors of white fruits, crisp apples, and fresh croissants to give good complexity and richness. **89** *—R.V. (12/1/2004)*

DELAMOTTE

Delamotte 1992 Blanc de Blancs (Champagne) $63. **84** *(12/15/1999)*

Delamotte NV Brut (Champagne) $44. Owned by Laurent-Perrier, this small house makes a great, toasty Chardonnay-dominated nonvintage blend. Rich, full bodied and elegant; an impressive wine. Imported by Wilson Daniels Ltd. **93** *—R.V. (12/1/2005)*

DELAS FRÈRES

Delas Frères 1999 Haute Pierre (Châteauneuf-du-Pape) $40. **85** *—M.S. (9/1/2003)*

Delas Frères 2001 Séléction Delas Merlot (Vin de Pays d'Oc) $8. **85** *—M.S. (9/1/2003)*

Delas Frères 2002 Rhône Red Blend (Côtes-du-Ventoux) $9. Smells okay, with soft Bing cherry aromas and hints of peppery spice. But the flavors don't quite measure up, turning excessively tart and lemony on the finish. **81** *—J.C. (3/1/2004)*

Delas Frères 2003 Rhône Red Blend (Côtes-du-Ventoux) $10. After a tough 2002 vintage, Delas has bounced back nicely with this wine, which shows uncommon depth and intensity for a humble Côtes du Ventoux. Bold scents of black cherries, blackberries, and earth rise from the glass and there's plenty of richness on the palate, even some slightly rustic tannins to help rein in all that fruit. Notes of licorice, tar, and earth on the finish make it more than a simple fruit bomb. **88 Best Buy** *—J.C. (11/15/2004)*

Delas Frères 2000 Domaine des Genets Rhône Red Blend (Vacqueyras) $19. Delas has made a Vacqueyras from the 61-acre Domaine des Genets since 1990, and the alluvial soil of the estate gives deep, plummy fruit with rich tannins and a fine layer of acidity. It is not a heavyweight, but is fine and elegant. **88** *—R.V. (3/1/2004)*

Delas Frères 1999 La Landonne (Côte Rôtie) $105. 94 *—R.V. (6/1/2002)*

Delas Frères 1998 Les Calcerniers Rhône Red Blend (Châteauneuf-du-Pape) $29. 91 Editors' Choice *(3/1/2002)*

Delas Frères 2001 Les Reinages Rhône Red Blend (Gigondas) $34. A broad-shouldered and extracted wine, it also has some hard edges that demand cellaring. Herbal and cherry scents mix with darker, plummier notes on the nose, while the palate folds in earthy nuances. The one concern is that the alcohol level comes through a bit on the finish. **88** *—J.C. (2/1/2005)*

Delas Frères 2000 Saint-Esprit Rhône Red Blend (Côtes-du-Rhône) $9. 87 *—R.V. (6/1/2002)*

Delas Frères 2000 Clos Boucher Rhône White Blend (Condrieu) $15. 90 *—R.V. (6/1/2002)*

Delas Frères 1997 Les Launes Rhône White Blend (Crozes-Hermitage) $15. 85 *—M.S. (5/1/2000)*

Delas Frères 2003 Saint-Esprit Rhône White Blend (Côtes-du-Rhône) $14. A bit cloudy in appearance, this richly textured, plump wine boasts rich aromas of ripe pears and dried spices alongside notes of lemon curd. Custardy on the palate, folding in hints of pear, citrus and minerals. The only quibble is that it finishes a little short. Drink now. **88** *—J.C. (2/1/2005)*

Delas Frères 2001 François de Tournon (Saint-Joseph) $27. An easy-drinking syrah from the northern Rhône, this medium-weight wine boasts aromas of horse sweat, black pepper, and roasted cherries, backed by flavors of black cherries and dried spices. It's plump and juicy, with a mouthwatering finish. Drink now–2010. **87** *(2/1/2005)*

Delas Frères 1997 Cuvée François de Tournon (Saint-Joseph) $20. 89 *(3/1/2002)*

Delas Frères 2002 Les Launes (Crozes-Hermitage) $19. Modest cherry and herbal-stemmy aromas give way to lean cherry flavors on the palate. It seems a little dilute and underripe, which could be a result of the vintage. Decent, but leaves one wishing for more power. **84** *—J.C. (2/1/2005)*

Delas Frères 1998 Les Launes (Crozes-Hermitage) $15. 88 Editors' Choice *(10/1/2001)*

Delas Frères 1998 Marquise de la Tourette (Hermitage) $54. 92 *—R.V. (6/1/2002)*

Delas Frères 2001 Sainte-Epine (Saint-Joseph) $53. With fruit coming from the Saint-Epine vineyard, this wine comes from the heart of the Saint-Joseph appellation. There is plenty of rich fruit, generous and packed with black plums and sweet jelly fruits. There is acidity and a streak of spicy wood which provides great balance. **89** *—R.V. (2/1/2005)*

Delas Frères 1998 Seigneur de Maugiron (Côte Rôtie) $25. 91 *—R.V. (6/1/2002)*

Delas Frères 2002 La Galopine (Condrieu) $51. 87 *(12/1/2004)*

Delas Frères 2001 La Galopine (Condrieu) $47. 89 *—S.H. (1/1/2002)*

DELBECK

Delbeck 1999 Brut (Champagne) $60. An elegant, medium-weight Champagne with a persistent bead, this is young but already beautiful to drink. Citrus and chalk notes dominate, buttressed by apple, mineral, and toast. Finishes long. **92** *—J.C. (12/1/2004)*

Delbeck 1990 Brut (Champagne) $51. 94 *(12/1/2000)*

Delbeck NV Brut Cramant (Champagne) $48. 84 *(12/31/2000)*

DEUTZ

Deutz 1998 Amour de Deutz Blanc de Blancs Brut (Champagne) $162. This frothy, exuberantly fresh young wine could have been held another few years prior to release. Right now, it's delicious but more about potential, like a beautiful yearling at the Keenland auctions. The flavors of toast, apples, and limes stand out brightly, needing some time to mellow into a harmonious glow. Try around 2010. **90 Cellar Selection** *—J.C. (12/1/2004)*

Deutz 1998 Blanc de Blancs Brut (Champagne) $95. In five years, this rating may look conservative, but right now the wine is youthful and aggressive—a bit tough to tackle. Spicy, gingery aromas war with toast and citrus; the finish is long, but not totally harmonious. All of this should be resolved by time, which will round off the edges and blend the flavors. **89** *—J.C. (12/1/2004)*

Deutz 1996 Blanc de Blancs Brut (Reims) $78. 93 *—J.C. (12/15/2003)*

Deutz 1995 Brut (Champagne) $52. 92 *—P.G. (6/1/2001)*

Deutz NV Brut Classic (Champagne) $49. Though it has mature, slightly toasty aromas, this wine also has great flavors of grapefruit, some lemon peel, and a vibrant white fruit character. It is dry, with the clean, fresh acidity going right through to the finish. **93 Editors' Choice** —*R.V. (12/1/2005)*

Deutz 1996 Brut Rosé (Champagne) $57. 92 —*S.H. (12/15/2002)*

Deutz 1996 Cuvée William Deutz (Champagne) $158. This is one of the most satisfying of the prestige cuvées, following the vintages closely. But this 1996 is exceptional, reflecting the exceptional character of the vintage. It is elegant, finely crafted, with acidity and structure, very pure in its flavors of gooseberries and white currants. This will develop well over the 5–10 years. The wine is named after the 19th century founder of Deutz. **93** —*R.V. (12/1/2004)*

Deutz 1990 Cuvée William Deutz (Champagne) $89. 96 —*E.D. (12/1/1999)*

Deutz 1997 Cuvée William Deutz Rosé (Champagne) $115. 92 —*R.V. (12/15/2003)*

Deutz 1995 Amour de Deutz (Champagne) $149. 86 *(12/15/2001)*

Deutz 1999 Rosé Brut (Champagne) $66. This has a seductive pink salmon color, and the delicious strawberry and red fruit flavors continue the theme. It is soft, very attractive, doing all the right things for an apéritif style of rosé, showing finesse and elegance more than power. **88** —*R.V. (12/1/2004)*

DEVAUX

Devaux NV Grande Réserve Brut (Champagne) $35. 87 *(6/1/2001)*

DIDIER DAGUENEAU

Didier Dagueneau 2003 Pur Sang (Pouilly-Fumé) $60. A little pretentious with the appellation (it could be Pouilly-Fumé), but nothing but great wine in the bottle. Aromas of grapefruit, apple, mustard, and wet stones are framed by gentle notes of cinnamon and toast. The palate is louder as it sizzles with razor-crisp orange, apple, peach, and grapefruit, all with a proper mineral, herbal edge. Rock solid, but cheerful and universally likable. **92** *(7/1/2005)*

DIEBOLT VALLOIS

Diebolt Vallois NV Blanc de Blancs Prestige (Champagne) $46. A full, ripe wine with a touch of toastiness. It is fresh, but it is also powered, rich and open. Yellow fruits give the extra fruitiness. The aftertaste is dry with ripe acidity. **89** —*R.V. (12/1/2004)*

DIVINUS DE CHÂTEAU BONNET

Divinus de Château Bonnet 2000 Bordeaux Blend (Bordeaux) $30. 90 —*R.V. (12/1/2002)*

DOMAINE A. CAILBOURDIN

Domaine A. Cailbourdin 2003 Les Cris (Pouilly-Fumé) $22. Apple and pine aromas are the highlights of the simple bouquet, while the mouth is big, heavy and weighted down by sweet fruit, particularly peach and mango. Seems a bit heavy and lacking in verve for a Loire Sauvignon, but that's 2003 for you. **85** *(7/1/2005)*

DOMAINE ALBERT MANN

Domaine Albert Mann 2002 Cuvée Albert Riesling (Alsace) $NA. From fruit growing around the village of Wettolsheim, this is a powerful, earthy style of wine. It may not have subtlety, but it makes up for this in its fresh impact, with flavors of lemon, grapefruit, and some minerality and a tannic structure. **86** —*R.V. (5/1/2005)*

DOMAINE AMIOT-SERVELLE

Domaine Amiot-Servelle 2000 Chambolle-Musigny $46. 87 —*R.V. (11/1/2002)*

Domaine Amiot-Servelle 2000 Les Amoureuses Premier Cru (Chambolle-Musigny) $100. 91 —*R.V. (11/1/2002)*

DOMAINE ANDRE BRUNEL

Domaine Andre Brunel 1999 Cuvée Sommelongue Rhône Red Blend (Côtes-du-Rhône) $10. 88 Best Buy —*J.C. (3/1/2001)*

DOMAINE ANTONIN GUYON

Domaine Antonin Guyon 2002 Clos du Village (Chambolle-Musigny) $48. A beautiful, silky wine that has smooth fruit and acidity. There are tannins and good aging potential, but at the moment it is vibrating with raspberry fruits. **90** —*R.V. (9/1/2004)*

Domaine Antonin Guyon 2002 Bressandes (Corton) $60. Gorgeous aromas of strawberry fruits lead to a palate of firm tannic fruit, balanced by luscious acidity and strawberry jelly flavors. It is rich, ethereal, and opulent all at the same time. **93** —*R.V. (9/1/2004)*

DOMAINE AUCHÈRE

Domaine Auchère 2004 Cuvée Calcaire (Sancerre) $21. Gritty and sweaty to start, although it finds a better groove with time. Shows basic citrus and herb on the palate, followed by lemon. Seems a bit salty on the finish. **84** *(7/1/2005)*

DOMAINE AUTHER

Domaine Auther 2003 Kirchweg Riesling (Alsace) $NA. With its tiny holdings scattered over many different vineyards, Domaine Auther is able to produce a bewildering array of wines. This riesling from the Kirchweg vineyard is ripe, full of the ripe, condensed flavors that come from a maceration of the whole fruits before fermentation, and just plain delicious. It will benefit from two more years' aging. **89** *—R.V. (5/1/2005)*

DOMAINE BARRAUD

Domaine Barraud 2003 En Buland (Pouilly-Fuissé) $NA. From 70-year-old vines at the base of Solutré, this is an exceptionally elegant, precise, and minerally rendering of Pouilly-Fuissé, especially so when seen in the context of the vintage. There's ample richness and length, with pear and spice notes, but the lingering impression is one of great minerality and finesse. **88** *—J.C. (11/15/2005)*

DOMAINE BEGUDE

Domaine Begude 2000 Chardonnay (Vin de Pays d'Oc) $10. 88 Best Buy *—D.T. (2/1/2002)*

DOMAINE BELLE

Domaine Belle 2002 Les Pierrelles (Crozes-Hermitage) $30. A ripe, full-bodied Crozes, with herbal aromas, and great smoky, leathery flavors. Red fruits add to the mix, which also shows some barnyard characters which don't offend and certainly add complexity. This is a well-made, good value wine. Drink now, and over 5 years. **88** *—R.V. (2/1/2005)*

DOMAINE BERTAGNA

Domaine Bertagna 1999 Premier Cru (Vougeot) $65. 88 *(10/1/2003)*

Domaine Bertagna 1999 Clos Vougeot $120. 92 *(10/1/2003)*

Domaine Bertagna 1998 (Marsannay) $21. 87 *—P.G. (11/1/2002)*

Domaine Bertagna 1998 Vosne-Romanée $NA. 89 *—P.G. (11/1/2002)*

Domaine Bertagna 1998 Clos Vougeot $107. 90 *—P.G. (11/1/2002)*

Domaine Bertagna 1998 Les Beaux Monts Premier Cru (Vosne-Romanée) $60. 89 *—P.G. (11/1/2002)*

Domaine Bertagna 1998 Les Murgers Premier Cru (Nuits-St.-Georges) $56. 89 *—P.G. (11/1/2002)*

Domaine Bertagna 1998 Premier Cru Les Cras (Vougeot) $25. 87 *—P.G. (11/1/2002)*

DOMAINE BERTHET-RAYNE

Domaine Berthet-Rayne 2003 Vieilli en Fut de Chêne Rhône Red Blend (Châteauneuf-du-Pape) $38. The year this wine spends in wood gives it a ripe, smooth feel. The tannins show both dry fruit and wood characteristics, while the freshness and acidity balance the black plum and cassis fruits. This wine, still young, will certainly age well. **89** *—R.V. (12/31/2005)*

DOMAINE BORIE DE MAUREL

Domaine Borie de Maurel 1999 Syrah (Minervois) $9. 84 *(10/1/2001)*

DOMAINE BOTT-GEYL

Domaine Bott-Geyl 2002 Burgreben de Zellenberg Riesling (Alsace) $20. The clay soil of the Burgreben produces a heavy style of Riesling, with some earthy flavors. But this wine also has fresh fruit, flavors of red apples and pears, along with a mineral streak that gives it a great lift on the finish. Leave it 3–4 years before drinking. **88** *—R.V. (11/1/2005)*

DOMAINE CAZES

Domaine Cazes 2003 Le Canon du Maréchal Rosé Grenache (Vin de Pays d'Oc) $16. A fresh, fruity style of rosé, with intense raspberry flavors, a touch of caramel, and just a touch of acidity. It's fresh enough to last until the next sunshine hits in the spring. **86** *—R.V. (4/1/2005)*

Domaine Cazes 2003 Le Canon du Maréchal Syrah-Merlot (Vin de Pays d'Oc) $13. The Cazes estate is the largest in Roussillon, in the driest area of France. This blend of Syrah and Merlot, dominated by spicy, peppery Syrah, is full of rich fruit, with just a hint of jammy Merlot to bring out the fruit. Great fruit flavors and a delicious juicy finish. **87** *—R.V. (4/1/2005)*

DOMAINE CHANTAL LESCURE

Domaine Chantal Lescure 2002 Clos Vougeot $100. A wine that reveals all the possibilities of great Clos de Vougeot. It is rich, spicy, packed with new wood but also with great fresh fruit. Underneath, there are huge, dense tannins. **94** *—R.V. (9/1/2004)*

DOMAINE CHANTE-PERDRIX

Domaine Chante-Perdrix 2003 Rhône Red Blend (Châteauneuf-du-Pape) $32. This great, solid, tannic wine is a huge statement of black fruits, pepper, and enormous ripe flavors. With its high alcohol (marked on the label as 15.5%), this is almost too much. It impresses, but is it drinkable? **88** *—R.V. (12/31/2005)*

DOMAINE CHARLES THOMAS

Domaine Charles Thomas 2002 Clos du Roi (Corton) $66. Firm, solid fruit, layers of concentrated black fruits and a touch of acidity. A firm, serious wine, which has good potential. **89** *—R.V. (9/1/2004)*

DOMAINE CHEVALIER PÈRE ET FILS

Domaine Chevalier Père et Fils 2003 Pinot Noir (Ladoix) $29. An intensely perfumed wine that shows freshness and light tannins along with vibrant red flavors and acidity. This is a fast-developing wine, and is ready to drink now. Imported by Robert Kacher Imports. **86** *—R. V. (9/1/2005)*

Domaine Chevalier Père et Fils 2003 Rognet (Corton) $79. Chevalier, based in Ladoix-Serigny, has made a light wine, with easy fresh red fruits. For a grand cru, this should have more backbone, but the tannins are there, and the fruit is red and sweet. **85** *—R. V. (9/1/2005)*

DOMAINE CLUSEL-ROCH

Domaine Clusel-Roch 1999 Côte Rôtie $NA. **93** *—R. V. (6/1/2002)*

Domaine Clusel-Roch 2003 Condrieu $52. From a small parcel of 12 acres of Condrieu on the steep slope of the Coteau de Chery, Gilbert Clusel and Brigitte Roch have made a beautifully crafted Condrieu, ripe and unctuous and with wood flavors from barrel fermentation and aging. Honey flavors dominate this delicious wine. **91** *—R. V. (2/1/2005)*

DOMAINE COMTE DE LAUZE

Domaine Comte de Lauze 2003 Rhône Red Blend (Châteauneuf-du-Pape) $40. An earthy style of wine, dominated by perfumed Grenache. The wine is rich, solid, and quite structured, with fine acidity penetrating through the dense tannins and rough Grenache flavors. **87** *—R. V. (12/31/2005)*

DOMAINE COMTE GEORGES DE VOGÜÉ

Domaine Comte Georges de Vogüé 2000 Chambolle-Musigny $100. **90** *—R. V. (11/1/2002)*

Domaine Comte Georges de Vogüé 2000 Premier Cru (Chassague-Montrachet) $NA. **91** *—R. V. (11/1/2002)*

DOMAINE CONFURON-COTETIDOT

Domaine Confuron-Cotetidot 2002 Chambolle-Musigny $NA. An intensely perfumed wine, with a smoky character. It is big and rich, but there is also sweet, juicy fruit, a hint of new wood and piercing acidity to finish. **88** *—R. V. (9/1/2004)*

Domaine Confuron-Cotetidot 1999 Chambolle-Musigny $35. **88** *—R. V. (11/1/2002)*

Domaine Confuron-Cotetidot 2002 Les Suchots Premier Cru (Vosne-Romanée) $NA. Raspberry fruit aromas and smoky wood give this wine an immediately appealing character. It is intense, too, and finishes with loads of toasty wood. **89** *—R. V. (9/1/2004)*

DOMAINE D'AUPILHAC

Domaine D'Aupilhac 1996 Montpeyroux Red Blend (Coteaux du Languedoc) $15. **92** *—L. W. (10/1/1999)*

DOMAINE DE BEAURENARD

Domaine de Beaurenard 2000 Rhône Red Blend (Châteauneuf-du-Pape) $27. **82** *—S.H. (1/1/2002)*

DOMAINE DE CHAMPAGA

Domaine de Champaga 2000 Cuvée Reserve Rhône Red Blend (Côtes-du-Ventoux) $8. **84** *—M.S. (2/1/2003)*

DOMAINE DE CHEVALIER

Domaine de Chevalier 2000 Bordeaux Blend (Pessac-Léognan) $60. **94** *—R. V. (6/1/2003)*

Domaine de Chevalier 2001 Bordeaux White Blend (Pessac-Léognan) $100. This is one of the legendary whites of Bordeaux. It lives up to its reputation. The 2001 vintage of the Domaine de Chevalier white (tasted from half bottle) is well-evolved, packed with flavors of almonds, toast, spice, fresh grapefruits, white fruits, and an impressive layer of acidity. It will age for a good 20 years or more. Expect a full bottle to be less evolved at this stage. **97** **Cellar Selection** *—R. V. (6/1/2005)*

DOMAINE DE COURTEILLAC

Domaine de Courteillac 2001 Bordeaux White Blend (Bordeaux) $11. **88** *—R. V. (12/1/2002)*

DOMAINE DE CRISTIA

Domaine de Cristia 2003 Renaissance Rhône Red Blend (Châteauneuf-du-Pape) $70. Alain and Baptiste Grangeon make this wine from a small, 3.7-acre plot of old vines. Aged in wood for 2–3 years, it shows definite vanilla characters, with intense, ripe black flavors, great concentration, and richness and flavors of cassis and spice. There is a delicious juicy aftertaste to this impressive wine. **95** **Editors' Choice** *—R. V. (12/31/2005)*

DOMAINE DE FONTAVIN

Domaine de Fontavin 2003 Rhône Red Blend (Châteauneuf-du-Pape) $33. With vines in Gigondas, Vacqueyras and Côtes-du-Rhône, the Chouvet family has 103 acres, with vinification being the charge of Helene Chouvet. This is a ripe, juicy, fruity, relatively soft style of wine, with some new wood, that only hints at the tannins and the earthy flavors that are beneath the surface. **88** *—R. V. (12/31/2005)*

Domaine de Fontavin 1999 Rhône Red Blend (Vacqueyras) $17. **87** *—M.S. (2/1/2003)*

DOMAINE DE FONTENILLE

Domaine de Fontenille 2000 Rhône Red Blend (Côtes du Luberon) $13. Fontenille is almost always a great value, and this 2000 is no exception, boasting concentrated raspberry aromas that leap from the glass. The intense fruit is nicely balanced by structure, and made complex by the addition of leather and dark chocolate notes on the lengthy finish. Drink now–2010. **90 Best Buy** *—J.C. (2/1/2005)*

DOMAINE DE L'AIGUELIÈRE

Domaine de L'Aiguelière 2002 Red Blend (Coteaux du Languedoc) $NA. A smooth, elegant wine, with fine fruit tannins and a touch of new wood which does not dominate. This wine, from 60-year old vines has intensity, concentration and some juicy fruit flavors to finish. **86** *—R.V. (12/1/2004)*

DOMAINE DE L'HARMAS

Domaine de L'Harmas 2000 Rhône Red Blend (Côtes-du-Rhône Brézème) $11. 88 Best Buy *—C.S. (11/15/2002)*

DOMAINE DE L'OLIVIER

Domaine de L'Olivier 2001 Chardonnay (Vin de Pays d'Oc) $6. 87 Best Buy *—D.T. (11/15/2002)*

DOMAINE DE LA BATARDIERE

Domaine de La Batardiere 2000 Muscadet Sèvre et Maine $9. 88 Best Buy *—S.H. (11/15/2002)*

DOMAINE DE LA BOUISSIÈRE

Domaine de La Bouissière 2001 Rhône Red Blend (Vacqueyras) $20. Enticing perfumes lead into a big, deeply colored wine with modern, polished fruit, layers of new wood and sweetly ripe, dark flavors. This wine should develop well over the next five years. **89** *—R.V. (3/1/2004)*

Domaine de La Bouissière 2001 La Font de Tonin Rhône Red Blend (Gigondas) $35. This wine is named after Thierry Maravel's father Antonin, who built a small fountain in the family vineyards. It is powered by wood at this stage in its life. But under the new wood tastes, there is powerful, dense fruit that will come through and dominate with its rich licorice and tar flavors. **92** *—R.V. (3/1/2004)*

DOMAINE DE LA CHARBONNIÈRE

Domaine de La Charbonnière 2003 Cuvée Vieilles Vignes Rhône Red Blend (Châteauneuf-du-Pape) $36. Ancient vines on the plateau of La Crau give a wine which is relatively soft, almost smooth in character, despite the dry tannins hiding in the background. This will develop more in the way of intense flavors, but it seems it will always be quite a subdued wine. **88** *—R.V. (12/31/2005)*

DOMAINE DE LA CÔTE DE L'ANGE

Domaine de La Côte de L'Ange 2003 Rhône Red Blend (Châteauneuf-du-Pape) $29. The label is fabulous, a 19th-century design that has survived. The wine is maybe less unusual, but is certainly finely made, with perfumed dusty tannins, sweet fruit, and solid wood flavors. This is a wine that will certainly last for 10 years. **89** *—R.V. (12/31/2005)*

DOMAINE DE LA COURTADE

Domaine de La Courtade 2001 L'Alycastre Rosé Blend (Côtes de Provence) $10. 81 *—M.S. (9/1/2003)*

DOMAINE DE LA GASQUI

Domaine de La Gasqui 2000 Le Vallat des Taches Red Blend (Vin de Pays de Vaucluse) $10. 85 *—R.V. (11/15/2003)*

DOMAINE DE LA JANASSE

Domaine de La Janasse 2001 Les Garrigues (Côtes-du-Rhône Villages) $30. A wine that is made from 100% Grenache, giving intense herbal aromas and concentrated, solid fruit. For a Côtes-du-Rhône, this is a big, powerful wine. **88** *—R.V. (3/1/2004)*

Domaine de La Janasse 2000 Terre de Buissière Red Blend (Vin de Pays de la Principauté d'Orange) $12. 86 *—R.V. (11/15/2003)*

Domaine de La Janasse 2002 Rhône Red Blend (Côtes-du-Rhône) $13. A simple, fresh wine, which has green fruit and some added complexity from being aged on the lees for six months. **84** *—R.V. (3/1/2004)*

Domaine de La Janasse 2003 Vieilles Vignes Rhône Red Blend (Châteauneuf-du-Pape) $100. From four parcels of vines, all giving different characteristics to the final blend. This is a beautifully structured wine, almost charming at first, and then packing an intense mouthful of fresh, balanced, and dangerously delicious fruit. There is a touch of new wood, but the fruit is the star of this great wine. **96 Editors' Choice** *—R.V. (12/31/2005)*

Domaine de La Janasse 2002 Rhône White Blend (Châteauneuf-du-Pape) $18. A blend of Grenache Blanc, Clairette, and Rousanne, fermented in wood. The result is a complete fruit salad of flavors: apricots, quince, and white peaches. Deceptively powerful and intensely aromatic. **88** *—R.V. (3/1/2004)*

DOMAINE DE LA LYRE

Domaine de La Lyre 2000 Rhône Red Blend (Côtes-du-Rhône) $10. 88 Best Buy *—M.S. (2/1/2003)*

DOMAINE DE LA PEPIÈRE

Domaine de La Pepière 2003 (Muscadet Sèvre et Maine) $10. The heat-drenched 2003 vintage has given this wine far more weight and flesh than is typical. Although this may turn off some Muscadet fans, it gives folks who haven't yet discovered Muscadet a relatively easy introduction to the genre. It's filled with soft stone fruit and melon flavors, but it still retains the briny, minerally soul of its appellation and a lingering finish. **87 Best Buy** *—J.C. (11/15/2004)*

DOMAINE DE LA POUSSE D'OR

Domaine de La Pousse d'Or 2002 Clos des 60 Ouvrées Premier Cru (Volnay) $60. Powerful rich fruit with flavors of chocolate and rich concentration make this a ripe, intense wine with delicious flavors of sweet acidity. **94** *—R.V. (9/1/2004)*

DOMAINE DE LA RENJARDE

Domaine de La Renjarde 2001 Rhône Red Blend (Côtes-du-Rhône Villages) $10. This wine boasts a tasty combination of white pepper and sweet, liqueur-like cherry aromas and flavors. The mouthfeel is smooth and viscous, the finish bolstered by crisp acidity. **87 Best Buy** *—J.C. (3/1/2004)*

DOMAINE DE LA RONCIÈRE

Domaine de La Roncière 2003 Louis Geoffrey Rhône Red Blend (Châteauneuf-du-Pape) $29. Jean-Louis Canto, owner of Domaine de la Roncière, produces this special cuvée, named after himself and his son, Geoffrey. It is densely perfumed, packed with black fruits and ripe tannins. Very pure juicy fruit is attractive, but the tannins promise a good development. **89** *—R.V. (12/31/2005)*

DOMAINE DE LA SAUVEUSE

Domaine de La Sauveuse 1999 Côtes de Provence Red Blend (Côtes de Provence) $13. **89 Best Buy** *—M.S. (2/1/2003)*

DOMAINE DE LA SOLITUDE

Domaine de La Solitude 1998 Rhône Red Blend (Châteauneuf-du-Pape) $21. **89** *—M.M. (12/31/2000)*

Domaine de La Solitude 1998 Rhône White Blend (Côtes-du-Rhône) $10. **86** *—M.M. (12/31/2000)*

DOMAINE DE LA VOUGERAIE

Domaine de La Vougeraie 2003 Clos Blanc de Vougeot (Vougeot) $120. A rich, spicy, new wood-flavored wine from a unique parcel of white grapes next to the famed Clos de Vougeot. The wine is big, rich, and densely flavored, packed with fresh apricots, and finishes with a hint of caramel. **90** *—R.V. (9/1/2005)*

Domaine de La Vougeraie 1999 Clos Blanc de Vougeot (Vougeot) $79. **91** *—R.V. (11/1/2001)*

Domaine de La Vougeraie 2003 Les Pierres Blanches (Côte de Beaune) $45. Planted directly onto a chalk substrate, this wine shows a great mineral character that complements flavors of white currants on the palate. **87** *—R.V. (9/1/2005)*

Domaine de La Vougeraie 2002 (Gevrey-Chambertin) $NA. A well-integrated wine that combines spice and black fruits in fine proportions. It is solid, but has delicious, approachable sweet fruit flavors. **89** *—R.V. (9/1/2004)*

Domaine de La Vougeraie 2003 Les Petits Noizon (Pommard) $80. A very dark, spicy wine with generous, rich fruit. This is powerful and concentrated, showing sweetness and openness. The structure is dry, a product of the stony soil of the vineyard. This will develop well over many years. **90** *—R.V. (9/1/2005)*

DOMAINE DE LALANDE

Domaine de Lalande 2000 Les Chevrières (Pouilly-Fuissé) $27. **89** *(10/1/2003)*

DOMAINE DE MARCOUX

Domaine de Marcoux 2000 Cuvée Classique Rhône Red Blend (Châteauneuf-du-Pape) $50. This beautiful, mouth-wateringly ripe wine has huge fruit, flavors of raspberries, soft tannins, and a rounded sweet tarry aftertaste. A gorgeous wine, it will age magnificently over the next 10 years. **90** *—R.V. (3/1/2004)*

DOMAINE DE NIZAS

Domaine de Nizas 2003 Red Blend (Coteaux du Languedoc) $16. The pale oyster pink color gives a freshness and liveliness to the wine. A blend of Grenache, Mourvédre, and Syrah, it has freshness along with a soft, strawberry-flavored finish. **85** *—R.V. (12/1/2004)*

Domaine de Nizas 2000 Red Blend (Coteaux du Languedoc) $20. With its elegant, ripe fruit, this wine flavors soft tannins and intense red fruit flavors. A touch of wood only adds complexity and does not dominate. This is a stylish wine, which works well with food. **89** *—R.V. (12/1/2004)*

Domaine de Nizas 1998 (Coteaux du Languedoc) $28. **92 Cellar Selection** *(11/1/2001)*

DOMAINE DE ROALLY

Domaine de Roally 2002 (Mâcon-Villages) $NA. Crisp and flavorful, with ripe apple, pear, and citrus flavors that turn slightly honeyed on the finish. Drink now–2010. **88** *—J.C. (11/15/2005)*

DOMAINE DE TREVALLON

Domaine de Trevallon 2001 Cabernet Sauvignon-Syrah (Vin de Pays de Vaucluse) $50. That the greatest wine produced in the Baux-en-Provence region should be designated a *vin de pays* shows how meaningless French appellation law can be. The reason is that this singular wine, produced from rocky vineyards where nothing should reasonably grow, is a blend of Cabernet Sauvignon and Syrah, which is not allowed under appellation rules. Forget the legality. Enjoy and admire the huge flavors of chocolate, spice, dark, brooding black fruits and lean tannins. This wine will age—give it 8 years. **94 Editors' Choice** *—R.V. (4/1/2005)*

DOMAINE DE VILLENEUVE

Domaine de Villeneuve 2003 Les Vieilles Vignes Rhône Red Blend (Châteauneuf-du-Pape) $NA. With its biodynamic viticulture, this is an exciting small domaine clos to Beaucastel. The pure fruit flavors, very direct and intense, attest to the quality of the grapes, while the vinification is simple, hands-off, leaving great flavors of ripe black plums, spices, fresh tannins, and a great openness. Give this wine 5 years of aging after it arrives, probably sometime next year. **93** *—R.V. (12/31/2005)*

DOMAINE DENIS GAUDRY

Domaine Denis Gaudry 1999 (Pouilly-Fumé) $20. **89** *—M.M. (11/1/2000)*

DOMAINE DES BERTHIERS

Domaine des Berthiers 2000 Pouilly-Fumé $24. **85** *(8/1/2002)*

DOMAINE DES BLAGUEURS

Domaine des Blagueurs 2000 Syrah (Vin de Pays d'Oc) $9. **89 Best Buy** *—S.H. (2/28/2003)*

DOMAINE DES COCCINELLES

Domaine des Coccinelles 2002 Red Blend (Côtes-du-Rhône) $10. Coccinelles are ladybugs, a reference to this domaine's use of organic farming. This light, simple wine should be consumed over the next six months while it still holds on to its delicate red plum and cherry fruit. **84** *—J.C. (3/1/2004)*

DOMAINE DES ENTREFAUX

Domaine des Entrefaux 1999 Crozes-Hermitage $13. **88** *—J.C. (12/31/2000)*

DOMAINE DES ESCARAVAILLES

Domaine des Escaravailles 2001 Cairanne Le Ventabren Rhône Red Blend (Côtes-du-Rhône Villages) $NA. Named after a high altitude portion of the Ferran vineyards, this wine is a blend of Grenache, Carignan, and Syrah, giving long tannins and juicy, sweet fruit flavors. **87** *—R.V. (3/1/2004)*

Domaine des Escaravailles 2002 Rhône White Blend (Côtes-du-Rhône) $NA. A 50-50 blend of Marsanne and Rousanne, this wine has a mineral character from the high elevation of the vineyard. This cool character give ripe, creamy fruit but also great acidity. **85** *—R.V. (3/1/2004)*

DOMAINE DES PERDRIX

Domaine des Perdrix 2003 Echézeaux $200. An opulent wine, full of very ripe fruit. The fruit is so big that the tannins seem to be overshadowed by them, until the finish, when acidity and fresh black fruit emerge. Structured yet open. **89** *—R.V. (9/1/2005)*

Domaine des Perdrix 2003 Nuits-St.-Georges $90. Typical of Nuits-Saint-Georges, this is a firm, dry wine, layered with tannins and dark fruits. It has a good intensity of flavor, with black fruits. Good acidity gives the finish a boost. **89** *—R.V. (9/1/2005)*

Domaine des Perdrix 2001 Echézeaux $107. **89** *—J.C. (10/1/2003)*

Domaine des Perdrix 2001 Vosne-Romanée $51. **88** *—J.C. (10/1/2003)*

Domaine des Perdrix 2002 Aux Perdrix Premier Cru Nuits-St.-Georges $93. An impressive peformance, this wine has pure flavors of ripe blackberries and bitter cherries along with dark tannins and solid, chunky fruit. **90** *—R.V. (9/1/2004)*

Domaine des Perdrix 1999 Aux Perdrix Premier Cru Nuits-St.-Georges $61. **91 Cellar Selection** *(1/1/2004)*

DOMAINE DES RELAGNES

Domaine des Relagnes 2003 Les Petits Pieds d'Armand Rhône Red Blend (Châteauneuf-du-Pape) $68. These pieds are the 100-year-old vines whose fruit goes into this wine. And Armand is the father of the present owner, Henri Boiron. With all that said, this is a fine wine, smooth, rich, generous, and full of juicy black plum and wood flavors as well as pepper. **94** *—R.V. (12/31/2005)*

DOMAINE DES REMIZIÈRES

Domaine des Remizières 2000 Cuvée Christophe (Crozes-Hermitage) $30. **88** *—R.V. (6/1/2002)*

Domaine des Remizières 2000 Cuvée Particulière (Crozes-Hermitage) $NA. **87** *—R.V. (6/1/2002)*

DOMAINE DES ROUET

Domaine des Rouet 1998 Chinon $11. **81** *—M.M. (1/1/2004)*

DOMAINE DU BOUSCAT

Domaine du Bouscat 1999 Cuvée Gargone Bordeaux Blend (Bordeaux Supérieur) $10. **85** *—R.V. (11/15/2003)*

DOMAINE DU DRAGON

Domaine du Dragon 2004 Hautes Vignes Red Blend (Côtes de Provence) $NA. It's hard not to be intrigued by the name of this wine, which derives from the hot, fiery soil of the 59-acre vineyard near Draguignan in the mountains north of the tourist-infested French Riviera. This wine, a blend of Cabernet Sauvignon, Syrah, and Grenache, gives an appropriately hot, spicy character, packed with sweet fruit, herbal flavors, and a touch of wood. Great with hearty meat dishes or hard cheeses. **88 Best Buy** *—R.V. (11/15/2005)*

DOMAINE DU GROS NORE

Domaine du Gros Nore 1999 Rosé Blend (Bandol) $20. **87** *—S.H. (2/1/2003)*

DOMAINE DU MONT SAINT-JEAN

Domaine du Mont Saint-Jean 2000 Aleatico (Vin de Pays de L'ile de Beaute) $8. **85** *—M.M. (2/1/2002)*

DOMAINE DU NIZAS

Domaine du Nizas 2003 Sauvignon Blanc (Vin de Pays d'Oc) $13. With winemaker Bernard Portet from Clos du Val in charge here, it's not surprising this is a finely crafted wine. It has ripe green fruits and a subtle layer of acidity over crisp, full, grassy flavors. It's delicious and definitely food oriented. **89 Best Buy** *—R.V. (12/1/2004)*

DOMAINE DU TARIQUET

Domaine du Tariquet 2001 Vinifie et Eleve en Fut de Chene Chardonnay (Vin de Pays des Côtes de Gascogne) $12. **85** *—M.S. (9/1/2003)*

Domaine du Tariquet 2001 Gros Manseng Premieres Grives (Vin de Pays des Côtes de Gascogne) $12. **85** *—M.S. (9/1/2003)*

DOMAINE DU TRAPADIS

Domaine du Trapadis 2001 Rasteau Rhône Red Blend (Côtes-du-Rhône Villages) $18. Serious tannins and dense black fruits make this anything but a simple Côtes-du-Rhône. It has long-lived flavors of dark fruits and intense herbs, alongside considerable elegance. **88** *—R.V. (3/1/2004)*

DOMAINE DU VIEUX TÉLÉGRAPHE

Domaine du Vieux Télégraphe 2003 La Crau Rhône Red Blend (Châteauneuf-du-Pape) $40. This classic wine from the Brunier family is certainly one of the best known names in Châteauneuf-du-Pape. It is also a very fine wine, full of perfumed fruit, dark, dry but rich tannins, flavors of oak, pepper and herbs, made in quite a traditional style. The name "La Crau" refers to the plateau on which the vines are planted. **92** *—R.V. (12/31/2005)*

DOMAINE FONT DE MICHELLE

Domaine Font de Michelle 2003 Rhône Red Blend (Châteauneuf-du-Pape) $35. This is a dusty, softly tannic wine that brings together very ripe fruit with some elegance. Flavors of wood strawberries, cherries, spice, and a hint of tobacco all give a sense of complexity. The tannins become dry in the mouth, hinting at ageworthiness. **89** *—R.V. (12/31/2005)*

DOMAINE FOUGERAY DE BEAUCLAIR

Domaine Fougeray de Beauclair 2000 Les Véroilles (Chambolle-Musigny) $NA. **88** *—R.V. (11/1/2002)*

DOMAINE GEORGES ROUMIER

Domaine Georges Roumier 2000 Chambolle-Musigny $45. **87** *—R.V. (11/1/2002)*

Domaine Georges Roumier 2000 Les Amoureuses Premier Cru (Chambolle-Musigny) $100. **91** *—R.V. (11/1/2002)*

DOMAINE GEORGES VERNAY

Domaine Georges Vernay 1999 Maison Rouge (Côte Rôtie) $45. **88** *—R.V. (6/1/2002)*

Domaine Georges Vernay 2002 Blonde de Seigneur (Côte Rôtie) $55. Blonde de Seigneur was first produced by Georges Vernay in 2000. It is a wine which shows up elegance rather than power, great black fruit expression with fine tannins. It has some dry tannic structure, but there is plenty of fruit here, perfumed and with layers of smoky wood. A really great wine from a medium vintage. **94 Cellar Selection** *—R.V. (2/1/2005)*

Domaine Georges Vernay 2002 Coteau de Vernon (Condrieu) $92. An exotic, perfumed wine, with aromas of violets and rosewater. To taste, this exoticism goes through to ripe, but elegant fruit. Along with all this, there is a freshness and fruitiness which makes the wine light, fragrant and vibrant. **92** *—R.V. (2/1/2005)*

DOMAINE GERARD TREMBLAY

Domaine Gerard Tremblay 1998 Chablis $NA. **84** *—R.V. (6/1/2001)*

DOMAINE GIRARD

Domaine Girard 2003 La Garenne (Sancerre) $20. Ripe and round, with aromas of almond, talcum powder, and plenty of melon and citrus. Quite standard but good, with full, attractive flavors of melon, orange, and custard. Not too racy, like almost every 2003 Sancerre we tried. **87** *(7/1/2005)*

DOMAINE GRAMENON

Domaine Gramenon 1998 Les Laurentides Rhône Red Blend (Côtes-du-Rhône) $16. 88 *—M.M. (12/31/2000)*

DOMAINE GRAND VENEUR

Domaine Grand Veneur 1998 Rhône Red Blend (Côtes-du-Rhône) $9. 86 *—J.C. (12/31/2000)*

DOMAINE GROS FRÈRE ET SOEUR

Domaine Gros Frère et Soeur 2002 Echézeaux $NA. A fine, perfumed wine, full of tannins, meaty flavors, and black fruit. A complex wine, which layers acidity, fruits, toast, and sweetness. 91 *—R.V. (9/1/2004)*

Domaine Gros Frère et Soeur 2002 Premier Cru (Vosne-Romanée) $NA. Aromas are of dark plums and tobacco. New wood gives a spicy, concentrated flavor to the wine, accenting its firm, solid fruit. 89 *—R.V. (9/1/2004)*

DOMAINE GROSSET

Domaine Grosset 2003 Cairanne Rhône Red Blend (Côtes-du-Rhône Villages) $16. With its dry, dusty mouthfeel and moderate tannins, this wine clearly calls for some cellaring, but the ingredients for a successful evolution are there: balanced measures of tannins, alcohol, fruit, and acidity. Leather, dried fruit, and chocolate notes lead the way, followed by ripe black cherries and a hint of anise on the finish. Drink 2007–2012. 87 *—J.C. (2/1/2005)*

DOMAINE HENRI PERROT-MINOT

Domaine Henri Perrot-Minot 2000 Vieilles Vignes (Mazoyeres-Chambertin) $109. 93 Cellar Selection *(10/1/2003)*

DOMAINE HERVÉ SIGAUT

Domaine Hervé Sigaut 1999 Les Sentiers Premier Cru (Chambolle-Musigny) $45. 90 *—R.V. (11/1/2002)*

DOMAINE HUET L'ECHANSONNE

Domaine Huet L'Echansonne 2003 Le Haut-Lieu Demi-Sec (Vouvray) $40. Flavors of fresh fruits, peaches, and layers of acidity dominate this wine from the 22-acre Haut-Lieu vineyard. This elegant wine is ripe, with a light sweetness. Try it with rich fish sauces or ripe blue cheese. 89 *—R.V. (4/1/2005)*

DOMAINE J-F MUGNIER

Domaine J-F Mugnier 1999 Musigny $179. 94 Editors' Choice *—R.V. (11/1/2002)*

Domaine J-F Mugnier 1999 Les Fuées Premier Cru (Chambolle-Musigny) $NA. 91 *—R.V. (11/1/2002)*

DOMAINE JACQUES PRIEUR

Domaine Jacques Prieur 2001 Clos de Mazeray (Meursault) $55. 91 *—J.C. (10/1/2003)*

Domaine Jacques Prieur 2002 Chambertin $192. Sweet fruit and layers of currants and berries give this wine an intense flavor. A touch of herbs adds complexity. Dry tannins and acidity finish a powerful, satisfying wine. 93 *—R.V. (9/1/2004)*

Domaine Jacques Prieur 1999 Champs Pimont Premier Cru (Beaune) $48. 92 *(1/1/2004)*

Domaine Jacques Prieur 2002 Clos Vougeot $135. Huge and serious wine with firm but very ripe tannins. This is wonderful and powerful, oozing rich black fruits and seduction. 94 *—R.V. (9/1/2004)*

Domaine Jacques Prieur 2002 Greves Premier Cru (Beaune) $61. A huge, sweet, silky wine with lovely acidity and firm tannins on the finish. It's big, rich, and seductive. 91 *—R.V. (9/1/2004)*

DOMAINE JACQUES PRIEUR & ANTONIN RODET

Domaine Jacques Prieur & Antonin Rodet 1999 Clos de Las Feguine Premier Cru (Beaune) $50. 89 *—P.G. (11/1/2002)*

DOMAINE JAMET

Domaine Jamet 2002 (Côte Rôtie) $88. This is old-style winemaking, but in the best sense. It is big, dominated at this stage by tannins. The fruit is dark, brooding, and intense. It has layers of wood (of which 20 percent was new), while the acidity still needs to soften out. This will age, maybe 10-12 years. 90 *—R.V. (2/1/2005)*

DOMAINE JEAN ROYER

Domaine Jean Royer 2003 Cuvée Prestige Rhône Red Blend (Châteauneuf-du-Pape) $70. A superb, very traditional wine, with big, brooding tannins and very dark flavors. Tastes of southern herbs come through the intense Grenache, while the dryness persists right to the end. This is a wine that just needs aging. 91 *—R.V. (12/31/2005)*

DOMAINE JEAN-MICHEL GERIN

Domaine Jean-Michel Gerin 1999 Champin Le Seigneur (Côte Rôtie) $27. 92 *—R.V. (6/1/2002)*

Domaine Jean-Michel Gerin 2000 La Loye (Condrieu) $24. 91 *—R.V. (6/1/2002)*

DOMAINE LA CHEVALIERE

Domaine La Chevaliere 1998 Reserve Syrah (Vin de Pays d'Oc) $10. 83 *—M.S. (11/1/2000)*

DOMAINE LA PRADE MARI

Domaine La Prade Mari 2001 Red Blend (Minervois) $NA. Rich, dusty tannins and concentrated sweet fruit give this wine a great start. Then pile in the balanced flavors of blackberry jelly and herbs and here is something that is very complete. Acidity to finish leaves freshness. **89** *—R.V. (12/1/2004)*

DOMAINE LA ROUBINE

Domaine La Roubine 2001 Rhône Red Blend (Gigondas) $NA. This is a beautiful, stylish, impressively elegant yet intensely powerful wine. It has juicy, sweet fruit, dusty intense tannins, and beautiful perfumed aroms. Herbs and black plums give depth of flavor to a wine that will age over many years. **94** *—R.V. (3/1/2004)*

DOMAINE LAFLAIVE

Domaine Laflaive 1997 Batard-Montrachet $NA. 93 *—S.H. (1/1/2002)*

Domaine Laflaive 1998 Les Folatieres Premier Cru (Puligny-Montrachet) $NA. **94** *—S.H. (1/1/2002)*

DOMAINE LAMARGUE

Domaine Lamargue 2000 Cabernet Sauvignon (Vin de Pays d'Oc) $13. 85 *—D.T. (2/1/2002)*

Domaine Lamargue 2000 Syrah (Vin de Pays d'Oc) $13. 83 *—M.M. (2/1/2002)*

DOMAINE LAROCHE

Domaine Laroche 1997 Les Blanchots (Chablis) $85. 92 *(11/15/2000)*

Domaine Laroche 2003 Les Clos Grand Cru (Chablis) $75. A big, fat, rich wine with great white currant and white peach flavors. This delicious wine still has fine acidity and just a touch of austerity to give it structure, depth and potental longevity. **91** *—R.V. (9/1/2005)*

Domaine Laroche 1997 Les Vaillons Viellies Vignes Premier Cru (Chablis) $46. 88 *—J.C. (11/1/2000)*

Domaine Laroche 2003 Premier Cru Les Fourchaumes (Chablis) $40. This is a complex, structured wine. With its rich white stone fruit flavors and touch of chalky minerality, this is going to be a great, complete Chablis. **90** *—R.V. (9/1/2005)*

Domaine Laroche 2003 Reserve de L'Obédience Grand Cru (Chablis) $100. A seductive wine, full of sweet peach and mirabelle flavors, which just hints at acidity. It has certainly gained richness and softness from the weather of 2003: It's round and generous, leaving just a streak of mineral acidity to remind us of its origins. **92** *—R.V. (9/1/2005)*

Domaine Laroche 2003 St. Martin (Chablis) $25. A bit fatter and softer than usual for this wine. Ripe apple and pear flavors dominate, but you still get hints of Chablisian minerality. **86** *—J.C. (9/1/2005)*

DOMAINE LE CLOS DU CAILLOU

Domaine Le Clos du Caillou 2003 Les Quartz Rhône Red Blend (Châteauneuf-du-Pape) $90. The top cuvée from the Domaine le Clos de Caillou takes its name from the stones of quartz which make up the vineyard. This is a deliciously rich wine, which shines with very ripe red fruits and layers of modern tannins. Although the aftertaste is dry, the fruit is already attractive. **90** *—R.V. (12/31/2005)*

DOMAINE LE COUROULU

Domaine Le Couroulu 2000 Rhône Red Blend (Côtes-du-Rhône) $12. A solid, finely crafted wine, with fleshy ripe fruit, sweet raspberry flavors and ripe tannins. Ready to drink now **86** *—R.V. (3/1/2004)*

Domaine Le Couroulu 2000 Vieilles Vignes Rhône Red Blend (Vacqueyras) $18. Guy Ricard's top cuvée has concentrated, soft tannins and rich, sweet fruit. With flavors of brambles and black berry fruits along with wild thyme and herbs, it looks set to age well over 10 years. **91** *—R.V. (3/1/2004)*

DOMAINE LES GOUBERT

Domaine Les Goubert 2000 Cuvée Florence (Gigondas) $50. This prestige cuvée gets the full barrel treatment, and it shows in its aromas of smoke, cedar, tobacco, and molasses. Some plum and earth flavors do poke through on the palate, giving us hope that its evolution will put it into a more balanced place. Hold 4–5 years. **88** *—J.C. (11/15/2005)*

DOMAINE LES HERITIERS DU COMTE LAFON

Domaine Les Heritiers du Comte Lafon 2003 Clos du Four (Mâcon-Milly Lamartine) $29. Smoky and minerally on the nose, surprisingly so for a 2003. Does have some pear and grapefruit on the palate, but overall it's steely and minerally, finishing long, with excellent cut and precision. A Mâcon that will probably age well for 5–8 years. **88** *—J.C. (11/15/2005)*

DOMAINE LONG-DEPAQUIT

Domaine Long-Depaquit 1998 Vaudsir (Chablis) $NA. **91** *—R.V. (6/1/2001)*

DOMAINE MACHARD DE GRAMONT

Domaine Machard de Gramont 1999 Les Nazoires (Chambolle-Musigny) $NA. 92 —*R.V. (11/1/2002)*

DOMAINE MARCEL DEISS

Domaine Marcel Deiss 2000 Gruenspiel (Alsace) $47. Hints of petrol on the nose open in this rich, intense wine, which has layers of smoky aromas over flavors of ripe lychees and smooth tannins. The finish seems to last forever. **90** —*R.V. (4/1/2005)*

Domaine Marcel Deiss 2001 Rotenberg Alsace (Alsace) $47. The 12-acre Rotenberg vineyard in Wintzenheim produces vibrant, racy wines, like this blend of Riesling and Pinot Gris. It is fresh and intense, with concentrated flavors of sweet white currants. **95** —*R.V. (4/1/2005)*

Domaine Marcel Deiss 2001 Bergheim Gewürztraminer (Alsace) $36. Bergheim is particularly noted for its Gewürztraminer, and it is not hard to see why with this concentrated, spicy example. The lychees and smoke aromas set the scene, and the flavors of spice, toast and exotic spices continue the story. It is relatively restrained at the moment, because it is young, but this will develop impressively over the next five years. **90** —*R.V. (4/1/2005)*

Domaine Marcel Deiss 2001 Saint Hippolyte Gewürztraminer (Alsace) $30. Saint-Hippolyte's vineyards have produced a fresh, light style of Gewürztraminer, which has simple spice and a soft, oily texture that sits well for early drinking. Well-crafted and very drinkable. **87** —*R.V. (4/1/2005)*

Domaine Marcel Deiss 2002 Bennwihr Pinot Blanc (Alsace) $17. A smooth, creamy wine, almost like Chardonnay in its rich butteriness. It has very ripe fruit and toasty accents. This is a delicious, full-bodied expression of Pinot Blanc. **88** —*R.V. (4/1/2005)*

Domaine Marcel Deiss 2002 Beblenheim Pinot Gris (Alsace) $27. Initially, this wine seems almost austere, with its lean acidity and tannic structure, which is surprising given Beblenheim's warm microclimate. It's rich, powerful, and superconcentrated, but needs a good many years (give it 10+) of aging. **90** —*R.V. (4/1/2005)*

Domaine Marcel Deiss 2000 Burlenberg Pinot Noir (Alsace) $34. This pure Pinot Noir is ripe, smoky, toasty, and with a touch of earthiness. Fresh acidity shows through the flavors of ripe strawberries and leaves vibrant red fruits on the palate. **89** —*R.V. (4/1/2005)*

Domaine Marcel Deiss 2000 Engelgarten Riesling (Alsace) $46. The Bergheim Engelgarten "Angel's garden" vineyard has fine, gravelly soil, ideally suited for Riesling. You can taste the minerality in this rich, steely wine. It's so fresh and so intense. Delicious flavors of white currants and acidity give it a lift. **94** —*R.V. (11/1/2005)*

FRANCE

DOMAINE MARECHAL-CAILLOT

Domaine Marechal-Caillot 1999 Ladoix (Cote de Beaune) $18. 88 —*P.G. (11/1/2002)*

Domaine Marechal-Caillot 1999 Pinot Noir (Bourgogne) $15. 87 —*P.G. (11/1/2002)*

DOMAINE MASSAMIER LA MIGNARDE

Domaine Massamier La Mignarde 2004 Cuvée des Oliviers Rosé Blend (Vin de Pays des Coteaux de Peyriac) $9. A rosé during winter? Certainly. Cool as an apéritif, but just as fine a combination with the winter turkey. This bone dry rosé, from vineyards close to Minervois in the Languedoc region of France, is a fine, crisp wine, with just a touch of caramel. It has freshness but also some weight and pepper for its role as a food partner. When the kitchen gets hot, reach for a glass. **87 Best Buy** —*R.V. (11/15/2005)*

DOMAINE MATHIEU

Domaine Mathieu 2003 Marquis Anselme Mathieu Rhône Red Blend (Châteauneuf-du-Pape) $35. A soft, fresh wine that is almost ready to drink. There are tannins, but the ripe red fruits, the fleshy richness and the dusty flavors suggest a wine that will develop quickly over the next 3-4 years. **87** —*R.V. (12/31/2005)*

DOMAINE MICHEL BROCK

Domaine Michel Brock 2003 Le Coteau (Sancerre) $20. Quite fruity, with tropical aromas of pineapple and citrus. Not much mineral or flint, but plenty of soft fruit like pink grapefruit, peach, and melon. A round, warming wine that may not have a ton of verve; yet another softie from 2003. **87** *(7/1/2005)*

DOMAINE MIQUEL

Domaine Miquel 2001 Viognier (Vin de Pays d'Oc) $15. 87 —*M.S. (9/1/2003)*

DOMAINE MOILLARD

Domaine Moillard 2003 (Chorey-lès-Beaune) $25. A fresh, perfumed wine with generous amounts of acidity along with red fruit flavors and dry tannins on the finish. **87** —*R.V. (9/1/2005)*

Domaine Moillard 2003 (Corton) $79. Coffee aromas mingle with red fruits at the complex start of this fine wine. The palate is rich and equally complex, showing spice and plum flavors, and an intense, rich structure. **91** —*R.V. (9/1/2005)*

Domaine Moillard 2002 Rouge (Savigny-lès-Beaune) $25. Lean and light, with tart cherries and cranberries that race to a crisply acidic finish. **82** —*J.C. (11/15/2005)*

Domaine Moillard 2003 Clos des Grandes Vignes Premier Cru (Nuits-St.-Georges) $55. A dark, brooding wine that is structured, firm and dry. Offers black fruit flavors, good acidity, and a very dry, tough finish which should soften out in time. **89** *—R.V. (9/1/2005)*

Domaine Moillard 2003 Epenots Premier Cru (Pommard) $65. All the power of a ripe, intense Pommard is in this wine. It is well-structured, dense and rich, balanced with juicy fruit and a solid, dry aftertaste. This is obviously a wine that will age well. **90** *—R.V. (9/1/2005)*

Domaine Moillard 2003 Rouge (Côte de Nuits-Villages) $28. A firm, dry style of wine with strong tannins and solid, dense fruits. Dark flavors of black plums and damsons are balanced with good acidity. **88** *—R.V. (9/1/2005)*

DOMAINE MONTHELIE-DOUHAIRET

Domaine Monthelie-Douhairet 1999 Clos Le Meix Garnier Monopole (Monthelie) $26. 87 *(10/1/2003)*

DOMAINE MOREY COFFINET

Domaine Morey Coffinet 2000 Les Caillerets Premier Cru (Chassagne-Montrachet) $51. 90 *(10/1/2003)*

DOMAINE OLIVIER MERLIN

Domaine Olivier Merlin 2003 (Saint-Véran) $23. A bit oaky, layered with vanilla and dried spices, but there's also ample richness and weight of fruit to help carry the wine forward. Spices intensify on the long, elegant finish. **88** *—J.C. (11/15/2005)*

DOMAINE OSTERTAG

Domaine Ostertag 2002 Fronholz Riesling (Alsace) $35. A fine, smooth wine, packed with mineral character and power. It also has fine acicity, but that's hard to find under the richness of the fruit. A fresh citric character gives a fine lift to the aftertaste. **89** *—R.V. (11/1/2005)*

Domaine Ostertag 2002 Heissenberg Riesling (Alsace) $39. A smooth, opulent Riesling, from a vineyard whose name literally means "hot mountain." It is hugely ripe, but still has some fine mineral character. The acidity is a little more in question; this could well be a wine that develops relatively quickly. **89** *—R.V. (11/1/2005)*

DOMAINE PASCAL BOUCHARD

Domaine Pascal Bouchard 1999 Vaudesir (Chablis) $NA. 86 *—R.V. (6/1/2001)*

DOMAINE PIERRE ANDRÉ

Domaine Pierre André 2003 Pinot Noir (Ladoix) $NA. A softly perfumed wine that has fresh, clean fruit, a lovely silky texture and just a touch of tannin. Will be ready to drink within two years. **87** *—R.V. (9/1/2005)*

Domaine Pierre André 2003 Aloxe-Corton Les Paulands Premier Cru (Aloxe-Corton) $NA. This wine balances tannins with full, red fruit flavors. Its dry tannins suggest that this wine could remain firm and solid rather than plush. But its perfumes are typically Pinot. An enticing and structured package over all. **87** *—R.V. (9/1/2005)*

Domaine Pierre André 2003 Clos des Guetottes Premier Cru Pinot Noir (Savigny-lès-Beaune) $NA. This vineyard has 30-year-old vines, which typically yield densely flavored wines. With the 2003 vintage, this density has been supplemented by great perfumes, and ripe, black fruit. Should develop well. **88** *—R.V. (9/1/2005)*

DOMAINE PIERRE MOREY

Domaine Pierre Morey 2002 Grands Epenots (Pommard) $83. A firm, tannic wine that promises long aging. The dry tannins are driven by ripe black fruits and flavors of spice and pure acidity. **86** *—R.V. (9/1/2004)*

DOMAINE PIERRE USSEGLIO ET FILS

Domaine Pierre Usseglio et Fils 2003 Cuvée Tradition Rhône Red Blend (Châteauneuf-du-Pape) $39. A traditional style of wine whose relatively light color shows the influence of 75% Grenache and classic vinification. But of its kind, this is a fine wine, with spice, red fruits and juicy flavors. **86** *—R.V. (12/31/2005)*

DOMAINE PUYDEVAL

Domaine Puydeval 2001 Red Blend (Vin de Pays d'Oc) $12. A blend of Cabernet Sauvignon, Syrah, and Merlot, this is a wood-aged wine from the south of France. Great spice and black currant aromas waft from this densely packed wine. To taste, it is equally bright but geneorus, with black, dry, and firm fruit. Layers of acidity combine with powerful fruit and wood flavors to complement rich food. **86 Best Buy** *—R.V. (11/15/2005)*

DOMAINE RAYMOND USSEGLIO ET FILS

Domaine Raymond Usseglio et Fils 2003 Cuvée Impériale Rhône Red Blend (Châteauneuf-du-Pape) $56. Century-old vines are the source of this top cuvée from a 5-acre parcel owned by Raymond Usseglio. It is ripe, with tarry and black fig flavors, along with thyme and herbes de Provence. The tannins are hugely dense, almost impenetrable at this stage, but this will develop into a great wine in 10 years. **93 Cellar Selection** *—R.V. (12/31/2005)*

DOMAINE ROBERT-DENOGENT

Domaine Robert-Denogent 2002 Cuvée Claude Denogent (Pouilly-Fuissé) $38. Very closed after its recent bottling, but shows even more length, minerality, and finesse than Robert-Denogent's other bottlings. I've no doubt it will emerge in several years even better. An incredible Pouilly-Fuissé. **92 Cellar Selection** *—J.C. (11/15/2005)*

Domaine Robert-Denogent 2002 Les Pommards (Saint-Véran) $28. From 45-year-old vines, this spent 20 months in second-use barrels, which imparted a delicate toastiness and vanilla to the concentrated fruit. Honey, apple, and citrus notes blend harmoniously with the ample oak. **89** *—J.C. (11/15/2005)*

Domaine Robert-Denogent 2002 Les Taches (Mâcon-Fuissé) $24. Despite 18 months in wood, the oak isn't that obvious. Instead, there's honey and pineapple, good richness for the Mâcon, and a long, crisp finish. **88** *—J.C. (11/15/2005)*

DOMAINE ROMANÉE CONTI

Domaine Romanée Conti 2000 (Echézeaux) $150. **89** *(10/1/2003)*

Domaine Romanée Conti 2000 La Tache $400. **97 Cellar Selection** *(10/1/2003)*

Domaine Romanée Conti 2000 Romanée-Conti $1200. **95** *(10/1/2003)*

DOMAINE SAINT VINCENT

Domaine Saint Vincent 2000 Syrah (Vin de Pays d'Oc) $8. **83** *(10/1/2001)*

DOMAINE SAINT-GAYAN

Domaine Saint-Gayan 2000 Rhône Red Blend (Gigondas) $23. A beautifully perfumed wine showing aromas of herbs and wild thyme. Rich, soft, with layers of ripe flavors, black fruits, and solid tannins. Open and soft, and ready to drink in three to five years. **89** *—R.V. (3/1/2004)*

Domaine Saint-Gayan 2000 Rhône Red Blend (Châteauneuf-du-Pape) $28. A tiny production of 3,000 bottles makes this a particularly rare wine, but one worth seeking out for its rich, sweet, strawberry flavors and its finely perfumed aromas. **91** *—R.V. (3/1/2004)*

DOMAINE SAINT-PRÉFERT

Domaine Saint-Préfert 2003 Réserve Auguste Favier Rhône Red Blend (Châteauneuf-du-Pape) $63. This super cuvée from one of the hottest vineyards in Châteauneuf is impressive, but also refreshingly elegant. The wine is full of dry tannins, as well as dark black fruits. A solid, intense wine, which promises many years of aging. **92** *—R.V. (12/31/2005)*

DOMAINE SALVAT

Domaine Salvat 2000 Red Blend (Vin de Pays Catalan) $8. **84** *—M.S. (2/1/2003)*

DOMAINE SERRES MAZARD

Domaine Serres Mazard 2001 Red Blend (Corbières) $28. Black tarry fruit aromas set the scene for a pungent, powerful, very southern wine. A blend of old-vine Carignan with Syrah, this is hugely intense, with big wood flavors as well as herbal, almost medicinal fruits. This needs time to age, over 5 years, but it is a powerful statement now. **90** *—R.V. (12/1/2004)*

DOMAINE SILENE DES PEYRAS

Domaine Silene des Peyras 2000 Red Blend (Coteaux du Languedoc) $20. **90** *—R.V. (11/15/2002)*

DOMAINE SOUMAIZE-MICHELIN

Domaine Soumaize-Michelin 2003 Clos Sur La Roche (Pouilly-Fuissé) $43. Seems a bit muted on the nose, offering little beyond the suggestion of honeyed fruit, but really takes off on the palate, exploding with floral notes and an intensity that belies its lightness of body. There's some buttered richness, but also fine minerality. **90** *—J.C. (11/15/2005)*

DOMAINE VALETTE

Domaine Valette 2002 Vieilles Vignes (Mâcon Chaintré) $25. Despite rich aromas of honey and oak, this wine is clean and crisp, with bright pear and citrus flavors and mouthwatering acids. Finishes long and lemony; the perfect foil to fish or poultry. **88** *—J.C. (11/15/2005)*

DOMAINE VINCENT GIRARDIN

Domaine Vincent Girardin 2001 Le Saint Jean (Santenay) $23. **87** *—J.C. (10/1/2003)*

Domaine Vincent Girardin 2000 Chapelle-Chambertin $92. **92** *—J.C. (10/1/2003)*

DOMAINE VINCENT SAUVESTRE

Domaine Vincent Sauvestre 2003 Chardonnay (Bourgogne) $11. A plump, medium-bodied Chardonnay with a trace of custardiness to its texture, this wine speaks of its origins, marrying ripe pear fruit with toasted nuts and mineral notes. Finishes clean and minerally, a good value in white Burgundy. **85** *—J.C. (11/15/2005)*

Domaine Vincent Sauvestre 2003 Clos des Tessons (Meursault) $48. **83** *—J.C. (11/15/2005)*

Domaine Vincent Sauvestre 2003 Pinot Noir (Bourgogne) $15. **84** *—J.C. (11/15/2005)*

Domaine Vincent Sauvestre 2003 Clos de La Platière (Pommard) $42. **88** *—J.C. (11/15/2005)*

Domaine Vincent Sauvestre 2002 (Savigny-lès-Beaune) $20. This supple, tender Savigny is ready to drink. Starts with slightly horsey, leather, and spice notes, then adds crisp cherry flavors to the mix before finishing tart and tangy. **85** —*J.C. (11/15/2005)*

DOMAINE WEINBACH

Domaine Weinbach 2002 Grand Cru Cuvée Ste Catherine L'Inédit Riesling (Alsace) $75. That Laurence Faller is able to conjure wonders from her family's great estate is an incontrovertible fact. But if further proof were needed, here it is in the shape of a fabulous Riesling from a small parcel of vines. It has enormous fruit, which is so pure, so steely and rich at the same time. It has hedgerow fruits, packing in behind finesse and elegance, with just the right touch of acidity. Give it 10 years at least. **95 Editors' Choice** —*R.V. (5/1/2005)*

DOMAINE WILLIAM FEVRE

Domaine William Fevre 1999 Les Clos (Chablis) $NA. **90** —*R.V. (6/1/2001)*

DOMAINE YVES CUILLERON

Domaine Yves Cuilleron 2000 Les Chaillets (Condrieu) $65. **90** —*R.V. (6/1/2002)*

DOMAINE ZIND-HUMBRECHT

Domaine Zind-Humbrecht 2002 Clos Windsbuhl Hunawihr Gewürztraminer (Alsace) $70. A smooth, rich, unctuous wine from the 13-acre Windsbuhl vineyard. It oozes charm, and hides its power underneath its seductive exterior. There is great fruit here, with some hints of acidity as well as flavors of lychees and pepper. **90** —*R.V. (4/1/2005)*

Domaine Zind-Humbrecht 2002 Grand Cru Goldert Gueberschwihr Vendange Tardive Gewürztraminer (Alsace) $123. An intensely sweet wine with layers of dry spice that give it balance. From the rich, fertile Goldert vineyard. This soil character gives it a richness and ripeness already, at this early stage in its development. Still the wine is structured and should age well over 10 years. **93** —*R.V. (4/1/2005)*

Domaine Zind-Humbrecht 2000 Grand Cru Hengst Gewürztraminer (Alsace) $68. **96** —*R.V. (10/1/2002)*

Domaine Zind-Humbrecht 2000 Heimbourg Gewürztraminer (Alsace) $54. **92** —*R.V. (10/1/2002)*

Domaine Zind-Humbrecht 2002 Herrenweg de Turckheim Gewürztraminer (Alsace) $43. A meaty, full-bodied style of wine, with concentrated, spicy flavors. It offers layers of tropical fruits, but the essence is pepper, bergamot, and some tannins. Finishes pleasantly fresh. This could certainly improve with age. **89** —*R.V. (4/1/2005)*

Domaine Zind-Humbrecht 2000 Turckheim Gewürztraminer (Alsace) $320. **88** —*R.V. (10/1/2002)*

Domaine Zind-Humbrecht 2000 Vendange Tardive Grand Cru Clos Saint Urbain Gewürztraminer (Alsace) $NA. **98** —*R.V. (10/1/2002)*

Domaine Zind-Humbrecht 2000 Wintzheim Gewürztraminer (Alsace) $32. **90** —*R.V. (10/1/2002)*

Domaine Zind-Humbrecht 2001 Clos Jebsal Séléction des Grains Nobles Pinot Gris (Alsace) $214. Smoky aromas followed by the explosion of sweet fruits, with flavors of ripe oranges, of wild flower honey and acidity. This is gorgeous now, but its sweetness should be tamed with aging. A fantastic wine. **96 Editors' Choice** —*R.V. (4/1/2005)*

Domaine Zind-Humbrecht 2000 Clos Windsbuhl Pinot Gris (Alsace) $58. **94** —*R.V. (10/1/2002)*

Domaine Zind-Humbrecht 2002 Clos Windsbuhl Hunawihr Vendange Tardive Pinot Gris (Alsace) $68. A huge, opulent wine that oozes botrytis flavors, yet is not overtly sweet; it's a fine package of richness, dryness, and sweetness. Balancing acidity shows through on the fresh finish. **94** —*R.V. (4/1/2005)*

Domaine Zind-Humbrecht 2002 Grand Cru Clos Saint-Urbain Rangen de Thann Pinot Gris (Alsace) $102. This is a wonderful wine, which comes from the vineyard in the south of Alsace that the Humbrechts brought back from obscurity. It has both intensity and also great elegance. It has flavors of currants, layers of orange zest, and some fresh acidity. But it also has spice which lies gently with the fruit flavors. The taste just goes on forever. **96** —*R.V. (4/1/2005)*

Domaine Zind-Humbrecht 2002 Heimbourg Turckheim Vendange Tardive Pinot Gris (Alsace) $123. Orange marmalade aromas set the scene for a fresh, intensely sweet wine. It has rich flavors of tropical fruit and coconut, but the acidity still ensures that the wine is in balance. However, it will continue to develop. Try again in 2015. **91** —*R.V. (4/1/2005)*

Domaine Zind-Humbrecht 2001 Rotenberg Pinot Gris (Alsace) $42. A smooth, fresh wine, with some sweetness but also great, easy flavors of spice, acidity, and tropical fruits. This is one of the less intense of Humbrecht's wines, which lets you enjoy it now. **88** —*R.V. (4/1/2005)*

Domaine Zind-Humbrecht 2002 Rotenberg Wintzenheim Vendange Tardive Pinot Gris (Alsace) $123. It may not be a Séléction des Grains Nobles, but this still has the intoxicating orange zest and honey aromas. Similiar notes echo on the palate; will need many years to develop. **90** —*R.V. (4/1/2005)*

Domaine Zind-Humbrecht 2000 Séléction des Grains Nobles Heimbourg Pinot Gris (Alsace) $NA. **97** —*R.V. (10/1/2002)*

Domaine Zind-Humbrecht 2000 Vendange Tardive Clos Jebsal Pinot Gris (Alsace) $75. **96** —*R.V. (10/1/2002)*

Domaine Zind-Humbrecht 2000 Vendange Tardive Herrenweg de Turckheim Pinot Gris (Alsace) $37. 92 *—R.V. (10/1/2002)*

Domaine Zind-Humbrecht 2000 Clos Hauserer Riesling (Alsace) $44. 93 *—R.V. (10/1/2002)*

Domaine Zind-Humbrecht 2000 Grand Cru Brand Riesling (Alsace) $85. 96 *—R.V. (10/1/2002)*

Domaine Zind-Humbrecht 2000 Grand Cru Brand Vendange Tardive Riesling (Alsace) $NA. 95 *—R.V. (10/1/2002)*

Domaine Zind-Humbrecht 2002 Grand Cru Clos Saint Urbain Rangen de Thann Riesling (Alsace) $103. With its tiny chapel, the Clos Saint Urbain is one of the great Alsace landmarks. On possibly the steepest vineyard in the region, the Humbrechts are able to make some of the greatest wines. It may be labeled Riesling, but the spiciness of this wine makes it almost like a Pinot Gris. It is so hugely rich that it is easy to lose track of its dryness and its fine structure, its acidity and its intense flavors of exotic fruits. **94** *—R.V. (11/1/2005)*

Domaine Zind-Humbrecht 2002 Heimbourg Riesling (Alsace) $57. From this Turckheim vineyard, close to the Brand grand cru vines, this is a big, rich wine, packed with great honeysuckle aromas, good acidity and spice accents. It is huge, but should age well. **90** *—R.V. (11/1/2005)*

Domaine Zind-Humbrecht 2000 Herrenweg de Turckheim Riesling (Alsace) $37. 92 *—R.V. (10/1/2002)*

Domaine Zind-Humbrecht 2000 Vendange Tardive Clos Windsbuhl Riesling (Alsace) $90. 93 *—R.V. (10/1/2002)*

Domaine Zind-Humbrecht NV Zind White Blend (Vin de Table Francais) $29. A blend of Chardonnay, Pinot Blanc, and Pinot Auxerrois which, under French law, is a Vin de Table because the Chardonnay is not permitted in Alsace. But Humbrecht makes sure you know the vintage by labeling it Z002 (get it?). It's a ripe wine, with very pure, concentrated fruit, a touch of spice and finishing acidity. **87** *—R.V. (4/1/2005)*

DOMAINES OTT

Domaines Ott 1997 Château De Selle Rouge Rhône Red Blend (Côtes de Provence) $34. 84 *—M.S. (5/1/2000)*

Domaines Ott 1998 Les Domaniers de Calignade Rhône Red Blend (Côtes de Provence) $11. 84 *—M.S. (5/1/2000)*

Domaines Ott 1998 Château De Selle Clair de Noir Rosé Blend (Côtes de Provence) $29. 89 *—M.S. (5/1/2000)*

DOMAINES SCHLUMBERGER

Domaines Schlumberger 1998 Cuvée Anne Sélection de Grains Nobles Gewürztraminer (Alsace) $75. 91 *—M.S. (12/31/2003)*

Domaines Schlumberger 2001 Cuvée Christine Vendanges Tardives Gewürztraminer (Alsace) $72. Dense and oily, with yellow peach and tropical fruit flavors, and an edge of fresh herb. Well-made, the wine has bergamot, dieselly aromas and a long finish. **90** *(6/1/2004)*

Domaines Schlumberger 2002 Fleur Gewürztraminer (Alsace) $22. Light and a bit more simple than the other Schlumberger wines, there's talc and lychee flavors on the palate and chalk/mineral notes on the finish. Smells like roses and apricots. Fleur is made from grapes of young grand cru vines. **85** *(6/1/2004)*

Domaines Schlumberger 2000 Fleur Gewürztraminer (Alsace) $21. 88 *—S.H. (1/1/2002)*

Domaines Schlumberger 2001 Grand Cru Kessler Gewürztraminer (Alsace) $32. Oily in texture and a trifle sweet, this luscious wine coats the palate with flavors of very ripe grapefruit and lychee. Aromas are more restrained, showing pear and melon, while it finishes long, with echoes of spice. **89** *—J.C. (2/1/2005)*

Domaines Schlumberger 2000 Grand Cru Kessler Gewürztraminer (Alsace) $32. 91 Editors' Choice *—M.S. (12/31/2003)*

Domaines Schlumberger 2000 Grand Cru Saering Gewürztraminer (Alsace) $32. 86 *—M.S. (12/31/2003)*

Domaines Schlumberger 2000 Pinot Blanc (Alsace) $14. 87 *—S.H. (1/1/2002)*

Domaines Schlumberger 1998 Cuvée Clarisse Sélection de Grains Nobles Pinot Gris (Alsace) $72. 87 *—M.S. (10/1/2003)*

Domaines Schlumberger 2000 Grand Cru Kitterlé Pinot Gris (Alsace) $38. Stumbles a little coming out of the gate, revealing hints of shoe polish and burnt rubber, but gathers itself midpalate with intense flavors of muskmelon and orange marmalade and finishes strong, ending on a hint of Earl Grey tea. **87** *—J.C. (2/1/2005)*

Domaines Schlumberger 1998 Grand Cru Kitterlé Pinot Gris (Alsace) $37. 90 *—M.S. (10/1/2003)*

Domaines Schlumberger 1999 Spiegel Pinot Gris (Alsace) $32. Smells of sunflowers and nuts, and tastes like flowers and honey in a glass, with peach fruit at the core. Finishes firm, with apricot flavors. **89** *(6/1/2004)*

Domaines Schlumberger 2001 Les Princes Abbés Pinot Noir (Alsace) $NA. Smells a bit leathery, with pleasant anise, sassafras, and sour cherry notes chiming in. It's a wine of intriguing spice complexity but ultimately not much fruity flesh. Drink now. **85** *—J.C. (2/1/2005)*

Domaines Schlumberger 1999 Grand Cru Kitterlé Riesling (Alsace) $29. Beydon-Schlumberger calls this a "serious, well-behaved grand cru," and it is an impressive wine, though not one that's showing much in the early term. Well-balanced and medium-weight, it shows appley, steely, minerally flavors, and a long, dry finish. Try after 2007. **90** *(6/1/2004)*

Domaines Schlumberger 1997 Grand Cru Kitterlé Riesling (Alsace) $30. 83 *—M.S. (12/1/2003)*

Domaines Schlumberger 2001 Grand Cru Saering Riesling (Alsace) $23. As the owner of more vineyards than any other Alsace producer, Schlumberger lords it over Guebwiller in the south of the region. This Riesling from the Saering vineyard is already showing petrol aromas, and the palate has lost some youthful acidity, replacing it with a light sweetness, flavors of currants, and even peaches. There is acidity, though, and this suggests it will mature further. **90** *—R.V. (5/1/2005)*

Domaines Schlumberger 1999 Grand Cru Saering Riesling (Alsace) $22. **90 Editors' Choice** *—M.S. (12/1/2003)*

Domaines Schlumberger 2002 Les Princes Abbés Riesling (Alsace) $16. Smells fresh—like lime and green apple, with a light floral component. It's dry in the mouth, with green apple flavors giving the wine a little tartness; mineral and citrus accompany the apple. **86** *(6/1/2004)*

Domaines Schlumberger 1998 Princes Abbés Riesling (Alsace) $16. **91** *—S.H. (1/1/2002)*

DOMIANE HOUCHART

Domiane Houchart 2000 Red Blend (Côtes de Provence) $11. 83 *—M.S. (9/1/2003)*

DOPFF & IRION

Dopff & Irion 2002 Les Sorcieres Gewürztraminer (Alsace) $23. There's a bit of rose petal on the nose, but this Gewurz tilts more to the lychee side of the taste spectrum, with spiced pears adding to the mix. Balanced and soft, with a gentle finish that fades a little too quickly. **85** *—J.C. (2/1/2005)*

Dopff & Irion 2002 Les Murailles Riesling (Alsace) $21. This is a large-scaled, structured Riesling that's loaded with minerals, boasting just hints of peach and apple. Starts with lime aromas but goes down like liquid rocks, capped of by a lingering, minerally finish. Nice wine, just not one full of fruit. **88** *—J.C. (2/1/2005)*

Dopff & Irion 2001 Les Murailles Riesling (Alsace) $21. One of the great names in Riquewihr, Dopff et Irion owns the Murailles property close to the Schoenenbourg Grand Cru. It has attractive fresh fruits, with layers of green acidity, and tannins to give structure. **87** *—R.V. (5/1/2005)*

Dopff & Irion 1997 Tokay Pinot Gris (Alsace) $16. **84** *(8/1/1999)*

Dopff & Irion 2003 Crustaces White Blend (Alsace) $11. As the name suggests, this would be a solid option with shellfish. Green apple and pear scents carry just a whiff of honey, while the body is light and the flavors spare and minerally, finishing with a touch of grapefruit. **85** *—J.C. (2/1/2005)*

DOPFF AU MOULIN

Dopff Au Moulin 1996 Reserve Tokay Pinot Gris (Alsace) $19. 86 *(8/1/1999)*

DOURTHE

Dourthe 2003 Numéro 1 Bordeaux White Blend (Bordeaux) $10. Dourthe's branded Bordeaux is one of the best around, and this white from vintage 2003 is no exception. With its ripe, honeyed fruit, it is delicious both as an apéritif and as a food wine. Layers of soft creaminess are backed by fine crisp acidity. **88 Best Buy** *—R.V. (6/1/2005)*

DUJAC FILS & PÈRE

Dujac Fils & Père 2001 (Meursault) $44. Nutty and toasty, but even those notes are muted and modest. Not much going on here—a real disappointment from a big name in Burgundy. **82** *—J.C. (12/1/2005)*

DULONG

Dulong 1999 Merlot (Vin de Pays d'Oc) $8. 84 *—D.T. (2/1/2002)*

DUVAL-LEROY

Duval-Leroy NV Brut (Champagne) $25. 87 *—K.F. (12/15/2002)*

Duval-Leroy 1995 Cuvée Femme (Champagne) $97. This is the second vintage of Femme, which has a 70% dominance of Chardonnay. From the generous, open 1995 vintage, this is a fine, rich wine with just a touch of wood. It is ripe, balanced, and open. This is a great value and a beautifully crafted wine. **90** *—R.V. (12/1/2004)*

Duval-Leroy 1996 Millesime (Champagne) $43. Reflecting the austere 1996 vintage, this wine has great structure with a fine aging potential. But it is also elegant, with finesse along with its mineral character. **89** *—R.V. (12/1/2004)*

Duval-Leroy NV Paris Brut (Champagne) $35. With evocative gold-painted Paris scenes decorating the bottle, this works beautifully as a light, vivacious wine, with deliciously clean, not quite green, fruit. **90** *—R.V. (12/1/2005)*

Duval-Leroy 1996 Blanc de Chardonnay (Champagne) $32. **90** *—P.G. (12/15/2002)*

Duval-Leroy NV Brut Rosé (Champagne) $32. **90** *—P.G. (12/15/2002)*

E. BARNAUT

E. Barnaut NV Grand Reserve Brut (Champagne) $20. **89** *—R.V. (12/1/2002)*

E. GUIGAL

E. Guigal 2001 Rhône Red Blend (Châteauneuf-du-Pape) $45. Smells leathery and a bit overripe, with scents of dried fruit outweighing freshness. The leather and dried-cherry flavors linger enticingly on the finish, but show a trace of alcoholic warmth as well. A solid wine, but a disappointing effort from the Rhône's most famous and reliable négociant. **86** *—J.C. (2/1/2005)*

E. Guigal 1999 Crozes-Hermitage $15. 89 *—R.V. (6/1/2002)*

E. Guigal 1999 Rhône Red Blend (Côtes-du-Rhône) $10. 88 *—R.V. (6/1/2002)*

E. Guigal 1999 Brune et Blonde (Côte Rôtie) $40. 94 *—R.V. (6/1/2002)*

E. Guigal 1998 Château d'Ampuis (Côte Rôtie) $90. 91 *—R.V. (6/1/2002)*

E. Guigal 1998 La Mouline (Côte Rôtie) $175. 96 *—R.V. (6/1/2002)*

E. Guigal 1999 Lieu-dit Saint-Joseph (St.-Joseph) $28. 93 *—R.V. (6/1/2002)*

E. Guigal 2000 Rhône White Blend (St.-Joseph) $26. 89 *—R.V. (6/1/2002)*

E. Guigal 1998 Rhône White Blend (Hermitage) $32. 91 *—R.V. (6/1/2002)*

E. Guigal 2000 Lieu-dit Saint-Joseph Rhône White Blend (St.-Joseph) $28. 90 *—R.V. (6/1/2002)*

E. Guigal 2001 (Crozes-Hermitage) $20. From its aromas of black pepper and cured meats, this wine screams Syrah. Of course, it tastes like syrah too, yielding flavors of blackberries, black pepper, and air-dried beef. A bit leaner and less generous on the palate than Guigal's Saint-Joseph, but still an impressive effort, with a firm structure and modest tannins on the finish. Drink 2006–2012. **87** *(2/1/2005)*

E. Guigal 2003 Condrieu $45. Lovely soft, easy fruit, show up the fresh, fragrant style of Condrieu, despite coming from the hot 2003 vintage. Spice and wood show through the flavors of apricots and honey, leaving a smooth, oily texture to finish. This would be great with Asian food. **90** *—R.V. (2/1/2005)*

ERIC & JOEL DURAND

Eric & Joel Durand 1999 Cornas $32. 93 *—R.V. (6/1/2002)*

Eric & Joel Durand 1999 Les Coteaux (St.-Joseph) $24. 88 *—R.V. (6/1/2002)*

ERIC TEXIER

Eric Texier 1999 Rhône Red Blend (Côtes-du-Rhône) $15. 82 *— (1/1/2004)*

ERNST BURN

Ernst Burn 1997 Tokay Pinot Gris (Alsace) $18. 88 *(8/1/1999)*

ESPRIT DE CHEVALIER

Esprit de Chevalier 2000 Bordeaux Blend (Pessac-Léognan) $35. 83 *—J.C. (6/1/2005)*

F. CHAUVENET

F. Chauvenet 2001 Pouilly-Fuissé $20. 84 *—J.C. (10/1/2003)*

FAIVELEY

Faiveley 1995 Aligoté (Bourgogne) $12. 85 *—S.H. (12/31/1999)*

Faiveley 2001 Puligny-Montrachet $NA. 87 *—S.H. (1/1/2002)*

Faiveley 2001 Georges Faiveley Chardonnay (Bourgogne) $NA. 86 *—S.H. (1/1/2002)*

Faiveley 1996 Vosne-Romanée $40. 87 *—S.H. (12/31/1999)*

Faiveley 1996 Clos des Myglands (Mercurey) $25. 88 *—S.H. (12/31/1999)*

Faiveley 1996 Clos Rochette Blanc (Mercurey) $29. 91 *—S.H. (12/31/1999)*

FERRATON PÈRE ET FILS

Ferraton Père et Fils 1998 Le Parvis (Châteauneuf-du-Pape) $29. 81 *—M.S. (9/1/2003)*

Ferraton Père et Fils 1999 Samorens (Côtes-du-Rhône) $10. 87 Best Buy *—M.S. (2/1/2003)*

Ferraton Père et Fils 2001 Le Grand Courtil (Crozes-Hermitage) $23. Ferraton is partly owned by Chapoutier, and affect to call their Crozes-Hermitage and Hermitage by the older spelling of Ermitage. But the important thing is the wine, and this Crozes is deliciously accessible with good acidity and some dry, but juicy fruit. The tannins and the wood play a good balancing role. **89** *—R.V. (2/1/2005)*

Ferraton Père et Fils 2000 Les Dionnières (Hermitage) $76. A powerful, dark, and tannic wine which reflects the power of this wine from 30-year old vines. It has great intense fruits, with some austerity at this young stage, but will ripen and richen over the next 5 years. Ferraton is partly owned by Chapoutier, and affect to call their Crozes-Hermitage and Hermitage by the older spelling of Ermitage. **90** *—R.V. (2/1/2005)*

FORTANT

Fortant 2003 Cabernet Sauvignon (Vin de Pays d'Oc) $6. A well-made wine which exhibits just the right amount of firm, dry tannic Cabernet structure to go with powerful black fruits. Good acidity gives balance, but the main impression is of great, ripe fruit. **88 Best Buy** *—R.V. (12/1/2004)*

Fortant 2003 Chardonnay (Vin de Pays d'Oc) $6. Smooth and soft, this wine has a touch of vanilla and apples and cream flavors. At the back, a freshness of acidity stops it being too rich or fat. It is well-made, well balanced and slips down easily **85 Best Buy** *—R.V. (12/1/2004)*

Fortant 1999 Chardonnay (Vin de Pays d'Oc) $10. 81 *—M.S. (4/1/2002)*

Fortant 2003 Merlot (Vin de Pays d'Oc) $6. Soft fruit, with a light jammy character characterizes this easy, fresh wine. It has light tannins and a firm, dry element which balanced the freshness. With some richness, it even manages a southern warmth **85 Best Buy** *—R.V. (12/1/2004)*

Fortant 2003 Sauvignon Blanc (Vin de Pays d'Oc) $6. There is lightweight, fresh fruit, flavors of crisp apples and grapefruit, along with a refreshing touch of acidity. The only downside is that it seems unfocused in its fruit flavors **82** *—R.V. (12/1/2004)*

FOURNIER PÈRE ET FILS

Fournier Père et Fils 2002 Grand Cuvée Fournier Vieilles Vignes (Sancerre) $25. Exotic and encouraging, with as much mineral and stone-like aromas as there are grapefruit, green melon, herb, and mustard seed scents. Citrus is definitely the lead soldier on the palate, which is tart and crisp. Tangerine and other citrus fruits carry the zesty finish to a pointed termination. **88** *(7/1/2005)*

FRANÇOIS COTAT

François Cotat 2003 Les Monts Damnés (Sancerre) $28. Fairly heavy and floral, with buttery, sweet aromas. That same bouquet weight carries onto the palate, where the ripe green melon and spiced-fruit flavors are meaty and broad. Finishes warm and chunky. **86** *(7/1/2005)*

FRANCOIS LABET

Francois Labet 2002 Corton-Charlemagne $135. Scents of cooked apples mingle with smoke and minerals on the nose. Lacks the power of Corton-Charlemagne, instead delivering apple and citrus flavors in a medium-weight format. Well-made but hard and ungenerous on the finish. **84** *—J.C. (4/1/2005)*

Francois Labet 2002 Clos Richemont Premier Cru (Meursault) $121. Light to medium in body, this lithe, citrusy wine delivers authentic white Burgundy flavor in a kosher package. Hints of smoke and grilled peaches highlight apple and citrus flavors. **86** *—J.C. (4/1/2005)*

FRANÇOIS MONTAND

François Montand NV Blanc de Blancs Brut (France) $12. Fairly neutral, with a bit of stony minerality. Very firm, on the cusp of sharp, with green apple and hint of pineapple for flavors. Quite tart on the back end, and lean throughout. **83** *—M.S. (12/31/2005)*

FREDERIC LORNET

Frederic Lornet NV Rosé Blend (Crémant de Jura Rosé) $10. 88 Best Buy *—C.S. (11/15/2002)*

G. H. MUMM

G. H. Mumm NV Brut Rosé (Champagne) $52. Rich and smoky, with a powerful blast of dustiness. Nectarine flavors carry the long, fresh palate to a clean, fruit-forward finish. Shows a tiny burnt, rustic character and isn't overly lively in terms of bead. Good for drinking this year and next. Imported by Allied Domecq Wines USA. **91** *—M.S. (12/31/2005)*

G. H. Mumm NV Carte Classique Extra Dry (Champagne) $41. Looking for a little sweetness in your bubbly, but not a full-blown dessert style? This offering from Mumm is a solid choice, bursting with a harmonious mix of pear and citrus fruit and topped off by dollops of toast, mineral, and smoky complexity. **87** *—J.C. (12/1/2004)*

G. H. Mumm NV Cordon Rouge Brut Champagne Blend (Champagne) $45. 86 *—M.S. (12/15/2003)*

G. H. Mumm NV Grand Cru Brut (Champagne) $60. Using only grapes from Mumm's own grand cru vineyards, winemaker Dominique Demarville has produced this impressive new cuvée. With a high proportion of reserve wines (from previous vintages), this is a well-integrated, elegant wine, with citrus characters and just a light touch of honey. **93** *—R.V. (12/1/2005)*

G. H. Mumm NV Mumm de Cramant Grand Cru Brut Chardonnay (Champagne) $61. Formerly known as Crémant de Cramant (a name now banned because it refers to sparkling wines from Burgundy, Alsace, the Loire and Limoux), Mumm continues to make this blanc de blancs, which is famed for its lightness. It is great to see they are also giving the wine some bottle age, which brings out delicious, toasty, nutty characters. **91** *—R.V. (12/1/2005)*

GABRIEL MEFFRE

Gabriel Meffre 2003 L'Orme Chaulé Rhône Red Blend (Châteauneuf-du-Pape) $33. An earthy wine that shows dark flavors. It has spice and herbal flavors leading to firm tannins. The aftertaste is very peppery and dry. Somewhere the fruit got lost. **84** *—R.V. (12/31/2005)*

Gabriel Meffre 2000 Laurus Rhône Red Blend (Vacqueyras) $17. Strawberry flavors dominate this big, hearty, fruity wine. It may not be hugely powerful, but the fruit is generous, spoilt by just a touch of alcoholic pepperiness. **86** *—R.V. (3/1/2004)*

Gabriel Meffre 2002 Laurus Rhône White Blend (Hermitage) $NA. Huge, spicy wood dominates this powerful wine. It also has good acidity, which gives it a lift and liveliness. At the moment, though, wood is right up front, leaving the apricot fruit flavors stuck in the background. Give it three or four years to develop. **87** *—R.V. (2/1/2005)*

Gabriel Meffre 2001 Laurus (Crozes-Hermitage) $NA. This is an earthy, traditional approach to Crozes-Hermitage. You need to like this style, with its barnyard flavors, its acidity and light oxidative character and its red fruits. It does need time to develop, and it will certainly be a great food wine. But it is an acquired taste. **86** *—R.V. (2/1/2005)*

Gabriel Meffre 2000 Laurus (Cornas) $NA. A surprisingly light Cornas, with fresh, juicy fruit, flavors of red currants and acidity. There is some wood, but the fruit is what makes this wine attractive, but developing fast. **85** *—R.V. (2/1/2005)*

GASTON CHIQUET

Gaston Chiquet 1997 Millésime Cuvée Club (Champagne) $60. Gaston Chiquet belongs to the Club Trésor de Champagne, a collection of growers who each produce a special cuvée which is approved at a tasting of the members. Chiquet's wine is beautifully made, with acidity, ripe fruits,flavors of yellow fruits and considerable mature richness. It should age well. **91** *—R.V. (12/1/2004)*

GEORGES DUBOEUF

Georges Duboeuf 2001 Prestige Cabernet Sauvignon (Vin de Pays d'Oc) $10. Earthy, farmyard aromas suggest the youth of this wine. The taste is much better, rich and full of black fruits with ripe flavors and a touch of pepper. **87 Best Buy** *—R.V. (12/1/2004)*

Georges Duboeuf 2001 (Pouilly-Fuissé) $19. **85** *—J.C. (10/1/2003)*

Georges Duboeuf 2002 Cépage Chardonnay (Vin de Pays d'Oc) $6. Soft, light and fresh, this wine has attractive acidity as well as crisp, green flavors. There's a touch of vanilla which broadens it out. It's a solid, ready-to-drink wine. **84 Best Buy** *—R.V. (12/1/2004)*

Georges Duboeuf 2002 Flower Label Chardonnay (Mâcon-Villages) $9. **85 Best Buy** *—J.C. (10/1/2003)*

Georges Duboeuf 2000 Mâcon Villages Chardonnay (Mâcon-Villages) $9. **82** *—D.T. (2/1/2002)*

Georges Duboeuf 2002 Prestige Chardonnay (Vin de Pays d'Oc) $10. Toast and nut aromas give this wine a sense of weight and importance. It is rich, toasty and creamy with ripe fruit that is maturing well for fall drinking. **87 Best Buy** *—R.V. (12/1/2004)*

Georges Duboeuf 2000 Saint-Véran $12. **84** *(2/1/2002)*

Georges Duboeuf 2003 (Régnié) $10. This gorgeous Beaujolais will stand up to whatever your picnic serves up, from roast chicken or ham to cold meatloaf and all the accompanying salads. The bouncy black cherry fruit is gulpable, so you won't have to bring back any unfinished wine. Put it in the fridge the night before, pack your basket that morning and by the time you reach your destination it will be at perfect serving temp. **88 Best Buy** *—J.C. (8/1/2005)*

Georges Duboeuf 2001 (Juliénas) $12. **86** *—M.M. (11/15/2002)*

Georges Duboeuf 2001 (Régnié) $9. **86 Best Buy** *—M.M. (11/15/2002)*

Georges Duboeuf 2001 (Fleurie) $14. **84** *—M.M. (11/15/2002)*

Georges Duboeuf 2000 Château de Nervers (Brouilly) $12. **85** *(1/1/2004)*

Georges Duboeuf 2001 Domaine des Quatre Vents (Fleurie) $14. **87** *—J.C. (11/15/2003)*

Georges Duboeuf 2001 Domaine des Rosiers (Moulin-à-Vent) $14. **83** *—J.C. (11/15/2003)*

Georges Duboeuf 2002 Flower Label (Régnié) $10. **86 Best Buy** *—J.C. (11/15/2003)*

Georges Duboeuf 2002 Grand Cuvée Flower Label (Brouilly) $11. **87 Best Buy** *—J.C. (11/15/2003)*

Georges Duboeuf 2001 Grande Cuvée (Brouilly) $11. **84** *—M.M. (11/15/2002)*

Georges Duboeuf 2001 Jean Descombes (Morgon) $12. **84** *—J.C. (11/15/2003)*

Georges Duboeuf 1997 Pisse Vieille (Brouilly) $11. **88** *—J.C. (11/15/1999)*

Georges Duboeuf 2000 Prestige (Moulin-à-Vent) $20. **87** *(1/1/2004)*

Georges Duboeuf 2002 Merlot (Vin de Pays d'Oc) $7. Here is a wine packed with light, fresh juicy red fruits. It has some dry tannins, flavors of herbs and a layer of acidity. This is a good wine for summer drinking. **82** *—R.V. (12/1/2004)*

Georges Duboeuf 1998 Domaine de Bordeneuve Merlot (Vin de Pays d'Oc) $8. **85** *—M.S. (12/31/1999)*

Georges Duboeuf 2001 Prestige Merlot (Vin de Pays d'Oc) $10. Ripe, juicy fruit with gentle tannins make this wine well-rounded. It has acidity and flavors of cranberry jelly along with herbs and young fruits. **86 Best Buy** *—R.V. (12/1/2004)*

Georges Duboeuf 1999 (Morgon) $12. **86** *—J.C. (11/1/2000)*

Georges Duboeuf NV GD Red Blend (Vin de Pays du Torgan) $5. **84** *—S.H. (1/1/2002)*

Georges Duboeuf 2000 Syrah (Vin de Pays d'Oc) $7. **82** *(10/1/2001)*

Georges Duboeuf 1999 Viognier (Vin de Pays d'Oc) $15. **87** *—M.S. (11/1/2000)*

GERARD BERTRAND

Gerard Bertrand 2003 Classic Chardonnay (Vin de Pays d'Oc) $10. No lack of weight here, but the heaviness isn't well balanced by big fruit or crisp acids. Instead you get modest pear and peach flavors and a short finish. **82** *—J.C. (12/1/2004)*

Gerard Bertrand 2003 Syrah (Vin de Pays d'Oc) $10. This youthful, vibrant purple wine is miles ahead of most insipid Vin de Pays d'Oc Syrahs. Scents of smoke and black pepper accent blackberry fruit, while supple tannins provide a smooth mouthfeel. It's a steak wine for a casual evening, uncomplicated but satisfying, with the requisite tannins and acids to handle red meat. **86 Best Buy** *—J.C. (12/1/2004)*

Gerard Bertrand 2003 Classic Viognier (Vin de Pays d'Oc) $10. A solid entry-level Viognier, with pear and ripe apple aromas leading into a full, viscous mouthfeel and ample pear and melon flavors. Finishes with a hint of spice. **85 Best Buy** *—J.C. (12/1/2004)*

GILLES ROBIN

Gilles Robin 1999 Cuvée Albéric Bouvet (Crozes-Hermitage) $20. **89 Cellar Selection** *(10/1/2001)*

GOSSET

Gosset 1998 Celebris Rosé (Champagne) $135. **89** *—P.G. (12/15/2003)*

Gosset NV Excellence Brut (Champagne) $40. Has some pleasant aromas of ginger and rising dough, followed by modest apple and citrus flavors. Medium-bodied, with a burst of lemon on the finish. **84** *—J.C. (12/1/2005)*

Gosset 1999 Grand Millésime Brut (Champagne) $85. The latest vintage from Gosset, this rich, intense wine is still young, its acidity showing through strongly. But it has great depth, complex green and white fruit flavors, a hint of toast just showing, and the promise of many years' aging. As it ages, it will reveal more and more flavors that will stand up to even the richest of foods. **94** *—R.V. (12/1/2005)*

Gosset NV Grand Rosé Brut (Champagne) $70. Strawberries and herbs mingle elegantly in this simply fruity, ultraclean Champagne. Finishes tart and crisp, like underripe berries with a squirt of lemon. **86** *—J.C. (12/1/2004)*

Gosset NV Grande Réserve Champagne Blend (Champagne) $60. **89** *—P.G. (12/15/2002)*

GRANDIN

Grandin NV Brut (France) $11. **84** *—M.M. (12/15/2001)*

Grandin NV Methode Tradtionnelle Brut (Loire) $12. **86 Best Buy** *—P.G. (12/15/2002)*

GUILLEMOT-MICHEL

Guillemot-Michel 2002 Quintaine (Mâcon-Villages) $30. Tasted at a closed stage in its evolution, the fruit was very much quiescent, showing merely hints of peach and citrus. More mineral than the richer 2003, with a long, mineral-and-grapefruit finish. Drink 2008–2015, maybe longer. A 1986 tasted at the domaine late in 2004 was still delicious (90 points). **88** *—J.C. (11/15/2005)*

GUSTAVE LORENTZ

Gustave Lorentz 2000 Grand Cru Kanzlerberg Riesling (Alsace) $39. The Gustave Lorentz style with its emphasis on pure fruit flavors really shines through with this wine. There is some petrol character, but the main impression is of pure grapefruit flavors, streaked through with acidity, with crisp, green fruits and a great refreshing bone dry aftertaste. **91** *—R.V. (5/1/2005)*

GUY CHARLEMAGNE

Guy Charlemagne NV Blanc de Blancs Reserve Brut (Champagne) $35. **89** *—R.V. (12/1/2002)*

Guy Charlemagne 1996 Brut (Champagne) $50. **92 Editors' Choice** *—R.V. (12/1/2002)*

H.GERMAIN

H. Germain NV Cuvée President (Champagne) $37. **91** *(12/31/2000)*

HEIDSIECK & CO MONOPOLE

Heidsieck & Co Monopole NV Blue Top Premiers Crus Brut (Champagne) $39. Round and mature, with yeasty, almost doughy aromas. Yet there's vivid fruit in the mouth, mostly apple and citrus. Finely textured, with a long, classy, complex finish featuring mild baked notes but also pulsating, acid-based fruit. **93** *—M.S. (12/15/2005)*

Heidsieck & Co Monopole NV Diamant Blanc Blanc de Blancs (Champagne) $50. **87** *—S.H. (12/15/2000)*

Heidsieck & Co Monopole 1995 Diamant Bleu Champagne Blend (Champagne) $120. Toasty and rich-smelling, like brioche, but it isn't one-dimensional, as it picks up fruitier notes of apple and citrus. Ends on a chalky note. **91** *—J.C. (12/1/2005)*

Heidsieck & Co Monopole 1988 Diamant Rosé Champagne Blend (Champagne) $70. **92** *—R.V. (12/15/2003)*

Heidsieck & Co Monopole NV Extra Dry (Champagne) $37. **87** *—M.S. (12/15/2003)*

Heidsieck & Co Monopole 1997 Gold Top (Champagne) $43. A blend dominated by 60% Chardonnay, this maturing wine has great yeasty, toasty aromas. But this maturity is supported by fresh fruit, with a touch of toastiness on the palate and fresh, crisp acidity. It is rich, weighty and would be a fine food wine. **89** *—R.V. (12/1/2004)*

Heidsieck & Co Monopole NV Red Top (Champagne) $27. Creamy and full-bodied, maybe even a little heavy, but shows solid aromas and flavors of toast, roasted-caramelized meat, soy, and wild mushrooms. A main-course Champagne. **87** *—J.C. (12/1/2004)*

Heidsieck & Co Monopole NV Rosé Top Brut (Champagne) $43. Like a big red wine, this is full-bodied and powerful, boasting scents of meat and leather and picking up berry and tobacco nuances on the palate. It's largish bead and lack of elegance hold it back, but this is one flavorful Champagne. **89** *—J.C. (12/1/2004)*

Heidsieck & Co Monopole NV Diamant Blanc Grands Crus (Champagne) $65. **87** *—J.C. (12/15/2003)*

Heidsieck Monopole NV Brut (Champagne) $35. **90** *—P.G. (12/15/2002)*

HENRI ABELE

Henri Abele NV 1757 Brut (Champagne) $28. A good value in Champagne, this nonvintage cuvée boasts delicate toast and citrus aromas followed up by tightly focused flavors of green apple, lemons, and limes. It's very different from Abele's vintage offering but delicious in a different way. Finishes with a crisp, youthful edge to its flavors. **89** *—J.C. (12/31/2004)*

Henri Abele NV Brut (Champagne) $25. **92 Best Buy** *—P.G. (12/15/2000)*

HENRI DE VILLAMONT

Henri de Villamont 1999 (Chambolle-Musigny) $48. **87** *—R.V. (11/1/2002)*

Henri de Villamont 2002 Clos des Guettes Premier Cru (Savigny-les-Beaune) $35. Aromatic fruit, with flavors of dark cherries and ripe plums, along with sweet wood notes. Good, solid tannins promise a long life ahead of it. **88** *—R.V. (9/1/2004)*

Henri de Villamont 2003 Les Baudes Premier Cru (Chambolle-Musigny) $NA. A wine that looks, from its dark color, to be supremely powerful, but which, to taste, shows much more of the elegance of Chambolle-Musigny. There are flavors of red peppers, red fruits, and a light amount of toast. It is delicious, fresh, and well-balanced. **91** *—R.V. (9/1/2005)*

Henri de Villamont 1999 Les Baudes Premier Cru (Chambolle-Musigny) $53. **90** *—R.V. (11/1/2002)*

Henri de Villamont 1999 Les Groseilles Premier Cru (Chambolle-Musigny) $53. **89** *—R.V. (11/1/2002)*

Henri de Villamont 1999 Premier Cru (Chambolle-Musigny) $49. **88** *—R.V. (11/1/2002)*

HENRIOT

Henriot 1989 Cuvée des Enchanteleurs Champagne Blend (Champagne) $NA. This is what mature Champagne should taste like. A fine, full-bodied wine, with ripeness and balancing toasty flavors. This is full of richness and flavors of almonds and mature fruit. A well-balanced wine which still has life ahead of it. **91** *—R.V. (12/1/2004)*

Henriot NV Brut Blanc de Blanc (Champagne) $50. Enticing aromas of white fruits set the scene for a wine that is very fresh, very crisp, the epitome of dry, clean, delicious Chardonnay. It has great acidity and a crisp, clear dry aftertaste. **91** *—R.V. (12/1/2005)*

HERON

Heron 1996 Red Blend (Vin de Pays d'Oc) $9. **85** *(11/15/1999)*

HERZOG SELECTION

Herzog Selection 1999 Chardonnay (Vin de Pays du Jardin de la France) $8. **84** *(4/1/2001)*

HIPPOLYTE REVERDY

Hippolyte Reverdy 2003 (Sancerre) $22. Full and fresh. Lots of mineral along with almond, white peach, and citrus on the nose. Zesty enough, with roundness as well. Flavors of melon, apple, peach, and more mix well together. Shows a bit of heat late, which folds into pithy bitterness at the very end. **90** *(7/1/2005)*

HUGEL

Hugel 2002 Gewürztraminer (Alsace) $20. Firmly in the house style, this Gewurz is restrained and minerally rather than dramatically flamboyant. Ripe melon and pear flavors are delivered in a medium-bodied format, finishing a bit short. **84** *—J.C. (2/1/2005)*

Hugel 1999 Gewürztraminer (Alsace) $19. **87** *(11/1/2001)*

Hugel 1997 Vendange Tardive Gewürztraminer (Alsace) $55. **91** *(11/1/2001)*

Hugel 1999 Cuvée Les Amours Pinot Blanc (Alsace) $12. **86** *(11/1/2001)*

Hugel 2000 Riesling (Alsace) $17. **85** *—R.V. (8/1/2003)*

Hugel 1998 Hommage à Jean Hugel Riesling (Alsace) $50. A wine that has been created to celebrate the continuing life of Jean Hugel, one of the great ambassadors for Alsace, this has fine petrol aromas, with a dry palate and great flavors of currants, toast, and some spice. It has structure, dryness, and fine perfumed flavors. **91** *—R.V. (5/1/2005)*

Hugel 1998 Jubilee Reserve Personelle Riesling (Alsace) $35. **89** *(11/1/2001)*

Hugel 1995 Vendage Tardive Riesling (Alsace) $65. **93 Cellar Selection** *(11/1/2001)*

Hugel 1997 Reserve Personelle Tokay Pinot Gris (Alsace) $35. **85** *— (8/1/1999)*

Hugel 2003 Gentil White Blend (Alsace) $11. This blended white combines fresh apple and pear fruit notes with minerally, petrolly nuances to give a surprisingly complex result. Finshes with a burst of lime. Drink now and over the next several months; this isn't built to age. **86 Best Buy** *—J.C. (2/1/2005)*

J DE TELMONT

J de Telmont 1993 Consécration (Champagne) $NA. A soft, mature but unfocused wine which has acidity and toast without the weight and richness to sustain it. It is enjoyable as an old wine, yes, but it's missed something along the way. **83** *—R.V. (12/1/2004)*

J de Telmont 2000 Grand Vintage (Champagne) $NA. This is one of the youngest vintages on the market currently, and it tastes like it. It is fresh and fruity, but isn't balanced yet between the sweetness of the dosage and the fruit and acidity of the Champagne. This could change, but it would certainly need four or five years' aging. **84** *—R.V. (12/1/2004)*

J. de Telmont NV Brut Rosé (Champagne) $39. **80** *—R.V. (12/15/2003)*

J. de Telmont NV Grande Réserve (Champagne) $30. **88** *(6/1/2001)*

J. & F. LURTON

J. & F. Lurton 2003 Les Fumées Blanches Sauvignon Blanc (Vin de Pays de Côtes du Tarn) $9. This simple acidic quaff blends grapefruit and gooseberry flavors in a tart, cleansing wine best served as an apéritif. **83** *—J.C. (12/1/2004)*

J. D. LAURENT

J. D. Laurent 2002 Cabernet Sauvignon (Bordeaux) $10. Offers up decent aromas of sour cherries, then folds in leather and earth notes on the palate. This is an easy-to-drink claret for immediate consumption—little tannin, some coffee, tart cherries for balance. **84** *—J.C. (6/1/2005)*

J. MOREAU & FILS

J. Moreau & Fils 2002 Bougros Grand Cru (Chablis) $55. This wine is all potential. Closed at this stage, it promises much. Green plums and crispness balance intense caramel flavors and a touch of tannins. **89** *—R.V. (9/1/2004)*

J. Moreau & Fils 2000 Bougros Grand Cru (Chablis) $45. **91** *—J.C. (10/1/2003)*

J. Moreau & Fils 1999 Cuvée Joyeaux Premier Cru (Chablis) $45. **89** *(6/1/2002)*

J. Moreau & Fils 2000 Les Clos Grand Cru (Chablis) $50. **92** *—J.C. (10/1/2003)*

J. Moreau & Fils 2000 Montmains Premier Cru (Chablis) $29. **91 Editors' Choice** *—J.C. (10/1/2003)*

J. Moreau & Fils 2001 Vaillons Premier Cru (Chablis) $29. **88** *—J.C. (10/1/2003)*

J. Moreau & Fils 1999 Vaucoupin Premier Cru (Chablis) $28. **88** *(6/1/2002)*

J. Moreau & Fils 2000 Vaucoupin Premier Cru (Chablis) $29. **87** *—J.C. (10/1/2003)*

J. Moreau & Fils 1999 Valmur Grand Cru (Chablis) $47. **90** *(6/1/2002)*

J. VIDAL FLEURY

J. Vidal Fleury 1998 Rhône Red Blend (Châteauneuf-du-Pape) $25. **86** *—M.S. (9/1/2003)*

J. Vidal Fleury 2000 Rhône Red Blend (Côtes-du-Rhône) $10. **88 Best Buy** *—M.S. (2/1/2003)*

J. Vidal Fleury 1998 Rhône Red Blend (Vacqueyras) $13. **85** *—D.T. (2/1/2002)*

J.J. VINCENT

J.J. Vincent 1997 Domaine des Morats (St.-Véran) $15. **89** *—M.S. (10/1/1999)*

J.J. Vincent 2001 Charmes (Morgon) $16. **86** *—J.C. (11/15/2003)*

J.L. CHAVE

J.L. Chave 1996 (Hermitage) $65. **94** *(11/15/1999)*

J.P. CHENET

J.P. Chenet 2000 Founder's Réserve Chardonnay (Vin de Pays d'Oc) $8. 85 Best Buy *—D.T. (2/1/2002)*

JACQUART

Jacquart NV Brut de Nominée (Champagne) $65. A 50/50 blend of Chardonnay and Pinot Noir, this is a full-bodied wine, with layers of toast and some good maturity. It has good nutty flavors, as well as white fruits, some bitter orange and a balanced, soft aftertaste. 88 *—R.V. (12/1/2005)*

Jacquart 1996 Brut Mosaique (Champagne) $36. A ripe, creamy blend of 50% Chardonnay with 50% of the two Pinots. There are spice, cinnamon and flavors of black currants, mingled together in a full-bodied blend. The freshness is laced with mature toastiness to give a wine of great complexity. 91 *—R.V. (12/1/2004)*

Jacquart NV Brut Mosaique Rosé (Champagne) $40. A simple, fresh rosé, which has some attractive toasty bottle age. There is also a yeasty character, which leaves the fruit submerged in the more autolytic flavors. This is a fine rosé for food. 86 *—R.V. (12/1/2005)*

Jacquart NV Brut Tradition (Champagne) $30. 86 *(12/15/1999)*

Jacquart NV Demi-Sec (Champagne) $30. 91 *(12/31/2000)*

Jacquart 1992 Mosaique Blanc de Blancs (Champagne) $38. 91 *—S.H. (12/31/2000)*

JACQUES HEURTIER

Jacques Heurtier 1998 Château Grand-Chene Red Blend (Cahors) $12. 81 *—M.S. (2/1/2003)*

JACQUESSON ET FILS

Jacquesson et Fils NV Brut Perfection (Champagne) $30. 93 *—R.V. (12/1/2001)*

Jacquesson et Fils 1995 Grand Vin Signature Rosé (Champagne) $110. An attractive onion skin colored wine with considerable acidity and maturity. This is very crisp, with flavors of red currants and hedgerow fruits, with a touch of mature toastines. A fine fresh wine from this medium-sized family company. 89 *—R.V. (12/1/2004)*

Jacquesson et Fils 1989 Non Dosé Blanc de Blancs (Champagne) $NA. From the exceptionally ripe 1989 vintage, Jacquesson decided to bottle a Champagne without any dosage of sugar. The wine was also kept on its lees in bottle and not disgorged until July 2004. The result is a wine with exceptional elegance and surprising freshness. It is approaching maturity but that is all. Flavors of green fruits and yeast are finely in balance with the acidity. 94 *—R.V. (12/1/2004)*

Jacquesson et Fils 1995 Signature Extra Brut (Champagne) $90. This Pinot Noir-dominated wine is rich and structured with waves of acidity passing through the white currant, toast, and a developing maturity. Extra richness comes from the oak fermentation, but, because of the low dosage, there is also an austerity and minerality about this wine that will find its best expression with food. 95 *—R.V. (12/1/2005)*

JAILLANCE

Jaillance NV Cuvée Impériale Tradition Muscat Blanc à Petit Grain (Clairette de Die) $15. This curiousity is a Rhône Valley wine made from Muscat grapes, not too dissimilar from Moscato d'Asti, but fully sparkling. As a result, it has flowery, tropical fruit aromas and flavors, and a touch of sweetness on a relatively light-bodied frame. 85 *—J.C. (12/1/2004)*

JEAN LAURENT

Jean Laurent NV Blanc de Blancs Brut (Champagne) $41. Light and delicate, this is a blanc de blancs worthy of the name. Toasty and biscuity on the nose, with flavors of citrus, green apple, and chalk dust. 88 *—J.C. (12/1/2005)*

JEAN-BAPTISTE ADAM

Jean-Baptiste Adam 2002 Grand Cru Wineck-Schlossberg Riesling (Alsace) $40. This wine is finely perfumed, with flavors of almonds, currants, and white berries. There is good intensity and the wine should age well over the next five years or more. 89 *—R.V. (11/1/2005)*

JEAN-CLAUDE BOISSET

Jean-Claude Boisset 2003 Chardonnay (Bourgogne) $16. Winemaker Patriat considers his Bourgognes the "most important wines in the range." This likeable Chardonnay melds ripe pear, melon, and honey notes with hints of spice and mineral. Only 5 percent new oak, with no battonage. 86 *(12/31/2005)*

Jean-Claude Boisset 2003 Pinot Noir (Bourgogne) $16. This blend of Pinots from Aloxe-Corton, Chorey, Savigny, and Marsannay is slightly lean and herbal. Has some nice black cherry fruit, then finishes on a teal-like note with some drying tannins. Try with rare beef or lamb. 84 *(12/31/2005)*

Jean-Claude Boisset 2002 Bressandes Premier Cru (Beaune) $NA. A very rich, concentrated wine that combines black fruits, dark tannins and sweetness. Hints of wood only give structure. The potential is there—give this 10 years at least. 93 *—R.V. (9/1/2004)*

Jean-Claude Boisset 2003 Clos de Verger Premier Cru (Pommard) $65. Supple and silky, this has a lovely texture for a Pommard. Black cherry and plum fruit is framed by vanilla and smoke, picking up some lingering meaty notes on the finish. **89** —*J.C. (12/31/2005)*

Jean-Claude Boisset 2003 Clos Rousseau Premier Cru (Santenay) $35. Shows surprising elegance for a wine from Santenay, with delicate black cherry flavors couched in layers of cinnamon and clove. Drink over the next 2–3 years. **87** *(12/31/2005)*

Jean-Claude Boisset 2003 Lavaut Saint-Jacques Premier Cru (Gevrey-Chambertin) $85. Gevrey is sometimes considered to confer a certain meatiness on its wines, and this wine shows that character, blending it with clove, allspice, and plummy fruit. It's full-bodied and soft, finishing on a tender note. **90** —*J.C. (12/31/2005)*

Jean-Claude Boisset 2003 Les Chaumes Premier Cru (Vosne-Romanée) $90. Big black cherry aromas upfront, framed by vanilla and cedar. Plummy, rich and chocolaty on the palate, verging on overripeness, but maintaining a precarious sense of balance on the soft, lingering finish. **90** —*J.C. (12/31/2005)*

JEAN-LUC COLOMBO

Jean-Luc Colombo 2001 Les Ruchets (Cornas) $86. Spice and black currant aromas are combined with solid tannins and powerful wood flavors to give a spectacular, polished style, a contrast to the often rustic wines that come from this appellation. The wine comes from 90-year old vines that are then aged in 70% new wood for 18 months. **91** —*R.V. (2/1/2005)*

Jean-Luc Colombo 1997 Les Ruchets (Cornas) $62. **94** *(11/15/1999)*

Jean-Luc Colombo 2003 Les Abeilles Rhône Red Blend (Côtes-du-Rhône) $11. The chocolate and dried cherry flavors seem a touch baked and dull. Still, it's a well-made example of Côtes-du-Rhône from a hot year. **83** —*J.C. (11/15/2005)*

Jean-Luc Colombo 2001 Les Pins Couchés Rhône Red Blend (Coteaux d'Aix-en-Provence) $20. A spicy, earthy wine, with ripe tannins and generous fruit. It is tannic, with dry spice and cranberry flavors, with acidity. This wine comes from Jean-Luc Colombo's family property near Aix-en-Provence. It will work well with spicy Mediterranean food flavors. **88** —*R.V. (2/1/2005)*

Jean-Luc Colombo 1999 Le Prieuré (St.-Joseph) $20. **86** *(10/1/2001)*

JEAN-MARC BOUILLOT

Jean-Marc Bouillot 2002 Batârd Montrachet $NA. Earth and spice aromas make this an unusual wine. It has woodland fruit flavors with white currants dominating. Fresh and crisp, it will age relatively quickly. **87** —*R.V. (9/1/2004)*

JEAN-MARC BROCARD

Jean-Marc Brocard 2002 (Sauvignon de St-Bris) $10. **86** —*R.V. (11/15/2003)*

JEAN-PAUL BRUN

Jean-Paul Brun 2002 Terres Dorees L'Ancien Vieilles Vignes (Beaujolais) $13. **88 Best Buy** —*J.C. (11/15/2003)*

JOSEPH BURRIER

Joseph Burrier 2003 Château de Beauregard (Fleurie) $22. **83** —*J.C. (11/15/2005)*

JOSEPH DROUHIN

Joseph Drouhin 2001 (Puligny-Montrachet) $42. **89** —*J.C. (10/1/2003)*

Joseph Drouhin 2001 (Chassagne-Montrachet) $41. **85** —*J.C. (10/1/2003)*

Joseph Drouhin 2001 (Meursault) $38. **90** —*J.C. (10/1/2003)*

Joseph Drouhin 2001 Folatières Premier Cru (Puligny-Montrachet) $60. **91** —*J.C. (10/1/2003)*

Joseph Drouhin 2001 Perrières Premier Cru (Meursault) $38. **86** —*J.C. (10/1/2003)*

Joseph Drouhin 2001 Vaudesir Grand Cru (Chablis) $51. **90** —*J.C. (10/1/2003)*

Joseph Drouhin 2003 Véro Chardonnay (Bourgogne) $20. Starts off perfumy and floral, then develops into a perfectly drinkable Chardonnay, with hints of toasted almond and vanilla but also pleasant peach, pear, and apple fruit. Not very mineral, but easy to like. **87** —*J.C. (11/15/2005)*

Joseph Drouhin 2001 (Brouilly) $15. **83** —*J.C. (11/15/2003)*

Joseph Drouhin 2001 (Fleurie) $19. **85** —*J.C. (11/15/2003)*

Joseph Drouhin 2000 Bonnes-Mares $119. **94 Editors' Choice** —*R.V. (11/1/2002)*

Joseph Drouhin 2003 (Chambolle-Musigny) $73. A soft, seductive wine that oozes ripe Pinot Noir. There are tannins there, but they are subsumed into the beautiful red fruit flavors. Will mature well, over 5 years at least. **88** —*R.V. (9/1/2005)*

Joseph Drouhin 2003 (Gevrey-Chambertin) $43. A big, solid wine, full of strawberry fruit flavors and solid tannins. Ripe and generous; earthy and juicy fruit flavors, and a layer of acidity, complete this delicious wine. **89** —*R.V. (9/1/2005)*

Joseph Drouhin 2001 (Chambolle-Musigny) $38. **83** —*J.C. (10/1/2003)*

Joseph Drouhin 2001 (Savigny-lès-Beaune) $20. **84** —*J.C. (10/1/2003)*

Joseph Drouhin 2001 (Côte de Beaune) $23. 84 —*J.C. (10/1/2003)*

Joseph Drouhin 2000 (Chambolle-Musigny) $39. 88 —*R.V. (11/1/2002)*

Joseph Drouhin 2002 Chambertin Clos de Bèze $NA. Power and tannins mark this smoky flavored wine. Chocolate and black fruit show through the dry flavors. This is a wine that needs at least 10 years in the bottle. **92** —*R.V. (9/1/2004)*

Joseph Drouhin 2001 Charmes-Chambertin $118. 90 —*J.C. (10/1/2003)*

Joseph Drouhin 2002 Clos des Mouches (Beaune) $57. This was the first Drouhin vineyard to become fully biodynamic, a process which now covers the entire domaine. The wine is full of rich, smoky plum fruit, cherries, and a touch of wood. **89** —*R.V. (9/1/2004)*

Joseph Drouhin 2002 Clos Sorbe Premier Cru (Morey Saint-Denis) $47. This wine has fine fruit and a soft, rich mouthfeel. Dusty tannins and nice acidity complete the picture. **89** —*R.V. (9/1/2004)*

Joseph Drouhin 2000 Le Musigny $139. 95 Cellar Selection —*R.V. (11/1/2002)*

Joseph Drouhin 2000 Les Amoureuses Premier Cru (Chambolle-Musigny) $96. 93 —*R.V. (11/1/2002)*

Joseph Drouhin 2002 Les Petits Monts Premier Cru (Vosne-Romanée) $104. This vineyard, owned by Veronique Drouhin, has produced a firm, serious wine, with solid structure. It is big and chunky, with chocolate flavors accenting the fruit. **91** —*R.V. (9/1/2004)*

Joseph Drouhin 1999 Marquis de Leguiche (Chassagne-Montrachet) $NA. 92 —*R.V. (11/1/2001)*

JOSEPH PERRIER

Joseph Perrier 1990 Cuvée Josephine (Champagne) $120. Aromas of walnuts and red fruits show that this is a still a young wine. And that is confirmed by the taste, which is full-bodied but still very fresh and, ripe rather than mature. With its blend of premier and grand cru wines from the hot 1990 vintage, it is almost more like a wine than a Champagne. **89** —*R.V. (12/1/2004)*

Joseph Perrier NV Cuvée Royale Brut (Champagne) $NA. This is a soft style of wine, quite full, with fresh, crisp layers. It has some bottle age, but also some good, pure fruit characters. Elegant and light, which makes this a good apéritif choice. **89** —*R.V. (12/1/2005)*

JOSMEYER

Josmeyer 2000 Cuvée des Folastries Gewürztraminer (Alsace) $32. 82 —*M.S. (6/1/2003)*

Josmeyer 2001 Pinot Blanc (Alsace) $15. 87 —*M.S. (10/1/2003)*

Josmeyer 2000 Mise du Printemps Pinot Blanc (Alsace) $18. 84 —*M.S. (12/31/2003)*

Josmeyer 2000 Le Fromenteau Pinot Gris (Alsace) $33. 85 —*M.S. (6/1/2003)*

Josmeyer 2001 Riesling (Alsace) $19. 84 —*M.S. (12/1/2003)*

Josmeyer 2002 Le Dragon Riesling (Alsace) $34. A crisp, fresh Riesling that manages to be lean without being mean, cushioning its racy acids with just enough lime and green apple fruit flavors. **86** —*J.C. (2/1/2005)*

Josmeyer 1996 Tokay Pinot Gris (Alsace) $20. 85 *(8/1/1999)*

Josmeyer 1989 Hengst Selection de Grains Nobles Tokay Pinot Gris (Alsace) $NA. 90 *(8/1/1999)*

Josmeyer 2001 L'Isabelle White Blend (Alsace) $16. 83 —*M.S. (12/1/2003)*

KRITER

Kriter NV Blanc de Blancs Brut (France) $9. This is a blend of white grapes from various parts of France, and thus ineligible for any appellation contrôlée. Yes, the bead is a little larger than it might be if the wine's second fermentation had been in the bottle, but the costs associated with that would price it well out of the value range. Still, it does ferment for seven months before aging on the lees for an additional nine, acquiring toasty, autolytic notes to complement its ripe fruit flavors. It's a soft, approachable bubbly ideal for large holiday crowds. **85 Best Buy** —*J.C. (12/1/2004)*

Kriter 2002 Brut Prestige Chardonnay (France) $11. Fruity and simple, with green apple and citrus aromas and flavors that are direct and satisfying, even if they're not particularly nuanced. Medium-weight; picks up some herbal notes on the finish. **84** —*J.C. (12/1/2004)*

Kriter NV Blanc de Blancs Brut (France) $13. Shows some smoke and other hard, burnt aromas in front of a bright apple-based palate that blends in pineapple, pear and mango. Good on the tongue, with clean, fresh flavors and balance. Tastes pure and lively. **86** —*M.S. (12/31/2005)*

KRUG

Krug 1990 Brut (Champagne) $224. A bit dark in color and lacking in bubbles, but when it comes to aromas and flavors it's out of this world. Vanilla, cinnamon, almond and apple scents are ethereal and mature as can be, while the palate deals layered apple and spice in multiple layers. Runs a mile long but soft on the finish. Unique in style; not the least bit zesty. **95** —*M.S. (12/31/2005)*

Krug NV Grande Cuvée Brut (Champagne) $172. This multivintage blend nails the essence of Krug, intense richness of fruit and flavor without weight. Meaty mushroom and soy aromas are balanced by rich red fruits, citrus, toast, and mineral notes. Long finish. **94** *—J.C. (12/1/2005)*

Krug NV Rosé (Champagne) $282. Krug Rosé has always been seen as the food rosé without rival. And so it remains. The secret is in the richness of the fruit, the layers of toastiness and the concentration of flavors. Fruit is there, but mature toastiness is more important in this wine, which layers acidity, and ripe fruit along with great style. **95 Editors' Choice** *—R.V. (12/1/2004)*

Krug 1988 Clos du Mesnil (Champagne) $370. **95 Cellar Selection** *(12/15/2001)*

KUENTZ-BAS

Kuentz-Bas 2000 Collection Riesling (Alsace) $20. **86** *—R.V. (8/1/2003)*

Kuentz-Bas 2000 Grand Cru Brand Riesling (Alsace) $42. A great, intense wine, probably the most impressive in the line-up of Kuentz-Bas grand crus. The structure, tannins and concentrated fruit all work together, while the toast and green apples combine to give it both depth and a lift. It should age as well, over the next 5–10 years. **91** *—R.V. (11/1/2005)*

Kuentz-Bas 2000 Grand Cru Pfersigberg Riesling (Alsace) $42. There's already some petrol character to this attractive wine, which also has great acidity and a fine, bone- dry feel. On the palate, there are some intense currant flavors. A great food wine with good concentration. **89** *—R.V. (11/1/2005)*

Kuentz-Bas 2002 Tradition Riesling (Alsace) $17. This simple, very attractive Riesling is a light, delicate wine, with dryness, fine acidity and flavors of grapefruit and green apples. It is fresh, crisp, and ready to drink now. **86** *—R.V. (11/1/2005)*

L'ORVAL

L'Orval NV Chasan Chardonnay (Vin de Pays d'Oc) $6. **80** *—M.M. (2/1/2002)*

L'OSTAL CAZES

L'Ostal Cazes 2002 Rhône Red Blend (Minervois La Liviniere) $30. This would be a nice everyday table wine if the price weren't so high. Vanilla, dried spices, and jammy berry fruit make a statement on the nose, but the fruit isn't as assertive in the mouth, yielding some stewed berries and bright, lemony acids. The vintage was a difficult one, so look for better things from this label next year. **84** *—J.C. (11/15/2005)*

LA BASTIDE SAINT DOMINIQUE

La Bastide Saint Dominique 2003 Rhône Red Blend (Châteauneuf-du-Pape) $30. A finely structured wine, with dusty tannins, delicious fresh, purple fruits, and fine acidity. Great perfumes set the scene for a poised, intense wine that is high in alcohol (15%) but does not taste like it. **90** *—R.V. (12/31/2005)*

LA BAUME

La Baume 2003 Chardonnay (Vin de Pays d'Oc) $8. Nectarines and melons are the dominant flavors in this rich, powerful, full-bodied Chardonnay. There aren't many punches pulled in this flavorful wine. A touch of wood completes the impact. The bottle has a screw cap. **87 Best Buy** *—R.V. (12/1/2004)*

La Baume 1999 Merlot (Vin de Pays d'Oc) $7. **82** *—D.T. (2/1/2002)*

La Baume 1998 Syrah (Vin de Pays d'Oc) $7. **82** *(10/1/2001)*

LA CHABLISIENNE

La Chablisienne 2004 (Chablis) $19. **86** *—J.C. (11/15/2005)*

La Chablisienne 2001 (Petit Chablis) $13. **84** *—J.C. (10/1/2003)*

La Chablisienne 2003 Côte de Léchet Premier Cru (Chablis) $28. **84** *—J.C. (11/15/2005)*

La Chablisienne 2001 Cuvée LC Chardonnay (Chablis) $16. **85** *—J.C. (10/1/2003)*

La Chablisienne 1999 Grenouille Grand Cru (Chablis) $NA. Lovely pure fruit aromas. This is a firm wine with excellent structure and rich fruit. The flavors are almost tropical, blending well with just a hint of wood, which becomes more obvious at the end. **88** *—R.V. (1/1/2004)*

La Chablisienne 2001 Le Chablis Premier Cru (Chablis) $24. **89** *—J.C. (10/1/2003)*

La Chablisienne 2001 Montmain Premier Cru (Chablis) $27. **87** *—J.C. (10/1/2003)*

La Chablisienne 2003 Vieilles Vignes (Chablis) $23. **86** *—J.C. (11/15/2005)*

LA COURTADE

La Courtade 2000 Red Blend (Côtes de Provence) $20. **88** *—M.S. (2/1/2003)*

LA CROIX MARTELLE

La Croix Martelle 2001 Petit Frère Pinot Noir (Vin de Pays d'Oc) $24. From the Boisset-owned Château la Croix Martelle, this Pinot Noir is something of a rarity for Languedoc. It is firm with dense wood tannins which cover the varietal character. The end is a fine, well-made wine which seems to have little varietal character. **84** *—R.V. (12/1/2004)*

LA FORGE ESTATE

La Forge Estate 1999 Syrah (Vin de Pays d'Oc) $12. 85 *(10/1/2001)*

LA POUSSIE

La Poussie 1998 (Sancerre) $24. 87 *—M.S. (11/1/2000)*

LA SAUVAGEONNE

La Sauvageonne 2002 Cabernet Sauvignon-Merlot (Vin de Pays de L'Aude) $23. A blend of Merlot and Cabernet Sauvignon from a cool year. It is a medium-bodied, wood dominated wine which lacks fruit weight for the wood. Spice, pepper, and some black fruits leave a dry aftertaste. **85** *—R.V. (12/1/2004)*

La Sauvageonne 2002 Pica Broca Red Blend (Coteaux du Languedoc) $18. The second label of La Sauvageonne, from a year when the first wine was not made because of the quality of the vintage. It has spicy, wood dominated aromas, and young, soft fruit. It's an attractive wine, with lightness and elegance rather than power. **87** *—R.V. (12/1/2004)*

LA SOUFRANDIÈRE

La Soufrandière 2003 Pouilly-Vinzelles $27. Impressive for what the Bret brothers modestly refer to as their young vine cuvée. Floral, mineral, and fresh pear aromas upfront, then layers of honeyed fruit on the palate, finishing with an extra flourish of minerals. Ready to drink. **89** *—J.C. (11/15/2005)*

LA VIEILLE FERME

La Vieille Ferme 2002 Lasira Grenache-Syrah (Costières de Nimes) $8. As the label states, this is a blend of 75% Syrah, 25% Grenache, 0% Cork. The slickly packaged, screw-capped wine is young and grapy, featuring bright bouncy fruit accented by peppery spice. Perhaps because of the vintage, it's rather light, yet shows firm tannins on the finish, making it a burger wine for drinking over the next year or so. **84** *—J.C. (3/1/2004)*

La Vieille Ferme 2000 Rhône Red Blend (Côtes-du-Ventoux) $9. 86 *—M.S. (2/1/2003)*

La Vieille Ferme 1999 Rhône Red Blend (Côtes-du-Ventoux) $8. 84 *—M.M. (2/1/2002)*

La Vieille Ferme 2004 Rhône White Blend (Côtes du Luberon) $8. A simple, fruity white best as an easy quaffer before dinner, this wine prominently features notes of tropical fruit and pineapple, with apple and pear flavors in support. Clean and fresh, if a little short on the finish. **84 Best Buy** *—J.C. (11/15/2005)*

La Vieille Ferme 2003 Rhône White Blend (Côtes du Luberon) $8. This clean, neutral white wine features modest aromas of apples and limes, a plump mouthfeel and a stony, citrusy finish. Try it with fish stew, sometime during the next several months. **84 Best Buy** *—J.C. (2/1/2005)*

FRANCE

La Vieille Ferme 2002 Rhône White Blend (Côtes du Luberon) $8. 84 *—J.C. (3/1/2004)*

LABOURÉ-ROI

Labouré-Roi 2003 Fourchaume Premier Cru (Chablis) $25. 84 *—J.C. (11/15/2005)*

Labouré-Roi 2003 Premier Cru (Montagny) $16. A crisp, fresh, medium-weight wine that starts off a little stinky and sulfurous before righting itself. Decant in advance to enjoy the apple and smoke aromas and flavors and refreshing finish. **85** *—J.C. (11/15/2005)*

Labouré-Roi 2002 (Corton) $52. Highly aromatic wine; fresh and very attractive at this stage, with fresh strawberry fruits. Has some good tannins, but will probably not age well. **87** *—R.V. (9/1/2004)*

Labouré-Roi 1998 (Gevrey-Chambertin) $28. 87 *(10/1/2001)*

Labouré-Roi 2002 Pinot Noir (Chassagne-Montrachet) $23. Dusty and herbal on the nose, with modest cherry fruit carrying peppery spice on the palate. Light and tart. **83** *—J.C. (11/15/2005)*

Labouré-Roi 2002 (Echézeaux) $65. Hollow, rather soft wine, which lacks definition. It has some pleasant, soft, raspberry fruits and light hints of tannin. **82** *—R.V. (9/1/2004)*

Labouré-Roi 2002 (Pommard) $32. Smells of dried spices and earth, but alsop shows hints of alcoholic warmth and sun-baked blackberries. Earth and tobacco flavors predominate on the palate, with a dried-fruit finish and some astringent tannins. Seems to be past peak already. **82** *—J.C. (11/15/2005)*

Labouré-Roi 1998 (Pommard) $28. 88 *(10/1/2001)*

Labouré-Roi 1998 Domaine Sirugue Clos La Belle Marguerite (Côte de Nuits-Villages) $19. 89 Editors' Choice *(10/1/2001)*

Labouré-Roi 1998 Blanc (Chassagne-Montrachet) $28. 89 *(10/1/2001)*

Labouré-Roi 1999 Domaine Rene Manuel Clos des Bouches Cheres Premier Cru (Meursault) $43. 90 *(10/1/2001)*

LACHETEAU

Lacheteau 2000 (Pouilly-Fumé) $17. 85 *(8/1/2002)*

LACOUR PAVILLON

LaCour Pavillon 1996 Bordeaux Blend (Bordeaux) $9. 86 *(11/15/1999)*

LALEURE-PIOT

Laleure-Piot 1998 Premier Cru Les Vergelesses (Pernand-Vergelesses) $33. 92 *—M.S. (11/1/2000)*

LAMBLIN & FILS

Lamblin & Fils 2001 Chardonnay (Bourgogne) $7. 83 *—J.C. (10/1/2003)*

Lamblin & Fils 2001 Vaillon Premier Cru (Chablis) $22. 86 *—J.C. (10/1/2003)*

LANGLOIS-CHÂTEAU

Langlois-Château 2003 Château de Fontaine-Audon (Sancerre) $22. Fleshy and clean, with a blast of smoke and mineral tightening up what is otherwise a basic nose of stone fruits and citrus. Orange/tangerine is the dominant flavor profile, but there's also some stony minerality to harden it up. Not terribly intense but good for a warm-vintage Sancerre. Imported by Dreyfus, Ashby & Co. **88** *(7/1/2005)*

Langlois-Château NV Brut (Crémant de Loire) $15. 87 Best Buy *—J.C. (12/15/2003)*

Langlois-Château NV Brut Rosé (Crémant de Loire) $16. 87 *—M.S. (12/15/2003)*

Langlois-Château 1999 Quadrille de Langlois Château Brut (Crémant de Loire) $35. Crisp and light, this is a refreshing apéritif-styled wine, with subtle toast aromas backed by apple, lime, and chalk flavors. **86** *—J.C. (12/1/2004)*

LANSON

Lanson NV Black Label Cuvée (Champagne) $28. 90 *(12/15/2001)*

Lanson 1996 Gold Label Brut (Champagne) $45. 85 *—P.G. (12/15/2003)*

Lanson 1995 Gold Label (Champagne) $45. 87 *(12/15/2001)*

Lanson 1989 Noble Cuvée Brut (Champagne) $120. 93 *—M.S. (12/15/2001)*

LARMANDIER-BERNIER

Larmandier-Bernier 1998 Vieilles Vignes de Cramant (Champagne) $50. 92 Editors' Choice *—R.V. (12/1/2002)*

Larmandier-Bernier NV Blanc de Blancs Premier Cru Brut (Champagne) $53. Produced from biodynamically cultivated vineyards. This wine gushes fruit, with great pure crisp flavors and deliciously clean acidity as part of the finish. **91 Editors' Choice** *—R.V. (12/1/2005)*

Larmandier-Bernier NV Terre de Vertus Premier Cru Brut (Champagne) $55. A 100% Chardonnay blanc de blancs that is presented without any dosage to soften the acidity. Yet it doesn't seem to matter, because this Champagne is deliciously ripe, packed with mature fruit flavors, a touch of almonds to go with the white currant tastes and a layer of toastiness. **94** *—R.V. (12/1/2005)*

LAURENS

Laurens 1996 Clos des Demoiselles Brut (Crémant de Limoux) $15. 89 Best Buy *—P.G. (12/15/2000)*

LAURENT COMBIER

Laurent Combier 2000 Cuvée L Rhône Red Blend (Côtes-du-Rhône) $13. 85 *—S.H. (1/1/2002)*

LAURENT-PERRIER

Laurent-Perrier 1993 Brut (Champagne) $50. 90 *—S.H. (12/15/2001)*

Laurent-Perrier NV Brut L-P (Champagne) $30. A good value in Champagne, Laurent-Perrier's basic cuvée boasts scents of ginger, soy, and mixed citrus fruits, It's medium in body and a little soft on the finish, but carries a complex flavor melange of spice, citrus, yeast, and minerals. **89 Editors' Choice** *—J.C. (12/1/2004)*

Laurent-Perrier NV Brut L-P Kosher (Champagne) $60. Quite nice, with pleasing hints of toast, pear, apple, spice, and floral notes. The wine has good body and finesse, ending with a supple roundness on a finish that's moderate in length. **88** *—J.M. (4/3/2004)*

Laurent-Perrier 1995 Brut Millésime (Champagne) $53. 91 *—M.S. (12/15/2003)*

Laurent-Perrier NV Cuvée Rosé Brut (Champagne) $60. With its bottle shape dating from the late 16th century, this is a traditionally made rosé, using color from macerating Pinot Noir grapes. It is full, ripe, flavored with strawberries and other sweet red fruits, with a layer of dryness. The wine finishes fresh and crisp. **90** *—R.V. (12/1/2005)*

Laurent-Perrier NV Cuvée Rosé Brut Kosher (Champagne) $70. Crisp, fresh, and clean, with a spicy center and hints of raspberry, cherry, lemon, grapefruit, minerals, and herbs. Sleek, with small bubbles and a good, long finish. **88** *—J.M. (4/3/2004)*

Laurent-Perrier NV Demi-Sec (Champagne) $30. Citrus and herbs on the nose, apple, pear, and honey flavors on the palate. A bit simple and short, this slightly sweet bubbly is clean and well made, just lacking for excitement. **85** *—J.C. (12/1/2004)*

Laurent-Perrier 1997 Grand Siècle (Champagne) $95. Crisp and refreshing, this a young vintage Champagne with a good future ahead of it. Toast and ripe fruit notes on the nose give way to apple, cherry, and herbal flavors on the palate. Zippy and clean on the finish. **89** *—J.C. (12/1/2004)*

Laurent-Perrier 1997 Grand Siècle Alexandra Rosè (Champagne) $110. Fresh yet toasty, with more smoke and slyness than overt fruit. The palate is driven by apricot and orange rind, while the mouthfeel is succulent and secure, with ample smoothness. Grows on you even as it impresses from the start. **92** *—M.S. (12/31/2005)*

Laurent-Perrier NV Grand Siècle La Cuvée Brut (Champagne) $79. 88 *—J.C. (12/15/2003)*

Laurent-Perrier NV Ultra-Brut (Champagne) $39. 86 *—M.S. (12/15/2003)*

LE CELLIER DE MARRENON

Le Cellier de Marrenon 2000 Château La Tour d'Aigues Rhône Red Blend (Côtes du Luberon) $16. 84 *—M.S. (9/1/2003)*

Le Cellier de Marrenon 2000 Grand Luberon Rhône Red Blend (Côtes du Luberon) $10. 88 Best Buy *—M.S. (9/1/2003)*

LE FAUX FROG

Le Faux Frog 1999 Apropos Syrah (Vin de Pays d'Oc) $8. 83 *(10/1/2001)*

LE GRAND NOIR

Le Grand Noir 2004 Black Sheep Chardonnay-Viognier (Vin de Pays d'Oc) $10. This unusual blend of Chardonnay and Viognier combines apple and pear fruit aromas with scents of honey and crushed stones. Plump and medium-bodied, with pear and mineral flavors that add a hint of butter on the finish. **85 Best Buy** *—J.C. (11/15/2005)*

LE ROUGE DE SAINT-LOUIS

Le Rouge de Saint-Louis 1998 Red Blend (Côtes de Provence) $11. 88 Best Buy *—J.C. (3/1/2001)*

LECHÈRE

Lechère NV Orient-Express (Champagne) $45. 85 *—M.M. (12/15/2001)*

LEON BEYER

Leon Beyer 2001 Riesling (Alsace) $9. 85 *—R.V. (8/1/2003)*

Leon Beyer 2001 Les Ecaillers Riesling (Alsace) $37. A great, fresh, clean Riesling that just demands to be drunk. The wine has freshness, crispness, green fruits, and balancing acidity. Not very complex, but still delicious. **88** *—R.V. (11/1/2005)*

Leon Beyer 1997 Tokay Pinot Gris (Alsace) $35. 80 *— (8/1/1999)*

LES AMIS DES HOSPICES DE DIJON

Les Amis des Hospices de Dijon NV Champagne Blend (Crémant de Bourgogne) $NA. 87 *—M.S. (6/1/2003)*

LES DOMANIERS

Les Domaniers 2003 Rosé Blend (Côtes de Provence) $17. Citrusy, minerally, and dropping fruit at a rapid rate, this light-bodied rosé should have been consumed already. Modest peach and citrus flavors are pleasant, but fading. **83** *—J.C. (11/15/2005)*

LES HÉRÉTIQUES

Les Hérétiques 2001 Red Blend (Vin de Pays de L'Herault) $8. 87 Best Buy *—J.C. (11/15/2002)*

LES JAMELLES

Les Jamelles 2001 Cabernet Sauvignon (Vin de Pays d'Oc) $9. 86 Best Buy *—M.S. (9/1/2003)*

Les Jamelles 2002 Chardonnay (Vin de Pays d'Oc) $8. A hint of butteriness, grilled nuts, and ripe peaches give this wine a bit of California-esque quality. It's plump and ripe in the mouth, then turns a bit tart and metallic on the finish. **84 Best Buy** *—J.C. (12/1/2004)*

Les Jamelles 2001 Chardonnay (Vin de Pays d'Oc) $9. Flowery, pungent and powerful, with a good level of perfume, sweet pear aromas, and outright appeal. A nicely fruited palate with roundness and creamy undertones leads you to a finish of sweet citrus and grapefruit. With a full mouthfeel and clean, bold flavors, this is a winner in its class. **88 Best Buy** *—M.S. (1/1/2004)*

Les Jamelles 2001 Cinsault (Vin de Pays d'Oc) $9. 85 *—M.S. (9/1/2003)*

Les Jamelles 2003 Special Réserve Grenache-Syrah (Vin de Pays d'Oc) $15. A plump, medium-weight wine with no rough edges, this easygoing blend of Grenache and Syrah boasts ample cherry flavors accented by vanilla and tobacco. Clean and fresh on the finish, with supple tannins. **86** *—J.C. (11/15/2005)*

Les Jamelles 2001 Merlot (Vin de Pays d'Oc) $9. 84 *—M.S. (9/1/2003)*

Les Jamelles 2000 Sauvignon Blanc (Vin de Pays d'Oc) $8. 85 *—M.M. (2/1/2002)*

Les Jamelles 1999 Syrah (Vin de Pays d'Oc) $8. 83 *(10/1/2001)*

LES MARIONETTES

Les Marionettes 2003 Chardonnay-Viognier (Vin de Pays d'Oc) $NA. The combination of Chardonnay and Viognier produces a ripe, full-bodied wine. It has flavors of almonds and ripe quince. A delicious layer of acidity gives it freshness. This is a great Mediterranean food wine. 86 *—R.V. (12/1/2004)*

Les Marionettes 2001 Syrah (Vin de Pays d'Oc) $NA. Soft, earthy, perfumed fruit with good acidity give this wine character. It is fresh, attractive, and layered with light tannins. 83 *—R.V. (12/1/2004)*

LES VIGNERONS DE CHUSCLAN

Les Vignerons de Chusclan 2001 La Ferme de Gicon Rhône Red Blend (Côtes-du-Rhône) $9. 84 *—M.S. (9/1/2003)*

Les Vignerons de Chusclan 2000 Les Monticauts Rhône Red Blend (Côtes-du-Rhône) $14. 89 Best Buy *—M.S. (9/1/2003)*

LES VIGNERONS DU MONT-VENTOUX

Les Vignerons du Mont-Ventoux 2001 Grange des Dames Rhône Red Blend (Côtes-du-Ventoux) $10. This is a gulpable, satisfying wine that shows plenty of ripeness. Full, soft flavors of ripe black cherries are balanced by notes of coffee and chocolate. Long and harmonious finish. 88 Best Buy *—J.C. (3/1/2004)*

LES VINS DE VIENNE

Les Vins de Vienne 2000 Les Pimpignoles Rhône Red Blend (Côtes-du-Rhône) $40. A big wine, but with many complex aromas, of vanilla, of black plums, of tar and violets. The flavors are equally varied, showing concentration and tannins, as well as new wood. 90 *—R.V. (3/1/2004)*

LES VINS SKALLI

Les Vins Skalli 1998 Edition Limitee Cabernet Sauvignon (Vin de Pays d'Oc) $17. 89 *—R.V. (11/15/2002)*

Les Vins Skalli 2000 Oak Aged Chardonnay (Vin de Pays d'Oc) $10. 87 *—R.V. (11/15/2002)*

Les Vins Skalli 1999 Oak Aged Syrah (Vin de Pays d'Oc) $10. 85 *—R.V. (11/15/2002)*

LOUIS BERNARD

Louis Bernard 2001 Rhône Red Blend (Côtes-du-Rhône Villages) $11. 81 *—J.C. (3/1/2004)*

Louis Bernard 1999 Rhône Red Blend (Châteauneuf-du-Pape) $28. 88 *(11/15/2001)*

Louis Bernard 2001 Grande Réserve Rhône Red Blend (Châteauneuf-du-Pape) $37. A blend of Grenache and Syrah, this wine is packed with black fruits and with spice. It is tarry, dense, and concentrated. Layers of licorice give complexity to the powerful fruit. 88 *—R.V. (3/1/2004)*

Louis Bernard 2003 Rhône Red Blend (Vacqueyras) $22. Not up to some of the other cuvées from Bernard, with understated berry aromas and simple black cherry and earth flavors. Full-bodied and low in acidity, it comes across as a bit heavy. 83 *—J.C. (11/15/2005)*

Louis Bernard 2001 Rhône Red Blend (Gigondas) $18. This is a big, dense wine, and full-bodied. It spares few punches, but delivers hugely on solid, dense, black fruits. It will be ready to drink in three to four years. 86 *—R.V. (3/1/2004)*

Louis Bernard 1999 Rhône Red Blend (Gigondas) $20. 87 *(11/15/2001)*

Louis Bernard 1999 Grande Reserve Rhône Red Blend (Côtes-du-Rhône) $10. 89 Best Buy *(12/12/2003)*

Louis Bernard 2003 (Crozes-Hermitage) $20. A good showing for this négociant Crozes, with dense black fruit on the nose followed by flavors of plum and black cherries over a firm, minerally core. It's full-bodied yet crisp in acidity, with a long, juicy finish and supple tannins. 89 Editors' Choice *—J.C. (11/15/2005)*

LOUIS BOUILLOT

Louis Bouillot NV Brut Blanc de Blancs (Bourgogne) $12. 86 *—P.G. (12/15/2002)*

Louis Bouillot NV Grand Réserve Extra Dry (Bourgogne) $12. 86 *—P.G. (12/15/2002)*

Louis Bouillot NV Perle de Nuit Blanc de Noirs Brut (Crémant de Bourgogne) $15. This deep-golden sparkler has some pleasantly toasty, faintly eggy aromas, medium body, and a relatively large bead. Finishes a little rough. 84 *—J.C. (12/1/2004)*

Louis Bouillot NV Perle d'Aurore Rosé Brut (Crémant de Bourgogne) $15. Pale salmon color; fine bead. Toasty, yeasty aromas add scents of cinnamon and plum. The fruit is even more apparent on the palate, where plum and straberry flavors predominate. It's fairly full-bodied and would work better with meat dishes than on its own. 86 *—J.C. (12/1/2004)*

LOUIS DE SACY

Louis de Sacy NV Brut (Champagne) $35. 88 *—P.G. (12/15/2003)*

Louis de Sacy NV Brut Rosé (Champagne) $39. 89 *—P.G. (12/15/2003)*

Louis de Sacy 1986 Cuvée de Tentation Demi-Sec (Champagne) $NA. 89 *(12/15/2001)*

LOUIS JADOT

Louis Jadot 2002 (Corton-Charlemagne) $70. While this wine shows huge amounts of toasty wood at this stage, its potential for balancing out is all there. The fruit under the wood is hugely ripe, combining sweetness with lemony acidity in a fine balance. Give it 10 years. **94** *—R.V. (9/1/2004)*

Louis Jadot 2000 (Mâcon-Villages) $12. 82 *—D.T. (2/1/2002)*

Louis Jadot 1998 (St.-Aubin) $22. 86 *—M.M. (1/1/2004)*

Louis Jadot 2000 Château des Jacques Grand Clos de Loyse Blanc (Beaujolais-Villages) $15. 87 Best Buy *—S.H. (11/15/2002)*

Louis Jadot 2003 (Corton-Charlemagne) $145. A hugely powerful wine that exudes dense, packed tropical fruit flavors. Yet, it is surprisingly delicate, its power tempered by a cocktail of green fruits, nuts, spice, and toasty new wood. Almost in balance already, it should still age well over many years. **95** *—R.V. (9/1/2005)*

Louis Jadot 2003 Le Clos Blanc Beaune Grèves Premier Cru (Beaune) $65. Le Clos Blanc is a rarity in the mainly red vineyards of Beaune, a patch of chalky soil that has long been planted with Chardonnay. This 2003 is an open wine, with touches of almond and toast flavors, leaving a fresh aftertaste of acidity and green plums. **90** *—R.V. (9/1/2005)*

Louis Jadot 2003 (Beaujolais) $10. Yes, I know Beaujolais Nouveau is out of favor, it's yesterday's wine. But this isn't Nouveau, this is the real stuff, the original up-front fruity wine. Made from the Gamay grape, it's packed with strawberries, cherries and soft, generous fruit. There's a slight earthy, mineral touch to it that stops it just being a fruit bomb, and turns it into an easy food wine, especially with salamis, sausages, or burgers. **85 Best Buy** *—R.V. (11/15/2004)*

Louis Jadot 2000 Château de Bellevue (Morgon) $16. 88 *—S.H. (11/15/2002)*

Louis Jadot 2000 Château des Jacques (Moulin-à-Vent) $20. 87 *—S.H. (11/15/2002)*

Louis Jadot 2000 Domaine du Monnet (Brouilly) $16. 86 *—S.H. (11/15/2002)*

Louis Jadot 2003 (Clos Saint-Denis) $182. Finesse and elegance are typical characteristics of the wines from this grand cru vineyard in the village of Morey-Saint-Denis. In this wine, those characteristics are combined with a richness and a chewy tannic core that come from the superripe 2003 vintage. At the same time, the pure red fruits have an enticing freshness, leaving a wonderful, complex wine. **96** *—R.V. (9/1/2005)*

Louis Jadot 1999 (Chambolle-Musigny) $37. 84 *—R.V. (11/1/2002)*

Louis Jadot 1995 (Marsannay) $20. 87 *(11/15/1999)*

Louis Jadot 2003 Beaune Theurons Premier Cru (Beaune) $42. Packed with toast and roasted coffee flavors, this is an exotic wine that is only just beginning to develop. This wine will mature slowly, revealing its huge red fruits and perfumes over many years. **91** *—R.V. (9/1/2005)*

Louis Jadot 2002 Chambertin Clos de Bèze Pinot Noir $140. This is one of the great Burgundies of 2002. It shows the power of the year, with huge black fruits and dense tannins. But it also shows the charm, with ripeness that promises a precocious development as well as long aging. **97** *—R.V. (9/1/2004)*

Louis Jadot 2002 Greves Premier Cru (Corton) $70. Black fruit flavors and ripe sweetness give this wine great character as well as richness. The acidity streaks through the rich fruit, leaving dark tannins to finish. **93** *—R.V. (9/1/2004)*

Louis Jadot 2002 Clos Saint-Jacques Premier Cru (Gevrey-Chambertin) $85. As so often with wines from Gevrey, this is huge and structured. It is packed with firm, dense, solid fruit, but tempered with ripe tannins. **94** *—R.V. (9/1/2004)*

Louis Jadot 1999 Les Baudes Premier Cru (Chambolle-Musigny) $61. 92 *—R.V. (11/1/2002)*

Louis Jadot 1999 Les Fuées Premier Cru (Chambolle-Musigny) $61. 89 *—R.V. (11/1/2002)*

Louis Jadot 2002 Clos des Chênes Premier Cru (Volnay) $29. This Volnay is so intense, so seductive. It has great structure, too, deeply flavored and rich, with pure, sweet fruits. **92** *—R.V. (9/1/2004)*

Louis Jadot 2003 Château des Jacques (Moulin-à-Vent) $22. 89 *—J.C. (11/15/2005)*

Louis Jadot 2001 Domaine du Monnet (Brouilly) $16. 83 *—J.C. (11/15/2003)*

Louis Jadot 1998 Les Demoiselles (Chevalier-Montrachet) $NA. 91 *—R.V. (11/1/2001)*

LOUIS LATOUR

Louis Latour 2003 (Corton-Charlemagne) $140. Latour's signature wine is huge in 2003—certainly less subtle and less grand than the 2002, but still a great wine. It is rich, ripe and creamy, with toast and wood nuances. The power is dominant, but there is still the recognizable elegance of a fine Corton-Charlemagne. **93** *—R.V. (9/1/2005)*

Louis Latour 2002 (Corton-Charlemagne) $100. Immense power lies behind the initially seductive nature of this wine. It is powerful, ripe, complex, full of tropical fruits, and still at first it seems to be restraining this intensity. Give it 10 years and it will be mind-blowing. **96** *—R.V. (9/1/2004)*

Louis Latour 2000 (Corton-Charlemagne) $90. 92 Cellar Selection *(8/1/2002)*

Louis Latour 2000 (Chassagne-Montrachet) $44. 88 *(8/1/2002)*

Louis Latour 2000 (Beaune) $26. 86 *(8/1/2002)*

Louis Latour 1998 (Chablis) $16. 84 *—P.G. (11/1/2000)*

Louis Latour 1997 (Pouilly-Fuissé) $20. 85 *—P.G. (11/1/2000)*

Louis Latour 2000 Château De Blagny Premier Cru (Meursault) $40. 89 *(8/1/2002)*

Louis Latour 2000 Goutte d'Or Premier Cru (Meursault) $54. 88 *(8/1/2002)*

Louis Latour 2000 Le Referts Premier Cru (Puligny-Montrachet) $55. 91 Editors' Choice *(8/1/2002)*

Louis Latour 2003 Les Demoiselles (Chevalier-Montrachet) $470. What a powerhouse of flavors: white and yellow fruit, herbs and spicy wood, but still exhibiting some of the finesse and elegance for which this grand cru vineyard is noted. Ripe fruit means that this is not a wine for long aging, but it will certainly give pleasure over the next several years. **94** *—R.V. (9/1/2005)*

Louis Latour 1998 Les Referts Premier Cru (Puligny-Montrachet) $55. 92 *—P.G. (11/1/2000)*

Louis Latour 1998 Morgeot Premier Cru (Chassagne-Montrachet) $48. 89 *—P.G. (11/1/2000)*

Louis Latour 2002 Premier Cru (Chassagne-Montrachet) $45. At this stage, this wine is quite closed, but the potential is there. When it opens out, over five years, it will have enticing layers of wood, sweet fruit and intense ripe fruit. **92** *—R.V. (9/1/2004)*

Louis Latour 2000 Sous Le Puits (Puligny-Montrachet) $44. 89 *(8/1/2002)*

Louis Latour 2003 (Aloxe-Corton) $45. A pleasingly ripe, rich wine that has very sweet fruit flavors. Red jelly is the dominant character, with some light tannic structure to hold it together. **87** *—R.V. (9/1/2005)*

Louis Latour 2003 Les Heritiers Latour (Chambertin) $220. A wine that explodes with powerful, ripe flavors. It offers complex black fruit flavors, and tons of spice plus ample acidity. This great wine should develop over many years. **93** *—R.V. (9/1/2005)*

Louis Latour 2002 Corton Grancy $NA. A lovely, juicy wine with black tannins and immense fruits. Watch this wine develop over 10 years. **91** *—R.V. (9/1/2004)*

Louis Latour 1996 Domaine Latour (Aloxe-Corton) $29. 90 *(11/15/1999)*

Louis Latour 2002 Le Chaillots Premier Cru (Aloxe-Corton) $NA. This wine has intense jammy fruit flavors and some tannins to give structure. It is powerful, but restrained. **89** *—R.V. (9/1/2004)*

Louis Latour 1995 Savigny-les-Beaune $20. 88 *(11/15/1999)*

LOUIS MOUSSET

Louis Mousset 1999 Prestige (Côtes-du-Rhône) $10. 80 *(10/1/2001)*

LOUIS ROEDERER

Louis Roederer 1997 Blanc de Blancs (Reims) $59. 90 *—P.G. (12/15/2003)*

Louis Roederer 1995 Blanc de Blancs (Champagne) $55. 91 Editors' Choice *—M.M. (12/15/2001)*

Louis Roederer 1993 Blanc de Blancs (Champagne) $55. 91 *—M.S. (12/1/1999)*

Louis Roederer NV Brut Premier Champagne Blend (Champagne) $45. Basic Champagne, but done exceedingly well, with toasty, yeasty aromas that dominate the nose, joined only by fleeting scents of lime. Medium in body, slightly creamy in the mouth, with more toast and citrus and even some chalky mineral notes on the finish. **89** *—J.C. (12/1/2004)*

Louis Roederer 1999 Brut Rosé (Champagne) $71. Chalk and mineral aromas are backed by hints of wheat and orange peel. Lively and young in the mouth, almost to the point of being jumpy, with nice orange flavors. Subtle on the finish, with some spiced apple and zest. **89** *—M.S. (12/31/2005)*

Louis Roederer 1994 Brut Rosé (Champagne) $55. 86 *—J.C. (12/15/2000)*

Louis Roederer 1996 Brut Vintage (Champagne) $63. Bold and toasty, but also boasts plenty of subtleties: mushrooms, a hint of butter, ripe apples. It's full-bodied, rich, and creamy; intensely flavored yet retains a sense of elegance throughout its long, vinous finish. It's a good value in vintage Champagne. **93 Editors' Choice** *—J.C. (12/1/2004)*

Louis Roederer 1994 (Champagne) $55. 95 *—S.H. (1/1/2002)*

Louis Roederer 1997 Cristal Brut (Champagne) $175. In its famous clear bottle, this is one of the best known prestige cuvées, and also the oldest, made first in 1876 for the Russian Tsars.This most recent vintage is a very fine wine in a great tradition, revealing elegance, flavors of red fruits and impressive complexity from the blending. The aftertaste is extraordinary, going on seemingly into the distant horizon. **94** *—R.V. (12/1/2004)*

Louis Roederer 1996 Cristal (Reims) $175. 92 *(12/15/2002)*

Louis Roederer 1995 Cristal (Champagne) $180. 92 *(12/15/2001)*

Louis Roederer 1996 Cristal Rosé (Champagne) $295. Perhaps this extravagantly priced bubbly just needs more time to fill out, because right now it's lean and light in body, strongly citrusy and tart on the finish. Toast and mushroom notes on the nose add complexity and hope for the future. **90** *—J.C. (12/1/2004)*

Louis Roederer 1998 Rosé (Champagne) $63. A rich, smooth, very pale rosé, with intense, concentrated raspberry and red currant flavors and layers of crispness over the rich fruit. This wine is beautifully blended showing elegance as well as richness, the ability to be an aperitif wine, but just as important, the ability to go with food. **92**
—R.V. (12/1/2004)

Louis Roederer 1996 Rosé (France) $55. **92** *—S.H. (12/15/2002)*

LOUIS SIPP

Louis Sipp 2001 Grand Cru Kirchberg de Ribeauvillé Riesling (Alsace) $28. This is a firm, closed wine, which shows how well the Rieslings from this grand cru vineyard can age. It is powerful, with a tight structure and green fruits. There are fine, green flavors as well as some hints of green plums. Wait 5 years before drinking. Imported by Baron François Collection. **90** *—R.V. (11/1/2005)*

LOUIS TÍTE

Louis Títe 2003 Gamay (Moulin-à-Vent) $18. **86** *—J.C. (11/15/2005)*

LUCIEN ALBRECHT

Lucien Albrecht 2001 Cuvée Marie Gewürztraminer (Alsace) $23. Off-dry and richly concentrated, without being over the top. Restrained lychee fruit flavors blend with another note that's reminiscent of corn oil. Finishes with decent length and a touch of spice. **87** *—J.C. (2/1/2005)*

Lucien Albrecht 2003 Réserve Gewürztraminer (Alsace) $16. Textbook Gewürztraminer, done well, starting with scents of rose petals and lychees, and moving through pear and melon flavors into a finish that shows a hint of bitterness. Medium-weight and just slightly off-dry. **87** *—J.C. (2/1/2005)*

Lucien Albrecht 2003 Cuvée Balthazar Pinot Blanc (Alsace) $12. This full-bodied Pinot Blanc is ripe and soft, boasting lots of round, melony fruit. Likeable and zaftig, but lacking nuance. Drink now. **86** *—J.C. (2/1/2005)*

Lucien Albrecht 2001 Cuvée Cecile Pinot Gris (Alsace) $23. Starts with scents of almond and unripe nectarine, then slowly unfurls to reveal flavors of honey and peach. A hint of sweetness makes this easier to drink now, but this cuvée could still use another few years of cellaring to give up the goods. **87** *—J.C. (2/1/2005)*

Lucien Albrecht 2003 Cuvée Romanus Pinot Gris (Alsace) $16. Surprisingly dry and steely for a 2003, with lime and green apples married to hints of almond and peach. Crisp acids and a dry, clean finish. **86** *—J.C. (2/1/2005)*

Lucien Albrecht 2000 Sélection de Grains Nobles Pinot Gris (Alsace) $67. Albrecht made only 25 cases of this SGN, but if you can find it, it's worth a try. Aromas of caramelized orange peel and ripe melon suggest sweetness—and the wine is sweet—just not dessert-sweet. It's oily and viscous on the palate, conveying an impression of great weight and richness along with flavors of dried spices and citrus. Pair with foie gras or cheeses. **92** *—J.C. (2/1/2005)*

Lucien Albrecht 2001 Amplus Pinot Noir (Alsace) $44. Undoubtedly an ambitious effort, Albrecht's Amplus is an impressively extracted Pinot that ends up coming across as too woody and too tannic for its modest cherry fruit. Lots of vanilla, cedar, and caramel if you like that sort of thing. **84** *—J.C. (2/1/2005)*

Lucien Albrecht 2001 Grand Cru Clos Schild Pfingstberg Riesling (Alsace) $96. Not a blockbuster, but a medium-weight Riesling that should age almost indefinitely on its taut spine of acidity. Smoke and mineral aromas add complexity to bold, peach-accented apples and a broad streak of lime. **90 Cellar Selection** *—J.C. (2/1/2005)*

Lucien Albrecht 2004 Réserve Riesling (Alsace) $16. Made in a relatively soft, friendly style, this wine starts off floral and citrusy, then turns honeyed and apple-y in the mouth. Plump and low acid, it's an easy introduction to Alsace's Riesling. **85** *—J.C. (11/1/2005)*

Lucien Albrecht 2000 Vendanges Tardives Riesling (Alsace) $41/375 ml. Scents of dried apricots and candied citrus leap from the glass, followed by flavors of honey, pear, and melon. This is slightly sweet, with a robust 13% alcohol that gives it heft on the palate. Try with rich appetizers or with the cheese course. **88** *—J.C. (2/1/2005)*

LUCIEN CROCHET

Lucien Crochet 2003 (Sancerre) $23. Immensely flowery, with pure honeysuckle and touches of melon on the summer-fresh nose. Rather full and big on the palate, with intense flavors of green melon, peach and spice. Only medium zest to the finish, but sneakily powerful. Imported by Rosenthal Wine Merchants. **90 Editors' Choice** *(7/1/2005)*

M ET F LAMARIE

M et F Lamarie 1999 Château Aiguilloux Cuvée des Trois Seigneurs Red Blend (Corbières) $11. **87 Best Buy** *—M.S. (2/1/2003)*

M. CHAPOUTIER

M. Chapoutier 2000 Beaurevoir (Tavel) $23. **84** *—M.M. (2/1/2002)*

M. Chapoutier 1999 Les Béatênes Red Blend (Coteaux d'Aix en Provence) $14. **81** *—M.M. (2/1/2002)*

M. Chapoutier 2000 (Cornas) $55. **85** *—M.S. (9/1/2003)*

M. Chapoutier 2001 Belleruche Rhône Red Blend (Côtes-du-Rhône) $14. 90 Best Buy *—M.S. (9/1/2003)*

M. Chapoutier 1999 Deschants(St.-Joseph) $34. 91 *—R.V. (6/1/2002)*

M. Chapoutier 2001 La Bernardine Rhône Red Blend (Châteauneuf-du-Pape) $37. This wine doesn't reveal that much of itself on the nose, showing just teasing hints of leather and cherries. But it oozes across the palate with dense, chocolate fudge flavors that carry cherry and dried spice notes. Rich and supple in the mouth, it finishes long and nuanced. Drink now-2010+. **90** *—J.C. (2/1/2005)*

M. Chapoutier 1999 Les Meysonniers (Crozes-Hermitage) $26. 85 *—M.S. (2/1/2003)*

M. Chapoutier 2001 Petite Ruche (Crozes-Hermitage) $23. 82 *—M.S. (9/1/2003)*

M. Chapoutier 2001 (Condrieu) $83. 88 *—M.S. (9/1/2003)*

M. Chapoutier 2000 (Condrieu) $75. 92 *—R.V. (6/1/2002)*

M. Chapoutier 1998 Belleruche Blanc (Côtes-du-Rhône) $11. 84 *—M.M. (11/1/2000)*

M. Chapoutier 1999 Chante Alouette (Hermitage) $80. 89 *—R.V. (6/1/2002)*

M. Chapoutier 2000 De L'Orée (Hermitage) $279. 92 Cellar Selection *—M.S. (9/1/2003)*

M. Chapoutier 1999 L'Ermite Rhône White Blend (Hermitage) $313. 90 *—M.S. (9/1/2003)*

M. Chapoutier 1999 Les Granits (St.-Joseph) $97. 90 *—R.V. (6/1/2002)*

M. Chapoutier 2001 Les Meysonnierres Rhône White Blend (Crozes-Hermitage) $26. 86 *—M.S. (9/1/2003)*

M. Chapoutier 2000 Les Beatines Rosé Blend (Coteaux d'Aix en Provence) $13. 85 *—M.M. (2/1/2002)*

M. Chapoutier 2000 La Mordoree (Côte Rôtie) $210. 93 *—M.S. (9/1/2003)*

M. Chapoutier 1997 La Sizeranne (Hermitage) $70. 89 *(7/1/2000)*

M. Chapoutier 2000 Le Méal (Hermitage) $317. 96 Cellar Selection *(9/1/2003)*

M. Chapoutier 1999 Les Bécasses (Côte Rôtie) $79. 94 Cellar Selection *(11/1/2001)*

M. Chapoutier 1999 Petite Ruche (Crozes-Hermitage) $19. 86 *(10/1/2001)*

MAILLY

Mailly NV Brut Réserve (Champagne) $38. A quite green style of Champagne, very clean and very crisp. From one of the Champagne cooperatives, this is a great value wine, with pleasing freshness. **86** *—R.V. (12/1/2005)*

Mailly NV Extra Brut (Champagne) $43. Yeasty aromas set the scene for a wine that is fresh, crisp, and not long in bottle. It is an attractive Champagne, and its grapefruit and lime flavors are refreshing. Pre-dinner drinks would be a good moment for this wine. **88** *—R.V. (12/1/2005)*

Mailly NV Grand Cru Brut Réserve (Champagne) $30. Seems very fruity and simple at first—offering little more than hints of peach and strawberry. But it picks up on the midpalate, turning toastier and more savory. Plump, yet finishes with a crisp burst of citrus. **87** *—J.C. (12/1/2004)*

MAISON CHAMPY

Maison Champy 2003 (Pernand-Vergelesses) $34. A powerful, rich wine that packs layers of ripe fruit and toast flavors, and some crisp tannins, into a voluptuous package. The acidity is there as well, to add complexity. **89** *—R.V. (9/1/2005)*

Maison Champy 2003 (Savigny-lès-Beaune) $32. A ripe, soft wine that is already well developed. With just a touch of caramel, this generous wine has attractive red fruits and a light layer of tannins. **87** *—R.V. (9/1/2005)*

Maison Champy 2003 Beaune Champs Pimont Premier Cru (Beaune) $50. A ripe, juicy wine with some fresh fruit flavors. Herbs and dry tannins complement the forward fruit. A dry finish suggests some aging potential. **87** *—R.V. (9/1/2005)*

Maison Champy 2003 Vieilles Vignes (Beaune) $34. Sweet and soft, with pleasant red flavors, light tannins and a touch of ripe acidity. **83** *—R.V. (9/1/2005)*

Maison Champy 2002 Pernand-Vergelesses Premier Cru Les Fichots (Pernand-Vergelesses) $30. A very soft wine, which has some pleasant red fruits and spice, but is rather too light. **82** *—R.V. (9/1/2004)*

Maison Champy 2002 Savigny-lès-Beaune Premier Cru Les Peuillets (Savigny-lès-Beaune) $43. Ripe fruit and solid tannins give a foursquare feel to this wine. There are flavors of dark plums and a layer of sweet acidity. **84** *—R.V. (9/1/2004)*

MAISON JAFFELIN

Maison Jaffelin 2001 Chardonnay (Mâcon-Villages) $9. 82 *—J.C. (10/1/2003)*

MAISON NICOLAS

Maison Nicolas 2000 Chardonnay (Vin de Pays d'Oc) $7. 83 *—D.T. (2/1/2002)*

MALESAN

Malesan 2001 Blanc Bordeaux Blend (Bordeaux) $9. 85 Best Buy *(9/1/2002)*

Malesan 1999 Fierte de Malesan Bordeaux Blend (Bordeaux) $11. 84 *(9/1/2002)*

Malesan 2001 Rosé Bordeaux Blend (Bordeaux) $9. 84 *(9/1/2002)*

Malesan 2000 Rouge Wood Bordeaux Blend (Bordeaux) $10. Malesan is the bestselling Bordeaux brand in France, and this wood-aged version shows the French have got it right. With the quality of the 2000 vintage to help it along, it is ripe, packed with black currant flavors and ripe acidity plus just a touch of wood. Anybody in Bordeaux should visit the Malesan cellar, which is like a football ground, with the tasting room set out on a stage in the central pitch, surrounded by tiers of barrels instead of spectators. **84 Best Buy** *—R.V. (11/15/2004)*

MARC BREDIF

Marc Bredif 2000 (Chinon) $16. 80 *—S.H. (1/1/2002)*

Marc Bredif 2000 (Vouvray) $15. 85 *—S.H. (1/1/2002)*

MARC KREYDENWEISS

Marc Kreydenweiss 1997 Kritt Gewürztraminer (Alsace) $23. 90 *—S.H. (12/31/1999)*

Marc Kreydenweiss 2001 Les Charmes Pinot Blanc (Alsace) $NA. 90 *—S.H. (1/1/2002)*

Marc Kreydenweiss 1997 Moenchberg Pinot Gris (Alsace) $35. 88 *—S.H. (12/31/1999)*

Marc Kreydenweiss 2001 Andlau Riesling (Alsace) $20. 92 *—S.H. (1/1/2002)*

Marc Kreydenweiss 2001 Clos Rebberg Aux Vignes Riesling (Alsace) $NA. 89 *—S.H. (1/1/2002)*

Marc Kreydenweiss 2002 Grand Cru La Dame Wiebelsberg Riesling (Alsace) $38. Packed with ripe, peach-flavored fruits, this intense wine is from the 29-acre grand cru Wiebelsberg vineyard in Andlau. Full, toasty and intense, it layers flowers and fruit with powerful flavors of walnuts and almonds. **91 Editors' Choice** *—R.V. (11/1/2005)*

Marc Kreydenweiss 2001 Grand Cru Moenchberg Le Moine Tokay Pinot Gris (Alsace) $NA. 93 *—S.H. (1/1/2002)*

MARCEL HEMARD

Marcel Hemard NV Premier Cru Brut (Champagne) $NA. A brand of the Union Champagne, one of the largest cooperatives in Champagne, this particular wine is produced in a limited release of 5,480 cases. It has some good bottle age, and ripe fruit, spoilt at the end by the relatively high dosage that is not well integrated. **86** *—R.V. (12/15/2005)*

MARQUIS DE CHASSE

Marquis de Chasse 1999 Réserve White Blend (Bordeaux) $9. 84 *—J.C. (3/1/2001)*

MARQUIS DE PERLADE

Marquis de Perlade NV Blanc de Blancs Brut (France) $11. 83 *—P.G. (12/15/2002)*

MAS DE DAUMAS GASSAC

Mas de Daumas Gassac 2002 Red Blend (Vin de Pays de L'Herault) $50. The big wine, the grand vin from Daumas Gassac is a blend of 80% Cabernet Sauvignon with more typical Languedoc varietals. It shows structure and impressive elegance to go along with its power. Flavors of dark plums and black fruits go along with the layer of wood. Considering the poor vintage, this doesn't miss a moment of richness. Ideally age for 10 years or more, but will be drinkable after 5. **93** *—R.V. (12/1/2004)*

Mas de Daumas Gassac 2003 Rhône White Blend (Vin de Pays de L'Herault) $50. This southern classic is full of ripe fruit, but tempered with complexities of herbal flavors, citrus and ripe fruit hanging on a summer day. It is beautifully integrated, and should age over 10 years. **90** *—R.V. (12/1/2004)*

MAS DE LA BARBEN

Mas de La Barben 1998 (Coteaux du Languedoc) $12. 85 *(10/1/2001)*

MAS VIALA

Mas Viala 1998 Cuvée T.S. Syrah (Vin de Pays d'Oc) $14. 85 *(10/1/2001)*

MICHEL GONET

Michel Gonet NV Blanc de Blancs (Champagne) $38. 89 *—R.V. (12/1/2002)*

Michel Gonet NV Brut Réserve (Champagne) $36. 86 *—R.V. (12/1/2002)*

MICHEL GROS

Michel Gros 1999 Aux Brulees (Vosne-Romanée) $65. **90** *—P.G. (1/7/2001)*

Michel Gros 1999 Les Chaliots (Nuits-St.-Georges) $37. **87** *—P.G. (1/7/2001)*

MICHEL LAROCHE

Michel Laroche 2002 Merlot (Vin de Pays d'Oc) $9. Mocha and black cherry aromas and followed by similar flavors graced by a touch of dried herbs. It's plump and fresh, a step up from most Pays d'Oc offerings. **85** *(2/1/2004)*

Michel Laroche 2000 La Croix Chevalière Red Blend (Vin de Pays d'Oc) $NA. Laroche's top Pays d'Oc cuvée isn't yet available in the U.S., but is worth a try if you stumble across a bottle while traveling. This blend of Syrah, Grenache, and Mourvèdre boasts powerful plum, blackberry, and vanilla flavors accented by a bit of tobacco on the finish. **89** *(2/1/2004)*

Michel Laroche 2000 Syrah (Vin de Pays d'Oc) $7. **86** *—R.V. (11/15/2003)*

MICHEL LYNCH

Michel Lynch 1998 Merlot (Bordeaux) $9. **81** *—J.C. (3/1/2001)*

MICHEL PICARD

Michel Picard 2001 Cabernet Sauvignon (Languedoc) $9. **81** *—M.S. (9/1/2003)*

Michel Picard 2001 (Pouilly-Fuissé) $20. **86** *—J.C. (10/1/2003)*

Michel Picard 2001 (Chablis) $20. **84** *—J.C. (10/1/2003)*

Michel Picard 1996 Château de Chassagne-Montrache Chardonnay (St.-Aubin) $26. **85** *(6/1/2000)*

Michel Picard 2002 Le Montrachet $325. A modern, high toast style of wine, it packs spice and creamy vanilla flavors over rich, intense, green plum and ripe, sweet apples. The wood dominates to finish, but will balance out over the next 5 years. **90** *—R.V. (9/1/2004)*

Michel Picard 1998 Beaujolais-Villages $11. **84** *—M.P. (6/1/2000)*

Michel Picard 2002 Pinot Noir (Bourgogne) $15. Sappy cherry and beet aromas lead the way, then gradually yield to overripe notes of dried fruit. It's light in body, yet finishes on a slightly heavy note, if that makes any sense. You could do better in Burgundy, but you could also do a lot worse. **83** *—J.C. (11/15/2005)*

Michel Picard 1996 Château de Chassagne-Montrache Pinot Noir (St.-Aubin) $23. **88** *(6/1/2000)*

Michel Picard 2000 Rhône Red Blend (Châteauneuf-du-Pape) $20. **86** *—M.S. (9/1/2003)*

Michel Picard 1999 Rhône Red Blend (Châteauneuf-du-Pape) $20. **87** *—M.S. (9/1/2003)*

Michel Picard 1999 Syrah (Vin de Pays d'Oc) $9. **83** *(10/1/2001)*

Michel Picard 1997 Syrah (Vin de Pays d'Oc) $10. **86** *—M.P. (6/1/2000)*

MICHEL REDDE

Michel Redde 2003 Les Tuilières (Sancerre) $22. Ripe and sun-baked, with heavy aromas of honey, white flowers and pink grapefruit. It's the antithesis of a lean, wispy wine in that it pushes substantial melon, citrus and peppery flavors. Finishes short and plump. **87** *(7/1/2005)*

MOËT & CHANDON

Moët & Chandon 1995 Brut Impérial (Champagne) $53. **87** *—P.G. (12/15/2002)*

Moët & Chandon NV Brut Impérial (Champagne) $38. Probably the best-selling Champagne brand in the world, with a production of over 30 million bottles a year, Moët's quality is consistent. It has a ripeness and richness, and in this bottle, some bottle age. This bottling is not hugely fruity, but it has more to offer than just fruit. Imported by Moët Hennessy USA. **89** *—R.V. (12/1/2005)*

Moët & Chandon NV Brut Impérial Rosé (Champagne) $42. Rather fruity, with scents of cherries and peaches that come together in a round, easy-to-drink style. A little simple perhaps, but this is a clean, fresh sparkler that won't disappoint. **87** *—J.C. (12/1/2004)*

Moët & Chandon 1995 Brut Impérial Rosé (Champagne) $65. **88** *—P.G. (12/15/2002)*

Moët & Chandon NV Brut Impérial Rosé (Champagne) $40. **90** *—M.S. (12/15/2003)*

Moët & Chandon 1995 Cuvée Dom Perignon (Champagne) $150. **92** *(12/15/2002)*

Moët & Chandon 1990 Cuvée Dom Perignon Oenothèque (Champagne) $260. Disgorged in 1993, this wine seems very youthful. Lovely aromas and flavors of smoke, toast, citrus fruit, and cream still need more time to develop the rich, nutty notes that characterize well-aged Dom. Although some purchasers will prefer this wine's freshness, I think I'd prefer a well-cellared example from the original release. Try holding this another 5–10 years. **90** *—J.C. (12/1/2004)*

Moët & Chandon 1990 Cuvée Dom Perignon Rosé (Champagne) $290. **94 Editors' Choice** *(12/15/2001)*

Moët & Chandon 1996 Dom Perignon (Champagne) $130. In some vintages, Dom can be difficult to judge when young, seeming a bit austere and calling for cellaring. The '96 appears to be a slightly riper, lusher vintage, and while it has plenty of toast, pencil shaving, and smoke notes that promise to age into nutty elegance, it is also creamier and more approachable in its youth. Finishines with ripe apples and a hint of coffee or bittersweet chocolate. **92** *—J.C. (12/1/2004)*

Moët & Chandon 1995 Dom Perignon Rosé (Champagne) $300. The 1990 Dom rosé remains one of the greatest rosé Champagnes I have tasted. While the 1995 doesn't reach those heights, I doubt anyone will be disappointed by what is in the bottle. Dry, wheat thin scents seamlessly blend with hints of strawberries, finishing on some lingering, slightly herbal notes. **91** *—J.C. (12/1/2004)*

Moët & Chandon NV Les Sarments d'Aÿ (Champagne) $85. 92 Cellar Selection *—M.M. (12/15/2001)*

Moët & Chandon 1996 Millésime Blanc (Champagne) $50. 89 *—J.C. (12/15/2003)*

Moët & Chandon 1996 Millésime Rosé (Champagne) $55. 92 *—M.S. (12/15/2003)*

Moët & Chandon NV Nectar Impérial (Champagne) $48. 86 *—S.H. (12/15/2001)*

Moët & Chandon 1999 Rosé Brut (Champagne) $65. Ripe and forward, with a bit of sweetness in the form of root beer and nutmeg. The palate is equally ripe, as it shows melon and red-apple flavors. Long on the back end, with a blend of cinnamon and vanilla. Fairly simple but classy. Imported by Moët Hennessy USA. **89** *—M.S. (12/15/2005)*

Moët & Chandon NV White Star (Champagne) $40. 84 *—M.S. (12/15/2003)*

MOILLARD

Moillard 1997 (Puligny-Montrachet) $40. 84 *—J.C. (9/1/1999)*

Moillard 1997 Les Violettes Rhône Red Blend (Côtes-du-Rhône) $7. 83 *—M.S. (10/1/1999)*

MOMMESSIN

Mommessin 2002 (Pouilly-Fuissé) $19. 87 *—J.C. (10/1/2003)*

Mommessin 2001 La Clé Saint Pierre Chardonnay (Bourgogne) $12. 84 *—J.C. (10/1/2003)*

Mommessin 2003 Nid D'Abeille Chardonnay (Vin de Pays d'Oc) $8. Decently made but modest Chardonnay, with melon flavors that turn tart and earthy, veering toward grapefruit on the finish. **83** *—J.C. (12/1/2004)*

Mommessin 2002 Old Vines Chardonnay (Mâcon-Villages) $10. 86 Best Buy *—J.C. (10/1/2003)*

Mommessin 2003 6 Terroirs (St.-Amour) $21. 87 *—J.C. (11/15/2005)*

Mommessin 2001 Domaine de Champ de Cour (Moulin-à-Vent) $13. 83 *—J.C. (11/15/2003)*

Mommessin 2001 Les Grumières (Brouilly) $12. 86 *—M.S. (11/15/2002)*

Mommessin 2000 Réserve (Fleurie) $15. 83 *—M.S. (11/15/2002)*

Mommessin 2003 Le Montagne Bleue (Côte de Brouilly) $19. 87 *—J.C. (11/15/2005)*

Mommessin 2001 Clos de Tart $138. 92 *—J.C. (10/1/2003)*

Mommessin 2001 Charmes-Chambertin $90. 92 *—J.C. (10/1/2003)*

Mommessin 2001 Clos Sainte Anne des Teurons Les Grèves Premier Cru (Beaune) $34. 87 *—J.C. (10/1/2003)*

Mommessin 2001 Les Suchots Premier Cru (Vosne-Romanée) $67. 83 *—J.C. (10/1/2003)*

Mommessin 2000 Oak Aged Pinot Noir (Bourgogne) $13. 84 *—P.G. (11/1/2002)*

Mommessin 2000 Les Charmes Premier Cru (Chambolle-Musigny) $57. 86 *—P.G. (11/1/2002)*

Mommessin 2000 Santenots Premier Cru (Volnay) $65. 87 *—P.G. (11/1/2002)*

Mommessin NV Red Blend (Vin de Pays d'Oc) $9. 81 *—M.M. (2/1/2002)*

Mommessin 1999 Château De Domazan Rhône Red Blend (Côtes-du-Rhône) $8. 84 *(3/1/2001)*

Mommessin 1998 Les Épices Rhône Red Blend (Châteauneuf-du-Pape) $26. 85 *—D.T. (2/1/2002)*

MONT SAINT-VINCENT

Mont Saint-Vincent 2000 Chardonnay (Vin de Pays du Jardin de la France) $7. 83 *—D.T. (2/1/2002)*

MONT TAUCH

Mont Tauch 1998 Red Blend (Fitou) $11. 80 *—J.C. (3/1/2001)*

MONTAUDON

Montaudon NV Brut (Champagne) $27. 87 *(12/15/2001)*

Montaudon 1995 Brut Millésime (Champagne) $36. **88** *(12/15/1999)*

Montaudon NV Chardonnay Premier Cru (Champagne) $39. **85** *—P.G. (12/15/2000)*

Montaudon NV Classe M (Reims) $40. Butterscotch, vanilla, and popcorn on the nose, which is followed by some mute green apple and a sharp, fairly weak finish. The color is overtly gold and there just isn't much character or pleasantness. **81** *—M.S. (1/1/2004)*

Montaudon NV Grande Rosé Brut (Champagne) $35. **88** *—P.G. (6/1/2001)*

Montaudon NV M 2000 Celebration (Champagne) $50. **81** *—M.S. (12/15/2001)*

MONTIRIUS

Montirius 2002 Rhône Red Blend (Vin de Pays de Vaucluse) $NA. A blend of 50 percent Grenache, 30 percent Syrah, and 20 percent Cinsault from a portion of the Montirius vineyard close to the river Ouvèze. The wine is fresh, earthy with spicy flavors and dark plum fruits. It is ready to drink now. **85 Best Buy** *—R.V. (4/1/2005)*

Montirius 2001 Rhône Red Blend (Vacqueyras) $22. A full-bodied wine with delicious flavors of perfumed fruits from the 30% Syrah and intense, brooding tannins from the 70% Grenache. This is a complex, minerally wine, which has intense concentration and purity of fruit. **89** *—R.V. (4/1/2005)*

Montirius 2000 Rhône Red Blend (Vacqueyras) $19. A solid, sweet, perfumed wine with dry tannins overlying red fruit and herbal flavors. What this wine lacks in power, it makes up for in the intensity of its pure fruit flavors. **87** *—R.V. (3/1/2004)*

Montirius 2002 Rhône White Blend (Vacqueyras) $21. Ripe quince and green plum flavors blend with crisp acidity. This is an excellent, well-structured wine with ripe but fresh fruit. **87** *—R.V. (3/1/2004)*

MOREY BLANC

Morey Blanc 2002 Les Renardes (Corton) $96. Light in color, rather lean, high acid fruit and firm tannins, this is a somewhat undernourished wine for a grand cru. **85** *—R.V. (9/1/2004)*

Morey Blanc 2002 Santenots Premier Cru (Volnay) $77. This fresh wine offers a nice balance of tannins and lively acidity. It is ripe and sweet with a dry finish. **89** *—R.V. (9/1/2004)*

MOULIN DE GASSAC

Moulin de Gassac 2003 Le Mazet Old World Red Blend (Vin de Pays de L'Herault) $11. This is a blend of all the typical varieties of Languedoc—Syrah, Grenache, Carignan, Alicante, and Cinsault. A rich, generous wine it is marked by a dusty tannic structure by flavors of blackberries and bitter cherries, and by a completeness from a well-judged blendin. **89** *—R.V. (12/1/2004)*

Moulin de Gassac 2003 Le Mazet Rosé Blend (Vin de Pays de L'Herault) $11. Grenache, Cinsault, and Syrah old clones have been blended into this pure, ripe, vanilla flavored wine. It has just a touch of tannin to give structure, but also has lovely soft strawberry flavors. A great food wine for the summer. **88** *—R.V. (12/1/2004)*

Moulin de Gassac 2003 Syrah (Vin de Pays de L'Herault) $11. Packed with herbal aromas, this wine from the Mas de Daumas Gassac estate is rich, southern and warm. It has power and dense fruit but that is well balanced with discreet tannins and acidity. **88** *—R.V. (12/1/2004)*

MOULIN DE LA DAME

Moulin de la Dame 1999 Rhône Red Blend (Coteaux d'Aix en Provence) $10. **84** *—M.M. (2/1/2002)*

MOUTON-CADET

Mouton-Cadet 2000 Rouge Bordeaux Blend (Bordeaux) $14. Quite herbal, with some green beans and anise up front. Black fruit takes a back seat but is there if you look for it. Blackberry and beach plums come to mind. The tannins are a bit rustic. Kosher. **84** *—J.M. (4/3/2004)*

NICOLAS FEUILLATTE

Nicolas Feuillatte NV Brut (Champagne) $40. **87** *(4/1/2001)*

Nicolas Feuillatte NV Brut Premier Cru (Champagne) $40. **86** *—K.F. (12/15/2002)*

Nicolas Feuillatte NV Brut Kosher Mevushal (Champagne) $40. **85** *(12/15/2001)*

Nicolas Feuillatte NV Chardonnay Blanc de Blancs (Champagne) $43. Very aromatic, this wine is made from Chardonnay which comes unusually from the Montagne de Reims, better known for its Pinot Noir. That gives the wine a fuller, richer style, packed with flavors of apples and ripe pears. **88** *—R.V. (12/1/2004)*

Nicolas Feuillatte 1996 Cuvée Palmes D'Or Brut Rosé (Champagne) $125. More orange than salmon in color, with impressively smooth aromas of melon, orange peel, and brown sugar. The palate deals a full hand of citrus, and there's a sweet quince-like undertone. The finish is bold, fruity and long, like a couple of minutes long. This is a pure wine; it would be nearly impossible not to enjoy it. **91** *—M.S. (1/1/2004)*

Nicolas Feuillatte 1999 Cuvée Palmes D'Or Brut Rosé Champagne Blend (Champagne) $175. Quite red in color and a tad unusual. The nose has rhubarb, berry, and beet, while the palate is jumpy and tastes like raspberry. Bubbly on the finish. **85** *—M.S. (12/15/2005)*

Nicolas Feuillatte 1995 Cuvée Speciale Premier Cru Brut (Champagne) $65. Rich and toasty, this has vanilla and soft ripe fruit flavors. Sweet white and yellow fruits dominate the palate, which has a butter layer from the malolactic fermentation of the Chardonnay in the blend. Good, well-balanced. **90** *(12/1/2004)*

Nicolas Feuillatte NV Premier Cru Blanc de Blancs Brut (Champagne) $40. **87** *—M.S. (12/15/2001)*

Nicolas Feuillatte NV Premier Cru Brut (Champagne) $40. **89** *—M.S. (12/15/2003)*

Nicolas Feuillatte NV Premier Cru Brut (Champagne) $33. Hints of vanilla and white chocolate on the nose; modest toast, herb, and citrus flavors. Creamy mouthfeel and a clean, fresh finish. This is solid Champagne at a good price. **87** *—J.C. (12/1/2004)*

Nicolas Feuillatte NV Premier Cru Rosé Brut (Champagne) $43. A solid value in rosé Champagnes, this wine offers delicate toasty scents alongside hints of chocolate and caramel—the impression is one of understated elegance. Adds some apple and berry flavors on the palate, finishing with a note of coffee. **90** *—J.C. (12/1/2004)*

Nicolas Feuillatte NV Réserve Particulière Brut (Champagne) $28. The cooperative that makes Nicolas Feuillatte is doing good things with this brand. This Réserve Particulière is elegantly made, with fine white fruit flavors along with a touch of toast. It is light, poised, and makes a good apéritif. **88** *—R.V. (12/1/2005)*

Nicolas Feuillatte NV Rosé Premier Cru Brut (Champagne) $35. **87** *(12/15/2000)*

Nicolas Feuillatte NV Brut Blanc de Blancs Premier Cru (Champagne) $35. **85** *—K.F. (12/15/2002)*

Nicolas Feuillatte 1997 Cuvée Palmes D'Or Rosé Brut (Champagne) $175. This is a rather soft style, attractive but without the acidity. It is clean and easy to drink. Flavors of white currants, of lychees, and of exotic fruits fill the wine out and give a final feeling of ripeness. **86** *—R.V. (12/1/2004)*

NICOLAS JOLY

Nicolas Joly 2002 Clos de la Bergerie (Savennières-Roche-Aux-Moines) $45. **88** *—J.C. (11/15/2005)*

Nicolas Joly 2002 Coulée de Serrant (Savennières-Coulée de Serrant) $79. **87** *—J.C. (11/15/2005)*

NICOLAS POTEL

Nicolas Potel 2003 (Savigny-lès-Beaune) $32. **86** *—J.C. (11/15/2005)*

Nicolas Potel 2001 (Nuits-St.-Georges) $38. **89** *—J.C. (10/1/2003)*

Nicolas Potel 2000 (Volnay) $30. **87** *—C.S. (11/1/2002)*

Nicolas Potel 2001 Maison Dieu Vieilles Vignes Pinot Noir (Bourgogne) $18. **83** *—J.C. (10/1/2003)*

Nicolas Potel 2003 Vieilles Vignes (Volnay) $40. Fairly big and tannic, with dusty, dried-herb aromatics and brooding flavors of black cherries and spice. Finishes long and supple, so hold another few years to experience the considerable upside of this currently chunky offering. **89** *—J.C. (11/15/2005)*

Nicolas Potel 2001 Vieilles Vignes (Côte de Nuits-Villages) $18. **86** *—J.C. (10/1/2003)*

NOËL VERSET

Noël Verset 1998 Syrah (Cornas) $45. **90** *(11/1/2001)*

OGIER

Ogier 2000 Les Allegories D'Antoine (Crozes-Hermitage) $28. Light, crisp and lemony, with notes of smoke, sour cherries and tobacco. Drink up. **83** *—J.C. (11/15/2005)*

OLIVIER LEFLAIVE

Olivier Leflaive 2001 (Meursault) $40. **86** *—J.C. (10/1/2003)*

Olivier Leflaive 2001 (Puligny-Montrachet) $42. **90** *—J.C. (10/1/2003)*

Olivier Leflaive 1998 (Puligny-Montrachet) $39. **88** *(6/1/2001)*

Olivier Leflaive 1998 Charmes Premier Cru (Meursault) $50. **90** *(6/1/2001)*

Olivier Leflaive 2003 Clos St. Marc Premier Cru (Chassagne-Montrachet) $58. A sophisticated, elegant wine, which shows white fruit, subtle wood flavors and a structure that promises good aging. It has acidity, and some fresh apples at this young age. The whole is much greater than the sum of its parts. **93** *—R.V. (9/1/2005)*

Olivier Leflaive 2001 Les Sétilles Chardonnay (Bourgogne) $15. **85** *—J.C. (10/1/2003)*

Olivier Leflaive 2001 Premier Cru (Rully) $20. **86** *—J.C. (10/1/2003)*

Olivier Leflaive 2003 Cuvée Margot Pinot Noir (Bourgogne) $20. **88** *—J.C. (11/15/2005)*

OLIVIER RAVIER

Olivier Ravier 2002 Domaine des Sables D'Or (Beaujolais) $9. **84** *—J.C. (11/15/2003)*

PANNIER

Pannier NV Brut Rosé (Champagne) $40. An attractive, salmon-pink-colored wine, which has flavors of ripe strawberries and a touch of caramel. The acidity is relatively light, and the impression is of a ripe wine. **87** *—R.V. (12/1/2005)*

Pannier NV Brut Tradition (Champagne) $NA. A soft, easy style of Champagne, with some earthy fruit flavors as well as lightness. This is a gentle, apéritif style with some fresh acidity and a touch of tannin to finish. **86** *—R.V. (12/1/2005)*

PASCAL & NICOLAS REVERDY

Pascal & Nicolas Reverdy 2000 (Sancerre) $24. 90 Editors' Choice *(8/1/2002)*

PASCAL JOLIVET

Pascal Jolivet 1998 (Sancerre) $19. 83 *—M.S. (7/1/2000)*

Pascal Jolivet 2003 (Sancerre) $20. Exceedingly pungent, with piercing aromas of cat pee and prickly pear cactus. Comes across a touch acidic and lean, with flavors of dry tangerine peel and green apple. Yet with all that noted it still seems pulpy and fat on the palate. Not bad but not great. **85** *(7/1/2005)*

Pascal Jolivet 2000 (Sancerre) $19. 86 *(8/1/2002)*

Pascal Jolivet 2000 Château du Nozay (Sancerre) $21. 86 *(8/1/2002)*

Pascal Jolivet 2000 Clos du Roy (Sancerre) $22. 86 *(8/1/2002)*

Pascal Jolivet 2003 Le Château du Nozay (Sancerre) $26. Lively, full, tangy and precise. Our tasting panel was unanimous in its support for this minerally, citrusy wine; we very much liked its fresh green apple, grapefruit, and white peach flavors, and we're sure it would be an excellent food wine, especially with fish. **89** *(7/1/2005)*

Pascal Jolivet 2000 Les Caillottes (Sancerre) $22. 90 Editors' Choice *(8/1/2002)*

PATRIARCHE PÈRE & FILS

Patriarche Père & Fils 2003 Chardonnay (Vin de Pays d'Oc) $8. Has buttery, baked-apple aromas, but lacks that same sense of richness on the palate, with tart apple and lemon flavors following. Citrusy and fresh on the finish. **83** *—J.C. (11/15/2005)*

Patriarche Père & Fils 2002 (Chablis) $21. 86 *—J.C. (11/15/2005)*

Patriarche Père & Fils 2003 (Gevrey-Chambertin) $39. 85 *—J.C. (11/15/2005)*

Patriarche Père & Fils 2003 (Beaujolais-Villages) $10. 82 *—J.C. (11/15/2005)*

PAUL BLANCK

Paul Blanck 2001 Pinot Blanc (Alsace) $11. 90 Best Buy *—C.S. (11/15/2002)*

Paul Blanck 2001 Grand Cru Schlossberg Riesling (Alsace) $33. This is one super-rich wine, with some light toast character and already a touch of petrol. It has freshness and spice, plus intense acidity and elegance. **92** *—R.V. (11/1/2005)*

Paul Blanck 2002 Patergarten Riesling (Alsace) $23. Situated in the floor of the Kaysersberg valley, this vineyard produces great ripe Rieslings. The 2002 from the Blanck family is a deliciously rich wine, with exotic fruits, flavors of star fruit and green plums, along with fine aromatic spices. This will be a short-term wine: drink over the next five years. **88** *—R.V. (5/1/2005)*

PAUL GOERG

Paul Goerg NV Brut Rosé (Champagne) $30. 85 *—P.G. (12/15/2002)*

PAUL JABOULET AÎNÉ

Paul Jaboulet Aîné 1999 Pierre Aiguille (Gigondas) $28. 89 *—M.S. (2/1/2003)*

Paul Jaboulet Aîné 1999 Parallèle 45 Rhône Red Blend (Côtes-du-Rhône) $9. 85 *—R.V. (6/1/2002)*

Paul Jaboulet Aîné 1996 Domaine de Thalabert (Crozes-Hermitage) $25. 90 *—M.S. (10/1/1999)*

Paul Jaboulet Aîné 1999 La Chapelle (Hermitage) $131. 94 *—R.V. (6/1/2002)*

Paul Jaboulet Aîné 1996 La Chapelle (Hermitage) $80. 93 *—M.S. (10/1/1999)*

Paul Jaboulet Aîné 2003 Le Paradou Rhône Red Blend (Beaumes-de-Venise) $16. Not that effusive on the nose, but the flavors sing on the palate, revealing black cherry, earth, and coffee flavors carried along on a supple, velvety mouthfeel. The fruit really comes through on the finish. Drink now, or anytime before 2012. **88** *—J.C. (2/1/2005)*

Paul Jaboulet Aîné 1998 Les Traverses Rhône Red Blend (Côtes-du-Ventoux) $9. 88 Best Buy *—M.S. (11/1/2000)*

Paul Jaboulet Aîné 1998 Domaine Raymond Roure Rhône White Blend (Crozes-Hermitage) $33. 90 *—R.V. (6/1/2002)*

Paul Jaboulet Aîné 2000 Les Savagères Rhône White Blend (Saint-Péray) $15. 86 *—R.V. (6/1/2002)*

Paul Jaboulet Aîné 2001 Domaine de Thalabert (Crozes-Hermitage) $30. Seems a little disjointed at this stage of its development, with components that don't seem completely integrated: caramel, cherries, pepper, and dusty earth notes. Supple mouthfeel bodes well, and if the pieces here come together, this rating may look stingy five years from now. **85** —*J.C. (2/1/2005)*

Paul Jaboulet Aîné 1999 Domaine de Thalabert (Crozes-Hermitage) $25. 89 —*R.V. (6/1/2002)*

Paul Jaboulet Aîné 1999 Les Jalets (Crozes-Hermitage) $14. 86 *(10/1/2001)*

PAUL JACQUESON

Paul Jacqueson 2003 (Rully) $30. A bit toasty and obviously woody, but underneath is adequate apple and melon fruit to support the oaking. The buttered popcorn notes are disconcertingly New World-ish, delivering broad, mouthfilling flavors that nevertheless finish clean and fresh. **86** —*J.C. (11/15/2005)*

PERRIER JOUËT

Perrier Jouët NV Blason Rosé (Champagne) $48. 87 —*R.V. (12/15/2003)*

Perrier Jouët 1997 Fleur de Champagne Rosé Brut (Champagne) $140. 91 —*R.V. (12/15/2003)*

Perrier Jouët 1996 Fleur de Champagne Brut (Champagne) $120. The famous Belle Epoque bottle design is based on a 1902 bottle of Emile Gallé. Today's blend of this prestige cuvée is a fine balance between Chardonnay and Pinot Noir, crisp and fresh in a ripe, mature apéritif style. It is lively but complex, showing some toasty flavors to complement the rich, ripe green fruit tastes. Great balance and elegance. **93** —*R.V. (12/1/2004)*

Perrier Jouët 1995 Fleur de Champagne Brut (Champagne) $120. 92 *(12/15/2001)*

Perrier Jouët 1993 Fleur de Champagne Blanc de Blancs Brut (Champagne) $125. 93 *(12/15/2001)*

Perrier Jouët NV Grand Brut (Champagne) $40. Frothy, vigorous, and youthful, with chalky-minerally nuances to its vibrant green apple and lime flavors. Finishes a bit softer than expected, but the chalky notes persist, giving a strong identity to the wine. **88** —*J.C. (12/1/2004)*

PERRIN & FILS

Perrin & Fils 2003 L'Andéol Rasteau (Côtes-du-Rhône Villages) $23. Impressively sized and full-bodied, but doesn't show the flesh or richness needed to rate higher. Roasted fruit, leather, and chocolate flavors finish on a slightly alcoholic note. Hold 2–3 years and hope it comes around. **85** —*J.C. (11/15/2005)*

Perrin & Fils 2003 Les Chrisitins (Vacqueyras) $19. Rather firmly tannic, but also packed with superripe fruit—it will be a close contest to see which lasts longest. Chocolate, brandied fruit cake and plums finish tough and chewy. Try it now with rare meats to help tame the tannins, or cross your fingers and wait. **88** —*J.C. (11/15/2005)*

Perrin & Fils 2000 Réserve Rhône Red Blend (Côtes-du-Rhône) $11. 87 —*M.S. (9/1/2003)*

Perrin & Fils 2000 Perrin L'Andéol Rasteau Rhône Red Blend (Côtes-du-Rhône) $16. 91 Editors' Choice —*M.S. (9/1/2003)*

Perrin & Fils 2000 Vinsobres Rhône Red Blend (Côtes-du-Rhône) $16. 84 —*M.S. (9/1/2003)*

Perrin & Fils 2002 Réserve Rhône White Blend (Côtes-du-Rhône) $10. 83 —*J.C. (3/1/2004)*

Perrin & Fils 2003 Les Cornuds Vinsobres Rhône Red Blend (Côtes-du-Rhône Villages) $23. The Perrin négociant business is now bottling a number of individual cuvées from the Côtes-du-Rhône. This one, a 50-50 blend of Syrah and Grenache, features plum and cherry fruit, with complex earth, spice and leather notes. Firmly structured, look for it to be at its peak from 2008–2012. **88** —*J.C. (11/15/2005)*

PHILIPPE GONET

Philippe Gonet NV Le Mesnil Sur Oger Réserve Brut (Champagne) $33. Toasty aromas follow through to a soft, creamy wine that has light acidity, ripeness and full Chardonnay flavors. This is a delicious, full-bodied wine, produced by a small family-owned firm in Le Mesnil Sur Oger. **90** —*R.V. (12/1/2005)*

Philippe Gonet NV Roy Soleil Grand Cru Blanc de Blancs (Champagne) $41. No doubt Le Roi Soleil (Louis XIV, the Sun King) would have downed plenty of Champagne given half a chance, so I'm surprised this is the first wine I have come across named after one of history's great hedonists. This is actually quite a delicate wine, crisp and fresh, with a deliciously clean streak of acidity. **91** —*R.V. (12/1/2005)*

PHILIPPONNAT

Philipponnat 1997 Réserve Brut (Champagne) $63. A blend of 70% Pinot Noir and 30% Chardonnay, this is a true food Champagne. "Our objective was to show how powerful Pinot Noir can get in our wines," says Charles Philipponnat, and he is right. It is rich but dry, concentrated, slightly spicy, with weight and intensity without losing freshness from the acidity. **93** —*R.V. (12/1/2005)*

Philipponnat NV Royale Réserve Brut (Champagne) $40. The dry style of Philipponnat, with its Pinot Noir dominance, demands bottle aging, which the bottle tasted had. It has good structure, and intense grapefruit and orange peel flavors. A finely made wine, which is also a good value. **91** —*R.V. (12/1/2005)*

PIERRE BESINET

Pierre Besinet 2003 Le Bosc Chardonnay-Sauvignon (Vin de Pays d'Oc) $NA. This wine is certainly fresh, but it has an artificial boiled sweets and banana flavor which gives a tartness. **80** —*R.V. (12/1/2004)*

Pierre Besinet 2003 Le Bosc Rosé Blend (Vin de Pays d'Oc) $NA. A blend of Cabernet Franc and Syrah, here is a delicious, soft wine which finishes with a little sweetness. It lacks acidity but makes up for that by its attractive fruit. **86** —*R.V. (12/1/2004)*

PIERRE COURSODON

Pierre Coursodon 2000 Le Paradis Saint-Pierre (St.-Joseph) $25. 89 —*R.V. (6/1/2002)*

PIERRE FRICK

Pierre Frick 2001 Grand Cru Steinert Gewürztraminer (Alsace) $43. Aromas of intense spice leave little to the imagination. This has to be Gewürz, and it comes from the Grand Cru Steinert in Pfaffenheim. It's concentrated and rich flavors of lychees, pepper, and a touch of honey are also intense. **88** —*R.V. (4/1/2005)*

Pierre Frick 2002 Cuvée Precieuse Tokay Pinot Gris (Alsace) $NA. A fresh style of Pinot Gris, with aromas of toast and chestnuts and flavors of ripe, juicy fruit. There is some acidity, but this is still rich, with some pepper and softness at the end. **86** —*R.V. (4/1/2005)*

PIERRE GIMMONET ET FILS

Pierre Gimmonet et Fils 1995 Oenophile Extra Brut (Champagne) $45. 91 Editors' Choice —*R.V. (12/1/2002)*

PIERRE JEAN

Pierre Jean 2000 Cabernet Sauvignon (Vin de Pays de L'Aude) $7. 83 —*D.T. (2/1/2002)*

PIERRE SPARR

Pierre Sparr 1997 Dynastie Brut Crémant Champagne Blend (Alsace) $18. 88 Best Buy —*M.M. (12/15/2001)*

Pierre Sparr 1999 Mambourg Gewürztraminer (Alsace) $23. 88 —*M.S. (6/1/2003)*

Pierre Sparr 2001 Réserve Gewürztraminer (Alsace) $15. 89 —*M.S. (6/1/2003)*

Pierre Sparr 2003 Réserve Pinot Blanc (Alsace) $12. Begins with ultraripe scents of melon and honey, and doesn't change much from start to finish. It's a plump, fairly weighty offering, low in acid, that leaves the mouth coated with flavor. Simple but satisfying. **86** —*J.C. (2/1/2005)*

Pierre Sparr 2003 Pinot Gris (Alsace) $15. Pear, honey, and pineapple notes on the nose give way to more melony flavors on the palate. Mouthfeel is slightly oily, leaving behind the suggestion of quince and honey on the finish. Not complex, but mouthfilling and well balanced. **85** —*J.C. (2/1/2005)*

Pierre Sparr 2003 Réserve Pinot Gris (Alsace) $17. Adds an extra level of richness compared to Sparr's regular Pinot Gris, but the flavors are similar: poached pears and ripe melons tinged with honey and pineapple. A smooth, harmonious expression of Pinot Gris that won't set you back a fortune. **87** —*J.C. (2/1/2005)*

Pierre Sparr 2004 Réserve Pinot Gris (Alsace) $17. A medium-bodied, food-friendly version of Pinot Gris, without the high residual sugar levels of some. Still, it is off-dry, with apple, pear, and honey notes buttressed on the finish by fresh acidity and a hint of minerality. **86** —*J.C. (11/1/2005)*

Pierre Sparr 2003 Riesling (Alsace) $11. A soft, simple, and fresh wine, with light fruit and some good acidity. It has flavors of apples which leave a good clean aftertaste. **84** —*R.V. (5/1/2005)*

Pierre Sparr 2001 Altenbourg Riesling (Alsace) $25. This Kientzheim vineyard is surrounded by Grand Cru vineyards and gives attractively fruity wines. With its aromas of tropical fruits, this is quite an exotic wine, but has plenty of acidity to balance. There are great layers of structure, flavors of grapefruits and mangoes, and plenty of indication that this will age for 5 years or more. **89** —*R.V. (5/1/2005)*

Pierre Sparr 2000 Grand Cru Schoenenbourg Riesling (Alsace) $35. This wine shows finesse, quality, and at the same time power. There are fine flavors of mint and grapefruit, with long-lasting acidity. **90** —*R.V. (11/1/2005)*

Pierre Sparr 2001 Réserve Riesling (Alsace) $13. 85 —*M.S. (12/1/2003)*

Pierre Sparr 2003 Réserve Riesling (Alsace) $16. A full-bodied wine, with aromas of apples and pears. It's dry, lively, and fresh, with great crisp fruit, flavors of grapefruits, and long-lasting acidity. It needs two years to develop. **87** —*R.V. (5/1/2005)*

Pierre Sparr 1997 Brand Tokay Pinot Gris (Alsace) $25. 89 *(8/1/1999)*

Pierre Sparr 1997 Réserve Tokay Pinot Gris (Alsace) $13. 91 Best Buy *(8/1/1999)*

Pierre Sparr 2003 One White Blend (Alsace) $12. Despite the name, this is a blend of five of Alsace's white varieties: Riesling, Pinot Blanc, Gewürztraminer, Muscat, and Pinot Gris. The result is a simple sipper destined for the apéritif course or perhaps a casual picnic. Pear and melon flavors finish with a spicy, grapefruity edge. **84**—*J.C. (2/1/2005)*

PIPER-HEIDSIECK

Piper-Heidsieck 1998 Brut (Champagne) $65. Round and mildly yeasty, with vanilla, pear and toast all wrapped into a welcoming whole. The palate is full and complex, with additional vanilla coating crisp apple. This is a fuller, mouthfilling style of Champagne, one with a broad, classy finish. That said, vital acidity should ensure a full lifespan. **92 Cellar Selection** —*M.S. (12/31/2005)*

Piper-Heidsieck NV Brut (Champagne) $35. Toasty aromas leap from the glass in this deliciously mature wine. It is soft but still very dry, with acidity tamed by both fine, mature fruit and a creamy texture that sits well in the mouth. This is a very fine, tasty wine. **92 Editors' Choice** —*R.V. (12/1/2005)*

Piper-Heidsieck NV Brut Rosé (Reims) $44. 91 —*P.G. (12/15/2003)*

Piper-Heidsieck 1995 Brut Vintage (Champagne) $50. 87 *(12/15/2001)*

Piper-Heidsieck NV Cuvée Jean-Paul Gaultier (Champagne) $100. Perhaps this wine is the ultimate in Champagne packaging—a leather outer sleeve around the bottle designed by couturier Jean-Paul Gaultier. Does the wine justify the hype? If you like very mature tasting wine, yes, because this is all toast and not much fruit. But it does work, with good acidity to crispen it at the end. **90** —*R.V. (12/1/2004)*

Piper-Heidsieck NV Cuvée Rare Réserve Brut (Champagne) $120. This is a bone dry, deliciously mature Champagne. The fruit aromas and flavors are now submerged beneath a layer of toast. A very fine wine, packed in a beautiful bottle designed by Van Cleef and Arpels. **95** —*R.V. (12/1/2005)*

Piper-Heidsieck NV Extra Dry (Reims) $35. 89 —*P.G. (12/15/2003)*

Piper-Heidsieck 1990 Rare Cuvée Réserve Brut (Champagne) $70. 91 *(12/15/2001)*

Piper-Heidsieck NV Rosé Sauvage (Champagne) $45. This is Piper's style of making extra dry wines. Its pale raspberry color suggests a party wine, but to taste it is more raw than pretty, with high acids and light green flavors. It doesn't hang together, with the fruit struggling to get through the acidity. **83** —*R.V. (12/1/2004)*

POL ROGER

Pol Roger 1995 Brut (Champagne) $59. 89 —*P.G. (12/15/2002)*

Pol Roger NV Brut Réserve (Champagne) $33. 92 —*R.V. (12/15/2001)*

Pol Roger 1995 Cuvée Sir Winston Churchill Brut (Champagne) $194. 90 —*J.C. (12/15/2003)*

Pol Roger 1993 Cuvée Sir Winston Churchill Brut (Champagne) $166. 89 *(12/15/2002)*

Pol Roger 1996 Extra Cuvée de Réserve Rosé Brut Champagne Blend (Champagne) $70. An enticing onion pink color draws you into this lively, full bodied rosé, which just demands a bowl of strawberries or a pair of star-struck lovers. It is packed with fresh red fruits and balancing acidity, not too dry, with a fresh raspberry element which fleshes out the flavors. **90** —*R.V. (12/1/2004)*

Pol Roger 1996 Extra Cuvée de Réserve Blanc De Chardonnay Brut (Champagne) $84. Made from Pol Roger's Grand Cru vineyards in the Côtes des Blancs, this is a finely crafted wine, full of mineral Chardonnay flavors and yellow fruits beneath a pure, intense acidity. There are just hints of toastiness, but this is still a young wine, which will benefit from many years aging. **93** —*R.V. (12/1/2004)*

POMMERY

Pommery 1995 Brut (Champagne) $55. 90 Editors' Choice *(12/1/2000)*

Pommery NV Brut Apanage Champagne Blend (Champagne) $38. 90 —*P.G. (12/15/2002)*

Pommery NV Brut Rosé (Champagne) $60. Quite seductive, with clear widespread appeal. It offers vanilla and peach aromas that draw a smile, while the ripe citrus and apricot flavors are really exact and tasty. Finishes with clever spice notes. Explosive throughout. Will age nicely for several years. **91 Editors' Choice** —*M.S. (12/31/2005)*

Pommery NV Brut Royal (Champagne) $37. Pommery's main brand has curious new wood and caramel aromas that don't sit well with the very light, fragrant taste that is this house style. The top wines from Pommery are performing well today, but this still needs improvement. **84** —*R.V. (12/1/2005)*

Pommery 1995 Louise (Champagne) $120. If you want purity of fruit, this is the wine for you. With its relatively low dosage, there is no compromise with the rich, but elegant fruit, very much following the Pommery style. At this stage, the wine is very young, leaving it somewhat unbalanced. But at the end of another 5 years, this will be a great wine. At this stage, decant before serving. **90** —*R.V. (12/1/2004)*

Pommery 1989 Louise (Champagne) $NA. A very toasty wine, with maturity but without the balancing elegance. Somehow the fruit seems to have been sidelined by the toastiness and the wine doesn't quite hold together. Pommery is supposed to be back on form now, so more recent vintage releases of Louise should be less disappointing than this. **83** —*R.V. (12/1/2004)*

Pommery 1992 Louise Rosé (Champagne) $240. 92 *(12/15/2001)*

Pommery NV Pink Pop Champagne Blend (Champagne) $13/187 ml. A light, fruity rosé, filled with berry and citrus flavors and made for the trendy party crowd. Clean and fresh on the finish. **87** —*J.C. (12/1/2004)*

PONT D'AVIGNON

Pont d'Avignon 2003 Rhône Red Blend (Côtes-du-Rhône) $15. Blackberry, plum, and tar aromas and flavors provide plenty of interest in this silky-textured, medium-bodied blend of Syrah and Grenache. Turns a bit drying on the finish, but also picks up intriguing hints of chocolate, leather, berries, and spice. Drink now–2008. **87** *—J.C. (11/15/2005)*

POTEL-AVIRON

Potel-Aviron 2000 Côte du Py Vieilles Vignes (Morgon) $17. **86** *(11/15/2002)*

Potel-Aviron 2000 Vieilles Vignes (Fleurie) $17. **85** *—J.C. (11/15/2003)*

Potel-Aviron 2000 Vielles Vignes (Moulin-à-Vent) $17. **85** *—M.M. (11/15/2002)*

Potel-Aviron 2001 Vieilles Vignes (Côte de Brouilly) $15. **85** *—J.C. (11/15/2003)*

PREMIUS

Premius 1998 Bordeaux Blend (Bordeaux) $10. **86 Best Buy** *—J.C. (3/1/2001)*

PROSPER MAUFOUX

Prosper Maufoux 1998 (Puligny-Montrachet) $55. **88** *(7/1/2001)*

Prosper Maufoux 1999 Mont de Milieu Premier Cru (Chablis) $29. **89 Editors' Choice** *(7/1/2001)*

Prosper Maufoux 1998 (Clos Vougeot) $65. **90** *(7/1/2001)*

Prosper Maufoux 1998 Arvelets (Pommard) $45. **91 Cellar Selection** *(7/1/2001)*

Prosper Maufoux 1997 Beaumonts Premier Cru (Vosne-Romanée) $57. **90** *(7/1/2001)*

Prosper Maufoux 1998 (Sancerre) $18. **84** *(5/1/2000)*

RAYMOND BECK

Raymond Beck NV Cuvée Prestige (Clairette de Die) $12. **87** *—P.G. (12/15/2000)*

RAYMOND HENRIOT

Raymond Henriot NV Brut (Champagne) $28. Yeasty, chalky, and vinous, this young, assertive NV boasts apple and citrus flavors layered atop a chalky substrate. While it may be a little agressive for some drinkers, this is a bold mouthful of flavor at a bargain price. **88 Editors' Choice** *—J.C. (12/1/2004)*

RED BICYCLETTE

Red Bicyclette 2003 Chardonnay (Vin de Pays d'Oc) $12. A light, fresh Chardonnay with minimal barrel influence, the debut vintage of Red Bicyclette boasts ample pear and citrus flavors, a stony minerality and hints of roasted nuts. At its commonly offered retail price of $10, this would be a Best Buy. **85** *(12/1/2004)*

Red Bicyclette 2004 French Rosé (Vin de Pays d'Oc) $11. Floral and perfumey, with apple blossom and pear flavors that finish clean. Tastes a bit like a medium-bodied white; try with poultry or seafood. **84** *—J.C. (11/15/2005)*

RÉGNARD

Régnard 1999 (Mâcon-Lugny) $15. **82** *—D.T. (2/1/2002)*

Régnard 1999 Pinot Noir (Bourgogne) $15. **80** *—J.C. (10/1/2003)*

REIGNAC

Reignac 2001 Bordeaux Blend (Bordeaux Supérieur) $NA. Hints at weediness on the nose, with otherwise well-ripened cassis joining with notes of caramel and graham crackers. Rather earthy and tobacco-driven on the palate, finishing with soft, relatively modest tannins. Drink now--2015. **88** *—J.C. (6/6/2005)*

REMY-PANNIER

Remy-Pannier 2000 (Chinon) $9. **87** *—S.H. (9/12/2002)*

Remy-Pannier 2000 (Vouvray) $8. **85** *—S.H. (9/12/2002)*

Remy-Pannier 2000 (Sancerre) $13. **86** *—S.H. (9/12/2002)*

RENE GEOFFROY

Rene Geoffroy NV Premier Cru Cuvée Sélectionee Brut (Champagne) $42. **80** *—R.V. (12/1/2002)*

RENÉ MURÉ

René Muré 2001 Riesling (Alsace) $18. **87** *—R.V. (8/1/2003)*

René Muré 2000 Domaine du Clos St Landelin Grand Cru Vorbourg Riesling (Alsace) $42. **91 Editors' Choice** *—M.S. (12/1/2003)*

RENE ROSTAING

Rene Rostaing 1998 (Côte Rôtie) $55. **90** *(11/1/2001)*

RÉSERVE ST. MARTIN

Réserve St. Martin 2003 Chardonnay (Vin de Pays d'Oc) $8. Supple, soft fruit gives this wine a simple easy-drinking character. It's great for apéritifs, rich enough for food, and just plain enjoyable. **84 Best Buy** *—R.V. (12/1/2004)*

Réserve St. Martin 2003 Sauvignon Blanc (Vin de Pays d'Oc) $8. Fresh creamy fruit gives this wine immediate appeal. It has tropical flavors, a light touch of green and fresh, crisp acidity. Great summer drinking. **84 Best Buy** *—R.V. (12/1/2004)*

RICHARD BOURGEOIS

Richard Bourgeois 2003 (Sancerre) $20. Like a textbook Loire white, it's minerally and crisp, with aromas of stone fruits, citrus and pink grapefruit. Not the deepest wine going, but what's here is solid. Look for stony flavors of grapefruit and orange, with a short, simple finish. **85** *(7/1/2005)*

RIEFLÉ

Rieflé 1997 Côte de Rouffach Tokay Pinot Gris (Alsace) $19. **88** *—M.M. (11/1/2000)*

Rieflé 1996 Steinert Tokay Pinot Gris (Alsace) $30. **89** *—J.C. (11/1/2000)*

RIVEFORT DE FRANCE

Rivefort de France 1997 Viognier (Vin de Pays d'Oc) $10. **81** *—J.C. (10/1/1999)*

ROBERT GIRAUD

Robert Giraud 2000 Cepages Cabernet Sauvignon (Vin de Pays d'Oc) $7. **81** *—M.S. (9/1/2003)*

ROC DE CAMBES

Roc de Cambes 1996 Bordeaux Blend (Côtes de Bourg) $29. **90** *—M.S. (12/31/1999)*

ROPITEAU

Ropiteau 2000 Les Perrieres Premier Cru (Meursault) $49. **90** *(10/1/2002)*

Ropiteau 2000 Les Tillets (Meursault) $37. **88** *(10/1/2002)*

Ropiteau 2000 Meursault de Ropiteau (Meursault) $32. **85** *(10/1/2002)*

Ropiteau 2000 Premier Cru (Rully) $18. **86** *(10/1/2002)*

Ropiteau 2000 Pinot Noir (Chassagne-Montrachet) $18. **84** *(10/1/2002)*

ROUX PÈRE ET FILS

Roux Père et Fils 2002 Chardonnay (Corton-Charlemagne) $NA. This is a full wine, showing all the majesty of Corton-Charlemagne. It powers with ripe, sweet, intense almond flavors and lemon acidity. At this stage, it is still coming together, but give it 5–10 years. **91** *—R.V. (9/1/2004)*

RUINART

Ruinart NV Brut (Champagne) $48. **88** *(12/1/2003)*

Ruinart 1993 Dom Ruinart (Champagne) $130. **92 Cellar Selection** *(12/31/2003)*

Ruinart 1990 Dom Ruinart Rosé (Champagne) $NA. The palest of onion skin pink colors is certainly the freshest part of this mature wine. The flavors are full of mature toast and will certainly appeal to those who like their Champagnes with bottle age. With the fruit less prominent, it is left to the richness and great style of the wine to carry the day. **91** *—R.V. (12/1/2004)*

Ruinart 1993 R de Ruinart Brut (Champagne) $72. **82** *(12/15/1999)*

Ruinart NV Rosé Brut (Champagne) $83. **87** *(12/1/2003)*

Ruinart 1990 Dom Ruinart Blanc de Blancs Brut (Champagne) $130. **86** *—J.C. (12/15/2001)*

SAINT-HILAIRE

Saint-Hilaire NV (Blanquette de Limoux) $10. **86** *(11/15/1999)*

SALON

Salon 1995 Le Mesnil Blanc de Blancs Brut (Champagne) $225. A thorough classic, with soda and mineral on the nose along with pineapple, apple, and other white fruits. The flavor profile is as pure and ethereal as it comes, with luscious apple, melon, and citrus. Lively and persistent on the finish, with a touch of toast. Feels just right; has great purity; will age nicely for another decade. **97** *—M.S. (12/31/2005)*

Salon 1990 Le Mesnil Brut Champagne Blend (Champagne) $200. **91** *(12/15/2001)*

SAUVION

Sauvion 2003 Baronne du Cléray (Muscadet Sèvre et Maine) $NA. Good green fruits, with some ripe acidity. A little fat, but it has some good green flavours at the back. **86** *—R.V. (1/1/2004)*

Sauvion 2001 (Sancerre) $15. **83** *(8/1/2002)*

SCHRÖDER ET SCHYLER

Schröder et Schyler 2003 Signatures en Bordeaux Bordeaux White Blend (Bordeaux) $NA. A soft wine which maybe lacks acidity but makes up for it with its rich flavors of tropical fruits and a generous food-friendly character. Serve it like a white Burgundy, not too cold. **84** —*R.V. (6/1/2005)*

SEIGNEURS DE BERGERAC

Seigneurs de Bergerac 2002 White Blend (Bergerac Sec) $8. Slightly grassy on the nose, along with hints of lime and green bean. On the palate, it's light in body, offering only watery green bean flavors. **80** —*J.C. (12/1/2004)*

SERGE MATHIEU

Serge Mathieu NV Blanc de Noirs Cuvée Tradition Brut (Champagne) $30. **89** —*R.V. (12/1/2002)*

Serge Mathieu 1997 Millésime Brut (Champagne) $35. **88** —*R.V. (12/1/2002)*

SIEUR D'ARQUES

Sieur d'Arques 2001 Vichon Mediterranean Chardonnay (Vin de Pays d'Oc) $7. **85 Best Buy** —*R.V. (11/15/2002)*

Sieur d'Arques NV Toques et Clochers (Crémant de Limoux) $15. The locals in Limoux say they created the method of secondary fermentation of a wine in bottle even before the guys up in Champagne. Maybe, but this blend of Chardonnay, Chenin Blanc, and Mauzac is deliciously easy and fresh, and cheaper than any Champagne. Flavors of apples and cream dominate a fine celebratory apéritif wine, which comes from the top cooperative of the region. **86** —*R.V. (11/15/2005)*

SIMONNET-FEBVRE

Simonnet-Febvre 1999 (Bourgogne) $15. **85** —*P.G. (11/1/2002)*

TAITTINGER

Taittinger NV Brut La Francaise Champagne Blend (Champagne) $35. **91** —*P.G. (12/15/2002)*

Taittinger 1998 Brut Millésime (Reims) $56. **88** —*M.S. (12/15/2003)*

Taittinger 1995 Brut Millésime (Champagne) $56. **92** —*P.G. (12/1/2000)*

Taittinger 1995 Comptes de Champagne Blanc de Blancs (Champagne) $130. **90** —*P.G. (12/15/2002)*

Taittinger 1994 Comtes de Champagne Blanc de Blancs (Champagne) $170. **89** *(12/31/2000)*

Taittinger 1995 Comtes de Champagne Brut Rosé (Champagne) $204. **95** —*M.S. (12/15/2000)*

Taittinger 1993 Comtes de Champagne Rosé Brut (Champagne) $206. **95** —*P.G. (12/15/2001)*

Taittinger NV Prélude Grands Crus Brut (Champagne) $70. A blend made entirely from grand cru vineyards, this is a superbly ripe, full wine; a very different, richer one from the normally light Taittinger style. A great Champagne, impressive and worth aging. **94 Cellar Selection** —*R.V. (12/1/2005)*

Taittinger NV Prestige Rosé Brut Champagne Blend (Reims) $52. **88** —*P.G. (12/15/2003)*

Taittinger NV Prestige Rosé Brut (Champagne) $70. This deep rose-colored Champagne is full-bodied with ripe, fresh fruit flavors. There is acidity but with the very fruity character of this wine, it is one which can be drunk relatively young and fresh. **89** —*R.V. (12/1/2005)*

TERRES NOIRES

Terres Noires 2003 Chardonnay (Vin de Pays d'Oc) $NA. Full-bodied flavors of tropical fruits give this wine richness and ripeness. It is simple, straightforward with immediately attractive depth of flavor. No complexity here. **83** —*R.V. (12/1/2004)*

THIERRY & GUY

Thierry & Guy 2003 Fat Bastard Chardonnay (Vin de Pays d'Oc) $11. Despite pleasant aromas of apple tinged with cinnamon, vanilla, and honey, the palate is hard, with grapefruit and sour apple flavors. **83** —*J.C. (11/15/2005)*

Thierry & Guy 2000 Fat Bastard Shiraz (Vin de Pays d'Oc) $10. **83** *(10/1/2001)*

TOQUES ET CLOCHERS

Toques et Clochers 2003 Clocher D'Ajac Réserve Jean-Pierre Bourret Vigneron (Limoux) $33. Slathered with spicy oak, sweet caramel, and blatant buttery notes, which largely overwhelm the modest apple and citrus fruit. If you like heavy oaking, you'll like this more than we did. **83** —*J.C. (11/15/2005)*

Toques et Clochers 2003 Red Blend (Limoux) $15. Half Merlot, with the balance a blend of 35% Syrah and 15% Grenache, this wine yields slightly baked fruit aromas, then delivers plenty of dried cherry and chocolate flavors. Shows good texture and length on the finish, so this large producer may be on to something special if they could just freshen up the aromatics. **86** —*J.C. (11/15/2005)*

TORTOISE CREEK

Tortoise Creek 2004 Chardonnay (Vin de Pays d'Oc) $9. A lightweight Chardonnay, with scents of apple, earth and flinty minerality.

Flavors run along the same lines, picking up riper pear notes before finishing with hints of quince. **84** *—J.C. (11/15/2005)*

Tortoise Creek 2004 Chardonnay-Viognier (Vin de Pays d'Oc) $8. Broad and mouthfilling, with apple, melon, and mineral flavors that fan out nicely across the palate. A nicely balanced table wine that could easily partner with fish or poultry. **85 Best Buy** *—J.C. (11/15/2005)*

Tortoise Creek 2003 Merlot (Vin de Pays d'Oc) $8. Medium-weight, with just enough supple tannins to provide a modicum of structure, this soft, easygoing Merlot boasts plummy fruit and notes of coffee and brown sugar. Finishes with hints of dried herbs and tea leaves. **86 Best Buy** *—J.C. (12/1/2004)*

Tortoise Creek 2003 Sauvignon Blanc (Vin de Pays d'Oc) $8. Ripe- and fresh-smelling—peach-like, with overtones of pink grapefruit. Plump and slightly viscous in the mouth, offering pink grapefruit and melon flavors. A bit low in acid, likely a result of the tremendously hot vintage, but still tasty. **84 Best Buy** *—J.C. (12/1/2004)*

TRIENNES

Triennes 1996 Syrah (Vin de Pays Var) $15. **89** *(11/15/1999)*

TRIMBACH

Trimbach 2000 Gewürztraminer (Alsace) $18. **86** *(1/1/2004)*

Trimbach 1994 Sélection de Grains Nobles Gewürztraminer (Alsace) $130. **92** *(1/1/2004)*

Trimbach 2001 Pinot Blanc (Alsace) $11. **85** *—R.V. (11/15/2003)*

Trimbach 2000 Réserve Pinot Gris (Alsace) $18. **87** *(1/1/2004)*

Trimbach 1996 Réserve Personnelle Pinot Gris (Alsace) $30. **87** *(8/1/1999)*

Trimbach 2000 Riesling (Alsace) $18. Two Rieslings produced by Trimbach—Clos Sainte-Hune and Cuvée Frédéric-Emile—are among the greatest in Alsace. But this much less expensive, dry wine has some reflected glory in its pure flavors of white fruits, of mineral and lemon. It will age well over five years or more. **86** *(1/1/2004)*

Trimbach 1998 Cuvée Frédéric Emile Riesling (Alsace) $40. **90** *(1/1/2004)*

Trimbach 1997 Cuvée Frédéric Emile Riesling (Alsace) $35. **90** *—S.H. (1/1/2002)*

VAL D'ORBIEU

Val d'Orbieu 2001 Réserve St. Martin Cabernet Sauvignon (Languedoc) $8. **82** *—M.S. (9/1/2003)*

Val d'Orbieu 2001 Réserve St. Martin Merlot (Languedoc) $8. **83** *—M.S. (9/1/2003)*

Val d'Orbieu 2001 Les Deux Rives Rouge (Corbières) $8. **84** *—M.S. (9/1/2003)*

Val d'Orbieu 2001 Réserve St. Martin Syrah (Languedoc) $8. **82** *—M.S. (9/1/2003)*

Val d'Orbieu 2001 Les Deux Rives Blanc (Corbières) $8. **84** *—M.S. (9/1/2003)*

VERBAU

Verbau 2001 Gewürztraminer (Alsace) $15. A year ago, this was much better (rated 87 points). Now, it's fading, blending slightly sweet lychee fruit with apples and pears. Low acid and flabby on the finish. **83** *—J.C. (4/1/2005)*

VEUVE CLICQUOT PONSARDIN

Veuve Clicquot Ponsardin 1999 Brut (Champagne) $60. The vintage wines from Clicquot are consistently richer and fuller than either the nonvintage or La Grande Dame. Toast and custard scents, followed by youthful notes of apple and citrus. Long, even a bit tannic-feeling, on the finish. Arrives this December, but the price was not available at press time. **89** *(12/1/2005)*

Veuve Clicquot Ponsardin NV Brut (Champagne) $50. The famous yellow label wine. This bottling contains mostly 2001-vintage base wine, and offers a round mouthfeel balanced by crisp acids and flavors of apple and citrus. **87** *(12/1/2005)*

Veuve Clicquot Ponsardin 1985 Brut Rosé (Champagne) $250. Tasted from a magnum disgorged in '97, this provides ample evidence that '85 was a great year for Clicquot. Toasty, but seems less evolved than the '85 Brut, with a deep copper color, meaty, savory aromas, berry flavors and a full, creamy texture. Long on the finish. It's made from the same base as the '85 Brut, but with 14.5% red from Bouzy added. **93** *(12/1/2005)*

Veuve Clicquot Ponsardin NV Demi-Sec Champagne Blend (Champagne) $50. One of the better sweeter-styled Champagnes, this has a degree of elegance that many do not. Toast and spice notes join honeyed apple and pear flavors that persist a long time on the finish. **87** *—J.C. (12/1/2004)*

Veuve Clicquot Ponsardin 1990 La Grande Dame Brut (Champagne) $135. **92** *—M.S. (12/1/1999)*

Veuve Clicquot Ponsardin 1996 La Grande Dame (Champagne) $150. In five years, this rating may look conservative, as this wine seems to have the building blocks upon which to age well. Right now, it's tight and citrusy, with some riper pear notes and a creamy midpalate. Expect this to develop richer toast and nut nuances, and for the grapefruity finish to soften and become more harmonious. **91 Cellar Selection** *—J.C. (12/1/2004)*

Veuve Clicquot Ponsardin 1989 La Grande Dame Brut (Champagne) $NA. The richest and ripest of the 1988–1990 trilogy, with notes of brioche and berry flavors. Round and full in the mouth, but without the same degree of elegance exhibited by the other two years. **90** *(12/1/2005)*

Veuve Clicquot Ponsardin 1995 La Grande Dame Brut Rosé (Champagne) $200. Like the regular Grande Dame, the aim here is finesse. It's softer and more elegant than Clicquot's vintage rosé, with delicate hints of cherry, toast, mushroom, and citrus. Long, tight, and tannic on the finish, this wine is worth cellaring. **92** *(12/1/2005)*

Veuve Clicquot Ponsardin 1995 Réserve Brut (Champagne) $68. 88 *(12/15/2001)*

Veuve Clicquot Ponsardin 1998 Rosé Réserve Brut (Champagne) $75. A fine Champagne, and already very easy to drink. Toast, milk chocolate, and caramel notes blend with flavors of ripe apples and berries, while a citrusy backbone keeps it focused. The creamy mouthfel and long, lipsmacking finish invite you back for another sip. **91** *—J.C. (12/1/2004)*

Veuve Clicquot Ponsardin 1995 Rosé Réserve Brut (Champagne) $80. 90 *(12/15/2001)*

Veuve Clicquot Ponsardin 1998 Vintage Réserve Brut (Champagne) $75. Just lightly toasty, with hints of green apple and lime also appearing on the nose. Vividly fresh fruit on the palate, with crisp acidity to give it bite on the finish. Tighter-knit and seemingly drier than the nonvintage stuff from Clicquot, this could use a little time in the cellar to plump up and gain richness. Try in 2008. **90** *—J.C. (12/1/2004)*

VEUVE DU VERNAY

Veuve du Vernay NV Blanc de Blancs Brut (France) $10. Apple and hay aromas get it going, followed by spicy, slightly cinnamon-tinged apple flavors. Finishes with toast and seems solid on the tongue. Nothing outrageous or offputting; right down the center as sparklers go. **85 Best Buy** *—M.S. (12/31/2005)*

VICHON

Vichon 1997 Mediterranean Cabernet Sauvignon (Vin de Pays d'Oc) $10. 83 *—S.H. (7/1/2000)*

Vichon 1997 Mediterranean Merlot (Vin de Pays d'Oc) $10. 81 *—S.H. (7/1/2000)*

VIEUX CHÂTEAU GAUBERT

Vieux Château Gaubert 2002 Bordeaux White Blend (Graves) $25. Lovely acidity dominates this wine, the top white wine from Dominique Haverlan's Vieux Château Gaubert. It is fresh and crisp, with wood underlying attractive apples and cream flavors. A fresh and lively, but also serious, wine. **89** *—R.V. (6/1/2005)*

VIEUX CHÂTEAU NÉGRIT

Vieux Château Négrit 1997 Bordeaux Blend (Montagne-Saint-Emilion) $15. 83 *—J.C. (3/1/2001)*

VIGNERONS DE BUZET

Vignerons de Buzet 2004 Le Lys Bordeaux Blend (Buzet) $NA. A simple, soft red with flavors of red berries and light tannins. This is a easy wine, which can be served slightly chilled, as well as working well with light meat dishes. **85** *—R.V. (9/1/2005)*

VIGNOBLES DE FRANCE

Vignobles de France 2000 Cabernet Sauvignon (Vin de Pays d'Oc) $6. 80 *—S.H. (7/1/2001)*

Vignobles de France 2000 Merlot (Vin de Pays d'Oc) $6. 82 *—S.H. (7/1/2001)*

Vignobles de France 2000 Sauvignon Blanc (Entre-Deux-Mers) $7. 83 *—S.H. (7/1/2001)*

VIGNOBLES JEAN & BERNARD DAURÉ

Vignobles Jean & Bernard Dauré 2000 Les Clos de Paulilles Rouge (Collioure) $20. 84 *—M.S. (9/1/2003)*

VILLA SYMPOSIA

Villa Symposia 2003 La Petite Sieste Rosé Blend (Coteaux du Languedoc) $12. A pale, salmon pink-colored wine, with herbal flavors and a fresh touch of acidity. This is an intensely flavored blend of Cinsault and Grenache, with pepper and rich fruit. **87 Best Buy** *—R.V. (12/1/2004)*

VINCENT DELAPORTE

Vincent Delaporte 2003 Chavignol (Sancerre) $26. Talcum powder, orange peel, and a bit of fresh-cut grass make for a pleasant bouquet. Quite forward and fully charged on the palate; there's melon, apple, and lemon as well as some softer peach flavors. Good and lively. **89** *(7/1/2005)*

VRANKEN

Vranken NV Cuvée de L'An 2000 Brut NV (Champagne) $60. 90 *(12/15/1999)*

Vranken 1995 Demoiselle Cuvée 21 (Champagne) $80. 86 *—P.G. (12/15/2003)*

Vranken NV Demoiselle E.O. Tete de Cuvée Brut (Champagne) $35. Light in body, but flavorful, with ginger and soy aromas yielding to mixed citrus and berry fruits and dark, meaty notes in the mouth. Crisp and vibrant on the finish. **87** *—J.C. (12/1/2004)*

Vranken NV Demoiselle Premier Choix de Cuvées Brut (Champagne) $30. 88 *—P.G. (12/15/2002)*

Vranken NV Demoiselle Rose Brut (Champagne) $38. 86 *—P.G. (12/15/2002)*

Vranken 1994 Demoiselle Tete de Cuvée (Champagne) $45. 87 *(12/15/1999)*

Vranken 1994 Demoiselle Tete de Cuvée Grand Réserve Brut (Champagne) $30. 85 *—P.G. (12/15/2002)*

Vranken NV La Demoiselle Brut Rosé (Champagne) $43. 86 *—P.G. (12/15/2003)*

Vranken NV La Demoiselle Grande Cuvée Brut Rosé (Champagne) $47. Dry and spicy, with aromatic notes of spiced ham and dried fruit. Berry and peach flavors are solid and fresh, and there's just enough broadness on the finish. Shows a modicum of complexity on a forward, easy foundation. **89** *—M.S. (12/15/2005)*

Vranken NV Tete de Cuvée Tradition Grande Réserve (Champagne) $22. 88 Editors' Choice *—P.G. (12/15/2003)*

WILLIAM FÈVRE

William Fèvre 1998 Valmur Grand Cru (Chablis) $56. 94 *—P.G. (12/31/2001)*

YVES CUILLERON

Yves Cuilleron 2003 Cuvée Saint-Pierre Rhône White Blend (Saint-Joseph) $44. Cuilleron's use of wood is subtle, leaving just a hint of caramel on this smooth, opulent wine. It is rich, fat, and full-bodied, with flavors more of apricots and white fruits. There's a light touch of acidity, but spices and ripe fruits dominate. **89** *—R.V. (2/1/2005)*

Yves Cuilleron 2003 Lyseras Rhône White Blend (Saint-Joseph) $36. An earthy wine, which has flavors of walnuts and spice, with a hint of ripe fruits, but more of herbs. At this stage, the wine hasn't yet struck a balance between the wood and other flavors. **87** *—R.V. (2/1/2005)*

Yves Cuilleron 2002 L'Amarybelle (Saint-Joseph) $38. The exuberance of this wine, full of ripe black fruits with great acidity, smoky wood and pure flavors, pushes Cuilleron's wines up to a new level. This is a solid, tannic wine which at the same time has vibrancy and great fruit. **92** *—R.V. (2/1/2005)*

Yves Cuilleron 2002 Les Serines (Saint-Joseph) $58. A serious style, big with tannins and dry fruit, this is still packed with perfumed Syrah flavors. It has a dark, brooding structure, with acidity and pure fruits. This is the pair to the more exuberant L'Amarybelle. **90** *—R.V. (2/1/2005)*

Yves Cuilleron 2002 Ayguets (Condrieu) $80. Condrieu also comes in a rarer, sweet style, and here it is, in a wine that is both opulent and exotic. This cuvée de prestige is sweet, certainly, but it has layers of dry botrytis which give it balance. There's also acidity to give the wine a final lift. **90** *—R.V. (2/1/2005)*

Yves Cuilleron 2003 Les Chaillets (Condrieu) $85. This is Cuilleron's top Condrieu, a voluptuous style of wine which is spiced with new wood and packed with flavors of honey, of treacle, and white peaches. There is acidity, but it only plays a walk-on part in this big, fat wine. **90** *—R.V. (2/1/2005)*

YVON MAU

Yvon Mau 2002 Yvecourt Bordeaux Blend (Médoc) $15. Quite minty and herbal, but balanced somewhat by cherry, blackberry, and vanilla flavors. A medium-weight quaffer with a fresh, cinnamon note to the finish. **84** *—J.C. (6/1/2005)*

Yvon Mau 2004 Yvecourt Bordeaux White Blend (Bordeaux) $10. This 100% Sauvignon Blanc is a fresh, delicious summer wine. It is light and clean, with flavors of mango and citrus and a flowery feel. Acidity gives it a great lift to the finish. **85** *—R.V. (6/1/2005)*

Yvon Mau 2004 Premius Sauvignon Blanc (Bordeaux) $10. Yvon Mau's branded white Bordeaux is a soft, full-bodied wine, with great citrus flavors. It has a good grassy character, freshness, and a long, crisp acidic finish. **85 Best Buy** *—R.V. (6/1/2005)*

ZOÉMIE DE SOUSA

Zoémie De Sousa NV Brut Précieuse Grand Cru (Champagne) $NA. Zoémie De Sousa is a négociant brand created by Erick de Sousa in 2004 to satisfy world demand for his wines. A 100% Chardonnay from the Côte des Blancs, this deliciously creamy Champagne has lightness, freshness and great flavors of crisp apples and grapefruit. A bonus with De Sousa Champagnes is the disgorgement date indication—the older, the better. **92** *—R.V. (12/1/2005)*

Germany

German wine labels can be intimidating: long foreign words and ornate gothic script are enough to make many consumers head for a different section of the wine shop. But for the initiated—and you'll qualify after reading this quick primer—German wine labels are among the most descriptive out there.

As on any wine label, you'll find the name of the producer, the vintage, the region, and sometimes the name of the grape.

Label on a bottle of Zimmermann-Graeff.

In addition to the grape-growing region (see below), most labels will show the names of the town and the vineyard in large type, such as Graacher Himmelreich (the town of Graach, Himmelreich vineyard). In much smaller type will be the terms Qualitätswein bestimmter Anbaugebiete (often just Qualitätswein, or QbA), indicating a "quality wine," or Qualitätswein mit Prädikat (QmP), denoting a quality wine picked at designated minimum ripeness levels that vary by grape variety and growing region. These ripeness levels will be indicated on the label as follows:

Kabinett The least ripe of the prädikat levels, and typically the lightest of a grower's offerings. With their low alcohol levels and touch of sweetness, these wines make ideal picnic quaffs and mouth-watering apéritifs. Most often consumed in their youth, they can last for ten years or more.

Spätlese Literally, "late picked." These grapes are generally only late-picked with respect to those grapes that go into Kabinett or QbA wines. If vinified dry (an increasingly popular style), they can still seem less than optimally ripe. Traditionally made, with some residual sugar left in, they are extremely food friendly. Try them with anything from Asian food to baked ham and roast fowl. Most should be consumed before age twenty.

Auslese Made from "select" bunches of grapes left on the vine until they achieve high sugar readings, these wines often carry a hint or more of botrytis (see Glossary). While some are sweet enough to serve with simple fruit desserts, others are best sipped alone. With age, some of the sugar seems to melt away, yielding wines that can ably partner with roast pork or goose. Thirty-year-old auslesen can smell heavenly, but sometimes fall flat on the palate. Enjoy them on release for their luscious sweet fruit, or cellar for ten to twenty years.

Beerenauslese "Berry select" wines are harvested berry by berry, taking only botrytis-affected fruit. While auslesen are usually sweet, this level of ripeness elevates the wine to the dessert-only category. Hold up to fifty years.

Trockenbeerenauslese These "dried berry select" wines are made from individually harvested, shriveled grapes that have been heavily affected by botrytis. Profoundly sweet and honeyed, their over-the-top viscosity and sweetness can turn off some tasters, while others revel in the complex aromas and flavors.

Eiswein Made from frozen grapes that are at least equivalent in sugar levels to beerenauslese, but which produce wines with much racier levels of acidity. The intense sugars and acids enable these wines to easily endure for decades.

Aside from the ripeness levels denoted by the QmP

system, you can expect to see the terms trocken and halbtrocken on some labels (their use is optional). Trocken, or dry, may be used on wines with fewer than 9g/L residual sugar (less than 0.9 percent); halbtrocken (half-dry) refers to wines with between 9 and 18g/L. Given the allowable ranges, these wines may be truly dry or verging on sweet, depending on acid-sugar balance.

In an effort to simplify German labels, a few relatively new terms have cropped up that supplement, replace, or partially replace the traditional labeling system. Erstes Gewächs wines, or "first growths," come only from designated sites in the Rheingau. Classic wines must be "harmoniously dry" and must omit references to specific villages or vineyards. Selection wines bear a single-vineyard designation on the label and must be dry.

GERMAN WINE REGIONS

Most of the classic German wine regions are closely identified with river valleys, the slopes of which provide the proper exposure for ripening grapes at this northern latitude. Virtually all of Germany's best wines come from the Riesling grape, but there are several exceptions, like the fine Gewürztraminers from Fitz-Ritter in the Pfalz and Valckenberg in Rheinhessen and the exquisite Rieslaners and Scheurebes from Müller-Catoir in the Pfalz.

Mosel-Saar-Ruwer The coolest of the German growing regions, and home to Germany's crispest, raciest, and most delicate Rieslings. Green apples, floral notes, and citrus are all likely descriptors, but the best wines also display fine mineral notes that express their slate-driven terroirs.

Rheingau Steep slate slopes and slightly warmer temperatures than found in the Mosel-Saar-Ruwer yield powerful, sturdy wines, with ripe fruit flavors underscored by deep minerality.

Rheinhessen Source for much of Germany's production, quality here can vary from generic liebfraumilch to fine single-estate wines.

Nahe This small side valley is the only rival to the Mosel-Saar-Ruwer for elegance and finesse, with Rieslings that balance lightness of body with mineral-based tensile strength.

Pfalz One of Germany's warmest winegrowing regions, with a great diversity of soils, microclimates, and grape varieties. Dry styles, whether made from Riesling or other white grapes, are more common here, and show better balance than those from cooler regions. Spätburgunder (Pinot Noir) is also more successful here than elsewhere.

Wines from other German winegrowing regions, such as the Ahr, Baden, Franken, and Württemberg are infrequently seen in the United States.

A. CHRISTMANN

A. Christmann 1997 Konigsbacher Idig Spätburgunder (Pfalz) $50. 93 *(12/31/2001)*

A. Christmann 2002 Königsbacher Idig Spätlese Trocken Riesling (Pfalz) $48. Heavy and a bit dull, with muted fruit flavors and a short finish. A major disappointment from this normally reliable producer. **83** *—J.C. (11/1/2004)*

A. Christmann 2001 QbA Riesling (Pfalz) $17. 88 *—J.C. (3/1/2003)*

A. Christmann 2003 Ruppertsberger Reiterpfad Auslese Riesling (Pfalz) $40. Rich, unctuous, and low-acid, this Auslese impresses for its weight and sucrosity. Aromas and flavors of marmalade, honey, dried apricot, and baked apple finish long and sweet. Despite the relatively low acids, it should age easily for at least the next decade. **91** *—J.C. (5/1/2005)*

A. Christmann 1999 Ruppertsberger Reiterpfad Auslese Riesling (Pfalz) $50. 94 Editors' Choice *—P.G. (12/31/2001)*

ADELSECK

Adelseck NV Juwel Brut Riesling (Nahe) $15. 84 *—P.G. (12/31/2002)*

ALFRED MERKELBACH

Alfred Merkelbach 2001 Ürziger Würzgarten Spätlese Fuder 11 Riesling (Mosel-Saar-Ruwer) $17. 90 Editors' Choice *—J.C. (3/1/2003)*

BALTHASAR RESS

Balthasar Ress 2001 Hattenheimer Engelmannsberg Eiswein Riesling (Rheingau) $160. Something of a disappointment from a top producer. The wine has rustic aromas and flavors which hide the obvious potential. There are hints of quince flavors and acidity, which could well make the wine come good. **85** *—R.V. (1/1/2004)*

Balthasar Ress 2001 Hattenheimer Nussbrunnen Beerenauslese Riesling (Rheingau) $120. 91 *—R.V. (4/1/2003)*

Balthasar Ress 2001 Hattenheimer Nussbrunnen Trockenbeerenauslese Riesling (Rheingau) $170. A blockbuster wine, hugely sweet and rich wine with powerful botrytis and honey. There are flavors of honey and acacia and an opulent layer of rich dryness. The underlying acidity gives the wine an enormous potential. **94** *—R.V. (1/1/2004)*

Balthasar Ress 2001 Rüdesheimer Berg Roseneck Auslese Riesling (Rheingau) $23. The Ress wines are made for early drinking, as this fragrant wine shows. It has aromas of cherry blossom, a light, fresh palate with layers of light sweetness overlaying fresh, spring fruit flavors. **90** *—R.V. (1/1/2004)*

Balthasar Ress 2001 Rüdesheimer Berg Rottland Spätlese Riesling (Rheingau) $19. Surprisingly light on its feet, with a spritely mouthfeel that complements tart lemon-lime and green apple flavors. Finishes long and crisp, wonderfully refreshing. **89** *—J.C. (8/1/2004)*

Balthasar Ress 2001 Schloss Reichartshausen Kabinett Riesling (Rheingau) $14. 88 *—R.V. (3/1/2003)*

BARON ZU KNYPHAUSEN

Baron zu Knyphausen 2001 Charta Kabinett Riesling (Rheingau) $18. This was probably not the best time to be sampling this wine, as it appeared lean and closed at this stage of its evolution. Lime and powdered mineral aromas and flavors finish extremely crisp and unforgiving. Give it another few years to loosen up and this rating may look downright stingy. **85** *—J.C. (5/1/2005)*

Baron zu Knyphausen 2001 Erbacher Steinmorgen Kabinett Riesling (Rheingau) $14. 86 *—J.C. (3/1/2003)*

Baron zu Knyphausen 2001 Erbacher Steinmorgen Spätlese Riesling (Rheingau) $22. 91 Editors' Choice *—J.C. (3/1/2003)*

Baron zu Knyphausen 2003 Hattenheimer Wisselbrunnen Riesling Auslese Riesling (Rheingau) $51. A bit discordant at this early stage of its evolution, combining rich, oily, minerally flavors with baked apples and pears and picking up bitter, peppery notes on the finish. Love the minerals, hate the finish, and it's not clear where this will go in the future. **85** *—J.C. (12/15/2004)*

Baron zu Knyphausen 2003 QbA Riesling (Rheingau) $13. This is a big, relatively high-alcohol Riesling, tipping the scales at 11.5%. Pear and pineapple flavors are bold, and still sweet enough to stand up to modestly spicy dishes, but it might work best with something substantial like roasted pork. **87** *—J.C. (12/15/2004)*

BEND IN THE RIVER

Bend In The River 2001 QbA Riesling (Rheinhessen) $10. 83 *—J.C. (3/1/2003)*

BERNHARD EIFEL

Bernhard Eifel 2003 Maximillian Classic Qualitätswein Riesling (Mosel-Saar-Ruwer) $16. An intriguing wine, one that balances aromas of peaches and spring flowers with minerally, oily flavors. It's fairly full-bodied, with a suggestion of oiliness to its texture as well. Finishes long and close to dry. **88** *—J.C. (11/1/2004)*

BLUE FISH

Blue Fish 2004 Estate Riesling (Pfalz) $10. From a Pfalz cooperative, this is a strong effort at a bargain price. It's not the most complex Riesling, but its aromas of cinnamon-dusted apples are followed by refreshing off-dry flavors of apple and melon. **86 Best Buy** *—J.C. (10/1/2005)*

BLUE NUN

Blue Nun 2001 QbA Riesling (Pfalz) $7. This ain't your father's Blue Nun. This is recognizably a Riesling, boasting modest green apple and pear flavors and a close-to-dry finish. A quantum leap beyond what Blue Nun used to be back in the 1970s and '80s. **84** *—J.C. (8/1/2004)*

CARL GRAFF

Carl Graff 2003 Erdener Pralat Auslese Riesling (Mosel-Saar-Ruwer) $25. Light in body but intense in flavor, with delicately floral aromas but bold pineapple, brown sugar, and cinnamon flavors. Ernst Loosen is now consulting for this label, and the positive results show. **89** *—J.C. (5/1/2005)*

Carl Graff 2001 Erdener Treppchen Spätlese Riesling (Mosel-Saar-Ruwer) $11. **85** *—J.C. (3/1/2003)*

Carl Graff 2003 Graacher Himmelreich Spätlese Riesling (Mosel-Saar-Ruwer) $15. Abundant apple and peach aromas presage the rush of fleshy fruit that cascades across the palate. There's a hint of unreleased CO2 to help enliven the relatively low-acid mouthfeel, and a bit of lime on the finish to help balance things out further. **86** *—J.C. (5/1/2005)*

Carl Graff 2001 Piesporter Goldtröpfchen Kabinett Riesling (Mosel-Saar-Ruwer) $12. **85** *—J.C. (3/1/2003)*

Carl Graff 2001 Piesporter Michelsberg Auslese Riesling (Mosel-Saar-Ruwer) $14. **86** *—J.C. (3/1/2003)*

Carl Graff 2003 Riesling Kabinett Riesling (Mosel-Saar-Ruwer) $11. A simple, lightweight Riesling that starts off a bit sulfury, then reveals tart flavors of green apples and grapefruit. Decent value, worth trying as an apéritif. **85** *—J.C. (12/15/2004)*

Carl Graff 2003 Ürziger Würzgarten Auslese Riesling (Mosel-Saar-Ruwer) $22. Lean and a bit ungenerous, especially for a 2003. Tart apple and citrus aromas and flavors shed some early sulfur but never really blossom, finishing hard. **84** *—J.C. (5/1/2005)*

Carl Graff 2001 Wehlener Sonnenuhr Spätlese Riesling (Mosel-Saar-Ruwer) $12. **87 Best Buy** *—J.C. (3/1/2003)*

CARL LOEWEN

Carl Loewen 2001 Thörnicher Ritsch Spätlese Riesling (Mosel-Saar-Ruwer) $20. **90 Editors' Choice** *—J.C. (3/1/2003)*

CARL SCHMITT-WAGNER

Carl Schmitt-Wagner 2001 Longuicher Maximiner Herrenberg Spätlese Riesling (Mosel-Saar-Ruwer) $19. **89** *—J.C. (3/1/2003)*

CLUSSERATH-WEILER

Clusserath-Weiler 2003 Trittenheimer Apotheke Spätlese Riesling (Mosel-Saar-Ruwer) $25. Most of the Clüsserath-Weiler wines had elevated levels of sulfur (burnt matchstick aromas) on the nose, which depressed their ratings. A shame, as otherwise the wines seemed to be of generally high quality. This one was no exception, with modest apple and pear scents partially overpowered, while the sulfur also seemed to detract from the finish, muting it. **85** *—J.C. (11/1/2004)*

Clusserath-Weiler 2003 Trittenheimer Apotheke Spätlese Trocken Riesling (Mosel-Saar-Ruwer) $24. Smoke, pear, and quince aromas on the nose, then the wine shows less fruit on the palate. It's a sip of liquid rocks—a bit hard to get at—without the normal friendliness of young Riesling, yet possessed of a certain intellectual pleasure. **86** *—J.C. (11/1/2004)*

DEINHARD

Deinhard 2003 Classic Pinot Blanc (Pfalz) $8. Although this doesn't exhibit the orange and tangerine notes often characteristic of Pinot Blanc, it is a lightweight, refreshing wine. Starts off with scents of earth and clay, then shows flavors of green apples and underripe melons before finishing with some zesty grapefruit. Probably best as an apéritif. **84 Best Buy** *—J.C. (11/1/2004)*

Deinhard 2002 Classic Riesling (Rheinhessen) $8. Earthy and tart, with modest citrus fruit competing with damp clay and hints of chalk dust. **82** *—J.C. (8/1/2004)*

Deinhard 2003 Green Label Qualitätswein Riesling (Mosel-Saar-Ruwer) $6. Rieslings drawn from Bereich Bernkastel, as this one is, are often floral, but this one is oddly floral, with a plasticy note to the flavors of apple and pear. **82** *—J.C. (11/1/2004)*

Deinhard 2003 Piesporter Qualitätswein Riesling (Mosel-Saar-Ruwer) $9. Classic lime, slate, and green apple aromas and flavors signal this budget-priced offering's origin. It's light and delicate, just as it should be; the only knock on this wine is its soft, short finish. Still, it's a fine example of how good some of the lower-priced wines can be in 2003. **85 Best Buy** *—J.C. (11/1/2004)*

Deinhard NV Feiner Fruchtiger Sekt Halbtrocken Sparkling Blend (Germany) $9. A bit sweet, with large bubbles and floral and toast aromas and flavors. Cleanly made. **83** *—J.C. (12/31/2004)*

Deinhard NV Rosé de Blanc et Noir Feiner Fruchtiger Sekt Halbtrocken Sparkling Blend (Germany) $8. Hints of toast and citrus on the nose give way to frankly sweet strawberry flavors. Yes, it's meant to be somewhat sweet, but this is verging on being unbalanced. **82** *—J.C. (12/31/2004)*

DES GRAFEN NEIPPERG

Des Grafen Neipperg 2001 Hemma QbA White Blend (Württemberg) $17. Oyster wine from Germany? That's the appropriate pairing for this lean, green wine that ends slightly bitter and pithy. **82** —*J.C. (1/1/2004)*

DOMDECHANT WERNER

Domdechant Werner 2002 Hochheim Domdechaney QbA Erstes Gewachs Riesling (Rheingau) $44. This remarkable (almost) dry Riesling is big and broad-shouldered, with intense, oily aromas paired with hints of Golden Delicious apples. It seems to expand in the mouth, flooding the senses with oily, minerally flavors that linger on the finish. **91** —*J.C. (8/1/2004)*

Domdechant Werner 1999 Hochheimer Domdechaney Auslese Riesling (Rheingau) $35. 90 *(8/1/2001)*

Domdechant Werner 1999 Hochheimer Domdechaney Spätlese Riesling (Rheingau) $24. 87 *(8/1/2001)*

Domdechant Werner 2001 Hochheimer Domdechaney Spätlese Riesling (Rheingau) $21. A stunningly intense wine, with ripe fruit with perfectly balanced, crisp acidity. At the moment, it is certainly young, but Werner estate, long-established in Hochheim, has made a wine that will develop slowly and beautifully over many years. **92** —*R.V. (1/1/2004)*

Domdechant Werner 1999 Hochheimer Domdechaney Trockenbeerenauslese Riesling (Rheingau) $227. 91 *(8/1/2001)*

Domdechant Werner 2003 Hochheimer Hölle Kabinett Riesling (Rheingau) $19. Typical in some ways for 2003, this is a soft, cuddly Riesling that boasts modest pear, apple, and melon flavors. Plump and easy to drink over the short term. **86** —*J.C. (5/1/2005)*

Domdechant Werner 1999 Hochheimer Hölle Kabinett Riesling (Rheingau) $14. 88 *(8/1/2001)*

Domdechant Werner 1999 Hochheimer Hölle Kabinett Trocken Riesling (Rheingau) $14. 89 Best Buy *(8/1/2001)*

Domdechant Werner 2003 Hochheimer Kirchenstück Beerenauslese 375 ml Riesling (Rheingau) $300. Wines like this are why 2003 has generated such buzz across Germany. Thick and oily-textured, and filled with flavors of superripe pears, peaches, and dried apricots, this is a monumental dessert wine. Yes, it's decadently rich, but it also boasts sufficient acidity to keep it from becoming cloying. Finishes long, with lingering notes of tropical fruit and citrus. One for the ages. **96 Cellar Selection** —*J.C. (5/1/2005)*

Domdechant Werner 2001 Hochheimer Kirchenstück Eiswein Riesling (Rheingau) $126. In keeping with this estate's reputation for elegance, this eiswein is finely poised, with some delicious acidity alongside the flavors of ripe quince jelly. It is certainly intense, but this is balanced by the complex layers of crisp, dry honey and acidity. **92** —*R.V. (1/1/2004)*

Domdechant Werner 2002 Hochheimer Kirchenstück QbA Erstes Gewachs Riesling (Rheingau) $44. Hints of smoke and powdered quartz add nuance to aromas of rainwater and green apple. It's an austere, aristocratic blend of hard minerals and tart apples barely softened by notes of softer, rounder fruits—peaches come to mind. **89** —*J.C. (8/1/2004)*

Domdechant Werner 2002 Hochheimer Kirchenstück Spätlese Riesling (Rheingau) $30. Sweet and relatively low in acidity, this spätlese boasts a lilac-like, perfumy nose followed by simple, fruit-juicy flavors. **84** —*J.C. (8/1/2004)*

Domdechant Werner 2003 Hochheimer Kirchenstuck Spätlese Trocken Riesling (Rheingau) $29. Subdued on the nose, where the sulfur is still very much in evidence. Pear and lemon fruit on the palate, gliding into a finish that seems a bit hard, with acids that jut out, interrupting the smooth flow of the wine. **84** —*J.C. (5/1/2005)*

DÖNNHOFF

Dönnhoff 2001 Schlossböckelheimer Kupfergrube Spätlese Riesling (Nahe) $42. 93 —*J.C. (3/1/2003)*

DR. BÜRKLIN-WOLF

Dr. Bürklin-Wolf 2001 Bürklin Estate Riesling (Pfalz) $16. 90 Editors' Choice —*J.C. (3/1/2003)*

Dr. Bürklin-Wolf 2002 Bürklin Estate Qualitätswein Riesling (Pfalz) $20. Smoky and earthy, with flavors of damp clay and just hints of pear and apple fruit. Lacks the acidity to make the flavors sing. **83** —*J.C. (11/1/2004)*

Dr. Bürklin-Wolf 2002 Qualitätswein Riesling (Pfalz) $12. Starts with sparkling aromas of fresh limes, hints of ripe apple and honey, but loses it on the palate, where it's fat and lacking in acidity. Finishes short. **83** —*J.C. (11/1/2004)*

Dr. Bürklin-Wolf 1998 Ruppertsberger Gaisböhl Spätlese Trocken Riesling (Pfalz) $37. 92 Cellar Selection *(8/1/2001)*

Dr. Bürklin-Wolf 2001 Ruppertsberger Gaisböhl Trocken Riesling (Pfalz) $37. 87 —*J.C. (3/1/2003)*

Dr. Bürklin-Wolf 1990 Wachenheimer Rechbächel 'R' Riesling (Pfalz) $44. 91 *(8/1/2001)*

Dr. Bürklin-Wolf 1998 Wachenheimer Rechbächel Spätlese Trocken Riesling (Pfalz) $28. 90 *(8/1/2001)*

DR. FISCHER

Dr. Fischer 2003 Ockfener Bockstein Kabinett Riesling (Mosel-Saar-Ruwer) $17. Slightly green aromas of fern fronds and citrus fruits start things off, and this wine stays light, lean and tart throughout. Mixed citrus fruits—tangerine, lime, and grapefruit—finish clean but short. **84** —*J.C. (11/1/2004)*

Dr. Fischer 2002 Wawerner Herrenberger Spätlese Riesling (Mosel-Saar-Ruwer) $20. Understated on the nose, with modest scents of petrol and apples. Medium-sweet on the palate, with flavors of corn oil layered over apples and pears. Finishes with a burst of citrus. **85** —*J.C. (11/1/2004)*

DR. H. THANISCH (MÜLLER-BURGGRAEF)

Dr. H. Thanisch (Erben Müller-Burggraef) 2002 Berncasteler Doctor Kabinett Riesling (Mosel-Saar-Ruwer) $29. Shows the wonderful mineral aromas of the Doctor site, along with apple, nectarine, and lime scents, but lacks the fine edge of racy acidity and lingering finish that can make this wine truly special. Plump, with sweet, oily flavors just balanced out by tart green apple notes. **86** —*J.C. (8/1/2004)*

Dr. H. Thanisch (Erben Müller-Burggraef) 2002 Berncasteler Doctor Spätlese Riesling (Mosel-Saar-Ruwer) $46. Rich and sweet, but a trifle low in acidity, this is a plump, succulent wine from a vineyard renowned for its raciness and delicacy. Apple, peach, and honey aromas and flavors dominate, melding together in a pleasant whole. **88** —*J.C. (8/1/2004)*

Dr. H. Thanisch (Erben Müller-Burggraef) 2002 Bernkasteler Badstube Kabinett Riesling (Mosel-Saar-Ruwer) $17. Light and a bit green, with fresh scents of green apples and limes followed by similar flavors and hints of mint and green plums. Fresh and clean on the finish. **86** —*J.C. (8/1/2004)*

Dr. H. Thanisch (Erben Müller-Burggraef) 2003 Brauneberger Juffer-Sonnenuhr Spätlese Riesling (Mosel-Saar-Ruwer) $24. Smells like ultra ripe nectarines or peaches, flesh practically oozing from the skins. In the mouth, it's big, rich, and enveloping, yet it finishes with a trace of bitter peach pit. **87** —*J.C. (5/1/2005)*

Dr. H. Thanisch (Erben Müller-Burggraef) 2002 Wehlener Sonnenuhr Kabinett Riesling (Mosel-Saar-Ruwer) $17. This large-scaled, fully ripe Riesling boasts aromas of mineral oil and baked apple backed by expansive, mouthfilling flavors of the same. It's certainly rounder and riper than a traditional kabinett, but it doesn't seem at all flabby. **89** —*J.C. (8/1/2004)*

DR. H. THANISCH (THANISCH)

Dr. H. Thanisch (Erben Thanisch) 2003 Bernkasteler Badstube Kabinett Riesling (Mosel-Saar-Ruwer) $23. Limes, minerals, and green apples dance on the nose of this lithe yet flavorful kabinett. Flavors lean heavily toward green apples and citrus, yet the acids are ripe on the finish, giving an impression of softness and early approachability. **88** —*J.C. (12/15/2004)*

Dr. H. Thanisch (Erben Thanisch) 2001 Bernkasteler Doctor Auslese Riesling (Mosel-Saar-Ruwer) $60. 93 —*R.V. (3/1/2003)*

Dr. H. Thanisch (Erben Thanisch) 2001 QbA Riesling (Mosel-Saar-Ruwer) $16. 86 —*J.C. (3/1/2003)*

DR. LOOSEN

Dr. Loosen 1999 Bernkasteler Lay Riesling (Mosel-Saar-Ruwer) $17. 84 —*C.S. (5/1/2002)*

Dr. Loosen 2002 Bernkasteler Lay Kabinett Riesling (Mosel-Saar-Ruwer) $17. Light in weight and possessed of a fine balance between sweetness and acidity, this is an ideal apéritif wine. Pungent lime and green apple aromas combine with green gage plum notes in a mouthwatering ensemble. **88** —*J.C. (8/1/2004)*

Dr. Loosen 1999 Bernkasteler Lay Kabinett Riesling (Mosel-Saar-Ruwer) $12. 87 *(8/1/2001)*

Dr. Loosen 2001 Dr. L QbA Riesling (Mosel-Saar-Ruwer) $10. 85 —*J.C. (3/1/2003)*

Dr. Loosen 2002 Erdener Prälat Auslese Riesling (Mosel-Saar-Ruwer) $48. In contrast to the delicate, ethereal nature of Loosen's '02 Ürziger Würzgarten auslese, this is a plump, rich wine filled with nectarine, honey, and lime flavors. Despite a modest finish, this wine has loads of up-front appeal. **90** —*J.C. (8/1/2004)*

Dr. Loosen 2003 Erdener Treppchen Auslese Riesling (Mosel-Saar-Ruwer) $40. Wonderfully clean and precise aromas of pear and honeydew give way to apple and lime flavors. This avoids excess weight or sugar, revealing a more classical structure than many of the 2003s. Long and fresh on the finish. **90** —*J.C. (5/1/2005)*

Dr. Loosen 2002 Erdener Treppchen Kabinett Riesling (Mosel-Saar-Ruwer) $18. A light-bodied, delicately flavored wine, filled with notes of flower-shop greens, ripe apples, and citrus. Finishes crisp and clean, with just a touch of sweetness, making it perfect to sip on its own as an apéritif. **87** —*J.C. (8/1/2004)*

Dr. Loosen 1999 Erdener Treppchen Kabinett Riesling (Mosel-Saar-Ruwer) $18. 90 Editors' Choice *(8/1/2001)*

Dr. Loosen 1999 Ürziger Würzgarten Riesling (Mosel-Saar-Ruwer) $25. 89 *(8/1/2001)*

Dr. Loosen 2003 Ürziger Würzgarten Auslese Riesling (Mosel-Saar-Ruwer) $40. Fresh and crisp, but it lacks a bit of intensity. An initial blast of sulfur fades readily enough, revealing simple apple and citrus flavors, but that's as far as this usually stellar bottling goes this year. **85** —*J.C. (5/1/2005)*

Dr. Loosen 2001 Ürziger Würzgarten Spätlese Riesling (Mosel-Saar-Ruwer) $25. 90 —*J.C. (3/1/2003)*

Dr. Loosen 2002 Ürziger Würzgarten Spätlese Riesling (Mosel-Saar-Ruwer) $25. Great Spätlese from Loosen, combining apple, citrus, pear, pineapple, and lime flavors into a seamless whole that defies such deconstructionist description. And while it has great aromatics and midpalate flavor, it's also lively, fresh, and long on the finish. **91 Editors' Choice** —*J.C. (8/1/2004)*

Dr. Loosen 1999 Wehlener Sonnenuhr Riesling (Mosel-Saar-Ruwer) $17. 88 *(8/1/2001)*

Dr. Loosen 2001 Wehlener Sonnenuhr Goldkapsel Auslese Riesling (Mosel-Saar-Ruwer) $33. 92 —*R.V. (3/1/2003)*

Dr. Loosen 2001 Wehlener Sonnenuhr Spätlese Riesling (Mosel-Saar-Ruwer) $25. **88** —*R.V. (3/1/2003)*

Dr. Loosen 2002 Wehlener Sonnenuhr Spätlese Riesling (Mosel-Saar-Ruwer) $25. This offering from Loosen manages to combine great minerality—an almost palpable sense of rock dust—with terrific fruit. Ripe apples and candied pineapple are sweet, but nicely balanced by crisp acids. **91 Editors' Choice** —*J.C. (8/1/2004)*

DR. PAULY BERGWEILER

Dr. Pauly Bergweiler 2003 Bernkasteler alte Badstube am Doctorberg Auslese Riesling (Mosel-Saar-Ruwer) $50. Full-bodied, sweet, and thick in the mouth, this is more like a beerenauslese than a true auslese. But evaluated on its own merits, it is a special wine: pear and honey scents give way to apricot preserves that finish sweet and lingering on the finish. **92** —*J.C. (11/1/2004)*

Dr. Pauly Bergweiler 2001 Bernkasteler alte Badstube am Doctorberg Auslese Riesling (Mosel-Saar-Ruwer) $36. **87** —*J.C. (3/1/2003)*

Dr. Pauly Bergweiler 2004 Bernkasteler alte Badstube am Doctorberg Kabinett Riesling (Mosel-Saar-Ruwer) $23. Firmly in the house style, with soft, fully ripe fruit flavors that caress the palate rather than awaken it. Peach and pear lead the way, backed by melon notes. **87** —*J.C. (10/1/2005)*

Dr. Pauly Bergweiler 2002 Bernkasteler alte Badstube am Doctorberg Kabinett Riesling (Mosel-Saar-Ruwer) $20. Like most of this producer's 2002s, this is a plump, succulent wine, amply endowed with fruit. What sets this one apart is its combination of baked apple, ripe peach, dried spices, and dusty minerality. **88** —*J.C. (8/1/2004)*

Dr. Pauly Bergweiler 2004 Bernkasteler alte Badstube am Doctorberg Spätlese Riesling (Mosel-Saar-Ruwer) $30. Big and sweet; broad and mouthfilling. It has decent complexity (pear, peach, dried spices, and fuel oil) but lacks delicacy and raciness. If you like your Rieslings on the heavy side, you'll rate this even higher. **87** —*J.C. (10/1/2005)*

Dr. Pauly Bergweiler 2002 Bernkasteler alte Badstube am Doctorberg Spätlese Riesling (Mosel-Saar-Ruwer) $26. Nicely balanced, if a little on the sweet side, with aromas of lime and stone dust rounded out in the mouth by flavors of honey, pineapple, and apricot. Plump and easy to drink. **90** —*J.C. (8/1/2004)*

Dr. Pauly Bergweiler 2001 Bernkasteler alte Badstube am Doctorberg Trockenbeerenauslese Riesling (Mosel-Saar-Ruwer) $150. **92** —*J.C. (3/1/2003)*

Dr. Pauly Bergweiler 2000 Bernkasteler alte Badtube am Doctober Kabinett Riesling (Mosel-Saar-Ruwer) $21. **85** —*J.C. (5/1/2002)*

Dr. Pauly Bergweiler 2003 Bernkasteler Badstube Auslese Riesling (Mosel-Saar-Ruwer) $30. Begins with scents of clover-blossom honey drizzled over supremely ripe apples and pears, then opens to show a dizzying array of fruits ranging from apricot to pineapple. Sweet, luscious and soft; don't expect a razor edge of acidity, just all-enveloping fruit. **91 Editors' Choice** —*J.C. (11/1/2004)*

Dr. Pauly Bergweiler 2003 Bernkasteler Badstube Eiswein Riesling (Mosel-Saar-Ruwer) $175. Absolutely incredible eiswein, with finely etched flavors of pear and pineapple that flow across the palate like fruit syrup borne on light-footed acids. Stunningly sweet, but with great balancing acidity and a finish that lingers for minutes. **96** —*J.C. (12/15/2004)*

Dr. Pauly Bergweiler 2001 Bernkasteler Badstube Eiswein Riesling (Mosel-Saar-Ruwer) $115. **89** —*J.C. (3/1/2003)*

Dr. Pauly Bergweiler 2003 Bernkasteler Badstube Kabinett Riesling (Mosel-Saar-Ruwer) $19. Sweet and plump, with ripe apple and pear flavors that glide easily across the palate, then finish tart and pineappley. Very fruity, not showing a lot of mineral character. **86** —*J.C. (11/1/2004)*

Dr. Pauly Bergweiler 2001 Bernkasteler Badstube Kabinett Riesling (Mosel-Saar-Ruwer) $14. Green apple and lime aromas are partially disguised by a moderate sulfur funk (think burnt matchstick). The flavors are clean but frankly sweet, showing notes of strawberries and candied apples. Soft on the finish. **84** —*J.C. (1/1/2004)*

Dr. Pauly Bergweiler 2004 Bernkasteler Badstube Spätlese Riesling (Mosel-Saar-Ruwer) $30. True to the style at Pauly-Bergweiler, this is a sweet, rich wine, with super-ripe apple, pear, and even tropical fruit notes. There's also a bit of diesel and slate and good acidity for balance. Finishes long and mouthwatering. **89** —*J.C. (10/1/2005)*

Dr. Pauly Bergweiler 2001 Bernkasteler Badstube Spätlese Riesling (Mosel-Saar-Ruwer) $18. **87** —*J.C. (3/1/2003)*

Dr. Pauly Bergweiler 2002 Erdener Treppchen Spätlese Riesling (Mosel-Saar-Ruwer) $25. Possesses a very clean, almost crystalline quality on the nose, highlighting apple and citrus notes that broaden out on the palate to include peach and pear. **87** —*J.C. (8/1/2004)*

Dr. Pauly Bergweiler 2001 Graacher Himmelreich Kabinett Riesling (Mosel-Saar-Ruwer) $14. **88** —*J.C. (3/1/2003)*

Dr. Pauly Bergweiler 2001 Noble House QbA Riesling (Mosel-Saar-Ruwer) $8. **88 Best Buy** —*J.C. (3/1/2003)*

Dr. Pauly Bergweiler 2003 Noble House Qualitätswein Riesling (Mosel-Saar-Ruwer) $11. Green apple and pear aromas, along with a bit of stone dust, but the flavors seem a little bland and understated, and the wine finishes short. Good, well-made wine at a reasonable price, just seems to lack a bit of intensity. **84** —*J.C. (11/1/2004)*

Dr. Pauly Bergweiler 2001 Ürziger Würzgarten Trockenbeerenauslese Riesling (Mosel-Saar-Ruwer) $265. **94 Cellar Selection** —*J.C. (3/1/2003)*

Dr. Pauly Bergweiler 2000 Wehlener Sonnehur Spätlese Riesling (Mosel-Saar-Ruwer) $23. **85** —*D.T. (5/1/2002)*

Dr. Pauly Bergweiler 2001 Wehlener Sonnenuhr Auslese Riesling (Mosel-Saar-Ruwer) $26. 87 *—J.C. (3/1/2003)*

Dr. Pauly Bergweiler 2003 Wehlener Sonnenuhr Kabinett Riesling (Mosel-Saar-Ruwer) $22. A bit simple and sweet, offering pineapple fruit, a bit of smoke, and a hint of flowers. Easy drinking, to be sure, but lacks acidity to give the flavors crispness and definition. **84** *—J.C. (11/1/2004)*

Dr. Pauly Bergweiler 2004 Wehlener Sonnenuhr Spätlese Riesling (Mosel-Saar-Ruwer) $30. A bit simple for a spätlese from such a storied site, but still an enjoyable wine. Sweet apple and pear flavors are paired with relatively low acids. It's mouthfilling; satisfying rather than refreshing. **86** *—J.C. (10/1/2005)*

Dr. Pauly Bergweiler 2002 Wehlener Sonnenuhr Spätlese Riesling (Mosel-Saar-Ruwer) $25. This light- to medium-bodied wine seems a little low in acidity, but offers a pleasant mouthful of baked apple flavors. A piney, resinous note persists throughout, extending onto the off-dry finish. **85** *—J.C. (8/1/2004)*

Dr. Pauly Bergweiler 2002 Wehlener Sonneuhr Kabinett Riesling (Mosel-Saar-Ruwer) $21. Plump and fruit-filled, this kabinett comes across more like a typical Spätlese, with ample sugar and alcohol giving a distinct impression of richness. Baked apple and pear flavors are balanced by just a hint of lime. **88** *—J.C. (8/1/2004)*

DR. WAGNER

Dr. Wagner 2003 Ockfener Bockstein Riesling Kabinett Riesling (Mosel-Saar-Ruwer) $18. This is textbook M-S-R Riesling, light-bodied and elegant, with green apple and lime flavors. It's slightly sweet yet refreshingly acidic, adding pear and citrus on the finish. **87** *—J.C. (12/15/2004)*

EGON MULLER

Egon Muller 2002 Scharzhof QbA Riesling (Mosel-Saar-Ruwer) $17. Light and zesty—but maybe a little too light, as the lemon-lime and gingery flavors don't come across with the strength and precision expected at this estate. Fresh, tart, and cleansing on the finish—a Riesling for shellfish. **84** *—J.C. (11/1/2004)*

Egon Müller-Scharzhof 2001 Kabinett Riesling (Mosel-Saar-Ruwer) $34. 92 Cellar Selection *—J.C. (3/1/2003)*

EILENZ

Eilenz 2001 Ayler Kupp Kabinett Riesling (Mosel-Saar-Ruwer) $12. 88 Best Buy *—J.C. (3/1/2003)*

Eilenz 2001 Ayler Kupp Spätlese Riesling (Mosel-Saar-Ruwer) $16. The tart, lemony flavors pack a petrol edge, but not a lot of weight or intensity. Pineapple and a hint of kerosene round out the package. **83** *—J.C. (1/1/2004)*

EUGEN WEHRHEIM

Eugen Wehrheim 2001 Niersteiner Bildstock Kabinett Riesling (Rheinhessen) $13. Raw oysters might be just the ticket to match with this lean, lemony kabinett. There's a bit of plumpness in the midpalate that comes across as a custardy quality, but the lengthy finish is extremely tart. **84** *—J.C. (1/1/2004)*

Eugen Wehrheim 2003 Niersteiner Orbel Riesling Spätlese Riesling (Rheinhessen) $16. Slightly rubbery at first, with notes of slate, diesel, and lime, then develops apple, pear, and citrus flavors on the palate. Light and spry; well-balanced. Finishes with hints of pith. **87** *—J.C. (12/15/2004)*

EYMANN

Eymann 2003 Classic Riesling (Pfalz) $12. Light, dry, and crisp, this is the perfect Riesling to enjoy with food. It has structure, acidity, flavors of green apples, and a lively, fresh finish. **87 Best Buy** *—R.V. (4/1/2005)*

Eymann 2001 Selektion Toreye Gönnheimer Sonnenberg Trocken Spätburgunder (Pfalz) $26. This is a very dry red wine, with flavors of fresh strawberries and just a touch of toast. It is lean and austere but there is still a lively juiciness to the fruit. Drink now. **86** *—R.V. (4/1/2005)*

FITZ-RITTER

Fitz-Ritter 2003 Dürkheimer Abtsfronhof Riesling Spätlese Halbtrocken Riesling (Pfalz) $18. For a halbtrocken, this is pretty darn dry. Grapefruit and green apple aromas give way to flavors of wet stone and lime, finishing tart and stony. There's just enough fruit to balance the elevated acids and low residual sugar. Probably best with seafood. **87** *—J.C. (12/15/2004)*

FORSTMEISTER GELTZ ZILLIKEN

Forstmeister Geltz Zilliken 2001 Saarburger Rausch Kabinett Riesling (Mosel-Saar-Ruwer) $NA. The 24-acre vineyard of Hans-Joachim Zilliken is in one of the best vineyard sites of the Saar. The style combines pleasing soft fruit with fresh, refreshing crisp, appley fruit flavors. It is finely poised, shot through with steel and acidity. **89** *—R.V. (1/1/2004)*

FRANZ KÜNSTLER

Franz Künstler 2001 Hochheimer Hölle Eiswein Riesling (Rheingau) $140. The intense sweetness of this may be one-dimensional, but what a dimension. With its deep gold color, the richness is overpowering and intensely opulent. A wine to savor in sips rather than gulps. **90** *—R.V. (1/1/2004)*

Franz Künstler 2001 Hochheimer Kirchenstück Eiswein Riesling (Rheingau) $150. This wine is the perfect example of the difference between the huge richness of a TBA and the relative delicacy of an Eiswein. Like pure syrup, it trickles through the palate, leaving flavors of ripe apricots, of orange marmalade, and of intense honey.

The intensity of the fruit flavors masks the high acidity but does show up the lightness that stays in the mouth. **94** *—R.V. (1/1/2004)*

Franz Künstler 2001 Hochheimer Reichestal Kabinett Riesling (Rheingau) $20. Caramel and warm straw aromas are not what makes this wine attractive. But the yeasty fruit, and full fat flavors with a touch of acidity certainly make it immediately drinkable. **84** *—R.V. (1/1/2004)*

FRED PRINZ

Fred Prinz 2001 Hallgartner Jungfer Spätlese Riesling (Rheingau) $NA. There is crisp, acidity with a nice concentration of fruit salad flavors. The wine still tastes young and fresh, but could develop. **87** *—R.V. (1/1/2004)*

Fred Prinz 2001 Hallgartner Jungfer Kabinett White Blend (Rheingau) $NA. Fred Prinz makes the most of his small Hallgarten vineyards. This wine, with its full, pure fruit and delicious acidity has intense piercing vibrant flavors of currants. It is delicious and intense. **92** *—R.V. (1/1/2004)*

FREIHERR HEYL ZU HERRNSHEIM

Freiherr Heyl zu Herrnsheim 2003 Baron Heyl Nierstein Kabinett Riesling (Rheinhessen) $16. Herrnsheim tends toward a drier style of wine without labeling it as such, so this kabinett is crisp and almost dry-tasting. Apple blossoms and limes on the nose are complemented by hints of diesel and a tart, steely finish. **86** *—J.C. (12/15/2004)*

Freiherr Heyl zu Herrnsheim 2001 Baron Heyl Nierstein Spätlese Riesling (Rheinhessen) $11. 87 Best Buy *—J.C. (3/1/2003)*

Freiherr Heyl zu Herrnsheim 2001 Nierstein Pettental QbA Trocken Riesling (Rheinhessen) $30. 88 *—J.C. (3/1/2003)*

FRIEDRICH-WILHELM-GYMNASIUM

Friedrich-Wilhelm-Gymnasium 2001 Graacher Himmelreich Auslese Riesling (Mosel-Saar-Ruwer) $24. The school vineyards of this high school (whose more famous alumni include Karl Marx) produce wines which are typically light. This wine is still very young, showing yeasty aromas, but the palate is creamy, with some yeast flavors on top of sweet acidity and flavors of green grapes. The aftertaste leaves a touch of citrus. **92** *—R.V. (1/1/2004)*

Friedrich-Wilhelm-Gymnasium 2001 Graacher Himmelreich Spätlese Riesling (Mosel-Saar-Ruwer) $18. The light, poised delicate character of this wine, with delicious fruit shows a fine, crisp style. With its fresh acidity, and flavors of apricots, it already makes an appealing glass of summer wine. **91** *—R.V. (1/1/2004)*

Friedrich-Wilhelm-Gymnasium 2001 Trittenheimer Apotheke Auslese Riesling (Mosel-Saar-Ruwer) $20. The wine has immediately attractive aromas of almonds, followed by full, nutty fruit with layers of acidity and sweet fruit. It is intense, immediately appealing, showing flavors of almond cakes. **90** *—R.V. (1/1/2004)*

Friedrich-Wilhelm-Gymnasium 2001 Trittenheimer Apotheke Spätlese Riesling (Mosel-Saar-Ruwer) $18. The minerally wines of the Trittenheim Apotheke vineyard have gained enormously in reputation in recent years. The character shows well in this creamy ripe wine, with its soft, delicate fruit flavors shot through with a crisp layer of tannin, which shows how young the wine is. Yeasty flavors show through. This will develop well over 5–10 years. **92** *—R.V. (1/1/2004)*

FÜRST VON METTERNICH

Fürst von Metternich NV Brut Riesling Sekt Riesling (Germany) $23. Fresh and apple-y from start to finish, with even a hint of spring flowers. Creamy and a bit soft in the mouth. This isn't complex, but is clean and tasty, easy-to-drink bubbly. **86** *—J.C. (12/31/2004)*

FÜRST ZU HOHENLOHE

Fürst zu Hohenlohe 2002 Verrenberger Verrenberg Butzen QbA Trocken Riesling (Württemberg) $13. Shows complexity and freshness, with scents of apple blossoms and citrus blending into flavors of pear and lime. Nicely balanced, dry without being austere, yet crisp and refreshing on the finish. **87** *—J.C. (8/1/2004)*

G. DICKENSHEID

G. Dickensheid 2003 Riesling Kabinett Riesling (Rheinhessen) $10. Apricot and tangerine aromas lead into flavors of ripe peaches and nectarines. This is a bit heavy and low in acid, but the richness is not so much from sugar as it is from high alcohol. **84 Best Buy** *—J.C. (12/15/2004)*

GEH. RAT DR. VON BASSERMANN-JORDAN

Geh. Rat Dr. von Bassermann-Jordan 2003 Deidesheimer Paradiesgarten Riesling Kabinett Riesling (Pfalz) $19. Intriguing notes of smoke and mineral on the nose raise hopes, but this medium-weight wine's soft, sweet pear fruit turns tart and sour on the finish. **84** *—J.C. (12/15/2004)*

Geh. Rat Dr. von Bassermann-Jordan 2001 Forster Jesuitengarten Spätlese Riesling (Pfalz) $26. 86 *—J.C. (3/1/2003)*

Geh. Rat Dr. von Bassermann-Jordan 2001 QbA Riesling (Pfalz) $14. Starts off just fine, with pear and quince aromas alongside a warm cinnamon note. Then in the mouth it's rich and soft upfront, yet overly tangy on the finish—a disconnect that never quite resolves. **83** *—J.C. (1/1/2004)*

Geh. Rat Dr. von Bassermann-Jordan 2001 QbA Trocken Riesling (Pfalz) $14. 85 *—J.C. (3/1/2003)*

GEORG BREUER

Georg Breuer 2003 Berg Schlossberg Trockenbeerenauslese Riesling (Rheingau) $250. There's a hint of volatility to the otherwise heady aromas of dried apricot and candied pineapple, but the flavors seem unaffected, delivering loads of sweet stone fruit and citrus. Thick and viscous on the palate, finishing long and sweet, if somewhat low in acidity. Approachable now, but should easily age for 20–30 years. **91** *—J.C. (5/1/2005)*

Georg Breuer 1999 GB Riesling (Rheingau) $13. 88 Best Buy *—P.G. (8/1/2001)*

Georg Breuer 1998 Rauenthal Nonnenberg Riesling (Rheingau) $36. 89 *(8/1/2001)*

Georg Breuer 2002 Rudesheim Berg Schlossberg QbA Riesling (Rheingau) $50. Slightly floral, with apple-blossom notes gracing pear and lime fruit, but a bit low acid and even heavy, showing a trace of sweetness. Good wine, but disappointing for this bottling. Tasted twice, with consistent results. **85** *—J.C. (11/1/2004)*

Georg Breuer 2001 Terra Montosa Riesling (Rheingau) $20. 90 Editors' Choice *—J.C. (3/1/2003)*

GRAFF

Graff 2004 Wehlener Sonnenuhr Kabinett Riesling (Mosel-Saar-Ruwer) $12. Star winemaker Ernie Loosen is now consulting for Graff, and the wines have taken a step up in quality. Leesy and a bit sulfury on the nose, but underneath are some wonderfully pure flavors of melon and mineral, finishing with a dusting of dried spices and powdered mineral over poached apple. Could be racier, but the broad, mouthfilling flavors are satisfying in a different way. **89 Best Buy** *—J.C. (10/1/2005)*

GRANS-FASSIAN

Grans-Fassian 2001 Trittenheimer Apotheke Riesling (Mosel-Saar-Ruwer) $21. 87 *—J.C. (3/1/2003)*

Grans-Fassian 2001 Trittenheimer Kabinett Riesling (Mosel-Saar-Ruwer) $14. 91 Best Buy *—J.C. (3/1/2003)*

GROEBE

Groebe 2003 Westhofener Kirchspiel Spätlese Riesling (Rheinhessen) $26. Nicely balanced, yet still reflects the vintage's hot character in its rounded acids and sweet finish. Rainwater, green apples, and limes provide a counterweight to the sugar and give the wine a light, airy feel. **87** *—J.C. (11/1/2004)*

GUNDERLOCH

Gunderloch 2002 Diva Spätlese Riesling (Rheinhessen) $20. Seems lacking in acidity, with slightly baked or cooked apple aromas and flavors that aren't unpleasant, just lacking an extra dimension of verve or stuffing. **85** *—J.C. (8/1/2004)*

Gunderloch 2002 Jean Baptiste Kabinett Riesling (Rheingau) $18. If not for a sulfury-yeasty note on the nose, this wine would have scored higher. Its citrus and mineral elements bring to mind limes and riverstones, picking up luscious peach notes on the finish while staying fresh and lively. Try decanting, or hold another year or two before opening. **86** *—J.C. (8/1/2004)*

GYSLER

Gysler 2004 Weinheimer Kabinett Riesling (Rheinhessen) $17. Starts off a bit tarry and rubbery—downright stinky, in fact. Just be patient, or decant vigorously, and you'll be amply rewarded by pineapple fruit so pure it seems almost crystalline in both flavor and structure. It's fleshy, yet sharply delineated and focused, ending in a laserbeam of vibrant citrus. **89** *—J.C. (10/1/2005)*

HANS LANG

Hans Lang 2001 Hallgartner Jungfer Eiswein Riesling (Rheingau) $NA. A deliciously fresh wine, with springtime ripeness and a vibrancy and life. Flavors of orange marmalade and crisp honey come with the lightness and freshness **91** *—R.V. (1/1/2004)*

Hans Lang 2001 Hattenheimer Wisselbrunnen Beerenauslese Riesling (Rheingau) $NA. The 45-acre Hans Lang estate is run by Johann Maximilian Lang from the winery in Hattenheim. With this Beerenauslese, he has been able to extract all the best elements of botrytis. It is beautifully intense, full of ripe, sweet fruit, with tangible flavors of raisins and honey. The palate is silky smooth, voluptuous, opulent. There is enormous intensity. **94** *—R.V. (1/1/2004)*

Hans Lang 2001 Kabinett Riesling (Rheingau) $NA. This is a classic, but it just misses greatness. There is sweetness at the start and the fruit is very ripe, balanced by a layer of tannin. Very pure fruit with thirst quenching acidity. **88** *—R.V. (1/1/2004)*

HEINRICH SEEBRICH

Heinrich Seebrich 2001 Niersteiner Hipping Spätlese Riesling (Rheinhessen) $13. 85 *—J.C. (3/1/2003)*

HELMUT HEXAMER

Helmut Hexamer 2004 Quarzit Meddersheimer Rheingrafenberg Qualitätswein Riesling (Nahe) $22. Racy and crisp, this wine showcases the balance that is a hallmark of the best '04s. Green apple and lime aromas segue easily into similar flavors, graced with touches of spring flowers and leafy greens, while the vibrant apple notes linger elegantly on the finish. **91 Editors' Choice** *—J.C. (10/1/2005)*

HENKELL

Henkell NV Rosé Feiner Sekt Trocken Rosé Blend (Germany) $11. Pale rose color. Really light-bodied, with modest lemon-lime flavors and a short finish. **83** *—J.C. (12/31/2004)*

HESS. STAATSWEINGÜTER

Hess. Staatsweingüter 2001 Rauenthaler Baiken Kabinett Riesling (Rheingau) $17. **88** *—J.C. (3/1/2003)*

Hess. Staatsweingüter 2001 Steinberger Spätlese Riesling (Rheingau) $34. **90** *—J.C. (3/1/2003)*

IMMICH-BATTERIEBERG

Immich-Batterieberg 2003 Kabinett Riesling (Mosel-Saar-Ruwer) $20. Starts with pineapple and apricot scents, then delivers mint and vanilla flavors to go along with citrus custard. Long on the finish, with soft acids, just lacks a bit of raciness. **89** *—J.C. (5/1/2005)*

J.L. WOLF

J.L. Wolf 2000 Forster Jesuitengarten Spätlese Trocken Riesling (Pfalz) $30. **87** *—J.C. (3/1/2003)*

J.L. Wolf 2001 Wachenheimer Riesling (Pfalz) $14. **86** *—J.C. (3/1/2003)*

J.L. Wolf 2003 Wachenheimer Belz Spätlese Riesling (Pfalz) $20. Citrusy and leaner than most spätlese in this vintage of unremitting heat, wih candied lime and green apple aromas and flavors, and a prickle of CO_2 on the palate. Turns a bit metallic and hard on the finish. **85** *—J.C. (5/1/2005)*

J.L. Wolf 2003 Wachenheimer Kabinett Riesling (Pfalz) $13. This wine features an unflattering dichotomy: soft, stewy fruit on one hand, and a hard, slightly metallic finish on the other. Passable, but lacks harmony. **82** *—J.C. (5/1/2005)*

J.U.H.A. STRUB

J.U.H.A. Strub 2001 Niersteiner Kabinett Riesling (Rheinhessen) $13. **87 Best Buy** *—J.C. (3/1/2003)*

JOH. HAART

Joh. Haart 2003 Piersporter Riesling (Mosel-Saar-Ruwer) $15. Nicely done for an entry-level wine, with lovely fresh notes of green apple, spring flowers, and lime on the nose, followed by apple, pear, and pineapple flavors. It's light in body, with a soft finish that maintains its focus without being excessively tart. **87** *—J.C. (5/1/2005)*

JOH. JOS. CHRISTOFFEL

Joh. Jos. Christoffel 2001 Erdener Treppchen Kabinett Riesling (Mosel-Saar-Ruwer) $23. **91 Editors' Choice** *—J.C. (3/1/2003)*

Joh. Jos. Christoffel 2004 Ürziger Würzgarten Kabinett Riesling (Mosel-Saar-Ruwer) $27. A bit tarry and rubbery on the nose, this plump kabinett boasts plenty of leesy pear and apple flavors allied to a slightly custardy texture. Not as impressive as in other recent vintages. **86** *—J.C. (10/1/2005)*

JOH. JOS. PRÜM

Joh. Jos. Prüm 2001 Wehlener Sonnenuhr Kabinett Riesling (Mosel-Saar-Ruwer) $25. **90** *—J.C. (3/1/2003)*

JOHANN HAART

Johann Haart 2001 Piersporter Goldtröpfchen Kabinett Riesling (Mosel-Saar-Ruwer) $17. **89** *—J.C. (3/1/2003)*

Johann Haart 2001 Piersporter Goldtröpfchen Spätlese Riesling (Mosel-Saar-Ruwer) $20. **91 Editors' Choice** *—J.C. (3/1/2003)*

JOHANN RUCK IPHOFEN

Johann Ruck Iphofen 2002 Iphofer Julius-Echter-Berg Spätlese Trocken Riesling (Franken) $36. Shows a rich, earthy note that runs through the wine, backed up by tart lime and grapefruit. Some green apple flavors add additional interest to this light-bodied, slightly off-dry offering. **85** *—J.C. (8/1/2004)*

JOHANNISHOF

Johannishof 2001 Charta QbA Riesling (Rheingau) $14. **90 Best Buy** *—J.C. (3/1/2003)*

Johannishof 2001 Johannisberger Goldatzel Kabinett Riesling (Rheingau) $11. **88 Best Buy** *—J.C. (3/1/2003)*

Johannishof 2003 Rudesheimer Berg Rottland Spätlese Riesling (Rheingau) $26. Stony and minerally on the nose, followed by gentler whiffs of honey, then finally broad, sweet flavors of ripe apples and pineapples. Mouthfilling and soft, but with balanced acidity and a long, complex finish. **92 Editors' Choice** *—J.C. (12/15/2004)*

JOSEF BIFFAR

Josef Biffar 2001 Wachenheimer Altenburg Spätlese Riesling (Pfalz) $32. **86** *—J.C. (3/1/2003)*

JOSEF LEITZ

Josef Leitz 2001 Rüdesheimer Berg Rottland Spätlese Trocken Riesling (Rheingau) $33. **90** *—J.C. (3/1/2003)*

Josef Leitz 2002 Rudesheimer Drachenstein Riesling QbA Riesling (Rheingau) $12. **90 Best Buy** *—J.C. (11/15/2003)*

JUL. FERD. KIMICH

Jul. Ferd. Kimich 2001 Deidecheimer Paradiesgarten Kabinett Halbtrocken Riesling (Pfalz) $15. Yellow-fruit aromas burst from the glass, followed by sweet pineapple and pear flavors. A slightly custardy mouthfeel adds plumpness to the midpalate, while a tangy edge of lemony acids keeps the fruit fresh and lively. **87** *—J.C. (1/1/2004)*

KARL ERBES

Karl Erbes 2001 Ürziger Würzgarten Kabinett Riesling (Mosel-Saar-Ruwer) $12. 88 Best Buy *—J.C. (3/1/2003)*

Karl Erbes 2003 Ürziger Würzgarten Riesling Spätlese Riesling (Mosel-Saar-Ruwer) $18. Nicely done spätlese—slightly sweet, yet well-balanced by acidity. Delicately etched pear and pineapple fruit carries hints of apple blossoms and vanilla. More length on the finish would have pushed the score higher. **88** *—J.C. (12/15/2004)*

KARTHAUSERHOF

Karthauserhof 2002 Kabinett Riesling (Mosel-Saar-Ruwer) $20. Rather full-bodied and slightly sweet, with mouthfilling mineral and tree-fruit flavors of apples and pears. Powdered quartz imparts a dusty quality to the nose, picking up lime notes on the finish. **88** *—J.C. (8/1/2004)*

KASSNER SIMON

Kassner Simon 2001 Freinsheimer Oschelkopf Spätlese Scheurebe (Pfalz) $16. Very aromatic, with aromas reminiscent of vanilla and spice. It's so aromatic, it even tastes floral, which may put off some tasters, but it's also ripe, full, and concentrated. The only quibble is an abbreviated finish, characteristic of the variety. **87** *—J.C. (1/1/2004)*

KIRSTEN

Kirsten 1998 Brut Riesling (Mosel-Saar-Ruwer) $16. 88 *—P.G. (12/31/2002)*

KNIPSER

Knipser 2003 Chardonnay & Weissburgunder Trocken White Blend (Pfalz) $27. It's roughly two-thirds Chardonnay, one-third Pinot Blanc, made in a dry style. Smells like vanilla and pears, but there's also a persistent vinegary note that creeps in and doesn't fade. Tasters less sensitive to this character will no doubt find more to like. **83** *—J.C. (5/1/2005)*

KOWERICH LUDWIG VON BEETHOVEN

Kowerich Ludwig von Beethoven 1998 Brut Riesling (Mosel-Saar-Ruwer) $17. 87 Best Buy *—P.G. (12/31/2002)*

KÜHL

Kühl 2003 Kabinett Riesling (Mosel-Saar-Ruwer) $9. Dusty and earthy on the nose, followed by pear and melon flavors that seema bit flabby and broad, lacking sharp definition. Picks up a canned sweet corn note on the finish. **83** *—J.C. (12/15/2004)*

KÜNSTLER

Künstler 2004 Hochheimer Reichestal Kabinett Riesling (Rheingau) $25. A broad, mouthfilling kabinett that's filled with green apple and plum fruit, with some riper peach notes sprinkled in as well. Plump and sweet, maybe a bit soft for some palates, but clean and very well made. **88** *—J.C. (10/1/2005)*

LANDSHUT

Landshut 2002 Qualitätswein Riesling (Mosel-Saar-Ruwer) $5. No, this is not a great, classic single-vineyard wine. But it is a clean, well-made blended Riesling that sells for a song. With its blend of melon, peach, cinnamon, and stone dust, you could do a lot worse for a fiver. **83 Best Buy** *—J.C. (11/1/2004)*

LOSEN-BOCKSTANZ

Losen-Bockstanz 2001 Wittlicher Lay Spätlese Riesling (Mosel-Saar-Ruwer) $18. An attractive wine with a sense of youth and freshness. Aromas of fresh hay, flavors of green fruits, and a restrained sweetness suggest this will go well with food. **86** *—R.V. (1/1/2004)*

LOTHAR FRANZ

Lothar Franz 2001 Hattenheimer Pfaffenberg Spätlese Riesling (Rheingau) $NA. Rich fruit with flavors of toffee apples and simple, but attractive ripeness. A layer of acidity gives balance, but this is not a complex wine. **86** *—R.V. (1/1/2004)*

LOUIS GUNTRUM

Louis Guntrum 2002 Oppenheimer Herrenberg Auslese Riesling (Rheinhessen) $23. This medium-bodied auslese has a rich, concentrated mouthfeel that perfectly suits its flavors of ripe apples, pears, and melons. Some slate notes on the nose add interest, while the finish is firmer than you might expect, suggesting decent ageability. Try now or in five years. **88** *—J.C. (12/15/2004)*

Louis Guntrum 2002 Oppenheimer Sackträger Riesling Spätlese Trocken Riesling (Rheinhessen) $19. Flint and mineral notes accent pineapple and lime aromas, while on the palate, the wine shows plenty of ripe, citrusy fruit flavors. Note that trocken wines can still have some residual sugar and this seems to have some, or perhaps it's just the very ripe-tasting fruit. Tangy acids on the long finish provide balance. **87** *—J.C. (12/15/2004)*

LUCASOF

Lucasof 2002 QbA Riesling (Pfalz) $11. Tart, lemony and earthy, but could be just the ticket on a hot summer day, when you're looking for something more complex than lemonade yet similarly refreshing. **84** *—J.C. (8/1/2004)*

MARKUS MOLITOR

Markus Molitor 2002 Bernkasteler Badstube Spätlese Feinherb Riesling (Mosel-Saar-Ruwer) $18. Sulfury on the nose, but behind that there's plenty of zesty lemon-lime fruit in a lean, dry format. Try with oysters and the like. **86** *—J.C. (12/15/2004)*

Markus Molitor 2001 Graacher Himmelreich Spätlese Riesling (Mosel-Saar-Ruwer) $16. Another mineral-laden wine from Markus Molitor, with a rich, oily texture balanced by a firm spine of acidity. Green apples, peaches, and citrus combine with stones and vegetable oil on the palate. Finishes long and crisp, like a good 2001 should. Good now, better in five years. **91** *—J.C. (12/15/2004)*

Markus Molitor 2002 QbA Trocken Riesling (Mosel-Saar-Ruwer) $12. Slightly sulfury and leesy on the nose, then lean and tart flavors of lemon curd and green apple on the palate. Light in body, very tart, and close to sour on the finish. **84** *—J.C. (12/15/2004)*

Markus Molitor 2002 Zeltinger Sonnenuhr Auslese * Feinherb Riesling (Mosel-Saar-Ruwer) $28. Aromas dominated by slate and diesel allow only a vague notion of fruit to show through, but the flavors are more apparent on the palate, where ripe peach emerges to complement the sense of slaty, minerally strength. Crisp acids turn a little grapefruity on the finish. **90** *—J.C. (12/15/2004)*

Markus Molitor 2002 Zeltinger Sonnenuhr Spätlese Riesling (Mosel-Saar-Ruwer) $20. Intensely minerally, this wine features an avalanche of stony flavors supported by baked apple notes for softness, and fresh-squeezed limes for backbone. Hints of diesel and oil shale dominate the nose. It's richly textured—almost chewy—yet crisp on the finish. Drink now–2010. **91** *—J.C. (12/15/2004)*

MAX FERD. RICHTER

Max Ferd. Richter 2001 Braueneberger Juffer Kabinett Riesling (Mosel-Saar-Ruwer) $20. **88** *—R.V. (4/1/2003)*

Max Ferd. Richter 2001 Braueneberger Juffer-Sonnenuhr Auslese Riesling (Mosel-Saar-Ruwer) $55. Dirk Richter makes wonderful, pure wines at this estate, which has been in his family for 300 years. Aromas of sweet honey and botrytis lead to an intensely flavored wine, filled with vibrant tastes of wild fruits and sweet apricots. **92** *—R.V. (1/1/2004)*

Max Ferd. Richter 2001 Graacher Himmelreich Kabinett Riesling (Mosel-Saar-Ruwer) $20. The palate of this wine is fresh, light and green, with dry, yeasty notes. Flavors of gooseberries and aromas of hedgerow fruits add a refreshing attractiveness. **87** *—R.V. (1/1/2004)*

Max Ferd. Richter 2001 Veldenzer Eisenberg Auslese Riesling (Mosel-Saar-Ruwer) $40. The light yeasty character is overlain with crisply sweet apple flavors and touches of orange peel. It is a wine which shows youth at this stage, but has a sense of great aging ability. **90** *—R.V. (1/1/2004)*

MAXIMIN GRÜNHÄUSER

Maximin Grünhäuser 2003 Abtsberg Beerenauslese Riesling (Mosel-Saar-Ruwer) $167. Heavily botrytized, this thick, unctuous wine virtually oozes with dried apricots and spiced applesauce aromas and flavors. So much going on it's hard to adequately describe, with a long, sticky finish. **95** *—J.C. (12/15/2004)*

Maximin Grünhäuser 2003 Abtsberg Riesling Auslese 155 Riesling (Mosel-Saar-Ruwer) $38. A mild disappointment, given the strong showing of so many of Von Schubert's other bottlings, the 2003 Auslese 155 is pleasantly light-bodied and nicely balances sugar and acidity. But unless I missed it, it doesn't show the same compelling complexity and minerality, instead relying on fruity-sweet flavors of ripe apples and pears. Hold 5–10 years, hoping for more detail to emerge with time. **88** *—J.C. (12/15/2004)*

Maximin Grünhäuser 2003 Abtsberg Spätlese Riesling (Mosel-Saar-Ruwer) $28. Good depth and richness here, yet balanced by soft acids, minerality, and spice. Hints of kerosene spark the aromas, which also boast ripe apple and pear notes. Baked tree fruit on the palate, wrapped in minerals and spice, yet not overly heavy. **90** *—J.C. (5/1/2005)*

Maximin Grünhäuser 2003 Herrenberg Riesling Kabinett Riesling (Mosel-Saar-Ruwer) $22. A bit sulfury at the moment, so give it some time in a decanter if opened in the next year or so. Once past that, it delivers apple, pear and orange-scented fruit in a plump, medium-weight package. Finishes long and a little soft, making it easy to drink now. **89** *—J.C. (12/15/2004)*

Maximin Grünhäuser 2003 QbA Riesling (Mosel-Saar-Ruwer) $19. Light in weight and crisper than many 2003s, with plenty of citrusy elements to support the ripe apple and pear flavors. There's also plenty of smoke and mineral notes to add complexity and a long finish that folds in touches of tangerine. **90** *—J.C. (12/15/2004)*

MÖNCHHOF

Mönchhof 2002 Astor Kabinett Riesling (Mosel-Saar-Ruwer) $18. The aromas burst from the glass, a bold kaleidoscope of limes, peaches, and minerals, but it's sweet and a bit soft on the palate, lacking cut and precision. Hold a few years, hoping it will emerge from this babyfat stage into a sleeker, more refined bottling. **85** *—J.C. (8/1/2004)*

Mönchhof 2004 Estate Qualitätswein Riesling (Mosel-Saar-Ruwer) $16. A delicate, racy wine, with attractive aromas of flint smoke, lime, and Granny Smith apple. Flavors are a bit simpler, reminiscent of crisp apples—tart but not hard-edged. Only quibble is that it finishes a bit short. **86** *—J.C. (10/1/2005)*

P.J. VALCKENBERG

P.J. Valckenberg 2001 QBA Gewürztraminer (Pfalz) $10. Next time you're looking for a solid Gewürz at a rock-bottom price, think twice before going straight for Alsace. This Pfalz version has all of the requisite elements—rose petals, lychee fruit, spice, and pears—in a round but not flabby package. **87 Best Buy** *—J.C. (1/1/2004)*

P.J. Valckenberg 2003 1808 Wormser Liebfrauenstift-Kirchenstück Riesling Spätlese Trocken Riesling (Rheinhessen) $27. Combines peach and lime scents with flavors that are more earthy and chalky. Medium-bodied and dry on the palate. Alternative closure fans will want to check out this bottling's cool Vino-Lok glass stopper from Alcoa. **85** *—J.C. (12/15/2004)*

P.J. Valckenberg 2001 Liebfrauenstift-Kirchenstück Kabinett Riesling (Rheinhessen) $14. **87** *—J.C. (3/1/2003)*

P.J. Valckenberg 2003 Liebfrauenstift-Kirchenstück Spätlese Riesling (Rheinhessen) $22. This is the flagship vineyard for the large Valckenberg firm, and one of their best wines, year in and year out. The 2003 shows yeasty, leesy, minerally aromas and flavors of pear, pineapple and talc, finishing on tart, grapefruity notes. Light in body; try as an apéritif. **87** *—J.C. (5/1/2005)*

P.J. Valckenberg 2003 QbA Riesling (Rheinhessen) $11. A bit floral on the nose, picking up green apple and grapefruit scents as well. Soft, pillowy fruit flavors are balanced by acidity that seems to build in strength on the finish. **84** *—J.C. (12/15/2004)*

P.J. Valckenberg 2001 QbA Trocken Riesling (Rheinhessen) $10. **89 Best Buy** *—J.C. (3/1/2003)*

P.J. Valckenberg 2003 Wormser Liebfrauenstift-Kirchenstück Kabinett Riesling (Rheinhessen) $16. Redolent with fresh, vibrant fruit aromas, but not nearly as exciting in the mouth, where the plump baked apple and pear flavors finish short. **84** *—J.C. (12/15/2004)*

PAZEN

Pazen 2001 Zeltinger Himmelreich Kabinett Riesling (Mosel-Saar-Ruwer) $14. **91 Best Buy** *—J.C. (3/1/2003)*

PETER JAKOB KUHN

Peter Jakob Kuhn 1999 Oestricher Lenchen Kabinett Riesling (Rheingau) $12. **87** *—S.H. (6/1/2001)*

PETER NICOLAY

Peter Nicolay 2001 Bernkasteler alte Badstube am Doctorberg Auslese Riesling (Mosel-Saar-Ruwer) $47. **87** *—R.V. (3/1/2003)*

Peter Nicolay 2001 Bernkasteler Badstube Spätlese Riesling (Mosel-Saar-Ruwer) $21. **87** *—R.V. (3/1/2003)*

Peter Nicolay 2001 Ürziger Goldwingert Spätlese Riesling (Mosel-Saar-Ruwer) $26. **92** *—R.V. (3/1/2003)*

PRINZ ZU SALM-DALBERG

Prinz zu Salm-Dalberg 2003 Johannisberg Wallhausen Auslese Riesling (Nahe) $50. Intensely minerally, with hints of fuel oil on the nose, then crushed stones and ripe melon flavors on the palate. This shows unusual balance and precision for a 2003, culminating in a long, mouthwatering finish.. **90** *—J.C. (5/1/2005)*

Prinz zu Salm-Dalberg 2003 Schloss Wallhausen Berg Roxheim Spätlese Riesling (Nahe) $29. If German wine labels are confusing to Americans, labels like this one are one reason why. Traditionally, this wine would be written as Roxheimer Berg, but for some reason this producer has written it Berg Roxheim. Green apple and diesel fuel aromas lead the way, followed by simple, fruity, apple flavors. Sweet and low in acidity, with a finish that's close to cloying. Try this as a dessert sipper with fresh fruit. **85** *—J.C. (5/1/2005)*

Prinz zu Salm-Dalberg 2001 Wallhäuser Johannisberg QbA Riesling (Nahe) $31. **90** *—J.C. (3/1/2003)*

REICHSGRAF VON KESSELSTATT

Reichsgraf von Kesselstatt 2001 Graacher QbA Trocken Riesling (Mosel-Saar-Ruwer) $NA. Von Kesselstatt's dry wine is a solid offering, but lacks the extra dimensions found in their more traditional bottlings. It's light, lean, and clean, combining green apples, Bartlett pears, and fresh lemons. **86** *—J.C. (1/1/2004)*

Reichsgraf von Kesselstatt 2001 Kaseler Nies'chen Kabinett Riesling (Mosel-Saar-Ruwer) $19. **86** *—J.C. (3/1/2003)*

Reichsgraf von Kesselstatt 2003 Piesporter Goldtröpfchen Riesling Kabinett Riesling (Mosel-Saar-Ruwer) $22. Smells great, with expansive floral notes that are reminiscent of roses. Yet that promise isn't fully fulfilled on the palate, where its relatively high (9.5%) alcohol levels make for an awkward balance with the guava and citrus flavors. Cellar it and hope for positive evolution, or drink up in the short term. **86** *—J.C. (12/15/2004)*

Reichsgraf von Kesselstatt 2001 RK QbA Riesling (Mosel-Saar-Ruwer) $9. **88 Best Buy** *—J.C. (3/1/2003)*

Reichsgraf von Kesselstatt 2002 Scharzhofberger Auslese Riesling (Mosel-Saar-Ruwer) $84. Smells like a mix of apricots, pineapples, and pears, with a judicious sprinkling of cinnamon. On the palate, the spice and earth components really kick in, adding richness to the fruit and honey flavors. Finishes with lingering sweetness. Approachable now, but should age beautifully. **92** *—J.C. (12/15/2004)*

Reichsgraf von Kesselstatt 2001 Scharzhofberger Spätlese Riesling (Mosel-Saar-Ruwer) $25. **90** *—J.C. (3/1/2003)*

ROBERT WEIL

Robert Weil 2002 QbA Trocken Riesling (Rheingau) $20. This is a fun, fresh, juicy wine, redolent of mixed citrus fruits. Lime, orange, and tangerine flavors bounce across the palate, finishing clean and refreshing. **86** *—J.C. (8/1/2004)*

RUDI WIEST

Rudi Wiest 2002 Rhein River QbA Riesling (Rheingau) $10. Importer Rudi Wiest has taken to selecting wines to bottle under his own label that offer fine quality for the price. This Rhine bottling blends peach and anise flavors in a medium-weight, off-dry wine that finishes strong. **85** *—J.C. (8/1/2004)*

S.A. PRÜM

S.A. Prüm 2003 Blue Slate Kabinett Riesling (Mosel-Saar-Ruwer) $16. Shows off the tropical nature of the vintage in impressive style, with mango, melon, and nectarine fruit overflowing the glass. It's big, relatively dry, and full-bodied, but it all works, capped off by super-ripe grapefruit on the finish. **88** *—J.C. (5/1/2005)*

S.A. Prüm 2001 Graacher Domprobst Eiswein Riesling (Mosel-Saar-Ruwer) $175. 90 *—J.C. (3/1/2003)*

S.A. Prüm 2001 Graacher Hammelreich Eiswein Riesling (Mosel-Saar-Ruwer) $165. 89 *—J.C. (3/1/2003)*

S.A. Prüm 1998 Graacher Himmelreich Eiswein Vat 28 Riesling (Mosel-Saar-Ruwer) $140. Dark in color for an eiswein, with intense, caramelized sugar, golden-raisin and dried-spice aromas. Tastes intensely sweet and sour, with sky-high acids and sugars that can't quite keep up. And it finishes with tart, quince-like notes. **84** *—J.C. (5/1/2005)*

S.A. Prüm 2001 Kabinett Halbtrocken Riesling (Mosel-Saar-Ruwer) $20. 89 *—J.C. (3/1/2003)*

S.A. Prüm 2001 Spätlese Trocken Riesling (Mosel-Saar-Ruwer) $23. 87 *—J.C. (3/1/2003)*

S.A. Prüm 2001 Wehlener Sonnenuhr Auslese Riesling (Mosel-Saar-Ruwer) $53. 87 *—J.C. (3/1/2003)*

S.A. Prüm 2001 Wehlener Sonnenuhr Spätlese Riesling (Mosel-Saar-Ruwer) $24. 86 *—J.C. (3/1/2003)*

S.A. Prüm 2001 Wehlener Sonnenuhr Spätlese Trocken Riesling (Mosel-Saar-Ruwer) $35. 87 *—J.C. (3/1/2003)*

SANDER

Sander 2002 Terravita Dornfelder (Rheinhessen) $18. A fresh, structured wine, with a touch of acidity, some wood and bitter chocolate flavors and a juicy, ripe aftertaste. This is a light red, very fersh and would work best at a cool cellar temperature. Like all Sander wines, the fruit was treated as gently as possible, with only small amounts of sulfites added. **85** *—R.V. (4/1/2005)*

Sander 2002 QbA Riesling (Rheinhessen) $13. Waxy and citrusy, this wine, made from organically grown grapes, is virtually dry, although not labeled as trocken. It's relatively heavy for a Riesling, finishing short. **84** *—J.C. (8/1/2004)*

Sander 2004 Metterheimer Sauvignon Blanc (Rheinhessen) $28. You don't find too many German Sauvignons, and maybe this wine tells us why. It's spritzy and artificially sweet, almost like lemon-lime soda pop. Could be better in the summer if served nicely chilled. **83** *(7/1/2005)*

Sander 2003 Trocken Weissburgunder (Rheinhessen) $13. A full-bodied, ripe wine with soft Pinot Blanc fruit and a touch of vanilla and caramel flavors. There are flavors of currants and a good layer of acidity with a full, but fresh aftertaste. **85** *—R.V. (4/1/2005)*

Sander 2003 Trio Terravita White Blend (Rheinhessen) $11. A fresh, uncomplicated light wine, with good clean and ripe fruit. This is a perfect apéritif wine, with good crisp pear and apple flavors. There is a touch of sweetness just to give it a lift. **84** *—R.V. (4/1/2005)*

SCHLOSS JOHANNISBERGER

Schloss Johannisberger 2003 QbA Riesling (Rheingau) $23. This is nicely balanced, with a relatively light body and sweet fruit, yet enough grapefruity acids on the finish to offset the residual sugar. Bright apple and pear flavors sing loudly, alongside hints of honey and citrus. **86** *—J.C. (12/15/2004)*

Schloss Johannisberger 2003 Riesling Kabinett Riesling (Rheingau) $28. Fairly full-bodied and quite dry, with low residual sugar levels and high alcohol (12%), this is an atypically muscular kabinett. Smoke and earth flavors are minerally and complex, backed by hints of peach and grapefruit, finishing tart. **86** *—J.C. (12/15/2004)*

SCHLOSS SAARSTEIN

Schloss Saarstein 2001 QbA Trocken Riesling (Mosel-Saar-Ruwer) $11. 88 Best Buy *—J.C. (3/1/2003)*

Schloss Saarstein 2003 Riesling Spätlese Trocken Riesling (Mosel-Saar-Ruwer) $26. This wine is for folks who bemoan the lack of acidity in the 2003s. Here's your acid fix: zippy, zesty lime-like acids are cushioned by just enough ripe peaches to make it enjoyable. Crisp and stone-dry on the finish. **87** *—J.C. (12/15/2004)*

Schloss Saarstein 2003 Serriger Schloss Saarsteiner Kabinett Riesling (Mosel-Saar-Ruwer) $20. Decently balanced for short-term drinking, this wine has managed to retain a sense of freshness to its finish that some 2003s are lacking. Apricot and pineapple aromas give way to apple and pear flavors and a lively, citrusy finish. **88** *—J.C. (5/1/2005)*

Schloss Saarstein 2003 QbA Weissburgunder (Mosel-Saar-Ruwer) $17. This is a dramatic contrast to the Rieslings from Schloss Saarstein, which tend to be delicate and racy. This Pinot Blanc is fat, with modest melon and baked apple flavors and a soft, short finish. **84** *—J.C. (12/15/2004)*

GERMANY

SCHLOSS SCHÖNBORN

Schloss Schönborn 2001 Erbacher Marcobrunn Kabinett Riesling (Rheingau) $14. **90** *—R.V. (3/1/2003)*

Schloss Schönborn 2001 Hattenheimer Pfaffenberg Kabinett Riesling (Rheingau) $12. **90** *—R.V. (3/1/2003)*

Schloss Schönborn 2001 Johannisberger Klaus Spätlese Riesling (Rheingau) $16. **87** *—R.V. (3/1/2003)*

Schloss Schönborn 2000 Rudesheimer Berg Rottland Auslese Riesling (Rheingau) $43. **93** *—R.V. (3/1/2003)*

SCHLOSS VOLLRADS

Schloss Vollrads 2003 Auslese Riesling (Rheingau) $50. Despite the inclusion of 25% botrytized fruit, this wine remains well-balanced; fresh, not heavy. Melon and green apple flavors offset riper notes of honey and orange marmalade. **90** *(8/1/2004)*

Schloss Vollrads 2002 Eiswein Riesling (Rheingau) $160. This wine's high acidity provides balance for the wine's intense sweetness, imparting a racy quality to the long, lemony finish. Aromas and flavors of "yellow" fruits—pineapple, citrus, and quince—predominate. **91** *(8/1/2004)*

Schloss Vollrads 2003 Kabinett Riesling (Rheingau) $17. Plump, medium-weight kabinett that features aromas of peach and apple blossom and flavors of peach and mango. Finishes a bit tart, giving it a nice sense of balance. **86** *(8/1/2004)*

Schloss Vollrads 2002 Kabinett Halbtrocken Riesling (Rheingau) $17. Starts off with a hint of diesel fuel, then merges seamlessly into green apples, pears, honey, and mineral notes. Finishes crisp and clean, picking up additional mineral flavors. **87** *(8/1/2004)*

Schloss Vollrads 2003 Kabinett Trocken Riesling (Rheingau) $17. Seems a bit disjointed right now, with aromas of ripe stone fruit and mineral that aren't obvious on the palate, where the flavors are grapefruity and sharp. Give it another six months to come into balance. **85** *(8/1/2004)*

Schloss Vollrads 2003 QbA Trocken Riesling (Rheingau) $15. Smells fresh and a bit yeasty and minerally, then follows through with rich fruit and grapefruity acids that finish on a razor-sharp edge. Try with shellfish. **86** *(8/1/2004)*

Schloss Vollrads 2003 Spätlese Riesling (Rheingau) $26. In an interesting twist, this wine actually seems lighter and crisper than the kabinett, pairing peach, apple, and pear flavors with a minerally finish that still retains the vintage's inherent softness. **89** *(8/1/2004)*

Schloss Vollrads 2003 Spätlese Halbtrocken Riesling (Rheingau) $26. This full-bodied, mostly dry Riesling features a rich, layered texture and a spicy finish. Slightly floral notes add nuance to solid pear, melon, and mineral flavors. **88** *(8/1/2004)*

SCHLOSS WALLHAUSEN

Schloss Wallhausen 2004 Kabinett Riesling (Nahe) $17. Plump, yet buttressed by firm acidity, Wallhausen's kabinett features strong minerality this year. My original notes on its aromas read: powdered mineral, apple, pear, mineral. Tastes like liquid rocks, with hints of green herbs. Finishes with a grapefruity flourish. **88** *—J.C. (10/1/2005)*

SCHMITGES

Schmitges 2003 Grauschiefer Qualitätswein Trocken Riesling (Mosel-Saar-Ruwer) $15. Smells fruity, with scents of apple, lime, pineapple, and pear that are echoed on the palate. Doesn't offer a lot of mineral complexity, but plenty of tart, lightbodied, almost completely dry fruit. **86** *—J.C. (11/1/2004)*

Schmitges 2003 QbA Riesling (Mosel-Saar-Ruwer) $17. Apple and pineapple on the nose, bolstered by scents of spring flowers. It's medium-bodied on the palate, with mineral-accented apple flavors and a long, crisply acidic finish. **88** *—J.C. (11/1/2004)*

SCHMITT SCHENK

Schmitt Schenk 2001 Ayler Kupp Auslese Riesling (Mosel-Saar-Ruwer) $14. **86** *—R.V. (3/1/2003)*

SCHMITT SOHNE

Schmitt Sohne 2001 Spätlese Riesling (Mosel-Saar-Ruwer) $9. **83** *—R.V. (3/1/2003)*

Schmitt Sohne 2001 Wehlener Sonnenuhr Kabinett Riesling (Mosel-Saar-Ruwer) $18. **86** *—R.V. (3/1/2003)*

SCHUMANN-NÄGLER

Schumann-Nägler 2001 Christopher Philipp QbA Riesling (Rheingau) $10. Simple apple and citrus aromas and flavors in a weightier-than-expected package. The lingering finish turns slightly sour at the end. **83** *—J.C. (1/1/2004)*

Schumann-Nägler 2001 Johannisberger Ertenbringer Riesling (Rheingau) $15. **86** *—J.C. (3/1/2003)*

SELBACH

Selbach 2001 Piesporter Michelsberg Riesling Kabinett Riesling (Mosel-Saar-Ruwer) $11. **87 Best Buy** *—D.T. (11/15/2002)*

SELBACH-OSTER

Selbach-Oster 2001 Zeltinger Sonnenuhr Auslese Riesling (Mosel-Saar-Ruwer) $33. **91** *—J.C. (3/1/2003)*

Selbach-Oster 2001 Zeltinger Sonnenuuhr Spätlese One Star Riesling (Mosel-Saar-Ruwer) $27. 91 *—J.C. (3/1/2003)*

ST. GABRIEL

St. Gabriel 2002 Auslese Riesling (Mosel-Saar-Ruwer) $9. Light-bodied, with sweet apple, lime, and peach fruit. Hints of kerosene mark the nose, while the finish is sweet but simultaneously crisp and grapefruity. 86 Best Buy *—J.C. (12/15/2004)*

St. Gabriel 2002 Qualitätswein Riesling (Pfalz) $6. Simple lime and apple flavors, lightly sweet and low in acidity, but supple, easy to drink and generally harmonious. A good by-the-glass choice at your local German restaurant. 84 Best Buy *—J.C. (11/1/2004)*

ST. URBANS-HOF

St. Urbans-Hof 2001 Ockfener Bockstein Auslese Riesling (Mosel-Saar-Ruwer) $16. The palate is clean, fresh, softly sweet rather than intense. Flavors of ripe plums and currants give it an attractive directness and simplicity. It could age, but only in the medium-term. 87 *—R.V. (1/1/2004)*

St. Urbans-Hof 2000 Ockfener Bockstein Kabinett Riesling (Mosel-Saar-Ruwer) $14. 86 *—J.C. (5/1/2002)*

St. Urbans-Hof 2000 Ockfener Bockstein Spätlese Riesling (Mosel-Saar-Ruwer) $18. 86 *—C.S. (5/1/2002)*

St. Urbans-Hof 2001 Piesporter Goldtröpfchen Kabinett Riesling (Mosel-Saar-Ruwer) $16. 88 *—J.C. (3/1/2003)*

St. Urbans-Hof 2000 Piesporter Goldtröpfchen Spätlese Riesling (Mosel-Saar-Ruwer) $21. 86 *—C.S. (5/1/2002)*

STAATSWEINGÜTER KLOSTER EBERBACH

Staatsweingüter Kloster Eberbach 1998 Rauenthaler Baiken Brut Riesling (Rheingau) $17. 86 *—P.G. (12/31/2002)*

Staatsweingüter Kloster Eberbach 2001 Steinberger Spätlese Riesling (Rheingau) $34. 89 *—R.V. (3/1/2003)*

STICH DEN BUBEN

Stich den Buben 1999 Kabinett Riesling (Baden-Baden) $13. 84 *(8/1/2001)*

SYBILLE KUNTZ

Sybille Kuntz 2001 Dreistern Lieser Niederberg-Helden Spätlese Trocken Riesling (Mosel-Saar-Ruwer) $NA. The dry style of this wine emphasizes the flavors of green plums and hedgerow fruits. Crisp, but full-bodied with its almond aromas, it is peppery and spicy and has some weight. 89 *—R.V. (1/1/2004)*

TESCH

Tesch 2001 Langenlonsheimer Löhrer Berg Auslese Riesling (Nahe) $30. 90 *—J.C. (3/1/2003)*

Tesch 2001 Langenlonsheimer Löhrer Berg Kabinett Halbtrocken Riesling (Nahe) $15. 89 *—J.C. (3/1/2003)*

Tesch 2001 Laubenheimer St. Remigiusberg Spätlese Trocken Riesling (Nahe) $23. 88 *—J.C. (3/1/2003)*

TWO PRINCES

Two Princes 2004 P2 Qualitätswein Riesling (Nahe) $10. Solid Riesling from the zu Salm family. Pear, pineapple, and melon scents waft from the glass, while the flavors take all of those and add dried-spice notes. Not the most intense or longest wine, but an enjoyable quaff. 85 Best Buy *—J.C. (10/1/2005)*

ULRICH LANGGUTH

Ulrich Langguth 2001 Piesporter Goldtröpfchen Spätlese Riesling (Mosel-Saar-Ruwer) $20. Full, and fat, with a layer of meaty flavors on top of light acidity and flavors of ripe green plums. 82 *—R.V. (1/1/2004)*

VILLA WOLF

Villa Wolf 2003 Kabinett Riesling (Pfalz) $12. This light-bodied wine shows impressive balance, it's just not that expressive at this early stage of its evolution. There's some lime and green apple notes, but also lots of beery, yeasty, leesy notes, with the true flavors still unformed. Try in six months. 87 Best Buy *—J.C. (5/1/2005)*

VON BEULWITZ

Von Beulwitz 1999 Kaseler Nies'chen Spätlese Riesling (Mosel-Saar-Ruwer) $12. 89 *—S.H. (6/1/2001)*

VON OTHEGRAVEN

Von Othegraven 2003 Kanzem Altenberg Auslese Riesling (Mosel-Saar-Ruwer) $50. A soft, mouthfilling wine that boasts impressive ripeness, Von Othegraven's Kanzem Altenberg Auslese oozes with spiced poached pear aromas and flavors that spread out across the palate to encompass cinnamon and vanilla in addition to the sweet fruit. Drink now–2010, but it may surprise you and last even longer. 88 *—J.C. (5/1/2005)*

Von Othegraven 2001 Kanzemer Altenberg Auslese Riesling (Mosel-Saar-Ruwer) $32. 90 *—R.V. (3/1/2003)*

Von Othegraven 2001 Kanzemer Altenberg QbA Riesling (Mosel-Saar-Ruwer) $27. 91 Editors' Choice *—J.C. (3/1/2003)*

Von Othegraven 2001 Maria v. O. Riesling (Mosel-Saar-Ruwer) $15. 90 Best Buy *—J.C. (3/1/2003)*

Von Othegraven 1999 Maximus Riesling (Mosel-Saar-Ruwer) $18. 87 *(8/1/2001)*

Von Othegraven 2001 Ockfen Bockstein Riesling (Mosel-Saar-Ruwer) $25. 90 *—J.C. (3/1/2003)*

Von Othegraven 2000 Kanzemer Berg Brut Sekt (Mosel-Saar-Ruwer) $35. An interesting sparkler, one that tastes like aged Riesling with a soft, creamy mousse. Sound excellent? It is, but the layers of toast and yeast piled on top don't fully mesh with the rest of the wine, making it merely good. **85** *—J.C. (12/31/2004)*

WILLI HAAG

Willi Haag 2003 Brauneberger Juffer Riesling Kabinett Riesling (Mosel-Saar-Ruwer) $18. Hints of ripe apples and pears are largely submerged under lots of dieselly aromas. On the palate, once past the cloud of terpenes, there is some lively ripe fruit, but it finishes a little soft. Drink now. **87** *—J.C. (12/15/2004)*

WITTMANN

Wittmann 2003 Trocken Riesling (Rheinhessen) $23. A light fresh style of wine, which is fruity, lively and easy drinking. There is a touch of tannic structure and flavors of green fruits, apples and gooseberries. This is a good food style of Riesling. **85** *—R.V. (4/1/2005)*

Wittmann 2003 Westhofen Morstein Trocken Riesling (Rheinhessen) $NA. A lively, crisp Riesling with enough rich fruit to give it weight as well as freshness. An intense wine, with floral aromas, and flavors of white currants, pears and fresh herbs. **88** *—R.V. (4/1/2005)*

Wittmann 2003 Westhofener Morstein Auslese S Riesling (Rheinhessen) $NA. Full of sweet fruit and balancing acidity, this is a light, fresh style of Auslese, with lively fruit and flavors of honey and quince jelly. **87** *—R.V. (4/1/2005)*

Wittmann 2003 Westhofener Morstein Trockenbeerenauslese Riesling (Rheinhessen) $NA. Aromas of pure, sweet, dry botrytis follow through to a wine of great richness, sweetness and acidity on the palate. Offers orange marmalade flavors and concentrated superripe fruit; at this stage, it is just beginning to come together—give it 10 years or more. **91** *—R.V. (4/1/2005)*

Italy

In ancient times, the Italian peninsula was commonly referred to as enotria, or "land of wine," because of its rich diversity of grape varieties and many acres dedicated to cultivated vines. In more ways than one, Italy became a gigantic nursery and a commercial hub fortuitously positioned at the heart of the Mediterranean for what would become western civilization's first "globally" traded product: wine.

Tenuta la Volta, near Barolo, Piemonte, Italy.

Italy's prominence in the global wine industry has in no way diminished despite millennia of history. The sun-drenched North-South peninsula that extends from the thirty-sixth to the forty-sixth parallel embodies pockets of geographical, geological, and climatic perfection between the Upper Adige and the island of Pantelleria for the production of quality wine. Italian tradition is so closely grafted to the vine that the good cheer and easy attitudes associated with wine culture are mirrored in the nation's temperament.

Despite Italy's long affinity with *Vitis vinifera*, the Italian wine industry has experienced an invigorating rebirth over the past three decades that truly sets it apart from other European wine nations. American baby boomers may still recall watery Valpolicella or Chianti Classico in hay-wrapped flasks at neighborhood New York eateries, or the generic "white" and "red" wines of Sicily's Corvo. Wines like those cemented Italy's reputation as a quantity (as opposed to quality, like in France) producer of wines sold at attractive prices. But as Italy gained confidence during the prosperous post-war years in the areas of design, fashion, and gastronomy, it demonstrated renewed attention to wine. Thanks to a small band of primarily Tuscan vintners, Italy launched itself with aggressive determination onto the world stage as a producer of some of the best wines ever produced anywhere: Amarone, Barolo, Brunello di Montalcino, and Passito di Pantelleria.

Like a happy epidemic, modern viticulture and enological techniques swept across the Italian peninsula throughout the 1980s and 1990s: Vertical shoot positioning and bilateral cordon trellising in vineyards; stainless steel, temperature-controlled fermentation, and barrique wood aging in wineries. As profits soared, producers reinvested in technology, personnel, and high-priced consultants, and a modern Italian wine revolution had suddenly taken place.

As it stands, Italy is the world's second-largest producer of wine after France. Each year, one in fifty Italians is involved with the grape harvest. And like France, Italy has adopted a rigorously controlled appellation system that imposes strict controls, with regulations governing vineyard quality, yields per acre, and aging practices among other things. There are over three hundred DOC (Denominazioni di Origine Controllata) and DOCG (Denominazioni di Origine Controllata e Garantita) wines today, and the classifications increase to over five hundred when IGT (Indicazioni Geografica Tipica) wines are factored in. Thanks to this system, Italy's fifty thousand wineries enjoy a competitive advantage when it comes to the production and sales of quality wines.

Interestingly, there is a second wine revolution underway that promises to unlock potential uniquely associated with Italy. It is the re-evaluation and celebration of Italy's rich patrimony of "indigenous" grapes. (Because some varieties actually originated outside Italy, producers often refer to them as "traditional" varieties instead.) These are grapes—like Nero d'Avola, Fiano, Sagrantino, and Teroldego—that only modern enotria can offer to world consumers. As a result, a rapidly increasing number of vintners from Italy's twenty winemaking regions are banking on "traditional" varieties to distinguish themselves in a market dominated by "international" varieties, such as Merlot, Cabernet Sauvignon, and Chardonnay.

NORTH

The Italian Alps butt against the long expanses of the Po River plains leaving tiny pockets and microclimates along the foot of the mountains that are each linked to their own special wine. Starting in northwestern Piedmont, Nebbiolo grapes form two tall pillars of Italy's wine legacy: Barolo and Barbaresco, named in the French tradition after the hilltop hamlets where the wines were born. Like in Burgundy, the exclusivity of these wines has a lot to do with the winemakers' battle against nature and the wine's extraordinary ability to age. Rare vintages like the stellar 1985 or 1990 Barolos are the darlings of serious wine collectors.

Further east, in the Veneto region, vintners follow an ancient formula in which wine is made from raisins dried on straw mats. With its higher concentration and alcohol, silky Amarone is Italy's most distinctive wine and can command record prices for new releases. The Veneto Trentino, Alto Adige, and Friuli-Venezia Giulia are celebrated for their white wines—such as the phenomenally successful Pinot Grigio. Italy's best sparkling wine is made in Trentino and the Franciacorta area of Lombardy (known as the "Champagne of Italy") under strict regulation with Pinot Noir and Chardonnay grapes.

CENTER

With its cypress-crested hills and beautiful stone farmhouses, Tuscany is the pin-up queen of Italian enology. The region's iconic dreamscape has helped promote the image of Italian wine abroad like no other. Within Tuscany's borders is a treasure-trove of excellent wines: Chianti Classico, Brunello di Montalcino, Vino Nobile di Montepulciano, San Gimignano whites, Bolgheri and Maremma reds. Italy's wine revolution started here when storied producers like Piero Antinori worked outside appellation regulations to make wines blended with international varieties such as Cabernet Sauvignon. These wines are known as Super Tuscans and are considered on par with the top crus of Bordeaux and California.

Central Italy delivers many more exciting wines, such as Sagrantino from the Umbrian town of Montefalco, dense and dark Montepulciano from Abruzzo, and white Verdicchio from Le Marche.

SOUTH AND ISLANDS

The regions of southern Italy, and the island of Sicily in particular, are regarded as Italy's enological frontier: Relaxed regulation and increased experimentation promise a bright future for vintners and investors alike. In many ways, Italy's south is a "new world" wine region locked within the confines of an "old world" wine reality. This unique duality has many betting on its enological promise.

Campania boasts wonderful whites, such as Fiano and Greco di Tufo that embody crisp, mineral characteristics from volcanic soils. Its red is Taurasi ("the Barolo of the south"), made from Aglianico. That same grape makes Basilicata's much-hyped Aglianico del Vulture. Puglia, the "heel" of the boot of Italy, was mostly a producer of bulk wine, but holds it own today among nascent wine regions with its powerhouse Primitivo and Negroamaro grapes.

Sicily has shown keen marketing savvy in bringing media attention to its native grapes like Nero d'Avola (red) and Grillo (a white once used in the production of fortified wine Marsala) and has done a great job of promoting the south of Italy in general. Some of Europe's most sensuous dessert wines, like the honey-rich Passito di Pantelleria, come from Sicily's satellite islands. The Mediterranean's other big island, Sardinia, is steadily working on its Cannonau and Vermentino grapes to raise the bar on quality there.

A-MANO

A-Mano 2003 Primitivo (Puglia) $11. A-Mano's solid, well-made Pimitivo has yet again delivered a winning hand despite the hot vintage. Ripe black cherry, cigar box, nutmeg, clove, and fruit roll-ups seem to dance in a circle right under your nose. There is slight jamminess that gets mopped up by the wine's fierce power and structure. **87 Best Buy** *—M.L. (9/1/2005)*

A-Mano 2001 Primitivo (Puglia) $10. 88 *—M.S. (11/15/2003)*

A-Mano 2003 Prima Mano Primitivo (Puglia) $28. California's Mark Shannon flexes his winemaking muscles in Puglia with this barrique-aged reserve wine. He pumps out dried rosemary, thyme, and smells that resemble those fish-shaped crackers backed by plenty of rich fruit. Tannins are forceful and the wine's alcohol and thick concentration might make it hard to pair with anything other than a thick slab of red meat. **88** *—M.L. (9/1/2005)*

AAA

AAA NV Montenisa Brut Satèn (Franciacorta) $46. The Antinori daughters have teamed up to make wine in Franciacorta, Italy's most exciting sparkling wine zone. This 100% Chardonnay offers aromas of citrus, peaches, some raspberry, and freshly cut grass. In the mouth it follows up with roasted nuts. **88** *—M.L. (12/15/2004)*

ABBAZIA MONTE OLIVETO

Abbazia Monte Oliveto 2000 Vernaccia (San Gimignano) $10. 87 *(12/31/2002)*

ABBAZIA SANTA ANASTASIA

Abbazia Santa Anastasia 1998 Litra Cabernet Sauvignon (Sicilia) $40. 88 *—C.S. (5/1/2002)*

Abbazia Santa Anastasia 2002 Nero d'Avola (Sicilia) $13. Good raisin and cherry aromas give way to chocolate and earth scents. Fairly snappy and lean in terms of fruit, but incredibly fresh and lively. Some bitter chocolate and coffee on the finish add character. Fine as an everyday offering. **87** *—M.S. (2/1/2005)*

Abbazia Santa Anastasia 1998 Montenero Nero d'Avola (Sicilia) $34. 90 Cellar Selection *(5/1/2002)*

Abbazia Santa Anastasia 2001 Passomaggio Red Blend (Sicilia) $14. 92 Best Buy *—M.S. (10/1/2003)*

Abbazia Santa Anastasia 2002 Bianco di Passomaggio White Blend (Sicilia) $14. 88 *—M.S. (11/15/2003)*

ABBONA

Abbona 1997 Papa Celso (Dolcetto di Dogliani) $16. 89 *(4/1/2000)*

ADRIANO MARCO & VITTORIO

Adriano Marco & Vittorio 1999 Nebbiolo (Barbaresco) $40. Mildly floral on the nose, with hints of cherry, leather, and chocolate that roll gently into supple cherry flavors. This wine's on the lighter side, but very pretty, and its modest tannins suggest early drinkability. Try 2005–2015. **88** *(4/2/2004)*

Adriano Marco & Vittorio 2000 Basarin Nebbiolo (Barbaresco) $40. Big, chewy, and expansive, with a blend of dark and milk chocolates, black cherries and plums. Picks up intriguing hints of anise and leather on the extended, finely textured finish. **92** *(4/2/2004)*

AGOSTINO PAVIA & FIGLI

Agostino Pavia & Figli 2000 Moliss (Barbera d'Asti) $14. 84 *—M.S. (12/15/2003)*

AGRICOLE VALLONE

Agricole Vallone 1997 Riserva Vigna Flaminio Red Blend (Salice Salentino) $10. 88 Best Buy *—M.S. (11/15/2003)*

AL BANO CARRISI

Al Bano Carrisi 1997 Negroamaro (Salice Salentino) $9. 83 *—C.S. (5/1/2002)*

ALBERTO LOI

Alberto Loi 1995 Grenache (Sardinia) $15. 84 *—C.S. (5/1/2002)*

ALBINO ARMANI

Albino Armani 2001 Pinot Grigio (Veneto) $17. 86 *—J.C. (7/1/2003)*

ALBINO ROCCA

Albino Rocca 1999 Vigneto Brich Ronchi Nebbiolo (Barbaresco) $65. Long and firmly tannic, the only question is whether it has enough fruit. Our money says it does—the hints of black cherries, leather, and citrus peel currently walled off by a veil of cedar and tannin should emerge by 2010. **91** *(4/2/2004)*

ALDO CONTERNO

Aldo Conterno 1999 (Barbera d'Alba) $40. 84 *—M.S. (11/15/2002)*

Aldo Conterno 1998 Bussia Soprana (Dolcetto d'Alba) $22. 83 *(4/1/2000)*

ALLEGRINI

Allegrini 1998 La Poja Corvina (Veronese) $85. 90 *(5/1/2003)*

Allegrini 2000 Red Blend (Amarone della Valpolicella Classico) $75. Dark and smoky, with a dab of charcoal along with prune, chocolate and herbs on the nose. Runs zesty and fast, with lively black cherry flavors and a touch of pepper. Definitely well made, with chewy richness. **90** *(11/1/2005)*

Allegrini 1999 La Grola Red Blend (Veneto) $20. **88** *(5/1/2003)*

Allegrini 1993 Recioto Superiore Red Blend (Amarone della Valpolicella Classico) $40. **94** *(11/15/1999)*

ALOIS LAGEDER

Alois Lageder 1998 Pinot Grigio (Alto Adige) $11. **87** *—M.S. (4/1/2000)*

ALTESINO

Altesino 2000 (Brunello di Montalcino) $55. Strangely this one has a nose of Italian bitters, anise, and pine. It's not a warm, ripe wine. What it does give is tight, dry cherry and berry flavors with layers of complexity and intrigue. Not very woody or chewy. More old school and an enigma among so many forward, fruity compatriots. **89** *—M.S. (7/1/2005)*

Altesino 1999 Riserva (Brunello di Montalcino) $90. Begins with a light touch of raisin, while the mouth feels soft, albeit a touch tannic. Further inspection unveils a deeper, meatier side, but also a touch of stewed fruit. Finishes solid, with coffee and chocolate as well as a medicinal hint. **90** *—M.S. (7/1/2005)*

AMINEA

Aminea 2004 Fiano (Fiano di Avellino) $19. Slightly reductive at the start, this lightly golden Fiano carries through with exotic fruit and dough-like notes. Ripe and viscous in the mouth with medium persistence. **84** *—M.L. (9/1/2005)*

ANERI

Aneri NV Brut (Prosecco di Valdobbiadene) $20. Fairly plump and wayward on the bouquet, with chalky, tart, green-apple flavors. A bit sulfuric and bitter toward the end, with dry lemon notes. Good enough in the mouth, but sort of short on fruit. **84** *—M.S. (12/15/2005)*

ANSELMA

Anselma 1996 (Barbera d'Alba) $15. **86** *(4/1/2000)*

ANSELMI

Anselmi 2001 Capitel Croce White Blend (Delle Venezie) $18. **91** *—R.V. (7/1/2003)*

Anselmi 2001 San Vincenzo White Blend (Veneto) $10. **84** *—J.C. (7/1/2003)*

ANTINORI

Antinori 1999 Pian delle Vigne (Brunello di Montalcino) $80. Lovely, with its own version of perfume exuding from the glass. Additional rose and berry notes lead to a silky palate featuring prune, flourless chocolate torte, and coffee. The back end is tighter and heavier than the front, which bodes well for its future. Made in the modern style. **93** *—M.S. (6/1/2004)*

Antinori 1995 Pian delle Vigne (Brunello di Montalcino) $60. **89** *—M.S. (9/1/2000)*

Antinori 2000 Guado al Tasso Blend (Bolgheri) $80. Probably not what you'd expect from this wine. It's a fair amount gamy, with caramel, warm earth, and some bacon on the nose. There's sweet berry fruit and licorice notes, but also a dry, peppery, woody character. Shows a young, willing attitude, but it's not the best "Guado" of the past few vintages. **89** *—M.S. (10/1/2004)*

Antinori 1999 Guado Al Tasso Red Blend (Bolgheri) $80. **95** *—M.S. (8/1/2002)*

Antinori 1997 Solaia Red Blend (Toscana) $115. **97 Editors' Choice** *(9/1/2001)*

Antinori 2001 Pèppoli (Chianti Classico) $21. A perfectly solid, well-made Chianti in every sense. The nose is spicy, with hints of wood smoke, barbecue sauce, cedar, and coconut. The palate delivers requisite berry, plum, cherry, and tea in a fine wrapping, while the finish is harmonious, with bits of espresso and chocolate. Not in-your-face, but still fairly forward. **89** *(4/1/2005)*

Antinori 1998 Pèppoli (Chianti Classico) $22. **89** *(4/1/2001)*

Antinori 2001 Santa Cristina (Toscana) $11. **86 Best Buy** *—M.S. (12/31/2002)*

Antinori 1998 Tenuta Marchese Antinori Riserva (Chianti Classico) $23. **92** *—R.V. (8/1/2002)*

Antinori 2000 Tignanello (Toscana) $70. Clearly not the greatest of Tignanellos, but still a fine wine in its own right. One of the founding super Tuscans, this rendition features chunky, grapy, flowery aromas backed by blackberry and black cherry flavors. It's plump, maybe a bit heavy and oaky, but still worthy of its reputation. **90** *—M.S. (10/1/2004)*

Antinori 1997 Villa Antinori Riserva (Chianti Classico) $21. **87** *(4/1/2001)*

Antinori 2001 Villa Antinori Tuscan Blend (Toscana) $23. An excellent blend of Sangiovese, Cabernet Sauvignon, Merlot, and Syrah. The bouquet is loaded with sweet fruit, lushness, and a deft dollop of oak. A masculine yet bright wine, with cassis, cherry, and the works. Finishes fresh, with chocolate notes. A value in its price range. **91 Editors' Choice** *—M.S. (10/1/2004)*

Antinori 2002 Tenuta Guado al Tasso Vermentino (Bolgheri) $18. Talk about a white wine with shine. This aromatic slugger offers a pretty luster, lovely almond and wildflower aromas and also touches of sea air and honey. Flavors of pineapple, lime, and banana are unadulterated, and the finish is clean. **90** *—M.S. (8/1/2004)*

Antinori 1999 Villa Antinori White Blend (Toscana) $11. 87 Best Buy *(9/1/2001)*

ANTONELLI

Antonelli 2000 Rosso (Montefalco) $14. Warm and bit stewy, with molasses and blackberry on the nose. Surprisingly, things go tangy on the palate. And that tartness remains throughout the finish. Nevertheless this is a good, solid Umbrian red for casual occasions. Needs food to show its stuff. **86** *—M.S. (10/1/2004)*

Antonelli 2001 (Sagrantino di Montefalco) $40. Filippo Antonelli is one of the forces that helped push Sagrantino into the international spotlight. His wine is ripe with black currant, cherry, cassis, vanilla, and a sweet and sour note that tastes like orange peel. Tannins are hefty. Imported by Laird & Company. **88** *—M.L. (9/1/2005)*

Antonelli 1999 Estate Bottled (Sagrantino di Montefalco) $34. A heavy wine with youthful tobacco, plum, and berry aromas. The bold plum and blackberry flavors are bruising, but the fruit is a kitten compared to the tannic structure of this wine, which hits like a sledgehammer. A very young and willing red, maybe not perfectly refined but powerful. **89** *—M.S. (10/1/2004)*

Antonelli 1997 Estate Bottled (Sagrantino di Montefalco) $30. 90 Editors' Choice *(4/1/2001)*

ANTONIO CAGGIANO

Antonio Caggiano 1997 Vigna Dei Gotti Aglianico (Taurasi) $42. 84 *(5/1/2002)*

ARAGOSTA

Aragosta 2003 (Vermentino di Sardegna) $13. Light and flowery, with aromas of gardenia, air freshener, and simple white fruits. Runs sweet and easy on the palate, if a bit watery. Flavors of apple and nectarine aren't dilute but they are thin. With a big lobster on the label, it seems targeted for waterside fish joints. **84** *—M.S. (7/1/2005)*

ARÈLE

Arèle 1994 Vin Santo (Trentino) $42. Made from the native Nosiola grape, which are dried on mats for several months before crushing, this golden wine is nicely balanced and not overly sweet. Apricot, candied oranges, and nuts are honeyed and rich, lightly sugary, yet balanced by crisp acids. Try with cheese or lightly sweetened biscotti. **90** *(4/1/2004)*

ARGIANO

Argiano 1999 (Brunello di Montalcino) $66. Full and open on the nose, showing fresh herbs, crushed berries and damp earth. A fruity wine, with plum and cherry carried on a chewy, clean frame. Good and generous, with just enough complexity. **90** *—M.S. (6/1/2004)*

ARGIOLAS

Argiolas 1996 Isola dei Nuraghi Red Blend (Sardinia) $9. 90 *(11/15/1999)*

Argiolas 2001 Perdera Red Blend (Isola dei Nuraghi) $12. 89 *—M.S. (11/15/2003)*

Argiolas 2000 Costamolino (Vermentino di Sardegna) $9. 86 *—J.C. (9/1/2001)*

ARNALDO CAPRAI

Arnaldo Caprai 2000 Poggio Belvedere Red Blend (Umbria) $14. 88 Best Buy *—C.S. (2/1/2003)*

Arnaldo Caprai 2001 25 Anni (Sagrantino di Montefalco) $110. Not a wine you will easily forget. Marketing-savvy Marco Caprai has taken a difficult, little-known variety and turned it into an international superstar. A made-to-please wine—meaning all nuts and bolts are screwed tight in terms of color, aromatics, and structure—it has tar, coffee, leather and velvety fullness in the mouth. **93 Cellar Selection** *—M.L. (9/1/2005)*

Arnaldo Caprai 2001 Collepiano (Sagrantino di Montefalco) $55. There's no mistaking that Caprai touch. Resin, dark chocolate, coffee bean, and new oak in layer after layer from the man who put Montefalco on the enological map. Big on tannins but carefully structured, balanced, and lacking the alcoholic burn of some of its contemporaries. Imported by Villa Italia. **90** *—M.L. (9/1/2005)*

Arnaldo Caprai 1998 Collepiano (Sagrantino di Montefalco) $48. 92 *—C.S. (2/1/2003)*

ARUNDA

Arunda 1995 Riserva Brut (Alto Adige) $27. Lean and dominated by tart apple aromas and flavors. Lemon and acid on the palate ensures a fresh, snappy feel, but with so much tang it's on the sour side. **82** *—M.S. (12/31/2004)*

ASTORIA

Astoria 2001 Pinot Grigio (Delle Venezie) $11. An interesting Grigio that blends nutty, herbal aromas with fleshier flavors of honey and tangerines. The weight in the mouth is reminiscent of some Alsatian Pinot Gris, while the tangy citrus on the finish is strong enough to cut through fatty appetizers. **85** *—J.C. (1/1/2004)*

Astoria 2004 18 Dry (Prosecco di Conegliano) $15. Lightly mineral, with lime on the nose along with sugared pastry. Mostly it's about ripe apple flavors along with lemon-lime, but along the way there's some wayward bitterness that wrestles with overt sweetness. Still, it's good overall. **86** *—M.S. (12/15/2005)*

Astoria 2004 Cuvée Tenuta Val de Brun (Prosecco di Valdobbiadene) $13. No surprises here; just good, clean fun. The nose is fresh as a spring garden and the palate delivers nothing but pure lemon-lime. The feel and bubble bead are lively and friendly, while the finish is crisp, smooth and somewhat long. Mildly sweet but not at all cloying. **88 Best Buy** *—M.S. (12/15/2005)*

Astoria 2002 Cuvée Tenuta Val di Brun (Prosecco di Valdobbiadene) $15. **86** *—J.C. (12/31/2003)*

Astoria 2002 Sedici Anni Dry (Prosecco di Conegliano) $15. **87** *—J.C. (12/31/2003)*

Astoria 1998 Rosso Croder Red Blend (Colli di Conegliano) $18. **89** *(5/1/2003)*

Astoria 2000 White Blend (Colli di Conegliano) $17. **85** *—J.C. (7/1/2003)*

ITALY

ATTEMS

Attems 2001 Pinot Grigio (Collio) $20. **81** *—J.C. (7/1/2003)*

Attems 2003 Sauvignon (Collio) $20. Very ripe Sauvignon for Collio, with only a hint of grassiness gracing a full-bodied, well-fruited wine. Bold notes of pink grapefruit and fig wrap around a sturdy melon core, and is that a hint of warmth on the finish? **88** *—J.C. (12/31/2004)*

ATTILIO GHISOLFI

Attilio Ghisolfi 1997 (Barbera d'Alba) $14. **91 Best Buy** *(4/1/2000)*

Attilio Ghisolfi 1997 Dolcetto (Dolcetto d'Alba) $13. **86** *(4/1/2000)*

Attilio Ghisolfi 1995 Bricco Visette Nebbiolo (Barolo) $42. **89** *(9/1/2000)*

AURELIO SETTIMO

Aurelio Settimo 1999 Rocche Nebbiolo (Barolo) $45. Artfully combines enormous power, complexity, and finesse. Aromas and flavors include tar, roses, orange peel, cherries, anise, dried spices, and earth, all in a rich, chewy wine that reveals the beginnings of elegance. Finishes long, with ripe tannins that need time to resolve. Try in 2015. **93 Cellar Selection** *—J.C. (11/15/2004)*

AVIGNONESI

Avignonesi 2002 Tuscan Blend (Vino Nobile di Montepulciano) $25. New-oak and raw-fruit aromas create a sharp, somewhat angular bouquet holding the slightest hint of vinegar. Airing reveals smoky notes and more richness. Plenty of cherry and berry on the palate mixed with cedar and vanilla. The mouthfeel, meanwhile, seems a little heavy. **86** *—M.S. (7/1/2005)*

AZELIA

Azelia 1999 San Rocco Nebbiolo (Barolo) $71. Modern, but it still tastes like Barolo underneath its veneer of toast, coffee, and coconut. Under the wood beats a heart of tar, molasses and dates nestled in soft, supple tannins and finishing with juicy acidity. **91** *(4/2/2004)*

AZIENDA AGRARIA SCACCIADIAVOLI

Azienda Agraria Scacciadiavoli 1998 (Sagrantino di Montefalco) $34. **88** *—C.S. (2/1/2002)*

AZIENDA AGRICOLA ADANTI

Azienda Agricola Adanti 2000 Arquata (Sagrantino di Montefalco) $40. This beautiful, 30-hectare vineyard surrounding a convent near Bevagna produces seven wines. This Sagrantino delivers whiffs of beef jerky, leather, and barnyard and is aged for three years. Sagrantino is not for everyone, although it works wonders with barbecued meats and cold weather. **87** *—M.L. (9/1/2005)*

AZIENDA AGRICOLA BORGNOT/VIRNA

Azienda Agricola Borgnot/Virna 1998 Cannubi Boschis Nebbiolo (Barolo) $35. This is a great value in Barolo. It's a big, somewhat rustic wine, with scents of horse sweat and leather intermingling with black cherries. Anise and intense, meaty flavors chime in on the long, firm finish. Try in 2008 or beyond. **92 Editors' Choice** *(4/2/2004)*

AZIENDA AGRICOLA COGNO

Azienda Agricola Cogno 1997 Vigna Elena Nebbiolo (Barolo) $75. **86** *—M.S. (11/15/2002)*

AZIENDA AGRICOLA PALOMBO

Azienda Agricola Palombo 1998 Cabernet Duca Cantelmi Red Blend (Lazio) $34. **85** *—M.S. (11/15/2003)*

AZIENDA AGRICOLA PUGNANE

Azienda Agricola Pugnane 1996 Vigna Villero Nebbiolo (Barolo) $39. **89** *(11/15/2002)*

AZIENDA AGRICOLA ROBERTO CERAUDO STRONGOLI

Azienda Agricola Roberto Ceraudo Strongoli 2003 Imyr Chardonnay (Val di Neto) $36. Off the charts in almost every way. First, it's a Calabrian Chardonnay with tons of hangtime and oak. Second, it hardly resembles Chardonnay as we know it. The nose is oily, with lemon, baked corn and quince. The palate is custardy, ultra ripe and borderline over the top. Finishes in complex ways, with peach, apricot, and nutmeg along with white pepper. More of a sommelier/explorer's wine. **89** *—M.S. (7/1/2005)*

Azienda Agricola Roberto Ceraudo Strongoli 2000 Petraro Red Blend (Val di Neto) $37. Rusty, with aromas of tar, sweet rubber, petrol, and dark chocolate. Call it funky, call it cooked, call it classic, call it Calabrian. Flavors of dried cherry, raisin, and toffee are sly; so is the spicy, sweet finish. There's a bit of Barbaresco spirit in this wine, but the real fuel is Gaglioppo and Cabernet. **91** *—M.S. (10/1/2004)*

AZIENDA AGRICOLA SUAVIA

Azienda Agricola Suavia 2001 Le Rive White Blend (Soave Classico) $37. Dark and gold, so you just know something's up. And that's the fact that this is over-the-top Soave, a heavyweight tipping the scale at 14%. Thus, there's butterscotch, honey, baked fruit, and a whole lot of extract and sweetness. Not for everyone, but maybe worth trying. **87** *—M.S. (10/1/2004)*

BADIA A COLTIBUONO

Badia a Coltibuono 1998 (Chianti Classico) $20. **87** *(4/1/2001)*

Badia a Coltibuono 1997 Cetamura (Chianti) $11. **90** *—M.S. (3/1/2000)*

Badia a Coltibuono 1999 Riserva (Chianti Classico) $31. Sweet and simple on the nose, with caramel and red licorice. Black cherry, raisin, and tobacco flavors don't carry much pop. Seems tired and empty, which it shouldn't be at this age. **83** *(4/1/2005)*

Badia a Coltibuono 1999 Roberto Stucchi (Chianti Classico) $20. **86** *(4/1/2001)*

BADIA DI MORRONA

Badia di Morrona 2002 I Sodi Del Paretaio (Chianti) $14. Sharp and volatile, with vegetal aromas mixed with candied fruit. Finishes salty and dull, with a blast of asparagus. **80** *(4/1/2005)*

Badia di Morrona 1997 N'Antia Tuscan Blend (Toscana) $30. **91** *—J.F. (9/1/2001)*

BADIOLO

Badiolo 2000 Riserva (Chianti) $14. Light and dilute, with strawberry aromas and then tangy fruit on the palate. Finishes clean, with more citrus and acids than meaty red-fruit notes. Made by Trambusti. **83** *—M.S. (10/1/2004)*

BANEAR

Banear 2001 RossoRosso Merlot (Colli Orientali del Friuli) $15. **83** *—M.S. (12/15/2003)*

Banear 2001 Pinot Grigio (Friuli Grave) $13. **87** *—J.C. (7/1/2003)*

BANFI

Banfi 2001 Rosa Regale (Brachetto d'Acqui) $23. **87** *—K.F. (12/31/2002)*

Banfi 1998 Principessa Gavia (Gavi) $11. **85** *—M.S. (4/1/2000)*

Banfi 2001 Centine Red Blend (Toscana) $11. This trattoria wine has it going on. The nose offers bacon and smoke at first, and then lots of red berry fruit and a bit of light wood. Snappy red fruit dominates the palate, while the zesty finish is lean and tight, with freshness and length. Great for pastas and pizza. **87 Best Buy** *—M.S. (10/1/2004)*

Banfi 2003 Rosa Regale (Brachetto d'Acqui) $23. Heavy on the rose petal and raspberry compote aromas, and also heavy on the palate. Yes, there's definitely a touch of cherry cough syrup to this red sparkler. To enjoy this you have to like yours sweet; maybe best with a custard dessert or vanilla ice cream. It's too sweet and candied for chocolate. **84** *—M.S. (12/15/2004)*

Banfi 2001 Riserva (Chianti Classico) $18. A fair amount of sweet character comes off the nose, primarily chocolate, berry jam, and sugar beet. In the mouth, there's additional milk chocolate alongside dried fruit, herbs and a hint of citrus. Finishes solid but with starchy tannins. There's also some marshmallow sweetness to the aftertaste. **87** *(4/1/2005)*

Banfi 1997 Riserva (Chianti Classico) $16. **87** *(4/1/2001)*

Banfi 2003 Centine Tuscan Blend (Toscana) $11. A succulent, chewy Sangiovese, Merlot, and Cabernet Sauvignon blend with a pretty ruby color and intense aromas of coffee, tar, leather, and toasted wood. The tannins are still a bit raw and beg for hearty meat. Tightly packed cherry and blackberry linger over a long finish. Castello Banfi performs the extraordinary vintage after vintage: It's almost a one million case per year winery and it continues to offer excellent quality on its lowest priced products. **87 Best Buy** *—M.L. (11/15/2005)*

Banfi 2002 Col di Sasso Tuscan Blend (Toscana) $9. Purple in the middle and light on the edges. A candied, sweet, simple red with plum, raisin, and chocolate flavors. Bold and basic. **83** *—M.S. (11/15/2004)*

BANOLIS

Banolis 1998 Pinot Grigio (Grave del Friuli) $13. **87** *(8/1/1999)*

BARBERANI

Barberani 2003 Villa Monticelli Grechetto (Umbria) $28. Fresh cut timber and woodshop aromas are distracting and ultimately leave a bitter taste that overpowers the wine's lean consistency in the mouth. But lovers of oak-aged whites will have success matching this wine with cream-based dishes or smoked foods. **82** *—M.L. (9/1/2005)*

BARBI

Barbi 2000 (Brunello di Montalcino) $50. Earthy on the nose, with hints of coffee. Tastes a bit sweet and candied, with cherry, plum and berry flavors—your standard three-pack. Not terribly deep, but tasty. Finishes smooth, if a bit simple. **88** *—M.S. (7/1/2005)*

BARONCINI

Baroncini 1999 (Chianti Colli Senesi) $9. 89 Best Buy *(4/1/2001)*

Baroncini 1999 (Chianti) $8. 86 Best Buy *(4/1/2001)*

Baroncini 1998 Le Mandorlae Tuscan Blend (Morellino di Scansano) $11. 80 *—M.S. (8/1/2002)*

Baroncini 1999 White Blend (Vernaccia di San Gimignano) $10. 86 *—J.C. (9/1/2001)*

BARONE FINI

Barone Fini 2002 Merlot (Trentino) $14. Straightforward, varietally correct Merlot, with aromas of black cherries, chocolate, tobacco, and a hint of vanilla. It's medium-weight, with soft tannins and crisp acids that leave your mouth watering. Solid stuff. **86** *—J.C. (12/31/2004)*

Barone Fini 2003 Pinot Grigio (Valdadige) $12. Plump in the mouth, with scents of blanched almonds and apple butter. Picks up dried spices on the palate to go along with apple-y fruit. It's low-acid nature correctly reflects the heat of the vintage. **84** *—J.C. (12/31/2004)*

Barone Fini 2001 Pinot Grigio (Valdadige) $10. A lightweight Pinot Grigio marked by dried spices and delicately-flavored apple fruit. **83** *—J.C. (1/1/2004)*

BARONE RICASOLI

Barone Ricasoli 2001 1141 (Chianti Classico) $15. 84 *—M.S. (11/15/2003)*

Barone Ricasoli 1998 1141 (Chianti Classico) $18. 86 *(4/1/2001)*

Barone Ricasoli 2002 Brolio (Chianti Classico) $22. Straight from the sawmill, this is one heavily oaked Chianti. The nose oozes espresso, burnt toast, marinade, and more. But do the depth of fruit and the level of flavor deserve such wood? We liked the size, texture, and pillowy tannins, but in giving this positive rating we still question the fruit at the foundation. You be the judge. **89** *(4/1/2005)*

Barone Ricasoli 2000 Castello di Brolio (Chianti Classico) $55. Inky and raw, but in the best way. This is an unbridled, unchained monster of a Chianti, one with impeccable depth and extraction but also one that doesn't sit on your palate like dead weight. Racy acids and firm tannins work in tandem to prop up the bulky dark fruit, creating a structured, delicious mass. Drink from 2007 through 2015. **92 Cellar Selection** *(4/1/2005)*

Barone Ricasoli 1999 Castello di Brolio (Chianti Classico) $45. 92 *—M.S. (11/15/2003)*

Barone Ricasoli 1998 Rocca Guicciarda Riserva (Chianti Classico) $18. 87 *—M.S. (12/31/2002)*

Barone Ricasoli 1997 Rocca Guicciarda Riserva (Chianti Classico) $22. 89 *(4/1/2001)*

Barone Ricasoli 2002 Campo Ceni Tuscan Blend (Toscana) $20. Ricasoli's easy-to-drink, "international" bottling blends cherry, tobacco, earth, and vanilla flavors in a soft, supple package that admirably achieves its goal. **87** *(12/15/2004)*

Barone Ricasoli 2000 Casalferro Tuscan Blend (Toscana) $40. 88 *—M.S. (11/15/2003)*

BARTENURA

Bartenura 1998 (Barbera d'Asti) $10. 87 *(4/1/2000)*

Bartenura 2000 Moscato (Moscato d'Asti) $10. 90 Best Buy *(4/1/2001)*

Bartenura 2000 Pinot Grigio (Veneto) $10. 82 *—J.C. (7/1/2003)*

Bartenura 1998 Pinot Grigio (Veneto) $10. 86 *—S.H. (9/1/2000)*

Bartenura NV (Prosecco di Valdobbiadene) $12. Crisp and clean, with a lemon and grapefruit core. Not complex, but dry and refreshing. Kosher. **85** *—J.M. (4/3/2004)*

Bartenura NV Asti Spumante $15. Bright and fresh, though sweet and spicy. A wonderful apéritif or dessert wine—low in alcohol (7%), but high in flavor, with hints of ginger, peach, apricot, pear, and vanilla notes. Kosher. **86** *—J.M. (4/3/2004)*

BASTÌA

Bastia 1998 Chardonnay (Langhe) $34. 86 *—M.M. (9/1/2001)*

BATASIOLO

Batasiolo 2001 (Barbera d'Alba) $12. 86 Best Buy *(4/1/2003)*

Batasiolo 2001 Sovrana (Barbera d'Alba) $18. 89 Editors' Choice *(4/1/2003)*

Batasiolo 2002 Serbato Chardonnay (Langhe) $12. 85 *—M.S. (12/15/2003)*

Batasiolo 2002 Granée Gavi del Comune di Gavi (Gavi) $15. 87 *—M.S. (12/15/2003)*

Batasiolo 2001 Bricco di Vergne (Dolcetto d'Alba) $14. 86 *(4/1/2003)*

Batasiolo 2001 Bosc d'la Rei (Moscato d'Asti) $12. 85 *(4/1/2003)*

Batasiolo 2000 Muscatel Tardi (Piedmont) $40. 86 *(4/1/2003)*

Batasiolo 1999 Nebbiolo (Barbaresco) $27. 89 *—M.S. (11/15/2002)*

Batasiolo 1998 Nebbiolo (Barolo) $32. 88 *(4/1/2003)*

Batasiolo 1997 Vigneto Bofani Nebbiolo (Piedmont) $52. 89 *—R.V. (11/15/2002)*

Batasiolo 1998 Vigneto Cerequio Nebbiolo (Barolo) $63. 90 *(4/1/2003)*

Batasiolo 1998 Vigneto Corda della Briccolina Nebbiolo (Barolo) $70. 91 Cellar Selection *(4/1/2003)*

BAVA

Bava 1996 Piano Alto Vigneti Bava d'Agl Barbera d'Asti Superiore $38. 84 *(4/1/2000)*

Bava 1998 Controvento (Dolcetto d'Asti) $13. 87 *(4/1/2000)*

Bava 1997 Barolo di Castiglione Falletto Nebbiolo (Barolo) $60. 89 *—R.V. (11/15/2002)*

BEGALI

Begali 1999 Monte Ca'Bianca Red Blend (Amarone della Valpolicella Classico) $75. Nice and sturdy on the bouquet, where dainty cedar notes blend perfectly with cola, gingerbread, and tree bark. Healthy and muscular, with intense cherry, plum, and raspberry flavors. Throughout there's power and pizzazz, and just enough sweet chocolaty notes to make it friendly. A winner with some kick. 91 *(11/1/2005)*

BELLA ROSA

Bella Rosa 2002 (Chianti) $13. Plum and berry fruit, but in candied form. The nose is like a hard sucking candy, while the palate is grapey and endowed with black cherry. Tangy and high-ended on the back end, but decently textured. 84 *(4/1/2005)*

BELLA SERA

Bella Sera 2002 Tre Venezie Pinot Grigio (Delle Venezie) $7. 84 *—J.C. (7/1/2003)*

BELLAVISTA

Bellavista 1991 Vittorio Moretti Reserve Cuvée (Franciacorta) $100. 83 *(12/31/2000)*

Bellavista NV Cuvée Brut (Franciacorta) $36. Snappy yet smooth, with subtle apple, toast, and vanilla aromas. Very good in terms of feel, with dry, spicy flavors of baked apple, white pepper, and herbs. Slightly mature notes of mushroom and Sherry rise up on the finish, lending this bubbly added complexity. 91 Editors' Choice *—M.S. (12/15/2005)*

Bellavista 1998 Gran Cuvée Brut (Franciacorta) $39. 89 *—J.C. (12/31/2003)*

Bellavista 1999 Gran Cuvée Brut Rosé (Franciacorta) $59. Firm on the nose, with mineral and underripe peach aromas. The palate is more plump, with riper peach flavors accenting cantaloupe. Shows good verve, but remains tame on the palate. Very dry and food-friendly. 88 *—M.S. (12/15/2004)*

Bellavista NV Gran Cuvée Satèn (Franciacorta) $59. Lightly scrambled egg, vanilla, and apple fruit all total a seductive, classy nose that's one part Champagne and one part Italian. Crisp but deep, with lovely apple and peach flavors. Quite zesty yet smooth, with serious aging potential; in fact, cellaring for a few years should really bring it to its peak. 93 Editors' Choice *—M.S. (12/15/2005)*

Bellavista 1998 Grand Cuvée Brut Rosé (Franciacorta) $45. 88 *—J.C. (12/31/2003)*

BELMONDO

Belmondo 1999 Pinot Grigio (Oltrepó Pavese) $5. 81 *—M.N. (12/31/2000)*

BENINCASA

Benincasa 2000 (Sagrantino di Montefalco) $NA. The aromas are dominated by monotone vibrant cherry lollipop and candied strawberry. Moderately intense in the mouth with solid structure but less power than your standard Sagrantino. 85 *—M.L. (9/1/2005)*

BERSANO

Bersano 1997 Cremosina Barbera (Barbera d'Asti) $17. 86 *(4/1/2000)*

Bersano 2001 Gavi (Gavi) $12. 88 Best Buy *—M.S. (12/15/2003)*

Bersano 2004 (Moscato d'Asti) $8. Not an intense nose, but an attractive one with floral and fruity layers. There's chalk, peach and generous cream in the mouth, which beg for all kinds of cream or custard-based desserts. 88 Best Buy *—M.L. (12/15/2005)*

Bersano 1997 Badarina Nebbiolo (Barolo) $49. 88 *—M.S. (12/15/2003)*

BERTANI

Bertani 1997 Red Blend (Amarone della Valpolicella Classico) $90. Dry and maturing, with aromatic notes of tea, toast, cherry, and earth. Not a ton of complexity or layering here. Instead it's straightforward and lean, with a hint of saline to the finish. 85 *(11/1/2005)*

Bertani 2000 Villa Arvedi Red Blend (Amarone della Valpolicella Valpantena) $54. Smooth, toasty, and solid even if it doesn't offer any one particular thing that will sear into your memory. The bouquet is toasty and fruity, with a bit of cedar. The mouth offers cherry, berry, and chocolate, the standard three of Amarone. Finishes steady, with some size. **88** *(11/1/2005)*

Bertani 2002 Due Uve White Blend (Delle Venezie) $13. **85** *—R.V. (7/1/2003)*

BERTELLI

Bertelli 1995 Montetusa (Barbera d'Alba) $13. **83** *(4/1/2000)*

BIONDI-SANTI

Biondi-Santi 1997 Il Greppo (Brunello di Montalcino) $120. **93 Cellar Selection** *—R.V. (8/1/2002)*

Biondi-Santi 1995 Sassoalloro Tuscan Blend (Toscana) $25. **91** *—M.G. (5/1/1999)*

BISOL

Bisol NV Crede (Prosecco di Valdobbiadene) $18. Not cheap by Prosecco standards, and that extra level of quality is evident at every checkpoint. The bouquet is exceedingly snappy, with pure lemon-lime aromas. Citrus, green apple, and white pepper flavors create a near-perfect palate, while the mouthfeel is excellent. About as good as Prosecco gets. **90 Editors' Choice** *—M.S. (6/1/2005)*

Bisol NV Crede Brut (Prosecco di Valdobbiadene) $18. Interesting from the start, where crushed vitamin, orange pulp, and some warm dust make for an atypical but solid bouquet. As always, the palate is forward and fresh, with nectarine and citrus pith. Solid on the back end, with a bit of lemony heft. **88** *—M.S. (12/15/2005)*

Bisol NV Jeio Brut (Prosecco) $15. Crisp, clean and correct—nothing more or less. The palate pumps pure tangerine and apple flavors on the heels of fine, inoffensive bubbles. Balanced and tasty, but nothing fancy. **87** *—M.S. (12/15/2005)*

BOLLA

Bolla 2001 Cabernet Sauvignon (Delle Venezie) $9. **82** *(5/1/2003)*

Bolla 1998 Creso Cabernet Sauvignon (Delle Venezie) $27. **84** *(5/1/2003)*

Bolla 2002 Merlot (Delle Venezie) $9. **83** *—M.S. (12/15/2003)*

Bolla 2000 Colforte Merlot (Delle Venezie) $15. **83** *(5/1/2003)*

Bolla 2001 Arcale Pinot Grigio (Collio) $10. **84** *—J.C. (7/1/2003)*

Bolla 2001 Red Blend (Valpolicella) $9. **81** *(5/1/2003)*

Bolla 1999 Red Blend (Valpolicella) $9. **84** *—J.C. (12/31/2000)*

Bolla 1998 Red Blend (Valpolicella) $8. **80** *(5/1/2003)*

Bolla 1996 Red Blend (Amarone della Valpolicella Classico) $50. **86** *—M.N. (12/31/2000)*

Bolla 2002 White Blend (Soave) $9. Lime, citrus peel, and apricot aromas are nice. The apple, pineapple, and mango fruit is on the sweet side. Finishes gritty, ultra sweet, and heavy. **83** *—M.S. (10/1/2004)*

Bolla 2000 Tufaie White Blend (Soave Classico Superiore) $8. **84** *—J.C. (7/1/2003)*

BOLLINI

Bollini 1998 Pinot Grigio (Trentino) $11. **87** *(8/1/1999)*

BORGO CONVENTI

Borgo Conventi 1997 Pinot Grigio (Collio) $22. **87** *(8/1/1999)*

Borgo Conventi 2002 Sauvignon Blanc (Collio) $15. **91** *—R.V. (7/1/2003)*

BORGO MAGREDO

Borgo Magredo 1997 Pinot Grigio (Grave del Friuli) $10. **83** *(8/1/1999)*

BORGO PRETALE

Borgo Pretale 1999 Riserva (Chianti Classico) $22. Weedy and sour, with grapefruit-like aromas and flavors. Out of whack. **81** *(4/1/2005)*

Borgo Pretale 1998 Borgato Tuscan Blend (Colli della Toscana Centrale) $50. Surprising to see a '98 coming onto the market now, but the wine is fine, raring and ready to go. Cola, charcoal, and sliced lemon carry the nose into a tangy, cherry-laden palate. The finish is long and liqueur-like. Some gritty tannins call out for food. **89** *—M.S. (11/15/2004)*

BORGO SALCETINO

Borgo Salcetino 2000 (Chianti Classico) $22. Aromas of leather and tar override the spicy fruit. In the mouth, raspberry and cherry flavors are forward and tight, propelled by generous acids and ample tannins. Ultimately kind of tart, hard and basic. **84** *—M.S. (10/1/2004)*

Borgo Salcetino 1999 Lucarello Riserva (Chianti Classico) $40. Quite funky at first, with leather, earth, and a certain murkiness that blows off after airing. Features ample black plum and chocolate on the palate, with minty, herbal notes to the finish. Seems mildly overoaked. **87** *—M.S. (10/1/2004)*

Borgo Salcetino 1999 Tuscan Blend (Chianti Classico) $18. **83** *—M.S. (11/15/2003)*

Borgo Salcetino 1998 RosSole Tuscan Blend (Chianti) $16. 84 *—M.S. (12/31/2002)*

BORGO SCOPETO

Borgo Scopeto 2000 (Chianti Classico) $15. This is a supple, medium-weight wine filled with the flavors of Chianti: cherries, earth, and tobacco. If the tannins are suppler than most and the fruit a shade darker and riper, it's probably because of the heat of this vintage, but the wine retains a crisply acidic bite on the finish. 86 *(3/1/2005)*

Borgo Scopeto 1999 Misciano Riserva (Chianti Classico) $35. A lush, medium-weight wine that shows some barrique influence in its aromas of vanilla, tobacco, smoke, and bacon. Soft and chewy on the finish, this is approachable now, but should be more food-friendly in a year or two. 90 *(3/1/2005)*

Borgo Scopeto 1998 Riserva (Chianti Classico) $28. 92 *—M.S. (8/1/2002)*

Borgo Scopeto 1998 Borgonero Tuscan Blend (Toscana) $35. 93 *—M.S. (8/1/2002)*

BOROLI

Boroli 1998 Nebbiolo (Barolo) $38. This well-priced offering got off to a slow start in our tasting. Gradually it opened up to reveal lots of oak influence—toast, vanilla, maple syrup, and even some dill. But what really impressed were flavors of black cherries and tar that glided across the palate upon masses of soft, enveloping tannins. 91 *(4/2/2004)*

BORTOLUZZI

Bortoluzzi 2001 Chardonnay (Isonzo del Friuli) $15. 82 *—J.C. (7/1/2003)*

Bortoluzzi 1997 Pinot Grigio (Isonzo del Friuli) $13. 82 *(8/1/1999)*

BOSCAINI

Boscaini 1999 La Cros Pinot Grigio (Valdadige) $12. 86 *—J.C. (9/1/2000)*

BOSCARELLI

Boscarelli 1996 Vino Nobile Di Montepulciano (Toscana) $27. 85 *—M.S. (7/1/2000)*

Boscarelli 2002 Tuscan Blend (Vino Nobile di Montepulciano) $33. Sharp on the nose, with background aromas of cola, cedar, and plum. Fairly tight and oaky on the palate, with a shot of lemon supporting plum and berry flavors. Sizable and solid, with some spice and red pepper on the finish. 86 *—M.S. (7/1/2005)*

Boscarelli 1999 35 Anni Tuscan Blend (Toscana) $51. 94 **Editors' Choice** *—M.S. (11/15/2003)*

Boscarelli 1999 Rosso Tuscan Blend (Toscana) $67. 89 *—M.S. (12/31/2002)*

BOTROMAGNO

Botromagno 2004 Gravina White Blend (Puglia) $10. A 60% Greco and 40% Malvasia blend from a surreal part of Puglia with long horizons and whole towns buried within deep ravines. Offers some buttery popcorn and peach and lots of yellow floral tones, like acacia. Nice tart finish. 87 **Best Buy** *—M.L. (9/1/2005)*

BOTTEGA VINAIA

Bottega Vinaia 2001 Chardonnay (Trentino) $20. Only 30% is barrel-fermented in French oak, the rest in stainless steel, so the wood component is understated, allowing lush pineapple and pear fruit to shine on the midpalate. Dried spices (clove and cinnamon) become more apparent on the finish, while the fruit fades away. 87 *(4/1/2004)*

Bottega Vinaia 2002 Lagrein (Trentino) $21. This is a big comedown after the stellar 2000 (we never received samples of the 2001), but still a solid effort. It shows earth and cassis flavors, relatively light weight on the palate and a crisp, herbal finish. 85 *—J.C. (12/31/2004)*

Bottega Vinaia 2000 Merlot (Trentino) $21. Plummy and chocolaty on the nose, with herbal notes that seem to grow stronger the longer the wine sits in the glass. It's structured and quite firm in the mouth, picking up increasing amounts of dried basil on the finish. 87 *(4/1/2004)*

Bottega Vinaia 2002 Pinot Grigio (Trentino) $20. A distinct step up from many Pinot Grigios, with floral and herbal nuances layered over a fresh-fruit core of peaches, pears, and white-fleshed melons. Tangerine and anise notes give a lift to the finish. 87 *(4/1/2004)*

Bottega Vinaia 2002 Teroldego (Rotaliano) $21. This exuberantly fruity wine boasts super-ripe, candied fruit aromas, smoke and vanilla from oak aging and a fun, bouncy personality. Blackberry and black cherry fruit finishes tart and "crunchy," showing great freshness. 86 *—J.C. (12/31/2004)*

BRAIDA DI GIACOMO BOLOGNA

Braida di Giacomo Bologna 2004 Vigna Senza Nome (Moscato d'Asti) $16. Honey and peach fills the mouth and is backed by lemon blossom, mineral, and chalky notes, apricot, and a distant dairy smell that blows off after a few swirls. A pleasant touch of acidity at the rear keeps the wine's floral freshness intact in the mouth. 88 *—M.L. (12/15/2005)*

BRANCAIA

Brancaia 2001 (Chianti Classico) $32. Big, bold, and boisterous, with deep fruit, lots of oak, and plenty of heft. The palate is loaded with black cherry and chocolate, while the finish settles down and fades away with subtlety and smoothness. Quite evolved and forward. A fine modern-style Chianti. **90** *—M.S. (10/1/2004)*

Brancaia 2001 Il Blu Tuscan Blend (Toscana) $72. This wine has great potential among casual drinkers. It's inky black, with a deep, charred nose that frames dark fruit and new oak. The palate is forward and lively, with blackberry and cola. Finishes clean and fairly short despite its immense color and size. **88** *—M.S. (10/1/2004)*

BROGAL VINI

Brogal Vini 2001 Antigniano (Sagrantino di Montefalco) $16. A dark, brooding beast with tar, coffee, and some barnyard. You can tell this is a big wine by the way it sits determined in your glass. The tannins will rip through your mouth like an 18-wheeler in the fast lane. Matured 18 months in French oak, a few more years of cellar aging should soften it up. **87** *—M.L. (9/1/2005)*

BRUNO FRANCO

Bruno Franco 2000 Nebbiolo (Nebbiolo d'Alba) $NA. **83** *—M.S. (12/15/2003)*

BRUNO GIACOSA

Bruno Giacosa 1996 Dino Nero Spumante (Piedmont) $36. **90** *—P.G. (12/15/2000)*

Bruno Giacosa 1997 Falletto di Serralunga (Dolcetto d'Alba) $19. **80** *(4/1/2000)*

Bruno Giacosa 1999 Falletto Nebbiolo (Barolo) $155. Big-boned but not showing much flesh, this wine didn't appear to be at its best when we tasted it, yet it was still impressive. Scents of rubber, tar, and prunes, flavors of red berries and cherry tomatoes. Long finish that builds in intensity is a positive sign for aging. Anticipated maturity: 2012–2020. **88** *(4/2/2004)*

Bruno Giacosa 1999 Santo Stefano Nebbiolo (Barbaresco) $160. After this wine's identity was revealed, we naturally wondered if we hadn't underrated it. It ranks among the best of the Barbarescos, but not at the very top as we had expected. Leather, Asian spices, and citrus peel, anise and dried cherries provide remarkable complexity and mouthfilling flavors without ever seeming overdone. Tannins cut short the finish, but they're chewy and rich, and will support this wine's growth for decades to come. **91** *(4/2/2004)*

BRUNO NICODEMI

Bruno Nicodemi 1998 Colline Teramane Riserva Montepulciano (Abruzzo) $23. **85** *—M.S. (11/15/2003)*

BRUNO ROCCA

Bruno Rocca 1997 (Barbera d'Alba) $32. **85** *(4/1/2000)*

Bruno Rocca 1999 Estate Bottled (Barbera d'Alba) $40. **90** *—M.S. (11/15/2002)*

Bruno Rocca 1996 Coparossa Nebbiolo (Barbaresco) $60. **89** *—J.C. (9/1/2000)*

Bruno Rocca 1999 Rabaj à Nebbiolo (Barbaresco) $85. Extraordinary stuff. The aromas practically defy description, packed with smoke, tobacco, cigar box, and cured meat, all wrapped around a deep, rich core of black cherries. Picks up even more complexity in the mouth, adding vanilla, plums and dates in an expansive, mouthfilling experience, then—wham—the tannins hit home, sending you reeling and wondering when this wine will finally blossom. Great now, great 20 years from now. **95 Editors' Choice** *(4/2/2004)*

BUCCI

Bucci 2002 Pongelli Red Blend (Rosso Piceno) $19. This 50-50 blend of Montepulciano and Sangiovese is fresh like sorbet but also sweet like a lollipop. Open red fruit greets you, followed by candied cherry and raspberry flavors. Zesty but a little sugary on the finish. **84** *—M.S. (6/1/2005)*

Bucci 1997 (Verdicchio dei Castelli di Jesi Classico) $16. **85** *(11/1/1999)*

Bucci 1994 Villa Bucci Riserva (Verdicchio dei Castelli di Jesi Classico) $22. **88** *(11/1/1999)*

BURCHINO

Burchino 1999 (Chianti Superiore) $13. **84** *—M.S. (12/31/2002)*

BUSSIA SOPRANA

Bussia Soprana 2000 (Dolcetto d'Alba) $18. **83** *—M.S. (12/15/2003)*

Bussia Soprana 1997 Bussia Nebbiolo (Barolo) $70. **87** *—R.V. (11/15/2002)*

Bussia Soprana 1998 Mosconi Nebbiolo (Barolo) $68. This Barolo is a bit light in weight, but elegant and complex, prettily combining leather, dried orange peel, cured meat, and floral notes. Finishes dry and tannic, so revisit it in 10 years. **89** *(4/2/2004)*

Bussia Soprana 2001 Vigne del Rio White Blend (Piedmont) $23. **87** *—M.S. (12/15/2003)*

CA' BIANCA

Ca' Bianca 2002 (Barbera d'Asti) $14. This oak-influenced Barbera manages to nicely integrate the tartness of fresh fruit with the vanilla and spices imparted by oak aging. Cherries mingle with cinnamon, clove, and vanilla, with a proper amount of acidity on the finish. Decent value, too. **88** *—J.C. (11/15/2004)*

Ca' Bianca 2000 (Gavi) $13. **84** *—M.S. (12/15/2003)*

Ca' Bianca 1999 Nebbiolo (Barolo) $36. Scents of mint and sweet hay give this wine's flavors a slightly greenish cast, without obliterating the sturdy dried fig and cherry flavors. Features a supple, evolved mouthfeel that makes it approachable now. Anticipated maturity: 2006–2012. **86** *(4/2/2004)*

Ca' Bianca 1997 Nebbiolo (Barbaresco) $33. **86** *—M.S. (11/15/2002)*

CA' BOLANI

Ca' Bolani 2000 Aquileia Pinot Grigio (Friuli Aquileia) $15. **86** *(12/31/2002)*

CA' BRUZZO

Ca' Bruzzo 2000 La Sperugola Merlot (Veneto) $15. **89 Editors' Choice** *(5/1/2003)*

CA' DEL BOSCO

Ca' del Bosco NV Carmenero (Italy) $126. This unusual table wine is a Carmenère, the aloof Bordeaux variety found almost exclusively in Chile. That it comes from an Italian sparkling wine producer is odd. As for the wine, it's got color and body along with strong vegetal aromas and flavors. Looks and feels right; smells and tastes not as good. **85** *—M.S. (11/15/2004)*

Ca' del Bosco 1997 Brut (Franciacorta) $65. **87** *—J.C. (12/31/2003)*

Ca' del Bosco NV Brut (Franciacorta) $32. **86** *—J.C. (12/31/2003)*

Ca' del Bosco 1994 Cuvée Annamaria Clementi (Franciacorta) $120. **91** *—J.C. (12/31/2003)*

Ca' del Bosco 1998 Dosage Zero (Franciacorta) $65. **91 Editors' Choice** *—J.C. (12/31/2003)*

Ca' del Bosco 1998 Rosé (Franciacorta) $67. **88** *—J.C. (12/31/2003)*

Ca' del Bosco 1993 Satèn (Franciacorta) $68. Round and nicely balanced, but the flavor profile falls short of thrilling. The nose deals yeasty cornflake and toast aromas that veer toward vanilla liqueur when given air time, but the finish is spiky and lemony. An "intellectual" wine that should strike different folks differently. **89** *—M.S. (12/15/2004)*

CA' DEL MONTE

Ca' del Monte 1994 (Amarone della Valpolicella Classico) $35. **84** *—J.C. (9/1/2000)*

Ca' del Monte 1995 Vigneto Scaiso Red Blend (Valpolicella Classico Superiore) $19. **86** *(5/1/2003)*

CA' DEL VISPO

Ca' del Vispo 2002 (Chianti Colli Senesi) $12. Lightweight, with innocuous aromas of pie cherry, tobacco, and earth. Mostly dried fruits on the palate, including cherry and red plum. Tangy and thin on the finish, but with a puncher's chance. **83** *(4/1/2005)*

CA' MARCANDA

Ca' Marcanda 2001 Magari Tuscan Blend (Toscana) $70. A silky, medium-weight wine that bears more than a slight resemblance to Right-Bank Bordeaux. Dried herbs, chocolate, and plum aromas and flavors finish long. Half Merlot, the rest evenly divided between Cabernet Sauvignon and Cabernet Franc. **88** *(7/1/2005)*

CA' RUGATE

Ca' Rugate 1999 Monte Fiorntine Soave Classico $13. **89 Best Buy** *—M.M. (9/1/2001)*

CA'NTELE

Ca'ntele 1999 Riserva Negroamaro (Salice Salentino) $11. Meaty and solid, with mineral and raisin aromas. Fresh more than stewed, with cherry and apple-skin flavors followed by a free flow of red fruits and acidity. It's almost a mouthwash with substance, something perfect for saucy pastas or chewy calzoni. **87 Best Buy** *—M.S. (2/1/2005)*

CA'ROME

Ca'Rome 1998 Nebbiolo (Barbaresco) $50. **88** *—M.M. (11/15/2002)*

Ca'Rome 2001 Maria di Brun Nebbiolo (Barbaresco) $83. Once past some funky burnt-matchstick scents, this wine really shines, mixing cherry, leather and dried spices together in a richly textured, creamy wine that finishes with masses of soft tannins. Should be approachable by 2008, and mature gracefully until 2016 or beyond. **90** *—J.C. (11/15/2004)*

Ca'Rome 2001 Söri Rio Sordo Nebbiolo (Barbaresco) $76. Having heard some promising buzz about the 2001 vintage, this wine—one of the first 2001 Barbarescos tasted—was a bit of a disappointment. The mint, citrus, and rhubarb aromas do open up and gain some chocolaty richness with air, but the finish remains tart, crisp, and astringent. **86** *—J.C. (11/15/2004)*

Ca'Rome 2000 Vigna Cerretta Nebbiolo (Barolo) $81. Oh baby. This wine has it all, from alluring scents of toast, black cherries, and cola to flavors of exotic spices and a big, plush, tannic framework that promises well for the future. Combines great power with a sense of proportion. Should reach its peak around 2015. **92 Cellar Selection** *—J.C. (11/15/2004)*

CADIS-CANTINA DI SOAVE

Cadis-Cantina di Soave 1997 Pinot Grigio (Veneto) $6. **83** *(8/1/1999)*

CAIREL

Cairel 1998 Vigneto del Mandorlo (Dolcetto d'Alba) $15. **83** *(4/1/2000)*

CAMIGLIANO

Camigliano 2000 (Brunello di Montalcino) $53. Ripe, snappy, alert, and forward, with aromas of toast and dried cherries. If you like a bit more red fruit than black in your Brunello, give this a shot. Cranberry, cherry, and red plum flavors dominate, while the finish is crisp, with hints of pepper and spice. Lively but not terribly deep. **90** *—M.S. (7/1/2005)*

Camigliano 2000 (Rosso di Montalcino) $19. **88** *—M.S. (11/15/2003)*

CAMPANILE

Campanile 2003 Pinot Grigio (Delle Venezie) $10. Light in body, fresh, and imbued with fruit, this offering from Beringer Blass boasts pear, apple, and almond notes alongside enough lemony acidity to keep it crisp and refreshing. **85 Best Buy** *—J.C. (12/31/2004)*

Campanile 2001 Pinot Grigio (Friuli Grave) $10. **87** *—S.H. (1/1/2002)*

CAMPO VERDE

Campo Verde 1996 Barrel Aged (Barbera d'Asti) $14. **84** *(4/1/2000)*

Campo Verde 1999 Nebbiolo (Barbaresco) $44. Starts off unexpressively yet reasonably complex, revealing only modest aromas of tobacco, earth, mushroom, and anise. Flavors are high acid, featuring tangy cherry, tar, and coffee. This is a difficult wine to figure, with its high acids and low tannins, yet the panel liked it for its earthy notes and complexity. Drink 2008–2020. **88** *(4/2/2004)*

CAMPOGIOVANNI

Campogiovanni 2000 (Brunello di Montalcino) $65. Fully charred, with a lot of leather and campfire to the nose. More dark and obscure than forward and fruity, with heavy plum flavors and a shot of pepper on the tail end. Smoky and brooding throughout. **88** *—M.S. (7/1/2005)*

CAMPOMAGGIO

Campomaggio 2000 (Chianti Classico) $14. A pretty good deal for a single-vineyard wine. The bouquet has nice baking-spice aromas, primarily cinnamon and nutmeg, while the flavor profile stocks foresty cherry-berry fruit. Smooth enough late, with vanilla and dried spices. The only fault is a strong acid streak that dominates the center. **87** *(4/1/2005)*

Campomaggio 1999 Riserva (Chianti Classico) $22. Ripe and fruity, with earth, leather, and plum aromas. The flavors drive toward strawberry and raspberry, while the finish is round and pleasant. Good quality; easy to drink. **88** *—M.S. (10/1/2004)*

Campomaggio 1997 Riserva (Chianti Classico) $24. **91** *(4/1/2001)*

Campomaggio 1999 Tuscan Blend (Toscana) $18. A single-vineyard Sangiovese with leather, dried fruit, and cedar aromas. Flavors of tight red fruit hit forcefully, propelled by zesty acidity. Definitely tangy and racy on the finish, but the strawberry and raspberry flavors are solid enough. With food it will do just fine. **86** *—M.S. (10/1/2004)*

CANALETTO

Canaletto 2000 Winemaker's Collection Chardonnay (Puglia) $9. **84** *(5/1/2001)*

Canaletto 1998 Pinot Grigio (Venezie) $7. **87** *(8/1/1999)*

Canaletto 2000 Winemaker's Collection Red Blend (Sicily) $9. **85** *(5/1/2002)*

CANALICCHIO

Canalicchio 1999 (Brunello di Montalcino) $75. Rock solid, with a pure nose that exudes leather, coffee, charred beef, and lots of prime red fruit. From the plum and cherry flavors riding the surface to the wine's deepest depths, there's nothing not to like. As a whole, this one is Brunello like it should be: lively, racy, and fun. Hold for several years for best results. **94** *—M.S. (6/1/2004)*

CANDIDO

Candido 1995 Duca D'Aragona Negroamaro (Salento) $25. **84** *—C.S. (5/1/2002)*

Candido 2000 Red Blend (Salice Salentino) $10. Here's a wine from Puglia that tastes like the sun-drenched southern region thanks to an aromatic assortment of Mediterranean oregano and sage, mint tea, dried hay, and ripe red fruit. Not a gigantically structured wine, but a lighter-hued blend of Negroamaro and Malvasia Nera that would bring out the best in pork or roasted chicken. **87 Best Buy** *—M.L. (11/15/2005)*

CANDONI

Candoni 2001 Pinot Grigio (Friuli Venezia Giulia) $13. **81** *—J.C. (7/1/2003)*

CANELLA

Canella NV (Prosecco di Conegliano e Valdobbiadene) $11. **87 Best Buy** *—P.G. (12/15/2000)*

Canella NV Extra Dry (Prosecco di Conegliano) $11. **90 Best Buy** *—M.S. (6/1/2003)*

CANEVELE

Canevele NV Brut (Prosecco di Valdobbiadene) $13. Crisp and precise; entirely clean and refreshing. Plenty of fruit throughout, with no interference. The palate pumps apple fruit in droves, with hints of apricot and white pepper. Finish notes of citrus and talc work like a charm. **89 Best Buy** *—M.S. (12/15/2004)*

CANNETO

Canneto 2002 (Vino Nobile di Montepulciano) $22. Raspberry and plum aromas are forward yet softened by a thick block of sweet oak. In the mouth, the wine shows serious ripeness, a bold cherry flavor, and raw but healthy tannins. With char and zest throughout, this is one of the better '02s you'll encounter. **88** *—M.S. (7/1/2005)*

CÁNTELE

Cántele 2003 Chardonnay (Salento) $11. This medium-bodied Chardonnay is nutty and pear-scented, with plump, ripe pear fruit balanced by a grapefruity undercurrent that turns a bit metallic on the finish. **83** *—J.C. (12/31/2004)*

Cántele 1996 Primitivo (Salice Salentino) $12. **89** *(11/15/1999)*

CANTINA

Cantina Bera 2001 (Moscato d'Asti) $10. **90 Best Buy** *—S.H. (11/15/2002)*

CANTINA DI CUSTOZA

Cantina di Custoza 2003 Trebbiano (Lugana) $12. Peach, kiwi, mango, grapefruit, and apricot merge with spring flowers and orange blossoms to accent a brilliantly colored wine with crisp tartness and concentrated flavor. It also has a unique consistency that is both chewy and sticky and promotes a long, polished finish. A wonderful leisurely lunch on the patio wine. **86 Best Buy** *—M.L. (11/15/2005)*

CANTINA DI MONTALCINO

Cantina di Montalcino 2003 (Chianti) $10. Smoky and masculine, with initial aromas of black cherry and coffee. Talk about perfect balance; this has it. The cherry and berry flavors glide on a wave of crisp acids and modest tannins. And while not velvety, the mouthfeel is lush. Worth more than a look. **90 Best Buy** *(4/1/2005)*

Cantina di Montalcino 2001 Riserva (Chianti) $15. Soy sauce is a major component of the aged, mature nose, while in the mouth you're looking at black cherry, leather, and vanilla, all with a slight citrusy kick. Short and somewhat tomato-based on the finish, with a tart, crisp feel. **85** *(4/1/2005)*

CANTINA GIACOMO MONTRESOR

Cantina Giacomo Montresor 1997 Rocca Bianca Pinot Grigio (Valdadige) $8. **85 Best Buy** *(8/1/1999)*

CANTINA SANTADI

Cantina Santadi 2002 Grotta Rossa (Carignano del Sulcis) $11. Chunky and ripe, with red fruit defining the nose. The palate is intense and tannic, with a reduced cherry-powder flavor. Finishes firm, with leather and drying tannins. Ideal for everyday drinking; best with food. **87 Best Buy** *—M.S. (2/1/2005)*

Cantina Santadi 2000 Rocca Rubia Riserva (Carignano del Sulcis) $25. Tight and a touch grassy on the nose, with hints of licorice, clove, and forest floor. The palate hits firmly with berry fruit and buttery oak, and that overt, creamy, woody flavor holds on into the finish, where it mixes with cola. Fairly rich and smooth, but the oak is heavy. **87** *—M.S. (11/15/2004)*

Cantina Santadi 1999 Terre Brune Superiore (Carignano del Sulcis) $63. This Sardinian red is a bit rough and raw despite its age, yet it's also quite masculine and enjoyable, a traditional wine in a field of newcomers. The fruit is candied and ripe, veering toward sugary. A finish full of raisin, butter, and carob offers a lot to chew on. Needs time to breathe; consider decanting. **88** *—M.S. (11/15/2004)*

Cantina Santadi 2002 Cala Silente (Vermentino di Sardegna) $16. Off-gold in color, but not overdone. This is a near-perfect rendition of Vermentino; it's powerful but restrained, with warm aromas that conjure memories of baked apple and spice. The palate is sly and dry, with cinnamon notes supporting lemon and pineapple. A rich, creamy finish cements this wine's reputation as a leader in its class. **91 Editors' Choice** *—M.S. (8/1/2004)*

CANTINA TERLANO

Cantina Terlano 2001 Lunare Gewürztraminer (Alto Adige) $43. **87** *—J.C. (7/1/2003)*

Cantina Terlano 2000 Vorberg Pinot Bianco (Alto Adige) $21. **88** *—J.C. (7/1/2003)*

Cantina Terlano 2001 Quarz Sauvignon Blanc (Alto Adige) $43. **90** *—J.C. (7/1/2003)*

Cantina Terlano 2001 Winkl Sauvignon Blanc (Alto Adige) $22. **89** *—J.C. (7/1/2003)*

Cantina Terlano 2002 Classico White Blend (Alto Adige) $15. **88 Editors' Choice** *—J.C. (7/1/2003)*

Cantina Terlano 2000 Classico White Blend (Alto Adige) $15. **83** *—J.C. (7/1/2003)*

CANTINA TRAMIN

Cantina Tramin 2004 Lagrein (Alto Adige) $33. A ruby-colored, purist take on Lagrein with a charming medley of forest berries, anise, violet, and menthol. Already expansive and expressive at a young age, this medium-bodied wine ends on a sour note. This could definitely use a few years in the cellar. **85** *—M.L. (9/1/2005)*

Cantina Tramin 2002 Pinot Grigio (Alto Adige) $13. **86** *—R.V. (7/1/2003)*

CANTINE GEMMA

Cantine Gemma 1997 Bricco Angelini (Barbera d'Alba) $14. **85** *(4/1/2000)*

CANTINE LUCIANI

Cantine Luciani 1997 (Brunello di Montalcino) $32. **84** *—M.S. (11/15/2003)*

CANTININO

Cantinino 2000 Cantinino de Renzis Sonnino Sangiovese (Tuscany) $30. **86** *—M.S. (11/15/2003)*

CAPANNELLE

Capannelle 1998 50 & 50 Tuscan Blend (Montepulciano) $112. **89** *—M.S. (12/15/2003)*

CAPESTRANO

Capestrano 2001 (Montepulciano d'Abruzzo) $10. This is what this wine style is all about. You get a sweet, syrupy, deep nose and then lots of fruit on the palate followed by an incredibly dense, dark, chocolaty finish. It's a full-force express, bold, zippy, and solid. **89 Best Buy** *—M.S. (10/1/2004)*

Capezzana 1999 Red Blend (Carmignano) $21. **91** *—M.S. (8/1/2002)*

Capezzana 2001 Barco Reale Red Blend (Carmignano) $15. **87** *—M.S. (11/15/2003)*

Capezzana 2000 Barco Reale Red Blend (Carmignano) $14. **86** *—M.S. (8/1/2002)*

Capezzana 1998 Ghiaie della Furba Red Blend (Toscana) $52. **88** *—J.C. (9/1/2001)*

Capezzana 1995 Riserva (Carmignano) $41. **91** *—M.S. (11/15/1999)*

CAPICHERA

Capichera 2002 Assajé Carignano (Isola dei Nuraghi) $42. Flush on the nose and loaded with leather, earth, and spicy plum fruit. The palate is warm and saturated with all sorts of berries framed by genuine, appropriate tannins. Then on the finish it turns smoky and coffee-like. Simply an excellent, juicy, satisfying red wine. **91 Editors' Choice** *—M.S. (2/1/2005)*

CAPPELLANO

Cappellano 1996 (Barbera d'Alba) $17. **89** *(4/1/2000)*

CAPRILI

Caprili 1997 (Brunello di Montalcino) $54. **90** *—R.V. (8/1/2002)*

CAPUTO

Caputo 1999 Zicorra Aglianico (Campania) $20. **84** *—C.S. (5/1/2002)*

Caputo 2002 Rosso (Lacryma Christi del Vesuvio) $11. Burnt and raw, with lean, tart red fruit on the nose. Equally tart raspberry in the mouth is pushed by fiery acidity. Call it a red-cherry snapper without much softness or character. **82** *—M.S. (11/15/2004)*

CARLO GANCIA

Carlo Gancia 2000 Cuvée del Fondatore Brut (Asti) $20. Extremely oaky for a sparkler, with a heavy, forceful nose that's dominated by toasted wood grain. The equally woody palate is round, with hints of apple and caramel. Smoky on the finish, with a smack of banana and lemon. **83** *—M.S. (12/15/2004)*

CARPINETO

Carpineto 1999 Farnito Cabernet Sauvignon (Toscana) $35. **89** *(11/1/2003)*

Carpineto NV Dolce Moscato (Tuscany) $17. **83** *—M.S. (6/1/2003)*

Carpineto 2001 (Chianti Classico) $20. A bit sparse in terms of fruit, but still jammy and ripe enough to please. Look for raspberry and black cherry flavors, and a fresh, fairly acidic finish. A snappy, crisp Chianti. **86** *—M.S. (10/1/2004)*

Carpineto 1999 (Chianti Classico) $19. **85** *(4/1/2001)*

Carpineto 1999 Riserva (Chianti Classico) $26. Floral, ripe and full of red fruit and lavender. It's big and tight on the tongue, with raspberry, plum, and cassis flavors. Very juicy and solid. Not showy, but defined and correct for Chianti. **88** *—M.S. (10/1/2004)*

Carpineto 1998 Riserva (Chianti Classico) $28. **87** *(11/1/2003)*

Carpineto 2001 Dogajolo Tuscan Blend (Toscana) $10. **86** *—M.S. (11/15/2003)*

Carpineto 1986 Farnito Vin Santo Tuscan Blend (Toscana) $55. **90** *(11/1/2003)*

Carpineto 1999 Poggio Sant'Enrico Tuscan Blend (Toscana) $70. 91 *(11/1/2003)*

Carpineto 1998 Riserva Tuscan Blend (Vino Nobile di Montepulciano) $33. 88 *(11/1/2003)*

Carpineto 2002 (Vernaccia di San Gimignano) $17. Pretty wildflower and honey aromas grace the bouquet of this yellow-gold wine, which tosses up flavors of citrus, under-ripe pineapple, and peach. Finishes dry and clean, and not too heavy. It's medium-bodied at best, however, and loses intensity with airing. 86 *—M.S. (8/1/2004)*

CASA ALLE VACCHE

Casa alle Vacche 1999 Cinabro Tuscan Blend (Chianti Colli Senesi) $20. 88 *—M.S. (11/15/2003)*

CASA BALOCCA

Casa Balocca 1997 Nebbiolo (Barbaresco) $64. Shows a bit of the vintage's hot character in its aromas of roasted, caramelized fruit; also a touch of smoked meat. Flavors veer toward stone fruits, evidencing a touch of sur-maturité. Drinkable now and over the next 5–10 years. 88 *—J.C. (11/15/2004)*

CASA GIRELLI

Casa Girelli 1998 Fontella Red Blend (Tuscany) $8. 85 Best Buy *(4/1/2001)*

CASA VINO

Casa Vino 2003 Nero d'Avola (Sicilia) $9. Fresh and fragrant, with a jumble of cherry, plum, and raspberry aromas. The palate is tight and snappy, with raspberry along with a sure-fire dose of lemon-based acidity. Quite tight and scouring, due to that aforementioned acidity. 85 Best Buy *—M.S. (7/1/2005)*

Casa Vino 2000 Riserva (Chianti) $13. Grapey and jammy on the nose, with blackberry and vanilla aromas. Hits firmly with cherry flavors, but the feel is a touch coarse, courtesy of hard tannins. At times the wine even throws off an artificial flavor, but it's hard to retrieve, so we've discounted it. 86 *(4/1/2005)*

CASALE DELLO SPARVIERO

Casale dello Sparviero 1997 (Chianti Classico) $16. 85 *(4/1/2001)*

CASALE TRIOCCO

Casale Triocco 2001 (Sagrantino di Montefalco) $NA. One notch down in aromatic intensity compared to the others, yet unbashful with ripe cherry, prunes, and blackberry. More cherry in the mouth and pucker-time tannins. 85 *—M.L. (9/1/2005)*

CASALFARNETO

Casalfarneto 2001 Grancasale (Verdicchio dei Castelli di Jesi Classico Superiore) $22. Bright gold in color, which is unusual for the variety. Aromas of ripe peach, apricot, and salty air are mature and chunky. The palate is equally ripe and forward, with flavors of honey, nuts, and corn flakes. Turns sweet and mildly cloying on the midpalate, with vanilla on the finish. Not for everyone, but has merits. 86 *—M.S. (8/1/2004)*

CASALI DI BIBBIANO

Casali di Bibbiano 2002 Montornello (Chianti Classico) $18. Dark and dense, with medicinal aromas of jerky, molasses, and fresh-cut wood. Runs bold and sweet on the palate, with candied plum and black cherry. Quite a lot of burnt sugar on the finish renders it moody and chewy. 86 *(4/1/2005)*

CASALOSTE

Casaloste 2000 (Chianti Classico) $30. The nose is grainy and dense, with short fruit aromas and iodine. The palate is grippy and loaded with dark, rubbery plum notes. Sharp and lean on the finish. 82 *—M.S. (10/1/2004)*

Casaloste 1998 (Chianti Classico) $26. 85 *(4/1/2001)*

Casaloste 1999 Riserva (Chianti Classico) $38. What begins as cheesy and astringent gains clarity with time. The nose ultimately turns toward bacon and cedar, while the toasty palate offers red plum and plenty of lemony oak. Intense and brightly fruity, but arguably a touch too zesty for its own good. 87 *(4/1/2005)*

Casaloste 1997 Riserva (Chianti Classico) $44. 88 *(4/1/2001)*

CASANOVA DI NERI

Casanova di Neri 1999 (Brunello di Montalcino) $70. Rich almost to the point of chunky; aromas of coffee and new oak announce its New World style, and then come blackberry, chocolate, and smoked-meat flavors. This wine is probably shocking to the old guard, but if tastes this good, drink it. 93 *—M.S. (6/1/2004)*

CASANUOVA DELLE CERBAIE

Casanuova delle Cerbaie 1999 (Brunello di Montalcino) $NA. Rich, lush, and Port-like, with tons of sweet fruit. The rush of dark plum and berry carried on the wavy, dense palate is hedonistic, and while it won't age forever, the bet here is that it'll prove irresistible to anyone who tries it. 92 *—M.S. (6/1/2004)*

CASANUOVA DI NITTARDI

Casanuova di Nittardi 1999 Riserva (Chianti Classico) $48. Roasted as if Starbucks got a hold of the grapes, and that charred character lasts from the deep nose, to the chewy palate, and finally through the smoky finish. Does it have the stuffing to support such copious oak? That's the million-dollar question, and some may say yes and others no. We liked the coffee and black-fruit characteristics but were less fond of the lemon-pushing wood. **88** *(4/1/2005)*

CASCINA BALLARIN

Cascina Ballarin 1996 Giuli (Barbera d'Alba) $16. **83** *(4/1/2000)*

CASCINA BONGIOVANNI

Cascina Bongiovanni 1998 (Dolcetto d'Alba) $18. **89** *(4/1/2000)*

Cascina Bongiovanni 2000 Nebbiolo (Barolo) $60. Tight and tannic, showing just glimpses of cherries, leather, and citrus peel, but gradually opens with air. It's a bit burly and rustic, and mouthdrying on the finish, but should show greater balance with several years' age. **89** *—J.C. (11/15/2004)*

Cascina Bongiovanni 1997 Nebbiolo (Barolo) $59. **88** *—M.S. (12/15/2003)*

Cascina Bongiovanni 2001 Faletto Red Blend (Langhe) $46. This intriguing wine is a blend of approximately 50% Barbera, 25% Nebbiolo, and 25% Cabernet Sauvignon, aged in barriques. A slight acetic note gives way to hints of pepper and sturdy blackberry and cassis fruit. It's dry and tannic, but possesses decent depth so it could develop into something interesting with 3–4 years of bottle age. **86** *—J.C. (11/15/2004)*

CASCINA CHICCO

Cascina Chicco 1997 Bric Loira (Barbera d'Alba) $26. **93** *(4/1/2000)*

CASCINA CUCCO

Cascina Cucco 1998 Cerrati Nebbiolo (Barolo) $64. **87** *—C.S. (11/15/2002)*

CASCINA LA GHERSA

Cascina La Ghersa 1999 Camparo-Superiore (Barbera d'Asti) $14. **88 Best Buy** *—M.S. (11/15/2002)*

Cascina La Ghersa 2004 Giorgia (Moscato d'Asti) $15. Here's a gem of a family-run winery and a refreshing discovery in the Asti area. Following a selection of international and local varieties in the producer's portfolio, the Giorgia Moscato d'Asti is thick with spring flowers, mimosa, and jasmine. Apricot and kiwi are tightly packed around a dessert wine with just enough acidity to keep it perky and interesting. **88** *—M.L. (12/15/2005)*

CASCINA LUISIN

Cascina Luisin 1998 Rabaja Nebbiolo (Barbaresco) $50. **91** *—M.M. (11/15/2002)*

Cascina Luisin 1998 Sori Paolin Nebbiolo (Barbaresco) $56. **88** *—M.S. (11/15/2002)*

CASCINACASTLE'T

Cascinacastle't 2004 (Moscato d'Asti) $13. Producer Maria Borio and her family have crafted an elegant Moscato d'Asti ripe with sticky white flowers, grapefruit, earthy tones, green herbs, and fresh-cut grass. That green theme continues in the mouth. A delightful wine with a colorful, child-painted label, it would be great for outdoor events like picnics and barbecues. **87** *—M.L. (12/15/2005)*

CASISANO COLOMBAIO

Casisano Colombaio 1999 (Brunello di Montalcino) $NA. Arguably a touch sugary and overdone, but still a good utility-level Brunello. The aromas of caramel and marshmallow suggest plenty of barrel influence, while on the palate the fruit veers toward candied cherry and raspberry. Good enough on the finish, and largely satisfying as a whole. **87** *—M.S. (6/1/2004)*

CASTELGIOCONDO

Castelgiocondo 1999 (Brunello di Montalcino) $NA. Frescobaldi's Montalcino estate produces this nicely extracted, fairly sweet and modern wine. The style is refined and highly polished, with fleshy cherry fruit and a smooth texture. Maybe too simple for the cognoscenti but possesses sure-fire restaurant and mass appeal. **90** *—M.S. (6/1/2004)*

CASTELL'IN VILLA

Castell'In Villa 1998 Poggio Delle Rosé Riserva Sangiovese (Chianti Classico) $75. After six plus years this wine still carries a huge whack of oak, so much so that the nose exudes menthol, cedar, and fir bark along with black cherry. Quite fresh and vertical on the palate, with clean cherry and vanilla flavors. Tannic for sure, but with enough cushion to handle it. **89** *(4/1/2005)*

Castell'In Villa 1997 Riserva (Chianti Classico) $48. Overall it's lovely on the nose, assuming you like cedary notes of tobacco, cinnamon, and wintergreen. Inordinately zesty on the tongue, with fiery tannins and live-wire acidity churning away. A little jagged and rough in terms of texture, but very much alive and kicking. **88** *(4/1/2005)*

CASTELLANI

Castellani 2000 Essenza Primitivo (Puglia) $9. **85 Best Buy** *—C.S. (5/1/2002)*

Castellani 2003 (Chianti) $7. Mildly sweet and grapey, with an herbal, almost spiced gumdrop character to the nose. Comes across a bit green on the palate, with a light-bodied crispness. Tangy and fresh on the finish. **84 Best Buy** *(4/1/2005)*

Castellani 1998 (Chianti Classico) $12. **87 Best Buy** *(4/1/2001)*

ITALY

Castellani 2000 Biagio (Toscana) $11. Dark and meaty, with a strong oak element. Cherry and plum flavors are full and roasted; the finish is spiky before going flat and heavy. Hammering tannins. **84** —*M.S. (10/1/2004)*

Castellani 1997 Burchino Vineyard (Chianti Superiore) $15. 87 *(4/1/2001)*

Castellani 1999 Poggio Al Casone (Chianti Superiore) $12. 86 Best Buy —*M.S. (12/31/2002)*

Castellani 1997 Riserva (Chianti) $12. 83 *(4/1/2001)*

Castellani 1998 Riserva (Chianti Classico) $18. 84 —*M.S. (12/31/2002)*

CASTELLARE

Castellare 2002 (Chianti Classico) $22. Wiry and tight, with leathery aromas sitting in front of tangy red fruit. Seems a bit vinegary and sharp, but not overwhelmingly so. Pumped up acidity means it's juicy and mouthwatering. **84** *(4/1/2005)*

Castellare 2000 Il Poggiale Riserva (Chianti Classico) $36. Soft on the nose, where you get mostly peanut brittle and graham cracker. Underneath you'll find a bit of green along with plum and berry. The wine has power, but it's also rather flat and alcoholic. Likely better in a more balanced vintage like 2001. **85** *(4/1/2005)*

CASTELLARIN

Castellarin 2001 Cabernet Sauvignon (Delle Venezie) $10. 82 *(5/1/2003)*

Castellarin 1998 Pinot Grigio (Venezia Giulia) $8. 86 Best Buy *(8/1/1999)*

CASTELLO BANFI

Castello Banfi 1999 (Brunello di Montalcino) $66. Rich, dark and muscular, with deep, jammy aromas of plum and blackberry. Banfi toes the line between modern and traditional, and this wine fits their model perfectly. It's a ripe, sizable mouthful, yet it has some true-life edges to it. Drink now through 2009. **91** —*M.S. (6/1/2004)*

Castello Banfi 1997 (Brunello di Montalcino) $59. 92 —*R.V. (8/1/2002)*

Castello Banfi 1994 (Brunello di Montalcino) $43. 88 —*M.S. (3/1/2000)*

Castello Banfi 1999 Poggio All'Oro Riserva (Brunello di Montalcino) $150. Smooth and lush, with a ton of berry, cherry, and smoke character. Supremely ripe and full, with chocolate and spice mixed into the prime cherry/berry palate. This is a wine for anyone who simply loves wine; maybe it isn't ultra-complex but there's no arguing about its polish and style. It's incredibly round and likable. **94 Cellar Selection** —*M.S. (7/1/2005)*

Castello Banfi 1997 Poggio All'Oro Riserva (Brunello di Montalcino) $125. 93 Cellar Selection —*M.S. (11/15/2003)*

Castello Banfi 2000 Poggio Alle Mura (Brunello di Montalcino) $75. Quite the fruit bomb with little to no vestiges of Old World red wine. It hits with broad, meaty aromas of black fruits and keeps that tone through the round, rich palate. Everything here is black and ripe, but there's enough acid to produce a juicy mouthfeel. Finishes with licorice, fudge, and mineral notes. **92** —*M.S. (7/1/2005)*

Castello Banfi 2000 Tavernelle Cabernet Sauvignon (Sant'Antimo) $41. 88 —*M.S. (11/15/2003)*

Castello Banfi 1996 Tavernelle Cabernet Sauvignon (Montalcino) $38. 87 —*M.S. (7/1/2000)*

Castello Banfi 1997 Excelsus Cabernet Sauvignon-Merlot (Montalcino) $73. 89 *(2/1/2001)*

Castello Banfi 2002 Fontanelle Chardonnay (Montalcino) $19. Aromas of lemon drop, butter, dust, and fresh-cut wood are sizable, as is the palate, which pushes mango, peach, and pineapple. It's a fairly big mouthful overall, with somewhat of a waxy feel. Good but only reaches modest heights. **85** —*M.S. (10/1/2004)*

Castello Banfi 1999 San Angelo Pinot Grigio (Toscana) $13. 88 Best Buy *(2/1/2001)*

Castello Banfi 1998 Colvecchio Syrah (Sant'Antimo) $36. 86 —*M.S. (8/1/2002)*

Castello Banfi 1998 (Rosso di Montalcino) $22. 89 *(2/1/2001)*

Castello Banfi 1999 Cum Laude Tuscan Blend (Sant'Antimo) $35. 87 —*M.S. (8/1/2002)*

Castello Banfi 1999 Summus Tuscan Blend (Sant'Antimo) $63. 94 Editors' Choice —*M.S. (11/15/2003)*

CASTELLO D'ALBOLA

Castello d'Albola 1992 Vin Santo del Chianti $50. A beautifully balanced vin santo—not too sweet and not too alcoholic. Combines hints of nuts and stone fruits on the nose, develops apricot, almond paste, and chestnut honey flavors on the palate, finishing with notes of candied orange peel. Yes, the 1992 is the current vintage of this delicious dessert wine. **91** *(3/1/2004)*

Castello d'Albola 2000 (Chianti Classico) $14. A solid, typical Chianti, with cherry, leather, and tobacco flavors. Largely supple, yet finishes with a tart, herbal edge. A blend of 95% Sangiovese and 5% Canaiolo. **86** *(3/1/2004)*

Castello d'Albola 1999 Le Ellere (Chianti Classico) $20. 88 *(12/31/2002)*

Castello d'Albola 1999 Riserva (Chianti Classico) $23. Shows some obvious oak influence on the nose, in hints of coffee, toast, and chocolate. These elements smooth out and integrate nicely with the rest of the wine on the palate, joined by bright cherries and an underlying note of finely tanned leather. Boasts a chewy, rich mouthfeel and a long, tart finish, anchored by black tea notes. **91 Editors' Choice** *(3/1/2004)*

Castello d'Albola 1997 Acciaiolo (Chianti Classico) $40. **87** *(9/1/2001)*

Castello d'Albola 1993 Acciaiolo Tuscan Blend (Toscana) $33. **92** *—M.G. (5/1/1999)*

CASTELLO DEI RAMPOLLA

Castello dei Rampolla 2000 (Chianti Classico) $29. Medium weight and medium intensity, with aromas of cherry tomato, flowers, leather, and bramble. Firm and simple, with dried cherry and a touch of sweet chocolate. Hardly exciting but clean and much better than bland. **86** *(4/1/2005)*

Castello dei Rampolla 1997 Riserva (Chianti Classico) $43. **88** *(4/1/2001)*

CASTELLO DEL POGGIO

Castello del Poggio 2004 (Moscato d'Asti) $12. Textbook appearance for a Moscato d'Asti with a thick layer of foam and a pale straw color. The nose is not super-intense but apricot, white blossoms, and fresh fruit are direct and clean as a whistle. Equally fresh and straightforward in the mouth. **87 Best Buy** *—M.L. (12/15/2005)*

Castello del Poggio NV Brachetto (Piedmont) $12. A bit heavy for Bracchetto, with slightly medicinal flavors of black cherries and sour herbs. Decent, just lacks finesse. **83** *—J.C. (12/15/2004)*

CASTELLO DEL TERRICCIO

Castello del Terriccio 1999 Tassinaia Red Blend (Toscana) $35. Lively aromas of plum, cherry, and vanilla are on the mark and inviting. Flavors of blackberry, cherry, and mineral are solid and complex. Finishes clean and proper. Simply a well-made, international-style red; round, ripe, and ready. **90** *—M.S. (10/1/2004)*

Castello del Terriccio 2000 Rondinaia Tuscan Blend (Toscana) $18. **91** *—M.S. (8/1/2002)*

CASTELLO DI AMA

Castello di Ama 1997 Al Poggio Chardonnay (Toscana) $27. **88** *—J.C. (11/15/1999)*

Castello di Ama 2000 (Chianti Classico) $38. Classy and precise. This is a wine that sooths and satisfies, but also is capable of playing at a pretty fast pace. The nose offers crisp red fruit, hints of orange, and plenty of dry leather. Snappy and secure on the palate, with structured cherry and raspberry. Proportion could be its middle name. **90 Editors' Choice** *(4/1/2005)*

Castello di Ama 1997 Chianti Classico (Chianti Classico) $39. **90** *—J.C. (11/15/1999)*

Castello di Ama 1995 Cru La Casuccia (Chianti Classico) $150. **91** *—J.C. (11/15/1999)*

Castello di Ama 1995 Il Chiuso Pinot Nero (Toscana) $47. **87** *—J.C. (11/15/1999)*

CASTELLO DI BOSSI

Castello di Bossi 2001 (Chianti Classico) $25. Dusty and moderately rich, with aromas of blackberry and a distant note of green bean. The mouthfeel is entirely on the mark, while the flavor profile consists of oak, plum, currant, and chocolate. Finishes tight and warm, with some bulk. A good food wine due to its correct balance. **88** *(4/1/2005)*

CASTELLO DI BROLIO

Castello di Brolio 1999 (Chianti Classico) $16. **88** *—M.S. (12/31/2002)*

Castello di Brolio 1997 (Chianti Classico) $40. **89** *(4/1/2001)*

CASTELLO DI CACCHIANO

Castello di Cacchiano 1998 (Chianti Classico) $21. **88** *(4/1/2001)*

CASTELLO DI FONTERUTOLI

Castello di Fonterutoli 2001 (Chianti Classico) $26. Deep, lush, and enchanting for what amounts to a basic Chianti Classico. The nose offers licorice, black plum, wild berry, and clove. The palate is equally nice, with cherry, plum, and oozing berry all rolled into one. Fine texture; good tannic grip; good balance; just what the doctor ordered. From Mazzei. **91** *—M.S. (10/1/2004)*

Castello di Fonterutoli 1997 Riserva (Chianti Classico) $49. **90** *(4/1/2001)*

CASTELLO DI GABBIANO

Castello di Gabbiano 2003 (Chianti) $10. Jagged cherry and leather aromas carry some egg scents as well, followed by light red-fruit flavors with a citrusy edge. Tart and tannic, but cleansing and fresh. Simple Chianti in its most mainstreet form. **84** *(4/1/2005)*

Castello di Gabbiano 2000 (Chianti Classico) $12. **85** *—S.H. (1/1/2002)*

Castello di Gabbiano 1999 Bellezza (Toscana) $30. Hints of mint, licorice, and cedar precede grassy, leathery aromas. The palate on this Sangiovese is simple and slightly woody, with raspberry and strawberry notes. Finishes a bit thin and drying, with notes of oak and vanilla. **86** *—M.S. (10/1/2004)*

Castello di Gabbiano 1999 Riserva (Chianti Classico) $17. 90 *—S.H. (12/31/2002)*

Castello di Gabbiano 1995 Riserva (Chianti Classico) $16. 86 *—M.S. (3/1/2000)*

Castello di Gabbiano 1999 Alleanza Tuscan Blend (Toscana) $35. Leather, mint, and raisin aromas define the bouquet, which is backed by a ripe palate full of tree fruits. Feels rather heavy on the tongue, with grabby, hard tannins. The blend is Sangiovese, Merlot, and Cab. 85 *—M.S. (10/1/2004)*

CASTELLO DI LISPIDA

Castello di Lispida 1999 Terraforte Red Blend (Veneto) $40. 89 *(5/1/2003)*

CASTELLO DI MELETO

Castello di Meleto 2000 (Chianti Classico) $20. 88 *—M.S. (11/15/2003)*

Castello di Meleto 1998 (Chianti Classico) $23. 89 *(4/1/2001)*

Castello di Meleto 1997 Riserva (Chianti Classico) $36. 90 *(4/1/2001)*

CASTELLO DI MONASTERO

Castello di Monastero 2001 (Chianti Classico) $17. Smooth and likable, with a touch of candy, licorice, and cedar on the nose. More cedar on the palate along with plum, chocolate, and leather. And finally you get tannins and some acid. Sound textbook? It is exactly that. And it's good. 89 *(4/1/2005)*

Castello di Monastero 2001 Montetondo (Chianti Superiore) $15. The real deal with a firm mouthfeel. From the start, where root beer and soy notes attach themselves to dry plum aromas, the mood is meaty. On the palate, it's almost hard. Tannin is in the lead, and it creates a gritty sensation on the tongue and cheeks. Best with food. 88 *(4/1/2005)*

Castello di Monastero 1999 Riserva (Chianti Classico) $30. Round and full-bodied, with a touch of prune to the otherwise foresty nose. Tastes a bit cooked, but not enough to be a detractor. Beyond that, the plum, raisin, and black-cherry flavors are deep and satisfying. Finishes expectedly rich, but with structure. Drink by the end of 2006. 90 *(4/1/2005)*

CASTELLO DI MONSANTO

Castello di Monsanto 1999 Nemo Cabernet Sauvignon (Tuscany) $44. 87 *—M.S. (12/31/2002)*

Castello di Monsanto 2002 Alaura (Chianti) $11. Normally a solid but unspectacular performer, Castello di Monsanto's "starter" Chianti struts its stuff in this down vintage (maybe some pedigreed grapes were declassified, thus making Alaura better). Regardless, it delivers spicy cola, leather, and tobacco aromas along with forward plum and berry fruit. The balance is correct and the feel is deeper than what we recall. **89 Best Buy** *(4/1/2005)*

Castello di Monsanto 1999 Fabrizio Bianchi (Tuscany) $39. 92 Editors' Choice *—M.S. (12/31/2002)*

Castello di Monsanto 1997 Il Poggio Riserva (Chianti Classico) $44. 87 *(4/1/2001)*

Castello di Monsanto 1999 Riserva (Chianti Classico) $23. 90 *—M.S. (12/31/2002)*

Castello di Monsanto 1997 Riserva (Chianti Classico) $22. 86 *(4/1/2001)*

Castello di Monsanto 1999 Il Poggio Riserva Tuscan Blend (Chianti Classico) $55. 92 *—M.S. (12/31/2002)*

Castello di Monsanto 1997 Tinscvil Tuscan Blend (Toscana) $34. 87 *(9/1/2001)*

CASTELLO DI MONTEPÓ

Castello di Montepó 1998 Schidione Tuscan Blend (Toscana) $125. 93 *(11/15/2003)*

CASTELLO DI NEIVE

Castello di Neive 1998 Messoirano (Dolcetto d'Alba) $12. 89 Best Buy *(4/1/2000)*

CASTELLO DI POPPIANO

Castello di Poppiano 2003 Il Cortile (Chianti Colli Fiorentini) $14. Sweet and creamy on the nose, with both caramel and vanilla accents. A touch candied on the palate, but chewy and wholesome. Maybe a little green if examined under a microscope, but if casually drunk with spaghetti or pizza it'll do the job. 86 *(4/1/2005)*

Castello di Poppiano 1999 Riserva (Chianti Colli Fiorentini) $18. There's plenty of body and stuffing to this fine Chianti. Also a good deal of cherry and plum fruit, some oak and vanilla, and a touch of earth. A plush, solid wine from a good Chianti vintage. Drinkable now through 2006. 90 *—M.S. (10/1/2004)*

Castello di Poppiano 2000 Conte Ferdinando Guicciardini Syrah (Colli della Toscana Centrale) $19. 81 *—M.S. (12/31/2002)*

Castello di Poppiano 2000 Tosco Forte Tuscan Blend (Colli della Toscana Centrale) $18. 84 *—M.S. (12/31/2002)*

Castello di Poppiano 1999 Tricorno Tuscan Blend (Colli della Toscana Centrale) $35. 92 Editors' Choice *—M.S. (11/15/2003)*

CASTELLO DI QUERCETO

Castello di Querceto 1999 Il Picchio Riserva Sangiovese (Chianti Classico) $33. Smooth and deep, with cherry, chocolate, and earth aromas. Quite typical and traditional, with maturity as well as verve. Plum, cherry, and raspberry flavors create a fruity but basic palate, while the zingy finish is propelled by a wash of refreshing acidity. **88** *(4/1/2005)*

CASTELLO DI SPESSA

Castello di Spessa 1997 Tocai (Collio) $22. **87** *(11/1/1999)*

CASTELLO DI TASSAROLO

Castello di Tassarolo 2002 Villa Rosa Gavi (Gavi) $17. **84** *—M.S. (12/15/2003)*

CASTELLO DI VERRAZZANO

Castello di Verrazzano 1998 (Chianti Classico) $21. **85** *(4/1/2001)*

Castello di Verrazzano 1997 Riserva (Chianti Classico) $38. **87** *(4/1/2001)*

CASTELLO DI VOLPAIA

Castello di Volpaia 2002 (Chianti Classico) $17. Red fruit carries this one, from the raw, leathery nose, through the cherry and red-plum palate, to the racy finish. Along the way are softening nuances of chocolate and cream. Modest tannins keep it from feeling too rough, so it should do well at the dinner table. **87** *(4/1/2005)*

Castello di Volpaia 2002 Borgianni (Chianti) $10. Not very clean, with a murky nose of caramel and wet dog. Once things clear a bit, you get jammy fruit, some pepper, and a bit of earth. **82** *(4/1/2005)*

Castello di Volpaia 1996 Classico (Toscana) $17. **84** *(2/1/2000)*

Castello di Volpaia 2000 Coltassala Riserva (Chianti Classico) $36. Begins granular, with intense aromas of iodine and leather. Gets its feet underneath it with time, showing plum and black cherry flavors prior to a long, mildly bitter finish. If one word describes the palate, it's tannic. This is a wine that drills hard, leaving the cheeks exhausted. **87** *(4/1/2005)*

Castello di Volpaia 2000 Riserva (Chianti Classico) $26. A bit bulky and roasted, but that brings with it tobacco, earth, and chocolate aromas. Expressive on the palate; the plum and berry fruit is exciting and braced by serious tannins. Those tannins are also a bit drying, so the finish seems tight as nails. Deserves air and time after opening. **90** *(4/1/2005)*

Castello di Volpaia 1999 Balifico Tuscan Blend (Toscana) $46. **91** *—M.S. (11/15/2003)*

Castello di Volpaia 2001 Borgianni (Chianti) $10. **88 Best Buy** *—M.S. (11/15/2003)*

Castello di Volpaia 1999 Riserva (Chianti Classico) $29. **89** *—M.S. (11/15/2003)*

CASTELLO MONTAÚTO

Castello Montaúto 2003 (Vernaccia di San Gimignano) $13. Sincerely aromatic, with scents of lilac, wild flower, and almond candy. All in all, the bouquet is anything but subtle, but it's still pretty. In the mouth, there's a ripe core of melon, papaya, and spice, while the finish is big and smooth. Seems like the warm '03 summer helped this wine out. **87** *—M.S. (8/1/2004)*

CASTELLO ROMITORIO

Castello Romitorio 1999 (Brunello di Montalcino) $59. A glorious Brunello, one overflowing with the scents of leather, tree bark, cherry tomato, and black cherry. One taste confirms the nose, and at every checkpoint it's full and rewarding. With its huge wingspan, there's flavor and texture at every turn. Hold for 3–10 years before drinking. **94** *—M.S. (6/1/2004)*

Castello Romitorio 1999 Riserva (Brunello di Montalcino) $65. Surprisingly sweet but lovable just the same. The nose offers sugared doughnut and marzipan aromas yet the palate has cut-through acidity that ensures that the wine is neither flabby nor dull. Big-time cherry and plum flavors are pure and exciting; all in all there isn't much more to ask for. **93** *—M.S. (7/1/2005)*

Castello Romitorio 1998 (Chianti Colli Senesi) $10. **88 Best Buy** *(4/1/2001)*

CASTELLO VICCHIOMAGGIO

Castello Vicchiomaggio 1998 Riserva La Prima (Chianti Classico) $25. **92 Editors' Choice** *—R.V. (12/31/2002)*

Castello Vicchiomaggio 1998 Riserva Petri (Chianti Classico) $24. **90** *—R.V. (12/31/2002)*

CASTELVERO

Castelvero 2003 Barbera (Piedmont) $9. From the region of Monferrato, this joyous wine just oozes youth, from its vivid purple hue to its fruity-perfumey aromas and bright flavors of cherries and plums. Sure, it's a little on the simple side, but it's fun to drink and would make a great pizza wine. **87 Best Buy** *—J.C. (11/15/2004)*

Castelvero 1998 (Barbera di Piemonte) $8. **88 Best Buy** *(4/1/2000)*

CASTIGLION DEL BOSCO

Castiglion del Bosco 1997 (Brunello di Montalcino) $NA. **89** *—R.V. (8/1/2002)*

CAVALLERI

Cavalleri NV Brut Blanc de Blancs (Franciacorta) $15. **86** *—J.C. (12/31/2001)*

Cavalleri NV Satèn Blanc de Blancs (Franciacorta) $18. 84 *(12/31/2001)*

CAVIT

Cavit 2000 Pinot Grigio (Trentino) $8. 84 *—S.H. (9/1/2001)*

Cavit 1999 Pinot Noir (Delle Venezie) $9. 82 *—S.H. (9/1/2001)*

CECCHI

Cecchi 2002 (Chianti Classico) $12. Herbal and leafy, with aromatics of damp earth, cherry, and leather. Snappy on the tongue, where apple skins and fresh red berries mix. Short on the finish, with mild tannins. Satisfactory, with no major bumps or dips. **85** *(4/1/2005)*

Cecchi 1998 Sangiovese (Toscana) $9. 83 *—J.C. (9/1/2001)*

Cecchi 2002 Arcano (Chianti Classico) $14. The nose leaks hard cheese and barnyard aromas at first, which are backed by notes of candied fruit and mint. Flavors veer toward cherry and raspberry, with finishing notes that are somewhat medicinal. **84** *—M.S. (10/1/2004)*

Cecchi 1997 Messr Pietro di Teuzzo Riserva (Chianti Classico) $28. 88 *(4/1/2001)*

Cecchi 2000 Teuzzo Riserva (Chianti Classico) $32. Cherry and raspberry aromas are sweet and easy, as is the palate, which sports black cherry, plum, and some kirsch. Finishes round, arguably a bit flat, with tannins that go thud. That said, aging isn't the ticket. Drink now with red meats. **87** *—M.S. (10/1/2004)*

Cecchi 2002 (Sangiovese di Toscana) $9. Light and smelling of cherry Kool-Aid. Candied on the palate and finish. **81** *—M.S. (11/15/2004)*

Cecchi 2003 Litorale Vermentino (Maremma) $17. Hugely aromatic, with sweet scents of flowers and candied licorice. Very big for a Tuscan white, a reflection of the warm region from which it hails as well as the warm summer in which it was born. On the back end, the finish pushes ripe apple and pear flavors. **88** *—M.S. (8/1/2004)*

Cecchi 2003 White Blend (Orvieto Classico) $10. Soft, with vanilla cream and pear aromas. Lemon and melon flavors create a zesty wash across the palate, while the finish is chunky, round and mildly spicy. **85 Best Buy** *—M.S. (11/15/2004)*

CENNATOIO

Cennatoio 1997 (Chianti Classico) $22. 87 *(4/1/2001)*

Cennatoio 1996 Riserva (Chianti Classico) $37. 85 *(4/1/2001)*

CERBAIA

Cerbaia 2000 (Brunello di Montalcino) $55. Charred; almost tastes as if you came across a field or briar patch on fire. In the mouth it holds on to that burnt character, and the tannins seem exceedingly hard. More age should soften it up, but in its relative youth it's a raw, tough wine with screeching tannins. **85** *—M.S. (7/1/2005)*

CERETTO

Ceretto 2002 Blange' Arneis (Piedmont) $20. 86 *—M.S. (12/15/2003)*

Ceretto 2002 Rossana (Dolcetto d'Alba) $19. Shows decent complexity on the nose in its aromas of leather, rhubarb, and fresh herbs, but comes across as light and lacking ripeness in the mouth. Modest cherry flavors carry a hint of weediness through the finish. **84** *—J.C. (11/15/2004)*

Ceretto 1999 Rossana (Dolcetto d'Alba) $19. 82 *—M.N. (9/1/2001)*

Ceretto 2003 I Vignaioli di Santo Stefano (Moscato d'Asti) $19. Shows some nice floral, almost lilacy aromas; on the palate there is restrained pineapple and orange fruit in a soft, low-acid format that's reflective of the hot vintage. **85** *—J.C. (11/15/2004)*

Ceretto 1998 Nebbiolo (Barbaresco) $111. 91 Cellar Selection *(9/1/2001)*

Ceretto 1998 Asij Nebbiolo (Barbaresco) $44. 88 *—M.S. (11/15/2002)*

Ceretto 2000 Bernardot Nebbiolo (Barbaresco) $67. Somewhat confusingly, Ceretto's estate wines from Barbaresco are now bottled under the name Bricco Asili, with Ceretto only in small letters. But the quality is in the bottle. Smoky, meaty aromas give way with air to dried cherries, leather, and a touch of citrus. Darker notes of asphalt and chocolate join in on the palate, which is big, muscular and chewy without being overdone. Finishes long, picking up flavors and a texture akin to cocoa powder. **93 Editors' Choice** *(4/2/2004)*

Ceretto 1998 Bernardot Nebbiolo (Piedmont) $74. 87 *(9/1/2001)*

Ceretto 2000 Bricco Asili Nebbiolo (Barbaresco) $122. Beautifully balanced and fragrant Barbaresco, with floral notes joining scents of leather and fresh cherries. Hints of milk chocolate and vanilla sneak in on the palate, but the emphasis remains on the fruit. The mouthwatering finish boasts supple tannins, suggesting midterm ageability; try 2008–2015. **91** *(4/2/2004)*

Ceretto 1995 Bricco Asili Nebbiolo (Barbaresco) $105. 90 *—M.S. (11/15/1999)*

Ceretto 1998 Bricco Rocche Nebbiolo (Piedmont) $221. 94 Editors' Choice *—R.V. (11/15/2002)*

Ceretto 1995 Bricco Rocche Nebbiolo (Piedmont) $140. 96 Cellar Selection *(3/1/2000)*

Ceretto 1998 Bricco Rocche Prapó Barolo Nebbiolo (Barolo) $90. 88 *—R.V. (11/15/2002)*

Ceretto 1997 Brunate Nebbiolo (Barolo) $74. 90 *(9/1/2001)*

Ceretto 1998 Fasít Nebbiolo (Barbaresco) $74. **90** *(9/1/2001)*

Ceretto 1995 Prapó Nebbiolo (Barolo) $70. **92** *—M.S. (7/1/2000)*

Ceretto 1997 Prapó Nebbiolo (Barolo) $74. **92** *(9/1/2001)*

Ceretto 1998 Zonchera Nebbiolo (Piedmont) $40. **93 Editors' Choice** *—R.V. (11/15/2002)*

CERRAIA

Cerraia 1996 (Vino Nobile di Montepulciano) $27. **83** *—M.S. (9/1/2000)*

CERRI DEL PALAGIO

Cerri del Palagio 2000 Riserva (Chianti Classico) $20. A bit over-ripe, with Port and sherry aromas, mushroom, and a whiff of anise. Black cherry and plum fruit seems plump at first but thins quickly. A touch lean and starchy, but mostly it's good to go. **84** *(4/1/2005)*

CESARI

Cesari 1998 Fiorile Pinot Grigio (Trentino) $11. **84** *(8/1/1999)*

Cesari 1998 Red Blend (Amarone della Valpolicella Classico) $40. **92 Editors' Choice** *(5/1/2003)*

Cesari 2000 Il Bosco Red Blend (Amarone della Valpolicella) $60. Ample toast and smoke announce plenty of barrique aging, but in this case it works like a charm because there's marzipan, baked fruit, and coffee playing second fiddle. Super deep in the mouth, with prune, date, and cinnamon notes. Finishes big and toasty, with succulence and supreme balance. **93** *(11/1/2005)*

Cesari 2000 Recioto della Valpolicella $30. **89** *(5/1/2003)*

CEUSO

Ceuso 2003 Scurati Nero d'Avola (Sicilia) $19. With deep, meaty red fruit, leather, and a natural, unadulterated sweetness to it, this is one likable Nero d'Avola. The palate is ripe and modern, but the flavors are traditional: spicy plum fruit, nutmeg, earth, and oak. Long and dessert-like on the finish, with vanilla and licorice notes. A prototype for the new Sicily. **91** *—M.S. (2/1/2005)*

Ceuso 2000 Fastaia Red Blend (Sicilia) $31. **88** *—M.S. (10/1/2003)*

CHIANTI TRAMBUSTI

Chianti Trambusti 1998 Celsus (Sangiovese di Toscana) $22. **84** *—M.S. (11/15/2003)*

Chianti Trambusti 1999 Il Perticato Tuscan Blend (Chianti Classico) $17. **86** *—M.S. (11/15/2003)*

CIACCI PICCOLOMINI D'ARAGONA

Ciacci Piccolomini d'Aragona 2000 (Brunello di Montalcino) $65. Red and jammy, with a lot of sweet raspberry on the bouquet. Not much meat or darkness here; instead it's overtly bright on the palate, where pie cherry, cranberry, and apple skins reign. Simple in its singular focus on red fruit. Could be perfect for those who don't want to taste a lot of oak. **87** *—M.S. (7/1/2005)*

CIELO

Cielo 2001 Pinot Grigio (Veneto) $8. **83** *—J.C. (7/1/2003)*

CIELO BLEU

Cielo Bleu 2001 (Vermentino di Sardegna) $14. Mildly oxidized and caramelized to the nose, but fresher on the tongue. Chunky apple, melon, and spice flavors are persistent, and while the wine lacks sex appeal and polish, it's mature and has its charms. **85** *—M.S. (8/1/2004)*

CITRA

Citra 2002 (Montepulciano d'Abruzzo) $5. **81** *—M.S. (11/15/2003)*

CLERICO

Clerico 1999 Ciabot Mentin Ginestra Nebbiolo (Barolo) $75. Long considered a member of Barolo's New Wave vanguard, Clerico's wines are still unabashedly oaky, featuring aromas of toast and vanilla liqueur and lush masses of soft tannins underneath. Drink now–2015. **90** *(4/2/2004)*

COL D'ORCIA

Col d'Orcia 2000 (Brunello di Montalcino) $49. Lighter bodied, with an emphasis on leather, pepper, and red fruit. Strawberry and raspberry flavors are front and center, while a bit of oak-based milk chocolate provides support. Hard to find fault here, but by the same token it's rather simple and antiseptic. Good in a clean, light way. **88** *—M.S. (7/1/2005)*

Col d'Orcia 1999 Banditella (Rosso di Montalcino) $18. **87** *—M.S. (12/31/2002)*

COL DE' SALICI

Col de' Salici NV Extra Dry (Prosecco di Valdobbiadene) $15. **87** *—S.H. (12/31/2000)*

COL DI LUNA

Col di Luna NV Cuvée Brut (Italy) $12. An unusual blend of 50% Prosecco and 50% Chardonnay; it smells very much like ginger ale, while the flavors trigger citrus, apple, and mild spice. Fairly clean and persistent; neither complex nor flawed. **85** *—M.S. (6/1/2005)*

ITALY

COLI

Coli 2000 (Montepulciano d'Abruzzo) $7. 84 Best Buy *(11/1/2002)*

Coli 2000 (Chianti Classico) $13. 85 *(11/1/2002)*

Coli 1998 (Chianti Classico) $10. 83 *(4/1/2001)*

Coli 1998 Pratale (Chianti Classico) $22. 86 *(11/1/2002)*

Coli 1999 Riserva (Chianti Classico) $18. 87 *—M.S. (11/15/2003)*

Coli 1997 Riserva (Chianti) $11. 86 *(4/1/2001)*

Coli 2001 (Orvieto) $7. 85 Best Buy *(11/1/2002)*

Coli 2003 (Vernaccia di San Gimignano) $10. Fairly mute, with light aromas of green melon and apple. For certain this is a simple, basic white, but its simplicity is its best attribute. Correct acidity and balance make it a worthwhile quaffer. Drink soon, and drink well-chilled. 85 *—M.S. (8/1/2004)*

COLLE S. MUSTIOLA DI FABIO CENNI

Colle S. Mustiola di Fabio Cenni 1999 Poggio Ai Chiari Sangiovese (Toscana) $48. 88 *—M.S. (12/31/2002)*

COLLI DELLA MURGIA

Colli della Murgia 1998 Selvato Red Blend (Apulia) $11. 84 *(9/1/2000)*

COLLOSORBO

Collosorbo 1999 Riserva (Brunello di Montalcino) $65. A bit lighter in color than most of the '99 riservas, but still a very nice wine offering easy drinkability. Toasty, foresty notes accent the nose, while the palate is sweet at the core with ripe plum and cherry. Excellent on its own; will certainly please. 91 *—M.S. (7/1/2005)*

COLOGNOLE

Colognole 1997 (Chianti Rufina) $12. 81 *(4/1/2001)*

COLONNARA

Colonnara 2003 Lyricus (Verdicchio dei Castelli di Jesi Classico) $11. The bouquet is razor clean, lucid, and smooth, with aromas of peach blossom and a hint of citrus. Fruity and less refined than the sensational Cuprese, with grapefruit and toasted almond controlling the palate. Finishes tight and sturdy. 88 Best Buy *—M.S. (8/1/2004)*

COLOSI

Colosi 2002 Red Blend (Sicilia) $11. Attractive on the nose, with plum, raisin, and chocolate. However, it's ultra-sweet and candied, as if some sugar were left in it. As for the finish, it's syrupy. 83 *—M.S. (2/1/2005)*

CÚLPETRONE

Cúlpetrone 1999 Red Blend (Montefalco) $14. 91 Best Buy *—M.S. (2/1/2003)*

COLSANTO

Colsanto 2002 (Sagrantino di Montefalco) $NA. Leather, tar, pencil shavings, graphite, and smoked wood from the Livon family of Friuli who recently acquired this Umbrian winery and 20 hectares of vineyard not far from Assisi. 87 *—M.L. (9/1/2005)*

COLUTTA

Colutta 2002 Friulano (Friuli) $17. A complex white wine that combines metallic mineral, lime zest, and white pepper flavors that are highlighted by high acidity. Bone dry, it will be a classy companion for a wide spectrum of foods. 86 *—S.H. (10/1/2004)*

CONCILIO

Concilio 2001 Riserva Merlot (Trentino) $10. Here's a single-varietal wine from Italy's northernmost Trentino region that boasts all the sensual roundness and softness of Merlot with the fresh forest berry and spicy acidity of cool climate growing conditions. Tobacco, mineral tones, dried hay, nutmeg, black pepper, and bay leaf render a wine of deep aromatic intensity that undergoes an impressive evolution in the glass. 88 Best Buy *—M.L. (11/15/2005)*

Concilio 1997 Single Vineyard Pinot Grigio (Trentino) $13. 85 *(8/1/1999)*

CONTADI CASTALDI

Contadi Castaldi 1998 Rosé (Terre di Franciacorta) $27. 83 *—M.S. (12/31/2002)*

Contadi Castaldi NV Chardonnay (Terre di Franciacorta) $11. 84 *—J.C. (9/1/2000)*

Contadi Castaldi 1999 Rosé (Franciacorta) $35. 84 *—J.C. (12/31/2003)*

CONTE DELLA VIPERA

Conte della Vipera 2001 Sauvignon Blanc (Umbria) $22. Interesting on the nose, where pineapple, licorice, and mint vie for attention. But in the mouth it's a low-acid flat-liner with pickled flavors and a sour aftertaste. 81 *—M.S. (10/1/2004)*

ITALY

CONTE FERDINANDO GUICCIARDINI

Conte Ferdinando Guicciardini 2001 Massi di Mandorlaia Riserva (Morellino di Scansano) $40. Incredibly rich and ripe, a total departure from traditional dry Morellino. Cola, chocolate, caramel, and blackberry aromas emanate from the bouquet, while the palate is loaded with black fruit and coffee. Finishes sweet, with fudge and mocha notes. A layered, meaty wine. **91** *—M.S. (11/15/2004)*

CONTERNO FANTINO

Conterno Fantino 1999 Vignota (Barbera d'Alba) $22. **87** *—M.N. (9/1/2001)*

Conterno Fantino 2000 Parussi Nebbiolo (Barolo) $81. Boasts knockout aromas of flowers and herbs—a haunting perfume that adds cherry and balsamic notes as it develops. It's not a blockbuster on the palate, but relies on silkiness and finesse to make an impression, its long finish couched in supple tannins. **92** *—J.C. (11/15/2004)*

Conterno Fantino 2000 Sorí Ginestra Nebbiolo (Barolo) $99. A softer, gentler Barolo, with Nebbiolo's hard edges tamed by a combination of the vintage, short, rotary fermentation and new oak. Yet as if to thwart critics of the modern style, it retains the essence of Nebbiolo in its floral, cherry, and leather aromas—vanilla plays only a small part. Firms up considerably on the finish, suggesting greater ageability than at first glance, picking up hints of citrus peel and tea leaves. **89** *—J.C. (11/15/2004)*

Conterno Fantino 2001 Monprá Red Blend (Langhe) $59. Starts off nicely, with aromatic notes of cinnamon, graham cracker, and mint. There's some solid cherry fruit in the mouth, but it gets a little swamped by oaky notes of cedar and vanilla, finishing with soft tannins and tart acids. The barrique-aged blend is approximately 50% Nebbiolo, 40% Barbera, and 10% Cabernet Sauvignon. **87** *—J.C. (11/15/2004)*

CONTI COSTANTI

Conti Costanti 1997 Riserva (Brunello di Montalcino) $97. **92** *—M.S. (11/15/2003)*

CONTI FORMENTINI

Conti Formentini 2000 Torre di Tramontana Chardonnay (Collio) $25. **89** *—R.V. (7/1/2003)*

Conti Formentini 2001 Pinot Grigio (Collio) $15. **84** *—J.C. (7/1/2003)*

Conti Formentini 1996 Pinot Grigio (Collio) $13. **84** *(8/1/1999)*

CONTINI

Contini 2002 (Vermentino di Sardegna) $15. Strong, smoky and meaty at first, and then giving way to more expressive and subtle fruit and sea notes. The palate offers a delicious mix of ripe apple, lemon, and papaya, while the finish is very full and complex. A good match for seafood or poultry. **88** *—M.S. (8/1/2004)*

CONTRATTO

Contratto 1997 Panta Rei (Barbera d'Asti) $15. **86** *(4/1/2000)*

COPPO

Coppo 1997 L'Avvocata (Barbera d'Asti) $14. **85** *(4/1/2000)*

Coppo 1997 Monteriolo Chardonnay (Piedmont) $43. **84** *(9/1/2000)*

CORDERO DI MONTEZEMOLO

Cordero di Montezemolo 1998 (Dolcetto d'Alba) $17. **88** *(4/1/2000)*

CORINO

Corino 1999 Vigneto Rocche Nebbiolo (Barolo) $70. Is this really Barolo? Tastes so exotic, featuring raspberry and blackberry liqueur splashed with oodles of vanilla, that Barolo origins seem questionable, yet try it the next day and more traditional Barolo flavors have emerged—cherries, tar, and tobacco. Crisp acids and firm tannins suggest cellaring until 2012. **88** *(4/2/2004)*

CORTE VECCHIA

Corte Vecchia 1997 Red Blend (Amarone della Valpolicella Classico) $45. **90** *(5/1/2003)*

CORTEFORTE

Corteforte 1998 Ripasso Red Blend (Valpolicella Classico Superiore) $17. **87** *(5/1/2003)*

CORVO

Corvo 2002 Rosso (Sicilia) $10. This Nero d'Avola is simple, light, and smooth, with aromatics of red fruits and leather. Plum and berry flavors are solid, while the finish offers integrated oak and vanilla. A correct, good-feel red for easygoing occasions. **86 Best Buy** *—M.S. (11/15/2004)*

Corvo 2000 Rosso (Sicilia) $10. **86 Best Buy** *—M.S. (10/1/2003)*

COSTANZA MALFATTI

Costanza Malfatti 2001 (Morellino di Scansano) $47. Heavily oaked, with cedar, mint, and lemon-rind aromas. Becomes more integrated with airing, showing ripe red fruit and a dose of chocolate. Plenty of open-grained wood, vanilla, and cocoa on the finish. A woody Sangiovese that can handle the bulk of its oak. **89** *—M.S. (11/15/2004)*

COTTANERA

Cottanera 2002 Barbazzale Inzolia (Sicilia) $18. 85 *—J.C. (10/1/2003)*

Cottanera 1999 L'Ardenza Mondeuse (Sicilia) $38. 89 *—C.S. (5/1/2002)*

Cottanera 2001 Fatagione Nerello Mascalese (Sicilia) $28. Forward all the way, with raspberry, cherry, and smoke aromas. The palate is round and broad, with virtually no edges. Thus it finishes heavy and meaty, without much subtlety. It's rugged, acidic, tannic and tasty. Patience is required. 87 *—M.S. (7/1/2005)*

Cottanera 2001 Barbazzale Red Blend (Sicilia) $19. 87 *—M.S. (10/1/2003)*

Cottanera 2001 L'Ardenza Red Blend (Sicilia) $45. Weighs in on the heavy side, and that's obvious from the color as well as the tomato and beet aromas. Yet just when you think it's too stewy, a blast of black plum and licorice hits and the wine is salvaged. Not a dancer; more of a plodder with local appeal. 85 *—M.S. (7/1/2005)*

Cottanera 1999 Sole Di Sesta Syrah (Sicilia) $38. 87 *—C.S. (5/1/2002)*

CUSUMANO

Cusumano 2001 Jalé Chardonnay (Sicilia) $28. 84 *—J.C. (10/1/2003)*

Cusumano 2001 Cubía Inzolia (Sicilia) $20. 84 *—J.C. (10/1/2003)*

Cusumano 2002 Nadaría Nero d'Avola (Sicilia) $10. 87 *—J.C. (10/1/2003)*

Cusumano 2001 Benuara Red Blend (Sicilia) $15. 88 *—J.C. (10/1/2003)*

Cusumano 2002 Angimbé Insolia-Chardonnay (Sicilia) $15. 86 *—J.C. (10/1/2003)*

D'ANGELO

D'Angelo 2001 Sacravite (Aglianico del Vulture) $12. A spicy, sun-baked Aglianico that deals cherry, bourbon, and piles of hard spice. The flavors of dried cherries and cinnamon are subtle and enticing, while the tight, hard finish offers raisin and other baked fruits. Not complex but good in a finite way. 88 Best Buy *—M.S. (2/1/2005)*

DA VINCI

Da Vinci 2003 (Chianti) $14. Smells really nice, with floral notes alongside black cherries, tobacco, and hint of graham cracker. Flavors are fully ripe, blending black cherry and plum, but retaining Chianti's essential leanness. Finishes a bit ungenerous and hard, or it would have scored higher. 85 *(12/31/2004)*

Da Vinci 2001 (Chianti Classico) $17. Attains a level of intensity not matched by the other Da Vinci wines, with bold aromas of tobacco, earth, and cedar matched on the palate by flavors of cherry, plum, and dried spices. This 100% Sangiovese possesses a long finish and supple tannins; it should drink well for 4–7 years. 88 *(12/31/2004)*

Da Vinci 2000 Riserva (Chianti) $20. Dark to the eye, with round plum and berry aromas jazzed up by a mix of chocolate and herbs. A forward palate presses ripe cherry/berry fruit, while the finish is collected and pure. Well-made and on the money. Of note, this is a Gallo project. 88 *—M.S. (10/1/2004)*

DAL FORNO ROMANO

Dal Forno Romano 1997 Red Blend (Valpolicella Superiore) $70. 90 *(5/1/2003)*

DALFIUME

Dalfiume 1999 Rubicone Sangiovese (Emilia-Romagna) $6. 87 Best Buy *—M.N. (12/31/2000)*

DAMILANO

Damilano 1999 Cannubi Nebbiolo (Barolo) $72. Like Damilano's Liste bottling, this one also has a strong vegetal streak to its aromas. Black cherry and coffee flavors are ripe and loaded with chewy tannins. If you can get past the green, you'll like this better than we did. Drink 2008–2015. 88 *(4/2/2004)*

Damilano 1999 Liste Nebbiolo (Barolo) $65. This wine has a persistent vegetal note to its aromas that may put some tasters off; others may not be bothered by it. Flavors are earthy and moderately rich, blending sweet notes of dried fruit with mushroom and tar. Long, tannic finish picks up hints of coffee beans. 85 *(4/2/2004)*

DANZANTE

Danzante 2001 Merlot (Sicilia) $11. Chunky and green, with caramel oak sitting on top as camouflage. Modest berry fruit leads into a lean, quick finish. Over and out. 81 *—M.S. (10/1/2004)*

Danzante 1999 Merlot (Sicilia) $11. 86 Best Buy *—C.S. (5/1/2002)*

Danzante 2001 Pinot Grigio (Delle Venezie) $10. 86 *(9/1/2002)*

Danzante 2000 Sangiovese (Marche) $11. 84 *(9/1/2002)*

DARDANO

Dardano 1997 Nebbiolo (Barolo) $23. 87 *—C.S. (11/15/2002)*

DEI

Dei 1999 (Rosso di Montepulciano) $15. 87 *—M.N. (9/1/2001)*

Dei 2001 Bossona Tuscan Blend (Vino Nobile di Montepulciano) $45. Super-tight yet smooth; this reserve-quality Sangiovese is exactly as it should be. Chocolate, raspberry, and leather aromas lead to a corpulent but structured body veiling ultra-pure red-fruit flavors. Neither tannic nor hard; hold for another 12 to 18 months. **91 Editors' Choice** *—M.S. (7/1/2005)*

DESSILANI

Dessilani 1997 Reserve Selection (Barbera di Piemonte) $16. **86** *(4/1/2000)*

DEZZANI

Dezzani 2004 I Morelli (Moscato d'Asti) $12. The nose is ripe with floral, fruit, honey, and those trademark soapy notes with rose petal, dried grass, and citrus in the mouth. A beautiful single-vineyard wine from Terzo d'Acqui with a creamy texture and a saccharine-sweet finish. **88 Best Buy** *—M.L. (12/15/2005)*

DI MAJO NORANTE

Di Majo Norante 2001 Contado Aglianico (Molise) $12. Deep, ripe and syrupy on the nose, with leather, brambly red fruit, and licorice. Seemingly on the ripe side, but still juicy and fresh. The plum and berry fruit is mature, while proper aging has added a smoky edge along with carob, earth, and coffee nuances. **89 Best Buy** *—M.S. (2/1/2005)*

Di Majo Norante 2002 Ramitello Red Blend (Terra degli Osci) $14. I am simply delighted with the latest releases from Molise's Di Majo Norante. This luscious red blend is made from two little-known, organically grown native varieties (85 percent Prugnolo and 15 percent Aglianico) and has been deftly transformed thanks to consulting enologist Riccardo Cotarella into a thick, inky garnet wine with black cherry, tar, leather, bitter chocolate, and never-ending layers of aromatic intensity. A gorgeously concentrated and velvety body leaves zesty spice in the mouth until you're ready for the next sip. **89 Best Buy** *—M.L. (11/15/2005)*

Di Majo Norante 2003 Sangiovese (Terra degli Osci) $10. Full and purple, with a meaty bouquet that dishes bacon, berry, and cookie dough. Great feel, assuming you like yours big. As for flavor, look for plum, blackberry, and spice cake. With modest tannins, this is a drink-me-now kind of red, perfect with pizza or pasta. **86 Best Buy** *—M.S. (2/1/2005)*

DI MEO

Di Meo 2004 G (Greco di Tufo) $NA. Winemaker Roberto Di Meo is one of those people you instinctively like. He laughs loud and loves practical jokes and his good cheer is reflected in the long portfolio of wines he produces from grapes native to the Campania region. This single varietal Greco di Tufo has tangible almond, creamy peach, and Golden Delicious apple and is round and full with mouth-puckering tartness on the finish. Elegant packaging makes for a handsome table presentation. **88 Best Buy** *—M.L. (11/15/2005)*

DIEVOLE

Dievole 2000 Novecento Riserva (Chianti Classico) $37. Exotic, luxurious, and lush; super-ripe and intense, but cuddly and lush, with a splendid texture. Aromas of smoked meats, cinnamon, and coffee are more savory than sweet. Tastes generous, with black fruit floating on ripe tannins. Finishes very long. **93 Editors' Choice** *(4/1/2005)*

DILEO

DiLeo 1996 Cabernet Sauvignon (Sicily) $22. **85** *—J.C. (10/1/2003)*

DiLeo 1999 Sangiovese (Sicily) $20. **84** *—J.C. (10/1/2003)*

DOMENICO DE BERTIOL

Domenico de Bertiol NV (Prosecco di Conegliano) $13. **86** *—J.C. (12/31/2003)*

DOMÍNI VENETI

Domíni Veneti 1997 Vigneti di Jago Corvina (Amarone della Valpolicella Classico) $52. Starts out with crusted red fruit and chocolate before turning decidedly more oaky. Aromas of molasses, tar, and wood grain take over, setting a path toward cherry and chocolate flavors. Finishes warm and quick, with softening tannins. The time to drink it is now. **88** *(11/1/2005)*

Domíni Veneti 2002 Red Blend (Amarone della Valpolicella Classico) $39. Dark as night, with touches of aged balsamic vinegar, black olive, and fruitcake on the rich, youthful bouquet. As a brand new Amarone, it's full of rock-hard tannins and intensity. Definitely chewy and big at this point, but with plenty of fruit in reserve. It should settle down in the years to come. **91 Editors' Choice** *(11/1/2005)*

Domíni Veneti 1999 La Casetta Ripasso Red Blend (Valpolicella Classico Superiore) $20. **91 Editors' Choice** *(5/1/2003)*

Domíni Veneti 1997 Vigneti di Lago Red Blend (Valpolicella Classico) $48. **89** *(5/1/2003)*

DON GATTI

Don Gatti NV Amabile Frizzante Malvasia Bianca (Colli Piacentini) $9. **82** *—M.S. (12/31/2002)*

DONATELLA CINELLI COLOMBINI

Donatella Cinelli Colombini 1999 (Brunello di Montalcino) $45. Nice and sweet to the nose, with black fruit, ample body, and modest tannins awaiting. This wine isn't hard to like; it's chewy and full, with simple, clean flavors. **88** *—M.S. (6/1/2004)*

Donatella Cinelli Colombini 2000 Prime Donne (Brunello di Montalcino) $65. A wine in which the grapes were selected by four women, hence the name. This version is more ripe and chewy than the normal, and it exhibits plum, raisin, chocolate, and licorice aromas and flavors. Very nice in its own right, but not quite as balanced and upright as the basic wine. Also, there's more barrique influence here. **90** *—M.S. (7/1/2005)*

DONNAFUGATA

Donnafugata 1999 Mille e Uno Notte Red Blend (Contessa Entellina) $65. **90** *—R.V. (10/1/2003)*

Donnafugata 2001 Tancredi Red Blend (Contessa Entellina) $25. **88** *—R.V. (10/1/2003)*

Donnafugata 2002 Anthìlia White Blend (Sicilia) $12. **84** *—R.V. (10/1/2003)*

DRAGANI

Dragani 1996 Selva de' Canonici (Montepulciano d'Abruzzo) $14. **87** *—J.F. (9/1/2001)*

DUCA DI SALAPARUTA

Duca di Salaparuta 2003 Colomba Platino Insolia (Sicilia) $18. Quite tropical on the nose, with floral aromas. Flavors of cantaloupe and papaya are reserved but fresh, while the finish is entirely refreshing. On the plump side, but still balanced and upright. A blend of Insolia and Grecanico. **87** *—M.S. (2/1/2005)*

Duca di Salaparuta 1999 Duca Enrico Nero d'Avola (Sicilia) $55. **89** *—R.V. (10/1/2003)*

Duca di Salaparuta 1999 Terre D'Agala Red Blend (Sicilia) $16. **87** *—M.S. (10/1/2003)*

Duca di Salaparuta 2002 Colomba Platino White Blend (Sicily) $15. **85** *—R.V. (10/1/2003)*

DUE TORRI

Due Torri 1998 Pinot Grigio (Veneto) $7. **85 Best Buy** *(8/1/1999)*

ECCO DOMANI

Ecco Domani 2003 Pinot Grigio (Delle Venezie) $10. Starts better than it finishes, with promising scents of pears, honey, and lemon rind. Light in body, which is fine, but the flavors are an unbalanced blend of ripe pears and stridently sour lemons, turning a bit metallic on the finish. **82** *—J.C. (12/31/2004)*

Ecco Domani 2001 Maso Canali Pinot Grigio (Trentino) $17. **84** *—J.C. (7/1/2003)*

ELENA WALCH

Elena Walch 2002 Castel Ringberg Chardonnay (Alto Adige) $18. **86** *—R.V. (7/1/2003)*

Elena Walch 2002 Kastelatz Gewürztraminer (Alto Adige) $25. **89** *—R.V. (7/1/2003)*

Elena Walch 2002 Kastelatz Pinot Bianco (Alto Adige) $23. **87** *—R.V. (7/1/2003)*

Elena Walch 2002 Pinot Grigio (Alto Adige) $12. **85** *—R.V. (7/1/2003)*

Elena Walch 1998 Castel Ringberg Pinot Grigio (Alto Adige) $20. **87** *(8/1/1999)*

Elena Walch 2001 Beyond the Clouds White Blend (Alto Adige) $40. **90** *—R.V. (7/1/2003)*

ELIO ALTARE

Elio Altare 1998 Dolcetto (Dolcetto d'Alba) $19. **89** *(4/1/2000)*

ELIO GRASSO

Elio Grasso 1996 Vigna Martini Barbera (Barbera d'Alba) $21. **87** *(4/1/2000)*

Elio Grasso 1999 Ginestra Vigna Casa Maté Nebbiolo (Barolo) $53. Turns the neat trick of being big and mouthfilling yet not heavy, packing in spiced prune and date flavors wrapped in dark chocolate and tar. The finish shows this wine's true potential, ending with big fruit, big tannins, mouthwatering acids, and great length. **93 Editors' Choice** *(4/2/2004)*

ELIO PERRONE

Elio Perrone 2004 Sourgal Moscato (Moscato d'Asti) $16. I liked this vineyard-designate wine better than the producer's Clartè Moscato d'Asti (from an east-facing vineyard) thanks to its truly gorgeous and feminine nose. It is delicate and floral and the word "pretty" sums it up just right. Great for a romantic picnic in the park. **87** *—M.L. (12/15/2005)*

ELISABETTA

Elisabetta 1999 Aulo Tuscan Blend (Toscana) $12. **86** *—M.S. (8/1/2002)*

ELORINA

Elorina 1998 Pachino Nero d'Avola (Sicily) $17. **84** *—M.S. (10/1/2003)*

ELVIO COGNO

Elvio Cogno 1997 Bricco del Merli (Barbera d'Alba) $30. **87** *(4/1/2000)*

Elvio Cogno 1998 Vigna del Mandorlo (Dolcetto d'Alba) $16. 88 *(4/1/2000)*

ENRICO

Enrico NV Brut (Prosecco di Valdobbiadene) $11. Crisp and natural, with some bread dough on the less than expressive nose. Distant citrus carries the flavor profile, while the finish is dry and natural. Washes the palate in fresh fashion. Made by Bellussi. 84 *—M.S. (12/15/2005)*

ENZO BOGLIETTI

Enzo Boglietti 1998 Brunate Nebbiolo (Piedmont) $60. 89 *—R.V. (11/15/2002)*

Enzo Boglietti 1998 Fossati Nebbiolo (Piedmont) $60. 90 *—R.V. (11/15/2002)*

ESPERTO

Esperto 2001 Pinot Grigio (Delle Venezie) $13. 86 *—J.C. (7/1/2003)*

F PRINCIPIANO

F Principiano 1996 La Romualda (Barbera d'Alba) $36. 87 *(4/1/2000)*

F Principiano 1997 Sant'Anna (Dolcetto d'Alba) $17. 90 *(4/1/2000)*

FABIANO

Fabiano 2000 Red Blend (Amarone della Valpolicella Classico) $37. Round with some prune-based aromas. The palate runs soft and smooth, but with good balance. Flavors dominated by black cherry are enlivened by a shot of citrus, but it's not an overly acidic wine. Fairly standard fare in the final analysis, but pleasant. 87 *(11/1/2005)*

Fabiano 1998 Red Blend (Amarone della Valpolicella Classico) $39. Charged up and a bit acidic, with aromas of smoke, under brush and leather along with some nicely integrated wood. Solid, with requisite dark-fruit and chocolate flavors. But there's no doubt that it's zesty, bordering on racy. Nice but could use more mouthfeel. 87 (11/1/2005)

Fabiano 1997 I Fondatori Red Blend (Amarone della Valpolicella Classico) $55. Fairly round and harmonious, with spice, leather, and some sweaty rubber on the nose. Comes along snappy once it hits the palate, thus the cherry and raspberry flavors are a touch sharp. Seems to have a touch of bretty character. 86 *(11/1/2005)*

FALCHINI

Falchini 2002 Vigna a Solatio (Vernaccia di San Gimignano) $14. Extremely lively, to the point of being spritzy. The nose is full of citrus and a hint of anise, while the palate, while not particularly complex, is zesty and deals active melon and mineral flavors. A likable wine, one from a single vineyard. 86 *—M.S. (8/1/2004)*

FALESCO

Falesco 2001 Vitiano Red Blend (Umbria) $10. 88 Best Buy *—C.S. (2/1/2003)*

Falesco 2003 Ferentano Roscetto (Lazio) $25. A pure expression of the little-known Roscetto grape skillfully worked by the talented Cotarella brothers. Intense peach, pineapple, toasted nuts, and a playful hint of aged Parmigiano cheese rind. Good length and depth on the body and perfectly integrated acidity. **90 Editors' Choice** *—M.L. (9/1/2005)*

FANTI

Fanti 1999 (Brunello di Montalcino) $80. Rich, dark and lush, with liqueur-like aromas wafting upward from a sea of purple. An obvious entry into the "modern" category of Brunello. There's jammy, mouthcoating fruit and only modest acidity. Detractors may find it heavy and bruising, but fans will adore its weight and creaminess. 92 *—M.S. (6/1/2004)*

Fanti 2000 Sangiovese (Sant'Antimo) $17. 88 *—M.S. (8/1/2002)*

FATTORIA CARPINETA FONTALPINO

Fattoria Carpineta Fontalpino 1997 Gioia Sangiovese (Chianti Colli Senesi) $13. 86 *(4/1/2001)*

FATTORIA CORONCINO

Fattoria Coroncino 2001 Il Coroncino (Verdicchio dei Castelli di Jesi Classico Superiore) $18. Full and fresh, with a little bit of youth. The nose is delightful as if offers almond, peach, and vanilla cream. The palate is equally nice, with its cashew, citrus, and spice notes. A lively white that's primed to run. 89 *—M.S. (8/1/2004)*

FATTORIA DEL CERRO

Fattoria Del Cerro 1999 Prugnolo Gentile (Rosso di Montepulciano) $14. 90 Best Buy *—M.S. (11/15/2003)*

Fattoria Del Cerro 1999 Tuscan Blend (Vino Nobile di Montepulciano) $30. Full and round, with plum, berry, and herbal aromas. The racy, mouthfilling palate features raspberry, cherry, and oak, while the finish delivers coffee and vanilla. A well-made Tuscan red. 87 *—M.S. (10/1/2004)*

Fattoria Del Cerro 1996 Vino Nobile Di Montepulciano $17. 82 *—J.C. (9/1/2000)*

FATTORIA DI BASCIANO

Fattoria di Basciano 2001 Riserva (Chianti Rufina) $22. Deceptively soft and easy, this creamy-textured wine also boasts a sense of wiry

ITALY

power underneath briary, blackberry-scented fruit. It's soft enough to drink on its own, yet the inner strength will allow it to pair with assertive flavors as well. **89** *(4/1/2005)*

FATTORIA DI FELSINA

Fattoria di Felsina 1995 Fontalloro (Tuscany) $60. **93** *(11/15/1999)*

FATTORIA DI LUCIGNANO

Fattoria di Lucignano 2002 (Chianti Colli Fiorentini) $12. Questionable cleanliness, with aromas of compost and peanuts. Tangy and thin, with notes of pickle. Does not offer much. **80** *(4/1/2005)*

FATTORIA IL PALAGIO

Fattoria il Palagio 2002 Chardonnay (Toscana) $15. This Tuscan wine has some cheesy aromas and loose fruit. It's zesty on the palate, with apple and white pepper. Finishes zingy, with overt acids. **83** *—M.S. (6/1/2005)*

Fattoria il Palagio 2001 Sauvignon Blanc (Toscana) $12. **88 Best Buy** *(12/31/2002)*

Fattoria Le Sorgenti 1998 (Chianti Colli Fiorentini) $12. **91 Best Buy** *(4/1/2001)*

FATTORIA POGGIOPIANO

Fattoria Poggiopiano 1998 (Chianti Classico) $21. **86** *(4/1/2001)*

FATTORIA RODANO

Fattoria Rodano 1999 Riserva Viacoste (Chianti Classico) $28. Talk about the perfect mouthfeel; this baby has it. But first you get a bouquet of fine herbs, molasses, forest floor, and meaty black fruit. Back to the mouth, there's pure, developed fruit, tobacco and earth notes; overall it's exactly what you want from a middle-age wine: minerality, smoothness, and deep flavors. **92 Editors' Choice** *(4/1/2005)*

FATTORIA SAN LORENZO

Fattoria San Lorenzo 2002 di Gino (Verdicchio dei Castelli di Jesi Classico) $10. Talk about a nose that reflects the ocean: Initial aromas of clam shells and sea foam are almost offputting, but once you taste the wine there's a good mix of papaya, green banana, and dried stone fruits. On the finish, cinnamon-spiced applesauce flavors mingle with hints of white pepper. Not bad, but a little shaky on the nose. **85** *—M.S. (8/1/2004)*

FATTORIA SONNINO

Fattoria Sonnino 2001 (Chianti Montespertoli) $12. **87** *—M.S. (11/15/2003)*

FATTORIE AZZOLINO

Fattorie Azzolino 2002 Chardonnay (Sicilia) $27. Gold in color, with a ton of oak. But you know what? It works. The resin and vanilla aromas over time become attractive, while the rich palate deals coconut, toffee, and baked white fruits. Yes, it's a barrique bomber from a hot climate, but it's interesting and should go well with roast fowl or foie gras. **87** *—M.S. (2/1/2005)*

Fattorie Azzolino 2001 Di'More Red Blend (Sicilia) $27. A touch scattered on the nose, with leather, oak, and bright berry fruit. Surprisingly tart on the palate, with plum, cherry, and berry flavors. A snappy wine with a good core of cherry, but ultimately more racy than classy. **86** *—M.S. (2/1/2005)*

FAUNUS

Faunus 1998 Riserva Red Blend (Salice Salentino) $11. Very dark, with damp earth, cola, and meaty fruit aromas. A bit pruny, with a fudge-like flavor. But for all its darkness and rich suggestions, it's surprisingly hard and tannic, with a mouthfeel that is tight and tough. **84** *—M.S. (1/1/2004)*

FAZI BATTAGLIA

Fazi Battaglia 1998 Passo Del Lupo Riserva Red Blend (Rosso Conero) $34. Saucy and spicy on the nose, and from that point on it never really gets better. The palate is jacked up with acidic plum and cherry fruit, and the finish is overt, apparently stuck in overdrive. **82** *—M.S. (10/1/2004)*

FAZI BATTAGLIA

Fazi Battaglia 2002 (Verdicchio dei Castelli di Jesi Classico) $10. Light and clean, with a proper level of nuttiness, peach, and flowers to the nose. Simple on the palate, with lime, pear, and peach flavors. With its clean finish, this wine is a good example of a functional, medium-weight Verdicchio. Likely good with seafood-based appetizers. **86 Best Buy** *—M.S. (8/1/2004)*

FELLINE

Felline 2000 Alberello Negroamaro (Salento) $15. **84** *(5/1/2002)*

Felline 2000 Vigna Del Feudo Red Blend (Puglia) $28. **88** *—C.S. (5/1/2002)*

Felline 1996 Berardenga (Chianti Classico) $18. **90** *—M.M. (5/1/1999)*

FELSINA

Felsina 2000 Berardenga Riserva (Chianti Classico) $32. Plenty of intensity, with a pleasant spice element that runs from the smooth berry nose onto the serious palate. Flavors of cherry and blackberry rise to the top level, while spice, chocolate, and medium tannins ensure easy drinkability. Not overly concentrated; drink now. **89** (4/1/2005)

FERRARI

Ferrari 1998 Perle' Chardonnay (Trento) $30. The complexity is intriguing and the overall impact on the nose and mouth denotes a wine of defined character. Notes of butterscotch, toast, and fresh croissants create a creamy and rich feeling in the mouth. Put this bubbly aside for a special occasion. **89** *—M.L. (12/15/2004)*

Ferrari 1994 Riserva del Fondatore Brut (Trento) $75. An excellent sparkler by any measure, with deep, rich aromas of toast, sauteed mushrooms, and hint of citrus. Creamy and full-bodied, the flavors expand to include apple and spice notes, finishing elegantly and long. **92** *(12/15/2004)*

FEUDI DI SAN GREGORIO

Feudi di San Gregorio 2000 Patrimo Aglianico (Irpinia) $115. 91 *(12/1/2002)*

Feudi di San Gregorio 1998 Selve di Luoti Aglianico (Taurasi) $36. 88 Cellar Selection *(12/1/2002)*

Feudi di San Gregorio 2000 Serpico Aglianico (Irpinia) $62. 89 *(12/1/2002)*

Feudi di San Gregorio 1997 Serpico Aglianico (Campania) $60. 92 Cellar Selection *—M.N. (9/1/2001)*

Feudi di San Gregorio 2000 (Fiano di Avellino) $20. 86 *—M.N. (9/1/2001)*

Feudi di San Gregorio 1999 Privilegio Fiano (Irpinia) $55. 90 *(12/1/2002)*

Feudi di San Gregorio 2001(Greco di Tufo) $21. 88 *(12/1/2002)*

Feudi di San Gregorio 2001 (Falanghina) $12. 87 Best Buy *—D.T. (11/15/2002)*

Feudi di San Gregorio 2000 Falanghina Sannio $15. 89 Editors' Choice *—M.N. (9/1/2001)*

Feudi di San Gregorio 2004 Campanaro (Fiano di Avellino) $40. A golden, intense wine that offers tiers of citrus from orange blossom to lemon pie. Dig in there with your nose and uncover honey and dried apricot as well. This barrel fermented and aged Fiano and Greco blend sees less oak than it did in past vintages. The mouthfeel is dense and persistent. **90** *—M.L. (9/1/2005)*

Feudi di San Gregorio 2001 Campanaro (Irpinia) $36. 87 *(12/1/2002)*

FEUDO ARANCIO

Feudo Arancio 2003 Chardonnay (Sicilia) $9. A low-oak Chard (15%, the rest sees only stainless), this wine boasts a plump, appealing texture and scents of pear and citrus. Brings in some peachy flavors, then turns tangy and fresh on the finish, folding in hints of orange and lemon. **85 Best Buy** *(2/1/2005)*

Feudo Arancio 2004 Grillo (Sicilia) $7. Lots of peach and honey aromas create a big, heavy bouquet. Golden Delicious apple and pineapple flavors are prominent, while the finish provides a full mix of apple and citrus notes. A bit sticky on the back palate, but good for the money. **86 Best Buy** *—M.S. (7/1/2005)*

Feudo Arancio 2002 Grillo (Sicily) $10. 84 *—J.C. (10/1/2003)*

Feudo Arancio 2001 Merlot (Sicilia) $9. Soft and easy, with plum and prune flavors that turn a bit dull on the finish. Decent but not up to the level of Arancio's other wines. **83** *(2/1/2005)*

Feudo Arancio 2003 Nero d'Avola (Sicilia) $7. This winery seems to have mastered the formula for making clean, approachable wines that have mass appeal while staying true to their roots. Here you get leather, plum, and pepper on the nose, with ripe black cherry and a touch of candied berry on the palate. Finishes with blueberry sweetness and just enough kick. Bargain hunters should buy this in quantity. **87 Best Buy** *—M.S. (7/1/2005)*

Feudo Arancio 2001 Nero d'Avola (Sicily) $10. 87 Best Buy *—M.S. (10/1/2003)*

Feudo Arancio 2001 Syrah (Sicily) $10. 88 Best Buy *—M.S. (10/1/2003)*

FEUDO MACCARI

Feudo Maccari 2003 Saia Nero d'Avola (Sicilia) $33. Here's a relatively new name in Sicilian viticulture to watch out for. Entrepreneur Antonio Moretti (owner of Tuscany's Sette Ponti) and consulting enologist Carlo Ferrini have created a blockbuster Nero d'Avola with big, round ripe cherry, smoked wood, firm tannins, and a velvety smooth finish. **91** *—M.L. (9/1/2005)*

FEUDO MONACI

Feudo Monaci 2000 Negroamaro (Salice Salentino) $9. 83 *—C.S. (5/1/2002)*

Feudo Monaci 2002 Primitivo (Puglia) $9. Pretty and light, with dried fruit, herbs, belt leather, and a distant woodsy scent. An example of a lighter-bodied wine made well; it's got life, structure and acidity, but nothing too demanding. A real pop and drop type of wine. **89 Best Buy** *—M.S. (2/1/2005)*

Feudo Monaci 2003 Red Blend (Salice Salentino) $9. Complex and inviting on the nose, which features hints of clove, leather, chocolate, and dried cherries. It's medium in body and fully dry, an authentic-tasting wine at a reasonable price. **87 Best Buy** *(8/1/2005)*

FEUDO PRINCIPI DI BUTERA

Feudo Principi di Butera 2000 San Rocco Cabernet Sauvignon (Sicilia) $60. 90 *(12/31/2002)*

Feudo Principi di Butera 2002 Inzolia (Sicilia) $20. Nutty and round, with plump tropical fruit on the nose and palate. Apple, melon, and spice flavors work well together, while the almond-packed finish is on the mark. Drink soon to enjoy the wine's balance. It won't wait around forever. 88 *—M.S. (2/1/2005)*

Feudo Principi di Butera 2001 Merlot (Sicilia) $26. Ripe, jelly flavors sit alongside a touch of barnyard aromas and tannins. The wine still needs to fully blend together, but it has great tannins and fruit, and should develop well. 84 *—R.V. (1/1/2004)*

Feudo Principi di Butera 2000 Calat Merlot (Sicilia) $60. 89 *—M.S. (10/1/2003)*

Feudo Principi di Butera 2000 Deliella Nero d'Avola (Sicilia) $60. 85 *—M.S. (10/1/2003)*

FIBBIANO

Fibbiano 2000 L'Aspetto Sangiovese (Tuscany) $14. 80 *—M.S. (12/31/2002)*

FILIPPO GALLINO

Filippo Gallino 1998 Superiore (Barbera d'Alba) $25. 84 *—M.S. (12/15/2003)*

FOFFANI

Foffani 2000 Pinot Grigio (Friuli Aquileia) $14. 86 *—J.C. (7/1/2003)*

Foffani 1999 Superiore Sauvignon Blanc (Friuli Aquileia) $13. 83 *(9/1/2001)*

FOLONARI

Folonari 2003 Pinot Grigio (Delle Venezie) $8. Light and seems a bit lacking in concentration, with modest spice aromas and flavors but not a lot else going on. Clean and fresh on the finish. 83 *—J.C. (12/31/2004)*

FONTALEONI

Fontaleoni 2003 (Chianti Colli Senesi) $12. Big and round, with a rubbery note to the forceful, heavy bouquet. Comes across snappy, with cherry and plum. Definitely this is a stuffed, big red, but it runs unwaveringly along one note. And it's stern and tannic come the finish. 86 *(4/1/2005)*

FONTANA

Fontana 1996 (Dolcetto d'Alba) $19. 84 *(4/1/2000)*

FONTANAFREDDA

Fontanafredda 2004 Moncucco (Moscato d'Asti) $23. You'll love the dried sage and chamomile tea aromatics with the peach cream texture of this golden hued semi-sparkler. The back offers tingling acidity that is perfect for cutting through cream-based desserts. 90 *—M.L. (12/15/2005)*

Fontanafredda 1998 La Rosa Nebbiolo (Piedmont) $68. 90 *—R.V. (11/15/2002)*

Fontanafredda 1998 Serralunga d'Alba Nebbiolo (Piedmont) $44. 89 *—R.V. (11/15/2002)*

FONTERUTOLI

Fonterutoli 2000 (Chianti Classico) $26. **93 Editors' Choice** —M.S. (11/15/2003)

Fonterutoli 1998 (Chianti Classico) $27. 86 *(4/1/2001)*

FONTEVECCHIA

Fontevecchia 1998 (Brunello di Montalcino) $40. Give this wine a few minutes and it'll display a fine bouquet of black cherry, sweet almond paste, and cedar. The palate veers a bit toward the lean, red-fruit spectrum of Brunello, but the more air and time it's given, the more open it becomes. Decant and drink slowly for best results. 89 *—M.S. (10/1/2004)*

FONTODI

Fontodi 2001 (Chianti Classico) $32. Begins with a blast of bright cherry fruit, backed by subtle leather and tobacco aromas, before subsiding into a creamy mouthful of cherries and vanilla. A slight herbal note adds complexity. Finish is rich and filled with supple tannins. 90 *(4/1/2005)*

FORADORI

Foradori 2002 Teroldego (Rotaliano) $23. Foradori's main cuvée doesn't come close to equaling its big brother, offering tobacco, herbs, and fresh cherries in a light to medium-bodied format. It's pleasant and quaffable, finishing on a herbal note. 84 *—J.C. (12/31/2004)*

FORTETO DELLA LUJA

Forteto della Luja 2004 Piasa Sanmaurizio (Moscato d'Asti) $18. With a slightly copperish hue and plenty of persistent effervescence, this Moscato d'Asti from Loazzolo smells of Golden Delicious apple, dried flowers, and lavender honey. It has a broader and less defined mouthfeel than other wines of its kind. 85 *—M.L. (12/15/2005)*

FOSS MARAI

Foss Marai NV Dry (Prosecco Superiore di Cartizze) $30. Perfectly fresh and open as a pasture of wild flowers in full bloom. Delicious, easy-to-take flavors of orange and pineapple are zesty and clean as a whistle. Excellent mouthfeel and tingly bubbles are the coup de grace. **90** *—M.S. (12/15/2005)*

Foss Marai NV Cuvée Vino Spumante Brut (Italy) $18. Apple and green herbs on the nose are more convincing than the flavor profile, which deals applesauce and buttered toast. Fairly weighty on the palate, but clean and correct as a whole. **85** *—M.S. (6/1/2005)*

FOURPLAY

Fourplay 2001 No 1 Red Blend (Sicily) $12. A wine from the minds of the local Saro di Pietro winery and Tuscany's Dievole. This blend of four Sicilian grapes is dark, cherry-laden, and just oaky enough to register. Good as an everyday pizza and pasta wine, with plenty of zest and forward character. Balanced but basic. **86** *—M.S. (7/1/2005)*

FRANZ HAAS

Franz Haas 2003 Lagrein (Alto Adige) $33. Known for excellent Pinot Nero from the slopes of the Cislon mountain in Alto Adige, this family-run estate also does a fine job with late ripener Lagrein. A spectacular, inky red color, the wine opens with multiple layers of mild cherry and wild fennel that will transform into coffee and black pepper with age. There's plenty of spice already but the structure is bony. **87** *—M.L. (9/1/2005)*

Franz Haas 2001 Manna Bianco di Mitterberg White Blend (Alto Adige) $24. **92** *—R.V. (7/1/2003)*

FRATELLI

Fratelli FICI 2000 Baglio Fici Syrah (Sicilia) $NA. **87** *(10/1/2003)*

FRATELLI BERLUCCHI

Fratelli Berlucchi 2000 Satèn (Franciacorta) $NA. A blanc de blancs (Chardonnay and Pinot Bianco) that boasts a slightly greenish tint with servings of apple and peach on the nose. The most mature grape clusters are selected to go into this beautifully rich wine. **88** *—M.L. (12/15/2004)*

Fratelli Berlucchi 2000 Brut (Franciacorta) $30. A beautiful wine with beautiful packaging to match (a truly museum-worthy bottle). Green apple, honeydew melon, and yeast reveal themselves after the creamy mousse has finished its show. Hits the palate with enough personality and precision to accompany a full meal. **90** *—M.L. (12/15/2004)*

Fratelli Berlucchi NV Cuvée Imperiale Brut (Franciacorta) $NA. The multiple layers of this wine are like the pages of an encyclopedia of tastes: from almond to nougat to baked apple tart to flinty minerality. There are no rough edges and the wine hits the mouth with sassy smoothness. **89** *—M.L. (12/15/2004)*

FRATELLI GANCIA

Fratelli Gancia 2002 Serenissima Pinot Grigio (Friuli) $22. Herbal and under-ripe on the nose, with green notes that translate into grapefruit and herb flavors on the palate. Does pick up some riper, peachier notes on the finish. **83** *—J.C. (12/31/2004)*

FRATELLI GIULIARI

Fratelli Giuliari 1998 Red Blend (Valpolicella Classico Superiore) $9. **84** *(5/1/2003)*

Fratelli Giuliari 1998 La Piccola Botte Red Blend (Recioto della Valpolicella Classico) $31. **85** *(5/1/2003)*

FRATELLI ZENI

Fratelli Zeni 1998 Red Blend (Bardolino Classico) $12. **84** *(5/1/2003)*

Fratelli Zeni 1998 Vigne Alte Red Blend (Valpolicella Classico) $11. **83** *(5/1/2003)*

FRATTA PASINI

Fratta Pasini 2002 Red Blend (Amarone della Valpolicella) $53. Begins with sweet, floral aromas of red fruit, which one of our tasters found to be a bit too much like perfume or nail polish. The rest of our panel liked the wine's berry flavors, no-fuss style, and length on the finish. "Size with stamina" was how one taster described the body. **89** *(11/1/2005)*

FULIGNI

Fuligni 1999 (Brunello di Montalcino) $82. Anyone who loves great Sangiovese should snap up this star-quality wine. Always a personal favorite, the '99 doesn't disappoint. It's lively and electric, with structure equal to the Tuscan fort in which it was tasted. As for flavors, look for overflowing blackberry, cola, mocha, and more. A wine that can probably last for 15 years. **95** *—M.S. (6/1/2004)*

Fuligni 1997 Riserva (Brunello di Montalcino) $100. **94 Editors' Choice** *—M.S. (11/15/2003)*

FURLAN

Furlan 2000 Castelcosa Pinot Grigio (Friuli) $12. **83** *—J.C. (7/1/2003)*

Furlan 2000 Cuvée Tai White Blend (Friuli) $14. **82** *—J.C. (7/1/2003)*

G D VAJRA

G D Vajra 1997 (Barbera d'Alba) $17. **88** *(4/1/2000)*

G D Vajra 1997 Coste & Fossati (Dolcetto d'Alba) $18. **87** *(4/1/2000)*

GABBIANO

Gabbiano 2003 Pinot Grigio (Delle Venezie) $10. Delicate peach and pear fruit carries a minerally or graphite note. Crisp and clean on the finish, this is a solid, harmonious wine that delivers what you expect for the price. **85 Best Buy** *—J.C. (12/31/2004)*

Gabbiano 2001 (Chianti Classico) $14. Vulcanized rubber, iodine, and molasses aromas, with simple berry flavors. Carries a bit of green on the palate, but finishes solid. **82** *(4/1/2005)*

GAGLIOLE

Gagliole 2001 Red Blend (Colli della Toscana Centrale) $56. **92 Editors' Choice** *—M.S. (11/15/2003)*

GAIERHOF

Gaierhof 2001 Pinot Grigio (Trentino) $11. **83** *—J.C. (7/1/2003)*

GAJA

Gaja 2001 Conteisa (Langhe) $205. Elegantly perfumed, with touches of cinnamon, ground pepper, and dusty earth accenting notes of black cherries and chocolate. On the palate, there's powerful plum and black cherry flavors, but also a strong minerality that adds an extra dimension to this compelling wine. Soft enough to begin drinking around 2010, it should keep for a couple of decades after that. **94** *(7/1/2005)*

Gaja 2003 Rossj-Bass (Langhe) $57. Mainly Chardonnay (with up to 5% Sauvignon Blanc) from several vineyards in Barbaresco and Serralunga, fermented in stainless, then matured in oak. The result is a mealy, toasty wine full of honeysuckle and pear fruit. Soft and round in the mouth, yet it firms up nicely on the finish. **89** *(7/1/2005)*

Gaja 2001 Sorí Tildín (Langhe) $350. Filled with intoxicating perfume reminiscent of dried spices, fine leather, exotic woods, then delivers bold black cherry, plum, and Asian spice flavors tightly wrapped in a velvety blanket of tannin. Long and richly chewy on the finish, yet minerally as well. Drink 2015–2030. **95** *(7/1/2005)*

GALLI & BROCCATELLI

Galli & Broccatelli 1998 (Sagrantino di Montefalco) $25. **85** *—C.S. (2/1/2003)*

GANCIA

Gancia NV Moscato d'Asti $13. Fruity and floral, with attractive apple, mango, and melon notes. It's like a trip to carbonated Fruitopia, a place where there's plenty of pop and pizzazz but not a whole lot of substance. This wine will tame the toughest sweet tooth. **85** *—M.S. (12/15/2004)*

Gancia NV Extra Dry Prosecco (Veneto) $10. Fresh and clean, like a forest after the rain. Flavors of apple, green melon, and celery are lean and crisp, while the finish deals nothing but citrus. Rather monotone in style, but good. **86 Best Buy** *—M.S. (12/15/2004)*

GAROFOLI

Garofoli 2001 Piancarda Montepulciano (Rosso Conero) $13. Simple red fruit from the berry and plum family defines the nose, which is a bit herbal as well. Black plum and raspberry flavors are tight, lean, and juicy due to lively acidity. Turns a little green in the midpalate as the fruit thins. Good for everyday drinking. **85** *—M.S. (6/1/2005)*

Garofoli 2002 Serra del Conte (Verdicchio dei Castelli di Jesi Classico) $8. Simple but hefty aromas of banana and lemon precede a clean but underwhelming palate of papaya and tangerine. Fairly reserved and lean, with proper acidity and a full finish. A good entry into the variety. **85 Best Buy** *—M.S. (8/1/2004)*

GATTAVECCHI

Gattavecchi 1998 (Chianti Colli Senesi) $11. **84** *(4/1/2001)*

Geretto 2001 Merlot (Delle Venezie) $10. **83** *(5/1/2003)*

GERMANO ETTORE

Germano Ettore 2001 Pra Di Po (Dolcetto d'Alba) $17. **86** *—M.S. (12/15/2003)*

GIACOMELLI

Giacomelli 1997 Pinot Grigio (Colli Orientali del Friuli) $10. **82** *—(8/1/1999)*

GIACOMO ASCHERI

Giacomo Ascheri 1997 Poderi di Sorano Nebbiolo (Barolo) $40. **87** *—R.V. (11/15/2002)*

Giacomo Ascheri 1999 Sorano Coste & Bricco Nebbiolo (Barolo) $55. This wine is nicely balanced, with a full, rich mouthfeel and supple tannins that admirably support the cherry and leather fruit. Traces of herbs and tobacco enhance the mouthwatering finish. Drink now–2015. **89** *(4/2/2004)*

GIACOMO BREZZA

Giacomo Brezza 1996 Cannubi Muscatel (Barbera d'Alba) $20. **90** *(4/1/2000)*

GIACOMO BREZZA & FIGLI

Giacomo Brezza & Figli 1997 Nebbiolo (Piedmont) $45. **91** *—R.V. (11/15/2002)*

Giacomo Brezza & Figli 1998 Sarmassa Nebbiolo (Piedmont) $55. 87 *—R.V. (11/15/2002)*

GIACOMO CONTERNO

Giacomo Conterno 1998 Cascina Francia (Dolcetto d'Alba) $22. 88 *(4/1/2000)*

GIACOMO MARENGO

Giacomo Marengo 2001 Castello Di Rapale (Chianti) $23. Browning, with unmistakable paint and lacquer aromas. Already thinning out, with staunch acids and tannins making for a hard ride. Not much on display, and from a standout vintage. 83 *(4/1/2005)*

Giacomo Marengo 1998 Tenuta del Fondatore La Commenda Riserva (Chianti) $33. Spiky hard and downright traditional, but still attractive in a modern way. The nose offers roasted fruit, cinnamon, and herbs, and the taste profile follows suit. Along the way come notes of mocha, coffee, and milk chocolate. If there's a pitfall, it's that it hits like a jackhammer on the palate. Begs for food. 87 *(4/1/2005)*

ITALY

GIACOMO MORI

Giacomo Mori 1999 (Chianti) $15. 87 *(4/1/2001)*

Giacomo Mori 1998 Castelrotto (Chianti) $26. 83 *(4/1/2001)*

GIANNI BRUNELLI

Gianni Brunelli 2000 (Brunello di Montalcino) $75. Plum, cranberry, and cherry—but not too much oak—make for a lovely nose, while the soft-ish palate is more round than blisteringly tannic. Midpalate and finishing flavors of espresso and chocolate seem oak-related, yet there's no woody resin flavors to detract from the purity. Meets all the standards of a fine wine without forcing it. 90 *—M.S. (7/1/2005)*

GIANNI DOGLIA

Gianni Doglia 2004 (Moscato d'Asti) $15. Bruno and Gianni Doglia oversee five hectares of vineyard with 20-year-old vines near Castagnole Lanze. This is interesting Moscato d'Asti, with unexpected hits of nutmeg, clove, gingerbread, and Indian spice backed by cream soda and lemon Fruit Loops. Thick and lathery in the mouth with layers of peach, jasmine, pear, and fig. **90 Editors' Choice** *—M.L. (12/15/2005)*

GIANNI VOERZIO

Gianni Voerzio 1996 Ciabot della Luna (Barbera d'Alba) $27. 88 *(4/1/2000)*

GIANNINA

Giannina 2002 (Vernaccia di San Gimignano) $11. From Giannina di Puthod, this is Vernaccia at its near best. The laser-beam nose offers lemon-lime to the max, and that's followed by a round palate with fresh citrus and green apple flavors. It's weighty but upright, with a dry-as-a-bone crystalline finish. **89 Best Buy** *—M.S. (8/1/2004)*

GIGI ROSSO

Gigi Rosso 1997 Cascina Rocca Giovino (Barbera d'Alba) $12. 87 *(4/1/2000)*

Gigi Rosso 1999 Arione Nebbiolo (Barolo) $48. Deeply earthy on the nose, with tobacco and dried fruits mixing with saddle leather, tar, and hints of citrus. Richly tannic, this wine deserves all the time you can give it; try in 2010 or beyond. 89 *(4/2/2004)*

GINI

Gini 1999 La Frosca Soave Classico Superiore $18. **90 Editors' Choice** *—M.N. (12/31/2000)*

Gini 1999 Villa Fortunato (Chianti) $7. **86 Best Buy** *(4/1/2001)*

Gini 2001 Contrada Salavrenza Vecchie Vigne (Soave Classico Superiore) $24. 91 *—R.V. (7/1/2003)*

Gini 2000 Soave Classico Superiore $12. **88 Best Buy** *—M.N. (9/1/2001)*

GIRIBALDI

Giribaldi 1997 (Barbera d'Asti) $10. 84 *(4/1/2000)*

Giribaldi NV Selezioni Rodellisa Dolce Brachetto (Piedmont) $15. **88 Best Buy** *—K.F. (12/31/2002)*

Giribaldi 2000 Vigna Cason (Dolcetto d'Alba) $14. 85 *—M.S. (12/15/2003)*

Giribaldi 1999 Nebbiolo (Barolo) $39. Supple and oaky, this modern-style Barolo boasts ample plum fruit that's backed by cinnamon, vanilla, and toast. A solid restaurant Barolo, not needing years to reach its peak. 86 *—J.C. (11/15/2004)*

Giribaldi 1997 Nebbiolo (Barolo) $30. 90 *—C.S. (11/15/2002)*

GIROLAMO DORIGO

Girolamo Dorigo 2000 Chardonnay (Colli Orientali del Friuli) $35. 87 *—R.V. (7/1/2003)*

Girolamo Dorigo 1999 Ronc di Juri Sauvignon Blanc (Friuli) $37. 82 *(1/1/2004)*

GIUNTI

Giunti 2001 Il Monte Riserva (Chianti) $25. Dark and intense, with a hint of paste or glue that eventually yields to leather, tree bark, and earth. Quite rich, with plum, baked berry, and coffee making for a manly flavor profile. Drinkable now, even with its mouth-coating tannins. **88** *(4/1/2005)*

GIUSEPPE CORTESE

Giuseppe Cortese 2000 Rabajá Nebbiolo (Barbaresco) $45. Scents of warm, roasted fruit emerge from the glass, along with notes of molasses, soy sauce, and leather. Prunes and dates in the mouth, nestled in soft tannins. Drink now–2015. **89** *(4/2/2004)*

GOTTARDO CASA VINICOLA

Gottardo Casa Vinicola 1997 Pinot Grigio (Veneto) $6. **83** *(8/1/1999)*

GRADIS'CIUTTA

Gradis'ciutta 2000 del Bratinus Bianco (Collio) $13. **81** *—J.C. (7/1/2003)*

GRASSO FRATELLI

Grasso Fratelli 1999 Bricco Spessa Nebbiolo (Barbaresco) $36. Features a complex and intriguing nose, filled with aromas of graham crackers, toast, and hints of cherries and herbs, but it's a bit grapy and unformed on the palate, with a loose structure that doesn't offer the structure expected of a top-flight Barbaresco. It's good and ready to drink, just doesn't fit the classic mold. **89** *(4/2/2004)*

GREPPONE MAZZI

Greppone Mazzi 1999 (Brunello di Montalcino) $65. From Ruffino, this Brunello is ripe yet earthy, with a touch of forest and moss to the nose. It may be softer and riper than many, but it's definitely balanced. Meanwhile, fine black cherry and plum fruit steals the palate, which also dishes hints of chocolate and fennel. Good tannins and grip ensure its longevity. **92** *—M.S. (6/1/2004)*

GUARNIERI

Guarnieri 1999 Le Masse di Greve (Chianti Classico) $19. **84** *—M.S. (12/31/2002)*

GUERRA

Guerra 1998 Pinot Grigio (Colli Orientali del Friuli) $11. **85** *—(8/1/1999)*

GUERRIERI RIZZARDI

Guerrieri Rizzardi 1997 Red Blend (Amarone della Valpolicella Classico) $59. **87** *(5/1/2003)*

Guerrieri Rizzardi 1995 Calcarole Red Blend (Amarone della Valpolicella Classico) $82. **87** *(5/1/2003)*

Guerrieri Rizzardi 2000 Pojega Red Blend (Valpolicella Classico Superiore) $15. **82** *(5/1/2003)*

GUICCIARDINI STROZZI

Guicciardini Strozzi 2003 Titolato (Chianti Colli Senesi) $10. To the nose, it's simultaneously soft and sweet while also smoky, leathery, and earthy. This one gives a little of this and that; the fruit is medium and bright, with full supporting tannins. But it also pours on the red fruit in doses, meaning it's snappy and sharp. **88 Best Buy** *(4/1/2005)*

GULFI

Gulfi 2000 Nero Ibleo Nero d'Avola (Sicilia) $16. **90 Editors' Choice** *—J.C. (10/1/2003)*

Gulfi 1999 Neroibleo Nero d'Avola (Sicilia) $12. **90** *—C.S. (5/1/2002)*

Gulfi 2000 Caricanti White Blend (Sicilia) $22. **85** *—J.C. (10/1/2003)*

HAUNER

Hauner 1999 Agave Red Blend (Sicilia) $15. **86** *(5/1/2002)*

I GIUSTI E ZANZA

I Giusti e Zanza 1999 Dulcamara Tuscan Blend (Toscana) $55. **88** *—M.S. (8/1/2002)*

IL CIRCO

Il Circo 2001 La Violetta Uva di Troia (Castel del Monte) $15. So Randall Grahm of Bonny Doon finally got to Southern Italy, and thus comes this berry and licorice red. It's all about color, zest, forward fruit, and tannins. Lots of backbone and boldness, and some chocolaty substance to the finish. **88** *—M.S. (10/1/2004)*

IL CONTE

Il Conte 2002 Marinus Red Blend (Rosso Piceno) $14. Violet in color, as if it were berry syrup. And that same thick, oozing character is noticeable on the sweet, gooey nose as well as the extracted, low-acid palate. Richness and sweetness are not in question; but overall balance is. Flavorful but a hard pill to swallow. **83** *—M.S. (7/1/2005)*

Il Conte 2003 Donello Sangiovese (Marche) $13. Dark in color, with sappy raisin and blackberry jam aromas. While it runs a bit reduced across the tongue, there's still more than enough quality plum flavors to save the day. Not a ton of nuance and subtleties here; it's more about ripe, dark fruit and some earth. **85** *—M.S. (7/1/2005)*

IL CONTE D'ALBA

Il Conte d'Alba NV (Moscato d'Asti) $10. I like this greenish-hued wine for its very linear and sharp mineral, graphite, green apple, and lemon-rind aromas. Those defined fragrances make it a perfect pair with cream- or butter-based desserts. **87 Editors' Choice** *—M.L. (12/15/2005)*

IL FALCHETTO

Il Falchetto 2004 Tenuta del Fant (Moscato d'Asti) $17. Delicate and feminine with tight peach and apricot weaved into an attractive aromatic embroidery. Extremely dense lather builds up each time you swirl your glass, making this wine perfect for dried or baked desserts. **86** *—M.L. (12/15/2005)*

IL FEUDUCCIO DI S. MARIA D'ORNI

Il Feuduccio Di S. Maria D'Orni 1998 Ursonia (Montepulciano d'Abruzzo) $31. **90** *—M.S. (11/15/2003)*

IL GRILLESINO

Il Grillesino 1999 Tuscan Blend (Morellino di Scansano) $14. **86** *—M.S. (8/1/2002)*

IL NURAGHE

Il Nuraghe 1999 Chio (Cannonau di Sardegna) $22. **88** *—M.S. (12/15/2003)*

Il Nuraghe 1998 Nabui (Monica di Sardegna) $21. **89** *—M.S. (12/15/2003)*

Il Nuraghe 2001 Vignaruja (Cannonau di Sardegna) $15. **87** *—M.S. (12/15/2003)*

IL PALAZZINO

Il Palazzino 1998 (Chianti Classico) $18. **90 Editors' Choice** *(4/1/2001)*

Il Palazzone 2000 (Brunello di Montalcino) $85. Excellent from the initial nosing through the polished palate and onto the hedonistic finish. This wine from the estate of Time Warner chairman Richard Parsons offers robust aromas of forest floor and black cherry, followed by a sleek, silky palate. Creamy and sweet on the finish, with chocolate and vanilla in spades. **92** *—M.S. (7/1/2005)*

IL POGGIOLINO

Il Poggiolino 1998 Riserva (Chianti Classico) $25. **87** *—R.V. (8/1/2002)*

IL POGGIONE

Il Poggione 1999 (Brunello di Montalcino) $62. This excellent wine represents a model for straddling the line between the past and current styles of Brunello. The cherry and raspberry fruit gets a kick from oak-based notes of charcoal and vanilla. Hold for at least four years, if possible. **93** *—M.S. (6/1/2004)*

Il Poggione 1997 (Brunello di Montalcino) $60. **91** *—R.V. (8/1/2002)*

Il Poggione 1997 Riserva (Brunello di Montalcino) $71. **92 Cellar Selection** *—M.S. (11/15/2003)*

Il Poggione 1999 (Rosso di Montalcino) $19. **90** *—M.S. (8/1/2002)*

IL TASSO

Il Tasso 1999 (Chianti) $11. **86** *(4/1/2001)*

IL VIGNALE

Il Vignale 1997 Pinot Grigio (Veneto) $10. **86** *(8/1/1999)*

INAMA

Inama 2001 Vulcaia Sauvignon Blanc (Delle Venezie) $21. **88** *—R.V. (7/1/2003)*

Inama 2001 Vigneti di Foscarino (Soave Classico Superiore) $19. **90** *—R.V. (7/1/2003)*

J. HOFSTATTER

J. Hofstatter 2002 Chardonnay (Alto Adige) $NA. **86** *—R.V. (7/1/2003)*

J. Hofstatter 1997 Pinot Grigio (Alto Adige) $18. **80** *— (8/1/1999)*

JERMANN

Jermann 2002 Mjzzu Blau & Blau Blaufränkisch (Delle Venezie) $36. Give it time to open and the vegetal, beet-like tones are replaced with warm earth, clove, and raspberry tart. Has a chewy, thick consistency and a rigid tannic backbone; would pair nicely with stewed or oven-roasted meats. Made with 90% Blaufrankisch and 10% Blauburgunder (Pinot Noir). **88** *—M.L. (9/1/2005)*

Jermann 2001 Chardonnay (Venezia Giulia) $27. **85** *—J.C. (7/1/2003)*

Jermann 2001 Pignacolusse Pignolo (Venezia Giulia) $52. A stellar example of the potential of Italian indigenous grapes this is 100% Pignolo, a small-clustered variety that faced almost certain extinction. This robust, succulent single-vineyard wine has blackberry, prunes, cigar box, and sticky melted milk chocolate aromas and flavors. Rich in soft tannins and fruity concentration. Delightful. **94 Editors' Choice** *—M.L. (9/1/2005)*

Jermann 2003 Pinot Grigio (Venezia Giulia) $32. Don't be put off by this wine's slightly coppery hue—it's from a short length of skin contact. Aromas of Red Delicious apples ease into flavors of fresh apples sprinkled with dried spices like cinnamon and clove. Medium-bodied, with a finish that shows hints of appleskin and some phenolic notes. **87** *—J.C. (12/31/2004)*

Jermann 2003 Sauvignon (Venezia Giulia) $33. Round and waxy on the nose, with an oily note alongside minerality and apple. Quite toasty and baked on the palate, with applesauce, grapefruit, and stone-fruit flavors. Very dry and long on the tail, with soda-cracker flavors. Ultra-textured. **87** *(7/1/2005)*

Jermann 2001 Vintage Tunina White Blend (Venezia Giulia) $49. **90** *—J.C. (7/1/2003)*

JERZU ANTICHI PODERI

Jerzu Antichi Poderi 1998 Josto Miglior Riserva (Cannonau di Sardegna) $32. **89** *—C.S. (5/1/2002)*

JOSÉ MARIA DA FONSECA

José Maria da Fonseca 1999 Alambre Moscatel (Abruzzo) $19. **88** *—R.V. (12/31/2002)*

KISMET CELLARS

Kismet Cellars 2002 (Montepulciano d'Abruzzo) $10. **84** *—M.S. (11/15/2003)*

KRIS

Kris 2003 Pinot Grigio (Delle Venezie) $11. Delicate and graceful, this Franz Haas selection is redolent of almonds and acacia flowers, lightly laced with green fruits and flowers. It is everything that Pinot Grigio can be and Pinot Gris rarely is: elegant and subtle, with flowers and honey, rather than barrels, adding the grace notes. Supple and balanced, it continues along a smooth path through a lingering finish. **90 Best Buy** *—P.G. (11/15/2004)*

LA BRACCESCA

La Braccesca 1996 (Vino Nobile di Montepulciano) $26. **86** *—J.C. (7/1/2000)*

LA CARRAIA

La Carraia 1999 Fobiano Red Blend (Umbria) $35. **89** *—C.S. (2/1/2003)*

LA CASA DELL'ORCO

La Casa Dell'Orco 1996 (Taurasi) $25. **83** *—C.S. (5/1/2002)*

LA COLOMBAIA

La Colombaia 2000 Red Blend (Amarone della Valpolicella) $50. Coffee is a dominant element of the raw bouquet, which comes across a touch burnt. Modest red fruit carries the somewhat tannic palate. More elegant than opulent, and ready to drink soon if not now. Of note: one reviewer did not like this wine, noting charred, grassy aromas and off flavors. **89** *(11/1/2005)*

LA COLOMBINA

La Colombina 1999 (Brunello di Montalcino) $NA. Dark and muscular up front, with aromas of tar, smoke, and charred beef. Below that brooding surface you'll find jammy fruit mixed with tobacco and herbs. Not a classic, but still a very good wine on the chunky side. **89** *—M.S. (6/1/2004)*

LA CORTE

La Corte 2004 Anfora Primitivo (Puglia) $14. A textbook fruit bomb from Southern Italy that is linear and one dimentional but nevertheless delivers the goods. Candied cherries and strawberries accent a wine made with grapes from 35-year-old vines. You'll taste its youth. **86** *—M.L. (9/1/2005)*

La Corte 2003 Re Red Blend (Salento) $49. A velvety, rich Negroamaro (65%) and Primitivo (35%) blend that has horse saddle, toasted coffee beans, and cloves. Definitely dark and brooding with a smoky, beefy finish. Ready to drink this winter. **87** *—M.L. (9/1/2005)*

LA FORTUNA

La Fortuna 2000 (Brunello di Montalcino) $48. Potent, tight, and condensed on the nose, with a blast of woody smoke. Brighter on the palate, where cherry and plum ride high and confident. This is a lively, fresh wine with an extended finish of cherry, plum, and licorice. It also shows a raw, leathery streak, good tannins, and solid aging ability. **90** *—M.S. (7/1/2005)*

LA FRANCESCA

La Francesca 2001 Cabernet Sauvignon (Veneto) $6. **80** *(5/1/2003)*

La Francesca 2002 Merlot (Veneto) $6. **84 Best Buy** *—M.S. (12/15/2003)*

La Francesca 2001 Pinot Grigio (Veneto) $6. **84 Best Buy** *—J.C. (7/1/2003)*

La Francesca 1998 Pinot Grigio (Veneto) $5. **86 Best Buy** *(8/1/1999)*

La Francesca 2001 Red Blend (Valpolicella) $6. **84** *(5/1/2003)*

LA GERLA

La Gerla 2000 (Brunello di Montalcino) $60. Dark and chunky, both in sight and smell. Nevertheless, it's fairly nice on the palate, but it's soft. The black plum, cherry, and licorice flavors are warm although not overly precise. Finishes with a decent kick as well as balancing flavors of fresh tomato and cherry. **88** *—M.S. (7/1/2005)*

La Gerla 1997 Brunello (Brunello di Montalcino) $55. **93 Editors' Choice** *—R.V. (8/1/2002)*

La Lastra 1999 (Chianti Colli Senesi) $12. **87 Best Buy** *(4/1/2001)*

LA MARCA

La Marca 2003 Winemaker's Collection Pinot Grigio (Piave) $11. Light and lemony, with hints of green peas and fresh apples. Finishes tart and clean. **83** *—J.C. (12/31/2004)*

LA MONACESCA

La Monacesca 2002 (Verdicchio di Matelica) $19. Gold in color, with mushroom and honey on the nose. Round in the mouth, with mild flavors of orange, grapefruit, and pineapple. Quite thick and substantive, with a big, grabbing finish. **85** *—M.S. (8/1/2004)*

LA NUNSIO

La Nunsio 1997 (Barbera d'Asti) $22. **89** *(4/1/2000)*

LA PODERINA

La Poderina 2000 (Brunello di Montalcino) $65. Downright purple in color, so much so that it looks more like Merlot than Sangiovese. Smells incredibly rich, but not stewy. Concentrated and extracted palate, with no hard tannins or acids. Very smooth but short on the finish. Good for near-term drinking. **90** *—M.S. (7/1/2005)*

La Poderina 1999 Poggio Banale (Brunello di Montalcino) $125. Beautiful on the nose, with density and power. Very tannic on the palate, but interspersed are pockets of delicious cherry and berry flavors. With great color, tightness, and pulsing acids, this is one for the cellar. Put it away and revisit in 2007 to 2010. **91** *—M.S. (6/1/2004)*

LA RONCAIA

La Roncaia 1999 Il Fusco Red Blend (Friuli Venezia Giulia) $50. **89** *(5/1/2003)*

LA SCOLCA

La Scolca 2002 Black Label (Gavi di Gavi) $42. I have to admit: I've never "gotten" this wine. This ne plus ultra of Gavi just doesn't do it for me. Vaguely sweaty aromas join almond and unripe peach scents on the nose, followed up by lemony, underripe flavors. **84** *—J.C. (11/15/2004)*

La Scolca 1999 (Gavi di Gavi) $19. **84** *(9/1/2001)*

La Scolca 2001 Il Valentino (Gavi) $13. **80** *—M.S. (12/15/2003)*

LA SERA

La Sera 1997 (Barbera del Monferrato) $12. **87** *(4/1/2000)*

LA SERENA

La Serena 2000 (Brunello di Montalcino) $NA. Pure violet in color, with a nose packed full of creamy oak, sweet plum, and blackberry. This is your prototypical modern-day bruiser. The palate offers a powder keg of sweet, chewy fruit, yet the acidity is right there corralling it all. Properly applied oak cuddles rather than overwhelms the fruit, while the full tannins make it a lion heart. Fabulous for a 2000 normale. Imported by Summa Vitis, Inc. **94 Editors' Choice** *—M.S. (7/1/2005)*

LA SPINETTA

La Spinetta 2004 Bricco Quaglia (Moscato d'Asti) $18. Pink grapefruit, peach, mint candy, rose petal, chamomile, mineral tones, and dried grass make for a surprisingly complex nose. Correct in every way, including bubble persistency, liveliness, and impact in the mouth. Watch out for this producer's excellent Moscato Passito and red wines as well. **88** *—M.L. (12/15/2005)*

LA SPINONA

La Spinona 1998 Vigneto Qualin (Dolcetto d'Alba) $15. **83** *(4/1/2000)*

LA VIARTE

La Viarte 2003 Sauvignon Blanc (Colli Orientali del Friuli) $20. Strange on the nose, with hints of cat box, crushed vitamins, iodine, and yeast. Quite rubbery and pithy on the palate, with papaya, green melon, and some vegetal notes. And it's spritzy across the tongue. **83** *(7/1/2005)*

LA VILLA VENETA

La Villa Veneta 2001 Pinot Grigio (Veneto) $8. **83** *—J.C. (7/1/2003)*

LA VIS

La Vis 2000 Ritratti Chardonnay (Trentino) $13. **84** *—J.C. (7/1/2003)*

La Vis 2001 Rosso dei Sorni Red Blend (Trentino) $15. **85** *—M.S. (12/15/2003)*

La Vis 2001 Bianco dei Sorni White Blend (Trentino) $15. **88** *—J.C. (7/1/2003)*

LAGARIA

Lagaria 2001 Chardonnay (Delle Venezie) $8. **87 Best Buy** *—J.C. (7/1/2003)*

Lagaria 2001 Pinot Grigio (Delle Venezie) $8. **83** *—J.C. (7/1/2003)*

Lagaria 1997 Pinot Grigio (Trentino) $8. **82** *— (8/1/1999)*

LAMBERTI

Lamberti 1998 Corte Rubini Red Blend (Amarone della Valpolicella) $30. **84** *(5/1/2003)*

LAMBORGHINI

Lamborghini 2000 Campoleone Red Blend (Umbria) $75. 91 *—C.S. (2/1/2003)*

LAMOLE DI LAMOLE

Lamole Di Lamole 2001 (Chianti Classico) $18. Simple yet reserved, with jammy aromas of black cherry and raisin. There is also a sharp element to the nose, which one of our tasters pegged as vinegar. Overall, however, the palate is racy and tight, with high-toned raspberry and strawberry flavors. Finishes snappy, with a touch of sugar beet. 86 *(4/1/2005)*

Lamole Di Lamole 2000 Riserva (Chianti Classico) $24. Slightly roasted on the nose, with pure saddle leather and a bit of prune. Runs a bit lean and tight across the palate, but it still delivers a juicy ride due to crisp acids and power tannins. More traditional, with a brick-colored tint. 89 *(4/1/2005)*

LANARI

Lanari 2002 Red Blend (Rosso Conero) $20. Forward and tight, with lean berry and plum flavors. Feels a touch hard, with strawberry and raspberry notes. Seems mildly burnt on the finish, and tannic. Too rustic and raw to rate higher. 83 *—M.S. (6/1/2005)*

LANCIOLA

Lanciola 2001 (Chianti Colli Fiorentini) $16. Funky at first, with an amalgam of lactic, meat, and smoke aromas. Seems a touch soft on the palate, where prune and coffee flavors match wits with black cherry. Minty green on the finish, which may be construed as tobacco. 86 *(4/1/2005)*

Lanciola 1998 (Chianti Colli Fiorentini) $12. 87 Best Buy *(4/1/2001)*

LE BELLERIVE

Le Bellerive NV Di Cartizze (Prosecco di Valdobbiadene Superiore) $47. Much more mature and round than your typical Prosecco, yet it doesn't necessarily hit the right chords. There's a wheaty, burnt-grass quality to the fruit, smoke, and toast, and then residual sugar. The goal here seems to be Champagne-like complexity and size, but the result is not fully convincing. 85 *—M.S. (12/15/2005)*

LE BOCCE

Le Bocce 1998 (Chianti Classico) $14. 87 *(4/1/2001)*

LE CALVANE

Le Calvane 1999 Trecione Riserva (Chianti Colli Fiorentini) $25. Jammy for starters, but with an attractive sweetness along with some chocolate. The epitome of a sugary berry ball. The palate is soft and easy, maybe borderline chunky, but there's enough tannin and acid to ensure an even flow. Drink now. 87 *(4/1/2005)*

LE CHIUSE

Le Chiuse 1999 (Brunello di Montalcino) $NA. Dense and reduced, with cola and root beer aromas. This is not the liveliest Brunello going, which is proven by the modest tannins and equally moderate acids. Nonetheless, it's not flabby or disproportionately flat. The flavors are good and the finish is long. But with a touch more zest it could be a high-flyer. 89 *—M.S. (6/1/2004)*

LE CINCIOLE

Le Cinciole 2000 Petresco Riserva (Chianti Classico) $33. Sour from the start, with grapey flavors and even some chemical. Bitter chocolate on the finish. Harsh on the palate. 80 *(4/1/2005)*

LE CORTE

Le Corte 2001 Anfora Zinfandel (Puglia) $11. 87 Best Buy *—R.V. (11/15/2002)*

LE CORTI

Le Corti 1999 Cortevecchia Riserva (Chianti Classico) $23. 86 *—M.S. (12/31/2002)*

Le Corti 2000 Marsiliana Tuscan Blend (Toscana) $15. 86 *—M.S. (12/31/2002)*

LE FILIGARE

Le Filigare 1997 (Chianti Classico) $19. 85 *(4/1/2001)*

LE FIORAIE

Le Fioraie 1998 Riserva Tuscan Blend (Toscana) $28. Fairly dull on the nose, with light tea and cherry aromas. On the palate, full strawberry and raspberry flavors precede a chunky, full finish. A bit of an awkward heavyweight, but friendly enough. 85 *—M.S. (10/1/2004)*

LE GINESTRE

Le Ginestre 1997 Pian Romaldo (Barbera d'Alba) $19. 85 *(4/1/2000)*

Le Ginestre 1999 Madonna di Como (Dolcetto d'Alba) $16. 88 *—M.N. (9/1/2001)*

Le Ginestre 1998 Nebbiolo (Barolo) $45. Already brick at the rim, this wine smells mature, yielding scents of cedar, leather, and hints of raisins and figs. Flavors are sweet and caramelized; the tannins supple. Drink now–2008. 87 *(4/2/2004)*

LE MACCHIOLE

Le Macchiole 1998 Paleo Cabernet Blend (Bolgheri) $84. 87 *—M.S. (8/1/2002)*

LE MICCINE

Le Miccine 2002 (Chianti Classico) $20. A fragile wine that doesn't seem meant for the cellar. In the meantime, enjoy the racy mouthfeel, red-cherry flavors and mild tobacco and citrus peel nuances that improve the lengthy finish **85** *(4/1/2005)*

Le Miccine 2000 (Chianti Classico) $22. **87** *—M.S. (11/15/2003)*

Le Miccine 2000 Don Alberto Riserva (Chianti Classico) $40. Heavily oaked; frankly too much so. It smells at first like ham hocks and tar spread over bacon-covered marmalade. Once it opens, there's only modest berry fruit to support the thick, lemony oak that's all over the palate and finish. Ultimately, it tastes resiny. **83** *—M.S. (10/1/2004)*

Le Miccine 1997 Don Alberto Riserva (Chianti Classico) $40. **89** *(9/1/2000)*

Le Miccine 2001 Riserva Don Alberto (Chianti Classico) $40. Very tight and woody, with aromas of charred hamburger, leather, and toast. Cherry, burnt bread crust, and smoked meat on the palate lead into a fresh but oaky finish, where popcorn is identifiable. Overall it's racy and tasty. A stand-up contender. **88** *(4/1/2005)*

LE RAGOSE

Le Ragose 1999 Estate Bottled Red Blend (Valpolicella Classico Superiore) $14. **89 Best Buy** *(5/1/2003)*

Le Ragose 1997 Estate Bottled Red Blend (Amarone della Valpolicella) $53. **89** *(5/1/2003)*

LE SALETTE

Le Salette 1999 Pergole Vece (Amarone della Valpolicella Classico) $120. Definitely smooth and woody, with plenty of toast, cedar, and coffee along with black cherry. Shows a lot of the right stuff throughout, from the broad palate that sports sweet notes of caramel, coffee, and root beer to the easy finish. Only a bit of hard tannin makes it firm; otherwise it registers as soft. **89** *(11/1/2005)*

Le Salette 2000 I Progni Red Blend (Valpolicella Classico Superiore) $25. **90** *(5/1/2003)*

Le Salette 1998 Pergole Vece Red Blend (Amarone della Valpolicella Classico) $115. **93 Cellar Selection** *(5/1/2003)*

LE VIGNE

Le Vigne 2003 (Chianti) $12. Somewhat lean, yet chunky enough. Aromas of candied berry and green tobacco lead to a plum and cherry palate with medium tannins and a mildly chewy feel. Short and dusty on the tail, but with ample acidity. **85** *(4/1/2005)*

LEONE DE CASTRIS

Leone de Castris 1996 Donna Lisa Riserva Negroamaro (Salice Salentino) $30. **86** *—C.S. (5/1/2002)*

Leone de Castris 1998 Riserva Negroamaro (Salice Salentino) $12. **85** *—C.S. (5/1/2002)*

LEPORE

Lepore 1996 Montepulciano (Colonella) $13. **85** *(9/1/2000)*

LIBRANDI

Librandi 1999 Gaglioppo (Ciró Classico) $10. **84** *—M.N. (9/1/2001)*

Librandi 1996 Gravello Gaglioppo (Calabria) $29. **88** *—M.N. (9/1/2001)*

Librandi 1999 Magno Megonio Magliocco (Calabria) $35. **85** *—C.S. (5/1/2002)*

LISINI

Lisini 2000 (Brunello di Montalcino) $69. Dark and masculine, with smoky black cherry notes carrying the sturdy bouquet. It pops with bright plum, black cherry, and chocolate flavors, and it has proper tannins that give it some edge. **90** *—M.S. (7/1/2005)*

LIVIO FELLUGA

Livio Felluga 1997 Esperto Chardonnay (Friuli) $16. **86** *(9/1/2000)*

Livio Felluga 2000 Vertigo Merlot-Cabernet Sauvignon (Friuli Venezia Giulia) $21. **89** *(5/1/2003)*

Livio Felluga 1999 Pinot Grigio (Friuli Venezia Giulia) $21. **90** *—M.S. (9/1/2000)*

Livio Felluga 2002 Pinot Grigio (Friuli Venezia Giulia) $23. **90** *—J.C. (7/1/2003)*

Livio Felluga 2000 Pinot Grigio (Friuli Venezia Giulia) $21. **88** *—M.M. (9/1/2001)*

Livio Felluga 1998 Tocai (Colli Orientali del Friuli) $20. **86** *(9/1/2000)*

Livio Felluga 2001 Tocai (Friuli Venezia Giulia) $24. **90 Editors' Choice** *—J.C. (7/1/2003)*

LIVON

Livon 1997 Pinot Grigio (Collio) $15. **85** *— (8/1/1999)*

LODOLA NUOVA

Lodola Nuova 2002 Tuscan Blend (Vino Nobile di Montepulciano) $22. Fairly full on the bouquet, with a dense roundness that cups charcoal and shoe polish aromas along with berry fruit. A bit more harsh than desirable on the palate, with sweetness lacking. That said, it pours on the plum, cherry, and cranberry in fist-like fashion. **84** *—M.S. (7/1/2005)*

LOSI

Losi 1997 Millennium Riserva (Chianti Classico) $30. Funky at first, then better. The nose deals stewed fruit dressed in mocha and a blast of char. Slightly muddled on the palate, with beefy, sugary red fruit that sports some bell pepper. Finishes crunchy and gritty, with a sweet-and-sour component. **85** *(4/1/2005)*

LUCCÍO

Luccío NV (Moscato d'Asti) $9. Bright, floral aromas give way to ripe stone fruit and tangerines. This is concentrated and flavorful, but not overly rich or heavy; sweet, yet balanced by orangy acids. **87 Best Buy** *—J.C. (11/15/2004)*

Luccío 2002 (Chianti) $7. Lean and drying on the bouquet, with rhubarb, campfire and citrus notes. Flavorwise, we're talking tart cherry and raspberry, while the finish is simple and mainstream in scope. **84 Best Buy** *(4/1/2005)*

LUCE

Luce 1999 della Vite Tuscan Blend (Toscana) $75. **90** *(9/1/2002)*

LUCENTE

Lucente 1999 Tuscan Blend (Toscana) $28. **85** *(9/1/2002)*

LUCIANO SANDRONE

Luciano Sandrone 2003 (Dolcetto d'Alba) $20. The 2003 Dolcettos have enough boldly flavored fruit to hang with your best blue-cheese burgers, enough spice to stand up to jerk chicken—and enough tannin to cut through the fattiest slab of ribs. What sets Sandrone's version apart is the sense of elegance that suggests it would be just as home on a white tablecloth as a rustic wooden table. **90** *—J.C. (8/1/2005)*

LUIANO

Luiano 2002 (Chianti Classico) $16. Cherry, open-cut wood, and rubber dominate the nose, which is backed by harsh, lemony fruit. Exceedingly tart, with a lean streak to the palate. **83** *(4/1/2005)*

Luiano 1999 Gold Label Riserva (Chianti Classico) $24. A bit of leather and raisin get it going, followed by berry, citrus and tannins. Comes on lean, where it resembles the whicker-basket wines of the old days. A touch too rudimentary and tart to score higher. **84** *(4/1/2005)*

Luiano 2000 Tuscan Blend (Chianti Classico) $16. **89** *—M.S. (11/15/2003)*

LUIGI EINAUDI

Luigi Einaudi 1997 Vigna Tecc (Dolcetto di Dogliani) $20. **89** *(4/1/2000)*

LUIGI RIGHETTI

Luigi Righetti 1995 Capitel de' Roari Red Blend (Amarone della Valpolicella) $25. **87** *—M.N. (12/31/2000)*

Luigi Righetti 1999 Campolieti Red Blend (Valpolicella Classico) $12. **87** *(5/1/2003)*

LUNA DI LUNA

Luna Di Luna 2002 White Blend (Veneto) $10. **83** *—J.C. (7/1/2003)*

LUNGAROTTI

Lungarotti 2001 Cabernet Sauvignon (Torgiano) $22. A Cab that amounts to a starter wine. It lacks the cassis and berry flavors and aromas of a big boy while pouring on red fruit and acidity. Fairly monotone in its approach, with big Umbrian tannins. **84** *—M.S. (11/15/2004)*

Lungarotti 2002 Aurente Chardonnay (Umbria) $40. Attractive apricot, peach and honey aromas vie with a strong dosing of oak on the bouquet. Second and third takes, however, unveil additional smoky nuances. Apple and melon flavors are true, while the finish is soft and smooth. Easygoing and textured; a positive example of high-end Umbrian Chardonnay. **89** *—M.S. (6/1/2005)*

Lungarotti 2000 Giubilante Red Blend (Umbria) $18. **85** *—M.S. (12/15/2003)*

Lungarotti 1998 Rubesco Red Blend (Torgiano) $15. **87** *—M.S. (2/1/2003)*

Lungarotti 1997 San Giorgio Red Blend (Umbria) $67. A classic, old-style blend of Sangiovese, Canaiolo, and Cab Sauvignon. It's dry, aging, and lighter in frame. Which isn't to imply that it's short of structure. It has bracing acidity and a racy mouthfeel. Along the way catch pure, oak-draped berry character. **88** *—M.S. (11/15/2004)*

Lungarotti 1990 San Giorgio Red Blend (Rosso dell'Umbria) $49. **90** *—M.S. (3/1/2000)*

Lungarotti 2002 Torre di Giano White Blend (Torgiano) $18. Simple, with bland citrus aromas and flavors. Finishes watery. **81** *—M.S. (10/1/2004)*

MACHIAVELLI

Machiavelli 1998 Riserva Fontalle (Chianti Classico) $NA. 85 *—R.V. (8/1/2002)*

MACULAN

Maculan 1999 Fratta Cabernet Sauvignon-Merlot (Veneto) $80. 91 Cellar Selection *(5/1/2003)*

Maculan 2002 Pino & Toi White Blend (Veneto) $10. 87 Best Buy *—J.C. (7/1/2003)*

Maculan 2001 Pinot & Toi White Blend (Veneto) $11. 88 Best Buy *—C.S. (11/15/2002)*

MALGRA

Malgra 2001 (Gavi di Gavi) $16. 85 *—M.S. (12/15/2003)*

MANDRAROSSA

MandraRossa 2004 Fiano (Sicilia) $9. A golden-hued wine with a thicker consistency that packs walnuts, peanut shell, and exotic fruit. The mouthfeel is buttery, fleshy, and smooth, making it an ideal match for spicy foods. Imported by Palm Bay Imports. 86 Best Buy *—M.L. (9/1/2005)*

MandraRossa 2004 Nero d'Avola (Sicilia) $9. A casual dinner wine with spunk, blackberry, coffee bean, and a straightforward, crowd-pleasing nose. There are some faint but typically Sicilian smells that come in the form of dried brush and sea breeze. Imported by Palm Bay Imports. 86 Best Buy *—M.L. (9/1/2005)*

MARCARINI

Marcarini 1998 Ciabot Camerano (Barbera d'Asti) $15. 86 *(4/1/2000)*

Marcarini 2003 (Moscato d'Asti) $16. This reliable Barolo producer has turned out a balanced Moscato from a ferociously hot vintage. Apricot, honey, and pink grapefruit aromas and flavors all swirl together in a harmonious whole that's not profound, simply very enjoyable. 87 *—J.C. (11/15/2004)*

Marcarini 1998 Brunate Nebbiolo (Barolo) $50. 89 *—C.S. (11/15/2002)*

Marcarini 1998 La Serra Nebbiolo (Barolo) $50. 92 *—C.S. (11/15/2002)*

MARCHESATO DEGLI ALERAMICI

Marchesato Degli Aleramici 2000 (Brunello di Montalcino) $45. Wonderful, almost flowery, perfume on the nose. There are also hints of men's cologne and lemon peel. Chewy and meaty across the palate, where black cherry and plum dominate. The finish shows ample oak, chocolate, and butter. Will be round and easy upon maturity, which should come in a couple of years. Imported by Lauber Imports. 91 *—M.S. (7/1/2005)*

Marchesato Degli Aleramici 1999 Riserva (Brunello di Montalcino) $60. Despite starting out a bit mute, what lurks below is nothing short of stellar. Fine black licorice and ripe, meaty fruit creates a dark, manly flavor profile, while the finish deals a layer cake's worth of fudge, vanilla, and espresso. Virtually anything you would want in a Brunello is here. 93 *—M.S. (7/1/2005)*

MARCHESE ANTINORI

Marchese Antinori NV Nature (Oltrepó Pavese) $25. This wine waltzes up to the nose with the most delicate steps to offer crisp aromas of roses, golden apples, and kiwi. It offers a pleasant balance that finishes on a dry and clean note. 87 *—M.L. (12/15/2004)*

MARCHESE CARLO GUERRIERI GONZAGA

Marchese Carlo Guerrieri Gonzaga 1998 Merlot di San Leonardo Estate Bottled Merlot (Trento) $18. 83 *—M.S. (12/15/2003)*

MARCHESI BISCARDO

Marchesi Biscardo 2000 Red Blend (Amarone della Valpolicella) $65. Saddle leather, horsehide and dried cherry comprise the lean, rustic nose. The flavors veer toward fresh fruits and spice, with a bit of chocolate hiding below the surface. Not that deep or complex, with a short, crisp, clean finish. 86 *(11/1/2005)*

MARCHESI DE' FRESCOBALDI

Marchesi de' Frescobaldi 1999 Castelgiocondo Riserva (Brunello di Montalcino) $100. Tight as nails on the nose before it explodes on the palate in a cacophony of cherry, cassis, black plum, tobacco, and chocolate. It's like the best cigar and a great red wine rolled into one. Yes, the tannins are hammering and yes, the acidity is forward. But that only means this brilliant Brunello should age for 15 years without batting an eyelash. 97 Cellar Selection *—M.S. (7/1/2005)*

Marchesi de' Frescobaldi 2002 Benefizio Bianco Chardonnay (Pomino) $27. Deep gold in color, with sunny aromas of peaches and flowers. In the mouth, however, it's shrill, with blasting acidity and a sour flavor profile. Disappointing because the nose seems promising. 83 *—M.S. (6/1/2005)*

Marchesi de' Frescobaldi 2001 Benefizio White Blend (Pomino) $NA. This fragrant white, with its boisterous bouquet of designer soap, perfume, and gardenia, is exotic, but it's hard to say that the palate that follows is as exciting. In fact, it's soft and bland, with banana, citrus and nutmeg flavors that don't come in layers but all at once. A blend that's mostly Chardonnay. 86 *—M.S. (10/1/2004)*

Marchesi de' Frescobaldi 1998 Lamaione Merlot (Toscana) $64. 92 Cellar Selection *—M.S. (12/31/2002)*

Marchesi de' Frescobaldi 2000 Castiglioni Red Blend (Chianti) $13. 85 *—M.S. (12/31/2002)*

Marchesi de' Frescobaldi 1999 Castiglioni (Chianti) $13. **89 Best Buy** *(4/1/2001)*

Marchesi de' Frescobaldi 1997 Montesodi Castello di Nipozzano (Chianti Rufina) $54. **92 Cellar Selection** *(4/1/2001)*

Marchesi de' Frescobaldi 1999 Montesodi Castello Di Nipozzano (Chianti Rufina) $40. **90** *—M.S. (12/31/2002)*

Marchesi de' Frescobaldi 2000 Nipozzano Riserva (Chianti Rufina) $22. One of the few ratings where unanimity was lacking. Part of the panel appreciated the wine's assertiveness, while finding a wiry blackberry foundation and character-adding herbal qualities, while the other part disapproved of the fruit quality, finding it stewed yet still too tannic. **86** *(4/1/2005)*

Marchesi de' Frescobaldi 1996 Nipozzano Riserva (Chianti Rufina) $20. **86** *—M.S. (7/1/2000)*

Marchesi de' Frescobaldi 2000 Remole Tuscan Blend (Toscana) $9. **83** *(9/1/2002)*

Marchesi de' Frescobaldi 1998 Remole (Toscana) $9. **87** *(11/15/1999)*

Marchesi de' Frescobaldi 1996 Pomino Rosso (Pomino) $25. **86** *—L.W. (3/1/2000)*

MARCHESI DI BAROLO

Marchesi di Barolo 1999 Le Lune Cortese (Gavi) $14. **86** *(3/1/2001)*

Marchesi di Barolo 1996 Nebbiolo (Barolo) $40. **89** *(3/1/2001)*

Marchesi di Barolo 1998 Cannubi Nebbiolo (Piedmont) $65. **90** *—R.V. (11/15/2002)*

Marchesi di Barolo 1998 Vigne di Proprieta Nebbiolo (Barolo) $45. Lush berry fruit and a plump, juicy mouthfeel scored big with our tasters, who also remarked on this wine's complex notes of meat, black cherries, and anise. Supple and easy on the finish, making it ready to drink now and over the next decade. **90** *(4/2/2004)*

MARCHESI DI GRESY

Marchesi di Gresy 2004 La Serra (Moscato d'Asti) $13. You can't beat the activity in the glass. Persistent bubbling and frothy mousse hint at what's to come: The zesty mineral and floral notes are so intense they are almost spicy in the mouth but soon yield to creamy softness and melted honey on the finish. **89 Editors' Choice** *—M.L. (12/15/2005)*

MARCHESI SPINOLA

Marchesi Spinola 1998 Fratelli Gancia Nebbiolo (Barolo) $35. Shows some oak on the nose, marked by vanilla and a hint of maple syrup. Lush plum fruit, some leather, and orange zest on the palate before the tannins clamp down on the anise-tinged finish. Try after 2008. **87** *(4/2/2004)*

MARCO BONFANTE

Marco Bonfante 2000 Nebbiolo (Nebbiolo d'Alba) $18. A bit disjointed, this wine offers alcoholic scents of brandy-soaked cherries, then follows that with flavors of anise, dried fruit, and a hint of soy sauce. Lightweight, without much depth, and finishes with a slight astringency. **83** *—J.C. (11/15/2004)*

MARCO DE BARTOLI

Marco de Bartoli 2003 Grappoli Del Grillo (Sicilia) $34. Clean and medium in weight, with apple, pineapple, and a shot of mineral to the nose. Pure citrus and sunshine in the mouth, with a finish of orange peel and pepper. Acidic and snappy, but crafty. Simple yet solid. **87** *—M.S. (7/1/2005)*

MAREGA

Marega 1998 Chardonnay (Collio) $15. **88 Best Buy** *(4/1/2001)*

Marega 1997 Merlot (Collio) $14. **87** *—M.S. (5/1/1999)*

Marega 1994 Holbar Red Blend (Friuli Venezia Giulia) $20. **91 Editors' Choice** *(4/1/2001)*

Marega 1995 Holbar White Blend (Friuli Venezia Giulia) $20. **89** *(4/1/2001)*

MARENCO

Marenco 2003 Scrapona (Moscato d'Asti) $17. A bit richer and sweeter than it might be in more typical vintages, Marenco's Moscato lacks the touch of acidity that would have focused its flavors more effectively. The honey, peach, and pineapple flavors are rich and concentrated, they just seem a bit heavier than they should. Serve well-chilled. **84** *—J.C. (11/15/2004)*

MARETIMA

Maretima 1999 Fabula Sangiovese (Tuscany) $16. **91 Editors' Choice** *—M.S. (11/15/2003)*

MARIO SCHIOPETTO

Mario Schiopetto 2001 Pinot Grigio (Collio) $32. **91** *—R.V. (7/1/2003)*

Mario Schiopetto 2001 Blanc des Rosis White Blend (Friuli Venezia Giulia) $31. **89** *—R.V. (7/1/2003)*

MARISA CUOMO

Marisa Cuomo 1997 Furore Riserva Piedirosso (Campania) $32. **91** *—C.S. (5/1/2002)*

MAROTTI CAMPI

Marotti Campi 2002 Luzano Classico (Verdicchio dei Castelli di Jesi Classico) $11. Slightly sweet on the nose, with whiffs of Bartlett pear followed by flavors of lemon, lime, soda cracker, and mineral. The mouthfeel is good and the finish is springy, with lively acidity and straightforward flavors. **86** *—M.S. (8/1/2004)*

MARTINI & ROSSI

Martini & Rossi NV Asti Spumante (Moscato d'Asti) $10. 87 *—S.H. (12/31/2000)*

MASCIARELLI

Masciarelli 2000 Villa Gemma (Montepulciano d'Abruzzo) $80. This is big wine in every sense. Scratch that: it's huge and inky black in color. Evolving aromatics include leather, vanilla, tobacco, toasted wood, and red fruit. Firmly cemented tannins balanced to alcohol and acidity make this a bold and brave protagonist of the Abruzzo region. **90 Cellar Selection** *—M.L. (9/1/2005)*

Masciarelli 2002 Marina Cvetic (Trebbiano d'Abruzzo) $55. This wine is named after Gianni Masciarelli's wife and is usually cited as the benchmark for Trebbiano. This vintage boasts a deep golden color with toasted almonds, apples, vanilla, and lots of new oak. Indeed, the woodshop aromas are just shy of too much. **89** *—M.L. (9/1/2005)*

MASI

Masi 1997 Brolo di Campofiorin (Rosso del Veronese) $NA. Seems a bit closed and in need of more cellaring. You can sense the depth of black cherry fruit rather than smell or taste it. Finishes long and tannic. Try in 2010. **89** *(12/1/2004)*

Masi 2001 Campofiorin (Rosso del Veronese) $16. Like the '98 Brolo, this is still showing some reductive notes of rubber on the nose, but boasts plenty of lush, ripe black cherries and dried spices on the palate. It goes down deceptively easy, yet should improve for another few years at least. **90 Editors' Choice** *(12/1/2004)*

Masi 1997 Campofiorin (Rosso del Veronese) $NA. Nearing maturity, but still fresh, showing brown sugar, black cherry and plum aromas and flavors. The tannins this vintage are very supple, with perhaps slightly less body. **88** *(12/1/2004)*

Masi 1993 Campofiorin (Rosso del Veronese) $NA. An understated vintage that seems to be tiring, with subtle notes of molasses and soy sauce, modest cherry fruit, and a finish that fades quickly. **86** *(12/1/2004)*

Masi 1983 Campofiorin (Rosso del Veronese) $NA. Shows a lot more fruit that the '77, packing cherry and brown sugar flavors onto a rounder, softer frame. Finishes with hints of tobacco and tea. Fully mature, or maybe a little past peak. **87** *(12/1/2004)*

Masi 1983 Campofiorin (Rosso del Veronese) $NA. 87 *(12/1/2004)*

Masi 2003 Bonacosta (Valpolicella Classico) $14. Veneto's classic Corvina, Rondinella, and Molinara blend has tart fruit like cranberry skins, white cherry, and crushed red rose petal with a subtle menthol endnote. Good companion for a full meal, from appetizer to the meat course. **86** *—M.L. (9/1/2005)*

Masi 2000 Colbaraca Soave Classico Superiore $12. 89 Best Buy *(9/1/2001)*

Masi 1999 Campolongo di Torbe Red Blend (Amarone della Valpolicella Classico) $110. Dried fruit with a lot of woody, spicy aromas make for an alluring, somewhat rustic nose. The palate, however, delivers round fruit flavors touched up by plenty of sweet mocha and vanilla notes. Finely textured, with a long, supple finish. Almost a no-brainer as goes Amarone. **91** *(11/1/2005)*

Masi 1993 Campolongo di Torbe Red Blend (Amarone della Valpolicella Classico) $62. 88 *(5/1/2003)*

Masi 1999 Costasera Red Blend (Amarone della Valpolicella Classico) $40. 91 *(5/1/2003)*

Masi 1999 Mazzano Red Blend (Amarone della Valpolicella Classico) $140. Exotic and mature, with a classic nose of prune, licorice, maple, and sweet sherry. The palate is quite round and generous, and it spreads out like a comfortable blanket on a feather bed. Finishing touches of smooth tannins and flavors of coffee and anise are ideal. **93** *(11/1/2005)*

Masi 1999 Serego Alighieri Red Blend (Valpolicella Classico Superiore) $17. 88 *(5/1/2003)*

Masi 1998 Serego Alighieri Red Blend (Valpolicella Classico Superiore) $15. 85 *(5/1/2003)*

Masi 1996 Serego Alighieri Vaio Red Blend (Amarone della Valpolicella) $55. 89 *(5/1/2003)*

Masi 2002 Classico White Blend (Soave) $15. 86 *—R.V. (7/1/2003)*

Masi 2002 Masianco White Blend (Delle Venezie) $12. 90 *—R.V. (7/1/2003)*

MASO POLI

Maso Poli 1997 Pinot Grigio (Trentino) $13. 85 *— (8/1/1999)*

MASOTTINA

Masottina 1997 Montesco Bordeaux Blend (Colli di Conegliano) $35. 87 *(5/1/2003)*

Masottina NV (Prosecco di Conegliano e Valdobbiadene) $14. 89 *—M.S. (6/1/2003)*

Masottina 1999 Vigneto Rizzardo White Blend (Colli di Conegliano) $25. 89 *—J.C. (7/1/2003)*

MASTROBERARDINO

Mastroberardino 2003 Aglianico (Irpinia) $22. Earthy and leathery, with aromas and flavors of black olives and dried cherries. It's medium-bodied, with a chewy tannic structure that calls for rare beef at this stage of its development. **87** *(12/1/2005)*

Mastroberardino 1995 Radici Aglianico (Taurasi) $42. **89** *(3/1/2000)*

Mastroberardino 2004 Falanghina (Sannio) $19. A stronger hue and heavy thickness in the glass make you think of anything but a flinty Campanian white. Despite volcanic soils and the use of steel tanks, flavors of candied orange peel and honey graham cracker come through nicely. Oiliness and lower acidity make it less exciting in the mouth although the overall structure suggests a good match for shellfish. **86** *—M.L. (9/1/2005)*

Mastroberardino 1998 Radici (Fiano di Avellino) $26. **89** *—M.M. (9/1/2001)*

Mastroberardino 1997 (Greco di Tufo) $25. **92** *(4/1/2000)*

Mastroberardino 1997 Red Blend (Aglianico d'Irpinia) $22. **91** *(11/15/1999)*

Mastroberardino 2000 Red Blend (Lacryma Christi del Vesuvio) $20. **86** *—C.S. (5/1/2002)*

Mastroberardino 1998 Red Blend (Lacryma Christi del Vesuvio) $23. **86** *—L.W. (3/1/2000)*

Mastroberardino 2000 Naturalis Historia Red Blend (Irpinia) $65. Mostly Aglianico, but its blended with approximately 15% Piedirosso from Vesuvio. This is Mastroberardino's luxury cuvée, so it's aged in barrique, but the influence isn't overdone. Rhubarb and mulling spices on the nose gradually deepen with air into cherry and plum, with hints of mint and olive adding complexity. Long and elegant on the finish. **90** *(12/1/2005)*

Mastroberardino 1997 Naturalis Historia Red Blend (Irpinia) $70. **90** *—C.S. (5/1/2002)*

Mastroberardino 1998 White Blend (Coda di Volpe d'Irpinia) $13. **88** *—L.W. (4/1/2000)*

Mastroberardino 1998 Sireum White Blend (Campania) $NA. **87** *—L.W. (4/1/2000)*

MASTROJANNI

Mastrojanni 1999 (Brunello di Montalcino) $55. A touch rusty and weathered given its young age, but classic on the nose, where there's tomato, pepper, and dried red fruit. This is very drinkable now, and after a few minutes in the glass it begins to show more. Traditional, and just perfect for restaurants and early drinking. **89** *—M.S. (6/1/2004)*

MASÚT DA RIVE

Masút Da Rive 2001 Sauvignon (Isonzo del Friuli) $22. The nose offers a bit of northern Italian funk, with aromas frighteningly close to smelling of garlic. The palate is a bit sour, with generic, mildly bitter flavors of pineapple and peach. Better weight and feel. **82** *(7/1/2005)*

MAURO MOLINO

Mauro Molino 1997 Vigna Gettere (Barbera d'Alba) $33. **89** *(4/1/2000)*

MAURO SEBASTE

Mauro Sebaste 1999 La Serra Nebbiolo (Barolo) $54. Coffee and tree-bark aromas lead into flavors of cola and tart cherries. This is interesting from a structural standpoint, with soft, supple tannins, but it has very high, tart acids. Finish picks up hints of hickory smoke and lemon. **87** *(4/2/2004)*

Mauro Sebaste 2001 Parigi Nebbiolo (Nebbiolo d'Alba) $32. **84** *—M.S. (12/15/2003)*

MAURO VEGLIO

Mauro Veglio 1998 Castelletto Nebbiolo (Barolo) $60. Toasty, showing some obvious new wood aromas, balanced by Porty scents—the densely packed fruit is on the verge of being overripe, yet there are also some faint green notes. Firm tannins cut the finish short, but should enable the wine to age for at least 5–10 years. **87** *(4/2/2004)*

MAZZEI

Mazzei 1999 Fonterutoli (Chianti Classico) $27. **91** *—M.S. (8/1/2002)*

MAZZINO

Mazzino 1998 (Barbera d'Alba) $12. **82** *—M.S. (12/15/2003)*

MELINI

Melini 1997 Coltri 2 Cabernet Blend (Tuscany) $33. **90** *—M.S. (11/15/2003)*

Melini 2002 Borghi d'Elsa (Chianti) $10. Sharp aromas of rhubarb, leather, and barnyard keep this one from blossoming. The palate, however, is light and fresh, with thin but pleasant strawberry and raspberry flavors preceding a peppery, mildly lemony finish. **84** *(4/1/2005)*

Melini 2000 Isassi (Chianti Classico) $16. Solid, with restrained red fruit, tea, fallen leaves, and leather on the nose. Old school all the way, with raspberry and black cherry flavors and little to no perceivable oak. It expands nicely on the finish, offering a glance into the lighter style of Chianti. **87** *—M.S. (11/15/2004)*

Melini 1997 Isassi (Chianti Classico) $13. **85** *(4/1/2001)*

Melini 1998 Laborel Riserva (Chianti Classico) $19. 85 —*M.S. (11/15/2003)*

Melini 1999 Riserva Massovecchio (Chianti Classico) $30. Jammy and broad, with cola and loud fruit aromas. With time it picks up focus, showing tangy cherry/berry fruit and a live-wire finish full of leather, smoke, tomato, and chocolate. Fairly complex yet ripe and forward. The best of both worlds. 90 —*M.S. (10/1/2004)*

Melini 1995 Massovecchio dai Vigneti Terrarossa Riserva Tuscan Blend (Chianti Classico) $35. 91 *(11/15/1999)*

Melini 2002 Le Grillaie (Vernaccia di San Gimignano) $20. A bit pricey for Vernaccia, especially when you consider that the wine doesn't really show more than the basics: citrus and melon notes, and some soda-cracker dryness along with white pepper. All in all, however, it's perfectly good and entirely traditional. 87 —*M.S. (8/1/2004)*

ITALY

MERK

Merk 2001 Pinot Bianco (Friuli Aquileia) $16. 86 —*J.C. (7/1/2003)*

Merk 2001 Tocai (Friuli Aquileia) $16. 87 —*J.C. (7/1/2003)*

MERONI

Meroni 1997 Il Velluto Riserva Red Blend (Amarone della Valpolicella Classico) $80. Slightly gaseous on the nose and losing freshness with each passing day. Zingy acids are keeping it alive but the flavors are slipping toward cranberry and tomato. Not much else is left. 83 *(11/1/2005)*

MEZZACORONA

Mezzacorona 2004 Chardonnay (Vigneti delle Dolomiti) $7. This bargain-priced Chardonnay delivers the goods. Hints of butter on the nose come from 25% barrel fermentation and malolactic, while the fresh pear and ripe apple flavors come straight from the fruit. Clean on the finish. 85 Best Buy *(6/1/2005)*

Mezzacorona 2002 Vigneti delle Dolomiti Chardonnay (Trentino) $8. 85 Best Buy —*J.C. (7/1/2003)*

Mezzacorona 2001 Merlot (Trentino) $8. 86 Best Buy —*M.S. (12/15/2003)*

Mezzacorona 1998 Pinot Grigio (Trentino) $8. 86 *(8/1/1999)*

Mezzacorona 1999 Pinot Grigio (Trentino) $7. 83 —*M.N. (12/31/2000)*

Mezzacorona 2002 Riserva Pinot Grigio (Trentino) $14. An oak-aged Pinot Grigio, with notes of cinnamon and buttered toast to complement the fruit elements of poached pears. In a world of tart, tangy Grigios, this one stands out. 85 —*J.C. (12/31/2004)*

Mezzacorona 2000 Riserva Superiore (Teroldego Rotaliano) $NA. A special bottling produced for the 100th anniversary of the cooperative, this is creamier and much more supple than the regular riserva, reviewed in our December 31, 2004 issue. Smoky, toasty and loaded with berry fruit on the nose, dusty and smooth on the finish, this wine shows what large co-ops can achieve but rarely accomplish. 89 *(6/1/2005)*

MICHELE CHIARLO

Michele Chiarlo 1997 (Barbera d'Asti) $12. 83 — *(4/1/2000)*

Michele Chiarlo 1996 La Court (Barbera d'Asti) $46. 87 *(4/1/2000)*

Michele Chiarlo 2001 Le Orme (Barbera d'Asti) $11. A tart, juicy, cherry-flavored wine, couched in nuances of leather and cinnamon from a year in oak. Picks up hints of chocolate on the finish. 86 Best Buy —*J.C. (11/15/2004)*

Michele Chiarlo 1995 Valle del Sole (Barbera d'Asti) $29. 88 *(4/1/2000)*

Michele Chiarlo 2002 Cortese (Gavi) $14. 87 —*M.S. (11/15/2003)*

Michele Chiarlo 2004 Nivole (Moscato d'Asti) $12. Good things come in little packages and this half bottle Moscato d'Asti is hugely satisfying. It boasted the most crystalline luminosity of all the wines I tasted and among the thickest, foamiest froths. I also loved the nose with limestone and peach notes backed by characteristic muskiness. 89 Best Buy —*M.L. (12/15/2005)*

Michele Chiarlo 1995 Nebbiolo (Barbaresco) $35. 88 —*M.M. (5/1/1999)*

Michele Chiarlo 1998 Brunate Nebbiolo (Piedmont) $81. 93 Cellar Selection —*R.V. (11/15/2002)*

Michele Chiarlo 1998 Cannubi Nebbiolo (Piedmont) $81. 92 —*R.V. (11/15/2002)*

Michele Chiarlo 1999 Cerequio Nebbiolo (Barolo) $84. Nicely balanced and already approachable, Chiarlo's '99 Cerequio boasts textbook aromatics and flavors of anise, cherries, leather, and asphalt. It's firmly structured, but not overbearing or too tannic. Drink 2008–2015. 88 *(4/2/2004)*

Michele Chiarlo 1995 Cerequio Nebbiolo (Barolo) $89. 88 *(7/1/2000)*

Michele Chiarlo 1995 Countacc Red Blend (Monferrato) $40. 91 —*M.M. (5/1/1999)*

MIONETTO

Mionetto NV Cartizze (Prosecco di Valdobbiadene) $47. 88 *(11/15/2002)*

Mionetto NV Frizzante (Soft White Wine) (Prosecco di Valdobbiadene) $12. 88 Best Buy —*M.M. (12/31/2001)*

Mionetto NV Sergio Extra Dry Spumante (Prosecco di Valdobbiadene) $16. 92 *(11/15/2002)*

Mionetto NV Spumante Brut (Prosecco di Valdobbiadene) $11. 89 Best Buy *(11/15/2002)*

Mionetto NV Il Moscato (Moscato delle Venezie) $10. **84** *—J.C. (12/31/2003)*

Mionetto NV Prosecco (Prosecco di Valdobbiadene) $13. In a bottle closed with the traditional string over the cork, this Prosecco is the lightest shade of gold with pearl-like strings of bubbles. There's pear, some citrus, white peach, and a dab of almond followed by a refreshing jolt of crispness. **85** *—M.L. (12/15/2004)*

Mionetto NV Brut Spumante (Prosecco di Valdobbiadene) $12. Juicy and clean, although you don't really pull much from the quiet nose. Round and citrusy on the tongue, with crisp apple flavors. Runs long and standard on the finish, with a mix of sweet and tart flavors. Easy to drink. **87 Best Buy** *—M.S. (6/1/2005)*

Mionetto NV Frizzante (Prosecco di Valdobbiadene) $12. Basic, but 100% good. This is a perfect cocktail-party drink, one with baked-apple aromas and a round, apple-and-citrus palate. Finishes fresh, long, and pure. Nothing sensational, just good, clean fun. **88 Best Buy** *—M.S. (6/1/2005)*

Mionetto NV Il Prosecco (Prosecco del Veneto) $11. Fresh and clean, with aromas of slate, citrus, and green herbs. The palate delivers lemon-lime flavors and a modest bubble bead that doesn't overwhelm. And when folks say packaging means nothing, ignore them. This one comes in a cool bowling pin-shaped bottle that's capped like a beer. The tagline on the label points out that Prosecco is the "gentle" sparkling wine. Yeah, gentle on your wallet. **86 Best Buy** *—M.S. (12/15/2004)*

Mionetto NV Sergio Extra Dry (Prosecco di Valdobbiadene) $18. There's a lot more flinty chalkiness in this wine, beyond the apple and melon, which makes it stand out from others. Prosecco, Chardonnay, Bianchetta, and Verdiso go into this wine, vinified without skin contact, which explains its pale, delicate hue. **87** *—M.L. (12/15/2004)*

Mionetto NV Sergio Extra Dry Spumante (Prosecco di Valdobbiadene) $18. Light and garden fresh, with apple-based aromas. Not excessively expressive, but still full of chunky green apple, citrus and honeydew melon flavors. Cleansing, with a sorbet quality. Off-dry but not sugary sweet. Shows decent style and precision. **88** *—M.S. (6/1/2005)*

MOCCAGATTA

Moccagatta 2000 Cole Nebbiolo (Barbaresco) $60. The wood on this wine is either permanently out of whack or just going through the ultimate awkward phase. Features big scents of burnt popcorn and earthy, charred flavors. Yet it finishes supple and long. Hmmm. **83** *(4/2/2004)*

MOLETTO

Moletto 1998 Merlot (Piave) $20. **87** *(9/1/2001)*

Moletto 2000 Pinot Grigio (Veneto) $10. **87 Best Buy** *(9/1/2001)*

Moletto 2000 Prosecco (Veneto) $10. **85** *(5/1/2002)*

Moletto NV Extra Dry (Prosecco di Valdobbiadene) $14. **84** *—J.C. (12/31/2003)*

Moletto NV Frizzante Prosecco (Marca Trevigiana) $13. Cotton candy on the nose indicates a sweet wine, and joining that sensation is wildflower and lemon-lime. Flavors of tangerine and papaya are relaxed, and there's some light banana to the finish, which is here one minute and gone the next. **87** *—M.S. (12/15/2004)*

MONASTERO DI CORIANO

Monastero di Coriano 1996 (Vin Santo del Chianti) $21. **84** *—S.H. (1/1/2002)*

MONCARO

Moncaro 2002 Terrazzo (Verdicchio dei Castelli di Jesi Classico Superiore) $13. Fat and heavy on the nose, with some initial barnyard/animal notes that raise questions about cleanliness. However, in the mouth it seems clean, with apple and spice notes preceding the potent finish. Of note, this is a well-packaged wine with a nice label. **84** *—M.S. (8/1/2004)*

MONDORO

Mondoro NV Moscato (Asti) $14. **82** *—J.C. (12/31/2001)*

MONTE ANTICO

Monte Antico 1998 Sangiovese (Toscana) $10. **85** *(10/1/2001)*

MONTE ROSSA

Monte Rossa NV Brut Satèn (Franciacorta) $30. **81** *—S.H. (6/1/2001)*

MONTENISA

Montenisa NV Brut (Franciacorta) $30. Nice and smooth, with pure green apple, citrus, and rosemary aromas. Bold in the mouth, with melon, pineapple, and subtle spice flavors. Finishes seductively dry, with stylish mushroom and toast flavors, almost like a good dry Sherry. **92 Editors' Choice** *—M.S. (12/15/2005)*

MONTEVETRANO

Montevetrano 1999 Montevetrano Red Blend (Campania) $70. **94 Cellar Selection** *—C.S. (5/1/2002)*

MONTI

Monti 1999 (Barbera d'Alba) $37. **92** *—M.N. (9/1/2001)*

Monti 2000 Bussia Nebbiolo (Barolo) $NA. Strong oak influence here, with toast, vanilla, and scorched wood dominating the nose at this point. But given the wine's core of cherry fruit, this should come into better balance within a couple of years. Finishes tart, with soft tannins, a short-term ager for the non-oak averse. **87** *—J.C. (11/15/2004)*

MONTICELLO VINEYARDS

Monticello Vineyards 2001 Riserva (Chianti Classico) $25. Starts out by pushing sweet cherry and tea aromas before shifting to leather and sawdust. Yes, it's oaky, but the wood falls into place on the palate, where it shares time with cherry and plum. Just shy of elaborate, with palate-friendly tannins and ample spice. Great for near-term drinking. **89** *(4/1/2005)*

MONTRESOR

Montresor 1999 CS del Veneto Campo Madonna Cabernet Sauvignon (Veneto) $17. **87** *(5/1/2003)*

Montresor 2002 La Colombaia Pinot Grigio (Valdadige) $13. **87** *—M.S. (11/15/2003)*

Montresor 1998 Recioto re Tiodorico Red Blend (Amarone della Valpolicella) $33. **89** *(5/1/2003)*

MORELLONE

Morellone 1999 Le Caniette Red Blend (Rosso Piceno) $23. **83** *—M.S. (12/15/2003)*

MORGANTE

Morgante 2002 Nero d'Avola (Sicilia) $15. **84** *—R.V. (10/1/2003)*

Morgante 2003 Don Antonio Nero d'Avola (Sicilia) $30. You can usually count Don Antonio as one of Sicily's very best Nero d'Avolas. But the 2003 heat seems to have left a slight jammy quality that butts awkwardly against the blackberry and crunchy toasted almond. The tannic structure is firm, which bodes well for its evolution over time. **87** *—M.L. (9/1/2005)*

Morgante 1999 Don Antonio Nero d'Avola (Sicily) $30. **90** *—C.S. (5/1/2002)*

MOTTA

Motta 1999 Tuscan Blend (Morellino di Scansano) $15. This solid Tuscan red comes from the seaside area of Tuscany, not the zone of our usual image of this historic region, but one of great recent activity. Dark cherry, earth, and spice aromas open to a full and ripe mouth, with rich dry cherry fruit, and moderate acidity. Finishes dry with a mild chalky element. Very drinkable now; should improve over one or two years. **89 Best Buy** *—M.M. (1/1/2004)*

MUSELLA

Musella 1999 Red Blend (Amarone della Valpolicella) $32. Finely textured with exemplary aromatics. The bouquet is graced by cola, black licorice, marzipan, pipe tobacco, and other alluring smells in addition to pure, dark fruit notes. Flashy and smooth in the mouth, where the berry and prune notes are touched up by leather and spice. Just right, with more potential if given a few more years of cellar time. **93 Editors' Choice** *(11/1/2005)*

MUSSO

Musso 1999 Bricco Rio Sordo Nebbiolo (Barbaresco) $38. Rio Sordo is acknowledged as a top cru, and Walter Musso has struck gold in 1999. Toasty hints of cedar blend harmoniously with succulent cherries, picking up notes of cured meat and vanilla. Long and richly textured on the finish, this should be approachable young, yet age well. Drink 2005–2015. **92** *(4/2/2004)*

MUZIC

Muzic 2001 Moresco Pinot Grigio (Collio) $NA. Bland and beery, with a slight spritz and some burnt-matchstick aromas. **81** *—J.C. (1/1/2004)*

NANDO

Nando NV Moscato (Asti) $9. Almost overly floral and sweet, with the palate showing an overdose of heavy citrus fruit. Finishes expectedly sweet, with a good mouthfeel. Attacks forcefully. **84** *—M.S. (12/15/2004)*

Nando 2001 Pinot Grigio (Isonzo del Friuli) $10. **83** *—J.C. (7/1/2003)*

Nando 2002 (Chianti Classico) $12. Dried cherry, leather, tomato, and spice make for a common, recognizable bouquet, while the palate offers fresh plum and raspberry with shadings of cedar and vanilla. Lighter tannins, decent acidity and good on the tongue. All in all, it does not push the envelope. **86** *(4/1/2005)*

Nando 2000 Sangiovese (Chianti Classico) $11. **89 Best Buy** *—M.S. (11/15/2003)*

Nando NV Spumanti (Asti) $9. Odd aromas of candy, Windex, and lime lead into an overtly sweet and cloying palate of lime and seedless white table grapes. Some Asti sparklers are good despite their sweetness, but this one is borderline acceptable. **80** *—M.S. (1/1/2004)*

NEIRANO

Neirano 1998 Le Croci Superiore (Barbera d'Asti) $24. **91** *—M.M. (11/15/2002)*

Neirano 2002 (Dolcetto d'Alba) $10. **85** *—M.S. (12/15/2003)*

Neirano 1995 Nebbiolo (Barolo) $18. **86** *(9/1/2000)*

NICOLIS

Nicolis 1998 Red Blend (Amarone della Valpolicella Classico) $50. 87 *(5/1/2003)*

Nicolis 1998 Ambrosan Red Blend (Amarone della Valpolicella) $75. 90 *(5/1/2003)*

Nicolis 2000 Seccal Red Blend (Valpolicella Classico Superiore) $20. 84 *(5/1/2003)*

NINO FRANCO

Nino Franco NV Brut (Prosecco di Valdobbiadene) $14. 83 *—D.T. (12/31/2001)*

Nino Franco 2000 Rive di San Floriano (Prosecco di Valdobbiadene) $15. 83 *—D.T. (12/31/2001)*

Nino Franco NV Rustico (Prosecco di Valdobbiadene) $12. 87 *—M.S. (12/31/2002)*

Nino Franco 2001 Rive di San Floriano Brut (Prosecco di Valdobbiadene) $17. 84 *—J.C. (12/31/2003)*

NINO NEGRI

Nino Negri 1995 Inferno Nebbiolo (Valtellina Superiore) $16. 88 *—R.V. (5/1/1999)*

NOCIANO

Nociano 1998 Red Blend (Umbria) $9. 90 *—M.S. (2/1/2003)*

NOZZOLE

Nozzole 2002 Le Bruniche Chardonnay (Toscana) $12. 86 *—M.S. (11/15/2003)*

Nozzole 2000 Riserva (Tuscany) $22. Starts with plum, berry, and light wood aromas. The flavor profile is pure red fruit, mostly plum, with nice acidity keeping things propped up. A bit of excess tannin on the finish roughs it up a bit, but with food that will not be an issue. Improves with airing. **88** *—M.S. (10/1/2004)*

OCONE

Ocone 2000 (Aglianico del Taburno) $12. Dark at first, with raspberry emerging. Throughout it's snappy, with red fruit dominant. Finishes clean, tight and crisp, with solid tannins that don't go overboard. An everyday, drink-me style of Aglianico. **86** *—M.S. (11/15/2004)*

Ocone 2003 Piedirosso (Taburno) $12. The prime red fruit here jolts your palate to attention. Even so, it's sweet and ripe at its center. The mouth deals light but fresh strawberry and cherry, while the minerally finish is sound. A tad bit jumpy and acidic, but still a real wine for real people. **87 Best Buy** *—M.S. (2/1/2005)*

OGNISSOLE

Ognissole 2003 (Primitivo Di Manduria) $22. Despite high expectations surrounding Feudi di San Gregorio's Puglia property, this nicely packaged Primitivo fails to deliver the goods. The nose is vegetal and stewy resembling minestrone. But the wine does improve in the mouth with spice and good length. **83** *—M.L. (9/1/2005)*

PALARI

Palari 1998 Rosso Del Soprano Red Blend (Sicily) $31. 91 *—C.S. (5/1/2002)*

PALAZZETTI

Palazzetti 1998 (Rosso di Montalcino) $23. 88 *—M.S. (11/15/2003)*

PALAZZO

Palazzo 2000 (Brunello di Montalcino) $69. Fairly heavy on the nose, with a whiff of wet pooch and damp earth. Somewhat stewy on the nose, while the palate features fat plum flavors and oversized tannins. Not quite up to snuff. **84** *—M.S. (7/1/2005)*

PALLADIO

Palladio 2003 (Chianti) $10. Sweet, earthy and largely clean, with some tart cherry and red plum flavors comprising the palate. Finishes largely fresh, with an acid-based crispness. **84** *(4/1/2005)*

PANZANELLO

Panzanello 2000 Riserva (Chianti Classico) $35. A dark, fully oaked, flavorful wine with aromas of blackberry, molasses, coffee, and smoke. Rich and woody on the palate, with black cherry, cedar, and vanilla. Runs a little sweet and soft, with noticeably soft tannins and modest acidity. Drink now for maximum pleasure. **90** *(4/1/2005)*

PAOLO SCAVINO

Paolo Scavino 1998 (Dolcetto di Diano d'Alba) $20. 91 *(4/1/2000)*

Paolo Scavino 1999 Bric dël Fiasc Nebbiolo (Barolo) $85. Slightly herbal or minty on the nose, but the palate is all that we've come to expect from Scavino, with wonderfully pure red fruits and subtle notes of mineral and sous bois for complexity. Tar and dark chocolate wrap up the supple finish. Drink 2005–2020. **91** *(4/2/2004)*

PARUSSO

Parusso 1998 Piani Noce (Dolcetto d'Alba) $15. 90 *(4/1/2000)*

Parusso 2001 Bricco Rovella Sauvignon Blanc (Langhe) $36. You don't come across too much Sauvignon Blanc from Piedmont, and this older example is mid-tier. The nose is smoky from oak aging, while the palate is primed with meaty, herbal flavors. An uncommon take on the grape that purists may not like. If you're experimental, it could work. **85** *(7/1/2005)*

PASQUA

Pasqua 1999 Sagramoso Red Blend (Valpolicella Classico Superiore) $NA. **86** *(5/1/2003)*

Pasqua 2002 Vigneti Del Sole (Montepulciano d'Abruzzo) $7. **85** *—M.S. (11/15/2003)*

PATERNOSTER

Paternoster 2000 Don Anselmo (Aglianico del Vulture) $47. May well be Basilicata's best wine with flinty, graphite notes derived from volcanic soils and loads of dried prunes, cassis, intense blackberry, leather, and toast. The aromas go on and on and constantly evolve in your glass. Aged in barrique and Slovenian casks, the mouthfeel is solid yet smooth, powerful yet elegant. **92 Cellar Selection** *—M.L. (9/1/2005)*

PATRIGLIONE

Patriglione 1994 Red Blend (Salento) $NA. **83** *—D.T. (5/1/2002)*

PE'RE ALESSANDRO

Pe're Alessandro 2000 Vigna Giaia Nebbiolo (Barbaresco) $55. Dull and earthy on the nose, with tree bark aromas and not a lot of fruit. Thankfully, it recovers on the palate, offering up intense black cherry flavors and a helping of dusty earth couched in supple tannins. Long and powerful on the finish. **89** *(4/2/2004)*

PECCHENINO

Pecchenino 2002 San Luigi (Dolcetto di Dogliani) $18. Among the 2002 Dolcettos we've sampled, the ones from Dogliani have stood out for their greater depth and intensity of flavor. This one boasts a dark purple hue and dense, plummy fruit. It's a supple mouthful of flavor that goes down easily yet retains a sense of structure and balance. **90 Editors' Choice** *—J.C. (11/15/2004)*

PERE ALESSANDRO

Pere Alessandro 2001 (Moscato d'Asti) $16. **87** *—M.S. (12/15/2003)*

Pere Alessandro 1997 Nebbiolo (Barolo) $44. **90** *—M.S. (12/15/2003)*

PETER ZEMMER

Peter Zemmer 1998 Pinot Grigio (Alto Adige) $11. **88** *(8/1/1999)*

PETRA

Petra 1998 Riserva Cabernet Sauvignon-Merlot (Toscana) $50. **95** *—M.S. (8/1/2002)*

PETROLO

Petrolo 1999 Terre di Galatrona Tuscan Blend (Toscana) $16. **87** *—M.S. (12/31/2002)*

PETRUSSA

Petrussa 2003 Sauvignon (Colli Orientali del Friuli) $27. Sulfuric and reductive to start, with heavy aromas of match stick, barnyard, and algae. But if you haven't tossed it aside after the first sniff or two, there's a lot below the surface. For starters, the richness and pungency of the melon and peach flavors is something. So is the briny character of the palate. But let it be noted: one of our panelists simply did not like this wine, proclaiming it "oily and dominated by salinity." **88** *(7/1/2005)*

PIAZZO ARMANDO

Piazzo Armando 2004 (Moscato d'Asti) $15. I really enjoyed this wine with its super thick froth, creamy peach, floral tones, intense fruit aromas and higher than normal (for a Moscato d'Asti) alcohol. A great aperitivo or dessert drink. **89** *—M.L. (12/15/2005)*

PICCINI

Piccini 2004 (Chianti) $8. Some situations simply demand solid, dependable Chianti that is rich in fruity notes but not too heavy in the mouth. Recognized by its eye-catching orange label, Piccini won't let you down. Red forest berries, clove, and cinnamon round off an extremely quaffable and affordable wine. Its lean consistency is accented by crispness and a fruit driven finish that would be an ideal match with cheese-topped pizza or pasta. **87 Best Buy** *—M.L. (11/15/2005)*

Piccini 2002 (Vernaccia di San Gimignano) $10. **85** *(7/1/2003)*

Piccini 2000 (Chianti Superiore) $10. **86** *(11/15/2001)*

Piccini 1999 (Chianti) $6. **82** *(4/1/2001)*

Piccini 2000 Riserva (Chianti) $10. **85** *(7/1/2003)*

Piccini 1997 Riserva (Chianti Classico) $13. **83** *(4/1/2001)*

Piccini 1999 Patriale Tuscan Blend (Toscana) $10. **86 Best Buy** *(7/1/2003)*

PIERO BUSSO

Piero Busso 1997 Vigna Majano (Dolcetto d'Alba) $19. **84** *(4/1/2000)*

Piero Busso 1999 Vigna Borgese Nebbiolo (Barbaresco) $57. The cedary, creamy, vanilla-laden nose comes across as a bit too "international." The mouthfeel is pleasantly chewy, but the flavors are limited to citrus and cedar, finishing with furry-textured wood tannins. **87** *(4/2/2004)*

PIEROPAN

Pieropan 2003 La Rocca (Soave) $43. This elaborate interpretation of Soave is made with late-harvest Garganega grapes fermented and aged in oak barrels to yield intense depth and a bigger, bolder body. Creamy butter, toasted nuts, and vanilla play supporting roles to a predominately fruity nose. **88** *—M.L. (9/1/2005)*

Pieropan 1997 Soave Classico Superiore $13. **84** *(11/1/1999)*

Pieropan 2003 Calvarino (Soave) $30. This Garganega-Trebbiano blend from the estate's original vineyard has a greenish tinge and more refreshing flowers, citrus and lime than the others in this portfolio. **87** *—M.L. (9/1/2005)*

Pieropan 2000 La Rocca (Soave Classico Superiore) $30. **89** *—J.C. (7/1/2003)*

Pieropan 1999 Soave Classico Superiore $15. **88** *—M.N. (12/31/2000)*

PIERPAOLO PECORARI

Pierpaolo Pecorari 2000 Isonzio Sauvignon Blanc (Friuli Venezia Giulia) $15. **82** *(8/1/2002)*

PIETRACOLATA

Pietracolata 2002 White Blend (Orvieto) $8. Floral and fresh, with melon and apple aromas. More melon, especially cantaloupe, on the palate. Well balanced and flavorful; a good quaffer. **84** *—M.S. (10/1/2004)*

PIETRAFITTA

Pietrafitta 2001 (Chianti Colli Senesi) $11. The bouquet of strawberry and plum is simple and open. The palate, meanwhile, is tangy, with raspberry and cherry flavors. A bit of licorice and wood spice on the finish adds character. Still, it's a lean, juicy, acidic red. **85** *—M.S. (10/1/2004)*

Pietrafitta 1999 La Sughera Sangiovese (San Gimignano) $18. **86** *—M.S. (12/31/2002)*

Pietrafitta 2000 Tuscan Blend (Chianti Colli Senesi) $11. **85 Best Buy** *—M.S. (12/31/2002)*

Pietrafitta 2002 Borghetto (Vernaccia di San Gimignano) $16. A bit yellow in color, with licorice gumdrop, anise, and mineral aromas. It offers a tight grip across the palate and good balance. Flavors of citrus and papaya are smooth, and the finish is drying. Overall, there's just the right amount of apple, mineral and soda cracker to warrant the thumbs up. **87** *—M.S. (8/1/2004)*

Pietrafitta 1992 Vin Santo (Colli della Toscana Centrale) $16. **90 Editors' Choice** *(4/1/2001)*

PIETRATORCIA

Pietratorcia 1998 Riserva Red Blend (Ischia) $36. **87** *—C.S. (5/1/2002)*

PIETRO BARBERO

Pietro Barbero 1996 La Vignassa Barbera D'Asti Superiore $35. **90** *(4/1/2000)*

PIEVE SANTA RESTITUTA

Pieve Santa Restituta 1999 Rennina (Brunello di Montalcino) $95. Doesn't seem that concentrated at first, but builds powerfully on the finish, giving it good promise for the future. Combines ripe cherries, tobacco, and leather with a silky mouthfeel in a classic Brunello style, finishing with firm tannins. Try in 2008. **92** *(7/1/2005)*

PIGHIN

Pighin 1997 Pinot Grigio (Collio) $13. **82** *— (8/1/1999)*

PINTAR

Pintar 1997 Single Vineyard Pinot Grigio (Collio) $20. **85** *— (8/1/1999)*

PIO CESARE

Pio Cesare 2000 Fides (Barbera d'Alba) $40. **90** *—M.S. (12/15/2003)*

Pio Cesare 1998 Chardonnay (Piedmont) $18. **88** *—M.S. (4/1/2000)*

Pio Cesare 2002 L'Altro Chardonnay (Piedmont) $20. **82** *—M.S. (12/15/2003)*

Pio Cesare 2001 Piodilei Chardonnay (Langhe) $40. **83** *—M.S. (12/15/2003)*

Pio Cesare 1998 (Cortese di Gavi) $20. **86** *(4/1/2000)*

Pio Cesare 2002 (Dolcetto d'Alba) $26. **86** *—M.S. (12/15/2003)*

Pio Cesare 2002 (Cortese di Gavi) $20. **83** *—M.S. (12/15/2003)*

Pio Cesare 2000 (Nebbiolo d'Alba) $23. **84** *—M.S. (12/15/2003)*

Pio Cesare 1999 Nebbiolo (Barbaresco) $71. This historic producer has developed into a reliable source for Barolo and Barbaresco, scoring uniformly well in our tastings. This offering boasts delicate aromas of cherries, leather, and tea. It's plump in the mouth, then finishes with firm tannins. Drink 2008–2016. **89** *(4/2/2004)*

Pio Cesare 1998 Nebbiolo (Barbaresco) $60. **89** *—M.S. (11/15/2002)*

Pio Cesare 1999 Il Bricco Nebbiolo (Barbaresco) $137. A rich, velvety wine that falls firmly into the modern camp without losing its regional or varietal identity. The 1999 Il Bricco boasts aromas of toast and vanilla layered against a backdrop of ripe cherries and plums, adding in notes of cinnamon and clove. It's rich and velvety in the mouth, with substantial, supple tannins on the long finish. **91** *—J.C. (11/15/2004)*

Pio Cesare 1999 Ornato Nebbiolo (Barolo) $110. A plush, soft Barolo, the '99 Ornato blends rich black cherry fruit with tobacco and dark earth. Coffee, hazelnut, and caramel notes add layers of sweetness without obscuring the fruit. Deceptively approachable, its best drinking probably lies between 2010 and 2020. **91** *(4/2/2004)*

Pio Cesare 1997 Ornato Nebbiolo (Barolo) $110. **90** *—R.V. (11/15/2002)*

Pio Cesare 1995 Ornato Nebbiolo (Barolo) $100. **87** *(7/1/2000)*

Pio Cesare 1998 Dolcetto D'Alba Piedmont Blend (Dolcetto d'Alba) $19. **85** *—L.W. (11/15/1999)*

ITALY

PLACIDO

Placido 1998 Pinot Grigio (Veneto) $8. **85 Best Buy** *(8/1/1999)*

Placido 1998 Sangiovese (Chianti) $8. **89 Best Buy** *(4/1/2001)*

PLANETA

Planeta 2001 Chardonnay (Sicilia) $16. **88** *—R.V. (10/1/2003)*

Planeta 1999 Merlot (Sicilia) $39. **87** *—C.S. (5/1/2002)*

Planeta 2003 Red Blend (Cerasuolo di Vittoria) $26. Exotic aromas of crushed lavender, violets, cherry, and molasses give hints as to what this wine is about. The palate, however, is a bit more mundane, albeit healthy in its own right. Bold plum and boysenberry is almost Zinfandel-like, while the finish is full and chewy. Drink now. **89** *—M.S. (7/1/2005)*

Planeta 2003 La Segreta Rosso (Sicilia) $17. Ripe and heady, with aromas of crushed cherry and berry jam. Tons of red fruit flows on the palate, and the result is a basket of unbridled, acid-jolted flavor. Finishes full, fruity and doused with chocolate. Very good as an everyday red. **87** *—M.S. (7/1/2005)*

Planeta 2002 La Segreta Rosso (Sicilia) $16. **88 Editors' Choice** *—M.S. (10/1/2003)*

Planeta 2001 Syrah (Sicilia) $38. **88** *—R.V. (10/1/2003)*

Planeta 2003 La Segreta Bianco (Sicilia) $17. Yellow in color and a touch syrupy on the nose, with plowing aromas of apricot and creamed corn. More tangy and leaner than expected in the mouth, with citrus and some vanilla oak. Not really going places, so drink now. **84** *—M.S. (7/1/2005)*

PLOZNER

Plozner 1999 Pinot Grigio (Friuli Grave) $10. **84** *—J.F. (9/1/2001)*

Plozner 1997 Pinot Grigio (Friuli Grave) $12. **84** *— (8/1/1999)*

PODERE IL PALAZZINO

Podere IL Palazzino 2002 Argenina (Chianti Classico) $20. Nicely smoked on the nose, with a leafy underbelly as well as leather and licorice. As a whole, it's a serious wine, with black cherry, vanilla and some tart cranberry comprising the palate. A touch rough around the edges, but overall it's pleasingly snappy and smooth. **88** *(4/1/2005)*

PODERE RUGGERI CORSINI

Podere Ruggeri Corsini 1999 Nebbiolo (Barolo) $45. Explosive aromatics are frankly a touch over the top, bursting with cherry, leather, and touches of cedar, vanilla, coffee, and maple syrup. It's very rich, big and bulky on the palate; gangly in its youth, it may settle down with some time in the bottle, but for now it's fruity and unformed. Try after 2009. **87** *(4/2/2004)*

PODERI ALASIA

Poderi Alasia 2000 Rive (Barbera d'Asti) $22. **91 Editors' Choice** *—M.S. (12/15/2003)*

Poderi Alasia 2003 Camillona Sauvignon Blanc (Monferrato) $28. Rather smoky and round, with aromas of baked peaches, melon, and cream. Adequately fruity on the palate, with mid-level flavors of grapefruit, melon, and peach. Finishes a little bit sticky, with a bitter note akin to citrus pith. **85** *(7/1/2005)*

PODERI ALDO CONTERNO

Poderi Aldo Conterno 1999 Cicala Nebbiolo (Barolo) $126. We found some inconsistency in the lineup from Aldo Conterno, but this wine flat-out rocks. The rich, intense aromas layer vanilla, coffee, and buttercream over a framework of tart cherries, which explode in the mouth into a panopoly of red fruits. The tannins are plentiful—creating a rich texture—yet supple, showing great ripeness on the finish. **93** *(4/2/2004)*

Poderi Aldo Conterno 1999 Colonello Nebbiolo (Barolo) $126. Dark plums, black cherries, and cola notes mingle effortlessly in this expressive offering. Tobacco, earth, and the merest hints of roasted meat add layers of complexity, while the mouthfeel is silky smooth without sacrificing any of the wine's fresh acidity. Drink 2005–2020. **91** *(4/2/2004)*

Poderi Aldo Conterno 1999 Monforte Bussia Nebbiolo (Barolo) $100. There's a lot to like in this wine: dried fruit and spices, leather and citrusy, floral aromatics. It's pump and relatively full-bodied, featuring cherry, cranberry, and milk chocolate flavors. Turns a bit too tart and citrusy on the finish, but it's a solid effort best consumed from 2008–2016. **87** *(4/2/2004)*

PODERI BRIZIO

Poderi Brizio 1998 (Brunello di Montalcino) $70. 91 *—M.S. (11/15/2003)*

PODERI COLLA

Poderi Colla 1997 (Barbera d'Alba) $18. 88 *(4/1/2000)*

Poderi Colla 1996 (Dolcetto d'Alba) $17. 83 *(4/1/2000)*

Poderi Colla 1999 Bussia Dardi Le Rose Nebbiolo (Barolo) $60. After revealing its identity, we confess to being slightly disappointed by this wine's showing. It was good, but not as good as we would have hoped. Modest cherry, tar, and earth flavors seem less concentrated than many of the other wines in the tasting, but the finish is long and complex, with intriguing notes of *sous-bois.* **86** *(4/2/2004)*

Poderi Colla 2000 Dardi Le Rosé Bussia Nebbiolo (Barolo) $64. A bit herbal on the nose, with other scents of cherries and dusty spices. It's more powerful in the mouth, where the cherries seem to expand and flow silkily across the palate. Finishes long and elegant, with a hint of chocolate. Uncommonly supple for Barolo, suggesting early drinkability. **89** *—J.C. (11/15/2004)*

Poderi Colla 2000 Roncaglie Nebbiolo (Barbaresco) $56. Hints of tea and flowers dress up the briary, berry-scented nose of this Barbaresco. Boasts fresh acidity, which accents the berry fruit flavors and offsets the rich notes of dark chocolate and tar. Drink now–2015. **87** *(4/2/2004)*

Poderi Colla 2000 Bricco del Drago Red Blend (Langhe) $35. This blend of 85% Dolcetto and 15% Nebbiolo is certainly soft and lush, but ends up tasting more like expensive oak than fruit. If vanilla, toast, and dried spices ring your chimes, go for it. **85** *—J.C. (11/15/2004)*

PODERI LUIGI EINAUDI

Poderi Luigi Einaudi 2002 (Dolcetto di Dogliani) $20. This is a solid Dolcetto, beginning with bold scents of plums and hints of surmaturité that are followed up on the palate by black, earthy flavors and more plummy fruit. Finishes long, with a dusting of fine tannins. **88** *—J.C. (11/15/2004)*

Poderi Luigi Einaudi 2000 Nebbiolo (Barolo) $73. Einaudi's 2000 Barolo is a big, mouthfilling wine, in keeping with the ripeness achieved that vintage. Boatloads of cherries and plums balance hints of vanilla and spice. Finishes with firm, yet fully ripe and supple tannins. Try after 2010. **90** *—J.C. (11/15/2004)*

Poderi Luigi Einaudi 1998 Nebbiolo (Barolo) $52. 91 *—C.S. (11/15/2002)*

Poderi Luigi Einaudi 1999 Costa Grimaldi Nebbiolo (Barolo) $81. Despite this wine's ample weight, it retains a remarkable sense of elegance and complexity, blending minor amounts of toast and vanilla with dried cherries, cinnamon, citrus peel, licorice, and dates. The tannins are well rounded and supple, the finish long. Drink now–2020. **91** *(4/2/2004)*

Poderi Luigi Einaudi 1999 Nei Cannubi Nebbiolo (Barolo) $93. Toast and vanilla aromas and flavors suggest a certain amount of new oak, but there are also ample quantities of cherry- and citrus-tinged fruit. Full-boded, with a tannic finish. Drink 2010–2020. **90** *(4/2/2004)*

Poderi Luigi Einaudi 2001 Luigi Einaudi Red Blend (Langhe) $73. An equiproportioned blend of Nebbiolo, Barbera, Cabernet Sauvignon, and Merlot, you can taste each of the components in the finished wine: earth, cherries, tobacco, and cassis, and plums, respectively. It's deceptively easy to drink, with broad, expansive tannins on the finish. You could drink it now, but it should be even better in a few years' time. **88** *—J.C. (11/15/2004)*

POGGIO AL MULINO

Poggio Al Mulino 1997 Pancarta Tuscan Blend (Toscana) $32. 91 *—M.S. (8/1/2002)*

POGGIO ANTICO

Poggio Antico 1999 (Brunello di Montalcino) $76. The color is literally purple, while the nose is layered with toasty oak and coffee atop pound cake and berry jam. The palate is powerful yet restrained, and with a mile-long finish propped up by jackhammer tannins, you just know it's built to last. This will drink fabulously in about six years. **94** *—M.S. (6/1/2004)*

Poggio Antico 1997 (Brunello di Montalcino) $60. 84 *—R.V. (8/1/2002)*

Poggio Antico 1999 Riserva (Brunello di Montalcino) $125. Here's a huge, stately wine with a brick-based structure and mounds of lovely oak that is already so well integrated you barely notice it. Quite tannic, and will require come cellaring. When you do drink it, expect warm flavors, liqueur-soaked berry fruit and a mile-long finish. Hold until 2010, at least. Imported by Empson (USA) Ltd. **95 Cellar Selection** *—M.S. (7/1/2005)*

Poggio Antico 2001 Madre (Toscana) $64. One sniff delivers heavenly aromas of liqueur, plum, and licorice. This 50/50 blend of Sangiovese and Cabernet represents the Super Tuscan concept at its best. The fruit is dynamite, the oak front and center, and the aging potential great. Hold for about five years then unleash an avalanche of class and flavor. **94 Editors' Choice** *—M.S. (10/1/2004)*

POGGIO BERTAIO

Poggio Bertaio 2000 Cimbolo Sangiovese (Umbria) $20. 90 *—M.S. (2/1/2003)*

POGGIO DEI POGGI

Poggio Dei Poggi 1997 (Chianti Classico) $13. 85 *(4/1/2001)*

POGGIO SALVI

Poggio Salvi 1998 (Chianti Colli Senesi) $15. 84 *(4/1/2001)*

POJER & SANDRI

Pojer & Sandri NV Cuvée Vino Spumante Extra Brut (Trento) $30. 82 *—M.S. (12/31/2002)*

Pojer & Sandri 2001 Traminer (Trentino) $18. 90 *—R.V. (7/1/2003)*

POLIZIANO

Poliziano 2002 Tuscan Blend (Vino Nobile di Montepulciano) $25. Smoky as a campfire, with heavy barrique-driven aromas along with lemon, bitter chocolate, and cherry. Model intensity, the hallmark of Poliziano, is on display across the palate, where firm tannins clamp down like a vise. Not a great wine, but plenty dark and manly. 87 *—M.S. (7/1/2005)*

Poliziano 2000 Tuscan Blend (Rosso di Montepulciano) $20. 87 *—M.S. (8/1/2002)*

Poliziano 1998 Asinone Tuscan Blend Vino Nobile di Montepulciano $45. 89 *(8/1/2002)*

Poliziano 1998 Tuscan Blend Vino Nobile di Montepulciano $29. 87 *(8/1/2002)*

POZZI

Pozzi 2001 Merlot (Delle Venezie) $9. 82 *(5/1/2003)*

Pozzi 2001 Rosso Nero d'Avola (Sicilia) $10. 83 *(10/1/2003)*

Pozzi 2001 Pinot Grigio (Delle Venezie) $10. 84 *—J.C. (7/1/2003)*

PRIMOSIC

Primosic 1997 Gmajne Pinot Grigio (Collio) $18. 85 *— (8/1/1999)*

PRINCIPESSA GAVIA

Principessa Gavia 2002 Cortese (Gavi) $12. 88 Best Buy *—M.S. (12/15/2003)*

PRINCIPIANO FERDINANDO

Principiano Ferdinando 1999 Boscareto Nebbiolo (Barolo) $60. Creamy and lush, this wine will be derided in some quarters for being too New Wave, but to us it strikes a fine balance between lush fruit and lavish oak without losing its identity as Barolo. Drink now–2015. 91 *(4/2/2004)*

PRODUTTORI COLTERENZIO

Produttori Colterenzio 1997 Pinot Grigio (Alto Adige) $12. 85 *(8/1/1999)*

Produttori Colterenzio 2001 Lafoa Sauvignon Blanc (Alto Adige) $35. 90 *—R.V. (7/1/2003)*

PRODUTTORI DEL BARBARESCO

Produttori del Barbaresco 1999 Nebbiolo (Barbaresco) $20. The region's famous co-op continues to turn out solid, traditionally styled wines. Although the crus are the ones to seek out, the blended wine is often a good value. This vintage seems built with firmer structure than in the past, finishing hard and tannic. Aromas and flavors are pretty amalgams of cherries, tea leaves, and stone fruits, but will they outlast the tannins? 86 *(4/2/2004)*

PROMESSA

Promessa 2003 Negroamaro (Puglia) $9. The sister project to A-Mano is a touch awkward, with loud aromas of red fruit and Kool-Aid. Luckily it finds its stride in the mouth, where you'll find berry liqueur, chocolate, and pepper. Slightly roasted on the finish. 86 Best Buy *—M.S. (2/1/2005)*

Promessa 2001 Rosso (Salento) $8. 88 Best Buy *—M.S. (12/15/2003)*

PROVOLO

Provolo 2001 Red Blend (Valpolicella) $12. 84 *(5/1/2003)*

Provolo 1997 Red Blend (Amarone della Valpolicella) $49. 89 *(5/1/2003)*

PRUNETO

Pruneto 1996 Riserva Sangiovese (Chianti Classico) $28. 82 *(4/1/2001)*

PRUNOTTO

Prunotto 1997 Pian Romualdo Barbera (Barbera d'Alba) $28. 90 *(4/1/2000)*

Prunotto 2004 (Moscato d'Asti) $21. An upfront and genuine dessert wine with a refreshing mineral prelude that yields to lush floral and stone fruit roundness. Zippy and slightly tart in the mouth with lots of foam and overall prettiness. Imported by Winebow. 88 *—M.L. (12/15/2005)*

Prunotto 1999 Nebbiolo (Barolo) $45. Tar and dried cherry aromas and flavors. This wine boasts a supple, creamy mouthfeel and a finish graced with notes of dark chocolate. Drink now–2010. 86 *(4/2/2004)*

Prunotto 1998 Bussia Nebbiolo (Piedmont) $70. 93 *—R.V. (11/15/2002)*

QUERCETO

Querceto 1997 (Chianti Classico) $11. 90 Best Buy *(7/1/2000)*

Querceto 2003 (Chianti) $9. Pleasant all the way, starting from the cedar, leather, and dark-fruit aromas, to the zippy cherry and raspberry palate, to the clean, spicy finish. Tart, linear, and refreshing, a Chianti in textbook proportions. 88 Best Buy *(4/1/2005)*

Querceto 2000 (Chianti Classico) $11. 83 *—M.S. (8/1/2002)*

Querceto 1996 Riserva (Chianti Classico) $18. 84 *(4/1/2001)*

Querceto 2001 Tuscan Blend (Chianti) $8. 86 Best Buy *—M.S. (11/15/2003)*

QUERCIAVALLE

Querciavalle 1999 Riserva Sangiovese (Chianti Classico) $28. Pungent and peppery, but also short on the nose and throughout. The palate offers herbs and tart cherry, while the one-note finish is gritty. Rather lean and snipped, with a slight pickled quality. 84 *(4/1/2005)*

QUINTARELLI

Quintarelli 1997 Red Blend (Amarone della Valpolicella Classico) $300. Big in alcohol at 16% and big in reputation; we liked this wine but did not really find it up to its icon status. The nose shows a bit of volatile acidity as well as a hint of horseradish, but it also delivers fine cherry and sugared cake notes. Rather intense in the mouth, with a touch of cherry skin and grit along with cola. Finishes long and correct. 89 *(11/1/2005)*

RAIMONDI

Raimondi 1998 Villa Monteleone Red Blend (Amarone della Valpolicella Classico) $49. Gets off the mark with some murk and earth, but clears up to display aromas of apple skin, horsehide, and dark fruits. Decent weight and only modest tannins create a chunky, almost syrupy personality that fosters flavors of chocolate, liqueur, and coffee. 88 *(11/1/2005)*

RASHI

Rashi 2003 (Moscato d'Asti) $11. Properly floral and orangey on the nose, with lightly sweet pineapple and orange juice flavors. Lacks a bit of vigor on the finish, but decent overall. 83 *—J.C. (4/1/2005)*

Rashi 1999 Select Nebbiolo (Barolo) $38. Quite toasty, with powdery tannins and moderate body. The wine holds back on the fruit, with a lean delivery. Herbs and hints of cherries are in evidence. Maybe cellaring will round things out. Kosher. 83 *—J.M. (4/3/2004)*

Rashi NV Kosher (Asti) $12. Neutral at first, and then a bit mealy and dusty. Sweet almost beyond belief, with over-ripe apricot and mango flavors. Lots of sugary sweetness at all points. A dessert wine (kosher) by default. 82 *—M.S. (6/1/2005)*

REMO FARINA

Remo Farina 2000 Red Blend (Amarone della Valpolicella Classico) $40. A touch piercing and spicy on the nose, with sweaty leather and wood notes. The flavor profile revolves around zesty red fruits like raspberry and strawberry, while the back end is mildly toasty. 86 *(11/1/2005)*

Remo Farina 1998 Corte Conti Cavalli Red Blend (Rosso del Veronese) $45. 88 *(5/1/2003)*

Remo Farina 2000 Ripasso Red Blend (Valpolicella Classico Superiore) $13. 87 Best Buy *(5/1/2003)*

Remo Farina 1999 Soave Classico Superiore $NA. The nose mixes aromas of Wrigley's spearmint gum and peaches. The body is on the full side, with bright white stone-fruit flavors, particularly white peaches. Some grapefruit works it's way in there, too. Although it's fairly nondescript, it offers all the traditional flavors of this regional white wine and vital acidity. Finishes warm and clean. 86 *—M.S. (1/1/2004)*

RENATO RATTI

Renato Ratti 1997 Torriglione (Barbera d'Alba) $14. 88 *(4/1/2000)*

Renato Ratti 1998 Conca Marcenasco Nebbiolo (Piedmont) $62. 95 Editors' Choice *—R.V. (11/15/2002)*

Renato Ratti 1998 Rocche Marcenasco Nebbiolo (Piedmont) $60. 96 Cellar Selection *—R.V. (11/15/2002)*

RENZO MASI

Renzo Masi 1999 (Chianti Rufina) $8. 85 Best Buy *(4/1/2001)*

RICCARDO ARRIGONI

Riccardo Arrigoni 2003 Ampelos Vermentino (Colli di Luni) $17. This Ligurian Vermentino is very clear and light, almost the polar opposite of the meaty, warmer styles that come from Sardegna or the Maremma. But still it pours on lime, mineral, and stony notes, and ultimately it's a healthy, crisp wine that will cut through vinaigrettes and garlic like a hot knife through butter. 86 *—M.S. (8/1/2004)*

RIECINE

Riecine 1997 Riserva (Chianti Classico) $35. 90 *(4/1/2001)*

RISECCOLI

Riseccoli 1997 Riserva (Chianti Classico) $26. 90 *(4/1/2001)*

RIVE DELLA CHIESA

Rive Della Chiesa NV Frizzante Prosecco (Colli Trevigiani) $10. 85 *—M.S. (6/1/2003)*

Rive Della Chiesa NV Spumante Extra Dry Prosecco (Montello e Colli Asolani) $14. Austere and minerally on the nose, with hints of yeastiness and citrus. This is much less fruity and floral than most Proseccos, yielding instead flavors of stones and limes. The slightly chalky finish is clean and refreshing. 87 *—J.C. (12/15/2004)*

RIVETTO

Rivetto 2002 Ercolino (Dolcetto d'Alba) $15. 86 *—M.S. (12/15/2003)*

Rivetto 1999 Giulin Nebbiolo (Barolo) $38. A pretty, delicate, feminine style of Barolo, with minty, herbal hints layered over black cherry fruit. The mouthfeel is supple, never overpowering, finishing with soft, chewy tannins. Drink now–2010. **88** *(4/2/2004)*

Rivetto 2001 Lirano (Nebbiolo d'Alba) $11. 85 *—M.S. (12/15/2003)*

RIZZI

Rizzi 2000 Boito Nebbiolo (Barbaresco) $45. This plump, moderately rich wine impressed with its complex scents of leather, asphalt, and fennel that accent plum and cherry fruit. Turns chewy and tarry on the finish, suggesting decent longevity; try after 2008. **92** *(4/2/2004)*

ROCCA

Rocca 2000 Mitico Red Blend (Salento) $22. Lots of alcohol as well as a syrupy, sweet red that is so rich and unctuous that it's tough to sip. For the prune flavor and outright size it's almost worth taking a look. But beware. **83** *—M.S. (10/1/2004)*

ROCCA DELLE MACÍE

Rocca delle Macíe 2002 (Chianti Classico) $16. The red fruit on the nose conjures memories of lollipops and/or Jell-O, and there's just enough herbal rusticity to offset the wine's candied nature. In the mouth, plum, raspberry, and black cherry flavors are textbook typical, while the finish is round and solid. **86** *(4/1/2005)*

Rocca delle Macíe 2000 Riserva (Chianti Classico) $22. More herbal and spicy than fruity, as the nose shows cumin and molasses in spades. Seems a touch stewed, with flavors of black-cherry jam, dates, and brown sugar. A heavyweight in that the palate is soft and the body creamy. **86** *(4/1/2005)*

Rocca delle Macíe 1997 Riserva (Chianti Classico) $21. 89 *(8/1/2001)*

Rocca delle Macíe 1997 Riserva di Fizzano (Chianti Classico) $25. 90 *(8/1/2001)*

Rocca delle Macíe 1999 Rubizzo Sangiovese (Toscana) $12. 87 Best Buy *(8/1/2001)*

Rocca delle Macíe 1999 Campomaccione Tuscan Blend (Morellino di Scansano) $14. 87 Best Buy *(8/1/2001)*

Rocca delle Macíe 2003 (Vernaccia di San Gimignano) $11. Light in color, with aromas of pear and applesauce. Fairly soft and bland on the palate, with a hint of white pepper. Also shows some apple and white grapefruit. **84** *—M.S. (8/1/2004)*

Rocca delle Macíe 1999 White Blend (Orvieto Classico) $10. 84 *(8/1/2001)*

ROCCA DI FABBRI

Rocca di Fabbri 1999 (Sagrantino di Montefalco) $35. 88 *—C.S. (2/1/2002)*

Rocca di Fabbri 2001 (Sagrantino di Montefalco) $NA. Under this leadership of the Vitali sisters, Rocca di Fabbri has released a gorgeous ruby red Sagrantino with loads of spice, tar, dried prunes and vanilla. This grape makes some of the most beautifully colored wines in Italy. Twelve months in stainless steel and 18 months in wood, of which 70% in oak and 30% in barrique. **88** *—M.L. (9/1/2005)*

ROCCA DI MONTEGROSSI

Rocca di Montegrossi 2001 (Chianti Classico) $23. The bouquet is good, with aromas of rubber, spice, leather, and plum-style fruit. Seems a little grippy and starchy on the palate, where big tannins take over and mask the rest of the show. Ultra-firm and tannic on the back end, where more grab than flavor is on display. **86** *(4/1/2005)*

Rocca di Montegrossi 1998 Riserva (Chianti Classico) $NA. 85 *—R.V. (8/1/2002)*

Rocca di Montegrossi 1999 Vigneto San Marcellino (Chianti Classico) $40. Dark and roasted on the nose, but short on the palate. The tannins are green and rock-hard, yet there's some meatiness and plum-based darkness to the flavors. In the end, however, it's a touch rough and unyielding. **84** *(4/1/2005)*

ROCCHE CASTAMAGNA

Rocche Castamagna 1997 Annunziata (Barbera d'Alba) $20. 86 *(4/1/2000)*

Rocche Castamagna 1996 Rocche delle Rocche (Barbera d'Alba) $27. 89 *(4/1/2000)*

Rocche Castamagna 2001 (Dolcetto d'Alba) $13. 90 Best Buy *—M.S. (12/15/2003)*

Rocche Castamagna 1998 Bricco Francesco Nebbiolo (Barolo) $50. Seems a bit leathery and potentially dull at first, but it really opens up nicely to reveal sweetly ripe black cherries and dried figs. Picks up hints of oranges and tea leaves on the finish. Drink 2005–2015. **87** *(4/2/2004)*

ROMOLO BUCCELLATO

Romolo Buccellato 1999 Tre Vigne Frappato (Sicily) $11. 82 *—M.S. (12/15/2003)*

RONCHI DI GIANCARLO ROCCA

Ronchi di Giancarlo Rocca 1999 Nebbiolo (Barbaresco) $40. Shows sturdy dried fruit—dates and prunes—but also fresher notes of cherries and orange peel along with a large helping of rich earthy complexity. Plump on the palate, but firm on the finish, where it shows ample tannins. Try in 2010 and beyond. **92** *(4/2/2004)*

RONCO DE TASSI

Ronco de Tassi 1997 Pinot Grigio (Colli) $15. 84 — *(8/1/1999)*

RONCO DEL GNEMIZ

Ronco del Gnemiz 2003 Sauvignon (Colli Orientali del Friuli) $23. Interesting on the nose because it mixes sweet, spicy elements with more standard citrus and mineral. Fairly ripe and rich across the palate, where melon, pineapple, and honey flavors run sweet. Has a bit of pop to the finish but not a ton. Hefty in terms of weight. 87 *(7/1/2005)*

ROSA DEL GOLFO

Rosa Del Golfo 1997 Portulano Red Blend (Salento) $15. 88 *—J.F. (5/1/2002)*

ROTARI

Rotari 2000 Brut Riserva (Trento) $14. Pungent and aggressive. The nose offers hints of hard cider and toast, while the palate is crisp and fresh. Good mouthfeel, but lacks depth of flavor. 84 *—M.S. (6/1/2005)*

Rotari 1995 Brut Riserva (Trento) $15. 87 Best Buy *(7/1/2000)*

Rotari 1998 Brut Riserva (Trento) $13. 86 *—J.C. (12/31/2003)*

Rotari NV Blanc de Noir Pinot Noir (Trento) $11. Pink in color, with a light, fading bubble bead. Simple in terms of aromatics, showing a hint of peach and berry. Zesty stone-fruit flavors are offset by some drying soda-cracker notes. Finishes clean and zesty. 86 Best Buy *—M.S. (12/15/2004)*

Rotari NV Arte Italiana Brut (Trento) $11. Gold in color, with aromas of wheat bread and Golden Delicious apples. Lots of fresh peach, apple, and tangerine on the palate make for a pleasing flavor profile, while it finishes full and toasty. Nothing overwhelming, but rock solid as a whole. 87 Best Buy *—M.S. (12/15/2005)*

Rotari NV Demi-Sec (Trento) $12. Definitely off-dry in character, with caramel corn, doughnut, and apples on the nose. Additional applesauce flavors blend with canned pear to create a sweet, sugary, lingering whole. Not bad but simple and candied. 84 *—M.S. (12/15/2005)*

RUFFINO

Ruffino 1997 Greppone Mazzi Brunello (Brunello di Montalcino) $60. 90 *—M.S. (8/1/2002)*

Ruffino 1998 La Solatia Chardonnay (Toscana) $20. 86 *(3/1/2002)*

Ruffino 2002 Lumina Pinot Grigio (Venezia Giulia) $13. Aromas of pear, anise, and lemondrops lead into a bracingly citric wine. A modest amount of spice-driven complexity makes it more than just a bracing mouthful of acid. Finishes tart and clean. 85 *—J.C. (1/1/2004)*

Ruffino 1997 Modus Red Blend (Toscana) $40. 88 *(3/1/2002)*

Ruffino 1997 Tenuta Lodola Nuova Red Blend (Vino Nobile di Montepulciano) $17. 88 Editors' Choice *(3/1/2002)*

Ruffino 2000 Fonte al Sole Sangiovese (Toscana) $8. 84 Best Buy *(3/1/2002)*

Ruffino 2001 Riserva Ducale Sangiovese (Chianti Classico) $27. Rubber, sulfur, and mushroom are tough starting aromas, but with time it opens to offer cherry, plum, and tomato. Fairly forward and edgy, with brisk tannins. Slightly green at the center. 85 *(4/1/2005)*

Ruffino 1997 Riserva Ducale Tan Label Sangiovese (Chianti Classico) $20. 89 *(4/1/2001)*

Ruffino 1997 Tenuta Santedame Sangiovese (Chianti Classico) $18. 87 *(4/1/2001)*

Ruffino 1998 Tenuta Santedame Tuscan Blend (Chianti Classico) $16. 85 *(3/1/2002)*

RUGGERI GIULIANO

Ruggeri Giuliano 2001 Giustino B. Extra Dry (Prosecco di Valdobbiadene) $20. 87 *—M.S. (6/1/2003)*

Ruggeri Giuliano 1999 Rosso (Montefalco) $15. 84 *—M.S. (2/1/2003)*

SALADINI PILASTRI

Saladini Pilastri 2003 White Blend (Falerio) $10. The Falerio DOC is in the Marches region of Italy. This white, a blend of Trebbiano, Pecorino, Passerina, and Chardonnay is rich and full-bodied, flavored with fresh almonds, peaches, and a touch of cilantro. There's very intense, ripe fruit here; the wine is perfect to serve with fish or white meat. 88 Best Buy *—R.V. (11/15/2004)*

SALICUTTI

Salicutti 1999 (Rosso di Montalcino) $33. 90 *—M.S. (8/1/2002)*

SALVATORE MOLETTIERI

Salvatore Molettieri 1996 Vigna Cinque Querce Aglianico (Taurasi) $32. 85 *—C.S. (5/1/2002)*

SALVIANO

Salviano 2003 White Blend (Orvieto Classico Superiore) $13. Fairly spicy for an Orvieto, with aromas of pepper, wasabi, and green herbs in addition to almond and mild white fruits. Nice on the palate, with just enough acid push so that it avoids blandness. Mild apple and peach flavors lead to a round, almondy finish. 85 *—M.S. (7/1/2005)*

SAN ANGELO

San Angelo 1998 Single Vineyard Pinot Grigio (Toscana) $13. 87 *(8/1/1999)*

SAN CARLO

San Carlo 1999 (Brunello di Montalcino) $NA. The closed nose offers a slight paint or chemical aroma that hopefully will subside with aging. Very tight and dry on the palate, with cherry notes and strong hints of black pepper. Fairly lean and basic Brunello, with medium-level oak. Of note: Very little of this wine (about 20 cases) makes it to the U.S. 86 *—M.S. (6/1/2004)*

SAN FABIANO

San Fabiano 1998 Sangiovese (Chianti) $8. 85 *(4/1/2001)*

SAN FABIANO CALCINAIA

San Fabiano Calcinaia 2001 Sangiovese (Chianti Classico) $23. 86 *—M.S. (11/15/2003)*

San Fabiano Calcinaia 1998 (Chianti Classico) $18. 87 *(4/1/2001)*

San Fabiano Calcinaia 1997 Riserva Cellole (Chianti Classico) $28. 87 *(4/1/2001)*

San Fabiano Calcinaia 2000 Cerviolo Rosso Tuscan Blend (Tuscany) $65. 88 *—M.S. (11/15/2003)*

San Fabiano Calcinaia 1999 Cerviolo (Toscana) $45. 90 *—M.S. (12/31/2002)*

San Fabiano Calcinaia 1997 Cerviolo Tuscan Blend (Toscana) $45. 90 *—J.F. (9/1/2001)*

SAN FELICE

San Felice 2000 (Chianti Classico) $18. 86 *(1/1/2004)*

San Felice 1999 Il Grigio Riserva (Chianti Classico) $26. 89 *(1/1/2004)*

San Felice 1999 Poggio Rosso Riserva (Chianti Classico) $50. Starts with attractive cherry, blackberry, and charred bacon aromas, but turns more monotone and tart than expected once you get down to drinking it. One of our panelists found "clipped, narrow" flavors and sharp "one-note" acids, while another was more positive, locking in on the wine's chewy tannins and power. 86 *(4/1/2005)*

SAN FRANCESCO

San Francesco 1999 Rosso Gaglioppo (Ciró Classico) $12. 80 *—C.S. (5/1/2002)*

SAN GIUSEPPE

San Giuseppe 2003 Pinot Grigio (Piave) $18. Minerally aromas, backed by modest pear fruit and flavors more reminiscent of earth and wet gravel. Tangy and clean on the finish. 83 *—J.C. (12/31/2004)*

San Giuseppe 2001 Pinot Grigio (Veneto) $9. 82 *—J.C. (7/1/2003)*

SAN GIUSTO A RENTENNANO

San Giusto a Rentennano 1998 (Chianti Classico) $19. 92 Editors' Choice *(4/1/2001)*

SAN MICHELE EPPAN

San Michele Eppan 2002 Sanct Valentin Pinot Bianco (Alto Adige) $30. 88 *—R.V. (7/1/2003)*

SAN PATRIGNANO

San Patrignano 2001 Montepirolo Cabernet Sauvignon (Colli di Rimini) $45. This Cabernet starts with mild but inoffensive coconut aromas that are backed by pungent red fruit and a hint of herbaceousness. Plum, blackberry, and chocolate flavors dominate, but there's a shock of oregano in there, too. Lasting on the finish, and saturated. Not stylish but sound. 87 *—M.S. (7/1/2005)*

San Patrignano 2001 Avi Sangiovese (Sangiovese di Romagna) $45. Spicy and sweet, with a full blast of oak on the nose. Palate flavors of vanilla, boysenberry, cinnamon, and cola work well as a team, while the textured finish offers leather, pepper, and some wayward oak. A chewy, chunky red that should satisfy on most occasions. 87 *—M.S. (7/1/2005)*

SAN QUIRICO

San Quirico 1999 (Chianti Colli Senesi) $12. 86 *(4/1/2001)*

SANDRA LOTTI

Sandra Lotti 2000 Saporita Tuscan Blend (Toscana) $23. The nose opens with a standard offering of leather, mint, and berries. The palate is plump in terms of fruit, but the feel turns skinny and firm. Has good flavors but seems a bit jumpy and hot. 86 *—M.S. (10/1/2004)*

SANGERVASIO

Sangervasio 1998 Le Stoppie (Chianti Colli Pisani) $9. 85 Best Buy *(4/1/2001)*

SANT' ELENA

Sant' Elena 1998 Pinot Grigio (Venezia Giulia) $15. 86 *(8/1/1999)*

SANT'EVASIO

Sant'Evasio 1995 Nebbiolo (Barolo) $34. **91** *—J.C. (9/1/2001)*

SANTA MARGHERITA

Santa Margherita 2003 Chardonnay (Veneto Orientale) $16. Simple and fruity, with modest aromas and flavors of pineapple and grapefruit. Finishes crisp and clean. **83** *—J.C. (12/31/2004)*

Santa Margherita 2001 Versato Merlot (Veneto) $21. Aromas are dominated by scents of coffee, chocolate, and tobacco, but this wine reveals more fruit on the palate, where tart cherries kick in. It's soft and light—a pretty wine, not a blockbuster, with modest tannins on the finish. Drink now. **85** *—J.C. (12/31/2004)*

Santa Margherita 2003 Pinot Grigio (Alto Adige) $25. America's most recognized brand of Pinot Grigio is crisply focused this year, with almond paste and ripe apple aromas backed by fresh apple and pear flavors. Clean and citrusy on the finish. **86** *—J.C. (12/31/2004)*

Santa Margherita 1998 Pinot Grigio (Valdadige) $19. **84** *— (8/1/1999)*

Santa Margherita NV Brut (Prosecco di Valdobbiadene) $21. The lemon-lime nose is true to form, and the palate is perfectly zesty, with citrus dominating a full package of Prosecco-like flavors. Slightly sweet later on, which carries the finish. Plucky and solid. **88** *—M.S. (12/15/2005)*

SANTA SOFIA

Santa Sofia 2000 Red Blend (Amarone della Valpolicella Classico) $55. Starts out sly and smooth and gains complexity as it opens. The bouquet is classy, with scents of black cherry, fine leather, and spice. Perfectly balanced on the palate, and sporting a classic mix of cherry, plum, and vanilla flavors. Feels great at all stops, with some chocolate to the ever-lasting finish. Can drink now or hold for up to 10 years. **92** *(11/1/2005)*

Santa Sofia 1998 Gioé Red Blend (Amarone della Valpolicella Classico) $72. Intriguing and complex, with alluring aromas of campfire, citrus peel, cinnamon, and cedar. Offers fine fruit and highly commendable balance, as the palate is juiced with acidity, cherry, and raspberry flavors, and more. Smoky on the finish, with a bit of sweet caramel. **92** *(11/1/2005)*

Santa Sofia 1998 Monte Gradella Red Blend (Valpolicella Classico Superiore) $20. **86** *(5/1/2003)*

SANTADI

Santadi 1998 Grotta Rossa (Cannonau di Sardegna) $10. **85 Best Buy** *—C.S. (5/1/2002)*

Santadi 1997 Shardana Red Blend (Valli di Porto Pino) $24. **90 Editors' Choice** *—C.S. (5/1/2002)*

SANTI

Santi 1999 Merlot (Delle Venezie) $10. **83** *(5/1/2003)*

Santi 2001 Sortesele Pinot Grigio (Trentino) $12. **83** *—J.C. (7/1/2003)*

Santi 1996 Proemio Red Blend (Amarone della Valpolicella) $51. **91** *—J.F. (9/1/2001)*

SANTINI

Santini NV Asti Spumante $7. **84** *—P.G. (12/31/2000)*

SARACCO

Saracco 2004 (Moscato d'Asti) $15. Boasts frothy mousse, good persistency, and a clearly defined mineral tenor backed by sweet green apple, honey, jasmine, and a touch of clove. Sweet peach cream in the mouth makes this semi-sparkler an ideal match for baked desserts. **90 Best Buy** *—M.L. (12/15/2005)*

SARTARELLI

Sartarelli 2003 (Verdicchio dei Castelli di Jesi Classico) $13. Opens with plump pear and peach aromas. Smooth in the mouth, with layered almond, pear, pepper, and ocean-influenced flavors. Quite deep and big on the finish, and as a whole it speaks well for the region and grape type. **87** *—M.S. (8/1/2004)*

SARTORI

Sartori 1991 Corte Bra (Amarone della Valpolicella) $40. **94** *—M.G. (5/1/1999)*

Sartori 1997 Merlot (Friuli Venezia Giulia) $9. **83** *—M.S. (9/1/2000)*

Sartori 2003 Pinot Grigio (Delle Venezie) $9. A pleasant, medium-weight cocktail white, Sartori's 2003 Pinot Grigio boasts hints of blanched almonds alongside more assertive flavors of peaches and pears. Picks up an anise note on the citrusy finish. **85 Best Buy** *—J.C. (12/31/2004)*

Sartori 2001 Red Blend (Amarone della Valpolicella) $34. Medium in force, with modest tannins and a lot of crispness. Approachable and easy, with date, dried cherry, and liqueur-like flavors. An unflappable, solid wine, but not overwhelming in any way. It's juicy, structured and pretty easy to wrap yourself around. **88** *(11/1/2005)*

Sartori 1995 Cent'Anni Red Blend (Valpolicella) $33. **84** *—M.S. (9/1/2000)*

SASSO

Sasso 1997 Covo dei Briganti (Aglianico del Vulture) $15. **85** *—C.S. (5/1/2002)*

SCARLATTA

Scarlatta 1997 Merlot (Veneto) $5. **81** *—M.S. (9/1/2000)*

SCARPA

Scarpa 1990 Tettimorra Nebbiolo (Barolo) $NA. **81** *—R.V. (11/15/2002)*

SCOPETANI

Scopetani 2003 Angelicus (Chianti) $8. Dark and manly from the get-go, with aromas of melted brown sugar, black cherry, and charbroiled beef. Next up you'll encounter fresh red fruit, peppy acids, and enough body to provide balance and a perceived creaminess. Very easy to like. **89 Best Buy** *(4/1/2005)*

SEGHESIO

Seghesio 1997 Vigneto della Chiesa (Barbera d'Alba) $30. **91** *(4/1/2000)*

SELLA & MOSCA

Sella & Mosca 1996 Raím Red Blend (Isola dei Nuraghi) $12. **85** *—M.N. (12/31/2000)*

Sella & Mosca 1995 Tanca Farra Red Blend (Sardinia) $16. **88** *—M.N. (12/31/2000)*

Sella & Mosca 2003 La Cala (Vermentino di Sardegna) $13. At less than 12% alcohol, this is a lighter-styled Vermentino. Nevertheless, it has forward aromas of tropical fruit and flowers, and then flavors of tangy apple, papaya, and lime. It's snappy on the tongue and clean. Very easygoing and solid. **87** *—M.S. (8/1/2004)*

SELVO DEL MORO

Selvo del Moro 2001 (Chianti Classico) $22. Leathery and lean, which makes it a bit dull. Generic plum and berry fruit flavors come across mildly tart, while the finish is open but unexciting. Standard stuff that doesn't offend. **85** *(4/1/2005)*

SETTE PONTI

Sette Ponti 2001 Crognolo Sangiovese (Toscana) $32. Huge and meaty, with round berry and plum aromas propped up by a healthy load of lumber. The palate is loaded with plum and chocolate, while the finish is ultra-rich and smooth, bordering on buttery. In the end it all comes together. Give this Sangiovese ample air and it's sure to please. **91 Editors' Choice** *—M.S. (10/1/2004)*

Sette Ponti 1999 Oreno Tuscan Blend (Toscana) $90. **91** *—M.S. (8/1/2002)*

SIGNANO

Signano 2002 (Vernaccia di San Gimignano) $17. The funky nose is hard to peg; there's some cantaloupe but not much else is recognizable. Fortunately, good acidity keeps the mouthfeel fresh, while flavors of orange, lemon and grapefruit are a bit high-toned. Decent on the finish. **84** *—M.S. (8/1/2004)*

SINFAROSA

Sinfarosa 1998 Zinfandel (Puglia) $24. **82** *—C.S. (5/1/2002)*

SIRO PACENTI

Siro Pacenti 1999 (Brunello di Montalcino) $NA. A stunningly complete, cool-as-can-be modern wine with great color, lush plum and berry fruit, and very little of the earth and leather notes that some Brunello-istas may be seeking. However, if you like texture, sublime flavors of chocolate and charcoal, and perfectly integrated oak, this is for you. Consider drinking in 2005 or 2006. **95** *—M.S. (6/1/2004)*

SOLARIA

Solaria 2000 (Brunello di Montalcino) $70. Stout but intoxicating, with floral aromas along with hints of maple, leather, and pepper. For some it might come across heavy, as the ultra-ripe plum and cherry fruit almost veers toward medicinal. Fortunately, however, it holds the line. Powerful and heady, but plenty elegant. **92** *—M.S. (7/1/2005)*

Solaria 2002 Sangiovese (Rosso di Montalcino) $29. This fine producer chose not to make Brunello in 2002 due to below-average harvest conditions, so its Rosso benefited. The wine delivers sweet prune and chocolate aromas prior to a stylish, delicious palate. This one is really easy to drink and should be a no-brainer for restaurateurs. **89** *—M.S. (6/1/2004)*

SOLDIMELA

Soldimela 1999 Sangiovese Grosso (Monteregio di Massa Maritima) $8. **87 Best Buy** *—M.M. (11/15/2001)*

SOLDO

Soldo 2001 Cabernet Sauvignon (Veneto) $6. **83** *(5/1/2003)*

Soldo 2001 Pinot Grigio (Veneto) $6. **83** *—J.C. (7/1/2003)*

Soldo 2000 Red Blend (Valpolicella) $6. **85 Best Buy** *(5/1/2003)*

SORELLE BRONCA

Sorelle Bronca NV Extra Dry (Prosecco di Valdobbiadene) $14. **86** *—J.C. (12/31/2003)*

SPADINA

Spadina 2002 Una Rosa Signature Nero d'Avola (Sicily) $15. Dark and intense, with lemony oak on the nose that you can't miss. In the mouth, licorice, plum, and pepper wrestle with some oakiness, but the whole is successful. Finishes with tight tannins that create a thinning sensation. More good than flawed. **88** *—M.S. (2/1/2005)*

SPANO

Spano 1996 Annata Red Blend (Salento) $40. 84 —*C.S. (5/1/2002)*

SPERI

Speri 2001 Red Blend (Amarone della Valpolicella Classico) $60. Pitch black and full of asphalt, tar, coffee, and meat aromas. The feel right now is a touch raw due to its youth, but as it sizzles and scours it shows masculine, smoky flavors and a lot of bitter chocolate. Comes on with guns blazing and full tannins. Needs several years to mellow out. **91** *(11/1/2005)*

Speri 2003 La Roverina Red Blend (Valpolicella Classico Superiore) $16. A garnet-red wine with a vegetal touch and some white mushroom backed by raspberry jam and red cherry. Sits well in the mouth with a medium build and finish but lower acidity. **86** —*M.L. (9/1/2005)*

Speri 1998 Sant'Urbano Red Blend (Valpolicella Classico Superiore) $22. 85 *(5/1/2003)*

SPORTOLETTI

Sportoletti 2004 Grechetto (Assisi) $12. Brilliant straw-yellow color and layers of delicate aromas that span cut grass, stone fruits, and white flowers. Elegance continues in the mouth but ends on a suddenly tart note that works well in this case. Vines benefit from reddish, calcium-rich soils. Fermented in steel tanks. Imported by Winebow. **87** —*M.L. (9/1/2005)*

Sportoletti 2000 Villa Fidelia Rosso Red Blend (Umbria) $55. **92 Editors' Choice** —*C.S. (2/1/2003)*

ST. MICHAEL EPPAN

St. Michael Eppan 2000 Sanct Valentin Sauvignon Blanc (Alto Adige) $28. 87 *(8/1/2002)*

STELLA

Stella 2000 Pinot Grigio (Umbria) $6. 87 —*P.G. (11/15/2001)*

STIVAL

Stival 2000 Cabernet Sauvignon (Veneto) $6. 85 *(5/1/2002)*

Stival 2000 Merlot (Veneto) $6. **86 Best Buy** *(5/1/2002)*

Stival 2003 Pinot Grigio (Veneto) $6. Hints of almond paste and nectarine on the nose are followed by clean, fruity flavors of stone fruits, oranges, and grapefruit. A bit low in acidity, but user-friendly, with notes of almond reprising on the finish. **84 Best Buy** —*J.C. (12/31/2004)*

STRACCALI

Straccali 2003 (Chianti) $9. Pungent and rubbery, with aromas of leather and pie cherry. Tart red fruit is about all you get from the palate, which has a stripped-down but solid texture. Juicy and simple, with serious acidity. **84** *(4/1/2005)*

Straccali 1999 Sangiovese (Chianti) $10. 85 *(4/1/2001)*

TALAMONTI

Talamonti 2004 Trebì (Trebbiano d'Abruzzo) $NA. Started in 2001, Cantine Talamonti is determined to put the spotlight on the region of Abruzzo and its native grapes. Winemaker Lucio Matricardi has produced a crisp white bursting with flowers, apples, and subtle mineral notes. **86** —*M.L. (9/1/2005)*

TALENTI

Talenti 1997 (Brunello di Montalcino) $NA. **95 Editors' Choice** —*R.V. (8/1/2002)*

Talenti 1999 Riserva (Brunello di Montalcino) $85. A touch of barnyard at first gives way to deep, dark fruit that's spun tight on the palate. As it opens, bigger berry and black cherry flavors emerge. Tight and tannic on the back palate, with an uncomplicated finish. An excellent wine, but one competing in a talented field. **90** —*M.S. (7/1/2005)*

TASCA D'ALMERITA

Tasca d'Almerita 1998 Cabernet Sauvignon (Sicily) $48. 85 —*C.S. (5/1/2002)*

Tasca d'Almerita 1998 Rosso Del Conte Nero d'Avola (Sicily) $42. 91 —*C.S. (5/1/2002)*

Tasca d'Almerita 1999 Cygnus Red Blend (Sicilia) $21. **90 Editors' Choice** *(6/1/2003)*

Tasca d'Almerita 2002 Regaleali Rosso Red Blend (Sicilia) $14. Nice and jammy; the quintessential ripe, easy quaffer. Plenty of black fruit and licorice cover the bouquet, followed by deep plum and black-cherry fruit. The finish is fat, full, and continuous. A fine effort among its type. **88** —*M.S. (2/1/2005)*

Tasca d'Almerita 2001 Regaleali Rosso Red Blend (Sicilia) $16. 84 —*R.V. (10/1/2003)*

Tasca d'Almerita 2000 Rosso del Conte Red Blend (Sicilia) $37. 91 —*R.V. (10/1/2003)*

Tasca d'Almerita 2001 Rosé di Regaleali Rosé Blend (Sicilia) $11. **90 Best Buy** *(6/1/2003)*

Tasca d'Almerita 2001 Leone d'Almerita White Blend (Sicilia) $15. 87 *(6/1/2003)*

Tasca d'Almerita 2004 Regaleali Bianco White Blend (Sicilia) $13. Delightful and delicately pale blend of three native Sicilian grapes: Insolia, Grecanico, and Catarratto. Hands off to the winemaker who extracted intense, jasmine and citrus blossom characteristics and pink grapefruit acidity in the mouth. An extremely feminine wine. **90 Best Buy** —*M.L. (9/1/2005)*

Tasca d'Almerita 2001 Regaleali Bianco White Blend (Sicilia) $11. 86 *(6/1/2003)*

Tasca d'Almerita 1998 Regaleali Bianco White Blend (Sicily) $10. 90 *(11/15/1999)*

TASSAROLO

Tassarolo 1996 Vigneto Alborina (Gavi) $30. 89 *(11/1/1999)*

TAURINO

Taurino 1998 Riserva Negroamaro (Salice Salentino) $10. 85 Best Buy —*C.S. (5/1/2002)*

Taurino 1996 Salice Salentino Riserva Red Blend (Apulia) $9. 90 *(11/15/1999)*

TENIMENTI ANGELINI

Tenimenti Angelini 2000 (Brunello di Montalcino) $64. Open knit, with raw cherry aromas. This wine has sweet and common flavors, with a fresh, fast mouthfeel. It's fairly chocolaty on the finish, with a hint of cherry cough drop. Good, but fails to stand out in a high-class field. **87** —*M.S. (7/1/2005)*

Tenimenti Angelini 1999 Vigna del Lago Riserva (Brunello di Montalcino) $134. Kicks off with a lot of maple, coffee, and espresso, and in the mouth the tannins are spiky and aggressive. Nonetheless, there's dynamite classic fruit here and structure to burn. A classic Brunello with a rugged edge. Needs five to ten years on its side. **92 Cellar Selection** —*M.S. (7/1/2005)*

Tenimenti Angelini 1999 San Leonino Riserva (Chianti Classico) $34. Plenty of wood to the nose, leaving aromas of smoke, cedar, leather, and lemon. That tangy, barrique-based lemon character lasts through the cherry-dominated palate and onto the juicy finish. With a bit less citrus and more harmony it would be right up there with the best. **87** *(4/1/2005)*

Tenimenti Angelini 2001 La Villa Tuscan Blend (Vino Nobile di Montepulciano) $41. Weighty yet bright, with aromas of charred hamburger, leather, and plum/berry jam. Complex and interwoven on the palate, with kirsch, cassis, red plum, and chocolate flavors. Finishes smooth and stylish. Textbook stuff; hold until 2007. **90** —*M.S. (7/1/2005)*

TENUTA A GREPPONE MAZZI

Tenuta a Greppone Mazzi 1997 (Brunello di Montalcino) $70. 89 —*R.V. (8/1/2002)*

TENUTA BELGUARDO

Tenuta Belguardo 1999 Sangiovese (Morellino di Scansano) $20. 89 —*M.S. (8/1/2002)*

Tenuta Belguardo 2001 Serrata di Belguardo Tuscan Blend (Maremma) $44. A rich and full wine, with raisin, licorice, and cassis on a semi-sweet nose. Plum and juicy berry define the palate. Finishes alive and fast, with ripe-edged fruit and some leathery tannins. Packed fairly full with Cabernet Sauvignon and Merlot, in addition to Sangiovese. Made by Marchese Mazzei. **90** —*M.S. (10/1/2004)*

TENUTA CAPARZO

Tenuta Caparzo 2001 (Rosso di Montalcino) $18. Supple and forward, just the way a good rosso should be, with cherry and tobacco aromas and flavors backed up by a plump mouthfeel and a long, softly tannic finish. Good value. **88** *(3/1/2005)*

Tenuta Caparzo 2000 (Brunello di Montalcino) $48. Stylish smoke and leather aromas combine with plum, cherry, and berry to create a fresh but monotone nose that is true Brunello. Snappy cherry and raspberry flavors appear on the palate along with accents of clove and spice. Upright on the finish. Forward and well made, but hardly complex. **89** —*M.S. (7/1/2005)*

Tenuta Caparzo 1997 (Brunello di Montalcino) $65. 92 —*R.V. (8/1/2002)*

Tenuta Caparzo 1999 La Vigna (Brunello di Montalcino) $66. Floral and round, and eminently approachable at this early stage. The bouquet is rosy and sweet, while the palate is easygoing and fresh. Yet once you think its aging potential might be short, the finish drives on for a long distance, tossing up coffee and earth notes. Drinkable now, but can last for at least a decade. **91** —*M.S. (6/1/2004)*

Tenuta Caparzo 2002 (Toscana) $10. A victim of the vintage, this light-bodied wine styled for early drinking shows decent cherry, earth, and tobacco flavors but comes up lean and drying on the finish. **83** *(3/1/2005)*

Tenuta Caparzo 2000 Sangiovese (Toscana) $14. 86 —*M.S. (11/15/2003)*

Tenuta Caparzo 1999 Borgo Scopeto Riserva Misciano (Chianti Classico) $35. 87 —*M.S. (11/15/2003)*

Tenuta Caparzo 1994 Ca del Pazzo Tuscan Blend (Toscana) $33. 87 —*J.C. (3/1/2000)*

Tenuta Caparzo 2000 La Grance White Blend (Sant'Antimo) $21. This kitchen-sink blend of Chardonnay, Trebbiano, Sauvignon, and Traminer shows a bit of toast and lemon custard on the nose, then leesy, minerally and citrus flavors on the palate. Finishes on mealy, toasty notes alongside a beam of bright acidity. **85** *(3/1/2005)*

Tenuta Carparzo 1997 Le Grance Sant'Antimo White Blend (Tuscany) $25. 91 —*M.M. (9/1/2001)*

TENUTA CARRETTA

Tenuta Carretta 2002 (Dolcetto d'Alba) $16. 83 *—M.S. (12/15/2003)*

Tenuta Carretta 1998 Cannubi Nebbiolo (Barolo) $NA. 89 *—R.V. (11/15/2002)*

TENUTA COCCI GRIFONI

Tenuta Cocci Grifoni 2000 Il Grifone Red Blend (Rosso Piceno Superiore) $48. Ample black fruit along with mint and herbs make for a solid if unusual bouquet. It's fairly ripe and sweet to the taste, with bold cherry and raspberry flavors. Textured on the finish, with zest. The only negative is that it's rowdy and unrefined, but hey, that's Rosso Piceno. 88 *—M.S. (7/1/2005)*

Tenuta Cocci Grifoni 1997 Il Grifone Sangiovese (Rosso Piceno Superiore) $36. 87 *(10/1/2001)*

TENUTA DEL NANFRO

Tenuta del Nanfro 2001 San Mauro Nero d'Avola (Sicilia) $18. 81 *—M.S. (10/1/2003)*

TENUTA DELL'ORNELLAIA

Tenuta dell'Ornellaia 2000 Ornellaia Cabernet Blend (Bolgheri) $145. 94 Cellar Selection *—M.S. (11/15/2003)*

Tenuta dell'Ornellaia 1996 Ornellaia Cabernet Blend (Bolgheri) $73. 92 *—M.S. (7/1/2000)*

Tenuta dell'Ornellaia 1995 Ornellaia Cabernet Blend (Toscana) $63. 96 *—M.S. (5/1/1999)*

Tenuta dell'Ornellaia 1996 Masseto Merlot (Bolgheri) $138. 93 *—R.V. (12/31/2001)*

TENUTA DI ARGIANO

Tenuta di Argiano 1997 (Brunello di Montalcino) $56. 92 Cellar Selection *—R.V. (8/1/2002)*

TENUTA DI RISECCOLI

Tenuta di Riseccoli 1999 (Chianti Classico) $12. 89 Best Buy *—M.S. (12/31/2002)*

TENUTA DI SESTA

Tenuta di Sesta 1997 (Brunello di Montalcino) $45. 94 Cellar Selection *—R.V. (8/1/2002)*

TENUTA FARNETA DI COLLATO

Tenuta Farneta di Collato 2003 Tenuta Farneta (Chianti Colli Senesi) $8. A bit reduced, with meaty black-fruit aromas accompanied by hints of grass and hay. The palate is spicy and full of plum and cherry, while the rest of the mouth and finish are carried by short acidity. Hits hard toward the back while scoring points along the way. 86 Best Buy *(4/1/2005)*

TENUTA IL BOSCO

Tenuta Il Bosco NV Philèo Brut (Oltrepó Pavese) $NA. An enjoyable sparkling wine with citrus, pears, and toasted almonds on the nose. Shows similar flavors on the palate, where it reveals a surprise splash of hazelnut. Refermented using the long charmat process, the bubble size and persistence makes you think it was done in the metodo classico. 84 *—M.L. (12/15/2004)*

TENUTA IL TESORO

Tenuta Il Tesoro 2000 La Fonte Red Blend (Toscana) $15. 86 *—M.S. (12/31/2002)*

TENUTA LA FUGA

Tenuta La Fuga 1999 Sangiovese (Rosso di Montalcino) $NA. 83 *—M.S. (8/1/2002)*

TENUTA LE QUERCE

Tenuta Le Querce 1999 Il Viola (Aglianico del Vulture) $11. 86 *—C.S. (5/1/2002)*

TENUTA MONACI

Tenuta Monaci 1997 Simposia Negroamaro (Puglia) $12. 85 *—C.S. (5/1/2002)*

TENUTA RAPITALA

Tenuta Rapitala 2002 Hugonis Red Blend (Sicilia) $39. A 50-50 blend of Nero d'Avola and Cabernet Sauvignon, this effort reveals attributes of both varieties: dense chocolate and plum fruit alongside mint and green pepper notes. It's big and fully extracted; firmly tannic on the finish. 88 *(8/1/2005)*

Tenuta Rapitala 2002 Nu-har Red Blend (Sicilia) $13. This is Rapitala 's entry-level red, a blend of 70% Nero d'Avola matured in stainless and 30% Cabernet Sauvignon matured in used oak. The result is a pleasantly structured red with notes of plum and chocolate accented by hints of mint and dusty earth. 87 *(8/1/2005)*

Tenuta Rapitala 2002 Solinero Syrah (Sicilia) $42. This dark, richly saturated in color Syrah features scents of baked plums, dusted with cinnamon, and white pepper. Oak aging for 18 months has imparted a silky texture to the mouthfilling fruit and a touch of vanilla on the finish. Has enough structure to suggest holding 3–5 years, but is approachable now. 89 *(8/1/2005)*

Tenuta Rapitala 2003 Casalj White Blend (Sicilia) $13. Don't be put off by the odd name: The J at the end is pronounced like an I. What's

ITALY

important is the wine itself, a blend of 70% Catarratto and 30% Chardonnay that boasts assertive aromas of orange blossom and honey. Tropical fruit notes mark the plump, mouthfilling palate, while the finish is citrusy with acidity. **88 Best Buy** *(8/1/2005)*

Tenuta Rapitala 2001 Casalj White Blend (Sicilia) $11. 83 *—R.V. (10/1/2003)*

TENUTA SAN GUIDO

Tenuta San Guido 2000 Guidalberto Red Blend (Bolgheri) $52. Starts with a confusing nose of tobacco, smoked ham, and overt leather and animal aromas; a staid, simple wine this is not. The palate, which has a feel that's thick and chewy, is bulked up with baked black fruits. The finish, meanwhile, is dark, with berry flavors and fading spice. The blend is Cabernet, Merlot, and Sangiovese. **89** *—M.S. (10/1/2004)*

TENUTA SANT'ANTONIO

Tenuta Sant'Antonio 1998 Capitello Chardonnay (Friuli) $27. 89 *—J.C. (7/1/2003)*

Tenuta Sant'Antonio 1998 Campo dei Gigli Red Blend (Amarone della Valpolicella) $64. 88 *(5/1/2003)*

Tenuta Sant'Antonio 2000 Selezione Antonio Castagnedi Red Blend (Amarone della Valpolicella) $50. This is one beautiful wine, something our tasting panel could agree on to a person. We loved the meaty, smoky nose along with the lush palate that oozes pure red fruit, vanilla, chocolate, and dried spices. It's everything you'd want in a young Amarone, and a little bit more. **93** *(11/1/2005)*

TENUTA SETTEN

Tenuta Setten 1999 Moresco (Raboso) $24. 84 *(5/1/2003)*

TENUTA VALDIPIATTA

Tenuta Valdipiatta 2002 Tuscan Blend (Vino Nobile di Montepulciano) $29. Straightforward and a touch sharp, with cherry, earth, and leather aromas. Red plum, pie cherry, and vanilla flavors carry the palate toward a peppery, lean finish. Fresh enough but not very loving. **84** *—M.S. (7/1/2005)*

TENUTE DEI VALLARINO

Tenute dei Vallarino 2001 Bricco Asinari Superiore (Barbera d'Asti) $36. Assertively oaky on the nose, with strong aromas of charred wood and cedar. But there's sufficient fruit to back it up, lending tart cherries and a lingering finish to the harmonious, medium-weight whole. **88** *—J.C. (11/15/2004)*

Tenute dei Vallarino 2004 Castello di Canelli (Moscato d'Asti) $15. A brilliant semi-sparkler with persistent bubbles, lush grassy notes, citrus, kiwi, lavender, honey, and peach. You can really taste the Moscato grape in the glass. The wine also delivers sweet lime pie, cream, and a medium finish. Tenute dei Vallarino is part of Fratelli Gancia, one of the grandfather companies of Italian sparkling wines. **88** *—M.L. (12/15/2005)*

TENUTE DETTORI

Tenute Dettori 2001 Badde Nigolosu Tenores Cannonau (Romangia) $91. Big and rubbery, with 17.5% alcohol and a backpalate burn that will bring you to the brink. Licorice, stewed fruit, and kirsch make for a heady nose. The palate is just as demanding, with reduced flavors of chocolate and raisins. Quite difficult to score; this burly Sardinian red needs a pungent sheep's milk cheese or something similar to show its best. **87** *—M.S. (7/1/2005)*

Tenute Dettori 2003 Badde Nigolosu Bianco Vermentino (Romangia) $40. This Sardinian white is so much the opposite of a quaffer that it actually suffers a bit. Lofty intentions and a warm vintage have produced excess weight and sweetness; the banana and vanilla flavors overwhelm. That said, some folks will appreciate the immense flavor and intensity of this Vermentino. **86** *—M.S. (7/1/2005)*

TENUTE SILVIO NARDI

Tenute Silvio Nardi 2000 (Brunello di Montalcino) $55. Exceptionally spicy on the nose, with forest floor, leather, and pepper as well as ample berry fruit. Round and likable, with plum, chocolate, vanilla, and toast flavors. What brings this wine up is that it has a few levels of complexity. The finish, for example, is at first juicy. But then it runs long and spicy. Rock-solid Brunello from a consistent producer. **91** *—M.S. (7/1/2005)*

Tenute Silvio Nardi 1997 (Brunello di Montalcino) $60. 92 *—R.V. (8/1/2002)*

Tenute Silvio Nardi 2002 Sangiovese (Rosso di Montalcino) $22. Wonderful in the nose, with snappy fruit and plenty of light but fragrant wood. The palate is nothing but red fruit, while the body is not too thick but substantive enough. It finishes smooth and easy, and it improves with airing. A perfect wine for cheeses or pasta, or with lunch. **90** *—M.S. (6/1/2004)*

TENUTE SOLETTA

Tenute Soletta 2002 Prestizu (Vermentino di Sardegna) $17. Modest flower blossom and earth aromas are a bit heavy, which is typical for the variety and region. Fairly full and round on the palate, with dry apple and papaya flavors. Not an overly expressive wine, but solid. **86** *—M.S. (8/1/2004)*

TERRABIANCA

Terrabianca 1999 Campaccio Red Blend (Toscana) $24. 89 *—M.S. (12/31/2002)*

Terrabianca 2000 Croce Riserva Sangiovese (Chianti Classico) $25. A bit of bramble and root beer add sweetness to the toasty, oaky nose. The palate is lush with plum, berry, and a slight hint of tomato.

ITALY

Finishes broad, but oak pops up, forming a soft carpet to this new-age Chianti. **90** *—M.S. (10/1/2004)*

Terrabianca 2001 La Fonte (Toscana) $20. More dry, toasty wood than fruit creates a modest, distant nose. The palate is quite lean and acid-packed, with cherry and apple skin carrying the flavor profile. More zesty and sharp than ideal; not caustic but raw. **85** *—M.S. (10/1/2004)*

Terrabianca 2002 Scassino (Chianti Classico) $22. Closed but a little spicy, with hints of cola, damp leather, and coffee. Modest in its force, with cherry and citrus creating a fresh, zesty palate feel. Stays mostly in the middle of the road, with supple tannins and a modest finishing flavor of root beer. **86** *(4/1/2005)*

Terrabianca 2000 Scassino (Chianti Classico) $20. 87 *(8/1/2002)*

Terrabianca 1999 Scassino (Chianti Classico) $14. 87 *—M.S. (12/31/2002)*

Terrabianca 2001 Campaccio Tuscan Blend (Toscana) $38. Interesting bouquet, with early lactic notes giving way to blueberry and then sawdust, root beer, and finally Christmas spice. A bit flat on the palate, but still pushing lively raspberry and strawberry flavors. Tight on the finish, with lively acidity and fierce tannins. **87** *—M.S. (11/15/2004)*

Terrabianca 1998 Ceppate Tuscan Blend (Tuscany) $22. 86 *—M.S. (12/31/2002)*

TERRALE

Terrale 2000 Primitivo (Puglia) $8. 85 Best Buy *(5/1/2002)*

Terrale 2000 Nero D'Avola-Syrah (Sicilia) $8. 86 Best Buy *(5/1/2002)*

Terrale 1998 Bianco White Blend (Sicilia) $5. 82 *—M.N. (12/31/2000)*

TERRE DA VINO

Terre da Vino 2004 La Gatta (Moscato d'Asti) $12. Here is a vineyard-designate wine bursting with floral notes: jasmine, honeysuckle, and orange blossom. Exotic fruit takes over in the mouth leaving a trail of kiwi, lime, and peach backed by thick, creamy mousse. **87 Editors' Choice** *—M.L. (12/15/2005)*

TERRE DEGLI SVEVI

Terre Degli Svevi 1999 Re Manfredi (Aglianico del Vulture) $30. Vital and tannic after a number of years, a testament to this grape's aging ability. The bouquet deals strawberry, raspberry, mint, and sage. In the mouth, hard tannins frame plum and cherry fruit, which is backed by a racy, no-holds-barred finish. Nothing out of place; well-structured. **90** *—M.S. (11/15/2004)*

TERRE DEL PRINCIPE

Terre del Principe 2002 (Vernaccia di San Gimignano) $13. Quite flowery on the nose, almost to the point of smelling like a tree grove in bloom. But beyond that there's little stuffing to this wine. It's got some lime and tangerine at its edges, but not too much at the core. A decent quaff; nothing faulty or off. **84** *—M.S. (8/1/2004)*

TERRE DI GENESTRA

Terre di Genestra 2002 Nero d'Avola (Sicilia) $13. 87 *—R.V. (10/1/2003)*

Terre di Ginestra 2002 Catarratto Chardonnay (Sicilia) $9. 87 *—R.V. (10/1/2003)*

TERREDORA

Terredora 1998 Il Principio (Aglianico d'Irpinia) $9. 85 Best Buy *—C.S. (5/1/2002)*

Terredora 1996 Fatica Contadina Red Blend (Taurasi) $38. 89 *—M.N. (12/31/2000)*

TERREDORA DI PAOLO

Terredora di Paolo 2003 Aglianico (Irpinia) $14. A young, chunky heavyweight is the only way to describe this black wine, which smells of fruitcake and herbs, and tastes of baked plums and chocolate. Rich and overflowing, and building to a tannic crescendo. One can see the mass appeal here. **87** *—M.S. (2/1/2005)*

Terredora di Paolo 1999 Fatica Contadina Red Blend (Taurasi) $49. A large, complex, forceful wine that requires time to show off. What starts out murky, heavy and clumsy becomes more lovable once it gets some air. Along the way come plum, chocolate, and raisin characteristics, and as expected, hammer-time tannins. Very hard on the cheeks, but such is Taurasi. **89** *—M.S. (2/1/2005)*

TERUZZI & PUTHOD

Teruzzi & Puthod 2004 (Vernaccia di San Gimignano) $13. Said to be the favorite après-sculpturing drink of Michelangelo, Vernaccia is one of Italy's oldest natives grapes. This version from a 235-acre vineyard near Tuscany's famed "city of towers" is not aromatically intense but it does offer nice melon and floral tones. Tart and flinty in the mouth. **85** *—M.L. (9/1/2005)*

Teruzzi & Puthod 2002 (Vernaccia di San Gimignano) $12. Aromas of stone fruits, particularly apricot, are light but nice. The palate offers lightweight lemon and tangerine, while the finish is dry and simple. Nicely textured but a bit weak on flavor. **85** *—M.S. (8/1/2004)*

Teruzzi & Puthod 1997 Terre di Tufi (Vernaccia di San Gimignano) $21. 86 *(11/1/1999)*

TIBERINI

Tiberini 1998 Podere le Caggiole (Montepulciano) $20. 86 *—M.S. (11/15/2003)*

ITALY

TIEFENBRUNNER

Tiefenbrunner 1999 Linticlarus Chardonnay (Alto Adige) $20. 89 —*R.V. (7/1/2003)*

Tiefenbrunner 2002 Feldmarschall von Fenner Vino da Tavola Müller-Thurgau (Alto Adige) $27. 87 —*R.V. (7/1/2003)*

Tieffenbrunner 2000 Pinot Bianco (Alto Adige) $12. 83 —*M.N. (9/1/2001)*

TIEZZI

Tiezzi 2000 (Brunello di Montalcino) $50. Red licorice, raspberry jam, and a hint of cherry tomato make for a modest but open bouquet. To the contrary, the palate is hard, with fierce tannins. As for flavors, the wine locks into that familiar black cherry, medicinal tune before finishing with vanilla and milk chocolate. 87 —*M.S. (7/1/2005)*

TIZIANO

Tiziano 2003 (Chianti) $10. Solid and chunky, with aromas of sawdust, cinnamon, and clove. Full enough, with strawberry, cherry, and spice flavors. A touch tart on the finish, but with enough length and weight to push it forward. Not profound but 100% likable. 87 Best Buy *(4/1/2005)*

Tiziano 1999 (Chianti) $7. 83 *(4/1/2001)*

Tiziano 2001 Riserva (Chianti) $12. Lots of leather, coffee, and campfire aromas are followed by tart plum, cherry, and hickory smoke flavors. A bit tangy, and not subtle in the least. There is also a whiff of green to the middle. 85 *(4/1/2005)*

TOLLOY

Tolloy 1998 Pinot Bianco (Alto Adige) $11. 86 *(7/1/2000)*

Tolloy 2003 Cantina Salorno Pinot Grigio (Alto Adige) $12. Shows decent weight and richness in the mouth, along with flavors of pear, melon, and fresh herbs. Picks up some Gewürz-like spice as well, giving it greater complexity than most inexpensive Grigios. Worth a try with unsweetened Asian dishes. 86 —*J.C. (12/31/2004)*

TOMMASI

Tommasi 2001 Vigneto Santa Cecilia Chardonnay (Valdadige) $9. 88 —*J.C. (7/1/2003)*

Tommasi 2001 Ripasso (Valpolicella Classico Superiore) $18. Starts off a bit horsey and leathery, but has ample depth of fruit lurking behind. Dark plum and earth flavors are tinged with meat on the palate. Shows good complexity and a long, supple finish. Drink now and over the next few years. 88 —*J.C. (12/31/2004)*

Tommasi 2003 Le Rosse Pinot Grigio (Delle Venezie) $10. This is a weighty, corpulent wine, enlivened by a dash of citrusy acidity. Bold melon, ripe apple, and dried spice flavors make for a satisfying mouthful that could pair with fish or light chicken dishes. 86 Best Buy —*J.C. (12/31/2004)*

Tommasi 2000 Red Blend (Amarone della Valpolicella Classico) $60. A full-bodied, corpulent Amarone, this doesn't have a great deal of grace just yet. Instead, its bold flavors of cinnamon and clove, cherry and plum plow ahead ruggedly, finshing long and tannic. This has all the right stuff, it just needs time to settle down; try after 2008. 90 —*J.C. (12/31/2004)*

Tommasi 2000 Il Sestante Vigneto Monte Masua (Amarone della Valpolicella Classico) $58. Fairly tight and snappy, but weighs in more rich than lean. The palate deals cherry, plum and earth, while the finish offers lavender, fudge, and pepper. Well-balanced stuff, and pretty easy to get into; this one doesn't need a ton of time in the cellar. 89 *(11/1/2005)*

Tommasi 1997 Ca'Florian Red Blend (Amarone della Valpolicella) $55. 93 Editors' Choice *(5/1/2003)*

Tommasi 2000 Crearo della Concaa d'Oro Red Blend (Veronese) $25. 89 *(5/1/2003)*

Tommasi 1998 Ripasso Red Blend (Valpolicella Classico Superiore) $30. 87 *(5/1/2003)*

Tommasi 2001 Vigneto San Martino White Blend (Lugana) $NA. 84 —*J.C. (7/1/2003)*

TORMARESCA

Tormaresca 2002 Chardonnay (Puglia) $10. Distant on the nose, offering only light banana and butterscotch. Simple flavors of lemon and apple are carried on a flat palate. 82 —*M.S. (10/1/2004)*

Tormaresca 2003 Torcicoda Primitivo (Salento) $20. Antinori's Puglia estate launches a powerful rocket that rips through the mouth leaving a smoldering trail of cassis, bitter chocolate, and black cherry preserves. The mouthfeel is equally intense with rounded tannins and a lingering taste of smoked ham. 88 —*M.L. (9/1/2005)*

Tormaresca 2000 Red Blend (Puglia) $11. 86 Best Buy —*C.S. (5/1/2002)*

TORRE DI LUNA

Torre di Luna 2003 Pinot Grigio (Delle Venezie) $13. This wine has plenty of mouthfilling pear and melon fruit, carried along by a broad, expansive mouthfeel and low acidity. Lacks a refreshing bite on the finish, probably because of the warm vintage. 84 —*J.C. (12/31/2004)*

TORRE DI MONTE

Torre di Monte 2001 Pinot Grigio (Umbria) $10. Light, with vanilla, banana, and caramel aromas. Not a zesty, snappy Pinot Grigio at all, and likely at the end of its life span. What's here is tasty, albeit dilute. 82 —*M.S. (10/1/2004)*

TORRE SVEVA

Torre Sveva 1998 Castel del Monte Red Blend (Apulia) $8. **85** *—L.W. (3/1/2000)*

TORREBIANCO

Torrebianco 2000 Fratelli Gancia Negroamaro (Salento) $8. Black cherry, caramel, and toffee create a sweet bouquet. Flavors of raspberry, smoke, and coffee work well together, and the mouthfeel is easy. However, it turns thin on the back palate and dilute on the back end. **85** *—M.S. (11/15/2004)*

Torrebianco 2002 Fratelli Gancia Red Blend (Sicilia) $6. Light red fruit throughout, and mostly soft and clean. Some strawberry and raspberry on the palate leads into a lightweight finish. Easygoing and inoffensive. **84 Best Buy** *—M.S. (10/1/2004)*

TORRESELLA

Torresella 2000 Cabernet Sauvignon (Veneto) $10. **82** *(5/1/2003)*

Torresella 2000 Merlot (Veneto) $10. **83** *(5/1/2003)*

Torresella 2001 Pinot Grigio (Veneto) $10. **83** *—J.C. (7/1/2003)*

TOSCOLO

Toscolo 2003 (Chianti) $11. Dark in color, with cherry, leather, and lemon to the nose. The palate also tastes of lemon, and there's some plum in there to soften things up. Snappy, simple, and lean; a wine that perpetuates everyday Chianti's pedestrian reputation. **84** *(4/1/2005)*

Toscolo 2000 (Chianti Classico) $19. Saucy and spicy to the nose, with hints of chocolate, mocha, and damp earth. Plum flavors and a smooth, moderately long finish keep this wine's head above water. Nonetheless, it's not real strong in the middle. **85** *—M.S. (10/1/2004)*

Toscolo 2000 Tuscan Blend (Chianti) $8. **84** *(10/1/2001)*

Toscolo 1999 Riserva Tuscan Blend (Chianti Classico) $24. A bit lean and chemical, with earth, chocolate, and blackberry aromas. Plum, berry and distant green notes define the palate. Tight and a touch bitter at the end, with coffee and cocoa. Heavily tannic. **84** *—M.S. (10/1/2004)*

TRABUCCHI

Trabucchi 2000 Red Blend (Amarone della Valpolicella) $50. A bit rooty and spicy, with aromatic notes of root beer, cinnamon, tea, and cedar. Features somewhat of a tannic, racy feel, with flavors running toward cherry. One taster found it a touch minty and leafy, but two-thirds of our panel approved of the wine's zesty, snappy characteristics. **89** *(11/1/2005)*

TRANCHERO OSVALDO

Tranchero Osvaldo 2004 Casot (Moscato d'Asti) $15. This vineyard-designated Moscato d'Asti didn't quite deliver the pizzazz and spunk we expected. The bubbles are large and not very frothy, but the nose had an interesting mix of charcoal, chalk, lavender, peach, soap and graham cracker. **84** *—M.L. (12/15/2005)*

TRAVAGLINI

Travaglini 1996 Riserva Nebbiolo (Gattinara) $35. **89** *—S.H. (11/15/2002)*

Travaglini 1995 Nebbiolo (Gattinara) $29. **92** *(11/15/1999)*

TREFIANO

Trefiano 1995 Carmignano Tuscan Blend (Toscana) $37. **88** *—M.S. (11/15/1999)*

TRIACCA

Triacca 1998 La Palaia (Chianti Classico) $NA. **84** *—M.S. (8/1/2002)*

UCCELLIERA

Uccelliera 2000 (Brunello di Montalcino) $62. One of the more unique, complex 2000s from Montalcino. Citrus peel, lavender, and basil are just some of the aromas that waft from the nose. In the mouth, there's good coverage and solid tannins. To that end, black cherry, plum, and other usual suspects make for a fine flavor profile, while the acidity is right for aging. **92 Editors' Choice** *—M.S. (7/1/2005)*

Uccelliera 1999 Riserva (Brunello di Montalcino) $90. Wonderfully toasted up front, with baked, but not cooked, fruit aromas. There's also plenty of coffee, earth, and leather to the bouquet. Initial livewire flavors settle to reveal marzipan and dried stone fruits, while the sly finish is so complex that the wine ultimately registers as a different breed. Drinking this is like navigating a maze. **94 Editors' Choice** *—M.S. (7/1/2005)*

UGO LEQUIO

Ugo Lequio 1999 Gallina Nebbiolo (Barbaresco) $49. This is a soft, silky, feminine Barbaresco that's already approachable. Pretty aromas of cherry preserves and spring flowers fold in vanilla notes on the palate. Drink now–2010. **88** *(4/2/2004)*

UMANI RONCHI

Umani Ronchi 2002 Villa Bianchi (Verdicchio dei Castelli di Jesi Classico Superiore) $12. Opens with full pear, tangerine, and flower aromas, which are backed by basic apple and melon flavors. It's a fairly plump, heavy wine in terms of mouthfeel, yet it finishes a touch hollow. Still, it's flavorful and true throughout. **86** *—M.S. (8/1/2004)*

VAGNONI

Vagnoni 2000 Riserva (Chianti Colli Senesi) $24. Candied cherry and raspberry aromas give off a jammy sensation, while the plum and berry fruit that carries the palate also brings with it some severely spiked acidity. Mainstream Chianti, with a slight scouring edge. **85** *(4/1/2005)*

Vagnoni 2002 (Vernaccia di San Gimignano) $15. Muddled and sulfuric at first, with matchstick aromas preceding a palate of citrus and apple. That heavy, burnt note burns off with time, leaving a tangy apple and citrus palate. Nothing spectacular, but better than initial impressions indicate. **84** *—M.S. (8/1/2004)*

VAL D'OCA

Val d'Oca NV Brut (Prosecco di Valdobbiadene) $14. A bit flat, with lime and cracker aromas. Mostly dry citrus on the palate, which puckers up your lips and cheeks. Finishes tart, with celery and green-apple notes. **85** *—M.S. (12/15/2004)*

Val d'Oca 2003 Millesimato Extra Dry (Prosecco di Valdobbiadene) $14. Dry and leafy, with aromatic notes of fresh spinach and green tobacco. As it opens it loses some of that green character and adopts a more typical stone fruit and apple personality. Finishes on the spot, with a good mouthfeel. **85** *—M.S. (12/15/2004)*

VAL DELLE ROSE

Val delle Rose 2003 Sangiovese (Morellino di Scansano) $15. Sweet, ripe, and welcoming, with aromas of cherry, cotton candy, and rubber. More cherry and raspberry come forward as you taste, while the finish is short and a bit tart. Pretty good, with snap, crackle, and pop. **84** *—M.S. (11/15/2004)*

Val delle Rose 1999 Sangiovese (Morellino di Scansano) $14. **88** *—M.S. (8/1/2002)*

Val delle Rose 1998 Riserva Sangiovese (Morellino di Scansano) $19. **88** *—M.S. (8/1/2002)*

VAL DI SUGA

Val di Suga 1993 Vigna del Lago (Brunello di Montalcino) $92. **93** *—M.S. (3/1/2000)*

Val di Suga 1999 Vigna Spuntali (Brunello di Montalcino) $50. A single-vineyard Brunello that's unconventional from the get-go. Not unkind aromas of mineral, peanut, and curry suggest unusual new-barrel oaking, while the palate beats fast with racy acids and broad, heavy tannins. The finish, meanwhile, is airy and long. Hold until 2008. **91** *—M.S. (6/1/2004)*

VALDICAVA

Valdicava 2000 (Brunello di Montalcino) $89. Pitch black, like midnight on a country road. Talk about saturated: The nose yields tar, char, and more, and in the mouth it has that mid-level intensity that many of the 2000s don't have. Earthy at one moment, polished the next. It finishes with a sweet blast of molasses, black cherry, and coffee. A head-turner, one that gets better with every sip. **93** *—M.S. (7/1/2005)*

Valdicava 1997 (Brunello di Montalcino) $90. **88** *—R.V. (8/1/2002)*

Valdipiatta 1998 Sangiovese (Rosso di Montepulciano) $15. **88** *—M.M. (9/1/2000)*

VALDO

Valdo NV Selezzione Oro Brut (Prosecco di Valdobbiadene) $14. **86** *—J.C. (12/31/2003)*

VALFIERI

Valfieri 2001 (Gavi di Gavi) $17. **85** *—M.S. (12/15/2003)*

VALIANO

Valiano 2001 (Chianti Classico) $15. **87** *(7/1/2003)*

Valiano 1999 Riserva (Chianti Classico) $25. **86** *(7/1/2003)*

Valiano 2000 Poggio Teo (Chianti Classico) $20. A raw, tight, ready wine with a spot of green on the nose along with leather and damp earth. Airing freshens it up, revealing berry fruit flavors with accents of soy. Crisp on the finish, with acids at work. **88** *(4/1/2005)*

Valiano 1999 Poggio Teo (Chianti Classico) $20. **87** *—J.C. (7/1/2003)*

Valiano 1998 Poggio Teo Riserva (Chianti Classico) $24. **91 Editors' Choice** *(11/15/2001)*

Valiano 1997 Vino in Musica Tuscan Blend (Toscana) $40. **88** *(7/1/2003)*

VALLE DELL'ACATE

Valle dell'Acate 2000 Il Moro Nero d'Avola (Sicilia) $23. **88** *—J.C. (10/1/2003)*

Valle dell'Acate 2001 Poggio Bidini Nero d'Avola (Sicilia) $9. **88 Best Buy** *—C.S. (11/15/2002)*

Valle dell'Acate 1999 Cerasuolo di Vittoria $24. **88** *—C.S. (5/1/2002)*

Valle dell'Acate 2000 Frappato (Sicily) $22. **84** *—C.S. (5/1/2002)*

VALLEBELBO

Vallebelbo 2004 (Moscato d'Asti) $11. A frothy, fun, and festive wine from one of the area's biggest producers. This wine shows grassy notes, mineral tones, generous peach, and honey. **86 Best Buy** *—M.L. (12/15/2005)*

VARALDO

Varaldo 1999 Bricco Libero Nebbiolo (Barbaresco) $62. Slightly herbal, but balanced by gobs of blackberry fruit and creamy vanilla oak. Coconutty notes on the palate are backed by rich berry flavors and lush, soft tannins. Drink now–2015. **90** *(4/2/2004)*

Varaldo 1995 Vigua di Aldo Nebbiolo (Barolo) $45. 87 *(11/15/2002)*

VASARI

Vasari 1998 (Chianti Colli Aretini) $11. 84 *(4/1/2001)*

VECCHIE TERRE DI MONTEFILI

Vecchie Terre di Montefili 1998 (Chianti Classico) $21. 87 *(4/1/2001)*

VENICA

Venica 2000 Bottaz Collio Refosco (Venezia Giulia) $30. This family-operated winery in Friuli is known for excellent Sauvignon. But their dedication to Italian natives is evident with this up-and-coming variety. Refosco has pizzazz that comes through as cinnamon spiciness and bitter cherry liqueur. Tannins are still a bit thorny. **86** *—M.L. (9/1/2005)*

VENTURINI MASSIMINO

Venturini Massimino 1998 Red Blend (Amarone della Valpolicella Classico) $42. 91 *(5/1/2003)*

VEZZANI

Vezzani 2000 Rosso Red Blend (Salice Salentino) $6. 82 *—C.S. (5/1/2002)*

Vezzani 2002 Bianco White Blend (Sicilia) $7. Mostly burnt aromas carry the nose. Lemon-lime and apple control the palate, with more of the same on the finish. Bland but basic in the mouth. **81** *—M.S. (10/1/2004)*

VIBERTI

Viberti 2001 Toni 'D Giuspin (Dolcetto d'Alba) $21. 87 *—M.S. (12/15/2003)*

Viberti 1998 Buon Padre Nebbiolo (Barolo) $42. Starts off shaky, with burnt matchstick and slightly herbal aromas. Yet it recovers nicely with air, losing the offending scents and developing lovely black cherry and hickory notes. Medium- to full-bodied, it boasts a creamy texture and dry, tea-like tannins on the finish. Drink 2010–2015. **88** *(4/2/2004)*

VICARA

Vicara 1999 Cantico della Crosia Barbera (Monferrato) $23. 88 *—M.S. (11/15/2002)*

VICCHIOMAGGIO

Vicchiomaggio 2002 La Lellera (Chianti Classico) $15. Stewed and reduced, with herbal/vegetal aromas of bell pepper and oregano. What saves this wine from a worse fate is the decent body and acceptable mouthfeel. Still, it's too scattered and baked to rate higher. **84** *(4/1/2005)*

Vicchiomaggio 2000 Petri Riserva (Chianti Classico) $27. Petri spends part of its maturation in barriques and part in larger oak to help preserve its fruit. The aromas are not particularly fruity, boasting tobacco and earth alongside dried herbs and mocha, but the palate shows dark fruit flavors and a bright beam of acidity before finishing with echoes of earth and tea. **89** *(11/15/2004)*

Vicchiomaggio 2000 Ripa delle Mandorle Tuscan Blend (Toscana) $20. Named for the little hill's almond trees, this modestly priced super Tuscan is a blend of 80% Sangiovese and 20% barrique-aged Cabernet Sauvignon. The Sangiovese provides black cherry and tobacco flavors, while the Cab contributes toasty, buttery oak and herbal notes. Drink now and over the next several years. **86** *(11/15/2004)*

VIE DE ROMANS

Vie de Romans 2001 Ciampaign Vieris Chardonnay (Friuli Isonzo) $24. 90 *—R.V. (7/1/2003)*

Vie de Romans 2001 Piere Sauvignon Blanc (Friuli Isonzo) $29. 86 *—R.V. (7/1/2003)*

VIETTI

Vietti 1996 La Crena (Barbera d'Asti) $30. 90 *(4/1/2000)*

Vietti 1998 Lazzarito (Dolcetto d'Alba) $19. 90 *(4/1/2000)*

Vietti 1998 Tre Vigne (Dolcetto d'Alba) $18. 86 *(4/1/2000)*

Vietti 1998 Brunate Nebbiolo (Piedmont) $84. 85 *—R.V. (11/15/2002)*

Vietti 1998 Rocche Nebbiolo (Piedmont) $84. 84 *—R.V. (11/15/2002)*

VIGNA PICCOLA

Vigna Piccola 1996 (Chianti Classico) $18. 83 *(4/1/2001)*

VIGNETI DI UMBERTO FRANCASSI RATTI MENTONE

Vigneti di Umberto Francassi Ratti Mentone 1998 Nebbiolo (Barolo) $47. This interesting wine is going brown at the rim already, yet still packs a tannic wallop. Aromas of fig and walnut give way to surprisingly delicate flavors of cherries and orange zest. Try in 2010. **90** *(4/2/2004)*

VILLA ABA

Villa Aba 1998 Pinot Grigio (Grave del Friuli) $13. 84 *— (8/1/1999)*

VILLA ARCENO

Villa Arceno 1999 Merlot (Toscana) $35. 86 *—S.H. (1/1/2002)*

Villa Arceno 1999 Syrah (Toscana) $20. 88 *—S.H. (1/1/2002)*

Villa Arceno 1999 Arguzzio Tuscan Blend (Toscana) $60. 91 *—S.H. (1/1/2002)*

Villa Arceno 1998 Arguzzio Tuscan Blend (Toscana) $50. 86 *—M.S. (12/31/2002)*

VILLA BANFIO

Villa Banfio 2000 Il Torrione Sangiovese (Tuscany) $20. 87 *—M.S. (11/15/2003)*

VILLA BORGHETTI

Villa Borghetti 1998 Grigio Luna Pinot Grigio (Valdadige) $9. 81 *(8/1/1999)*

VILLA CAFAGGIO

Villa Cafaggio 1998 (Chianti Classico) $17. 88 *(4/1/2001)*

Villa Cafaggio 1997 San Martino (Tuscany) $50. 91 Cellar Selection *(5/1/2001)*

VILLA CALCINAIA

Villa Calcinaia 2001 Riserva (Chianti Classico) $24. Fairly oaky, with strong aromas of sawdust morphing into vanilla and butter. Fortunately there's plenty of fruit backing it up. In the mouth, it's firm, with bright cherry and plum; then even more vanilla shows up. Finishes with rubbery tannins and the flavor of black tea. 89 *(4/1/2005)*

VILLA CARRA

Villa Carra 2001 Selection Castellarin Merlot (Delle Venezie) $7. 80 *(5/1/2003)*

VILLA CERNA

Villa Cerna 2001 Riserva (Chianti Classico) $22. Big and brawny, with a strutting bouquet that spills earth, leather, coffee, and cedar-lined cigar box. The fruit is fine and dandy as well, with black cherry, plum, and raspberry dominating. Finishes solid, warm, and mildly tannic. Quite tasty and satisfying as a whole. 90 Editors' Choice *(4/1/2005)*

Villa Cerna 1997 Riserva (Chianti Classico) $21. 89 *(4/1/2001)*

VILLA DANTE

Villa Dante 1995 Sangiovese (Vino Nobile di Montepulciano) $18. 84 *(7/1/2000)*

VILLA DI BAGNOLO

Villa di Bagnolo 1997 Marchesi Pancrazi Pinot Noir (Toscana) $43. 86 *—M.S. (8/1/2002)*

VILLA GIADA

Villa Giada 2004 Andrea (Moscato d'Asti) $15. Classic Muscat muskiness greets the nose and is followed by grass, citrus, dried flowers and rubber. The dried flower notes are particularly attractive and beg for hazelnut tarts, as producer Andrea Faccio suggests. Imported by Vin Divino. 86 *—M.L. (12/15/2005)*

VILLA GIULIA

Villa Giulia 2001 Alaura (Chianti) $10. 85 *—M.S. (11/15/2003)*

Villa Giulia 1998 Alaura (Chianti) $10. 86 *—M.S. (3/1/2000)*

VILLA ILARIA

Villa Ilaria 2000 Nebbiolo (Barbaresco) $18. Seems a bit green and under-ripe, with aromas that range from tobacco to herb to green bean, but slightly more generous on the palate, where tart cherries come into play. Picks up hints of anise and citrus on the finish. 85 *—J.C. (11/15/2004)*

VILLA LA SELVA

Villa La Selva 1997 Selvamaggio Cabernet Sauvignon (Toscana) $27. 88 *—M.S. (8/1/2002)*

Villa La Selva 1999 Feliciaia Sangiovese (Toscana) $23. Chunky and meaty, with broad fruit spread across a full bouquet. The palate deals a wave of cherry-cola and plum before a clean, fruity finish. An upright wine with snappy acids and tasty core flavors. A good food wine for sure. 88 *—M.S. (10/1/2004)*

Villa La Selva 1998 Selvamaggio Tuscan Blend (Toscana) $27. 86 *—M.S. (12/31/2002)*

VILLA LANATA

Villa Lanata 2004 Cardinale Lanata (Moscato d'Asti) $13. From one of Asti's biggest and most established producers. Good mousse and green notes on the nose, such as lemon rind, bay leaf, fresh grass, and dried mint, round off a perky dessert wine ripe with honey and peach. 87 *—M.L. (12/15/2005)*

VILLA MAISANO

Villa Maisano 1997 Questo (Chianti Classico) $30. 90 *(4/1/2001)*

VILLA MATILDE

Villa Matilde 1999 Aglianico (Falerno del Massico) $15. 84 *—C.S. (5/1/2002)*

Villa Matilde 2004 Falanghina (Falerno del Massico) $15. A luminous, linear and crisp white wine that offers Campania's trademark mineral tones, white flowers and stone fruit. Its intensity and body could be edged up a notch although the mouth-cleansing acidity is there. **86** *—M.L. (9/1/2005)*

Villa Matilde 2003 Tenuta Rocca dei Leoni (Falanghina del Beneventano) $14. Moderate vanilla and flower aromas are unconvincing, while the palate is lemony and overdosed with pineapple. Barely in balance, with a beam of acidity in the midpalate but nothing to the edges. **82** *—M.S. (7/1/2005)*

Villa Matilde 1999 Cecubo Red Blend (Campania) $28. **87** *—C.S. (5/1/2002)*

VILLA PATRIZIA

Villa Patrizia 2000 Orto di Boccio Tuscan Blend (Montecucco) $36. **88** *—M.S. (11/15/2003)*

VILLA PILLO

Villa Pillo 1998 Vivaldaia Cabernet Franc (Toscana) $16. **84** *—M.S. (12/31/2002)*

Villa Pillo 2000 Sant' Adele Merlot (Toscana) $23. **83** *—M.S. (12/31/2002)*

Villa Pillo 1998 Syrah (Tuscany) $15. **87 Editors' Choice** *(10/1/2001)*

Villa Pillo 2000 Borgoforte Tuscan Blend (Tuscany) $12. **89** *—M.S. (11/15/2003)*

VILLA POGGIO SALVI

Villa Poggio Salvi 1999 (Brunello di Montalcino) $NA. A bit lean throughout but with its good points. Mild aromas of tobacco and greens suggest some under-ripeness, but there's also good raspberry and strawberry flavors. The proper tannic structure makes it crisp and precise on the finish. From Biondi Santi. **87** *—M.S. (6/1/2004)*

VILLA RUSSIZ

Villa Russiz 2002 Pinot Bianco (Collio) $22. **88** *—R.V. (7/1/2003)*

Villa Russiz 2001 Pinot Grigio (Collio) $22. **86** *—J.C. (7/1/2003)*

Villa Russiz 2002 Sauvignon (Collio) $28. Grassy and herbal on the nose. On the palate there's peachy fruit to counter the green, herbal elements, and a strong foundation built upon grapefruit. Herbal notes reprise on the finish. **86** *—J.C. (12/31/2004)*

Villa Russiz 2001 Sauvignon de la Tour (Collio) $38. **87** *—J.C. (7/1/2003)*

Villa Russiz 2002 Tocai (Collio) $22. **90** *—R.V. (7/1/2003)*

VILLA SANDI

Villa Sandi 1998 Marinali Rosso Cabernet Blend (Veneto) $20. **86** *(5/1/2003)*

Villa Sandi 2003 Pinot Grigio (Piave) $12. Medium-bodied, with decent depth and complexity. Bold pear and apple flavors accented by intriguing dried-spice notes elevate this to a level above basic Pinot Grigio. **86** *—J.C. (12/31/2004)*

Villa Sandi NV Brut (Prosecco di Valdobbiadene) $12. Lemonade-like sweetness on the nose is enhanced by notes of green herbs. Flavors of pineapple and nectarine carry the palate, while the finish is quick and clean. Adequately round and thorough. Solid and entirely functional. **87 Best Buy** *—M.S. (12/15/2005)*

Villa Sandi NV Extra Dry (Prosecco di Valdobbiadene) $12. This is the quintessentially perky wine: Crisp and snappy with bursting citrus notes including lemon drop, pink grapefruit, and candied orange peel backed by delicate floral and jasmine aromas. Chalky, mineral notes round off a gorgeous nose. Designed according to Palladian principals in 1622, Villa Sandi is one of the most beautiful estates near Treviso. Owned by shoemaker Giancarlo Moretti Polegato, it has a one-kilometer long underground 17th-century gallery for red wine barrique aging. **89 Best Buy** *—M.L. (11/15/2005)*

Villa Sandi 2000 Marinali Bianco White Blend (Marca Trevigiana) $20. **84** *—J.C. (7/1/2003)*

VILLA SPARINA

Villa Sparina 1996 Rivalta (Barbera del Monferrato) $40. **85** *(4/1/2000)*

Villa Sparina 1997 D Giusep (Dolcetto d'Acqui) $11. **88** *(4/1/2000)*

VILLABELLA

Villabella 2000 Red Blend (Amarone della Valpolicella Classico) $20. Earthy for certain, with clear scents of tobacco, dry leaves, and dried cherry. Much more mature than its age might indicate, with a lean flavor profile and a lot of savory flavors. More of a drink-now kind of wine, and snappy enough to offset meats and other rich foods. **86** *(11/1/2005)*

VILLADORIA

Villadoria 2000 (Roero Arneis) $9. **80** *—M.S. (12/15/2003)*

Villadoria 1997 Superiore (Barbera d'Alba) $10. **87** *(1/1/2000)*

Villadoria 1997 Nebbiolo (Barolo) $23. **88** *—C.S. (11/15/2002)*

Villadoro 2002 (Montepulciano d'Abruzzo) $12. The murky nose deals mushroom, soy, and earth, while the palate mixes hints of green vegetables with limited red fruit. Finishes tangy and sharp. **83** *—M.S. (10/1/2004)*

VINAGRI PUGLIA SRL

Vinagri Puglia SRL 2000 Limitone Dei Greci Primitivo (Salento) $30. 84 *—M.S. (12/15/2003)*

VITICCIO

Viticcio 1998 (Chianti Classico) $12. 88 Best Buy *(4/1/2001)*

Viticcio 1998 Riserva (Chianti Classico) $18. 85 *—M.S. (8/1/2002)*

Viticcio 2000 Rosarossa Sangiovese (Toscana) $9. 85 *—M.S. (8/1/2002)*

VOLPE PASINI

Volpe Pasini 2001 Ipso Pinot Grigio (Friuli Venezia Giulia) $18. 91 *—R.V. (7/1/2003)*

Volpe Pasini 2002 Zuc de Volpe Ribolla Gialla (Colli Orientali del Friuli) $18. 86 *—R.V. (7/1/2003)*

WALTER FILIPUTTI

Walter Filiputti 1997 Pinot Grigio (Venezia Giulia) $24. 83 *— (8/1/1999)*

ZARDETTO

Zardetto NV Zeta (Prosecco di Conegliano) $19. Sweet and floral, with lime and gardenia on the nose. Nice lemon-lime flavors are tasty and just crisp enough. Finishes a touch like Sprite, with lingering tangerine and pineapple flavors. 87 *—M.S. (12/15/2005)*

ZENATO

Zenato 1998 Pinot Grigio (Delle Venezie) $10. 85 *— (8/1/1999)*

Zenato 1998 Red Blend (Amarone della Valpolicella Classico) $50. 91 *(5/1/2003)*

Zenato 2001 San Benedetto Trebbiano (Lugana) $10. 87 Best Buy *—R.V. (11/15/2002)*

ZONIN

Zonin NV Brut Chardonnay (Italy) $10. Perfectly fine bubbly, with a pale color and fine bead, citrusy, gingery flavors and a short, dry finish. Best as an apéritif. 85 Best Buy *—J.C. (12/15/2004)*

Zonin 2002 Podere Il Giangio Garganega (Gambellara Classico) $NA. 86 *—R.V. (7/1/2003)*

Zonin 2000 Terre Mediterranee Insolia (Sicilia) $NA. 84 *—J.C. (10/1/2003)*

Zonin 2000 (Montepulciano d'Abruzzo) $7. 85 Best Buy *—M.S. (11/15/2003)*

Zonin NV Dolce Moscato (Italy) $10. This one is out there in terms of its sweet lemon-lime character. Alongside that you'll get dried mango and other sweet fruits. Good in terms of feel, with no residue or cloying character. But it's supersweet, hence the "dolce" designation. And even for Moscato it's like liquid sugar. 84 *—M.S. (12/15/2005)*

Zonin 2003 Pinot Grigio (Delle Venezie) $9. Has some odd pine resin notes that creep in on the nose and palate, joining predominantly simple apple flavors. Finshes clean and citrusy. 83 *—J.C. (12/31/2004)*

Zonin NV Brut Prosecco (Italy) $10. Aggressive in a soda-like fashion, with light fruit aromas and plenty of warm, dusty qualities. Apple and peach carry the palate, while the finish is fresh in terms of feel but a touch mealy as far as flavor. 84 *—M.S. (12/15/2005)*

Zonin NV Special Cuvée Brut Prosecco (Italy) $10. The best bubbly in the Zonin portfolio. The nose is yeasty, with moderate richness and enough apple, and citrus to register. The palate features green melon, apple and toast, while the finish is mildly yeasty and fairly full. Satisfying as it fills the mouth. 87 Best Buy *—M.S. (12/15/2005)*

Zonin 1999 Red Blend (Amarone della Valpolicella) $35. Round, smoky, and solid, with all components in their proper places. We liked this wine's ripe black cherry and plum flavors and found the mouthfeel to be rock solid and the acid-tannin balance just right. Maybe it doesn't stand out, but it will fit the bill with nary a problem. 90 *(11/1/2005)*

Zonin 1997 Red Blend (Amarone della Valpolicella) $35. 89 *(5/1/2003)*

Zonin NV Spumante (Asti) $10. Features floral, muscat aromas and tropical fruit and citrus flavors. Finishes short; a pleasant quaff but lacking in concentration. 83 *—J.C. (12/15/2004)*

New Zealand

In recent years, the New Zealand wine industry has mushroomed in size like no other. New Zealand now boasts more than five hundred wineries in a country with a total human population of only four million. The reason behind this growth has been exports. From 1995 to 2005, United States imports of New Zealand wine went from just over NZ$1 million to more than NZ$113 million. The result is that consumers in the United States are seeing more and more New Zealand wines on store shelves and restaurant wine lists. Thankfully, quality has remained generally excellent, thanks to a rigorous export certification process, a solid technological base, and a rapidly expanding understanding of viticulture.

Fairhall Downs Estate produces wine in the Brancott Valley, Marlborough, New Zealand.

NEW ZEALAND WINE REGIONS

Marlborough The engine driving New Zealand's growth, Marlborough wine production is dominated by Sauvignon Blanc. With its crisp, grassy, herbal-yet-tropical style, it has become the hallmark of New Zealand. Yet Marlborough is also capable of making other fine aromatic white wines, as well as Pinot Noir and Chardonnay.

Hawkes Bay Known for its Bordeaux-style reds from Merlot and Cabernet Sauvignon, which can be very fine in warm vintages, but excessively herbal in others. Alternative reds, such as Malbec and Syrah, are gaining in popularity, with Syrah in particular likely to emerge as a star.

Martinborough Together with the surrounding Wairarapa, Martinborough is Pinot Noir country. The wines marry cherry fruit with an often intense, wiry-herbal character that adds character and staying power.

Central Otago The world's southernmost winegrowing region has gained a reputation for its bold, dramatically fruity Pinot Noirs, but also makes some surprisingly good Rieslings.

Other important parts of New Zealand include Waipara for Riesling and Burgundy varieties, Gisborne for Chardonnay, and Nelson for a spectrum of grape varieties similar to Marlborough's.

AKARUA

Akarua 2003 The Gullies Pinot Noir (Central Otago) $33. Charred and cola-laden on the nose, then delivers crisp, tart berry and roasted beet flavors on the palate. Solid but not terribly distinguished. **85** *—J.C. (12/1/2005)*

ALEXANDRA WINE COMPANY

Alexandra Wine Company 2002 Davishon Pinot Noir (Central Otago) $35. Herbal and minty up front, but then some pleasant cherry flavors take over. Turns a bit hard and drying on the finish. **84** *—J.C. (12/1/2005)*

Alexandra Wine Company 2001 Cragan Oir Alexandra Riesling (Central Otago) $20. **88** *—J.C. (8/1/2003)*

ALEXIA

Alexia 2002 Sauvignon Blanc (Nelson) $18. **87** *—J.C. (9/1/2003)*

ALLAN SCOTT

Allan Scott 1999 Chardonnay (Marlborough) $18. **88** *—J.C. (5/1/2001)*

Allan Scott 2002 Pinot Noir (Marlborough) $24. A poster boy for what is wrong with New Zealand Pinot Noir, the 2002 Allan Scott takes some delicate cherry fruit and covers it with oak that tastes like caramel or toasted marshmallows. Finishes short. It's not bad, but could have been so much better. **83** *—J.C. (7/1/2005)*

Allan Scott 2001 Riesling (Marlborough) $14. **87** *—J.C. (8/1/2003)*

Allan Scott 2000 Sauvignon Blanc (Marlborough) $15. **87** *—J.C. (5/1/2001)*

ALPHA DOMUS

Alpha Domus 2000 The Aviator Bordeaux Blend (Hawke's Bay) $37. Smoky and toasty at first, slowly giving up hints of Provençal herbs and dark fruit. Opens on the palate to show bright, concentrated berry fruit underscored by smoky oak and a bed of dried herbs. Crisp and fresh on the palate, this Bordeaux Blend could age into something interesting, or it could lose its fruit and show more tart-edged acids. Drink now. **88** *—J.C. (4/1/2004)*

Alpha Domus 2004 Chardonnay (Hawke's Bay) $13. Simple, fruity and fresh—not the stuff legends are made of, but a fine everyday Chard that should please most everyone. Tangy tropical and citrus fruit flavors carry a bit of weight, yet end crisp and tart. **86** *—J.C. (7/1/2005)*

Alpha Domus 2001 Chardonnay (North Island) $14. **85** *—J.C. (7/1/2002)*

Alpha Domus 2004 Sauvignon Blanc (Hawke's Bay) $13. This plump, medium-weight Sauvignon Blanc features simple grapefruit aromas and flavors. Turns a little tart, almost metallic, on the finish. **84** *—J.C. (7/1/2005)*

AMISFIELD

Amisfield 2004 Pinot Noir (Central Otago) $32. Very cleanly made and modern in style, with pure cherry flavors accented by vanilla and dried spices from new oak. This is a creamy, medium-bodied wine that isn't Burgundian by any measure, but represents textbook New World Pinot Noir. **88** *—J.C. (12/1/2005)*

Amisfield 2004 Sauvignon Blanc (Central Otago) $20. Shows all the requisite pea, pepper, and tropical fruit in front of an intense palate that comes on like an explosion of melon, nectarine, and grapefruit. On the finish it runs calmer, and the flavors and feel are harmonious. Says a lot for New Zealand, at least their Sauvignon Blanc. **91 Editors' Choice** *(7/1/2005)*

ATA RANGI

Ata Rangi 2003 Pinot Noir (Martinborough) $39. Worth decanting if you open a bottle now, as this wine really blossoms with time in the glass, opening to reveal floral, rose-petal notes. Mouthfeel is big, but buffered by soft tannins and cherry, cola, and herb flavors. Finishes long, with tangy acidity and dusty tannins. Hold 3–4 years. **90 Cellar Selection** *—J.C. (12/1/2005)*

Ata Rangi 1999 Célèbre Red Blend (Martinborough) $36. **87** *—J.C. (12/15/2003)*

BABICH

Babich 1996 Irongate Chardonnay (Hawke's Bay) $22. **91** *—S.H. (8/1/1999)*

Babich 1998 Sauvignon Blanc (Marlborough) $10. **87 Best Buy** *—S.H. (8/1/1999)*

BANNOCK BRAE

Bannock Brae 2002 Barrel Selection Pinot Noir (Central Otago) $38. Starts off with scents of toast, black cherries, and cola, while the flavors follow along, picking up hints of chocolate and plum. Supple and ready to drink. **87** *—J.C. (7/1/2005)*

BLADEN

Bladen 2000 Riesling (Marlborough) $11. **86** *—J.C. (8/1/2002)*

BLIND RIVER

Blind River 2003 Sauvignon Blanc (Marlborough) $13. A recent entrant into the U.S. market, the wines here are made under the direction of John Belsham, long-time wine judge and proprietor of his own Foxes Island label. This bargain-priced offering features ripe notes of melons, nectarines, and figs, with a touch of smoke and mineral for complexity. Lingers on the finish. **89 Best Buy** *—J.C. (8/1/2004)*

BRANCOTT

Brancott 1997 Fairhall Estate Cabernet Sauvignon (Marlborough) $22. 87 *—J.C. (5/1/2001)*

Brancott 2000 Chardonnay (Gisborne) $10. 85 Best Buy *—J.C. (5/1/2001)*

Brancott 1998 Ormond Estate Chardonnay (Gisborne) $25. 88 *—J.C. (5/1/2001)*

Brancott 1999 Reserve Chardonnay (Gisborne) $17. 88 *—D.T. (12/15/2001)*

Brancott 1998 Reserve Chardonnay (Gisborne) $15. 84 *—J.C. (5/1/2001)*

Brancott 1999 Reserve Merlot (Marlborough) $17. 86 *—J.C. (5/1/2001)*

Brancott 2002 Pinot Noir (Marlborough) $11. A plump, corpulent wine with just enough tannin to give it structure in the face of relatively low acidity. It's lush and chocolaty, adding hints of vanilla and dried spices. Drink now. **86 Best Buy** *—J.C. (8/1/2004)*

Brancott 1999 Reserve Pinot Noir (Marlborough) $17. 88 Best Buy *—J.C. (5/1/2001)*

Brancott 2002 Terraces Estate Pinot Noir (Marlborough) $22. A big step up from Brancott's basic Pinot Noir, this offers substantially more richness and concentration, a smoother, creamier mouthfeel and more intense and complex flavors. Smoke, cola, and earth aromas give way to black cherries and vanilla, finishing with a subtle note of dried spice and tea leaves. **88** *(12/31/2004)*

Brancott 2003 Sauvignon Blanc (Marlborough) $11. Shows some sweaty notes, but also plenty of zippy, peppery fruit backed by ripe melon flavors. It's surprisingly weighty for an entry-level bottling, its slightly oily texture offset by a tangy finish. **86** *—J.C. (8/1/2004)*

Brancott 2000 Sauvignon Blanc (Marlborough) $22. 86 Best Buy *—J.C. (5/1/2001)*

Brancott 1998 Brancott Estate Sauvignon Blanc (Marlborough) $25. 87 *—J.C. (5/1/2001)*

Brancott 2004 Reserve Sauvignon Blanc (Marlborough) $18. More pungent and powerful than the regular bottling, this wine shows more grass, more asparagus and yet more ripe stone fruit flavors. Fuller and richer on the palate, with a hint of oiliness to its texture and a slightly peppery aspect to the grapefruity finish. **89** *(12/31/2004)*

Brancott 2001 Reserve Sauvignon Blanc (Marlborough) $18. 88 *(8/1/2002)*

BURINGS

Burings 2004 Pinot Noir (Martinborough) $NA. Blends cola and cherry in a medium-bodied format that turns a bit lean and astringent on the finish. **84** *—J.C. (12/1/2005)*

CADWALLADERS RIVERSIDE

Cadwalladers Riverside 2004 Sauvignon Blanc (Hawke's Bay) $15. Less vegetable and more stone fruit suggests a slightly warmer climate, or a later harvest than a typical Marlborough Sauvignon Blanc. Nectarine and lime flavors are medium-weight and tangy on the finish—a bit simple, but appealing. **86** *—J.C. (7/1/2005)*

CAIRNBRAE

Cairnbrae 1999 Chardonnay (Marlborough) $15. 85 *—J.C. (5/1/2001)*

Cairnbrae 2000 Old River Riesling (Marlborough) $12. 87 Best Buy *—J.C. (5/1/2001)*

Cairnbrae 2003 The Stones Sauvignon Blanc (Marlborough) $13. Smells of pineapple and grapefruit at first, laced with plenty of herbal nuances. But the flavors are solid, citrusy at the core, and garnished by riper melon notes. Racy throughout, finishing with zippy acids. **87** *—J.C. (4/1/2004)*

Cairnbrae 1999 The Stones Sauvignon Blanc (Marlborough) $13. 86 *—J.C. (5/1/2001)*

CANTERBURY HOUSE

Canterbury House 2000 Pinot Gris (Waipara) $14. 82 *—J.C. (8/1/2002)*

Canterbury House 1999 Riesling (Waipara) $13. 84 *—J.C. (8/1/2002)*

CAROLINE BAY

Caroline Bay 2000 Cabernet Sauvignon (Hawke's Bay) $20. 85 *—J.C. (8/1/2002)*

Caroline Bay 2003 Sauvignon Blanc (Marlborough) $18. Plump, rounded, and a bit soft overall, with musky, ripe melon and stone fruits. A pleasant mouthful that lacks the zip and freshness of the very best examples. **86** *—J.C. (8/1/2004)*

Caroline Bay 2001 Sauvignon Blanc (Marlborough) $16. 90 Editors' Choice *(8/1/2002)*

CARRICK

Carrick 2002 Pinot Noir (Central Otago) $40. Delicately herbal on the nose, with dry, dusty scents of earth that accent pretty cherry aromas. Not a blockbuster, this is a more delicate, feminine style of wine from Central Otago. Finishes with a silky flourish. **89** *—J.C. (12/1/2005)*

Carrick 2001 Bannockburn Riesling (Central Otago) $20. 90 Editors' Choice *—J.C. (8/1/2003)*

CHANCELLOR ESTATES

Chancellor Estates 2000 Mt. Cass Road Pinot Noir (Waipara) $24. 83 *—J.C. (8/1/2002)*

Chancellor Estates 2000 Mt. Cass Road Sauvignon Blanc (Waipara) $15. 88 *(8/1/2002)*

CHARLES WIFFEN

Charles Wiffen 2000 Riesling (Marlborough) $12. 85 *—M.S. (12/15/2001)*

Charles Wiffen 2000 Sauvignon Blanc (Marlborough) $14. 89 *—D.T. (12/15/2001)*

CLEARVIEW

Clearview 2001 Reserve Chardonnay (Hawke's Bay) $45. Buttery and lactic, with big aromas of caramel-laced baked apples. It's sweet-tasting and laden with vanilla and dried spices, then turns tangy and citrusy on the finish, no doubt intended to balance the sensations of sweetness and butter. **83** *—J.C. (4/1/2004)*

CLOS MARGUERITE

Clos Marguerite 2003 Sauvignon Blanc (Marlborough) $17. An interesting rendition of Marlborough Sauvignon Blanc that comes close, but doesn't quite cross the line into vegetal. Tart, almost sour, passion fruit flavors are joined by piquant citrus and pungent earth notes. **86** *—J.C. (7/1/2005)*

CLOUDY BAY

Cloudy Bay 2002 Chardonnay (Marlborough) $29. This well-balanced example of cool-climate Chard features aromas of buttered cashews balanced by ample flavors of pear and melon. It's restrained and elegant, ending on lingering notes of smoke and nuts. **88** *—J.C. (8/1/2004)*

Cloudy Bay 2003 Pinot Noir (Marlborough) $29. With a core fashioned from older clonal material, this wine doesn't have quite the same vibrancy and fruit of some flashier counterparts. What it does have is some wonderful underbrushy complexity: earth, mushrooms, bracken, and spice, balanced by just enough cola and cherry fruit. Finishes wiry and a bit herbal. **88** *(12/15/2005)*

Cloudy Bay 2005 Sauvignon Blanc (Marlborough) $25. This is the highest this benchmark wine has ever scored with our tasters, from what is beginning to look like an excellent year for Marlborough Sauvignon Blanc. It's still in an early estery phase right now, marked by honeyed tropical fruits, nectarines and grapefruit, but you can sense the herbal-jalapeño flavors lurking in the background. Rich and powerful on the palate, long on the finish, with this wine, Cloudy Bay is on top of its game. **91** *(12/15/2005)*

Cloudy Bay 2003 Sauvignon Blanc (Marlborough) $29. Marlborough's standard bearer is always reliable, even if it no longer stands far above the pack. The 2003 is a worthy effort, combining grassy, herbal notes with a core of grapefruit and gooseberry flavors. A safe, solid choice, with enough weight in the mouth to pair with a variety of foods. **88** *—J.C. (8/1/2004)*

Cloudy Bay 2000 Sauvignon Blanc (Marlborough) $24. 90 Editors' Choice *—J.C. (5/1/2001)*

COOPERS CREEK

Coopers Creek 1998 Reserve Cabernet Sauvignon-Merlot (Hawke's Bay) $24. 88 *—J.C. (5/1/2001)*

Coopers Creek 1998 Merlot (Hawke's Bay) $14. 86 *—J.C. (5/1/2001)*

Coopers Creek 2000 Riesling (Hawke's Bay) $12. 87 Best Buy *—J.C. (5/1/2001)*

Coopers Creek 2000 Sauvignon Blanc (Marlborough) $10. 86 *—J.C. (5/1/2001)*

Coopers Creek 1999 Reserve Sauvignon Blanc (Marlborough) $18. 90 *—J.C. (5/1/2001)*

CORBANS

Corbans 1998 Winemaker's Private Bin Bordeaux Blend (Hawke's Bay) $20. 88 *—J.C. (5/1/2001)*

Corbans 1999 Winemaker's Selection Chardonnay (East Coast) $13. 85 *—J.C. (5/1/2001)*

Corbans 1999 Winemaker's Private Bin Sauvignon Blanc (Marlborough) $18. 83 *—J.C. (5/1/2001)*

COURTNEY'S POST

Courtney's Post 2002 Sauvignon Blanc (Marlborough) $16. Starts off with cat pee and asparagus, but also some honey-laced grapefruit. Medium-weight, with more grapefruit on the finish. A bit green, but okay. **84** *—J.C. (4/1/2004)*

CRAGGY RANGE

Craggy Range 2002 Les Beaux Cailloux Chardonnay (Hawke's Bay) $50. A full-bodied Chard (14.9% alcohol), but one that boasts a lush softness, delivering layers of toast, cinnamon, and lusciously ripe peaches. Has a mealy, leesy side to its character, and a hint of butter on the finish. Goes down easy, without a trace of heat. **89** *—J.C. (7/1/2005)*

Craggy Range 2002 Gimblett Gravels Vineyard Merlot (Hawke's Bay) $35. Starts off promising, with scents of blackberries, vanilla, and graham crackers, but does not live up to that promise on the palate. It's big, black and softly tannic, with coffee and vanilla shadings but not that much fruit or minerality. **86** *—J.C. (8/1/2004)*

Craggy Range 2003 Te Muna Block 1 Doug Wisor Memorial Pinot Noir (Martinborough Terrace) $60. Full-bodied, yet soft and enveloping, this silky-smooth wine seduces with its lush mouthfeel and ripe, plummy fruit, then layers on spice and savory complexities including hints of coffee, game, cola, and earth. Just 42 cases imported. **93** *—J.C. (12/1/2005)*

Craggy Range 2001 Old Renwick Vineyard Sauvignon Blanc (Marlborough) $17. **90 Editors' Choice** *(8/1/2002)*

Craggy Range 2003 Te Muna Road Vineyard Sauvignon Blanc (Martinborough) $18. This is a full, ripe style of Sauvignon Blanc, one that layers generous peach and nectarine flavors over a citrusy core. There's a hint of honeyed ripeness, and the finish is refreshingly zingy without being overly acidic. Beautifully balanced. **90 Editors' Choice** *—J.C. (4/1/2004)*

CROSSROADS

Crossroads 2004 Destination Series Sauvignon Blanc (Marlborough) $14. This Hawke's Bay winery has turned a credible example of Marlborough Sauvignon Blanc. Medium-weight, likely fattened up by a hint of residual sugar, but the flavors are sure: celery leaf and bell pepper joined by grapefruit and red berries. Tart and tangy on the finish. **85** *—J.C. (7/1/2005)*

DANIEL SCHUSTER

Daniel Schuster 2002 Omihi Hills Vineyard Selection Pinot Noir (Waipara) $30. Schuster's top wine comes from a single estate vineyard planted 20 years ago—ancient by New Zealand standards. Aromas are floral, layered over earthier notes of mushroom and sous bois, then flavors add black cherries to the mix. Still firm enough to warrant cellaring. Drink 2006–2012. **90** *—J.C. (12/1/2005)*

DASHWOOD

Dashwood 2001 Sauvignon Blanc (Marlborough) $NA. **88** *—S.H. (11/15/2002)*

DOMAINE GEORGES MICHEL

Domaine Georges Michel 2000 Golden Mile Chardonnay (Marlborough) $16. **88** *—J.C. (9/1/2003)*

Domaine Georges Michel 2002 Golden Mile Sauvignon Blanc (Marlborough) $15. **83** *—J.C. (9/1/2003)*

DRYLANDS

Drylands 2004 Pinot Noir (Marlborough) $14. Fairly priced, this entry-level New Zealand Pinot offers herbal and black cherry aromas and flavors. It's a bit simple and fruity, but finishes clean, with crisp acids. **86** *—J.C. (12/1/2005)*

DRYSTONE

Drystone 2003 Pinot Noir (Central Otago) $30. Supple, silky, and lush on the palate, with complex aromas and flavors of cola, cherries, and peppery-minty herbs, like wintergreen and sassafras. There's a dusting of cinnamon and clove as well, and a long, graceful finish. **90** *—J.C. (12/1/2005)*

DYED-IN-THE-WOOL

Dyed-In-The-Wool 2003 Unchangeable Pinot Noir (Canterbury) $14. Light in color and already showing some disturbing bricking at the rim, this Pinot is rather light-bodied, with dusty, earthy scents and flavors of cherries, herbs, and crushed pepper. Finishes with crisp acidity. **83** *—J.C. (12/1/2005)*

Dyed-In-The-Wool 2003 Unchangeable Ram's Reserve Pinot Noir (Marlborough) $20. Herbs and pie cherries form the base flavors for this modestly priced reserve bottling. Full-bodied, with soft tannins, yet turns crisp and tangy on the finish. **85** *—J.C. (12/1/2005)*

Dyed-In-The-Wool 2003 Unchangeable Sauvignon Blanc (Marlborough) $12. Grassy notes are nicely balanced by stone fruit and melon in this medium-weight wine that offers good length. A grapefruity tang on the finish gives it a refreshing feel. **87 Best Buy** *—J.C. (8/1/2004)*

ELSTREE

Elstree 1998 Reserve Riesling (Marlborough) $20. **90** *—S.H. (8/1/1999)*

ESCARPMENT

Escarpment 2001 Station Bus Vineyard Pinot Gris (Martinborough) $23. **85** *—J.C. (9/1/2003)*

Escarpment 2003 Pinot Noir (Martinborough) $45. Starts with a dusty, savory, spicy bouquet, then unfurls ripe black cherry flavors on the palate. Shows some slightly animale and sous-bois notes on the finish. Firmly structured, this should age well for the next five years or so. **88** *—J.C. (12/1/2005)*

Escarpment 2003 Kupe Pinot Noir (Martinborough) $60. Impressively big, rich, and well-extracted, with bold black cherry flavors, but also complex hints of cinnamon and other spices, floral notes and a pleasant herbal tinge to the softly tannic finish. Approachable now, but probably better in 3–4 years. Just 500 cases produced. **93** *—J.C. (12/1/2005)*

ESK VALLEY

Esk Valley 2000 Red Blend (Hawke's Bay) $15. 84 *—J.C. (12/15/2003)*

Esk Valley 2002 Riesling (Hawke's Bay) $19. 90 *—J.C. (8/1/2003)*

Esk Valley 2001 Sauvignon Blanc (Hawke's Bay) $19. 89 *(8/1/2002)*

FAIRHALL DOWNS

Fairhall Downs 2004 Pinot Noir (Marlborough) $NA. Darn tasty, combining cherry and cola flavors with dried spices. Plump and soft in the mouth, with a creamy, caressing mouthfeel, it's surprisingly long on the finish as well. Bravo. **90** *—J.C. (12/1/2005)*

Fairhall Downs 2000 Sauvignon Blanc (Marlborough) $18. 88 *—J.C. (5/1/2001)*

FELTON ROAD

Felton Road 2000 Barrel Fermented Chardonnay (Central Otago) $30. 88 *—J.C. (7/1/2002)*

Felton Road 2004 Pinot Noir (Central Otago) $44. Herbal on the nose, with hints of mint and spice, yet it also boasts full-bodied black cherry and plum flavors. Supple, velvety tannins provide a great mouthfeel, with little oak in evidence. Drink now–2010. **90** *—J.C. (12/1/2005)*

Felton Road 2000 Pinot Noir (Central Otago) $40. 90 *—J.C. (8/1/2002)*

Felton Road 2004 Block 3 Pinot Noir (Central Otago) $60. Adds a meaty, bacony edge to broad, mouthfilling flavors of black cherries and herbs. There's plenty of concentration in this wine, more than in many '04s, and some silky tannins on the finish that ideally deserve another 2–3 years of cellaring. Another winner from Felton Road. **91** *—J.C. (12/1/2005)*

Felton Road 2000 Block 3 Pinot Noir (Central Otago) $50. 89 *—J.C. (8/1/2002)*

Felton Road 2003 Block 5 Pinot Noir (Central Otago) $62. Yes, it's expensive, and no, it's not showing its full potential right now; prospective purchasers should be prepared to wait 2–3 years before opening. That said, it's an excellent wine, combining dried spices, a wiry, herbal note, and vibrant red cherries. An undercurrent of earth and chocolate provides the bass. Firmly structured, it's built to age. **91 Cellar Selection** *—J.C. (12/1/2005)*

Felton Road 2002 Riesling (Central Otago) $23. **91 Editors' Choice** *—J.C. (8/1/2003)*

Felton Road 2002 Block 1 Riesling (Central Otago) $25. 90 *—J.C. (8/1/2003)*

Felton Road 2000 Dry Riesling (Central Otago) $21. **91 Editors' Choice** *—J.C. (5/1/2001)*

FIRSTLAND

Firstland 2002 Sauvignon Blanc (Marlborough) $19. 86 *—J.C. (9/1/2003)*

FOREFATHERS

Forefathers 2002 Sauvignon Blanc (Marlborough) $13. 90 *—J.M. (1/1/2003)*

Forefathers 1999 Sauvignon Blanc (Marlborough) $14. 84 *—J.C. (5/1/2001)*

FORREST ESTATE

Forrest Estate 1997 Chardonnay (Marlborough) $15. 90 *—S.H. (8/1/1999)*

Forrest Estate 2001 Pinot Noir (Marlborough) $20. Quite oaky, but classy nonetheless, with cinnamon, cedar, and a hint of hickory playing leading roles in shaping the modest cherry fruit. The mouthfeel is the star, boasting a wonderfully supple texture that's the goal of every Pinot maker. **88** *—J.C. (4/1/2004)*

Forrest Estate 1997 Sauvignon Blanc (Marlborough) $15. 88 *—S.H. (8/1/1999)*

Forrest Estate 2001 Sauvignon Blanc (Marlborough) $19. 88 *—S.H. (11/15/2002)*

FOXES ISLAND

Foxes Island 2002 Chardonnay (Marlborough) $30. Intensely smoky on the nose, with powerful grilled-fruit aromas that echo on the palate. These grilled-peach flavors are tasty on their own, then pick up an added citrusy dimension on the tart, lemony finish. **87** *—J.C. (7/1/2005)*

Foxes Island 2000 Chardonnay (Marlborough) $26. 85 *—J.C. (9/1/2003)*

Foxes Island 1998 Chardonnay (Marlborough) $28. 83 *—J.C. (5/1/2001)*

Foxes Island 2001 Pinot Noir (Marlborough) $38. A delicately flavored, yet impressively plush wine, with scents of woodsmoke, black cherries and mushrooms echoed on the palate with added notes of sous bois and plums. **89** *—J.C. (8/1/2004)*

Foxes Island 1999 Pinot Noir (Marlborough) $24. 88 *—J.C. (8/1/2002)*

FRAMINGHAM

Framingham 2000 Chardonnay (Marlborough) $16. 87 *—D.T. (12/15/2001)*

Framingham 2001 Classic Riesling (Marlborough) $15. 88 *—J.C. (8/1/2002)*

FROMM WINERY

Fromm Winery 2002 Clayvin Vineyard Pinot Noir (Marlborough) $49. With its medium body and supple texture, this is harmonious, solid stuff. Aromas and flavors of cola, cherries, and earth are true to the variety, finishing on a herbal, tea-like note. Savor the mouthfeel, which comes as close to silk as vinously possible. 88 *—J.C. (7/1/2005)*

Fromm Winery 2002 La Strada Pinot Noir (Marlborough) $36. Seems a bit too oaky, with cedar and mint aromas covering the fruit, while the flavors veer toward chocolate and plum. Finishes tart and crisp, with bright acidity. 85 *—J.C. (7/1/2005)*

GIBBSTON VALLEY

Gibbston Valley 2000 Pinot Noir (Central Otago) $30. 88 *—S.H. (1/1/2002)*

GIESEN

Giesen 1999 Reserve Barrel Selection Chardonnay (Marlborough) $20. 88 *—J.C. (5/1/2001)*

Giesen 1999 Pinot Noir (Canterbury) $16. 85 *—J.C. (5/1/2001)*

Giesen 1999 Noble School Road Late Harvest Riesling (Canterbury) $18. 88 *—J.C. (5/1/2001)*

Giesen 2003 Single Vineyard Selection Sauvignon Blanc (Marlborough) $20. Lime and lemon zest along with green pepper on the nose, and then sour fruit and too much canned pea flavor on the palate. Hard to describe other than to say that it lacks fruit. 82 *(7/1/2005)*

GLAZEBROOK

Glazebrook 2000 Chardonnay (Gisborne) $11. 87 *—J.C. (7/1/2002)*

Glazebrook 1999 Merlot-Cabernet Sauvignon (Hawke's Bay) $19. 87 *—J.C. (5/1/2001)*

Glazebrook 2002 Sauvignon Blanc (Marlborough) $13. 88 Best Buy *—J.C. (9/1/2003)*

GOLDWATER

Goldwater 1998 Bordeaux Blend (Waiheke Island) $60. 89 *—J.C. (5/1/2001)*

Goldwater 2002 Roseland Chardonnay (Marlborough) $24. Displays copious amounts of tropical fruit, all underscored by delicate buttered-toast notes. It's medium-weight and plump on the palate, showing pear, vanilla, and toast on the moderately long finish. 89 *—J.C. (4/1/2004)*

Goldwater 1999 Roseland Chardonnay (Central Otago) $27. 90 *—J.C. (5/1/2001)*

Goldwater 2002 Zell Chardonnay (Waiheke Island) $40. Nicely done, with toasty, mealy notes that are balanced by ripe pear and peach fruit. Hints of grilled fruit and roasted nuts complete the picture, finishing with lingering echoes of smoke. 90 *—J.C. (8/1/2004)*

Goldwater 2002 Esslin Merlot (Waiheke Island) $100. This particular bottling from Goldwater continues to be an enigma. Despite the wine's fame (and price), I've never been moved by it. The 2002 shows pretty, Bordeaux-like nuances of earth and tobacco on the nose, then charming cherry and vanilla flavors on the palate. Yet it never really fleshes out, and it turns a bit herbal and lean on the finish. 86 *—J.C. (7/1/2005)*

Goldwater 1998 Esslin Merlot (Waiheke Island) $99. 87 *—J.C. (5/1/2001)*

Goldwater 2002 Dog Point Sauvignon Blanc (Marlborough) $20. 89 *—J.C. (9/1/2003)*

Goldwater 2004 New Dog Sauvignon Blanc (Marlborough) $20. Big-time vegetal, with aromas of cooked asparagus and canned peas. In the mouth, you'll find citrus, but on the finish that vegetal character comes back with vengeance. 84 *(7/1/2005)*

GREENHOUGH

Greenhough 2000 Riesling (Nelson) $12. 86 *—M.S. (12/15/2001)*

GROVE MILL

Grove Mill 2001 Chardonnay (Marlborough) $18. 87 *—J.C. (9/1/2003)*

Grove Mill 2002 Pinot Gris (Marlborough) $18. 86 *—J.C. (9/1/2003)*

Grove Mill 2004 Pinot Noir (Marlborough) $25. This winery is normally pretty reliable, so one has to wonder what happened here. Brown sugar and mushroom aromas give way to earthy flavors and not much fruit. Tasted twice, with consistent results. 82 *—J.C. (12/1/2005)*

Grove Mill 2001 Pinot Noir (Marlborough) $23. 90 *—J.C. (9/1/2003)*

Grove Mill 2002 Riesling (Marlborough) $15. The medium-weight, off-dry Riesling boasts fresh aromas of pear and quince, enriched by a touch of honey. The flavors of baked apples and poached pears are bolstered by firm, lime-like acids that impart a refreshing quality to the finish. 89 *—J.C. (8/1/2004)*

Grove Mill 2000 Riesling (Marlborough) $16. 88 *—J.C. (5/1/2001)*

Grove Mill 2000 Sauvignon Blanc (Marlborough) $17. 87 *—J.C. (5/1/2001)*

GUNN ESTATE

Gunn Estate 1998 Woolshed Merlot-Cabernet Sauvignon (Ohiti Valley) $17. **86** *—J.C. (5/1/2001)*

GYPSY DANCER

Gypsy Dancer 2003 Gibbston Home Estate Vineyard Pinot Noir (Central Otago) $50. From Gary Andrus's NZ venture, this is a plump, appealing Pinot that boasts scents of smoke and black cherries, followed by flavors of woodsmoke and plum. A bit astringent on the finish, with firm tannins that deserve to be cellared 2–3 years. **88** *—J.C. (7/1/2005)*

HERZOG

Herzog 1999 Bordeaux Blend (Marlborough) $45. This Bordeaux-inspired blend seems a touch overdone—the fruit has a dried quality to it, reminiscent of prunes and dates; the oak is chocolaty and rich. Seems supple enough on the palate, then firm tannins grab on the finish. **85** *—J.C. (4/1/2004)*

Herzog 2001 Montepulciano-Cabernet Fanc (Marlborough) $34. When you need to stump your wine-geek friends in a blind tasting, here's the perfect choice. After all, how many of them even know that Montepulciano is grown outside Italy? It's even pretty palatable, if somewhat heavy and low acid. Blackberry, blueberry, and chocolate flavors are chewy and mouthfilling. **86** *—J.C. (4/1/2004)*

NEW ZEALAND

HIGHFIELD ESTATE

Highfield Estate 2001 Pinot Noir (Marlborough) $23. This pretty, relatively lightweight Pinot boasts a skinny thread of red cherry fruit wrapped in layers of root beer, dried spices, and brown sugar. Finishes with some woody notes of dark coffee and chocolate. **86** *—J.C. (8/1/2004)*

Highfield Estate 2004 Sauvignon Blanc (Marlborough) $20. Always a nice wine, the '04 succeeds by pushing steely, sharp aromas of nettles, grapefruit and citrus, and then following that up with passion fruit, grapefruit and melon flavors. Basically, it tastes as it smells, and it finishes crystal clean if a tiny bit short. **89** *(7/1/2005)*

Highfield Estate 2001 Sauvignon Blanc (Marlborough) $NA. **90** *—S.H. (11/15/2002)*

HOLMES

Holmes 2003 Pinot Noir (Nelson) $25. Leathery and leafy on the nose, although the bouquet also incorporates some cherry scents. It's a lean, focused wine, one that finishes tart and zingy. **84** *—J.C. (12/1/2005)*

HOUSE OF NOBILO

House of Nobilo 2004 Regional Collection Chardonnay (East Coast) $12. Well-crafted and well-priced, with gentle scents of toasted nuts and grilled peaches picking up additional notes of pear and melon. Medium-weight, with a soft, easy finish. **87 Best Buy** *—J.C. (7/1/2005)*

House of Nobilo 2002 Icon Pinot Noir (Marlborough) $20. Don't look for big fruit in this wine—you'll be disappointed. What you will find is plenty of earthy, spicy complexity. The flavors are slightly herbal and mushroomy, yet with a supple, rich texture. A bit tannic right now, so give it a year or two before pulling the cork. **88** *—J.C. (4/1/2004)*

House of Nobilo 2000 Fall Harvest Sauvignon Blanc (Marlborough) $10. **86 Best Buy** *—J.C. (5/1/2001)*

House of Nobilo 2004 Icon Sauvignon Blanc (Marlborough) $20. A wine that evoked no consensus among our tasters. Is more less or is it more? The nose is rich and packed full of asparagus, canned pea, and pickled bell pepper, and the palate is thick and syrupy. One reviewer called it "good within the paradigm"; another found it mushy and lacking in balance. **85** *(7/1/2005)*

HUIA

Huia 2003 Gewürztraminer (Marlborough) $19. Subtly flowery on the nose, with hints of pear and spice, Claire and Mike Allen's Gewürz is more restrained and controlled than many. Understated poached pears feature only a modicum of spice. Gewürztraminer is one grape that can benefit from full volume, and this one is just too quiet. **85** *—J.C. (7/1/2005)*

Huia 2004 Pinot Gris (Marlborough) $19. This off-dry rendition of Pinot Gris (the "it" grape in NZ right now) boasts a lovely, rich mouthfeel. Aromas of pear, almond, and apple, then more of the same on the palate, picking up some pineapple notes on the finish. Not complex enough to rate higher, but a very pleasing wine. **86** *—J.C. (7/1/2005)*

Huia 2002 Pinot Noir (Marlborough) $27. Plump and juicy, but missing some of the velvety texture that has marked this wine in the past. Roasted cherries and fresh herbs join dark chocolate, coffee, and caramel flavors. **86** *—J.C. (8/1/2004)*

Huia 2000 Pinot Noir (Marlborough) $24. **90** *—J.C. (8/1/2002)*

Huia 2002 Riesling (Marlborough) $15. **89** *—J.C. (8/1/2003)*

Huia 2003 Sauvignon Blanc (Marlborough) $18. Concentrated, racy, and intense, packed with everchanging notes of fruit that range from peach and melon to passion fruit, pineapple, and grapefruit. The long, tangy finish reverberates across the palate long after the wine is gone. **91 Editors' Choice** *—J.C. (4/1/2004)*

Huia 2000 Brut (Marlborough) $33. Disjointed, with ample toast, eggs, and baked apple flavors but also a citrusy note that turns metallic on the finish. A disappointing effort from one of NZ's artisanal producers, or just a badly handled batch of bubbly? Tasted twice. **83** *—J.C. (6/1/2005)*

HUNTAWAY

Huntaway 1998 Reserve Chardonnay (North Island) $15. 82 *—J.C. (5/1/2001)*

HUNTER'S

Hunter's 2003 Pinot Noir (Marlborough) $18. Relatively light in color, but very nicely perfumed and floral on the nose. Flavors are a bit simpler, focusing on cherries and vanilla. This soft, easy-drinking wine would make a fine accompaniment to delicate salmon dishes. **87** *—J.C. (12/1/2005)*

Hunter's 1999 Sauvignon Blanc (Marlborough) $12. 90 *—S.H. (6/1/2001)*

ISABEL ESTATE

Isabel Estate 1997 Chardonnay (Marlborough) $20. 91 *—S.H. (8/1/1999)*

Isabel Estate 2001 Pinot Noir (Marlborough) $30. 86 *—J.C. (9/1/2003)*

Isabel Estate 2000 Riesling (Marlborough) $18. 90 *—J.C. (5/1/2001)*

Isabel Estate 2004 Sauvignon Blanc (Marlborough) $21. Hits this country's style like an arrow to the bull's eye. Fragrant as can be, with aromas of pineapple, passion fruit, tomatillo, fresh pea, and wheat grass. If that's not enough, the palate is round and spotless, with a tropical overload of sweet and tart tastes. Finishes long and precise, with radiant zest. **91 Editors' Choice** *(7/1/2005)*

Isabel Estate 2001 Sauvignon Blanc (Marlborough) $18. 92 *—S.H. (11/15/2002)*

Isabel Estate 1999 Noble Sauvage Sauvignon Blanc (Marlborough) $35/375 ml. 92 *—J.C. (5/1/2001)*

JACKSON ESTATE

Jackson Estate 1998 Reserve Chardonnay (Marlborough) $25. 84 *—J.C. (5/1/2001)*

Jackson Estate 2001 Unoaked Chardonnay (Marlborough) $15. 82 *—J.C. (11/15/2002)*

Jackson Estate 2000 Dry Riesling (Marlborough) $15. 87 *—J.C. (8/1/2003)*

Jackson Estate 2004 Sauvignon Blanc (Marlborough) $13. Citrusy and grassy on the nose, picking up hints of boxwood on the way to a surprisingly plump yet neutral midpalate. Tangy on the finish. **85** *—J.C. (7/1/2005)*

Jackson Estate 2002 Sauvignon Blanc (Marlborough) $17. 90 Editors' Choice *—J.C. (9/1/2003)*

KAHURANGI

Kahurangi 2004 Pinot Noir (Nelson) $24. Aims at a perfumed, elegant style and partially succeeds. There's a bright, floral bouquet, but the flavors are tart, with shadings of cherry and chocolate that finish short. **84** *—J.C. (12/1/2005)*

KATHY LYNSKEY

Kathy Lynskey 2003 Godfrey Reserve Chardonnay (Marlborough) $29. Starts off a bit floral, then picks up hints of toast and lemon curd on the nose. In the mouth, it's a plump, medium-weight wine, with crisp citrus flavors that linger on the finish. **87** *—J.C. (7/1/2005)*

Kathy Lynskey 2004 Single Vineyard Pinot Gris (Marlborough) $25. Starts with a nutty, almond-like note, then delivers lots of ripe melon flavors in a plump, appealing format. Slightly off-dry, but well balanced, without any cloying sweetness on the finish. **87** *—J.C. (7/1/2005)*

Kathy Lynskey 2004 Vineyard Select Sauvignon Blanc (Marlborough) $19. A bit richer than most NZ SBs, this wine also incorporates chalky-minerally notes that elevate it above the crowd. Take complex aromas of peach, apple, grapefruit, and mineral, add nectarine flavors and a long finish, and you've got a winning recipe. Drink over the next year or so. **90 Editors' Choice** *—J.C. (7/1/2005)*

KIM CRAWFORD

Kim Crawford 1996 Rory Brut (Marlborough) $NA. 87 *—J.C. (5/1/2001)*

Kim Crawford 2000 Tietjen Chardonnay (Gisborne) $20. 91 Editors' Choice *—J.C. (5/1/2001)*

Kim Crawford 2000 Unoaked Chardonnay (Marlborough) $17. 88 *—J.C. (5/1/2001)*

Kim Crawford 1998 Unoaked Chardonnay (Marlborough) $15. 90 *(11/15/1999)*

Kim Crawford 1999 Te Awanga Merlot (Hawke's Bay) $21. 88 *—J.C. (5/1/2001)*

Kim Crawford 2000 Boyzown Vineyard Pinot Gris (Marlborough) $18. 88 *—J.C. (5/1/2001)*

Kim Crawford 2002 Pinot Noir (Marlborough) $14. For the price, this is a good introduction to NZ Pinot Noir, showing a smooth mouthfeel and smoky, briary complexities layered over tangy beet and cherry fruit. **86** *—J.C. (4/1/2004)*

Kim Crawford 2000 Anderson Vineyard Pinot Noir (Marlborough) $35. 90 *—M.S. (12/15/2001)*

Kim Crawford 2000 Dry Riesling (Marlborough) $16. 90 Editors' Choice *—J.C. (5/1/2001)*

Kim Crawford 1998 Sauvignon Blanc (Wairau) $15. 88 —*S.H. (8/1/1999)*

Kim Crawford 2002 Sauvignon Blanc (Marlborough) $18. 89 —*S.H. (1/1/2002)*

Kim Crawford 1999 Sauvignon Blanc (Marlborough) $15. 92 —*L.W. (4/1/2000)*

KINGSLEY ESTATE

Kingsley Estate 2000 Cabernet Sauvignon-Merlot (Hawke's Bay) $55. American consumers benefit from the late arrival of this wine on the market, as initial reports out of New Zealand suggested it was a tannic beast. Now, the wine is ready to drink, with dark, earthy flavors of plum and tobacco riding atop soft, enveloping tannins. Drink now or hold another 2–3 years. 88 —*J.C. (7/1/2005)*

KOURA BAY

Koura Bay 2001 Whalesback Awatere Valley Sauvignon Blanc (Marlborough) $18. 85 —*S.H. (11/15/2002)*

KUMEU RIVER

Kumeu River 2003 Chardonnay (Kumeu) $32. Just a bare step behind Kumeu's Mate's Vineyard, the regular Chardonnay is still a special wine. The aromas meld smoke, butter, and tropical fruit, while the palate is a bit hard-edged at this stage, yielding mostly crisp, citrusy flavors. Give it a year or two in the bottle to soften. 89 —*J.C. (7/1/2005)*

Kumeu River 1999 Chardonnay (Kumeu) $23. 90 Editors' Choice —*J.C. (5/1/2001)*

Kumeu River 2003 Mate's Vineyard Chardonnay (Kumeu) $37. One of New Zealand's perennial award-winners, the 2003 Mate's Chard features wonderfully complete aromas that combine scents of smoke and toasted oats with grilled fruit and nut meat. It's full-bodied, drenching the palate with grilled-nut and citrus flavors, before finishing on a long, harmonious note. 91 Editors' Choice —*J.C. (7/1/2005)*

Kumeu River 1997 Matés Vineyard Chardonnay (Kumeu) $40. 90 —*J.C. (10/1/2000)*

Kumeu River 2002 Pinot Noir (Kumeu) $30. A lightweight, delicate style, with slightly stinky, smoky and cedary aromas that give way only stubbornly to cherry and herb flavors. Tart and clean on the finish. 86 —*J.C. (6/6/2005)*

Kumeu River 1998 Pinot Noir (Kumeu) $18. 87 —*M.S. (10/1/2000)*

Kumeu River 1997 Sauvignon Blanc (Kumeu) $17. 88 —*S.H. (8/1/1999)*

NEW ZEALAND

KUSUDA

Kusuda 2003 C Pinot Noir (Martinborough) $NA. The "C" stands for clay, the predominant soil type in the vineyard. Well-oaked, with smoke and berry aromas and flavors and a wiry, herbal thread wrapped around a core of bright boysenberry fruit. Shows some sturdy tannins on the finish, so hold 2–3 years. 89 —*J.C. (12/1/2005)*

LAKE CHALICE

Lake Chalice 2003 Pinot Noir (Marlborough) $20. A big-bodied, somewhat beefy Pinot, with rustic herbal tendrils giving the cherry fruit an earthy, beet-like nuance. Delivers a mouthful of flavor, but it's missing the silky mouthfeel of great Pinot. 86 —*J.C. (7/1/2005)*

Lake Chalice 2004 Riesling (Marlborough) $16. Reasonably full-bodied despite only 12.5% alcohol, this off-dry Riesling features aromas and flavors of ripe peaches and vanilla, while a shot of grapefruit cleans things up nicely, adding needed delineation to the finish. 87 —*J.C. (7/1/2005)*

Lake Chalice 2001 Falcon Vineyard Late Harvest Riesling (Marlborough) $17. 83 —*J.C. (8/1/2003)*

Lake Chalice 2001 Sauvignon Blanc (Marlborough) $15. 84 *(8/1/2002)*

LAWSON'S DRY HILLS

Lawson's Dry Hills 2004 Gewürztraminer (Marlborough) $16. Rather honeyed and peachy, with lychee and some extremely ripe grapefruit scents that presage broad, mouthfilling flavors of lychee, stone fruits, and citrus. Shows good weight and concentration on the palate and a long, spicy finish. Even the price is right. What's not to like? 90 Editors' Choice —*J.C. (7/1/2005)*

Lawson's Dry Hills 2004 Pinot Noir (Marlborough) $22. Yet another well-priced offering from Marlborough, Lawson's Pinot is a plump, fruity wine framed by ample oak. Toasty and cedary on the nose, it finishes with some dry wood tannins. Give it another year to smooth out. 87 —*J.C. (12/1/2005)*

Lawson's Dry Hills 2004 Sauvignon Blanc (Marlborough) $16. Smells just right, with bits of passion fruit and grassy notes, and also riper hints of apricot. But it just delivers on the palate, where it seems a bit light and hollow before finishing tart and shrill. A wine of unfulfilled promise. 84 —*J.C. (7/1/2005)*

Lawson's Dry Hills 2002 Sauvignon Blanc (Marlborough) $16. Yet another fine effort from this Marlborough winery, the 2002 Sauvignon Blanc is a big, rich, mouthfilling wine. Hints of honey and smoke accent gooseberries and nectarines. Drink now. 88 —*J.C. (4/1/2004)*

LEGRYS

LeGrys 2000 Adam's Estate Pinot Noir (Marlborough) $26. 83 —*J.C. (9/1/2003)*

LINACRE LANE

Linacre Lane 2003 Pinot Noir (Martinborough) $NA. Herbal, with green aromas that come awfully close to green bean. Earthy and mushroomy on the palate, with a short finish. **83** *—J.C. (12/1/2005)*

LINDEN ESTATE

Linden Estate 2000 Merlot (Hawke's Bay) $13. **83** *—J.C. (12/15/2003)*

LONGRIDGE

Longridge 1999 Chardonnay (Hawke's Bay) $10. **81** *—J.C. (5/1/2001)*

LYNSKEYS WAIRAU PEAKS

Lynskeys Wairau Peaks 2002 Chardonnay (Marlborough) $25. **90** *—J.C. (9/1/2003)*

Lynskeys Wairau Peaks 2001 Reserve Chardonnay (Marlborough) $25. **87** *—J.C. (9/1/2003)*

Lynskeys Wairau Peaks 2000 Gewürztraminer (Marlborough) $17. **87** *—J.C. (5/1/2001)*

Lynskeys Wairau Peaks 2001 Merlot (Marlborough) $45. **88** *—J.C. (12/15/2003)*

Lynskeys Wairau Peaks 2002 Pinot Noir (Marlborough) $33. This is a sturdy, chunky NZ Pinot with plenty of black cherry fruit. It's also marked by distinctive herb and smoke shadings that give it a welcome degree of complexity. Despite the relatively short finish, it's a strong effort overall. **87** *—J.C. (4/1/2004)*

Lynskeys Wairau Peaks 1999 Pinot Noir (Marlborough) $33. **82** *—J.C. (5/1/2001)*

Lynskeys Wairau Peaks 2001 Sauvignon Blanc (Marlborough) $17. **87** *(8/1/2002)*

Lynskeys Wairau Peaks 2003 Vineyard Select Sauvignon Blanc (Marlborough) $19. Seems light and a little dilute for this bottling, with pleasant aromas of passion fruit, pineapple, bell peppers, and a hint of asparagus, but relatively neutral flavors, ending clean and fresh. **84** *—J.C. (8/1/2004)*

MAIN DIVIDE

Main Divide 2004 Pinot Noir (Canterbury) $25. From the folks at Pegasus Bay, this is a blend of purchased and estate fruit. Cherry notes blend with hints of mint, giving a bit of a medicinal edge to the flavors. Supple, but picks up a touch more green on the finish. **86** *—J.C. (12/1/2005)*

MARGRAIN

Margrain 2003 Pinot Noir (Martinborough) $25. Toasty and bacony on the nose, but there's also a helping of black cherries. Shows more mushroom and forest-floor character with time in the glass, and the fruit moves toward the background. **86** *—J.C. (12/1/2005)*

MARLBOROUGH WINES

Marlborough Wines 2003 Sauvignon Blanc (Marlborough) $16. Plump and welcoming, this is an easy-to-drink introduction to New Zealand Sauvignon. Slightly grassy on the nose, but not aggressive, with a core of ripe nectarine and pink grapefruit flavors. Drink now. **88** *—J.C. (7/1/2005)*

MARTINBOROUGH VINEYARD

Martinborough Vineyard 2003 Pinot Noir (Martinborough) $40. Favors a meaty, savory style, with ample dried spice and underbrush character. There's enough cherry fruit to support the other elements, along with an herbal edge on the finish. **85** *—J.C. (12/1/2005)*

Martinborough Vineyard 1999 Late Harvest Riesling (Martinborough) $29. **93** *—J.C. (5/1/2001)*

MATAHIWI

Matahiwi 2004 Holly Pinot Noir (Wairarapa) $NA. Darker and toastier than Matahiwi's regular bottling, but not appreciably more likable, with black cherry fruit and a slightly herbal note on the finish. **86** *—J.C. (12/1/2005)*

MATARIKI

Matariki 1999 Chardonnay (Hawke's Bay) $22. **89** *—J.C. (5/1/2001)*

Matariki 1999 Merlot (Hawke's Bay) $25. **83** *—J.C. (5/1/2001)*

Matariki 2000 Late Harvest Riesling (Hawke's Bay) $30. **87** *—J.C. (8/1/2003)*

Matariki 2004 Sauvignon Blanc (Hawke's Bay) $18. This Sauvignon has moved toward a grassier style in recent vintages, but it's still darn good. Lime and herb notes dominate the nose, but it adds just enough chalk and grapefruit nuances on the palate to give it needed complexity. Plump yet crisply acidic at the same time, ending on racy grapefruit notes that finish without any trace of harshness. **90** *—J.C. (7/1/2005)*

Matariki 2002 Sauvignon Blanc (Hawke's Bay) $14. **84** *—J.C. (9/1/2003)*

Matariki 2000 Sauvignon Blanc (Hawke's Bay) $16. **87** *—J.C. (5/1/2001)*

Matariki 2001 Syrah (Hawke's Bay) $30. Shows the characteristic herbal and peppery notes of Rhône-style Syrah, accenting crisp blackberry fruit. Complex on the palate, wrapping the herbs and peppers tightly around rich fruit to the point that they're really inseparable. **89** *—J.C. (4/1/2004)*

MATUA VALLEY

Matua Valley 1998 Bordeaux Blend (Hawke's Bay) $16. 87 *—J.C. (10/1/2000)*

Matua Valley 1998 Matheson Vineyard Bordeaux Blend (Hawke's Bay) $20. 87 *—J.C. (10/1/2000)*

Matua Valley 2001 Ararimu Cabernet Sauvignon-Merlot (Hawke's Bay) $23. 86 *—J.C. (12/15/2003)*

Matua Valley 2004 Chardonnay (Gisborne) $12. Starts with plenty of buttered toast or popcorn on the nose, then reveals leaner pear and citrus flavors on the palate. This medium-bodied wine finishes crisp and tart, making it suitable as an apéritif. **84** *—J.C. (12/1/2005)*

Matua Valley 1999 Chardonnay (Eastern Bays) $15. 86 *—J.C. (5/1/2001)*

Matua Valley 2002 Judd Estate Chardonnay (Gisborne) $17. An excellent example of Gisborne Chardonnay, with lush peach and tropical fruit framed by warm vanilla oak. Finishes with flourishes of butter, honey, and caramel, along with bracing tartness. **89** *—J.C. (4/1/2004)*

Matua Valley 1998 Judd Estate Chardonnay (Gisborne) $18. 89 *—J.C. (10/1/2000)*

Matua Valley 1998 Judd Estate Innovator Handpicked Chardonnay (Gisborne) $45. 90 *—J.C. (5/1/2001)*

Matua Valley 2002 Bullrush Merlot (Hawke's Bay) $20. Slightly jammy on the nose, blending in hints of graham cracker. This low-tannin, fruit-forward wine is a decent cocktail Merlot, laden with sweet black cherries but without a strong backbone from which to hang all of its flesh. **85** *—J.C. (4/1/2004)*

Matua Valley 1996 Smith-Dartmoor Estate Merlot (Hawke's Bay) $18. 82 *—J.C. (10/1/2000)*

Matua Valley 2000 Late Harvest Muscat (Eastern Bays) $13. 86 *—J.C. (5/1/2001)*

Matua Valley 2004 Pinot Gris (Marlborough) $12. Finding good Pinot Gris at this price is a challenge, but Matua Valley, part of Beringer-Blass Wine Estates, has hit a home run with its fresh herb- and citrus-laced 2004. There's just enough plumpness to make it satisfying in the mouth, while the flavors of pear and apple end on a clean, refreshing note. **87 Best Buy** *—J.C. (7/1/2005)*

Matua Valley 2002 Pinot Noir (Marlborough) $11. It's supple, smooth and the price is right, but the flavors are herbaceous and menthol-like, with sour cherry fruit and white gumdrop notes. **83** *—J.C. (8/1/2004)*

Matua Valley 2005 Sauvignon Blanc (Marlborough) $12. Bursting with ripe tropical flavors, lush and fruity. There's just a hint of green herb—enough so that you know it's Sauvignon Blanc—but the emphasis here is on forward fruit. Finishes with crisp acids and more and more fruit. **88 Best Buy** *—J.C. (12/1/2005)*

Matua Valley 2002 Sauvignon Blanc (Hawke's Bay) $11. 88 Best Buy *—S.H. (11/15/2002)*

Matua Valley 1999 Matheson Vineyard Sauvignon Blanc (Hawke's Bay) $15. 88 *—J.C. (5/1/2001)*

MEBUS

Mebus 2000 Dakins Road Bordeaux Blend (Wairarapa) $25. 87 *—J.C. (12/15/2003)*

MILLS REEF

Mills Reef 1999 Reserve Chardonnay (Hawke's Bay) $17. 84 *—J.C. (5/1/2001)*

Mills Reef 2002 Elspeth One Red Blend (Hawke's Bay) $35. Big, black and dense—who knew that New Zealand could make wines this big and burly? It's grapy and concentrated, with hints of licorice and mouthdrying tannins. Could improve with age, hopefully picking up some grace and nuance. Drink now–2010+. **87** *—J.C. (8/1/2004)*

Mills Reef 1998 Sauvignon Blanc (Hawke's Bay) $13. 87 *—S.H. (8/1/1999)*

Mills Reef 2002 Reserve Sauvignon Blanc (Hawke's Bay) $14. 87 *—J.C. (9/1/2003)*

Mills Reef 2000 Reserve Sauvignon Blanc (Hawke's Bay) $14. 83 *—J.C. (5/1/2001)*

Mills Reef 1998 Reserve Sauvignon Blanc (Hawke's Bay) $13. 90 *—L.W. (8/1/1999)*

Mills Reef 2000 Mere Road Elspeth Syrah (Hawke's Bay) $30. 92 Editors' Choice *—S.H. (11/15/2002)*

MONKEY BAY

Monkey Bay 2004 Sauvignon Blanc (Marlborough) $10. Ripe, not bracing, this new star in the Constellation portfolio boasts subtle aromas of stone fruit and citrus that become more apparent on the palate, emerging as nectarine and pink grapefruit. Plump and easy to drink; a real crowd-pleaser at a crowd-pleasing price. **87 Best Buy** *—J.C. (7/1/2005)*

MORWORTH ESTATE

Morworth Estate 1999 Pinot Noir (Canterbury) $NA. 82 *—J.C. (8/1/2002)*

Morworth Estate 2001 Sauvignon Blanc (Marlborough) $11. 85 *—J.C. (9/1/2003)*

MOUNT EDWARD

Mount Edward 2003 Pinot Noir (Central Otago) $39. Relatively light in color, but long on flavor, this is a light-bodied, silky wine that comes across as very Burgundian. Subtle herb and spice notes accent delicate cherry flavors, and there's a wiry, tensile strength to it despite the softness of the tannins. **89** *—J.C. (12/1/2005)*

MOUNT RILEY

Mount Riley 2001 Chardonnay (Marlborough) $13. 91 Best Buy *—S.H. (11/15/2002)*

Mount Riley 2001 Pinot Noir (Marlborough) $20. 87 *—J.C. (9/1/2003)*

Mount Riley 2001 Sauvignon Blanc (Marlborough) $15. 90 Editors' Choice *(8/1/2002)*

MT. DIFFICULTY

Mt. Difficulty 1999 Chardonnay (Central Otago) $17. 88 *—J.C. (5/1/2001)*

Mt. Difficulty 2003 Pinot Noir (Central Otago) $30. A much better value than the more complex Target Gully bottling, this Bannockburn Pinot offers up dark chocolate and cola flavors, blended with treebark and plum. Dark, earthy notes are borne on a plump, medium-bodied mouthfeel that maintains decent structure. Drink or hold through 2010. **88** *—J.C. (12/1/2005)*

Mt. Difficulty 2004 Roaring Meg Pinot Noir (Central Otago) $20. Mt. Difficulty's entry-level Pinot is from young vines. It features perfumed scents of cherries and a plump, juicy, fruit-laden midpalate, then thins out a bit on the finish, where it picks up some herbal notes. **86** *—J.C. (12/1/2005)*

Mt. Difficulty 2000 Riesling (Central Otago) $15. 84 *—D.T. (12/15/2001)*

Mt. Difficulty 2000 Sauvignon Blanc (Central Otago) $13. 88 *—J.C. (5/1/2001)*

MUD HOUSE WINE COMPANY

Mud House Wine Company 1999 Black Swan Reserve Merlot (Marlborough) $25. 82 *—J.C. (12/15/2003)*

Mud House Wine Company 2002 Sauvignon Blanc (Marlborough) $16. 83 *—J.C. (9/1/2003)*

MUDDY WATER

Muddy Water 2003 Pinot Noir (Waipara) $31. Crisp and relatively high in acidity, but that's partially offset by soft, supple tannins. Tangy cherry flavors pick up meaty, leathery nuances. **84** *—J.C. (12/1/2005)*

MURDOCH JAMES

Murdoch James 2004 Pinot Noir (Martinborough) $20. A bit on the simple side, but lively, fresh and ultimately satisfying. Impressively pure black cherry fruit does pick up a hint of spice on the finish. A nice introduction to NZ Pinot that should drink well from now through 2010. **87** *—J.C. (12/1/2005)*

Murdoch James 2001 Waiata Pinot Noir (Martinborough) $27. 86 *—J.C. (9/1/2003)*

Murdoch James 2001 Syrah (Martinborough) $27. 82 *—J.C. (12/15/2003)*

NAUTILUS

Nautilus 1999 Chardonnay (Marlborough) $18. 86 *—J.C. (5/1/2001)*

Nautilus 2001 Pinot Gris (Marlborough) $18. 88 *—S.H. (11/15/2002)*

Nautilus 2001 Pinot Noir (Marlborough) $20. 89 *—J.C. (9/1/2003)*

Nautilus 1999 Sauvignon Blanc (Marlborough) $16. 86 *—M.M. (10/1/2000)*

Nautilus 2001 Sauvignon Blanc (Marlborough) $18. 88 *(8/1/2002)*

NEUDORF

Neudorf 2003 Moutere Chardonnay (New Zealand) $53. Toasty, but with the fruit to back it up. Peach and caramel scents on the nose, then layers of ripe tropical and citrus fruit on the palate that keep pumping out flavor through the long finish. Another top effort for one of New Zealand's benchmark Chardonnays. **90 Editors' Choice** *—J.C. (7/1/2005)*

Neudorf 2003 Pinot Noir (Moutere) $46. Shows that great wines can be made from the 10/5 clone, with lots of dried spice and leather aromas that are balanced on the palate by a rich, sturdy core of ripe cherries. Great persistence on the finish adds another dimension. **91** *—J.C. (12/1/2005)*

Neudorf 2003 Home Vineyard Pinot Noir (Moutere) $NA. Based on old (20–25-year-old) plantings of Pommard clone, this fabulous wine blends savory, spicy scents with floral elements on the nose, then delves deep into black cherries in the mouth. Rich and velvety on the palate, with powerful fruit and the structure to age. One of the best New World Pinots I've ever tasted. **94** *—J.C. (12/1/2005)*

Neudorf 2003 Sauvignon Blanc (Nelson) $23. A big, ripe style of Sauvignon Blanc, one that sacrifices herbal notes in favor of peach, melon, and fig flavors. This full-bodied wine comes across as rich and honeyed, yet dry and persistent on the finish. **89** *—J.C. (8/1/2004)*

NEVIS BLUFF

Nevis Bluff 2003 Pinot Noir (Central Otago) $24. Doesn't have the richness, mouthfeel or intensity of the winery's 2002, but the vintage was more challenging. Crisp cherry fruit boasts hints of celery seed and a long, tart finish. **87** *—J.C. (12/1/2005)*

NGA WAKA

Nga Waka 2000 Chardonnay (Martinborough) $30. 86 *—J.C. (7/1/2002)*

Nga Waka 2003 Pinot Noir (Martinborough) $NA. Seems to have a bit of a volatile acidity issue, with lifted aromas and a slightly pickle-y taste that distract from the cherry fruit. **81** *—J.C. (12/1/2005)*

Nga Waka 2001 Riesling (Martinborough) $20. 87 *—J.C. (8/1/2003)*

Nga Waka 2001 Sauvignon Blanc (Martinborough) $20. 87 *(8/1/2002)*

NGATARAWA

Ngatarawa 2004 Glazebrook Sauvignon Blanc (Marlborough) $14. Grassy and herbal-smelling, but there's also lots of grapefruit and nectarines to provide a fruity counterbalance. Light in weight, with a hint of unreleased CO_2 to provide additional freshness, this is a mouthwatering summer refresher. **87** *—J.C. (7/1/2005)*

NO 1 FAMILY ESTATE

No 1 Family Estate NV Cuvée Number Eight Brut (Marlborough) $20. 90 Editors' Choice *—J.C. (12/15/2003)*

NOBILO

Nobilo 2000 Fall Harvest Chardonnay (Gisborne) $10. 83 *—J.C. (5/1/2001)*

Nobilo 2003 Icon Pinot Gris (Marlborough) $20. A big, ripe, slightly alcoholic wine, this is meant to make a statement. The color is coppery, suggesting some skin contact and there are even some red fruit flavors mixed in with the layers of peaches and honey. Slightly off-dry and low in acidity, this rich Pinot Gris would be lovely by itself on a lazy, late-summer day. **87** *—J.C. (8/1/2004)*

Nobilo 2003 Sauvignon Blanc (Marlborough) $12. A fine value, Nobilo's latest SB shows a fine bouquet of musk, lime, and passion fruit paired with flavors of pink grapefruit and white currants. The slightly creamy texture glides into a zesty, clean, refreshing finish. **88 Best Buy** *—J.C. (4/1/2004)*

Nobilo 2000 Fall Harvest Sauvignon Blanc (Marlborough) $10. 86 Best Buy *—J.C. (5/1/2001)*

Nobilo 1999 Icon Series Sauvignon Blanc (Marlborough) $NA. 89 *—J.C. (5/1/2001)*

Nobilo 2004 Regional Collection Sauvignon Blanc (Marlborough) $12. Fits the New Zealand stereotype to a T, boasting pungent, earthy aromas, then a burst of passion fruit and citrus on the palate. Zippy and fresh, this is a wine to gulp down over the hot summer months. No food necessary, although a bowl of *moules* would seem appropriate. **87 Best Buy** *—J.C. (7/1/2005)*

OLSSENS

Olssens 2004 Jackson Barry Pinot Noir (Central Otago) $33. Kicks off with lovely herbal, floral, and spice elements, creating an intriguing bouquet, then adds bass notes of flavor—cherries and chocolate. Finishes well, picking up hints of cola. **88** *—J.C. (12/1/2005)*

Olssens 2003 Slap Jack Creek Pinot Noir (Central Otago) $48. From its lovely dusty, dried-spice aromas to its pretty cherry flavors, this is all Pinot. Medium in body, it's neither too heavy nor too light, ending with a delicate overlay of fine tannins. **89** *—J.C. (12/1/2005)*

OMAKA SPRINGS

Omaka Springs 2002 Chardonnay (Marlborough) $18. 85 *—J.C. (9/1/2003)*

Omaka Springs 2002 Winemaker's Selection Chardonnay (Marlborough) $24. Buttery on the nose, but nicely balanced, with scents of honey, peaches, and limes giving way to apple, peach, and citrus flavors. Plump in the mouth without being heavy, and it even picks up a hint of chalky minerality on the finish. Imported by T.G.I.C. Importers. **90 Editors' Choice** *—J.C. (7/1/2005)*

Omaka Springs 1999 Merlot (Marlborough) $15. 85 *—J.C. (5/1/2001)*

Omaka Springs 1998 Reserve Pinot Noir (Marlborough) $NA. 85 *—J.C. (5/1/2001)*

Omaka Springs 2004 Riesling (Marlborough) $17. Made in a lean, racy style, this Marlborough Riesling combines moderate alcohol (12.5%) with minimal residual sugar to make a crisp, refreshing wine well suited to washing down shellfish. Scents of stones (flint) and lime pick up hints of nectarine before finishing tart and clean. **88** *—J.C. (7/1/2005)*

Omaka Springs 2002 Riesling (Marlborough) $15. 85 *—J.C. (8/1/2003)*

Omaka Springs 1998 Riesling (Marlborough) $NA. 85 *—J.C. (5/1/2001)*

Omaka Springs 2003 Sauvignon Blanc (Marlborough) $17. This slightly clumsy, heavyhanded wine boasts a sweet, honeyed attack that turns tart and grapefruity somewhere midpalate, resulting in a sweet-and-sour combination that's not entirely convincing. **83** *—J.C. (4/1/2004)*

Omaka Springs 2001 Sauvignon Blanc (Marlborough) $17. 89 *(8/1/2002)*

ORIGIN

Origin 2004 Sauvignon Blanc (Marlborough) $14. Shows some flinty-chalky notes that resemble a decent Pouilly-Fumé alongside grapefruit and bell pepper fruit. Light in body, with a long, citrusy finish. Ideal with shellfish or simple fish dishes. **88** *—J.C. (7/1/2005)*

OYSTER BAY

Oyster Bay 2004 Pinot Noir (Marlborough) $17. Starts off a bit muted on the nose, then delivers sweet cherry flavors upfront. The flavors veer toward cola and spice on the finish, where the tannins turn a bit drying. Imported by Lauber Imports. **85** *—J.C. (12/1/2005)*

PALLISER ESTATE

Palliser Estate 2004 Pinot Gris (Martinborough) $19. Seems just the tiniest bit heavy, but offers ample compensation by way of bold pear and black pepper aromas, apple and spice flavors and an orangey citrus finish. Off dry. **86** *—J.C. (7/1/2005)*

Palliser Estate 2000 Pinot Gris (Martinborough) $20. 85 *—J.C. (5/1/2001)*

Palliser Estate 2003 Pinot Noir (Martinborough) $27. Complex and meaty on the nose, blending layers of dried spices, roasted meat, and spring flowers. Adds cola, clove and crisp cherry flavors on the palate before finishing firm, almost tough. Give it a few years. **86** *—J.C. (12/1/2005)*

Palliser Estate 1999 Pinot Noir (Martinborough) $26. 88 *—J.C. (5/1/2001)*

Palliser Estate 2002 Pencarrow Pinot Noir (Martinborough) $18. Looks and tastes tired, with a light, rusty hue and leafy, tomatoey flavors. **81** *—J.C. (12/1/2005)*

Palliser Estate 2000 Riesling (Martinborough) $NA. 87 *—J.C. (5/1/2001)*

Palliser Estate 2004 Sauvignon Blanc (Martinborough) $19. Bold peach and apricot notes on the nose, with only a trace of herbaceousness. Plump and medium-weight on the palate, with more stone fruit flavors that finish a trifle short. Drink now. **87** *—J.C. (12/1/2005)*

Palliser Estate 2001 Sauvignon Blanc (Marlborough) $18. 91 *—S.H. (11/15/2002)*

Palliser Estate 2002 Pencarrow Sauvignon Blanc (Martinborough) $13. 86 *—J.C. (9/1/2003)*

PEGASUS BAY

Pegasus Bay 2004 Chardonnay (Waipara) $35. Toasty on the nose, but not as rich or opulently fruity as some previous vintages. Instead, it's a leaner style, with tart, grapefruity flavors that finish long and intense. **88** *—J.C. (12/1/2005)*

Pegasus Bay 2000 Chardonnay (Waipara) $30. 91 *—J.C. (7/1/2002)*

Pegasus Bay 2003 Pinot Noir (Waipara) $40. Seems a bit tight and sinewy, with dried spices and black cherries at the fore. Earth, sous bois, and chocolate provide the underpinnings, while crisp cranberry notes emerge on the finish. **87** *—J.C. (12/1/2005)*

Pegasus Bay 1999 Pinot Noir (Waipara) $39. 91 *—J.C. (5/1/2001)*

Pegasus Bay 2001 Prima Donna Pinot Noir (Waipara) $88. For the second consecutive release, I've rated Prima Donna lower than the regular Pinot from Peg Bay. Maybe it's just more closed at this stage, or maybe I'm looking for something different in Pinot than this wine's architects have in mind. It's nice enough, offering plenty of spice and earthy complexity, but also a dark, brooding character reminiscent of coffee and dark chocolate. Try in 2008. **88** *—J.C. (8/1/2004)*

Pegasus Bay 2004 Riesling (Waipara) $24. Smells fresh enough to make your mouth water, filled with scents of lime zest and green apples. On the palate, it's nicely balanced, not as rich or sweet as a tank sample of the '05, but crisp and elegant, with superb concentration. **90** *—J.C. (12/1/2005)*

Pegasus Bay 2002 Riesling (Waipara) $24. 90 **Editors' Choice** *—J.C. (8/1/2003)*

Pegasus Bay 2004 Sauvignon Blanc (Waipara) $24. There's 15% Sémillon blended into this wine, which helps add a bit of creaminess to the texture. It's reasonably rich on the palate as a result, with ripe stone fruit flavors that taper off toward grapefruit on the finish. **87** *—J.C. (12/1/2005)*

Pegasus Bay 2001 Sauvignon Blanc (Waipara) $19. 88 *—J.C. (9/1/2003)*

Pegasus Bay 1999 Sauvignon Blanc (Waipara) $20. 85 *—J.C. (5/1/2001)*

PENINSULA ESTATE WINES

Peninsula Estate Wines 2000 Zeno Syrah (Waiheke Island) $40. A decent quaff—a bit light and herbal—but probably tasty with grilled lamb chops. Its leafy, eucalyptus aromas and light red cherry fruit are pleasant enough and would complement simply prepared grilled meats. **85** *—J.C. (8/1/2004)*

PEREGRINE

Peregrine 2002 Pinot Gris (Central Otago) $19. 88 *—J.C. (9/1/2003)*

Peregrine 2002 Pinot Noir (Central Otago) $34. This is a big, burly Pinot, with bold black cherry aromas marked by some herbal, beet-like notes. Broadens out with air to show deeper, darker flavors, including plums, earth, and coffee grounds. Give it 2–3 years in the cellar, then drink it over the next five. **89** *—J.C. (8/1/2004)*

PHEASANT GROVE

Pheasant Grove 2004 Sauvignon Blanc (Marlborough) $15. Fresh and snappy, with green pea, celery, and nectarine/peach to the bouquet. This is a pleasing, smooth wine with quite a bit of natural sweetness. Finishes slightly chalky, but with enough zest to prevent any stickiness. Imported by Robert Bath Imports. **88** *—J.C. (7/1/2005)*

POND PADDOCK

Pond Paddock 2003 Hawk's Flight Pinot Noir (Martinborough) $NA. Crisply acidic, with tart cherry notes alongside mushroom and spice. Turns tea-like on the finish—a bit leafy and drying. **85** *—J.C. (12/1/2005)*

QUARTZ REEF

Quartz Reef 2003 Pinot Noir (Central Otago) $30. Starts off a bit herbal or hay-like on the nose, but gradually develops in the glass to reveal ripe cherry scents. Supple; less dense and powerful than the 2002, but still a very pretty wine. **87** *—J.C. (12/1/2005)*

Quartz Reef 2003 Bendigo Estate Vineyard Pinot Noir (Central Otago) $NA. Like the regular 2003 bottling, there's a slightly herbal or hay-like note on the nose of this wine, but also floral hints and bright cherry aromas. Lacks the depth and drama of the superb 2002, but still a nice wine. Finishes with some drying tannins, so hold a couple of years before opening. **88** *—J.C. (12/1/2005)*

REBECCA SALMOND

Rebecca Salmond 2001 Reserve Chardonnay (Gisborne) $25. **84** *—J.C. (9/1/2003)*

Rebecca Salmond 2001 Sauvignon Blanc (Marlborough) $15. **83** *—J.C. (9/1/2003)*

RED HILL (NZ)

Red Hill (NZ) 2001 Sauvignon Blanc (Marlborough) $11. **83** *—M.M. (12/15/2001)*

RIMU GROVE

Rimu Grove 2004 Pinot Gris (Nelson) $19. Reductive on the nose, with tar, rubber, and chocolate notes that make the flavors challenging to find. There are some modest citrus notes on the finish. Try vigorous decanting to help it along. **82** *—J.C. (7/1/2005)*

Rimu Grove 2001 Pinot Noir (Nelson) $35. Black cherry and vanilla start strong enough, and touches of herbs and black pepper add complexity to the nose. The palate is a bit candied and simple, turning very tangy on the finish. **84** *—J.C. (4/1/2004)*

RIVER FORD

River Ford 1999 Saint Clair Estate Sauvignon Blanc (Marlborough) $16. **87** *—M.M. (10/1/2000)*

RIVERSIDE

Riverside 1997 Reserve Chardonnay (Stirling) $20. **83** *—J.C. (10/1/2000)*

ROARING MEG

Roaring Meg 2002 Pinot Noir (Central Otago) $25. Seems a little underripe—surprising for a 2002 wine from Central Otago. Ashy, peppery aromas and flavors mix with sour cherries and earth. Herb-crusted meat dishes will help bring out the fruit and tame the wine's dry tannins. **84** *—J.C. (8/1/2004)*

ROCKBURN

Rockburn 2002 Pinot Noir (Central Otago) $38. A big, extracted Pinot with lots of dusty earth and dried spice components. Cola, coffee, and plum flavors round it out, wrapped in firm tannins. Give it a few years to mellow. **89** *—J.C. (8/1/2004)*

ROWLAND

Rowland 2000 Jill's Vineyard Pinot Noir (Central Otago) $28. **87** *—J.C. (8/1/2002)*

Rowland 1998 Jill's Vineyard Pinot Noir (Central Otago) $22. **86** *—J.C. (10/1/2000)*

SACRED HILL

Sacred Hill 1998 Helmsman Cabernet Sauvignon (Hawke's Bay) $40. **87** *—J.C. (5/1/2001)*

Sacred Hill 1998 Barrel Fermented Chardonnay (Hawke's Bay) $20. **88** *(9/1/2000)*

Sacred Hill 1999 Rifleman's Chardonnay (Hawke's Bay) $36. **90** *—J.C. (5/1/2001)*

Sacred Hill 1998 Whitecliff Chardonnay (Marlborough & Hawkes Bay) $16. **89** *(9/1/2000)*

Sacred Hill 1999 Whitecliff Merlot (Hawke's Bay) $16. **87** *(9/1/2000)*

Sacred Hill 1997 Barrel Fermented Sauvignon Blanc (Hawke's Bay) $20. **88** *(9/1/2000)*

Sacred Hill 1999 Whitecliff Sauvignon Blanc (Hawke's Bay) $13. 88 *(9/1/2000)*

SAINT CLAIR ESTATE

Saint Clair Estate 2002 Vicar's Choice Pinot Noir (Marlborough) $15. This is a big, bulky wine with a slightly syrupy mouthfeel, yet it doesn't show much in the way of fruit. Instead, it's minty and herbal, with wintergreen and cherry cough medicine flavors. 83 *—J.C. (4/1/2004)*

Saint Clair Estate 2002 Sauvignon Blanc (Marlborough) $13. 87 *—J.C. (9/1/2003)*

SANDIHURST

Sandihurst 2004 Pinot Noir (Canterbury) $18. Spicy and floral, with a light, silky mouthfeel and flavors of cranberries, cherries, and hints of mushroom. This is a pretty style, best paired with chicken or salmon rather than heavier meats. 87 *—J.C. (12/1/2005)*

SCHUBERT

Schubert 1999 Cabernet Sauvignon (Hawke's Bay) $40. 85 *—J.C. (12/15/2003)*

Schubert 1999 Syrah (New Zealand) $24. 90 Editors' Choice *—J.C. (12/15/2003)*

SEIFRIED

Seifried 2002 Bordeaux Blend (Nelson) $16. 87 *—J.C. (8/1/2004)*

Seifried 2003 Unoaked Chardonnay (Nelson) $16. Packs boatloads of tropical fruit into a medium-weight package that's clean and fresh, if somewhat fruity and simple. Good party Chardonnay. 85 *—J.C. (8/1/2004)*

Seifried 2002 Pinot Noir (Nelson) $25. This pretty, delicately scented wine blends notes of cherries, leather, and cinnamon into a promising nose, followed by herbal, mushroomy flavors. Lithe, and a bit lean in texture, finishing with hints of coffee and charred wood. 86 *—J.C. (8/1/2004)*

Seifried 2004 Riesling (Nelson) $15. From the little-known region of Nelson, this Riesling bursts with petrol and lime scents. Quite full-bodied for a Riesling, with a touch of residual sugar and plenty of alcohol (12.5%), yet it retains a sense of grace and a finely developed minerality not often found in New World Riesling. 90 Best Buy *—J.C. (7/1/2005)*

Seifried 2004 Sauvignon Blanc (Nelson) $17. A riper style of SB, built around a core of passion fruit. Ripe fig and melon notes accent the strident tropical fruit, while the harmonious finish picks up hints of grapefruit. Medium-to-full-bodied; richer than most despite having only 12.5% alcohol. 89 *—J.C. (7/1/2005)*

SELAKS

Selaks 2000 Chardonnay (Marlborough) $15. 88 Best Buy *—J.C. (5/1/2001)*

Selaks 1999 Drylands Merlot (Marlborough) $NA. 86 *—J.C. (5/1/2001)*

Selaks 2000 Drylands Pinot Gris (Marlborough) $NA. 88 *—J.C. (5/1/2001)*

Selaks 1999 Riesling (Marlborough) $NA. 85 *—J.C. (5/1/2001)*

Selaks 2000 Sauvignon Blanc (Marlborough) $11. 88 Best Buy *—J.C. (5/1/2001)*

Selaks 1998 Founders Reserve Sauvignon Blanc (Marlborough) $NA. 90 *—J.C. (5/1/2001)*

SERESIN

Seresin 2001 Sauvignon Blanc (Marlborough) $20. 91 *(8/1/2002)*

SEVEN TERRACES

Seven Terraces 2004 Sauvignon Blanc (Marlborough) $15. A bit reined in aromatically, with modest passion fruit scents. But this wine is very bold and assertive on the palate, combining bright citrus and tropical fruit with hints of bell pepper. Good value. 88 *—J.C. (12/1/2005)*

SHAKY BRIDGE

Shaky Bridge 2003 Pinot Noir (Central Otago) $36. Shows lovely complexity on the nose, blending floral notes with spice and herbs. This is light on its feet, verging on delicate, yet delivers plenty of flavor. Silky tannins and a long finish suggest this has the balance to age, despite not being a massive blockbuster. Elegant. 90 *—J.C. (12/1/2005)*

SHEPHERDS RIDGE

Shepherds Ridge 2002 Sauvignon Blanc (Marlborough) $15. 86 *—J.C. (9/1/2003)*

SHERWOOD ESTATE

Sherwood Estate 2000 Reserve Chardonnay (Canterbury) $20. 89 *—J.C. (7/1/2002)*

SHINGLE PEAK

Shingle Peak 2001 Sauvignon Blanc (Marlborough) $12. 90 *—S.H. (11/15/2002)*

SPY VALLEY

Spy Valley 2003 Chardonnay (Marlborough) $25. A plump, fleshy Chardonnay that delivers plenty of pear and peach aromas and flavors. It's pleasing, if a bit simple, with just some modest hints of smoke and popcorn on the finish to add complexity. **86** *—J.C. (7/1/2005)*

Spy Valley 2001 Gewürztraminer (Marlborough) $12. **88** *—J.C. (8/1/2002)*

Spy Valley 2004 Pinot Gris (Marlborough) $20. There's a hint of rubber on the nose at first, but it quickly dissipates in favor of ripe pear aromas. Off-dry and reasonably weighty on the palate, it has flavors of spiced honey drizzled over poached pears before finishing fresh and clean. **87** *—J.C. (7/1/2005)*

Spy Valley 2004 Riesling (Marlborough) $14. Wonderfully clean and pure, with aromas of peaches, limes, and wet stones. On the palate, there's soft, ripe stone fruit, but also powerful citrus notes to provide focus. Finishes dry and tart, crisp, and refreshing. **90 Best Buy** *—J.C. (7/1/2005)*

Spy Valley 2001 Sauvignon Blanc (Marlborough) $13. **88 Best Buy** *—S.H. (11/15/2002)*

STONECROFT

Stonecroft 2000 Chardonnay (Hawke's Bay) $22. **89** *—J.C. (7/1/2002)*

STONELEIGH

Stoneleigh 2003 Chardonnay (Marlborough) $15. Nicely balanced and harmonious, with toast and yellow fruits mingling easily on the nose before giving way to pineapple and melon flavors that seem to have no sharp edges. There's a hint of caramel from oak on the finish, but it doesn't overwhelm. **88** *—J.C. (7/1/2005)*

Stoneleigh 2004 Pinot Noir (Marlborough) $16. The higher yields of 2004 seem to have lightened this wine compared to the same bottling in 2003, but it's still a charming wine, featuring lightweight cherry fruit coupled with briary nuances. Silky tannins grace the finish. **85** *—J.C. (12/1/2005)*

Stoneleigh 1999 Pinot Noir (Marlborough) $15. **83** *—J.C. (5/1/2001)*

Stoneleigh 2003 Riesling (Marlborough) $15. Shows some fine minerally notes on the slaty nose, while the flavors are fruitier and more accessible. Apple and citrus flavors, a slightly oily mouthfeel and a hint of residual sugar give it a sense of ripeness. Clean and refreshing, thanks to a squirt of lemon on the finish. **87** *—J.C. (7/1/2005)*

STRATFORD

Stratford 2003 Pinot Noir (Martinborough) $40. Peppery and mushroomy on the nose, this wine also features earthy, leathery notes that call to mind the Rhône. It's a pleasant drink in a rustic red sort of way, distinctive for NZ Pinot. **86** *—J.C. (12/1/2005)*

SYREN

Syren 2001 Pinot Noir (Central Otago) $27. **89** *—J.C. (9/1/2003)*

TE AWA FARM

Te Awa Farm 1999 Longlands Bordeaux Blend (Hawke's Bay) $16. **87** *—J.C. (5/1/2001)*

Te Awa Farm 2000 Longlands Chardonnay (Hawke's Bay) $14. **87 Best Buy** *—M.M. (12/15/2001)*

Te Awa Farm 1999 Longlands Merlot (Hawke's Bay) $16. **88** *—J.C. (5/1/2001)*

Te Awa Farm 2000 Frontier Sauvignon Blanc (Hawke's Bay) $20. **89** *—J.C. (5/1/2001)*

Te Awa Farm 2000 Longlands Syrah (Hawke's Bay) $21. **89** *(11/1/2001)*

TE KAIRANGA

Te Kairanga 1999 Cabernet Sauvignon (Martinborough) $15. **80** *—J.C. (5/1/2001)*

Te Kairanga 1999 Reserve Chardonnay (Martinborough) $20. **88** *—J.C. (5/1/2001)*

Te Kairanga 2002 Pinot Noir (Martinborough) $26. Supple and smooth in the mouth, this relatively light-hued Pinot shows elegant aromas of tea, cinnamon, vanilla, and sour cherries. Finishes with tart berry and citrus flavors. **87** *—J.C. (4/1/2004)*

Te Kairanga 2003 Reserve Pinot Noir (Martinborough) $42. Nails Pinot's texture, boasting a supple, velvety mouthfeel; also its complexity, blending savory spice and mushroom notes with bright pie cherry flavors. There's also an earthy, slightly vegetal beet nuance. **88** *—J.C. (12/1/2005)*

Te Kairanga 2001 Sauvignon Blanc (Martinborough) $14. **93 Best Buy** *—S.H. (11/15/2002)*

TE MATA

Te Mata 2002 Woodthorpe Sauvignon Blanc (Hawke's Bay) $18. **86** *—J.C. (9/1/2003)*

TERRACE ROAD

Terrace Road 2001 Sauvignon Blanc (Marlborough) $17. **91** *—S.H. (11/15/2002)*

TERRAVIN

Terravin 2003 Hillside Selection Pinot Noir (Omaka Valley) $59. Lovely Pinot aromas, with layers of flowers and herbs atop black cherry. Smooth, supple fruit, but not superficial, as there's also a deeper core of earth and chocolate. Velvety on the finish. Drink now–2010. **88** *—J.C. (12/1/2005)*

THE CROSSINGS

The Crossings 2003 Pinot Noir (Marlborough) $20. Powerful aromas of black cherries and anise make a big initial impression, followed by waves of big, soft fruit. Rich black plum and cherry flavors firm up a little on the finish, making this a wine that's more about immediately satisfying fruit than structure or complexity. **88** *—J.C. (8/1/2004)*

The Crossings 2003 Sauvignon Blanc (Marlborough) $16. Ripe notes of honey and peaches are balanced on the nose by celery, dill-like, herbal qualities. The palate features mouthfilling flavors of white nectarines, melons, and figs that fade gently into smoky complexity on the finish. **90 Editors' Choice** *—J.C. (8/1/2004)*

The Crossings 2001 Awatere Valley Sauvignon Blanc (Marlborough) $16. 90 Editors' Choice *(8/1/2002)*

THE JIBE

The Jibe 2004 Pinot Noir (Marlborough) $15. Light and crisp, with plenty of cherry fruit. This is a bit simple, but tasty, and reasonably priced. **85** *—J.C. (12/1/2005)*

THORNBURY

Thornbury 2003 Pinot Noir (Marlborough) $NA. Bold and fresh, but also a bit rough and loud. Has some grassy elements on the nose, along with chocolate and carob flavors and some zesty, lemony acids on the finish. **83** *—J.C. (12/1/2005)*

Thornbury 2004 Sauvignon Blanc (Marlborough) $19. Mildly grassy and grapefruity on the low-intensity nose, this effort from winemaker Steve Bird lacks some of the vigor that has characterized his previous efforts. Modest herbal and citrus flavors pick up riper, stone-fruit accents on the crisp finish. **85** *—J.C. (7/1/2005)*

Thornbury 2001 Sauvignon Blanc (Marlborough) $17. 87 *(8/1/2002)*

TOHU

Tohu 2001 Chardonnay (Gisborne) $15. 88 *(9/1/2003)*

Tohu 2002 Reserve Chardonnay (Gisborne) $22. 88 *(9/1/2003)*

Tohu 2003 Unoaked Chardonnay (Gisborne) $10. One of the best unoaked Chards I've tried, with enough leesy, mealy notes to impart complexity to the waves of pear and melon fruit. Nicely balanced, with enough weight to match with food and enough freshness to serve alone. A versatile wine that's worth keeping on hand for any occasion. **88 Best Buy** *—J.C. (8/1/2004)*

Tohu 2001 Pinot Noir (Marlborough) $25. 91 *(9/1/2003)*

Tohu 2002 Sauvignon Blanc (Marlborough) $14. 89 Best Buy *(9/1/2003)*

Tohu 1999 Sauvignon Blanc (Marlborough) $15. 88 *—M.S. (10/1/2000)*

TORLEESE

Torleese 2002 Sauvignon Blanc (Waipara) $16. 87 *—J.C. (9/1/2003)*

Torlesse 2002 Pinot Noir (Canterbury) $18. A light, quaffable Pinot, with cola and caramel dominating the nose. Flavors are similar, picking up earth and herb nuances; this is not a terribly fruity wine, but delivers some interesting flavors nonetheless. **84** *—J.C. (7/1/2005)*

Torlesse 2004 Sauvignon Blanc (Waipara) $15. Starts with promise, showing fresh scents of stone fruit, melon, passion fruit, and green pepper, but they don't quite blend properly on the palate, where there's juicy tropical fruit but also a crisp, hard layer of acidity that tastes metallic on the finish. **84** *—J.C. (7/1/2005)*

TRINITY HILL

Trinity Hill 1998 Gimblett Road Chardonnay (Hawke's Bay) $30. 90 *—J.C. (5/1/2001)*

Trinity Hill 2003 High Country Pinot Noir (Hawke's Bay) $30. From a region of New Zealand better known for its Bordeaux varieties and gaining a growing reputation for Syrah, this Pinot delivers smoky, charred scents, meaty, plum, and black cherry flavors and a finish that's surprisingly firm given the softness of the mouthfeel. **87** *—J.C. (12/1/2005)*

TROUT VALLEY

Trout Valley 2001 Chardonnay (Marlborough) $14. This seems to be tiring, with lactic notes, sour fruit and toasty oak starting to dominate its bouquet. Yet it's much better on the palate, with powdered cinnamon and cloves sprinkled over buttered toast and orange marmalade. Drink up. **84** *—J.C. (8/1/2004)*

TUATARA

Tuatara 2001 Chardonnay (Nelson) $16. 85 *—J.C. (9/1/2003)*

Tuatara 2002 Sauvignon Blanc (Nelson) $12. 86 *—J.C. (9/1/2003)*

TWIN ISLANDS

Twin Islands 2002 Sauvignon Blanc (Marlborough) $12. 85 *—S.H. (1/1/2002)*

UNISON VINEYARD

Unison Vineyard 1999 Unison Red Blend (Hawke's Bay) $25. **83** *—J.C. (12/15/2003)*

VAVASOUR

Vavasour 1999 Awatere Valley Chardonnay (Marlborough) $23. **90** *—J.C. (5/1/2001)*

Vavasour 1999 Awatere Valley Sauvignon Blanc (Marlborough) $19. **89** *—J.C. (5/1/2001)*

VILLA MARIA

Villa Maria 2001 Cellar Selection Cabernet Sauvignon-Merlot Cabernet Blend (Hawke's Bay) $20. Think cru bourgeois from a ripe vintage: smoke, dried herbs and cassis, medium body and a lingering finish that picks up touches of earth and vanilla. **88** *—J.C. (8/1/2004)*

Villa Maria 2000 Cellar Selection Cabernet Sauvignon-Merlot (Hawke's Bay) $23. **86** *—J.C. (12/15/2003)*

Villa Maria 2000 Private Bin Cabernet Sauvignon-Merlot (Hawke's Bay) $19. **88** *—J.C. (8/1/2002)*

Villa Maria 2003 Private Bin Chardonnay (Marlborough) $13. Clean, fruity, and tropical, with a slightly creamy mouthfeel and hints of vanilla, mint, and flowers. This is a solid everyday Chardonnay at an everyday price. **85** *—J.C. (7/1/2005)*

Villa Maria 2001 Private Bin Chardonnay (Marlborough) $15. **87** *—J.C. (7/1/2002)*

Villa Maria 1999 Private Bin Chardonnay (East Coast) $15. **86** *—J.C. (5/1/2001)*

Villa Maria 2002 Cellar Selection Pinot Noir (Marlborough) $28. Not that dissimilar from Villa's reserve Pinot, just scaled back a bit, with the same black cherry-cola flavor profile, just less weight, texture and body. **87** *(8/1/2004)*

Villa Maria 2002 Reserve Pinot Noir (Marlborough) $35. The 2002 vintage was kind to Marlborough Pinot Noir, and this wine shows the beneficence of the weather in its plump, rounded flavors and supple tannins. Boasts ample black cherry, earth, and cola and root beer flavors. **88** *—J.C. (8/1/2004)*

Villa Maria 2002 Botrytis Selection Reserve Noble Riesling (Marlborough) $45. Fairly full-bodied and a bit alcoholic, testament to the immense ripeness achieved. Apricot, pineapple, and lime notes provide a fruit salad of flavors that linger on the finish. **90** *(8/1/2004)*

Villa Maria 2004 Private Bin Riesling (Marlborough) $13. This Riesling packs in a lot of character at a modest price. The fern-scented bouquet of warm stones and ripe apples is enticing, the weight—not too heavy, not too light—is just right, and the flavors of apple, lime, and peach hit the pleasure buttons. Finishes fresh and clean. **89 Best Buy** *—J.C. (7/1/2005)*

Villa Maria 2001 Private Bin Riesling (Marlborough) $15. **86** *—J.C. (8/1/2002)*

Villa Maria 1999 Private Bin Riesling (Marlborough) $12. **87** *—M.S. (10/1/2000)*

Villa Maria 2003 Cellar Selection Sauvignon Blanc (Marlborough) $19. Starts off with some sweaty, passion fruit scents, then glides into passion fruit and pineapple flavors. Feels creamy and supple on the palate, finshing with some soft spice notes. **88** *—J.C. (8/1/2004)*

Villa Maria 2001 Cellar Selection Sauvignon Blanc (Marlborough) $22. **86** *(8/1/2002)*

Villa Maria 2004 Clifford Bay Reserve Sauvignon Blanc (Marlborough) $32. Like so many New Zealand wines, this one blends vegetal notes of peas and beans with tropical fruit, and the whole is quite nice. Along the way there's some sweat, a bit of salt, and a touch of grass. Lengthy on the finish, with grapefruit and a certain sweetness. **88** *(7/1/2005)*

Villa Maria 2002 Clifford Bay Reserve Sauvignon Blanc (Marlborough) $30. **88** *—J.C. (9/1/2003)*

Villa Maria 2004 Private Bin Sauvignon Blanc (Marlborough) $13. This workhorse NZ Savvy delivers just what you'd expect: an initial blast of pungent herbal and passion fruit scents, followed by bright tropical fruit on the palate and a crisp, clean finish. Good value. **86** *—J.C. (7/1/2005)*

Villa Maria 2002 Private Bin Sauvignon Blanc (Marlborough) $13. **86** *—J.C. (9/1/2003)*

Villa Maria 2000 Private Bin Sauvignon Blanc (Marlborough & Hawkes Bay) $12. **86** *—J.C. (5/1/2001)*

Villa Maria 1998 Reserve Sauvignon Blanc (Clifford Bay) $25. **89** *—S.H. (8/1/1999)*

VOSS

Voss 2002 Pinot Noir (Martinborough) $41. A bit of a come-down after this winery's outstanding 2001, but still a very good effort, with black cherry and mushroom notes intertwined with strands of coffee and earth. Finishes long, with hints of tea and black pepper. **87** *—J.C. (8/1/2004)*

VYNFIELDS

Vynfields 2003 Reserve Pinot Noir (Martinborough) $NA. Amply oaked, but it works well in the context of this wine, adding hints of bacon and wood dust to the lovely rose petal and cherry aromas. Medium-bodied, with silky tannins on the finish that add just enough structure for balance. **89** *—J.C. (12/1/2005)*

WAIRAU RIVER

Wairau River 1998 Chardonnay (Marlborough) $25. 84 *—J.C. (7/1/2002)*

Wairau River 1997 Reserve Chardonnay (Marlborough) $22. 89 *—J.C. (5/1/2001)*

Wairau River 1998 Reserve Botrytised Riesling (Marlborough) $58. 90 *—J.C. (5/1/2001)*

Wairau River 2001 Sauvignon Blanc (Marlborough) $17. 87 *(8/1/2002)*

Wairau River 2002 Reserve Sauvignon Blanc (Marlborough) $25. Extremely green, with aromas of pole beans and asparagus along with faint whiffs of lime. In the mouth it's hard to wade through the pea and green bean flavors, but if you're intrepid you will find some grassy citrus notes. **83** *(7/1/2005)*

Wairau River 2000 Reserve Sauvignon Blanc (Marlborough) $24. 89 *(8/1/2002)*

Wairau River 1998 Reserve Sauvignon Blanc (Marlborough) $24. 86 *—J.C. (5/1/2001)*

WHITEHAVEN

Whitehaven 2002 Pinot Noir (Marlborough) $29. This pretty wine artfully blends earth and fruit—cherries and beets with sous bois and leather—but the best part is its mouthfeel, silky and caressing, lingering delicately on the finish. **89** *—J.C. (8/1/2004)*

Whitehaven 2001 Estate Grown Pinot Noir (Marlborough) $24. 87 *—J.C. (9/1/2003)*

Whitehaven 2003 Sauvignon Blanc (Marlborough) $17. Light to medium in body, but with a suggestion of oiliness to its flavors, which boast a solid core of melon and stone fruit wrapped in layers of green. Herbs and jalapeños can be sharp, but in this wine they actually finish quite easy and soft. **87** *—J.C. (8/1/2004)*

Whitehaven 2000 Sauvignon Blanc (Marlborough) $15. 80 *—M.M. (1/1/2004)*

WILLOW CREEK

Willow Creek 2000 Pinot Noir (Canterbury) $16. 80 *—J.C. (9/1/2003)*

WITHER HILLS

Wither Hills 2004 Pinot Noir (Marlborough) $36. Just after bottling, but this seems to have recovered from that shock nicely, with lush cherry-berry fruit that picks up some darker earth and cola notes that extend through the finish. **88** *—J.C. (12/1/2005)*

Wither Hills 2004 Sauvignon Blanc (Marlborough) $23. Tons of passion fruit, melon, celery, nettles, and grass create that telltale N.Z. bouquet. In the mouth, fresh acidity pushes ripe citrus, mango, and melon flavors. Quite healthy, with a solid, satisfying mouthfeel. Razor clean and crisp. **89** *(7/1/2005)*

WOOLLASTON

Woollaston 2004 Pinot Noir (Nelson) $30. 86 *—J.C. (12/1/2005)*

Woollaston 2001 Sémillon-Sauvignon Blanc (Nelson) $14. 82 *—J.C. (9/1/2003)*

Portugal

Portugal has always had Port. Vintage Port and Late Bottled Vintage Port are the best sellers in the United States, but aged tawnies should command increasing interest. With the great strides in winemaking techniques and the results of great research into grape varieties and vineyard sites being put into practice, Portugal's Port is entering a golden age.

What makes Portugal so exciting at the moment is that the same can now be said of Portuguese table wines. The days of Portugal being known for only lightly sparkling Rosé are long gone, although the wines themselves are still widely available. Increasingly, wines with the quality to be poured at the top international tables are arriving in America from Portugal, and the number of these wines is increasing with each new harvest.

Terraced vineyards at Taylor's Quinta da Vargellas, high in the Douro Valley east of Pinhão, Portugal.

Encouragingly, Portugal has not copied the rest of the world. As with the Italians, Portuguese winemakers have not capitulated to international grape varieties and tastes. But, unlike the Italians, who enjoy playing with Cabernet, Chardonnay, and have acres of Merlot, Portuguese vineyards are still almost entirely planted with the great native varietals.

The boiler house of new developments in Portugal is the Douro Valley. Many of the same people who also make Port are making the greatest table wines. They use Portugal's greatest red grape varieties, Touriga Nacional, Tinta Roriz, Tinta Franca, Souzão, Tinta Cão, and Tinta Barroca, generally blended, invariably wood aged (although often in large wood barrels). The tastes are powerful, intense, tannic; the wines are long-lived.

South of the Douro, the Dão region also makes reds, which can be ageworthy (see Glossary). The Dão, lacking the same wealth of winemaking talent, has lagged behind, but there are now enough producers of quality to show that the style of the reds is going to be less intense than the Douro, more mineral, more herbal.

But Portugal is not only a red wine country. One of the country's most famous wines, Vinho Verde, produced in the far north of the country, is normally seen overseas in its white version (the tart, acid red stays at home and is drunk with sardines). At its best, Vinho Verde can equal some of the whites of the Rias Baixas region of Spain.

More southerly regions of Portugal bring us back to red wine. The Alentejo, the Ribatejo, and Estremadura are three vineyards that straddle the center of the country. These are the good value areas, which can often reach fascinating heights of quality. Warmer and softer wines than the tannic giants of the Douro are produced in greater quantities, making these regions the best way of starting into the adventure of today's Portuguese wines.

ADEGA COOPERATIVA DE VILA NOVA DE TAZEM

Adega Cooperativa de Vila Nova de Tazem 2000 Alfrocheiro Red Blend (Dão) $18. 86 —*J.C. (11/15/2003)*

ALTANO

Altano 2001 Tinta Roriz-Touriga Franca (Douro) $7. This wine from the Symington Port company is ripe, juicy, and packed with red fruits. It is designed for early drinking, with its fresh bright flavors and light acidity. **85 Best Buy** —*R.V. (11/1/2004)*

Altano 1999 Portuguese Red (Douro) $8. 82 —*D.T. (12/31/2001)*

AVELEDA

Aveleda 2000 Alvarinho (Vinho Verde) $11. 85 —*J.C. (12/31/2001)*

Aveleda NV White Blend (Vinho Verde) $6. 86 **Best Buy** —*D.T. (12/31/2001)*

BARÃO DE VILAR

Barão de Vilar 2003 Vintage Port (Port) $38. Owned by the Kopke and Van Zeller families (Fernando van Zeller is Baron de Vilar), this Port comes from vineyards in Moncorvo and San João de Pesqueira. It is a beautifully perfumed wine, with solid tannins, balancing rich fruit with a firm structure. **90** —*R.V. (11/15/2005)*

BARROS

Barros NV 20 Years Old Port $35. 90 —*J.C. (11/15/2003)*

Barros NV Hutcheson Porto Rocha Vintage Character Port $17. The wine is perfumed with violets and a touch of nutmeg, but that is counterbalanced by its stalkiness. To taste, it is soft, but rather green and lightweight. It is pleasant enough, but doesn't have much character. **83** —*R.V. (3/1/2005)*

Barros 1996 LBV Bottled 2001 Port $20. 85 —*J.C. (11/15/2003)*

Barros NV Special Reserve Port $NA. An easy drinking, ready to drink Port, with few pretensions. But it is soft and pleasant enough, with its flavors of gum arabic and soft, rich fruit. Some bitterness in the aftertaste lets the wine down. **84** —*R.V. (3/1/2005)*

BLANDY'S

Blandy's NV Alvada 5 Year Old Rich Madeira $15. Amber-colored, with a green tinge to the rim, this is a medium-weight, not-terribly-sweet Madeira imbued with flavors of walnuts and dried figs. Lots of acidity on the finish. **86** —*J.C. (3/1/2005)*

BORGES

Borges 2003 Vintage Port $30. Over-floral and overperfumed aromas lead to a Port that is lean, with rather too many green flavors. The dry tannins are too much for the fruit. **81** —*R.V. (11/15/2005)*

Borges NV Gatão White Blend (Vinho Verde) $6. 83 —*R.V. (8/1/2004)*

BURMEISTER

Burmeister NV Sotto Voce Port $NA. This really fits the bill for an easy-drinking, rich style of Port. Packed with aromatic fruit, herbs, chocolate, and tannins, it combines sweetness with ripeness and structure. There is a dark, dry aftertaste that adds complexity. **90** —*R.V. (3/1/2005)*

CALÇOS DO TANHA

Calços do Tanha 1997 Reserva Portuguese Red (Douro) $19. 86 —*M.S. (12/31/2001)*

Calços do Tanha 1999 Touriga Francesa Portuguese Red (Douro) $26. 86 —*J.C. (12/31/2001)*

CÁLEM

Cálem 1994 LBV Bottled 1998 Port $19. 89 —*R.V. (3/1/2003)*

Cálem NV Reserva Ruby Port $NA. A soft ripe wine, with caramel aromas, dense perfumed fruit and considerable sweetness. It has good, intense flavors, but is not hugely fruity, showing maturity instead. This is in the same soft style as Cálem's tawny Ports. **86** —*R.V. (3/1/2005)*

CALHEIROS CRUZ

Calheiros Cruz 1999 Touriga Nacional-Tinta Roriz (Douro) $26. 87 —*D.T. (12/31/2001)*

CAMPO ARDOSA

Campo Ardosa 2000 Quinta da Carvalhosa Red Blend (Douro) $28. 94 —*R.V. (12/31/2002)*

CANTANHEDE

Cantanhede 2001 Marquês de Marialva Baga Reserva Seleccionada (Bairrada) $17. 86 —*R.V. (12/31/2002)*

Cantanhede 2001 Marquês de Marialva White Blend (Bairrada) $NA. 85 —*R.V. (8/1/2004)*

CARDOSO DE MENEZES

Cardoso de Menezes 1998 Quinta da Murqueira-Reserva Red Blend (Dão) $NA. 83 —*R.V. (12/31/2002)*

Cardoso de Menezes 2001 Quinta da Murqueira Reserva White Blend (Dão) $5. **87** *—R.V. (8/1/2004)*

CASA DE SANTAR

Casa de Santar 2001 Outono de Santar Vindima Tardia Encruzado (Dão) $14. An unique dessert wine, this is a late-harvest effort made from Encruzado grapes. Its deep golden color and scents of burnt orange peel and honey lead into a wine that's not very sweet—and so best paired with foie gras or a cheese course. Traces of nuts, oranges, and honey finish a bit short. **87** *—J.C. (3/1/2005)*

Casa de Santar 2000 Reserva Portuguese Red (Dão) $20. A very perfumed wine with great sweet ripe tannins, packed with rich fruit. The wood and fruit balance gives the wine complexity, directness and the potential of aging over at least 10 years. A classic. **92** *—R.V. (11/1/2004)*

Casa de Santar 2001 Castas de Santar Red Blend (Dão) $8. **86 Best Buy** *—J.C. (11/15/2003)*

Casa de Santar 1999 Reserva Red Blend (Dão) $15. **90** *—R.V. (12/31/2002)*

Casa de Santar 2000 Touriga Nacional (Dão) $43. **91** *—J.C. (11/15/2003)*

Casa de Santar 2001 Castas de Santar Touriga Nacional (Dão) $10. A finely constructed wine which shows rich herbal flavors, dry tannins, and also solid, structured fruit. With its black fruits, its dense texture and its dark acidity, this is a wine which will age well, over 4–5 years. **88 Best Buy** *—R.V. (11/1/2004)*

CASA DE SEZIM

Casa de Sezim 2003 Portuguese White (Vinho Verde) $NA. Light, delicate, and fresh, this wine is classic bone dry Vinho Verde. It has a touch of tannin from the green grapes, the acidity is very present, but it makes a great, refreshing summer drink. **87** *—R.V. (8/1/2005)*

CASA DE VILA VERDE

Casa de Vila Verde 2004 Alvarinho (Minho) $14. A single-vineyard wine made from the sought after Alvarinho grape. It's fuller than the average Vinho Verde, packed with ripe green fruits and flavors of pink grapefruit and white peaches. Drink now. **90 Best Buy** *—R.V. (8/1/2005)*

Casa de Vila Verde 2004 Estate White Blend (Vinho Verde) $10. Floral and apple-y, with overtones of smoke and slate that add an intriguing mineral component. Green apple, citrus, and chalk flavors finish, short and clean. **84** *—J.C. (12/31/2005)*

CASA FERREIRINHA

Casa Ferreirinha 1991 Barca Velha Red Blend (Douro) $80. **90** *(10/1/2000)*

Casa Ferreirinha 1989 Reserva Red Blend (Douro) $46. **87** *(10/1/2000)*

CASA SANTOS LIMA

Casa Santos Lima 2000 Palha-Cana Vinho Tinto Red Blend (Estremadura) $9. **85 Best Buy** *—D.T. (11/15/2002)*

CASAL DE VALLE PRADINHOS

Casal de Valle Pradinhos 2000 Valle Pradinhos Red Blend (Trás-os-Montes) $15. At first glance, this wine, with its modest cherry and cedar aromas and flavors seems too acidic and too tannic. But it seems to fill out a little as it sits in the glass, giving some hope that it will evolve in a positive direction. **85** *—J.C. (3/1/2004)*

CAVES ALIANÇA

Caves Aliança 2004 Galeria Bical (Bairrada) $8. A fresh green wine that shows good, crisp acidity. The Bical grape, the standard white of Bairrada, gives a good tannic structure, as well as flavors of gooseberries and hedgerow fruits. **85 Best Buy** *—R.V. (8/1/2005)*

Caves Aliança 2001 Alabastro Reserva Portuguese Red (Alentejano) $13. A selection of grapes from the Quinta de Terrugem, including Cabernet Sauvignon. Eight months barrel aging give this wine richness and layers of toast, as well as solid tannins. Underneath ripe, generous fruit, there is a layer of dryness which indicates it will age 5 years or more. **89** *—R.V. (12/1/2004)*

Caves Aliança 1996 Particular Portuguese Red (Dão) $11. **87 Best Buy** *—M.S. (10/1/1999)*

Caves Aliança 2001 Quinta das Baceladas Portuguese Red (Beiras) $25. With consultant Michel Rolland on board, it's hardly surprising that this is a supremely polished wine. It emphasizes elegance, new wood, and ripe fruit. The Merlot and Cabernet Sauvignon in the blend meld well with the local Baga grape to form a structured, generous wine. **91** *—R.V. (11/1/2004)*

Caves Aliança 2001 T da Terrugem Portuguese Red (Alentejo) $60. Consultant Michel Rolland and Caves Aliança winemaker Francisco Atunes have produced a rich, smooth, polished blend of Aragonês and Trincadeira. Flavors of wood, chocolate, spice, and deep black fruits combine richly and with intensity. This is a limited production of 21,000 bottles. **90** *—R.V. (12/1/2004)*

Caves Aliança 1998 Alianca Classico Reserva Red Blend (Beiras) $9. **87** *—R.V. (12/31/2002)*

Caves Aliança 1999 Alianca Particular Red Blend (Palmela) $15. **88** *—R.V. (12/31/2002)*

Caves Aliança 1998 Alianca Reserva Red Blend (Dão) $7. **82** *—R.V. (12/31/2002)*

Caves Aliança 1995 Floral Grande Escolha Red Blend (Douro) $13. **87** *(11/15/1999)*

Caves Aliança 1997 Quinta da Terrugem Red Blend (Alentejo) $20. **90** —*R.V. (12/31/2002)*

Caves Aliança 1999 Quinta dos Quatro Ventos Red Blend (Douro) $30. **88** —*R.V. (12/31/2002)*

CAVES DO SOLAR DE SÃO DOMINGOS

Caves do Solar de São Domingos 2000 Prestigio Red Blend (Beiras) $14. **81** —*J.C. (11/15/2003)*

CAVES MESSIAS

Caves Messias 2003 Vintage Port $NA. A ripe, open style of wine, generous and fruity. This is not a Port for the long-term, but for the next 5–10 years it will be a delicious, enjoyable wine. **86** —*R.V. (11/15/2005)*

CHARAMBA

Charamba 1999 Portuguese Red (Douro) $6. **84 Best Buy** —*M.M. (12/31/2001)*

CHURCHILL'S

Churchill's NV Finest Vintage Character Port $17. A sweet, slightly spirity Port that lacks any real depth or complexity, yet still provides a modicum of pleasure in its sugary, cooked-fruit flavors of prunes, dates, and raisins. **83** —*J.C. (12/1/2004)*

Churchill's 1996 LBV Port $24. **89** —*M.S. (11/15/2002)*

Churchill's 1998 Quinta Da Agua Alta Port $60. **89** —*M.S. (11/15/2002)*

Churchill's 2003 Quinta da Gricha Vintage Port $85. Bought by Churchill in the 1990s, this is a single-quinta wine kept apart from the firm's true vintage. It is a rustic, earthy wine, and the fruit cannot break through that rusticity. Hints of potential, but not enough. **83** —*R.V. (11/15/2005)*

Churchill's 2000 Quinta da Gricha Vintage Port $83. **87** —*J.C. (11/15/2003)*

Churchill's NV Tawny Ten Years Old Port $30. **87** —*M.S. (7/1/2002)*

Churchill's 2003 Vintage Port $95. An impressive, finely tannic Port with solid, ripe fruits and great black jelly and fig flavors. **92** —*R.V. (11/15/2005)*

Churchill's 2000 Vintage Port $82. **93 Cellar Selection** —*J.C. (11/15/2003)*

Churchill's NV White Port $17. **83** —*M.S. (11/15/2002)*

COCKBURN'S

Cockburn's 1996 Late Bottled Vintage Port $20. Successfully marries young, grapy aromas with notes of maple syrup. The flavors are slightly pruny and raisiny, but an elegant overlay of caramel smoothes things out. This is a supple, easy-to-drink LBV for current consumption. **85** —*J.C. (3/1/2004)*

Cockburn's 2001 Quinta dos Canais Vintage Port $NA. The blackest, inkiest wine of the tasting, it's incredibly rich and dense. Round and mouthfilling, packed with mixed berries and chocolate. The vintage's flesh is obscuring the wine's structure for the moment, but this should age magnificently. Drink 2011–2040. **93** —*J.C. (3/1/2004)*

Cockburn's 1999 Quinta dos Canais Vintage Port $NA. Dark, close to inky in color. Intense, youthful aromas of plums and berries are firmly backed by a chocolaty core. Soft and full in the mouth, the masses of ripe fruit make this wine almost approachable. Hold a few more years, and try it in 2009. **92** —*J.C. (3/1/2004)*

Cockburn's 1995 Quinta dos Canais Vintage Port $55. **90** —*J.C. (3/1/2000)*

Cockburn's NV Special Reserve Port $14. **85** —*M.S. (7/1/2002)*

Cockburn's 2000 Vintage Port $90. Incredibly juicy and fruit-filled, with mixed berries leading the charge, backed by cocoa, chocolate and dried spices. It's deceptively easy to drink now, but the structure should become more obvious in time. Côrte-Real considers it "one of the best vintages ever made." Worth cellaring some for 50 years to see how it compares with the '27 and '55. Hold. **92** —*J.C. (3/1/2004)*

Cockburn's 1994 Vintage Port $NA. This seems lighter in weight than expected, despite an impressively dark, saturated color. Lots of cherries and dried spices on the palate, along with aromas of walnuts and smoked meat. "Passing through some middle-age disturbances," as Côrte-Real said, or just very good Port, not great? Hold. **88** —*J.C. (3/1/2004)*

Cockburn's 1970 Vintage Port $NA. Ruby color, with just a hint of brick at the rim. Mouthfilling red berries and plums, finishing with chocolate and peppery spice. Overall, it's a bit austere, but pretty, and capable of another decade or two of further aging. Drink or hold. **91** —*J.C. (3/1/2004)*

Cockburn's 1955 Vintage Port $NA. Slightly deeper and richer in color than the 1947, featuring rich cassis aromas, violets, and dried spices. It's wonderfully rich in the mouth—expansive and mouthfilling, yet not lacking at all for nuance or complexity. Tannins are resolved, but the wine is still sturdy and holding well. Drink now or, based on the strength of the '27, hold up to 20 more years. **96** —*J.C. (3/1/2004)*

Cockburn's 1935 Vintage Port $NA. Entirely amber colored, this has taken on many qualities of a fine old tawny, boasting aromas of toffee and citrus peel, flavors that include nuts and maple syrup. The fruit is tired, but the wine still shows beautiful tawny character. Drink up. **88** —*J.C. (3/1/2004)*

Cockburn's 1912 Vintage Port $NA. Côrte-Real brought six of the company's last 12 bottles to the U.S. for these tastings, making this vintage by far the scarcest of those tasted. It is translucent throughout, but still shows some ruby color at its core, with amber at the rim. Slightly spirity on the nose, with delicate notes of dried cherries and leather. In the mouth, it's full-bodied, with pepper, nut and toffee flavors. A bit hot on the long, mouthcoating finish, the tannins fully resolved. The fruit has almost faded away, yet the wine still seems vigorous. Drink up. **89** *—J.C. (3/1/2004)*

Cockburn's NV 20 Years Old Tawny Port $50. **91** *—J.C. (11/15/2003)*

Cockburn's NV Special Reserve Port $16. Modest earth and prune flavors are largely overshadowed by a fiery, spirity finish. **82** *—J.C. (3/1/2004)*

COMPANHIA DAS QUINTAS

Companhia das Quintas 2000 Cado Portuguese Red (Douro) $14. With its well-integrated scents of cedar, plum, and tobacco, this is a medium-weight wine whose hallmark is its balance. Vanilla and dried spices meld nicely with cherry and plum fruit, finishing smooth, with modest tannins. Drink now–2008. **87** *—J.C. (3/1/2005)*

Companhia das Quintas 2004 Quinta do Cardo Portuguese White (Beira Interior) $6. Grapefruit and other citrus dominates this cool, fresh wine. It's not delicate, but is packed with crisp, white fruits and green acidity. This is a great fish or seafood wine, in the style of a good Muscadet. **88 Best Buy** *—R.V. (8/1/2005)*

Companhia das Quintas 2000 Aristocrata Red Blend (Estremadura) $6. **82** *—R.V. (12/31/2002)*

Companhia das Quintas 1999 Fronteira Reserva Red Blend (Douro) $NA. **89** *—R.V. (12/31/2002)*

Companhia das Quintas 2000 Tradicao Red Blend (Palmela) $6. **85** *—R.V. (12/31/2002)*

Companhia das Quintas 1999 Quinta do Cardo Touriga Nacional (Beira Interior) $14. **88** *—R.V. (12/31/2002)*

Companhia das Quintas 2001 Calhandriz White Blend (Estremadura) $NA. **82** *—R.V. (8/1/2004)*

PORTUGAL

COOPERATIVA AGRICOLA DE SANTO ISIDRO DE PEGOES

Cooperativa Agricola de Santo Isidro de Pegoes 2000 Fontanario de Pegoes Portuguese Red (Palmela) $NA. **88** *—R.V. (12/31/2002)*

Cooperativa Agricola de Santo Isidro de Pegoes 2001 Adega de Pegoes Colheita Seleccionada White Blend (Terras do Sado) $NA. **90** *—R.V. (8/1/2004)*

CORTES DE CIMA

Cortes de Cima 2001 Portuguese Red (Alentejano) $18. A firm, tarry wine with ripe blackberry juicy fruits, layering fresh acidity and tannins. This has some wood flavors and fresh fruits. It is ready to drink now, but would repay cellaring for three to four years. **88** *—R.V. (12/1/2004)*

Cortes de Cima 2001 Red Blend (Alentejo) $21. Jammy blackberries blend with vanilla-scented oak in this rather New World-styled wine. It's supple and fully ripe, with smooth tannins and very berry fruit. Might pass for a Zin in a blind tasting. Drink now–2008. **89** *—J.C. (3/1/2004)*

Cortes de Cima 2000 Chamine Red Blend (Alentejo) $12. This blend of Aragonís and Trincadeira boasts hints of smoke, herbs, pepper, and meat on the nose, along with plenty of cherry-scented fruit. Although it sounds like a cacophony, the reality is harmonious and smooth, finishing with a twist of peppery spice. Drink now. **87 Best Buy** *—J.C. (1/1/2004)*

Cortes de Cima 2002 Incógnito (Alentejano) $NA. A smooth, rich wine, full of young berries and lively acidity. There are tannins but they are covered with the ripe, jammy fruits which are so full and delicious. **88** *—R.V. (12/1/2004)*

Cortes de Cima 2001 Incógnito (Alentejo) $37. This cleverly packaged Syrah (check the back label) tastes more like an Aussie Shiraz than a Northern Rhône, but given Alentejo's climate, that's to be expected. Vanilla-laced oak frames big blackberry flavors that finish with a slight sensation of sweetness. It's a mouthfilling, fruity wine that doesn't lack for flavor. **88** *—J.C. (1/1/2004)*

Cortes de Cima 2000 Incógnito (Alentejano) $33. **88** *—R.V. (12/31/2002)*

CROFT

Croft NV Distinction Special Reserve Port $17. Now under the same ownership as Taylor and Ferreira, Croft Ports have taken on a new lease of life. This is a classic Port from a classic name, with its ripe fruit and structure. It has flavors of dried raisins, figs, and dark chocolate, along with firm, dusty tannins and a dry aftertaste. **88** *—R.V. (3/1/2005)*

Croft 1983 Quinta da Roeda Port $56. **82** *—M.S. (11/15/2002)*

DÃO SUL

Dão Sul 2002 Quinta das Tecedeiras Reserva Portuguese Red (Douro) $20. Produced in conjunction with Dão Sul, this Douro wine is rich and finely balanced. It has all the power of a top Douro wine, with immediate accessibility. There are lovely ripe black fruits, flavors of herbs and rich, soft tannins. Drink over the next 5 years. **89** *—R.V. (11/1/2004)*

Dão Sul 2000 Quinta de Cabriz Reserva Portuguese Red (Dão) $14. Sweet, ripe fruit with supporting acidity go with the dark, brooding tannins in this wine. It is rich, almost opulent, and packed with ripe, generous fruit. From the ripe 2000 vintage, this shows great potential. Give it at least 5 years before drinking. **91 Best Buy** —*R.V. (11/1/2004)*

Dão Sul 2000 Quinta da Cabriz Colheita Seleccionada Red Blend (Dão) $6. 89 —*R.V. (12/31/2002)*

Dão Sul 2000 Quinta de Cabriz Touriga Nacional (Dão) $19. 91 —*R.V. (12/31/2002)*

DELAFORCE

Delaforce 1992 LBV Port (Douro) $19. 87 —*M.S. (11/15/2002)*

Delaforce 2003 Vintage Port (Port) $58. Now under the same ownership as Taylor Fladgate and Fonseca, this is the best Delaforce vintage Port in many years. It is a big, ripe, full-flavored Port with bitter chocolate and solid black fruit flavors. The dry finish suggests good aging potential. Imported by Kobrand. **89** —*R.V. (11/15/2005)*

DFJ VINHOS

DFJ Vinhos 2000 DJF Cabernet Blend (Estremadura) $9. 90 —*R.V. (12/31/2002)*

DFJ Vinhos 1999 Grand Arte Caladoc (Estremadura) $20. 86 —*R.V. (12/31/2002)*

DFJ Vinhos 2000 Grand Arte Touriga Franca (Estremadura) $20. 88 —*R.V. (12/31/2002)*

DFJ Vinhos 2000 DFJ Touriga Nacional Blend (Estremadura) $23. 90 —*R.V. (12/31/2002)*

DOMINGOS ALVES DE SOUSA

Domingos Alves de Sousa 2003 Quinta da Gaivosa Port (Port) $42. A rare vintage Port from a producer, normally known for table wines, in the Baixo Corgo region (the most westerly Port area). This is a success, a rich Port with plenty of sweet fruit, flavors of black currants, and sweet tannins. At this stage though, the spirit is still not fully integrated. **89** —*R.V. (11/15/2005)*

DOW'S

Dow's 1992 Colheita Port (Port) $30. Caramelly and sweet, without the usual complexity or elegance that are Dow's hallmarks. Smoother and silkier than run-of-the-mill tawnies, but a disappointing effort given the house's fine track record. **84** —*J.C. (12/1/2004)*

Dow's 1998 Late Bottled Vintage Port (Port) $19. Shows good complexity for an LBV, with aromas of smoke, herb, and black cherries. Tobacco, dark chocolate, and tea notes emerge on the palate, which is drier than most LBVs and in keeping with the house style. **85** —*J.C. (12/1/2004)*

Dow's 1997 LBV Porto Port (Portugal) $18. 89 Editors' Choice —*J.C. (11/15/2003)*

Dow's 2001 Senhora da Ribeira Vintage Porto Port (Douro) $50. 92 —*J.C. (11/15/2003)*

Dow's 2003 Vintage Port (Port) $80. A dark, dense wine, packed with dry fruits and firm tannins. There are coffee and bitter cherry flavors. All these elements come together to produce a dry but fruity style of wine, which, like all Dow wines, is sure to age well. Imported by Premium Port Wines, Inc. **93** —*R.V. (11/15/2005)*

ENCOSTAS DO DOURO

Encostas do Douro 2001 Vinha Palestra Portuguese Red (Douro) $NA. A light, fresh, perfumed wine that has good, dry tannins along with bright red fruits. This is ripe, easy drinking, and ready to go now. **84** —*R.V. (11/1/2004)*

EVEL

Evel 2004 White Portuguese White (Douro) $9. Smells of honey, nectarine, and apricot. Medium- to full-bodied, with ripe melon flavors and a finish that's seemingly off-dry, spicy and long. With its apparent sweetness, it might work well with Asian dishes. Imported by Admiral Wine Imports. **86 Best Buy** —*J.C. (12/31/2005)*

Evel 2002 Vinho Branco White Blend (Douro) $NA. A blend of four indigenous Douro grape varieties, this wine blends pineapple and lychee aromas and flavors in medium-weight package. Picks up hints of wet stones as well, adding a welcome layer of minerality, but finishes slightly bitter, with a note of citrus pith. **85** —*J.C. (1/1/2004)*

FALDAS DA SERRA

Faldas da Serra 2000 Quinta das Maias Jaen Red Blend (Dão) $22. 91 —*R.V. (12/31/2002)*

Faldas da Serra 2001 Quinta das Maias Malvasia Fina White Blend (Dão) $14. 88 —*R.V. (8/1/2004)*

FEIST

Feist NV 10 Years Old Port (Douro) $19. 89 Best Buy *(3/1/2000)*

Feist 2003 Vintage Port (Port) $NA. Part of the large Barros Almeida group, Feist is one of those names that has an illustrious history in Port. This 2003 is a fine, ripe wine with plenty of rich, dark fruit flavors. There is a pronounced dry character as well, which promises well for the future. **90** —*R.V. (11/15/2005)*

FERREIRA

Ferreira NV Dona Antonia Personal Reserve Port (Port) $22. 83 —*M.S. (7/1/2002)*

Ferreira NV Tawny Port (Port) $14. 86 —*M.S. (7/1/2002)*

Ferreira 2003 Vintage Port (Port) $78. Caramel aromas give a strange, unbalanced nature to this wine. It is soft, with ripe, but unfocused fruit. Imported Broadbent Selections, Inc. 82 —*R.V. (11/15/2005)*

FONSECA

Fonseca 1984 Guimaraens Port (Portugal) $44. 90 —*M.S. (11/15/2002)*

Fonseca 2001 Quinta Do Panascal Port (Port) $50. A strong candidate for Port of the vintage, Fonseca's 2001 Quinta do Panascal boasts a nose filled with rich, dense, brooding fruit. Blackberries and plums rush the palate; it's lush and fruity, yet given shape by some dusty tannins. Turns chocolaty on the finish. Likely to be an early-maturing vintage; drink 2010–2020, possibly beyond. **91 Cellar Selection** —*J.C. (12/1/2004)*

FRANCISCO NUNES GARCIA

Francisco Nunes Garcia 1999 Colheita Seleccionada AragonÍs (Alentejo) $45. Clearly made with lofty aims, this wine displays great intensity. The aromas of fresh-sawn wood and vanilla are nearly overpowering, while the fruit is concentrated and plummy, with a large dose of tannins that dry out the finish. Give it a few years to settle down and it will be more approachable and hopefully more complex as well. 87 —*J.C. (3/1/2004)*

GOULD CAMPBELL

Gould Campbell 1996 LBV Bottled 2002 Port (Douro) $20. 91 —*R.V. (3/1/2003)*

HERDADE DA CALADA

Herdade da Calada 2000 Baron de B Reserva Red Blend (Alentejo) $25. 85 —*J.C. (11/15/2003)*

HERDADE DA MADEIRA

Herdade da Madeira 1999 Roquevale Red Blend (Alentejo) $16. 82 —*R.V. (12/31/2002)*

HERDADE DE ESPORÃO

Herdade de Esporão 2002 Aragonís (Alentejano) $20. The Aragonís is the Alentejo's name for the Spanish Tempranillo.This 100% version, with its huge, solid tannins, and layers of spicy wood, is definitely a hot climate wine. It has richness and ripe, almost new world flavors, while still preserving some element of tannin and dryness which would support some aging. **89 Best Buy** —*R.V. (12/1/2004)*

Herdade de Esporão 2001 Esporão Reserva Portuguese Red (Alentejo) $17. Of the many wines from Esporão, this is the most traditionally Portuguese in its dark black tannins, acidity and leather and spice aromas. It is powerful, at 14.5% alcohol, and a touch hot but it is a great wine with richly flavored dishes. 88 —*R.V. (12/1/2004)*

Herdade de Esporão 2003 Monte Velho Portuguese Red (Alentejano) $8. A powerful, tannic wine which shows big spice and ripe berry flavors. From the 1500 acre Esporão vineyard, this wine has layers of dark fruits and richness. There is a juicy element which gives freshness, but this is a wine which needs another 3-4 years before drinking. 85 —*R.V. (12/1/2004)*

Herdade de Esporão 2004 Monte Velho Portuguese White (Alentejano) $8. A smooth, creamy ripe wine from the 1,500-acre Esporão estate, this blended wine has richness, and almond and green plum flavors. It is intense, dense and polished, with good acidity. **90 Best Buy** —*R.V. (11/15/2005)*

Herdade de Esporão 2004 Vinha da Defesa Portuguese White (Alentejo) $11. A blend of Antão Vaz, Arinto, and Roupeiro, this full-bodied white is ripe and modern, with delicious tropical fruit and lime flavors. It makes a great accompaniment to fish or chicken. **87 Best Buy** —*R.V. (8/1/2005)*

Herdade de Esporão 2001 Monte Velho Tinto Red Blend (Alentejano) $6. 84 —*R.V. (12/31/2002)*

Herdade de Esporão 2000 Vinha da Defesa Red Blend (Alentejano) $14. 85 —*R.V. (12/31/2002)*

Herdade de Esporão 2002 Touriga Nacional (Alentejano) $22. Aged in half and half French and American oak, this intense wine has aromas of violets, spice, and flavors of black fruits. It has more power than elegance, but it still has class from the balancing tannins, acidity, and dry fruit flavors. Age for 5 years. 88 —*R.V. (12/1/2004)*

Herdade de Esporão 2000 Trincadeira (Alentejano) $14. 86 —*R.V. (12/31/2002)*

Herdade de Esporão 2001 Reserva White Blend (Alentejo) $14. 86 —*J.C. (11/15/2003)*

HERDADE DOS COELHEIROS

Herdade dos Coelheiros 2001 Tapada de Coelheiros Chardonnay (Alentejano) $NA. 81 —*R.V. (8/1/2004)*

Herdade dos Coelheiros 1999 Tapada de Coelheiros Garrafeira Red Blend (Alentejano) $42. 90 —*R.V. (12/31/2002)*

Herdade dos Coelheiros 2001 Tapada de Coelheiros White Blend (Alentejano) $NA. 83 —*R.V. (8/1/2004)*

HUTCHESON FEUERHEERD

Hutcheson Feuerheerd 2003 Vintage Port $NA. This is one of the brands owned by Barros Almeida. This vintage Port has hints of volatile acidity, which leaves dirty flavors. Has tannins and some fine blackberry flavors, but overall, it's not an impressive wine. **83** —*R.V. (11/15/2005)*

J. H. ANDRESEN

J. H. Andresen 2003 Vintage Port $32. Founded in 1845 by a Danish sea captain, Andresen remains a tiny, independent shipper, run by the Santos family. It certainly knows how to make some good vintage Port, with its fragrant flavors, big, dark fruits and rich raisins. There is a fine mélange of fruit flavors, balanced with a touch of acidity. **90** —*R.V. (11/15/2005)*

J.P. VINHOS

J.P. Vinhos 2000 Quinta da Bacalhôa Cabernet Blend (Terras do Sado) $27. The beautiful vineyard of Quinta da Bacalhôa was established along with the palace in the 15th century. It was replanted with Cabernet Sauvignon and Merlot by American owners in the 1970s. This 2000 vintage is as good as ever, rich and tannic, with dark fruits and intensity along with wood flavors. A great wine for short-term aging, it is very drinkable already. **89** —*R.V. (11/1/2004)*

J.P. Vinhos 1999 Herdade de Santa Marta Portuguese Red (Alentejano) $10. A big round, juicy wine which is a perfect barbecue wine. Packed with berry and herbal flavors, it is soft, ripe, with a light layer of tannins. From a blend of local grapes, this is ready to drink now. **84** —*R.V. (12/1/2004)*

J.P. Vinhos 2003 Santa Fé de Arraiolos Portuguese Red (Alentejano) $9. Smells slightly roasted or caramelized, then picks up dried cherries, citrus fruit, and herbs in the mouth. A smooth, rounded mouthfeel adds interest. Chocolate and raisin notes on the finish suggest pairing with hard cheeses at the end of a meal. **85 Best Buy** —*J.C. (12/31/2005)*

J.P. Vinhos 1994 Tinto da Anfora Portuguese Red (Alenteo) $11. 87 Best Buy *(10/1/1999)*

J.P. Vinhos 2004 Catarina Portuguese White (Terras do Sado) $9. Musky on the nose, picking up hints of honey and peaches with air. Smells as if it might taste sweet, but it's dry on the palate, with floral, spicy, and melon flavors that finish short and clean. **86 Best Buy** —*J.C. (12/31/2005)*

J.P. Vinhos 2003 J.P. Branco Portuguese White (Terras do Sado) $7. A soft, gentle, honey-and-spice wine that gives immediate pleasure as an apéritif. There is just a touch of acidity to keep it all in balance. **83** —*R.V. (8/1/2005)*

J.P. Vinhos 2003 Serras de Azeitão Portuguese White (Terras do Sado) $8. This white wine is a blend of Fernão Pires and Moscatel, giving an aromatic style which has attractive apples and cream flavors. It is fresh, rich, and soft, with a touch of tropical fruits to round it off. **85 Best Buy** —*R.V. (11/1/2004)*

J.P. Vinhos 1995 J.P. Garrafeira Red Blend (Palmela) $10. 91 —*R.V. (12/31/2002)*

J.P. Vinhos 2001 Monte das Anforas Vinho Tinto Red Blend (Alentejano) $8. This starts off with pure cherry aromas, but they quickly turn more herbal as the wine sits in the glass. In the mouth, the candied, brandied cherries compete with a broad swathe of herbal flavors, finally finishing a tart, sour cherry finale. Shows good concentration, a smooth mouthfeel and unique flavors. **84** —*J.C. (3/1/2004)*

J.P. Vinhos 2001 Tinto da Anfora Red Blend (Alentejano) $12. Sure, purists may quibble that it's international, but so what? It tastes good. Vanilla and chocolate notes from the oak caress blueberry and blackberry flavors in a smooth, creamy embrace that goes down easily. The finish echoes with vanilla, spice and fruit. No point in aging this puppy—drink it now. **90 Best Buy** —*J.C. (3/1/2004)*

J.P. Vinhos 1999 Tinto da Anfora Grande Escohla Red Blend (Alentejano) $30. 90 —*R.V. (12/31/2002)*

J.P. Vinhos 2002 Catarina White Blend (Terras do Sado) $8. A light-weight wine with aromas of apple, anise, and a hint of fresh greens. The delicate flavors evoke rainwater seasoned with touches of green apples and lime, finishing tart and clean. A blend of Fernão Pires, Tamarez, Rabo de Ovelha, and—finally a grape variety we all know—Chardonnay. **85** —*J.C. (3/1/2004)*

JOÃO PIRES

João Pires 1997 Muscat (Terras do Sado) $11. 85 *(10/1/1999)*

João Pires 1998 Muscat (Terras do Sado) $7. 87 Best Buy —*J.C. (12/15/2000)*

João Pires 2001 Muscat of Alexandria Muscat (Terras do Sado) $10. 87 —*J.C. (7/1/2003)*

JOÃO PORTUGAL RAMOS

João Portugal Ramos 2002 Conde de Vimioso Portuguese Red (Ribatejano) $8. A blend in which Portuguese varieties meld with Cabernet Sauvignon, here is a wine that gives depth of flavor and tannins as well as good, fresh red fruits. It is spicy, with a touch of wood and ripe flavors. **87 Best Buy** —*R.V. (11/1/2004)*

João Portugal Ramos 1999 Marquês de Borba Portuguese Red (Alentejo) $11. 86 —*J.C. (12/31/2001)*

João Portugal Ramos 1999 Marquês de Borba Reserva Portuguese Red (Alentejo) $45. 88 —*M.S. (12/31/2001)*

João Portugal Ramos 1999 Sinfonia Portuguese Red (Alentejo) $9. 86 Best Buy —*J.C. (12/31/2001)*

João Portugal Ramos 2004 Antão Vaz Portuguese White (Alentejano) $10. Delicious, fresh, fruity, and clean; great acidity, creamy flavors and aromas of summer hedgerow flowers. **87 Best Buy** —*R.V. (8/1/2005)*

João Portugal Ramos 2001 Aragonês Red Blend (Alentejano) $18. 88 *—R.V. (12/31/2002)*

João Portugal Ramos 2001 Marquês de Borba Red Blend (Alentejo) $10. 85 *—J.C. (11/15/2003)*

João Portugal Ramos 2001 Tinta Caiada Red Blend (Alentejano) $18. 89 *—R.V. (12/31/2002)*

João Portugal Ramos 2001 Vila Santa Red Blend (Alentejano) $20. 90 *—R.V. (12/31/2002)*

João Portugal Ramos 2001 Syrah (Alentejano) $18. 90 *—R.V. (12/31/2002)*

JOSÉ MARIA DA FONSECA

José Maria da Fonseca 2001 Periquita Castelão (Palmela) $7. This is J.M. da Fonseca's big brand, the name meaning "little parrot," from the plot of vines that went into the original blend back in the 19th century. Made from the Castelão grape, it is soft, juicy, and impressively easy to drink. **85 Best Buy** *—R.V. (11/1/2004)*

José Maria da Fonseca NV Alambre 20 Years (Moscatel de Setúbal) $62. A classic fortified wine from just south of Lisbon, this Moscatel de Setúbal is a beautifully smooth, nutty wine, with acidity and freshness along with sweetness. Surprisingly light, despite its 18% alcohol, its closest parallel is Madeira rather than Port.. **92** *—R.V. (11/15/2005)*

José Maria da Fonseca NV Moscatel Roxo 20 Years (Moscatel de Setúbal) $NA. Called Moscatel Roxo because of the slight red tinge to the old gold color of the wine, this is a stunning, mature wine, whose youngest component is 20 years old. It is deep, with a tannic element, and a dry, acidic streak over the intense sweetness. This is a beautiful wine, one of the world's classics. **94** *—R.V. (11/15/2005)*

José Maria da Fonseca 2001 Domini Portuguese Red (Douro) $14. A joint venture between J.M. da Fonseca chief winemaker Domingos Soares Franco and Cristiano van Zeller, this wine packs ripe, toasty fruit and flavors of dark plums, herbs, and bitter cherries. It is rich, ripe, but juicy, and so elegant. **89** *—R.V. (11/1/2004)*

José Maria da Fonseca 2001 DPT Garrafeira Portuguese Red (Palmela) $NA. J.M. da Fonseca is renowned for its Garrafeira wines, every one different, every one with its own three-letter code. This wine lives up to the reputation, full of dark, tarry fruit, dusty tannins and intense flavors. This is great, a link with the positive past of Portuguese wines. **92** *—R.V. (11/1/2004)*

José Maria da Fonseca 1999 Garrafeira CO Portuguese Red (Palmela) $20. A Garrafeira (special selection) from the Castelão grape, aged in wood and tank for four years. It has dense tannins and shows a completely different view of a grape equally at home in fresh, juicy wines. Big and powerful, it should age well over 5–7 years, maybe more. **89** *—R.V. (11/1/2004)*

José Maria da Fonseca 2003 Jose de Sousa Portuguese Red (Alentejano) $NA. A wine from the Jose de Sousa estate in Alentejo, now owned by J.M. da Fonseca. Fermented partly in traditional clay pots, and then aged in wood, it is a generous, fruity wine with just a touch of tobacco and firm but soft tannins. **88** *—R.V. (11/15/2005)*

José Maria da Fonseca 2001 Periquita Portuguese Red (Terras do Sado) $10. One of the classic Portuguese red wine brands, with a production of around 4.5 million bottles, this has flavors of ripe red berries, spice and soft balanced acidity. This is a wine that does not need any aging, but is great for everyday drinking. **87 Best Buy** *—R.V. (11/15/2005)*

José Maria da Fonseca 1996 Primum Portuguese Red (Terras do Sado) $11. 89 *(11/15/1999)*

José Maria da Fonseca 2000 Domini Red Blend (Douro) $15. 89 *—R.V. (12/31/2002)*

José Maria da Fonseca 1999 Periquita (Azeitao) $8. 85 Best Buy *—D.T. (11/15/2002)*

José Maria da Fonseca 2000 Primum Touriga Nacional Blend (Terras do Sado) $13. 88 *—R.V. (12/31/2002)*

José Maria da Fonseca 2002 Primum Sauvignon-Arinto White Blend (Terras do Sado) $15. 87 *—J.C. (11/15/2003)*

KOPKE

Kopke 2003 Vintage Port $NA. An attractive, fresh wine from one of the oldest Port companies, founded in 1638. The fruit is ripe and forward; this is a Port that will develop quickly. There are good tannins to round off an attractive wine. **86** *—R.V. (11/15/2005)*

LAVRADORES DE FEITORIA

Lavradores de Feitoria 2001 Portuguese Red (Douro) $9. Lavradores is an innovative project that brings together 15 growers (lavradores) and estate owners in the Douro to make and market their own wine. This first vintage, an amazing bargain at the price, justifies the innovation. It has a fine, earthy character, with rich, dark tannic fruit and big blackberry fruit flavors. A powerful and impressive wine which talks of schist rocks and mountain vineyards. **90 Best Buy** *—R.V. (11/15/2005)*

LUIS PATO

Luis Pato 2003 Vinha Formal Bical (Beiras) $19. A full-flavored, wooded wine that shows flavors of ripe grapefruit, white currants, and a generous richness. Made from the local Bical grape, this is Luis Pato's top white. **90** *—R.V. (8/1/2005)*

Luis Pato 2001 Quinta do Ribeirinho Primeira Escolha Portuguese Red (Beiras) $20. This is a single-vineyard blend of Baga and Touriga Nacional, making an intensely dense and rich wine, packed with sweet tannins and great ripe fruit. There is a juicy element that suggests it will age relatively quickly, but those dark, dry tannins should give it a long life. This is a fine wine, to be drunk after 5 years. **89** *—R.V. (11/1/2004)*

Luis Pato 2001 Vinha Pan Portuguese Red (Beiras) $50. Named after the village of Panasqueira, where the vineyard is situated, this wine is made from the local Baga grape. Packed with rich black fruits, ripe but firm tannins, and layers of wood, this is an intense wine that would repay cellaring. Pato believes the Baga softens and becomes more like Pinot Noir as it ages—give it 10 years. **91** —*R. V. (11/1/2004)*

Luis Pato 2004 Maria Gomes Portuguese White (Beiras) $8. Green fruits dominate this wine, with their tannins and lime and citric flavors. It's fresh, crisp, and acidic, with just a touch of toast. **86 Best Buy** —*R. V. (8/1/2005)*

Luis Pato 2000 Red Blend (Beiras) $13. 86 —*R. V. (12/31/2002)*

Luis Pato 1999 Quinta do Moinho Red Blend (Beiras) $45. 88 —*R. V. (12/31/2002)*

Luis Pato 2000 Quinta do Ribeirinho Red Blend (Beiras) $30. 85 —*R. V. (12/31/2002)*

Luis Pato 2000 Vinha Barrio Red Blend (Beiras) $29. 87 —*R. V. (12/31/2002)*

Luis Pato 2000 Vinha Pan Red Blend (Beiras) $13. 90 —*R. V. (12/31/2002)*

Luis Pato 1997 Vinhas Velhas Red Blend (Bairrada) $20. 90 *(11/15/1999)*

Luis Pato 2000 Vinha Formal White Blend (Beiras) $NA. 87 —*R. V. (11/1/2004)*

MARGARIDA CABACO

Margarida Cabaco 2001 Monte dos Cabacos Portuguese Red (Alentejano) $19. Like many of the Alentejano wines, this one is a blend of several grape varieties. In this case, it's Syrah, Cabernet Sauvignon, Touriga Nacional, and Alicante Bouschet. The result is a broad, mouthfilling wine but one that lacks depth or richness. Black cherry and leather flavors are pleasant enough for washing down weeknight burgers. **84** —*J.C. (12/31/2005)*

MARQUÊS BE BORBA

Marquês be Borba 2000 White Blend (Alentejo) $11. 85 —*D. T. (12/31/2001)*

MARQUÊS DE GRIÑON

Marquês de Griñon 2001 Durius White Blend (Douro) $9. 83 —*D. T. (4/1/2003)*

MARTINEZ GASSIOT

Martinez Gassiot 1995 Quinta da Eira Velha Port $43. 89 —*J.C. (3/1/2000)*

NIEPOORT

Niepoort 1997 LBV Bottled 2001 Port $22. 90 —*R. V. (3/1/2003)*

Niepoort 2003 Secundum Vintage Port $58. This may be called "Secundum," or "second wine," but this is as fine a vintage Port as many so-called first wines. The tannins are huge, dense, dry, and designed for the long haul. The Port is packed with ripe fruit, cassis flavors, and an herbal layer. The style is big and opulent, backed up with tannins. **93** —*R. V. (11/15/2005)*

Niepoort NV Vintage Character Port $18. A well-balanced Port from master winemaker Dirk Niepoort. It is soft, with delicate flavors of black cherries, and young, fresh fruit. In keeping with what a Reserve Port should be, this is easy to drink, just hinting at a tannic structure. **88** —*R. V. (3/1/2005)*

Niepoort 2001 Batuta Portuguese Red (Douro) $71. A great wine, which has the richness and the intense concentration of the Douro with a world-class style. This blend of Douro grapes is full of black fruits, of new wood flavors, of solid, dry tannins. But it also has tastes of prunes, of brooding dark fruits, and balancing acidity. This is undoubtedly one of the greatest wines from the Douro. **94** —*R. V. (11/1/2004)*

Niepoort 2001 Vertente Portuguese Red (Douro) $26. A rich, smooth, concentrated wine that shows great juicy fruit along with soft, cigar box tannins. It has vibrant fruit along with dark black flavors. This wine, from the hands of Douro master winemaker Dirk van Niepoort, could well be drunk now, but would certainly benefit from 5 years'cellaring. **89** —*R. V. (11/1/2004)*

Niepoort 1999 Redoma Red Blend (Douro) $41. 92 —*R. V. (12/31/2002)*

NOVAL

Noval NV LB Finest Reserve Port $18. Freshness and fruitiness are the hallmarks of this wine, from French-owned Noval. It is easy and simple, but some herbal flavors add an edge of interest and there is structure as well. The bitter aftertaste spoils the rest of the wine. **85** —*R. V. (3/1/2005)*

OFFLEY

Offley NV Baron de Forrester Reserva Port $NA. Aromas of raisins lead to sweet fruit and intense ripe flavors. The wine has richness but the main impression is of smoothness and softness, along with sweetness. Now owned by Portugal's largest wine company (also owner of Ferreira, Sandeman, and Mateus Rose Offley Ports bear the name of Baron Forrester, the Englishman who created the modern style of Port in the 19th century. **87** —*R. V. (3/1/2005)*

Offley 2003 Boa Vista Vintage Port $50. A fine, structured wine from one of the Port houses now owned by Sogrape (Portugal's largest wine producer). It is in a relatively fast maturing style, but the Port has great, ripe blackberry jelly flavors, some dry tannins and a full, fleshy feel. **90** —*R.V. (11/15/2005)*

OSBORNE

Osborne NV 10 Years Old Tawny Port $25. **84** —*J.C. (11/15/2003)*

Osborne 1997 Late Bottled Vintage Port $16. Shows floral aromas alongside fresh black cherries, leather, and anise. It's a pretty Port, much like Osborne's 2000 vintage wine, without bonecrushing concentration or extract yet possessed of an easy harmony. **86** —*J.C. (3/1/2004)*

Osborne 1997 LBV Port (Douro) $16. **86** —*M.S. (11/15/2002)*

Osborne 2003 Vintage Port $50. A disappointing Port from a firm that is better known for its Sherries and brandies. The fruit is highly perfumed, with aromas of geraniums, but is not at all structured. Instead, it is much more in a light, fresh style. **84** —*R.V. (11/15/2005)*

Osborne 2000 Vintage Port $45. A solid, medium-weight offering that boasts supple tannins and pretty floral notes. Not a blockbuster, but a fruity vintage Port that should mature relatively quickly and provide ample enjoyment while you wait for the big boys to shed their massive tannins. **87** —*J.C. (3/1/2004)*

PINTAS

Pintas 2002 Portuguese Red (Douro) $NA. Tasted as a cask sample, this wine was packed with new wood and red fruit flavors. It will not be as powerful, or as long-lasting as the 2001, but it has the potential for great drinkability within 5 years **88** —*R.V. (11/1/2004)*

POÇAS

Poças 2003 Director's Choice Vintage Port $19. A big, perfumed, delicious wine that seduces with its opulence and generosity. It also offers some dry tannins which beautifully frame the ripe, red fruits. Imported by Signature Imports. **91** —*R.V. (11/15/2005)*

PORCA DE MURCA

Porca de Murca 2000 Reserve Red Blend (Douro) $16. Leathery, with slightly raisiny fruit flavors reminiscent of prune or dried cherries. The tough tannins are mouthdrying and may not have the fruit behind them to support extended aging. Drink now with hearty foods that need an austere counterpoint. **83** —*J.C. (3/1/2004)*

Porca de Murca 2002 Branco Reserva White Blend (Douro) $10. This unique blend of 50% Sémillon, 25% Gouveio, and 25% Cerceal (Sercial) is plump and aromatic enough (pears, tropical fruit) but the flavors are less pronounced. Finishes on a tart, grapefruity note. **84** —*J.C. (3/1/2004)*

PORTAL DO FIDALGO

Portal do Fidalgo 2004 Alvarinho (Vinho Verde) $15. From the subregion of Monção, this is a richly fruity Alvarinho, featuring pineapple and pears. It's ultimately a little simple, but satisfying and cleanly made. **84** —*J.C. (12/31/2005)*

PORTO POÇAS

Porto Poças NV 10 Year Old Tawny Port $35. Interesting contrast to the 20 Years Old from the same house, yielding similar walnut and caramel scents and also a touch of spirit on the nose. But quite different in the mouth, where it is blockier and more intense, with robust berry flavors. Finishes a little coarse and rustic. **87** —*J.C. (3/1/2005)*

Porto Poças NV Director's Choice Tawny Port $20. Starts with aromas of dried cherries, a slight nuttiness, and hints of smoke. Elegant and smooth in the mouth, its lovely nutty flavors buffered by dried cherries and honey. Finishes long, just a touch on the tart side. **89** —*J.C. (3/1/2005)*

Porto Poças NV Quinta Vale de Cavalos Special Reserve Ruby Port $19. A single quinta Reserva, which is young and seems to have the potential to age in bottle. The aromas are fresh and lightly stalky. It is well-made and fruity with layers of tannins along with firm fruit flavors. It would be worth buying this now and keeping it until the end of the year. **88** —*R.V. (3/1/2005)*

Porto Poças NV Tawny Port $14. Earthy and a bit simple, with modest dried-fruit flavors and hints of candied orange peel. Lacks concentration, making it seem a little warm on the finish, but it's a solid performer in its class. **84** —*J.C. (3/1/2005)*

PRATS & SYMINGTON LDA

Prats & Symington LDA 2001 Chryseia Red Blend (Douro) $45. **91** —*J.C. (7/1/2003)*

QUARLES HARRIS

Quarles Harris 2003 Vintage Port (Port) $NA. A dry, power-packed Port from one of the Symington-owned brands. The wine is dense, structured, and full of big, firm fruit flavors. A touch of stalkiness is a discordant note. **88** —*R.V. (11/15/2005)*

QUINTA D'AGUIEIRA

Quinta d'Aguieira 2001 Touriga Nacional-Cabernet Sauvignon (Beiras) $13. This blend is 60% Cabernet Sauvignon, and it really dominates the wine, imparting black olive and bell pepper aromas that merge with cherry fruit and sweet oak on the palate. Supple and chewy, finishing with dry oak and firm tannins. **84** *(1/1/2004)*

Quinta d'Aguieira 2000 Touriga Nacional-Cabernet Sauvignon (Beiras) $16. **84** —*R.V. (12/31/2002)*

Quinta d'Aguieira 2002 White Blend (Beiras) $8. **86 Best Buy** *(12/15/2003)*

QUINTA DA AVELEDA

Quinta da Aveleda 2002 Alvarinho (Vinho Verde) $12. 86 *(12/15/2003)*

Quinta da Aveleda 2000 Alvarinho (Vinho Verde) $12. 88 *—R. V. (8/1/2004)*

Quinta da Aveleda 2000 Aveleda Red Blend (Estremadura) $6. 86 *—R. V. (12/31/2002)*

Quinta da Aveleda 1999 Charamba Red Blend (Douro) $7. 83 *—R. V. (12/31/2002)*

Quinta da Aveleda 2002 Aveleda Trajadura (Vinho Verde) $8. 84 *(12/15/2003)*

Quinta da Aveleda NV Aveleda White Blend (Vinho Verde) $6. 83 *(12/15/2003)*

Quinta da Aveleda NV Casal Garcia White Blend (Vinho Verde) $6. 84 *(12/15/2003)*

Quinta da Aveleda 2000 Grinalda White Blend (Vinho Verde) $9. 84 *—J.C. (12/31/2001)*

Quinta da Aveleda 2001 Quinta de Aveleda White Blend (Vinho Verde) $7. 88 *—R. V. (8/1/2004)*

QUINTA DA CARVALHOSA

Quinta da Carvalhosa 2001 Campo Ardosa Portuguese Red (Douro) $30. Matured in new oak, this shows how the Douro is capable of great elegance. Flavors of dark fruits balance dry tannins and spice. This wine will age, for 10 years or more. **94 Editors' Choice** *—R. V. (11/1/2004)*

QUINTA DA CORTEZIA

Quinta da Cortezia 1997 Touriga Nacional (Estremadura) $33. 91 *(10/1/1999)*

QUINTA DA FOZ

Quinta da Foz 1996 Vintage Port $50. This 1996 is finely poised, elegant, and has a sweetness and richness that makes it immediately appealing. But its fruit is shot through with tannins that suggest 10 years' aging potential. 90 *—R. V. (3/1/2004)*

QUINTA DA MANUELA

Quinta da Manuela 2000 Portuguese Red (Douro) $61. Starts off with lovely mixed-berry scents, including hints of raspberry, blackberry, and mulberry, accented by hints of toast and cedar. Darker fruit flavors emerge on the palate, adding earth, anise, and chocolate notes. For a full-bodied wine, it shows remarkable poise, balanced by modest tannins and decent acidity. Drink now–2010, possibly longer. 90 *—J.C. (3/1/2005)*

QUINTA DA MIMOSA

Quinta da Mimosa 2000 Tinto Red Blend (Palmela) $15. 88 *—J.C. (7/1/2003)*

QUINTA DA ROMEIRA

Quinta da Romeira 2003 Arinto (Bucelas) $9. Lime and chalk dust aromas ease into flavors of green apples and minerals. Finishes with mild citrus flavors that seem a bit softer than usual for this wine, giving it an atypically plump mouthfeel. **85 Best Buy** *—J.C. (3/1/2005)*

Quinta da Romeira 2001 Estate Bottled Arinto (Bucelas) $7. 83 *—J.C. (7/1/2003)*

Quinta da Romeira 1999 Morgado de Sta. Catherina Arinto (Bucelas) $13. 83 *—J.C. (12/31/2001)*

Quinta da Romeira 2003 Morgado de Santa Catherina Portuguese White (Bucelas) $NA. A finely poised wine from this appellation close to Lisbon. Made from the Arinto grape, it is delicate, but still has a creaminess almost like Chardonnay, from the wood aging and lees stirring during and after fermentation. 88 *—R. V. (8/1/2005)*

Quinta da Romeira 1999 Tradicão Red Blend (Palmela) $7. **87 Best Buy** *—J.C. (12/15/2000)*

QUINTA DAS BALDIAS

Quinta das Baldias 2003 Vintage Port $NA. José and Manuel Vizeu have been grape growers for three generations, and have been bottling their own wine since the 1980s. This is a dense, deep powerful Port, with firm tannins. It is sweet, structured, and impressive. 93 *—R. V. (11/15/2005)*

QUINTA DAS MAIAS

Quinta das Maias 2001 Portuguese Red (Dão) $18. This wine offers great power, despite the relatively low (12.5%) alcohol. That gives it balance, and drinkability, which makes it a pleasure. Rich, earthy fruit flavors are balanced by some dry tannins and soft acidity. Definitely food friendly. 89 *—R. V. (11/1/2004)*

Quinta das Maias 2000 Reserva Portuguese Red (Dão) $29. From 70-year-old vines, this is a ripe wine, packed with fruit and soft, dusty tannins. Aged 12 months in wood; a blend of Tinta Amarela, Tinta Roriz, and Touriga Nacional, this has lovely, generous, opulent flavors, and yet remains restrained in its alcohol (13%). 90 *—R. V. (11/1/2004)*

QUINTA DAS TECEDEIRAS

Quinta das Tecedeiras 2003 Vintage Port $35. Owned by Dão Sul, well known as table wine producers, this is a fragrant, floral wine with soft, easy, raisiny flavors. There are some good dusty tannins, but this is a wine for early, enjoyable drinking. 88 *—R. V. (11/15/2005)*

QUINTA DE CABRIZ

Quinta de Cabriz 2000 Colheita Seleccionada Red Blend (Dão) $20. **85** *—J.C. (11/15/2003)*

QUINTA DE COVELA

Quinta de Covela 2001 Colheita Seleccionada Portuguese Red (Portugal) $NA. This oak-aged wine, a blend of Touriga Nacional, Cabernet Sauvignon, and Merlot, is a successful balancing act between ripe acidity and cool-climate fruit. It has red fruits, lively flavors, and just a touch of wood, which certainly doesn't detract from the fruit. **87** *—R.V. (11/1/2004)*

Quinta de Covela 2003 Branco Escolha Portuguese White (Portugal) $NA. This unoaked wine follows the same blend of Avesso and Chardonnay as Covela's oaked Colheita Seleccionada. Lighter in style and fresh, it is an equal success with its ripe apple flavors and full richness, a reflection of the warm 2003 vintage. **88** *—R.V. (11/1/2004)*

Quinta de Covela 2004 Covela Portuguese White (Minho) $21. This floral wine is a successful blend of Gewürztraminer, Chardonnay and the local Avesso. It is perfumed, but also full-bodied with a great layer of acidity. Drink by 2006. **86** *—R.V. (8/1/2005)*

Quinta de Covela 2003 Covela Fantástico Portuguese White (Minho) $NA. A hugely toasty, woody wine at this stage, but there is also ripe fruit with flavors of ripe quince, lychees, and spice. Made from a selection of wines, this is the Reserve wine from Quinta de Covela. **90** *—R.V. (8/1/2005)*

QUINTA DE LA ROSA

Quinta de la Rosa NV 10-Year-Old Tawny Port $37. This deliciously nutty tawny has old wood and concentrated flavors. They balance against fresh, sweet fruit, and coffee flavors, along with some acidity and elegance. **88** *—R.V. (3/1/2004)*

Quinta de la Rosa 1997 LBV Bottled 2002 Port $26. **87** *—R.V. (3/1/2003)*

Quinta de la Rosa 2003 Vintage Port $NA. Owned by the Bergqvist family, this stunning quinta, on the banks of the Douro near Pinhão, produces both Port and table wines. This 2003 vintage is a fine, firmly tannic wine, which also manages to push through with sweet fruit. The structure and the aging potential are both excellent. **94** *—R.V. (11/15/2005)*

Quinta de la Rosa 2001 Portuguese Red (Douro) $NA. Rich, juicy fruit with great acidity and firm, but not overpowering, tannins. It has tarry and juicy black fruits which give concentration. The finishing acidity and the wood flavors give it complexity. **89** *—R.V. (11/1/2004)*

QUINTA DE PARROTES

Quinta de Parrotes 2001 Red Blend (Alenquer) $9. Tastes more than a little like a decent cru bourgeois, with scents of leather and cedar and flavors of tea, tobacco, and cassis. Medium-weight and surprisingly elegant. A blend of Castelão and Cabernet Sauvignon. **86 Best Buy** *—J.C. (11/1/2004)*

QUINTA DE RORIZ

Quinta de Roriz 2003 Vintage Port $57. Jointly owned by the Symington family and João van Zeller, this Port is charming, with balanced, attractive, open fruit. If there is a touch of greenness in the wine from the tannins, it is still going to be a delicious Port. **87** *—R.V. (11/15/2005)*

Quinta de Roriz 2001 Vintage Porto $48. **92 Editors' Choice** *—J.C. (11/15/2003)*

Quinta de Roriz 2002 Prazo de Roriz Portuguese Red (Douro) $13. The second label of Quinta de Roriz, from the lighter 2002 vintage, is a wine for early drinking. It has fresh red fruits, soft tannins and good balancing acidity. The word "prazo," meaning "lease," was the name given to the quinta in the 18th century. **85** *—R.V. (11/1/2004)*

Quinta de Roriz 2001 Prazo de Roriz Portuguese Red $13. **88** *—R.V. (12/31/2002)*

Quinta de Roriz 2001 Reserva Portuguese Red (Douro) $23. A joint venture between the quinta's owner João van Zeller and the Symington family, this wine was aged in new oak for 12 months. The result is rich, with sweet but firm tannins, with flavors of red currant fruits and sweet figs. It could well age for 10 years or more, with its dark, intense aftertaste. **90 Editors' Choice** *—R.V. (11/1/2004)*

QUINTA DE SAES

Quinta de Saes 1996 Vinho Tinto Red Blend (Dão) $25. **87** *(10/1/1999)*

QUINTA DE VENTOZELO

Quinta de Ventozelo 2000 Portuguese Red (Douro) $12. Not for the oak-averse, this is layered in cedar and vanilla, yet remains lean and focused, with roasted plum flavors supporting the oak. Finishes on a tart note, couched in soft, woody tannins. **86** *—J.C. (12/1/2004)*

Quinta de Ventozelo 2001 Cister da Ribeira Portuguese Red (Douro) $9. Presents admirably pure black cherry fruit in a medium-bodied format. What it lacks in weight and texture it makes up for in flavor, delivering fruit, mineral, and spice in a harmonious package that builds in intensity on the finish. **87 Best Buy** *—J.C. (12/31/2005)*

Quinta de Ventozelo 2001 Reserva Portuguese Red (Douro) $22. Another winner from Quinta de Ventozelo, the 2001 Reserva features complex, Rhône-like scents of leather, game, and spice alongside bold cherry flavors. Smooth and supple, with a long, piquant finish endowed with crisp acids and soft tannins. **89** *—J.C. (12/31/2005)*

Quinta de Ventozelo 2003 Touriga Franca (Douro) $16. Smoky, toasty, and vanilla-laden on the nose, but turns juicy and filled with cherry-berry fruit in the mouth. Medium-bodied, with more vanilla and some dry, woody notes on the finish. Good, if somewhat oaky. **86** *—J.C. (12/31/2005)*

QUINTA DO CARMO

Quinta do Carmo 2001 Red Blend (Alentejano) $30. This Lafite-owned venture in the south of Portugal has turned out a round, softly fruity wine dominated by chocolate and plum aromas and flavors. A blend of Aragonís, Alicante Bouschet, Trincadeira, Castelão, Cabernet Sauvignon, and Syrah. **86** *—J.C. (12/31/2005)*

Quinta do Carmo 2000 Red Blend (Alentejano) $25. 86 *—J.C. (12/10/2003)*

Quinta do Carmo 1998 Red Blend (Alentejo) $30. 85 *—M.S. (11/15/2002)*

Quinta do Carmo 2001 Dom Martinho Red Blend (Alentejano) $11. This is the second wine of the Rothschild-owned Quinta do Carmo. It is soft and supple with dry tannins and fresh, juicy fruit flavors. The tannins suggest it could age, but it is not a complex wine and is good to drink now. **84** *—R.V. (12/1/2004)*

Quinta do Carmo 1999 Dom Martinho Red Blend (Alentejano) $10. 82 *—R.V. (12/31/2002)*

Quinta do Carmo 2002 Reserva Red Blend (Alentejano) $40. Strongly scented of oak, with toasty, mentholated scents alongside vanilla, cinnamon, and clove. The texture is creamy, with vanilla and tobacco flavors backed by soft black cherries. Should integrate better in another year or two but there's no need to hide this away. Drink now–2010. **87** *—J.C. (12/31/2005)*

Quinta do Carmo 2000 Reserva Red Blend (Alentejano) $NA. 87 *—J.C. (7/1/2003)*

QUINTA DO CASAL BRANCO

Quinta do Casal Branco 2002 Falcoaria Fernão Pires (Ribatejo) $9. This is the estate wine from the huge property of the Vasconcellos family. It is rich, creamy, and toasty, with good acidity. The name comes from a dovecote on the estate. **87 Best Buy** *—R.V. (8/1/2005)*

Quinta do Casal Branco 1999 Falcoaria Portuguese Red (Ribatejo) $15. A blend of Trincadeira and Castelão, named after a dovecote on the estate, this wine is soft, with smoky tannins and some mature fruit. This is certainly ready to drink, and, with its light, drinkable acidity, goes well with pasta or oily foods. **85** *—R.V. (11/1/2004)*

Quinta do Casal Branco 2000 Globus Portuguese Red (Ribatejano) $NA. A soft, mature wine, with some ripe black fruits, this has layers of wood to give some complexity. From the good 2000 vintage, it has richness in its blend of Castelão and Trincadeira. The tannins are dry and firm. **86** *—R.V. (11/1/2004)*

Quinta do Casal Branco 2003 Portuguese White (Ribatejano) $6. This is a serious, complex wine, from the Casal Branco estate. It has aromas of wood, spice, toast, and white fruits. The palate is packed with intense, dense fruit, shot through with fresh acidity and wood. Ageworthy, it should mature for 5 years or more. **91 Best Buy** *—R.V. (11/15/2005)*

Quinta do Casal Branco 1999 Falcoaria Red Blend (Ribatejo) $15. 90 *—R.V. (12/31/2002)*

QUINTA DO CÙTTO

Quinta do Cùtto 2002 Paço de Texeiró Avesso (Minho) $26. From the local Minho grape Avesso, this is a full-bodied white, with some crisp acidity. Flavors of green plums, white currants, and a touch of grassiness make this a great wine to drink with white fish. **87** *—R.V. (11/1/2004)*

Quinta do Cùtto 2002 Portuguese Red (Douro) $19. Soft, warm, spicy aromas give this wine immediate attraction. Produced from one of the original Douro top table wine quintas, this 2002 shows the lighter side of the vintage, but still manages to have great flavors of sweet fruits and dry tannins. Drink over 5 years. **87** *—R.V. (11/1/2004)*

QUINTA DO CRASTO

Quinta do Crasto 1996 LBV Bottled 2000 Port $20. 90 *—R.V. (3/1/2003)*

Quinta do Crasto 2003 Vintage Port $94. This beautiful quinta, high above the Douro, has produced a generous, raisin and black fig-flavored Port. It is ripe, plummy, and sweet in style, although the tannins at the end show good structure. **88** *—R.V. (11/15/2005)*

Quinta do Crasto 2001 Vintage Port $63. It is still very young, but this wine has enormous potential, with its black fruit, flavors of crushed blackberries, and wild cherries and layers of dense tannins. Give it at least 15 years. **90** *—R.V. (3/1/2004)*

Quinta do Crasto 2002 Portuguese Red (Douro) $15. A fine, fresh wine, from the light 2002 vintage, which has fresh red fruit flavors and a touch of wood. It is not powerful, but it will be very drinkable over the next 4–5 years. **86** *—R.V. (11/1/2004)*

Quinta do Crasto 2001 Reserva Old Vines Portuguese Red (Douro) $33. A smooth, spicy, juicy wine that is packed with ripe, fresh, black fruit flavors. It has dry tannins but these are balanced by the acidity and forward fruit. Quinta do Crasto, was one of the first estates on the Douro to make top-class table wines, and it still sets a benchmark. **90** *—R.V. (11/1/2004)*

Quinta Do Crasto 1997 Reserva Red Blend (Douro) $22. 89 *—J.C. (10/1/2000)*

Quinta Do Crasto 1998 Vinho Tinto Red Blend (Douro) $14. 86 *—J.C. (10/1/2000)*

QUINTA DO ESTANHO

Quinta do Estanho 1996 Vintage Port $28. Situated in the heart of the Pinhão Valley, Estanho began to produce good vintage Port in the 1990s. This 1996 shows the style well. Big and ripe, quite dry with acidity and solid tannins, it is built for long aging. **88** *—R.V. (3/1/2004)*

QUINTA DO FOJO

Quinta do Fojo 1999 Vinha do Fojo Portuguese Red (Douro) $51. Smells a bit under-ripe, with weedy, green notes that ride atop sour cherries.

Tart and sour-tasting, yet it does pick up an intriguing licorice note on the finish. Not bad, but not worthy of its reputation. **84** *—J.C. (3/1/2005)*

QUINTA DO INFANTADO

Quinta do Infantado 1998 Late Bottled Vintage Port $23. An opulent, fruity LBV, full of black fruits and layers of tannins over the sweetness. It is young and will develop some good bottle age, giving elegance as well as richness. **87** *—R.V. (3/1/2004)*

Quinta do Infantado 2000 Vintage Port $50. One of the pioneers of single-quinta Ports under the ownership of the Roseira family, Infantado's wines can be impressively powerful. This wine from the great 2000 vintage has power, but it also has great structured tannins, piled with firm, ripe fruit. It's packed with potential to age over the next 10–15 years. **91** *—R.V. (3/1/2004)*

Quinta do Infantado 1995 Vintage Port $NA. Infantado has produced a 1995 full of ripe tannins, powerful black fruits, and sweetness. There is a layer of dryness but the ripeness and sweetness means the wine is ready to drink now. **89** *—R.V. (3/1/2004)*

QUINTA DO NOVAL

Quinta do Noval 1971 Colheita Port $40. **85** *—M.S. (3/1/2000)*

Quinta do Noval 2000 Silval Vintage Port (Port) $37. **90** *—J.C. (11/15/2003)*

Quinta do Noval 2003 Vintage Port $95. A pure fruited wine, with an unusual touch of toast and new wood. The fruit is well structured with flavors of thyme and rosemary. This is a smooth, polished Port, which is definitely in a modern style of winemaking. **90** *—R.V. (11/15/2005)*

QUINTA DO PASSADOURO

Quinta do Passadouro 2000 Vintage Port $70. **91** *(11/15/2003)*

QUINTA DO PORTAL

Quinta do Portal 1994 Colheita Port $28. A rare category, Colheita Ports are vintage wines aged in barrel (this was aged for eight years before bottling in 2002). This gives a wine with huge concentration, dense flavors of sweet plums. The wood aging has softened the tannins, meaning that it is ready to drink. **90** *—R.V. (3/1/2004)*

Quinta do Portal 2000 Portal Vintage Port $33. This is a densely concentrated wine, powering through with tannins and dry concentration over the young black fruits. It's young, showing sweetness and acidity still coming into balance, but over the next 10 years it will develop well. **89** *—R.V. (3/1/2004)*

Quinta do Portal NV Tawny Reserve Port $14. **87** *—J.C. (11/15/2003)*

Quinta do Portal NV Twenty Year Old Aged Tawny Port $49. **87** *—J.C. (11/15/2003)*

Quinta do Portal 2003 Vintage Port $60. Potentially one of the best wines of the vintage, this is an extraordinary performance from a producer not previously noted for making such high-quality Vintage Ports. The wine—a special selection that at this stage, has no name—has great ripe fruit and huge tannins combined to make a dense, intense wine. It is dark, brooding, and rich. There are also layers of dryness which shows the aging potential of this great wine. **95** *—R.V. (11/15/2005)*

Quinta do Portal 1995 Vintage Port $33. **89** *—J.C. (11/15/2003)*

Quinta do Portal 2000 Grande Reserva Portuguese Red (Douro) $35. The top wine from Quinta do Portal, only made in the best years, this has great ripe flavors and delicious richness. It is packed with sweet tannins and red fruits, along with flavors of wood and tastes of rich currants. It is still young, and will benefit from at least 7–8 years bottle age. **90** *—R.V. (11/1/2004)*

Quinta do Portal 2000 Reserva Portuguese Red (Douro) $17. With the 2000 vintage, Portal was able to make a Grande Reserva as well as this Reserva. It has fine, ripe fruit, but is a wine for early drinking. The tannins and the wood flavors are there, but it is the fruit, rich, red and generous, that makes this wine so attractive. **88** *—R.V. (11/1/2004)*

Quinta do Portal 1996 Mural Red Blend (Douro) $7. **84** *—J.C. (11/15/2003)*

Quinta do Portal 1999 Quinta do Portal Reserva Red Blend (Douro) $NA. **90** *—R.V. (12/31/2002)*

Quinta do Portal 2001 Touriga Franca (Douro) $35. The first varietal release of Touriga Franca from Quinta do Portal is packed with cedar and coffee aromas, and flavors ripe figs and red plums. This is rich, but balanced with some wood flavors balancing the ripe fruit. Good tannins suggest aging potential. **89** *—R.V. (11/1/2004)*

QUINTA DO TEDO

Quinta do Tedo NV Finest Reserve Port $NA. This wine from the single quinta Quinta do Tedo, owned by Napa-based Vincent Bouchard, is sweet and soft, but has good flavors of raisins and a solid structure. The black fruit tastes are fresh, juicy, and lively. A classic, easy drinking Reserve style. **85** *—R.V. (3/1/2005)*

Quinta do Tedo 2000 Savedra Vintage Port $55. From a small parcel of old vines, this wine is dense, very firm, and closed. It is in a dry style, layering richness rather than sweetness, with solid black fruit. Give this wine at least 10 years. **88** *—R.V. (3/1/2004)*

Quinta do Tedo 2000 Vintage Port $45. Rich, soft, and seductive, this Port has aromas of caramel, and ripe, sweet tannins. It's very attractive, but likely to age fast. **85** *—R.V. (3/1/2004)*

QUINTA DO VALE MEÃO

Quinta do Vale Meão 2000 Vintage Port $45. **92 Editors' Choice** *—J.C. (11/15/2003)*

Quinta do Vale Meão 2002 Portuguese Red (Douro) $50. A bit crisper and lighter in weight than top vintages of this wine, but pleasing nevertheless, with cedar, herb, and cherry flavors that merge harmoniously on the finish. **88** *—J.C. (12/31/2005)*

Quinta do Vale Meão 2003 Meandro Portuguese Red (Douro) $20. Rich and thickly textured on the palate, this is a big, ripe, jammy wine filled with blackberries and dried spices. Long, tannic, and layered on the finish. Hard to believe this is a second label. **91 Editors' Choice** *—J.C. (12/31/2005)*

Quinta do Vale Meão 2001 Meandro Portuguese Red (Douro) $19. The second wine of Quinta do Vale Meão is inevitably much less powerful than the estate wine. It has ripe, earthy fruit, with flavors of spices and warm, southern herbs. The tannins are there, but only serve to balance the wine's immediate drinkability. **87** *—R.V. (11/1/2004)*

Quinta do Vale Meão 2000 Meandro Portuguese Red (Douro) $19. **90 Editors' Choice** *—J.C. (11/15/2003)*

QUINTA DO VALLADO

Quinta do Vallado 2003 Portuguese White (Douro) $18. A highly perfumed wine, with spice and melon flavors. There is just a hint of spicy wood. The wine comes from a top Douro estate, close to Regua. **89** *—R.V. (8/1/2005)*

QUINTA DO VESUVIO

Quinta do Vesuvio 2000 Vintage Port $NA. Quinta do Vesuvio is owned by the Symington family but managed separately from the family's shipping brands (Dow, Graham, Warre). Vesuvio's immense terraces and vast open lagares for fermentation, have produced a suitably dense, dark, brooding 2000, perfumed with violets and bursting with solid tannins. This is a great vintage wine.- **93** *—R.V. (3/1/2004)*

Quinta do Vesuvio 1998 Vintage Port $50. **90** *—R.V. (2/1/2001)*

QUINTA DOS ACIPRESTES

Quinta dos Aciprestes 2001 Portuguese Red (Douro) $12. A wine from old vines grown across the river from Tua in the upper Douro, owned by the Royal Oporto company. With its ripe, juicy fruits, flavors of firm, solid tannins and attractive herbal flavors, this is a wine that could be drunk soon, but will age well over 5 years. **87 Best Buy** *—R.V. (11/1/2004)*

QUINTA DOS ROQUES

Quinta dos Roques 2000 Garrafeira Portuguese Red (Dão) $39. The idea of a Garrafeira is a special selection, and this wine from Quinta dos Roques, with its smooth, rich tannins and intense fruit flavors, is certainly special. Aged in wood for 13 months, it is packed with ripe black fruits, leaving sweet acidity and a dry aftertaste. Has good aging potential. **91** *—R.V. (11/1/2004)*

Quinta dos Roques 2003 Encruzado Portuguese White (Dão) $18. A hearty, ripe wine, packed with flavors of green plums, layers of wood, spice and a complex herbal character. This is rich, intense and full-bodied, great with food. **90** *—R.V. (8/1/2005)*

Quinta dos Roques 2000 Alfrocheiro Preto Red Blend (Dão) $22. **88** *—R.V. (12/31/2002)*

Quinta dos Roques 2000 Tinta Roriz (Dão) $22. **90** *—R.V. (12/31/2002)*

Quinta dos Roques 2000 Touriga Nacional (Dão) $22. **89** *—R.V. (12/31/2002)*

QUINTA SEARA D'ORDENS

Quinta Seara d'Ordens 2003 Vintage Port $NA. A quinta on the western edge of the Port region, owned by the Moreira family, who also produce a Douro table wine. New wood aromas are unusual for a vintage Port, and the wood dominates the black fruit flavors. This is an unusual, modern style of Port, one that doesn't quite come off. **83** *—R.V. (11/15/2005)*

QUINTA VALE D. MARIA

Quinta Vale D. Maria 2003 Vintage Port $NA. A dry, ripe wine with some firm tannins. Flavors of raisins and dry figs lead to a dry finish. At this stage in its development, the spirits element dominates. **85** *—R.V. (11/15/2005)*

Quinta Vale D. Maria 2001 Portuguese Red (Douro) $NA. A spicy, elegant wine, that has all the hallmarks of great style as well as power. From the hot valley of the Torto, a tributary of the Douro, the wine still manages to retain dry tannins along with plums and sultana fruit flavors. It is designed for aging, but drinkable in 4–5 years. **90** *—R.V. (11/1/2004)*

QUINTAS DE MELGACO

Quintas de Melgaco 1998 QM Alvarinho (Vinho Verde) $11. **82** *—J.C. (12/15/2000)*

RAMOS-PINTO

Ramos-Pinto NV 30 Year Tawny Port $90. Like so many of the Portuguese houses, Ramos-Pinto takes special pride in its tawnies, with the 30-year being the crowning glory. It's a delicate wine, one that has gained many times in complexity what it has lost in weight. Almeida likens it to "an aged person who has a lot of things to tell you." Hazelnuts and walnuts, dried apricots, and citrus fruits, honey, the list of descriptors goes on and on. **92** *(10/1/2004)*

Ramos-Pinto NV Collector Reserva Port $19. This basic Port is well-balanced for its type, not syrupy or hot, but blessed with grapy prune and chocolate flavors and a smooth, not-too-sweet finish. **86** *—J.C. (3/1/2004)*

Ramos-Pinto 1998 LBV Port (Douro) $18. **86** *—R.V. (3/1/2003)*

Ramos-Pinto 1997 LBV Port $21. Fairly big and chunky, a solid mouthful of Port that packs in leather, chocolate, prune, and blackberry flavors. Fruit-forward, but with enough complexity to keep it from becoming tiring. **88** *(10/1/2004)*

Ramos-Pinto 1996 LBV Port $19. **89** *—M.S. (11/15/2002)*

Ramos-Pinto NV Quinta do Bom Retiro 20 Year Tawny Port $67. Lush and creamy-textured, with nuances that bring to mind an old shipping office: worn leather furniture, a bowl of nuts, a faint haze of cigar smoke. Hints of lemon zest peak through on the finish. **90** *(10/1/2004)*

Ramos-Pinto NV Urtiga Vintage Character Port (Port) $16. **88** *—M.S. (11/15/2002)*

Ramos-Pinto 2000 Vintage Port $63. Showing slightly better than it did a year ago when last reviewed, the 2000 boasts sweet plum fruit, ample earthiness, and refined spice flavors. As vintage Ports go, it's not the biggest or most concentrated, but shows a fine sense of harmony and balance. **91** *(10/1/2004)*

Ramos-Pinto 1997 Vintage Port $50. **86** *—J.C. (11/15/2003)*

Ramos-Pinto 1983 Vintage Port $NA. Almeida refers to this vintage as playing Mozart compared to the 1994's Beethoven and 2000's Bach. At 20 years of age, it seems pretty much mature, with hints of coffee and maple syrup adding complexity to plum and cherry fruit. Drink now–2015. **91** *(10/1/2004)*

Ramos-Pinto 2003 Adriano Estate Bottled Red Wine (Douro) $15. A bit herbal and resiny, but those elements are mostly balanced by cherry fruit, giving it a slightly medicinal aspect. Supple in texture and medium-bodied, it finishes crisply, with hints of cocoa and citrus. **86** *—J.C. (12/31/2005)*

Ramos-Pinto 2001 Duas Quintas Red Blend (Douro) $NA. This blend of Tinta Roriz, Touriga Francesa, and Touriga Nacional is appreciably lighter than the Touriga Nacional-dominated Reserva, but similar in flavor, with dark fruit and baking spices enlivened by a beam of bright acidity on the finish. **86** *(10/1/2004)*

Ramos-Pinto 1999 Duas Quintas Red Blend (Douro) $12. **85** *—M.S. (11/15/2002)*

Ramos-Pinto 1999 Duas Quintas Reserva Red Blend (Douro) $34. **91** *—R.V. (12/31/2002)*

Ramos-Pinto NV Quinta da Ervamoira 10 Year Tawny Port $38. This shows its alcohol a bit, a warm undercurrent to the flavors of nuts, dried cherries, and maple syrup. Like all of the Ramos-Pinto tawnies, it tends to the drier side of the genre. **87** *(11/1/2004)*

Ramos-Pinto NV Fine White Port $14. We don't see much white Port in this country, but in Portugal it's often served as an apéritif. This is a fine example, a little sweet but also possessing bracing acidity for balance. Mouthwatering aromas and flavors run toward nuts and stone fruits, with a hint of honey. **88 Editors' Choice** *—J.C. (3/1/2004)*

PORTUGAL

REAL COMPANHIA VELHA

Real Companhia Velha 2002 Quinta de Cidró Chardonnay (Trás-os-Montes) $12. The cooler climate of the far north-east of Portugal allows this creamy Chardonnay to also have good fresh acidity balancing its layers of wood. It is not complex, but is a fine, well-made, lively wine. **87 Best Buy** *—R.V. (12/1/2004)*

Real Companhia Velha 2001 Grantom Reserva Portuguese Red (Trás-os-Montes) $40. This was once one of Portugal's famous wine brands, which disappeared 15 years ago. Now revived by Real Companhia Velha, it is a blend of Cabernet Sauvignon, Touriga Nacional, and Touriga Franca. With 18 months in Portuguese oak, this is a powerful wine with dark fruits, vanilla, and chocolate flavors. **89** *—R.V. (11/1/2004)*

Real Companhia Velha 2004 Quinta de Cidró Sauvignon Blanc (Trás-os-Montes) $10. High up above the Douro Valley, Quinta de Cidró is a large estate on the plateau. This Sauvignon Blanc, taking advantage of the high altitude, is green, ripe and clean. Finishes crisp and light. **85 Best Buy** *—R.V. (8/1/2005)*

REAL VINICOLA

Real Vinicola 1998 Porca de Murça Reserva Red Blend (Douro) $17. **89** *(10/1/1999)*

ROBEREDO MADEIRA

Roberedo Madeira 2000 Carm Classico Red Blend (Douro) $18. **87** *—J.C. (11/15/2003)*

Roberedo Madeira 2000 Carm Reserva Touriga Nacional (Douro) $23. **90 Editors' Choice** *—J.C. (11/15/2003)*

ROQUEVALE

Roquevale 1999 Redondo Portuguese Red (Alentejo) $6. **83** *—M.M. (12/31/2001)*

ROZES

Rozes NV Infanta Isabel 10 Year Tawny Port $25. **87** *(3/1/2000)*

Rozes 1994 Reserve Edition Late Bottled Port $19. **86** *—M.S. (3/1/2000)*

Rozes 1997 Vintage Port $60. **92 Cellar Selection** *—M.S. (11/15/2002)*

SANDEMAN

Sandeman NV Founder's Reserve Port $16. This is a sturdy, warming drink that boasts plenty of dark, raisiny, tarry fruit that brings to mind prunes and dark chocolate. Finishes spicy and a bit hot. **84** *—J.C. (3/1/2004)*

Sandeman NV Founders Reserve Port $17. Standard, simple Port, with flavors of dates, blackberry jam, and a hint of mint or straw. Good balance for a a wine in his category. **84** *—J.C. (12/1/2004)*

Sandeman 2000 Vau Vintage Port $45. **90** *—J.C. (11/15/2003)*

Sandeman 1997 Quinta do Vau Vintage Port $38. **93** *(12/15/1999)*

Sandeman NV Tawny 20 Years Old Port $48. **84** *—J.C. (11/15/2003)*

Sandeman 2003 Vintage Port $60. A wine which, to smell, has a rustic, earthy character. The taste is cleaner, fresher, more solid, and with attractive raspberry and wild strawberry flavors vying with acidity. **87** *—R.V. (11/15/2005)*

SAO PEDRO

Sao Pedro 1995 das Águias Late Bottled Vintage Port $NA. **84** *—J.C. (11/15/2003)*

SENHORA DO CONVENTO

Senhora do Convento 2003 Vintage Port $NA. A rich wine with a touch of new wood. The fruit is huge but restrained, giving ripeness and black jelly sweetness. This is a fine wine that will age well. **89** *—R.V. (11/15/2005)*

SILVA & COSENS

Silva & Cosens 2001 Chryseia Portuguese Red (Douro) $25. The joint venture between Bruno Prats, formerly of Cos d'Estournel in Bordeaux, and the Symington family has already produced some great wines. This latest release of Chryseia, a blend of classic Douro varieties, is packed with intense cigar box aromas, with elegant tannins and with flavors of ripe, almost juicy red fruits. A herbal character is also in the blend to give a warm feel to what is a sophisticated wine. **91 Editors' Choice** *—R.V. (11/1/2004)*

Silva & Cosens 2000 Altano Red Blend (Douro) $8. **87** *—R.V. (12/31/2002)*

SMITH WOODHOUSE

Smith Woodhouse 1986 Colheita Port $41. On the nose, nuts and caramel dominate, but in the mouth enough stone fruits emerge to bring to mind peaches and cherries drizzled with the liquid nuts from the ice cream parlor. It's elegant—almost delicate—bringing complexity and flavor without heaviness, and it ends on a lingering smoky, coffee-like note. **90 Editors' Choice** *—J.C. (12/1/2004)*

Smith Woodhouse 1992 Late Bottled Vintage Port $25. Bottled in 1996, but just being released to the U.S. market, this is a relatively mature LBV, with aromatic notes of caramel and dried cherries. Flavors are a bit simple and sweet, revolving around dates, figs, and cherries, while the mouthfeel is soft and jammy right up until the finish, which picks up a scour of acidity. **85** *—J.C. (12/1/2004)*

Smith Woodhouse 1990 LBV Port $27. **88** *—R.V. (3/1/2003)*

Smith Woodhouse 1999 Quinta de Madelena Port $32. **87** *—M.S. (11/15/2002)*

SOGRAPE

Sogrape 1998 Morgadio da Torre Alvarinho (Vinho Verde) $13. **87 Best Buy** *—M.S. (10/1/1999)*

Sogrape 2003 Callabriga Portuguese Red (Alentejo) $NA. Named after the old Roman name for a fortified settlement in northeast Portugal, there are two wines in this new range from Portugal's largest producer, Sogrape. Both are based on the Tinta Roriz grape. This wine from the southern Alentejo shows the rich, ripe, open character of many southern Italian wines. Great fruit, great value. **89** *—R.V. (11/15/2005)*

Sogrape NV Duque du Viseu Portuguese Red (Dão) $11. **87 Best Buy** *—M.S. (10/1/1999)*

Sogrape 1996 Reserva Portuguese Red (Douro) $13. **87** *—M.S. (10/1/1999)*

Sogrape 1997 Vinha do Monte Portuguese Red (Alentejo) $10. **85** *—M.S. (10/1/1999)*

Sogrape 1999 Duque de Viseu Red Blend (Dão) $11. **85** *—R.V. (12/31/2002)*

Sogrape 2000 Vinha do Monte Red Blend (Alentejano) $11. **87 Best Buy** *—R.V. (12/31/2002)*

Sogrape 2001 Duque de Viseu White Blend (Vinho Verde) $11. **85** *—R.V. (8/1/2004)*

TAYLOR FLADGATE

Taylor Fladgate 1997 LBV Port $21. **89** *—R.V. (3/1/2003)*

Taylor Fladgate 1998 Quinta de Vargellas Port $42. **90** *—R.V. (2/1/2001)*

Taylor Fladgate 2000 Vargellas Vinha Velha Port $NA. The youngest of Taylor Fladgate's Vargellas old vines bottling offers considerable aging potential. It's richly tannic and chewy in the mouth; firm on the finish. The noble structure amply supports dried spices, chocolate, amid plum flavors. Try after 2015. **95 Cellar Selection** *—J.C. (12/1/2004)*

Taylor Fladgate 2003 Vintage Port $92. Hugely ripe fruit dominates this wine. But, as so often with a Taylor Fladgate Port, this fruit is balanced out with beautiful perfumes, elegant tannins, and complex layers of dryness, sweetness and acidity. This is a great wine, maybe not as long-lived as some Taylor Fladgate vintages of the past, but certainly destined for many years of aging. **95** *—R.V. (11/15/2005)*

TERRACOTA

Terracota 2001 Portuguese Red (Ribatejo) $NA. An impressive blend of Cabernet Sauvignon and Castelão, this is richly wood aged. With its juicy, jelly tastes (from the Castelão) and the tannins from the Cabernet, this has power as well as immediate drinkability. **86** *—R.V. (11/1/2004)*

VALLEGRE

Vallegre 2003 Valle Longo Port $NA. Shows a somewhat earthy character, which leaves it unfocused and dominated by rustic perfumes. **82** *—R.V. (11/15/2005)*

VEIGA TEIXEIRA

Veiga Teixeira 2001 Horta da Nazaré Castelão Red Blend (Ribatejo) $13. A powerful, tannic wine that deserves to be cellared 2–3 years, or served alongside some rare lamb or beef to help tame the tannins. There's a blast of black cherries, graham crackers, and vanilla right out of the glass, and plenty of weight to support the hearty flavors. **88 Best Buy** *—J.C. (11/1/2004)*

Veiga Teixeira 2003 Quinta de Santo André White Blend (Ribatejo) $8. A bit similar to a white Rhône in style, with delicate floral aromas combined with nutty scents, then chunky, slightly neutral flavors on the palate of melon and spice. Full enough to handle delicate cream sauces. **84 Best Buy** *—J.C. (11/1/2004)*

VINHOS JUSTINO HENRIQUES, FILHOS

Vinhos Justino Henriques, Filhos 1996 Colheita Sweet Madeira $25. Plump and sweet, this single-vintage Madeira boasts slightly nutty aromas allied to scents of dried figs and dates. The sweet dried-fruit and Christmas-spice flavors come on strong on the palate, balanced by tangy acids on the long finish. **88** *—J.C. (3/1/2005)*

VINHOS MESSIAS

Vinhos Messias 1999 Quinta do Cachão Touriga Nacional (Douro) $5. 85 Best Buy *—J.C. (12/31/2001)*

Vinhos Messias 2001 Quinta do Valdoeiro Touriga Nacional (Beiras) $20. 87 *—R.V. (12/31/2002)*

VISTA ALEGRE

Vista Alegre 1995 LBV Port $NA. This is dry, dense, and raisiny, with dry tannins and acidity. Towards the aftertaste, the solidity of the wine is spoilt by a touch of green tannin. The name of the wine comes from the principal quinta owned by Barros Agricola near Pinhão. **86** *—R.V. (11/1/2004)*

Vista Alegre 2003 Single Estate Vintage Port $NA. From the Vista Alegre vineyard in the Pinhão valley, this Port is powerfully perfumed, with great black-cherry flavors and acidity. It has good structure, but is generally relatively simple and easy to appreciate. **88** *—R.V. (11/15/2005)*

W. & J. GRAHAM'S

W. & J. Graham's NV Aged 20 Years Finest Cask Matured Tawny Port (Port) $45. 90 *—J.C. (11/15/2003)*

W. & J. Graham's 1995 LBV Port $20. 88 *—R.V. (3/1/2003)*

W. & J. Graham's NV Six Grapes Reserve Port $21. W & J Graham makes one of the best-known Reserve Port brands. And a great wine it is, too. It is soft, but there are tannins. It is fruity, but there is good concentration. And with its flavors of ripe black figs and dark chocolate, it is an immediately appealing wine. **89** *—R.V. (3/1/2005)*

W. & J. Graham's 2003 Vintage Port $100. This is a great Port, from a great brand. It is packed with solid, structured, rich, and intense black fruit flavors. Its tannins show considerable aging potential. It is a big, ripe wine, balanced by a long, lingering dark aftertaste. **96** *—R.V. (11/15/2005)*

WARRE'S

Warre's 1992 LBV Port $23. 92 *—R.V. (3/1/2003)*

Warre's NV Otima 20 Year Old Tawny Port $40. A lush, soft Port, with nutty aromas rounded out by scents of coffee and caramel. Caresses the palate with flavors of coffee and crème caramel, blending in a bit of orange peel on the finish. There's not a rough edge to be found. **90 Editors' Choice** *—J.C. (12/1/2004)*

Warre's 1987 Reserve Tawny Port $28. A knockout of a 12-year-old tawny, with heavy, inviting caramel aromas and flavors. The color is still slightly rosy, showing that this wine has retained its fruity roots. Structured and weighty in the mouth, with notes of cloves and ginger throughout. **93** *(1/1/2004)*

Warre's 2003 Vintage Port $82. A fine, perfumed wine with great fruit. It's ripe, with lovely rich flavors and a backbone of firm tannins. This is a good, solid, classic wine. **90** *—R.V. (11/15/2005)*

WIESE & KROHN

Wiese & Krohn 2003 Vintage Port $NA. Normally known for relatively soft vintages, Wiese & Krohn have changed style with this 2003. This Port is firm, solid with intense fruits, black figs, and fine tannins. It should have a good, medium-term future. **89** *—R.V. (11/15/2005)*

South Africa

After a slow start, South Africa's wines have reached international heights. The wines are sold at an impressively good value, and the country offers styles and tastes that are special and—importantly—enjoyable.

South Africa has been producing wine since the first vineyards were planted by the French in the seventeenth century, brought to the country by the Dutch governors of Cape Colony. At one time, the sweet wine of Constantia was the most prized in the world. For decades, South Africa, as part of the British Empire, sent shiploads of fortified wines to London.

Boschendal Estate, Groot Drakenstein Valley, Franschhoek, Cape Province, South Africa.

This luxurious past can still be seen in the stunningly beautiful Cape vineyards, and the elegant, gabled Dutch Cape houses that form the centerpieces of many wine estates. But the future has also made its mark in South Africa's vineyards, where local winemakers (joined by an increasing number of European and American winemakers and investors) are creating a new generation of wines.

The style, the character of the wines, is somewhere between California or Australia and Europe. Food friendly and equally elegant and powerful, there are many wines here for drinkers tired of alcoholic blockbusters.

All South Africa's vineyards are within an hour or three of Cape Town, in the southwest corner of the country. South Africa has its own appellation system, Wine of Origin, which is indicated on the label and on a government-issued neck sticker.

The most important quality wine areas are around the two cities of Stellenbosch and Paarl. All wine styles are made here: the country's greatest reds are from Stellenbosch, but Paarl's sub-district of Franschhoek runs a close second. Increasingly, other areas are being developed: the west coast, which makes great cooler-climate Sauvignon Blanc and red wines under the Darling and Swartland Wine of Origin, and the south coast at Walker Bay and Elgin, from which the country's best Pinot Noir comes.

The other famed quality area (although tiny in volume) is Constantia, almost in the suburbs of Cape Town. The original Cape vineyards now make impressive reds and whites in the country's most historic wine estates.

Larger-volume areas are further north and east than these classic heartland areas: Robertson, known for its Chardonnay, Worcester, for inexpensive volume wines, and Oliphants River, better known for reds and fortified wines.

South Africa's wine styles are evolving. Chenin Blanc, the local white workhorse grape, is also capable of making some impressive dry and sweet wines. Sauvignon Blanc has the potential to be more exciting than Chardonnay.

For reds, Pinotage, South Africa's own red grape (a cross between Pinot Noir and Cinsaut) still leaves wine critics divided, but can make great things, especially if found in Cape Blend wines (Pinotage blended with other red grapes). Shiraz is seen as the new hope for red wine, but Cabernet Sauvignon, Merlot, and Bordeaux blend wines are still the country's top reds.

ALEXANDERFONTEIN

Alexanderfontein 2003 Chenin Blanc (Coastal Region) $10. A classy Chenin Blanc that offers an intriguing profile with smoke and mineral notes over a dry green apple and citrus foundation. It's restrained, but shows good fruit intensity. Tasty and long, it will pair beautifully with lobster or a fleshy, white fish like sea bass, and is delicious on its own. **88 Editors' Choice** *—M.M. (7/1/2005)*

AMBELOUI 2000

Ambeloui 2000 Valley Road Hout Bay Christo (Constantia) $20. **84** *—S.H. (12/1/2002)*

ARNISTON BAY

Arniston Bay 2003 Merlot-Shiraz (Western Cape) $11. Not your usual red blend, this light wine has a red berry and rhubarb profile. The feel is easy, but with slightly high-strung fruit and acidity, and some peppery tannins on the close. **82** *—M.M. (7/1/2005)*

ASHANTI

Ashanti 2001 Chiwara Red Blend (Paarl) $24. **87** *—K.F. (9/1/2003)*

Ashanti 2001 Nicole's Hat White Blend (Paarl) $10. **85** *—K.F. (9/1/2003)*

BACKSBERG

Backsberg 2002 Cabernet Sauvignon (Paarl) $12. Medium weight with good flavor and varietal character after a slightly muddy opening. The wine expands, improving in the glass where the dark berry fruit and tobacco, earth, and toasty oak accents gain focus. Solid, basic Cabernet with a decently long finish. **86** *—M.M. (11/15/2004)*

Backsberg 2002 Klein Babylons Toren Cabernet Sauvignon-Merlot (Paarl) $15. Opaque and hard to read, with deep, toasty, menthol-tinged oak over dark and dense fruit. Built for the cellar. Taut structure and firm tannins here demand keeping both the wine until 2006–7. **87** *—M.M. (11/15/2004)*

Backsberg 1998 Klein Babylons toren Merlot-Cabernet Sauvignon (Paarl) $18. **87** *—M.S. (4/1/2002)*

Backsberg 2001 Chardonnay (Paarl) $13. **84** *—M.M. (4/1/2002)*

Backsberg 1999 Chardonnay (Paarl) $14. **82** *—M.N. (3/1/2001)*

Backsberg 2003 Chenin Blanc (Paarl) $10. An interesting wine that's dry, yet shows some distinctly sweet notes. The apple-grape front end is fruity, somewhat Riesling-like. The appealing, tart green apple close turns crisper and drier. Light weight with good acidity, a good choice for moderately spicy foods, and pretty tasty on its own. **86** *—M.M. (7/4/2004)*

Backsberg 2003 Sauvignon Blanc (Western Cape) $10. Round with perfectly accurate, varietally correct aromas and flavors. Bright without being sharp, showing sweet-sour fruit and pepper hints on the close. Quite drinkable and quite mainstream. **85 Best Buy** *—M.M. (11/15/2004)*

Backsberg 1998 Shiraz (Paarl) $14. **82** *(10/1/2001)*

Backsberg 2003 Babylons Toren Viognier (South Africa) $25. This tasty Viognier hits all the right notes, presenting very appealing honeysuckle-spice aromas and flavors. It's not heavy or sappy, and good acidity supports the fruit. Finishes long and with a very nice blend of spice and mineral notes. **88** *—M.S. (11/15/2004)*

BAOBAB

Baobab 2001 Chenin Blanc (Western Cape) $7. **85** *—S.H. (4/1/2002)*

Baobab 2002 Merlot (Western Cape) $8. Nicely opposed berry, earth, and smoke elements riff in this tasty overachiever. Bordeaux-like, with solid dry fruit, earth, and herb accents. Shows good length and even a touch of elegance. Outperforms most value Merlots, regardless of origin. **87 Best Buy** *—M.M. (11/15/2004)*

Baobab 2001 Pinotage (Western Cape) $10. **88 Best Buy** *—K.F. (4/1/2003)*

BEAUMONT

Beaumont 2001 Ariane Bordeaux Blend (Walker Bay) $20. **87** *—K.F. (8/1/2003)*

Beaumont 2004 Hope Marguerite Chenin Blanc (Walker Bay) $21. Named after winemaker Sebastian Beaumont's grandmother, this is a fine, barrel-fermented Chenin that balances elegant citrus fruit with spice and fresh toast. A delicious, dry food style of Chenin. **91** *—R.V. (11/15/2005)*

BERGSIG

Bergsig 2001 Pinotage (South Africa) $12. **87** *—K.F. (4/1/2003)*

BEYERSKLOOF

Beyerskloof 2000 Pinotage (Stellenbosch) $10. **89 Best Buy** *(9/1/2001)*

BILTON

Bilton 2002 Shiraz (Stellenbosch) $25. Shows a hint of volatility in its high-toned, mixed-berry, and pie crust aromas, then settles down a bit on the palate, where the predominant flavors are of tart cherries and cranberries. Finishes with flourishes of toast and vanilla. **85** *—J.C. (11/15/2005)*

BLACK ROCK

Black Rock 2004 White Blend (Swartland) $24. A blend of 75% Chenin Blanc with some Chardonnay and Viognier, the fruit for this wine comes from cool, dry-farmed vineyards in Swartland. It has a great, pure fruit character, and it's ripe and generous, balancing wood and acidity along with white fruit flavors, peaches, and green plums. A touch of minerality completes the picture. **91** *—R.V. (11/15/2005)*

BOSCHENDAL

Boschendal 2000 Reserve Cabernet Sauvignon (Coastal Region) $20. The oak is dark and heavy here, but the fruit core is strong and not entirely obscured. This medium-to-full-bodied red shows nice weight and good tannic structure, plus a long close. Tasty now in a woody way, it will be better after 2006 and hold well to 2010+. **88** *—M.M. (7/1/2005)*

Boschendal 2000 Chardonnay (Coastal Region) $NA. **85** *—R.V. (7/1/2002)*

Boschendal 2001 Reserve Merlot (Coastal Region) $20. A tart berry profile prevails in this firm red. It's structured and Bordeaux-inspired, with some earth and mineral accents. Hard and very dry. Try with grilled meats. **84** *—M.M. (7/1/2005)*

Boschendal 2004 Sauvignon Blanc (Coastal Region) $12. Quite pale, but shows its substance quickly with a lively green apple, grass, and mild tropical fruit bouquet. Seems like it might be sweet, but turns considerably more citrusy and spritzy on the tongue. A surprise that closes clean, refreshingly tart-sweet, and tangy. **86** *—M.M. (4/1/2005)*

Boschendal 2003 Grand Cuvée Sauvignon Blanc (Franschhoek) $14. Everything's in place as the complex grapefruit, pineapple, and tangy-spice nose opens to a full, similarly flavored palate. The feel is ripe and full yet alive with vibrant acidity, the finish long and clean with zesty pepper notes. **90 Editors' Choice** *—M.M. (4/1/2005)*

Boschendal 2002 Grande Cuvée Sauvignon Blanc (Coastal Region) $14. Dusty hay, citrus, and butter icing stretch from the nose to the palate in lovely layers. The flavors are full and sweet, like cantaloupe rind, but are never cloying, thanks to the spritzy acidity. Finishes dry and faintly chalky with herbs. This is a lightweight and warm style with fine depth. **89** *—K.F. (1/1/2004)*

Boschendal 2004 Le Pavillon Sémillon-Chardonnay (Western Cape) $9. The vanilla and pear nose shows this white's ripe easy style up front. Unexpectedly turns too sweet and soft on the tongue. Good fruit, but simple, and to this palate cloying, though it could have broad appeal in our sweet-tooth nation. The clean close shows some spice. Try with spicy chicken dishes. **83** *—M.M. (4/1/2005)*

Boschendal NV Le Grand Pavillon Brut Champagne Blend (Coastal Region) $13. **87** *—M.M. (3/1/2004)*

Boschendal 2001 Grand Pavillon Sparkling Blend (Franschhoek) $15. **86** *—K.F. (12/1/2003)*

BOSCHKLOOF

Boschkloof 1998 Reserve Cabernet Sauvignon-Merlot (Vlootenburg) $20. **85** *—K.F. (4/1/2003)*

BOUCHARD FINLAYSON

Bouchard Finlayson 2000 Crocodile's Lair/Kaaimansgat Chardonnay (Overberg) $20. **88** *—K.F. (4/1/2003)*

Bouchard Finlayson 2001 Blanc de Mer Meritage (Hemel en Aarde) $12. **87** *—K.F. (4/1/2003)*

Bouchard Finlayson 2001 Hannibal Cuvée Red Blend (Walker Bay) $30. **87** *—K.F. (9/1/2003)*

BOWE JOUBERT VINEYARD & WINERY

Bowe Joubert Vineyard & Winery 2001 Cabernet Sauvignon (Stellenbosch) $18. **88** *—K.F. (4/1/2003)*

Bowe Joubert Vineyard & Winery 2001 Cuvée Emmerentia Chardonnay (Stellenbosch) $15. **85** *—K.F. (4/1/2003)*

Bowe Joubert Vineyard & Winery 2001 Merlot (Stellenbosch) $18. **87** *—K.F. (4/1/2003)*

Bowe Joubert Vineyard & Winery 2003 JB Sauvignon Blanc (Stellenbosch) $12. Tasty Sauvignon, with grass, grapefruit, and slate elements in nice balance. It's crisp without being sharp, as too many are, and just slightly tangy on the tongue. An attractive wine with a spicy satisfying finish. **88 Best Buy** *—M.M. (3/1/2004)*

BRADGATE

Bradgate 2002 White Blend (Stellenbosch) $9. **85** *—K.F. (4/1/2003)*

BRAHMS

Brahms 2004 Chenin Blanc (Paarl) $17. Two Cape Town lawyers hung up their robes and bought vineyards in Paarl in 1989. Their winery produces a well-made Chenin from a single vineyard on Paarl mountain, which gives a nutty aroma, flavors of salted peanuts, as well as a touch of apple fruits. This wine needs to age for another year. **87** *—R.V. (11/15/2005)*

BRAMPTON

Brampton 2001 Red Blend (Stellenbosch) $15. **84** *—K.F. (4/1/2003)*

BUITENVERWACHTING

Buitenverwachting 2001 Chardonnay (Constantia) $15. **85** *—K.F. (9/1/2003)*

CAMBERLEY

Camberley 2000 Cabernet Sauvignon-Merlot (Stellenbosch) $18. **85** *—K.F. (8/1/2003)*

CAPE INDABA

Cape Indaba 1998 Chardonnay (Western Cape) $10. **82** *(9/1/1999)*

Cape Indaba 1998 Sauvignon Blanc (Robertson) $8. **82** *(9/1/1999)*

CAPE VIEW

Cape View 1999 Pinotage (Stellenbosch) $28. **84** *—K.F. (4/1/2003)*

CATHEDRAL CELLAR

Cathedral Cellar 1999 Cabernet Sauvignon (Coastal Region) $15. **88** *—K.F. (4/1/2003)*

Cathedral Cellar 2003 Chardonnay (Coastal Region) $17. Solid mainstream Chardonnay whose ripe nose shows apple-pear fruit and oak-butterscotch accents. Medium-full in feel, with maybe just a touch of alcoholic heat, its broad, friendly profile will enjoy wide appeal. Direct rather than complex, and rich and flavorful, closing with good length. **87** *—M.M. (4/1/2005)*

Cathedral Cellar 2001 Chardonnay (Western Cape) $12. **90 Best Buy** *—R.V. (7/1/2002)*

Cathedral Cellar 1996 Merlot (Coastal Region) $15. **86** *(9/1/2001)*

Cathedral Cellar 2001 Sauvignon Blanc (Western Cape) $15. **87** *—K.F. (4/1/2003)*

Cathedral Cellar 1998 Shiraz (Coastal Region) $15. **83** *(10/1/2001)*

CEDERBERG

Cederberg 2002 Cabernet Sauvignon (South Africa) $25. Elegant wine with an attractive bouquet of dark fruit, Oriental spice, cinnamon, and cocoa. Quite dry, with a similar palate profile. This has Tuscan manners—it's solid, tasty, and firm—and demands food. Possible big league potential with greater depth of fruit and a bit more back-end length. Keep your eye on this producer. **88** *—M.M. (12/15/2004)*

Cederberg 2004 Chenin Blanc (South Africa) $15. This rich, almost Viognier-like Chenin Blanc offers lots of melon, apricot, tropical fruit, and citrus on the nose and palate. The nose is slightly oversweet, but the wine turns more tangy and spicy on the tongue. Try this flavorful, persistent white with grilled pork chops. **86** *—M.M. (7/1/2005)*

Cederberg 2003 Five Generations Chenin Blanc (Cederberg) $35. Five generations of the Nieuwoud family have run the Cederberg farm, and this wine, along with a Cabernet Sauvignon, are here to commemorate. This is a great full-bodied white, showing a successful marriage of wood and peachy, aromatic fruit, layered with acidity. A delicious wine with aging potential. Imported by Global Vineyard Importers. **93** *—R.V. (11/15/2005)*

Cederberg 2002 Shiraz (South Africa) $25. Deep and fairly tightly wound, with ripe berry, leather, and tobacco aromas and flavors. Stylish herb and mildly metallic notes yield a very Rhônish character once it breathes some. Starts dry—almost hard—then opens, developing nicely in the glass. Firm now, structured and handsome, and can age for three to six years. **88** *—M.M. (12/15/2004)*

CHAMONIX

Chamonix 1998 Chardonnay (Franschhoek) $16. **85** *—K.F. (9/1/2003)*

Chamonix 2000 Pinot Noir (Franschhoek) $25. **85** *—K.F. (9/1/2003)*

CLOS MALVERNE

Clos Malverne 1998 Cabernet-Pinotage (Stellenbosch) $17. **85** *—K.F. (4/1/2003)*

Clos Malverne 2002 Cabernet Sauvignon-Shiraz (Stellenbosch) $16. Suave and dark, with blackberry-licorice aromas and flavors, a full mouthfeel and substantial tannins. If this comes off as slightly facile due to the very pronounced oak, it still has great appeal. Finishes long and smooth, with black coffee and espresso notes, and the structure to age for a few years. **88** *—M.M. (4/1/2005)*

Clos Malverne 2001 Pinotage (Stellenbosch) $16. Sharp, with tart red fruit, green tobacco, and a deep elefunkiness that doesn't let go. The modest fruit is overwhelmed by the earthiness and harder, more bitter metallic elements that ascend on the finish. **82** *—M.M. (4/1/2005)*

Clos Malverne 2000 Reserve Pinotage (Stellenbosch) $17. **84** *—K.F. (9/1/2003)*

Clos Malverne 1999 Auret Red Blend (Stellenbosch) $17. A pleasant, full nose of earth, hickory, apple, and a note reminiscent of rum-raisin does not extend to the toasty, brown sugar palate. The eucalyptus-laden finish is sharp and minty. **84** *—K.F. (1/1/2004)*

Clos Malverne 1999 Shiraz (Stellenbosch) $13. **83** *(10/1/2001)*

DARLING CELLARS

Darling Cellars 1999 Onyx Cabernet Sauvignon (Groenekloof) $20. **82** *—K.F. (4/1/2003)*

Darling Cellars 1999 Onyx Chardonnay (Groenekloof) $15. **85** *—K.F. (9/1/2003)*

Darling Cellars 1999 DC Pinotage (Coastal Region) $22. **85** *—K.F. (4/1/2003)*

Darling Cellars 2001 Onyx Kroon Red Blend (Groenekloof) $25. **85** *—K.F. (9/1/2003)*

DASHBOSCH

Dashbosch 2005 Chenin Blanc (Worcester) $NA. A floral, fresh wine, very aromatic, with flavors of pears. From the Dashbosch winery in Worcester, this is an attractive, ripe and soft wine, fruity and easy. **85** —*R.V. (11/15/2005)*

DAVID FROST

David Frost 2000 Chardonnay (Western Cape) $NA. **87** —*S.H. (1/1/2002)*

DC

DC 1999 Shiraz (Coastal Region) $23. **88** —*K.F. (4/1/2003)*

DE MEYE

De Meye 2000 Shiraz (South Africa) $16. **86** —*K.F. (4/1/2003)*

DE TRAFFORD

De Trafford 2004 Chenin Blanc (Stellenbosch) $25. A wood-aged style that works, and works well. Balanced with its touch of spice and some vanilla flavors from the American wood, there is fresh fruit, delicious acidity, and flavors of apples. De Trafford is a top quality, small-scale producer, high up in the mountains above Stellenbosch. **91** —*R.V. (11/15/2005)*

De Trafford 2001 Straw Wine Chenin Blanc (Helderberg) $25. **88** —*K.F. (12/1/2003)*

De Trafford 2000 Shiraz (Helderberg) $40. **88** —*K.F. (8/1/2003)*

DE WETSHOF

De Wetshof 2000 Bateleur/Danie de Wet Chardonnay (Robertson) $31. **88** —*K.F. (4/1/2003)*

De Wetshof 2001 Bon Vallon Chardonnay (Robertson) $12. **90 Best Buy** —*R.V. (7/1/2002)*

De Wetshof 2002 D'Honneur Chardonnay (Robertson) $24. Danie De Wets has steadily demonstrated both what he and the Robertson region—for many still an unknown—can deliver. He does it again in this convincing white, built (of course) on a solid Chardonnay fruit core. Rich but not sappy, it offers abundant flavor, a solid mouthfeel, elegant style, and a spicy, long finish. An impressive white with balance and finesse well beyond its price and rustic origins. **91 Editors' Choice** —*M.M. (4/1/2005)*

De Wetshof 2001 Lesca Chardonnay (Robertson) $14. **87** —*R.V. (7/1/2002)*

De Wetshof 2002 Rhine Riesling (Robertson) $12. **85** —*K.F. (8/1/2003)*

DEWAAL/VITERWYK ESTATE

DeWaal/Viterwyk Estate 2001 Top of the Hill Pinotage (Stellenbosch) $45. **88** —*K.F. (4/1/2003)*

DIEU DONNE

Dieu Donne 1999 Merlot (Franschhoek) $17. **88** —*K.F. (4/1/2003)*

Dieu Donne 2001 Sauvignon Blanc (Franschhoek) $15. **87** *(8/1/2002)*

DU PREEZ ESTATE

Du Preez Estate 2001 Sauvignon Blanc (Goudini) $9. **88 Best Buy** —*K.F. (4/1/2003)*

Du Preez Estate 1999 Hanepoot Estate Wine White Blend (South Africa) $10. **86** —*K.F. (11/15/2003)*

DURBANVILLE HILLS

Durbanville Hills 2002 Sauvignon Blanc (Durbanville) $12. **86** —*K.F. (4/1/2003)*

Durbanville Hills 2001 Shiraz (South Africa) $15. **87** —*K.F. (4/1/2003)*

EIKENDAL

Eikendal 2003 Chardonnay (Stellenbosch) $22. Ample toasty oak here, but it doesn't entirely bury the sweet apple-pear-and tropical fruit. Styled like many New World Chardonnays, and fits comfortably in that league. If woody, it's tasty and well-made. Shows potential to be a serious player, with some fine tuning and restraint on the wood. **87** —*M.M. (12/15/2004)*

EXCELSIOR

Excelsior 2002 Estate Chardonnay (Robertson) $8. **85** —*K.F. (9/1/2003)*

FAIRVIEW

Fairview 2001 Pegleg Carignane (Paarl) $25. **89** —*K.F. (4/1/2003)*

Fairview 2001 Pinotage (Coastal Region) $13. **87** —*K.F. (4/1/2003)*

Fairview 2001 Goat-Roti Red Blend (Western Cape) $17. **86** —*K.F. (9/1/2003)*

Fairview 2002 Sauvignon Blanc (Coastal Region) $10. **85** —*K.F. (4/1/2003)*

Fairview 2001 Shiraz (Paarl) $13. Solid, medium-weight Shiraz with some structure. Displays briary, dark fruit with pepper and toasty oak accents. Very drinkable, with good fruit, not at all overly sweet or jammy, and mildly tangy tannins on the close. **86** —*M.M. (11/15/2004)*

Fairview 2002 Beacon Shiraz (Paarl) $28. Opaque and very dense on the nose with deep, focused, black plum and berry fruit. Toasty oak is nicely melded with the strong fruit, adding smoke and tobacco notes. A chewy mouthfeel and long dark finish complete the package. Should improve through 2006, and hold well beyond that. **90 Cellar Selection** —*M.M. (11/15/2004)*

Fairview 2001 Cyril Back Shiraz (Paarl) $26. Even and smooth yet somewhat thin, this is light in feel but with dark aromas and flavors. The tart blackberry-currant fruit wears dense, oak-derived espresso-black coffee accents. Still this vintage doesn't deliver the weight or depth I had hoped for. **85** —*M.M. (11/15/2004)*

Fairview 2000 Cyril Back Shiraz (Paarl) $20. 85 —*K.F. (4/1/2003)*

Fairview 2001 Solitude Shiraz (Paarl) $20. 87 —*K.F. (4/1/2003)*

Fairview 2002 Viognier (Paarl) $18. 83 —*K.F. (9/1/2003)*

FALSE BAY

False Bay 2000 Chenin Blanc (Coastal Region) $9. 84 —*M.S. (4/1/2002)*

False Bay 2002 Pinotage (South Africa) $NA. Flavorful, uncomplicated Pinotage showing good depth of fruit with solid berry and tart cherry flavors. Leather and metallic notes creep in towards the finish, but don't predominate. A good basic version of this South African Pinot Noir-Cinsault hybrid. **85** —*M.M. (7/4/2004)*

False Bay 2000 Rhône Red Blend (Coastal Region) $9. 85 —*M.M. (4/1/2002)*

FLAMINGO BAY

Flamingo Bay 2001 Red Blend (Coastal Region) $7. 84 —*K.F. (4/1/2003)*

FLEUR DU CAP

Fleur du Cap 1992 Cabernet Sauvignon (Coastal Region) $12. 84 *(9/1/1999)*

Fleur du Cap 1998 Cabernet Sauvignon (Stellenbosch) $10. 84 *(11/15/2002)*

Fleur du Cap 1998 Unfiltered Cabernet Sauvignon (Coastal Region) $23. 84 —*K.F. (8/1/2003)*

Fleur du Cap 2001 Chardonnay (Stellenbosch) $9. 85 *(11/15/2002)*

Fleur du Cap 2000 Unfiltered Chardonnay (Coastal Region) $15. 86 —*K.F. (9/1/2003)*

Fleur du Cap 2003 Chenin Blanc (Stellenbosch) $10. A heavily wooded, spicy wine that has little connection with Chenin Blanc. Imported by Distell USA Inc. **83** —*R.V. (11/15/2005)*

Fleur du Cap 2000 Merlot (Stellenbosch) $10. 84 *(11/15/2002)*

Fleur du Cap 2000 Unfiltered Merlot (Stellenbosch) $15. 86 *(11/15/2002)*

Fleur du Cap 1993 Pinotage (Coastal Region) $12. 83 *(9/1/1999)*

Fleur du Cap 2004 Sauvignon Blanc (Coastal Region) $11. Clean and well-defined with abundant green apple, herbgrass, and mineral notes. It's subtle, with a fine, high strung balance, becoming more impressive with time in the glass. A brisk finish closes this tasty, affordable example of the elevated confidence and performance so many Cape wineries now demonstrate with Sauvignon Blanc. **87 Best Buy** —*M.M. (4/1/2005)*

Fleur du Cap 2002 Sauvignon Blanc (Stellenbosch) $9. 86 Best Buy — *(11/15/2002)*

Fleur du Cap 2002 Unfiltered Sauvignon Blanc (Stellenbosch) $15. 87 *(11/15/2002)*

Fleur du Cap 2000 Shiraz (Coastal Region) $15. 85 —*K.F. (4/1/2003)*

FORRESTER'S

Forrester's 2002 Petit Chenin Blanc (Stellenbosch) $9. 87 Best Buy —*K.F. (4/1/2003)*

GENERAL BILIMORIA

General Bilimoria 2002 Pinotage (Stellenbosch) $11. Creamy oak mingles here with tart dry berry fruit and the usual earth-iron-iodine element. Straightahead Pinotage, and you'll like it or not, depending upon how you react to the earth-metal component. The tart berry finish has tangy tannins. **84** —*M.M. (7/4/2004)*

General Bilimoria 2003 Olifants River White Blend (Olifants River) $8. This Colombard-Chardonnay blend has a chewing gum-like quality. Might work with South Asian cuisine or as a quaff for casual circumstances. But the cheap-perfume notes are hard to get past. **82** —*M.M. (7/4/2004)*

GILGA

Gilga 2000 Shiraz (Stellenbosch) $45. 87 —*K.F. (8/1/2003)*

GLEN CARLOU

Glen Carlou 2000 Chardonnay (Paarl) $14. 86 —*R.V. (7/1/2002)*

GOATS DO ROAM

Goats do Roam 2003 Red Blend (Western Cape) $10. Red currant flavors, earth, and toast prevail in this medium weight Cape Rhône blend. Undeniably tasty, if a bit woody and slightly one- dimensional, though it improves in the glass. Decent everyday wine, if less dynamic and impressive than some other Goats do Roam offerings. **85 Best Buy** *—M.M. (4/1/2005)*

Goats do Roam 2003 Rosé Blend (South Africa) $10. Full bodied, darker in hue than many rosés, this is tasty and substantial, with full dry cherry and mineral aromas and flavors. There's more positive things going on here than in many light reds. Very good job, showing again why this Fairview brand has been the biggest South African success to date in the U.S. **87 Best Buy** *—M.M. (12/15/2004)*

Goats do Roam 2003 in Villages White Blend (Western Cape) $14. This attractive white's dry mineral-herb nose, round, full feel, and tasty pear-spice flavors add up to a winner. Yet another very credible pseudo-Rhône Capester from Charles Back and the Fairview crew. French authorities should lighten up on their (serious) case against his harmless, tongue-in-cheek name, while Rhône winemakers ought to note it as an homage and laud Back's good work with their native grapes. **87** *—M.M. (4/1/2005)*

GÔIYA

Gôiya 2004 Chardonnay-Sauvignon (Olifants River) $7. This 50-50 blend is dominated by the Sauvignon Blanc, but tamed by the Chardonnay. Smoky and flinty on the nose, with mineral and fresh herb flavors, and a citrusy finish. It's light in weight, without a lot of intensity, but what did you expect for $7? Imported by Hemingway and Hale. **84 Best Buy** *—J.C. (11/15/2005)*

Gôiya 2004 Shiraz (Western Cape) $7. Starts with some rather baked fruit aromas, but quickly settles down to deliver balanced plum and cherry fruit on a medium-bodied frame. Dry and slightly peppery on the finish. Imported by Hemingway and Hale. **85 Best Buy** *—J.C. (11/15/2005)*

GOLDEN KAAN

Golden Kaan 2004 Chardonnay (Western Cape) $10. This medium-bodied Chardonnay opens with understated scents of apples and honey, then follows with earthy, minerally flavors that fold in hints of apple, citrus, and pear. Imported by Golden Kaan USA. **84** *—J.C. (11/15/2005)*

Golden Kaan 2003 Merlot (Western Cape) $10. Herbal, with aromas reminscent of dried grass alongside modest cherry flavors. A lightweight. **82** *—J.C. (11/15/2005)*

Golden Kaan 2004 Sauvignon Blanc (Western Cape) $10. This crisp Sauvignon doesn't wow with intensity, weight, or complexity. But it is a clean, well-crafted wine at an excellent price. Snappy grapefruit flavors are buttressed by hints of honeyed peach and a refreshing finish. Imported by Golden Kaan USA. **84** *—J.C. (11/15/2005)*

Golden Kaan 2003 Shiraz (Western Cape) $10. Attractive everyday wine with a red berry-spice profile, and a nice mouthfeel—neither too soft or hard. Shows good if slightly candied fruit with leather-herb accents. Uncomplicated, enjoyable. This relatively unknown brand delivers dependable quality in this price range. **85 Best Buy** *—M.M. (12/15/2004)*

GRANGEHURST

Grangehurst 1997 Cabernet Sauvignon-Merlot (Stellenbosch) $30. **84** *—M.S. (4/1/2002)*

GREAT WHITE WINES

Great White Wines 2004 Chenin Blanc (Western Cape) $9. This dry, refreshing white might surprise many tasters, as it did this reviewer. Expecting another undistinguished (to be generous) animal-label wine, found really unexpected flavorful, lively Chenin Blanc fruit and a crisp, cleansing palate feel. 10% of proceeds go to preserve this top-of-the-food-chain predator. **86 Best Buy** *—M.M. (12/15/2004)*

GROENLAND

Groenland 2000 Cabernet Sauvignon (Stellenbosch) $13. **84** *—K.F. (9/1/2003)*

GROOT CONSTANTIA

Groot Constantia 2001 Cabernet Sauvignon (Constantia) $14. This historic property's 2001 Cabernet is lean and tart, with aromas and flavors more mineral, iodine, and even animal, than of fruit or tobacco. A little barnyardiness can add complexity, but the forward elements here will overtly challenge most palates. **81** *—M.M. (3/1/2004)*

Groot Constantia 2001 Merlot (Constantia) $17. Faint hints of underlying [and under-ripe] fruit here are swamped by a dominant earth-metal profile and hard tannins. Yes, this shows some interesting smoke and saddle-leather notes, but overall it's tough, closing with fairly bitter metallic notes. **82** *—M.M. (7/1/2005)*

Groot Constantia 2003 Sauvignon Blanc (Constantia) $16. Lean and green, showing the same tang seen in many New Zealand Sauvignon Blancs. Lime and bright green pepper notes abound and bracing acidity wakes up the taste buds. Quite tart, but decently made, and will appeal to fans of the style. **86** *—M.M. (3/1/2004)*

Groot Constantia 1997 Shiraz (Constantia) $12. **82** *—M.S. (5/1/2000)*

Groot Constantia 1999 Shiraz (Constantia) $13. **82** *(10/1/2001)*

GROOTE POST

Groote Post 2002 Darling Hills Road Chenin Blanc (Coastal Region) $13. **86** *—K.F. (4/1/2003)*

GUARDIAN

Guardian 2002 Chardonnay (Western Cape) $7. **85** *—K.F. (9/1/2003)*

GUARDIAN PEAK

Guardian Peak 2002 Frontier Red Blend (Western Cape) $13. Though lightweight and smooth with dry, even tannins, the modest tart red fruit of this blend is overpowered by unrelenting, intense funky earth, game and metallic notes, rendering it out of balance. **82** *—M.M. (4/1/2005)*

HAMILTON RUSSELL

Hamilton Russell 2003 Chardonnay (Walker Bay) $25. A taut and fine-tuned, yet large-scale, lavishly-oaked white that projects suave appeal and will wow fans of the WTNFO (well-toasted new French oak) style. Lives up to its bold Burgundian pretensions with a lean, angular stance and long, stylish finish. The persistent, intense wood leads one to ponder which shines more brightly—the fruit or the classy oak suit it wears. But tasty? Oh, yes indeed. **88** *—M.M. (4/1/2005)*

HAVANA HILLS

Havana Hills 2000 Merlot (Western Cape) $33. Salad greens, like chicory and endive, carry through this wine from start to finish in a strangely pleasant fashion. The fresh red plum, toast, earth, and dusty cocoa fill out the palate. **85** *—K.F. (1/1/2004)*

Havana Hills 2000 Sauvignon Blanc (Western Cape) $15. **84** *—K.F. (9/1/2003)*

Havana Hills 1999 Shiraz (Western Cape) $33. **86** *—K.F. (8/1/2003)*

HELDERBERG

Helderberg 2000 Chardonnay (Stellenbosch) $8. **81** *—R.V. (1/1/2003)*

Helderberg 1999 Shiraz (Stellenbosch) $9. **86 Best Buy** *(1/1/2003)*

HOOPENBURG

Hoopenburg 1998 Winemaker's Selection Cabernet Sauvignon (Stellenbosch) $18. **86** *—K.F. (4/1/2003)*

INDABA

Indaba 2002 Chardonnay (Western Cape) $9. **84** *—K.F. (9/1/2003)*

Indaba 2002 Sauvignon Blanc (Western Cape) $8. **83** *—K.F. (9/1/2003)*

JACOBSDAL

Jacobsdal 1996 Pinotage (Stellenbosch) $15. **83** *(3/1/2001)*

JARDIN

Jardin 1999 Fumé Blanc (Stellenbosch) $13. **88** *—M.M. (3/1/2001)*

Jardin 2002 Sauvignon Blanc (Stellenbosch) $12. **85** *—K.F. (9/1/2003)*

JEAN TAILLEFERT

Jean Taillefert 2001 Shiraz (Paarl) $66. Well-built, with deep tart-sweet fruit and hefty American oak. Perhaps Aussie-inspired, but the subtle hints of typical Cape earthiness are a plus here, adding unique character. Closes long and very smooth with polished cocoa, smoke, and dark cherry-plum notes. **90** *—M.M. (11/15/2004)*

KANONKOP

Kanonkop 2000 Cabernet Sauvignon (Stellenbosch) $30. This claret-like Cabernet with Cape accents shows tea, plum, berry, and tobacco on the nose, which opens to a solid fruit core accented by spice, dark chocolate, and earth-mineral tones. Crisp acidity recommends it as a food wine, while the ripe fruit and good tannic structure suggest it will improve with age. Best after 2005. **89** *—M.M. (3/1/2004)*

Kanonkop 2000 Pinotage (Stellenbosch) $27. Jerked meat aromas herald toasty red plum that follows through to the palate. This has a lean, herbal finish, but the fine tannins and firm acids make it rather agreeable. **86** *—K.F. (1/1/2004)*

Kanonkop 2000 Paul Sauer Red Blend (Stellenbosch) $35. A brooding and serious wine, showing very good depth and intense dark cherry and cassis fruit on a nicely structured frame. There's tobacco and cocoa hints throughout, as well as oak. Finishes long, with firm tannins. Best cellared three or four years, and could easily hold for 10–15. **90 Cellar Selection** *—M.M. (3/1/2004)*

KANU

Kanu 2004 Limited Release Wooded Chenin Blanc (Stellenbosch) $18. This is Kanu's signature wine, with its soft toast and wooded character layering with perfumed, crisp gooseberry, and tropical fruit flavors. New winemaker Richard Kershaw dropped the 2003 vintage while he settled in, but now the wine is back, and very much on form. **91** *—R.V. (11/15/2005)*

KEN FORRESTER

Ken Forrester 2003 Forrester Meinert Chenin Blanc (Stellenbosch) $65. A rich, nutty style of wine, which has 12 months of barrel aging. Added complexity comes from the addition of some noble late harvest (botrytis) fruit to the blend. Apple and cream flavors make the wine very attractive. **88** *—R.V. (11/15/2005)*

Ken Forrester 2004 Petit Chenin Blanc (Stellenbosch) $9. "Petit" in the case of this wine refers to the fact that this is the good-value Chenin from Forrester Vineyards. With its flowery aroma, ripeness, mature fruit, layers of nuts, and just a hint of a soft aftertaste, this is a great value wine. **90 Best Buy** *—R.V. (11/15/2005)*

Ken Forrester 2000 Helderberg Grenache-Syrah (Stellenbosch) $20. **86** *—K.F. (4/1/2003)*

Ken Forrester 2002 Sauvignon Blanc (Stellenbosch) $14. **86** *—K.F. (4/1/2003)*

KLEINE ZALZE

Kleine Zalze 2004 Bush Vines Chenin Blanc (Stellenbosch) $NA. A fascinating wine from this new Stellenbosch estate. It has ripeness, almost sweetness, certainly weight, which comes through as a creamy character, and just a touch of botrytis to give a honey edge to the wine. **89** *—R.V. (11/15/2005)*

KUMALA

Kumala 2004 Chardonnay (Western Cape) $9. South Africa has emerged as a top source for bargain-priced wines, but remains a bit of a minefield, as many of the less expensive wines continue to exhibit various winemaking faults. Not so this wine, part of the Vincor portfolio. This plump, easy-to-drink Chardonnay boasts oodles of tropical and citrus fruit flavors that finish clean and fresh. It's in the uncomplicated fruit-cocktail style popularized by mass market Australian brands, but remarkably well done. **85 Best Buy** *—J.C. (11/15/2005)*

Kumala 2004 Shiraz (Western Cape) $9. Earthy and dry, with flavors reminiscent black cherries covered in fine, wind-borne dust. **83** *—J.C. (11/15/2005)*

KUMKANI

Kumkani 2004 Sauvignon Blanc (Stellenbosch) $12. Clean and taut, with a citrus-floral-herb nose opening to a very dry, minerally mouthfeel. It's bright, bracing, and palate-cleansing, though some might find it sharp-edged. Will shine with shellfish or a salad. **86** *—M.M. (7/1/2005)*

Kumkani 2002 Shiraz (Stellenbosch) $15. This medium-weight, supple wine stood apart from the other South African Shirazes in its flight for its dark, meaty aromas and flavors. Roast beef-like flavors add coffee and plum notes, then finish crisp. **85** *—J.C. (11/15/2005)*

Kumkani 2002 Shiraz-Cabernet (Stellenbosch) $13. An outgoing wine well-poised to make friends for South African wine in general. It's tasty, even, and stylish, if not that deep. Yes, it could lack much Cape "typicity," if you accept that sort of stuff—and I do. But at at this price, just enjoy the tasty dark fruit, smoke-earth accents, and supple feel. **87 Best Buy** *—M.M. (7/1/2005)*

KWV

KWV 2002 Cabernet Sauvignon (Western Cape) $10. Medium berry flavors, a slight juiciness, and easy palate feel make this a very likeable wine. Oak is used gently on this pleasant, entry-level South African. Though not complex, the wine has good balance and a dry finish with even tannins. **85** *—M.M. (3/1/2004)*

KWV 2000 Cabernet Sauvignon (Western Cape) $10. 90 Best Buy *—K.F. (4/1/2003)*

KWV 2003 Chardonnay (Western Cape) $10. A simple, easy-drinker, offering mild citrus and tropical fruit on a light frame. The soft palate shows a melony quality, in both flavor and texture. On the sweet side, this should have mainstream appeal. **83** *—M.M. (3/1/2004)*

KWV 2004 Steen Chenin Blanc (Western Cape) $8. Ripe fruit and bubblegum hints open this clean, angular white. Quickly turns much less sweet than expected, its ample melon and tropical fruit supported by brisk acidity. A refreshing value Chenin Blanc (Steen in South Africa) that closes very clean, surprisingly long. **85 Best Buy** *—M.M. (4/1/2005)*

KWV 2002 Steen Chenin Blanc (Western Cape) $8. 85 *—K.F. (4/1/2003)*

KWV 2001 Merlot (Western Cape) $10. 88 Best Buy *—K.F. (4/1/2003)*

KWV 2001 Pinotage (Western Cape) $10. 85 *—K.F. (9/1/2003)*

KWV 1999 Pinotage (Western Cape) $9. 86 *(9/1/2001)*

KWV NV Full Tawny Port (Western Cape) $9. 87 *—K.F. (12/1/2003)*

KWV 2002 Shiraz (Western Cape) $10. Simple dark juice, though not sappy and sweet like so much value Shiraz. Undefined dark fruit is accented by toast and leather notes in this tangy, lean lightweight. **84** *—M.M. (4/1/2005)*

KWV 1999 Shiraz (Western Cape) $9. 84 *(10/1/2001)*

L'AVENIR

L'Avenir 2005 Chenin Blanc (Stellenbosch) $NA. This estate is widely reputed for its Chenin Blanc. And no wonder, with this very dry, ripe character wine spiced with cinnamon and citrus. This is a full, creamy style, which matures well, and will certainly be even more impressive in 8–9 years. **91** *—R.V. (11/15/2005)*

LABORIE

Laborie 2001 Estate Cabernet Sauvignon (Paarl) $12. Focused, lush aromas and flavors of ripe black plum, apple peel, star anise, and woodsmoke are well-balanced and unwavering. Finishes with a cozy hint of fresh bread. Satisfies the senses and the budget. **89 Best Buy** *—K.F. (1/1/2004)*

Laborie 1995 Cap Classique Brut Champagne Blend (Paarl) $18. 85 *—J.M. (12/1/2002)*

Laborie 2001 Chardonnay (Paarl) $11. 84 *—R.V. (7/1/2002)*

Laborie 2001 Estate Wine Merlot-Cabernet Sauvignon (Paarl) $12. 85 *—K.F. (9/1/2003)*

Laborie 2003 Sauvignon Blanc (Paarl) $11. The opening bouquet has an almost quinine-like perfume. On the tongue it's a bit thin, with green pepper and citrus notes that fail to mesh in a complimentary manner. A Cape Sauvignon Blanc that aims high, for a point somewhere between Sancerre and Marlborough, but veers off course. **84** *—M.M. (3/1/2004)*

Laborie 1999 Blanc de Noir Sparkling Blend (Paarl) $13. 87 **Best Buy** *—K.F. (12/1/2003)*

LAMMERSHOEK

Lammershoek 2001 Red Blend (Coastal Region) $13. This 60% Shiraz/40% Carignan blend shows a decidedly Rhônish profile with a (challenging?) mix of sweet lavender and vanilla with some very gamy notes accenting the dry red fruits. Medium weight, with decent acidity, this is no juiceball or fruitbomb, but shows a reserved slight tartness throughout, with even a traditional bitter herb touch at the close. **84** *—M.M. (3/1/2004)*

LANDSKROON

Landskroon 2001 Cabernet Sauvignon (Paarl) $15. Light but quite tasty with red berry, black plum, herb, and licorice aromas and flavors. An even mouthfeel and mild, smooth tannins complete the profile in this very drinkable, claret-like wine. **85** *—M.M. (11/15/2004)*

Landskroon 2000 Merlot (Paarl) $16. 86 *—K.F. (4/1/2003)*

Landskroon 1999 Pinotage (Paarl) $15. 83 *—K.F. (4/1/2003)*

Landskroon 2002 Shiraz (Paarl) $16. Even and medium weight, with sweet berry-plum fruit, plus nice oak. The wine is not terrifically complex, but is handsomely balanced. All components are in harmony—including a modest dose of South African earthiness, closing with smooth, dry tannins. **86** *—M.M. (11/15/2004)*

LANZERAC

Lanzerac 1998 Cabernet Sauvignon (Stellenbosch) $27. The slight brown edge reads age, which this has. Plus handsome dried raspberry, cedar, leather, and cigar box aromas and flavors. Elegantly constructed, this shows many admirable qualities of mature Bordeaux, but also a large dose of greenness. **86** *—M.M. (11/15/2004)*

Lanzerac 1999 Chardonnay (Stellenbosch) $22. 85 *—K.F. (4/1/2003)*

Lanzerac 2004 Sauvignon Blanc (Stellenbosch) $21. A goodly amount of stoniness and mineral offset any candied fruit element, and the whole is largely on the money. Flavors of ripe melon, grapefruit, and other citrus fruits are sweet but pleasant, while the finish is concentrated and forward, with ample pith and zesty dryness. **87** *(7/1/2005)*

LE BONHEUR

Le Bonheur 1997 Cabernet Sauvignon (Stellenbosch) $18. Intense aromatics of field greens and rhubarb seem indicative of unripe fruit. That impression is echoed by the palate, where there's cherry cola and root-like qualities. As a package, it's unbalanced, with a berry-syrup quality dominating the core. **82** *—M.S. (1/1/2004)*

Le Bonheur 2003 Chardonnay (Simonsberg Stellenbosch) $13. Pale gold, with pear-tangerine fruit and a sweet, almost juicy-fruit-gum note that persists all the way through. This round, easy-drinking mid-weight Chardonnay's candied edge is more like a value white than what an estate wine could deliver. **84** *—M.M. (4/1/2005)*

Le Bonheur 2001 Landgoed Chardonnay (Stellenbosch) $12. The aromas of lemon-infused honey and creamy toffee are tied in with a waft of alcohol. The palate is almost unflavored, with thin lemon and toast that trail off on the finish. This lacks depth of flavor, weight, and acidity, but the aromas are nice. **83** *—K.F. (9/1/2004)*

Le Bonheur 1999 Prima Merlot-Cabernet Sauvignon (Stellenbosch) $15. Though a Merlot-Cabernet blend, this wine's pronounced tart cherry and spice elements call to mind a Chianti. Then again, it's named Prima, so maybe the Italian profile was intended. It's flavorful and fairly light-bodied, with licorice and earth accents. Finishes with even tannins and a mineral note. **87** *—M.M. (3/1/2004)*

Le Bonheur 2003 Sauvignon Blanc (Stellenbosch) $11. Light and even with mild citrus herb and grass elements throughout. A slightly too-green note showed early on the nose, but was not on the palate. A good, straightforward example that's lean but not sharp, and finishes clean. **84** *—M.M. (11/15/2004)*

Le Bonheur 2004 Landgoed Sauvignon Blanc (Simonsberg Stellenbosch) $13. Tasty juice with ample tangy citrus-herb tones over ripe melon and tropical fruit aromas and flavors. Has pizzazz, but no sharp edges, and finishes long with nice spicy notes. Easy to like and easy to drink, with good balance and some complexity. **87** *—M.M. (4/1/2005)*

LE RICHE

Le Riche 1999 Reserve Cabernet Sauvignon (Stellenbosch) $30. 86 *—M.M. (3/1/2001)*

LEIDERSBURG

Leidersburg 2003 Vintner's Reserve Sur Lie Sauvignon Blanc (Coastal Region) $19. This even, elegant white is medium-weight and balanced, with a gentle citrus-hay bouquet. Shows poise, if less depth than the sur lie designation might suggest. A tasty and attractively tangy wine, with lemon-lime flavors and a dry, minerally close. **85** *—M.M. (7/1/2005)*

LONG NECK

Long Neck 2003 Chardonnay (Western Cape) $8. Vaguely sweet and perfumy on the nose, but also shows nice mild tropical fruit and avoids cloying sweetness on the tongue. A modest but enjoyable simple Chardonnay, with a smooth feel and clean finish. An off-the-beaten- track choice for an inexpensive by-the-glass pour. **84 Best Buy** *—M.M. (12/15/2004)*

Long Neck 2003 Shiraz (Western Cape) $8. Nose mostly mute; light in feel, it lacks fruit presence and flavor. Very mild red berry, cocoa, and toasty oak shadings show, mostly on the finish. Yes, it's a simple value wine, but where's the fruit? **82** *—M.M. (12/15/2004)*

LONGRIDGE

Longridge 1999 Bay View Merlot (Stellenbosch) $10. 87 Best Buy *(3/1/2001)*

Longridge 1999 Bayview Pinotage (South Africa) $10. 86 *(3/1/2001)*

Longridge 1999 Chardonnay (Stellenbosch) $19. 87 *—M.M. (3/1/2001)*

LOST HORIZONS

Lost Horizons 2001 Cabernet Sauvignon-Merlot (Western Cape) $8. 85 *—K.F. (4/1/2003)*

MALAN

Malan 2000 Family Vinter's Chardonnay (Stellenbosch) $8. 86 Best Buy *—R.V. (7/1/2002)*

Malan 2001 Family Vinters Sauvignon Blanc (Stellenbosch) $8. 89 Best Buy *—M.M. (4/1/2002)*

MAS NICOLAS

Mas Nicolas 2000 Cape Shiraz-Cabernet (Stellenbosch) $34. 86 *—K.F. (8/1/2003)*

MEERLUST

Meerlust 1997 Rubicon Red Blend (Stellenbosch) $28. 87 *—K.F. (9/1/2003)*

MEINERT

Meinert 2000 Merlot (Devon Valley) $20. 84 *—K.F. (8/1/2003)*

MIDDELVLEI

Middelvlei 1995 Cabernet Sauvignon (Stellenbosch) $17. 87 *—M.N. (3/1/2001)*

Middelvlei 1998 Red Blend (Stellenbosch) $16. 86 *(3/1/2001)*

MISSIONVALE

Missionvale 2000 Walker Bay Chardonnay (South Africa) $NA. 91 *—R.V. (9/10/2002)*

MONTESTELL

Montestell 2000 Reserve Cabernet Sauvignon (Paarl) $20. 88 *—K.F. (4/1/2003)*

Montestell 2000 Reserve Pinotage (Paarl) $16. 84 *—K.F. (4/1/2003)*

MOOIUITZICHT

Mooiuitzicht NV Old Tawny Port (Western Cape) $16. Light tawny in color, with dried fruits and caramel on the nose and palate. Not heavy in feel, but a touch hot with some tangy tannins. 85 *—M.M. (11/15/2004)*

MÔRESON

Môreson 1997 Cabernet Sauvignon (Franschhoek) $25. 88 *—K.F. (4/1/2003)*

Môreson 2001 Chenin Blanc (Franschhoek) $13. 86 *—K.F. (4/1/2003)*

Môreson 1999 Magia Red Blend (Coastal Region) $25. 87 *—K.F. (9/1/2003)*

MORGENHOF

Morgenhof 1997 Premiere Selection Cabernet Blend (Stellenbosch) $20. 90 Editors' Choice *—M.M. (4/1/2002)*

Morgenhof 1998 Merlot (Stellenbosch) $16. 88 *—M.M. (4/1/2002)*

MOUNTAIN GATE

Mountain Gate 2000 Cabernet Sauvignon (Stellenbosch) $15. Accessible, medium-weight, and in the international style. The typical South African earth and iodine notes are nicely tamed here. They compliment rather than obscure the dry, dark berry fruit, offering just enough character to keep this from being generic. Finishes with cocoa hints. 86 *—M.M. (3/1/2004)*

MULDERBOSCH

Mulderbosch 1999 Barrel Fermented Chardonnay (Stellenbosch) $23. 91 *—R.V. (7/1/2002)*

NATURAL STATE

Natural State 1999 Cape Soleil Shiraz (Coastal Region) $12. 82 *(10/1/2001)*

NEDERBURG

Nederburg 2001 Cabernet Sauvignon (Western Cape) $11. A light Cabernet Sauvignon, with tart cherry and cranberry aromas and flavors. Not unlike the estate's Private Bin wine, but with less weight, texture, and length . . . and price. Closes with wood-mineral accents over dry fruit. 82 *—M.M. (3/1/2004)*

Nederburg 2002 Edelrood Cabernet Sauvignon-Merlot (Western Cape) $11. This simple Bordeaux blend opens with an attractive red berry-rhubarb and toast nose, but not much follows. It's lightweight and not amply fruited, closing tart with quite drying tannins. 83 *—M.M. (4/1/2005)*

Nederburg 2003 Paarl Riesling (Western Cape) $10. Light and taut, with bright acidity underlying grass and mineral aromas and flavors, plus kerosene hints. The light lemon and grape flavors are appealing. An attractive, inexpensive white for sipping or light dining. **85 Best Buy** *—M.M. (7/1/2005)*

Nederburg 2003 Private Bin Sauvignon Blanc (South Africa) $15. Shows an angular profile, with amped-up grassy-gooseberry-cat pee elements, though warmer spice notes appear on the close. Different and more intense, but not necessarily better than the winery's regular bottling—it's more a matter of style. **87** *—M.M. (3/1/2004)*

Nederburg 2001 Private Bin Shiraz (South Africa) $18. Why does the perception that more oak makes a better wine persist? This basic, solid wine, like too many others, suffers from an excess of oak. The sound black plum fruit, with its nice earthy accents, struggles to assert itself. When it peeks through, it's lovely. Black pepper notes show on the even finish. **85** *—M.M. (3/1/2004)*

Nederburg 2003 Special Late Harvest White Blend (Western Cape) $10. A tasty, vaguely spritzy and ethereal dessert wine that opens with faint white peach and apricot-lemon aromas. Lacks body, but has tasty sweet apricot, baked apple, and honey flavors. It's not very complex but also avoids being cloying. Finishes with a drier mineral undertone. **85 Best Buy** *—M.M. (4/1/2005)*

NEIL ELLIS

Neil Ellis 2002 Cabernet Sauvignon-Merlot (Stellenbosch) $15. A 61% Cabernet Sauvignon and 39% Merlot black beauty with some intriguing tart berry, Indian spices, popcorn, and licorice whiffs on the nose. It's quite dark, adding espresso and smoke notes on the palate and a very dry, briskly tannic finish. **86** *—M.M. (11/15/2004)*

Neil Ellis 2000 Elgin Chardonnay (South Africa) $20. **91** *—R.V. (7/1/2002)*

Neil Ellis 2003 Sauvignon Blanc (Groenekloof) $14. Starts with soft ripe melon, pear, and tropical fruit notes. Turns crisper and more typically Sauvignon Blanc on the tongue, where satisfying grapefruit flavors show classic herb and pepper accents and a fairly full yet crisp feel. **88** *—M.M. (11/15/2004)*

Neil Ellis 2000 Sauvignon Blanc (Groenekloof) $15. **90** *—M.M. (3/1/2001)*

NEW WORLD

New World 2002 Sémillon-Chardonnay (Western Cape) $9. **85** *—K.F. (4/1/2003)*

NIEL JOUBERT

Niel Joubert 2001 African Tradition Collection Leopard Cabernet Sauvignon (Paarl) $12. **86** *—K.F. (8/1/2003)*

Niel Joubert 2000 African Tradition Collection Lion Merlot (Paarl) $12. **87** *—K.F. (8/1/2003)*

Niel Joubert 2000 African Tradition Collection Elephant Shiraz (Paarl) $12. **86** *—K.F. (8/1/2003)*

NITÍDA

Nitída 2003 Sauvignon Blanc (Durbanville) $15. Clean and fresh, with lime-herb aromas and flavors. Taut mineral and sour grass elements here are on a par with solid Loire or New Zealand Sauvignon Blanc. A firm acid backbone sits over lurking ripe tropical fruit notes. This begs for grilled seafood or pork in a lime marinade. **88** *—M.M. (12/15/2004)*

OMNIA

Omnia 2005 Arniston Bay Bush Vines Chenin Blanc (Coastal Region) $NA. One of South Africa's successful brands, especially in the British market, this wine goes for the gooseberry spectrum of Chenin Blanc, emphasizing green flavors along with its sweetness. It is well-made, but does lack some character. **84** *—R.V. (11/15/2005)*

ORACLE

Oracle 2002 Cabernet Sauvignon (Western Cape) $8. Curious, with some dark sweet fruit and spice accents, but also a less enjoyable, sharp tart note that really takes over. Shows decent mouthfeel and even tannins, but the bitter element predominates, leaving a strong sour aftertaste. **81** *—M.M. (11/15/2004)*

Oracle 2003 Sauvignon Blanc (Western Cape) $8. Impressive, with good tang and surprising persistence. Tends towards the crisper Sauvignon Blanc style in aromas and flavors, but a fairly round, smooth mouthfeel provides a nice counterpoint, and subtle figgy notes keep the sharper elements in check. Focused and tasty. **88** *—M.M. (7/4/2004)*

OUT OF AFRICA

Out of Africa 2002 Cabernet Sauvignon (Western Cape) $9. Light, with typical berry and herb elements, but with an overwhelming greenish, seemingly under-ripe edge. Smooth and even-textured, but lacking concentration or depth of fruit to overcome the green. **82** *—M.M. (11/15/2004)*

Out of Africa 2002 Pinotage (Western Cape) $9. Tasty wine similar to a basic Bordeaux. The very dry tart berry fruit wears a dose of earthiness, but it comes off less overtly South African as the iron-iodine element is suppressed here. As such, it's less typical of its origins. Putting whether that's a plus or minus aside, it should afford the wine wider mainstream appeal. **85** *—M.M. (7/4/2004)*

Out of Africa 2003 Shiraz (Western Cape) $9. Solid and inky, with an earthy, slightly metallic South African typicity on the dark berry-licorice Shiraz fruit. Has good flavors and medium-weight feel. Closes with some dry tannins, making it a good companion to grilled meat. **86** *—M.M. (7/4/2004)*

PEARLY BAY

Pearly Bay NV Celebration Champagne Blend (South Africa) $7. **84** *—J.M. (12/1/2002)*

PINE CREST

Pine Crest 2000 Chardonnay (Franschhoek) $13. **88** *—K.F. (4/1/2003)*

PLAISIR DE MERLE

Plaisir De Merle 1998 Merlot (Paarl) $22. **86** *—K.F. (8/1/2003)*

PORCUPINE RIDGE

Porcupine Ridge 2003 Merlot (Coastal Region) $11. An opening display of solid berry and plum fruit is overtaken by wood. The wine turns astringent rather quickly, with drying tannins and difficult earth and vitamin-tablet notes predominating. **83** *—M.M. (11/15/2004)*

Porcupine Ridge 2003 Sauvignon Blanc (Western Cape) $9. With a light, even feel, this is rather unique for its mix of typical high-strung citrus with dense floral notes. Tangy and round at once, with good fruit, this finishes bright, tasty and refreshing, with a lot of appeal. **86 Best Buy** *—M.M. (11/15/2004)*

Porcupine Ridge 2003 Syrah (Coastal Region) $11. A tart cranberry-rhubarb and stewed tomato bouquet opens this lean wine. As it opens, a predominant green quality ascends on the palate and takes over. This simply seems under-ripe. **82** *—M.M. (11/15/2004)*

POSITIVELY ZINFUL

Positively Zinful 2001 Zinfandel (Coastal Region) $10. **87** *—K.F. (11/15/2003)*

PROSPECT 1870

Prospect 1870 1998 Cabernet Sauvignon (Robertson) $30. **85** *—K.F. (8/1/2003)*

RAATS FAMILY

Raats Family 2004 Original Chenin Blanc (Stellenbosch) $13. Bruwer Raats is a Loire wine lover, and he expresses this love in two distinct styles of Chenin Blanc. The unwooded Original is packed with apples, almonds, and nuts, as well as flinty mineral character. It is almost bone dry, and is crisp and fresh. **89 Best Buy** *—R.V. (11/15/2005)*

RAWSON'S

Rawson's 2001 Pinotage (Breede River Valley) $10. **85** *—K.F. (9/1/2003)*

Rawson's 2001 Revelry White Blend (Worcester) $8. **86** *—K.F. (4/1/2003)*

RIETVALLEI ESTATE WINE

Rietvallei Estate Wine 2002 Cabernet Sauvignon (Robertson) $13. A light-weight red with good fruit-acid balance and some even, dusty tannins. Displays a rather neo-Tuscan profile—the fruit is sour cherry, with dry leather tones. Not typical Cabernet, but with individual character. **86** *—M.M. (11/15/2004)*

Rietvallei Estate Wine 2003 Gewürztraminer (Robertson) $10. Mild spice and some faint tangy fruit on the nose introduce this as Gewürztraminer, but straightaway a cloying sweetness takes over. It's just too soft and sweet, a cross between tropical fruit juice and drugstore perfume. Needs both more spine and concentration. **82** *—M.M. (12/15/2004)*

Rietvallei Estate Wine 2002 Shiraz (Robertson) $15. Some handsome, dense fruit shows through this wine's overall rather inky, toasty facade. Oaky? Yes, but a black beauty with a still healthy, positive Shiraz fruit presence, right through the long, even finish. **87** *—M.M. (11/15/2004)*

RIJK'S PRIVATE CELLAR

Rijk's Private Cellar 2004 Chenin Blanc (Tulbagh) $NA. This barrel-fermented wine shows great wood flavors, but very little fruit. Caramel and vanilla elements dominate, along with spice and pepper. The aftertaste is creamy and soft. Imported by wine@34south. **85** *—R.V. (11/15/2005)*

ROBERT'S ROCK

Robert's Rock 2004 Cabernet Sauvignon-Merlot (Western Cape) $8. This self-proclaimed "lifestyle brand" from giant South African wine company KWV boasts the usual trappings: brightly colored label, flanged top. What's unusual is that the wine in the bottle is pretty good. Cherry, leather, and chocolate notes provide a modicum of complexity, while the finish is soft and clean. A solid choice to accompany burgers on the patio. Imported by 57 Main Street Wine Co. **84 Best Buy** *—J.C. (11/15/2005)*

Robert's Rock 2002 Cabernet Sauvignon-Merlot (Western Cape) $8. **84** *—K.F. (8/1/2003)*

Robert's Rock 2003 Chenin Blanc-Chardonnay (Western Cape) $8. Pleasingly plump, this soft white grape blend shows pear and melon aromas and flavors. Definitely low-acid, but this vaguely Viognier-like wine finishes drier and longer than expected. **85 Best Buy** *—M.M. (3/1/2004)*

Robert's Rock 2003 Shiraz-Malbec (Western Cape) $9. Simple, yet with plenty of straightforward appeal, this attractive wine is a credible light red (read Beaujolais-style) alternative. Ample strawberry-raspberry aromas and flavors prevail, while a smooth feel and clean finish complete this modest yet attractive offering. **85 Best Buy** *—M.M. (4/1/2005)*

Robert's Rock 2000 White Blend (Western Cape) $6. **84** *(9/1/2001)*

ROBERTSON WINERY

Robertson Winery 2002 Cabernet Sauvignon (Robertson) $10. 87 *—K.F. (8/1/2003)*

Robertson Winery 2003 Chardonnay (Robertson) $10. On the sweet side, with a floral nose followed by apple and tropical fruit flavors. Too candied for my taste, but will have its fans. **82** *—M.M. (7/4/2004)*

Robertson Winery 2003 Kings River Chardonnay (Robertson) $19. Solid Chardonnay with tasty citrus-apple-pear fruit that's nicely wrapped in oak. Subdued toffee-butterscotch notes add appeal. Shows a nice chewiness, with an almost grain-like, oaty flavor and feel on the finish. **87** *—M.M. (7/4/2004)*

Robertson Winery 2004 Chenin Blanc (Robertson) $10. Ripe, fruity, slightly sweet Chenin Blanc—think Vouvray—with a bright feel. Ample chalk-mineral notes on the fruit keep it refreshing. Solid as an apéritif or with light foods. **84** *—M.M. (12/15/2004)*

Robertson Winery 2004 Special Late Harvest Gewürztraminer (Robertson) $10. Quite similar to the tasty 2003, if a little less concentrated. Light on the tongue with an attractive lychee-citrus-pineapple profile. Closes drier than expected. Again, an interesting, affordable surprise and a perfectly sufficient dessert wine for many situations. **85 Best Buy** *—M.M. (12/15/2004)*

Robertson Winery 2003 Merlot (Robertson) $10. Bricking already at this young age, with herbal notes and dried-out fruit. Light and inoffensive, but surprisingly past its prime. **80** *—J.C. (11/15/2005)*

Robertson Winery 2001 Merlot (Robertson) $10. 84 *—K.F. (8/1/2003)*

Robertson Winery 2002 Pinotage (Robertson) $10. 84 *—K.F. (9/1/2003)*

Robertson Winery 2004 Sauvignon Blanc (Robertson) $10. A soft wine with faint, sweet perfume notes on the nose. Tastes more like a Chardonnay or white blend. Simple, and could have some mainstream appeal with its slightly overripe hints and short, clean finish. **83** *—M.M. (12/15/2004)*

Robertson Winery 2002 Sauvignon Blanc (Robertson) $9. 84 *—K.F. (9/1/2003)*

Robertson Winery 2003 Shiraz (Robertson) $10. Shows plenty of character, but it's not always entirely pleasant, combining leather, horse sweat, and Band-Aid aromas with a smooth, medium-weight mouthfeel. Imported by Indigo Wine Group. **82** *—J.C. (11/15/2005)*

Robertson Winery 2003 Wolfkloof Shiraz (Robertson) $20. Presents tasty dark berry fruit accented by mocha and dense oak. The hints of earthiness are modest and controlled, adding positively to the sensory mix. Closes with full coffee-chocolate notes and some spicy, tangy tannins. Good wine, if a bit on the oaky side. **86** *—M.M. (12/15/2004)*

RODEBERG

Roodeberg 2002 Red Blend (Western Cape) $13. A sprightly red blend—light, tangy, and flavorful. Sour cherry fruit abounds, accented by leather, toast, cocoa, and earth. Quite dry and slightly tart on the close. **87** *—M.M. (3/1/2004)*

Roodeberg 1998 Red Blend (Western Cape) $11. 88 *(9/1/2001)*

RUDERA

Rudera 2004 Chenin Blanc (Stellenbosch) $20. This could be an impressive wine, but the overwhelming wood element makes it hard to taste the fruit. There are just hints of ripe spice and creamy apples, and the aftertaste is just off dry. **89** *—R.V. (11/15/2005)*

RUPERT & ROTHSCHILD

Rupert & Rothschild 1999 Baron Edmund Bordeaux Blend (Coastal Region) $45. This Cabernet-based blend opens with deep cassis and herb aromas. A svelte, evenly textured palate follows, with dark berry and plum flavors sporting tobacco accents. Finely balanced, it finishes long, with full, even tannins. **88** *—M.M. (12/15/2004)*

Rupert & Rothschild 2000 Classique Bordeaux Blend (Coastal Region) $20. Cassis, leather, spice, and faint creamy notes open this nicely balanced claret-like red. The dry cherry, licorice, and earth palate, very even tannins, and lingering finish offer plenty of appeal, and it's built to be consumed within the next few years. **88** *—M.M. (3/1/2004)*

Rupert & Rothschild 2001 Baron Edmond Cabernet Sauvignon-Merlot (Coastal Region) $45. 88 *—J.C. (7/1/2005)*

Rupert & Rothschild 1999 Baroness Nadine Chardonnay (Coastal Region) $26. 89 *(2/1/2002)*

RUST EN VREDE

Rust en Vrede 1998 Estate Wine Bordeaux Blend (Stellenbosch) $33. Earthy, meaty, and full of smashed berries. Red currant and plum flavors dominate, with a touch of green pepper in there as well. It's a brawny wine that's more rustic than refined. The balance and acid structure, however, is right on. The blend is Cabernet Sauvignon, Shiraz, and Merlot, in descending order. —M.S. **87** *—M.S. (1/1/2004)*

Rust en Vrede 1999 Estate Wine Cabernet Sauvignon (Stellenbosch) $20. 83 *—K.F. (4/1/2003)*

Rust en Vrede 1998 Shiraz (Stellenbosch) $22. 87 *(11/1/2001)*

RUSTENBERG

Rustenberg 1999 Five Soldiers Chardonnay (Stellenbosch) $33. 91 *—R.V. (7/1/2002)*

SAXENBURG ESTATE

Saxenburg Estate 1998 Merlot (Coastal Region) $15. 82 *—M.M. (3/1/2001)*

Saxenburg Estate 1999 Private Collection Sauvignon Blanc (Stellenbosch) $14. 85 *—M.N. (3/1/2001)*

SCALI

Scali 1999 Pinotage (Paarl) $25. 86 *—K.F. (4/1/2003)*

SEIDELBERG

Seidelberg 2001 Chardonnay (Paarl) $15. 87 *—K.F. (4/1/2003)*

Seidelberg 2001 Roland's Reserve Estate Wine Pinotage (Paarl) $32. 89 *—K.F. (4/1/2003)*

Seidelberg 2001 Roland's Reserve Estate Wine Syrah (Paarl) $32. 88 *—K.F. (4/1/2003)*

SERENGETI

Serengeti 2003 Shiraz (Coastal Region) $13. A trifle soft, but otherwise very drinkable, this medium-bodied Shiraz boasts ample red raspberry and vanilla flavors sure to please most drinkers. Shows more elegance and better integration of components than many of its brethren, ending on a supple, harmonious note. Imported by Hemingway and Hale. 87 *—J.C. (11/15/2005)*

SIGNAL HILL

Signal Hill 2000 Gamay Noir (Stellenbosch) $10. 87 *—K.F. (9/1/2003)*

SIMONSIG

Simonsig 1996 Tiara Bordeaux Blend (Stellenbosch) $25. 86 *—M.S. (5/1/2000)*

Simonsig 1998 Cabernet Sauvignon (Stellenbosch) $15. 93 Editors' Choice *—M.N. (3/1/2001)*

Simonsig 1998 Chenin Blanc (Stellenbosch) $8. 87 *—M.S. (11/15/1999)*

Simonsig 2004 Chenin Blanc (Stellenbosch) $10. Attractive in an overripe way with a core of tangerine and papaya fruit and lime-herb accents. It's rich, with botrytis-like notes, yet shows a faint petillance. Turns drier on the finish, where lemony notes ascend. This is a fine match for spicy foods. **86 Best Buy** *—M.M. (7/1/2005)*

Simonsig 2001 Estate Wine Chenin Blanc (Stellenbosch) $7. 85 *—M.S. (4/1/2002)*

Simonsig 2001 Estate Wine Sauvignon Blanc (Stellenbosch) $11. 84 *—M.S. (4/1/2002)*

Simonsig 1998 Merindol Shiraz (Stellenbosch) $45. 86 *(11/1/2001)*

SIMONSVLEI

Simonsvlei 2005 Premier Chenin Blanc (Western Cape) $NA. From fruit mainly grown on the eastern slopes of the Pederberg mountain in Swartland, this is a toasty-edged wine, with fat spicy fruit and light acidity. Because of its dry style, this is a wine which should age, for a couple of years at least. 86 *—R.V. (11/15/2005)*

SINNYA

Sinnya 1998 Chardonnay (Robertson) $11. 82 *(9/1/1999)*

Sinnya 2001 Merlot-Cabernet Sauvignon (Robertson) $10. 84 *—K.F. (8/1/2003)*

SIYABONGA

Siyabonga 2001 Cabernet Sauvignon-Merlot (Western Cape) $28. Toast, breadiness, and simple cherry read a bit thin on the nose and palate. This is lightweight, with gripping tannins and a eucalyptus trail to the finish. 84 *—K.F. (1/1/2004)*

SLALEY

Slaley 1999 Hunting Family Shiraz (Stellenbosch) $28. 89 *(11/1/2001)*

SLANGHOEK

Slanghoek 2002 Private Reserve Sauvignon Blanc (South Africa) $11. 86 *—K.F. (11/15/2003)*

Slanghoek NV Vin Doux Sparkling Blend (South Africa) $14. 86 *—K.F. (12/1/2003)*

SOUTHERN RIGHT

Southern Right 2003 Sauvignon Blanc (Western Cape) $10. Grass, lime, even asparagus notes show in this decidedly Kiwi-inspired Sauvignon Blanc. Lean and tangy to the max. **87 Best Buy** *—M.M. (11/15/2004)*

SPICE ROUTE

Spice Route 2000 Flagship Merlot (Swartland) $35. 88 *—K.F. (4/1/2003)*

Spice Route 1999 Shiraz (Swartland) $20. 80 *(10/1/2001)*

Spice Route 1999 Flagship Syrah (Swartland) $35. 88 *(11/1/2001)*

SPIER

Spier 2005 Discover Steen (Western Cape) $7. A tropical fruit style of Chenin, marketed as Steen, the old South African name for the grape. This version has too much weight. With green plum flavors and only a touch of crispness, it ends up being rather too full and fat. **83** *—R.V. (11/15/2005)*

STELLENRYCK

Stellenryck 1996 Cabernet Sauvignon (Coastal Region) $16. **87** *—M.M. (3/1/2001)*

STELLENZICHT

Stellenzicht 2001 Golden Triangle Pinotage (Stellenbosch) $18. Elegant Pinotage, smooth but not heavy, classily oaked and rather Pinot Noir-like—of course, that's 50% of its lineage. This is an appealingly tasty, if overtly woody, example. There's very good fruit here; in time I think the elements will resolve positively. Impressive structure too, with back-end tannins to lose. Time will surely tell. Enticing now, best 2006–2010. **88** *—M.M. (7/4/2004)*

Stellenzicht 2002 Reserve Sémillon (Stellenbosch) $25. Delicious and full bodied with fine depth of flavor and excellent texture. Ample oak compliments dry pear, herb-tinged fruit aromas and flavors. Most Chardonnays don't offer this elegance, structure, or food-friendliness. Will cellar well for 4–8 years. **90 Editors' Choice** *—M.M. (11/15/2004)*

Stellenzicht 2000 Syrah (Stellenbosch) $60. The tart-sweet fruit says Syrah, and the potent earthiness is distinctively South African. But the game-earth notes are overpowering here. Neither the fruit nor the texture offer enough positive counter-balance in this shot at a serious Syrah gone awry. **83** *—M.M. (11/15/2004)*

SWARTLAND

Swartland 1997 Chardonnay (Swartland) $10. **81** *(9/1/1999)*

Swartland 2005 Indalo Chenin Blanc (Swartland) $NA. From the highly rated Swartland cooperative, this wine has fresh fruit, a touch of softness, and ripe, clean apple flavors. It balances richness and freshness very easily. **86** *—R.V. (11/15/2005)*

Swartland 1997 Shiraz (Swartland) $10. **86** *(9/1/1999)*

THANDI

Thandi 2001 Cabernet Sauvignon (Coastal Region) $14. Nice accents show here, including some associated with expensive red wines—leather, tobacco, cedar, shoepolish. But the modest red fruit is overpowered by the amount of oak used, making this overly drying. Some good parts, but the whole is less than the sum. **83** *—M.M. (12/15/2004)*

Thandi 2002 Pinot Noir (Elgin) $15. A tangy cherry and smoke bouquet opens this light, attractively balanced wine. Shows interesting chalk hints, but also too much of a green element for it to really sing. Still, they've gotten the feel just right, hard enough with Pinot Noir. Deeper, more focused fruit could make this an impressive contender. I hope the Thandi team stays with it in upcoming vintages. **84** *—M.M. (12/15/2004)*

THE BIG FIVE COLLECTION

The Big Five Collection 2004 Leopard Chardonnay (Western Cape) $10. This attractive white opens with a handsome peach and herb nose. The even palate's good fruit/acid balance supports solid fruit in the style of the bouquet. Closes clean with drier mineral notes. Flavorful, with some unique character, and commendably off the predictable track. **87 Best Buy** *—M.M. (4/1/2005)*

The Big Five Collection 2004 Rhino Sauvignon Blanc (Western Cape) $10. Opens with a soft mineral-herb bouquet. The rounder style continues on the palate, but ample citrus and white pepper notes keep it from being flaccid or mushy. Closes fairly long with a nice reprise of the early mineral notes. An appealing, well-done mainstream white. **85 Best Buy** *—M.M. (4/1/2005)*

THE WOLFTRAP

The Wolftrap 2003 Red Blend (Western Cape) $10. There's ample cherry fruit in this simple, juicy, tasty red from Boekenhoutskloof. The soft, ripe feel will be a crowd pleaser, and slight hints of funkiness are positive here, preventing this from being just another bland blend. Closes drier, showing its Rhônish roots with slight herb-metal notes and modest tannins. **85 Best Buy** *—M.M. (12/15/2004)*

THELEMA

Thelema 2000 Chardonnay (Stellenbosch) $25. **90** *—R.V. (7/1/2002)*

TRIBAL

Tribal 2003 Chardonnay (Western Cape) $7. Simple Chardonnay with a pleasant, smooth feel that avoids being cloying. Shows a little heat on the nose at first but evens out on the palate. Ends with mild apple and cream notes. **83** *—M.M. (7/4/2004)*

Tribal 2003 Pinot Noir (Western Cape) $7. Shows sour cherry fruit, some oak, and a dose of that metallic earthiness Cape wines often show. A little lighter in weight, but not far from a Pinotage in manner—then again, it is a parent grape (with the Rhône's Cinsault) to that South African hybrid. **83** *—M.M. (7/4/2004)*

TUKULU

Tukulu 2003 Chenin Blanc (Groenekloof) $12. Dry and very refreshing, a fine example of the potential of Cape Chenin Blanc. Slate and mineral notes over fine dry white peach and citrus fruit make for a tasty, refreshing wine. **87 Best Buy** *—M.M. (11/15/2004)*

TUMARA

Tumara 2002 Malbec (Stellenbosch) $13. Good fruit meets intense ele-funkiness (my term for that Cape earthy element) in this even, mid-weight red. Black raspberry, licorice, toast, and asphalt notes play on the palate. But on the back end, full, spiky tannins and fierce funk prevail. Still, it's interesting, atypical, and feels like it may show improved focus and balance with a little age. **85** *—M.M. (4/1/2005)*

Tumara 2001 Bellevue Estate Pinotage (Stellenbosch) $13. Plenty of flavor shows in this zingy Pinotage from the first estate to ever plant the grape commercially. Dry, sour cherry fruit is offset by toast and herb accents. **85** *—M.M. (3/1/2004)*

TWO OCEANS

Two Oceans 2002 Chardonnay (Western Cape) $7. **87 Best Buy** *—K.F. (4/1/2003)*

Two Oceans 2001 Shiraz (Western Cape) $7. **88 Best Buy** *—K.F. (4/1/2003)*

UITKYK

Uitkyk 1999 Estate Cabernet Sauvignon (Stellenbosch) $18. Oak runs rampant here, swamping the dark red berry fruit with ashphalt, licorice and toast, toast, toast. The modest fruit is hard to find. Quite dry and not well-balanced, with overtly woody tannins. **83** *—M.M. (4/1/2005)*

Uitkyk 2001 Chardonnay (Stellenbosch) $17. **85** *—K.F. (4/1/2003)*

Uitkyk 2002 Sauvignon Blanc (Stellenbosch) $11. **84** *—K.F. (9/1/2003)*

UMKHULU

Umkhulu 2004 Dry White Blend (Stellenbosch) $NA. A wine with a fine, nutty complexity over ripe fruit, with a touch of toast and a full, buttery flavor. This is developing well, but could age another 18 months. **89** *—R.V. (11/15/2005)*

URBANE

Urbane 2002 Sauvignon Blanc (Stellenbosch) $10. The aromas and flavors here are green, in the Kiwi (that's New Zealand) style, but the mouthfeel is much softer than most wines of this profile. It's clean from start to finish, and for drinking near term. And soon after opening—it softened up too much, too quickly. **83** *—M.M. (3/1/2004)*

VAN LOVEREN

Van Loveren 2003 Reserve Chardonnay (Robertson) $15. A nose of hay and sweet perfume opens to over-ripe and slightly oxidized flavors. Just too soft and too sweet. **80** *—M.M. (11/15/2004)*

Van Loveren 2001 Reserve Chardonnay (Robertson) $16. **84** *—K.F. (4/1/2003)*

Van Loveren 2003 Sauvignon Blanc (Robertson) $10. Sauvignon Blanc with unusual acacia wood-like aromatics and a slightly over-ripe fruit quality. The feel is easy, almost plush, and on the sweet and soft side for a grape known more for zesty acidity and tangy flavors. Could have everyday appeal as a Chardonnay alternative. **83** *—M.M. (12/15/2004)*

VEENWOUDEN

Veenwouden 1998 Merlot (Paarl) $37. **90** *—M.S. (4/1/2002)*

VERGELEGEN

Vergelegen 2004 Sauvignon Blanc (Western Cape) $22. Citrus, flint, and stone scents join riper peach and melon aromas to create a full, solid bouquet. The palate is plump, a bit pithy, and overall the wine is a straightforward, well-made easy drinker. Nothing weird or wild, just a pure wine with mass appeal. Imported by 57 Main Street Wine Co. **87** *(7/1/2005)*

VERGENOEGD

Vergenoegd 2000 Estate Merlot (Stellenbosch) $31. Red berry fruit fights to show through a heavy cloak of toasty-oak. The smooth mouthfeel and even finish are-appealing, but the overall profile is too indistinct. Lovers of dark, lavishly oaky wines will find lots to like and my score stingy, but I prefer the fruit more forward. **84** *—M.M. (11/15/2004)*

Vergenoegd 2000 Estate Shiraz (Stellenbosch) $40. Nice parts try to surface here, showing hints at a serious Shiraz: Very dark, tart, sweet fruit, herb and tar accents, and a mouthfilling, if dryly woody feel. The problem? Massive, overbearing oak that envelops and submerges all else, even after an hour of breathing. **82** *—M.M. (12/15/2004)*

VILAFONTÉ

Vilafonté 2003 Series M Bordeaux Blend (Paarl) $50. Rounder and softer in the mouth than the Series C, with plump plum and chocolate flavors that pick up hints of caramel, toast, and dried herbs on the finish. Soft but not unstructured, this is immediately likeable. Drink now–2010. It might last longer, but why chance it? **91** *(11/15/2005)*

VILLIERA

Villiera 2005 Chenin Blanc (Stellenbosch) $12. One of the top wineries of Stellenbosch, the Villiera winery has a fine reputation for strongly terroir-based wines. This Chenin, with its mineral character, shows good structure to go with the tropical fruit flavors, the almonds and some citrus. **89** *—R.V. (11/15/2005)*

VINAY

Vinay NV Rosé (South Africa) $12/1L. A very cherry bouquet opens this surprisingly flavorful rosé. The tangy mouthfeel, spicy cherry flavors, and meaty accents have appeal. Though a touch metallic on the close, it's far ahead of most white zins as a tasty, inexpensive quaff. Non vintage and in a 1-liter bottle, to boot. **84** *—M.M. (3/1/2004)*

VINUM CELLARS

Vinum Cellars 2004 Chenin Blanc (Stellenbosch) $12. Just a hint of wood from a small percentage of barrel aging gives this wine an open, buttery character. From vines on the slopes of the Helderberg mountain outside Stellenbosch, the wine lacks pure Chenin varietal character, but there are great, ripe flavors. **89 Best Buy** *—R.V. (11/15/2005)*

WARWICK

Warwick 2002 Reserve Bordeaux Blend (Stellenbosch) $32. A firm, dry and elegant red whose earth and mineral notes accent a solid, dark cherry-berry fruit core. A modest amount of typical South African funkiness shows. But well-handled here, rather than detracting, it adds complexity. Closes long, with good tannic structure. Should improve through this decade. **90** *—M.M. (7/1/2005)*

Warwick 1999 Chardonnay (Stellenbosch) $18. **89** *—R.V. (9/10/2002)*

Warwick 1997 Merlot (Stellenbosch) $18. **87** *—M.N. (3/1/2001)*

Warwick 1999 Old Bush Vines Pinotage (Stellenbosch) $17. **89** *—M.M. (4/1/2002)*

Warwick 2001 Three Cape Ladies Red Blend (Simonsberg Stellenbosch) $21. The three Cape ladies are the Cabernet Sauvignon, Merlot, and Pinotage in this tasty, accessible blend. Shows attractive dry berry fruit, tobacco, and forest floor accents, and very good fruit/acid balance. Drink through 2007–8. **86** *—M.M. (11/15/2004)*

Warwick 2004 Professor Black Sauvignon Blanc (Simonsberg Stellenbosch) $18. Initially rather simple and sweet, offering ripe tropical-citrus fruit plus a round, soft feel, behind that veneer lurked an impressive wine. With time emerged Sauvignon Blanc's brighter citrus and grass tanginess, and much higher apparent acidity. It's full yet crisp, closing long with rich fruit and mild pepper notes. Grab now, but wait until 2005 to drink. **90 Editors' Choice** *—M.M. (11/15/2004)*

WATERFORD

Waterford 2000 Cabernet Sauvignon (Stellenbosch) $22. **87** *—K.F. (4/1/2003)*

Waterford 2005 Pecan Stream Chenin Blanc (Stellenbosch) $14. One of South Africa's star winemakers, Kevin Arnold, has produced an impressive, dry wine, with intense apple and grapefruit flavors. It is crisp, with a delicious lift at the end, and a dry, green aftertaste. **90 Best Buy** *—R.V. (11/15/2005)*

Waterford 1999 Kevin Arnold Shiraz (Stellenbosch) $30. **88** *—M.M. (3/1/2001)*

WEBERSBURG

Webersburg 1999 Cabernet Sauvignon (Stellenbosch) $35. This plump, medium-bodied wine boasts plenty of briary, blackberry flavors laced with notes of beefy meatiness and vanilla. Despite its age, it's still relatively youthful, with dry tannins on the finish that may never fully integrate. Drink now. **84** *—J.C. (11/15/2005)*

WILD RUSH

Wild Rush 2003 Cape White Blend (Robertson) $8. A blend of Chenin Blanc, Colombard, Sauvignon Blanc, and Chardonnay, this easy-drinking white recalls many everyday Pinot Grigios. It's a little sweet, with a mild citrus, grass, and herb profile. This uncomplicated refresher is best served well-chilled. **83** *—M.M. (11/15/2004)*

WILDEKRANS

Wildekrans 2001 Reserve Estate Wine Chenin Blanc (Walker Bay) $9. **85** *—K.F. (4/1/2003)*

Wildekrans 2001 Estate Wine Pinotage (Walker Bay) $15. **87** *—K.F. (9/1/2003)*

Wildekrans 2000 Warrant Estate Wine Red Blend (Walker Bay) $25. **84** *—K.F. (9/1/2003)*

Wildekrans 2001 Estate Wine Sémillon (Walker Bay) $15. **84** *—K.F. (4/1/2003)*

ZELPHI WINES

Zelphi Wines 2001 Simunye Sauvignon Blanc (Coastal Region) $17. **85** *—K.F. (4/1/2003)*

ZONNEBLOEM

Zonnebloem 2003 Chardonnay (Western Cape) $10. Tasty apple-pear aromas and flavors, fine balance, and good fruit-acid balance are a winning combination (as always) in this appealing mid-weight white. Tasty and surprisingly stylish at the price, with (again, as always) good fruit at the core. Worth seeking out, the equal of many more costly Chardonnays of diverse origin. **87 Best Buy** *—M.M. (4/1/2005)*

Zonnebloem 2002 Shiraz (Stellenbosch) $10. Juicy, ripe Shiraz fruit is accented by ample toasty oak and a lively citrus note in this tasty, even welterweight. There's more tangy acidity and tannins here than is usually found in a value red. Closes dry with espresso and black fruit notes. **85 Best Buy** *—M.M. (4/1/2005)*

Spain

Among European countries with long winemaking histories, no country has come further in recent years than Spain. As the nation with more acreage under vine than any of its continental mates, Spain is no longer simply a producer of overcropped, basic wines destined for domestic consumption. Just the opposite: in less than two decades, Spain has evolved into one of Europe's most exciting and progressive wine producers.

Today, Spanish winemakers are making sought-after wines at almost every price point and quality level, and in most of the country's sixty-plus denominated regions. From everyday reds made from grapes including Tempranillo, Monastrell, and Garnacha, to crisp whites like Albariño and Verdejo, to frothy Cava and some of the world's finest and richest red and dessert wines, Spain is offering the consumer variety and value at almost every turn.

Harvesting Xarel-lo grapes in a vineyard at Cavas Chandon, the Spanish branch of Moët et Chandon.

Talk about a 180-degree turnabout; twenty years ago, nobody thought much of Spain's wines. In those early post-Franco years, the country featured one collectable red—the idiosyncratic and esoteric Vega Sicilia (still one of the world's great red wines). Meanwhile, Rioja boasted a few highly traditional wines (read: not that fruity, with a lot of American oak flavor) in López de Heredia's Viña Tondonia, Marqués de Riscal, and CUNE, among others. Beyond that, there wasn't much to talk about besides Torres' Sangre de Toro and the dry and sweet fortified wines coming from Jerez in the south.

By the middle of the 1990s and into the twenty-first century, however, the world's thirst for better, more distinctive wines gave Spain the necessary spur in the side that it needed to push the envelope. Younger winemakers, many trained outside the country, started to replace their more traditional predecessors. Older regions that had fallen out of style were invigorated with new plantings and the construction of modern wineries. And almost before you could say Olé, quality wines were emerging from all four corners of the country and quite a few places in between.

SPAIN'S WINES AND REGIONS

There are currently more than sixty regulated wine regions in Spain. The most prominent denominaciones de origen, as the regions are called, have been around for decades if not longer; places like Rioja, Ribera Del Duero, Jerez, Rias Baixas, Priorat, Penedès, Navarra, La Mancha, and Valdepeñas. Others have risen to prominence during the aforementioned growth boom: Rueda, Bierzo, Toro, Cigales, Somontano, Yecla, Jumilla, and Montsant, while not all young, fit the mold of up and coming. And there are still a few DOs that seem stuck in time; outposts like Extremadura, located along the border with

Portugal, and Utiel-Requena (inland from Valencia) that may have their day down the line.

Among red-wine regions, the spotlight is shining brightest on Rioja, Ribera Del Duero, Priorat, and, to a lesser degree, Toro and Bierzo. Rioja is one of Spain's larger DOs, and the focus here is on Tempranillo. Rioja came to prominence in the 1800s when French winemakers fled their country's phylloxera (see Glossary) epidemic, and over time three main styles of red wine have evolved: crianzas, which are wood-aged wines generally of lighter stature; reservas, which spend extended time in barrel; and gran reserva, theoretically the ripest and most age-worthy of wines. Look for modern, extracted, flavorful wines from the likes of Allende, LAN, Muga, Remelluri, Remírez de Ganuza, Roda, and a host of other newcomers. Marqués de Murrieta, Marqués de Cáceres, Montecillo, and the previously mentioned CUNE and Riscal comprise the respected old guard.

Ribera Del Duero, Toro, Cigales, and other sections of Castilla y León province are also prime Tempranillo areas. Modern wineries like Alion, Pingus, Viña Sastre, and others in Ribera, as well as Numanthia-Termes in Toro are the new-wave leaders, while Vega Sicilia, Pesquera, Protos, and Pérez Pascuas have been plying their trade in Ribera for longer, with commendable results.

Just to the southwest of Barcelona lies Penedès, the heart of Spain's sparkling wine industry. Here wineries harvest the white grapes Macabeo, Parellada, and Xarello before blending them into what's known as Cava. This sparkling wine is made similarly to Champagne but is lighter and far less complex than France's prized bubbly. Penedès is also home to Miguel Torres S.A., one of Spain's preeminent wineries, a survivor of the Spanish Civil War, and for many years when Spain was overlooked, a major exporter to the United States.

A little further southwest of Penedès are Priorat and Montsant, regions that can trace their winemaking roots back to the Romans and later Carthusian monks. Here Garnacha and old Cariñena vines yield powerful wines, and the current crop of winemakers is, almost to a person, young, ambitious, and iconoclastic. Today Priorat is producing some of the world's finest red wines, ones that compare with the best of France, Italy, and California.

Lastly, Sherry is the fortified sipper of Andalusia. From crisp fino and manzanilla up to richer, nuttier amontillado and oloroso, Sherry is a unique wine for either before a meal or after. Sherry predates Spain's vinous renaissance by centuries, but never has it gone out of style.

AALTO

Aalto 2001 PS Tinto del Pais (Ribera del Duero) $105. Aalto is one of several smaller projects being led by former Vega Sicilia head winemaker Mariano Garcla, and we think this 2001 Pagos Seliccionados (PS) is his best effort to date. The wine is dark, with charcoal, lemon, and pure black-fruit aromas. It features a brilliant luster and deep, rich, syrupy flavors of maple, boysenberry, and black cherry. Shows a beautiful finish and amazing depth. Hold until 2006–07. **95 Editors' Choice** *—M.S. (6/1/2005)*

ABADIA RETUERTA

Abadia Retuerta 1998 Red Blend (Sardon de Duero) $10. 86 *—M.M. (8/1/2000)*

Abadia Retuerta 2000 Primicia Red Blend (Viño de la Tierra de Castilla y León) $10. 87 Best Buy *—J.C. (11/1/2001)*

Abadia Retuerta 1998 Selecci—n Especial Red Blend (Viño de Mesa de Castilla y León) $24. 87 *—J.C. (11/1/2001)*

Abadia Retuerta 1997 Cuvée El Campanario Tempranillo (Sardon de Duero) $50. 95 *—M.M. (8/1/2000)*

Abadia Retuerta 1996 Pago Negralada Tempranillo (Sardon de Duero) $140. 90 *(8/1/2000)*

Abadia Retuerta 1998 Cuvée El Palomar Tempranillo-Cabernet (Viño de Mesa de Castilla y León) $45. 89 *—J.C. (11/1/2001)*

Abadia Retuerta 1997 Cuvée El Palomar Tempranillo (Sardon de Duero) $48. 89 *—M.M. (8/1/2000)*

Abadia Retuerta 1999 Rivola Tempranillo-Cabernet (Viño de Mesa de Castilla y León) $11. 89 Editors' Choice *—J.C. (11/1/2001)*

ABRAZO

Abrazo 2003 Garnacha (Cariñena) $7. Sharp and edgy, with burnt leather on the piquant nose. Some red fruit and also a lot of spicy, green notes. Finishes swift and peppery. **81** *—M.S. (12/31/2004)*

Abrazo 1999 Crianza Garnacha-Tempranillo Red Blend (Cariñena) $8. Sharp and rubbery on the nose, with a racy, spirited red-cherry character. Trouble is, the acidity is piercing and the fruit, if there ever was any, is quickly exiting stage left. **81** *—M.S. (6/1/2005)*

Abrazo 1996 Gran Reserva Red Blend (Cariñena) $11. 86 *—S.H. (1/1/2002)*

ADEGAS GALEGAS

Adegas Galegas 2003 O Deus Dionisos Albariño (Rias Baixas) $22. Light and easy, with simple aromas of lemon and wildflowers. Fairly forward and pronounced in terms of fruit; the lemon, pineapple, and peach are all right there and lively. Finishes smooth and easy, if maybe a touch watery. **86** *—M.S. (9/1/2004)*

AGREST DE GUITARD

Agrest de Guitard 2003 Cabernet Sauvignon-Merlot (Penedès) $10. Quite raw and rubbery, with loud aromas that offer more power than harmony. In the mouth, strawberry fruit precedes a tight, hard finish. **82** *—M.S. (3/1/2005)*

AGRO DE BAZÁN

Agro de Bazán 1999 Granbazán Albariño (Rias Baixas) $13. Nearly the color of Sherry, this is pure burnished gold, which announces oxidation and/or some heavy oaking. Aromas of butterscotch and baked apples are momentarily intriguing, but in the mouth the wine is lean and acidic, with a fiery quality. Safe to say this is not the Albariño most of us are seeking. **83** *—M.S. (3/1/2004)*

AGUSTÍ TORELLÓ

Agustí Torelló 1999 Barrica Reserva Extra Brut (Penedès) $25. 89 *—M.S. (12/31/2002)*

Agustí Torelló 1999 Brut Riserva (Penedès) $12. 88 Best Buy *—M.S. (12/31/2002)*

Agustí Torelló 1997 Kripta Extra Brut (Penedès) $45. 91 Editors' Choice *—M.S. (12/31/2002)*

ALABANZA

Alabanza 1999 Reserva Tempranillo (Rioja) $24. Herbal on the nose, with tobacco, mushroom, and tomato aromas. Quite juicy, sharp and tannic, yielding apple-skin and red plum flavors. Gets better with airing, as tobacco, almond, and plum flavors emerge. Struggles for the right mouthfeel and texture, but has its moments and virtues. **86** *—M.S. (8/1/2005)*

ALBA DE BRETON

Alba de Breton 2001 Reserva Tempranillo (Rioja) $54. For a full-priced Rioja, it's rather scattered and scouring. The nose is mildly green, while the palate and finish are both fast and raw, bolstered by a pushy streak of core acidity. From the start it strikes an acidic, razor-sharp note, and the finish is mostly defined by oak. **83** *—M.S. (11/15/2005)*

ALBADA

Albada 2000 Garnacha (Calatayud) $8. 81 *—M.S. (10/1/2003)*

ALBET I NOYA

Albet I Noya 1999 Brut Reserva (Cava) $14. 84 *—J.C. (12/31/2003)*

SPAIN

ALDOR

Aldor 2003 Verdejo (Rueda) $11. Moderate cinnamon spice notes to the nose, with thick, soft apple flavors on the palate. Not the most forward wine, with a leaden mouthfeel. Fails to improve in the glass. Imported by Table 31 Imports. **83** *—M.S. (8/1/2005)*

ALIDIS

Alidis 2000 Crianza Tempranillo (Ribera del Duero) $22. Funky and gassy at first, but with time leather and wild berries emerge on the nose. The mouth offers red plum and blackberry, while the lean, starchy finish is tight, tannic, and oaky. Very zippy and alive, with raisin and chocolate nuances. **86** *—M.S. (3/1/2004)*

Alidis 2001 Tinto Roble Tempranillo (Ribera del Duero) $15. A bit horsey and scattered at first, but it improves with time. Flavors of blackberry and raspberry are attractive in the glass, as is the smooth finish that comes with some bitter coffee. Very young and aggressive. Bright wine, although some might view it as slightly thin and sour. **85** *—M.S. (3/1/2004)*

ALION

Alion 1996 Crianza Tempranillo (Ribera del Duero) $45. **95** *(8/1/2000)*

ALTANZA

Altanza 1999 Lealtanza Reserva Tempranillo (Rioja) $25. Subtlety is not in the calling here. The nose is chunky, with leather and scattered fruit. Sweet plum and berry fruit is bolstered by forward acidity. Condensed and short, but undoubtedly lively. **85** *—M.S. (3/1/2005)*

Altanza 1998 Reserva Tempranillo (Rioja) $47. Meaty on the nose, with chunky leather aromas along with mature fruit. In the mouth, it's a touch racy and acidic, which serves to bolster its raspberry and pie-cherry personality. Pretty good overall, with a sizable allotment of zest. **86** *—M.S. (6/1/2005)*

ALTOS DE TAMARON

Altos de Tamaron 2003 Tinto del Pais (Ribera del Duero) $10. Toasty and rough at first, but it settles. Flavors of root beer and jammy fruit are carried on a creamy palate. Solid and round if given time, with some syrupy sweetness courtesy of the hot vintage. **85 Best Buy** *—M.S. (11/15/2005)*

ALVAREZ Y DIEZ

Alvarez y Diez 2002 Nava Real Verdejo (Rueda) $11. The nose offers some applesauce and a touch of pickle. The palate is also a bit off; popcorn and burnt toast seem to dominate. Heavy and clumsy, but not necessarily bad. **83** *—M.S. (9/1/2004)*

ALVARO PALACIOS

Alvaro Palacios 2003 L'Ermita Red Blend (Priorat) $440. Super pricey but this is a knock-your-socks-off wine with a gorgeous bouquet that shows not even a hint of syrup or jam. The palate is like a nova; it bursts with plum, blackberry, and cinnamon. No harshness, not too tannic, and splendid on the finish, where toast and chocolate appear and stick around for a long time. It's 80% old-vines Garnacha and 20% Cabernet, and there just aren't enough superlatives to describe it. Only 300 cases made. **98** *—M.S. (10/1/2005)*

ALVEAR NV SOLERA

Alvear NV Solera 1830 Pedro Ximénez (Montilla-Moriles) $NA. A bit more easygoing than the PX wines of Jerez, as it delivers white raisin, milk chocolate, and brown-sugar aromas and flavors. The palate is far from aggressive; in fact, it's a little low in acidity, which results in a soft mouthfeel and a short finish. Excellent stuff; just not a classic. **90** *—M.S. (6/1/2005)*

ALZANIA

Alzania 2002 Selección Privada Red Blend (Navarra) $70. Potent to start, with heavy oak notes that conjure memories of pickle barrel and malt vinegar. Airing opens it up, and below there's black cherry, cassis, and a lot of sticky, hard tannins. Patience and hearty food are needed, but it has its qualities. Suavity, however, is not among them. **88** *—M.S. (10/1/2005)*

ANTAÑO

Antaño 1997 Crianza Red Blend (Rioja) $10. **80** *—M.M. (9/1/2002)*

ARADON

Aradon 2004 Rosado Tempranillo Blend (Rioja) $10. Some measurable weight to the nose, but mostly it's light and clean. Aromas of powdered drink mix and wet stones are solid, as is the raspberry, cherry, and peach flavors. Spicy and juicy, with enough body to tip the scales as a middleweight. Nice Riojano rosé. **86 Best Buy** *—M.S. (8/1/2005)*

ARBANTA

Arbanta 2002 Tempranillo (Rioja) $10. Leather and tar up front, followed by sweet fruit with adequate depth and plenty of plum and berry. A bit soft, touching on over-ripe, but pretty good despite some burnt, rubbery notes to the finish. **85** *—M.S. (9/1/2004)*

ARRIBEÑO

Arribeño 2003 Roble Tempranillo (Ribera del Duero) $9. Murky aromas of milk chocolate and cherry don't forecast the tart, snappy boysenberry flavors that follow. Very jumpy and acidic, with a shrill mouthfeel. **81** *—M.S. (11/15/2005)*

ARROYO

Arroyo 1995 Reserva Red Blend (Ribera del Duero) $18. **85** *—J.C. (11/1/2001)*

ARTADI

Artadi 2002 Pagos Viejos Tempranillo (Rioja) $70. A poster child for modern Rioja. Seriously extracted, with saturated blackberry, cola, and chocolate aromas. Features excellent texture and a fine, tannic finish. If it could offer anything else, it would be additional complexity and variety. It locks onto that fruit-and-chocolate combination and doesn't let go. **91** *—M.S. (6/1/2005)*

ARX

Arx 2003 Tempranillo-Cabernet (Navarra) $12. Smells like sweaty leather, with a certain salty, grassy quality. The mouth offers tart cherry and raspberry, quickened by mild tannins and starchy acidity. **82** *—M.S. (10/1/2005)*

ARZUAGA

Arzuaga 1995 Crianza Tempranillo (Ribera del Duero) $23. **92** *—S.H. (11/15/1999)*

Arzuaga 1995 Reserva Tempranillo (Ribera del Duero) $60. **89** *—S.H. (11/15/1999)*

AURUS

Aurus 1996 Aurus Tempranillo (Rioja) $130. **96** *—M.M. (8/1/2000)*

AVINYÓ

Avinyó NV Cava Brut Sparkling Blend (Penedès) $13. **86** *—J.C. (12/31/2003)*

BALBAS

Balbas 2003 Tradición Tempranillo (Ribera del Duero) $17. Features a nice mix of mint, herbs, spice, and black fruit. It's a touch sharp and hard, but overall the cherry and strawberry flavors work. Tannic and clean on the finish, with balance. Nothing complex or regal, but easily fits the bill. **86** *—M.S. (11/15/2005)*

BARON DE CHIREL

Baron de Chirel 2001 Reserva Red Blend (Rioja) $50. Dark violet in color, with plenty of wood smoke and earth to the nose, which also offers tobacco and mushroom. Dynamic on the palate, with ripe cherry and blackberry flavors. Sort of airy on the finish, with mocha and chocolate. Hefty throughout, with nice tannins. From Marqués de Riscal. **91** *—M.S. (10/1/2005)*

Baron de Chirel 1999 Rioja Reserva Tempranillo Blend (Rioja) $60. Firmly structured and ageworthy, with loads of vanillin oak but also masses of dark fruit, earth, molasses, and tobacco flavors that linger on the finish. In contrast to the rest of Riscal's offerings, this one needs time in the cellar. Try in 2008 or so. **90** *(12/31/2004)*

BARON DE LEY

Baron De Ley 1995 Gran Reserva Tempranillo (Rioja) $32. **81** *—M.S. (10/1/2003)*

Baron De Ley 2001 Finca Monasterio Tempranillo-Cabernet (Rioja) $45. Begins with cola and root beer aromas before going decidedly stewy. Ultra-lemony on the palate, a combination of thin but cooked fruit along with over-aggressive oak. Finishes reedy, with tomato notes. A wine with greater intentions that doesn't click. **83** *—M.S. (8/1/2005)*

BARZAGOSO

Barzagoso 2001 Crianza Tempranillo Blend (Rioja) $14. Rose-colored, with subdued aromas of cherry tomato, dried red fruits, mint, and leather. By modern standards, it's light and starchy, but the cherry and raspberry flavors are solid and easy to like. Better than inoffensive even if it's ultimately a simple, clean wine and nothing more. **87** *—M.S. (10/1/2005)*

BENJAMIN ROMEO

Benjamin Romeo 2001 La Viña de Andrés Romeo Tempranillo (Rioja) $140. Here's another full-force Tempranillo made in the modern style. The fruit is from older vines, and the oak regimen lasted 20 months. The nose features a mix of tree fruits along with earth and wood, and the palate is round and tannic, with a fairly thin midsection and a sweet finish of marzipan, coffee, and plum. **90** *—M.S. (9/1/2004)*

BERBERANA

Berberana 2002 Dragón Tempranillo (Rioja) $10. Hits the ground running with berry and spice notes courtesy of ample oak. The mouth is equally spicy, with mid-level plum and berry fruit. Finishes fairly long, and again with a shot of oakiness that is not fully integrated. **85** *—M.S. (5/1/2004)*

Berberana 2000 Dragón Tempranillo (Rioja) $8. **85** *—D.T. (4/1/2003)*

Berberana 2001 Vina Alarde Reserva Tempranillo (Rioja) $18. Light in color, with Old-World aromas of leaves, dried cherries, and leather. It's a clean, easy wine with cherry and cranberry flavors coming in front of a dry, spicy finish. With proper acids and balance, its traditional qualities are admirable. **85** *—M.S. (3/1/2004)*

SPAIN

BLASÓN DE SAN JUAN

Blasón de San Juan 2000 Crianza Tinto del Pais (Ribera del Duero) $19. Plump and fruity, with aromatics of tobacco, leather, and dark fruits. Features sweet, sturdy black cherry and plum flavors before a finish of warm earth, plum, and vanilla. Very straightforward in its approach, but solid on all accounts. **87** *—M.S. (6/1/2005)*

Blasón de San Juan 1999 Reserva Tinto del Pais (Ribera del Duero) $27. If it seems dirty at first, time will reveal tobacco and leather aromas along with black plum and coffee. Seems more sour than you might expect, with pie cherry and rhubarb flavors. Really high-toned on the finish, where it teeters on the brink of sour. Not bad but not endearing. **84** *—M.S. (6/1/2005)*

BLECUA

Blecua 2001 Vino Tinto Red Blend (Somontano) $NA. An eye-opening, intriguing wine from Somontano, at the foot of the Pyrenees. The bouquet is quite interesting, as it offers herbs, ripeness, and intensity. Super dense in the mouth, with pure blackberry and chocolate flavors floating atop dynamite tannins. Tons of flavor; from the Viñas del Vero group. **91** *—M.S. (6/1/2005)*

BODEGAS ABEL DE MENDOZA

Bodegas Abel de Mendoza 1999 Jarrarte Tempranillo (Rioja) $26. Pretty berry and chocolate aromas lead you to a palate that's round and pure. Right away this wine impresses; it's got all the requisite fruit as well as some peppery kick. The finish is massive, with a bitter espresso edge. Wholly modern in style, with a chewy, delicious feel/flavor combination. **91** *—M.S. (3/1/2004)*

BODEGAS AGAPITO RICO

Bodegas Agapito Rico 2000 Carchelo Red Blend (Jumilla) $8. **85 Best Buy** *—M.M. (9/1/2002)*

Bodegas Agapito Rico 1999 Carchelo Syrah (Jumilla) $13. **84** *—M.S. (8/1/2000)*

BODEGAS ANGEL LORENZO CACHAZO

Bodegas Angel Lorenzo Cachazo 2002 Las Brisas White Blend (Rueda) $9. Angel Lorenzo Cachazo is behind this open, piquant, vibrant white that really pours on the Sauvignon character. The aromas are more to peach and pear, yet the high-voltage palate is all grapefruit and other citrus. Very refreshing, with some pepper on the finish. **89 Best Buy** *—M.S. (3/1/2004)*

BODEGAS ARAGONESAS

Bodegas Aragonesas 2001 Coto de Hayas "Fagus" Garnacha (Campo de Borja) $30. This huge, ultra-sweet Garnacha knows no boundaries. It's full of candied cherry, milk chocolate, and out-of-whack tannins. A fast ride with no guard rails. Beware! **83** *—M.S. (9/1/2004)*

Bodegas Aragonesas 1998 Coto de Hayas Reserva Garnacha (Campo de Borja) $13. Lots of sweet mocha and milk chocolate coats the nose of this basic, chunky red. The palate offers adequate strawberry and raspberry, while the finish turns high-wire and tart. A bit syrupy in terms of mouthfeel. **84** *—M.S. (9/1/2004)*

Bodegas Aragonesas 2002 Crucillon Tinto Garnacha (Campo de Borja) $5. This Garnacha has a strong berry nose with hints of leather, but it doesn't hold up to airing. Within the basics, look for loud, juicy fruit that tastes like plum, strawberry, and cherry mixed together. Seems most complete on the finish. **85 Best Buy** *—M.S. (5/1/2004)*

Bodegas Aragonesas 1998 Duque de Sevilla Reserva (Campo de Borja) $11. A Garnacha-Tempranillo mix that's sweet and syrupy, with stewed fruit and a fair amount of wood. Aromas of cola and root beer lead into a thick palate that's sugary in the middle and tangy on the edges. **83** *—M.S. (9/1/2004)*

Bodegas Aragonesas 2000 Castillo de Fuendejalon Crianza Red Blend (Campo de Borja) $7. The odd yellow paper wrapping might draw attention to this modest red, which features wood spice and cinnamon atop a soft, lean core of red fruit. Flavors of cherry extract and artificial drink mix lack integrity but could please fans of sweet, simple wines. **84** *—M.S. (5/1/2004)*

Bodegas Aragonesas 2002 Coto de Hayas Tinto Joven Red Blend (Campo de Borja) $6. Racy and juicy, with forward strawberry, raspberry and leather aromas followed by a zesty, bold mouthful of plum fruit and black pepper. Long and deep for a youngster, with warmth and spice. **87 Best Buy** *—M.S. (5/1/2004)*

Bodegas Aragonesas 2002 Coto de Hayas Tempranillo-Cabernet (Campo de Borja) $9. At 85% Tempranillo, it could be labeled as such. Regardless, look for a bouquet of fat black fruit and touches of earth and smoke. Flavors of plum and blackberry are warm and full, while both the back end and overall impression are positive and lusty. **87 Best Buy** *—M.S. (5/1/2004)*

BODEGAS ARTESANAS

Bodegas Artesanas 2000 Campo Viejo Crianza Red Blend (Rioja) $9. Some raspberry jam on the nose, but also dried leaves, pickle barrel, and tea. Flavors of cherry and buttery oak carry the palate into a broad, bland finish. Simple and plump, and ultimately a decent baby Rioja. **84** *—M.S. (3/1/2004)*

Bodegas Artesanas 1997 Campo Viejo Reserva Red Blend (Rioja) $15. **83** *—D.T. (4/1/2003)*

BODEGAS BALCONA

Bodegas Balcona 1999 Partal Crianza Red Blend (Bullas) $23. Chances are you don't know this tasty little Crianza from near Murcia, which is close to Alicante. The wine has plum and earth aromas along with some wood smoke and citrus peel. A palate loaded with cherry, raspberry, and other red fruits is smooth, open and lively. Nice and racy throughout, with the right mouthfeel, one that's neither too much nor too little. **88** *—M.S. (3/1/2004)*

BODEGAS BILBAINAS

Bodegas Bilbainas 1994 Viña Pomal Reserva Red Blend (Rioja Alta) $15. **86** *(8/1/2000)*

Bodegas Bilbainas 1999 La Vicalanda de Viña Pomal Reserva Tempranillo (Rioja) $20. Super old school, featuring aromas of mint, rubber, dried red fruits, and wood smoke. Turns more reduced and hard on the palate, where cherry and raspberry shift toward medicinal: think cough drops. Finishes solid, with light oak notes. **86** *—M.S. (8/1/2005)*

Bodegas Bilbainas 1999 La Vicalanda Reserva Tempranillo Blend (Rioja) $22. Dark in color, with aromas of black plum, raisin, and spice. Fairly plump and easy, with modest richness, medium tannins, and a fair amount of sweet, chocolaty oak on the finish. **87** *—M.S. (9/1/2004)*

Bodegas Bilbainas 1998 Viña Pomal Reserva Tempranillo Blend (Rioja) $16. Starts with a blast of coconut backed by dill and crystallized red fruit. Cherry, berry, and spice on the palate, with back notes of cherry tomato and green herbs. Oaky but tight, with a lot of acidity. **86** *—M.S. (8/1/2005)*

Bodegas Bilbainas 1997 Viña Pomal Reserva Tempranillo Blend (Rioja) $10. This wine only spends a year in oak, so it's no newbie. It's rather distinguished, with cherry and plum on the nose and clean fruit that tastes right and ripe, not covered with wood it can't handle. Refined and light, not dissimilar to a good Burgundy. Old school but good. **88 Best Buy** *—M.S. (9/1/2004)*

Bodegas Bilbainas 1996 La Vicalanda Reserva Tempranillo Blend (Rioja) $20. **88** *—D.T. (4/1/2003)*

BODEGAS BRETON

Bodegas Breton 1998 Loriñon Reserva Red Blend (Rioja) $14. **85** *—M.S. (10/1/2003)*

Bodegas Breton 1996 Alba de Breton Tempranillo (Rioja) $55. **90** *— (9/1/2002)*

BODEGAS CAMPANTE

Bodegas Campante 2003 Gran Reboreda White Blend (Ribeiro) $16. Ultra-sweet and candied up front, with bulky apple and melon flavors. Finishes thick, grapey and innocuous. Lots of holes and flaws where they shouldn't be. **83** *—M.S. (9/1/2004)*

BODEGAS CARMELO RODERO

Bodegas Carmelo Rodero 2000 Tempranillo (Ribera del Duero) $13. **86** *—D.T. (4/1/2003)*

BODEGAS CASTEJÓN

Bodegas Castejón 2002 NOBUL Red Tempranillo (Madrid) $7. Flat up front, with a gassy nose. The flavor profile offers modest red fruit and a touch of green. Lots of wood grain rears up on the finish. Covers the easy bases but goes no further. **83** *—M.S. (9/1/2004)*

Bodegas Castejón 2001 Viña Rey Tempranillo (Madrid) $8. **83** *—D.T. (4/1/2003)*

BODEGAS CERROSAL

Bodegas Cerrosal 2000 Verdejo (Rueda) $9. **84** *—M.M. (9/1/2002)*

Bodegas Cerrosal 2001 Verdejo (Rueda) $9. There are a number of sensational Verdejo-based whites from this region, but this isn't one of them. The nose is heavy and creamy, while the palate is overdone yet bland. The dry, acidic palate is fresh enough, but where's the flavor? Not terrible, but not very good. **80** *—M.S. (3/1/2004)*

BODEGAS CONDE

Bodegas Conde 2001 Neo Punta Esencia Tinto del Pais (Ribera del Duero) $96. Inky dark, with coconut, baking spice, and leather on the otherwise fruity nose. There's a lumber yard's worth of oak here, but overall it works. The spice element is undeniable, while the quality of the fruit supercedes any raw wood quality. A bit simple and forward, but nothing to take issue with. **91** *—M.S. (6/1/2005)*

BODEGAS DIOS BACO S.L.

Bodegas Dios Baco S.L. NV Pedro Ximénez (Jerez) $20. Black like oil, with huge prune, coffee, licorice, and root aromas. It's a touch overbearing if you get too close, so sniff and taste lightly to reap in all the caramel, nutmeg, butter cream, and raisin this wine has to offer. It's thick, slick and delivers a kick. Great over vanilla ice cream. **92** *—M.S. (12/31/2004)*

Bodegas Dios Baco S.L. NV 20 Year Imperial Amontillado Sherry (Jerez) $75. Dark in color and extremely nutty. Along the way there are notes of seawater and white plum. The palate is a bit tangy and sharp, with orange peel, almond, and butter. Oily and complex on the finish, with a buttery tail and plenty of palate presence. **90** *—M.S. (10/1/2005)*

Bodegas Dios Baco S.L. NV Amontillado Sherry (Jerez) $20. Pristine aromas of caramel, orange peel, and leather are both powerful and pure. Flavors of toffee, cinnamon, cheddar cheese, and raisin are first-rate, while the sum of the parts is brightened and heightened by perfect acidity. A fine Amontillado that should please anyone with a fondness for good Sherry. **91** *—M.S. (10/1/2005)*

Bodegas Dios Baco S.L. NV Cream Sherry (Jerez) $20. $20. Sweet and a bit unusual, with aromatic notes of cheddar cheese and barnyard along with more typical toffee and caramel. The palate is confectionary and sturdy, with vanilla, maple, and mushroom flavors. Plump and rich on the finish. **90** *—M.S. (10/1/2005)*

Bodegas Dios Baco S.L. NV Fino Sherry (Jerez) $15. **88** *—M.S. (8/1/2003)*

Bodegas Dios Baco S.L. NV Oloroso Sherry (Jerez) $20. Dark in color, with round, malty aromas that run deep. The palate is a bit sweet as well as a bit sharp; think citrus mixed with caramel. And along with that there's pumpkin pie and allspice. Flavorful and nicely balanced. **89** *—M.S. (10/1/2005)*

BODEGAS EL MOLAR

Bodegas El Molar 2001 Araviñas Semi-Crianza Tempranillo (Ribera del Duero) $14. Light and flowery in the nose, with delicate notes of lavender and smoke. The palate, however, is compact and intense. The cherry fruit is so acid-driven and reduced that it tastes a bit like a powdered drink mix. Probably best with burgers or steak. **86** *—M.S. (3/1/2004)*

BODEGAS FONTANA

Bodegas Fontana 2001 Fontal Roble Tempranillo (La Mancha) $9. Full and convincing at first, but with airing some of the wine's holes become apparent. Nevertheless, this oak-aged Tempranillo delivers good plum and raspberry fruit and a smoky, woody finish. Solid and flavorful, but with a thin midsection. **86** *—M.S. (5/1/2004)*

BODEGAS FUENTESPINA

Bodegas Fuentespina 2001 Tempranillo (Ribera del Duero) $12. Jammy and sweet up front, and almost like a fruit roll-up as far as aromatics go. The palate is chewy and sweet, with boysenberry and plum flavors. Pretty nice in terms of mouthfeel, and for the most part it's right there. This is ultimately a basic Tempranillo, just the right wine for everyday drinking. **87** *—M.S. (3/1/2004)*

Bodegas Fuentespina 1999 Crianza Tempranillo Blend (Ribera del Duero) $22. Cool and collected, with a deeply fruity nose. The palate pours forth with red fruit, particularly cherry and raspberry, with some vanilla shadings to prop it all up. Fairly lush and chocolaty, with a fine transition from palate to finish. **90** *—M.S. (3/1/2004)*

Bodegas Fuentespina 1998 Crianza Tempranillo Blend (Ribera del Duero) $17. **85** *—J.C. (11/1/2001)*

Bodegas Fuentespina 1998 Crianza Tempranillo Blend (Ribera del Duero) $17. **85** *—J.C. (11/1/2001)*

Bodegas Fuentespina 1998 Reserva Especial Tempranillo Blend (Ribera del Duero) $72. Rich and attractive to the nose, with hints of smoked meat, tobacco, and black fruit. The palate is both developed and enveloping; it blends meat, berries, earth, and spice into a whole that's beyond the ordinary. The finish drives on for minutes with mocha, coffee, and charred meat. This has all the right components in all the right places. **92** *—M.S. (3/1/2004)*

Bodegas Fuentespina 1996 Reserva Especial Tempranillo Blend (Ribera del Duero) $65. **87** *—J.C. (11/1/2001)*

BODEGAS GODEVAL

Bodegas Godeval 2001 Viña Godeval Godello (Valdeorras) $14. One of Rueda's top producers strikes gold here. Brilliant peach and pear aromas carry a hint of fresh cream, and the palate of pure apple and white pepper is dynamite. Some lemon and hard spice create a firm, biting and lasting finish. Drink this one up while it lasts. **90 Best Buy** *—M.S. (3/1/2004)*

BODEGAS GUELBENZU

Bodegas Guelbenzu 1999 Guelbenzu EVO Cabernet Blend (Navarra) $22. **89** *—C.S. (4/1/2002)*

Bodegas Guelbenzu 1999 Guelbenzu Azul Tempranillo Blend (Navarra) $13. Starts off a little slow, taking a few minutes to open from dull, forest-floor aromas into a mix of dried spices and vanilla. Where it starts to sing is on the palate, with berry and black cherry flavors that mingle enticingly with notes of pepper, smoke, and herb. Finishes with tobacco flavors and enough ripe tannins to carry it through 2004. **88 Best Buy** *(1/1/2004)*

BODEGAS GUTIÉRREZ DE LA VEGA

Bodegas Gutiérrez de la Vega 2003 Casta Diva Cosecha Miel Muscat (Alicanté) $25. Funky to say the least, with aromas of canned pear and pumpkin pie. Big and sweet on the palate; like candy in a cup. Clunky and chunky, but pretty good if you're taking one nicely chilled glass with a fruit dessert. **85** *—M.S. (8/1/2005)*

BODEGAS HIDALGO

Bodegas Hidalgo NV La Gitana Manzanilla Sherry (Jerez) $10. The benchmark among fino-style Sherries is La Gitana. Simply put, it's a classic. Pour yourself a copita of this beauty and sip it while munching some olives, peanuts, or pistachios. Shazzam! You're transported to a whitewashed village in Andalusia. Aromas of mushroom and yeast are just as they should be. And deep within are subtle flavors of marzipan and citrus. The long, salty, bone-dry finish cleanses the palate and primes your appetite for better things to come. **89 Best Buy** *—M.S. (11/15/2004)*

BODEGAS INVIOSA

Bodegas Inviosa 1998 Lar de Barros Crianza White Blend (Ribera del Guadiana) $10. 87 Best Buy *—C.S. (4/1/2002)*

BODEGAS LA CERCA

Bodegas La Cerca 2000 Milino Viejo Crianza Red Blend (Mentrida) $18. This wine from the La Cerca winery hails from near Toledo. It's dark and ripe, with plum, currant, and oak on the nose. Syrupy cassis notes carry the palate toward and extracted, tannic finish. Quite deep and rich, but arguably a touch grapy. Worth a look. 87 *—M.S. (3/1/2004)*

BODEGAS LAN

Bodegas LAN 2000 Crianza Tempranillo (Rioja) $10. A little heavier than ideal, with a touch of raisin along with candied black cherry on the bouquet. Better in the mouth, where it comes to life on the wings of good acids, modest tannins, and simple but proper berry fruit flavors. 84 *—M.S. (6/1/2005)*

Bodegas LAN 1999 Crianza Tempranillo (Rioja) $11. Sweet on the nose, with aromas of molasses, burnt sugar, and fresh-cut wood. The palate runs tart, with spiky red-berry flavors. Firm on the finish, with genuine tannins. Still, it seems diluted. 83 *—M.S. (6/1/2005)*

Bodegas LAN 2002 Edición Limitada Tempranillo (Rioja) $38. Ultra-sweet and intriguing; you'd have to say, given the vintage, that LAN has done a great job with this prestige wine. It's loaded with sandalwood, plum and cassis aromas. Best of all, it's fresh and lively, not a dull heavyweight that trips over itself. As for flavors, look for dark plum, coffee and black currant. 91 *—M.S. (3/1/2005)*

Bodegas LAN 1996 Viña Lanciano Reserva Tempranillo (Rioja) $30. Sly and expressive, with traditional aromas of wood, earth, and leather along with telltale dried fruit. The palate is racy and reduced, a combination of apple skins, cherry, and red plum. Finishes tight and concentrated before giving way to mature chocolaty notes. Drink or continue to hold. 89 *—M.S. (3/1/2005)*

Bodegas LAN 1996 Edición Limitada Reserva Tempranillo Blend (Rioja) $39. Some Russian oak was used on this wine, which is 80% Tempranillo, and it has a nose of bell pepper and dill that could stem from that. The body, however, is good as is the acidity, but the flavor profile comes up midland. From the older school and Bodegas LAN, and in essence lost in space. 86 *—M.S. (9/1/2004)*

Bodegas LAN 1999 Viña Lanciano Tempranillo Blend (Rioja) $30. Dark and saturated, like a New World wine should be. The nose is lush and smoky, with deep prune, violet, and rubber aromas. Rich and lusty on the palate, with bacon, mustard green, clove and cinnamon. Finishes with brown sugar, licorice, and coffee. Very easy to drink; a likely crowd favorite. 90 *—M.S. (6/1/2005)*

BODEGAS LEDA

Bodegas Leda 2002 Viñas Viejas Tempranillo (Viño de la Tierra de Castilla y León) $60. Round up front, although not terribly fragrant. The nose shows only subtle berry and game aromas, with a hint of bacon. Very tannic, with a foundation of bitter chocolate and earth. Tastes good, as it should, but still not the best Leda in terms of depth and mouthfeel. 89 *—M.S. (6/1/2005)*

BODEGAS LUZON

Bodegas Luzon 2004 Verde Monastrell (Jumilla) $8. Smells like fruit bubble gum and even though it settles down with time in the glass, it really doesn't offer much besides jumpy fruit. Devoid of complexity despite being clean and juicy. 82 *—M.S. (11/15/2005)*

BODEGAS MARTINEZ PAYVA

Bodegas Martinez Payva 2003 Payva Tempranillo (Ribera del Guadiana) $8. This hot-climate chunkster hails from Extremadura, and you can tell it's warm there by the wine's heavy color and nose. It's fairly soft on the palate, however, with flavors of cough syrup, wood, and brandied fruit. Some pepper and spice on the finish add a rustic touch. 84 *—M.S. (9/1/2004)*

BODEGAS MAURO

Bodegas Mauro 1998 Vendimmia Seleccionada Red Blend (Viño de la Tierra de Castilla y León) $90. 91 Cellar Selection *—J.C. (11/1/2001)*

BODEGAS MURIEL

Bodegas Muriel 1995 Reserva Tempranillo (Rioja) $13. 86 *(8/1/2000)*

BODEGAS MURVIEDRO

Bodegas Murviedro 2000 Los Monteros Crianza Monastrell (Valencia) $11. 85 *—D.T. (4/1/2003)*

Bodegas Murviedro 1999 Tinto Crianza Red Blend (Valencia) $10. 83 *—D.T. (4/1/2003)*

Bodegas Murviedro 2001 Agarena Tempranillo-Cabernet (Utiel-Requena) $8. 87 Best Buy *—D.T. (4/1/2003)*

BODEGAS NAIA

Bodegas Naia 2004 Las Brisas White Blend (Rueda) $10. Amazingly expressive stuff from Spain. A mix of Verdejo, Sauvignon Blanc, and Viura that delivers a cornucopia of citrus. Grapefruit, passion fruit, and lime aromas and flavors abound, and the finish is so fresh and scouring that it can't help but quench your thirst. A superb summer sipper from the constantly improving Rueda region. 89 Best Buy *—M.S. (8/1/2005)*

BODEGAS NEKEAS

Bodegas Nekeas 2001 Vega Sindoa Cabernet Sauvignon-Tempranillo (Navarra) $11. This wine from Bodegas Nekeas is overtly green. It smells and tastes of bell peppers and green beans, and despite a perfectly good mouthfeel and tannic structure, the under-ripe aromas and flavors drag it down. **82** *—M.S. (3/1/2004)*

Bodegas Nekeas 2001 Vega Sindoa El Chaparral, Old Vines Garnacha (Navarra) $11. Racy and rambunctious, with a potent yet pretty nose featuring tons of red licorice and cassis. This is old-vines Garnacha, and it has some tannins that could use a few years to settle in. Nonetheless the chocolate and coffee flavors are fine, and there's a sweetness that grows on you. Drink beginning in late 2004. **89 Best Buy** *—M.S. (3/1/2004)*

Bodegas Nekeas 2002 Vega Sindoa Rosé (Navarra) $7. Such a pretty pink is this little Garnacha/Cabernet mix; and it tastes and smells great, too. Fruity raspberry aromas blend into the flowery bouquet, while the palate is streamlined by watermelon notes that prime the peach flavors that dominate. A mild dose of pepper on the finish is nice. **88 Best Buy** *—M.S. (3/1/2004)*

BODEGAS ONTANON

Bodegas Ontanon 1998 Crianza Tempranillo (Rioja) $NA. **86** *—M.M. (9/1/2002)*

BODEGAS ORVALAIZ

Bodegas Orvalaiz 1998 Cabernet Sauvignon (Navarra) $8. Funky aromas of red cabbage, green herbs, and sweet cherries lead into a lean, herbaceous wine that finishes on a metallic note. Tasters' views were more consistent on this wine than on this winery's Merlot. **82** *(1/1/2004)*

Bodegas Orvalaiz 1999 Tempranillo (Navarra) $8. **85** *—C.S. (4/1/2002)*

BODEGAS OTTO BESTUE

Bodegas Otto Bestue 2002 Finca Rableros Tempranillo-Cabernet (Somontano) $13. The country-style nose deals beets and crystallized fruit at first, and then comes sweaty leather and earth notes. In the mouth, raspberry, strawberry, and spice come in layers, while the finish is plump and shows some muscle. Bold and satisfying, yet somewhat rustic. **87** *—M.S. (5/1/2004)*

BODEGAS PALACIO

Bodegas Palacio 2000 Glorioso Reserva Tempranillo (Rioja) $15. A wine that very much fits the bill. The aromas are rubbery and smoky, with plenty of dark, ripe fruit filling in the voids. In the mouth, cherry and plum runneth over, while the finish is potent. Fruit is front and center, all supported by spicy oak. Very good in a mainstream, approachable way. **88 Best Buy** *—M.S. (12/31/2004)*

BODEGAS PALACIOS REMONDO

Bodegas Palacios Remondo 2001 Propiedad Herencia Remondo Red Blend (Rioja) $28. Alvaro Palacios is indeed a great winemaker, as is evidenced by this blend of Garnacha, Tempranillo, Graciano, and Mazuelo. Aromas of bright cherry signify power and structure, yet it's easy as sin to drink. Shows model integration, bursting berry flavors and ripe tannins. Tasted several times during the past year but not rated until now; this wine just keeps getting better. **92** *—M.S. (6/1/2005)*

BODEGAS PIRINEOS

Bodegas Pirineos 2001 Moristel (Somontano) $13. Scattered and woody, with grainy notes to the red-fruit nose. This is Mourvèdre, or if you prefer, Monastrell, but any way you cut it the fruit is big and ripe yet somewhat sour, with a lot of dry oak in support. Promising at first but it doesn't hit with much force. **84** *—M.S. (3/1/2004)*

Bodegas Pirineos 1999 Marboré Red Blend (Somontano) $28. **86** *—D.T. (4/1/2003)*

Bodegas Pirineos 2000 Marboré Red Blend (Somontano) $28. Very woody, with overt menthol and lemony aromas that cover up what black cherry fruit there is. The palate is fairly lean and sour, and with that funky lemon-tinged oak, it tastes almost of citrus. A five-grape blend with hard tannins and bite. **82** *—M.S. (3/1/2004)*

Bodegas Pirineos 2002 Montesierra Rosado Rosé Blend (Somontano) $10. Heavy, forceful aromas make it tough and rough to get into, but with time it opens to display tea, raspberry, and nutty flavors. The finish is clean and the weight throughout is good. But when you get down to it it's fairly innocuous. Made by Bodega Pirineos. **83** *—M.S. (3/1/2004)*

BODEGAS REMIREZ DE GANUZA

Bodegas Remirez de Ganuza 1998 Reserva Tempranillo Blend (Rioja) $65. Dark in color, with dynamite bacon, boysenberry, and lavender aromas. Quite a saturated wine, with smoke and earth surrounding cola and dried fruit. This is killer Rioja, one with all the trimmings. There's racy spice, pencil lead, and push. Sensationally snazzy and stylish. **92 Cellar Selection** *—M.S. (3/1/2004)*

BODEGAS RODA

Bodegas Roda 1998 Cirsion Tempranillo (Rioja) $215. **94** *(8/1/2000)*

Bodegas Roda 2000 Roda I Tempranillo Blend (Rioja) $60. It's hard to imagine the subsequent vintage surpassing this purring monster, but it could and probably will. That said, the current 2000 is magnificent in its dark masculinity and layered complexity. The fruit aromas are perfect, the spice notes exotic, and overall it's just a blast to drink. Lots of sweet oak is still front and center, so give it until

2006 for it to show even better. **95 Cellar Selection** —*M.S. (9/1/2004)*

BODEGAS VALDEÁGUILA

Bodegas Valdeáguila 2003 Viña Salamanca Verdejo (Sierra de Salamanca) $8. Candle wax, vanilla, and a foxy, wet-animal aroma define the nose. Starts off spicy and racy but doesn't hold the pace. Finishes creamy and modestly thick. **82** —*M.S. (9/1/2004)*

BODEGAS VIDAL SOBLECHERO

Bodegas Vidal Soblechero 2001 Viña Clavidor Tempranillo (Rueda) $11. Dark like crude oil, with a rich, raisiny nose that conveys thickness. This is pure Tempranillo, made ripe and sweet. Flavors of prunes and blackberry are full and forward. The tannins are soft. Not overly complex, but chewy and of a certain style. **88 Best Buy** —*M.S. (5/1/2004)*

BODEGAS Y VINEDOS DE JALÓN

Bodegas y Viñedos de Jalón 2002 Viña Alarba Old Vines Grenache Grenache (Catalonia) $6. Sweet and grapey, but pleasurable and well made. The candied palate of sugar beets, raspberry, and mocha is juicy, and there's decent grip to the mouthfeel. The tail end then fans out and showcases nice acidity, integrated tannins and a juicy personality. Drink now and throughout the year. **87** —*M.S. (3/1/2004)*

BODEGAS Y VIÑEDOS DEL JARO

Bodegas y Viñedos del Jaro 2001 Sed de Caná Tinto del Pais (Ribera del Duero) $NA. My first look at this fledgling project from the folks at Osborne left me impressed. Sed de Caná is a well-toasted, masculine Tempranillo with raw, smoky aromas and a broad-shouldered palate. It toes the line between spunky and tannic, but there's so much forward fruit thrown in that you can't help but like it. Needs several years to settle; best by 2008. 145 cases made. **92** —*M.S. (6/1/2005)*

BOHIGAS

Bohigas 2000 Chardonnay (Catalonia) $12. **80** —*M.M. (9/1/2002)*

Bohigas 1999 Tempranillo Blend (Catalonia) $10. **88** —*C.S. (4/1/2002)*

BORSAO

Borsao 2002 (Campo de Borja) $6. The essence of mint and orange peel add character to the youthful red fruit that defines the bouquet of this 100% Garnacha. Cherry, plum skin, and red licorice flavors come in front of a zesty, sharp, lean finish. There's not much fat or waste to this wine; it's precise and racy, and eminently tasty. It's a fine starter Garnacha. **87 Best Buy** —*M.S. (3/1/2004)*

BUIL & GINÉ

Buil & Giné 2002 17-XI Red Blend (Montsant) $23. Quite sweet and borderline raisiny on the nose, yet red and tart in the mouth, with pie cherry and red raspberry flavors. Quite basic and straightforward, with a touch of green spiciness to the racy finish. **84** —*M.S. (10/1/2005)*

Buil & Giné 2004 Nosis Verdejo (Rueda) $19. Pungent and grassy, with a scrappy sharpness that softens with time. Flavors of passion fruit and orange create a juice-like palate, while sweet and tart flavors carry the finish. Nice Verdejo but not quite up there with the region's best. **86** —*M.S. (10/1/2005)*

CALDERONA

Calderona 1999 Crianza Red Blend (Cigales) $12. **86** —*D.T. (4/1/2003)*

CAMPILLO

Campillo 1994 Gran Reserva Tempranillo (Rioja) $32. This shows some advanced aromatics of decayed fruit, coffee, and tobacco, but at the same time it tastes robust and youthful, with plum and dark chocolate dominating the flavor profile. Finishes long and earthy, picking up notes of tar and vanilla. **88** *(5/1/2004)*

Campillo 1996 Reserva Tempranillo (Rioja) $24. Across the board, the Campillo wines are bigger and more robust than their Faustino stablemates. This reserva shows plenty of coffee and caramel aromas, allied to black cherry, plum, and tobacco flavors. Smooth in the mouth, with a long, tart finish. **88** *(5/1/2004)*

Campillo 1995 Rioja Reserva Tempranillo (Rioja) $24. **90** *(5/1/2001)*

CAMPO ELISEO

Campo Eliseo 2002 Tinta de Toro (Toro) $50. Big and ripe, with tobacco, blackberry, and fresh-cut lumber on the nose. This big boy weighs in at 15%, so the chocolate, cassis, and rich blackberry flavors on the palate should not come as a surprise. Toasty and plush; a model New World red from Jacques and François Lurton and partner Michel Rolland. **91** —*M.S. (10/1/2005)*

CAMPO VIEJO

Campo Viejo 1994 Gran Reserva Red Blend (Rioja) $25. **88** —*M.M. (9/1/2002)*

CAMPOS REALES

Campos Reales 2004 Tempranillo (La Mancha) $6. Pretty darn good red wine for what it costs. Smells like pure raspberries and black cherries, with nothing mucking it up. Has balance and acid, a solid mouthfeel, and no abnormal funk or green. In its price category it's as good as you could ask for. **84 Best Buy** —*M.S. (11/15/2005)*

CAPÇANES

Capçanes 2001 Cabrida Garnacha (Priorat) $60. Pure Garnacha, which is anathema in the region. Savory on the nose, with roasted meat and spice notes as much as fruit. Once it hits the palate, however, the plum and berry flavors explode. Turns elegant as it opens, while retaining intensity. Flashy stuff. **91** —*M.S. (10/1/2005)*

Capçanes 2003 Mas Donís Barrica Red Blend (Montsant) $12. This wine is a custom cuvée made by Montsant's trend-setting co-operative for American importer Eric Solomon. It's a bit like a Côtes du Rhône, but with more color, dark fruit and body. And it displays some of the region's patented terroir, meaning it has that graphite-schist quality along with peppery notes. **86** —*M.S. (10/1/2005)*

CARCHELO

Carchelo 2004 Monastrell (Jumilla) $9. This has become a popular by-the-glass wine, and deservedly so. The color is pure, the nose a nice mix of leather, earth, and dark but healthy plum and blackberry. Hails from a hot climate, but shows balance via bright acidity and firm tannins. Finishes with a fat, spicy finish. A country wine but a good one. **87 Best Buy** —*M.S. (10/1/2005)*

CARE

Care 2001 Tinto Red Blend (Cariñena) $20. Tons of color but the nose is a bit soupy, with aromas of heavy oak, black fruit, tomato, and herbs. A blend of 60% Garnacha and 40% Cabernet Sauvignon that's solid but shrill. Hits with extract and tannins, but the integration and flavors don't quite achieve the next level. **84** —*M.S. (6/1/2005)*

CARMELO RODERO

Carmelo Rodero 2000 Crianza Tempranillo (Ribera del Duero) $24. Strong and oaky, without much finesse to the fast-paced nose and palate. Basic red fruit and sharp-cutting acidity defines the mouth. Rounds out some late in the game, but still it only goes so far. **84** —*M.S. (9/1/2004)*

Carmelo Rodero 1999 Reserva Tempranillo (Ribera del Duero) $45. Sweet and solid, with true-form tree bark, root vegetable, and black fruit aromas. Ripe strawberry and raspberry carry the healthy palate toward a smooth, juicy, satisfying finish. Very well-balanced and correct at all major checkpoints. **90** —*M.S. (9/1/2004)*

Carmelo Rodero 2002 Roble Tempranillo (Ribera del Duero) $17. An oak-aged vino joven with a nose of cherry, rubber, and raspberry. At first taste, it seems overtly buttery, as if the young oak were sitting atop the wine. As you get into it, that oak seems less obvious and more integrated. Still, it's a touch bland, yet competent. **85** —*M.S. (9/1/2004)*

CASA SOLAR

Casa Solar 2000 Plata Red Blend (Rioja) $6. **83** —*M.S. (10/1/2003)*

Casa Solar 1997 Tempranillo (Bajo Aragon) $4. **84** *(3/1/2000)*

Casa Solar 1994 Plata Tempranillo (Sacedon-Mondejar) $5. **86** *(3/1/2000)*

CASAL CAEIRO

Casal Caeiro 2003 Albariño (Rias Baixas) $16. Yellow in color, with a round, yeasty, corn-tinged nose. That roundness is maintained on the palate, where flavors of orange, lemon, and peach lead to a mild, buttery finish. Good but a bit chunky. **85** —*M.S. (8/1/2005)*

CASTAÑO

Castaño 2000 Monastrell (Yecla) $9. **87 Best Buy** —*J.C. (11/15/2002)*

CASTELL DE FALSET

Castell de Falset 1998 Tempranillo Blend (Tarragona) $19. **86** —*M.M. (4/1/2002)*

CASTELLBLANCH

Castellblanch NV Cristal SemiSeco (Cava) $10. Kicks off with aromas of licorice gumdrop, wild flower, and light stone fruits. Offers lime and sugared candy in the mouth along with a touch of banana and ripe apple. Finishes sweet, almost as if it were dessert. Fortunately some lively acidity keeps it fresh. **86** —*M.S. (5/1/2004)*

Castellblanch NV Rosado Seco (Cava) $10. Dark and rosy, with a sweet strawberry fizz-like bouquet. The palate is firm and the flavor package delivers a full shot of ripe tangerine and nectarine. Yes, it tastes somewhat like a confection, meaning it's rather sweet, but the balance and acids are right there, so it goes down well. **85** —*M.S. (5/1/2004)*

CASTELLFLORIT

Castellflorit 1999 Tinto Garnacha (Priorat) $17. **84** —*M.S. (11/1/2002)*

CASTILLO DE ALMANSA

Castillo de Almansa 1994 Reserva Cencibel (Almansa) $10. **87** —*J.C. (8/1/2000)*

Castillo de Almansa 1993 Reserva Tempranillo (Almansa) $10. **87 Best Buy** —*J.C. (11/15/1999)*

CASTILLO DE JUMILLA

Castillo de Jumilla 1999 Reserva Red Blend (Jumilla) $17. Seems overripe and stewy at first; airing brings it into better form, but there's still a lot of overt oak sitting on the bouquet. Flavors of raisins, cherries, and plums are dark and chewy, while the finish offers vanilla and lively acids. Not dull but clumsy and heavy. **84** *—M.S. (10/1/2005)*

CASTILLO DE MONJARDIN

Castillo de Monjardin 2002 Unoaked Chardonnay (Navarra) $11. Unoaked and forward, with a shot of butterscotch and fresh herbs to the nose. Banana, mango, and cucumber flavors lead toward a thin, citrusy finish. The acidity is lively but constrained. **86** *—M.S. (5/1/2004)*

Castillo de Monjardin 2000 Deyo Merlot (Navarra) $15. Delightfully round and pleasant, with aromas of plum, earth, pencil lead, and redwood shavings. The palate is deep and developed, with a full allotment of berry fruits and sweet strawberry working the layer below. Finishes leathery and dry, but not drying. A centered, classy Merlot from Navarra. **91 Best Buy** *—M.S. (5/1/2004)*

CASTILLO DE MONSERAN

Castillo de Monseran 2002 Garnacha (Cariñena) $7. Ruby in color and sweet on the nose. Yes, it's a candied Grenache from central Spain, and while it doesn't overwhelm, it's steady as she goes. Plenty of raspberry and cherry on the palate is backed by a clear, focused finish. A tasty, upright, semisweet red. **85 Best Buy** *—M.S. (9/1/2004)*

CASTILLO DE PERELADA

Castillo de Perelada NV Cresta Rosa (Emporadà-Costa Brava) $18. This oddball from near Girona is a sparkling dry wine with hardly any flavor other than dried fruit and burnt toast. It isn't particularly good or bad, and finding its target market seems impossible. But what the heck, here it is, a bone-dry Rosado sparkler. Go figure. **81** *—M.S. (9/1/2004)*

CASTILLO DE URTAU

Castillo de Urtau 2001 Crianza Tempranillo (Ribera del Duero) $34. Initial aromas of tree bark, root beer, and leather give way to stronger, obvious oak notes. Very snappy on the palate; in fact, it's downright sharp and acidic in the midpalate. Has its positives but is too racy and shrill in the middle. Imported by Haro Imports. **84** *—M.S. (8/1/2005)*

CATALINO

Catalino 2003 Tempranillo-Cabernet (Catalunya) $10. Smoke and rubber aromas along with soy carry the nose. Raspberry and spice, mainly clove, kick in on the palate. Finishes sharp and juicy, with a lot of acidity. Also plenty of drawn out, unflinching wood. **84** *—M.S. (8/1/2005)*

CAVAS HILL

Cavas Hill 2001 Gran Civet Hill Crianza Red Blend (Penedès) $10. Smoky and dry, with strong aromas of cherry and forest floor. Flavors of raspberry and cherry blend with greener tomato and basil notes, while the finish is tight and tannic. Very standard; like something you've tasted many times before. **85 Best Buy** *—M.S. (8/1/2005)*

Cavas Hill 1999 Gran Civet Hill Crianza Red Blend (Penedès) $8. **83** *—M.S. (11/1/2002)*

Cavas Hill 1997 Gran Toc Hill Reserva Red Blend (Penedès) $13. **83** *—M.S. (11/1/2002)*

CELLAR MARTI FABRA CARRERAS

Cellar Marti Fabra Carreras 1999 Masia Carreras Red Blend (Emporadà-Costa Brava) $29. Anyone who favors sweet, extracted, rich bruisers should snap this up. It's thick and chewy, with caramel and chocolate jazzing up deep plum and boysenberry fruit. You might think that this baby was spiked; it has kirsch and brandied fruit at its core. Fans of more traditional styles, however, should probably steer clear. **87** *—M.S. (3/1/2004)*

CELLERS UNIO

Cellers Unio 1999 Tendral Red Blend (Priorat) $22. Very sweet and round in the nose—a true whiff of Spanish Garnacha if there ever was one. The palate feels chewy as it delivers earthy, sweet flavors that don't really fit any one particular flavor profile. In its favor, the wine has size and guts. But it also seems a tad over-ripe and raisiny. **84** *—M.S. (3/1/2004)*

CLOS CYPRES

Clos Cypres 2002 Tinto Red Blend (Priorat) $48. Lively and loaded with smoky aromas of beef jerky, sandalwood, and leather. Distant blackberry along with vanilla and tobacco carry the palate, while the finish is wide and smooth. Very drinkable if not a classic. **86** *—M.S. (10/1/2005)*

CLOS DE L'OBAC

Clos de L'Obac 2000 Dolç de L'Obac Red Blend (Priorat) $100. **91** *—M.N. (3/1/2003)*

CLOS ERASMUS

Clos Erasmus 1996 Grenache (Priorat) $50. **94** *(11/15/1999)*

CLOS FIGUERAS

Clos Figueras 2002 Font de la Figuera Red Blend (Priorat) $30. A lot of leather and rubber join jammy red-fruit scents on the bouquet. The palate is loaded with zesty, fairly lean raspberry and plum flavors, while the finish sports vanilla, spice, and tannin. A bit harsh and acid-driven, but still a good wine from a less-than-ideal year. **86** *—M.S. (10/1/2005)*

CLOS MOGADOR

Clos Mogador 2001 Manyetes Red Blend (Priorat) $70. This monster is intensely mineral, with aromas of crushed stones mixed with leather, lavender, pepper, and cherry. In the mouth, it's heady with maple, leather, asphalt, and cola. Comes at you in layers, the last of which is a finishing flow of espresso. Aged 20 months in new 500-liter barrels, not barriques. **91** *—M.S. (10/1/2005)*

Clos Mogador 2002 Viño Tinto Red Blend (Priorat) $75. René Barbier, the pioneer of Priorat, pulled together a beautiful wine in what was, at best, a mediocre vintage. Admittedly, it starts out coarse and grainy, but airing shows juicy red fruit and a level of complexity that's up there. More the total package than a collection of spare parts; as a result, it'll drink wonderfully around 2006-07. A mix of Cabernet, Cariñena, Garnacha, and Syrah. **93** *—M.S. (6/1/2005)*

CODICE

Codice 1999 Red Blend (Viño de la Tierra de Manchuela) $9. **87** *—M.M. (4/1/2002)*

CODORNIÚ

Codorniú NV Cuvée Raventós Brut (Cava) $11. Dry and toasty, with corn-like aromas. The palate is thin and overly simple, with bare hints of apple, apricot, and grapefruit. The finish is dull and weak. Definitely a wine that lacks soul. **81** *—M.S. (1/1/2004)*

Codorniú NV Brut Pinot Noir (Cava) $14. **86** *—R.V. (12/31/2003)*

Codorniú NV Brut Rosado Pinot Noir (Cava) $NA. Maybe Pinot Noir isn't meant to be in Catalonia. This has a burnt nose, with medicinal cherry and cranberry aromas and flavors. Starts sweet then goes a bit raspy. Unusual. **84** *—M.S. (6/1/2005)*

Codorniú NV Jaume de Codorniú Brut (Cava) $NA. More mature and minerally than most, with some earthy notes as well as a sharp smokiness. Apple, citrus, and grapefruit flavors dominate the developed, smooth-textured palate. Nice overall, with good body. A stand-up cava. **89** *—M.S. (6/1/2005)*

CONDADO DE HAZA

Condado de Haza 1999 Estate Bottled Tempranillo (Ribera del Duero) $20. **88** *—C.S. (11/1/2002)*

CONDE DE LA SALCEDA

Conde de La Salceda 1998 Reserva Tempranillo Blend (Navarra) $49. **86** *(4/1/2003)*

CONDE DE VALDEMAR

Conde de Valdemar 2001 Crianza Tempranillo Blend (Rioja) $12. Clean but rugged, with meaty, solid aromas. Cherry, berry, and cola create a sturdy, fruity attack, while the finish is round and medium in size. A pedestrian, good red for everyday drinking. **86** *—M.S. (9/1/2004)*

Conde de Valdemar 1998 Reserva Tempranillo Blend (Rioja) $15. Big and broad, with aromas of burnt sugar, leather, tomato, and mocha. The palate delivers ample raspberry and plum flavors amid meaty tannins and healthy acidity. Finishes lively and tannic. **87** *—M.S. (9/1/2004)*

CONDES DE ALBAREI

Condes de Albarei 1999 Albariño (Rias Baixas) $13. **86** *(8/1/2000)*

Condes de Albarei 2003 Albariño (Rias Baixas) $12. Attractive enough, with buttercup, cashew, citrus, and canned pineapple aromas. Fairly focused and controlled on the palate, with basic apple and peach flavors. Finishes a bit chunky, with a sweet pineapple-driven roundness. **86** *—M.S. (12/31/2004)*

CONDESA DE LEGANZA

Condesa de Leganza 2001 Crianza Tempranillo (La Mancha) $10. Typical and likable, with aromas of dark fruit, rubber, leather, and spice. Fairly broad and easy on the palate, where simple raspberry and cherry flavors lead to a light, airy finish. Solid and juicy stuff. **86** *—M.S. (8/1/2005)*

Condesa de Leganza 1999 Crianza Estate Bottled Finca los Trenzones Tempranillo (La Mancha) $9. **88 Best Buy** *—M.S. (8/1/2003)*

CONRERIA D'SCALA DEI

Conreria d'Scala Dei 2004 Les Brugueres (Priorat) $25. Immediately this white Garnacha registers as something totally different, but more importantly, it's really good. A mere 108 vines yield this lovely anomaly, almost all of which is imported into the U.S. Look for melon and apricot aromas and flavors, along with accents ranging from almond to peach pit to bee's wax. Spectacular texture. 375 cases made. **90** *—M.S. (10/1/2005)*

CONTINO

Contino 1996 Gran Reserva Tempranillo (Rioja) $50. Very healthy and lively, and positively a traditional in style Rioja. Leather, caramel, and chocolate aromas precede a dry, acid-packed palate of cherries and raspberries. The finish is tart at first, then opens into vanilla and spice. With its exciting flavor accents, this is like taking a trip back to a bygone winemaking era. **90** *—M.S. (3/1/2004)*

Contino 1999 Reserva Tempranillo (Rioja) $42. Open and downright fruity for an old-school wine. The bouquet is sweet and rubbery, while the palate delivers plum and blackberry along with chocolate and vanilla. Big tannins are firm but friendly, and the body is sturdy. Not sharp but modestly aggressive. **89** *—M.S. (8/1/2005)*

Contino 2001 Viña del Olivo Tempranillo Blend (Rioja) $120. With density and purity, this is yet another fine Rioja from 2001. Contino is CUNE's so-called "modern" label, and the wine delivers ripe plum and cherry, with oak-driven cinnamon, nutmeg, and chocolate playing supporting roles. A textbook 21st-century wine, with all the right parts in all the right places **90** *—M.S. (6/1/2005)*

COOPERATIVO SAN ISIDRO

Cooperativo San Isidro 2001 Campo de Camarena Garnacha (Mentrida) $9. **85** *—D.T. (4/1/2003)*

CORONILLA

Coronilla 2002 Crianza Bobal (Utiel-Requena) $12. The bouquet kicks up aromas of black fruit, bacon, and rubber. The grape type is Bobal, and the wine is grabby and rubbery, with piercing tannins supporting black cherry and pepper flavors. Tangy but not shrill on the finish. **85** *—M.S. (8/1/2005)*

Coronilla 2000 Crianza Red Blend (Utiel-Requena) $15. **85** *—D.T. (4/1/2003)*

COSME PALACIO Y HERMANOS

Cosme Palacio y Hermanos 2001 Tempranillo (Rioja) $12. Heavy and sweaty at first, with a fat texture and forward fruit. It takes this wine a couple of minutes to show its black core and some spicy heat. Finishes with obvious flavors of oak and coffee. **85** *—M.S. (9/1/2004)*

Cosme Palacio y Hermanos 2003 Viura (Rioja) $12. Flat and gassy. Bland apple flavors carry the palate, followed by a short, low-acid finish. **81** *—M.S. (11/15/2005)*

COSTERS DEL SIURANA

Costers del Siurana 2001 Clos de L'Obac Red Blend (Priorat) $67. Plenty of smoked meat, hard spice, and pulsating fruit to the nose, which evolves greatly if given time. If there's anything to take issue with, it's that the wine is almost too much of a straight-shooter: It's a touch racy and acidic, with a single beam of bright flavors off of which it doesn't vary. **90** *—M.S. (10/1/2005)*

Costers del Siurana 2001 Miserere Red Blend (Priorat) $60. Sleek and fruity, with round, mature aromas and flavors of strawberry and raspberry. Pleasant more than complex, with some acidic verve and a core of healthy fruit. Easy to like, with a lot of flavor. Drink now through 2006. **88** *—M.S. (10/1/2005)*

COTO DE HAYAS

Coto de Hayas 1998 Crianza Red Blend (Campo de Borja) $7. **85 Best Buy** *—M.S. (11/1/2002)*

COTO DE IMAZ

Coto de Imaz 1994 Gran Reserva Tempranillo (Rioja) $29. **87** *—M.M. (9/1/2002)*

CRISTALINO

Cristalino NV Brut (Cava) $9. Light aromas of petrol and lemon-lime are entirely correct for cava, and the palate pushes fresh fruit in the tangerine and grapefruit realm. Has a bit of heft and zap, with a dry, largely clean finish. Fine on its own; maybe better in a Spanish-style mimosa. **85 Best Buy** *—M.S. (12/15/2005)*

Cristalino 1998 Brut Nature (Cava) $12. **85** *—J.C. (12/31/2003)*

Cristalino NV Extra Dry (Cava) $9. Aromas of apple are sweetened by hints of toffee and caramel. The fruit on the palate is bright enough, albeit sweet: the apple, pear, and peach flavors are ripe. Finishes lively yet still a tad bit creamy. Stylish for the price. **87 Best Buy** *—M.S. (12/15/2004)*

Cristalino NV Rosé Brut (Cava) $9. A bit gaseous and funky, with simple dried-cherry and slightly mealy citrus flavors. Gets better with time but never really impresses. Not musty but definitely less than fresh. **81** *—M.S. (12/15/2005)*

CRUZ DE PIEDRA

Cruz de Piedra 2002 Garnacha (Calatayud) $7. Plump and grapey, with sharp raspberry and pepper controlling the palate. Fairly tart and condensed, but mostly clean. Spice on the finish, but never all that much texture. **84** *—M.S. (12/31/2004)*

CULMAN DE LAN

Culman de LAN 1994 Reserva Tempranillo (Rioja) $162. **89** *— (9/1/2002)*

CUNE

CUNE 2001 Rosado Grenache (Rioja) $11. **82** *—D.T. (4/1/2003)*

CUNE 1996 Imperial Reserva Tempranillo (Rioja) $31. **87** *—D.T. (4/1/2003)*

CUNE 2001 Pagos de Viña Real Tempranillo (Rioja) $119. Perfect color; built like a house. The bouquet is telling, as one whiff delivers cherry, cola, tobacco, and almond paste. Much to ponder on the palate, as red berry and cassis flavors are puffed up by woody waves of coconut and cream. And then there are those tight, driving tannins. You can't miss them. Hold for several years, if you can. **91 Cellar Selection** *—M.S. (8/1/2005)*

CUNE 2000 Viña Real Oro Reserva Tempranillo (Rioja) $33. Starts out rather simple, with cherry, tomato, and dill notes. Picks up complexity and style as it airs, revealing plum and raspberry flavors along with herbs and leather. Toasty, with flavors of coconut to the finish. Acidic still, so serve with food. **87** *—M.S. (8/1/2005)*

CUNE 1996 Viña Real Reserva Tempranillo (Rioja) $29. **86** *—D.T. (4/1/2003)*

CUNE 2000 Real de Asúa Reserva Tempranillo Blend (Rioja) $120. Concentrated but not too heavy, at least not compared to some new-age Riojanos. Asúa shows smoky, toasty aromas and some bright cherry fruit. In the mouth, she's fresh and upright, with just a hint of Bordeaux-style leafiness but zero under ripeness. Toward the finish cola and red licorice flavors come up. Lovely and more subtle than the competition. **92** *—M.S. (6/1/2005)*

DAMALISCO

Damalisco 1999 Reserva Tempranillo Blend (Toro) $26. Fairly soft and fruity on first inspection, with some dusty notes to the nose along with a hint of wood. The palate shows cherry, plum, and tangy acids. It finishes dry and a bit oaky. Not a complex red, but solid enough. **86** *—M.S. (9/1/2004)*

DARIEN

Darien 2000 Crianza Tempranillo Blend (Rioja) $14. Slightly buttery and unstable on the nose, with popcorn and light raspberry aromas. More lightweight berry fruit comes forth on the palate, which is dominated by a dry tea-like quality. Clean but underwhelming. **84** *—M.S. (5/1/2004)*

Darien 2000 Selección Tempranillo Blend (Rioja) $32. Open and simple, with fresh red-fruit flavors prior to a soft but tart finish. There's just enough stuffing here to keep things afloat, yet it's best initially and thins as it opens up. **86** *—M.S. (5/1/2004)*

DE MULLER

De Muller 1998 Legitim Red Blend (Priorat) $15. **80** *—D.T. (4/1/2003)*

DESCENDIENTES DE J. PALACIOS

Descendientes de J. Palacios 2001 Corullón Villa Mencía (Bierzo) $40. This rather unique wine (made from Mencía) is at the vanguard of the Bierzo revival. It's earthy and leafy, with aromas of red plums and natural spice. The mouthfeel is perfect, as it's just lush and firm enough. Nearly explodes in the mouth, with fine French oak softening the blow. **92** *—M.S. (6/1/2005)*

DIEGO DE ALMAGRO

Diego de Almagro 1991 Gran Reserva Tempranillo (Valdepeñas) $19. **87** *—J.C. (8/1/2000)*

DINASTÍA VIVANCO

Dinastía Vivanco 1998 Reserva Tempranillo Blend (Rioja) $20. This new, showy winery in the heart of Rioja was founded by bulk brokers, and this wine still tastes as if were from the old stock. Some spice and leather aromas and then tart pie cherry and raspberry in the mouth. Not a sour, bad wine, but dull. **84** *—M.S. (9/1/2004)*

DO FERREIRO

Do Ferreiro 2003 Cepas Vellas Albariño (Rias Baixas) $33. From the outset, this beauty oozes character. The whole exceeds the parts by a sum of three, as the wine delivers full flavors, complexity, and a near Burgundian minerality. This is what great Albariño is about, even if it's from a hot vintage. Spicy yet thumping with guava, banana, and citrus. Simply delicious. **92 Editors' Choice** *—M.S. (6/1/2005)*

DOMECQ

Domecq NV La Ina Fino Sherry (Jerez) $14. La Ina always has its own likable style. It's fresh, with plenty of apple character, and always dry as a bone. Maybe it won't overwhelm or surprise, but if served properly chilled, La Ina always satisfies. A quintessential apéritif with tapas and finger foods. **88** *—M.S. (6/1/2005)*

DOMINIO DE ATUATA

Dominio de Atuata 2000 Tempranillo (Ribera del Duero) $30. Dense and meaty, with cured ham and earthy mineral notes. The rustic, untamed nose draws you in, but once you get inside things calm down. Yes, the palate's saturated, but it stops short of bowling you over. On the finish, cherry and chocolate flavors bring it home. From a Spanish owner/French winemaker duo. **89** *—M.S. (3/1/2004)*

DOMINIO DE EQUREN

Dominio de Equren 2001 Codice Tempranillo (Tierra Manchuela) $9. Overly sweet and syrupy you might say, but maple, caramel, and chocolate are often the types of flavors folks are seeking. The tannins are gritty, so much so that they almost run roughshod over some of the sublime characteristics hidden within. **85** *—M.S. (3/1/2004)*

Dominio de Equren 2001 Protocolo Tempranillo (Tierra Manchuela) $6. Subdued and earthy, with cool, compact red-fruit aromas. The palate offers brandied cherry, plum, and apple skin flavors. The finish is long, with coffee and chocolate along with some fatty oak. Has a lot going for it, but could use more focus. **86 Best Buy** *—M.S. (3/1/2004)*

Dominio de Equren 1999 Protocolo Blanca White Blend (Tierra Manchuela) $6. 86 *—M.M. (8/1/2000)*

DOMINIO DE PINGUS

Dominio de Pingus 2001 Flor de Pingus Tinto del Pais (Ribera del Duero) $50. Barely a step down from the more rare and pricey Pingus, the '01 Flor should fly off store shelves and restaurant wine lists. It's that good, starting with the intoxicating nose and moving through the pure palate and onto the marvelous finish. A wine that goes all the way, with spice, leather, and mounds of rich, ripe fruit. 93 Editors' Choice *—M.S. (6/1/2005)*

DOMINIO DE TARES

Dominio de Tares 2003 Mencía (Bierzo) $16. A real-deal, modern wine. Among the many imposters coming out of Spain, this beefy, ripe, muscled red tosses up cinnamon and earth before a free flow of plum, black cherry, and berry fruit. Thick, chewy, and balanced, with mounds of coffee and fudge waiting on the finish. Not subtle but a lot of fun to drink, especially given the price. 90 Editors' Choice *—M.S. (6/1/2005)*

Dominio de Tares 2002 Bembibre Mencía (Bierzo) $45. Lush on the nose, with wild game, smoke, and blackberry filling every void. Almost Syrah-like in its weight, more so than the other Mencía wines that are making a statement. Which only means that it's chewy, chocolaty, and creamy. Finishes slightly short, with bitter fudge and vanilla shadings. 91 *—M.S. (6/1/2005)*

DON PEDRO DE SOUTOMAIOR

Don Pedro de Soutomaior 2002 Albariño (Rias Baixas) $19. The dainty nose offers pound cake, citrus, and a laudable freshness, while the palate is forward and blasting with citrus and melon. Finishes with more melon. Possibly a touch flabby at the end, but still a good example of the type. 87 *—M.S. (9/1/2004)*

DON RAMÓN

Don Ramón 2002 Tempranillo (Rioja) $15. This co-op wine is almost a good deal, but ultimately it does not show enough depth or elegance to reach the next level. The nose is a touch stewy and lifeless, while the palate offers chewy raisin, plum, and berry. Flat on the finish, with a syrupy feel. 83 *—M.S. (6/1/2005)*

EL COPERO

El Copero 2004 Tinto Bobal (Valencia) $6. Simple and fruity, with red-cherry and candied aromas. The palate offers pie cherry and raspberry with a streak of acidity running through the center. Finishes light and zesty. Not much to it, but not bad. 83 *—M.S. (8/1/2005)*

El Copero 2001 White Blend (Valencia) $7. 82 *—D.T. (4/1/2003)*

EL COTO

El Coto 2001 Rosado Rosé Blend (Rioja) $9. 82 *—M.S. (10/1/2003)*

El Coto 1997 Coto de Imaz Reserva Tempranillo (Rioja) $18. 88 *—D.T. (4/1/2003)*

El Coto 2000 Crianza Tempranillo (Rioja) $12. 87 Best Buy *—M.S. (10/1/2003)*

El Coto 1998 Crianza Tempranillo (Rioja) $12. 85 *—M.M. (9/1/2002)*

El Coto 2001 Viura (Rioja) $9. 84 *—M.S. (10/1/2003)*

EL VINCULO

El Vinculo 1999 Red Blend (La Mancha) $21. 85 *—D.T. (4/1/2003)*

El Vinculo 2000 Crianza Tempranillo (La Mancha) $27. Aromas of charred beef, pepper, and raspberry start it off before giving way to a questionable grassiness. Flavors of blackberry, plum, and cassis carry the forward palate, which is nothing if not power-packed and forward. Ripe tannins are highly evident but they don't pound away. 87 *—M.S. (3/1/2004)*

El Vinculo 1999 Reserva Tempranillo (La Mancha) $19. This is a new wine made by Alejandro Fernandez of Pesquera in Ribera del Duero. It's clear, defined, and ripe, with earthy, spicy undercurrents supporting potent blackberry fruit. The chewy, deep palate is solid and saturated, leading into a coffee-tinged finish that carries echoes of chocolate. The tannins get larger with each passing minute; drink this with food. 88 *—M.S. (3/1/2004)*

EMILIO MORO

Emilio Moro 1997 Crianza Tempranillo (Ribera del Duero) $25. 89 *—M.M. (8/1/2000)*

Emilio Moro 2000 Crianza Tinto del Pais (Ribera del Duero) $28. Chunky and ripe, with natural leather and barnyard notes along with a bit of surface-sitting oak. The palate is jacked up and exciting, with deep black fruit, firm tannins and plenty of length. The finish is long and wide, with a burnt flavor note. Big-time verve and kick should maintain its following. 89 *—M.S. (3/1/2004)*

Emilio Moro 2002 Malleolus de Valderramiro Tinto del Pais (Ribera del Duero) $166. Undoubtedly powerful, but lovable. The nose is wholesome and complete, a blend of earth, coffee, and heavy black cherry and plum aromas. Broad on the palate, with deep levels of dark fruit mixed with copious French oak. A big-time success in '02, and proof that good wines can come from marginal vintages. 92 *—M.S. (6/1/2005)*

EMILIO ROJO

Emilio Rojo 2003 Blanco White Blend (Ribeiro) $35. A blend of four white grapes, including Albariño; this is an unconventional wine made in small quantities. Starts with cinnamon and anise aromas that morph toward curry. Plenty of full-bodied spiced pear and banana flavors in the center. Unlike most everything else; could even be better in a cooler vintage like the upcoming 2004. **89** *—M.S. (6/1/2005)*

ENATE

Enate 2002 Fermentado en Barrica de Roble Chardonnay (Somontano) $NA. Rich and creamy, but lacks zest and drive. The nose and palate offer sweet banana and oak, while the feel is almost too pillowy. Tastes more like a dessert than a dry white should. Still, it's neither bad nor poorly made. **85** *—M.S. (6/1/2005)*

ENRIQUE MENDOZA

Enrique Mendoza 2000 Reserva Santa Rosa Red Blend (Alicanté) $35. Dark and intense is this Cabernet-Merlot-Syrah blend. The nose offers smoky leather and hot earth, but also a sweet perfume dominated by violets. Quite drinkable now, with soft tannins and easygoing black fruit. Best to get this one over the next year or two, before the fruit fades. **90** *—M.S. (6/1/2005)*

ESPERANZA

Esperanza 2003 Verdejo (Rueda) $10. A bit fuller than the Verdejo-Viura blend but every bit as functional and satisfying. Melon, pineapple, and passion fruit aromas are full rather than crisp, while the grapefruit and orange flavors sizzle. More than decent length, structure, and finish. **87** *—M.S. (12/31/2004)*

ESTOLA

Estola 1991 Gran Reserva Red Blend (La Mancha) $16. **86** *—M.S. (11/1/2002)*

FAUSTINO

Faustino 1994 Faustino de Autor Reserva Tempranillo (Rioja) $50. A lean, structured wine of great elegance and finesse. Begins with aromas of leather and vanilla, folding hints of plum, coffee, earth, and pepper. Tarter and redder on the finish, with cranberry and herb notes lingering delicately. Substantially better than a bottle reviewed in the March issue. **91** *(5/1/2004)*

Faustino 1999 Faustino de Crianza Tempranillo (Rioja) $12. There's much to dig into here; poised berry fruit dominates the palate, with some plum and raspberry flavors present. Vanilla and chocolate notes grace the finish, which is lasting and sturdy. **86** *—M.S. (3/1/2004)*

Faustino 1999 Faustino V Reserva Tempranillo (Rioja) $19. Rusting in color, but showing some of the positive signs of maturing Rioja. For instance, the bouquet provides spiced raisin, dried plum, and cinnamon, and together the nose is as old-fashioned as it comes. Dried cherry and apricot flavors mix with pepper and tobacco on the palate, while the finish is warm and accented by vanilla. **87** *—M.S. (10/1/2005)*

Faustino 2003 Faustino VII Tempranillo Blend (Rioja) $11. A bit leafy and smoky, with snappy red fruit and basic spice notes. Very simple and traditional, with firm acidity. Will cut through most foods like a hot knife through butter, and it's fresh. **84** *—M.S. (10/1/2005)*

Faustino 1994 Faustino I Rioja Gran Reserva Tempranillo (Rioja) $26. **92** **Editors' Choice** *(5/1/2001)*

Faustino 1970 Faustino I Rioja Gran Reserva Tempranillo (Rioja) $125. **92** *(5/1/2001)*

Faustino 1999 Faustino V Rosado (Rioja) $12. **84** *(5/1/2001)*

Faustino 1995 Faustino V Rioja Riserva Tempranillo (Rioja) $17. **89** *(5/1/2001)*

Faustino 2003 Faustino V Blanco Seco Viura (Rioja) $10. Dry and clean, with apple and tarragon on the nose. The palate deals crisp green apple and nectarine, with a hint of butterscotch and corn. Finishes crisp and generally fresh, with touches of butter and citrus rind. **85** **Best Buy** *—M.S. (11/15/2005)*

Faustino 2000 Faustino VII Tempranillo (Rioja) $10. Spicy and lean, with light pickled notes. In the mouth, however, it's got pure fruit and adequate spice. It's on the basic side, but the mouthfeel is good and it tastes fresh and lively. **86** *—M.S. (3/1/2004)*

FELIX CALLEJO

Felix Callejo 2002 Selección de Vinedos de La Familia Tempranillo (Ribera del Duero) $108. The bouquet starts out with promising whiffs of molasses, bacon, and black fruit but it loses form quickly, resulting in aromas of menthol and funky beet. In the mouth, it's ultra-sweet and candied, and the tannins are jackhammer hard. **84** *—M.S. (11/15/2005)*

FELIX SOLIS

Felix Solis 2001 Los Molinos Tempranillo (Valdepeñas) $7. **85** **Best Buy** *—M.S. (11/1/2002)*

Felix Solis 1998 Viña Albali Los Molinos Crianza Tempranillo (Valdepeñas) $9. **82** *—M.S. (11/1/2002)*

FILLABOA

Fillaboa 2002 Finca Monte Alto Albariño (Rias Baixas) $27. Floral and mildly leesy, with pungent aromas of green apple, citrus, and honey. For anyone looking for steely, pure Albariño, the single-vineyard Fillaboa Monte Alto is the ticket. The fruit is crisp and zesty, the acidity just right. And the finish runs a mile long. **91** **Editors' Choice** *—M.S. (6/1/2005)*

FINCA ALLENDE

Finca Allende 2001 Aurus Tempranillo (Rioja) $184. Miguel Angel de Gregorio makes wines that match his exuberant personality, and Aurus, with 85% old-vine Tempranillo and 15% Graciano, is his premier offering. The 2001's exotic nose pumps licorice, clove, nutmeg, and vanilla on top of the ripest black-fruit aromas going. With pillowy tannins, unmatched breadth and huge flavors of blackberry, plum, and chocolate, there's no denying this wine's quality and stature. **96 Editors' Choice** —*M.S. (6/1/2005)*

Finca Allende 2001 Calvario Tempranillo Blend (Rioja) $88. Yet another portly, gorgeous wine from Allende, one that well serves the single-vineyard train of thought. Entirely international in style, with pure plum, blackberry, and vanilla aromas and flavors. Super concentrated and unctuous, with soft tannins and an all-out finish. And the acidity is as integrated and proper as possible. **94 Editors' Choice** —*M.S. (6/1/2005)*

Finca Allende 1997 Aurus Red Blend (Rioja) $155. 91 —*M.M. (11/1/2002)*

Finca Allende 1999 Tempranillo (Rioja) $20. High-toned and forward, with lilac and nutmeg adding to the gorgeous bouquet. The palate is huge and ripe, with ample plum, blackberry, and coffee flavors. Finishes round with enveloping yet soft tannins. If you like your reds big and polished, than proceed happily and without caution. **91 Editors' Choice** —*M.S. (3/1/2004)*

Finca Allende 2000 Calvario Tempranillo (Rioja) $50. Inky and saturated, which makes sense given that it's from vines planted more than 50 years ago. Condensed blackberry aromas are a hint that big fruit is to come. And it does, in the form of a berry cornucopia accented by lavender and clove. Some might find it a touch syrupy and jacked up. But if you like big-shouldered modern wines, you'll be all over this. **91** —*M.S. (3/1/2004)*

Finca Allende 2000 Special Reserve Dealu Mare Ploiesti White Blend (Rioja) $18. Golden in color, with a waxy nose that's on the rich, creamy side. The mouth deals some lemon and apple, a hint of green herb, and butter. The finish is moderate and enveloping, with a soft feel. Good but fading; maybe it's best to wait for the 2001. **86** —*M.S. (3/1/2004)*

FINCA ANTIGUA

Finca Antigua 2001 Crianza Red Blend (La Mancha) $10. Not too refined, but still pretty tasty. The palate offers chewy cherry and raspberry fruit, while the finish is spicy and zesty to the point that it creates a tingle. Somewhat sugary, but definitely an easy one to drink. **84** —*M.S. (6/1/2005)*

Finca Antigua 2003 Tempranillo (La Mancha) $10. Good size but struggles a bit. The nose is a touch green and murky, but below the surface there's solid raspberry and plum fruit. Shows some oak and barnyard throughout, and runs fairly smooth through the finish. **83** —*M.S. (11/15/2005)*

FINCA LUZÓN

Finca Luzón 2002 Merlot (Jumilla) $8. For several years we've been impressed with this under-$10 Merlot, and this year the quality and purity are once again exemplary. Aromas of smoke, mineral and sweet leather set the stage for amplified cherry, raspberry, plum and chocolate flavors. A medium-bodied but healthy and spicy finish secures the final favorable votes. **88 Best Buy** —*M.S. (3/1/2004)*

Finca Luzón 2000 Merlot (Jumilla) $10. 86 —*M.M. (4/1/2002)*

Finca Luzón 2002 Altos de Luzón Red Blend (Jumilla) $10. This wine comes in two waves. The first is youthful and aggressive; it carries maple and sawdust aromas, and tons of powerful plum, cassis, and smoky oak. The next wave is textured and chocolaty, and a little bit dark. Overall, it might not ooze elegance, but it's certainly lively and big. The blend is Monastrell, Cabernet, and Tempranillo. **89 Best Buy** —*M.S. (3/1/2004)*

FINCA MINATEDA

Finca Minateda 2001 Tinto Roble Garnacha (Viño de la Tierra de Castilla) $13. Sweet and marinated at first, with a certain stewy richness. The palate is round and plump, with good berry and plum characteristics. Open-grained wood and vanilla notes dominate the finish. **85** —*M.S. (10/1/2005)*

FINCA SANDOVAL

Finca Sandoval 2002 Viño Tinto Syrah (Tierra Manchuela) $39. Local wine critic Victor de la Serna is the man behind this Syrah from central Spain, and you have to admire its bright purple color and sweet plum and black-cherry flavor profile. Leaner in the middle than the downright gooey 2001, which means it's less jammy and more racy. With 7% Monastrell. **90** —*M.S. (6/1/2005)*

FINCA ZUBASTÌA

Finca Zubastìa 2003 ADA Tempranillo Blend (Navarra) $10. Extracted and raw, but with enough rustic country charm to make it worth a go. Four major grapes were thrown together, yielding cherry, beet, and tomato aromas. The palate is ripe and edgy, with red plum and herb flavors. A tight, basic wine with ample tannin and acid. **86 Best Buy** —*M.S. (6/1/2005)*

FLEUR DE NUIT

Fleur de Nuit NV Brut (Cava) $7. Pedestrian yet entirely solid, with nice citrus and apple flavors. A very easy wine to understand, with seltzer and grapefruit on the finish along with a slight twinge of mushroom. Good cava that will go down easy. **85 Best Buy** —*M.S. (12/15/2005)*

SPAIN

FORTIUS

Fortius 1999 Tierra de Estella Merlot (Navarra) $12. **85** *—M.S. (8/1/2003)*

FRA GUERAU

Fra Guerau 2002 Red Blend (Montsant) $12. This well-priced red from Tarragona shows a glimpse of what the Montsant region can produce. The nose is all red fruit, with a splinter of oak. The palate is chunky and easy as it deals blackberry and raspberry in spades. Chocolate and mocha on the thick finish should please the sugar mavens. **87 Best Buy** *—M.S. (6/1/2005)*

FRANCESC SANCHEZ BAS

Francesc Sanchez Bas 2001 Montgarnatx Garnacha (Priorat) $38. Open, round, and clean, with a lovely bouquet and an even better palate that offers strawberry, plum, and a full blast of creamy oak. Turns soft and friendly upon airing, and overall it provides complexity along with straightforward likeability. **91** *—M.S. (5/1/2004)*

Francesc Sanchez Bas 2000 Montsalvat Red Blend (Priorat) $60. A typically masculine Priorat red, one with beef jerky, leather, and reduced blackberry on the nose, and then a fully jazzed palate with lively berry fruit, chocolate, and mocha. It's not soft, but it remains round and lush, and the finish is warm and spunky. **92** *—M.S. (5/1/2004)*

FREIXENET

Freixenet NV Brut de Noirs (Cava) $8. **84** *—J.C. (12/31/2003)*

Freixenet 1999 Brut Nature (Cava) $NA. Tart and sour, with unripe apple flavors joined by earth and saddle leather. **81** *—J.C. (1/1/2004)*

Freixenet NV Carta Nevada Brut (Cava) $9. Neutral yet clean, with pineapple and lemon-lime on both the nose and palate. Nothing out of the ordinary here. It's exactly as it has been for years: bubbly, a touch sweet, and satisfying. **86 Best Buy** *—M.S. (12/15/2005)*

Freixenet NV Carta Nevada Semi-Dry (Cava) $9. The sweet and waxy aromas are similar to what you might get from an aromatized candle. The palate is sugary and soda-like, with flavors of sweetened lime and apple wedges. And the finish seems a bit like 7-Up. Best for those who like a sweeter bubbly. **86 Best Buy** *—M.S. (12/15/2004)*

Freixenet NV Cordon Negro Brut (Cava) $9. **85 Best Buy** *—J.C. (12/31/2003)*

Freixenet NV Cordon Negro Extra Dry (Cava) $10. For a well-made sparkling wine with balance, flavor, and a bit of sweetness, look no further. This one features pretty apple, lemon, and yeast aromas prior to honey, melon, and apple flavors. Finishes smooth and stylish, proving that a cava can be slightly sweet yet rock solid. **88 Best Buy** *—M.S. (12/15/2004)*

Freixenet NV Spumante Doux (Cava) $10. Sweet and artificial, with a strong hint of Dijon mustard, which seems totally out of place. Not sure who this is aimed at. **80** *—M.S. (12/15/2005)*

FUENTE DEL CONDE

Fuente del Conde 2002 Rosado (Cigales) $9. Minty-fresh, with aromatic hints of herbs, peach, and bread dough. With a round palate propped up by citrus, berry flavors, and modest acidity, this wine delivers the goods—but only for the short term. Drink this Tempranillo-based rosé now. **86 Best Buy** *—M.S. (3/1/2004)*

FUENTES

Fuentes 2000 Gran Clos de J.M. Fuentes Red Blend (Priorat) $50. A massive wine with lovely black fruit wrapped is a veneer of classy charred oak. A bomber but a precision one. The plum and blackberry fruit is vital and forceful, while the finish is big, aggressive, supremely built, and long-lasting. The epitome of brickyard Priorat, so give it a year or two before opening. **93 Editors' Choice** *—M.S. (3/1/2004)*

GAGO

Gago 2000 Dehesa Gago Tinta de Toro (Toro) $12. **88** *—M.M. (4/1/2002)*

GONDOMAR DEL REINO

Gondomar Del Reino 1996 Gran Reserva Tempranillo (Ribera del Duero) $43. Hard to penetrate, with some funk. Airing reveals unchained fruit with some green flavors at the core. Stays hard and medicinal, with cherry, spice, and burnt grass. Not in line with the best of the region. **83** *—M.S. (10/1/2005)*

GONZALEZ BYASS

Gonzalez Byass NV Noe Muy Viejo Pedro Ximénez (Jerez) $NA. The crude oil of PX Sherries, Noe won't appeal to everyone. For starters, it's thick as molasses, with heavy caramel and toffee aromas and flavors. And while there's nothing not to like about caramel and toffee, this wine is fat and chewy, arguably too viscous to drink with ease. **88** *—M.S. (6/1/2005)*

GOSALBEZ ORTI

Gosalbez Orti 2001 Qubel Barrica Tempranillo Blend (Viños de Madrid) $47. Pure blueberry and blackberry pour forth from this dark-as-night Tempranillo, one of tiny production made in organic fashion. Wonderful texture, excellent fruit, and a smoky, rubbery finish announce it as a major leaguer. Not overly expansive on the finish, but lovely and serious throughout. **92 Editors' Choice** *—M.S. (9/1/2004)*

GRAMONA

Gramona 1998 III Lustros Gran Reserva (Cava) $NA. It is said that at five years a good cava starts to change for the better, and this seems to be an example of that. Classic aromas of petrol, baked apple, and spiced ham precede a sly palate that's both soft and deep. Mild citrus flavors are topped by vanilla and white pepper. Mature. **91** *—M.S. (6/1/2005)*

GRAN CERMEÑO

Gran Cermeño 1996 Reserva Tinta de Toro (Toro) $19. **91 Editors' Choice** *—M.M. (9/1/2002)*

GRAN METS

Gran Mets 2001 Red Blend (Montsant) $15. A fine blend of Cabernet Sauvignon, Merlot, and Tempranillo. Aromas of cherry, licorice, and nutmeg are inviting, as is the palate of tobacco, cherry, and blackberry. The finish is tight and fundamentally sound, with a hint of creaminess. **88** *—M.S. (5/1/2004)*

GRAN ORISTAN

Gran Oristan 1995 Gran Reserva Red Blend (La Mancha) $14. **85** *—D.T. (4/1/2002)*

GRAN VEREMA

Gran Verema 2000 Old Vines Reserva Tempranillo (Utiel-Requena) $9. Light and dry, with mild aromas of mint and red fruit. Forward and tart, with lively berry and cherry flavors. Not thrilling, but solid and balanced. From the Gandia family. **84** *—M.S. (10/1/2005)*

GRANJA NTRA, SRA. DE REMELLURI

Granja Ntra, Sra. de Remelluri 2001 Remelluri Blanco White Blend (Rioja) $40. Flowery, with a nice mix of sweetness, dried apricots, and vanilla. Flavors of banana, papaya, and apple dominate a textured, modestly rich palate. Remelluri blends about a half-dozen grapes together for its white Rioja, and the result is smooth, albeit not overly powerful. **88** *—M.S. (3/1/2004)*

GUELBENZU

Guelbenzu 2001 Azul Red Blend (Navarra) $13. Clean and bouncy, with fresh berry aromas. This is a pretty, lighter-framed red with expressive cherry, plum, and oak all in a row. It finishes chewy and rich enough, but it's still in balance and not overpowering. All in all, it's a good blend with proper feel and a full taste. **87** *—M.S. (3/1/2004)*

Guelbenzu 2001 EVO Red Blend (Navarra) $20. Broad-shouldered and bold, but like all Guelbenzu wines, it applies the brakes where necessary. Herbal, terroir-driven characteristics pop up in between the red berry, plum and oak flavors, giving it some boost and nuance. And it gets better with airing, as it delivers coffee and buttery oak at the end. **88** *—M.S. (3/1/2004)*

Guelbenzu 1998 EVO Red Blend (Navarra) $22. **89** *—C.S. (4/1/2002)*

Guelbenzu 1998 Tempranillo Blend (Navarra) $13. Toasty and smoky, this is a big, bulky wine loaded with burnt sugar and oak. The black cherry flavors blend in vanilla, cinnamon, and allspice, along with earth and herbs on the finish. It has nice components; they just aren't all going the same direction. **84** *(1/1/2004)*

GUITIÁN

Guitián 2002 Sobre Lias Godello (Valdeorras) $NA. An example of a richer-styled Godello, a grape you'll only find in this small region. The nose and body are both full, and despite no oak aging, there are licorice and vanilla shadings to the ripe apple and banana flavors. Something to chew on. Unique. **90** *—M.S. (6/1/2005)*

HACIENDA LA CONCORDIA

Hacienda La Concordia 1999 Reserva Tempranillo (Rioja) $25. Soft and simple, with a dry, spicy nose that's ultimately light. Adequate raspberry, cherry, and plum-skin flavors turn astringent and sour as the acidity rears up toward the finish. **83** *—M.S. (5/1/2004)*

HACIENDA MONASTERIO

Hacienda Monasterio 1995 Crianza Tempranillo (Ribera del Duero) $30. **92** *(11/15/1999)*

HACIENDAS DURIUS

Haciendas Durius 2003 Alto Duero Viura-Sauvignon Blanc (Viño de la Tierra de Castilla y León) $13. Quite light in color and mute on the nose, with faint apple and honeydew flavors on the smooth but soft palate. Lacks the drive normally associated with these grapes. Despite that, it tastes okay. **84** *—M.S. (3/1/2005)*

HEREDEROS DE MARQUÉS DE RISCAL

Herederos de Marqués de Riscal 2004 Sauvignon (Rueda) $8. Moderately forward, with smooth, floral, comfortable aromas. The palate is loaded with citrus, mostly lime but also some grapefruit. Rock solid on the finish, with acidic snap and mineral notes. A perfect apéritif white. **87** *—M.S. (10/1/2005)*

HERENCIA ANTICA

Herencia Antica 2000 Reserva Tempranillo (Utiel-Requena) $8. Brambly and pickled, with monotone flavors. Juicy on the palate, but unrefined. Overall there's a lot of acid and not much clarity or depth. **81** *—M.S. (10/1/2005)*

SPAIN

HERMANOS LURTON

Hermanos Lurton 2004 Rosado Tempranillo Blend (Viño de la Tierra de Castilla y León) $11. The fresh berry, red licorice, and cherry Lifesaver aromas will make you think you've placed your nose in a bushel of summer fruit, and while this rosé from the warm plains of central Spain looks more red than pink, it shows a bit of stoniness and a ton of clean, attractive flavors. It's a blend of Garnacha and Tempranillo from vineyards around Valladolid, and it will appeal to those who prefer a bit of meat on the bones of their dry pink wines. **88 Best Buy** *—M.S. (11/15/2005)*

HERMANOS SASTRE

Hermanos Sastre 2000 Roble Tempranillo (Ribera del Duero) $14. 88 Best Buy *—C.S. (11/1/2002)*

HUGUET DE CAN FEIXES

Huguet de Can Feixes 1999 Brut Nature Cava Reserve (Cava) $18. 85 *—M.S. (12/31/2002)*

Huguet de Can Feixes 2000 Negre Selección Red Blend (Penedès) $22. Compact and pungent, and borderline ungenerous at first. Once it opens up, there's ripe cherry and berry fruit pumped forward by zippy acidity. Toward the back it grows darker and more masculine, and at the very end the tannins get tough. **86** *—M.S. (3/1/2004)*

IBERNOBLE

Ibernoble 1995 Reserva Tempranillo (Ribera del Duero) $42. 87 *—J.C. (11/1/2001)*

IGLESIA VIEJA

Iglesia Vieja 1997 La Purisima Red Blend (Yecla) $13. 87 *—D.T. (4/1/2002)*

INFINITUS

Infinitus 2004 Syrah (Viño de la Tierra de Castilla) $7. Purple in color, but clumsy from start to finish. The nose is oily and loaded with balsamic notes along with berry jam. Prune and chocolate flavors are awkward and aggressive. Extract over balance is the formula. **81** *—M.S. (11/15/2005)*

INURRIETA

Inurrieta 2002 Norte (Navarra) $13. This wine is making its American debut this fall. It's a blend of Merlot and Cabernet, with ripe plum and blackberry aromas along with balsamic notes. Flavor-packed and round; a wine to keep in mind when "value" is what you're after. **88** *—M.S. (10/1/2004)*

J. & F. LURTON

J. & F. Lurton 2001 El Albar Excelencia Tempranillo (Toro) $43. Made in the modern, ripe, soft, extracted style. The nose exudes maple, cinnamon, and chocolate but not as much fruit as you might hope for. Big plum and chocolate flavors along with a thick, smoky palate make for an easygoing, 21st-century wine. Not flawless, but real nice. **89** *—M.S. (8/1/2005)*

J. & F. Lurton 2001 Campo Eliseo Tinta de Toro (Toro) $50. A new wine from François and Jacques Lurton and partners Michel and Dany Rolland. It's expectedly dark, with exotic spice aromas, stewed stone fruits, and a certain sauciness to the nose. Very dense and textured, with plum, blackberry, and fudge flavors. Finishes thick but short, with some bitterness at the end. **88** *—M.S. (9/1/2004)*

JANÉ VENTURA

Jané Ventura 2000 Finca Els Camps Macabeo (Penedès) $21. 82 *—M.S. (11/1/2002)*

JARRARTE

Jarrarte 1998 Red Blend (Rioja) $24. 89 *—M.M. (11/1/2002)*

JAUME LLOPART ALEMANY

Jaume Llopart Alemany NV Artesanal Brut Nature (Cava) $14. 83 *(12/31/2001)*

JAUME SERRA

Jaume Serra NV Seco Reserva (Penedès) $9. 82 *(12/15/2000)*

Jaume Serra 2000 Estate Bottled Chardonnay (Penedès) $9. 82 *—M.S. (11/1/2002)*

JEAN LEÓN

Jean León 1998 Cabernet Sauvignon (Penedès) $26. Attractive to the nose, as it offers a smooth, integrated blend of dry fruit, vanilla, and spice. Equally dry on the palate, with cherry and plum and whole lot of hammering tannins. Fairly interesting and rustic, and firm. While not old or fading it's probably not improving either. **87** *—M.S. (12/31/2004)*

Jean León 1996 Reserva Cabernet Sauvignon (Penedès) $23. 88 *(2/1/2003)*

Jean León 2002 Chardonnay (Penedès) $26. Gold in color, with a cheese-filled nose that offers only a modicum of pear and butter. Tastes lemony and bland, with citrus on the palate and finish. **81** *—M.S. (12/31/2004)*

Jean León 2002 Terrasola Chardonnay (Catalonia) $14. Funky and strange is this blend of 85% Chardonnay and 15% Garnacha

Blanca. On the tongue it's lean and citrusy, without much composition. **80** *—M.S. (12/31/2004)*

Jean León 2001 Merlot (Penedès) $26. Big and round, with heavy aromas of smoke and tar. Lively, with wild cherry and berry flavors, full tannins and ample zest. Chocolaty on the finish, and oaky throughout. **86** *—M.S. (12/31/2004)*

JM ORTEA

JM Ortea 2000 Crianza Tempranillo (Ribera del Guadiana) $23. Cola, mushroom, and some cheesy oak make for a scattered nose. Better in the mouth, where plum and berry flavors are full if a bit heavy. Sort of roasted and reduced, but with air it softens and ultimately rounds into form. **83** *—M.S. (10/1/2005)*

JOAN D'ANGUERA

Joan D'Anguera 2002 Finca L'Argata Red Blend (Montsant) $25. Dark as night, with smooth, deep aromas of earth, leather, and black fruit. It's a blend of four fairly common red grapes, and together they yield pleasant plum, blackberry, and other dark-fruit flavors. Sizable and tannic, but impressive for its clarity and simplicity. **88** *—M.S. (10/1/2005)*

Joan D'Anguera 2000 Finca L'Argatà Red Blend (Montsant) $21. Full-force blackberry, cherry, and licorice create a lovely bouquet, which is followed nicely by cherry, plum, and additional berry flavors. The finish is broad, meaty, and firm, with fine tannins. **90 Editors' Choice** *—M.S. (3/1/2004)*

Joan D'Anguera 2002 La Planella Red Blend (Montsant) $19. Saturated and dense, but youthful as well as a few shades shy of refined. There's herbal essence to the flavor profile, but there's also bold and tasty cassis and black plum. The finish is chewy and a bit spicy, and overall you'd have to label it rich and full. **87** *—M.S. (3/1/2004)*

Joan D'Anguera 1998 Vi Dolç Red Blend (Tarragona) $70. **88** *—C.S. (4/1/2002)*

Joan D'Anguera 2000 El Bugader Syrah (Montsant) $50. Here's an excellent wine from a high-flying subsection of Tarragona. It's rich, inky, and thick, but impeccably balanced. Pulsating dark-berry fruit carries the nose and palate, while chocolate comes on late. Polished and intense, with all elements squarely in place. **92** *—M.S. (3/1/2004)*

JOAN SIMÓ

Joan Simó 2000 Les Eres Vinyes Velles Red Blend (Priorat) $59. This blend is 55% old-vines Garnacha, 30% ancient Carignan, and the rest Cabernet. It's sweet and rich, with aromas of red fruit and a hint of coconut. The palate is classic old-vines stuff: cassis, red plum, beet, and plenty of persistence. Yet despite it's old-vines status, it still tastes young and snappy. **89** *—M.S. (3/1/2004)*

JULIA ROCH E HIJOS

Julia Roch e Hijos 2000 Las Gravas Red Blend (Jumilla) $19. Deep and exotic, with fine black fruit and perfume on the nose. Flavors of black cherry and blackberry sing a pretty song, while the finish is racy and firm, and arguably a bit lean. Among all the big bruisers out there, it's nice to see a juicier, fruitier wine that doesn't hit like a battering ram. That said, this is no lightweight. **89** *—M.S. (3/1/2004)*

JULIÁN CHIVITE

Julián Chivite 2000 Colección 125 Chardonnay (Navarra) $50. **90** *(4/1/2003)*

Julián Chivite 2002 Colección 125 Vendimia Tardìa Moscatel (Navarra) $40. The epitome of freshness and complexity is on offer in this delicious late-harvest Moscatel from Navarra's most innovative bodega. Lemon peel, wild flowers, and piercing apricot and peach aromas carry the ultra pure nose. There's nothing funky or odd about this barrel-fermented wine; it will appeal to almost everyone who likes a well-made sweet white. **92** *—M.S. (6/1/2005)*

Julián Chivite 2001 Colección 125 Reserva Tempranillo Blend (Navarra) $NA. A masterful mixture of Tempranillo, Merlot, and Cabernet Sauvignon. Aromas of wood smoke, blackberry, and plum. An open wine for near-term drinking. Sweet and rich at the core, while pure cacao darkens the tail end. **92** *—M.S. (10/1/2004)*

Julián Chivite 1999 Colección 125 Reserva Tempranillo Blend (Navarra) $46. **90** *(4/1/2003)*

Julián Chivite 2000 Señorio de Arinzano Tempranillo Blend (Navarra) $NA. **93 Cellar Selection** *(4/1/2003)*

JUVÉ Y CAMPS

Juvé y Camps NV Reserva de La Familia Brut Nature (Penedès) $17. **86** *—S.H. (12/15/2000)*

Juvé y Camps 1995 Reserva de La Familia Natural (Penedès) $18. **90** *—G.D. (12/15/1999)*

Juvé y Camps 2001 Reserva de La Familia Brut Nature(Cava) $20. Quite hard on the nose, with classic petrol aromas that almost smell of rubber cement. Tough and tight on the palate; it takes some effort to penetrate. Once inside there's crisp apple and lime zest. A true "nature" in every sense. **87** *—M.S. (6/1/2005)*

LA LEGUA

La Legua 1998 Reserva Tempranillo (Cigales) $19. **89** *—M.S. (8/1/2003)*

SPAIN

LA RIOJA ALTA

La Rioja Alta 1994 Gran Reserva 904 Tempranillo (Rioja) $53. Leaner than ideal on the nose, with hot aromas of leather, earth, and peach pit. A bit sharp in flavor, showing more pie cherry and apricot than anything else. Still a classic, however, but best be prepared for tea and juice notes more than beef and brawn. **88** *—M.S. (9/1/2004)*

La Rioja Alta 1998 Vina Alberdi Reserva Tempranillo (Rioja) $23. Rather thin and transparent to the eye, but that lightness doesn't translate into it being a thin, nothing wine. Just the opposite: It's loaded with leather, cranberry, and tea aromas and brisk cherry and cranberry flavors. Some chocolate on the finish adds heft to this old-school wine that really seems to have been made to go with food. **88** *—M.S. (3/1/2004)*

La Rioja Alta 1990 Vina Ardanza Reserva Tempranillo (Rioja) $27. **86** *—J.C. (11/15/1999)*

LACATUS

Lacatus 2001 Tempranillo (Penedès) $7. The nose kicks up some acetone, and beyond that it's all about piercing raspberry aromas. The palate is simple and drying, mostly due to hard tannins that overwhelm the fruit. The finish, thus, is just as hard and tough to fight through. **81** *—M.S. (3/1/2004)*

Lacatus NV Semi Seco (Cava) $12. Clean but quiet aromas lead to sweet flavors, predominantly candied peach, cantaloupe, and dried apricot. Fairly lively in the mouth, almost to the point of being too bubbly. Overall it tastes good even if it's jumpy. **85** *—M.S. (12/15/2005)*

LAS GRAVAS

Las Gravas 1999 Red Blend (Jumilla) $18. **85** *—M.M. (4/1/2002)*

LAURONA

Laurona 2000 6 Vinyes de Laurona Red Blend (Montsant) $45. A millennium wine that's now in fine form. It's a typical Garnacha-Cariñena blend that runs heavy on Garnacha. The bouquet is strong and evolved, with leather and mineral along with aromas of crushed flower petals, asphalt, and earth. Excellent fruit quality in the mouth; vivid with raspberry and black pepper. 800 cases made. **90** *—M.S. (10/1/2005)*

LEALTANZA

Lealtanza 2001 Crianza Tempranillo (Rioja) $20. Roasted and leathery but not that bright. The palate is zesty and chock full of nondescript red fruit. The finish is similar, while overall that tannins are firm if a bit spiky. **84** *—M.S. (11/15/2005)*

LEGARIS

Legaris 2002 Crianza Tinto Fino (Ribera del Duero) $17. Jammy aromas with a lot of bramble make for a jumbled nose. The palate is thin and racy, with nondescript flavors that veer toward cherry. Finishes overtly buttery and cheesy, a result of too much oak being applied to a wine that couldn't handle it. **83** *—M.S. (10/1/2005)*

Legaris 2000 Crianza Tempranillo (Ribera del Duero) $15. Sweet and ripe, and a touch aggressive. That said, the spicy pepper and blackberry palate is satisfying. The finish offers vanilla, black pepper, and wood resin. Very plump and fruity, with chocolaty edges. Definitely a good Ribera red, even if it comes in below the cream of the region. **87** *—M.S. (3/1/2004)*

LLOPART

Llopart 1994 Brut Leopardi (Cava) $26. **85** *(12/31/2001)*

LORIÑON

Loriñon 1997 Gran Reserva Tempranillo (Rioja) $34. Lean yet still fresh, with punchy herbal aromas of tree bark, dried fruits, and burnt grass. A bit stripped of its power by now, but still tossing up strawberry and cherry flavors in front of snappy finishing notes of nectarine and pie cherry. An old-style wine with more acidity than flesh. **86** *—M.S. (10/1/2005)*

Loriñon 2001 Crianza Tempranillo Blend (Rioja) $13. From Bodegas Bretón, this medium-weight red is a touch stewy, with peanut and black-olive aromas along with red licorice and Tootsie Roll. The palate offers strawberry and red cherry, while the finish is surprisingly tangy, with a shock of overt acidity. **85** *—M.S. (6/1/2005)*

LOS MONTEROS

Los Monteros 2004 Blanco White Blend (Valencia) $10. Offers big floral aromas along with scents of honeysuckle and lemon zest. Mango, pineapple, and lime flavors are crisp and clean, while the palate is a bit acidic and sharp, but entirely refreshing. **86 Best Buy** *—M.S. (8/1/2005)*

LUSCO

Lusco 2003 Pazo Piñeiro Albariño (Rias Baixas) $35. Impeccably clean, with light tropical fruit gracing the bouquet. A wine that's better than the sum of its parts; the palate is lemony fresh and satisfying, while the overall impression is that of elegance and simplicity. Perfectly good but not overly flavorful. **88** *—M.S. (6/1/2005)*

LUSCO DO MIÑO

Lusco do Miño 2000 Albariño (Rias Baixas) $20. **89** *—M.M. (9/1/2002)*

MAJAZUL

Majazul 1999 Crianza Tempranillo (Mentrida) $13. **82** *—D.T. (4/1/2003)*

MANYANA

Manyana 2003 Tempranillo (Cariñena) $7. Weedy and leafy, with penetrating aromas of rhubarb and burning hayfield. Never finds much fruit or style, as it finishes with a bland, raspy burn. **80** *—M.S. (8/1/2005)*

MARQUÉS DE ALELLA

Marqués de Alella 1999 White Blend (Alella) $10. **87** *(8/1/2000)*

MARQUES DE ARIENZO

Marqués de Arienzo 1999 Crianza Tempranillo (Rioja) $10. The bouquet is mostly sweet and fresh, with just the slightest hint of field greens. Adequate strawberry and raspberry fruit carries the palate toward a rubbery, spicy finish that brings pepper at the end. Easy and lean, with a good enough mouthfeel. **85** *—M.S. (3/1/2004)*

Marqués de Arienzo 1994 Gran Reserva Tempranillo (Rioja) $25. **90 Editors' Choice** *—M.M. (9/1/2002)*

Marqués de Arienzo 1996 Reserva Tempranillo (Rioja) $16. **84** *—M.M. (9/1/2002)*

MARQUÉS DE CÁCERES

Marqués de Cáceres 1992 Rioja Reserva Tempranillo (Rioja) $18. **88** *—J.C. (11/15/1999)*

Marqués de Cáceres 2004 Dry Rosé Tempranillo Blend (Rioja) $8. Chill it down and let it flow. That's the one and only secret to enjoying this textbook, inexpensive rosado from Spain. Aromas of red licorice, dried cherries, and strawberries are fresh and lucid, as is the crystal-clean palate. Spicy and wispy on the finish; will work with almost any salad or sandwich in your picnic basket. **88 Best Buy** *—M.S. (8/1/2005)*

Marqués de Cáceres 1998 Tempranillo Blend (Rioja) $12. **89 Best Buy** *—S.H. (11/15/2002)*

Marqués de Cáceres 1999 Rosé (Rioja) $7. **84** *—M.M. (8/1/2000)*

Marqués de Cáceres 2003 Dry Rosé (Rioja) $7. Round and fleshy, with bold aromatic notes of strawberry and watermelon candies. Finishes short. **84** *(10/1/2004)*

Marqués de Cáceres 1996 Gaudium Gran Viño Tempranillo Blend (Rioja) $60. Cáceres's alta expressión wine gets the Full Monty: old vines (averaging 70 years of age), malolactic fermentation in new French oak, microxygenation. The result is a creamy, supple, thoroughly modern wine that blends black cherries with hints of tobacco and vanilla. **90** *(10/1/2004)*

Marqués de Cáceres 1994 Gran Reserva Tempranillo Blend (Rioja) $25. One of the big differences between Cáceres and its competitors is a reliance on French rather than American oak. This gran reserva spent more than two years in barrel, and it shows wonderful leather, vanilla, and tobacco shadings layered over red plum fruit. A fully mature Rioja that offers good value. **90 Editors' Choice** *(10/1/2004)*

Marqués de Cáceres 1995 Reserva Tempranillo Blend (Rioja) $21. Back into traditional mode, this wine stayed in barrel for 2 years, then in bottle for 6 years before being released. The result is an earthy, tobacco-scented wine that still retains underpinnings of fresh blackberries. Finishes with elegant flourishes of smoke and vanilla. **89** *(10/1/2004)*

Marqués de Cáceres 2003 Viura (Rioja) $7. Made from 100% Viura, fermented in stainless steel, this is a plump, quaffable wine laced with melon and fig flavors. **84** *(10/1/2004)*

Marqués de Cáceres 2002 Blanco Viura (Rioja) $7. **85** *—M.S. (11/15/2003)*

Marqués de Cáceres 2003 Antea White Blend (Rioja) $10. A heavy, awkward, rather tasteless blend of Viura and Malvasia. And it's barrel fermented from a hot year. So just imagine the weight. The opposite of a refreshing Spanish white, this is an oily wine with distant notes of dried apricot and vanilla. **81** *—M.S. (8/1/2005)*

Marqués de Cáceres 2001 Antea White Blend (Rioja) $9. **87** *—M.S. (11/1/2002)*

Marqués de Cáceres 2000 Blanco White Blend (Rioja) $7. **85 Best Buy** *—M.M. (9/1/2002)*

Marqués de Cáceres 2001 Satinela White Blend (Rioja) $9. **84** *—D.T. (4/1/2003)*

Marqués de Cáceres 2004 Satinela Medium Sweet White Blend (Rioja) $8. This medium-sweet wine has a lot of issues. First off, it smells like cooked bananas. Next, the palate is like mango cotton candy. Third, the juice itself will take a coat of enamel off your teeth. Need more? **80** *—M.S. (8/1/2005)*

MARQUÉS DE GRIÑON

Marqués de Griñon 2001 Dominio de Valdepusa Cabernet Sauvignon (Toledo) $35. Tar, rubber, and a light chemical note turn the nose down, while rhubarb and cranberry mix with cola on the palate. Finishes sweet, with stewed fruit and carob. It's also a touch green. **83** *—M.S. (12/31/2004)*

Marqués de Griñon 1999 Dominio de Valdepusa Cabernet Sauvignon (Viño da Mesa de Toledo) $28. **84** *—M.M. (9/1/2002)*

Marqués de Griñon 2000 Emeritus Red Blend (Viño da Mesa de Toledo) $60. As you might expect from a wine from Spain's central plains, this is dark, stewy, and heavy. But it's also loaded with exotic gumdrop, spice, and plum syrup aromas, saturated deep-fruit flavors, and ultimately an ending flow of coffee and fudge. It's like drinking a confection, but one crafted for adults. **90** *—M.S. (3/1/2005)*

Marqués de Griñon 1999 Enartis Red Blend (Rioja) $30. 85 *—D.T. (4/1/2003)*

Marqués de Griñon 1999 Dominio de Valdepusa Syrah (Viño da Mesa de Toledo) $34. 83 *(11/1/2001)*

Marqués de Griñon 1997 Colección Personal Reserva Tempranillo (Rioja) $26. 88 *—D.T. (4/1/2003)*

MARQUÉS DE LA CONCORDIA

Marqués De La Concordia 2001 Hacienda de Susar Tempranillo (Rioja) $15. Offers an attractive mix of herb, oak, and ripe fruit aromas. The palate is sunny, and thus bright fruit in the form of raspberry and cherry shines. Full and lengthy on the finish, with chocolate as the lasting flavor. **87** *—M.S. (6/1/2005)*

MARQUÉS DE MONISTROL

Marqués de Monistrol 2000 Cabernet Sauvignon-Tempranillo (Penedès) $7. 88 Best Buy *—D.T. (4/1/2003)*

Marqués de Monistrol NV Masia Monistrol Champagne Blend (Cava) $7. 86 Best Buy *—M.S. (12/31/2002)*

Marqués de Monistrol 1999 Reserva Privada Sparkling Blend (Cava) $17. Notes of scrambled eggs, apple, and melon create a yeasty, full bouquet. Flavors of lime and kiwi are clean and exact, while the finish is moderately long and nuanced with hints of smoke and slate. Very nice on the palate, with good bead. **88** *—M.S. (12/15/2004)*

MARQUÉS DE MURRIETA

Marqués de Murrieta 1989 Castillo Ygay Gran Reserva Esp Red Blend (Rioja) $35. 89 *(2/1/2000)*

Marqués de Murrieta 1997 Colección 2100 Tinto Red Blend (Rioja) $10. 83 *(2/1/2000)*

Marqués de Murrieta 1995 Prado Lagar Reserva Especial Red Blend (Rioja) $27. 89 *(2/1/2000)*

Marqués de Murrieta 1995 Castillo Ygay Gran Reserva Tempranillo (Rioja) $45. This is a single-vineyard wine with pedigree. The tint is toward orange, with a brick center. The nose deals intoxicating vanilla, marzipan, and sweet leather, while the palate picks up the pace with fruit, density, and subtlety. Wonderful texture; drink over next five years. **91** *—M.S. (9/1/2004)*

Marqués de Murrieta 2000 Dalmau Reserva Tempranillo Blend (Rioja) $NA. This wine shows that old dogs can be taught new tricks. Murrieta is about as traditional as they come in Rioja yet Dalmau is ultra modern. The nose is a smooth mix of plum, raspberry, and tobacco, while the sizable palate pushes oak-backed berry fruit. Runs racy but not particularly aggressive. Long and satisfying on the finish. **92** *—M.S. (6/1/2005)*

MARQUÉS DE REALA

Marqués de Reala 2003 Tinto Grenache (Campo de Borja) $7. Very sweet, with cherry cola and licorice nibs comprising the nose. It's nothing more than simple Garnacha, which means it's all about red fruit and sunshine. Not a fine wine, but good for those with a sweet tooth. **84 Best Buy** *—M.S. (6/1/2005)*

MARQUÉS DE RISCAL

Marqués de Riscal 1996 Gran Reserva Red Blend (Rioja) $36. 92 *—M.S. (10/1/2003)*

Marqués de Riscal 1998 Reserva Red Blend (Rioja) $15. 86 *—C.S. (11/1/2002)*

Marqués de Riscal 2000 Reserva Tempranillo Blend (Rioja) $17. Starts off a little shaky, but just needs a little time in a decanter to right itself and blow off some dusty aromas. Underneath that is some toasty oak, along with cherry, vanilla, and tobacco flavors. It's relatively light, supple, and ready to drink tonight with roast lamb. **87** *(12/31/2004)*

Marqués de Riscal 2000 White Blend (Rueda) $9. 85 *—M.M. (9/1/2002)*

MARQUES DE TOMARES

Marqués de Tomares 1995 Gran Reserva Red Blend (Rioja) $50. Root beer, cola nut, red pepper, and saddle leather together form a classic aged Rioja bouquet. Bright cherry and red currant on the palate is followed by a finish graced by vanilla and cherry tomato. Some minty, herbal nuances make it extra interesting. **89** *—M.S. (12/31/2004)*

Marqués de Tomares 1999 Crianza Tempranillo Blend (Rioja) $19. Smoky and saucy on the nose, with a hint of oak-based caramel. The palate features tart raspberry and light oak, while the thin, tight finish carries with it a bit of milk chocolate. Not dense or layered; mildly leafy. **84** *—M.S. (12/31/2004)*

MARQUÉS DE VARGAS

Marqués de Vargas 1998 Reserva Tempranillo Blend (Rioja) $70. Full-bodied and earthy, with red plum, cola, and tomato aromas. The palate mixes leafy, herbal flavors with candied cherry, and the combination proves to have issues. Finishes gritty, with hard tannins. More traditional than modern in style. **86** *—M.S. (3/1/2005)*

MARQUÉS DE VILLAMAGNA

Marqués de Villamagna 1997 Gran Reserva Tempranillo (Rioja) $NA. Fairly dark, with black raspberry and pepper aromas. Shows decent length and depth, with standard old-Rioja smoke and leather. Cut from the classic mold, made simply and clean by Juan Alcorta Bodegas, part of the Allied Domecq group. **87** *—M.S. (9/1/2004)*

MARQUÉS DEL PUERTO

Marqués del Puerto 1991 Gran Reserva Red Blend (Rioja) $21. **84** *(8/1/2000)*

Marqués del Puerto 1995 Reserva Red Blend (Rioja) $17. **85** *(8/1/2000)*

Marqués del Puerto 1996 Selección Especial MM Reserva Red Blend (Rioja) $40. **90** *(11/1/2002)*

Marqués del Puerto 2002 Rosado Rosé Blend (Rioja) $9. **83** *—M.S. (10/1/2003)*

Marqués del Puerto 1999 Crianza Tempranillo (Rioja) $12. **89** *—C.S. (11/1/2002)*

Marqués del Puerto 1999 Rosado Tempranillo (Rioja) $10. **85** *(8/1/2000)*

Marqués del Puerto 2003 Blanco Viura (Rioja) $9. This 100% Viura is fresh and forward but not overly expressive in terms of aromas or flavors. Simple white fruits like grapes and peach carry the palate, while the finish is heavy with the aftertaste of citrus pith. **83** *—M.S. (12/31/2004)*

Marqués del Puerto 2000 Cosecha White Blend (Rioja) $17. **81** *—M.S. (11/1/2002)*

MARQUES DEL REAL TESORO

Marqués del Real Tesoro NV Pedro Ximénez Viejo Sherry (Jerez) $16. A bit separated and orange at the edges, but full of raisin, hard spice, and power. Flavors of dried fruit, cinnamon, and brown sugar are sweet as daylights, but there's enough piercing acidity and savory qualities on keep it on line. **88** *—M.S. (12/31/2004)*

MARTIN CODAX

Martin Codax 1999 Albariño (Rias Baixas) $13. **88 Best Buy** *—M.M. (8/1/2000)*

Martin Codax 1998 Organistrum Albariño (Rias Baixas) $17. **87** *—M.M. (8/1/2000)*

MARTINEZ BUJANDA

Martinez Bujanda 1997 Conde de Valdemar Reserva Garnacha (Rioja) $26. **82** *—M.S. (10/1/2003)*

Martinez Bujanda 2002 Valdemar Viño Rosado Garnacha (Rioja) $8. **85 Best Buy** *(11/1/2003)*

Martinez Bujanda 1994 Conde de Valdemar Gran Reserva Tempranillo (Rioja) $21. **89** *—M.M. (9/1/2002)*

Martinez Bujanda 2001 Finca Antigua Tempranillo (La Mancha) $9. **87 Best Buy** *(11/1/2003)*

Martinez Bujanda 1998 Conde de Valdemar-Crianza Tempranillo Blend (Rioja) $10. **86** *—M.M. (9/1/2002)*

Martinez Bujanda 1999 Finca Valpiedra Reserva Tempranillo Blend (Rioja) $32. A stand-alone project from Martìnez-Bujanda that is spicy, leafy and not unlike good Bordeaux. The wine is a Tempranillo-dominated blend that includes some Cabernet. It has herbal, leafy, aromas along with cherry and vanilla, and then zest, acidity and tannin on the palate. Well made and ready for the dinner table. **90** *—M.S. (9/1/2004)*

Martinez Bujanda 1998 Finca Valpiedra Reserva Tempranillo Blend (Rioja) $32. This single-vineyard wine is beefy and bold, with a thick mouthfeel and lots of extract. Blackberry and pepper control the palate, while the finish is heavy and smoky. If there's a fault, it's that the wine is lacking in edginess. It's a tiny bit grapy and soft. Otherwise, everything else is a go. **87** *—M.S. (3/1/2004)*

Martinez Bujanda 1997 Finca Valpiedra Reserva Tempranillo Blend (Rioja) $30. **87** *(11/1/2003)*

MARTINSANCHO

Martinsancho 2004 Verdejo (Rueda) $15. Crisp and green on the nose, with aromas of celery, green pepper, and passion fruit. Tight and juicy across the palate, with peach and lime flavors. Dry as a soda cracker on the finish, yet firm and food friendly. **86** *—M.S. (8/1/2005)*

Martinsancho 2002 Verdejo (Rueda) $12. Sharp and siren-like in the nose, with snappy green pepper and passion fruit aromas. Based on the bouquet, you'd think it Sauvignon Blanc. And the peppery, grapefruit palate wouldn't steer you away from that perception. It's not spritzy, but almost so. A real live-wire act. **85** *—M.S. (3/1/2004)*

MARTIVILLI

Martivilli 2000 Verdejo (Rueda) $10. **87 Best Buy** *—M.M. (4/1/2002)*

MAS DOIX

Mas Doix 2002 Doix Costers de Vinyes Velles Red Blend (Priorat) $85. Like a freight train, this wine from the village of Poboleda hits with force. From Joan Doix and his winemaking nephew, Ramón Llagostera, it deftly delivers both red and black fruit notes, all on a lightly tannic frame. To call it lip-smacking and juicy would be correct. The blend is 51% old-vines Garnacha, 46% Cariñena and 3% Merlot. 500 cases made. **91** *—M.S. (10/1/2005)*

MAS IGNEUS

Mas Igneus 2001 Barranc Dels Closos Red Blend (Priorat) $15. Word has it that 2001 is a benchmark year for Priorat, and this early bird seems like a positive indicator. It has some earth and mushroom on the nose, but also plenty of sweet fruit and cinnamon. The palate is chunky and unbridled, with all the plum, berry, and apple skin one could ask for. A chewy finish with a creamy chocolate base seals the deal in a winning way. **91 Editors' Choice** *—M.S. (3/1/2004)*

Mas Igneus 1999 FA 104 Blanco White Blend (Priorat) $19. 88 *—M.M. (4/1/2002)*

MAS MARTINET

Mas Martinet 2002 Clos Martinet Red Blend (Priorat) $58. Elevated from the first nosing through the multilevel palate and then out the door. Fragrant like an aromatic magnet, with red licorice, wild flower, and jammy fruit. A potent brew, with some medicinal cherry to the toasty finish. Super healthy, with an aggressive personality. Could use a year or two to settle because now it's rather tannic. **92** *—M.S. (10/1/2005)*

MASET DEL LLEÓ

Maset del Lleó NV Semi-Dulce Rosé (Penedès) $11. Out of the ordinary, so it's hard to gauge. To enjoy this you have to appreciate the off-dry style that features residual sugar and overt sweetness. In that sense, it's a lot like White Zin. Assuming that's not your bag, it won't score big. **83** *—M.S. (8/1/2005)*

Maset del Lleó NV Brut Nature (Cava) $14. The bouquet is flowery, with a full note of lime. The mouthfeel is a touch heavy and sticky, but the citrus (primarily orange) flavors are good. A light and easy cava. **84** *—M.S. (12/15/2004)*

Maset del Lleó NV Brut Reserva (Cava) $15. A bit fizzy, with a nose reminiscent of lemon-lime soda. Yet while it tickles, it manages to please. The palate offers nice honeydew and nectarine flavors, which are backed by a frothy, creamy finish. Fresh and balanced. **87** *—M.S. (12/15/2004)*

Maset del Lleó NV Semi-Seco Reserva (Cava) $14. Dosed heavily to be sweet, but still very nice. Look for ripe melon and sugared citrus on the palate, followed by a thick finish that toes the line on cloying but manages to avoid stepping on it. Not quite as clean as the bodega's normal semisweet cava. **87** *—M.S. (12/15/2004)*

MASIA BACH

Masia Bach 1997 Bach Cabernet Sauvignon (Catalonia) $12. 86 *—RV (11/1/1999)*

Masia Bach 1996 Bach Tempranillo (Catalonia) $8. 89 Best Buy *—RV (11/1/1999)*

MATARROMERA

Matarromera 1998 Reserva Tempranillo (Ribera del Duero) $49. Sweet aromas hint of grassy meadows and cherry cola. The palate is open and ripe, but there's also a firm, tannic foundation to support all the ripe flavors. Time in the cellar should permit this powerhouse to shed some of its tannins. Hold for another year or so. **90** *—M.S. (3/1/2004)*

MAYORAL

Mayoral 2000 Cosecha Tempranillo Blend (Jumilla) $7. 87 Best Buy *—M.M. (9/1/2002)*

MEDERAÑO

Mederaño 2001 White Blend (Tierra de Castilla) $7. 80 *—D.T. (4/1/2003)*

MERUM

Merum 2002 Unico Monastrell (Jumilla) $27. A Monastrell with 10% Cabernet, and it is heavily minty and woody, with leaner than expected fruit and a whole lot of resin and vanilla setting things off. Decent structure and mouthfeel, and with plenty of oak. Not bad but nothing too exciting. **84** *—M.S. (6/1/2005)*

Merum 1999 Crianza Tempranillo (Madrid) $10. Aromas of coffee, balsamic vinegar, and cedar, but not much fruit, send this wine on its way. Flavors of plum and cherry are standard but clean, while the finish is fruity and offers hints of licorice. A touch sharp but likable. **86 Best Buy** *—M.S. (9/1/2004)*

MM MASIA L'HEREU

MM Masia L'Hereu 1999 1882 Reserva Privada Red Blend (Penedès) $10. Dense and fruity, but not as defined or enriched as the 2000. The bouquet delivers red fruit, foresty aromas, and chocolate. Next in line is a palate of brandied berries, earth, and a touch too much acidity. No complaints as a whole, but it shows some leanness in the middle. **88 Best Buy** *—M.S. (5/1/2004)*

MONT MARÇAL

Mont Marçal NV Brut (Cava) $11. 89 *(11/15/1999)*

Mont Marçal 1999 Reserva Brut (Cava) $9. 86 *—K.F. (12/31/2002)*

Mont Marçal NV Reserva Rosé Brut (Cava) $15. Colorful stuff, like the flesh of a wild King salmon. The nose offers dried cherry, nectarine, and some carbon dioxide. Fresh and tangy in the mouth, with pink grapefruit as the primary flavor despite its Pinot Noir DNA. Good enough to sip on a summer day, but not what you'd call elevated. **86** *—M.S. (12/15/2005)*

MONTALVO WILMONT

Montalvo Wilmont 2003 Tempranillo-Cabernet (La Mancha) $11. Adequately smoky and raw, with rubber, cassis, and black cherry. A bit unfocused and clumsy, but good in a natural, no-frills kind of way. Finishes easy, with oak and some earthy mushroom. **84** *—M.S. (8/1/2005)*

MONTE PINADILLO

Monte Pinadillo 1997 Crianza Tempranillo (Ribera del Duero) $20. **82** *—J.C. (11/1/2001)*

MONTECILLO

Montecillo 1994 130 Edición Limitada Gran Reserva Tempranillo (Rioja) $50. Aromas of warm cedar planks, tobacco, and mushroom turn more murky and leafy with air. Quite acidic, which is why the wine is still kicking and screaming. The fruit is slick and racy, while the finish is hot, fiery and bitter like espresso. **83** *—M.S. (8/1/2005)*

Montecillo 1998 Crianza Tempranillo (Rioja) $10. **85** *—M.M. (9/1/2002)*

Montecillo 1997 Reserva Tempranillo (Rioja) $17. **86** *—M.M. (11/1/2002)*

Montecillo 1991 Selección Especial Gran Reserva Tempranillo (Rioja) $65. More red still than orange, with classic aromas of leather, molasses, and tobacco. Rich and developed in the mouth, with black cherry and caramel leading to a finish of chocolaty complexity. Has it now and will age for another 10 to 20 years if properly stored. **92 Cellar Selection** *—M.S. (12/31/2004)*

Montecillo 1982 Selección Especial Gran Reserva Tempranillo (Rioja) $75. Orange in color, with dark, burnt aromas that turn from sweet and saucy to tobacco and leaves in no time. Quite forward and zesty, with apricot, dried cherry, and tobacco flavors. Finishes a bit dry and salty, but with an undercurrent of toffee to save it. **90** *—M.S. (12/31/2004)*

Montecillo 2002 Viura (Rioja) $10. This basic Viura has a waxy nose with hints of mineral and banana. The palate deals tart apple and lemon juice, while the finish is tight and sharp. Needs salty, basics to pump it up, something like green olives. **84** *—M.S. (9/1/2004)*

Montecillo 2003 Blanco Viura (Rioja) $8. Bland apple and tart citrus with very little body. Not much here. **80** *—M.S. (12/31/2004)*

MONTEGAREDO

Montegaredo 2000 Piramide Red Blend (Ribera del Duero) $20. **83** *—C.S. (11/1/2002)*

Montegaredo 1999 Tinto Tempranillo (Ribera del Duero) $13. **88 Best Buy** *—K.F. (11/1/2002)*

MONTSARRA

Montsarra NV Brut Sparkling Blend (Cava) $15. Nice in terms of texture, but a bit strange and hard to identify as far as aromas and flavors go. The nose tosses up Sherry and syrup notes, while the flavors run toward Granny Smith apples and lime. Shockingly, the finish is sweet. Confounding and hard to appreciate, but not a bad cava. **84** *—M.S. (6/1/2005)*

MORGADIO

Morgadio 2003 Albariño (Rias Baixas) $19. A touch prickly and odd at first, with cactus and canned peaches on the nose. More canned, sweet fruit appears on the palate, which is soft and modest from front to finish. Ends with the flavor of pineapple Lifesavers. **86** *—M.S. (9/1/2004)*

Morgadio 2000 Albariño (Rias Baixas) $19. **85** *—M.M. (9/1/2002)*

MORLANDA

Morlanda 2001 Criança Red Blend (Priorat) $48. Light in color, with some cloudiness. On the nose it's fairly lean and herbal, more similar to French Cabernet Franc or Pinot Noir than your typical muscular Priorat. Flavorwise, expect raisin and raspberry notes before a short, spicy finish. **84** *—M.S. (3/1/2005)*

Morlanda 2002 Vi de Guarda Red Blend (Priorat) $48. Hard and rubbery at first; the nose requires a lot of patience. Those who have it will be rewarded with candied red fruit and a buttery, oaky finish. Somewhat of a unique, odd style for Priorat, with a broader, less mineral character. **85** *—M.S. (10/1/2005)*

MUGA

Muga 1996 Reserva Red Blend (Rioja) $17. **89** *—M.M. (8/1/2000)*

Muga 1999 Rosada Rosé Blend (Rioja) $10. **87** *—M.M. (8/1/2000)*

Muga 1994 Reserva Selección Especial Tempranillo (Rioja) $29. **91** *—M.M. (8/1/2000)*

Muga 2001 Aro Tempranillo Blend (Rioja) $179. A compact red with aromatic hints of tobacco, violets, and dark berries. Fueled in high-octane fashion, meaning it's tight, tannic, and forward. While it needs five years to loosen up, now you get refined black cherry and chocolate. A stern drink for those who favor big reds. Tempranillo with 30% Graciano. **90** *—M.S. (6/1/2005)*

Muga 1999 Reserva Tempranillo Blend (Rioja) $19. Sweet, ripe, and full, which is pretty much the Muga style. One whiff tells you a lot: there's nice plum and cherry, with depth. The finish lingers for a while, delivering vanilla and ample wood. This is so easy to like, and equally easy to drink. **89** *—M.S. (3/1/2004)*

Muga 1998 Torre Muga Tempranillo Blend (Rioja) $45. Deep and earthy, and packing more than a punch. This is big-time modern Rioja in brash form. The nose is gorgeous, dealing milk chocolate

SPAIN

and fresh soil. The palate is a tight blend of tannins, acids, and zesty flavors. Big and hedonistic for sure, but you'll love the plum, pepper, and espresso flavors. Still feverishly tannic; hold at least until 2005. **93 Editors' Choice** *—M.S. (3/1/2004)*

Muga 2002 Muga Blanco White Blend (Rioja) $11. Elegant and fragrant on the nose, with wild flower, honey, and apple/pear aromas. Flavors of green apple and lemon are surprisingly tart given the barrel-fermented status of the wine. Solid and tasty for the style. **87** *—M.S. (3/1/2004)*

MURUVE

Muruve 1996 Crianza Tinta de Toro (Toro) $13. **91 Best Buy** *—M.S. (8/1/2000)*

MUSEUM

Museum 2000 Real Reserva Tempranillo (Cigales) $23. Decent aromas of sun-baked fruit, leather, and oak is a known trio that spells out Spanish Tempranillo. The palate offers tangy cherry and red plum, while the finish is buttery. Piercing acidity sort of sneaks up on you as you get into it. Pretty good but lacking in mouthfeel. **86** *—M.S. (8/1/2005)*

NAIA

Naia 2003 Verdejo (Rueda) $13. An aggressive example of Verdejo, one that wants to be grapefruit juice and comes very close to tasting like it. Along with the pulsating pink grapefruit aromas and flavors there's some passion fruit and pith. But you'll be hard pressed to go beyond these dominating characteristics. A proverbial one-noter, but a good one. **86** *—M.S. (8/1/2005)*

NORA

Nora 2003 Albariño (Rias Baixas) $16. Shows all the typical outward signs of the variety, including melon, peach, and citrus aromas followed by pear, orange, and biscuit-like flavors. There's just enough slate and mineral on the palate to offer some complexity, while the finish is clean and light. A satisfying Spanish white. **88** *—M.S. (8/1/2005)*

Nora 2002 Albariño (Rias Baixas) $13. This Galician white is clean and properly acidic; it'll take the coating off your palate like liquid sorbet. In the nose, aromas of lemon-lime dominate, while in the mouth, lemon, green apple, and white pepper take over. While it's a touch thin, it's fresh and likable. **86** *—M.S. (3/1/2004)*

NUMANTHIA-TERMES, S.L.

Numanthia-Termes, S.L. 2000 Numanthia Tinta de Toro (Toro) $45. Tight as nails, with earth and mint aromas leading you toward plum, black cherry, and leather-like flavors. This is fiercely tannic right now, with a hint of bitterness. But it's also a high-voltage, new-age wine with copious oak, cola, and earth characteristics. Shows good aging potential. Hold until 2005 or 2006. **89** *—M.S. (3/1/2004)*

Numanthia-Termes, S.L. 1999 Termes Tinta de Toro (Toro) $21. Less concentrated and oaky than its big brother, Numanthia, but definitely more approachable, and arguably more likable. Some earth and leather deepen and darken the nose, while in the mouth, chunky black fruit kicks up notes of cola and chocolate. Very smooth and sweet, with firm tannins but not the jack-hammer type. **90** *—M.S. (3/1/2004)*

OCHOA

Ochoa 2003 Viura-Chardonnay White Blend (Navarra) $10. Expressive, with a fresh, flowery, Moscato-like nose. Bursts with apple and grapefruit, and then a wave of pineapple. It has spine, zest, and style. A good everyday white that's balanced. **87 Best Buy** *—M.S. (10/1/2004)*

OLIVER CONTI

Oliver Conti 1998 Bordeaux Blend (Emporadà-Costa Brava) $39. **89** *—M.M. (4/1/2002)*

ORBALLO

Orballo 2003 Albariño (Rias Baixas) $17. A bit sweet and ripe, with aromas of pineapple, canned pear, and sugared doughnuts. Round pineapple, nectarine, and apple flavors lead toward a satisfying, smooth finish. Reserved but still carries some kick. **87** *—M.S. (8/1/2005)*

ORIEL

Oriel 2003 Setena Red Blend (Terra Alta) $18. This five-grape blend hails from outside Barcelona. It's mute on the nose, with hints of horseradish and vinaigrette. Seems pickled on the palate, with rubbery tannins and flavor notes of salsa and wasabi. **81** *—M.S. (10/1/2005)*

ORIGIN

Origin 1998 Reserva Tempranillo Blend (Rioja) $24. A bit sweet on the nose, with notes of caramel, blackberry, and earth. Better at first, where it comes on ripe. But then it turns a little sluggish and heavy as it opens. Still, it's largely a good Rioja, maybe more in the "modern" style than old-school. **85** *—M.S. (6/1/2005)*

ORISTAN

Oristan 1995 Reserva Cencibel (La Mancha) $10. **83** *(8/1/2000)*

OSBORNE

Osborne NV Rare Sherry Pedro Ximénez Viejo Pedro Ximénez (Jerez) $120. Fairly typical of a quality PX, with prune, fudge, and leather on the nose. Runs a touch syrupy, but the flavors are excellent: the chocolate, raisin, and coffee tastes are all precise and stellar. Shows some raw power at times, but also remains subdued. **91** *—M.S. (6/1/2005)*

Osborne NV Bailen Dry Oloroso Sherry (Jerez) $14. Offers all the requisite almond and dried stone fruits one could ask for. The spicy palate is racy as can be, with flavors of mushroom, almond, sea salt, and white pepper. The finish is long and powerful, and overall it is a serious Sherry with no cracks or flaws. **90 Best Buy** *—M.S. (10/1/2005)*

Osborne NV Manzanilla Sherry (Jerez) $14. Petrol and crisp sea air control the nose, while the palate has saline, lemon, and bitter almond flavors. Chalky and tight on the finish, with some mushroom and vanilla nuance. **87** *—M.S. (8/1/2005)*

Osborne NV Pale Dry Fino Sherry (Jerez) $10. Heavier in color, with a bit of yellow to the tint. Salted nut, popcorn, and light fruit flavors are solid, as is the mouthfeel. Finishes crisp and solid, but without much elegance. Sizable and weighty for a fino. **87 Best Buy** *—M.S. (8/1/2005)*

Osborne NV Solera AOS Rare Amontillado Sherry (Jerez) $60. Dark and mature, with iodine and roasted nuts on the nose. Very salty and aggressive on the palate, almost too much so. Finishes with popcorn, clarified butter, and peanuts. Better aromatics than flavors; comes off the nose and hits the wall before slumping. **87** *—M.S. (8/1/2005)*

Osborne 2003 Solaz Tempranillo Blend (Tierra de Castilla) $8. With some leather, bramble, and smoky dark fruit, this Cabernet-Tempranillo blend scores as an everyday steady. But to take it farther brings caveat emptor into play. Flavorwise, it's got nice cherry and raspberry, and the finish deals vanilla and chocolate. Pleasant in every way. **86 Best Buy** *—M.S. (10/1/2005)*

Osborne 2000 Solaz Blend (Tierra de Castilla) $7. **85 Best Buy** *—M.M. (11/1/2002)*

Osborne 1999 Solaz Tempranillo Blend (Tierra de Castilla) $7. **82** *—M.M. (9/1/2002)*

OSBORNE SELECCIÓN

Osborne Selección 2002 Dominio de Malpica Cabernet Sauvignon (Viño de la Tierra de Castilla) $15. A lightweight specimen with tomato, earth, leaves, and leather on the nose. Cherry and cola flavors are distant but solid, while the acidity is out there, bordering on scouring. Modest in scope, with some appeal. **84** *—M.S. (11/15/2005)*

OSTATU

Ostatu 2000 Crianza Tempranillo (Rioja) $16. Aromas of strawberry and plum lead into a fruity, lightly sugared palate that pours on the friendly red fruit. Well made and perfectly drinkable. What a simple, modern Rioja can and should be. **87** *—M.S. (3/1/2004)*

OTAZU

Otazu 2000 Chardonnay (Navarra) $11. **86** *—C.S. (4/1/2002)*

Otazu 2002 Palacio de Otazu Chardonnay (Navarra) $14. Not a great quality-to-price ratio, but still a fresh Chardonnay with citrus, green apple, and tropical-fruit. Tight and lean because it's unoaked, with white pepper on the finish. Good in a scaled-back manner. **86** *—M.S. (10/1/2004)*

Otazu 1997 Palacio de Otazu Crianza Red Blend (Navarra) $16. **86** *—C.S. (11/1/2002)*

PAGO DE LOS CAPELLANES

Pago de Los Capellanes 1996 Crianza Red Blend (Ribera del Duero) $25. **88** *—J.C. (11/1/2001)*

Pago de Los Capellanes 1998 Reserva Tempranillo (Ribera del Duero) $22. **90 Editors' Choice** *—M.S. (11/1/2002)*

Pago de Los Capellanes 1999 Tinto Jóven Tinto Fino (Ribera del Duero) $13. **84** *—J.C. (11/1/2001)*

PALACIO DE LA VEGA

Palacio de La Vega 2000 Conde de La Vega Selección Privada Cabernet Blend (Navarra) $20. Aromas of plum, cherry, and licorice are good, although some obvious bell pepper gets in there as well. Raspberry and cherry carry the palate, but again there's an infusion of green, which one frequently sees in the wines of Navarra. Carob and earth soften the electric, high-wire finish. **86** *—M.S. (12/31/2004)*

Palacio de La Vega 2000 Crianza Cabernet Sauvignon-Tempranillo (Navarra) $9. Rusty and flat, with aromas of lettuce, celery, and other dry greens. Some cherry and plum carry the palate, while the finish is dry and simple. Starchy in terms of feel. **82** *—M.S. (12/31/2004)*

PALACIO DE VILLACHICA

Palacio de Villachica 2003 3T Tinta de Toro (Toro) $12. Lots of color and aggressiveness, but no polish or poise. The nose is gassy and harsh, while the palate is surprisingly boring, with little to no flavor. Finishes short and clipped, with tannins that drill your cheeks. **82** *—M.S. (10/1/2005)*

Palacio de Villachica 2001 5T Tinta de Toro (Toro) $19. Aromas of dill, char, and vanilla mix with red fruit to create a recognizable, inviting bouquet. Black cherry and plum flavors are firm and spicy, however the back palate is a bit short, verging on hollow. With gritty tannins and forward acidity, this is no slouch. **87** *—M.S. (10/1/2005)*

PAÑUELO

Pañuelo 2002 Merlot-Cabernet Sauvignon (Navarra) $11. Heavy and a bit closed, with smoky bacon notes, olive, and green pepper on the nose. The plum and cherry flavors are big but awkward, while the finish steers you to the tannic side. Still, it's a decent wine from a marginal vintage. **84** *—M.S. (10/1/2005)*

PÁRAMO DE GUZMÁN

Páramo de Guzmán 2000 Crianza Tempranillo (Ribera del Duero) $31. Looks good in the glass, and smells pretty nice despite a hint of barnyard. In addition, there's cola, vanilla, and plum to consider. Fairly meaty in terms of feel, but not overly expressive and not quite reaching the upper echelon. Finishes with some gritty, hard-fighting tannins. **87** *—M.S. (6/1/2005)*

PARTAL

Partal 1998 Crianza Monastrell (Bullas) $25. **88** *—M.M. (4/1/2002)*

PARXET

Parxet NV Brut (Penedès) $14. **84** *—P.G. (12/15/2000)*

Parxet NV Brut Nature (Cava) $17. **87** *—G.D. (12/15/1999)*

Parxet NV Brut Pinot Noir (Cava) $24. Rusty orange in color, with sweet-and-sour aromas mixed with orange peel. Quite dry and earthy, with a spicy hot-sauce element. Finishes scattered and burnt. Unconventional to say the least. **82** *—M.S. (12/15/2004)*

Parxet NV Aniversario PA 84 Brut Nature (Cava) $70. Lean on the bouquet; there's almost zero yeast or lees character. But there is an interesting smoked-meat aroma that conjures memories of sausage or ballpark franks. Aggressive in the mouth, with green herbs and paprika. An unusual cava with confusing characteristics. **86** *—M.S. (6/1/2005)*

Parxet 1999 Tionio Crianza Tinto Fino (Ribera del Duero) $20. **87** *—D.T. (4/1/2003)*

Parxet NV Cuvée 21 Brut (Cava) $10. **85** *—M.S. (12/31/2002)*

PASANAU GERMANS

Pasanau Germans 2002 Finca La Planeta Cabernet Sauvignon (Priorat) $46. From the village of La Morera, this is a jumpy, spiky wine with lively acidity and a racy personality. Aromas of lemon peel, black olive, and rock quarry precede a chiseled palate that's quite tannic. Pent-up power for sure, with a blast of toasty vanilla on the finish. Possibly a touch green at its core. **88** *—M.S. (10/1/2005)*

Pasanau Germans 2001 Finca La Planeta Cabernet Sauvignon (Priorat) $46. Aromas of dark fruits are distinct and defined, while hints of perfume soften the bullish, rather earthy nose. Classy berry fruit rests comfortably on the palate, while the feel is juicy and tight. Finishes strong, maybe a little sharp, but with full flavors. 100% Cabernet. **88** *—M.S. (3/1/2005)*

Pasanau Germans 2000 Finca La Planeta Red Blend (Priorat) $34. Giant and muscled, with potent aromas of smoke, tar, maple, and prune. At 14% alcohol, not much is held back; the palate is at first sweet and rich, with the full allotment of plum, raisin, and black cherry. On the finish comes mammoth tannins and some of the toastiest, burnt coffee notes you'll find. A real bruiser with a full tank of fuel behind it. **92 Editors' Choice** *—M.S. (3/1/2004)*

Pasanau Germans 2001 La Morera de Montsant Red Blend (Priorat) $34. This wine will stick to your ribs, and it'll grab your palate on the way down, leaving quite an impression. Red fruit, leather, and toast create a rock-solid, ideal nose. Moderately syrupy and full-bodied, with smooth berry flavors and plenty of vanilla. Finishes long and classy. **90** *—M.S. (10/1/2005)*

PAUL CHENEAU

Paul Cheneau NV 25th Anniversary Brut (Cava) $10. **83** *—M.M. (12/31/2001)*

Paul Cheneau 1994 Grande Reserve Brut (Penedès) $20. **88** *—G.D. (12/15/1999)*

Paul Cheneau NV Brut (Cava) $9. This simple sparkler shows hints of toast on the nose, then plenty of ripe apple flavors. But that's it, and then it finishes slightly soft and sweet. **83** *—J.C. (1/1/2004)*

PAZO DE EIRAS

Pazo de Eiras 2003 Albariño (Rias Baixas) $25. Floral and super clean, with pretty overall aromas of mineral and lemon. Round and zesty, with a modest hint of almond oil softening up vibrant orange and lemon flavors. Refreshing but hefty, with a warm finish and lots of citrus peel. **89** *—M.S. (8/1/2005)*

PAZO SAN MAURO

Pazo San Mauro 2003 Albariño (Rias Baixas) $17. Clean and sweet, with an aromatic touch of cookies and cream. In the mouth, it's more of the standard lemon, apple, and mineral that you expect from this Galician white. Finishes easy and nice, but not too crisp. **87** *—M.S. (3/1/2005)*

Pazo San Mauro 2001 Albariño (Rias Baixas) $17. **86** *—D.T. (4/1/2003)*

PEDROSA

Pedrosa 1995 Gran Reserva Red Blend (Ribera del Duero) $79. **90 Cellar Selection** *—J.C. (11/1/2001)*

Pedrosa 1998 Crianza Tempranillo (Ribera del Duero) $28. **88** *—J.C. (11/1/2001)*

PENASCAL

Penascal 2002 Sauvignon Blanc (Viño de la Tierra de Castilla y León) $7. Who knew that crisp, varietally correct Sauvignon Blanc was being made on the plains of central Spain? The nose deals pine and bell pepper, while the palate is zippy and zesty, but filled with apple and banana flavors. A tangy, precise finish with tangerine notes is the final act. **88 Best Buy** *—M.S. (3/1/2004)*

Penascal 2000 Tempranillo (Viño de la Tierra de Castilla y León) $7. A little funky and "country style" in the nose, with some cherry lurking in the background. Raspberry and pepper are the predominant flavors, while the finish is broad, with more than a touch of wood. Fairly modest in strength, but more than adequate. **85 Best Buy** *—M.S. (3/1/2004)*

PESQUERA

Pesquera 1995 Gran Reserva Tempranillo Blend (Ribera del Duero) $99. **91 Cellar Selection** *—J.C. (11/1/2001)*

Pesquera 2001 Reserva Tempranillo Blend (Ribera del Duero) $44. Full, tight, and entering its prime, this classic Spanish red offers big aromas of leather, blackberry, violets, and dried brush. Dense on the palate, with flavors of black olive, tobacco, and racy black fruit. Chewy and chocolaty on the finish, with a wash of real-deal tannins. Will age well for at least another five years. **91** *—M.S. (10/1/2005)*

Pesquera 1999 Tinto Reserva Tempranillo Blend (Ribera del Duero) $40. Deep and packed with aromas of cola, earth, and violets. It's open from the gun, with a round, plummy texture, bright fruit, and nuances of chocolate and coffee. Very full and balanced, with a good attack, middle, and finish. Drink now or hold for several years. **90** *—M.S. (3/1/2004)*

Pesquera 1997 Reserva Tempranillo (Ribera del Duero) $40. **89** *—J.C. (11/1/2001)*

Pesquera 2002 Tinto Crianza Tinto del Pais (Ribera del Duero) $27. Gritty and tight, with black cherry, kirsch, and wood on the nose. The palate features cranberry on top with deeper fruit notes below. Last but not least, toffee, coffee, and vanilla carry the finish. More than adequate, but a bit under-developed. **86** *—M.S. (10/1/2005)*

Pesquera 1999 Tinto Crianza (Ribera del Duero) $23. **85** *—K.F. (11/1/2002)*

PIRAMIDE

Piramide 1999 Piramide Crianza Red Blend (Ribera del Duero) $20. **86** *—K.F. (11/1/2002)*

PONTALIE

Pontalie 1998 Crianza Red Blend (Mentrida) $17. **82** *—D.T. (4/1/2003)*

PRADO REY

Prado Rey 1999 Real Sitio Red Blend (Ribera del Duero) $NA. **91** *—J.C. (11/1/2001)*

Prado Rey 1999 Roble Red Blend (Ribera del Duero) $11. **86** *—J.C. (11/1/2001)*

Prado Rey 1997 Crianza Tempranillo (Ribera del Duero) $17. **88** *—M.M. (8/1/2000)*

Prado Rey 1999 Reserva Tempranillo (Ribera del Duero) $35. Earth and leather control the nose along with some barnyard. All in all, it's an old-school wine, one with plum fruit, dryness, and plenty of acidity. In the long run it's not that exciting. **83** *—M.S. (6/1/2005)*

Prado Rey 1998 Roble Tempranillo (Ribera del Duero) $11. **85** *—M.M. (8/1/2000)*

Prado Rey 1999 Crianza Tinto Fino (Ribera del Duero) $18. **83** *—M.S. (8/1/2003)*

PRINCIPE DE VIANA

Principe de Viana 1996 Tempranillo (Navarra) $11. **85** *—J.C. (11/15/1999)*

PROTOS

Protos 2000 Jóven Roble Tempranillo (Ribera del Duero) $11. **87 Best Buy** *—J.C. (11/1/2001)*

PUERTA DE GRANADA

Puerta de Granada 1996 Puerta de Granada Reserva Monastrell (Jumilla) $20. **82** *—D.T. (4/1/2003)*

PUERTA DEL SOL

Puerta Del Sol 2002 Blanco Fermentado en Roble Malvar (Madrid) $16. From Vinos Jeromìn, this heavily oaked white smells of wood char and popcorn, while it tastes of coconut, more popcorn, and some hard-to-peg white fruit. Weighs a ton; hard to identify and embrace. **81** *—M.S. (12/31/2004)*

PUERTA PALMA

Puerta Palma 2000 Viño Tinto Tempranillo (Ribera del Guadiana) $NA. **87** *—M.S. (11/1/2002)*

Puerta Palma 2000 Finca El Campillo Reserva de La Familia Tempranillo Blend (Ribera del Guadiana) $12. Seemingly fading, with murky cedar and mint aromas and not too much fruit. Fairly gritty and tight on the back palate. A country wine that might do best with beef or lamb. **82** *—M.S. (12/31/2004)*

SPAIN

R. LÓPEZ DE HEREDIA

R. Lopez de Heredia 1996 Viña Bosconia Reserva Tempranillo Blend (Rioja) $32. The poster-boy wine for old Rioja is indeed tasting and acting old, even more so than its eight years. It's orange in color, with nothing but acidity on the palate. The best part is the intriguing nose, which offers vanilla, citrus peel, and saddle leather. Unfortunately, there's nothing left of this wine's body. It's emaciated. **84** *—M.S. (9/1/2004)*

R. López de Heredia Viña Tondonia 1997 Viña Tondonia Reserva Tempranillo Blend (Rioja) $39. Typically amber in color, with aromas of dried cherries merging into apricots. Tangy and sharp on the palate, as is standard. Neither fruity nor deep, even according to Tondonia's track record. Newcomers may not be impressed. **86** *—M.S. (6/1/2005)*

RAIMAT

Raimat 1994 El Moli Cabernet Sauvignon (Costers del Segre) $29. **93** *—R.V. (11/1/1999)*

Raimat 1995 Mas Castell Reserva Cabernet Sauvignon (Costers del Segre) $20. **81** *—D.T. (4/1/2003)*

Raimat 2003 Chardonnay (Costers del Segre) $9. Rather dull and oily, with lemon and apple flavors. Feels good on the palate, but lacks style and clarity. Limited in its merits. **82** *—M.S. (12/31/2004)*

Raimat 1996 Merlot (Costers del Segre) $12. **88** *—R.V. (11/1/1999)*

Raimat 2000 Tempranillo (Costers del Segre) $14. The nose tosses up hints of tobacco, tree bark, and root beer. Flavors of cherry and strawberry carry a sugary beam, and the finish turns rather candied. Not the easiest wine to wrap yourself around; it has some Old-World style but also some clumsy sweetness. **85** *—M.S. (3/1/2004)*

Raimat 1999 Abadia Tempranillo-Cabernet (Costers del Segre) $10. **85** *—D.T. (4/1/2003)*

RAMIREZ DE LA PISCINA

Ramirez de La Piscina 1999 Crianza Tempranillo (Rioja) $12. Call it rustic, barnyardy, or pickled, but no matter how you slice it, it comes out rather green. At first the fruit seems too dilute to matter, but with airing it develops some personality. A good mouthfeel is the high point, while too much in the way of pickle and cabbage notes is the main detractor. **83** *—M.S. (3/1/2004)*

Ramirez de La Piscina 1995 Reserva Tempranillo (Rioja) $21. **90** *—M.M. (8/1/2000)*

RAMÓN BILBAO

Ramón Bilbao 1999 Tempranillo (Rioja) $10. **88 Best Buy** *—D.T. (4/1/2003)*

Ramón Bilbao 1995 Gran Reserva Tempranillo (Rioja) $20. **84** *—D.T. (4/1/2003)*

Ramón Bilbao 1999 Mirto Unfiltered Tempranillo (Rioja) $37. Lush and masculine, and every bit made to emphasize extract and oak. It's dark, with heavy berry fruit, density, and ripeness. On the finish it turns even darker, with bitter chocolate and wood smoke. Arguably better at first; airing seems to close it up rather than expanding it. Drink now or cellar for up to five years. **88** *—M.S. (3/1/2004)*

Ramón Bilbao 1996 Reserva Tempranillo (Rioja) $15. **84** *—D.T. (4/1/2003)*

Ramón Bilbao 2001 Mirto Tempranillo Blend (Rioja) $37. Clean and polished, but not as expressive as the company it's running with. The nose is spicy, forward and full of plum and berry. A bit acidic and racy, with good flavors of cherry, mint and oak. Finishes swift but snappy. Very good but playing in a tough division. **89** *—M.S. (9/1/2004)*

RAMÓN CARDOVA

Ramón Cardova 2001 Tempranillo (Rioja) $10. **82** *—M.S. (10/1/2003)*

RAVENTÓS I BLANC

Raventós I Blanc 1998 Gran Reserva Personal Brut Nature (Cava) $NA. Harmonious and a bit creamy to the nose, with apple, citrus and lees. More citrus, and apple on the palate, with an almondy kick. Shows fine depth on the finish, where orange notes take over. An excellent, mature cava that still has some grit. **90** *—M.S. (6/1/2005)*

REGINA VIDES

Regina Vides 1998 Tempranillo (Ribera del Duero) $175. **93** *(4/1/2003)*

RENÉ BARBIER

René Barbier 2002 Cabernet Sauvignon (Penedès) $7. Initial off aromas never really find their way, leaving lasting notes of red cabbage and pickle barrel. The mouth is sharp and grapey, and there isn't much charm or Cabernet-related richness. Very pedestrian. **82** *—M.S. (3/1/2004)*

René Barbier 2002 Chardonnay (Penedès) $7. A zesty, lean wine, one that's not really identifiable as mainstream Chardonnay but which will go well with seafood due to its racy mouthfeel. The nose, meanwhile, is thin and prickly, while the palate offers lean apple and melon. **84** *—M.S. (3/1/2004)*

René Barbier 1999 Selección Chardonnay (Penedès) $14. **83** *—M.M. (9/1/2002)*

René Barbier 2002 Tempranillo (Penedès) $7. Bulky and simple on the bouquet, with some plum and blackberry. Flavors of cherry, plum, and berry are standard fare and clean, while the mouthfeel is a touch racy as it toes the line of sharpness. A bit of chocolaty oak adds sweetness to the zesty, acid-strong finish. **84** *—M.S. (3/1/2004)*

René Barbier NV Mediterranean White White Blend (Catalunya) $6. This simple summer sipper is clean, fresh, and grassy, with aromas of apple and green melon. Surprisingly mouthfilling for something so easygoing, but still packed with melon and citrus flavors. Fresh and zesty, and just right for patio parties. **85 Best Buy** *—M.S. (10/1/2005)*

RIMARTS

Rimarts 2002 Merlot Rosé Blend (Penedès) $11. Powerful and beefy on the nose, but lacking in refinement. And overall the bouquet seems slightly pickled and prickly, while there's little identifiable fruit to the palate. Mostly it's thin and just mildly peachy. **82** *—M.S. (5/1/2004)*

Rimarts 1996 Brut Nature Gran Reserva (Cava) $21. Savory, with a hint of anise and not much fruit remaining, this aged Cava finishes on a slightly sweet-and-sour note. This is the red label Gran Reserva; no vintage is indicated on the bottle, but the 1996 is the current release. **83** *—J.C. (1/1/2004)*

RIOJA VEGA

Rioja Vega 2000 Red Blend (Rioja) $8. **87 Best Buy** *—D.T. (4/1/2003)*

RISCAL

Riscal 2001 1860 Tempranillo (Viño de la Tierra de Castilla y León) $9. Tobacco and berries join with brown sugar, cinnamon, and spice—all of the things that make oak nice. Smooth and supple, with modest plum and berry fruit layered with vanilla. **86 Best Buy** *(12/31/2004)*

ROQUERO

Roquero 1995 Reserva Monastrell (Jumilla) $12. **83** *—M.M. (9/1/2002)*

Roquero 1998 Tinto Monastrell (Jumilla) $9. **87** *—J.C. (8/1/2000)*

ROTLLAN TORRA

Rotllan Torra 1998 Amadis Red Blend (Priorat) $45. **93 Editors' Choice** *—K.F. (11/1/2002)*

Rotllan Torra 1997 Reserva Red Blend (Priorat) $15. **89 Best Buy** *—C.S. (11/15/2002)*

Rotllan Torra 2002 Tirant Red Blend (Priorat) $75. Ripe and rich; it pushes the limit toward raisiny but doesn't cross the boundary. As a result, the sweet bouquet oozes kirsch, licorice, and spice. Stays thick on the palate, but not particularly heavy. Flavors of baked black fruit, mocha, and espresso impress, with accents of cinnamon and herbs popping through. Complex and out of the ordinary. **91** *—M.S. (10/1/2005)*

RUBIEJO

Rubiejo 2003 Oak Aged Tempranillo (Ribera del Duero) $17. This young RdD was aged only five months in barrel, yet it has weight, softness, and vanilla shadings as well as pure, unadulterated dark fruit. In a word, it's delicious; the round blackberry and cherry flavors are great and the chocolate and smoke that sneak up on the finish seal the deal. A bit too expensive to be a Best Buy, but still a very good deal. **89** *—M.S. (11/15/2005)*

Rubiejo 2003 Jóven Tinto del Pais (Ribera del Duero) $13. Seductively rich, with blackberry and vanilla aromas. Ripe and chewy, with plum, vanilla, and subtle spice in the background. Nice doses of licorice and bitter chocolate solidify the finish. Quite meaty and modern, if a bit pricy for a youngster from a hot year. **88 Best Buy** *—M.S. (10/1/2005)*

S'FORNO

S'forno 2003 Estate Godello (Valdeorras) $15. Reeks of burnt matchstick on the nose, and the sensation permeates the wine, turning the modest apple and mineral flavors acrid on the finish. Might be acceptable with long decanting. **80** *—J.C. (4/1/2005)*

S. ARROYO

S. Arroyo 2001 Tinto Jóven Tempranillo (Ribera del Duero) $9. A monster with a forceful nose that reeks of earth, coffee grounds, and leather. Underneath is a bruiser that pumps high-octane licorice and blackberry. Along the way the tannins are young and fierce. This is not a smooth, cuddly wine. Best for fans of tannic, lusty reds. **86 Best Buy** *—M.S. (3/1/2004)*

SAN PEDRO

San Pedro 1999 Vallobera Crianza Tempranillo (Rioja) $15. **87** *—M.S. (8/1/2003)*

SAN VICENTE

San Vicente 2001 Tempranillo (Rioja) $51. Smoky and rich, with hints of raisin, black cherry, and chocolate scurrying about the nose. Meaty plum, cherry, and blackberry flavors form a seamless palate that slides easily onto the coffee-filled finish. Everything evolves beautifully here, and it will satisfy anyone with an unbridled craving for chocolaty hedonism. **94 Editors' Choice** *—M.S. (8/1/2005)*

SANCHEZ ROMATE

Sanchez Romate NV Cardenal Cisneros Reservas Pedro Ximénez (Jerez) $15. This reserve-level P.X. sets the gold standard for excellence in sweet sherry. The lovely bouquet straddles the line between unadulterated sweetness and impeccable slyness. The flavors of fig, chocolate, caramel, browned butter, and cinnamon are amazing. So chewy and thick, but balanced by firm acids. Brilliant. **94 Best Buy** *—M.S. (10/1/2005)*

Sanchez Romate NV Iberia Cream Sherry (Jerez) $15. It's rare that a sweet sherry reaches such heights, but here's a case in point. Iberia has impeccable prune and raisin aromas along with intoxicating scents of toffee and cane sugar. All in all, the bouquet is excellent. The palate, meanwhile, is seamless as it deals raisin, vanilla, and mocha. Spot on for a dessert elixir, with a ceaseless finish. **93 Editors' Choice** *—M.S. (10/1/2005)*

Sanchez Romate NV NPU Amontillado Sherry (Jerez) $17. Pure and nutty, with aromas of dried apricot and sea air. In the mouth you get lots of almond and butter, while the A-rate finish is buttery but also quite complex. A classic, refined wine that dances across your tongue like a ballerina. **92** *—M.S. (10/1/2005)*

SANDEMAN

Sandeman NV Royal Ambrosante Aged 20 Years Old Solera Pedro Ximénez (Jerez) $24. Sandeman excels with its reserve-level sherries, as is exemplified by this stand-out PX. Figs and raisins are front and center throughout, but it never sits heavily on your palate. Just the opposite, there's plow-through acidity that creates a brilliant mouthfeel and the sensation of freshness. Fabulous by itself or on top of vanilla ice cream. **93 Editors' Choice** *—M.S. (6/1/2005)*

Sandeman NV Royal Esmeralda Fine Dry Amontillado Sherry (Jerez) $25. **91** *—M.S. (8/1/2003)*

SANTANA

Santana 1998 Tempranillo (Rioja) $7. **84** *(5/1/2001)*

SCALA DEI

Scala Dei 2002 Negre Garnacha (Priorat) $13. Catchy aromas such as violet and exotic candle wax are encouraging, maybe a bit more so than the tangy palate, which runs toward red-apple skins and cherry. Light in the middle but tannic on the edges. Fresh and spry, but lean. **85** *—M.S. (12/31/2004)*

Scala Dei 2003 Negre Grenache (Priorat) $15. Sweet and raisiny, with a heavy profile as well as some unexpected aromatic sharpness. The fruit is more brambly and baked than usual, and there's some murkiness. Not the best example of this wine, which was not oaked; it was better in previous vintages. **83** *—M.S. (10/1/2005)*

Scala Dei 2001 Cartoixa Red Blend (Priorat) $30. Pure and cerebral, but with enough natural liveliness that you can't help but love it. Aromas of schist, lavender, and plum mix with oak-driven bacon and chocolate to create a welcoming whole. Sizable cherry and plum flavors are round but also precise and firm. Looming tannins suggest some cellaring may be warranted. The blend is Garnacha followed by Syrah and Cabernet Sauvignon. **91** *—M.S. (10/1/2005)*

Scala Dei 1998 Cartoixa Reserva Red Blend (Priorat) $22. **86** *—D.T. (4/1/2003)*

SEGURA VIUDAS

Segura Viudas NV Aria Brut Rosé (Cava) $12. Plump and nice, with watermelon aromas that match the wine's watermelon hue. Made from Pinot Noir, Aria carries a mild hint of sweetness along with drier berry and peach-pit flavors. And on the finish you get a clear smack of Pinot-driven cherry skin to offset its richness. Perfect for brunch, as an accompaniment to a mushroom-and-cheese omelet, while that noted touch of sweetness gives it the versatility to go with dessert. **87** *—M.S. (11/15/2005)*

Segura Viudas NV Aria Estate Brut (Cava) $12. Light and mildly yeasty, with aromatic hints of campfire marshmallow and scrambled eggs. Primed across the palate, with lively acids propelling pure tangerine and lemon-pith flavors. Finishes clean and crisp, with even more citrus. **88 Best Buy** *—M.S. (12/15/2004)*

Segura Viudas NV Aria Estate Extra Dry (Cava) $12. Plump and yeasty, with some sweet pastry aromas. Flavors of apple, nectarine, and melon are ripe, bordering on sugary. Sits rather flat in the glass but becomes frothy once it hits the palate. Simple and tasty, with a candied edge. **86** *—M.S. (12/15/2004)*

Segura Viudas NV Brut Heredad Reserva (Cava) $20. Clearly more serious than average, with light apple and honey aromas that are followed nicely by lime, apple, and white-pepper flavors. Rather round, with freshness and a solid mouthfeel. For cava this is fairly classy and elevated. Imported by Freixenet USA. **88** *—M.S. (12/15/2005)*

Segura Viudas NV Brut Reserva (Cava) $10. Aromas of stone fruits, lemon-lime, and ripe citrus are crisp and welcoming. The palate follows the nose, offering lemon, lime, and orange. Zesty yet easy-going; the quintessential cava quaff. Good for parties and receptions because it tastes right yet costs only 10 bills. **87 Best Buy** *—M.S. (12/15/2004)*

Segura Viudas 2000 Torre Galimany Brut Nature (Cava) $NA. Begins with mature aromas of toast, sugared pastry, and yeast. Ultra-dry in the mouth but flavorful, with almost sterile apple and spice flavors. Crisp but forgiving on the finish; a good match for poultry. **88** *—M.S. (6/1/2005)*

Segura Viudas 1997 Mas D'Aranyó Riserva Tempranillo (Penedès) $15. **83** *—M.M. (9/1/2002)*

Segura Viudas 2004 Creu de Lavit Xarel-lo (Penedès) $15. This one takes some getting used to. The nose begins in crystallized, granular fashion, much like a powdered drink mix. The palate offers citrus, apple, and some oak, because it was barrel fermented. Medium in depth, with tang across the tongue. Good for Penedès white table wine. **86** *—M.S. (10/1/2005)*

Segura Viudas 2002 Creu de Lavit Xarel-lo (Penedès) $15. Waxy on the nose, with barrel hints as well as buttered toast and vanilla. Fairly limited in scope, but nicely textured. Flavors of apple, banana, and custard lead into a lemon and pineapple finish. **84** —*M.S. (9/1/2004)*

Segura Viudas 2001 Creu de Lavit Estate Bottled Xarel-lo (Penedès) $15. **87** —*D.T. (4/1/2003)*

SEÑORÌO DE CUZCURRITA

Señorìo de Cuzcurrita 2001 Tempranillo Blend (Rioja) $39. Bright in color and aromas, with pure cherry, leather, and yeast on the nose. Medium-bodied, not thick, but pretty full in terms of flavors, tannins, and feel. Being young, it's rambunctious, hot and spicy, but all bets are that it will settle down well over the next year or two. **90** —*M.S. (9/1/2004)*

SEÑORÌO DE SARRIA

Señorìo de Sarria 1996 Cabernet Sauvignon (Navarra) $12. **86** —*D.T. (4/1/2003)*

Señorìo de Sarria 2001 Vinedo No 7 Graciano (Navarra) $15. **81** —*D.T. (4/1/2003)*

Señorìo de Sarria 1997 Reserva Red Blend (Navarra) $18. **88 Best Buy** —*D.T. (4/1/2003)*

SEÑORIO DEL AGUILA

Señorìò del Aguila 1994 Reserva Tempranillo Blend (Cariñena) $12. **84** —*M.M. (9/1/2002)*

SERRA DA ESTRELA

Serra da Estrela 2003 Albariño (Rias Baixas) $15. Fairly thick and creamy for the style, probably due to the hot vintage. The bouquet is sweet, with buttered corn and wildflower aromas. More citrusy on the palate, with flavors of orange, tangerine, and nectarine. Well made and textured; just a little more ripe than usual. **88** —*M.S. (12/31/2004)*

SESTERO

Sestero 2003 Tempranillo-Cabernet (Navarra) $7. Smells like powdered cherry drink mix, and tastes like candied cherries, tomato, and spice. Very familiar in its style; there's sweet fruit, jumpy acidity and lots of drying oak. Not polished. **83** —*M.S. (10/1/2005)*

SIERRA CANTABRIA

Sierra Cantabria 2002 Tempranillo (Rioja) $9. Ask for a glass of simple, modern Rioja and hopefully you'll get something like this. Red fruit and rubber on the nose, flavors of cherry, plum, and cotton candy, and finally some chocolate, coffee, and vanilla on the finish. Healthy, with big tannins and full acids. **87 Best Buy** —*M.S. (9/1/2004)*

Sierra Cantabria 2001 Amancio Tempranillo (Rioja) $138. The color tells you everything you need to know; saturation overload is what this is about, with aromas of licorice, leather, pepper, and dark, masculine fruit. It comes from Sierra Cantabria, a winery known for modern-style reds. And this one fits the bill with its firm tannins, vanilla shadings, and insurmountable wall of spice on the finish. **93** —*M.S. (8/1/2005)*

Sierra Cantabria 1998 Crianza Tempranillo (Rioja) $13. Smooth and fresh, with bright berry on the nose and also some well-applied oak. In the mouth, raspberry and cherry flavors are spiced up with a note of black pepper. Lean, clean and moderately tangy; a basic but good Rioja in the truest sense. **86** —*M.S. (3/1/2004)*

Sierra Cantabria 2002 El Bosque Tempranillo (Rioja) $138. Hard and tannic to start with, so it really needs time. Aromas of beef bullion, jerky, and soy convey a certain smokiness, which is more geared to the nose than the palate. As for taste, it's laced with black cherry, cinnamon, vanilla, and chocolate. Very tight and firm, so hold for another three years. **91** —*M.S. (6/1/2005)*

Sierra Cantabria 1996 Reserva Tempranillo (Rioja) $19. The bouquet of this aging Rioja features a good mix of berry fruit, tree bark, and earth. Across the palate flows a stream of strawberry, cherry, and coffee. Firm tannins create a masculine mouthfeel, while the finish is dry with a tad of buttery oak. Gets better with airing and patient swirling. **88** —*M.S. (3/1/2004)*

Sierra Cantabria 2001 Organza White Blend (Rioja) $17. A bit awkward, with mild corn and wheat aromas in addition to melon and banana. The overall feel is flat, yet there's just enough acid to keep it lively. Finishes toasty, with a leesy, vanilla character. **85** —*M.S. (3/1/2004)*

SIGLO SACO

Siglo Saco 2001 Crianza Tempranillo (Rioja) $NA. This basic red from Bodegas y Bebidas is fresh and offers ample pop across the palate. With some wood and acidity, it's a well-made everyday red with tasty fruit and mildly sharp edges. **84** —*M.S. (9/1/2004)*

SOLABAL

Solabal 1997 Reserva Tempranillo (Rioja) $20. **89** —*M.M. (8/1/2000)*

SOLAR DE LA VEGA

Solar de La Vega 2004 Verdejo (Rueda) $8. Aggressive on the nose, with white grapefruit and scallion aromas. There's some lemon-lime and lychee to the flavor profile, but it finishes mildly bitter, with a heavy whack of citrus peel. **83** —*M.S. (10/1/2005)*

TELMO RODRÍGUEZ

Telmo Rodríguez 2002 Molino Real Mountain Wine Moscatel (Málaga) $50. More concentrated than the MR, but not necessarily better. Candle and body oil on the nose, with notes of pineapple and spice. Quite big and ripe, with intense flavors of honey, candied yams, and dripping mango. Long on the finish and persistent in its emphasis on vanilla.. **90** —*M.S. (8/1/2005)*

Telmo Rodríguez 2003 MR Mountain Wine Moscatel (Málaga) $19. Even if this Moscatel begins with waxy aromas and whiffs of hard cheese, it is one excellent elixir. The palate will please with its honey, sweet melon, and guava flavors, while the additional notes of white pepper and green melon add foundation. Excellent for the price, and it won't require a Master's degree in wine to enjoy. **90** —*M.S. (8/1/2005)*

Telmo Rodríguez 1998 Altos Lanzaga Tempranillo (Rioja) $20. 91 —*M.M. (8/1/2000)*

Telmo Rodríguez 2000 Lanzaga Tempranillo (Rioja) $20. Simply lovely in the nose, with lavender, violets, berries, and cedary wood. This is quite the heavyweight, with a candied, oaky palate that offers plenty of vanilla. The mouthfeel is a touch creamy, but once you dig in, the wine shows its nuances and stuffing. Smoothness is definitely what you get here, plus major-league richness and extract. **90** —*M.S. (3/1/2004)*

Telmo Rodríguez 2002 G Dehesa Gago Tinta de Toro (Toro) $13. The initial aromas are of barnyard and medicine. But with time raspberry and blackberry emerge, and across the palate a wide blanket of tannins spreads out. Espresso, earth, and char make for a masculine, tantalizing finish. **86** —*M.S. (3/1/2004)*

Telmo Rodríguez 1999 Basa White Blend (Rueda) $8. 88 Best Buy —*M.M. (8/1/2000)*

TEOFILO REYES

Teofilo Reyes 1998 Tempranillo (Ribera del Duero) $36. 89 —*M.M. (8/1/2000)*

TERRAS GAUDA

Terras Gauda 2004 O Rosal Albariño (Rias Baixas) $20. Gold in color, with a chunky, oversized nose weighted down by apple and orange aromas. A lot of bulky citrus flavors carry the palate, but there isn't much balance or zest. Tastes okay but feels a bit mealy. **83** —*M.S. (12/31/2005)*

TINAR

Tinar 2000 Crianza Tempranillo (Ribera del Duero) $32. Solid but unspectacular. The nose deals earth, leather, and blackberry in front of an austere palate defined by apple skin and cherry. Finishes with some buttery oak, soy, and chocolate. Entirely drinkable but where's the bang for the buck? **85** —*M.S. (8/1/2005)*

TIONIO

Tionio 1998 Crianza Tempranillo (Ribera del Duero) $17. 86 —*J.C. (11/1/2001)*

TORRE ORIA

Torre Oria NV Brut Nature (Cava) $20. 85 —*M.M. (12/31/2001)*

Torre Oria NV Brut (Cava) $11. Toast, butterscotch, and oxidized apple aromas precede a heavy, nearly over-ripe palate loaded down with sticky apple, nectarine, and banana. Where it does well is in texture, which is correct and pleasant. Finishes long and heavy. A different breed. **85** —*M.S. (6/1/2005)*

Torre Oria 1996 Reserva Tempranillo (Utiel-Requena) $15. Smells old and dirty, with peanut and barnyard grass on the nose. Dry and fading is the palate, and it's also rather murky. Acidity and some flesh in the middle is all that's keeping this one afloat. **80** —*M.S. (9/1/2004)*

TORRES

Torres 2000 Reserva Real (Penedès) $150. This Bordeaux-style blend features enticing aromas of molasses, licorice, leather, and plum, and while the palate satisfies, it doesn't quite live up to the hype built by the bouquet. The feel is soft, as if the edges had slipped away. Still, it offers good mouthfeel and decent depth. **88** —*M.S. (3/1/2005)*

Torres 1999 Gran Coronas Reserva Cabernet Sauvignon (Penedès) $20. The nose is nice; there's cherry, blackberry, and mint. Loads of ripe berry fruit draw raves, and the finish is warm, with notes of cream-filled coffee. Tight and firm in terms of feel. **88** —*M.S. (3/1/2004)*

Torres 2001 Mas La Plana Cabernet Sauvignon (Penedès) $50. This icon Spanish Cabernet hails from a 72-acre plot in Penedès. It's 100% Cabernet, aged in new French oak for 18 months. It has a roasted charcoal and lemon-peel nose, followed by herbs, cherry, and cassis flavors. It has mouthfeel and structure, with fine coffee and chocolate finishing notes. Best around 2009–2112. **91 Cellar Selection** *(11/15/2005)*

Torres 1998 Mas La Plana Cabernet Sauvignon (Penedès) $49. The nose is generally sweet and likable, yet there's some medicinal character in there too. Very ripe and dynamic, with mint and chocolate flavors along with fast-moving currant and cherry. A bit racy and unbridled for Cabernet. **87** —*M.S. (3/1/2004)*

Torres 1995 Gran Coronas Cabernet Sauvignon-Tempranillo (Penedès) $18. 87 —*J.C. (8/1/2000)*

Torres 2002 Gran Viña Sol Chardonnay (Penedès) $14. Oak is a key feature. The nose carries some sawdust and vanilla, while the plate is creamy, with banana and pear flavors. Vanilla is also present on the oaky, airy finish. Thick and woody, but healthy and honest. **86** —*M.S. (3/1/2004)*

Torres 2002 Milmanda Chardonnay (Conca de Barberà) $47. Soft and buttery on the nose, with a touch of pear. Shy pear and apple flavors drive toward a modest finish that's dry and almondy. Smooth on the palate, but not dynamic. This is intended to be a prestige Chardonnay, yet while it has mouthfeel there's not a whole lot of zest or character. **86** —*M.S. (12/31/2004)*

Torres 2000 Milmanda Chardonnay (Conca de Barberà) $50. **86** —*M.S. (11/1/2002)*

Torres 2003 Atrium Merlot (Penedès) $16. Aggressive and candied, with boiled beet, red plum, and carob flavors. Bulky and grapey. **82** —*M.S. (12/31/2004)*

Torres 1999 Atrium Merlot (Penedès) $14. **86** —*M.S. (11/1/2002)*

Torres 2003 Viña Sol Paralleda (Catalonia) $9. Light and floral, with an attractive overall nose that conveys freshness. Light citrus and melon notes on the palate are pushed by good acidity, while the lemony finish is tight and right. **85 Best Buy** —*M.S. (12/31/2004)*

Torres 2002 Mas Borras Pinot Noir (Penedès) $30. Hazy in color, with funky aromas of cranberry, leather, and pickle. The fruit is bland, and the feel is sticky and forced. Spain has never offered much in the way of Pinot Noir, and here you see why. **82** —*M.S. (6/1/2005)*

Torres 2001 Mas Borràs Pinot Noir (Penedès) $32. A burly bomber, with a heavily barrel-influenced nose. The palate is broad and chunky, and while undeniably ripe, it's a stretch finding true Pinot Noir characteristics, say something a Burgundian would recognize. Nonetheless, it's got a rich feel and it's definitely not unripe. **85** —*M.S. (3/1/2004)*

Torres 2001 Gran Sangre de Toro Red Blend (Catalunya) $15. A blend of Garnacha, Cariñena, and Syrah that starts with leather, plum, and cherry aromas. Runs a bit racy and snappy on the palate and then settles into a fairly nice groove. Still, it's kind of a spunky wine that will do better with food than as a solo sipper. **86** —*M.S. (11/15/2005)*

Torres 1998 Gran Sangre de Toro Red Blend (Catalonia) $13. **87 Best Buy** —*D.T. (4/1/2002)*

Torres 1995 Gran Sangre de Toro Reserva Red Blend (Penedès) $11. **90** —*R.V. (11/1/1999)*

Torres 1998 Grans Muralles Red Blend (Conca de Barberà) $106. **87** —*D.T. (4/1/2003)*

Torres 2002 Nerola Red Blend (Catalonia) $20. As we noted in an earlier article, this wine represents Torres' attempt at the so-called "modern Mediterranean" style. It features 80% Syrah and 20% Monastrell, and it comes across as successfully New World. The color is violet, the nose sweet and young, with a hint of toffee and marshmallow. The plump palate and chocolaty finish should please those who crave size and ripeness from their red wine. **88** —*M.S. (12/31/2004)*

Torres 2003 Nerola White Blend (Catalunya) $18. Half of the wine here was fermented in barrel, and that yields buttercup and vanilla aromas along with lighter peach and melon notes. The flavor profile, however, is more lemony crisp. With a Gaudi-inspired label, this is a wine aimed at younger wine consumers. **85** *(11/15/2005)*

Torres 2003 50th Aniversario Sangre de Toro Red Blend (Catalonia) $10. Earthy and ripe, with jammy, borderline stewy fruit that carries a meaty edge. Fairly one-line in terms of complexity, but it stands on its feet and tastes pretty solid. With some rustic character, it'll do the job. **85 Best Buy** —*M.S. (6/1/2005)*

Torres 2002 Sangre de Toro Red Blend (Catalonia) $10. Open and a bit hot, with raspberry, cherry, and bold acidity. The body is full, bordering on chunky and big. There's little in the way of nuance in this bistro-style red, but it tastes nice and will wash down munchies like chorizo or pizza with no problem. **84** —*M.S. (3/1/2004)*

Torres 1999 Sangre de Toro Red Blend (Catalonia) $11. **83** —*D.T. (4/1/2002)*

Torres 2003 Fransola Sauvignon Blanc (Penedès) $26. Grassy on the nose, with a touch of green apple to help it along. Melon, canned peach, and banana flavors indicate that it was too hot in 2003 for Sauvignon Blanc. Lacks the piquant, zesty quality the wine in known for. **83** —*M.S. (3/1/2005)*

Torres 2001 Fransola Sauvignon Blanc (Penedès) $25. **87** —*D.T. (4/1/2003)*

Torres 1998 Fransola Sauvignon Blanc (Penedès) $22. **84** *(8/1/2000)*

Torres 2002 Coronas Tempranillo (Catalonia) $10. Initially it is harsh and on the verge of caustic, although time settles it down. Nevertheless, this basic Tempranillo has medicinal flavors along with chunky black cherry and raspberry notes. Gets better with time but fails to make its mark. **83** —*M.S. (6/1/2005)*

Torres 2000 Coronas Tempranillo (Penedès) $10. **87 Best Buy** —*M.S. (11/1/2002)*

Torres 1999 Coronas Tempranillo (Catalonia) $11. **85** —*D.T. (4/1/2002)*

Torres 2001 Viña Esmeralda White Blend (Penedès) $13. **87 Best Buy** —*M.S. (11/1/2002)*

Torres 2001 Viña Sol White Blend (Penedès) $10. **85** —*M.S. (11/1/2002)*

TORRES DE ANGUIX

Torres de Anguix 2000 A Tinto del Pais (Ribera del Duero) $20. Reduced, sweet aromas lead into a chunky red-fruit palate that lacks structure but remains wet and juicy. Finishes mildly hot and spicy, but without much stuffing. **83** —*M.S. (6/1/2005)*

Torres de Anguix 2003 Tinto del Pais (Ribera del Duero) $10. Black in color and saturated with plum, fruit cake, and vanilla aromas. Big in the mouth but clumsy, with dense, thumping black cherry and blackberry flavors. In fact, everything about the wine is black, including the burnt, licorice-tinged finish. Ponderous in the long run. **84** —*M.S. (6/1/2005)*

TRAVITANA

Travitana 2003 Old Vines Monastrell (Alicanté) $10. Jumpy raspberry and strawberry aromas greet you, followed by plump, buttery red-fruit flavors of cherry and plum. Turns a bit hard and gritty, with woody tannins. Fortunately there are also some chocolate and juicy, sweet flavors to keep it on an even keel. Imported by Tasman Imports, Ltd. **85 Best Buy** —*M.S. (8/1/2005)*

TXOMÍN ETXANÍZ

Txomín Etxaníz 1999 Txakoli (Getariako Txakolina) $17. 87 —*M.M. (8/1/2000)*

Txomín Etxaníz 2000 Txakoli (Getariako Txakolina) $16. 85 —*M.M. (4/1/2002)*

VAL DE LOS FRAILES

Val de Los Frailes 2003 Jóven Tempranillo (Cigales) $8. Sharp, with harsh, reduced aromas of tar, rhubarb, and molasses. A lot of heavy plum and berry flavors raise hopes, but in the end it's just not that thrilling. Authentic, however. **83** —*M.S. (8/1/2005)*

Val de Los Frailes 2001 Vendimia Seleccionada Tempranillo (Cigales) $15. Piercing and reduced, with cherry and red currant flavors. Quite tannic and acidic, with a tough personality. But the overall take remains positive and the wine seems healthy and live-wire. For best results pour with chorizo or jamón Serrano. The salt will soften it up. **86** —*M.S. (8/1/2005)*

VAL SOTILLO

Val Sotillo 1995 Gran Reserva Red Blend (Ribera del Duero) $75. 89 —*J.C. (11/1/2001)*

Val Sotillo 1997 Tempranillo (Ribera del Duero) $29. 88 —*M.M. (8/1/2000)*

VALCORTES

Valcortes 2001 Crianza Tempranillo (Rioja) $15. Plump and a bit stewy, but the flavors manage to take over in a fairly positive way. Upon sipping you take in blackberry and prune, but also some murkiness. Not much in the midpalate, but decent around the edges. **84** —*M.S. (6/1/2005)*

VALDEGRACIA

Valdegracia 1998 Tinto Crianza Tempranillo (Ribera del Guadiana) $14. 87 —*M.M. (9/1/2002)*

VALDELANA

Valdelana 1999 Crianza Red Blend (Rioja) $11. 84 *(11/1/2002)*

VALDEMORAL

Valdemoral 1998 Tinto Fino (Ribera del Duero) $17. 85 —*W.E. (8/1/2000)*

VALDETAN

Valdetan 2001 Tinto Red Blend (Cigales) $NA. 87 —*M.S. (8/1/2003)*

VALDUBÓN

Valdubón 1999 Tempranillo (Ribera del Duero) $14. 85 —*J.C. (11/1/2001)*

Valdubón 2002 Crianza Tempranillo (Ribera del Duero) $18. Smooth and round, with chunky red-fruit aromas touched up by cinnamon. Tangy on the tongue, with plum and cherry balanced by firm tannins and lively acidity. Not flashy but plenty good enough to enjoy on an everyday basis. **87** —*M.S. (11/15/2005)*

Valdubón 1999 Crianza Tempranillo (Ribera del Duero) $18. 86 —*D.T. (4/1/2003)*

Valdubón 2000 Reserva Tempranillo (Ribera del Duero) $24. Kicks off with a bouquet akin to chocolate-covered cherries before moving on to cured meat and bacon. Strawberry and cherry flavors are touched up by buttery oak, while the finish is so broad that it seems like pulled dough. Shows much of what's good about this appellation. **87** —*M.S. (6/1/2005)*

VALENCISO

Valenciso 2000 Reserva Tempranillo (Rioja) $34. Broad and rubbery, with ripe black fruit and citrus peel on the nose. Good on the tongue, with a solid mouthfeel. And the finish is attractively marinated, offering hints of soy sauce, molasses, and sea salt. Fresh enough, and definitely forward in thrust. **87** —*M.S. (6/1/2005)*

VALL LLACH

Vall Llach 2002 Embruix Red Blend (Priorat) $33. More of an approachable Priorat, with plump fruit and modest tannins. It's a blend of five grapes, mostly from vineyards planted in the 1990s, and the aging takes place in one-year-old French oak. Ripe and rich enough to go with hearty foods, but it's not a full-force bruiser. Look for boysenberry and blackberry flavors, hints of cocoa, and a smooth finish. **88** —*M.S. (10/1/2005)*

Vall Llach 1998 Embruix Red Blend (Priorat) $80. 87 —*M.M. (4/1/2002)*

Vall Llach 2002 Viño Tinto Red Blend (Priorat) $94. More jammy than previous vintages, with blackberry aromas and notes of bitter dark chocolate. Like any young Priorat stud, it hits firmly with jackhammer tannins, but there's also a likable, soft underside to it. Starts to sing with air and swirling, indicating a bright future. Hold a few years, if possible. **91** —*M.S. (6/1/2005)*

VALLOBERA

Vallobera 1998 Reserva Tempranillo (Rioja) $20. Starts with a big, dusty nose of cherry, blackberry, and forest notes. Fresh and proper on the palate, with plum and boysenberry. Finishes with vanilla and toffee, while the feel is warm and round. Very functional and moderately complex. **88** *—M.S. (6/1/2005)*

Vallobera 2002 Pago Malarina Tempranillo Blend (Rioja) $10. Murky and leathery at first, with spice, stewed meat, and herbal aromas. Chunky but mostly in balance. The thick palate offers baked plum and black raspberry, while the finish is full and earthy. Best with tapas, ideally chorizo. **85 Best Buy** *—M.S. (10/1/2005)*

VALSACRO

Valsacro 2001 Dioro Tempranillo Blend (Rioja) $36. This is a very new wine, but one worth getting if you like the modern style Spanish red. Made from 70-year old Tempranillo as well as some Mazuelo, Graciano and Garnacha, you'll be digging into a massively roasted, well-oaked bruiser. Caramel, mocha, and chocolate mix with full berry fruit to yield a wine of concentration and body. Thick and manly; mature and ready by 2008. **93** *—M.S. (9/1/2004)*

VEGA PRIVANZA

Vega Privanza 1999 Tinto Jóven Tempranillo (Ribera del Duero) $11. **83** *—J.C. (11/1/2001)*

VEGA RIAZA

Vega Riaza 2002 Roble Tempranillo (Ribera del Duero) $15. Spicy and rubbery on the nose, with a touch of heavy fruit providing the base. Shows ample cherry and berry flavors, but that fruit is a bit high-toned, meaning the back palate is mildly acidic and slightly sour. Needs food, with which it should fit the bill. **85** *—M.S. (5/1/2004)*

VEGA SAUCO

Vega Sauco 1998 Adoremus Reserva Tinta de Toro (Toro) $22. A bit tart and leathery at first, but airing reveals plum, raspberry, and chocolate. It's a well-oaked, fairly mature wine, probably at its best right now. The finish is lean, acid-packed and spicy. **87** *—M.S. (9/1/2004)*

Vega Sauco 2001 Roble Tinta de Toro (Toro) $10. A touch heavy and sulfuric at first, but better with airing. Aromas of licorice and black plum come right off the bat, followed by flavors of raspberry, spice, and pepper. Finishes smooth and in a couple of layers, with a coffee-like bitterness at the very end. Limited but a gritty contender. **86 Best Buy** *—M.S. (9/1/2004)*

VEGA SICILIA

Vega Sicilia 1994 Unico Gran Reserva Tempranillo Blend (Ribera del Duero) $325. Who else but Vega holds wines for more than 10 years before their release? This gorgeous/nico spent 104 months in large casks and smaller barrels, yet there's virtually no overt wood. The nose is foresty and complex, with hints of tomato, leather, and licorice. Flavors of plum, cherry, and vanilla are otherworldly, and there's enough tobacco to conjure memories of a fine cigar. A Tempranillo-Cabernet-Merlot blend worthy of its reputation. **95 Editors' Choice** *—M.S. (6/1/2005)*

Vega Sicilia 1987 Unico Gran Reserva Tempranillo Blend (Ribera del Duero) $200. **90** *—J.C. (11/1/2001)*

VEGA SINDOA

Vega Sindoa 1998 Cabernet Sauvignon-Tempranillo (Navarra) $7. **84** *—M.M. (8/1/2000)*

Vega Sindoa 1999 Barrel Fermented Chardonnay (Navarra) $10. **86** *—M.M. (8/1/2000)*

Vega Sindoa 2002 Merlot (Navarra) $8. A good, affordable Merlot. Leather, plum, and cherry notes mix with a touch of green pepper to yield a friendly, mostly sweet red with a nice mouthfeel. Mocha, vanilla, and fudge on the finish make for a tasty end. **87 Best Buy** *—M.S. (10/1/2004)*

Vega Sindoa 1996 Reserva Red Blend (Navarra) $16. **86** *—M.M. (8/1/2000)*

Vega Sindoa 2000 Rosé Blend (Navarra) $7. **87** *—M.M. (4/1/2002)*

Vega Sindoa 2002 Tempranillo-Merlot (Navarra) $7. **86 Best Buy** *—M.S. (11/15/2003)*

Vega Sindoa 2000 White Blend (Navarra) $7. **86 Best Buy** *—M.M. (4/1/2002)*

VEGAVAL PLATA

Vegaval Plata 1996 Crianza Cencibel (Valdepeñas) $10. **86** *—J.C. (8/1/2000)*

Vegaval Plata 1993 Reserva Tempranillo (Valdepeñas) $12. **82** *—J.C. (11/15/1999)*

VEIGADARES

Veigadares 2002 White Blend (Rias Baixas) $18. More action on the nose than the palate, as the bouquet pushes toasted wood along with pear. Meanwhile, the mouth is dilute, with modest apple and pineapple flavors. Finishes on the thin side, but with heavy barrel notes. An oak-aged blend of Albariño, Treixadura, and Loureiro. **84** *—M.S. (12/31/2004)*

VICENTE GANDIA

Vicente Gandia 2001 Generación 1 Red Blend (Utiel-Requena) $19. Composed of 50% Bobal, a rubbery, hard-tannin grape, and Cabernet Sauvignon; to call this wine shrill would be an understatement. The color is purple, the nose dense but quiet. Black

SPAIN

cherry flavors with unforgiving acidity and tannins create a grabby, squelching palate feel. **83** *—M.S. (6/1/2005)*

Vicente Gandia 2000 Hoya De Cadenas Reserva Prevada Tempranillo-Cabernet (Utiel-Requena) $11. More minty oak than fruit on the nose, with simple but clean candied fruit flavors. A bit short on depth and complexity, but totally drinkable, especially after some airing. Decent texture to the finish, with leftover spice and wood-based flavors. **85** *—M.S. (6/1/2005)*

VILLACEZAN

Villacezan 2003 Molendores Prieto Picudo (Viño Tierra de León) $12. Dark in color, with questionable cleanliness. In the mouth, it's meaty, big, and unbalanced. Finishes with slight mushroom and sherry notes. The grape used is Prieto Picudo. **80** *—M.S. (3/1/2005)*

Villacezan 2001 Doce Meses Red Blend (Viño Tierra de León) $17. Muddled to start, with chocolate and earth aromas along with heavy, seemingly chewable berry fruit. Big on the palate, with slightly over-ripe plum backed by overt vanilla and brown sugar. A three-grape mix of Prieto Pecudo, Mencìa, and Tempranillo. **84** *—M.S. (6/1/2005)*

Villacezan 2003 Elverite Verdejo (Viño de la Tierra de Castilla y León) $11. Lightweight and flaccid, with distant melon and citrus rind flavors. Short and simple, but not at all offensive. **82** *—M.S. (12/31/2004)*

VIÑA ALBALI

Viña Albali 1998 Gran Reserva Tempranillo (Valdepeñas) $11. Light and dry, with a touch of raisin, mint, and butter on the nose. Tomato and red cherry are the prime flavors, and the finish is fresh and lean. **83** *—M.S. (10/1/2005)*

VIÑA ARNÁIZ

Viña Arnáiz 1999 Crianza Red Blend (Ribera del Duero) $19. **87** *—C.S. (11/1/2002)*

VIÑA BORGIA

Viña Borgia 2000 Garnacha (Campo de Borja) $6. **86 Best Buy** *—M.M. (4/1/2002)*

VIÑA CANCHAL

Viña Canchal 2001 Crianza Tempranillo (Ribera del Guadiana) $9. A commonplace yet good Tempranillo, with red-fruit aromas and some leather. Cherry and strawberry grace the racy palate, which is carried by hard tannins and raw acids. Tastes good but the mouth-feel is rough. A true country wine in every sense of the word. **86 Best Buy** *—M.S. (3/1/2005)*

VIÑA CAROSSA

Viña Carossa NV Tinto Red Blend (Spain) $6. The ultimate Spanish table wine in that it has no vintage and is likely a blend of bulk wines from various regions. Yet it's not bad; raspberry and cherry aromas and flavors are decent, while the finish is crisp, dry, and fairly clean. **83** *—M.S. (5/1/2004)*

Viña Carossa NV Brut White Blend (Spain) $5. **84** *—M.S. (12/31/2002)*

VIÑA CONCEJO

Viña Concejo 1999 Crianza Tempranillo (Cigales) $20. This crianza has some stuffing and it's definitely still kicking. The nose is meaty, robust, and full of spice, leather, and black fruit. The plate pours forth with blackberry and some powerful wood notes, while the finish remains woody but flows cleanly. Solid, warm, and ready to drink. **87** *—M.S. (12/31/2004)*

VIÑA GODEVAL

Viña Godeval 2000 White Blend (Valdeorras) $16. **89** *—M.M. (4/1/2002)*

VIÑA IJALBA

Viña Ijalba 1998 Reserva Tempranillo Blend (Rioja) $20. The nose contains beet, fir, and air freshener aromas, while the acidic palate pumps red plum and raspberry without any restraint. Tannic, racy and hard. **82** *—M.S. (10/1/2005)*

VIÑA IZADI

Viña Izadi 1998 Expresión Tempranillo (Rioja) $60. **91** *—K.F. (11/1/2002)*

Viña Izadi 1997 Selección Tempranillo (Rioja) $45. **89** *—M.M. (9/1/2002)*

Viña Izadi 2001 White Blend (Rioja) $14. **83** *—M.S. (10/1/2003)*

VIÑA MAGAÑA

Viña Magaña 2001 Baron de Magaña Merlot (Navarra) $22. Full and heavy, with a smack of berry, oak, and bouillon on the nose. Big blackberry and espresso notes on the palate seem warm and raw, while the tannins force the finish toward the bitter side. **83** *—M.S. (12/31/2004)*

Viña Magaña 1998 Dignus Red Blend (Navarra) $12. Not very pleasant as the nose offers sour, burnt aromas. Then comes a palate that's weedy and tart. Some cherry and cola flavors are present, but it's still fiery and awkward. **82** *—M.S. (9/1/2004)*

VIÑA MAYOR

Viña Mayor 1996 Reserva Red Blend (Ribera del Duero) $16. **84** *—J.C. (11/1/2001)*

Viña Mayor 2000 Crianza Tempranillo (Ribera del Duero) $13. Dry and lean, with apple-skin aromas. Light and fruity on the palate, with some fading raspberry and strawberry flavors. Pretty much a one-note tune. **83** *—M.S. (12/31/2004)*

Viña Mayor 1996 Gran Reserva Tempranillo (Ribera del Duero) $30. Saucy and mildly seductive, with aromas of herbs, leather, and exotic spices. In the mouth, however, things seem a touch rustic and burnt. The palate carries some serious zing and spice, but to call it smooth would be a stretch. **86** *—M.S. (6/1/2005)*

VIÑA MEIN

Viña Mein 2001 White Blend (Ribeiro) $16. Touches of nectarine, apricot, and wildflower grace the nose. The plate is equally floral and nice, and the finish is soft and mildly nutty. Where it takes a hit, however, is in the mouthfeel: it seems flat, like an older Alsatian wine or something similar. **86** *—M.S. (3/1/2004)*

Viña Mein 2000 Blanco White Blend (Ribeiro) $16. **86** *—M.M. (4/1/2002)*

VIÑA PRÓDIGUS

Viña Pródigus 2001 Roble Tinta de Toro (Toro) $18. Starts with strong scents of cured meat and marinade, before turning toward hard-smoked rubber. A bit tart in the mouth, with red raspberry and green pepper notes. Not terribly ruity, with a raw feel. But overall it has more positives than negatives, and it should go well with grilled meats. **85** *—M.S. (10/1/2005)*

VIÑA SARDASOL

Viña Sardasol 2004 Tempranillo (Navarra) $7. Foresty and smoky, with berry and earthy plum flavors. Soft in the mouth, with only mild tannins. Overall it's plump and generous, although the complexity and depth are moderate at best. **84 Best Buy** *—M.S. (11/15/2005)*

Viña Sardasol 2000 Reserva Tempranillo Blend (Navarra) $11. A bit rubbery at first, but then it picks up steam and clarity. Raspberry, cherry, and earth flavors are good, as is the light finish that shows touches of citrus and vanilla. Nothing special but absolutely nothing to take issue with. **85** *—M.S. (11/15/2005)*

VIÑA SASTRE

Viña Sastre 1999 Pago de Santa Cruz Tempranillo (Ribera del Duero) $85. **92** *(4/1/2003)*

Viña Sastre 1996 Pago de Santa Cruz Gran Reserva Tempranillo (Ribera del Duero) $175. **90** *(4/1/2003)*

Viña Sastre 1999 Pesus Tempranillo Blend (Ribera del Duero) $375. **94 Cellar Selection** *(4/1/2003)*

VIÑA SILA

Viña Sila 2003 Naia Des Verdejo (Rueda) $28. A barrel-fermented Verdejo, which will work for some and seem wrong to others. The nose is wood-heavy, with smoke, butterscotch, and licorice. In the mouth, it's ripe and full of spiced pear and vanilla flavors. A one-trick pony in that it's dominated by oak. Still, the quality of the fruit and oak is solid. **88** *—M.S. (6/1/2005)*

VIÑA SOLORCA

Viña Solorca 1999 Roble Tempranillo (Ribera del Duero) $12. **85** *—C.S. (11/1/2002)*

VIÑALCASTA

Viñalcasta 2000 Crianza Tempranillo (Toro) $14. Thick and saucy, with a nose akin to BBQ. Along the way are chocolate, stewed prune, and bacon. The mouth sports rich, ripe cherry, and berry fruit while the easygoing finish yields more of that oaky bacon found on the nose. On the heavier but not too much so. **86** *—M.S. (12/31/2004)*

VIÑAS DEL CENIT

Viñas del Cenit 2003 Venta Mazzaron Tempranillo (Viño de la Tierra de Manchuela) $15. This modern-style wine could be designated as Toro, but it comes from a village that predates the Toro D.O. so it keeps the "Vino de la Tierra" moniker. That said, it's a first-ever Tempranillo made by the New Zealand enologist Amy Hopkinson, and like many new-wave Spanish bruisers five times pricier it pours on the smoky aromas in front of a textured, extracted palate. In terms of sheer flavor per dollar, you'll be hard pressed to do better. **90 Best Buy** *—M.S. (11/15/2005)*

VIÑAS DEL VERO

Viñas del Vero 2003 Clarion White Blend (Somontano) $NA. Hailing from a more obscure mountainous region, this Chardonnay-based white blend is a potent brew. The nose offers pointed lime, citrus, and cream aromas, which are followed by vanilla-tinged pear and spice flavors. Big boned yet clean, with a piquant finish. **88** *—M.S. (6/1/2005)*

VINOS JEROMIN

Viños Jeromin 1999 Cosecha de Familia Félix Martinez Reserva Red Blend (Viños de Madrid) $45. On one hand it shows black cherry, plum, and licorice. On the other there are green, lettuce-like aromas and flavors. Along the way is some tang on the palate, length to the herbal finish, and an adequate mouthfeel. **84** *—M.S. (6/1/2005)*

VINOS SANZ

Viños Sanz 2004 Finca La Colina Sauvignon Blanc (Rueda) $NA. In Rueda, sometimes the Sauvignon Blanc and Verdejo taste similar. But in this case there's no mistaking things. This S.B. is sharp, with

SPAIN

teeth to the nose and palate. Classic sweaty gooseberry aromas lead to pure citrus, slate, and grass on the tongue. As good as you're going to find in Spanish Sauvignon. **90** —*M.S. (6/1/2005)*

VIONTA

Vionta 2000 Albariño (Rias Baixas) $12. 81 —*M.M. (9/1/2002)*

Vionta 2003 Single Vineyard Albariño (Rias Baixas) $18. Yellow in color, with a heavy disposition. The nose yields sweet and ripe mango, melon, and Lemon Pledge aromas. Additional lemon and tangerine carries the monoline palate. Best as a simple shellfish wine. **84** —*M.S. (12/31/2004)*

VITICULTORES BERCIANOS

Viticultores Bercianos 2001 Gran Riocua Mencia (Bierzo) $65. A strange brew. Starts off with charred espresso aromas, not really the way elegant Bierzo wines usually go. Lots of oak throughout, with a stewy personality. Bold but bumbling. **80** —*M.S. (6/1/2005)*

VIZCONDE DE AYALA

Vizconde de Ayala 1999 Crianza Tempranillo (Rioja) $12. Thin, with flavors of cherry skins and lemon juice. Not nearly enough flesh to support the acidity. **81** —*M.S. (8/1/2005)*

YLLERA

Yllera 1986 Black Label Red Blend (Viño da Mesa de Toledo) $28. 86 —*J.C. (11/1/2001)*

Yllera 1999 Oak Selection Tempranillo (Viño de Mesa de Castilla y León) $9. 87 Best Buy —*J.C. (11/1/2001)*

ZUMAYA

Zumaya 1999 Crianza Tempranillo (Ribera del Duero) $17. Light cherry, earth, and smoke notes are more encouraging than the tart, pointed palate, which features sour cherry and berry fruit. On the finish, you get lemony oak and some grabby tannins. **83** —*M.S. (12/31/2004)*

Zumaya 1998 Reserva Tempranillo (Ribera del Duero) $25. Raw and woody, with thin cherry fruit and hints of tangy, almost sour strawberry. Lightweight yet gritty. **80** —*M.S. (1/1/2005)*

Other International

BULGARIA AND ROMANIA

As they prepare for admission to the European Union in 2007, these two countries have been upgrading their vineyards and wineries. Bulgaria has some 200,000 acres of vinifera vines in production, Romania has about the same. Look for good-value Chardonnays, Merlots, and Cabernets from Bulgaria in particular. Merlot and Cabernet show promise in Romania, along with indigenous reds such as Feteasca Neagra.

CANADA

The Canadian wine industry divides neatly in half. In eastern Canada, the Niagara Peninsula north of Lake Ontario produces the vast majority of the region's wines. The government-funded switch to vinifera vines in the early 1990s revolutionized the region, which produces roughly four-fifths of Canada's wine grapes. Though a wide range of varietal white and red wines are made, it is the region's ice wines, marketed in super-tall, slim, 375 ml bottles, that have brought it global acclaim. Meanwhile, British Columbia has been quietly building a substantial wine industry of its own, especially on the bluffs surrounding Lake Okanagan, where a compelling blend of wine and recreational tourism draws visitors year-round. Everything from Germanic Rieslings to Burgundian Pinots to Bordeaux-style red wines and even Syrah can be ripened here. More than one hundred wineries call British Columbia home, with more opening every month.

CROATIA

Original homeland to Zinfandel—known on the Dalmatian coast as Crljenik Kasteljanski. Plavac Mali is a similar grape, making sometimes tough, tannic wines.

GREECE

Greece's best, most distinctive wines are indigenous grape varieties that are unknown elsewhere. Moschofilero is Greece's answer to Pinot Grigio—a light, attractively fruity white that can be charming when cleanly made. Reds tend to be more rustic, whether made from Agiorgitiko or Xinomavro.

HUNGARY

Although home to the storied wines of Tokaji and Egri Bikaver (Bull's Blood), quality was stunted by the chaos that supplanted Communism. Western investment and heroic individual efforts are just beginning to bear fruit.

ISRAEL

High-tech farming is a hallmark of Israeli agriculture, and grape growing is no different, with carefully metered irrigation of international grape varieties the rule rather than the exception. A new generation of carefully sculpted reds is raising the bar.

LEBANON

For years, Lebanese wine was synonymous with Château Musar, but now other names have joined the Hochar family in making wine amidst the ruins. Reds show the most promise.

SLOVENIA

Bordering Italy's Collio region, Slovenia produces many of the same grape varieties, including pungent Sauvignon and classy Tocai, as well as blended whites.

URUGUAY

Uruguay is South America's fourth-largest wine producer (behind Chile, Argentina, and Brazil), and, in global wine terms, is best described as an emerging market.

With a couple hundred years of grape-growing history to its name, and 135 years of commercial winemaking history, Uruguay has never quite caught on the way Argentina and Chile have. Nonetheless, many vinifera grapes, most imported from France, are grown in Uruguay, including Cabernet Sauvignon, Merlot, Pinot Noir, Riesling, and Gewürztraminer. That said, the calling-card grape for the country is Tannat, a rustic variety hailing from Madiran, in southwest France. Somewhat of a chameleon, Uruguayan Tannat can be made in a racier, fruity style or in a more international, barrel-aged style.

BRAZIL

SALTON

Salton NV Demi-Sec (Brazil) $7. This blend of Chardonnay and Riesling from southern Brazil is sweet and a touch green. The feel is respectable and the flavors are more or less candy in a glass: look for sugary lime and melon. **84 Best Buy** *—M.S. (12/31/2005)*

BULGARIA

DAMIANITZA

Damianitza 2002 Reserva (Melnik) $10. Light in body and lacking flesh to cover its dry, scratchy tannins. Modest cherry flavors can't compete with dull cedar and leather notes. **81** *—J.C. (6/1/2005)*

KANOV VINEYARD

Kanov Vineyard 2003 Reserve Unfiltered Cabernet Sauvignon (Danube Hills Valley) $15. A very drinkable wine that could pass for a well-made cru bourgeois, this Cabernet was a nice surprise. Scents of smoke, cedar, and leather; crisp cherries accented by meaty, earthy notes on the palate. Claret-weight, with soft tannins. Drink now. **86** *—J.C. (6/1/2005)*

SUN VALLEY

Sun Valley 2003 Merlot (Bulgaria) $10. Fresh and bouncy, with grapy, fruit-juicy flavors that lack true depth or richness. Still, it's cleanly made, young, and has some appeal. **83** *—J.C. (6/1/2005)*

VINI

Vini 2002 Cabernet Sauvignon (Sliven) $7. Lacks intensity, giving up modest earth and tart cherry flavors. **82** *—J.C. (6/1/2005)*

CANADA

CAVE SPRING

Cave Spring 1997 Gamay (Niagara Peninsula) $9. **84** *—J.C. (8/1/1999)*

Cave Spring 1999 Ice Wine Riesling (Niagara Peninsula) $50. **88** *—J.C. (3/1/2001)*

Cave Spring 1997 Indian Summer Riesling (Niagara Peninsula) $18. **92** *—J.C. (8/1/1999)*

COLIO

Colio 1998 Icewine Riesling (Lake Erie) $NA. **90** *—J.C. (3/1/2001)*

HENRY OF PELHAM

Henry of Pelham 1998 Botrytis Affected Riesling (Niagara Peninsula) $30. **88** *—J.C. (3/1/2001)*

Henry of Pelham 1998 Select Late Harvest Riesling (Niagara Peninsula) $23. **87** *—J.C. (3/1/2001)*

INNISKILLIN

Inniskillin 2003 Ice Wine Riesling (Niagara Peninsula) $80. Lovely icewine, balancing orange-marmalade sweetness against zesty acidity. Not overly heavy, yet completely mouthfilling, with hints of apple and orange blossoms on the nose. Imported by Vincor USA. **92** *—J.C. (9/1/2005)*

Inniskillin 1997 Oak Aged Ice Wine Vidal Blanc (Niagara Peninsula) $80. **89** *—J.C. (3/1/2001)*

Inniskillin 2002 Sparkling Ice Wine Vidal Blanc (Niagara Peninsula) $90. Perfumey aromas of corn, melon, and ginger set the stage for one of the more unique wines on the market. It's a true dessert-level ice wine, but one with a creamy mouthfeel, thanks to the multitude of tiny bubbles that seem to aid in balancing the sweetness. Strange at first, but tasty. **91** *—J.C. (9/1/2005)*

JACKSON-TRIGGS

Jackson-Triggs 2002 Proprietor's Reserve Cabernet Sauvignon (Okanagan Valley) $15. This round, supple Cabernet boasts easy-to-drink flavors of black cherries, earth, and tobacco. Notes of vanilla add interest, while the soft tannins on the finish give it just enough structure. **85** *—J.C. (9/1/2005)*

Jackson-Triggs 1998 Proprietor's Grand Reserve Ice Wine Riesling (Okanagan Valley) $60. **92** *—J.M. (12/1/2002)*

Jackson-Triggs 2003 Proprietor's Reserve Icewine (187mL) Vidal Blanc (Niagara Peninsula) $20. The smaller bottle size makes this perfect for more intimate gatherings. Peach and creamed corn aromas give way to mouthfilling honey flavors. Fat, but not that complex or long. **87** *—J.C. (9/1/2005)*

Mission Hill 1999 Bin 99 Pinot Noir (Okanagan Valley) $8. **85** *—P.G. (12/31/2001)*

Osoyoos Larose 2002 Le Grand Vin Bordeaux Blend (Okanagan Valley) $35. The second vintage of this heralded joint venture between Vincor (owner of Jackson-Triggs) and Groupe Taillan of Bordeaux is an intriguing wine that starts with vibrant red berries, dried herbs, and cracked-pepper notes but thins out a bit on the finish. Credit the creamy midpalate to consulting enologist Michel Rolland. **87** *—J.C. (9/1/2005)*

Croatia

FERA VINO

Fera Vino NV Grasevina (Slavonija) Welschriesling (Croatia) $9. From the grape also known as Welschriesling, an aromatic, fragrant wine brimming with peach, mineral, wildflower, and citrus. Bone dry and tart with high acidity, this refreshing sipper is like a cross between Sauvignon Blanc and Riesling. **86** *—S.H. (10/1/2004)*

Greece

A. BABATZIM

A. Babatzim 2002 Domaine Anestis Babatzimopoulos Malvasia Bianca (Vin de Pays de Macedoine) $22. If you know Italian Malvasia, you know what to expect from this version—bland melon and pear flavors. What you might not expect is for the wine to be slightly off-dry and to finish with a perky tang, making it a candidate to pair with Asian dishes. **84** *—J.C. (9/2/2004)*

ACHAIA CLAUSS

Achaia Clauss 1996 Mavrodaphne of Patras Reserve (Peloponnese) $20. Made much like tawny Port, this russet-brown wine features aromas of coffee, toffee, and walnuts. It's sweet but not overly so, with hints of maple syrup that add a sense of refinement to the straightforward flavors. **86** *—J.C. (9/2/2004)*

Achaia Clauss NV Muscat de Patras (Patras) $9. 84 *—J.C. (9/1/2004)*

AGROS

Agros 2003 Assyrtiko (Santorini) $14. Peach, anise, and citrus aromas set the stage for this light, tart wine whose flavors turn lemony and crisp. Really zingy on the finish. **85** *—J.C. (9/2/2004)*

ALEXANDROS MEGAPANOS

Alexandros Megapanos 2002 Savatiano (Spata) $8. Light in body and flavor intensity, but boasts a helping of stone-dust minerality to go along with its clean pineapple, pear, and apple flavors. **85 Best Buy** *—J.C. (9/2/2004)*

ANTONOPOULOS

Antonopoulos 2002 Chardonnay in New Oak (Greece) $25. 83 *—J.C. (9/2/2004)*

Antonopoulos 2003 Collection White Dry Table Wine (Greece) $15. Shows some toasty, caramel-popcorm scents, but also pleasant enough peach, pineapple, and lemon flavors. Finishes intensely citrusy, with mouthpuckering acids that scream for food. **86** *—J.C. (9/2/2004)*

ARGYROS

Argyros NV Atlantis White Blend (Santorini) $15. Starts out plump-seeming, then finishes with powerful acidity. In between you get flavors of apples, pears, and citrus fruits, also hints of fresh herbs. **85** *—J.C. (9/2/2004)*

BOUTARI

Boutari 2003 Assyrtiko (Santorini) $15. Not only is this 100% Assyrtiko, it's fermented and aged entirely in stainless steel, which completely preserves its biting acidity. It has some waxy, citrusy aromas and flavors, but they are secondary to the wine's dominating acids, which leave the mouth clean and tingling after each taste. **85** *—J.C. (9/2/2004)*

Boutari 2002 Kallisti Assyrtiko (Santorini) $19. This is 100% Assyrtiko from Santorini, barrel-fermented in French oak. As a result, it shows some nutty, toasty elements on the nose, some softer peach fruit on the palate, and then shows trademark Assyrtiko acids on the finish, finishing a bit hard and tart. **87** *—J.C. (9/2/2004)*

Boutari 2003 Moschofilero (Mantinia) $15. Moschofilero is a grape that the Boutari company has high hopes for, as sales of the wine have skyrocketed in the U.S. Pleasant floral aromas lead into a wine with peach, strawberry, and herb flavors. The mouthfeel is plump, the finish virtually dry. A pleasant cocktail-hour white when you're looking for something a little different. **86** *—J.C. (9/2/2004)*

Boutari NV Muscat (Samos) $14. With only one winery on the island of Samos, the quality of this bottling depends on the Boutari company's selection of lots. This orangey, honeyed bottling was one of the best basic Muscats of Samos we tried, balancing sugar, acid, and alcohol very well. **87** *—J.C. (9/2/2004)*

Boutari 1999 Xinomavro Merlot Red Blend (Imathia) $18. 86 *—(11/15/2002)*

Boutari 2003 Fantaxometocho White Blend (Paros) $20. This intriguing blend of 70% barrel-fermented Chardonnay and 30% stainless steel-fermented Vilana comes from the island of Crete. The Chardonnay component provides toasty, nutty, and peachy nuances, while the Vilana gives fine acidity and bright green apple flavors. Give it a few months in the bottle to come together. **88** *—J.C. (9/2/2004)*

CHÂTEAU JULIA

Château Julia 2000 Merlot (Adriani) $23. 87 *—C.S. (11/15/2002)*

DOMAINE CONSTANTIN LAZARIDI

Domaine Constantin Lazaridi 1998 Amethystos Cabernet Sauvignon (Drama) $30. 89 *—C.S. (11/15/2002)*

DOMAINE COSTA LAZARIDI

Domaine Costa Lazaridi 2002 Oenodea Cabernet Blend (Vin de Pays de Macedoine) $10. 84 *—J.C. (9/2/2004)*

Domaine Costa Lazaridi 2003 Amethystos White Blend (Vin de Pays de Macedoine) $14. This open and welcoming blend of Sauvignon Blanc, Sémillon, and Assyrtiko starts off with pear and apple scents that glide easily into plump stone-fruit flavors. A bit of white-peppery spice kicks it up a notch on the finish. 86 *—J.C. (9/2/2004)*

DOMAINE MERCOURI

Domaine Mercouri 1999 Refosco Red Blend (Ilias) $15. 89 *—(11/15/2002)*

GAIA ESTATE

Gaia Estate 2003 14-18h Agiorgitiko (Peloponnese) $10. 83 *—J.C. (9/2/2004)*

Gaia Estate 2002 Notios Agiorgitiko (Peloponnese) $11. 86 *—M.S. (11/15/2003)*

GENTILINI

Gentilini 2003 Robola (Cephalonia) $15. Tart, lemony, and refreshing, with scents of green apples and lime alongside hints of peach and almond. It's a harmonious, lightweight blend of stone fruits and citrus with not an off note to be found. 87 *—J.C. (9/2/2004)*

GEROVASSILIOU

Gerovassiliou 2003 Malagauzia (Greece) $22. Not profoundly complex, but juicy and satisfying, this single-varietal Malagousia's aromas and flavors bring to mind nectarines and clementines harmoniously bound together with great balance and length. 88 *—J.C. (9/2/2004)*

GLINAVOS

Glinavos 1999 Red Velvet Red Blend (Greece) $17. 82 *—J.C. (9/2/2004)*

HAGGIPAVLU

Haggipavlu 2000 Agiorgitiko (Corinth) $14. 84 *—J.C. (9/2/2004)*

HARLAFTIS

Harlaftis 2001 Argilos Agiorgitiko (Corinth) $12. 81 *—J.C. (9/2/2004)*

HATZI MICHALIS

Hatzi Michalis 2002 Chardonnay (Atalanti Valley) $15. 83 *—J.C. (9/2/2004)*

HELIOPOULOS

Heliopoulos 2003 White Blend (Santorini) $16. Perhaps it's a trick of this wine's slightly coppery hue, but it seems to have some peach and strawberry scents along with intense pink grapefruit flavors. Its medium weight gives the impression of ripe fruit balanced by racy acids, finishing clean and crisp. 87 *—J.C. (9/2/2004)*

KARYDA

Karyda 2001 Xinomavro (Naoussa) $20. At first glance, this Xinomavro seems overly tannic, but come back to it later, and the tannins have started to smooth out. Tough, leathery fruit backs sturdy, roasted plum flavors. Finishes with hints of tea and coffee. Decant in advance, or age 3–5 years. 88 *—J.C. (9/2/2004)*

KEO

Keo NV Domaine D'Ahera Mavro Red Blend (Cyprus) $11. 84 *—(11/15/2002)*

KIR-YIANNI

Kir-Yianni 2003 Akakies Rosé Blend (Amyntaion) $11. Boldly flavored and assertive, with distinctive aromas and flavors of strawberries, cherry tomatoes, and herbs like oregano and basil. This highly individual rosé would be a good match to various summery main-course salads. 87 *—J.C. (9/2/2004)*

KOUROS

Kouros 2000 Agiorgitiko (Corinth) $9. 80 *—J.C. (9/2/2004)*

Kouros 2002 Roditis (Patras) $9. Not really, but it shows some similarities in its lemon-lime and ginger aromas and lightbodied, stony, minerally flavors. Made from Roditis grapes, a main component of Retsina. 84 *—J.C. (9/2/2004)*

KTIMA VOYATZI

Ktima Voyatzi 2001 Red Blend (Greece) $24. First, this wine has fruit—big fruit. Black cherries, even some grapiness. Second, the wine also has tannins—big tannins. Mouthstarching tannins. Will age bring this wine balance and harmony? Frankly, the score is a hedge—this is uncharted territory for us. 85 *—J.C. (9/2/2004)*

LATHAZANNI

Lathazanni 2003 Roditis (Corinth) $10. Lacks a bit of concentration, but showcases cleanly made pear and peach fruit on a lightweight frame. Refreshing. 85 *—J.C. (9/2/2004)*

MANOLESAKI ESTATE

Manolesaki Estate 2001 Cabernet Sauvignon (Drama) $23. Strawberry isn't a typical Cabernet descriptor, but it applies to this wine, which also boasts more classic notes of dried herbs, leather, and cedar.

Supple tannins make this Cab instantly approachable. **87** *—J.C. (9/2/2004)*

Manolesaki Estate 2002 Sauvignon Blanc-Chardonnay (Drama) $22. This interesting blend boasts aromas of preserved lemons and fresh herbs, then turns a bit plumper in the mouth, with nectarine flavors joining in. Tart and high-acid on the finish, making it a natural with oily seafood dishes like fresh sardines. **85** *—J.C. (9/2/2004)*

MINOS

Minos 2002 Vilana (Crete) $16. Smells buttery and caramelly, then shows clean apple, pear, and citrus fruit on the palate. Medium-weight, with a finish that turns more tropical, developing hints of pineapple, melon, and citrus. Vilana is the grape variety. **85** *—J.C. (9/2/2004)*

NASIAKOS

Nasiakos 2003 White Blend (Mantinia) $16. **84** *—J.C. (9/2/2004)*

NICO LAZARIDI

Nico Lazaridi 1999 Magic Mountain Red Bordeaux Blend (Drama) $50. An ambitious effort, with plenty of tasty oak influence in the form of coffee and vanilla aromas and flavors. Fruit is ripe and soft; tannins are supple and harmonious, giving the impression of immediate drinkability. **86** *—J.C. (9/2/2004)*

Nico Lazaridi 2001 Moushk Muscat d'Alexandrie (Drama) $23. Strongly floral, but also marked by a hint of nail polish. Once past that, it's sweet but well-balanced by tart acids and dominated by its powerful floral quality—clover blossoms? **85** *—J.C. (9/2/2004)*

Nico Lazaridi 2002 Magic Mountain White Sauvignon Blanc (Drama) $33. A valiant effort at making a full-bodied, barrel-fermented Sauvignon Blanc that falls just short. The toast and butter noes dominate the pear and peach fruit. **84** *—J.C. (9/2/2004)*

PALIVOU

Palivou 2001 St. George Agiorgitiko (Corinth) $13. With its firm acids and modest tannins, tart cherries, and worn leather, this is a natural burger wine—something assertive enough to pair with strong, simple flavors without being overwhelmed, yet not so complex as to demand finer fare. **85** *—J.C. (9/2/2004)*

Palivou 2001 Chardonnay (Corinth) $16. This well-oaked Chardonnay is plump and custardy in the mouth, with standard pear, cinnamon and butter flavors all enveloped in a large helping of vanilla. **85** *—J.C. (9/2/2004)*

PAPAGIANNAKOS

Papagiannakos 2000 St. George Agiorgitiko (Attica) $18. **84** *—J.C. (9/2/2004)*

PAVLIDIS

Pavlidis 2001 Cabernet Blend (Drama) $18. This blend of 70% Cabernet Sauvignon, 20% Merlot, and 10% Limnio offers a rush of cherries and sweet vanilla upfront, but not a lot of richness to back it up. Dry and astringent on the finish; try in a couple of years. **85** *—J.C. (9/2/2004)*

PORTO CARRAS

Porto Carras 2003 Melisanthi Assyrtiko (Côtes de Meliton) $15. **83** *—J.C. (9/2/2004)*

Porto Carras 2001 Lidia (Côtes de Meliton) $15. **84** *—J.C. (9/2/2004)*

Porto Carras 1999 Syrah (Halkidiki) $80. This is a brawny, ripe wine, with fruit flavors that veer toward prune and molasses while folding in dark earthy notes. Big and bulky, with full tannins that need 3–5 years to resolve. **86** *—J.C. (9/2/2004)*

PROVENZA

Provenza 2001 White Blend (Naoussa) $12. **84** *—J.C. (7/1/2003)*

SAMOS

Samos 2000 Grand Cru Vin Doux Naturel White Blend (Samos) $10. **88** *— (11/15/2002)*

SPYROS HATZIYIANNIS

Spyros Hatziyiannis 2002 White Blend (Cyclades) $10. Anise, pear, and mineral aromas and flavors imbue this wine with a fine degree of complexity. It's also richer than most of the whites from Santorini, yet it still retains a refreshing bite on its tart, minerally finish. **88 Best Buy** *—J.C. (9/2/2004)*

TSANTALI

Tsantali 2002 Athiri (Vin de Pays de Macedoine) $10. Another light-bodied, seafood white, Athiri is most often blended with Assyrtiko. In this stand-alone version, you get hints of pear and citrus on the nose, then lime zest dusted with minerals on the finish. **84** *—J.C. (9/2/2004)*

Tsantali 1999 Metoxi of Mt. Athos Cabernet Blend (Greece) $22. This blend of Cabernet Sauvignon and the indigenous Limnio shows the great improvement in Greek winemaking over recent years. While the '96 version is thinning out a bit, yet stubbornly tannic, this '99 is round and supple, packed with plum, black cherry, and vanilla flavors and finishes long. **89** *—J.C. (9/2/2004)*

Tsantali 2000 Organics Cabernet Sauvignon (Halkidiki) $24. Right now this vibrant, dark purple wine is closed up and dominated by toasty new oak—vanilla and cedar notes take the lead. But the wine appears to have the structure to support this ambitious oak treatment, the fruit just needs some time to re-emerge. Try in 2008. **88** *—J.C. (9/2/2004)*

Tsantali 2000 Halkidiki Vineyards Merlot (Halkidiki) $12. This simple, supple, modern Merlot blends black cherries and vanilla. It's well made, straightforward, and easy to drink. **86** *—J.C. (9/2/2004)*

Tsantali 1998 Epilegmenos Reserve Red Blend (Rapsani) $18. This light- to medium-weight wine exhibits fine complexity, blending earth, tobacco, mint, and red berries on the nose, then adding in hints of vanilla and orange peel on the long, layered finish. Drink now–2010. **88** *—J.C. (9/2/2004)*

Tsantali 1997 Epilegmenos Reserve Red Blend (Rapsani) $13. **88** *—(11/15/2002)*

Tsantali 1992 Rapsani Grand Reserve Red Blend (Rapsani) $43. **83** *—J.C. (9/2/2004)*

Tsantali 1999 Syrah (Greece) $17. Herbal, peppery overtones mark this Syrah, but the slightly creamy core of this wine is built around bright, bouncy cherry, and vanilla flavors. Turns a bit green and peppery again on the finish. **85** *—J.C. (9/2/2004)*

Tsantali 2003 Ambelonas White Blend (Halkidiki) $23. This blend of Sauvignon Blanc and the local Assyrtiko has medium intensity and some unusual aromas of acrylic dust, lemon grass, and honey. The palate has a meaty, cured-ham quality along with flavors of grapefruit and nectarine. Lengthy enough on the finish, but a bit bland. From Greece. **86** *(7/1/2005)*

Tsantali 2002 Chromitsa White Blend (Mount Athos) $16. **84** *—J.C. (9/2/2004)*

TSELEPOS

Tselepos 2000 Agiorgitiko Red Blend (Corinth) $15. **90** *—(11/15/2002)*

UNION DE COOPERATIVES VINICOLES DE SAMOS

Union de Cooperatives Vinicoles de Samos 1999 Nectar Vin de Paille Muscat (Samos) $20. Brown sugar, honey, caramelized nuts—what comforting, warming scents waft from the glass. It's plump but not overly sweet, more nutty and honeyed, with citrusy notes that give it a sense of structure. Made from sun-dried Muscat grapes, then aged in oak for three years. **90 Editors' Choice** *—J.C. (9/2/2004)*

VATISTAS

Vatistas 2002 Assyrtiko (Peloponnese) $20. **84** *—J.C. (9/2/2004)*

Vatistas 2001 Cabernet-Aghiorgitiko (Peloponnese) $15. **83** *—J.C. (9/2/2004)*

Vatistas 2000 Regional Wine Red Blend (Peloponnese) $14. **82** *—J.C. (9/2/2004)*

HUNGARY

OREMUS

Oremus 2000 Furmint (Tokaji) $10. **89 Best Buy** *—R.V. (11/15/2002)*

ISRAEL

BARKAN

Barkan 2000 Reserve Cabernet Sauvignon (Galil) $20. With its tobacco and earth notes, this Israeli Cab could almost pass for Bordeaux, except that it also oozes cassis fruit and has the ripe, supple mouthfeel that says warm climate. Finishes with gentle tannins, hints of coffee and vanilla and a bit of lemony tartness. Drink now. **88** *—J.C. (4/1/2005)*

Barkan 2000 Superieur Cabernet Sauvignon (Galilee) $75. Full-bodied and firm textured, with ripe, smooth tannins. The wine serves up a fine blend of blackberry, cassis, coffee, toast, and herb flavors. On the finish, it's long, with a tangy citrus edge. Kosher. **89** *—J.M. (4/3/2004)*

Barkan 1998 Reserve Chardonnay (Galil) $8. **84** *(4/1/2001)*

BINYAMINA

Binyamina 2002 Special Reserve Chardonnay (Galilee) $15. Bland on the palate, with burnt, acrid notes on the nose and a lemony finish. **81** *—J.C. (4/1/2005)*

CARMEL

Carmel 2002 Ben Zimra Single Vineyard Cabernet Sauvignon (Upper Galilee) $25. The biggest and most muscular of Carmel's single-vineyard Cabs, this wine blends hints of green bean and smoke with ripe cassis and blackberry. Extracted and tannic, and just a little rough on the finish. Try in 2007. **87** *—J.C. (4/1/2005)*

Carmel 1998 Private Collection Cabernet Sauvignon (Galil) $12. **81** *—M.S. (4/1/2002)*

Carmel 2002 Zarit Single Vineyard Cabernet Sauvignon (Upper Galilee) $25. Herbal and earthy, but this Carmel effort also features soft, slightly chewy tannins and nice cherry fruit. **85** *—J.C. (4/1/2005)*

Carmel 2002 Kerem Single Vineyard Merlot (Shomron) $25. Richly textured and dense, but the flavors are a touch herbal, leaning toward cherry tomatoes rather than cherries or plums. Chewy, even a bit meaty, on the finish. **87** *—J.C. (4/1/2005)*

Carmel 1999 Valley Wines Petite Sirah (Shomron) $9. **83** *(4/1/2001)*

Carmel 1998 Vineyards Selected Shiraz (Shomron) $12. **82** *(4/1/2001)*

CASTEL

Castel 1996 Grand Vin Cabernet Sauvignon-Merlot (Haut-Judeé) $41. **91** *(11/15/2002)*

DALTON

Dalton 2002 Reserve Chardonnay (Galilee) $21. Smooth and viscous, with some pretty high-toned toast upfront. Vanilla, peach, apple, pear, and Mandarin orange are at the core, finishing with a bright punch. Kosher. **87** *—J.M. (4/3/2004)*

Dalton 2000 Reserve Merlot (Galilee) $37. A bright wine with a cherry core framed by firm tannins. Herbal overtones, licorice, coffee, and tea notes add interest. On the finish, it remains fairly bright. Kosher. **86** *—J.M. (4/3/2004)*

Dalton 2002 Reserve Sauvignon Blanc (Galilee) $18. A full-bodied wine that serves up zippy acidity. The flavors are bright, with hints of pineapple, lemon, and grapefruit. A touch of sourness mars the finish. Kosher. **81** *—J.M. (4/3/2004)*

GALIL MOUNTAIN

Galil Mountain 2001 Yiron Cabernet Sauvignon-Merlot (Galilee) $26. A blend of 78% Cabernet Sauvignon and 22% Merlot, this wine displays decent aromas of cherries, earth, and herbs, but fails to develop a sense of verve or energy on the palate, ending on dull notes of coffee and dark chocolate. **84** *—J.C. (4/1/2005)*

GAMLA

Gamla 2000 Cabernet Sauvignon (Galilee) $16. Plum, blackberry, and graham-cracker notes start this wine off on the right foot, but it's tart and racy on the palate, with only modest black-cherry flavors. **83** *—J.C. (4/1/2005)*

Gamla 1998 Chardonnay (Galilee) $12. **84** *(4/1/2001)*

GOLAN HEIGHTS

Golan Heights 2003 Golan Chardonnay (Galilee) $15. This unwooded Chardonnay delivers a mouthful of low-acid, low-intensity fruit, ranging from pears and lemons to tropical and citrus fruits. Soft finish. **84** *—J.C. (4/1/2005)*

Golan Heights 2003 Golan Emerald Riesling (Galilee) $11. Smells nice, with fresh apple and citrus scents, but the flavors seem cooked and slightly sweet, finishing on a dull note without the requisite balancing acidity. **81** *—J.C. (4/1/2005)*

GUSH ETZION

Gush Etzion 2000 Cabernet Sauvignon-Merlot (Judean Hills) $27. This 70-30 blend boasts attractive aromas of cherries, menthol, and vanilla, then delivers cassis and vanilla flavors tinged with hints of green bell pepper. Supple and easy on the palate. **86** *—J.C. (4/1/2005)*

SEGAL'S

Segal's 2002 Unfiltered Cabernet Sauvignon (Galil) $60. Fans of oak should lap up this wine, but this reviewer found it overly-wooded, with dominant dill and vanilla notes that taste good, yet obscure the underlying fruit. An ambitious effort. **84** *—J.C. (4/1/2005)*

Segal's 2000 Special Reserve Merlot (Galilee) $15. Segal's hit it out of the park in 2000, delivering a Best Buy Special Reserve Cab, and this Merlot, which isn't far behind. Cedar, black cherry, and herb aromas lead into a supple, richly textured palate loaded with balanced coffee and black cherry flavors. Long and harmonious on the finish. **89 Editors' Choice** *—J.C. (4/1/2005)*

TISHBI ESTATE

Tishbi Estate 2000 Baron Chenin Blanc (Galilee) $9. **82** *— (11/15/2002)*

YARDEN

Yarden 1998 Cabernet Sauvignon (Galilee) $26. **87** *— (11/15/2002)*

Yarden NV Brut (Galilee) $20. **86** *(4/1/2000)*

Yarden 2000 Chardonnay (Galilee) $17. **85** *— (11/15/2002)*

Yarden 1998 Blanc de Blancs Chardonnay (Galilee) $20. Light, lean, and crisp, this is a surprisingly racy bubbly from Israel. The toast and lime aromas and flavors are clean and refreshing. And yes, it's kosher, if that's important to you. **86** *—J.C. (12/31/2004)*

Yarden 2002 Odem Organic Vineyard Chardonnay (Galilee) $19. Smells toasty and smoky, with a plump, medium-weight mouthfeel and smoky, leesy flavors. Finishes long, and—you guessed it—smoky. An oak-lover's wine; well made and tasty. Imported by Yarden. **88** *—J.C. (4/1/2005)*

Yarden 1999 Yarden Merlot (Galilee) $23. **86** *—M.S. (11/15/2002)*

Yarden 1998 Mt. Hermon Red Blend (Galilee) $11. **87** *(4/1/2000)*

YATIR

Yatir 2001 Cabernet Sauvignon-Merlot (Judean Hills) $30. Earthy and dull, a flat, boring wine that features modest fruit and a medicinal note. Imported by Royal Wine Corporation. **81** *—J.C. (4/1/2005)*

LEBANON

CHÂTEAU KEFRAYA

Château Kefraya 1997 Cabernet Blend (Bekaa Valley) $23. **91** —*(11/15/2002)*

CHÂTEAU MUSAR

Château Musar 1997 Red Blend (Bekaa Valley) $49. **88** —*J.C. (4/1/2005)*

Château Musar 1998 White Blend (Bekaa Valley) $28. Sherried-smelling, picking up nuances of anise, lacquer, and stone dust, and finishing on a lemony note. An acquired taste. **82** —*J.C. (4/1/2005)*

TISHBI ESTATE

Tishbi Estate 2000 Tishbi Vineyards Cabernet Sauvignon (Bekaa Valley) $16. **90** — *(11/15/2002)*

MEXICO

L.A. CETTO

L.A. Cetto 1996 Private Reserve Cabernet Sauvignon (Valle de Guadalupe) $18. **87** *(7/1/2003)*

L.A. Cetto 2000 Private Reserve Chardonnay (Valle de Guadalupe) $14. **84** *(7/1/2003)*

L.A. Cetto 1999 Petite Sirah (Valle de Guadalupe) $8. **83** *(7/1/2003)*

MOLDOVA

CRICOVA ACOREX

Cricova Acorex 1999 Riesling (Moldova) $6. **82** *(9/1/2004)*

MOROCCO

HICKORY RIDGE

Hickory Ridge 1999 Special Cuvée Shiraz (Beni M'Tir) $6. **82** *(10/1/2001)*

ROMANIA

TERRA ROMANA

Terra Romana 2003 Muscat Ottonel (Tarnave) $10. This Muscat is best served with mildly spicy Asian dishes, where its floral, off-dry flavors will offset some chili heat, while the refreshing acids on the finish will clean the palate. Lychee, melon, and tangerine flavors add exotic notes. **84** —*J.C. (6/1/2005)*

Terra Romana 2000 Reserve Red Blend (Dealu Mare) $9. Fading and already brick in color, this dull, earthy wine finishes tart and watery. **80** —*J.C. (6/1/2005)*

SLOVENIA

MOVIA

Movia 2002 Sauvignon (Brda) $24. This Slovenian white shows exotic, unconventional aromas that land squarely in the realm of tropical fruit and flowers. Soft and creamy on the palate, with melon, honeycomb, and just a spritz of lemon. Subtle and sleek on the finish as it gently drifts away. Quite interesting and satisfying. **89** *(7/1/2005)*

URUGUAY

ARIANO

Ariano 2002 Cabernet Sauvignon (Canelones) $7. Peanut and leather aromas, with a candied sweetness to the palate. Sweet and sugary, maybe a likable trait for some. **80** *—M.S. (11/15/2004)*

Ariano 2003 Selección Red Blend (Canelones) $10. Among the Ariano line, this Tannat, Cab Franc, and Syrah blend is the best. Yet it's still light, with caramel aromas along with hints of berry fruit. Mild strawberry and plum on the palate before a finish with kick. **83** *—M.S. (11/15/2004)*

BODEGONES DEL SUR

Bodegones Del Sur 2003 Sauvignon Blanc (Juanico) $9. Mild citrus aromas are clouded by the scent of green pepper and peas. Flavors of apple, pineapple, and citrus are ultimately sour, as is the finish. Not much nuance is on display, and in the wide world of Sauvignon Blanc, you can surely do better. **82** *—M.S. (9/1/2004)*

Bodegones Del Sur 2000 Reserve Tannat (Juanico) $12. Like all the wines from Uruguay, this one has rock-hard tannins that clamp down on the palate. But the nose of cool earth, leather, and black fruit is nice, and the flavor profile is nothing to take issue with. The cherry and raspberry flavors are full and healthy, and the wine's acidity forms a nice base for the fruit. Drink with food due to the firm tannins. **86** *—M.S. (9/1/2004)*

DELUCCA

DeLucca 2000 Tannat (El Colorado) $10. Round and tight, like Tannat is known to be, with burly black-fruit aromas and flavors. There's detectable cassis and raisin notes prior to a spicy, tannic finish that deals licorice and coffee. Pretty heavy, full-bodied stuff for sure, but a decent rendition of Tannat. Very much worth a go. **85** *—M.S. (1/1/2004)*

STAGNARI

Stagnari 2000 Salto Premier Tannat (Uruguay) $12. Almost over the top, but not quite. The nose seems a bit burnt and meaty, but the palate is all plum and blackberry fruit. There's good balance here and the tannins are not too wicked. But the finish is short and the early impression left by the wine exceeds the final impression by a healthy distance. **84** *—M.S. (1/1/2004)*

TOSCANINI

Toscanini 2003 Sauvignon Blanc (Canelones) $8. Not great, but shows some banana and pear flavors and aromas. Weak and watery; inoffensive. **80** *—M.S. (10/1/2004)*

Toscanini 1999 Reserve Tannat (Canelones) $13. If this five-year-old wine is an indication, then Tannat doesn't age that well. This example is rusty and orange at the rim, with dried fruit, caramel and earth on the nose. Over the hill. **80** *—M.S. (10/1/2004)*

VIÑA PROGRESO

Viña Progreso 2003 Reserve Chardonnay (Uruguay) $19. Butterscotch in color and aromas, with apple as the core flavor. Full and interesting, with a long, warm finish. A good deal of zest and attitude. Millions of miles away from Burgundy, but not bad. **85** *—M.S. (10/1/2004)*

VIÑEDO DE LOS VIENTOS

Viñedo de los Vientos 2000 Eolo Gran Reserva Red Blend (Atlantida) $15. The bouquet has a strong lemony scent, one that seems to come from the wood treatment it went through. But there's also saturated black fruit, boysenberry flavors, and, of course, huge, drying tannins. This is not an ordinary wine, or an ordinary Tannat. It certainly brings some zing to the table. **84** *—M.S. (1/1/2004)*

VINSON RICHARDS

Vinson Richards 2000 Merlot (Juanico) $9. The bouquet of cherry, vanilla, and leather is fairly complete and nice. Flavors of dried fruits, brandy, and chocolate pave the way to a quiet, simple, and clean finish. With a fair amount of Piedmontese character, this one has a bit in common with Nebbiolo. It's definitely leathery and tight, but the flavors are good. **85** *—M.S. (9/1/2004)*

Vinson Richards 2000 Reserve Tannat (Juanico) $17. Inky and saturated in the nose, with aromas of chocolate, coffee, and red berries. The palate kicks up cherry, plum and chocolate, and the finish is typically dry and tannic. But it's also tasty and comes in a couple of layers. This wine shows more style than most from Uruguay and would be worth a go with grilled steak. **86** *—M.S. (9/1/2004)*

US-FRANCE

DEUX C

Deux C 2002 Viognier (Santa Barbara County-Condrieu) $50. Defies categorization, in more ways than one. The wine is a joint venture between Cold Heaven's Morgan Clendenen and Condrieu winemaker Yves Cuilleron, and is a 50-50 blend of their wines. The wine has California's sunny flavors (sunflowers, hay, pretty yellow fruit), and a full, rich, viscous Condrieu texture. **88** *(11/15/2004)*

The United States

California

California wines account for a sixty-four percent share of the United States wine market, according to the Wine Institute, the venerable trade and lobbying group whose membership includes 840 wineries. However, Wine Business Monthly, a trade magazine, estimates that there are 2,445 wineries doing business in California.

Whatever the number, in 2004 California wineries produced wine grown on 440,296 acres of vineyards, about sixty percent of them planted with red or black grapes. The most widely planted major varietals, not surprisingly, are Chardonnay and Cabernet Sauvignon, although the latter has seen a slight percentage drop in recent years, as more Syrah and Pinot Noir have been planted.

Vineyard on the western slopes of the Napa Valley, Oakville, Napa County, California.

The Central Valley of California contains the majority of plantings, but grapes from this hot inland region are seldom if ever included in premium bottlings. California's reputation for world-class wine rests almost entirely on coastal bottlings, "coastal" being defined as anywhere a true maritime influence penetrates the land, through gaps in the Coast Ranges that run from Oregon down to below Los Angeles. The Pacific Ocean is a chilly body of water, even in high summer. Without the gaps, California's coastal valleys would be almost as hot as the Central Valley, and incapable of producing fine, dry table wine. With the gaps, however, come the cooling winds and fogs that make for premium grape growing.

PREDOMINANT VARIETIES

Cabernet Sauvignon The great grape of the Médoc, in France's Bordeaux region, which has been the model—and point of departure—for California claret-style wines for more than a century. Napa County dominates statewide acreage of Cabernet, as well as quality. The great estates of Napa Valley have been joined by scores of small, ambitious boutique wineries on the cutting edge of viticultural and enological—and pricing—practices. California Cabernet is rich, full-bodied, opulent, fruity, and hedonistic, matching supreme power with a velvety elegance. The best will easily age for a decade or two.

Pinot Noir Undoubtedly the great varietal success story of the late twentieth century in California wine, red or white, Pinot Noir continues to make the most astounding advances. It favors the coolest climates available, although if growing conditions are too chilly, the grapes fail to ripen. Pinot Noir is far more demanding to grow than almost any other wine grape, but when conditions are right, the wines can be majestic: lush, silky, complex, and (to use an overworked but useful word) seductive.

Chardonnay For at least fifty years, Chardonnay has been California's greatest dry white wine. Although in the 1990s the media touted an "A.B.C." phenomenon—anything but Chardonnay—the wine remains a triumph. Like Pinot Noir, Chardonnay is best grown in cool coastal conditions, although it is more forgiving, and the odd bottling from anywhere can gain praise. Full-throttle Burgundian winemaking is the norm, but lately, Australian-style unoaked Chardonnay has been enjoying favor.

Zinfandel Historians still quibble about when exactly this varietal came to California. It has been here for at least one-hundred-and-fifty years, and always has had its admirers. Zinfandel comes into and goes out of fashion, and has been made in styles ranging from sweet and Porty to dry and tannic to "white." The current thinking leans toward balance, in the model of a good Cabernet. The best Zinfandels come from cool coastal regions, especially old vines, most usually in Sonoma and Napa, but the Sierra Foothills have many old vineyards that produce great bottlings. Paso Robles occasionally comes up with a masterpiece.

Sauvignon Blanc This great grape of Sancerre and Pouilly-Fumé, in the Loire Valley, similarly produces a dry, crisp, pleasantly clean wine in California. It can be tank fermented and entirely unoaked, or just slightly oaked, in order to preserve the variety's fresh, citrusy flavors. Some producers look to Bordeaux to craft richer, barrel-fermented wines, often mixed with Sémillon, or even Viognier. "Fumé" Blanc is a synonym. If overcropped or unripe, the wines can have unpleasant aromas.

Merlot This other great grape of Bordeaux was greeted with fanfare by critics in the 1980s and 1990s, but Merlot never really reached Cabernet's superstardom. Merlot was said to be the "soft" Cabernet, but with modern tannin management, it's no softer than Cabernet, and, in fact can be quite hard. The wines, though, can be exceptional, especially in Napa Valley, Carneros, and parts of Sonoma County and Santa Barbara.

Syrah and Rhône Varieties Plantings of Syrah have increased, as consumers and critics alike welcome these deeply fruity, richly balanced wines. Syrah grapes are remarkably adaptable, and grow well almost everywhere. The wines tend to be organized into cool-climate and warm-climate bottlings, the former drier and more tannic, the latter often soft and jammy. The other red Rhône varieties, especially Mourvèdre and Grenache, are still exotic specimens, tinkered with lovingly by a coterie of Rhône Rangers.

Other Dry Whites Viognier, the darling of the Northern Rhône, grew in popularity in the 1990s. The wine achieved fame for its exotic, full-throttle fruit, floral, and spice flavors, but proved surprisingly elusive when it came to balance. An emerging handful display true Alsatian richness and complexity. The best are from cool coastal valleys, but if the climate is too cold, the wines turn acidic and green.

MAJOR CALIFORNIA WINE REGIONS

American grape-growing regions are authorized by the federal government, upon petitioning from individuals, and are called "American Viticultural Areas" (AVAs), or "appellations." Currently, there are ninety-five AVAs in California, with more petitions filed everyday.

Napa Valley The state's oldest AVA is its most famous. Napa Valley (established in 1981), at 225,000 acres, is so large that over the years, it has developed fourteen appellations within the larger one. Napa always has been home to California's, and America's, greatest Cabernet Sauvignons and blends, an achievement not likely to be upset anytime soon. In all other varieties, it strives, usually successfully, to compete.

Sonoma County Sonoma is California's most heterogeneous wine county. So diverse is its climate, from hot and sunny inland to cool, foggy coastal, that every grape varietal in the state is grown somewhere within its borders, often as not to good effect. In warm Alexander Valley and Dry Creek Valley, Zinfandel finds few peers. Out on the coast, and the adjacent Russian River Valley, Pinot Noir first proved that California could compete with Burgundy, and Pinot's huge improvements continue to startle. Chardonnay excels everywhere; Syrah is dependable. Old-vine field blends, comprised often of obscure French varieties, have their admirers. Meanwhile, Alexander Valley Cabernet, especially from the steep, rugged west-facing slopes of the Mayacamas Mountains, is showing continuing improvement.

Monterey County This large, cool growing area originally was planted with huge vineyards, making inexpensive wine in industrial-sized quantities. Serious, boutique-oriented adventurers sought out nooks and crannies where they could produce world-class wine, and the Santa Lucia Highlands AVA (1992) has been the most noteworthy result. Its slopes and benches are home to ripe, full-bodied, high-acid Pinot Noir, Chardonnay, and, increasingly, Syrah.

San Luis Obispo County Sandwiched between Monterey to the north and Santa Barbara to the south, this coastal county often is overlooked. But its twin AVAs, Edna Valley and Arroyo Grande Valley, arguably produce some of California's most distinguished Pinots and Chardonnays. A few vintners have made enormous strides with cool-climate Syrah and other Rhône varieties.

Santa Barbara County If any county deserves the honor for greatest achievements in winemaking over the last twenty years, it is this South-Central Coast region. The action began in the inland Santa Ynez Valley, a warmish-to-hot AVA. Years of experiments have shown the valley's aptitude for lush, complex red Rhône wines and Sauvignon Blanc. Merlot has been an unexpected star; Cabernet Sauvignon has not yet shown greatness. Closer to the ocean, the newest AVA, Santa Rita Hills (2001), was on critics' radar for Pinot Noir for showing lush fruit with an acidity found in few other regions. Chardonnay follows the same pattern. As in most cool-climate growing areas, determined winemakers tinker with Syrah, often excitingly.

Mendocino County Inland Mendocino is hot and mountainous. Beyond an individual winery here and there, it has yet to make a name for itself. The county's cool AVA is Anderson Valley, which has shown great promise in Pinot Noir.

The Sierra Foothills This enormous, multi-county region sprawls along the foothills of the Sierra Nevada Mountains. At their best, Foothills wines can be varietally pure, with Zinfandel taking the lead, although Cabernet Franc has been an unexpected star. Too many Foothills vintners, unfortunately, produce wines whose rusticity and high alcohol outweigh their charm.

WASHINGTON

In barely three decades, the Washington wine industry has risen from a half-dozen wineries trying their hand at a bit of Riesling, Gewürztraminer, and experimental plots of Pinot Noir and Cabernet, to become a global player. The state now boasts more than 375 wineries, 30,000 vineyard acres, and a track record for producing crisply etched, vibrantly fruity Rieslings; sleek and polished Chardonnays; ripe and flavorful Sémillons; bold, luscious Merlots; well-defined, muscular Cabernets; and vivid, smoky, saturated Syrahs.

Though a distant second to California in terms of total production, Washington wines get more medals and higher scores and sell for lower average prices on a percentage basis. There are seven appellations, all but one (the Puget Sound AVA) lying east of the Cascade mountains. The largest AVA by far is the Columbia Valley, a vast area of scrubby desert, punctuated by irrigated stretches of farmland with row crops, hops, orchards, and vineyards. The Cascade Mountains protect this inland desert from the cool, wet maritime climate of western Washington. Eastern Washington summers are hot and dry, and during the growing season, the vines average two extra hours of sunlight per day.

Inside the Columbia Valley AVA are the smaller appellations of Yakima Valley, Walla Walla Valley, Red Mountain, and Horse Heaven Hills. A sixth, the Columbia Gorge AVA, lies just to the west along the Columbia river.

Mount Rainier viewed over vineyards near Zillah, Washington.

Several factors account for Washington's unique wine-growing profile. Its vines are planted on their own roots, as phylloxera (see Glossary) has not been a problem in the state. Most vineyards are irrigated, and the scientifically timed application of precise amounts of water has become an important aspect of grape-growing and ripening. The lengthy fall harvest season, which can run from late August into early November, is marked by warm days and very cool nights. The 40 to 50 degree Fahrenheit daily temperature swings keep acids up as sugars rise, which means that in many vintages, no acidification is necessary. Alcohol levels for finished wines have risen, but are still below the numbers for California.

The exploration of Washington terroir is well underway, and the state actually has plantings of Cabernet as old or older than any in California, where vines have been ravaged by disease. Red Mountain in particular has proven itself as a spectacular region for Merlot and Cabernet, and the Red Mountain vineyards of Klipsun and Ciel du Cheval provide grapes to dozens of Washington's best boutique wineries.

Walla Walla has become an important tourist destination, with more than eighty wineries, 1,200 acres of vineyard, year-round recreational activities, and an active and fun-loving wine community. Pioneered in the early 1980s by Leonetti Cellar, L'Ecole No 41, and Woodward Canyon, the valley is now home to dozens of wineries producing small lots of rich, oaky red wines and ripe, succulent whites. Syrah does particularly well.

Eastern Washington has periodically suffered from arctic blasts that can devastate vineyards. The most recent, early in 2004, all but eliminated that year's harvest in Walla Walla. But much is being learned about Washington viticulture, and new plantings are better sited to survive the occasional frigid winters. Additionally, established vineyards are maturing, and older vines with deeper roots are far less likely to be killed by even severe cold.

Most of Washington's wineries produce fewer than two thousand cases of wine annually, and awareness of the state's best wines has been hampered by this lack of production. Additionally, there have been very few wineries large enough to produce soundly-made, inexpensive "supermarket" wines, the kind that help establish a national presence. The wines of Columbia Crest, Covey Run, and Precept brands are beginning to change that, challenging the huge California conglomerates with budget bottles that don't skimp on either character or quality.

USA

OREGON

Unlike Washington, where vineyards are scattered throughout the east, most Oregon vineyards lie in the state's western half. They are somewhat protected from ocean fogs and cloud cover by the coastal mountain range. The farther south you go, the hotter it gets. In the Rogue Valley appellation, centered around the town of Ashland, Syrah and Cabernet can be ripened, though with rather tough, chewy tannins. But it is the Pinot Noirs of the northern Willamette valley that have brought Oregon to the attention of the world.

Oregon became known as the Pinot Noir state at a time when decent Pinot was hard to come by outside of Burgundy. Pioneered by David Lett, David Adelsheim, Dick Ponzi, and Dick Erath, Oregon Pinot in the early years was indeed Burgundian, elegant and light, with modest color and relatively low alcohol levels.

Over the years, as viticulture improved and winemakers learned new techniques, Oregon Pinot became thicker, darker, more jammy, and hot in the ripe years; and more tannic and earthy in the cool ones. Recently, as Pinot Noirs from California, New Zealand, and elsewhere have risen in quality, Oregon vintners have begun turning their attention to other varietals. The Willamette Valley's two hundred-plus wineries still predominantly produce Pinot, but some of the state's most interesting wines are coming from other grapes grown outside the region.

The big challenges for Oregon Pinot are two-fold. First,

Vineyards of Domaine Serene, Dayton, Oregon.

vintage variation is a fact of life, and wines can range from thin, harsh, and weedy to hot, ripe, and impenetrable. Unlike California and Washington, where vintages are far more consistent, Oregon vintners can expect something different every year. Hail, rain, extreme heat, humidity, drought, and vast temperature swings during harvest are the norm, not the exception.

To some degree, this is a good thing, because it suggests that Oregon, like a handful of other winemaking regions scattered across the globe, has the ability to put its own distinct stamp on its wines. The plus side of vintage variation is that each harvest is unique, and imparts specific, unique qualities to the wines of that vintage. The minus side is that not every vintage is all that good, especially where Pinot Noir is concerned.

The second challenge is that there is no longer a generally identifiable Oregon Pinot "style." Some vintners make elegant, light, tannic Pinots that require years to open up, while others make wines so dark and jammy, they are dead ringers for Syrah. And finally, while there are plenty of pricey, single-vineyard Pinots being produced, it is still difficult for consumers to find drinkable, good value, every day bottles.

Oregon's Rieslings and Gewürztraminers remain well-kept secrets. These are lively, juicy, floral, and fragrant wines that are always good value. The state's signature white is Pinot Gris, and it's made in a lush, fruity style that tastes of fresh-cut pears and goes easy on the new oak. The Chardonnays, once clumsy and fat, have dramatically improved with the introduction of Dijon clones.

Some producers have demonstrated remarkable success with grapes not generally associated with Oregon. Syrah is grown in the south, and makes a big, tannic, rough-hewn red wine. At Abacela in central Oregon, Tempranillo has proved surprisingly good, and the old-vine Zinfandels of Sineann, from an eastern Oregon vineyard, are superb. Oregon has added several new AVAs in the past couple of years, but what is most exciting are these new wines from different grapes that promise to open up Oregon to its full potential in the decades ahead.

2820 WINE CO.

2820 Wine Co. 1998 Cabernet Sauvignon (Napa Valley) $32. **91** *—J.M. (12/1/2001)*

2820 Wine Co. 1999 Tain't Hermitage Syrah (Napa Valley) $36. **88** *(11/1/2001)*

6TH SENSE

6th Sense 2003 Syrah (Lodi) $17. Downgraded by one reviewer for being sweet, this Lodi wine did have enough positives to merit a Good rating, starting with hints of wintergreen on the nose and flowing into baked berry flavors. **83** *(9/1/2005)*

A.S. KIKEN

A.S. Kiken 2001 Estate Cabernet Blend (Diamond Mountain) $30. Kind of pricy for a not-so-ripe Cab with green peppercorn and cherry flavors. There's a ton of oak, and the wine is dry, with chunky tannins. From Reverie. **84** *—S.H. (10/1/2005)*

ABACELA

Abacela 2002 Cabernet Franc (Oregon) $24. I'm a big fan of Abacela's wines, and appreciate the effort to do a varietal cab franc, but this wine could benefit from a bit of blending. Tart, spicy, and slightly sweaty, it has the expected blueberry fruit and leathery tannins of cab franc, but the tannins are so dry and dominant that they undercut the middle of the wine and skew the finish. Interesting but not entirely complete. **86** *—P.G. (2/1/2005)*

USA

Abacela 2000 Cabernet Franc (Oregon) $20. **86** *—P.G. (8/1/2003)*

Abacela 2003 Dolcetto (Oregon) $18. There is not a great deal of dolcetto grown in the Northwest, but this is the best version I've yet seen. Its vivid, spicy fruit core expresses the soil, the plant, and the grape in equal proportion. Sappy flavors of spiced plum and wild berry hold the fort; it's built like a race car, sleek, and stylish, with a powerful, tannic frame. **88** *—P.G. (2/1/2005)*

Abacela 2000 Dolcetto (Umpqua Valley) $18. **88** *—P.G. (8/1/2002)*

Abacela 2003 Malbec (Southern Oregon) $23. Black and inky, this aromatic potpourri sends up scents of wet earth, truffle, spice, wild berries, and even a bit of Provençal garrigue. Concentrated and tannic, it adds elements of raw meat, leaf, and forest floor as it rolls across the tongue. Just a bit hot in the finish. **89** *—P.G. (11/15/2005)*

Abacela 2001 Malbec (Umpqua Valley) $20. The 2000 was a stunningly good Malbec; this is just a notch lighter. Mountain-grown fruit flavors dominate: plum, berry, and spice on the palate, with plenty of lip-smacking acids in the back end. What's missing is the weight of deep, dense fruit, but 2001 was a lighter vintage. **90** *—P.G. (5/1/2004)*

Abacela 1999 Malbec (Umpqua Valley) $15. **85** *—P.G. (8/1/2002)*

Abacela 2002 Merlot (Oregon) $18. Oregon Merlot can be extremely hard, green, and tannic, but this complex bottle shows that it need not be. Fruits and spices mingle perfectly, with scents of sandalwood, toffee, smoke, and leather providing depth. Plenty of serious heft to this wine, but the tannins are smoothed out and balanced. **89** *—P.G. (8/1/2005)*

Abacela 2000 Merlot (Umpqua Valley) $18. **88** *—P.G. (8/1/2003)*

Abacela NV Vintner's Blend #6 Red Blend (Oregon) $15. When Abacela does a kitchen sink blend, they don't hold anything back. Thirteen varieties from seven vineyards go into this gem, but rather than creating an unfocused mélange, the result is a lush, fragrant, fruit salad of a red, with some nice new oak and a solid core of berries and plums. **88 Best Buy** *—P.G. (8/1/2005)*

Abacela 2002 Syrah (Oregon) $29. A blend of Umpqua and Applegate valley fruit, this spicy, tannic wine sports a bit of citrus peel, anise, earth, and vanilla for added interest. Tannins are characteristically hard and tight, and it is quite angular at this time, showing some green tea in the tannins. Air it out. **90** *—P.G. (8/1/2005)*

Abacela 2000 Syrah (Umpqua Valley) $25. **90** *—P.G. (9/1/2003)*

Abacela 2002 Tempranillo (Umpqua Valley) $20. The winery has staked its reputation on Tempranillo of all things, and consistently over a half dozen vintages it has surprised and delighted me with the results. Good color for this pale grape, and decent varietal character, though the estate bottling is clearly superior. **87** *—P.G. (8/1/2005)*

Abacela 1999 Tempranillo (Umpqua Valley) $29. **89** *—P.G. (8/1/2002)*

Abacela 2002 Estate Grown Tempranillo (Umpqua Valley) $30. This is from Abacela's own grapes, which were planted in Oregon's Umpqua Valley because the winery's founders believed it was the best place in America to grow Tempranillo. So far, no one has proved them wrong. Concentrated, almost black, bursting with smoke, leather, tar, blackberry, black cherry, graphite, and more. Big, chewy, and firm. **91** *—P.G. (8/1/2005)*

Abacela 2003 Viognier (Oregon) $25. A high test version at 15% alcohol, this successfully skirts the problems that can plague such wines. The high-toned, complex aromas of rose petals, spice, and citrus avoid going volatile; the tropical fruit core never descends into bubble gum, and the bitter citrus rind finish manages to hold onto a sense of appropriate balance. Whew! **88** *—P.G. (2/1/2005)*

ABIOUNESS

Abiouness 2000 Stanly Ranch Pinot Noir (Carneros) $40. From a Lebanese winemaker, a jammy Pinot tasting of cherries, blueberries, black raspberries, and dusty oriental spices, especially clove. It is dry, with lively acids and silky tannins. **87** *—S.H. (2/1/2004)*

ABUNDANCE VINEYARDS

Abundance Vineyards 2000 Talmage Block Viognier (Mendocino County) $18. 88 *—J.M. (12/15/2002)*

ACACIA

Acacia 1993 Brut Champagne Blend (Carneros) $35. 91 *—S.H. (6/1/2001)*

Acacia 2002 Chardonnay (Carneros) $20. A flamboyant style that emphasizes well-ripened fruit flavors, including tangerine and pineapple, and quite a bit of smoky oak. Bold, rich, and opulent, with a creamy, honeyed texture. **90** *—S.H. (6/1/2004)*

Acacia 1998 Chardonnay (Carneros) $21. 87 *(6/1/2000)*

Acacia 2002 Sangiacomo Vineyard Chardonnay (Carneros) $30. Here's a deliciously drinkable Chard, sweet with pineapple and mango flavors and well-oaked, and with the excellent acidity to make it clean and bright. Lasts for a long time on the finish, turning spicy and reprising the mango theme. **90** *—S.H. (10/1/2004)*

Acacia 2003 Pinot Noir (Carneros) $20. Pretty full-bodied and rich for a Pinot, and dark, too. The flavors veer toward black cherries, coffee, and spice, and are very dry. Fortunately it's a silky wine, with zesty acids. Drink now with rich fare, like pork tenderloin. **87** *—S.H. (10/1/2005)*

Acacia 2000 Pinot Noir (Carneros) $27. 89 *(10/1/2002)*

Acacia 1998 Pinot Noir (Napa Valley) $25. 90 *—S.H. (5/1/2000)*

Acacia 1999 Beckstoffer Las Amigas Vineyard Pinot Noir (Carneros) $60. 86 *(10/1/2002)*

Acacia 1996 Beckstoffer Vineyard Reserve Pinot Noir (Carneros) $42. 90 *—M.S. (6/1/1999)*

Acacia 2000 DeSoto Vineyard Pinot Noir (Napa Valley) $52. 91 Cellar Selection *(10/1/2002)*

Acacia 2002 Field Blend Estate Vineyard Pinot Noir (Carneros) $50. Solid scores from tasters for this easy, fresh Pinot. Shows straightforward flavors of coffee, cola, cherries, and anise in a dry, supple wine with a spicy finish. **86** *(11/1/2004)*

Acacia 1999 Lee Vineyard Pinot Noir (Carneros) $50. 87 *(10/1/2002)*

Acacia 1996 Reserve Pinot Noir (Carneros) $32. 89 *(11/15/1999)*

Acacia 2001 St. Clair Vineyard Pinot Noir (Carneros) $50. Rather tannic and earthy, and hard to discern much beyond the tobacco, herb, coffee, and bitter chocolate flavors. Those tannins are tough and gritty. May soften and sweeten in a year or two. **86** *—S.H. (3/1/2004)*

Acacia 1999 St. Clair Vineyard Pinot Noir (Carneros) $50. 86 *(10/1/2002)*

ACORN

Acorn 2002 Alegria Vineyards Dolcetto (Russian River Valley) $22. Bone-dry, earthy, and gritty yet not really tannic, this is one of those wines that goes with almost anything calling for a dry red. There's a cherry tone and peppery finish that suggest tender beef. **84** *—S.H. (8/1/2005)*

Acorn 1999 Alegria Vineyards Dolcetto (Russian River Valley) $20. 82 *—S.H. (11/15/2001)*

Acorn 2001 Alegria Vineyards Medley Rhône Red Blend (Russian River Valley) $22. There are too many varietals to name, but it's sort of a Rhône blend. Drinks dry, rich, and earthy, with a tobaccoey, peppery edge to the cherries and herbs. The tannins are chewy but soft. This is a nice modern-day version of an old field blend. **87** *—S.H. (10/1/2004)*

Acorn 2002 Alegria Vineyards Sangiovese (Russian River Valley) $22. Rather sweetish in ripe, extracted jammy cherry, with a chocolaty finish, yet basically dry, with good acidity and silky tannins. Easy to drink with anything from pizza to vanilla ice cream. **84** *—S.H. (8/1/2005)*

Acorn 2001 Alegria Vineyards Sangiovese (Russian River Valley) $20. This is a medium-bodied, with soft tannins and cherryish fruit. Has good acidity and a cinnamony finish. Easy to drink and easy to like. **87** *—S.H. (10/1/2004)*

Acorn 2002 Alegria Vineyards Axiom Syrah (Russian River Valley) $28. Does a good job at the Syrah thing, namely, a full-bodied red wine, dry and rich in fruit, and soft in tannins and acids. Rises into complexity with the melange of coffee, cocoa, and spice flavors. **86** *—S.H. (8/1/2005)*

Acorn 2000 Alegria Vineyards Axiom Syrah Cuvée Syrah (Russian River Valley) $20. 90 Editors' Choice *—S.H. (12/15/2003)*

Acorn 1998 Alegria Vineyards Heritage Vin Zinfandel (Russian River Valley) $25. 86 *—S.H. (12/1/2000)*

Acorn 2000 Heritage Vines Alegria Vineyards Zinfandel (Russian River Valley) $28. 91 *—S.H. (7/1/2003)*

ADASTRA

Adastra 2003 Chardonnay (Carneros) $30. This toothpicky wine tastes overly oaked by far, and you have to wonder why they plastered it on, since the underlying fruit seems fine, even with the acid. Makes you appreciate the "unoaked" Chardonnay phenomenon. **83** *—S.H. (12/31/2005)*

Adastra 2000 Chardonnay (Carneros) $28. 86 *—S.H. (5/1/2002)*

ADEA

Adea 2000 Chardonnay (Willamette Valley) $20. 85 *—P.G. (9/1/2003)*

Adea 1999 Pinot Gris (Willamette Valley) $15. 85 *—P.G. (2/1/2002)*

Adea 2000 Pinot Noir (Willamette Valley) $35. 85 *—P.G. (4/1/2003)*

Adea 2002 Coleman Vineyard Pinot Noir (Willamette Valley) $35. Fragrant with diverse, interesting, unusual floral, and chocolate scents. The chocolaty oak, though appealing, runs over the light, citrus and cherry fruit, which can't stand up to it. **87** *(11/1/2004)*

Adea 2000 Reserve Pinot Noir (Willamette Valley) $42. 85 *—P.G. (4/1/2003)*

ADELAIDA

Adelaida 2001 Viking Port Cabernet Sauvignon (Paso Robles) $30. Sweet, heavy, and full-bodied, with rich chocolate and blackberry flavors. Turns a little cloying on the soft finish. **84** *—S.H. (8/1/2005)*

Adelaida 2002 HMR Estate Chardonnay (Paso Robles) $30. Not showing much to savor now, a flat, simple wine with earthy, vegetal flavors. **83** *—S.H. (7/1/2005)*

Adelaida 2002 HMR Estate Pinot Noir (Paso Robles) $25. From the cooler western hills of the appellation, a full-bodied Pinot that's smooth, dry and fruity. The pretty flavors of cherries and oak have an edge of tannins that will play well off goat cheese, steak or salmon. **88** *—S.H. (4/1/2005)*

USA

Adelaida 2003 Vin Gris de Pinot Noir (Paso Robles) $15. Dry and fruity, with peach, wild blackberry, and spice flavors, this is a crisp blush wine that has subtlety and complexity. It's fairly full-bodied, with a nice, curranty finish. Try with bouillabaisse. **85** *—S.H. (7/1/2005)*

Adelaida 1996 Syrah (Paso Robles) $24. 88 *—S.H. (10/1/1999)*

Adelaida 1997 Zinfandel (Paso Robles) $20. 83 *—S.H. (5/1/2000)*

Adelaida 2001 Reserve Zinfandel (Paso Robles) $35. 86 *(11/1/2003)*

ADELSHEIM

Adelsheim 2000 Chardonnay (Oregon) $14. 85 *—P.G. (4/1/2002)*

Adelsheim 1996 Stoller Vineyard Chardonnay (Yamhill County) $30. 90 *—P.G. (4/1/2002)*

Adelsheim 2000 Pinot Blanc (Oregon) $12. 91 Best Buy *—P.G. (4/1/2002)*

Adelsheim 1998 Pinot Grigio (Oregon) $14. 82 *(8/1/1999)*

Adelsheim 2000 Pinot Noir (Oregon) $22. 87 *—P.G. (4/1/2002)*

Adelsheim 1998 AVS Pinot Noir (Willamette Valley) $40. 91 *—M.M. (12/1/2000)*

Adelsheim 1998 Bryan Creek Vineyard Pinot Noir (Willamette Valley) $40. 88 *—M.S. (12/1/2000)*

Adelsheim 1999 Elizabeth's Reserve Pinot Noir (Oregon) $36. 91 Editors' Choice *—P.G. (4/1/2002)*

Adelsheim 1999 Goldschmidt Vineyard Pinot Noir (Yamhill County) $36. 90 *—P.G. (4/1/2002)*

Adelsheim 2002 Ribbon Springs Vineyard Pinot Noir (Yamhill County) $45. Earthy, lightly horsey aromas lend accents of leather, bacon, and coffee. There is some sweet, young, grapy fruit, but overall it seems one-dimensional. **84** *(11/1/2004)*

Adelsheim 1996 Seven Springs Vineyard Pinot Noir (Polk County) $30. 86 *(10/1/1999)*

ADLER FELS

Adler Fels 2001 Gewürztraminer (Russian River Valley) $10. 87 Best Buy *—S.H. (11/15/2002)*

Adler Fels 1998 Sauvignon Blanc (Russian River Valley) $11. 86 *—S.H. (11/15/2000)*

ADOBE CREEK

Adobe Creek 2001 Pinot Gris (Sonoma County) $14. 83 *—S.H. (12/1/2003)*

ADOBE ROAD

Adobe Road 2000 Cabernet Sauvignon (Alexander Valley) $39. Raw, unripe and unlikeable, with a bitter finish. Whatever were they thinking when they set the price? **81** *—S.H. (8/1/2005)*

Adobe Road 2001 Zinfandel (Alexander Valley) $32. Opens with the veggies, like canned aspraragus, and drinks a little richer, with black cherries flavors and firm tannins. Okay Zin, but kind of pricey. **83** *—S.H. (8/1/2005)*

AGRARIA

Agraria 1999 Big Barn Red Cabernet Sauvignon (Dry Creek Valley) $52. This wine has a weird aroma of cough drops and varnish, and is sharp in acids, with a medicinal cherry taste that finishes a little sweet. Tasted twice, with consistent results. **82** *—S.H. (10/1/2004)*

AHLGREN

Ahlgren 1997 Harvest Moon Vyd Cabernet Sauvignon (Santa Cruz Mountains) $33. 82 *(11/1/2000)*

AIRLIE

Airlie 2002 Gewürztraminer (Willamette Valley) $10. Bone dry style, which puts the emphasis on dusty, dried spices rather than flowers. There are concentrated fruit flavors of cantaloupe, citrus, pear, and honey, lending the impression of sweetness. Unusual and rich. 87 Best Buy *—P.G. (2/1/2005)*

Airlie 2002 Two Vineyard-Old Vines Pinot Noir (Willamette Valley) $20. Young, full, and forward, this delivers a big burst of nice, ripe fruit right off the top. It's cherries and chocolate, all good, but it loses some points for a gritty, tannic finish. 88 *—P.G. (2/1/2005)*

AJB VINEYARDS

AJB Vineyards 1997 Syrah (Paso Robles) $21. 90 *—S.H. (7/1/2002)*

ALAPAY

Alapay 2000 Viognier (Santa Barbara County) $19. 88 *—S.H. (9/1/2002)*

Alba 1998 East Coast Chardonnay (New Jersey) $10. 83 *—J.C. (1/1/2004)*

ALBAN

Alban 1993 Estate Grenache (Edna Valley) $NA. The bouquet of this wine made me very happy. Pure, intense raspberry-cherry, with spicy clove, cinnamon, vanilla. Fine and alluring. Tons of raspberry fruit in the mouth, with a roast coffee earthiness. Dry, clean, supple, elegant. A chef's dream. Delicate, powerful, uplifted. 94 *—S.H. (6/1/2005)*

Alban 2000 Roussanne (Central Coast) $25. 90 *—S.H. (6/1/2003)*

Alban 1998 Lorraine Syrah (Edna Valley) $45. 89 *(11/1/2001)*

Alban 1992 Reva Syrah (Edna Valley) $NA. Still a good color. Pepper, earth, blackberry, roasted coffee aromas. Still some sturdy tannins to shed. Tight now, with blackberry and cherry flavors, but closed, austere. Could re-emerge from its cocoon. Drink now-2010. 90 *—S.H. (6/1/2005)*

Alban 2000 Costello T.B.A. Viognier (Edna Valley) $65. 95 *—S.H. (6/1/2003)*

ALBEMARLE

Albemarle 2002 Simply Red Bordeaux Blend (America) $22. This blend of 51% Merlot, 30% Cabernet Sauvignon, and 19% Cabernet Franc carries a label designation as American Red Wine, which means the grapes could be from anywhere, but they were made into wine in Virginia. Pleasant spice, tobacco, and red berry flavors thin out on the finish. 83 *—J.C. (9/1/2005)*

ALDERBROOK

Alderbrook 2003 Chardonnay (Russian River Valley) $18. There's plenty of ripe fruit here, but the wine has too much oak, and has a weird salty flavor. The varietal identity is proper. 83 *—S.H. (11/1/2005)*

Alderbrook 2000 Chardonnay (Dry Creek Valley) $NA. 85 *— (6/1/2003)*

Alderbrook 1997 Dorothy's Vineyard Chardonnay (Dry Creek Valley) $22. 88 *(6/1/2000)*

Alderbrook 2002 Pinot Noir (Russian River Valley) $24. Earthy, simple, and light, with modest cherry and herb flavors. Finishes dry, with a silky mouth feel. 84 *—S.H. (3/1/2005)*

Alderbrook 1999 Pinot Noir (Russian River Valley) $22. 85 *(10/1/2002)*

Alderbrook 2000 Sauvignon Blanc (Dry Creek Valley) $NA. 87 *—S.H. (9/1/2003)*

Alderbrook 2002 Syrah (Dry Creek Valley) $24. Polished and soft in texture, with decent cherry, earth, and cocoa flavors. Could use more intensity. 84 *—S.H. (3/1/2005)*

Alderbrook 2002 Old Vine Zinfandel (Dry Creek Valley) $19. This is great Zin, filled with personality. Showcases the briary, brambly wild blackberry and blueberry flavors, spices, and dusty tannins this appellation is famous for. Finishes dry and smooth. Beautiful and compelling now. 91 *—S.H. (3/1/2005)*

Alderbrook 2000 OVOC Zinfandel (Dry Creek Valley) $25. 85 *—J.M. (3/1/2002)*

Alderbrook 1997 OVOC Zinfandel (Sonoma County) $16. 90 *—L.W. (9/1/1999)*

Alderbrook 2001 Reserve Zinfandel (Dry Creek Valley) $39. 87 *(11/1/2003)*

Alderbrook 2000 Reserve Zinfandel (Russian River Valley) $39. 91 *—P.G. (3/1/2002)*

ALEX SOTELO CELLARS

Alex Sotelo Cellars 2002 Dalraddy Vineyard Zinfandel (Napa Valley) $28. The front label says it's unfiltered, which may explain the spoiled, vegetal aroma. 81 *—S.H. (6/1/2005)*

ALEXANDER

Alexander 1998 Petite Sirah (Monterey) $23. 84 *—S.H. (12/31/2003)*

ALEXANDER VALLEY VINEYARDS

Alexander Valley Vineyards 2000 Cyrus Cabernet Blend (Alexander Valley) $50. Light and oaky but delicious, like a sweet confection. Intricately laced flavors of blackberry scone, vanilla, crème de cassis, and toast are encased in an airy texture. The tannins are gentle but rich, lending a silken quality to this delicate wine. 89 *—S.H. (6/1/2004)*

Alexander Valley Vineyards 2000 Estate Bottled Cabernet Sauvignon (Alexander Valley) $20. 86 *— (11/15/2002)*

Alexander Valley Vineyards 1998 Estate Bottled Chardonnay (Sonoma County) $15. 85 *(6/1/2000)*

Alexander Valley Vineyards 2001 Wetzel Family Estate Estate Bottled Chardonnay (Alexander Valley) $15. 85 *—S.H. (12/15/2002)*

Alexander Valley Vineyards 1997 Wetzel Family Reserve Chardonnay (Sonoma County) $24. 87 *(6/1/2000)*

Alexander Valley Vineyards 2000 Gewürztraminer (Alexander Valley) $9. 87 Best Buy *—J.M. (12/15/2001)*

Alexander Valley Vineyards 2002 New Gewurz Gewürztraminer (North Coast) $9. 84 *—S.H. (12/31/2003)*

Alexander Valley Vineyards 1997 Estate Bottled Merlot (Sonoma County) $18. 86 *—L.W. (12/31/1999)*

Alexander Valley Vineyards 2000 Wetzel Family Estate Estate Bottled Merlot (Alexander Valley) $20. 85 *—S.H. (11/15/2002)*

Alexander Valley Vineyards 2002 Wetzel Family Estate Pinot Noir (Alexander Valley) $20. A pretty wine with nice flavors of raspberry cola, cherries, vanilla, and sweet oak. It's soft and silky in the mouth, yet has firm acidity. Lots of elegance and style. 88 *—S.H. (3/1/2005)*

Alexander Valley Vineyards 1999 Syrah (Sonoma County) $18. 87 *(10/1/2001)*

Alexander Valley Vineyards 2000 Wetzel Family Estate Syrah (Alexander Valley) $18. 85 *—S.H. (12/1/2002)*

Alexander Valley Vineyards 2001 Redemption Zin Zinfandel (Dry Creek Valley) $30. 88 *(11/1/2003)*

Alexander Valley Vineyards 2001 Sin Zin Zinfandel (Alexander Valley) $20. 86 *(11/1/2003)*

USA

ALEXANDRIA NICOLE

Alexandria Nicole 2001 Lemberger (Columbia Valley (WA)) $21. A clean, bright Lem, pushing up loads of raspberry and sweet blackberry aromas, and framing the fruit with crisp natural acid. It might be mistaken for Grenache, meaty but less rustic than most Lembergers. Laying off the new oak helps; this got just four months in neutral barrels. 55 cases made. 88 *—P.G. (12/15/2005)*

Alexandria Nicole 2004 Destiny Ridge Vineyard Shepard's Mark White Rhône White Blend (Columbia Valley (WA)) $18. Barrel-fermented in neutral oak, this Roussanne/Viognier/Marsanne blend is full and pungent with apricot, peach, and cooked pear flavors. The fruit is nicely set off against cinnamon spice; it's a bit like drinking a baked apple tart, without the sugar. There is some kick to the finish. 88 *—P.G. (12/15/2005)*

Alexandria Nicole 2002 Destiny Ridge Vineyards Syrah (Columbia Valley (WA)) $27. After some initial burnt matchstick aromas blow off, this wine reveals pretty scents of raspberries, blackberries, and minerals. Juicy and medium-bodied, it picks up cedary nuances on the finish. 86 *(9/1/2005)*

Alexandria Nicole 2003 Destiny Ridge Vineyards Viognier (Columbia Valley (WA)) $16. This is a producer to watch closely, as the plans include a destination winery and inn in the heart of eastern Washington wine country, and the Destiny Ridge vineyard is already showing signs of greatness, despite its youth. Plump, thick, viscous, unctuous even, this wine is packed with ripe pear, citrus, and tropical fruit, and finishes with some sweetness, but no rough edges or heat. 90 *—P.G. (12/15/2004)*

ALIENTO DEL SOL

Aliento Del Sol 1998 Bien Nacido Vineyard Chardonnay (Santa Maria Valley) $25. 85 *(6/1/2000)*

Aliento Del Sol 1999 Loma Vista Pinot Noir (California) $25. 88 *(10/1/2002)*

Aliento Del Sol 2002 Sarmento Vineyard Pinot Noir (Santa Lucia Highlands) $28. Well-made and tasty, a good example of cool-climate Pinot, with its fresh, citrusy acidity and layers of cherry, cola, toasty oak, and spice flavors. Juicy and nice. 86 *(11/1/2004)*

ALLORA

Allora 1999 Cielo Red Blend (Napa Valley) $45. 86 *—S.H. (8/19/2003)*

ALTAMURA

Altamura 2001 Cabernet Sauvignon (Napa Valley) $60. Showcases the positive qualities of '01 Napa Cabs in the well-ripened tannins and ripe cherry and cocoa flavors. Could use more depth and seriousness, but it's a lovely wine to drink now. 88 *—S.H. (10/1/2005)*

Altamura 1999 Cabernet Sauvignon (Napa Valley) $60. 89 *—M.S. (5/1/2003)*

Altamura 2001 Sangiovese (Napa Valley) $30. Quite a nice wine, dry and soft, with a lush, generous mouthfeel that conveys rich cherry, chocolate, and oak flavors. There's a touch of over-ripe raisins, and the finish is a bit hot. **88** *—S.H. (6/1/2005)*

ALTERRA

Alterra 1998 Syrah (Russian River Valley) $18. 84 *(10/1/2001)*

AMADOR FOOTHILL WINERY

Amador Foothill Winery 2001 Fumé Blanc (Shenandoah Valley (CA)) $10. 86 *—S.H. (9/1/2003)*

Amador Foothill Winery 1999 Fumé Blanc (Shenandoah Valley (CA)) $10. 85 *—S.H. (8/1/2001)*

Amador Foothill Winery 2004 Rosato of Sangiovese Rosé Blend (Amador County) $10. I wish I liked this wine more. It's bone dry, with herbal, peppery notes, and a little bit of strawberry. Turns watery thin and acidic on the finish. **83** *—S.H. (10/1/2005)*

Amador Foothill Winery 2001 Barrel Select Sangiovese (Shenandoah Valley (CA)) $18. From a winery that's worked hard to get this tough variety, a dry, cherry-infused wine that, despite the light body, has some hefty tannins. Calls for cheeses, olive oil, and rich meats. **86** *—S.H. (11/15/2004)*

Amador Foothill Winery 2000 Grand Reserve Sangiovese (Shenandoah Valley (CA)) $30. 89 *—S.H. (9/1/2003)*

Amador Foothill Winery 2002 Rosato Sangiovese (Amador County) $10. 88 Best Buy *—S.H. (9/1/2003)*

Amador Foothill Winery 2004 Sauvignon Blanc (Shenandoah Valley (CA)) $11. This winery often turns up real jewels. Fans of dry Sauvignon Blancs need to stock up on this one by the case. It has New Zealand-like gooseberries and citrus flavors and a long, rich, spicy finish. **88 Best Buy** *—S.H. (12/31/2005)*

Amador Foothill Winery 2000 Hollander Vineyard Syrah (Sierra Foothills) $20. 84 *—S.H. (9/1/2002)*

Amador Foothill Winery 2001 Clockspring Vineyard Zinfandel (Shenandoah Valley (CA)) $13. 88 *(11/1/2003)*

Amador Foothill Winery 1999 Clockspring Vineyard Zinfandel (Amador County) $13. 84 *—S.H. (11/15/2001)*

Amador Foothill Winery 2002 Esola Vineyard Zinfandel (Shenandoah Valley (CA)) $15. I've been a critic of over-ripeness in red wines, but here, the raisiny flavors complement rather than hinder the fresh wild berries, lending a black currant complexity. It's high in alcohol, but totally dry, and besides, what else would you expect from a high-country Zin? **88** *—S.H. (8/1/2005)*

Amador Foothill Winery 2001 Esola Vineyard Zinfandel (Shenandoah Valley (CA)) $18. 87 *(11/1/2003)*

Amador Foothill Winery 2001 Ferrero Vineyard Zinfandel (Shenandoah Valley (CA)) $15. Extracted and jammy in black cherries and black raspberries, with hints of cocoa, this wine is fully dry and balanced. It tasty through the smooth finish. **87** *—S.H. (3/1/2005)*

AMAVI CELLARS

Amavi Cellars 2003 Syrah (Walla Walla (WA)) $25. Lays on a thick layer of caramel and toast, then moves into tart red berry fruit. Raspberries and vanilla on the palate, finishing with crisp acidity and a sense of elegance. **84** *(9/1/2005)*

AMBERHILL

Amberhill 2000 Cabernet Sauvignon (California) $9. 86 Best Buy *—S.H. (10/1/2003)*

Amberhill 2001 Chardonnay (California) $7. 81 *—S.H. (10/1/2003)*

AMETHYST

Amethyst 2001 Cabernet Sauvignon (Napa Valley) $36. This good, rich Cabernet brims with fancy, ripe black currant, and cassis flavors, well-oaked, that are framed in suave tannins. Feels lush and creamy in the mouth, and for all the fruitiness, it's completely dry. **90** *—S.H. (2/1/2004)*

Amethyst 1998 Vinalia Tuscan Blend (Napa Valley) $17. A wine strong in aromas and flavors, suggesting ripe plums, blackberries, tobacco, leather, and herbs. It's dry as they come, with the kind of sturdy tannins and acids that will stand up to a great big cheesy lasagna. A Nebbiolo-Sangiovese blend. **88** *—S.H. (3/1/2004)*

AMICI

Amici 2001 Cabernet Sauvignon (Napa Valley) $38. Smooth and elegant, with ripe cherry and plum flavors and soft, gentle tannins. Generously oaked, this pretty wine is drinking beautifully now. **90** *—S.H. (10/3/2004)*

Amici 2000 Meritage (Napa Valley) $45. Here's a muscular, intense Bordeaux blend, whose proportion of hillside fruit lends it firm, dusty tannins. The explosive cherry-berry fruit and lush, sweet oak give it a savor that's drinkable now, but the balance and harmony suggest the ability to age for a long time. **92** *—S.H. (11/15/2004)*

Amici 2002 Pinot Noir (Mendocino) $35. Simple, dry, and robust for a Pinot, with a heavy mouth feel. You'll find some tannins underlying the plum and coffee flavors. **84** *—S.H. (4/1/2005)*

AMICUS

Amicus 2002 Cabernet Sauvignon (Napa Valley) $49. This is a big, sweetly ripe 100% Cab, a blend of Yountville and Spring Mountain fruit. It's considerably more acidic and tannic than your usual Napa Cab, but the black currant flavors are as huge as anywhere. Despite the tannins it's best now and for a couple more years. **89** *—S.H. (12/31/2005)*

AMITY

Amity 1999 Gewürztraminer (Oregon) $12. **88** *—P.G. (11/15/2001)*

Amity 2000 Dry Gewürztraminer (Oregon) $12. **91 Best Buy** *—P.G. (12/1/2003)*

Amity 2003 Pinot Blanc (Willamette Valley) $14. The winemaking is stainless steel all the way, and the wine delivers crisp aromatics that mix rose petals, citrus, peach, and honeysuckle. It's all very appealing, with a hint of spritz to add life and lift to the finish. **88** *—P.G. (2/1/2005)*

Amity 1999 Pinot Blanc (Willamette Valley) $12. **85** *—D.T. (11/1/2001)*

Amity 1999 Pinot Noir (Willamette Valley) $20. **87** *(10/1/2002)*

Amity 1997 Pinot Noir (Willamette Valley) $16. **83** *(11/15/1999)*

Amity 1999 Eco Wine Cattrall Brothers Pinot Noir (Oregon) $14. **80** *—M.S. (12/1/2000)*

Amity 2000 Eco-Wine Pinot Noir (Oregon) $15. **85** *—P.G. (4/1/2003)*

Amity 1999 Estate Pinot Noir (Willamette Valley) $30. **90** *—P.G. (12/1/2003)*

Amity 2000 Schouten Vineyard Pinot Noir (Willamette Valley) $15. **89** *—P.G. (4/1/2003)*

Amity 2002 Sunnyside Pinot Noir (Willamette Valley) $30. Plum, cola, cocoa. Weak coffee and cherry flavors. Tart, tannic finish. **85** *(11/1/2004)*

Amity 1998 Winemaker's Reserve Pinot Noir (Willamette Valley) $40. **85** *—M.S. (9/1/2003)*

Amity 2002 Select Cluster Riesling (Oregon) $40. **90** *—P.G. (12/1/2003)*

Amity 2002 Crown Jewel Reserve White Blend (Willamette Valley) $16. **88** *—P.G. (12/1/2003)*

AMIZETTA

Amizetta 1999 Estate Bottled Vigneto del Tacchino Selvatico Cabernet Sauvignon (Napa Valley) $75. **91** *(8/1/2003)*

Amizetta 2002 Complexity Meritage (Napa Valley) $38. A little rough and ready to drink now. Sturdy and dry, with good acidity framing berry flavors; has a nice finish. **86** *—S.H. (10/1/2005)*

AMPHORA

Amphora 2003 Mounts Vineyard Merlot (Dry Creek Valley) $35. Easy does it with this Merlot, with its flavors of blackberries and chocolate. But it's too sweet on the finish, smacking of sugar. **83** *—S.H. (10/1/2005)*

Amphora 2001 Mounts Vineyard Petite Sirah (Dry Creek Valley) $30. **82** *(4/1/2003)*

Amphora 2002 Mounts Vineyard Syrah (Dry Creek Valley) $30. Rich and spicy, with an exuberant peacock's tail of wild berry, cherry, mocha, and sweet roasted coconut spreading across the palate. The lush fruit is wrapped in easy tannins. **86** *—S.H. (12/1/2004)*

AMUSANT

Amusant 2002 Cabernet Sauvignon (Napa Valley) $30. Textbook Napa Cabernet, with its rich, sweet, soft but complicated tannic structure, dry finish, and exuberantly ripe mélange of flavors. They include classic black currants and cassis, roasted coffee-bean, bitter dark chocolate, and sweet, toasty oak. **91** *—S.H. (8/1/2005)*

Amusant 2002 Chardonnay (Napa Valley) $16. This is an earthy Chardonnay, with restrained peach and spice flavors and a kiss of oak. It's also very dry. Has some real complexity in the structure and the finish. **84** *—S.H. (8/1/2005)*

AMUSE BOUCHE

Amuse Bouche 2002 Merlot-Cabernet Franc (Napa Valley) $200. Winemaker-owner Heidi Peterson Barrett (Screaming Eagle, La Sirena, others) chose only Merlot and Cab Franc for this first release, obviously meant to make a statement with its fancy graphics, rock-heavy bottle, and price. The wine is delicious, but so ethereal, you wonder if it wouldn't benefit from a little Cabernet. **90** *—S.H. (10/1/2004)*

ANAPAMU

Anapamu 2001 Chardonnay (Monterey County) $16. **87** *—S.H. (8/1/2003)*

Anapamu 2003 Pinot Noir (Monterey County) $16. Kind of thin, especially considering the price, but it's basically okay. The wine is totally dry and fairly acidic, with cherry flavors and a smooth, silky mouthfeel. **83** *—S.H. (12/15/2005)*

Anapamu 2001 Pinot Noir (Monterey County) $16. **86** *—S.H. (7/1/2003)*

Anapamu 2001 Riesling (Monterey County) $16. 87 *—J.M. (8/1/2003)*

Anapamu 2001 Syrah (Paso Robles) $22. 84 *—S.H. (12/15/2003)*

Anapamu 1999 Syrah (Central Coast) $16. 88 Editors' Choice *(10/1/2001)*

ANCIEN

Ancien 2000 Pinot Noir (Carneros) $32. 87 *(10/1/2002)*

ANDRE

Andre NV Extra Dry Champagne Blend (California) $4. 80 *—S.H. (12/15/1999)*

ANDRETTI

Andretti 2002 Cabernet Sauvignon (Napa Valley) $30. There's something about this lush Cab that keeps you reaching for more. It's soft and velvety, with just enough tannins to keep things perky, but best of all are the flavors. Blackberries and cherries, dusted with cocoa, sprinkled with a dash of cinnamon, and drizzled with crème de cassis. Yummy. **90** *—S.H. (12/1/2005)*

Andretti 2000 Cabernet Sauvignon (Napa Valley) $28. 89 *—S.H. (11/15/2003)*

Andretti 2001 Selection Series Cabernet Sauvignon (North Coast) $12. 85 *—S.H. (11/15/2003)*

Andretti 2004 Chardonnay (Napa Valley) $19. Here's a full-flavored Chardonnay in which toasty oak plays side by side with big, lush tropical fruit flavors to give plenty of mouth satisfaction. There's a vanilla custard and tapioca spice flavor on the finish that's especially rich. **87** *—S.H. (12/1/2005)*

Andretti 2001 Chardonnay (Napa Valley) $16. 90 Editors' Choice *—S.H. (12/15/2002)*

Andretti 2004 Selections Chardonnay (Central Coast) $12. This simple and dry Chard has watered down peach and apple flavors and a touch of oak. Acidity is fine. **83** *—S.H. (12/1/2005)*

Andretti 2001 Merlot (Napa Valley) $24. This beautifully crafted Merlot shows a near-perfect balance of ripe plum, cherry, and cassis-accented fruit with deeper notes of herbs, coffee, and dark unsweetened chocolate. It glides across the palate with a velvety texture and finishes long. Could use a tad more concentration, but it's a lovely wine. **90** *—S.H. (4/1/2004)*

Andretti 1999 Merlot (Napa Valley) $20. 91 *—S.H. (6/1/2002)*

Andretti 2004 Pinot Noir (Napa Valley) $20. For a winery known for Cabernet, Merlot, and Chardonnay, this Pinot is surprisingly good. It's rich in cherry, coffee, unsweetened chocolate, and spice flavors, wrapped in a silky but full-bodied texture. Try with rosemary-grilled lamb chops. **88** *—S.H. (12/1/2005)*

Andretti 2001 Sangiovese (Napa Valley) $18. Explores a nice side of this emerging varietal, with soft acids and brisk tannins that frame cherry, espresso, and herb flavors. This wine strikes the palate as dry and austere, but locked in its core is a potential sweetness that needs only cheese or fatty proteins to make it companionable at the table. **88** *—S.H. (4/1/2004)*

Andretti 2004 Sauvignon Blanc (Napa Valley) $16. The green grass, newly mown hay, lemon, and lime and melon aromas and flavors jump right out of the glass. Crisp acidity, a round, creamy texture, and a dryish finish. **86** *—S.H. (12/1/2005)*

Andretti 2001 Sauvignon Blanc (Napa Valley) $14. 89 *—S.H. (7/1/2003)*

Andretti 2004 Selections Zinfandel (California) $15. Try this rustic wine with rich meats and cheeses, as it's rather sharp in acids, with a racy, raw mouthfeel. The flavors are ripe and strong in berries, chocolate and tangy spices. **84** *—S.H. (12/1/2005)*

ANDREW GEOFFREY

Andrew Geoffrey 2000 Cabernet Sauvignon (Diamond Mountain) $85. 88 *—S.H. (11/15/2003)*

ANDREW MURRAY

Andrew Murray 2001 Esperance Rhône Red Blend (Santa Ynez Valley) $22. A happy wine, easy to slurp, but with some real character. Complexly fruity, with plum, blackberry, tangerine rind, and floral notes. Beautifully lush on the palate, with soft tannins and yet a crisp mouthfeel leading to a spicy finish. A blend of Grenache, Syrah, and Mourvedre. **88** *—S.H. (3/1/2004)*

Andrew Murray 1997 "Roasted Slope" Syrah (Santa Barbara County) $18. 88 *—S.H. (6/1/1999)*

Andrew Murray 2001 Estate Grown Syrah (Santa Ynez Valley) $20. The first estate-labelled Syrah off this fine property is eccentric. It has a Porty aroma with underlying currents of sweet cured tobacco, and while it is bone dry, it has a hot mouthfeel that's thin in fruit, leaving the alcohol and tannins front and center. A big disappointment. **84** *—S.H. (3/1/2004)*

Andrew Murray 1996 Hillside Reserve Syrah (Santa Barbara County) $25. 92 *—S.H. (6/1/1999)*

Andrew Murray 1999 Les Coteaux Syrah (Santa Ynez Valley) $25. 90 *—S.H. (7/1/2002)*

Andrew Murray 2001 Roasted Slope Syrah (Santa Ynez Valley) $32. For all its obvious power, this wine is elegant and stylish. The sweet cherry fruit is wrapped in a layer of lavender, thyme, and sweet oak. The flavors coat the mouth and last for a long time. The underlying strength and staying power of this wine shows in the tannic finish. Best after 2007. **93 Editors' Choice** *—S.H. (12/1/2004)*

Andrew Murray 1999 Roasted Slope Vineyard Syrah (Santa Ynez Valley) $30. 85 *(11/1/2001)*

Andrew Murray 2003 Westerly Vineyard Syrah (Santa Ynez Valley) $36. A crisp, structured wine at first blush, one that exhibits high-toned red-berry and herb aromas and flavors. With air it takes on overripe aromas, and accents of chocolate on the palate. Lipsmacking finish. **86** *(9/1/2005)*

Andrew Murray 1997 Viognier (Santa Barbara County) $25. 90 *—S.H. (6/1/1999)*

Andrew Murray 2000 Viognier (Santa Ynez Valley) $25. 87 *—S.H. (12/1/2001)*

Andrew Murray 2001 Enchanté White Blend (Santa Ynez Valley) $22. 90 *—S.H. (12/1/2003)*

ANDREW RICH

Andrew Rich 1998 Les Vigneaux Corral Creek Vyd Pinot Noir (Willamette Valley) $25. 88 *—M.S. (12/1/2000)*

ANDREW WILL

Andrew Will 2002 Champoux Vineyard Red Wine Bordeaux Blend (Columbia Valley (WA)) $55. Springs from the glass with a ripe, juicy nose of berry liqueur, hints of mocha and a whiff of fresh cut hay. There are some whiskey barrel esters as well, and the alcohol registers a bit hot, almost like a whiff of scotch. But the tight, concentrated fruit just needs breathing time and/or decanting, and then it more than holds up to the heat. The blend is 62% Cabernet Sauvignon, 21% Merlot, 11% Petit Verdot, and 4% Cab Franc. **91** *—P.G. (12/15/2004)*

Andrew Will 2002 Ciel du Cheval Vineyard Red Wine Bordeaux Blend (Red Mountain) $55. Gloriously structured, this extraordinary effort blends 44% Merlot, 28% Cab Franc, 18% Cab Sauvignon, and 10% Petit Verdot into a wine that reveals itself in sculpted layer upon layer of scent and flavor. Citrus peel, plum, wild berry, red currant, and spice are set upon a base of rich mineral and rock, with precisely cut tannins. Hold 8–10 years. **95 Cellar Selection** *—P.G. (12/15/2004)*

Andrew Will 2002 Klipsun Vineyard Cabernet Sauvignon (Red Mountain) $45. An unusual nose sends up floral and citrus scents along with the expected wild berry and black currant. There is plenty of very ripe fruit here, but Klipsun Cab also has some of the darkest, chewiest tannins in the state, and here they are still slightly out of proportion with the fruit, which needs a lot of breathing time to catch up. The finish is a bit tough; chalk it up to youth and put this one away for a few years. **92** *—P.G. (12/15/2004)*

Andrew Will 2000 Ciel du Cheval Vineyard Merlot (Washington) $40. 93 *—P.G. (9/1/2002)*

Andrew Will 2002 Cuvée Lucia Merlot (Washington) $30. The Cuvée Lucia lineup takes advantage of barrels not included in the winery's new single vineyard program. But what great juice! This is a taut, muscular, tannic wine with somewhat rough, grainy tannins. Delicious, tart, berry-flavored fruit is at the core. **89** *—P.G. (7/1/2004)*

Andrew Will 2002 Klipsun Vineyard Merlot (Red Mountain) $45. Is this the finest single-vineyard Merlot in the country? It certainly can stake a claim to that distinction, with its bright, dense, vibrant scents of berry and cherry, its muscular tannins, and deeply concentrated fruit flavors enhanced with the dark notes of earth and iron from Klipsun soil and the relentless wind that toughens the grape skins. Decant this one early. **94** *—P.G. (12/15/2004)*

Andrew Will 1998 Klipsun Vineyard Merlot (Washington) $45. 92 *—P.G. (9/1/2000)*

Andrew Will 2000 Pepper Bridge Vineyard Merlot (Washington) $36. 91 *—P.G. (9/1/2002)*

Andrew Will 1999 Seven Hills Merlot (Washington) $36. 87 *—P.G. (6/1/2001)*

Andrew Will 1998 Seven Hills Vineyard Merlot (Walla Walla (WA)) $45. 89 *—P.G. (9/1/2000)*

Andrew Will 2002 Seven Hills Vineyard Red Wine Merlot-Cabernet Sauvignon (Walla Walla (WA)) $55. This 62% Merlot, 38% Cabernet blend is the softest and most approachable of the new lineup from Andrew Will, showing tart cherry/berry fruit, notes of wild berry, cocoa, pepper, and coffee grounds. Nice entry into the midpalate, and then a gentle fade, rather than a drop off, as the flavors echo like distant music. **90** *—P.G. (12/15/2004)*

Andrew Will 1999 Ciel du Cheval Sangiovese (Yakima Valley) $23. 90 *—P.G. (11/15/2000)*

Andrew Will 1999 Pepper Bridge Sangiovese (Walla Walla (WA)) $23. 91 *—P.G. (11/15/2000)*

ANDRUS

Andrus 1997 Reserve Bordeaux Blend (Napa Valley) $125. 94 *(11/1/2000)*

ANGELO'S

Angelo's 2001 Cabernet Sauvignon (Columbia Valley (WA)) $21. Tough and chewy, with tart berry fruit leading into very thick, heavy tannins. Could be just fine with a grilled steak. **84** *—P.G. (1/1/2004)*

Angelo's 2001 Merlot (Columbia Valley (WA)) $21. Strong scents of bark and dill, with a powerfully earthy flavor. The wine is quite light bodied, with chalky, unripe tannins. **83** *—P.G. (1/1/2004)*

USA

ANNE AMIE

Anne Amie 2002 Deux Vert Vineyard Pinot Noir (Willamette Valley) $35. Plum, cola, dried spices. Briary, burnt, harsh finish. **85** *(11/1/2004)*

Anne Amie 2001 Doe Ridge Vineyard Pinot Noir (Willamette Valley) $40. **89** *—P.G. (12/1/2003)*

Anne Amie 2001 Hawks View Vineyard Pinot Noir (Willamette Valley) $40. **88** *—P.G. (12/1/2003)*

Anne Amie 2001 Laurel Vineyard Pinot Noir (Willamette Valley) $40. **88** *—P.G. (12/1/2003)*

Anne Amie 2001 Yamhill Springs Vineyard Pinot Noir (Willamette Valley) $40. **86** *—P.G. (12/1/2003)*

ANTHONY ROAD

Anthony Road 2002 Semi-Dry Spring Riesling (Finger Lakes) $12. **82** *—J.C. (8/1/2003)*

ANTICA TERRA

Antica Terra 2002 Pinot Noir (Willamette Valley) $35. A horsey nose that suggests leather and barnyard more than fruit. This may appeal to some more than others, but it renders the wine quite harsh and tannic, and kills the fruit. **83** *(11/1/2004)*

APEX

Apex 1998 Cabernet Sauvignon (Columbia Valley (WA)) $30. **87** *—P.G. (6/1/2002)*

Apex 2001 Outlook Vineyard Chardonnay (Yakima Valley) $25. A big, open, plush style, with the butterscotch fruit married to toasty oak. Nothing complicated, but quite tasty. **88** *—P.G. (9/1/2004)*

Apex 1998 Kestrel Vineyard Merlot (Yakima Valley) $60. **88** *—P.G. (9/1/2002)*

Apex II 2001 Cabernet Sauvignon (Yakima Valley) $16. Yakima valley cab can often have a distinct herbal edge. This wine skates on that border, but never strays too far over it. Medium weight and relatively soft, it has light cranberry fruit and hints of mushroom and woodsy flavors. **87** *—P.G. (4/1/2005)*

Apex II 2002 Merlot (Yakima Valley) $16. Fragrant and expressive, this soft, very approachable wine offers sweet blackberry fruit stylishly arrayed against a 50/50 blend of French and American oak. Smooth, silky, and ripe, it is a can't miss crowd pleaser. **88** *—P.G. (4/1/2005)*

Apex II 2002 Syrah (Yakima Valley) $16. Nice enough right out of the bottle, with pretty scents of raspberry and blueberry. It's clean and pleasant, but a bit insubstantial, without real definition or depth. Still, at this modest price, it's a very nice bottle. **86** *—P.G. (4/1/2005)*

AQUINAS

Aquinas 2002 Cabernet Sauvignon (Napa Valley) $10. Shows a hint of sur-maturité in its plum and prune flavors, but also pleasant earthiness and a soft, medium-bodied mouthfeel. Finishes with a slight rusticity of tannins that give it added character. **85 Best Buy** *(12/1/2004)*

Aquinas 2003 Chardonnay (Napa Valley) $13. Packs as much flavor as you can fit in a glass. Ultra-ripe pineapples and peaches, caramelized oak, toasty meringue, vanilla, the works. Plus, it's creamy, smooth, and crisp. **90 Best Buy** *—S.H. (6/1/2005)*

Aquinas 2002 Merlot (Napa Valley) $10. Not a fruity wine, but one with various nuances of tobacco, coffee, and earth wrapped in a soft, supple mouthfeel. This easy-going red is very drinkable on its own. **84** *(12/1/2004)*

ARBIOS

Arbios 2000 Cabernet Sauvignon (Alexander Valley) $30. You'll like this wine for its easy drinkability. The texture is soft and luscious, with rich, fine tannins. Flavors of black currants, mocha, and sweet spices entice the palate. Shows complexity and finesse throughout. **90** *—S.H. (11/15/2004)*

Arbios 1997 Cabernet Sauvignon (Sonoma County) $35. **88** *(11/1/2000)*

USA

ARBOR CREST

Arbor Crest 2001 Cabernet Sauvignon (Columbia Valley (WA)) $28. Pungent aromas mix blackberries with cracker and a bit of band-aid. The wine enters the palate quite hot; it actually burns, then shows a brief burst of cherry fruit before the alcohol and tannins take over and the flavors fade. **86** *—P.G. (12/1/2004)*

Arbor Crest 1999 Cabernet Sauvignon (Columbia Valley (WA)) $25. **84** *—P.G. (12/31/2001)*

Arbor Crest 1999 Chardonnay (Columbia Valley (WA)) $10. **88 Best Buy** *—P.G. (6/1/2001)*

Arbor Crest 1999 Conner Lee Vineyard Chardonnay (Columbia Valley (WA)) $18. **85** *—P.G. (7/1/2002)*

Arbor Crest 2000 Dionysus Meritage (Columbia Valley (WA)) $48. Concentrated scents of raspberry liqueur, with just a hint of fresh mushroom, stand out in this Bordeaux blend. The winery has held it back a bit longer than most, and consequently it is nicely softened, with maturing fruit, though the tannins are quite dry and chalky. **87** *—P.G. (12/1/2004)*

Arbor Crest 2001 Merlot (Columbia Valley (WA)) $20. This is quite stiff, tannic, hard, and herbal; definitely a bigger style of merlot with chewy tannins and dark chocolate over hard cassis and black cherry fruit. Give it plenty of breathing time. **86** *—P.G. (4/1/2005)*

Arbor Crest 2002 Sauvignon Blanc (Columbia Valley (WA)) $12. Arbor Crest has long been known for its sauvignon blancs, but this new release is a bit of a let-down. The fruit is ripe to the point of losing its focus, replacing crisp flavors with soft peach and tropical. But there is also a very noticeable nail polish scent, and it can also be tasted through the fruit. That's just too much volatility for some tasters. **85** *—P.G. (12/1/2004)*

Arbor Crest 2000 Sauvignon Blanc (Columbia Valley (WA)) $10. 86 *—P.G. (9/1/2002)*

Arbor Crest 2001 Syrah (Columbia Valley (WA)) $28. Sappy, ripe fruit, packed with juicy berry flavors, gets this wine going. Clearly the right things were happening in the vineyard. But more than subtle notes of vinegar and nail polish get in the way of the fruit, and keep this wine from being all it could be. **87** *—P.G. (12/1/2004)*

ARCADIAN

Arcadian 2000 Bien Nacido Vineyard Chardonnay (Santa Maria Valley) $25. Seems a bit tired, with the fruit flavors turning to herbs, dried leaves, and mushroom. Finishes dry and clean, with some green-apple notes. **84** *—S.H. (5/1/2005)*

USA

Arcadian 2001 Sleepy Hollow Vineyard Chardonnay (Monterey) $30. One of the more distinctive Chards I've had this year, notable especially for its very high acidity and mineral and lime complex. The lime tastes like a cool custard, flavored with vanilla, while the minerals bring to mind liquid steel. One hundred percent new French oak slathers it all with buttered toast. **90** *—S.H. (6/1/2005)*

Arcadian 2001 Francesca Pinot Noir (Central Coast) $75. Dark, dry, heavy, and rough in tannins, with plummy, herbal flavors. Isn't offering much now. Tasted twice. **84** *—S.H. (5/1/2005)*

Arcadian 1999 Pisoni Pinot Noir (Monterey County) $80. 91 Cellar Selection *(10/1/2002)*

Arcadian 2002 Sleepy Hollow Vineyard Pinot Noir (Santa Lucia Highlands) $45. I actually prefer this to Arcadian's 2001 Pinots, with which it was released, for its clean, pure framework of acidity and fruit. It's certainly a lively, brisk wine, with cool-climate flavors of cola, cherries, rhubarb, and oak. Showcases the delicacy yet sexiness of a fine Pinot Noir. **90** *—S.H. (6/1/2005)*

Arcadian 1999 Gary's Vineyard Syrah (Monterey) $50. 90 *(11/1/2001)*

ARCHERY SUMMIT

Archery Summit 2000 Vireton Pinot Gris (Oregon) $26. 89 *—P.G. (2/1/2002)*

Archery Summit 2000 Arcus Estate Pinot Noir (Oregon) $53. 87 *—P.G. (4/1/2003)*

Archery Summit 1997 Arcus Estate Pinot Noir (Oregon) $59. 89 *(10/1/1999)*

Archery Summit 1999 Premier Cuvée Pinot Noir (Willamette Valley) $45. 89 *(10/1/2002)*

Archery Summit 1999 Red Hills Estate Pinot Noir (Willamette Valley) $75. 86 *(10/1/2002)*

Archery Summit 2000 Renegade Ridge Estate Pinot Noir (Oregon) $60. 90 *—M.S. (9/1/2003)*

ARCIERO

Arciero 1998 Merlot (Central Coast) $12. 82 *—S.H. (5/1/2001)*

Arciero 1998 Estate Bottled Pinot Grigio (Paso Robles) $12. 86 Best Buy *(8/1/1999)*

ARDENTE

Ardente 2000 Estate Cabernet Sauvignon (Atlas Peak) $45. A tense, tight, tannic mountain wine that's pretty closed and rough at this time. Shows herbal and blackberry flavors and is very dry. Could develop a bit with short-term aging. **85** *—S.H. (11/15/2004)*

ARGER-MARTUCCI

Arger-Martucci 2000 Cabernet Sauvignon (Napa Valley) $50. From 1,500 feet up near Atlas Peak, another mountain wine that's closed and muted now with dense, hard tannins, and cherry flavors and herbal notes. **85** *—S.H. (11/15/2004)*

Arger-Martucci 2002 Chardonnay (Carneros) $22. Crisp, silky, and elegant, a wine of bright acidity that cleans the palate. Then there are the flavors, which are rich and explosive. They range from citrus fruits through apples and peaches to mango, and are well-oaked. **91** *—S.H. (12/15/2004)*

Arger-Martucci 2000 Pinot Noir (Carneros) $40. 85 *—S.H. (4/1/2003)*

ARGYLE

Argyle 2000 Brut (Willamette Valley) $21. Argyle vintage dates its brut, a mark of extra care and quality. As with the '99 when it was first released, this is still tight and showing crisp green apple flavors, but it opens gently into a smooth, yeasty wine with hints of toast. The blend is 55% Chardonnay and 45% Pinot Noir. **90** *—P.G. (11/15/2005)*

Argyle 1999 Brut (Willamette Valley) $21. Argyle vintage dates its brut, a mark of extra care and quality. This is still green apple young; at first sip it could almost be hard cider. Tart, bracing, and concentrated, it tastes of fresh cut apples, pears, and yeast. **88** *—P.G. (12/31/2004)*

Argyle 1996 Brut (Willamette Valley) $22. 87 —*S.H. (12/1/2000)*

Argyle 1994 Extended Tirage (Willamette Valley) $34. A thrilling success, with beautifully developed aromas of vanilla and buttered toast. Gorgeous mousse, and perisistent, nutty, complex flavors that show hints of candied tropical fruits and sweet butterscotch. Maybe the best Argyle ever. **91 Editors' Choice** —*P.G. (12/31/2004)*

Argyle 1991 Extended Tirage Disgorged on Demand (Willamette Valley) $22. 88 —*K.F. (12/1/2002)*

Argyle 1989 Extended Tirage Brut (Willamette Valley) $30. 87 —*P.G. (12/1/2001)*

Argyle 1998 Knudsen Vineyard Brut Sparkling Blend (Willamette Valley) $30. Amylic, showing rather awkward tropical fruit/bubblegum character, with banana-like softness. Blowsier than the rest of the lineup, this is perfectly drinkable but less elegant (and more expensive) than Argyle's fine vintage brut. **86** —*P.G. (12/31/2005)*

Argyle 1997 Knudsen Vineyard Brut (Willamette Valley) $30. This is 100% barrel-fermented, an 80% pinot/20% chardonnay blend, and at this age it is already showing lovely sherry notes and lightly oxidized fruit. Yet it retains enough youthful juice to be quite refreshing, with a finish that suggests toast and slightly oily nuts, layer upon layer. **90** —*P.G. (12/31/2004)*

Argyle 1996 Knudsen Vyd Julia Lee's Block Blanc de Blancs (Willamette Valley) $30. 87 —*P.G. (12/1/2000)*

Argyle 1996 Knutsen Vineyard Blanc de Blancs (Willamette Valley) $30. 88 —*P.G. (12/1/2001)*

Argyle 1999 Nuthouse Chardonnay (Willamette Valley) $28. 89 —*P.G. (8/1/2002)*

Argyle 1999 Reserve Chardonnay (Willamette Valley) $20. 90 —*P.G. (7/1/2002)*

Argyle 2004 Pinot Noir (Willamette Valley) $20. An early release is often good for Oregon Pinot, bringing out the young varietal flavors with bracing freshness. Here an extended maceration, both before and after fermentation, gives it a nice mix of cherry/grapy fruit with a good tannic structure. Comes on like a cru Beaujolais, with surprising weight and length for such a young wine. **88** —*P.G. (11/15/2005)*

Argyle 1998 Pinot Noir (Willamette Valley) $16. 87 Best Buy —*P.G. (9/1/2000)*

Argyle 2000 Nuthouse Pinot Noir (Willamette Valley) $40. 88 *(10/1/2002)*

Argyle 1997 Nuthouse Pinot Noir (Willamette Valley) $35. 91 *(10/1/1999)*

Argyle 2002 Reserve Pinot Noir (Willamette Valley) $30. Good concentration and noticeable density, with intriguing, briary flavors that mix candied fruit with dusty herbs, cinnamon, and cocoa. **87** *(11/1/2004)*

Argyle 1997 Reserve Pinot Noir (Willamette Valley) $35. 86 *(10/1/1999)*

Argyle 1998 Spirit House Pinot Noir (Willamette Valley) $50. 88 —*J.C. (12/1/2000)*

ARMIDA

Armida 1997 Chardonnay (Russian River Valley) $12. 87 —*J.C. (10/1/1999)*

Armida 2004 Sauvignon Blanc (Russian River Valley) $20. Herbal and bulky, with sweet apple, pear, and pineapple flavors. Quite heavy on the tongue, with soft acids. Seems a bit gummy and candied, and just not that precise, despite delivering some rich flavors. **84** *(7/1/2005)*

Armida 2001 Maple Vineyard Zinfandel (Dry Creek Valley) $30. 87 *(11/1/2003)*

ARNS

Arns 2000 Cabernet Sauvignon (Napa Valley) $60. 92 —*J.M. (11/15/2003)*

ARROWOOD

Arrowood 2001 Cabernet Sauvignon (Sonoma County) $45. Master vintner Dick Arrowood has crafted a sensational wine from a sensational vintage. A blend from throughout the county, it shows his discernment in the overall balance, harmony, and charm. Black currants, chocolate, green olives, sweet sage, and vanilla-scented oak flavors come together in a lush, smooth, intricately structured wine that will probably hold for 10 years, but is best in its flamboyant, exuberant youth. **93 Editors' Choice** —*S.H. (12/1/2005)*

Arrowood 2001 Grand Archer Cabernet Sauvignon (Sonoma County) $22. Plays it safe with a good varietal profile. Very dry, with a harmony of fruit, oak, tannins, and acidity, a regional Cabernet with some fanciness. Might improve with a few years in bottle. **86** —*S.H. (10/1/2004)*

Arrowood 1999 Grand Archer Cabernet Sauvignon (Sonoma County) $22. 87 —*S.H. (7/1/2002)*

Arrowood 2002 Chardonnay (Sonoma County) $29. Here's a powerful Chard that never loses its sense of balance. It is rich in pear, pineapple, and mango flavors accompanied by notes of smoky oak and creamy lees. Feels fat and plush in the mouth. **90** —*S.H. (9/1/2004)*

Arrowood 1998 Chardonnay (South Coast) $25. 91 —*S.H. (12/1/2001)*

Arrowood 2001 Grand Archer Chardonnay (Sonoma County) $18. 87 *—S.H. (8/1/2003)*

Arrowood 1998 Reserve Speciale Cuvée Michel Berthoud Chardonnay (Sonoma County) $38. 91 *(7/1/2001)*

Arrowood 2002 Saralee's Vineyard Gewürztraminer (Russian River Valley) $20. 86 *—S.H. (7/1/2003)*

Arrowood 2001 Grand Archer Merlot (Sonoma County) $16. This Merlot straddles that interesting line between easy, everyday drinking and real complexity. It's dry and richly tannic, and is the sort of wine that won't win a blind tasting, but leaves you reaching for a third glass with that steak. **87** *—S.H. (12/1/2005)*

Arrowood 1999 Grand Archer Merlot (Sonoma County) $20. 90 *—S.H. (9/1/2002)*

Arrowood 2001 Select Late Harvest White Riesling (Alexander Valley) $25. 84 *—S.H. (12/1/2003)*

Arrowood 1999 Syrah (Sonoma Valley) $55. 85 *—J.M. (12/1/2002)*

Arrowood 2001 Le Beau Melange Syrah (Sonoma Valley) $35. Arrowood's blended Syrah is a clean, well-made wine that won't disappoint many Syrah lovers. Aromas of vanilla, herb, and spice add mixed berries and pepper flavors on the palate. A bit less lush than the Saralee's Vineyard bottling, but still creamy and elegant. **88** *(9/1/2005)*

USA

Arrowood 1999 Saralee's Vineyard Syrah (Russian River Valley) $62. 88 *—J.M. (12/1/2002)*

Arrowood 2000 Saralee's Vineyard Unfined & Unfiltered Syrah (Russian River Valley) $35. 86 *—S.H. (12/1/2003)*

Arrowood 1997 Viognier (Russian River Valley) $30. 91 *—S.H. (6/1/1999)*

Arrowood 2001 Saralee's Vineyard Viognier (Russian River Valley) $30. 88 *—S.H. (6/1/2003)*

ARTESA

Artesa 2001 Elements Bordeaux Blend (Sonoma-Napa) $20. This is a rather rustic blend. It has lots of fruit and berry flavors, ripe and round, with firm acids and soft tannins. Easy to drink, and versatile with a wide range of food. **85** *—S.H. (5/1/2005)*

Artesa 1998 Cabernet Sauvignon (Napa Valley) $30. 92 *—S.H. (11/15/2002)*

Artesa 1997 Reserve Cabernet Sauvignon (Napa Valley) $70. 90 *—S.H. (6/1/2002)*

Artesa 2000 Chardonnay (Carneros) $23. 86 *—S.H. (2/1/2003)*

Artesa 1999 Chardonnay (Napa Valley) $23. 87 *—S.H. (12/1/2001)*

Artesa 1999 Reserve Chardonnay (Carneros) $30. 90 *—S.H. (12/1/2001)*

Artesa 1999 Select Late Harvest Gewürztraminer (Russian River Valley) $28. 87 *—J.M. (12/1/2002)*

Artesa 1997 Merlot (Sonoma Valley) $24. 88 *—S.H. (12/1/2001)*

Artesa 1999 Reserve Merlot (Sonoma Valley) $60. Slightly herbal on the nose, with caramel and vanilla scents accenting cherries and tomatoes. On the palate, alcohol is evident, matched by strident oak. Finishes lean and tart. A good wine, but something of a disappointment. **86** *(5/1/2004)*

Artesa 2002 Pinot Noir (Carneros) $22. An immensely enjoyable Pinot for its smoky, vanilla-infused aromas and flavors of red cherries, mint, and mocha, and the delicate, silky mouthfeel. The finish is long and tart in cherry fruit. **88** *(11/1/2004)*

Artesa 2000 Pinot Noir (Russian River Valley) $24. 89 *(10/1/2002)*

Artesa 1999 Pinot Noir (Santa Barbara County) $24. 89 *—S.H. (12/15/2001)*

Artesa 1999 Pinot Noir (Carneros) $24. 87 *—S.H. (12/15/2001)*

Artesa 2000 Reserve Pinot Noir (Carneros) $38. 88 *(10/1/2002)*

Artesa 2002 Reserve Sauvignon Blanc (Napa Valley) $20. Quite weighty, with a gold tint, enormous oak-based aromas, and heavy flavors that veer toward creamed corn, cantaloupe, and guava. Finishes with yet another monstrous blast of oak, and thus lingering notes of vanilla and buttered toast. Not a poor wine by any stretch, but too oaky for us to rate higher. **86** *(7/1/2005)*

Artesa 2001 Syrah (Sonoma Valley) $16. Features a generous overlay of caramel and vanilla atop tart berry flavors. Plenty of herb and spice nuances, ending on a cranberry note. Seems a tad under-ripe by California standards. **84** *(9/1/2005)*

ARTEVINO

Artevino 2001 Zinfandel (North Coast) $22. 84 *(11/1/2003)*

ASH HOLLOW

Ash Hollow 2002 Estate Blend (Walla Walla (WA)) $30. The vineyard was wiped clean in the freeze of '04, but this fragrant, chocolatey wine suggests that it holds real potential if it can be adequately protected. Crisp cranberry and strawberry fruits are underscored with smooth, chocolatey oak flavors. The style is Walla Walla all the way; broadly accessible, smooth, and seamless. **88** *—P.G. (4/1/2005)*

ASHLAND VINEYARDS

Ashland Vineyards 1999 Chardonnay (Rogue Valley) $8. 83 *—P.G. (8/1/2002)*

ASTRALE E TERRA

Astrale e Terra 2001 Arcturus Cabernet Blend (Napa Valley) $39. What a nice '01 this is. It exemplifies the ripe style, rich in black currants and cassis, and the smooth, sweet tannins of this great Napa vintage. Finishes with an edge of cocoa, anise, and oak. Drink now or over the next several years. **91** *—S.H. (10/1/2005)*

ATALON

Atalon 1998 Beckstoffer Vineyard Cabernet Blend (Oakville) $NA. Not half the wine of the remarkable '97. Smells oaky and of black cherries. Taste of dried herbs, cherries, coffee. Dry, with a chunky, chewy mouhtfeel and unresolved, awkward tannins. Shows some elegance and finesse. Probably best now-2008. **87** *—S.H. (6/1/2005)*

Atalon 2000 Cabernet Sauvignon (Napa Valley) $35. **90** *—S.H. (12/31/2003)*

Atalon 1999 Beckstoffer Tokalon Vineyard Cabernet Sauvignon (Napa Valley) $NA. Rich, dusty cocoa, black currant, cherry aromas. Very rich, ripe, pure. Fabulously soft and smooth in the mouth, complex. Rich, sweet tannins. Dry and rich, with a very long, satisfying finish. Now-2020. **94 Cellar Selection** *—S.H. (6/1/2005)*

ATELIER

Atelier 2003 Syrah (Alexander Valley) $28. There are lovely aromas in this wine. The scents of ripe blackberries, freshly ground French roast, cocoa dustings, and white pepper are so inviting. But the wine is way too soft. It has nice flavors, but is flat in the mouth. **83** *—S.H. (12/1/2005)*

ATLAS PEAK

Atlas Peak 1996 Consenso Vineyard Cabernet Sauvignon (Napa Valley) $30. **84** *—S.H. (2/1/2000)*

Atlas Peak 2001 Chardonnay (Atlas Peak) $16. **87** *—S.H. (6/1/2003)*

Atlas Peak 2000 Atlas Peak Chardonnay (Atlas Peak) $16. **86** *—S.H. (12/31/2001)*

Atlas Peak 2000 Sangiovese (Atlas Peak) $16. **86** *—S.H. (2/1/2003)*

Atlas Peak 1999 Sangiovese (Napa Valley) $16. **87** *—S.H. (11/15/2001)*

Atlas Peak 2000 Reserve Sangiovese (Atlas Peak) $30. **87** *—S.H. (9/1/2003)*

AU BON CLIMAT

Au Bon Climat 1997 Alban Vineyard Chardonnay (Edna Valley) $35. **92** *—S.H. (10/1/1999)*

Au Bon Climat 1997 Le Bouge D'a Côte Chardonnay (Santa Maria Valley) $25. **90** *—S.H. (10/1/1999)*

Au Bon Climat 1999 Sanford & Benedict Chardonnay (Santa Ynez Valley) $35. **86** *(7/1/2001)*

Au Bon Climat 1995 Sanford & Benedict Vineyard Reserve Chardonnay (Santa Ynez Valley) $NA. Lovely, fresh, clean, with pure apricot, honey, sweet-sour pineapple, caramel, smoke, vanilla aromas. Fresh and creamy, fruity, oaky. Notable for bright acidity. Finishes complex and spicy. **91** *—S.H. (6/1/2005)*

Au Bon Climat 1998 Talley Vyd "Rincon" Chardonnay (Arroyo Grande Valley) $25. **89** *(6/1/2000)*

Au Bon Climat 1999 Knox Alexander Pinot Noir (Santa Maria Valley) $45. **93** *—J.M. (7/1/2002)*

Au Bon Climat 1997 La Bauge Au Dessus Pinot Noir (Santa Maria Valley) $25. **88** *(10/1/1999)*

Au Bon Climat 2002 Sanford & Benedict Vineyard Pinot Noir (Santa Ynez Valley) $35. Still rather young and aggressive in tannins and acids, with pronounced cherry, pomegranate, coffee, and spice flavors, as well as an overlay of toasty oak. Very dry, with good structure. Not a blockbuster, but elegant and charming. Best 2005–2008. **89** *—S.H. (6/1/2005)*

Au Bon Climat 2000 Sanford & Benedict Vineyard Pinot Noir (Santa Ynez Valley) $NA. Alcohol: 13.5%. Fairly pale. Smells young, fresh, clean, piquant in Pinot aroma. Cherries, sweet beet, toast, sweet oriental spice, gingerbread. Acids, tannins, and oak up front now, or is the fruit thin? Delicately structured, silky. **89** *—S.H. (6/1/2005)*

Au Bon Climat 1996 Sanford & Benedict Vineyard Pinot Noir (Santa Ynez Valley) $NA. Alcohol only 13.0%. Pale, ruby-orange color. Succulent in sweet char, vanilla, cherry-raspberry meringue, nutmeggy spice, smoke. Filled with life and zest due to crisp acidity and fresh flavors. Cherries, pomegranates, sweet herbal tea. Dry, balanced, elegant. A bit sharp in the finish, though. **89** *—S.H. (6/1/2005)*

AUDELSSA

Audelssa 2001 Mountain Terraces Cabernet Sauvignon (Sonoma Valley) $33. Made by the legendary Richard Arrowood, a very fine Cab. Rich and complex in black currants and oak, it shows sturdy tannins that are perfectly drinkable now, but will enable this wine to age well through the decade. **92** *—S.H. (3/1/2005)*

Audelssa Sonoma 2002 Mountain Terraces Syrah (Sonoma Valley) $32. What happened? This winery, which has impressed with its first few releases, seems to have stumbled here. Despite a decent alcohol number (14.5%), the wine tastes under-ripe and thin, dominated by green, leafy and bell pepper flavors. **80** *(9/1/2005)*

AUDUBON CELLARS

Audubon Cellars 1997 Graeser Vineyards Cabernet Sauvignon (Napa Valley) $18. 88 *—S.H. (9/1/2000)*

Audubon Cellars 1997 Sangiacomo Vineyard Chardonnay (Sonoma) $15. 84 *(6/1/2000)*

Audubon Cellars 2000 Juliana Vineyards Sauvignon Blanc (Napa Valley) $12. 83 *—S.H. (11/15/2001)*

Audubon Cellars 1997 Picnic Hill Vineyard Late Harvest Zinfandel (Amador County) $14. 82 *—S.H. (12/31/2000)*

AUGUST BRIGGS

August Briggs 1997 Cabernet Sauvignon (Napa Valley) $50. 91 *(11/1/2000)*

August Briggs 2002 Pinot Noir (Russian River Valley) $32. Shows textbook Russian River notes of cherries and sweet cola, with a silky texture and good acids. Feels a little rough around the edges, with a candied finish. Toasty oak completes the picture. **85** *—S.H. (8/1/2005)*

August Briggs 1997 Pinot Noir (Russian River Valley) $28. 90 *(10/1/1999)*

August Briggs 2000 Dijon Clones Pinot Noir (Napa Valley) $35. 87 *(10/1/2002)*

August Briggs 2001 Zinfandel (Napa Valley) $32. 89 *(11/1/2003)*

AUSTIN ROBAIRE

Austin Robaire 2000 Cabernet Sauvignon (Columbia Valley (WA)) $55. 88 *—P.G. (9/1/2003)*

Austin Robaire 2002 Klipsun Vineyard Cabernet Sauvignon (Red Mountain) $55. Though Klipsun is widely regarded as an iconic vineyard for Washington, this wine smells more of raisins and prunes than of fresh, ripe grapes. The flavors are broad, baked, and pruny; yet the tannins remain a bit green and chalky. The wine doesn't knit together and seems unlikely to do so in the future. **85** *—P.G. (6/1/2005)*

Austin Robaire 2001 Ward Family Vineyard Pinot Noir (Washington) $26. 84 *—P.G. (9/1/2003)*

Austin Robaire 2002 La Petite Fille Syrah (Columbia Valley (WA)) $18. Sweet cracker and strawberry jam are the main notes struck here, with a whiff of leather. The leather and barnyard flavors seem to gather strength, along with smoke and licorice. Some tasters will find this wine too rustic; others will love it. **85** *—P.G. (6/1/2005)*

AUTUMN HILL

Autumn Hill 1997 Cabernet Sauvignon (Monticello) $16. 85 *—J.C. (8/1/1999)*

AVENUE

Avenue 2003 Cabernet Sauvignon (California) $11. Rough-and-ready Cab, with earthy, coffee-berry flavors that turn fruity and tannic on the finish. **83** *—S.H. (5/1/2005)*

Avenue 2003 Merlot (California) $11. Fruity and rustic, dry and balanced, with chocolate-cherry flavors and a good finish. **84** *—S.H. (5/1/2005)*

AVERY LANE

Avery Lane 2001 Cabernet Sauvignon (Columbia Valley (WA)) $8. 87 Best Buy *—P.G. (12/31/2003)*

Avery Lane 2001 Chardonnay (Columbia Valley (WA)) $8. 85 Best Buy *—P.G. (12/31/2003)*

Avery Lane 2002 Gewürztraminer (Columbia Valley (WA)) $7. 87 Best Buy *—P.G. (12/31/2003)*

Avery Lane 2001 Merlot (Columbia Valley (WA)) $8. 85 Best Buy *—P.G. (12/31/2003)*

Avery Lane 2002 Sauvignon Blanc (Washington) $7. Pungent with pine resin and pineapple scents. Sharp, aggressive, and herbal, with a bit of vitamin-pill flavor on the finish. **85** *—P.G. (7/1/2004)*

Avery Lane 2001 Syrah (Washington) $8. There is a bitter start to this light, innocuous, generic red wine. Some hints of graham cracker in the midpalate, and a finish that is both tarry and tannic. **82** *—P.G. (7/1/2004)*

AVILA

Avila 2002 Cabernet Sauvignon (Santa Barbara County) $11. On the overly sweet side, and soft to the point of flaccid. The fruit's ripe in cherries and black raspberries. **83** *—S.H. (2/1/2005)*

Avila 2000 Cabernet Sauvignon (Santa Barbara County) $12. 88 Best Buy *—S.H. (11/15/2002)*

Avila 2000 Chardonnay (San Luis Obispo County) $12. 85 *—S.H. (12/15/2002)*

Avila 2001 Merlot (Santa Barbara County) $13. Tough, herbal, and weedy, a dryly tannic wine with modest flavors of cherries that offers little pleasure now. **83** *—S.H. (4/1/2004)*

Avila 2003 Pinot Noir (San Luis Obispo County) $11. Starts off a little rough and raw, with some dry, chewy tannins, but when the ripe cherry and roasted coffee flavors hit mid-palate, it turns pretty. The fruit really kicks in on the finish. **85** *—S.H. (12/15/2004)*

Avila 2001 Pinot Noir (San Luis Obispo County) $10. 86 *—J.M. (11/15/2003)*

Avila 2001 Cote d'Avila Rhône Red Blend (Santa Barbara County) $13. 82 *—S.H. (5/1/2003)*

Avila 2003 Syrah (Santa Barbara County) $13. Here's a rough, somewhat rustic Syrah, with penetrating blackberry pie aromas but flavors that seem a bit herbal. Crisp on the finish, picking up spice and tea-like notes. **84** *(9/1/2005)*

B.R. COHN

B.R. Cohn 1996 Olive Hill Cabernet Sauvignon (Sonoma Valley) $35. 92 *(12/31/1999)*

B.R. Cohn 1999 Olive Hill Estate Vineyards Special Selection Cabernet Sauvignon (Sonoma Valley) $100. 86 *(8/1/2003)*

B.R. Cohn 1997 Olive Hill Estate Vyds Cabernet Sauvignon (Sonoma Valley) $38. 91 *(12/31/1999)*

B.R. Cohn 2001 Silver Label Cabernet Sauvignon (Central Coast) $20. Rough and unbalanced, with over-ripe raisiny flavors right next to under-ripe weedy ones. Overpriced for what you get. A mix of San Luis Obispo and Sonoma county grapes. **83** *—S.H. (10/1/2004)*

B.R. Cohn 2001 Chardonnay (Carneros) $35. Firm and bright, with a clean, clear focus that features mineral, lemon, green apple, and grapefruit. Fresh on the finish. **87** *—J.M. (2/1/2004)*

B.R. Cohn 1997 Reserve Joseph Herman Vyd. Chardonnay (Carneros) $24. 93 *—M.S. (2/1/2000)*

B.R. Cohn 2000 Merlot (Sonoma Valley) $28. Fairly bright, with zippy cherry notes at the center. Tannins are soft and the body is moderate in weight. There's a weedy, herbal core that permeates, so this might not be for everyone. But interesting, nonetheless. **87** *—J.M. (2/1/2004)*

BABCOCK

Babcock 1999 Fathom Bordeaux Blend (Santa Barbara County) $35. 93 Editors' Choice *—S.H. (12/1/2001)*

Babcock 2002 Cabernet Sauvignon (Central Coast) $19. Has sharp acids and a tart flavor of sour cherries, but the smooth tannins and pretty oak soften and sweeten. **85** *—S.H. (10/1/2004)*

Babcock 1997 Chardonnay (Santa Ynez Valley) $25. 92 *—S.H. (10/1/1999)*

Babcock 2001 Chardonnay (Santa Barbara County) $17. 93 Editors' Choice *—S.H. (12/15/2002)*

Babcock 2000 Chardonnay (Santa Ynez Valley) $25. 90 *—S.H. (9/1/2002)*

Babcock 1998 Chardonnay (Santa Barbara County) $18. 85 *(6/1/2000)*

Babcock 2002 Grand Cuvée Chardonnay (Santa Ynez Valley) $30. Crisp in acids, and not showing a lot of flavor now, except for oak. Reveals modest tree fruits in dry package. Elegant rather than opulent. **84** *—S.H. (12/31/2004)*

Babcock 1999 Grand Cuvée Chardonnay (Santa Barbara County) $25. 89 *—S.H. (12/1/2001)*

Babcock 1996 Grand Cuvée Chardonnay (Santa Ynez Valley) $30. 91 *—S.H. (7/1/1999)*

Babcock 1998 Mt. Carmel Vineyard Chardonnay (Santa Ynez Valley) $35. 86 *(7/1/2001)*

Babcock 2004 Rita's Earth Cuvée Chardonnay (Santa Rita Hills) $20. The first bottling of this particular cuvée, this Chardonnay is a great expression of Santa Barbara terroir, fresh, young, and racy. The flavors are explosive and complex, suggesting wildly ripe tropical fruits and key lime pie, with refreshingly bright acidity and rich oak and lees nuances. It's a big, assertive New World Chard, and a great value. **91 Editors' Choice** *—S.H. (12/31/2005)*

Babcock 2001 Pinot Grigio (Santa Barbara County) $14. 88 Best Buy *—S.H. (9/1/2002)*

Babcock 2001 Pinot Noir (Santa Barbara County) $23. 91 Editors' Choice *—S.H. (2/1/2003)*

Babcock 2002 Cargasacchi Pinot Noir (Santa Ynez Valley) $40. Pleasant and clean rather than complex, with pretty black and red cherry flavors and a bit of coffee and herb. Light- to medium-bodied, this wine is good, but wants a little more concentration. **86** *(11/1/2004)*

Babcock 2001 Grand Cuvée (Santa Ynez Valley) $35. A simple, unbalanced wine. It opens with aromas of cola, cherries and earth that are pretty good, and the flavors of cherries are ripe and tasty. But there is a sweetness that is out of place, and the wine has little depth. **84** *—S.H. (2/1/2004)*

Babcock 2001 Grand Cuvée Pinot Noir (Santa Ynez Valley) $30. This is a big, dark, rich, interesting Pinot Noir. Flavorwise, it shows black cherries, blueberries, pomegranates, and sweet rhubarb, and an edge of coffee, with an earthy, slightly bitter acidity. In the mouth it is soft and lush yet firm and assertive. **92** *—S.H. (4/1/2004)*

Babcock 1997 Mt. Carmel Vineyard Pinot Noir (Santa Ynez Valley) $35. 91 *(10/1/1999)*

Babcock 1997 Fathom Red Table Wine Red Blend (Santa Barbara County) $30. 90 *—J.C. (11/15/1999)*

Babcock 1997 Eleven Oaks Sangiovese (Santa Ynez Valley) $30. 90 *(10/1/1999)*

Babcock 2001 Eleven Oaks Sauvignon Blanc (Santa Barbara County) $23. 86 *(8/1/2002)*

Babcock 2003 Eleven Oaks Cuvée Sauvignon Blanc (Santa Ynez Valley) $25. Always complex and interesting, and this year shows plenty of upfront spearmint, fig, and melon flavors wrapped in a rich, creamy texture. There are oak and lees shadings that show up on the finish. **90** *—S.H. (12/31/2004)*

Babcock 2000 Syrah (Santa Barbara County) $23. 90 *—S.H. (7/1/2002)*

Babcock 2000 Black Label Cuvée Syrah (Santa Barbara County) $40. 93 Editors' Choice *—S.H. (12/1/2002)*

Babcock 1997 Black Label Cuvée Syrah (Santa Barbara County) $40. 91 *(10/1/1999)*

Babcock 2003 Nook & Cranny Syrah (Santa Rita Hills) $50. Herbal and peppery on the nose, but also shows plenty of fruit, which really expands on the palate to deliver a mouthful of creamy-textured cherries and vanilla. Yet the flavors remain complex, incorporating pepper and herb notes. Ends in a long, spice-driven finish. **90** *(9/1/2005)*

USA

BACIO DIVINO

Bacio Divino 2000 Red Blend (Napa Valley) $80. 85 *—S.H. (12/31/2003)*

Bacio Divino 1999 Red Blend (Napa Valley) $75. 91 *—M.S. (11/15/2003)*

BADGER MOUNTAIN

Badger Mountain 1998 Cabernet Franc (Columbia Valley (WA)) $12. 82 *—P.G. (6/1/2002)*

Badger Mountain 1999 N.S.A. Cabernet Sauvignon (Columbia Valley (WA)) $14. 84 *—P.G. (6/1/2002)*

Badger Mountain 2000 N.S.A. Chardonnay (Columbia Valley (WA)) $10. 86 *—P.G. (7/1/2002)*

Badger Mountain 1999 Merlot (Columbia Valley (WA)) $14. 82 *—P.G. (12/31/2001)*

Badger Mountain 2000 N.S.A Merlot (Columbia Valley (WA)) $14. 86 *—P.G. (6/1/2002)*

Badger Mountain 2001 N.S.A. Riesling (Columbia Valley (WA)) $8. 86 Best Buy *—P.G. (6/1/2002)*

Badger Mountain 2000 Seve White Blend (Columbia Valley (WA)) $8. 84 *—P.G. (6/1/2002)*

BAILEYANA

Baileyana 1997 Chardonnay (Edna Valley) $22. 86 *(6/1/2000)*

Baileyana 2002 55% San Luis Obispo County/45% Monterey County Chardonnay (California) $18. Way too much oak on this rustic wine, and rather insipid, too, with its too-soft mouthfeel and slightly sweet, Lifesaver flavors. **83** *—S.H. (8/1/2005)*

Baileyana 1999 Firepeak Vineyard Chardonnay (Edna Valley) $30. 88 *(7/1/2001)*

Baileyana 2003 Grand Firepeak Cuvée Chardonnay (Edna Valley) $30. The acidity and asperity of this Chard are a bit beyond my comfort zone, but that's Edna Valley for you. It's certainly a distinctive wine, a best-blocks selection rich in lemon, lime, and mineral flavors, to which the winemaker has added a filigree of toasted oak. **86** *—S.H. (12/15/2005)*

Baileyana 2000 Pinot Noir (Edna Valley) $23. 88 *(10/1/2002)*

Baileyana 2002 El Pico Firepeak Vineyard Clone 115 Pinot Noir (Edna Valley) $30. Very dry and a little disjointed now, but has great potential. The dry flavors suggest coffee, rhubarb pie, red cherries, and mushrooms. The earthiness is relieved by smoky oak that turns sweet in the finish. Give it a year or two to come together. **90 Editors' Choice** *—S.H. (11/1/2004)*

Baileyana 2001 Firepeak Vineyard Pinot Noir (Edna Valley) $38. A single-vineyard Pinot that shows signs of those green tomato Central Coast flavors complexed with riper black cherry notes and a rich, espresso finish. It's very dry and soft in tannins, although the tart acidity stimulates the taste buds. May soften and sweeten in a few years, but is best consumed now. **87** *—S.H. (4/1/2004)*

Baileyana 2000 Firepeak Vineyard Estate Bottled Pinot Noir (Edna Valley) $38. 87 *(10/1/2002)*

Baileyana 2002 Halcon Rojo Firepeak Vineyard Pommard Clone Pinot Noir (Edna Valley) $30. Dry, earthy, and not fully ripe, with beetroot, tomato and rhubarb flavors. Feels rich and earthy in the mouth, a chunky wine with crisp acids. Probably at its best now. **87** *—S.H. (11/1/2004)*

Baileyana 2002 La Entrada Firepeak Vineyard Clone 777 Pinot Noir (Edna Valley) $30. Riper by a hair than its Pommard Clone neighbor, showing tart red cherry flavors. Dry and crisp in acids, with a silky, velvety texture, this medium-bodied wine has good balance. Drink now with rich meats. **89** *—S.H. (11/1/2004)*

Baileyana 2002 Paragon Vineyard Sauvignon Blanc (Edna Valley) $13. From a cool coastal appellation, an herbal, green wine with grassy, citrusy flavors. It's very dry and backed up with firm acids, but there's a slight vegetal note that detracts from the enjoyment. **84** *—S.H. (4/1/2004)*

Baileyana 1999 Syrah (Paso Robles) $18. 87 *(10/1/2001)*

Baileyana 1999 Firepeak Vineyard Syrah (Edna Valley) $38. 89 *(11/1/2001)*

Baileyana 1998 Zinfandel (Paso Robles) $18. 86 *—D.T. (3/1/2002)*

BALCOM & MOE

Balcom & Moe 1997 Cabernet Sauvignon (Washington) $20. 83 *—P.G. (10/1/2001)*

BALDACCI

Baldacci 2002 Cabernet Sauvignon (Stags Leap District) $44. This is a classic young Napa Cabernet. It's very forward in ripe black currant and mocha flavors, with thoroughly sweet tannins and a soft, luxurious mouthfeel. The fruit flatters the palate from entry to long finish. Drink now and for the next two years. **90** *—S.H. (12/15/2005)*

Baldacci 2002 Brenda's Vineyard Cabernet Sauvignon (Stags Leap District) $70. Tasted alongside Baldacci's regular '02 Cab, this one's more tannic, and also more deeply flavored. There's an explosion of black currant, cherry, and mocha fruit, backed up with a firm dustiness that provides structure and balance. The wine will probably benefit from short-term aging. Drink 2006 and 2007. **92 Cellar Selection** *—S.H. (12/15/2005)*

BALLATORE

Ballatore NV Gran Spumante Champagne Blend (California) $7. 86 Best Buy *—S.H. (12/1/2002)*

Ballatore NV Rosso Champagne Blend (California) $8. 85 *—S.H. (12/1/2002)*

Ballatore NV Rosso Red Spumante Sparkling Blend (California) $6. Red in color, sugary sweet, this sparkler will have its fans, but it's really kind of cloying. **82** *—S.H. (12/31/2005)*

BALLENTINE

Ballentine 2002 Pocai Vineyard Cabernet Franc (Napa Valley) $24. Soft and juicy in berry flavors with a streak of herbaceousness. Finishes dry, with notes of oak. **84** *—S.H. (12/31/2004)*

Ballentine 2001 Merlot (Napa Valley) $22. Ripe and fruity in upfront blackberries, currants and oak, with a hint of cocoa, this wine also shows firm tannins. It's young, and finishes with that raw quality of a juvenile Cab. Fine now with rich fare, but should mellow for a few years. Now through 2008. **88** *—S.H. (6/1/2005)*

Ballentine 1997 Estate Grown Merlot (Napa Valley) $20. 87 *—J.C. (7/1/2000)*

Ballentine 2003 Zinfandel Port (Napa Valley) $40. Smooth in texture and very sweet, with flavors of cherry and black raspberry marmalade, chocolate pie, and spices. For immediate drinking. **85** *—S.H. (12/15/2005)*

Ballentine 1999 Syrah (Napa Valley) $28. 91 *—S.H. (12/1/2002)*

Ballentine 2003 Betty's Vineyard Syrah (Napa Valley) $22. Unanimously admired by our panel, Ballentine's Syrah boasts a big mouthful of cocoa, plum, and black cherry flavors, backed by firm acids and tannins. Has some faint rubbery notes, but they should fade with time or a brisk decanting. **88** *(9/1/2005)*

Ballentine 1999 Bg Reserve Zinfandel (Napa Valley) $28. 90 *—S.H. (12/1/2002)*

Ballentine 2000 Block 9 Zinfandel (Napa Valley) $27. This wine shows all the class and elegance of a fine Napa Cab, except it's indisputably Zin, with its brambly fruit flavors and spicy, peppery edge. The oak is rich and charred, the tannins sweet and ripe, the texture as smooth as velvet. Pretty much the best that Napa can do with Zinfandel. **92** *—S.H. (9/1/2004)*

Ballentine 2001 Old Vines Zinfandel (Napa Valley) $18. 88 *(11/1/2003)*

BANDIERA

Bandiera 2000 Vineyard Reserve Cabernet Sauvignon (California) $10. 84 *—S.H. (11/15/2002)*

Bandiera 1999 Vineyard Reserve Chardonnay (California) $10. 83 *—S.H. (5/1/2001)*

Bandiera 1998 Vineyard Reserve Merlot (California) $10. 82 *—S.H. (8/1/2001)*

BANNISTER

Bannister 1999 Porter-Bass Chardonnay (Russian River Valley) $38. 87 *—S.H. (12/15/2002)*

Bannister 2002 Rochioli & Allen Vineyards Chardonnay (Russian River Valley) $28. This Chard, from two famous vineyards, is a little too tart now for enjoyment. It has a roughness that detracts from the underlying fruit, while the oak sticks out. My hunch is that three or four years will reward your patience. **88** *—S.H. (10/1/2005)*

Bannister 1999 Floodgate Vineyard Pinot Noir (Anderson Valley) $30. 87 *—S.H. (2/1/2003)*

BARBOURSVILLE

Barboursville 1998 Chardonnay (Virginia) $12. 83 *—J.C. (8/1/1999)*

Barboursville 1998 Pinot Grigio (Monticello) $13. 86 *(8/1/1999)*

Barboursville 1998 Riesling (Monticello) $10. 82 *—J.C. (8/1/1999)*

BAREFOOT BUBBLY

Barefoot Bubbly NV Premium Extra Dry Chardonnay Champagne Sparkling Blend (California) $7. Frankly sweet, with sugared peach pie flavors, including the toasted crust, this sparkling wine is clean and smooth in texture. It's a good value. **84 Best Buy** *—S.H. (12/31/2005)*

BAREFOOT CELLARS

Barefoot Cellars 2001 Reserve Cabernet Sauvignon (Dry Creek Valley) $17. This nice, fruity wine offers pleasure and complexity in a full-bodied red, with its plum, raspberry, blackberry, and tobacco flavors. The youthful tannins are sweet and chewy. Best now through 2006. **86** *—S.H. (5/1/2004)*

Barefoot Cellars NV Barefoot Bubbly Champagne Blend (California) $7. **81** *—S.H. (12/1/2000)*

Barefoot Cellars NV Bubbly Brut Cuvée Champagne Blend (California) $7. **81** *—S.H. (12/1/2002)*

Barefoot Cellars NV Cuvée Brut Champagne Blend (California) $8. **82** *(12/1/2001)*

Barefoot Cellars NV Brut Cuvée Chardonnay (California) $7. **84** *—S.H. (12/1/2003)*

Barefoot Cellars 2003 Reserve Chardonnay (Russian River Valley) $15. Similar to Barefoot's non-vintage Chard bottling, with apple flavors and dry, crisp acids. There's a little more oak, and a fuller body. **84** *—S.H. (10/1/2005)*

Barefoot Cellars 2000 Reserve Impression Meritage (Alexander Valley) $18. **86** *—S.H. (11/15/2003)*

Barefoot Cellars 2000 Reserve Merlot (Russian River Valley) $17. **86** *—S.H. (2/1/2003)*

Barefoot Cellars 2001 Pinot Noir (Russian River Valley) $15. **85** *—S.H. (2/1/2003)*

Barefoot Cellars 2003 Reserve Pinot Noir (Russian River Valley) $15. You get a lot of Pinot character in this cool-climate wine, with its brisk acids, light, silky texture and pleasant flavors of cherries, raspberries, cola and spices. Those fruity flavors sink down deep and last a long time. **87** *—S.H. (11/15/2005)*

Barefoot Cellars 2000 Reserve Pinot Noir (Sonoma County) $NA. **87** *(5/1/2002)*

Barefoot Cellars 2001 Sauvignon Blanc (California) $6. A brisk, tart white wine that scours the palate with lemony flavors and leaves the throat feeling fresh and clean. The vibrancy of its lines, and the sleek, acidic structure are softened by a very slight residual sugar in the finish. **87 Best Buy** *—S.H. (1/1/2004)*

Barefoot Cellars 2002 Reserve Sauvignon Blanc (Alexander Valley) $15. **83** *—S.H. (12/31/2003)*

Barefoot Cellars NV Extra Dry Sparkling Blend (California) $7. **86 Best Buy** *—S.H. (12/1/2003)*

Barefoot Cellars NV Syrah (California) $6. Stinky and funky, with watery berry flavors and astringent tannins. **80** *—S.H. (3/1/2004)*

Barefoot Cellars NV Zinfandel (California) $6. **83** *—P.G. (3/1/2001)*

Barefoot Cellars 1998 Reserve Zinfandel (Sonoma County) $17. **85** *—S.H. (12/15/2001)*

BARGETTO

Bargetto 2000 Chardonnay (Central Coast) $NA. **84** *—S.H. (9/12/2002)*

Bargetto 2001 Regan Vineyards Chardonnay (Santa Cruz Mountains) $18. **86** *—S.H. (6/1/2003)*

Bargetto 2000 Dry Gewürztraminer (Santa Cruz Mountains) $12. **90** *—S.H. (9/12/2002)*

Bargetto 2000 Merlot (California) $12. **84** *—S.H. (4/1/2003)*

Bargetto 1998 Reserve Merlot (Santa Cruz Mountains) $30. **81** *—S.H. (9/12/2002)*

Bargetto 2001 Pinot Grigio (California) $16. **84** *—S.H. (9/1/2003)*

Bargetto 2001 Regan Vineyards Pinot Noir (Santa Cruz Mountains) $20. Shows lots of finesse in addition to the pretty cherry, raspberry, and herb flavors that are wrapped in a delicately fine structure. Silky tannins and crisp acids provide the balance and strength to make this a versatile food wine. **87** *—S.H. (12/15/2004)*

Bargetto 1999 Regan Vineyards Pinot Noir (Santa Cruz Mountains) $30. **84** *(10/1/2002)*

Bargetto 1999 La Vita Regan Vineyards Red Blend (Santa Cruz Mountains) $50. Raspingly dry and tannic, with earthy, herbal flavors and a hint of dark berry fruit, this blend of Dolcetto, Refosco, Nebbiolo, and Merlot may develop complexity with age. From Bargetto. **84** *—S.H. (12/15/2004)*

Bargetto 2002 Zinfandel (Lodi) $14. Big in berry-cherry fruit, dry, spicy, and life-affirming, it has that wild and woolly edge of an authentic country wine. **86** *—S.H. (11/15/2004)*

BARLOW

Barlow 2001 Red Table Wine Cabernet Blend (Napa Valley) $30. One for the cellar. It opens with a swift kick of dusty tannins that numb the palate to the sweet black currant and cherry fruit buried far below. On the finish, tannins and oak dominate. But such is the overall balance, and the core of fruit, that putting it away for 10 years is no gamble at all. Cabernet Sauvignon (80%) and Merlot. **90** *—S.H. (6/1/2004)*

Barlow 2001 Cabernet Sauvignon (Napa Valley) $39. Ripe in black currant fruit and nicely balanced in rich tannins and good acids. Just oozes flavor and character. Almost a food group of its own. Keep the food pairing simple, like a grilled steak or rib roast. **92 Editors' Choice** *—S.H. (10/1/2004)*

Barlow 2002 Merlot (Napa Valley) $32. Takes the usual formula of cherries, blackberries, cocoa, and oak and kicks it up a notch. It has all that, but the extra layers of dusty oriental spices and a wonderful integration of oak with ripe tannins add interest. The bottom line is elegance. **91** *—S.H. (4/1/2005)*

Barlow 2000 Merlot (Napa Valley) $28. 91 *—S.H. (8/1/2003)*

Barlow 2001 Zinfandel (Napa Valley) $19. 87 *(11/1/2003)*

BARNARD GRIFFIN

Barnard Griffin 2003 Cabernet Sauvignon (Columbia Valley (WA)) $14. Middle of the road, simple, and clean, with light herbs and a food-friendly lightness and balance at 13.8% alcohol. **87** *—P.G. (12/15/2005)*

Barnard Griffin 1999 Cabernet Sauvignon (Columbia Valley (WA)) $18. 85 *—P.G. (12/31/2001)*

Barnard Griffin 2000 Reserve Chardonnay (Columbia Valley (WA)) $19. 88 *—P.G. (7/1/2002)*

Barnard Griffin 2004 Fumé Blanc (Columbia Valley (WA)) $9. This dry sauvignon blanc, all stainless fermented, represents a change in style for B-G that puts it more in line with the lime/citrus flavors of New Zealand. Gone are the herbaceous notes; here the flavor is all about citrus zest, providing sharp relief around the good, juicy fruit. Barnard Griffin is one of the largest family-owned wineries in Washington, and winemaker Rob Griffin has been making wine in the state since 1976. "We're too available to be cultish," he modestly explains. But if there were $9 cult wines, this would qualify. **88 Best Buy** *—P.G. (11/15/2005)*

Barnard Griffin 2002 Fumé Blanc (Columbia Valley (WA)) $8. A rich, creamy, textured wine; with luscious fig and melon flavors. The blend includes about 18% Sémillon, which gives it breadth. The modest, 12.6% alcohol makes it a better balanced wine as well. **89 Best Buy** *—P.G. (5/1/2004)*

Barnard Griffin 2001 Merlot (Columbia Valley (WA)) $15. Straight-ahead, no frills Merlot, with plenty of up-front strawberry/cherry lifesaver fruit flavors. There are some stiff, slightly weedy tannins as well, and the finish is quite astringent. This Pomerol wannabe would taste best with a nice cut of beef. **87** *—P.G. (9/1/2004)*

Barnard Griffin 1998 Merlot (Columbia Valley (WA)) $17. 90 *—P.G. (6/1/2000)*

Barnard Griffin 2002 Caroway Vineyard Sémillon (Columbia Valley (WA)) $NA. Round and full, voluptuous even, this lip-smacking Sémillon blends in notes of honey and hay to expand upon its ripe peach and papaya flavors. Citrus rind completes the tangy finish. **90** *—P.G. (9/1/2004)*

Barnard Griffin 2002 Syrah (Columbia Valley (WA)) $14. A young, grapey, deliciously spicy Syrah with plenty of bright, juicy berry flavors. It clocks in at 14.2% alcohol, easily supported by the dense, deep fruit. Great now, or cellar it as you would a great Zinfandel. **91 Best Buy** *—P.G. (5/1/2004)*

Barnard Griffin 1999 Syrah (Columbia Valley (WA)) $30. 85 *(11/1/2001)*

BARNETT

Barnett 2002 Cabernet Sauvignon (Spring Mountain) $60. Here's a textbook Napa Cab. It's concentrated in black currant flavors, with the best tannic structure money can buy. Soft and elegant in the mouth, with a long, elegant finish. Could use some individuality, though, as it's firmly in the international style. **91** *—S.H. (10/1/2005)*

Barnett 2000 Chardonnay (Napa Valley) $25. 88 *—J.M. (5/1/2002)*

Barnett 2000 Sleepy Hollow Vineyard Pinot Noir (Santa Lucia Highlands) $40. 90 *(10/1/2002)*

BARNWOOD

Barnwood 2002 Cabernet Sauvignon (Santa Barbara County) $22. Ripe in juicy blackberry and cherry flavors, with an edge of sweet dried herbs and some oak, this polished Cab is soft and gentle. Has enough acidity to keep it brisk. **85** *—S.H. (2/1/2005)*

Barnwood 2000 Cabernet Sauvignon (Santa Barbara County) $22. 86 *—S.H. (6/1/2003)*

Barnwood 2002 Trio Red Blend (Santa Barbara County) $35. An interesting blend that combines ripe, juicy fruit with fairly firm tannins to make for balance. The blackberry, cherry, and coffee flavors will complement a nice steak. Cabernet, Merlot, Syrah. **85** *—S.H. (2/1/2005)*

Barnwood 2003 Sauvignon Blanc (Santa Barbara County) $14. Bright in acids and refreshing, this wine features straightforward flavors of ripe citrus fruits, figs, melons, and a hint of papaya on the finish. Try with fish or pork with a fruity salsa. **86** *—S.H. (2/1/2005)*

Barnwood 2000 Sauvignon Blanc (Santa Barbara County) $14. 87 *—S.H. (11/15/2001)*

BARON HERZOG

Baron Herzog 1997 Cabernet Sauvignon (California) $13. 85 *—S.H. (7/1/1999)*

Baron Herzog 1999 Cabernet Sauvignon (California) $13. 82 *—M.S. (4/1/2002)*

Baron Herzog 1998 Chardonnay (California) $13. 85 *—S.H. (10/1/2000)*

Baron Herzog 1999 Chardonnay (California) $13. 80 *—M.S. (4/1/2002)*

Baron Herzog 2003 Chenin Blanc (Clarksburg) $7. Fans of slightly sweet white wines will enjoy the apple sauce and lemon custard flavors of this wine, which fortunately has excellent acidity. Finishes clean. **84 Best Buy** *—S.H. (7/1/2005)*

Baron Herzog 2000 Chenin Blanc (Clarksburg) $7. 83 *—S.H. (11/15/2001)*

Baron Herzog 1999 Sauvignon Blanc (California) $13. 80 *—M.S. (4/1/2002)*

Baron Herzog 1997 Zinfandel (California) $13. 83 *—S.H. (9/1/1999)*

Baron Herzog 2001 Old Vine Zinfandel (Lodi) $13. Fruity and intense in blackberries, black cherries, leather, sweet cocoa, and peppery spices, and totally dry, this is a mouth-filling Zin. It's soft and gentle, with a finish that's just slightly sweet. **86** *—S.H. (8/1/2005)*

USA

BARRA

Barra 2001 Cabernet Sauvignon (Mendocino) $22. Juicy and sweet. You can taste the sunny ripeness with every sip of the blackberry, cherry, and blueberry fruit. Oak plays a supporting role. This dry wine, with its sweet, gentle tannins is delicious. **87** *—S.H. (4/1/2004)*

Barra 1999 Petite Sirah (Mendocino) $27. 84 *(4/1/2003)*

Barra 1999 Pinot Blanc (Mendocino) $14. 87 *—S.H. (5/1/2002)*

Barra of Mendocino 2002 Pinot Noir (Mendocino) $16. Not a whole lot going on in this simple wine. It's pale and light-bodied, with flavors of tea and watermelon. Turns watery on the finish. **83** *(11/1/2004)*

BARRELSTONE

Barrelstone 2003 Syrah (Columbia Valley (WA)) $10. An easy quaffer, not that dissimilar from a light-bodied Australian Shiraz. Candied berry and vanilla fruit, smooth mouthfeel and a hint of herbs make this a nice summer-weight Syrah that you could even serve slightly chilled, à la Beaujolais. **85 Best Buy** *(9/1/2005)*

BARRISTER

Barrister 2002 Cabernet Franc (Columbia Valley (WA)) $24. This new producer grabbed a "Best Limited Production Wine" award at the La County Fair for this herbal and flavorful effort. Once you rip past the bell pepper scents and dig into the wine, it's got dark cab franc fruit flavors, accented with ground coffee and plenty of smoky oak. The mid-palate is fleshy and concentrated, loaded with sweet fruit, while the finish lingers like smoke from a barbecue. **89** *—P.G. (12/1/2004)*

BARTHOLOMEW PARK

Bartholomew Park 1997 Alta Vista Vyds Cabernet Sauvignon (Sonoma Valley) $36. 89 *(11/1/2000)*

Bartholomew Park 1997 Kasper Vyd Cabernet Sauvignon (Sonoma Valley) $41. 88 *(11/1/2000)*

Bartholomew Park 1996 Weiler Vineyard Chardonnay (Sonoma Valley) $21. 86 *—S.H. (11/1/1999)*

BASEL CELLARS

Basel Cellars 2002 Merriment Red Wine Bordeaux Blend (Walla Walla (WA)) $48. A Bordeaux blend of 50% cabernet sauvignon, 40% merlot, and the rest cab franc; all free run juice given the full tilt new oak treatment. Big and fruity, it's immediately delicious, though the acidification sticks out a bit and tangles up the finish. **88** *—P.G. (4/1/2005)*

Basel Cellars 2002 Syrah (Columbia Valley (WA)) $48. An excellent example of spicy, peppery Washington syrah, this has a lifted bouquet of herb, pepper, and toast, tart cherry/cranberry fruit, and fine grained tannins. Scents and flavors of coffee and toast are beginning to integrate into the body of the wine, which may well merit a higher score with another few months of bottle age. **88** *—P.G. (4/1/2005)*

BATES CREEK

Bates Creek 1999 Cabernet Sauvignon (Napa Valley) $25. 92 Editors' Choice *—S.H. (11/15/2002)*

BAYSTONE

Baystone 2000 Saralee's Vineyard Chardonnay (Russian River Valley) $20. 87 *—S.H. (6/1/2003)*

Baystone 1999 Shiraz (Dry Creek Valley) $24. 86 *(11/1/2001)*

BAYWOOD

Baywood 1997 Merlot (Monterey) $18. 90 Editors' Choice *—S.H. (5/1/2001)*

Baywood 1999 Late Harvest Symphony White Blend (California) $35. 89 *(8/1/2001)*

BEAR CREEK

Bear Creek 2000 Petite Sirah (Lodi) $18. 84 *(4/1/2003)*

Bear Creek 2000 Zinfandel (Lodi) $18. 84 *—S.H. (2/1/2003)*

BEARBOAT

Bearboat 2002 Chardonnay (Russian River Valley) $15. Heavily oaked with well-charred wood, so you get lots of upfront toast. Below is a nice Chard with pleasant peach and apple flavors. Finishes dry and spicy. **84** *—S.H. (8/1/2005)*

Bearboat 2002 Pinot Noir (Russian River Valley) $19. Nice and delicately structured in the mouth, an elegant wine with fine acidity and a silky finish. The classic Russian River flavors suggest cherries, cola, mocha, and cinnamon spice. **86** *—S.H. (8/1/2005)*

BEAUCANON

Beaucanon 2000 Trifecta Cabernet Blend (Napa Valley) $27. Tastes old, tired, with flattening acids and still some sticky tannins. The flavors are of blackberries and oak, with a medicinal taste in the finish. **82** *—S.H. (10/1/2005)*

Beaucanon 1998 Jacques de Connick Cabernet Sauvignon (Napa Valley) $65. 92 *—S.H. (6/1/2002)*

Beaucanon 1999 Reserve Cabernet Sauvignon (Napa Valley) $20. 84 *—S.H. (6/1/2002)*

Beaucanon 2002 Chardonnay (Napa Valley) $15. A little earthy, with creamy apple sauce flavors dusted with cinnamon and nutmeg, but dry. There's a rough texture through the finish. **84** *—S.H. (10/1/2005)*

Beaucanon 1997 Jacques De Coninck Chardonnay (Napa Valley) $30. 85 *(6/1/2000)*

Beaucanon 2001 Selection Reserve Jacques de Coninck Chardonnay (Napa Valley) $27. Rather earthy for a Chardonnay, but it's extremely rich earth, with suggestions of apples, clover honey, butterscotch, and toast. Something about this wine makes you reach for a second glass. **87** *—S.H. (10/1/2005)*

Beaucanon 1998 Jacques de Connick Merlot (Napa Valley) $75. 91 *—S.H. (6/1/2002)*

Beaucanon 1999 Selection Reserve Jacques de Conink Merlot (Napa Valley) $47. 88 *—J.M. (8/1/2003)*

BEAULIEU VINEYARD

Beaulieu Vineyard 1997 Tapestry Reserve Red Table Win Bordeaux Blend (Napa Valley) $50. 92 *(11/1/2000)*

Beaulieu Vineyard 2002 Cabernet Sauvignon (Napa Valley) $17. This ripe, fruity blended Cab is bursting with cassis, mocha, and smoky oak flavors. The tannins are very smooth and ripe. A minor quibble is the alcoholic heat throughout. **85** *—S.H. (12/1/2005)*

Beaulieu Vineyard 2001 Cabernet Sauvignon (Rutherford) $25. Classic BV Rutherford, with its thick, dusty tannins, black currant flavors, dryness and overall balance. Those tannins really hit in the finish, suggesting midterm aging. Good now, but should improve by the end of the decade. **87** *—S.H. (5/1/2005)*

Beaulieu Vineyard 2000 Cabernet Sauvignon (Napa Valley) $17. BV does it again with this solid effort. It's as good as many Napa Cabs costing far more, with its currant, plum, and herb and lush, sweet tannins. Lots of finesse and complexity. Drink now. **88** *—S.H. (6/1/2004)*

Beaulieu Vineyard 1999 Cabernet Sauvignon (Rutherford) $25. 90 *—S.H. (11/15/2002)*

Beaulieu Vineyard 1998 Cabernet Sauvignon (Napa Valley) $17. 84 *—S.H. (8/1/2001)*

Beaulieu Vineyard 2001 Clone 4 Cabernet Sauvignon (Rutherford) $130. Soft and lush in texture, with cedar- and vanilla-scented oak, vibrant cassis fruit and hints of dried spices. A delicious wine, but one that needs more depth, structure, and complexity to push it into Cabernet's upper echelons. **89** *(12/1/2005)*

Beaulieu Vineyard 1995 Clone 4 Cabernet Sauvignon (Rutherford) $100. 97 Cellar Selection *(6/1/1999)*

Beaulieu Vineyard 1997 Clone 6 Cabernet Sauvignon (Napa Valley) $130. 92 *(11/1/2000)*

Beaulieu Vineyard 2002 Georges de Latour Private Reserve Cabernet Sauvignon (Napa Valley) $95. It's young, dry, tight, and tannic, although there's obviously a core of ripe black currant and cherry fruit. To evaluate this wine properly, you have to know its history as one of Napa's most ageable Cabernets. Still, it's not a great Georges. Hold until 2008 through 2010, but it could surprise. **92 Cellar Selection** *—S.H. (12/1/2005)*

Beaulieu Vineyard 2000 Georges de Latour Private Reserve Cabernet Sauvignon (Napa Valley) $85. Beaulieu's flagship wine does not have the volume of the best vintages, but it is still a beautiful wine, oozing black currant and cigar-box flavors. The dusty tannins create a lush, velvety texture that displays great balance and charm. **92** *(2/1/2004)*

Beaulieu Vineyard 1999 Georges de Latour Private Reserve Cabernet Sauvignon (Napa Valley) $100. 89 *—J.M. (10/1/2003)*

Beaulieu Vineyard 1997 Georges de Latour Private Reserve Cabernet Sauvignon (Napa Valley) $100. 94 *(11/1/2000)*

Beaulieu Vineyard 2001 Dulcet Reserve Cabernet Sauvignon-Syrah (Napa Valley) $35. First produced in the 2000 vintage, this Cabernet-Syrah blend is dramatically ripe and oaky. It shows huge aromas of black currants, violets, chocolate, and smoke, and is almost sweet, but it's technically dry. Balanced with rich tannins and good acidity, it will develop complexity through the years. **92 Editors' Choice** *—S.H. (10/1/2004)*

Beaulieu Vineyard 2003 Chardonnay (Carneros) $18. Joins very ripe, tropical fruits (like guavas and papayas) to vanilla-tinged, smoky oak to produce a likeable, flavorful Chard. Has a rich, almost thick, creamy texture that finishes with a swirl of spices. **86** *—S.H. (6/1/2005)*

Beaulieu Vineyard 2000 Chardonnay (Carneros) $18. 91 Editors' Choice *—S.H. (12/15/2002)*

Beaulieu Vineyard 2000 Coastal Chardonnay (California) $11. 85 *—S.H. (12/31/2001)*

Beaulieu Vineyard 2003 Coastal Estates Chardonnay (California) $11. There's a lot of Chard character here, in the flavors of peaches, pears, Asian spices, buttery toast, and cream. A large proportion of the grapes came from Monterey, which also helps explain the crispness. **85** *—S.H. (12/1/2005)*

Beaulieu Vineyard 1999 Reserve Chardonnay (Carneros) $30. 87 *(7/1/2001)*

Beaulieu Vineyard 1996 Merlot (Napa Valley) $16. 86 *—J.C. (7/1/2000)*

Beaulieu Vineyard 2001 Merlot (Napa Valley) $17. This wonderfully supple and rewarding Merlot offers satisfaction throughout. It's richly colored, with a velvety texture that carries waves of currant, olive, chocolate, and sweet oak flavors wrapped in soft tannins. **90** *—S.H. (5/1/2005)*

Beaulieu Vineyard 1999 Merlot (Napa Valley) $18. 90 *(11/15/2002)*

USA

Beaulieu Vineyard 1999 Coastal Merlot (California) $12. 88 Best Buy *—S.H. (12/31/2001)*

Beaulieu Vineyard 1997 Signet Collection Pinot Gris (Central Coast) $16. 85 *(8/1/1999)*

Beaulieu Vineyard 2002 Pinot Noir (Carneros) $18. Simple and refreshing, a light-bodied wine with some black cherry, cranberry, and vanilla aromas and flavors. Tight in acidity, with a silky texture and a hint of orange peel on the finish. **85** *(11/1/2004)*

Beaulieu Vineyard 1999 Pinot Noir (Carneros) $18. 86 *(10/1/2002)*

Beaulieu Vineyard 2001 Coastal Pinot Noir (California) $11. 85 *—S.H. (7/1/2003)*

Beaulieu Vineyard 2004 Coastal Estates Pinot Noir (California) $11. Hot and rubbery, with dried-out tannins and herbal, peppery flavors. **81** *—S.H. (12/1/2005)*

Beaulieu Vineyard 2003 Reserve Pinot Noir (Carneros) $39. A little light in flavor and length, this Pinot comes down more on the elegant side than the powerful. It's silky and dry, with pleasant raspberry-cherry, mocha, vanilla, and Asian spice flavors. **87** *—S.H. (12/15/2005)*

Beaulieu Vineyard 2000 Reserve Pinot Noir (Carneros) $32. 87 *(10/1/2002)*

Beaulieu Vineyard 1997 Reserve Carneros Pinot Noir (Carneros) $30. 90 *(10/1/1999)*

Beaulieu Vineyard 1999 Reserve Tapestry Red Blend (Napa Valley) $50. 89 *—M.S. (3/1/2003)*

Beaulieu Vineyard 1997 Signet Collection Beauzeaux Rhône Red Blend (California) $20. 88 *—J.C. (11/1/1999)*

Beaulieu Vineyard 1996 Signet Collection Ensemble Rhône Red Blend (California) $25. 86 *—J.C. (11/1/1999)*

Beaulieu Vineyard 1996 Signet Collection Sangiovese (Napa Valley) $16. 86 *(10/1/1999)*

Beaulieu Vineyard 2004 Coastal Estates Sauvignon Blanc (California) $11. Here's a bone-dry Sauvignon Blanc that's perfect as an everyday cocktail sipper, and versatile with food. It has citrus flavors and bright acidity. **84** *—S.H. (12/1/2005)*

Beaulieu Vineyard 2003 Syrah (Napa Valley) $15. A ripe, easy-drinking Syrah from a big brand, this has all the earmarks of commercial success. Jammy raspberries mingle with deft touches of vanilla, while the finish features just enough acid and tannin to remind you that you're drinking a red wine. Drink now. **85** *(9/1/2005)*

Beaulieu Vineyard 1999 Syrah (California) $15. 85 *—S.H. (10/1/2001)*

Beaulieu Vineyard 1996 Signet Collection Syrah (North Coast) $25. 87 *—J.C. (11/1/1999)*

Beaulieu Vineyard 1997 Signet Collection Tocai (Monterey County) $15. 80 *—J.C. (11/1/1999)*

Beaulieu Vineyard 2001 Signet Collection Viognier (Carneros) $17. 87 *—M.S. (3/1/2003)*

Beaulieu Vineyard 1996 Zinfandel (Napa Valley) $16. 87 *—S.H. (5/1/2000)*

Beaulieu Vineyard 2002 Zinfandel (Napa Valley) $14. Nice wine for this price. It's dry and full-bodied, and rich in plum, coffee, and herb flavors. Very balanced. The sturdy tannins call for rich fare. **86** *—S.H. (5/1/2005)*

Beaulieu Vineyard 2000 Zinfandel (Napa Valley) $15. 90 Best Buy *—S.H. (11/1/2002)*

Beaulieu Vineyard 1997 Zinfandel (Napa Valley) $16. 88 *—P.G. (3/1/2001)*

Beaulieu Vineyard 1997 Coastal Zinfandel (California) $10. 88 Best Buy *—P.G. (11/15/1999)*

Beaulieu Vineyard 1999 Signet Collection Zinfandel (Napa Valley) $28. 85 *—D.T. (3/1/2002)*

BEAUREGARD

Beauregard 2002 Beauregard Ranch Vineyard Chardonnay (Santa Cruz Mountains) $25. Rich and ripe in pineapple, mango, vanilla, spice, and buttered toast, a smooth, succulent wine that finishes long and spicy. A tad soft and simple, but polished. **87** *—S.H. (2/1/2005)*

Beauregard 2002 Beauregard Ranch Vineayrd Zinfandel (Santa Cruz Mountains) $25. Very ripe, verging on raisins, and strong in brambly fruit, this Zin is very dry and medium-bodied. Along with the raisins you get an array of late-summer wild berries and tannins. **85** *—S.H. (2/1/2005)*

BEAUX FRERES

Beaux Freres 2000 Pinot Noir (Willamette Valley) $75. 92 Cellar Selection *(10/1/2002)*

BECKMEN

Beckmen 1997 Atelier Bordeaux Blend (Santa Barbara County) $20. 91 *(3/1/2000)*

Beckmen 1999 Cabernet Sauvignon (Santa Barbara County) $24. 85 *—S.H. (11/15/2002)*

Beckmen 2001 Purisima Mountain Vineyard Grenache (Santa Ynez Valley) $14. 86 *—S.H. (9/1/2003)*

Beckmen 2002 Purisima Mountain Vineyard Marsanne (Santa Ynez Valley) $16. A bit flabby and thick in the mouth despite the peach, apricot, melon, and wildflower flavors. Sits on the palate with a heavy bodiedness, and then turns slightly bitter on the short finish. **85** *—S.H. (3/1/2004)*

Beckmen 1998 Purisima Mountain Vineyard Marsanne (Santa Ynez Valley) $14. 90 *—S.H. (10/1/1999)*

Beckmen 2000 Cuvée Le Bec Red Blend (Santa Barbara County) $14. 84 *—S.H. (12/1/2002)*

Beckmen 2002 Purisima Mountain Vineyard Roussanne (Santa Ynez Valley) $16. An effusively fruity wine, with upfront flavors of peaches and cream, figs, nectarines, and even some tropical pineapple notes. It has a nice acidity that uplifts the flavors and makes the wine bright. At the same time, it's basically a simple, fruit cocktaily sipper. **85** *—S.H. (3/1/2004)*

Beckmen 2001 Purisima Mountain Vineyard Sauvignon Blanc (Santa Ynez Valley) $20. 87 *—S.H. (12/15/2003)*

Beckmen 2000 Syrah (Santa Ynez Valley) $24. 88 *—S.H. (12/1/2002)*

Beckmen 1997 Syrah (Santa Barbara County) $20. 92 *(3/1/2000)*

Beckmen 2001 Estate Syrah (Santa Ynez Valley) $22. 91 Editors' Choice *—S.H. (12/1/2003)*

Beckmen 2001 Purisima Mountain Vineyard Syrah (Santa Ynez Valley) $38. 94 *—S.H. (12/1/2003)*

Beckmen 2003 Purisima Mountain Vineyard Block Six Syrah (Santa Ynez Valley) $42. With Beckmen's Syrah seemingly back on form after a disappointing 2002 vintage, this flagship wine shows penetrating raspberry scents alongside hints of dark chocolate, blueberries, and blackberries. It's a big-body, big-fruit wine, with hints of oak and spice to add nuance. The long, firmly tannic finish suggests cellaring 2–3 years. **89** *(9/1/2005)*

Beckmen 2001 Purisima Mountain Vineyard Clone #1 Syrah (Santa Ynez Valley) $40. 95 Editors' Choice *—S.H. (12/1/2003)*

BEDELL

Bedell 1997 Cabernet Sauvignon (North Fork of Long Island) $25. 87 *—J.C. (4/1/2001)*

Bedell 1998 Gewürztraminer (North Fork of Long Island) $13. 83 *—J.C. (4/1/2001)*

Bedell 1997 Merlot (North Fork of Long Island) $18. 86 *—J.C. (4/1/2001)*

Bedell NV Main Road Red Merlot-Cabernet Sauvignon (North Fork of Long Island) $14. 80 *—J.C. (10/2/2004)*

Bedell 2001 Late Harvest Riesling (North Fork of Long Island) $35. 88 *—J.C. (8/1/2003)*

BEDFORD THOMPSON

Bedford Thompson 2000 Thompson Vineyard Cabernet Franc (Santa Barbara County) $20. Nice and polished, an elegant wine with flavors of cherries and oak. It's medium in body, with smooth tannins and a silky finish, and quite dry. **85** *—S.H. (12/15/2004)*

Bedford Thompson 2002 Thompson Vineyard Chardonnay (Santa Barbara County) $20. A bit raw and green, with peach, apple, and oak flavors. Feels rough through the finish. **84** *—S.H. (12/15/2004)*

Bedford Thompson 2000 Thompson Vineyard Grenache (Santa Barbara County) $20. Light in body and flavor, a simple little wine with herbal, mushroomy flavors and puckery tannins. Feels dry and astringent because there's not enough ripe fruit to soften. **83** *—S.H. (3/1/2004)*

Bedford Thompson 2001 Thompson Vineyard Petite Sirah (Santa Barbara County) $45. Very dry and thick in tannins, with powerful plum, coffee, and chocolate fruit and crisp acids. Those tannins really kick in and numb the palate, leading to a dry, astringent finish. **84** *—S.H. (12/15/2004)*

Bedford Thompson 2000 Thompson Vineyard Syrah (Santa Barbara County) $22. 88 *—S.H. (12/1/2003)*

BEHRENS & HITCHCOCK

Behrens & Hitchcock 2001 Beckstoffer Tokalon Vineyard Cabernet Sauvignon (Napa Valley) $65. Black in color with well-charred oak, caramel, and toast flavors. Raisins, currants, and blackstrap molasses flavors. Big, Port-like in size, but dry. Finishes hot. **85** *—S.H. (6/1/2005)*

BEL ARBOR

Bel Arbor 1999 Cabernet Sauvignon (California) $6. 86 Best Buy *—S.H. (12/15/2000)*

Bel Arbor 2000 Chardonnay (Mendocino County) $6. 84 *—S.H. (5/1/2002)*

Bel Arbor 2000 Merlot (Mendocino County) $6. 83 *—S.H. (7/1/2002)*

BEL GLOS

Bel Glos 2000 Pinot Noir (Santa Maria Valley) $30. 88 *—J.M. (2/1/2003)*

BELFORD SPRINGS

Belford Springs 2000 Pinot Noir (California) $8. 84 *—S.H. (4/1/2003)*

Belford Springs 2001 Zinfandel (California) $6. 85 Best Buy *(11/1/2003)*

USA

BELL

Bell 2000 Cabernet Sauvignon (Napa Valley) $35. 85 *—S.H. (11/15/2003)*

Bell 1999 Baritelle Vineyard Cabernet Sauvignon (Rutherford) $60. 92 Editors' Choice *—S.H. (12/31/2002)*

Bell 1998 Baritelle Vineyard Jackson Clone Cabernet Sauvignon (Rutherford) $55. 93 *—S.H. (6/1/2002)*

Bell 1997 Baritelle Vyd Cabernet Sauvignon (Rutherford) $60. 90 *(11/1/2000)*

Bell 1999 Talianna Cabernet Sauvignon (Rutherford) $35. 92 *—S.H. (6/1/2002)*

Bell 1998 Aleta's Vineyard Chardonnay (Yountville) $24. 82 *(6/1/2000)*

Bell 1999 Aleta's Vineyard Merlot (Yountville) $35. 88 *—S.H. (6/1/2002)*

Bell 2003 Canterbury Vineyard Syrah (Sierra Foothills) $24. Slightly herbal and spicy, but this wine is mostly about the fruit, which one taster described as ripe while another called it stewed. There's a backbone of chocolate and prune that's undeniably rich and gives it strength. **87** *(9/1/2005)*

Bell 1999 Canterbury Vineyard Syrah (Sierra Foothills) $28. 88 *(11/1/2001)*

Bell 2000 T&A Vineyard Viognier (Santa Cruz County) $28. 88 *—J.M. (12/15/2002)*

BELLA

Bella 2002 Lily Hill Estate Syrah (Dry Creek Valley) $34. This soft Syrah is forward in ripe cherries, raspberries, pomegranates, coffee, and wood spice flavors. It has an apparent sweetness that comes from the interplay of ripeness, alcohol, and oak. Feels limpid, soft, and voluptuous on the palate. **88** *—S.H. (11/1/2005)*

Bella 2002 Belle Canyon Estate Zinfandel (Dry Creek Valley) $30. This fine example of a Dry Creek Zin is very forward in ripe cherries and raspberries, but possesses great structure from rich tannins. Deeply satisfying, it has a fine, claret-like balance and elegance. **90** *—S.H. (11/1/2005)*

Bella 2002 Big River Ranch Zinfandel (Alexander Valley) $34. Almost Port-like in the black-purple color. Aromas are of caramel, baked brown sugar and blueberries. This is a dry wine, but an enormously fruity one, with rich, thick, soft, elaborate tannins. The blackberries reprise on the finish, ripe with sunny sweetness. **88** *—S.H. (10/1/2005)*

Bella 2002 Estate Zinfandel (Dry Creek Valley) $24. With more than 15% alcohol and new oak, this Zin adds sweetness to the cherry and black raspberry flavors, but there's a good grip of acids and tannins to balance. Try with the best beef you can get. **87** *—S.H. (11/1/2005)*

Bella 2001 Lily Hill Estate Zinfandel (Dry Creek Valley) $28. 86 *(11/1/2003)*

BELLE GLOS

Belle Glos 2001 Pinot Noir (Santa Maria Valley) $30. 90 *—S.H. (7/1/2003)*

Belle Glos 2002 Clark & Telephone Vineyard Pinot Noir (Santa Maria Valley) $38. This spectacular Pinot, which defines its South Coast terroir, is a great wine. The extracted fruit is massive, flooding the palate with cherries and raspberries, and the wine is well-oaked. Yet it combines its power with regal grace, which is what Pinot is supposed to do. Finishes with a silky, velvety harmony. Really an eye-opening wine, superb in every respect. **95** *—S.H. (5/1/2005)*

Belle Glos 2002 Taylor Lane Vineyard Pinot Noir (Sonoma Coast) $50. This is a good wine, but it's really tannic and heavy for Pinot Noir. With the black color and peppery aroma, you might mistake it for Syrah. Perhaps it will age. Meanwhile, it defines a current trend in Sonoma for weighty Pinots, so be forewarned. **87** *—S.H. (4/1/2005)*

BELLE VALLÉE

Belle Vallée 2002 Reserve Pinot Noir (Oregon) $30. Cranberries and tart cherry fruit is awash in new oak; tannic and awkward at the moment. If the tannins smooth out, this could merit a significantly higher score. **86** *(11/1/2004)*

BELO

Belo 1999 Muscat Gris Muscat (California) $16. 89 *—S.H. (9/1/2003)*

Belo 1999 Touriga Nacional Vintage Reserve Port (Napa Valley) $40. 96 Cellar Selection *—S.H. (12/1/2002)*

BELVEDERE

Belvedere 1998 Chardonnay (Russian River Valley) $18. 89 *(6/1/2000)*

Belvedere 2002 Chardonnay (Russian River Valley) $20. More manipulated than Belvedere's Healdsburg Ranches bottling, showing the impact of sur lie aging in the slightly sour note that lends complexity to the oak and fruit. Dry and well-acidified, this needs something like cracked Dungeness crab to make it sing. **88** *—S.H. (8/1/2005)*

Belvedere 2003 Healdsburg Ranches Chardonnay (Sonoma County) $14. Well-oaked, brimming with vanilla, buttered toast, and sweet wood flavors, but the fruit below is big enough to take it. Spicy mango, guava, pineapple, and honey, in a creamy, full-bodied texture. Not a bad price for a wine of this quality. **88** *—S.H. (8/1/2005)*

Belvedere 2000 Pinot Noir (Russian River Valley) $30. 91 *—S.H. (5/1/2002)*

Belvedere 1998 Syrah (Dry Creek Valley) $22. 87 *(11/1/2001)*

Belvedere 1999 Zinfandel (Dry Creek Valley) $NA. 89 *—D.T. (3/1/2002)*

BENESSERE

Benessere 2003 Pinot Grigio (Carneros) $22. Smooth-textured and firm, yet with just the right touch of acidity. The wine shows complexity, with layered notes of melon, lemon, herbs, and a touch of peach. Medium-bodied with a finish that's moderate in length. **88** *—J.M. (10/1/2004)*

Benessere 2000 Pinot Grigio (Napa Valley) $20. 88 *—J.M. (11/15/2001)*

Benessere 1996 Sangiovese (Napa Valley) $25. 87 *—M.S. (6/1/1999)*

Benessere 2000 Sangiovese (Napa Valley) $25. A smoky, charry edge frames the black cherry, cassis, blackberry, licorice, and spice flavors here. The wine is smooth textured, though it ends with a touch of bitterness. **87** *—J.M. (4/1/2004)*

Benessere 1998 Sangiovese (Napa Valley) $28. 92 Editors' Choice *—J.M. (12/1/2001)*

Benessere 2003 Syrah (Napa Valley) $40. Limited production (under 200 cases), but worth seeking out. Features bold blackberries accented by hints of savory dried herbs, pepper, and dried spices, all buoyed by a creamy, supple, mouthfeel. The long, berry-filled finish boasts hints of coffee and vanilla. Nicely done. **89** *(9/1/2005)*

Benessere 1999 Benessere Estate Black Glass Vyd Zinfandel (Napa Valley) $35. 92 Editors' Choice *—J.M. (12/15/2001)*

Benessere 2001 Black Glass Vineyard Zinfandel (Napa Valley) $35. 91 *(11/1/2003)*

BENNETT LANE

Bennett Lane 2002 Maximus Cabernet Blend (Napa Valley) $28. A Bordeaux blend with a good chunk of Syrah added, this wine is soft and luscious. Although it's a little sweet and not an ager, the blackberry, coffee, and cocoa flavors make you want another glass. **87** *—S.H. (10/1/2005)*

BENSON FERRY

Benson Ferry 2001 Select Chardonnay (North Coast) $9. 86 Best Buy *—S.H. (6/1/2003)*

Benson Ferry 2001 Old Vines Zinfandel (Lodi) $13. 88 *(11/1/2003)*

BENTON-LANE

Benton-Lane 2002 Pinot Noir (Willamette Valley) $21. Quite similar to the winery's "First Class" bottling, this too offers very tart, sour red fruits, and a thin, watery texture. The herbal flavors carry into some forest floor, mushroomy notes. **84** *(11/1/2004)*

Benton-Lane 1998 Pinot Noir (Willamette Valley) $17. 82 *—M.S. (12/1/2000)*

Benton-Lane 1999 Reserve Pinot Noir (Oregon) $30. 89 *—P.G. (12/31/2001)*

Benton-Lane 1999 Sunnymount Cuvée Pinot Noir (Willamette Valley) $65. Good texture and more flesh than the B-L reserve from the same excellent vintage. This is a beautifully-crafted and balanced wine that could pass for a good Gevrey-Chambertin. Flavors of beetroot, herb, leaf, cherry, and spicy oak; will certainly improve with further cellar time. Just 100 cases were produced. **91 Cellar Selection** *—P.G. (2/1/2004)*

Benton-Lane 1998 Sunnymount Cuvée Pinot Noir (Oregon) $50. 88 *—P.G. (12/31/2001)*

BENZIGER

Benziger 2001 Cabernet Sauvignon (Sonoma County) $19. Balance and user-friendliness are what this wine is all about. The blackberry and herb flavors aren't overdone. The tannins are thick and dusty, but negotiable. There's a dab of smoky oak, but just enough to season. The result is a very good dinner wine, from fast food to cookbook special. **89** —*S.H. (6/1/2004)*

Benziger 1999 Cabernet Sauvignon (Sonoma County) $19. 86 —*S.H. (12/15/2003)*

Benziger 1997 Blue Rock Vineyards Cabernet Sauvignon (Alexander Valley) $50. 90 —*S.H. (12/31/2001)*

Benziger 1998 Estate Cabernet Sauvignon (Sonoma Mountain) $60. 88 —*S.H. (12/31/2001)*

Benziger 2001 Reserve Cabernet Sauvignon (Sonoma County) $42. This is a big, flamboyant Cab that floods the mouth with ripe, juicy flavors, but it's balanced despite the size. Blackberries, cherries, sweet red plums, cocoa, and spices, with soft, sweet tannins and a long, fruity finish. **89** —*S.H. (3/1/2005)*

Benziger 1998 Reserve Cabernet Sauvignon (Sonoma County) $45. 91 —*S.H. (12/1/2001)*

Benziger 2001 Stone Farm Vineyard Cabernet Sauvignon (Sonoma Valley) $27. Drinks beautifully now for its rich, smooth tannins, dry balance, and complex melange of black currant, oak, coffee, and spice flavors. Easy to toss back, but has extra layers of complexity and nuance. **91** —*S.H. (3/1/2005)*

Benziger 2002 Chardonnay (Carneros) $16. A pretty wine, spicy and rich, with an array of vibrantly fruity flavors ranging from sweet citrus through apples and peaches to exotic mango. Winemaker bells and whistles such as barrel fermentation and lees add creamy, vanilla, buttered toast notes. **87** —*S.H. (11/15/2004)*

Benziger 2000 Chardonnay (Carneros) $16. 86 —*S.H. (5/1/2002)*

Benziger 2002 Reserve Chardonnay (Carneros) $27. This is an oaky Chard, brimming with vanilla, honey, and smoky char, with underlying flavors of peaches and tropical fruits. There's also an earthy edge suggesting sweet dried herbs that suggests careful food pairing. A butter-sauteed filet of sole will be fine. **87** —*S.H. (3/1/2005)*

Benziger 2002 Ricci Vineyard Chardonnay (Carneros) $25. Oaky and sweet in honey, mango, papaya, and pear flavors, swirled with vanilla. Fortunately there's a good grip of acidity to balance the sweetness. **86** —*S.H. (3/1/2005)*

Benziger 2001 Sangiacomo Vineyards Reserve Chardonnay (Carneros) $27. 92 —*S.H. (12/15/2003)*

Benziger 2003 Fumé Blanc (North Coast) $13. Fruity and a little sweet, with apple and fig flavors and good acidity. Finishes clean and zesty. **84** —*S.H. (3/1/2005)*

USA

Benziger 2001 Merlot (Sonoma County) $19. Benziger keeps the good wines coming. This one straddles the line between ripe cherry and berry fruit flavors and earthier notes of mushrooms and dried herbs. Oak provides the bass. It's dry and tannic, and cries out for fine, rich meats and cheeses. **88** —*S.H. (6/1/2004)*

Benziger 1999 Merlot (Sonoma County) $19. 91 —*S.H. (7/1/2002)*

Benziger 2000 Blue Rock Vineyard Merlot (Alexander Valley) $30. A fat, strong, rich Merlot with potent flavors and lavish oak. When you sniff it, you get equal parts smoky, spicy vanillins from barrels and the underlying black currant of the grape. Drinks dense and refined, with creamy sweet tannins and a lavish mouthfeel. **91** —*S.H. (4/1/2004)*

Benziger 2000 Reserve Merlot (Sonoma County) $42. Lovely and soft in the modern red style, a full-bodied wine that glides like velvet over the palate. The flavors satisfy with plums, blackberries, cocoa, and oak. **90** —*S.H. (8/1/2005)*

Benziger 1997 Reserve Merlot (Sonoma County) $41. 91 *(6/1/2001)*

Benziger 1999 McNab Ranch Petite Sirah (Mendocino County) $21. 83 *(4/1/2003)*

Benziger 1997 Pinot Noir (California) $15. 87 *(11/15/1999)*

Benziger 2000 Pinot Noir (Sonoma County) $21. 86 —*S.H. (7/1/2003)*

Benziger 1999 Bien Nacido Pinot Noir (Santa Maria Valley) $33. 86 *(10/1/2002)*

Benziger 2000 Bien Nacido Vineyard Pinot Noir (Santa Maria Valley) $33. 87 —*S.H. (7/1/2003)*

Benziger 1997 Reserve Pinot Noir (California) $40. 90 —*S.H. (12/15/2001)*

Benziger 2001 Tribute Red Blend (Sonoma Mountain) $65. Made from biodynamically grown estate grapes, this Cabernet-based wine is as massive as any I've tasted from this great vintage. It's like drinking liquid steel, with deep, ripe flavors of black currants, chocolate, and cherries, and plenty of new oak. Despite the size, the texture is gentle and velvety, but it's an ager if you want. Now through 2015. **94 Cellar Selection** *(4/1/2005)*

Benziger 2004 Paradiso de Maria Sauvignon Blanc (Sonoma Mountain) $27. This is a very fine Sauvignon Blanc that has great elegance and finesse as well as power. To begin with, it's delicately structured, with a steely minerality and fine acidity, and is fully dry. The flavors are a mélange of lime, alfalfa, honeydew melon, fig, and white pepper. **91 Editors' Choice** —*S.H. (12/1/2005)*

Benziger 2000 Syrah (California) $22. 85 —*S.H. (10/1/2003)*

Benziger 1998 Bien Nacido Vineyard Syrah (Santa Maria Valley) $24. 90 —*S.H. (7/1/2002)*

Benziger 1997 Viognier (Sonoma County) $18. 89 —*S.H. (6/1/1999)*

BERAN

Beran 2002 Pinot Noir (Willamette Valley) $30. Some stemmy, vegetal notes start things off roughly, but then the wine opens up with pleasing citrus, rosewater, and watermelon flavors. Very light, elegant and polished through the finish. **86** *(11/1/2004)*

BERESAN

Beresan 2002 Cabernet Sauvignon (Walla Walla (WA)) $25. Extremely likeable and accessible, this cab includes 15% syrah and 5% cab franc. It's loaded with butterscotch and mocha, but the ripe, not over-ripe fruit gives it a clear, clean focus right down the middle. **90** *—P.G. (4/1/2005)*

Beresan 2002 Stone River Red Wine Red Blend (Walla Walla (WA)) $28. Sophisticated winemaking meets gorgeous fruit in this unusual blend: 30% Cabernet Sauvignon, 30% Syrah, 20% Merlot, and 20% Cab Franc. The Syrah's fresh citrus flavors are perfect in the context of the sappy Merlot and harder Cabs, making a wonderful blend that is immediately accessible with sweet, round fruit; then lingers into a long, textured, lively finish. **95 Editors' Choice** *—P.G. (11/15/2004)*

BERGEVIN LANE

Bergevin Lane 2002 Cabernet Sauvignon (Columbia Valley (WA)) $25. Spicy and tart, with sharp, stiff, tight cranberry/currant-flavored fruit. The wine feels attenuated; it hits a wall and stops, and after 24 hours of breathing time opens only slightly more. **86** *—P.G. (4/1/2005)*

Bergevin Lane 2003 Calico Red (Columbia Valley (WA)) $16. A "kitchen sink" blend of Cabernet Sauvignon, Cab Franc, Merlot, Syrah, and Zinfandel, it somehow knits itself together and avoids the broad, generic red syndrome of most cheap blends. This has sappy, sweet fruit built upon juicy berries, and that concentrated core carries right through the clean, spicy finish. **90** *—P.G. (6/1/2005)*

Bergevin Lane 2003 Syrah (Columbia Valley (WA)) $25. Among a bevy of Columbia Valley bottlings, Bergevin Lane's stood out for its complex nose of black cherry, cracked pepper, dried spices, and herbs and for its smooth, silky mouthfeel. Drink now. **88** *(9/1/2005)*

Bergevin Lane 2004 Viognier (Columbia Valley (WA)) $25. Thick and peachy, with the weight of Roussanne (19%) married to the elegance of the Viognier (81%), this barrel-fermented, oak-aged wine displays intense fruit flavors of apricot, white peach, and citrus. Round and fleshy, it retains sufficient acid to prevent a flabby impression. A nice kiss of vanilla sends it on its way. **90** *—P.G. (12/15/2005)*

BERGSTRÖM

Bergström 2001 Chardonnay (Willamette Valley) $28. **90** *—S.H. (9/1/2003)*

Bergström 2000 Pinot Gris (Willamette Valley) $16. **87** *—S.H. (8/1/2002)*

Bergström 2000 Pinot Noir (Willamette Valley) $35. **91** *—S.H. (12/31/2002)*

Bergström 2001 Arcus Vineyard Pinot Noir (Willamette Valley) $50. **93 Cellar Selection** *—S.H. (12/1/2003)*

BERINGER

Beringer 2001 Alluvium Bordeaux Blend (Knights Valley) $30. Tastes a little raw, with still-youthful acids, although there's a softness that frames the cherry and blackberry flavors. But this isn't an ager. It's a pleasant, clean Cabernet blend that's drinkable now and through 2006. **86** *—S.H. (12/15/2005)*

Beringer 1996 Alluvium Bordeaux Blend (Knights Valley) $30. **87** *(3/1/2000)*

Beringer 2001 Cabernet Sauvignon (Napa Valley) $35. Shows off the best of Napa Cab with aromas of cassis and toasty oak. Turns rich and dry in the mouth, classically structured, with firm tannins and a finish of pure black currants and sweet oak. **90** *—S.H. (3/1/2005)*

Beringer 1999 Cabernet Sauvignon (Knights Valley) $26. **87** *—S.H. (2/1/2003)*

Beringer 1999 Appellation Collection Reserve Cabernet Sauvignon (Knights Valley) $50. **84** *—S.H. (12/15/2003)*

Beringer 1998 Chabot Vineyard Cabernet Sauvignon (St. Helena) $80. **91** *—S.H. (11/15/2003)*

Beringer 2000 Founders' Estate Cabernet Sauvignon (California) $12. **85** *—S.H. (3/1/2003)*

Beringer 1997 Founders' Estate Cabernet Sauvignon (California) $11. **87** *(11/15/1999)*

Beringer 2000 Private Reserve Cabernet Sauvignon (Napa Valley) $100. Not the greatest Beringer PR of late, this wine showcases the weakness of the vintage. It's earthy and tannic, with only a suggestion of cherries and blackberries. It's a wine to drink now and over the next few years. **86** *—S.H. (5/1/2005)*

Beringer 1997 Private Reserve Cabernet Sauvignon (Napa Valley) $100. **93** *—S.H. (12/31/2001)*

Beringer 1995 Private Reserve Cabernet Sauvignon (Napa Valley) $75. **95** *—S.H. (7/1/2000)*

Beringer 1998 St. Helena Home Vineyard Cabernet Sauvignon (St. Helena) $80. **92** *—S.H. (11/15/2003)*

Beringer 1998 Tre Colline Cabernet Sauvignon (Howell Mountain) $80. **91** *—S.H. (11/15/2003)*

Beringer 1998 Chardonnay (Napa Valley) $16. 86 *(6/1/2000)*

Beringer 2002 Chardonnay (Napa Valley) $16. Bright in acidity, with nice apple, peach, and sweet oak flavors. Finishes with butter, spice, and vanilla. **86** *—S.H. (3/1/2005)*

Beringer 2000 Appellation Collection Chardonnay (Napa Valley) $16. 92 *—S.H. (12/15/2002)*

Beringer 2001 Founders' Estate Chardonnay (California) $12. 85 *—S.H. (6/1/2003)*

Beringer 2002 Private Reserve Chardonnay (Napa Valley) $35. Another great PR from Beringer. Stays the course with lushly ripe fruit and lavish oak. Big and bold, but elegant and balanced, with mouthwatering acidity and a sense of harmony. **91** *—S.H. (12/15/2004)*

Beringer 2000 Private Reserve Chardonnay (Napa Valley) $35. 91 *—S.H. (5/1/2003)*

Beringer 1998 Private Reserve Chardonnay (Napa Valley) $36. 89 *(10/1/2000)*

Beringer 2001 Sbragia Limited Release Chardonnay (Napa Valley) $40. 92 *—S.H. (12/1/2003)*

Beringer 1999 Sbragia-Limited Release Chardonnay (Napa Valley) $40. 91 *(7/1/2001)*

Beringer 2002 Chenin Blanc (California) $6. 83 *—S.H. (12/15/2003)*

Beringer 2002 Gewürztraminer (California) $6. 84 *—S.H. (12/31/2003)*

Beringer 2002 Johannisberg Riesling (California) $6. 85 Best Buy *—S.H. (12/31/2003)*

Beringer 2001 Merlot (Napa Valley) $19. It's surprising to see a four-year-old wine released at such an inexpensive price. Maybe Beringer was hoping it would come around. Instead, it's just tired. Already losing fruit, it's dry and brittle. **83** *—S.H. (11/15/2005)*

Beringer 1997 Bancroft Ranch Merlot (Howell Mountain) $75. 89 *(6/1/2001)*

Beringer 2002 Founders' Estate Merlot (California) $11. This wine has earth, blackberry, herb, and spice flavors that finish dry, with a cleansing, slightly bitter scour of acidity like the aftertaste on espresso. **83** *—S.H. (11/15/2005)*

Beringer 2000 Founders' Estate Merlot (California) $12. 87 Best Buy *—S.H. (10/1/2003)*

Beringer 2000 Private Reserve Howell Mountain Merlot (Napa Valley) $50. Hits with harsh, stinging tannins and a tantalizing hint of cherries, and quickly numbs the palate. Hard to tell where it's going. **86** *—S.H. (5/1/2005)*

USA

Beringer 2003 Pinot Grigio (California) $7. Bone dry and very tart in acids and grapefruit flavors. This clean wine gets the job done when you need a serviceable white. **83** *—S.H. (10/1/2004)*

Beringer 2004 Pinot Noir (Napa Valley) $16. Pleasant and uncomplicated, this is an easy Pinot to understand. Plays it straight down the middle, a gently silky wine with cola, cherry, vanilla, cocoa, and spice flavors. **84** *—S.H. (11/15/2005)*

Beringer 2002 Pinot Noir (Carneros) $16. Textbook example of a charming, young, cool-climate Pinot that's fresh and flavorful. Packs the cherry, white pepper, sweet tobacco, vanilla, and smoky tastes into soft, creamy tannins backed by a burst of clean acidity. **87** *(11/1/2004)*

Beringer 1999 Pinot Noir (North Coast) $16. 83 *(10/1/2002)*

Beringer 2001 Founders' Estate Pinot Noir (California) $12. 86 Best Buy *—S.H. (12/1/2003)*

Beringer 2002 Stanly Ranch Pinot Noir (Carneros) $30. Dramatically delicious, a complex wine of great depth and interest. It takes the minty, tutti-fruity flavors of simpler Carneros Pinots and elevates them, adding swirls of cherry liqueur, kid leather, veal and, on the finish, intense cassis. Maintains essential silkiness, dryness, delicacy, and crispness. **92 Editors' Choice** *—S.H. (11/1/2004)*

Beringer 1999 Stanly Ranch Pinot Noir (Napa Valley) $30. 92 Editors' Choice *(10/1/2002)*

Beringer 1998 Alluvium Red Blend (Knights Valley) $30. 88 *—J.M. (11/15/2002)*

Beringer 2002 Riesling (Napa Valley) $16. Aromatic and pretty, a light, delicate wine that offers up plenty of flavor. White peach, honeysuckle, smoky vanilla, gingerbread, flowers, and spices mingle in complex waves. Dry, but finishes with honeyed richness **87** *—S.H. (9/1/2004)*

Beringer 1998 Rosé de Saignee Rosé Blend (California) $16. 86 *—J.C. (8/1/2000)*

Beringer 2004 Sauvignon Blanc (Napa Valley) $12. Made in a bone dry style with green pepper, feline spray, and gooseberry flavors, this will appeal to those who like this type. It has a soft, creamy texture. **83** *—S.H. (11/15/2005)*

Beringer 2002 Sauvignon Blanc (Napa Valley) $12. 85 *—S.H. (12/31/2003)*

Beringer 2002 Founders' Estate Sauvignon Blanc (California) $11. Beringer's FE line does a good job of producing clean, varietally correct wines at fair prices. This white wine is sprightly and ripe with juicy citrus, fig, melon, and vanilla flavors. It's a bit sweet, but has good acidity for balance. **85** *—S.H. (8/1/2004)*

Beringer 2000 Founders' Estate Sauvignon Blanc (California) $11. 84 *—S.H. (12/15/2001)*

Beringer 2001 Alluvium Blanc Sémillon-Sauvignon Blanc (Knights Valley) $16. 84 *—S.H. (7/1/2003)*

Beringer 2000 Nightingale Sémillon-Sauvignon Blanc (Napa Valley) $35. 86 *—S.H. (12/1/2003)*

Beringer 2003 Founders' Estate Shiraz (California) $11. An easy-drinking, pleasing Shiraz. Very ripe plum, cinnamon, and vanilla aromas are echoed on the palate, where the wine also shows hints of chocolate. Medium-bodied; falls flat on the finish. **85** *(9/1/2005)*

Beringer 2001 Marston Vineyard Syrah (Spring Mountain) $35. Really ripe-smelling, with elements of pruny fruit intertwined with hickory smoke and graham cracker on the nose. The fruit freshens up on the palate, turning plummy and velvety. Sturdy, this wine shows its mountain origins without being overly tough. **89** *(9/1/2005)*

Beringer 2004 Viognier (Napa Valley) $16. Soft, simple, and clean, this is a big-fruit wine that appeals for its super-ripe peach, mango, pineapple, honeysuckle, and citrus flavors and creamy texture. It has just enough acidity to have a balanced mouthfeel. **84** *—S.H. (11/15/2005)*

Beringer 2002 Viognier (Napa Valley) $16. Drinks dry and tart, not the fruitiest Viognier ever, but a nice, calm one. Reins in the peach, citrus, and apple flavors with firm acidity and a steely clean finish. **85** *—S.H. (9/1/2004)*

Beringer 2000 Alluvium Blanc White Blend (Knights Valley) $16. 87 *—J.M. (12/15/2002)*

Beringer 1998 Alluvium Blanc White Blend (Knights Valley) $16. 89 *—S.H. (5/1/2001)*

Beringer 1996 Nightingale White Blend (North Coast) $30. 93 *—S.H. (12/31/2000)*

Beringer 2001 Zinfandel (California) $12. 82 *(11/1/2003)*

Beringer 1999 Appellation Collection Zinfandel (Clear Lake) $14. A difficult Zin to like. Opens with funky aromas of socks and that offputting smell doesn't blow off. In the mouth, it's jammy and unnaturally sweet. **81** *—S.H. (3/1/2004)*

Beringer 2003 Founders' Estate Old Vine Zinfandel (California) $11. There's a ton of juicy Zin character in this pleasant wine. It has big-time cherry, black raspberry, and blackberry flavors with a rich chocolate streak, and a raw, acidic edginess that cries out for food. **85** *—S.H. (11/15/2005)*

BERNARDUS

Bernardus 2001 Marinus Cabernet Sauvignon (Carmel Valley) $46. From this sheltered valley in Monterey, a lovely Cab that features ripe cassis and black currant flavors. The tannins invite a comparison to Napa Valley. They're firmer, but the wine is drinkable now. Finishes with a chocolaty taste. Mainly Cabernet Sauvignon. **90** *—S.H. (4/1/2005)*

Bernardus 2003 Chardonnay (Monterey) $20. Here's one of the more complex Chards at this price. It has much in common with what California does best, namely, well-ripened fruit, with fresh, keen acidity. The winemaker bells and whistles have been tastefully applied. **91 Editors' Choice** *—S.H. (11/1/2005)*

Bernardus 2001 Chardonnay (Monterey County) $20. 90 Editors' Choice *—S.H. (8/1/2003)*

Bernardus 1996 Bien Nacido Reserve Chardonnay (Santa Barbara County) $32. 84 *(7/1/2001)*

Bernardus 1996 Sangiacomo Vineyards Reserve Chardonnay (Sonoma County) $30. 87 *(7/1/2001)*

Bernardus 1996 Merlot (Carmel Valley) $30. 89 *—J.C. (7/1/2000)*

Bernardus 2000 Bien Nacido Vineyard Pinot Noir (Santa Barbara County) $48. 87 *—S.H. (12/1/2003)*

Bernardus 2004 Sauvignon Blanc (Monterey County) $15. An intensely flavored white wine, totally dry and tart in zesty citrus rind and gooseberry, with shadings of fig, melon, and vanilla. It's a really good wine, fun to drink, and versatile across a range of food. **88** *—S.H. (11/1/2005)*

Bernardus 2001 Sauvignon Blanc (Monterey County) $15. 89 *—S.H. (7/1/2003)*

Bernardus 2004 Griva Vineyard Sauvignon Blanc (Arroyo Seco) $20. Three cheers for this Sauvignon Blanc. It triangulates perfectly between the variety's grassy, green apple character, richer, riper fig and peach flavors, and an oaky veneer. But it never loses sight of its crisp, cleansing, and vital acidity. **90** *—S.H. (11/1/2005)*

Bernardus 2001 Griva Vineyard Sauvignon Blanc (Arroyo Seco) $20. 89 *—S.H. (10/1/2003)*

BETHEL HEIGHTS

Bethel Heights 1999 Estate Grown Chardonnay (Willamette Valley) $15. 89 Best Buy *—P.G. (4/1/2002)*

Bethel Heights 2002 Pinot Blanc (Willamette Valley) $12. 88 Best Buy *—P.G. (12/1/2003)*

Bethel Heights 2000 Pinot Gris (Willamette Valley) $12. 86 *—P.G. (4/1/2002)*

Bethel Heights 1997 Pinot Gris (Willamette Valley) $12. 83 *(8/1/1999)*

Bethel Heights 2002 Pinot Noir (Willamette Valley) $15. Despite its soft, pretty opening scents, this wine simply lacks fruit. The middle drops out completely, resolving in some dry tannins. Bottle shock? **84** *(11/1/2004)*

Bethel Heights 2000 Pinot Noir (Willamette Valley) $25. 86 *(10/1/2002)*

Bethel Heights 1997 Estate Pinot Noir (Eola Hills) $22. 84 *(10/1/1999)*

Bethel Heights 2002 Flat Block Reserve Pinot Noir (Willamette Valley) $38. Perhaps just young and closed up, but this reserve did not seem to show the extra dimensions that a reserve generally should. A mix of berry/cherry fruits, snappy acids, and a hint of new oak. Good, standard fare. 85 *(11/1/2004)*

Bethel Heights 2000 Flat Block Reserve Pinot Noir (Willamette Valley) $35. 87 *(10/1/2002)*

Bethel Heights 2002 Freedom Hill Vineyard Pinot Noir (Willamette Valley) $30. Hard and stemmy, oaky, and tannic. A lot of tough, chewy flavors here, augmented with herbs and tobacco. Time may take some of the bitterness away, but it's tough sledding right now. 86 *(11/1/2004)*

Bethel Heights 1998 Freedom Hill Vineyard Pinot Noir (Willamette Valley) $30. 89 *—M.M. (12/1/2000)*

Bethel Heights 2002 Nysa Vineyard Pinot Noir (Willamette Valley) $30. Very dark, purple, and extracted looking, with big, dense, plummy blue fruits beginning to show. Right now this is in a dumbed-down phase, and the reduced flavors, along with some volatile acidity, bring down the score. Has the potential to improve significantly. 86 *(11/1/2004)*

USA

Bethel Heights 2000 Nysa Vineyard Pinot Noir (Willamette Valley) $30. 87 *(10/1/2002)*

Bethel Heights 1998 Nysa Vineyard Pinot Noir (Willamette Valley) $25. 87 *—M.S. (12/1/2000)*

Bethel Heights 2002 Seven Springs Vineyard Pinot Noir (Willamette Valley) $38. A full, meaty style, mixing exotic fruits, tree bark, and smoky mocha. Tart, herbal, and sharp-edged, but characterful with a lively mix of layered flavors. 87 *(11/1/2004)*

Bethel Heights 2000 Southeast Block Reserve Pinot Noir (Willamette Valley) $40. 87 *(10/1/2002)*

Bethel Heights 1998 Southeast Block Reserve Pinot Noir (Willamette Valley) $35. 90 *—M.S. (12/1/2000)*

Bethel Heights 1998 Wadenswil Block Reserve Pinot Noir (Willamette Valley) $35. 89 *—M.S. (12/1/2000)*

Bethel Heights 2001 West Block Reserve Pinot Noir (Willamette Valley) $38. 88 *—P.G. (12/1/2003)*

BETZ FAMILY WINERY

Betz Family Winery 2002 Clos de Betz Bordeaux Blend (Columbia Valley (WA)) $29. Master of Wine Bob Betz has refined his winemaking to a style that is breaking new ground for the region. The Merlot-centric Clos de Betz (57% Merlot, 33% Cabernet Sauvignon, 10% Cab Franc) is incredibly dense, concentrated, and inky, yet retains amazing elegance. Its silky mouthfeel, brightness, and finesse support supple, ripe, immaculate fruit. It's all wrapped in pillowy tannins. **93 Editors' Choice** *—P.G. (6/1/2005)*

Betz Family Winery 2003 Bésolei Grenache (Columbia Valley (WA)) $35. Béso is kiss, soleil is sun; the name is made up to signify "sun-kissed." The grapes are from Alder Ridge, with 14% Syrah from Red Mountain blended in. Just 82 cases were made. It's a juicy, delicious tangle of red fruits and berries, with a spicy highlight. As it unfolds you notice the fruit is lined with citrus, orange peel, and clove, then finished with sweet oak. 91 *—P.G. (12/15/2005)*

Betz Family Winery 2002 La Cote Rousse Syrah (Red Mountain) $41. The second Syrah from Betz Family relies on Red Mountain fruit, and makes a fascinating contrast to the much more open and sappy La Serenne. This wine is tight, vertically structured, with far less immediate breadth. The nose grudgingly reveals cassis and sweet, toasted cracker, along with classic Red Mountain flavors of mineral and earth. Tight as a drum, the wine finishes with a hard shell of tannin, that will certainly require some years to smooth out. But the compact, dark, mysterious fruit core promises that it will be worth the wait. 92 *—P.G. (12/15/2004)*

Betz Family Winery 2002 La Serenne Syrah (Columbia Valley (WA)) $41. Dense and plush with exotic scents of roasted coffee, smoke, toast, cedar, and blackberry jam, this is very young, showing mostly primary fruits and lots of new wood. But the ripe, sappy fruit, from an exceptional block in the Boushey vineyard, stands out, seamless and pure. Like a racehorse, this wine is sleek, powerful, and perfectly proportioned. It offers immense enjoyment as soon as the cork is popped, but will go for a good 10 years in the cellar. 94 *—P.G. (12/15/2004)*

BIANCHI

Bianchi 2004 Signature Selection Sauvignon Blanc (Central Coast) $16. Grassiness and cat pee mark this wine, with clean grapefruit juice and lemon zest on the finish. It's absolutely dry, with crisp, cool-climate acidity. 84 *—S.H. (12/31/2005)*

BIG FIRE

Big Fire 2001 Pinot Gris (Oregon) $14. 88 *—P.G. (12/31/2002)*

BIGHORN

Bighorn 2001 Cabernet Sauvignon (Napa Valley) $29. Starts off with a musty aroma that decanting should take care of. In the mouth, this Cab tastes good. It's sweetish-dry and very smooth, with rich cherry and blackberry flavors that veer into chocolate. 86 *—S.H. (11/1/2005)*

Bighorn 1998 Coombsville Cabernet Sauvignon (Napa Valley) $39. 93 *—S.H. (11/15/2002)*

Bighorn 2000 Grand Reserve Cabernet Sauvignon (Napa Valley) $49. Nearly five years of aging has not helped this wine. It's hot and awkward, with low acids and an herbal edge to the blackberry fruit. **83** *—S.H. (11/1/2005)*

Bighorn 2002 Chardonnay (Carneros) $18. Surprisingly thin and watery for such a nice appellation, with a weak aroma and equally unimpressive citrus flavors. Seems like the vines were overcropped. **83** *—S.H. (6/1/2004)*

Bighorn 2001 Chardonnay (Carneros) $17. From the Napa side, a bells and whistles wine bursting with notes of spent lees and toasty oak. The underlying fruit veers toward ripe peaches and green apples. Clean, complex, and nuanced. **89** *—S.H. (12/15/2004)*

Bighorn 2001 Coombsville Vineyard Chardonnay (Napa Valley) $15. For all its heft, and this is a heavyweight Chardonnay, it never loses its balance and harmony. Bigtime tropical fruit and spicy fig flavors are wrapped in succulently sweet, smoky oak. The creamy texture and long, rich finish make this a great wine. **93 Best Buy** *—S.H. (12/15/2004)*

Bighorn 2003 Broken Rock Vineyard Merlot (Napa Valley) $30. There's lots to like in this ripe, juicy wine. The flavors are forward and ripe in black cherries and cocoa, and the tannic structure is sturdy, dry, and clean, with a long, fruity-spicy finish. It's an easy wine with some real elegance. **87** *—S.H. (12/15/2005)*

BINK

Bink 2002 Hawks Butte Vineyard Syrah (Mendocino) $40. Focused, lean, and light in body, with strong herbal overtones of basil and oregano that aren't unattractive. Shows enough cherry fruit on the midpalate to appeal, with a long, intense finish. With only 13% alcohol, crisp acids, and herbal notes, this is in many ways a non-Californian Syrah. **87** *(9/1/2005)*

BISHOP'S PEAK

Bishop's Peak 2002 Cabernet Sauvignon (Paso Robles) $16. Juicy enough in cassis and oak, but with a stubborn green streak, and a rather aggressive texture. **83** *—S.H. (10/1/2005)*

Bishop's Peak 2003 Chardonnay (Edna Valley) $14. Brings the Talley touch to a high-acid Chard that has bright flavors of passionfruit and lime. The structure is great, but the finish is a little thin. **84** *—S.H. (10/1/2005)*

Bishop's Peak 2000 Chardonnay (Central Coast) $13. **85** *—S.H. (2/1/2003)*

Bishop's Peak 2001 Pinot Noir (Central Coast) $16. A nice country-style Pinot, a bit rough and earthy, but okay as a substitute for more expensive versions. Dry, with silky tannins and cherry flavors. Second label from Talley. **84** *—S.H. (6/1/2004)*

Bishop's Peak 2001 Syrah (Edna Valley) $15. This is a seriously good wine and how the parent company, Talley, sells it at this price is a miracle. Smells grandly Rhoniste, with a burst of white pepper, blackberry, and leather. It doesn't have the density of a supreme wine, but this great value showcases Central Coast Syrah. **89** *—S.H. (12/1/2004)*

Bishop's Peak 2001 Zinfandel (Paso Robles) $14. A decent Zin with some good points and some not so good ones. There's plenty of fresh, succulent cherry berry fruit and spice, but also some residual sweetness that makes it taste a little like cough medicine. **84** *—S.H. (6/1/2004)*

BLACK BOX

Black Box 2002 Cabernet Sauvignon (Paso Robles) $20. Four bottles in one box, but what you get is pretty harsh and lean. Not much going on except acidity, tannins, and a harsh mouthfeel. **82** *—S.H. (8/1/2004)*

Black Box 2003 Chardonnay (Monterey County) $20. From a box that holds the equivalent of four regular bottles, a nice, rich Chard. It's all about ripe tropical fruits, peaches and cream, and Asian spices. Finishes long and flavorful. **86 Best Buy** *—S.H. (8/1/2004)*

BLACK COYOTE

Black Coyote 2002 Bates Creek Vineyard Cabernet Sauvignon (Napa Valley) $30. There's a good Cab in here, but it's surrounded by overripe raisined fruit that makes the wine drink hot. There's no quibbling with the deliciousness factor, though. **85** *—S.H. (11/1/2005)*

BLACK CREEK

Black Creek 2000 Bates Creek Vineyard Cabernet Sauvignon (Napa Valley) $25. Modest aromas of blackberries and oak lead to a thinly-flavored wine. There are some berry notes, but the oak and tannins are really the stars. Drink now. **84** *—S.H. (2/1/2004)*

BLACK SHEEP

Black Sheep 2002 Sémillon (Calaveras County) $13. Starts with a barnyardy smell, then turns rich and creamy in the mouth, vibrant in vanilla, butterscotch, peach and floral flavors. **84** *—S.H. (3/1/2005)*

Black Sheep 1997 Zinfandel (Amador County) $14. **87 Best Buy** *—S.H. (5/1/2000)*

BLACKJACK

Blackjack 1997 Harmonie Bordeaux Blend (Santa Barbara County) $32. **91** *(11/1/2000)*

BLACKRIDGE CANYON

Blackridge Canyon 2001 Pinot Noir (Napa Valley) $20. A polished Pinot with good varietal character, it's showing cherry liqueur, mocha, and spicy flavors, in a delicately oaked, lightly elegant texture. **87** *—S.H. (8/1/2005)*

BLACKSTONE

Blackstone 2002 Cabernet Sauvignon (California) $12. Smells of toast, vanilla, and cream. On the palate, tobacco is the dominant flavor, and earth and black currants take a backseat. Finishes lean and herbal. **83** *(6/1/2004)*

Blackstone 2002 Cabernet Sauvignon (California) $12. Kind of unripe and hard in tannins, a thin, green wine with very little fruit. Finishes dry and tough. **83** *—S.H. (8/1/2004)*

Blackstone 2002 Reserve Cabernet Sauvignon (Dry Creek Valley) $28. The pretty aroma mingles well-toasted, caramelly oak with ripe black currant fruit. In the mouth, turns rather bitter and astringent in rugged tannins. A year or two of aging could soften it up. **85** *—S.H. (10/1/2005)*

Blackstone 2004 Chardonnay (Monterey County) $11. This isn't a bad price for a nice, everyday Chardonnay with some pleasant peach, lemon rind, pineapple, and vanilla-oaky flavors that finish clean and dry. **84** *—S.H. (12/31/2005)*

Blackstone 2003 Chardonnay (Monterey County) $10. There's a firmness in the mouth with this Chard. The fruit is ripe and spicy, the oak is just right, and the acidity is high, leading to a tart, dry finish. **85 Best Buy** *—S.H. (10/1/2005)*

USA

Blackstone 2002 Chardonnay (Sonoma County) $16. Balanced and harmonious, blending nice flavors of apples, peaches, and pears with a touch of spicy oak. Feels creamy and rich in the mouth, and especially nice on the long finish. **86** *—S.H. (9/1/2004)*

Blackstone 1999 Chardonnay (Monterey County) $10. **82** *—S.H. (5/1/2001)*

Blackstone 2004 Gewürztraminer (Monterey County) $11. Floral, spicy, and dry, this Gewürz shows forward flavors of pink grapefruit, with a peppery finish. It has good acidity and a clean finish. **84** *—S.H. (10/1/2005)*

Blackstone 2003 Merlot (Sonoma County) $16. A nice, simple Merlot, with pleasant blackberry and cherry flavors. It's fully dry, with good tannic support, and finishes with rich, ripe fruit. **85** *—S.H. (7/1/2005)*

Blackstone 2002 Merlot (Monterey County) $17. A bit on the herbal side, showing green, woody notes. Turns tannic in the mouth, with blackberry and coffee flavors, and finishes dry. **84** *—S.H. (12/31/2004)*

Blackstone 2002 Merlot (California) $12. Very dry, somewhat tannic, and with jammy plum, currant, and herb flavors, this wine is a good value in a full-bodied dinner red. It's balanced and fresh, and the somewhat sharp acids will cut through lamb or steak. **85** *—S.H. (9/1/2004)*

Blackstone 2002 Merlot (Napa Valley) $17. Simple and fruity in blackberries and coffee, this wine is dry and sharp, with some stalky notes. **83** *—S.H. (5/1/2005)*

Blackstone 1999 Merlot (California) $10. **84** *—S.H. (11/15/2001)*

Blackstone 1998 Merlot (Napa Valley) $18. **89** *—S.H. (5/1/2001)*

Blackstone 2000 Reserve Merlot (Napa Valley) $28. Nose has an herbal edge and stewy fruit aromas. Dry, woody tannins show on the palate, where the flavors are of taut plum fruit, tree bark, and a hint of stem. Finishes dry and rough. **85** *(6/1/2004)*

Blackstone 2003 Pinot Noir (Monterey County) $12. Good value in a dry Pinot with real Salinas quality. Delicately structured and elegantly crisp, with silky tannins and cherry, cola, and herb flavors. **85** *—S.H. (5/1/2005)*

Blackstone 2001 Pinot Noir (Monterey County) $12. Varietally correct in the soft, silky tannins, crisp acids, and notes of berries. This simple wine also has a baked edge and finishes hot. **83** *—S.H. (9/1/2004)*

Blackstone 2002 Reserve Pinot Noir (Santa Lucia Highlands) $28. On the nose, cherry aromas are accented by tea and root beer notes. It's a bit light in weight on the palate, with flavors of cherry, tree bark, and beet. Tart and moderately long on the finish. 900 cases made. **86** *(6/1/2004)*

Blackstone 2004 Sauvignon Blanc (Monterey County) $10. This is a crisply tart, dry wine, light in body, with pleasant flavors of green apples and peaches. There's a lingering finish of tangerine that adds nuance. **85 Best Buy** *—S.H. (10/1/2005)*

Blackstone 2003 Sauvignon Blanc (Monterey County) $11. Oodles of almost sweet citrus, melon, and fig flavors are wrapped in crisp acids that make this easy wine clean and zesty. There's an edge of cat pee that may put some people off. **84** *—S.H. (9/1/2004)*

Blackstone 2002 Syrah (Sonoma County) $16. Big-bodied yet silky-smooth, this Syrah has a slight rusticity, yet also shows some elegance and finesse, courtesy of vanilla and toast accents. With its fruit and herb flavors, it should be fine with rich fare like roast lamb with olive tapenade. **86** *(9/1/2005)*

Blackstone 2002 Hamilton Vineyards Reserve Syrah (Dry Creek Valley) $28. Earthy and sharp, with coffee and berry flavors that finish dry and harsh. **82** *—S.H. (12/31/2005)*

Blackstone 2003 Zinfandel (Sonoma County) $16. Textbook Zin 101 here, a dry, full-bodied wine with flavors of wild berries, cherries, raisins, and tobacco, and rich, edgy tannins. Take advantage of the acids and try this with rich cheeses and sauces. **86** *—S.H. (12/15/2005)*

Blackstone 2002 Zinfandel (Sonoma County) $16. The wine is round and soft in the mouth, with juicy plum fruit jazzed up with a little herb. Finishes with rustic black-pepper and tree-bark flavors. **87** *(6/1/2004)*

BLISS

Bliss 2002 Heritage Series Cabernet Sauvignon (Mendocino) $11. Raw, harsh, and medicinal in berry flavors, this Cabernet is just barely acceptable. **80** *—S.H. (12/15/2005)*

Bliss 2002 Heritage Series Merlot (Mendocino) $25. Juicy-ripe, with tasty cherry, black raspberry, and blackberry flavors wrapped in angular tannins, and with a sharpness throughout. A pleasant, country-style wine. **83** *—S.H. (12/15/2005)*

BLOCKHEADIA RINGNOSII

Blockheadia Ringnosii 2001 Zinfandel (Mendocino) $24. 90 *(11/1/2003)*

BOCAGE

Bocage 2001 Chardonnay (Monterey) $11. 86 *—S.H. (12/15/2002)*

Bocage 2003 Unoaked Chardonnay (Monterey) $11. With no oak, what you get in the aroma are the prettiest, cleanest scents of ripe apples, peaches, pears, and spices. Would earn a higher score if it weren't soft and syrupy-sweet. **85** *—S.H. (3/1/2005)*

BOCCE

Bocce 2001 Rosso Red Blend (California) $6. As the name implies, an old-style Italian-American type wine, full-bodied and robust but gentle in tannins. Fully dry, with earthy-berry flavors. Mix of 7 common varietals. **84 Best Buy** *—S.H. (3/1/2005)*

BOEGER

Boeger 1998 Barbera (El Dorado) $14. 89 *—S.H. (8/1/2001)*

Boeger 1999 Reserve Petite Sirah (El Dorado) $25. 85 *(4/1/2003)*

Boeger 1999 Reserve Pinot Noir (El Dorado) $25. 85 *—S.H. (2/1/2003)*

Boeger 1998 Reserve Tempranillo (El Dorado) $25. 86 *—S.H. (5/1/2002)*

Boeger 1997 Estate Zinfandel (El Dorado) $15. 87 *—P.G. (3/1/2001)*

Boeger 1998 Walker Vineyard Zinfandel (El Dorado County) $18. 86 *—S.H. (5/1/2000)*

BOGLE

Bogle 2002 Cabernet Sauvignon (California) $12. A little rustic and pruny, but not a bad little wine. The flavors are of blackberries and chocolate, and the finish is dry. **83** *—S.H. (10/1/2005)*

Bogle 2004 Chardonnay (California) $9. This inexpensive Chard tastes herbal, with dill and thyme flavors that turn mildly peachy and appley on the finish. **83** *—S.H. (11/1/2005)*

Bogle 1998 Colby Ranch Reserve Chardonnay (Clarksburg) $18. 86 *(6/1/2000)*

Bogle 2003 Chenin Blanc (Clarksburg) $7. Easily earns its Best Buy status with its rich, fruity flavors and high acidity. Seems to have a little residual sugar, but those acids really balance. Try as an alternative to Sauvignon Blanc, Viognier. **86 Best Buy** *—S.H. (7/1/2005)*

Bogle 1998 Petite Sirah (California) $10. 87 *—J.C. (11/15/1999)*

Bogle 2001 Petite Sirah (California) $10. 84 *(4/1/2003)*

Bogle 1998 Sauvignon Blanc (California) $7. 85 *—L.W. (3/1/2000)*

Bogle 2003 Old Vine Zinfandel (California) $11. Ripe enough in berry fruit and totally soft, this wine is a little too sweet for me, suggesting as it does a dessert confection, although it's probably technically dry. **83** *—S.H. (10/1/2005)*

Bogle 1997 Old Vine Cuvée Zinfandel (California) $10. 90 Best Buy *—P.G. (11/15/1999)*

BOITANO

Boitano 2002 Port (Sierra Foothills) $14. Mute aroma, but turns sweet and chocolatey-cherry in the mouth, with good acidity, and very clean. A pleasant dessert quaffer. **86** *—S.H. (2/1/2005)*

Boitano 2002 Mokelumne Hill Sangiovese (Calaveras County) $24. Here's a Chianti-style wine, silky and acidic, with cherry-earthy flavors that drink very dry. It's pretty oaky, too. **84** *—S.H. (3/1/2005)*

BOKISCH

Bokisch 2002 Albariño (Lodi) $16. This Spanish variety, rare in California, is distinctive. It's full-bodied, with a thick texture and dense weight that carry rich, almost syrupy, flavors of peaches and apricots. But brilliant acidity keeps it all lively, and it's fully dry. **88** *—S.H. (2/1/2004)*

Bokisch 2003 Graciano (Lodi) $26. Simple and soft, this rustic wine has ripe red cherry flavors. It's very dry, with all kinds of oaky, peppery spices. It's not an insult to say it's the perfect upscale cheeseburger red. **84** *—S.H. (12/31/2005)*

Bokisch 2003 Tempranillo (Lodi) $21. Tempranillo continues to struggle to find a California identity. This warm-climate version strikes one path, in the direction of a soft, dry and fruity wine, with cherry flavors and an earthy, dried herb edge. The next step is for depth and complexity. **84** *—S.H. (12/31/2005)*

BONACCORSI

Bonaccorsi 2003 Sanford & Benedict Vineyard Pinot Noir (Santa Rita Hills) $42. Jammy and fat. All primary fruit (cherries) and loads of toast. It's rich and ripe, with loads of cherry fruit flavor, scads of sweet oak. Juicy acidity. Best 2006–2012. **92** —*S.H. (6/1/2005)*

BONAIR

Bonair 1998 Merlot (Yakima Valley) $18. **89** —*P.G. (9/1/2002)*

BOND

Bond 2000 Vecina Bordeaux Blend (Napa Valley) $150. Softly textured, gentle, and feminine, although rather light in body, with smooth-drinking cherry, tobacco, and dill flavors. The fruit is sweet and refined, and the wine finishes with some tannins. **89** —*S.H. (12/1/2004)*

Bond 2001 St. Eden Cabernet Blend (Napa Valley) $210. From Oakville, a wine quite different from Bond's Melbury. Not as immediately lush and flamboyant, it's a trace more reserved. Darker, too, more tannic and closed. Starts with an earthiness. Airing brings out cherries and cassis. There is great balance and integrity here, even though it is in desperate need of cellaring. Drink 2009. **95** —*S.H. (6/1/2005)*

Bond 2000 Melbury Red Blend (Napa Valley) $150. This wine opens with gorgeous aromatics, a waft of smoky vanilla and spicy, cherry compote that's irresistible. It's also tasty and sweetly plump, with savory cherry and blackberry flavors. On the light side, but polished and refined. **89** —*S.H. (11/15/2004)*

Bond 1999 Vecina Red Blend (Napa Valley) $150. **93** —*J.M. (7/1/2003)*

BONNY DOON

Bonny Doon 2001 Freisa (Monterey County) $18. Tastes like a workhorse wine, a dry, rustic red with earth, berry, and herb flavors and rugged tannins. Finishes with a bite of acidity. **84** —*S.H. (11/15/2004)*

Bonny Doon 2003 Clos de Gilroy Grenache (California) $12. As light in body and texture as a Pinot Noir, almost rosé, a Provençal-style wine with the rich earthiness of herbs and leaves. Finishes dry, with sour cherry and tannins. Value in a dry blush wine. **86** —*S.H. (10/1/2004)*

Bonny Doon 2001 Vin de Glacière Muscat (California) $17. It's a blast of apricot chutney sweetened with smoky honey and a sprinkle of vanilla. The texture is glyceriney and creamy. It's very sweet, but has orange-zesty acidity that keeps it from being cloying. **92** —*S.H. (6/1/2004)*

Bonny Doon 2003 Barbera Arneis Red Blend (Monterey County) $18. With 87 percent Barbera, you get a full-bodied, dry and pretty tannic red wine, with earthy, coffee and berry flavors. The Arneis, a white grape, seems to bring much-needed acidity, as well as a floral note. Still, it's a fringe wine, a better concept than reality. **84** —*S.H. (11/1/2005)*

Bonny Doon NV Framboise Red Blend (California) $11. The ultimate chocolate liqeur. Winemaker Randall Grahm calls this "an infusion" that's been boosted with brandied fruit that brings it to 17% alcohol. It's gooey in raspberry essence finished with a chocolate dust, but a brilliant squeeze of lime adds life and zest. **92** —*S.H. (8/1/2004)*

Bonny Doon 2000 Le Cigare Volant Red Blend (California) $32. **91** —*S.H. (12/1/2002)*

Bonny Doon 1995 Le Cigare Volant Red Blend (California) $20. **90** —*M.S. (6/1/1999)*

Bonny Doon 2002 Le Cigare Volant Rhône Red Blend (California) $32. A shade off prior vintages. Very dry, somewhat herbal, with modest cherry and tobacco flavors. Finishes clean and tannic, and will bounce well off a steak. **86** —*S.H. (8/1/2005)*

Bonny Doon 1998 Dry Pacific Rim Riesling (California-Washington) $10. **90 Best Buy** —*M.S. (11/15/1999)*

Bonny Doon 2002 Pacific Rim Riesling (America) $10. Zippy, zingy, zesty sipping with this delightfully crisp, slightly sweet white wine. It has pretty flavors of apples, peaches, and honeysuckle, with a minerally tang. **86** —*S.H. (2/1/2004)*

Bonny Doon 2003 The Heart Has Its Rieslings Riesling (Washington) $15. Has an off-dry sweetness that's a little cloying. It would be nice to have richer, brighter acidity. Beyond that, you'll find the flavors of apricots and ripe peaches. **84** —*S.H. (11/15/2004)*

Bonny Doon 2004 Vin Gris de Cigare Rosé Blend (California) $11. Randall Grahm is at the top of his game, producing Rhône wines that are inexpensive, yet incredibly complex and rewarding. This year's Cigare is bone dry, and the richest yet. With its zesty burst of acidity, the subtle flavors are of cherries, raspberries, rose petals, dried Provençal herbs, and pepper. This complex wine is a blend of Grenache, Mourvèdre, Roussanne, Cinsault, Syrah, and Marsanne. **90 Best Buy** —*S.H. (11/15/2005)*

Bonny Doon 2002 Vin Gris de Cigare Rosé Blend (California) $10. **89 Best Buy** —*S.H. (11/15/2003)*

Bonny Doon 2001 Syrah (California) $18. Made the way Randall Grahm likes Syrah, which is a dry, peppery wine with rich outbursts of sweet cherry fruit. It must be in the blending, but this wine seems to possess both warm- and cool-climate aspects, which is often what works best in a California Syrah. It's rich but dry, fruity but elegant, a Euro-wine of instant, and international, appeal. **91 Editors' Choice** —*S.H. (6/1/2004)*

Bonny Doon 2002 Le Pousseur Syrah (California) $15. Leans toward the red-fruit side of the Syrah fruit continuum, with raspberry and strawberry flavors strongly marked by herbal, peppery, menthol notes. Well made, but a bit too green for our tastes, with some hard tannins on the finish. **83** *(9/1/2005)*

Bonny Doon 2002 Viognier Doux Viognier (Paso Robles) $18. This interesting wine has the tropical fruits and exotic wildflower aromatics you associate with Viognier. But it's sweet as honey, with a white chocolate truffle, meringue flavor on the finish. Fortunately, there's good, clean acidity. **89** *—S.H. (6/1/2004)*

Bonny Doon 2003 Le Cigare Blanc White Blend (California) $20. Rhônemeister Randall Grahm's companion to his celebrated red Rhône wine, this is mainly Roussanne with a drop of Grenache Blanc. It's a very fine and interesting wine that combines white and yellow tree-fruit flavors with melons, flowers and a refreshing minerality. **91** *—S.H. (8/1/2005)*

Bonny Doon 2000 Cardinal Zin Zinfandel (California) $20. **86** *—S.H. (12/15/2001)*

Bonny Doon 2001 Cardinal Zin/Beastly Old Vines Zinfandel (California) $20. **87** *—J.M. (11/1/2003)*

BONTERRA

Bonterra 1999 Chardonnay (Mendocino County) $12. **87** *—P.G. (10/1/2000)*

Bonterra 1997 Chardonnay (Mendocino County) $11. **89 Best Buy** *—S.H. (10/1/1999)*

Bonterra 2000 Chardonnay (Mendocino County) $15. **88** *—S.H. (5/1/2002)*

Bonterra 2002 Merlot (Mendocino County) $15. Rich and deep are the words that come to mind for this intensely flavorful Merlot. It's as full-bodied as a Cab, with the prettiest cherry and chocolate flavors and a smooth finish that turns blueberry. **90 Best Buy** *—S.H. (12/15/2005)*

Bonterra 1998 Merlot (Mendocino County) $16. **85** *—S.H. (5/1/2002)*

Bonterra 1997 Roussanne (Mendocino) $17. **91** *—L.W. (10/1/1999)*

Bonterra 1999 Lakeview Vineyards Roussanne (Mendocino County) $19. **87** *—S.H. (8/1/2001)*

Bonterra 1998 Syrah (Mendocino) $19. **89 Editors' Choice** *(10/1/2001)*

Bonterra 2004 Viognier (Mendocino County) $18. Organically grown, this wine is clean and vibrant, with bright acidity and a dry, crisp mouthfeel. It doesn't show Viognier's usual flamboyant, exotic flavors, but instead shows a lean, citrus and floral elegance. **85** *—S.H. (12/15/2005)*

Bonterra 1999 Viognier (Mendocino County) $19. **88 Editors' Choice** *(8/1/2001)*

BOOKWALTER

Bookwalter 1998 Cabernet Sauvignon (Columbia Valley (WA)) $35. **87** *—P.G. (6/1/2001)*

Bookwalter 1997 Vintner's Select Chardonnay (Washington) $20. **88** *—P.G. (11/15/2000)*

Bookwalter 2001 Merlot (Columbia Valley (WA)) $NA. Powerful, pungent, ripe black cherry fruit assaults the nostrils, leading into a taut, slightly gamey, muscular, and dense with layers of fruit, tar, smoke, and earth. Give it 6 to 8 years to unwrap and it will be sensational. **91 Cellar Selection** *—P.G. (1/1/2004)*

BOUCHAINE

Bouchaine 1998 Chardonnay (Carneros) $20. **89** *(6/1/2000)*

Bouchaine 2001 Chardonnay (Carneros) $18. **88** *—S.H. (6/1/2003)*

Bouchaine 1999 B Chardonnay (Napa Valley) $13. **82** *—S.H. (9/1/2002)*

Bouchaine 2003 Pinot Noir (Carneros) $25. Seems a bit thin for this price. You get modest cherry and cola flavors in a very dry wine that actually has some tannins. Finishes dry and tart. **85** *—S.H. (10/1/2005)*

Bouchaine 2000 Pinot Noir (Carneros) $18. **84** *—S.H. (7/1/2003)*

Bouchaine 1996 Pinot Noir (Carneros) $20. **81** *(10/1/1999)*

Bouchaine 2000 B Pinot Noir (California) $15. **82** *(10/1/2002)*

Bouchaine 2003 Estate Vineyard Pinot Noir (Carneros) $35. A bit richer and fruitier than Bouchaine's regular '03, this dry wine shows cherry, earth, and coffee flavors. It won't astonish you, but it's a well-made, somewhat complex Pinot. **87** *—S.H. (10/1/2005)*

BOUDREAUX CELLARS

Boudreaux Cellars 2002 Cabernet Sauvignon (Walla Walla (WA)) $40. Seven Hills (Walla Walla) fruit, with an edgy, slightly herbal, tannic structure. The fruit is a mix of red berries, and there is lots of mixed clove and cinnamon spice from the barrels. It's nicely blended, and layered, though probably not for the long haul. Just 80 cases were made. **89** *—P.G. (4/1/2005)*

Boudreaux Cellars 2002 Chardonnay (Washington) $20. This new winery, with excellent grape sources, jumps in with a soft, plush, buttery Chardonnay. Substantial flavors of ripe tropical fruits—bananas, peaches, and melon—are melded to buttered nuts and toast. **88** *—P.G. (11/15/2004)*

Boudreaux Cellars 2002 Syrah (Walla Walla (WA)) $32. From the Pepper Bridge and Seven Hills vineyards, this compelling syrah offers more than just crisp red fruits. I love the citrus rind, the floral lift, the hints of cinnamon, and spice. It's a testament to sensitive winemaking, and grapes that were not pushed too far. **91** *—P.G. (4/1/2005)*

BOURASSA VINEYARDS

Bourassa Vineyards 2002 Harmony 3 Bordeaux Blend (Napa Valley) $52. Quite clean, vibrant, and forward in cassis and cherry aromas, this generously oaked wine has smooth tannins and is fairly high in acidity. It might soften and improve with several years of aging. **86** *—S.H. (5/1/2005)*

Bourassa Vineyards 2003 Sauvignon Blanc (Napa Valley) $16. Aggressive in green grass, wheatberry, and gooseberry aromas and flavors, but has a creamy edge of fig and melon to soften. Appealing for its crisp acidity and balance and lingering finish. **87** *—S.H. (12/31/2004)*

Bourassa Vineyards 2003 Viognier (Napa Valley) $24. Fruity and simple, with a buttercream thick texture and flavors of peaches and oak. A bit soft in acidity, and with a long, fruity finish. **85** *—S.H. (12/31/2004)*

BOYER

Boyer 2004 Riesling (Monterey) $14. What a delightful wine. It's low in alcohol but completely dry, with acidity that thoroughly cleanses the palate. The complex flavors suggest lime zest, pineapple, flowers, and tangy metals, and last for a long time on the finish. **89 Best Buy** *—S.H. (12/1/2005)*

USA

BRADFORD MOUNTAIN

Bradford Mountain 1999 Grist Vineyard Zinfandel (Dry Creek Valley) $30. 89 *—T.H. (3/1/2002)*

Brandborg 2001 Pinot Noir (Anderson Valley) $23. Offers some good varietal pleasure, with its silky texture and flavors of cherries, coffee, and herbs. It's a bone-dry wine and a bit acidic, and turns dustily tannic on the tart finish. Drink now. **85** *—S.H. (4/1/2004)*

BRANDBORG

Brandborg 2002 Northern Reach Pinot Noir (Umpqua Valley) $23. Blue fruits and mixed, peppery spices set the stage for this taut, supple wine. There's a fruit-salad quality to the grapes, but the winemaking is polished and appealing. **87** *(11/1/2004)*

Brandborg 2003 Syrah (Umpqua Valley) $25. A bit volatile and Port-y, yet it seems to lack richness and depth at the same time. The black cherry flavors are solid and the charred oak adds a welcome touch of complexity, so it's not without some good points. **84** *(9/1/2005)*

BRANDER

Brander 2001 Bouchet (Santa Ynez Valley) $30. 86 *—S.H. (12/31/2003)*

Brander 2003 Cabernet Sauvignon (Santa Ynez Valley) $20. An awkward wine. It's very dry, with some decent blackberry flavors, but doesn't seem altogether ripe. There's some tough acidity and a peppery, bitter coffee finish. **83** *—S.H. (12/1/2005)*

Brander 2002 Reserve Cabernet Sauvignon (Santa Ynez Valley) $45. If I'd never tasted a Napa Cab I would think this was a nice California wine. But comparisons are inevitable. There's certainly a lot of ripe fruit here, but also a sharpness and rustic tannic structure that's disturbing, especially at this price. **84** *—S.H. (12/1/2005)*

Brander 2003 Merlot (Santa Ynez Valley) $20. This is a very dry, tannic wine, with a simple structure. But it has well-developed black cherry and mocha flavors, and is soft in acids, making it pleasant now with something rich, like short ribs of beef. **86** *—S.H. (10/1/2005)*

Brander 1999 Merlot (Santa Ynez Valley) $18. 85 *—S.H. (5/1/2001)*

Brander 2003 Sauvignon Blanc (Santa Ynez Valley) $12. Redolent of citrus, melon, herb, and grass, the wine is clean and fresh, with a finish that is moderate in length. Good wine at a good price. **87** *—J.M. (8/1/2004)*

Brander 2003 Au Naturel Sauvignon Blanc (Santa Ynez Valley) $30. Sharp and minerally at first, with aromas of cat pee, nectarine, melon, and cucumber. Rather big and meaty on the tongue, with enough tangy gooseberry and citrus to balance out the larger peach and pear flavors. Thorough and healthy as a whole, with adequate acidity and girth. **89** *(7/1/2005)*

Brander 2004 Cuvée Natalie Sauvignon Blanc (Santa Ynez Valley) $16. Opens with a clean, citrus, and grass aroma, with just a hint of vanilla and toast, promising a dry wine. But it turns unexpectedly sweet, although acids are balancing. The 13 percent of Riesling in this Sauvignon Blanc-dominated wine really shows. **84** *—S.H. (10/1/2005)*

Brander 2004 Cuvée Nicolas Sauvignon Blanc (Santa Ynez Valley) $26. Shows a return to form after the '03, with brilliantly ripe guava, nectarine, and herb-infused citrus flavors and clean, crisp acids. Totally dry, the wine has a good chunk of new French oak, which assists with a creamy texture, but doesn't take over. This is great California SB. **92 Editors' Choice** *—S.H. (12/1/2005)*

Brander 2004 Early Release Sauvignon Blanc (Santa Ynez Valley) $12. The first wine I've had from the new vintage is clean, crisp, and totally enjoyable. It has a raw, juicy quality, like biting into a fresh lime, and is dry, with a long, citrus-and-vanilla aftertaste. **87 Best Buy** *—S.H. (5/1/2005)*

Brander 2001 Sauvignon Au Naturel Sauvignon Blanc (Santa Ynez Valley) $30. 91 *—S.H. (10/1/2003)*

Brander 2003 Cuvée Natalie White Blend (Santa Ynez Valley) $16. Here's a fun and refreshing wine that's a mélange of Sauvignon Blanc, Riesling, Pinot Gris, and Pinot Blanc. In this warm appellation the melon, fig, and citrus flavors are ripe and slightly sweet, but crisp acidity balances. **86** *—S.H. (12/1/2004)*

BRAREN PAULI

Braren Pauli 1999 Busch Creek Vineyard Chardonnay (Mendocino County) $12. **83** *—S.H. (5/1/2002)*

Braren Pauli 1999 Roar Vineyard Pinot Noir (Mendocino) $14. **85** *—S.H. (5/1/2002)*

BRASSFIELD

Brassfield 2003 Pinot Grigio (Clear Lake) $16. Fruity and crisp, with fresh apple, lime, and fig flavors that are balanced with brisk acids. An easy sipper that finishes slightly sweet. **85** *—S.H. (3/1/2005)*

Brassfield 2003 Sauvignon Blanc (Clear Lake) $15. A juicy Sauvignon Blanc, rich in ripe fig, lemon, and lime and spicy melon flavors, and well acidified. Finishes with a clean, fruity note. **84** *—S.H. (8/1/2005)*

Brassfield 2004 Serenity White Blend (Clear Lake) $15. This blend of Sauvignon Blanc, Pinot Grigio, and Gewürztraminer is simple and easy, a dry, fruity wine that finishes slightly sweet. It's picnic-style wine. **83** *—S.H. (12/15/2005)*

BRAVANTE

Bravante 2001 Merlot (Howell Mountain) $35. This is a sturdy, closed young wine. It's bone dry, with powerful tannins and subtle berry, cassis, and earth flavors. It has enough fruit in the finish to warrant another glass, but won't age for a long time. Best now through 2006. **85** *—S.H. (8/1/2005)*

BRICE STATION

Brice Station 2003 Gold Rush Cabernet Franc (Calaveras County) $18. A nice everyday sort of red, medium-bodied, with gentle, soft tannins and blackberry flavors. Finishes dry and clean. **86** *—S.H. (3/1/2005)*

Brice Station 2003 Chardonnay (California) $17. Rustic and sharp, and very fruit. Finishes with a blast of oak and spices. **83** *—S.H. (2/1/2005)*

BRICELAND

Briceland 2000 Phelps Vineyard Pinot Noir (Humboldt County) $22. **83** *—S.H. (2/1/2003)*

BRICK HOUSE

Brick House 2002 Clos Ladybug Pinot Noir (Willamette Valley) $20. Pungent and minty, with tart flavors of not-quite-ripe berries. Not a big wine, but lively with crisp, cutting acids. **86** *(11/1/2004)*

Brick House 2002 Evelyn's Pinot Noir (Willamette Valley) $40. Organically grown and made, this is a crisp, appealing bottle with fresh, round flavors of strawberry jam, vanilla, and a touch of herb. Shows some nice complexity and texture. **87** *(11/1/2004)*

BRIDGEVIEW

Bridgeview 2001 Cabernet Sauvignon-Merlot (Oregon) $10. **84** *—P.G. (8/1/2002)*

Bridgeview 1999 Chardonnay (Oregon) $7. **85 Best Buy** *—P.G. (11/1/2001)*

Bridgeview 1999 Blue Moon Chardonnay (Oregon) $10. **86** *—P.G. (11/1/2001)*

Bridgeview 2000 Merlot (Oregon) $10. **85** *—P.G. (8/1/2002)*

Bridgeview 1997 Black Beauty Merlot (Oregon) $15. **83** *—P.G. (11/1/2001)*

Bridgeview 2000 Reserve Pinot Gris (Oregon) $16. **89 Editors' Choice** *—P.G. (8/1/2002)*

Bridgeview 1999 Pinot Noir (Oregon) $12. **84** *—P.G. (11/1/2001)*

Bridgeview 2000 Blue Moon Pinot Noir (Oregon) $15. **84** *(10/1/2002)*

Bridgeview 1998 Oregon Pinot Noir (Oregon) $11. **88 Best Buy** *(11/15/1999)*

Bridgeview 1999 Reserve Pinot Noir (Rogue Valley) $18. **87** *—P.G. (8/1/2002)*

Bridgeview 2002 Blue Moon Riesling (Oregon) $8. **87** *—P.G. (8/1/2003)*

Bridgeview 2000 Blue Moon Riesling (Oregon) $7. **86 Best Buy** *—P.G. (11/1/2001)*

BRIDGMAN

Bridgman 2002 Chardonnay (Columbia Valley (WA)) $10. Here there is plenty of oak, laid on a bit thick, and a hot, tannic and buttery finish. **87** *—P.G. (9/1/2004)*

Bridgman 1999 Merlot (Columbia Valley (WA)) $17. **84** *—P.G. (6/1/2002)*

Bridgman 2000 Sauvignon Blanc (Yakima Valley) $11. **85** *—P.G. (6/1/2002)*

Bridgman 2001 Syrah (Yakima Valley) $13. Front-loaded flavors show clean berry fruit, but the wine stops short in the middle and quickly cuts off, finishing with somewhat green, herbal tannins. **86** *—P.G. (9/1/2004)*

Bridgman 1999 Syrah (Yakima Valley) $18. 85 *(10/1/2001)*

BRIDLEWOOD

Bridlewood 1997 Cabernet Franc (Central Coast) $28. 88 *—S.H. (7/1/2000)*

Bridlewood 2000 Chardonnay (Edna Valley) $16. 81 *—S.H. (9/1/2003)*

Bridlewood 1998 Chenin Blanc (Santa Barbara County) $10. 86 *—J.C. (10/14/2003)*

Bridlewood 1999 Merlot (Central Coast) $22. 84 *—S.H. (8/1/2003)*

Bridlewood 1999 Arabesque Rhône Red Blend (California) $14. 85 *—S.H. (12/15/2001)*

Bridlewood 1998 Saddlesore Rose Rhône Red Blend (California) $12. 85 *—M.S. (8/1/2000)*

Bridlewood 2000 Sauvignon Blanc (Santa Ynez Valley) $12. 87 *—S.H. (7/1/2003)*

Bridlewood 2001 Syrah (Central Coast) $20. This Syrah is grapy and raw, although there's no denying the wine's size and fruit-forward nature. It could use more complexity, finesse, and length. 83 *(9/1/2005)*

Bridlewood 1999 Syrah (Central Coast) $20. 89 *(10/1/2001)*

Bridlewood 1998 Winners Circle Syrah (Central Coast) $25. 90 *—S.H. (11/15/2000)*

Bridlewood 2001 Estate Reserve Zinfandel (Santa Ynez Valley) $24. 90 Editors' Choice *(11/1/2003)*

USA

BROADFIELDS

Broadfields 2001 Merlot (North Fork of Long Island) $NA. 86 *—J.C. (10/2/2004)*

BROADLEY

Broadley 1997 Reserve Pinot Noir (Willamette Valley) $23. 82 *(11/15/1999)*

BROLL MOUNTAIN VINEYARDS

Broll Mountain Vineyards 2002 Merlot (Calaveras County) $32. There's a nice peppermint patty note to the cherries, cocoa, and smoky vanilla. Drinks a bit soft, but dry, with pleasant earthy-berry flavors. 85 *—S.H. (2/1/2005)*

Broll Mountain Vineyards 2002 Syrah (Calaveras County) $31. A wonderfully drinkable Syrah, dry and balanced, with tart plum, blackberry, and coffee flavors and a deeper undertow of rich earth. The tannins are sizable, but smooth. Has lots of class. 89 *—S.H. (7/1/2005)*

BROMAN

Broman 1999 Cabernet Sauvignon (Napa Valley) $54. There's a weedy, cigarette ash scent here. The fruity flavors aren't bad, but there's a rough, tannic edge all the way through the finish. Tasted twice, with consistent results. 83 *—S.H. (10/1/2004)*

BROOKDALE VINEYARDS

Brookdale Vineyards 2002 Cabernet Sauvignon (Napa Valley) $52. With its dark purple color, dramatic aroma of ripe black currants and oak, and appealing mouthfeel, this fine Cabernet expresses very good Napa character. The black currant flavors are framed in rich, sweet, smooth tannins. Probably best now and through 2006. 90 *—S.H. (12/15/2005)*

Brookdale Vineyards 2000 Cabernet Sauvignon (Napa Valley) $48. 91 *—J.M. (6/1/2003)*

BROOKS

Brooks 2002 Pinot Noir (Oregon) $20. Light floral and tea scents, with notes of spice, herb, anise, and flowers on the palate. A quiet, delicate wine. 85 *(11/1/2004)*

Brooks 2002 Amycas White (Willamette Valley) $13. 90 Best Buy *—P.G. (12/1/2003)*

BROPHY CLARK

Brophy Clark 2000 Pinot Noir (Santa Maria Valley) $22. 86 *(10/1/2002)*

Brophy Clark 1998 Pinot Noir (Santa Maria Valley) $20. 85 *—M.M. (12/15/2000)*

Brophy Clark 2001 Ashley's Vineyard Pinot Noir (Santa Rita Hills) $24. From a cooler part of this cool appellation, a tart, crisp young wine, sharp with citrusy acids but ripe in bright cherry fruit. It's young and untogether now, but a year or so should bring more complexity and finesse. 87 *—S.H. (12/1/2004)*

Brophy Clark 2002 Valley View Vineyard Sauvignon Blanc (Santa Ynez Valley) $13. A crisp, clean wine, high in acidity, with pretty flavors of ripe citrus fruits, figs, and spice. It's a little sweet, and finishes long and honeyed. 85 *—S.H. (9/1/2004)*

Brophy Clark 1999 Syrah (Santa Ynez Valley) $18. 83 *(10/1/2001)*

Brophy Clark 2002 Rodney Shull Vineyard Syrah (Santa Ynez Valley) $18. Leathery notes and a whole panoply of herbs and spices—cinnamon, pepper, lavender, and fennel—make for a lovely bouquet. In the mouth, however, the wine is not quite as impressive, yielding up tart cherry flavors and a lean mouthfeel. Finishes on dry, herbal notes. 86 *(9/1/2005)*

Brophy Clark 2001 Lone Oak Vineyard Zinfandel (Paso Robles) $17. 85 *(11/1/2003)*

BROWN ESTATE

Brown Estate 2001 Zinfandel (Napa Valley) $32. A classy wine. Sleek, firm, and beautifully structured with lovely bright cherry, spice, chocolate, plum, and anise flavors. Clean and long at the end, the wine comes from a relatively new winery that consistently pumps out high quality. **92** *—J.M. (3/1/2004)*

BRUTOCAO

Brutocao 1997 Brutocao Vineyards Cabernet Sauvignon (Mendocino) $18. **88** *—P.G. (12/15/2000)*

Brutocao 2002 Riserva d'Argento Cabernet Sauvignon (Mendocino) $34. Clearly a step up from Brutocao's regular '02, this interesting wine has distinct features of its own. It's very soft and creamy, and intricate in flavors, suggesting macaroons soaked in rum and crème de cassis. But it's dry. **88** *—S.H. (11/1/2005)*

Brutocao 2002 Vineyard Select Cabernet Sauvignon (Mendocino) $25. Properly made in every respect, this Cab shows its warm origins in the raisiny flavors that accompany the blackberries, cherries, and oak. That slightly baked edge could actually make it a good match with a smoky barbecue sauce. **85** *—S.H. (11/1/2005)*

Brutocao 1997 Bliss Vineyard Reserve Chardonnay (Mendocino) $23. **86** *—P.G. (10/1/2000)*

Brutocao 2004 Feliz Vineyard Dolcetto (Mendocino) $18. Rustic and ready, this is a wine for spaghetti and meatballs. It's fruity, bold, and ripe, with rich, thick tannins. **83** *—S.H. (12/15/2005)*

Brutocao 1996 Brutocao Vineyards Merlot (Mendocino) $18. **90** *—S.H. (3/1/2000)*

Brutocao 1998 Riserva d'Argento Merlot (Mendocino) $32. **90** *—S.H. (5/1/2002)*

Brutocao 2003 Riserva d'Argento Pinot Noir (Anderson Valley) $32. This is a super-drinkable Pinot. It's delicately structured, silky, and dry, with complex flavors of cherries, cola, and spices and a rich coat of smoky oak. The finish is long in sweet raisins and cassis. Each sip makes you want another. **91** *—S.H. (11/1/2005)*

Brutocao 2002 Contento Vineyard Primitivo (Mendocino) $18. An herbal wine, with flavors redolent of dried thyme and sage. Tart cherry, raspberry, plum, and citrus flavors are also in evidence, unfolding with some length at the end. **86** *—J.M. (10/1/2004)*

Brutocao 2001 Sauvignon Blanc (Mendocino County) $12. **84** *—J.M. (10/1/2003)*

Brutocao 2003 Bliss Vineyards Sauvignon Blanc (Mendocino) $12. A lemony bright wine that serves up hints of herb and melon. Crisp, simple, and clean. **84** *—J.M. (10/1/2004)*

Brutocao 2003 Feliz Vineyard Select Syrah (Mendocino) $25. A bit funky, meaty, and gamy, but also unfurls in the glass to reveal jammy berry scents and a hint of coffee. Full-bodied, yet zips up the finish with citrusy notes. Rustic but enjoyable. **86** *(9/1/2005)*

Brutocao 2001 Zinfandel (Mendocino) $18. **80** *(11/1/2003)*

Brutocao 1996 Bliss Vineyard Zinfandel (Mendocino) $15. **87** *—J.C. (5/1/2000)*

Brutocao 1998 Brutocao Vineyards Zinfandel (Mendocino) $18. **85** *—P.G. (3/1/2001)*

BUCKLIN

Bucklin 2001 Old Hill Ranch Zinfandel (Sonoma Valley) $30. **88** *(11/1/2003)*

BUEHLER

Buehler 2000 Reserve Chardonnay (Russian River Valley) $30. **86** *—S.H. (2/1/2003)*

Buehler 1997 Estate Zinfandel (Napa Valley) $18. **89** *—P.G. (11/15/1999)*

BUENA VISTA

Buena Vista 2000 Cabernet Sauvignon (California) $9. **85 Best Buy** *—S.H. (11/15/2002)*

Buena Vista 1997 Cabernet Sauvignon (Carneros) $18. **90 Editors' Choice** *—S.H. (5/1/2001)*

Buena Vista 1995 Grand Reserve Cabernet Sauvignon (Carneros) $27. **90** *—M.M. (6/1/1999)*

Buena Vista 1999 Chardonnay (Carneros) $18. **88** *—S.H. (2/1/2003)*

Buena Vista 1997 Chardonnay (Carneros) $15. **89 Best Buy** *—S.H. (6/1/2000)*

Buena Vista 1997 Grand Reserve Chardonnay (Carneros) $28. **89** *(6/1/2000)*

Buena Vista 2003 Ramal Vineyard Chardonnay (Carneros) $32. Take either of Buena Vista's clonal bottlings of Chardonnay from this vineyard and kick them down a notch, and you get this wine. It's not quite as complex, but still a rich, supple Chard, a little soft but flamboyant in tropical fruit, oak, and buttercream. **89** *—S.H. (12/15/2005)*

Buena Vista 2003 Ramal Vineyard Clone 96 Chardonnay (Carneros) $32. From the Sonoma side of Carneros. It satisfies all around, from the rich tropical fruit and spice flavors to the creamy texture and refreshingly crisp mouthfeel to the deliciously long finish. **92** *—S.H. (12/15/2005)*

Buena Vista 1999 Merlot (Carneros) $22. **86** *—S.H. (2/1/2003)*

Buena Vista 1998 Merlot (California) $10. 86 Best Buy —*S.H. (5/1/2001)*

Buena Vista 2000 Pinot Noir (Carneros) $22. 86 —*S.H. (2/1/2003)*

Buena Vista 1998 Pinot Noir (Carneros) $17. 89 —*S.H. (5/1/2001)*

Buena Vista 1996 Grand Reserve Pinot Noir (Carneros) $26. 92 —*M.M. (6/1/1999)*

Buena Vista 2003 Ramal Vineyard Pommard Clone 5 Pinot Noir (Carneros) $38. What a pretty Pinot Noir. It's distinctly cool climate, with tangy acidity and a silky texture that frames good varietal flavors of cola, cherries, rhubarb, coffee, and cinnamon spice. Despite the light, airy texture, this wine leaves a seriously fruity aftertaste. **89** —*S.H. (12/15/2005)*

Buena Vista 2001 Sauvignon Blanc (Lake County) $7. 90 —*S.H. (9/1/2003)*

Buena Vista 1999 Sauvignon Blanc (California) $9. 87 Best Buy —*S.H. (5/1/2001)*

Buena Vista 2001 Zinfandel (California) $9. 87 Best Buy *(11/1/2003)*

USA

BUFFALO RIDGE

Buffalo Ridge 1999 French Camp Vineyard Chardonnay (Central Coast) $13. 87 —*S.H. (11/15/2001)*

Buffalo Ridge 1999 French Camp Vineyard Syrah (Central Coast) $12. 83 *(10/1/2001)*

Buffalo Ridge 1999 French Camp Vineyard Zinfandel (Central Coast) $12. 84 —*D.T. (3/1/2002)*

BURFORD & BROWN

Burford & Brown 2002 Barbera (Dry Creek Valley) $15. Pours black and dense, a young, tough wine marked with plum and blackberry flavors. You can taste the grape skins in the tannic astringency that numbs the lips. **86** —*S.H. (9/1/2004)*

BURGESS

Burgess 1997 Cabernet Sauvignon (Napa Valley) $33. 88 *(11/1/2000)*

Burgess 1998 Enveiere Cabernet Sauvignon (Napa Valley) $75. 90 —*D.T. (6/1/2002)*

Burgess 2000 Vintage Selection Cabernet Sauvignon (Napa Valley) $39. 85 —*S.H. (11/15/2003)*

Burgess 1998 Chardonnay (Napa Valley) $18. 91 *(6/1/2000)*

Burgess 2002 Merlot (Napa Valley) $20. Dark and fleshy, this is a ripe, extracted Merlot that's big in cherry and cocoa flavors, with a sweet oaky covering. It's quite soft in the mouth, and has rich, dusty tannins. Will be lovely now with a steak, and should improve over the next year or two. **88** —*S.H. (7/1/2005)*

Burgess 1999 Merlot (Napa Valley) $28. 91 —*S.H. (9/12/2002)*

Burgess 2001 Syrah (Lake County) $19. Spice and anise notes pepper stewed fruit on the nose. The palate delivers straightforward, soft red fruit couched in a dusty blanket. Soft and supple; an easy drinker. **85** *(9/1/2005)*

Burgess 2000 Syrah (Lake County) $22. 87 —*S.H. (10/1/2003)*

Burgess 1997 Zinfandel (Napa Valley) $16. 86 —*S.H. (5/1/2000)*

Burgess 1999 Zinfandel (Napa Valley) $22. 90 —*S.H. (9/12/2002)*

BURRELL SCHOOL VINEYARDS

Burrell School Vineyards 2002 Valedictorian Cabernet Blend (Santa Cruz Mountains) $50. A very nice Bordeaux blend that will complement food rather than overwhelm it. Shows blackberry and herb flavors. A dry, smooth wine with a spicy finish. **87** —*S.H. (10/1/2005)*

Burrell School Vineyards 2001 Ryan Oaks Vineyard Zinfandel (Amador County) $20. 83 *(11/1/2003)*

BUTTERFIELD STATION

Butterfield Station 2001 Chardonnay (California) $7. 84 —*S.H. (12/15/2002)*

Butterfield Station 2000 Merlot (California) $8. 81 —*S.H. (12/31/2002)*

BUTTONWOOD FARM

Buttonwood Farm 1997 Trevin Bordeaux Blend (Santa Ynez Valley) $30. 87 —*S.H. (4/1/2003)*

Buttonwood Farm 1999 Cabernet Franc (Santa Ynez Valley) $18. 85 —*S.H. (5/1/2003)*

Buttonwood Farm 1995 Cabernet Franc (Santa Ynez Valley) $18. 84 —*S.H. (9/1/1999)*

Buttonwood Farm 2000 Cabernet Sauvignon (Santa Ynez Valley) $24. They couldn't keep a stubborn streak of green stalkiness out of this wine. But that mintiness is just one flavor in a spectrum of cherries, blackberries, and spices. Easy drinking. **85** —*S.H. (11/15/2004)*

Buttonwood Farm 1997 Cabernet Sauvignon (Santa Ynez Valley) $18. 86 —*S.H. (12/15/2000)*

Buttonwood Farm 2002 Marsanne (Santa Ynez Valley) $12. Smooth and polished, with herb, peach, and sweet tobacco flavors and a swirl of spicy oak. Very dry and clean, with a soft, buttercream mouth feel. Try as an alternative to Chardonnay. **86** *—S.H. (12/15/2004)*

Buttonwood Farm 1998 Marsanne (Santa Ynez Valley) $12. 87 *—S.H. (11/15/2000)*

Buttonwood Farm 1995 Merlot (Santa Ynez Valley) $18. 88 *—S.H. (9/1/1999)*

Buttonwood Farm 2000 Merlot (Santa Ynez Valley) $18. This is the kind of wine that shows better with food than it does on its own. Its modulated balance is understated, but the polished cherry, tobacco, and herb flavors, easy tannins and gentle oak make it perfect for the table. **88** *—S.H. (9/1/2004)*

Buttonwood Farm 1998 Merlot (Santa Ynez Valley) $18. 88 *—S.H. (6/1/2002)*

Buttonwood Farm 1999 Trevin Merlot (Santa Ynez Valley) $30. A blend of 60% Merlot, 30% Cabernet Franc, and 10% Cabernet Sauvignon, this wine has waited a long time to see the light of day. Smoky rich and fairly smooth, it's got pretty plum, black cherry, chocolate, spice, herb, and mocha notes. **88** *—J.M. (4/1/2004)*

Buttonwood Farm 1998 Sauvignon Blanc (Santa Ynez Valley) $12. 86 *—S.H. (9/1/1999)*

Buttonwood Farm 2002 Sauvignon Blanc (Santa Ynez Valley) $14. From an appellation that's proved itself to be a natural home to this variety and a winery that's clearly mastered it, a terrific white wine. Retains the grape's grass and citrus profile while taming it with Sémillon and oak to create a lush, complex wine. **90** *—S.H. (9/1/2004)*

Buttonwood Farm 2000 Sauvignon Blanc (Santa Ynez Valley) $12. 86 *—S.H. (12/15/2001)*

Buttonwood Farm 2001 Devin Sauvignon Blanc-Sémillon (Santa Ynez Valley) $16. A mild-mannered wine that sports a subtle, mineral-like core framed in hints of citrus, melon, and herbs. Moderate length at the end, with a tangy edge. **86** *—J.M. (6/1/2004)*

Buttonwood Farm 2001 Syrah (Santa Ynez Valley) $22. Earthy and lean, with tobaccoey flavors, but there are some pretty cherry notes. This dry wine may soften and improve with a year or two of bottle age. **85** *—S.H. (12/15/2004)*

Buttonwood Farm 2003 Rosé Syrah (Santa Ynez Valley) $16. What a pretty copper-onion skin color. Opens with a blast of raspberry, vanilla, and smoky aromas leading to a medium-bodied, dry wine with strawberry-raspberry flavors and crisp acidity. Has some real complexity and nuance. **86** *—S.H. (12/15/2004)*

Buttonwood Farm 1999 Devin White Blend (Santa Ynez Valley) $16. 88 *—S.H. (12/15/2001)*

BUTY

Buty 2001 Columbia Rediviva Cabernet Sauvignon-Syrah (Columbia Valley (WA)) $40. Not to be confused with the Walla Walla Syrah-Cabernet Sauvignon blend called Rediviva of the Stones. This wine is made from Champoux Cab and Boushey Syrah, rather than all Cailloux, as with its sibling. It's a good effort, well-made, but the component parts seem to leave a hole in the mid-palate. There is some nice berry-flavored fruit and espresso-flecked tannins. **87** *—P.G. (6/1/2005)*

Buty 2002 Roza Bergé Chardonnay (Yakima Valley) $25. This is prime old-vine fruit, planted in 1972, and previously showcased in Woodward Canyon's great Chardonnays. Ripe, buttery, and round, this is perfect for those who love lush tropical fruit flavors and plenty of butterscotchy oak. **89** *—P.G. (11/15/2004)*

Buty 2003 Merlot-Cabernet Franc Red Blend (Columbia Valley (WA)) $35. Not the catchiest name for this superb red blend, but Buty doesn't go for flash. They go for sleek, sophisticated, terroir-driven style. This is a smooth and substantial wine that opens slowly but surely. From a stiff start, with acid and tannin driving the bus, the wine's cassis and cherry and wild berry fruit begins to show, along with hints of stone, coffee, anise, and green tea. The French oak is used subtly and the winemaking is spot on. **91** *—P.G. (12/15/2005)*

Buty 2002 Rediviva of the Stones Syrah (Walla Walla (WA)) $40. One of those interesting Syrahs that seems to blend ripe and underripe fruit—in this case, herbal, wiry flavors and jammy, black cherry and chocolate fudge notes.There's also a hint of funk to the aromas that will intrigue some tasters and put off others. **85** *(9/1/2005)*

Buty 2000 Sémillon-Sauvignon Blanc White Blend (Columbia Valley (WA)) $18. 88 *—P.G. (9/1/2002)*

BYINGTON

Byington 2001 Smith-Riechel Vineyard Cabernet Sauvignon (Alexander Valley) $29. Softly fruity and rather herbal, with a pleasant mixture of cherry and dill flavors and gentle tannins. This dry, balanced wine has lots of finesse, and will accompany food without overshadowing it. **86** *—S.H. (10/1/2004)*

Byington 1997 Chardonnay (Santa Cruz Mountains) $17. 83 *—L.W. (11/15/1999)*

Byington 2002 Chardonnay (Santa Cruz Mountains) $22. A very fine Chard with special features that come from the appellation. The fruit is a mélange of key lime pie and white peach, drizzled with vanilla and cinnamon, with hints of smoky oak. These mountains always seem to develop a firm, steely acidity that makes the wines ultra-clean. **90** *—S.H. (12/1/2004)*

Byington 2002 Hastings Ranch Pinot Noir (Paso Robles) $24. Consistent scores for this problematic wine. It's medicinal, with a syrupy texture. **81** *(11/1/2004)*

Byington 2002 Alliage Red Blend (Sonoma County) $24. This year Byington blended in some Syrah with the Cabernet Sauvignon, to good effect. I wish the wine were crisper and better structured, but there's no denying the deliciousness factor. The black currant pudding, cherry pie, and vanilla-sprinkled mocha flavors are irresistible. **87** *—S.H. (12/1/2005)*

BYRON

Byron 1998 Chardonnay (Santa Maria Valley) $20. **87** *(6/1/2000)*

Byron 2002 Chardonnay (Santa Maria Valley) $25. A lovely Chardonnay brimming with tropical fruits, roasted hazelnut, sweet buttercream, and gingery spices, with a good framework of oak. For all the flavor, there's a streamlined sleekness to the acids that keeps the mouthfeel clean and refreshing. **90** *—S.H. (12/15/2004)*

Byron 1997 Byron Vineyard Chardonnay (Santa Maria Valley) $32. **90** *—S.H. (2/1/2001)*

Byron 1999 Neilson Vineyard Chardonnay (Santa Maria Valley) $40. **93** *—S.H. (12/15/2002)*

Byron 2001 Nielson Vineyard Chardonnay (Santa Maria Valley) $30. Continues the Nielson tradition of lushly ripe, opulently textured Chards. It's rich in papaya and pear flavors that are swimming in toasty oak, with a creamy texture. Smooth and long, and completely satisfying. **92** *—S.H. (2/1/2005)*

USA

Byron 1998 Nielson Vineyard Chardonnay (Santa Maria Valley) $35. **90** *(7/1/2001)*

Byron 2000 Sierra Madre Chardonnay (Santa Maria Valley) $30. Tastes like the lemon zest. There are pineapple flavors, too, and smoky oak. Coastal acidity brings a steely mineral spine. A magnificent food wine. **91** *—S.H. (9/1/2004)*

Byron 1999 Sierra Madre Vineyard Chardonnay (Santa Maria Valley) $35. **93** *—S.H. (12/15/2002)*

Byron 2003 Pinot Noir (Santa Maria Valley) $25. Byron can always be counted on to come up with interesting, terroir-driven wines. This Pinot, clearly from a cool climate, is dry and tart in acids, with a silky texture and ripe, pleasing cherry, cola, and mocha flavors, as well as a complex woodspice taste that lasts through the long finish. **89** *—S.H. (12/15/2005)*

Byron 2000 Pinot Noir (Santa Maria Valley) $25. **83** *(10/1/2002)*

Byron 1997 Pinot Noir (Santa Maria Valley) $20. **88** *(10/1/1999)*

Byron 1996 Byron Estate Vineyard Pinot Noir (Santa Maria Valley) $40. **89** *(10/1/1999)*

Byron 2001 Nielson Vineyard Pinot Noir (Santa Maria Valley) $40. Dark in color, immense in structure, deep in flavor, this is a blockbuster. The deep color only hints at the intense flavors of sweet black cherry, mocha, roasted coffee, smoky oak, sweet tobacco, and Oriental spices. As big as it is, it's a silky wine that glides across the palate. With Chinese roast duck, a marriage made in heaven. **93** *—S.H. (12/15/2004)*

Byron 1999 Nielson Vineyard Pinot Noir (Santa Maria Valley) $45. **90** *(10/1/2002)*

Byron 1997 Sierra Madre Vineyard Pinot Noir (Santa Maria Valley) $32. **90** *—S.H. (12/15/2000)*

C. G. DI ARIE

C. G. di Arie 2004 Rosé (Sierra Foothills) $13. Simple, rustic, and slightly sweet in the finish, with vanilla, char, raspberry, and cherry flavors and decent acidity. **83** *—S.H. (12/1/2005)*

C. G. di Arie 2002 Syrah (Sierra Foothills) $25. Harsh, hot, and rather medicinal, with astringent tannins. **82** *—S.H. (4/1/2005)*

C. G. di Arie 2002 Zinfandel (Shenandoah Valley (CA)) $25. Rich and ripe in blackberry, pudding, and chocolate flavors, with a briary, peppery edge, this mountain Zin wisely avoids both excessive alcohol and residual sugar. Sit back and enjoy the fruit. **87** *—S.H. (8/1/2005)*

C. G. di Arie 2003 Southern Exposure Zinfandel (Sierra Foothills) $30. This Zin satisfies for its fruit-forward character and smooth, gentle texture. It's very soft for a mountain Zin, with a velvety feel that carries rich flavors of wild cherries and berries, milk chocolate, licorice, and vanilla. **86** *—S.H. (12/1/2005)*

C.R. SANDIDGE

C.R. Sandidge 2000 Minick Vineyard Syrah (Yakima Valley) $28. **89** *—P.G. (12/31/2002)*

CA'NA

Ca'Na 2001 Syrah (Contra Costa County) $30. Shows decent concentration and a creamy, syrupy mouthfeel, but the aromas and flavors are dominated by an excessively vegetal streak reminiscent of green beans. **82** *(9/1/2005)*

Ca'Na 1999 Syrah (Contra Costa County) $21. **86** *(11/1/2001)*

CA' DEL SOLO

Ca' del Solo 2002 Barbera (Monterey) $15. Tough and gritty, this robust wine plays the same workhorse role here as in Italy. It's tannic and dry, with earthy flavors. Yet it has a balance and cleanness that's admirable. **85** *—S.H. (10/1/2004)*

Ca' del Solo 2001 La Farfalla Charbono (California) $15. They used to make Charbono fruity, dry (when "dry" meant dry) and tannic. It lived forever, softening and sweetening in the bottle. Nowadays, no one feels like aging a wine for a dozen years, but if you've got the time, this one will entertain you. **88** *—S.H. (6/1/2004)*

Ca' del Solo 2000 Freisa (Frizzante) Freisa (Monterey County) $15. 87 Editors' Choice *—M.M. (12/1/2001)*

Ca' del Solo 2002 Malvasia Bianca (Monterey) $13. A unique interpretation of a unique varietal in California, this wine brims with the aromas of apricots, orange blossoms, peaches, and buttery vanilla. You expect it to explode in sweetness in the mouth, but it doesn't. It is very dry and intense, and very tart with acidity, so that after the initial shock wears off, you find yourself savoring it, right through the long finish. **88** *—S.H. (3/1/2004)*

Ca' del Solo 2004 San Bernabe Vineyard Malvasia Bianca (Monterey) $13. From this big vineyard in the southern part of the Salinas Valley, a wine amazingly high in acidity, with bright lime, grapefruit, passionfruit, melon, and hay flavors. The alcohol is well under 13 percent, but the wine is absolutely dry. Try as an alternative to Sauvignon Blanc. **89** *—S.H. (11/15/2005)*

Ca' del Solo 2000 Moscato del Solo Moscato (Santa Cruz County) $15. 86 *—S.H. (12/1/2001)*

Ca' del Solo 2003 Big House Red (California) $10. This is the kind of wine you'd happily drink with almost any fast food and make an upscale dinner of it. It's ridiculously fruity in cherries, with rich tannins and good acidity. **85 Best Buy** *—S.H. (10/1/2005)*

Ca' del Solo 2001 Big House Red (Santa Cruz County) $10. 90 Best Buy *—S.H. (11/15/2002)*

Ca' del Solo 1999 Big House Red (California) $10. 86 *—D.T. (11/15/2001)*

Ca' del Solo 2003 Sangiovese (Monterey) $15. An unbalanced wine, high in alcohol, with some residual sugar, and sharp in acids. Should not have been released. **81** *—S.H. (10/1/2005)*

Ca' del Solo 1997 Il Fiasco Tuscan Blend (California) $15. 87 *—M.S. (10/1/1999)*

Ca' del Solo 2003 Big House White (California) $10. Too many varieties to mention went into this wine, but Sauvignon Blanc contributes acidity and grassiness, Riesling a floral note, and Chenin Blanc a melony, wax-bean quality. The wine seems slightly off-dry. **84** *—S.H. (11/15/2005)*

Ca' del Solo 2002 Big House White (California) $10. Randall Grahm took eight different varieties from the cool Central Coast, carefully blended them together with no oak, and finished the wine dry. The result is amazingly nuanced despite the mélange of tree fruit, melon, and floral flavors. **87** *—S.H. (2/1/2004)*

CADENCE

Cadence 2002 Bel Canto Bordeaux Blend (Red Mountain) $60. The winery's selection of its best barrels, excluding Cabernet Sauvignon. This is 48% Ciel Cab Franc, 48% Tapteil Merlot, and 4% Petit Verdot. Firm and laden with the coffee and espresso scents of Cab Franc. Smoke, liqueur, cherries, and tobacco leaf scents lead into a plummy, yummy, big, and broad-shouldered wine that finishes with butterscotchy barrel flavors. **90** *—P.G. (12/15/2005)*

Cadence 2003 Coda Bordeaux Blend (Columbia Valley (WA)) $22. About 300 cases were made of this satiny red blend, roughly two-thirds Cabernet Franc and the rest Cabernet Sauvignon. A pretty, softly fruity nose is accented with barrel scents of toasted coconut. It has all the charm and vibrant fruit flavor of a young wine, nicely wrapped in new oak. **89** *—P.G. (12/15/2005)*

Cadence 2001 Ciel du Cheval Vineyard Red Blend (Red Mountain) $35. A whiff of sweaty saddle in the nose, followed by this exemplary vineyard's beguiling mix of stone, mineral, earth, and tart blueberry flavors. The complexity and elegance come through despite the huge (14.9%) alcohol; but perhaps this is pushing the ripeness just a bit too far. The distinctive character of the vineyard is close to being masked. **91** *—P.G. (5/1/2004)*

Cadence 2001 Klipsun Vineyard Red Blend (Red Mountain) $35. The penetrating bouquet of raspberries, blackberries, and bitter chocolate, and a purple inkiness that seems to stain the glass, suggest the power in this wine, a Merlot-dominated Bordeaux blend. It reminds me of some of the very best Ridge wines; intensely sappy fruit, powerful and alcoholic, dominates, while the presence of oak is minimized. **90** *—P.G. (5/1/2004)*

Cadence 2002 Tapteil Vineyard Red Wine Red Blend (Red Mountain) $37. Chunky, solid effort showing aggressive whiskey barrel scents and some heat in the finish. Young, tannic, and chewy. At this point the Ciel shows more elegance and integration, but the Tapteil is distinctive and ageworthy. **88** *—P.G. (12/15/2005)*

CAERNARVON CELLARS

Caernarvon Cellars 2002 Rio San Lucas Vineyard Pinot Noir (San Lucas) $25. This wine is quite dry, with a good grip of dusty tannins and a silky mouthfeel. It has cherry-berry and cocoa flavors and a long, fruity finish. Drinking well now, it should be consumed in the next year to preserve vibrancy. **86** *—S.H. (6/1/2005)*

Caernarvon Cellars 1999 Cuvée Frank Zinfandel (Monterey) $23. 85 *—J.M. (2/1/2003)*

Caernarvon Cellars 2001 Cuvée Frank Zlahtina Zinfandel (Paso Robles) $NA. A richly textured, viscous wine, with big, deep black plum, smoke, toast, cherry, licorice, and spice flavors. It falters a bit on the palate, as it finishes a bit short and a touch tannic. Nonetheless, it offers plenty of pleasure. **88** *—J.M. (10/1/2004)*

CAFARO

Cafaro 2000 Syrah (Napa Valley) $32. 85 *—S.H. (12/1/2002)*

CAIN

Cain 2001 Concept Bordeaux Blend (Napa Valley) $46. This blend is very tannic and disagreeably harsh at the moment, unlike many '01s that are so soft and chocolaty. It's a good bet for the cellar because it's balanced and streamlined and has a full well of berry and cherry fruit. Try beyond 2010. **89** *—S.H. (5/1/2005)*

Cain NV Cuvée NVO Bordeaux Blend (Napa Valley) $24. Herbal and lean in fruit, with earthy, tobacco flavors and a hint of blackberries and cherries. But the tannin-acid balance gives it a nice structure that will assist good food. A blend of 2000 and 2001. **84** *—S.H. (10/1/2004)*

Cain 1999 Cain Five Cabernet Blend (Napa Valley) $85. 88 *—S.H. (5/1/2003)*

Cain 1999 Concept Cabernet Sauvignon (Napa Valley) $46. 88 *—S.H. (11/15/2002)*

Cain 2002 Ventana Vineyard Musqué Sauvignon Blanc (Arroyo Seco) $23. With this vintage, Cain announces the end of their Musqué bottling, after 14 years, and consumers are the losers. This wonderful wine always is crisp and clean, dry, and intricately detailed with lime and gooseberry flavors. **91** *—S.H. (6/1/2005)*

Cain 1998 Ventana Vineyards Musqué Sauvignon Blanc (Monterey County) $20. 89 *—M.S. (2/1/2000)*

CAKEBREAD

Cakebread 1997 Cabernet Sauvignon (Napa Valley) $37. 93 *(11/1/2000)*

Cakebread 2000 Benchland Select Cabernet Sauvignon (Napa Valley) $90. Shows what a good winery can do in a challenging vintage. This wine is elegant rather than profound, opening with beautiful scents of cedar, toast, herbs, and cherries. It's light-bodied, and finishes with a gentle scour of tannins. **88** *—S.H. (11/15/2004)*

Cakebread 1999 Three Sisters Cabernet Sauvignon (Napa Valley) $90. 92 *—J.M. (2/1/2003)*

Cakebread 1997 Vine Hill Ranch Cabernet Sauvignon (Napa Valley) $70. 90 *—J.M. (9/10/2003)*

Cakebread 1999 Chardonnay (Napa Valley) $32. 91 *(7/1/2001)*

Cakebread 2002 Merlot (Napa Valley) $48. There's a firm structure of tannins and acids to this wine, which lends architecture to the black cherry and cocoa flavors. It has additional complexities from oak and all sorts of spices and herbs. It's really a very fine Merlot, powerful, yet pliant. **91** *—S.H. (11/15/2005)*

Cakebread 1998 Sauvignon Blanc (Napa Valley) $16. 86 *(3/1/2000)*

Cakebread 2002 Sauvignon Blanc (Napa Valley) $17. 86 *—S.H. (12/15/2003)*

Cakebread 2000 Syrah (Carneros) $45. 92 *—J.M. (2/1/2003)*

CALCAREOUS

Calcareous 2002 Cabernet Sauvignon (Paso Robles) $24. Opens with a strong cabernet nose of ripe black currants, with a hint of raisins, then turns soft and rich in the mouth. The gentle texture carries flavors of blackberry marmalade, chocolate, and oak. This polished wine has a long, sweet finish. **90 Editors' Choice** *—S.H. (8/1/2005)*

Calcareous 2003 Syrah (Paso Robles) $24. Tremendously forward in fruit, this soft, dry wine has black cherry, blackberry, and chocolate flavors wrapped in smooth, rich tannins, and a peppery aftertaste. **87** *—S.H. (12/31/2005)*

Calcareous 2004 Viognier (Paso Robles) $24. Here's a tasty, tangy Viognier with lots of nice fruit and wildflower flavors, a richly creamy texture and an oaky veneer. It's very well-balanced, and strikes just the right tone for this often exotic variety. **87** *—S.H. (12/31/2005)*

CALE

Cale 1998 Sangiacomo Vineyards Chardonnay (Carneros) $24. 88 *(6/1/2000)*

Cale 1997 Sangiacomo Vineyards Pinot Noir (Carneros) $24. 83 *(10/1/1999)*

CALERA

Calera 2002 Chardonnay (Central Coast) $14. Full-bodied and dry, this 3-year-old Chard is picking up dried fruit notes, although it's still rich in peaches and pineapples. The high acidity has carried the wine this far, but it should be consumed now. **86** *—S.H. (12/15/2005)*

Calera 2000 Chardonnay (Central Coast) $18. Getting old and tired, and the fruit, which once must have been all peaches and cream, is fading. So is the acidity. There's still plenty of oak, though. **82** *—S.H. (10/1/2004)*

Calera 1999 Chardonnay (Mount Harlan) $34. I am at a loss to explain why this wine has been held back so long. It's no longer fresh, but hasn't developed interesting bottle qualities either. Instead, it's a tired, old wine.Tasted twice. **83** *—S.H. (11/15/2004)*

Calera 1997 Chardonnay (Mount Harlan) $38. 89 *(7/1/2001)*

Calera 2001 Pinot Noir (Central Coast) $20. Decent, with a light, silky texture and good acidity framing modest cherry and spice flavors. Finishes dry. **84** *—S.H. (12/1/2004)*

Calera 1999 Pinot Noir (Central Coast) $20. 87 *—S.H. (7/1/2002)*

Calera 2000 Jensen Vineyard Pinot Noir (Mount Harlan) $50. This is one tough wine to evaluate. It's not showing much of anything now beyond an oaky earthiness with hints of spicy cherry pie. A hit of tannins numbs the palate. Tasted twice, with consistent result. **84** *—S.H. (12/1/2004)*

Calera 1997 Melange Pinot Noir (Mount Harlan) $40. 90 *—S.H. (7/1/2002)*

Calera 2000 Mills Pinot Noir (Mount Harlan) $40. My preference over Calera's Selleck. It's more typical and not as eccentric, with lush cherry, coffee, cocoa, and spice flavors balanced with vital acidity. Turns astringently tannic in the finish, but this is a classically structured Pinot that should mature. Drink now through 2008. **91** *—S.H. (12/15/2004)*

Calera 2001 Reed Vineyard Pinot Noir (Mount Harlan) $45. Similar to Calera's Jensen bottling, a youthful, tough wine with cherry, cola, and oak flavors and high acids and tannins. Not showing well now, although it has plenty of finesse. Best to age it for a few years. **88** *—S.H. (8/1/2005)*

Calera 1999 Reed Vineyard Pinot Noir (Mount Harlan) $45. 91 *—M.S. (12/1/2003)*

Calera 2001 Selleck Pinot Noir (Mount Harlan) $55. This is the most accessible of Calera's current single-vineyard releases, a real charmer with its creamy cherry, mocha, and oaky vanilla flavors. But don't be misled, it's an ager. Acidity is big, tannins are sturdy, balance is fine. As with all Calera Pinots, this wine is elegantly structured. **91** *—S.H. (12/15/2005)*

Calera 1996 Selleck Vineyard Pinot Noir (Mount Harlan) $80. 91 *(10/1/1999)*

Calera 2003 Viognier (Mount Harlan) $36. The first great California Viognier I ever had was Calera's, and I've admired it ever since. The tight acids do a good job of controlling the flamboyant, tropical fruit, white peach, and wildflower side. Like a combination of a rich Chardonnay and a crisp Sauvignon Blanc, elegant and delicious. **91** *—S.H. (8/1/2005)*

CALISTOGA CELLARS

Calistoga Cellars 2002 Cabernet Sauvignon (Napa Valley) $30. Fairly tannic, but there's a smooth, milk-chocolate texture that flatters the palate. The blackberry fruit is a bit thin in the middle through the finish, but the wine has lots of elegance. **86** *—S.H. (6/1/2005)*

Calistoga Cellars 2002 Merlot (Napa Valley) $26. Lots to like about the smooth, tannic structure, and the way the sweet black cherry fruit spreads across the palate. But it could use greater concentration and density. **85** *—S.H. (6/1/2005)*

Calistoga Cellars 2001 Zinfandel (Napa Valley) $22. 90 Editors' Choice *(11/1/2003)*

CALIX

Calix 2003 Parmalee-Hill Vineyard Syrah (Sonoma County) $33. A new discovery for me, and a fabulous one, for with this wine Calix enters the ranks of super-Syrah players. The vineyard is southwest of Sonoma Town, by the Carneros and thus not too hot. Good acidity backs up the black cherry flavors. The wine is balanced, complex, and totally delicious. **92** *—S.H. (12/31/2005)*

CALLAWAY

Callaway 1999 Coastal Cabernet Sauvignon (California) $11. 84 *—S.H. (11/15/2001)*

Callaway 2000 Coastal Winemaker's Reserve Cabernet Sauvignon (Paso Robles) $35. 83 *—S.H. (11/15/2003)*

Callaway 2000 Coastal Chardonnay (California) $11. 86 Best Buy *—S.H. (12/15/2002)*

Callaway 2000 Coastal Reserve Chardonnay (Santa Maria Valley) $16. 85 *—S.H. (5/1/2003)*

Callaway 1998 Chenin Blanc (California) $8. 86 Best Buy *—S.H. (9/1/1999)*

Callaway 2000 Coastal Chenin Blanc (California) $8. 83 *—S.H. (11/15/2001)*

Callaway 1997 Special Collection Dolcetto (Temecula) $15. 85 *(11/1/1999)*

Callaway 1999 Coastal Merlot (California) $11. 85 *—S.H. (11/15/2001)*

Callaway 1999 Coastal Reserve Merlot (California) $16. 84 *—S.H. (9/1/2003)*

Callaway 1998 Special Collection Pinot Gris (Temecula) $14. 86 *—S.H. (3/1/2000)*

Callaway 2000 Coastal Sauvignon Blanc (California) $8. 86 *—S.H. (9/1/2003)*

Callaway 1999 Coastal Syrah (California) $12. 84 *(10/1/2001)*

Callaway 2000 Coastal Reserve Viognier (California) $15. 85 *—S.H. (11/15/2001)*

Callaway 1998 Special Collection Viognier (Temecula) $15. 85 *—S.H. (11/1/1999)*

CAMARADERIE CELLARS

Camaraderie Cellars 2001 Cabernet Sauvignon (Columbia Valley (WA)) $25. 92 Cellar Selection *—P.G. (12/31/2003)*

Camaraderie Cellars 2001 Merlot (Columbia Valley (WA)) $25. 89 *—P.G. (12/31/2003)*

Camaraderie Cellars 2002 Sauvignon Blanc (Washington) $10. 87 Best Buy *—P.G. (12/31/2003)*

CAMBRIA

Cambria 2000 Bench Break Vineyard Chardonnay (Santa Maria Valley) $25. 87 *—S.H. (8/1/2003)*

Cambria 1999 Experimental Clone 4 Chardonnay (Santa Maria Valley) $40. 91 *(10/1/2002)*

Cambria 1999 Katherine's Vineyard Chardonnay (Santa Maria Valley) $22. 87 *(10/1/2002)*

Cambria 1997 Katherine's Vineyard Chardonnay (Santa Maria Valley) $20. 91 *—S.H. (7/1/1999)*

Cambria 1999 Rae's Chardonnay (Santa Maria Valley) $41. 91 *(7/1/2001)*

Cambria 1999 Bench Break Vineyard Pinot Noir (Santa Maria Valley) $42. 86 *(10/1/2002)*

Cambria 2000 Experimental Clone 115 Pinot Noir (Santa Maria Valley) $50. 93 *(10/1/2002)*

Cambria 2000 Experimental Clone 2A Pinot Noir (Santa Maria Valley) $50. 92 *(10/1/2002)*

Cambria 1999 Julia's Pinot Noir (Santa Maria Valley) $26. 83 *(10/1/2002)*

Cambria 2000 Rae's Estate Bottled Pinot Noir (Santa Maria Valley) $50. 92 *—S.H. (12/1/2003)*

Cambria 1999 Tepusquet Vineyard Syrah (Santa Maria Valley) $22. 87 *(11/1/2001)*

Cambria 1997 Tepusquet Vineyard Syrah (Santa Maria Valley) $22. 89 *—L.W. (2/1/2000)*

Cambria 1997 Tepusquet Vineyard Viognier (Santa Maria Valley) $16. 91 Best Buy *—S.H. (6/1/1999)*

CAMELLIA

Camellia 1999 Lencioni Vineyard Cabernet Sauvignon (Dry Creek Valley) $45. 81 *—S.H. (11/15/2002)*

Camellia 2001 Diamo Grazie Red Wine Cabernet Sauvignon-Sangiovese (Dry Creek Valley) $42. Dry, tannic, and ungenerous in fruit, leaving behind a puckery, astringent feeling in the mouth. Sangiovese, Cabernet Sauvignon, and Petite Sirah. **82** *—S.H. (8/1/2004)*

Camellia 2001 Merlo Vineyards Sangiovese (Dry Creek Valley) $24. Smells like bacon frying in the pan, and if there's fruit in this wine, it's effectively buried, so what you get is heat and tannins. **81** *—S.H. (8/1/2004)*

Camellia 1999 Merlo Vineyards Sangiovese (Dry Creek Valley) $28. 86 *—S.H. (12/15/2001)*

Camellia 1999 Lencioni Vineyard Zinfandel (Dry Creek Valley) $22. 86 *—S.H. (12/15/2001)*

CAMELOT

Camelot 2001 Cabernet Sauvignon (California) $7. Fruity-earthy, with pleasant blackberry and cherry flavors diffused with herbs and tobacco. A little sharp in acidity, and very dry. **84** *—S.H. (10/1/2004)*

Camelot 1997 Chardonnay (California) $13. 87 *—L.W. (10/1/1999)*

Camelot 2000 Chardonnay (California) $10. 82 *—S.H. (5/1/2002)*

Camelot 2001 Merlot (California) $7. This is a wine to stock up on by the case if you like a pretty good, full-bodied red at this price—and who doesn't? It's polished with cherry, tobacco, and spice flavors, and is dry and balanced. **85 Best Buy** *—S.H. (12/15/2004)*

Camelot 1997 Merlot (California) $10. 82 *(2/1/2001)*

Camelot 2002 Pinot Noir (California) $7. A little over-ripe and pruny, but dry and decently made. Shows some plump fruit, and also some herbal, coffee notes, leading to a finish of bitter tannins. **84 Best Buy** *(11/1/2004)*

Camelot 2000 Pinot Noir (California) $10. 84 *—S.H. (12/15/2001)*

Camelot 2004 Sauvignon Blanc (California) $8. Picture perfect Sauvignon Blanc, and at a nice price, too. It seems to come from coastal grapes, to judge from the lime-tart crispness. The tangy flavors are of spiced figs and vanilla, and finish a bit sweet. **85 Best Buy** *—S.H. (12/1/2005)*

Camelot 2002 Shiraz (California) $7. A nice wine, especially for the price. Dark, full-bodied, and dry, with rich, spicy flavors of plums and blackberries, and a sweet coating of oak. **86 Best Buy** *—S.H. (6/1/2005)*

Camelot 2002 Zinfandel (California) $7. Sweet oak and sweet raspberry merge to create a drink resembling a candy confection, with a sugary finish. **83** *—S.H. (6/1/2005)*

CAMPION

Campion 2001 Pinot Noir (Edna Valley) $35. Interesting and complex, and delicious to drink. Cherries, raspberries, and blackberries are spiced up with toasty oak and vanillins, while the mouthfeel is silky, seductive, and crisp. The light, airy texture is enjoyable. **87** *—S.H. (3/1/2004)*

Campion 2000 Pinot Noir (Santa Lucia Highlands) $32. Light in color and in body, almost ethereal, with a smooth, silky texture and bright acids. The pretty flavors include cola and rhubarb, and sweeter notes of raspberries and cherries. **86** *—S.H. (4/1/2004)*

CAMPUS OAKS

Campus Oaks 1998 Cabernet Sauvignon (Mendocino) $12. **82** *—S.H. (6/1/2002)*

Campus Oaks 1999 Chardonnay (California) $8. **83** *—S.H. (5/1/2002)*

Campus Oaks 1998 Merlot (California) $9. **84** *—S.H. (6/1/2002)*

Campus Oaks 1999 Syrah (California) $9. **82** *(10/1/2001)*

Campus Oaks 1999 Old Vine Zinfandel (California) $10. **84** *—S.H. (7/1/2002)*

CANA'S FEAST

Cana's Feast 2000 Del Rio Vineyard Bordeaux Blend (Rogue Valley) $30. **89** *—M.S. (8/1/2003)*

Cana's Feast 2002 Meredith Mitchell Vineyard Pinot Noir (Willamette Valley) $40. Done in a very sweet, juicy, slightly over-ripe mode, it offers varietally correct flavors in a smooth, everyday style. A couple of extra years in bottle should soften up the tannins sufficiently. **87** *(11/1/2004)*

CANOE RIDGE

Canoe Ridge 2001 Cabernet Sauvignon (Columbia Valley (WA)) $20. Broad and roughly tannic, this chewy Cab really needs grilled meat to soften it up and bring out the cherry fruit. That said, it offers a clean, firm slice of Horse Heaven Hills Cabernet Sauvignon terroir, with a long, appealing finish. **87** *—P.G. (7/1/2004)*

Canoe Ridge 1998 Cabernet Sauvignon (Columbia Valley (WA)) $25. **89** *—P.G. (6/1/2001)*

Canoe Ridge 1996 Cabernet Sauvignon (Columbia Valley (WA)) $25. **91** *—S.H. (7/1/1999)*

Canoe Ridge 2001 Chardonnay (Columbia Valley (WA)) $19. **87** *—M.S. (6/1/2003)*

Canoe Ridge 2000 Chardonnay (Columbia Valley (WA)) $19. **86** *—J.M. (5/1/2002)*

Canoe Ridge 2002 Oak Ridge Vineyard Gewürztraminer (Washington) $13. The winery always does well with this tricky grape, somehow walking the line between floral and oily, sweet and dry, and coming up with intensity that doesn't tire out the palate. Complex and lingering, it's perfect for southeast Asian cuisine. **90 Best Buy** *—P.G. (5/1/2004)*

Canoe Ridge 2001 Merlot (Columbia Valley (WA)) $15. This is a transition wine for Canoe Ridge, whose talented winemaker, John Abbott, did the crush but left before finishing it. It's a good effort, but not as lush as previous vintages. The fruit is pretty and the wine balanced, with nice flavors of plum and dried cherries, and intriguing hints of tobacco leaf in the finish. **88** *—P.G. (9/1/2004)*

Canoe Ridge 1999 Merlot (Columbia Valley (WA)) $14. **86** *—C.S. (12/31/2002)*

Canoe Ridge 1997 Merlot (Columbia Valley (WA)) $19. **90** *—S.H. (11/1/1999)*

Canoe Ridge 1999 Reserve - Lot No. 10 Merlot (Columbia Valley (WA)) $45. **91** *—P.G. (6/1/2002)*

Canoe Ridge 1998 Red Table Wine Merlot-Cabernet Sauvignon (Columbia Valley (WA)) $14. **87** *—P.G. (11/15/2000)*

CANON DE SOL

Canon de Sol 2000 Meritage (Columbia Valley (WA)) $28. **88** *—P.G. (9/1/2003)*

Canon de Sol 1999 Merlot (Columbia Valley (WA)) $24. **86** *—P.G. (9/1/2003)*

CANTIGA WINEWORKS

Cantiga Wineworks 2000 Cabernet Sauvignon-Shiraz (Central Coast) $18. **84** *—J.M. (4/1/2003)*

Cantiga Wineworks 2000 Oakless Chardonnay (Monterey) $20. **85** *—J.M. (2/1/2003)*

Cantiga Wineworks 2000 Shiraz (Monterey) $24. **86** *—J.M. (2/1/2003)*

CANYON ROAD

Canyon Road 2003 Cabernet Sauvignon (California) $9. This is a great price for an everyday Cab that offers lots of pleasure. It's dry and fairly tannic, with good blackberry flavors and a long finish. **85 Best Buy** *—S.H. (10/1/2005)*

Canyon Road 2001 Cabernet Sauvignon (California) $10. Tastes like it came from overcropped vines, with thin, watery berry flavors and a distinct earthiness. Alcohol, acidity, and tannins take front and center, offering little in the way of pleasure. **83** *—S.H. (6/1/2004)*

Canyon Road 1998 Cabernet Sauvignon (California) $8. **87** *(11/15/1999)*

Canyon Road 2003 Chardonnay (California) $10. Has all the elements of a top Chard, from the ripe fruit to the oak. It's just a little more modest, and a lot less expensive. **84** *—S.H. (12/31/2004)*

Canyon Road 2001 Chardonnay (California) $9. 86 *—S.H. (12/15/2002)*

Canyon Road 1998 Chardonnay (California) $8. 84 Best Buy *—J.C. (10/1/1999)*

Canyon Road 2002 Merlot (California) $10. A very well-behaved Merlot that offers plenty of sprightly, jammy blackberry and cherry flavors. It's a bit rough and ready, but that bright fruit and clean, dry finish make it a good value. **85** *—S.H. (9/1/2004)*

Canyon Road 2000 Merlot (California) $10. 86 Best Buy *—S.H. (6/1/2002)*

Canyon Road 1998 Merlot (California) $8. 81 *—S.H. (12/31/1999)*

Canyon Road 2003 Sauvignon Blanc (Alexander Valley) $9. Another in a series of fresh, clean wines with citrus zest, grassy, eau de chat (get it?), and pepper flavors. It gets the job done with its easy appeal. **84** *—S.H. (9/1/2004)*

Canyon Road 2001 Sauvignon Blanc (California) $9. 86 Best Buy *—S.H. (9/1/2002)*

Canyon Road 1999 Sauvignon Blanc (California) $8. 86 *—S.H. (9/1/2000)*

Canyon Road 2002 Shiraz (California) $10. Oozes cherry-cocoa flavor, with rich oaky-vanilla overtones. This dry, soft wine is as ripe as they come, but balanced. **84** *—S.H. (12/31/2004)*

Canyon Road 2000 Shiraz (California) $10. 85 *—S.H. (9/1/2002)*

USA

CAPAROSO

Caparoso 2001 Cabernet Sauvignon (Central Coast) $10. 86 *—S.H. (11/15/2003)*

CAPAY VALLEY

Capay Valley 2000 Syrah (California) $16. On the simple, watery side, with thinned-down cherry flavors and a scour of tough tannins. Way too expensive for what you get. **83** *—S.H. (12/1/2004)*

Capay Valley 2002 Tempranillo (California) $15. Tastes raw, sharp, and herbal, a thin, tough wine that seems to have mostly tannins going for it. **82** *—S.H. (12/15/2004)*

Capay Valley 2003 Viognier (California) $15. From a very warm appellation, a wine soft in acidity but high in sweet, ripe fruity flavor. Swarms of lemon and lime, melon, fig, and even pineapple cover the palate. If easy fruit is your thing, this one's got plenty of it. **84** *—S.H. (11/15/2004)*

CAPELLO

Capello 1999 Chardonnay (California) $9. 84 *—S.H. (6/1/2003)*

CAPIAUX

Capiaux 2000 Pisoni Vineyard Pinot Noir (Santa Lucia Highlands) $45. 90 *(10/1/2002)*

CARABELLA

Carabella 2002 Dijon 76 Clone Chardonnay (Willamette Valley) $23. Light style, that hints at butterscotch, with clean and transparent flavors. The fruit is elegant and pleasant, but seems overmatched by the alcohol. **85** *—P.G. (2/1/2005)*

Carabella 2002 Pinot Gris (Willamette Valley) $14. A concentrated, pear-scented wine that tastes quite ripe and fleshy, with ripe pear flavors coming through, and a hint of honey. Enough tannin to be felt. **87 Best Buy** *—P.G. (2/1/2004)*

Carabella 2002 Pinot Noir (Willamette Valley) $35. This is a good example of Willamette valley pinot, with strong flavors of tomato mixed with pretty plum/cherry fruit. Medium ripe, good tannic grip, and a little bit of heat in the finish. Simple but tasty. **86** *—P.G. (2/1/2005)*

Carabella 1999 Pinot Noir (Willamette Valley) $33. 86 *—P.G. (12/31/2001)*

Carabella 2001 Les Meres Pinot Noir (Willamette Valley) $19. Aging quickly, drinking well, with round, slightly oxidized flavors that show soft cherry fruit and lots of smooth vanilla. Good value and ready to go. **87** *—P.G. (2/1/2004)*

CARDINALE

Cardinale 2000 Cabernet Sauvignon (Napa-Sonoma) $120. 89 *—S.H. (12/31/2003)*

CARHARTT VINEYARD

Carhartt Vineyard 2002 Estate Merlot (Santa Ynez Valley) $29. There's a note of chocolate peppermint alongside the blackberry and oak aromas that's intriguing, and it's echoed in the mouth. This is a deliciously flavored wine, but it's rather soft in both acids and tannins. **84** *—S.H. (6/1/2005)*

Carhartt Vineyard 2001 Syrah (Santa Ynez Valley) $30. A dark, full-bodied and very extracted wine with powerful fruit flavors. The currant, blackberry, plum, and cherry flavors have a peppery note, especially in the aroma, and the texture is dry and lush. This young wine has lots of baby fat, but is charming now for its opulence. **90** *—S.H. (3/1/2004)*

CARINA CELLARS

Carina Cellars 2001 Syrah (Santa Barbara County) $16. 89 Editors' Choice *—S.H. (10/1/2003)*

CARLISLE

Carlisle 2001 Petite Sirah (Dry Creek Valley) $36. 89 *(4/1/2003)*

Carlisle 2001 Two Acres Red Blend (Russian River Valley) $36. 93 *—S.H. (12/31/2003)*

Carlisle 2001 Three Birds Rhône Red Blend (Sonoma County) $23. 89 *—S.H. (12/1/2003)*

Carlisle 2000 Syrah (Dry Creek Valley) $40. 93 Editors' Choice *—S.H. (6/1/2003)*

Carlisle 2001 Zinfandel (Sonoma County) $23. 88 *(11/1/2003)*

Carlisle 2001 Carlisle Vineyard Zinfandel (Russian River Valley) $35. 89 *(11/1/2003)*

CARMENET

Carmenet 1995 Moon Mountain Estate Reserve Bordeaux Blend (Sonoma) $40. 89 *—S.H. (7/1/1999)*

Carmenet 2001 Cabernet Sauvignon (Lake County) $18. The cherry-berry flavors and oaky notes are backed by firm, tough tannins. Finishes with a gritty scour. May soften with a year or so of bottle age. 84 *—S.H. (5/1/2004)*

Carmenet 2000 Cellar Selection Cabernet Sauvignon (California) $8. 84 *—S.H. (11/15/2003)*

Carmenet 1997 Dynamite Cabernet Sauvignon (North Coast) $20. 88 *—S.H. (7/1/1999)*

Carmenet 1997 Moon Mountain Reserve Cabernet Sauvignon (Sonoma Valley) $48. 93 *(11/1/2000)*

Carmenet 2002 Chardonnay (Napa Valley) $16. This wine is fresh and clean, with bright acids that cleanse the palate. It's not especially powerful in fruit, with suggestions of citrus, apple, and peach, and snaps to an abrupt finish. 84 *—S.H. (2/1/2004)*

Carmenet 2001 Cellar Selection Chardonnay (California) $8. 84 *—S.H. (12/1/2003)*

Carmenet 2001 Merlot (Sonoma County) $20. This solid Merlot pleases for its ripe blackberry and chocolate flavors and sweetly rich tannins. It's a big wine, but easy to drink, especially with a perfectly grilled ribeye steak. May even benefit from a year or two in the cellar. 87 *—S.H. (5/1/2004)*

Carmenet 2000 Cellar Selection Merlot (California) $8. 85 Best Buy *—S.H. (12/31/2003)*

Carmenet 2002 Cellar Selection Sauvignon Blanc (California) $8. 86 Best Buy *—S.H. (10/1/2003)*

Carmenet 1999 Paragon Vineyard Reserve Sauvignon Blanc (Edna Valley) $16. 88 *—S.H. (8/1/2001)*

Carmenet 1999 Evangelho Vineyard Zinfandel (Contra Costa County) $25. 90 *—S.H. (9/1/2002)*

Carmenet 1997 Evangelho Vineyard Old Vines Zinfandel (Contra Costa County) $17. 85 *—S.H. (5/1/2000)*

CARMICHAEL

Carmichael 2002 Sur le Pont Rhône Red Blend (Monterey County) $18. This blend of Syrah, Mourvédre, Carignane, and Grenache, which comes from California's Côtes-du-Rhône in southern Monterey as it approaches Paso Robles, is soft, fruity, and simple. It will be good with a rich bouillabaisse or lamb stew. 86 *—S.H. (2/1/2005)*

CARMODY MCKNIGHT

Carmody McKnight 1997 Chardonnay (Paso Robles) $15. 85 *(6/1/2000)*

CARNEROS CREEK

Carneros Creek 2001 Gavin Vineyard Chardonnay (Carneros) $20. 84 *—S.H. (12/31/2003)*

Carneros Creek 2000 Pinot Noir (Carneros) $24. 90 Editors' Choice *(10/1/2002)*

Carneros Creek 2000 Cote de Carneros Pinot Noir (Carneros) $17. 87 Best Buy *(10/1/2002)*

Carneros Creek 2002 Grail Pinot Noir (Carneros) $40. This wine is rather earthy, austere, and dry, but who knows, it could surprise in a few years. 86 *—S.H. (10/1/2005)*

Carneros Creek 2002 Los Carneros Reserve Pinot Noir (Carneros) $25. The acidity is high here, leading to a citrus peel tartness partially enriched with oak, cherry, and tobacco flavors. Silky in texture, soft in tannins, this dry, gentle wine is uncomplicated and versatile at the table. 85 *—S.H. (11/1/2004)*

Carneros Creek 2001 Mahoney Vineyard Pinot Noir (Carneros) $40. This is a bigger wine than the Las Brisas bottling, by a hair. It shares many of the same qualities, like raspberry and cherry cola flavors, soft tannins and a silky texture. Quite dry, and finishes with a flourish of sweet fruit, oak, and spice. 90 *—S.H. (2/1/2004)*

CAROL SHELTON

Carol Shelton 2002 Cox Vineyard Old Vines Wild Thing Zinfandel (Mendocino County) $28. Only in California. 16-1/2 percent alcohol, and fully dry. So rich, so ripe in berry fruit it's turned into chocolate decadence with a drizzle of cassis. For all the size it's balanced and even harmonious. Yummy with ribs or vanilla ice cream. 90 *—S.H. (12/31/2004)*

Carol Shelton 2002 Lopez Vineyard Old Vines MongaZin Zinfandel (Cucamonga Valley) $24. Tannic, full-bodied, and very dry. The blackberry, coffee, and spice flavors are rewarding, and the wine is nicely balanced with acidity. This is a classic warm country California Zin, and will likely age. **87** *—S.H. (12/31/2004)*

Carol Shelton 2002 Rock Pile Ridge Vineyard Rocky Reserve Zinfandel (Dry Creek Valley) $32. Shelton shows a deft hand in balancing Zin's over-the-edge tendencies with a more elegant approach. This wine is big in wild berry and spice flavors, and rather alcoholic, but never loses its sense of proportion. **88** *—S.H. (12/31/2004)*

Carol Shelton 2002 Rue Vineyard Old Vines KarmaZin Zinfandel (Russian River Valley) $30. This is one big Zin. It's dark as night and full of weight and fruit, and dry as dust. Yet the tannins are sweet and ripe, and they frame intense blackberry, coffee, and chocolate flavors. Try this balanced wine with short ribs or a roast chicken. **89** *—S.H. (12/31/2004)*

CARPE DIEM

Carpe Diem 2002 Firepeak Vineyard Chardonnay (Edna Valley) $25. Here's a crisp and elegantly structured wine. The citrus and apple flavors have an earthy, mineral edge and are accompanied by good acidity, leading to a clean and vibrant mouthfeel. There is, however, an almost excessive dryness. **87** *—S.H. (8/1/2004)*

Carpe Diem 2000 Firepeak Vineyard Chardonnay (Edna Valley) $25. 92 Editors' Choice *—S.H. (12/15/2002)*

Carpe Diem 2001 Firepeak Vineyard Pinot Noir (Edna Valley) $31. A smooth, complex Pinot whose silky texture is nicely balanced with rich flavors. Raspberries and cherries, Oriental spices, smoke, vanilla, and toast coalesce into a gently fruity impression backed up by soft, ripe tannins. Perfect with roast chicken. **90** *—S.H. (3/1/2004)*

CARPENTER CREEK

Carpenter Creek 2002 Chardonnay (Washington) $14. Simple, tart, green apple fruit awkwardly married to hard, tannic oak. Nothing comes together; the fruit seems thin and the oak tags a bitter, woody finish onto it. **83** *—P.G. (1/1/2004)*

Carpenter Creek 2002 Sauvignon Blanc (Washington) $13. Grassy and herbaceous style, showing light, lemony fruit and mouth-puckering acid. **83** *—P.G. (1/1/2004)*

Carpenter Creek 2002 Signature Series Syrah (Yakima Valley) $38. Clearly an ambitious effort, but one that's raisiny and roasted, with pruny, burnt flavors and a healthy dose of astringency. **82** *(9/1/2005)*

CARR

Carr 2002 Ashley's Vineyard Pinot Noir (Santa Rita Hills) $NA. Identical scores from all tasters for this big, dark, rich wine, which is filled with oaky, blackberry, and mocha flavors. It's big, tannic, and dense now, heavy in the mouth, but is likely to soften and turn supple with a few years in the bottle. **87** *(11/1/2004)*

CARTER

Carter 2001 Beckstoffer Vineyards Cabernet Sauvignon (Oakville) $75. Made from grapes grown in the Tokalon Vineyard, this Cab showcases both its terroir and the amazing vintage. It's dry, ripe in currants and cherries, lush in tannins yet expressive and forward. Very drinkable now, with good grip, a dry finish and plenty of elegance. **93** *—S.H. (8/1/2005)*

Carter 1999 Fortuna Block Cabernet Sauvignon (Napa Valley) $60. 92 *—J.M. (11/15/2002)*

Carter 2001 Truchard Vineyards Merlot (Napa Valley) $38. A sleek, smooth wine that serves up plenty of cinnamon and spice flavor backed by a core of blackberry, raspberry, anise, herb, and coffee flavors. It's complex and elegant, showing good length on the finish. **90** *—J.M. (8/1/2004)*

CARTLIDGE & BROWN

Cartlidge & Brown 2000 Chardonnay (California) $10. 85 *—S.H. (12/15/2002)*

Cartlidge & Brown 2000 Merlot (California) $10. 86 Best Buy *—S.H. (12/31/2002)*

Cartlidge & Brown 2001 Zinfandel (California) $10. 85 *(11/1/2003)*

CARVER SUTRO

Carver Sutro 1999 Palisades Vineyard Petite Sirah (Napa Valley) $92. 82 *(12/31/2003)*

CASA BARRANCA

Casa Barranca 2003 Craftsman Red Cabernet Sauvignon (Central Coast) $15. Rather tough and rustic, this Cab has a raw, sharp mouthfeel, although the fruit is very ripe and almost sweet in blackberries, cherries, and mocha. **83** *—S.H. (12/1/2005)*

Casa Barranca 2003 Bungalow Red Syrah-Grenache Rhône Red Blend (Santa Barbara County) $15. Kind of rustic in style, with an edgy, sharp mouthfeel and a finish that's too sweet. But there's plenty of tasty wild berry and red stone fruit flavor. **83** *—S.H. (12/1/2005)*

Casa Barranca 2003 Reserve Syrah (Santa Barbara County) $19. Opens with intriguing aromas of intense white pepper, freshly picked blackberries and mocha, butin the mouth, the wine turns overly soft and a bit cloying. **83** *—S.H. (12/1/2005)*

CASA CASSARA

Casa Cassara 2001 Burning Creek Vineyard Pinot Noir (Santa Rita Hills) $46. A little pruny or raisiny, and also hot, although there are some succulent black cherry flavors in the middle. But there's something tough and rugged about this wine, and it does leave a burn behind. **85** *—S.H. (12/1/2004)*

Casa Cassara 2001 Syrah (Santa Ynez Valley) $24. Very dry, rather tart and acidic, but the polished cherry and blackberry flavors are juicy and enjoyable, and are sweetened with a dash of oak. This wine desperately needs a big, thick cut of meat to tame it. Try with a sirloin steak. **86** *—S.H. (12/1/2004)*

CASA DE CABALLOS

Casa de Caballos 2002 Choclate Lily Cabernet Sauvignon (Paso Robles) $30. Soft in tannins, but sharp in acidity, with a raw, sandpapery flavor. **82** *—S.H. (2/1/2005)*

Casa de Caballos 2002 Ultra Violet Merlot (Paso Robles) $26. There's good, ripe fruit flavor here, but the wine hits the mouth with a raw feeling. Finishes sharp and disagreeably harsh. **83** *—S.H. (2/1/2005)*

Casa de Caballos 2000 Maggie May El Nino Red Pinot Noir (Paso Robles) $17. **82** *(10/1/2002)*

CASA NUESTRA

Casa Nuestra 2000 Reserve Chenin Blanc (Napa Valley) $22. **88** *—S.H. (9/1/2002)*

CASTALIA

Castalia 2003 Rochioli Vineyard Pinot Noir (Russian River Valley) $45. Rochioli's winemaker has crafted a fine, silky Pinot. The flavors veer toward red cherries and cola, with an edge of sweet oak, while acidity is tart. The wine finishes sharp, but should soften and improve with five to seven years in the cellar. **90** *—S.H. (12/1/2005)*

CASTELLETTO

Castelletto 1997 Trovato Red Blend (Temecula) $15. **90 Best Buy** *—S.H. (11/15/2001)*

Castelletto 1999 Trovato Tuscan Blend (Temecula) $15. **90** *—S.H. (4/1/2002)*

CASTELLO DI BORGHESE

Castello di Borghese 2001 Ovation Private Reserve Bordeaux Blend (North Fork of Long Island) $75. **82** *—J.C. (10/2/2004)*

Castello di Borghese 1998 Hargrave Vineyard Cabernet Franc (North Fork of Long Island) $17. **85** *—J.C. (4/1/2001)*

Castello di Borghese 1998 Hargrave Vineyard Reserve Cabernet Sauvignon (North Fork of Long Island) $32. **86** *—J.C. (4/1/2001)*

Castello di Borghese 2001 Hargrave Vineyard Barrel-Fermented Chardonnay (North Fork of Long Island) $22. **83** *—J.C. (10/2/2004)*

Castello di Borghese 1998 Hargrave Vineyard Reserve Chardonnay (North Fork of Long Island) $18. **88** *—J.C. (4/1/2001)*

Castello di Borghese 2000 Hargrave Vineyard Merlot (North Fork of Long Island) $19. **81** *—J.C. (10/2/2004)*

Castello di Borghese 2000 Hargrave Vineyard Reserve Merlot (North Fork of Long Island) $25. Tree bark, bell pepper, and alcohol mar the nose on this offering, which has some good points but also some things that hold it back. For instance, there is some fresh strawberry on the flavor profile but also a hindering note of green. Then there's the finish, which is round and creamy but also hot and clumsy. **84** *—M.S. (1/1/2004)*

Castello di Borghese 1999 Hargrave Vineyard Pinot Blanc (North Fork of Long Island) $10. **82** *—J.C. (4/1/2001)*

Castello di Borghese 1998 Hargrave Vineyard Pinot Noir (North Fork of Long Island) $35. **84** *—J.C. (4/1/2001)*

Castello di Borghese NV Chardonette White Blend (North Fork of Long Island) $7. **83** *—J.C. (4/1/2001)*

CASTLE

Castle 1998 Chardonnay (Sonoma Valley) $18. **84** *(6/1/2000)*

Castle 1999 Chardonnay (Sonoma Valley) $17. **89 Best Buy** *—S.H. (12/31/2001)*

Castle 2000 Merlot (Sonoma Valley) $20. Soft and tired, with leathery, funky smells and flavors. Not going anywhere. **82** *—S.H. (5/1/2005)*

Castle 1998 Merlot (Sonoma Valley) $20. **90** *—S.H. (12/31/2001)*

Castle 1999 Sangiacomo Vineyard Merlot (Carneros) $24. Time has not helped this vegetal wine, which smells and tastes of canned asparagus. Whatever fruit there was is largely gone. **82** *—S.H. (5/1/2005)*

Castle 2001 Pinot Noir (Carneros) $24. Cola, cherry, mocha, and vanilla flavors, in a light-bodied, silky wine, with pronounced acidity. Finishes dry. A bit rustic, but offers good Pinot character. **85** *—S.H. (5/1/2005)*

Castle 1999 Pinot Noir (Carneros) $24. **86** *—S.H. (12/15/2001)*

Castle 1997 Durell Vineyard Pinot Noir (Carneros) $30. **90** *(10/1/1999)*

Castle 1999 Sangiacomo Vineyard Pinot Noir (Carneros) $30. **90 Editors' Choice** *(10/1/2002)*

Castle 2001 Syrah (Sonoma Valley) $24. Rich and ripe, maybe a bit over-oaked, but that doesn't stop the plum, blackberry, hung meat, rum, and coffee flavors from running all over the palate. Finishes firmly dry, with a long aftertaste of spice. **89** *—S.H. (8/1/2004)*

Castle 2001 Port Syrah (Carneros) $28. This country-style wine sure is sweet in chocolate and cassis, but it lacks distinction and balance, and feels rough. **83** *—S.H. (5/1/2005)*

Castle 2000 Viognier (California) $19. 86 *—S.H. (12/15/2001)*

Castle 2001 Zinfandel (Sonoma Valley) $19. 88 *—J.M. (11/1/2003)*

Castle 1998 Zinfandel (Sonoma Valley) $19. 89 *—P.G. (3/1/2001)*

Castle 1997 Zinfandel (Sonoma Valley) $18. 90 *—S.H. (5/1/2000)*

CASTLE ROCK

Castle Rock 2002 Cabernet Sauvignon (Sonoma County) $11. Clean and varietally correct, this is an inexpensive Cabernet with pleasant flavors of blackberries and oak. It's thoroughly dry, and easy to drink. The sturdy tannins will stand up to rich meats and cheese. **84** *—S.H. (8/1/2005)*

Castle Rock 2000 Cabernet Sauvignon (Columbia Valley (WA)) $10. 87 Best Buy *—D.T. (12/31/2002)*

Castle Rock 2003 Reserve Chardonnay (Napa Valley) $15. This is one of those earthy Chards, the kind that bring to mind dusty brown spices. It's got appley and smoky, woody flavors, and is dry. **84** *—S.H. (8/1/2005)*

Castle Rock 2003 Reserve Petite Sirah (Napa Valley) $15. Rich and soft in blackberry, mocha, and sweet leather flavors, with lots of oak and a long aftertaste. As much as I like this wine, it is too sweet. The finish turns as sugary as a chocolate truffle, although the wine is no doubt technically dry. **87** *—S.H. (8/1/2005)*

Castle Rock 2003 Pinot Noir (Mendocino County) $11. A weird and disturbing aroma suggesting a chemical flaw ruins this wine's otherwise decent flavors and texture. **82** *—S.H. (2/1/2005)*

Castle Rock 2002 Pinot Noir (Russian River Valley) $11. Strictly average, showing tomato, cherry, and oaky aromas and tastes. Feels soft and a little tough in tannins. **84** *(11/1/2004)*

Castle Rock 2001 Pinot Noir (Russian River Valley) $10. 87 *—M.S. (12/1/2003)*

Castle Rock 2003 Syrah (Central Coast) $9. This cool-climate Syrah brims with bright white pepper, cassis, and coffee flavors, while the tannins are rich, ripe and fine. It's a bone-dry wine with plenty of style and complexity. **87 Best Buy** *—S.H. (8/1/2005)*

Castle Rock 1999 California Cuvée Syrah (California) $10. 82 *(10/1/2001)*

Castle Rock 1999 California Cuvée Zinfandel (California) $10. 83 *—D.T. (3/1/2002)*

USA

CASTORO

Castoro 2003 Cabernet Sauvignon (Paso Robles) $15. Shows good Cabernet character in the full-bodied flavors of black currants, coffee, and cocoa, and also shows Paso structure in the softness and low acids. Paso struggles to define its own style and Castoro is trying hard. **85** *—S.H. (12/1/2005)*

Castoro 2000 Cabernet Sauvignon (Paso Robles) $14. 85 *—S.H. (6/1/2003)*

Castoro 2003 Chardonnay (Central Coast) $13. Here's a dry Chard marked by creamy lees, oak, and an array of yellow and red tree stone fruits. It's a little soft, with a creamy texture. Will go well with food. **85** *—S.H. (2/1/2005)*

Castoro 2001 Due Mila Tre Meritage (Paso Robles) $33. Harsh and tannic, with burnt-coffee and plum flavors that finish dry and astringent. **82** *—S.H. (5/1/2005)*

Castoro 2002 Merlot (Paso Robles) $14. You'll find cherry-berry flavors mingled with herbs and tobacco in this dry wine. It has a balance of acids and tannins and will pair with rich red meats. **85** *—S.H. (12/15/2004)*

Castoro 2003 Late Harvest Muscat Canelli (Paso Robles) $17. Sweet in orange blossom and apricot flavors, with a good balance of acidity, this is a basic California late-harvest wine, satisfying due to its sweet fruit. Good with vanilla ice cream topped with peaches, with a sugar cookie. **85** *—S.H. (12/1/2005)*

Castoro 2002 Stone's Throw Reserve Petite Sirah (Paso Robles) $18. Smells disturbingly funky or bretty, and seems shut down. Barely acceptable. **80** *—S.H. (5/1/2005)*

Castoro 2000 Reserve Pinot Noir (Central Coast) $18. 82 *(10/1/2002)*

Castoro 2000 Syrah (Paso Robles) $18. 84 *—S.H. (6/1/2003)*

Castoro 2001 Reserve Syrah (Paso Robles) $18. Opens with a super-leathery, funky note that could be brett or a clonal attribute. Once past the odor, it's dry, soft and herbal-plummy. **84** *—S.H. (5/1/2005)*

Castoro 2002 Reserve Tempranillo (California) $16. Fully dry and medium-bodied, this is quite a good wine for a varietal no one really knows how to make in California. It has a mélange of berry, herb, spice, and coffee flavors, and is drinkable now. Try as an alternative to Zinfandel. **87** *—S.H. (4/1/2005)*

Castoro 2004 Stone's Throw Vineyard Viognier (Paso Robles) $18. Displays all the exotic wildflower and tropical fruit aromas and flavors Viognier is famous for, in a dry, soft wine with a honeyed finish. It could be a little more concentrated, though. **85** *—S.H. (12/1/2005)*

Castoro 2001 Zinfandel (Paso Robles) $14. A solid effort from a southland appellation, fully ripened with brambly wild blackberry and cherry-pepper flavors, but balanced in alcohol and without any residual sweetness. A distinctly California wine. **87** *—S.H. (4/1/2004)*

Castoro 2001 Cobble Creek Zinfandel (Paso Robles) $20. **82** *—J.M. (11/1/2003)*

Castoro 2000 Giubbine Zinfandel (Paso Robles) $18. A nice Zin with blackberry and cassis flavors and a fine, dry mouthfeel. If there's a fault, it's a streak of over-ripe raisins that grows stronger through the finish. **85** *—S.H. (4/1/2004)*

Castoro 2001 Late Harvest Zinfandel (Paso Robles) $16. **85** *—S.H. (12/1/2003)*

Castoro 2001 Vineyard Tribute Zinfandel (Paso Robles) $19. **86** *(11/1/2003)*

Castoro 2003 Zinfusion Reserve Zinfandel (Paso Robles) $19. Here's a rustic, country-style Zin with ripe berry flavors that are good enough to accompany a pizza or cheeseburger. It's dry, with a fruity finish. **83** *—S.H. (12/1/2005)*

CATACULA

Catacula 2001 Napa Valley Cabernet Sauvignon (Napa Valley) $19. Very ripe and opulent in fruit. Has flavors of black currant and cassis; so rich and extracted, it's almost a liqueur. Fortunately, adequate acidity brings life, and oak adds nuances of vanilla and toast. **88** *—S.H. (10/1/2004)*

Catacula 2004 Sauvignon Blanc (Napa Valley) $12. Green-grassy and citrusy, with spearmint, alfalfa, and fig flavors, this wine finishes a little sweet and cloying, with a honeyed aftertaste. **83** *—S.H. (12/15/2005)*

Catacula 2000 Sauvignon Blanc (Napa Valley) $11. **86** *—S.H. (7/1/2003)*

Catacula 2001 Zinfandel (Napa Valley) $15. Super-ripe, almost raisiny, with soft tannins and acidity. The softness accentuates the cherries, blackberries, chocolate and raisins and makes the wine drink syrupy, but it sure does tastes good. **85** *—S.H. (9/1/2004)*

CATANA

Catana NV Reserve Quintetta Port (California) $26. This California Port, made with traditional varieties, is from Calaveras County, and you can taste the sun in the super-ripe chocolate, cassis, and blackberry pie flavors. It's gooey and lip-smackingly delicious, with enough acidity to cut through the sweetness. **91** *—S.H. (12/1/2004)*

CATERINA

Caterina 1998 Cabernet Sauvignon (Washington) $24. **87** *—P.G. (10/1/2001)*

Caterina 1999 DuBrul Vineyard Cabernet Sauvignon (Yakima Valley) $28. **89** *—P.G. (12/31/2002)*

Caterina 1998 Willard Family Vineyard Cabernet Sauvignon (Columbia Valley (WA)) $30. **90** *—P.G. (10/1/2001)*

Caterina 1999 Merlot (Columbia Valley (WA)) $20. **88** *—P.G. (12/31/2002)*

Caterina 1997 Merlot (Columbia Valley (WA)) $19. **86** *—S.H. (11/15/2000)*

Caterina 1999 Willard Family Vineyard Merlot (Yakima Valley) $28. **89** *—P.G. (12/31/2002)*

Caterina 1999 Rosso Red Blend (Washington) $15. **88** *—P.G. (6/1/2002)*

Caterina 2000 Sauvignon Blanc (Columbia Valley (WA)) $10. **88 Best Buy** *—P.G. (6/1/2002)*

CATHY MACGREGOR

Cathy MacGregor 1998 Benito Dusi Vineyard Zinfandel (Paso Robles) $26. **84** *—D.T. (3/1/2002)*

CAVE B

Cave B 2003 Janine's Vineyard Chardonnay (Columbia Valley (WA)) $20. Light and buttery, with baked apple fruit and notes of cinnamon; it sounds more like a breakfast pastry than a wine but the flavors are soft and pleasant and it all hangs together well. **87** *—P.G. (12/15/2005)*

Cave B 2002 Famiglia Vineyards Merlot (Columbia Valley (WA)) $30. This wine shows some stuffing, with black cherry/black olive flavors and thick, rough tannins. Notes of moist earth, barnyard, and alcohol burn through the finish. Though the label says 14% alcohol, it feels higher. **85** *—P.G. (12/15/2005)*

Cave B 2002 Cuvée du Soleil Red Blend (Columbia Valley (WA)) $35. The best of the winery's new releases, this 45% Cab, 45% Merlot, 10% Cab Franc blend has more nuanced fruit, mixing black cherry, plum, ripe hints of raisin and prune with whiffs of spice and smoke. The rough edges have been smoothed, and the long finish includes pleasing streaks of vanilla. **88** *—P.G. (12/15/2005)*

Cave B 2001 Kimberley's Vineyard Sémillon (Columbia Valley (WA)) $35. Lots of brash new oak evident here, masking the light, melony fruit with big, toasty graham cracker flavors. Just 173 cases produced. **85** *—P.G. (1/1/2004)*

CAYMUS

Caymus 2002 Cabernet Sauvignon (Napa Valley) $70. Manages to feel both soft and tannic at the same time, which means it's fine now but should age for a few years. The black currant and smoky oak flavors are harmonious, with sweet fruit lasting through a long finish. **90** *—S.H. (3/1/2005)*

Caymus 1999 Cabernet Sauvignon (Napa Valley) $70. **93** *—M.S. (11/15/2002)*

Caymus 2002 Special Selection Cabernet Sauvignon (Napa Valley) $136. This young wine is fairly tough now, and the fruit is hiding behind the oak and tannins. Like many keepers, it's in a trough, and will go through its ups and downs. Eventually, the cherries and blackberries should emerge, but it doesn't seem like one of the great Special Selections. **91** *—S.H. (10/1/2005)*

Caymus 2000 Special Selection Cabernet Sauvignon (Napa Valley) $136. **93** *—J.M. (12/15/2003)*

Caymus 2001 Conundrum White Blend (California) $24. **89** *—J.M. (2/1/2003)*

CAYUSE

Cayuse 2002 Cailloux Vineyard Syrah (Walla Walla (WA)) $55. Even more herbal, and more tart, than the winery's En Cerise bottling. Offers peppery aromas and sour red fruit and chocolate flavors, and is streaked with green through and through. Mouthfeel is creamy, but the finish is tart. **85** *(9/1/2005)*

Cayuse 2000 Cailloux Vineyard Viognier (Walla Walla (WA)) $28. **92** *—P.G. (10/1/2001)*

USA

CE2V

CE2V 2000 Meritage (Napa Valley) $75. A soft, cuddly sort of wine. A core of ripe fruit nestles inside layers of toast, caramel, and dried spices; it's supple and easy from start to finish. **88** *—J.C. (5/1/2004)*

CE2V 2000 Sauvignon Blanc (Napa Valley) $25. **87** *—S.H. (12/1/2001)*

CEAGO VINEGARDEN

Ceago Vinegarden 2001 Camp Masut Cabernet Sauvignon (Mendocino) $32. Here's a wine that strikes you as pretty good as far as it goes, but the palate yearns for greater complexity. It's dry and polished, with rich tannins and a fine balance, but those cherry and blackberry flavors finish a tad thin, especially considering the price. **84** *—S.H. (12/15/2005)*

Ceago Vinegarden 2004 Jeriko Vineyard Chardonnay (Mendocino) $18. This powerfully flavored Chardonnay is laserlike in the intensity of its fruit. Mangoes, pineapples, and lemon custard assault the palate, wrapped in a creamy smooth texture. Not particularly subtle, and not for the faint-hearted, this is a quintessentially ripe California wine. **87** *—S.H. (12/15/2005)*

Ceago Vinegarden 2001 Camp Masut Merlot (Mendocino) $25. This ambitious brand continues to struggle, in its organic-biodynamic way, to master its Mendocino terroir. This Merlot is clean, dry, and very pure, with cherry flavors, yet it needs greater intensity and complexity, and a longer finish. **84** *—S.H. (12/15/2005)*

Ceago Vinegarden 2000 Petite Sirah (Mendocino County) $30. **92** *—S.H. (12/31/2003)*

Ceago Vinegarden 2001 Kathleen's Vineyard Sauvignon Blanc (Mendocino County) $19. **88** *—S.H. (7/1/2003)*

CECCHETTI SEBASTIANI CELLAR

Cecchetti Sebastiani Cellar 1999 Pinot Noir (Central Coast) $14. **82** *(10/1/2002)*

CEDAR MOUNTAIN

Cedar Mountain 1997 Duet Bordeaux Blend (Livermore Valley) $22. **86** *—M.S. (9/1/2000)*

Cedar Mountain 1999 Blanches Vineyard Cabernet Sauvignon (Livermore Valley) $22. **81** *—S.H. (11/15/2003)*

Cedar Mountain 1999 Estate Reserve Blanches Vineyard Cabernet Sauvignon (Livermore Valley) $50. **82** *—S.H. (11/15/2003)*

Cedar Mountain 1998 Blanches Vineyard Chardonnay (Livermore Valley) $18. **84** *(6/1/2000)*

Cedar Mountain 1997 One Oak Vineyard Merlot (Livermore Valley) $21. **84** *—S.H. (8/1/2003)*

Cedar Mountain 1997 Vintage Port (Amador County) $21. **87** *—S.H. (9/1/2003)*

Cedar Mountain 2004 Del Arroyo Vineyard Sauvignon Blanc (Livermore Valley) $12. A solid effort in an easy-drinking, cocktail white wine. It's clean in acidity and has proper lemon and lime flavors, and is basically dry, although you'll pick up on some fruity sweetness in the finish. **84** *—S.H. (8/1/2005)*

Cedar Mountain 1999 Zinfandel (Amador County) $18. **83** *—S.H. (9/1/2003)*

CEDARVILLE

Cedarville 2001 Zinfandel (El Dorado) $22. **82** *(11/1/2003)*

Cedarville Vineyard 2002 Estate Syrah (El Dorado) $25. A bit funky on the nose, with hints of game and dried herbs alongside pepper, plum, and coffee aromas. The mouthfeel is smooth and medium-weight, while the finish turns tannic and a bit rustic. Solid Foothills Syrah. **85** *(9/1/2005)*

CEJA

Ceja 2002 Syrah (Sonoma Coast) $28. Big disagreement over this wine, with West Coast Editor Steve Heimoff lauding it for its balance and ripe black cherry flavors, while Tasting Director Joe

Czerwinski found it a bit vegetal (green bean). It does have a supple, creamy mouthfeel and a pleasant finish of coffee and herb. **87** *(9/1/2005)*

CELADON TV

Celadon TV 2002 Esperanza Vineyard Grenache (Clarksburg) $20. A lovely, fresh, and focused white wine that offers a classy blend of melon, peach, apple, apricot, herb, and mineral flavors. These are layered in a complex, yet easy-to-drink manner. Smooth yet firm, it's got great balance and a good finish. **90** *—J.M. (10/1/2004)*

CELLAR NO. 8

Cellar No. 8 2001 Merlot (North Coast) $14. A nice Merlot with polished flavors of plums, blackberries, and coffee, and a good overlay of smoky oak. It's very dry, but the fruit is ripe and sweet. Finishes with a rich mouthfeel and some acidity. **85** *—S.H. (5/1/2004)*

Cellar No. 8 2001 Zinfandel (North Coast) $14. This is yummy Zin, packed with rich, ripe cherry-berry fruit, tobacco, spice, and chocolate, and it's bone dry and moderate in alcohol. It's a big, flavorful wine, yet has balance and charm. Finishes with a scour of acids and astringent tannins, suggesting barbecued steak or roast lamb. **89** **Best Buy** *—S.H. (5/1/2004)*

CENAY

Cenay 2000 Blue Tooth Vineyard Cabernet Sauvignon (Napa Valley) $30. **89** *—S.H. (12/15/2003)*

Cenay 2000 Rodger's Vineyard Pinot Noir (Napa Valley) $26. **88** *(10/1/2002)*

Cenay 2001 Rodgers Vineyard Pinot Noir (Napa Valley) $26. **84** *—S.H. (7/1/2003)*

Century Oak 2002 Cabernet Sauvignon (Lodi) $13. Here's a soft, simple Cabernet with decent flavors of cherries, blackberries, and coffee. It's dry and balanced, with a polished finish. **83** *—S.H. (12/31/2005)*

CENTURY OAK

Century Oak 2001 Reserve Cabernet Sauvignon (Lodi) $20. Nice texture, rich and soft in tannins, yet not offering much in the way of flavor. Drinks very dry, with modest berry and earth notes. **84** *—S.H. (3/1/2005)*

CERRO CALIENTE

Cerro Caliente 2001 Cabernet Sauvignon (Paso Robles) $19. **83** *—S.H. (12/15/2003)*

Cerro Caliente 2001 Chardonnay (Edna Valley) $18. **83** *—S.H. (10/1/2003)*

Cerro Caliente 2002 Pinot Grigio (Edna Valley) $16. **84** *—S.H. (12/1/2003)*

CHADDSFORD

Chaddsford 2001 Cabernet/Chambourcin Cabernet Blend (Pennsylvania) $15. **83** *—M.S. (3/1/2003)*

Chaddsford 1999 Cabernet Franc (Pennsylvania) $14. Light to the point of being watery, with hints of cherry and green veggies. Sweet-tasting on the finish. **80** *—J.C. (1/1/2004)*

Chaddsford 1998 Seven Valleys Vineyard Chambourcin (Pennsylvania) $16. **83** *—J.C. (8/1/1999)*

Chaddsford 2000 Philip Roth Vineyard Chardonnay (Pennsylvania) $33. **91** *—J.C. (7/1/2002)*

Chaddsford 1998 Pinot Grigio (Pennsylvania) $15. **87** *(8/1/1999)*

Chaddsford 2002 Barrel Select Pinot Noir (Pennsylvania) $25. Very pale in color and light in body, with pretty tea, rose, cola, and spice flavors that pick up sweet raspberries on the finish. **84** *(11/1/2004)*

Chaddsford 1999 Merican Red Blend (Pennsylvania) $35. **85** *—M.S. (3/1/2003)*

Chaddsford 2000 Proprietor's Reserve White Blend (Pennsylvania) $10. This blend of hybrid grapes (40% Seyval Blanc, 39% Vidal Blanc, 21% Vignoles) yields scents of lime, tonic, and green corn husks. Sweet corn flavors fight with sour lime elements on the finish. **80** *—J.C. (1/1/2004)*

Chaddsford 1998 Spring Wine White Blend (Pennsylvania) $9. **83** *—J.C. (8/1/1999)*

CHALK HILL

Chalk Hill 2001 Cabernet Sauvignon (Chalk Hill) $66. Compared to a lush Napa Cab, this has a distinct green olive and French-cured olive character. It must be the terroir, but oak, toasted and spicy, plays an important part. Finally, there's Cabernet's inherent currant flavor. The wine is thoroughly dry and balanced, with smooth tannins. It's a unique Cabernet, but in its own way, very fine. **90** *—S.H. (12/1/2005)*

Chalk Hill 1999 Cabernet Sauvignon (Chalk Hill) $64. **90** *—S.H. (2/1/2003)*

Chalk Hill 2002 Chardonnay (Chalk Hill) $36. A well-behaved Chard with a streak of minerality that uplifts the apple and peach flavors, as well as lees and oak. Finishes a bit rough and earthy, with tobacco leaf acidity. **86** *—S.H. (12/1/2005)*

Chalk Hill 1999 Estate Bottled Chardonnay (Chalk Hill) $42. **92** *—S.H. (12/1/2001)*

Chalk Hill 2002 Estate Vineyard Selection Chardonnay (Chalk Hill) $67. This ultraexpensive Chardonnay comes down along mineral, steel, and wet stone flavors. It's well-oaked, although you'll find tropical fruit, subtly, on the finish. It's extremely elegant, with a long draw of acidity and a classic structure. **90** *—S.H. (12/1/2005)*

Chalk Hill 2000 Merlot (Chalk Hill) $43. This blend of Merlot, Malbec, Cab Franc, and Petit Verdot is layered with blackberry and Indian pudding flavors, generously laced with oriental spices and coffee. It's dry, but the ripeness of the fruit feels sweet through the finish. Soft in acids and tannins; it's instantly drinkable. **89** *—S.H. (12/15/2004)*

Chalk Hill 1998 Adele's Merlot (Chalk Hill) $100. 86 *—S.H. (11/15/2002)*

Chalk Hill 2000 Estate Vineyard Selection Pinot Gris (Chalk Hill) $40. 86 *—S.H. (9/1/2003)*

Chalk Hill 2001 Sauvignon Blanc (Chalk Hill) $24. 90 *—S.H. (10/1/2003)*

Chalk Hill 2003 Estate Sauvignon Blanc (Chalk Hill) $25. Lemony and grassy, this very dry, tart wine is refreshing and zesty. *Sur lie* aging has given it body and structure, while a good proportion of new oak gives complex notes of smoke and vanilla. Totally dry. **88** *—S.H. (12/1/2005)*

CHALONE

Chalone 2003 Chardonnay (Chalone) $30. Here's a soft, full-bodied Chardonnay that has a distinct tang of minerality to it. It's also rich in green apple and white peach flavors, with a coat of toasty oak and a lingering trace of dried herbs on the finish. **88** *—S.H. (12/1/2005)*

Chalone 2001 Chardonnay (Chalone) $25. 91 *—S.H. (12/1/2003)*

Chalone 1998 Chardonnay (Chalone) $31. 90 *—S.H. (10/1/2000)*

Chalone 2003 Chenin Blanc (Chalone) $22. Chalone is one of a handful of California wineries that continues to take Chenin Blanc seriously. This is a dry, young wine, balanced and tart in grapefruit flavors. The acidity is quite high. Try as an alternative to Sauvignon Blanc. **86** *—S.H. (7/1/2005)*

Chalone 2000 Chalone Chenin Blanc (Chalone) $22. 93 *—J.M. (9/1/2003)*

Chalone 2003 Grenache (Chalone) $22. This Rhône variety, when well-made in California, is infused with pure cherry flavors, and so it is here. Very dry, rather pale in color, and light in texture and body, it's well-acidified, with some herbal complexities. Best with Provençal or Mediterranean fare. **88** *—S.H. (8/1/2005)*

Chalone 2001 Pinot Blanc (Chalone) $22. A full-bodied, polished wine, a lot like a big Chard with its creamy, leesy texture and peach and pear flavors. But shows its varietal character with a spicy melon note, and has a nice firm backbone of acidity that makes it an ager. **89** *—S.H. (2/1/2004)*

Chalone 1999 Pinot Blanc (Chalone) $24. 91 *—S.H. (2/1/2001)*

Chalone 1997 Reserve Pinot Blanc (Monterey County) $22. 92 *—L.W. (3/1/2000)*

Chalone 2001 Pinot Noir (Chalone) $25. Chalone's flagship wine in its youth is dark, dense, heavy and tannic. It doesn't show much finesse, and is almost Rhône-like. The winemaker marches to the beat of a drummer who is out of sync with light, delicate Pinot Noirs, but aficionados will stick it in their cellars anyway and keep their fingers crossed. **86** *—S.H. (2/1/2004)*

Chalone 1998 Pinot Noir (Chalone) $35. 85 *—S.H. (10/1/2000)*

Chalone 2001 Gavilan Rhône Red Blend (Chalone) $30. 84 *—S.H. (12/1/2003)*

Chalone 2002 Syrah (Chalone) $25. Starts out with a complex mélange of aromas, including smoky oak and bacon, then quickly turns fruity in the mouth. Blackberries and cherries co-star, sweet and ripe and pure. Soft tannins make this interesting wine drinkable right away. **88** *—S.H. (12/31/2004)*

Chalone 2000 Syrah (Chalone) $30. 91 *—J.M. (12/1/2002)*

CHAMELEON

Chameleon 2002 Barbera (Lake County) $15. This is a rustic wine, country-style in its fairly aggressive tannins, the kind of red to down without being too fussy. It's totally dry, with berry, coffee, and earth flavors. Might improve with age, if you care to cellar it. **84** *—S.H. (8/1/2005)*

Chameleon 1997 Sangiovese (North Coast) $18. 86 *—J.C. (10/1/1999)*

Chameleon 2002 Syrah (Napa Valley) $25. West Coast Editor Steve Heimoff found this wine thin and unripe, but our other reviewers praised its briary, herbal notes balanced by bright cherry fruit, calling it complex and elegant. Picks up hints of bacon and spice on the long finish. **89** *(9/1/2005)*

CHANDLER REACH

Chandler Reach 2000 Monte Regale Bordeaux Blend (Yakima Valley) $22. 86 *—P.G. (9/1/2003)*

Chandler Reach 2001 Syrah (Yakima Valley) $26. 89 *—P.G. (9/1/2003)*

CHANDON

Chandon NV Blanc de Noirs Champagne Blend (California) $17. 86 *—S.H. (12/1/2002)*

Chandon NV Brut Classic Champagne Blend (California) $17. Heads right down the middle, a popular style of bubbly with a little some-

USA

thing for everyone. Dry, with suggestions of lime, dough, and sweet oak, and nicely effervescent. Finishes with a clean, racy acidity. **87** *—S.H. (12/31/2004)*

Chandon NV Brut Classic 198 Champagne Blend (California) $16. 86 *—J.M. (12/1/2002)*

Chandon NV Étoile Champagne Blend (Napa-Sonoma) $35. 88 *(12/1/2001)*

Chandon NV Étoile Brut Champagne Blend (California) $35. 93 *—S.H. (12/1/2000)*

Chandon NV Étoile Brut Sur Lees 1999 Champagne Blend (Napa-Sonoma) $35. Drier than the '96 brut, and the better for it. This is an austere, tight wine of finesse. It displays citrus, herb, smoke, and yeast flavors, and good acidity. It is very elegant, the kind of wine made for toasts. **90** *—S.H. (12/31/2004)*

Chandon NV Étoile Rosé Champagne Blend (California) $40. 85 *—J.C. (12/1/2001)*

Chandon NV Étoile Rosé Sur Lees 1999 Champagne Blend (Napa-Sonoma) $40. There's a good wine in here and it should emerge in some years. Right now, it's full-bodied, rough, and acidic, with suggestions of cherries, limes, and yeasty smoke. It would be a shame to drink it now. Best after 2007. **90** *—S.H. (12/31/2004)*

Chandon NV Reserve Blanc de Noirs Champagne Blend (Sonoma-Napa) $24. Full-bodied and brisk, a big sparkler that showcases its strawberry-raspberry flavors. Fundamentally dry, although you'll detect some sweetness on the finish. **87** *—S.H. (12/31/2004)*

Chandon NV Reserve Brut Champagne Blend (Napa-Sonoma) $24. Delicate, refined and very dry. This is one of the more elegant bruts around, with a silky mouth feel and very fine texture. Seems to float in the mouth, with gentle lime and vanilla flavors. **92 Editors' Choice** *—S.H. (12/31/2004)*

Chandon NV Reserve Brut Champagne Blend (Napa County) $24. 89 *—S.H. (12/1/2000)*

Chandon 1995 Vintage Brut Champagne Blend (California) $50. 86 *(12/1/2001)*

Chandon 1996 Blanc de Blancs Mt. Veeder Ranch Chardonnay (Mount Veeder) $60. 88 *(12/1/2001)*

Chandon 2000 Pinot Noir (Carneros) $29. 89 *— (9/1/2002)*

Chandon NV Blanc de Noirs Sparkling Blend (California) $17. 88 *—S.H. (12/1/2003)*

Chandon NV Étoile Sparkling Blend (Napa-Sonoma) $35. 90 *—S.H. (12/1/2003)*

Chandon NV Extra-Dry Riche Sparkling Blend (California) $17. 87 *—S.H. (12/1/2003)*

Chandon NV Reserve Sparkling Blend (Sonoma-Napa) $24. 91 Editors' Choice *—S.H. (12/1/2003)*

CHANGALA

Changala 1999 Syrah (Paso Robles) $16. 86 *—S.H. (12/1/2002)*

CHANNING DAUGHTERS

Channing Daughters 1999 Scuttlehole Chardonnay (Long Island) $13. 84 *—J.C. (4/1/2001)*

Channing Daughters 1999 Fresh Red Red Blend (Long Island) $15. 84 *—J.C. (4/1/2001)*

CHANNING PERRINE

Channing Perrine 1999 Mudd Vineyard Fleur de Terre Merlot (North Fork of Long Island) $16. 83 *—J.C. (4/1/2001)*

CHANTICLEER

Chanticleer 2001 Cabernet Sauvignon (Napa Valley) $45. A complex wine, brimming with cinnamon and spice flavors and redolent of coffee, chocolate, black cherry, black currant, raspberry, herb, and anise flavors. The tannins are firm but ripe, and the finish is quite long. A first release from winemaker Chris Dearden. **91** *—J.M. (12/31/2004)*

CHAPPELLET

Chappellet 2002 Pritchard Hill Estate Vineyard Cabernet Sauvignon (Napa Valley) $120. Stands out not just because of its size, but also for its balance. It's a big wine, bursting with flamboyant black currant, cassis, mocha, and smoky oak flavors with rich, thick, and sweetly ripe tannins. The finish lasts for a very long time. So good now, you might miss its youthful character if you cellar it too long. **95** *—S.H. (12/15/2005)*

Chappellet 1999 Pritchard Hill Estate Vineyard Cabernet Sauvignon (Napa Valley) $110. 92 Cellar Selection *(8/1/2003)*

Chappellet 1997 Signature Cabernet Sauvignon (Napa Valley) $35. 90 *(11/1/2000)*

Chappellet 2003 Chardonnay (Napa Valley) $28. With apple and pear flavors and some oak, this is a clean Chard with mineral overtones. Nothing really stands out or clobbers you sidewise. It's just a well put-together wine, tasteful and understated. **90** *—S.H. (5/1/2005)*

Chappellet 2000 Signature Chardonnay (Napa Valley) $35. 90 *—S.H. (2/1/2003)*

Chappellet 2003 Dry Chenin Blanc (Napa Valley) $15. This is about as well as Chenin can do in California. This bone dry, medium-bodied wine is tart in acids, and has herbaceous, apple and wax bean flavors and a clean finish. **87** *—S.H. (12/15/2005)*

Chappellet 1997 Old Vine Cuvée Chenin Blanc (Napa Valley) $14. 92 Best Buy *—M.S. (12/15/2003)*

Chappellet 2001 Merlot (Napa Valley) $28. Not a blockbuster, but absolutely lovely. Well-balanced with sweet tannins and crisp acidity, the flavors veer include cherries and rich, sweet fresh herbs. The dryness is nicely contrasted with a long, sweet oaky-fruity finish. 90 *—S.H. (12/15/2004)*

Chappellet 1996 Sangiovese (Napa Valley) $23. 91 *—S.H. (11/1/1999)*

CHARIOT

Chariot 2000 Sangiovese (Central Coast) $15. 88 *—J.M. (5/1/2002)*

CHARLES CREEK

Charles Creek 2001 Hawk Hill Vineyard Chardonnay (Russian River Valley) $22. 85 *—S.H. (6/1/2003)*

Charles Creek 2003 Las Abuelas Hyde Vineyard Chardonnay (Carneros) $39. Impresses for the sheer volume of the fruit. Flamboyant tropical pineapple, mango, guava, lots of dusty spices, rich oak, but manages to hold onto balance, dryness and even a sense of finesse all the way through the long finish. 92 *—S.H. (6/1/2005)*

Charles Creek 2002 Vista del Halcon Chardonnay (Russian River Valley) $22. Oaky, with a raw, acidic mouthfeel that accentuates the lean, citrusy fruit. The wine's got knuckles. 83 *—S.H. (6/1/2004)*

Charles Creek 2001 Miradero Merlot (Sonoma-Napa) $22. 90 *—S.H. (12/31/2003)*

CHARLES KRUG

Charles Krug 1996 Generations Bordeaux Blend (Napa Valley) $34. 89 *(4/1/2001)*

Charles Krug 2002 Family Reserve Generations Cabernet Blend (Napa Valley) $42. Here's a well-oaked Cab that shows the winery's traditional preference for balance over power. It's not a blockbuster Napa Cab, but a subtle, harmonious one, with an elegant interplay of fruit and tannins. Drink now and over the next several years. 89 *—S.H. (11/15/2005)*

Charles Krug 2002 Peter Mondavi Family Cabernet Sauvignon (Napa Valley) $24. World-Class Cabernet, made in the modern style. It's softly textured, with melted tannins and low acidity. Black currants, cassis, cherries, milk chocolate, and spices come together and last through a long finish. 88 *—S.H. (11/15/2005)*

Charles Krug 1996 Peter Mondavi Family Cabernet Sauvignon (Napa Valley) $16. 86 *—S.H. (9/1/1999)*

Charles Krug 2002 Vintage Selection Cabernet Sauvignon (Napa Valley) $51. A ripe but firm, balanced Cabernet. The black currant and cassis flavors mesh well with the oak and soft tannins, leading to real elegance. Drinks well now, but should hold for a good 10 years, if not longer. 92 Cellar Selection *—S.H. (11/15/2005)*

Charles Krug 1995 Vintage Selection Cabernet Sauvignon (Napa Valley) $47. 89 *(12/15/1999)*

Charles Krug 2001 Chardonnay (Napa Valley) $17. 88 *—S.H. (6/1/2003)*

Charles Krug 1999 Family Reserve Chardonnay (Carneros) $21. 88 *—S.H. (12/1/2001)*

Charles Krug 2002 Peter Mondavi Family Chardonnay (Napa Valley) $17. Tight, with citrus, apple, and pear flavors and high acidity. It's a bracing wine that stimulates the taste buds. Winemaker effects include plenty of sweet oak, but it's still lean and angular. 85 *—S.H. (2/1/2004)*

Charles Krug 1999 Family Reserve Generations Meritage (Napa Valley) $35. 91 *—S.H. (3/1/2003)*

Charles Krug 1999 Merlot (Napa Valley) $21. 90 Editors' Choice *—S.H. (8/1/2003)*

Charles Krug 1997 P.Mondavi Family Reserve Merlot (Napa Valley) $25. 91 Editors' Choice *(6/1/2001)*

Charles Krug 1996 Pinot Noir (Carneros) $16. 90 Best Buy *—S.H. (6/1/1999)*

Charles Krug 1999 Pinot Noir (Carneros) $18. 88 *(10/1/2002)*

Charles Krug 1998 Peter Mondavi Family Pinot Noir (Napa Valley) $17. 87 *—S.H. (11/15/2001)*

Charles Krug 2002 Peter Mondavi Family Pinot Noir (Carneros) $20. Light, silky and elegant. Has a soft, pliant mouth feel, with pleasant cherry, herb, and cola flavors. 85 *—S.H. (2/1/2005)*

Charles Krug 1999 Family Reserve Sangiovese (Napa Valley) $20. 90 Editors' Choice *—S.H. (12/1/2002)*

Charles Krug 1998 Sauvignon Blanc (Napa Valley) $13. 88 *—M.S. (11/15/1999)*

Charles Krug 1999 Sauvignon Blanc (Napa Valley) $13. 86 *(4/1/2001)*

Charles Krug 2003 Peter Mondavi Family Sauvignon Blanc (Napa Valley) $16. Comes down firmly on the grassy, lime and gooseberry side, a bone dry, tart wine with high acidity. Very clean and proper, a refreshing apéritif, and will go well with a wide variety of food. 86 *—S.H. (10/1/2004)*

Charles Krug 2001 Zinfandel (Napa Valley) $15. 88 *(11/1/2003)*

Charles Krug 1998 Zinfandel (Alexander Valley) $12. 89 Best Buy *(4/1/2001)*

Charles Krug 2003 Peter Mondavi Family Zinfandel (Napa Valley) $20. Here's a balanced, warming Zin that shows what the variety can achieve when carefully monitored. While not a blockbuster, the wine's berry and cherry flavors have a hearty finish, with some dusty tannins. **87** *—S.H. (11/15/2005)*

Charles Krug 2000 Peter Mondavi Family Zinfandel (Napa Valley) $15. A thin, scraggly Zin, marked with faint berry flavors and dry tannins. Finishes astringent and watery. **82** *—S.H. (5/1/2004)*

CHÂTEAU BENOIT

Château Benoit 2000 Pinot Noir (Oregon) $18. 83 *(10/1/2002)*

Château Benoit 2000 Kestrel Vineyard Pinot Noir (Willamette Valley) $40. **87** *(10/1/2002)*

CHÂTEAU BIANCA

Château Bianca 2000 Barrel-Fermented Chardonnay (Willamette Valley) $10. **81** *—P.G. (8/1/2003)*

Château Bianca 2001 Estate Reserve Chardonnay (Willamette Valley) $20. A real letdown. This is a winery with some wonderful, elegant white wines, but here there is harsh, hot, tannic, raw new oak, and banana-flavored fruit. **83** *—P.G. (10/1/2004)*

Château Bianca 2000 Winery Estate Reserve Chardonnay (Willamette Valley) $20. **81** *—P.G. (8/1/2003)*

Château Bianca 2001 Estate Bottled Gewürztraminer (Willamette Valley) $9. **83** *—P.G. (12/31/2002)*

Château Bianca 2002 Estate Pinot Blanc (Willamette Valley) $12. If you don't mind a healthy dose of honey flavor in your Pinot Blanc, this is a wine to admire. The elegant fruit nicely blends white peaches and kiwi, and the kiss of honey smoothes out the middle into a very satisfying finish. **88 Best Buy** *—P.G. (10/1/2004)*

Château Bianca 2001 Wetzel Family Estate Pinot Blanc (Willamette Valley) $18. **85** *—P.G. (8/1/2003)*

Château Bianca 2002 Pinot Gris (Willamette Valley) $10. Pears leap out of the glass, ripe, round and softly seductive. This wine shows a lovely balance and a wonderful mouthfeel, with flavor that seems to gather strength through the middle. **88 Best Buy** *—P.G. (10/1/2004)*

Château Bianca 2001 Pinot Noir (Willamette Valley) $12. There's not much going on here. Pale, with scents of wild strawberry, it slips into a very light, herbal set of flavors and glides quietly away. Soundly made, and for the price, it does the job. **85** *—P.G. (10/1/2004)*

Château Bianca 1999 Pinot Noir (Oregon) $10. **83** *—P.G. (4/1/2002)*

Château Bianca 2001 Cellar Select Pinot Noir (Willamette Valley) $16. This is clearly, identifiably Pinot, and it displays a broadly accessible palate of varietal flavors. Beetroot, cranberry, some sassafras and cola, with well-modulated tannins and a nice, svelte, varietal finish. Nothing spectacular, but a very nice effort for the money. **87** *—P.G. (10/1/2004)*

Château Bianca 1997 Estate Reserve Pinot Noir (Willamette Valley) $25. **85** *—P.G. (11/1/2001)*

Château Bianca 2003 Riesling (Willamette Valley) $9. Quite a lovely wine, with a beguiling nose that sends up sweet floral/citrus blossom scents that lead into a core of crisp tangerine/orange peel fruit. There is a very nice grip and concentration to the midpalate, and this is one of those wines that you want to return to again and again. **89 Best Buy** *—P.G. (10/1/2004)*

CHÂTEAU FELICE

Château Felice 2002 Acier Chardonnay (Russian River Valley) $16. **84** *—S.H. (12/1/2003)*

Château Felice 2001 Syrah (Chalk Hill) $22. **82** *—S.H. (12/1/2003)*

Château Felice 2001 Zinfandel (Chalk Hill) $16. **83** *(11/1/2003)*

CHÂTEAU FRANK

Château Frank 1995 Blanc de Blancs Champagne Blend (Finger Lakes) $25. **83** *—P.G. (6/1/2001)*

Château Frank 1996 Blanc de Noirs Red Blend (Finger Lakes) $25. **87** *—M.M. (12/1/2001)*

CHÂTEAU JULIEN

Château Julien 1999 Cabernet Sauvignon (Monterey County) $10. **80** *—S.H. (9/12/2002)*

Château Julien 1998 Barrel Aged Cabernet Sauvignon (Monterey County) $10. **87 Best Buy** *—S.H. (5/1/2001)*

Château Julien 1998 Estate Vineyard Cabernet Sauvignon (Monterey County) $22. **86** *—S.H. (12/1/2001)*

Château Julien 2001 Private Reserve Cabernet Sauvignon (Monterey County) $36. Combines ultra-ripe black currant, cassis, cherry, and coffee flavors with some oak, wrapped in a tart, dry texture that finishes with a sharp edge of tannins. Best to let this still-young wine sit for a year or two. **85** *—S.H. (12/1/2005)*

Château Julien 1999 Private Reserve Cabernet Sauvignon (Monterey County) $36. **87** *—S.H. (10/1/2003)*

Château Julien 1996 Private Reserve Cabernet Sauvignon (Monterey County) $28. **87** *(2/1/2000)*

Château Julien 2001 Chardonnay (Monterey County) $10. **85** *—S.H. (2/1/2003)*

Château Julien 2000 Estate Chardonnay (Monterey County) $22. 89 *—S.H. (12/15/2002)*

Château Julien 1999 Estate Vineyard Chardonnay (Monterey County) $22. 88 *(8/1/2001)*

Château Julien 2000 Private Reserve Sur Lie Chardonnay (Monterey County) $30. 86 *—S.H. (2/1/2003)*

Château Julien 1997 Private Reserve Sur Lie Chardonnay (Monterey County) $20. 91 Editors' Choice *(2/1/2000)*

Château Julien 2001 Barrel Aged Merlot (Monterey County) $10. A little green and sharp, but clean and dry, with slight cherry-berry flavors and firm tannins. **82** *—S.H. (3/1/2005)*

Château Julien 1998 Barrel Aged Merlot (Monterey County) $10. 85 Best Buy *—S.H. (5/1/2001)*

Château Julien 1999 Estate Merlot (Monterey County) $22. 85 *—S.H. (11/15/2002)*

Château Julien 2001 Estate Vineyard Merlot (Monterey County) $22. Smells and tastes a little hot and over-ripe, as if some shriveled berries ended up in the hopper. Beyond that, dry and soft, with blackberry and cocoa flavors. **84** *—S.H. (3/1/2005)*

Château Julien 2001 Private Reserve Merlot (Monterey County) $36. Soft, fruity, and simple, with cherry-chocolate flavors, this dry red wine simply lacks vivacity. **82** *—S.H. (12/1/2005)*

USA

Château Julien 1999 Private Reserve Merlot (Monterey County) $30. 86 *—S.H. (12/31/2003)*

Château Julien 1997 Private Reserve Merlot (Monterey County) $20. 86 *—S.H. (5/1/2001)*

Château Julien 2003 Pinot Grigio (Monterey County) $10. Juicy and refreshing, a nice afternoon apéritif. You'll relish the ripe fig, melon, and spice flavors and crispness. **84** *—S.H. (12/15/2004)*

Château Julien 2002 Barrel Aged Pinot Grigio (Monterey County) $10. A fun wine with lemon-and-lime flavors, grassy hay, and a flourish of ripe fig. Very, very dry, with a crisp, tart acidity that cleanses the palate and prepares it for food. **85** *—S.H. (2/1/2004)*

Château Julien 1997 Sangiovese (California) $13. 87 *(2/1/2000)*

Château Julien 2001 Barrel Aged Sangiovese (Monterey County) $10. An easy-drinking wine marked by cherry, herb, and tobacco flavors, a silky texture, and crisp acidity. Has just a tiny too much sweetness, which gives it a cough-mediciney note, but offers pretty good bang for your buck. **85** *—S.H. (3/1/2004)*

Château Julien 2001 Sauvignon Blanc (Monterey County) $9. 84 *—S.H. (9/1/2003)*

Château Julien 1998 Barrel Aged Sauvignon Blanc (Monterey County) $8. 84 *(2/1/2000)*

Château Julien 2002 Syrah (Monterey County) $22. Must come from a warmer part of the county, because the fruit is very ripe and elaborate. Delicious in peppery blackberry, leather, and plum flavors, and dry, with rich, complex tannins. A wine to watch. **89** *—S.H. (10/1/2004)*

Château Julien 1999 Syrah (Monterey County) $15. 85 *(10/1/2001)*

Château Julien 2000 Barrel Aged Zinfandel (Monterey County) $10. 85 *(11/1/2003)*

CHÂTEAU LAFAYETTE RENEAU

Château Lafayette Reneau 1999 Owner's Reserve Cabernet Sauvignon (Finger Lakes) $45. 86 *—M.S. (3/1/2003)*

Château Lafayette Reneau 2000 Barrel-Fermented Chardonnay (Finger Lakes) $13. 84 *—J.M. (1/1/2003)*

Château Lafayette Reneau 2001 Johannisberg Riesling (Finger Lakes) $12. 85 *—J.C. (8/1/2003)*

CHÂTEAU MONTELENA

Château Montelena 1998 Chardonnay (Napa Valley) $30. 87 *(7/1/2001)*

Château Montelena 1996 Chardonnay (Napa Valley) $29. 90 *—S.H. (6/1/1999)*

Château Montelena 2000 Zinfandel (Napa Valley) $25. 87 *—S.H. (9/1/2003)*

CHÂTEAU POTELLE

Château Potelle 1997 V.G.S. Cabernet Sauvignon (Mount Veeder) $63. 92 *(11/1/2000)*

Château Potelle 2002 VGS Chardonnay (Mount Veeder) $35. This huge wine captures the essence of mountain fruit. Dense and concentrated in ripe pear, tropical fruit, and spice flavors, it also oozes elaborate honey, marzipan, and buttered toast from oak. Has the weight and intensity of a great white Burgundy. **93** *—S.H. (5/1/2005)*

Château Potelle 1998 VGS Chardonnay (Mount Veeder) $39. 94 *—S.H. (9/1/2002)*

Château Potelle 2002 Riviera Red Blend (Paso Robles) $15. 85 *—S.H. (11/15/2003)*

Château Potelle 2001 Sauvignon Blanc (Napa Valley) $15. 90 Best Buy *—S.H. (10/1/2003)*

Château Potelle 2001 Syrah (Paso Robles) $24. Made in the firm, grippy style typical of Potelle's reds, this Syrah could use a couple of years to settle down. But once it does, it'll be fine, with herbal, pepper, and meat accents to the chewy berry fruit. **88** *(9/1/2005)*

Château Potelle 2001 Zinfandel (Paso Robles) $22. 90 Editors' Choice *(11/1/2003)*

Château Potelle 1999 Old Vines Zinfandel (Amador County) $18. 87 *—S.H. (7/1/2002)*

Château Potelle 1999 V.G.S. Zinfandel (Mount Veeder) $50. 90 *—S.H. (9/1/2002)*

Château Potelle 1997 V.G.S. Zinfandel (Mount Veeder) $43. 86 *—J.C. (2/1/2000)*

Château Potelle 2000 VGS Zinfandel (Mount Veeder) $53. 91 *—S.H. (3/1/2003)*

CHÂTEAU SOUVERAIN

Château Souverain 1996 Cabernet Sauvignon (Sonoma County) $17. 91 *(11/15/1999)*

Château Souverain 2001 Cabernet Sauvignon (Alexander Valley) $20. Shows the balance and elegance this winery and region are known for, with modest cherry-blackberry flavors and a touch of smoky oak. Very dry, with a good grip of tannins, this is a nice restaurant wine. **86** *—S.H. (3/1/2005)*

Château Souverain 1999 Cabernet Sauvignon (Alexander Valley) $20. 87 *—S.H. (8/1/2003)*

Château Souverain 2000 Winemaker's Reserve Cabernet Sauvignon (Alexander Valley) $35. Offers lush, intricate flavors of blackberries, cassis, roasted coffeebean, sweet milk chocolate, and toasty oak in a soft, gentle wine that has complexity and interest. Not an ager, but a real beauty. **91** *—S.H. (11/15/2004)*

Château Souverain 1997 Winemaker's Reserve Cabernet Sauvignon (Alexander Valley) $35. 92 Editors' Choice *—S.H. (12/1/2001)*

Château Souverain 2003 Chardonnay (Sonoma County) $14. Lots to like in this wine. It has ripe peach and pear flavors, with a blast of smoky oak, buttered toast, and lees. Finishes rich in honeyed fruit. **86** *—S.H. (3/1/2005)*

Château Souverain 2001 Chardonnay (Sonoma County) $14. 86 *—S.H. (6/1/2003)*

Château Souverain 1999 Chardonnay (Sonoma County) $14. 85 *—S.H. (5/1/2001)*

Château Souverain 2003 Winemaker's Reserve Chardonnay (Russian River Valley) $30. This barrel-fermented wine was aged in 76% new French oak. The Chardonnay has a spicy vanilla character of its own. That double whammy drowns out the tropical fruit, making the wine all toast and sweet vanilla. **82** *—S.H. (11/15/2005)*

Château Souverain 2000 Winemaker's Reserve Chardonnay (Alexander Valley) $25. 87 *—J.M. (12/15/2002)*

Château Souverain 1997 Merlot (Sonoma County) $17. 87 *—J.C. (7/1/2000)*

Château Souverain 2000 Merlot (Alexander Valley) $18. 89 *—S.H. (8/1/2003)*

Château Souverain 1997 Sauvignon Blanc (Sonoma County) $9. 87 Best Buy *—S.H. (9/1/1999)*

Château Souverain 2002 Sauvignon Blanc (Alexander Valley) $14. Grassy, citrusy, and tart, but those who like this slightly aggressive style will love it. It's dry as dust, with big acids. The winemaker barrel fermented it in order to bring sweeter, softer features, and has succeeded. **87** *—S.H. (2/1/2004)*

Château Souverain 2000 Sauvignon Blanc (Sonoma County) $12. 84 *—S.H. (11/15/2001)*

Château Souverain 2000 Syrah (Alexander Valley) $20. 87 *—S.H. (2/1/2003)*

Château Souverain 1997 Zinfandel (Dry Creek Valley) $13. 86 *—J.C. (5/1/2000)*

Château Souverain 2001 Zinfandel (Dry Creek Valley) $18. 87 *(11/1/2003)*

Château Souverain 1998 Winemaker's Reserve Zinfandel (Dry Creek Valley) $25. 89 *—P.G. (3/1/2001)*

CHÂTEAU ST. JEAN

Château St. Jean 2001 Estate Vineyard Cabernet Franc (Sonoma Valley) $50. As good as this wine is, in my opinion Cabernet Franc by itself cannot make a great wine. It's certainly delicious, with cherry, currant, pecan pie, and vanilla flavors, and the tannins are soft, sweet and complex. But it lacks the depth that a darker varietal, like Cabernet, brings to the table. **88** *—S.H. (3/1/2005)*

Château St. Jean 2002 Cabernet Sauvignon (Sonoma County) $27. Easy, gentle, and soft, this is a simple, fairly thin Cab that's balanced and harmonious. The blackberry and currant flavors, accented by oak, will go well with a juicy steak. **84** *—S.H. (12/31/2005)*

Château St. Jean 2001 Cabernet Sauvignon (Sonoma County) $27. Here's a big, bold wine, made with super-ripe grapes that achieved intense, although varietally correct, flavors. It's also very oaky. Dry, with a creamy texture and a very long finish in which the cassis sinks into the tongue and stays there. It will develop nicely through 2007. **89** *—S.H. (8/1/2004)*

Château St. Jean 1996 Cinq Cepages Cabernet Sauvignon (Sonoma County) $33. 92 *—J.C. (2/1/2000)*

Château St. Jean 2000 Cinq Cepages Cabernet Sauvignon (Sonoma County) $70. This fine wine, which is at its best now, offers polished flavors of currants, blackberries, and herbs, with smoky nuances from oak. It is smooth and polished in the mouth, with a good balance of acids and tannins. Not an ager, but complex and elegant. **90** *—S.H. (5/1/2004)*

Château St. Jean 1998 Cinq Cepages Cabernet Sauvignon (Sonoma Valley) $70. 90 *(6/1/2002)*

Château St. Jean 1999 Reserve Cabernet Sauvignon (Sonoma Valley) $90. Oh, how tough this wine is now. It's like a mummy, wrapped in tannins. It would be easy to pass it by until you notice the intensity of cherry-blackberry fruit. Despite its age, the wine is still aggressively young. Will it soften and improve with cellaring? Probably. Try in 2009. **90** *—S.H. (11/15/2004)*

Château St. Jean 1998 Chardonnay (Sonoma County) $12. 88 *—L.W. (3/1/2000)*

Château St. Jean 2003 Chardonnay (Sonoma County) $14. Rich and intricate, a Chard that satisfies with its array of white peach, pineapple, mango, buttercream, and spice flavors. Finishes with a slightly sweet, vanilla ice cream flavor. **86** *—S.H. (5/1/2005)*

Château St. Jean 2000 Chardonnay (Sonoma County) $14. 87 *—J.M. (12/15/2002)*

Château St. Jean 2001 Belle Terre Vineyard Chardonnay (Alexander Valley) $24. Very rich and compelling, a beautiful wine with layers of tropical fruit, pear, buttered toast, vanilla, and spicy aromas and flavors that mingle on the palate. The creamy texture leads to a honeyed finish. **90** *—S.H. (2/1/2004)*

USA

Château St. Jean 1999 Belle Terre Vineyard Chardonnay (Alexander Valley) $22. 89 *—S.H. (12/1/2001)*

Château St. Jean 1997 Durell Vineyard Chardonnay (Carneros) $24. 89 *—L.W. (11/1/1999)*

Château St. Jean 1998 Reserve Chardonnay (Sonoma County) $45. 91 *(7/1/2001)*

Château St. Jean 2001 Robert Young Vineyard Chardonnay (Alexander Valley) $25. From this famed vineyard, an exciting wine. It's lush in ripe tropical fruit, peach, crème brulée, and Oriental spice flavors, with a firmly mineral spine. The texture is rich and creamy. Brisk acidity perfectly counterpoints the fruit. **92** *—S.H. (12/15/2004)*

Château St. Jean 1999 Robert Young Vineyard Chardonnay (Alexander Valley) $25. 90 *—J.M. (12/15/2002)*

Château St. Jean 1996 Robert Young Vyd Reserve Chardonnay (Sonoma County) $24. 88 *(6/1/2000)*

Château St. Jean 2003 Fumé Blanc (Sonoma County) $13. This is a very nice wine, rich and fruity, but crisp and clean all the way through the long finish. Brims with ripe lemon and lime, fig, and vanilla flavors. **87** *—S.H. (5/1/2005)*

Château St. Jean 2001 Fumé Blanc (Sonoma County) $13. 87 *—J.M. (7/1/2003)*

Château St. Jean 2003 La Petite Étoile Vineyard Fumé Blanc (Russian River Valley) $20. In every vintage you can predict one thing about this wine: that it will be extremely oaky. Here the aromas are so toasted they almost cover the peach and melon lurking below. The palate offers lots of spice and white pepper along with peach, apple, and herbs. The intensity of the fruit and the natural acidity save it from falling into the category of "severely overoaked." **87** *(7/1/2005)*

Château St. Jean 2000 La Petite Étoile Vineyard Fumé Blanc (Russian River Valley) $20. 84 *(8/1/2002)*

Château St. Jean 2003 Gewürztraminer (Sonoma County) $15. Fans of the variety will cheer the intense oriental spiciness that seasons the flowery, fruity flavors. Made Alsatian style, the wine is pretty dry, with a hint of honey on the finish. **84** *—S.H. (10/1/2004)*

Château St. Jean 2004 Johannisberg Riesling (Sonoma County) $15. Watery and sweet, this wine isn't offering much, especially at this price. It has simple syrup flavors and is low in acids. **81** *—S.H. (12/1/2005)*

Château St. Jean 2002 Johannisberg Riesling (Sonoma County) $15. 87 *—J.C. (8/1/2003)*

Château St. Jean 1995 Belle Terre Vyds Special Select Johannisberg Riesling (Sonoma County) $30. 90 *—J.C. (12/31/1999)*

Château St. Jean 2001 Reserve Malbec (Sonoma County) $55. Decent, but you'll do way better in Argentina, and save lots of bucks. Semi-unripe, with green, herb, and cherry flavors. **83** *—S.H. (7/1/2005)*

Château St. Jean 2002 Merlot (California) $15. Ripe, with cherry and blackberry flavors and a dose of smoky oak. Finishes dry. Shows some elegance in the smooth texture and balance. **85** *—S.H. (2/1/2005)*

Château St. Jean 2001 Merlot (Sonoma County) $25. Balanced, graceful and elegant, a wine with smooth, dusty tannins that's easy to drink, but has complexity and style. Has polished flavors of blackberries, green olives, dried herbs and vanilla. Rich and satisfying. **88** *—S.H. (8/1/2004)*

Château St. Jean 1997 Merlot (Sonoma County) $18. 92 *(11/15/1999)*

Château St. Jean 2000 Reserve Merlot (Sonoma County) $90. Held back unusually long for a Merlot. The tannins are still big and dusty. Yet there's a core of black cherry fruit, and a softness that makes the wine beguiling. Probably best now, with lamb. **89** *—S.H. (10/1/2005)*

Château St. Jean 1997 Reserve Merlot (Sonoma County) $100. 93 Cellar Selection *—J.M. (11/15/2002)*

Château St. Jean 2002 Pinot Noir (Sonoma County) $19. A textbook Pinot that tastes like it has plenty of Russian River Valley grapes inside. Light and silky in texture, but with rich, complex varietal flavors of cherries, cola, rhubarb, vanilla, and mocha. **88** *—S.H. (11/1/2004)*

Château St. Jean 2002 Durell Vineyard Pinot Noir (Sonoma Valley) $45. All tasters praised this wine for its plushness of flavor, delicate body and long, complex finish. Heaps of ripe cherries, toffee, vanilla, and chocolate wrapped in a smooth, creamy-crisp texture. **88** *(11/1/2004)*

Château St. Jean 1999 Durell Vineyard Pinot Noir (Carneros) $38. 87 *(10/1/2002)*

Château St. Jean 1997 La Petite Étoile Sauvignon Blanc (Sonoma) $13. 84 *—M.M. (9/1/1999)*

CHÂTEAU STE. MICHELLE

Château Ste. Michelle 2002 Cabernet Sauvignon (Columbia Valley (WA)) $16. Odd, disjointed, and chalky, It tastes as if it's been softened up a bit, but nothing knits together and there is neither depth nor definition to the fruit. The unusual blend includes 6% Sangiovese and 2% Syrah. **84** *—P.G. (12/15/2005)*

Château Ste. Michelle 1999 Cabernet Sauvignon (Columbia Valley (WA)) $15. 87 *—P.G. (6/1/2002)*

Château Ste. Michelle 2002 Canoe Ridge Cabernet Sauvignon (Columbia Valley (WA)) $22. Soft, light strawberry/cherry flavors suggest a much cheaper wine. Beyond the simple fruit it turns tart and astringent, with very little midpalate. **85** *—P.G. (12/15/2005)*

Château Ste. Michelle 2000 Canoe Ridge Estate Vineyard Cabernet Sauvignon (Columbia Valley (WA)) $24. 89 *—P.G. (12/31/2003)*

Château Ste. Michelle 1999 Canoe Ridge Estates Cabernet Sauvignon (Columbia Valley (WA)) $24. 90 *—P.G. (9/1/2002)*

Château Ste. Michelle 2001 Cold Creek Vineyard Cabernet Sauvignon (Columbia Valley (WA)) $29. From one of Washington's best vineyards, this is a complex, Bordeaux-like wine that mixes fruit, mineral, and barrel flavors with an even hand. Lightly spiced with fresh herbs, back-loaded with cocoa/espresso flavors, this is well-defined, with firm, ripe but not at all unctuous fruit. Hold 6–10 years. **91 Cellar Selection** *—P.G. (12/15/2004)*

Château Ste. Michelle 1999 Cold Creek Vineyard Cabernet Sauvignon (Columbia Valley (WA)) $29. 88 *—P.G. (12/31/2002)*

Château Ste. Michelle 1996 Cold Creek Vineyard Cabernet Sauvignon (Columbia Valley (WA)) $25. 91 *—L.W. (2/1/2000)*

Château Ste. Michelle 2001 Reserve Cabernet Sauvignon (Columbia Valley (WA)) $33. Thin and aggressively tannic, this wine does not seem to have to fruit intensity to overcome its stubbornly hard, tough tannins. **86** *—P.G. (4/1/2005)*

Château Ste. Michelle 2003 Chardonnay (Columbia Valley (WA)) $12. Pleasing pear and light vanilla aromas lead into a nicely textured, lively, and distinctly un-flabby chardonnay. This is the least expensive of five chardonnays from Ste. Michelle that all showcase winemaker Bob Bertheau's elegant, light touch. Happily, there is no reliance on buttered popcorn flavors or excessive new toasty oak to make the flavors pop; this is a great food wine, way ahead of most budget bottles from California. **88 Best Buy** *—P.G. (11/15/2005)*

Château Ste. Michelle 2000 Chardonnay (Columbia Valley (WA)) $13. 89 Best Buy *—P.G. (7/1/2002)*

Château Ste. Michelle 1999 Barrel-Fermented Chardonnay (Columbia Valley (WA)) $13. 90 Best Buy *—P.G. (6/1/2001)*

Château Ste. Michelle 2003 Canoe Ridge Estate Chardonnay (Columbia Valley (WA)) $20. This explodes with full-flavored fruit. A big boy, juicy and concentrated with ripe apple/citrus fruits, and well-integrated streaks of vanilla, hazelnut, and butterscotch. **92 Editors' Choice** *—P.G. (12/15/2005)*

Château Ste. Michelle 1999 Canoe Ridge Estate Vineyard Chardonnay (Columbia Valley (WA)) $20. 87 *—P.G. (6/1/2001)*

Château Ste. Michelle 2001 Cold Creek Vineyard Chardonnay (Columbia Valley (WA)) $26. 91 *—P.G. (12/31/2003)*

Château Ste. Michelle 1998 Cold Creek Vineyard Chardonnay (Columbia Valley (WA)) $25. 91 *—P.G. (10/1/2001)*

Château Ste. Michelle 2003 Indian Wells Chardonnay (Columbia Valley (WA)) $17. Peaches and apricots fill the mouth. The wine has a supple, rich midpalate, and a nice smack of butterscotch to finish. **89** *—P.G. (12/15/2005)*

Château Ste. Michelle 1999 Indian Wells Vineyard Chardonnay (Columbia Valley (WA)) $22. 88 *—P.G. (10/1/2001)*

Château Ste. Michelle 2001 Reserve Chardonnay (Columbia Valley (WA)) $29. Not much differentiates this from its "Cold Creek" brother; both show new oak scents and flavors, so much so that the fruit is buried. Here the alcohol is a moderate 13%. Moderate levels of acid and the light, pleasant fruit suggest near-term drinking. **89** *—P.G. (5/1/2004)*

Château Ste. Michelle 1997 Reserve Chardonnay (Columbia Valley (WA)) $29. 87 *(4/1/2000)*

Château Ste. Michelle 2001 Gewürztraminer (Columbia Valley (WA)) $8. 87 *—P.G. (9/1/2002)*

Château Ste. Michelle 2001 Johannisberg Riesling (Columbia Valley (WA)) $8. 85 *—M.S. (12/31/2003)*

Château Ste. Michelle 2002 Artist Series Meritage (Columbia Valley (WA)) $48. This Meritage blend includes 10% Merlot and 20% Malbec. It is a soft, chocolaty wine with bright raspberry/cherry fruit and plenty of new oak flavors. The oak is still tough and bitter; it has not had sufficient time to soften. 1,500 cases made. **88** *—P.G. (12/15/2005)*

Château Ste. Michelle 1997 Merlot (Columbia Valley (WA)) $18. 87 *(4/1/2000)*

Château Ste. Michelle 2002 Merlot (Columbia Valley (WA)) $16. Dark and plum-colored, the aromas suggest green, herbal fruit. In the mouth it tastes soft, stripped, over filtered; yet finishes with awkward, astringent green tannins and a lingering bit of alcoholic heat. **84** *—P.G. (12/15/2005)*

Château Ste. Michelle 2000 Merlot (Columbia Valley (WA)) $16. 88 *—P.G. (12/31/2003)*

Château Ste. Michelle 2002 Canoe Ridge Estate Merlot (Columbia Valley (WA)) $24. Lots of chocolatey oak over light cherry fruit; here again the dry, abrasive tannins stick out and give the wine a disjointed mouthfeel, despite the good fruit. **87** *—P.G. (4/1/2005)*

Château Ste. Michelle 1999 Canoe Ridge Estate Merlot (Columbia Valley (WA)) $23. 90 *—P.G. (6/1/2002)*

Château Ste. Michelle 1996 Canoe Ridge Estate Vyd Merlot (Columbia Valley (WA)) $32. 89 *—L.W. (9/1/1999)*

Château Ste. Michelle 2002 Cold Creek Vineyard Merlot (Columbia Valley (WA)) $33. Thin, watery, and acidic, this is not at all representative of what this outstanding vineyard can produce. Uncharacteristically lean and unyielding, this is a disappointment. **85** *—P.G. (4/1/2005)*

Château Ste. Michelle 1998 Cold Creek Vineyard Merlot (Columbia Valley (WA)) $32. 91 *—P.G. (12/31/2001)*

Château Ste. Michelle 2001 Indian Wells Merlot (Columbia Valley (WA)) $18. Formerly one of the winery's single-vineyard bottlings, Indian Wells is now part of a new "District Series" from CSM. Here are smooth, cherry-dominated flavors, with a bit of cocoa and a finishing edge of acid. Simple and a bit formulaic, but good nonetheless. **87** *—P.G. (5/1/2004)*

Château Ste. Michelle 1998 Indian Wells Vineyard Merlot (Columbia Valley (WA)) $31. 90 *—P.G. (10/1/2001)*

Château Ste. Michelle 2001 Reserve Merlot (Columbia Valley (WA)) $37. Surprisingly tough and chewy, the tannins at this point overwhelm the fruit, which itself seems hard and impenetrable. The tight, unyielding core of cherry/berry fruit is ensconced in rough, ragged tannins that will need some years to smooth out. **87** *—P.G. (12/15/2004)*

Château Ste. Michelle 1999 Reserve Merlot (Columbia Valley (WA)) $37. 92 *—P.G. (9/1/2002)*

Château Ste. Michelle 2003 Pinot Gris (Columbia Valley (WA)) $13. A perfect marriage of fresh-cut pears, cinnamon, orange, and a finishing kiss of honeysuckle. Lingers deliciously on the finish. **88 Best Buy** *—P.G. (9/1/2004)*

Château Ste. Michelle 1998 Artist Series Meritage Red Wine Red Blend (Columbia Valley (WA)) $50. 91 *—P.G. (12/31/2001)*

Château Ste. Michelle 2003 Cold Creek Vineyard Riesling (Columbia Valley (WA)) $14. There is a lovely textural quality to Cold Creek Vineyard Riesling, which supports the flavors of grapefruit and white peaches with a minerality through the back half. Offers good grip and a racy, tangy finish, despite its off-dry rating. **91** *—P.G. (9/1/2004)*

Château Ste. Michelle 2001 Cold Creek Vineyard Riesling (Columbia Valley (WA)) $14. 90 Best Buy *—P.G. (12/31/2002)*

Château Ste. Michelle 2001 Dr. Loosen Eroica Riesling (Columbia Valley (WA)) $20. 92 Cellar Selection *—P.G. (9/1/2002)*

Château Ste. Michelle 2001 Dry Riesling (Columbia Valley (WA)) $8. 90 *—P.G. (9/1/2002)*

Château Ste. Michelle 2002 Eroica Riesling (Columbia Valley (WA)) $20. 91 *—P.G. (12/31/2003)*

Château Ste. Michelle 2003 Sauvignon Blanc (Columbia Valley (WA)) $10. More stainless steel fermentation than in previous vintages brings out the bright, round, fruity character. Winemaker Bob Bertheau shows his California palate, shying away from the grassy, pungent side of the grape, building instead a crisp, fragrant, and lightly spiced white wine with popular appeal. **88 Best Buy** *—P.G. (12/15/2005)*

Château Ste. Michelle 2000 Sauvignon Blanc (Columbia Valley (WA)) $10. 85 *—S.H. (9/12/2002)*

Château Ste. Michelle 2003 Horse Heaven Vineyard Sauvignon Blanc (Columbia Valley (WA)) $15. Nicely crafted and a bit riper than the regular Sauvignon, this fruit-driven wine adds light butterscotch and hints of wood spice to the basic citrus and apple flavors. The acids taste like fresh-squeezed Meyer lemons. **88** *—P.G. (12/15/2005)*

Château Ste. Michelle 2000 Horse Heaven Vineyard Sauvignon Blanc (Columbia Valley (WA)) $14. 90 *—P.G. (2/1/2002)*

Château Ste. Michelle 1997 Horse Heaven Vineyard Sauvignon Blanc (Columbia Valley (WA)) $14. 88 *—L.W. (9/1/1999)*

Château Ste. Michelle 2003 Sémillon (Columbia Valley (WA)) $9. A mirror image of the Sauvignon Blancs; here the proportions reversed (the Sauv Blanc is at 24%) and consequently the wine has a bit of the woody/woolly mid-palate reediness of Sémillon. Balanced and crisply ripe. **87 Best Buy** *—P.G. (12/15/2005)*

Château Ste. Michelle 1998 Sémillon (Columbia Valley (WA)) $8. 85 *—P.G. (11/15/2000)*

Château Ste. Michelle 2002 Syrah (Columbia Valley (WA)) $15. Has some interesting herbal, peppery overtones to the nose, but the flavors are simple and fruity, a blend of blackberry and cherry, finishing short. **84** *(9/1/2005)*

Château Ste. Michelle 2000 Syrah (Columbia Valley (WA)) $15. 88 Best Buy *—P.G. (12/31/2002)*

USA

Château Ste. Michelle 2001 Reserve Syrah (Columbia Valley (WA)) $29. Spicy, tart, smooth, and polished, with roasted coffee accents that fall just a tad to the green side. Augmented with hints of citrus peel, it centers on penetrating raspberry/black cherry fruit, finishing with licorice and substantial tannins. **89** *—P.G. (12/15/2004)*

Château Ste. Michelle 1999 Reserve Syrah (Columbia Valley (WA)) $29. **90** *—P.G. (9/1/2002)*

CHÂTEAU WOLTNER

Château Woltner 1997 Private Reserve Bordeaux Blend (Howell Mountain) $50. **85** *(11/1/2000)*

CHATOM

Chatom 1999 Cabernet Sauvignon (Calaveras County) $18. **83** *(9/1/2002)*

Chatom 2002 Chardonnay (Calaveras County) $14. **84** *—S.H. (12/1/2003)*

Chatom 2003 Sauvignon Blanc (Calaveras County) $18. Ripely sweet in fig, melon, and the prettiest white peach, with vanilla and smoky notes. Drinks rich and creamy, with a long, spicy finish. Contains some Sémillon. **87** *—S.H. (2/1/2005)*

Chatom 2002 Sémillon (Calaveras County) $11. **84** *—S.H. (12/1/2003)*

Chatom 1999 Syrah (Calaveras County) $18. **88** *(10/1/2001)*

Chatom 2001 Zinfandel (Calaveras County) $16. **84** *(11/1/2003)*

CHATOM VINEYARDS

Chatom Vineyards 2002 Syrah (Calaveras County) $22. Polished and smooth, with fancy cocoa, blackberry, cherry, and coffee flavors that are well-ripened and long-lasting. The tannins are gentle, with good acidity. Turns candy sweet on the finish. **86** *—S.H. (8/1/2005)*

Chatom Vineyards 2002 Zinfandel (Calaveras County) $16. Try this charmingly rustic wine with almost anything that calls for a very dry red wine. It has earthy, fruity flavors, and the tannins are firm and dusty. **84** *—S.H. (8/1/2005)*

CHATTER CREEK

Chatter Creek 2003 Alder Ridge Vineyard Cabernet Franc (Columbia Valley (WA)) $20. Clean and ripe, with young, grapy fruit taking center stage. The wine has the firm, tannic grip of the Cab Franc grape, but the tannins are well managed, smooth and unencumbered with new oak. **88** *—P.G. (6/1/2005)*

Chatter Creek 2000 Alder Ridge Vineyard Cabernet Franc (Washington) $18. **86** *—P.G. (6/1/2002)*

Chatter Creek 1999 Alder Ridge Vineyard Cabernet Sauvignon (Washington) $20. **88** *—P.G. (10/1/2001)*

Chatter Creek 2003 Pinot Gris (Columbia Valley (WA)) $12. This is clean and crisp, a bit softer and rounder than many from Washington, with varietal flavors of pear and cut apple. **87** *—P.G. (6/1/2005)*

Chatter Creek 2002 Clifton Hill Vineyard Syrah (Columbia Valley (WA)) $30. A young, spicy Syrah, this shows unusually bright and intense fruit, a mix of purple plums and blackberries. There are unusual candied citrus highlights, hints of herb and spice. Top-shelf juice. **91** *—P.G. (6/1/2005)*

Chatter Creek 2000 Jack Jones Vineyard Syrah (Washington) $20. **89** *—P.G. (6/1/2002)*

Chatter Creek 2000 Lonesome Spring Ranch Syrah (Yakima Valley) $20. **91 Editors' Choice** *—P.G. (6/1/2002)*

CHEAPSKATE

Cheapskate 2003 Miser Cabernet Blend (California) $8. With Cab Franc added to the Cab Sauvignon, this wine is soft and cherryish, with a fine dusting of dry tannins and a clean, spicy finish. It's not terribly complex, but is a really good value. **84 Best Buy** *—S.H. (11/1/2005)*

Cheapskate 2002 Pinot Noir (California) $8. Pretty rude stuff, a harsh, hot wine that's recognizably Pinot Noir with its silky structure and cherry flavors, but that's about it. **82** *—S.H. (11/1/2005)*

CHEHALEM

Chehalem 2000 Chardonnay (Willamette Valley) $19. **90** *(8/1/2002)*

Chehalem 1999 Ian's Reserve Chardonnay (Willamette Valley) $32. **89** *—P.G. (2/1/2002)*

Chehalem 2001 Pinot Gris (Willamette Valley) $15. **89 Best Buy** *—P.G. (12/31/2002)*

Chehalem 1997 Pinot Gris (Willamette Valley) $19. **80** *(8/1/1999)*

Chehalem 1998 3 Vineyard Pinot Noir (Willamette Valley) $25. **90** *—M.S. (12/1/2000)*

Chehalem 2002 Corral Creek Vineyard Pinot Noir (Willamette Valley) $39. This bottle showed some signs of reduction. Stubbornly closed down, with some funky rubber ball aromas, its core of black cherry fruit was virtually invisible. Grainy tannins and some bitter chocolate marked the finish. Should improve with bottle age. **84** *(11/1/2004)*

Chehalem 2002 Reserve Pinot Noir (Willamette Valley) $50. It almost tastes like a Beaujolais, with grapy, spicy, whole-cluster flavors out in front, but nothing substantial following. Balanced, clean, and fruity. **84** *(11/1/2004)*

Chehalem 2000 Ridgecrest Vineyards Pinot Noir (Willamette Valley) $39. 87 *(10/1/2002)*

Chehalem 2000 Rion Reserve Pinot Noir (Willamette Valley) $50. 92 Editors' Choice *(10/1/2002)*

Chehalem 2002 Stoller Vineyard Pinot Noir (Dundee Hills) $39. Quite dark and dense, with heavy tannins. Strong scents of tomato leaf and beetroot give the wine a tough, herbal set of flavors; ungenerous and unyielding, at least for now. 85 *(11/1/2004)*

Chehalem 1997 Stoller Vineyards Pinot Noir (Willamette Valley) $28. 86 *(10/1/1999)*

Chehalem 1997 Three Vineyards Pinot Noir (Willamette Valley) $18. 90 *(10/1/1999)*

CHELAN ESTATE

Chelan Estate 2002 Cabernet Sauvignon (Columbia Valley (WA)) $25. A Cab/Merlot blend from Red Mountain grapes, this young wine has great color and good, tart, tight fruit. Flavors run to cranberry, sour cherry, and more, done in a firm, tannic, herbal style. 87 *—P.G. (9/1/2004)*

CHEVAL SAUVAGE

Cheval Sauvage 2002 Ashley Vineyard Pinot Noir (Santa Rita Hills) $50. This full-bodied, round Pinot boasts distinctive cola, coffee, and roasted meat aromas, then follows up with flavors of black cherries, earth and a hint of wintergreen. Finishes with supple tannins; drink now–2010. 90 *(10/1/2005)*

CHIMERE

Chimere 2002 Angelica Orange Muscat (Santa Barbara County) $14. Sweet in apricot, orange honey, and vanilla flavors, and with a gooey texture, this dessert wine nonetheless is balanced with crisp acidity, and is very refreshing. The flavors are addictively good, especially after a rich meal. 92 *—S.H. (3/1/2005)*

Chimere 2002 Paragon Vineyard Pinot Noir (Edna Valley) $30. Smells Porty and caramelized, and drinks hot and dry. 82 *—S.H. (3/1/2005)*

Chimere 1997 Paragon Vineyard Pinot Noir (Edna Valley) $22. 84 *—J.C. (12/15/2000)*

CHIMNEY ROCK

Chimney Rock 1997 Elevage Bordeaux Blend (Stags Leap District) $52. 89 *(11/1/2000)*

Chimney Rock 2002 Elevage Cabernet Blend (Stags Leap District) $76. If Tchelistcheff were still here, he might describe this Cab as an iron fist in a velvet glove. It's inviting in rich cassis, blueberry, and chocolate flavors, with a soft mouthfeel. But the softness is deceptive; this is a big, deeply structured wine. Drink now through 2012. 92 *—S.H. (12/1/2005)*

Chimney Rock 1997 Cabernet Sauvignon (Napa Valley) $40. 91 *(11/1/2000)*

Chimney Rock 2002 Cabernet Sauvignon (Napa Valley) $49. A little rough in texture, and with plenty of tannins, this Cab nonetheless satisfies with lots of ripe blackberry and cherry flavors. It's totally dry. Calls for powerful steaks and chops. 87 *—S.H. (10/1/2005)*

Chimney Rock 2001 Cabernet Sauvignon (Stags Leap District) $49. Seductively sweet, with ripe currant and cherry fruit framed by fancy oak, yet the underlying tannins kick in midway. Nowhere near its maximum integration; best left alone through 2008 to develop nuance. 93 *—S.H. (10/1/2004)*

Chimney Rock 1999 Cabernet Sauvignon (Stags Leap District) $45. 88 *—C.S. (11/15/2002)*

Chimney Rock 2001 Reserve Cabernet Sauvignon (Stags Leap District) $107. A great Cab showcasing everything good about Napa's fabulous '01 Cabs. It's rich, vibrant, and complex, with layers of cassis, cocoa, and roasted coffee flavors, and a deft touch of smoky oak. The tannins are sweet, ripe, and subtle. Doesn't clobber you sideways with fruit, but offers elegant, sophisticated drinking. 93 *—S.H. (7/1/2005)*

Chimney Rock 1997 Reserve Cabernet Sauvignon (Stags Leap District) $80. 88 *(11/1/2000)*

Chimney Rock 2000 Fumé Blanc (Napa Valley) $18. 85 *(8/1/2002)*

Chimney Rock 2000 Elevage Red Blend (Stags Leap District) $60. 88 *—S.H. (11/15/2003)*

Chimney Rock 2004 Rosé of Cabernet Franc Rosé Blend (Stags Leap District) $21. This is a Beaujolais-like California rosé. It's light in body, aromatic, clean, and zippy in acids and fruity, with raspberry, strawberry, vanilla cream, and nutmeg flavors. Chill it and then watch how it changes as it warms up on the table. 89 *—S.H. (12/1/2005)*

CHINOOK

Chinook 1998 Merlot (Yakima Valley) $28. 90 *—P.G. (9/1/2002)*

Chinook 2000 Sémillon (Yakima Valley) $14. 88 *—P.G. (9/1/2002)*

CHOUINARD

Chouinard NV Brut Sparkling Blend (California) $13. 84 *—S.H. (12/1/2003)*

CHRISTOPHE

Christophe 2000 Pinot Noir (Monterey) $10. 82 *(10/1/2002)*

CHRISTOPHER CREEK

Christopher Creek 2001 Zinfandel (Dry Creek Valley) $22. 84 *(11/1/2003)*

CHUMEIA

Chumeia 2002 Cabernet Sauvignon (California) $12. Smells burnt, and tastes sharp in tannins and herbaceousness. Unpleasant. 81 *—S.H. (2/1/2005)*

Chumeia 2000 Cabernet Sauvignon (California) $10. 85 Best Buy *—S.H. (8/1/2003)*

Chumeia 2004 Simpson Vineyard Chardonnay (Madera) $11. Soft, simple, and rather sweet, this Central Valley Chard has flavors of canned peaches and apricots. 82 *—S.H. (12/31/2005)*

Chumeia 2001 Simpson Vineyard Chardonnay (California) $10. 85 *—S.H. (6/1/2003)*

Chumeia 2002 Simpson Vineyard Merlot (California) $12. A full-bodied, rich wine for those looking for a value. The blackberry, blueberry, and cherry-chocolate flavors are melded into soft tannins, and finish long and spicy. 86 Best Buy *—S.H. (12/31/2004)*

Chumeia 2000 Pinot Blanc (Monterey County) $14. Smells fragrant and inviting, with aromas of peach, vanilla, smoke, and a pretty wildflower streak. In the mouth, the wine seems dominated by high acidity and lees, making it rather tart and sour despite the fruity flavors. 84 *—S.H. (3/1/2004)*

Chumeia 2001 Pinot Noir (Santa Lucia Highlands) $28. I preferred this winery's less costly Central Coast bottling to this one, which has an odd, raw meat smell and is too oaky. Although it has polished cherry flavors and good acids, it's odd. 84 *—S.H. (2/1/2005)*

Chumeia 2003 Silver Nectar Muscat-French Columbard (California) $10. Okay for an everyday sweetie, with canned fruit and honey flavors and some brightness. 84 *—S.H. (2/1/2005)*

Chumeia 2000 Viognier (California) $10. 83 *—S.H. (5/1/2003)*

Chumeia 2001 Dante Dusi Vineyard Zinfandel (Paso Robles) $22. 89 *—J.M. (11/1/2003)*

CINERGI

Cinergi 2000 Red Blend (Napa Valley) $18. 86 *—S.H. (12/1/2002)*

CINNABAR

Cinnabar 2000 Mercury Rising Bordeaux Blend (California) $17. 88 *—S.H. (8/1/2003)*

Cinnabar 2001 Estate Cabernet Sauvignon (Santa Cruz Mountains) $40. A beautiful Cab showcasing flamboyant cassis, cocoa, and smoky oak flavors, enhanced by firm, sweetly ripe tannins and a touch of oak. It's delicious, but has enough firmness and complexity to make it noteworthy. 90 *—S.H. (2/1/2005)*

Cinnabar 2003 Chardonnay (Monterey) $18. Unusually tropically, even for California Chard. Big time flavors of ripe, juicy papayas, and mangoes that are well oaked. Tasty, but a little syrupy-soft. 86 *—S.H. (2/1/2005)*

Cinnabar 2001 Chardonnay (Santa Cruz Mountains) $25. This mountain wine is taut with crisp acidity and a minerally spine. It's also well-oaked and leesy, and the oak has lots of char. This firm structure frames flavors of citrus fruits. It's a good wine, but could possess more fruity opulence. 86 *—S.H. (8/1/2004)*

Cinnabar 1999 Quicksilver Chardonnay (Central Coast) $18. 89 *—S.H. (5/1/2001)*

Cinnabar 2000 Sleepy Hollow Vineyard Chardonnay (Santa Lucia Highlands) $25. 92 *—S.H. (8/1/2003)*

Cinnabar 2001 Merlot (Paso Robles) $19. 87 *—S.H. (12/1/2003)*

Cinnabar 1999 Pinot Noir (Santa Cruz Mountains) $38. 89 *—S.H. (9/1/2002)*

Cinnabar 1999 Watts-Borden Ranch Syrah (Lodi) $17. 91 *—S.H. (11/15/2001)*

CK MONDAVI

CK Mondavi 2002 Wildcreek Canyon Cabernet Sauvignon (California) $10. Sure is ripe, with its flood of blackberries and cherries, and it's also dry and rich in tannins. It's rather sharp, though, in jammy acids. An affordable sipper at a fair price. 84 *—S.H. (11/15/2004)*

CK Mondavi 1999 Chardonnay (California) $8. 84 *—S.H. (5/1/2001)*

CK Mondavi 1999 Merlot (California) $9. 84 *—S.H. (5/1/2001)*

CK Mondavi 2001 Merlot-Cabernet Sauvignon (California) $8. 86 Best Buy *—S.H. (5/1/2003)*

CK Mondavi 2003 Sauvignon Blanc (California) $6. Rather vegetal, and dry and tart in acidity. Finishes with some black currant flavors. 82 *—S.H. (10/1/2004)*

CK Mondavi 2001 Zinfandel (California) $7. 86 *—S.H. (9/1/2003)*

CK Mondavi 2002 Wildcreek Canyon Zinfandel (California) $10. Rather lean and sharp, with an edge of over-ripe raisins. Fine for everyday occasions and gatherings. 82 *—S.H. (12/15/2004)*

CL

CL 2000 Armagh Vineyard Pinot Noir (Sonoma Coast) $35. 90 *—S.H. (2/1/2003)*

CLAAR

Claar 1999 White Bluffs Estate Grown & Bottled Cabernet Sauvignon (Columbia Valley (WA)) $21. 82 *—M.S. (8/1/2003)*

CLAIBORNE & CHURCHILL

Claiborne & Churchill 2000 Dry Gewürztraminer (Central Coast) $14. 88 *—S.H. (9/1/2003)*

Claiborne & Churchill 2002 Pinot Noir (Edna Valley) $16. What a lovely wine. It showcases the success that Edna Valley enjoyed this vintage. Rich, oaky forest floor, mushroom, hard spice, and tomato notes. Red stone fruits also star in the complex flavors. Fairly tannic and bone dry, with great balance, this is a wine that will benefit from mid-term aging or decanting. 90 *(11/1/2004)*

Claiborne & Churchill 2000 Runestone Pinot Noir (Edna Valley) $29. 82 *(10/1/2002)*

Claiborne & Churchill 2002 Runestone Barrel Select Pinot Noir (Edna Valley) $26. A pretty good wine and an easy sipper. It's a little overripe, with notes of stewed prunes, but they add interest to the cherry and tea flavors. Very dry and rather tannic. Try decanting for several hours before serving. 86 *(11/1/2004)*

Claiborne & Churchill 2002 Dry Riesling (Central Coast) $14. One of the nicer Rieslings in California, from specialists in the Alsatian style. It's fully dry, yet with ripe, delicious flavors of crisp apples and peaches, and a tangy aftertaste of minerals and petrol. Bright acidity makes this wine clean and zesty. 87 *—S.H. (2/1/2004)*

CLARK-CLAUDON

Clark-Claudon 1997 Cabernet Sauvignon (Napa Valley) $78. 92 *(11/1/2000)*

CLAUDIA SPRINGS

Claudia Springs 1999 Pinot Noir (Anderson Valley) $25. 87 *—S.H. (5/1/2002)*

Claudia Springs 1998 Clone 115 Vidmar Vineyard Pinot Noir (Mendocino) $25. 90 *—P.G. (12/15/2000)*

Claudia Springs 2000 Lolonis Vineyard Viognier (Redwood Valley) $24. 93 *—P.G. (5/1/2002)*

Claudia Springs 2000 Eaglepoint Ranch Zinfandel (Mendocino) $20. 88 *(11/1/2003)*

Claudia Springs 1999 Rhodes Vineyard Zinfandel (Redwood Valley) $26. 86 *—S.H. (5/1/2002)*

Claudia Springs 1997 Rhodes Vineyard Zinfandel (Redwood Valley) $24. 86 *—S.H. (5/1/2000)*

CLAY STATION

Clay Station 2003 Malbec (Lodi) $13. This is a junior version of those big, rich Argentine Malbecs. It's something like a California Zinfandel, medium- to full-bodied and dry, with brambly berry flavors and a robust, gritty mouthfeel. 83 *—S.H. (12/15/2005)*

Clay Station 2001 Cabernet-Petite Sirah Red Blend (Lodi) $13. This fruity wine has some rough tannins and is a bit jagged, but the blackberry, coffee, and chocolate flavors are delicious. Fully dry, but finishes with lots of ripe fruit. 84 *—S.H. (12/15/2004)*

Clay Station 2004 Viognier (Lodi) $13. This is one of those almost over-the-top Viogniers that has every fruit flavor you can think of. It drinks soft in texture and honeyed sweet on the finish, and is a simple quaffer. 83 *—S.H. (12/15/2005)*

Clay Station 2004 Old Vine Zinfandel (Lodi) $13. Dark, jammy, thick on the tongue and bursting with fresh fruit, this Zin is likeable from the get go. It's not subtle about the way it delivers its no-holds-barred blueberry, blackberry, and cherry flavors, wrapped in rich tannins. 85 *—S.H. (12/15/2005)*

CLAYHOUSE

Clayhouse 2004 Sauvignon Blanc (Paso Robles) $12. A dry, tartly acidic, citrusy wine. There's a strong greenness to it, a peppery, chlorophylly taste that gets those tastebuds going. 84 *—S.H. (12/31/2005)*

CLAYTON

Clayton 1999 Estate Vineyard Old Vine Petite Sirah (Lodi) $29. 89 *(4/1/2003)*

Clayton 2000 Zinfandel (Lodi) $19. 91 Editors' Choice *—J.M. (9/1/2003)*

CLIFF LEDE

Cliff Lede 2002 Claret Bordeaux Blend (Stags Leap District) $32. It's not made in the flashy, fleshy New World style, but has an earthy, herbal flavor, with a hint of blackberry. Oak is not at all prominent in this dry, balanced wine. 90 *—S.H. (12/15/2005)*

Cliff Lede 2001 Cabernet Sauvignon (Stags Leap District) $50. From S. Anderson, of sparkling wine fame, this wine has that seductively lush Stags Leap quality of a velvety mouthfeel and mouth-filling warmth. But then those iron-fist-in-a-velvet-glove tannins kick in, lending astringency to the polished blackberry flavors. Will develop gracefully for years. 92 *—S.H. (10/3/2004)*

Cliff Lede 2001 Poetry Cabernet Sauvignon (Stags Leap District) $100. A stunning wine that shows off the excellence of its origin and the vintage. Long and deep in cherry, currant, and mocha, with a round, creamy texture and plenty of smoky oak. The spicy finish lasts for a long time. So polished and delicious, it's hard to resist now, but will age gracefully for many years. Note, though, that the

Cliff Lede name appears only on the back of the label. **94** *—S.H. (10/1/2004)*

Cliff Lede 2004 Sauvignon Blanc (Napa Valley) $18. Rich in fig, gooseberry, lemon and lime, chamomile, and spice flavors, this bone-dry wine is impressively deep. It displays an elegance and finesse, as well as a power seldom found in California Sauvignon Blanc. **90** *—S.H. (12/15/2005)*

CLINE

Cline 1998 Marsanne (Carneros) $18. **89** *—S.H. (6/1/1999)*

Cline 1997 Ancient Vines Mourvèdre (Contra Costa County) $18. **87** *—S.H. (10/1/1999)*

Cline 1997 Small Berry Mourvèdre (Contra Costa County) $24. **91** *—S.H. (10/1/1999)*

Cline 2002 Oakley Five Reds Red Blend (California) $11. A rather exotic blend of Mourvèdre, Grenache, Carignane, Zinfandel, and Syrah, and a nice dry red. Smooth and polished, with cherry, herb and earthy flavors. Shows real finesse. **86 Best Buy** *—S.H. (4/1/2005)*

Cline 1997 Syrah (Carneros) $20. **88** *—S.H. (6/1/1999)*

Cline 2002 Syrah (California) $11. Here's a rustic, country-style wine that's very well made, and offers lots to like. It's a bit rough in the mouth, but has flavors of dark stone fruits. Finishes dry and balanced. **85** *—S.H. (4/1/2005)*

Cline 2001 Syrah (Sonoma County) $14. Lusciously sweet, a deeply colored wine saturated with ripe flavors of plums, blackberries, and mocha. There are some well-etched tannins and a crisp streak of acidity to help it cut through a well-marbled steak or prime rib. **87** *—S.H. (6/1/2004)*

Cline 2000 Syrah (Sonoma County) $15. **87** *—S.H. (12/1/2002)*

Cline 2000 Syrah (California) $8. **83** *—S.H. (12/1/2002)*

Cline 1999 Los Carneros Syrah (Carneros) $23. **88** *(11/1/2001)*

Cline 2004 Viognier (Sonoma County) $10. At this price, fans of Viognier's exotic side will stock up by the case. Shows an array of tropical fruit, wildflower, and spice flavors that finish in a crisp, honeyed aftertaste. Drink very cold. **85 Best Buy** *—S.H. (11/1/2005)*

Cline 2000 Viognier (Sonoma County) $18. **80** *—J.M. (12/15/2002)*

Cline 2000 Oakley Vin Blanc White Blend (California) $9. **84** *—J.M. (11/15/2001)*

Cline 2001 Zinfandel (California) $10. **86 Best Buy** *(11/1/2003)*

Cline 2004 Ancient Vines Zinfandel (California) $18. From vineyards in Lodi and Contra Costa County, an enormously enjoyable Zin that shows its hot climate origins, but maintains balance and integrity. The cassis, cherry, chocolate, and oatmeal-raisin cookie flavors finish in a swirl of acidity and dusty tannins. **90** *—S.H. (11/1/2005)*

Cline 1999 Ancient Vines Zinfandel (California) $23. **84** *—D.T. (3/1/2002)*

Cline 1997 Ancient Vines Zinfandel (Contra Costa County) $18. **89** *—S.H. (9/1/1999)*

Cline 2001 Big Break Zinfandel (Contra Costa County) $28. **88** *(11/1/2003)*

Cline 1998 Big Break Vineyard Zinfandel (Contra Costa County) $28. **93** *—P.G. (3/1/2001)*

Cline 2001 Bridgehead Zinfandel (Contra Costa County) $28. **90** *(11/1/2003)*

Cline 1999 Fulton Road Vineyard Zinfandel (Russian River Valley) $28. **87** *—D.T. (3/1/2002)*

Cline 2001 Live Oak Zinfandel (Contra Costa County) $28. **89** *(11/1/2003)*

Cline 1998 Live Oak Vineyard Zinfandel (Contra Costa County) $28. **93** *—P.G. (3/1/2001)*

CLINTON

Clinton 1999 Seyval Blanc (Hudson River Region) $13. Features unusual aromas of white root vegetables. Dry, sour-earth flavors of parsnips and rutabegas finish crisp and lemony. Try with oysters on the half shell. **83** *—J.C. (1/1/2004)*

CLONINGER

Cloninger 1998 Quinn Vineyard Cabernet Sauvignon (Carmel Valley) $18. **86** *—S.H. (5/1/2001)*

Cloninger 2000 Estate Grown Chardonnay (Santa Lucia Highlands) $16. **88** *—S.H. (5/1/2003)*

Cloninger 1997 Jardini Vyd. Pinot Noir (Monterey County) $22. **81** *(10/1/1999)*

CLOS DU BOIS

Clos du Bois 1996 Marlstone Vineyard Bordeaux Blend (Sonoma County) $30. **84** *(7/1/2000)*

Clos du Bois 2001 Marlstone Cabernet Blend (Alexander Valley) $50. After two years in French oak, the tannins are soft, but the acids still evident. Has pretty aromas and flavors of vanilla, tobacco, smoke, and cassis, just seems a bit hard-edged on the finish. A blend of 75% Cabernet Sauvignon, 14% Merlot, 8.5% Malbec, 1.5 % Cabernet Franc, and 1% Petit Verdot. **87** *(6/1/2005)*

Clos du Bois 2000 Cabernet Sauvignon (Sonoma County) $17. 85 —*S.H. (4/1/2003)*

Clos du Bois 1996 Cabernet Sauvignon (Sonoma County) $15. 83 —*S.H. (7/1/1999)*

Clos du Bois 2001 Briarcrest Cabernet Sauvignon (Alexander Valley) $40. Solid California Cabernet, with textbook aromas of toast, cassis, cigar box, and vanilla. It's medium- to full-bodied in the mouth, with the vanilla and cassis flavors easily flowing across the palate. **89** *(6/1/2005)*

Clos du Bois 2002 Reserve Cabernet Sauvignon (Alexander Valley) $22. This Cab is dry, fruity, soft, and gentle, with extra nuances of complexity. It's deep in blackberry and chocolate flavors, and an intricately detailed balance of acids, tannins, alcohol and oak. Not an ager, but absolutely delicious from the get-go. **90** —*S.H. (12/1/2005)*

Clos du Bois 1997 Reserve Cabernet Sauvignon (Sonoma County) $20. 87 —*S.H. (2/1/2000)*

Clos du Bois 1995 Winemaker's Reserve Cabernet Sauvignon (Sonoma County) $50. 88 —*J.C. (7/1/1999)*

Clos du Bois 2003 Chardonnay (North Coast) $12. This white has nice, ripe flavors of peaches and tropical fruits, and good oak. Rich and creamy, this Chard offers lots of pleasure at a good price. **85** —*S.H. (5/1/2005)*

Clos du Bois 2001 Chardonnay (Sonoma County) $14. 86 —*S.H. (12/15/2002)*

Clos du Bois 1999 Chardonnay (Sonoma County) $14. 86 —*S.H. (11/15/2000)*

Clos du Bois 1998 Chardonnay (Sonoma County) $16. 87 —*L.W. (12/31/1999)*

Clos du Bois 2000 Calcaire Chardonnay (Alexander Valley) $22. 90 —*S.H. (2/1/2003)*

Clos du Bois 1999 Flintwood Chardonnay (Dry Creek Valley) $22. 91 Editors' Choice —*S.H. (2/1/2003)*

Clos du Bois 2003 Reserve Chardonnay (Russian River Valley) $16. All of this is barrel-fermented, 45% in new French oak, and it shows in the toasty, nutty scents. Buttery and creamy on the palate, with a plump mouthfeel and layered flavors of ripe pears and dried spices. Long and pineapple-y on the finish. **87** *(6/1/2005)*

Clos du Bois 1999 Reserve Chardonnay (Sonoma County) $16. 84 —*S.H. (2/1/2001)*

Clos du Bois 2000 Merlot (Sonoma County) $18. 87 —*S.H. (4/1/2003)*

Clos du Bois 1998 Merlot (Sonoma County) $17. 84 —*J.C. (6/1/2001)*

Clos du Bois 2002 Reserve Merlot (Alexander Valley) $22. Like many of the Clos du Bois wines, this is textbook. There's everything you expect in a Merlot—black cherries, vanilla, toast, dried herbs, coffee. On the other hand, also like a textbook, it lacks the drama and excitement to push it into the next class. **87** *(6/1/2005)*

Clos du Bois 1997 Reserve Merlot (Sonoma County) $22. 85 —*S.H. (3/1/2000)*

Clos du Bois 2003 Pinot Noir (Sonoma County) $16. Light and crisp, this tart little Pinot boasts just enough cola and black cherry flavors to make it a worthwhile match with roast chicken, or perhaps grilled salmon. **85** *(6/1/2005)*

Clos du Bois 2000 Pinot Noir (Sonoma County) $17. 86 —*S.H. (12/15/2001)*

Clos du Bois 2003 Reserve Pinot Noir (Sonoma Coast) $22. Plump and smooth, with piquant briary, herbal accents to the strawberry and raspberry flavors. Picks up coffee and chocolate on the finish, along with just a hint of bitterness. A promising effort. **88** *(6/1/2005)*

Clos du Bois 2001 Sauvignon Blanc (North Coast) $10. 85 —*S.H. (3/1/2003)*

Clos du Bois 1998 Sauvignon Blanc (Sonoma County) $9. 84 —*S.H> (9/1/1999)*

Clos du Bois 2002 Shiraz (Sonoma County) $12. This is a rather light, bouncy Syrah, made in American oak. Pretty berry and vanilla notes on the nose turn slightly herbal—almost dill-like—by the finish. **85** *(9/1/2005)*

Clos du Bois 1998 Reserve Shiraz (Sonoma County) $16. 85 *(10/1/2001)*

Clos du Bois 2002 Reserve Tempranillo (Alexander Valley) $22. Winemaker Erik Olsen says the Tempranillo needs really careful tannin management—he even blends in Cabernet Sauvignon to soften this wine. The result is a medium-bodied wine filled with tobacco, vanilla, and blackberry nuances and boasting a tart, juicy finish. **88** *(6/1/2005)*

Clos du Bois 1997 Zinfandel (Sonoma County) $14. 84 *(2/1/2000)*

Clos du Bois 1999 Reserve Zinfandel (Dry Creek Valley) $22. 90 —*S.H. (7/1/2002)*

CLOS DU LAC

Clos du Lac 2001 Sangiovese (Amador County) $14. Dry and rough, with a burn on the finish, this wine has cherry and earth flavors. **83** —*S.H. (12/15/2004)*

Clos du Lac 1997 Syrah (California) $12. 88 *(5/1/2000)*

Clos du Lac 2001 Ghirardelli Vineyard Zinfandel (Calaveras County) $20. Deeper, richer, and more delicious than the Kane bottling, with great heaps of blackberries and black raspberries wrapped in dry, soft tannins. You'll like this fresh, vibrant wine for its youthful fruitiness and easy drinkability. **87** *—S.H. (12/15/2004)*

Clos du Lac 2002 Potter Vineyard Zinfandel (Shenandoah Valley (CA)) $20. Good Zin character, with brambly berry flavors and smooth tannins, but a little too sweet **84** *—S.H. (3/1/2005)*

Clos du Lac 2001 Reserve Blend Zinfandel (Amador County) $16. Unmistakably California Zin, with its briary, brambly flood of wild berry and peppery spice flavors that finish dry and tannic. It's not a heavy wine, but has a silky lightness that makes it super-drinkable. **87** *—S.H. (12/15/2004)*

CLOS DU VAL

Clos du Val 2001 Reserve Cabernet Franc (Stags Leap District) $85. Polished in red cherry, cocoa, vanilla, cinnamon, and oaky smoke, with smooth tannins and a long finish, this wine is medium-bodied and gentle. Its delicacy suggests veal or pork, not beef. **89** *—S.H. (12/31/2004)*

Clos du Val 1995 Cabernet Sauvignon (Napa Valley) $24. **85** *—S.H. (6/1/1999)*

Clos du Val 2001 Cabernet Sauvignon (Napa Valley) $28. Like its companion '01 Merlot release, this Cab needs time to come together, but when that happens, it will be a lovely drink. The firm, chunky tannins will hold the black currant and herb flavors through this decade. **90** *—S.H. (11/15/2004)*

Clos du Val 1999 Cabernet Sauvignon (Napa Valley) $29. **88** *—J.M. (6/1/2002)*

Clos du Val 2001 Oak Vineyard Cabernet Sauvignon (Stags Leap District) $62. Clos du Val continues to march to a different drummer. It's always been a youthfully shy, dry wine that stresses elegance over flamboyance. This wine has great black currant and herb flavors, but stresses its structure with an acidic, tannic emphasis. It should age for many years. **91** *—S.H. (10/3/2004)*

Clos du Val 1999 Palisade Vineyard Cabernet Sauvignon (Stags Leap District) $62. **92** *—C.S. (11/15/2002)*

Clos du Val 2000 Reserve Cabernet Sauvignon (Napa Valley) $95. Clos du Val fans always have appreciated the elegance and ageability of its Cabs, and this release continues the tradition. It's been getting riper and softer every year, yet still has that edge of herbs and tannins, and in this vintage, a hint of smoked meat. Now through 2015. **91** *—S.H. (12/31/2004)*

Clos du Val 1998 Reserve Cabernet Sauvignon (Napa Valley) $95. **91** *—S.H. (11/15/2002)*

Clos du Val 1995 Reserve Cabernet Sauvignon (Napa Valley) $65. **92** *—L.W. (10/1/1999)*

Clos du Val 1997 Vineyard Georges III Cabernet Sauvignon (Rutherford) $48. **94** *(11/1/2000)*

Clos du Val 2002 Chardonnay (Napa Valley) $21. Lots of apple, pear, and tropical fruit flavors are bathed in toasty oak, and the texture is rich and creamy. For me, the drawback of this wine is that it lacks crispness and so has a syrupy taste and feeling. **85** *—S.H. (11/15/2004)*

Clos du Val 2000 Chardonnay (Napa Valley) $23. **88** *—J.M. (5/1/2002)*

Clos du Val 2000 Reserve Chardonnay (Carneros) $39. **92** *—S.H. (12/15/2002)*

Clos du Val 2002 Merlot (Napa Valley) $25. This is an elegant, sexy wine, softly luxurious and velvety, with impressive flavors of blackberries, chocolate, plums, and oak. It's fairly tannic, and should improve over the next five years. **88** *—S.H. (10/1/2005)*

Clos du Val 2000 Merlot (Napa Valley) $25. **88** *—S.H. (8/1/2003)*

Clos du Val 2003 Pinot Noir (Napa Valley) $24. There are some good features in this wine, namely the pretty cherry flavor, gentle mouthfeel and light dusting of oak. There's also a cloying sweetness throughout that diminishes the score. **84** *—S.H. (10/1/2005)*

Clos du Val 2002 Pinot Noir (Napa Valley) $24. Pleasant cherry, raspberry, and smoky vanilla flavors make this wine polished and easy to sip. It's medium-bodied in weight, and while it could use a bit more delicacy for a Pinot Noir, it's quite delicious. **86** *—S.H. (11/1/2004)*

Clos du Val 2001 Carneros Vineyard Pinot Noir (Napa Valley) $38. A pleasant Pinot that takes its well-ripened cherry and raspberry flavors and saturates them with oaky seasonings of vanilla, smoke, and sweet tannins. Silky in the mouth, with a short finish. **86** *—S.H. (2/1/2004)*

Clos du Val 2002 Ariadne Sémillon-Sauvignon Blanc (Napa Valley) $32. A creamy, smooth blend of Sémillon and Sauvignon Blanc. The wine serves up hints of melon, hay, mineral, herbs, and citrus flavors. Acidity is a bit low for these varieties, but the wine shows elegance, finishing long. **89** *—J.M. (10/1/2004)*

Clos du Val 2000 Ariadne White Blend (Napa Valley) $32. **90** *—S.H. (12/15/2002)*

Clos du Val 1999 Palisade Vineyard Zinfandel (Stags Leap District) $28. **88** *—S.H. (12/15/2001)*

Clos du Val 1997 Palisade Vyd Zinfandel (Stags Leap District) $17. **80** *—P.G. (11/15/1999)*

CLOS LA CHANCE

Clos La Chance 2000 Cabernet Franc (Central Coast) $35. **86** *—S.H. (11/15/2003)*

Clos La Chance 1997 Cabernet Sauvignon (Santa Cruz Mountains) $21. **91** *—S.H. (7/1/2000)*

Clos La Chance 2001 Cabernet Sauvignon (Napa Valley) $25. Simple and rather hot, with a thick, heavy texture that conveys jammy cherry flavors through a slightly sweet finish. Lacks the breeding you expect from this appellation. **84** *—S.H. (6/1/2004)*

Clos La Chance 1998 Chardonnay (Santa Cruz Mountains) $19. 87 *(6/1/2000)*

Clos La Chance 1997 Chardonnay (Santa Cruz Mountains) $19. 90 *—J.C. (11/15/1999)*

Clos La Chance 2003 Chardonnay (Santa Cruz Mountains) $19. This is a very hands-on winemaker wine. It's strong in lees and oak, and feels a bit manipulated. The underlying wine seems very cool-climate, suggesting green apples and cinnamon-laced coffee, with tart acids. **85** *—S.H. (11/15/2005)*

Clos La Chance 2001 Chardonnay (Santa Cruz Mountains) $18. 91 Editors' Choice *—S.H. (10/1/2003)*

Clos La Chance 2000 Chardonnay (Napa Valley) $18. 90 Editors' Choice *—S.H. (12/15/2002)*

Clos La Chance 2002 Vanumanutagi Vineyard Chardonnay (Santa Cruz County) $30. Lemondrop candy, fresh ripe papaya, sun-ripened peach, toasted and sweetened coconut, cinnamon spice—there's enough flavor to go around a dozen wines. There's also lots of oak. This flashy, flamboyant wine has all that, but it's a little soft and one-dimensional. **87** *—S.H. (6/1/2004)*

USA

Clos La Chance 1999 Vanumanutagi Vineyard Chardonnay (Santa Cruz Mountains) $30. 89 *—J.M. (5/1/2002)*

Clos La Chance 2003 Grenache (Central Coast) $29. Showcases Grenache's cherry flavors very well, with the fruit standing front and center in this soft, dry wine with an edge of sweet oak. It could use greater structure, but sure is a tasty sipper. **86** *—S.H. (12/31/2005)*

Clos La Chance 1997 Merlot (Central Coast) $17. 88 *—M.M. (3/1/2000)*

Clos La Chance 2001 Merlot (Central Coast) $18. 91 Editors' Choice *—S.H. (10/1/2003)*

Clos La Chance 2003 Petite Sirah (Central Coast) $35. Soft, super-fruity, and dry, this is built along Cabernet lines, with ripe flavors of blackberries, cherries, and blueberries, and deliciously sweet oak. The tannins are lush, the acids are soft, and the finish has wild herbs sprinkled with white pepper. **88** *—S.H. (12/31/2005)*

Clos La Chance 2001 Pinot Noir (Santa Cruz County) $28. 88 *—S.H. (7/1/2003)*

Clos La Chance 1997 Pinot Noir (Santa Cruz Mountains) $24. 93 *(10/1/1999)*

Clos La Chance 2001 Erwin Vineyard Pinot Noir (Santa Cruz Mountains) $35. Forward in new oak, this wine opens with a burst of vanilla and toast, but it's big enough to shoulder all that wood. The ripe cherry, pomegranate, and coffee flavors are dry, wrapped in soft, silky tannins. You find yourself wishing it had more concentration, though. **89** *—S.H. (2/1/2005)*

Clos La Chance 2004 Rosé Wine (Central Coast) $14. Here's an easy, Rhône-style blush wine that's dry enough to have with a bouillabaisse-type dish, or grilled sausages and veggies. It has polished strawberry, cherry, and pepper flavors, boosted by bright acids. **85** *—S.H. (11/15/2005)*

Clos La Chance 2004 Estate Sauvignon Blanc (Central Coast) $16. Textbook coastal Sauvignon Blanc, a bone dry wine with brisk acidity, and flavors of grapefruit, lime, fig, and honeydew melon. There's a fine, peppery note on the finish. **87** *—S.H. (11/15/2005)*

Clos La Chance 2001 Syrah (Central Coast) $20. 85 *—S.H. (12/15/2003)*

Clos La Chance 2003 Viognier (Central Coast) $18. Kind of earthy and a bit disjointed, with herb, tobacco, and peach flavors and fairly high acidity. It's also a very dry wine. Almost Sauvignon Blanc-like in dryness and tartness; unusual for Viognier, but a good, crisp drink. **85** *—S.H. (8/1/2005)*

Clos La Chance 2002 Zinfandel (El Dorado County) $18. Very ripe in berry fruit, but dry, with a firm, tannic texture, and turns sweetish on the finish, like the aftertaste of a cherry tart. A bit rough overall, but a good Zin with extra features. **87** *—S.H. (5/1/2005)*

Clos La Chance 1997 Zinfandel (El Dorado County) $17. 88 *(5/1/2000)*

CLOS MIMI

Clos Mimi 2001 Bunny Slope Vineyard Syrah (Paso Robles) $50. Do we just not get this wine? Aromas are nice enough, starting with floral, minty scents and then delivering some mushroomy notes later on, but the flavors are sour and lean, finishing tangy and herbal. **83** *(9/1/2005)*

Clos Mimi 2003 Petite Rousse Syrah (Paso Robles) $17. Smells pretty Rhônish, with peppery, floral and meaty notes layered over blackberry fruit. Winemaker Tim Spear's entry-level Syrah boasts 16% alcohol but it's not all that noticeable, balanced by just enough raspberry, blackberry, and vanilla flavors. **85** *(9/1/2005)*

CLOS PEGASE

Clos Pegase 1997 Cabernet Sauvignon (Napa Valley) $30. 90 *(11/1/2000)*

Clos Pegase 2001 Cabernet Sauvignon (Napa Valley) $32. So ripe, it's gooey in currant, cocoa, and cassis flavors that have been lavishly oaked. This is a soft, smooth wine, with velvety tannins, and has enough complexity and nuance to merit its score. **91** *—S.H. (3/1/2005)*

Clos Pegase 2000 Graveyard Hill Cabernet Sauvignon (Carneros) $60. You can smell the new oak a mile away, powerful in char and smoky vanilla. Then the cassis hits you and the mind thinks, Great Cab. Rich, ripe, and intense, dripping with black currants and chocolate, but with firm tannins. Should be a keeper for years, but hard to resist its immediate charms. **92** *—S.H. (3/1/2005)*

Clos Pegase 2001 Hommage Cabernet Sauvignon (Napa Valley) $75. Clos Pegase has really hit its stride in recent years, as this fine Cabernet shows. It's true to the vintage, being supremely ripe and balanced, with pure, intense black currant flavors and quite a bit of new oak. I would cellar this wine for a good five years to let it all come together, and it should hold for several years. **91** *—S.H. (11/15/2005)*

Clos Pegase 1999 Palisades Vineyard Cabernet Sauvignon (Napa Valley) $60. 91 *—S.H. (6/1/2003)*

Clos Pegase 2001 Hommage Mitsuko's Vineyard Chardonnay (Carneros) $36. Enormously oaky, but it sure is delicious. Dominated by the taste of sweet caramelly char, honey, and vanilla. Underneath you'll find ripe flavors of sauteed banana, spicy mango, and peach cobbler. This flamboyant wine is heady. Try with scallops in a coconut milk and curry sauce **92** *—S.H. (3/1/2005)*

Clos Pegase 2002 Mitsuko's Vineyard Chardonnay (Carneros) $21. Tutti-frutti and jammy flavors mingle with plenty of toasty oak to provide for a rich, satisfying Chard. You'll find peaches and pears, apples and pineapples, and lots of spices, especially in the long, crisp finish. **88** *—S.H. (4/1/2004)*

Clos Pegase 2002 Mitsuko's Vineyard Hommage Chardonnay (Carneros) $36. Everything about this Chard is brilliantly crafted, but the parts haven't come together. It's all fine charred oak, creamy, yeasty lees and primary peach, pear and tropical fruit, battling it out. But it's a very fine wine, and simply needs a while to coalesce. Try in a few months. **92** *—S.H. (12/15/2005)*

Clos Pegase 2001 Mitsuko's Vineyard Merlot (Carneros) $25. This is the kind of Merlot that shows how well Carneros can ripen the variety. It's a big, rich wine, almost fat in gooey black cherry, mocha, and anise flavors, but is fortunately balanced with rich, furry tannins. It's a bit soft, but very tasty. **87** *—S.H. (12/15/2005)*

Clos Pegase 2000 Mitsuko's Vineyard Merlot (Carneros) $25. Not as rich as in the past, a wine marked with lean herbal flavors and tough, green tannins. The new French oak helps to provide sweet, fancy notes, but the final impression is astringent and short. **85** *—S.H. (5/1/2004)*

Clos Pegase 2001 Mitsuko's Vineyard Pinot Noir (Carneros) $30. Polished and delicious, just starting to come into its own. Has shed its youthful tannins to reveal a silky, fleshy wine of charm and nuance. Raspberry, cherry, nutmeg, cola, cocoa, and smoky oak flavors unfold in waves, leading to a soft, spicy finish. **92** *—S.H. (3/1/2005)*

Clos Pegase 2004 Mitsuko's Vineyard Sauvignon Blanc (Carneros) $19. Gooseberries, juniper, and lemon rind—those are the sorts of things that come to mind with this intensely dry wine. Yet it has an elegant balance, an inherent finesse that lifts it out of the ordinary into the realm of complexity. Try with shellfish in cream sauce. **90** *—S.H. (12/31/2005)*

Clos Pegase 2002 Mitsuko's Vineyard Sauvignon Blanc (Carneros) $18. Aromas of peach, pear, citrus and vanilla-smoke lead to a rich, complex wine, filled with lovely fruit flavors and spices. The texture is creamy smooth, with bright acids that make the wine lively and fresh. Long on the finish, and perfect with grilled shrimp. **88** *—S.H. (2/1/2004)*

CLOS PEPE

Clos Pepe 2002 Homage to Chablis Chardonnay (Santa Rita Hills) $25. A big, bracing, exotic Chard with a gunmetal and mineral spine plus, tangy flavors of candied grapefruit, mango, and papaya. High in acidity, yet well oaked. Very companionable for food; should age gracefully for several years. **91** *—S.H. (9/1/2004)*

Clos Pepe 2000 Pinot Noir (Santa Rita Hills) $35. 89 *(10/1/2002)*

CLOUD 9

Cloud 9 2001 Composition Red Blend (California) $35. Dramatically rich and smooth, with very ripe flavors of black cherries, red plums, mocha and sweet herbs, this complex wine also has supple tannins that are thick, but gentle. The finish is long and harmonious. Definitely one of the best "California" appellation reds out there. **91** *—S.H. (11/15/2005)*

Cloud 9 2003 Seity Zinfandel (Amador County) $35. The winery claims the wine comes from "the oldest Zinfandel vines on earth." Certainly this is an intensely flavored, densely structured Zin. The flavors go beyond cherry, raspberry, and cocoa fruit into the area of dessert pastries, with toasted pie dough and meringue. But the wine is fully dry, at the price of high alcohol, 15.4%. **90** *—S.H. (12/31/2005)*

CLOUD VIEW

Cloud View 2001 Red Wine Bordeaux Blend (Napa Valley) $60. Smoky and tarry at first, later opening into black cherry and tobacco notes. Long, intense, and tannic on the finish; needs time. Try around 2010. A blend of 57% Merlot and 43% Cabernet Sauvignon. **91** *(6/6/2005)*

COASTAL RIDGE

Coastal Ridge 2001 Cabernet Sauvignon (California) $7. Take a good '01 Cab, thin it down, and that's what you get with this affordably drinkable wine. It's dry and balanced, with pleasant berry flavors. **84 Best Buy** *—S.H. (4/1/2005)*

Coastal Ridge 1999 Cabernet Sauvignon (California) $7. 85 *—S.H. (6/1/2002)*

Coastal Ridge 2002 Chardonnay (California) $7. Drinks rustic in texture and sharp, with citrus and peach flavors and an edge of oak. If you need something quick to serve at your next block party, it's a good candidate. **83** *—S.H. (11/15/2004)*

Coastal Ridge 2000 Barrel Aged Chardonnay (Napa County) $7. **84** *—S.H. (12/15/2002)*

Coastal Ridge 2004 Johannisberg Riesling (California) $7. This is the kind of semisweet wine that vast numbers of Americans enjoy. It's clean, fruity, and affordable, with peach and honey flavors. **83 Best Buy** *—S.H. (12/1/2005)*

Coastal Ridge 2002 Merlot (California) $7. Jammy, juicy, and a little sweet, but easy enough, with cherry and cola flavors. **83** *—S.H. (4/1/2005)*

Coastal Ridge 1998 Merlot (California) $7. **84 Best Buy** *—S.H. (5/1/2001)*

Coastal Ridge 2003 Pinot Noir (California) $7. If you like Pinot's dry, silky elegance, this is a good everyday wine. It has a delicate mouthfeel, with crisp acids framing modest cherry, berry, and spice flavors in a creamy, oak-tinged texture. **84 Best Buy** *—S.H. (12/31/2005)*

Coastal Ridge 2001 Shiraz (California) $7. Smells pleasant, with plum, blackberry and oak notes, but turns rather thin and tannic in the mouth. Very dry, with some fruit and herb flavors. **83** *—S.H. (12/1/2004)*

Coastal Ridge 1999 Shiraz (California) $7. **83** *(10/1/2001)*

USA

COBBLESTONE

Cobblestone 1997 Chardonnay (Arroyo Seco) $23. **87** *(6/1/2000)*

Cobblestone 1999 Chardonnay (Arroyo Seco) $22. **87** *—S.H. (12/31/2001)*

COEUR D'ALENE CELLARS

Coeur d'Alene Cellars 2002 Syrah (Washington) $25. Blackberries and blueberries on the nose, but not a simple fruit bomb, as it picks up greater depth and spice on the palate, adding layers of pepper and anise to the mix. Full-bodied, yet supple, with hints of coffee on the long finish. **90 Editors' Choice** *(9/1/2005)*

COLD HEAVEN

Cold Heaven 2001 Le Bon Climate Viognier (Santa Barbara County) $25. Nothing heavenly about this wine. It's too old. Smells vegetal, tastes flat, end of story. **81** *—S.H. (8/1/2005)*

Cold Heaven 2000 Sanford & Benedict Vineyard Viognier (Santa Ynez Valley) $25. **88** *—J.M. (12/15/2002)*

COLEMAN

Coleman 2002 Estate Pinot Noir (Willamette Valley) $19. A strong cinnamon scent, along with orange peel and citrus, stands out. The fruit is juicy blackberry, with a smooth, somewhat lean, tannic finish. **87** *(11/1/2004)*

COLGIN

Colgin 1999 Herb Lamb Vineyard Cabernet Sauvignon (Napa Valley) $150. **96** *—J.M. (6/1/2002)*

COLLEGE CELLARS

College Cellars 2003 Minick Vineyards Syrah (Yakima Valley) $18. Some tasters will dislike this wine, while others will enjoy it. You might find it the proper blend of herb and spice to go with the tart red berries, or you might find it overtly vegetal—it will depend on your tolerance for green stuff in your wine. **85** *(9/1/2005)*

COLLIER FALLS

Collier Falls 2000 Hillside Estate Cabernet Sauvignon (Dry Creek Valley) $36. **89** *—S.H. (12/31/2003)*

Collier Falls 2002 Zinfandel (Dry Creek Valley) $26. One of the fruitier Zins around, or maybe the light tannins let the fruit shine through. Either way, it's a flavorful wine, showing blackberry, plum, and cherry flavors, with dry, plum skin-bitter tannins. This is a good, all-purpose Zin. **87** *—S.H. (11/1/2005)*

Collier Falls 2001 Private Reserve Zinfandel (Dry Creek Valley) $28. **83** *(11/1/2003)*

Collier Falls 1998 Private Reserve Zinfandel (Dry Creek Valley) $21. **91 Editors' Choice** *—P.G. (3/1/2001)*

COLUMBIA CREST

Columbia Crest 2001 Walter Clore Reserve Red Bordeaux Blend (Columbia Valley (WA)) $35. This sophisticated blend offers complex flavors of mixed red fruits, nicely textured and layered. You can pick out distinct pomegranate, cranberry, red berry, and cherry flavors; there's nothing monolithic about it. There are also some hints of olive and herb, and substantial tannins. **90** *—P.G. (4/1/2005)*

Columbia Crest 1997 Cabernet Sauvignon (Columbia Valley (WA)) $9. **88** *—P.G. (6/1/2000)*

Columbia Crest 1996 Estate Series Cabernet Sauvignon (Columbia Valley (WA)) $15. **88** *—P.G. (6/1/2000)*

Columbia Crest 2001 Grand Estates Cabernet Sauvignon (Columbia Valley (WA)) $11. A lovely blend of fruit from the Wahluke Slope, which lends aromatics and steely structure, and the Horse Heaven Hills, which gives it a broad, sweet core of jammy preserves. Very smooth, accessible, and surprisingly focused, this wine is perfectly aged and blended for near-term enjoyment. **87** *—P.G. (7/1/2004)*

Columbia Crest 2002 Reserve Cabernet Sauvignon (Columbia Valley (WA)) $30. Aromatic with black olive, herb, and cocoa wrapped around tight raspberry/cassis fruit. The fruit is nicely concentrated, then splays into a broad, chocolaty, softly tannic midpalate. At this stage of life the wine remains angular, woody, and unintegrated; with another six to twelve months in bottle it could improve its score by a point or two. **89** *—P.G. (12/15/2005)*

Columbia Crest 1999 Reserve Cabernet Sauvignon (Columbia Valley (WA)) $28. **92** *—P.G. (9/1/2002)*

Columbia Crest 2002 Two Vines Cabernet Sauvignon (Columbia Valley (WA)) $8. In keeping with the Two Vines style, this shows plenty of bright cherry fruit; but that's not the end of it. In fact it is surprisingly deep, polished and supple with good, juicy fruit and real concentration. There's nothing vegetal, or earthy, or rough; it's a smooth and polished effort but not at all spineless. Where else in the world can they make an $8 cab this good? **88 Best Buy** *—P.G. (4/1/2005)*

Columbia Crest 1999 Cabernet Sauvignon-Merlot (Columbia Valley (WA)) $30. **92** *—P.G. (9/1/2002)*

Columbia Crest 1998 Chardonnay (Columbia Valley (WA)) $8. **87** *—P.G. (6/1/2000)*

Columbia Crest 1999 Chardonnay (Columbia Valley (WA)) $12. **86** *(6/1/2001)*

Columbia Crest 2002 Grand Estates Chardonnay (Columbia Valley (WA)) $11. Bigger, with more obvious oak than the CC "regular," this gets special treatment (hand-stirred for nine months once a week) and 1/4 new oak. It's nicely integrated, big and buttery, with pleasing layers of caramelized sugar and baked apple. A home run. **90 Best Buy** *—P.G. (4/1/2005)*

Columbia Crest 1999 Grand Estates Chardonnay (Columbia Valley (WA)) $13. **89 Best Buy** *—P.G. (6/1/2001)*

Columbia Crest 2002 Reserve Chardonnay (Columbia Valley (WA)) $30. The biggest and richest of the three CC chards, this is decadently rich, supple, and smooth. It tastes lightly of butter; more of butterscotch. Powerful and expressive. **90** *—P.G. (4/1/2005)*

Columbia Crest 1997 Reserve Chardonnay (Columbia Valley (WA)) $18. **88** *—P.G. (6/1/2000)*

Columbia Crest 2002 Two Vines Chardonnay (Columbia Valley (WA)) $8. Fruity and soft and approachable, a mass-produced wine that still shows hand-crafted flavors. For the price this may well be the country's top chardonnay. **88 Best Buy** *—P.G. (4/1/2005)*

Columbia Crest 2000 Gewürztraminer (Columbia Valley (WA)) $8. **87** *—P.G. (12/31/2001)*

Columbia Crest 2003 Two Vines Gewürztraminer (Columbia Valley (WA)) $8. Fragrant yet tangy, with flat-out lovely fruit that showcases the candied citrus side of the grape. Penetrating and long. **88 Best Buy** *—P.G. (6/1/2005)*

Columbia Crest 1997 Merlot (Columbia Valley (WA)) $11. **88** *—P.G. (6/1/2000)*

Columbia Crest 1996 Estate Series Merlot (Columbia Valley (WA)) $16. **87** *—P.G. (8/19/2003)*

Columbia Crest 2001 Grand Estates Merlot (Columbia Valley (WA)) $11. Smooth, supple, full, and ripe, with a classic chocolate/cherry character. The merlot hits the palate a bit broader than the cab, which is more precise but not as weighty. It is unquestionably is a very seductive wine, broad yet medium deep, with dark berry and chocolatey flavors wrapped together, finishing with a very French hint of herb. **89 Best Buy** *—P.G. (4/1/2005)*

Columbia Crest 1999 Grand Estates Merlot (Columbia Valley (WA)) $11. **87** *—P.G. (9/1/2002)*

Columbia Crest 2001 Reserve Merlot (Columbia Valley (WA)) $30. Tight, dry, and tannic, the flavor mixes good, clean, well-ripened fruit and lots of woodsy, leafy nuances. There are some darker streaks of smoke and char, and beautiful tannin integration. **91** *—P.G. (4/1/2005)*

Columbia Crest 1999 Reserve Merlot (Columbia Valley (WA)) $28. **90** *—P.G. (9/1/2002)*

Columbia Crest 1999 Merlot-Cabernet Sauvignon (Columbia Valley (WA)) $10. **87 Best Buy** *—P.G. (6/1/2002)*

Columbia Crest 1997 Reserve Red Blend (Columbia Valley (WA)) $24. **90** *—P.G. (6/1/2001)*

Columbia Crest 2002 Walter Clore Reserve Red Red Blend (Columbia Valley (WA)) $35. The house style is readily apparent here: red fruits, whiffs of cocoa, light herb, and a hint of pickle barrel. Tastes good, comes together well, but hard to distinguish from the reserve cab, which seems to have just a bit more stuffing. **88** *—P.G. (12/15/2005)*

Columbia Crest 2003 Two Vines Riesling (Columbia Valley (WA)) $8. A new line for value leader Columbia Crest, this exceptionally fragrant, off-dry Riesling bursts with honeysuckle scents and tropical fruit flavors. There's enough crispness to support the residual sugar and keep the wine poised and vivid. **89 Best Buy** *—P.G. (7/1/2004)*

Columbia Crest 2002 Two Vines Sauvignon Blanc (Columbia Valley (WA)) $8. Crisp and clean, nice and refreshing, with plump, tangy green and yellow fruits. Apples and limes up front, while good crisp acids keep it lifted and great with food. **87 Best Buy** *—P.G. (4/1/2005)*

Columbia Crest 1998 Reserve Ice Wine Sémillon (Columbia Valley (WA)) $28. **92** *—P.G. (6/1/2000)*

Columbia Crest 2000 Sémillon-Chardonnay (Columbia Valley (WA)) $6. **87** *—P.G. (2/1/2002)*

Columbia Crest 2003 Two Vines Shiraz (Columbia Valley (WA)) $8. Slightly candied, bright cherry fruit and a healthy dose of vanilla give this easy-to-drink Shiraz all the prerequisites for commercial success. The creamy mouthfeel shows very little tannin, while the juicy, mouthwatering finish picks up enough hints of complexity to keep it interesting. With 100,000 cases made, should be plenty easy to find. **85 Best Buy** *(9/1/2005)*

Columbia Crest 2002 Grand Estates Syrah (Columbia Valley (WA)) $11. Delicious boysenberry fruit dominates this wine, but it doesn't carry through very far. It needs breathing time; when given a few hours, it does seem to expand. Overall, it's a pure and sweet and delicious expression of syrah, giving lots of flavor for the price. **88 Best Buy** *—P.G. (4/1/2005)*

Columbia Crest 2003 Reserve Syrah (Columbia Valley (WA)) $30. A bit of a disappointment after the exceptional 2002, this young, hard wine brings scents of citrus, white pepper, and green coffee beans into play, with rather aggressive notes of American oak. The pickle-barrel character is a bit of a detraction, and the wine is tart, chewy, and still awkward with unresolved tannins. Needs time. **87** *—P.G. (12/15/2005)*

Columbia Crest 2001 Reserve Syrah (Columbia Valley (WA)) $30. Much more concentrated and powerfully fragrant than the previous vintage, this is a keeper. It's sinfully dark and bursting with pepper, coffee, and berry scents. In the mouth it explodes with vivid fruit intensity, yet retains an elegance, keeping alcohol at a sensible 14%. **90 Editors' Choice** *—P.G. (1/1/2004)*

Columbia Crest 1999 Reserve Syrah (Columbia Valley (WA)) $28. **89** *—P.G. (6/1/2002)*

Columbia Crest 1997 Reserve Syrah (Columbia Valley (WA)) $25. **80** *—P.G. (9/1/2000)*

Columbia Crest 1998 White Blend (Columbia Valley (WA)) $8. **85** *—P.G. (11/15/2000)*

COLUMBIA WINERY

Columbia Winery 1996 Millennium Bordeaux Blend (Columbia Valley (WA)) $75. **89** *(4/1/2000)*

Columbia Winery 2001 Red Willow Cabernet Franc (Yakima Valley) $23. **85** *—P.G. (12/31/2003)*

Columbia Winery 1997 Red Willow Vineyard Cabernet Franc (Yakima Valley) $24. **88** *—P.G. (6/1/2001)*

Columbia Winery 1998 Signature Series Red Willow Vineyard Cabernet Franc (Columbia Valley (WA)) $22. **89** *—P.G. (12/31/2001)*

Columbia Winery 2000 Cabernet Sauvignon (Columbia Valley (WA)) $15. **87** *—P.G. (12/31/2003)*

Columbia Winery 1998 Cabernet Sauvignon (Columbia Valley (WA)) $15. **85** *—P.G. (10/1/2001)*

Columbia Winery 2000 Otis Vineyard Cabernet Sauvignon (Yakima Valley) $25. A relatively round, fruity and approachable wine with good cherry/plum flavors when first released, it has recently turned tight and dryly tannic. Shows the classic black pepper and dried sage character of the Otis vineyard. Otis Cabs are best cellared for a number of years in order to reveal their subtlety. **89** *—P.G. (12/15/2005)*

Columbia Winery 1997 Otis Vineyard Cabernet Sauvignon (Yakima Valley) $26. **89** *—P.G. (12/31/2002)*

Columbia Winery 1998 Red Willow Cabernet Sauvignon (Yakima Valley) $29. **90 Cellar Selection** *—P.G. (12/31/2003)*

Columbia Winery 2000 Red Willow Vineyard Cabernet Sauvignon (Yakima Valley) $23. Lots of ripe boysenberry, cranberry, and sour cherry fruit to start, with a strong foundation of tar, espresso, and bitter chocolate. This could pass for a Super Tuscan in a blind tasting. It unfolds slowly, with an interesting herbal/olive edge to it, and will reward additional cellaring. **91 Cellar Selection** *—P.G. (4/1/2005)*

Columbia Winery 1998 Sagemoor Cabernet Sauvignon (Columbia Valley (WA)) $29. **88** *—P.G. (12/31/2003)*

Columbia Winery 1997 Sagemoor Vineyard Cabernet Sauvignon (Columbia Valley (WA)) $29. **89** *—P.G. (6/1/2002)*

Columbia Winery 1999 Otis Vineyard Chardonnay (Yakima Valley) $24. **88** *—P.G. (10/1/2001)*

Columbia Winery 1999 Otis Vineyard-Block 6 Chardonnay (Columbia Valley (WA)) $40. **89** *—P.G. (7/1/2002)*

Columbia Winery 1999 Woodburne Cuvée Chardonnay (Columbia Valley (WA)) $14. **86** *—P.G. (6/1/2001)*

Columbia Winery 2000 Wyckoff Chardonnay (Yakima Valley) $19. This gets the full-blown barrel treatment (fermented and aged in French oak, lees-stirring, full malolactic fermentation), and it shows rather more than the fruit. Buttery, richly textured and spice-scented (clove and cinnamon), with only modest levels of yellow fruit flavors that include hints of pineapple and Golden Delicious. **87** *(1/1/2004)*

Columbia Winery 2002 Wyckoff Vineyard Chardonnay (Yakima Valley) $19. Butterscotch, vanilla, and spicy anise light up this Burgundian-style chardonnay. Its not-too-ripe fruit flavors of melon and citrus keep it crisp and well-defined, and winemaker David Lake has added just the right amount of toasty new oak. **90** *—P.G. (4/1/2005)*

Columbia Winery 1999 Wyckoff Vineyard Chardonnay (Yakima Valley) $19. **88** *—P.G. (12/31/2002)*

Columbia Winery 1997 Wyckoff Vyd Chardonnay (Yakima Valley) $21. 88 *—P.G. (4/1/2000)*

Columbia Winery 2003 Gewürztraminer (Columbia Valley (WA)) $9. This is a real success for the winery, made bracingly fresh and crisp despite its 3% residual sugar. Bright flavors of pink grapefruit dominate the palate, filling out a pristine, crisp and deliciously fresh finish. **90 Best Buy** *—P.G. (4/1/2005)*

Columbia Winery 1997 Merlot (Columbia Valley (WA)) $15. 88 *—P.G. (4/1/2000)*

Columbia Winery 1999 Merlot (Columbia Valley (WA)) $15. 87 *—P.G. (9/1/2002)*

Columbia Winery 1999 Red Willow Milestone Merlot (Yakima Valley) $29. 89 *—P.G. (12/31/2003)*

Columbia Winery 2002 Pinot Gris (Yakima Valley) $10. As is usually the style with David Lake's white wines, this is taut, clean, and very crisp, showing light mixed fruit flavors of fig and melon. Just a slight taste of cardboard shows up in the finish. **86 Best Buy** *—P.G. (12/1/2004)*

Columbia Winery 1998 Pinot Gris (Yakima Valley) $9. 84 *—P.G. (11/15/2000)*

Columbia Winery 2001 Red Willow Sangiovese (Yakima Valley) $20. 84 *—P.G. (12/31/2003)*

Columbia Winery 2002 Red Willow Vineyard Sangiovese (Yakima Valley) $25. This wine, though done in the understated style of winemaker David Lake, has an immensely appealing bouquet of spicy red fruits enhanced with cinnamon and toast. A firm, confident entry, that shows fruit that is ripe, not at all jammy, and focuses in on a clean core of pretty cherry. The back palate features a nice mix of cocoa, cinnamon and baking spices. **90** *—P.G. (12/1/2004)*

Columbia Winery 2001 Sémillon (Columbia Valley (WA)) $8. 90 Best Buy *—P.G. (12/31/2003)*

Columbia Winery 1997 Syrah (Yakima Valley) $14. 90 *—P.G. (4/1/2000)*

Columbia Winery 2000 Syrah (Columbia Valley (WA)) $15. 88 Best Buy *—P.G. (12/31/2002)*

Columbia Winery 1998 Syrah (Yakima Valley) $15. 88 *—P.G. (11/15/2000)*

Columbia Winery 2000 Red Willow South Chapel Block Syrah (Yakima Valley) $50. 89 *—P.G. (12/31/2003)*

Columbia Winery 1998 Red Willow Vineyard Syrah (Yakima Valley) $35. 86 *(11/1/2001)*

Columbia Winery 1997 Reserve Syrah (Columbia Valley (WA)) $32. 92 *—S.H. (11/1/1999)*

Columbia Winery 2000 Red Willow Viognier (Yakima Valley) $23. 85 *—P.G. (12/31/2001)*

COLVIN VINEYARDS

Colvin Vineyards 2001 Allégresse Bordeaux Blend (Walla Walla (WA)) $36. This Bordeaux blend includes a small amount of carmenère, for which this winery has built a reputation, and it is done in a style that has garnered a lot of positive attention. This reviewer finds that the overwhelming presence of brettanomyces, which lends a very horsey, leathery scent and flavor, detracts from everything else. It almost completely kills the fruit. **85** *—P.G. (12/1/2004)*

COM E BELLA

Com e Bella 2000 Cabernet Sauvignon (Calaveras County) $30. Sulfury, soft and sweet. **82** *—S.H. (3/1/2005)*

COMPASS

Compass 2000 Merlot (Napa Valley) $12. 86 *—S.H. (12/31/2003)*

COMTESSE THÉRÈSE

Comtesse Thérèse 2001 Château Reserve Merlot (North Fork of Long Island) $25. 88 *—J.C. (10/2/2004)*

CONCANNON

Concannon 2002 Reserve Assemblage Red Cabernet Blend (Livermore Valley) $24. Dry, soft, and a little rustic, with earthy, berry, and coffee flavors. Finishes rough in acids and tannins. **84** *—S.H. (6/1/2005)*

Concannon 2000 Reserve Limited Release Cabernet Sauvignon (Livermore Valley) $24. This wine will strike some as impossibly tannic and earthy, and it's true it's not particularly fruity. But it's like a fresh young Bordeaux, a Cabernet that needs time. There's a sweet core of blackberry and cherry flavor that's best cellared until 2008. **88** *—S.H. (6/1/2004)*

Concannon 2002 Selected Vineyard Cabernet Sauvignon (Central Coast) $12. Tough and tannic, this wine tastes cooked. It has flavors of grapes that burnt and shrivelled in the heat, with a raisiny finish. **81** *—S.H. (12/1/2005)*

Concannon 1997 Reserve Chardonnay (Central Coast) $20. 83 *(6/1/2000)*

Concannon 2002 Reserve Limited Release Chardonnay (Edna Valley) $18. The grapes struggled to get ripe, and you can taste the ocean climate in the green, citrusy flavors that just barely veer into white peach. Acidity is high, and oak has been kept strictly as a light seasoning. **86** *—S.H. (6/1/2004)*

Concannon 2003 Selected Vineyards Chardonnay (Central Coast) $12. A zesty, vibrant Chard, filled with acids, with flavors ranging from ripe citrus to peach. There's very little oak, so the fruit and crispness star. Long, spicy finish, and terrifically food-friendly. **86** *—S.H. (2/1/2005)*

Concannon 2001 Reserve Limited Release Merlot (Livermore Valley) $24. Red Bordeaux varieties can do very well in this appellation if they're well cared for, and Concannon has done a terrific job with this ripe, fancy Merlot. It has some big tannins, but they're the soft, dusty kind that are drinkable now with rich foods. The blackberry flavors break out into currants and cassis. **91** *—S.H. (6/1/2004)*

Concannon 2003 Selected Vineyards Merlot (Central Coast) $10. From cool-climate vineyards comes this hearty country red. It gets the job done with cherry-berry and earthy-spicy flavors, in a nicely dry and balanced package. Has the personality for everything from cheeseburgers to a sizzling steak. **85 Best Buy** *—S.H. (12/31/2005)*

Concannon 2000 Petite Sirah (Central Coast) $12. 86 *(4/1/2003)*

Concannon 2001 Heritage Petite Sirah (Livermore Valley) $40. From the winery that claims to have introduced Petite Sirah as a varietal wine comes this dynamic bottling. It's full-bodied, dry, and tannic, with a deep undertow of blackberry, cherry, plum, and coffee flavors, and has a complex structure. Will be beautiful with a grilled steak, but this is a wine you can stash away for at least a decade. **92 Cellar Selection** *—S.H. (12/1/2005)*

Concannon 2002 Reserve Petite Sirah (Livermore Valley) $30. Classic Pet, tough in tannins, bone dry, full-bodied, and with a big, hearty core of cherries, blackberries, leather, and spices. You can drink it now, but it should soften and sweeten through the decade. **90** *—S.H. (6/1/2005)*

Concannon 1995 Reserve Petite Sirah (Central Coast) $23. 90 *—J.C. (11/1/1999)*

Concannon 2002 Selected Vineyard Petite Sirah (Central Coast) $12. Quintessential Pet, inky black, rich in thick, dusty tannins, absolutely dry, and bursting with blackberry, plum, dark chocolate, and spicy, peppery flavors. Beautiful in its own way, and a super value. **88 Best Buy** *—S.H. (11/15/2004)*

Concannon 2002 Limited Release Pinot Noir (Edna Valley) $24. Hard to like this difficult wine. It's partially unripe, with herbal notes veering toward vegetal. **82** *—S.H. (6/1/2005)*

Concannon 2002 Stampmaker's Red Wine Rhône Red Blend (Livermore Valley) $24. Very fruit forward in cherries and pomegranates, with rich tannins that grip the palate. Feels dry all the way to the finish, when it turns cough-mediciney sweet. **84** *—S.H. (6/1/2005)*

Concannon 2004 Limited Release Assemblage White Wine Sauvignon Blanc (Central Coast) $15. So dry, so tart is this citrusy, high-acid wine that the palate begs for some morsel to soften it. Goat cheese will do exactly that, or grilled veggies, or a nice halibut sautéed in butter and olive oil. A heck of a good food wine. **87** *—S.H. (12/15/2005)*

Concannon 2002 Reserve Limited Release Sauvignon Blanc (Monterey) $18. 89 *—S.H. (12/1/2003)*

Concannon 2004 Selected Vineyards Sauvignon Blanc (Central Coast) $10. Bone dry and acidic, with lemon-and-lime and mineral flavors enriched with a lush streak of nectarine, this is not only a fun Sauvignon, but quite an elegant one. It's hard to imagine a dry white wine more versatile with food. **86 Best Buy** *—S.H. (12/15/2005)*

Concannon 1997 Syrah (Livermore Valley) $20. 86 *(10/1/2001)*

Concannon 2003 Selected Vineyard Syrah (Central Coast) $10. There's plenty of fruit in this country-style wine. It's jam-packed with blackberries, cherries, plums, and roasted coffee flavors, and is thoroughly dry, with full-bodied tannins and tart acidity. **84** *—S.H. (12/31/2005)*

Concannon 2001 Selected Vineyard Syrah (Central Coast) $12. A good everyday wine that scores with its nice, dry tannins and good balance. A bit thin in fruit, but you'll find some plummy, blackberry flavors with a touch of smoked meat. **85** *—S.H. (12/1/2004)*

Concannon 2004 Limited Release Stampmaker's Viognier (Central Coast) $15. If you're looking for an exotic, lush Viognier, this isn't the one. It's a tight, crisp, cool-climate wine, with citrus flavors and especially well-ripened limes, set off by mouthwatering acidity. It's also a very elegant, well-tailored wine. **87** *—S.H. (12/15/2005)*

CONN CREEK

Conn Creek 1996 Anthology Bordeaux Blend (Napa Valley) $44. 91 *(7/1/2000)*

Conn Creek 2000 Anthology Cabernet Blend (Napa Valley) $54. Absolutely delicious, a fat, sumptuous wine that flatters the palate from beginning to end. Smells plush, brimming with currants and fancy oak trimmings, and turns lush and complex with fruit in the mouth. Best to drink it soon, in the fullness of youth. **92** *—S.H. (6/1/2004)*

Conn Creek 1999 Limited Release Cabernet Franc (Napa Valley) $25. 93 Editors' Choice *—S.H. (9/1/2002)*

Conn Creek 2001 Limited Release Cabernet Sauvignon (Napa Valley) $28. This is a tight young wine, a little closed in with tannins, but with ripe blackberry and cherry flavors, and a chocolaty finish. It's probably giving all it has now, but is polished enough for a nice dinner. **87** *—S.H. (10/1/2005)*

Conn Creek 1998 Limited Release Cabernet Sauvignon (Napa Valley) $25. 90 *—S.H. (6/1/2002)*

Conn Creek 1999 Limited Release Merlot (Napa Valley) $25. 91 —*S.H. (6/1/2002)*

CONN VALLEY

Conn Valley 1997 Estate Reserve Cabernet Sauvignon (Napa Valley) $55. 90 *(11/1/2000)*

Conn Valley 1999 Dutton Ranch Pinot Noir (Russian River Valley) $48. 83 *(10/1/2002)*

Conn Valley 1997 Valhalla Vineyard Pinot Noir (Napa Valley) $45. 87 *(10/1/1999)*

CONSILIENCE

Consilience 2000 Petite Sirah (Santa Barbara County) $21. 86 *(4/1/2003)*

Consilience 2002 Roussanne (Santa Barbara County) $22. Here's a rich, full-bodied wine with the weight and density of an oaky Chard. Has flavors of ripe white peaches, bananas, and tapioca, with a trace of white chocolate on the finish, but it's dry. 86 —*S.H. (5/1/2005)*

Consilience 2001 Syrah (Santa Barbara County) $17. Very good wine, with cherry-berry-mocha fruit and a dusty tinge of spice. It's the quality of the tannins and the overall balance that lend this wine harmony and power. 91 —*S.H. (9/1/2004)*

Consilience 2002 Great Oaks Vineyard Syrah (Santa Barbara County) $28. This is a young, immature Syrah you'll want to have with something big and rich, to help tame the somewhat woody-tasting tannins. Berry, coffee, and vanilla flavors are mouthfilling and intense, but will they measure up to the tannins in the long run? 86 *(9/1/2005)*

Consilience 2001 Rodney Shull Vineyard Syrah (Santa Barbara County) $24. Perplexing wine, with promising hints of smoke, chocolate, plums, and blackberries, but also a distressing lack of depth and texture. 82 *(9/1/2005)*

Consilience 2000 Rodney's Vineyard Syrah (Santa Barbara County) $30. A deep, dark and impressive wine made from Fess Parker's estate, in the Santa Ynez Valley. It has opening aromas of blackberry, dark plum, smoke, and oak and a note of cheddar, and drinks intense in fruity flavor and tannins. It's a young, firm wine but a pliant one, and will be beautiful now with a grilled T-bone steak. 90 —*S.H. (2/1/2004)*

Consilience 2002 Viognier (Santa Barbara County) $21. There may be some botrytis here, it's so unctuous and sweet with apricot and honey flavors. It's good, crisp stuff, but it's not a dry table wine. 84 —*S.H. (5/1/2005)*

Consilience 2000 Viognier (Santa Barbara County) $21. 90 —*J.M. (12/15/2002)*

Consilience 1999 Rhodes Vineyard Zinfandel (Redwood Valley) $30. 84 —*D.T. (3/1/2002)*

CONSTANT

Constant 2001 Diamond Mountain Vineyard Cabernet Franc (Napa Valley) $45. Imagine a rich, ripe mountain Cabernet without the edgy tannins and spicy currant flavor of the Sauvignon. Complex in cherry and oak flavor, with a smooth texture and an explosion of spice. It has a chocolaty finish, and is lip-smackingly delicious. 90 —*S.H. (12/15/2004)*

Constant 2001 Estate Cabernet Sauvignon (Napa Valley) $85. A massive wine that floods the palate with ripe flavors of blackberries and chocolate and sweet, smoky oak. Ripe, sweet tannins make for a good grip. Finishes lush and opulent, and a little soft. 89 —*S.H. (10/1/2004)*

COOK'S

Cook's NV Blush (California) $7. 82 —*S.H. (12/15/1999)*

Cook's NV Brut (California) $7. 82 —*J.M. (12/1/2002)*

Cook's NV Grand Spumante (California) $7. 84 Best Buy —*J.M. (11/15/2002)*

Cook's NV Spumante (California) $7. 84 —*S.H. (6/1/2001)*

COOKE

Cooke Cellars 2000 Sangiovese (Paso Robles) $24. 82 —*S.H. (2/1/2003)*

COOPER MOUNTAIN

Cooper Mountain 1999 Chardonnay (Willamette Valley) $12. 88 Best Buy —*P.G. (4/1/2002)*

Cooper Mountain 2000 Estate Bottled Pinot Gris (Willamette Valley) $15. 87 —*P.G. (4/1/2002)*

Cooper Mountain 1998 20th Anniversary Pinot Noir (Willamette Valley) $25. 88 —*M.S. (12/1/2000)*

Cooper Mountain 2002 Reserve Pinot Noir (Willamette Valley) $18. Unpleasant aromas lead into a light, grapy, simple, and tannic wine. 84 *(11/1/2004)*

COOPER-GARROD

Cooper-Garrod 1995 Cabernet Sauvignon (Santa Cruz Mountains) $28. 92 —*S.H. (2/1/2000)*

COPAIN WINES

Copain Wines 2001 Eaglepoint Ranch Syrah (Mendocino County) $35. **93 Editors' Choice** *—S.H. (12/1/2003)*

COPELAND CREEK

Copeland Creek 2001 Pinot Noir (Sonoma Coast) $30. Awful, with garbagey smells and no flavor. **81** *—S.H. (2/1/2005)*

CORBETT CANYON

Corbett Canyon 1997 Reserve Chardonnay (Santa Barbara County) $10. **84** *(10/1/2000)*

Corbett Canyon 1997 Reserve Merlot (North Coast) $10. **84** *(11/15/2000)*

CORE WINERY

Core Winery 2001 Rhône Red Blend (Santa Barbara County) $24. From 3,200 feet up in the Sierra Madre Mountains, a first-release Rhône blend of Mourvèdre, Syrah, and Grenache from a promising new vintner. Very good extraction, lots of focus and intensity in the ripe fruit, but balanced, without being overly hot. Delicate tannins and firm acidity provide great structure. **90** *—S.H. (3/1/2004)*

COREY CREEK

Corey Creek 1999 Chardonnay (North Fork of Long Island) $15. A thick, buttery, and smoky style that may be too much for some tasters. Over-ripe and grilled peaches lack a bit of depth, yet finish long, lemony and tart, with buttered-popcorn overtones. **85** *—J.C. (1/1/2004)*

Corey Creek 2001 Reserve Chardonnay (North Fork of Long Island) $21. **87** *—J.C. (10/2/2004)*

Corey Creek 2002 Gewürztraminer (North Fork of Long Island) $23. **83** *—J.C. (10/2/2004)*

Corey Creek 1998 Rosé Blend (North Fork of Long Island) $11. **83** *—J.C. (4/1/2001)*

CORISON

Corison 1996 Cabernet Sauvignon (Napa Valley) $45. **94** *—S.H. (2/1/2000)*

Corison 2001 Kronos Vineyard Cabernet Sauvignon (Napa Valley) $90. This single-vineyard beauty is Corison's cellar bet. Tasted beside her regular '01 Napa Cab, it's much deeper, darker, and more brooding. It's also far more tannic. It's a big, flavorful wine, packed with plums, blackberries, currants, and mocha, as well as a coating of sweet oak. This classic Cab should begin to soften in a few years and will drink well through 2012. **94** *—S.H. (12/1/2005)*

CORLEY RESERVE

Corley Reserve 2002 Cabernet Sauvignon (Napa Valley) $65. Where Corley's '02 Proprietary Red Wine is all elegance and harmony, this Cab is pure, unalloyed power. What an excellent wine it is, a detonation of cassis—rich, full-bodied, and dry. Despite the great intensity, there's balance, which is a real achievement. **94 Editors' Choice** *—S.H. (12/15/2005)*

CORNERSTONE

Cornerstone 2002 Cabernet Sauvignon (Napa Valley) $60. Although the official alcohol reading is 14.5%, this wine has pronounced flavors of raisins and dessicated berries that mar it. There's a hot, harsh feeling throughout. **82** *—S.H. (12/31/2005)*

COSTA DE ORO

Costa de Oro 1999 Reserva Dorada Gold Coast Vineyard Chardonnay (Santa Maria Valley) $30. **89** *(7/1/2001)*

COTTONWOOD CANYON

Cottonwood Canyon 2000 Bistro Classic Chardonnay (Santa Maria Valley) $20. **86** *—J.M. (12/15/2002)*

Cottonwood Canyon 1999 Estate Pinot Noir (Santa Maria Valley) $32. **86** *(10/1/2002)*

COTURRI WINERY

Coturri Winery 2001 Zinfandel (Sonoma Mountain) $20. **82** *(11/1/2003)*

COUGAR CREST

Cougar Crest 2001 Syrah (Walla Walla (WA)) $30. **87** *—P.G. (9/1/2003)*

COUGAR RIDGE

Cougar Ridge 1999 Cabernet Sauvignon (Paso Robles) $18. **82** *—S.H. (4/1/2003)*

Cougar Ridge 1999 Merlot (Paso Robles) $18. **83** *—S.H. (4/1/2003)*

COULSON ELDORADO

Coulson Eldorado 2001 Koel Vineyard Mataro Mourvèdre (El Dorado) $15. **85** *—S.H. (12/1/2003)*

Coulson Eldorado 1999 Johnson Vineyard Syrah (El Dorado County) $16. **81** *(10/1/2001)*

COURTNEY BENHAM

Courtney Benham 2002 Cabernet Sauvignon (Sonoma County) $25. The winery released their '02 Napa Cab almost a year ago and is only now releasing this one. Was it the tannins? It's still a pretty gritty wine. But it has lively and appealing blackberry and cherry flavors that make it a good partner for barbecued steak or chicken, or just a decadent cheeseburger. **87** *—S.H. (12/31/2005)*

COURTNEY BENHAM

Courtney Benham 2003 Sauvignon Blanc (Napa Valley) $14. Dry, clean, and crisp, this is a refreshing, lemon-cream wine that will go well with a wide variety of foods. **85** *—S.H. (6/1/2005)*

COVEY RUN

Covey Run 2002 Cabernet Sauvignon (Washington) $9. Like the '01, this beautifully structured wine is supple and racy, with tart zippy fruit. It shows classic Washington berry flavors, with cassis, bright acid, and a hint of licorice. Absolutely clean and varietal, with the extra dimension rarely found in wines at this price. **89 Best Buy** *—P.G. (11/15/2004)*

Covey Run 1999 Cabernet Sauvignon (Washington) $9. 86 *—P.G. (9/1/2002)*

Covey Run 1998 Barrel Select Cabernet Sauvignon (Yakima Valley) $15. 85 *—P.G. (12/31/2001)*

Covey Run 2002 Winemaker's Collection Cabernet Sauvignon (Columbia Valley (WA)) $13. Unblended, this is sourced from three different vineyards, half from the famous Champoux vineyard above the Columbia River in the Horse Heaven AVA. Chewy, dusty, and aromatic, its herbal notes, offset with clean red fruits, suggest a Bordeaux more than a Napa style. **87** *—P.G. (12/15/2005)*

Covey Run 2002 Cabernet Sauvignon-Merlot (Columbia Valley (WA)) $9. Pleasant, not too stemmy, with good color and well-managed tannins. The addition of 15% Cab Franc gives it a more substantial, dry, slightly dusty finish. 31,350 cases made. **86 Best Buy** *—P.G. (12/15/2005)*

Covey Run 2000 Cabernet Sauvignon-Merlot (Washington) $9. 85 *—P.G. (9/1/2002)*

Covey Run 1997 Chardonnay (Washington) $10. 86 *—M.M. (11/1/1999)*

Covey Run 2002 Chardonnay (Washington) $9. Another wonderful effort from Covey Run, showing bright, spicy fruit from mostly Yakima Valley vineyards. A portion was barrel fermented and left on the lees, adding unusual complexity and pushing the wine past "simple, fresh, and fruity" status. This is genuinely complex and delicious. **88 Best Buy** *—P.G. (11/15/2004)*

Covey Run 2000 Chardonnay (Washington) $9. 86 Best Buy *—P.G. (12/31/2003)*

Covey Run 1998 Chardonnay (Columbia Valley (WA)) $10. 88 Best Buy *—P.G. (11/15/2000)*

Covey Run 2002 Reserve Chardonnay (Yakima Valley) $22. Rich, oaky, barrel-fermented flavors accent sweet/tart fruit. Nicely done, soft, and round, but avoiding the over-the-top heat and heaviness of comparable California bottlings. **88** *—P.G. (9/1/2004)*

Covey Run 2004 Winemaker's Collection Chardonnay (Columbia Valley (WA)) $13. Rich and round, this young wine is still showing the edges of its new oak, but offers crisp apple and pear flavors along with the vanilla, toast, and hazelnut of the wood, and balanced acidity. The sharpness should smooth out with additional bottle age. **88 Best Buy** *—P.G. (12/15/2005)*

Covey Run 2002 Chenin Blanc (Washington) $7. 86 Best Buy *—P.G. (12/31/2003)*

Covey Run 1997 Fumé Blanc (Washington) $7. 89 Best Buy *—M.S. (9/1/1999)*

Covey Run 2001 Fumé Blanc (Washington) $9. 85 *—P.G. (12/31/2003)*

Covey Run 1998 Gewürztraminer (Washington) $7. 80 *(4/1/2000)*

Covey Run 2003 Gewürztraminer (Washington) $7. Fresh and bracing, a nice mix of floral and citrus rind aromas, with spicy, semi-tropical fruit flavors. There's a splash of Muscat Canelli in the blend to bring out the orange blossom and tangerine notes. **86** *—P.G. (7/1/2004)*

Covey Run 2000 Gewürztraminer (Columbia Valley (WA)) $8. 86 *(5/1/2002)*

Covey Run 2000 Lemberger (Yakima Valley) $7. 87 *—P.G. (9/1/2002)*

Covey Run 2002 Merlot (Columbia Valley (WA)) $9. Covey's baseline Merlot is more authoritative than you would expect at this price. Tannic and chewy, it carries some real weight on the palate and delivers strong, herbal flavors that taste like wine, not watered-down punch. **87 Best Buy** *—P.G. (6/1/2005)*

Covey Run 1999 Merlot (Washington) $9. 88 *—P.G. (9/1/2002)*

Covey Run 2000 Barrel Select Merlot (Washington) $13. A blend that includes some Cabernet Sauvignon (11%) and Cab Franc (3%), which add a little muscle to a somewhat soft, forward Merlot vintage. Definitely aging quickly, and probably drinking its best right now. Soft cherry fruit with tomato leaf/herbal notes, and a chocolaty finish. **87** *—P.G. (9/1/2004)*

Covey Run 2001 Reserve Merlot (Columbia Valley (WA)) $22. A serious effort, with stiff tannins over firm fruit. Tightly wrapped in layers of tar, smoke and espresso, the fruit has a piercing cranberry/cherry character that will pair well with grilled meats. **88** *—P.G. (9/1/2004)*

Covey Run 2002 Morio Muskat (Washington) $7. What on earth, you may wonder, is Morio Muskat? Not a Muscat at all—it's a hybrid cross of Sylvaner and Pinot Blanc. Off-dry and full of ripe peachy fruit flavors, it rises above plodder status with a sweet, lifted honeysuckle finish. Pair with soft cow's cheese and a hot summer day. **85** *—P.G. (9/1/2004)*

Covey Run 2004 Riesling (Columbia Valley (WA)) $7. There is an embarrassment of riches in Oregon and Washington when it comes to crisp, seductive Rieslings, but most of the good ones cost double this amount. Wonderfully fresh, lively, and fruity, it delivers surprising complexity, with some sweetness (2.7% residual) but nothing sugary or cloying. 57,750 cases were made. The winery also markets (regionally) a limited-edition "Dry Riesling" which still clocks in at an off-dry-ish 1.5% residual. The regular version is the better of the two. **89 Best Buy** *—P.G. (11/15/2005)*

Covey Run 2000 Riesling (Washington) $7. **89 Best Buy** *—P.G. (12/31/2001)*

Covey Run 2004 Dry Riesling (Columbia Valley (WA)) $7. Floral, fragrant, and smelling of peaches and apricots, accented with honeysuckle. The addition of just 1% Gewürz may have lifted the nose a bit. Though it's labeled dry, it is in fact off-dry, at 1.5% residual sugar. Full-bodied, flavorful, and blessed with a long finish of mint, flowers, and lime. **88 Best Buy** *—P.G. (12/15/2005)*

USA

Covey Run 2002 Dry Riesling (Washington) $7. **88 Best Buy** *—P.G. (12/31/2003)*

Covey Run 2003 Late Harvest Riesling (Washington) $9. A nicely balanced wine that might compare to a particularly ripe spätlese, with just a hint of honeyed botrytis. A balanced palate mixing citrus blossom, apples, and lightly roasted almonds. **87 Best Buy** *—P.G. (11/15/2004)*

Covey Run 2004 Winemaker's Collection Late Harvest Riesling (Columbia Valley (WA)) $13. There is not much botrytis character in 2004, but this is a solidly made late harvest wine whose 5.6% residual sugar is neither sugary nor jagged. Substantial and lined with citrus zest, the round, peachy fruit holds down the center and finishes with a smooth, not fat, lick of sweetness. **88 Best Buy** *—P.G. (12/15/2005)*

Covey Run 2002 Sémillon-Chardonnay (Washington) $7. The blend is 60-40; the figgy flavors and slightly woolly texture of the Sémillon matches nicely to the crisp Chardonnay green apple fruit. A pleasant, soundly made quaffer. **85** *—P.G. (9/1/2004)*

Covey Run 2003 Syrah (Columbia Valley (WA)) $9. A bit candied, but not bad for the price, with bubblegum and raspberry flavors joined by lashings of vanilla. No structure to speak of, so drink now. **83** *(9/1/2005)*

Covey Run 2001 Barrel Select Syrah (Columbia Valley (WA)) $13. This starts off well, with deep, saturated colors and scents of blood and beef. Not much flavor though; it's a tart, thin wine, tannic, and unyielding. **85** *—P.G. (7/1/2004)*

Covey Run 1998 Barrel Select Syrah (Yakima Valley) $15. **89** *(5/1/2002)*

Covey Run 2002 Winemaker's Collection Syrah (Columbia Valley (WA)) $13. Pungent and assertive with spice, pepper, juniper, and lemon oil, this is a potent style of Syrah, lifted and high toned, that may not have universal appeal. Distinctive, tannic, and clearly showing its Viognier and Roussanne components, this leaves a lingering impression of orange peel and white pepper. **88 Best Buy** *—P.G. (12/15/2005)*

COYOTE CANYON

Coyote Canyon 2002 Chenin Blanc (Santa Lucia Highlands) $15. Bitter in acidity and bone dry, this wine has lemon and lime, vanilla, and herb flavors. Finishes acidic and clean. Needs food. **84** *—S.H. (12/31/2004)*

Coyote Canyon 2002 Pinot Noir (Santa Lucia Highlands) $18. Pale in color, with delicate but spicy aromas of cola, gingerbread, cherries, and smoky oak, this is really a pleasant wine. It's silky and light in texture, with good flavors of red berries and spices, and is dry and crisp. Finishes with an elegant flourish of spicy oak. **87** *—S.H. (11/1/2004)*

Coyote Canyon 2002 Reserve Pinot Noir (Santa Cruz Mountains) $32. A lovely Pinot, lightly colored, delicate, silky, and elegant. You'll find pretty flavors of cherries, cola, peppery spices, and herbs, with gentle oak shadings. **87** *—S.H. (11/1/2004)*

Coyote Canyon 2001 Sangiovese (Russian River Valley) $30. **90** *—S.H. (9/1/2003)*

COYOTE CREEK

Coyote Creek 1999 Syrah (Paso Robles) $17. **81** *(10/1/2001)*

CRANE BROTHERS

Crane Brothers 2002 Syrah (Napa Valley) $40. A controversial wine, with one reviewer calling it polished and easy to drink, while another downgraded it for hints of volatility and brett. Worth trying, as you might find its herbal, peppery notes accenting blackberry fruit appealing and its long finish to pick up vanilla and spice notes, or just simple and watery, as another reviewer did. **86** *(9/1/2005)*

CRANE FAMILY

Crane Family 2000 Don Raffaele Estate Merlot (Napa Valley) $39. **86** *—S.H. (8/1/2003)*

Crane Lake 2003 Chardonnay (California) $5. Clean, with apple, tangerine, and peach flavors and an overlay of oak. Has a pleasantly spicy finish. **84 Best Buy** *—S.H. (12/15/2004)*

CRAWFORD

Crawford 2003 Sauvignon Blanc (Napa Valley) $22. Bright, crisp, fresh, and lemony. This zippy wine also serves up a fine core of melon, herb, and grapefruit flavors, while finishing with a clean, mineral ending. **88** *—J.M. (10/1/2005)*

CRICHTON HALL

Crichton Hall 1997 Chardonnay (Napa Valley) $22. **91** *—M.S. (6/1/1999)*

Crichton Hall 2001 Chardonnay (Napa Valley) $28. You'd almost think this was apple cider, so pure in sweet green and red apple flavors is it. Whether that's due to oak, glycerine, or sugar, it's too sweet, and low in acidity to boot. **85** *—S.H. (11/15/2004)*

Crichton Hall 2001 Merlot (Napa Valley) $32. Very extracted and jammy, just oozing with sweet cherry, plum, and blackberry flavors. The smoky, vanilla-packed oak also is pronounced. As tasty as this wine is, it could use more balance and restraint of these powerful elements in order to achieve harmony. **87** *—S.H. (12/15/2004)*

Crichton Hall 2001 Reflexion Merlot-Cabernet Sauvignon (Napa Valley) $75. This stunningly rich and good Merlot-Cabernet blend has a splash of Cab Franc and Syrah, but it's very tannic. Yet beneath the tannins is a solid vein of black cherry, currant, plum, chocolate, and spice flavors. Enjoy it now in its youth, or age past 2010. **93** *—S.H. (11/15/2004)*

Crichton Hall 1995 Pinot Noir (Napa Valley) $26. **88** *—M.S. (6/1/1999)*

Crichton Hall 2001 Truchard Vineyard Pinot Noir (Carneros) $32. You can tell from the pale color that this is a delicate, light-bodied wine, and it is. It's silky and crisp, and feels weightless on the palate. The flavors? Ripe cherries and raspberries, drizzled with vanilla. The sweetness of the fruit creates weight of its own. **89** *—S.H. (12/1/2004)*

CRISTOM

Cristom 1998 Oregon/Washington Pinot Gris (Oregon) $15. **92 Editors' Choice** *—P.G. (11/1/2001)*

Cristom 2000 Eileen Vineyard Pinot Noir (Willamette Valley) $39. **86** *(10/1/2002)*

Cristom 2000 Louise Vineyard Pinot Noir (Willamette Valley) $39. **91 Editors' Choice** *(10/1/2002)*

Cristom 1997 Louise Vineyard Pinot Noir (Willamette Valley) $32. **90** *(10/1/1999)*

Cristom 1997 Marjorie Vineyard Pinot Noir (Willamette Valley) $32. **89** *—P.G. (9/1/2000)*

Cristom 2000 Mt. Jefferson Cuvée Pinot Noir (Willamette Valley) $24. **83** *— (10/1/2002)*

Cristom 1998 Mt. Jefferson Cuvée Pinot Noir (Willamette Valley) $25. **87** *(12/1/2000)*

Cristom 2002 Reserve Pinot Noir (Willamette Valley) $35. Cristom's reserve is a blend of 11 different vineyards, and makes a strong case for this approach over the single vineyard mania that has gripped Oregon for years. This is a big, concentrated wine, still hard and tight, with raspberry/blackberry fruit focused and lifted by tart acids. Just a light touch of oak balances it out. **91** *—P.G. (2/1/2005)*

Cristom 1998 Reserve Pinot Noir (Willamette Valley) $36. **91** *(12/1/2000)*

Cristom 2003 Viognier (Willamette Valley) $25. From 100% estate-grown fruit, this barrel-fermented viognier proves that Oregon has real potential with the grape. This is a big, thick wine, lusciously packed with lime and citrus fruit and rind. Big, alcoholic, and fruit-driven, it's definitely a drink-now style. **88** *—P.G. (2/1/2005)*

CROCKER & STARR

Crocker & Starr 2003 Sauvignon Blanc (Napa Valley) $23. Clean and pretty with some weight to the stone-fruit dominated nose. Clearly from the meaty, ripe-fruit school of thought, with honeysuckle, spiced pear, citrus, and minerality molding the palate. Lengthy and large on the finish, with anisette and a hint of alcohol. **89** *(7/1/2005)*

CROOKED VINE

Crooked Vine 2001 Sangiovese (Livermore Valley) $30. **85** *—S.H. (12/1/2003)*

CROSSPOINT

Crosspoint 2002 Pinot Noir (Monterey County) $12. Starts out with cherry candy aromas and some funky, leathery notes, then turns very fruity in the mouth. Red and black cherries, smoky oak, and orange peel flavors drink supple and long, with good acidity. **88 Best Buy** *(11/1/2004)*

CROZE

Croze 2004 Rosé of Cabernet Sauvignon (Suisun Valley) $14. Dark for a rosé, full-bodied and very dry, with flavors of roses and blackberry tea. There's a rich, intense finish of berries. **85** *—S.H. (11/1/2005)*

CRYSTAL BASIN CELLARS

Crystal Basin Cellars 2001 Reserve Mourvèdre (El Dorado) $25. 90 *—S.H. (12/1/2003)*

CRYSTAL VALLEY CELLARS

Crystal Valley Cellars 2002 Cabernet Sauvignon (California) $16. A nice, easy drinking wine with some extra features that make it worth your while. Soft in texture, it's loaded with ripe black currant, dark chocolate, and oak flavors. Makes you want to keep on sipping. **88** *—S.H. (10/1/2005)*

Crystal Valley Cellars 2002 Chardonnay (California) $14. Part of the huge wave of statewide appellation Chards now hitting the market. This one is strictly down the middle, offering modest peach and apple flavors and a good texture. **84** *—S.H. (8/1/2004)*

Crystal Valley Cellars 2000 Chardonnay (California) $14. 87 *—S.H. (11/15/2001)*

Crystal Valley Cellars 2004 The Chard Chardonnay (California) $16. Made primarily from Delta and Lodi grapes, this is an innocently good Chardonnay, rustic in character, but likeable for its fruit, touch of oak, and thoroughly dry character. It finishes with a rich streak of vanilla-drizzled peaches and cream. **85** *—S.H. (12/15/2005)*

Crystal Valley Cellars 2001 Reserve Merlot (California) $16. 84 *—S.H. (12/31/2003)*

Crystal Valley Cellars 1999 Reserve Merlot (California) $18. 84 *—S.H. (12/31/2001)*

Crystal Valley Cellars 2000 Pinot Noir (California) $16. 84 *(10/1/2002)*

Crystal Valley Cellars 2000 Mohr-Fry Ranch Sauvignon Blanc (California) $13. 86 *—S.H. (11/15/2001)*

Crystal Valley Cellars 2002 Syrah (Lodi) $16. Smells raw and minty, and tastes tart in green tannins and acids, turning cherryish on the finish. Perhaps the winemaker was trying to avoid super-ripeness, but this wine is too sharp to enjoy. **82** *—S.H. (9/1/2005)*

Crystal Valley Cellars 2000 Syrah (California) $16. 91 Best Buy *—S.H. (12/1/2002)*

Crystal Valley Cellars 2004 Cigar Zin Zinfandel (California) $27. Maybe a few puffs on a cigar would make this taste better, but it seems herbal, hot, and flat to me. There's a core of Zinny cherry-berry, but the finish is uninteresting. **83** *—S.H. (12/15/2005)*

CUNEO

Cuneo 2001 Two Rivers Bordeaux Blend (Washington) $25. This is interesting: a 55% Oregon/45% Washington Bordeaux blend from top vineyards in both states (the two rivers being the Columbia and the Rogue). I like the concept, but both the Red Mountain and the Rogue Valley fruit create similarly tough, chewy tannins, so neither side modulates the other. Very tannic and hard, it's tough sledding. **85** *—P.G. (9/1/2004)*

Cuneo 2002 Pinot Noir (Willamette Valley) $25. Cuneo's Willamette Valley bottling is one smooth customer, classically styled with cherry-flavored fruit and lots of oaky vanilla. Solid, simple, and leans just a bit to the alcoholic side. **87** *(11/1/2004)*

Cuneo 2000 Ciel du Cheval Vineyard Sangiovese (Red Mountain) $30. 82 *—M.S. (6/1/2003)*

CURTIS

Curtis 2002 Heritage Cuvée Rhône Red Blend (Santa Barbara County) $14. A bit rustic in texture and structure, with herb and berry flavors, and very dry. This is a good everyday wine. **84** *—S.H. (10/1/2005)*

Curtis 2000 Heritage Cuvée Rhône Red Blend (Central Coast) $14. 88 *—S.H. (6/1/2003)*

Curtis 2001 Heritage Blanc Rhône White Blend (Santa Barbara County) $14. An easy to like wine bursting with all sorts of fresh, fruity flavors, especially peaches. There's also a rich, smoky taste of wildflowers and honey. A creamy texture and smooth finish round off this blend of Viognier, Roussanne and Chenin Blanc. **86** *—S.H. (2/1/2004)*

Curtis 2002 Ambassador's Vineyard Syrah (Santa Barbara County) $25. Another love-it-or-hate-it wine whose reviewers' disparate ratings get turned into a middle-of-the-road score. Tasting Director Joe Czerwinski liked this wine's bold blackberry flavors and supple tannins, which he admitted bordered on being over-ripe, while the other reviewers criticized it for being jammy and over-ripe. **85** *(9/1/2005)*

Curtis 1998 Ambassador's Vineyard Syrah (Santa Barbara County) $20. 87 *(10/1/2001)*

Curtis 2000 Crossroads Vineyard Syrah (Santa Ynez Valley) $32. 87 *—S.H. (6/1/2003)*

Curtis 2000 Vogelzang Vineyard Syrah (Santa Ynez Valley) $18. 86 *—S.H. (6/1/2003)*

Curtis 2003 Viognier (Santa Barbara County) $18. Nothing shy about this wine. It's all about peaches, mangoes, spicy pears, and even cotton candy with a minty taste. It's also oaky and almost sweet. **84** *—S.H. (10/1/2005)*

Curtis 2001 Viognier (Santa Barbara County) $18. 85 *—S.H. (6/1/2003)*

CUVAISON

Cuvaison 1997 Cabernet Sauvignon (Napa Valley) $32. 91 *(6/1/2000)*

Cuvaison 1999 Cabernet Sauvignon (Napa Valley) $40. 90 *—S.H. (8/1/2003)*

Cuvaison 2003 Chardonnay (Carneros) $22. From a winery that's excelled at Chardonnay for many years comes this impressive wine. It's explosive in tangerines, mangoes, pineapples, cinnamon, vanilla, buttercream, and toast, with a long finish of roasted hazelnuts and smoky honey. Absolutely delicious. **92 Editors' Choice** *—S.H. (12/1/2005)*

Cuvaison 2001 Chardonnay (Carneros) $22. 91 *—S.H. (6/1/2003)*

Cuvaison 1997 Chardonnay (Carneros) $17. 93 *—S.H. (12/31/1999)*

Cuvaison 1996 ATS Selection Chardonnay (Carneros) $43. 93 *—S.H. (6/1/1999)*

Cuvaison 2000 Estate Selection Chardonnay (Carneros) $34. 88 *—J.M. (12/15/2002)*

Cuvaison 1998 Reserve Chardonnay (Carneros) $32. 90 *(6/1/2000)*

Cuvaison 2001 Merlot (Carneros) $32. Rich and chocolaty, but goes beyond candied simplicity with real complexity of structure. There are cross-currents of the ripest cherries and black raspberries, and a dash of coffee. That structure is built of ripe, smooth tannins, edgy acids and oak shadings, all kept in balance. **91** *—S.H. (12/15/2004)*

Cuvaison 2003 Pinot Noir (Carneros) $25. There's extracted over-ripeness here, in the chocolate-coated raisiny edge that completes the cherry fruit and oak flavors, but the wine has a nice Pinot Noir silkiness. Try with grilled lamb. **85** *—S.H. (12/15/2005)*

Cuvaison 2001 Pinot Noir (Carneros) $29. 89 *—S.H. (7/1/2003)*

Cuvaison 1998 Eris Vineyard Pinot Noir (Carneros) $20. 90 *(6/1/2000)*

Cuvaison 2002 Estate Selection Pinot Noir (Carneros) $42. A pretty wine, showing bigtime black cherry, plum, and chocolate flavors in a fresh, young body with good acidity and tannins. Finishes a bit hot. **84** *(11/1/2004)*

Cuvaison 2004 Sauvignon Blanc (Carneros) $19. What a refreshing wine. It's a little sweetish in lemon and lime Lifesaver flavors, but crisp and clean in balancing acidity. Turns rich in vanilla and peppery spice on the finish, with a reprise of the ripe citrus fruit. **88** *—S.H. (12/1/2005)*

Cuvaison 2001 Syrah (Carneros) $29. I love this wine, it's so balanced and easy. Flows like silk and velvet, with sweetly rich tannins and wonderfully modulated plum, blackberry, and coffee that mingle in a complex swirl of flavor. Firmly in the Cuvaison style of harmony, balance, and elegance. **91** *—S.H. (8/1/2004)*

CYPRESS

Cypress 2001 Cabernet Sauvignon (California) $10. 84 *—S.H. (12/31/2003)*

Cypress 2002 Merlot (California) $10. Unripe, with canned asparagus aromas and a raw mouthfeel to the modest cherry flavors. **82** *—S.H. (3/1/2005)*

Cypress 2002 Shiraz (California) $10. There's a flood of well-crafted wines such as this these days that are giving consumers the best values in history. This one's juicy and full-bodied, with plumy, spicy flavors and a hint of bacon. **85 Best Buy** *—S.H. (4/1/2005)*

CYRUS

Cyrus 1998 Bordeaux Blend (Alexander Valley) $50. 91 *—J.M. (6/1/2002)*

D'ANBINO

D'Anbino 2002 Syrah (Paso Robles) $24. Unusually light in color and body for a Syrah, almost a dark rose. Yet its very distinctive in the dry complexity of the Provencal wild herb, licorice, tart cherry, and olive tapenade flavors. **90** *—S.H. (12/1/2004)*

D'ARGENZIO

D'Argenzio 2002 Pinot Noir (Russian River Valley) $32. Rich, intricate, and rather heavy, like a Persian carpet, with a tapestry of cherry, cola, spice, and mocha flavors that are really quite delicious. This wine would benefit from greater acidity, to make all this richness shine, but it's a nice drink. **86** *—S.H. (8/1/2005)*

D'Argenzio 2001 Dutton Ranch Pinot Noir (Russian River Valley) $30. Displays classic RRV characteristics of cola, rhubarb, tart pomegranate, and cherry, with firm acidity and a silky texture, without showing a whole lot of depth. Still, the ride is a jazzy one. **86** *—S.H. (12/1/2004)*

D-CUBED CELLARS

D-Cubed Cellars 2001 Zinfandel (Howell Mountain) $35. 91 *(11/1/2003)*

D.R. STEPHENS

D.R. Stephens 2000 Moose Valley Cabernet Sauvignon (Napa Valley) $90. Stylish and plump, a delicious Cab with polished flavors of red stone fruits and berries, and a sweet veneer of toasty oak. Well-balanced, this charmer finishes with complexity. **90** *—S.H. (11/15/2004)*

DALLA VALLE

Dalla Valle 2001 Cabernet Sauvignon (Oakville) $100. What a treat. This is the quintessence of Oakville Cab, with an impressively firm structure, ripe tannins, smooth, supple mouthfeel and long, spicy finish. And what fruit! Scads of rich cassis, chocolate, and oak, yet thoroughly dry. Drink now through 2012. **94** *—S.H. (11/1/2005)*

USA

Dalla Valle 1999 Maya Red Blend (Napa Valley) $120. **96** *—J.M. (6/1/2002)*

DANIEL GEHRS

Daniel Gehrs 2000 Cabernet Sauvignon (Santa Ynez Valley) $24. **85** *—S.H. (11/15/2003)*

Daniel Gehrs 1999 Merlot (Santa Ynez Valley) $20. **90 Editors' Choice** *—S.H. (11/15/2001)*

Daniel Gehrs 2000 Careaga Pinot Noir (Santa Barbara County) $25. **86** *(10/1/2002)*

Daniel Gehrs 2000 Goodfellow Pinot Noir (Santa Maria Valley) $25. **87** *(10/1/2002)*

Daniel Gehrs 2001 Syrah (Santa Barbara County) $25. There are some tough acids and tannins framing the cherry and blackberry flavors in this elegant, well-crafted wine. If you're into food pairing, it suggests butter, olive oil, fatty lamb, and cheese. Under those softening influences, this will be a fabulous partner. **88** *—S.H. (5/1/2004)*

Daniel Gehrs 1999 Syrah (Paso Robles) $20. **89** *(10/1/2001)*

Daniel Gehrs 2001 Harmon Syrah (Santa Ynez Valley) $25. A medium-weight, good wine, but one whose primary flavors are of the cedar/cigar box/vanilla ilk. Has similar aromas; overall, we wish that fruit played more of a starring role here. **85** *(9/1/2005)*

Daniel Gehrs 2000 Viognier (Santa Ynez Valley) $18. **88** *—J.M. (11/15/2001)*

DARCIE KENT VINEYARDS

Darcie Kent Vineyards 2001 Merlot (Livermore Valley) $18. There's a good wine in here somewhere, with the fine dusty tannins and underlying flavors of plum and blackberry, but the wine is marred by a musty aroma that carries through a taste of mushrooms sauteed in soy sauce. **84** *—S.H. (2/1/2004)*

DARIOUSH

Darioush 1999 Chardonnay (Napa Valley) $34. **93 Editors' Choice** *(7/1/2001)*

Darioush 2000 Merlot (Napa Valley) $44. **91** *—J.M. (6/1/2003)*

Darioush 2002 Signature Shiraz (Napa Valley) $64. Tasty if a bit overpriced, with bright cherry and mint flavors accented by toast, coffee, and earth nuances. Seems a bit tough and hard on the finish, but one reviewer felt it would soften nicely in a year or two. **86** *(9/1/2005)*

DARK STAR

Dark Star 2001 Ricordati Cabernet Blend (Paso Robles) $20. Dry, rough, and earthy, with an astringent mouthfeel. Decanting overnight will bring out the cherries and berries, and the wine is good with barbecue. **84** *—S.H. (6/1/2005)*

Dark Star 2001 Cabernet Sauvignon (Paso Robles) $20. Dry, raw, and simple, with pruny flavors and a hot feeling through the finish. **83** *—S.H. (6/1/2005)*

Dark Star 2001 Anderson Road Cabernet Sauvignon-Syrah (Paso Robles) $15. Nice and fruity in cherries, plums, and blackberries, and with drier, more complex notes of roasted coffeebean and Asian spices. Overall, this is a dry, layered wine, with a fair amount of gritty tannins. **86** *—S.H. (6/1/2005)*

Dark Star 2001 Merlot (Paso Robles) $18. This score is perhaps charitable for this wine. It has vegetal-berry aromas, and is very dry and herbaceous in the mouth, with rough tannins. But it's clean. **83** *—S.H. (6/1/2005)*

Dark Star 1997 Ricordati Red Blend (Paso Robles) $24. **83** *—S.H. (7/1/2000)*

Dark Star 2001 Meeker Vineyard Syrah (Paso Robles) $10. A dry, tough wine, with funky notes. **80** *—S.H. (6/1/2005)*

Dark Star 2001 Zinfandel (Paso Robles) $18. There are some lovely cherry and coffee flavors and rich tannins in this wine, but it suffers from a raisiny, Porty aroma. Best with ribs or chicken smothered in a slightly sweet barbecue sauce. **84** *—S.H. (6/1/2005)*

DASHE CELLARS

Dashe Cellars 1999 Sangiovese (Sonoma County) $18. **87** *—S.H. (2/1/2003)*

Dashe Cellars 2001 Zinfandel (Dry Creek Valley) $20. **89** *(11/1/2003)*

Dashe Cellars 1999 Zinfandel (Dry Creek Valley) $20. **89** *—P.G. (3/1/2002)*

Dashe Cellars 2001 Louvau Vineyard, Old Vines Zinfandel (Dry Creek Valley) $28. **89** *(11/1/2003)*

Dashe Cellars 2000 Todd Brothers Ranch Zinfandel (Alexander Valley) $25. **92 Editors' Choice** *—S.H. (2/1/2003)*

Dashe Cellars 1998 Todd Brothers Ranch Zinfandel (Alexander Valley) $25. **91** *—P.G. (3/1/2002)*

DAVID BRUCE

David Bruce 1997 Pinot Noir (Chalone) $35. **88** *(11/15/1999)*

David Bruce 2000 Pinot Noir (Central Coast) $20. **86** *(10/1/2002)*

David Bruce 2000 Pinot Noir (Russian River Valley) $35. 90 *(10/1/2002)*

David Bruce 1997 Pinot Noir (Sonoma County) $24. 91 *(10/1/1999)*

DAVID COFFARO

David Coffaro 2001 Zinfandel (Dry Creek Valley) $22. 85 *(11/1/2003)*

David Coffaro 2003 My Zin Zinfandel (Dry Creek Valley) $22. A nice interpretation of Dry Creek Zin, showing pepper, herb, tobacco, and cherry flavors that are fully dry and not overly alcoholic. Gives pleasure while showing some real complexity. **87** *—S.H. (11/1/2005)*

DAVID GIRARD

David Girard 2003 Syrah (El Dorado) $28. Shows refinement in the well-managed tannins that lead to a soft, richly complex mouthfeel. The flavors are ripe and tasteful, suggesting blackberry tea, wild cherries, cocoa, and cinnamon, with a sweet tang of oak. This is an easy wine to savor. **88** *—S.H. (12/15/2005)*

DAVID HILL

David Hill 2002 Gewürztraminer (Willamette Valley) $12. 81 *—P.G. (12/1/2003)*

David Hill 2002 Pinot Gris (Willamette Valley) $12. 85 *—P.G. (12/1/2003)*

David Hill 2002 Cuvée Anna-Lara Pinot Noir (Willamette Valley) $18. Odd, stalky, smelling of grass, herbs and orange pekoe tea. This is exceptionally thin, and non-varietal. **83** *(11/1/2004)*

David Hill 2002 Estate Reserve Pinot Noir (Willamette Valley) $30. Very light and leafy, with a pale brick color and tart, tea-like flavors. Tannic and earthy, yet insubstantial, and lacking sweet fruit. **84** *(11/1/2004)*

David Hill 2002 Late Harvest Riesling (Willamette Valley) $15. 85 *—P.G. (12/1/2003)*

DAVIS BYNUM

Davis Bynum 1997 Hedin Vineyard Cabernet Sauvignon (Russian River Valley) $30. 92 *(11/1/2000)*

Davis Bynum 1998 Limited Edition Chardonnay (Russian River Valley) $25. 90 *(6/1/2000)*

Davis Bynum 1999 Westside Road Meritage (Sonoma County) $35. 87 *—S.H. (11/15/2003)*

Davis Bynum 1997 Laureles Merlot (Russian River Valley) $28. 89 *—S.H. (6/1/2001)*

Davis Bynum 2001 Pinot Noir (Russian River Valley) $28. A nice Pinot with good black cherry, spice, and earthy-coffee flavors and a bright burst of acidity. Smooth tannins complete the ride. **86** *—S.H. (10/1/2004)*

Davis Bynum 2001 3 Vineyards Pinot Noir (Russian River Valley) $50. Silky and very dry, an austere Pinot that has some tannins to resolve. The flavors suggest earth, tobacco, and bitter cherry, with just a hint of blueberry. Oak plays a supporting role. Might improve in a few years. **86** *—S.H. (10/1/2004)*

Davis Bynum 2001 Allen Vineyard Pinot Noir (Russian River Valley) $50. The winery seems to be picking earlier than most, so that the wine from this celebrated vineyard, in this wonderful vintage, is tough and tannic. You can taste the underlying cherry fruit, but it's hard. The gamble is on ageability. Giving it the benefit of the doubt, try after 2006. **88** *—S.H. (10/1/2004)*

Davis Bynum 1999 Bynum & Moshin Vineyards Pinot Noir (Russian River Valley) $45. 91 *(10/1/2002)*

Davis Bynum 2001 Lindley's Knoll Pinot Noir (Russian River Valley) $50. Very dry, pretty tannic, a Pinot that's too young to fully enjoy now, although a good lamb chop will soften it. Those tannins shut down the palate, barely allowing the cherry-berry flavors to emerge. Best after 2005. **87** *—S.H. (10/1/2004)*

Davis Bynum 1999 Lindley's Knoll Best 4 Barrels Pinot Noir (Russian River Valley) $90. 91 *(10/1/2002)*

Davis Bynum 2001 Rochioli Vineyard Le Pinot Pinot Noir (Russian River Valley) $80. There's a good Pinot in here waiting to get out, and three or four years may do it. Young and angular, with ripe cherry fruit and a rich earthiness suggesting sweet pipe tobacco, this well-oaked wine is dry, with an elegant, silky texture. **89** *—S.H. (6/1/2005)*

Davis Bynum 1999 Rochioli Vineyard Le Pinot Pinot Noir (Russian River Valley) $NA. A little too porty and raisiny for my tastes. Drinking dry and somewhat tannic, although the alcohol is a modest 13.9 percent. Drink now. **86** *—S.H. (6/1/2005)*

DAVIS FAMILY

Davis Family 2001 Cabernet Sauvignon (Napa Valley) $40. Shows the hallmarks of a fine Napa Cab, with ripe black currant and black cherry fruit. It also offers elaborately soft, integrated tannins, fine acidity, and a solid overlay of good oak. Drinks dry, round, and polished, with a milk chocolate finish. **89** *—S.H. (8/1/2005)*

Davis Family 2002 Dutton Ranch Chardonnay (Russian River Valley) $30. This ripe and oaky Chard shows crisp acids and subtlely charred oak, with flavors of apples and pears and a leesy finish. It's classically New World, with its obvious likeability and uncomplicated drinking. **87** *—S.H. (8/1/2005)*

Davis Family 2001 Zinfandel (Russian River Valley) $25. 88 *(11/1/2003)*

DE LOACH

De Loach 1998 Los Amigos Ranch Cabernet Sauvignon (Russian River Valley) $22. 87 —*S.H. (9/1/2003)*

De Loach 2000 OFS Cabernet Sauvignon (Russian River Valley) $30. A nice Cab that mingles its polished berry-cherry flavors with earthy tobacco and mocha to make for a dry, very drinkable wine. **87** —*S.H. (11/15/2004)*

De Loach 1998 Chardonnay (Russian River Valley) $18. 91 —*S.H. (2/1/2000)*

De Loach 2002 Chardonnay (Russian River Valley) $16. Rather light in weight, but pretty, with delicate, smoke-tinged pear and citrus flavors that gather focus on the crisp finish. **86** *(8/1/2005)*

De Loach 2000 Chardonnay (Russian River Valley) $18. 86 —*S.H. (12/15/2002)*

De Loach 2003 OFS Chardonnay (Russian River Valley) $26. Smoke, pear, and citrus notes dominate this wine's nose, while the palate features flavors that lean more toward apple and pineapple. It's not a heavy, thick California Chardonnay, but rather one that exhibits good balance and a sense of elegance to its lemon-curd finish. **89** *(8/1/2005)*

De Loach 1999 Olivet Ranch Chardonnay (Russian River Valley) $22. 90 —*S.H. (12/15/2002)*

De Loach 2000 Fumé Blanc (Russian River Valley) $14. 87 —*S.H. (9/1/2003)*

De Loach 2000 Early Harvest Gewürztraminer (Russian River Valley) $14. 86 —*J.M. (6/1/2002)*

De Loach 1999 Estate Bottled Merlot (Russian River Valley) $20. 89 —*S.H. (11/15/2002)*

De Loach 2001 Pinot Gris (Sonoma County) $14. 87 —*S.H. (9/1/2003)*

De Loach 2000 Pinot Noir (Russian River Valley) $18. 87 *(10/1/2002)*

De Loach 2001 Estate Pinot Noir (Russian River Valley) $18. A fine communal wine, with its pretty flavors of cherries and raspberries and an edge of cinnamon-spiked coffee. With its delicately silky mouthfeel, it's a versatile food wine. **86** —*S.H. (12/1/2004)*

De Loach 1997 O.F.S Pinot Noir (Russian River Valley) $32. 87 *(11/15/1999)*

De Loach 2002 OFS Pinot Noir (Russian River Valley) $29. Finely scented, with cherries, raspberries, rose petals, and smoky oak, and nicely delicate, dry, and light in the mouth. Could use more intensity, though. **85** —*S.H. (5/1/2005)*

De Loach 1999 OFS Pinot Noir (Russian River Valley) $44. 88 *(8/1/2001)*

De Loach 2000 Los Amigos Ranch Sangiovese (Russian River Valley) $28. 87 —*S.H. (12/1/2002)*

De Loach 2001 Viognier (Russian River Valley) $20. 88 —*S.H. (3/1/2003)*

De Loach 2001 Zinfandel (Russian River Valley) $20. 86 *(11/1/2003)*

De Loach 1999 Zinfandel (Russian River Valley) $20. 90 Editors' Choice —*S.H. (11/15/2001)*

De Loach 2001 Barbieri Ranch Zinfandel (Russian River Valley) $25. Dark, lush, and magnificent Zinfandel, but be warned, the tannins pack a punch. Opens with youthfully earthy aromas that suggest cassis and black cherries, and turns luscious and fruity in the mouth. Perfect now with ribs and such, but best to cellar it for four years or so. **92** —*S.H. (3/1/2004)*

De Loach 1999 Barbieri Ranch Zinfandel (Russian River Valley) $30. 90 Editors' Choice *(8/1/2001)*

De Loach 1997 Barbieri Ranch Zinfandel (Russian River Valley) $20. 88 —*P.G. (11/15/1999)*

De Loach 1997 Estate Zinfandel (Russian River Valley) $18. 87 —*P.G. (11/15/1999)*

De Loach 1998 Estate Bottled Zinfandel (Russian River Valley) $18. 90 —*S.H. (2/1/2000)*

De Loach 2001 Gambogi Ranch Zinfandel (Russian River Valley) $25. An excellent Zin that testifies to the greatness of the vintage for this varietal. Huge flavors of black raspberries, chocolate, and wild blackberries are wrapped in beautiful tannins. In fact the tannins don't get much better, rich, soft, dusty and complex. Feels just great in the mouth. But it has a youthful pertness, so drink with red meat or cellar. **92** —*S.H. (3/1/2004)*

De Loach 1999 Gambogi Ranch Zinfandel (Russian River Valley) $30. 88 *(8/1/2001)*

De Loach 1997 Gambogi Ranch Zinfandel (Russian River Valley) $20. 89 —*P.G. (11/15/1999)*

De Loach 1998 O.F.S. Zinfandel (Russian River Valley) $35. 93 —*S.H. (2/1/2000)*

De Loach 2000 OFS Zinfandel (Russian River Valley) $50. 87 —*S.H. (9/1/2003)*

De Loach 2001 Papera Ranch Zinfandel (Russian River Valley) $25. Another fine single-vineyard Zin from De Loach. It's more tannic than the others and is palate-numbing, but there's a rich, thick core of blackberry fruit that wants to come out. Very fine wine, but cellar through 2005. **90** —*S.H. (3/1/2004)*

De Loach 1999 Papera Ranch Zinfandel (Russian River Valley) $30. 88 *(8/1/2001)*

USA

De Loach 2000 Pelletti Ranch Zinfandel (Russian River Valley) $28. 91 *—S.H. (11/1/2002)*

De Loach 1998 Pelletti Ranch Zinfandel (Russian River Valley) $22. 91 *—S.H. (2/1/2000)*

De Loach 2001 Saitone Ranch Zinfandel (Russian River Valley) $25. Inky purple and black, a youthful wine with gorgeous aromas of plums and blackberry pie, dark chocolate, mincemeat, sweet compost, and white pepper. Drinks as complex as it sounds, bone dry, with beautiful tannins that are firm and complex but completely accessible. This is terrific, classic Zinfandel. **93 Editors' Choice** *—S.H. (3/1/2004)*

De Loach 1999 Saitone Ranch Zinfandel (Russian River Valley) $30. 88 *(8/1/2001)*

De Loach 1997 Saitone Ranch Zinfandel (Russian River Valley) $20. 90 *—P.G. (11/15/1999)*

DE SANTE

De Sante 2001 Calder Cabernet Sauvignon (Napa Valley) $40. Largely Howell Mountain Cabernet Sauvignon, this is a tough, young bruiser. It's very tannic now, but very fruity, with balancing acidity. Should purr along nicely for 10 years or so. **87** *—S.H. (5/1/2005)*

De Sante 2001 Sauvignon Blanc (Napa Valley) $18. 90 *—S.H. (10/1/2003)*

DEAVER

Deaver 2002 Zinfandel (Amador County) $25. Starts with a beautiful aroma that's dramatically chocolatey and oaky, then reveals layers of cherries and black raspberries. Lush, creamy, long in the mouth, with a claret-like balance, but the power of mountain Zin. **92** *—S.H. (3/1/2005)*

DEERFIELD RANCH

Deerfield Ranch 2000 Cabernet Sauvignon (Napa Valley) $50. There's a firm structure to the fruit, which is elaborate in plummy, blackberry and mocha flavors. Will hold for a few years, but it's best to drink it in its youthful freshness. **87** *—S.H. (11/15/2004)*

Deerfield Ranch 2002 Chardonnay (Sonoma Valley) $25. Tastes a bit old for a Chard, with the fruit fading. It's still lively in acids, and has enough pear and apple flavors to satisfy. Finishes quick, and overall, it's not what it should be. **84** *—S.H. (8/1/2005)*

Deerfield Ranch 1999 Labbe Vineyard Chardonnay Chardonnay (Sonoma Valley) $30. 91 *—S.H. (9/1/2002)*

Deerfield Ranch 1999 DRX Meritage (North Coast) $100. 85 *—S.H. (11/15/2003)*

Deerfield Ranch 2000 Roumiguiere Vineyard Merlot (Clear Lake) $24. 87 *—S.H. (9/1/2003)*

Deerfield Ranch 1999 Russian River Vineyards Merlot (Russian River Valley) $32. 90 *—S.H. (9/1/2002)*

Deerfield Ranch 2001 Pinot Noir (Carneros) $25. Nice and silky in texture, with soft, gentle tannins balanced by crisp acids. The flavors veer toward cola, rhubarb, and cherry, and they're a bit simple. Oak helps, especially in the smoky, spicy aftertaste. **85** *—S.H. (4/1/2004)*

Deerfield Ranch 2000 Cohn Vineyard Pinot Noir (Russian River Valley) $48. 86 *—S.H. (2/1/2003)*

Deerfield Ranch 2002 Jemrose Vineyard Pinot Noir (Bennett Valley) $40. From this newish AVA, a polished wine with tart cherry, beet, and oak notes, and quite crisp acidity. You'll find good penetration and length. Finishes with astringency, but nice with meats or cheeses. **87** *(11/1/2004)*

Deerfield Ranch 2002 Super T Red Blend (North Coast) $40. A blend of Sangiovese, Cab Franc, Cab Sauvignon, and Dolcetto. Rustic, dry and tannic, with earthy-berry flavors. **84** *—S.H. (8/1/2005)*

Deerfield Ranch 2001 Roumiguiere Vineyard Sangiovese (Clear Lake) $22. There's something nicely attractive about this dry, crisp red wine, with its flavors of cherries and tobacco. It shows a balance and harmony you don't always find in California Sangioveses. Has some real complexity. **84** *—S.H. (8/1/2005)*

Deerfield Ranch 2002 Sauvignon Blanc (North Coast) $18. A little bit on the sweet side, with the taste of a stick of spearmint chewing gum and pineapple juice. But there's some good, crisp acidity to make it bright and clean. Perfect for a late afternoon apéritif. **85** *—S.H. (4/1/2004)*

Deerfield Ranch 2001 Peterson Vineyard Sauvignon Blanc (Sonoma Valley) $18. 89 *—S.H. (7/1/2003)*

Deerfield Ranch 2002 Ladi's Vineyard Syrah (Sonoma County) $40. Brutal at first, with aromas variously described as stinky, murky, and burnt shrimp shells. Thankfully, the stinks do seem to lessen with air, revealing a dry, cedary Syrah with modest cherry-vanilla flavors. **82** *(9/1/2005)*

Deerfield Ranch 2000 Ladi's Vineyard Syrah (Sonoma County) $40. 94 *—S.H. (9/1/2002)*

Deerfield Ranch 2000 Old Vine Buchignani Vineyard Zinfandel (Dry Creek Valley) $40. 91 *—S.H. (9/1/2003)*

DEHLINGER

Dehlinger 1997 Chardonnay (Russian River Valley) $26. 91 *—J.C. (11/1/1999)*

Dehlinger 1999 Goldridge Vineyard Pinot Noir (Russian River Valley) $40. 89 *(10/1/2002)*

Dehlinger 1998 Syrah (Russian River Valley) $35. 94 Editors' Choice *(11/1/2001)*

DELECTUS

Delectus 2000 Stanton Vineyard Merlot (Oakville) $42. Starts off fruity and rich, with thick, jammy cherry, blackberry, and chocolate flavors that coat the palate. Feels soft and round in the mouth, like liquid velvet. Yet there's an herbal note that strikes midway and lasts into the finish, where the wine turns astringent with green tannins. **86** *—S.H. (5/1/2004)*

Delectus 2000 Argentum Red Blend (Napa Valley) $20. A schizy wine, with cherry aromas joined to weedy, stalky ones. Drinks thin in fruity flavor, although there's a core of cherry and an overlay of smoky oak. Drink now. **84** *—S.H. (6/1/2004)*

Delectus 1999 Terra Alta Vineyard Syrah (California) $29. 87 *(11/1/2001)*

DELICATO

Delicato 2003 Chardonnay (California) $7. Has lots in common with more expensive Chards, such as ripe pear and tropical fruit flavors, dusty spices, smoky oak, and a creamy texture. Finishes a little sweet. This is a great price. **85 Best Buy** *—S.H. (3/1/2005)*

Delicato 2003 Merlot (California) $7. Clean, dry, and fruity, an easy drinking wine with cherry and oak flavors that will go with a wide variety of food. **83** *—S.H. (3/1/2005)*

USA

Delicato 1998 Merlot (California) $6. 83 *(9/1/2000)*

Delicato 2001 San Bernabe Vineyard Monterey Vine Select Merlot (Monterey County) $25. This vast vineyard, in the southern Salinas Valley, has proven itself increasingly capable of producing fine wines from most varieties. Now it shows its hand at Merlot. More work is needed, but this wine is ripe, dry, and complex, although a little too oaky. **86** *—S.H. (11/15/2005)*

Delicato 2004 Shiraz (California) $7. Soft and medium-bodied in the mouth, this Calfornia Shiraz has tarry, earthy notes on the nose that join plum fruit on the palate. A good, simple, easy drinker. **85 Best Buy** *(9/1/2005)*

Delicato 2002 Shiraz (California) $6. 90 Best Buy *—S.H. (11/15/2003)*

Delicato 2003 3 Liter Shiraz (California) $18. What a great value this boxed wine is. It's dry and balanced, with rich tannins and blackberry, cherry, cocoa, and spice flavors. Perfect for a large occasion when you don't want to spend a lot of money. **85 Best Buy** *—S.H. (3/1/2005)*

Delicato 1998 Syrah (California) $6. 84 Best Buy *(2/1/2000)*

Delicato Monterey Vine Select 1998 San Bernabe Vineyard Merlot (Monterey) $40. 88 *(9/1/2000)*

Delicato Monterey Vine Select 1998 San Bernbe Vineyard Syrah (Monterey) $40. 89 *(9/1/2000)*

DELILLE CELLARS

DeLille Cellars 2001 Chaleur Estate Bordeaux Blend (Red Mountain) $60. One of Washington's best wines in vintage after vintage, the 2001 Chaleur Estate blends four classic Bordeaux grapes in a complex, layered, spicy red wine. Disarmingly soft and approachable, yet layered with mixed red fruits and lovely hints of leaf and herb. **92** *—P.G. (9/1/2004)*

DeLille Cellars 2001 D2 Bordeaux Blend (Yakima Valley) $32. This is DeLille's second-tier Bordeaux blend. Still, the list of contributing vineyards reads like a who's who of Washington viticulture. The Merlot-based wine delivers classic black cherry and plum fruit, hints of herb, and plenty of power. Most wineries would kill for a flagship wine this good. **90** *—P.G. (7/1/2004)*

DeLille Cellars 1997 Harrison Hill Bordeaux Blend (Yakima Valley) $40. 92 *—P.G. (6/1/2000)*

DeLille Cellars 2002 D2 Merlot (Columbia Valley (WA)) $36. This is the winery's Merlot-driven second wine, generally composed of barrels not used in the flagship Chaleur Estate. In this vintage it comes out a bit on the funky side, with scents that might be interpreted as reminiscent of truffles, leather, and earth. Cedar, lead pencil, and black fruits suggest its pedigreed sibling. Very tannic, earthy, and substantial compared with previous vintages of D2. **89** *—P.G. (6/1/2005)*

DeLille Cellars 1998 Chaleur Estate Red Blend (Yakima Valley) $45. 91 *—P.G. (6/1/2001)*

DeLille Cellars 1998 D2 Red Blend (Yakima Valley) $30. 89 *—P.G. (6/1/2001)*

DeLille Cellars 2001 Harrison Hill Red Blend (Yakima Valley) $60. This single-vineyard wine from DeLille is a rare evocation of old-vine, classic Washington fruit. Perfectly ripe, plummy fruit is backed with layers of iron and earth; the fruit has mixed elements of herb and tart red fruits. This is special. **91** *—P.G. (9/1/2004)*

DeLille Cellars 1998 Harrison Hill Red Blend (Yakima Valley) $45. 90 *—P.G. (6/1/2001)*

DeLille Cellars 2001 Doyenne Syrah (Yakima Valley) $40. Smooth, supple, and ripe, this lovely wine combines power and elegance in one concentrated package. Aromas of berries and jam, white pepper and bacon fat, along with floral notes. Complex and potent. **92** *—P.G. (7/1/2004)*

DeLille Cellars 1998 Doyenne Syrah (Yakima Valley) $38. 93 *—P.G. (6/1/2001)*

DeLille Cellars 2000 Chaleur Estate White Blend (Columbia Valley (WA)) $25. 92 Editors' Choice *—P.G. (6/1/2002)*

DeLille Cellars 1999 Chaleur Estate White Wine White Blend (Columbia Valley (WA)) $28. 93 *—P.G. (6/1/2001)*

DELORIMIER

DeLorimier 2001 Mosaic Meritage Cabernet Blend (Alexander Valley) $35. Primarily Cabernet Sauvignon, this blend hits with black currant flavors and is very dry. Has a good backbone of tannins and acidity, and enough of a balance to cellar for a few years. **88** *—S.H. (10/1/2005)*

DeLorimier 2002 Clonal Select Chardonnay (Alexander Valley) $24. A good, honest, and earthy Chardonnay that smacks of terroir. Shows apple, pear and herb flavors, with soft acids and a long, oaky-sweet finish. Finishes balanced and elegant. **90 Editors' Choice** *—S.H. (11/1/2005)*

DeLorimier 2000 Mosaic Meritage (Alexander Valley) $30. **85** *—S.H. (11/15/2003)*

DeLorimier 2000 Merlot (Alexander Valley) $20. **91 Editors' Choice** *—S.H. (12/15/2003)*

DeLorimier 2002 Sauvignon Blanc (Alexander Valley) $10. Here's a very nice value in a coastal Sauvignon Blanc. It's very fruity, with flavors of ripe green apples, figs, and spearmint, and finishes a bit sweet. Good acidity keeps it clean and refreshing. **85** *—S.H. (6/1/2004)*

DeLorimier 2002 Lace Sauvignon Blanc (Alexander Valley) $20. This late-harvest Sauvignon Blanc is very pale in color, though very sweet. Like drinking honey infused with apricots, with delicious suggestions of sweetened coconut, meringue, and smoky caramel. Finishes a little quick, but try with a dessert with vanilla and lots of butter. **89** *—S.H. (6/1/2004)*

DeLorimier 2000 Spectrum Reserve Sauvignon Blanc (Alexander Valley) $16. **85** *—S.H. (10/1/2003)*

DEMUTH

Demuth 2002 Pinot Noir (Anderson Valley) $40. Deliciously ripe in cherry, mocha, and spice flavors, and balanced in good acids and smooth tannins. Not only tasty, but also complex and nuanced. Best now. **90** *—S.H. (5/1/2005)*

DEROSE

DeRose 2002 Vintner's Reserve Merlot (Livermore Valley) $23. Ultra-dry, tart with acids and tannic, this tough wine has herb and coffee flavors just barely nudging into cherries. **83** *—S.H. (10/1/2004)*

DeRose 2002 Miller Family Vineyard Negrette (Cienega Valley) $23. Firmly tannic, very dry, and rugged in the way of country wines. Offers up ripe plum, coffee and sweet oak flavors, rather like a Barbera. **84** *—S.H. (11/15/2004)*

DeRose NV Hollywood Red Red Blend (Cienega Valley) $16. **81** *—S.H. (5/1/2003)*

DeRose 2002 Al DeRose Vineyard Viognier (Cienega Valley) $26. Rich, juicy, and as intricate as a tapestry, with ripe mango, breadfruit, white peach, butterscotch, and vanilla flavors interwoven with smoky oak. A crisp spine of acidity provides a clean finish. **88** *—S.H. (11/15/2004)*

DeRose 2002 Nick DeRose Sr. Vineyard Zinfandel (Cienega Valley) $21. Very dry and rather tannic, with a burst of Zinny wild berry, pepper, and earth flavors. A fun wine that will go well with anything Italian. **84** *—S.H. (11/15/2004)*

DESERT WIND

Desert Wind 1999 Cabernet Sauvignon (Columbia Valley (WA)) $13. Charred, horsey scents of burnt leather dominate the attack. This is a dark, tannic wine, chewy and mouth-scraping dry; inside is a core of black cherry fruit, but it's overwhelmed by all the tar and smoke. **84** *—P.G. (9/1/2004)*

Desert Wind 1999 Desert Wind Vineyard Merlot (Columbia Valley (WA)) $20. **85** *—P.G. (12/31/2001)*

Desert Wind 2002 Sémillon (Columbia Valley (WA)) $13. An aggressive, alcoholic wine, it shows unusual dark gold tones and smells of hay and oak barrels. Spicy, oaky, and hot, its 14.5% alcohol is felt as a burning sensation all the way down the throat. **84** *—P.G. (9/1/2004)*

DESOLATION FLATS

Desolation Flats 2000 Cabernet Sauvignon (San Lucas) $17. A good, rustic wine with blackberry flavors and firm tannins. It's nicely dry, and has firm acidity. A very nice Cab for everyday drinking. **84** *—S.H. (7/1/2005)*

DETERT FAMILY VINEYARDS

Detert Family Vineyards 2000 Cabernet Franc (Oakville) $30. **87** *—J.M. (12/1/2002)*

DEUX AMIS

Deux Amis 2002 Vyborny Vineyards Petite Sirah (Alexander Valley) $25. Petite Sirah at its best aspires to be rich, full-bodied and opulent. This is that kind of wine. It has flavors of red stone fruits and berries, thick, dusty, ageworthy tannins, and is bone dry. It also can't quite shake its basically rustic nature, which this wine celebrates instead of trying to hide. **88** *—S.H. (12/31/2005)*

Deux Amis 2001 Zinfandel (Sonoma County) $21. **86** *(11/1/2003)*

Deux Amis 2002 Belle Canyon Vineyards Zinfandel (Dry Creek Valley) $25. If you're looking for elegance, look elsewhere. But if you like hefty, big-shouldered Zins, pick up this one and try it with a grilled pork chop. It's a dry, tannic, balanced wine, with a classically feral Zin profile. **89** *—S.H. (12/31/2005)*

Deux Amis 2001 Rued Vineyard Zinfandel (Dry Creek Valley) $20. **89** *(11/1/2003)*

Deux Amis 1997 Rued Vineyards Zinfandel (Dry Creek Valley) $24. **90** *—P.G. (11/15/1999)*

DI STEFANO

Di Stefano 1999 Cabernet Sauvignon (Columbia Valley (WA)) $25. **85** *—P.G. (12/31/2002)*

Di Stefano 1998 Cabernet Sauvignon (Columbia Valley (WA)) $25. **87** *—J.C. (6/1/2001)*

Di Stefano 1999 Merlot (Columbia Valley (WA)) $28. **85** *—P.G. (12/31/2002)*

Di Stefano 2000 Meritage Red Blend (Columbia Valley (WA)) $NA. A strange wine that doesn't knit together. The high alcohol, super-ripe fruit and nutty, oxidized flavors suggest that it will have a brief lifespan. Flavors of preserves, raisins, prunes, and carmelized sugars. **86** *—P.G. (9/1/2004)*

Di Stefano 2000 Sauvignon Blanc (Columbia Valley (WA)) $12. **87** *—P.G. (12/31/2002)*

Di Stefano 2002 R Syrah (Columbia Valley (WA)) $32. Restrained on the nose, with subtle herb and spice accents and understated blackberries. Classic, elegant, and similarly restrained on the palate, finishing with soft tannins and hints of caramel and minerals. Pretty, but lacks the intensity to score higher. **87** *(9/1/2005)*

USA

DIABLO CREEK

Diablo Creek 2002 Chardonnay (California) $10. The apple and peach flavors have an oaky undercurrent of vanilla and smoke, wrapped in a nice texture. Fine with easy foods. **83** *—S.H. (2/1/2004)*

DIAMOND CREEK

Diamond Creek 2000 Gravelly Meadow Cabernet Sauvignon (Napa Valley) $175. Smooth and elegant, with a fine tuned core of black cherry, raspberry, blueberry, cedar, spice, coffee, chocolate, herbs, and licorice notes. Tannins are firm yet delicate, supporting a long, bright finish redolent of cocoa, vanilla, toast, and tangy berries. This is an elegant wine, neatly balanced and downright delicious to the end. **93** *—J.M. (4/1/2004)*

Diamond Creek 2000 Volcanic Hill Cabernet Sauvignon (Napa Valley) $175. Rich, ripe aromas of black cherry, spice, vanilla, and smoke lead the way here. On the palate, it's dark and sleek, with blackberry, tar, more smoke, licorice, cassis, raspberry, and herb notes that give it great complexity. The tannins are ripe and smooth, supporting the wine with fine, lush structure. **94** *—J.M. (4/1/2004)*

DIAMOND OAKS

Diamond Oaks 2002 Pinot Noir (Carneros) $21. A solid effort, with consistent scores. Quite extracted in black cherries and plums, but balanced in tannins and acids, with a silky texture. This pleasant wine will go well with roasted meats. **87** *(11/1/2004)*

DIAMOND OAKS DE MANIAR

Diamond Oaks de Maniar 2001 Chardonnay (Carneros) $14. **85** *—S.H. (12/15/2003)*

Diamond Oaks de Maniar 2002 Merlot (Carneros) $19. Rough in texture, with a combination of over-ripe and unripe flavors. **83** *—S.H. (5/1/2005)*

DIAMOND RIDGE

Diamond Ridge 2000 Merlot (Russian River Valley) $20. **85** *—S.H. (11/15/2002)*

DIAMOND TERRACE

Diamond Terrace 2001 Cabernet Sauvignon (Diamond Mountain) $50. An intense and concentrated Cabernet that's dominated now by its sheer tannic power. Tight and young, it has a rich, sweet core of black currant fruit modulated by dried herbs and sweet oak. Best after 2008 and beyond. **91 Cellar Selection** *—S.H. (10/1/2004)*

DIERBERG

Dierberg 2002 Pinot Noir (Santa Maria Valley) $33. Tasters all praised this wine's clean, polished black cherry, beet, and vanilla flavors and polished, supple mouthfeel. Could use more strength mid-palate, but the cherry and raspberry finish turns rich with charcoal and vanilla. **87** *(11/1/2004)*

DOBBES FAMILY ESTATE

Dobbes Family Estate 2002 Black Label Pinot Noir (Willamette Valley) $50. A big, forceful wine, which comes on strong with powerful aromas of earth, root, herb, and cherry. Plenty of black cherry fruit at the core, along with spicy, resiny, pine-needle pungency. The flavors are complex, long and sustain beautifully through the finish. **90** *(11/1/2004)*

Dobbes Family Estate 2002 Skipper's Cuvée Pinot Noir (Rogue Valley) $35. Despite some initial VA, this offers bright cherry fruit flavors and nuances of fresh-cut tobacco. Forward, flavorful, and well rounded, its tannins are nicely managed and it shows good balance all around. **88** *(11/1/2004)*

Dobbes Family Estate 2002 Grande Assemblage Syrah (Rogue Valley) $26. This wine has an earthy, sensual nose that mixes leather, barnyard, pepper and dense, concentrated dark fruits. Rhône-like and potent, it promises a bit more than it delivers, but for the price it's a heckuva good bottle. Lots of toast, smoke, and barrel flavors sweep through the finish. **88** *—P.G. (8/1/2005)*

DOCE ROBLES

Doce Robles 1999 Syrah (Paso Robles) $20. **83** *—S.H. (12/1/2002)*

DOG HOUSE

Dog House 2004 Charlie's Chard Chardonnay (California) $9. Amazing how they get wines this nice out at this everyday price. While not a blockbuster, this easy sipper has the peach and pineapple fruit, spice and yummy cream you want in a Chard. **86 Best Buy** —*S.H. (11/15/2005)*

DOGWOOD

Dogwood 2003 Zinfandel (Mendocino) $28. This is one of those high-alcohol, Porty Zins. With nearly 16% alcohol, it's like a mocha chocolate drink infused with cassis, black cherries, and raspberries, then sprinkled with cinnamon and nutmeg. Thankfully it's dry, which makes it worthy of recommendation. **86** —*S.H. (12/15/2005)*

DOLCE

Dolce 2001 Late Harvest (Oakville) $75. This Sémillon and Sauvignon Blanc blend continues the Dolce tradition of being among the finest dessert wines in California. The wine as usual is rich and unctuous, a glycerinev sweetie packed with apricot, peach, honey, vanilla, and crème brulée flavors offset by crisp acidity. It's sweet, but not too sweet. **93** —*S.H. (10/1/2005)*

Dolce 2000 Late Harvest (Napa Valley) $75. This flamboyant wine is drenched in new oak the way Hollywood stars used to wrap themselves in mink. It's fabulous, gooey-sweet in apricots, honey, vanilla, peaches and cream, and ripe, sweet bananas sautéed in butter. It's all folded into the most unctuous, butter cream texture. Thank goodness for the acids. Deliriously addictive. Mostly Sémillon, with Sauvignon Blanc. **96 Editors' Choice** —*S.H. (2/1/2005)*

DOMAINE ALFRED

Domaine Alfred 2003 Chamisal Vineyards Califa Chardonnay (Edna Valley) $38. I tasted this alongside the winery's regular Chamisal Chard, and actually preferred the latter. They seem to have applied more oak to this wine, which doesn't make it better, only oakier. Not only that, but the oak takes away from the beautiful fruit. **89** —*S.H. (11/15/2005)*

Domaine Alfred 2002 Califa Chamisal Vineyard Estate Bottled Pinot Noir (Edna Valley) $48. This winery's Califa bottling is richer and more sophisticated than its regular Chamisal, and showcases the strengths of its Central Coast terroir. Vibrant acidity and a light, silky texture frame cola, cherry, cranberry, rhubarb, and coffee flavors. Bone-dry, with some astringency on the finish. Probably best now. **91** —*S.H. (8/1/2005)*

Domaine Alfred 1999 Chamisal Pinot Noir (Edna Valley) $28. 89 *(10/1/2002)*

Domaine Alfred 2000 Chamisal Vineyard Pinot Noir (Edna Valley) $28. 87 *(10/1/2002)*

Domaine Alfred 1999 Chamisal Vineyards Califa Pinot Noir (Edna Valley) $42. 91 Editors' Choice *(10/1/2002)*

Domaine Alfred 2003 Da Red Red Blend (Edna Valley) $18. The winery doesn't say what the blend is, but this wine is very dry, thick, and dusty in tannins, with cherry and chocolate flavors. It's perfectly fine, a nice everyday sort of semi-fancy table wine **86** —*S.H. (11/15/2005)*

Domaine Alfred 2004 Chamisal Vineyards Rosé of Syrah (Edna Valley) $24. Opens with an inviting aroma of raspberry purée, white pepper, and cocoa powder, then turns very fruity and crisp in the mouth. It's definitely on the sweetish side, but that nice acidity provides balance. **85** —*S.H. (11/15/2005)*

DOMAINE CARNEROS

Domaine Carneros 2002 Brut Cuvée (Carneros) $25. A little rough and scoury around the edges, but gets the job done with some nice doughy, citrus fruit flavors and a dry, crisp finish. Drink now. **85** —*S.H. (12/31/2005)*

Domaine Carneros 1999 Brut (Carneros) $24. 88 —*M.S. (6/1/2003)*

Domaine Carneros 1995 Brut Cuvée (Napa Valley) $20. 89 —*S.H. (12/15/1999)*

Domaine Carneros 1994 Brut (Carneros) $20. 90 Best Buy —*J.C. (12/1/1999)*

Domaine Carneros 1999 La Reve Blanc de Blancs Sparkling Blend (Carneros) $59. At five years, this bubbly is drinkable, but it needs further cellaring. The acidic texture roughhouses the mouth, creating that pins and needles sensation. The wine is balanced enough to stick away in a cool cellar through 2008, by which time it ought to be smooth and approachable. **90** —*S.H. (12/31/2005)*

Domaine Carneros 1997 Le Reve Brut (Carneros) $55. Basically a blanc de blancs, this 100% Chardonnay is delicate, fine, and delicious. It is pale straw in color, with a storm of small, fine bubbles and pretty aromas of lime, smoke, yeast, and vanilla. In the mouth, you'll find rich flavors of lime and peach, in a dry wine that's light and clean. It's also firm and crisp enough to warrant a decade in the cellar. **92** —*S.H. (12/31/2004)*

Domaine Carneros 1996 La Reve (Carneros) $55. 89 —*S.H. (12/1/2002)*

Domaine Carneros 1993 Le Reve (Carneros) $55. 91 —*S.H. (12/15/1999)*

Domaine Carneros 2003 Pinot Noir (Carneros) $28. This lovely wine showcases how well beautifully Carneros's terroir can develop Pinot Noir. The wine is gentle and soft, with a silky texture that carries waves of cherry, cola, and spice flavors through a satisfying finish. **90** —*S.H. (12/15/2005)*

Domaine Carneros 2000 Pinot Noir (Carneros) $34. 85 *—K.F. (2/1/2003)*

Domaine Carneros 2002 Avant Garde Pinot Noir (Carneros) $18. Four identical scores on this simple, light wine. It's delicately structured, with pleasant flavors of strawberry, root beer, and vanilla. **84** *(11/1/2004)*

Domaine Carneros 2001 The Famous Gate Pinot Noir (Carneros) $50. This pretty wine is light in body, almost ethereal, but so rich and intricately detailed. Like a medieval tapestry, it has interwoven notes of cherry, mocha, oriental spices, smoky oak, and a foresty, pine-nut sharpness. Probably not an ager, but beautiful now for its refinement and complexity. **91** *—S.H. (12/1/2004)*

Domaine Carneros NV Brut Rosé Cuvée de La Pompadour Sparkling Blend (Carneros) $34. The aromas and flavors of this bubbly are great. Sweet vanilla, smoky char, and yeast, and the cherries and raspberries are ripe and delicious. The wine is a little rough and scoury, though. **86** *—S.H. (12/31/2004)*

DOMAINE CHANDON

Domaine Chandon 2002 Chardonnay (Carneros) $19. Tart and refreshing for its clean acids and silky mouth feel. You'll find mineral, lime sorbet, and plenty of oaky, vanilla, and smoke flavors. This balanced, elegant wine is a natural for food. **87** *—S.H. (12/31/2004)*

USA

Domaine Chandon 2003 Pinot Meunier (Carneros) $29. Like a Pinot Noir without the noble structure, this pretty red is medium-bodied and dry, with silky tannins and cola, cherry, and mushroom flavors. It has an especially nice, long and spicy finish. **87** *—S.H. (12/15/2005)*

Domaine Chandon 2001 Pinot Meunier (Carneros) $29. Similar to Pinot Noir, with the same silky tannins and light body. But the cherry flavors veer in an herbal direction, suggesting oregano and sage. This wine is very dry and a bit austere, although it's elegant. **86** *—S.H. (5/1/2004)*

Domaine Chandon 2003 Ramal Road Reserve Pinot Noir (Carneros) $45. The winery's regular Pinot, which was released at the same time, is a light, fruity wine. This one's darker, deeper, more ominous. It's a controlled explosion of black cherry, mocha, spice, and char in the mouth, enormously attractive and sensual. **92** *—S.H. (12/15/2005)*

Domaine Chandon NV Blanc de Noirs (California) $18. Pale in color despite a majority of Pinot Noir, but full-bodied, those cherry and strawberry flavors leap right out of the glass on this bubbly. The wine is dry and a little rough in texture. **85** *—S.H. (12/31/2005)*

Domaine Chandon 1999 L'Etoile Brut (Napa-Sonoma) $37. Years of lees contact have made this bubbly soft, creamy, and complex, although it still has a crisp spine of acidity. The flavors are rich and doughy, with a ripe finish of strawberries and peaches. It's a little sweet, and should hold well for several years. **87** *—S.H. (12/31/2005)*

Domaine Chandon 2000 Mt. Veeder Single Vineyard Blanc de Blancs (Mount Veeder) $45. Rich as sin, and packed with white peach and vanilla flavors, this dry wine shows the finesse, lightness, and elegance of a Chardonnay-based sparkling wine. The mousse is creamy, the finish long and decadent. Will be lovely with cracked crab and sourdough bread. **92 Editors' Choice** *—S.H. (12/31/2005)*

Domaine Chandon 1997 Vintage Brut (Napa-Sonoma) $50. Still young, acidic, and rough, this bubbly isn't showing its best now. But all indications are in favor of cellaring for five years. The wine has a solid core of peach and strawberry fruit, a fine, clean doughy taste, brilliant acidity, a long, powerful finish and the balance and finesse to develop bottle complexity. **91 Cellar Selection** *—S.H. (12/31/2005)*

DOMAINE COTEAU

Domaine Coteau 2002 Reserve Pinot Noir (Yamhill County) $34. The cola scents characteristic of Oregon Pinot dominate the nose, leading into firm, plummy fruit with interesting layers of black raspberry and black cherry. Turns thin and tannic. **87** *(11/1/2004)*

DOMAINE DANICA

Domaine Danica 1999 Pinot Noir (Carneros) $32. 85 *—S.H. (7/1/2003)*

Domaine Danica 2000 Salzgeber Vineyard Zinfandel (Russian River Valley) $32. 84 *—S.H. (7/1/2003)*

DOMAINE DE LA TERRE ROUGE

Domaine de la Terre Rouge 2002 Mourvèdre (Sierra Foothills) $22. An interesting and complex wine, dry and medium-bodied, and with soft, sweet tannins. The flavors suggest raspberries, cherries, chocolate, and herbs, and there's a soft sweetness to the finish, as opposed to the harder feel of Syrah. **87** *—S.H. (8/1/2005)*

Domaine de la Terre Rouge 2000 Muscat a Petits Grains Muscat (Shenandoah Valley (CA)) $15. 87 *—S.H. (12/1/2002)*

Domaine de la Terre Rouge 1998 Noir Rhône Red Blend (Sierra Foothills) $22. 87 *—S.H. (6/1/2003)*

Domaine de la Terre Rouge 1995 Noir Grande Année Rhône Red Blend (Sierra Foothills) $20. 91 *—S.H. (10/1/1999)*

Domaine de la Terre Rouge 2001 Tete-a-Tete Rhône Red Blend (Sierra Foothills) $13. 86 Best Buy *—S.H. (6/1/2003)*

Domaine de la Terre Rouge 2003 Vin Gris d'Amador Rosé Blend (Sierra Foothills) $13. This enjoyable blush wine is dry, crisp, and stylish. It shows subtle flavors of cherries, orange zest, rosehip tea, and dried herbs. Fairly full-bodied. Try with bouillabaise, herb-rubbed roast chicken. **85** *—S.H. (8/1/2005)*

Domaine de la Terre Rouge 2001 Roussanne (Sierra Foothills) $22. 87 *—S.H. (6/1/2003)*

Domaine de la Terre Rouge 2000 Syrah (Sierra Foothills) $24. 90 *—S.H. (6/1/2003)*

Domaine de la Terre Rouge 2000 Ascent Syrah (Sierra Foothills) $75. 94 Cellar Selection *—S.H. (6/1/2003)*

Domaine de la Terre Rouge 2003 Les Côtes de L'Ouest Syrah (California) $15. One taster found this wine a bit herbal, but the others found it a pleasant mix of berry and cherry fruit, tinged with vanilla and savory, meaty notes. Drink now–2010. 85 *(9/1/2005)*

Domaine de la Terre Rouge 2001 Les Cotes de l'Ouest Syrah (California) $15. 84 *—S.H. (12/15/2003)*

Domaine de la Terre Rouge 2000 Sentinel Oak Vineyard Pyramid Block Syrah (Shenandoah Valley (CA)) $35. 92 Editors' Choice *—S.H. (6/1/2003)*

Domaine de la Terre Rouge 2003 Viognier (Shenandoah Valley (CA)) $30. Lots of toasty, spicy richness in this flamboyantly fruity wine. Shows big, juicy flavors of peach tart, pineapple custard, tapioca, and butterscotch, making it almost sweet. Fortunately, the fresh acidity gives it flair and balance. 88 *—S.H. (8/1/2005)*

Domaine de la Terre Rouge 2003 Enigma White Blend (Sierra Foothills) $20. Made from white Rhône grapes, this is a flashy, fleshy blend that's as rich as a fruity dessert wine, yet it's dry and balanced. The creamy texture carries vanilla, banana cream pie, peach, and mocha flavors. 87 *—S.H. (8/1/2005)*

Domaine de la Terre Rouge 1996 Vin Gris d'Amado White Blend (California) $9. 88 *—S.H. (6/1/1999)*

DOMAINE DROUHIN

Domaine Drouhin 2002 Pinot Noir (Willamette Valley) $40. The regular DDO has plump, ripe fruit, bright and vivid, and the fresh, simple appeal of Beaujolais. What is missing is the midpalate, which falls off precipitously and never quite recovers. 86 *(11/1/2004)*

Domaine Drouhin 1999 Pinot Noir (Oregon) $45. 90 *—P.G. (12/31/2001)*

Domaine Drouhin 1999 Laurene Pinot Noir (Willamette Valley) $55. 88 *(10/1/2002)*

Domaine Drouhin 1996 Laurene Pinot Noir (Willamette Valley) $45. 85 *(10/1/1999)*

Domaine Drouhin 1999 Louise Drouhin Pinot Noir (Oregon) $45. 95 Cellar Selection *—P.G. (8/1/2002)*

DOMAINE M

Domaine M 2001 Cabernet Sauvignon (Napa Valley) $25. Rich and fruity in blackberry, cherry, and chocolate flavors, with a very soft texture and slight sweetness on the finish that's almost medicinal. Still, offers immediate drinking pleasure. 85 *—S.H. (8/1/2005)*

DOMAINE MERIWETHER

Domaine Meriwether 2002 Pinot Noir (Willamette Valley) $28. There is a lot of smoky, charred new wood here, layered upon tangy cherry and cranberry fruit. An astringent, crisp style that drew mixed reviews from our panel. Should improve with time. 88 *(11/1/2004)*

Domaine Meriwether 1998 Fort Clatsop Cuvée Blanc de Blancs (Oregon) $25. 81 *—J.C. (12/1/2003)*

DOMAINE SAINT GREGORY

Domaine Saint Gregory 1999 Pinot Blanc (Mendocino) $13. 83 *—S.H. (5/1/2002)*

Domaine Saint Gregory 1999 Pinot Noir (Mendocino) $18. 84 *—S.H. (5/1/2002)*

Domaine Saint Gregory 1998 Reserve Pinot Noir (Anderson Valley) $28. 85 *—P.G. (12/15/2000)*

DOMAINE SANTA BARBARA

Domaine Santa Barbara 2002 Chardonnay (Santa Barbara County) $15. Simple and one-dimensional, this Chard offers sweet fruit flavors. Finishes rough. 82 *—S.H. (5/1/2005)*

Domaine Santa Barbara 2002 Pinot Gris (Santa Barbara County) $12. Richer and fuller-bodied than your average California Pinot Gris, this one's got full-throttle flavors of spiced apples and figs, and whistle-clean acidity. It's delicious and complete, a fine complement to poached salmon with a fruity salsa topping. 87 *—S.H. (9/1/2004)*

Domaine Santa Barbara 1999 Pinot Noir (Santa Barbara County) $17. 83 *(10/1/2002)*

Domaine Santa Barbara 2003 Great Oaks Ranch Syrah (Santa Barbara County) $25. Heavy, soft and tannic, this wine shows black cherry, blackberry flavors, and coffee, and is very dry. The cherry finish is attractive, though. 84 *—S.H. (5/1/2005)*

DOMAINE SERENE

Domaine Serene 2000 Clos du Soleil Vineyard Chardonnay (Willamette Valley) $35. 88 *—P.G. (8/1/2002)*

Domaine Serene 2000 Côte Sud Chardonnay (Willamette Valley) $38. 87 *—P.G. (12/1/2003)*

Domaine Serene 2000 Evenstad Reserve Pinot Noir (Willamette Valley) $47. 88 *—P.G. (12/1/2003)*

Domaine Serene 2002 Fleur de Lis Vineyard Pinot Noir (Willamette Valley) $47. The first impression is of a very attractive mix of dusty cocoa, earth, tar, and vanilla. Fruit flavors are clean, precise, and tart, with youthful vitality and lots of acid. More time could flesh it out and up the score. **88** *(11/1/2004)*

Domaine Serene 1999 Mark Bradford Vineyard Pinot Noir (Willamette Valley) $75. 90 Cellar Selection *(10/1/2002)*

Domaine Serene 2002 Yamhill Cuvée Pinot Noir (Willamette Valley) $33. Though one-dimensional, this is a powerful wine with black cherry fruit and generous oak, expressed as roasted coffee scents and espresso flavors. **85** *(11/1/2004)*

DOMAINE ST. GEORGE

Domaine St. George 2001 Barrel Reserve Cabernet Sauvignon (Sonoma County) $10. There are some pretty blackberry and olive tapenade flavors alongside a streak of greenish bell pepper. Drinks sharp in acidity and a little thin, but fundamentally sound and serviceable. **84** *—S.H. (6/1/2004)*

Domaine St. George 2000 Coastal Cabernet Sauvignon (California) $7. Simple blackberry and cherry flavors drink rough and ready. It's fully dry. With takeout pizza or a quick burger, it's fine. **83** *—S.H. (3/1/2004)*

USA

Domaine St. George 2000 Chardonnay (Chalk Hill) $14. Tastes raw and acidic, a tough wine that has traces of citrus fruit flavors. You might think it was a Sauvignon Blanc, it's so dry and tart. **82** *—S.H. (5/1/2004)*

Domaine St. George 2003 Coastal Chardonnay (California) $8. Way too sugary, with cloying, candy flavors. **81** *—S.H. (6/1/2005)*

Domaine St. George 2000 Coastal Chardonnay (California) $7. 81 *—S.H. (6/1/2003)*

Domaine St. George 2001 Merlot (Sonoma County) $10. Good, serviceable Merlot, with ripe flavors of cherries and blackberries that last through the swallow. It's dry and soft, and has accents of oak. **84** *—S.H. (5/1/2004)*

Domaine St. George 2001 Coastal Merlot (California) $8. This easy-drinking wine is full bodied, with flavors of cherries and a touch of chocolatey Kahlúa. It offers plenty of pleasure in a dry, balanced red wine, and is fairly priced. **84** *—S.H. (6/1/2004)*

Domaine St. George 2002 Sauvignon Blanc (California) $6. Smells like dried hay and grapefruit juice, and is completely watery. Acceptable but not recommended. **81** *—S.H. (5/1/2004)*

Domaine St. George 2002 White Zinfandel (California) $5. Apricot and strawberry aromas drink fruity and zesty. Not much more to say except that it's dry. **83** *—S.H. (5/1/2004)*

DOMAINE STE MICHELLE

Domaine Ste Michelle NV Cuvée Brut (Columbia Valley (WA)) $12. Bigger and more obviously fruity than the Blanc de Blancs, it is a simple, clean, pleasant, but nondescript bubbly. **86** *— P.G. (12/31/2004)*

Domaine Ste Michelle NV Blanc de Blancs Chardonnay (Columbia Valley (WA)) $12. Soundly-made, attractively packaged, lightweight bubbly. Crisp green apple aromas lead into a clean and refreshing sparkler, with some citrusy tang. **86** *—P.G. (12/31/2004)*

Domaine Ste Michelle NV Blanc de Noirs (Columbia Valley (WA)) $12. This is one of the Ste. Michelle Estates brands, and the only producer of inexpensive sparkling wines in the region. They make four at the $12 price point: a Blanc de Blancs, a Brut, a Blanc de Noirs, and an Extra Dry. All are non-vintage and 100% méthode Champenoise. The Blanc de Noirs is consistently the best of the lineup; some of the others can be excessively foamy and a bit chalky through the finish. But the Blanc de Noirs is a pretty, pale copper; lightly Pinot-scented, and a good quaffer that really works well with turkey. **85** *—P.G. (11/15/2005)*

Domaine Ste Michelle NV Extra Dry (Columbia Valley (WA)) $11. 83 *—J.C. (12/1/2003)*

DOMINARI

Dominari 2001 Cabernet Sauvignon (Napa Valley) $75. Very young, with a cut of acidity that has yet to be integrated into the oaky, rather flamboyant flavors of cassis and blackberries. It's all there, including lush tannins, but needs a few years to come together. Best after 2005. A new label from Atlas Peak. **88** *—S.H. (10/1/2004)*

Dominari 2001 Merlot (Napa Valley) $45. This complete and fulfilling Merlot has lots of stuffing. The flavors run toward ripe plums and blackberries, with an undertow of green olive, coffee, and chocolate. Oak brings smoky vanillins and adds its own sort of sweetness. But the real wonder are the tannins, which are rich, ripe, and complex. **92** *—S.H. (9/1/2004)*

DOMINUS

Dominus 2001 Estate Bottled Bordeaux Blend (Napa Valley) $109. As good as the 2001 Napanook is, this wine is more intense. The fruit is lusher, the oak newer, the control more complete, but the kicker is the tannins. They're powerful and dusty, and conceal the flamboyance, for now. Needs time; hold until 2010 and beyond. **94 Cellar Selection** *—S.H. (10/1/2004)*

Dominus 2000 Estate Bottled Red Wine Bordeaux Blend (Napa Valley) $95. 90 *—S.H. (12/10/2003)*

Dominus 1996 Napanook Bordeaux Blend (Napa Valley) $30. 91 *—L.W. (7/1/1999)*

Dominus 2002 Napanook Cabernet Blend (Napa Valley) $39. There's a hardness, a tannic greenness to this Cab-based wine that time may or may not address. It's hard to tell. Meanwhile, the flavors of cassis, blackberries, black cherries, blueberries, and smoky oak finish with a dry, peppery spiciness. **85** *—S.H. (12/31/2005)*

Dominus 1999 Red Blend (Napa Valley) $117. **91** *—S.H. (11/15/2002)*

DOÑA SOL

Doña Sol 2001 Cabernet Sauvignon (California) $5. Lots of Cabernet character, with ripe black currant, spice, and oaky aromas and flavors and a dry finish. Drinks easy, with firm tannins. **84 Best Buy** *—S.H. (10/1/2004)*

DONUM ESTATE

Donum Estate 2002 Pinot Noir (Carneros) $60. Tasting this wine brings visions of the foggy, wind-swept, rolling hills of the appellation. The coolness has yielded an intensely herbal wine, with flavors of dried herbs such as sage and oregano. The acidity is vibrant, the tannins dusty. It's a well-tailored wine, but I wish there was more fruit. **88** *—S.H. (6/1/2004)*

DOUGLAS HILL

Douglas Hill 1997 Chardonnay (Napa Valley) $16. **82** *—M.S. (10/1/1999)*

DOVER CANYON

Dover Canyon 1998 Chequera Vineyard Roussanne (Central Coast) $19. **83** *—S.H. (10/1/1999)*

Dover Canyon 1999 Reserve Syrah (Paso Robles) $35. **85** *(11/1/2001)*

DOWNING FAMILY

Downing Family 2001 Zinfandel (Oakville) $30. **90** *(11/1/2003)*

DR. KONSTANTIN FRANK

Dr. Konstantin Frank 1999 Reserve Cabernet Sauvignon (Finger Lakes) $40. **83** *—M.S. (3/1/2003)*

Dr. Konstantin Frank 2001 Gewürztraminer (Finger Lakes) $16. **86** *—J.M. (1/1/2003)*

Dr. Konstantin Frank 2000 Dry Johannisberg Riesling (Finger Lakes) $12. **83** *—J.C. (3/1/2002)*

Dr. Konstantin Frank 2001 Semi Dry Johannisberg Riesling (Finger Lakes) $13. **83** *—J.C. (8/1/2003)*

Dr. Konstantin Frank 1999 Limited Release Merlot (Finger Lakes) $20. **84** *—J.C. (3/1/2002)*

Dr. Konstantin Frank NV Fleur de Pinot Noir (Finger Lakes) $12. **84** *—J.C. (3/1/2002)*

Dr. Konstantin Frank 1996 Old Vines Pinot Noir (Finger Lakes) $19. **82** *(10/1/1999)*

Dr. Konstantin Frank 2000 Limited Release Rkatsiteli (Finger Lakes) $15. **86** *—J.C. (3/1/2002)*

DREW

Drew 2003 Morehouse Vineyard Syrah (Santa Ynez Valley) $40. Crisp and medium-weight in the mouth, Drew's Morehouse has a profile in which herbal notes and tart cherry and berry flavors are front and center. Another reviewer remarked on the wine's black peppery accents. Distinctive, tight, tart, and not for everyone. **87** *(9/1/2005)*

Drew 2003 Rodney's and Larner Vineyards Syrah (Santa Ynez Valley) $32. Panelists applauded this Syrah's herbal-peppery aromas and flavors, and its tight, blueberry-black cherry fruit core. As mouthfilling and enjoyable as it is, all panelists mentioned that the texture was not quite as rich or complex as we'd have liked. Very good; has potential for excellence. **88** *(9/1/2005)*

DREYER SONOMA

Dreyer Sonoma 1998 Cabernet Sauvignon (Sonoma County) $14. **88 Best Buy** *—S.H. (12/15/2000)*

Dreyer Sonoma 2001 Chardonnay (Sonoma County) $10. **89 Best Buy** *—S.H. (12/1/2003)*

Dreyer Sonoma 1999 Chardonnay (Sonoma County) $10. **86** *—S.H. (2/1/2001)*

DRY CREEK VINEYARD

Dry Creek Vineyard 1998 Meritage Bordeaux Blend (Sonoma County) $28. **90** *—S.H. (2/1/2001)*

Dry Creek Vineyard 2002 Cabernet Sauvignon (Dry Creek Valley) $19. This is DCV's first Cab made entirely of Dry Creek fruit. It's a big, dark, dry wine, rich in dusty tannins, with an astringent finish. Doesn't seem drinkable now, but such is the core of dark stone fruits, I suspect it has a great future. Hold beyond 2007. **91** *—S.H. (11/15/2005)*

Dry Creek Vineyard 1999 Cabernet Sauvignon (Sonoma County) $21. **87** *—S.H. (11/15/2002)*

Dry Creek Vineyard 1998 Endeavour Cabernet Sauvignon (Dry Creek Valley) $50. **91** *(12/31/2003)*

Dry Creek Vineyard 1997 Epoch II Millenium Cuvée Cabernet Sauvignon (Dry Creek Valley) $60. **87** *—S.H. (2/1/2001)*

Dry Creek Vineyard 1998 Reserve Cabernet Sauvignon (Dry Creek Valley) $35. 88 *—S.H. (7/1/2002)*

Dry Creek Vineyard 2003 Chardonnay (Russian River Valley) $16. There's an earthy, herbal quality to the entry of this wine that make you wish it had more fruit. It's dry, oaky, and soft, with moderate peach and spice flavors that show up midpalate. **84** *—S.H. (12/1/2005)*

Dry Creek Vineyard 2000 Chardonnay (Sonoma County) $16. 86 *—S.H. (12/15/2002)*

Dry Creek Vineyard 1998 Barrel-Fermented Chardonnay (Sonoma County) $16. 87 *(6/1/2000)*

Dry Creek Vineyard 2000 Reserve Chardonnay (Russian River Valley) $22. 87 *—S.H. (12/15/2003)*

Dry Creek Vineyard 1998 Reserve Chardonnay (Dry Creek Valley) $22. 89 *(6/1/2000)*

Dry Creek Vineyard 2002 Saralee's Vineyard Chardonnay (Russian River Valley) $25. Walks a tightrope. Starts with a tease of ripe pineapple and mango, and then the acids and alcohol take over, leaving an impression of tart leanness. You can't quite decide if it's a big wine, or just well-balanced. The right food, such as sea bass seared in butter and served with a fruit salsa, will be perfect. **89** *—S.H. (12/31/2004)*

Dry Creek Vineyard 2003 Dry Chenin Blanc (Clarksburg) $9. Always a benchmark for bone-dry Chenins, this year's release is fragrant with peach, wildflower, and vanilla, and a slightly sour flavor of lemondrop. It's so high in acidity, it practically tingles. **85 Best Buy** *—S.H. (10/1/2004)*

Dry Creek Vineyard 2001 Dry Chenin Blanc (Clarksburg) $9. 85 *—S.H. (9/1/2003)*

Dry Creek Vineyard 2003 Fumé Blanc (Sonoma County) $13. Crisp and clean, this wine refreshes with its bright citrus and fig flavors and acidity. It has a good body and a touch of cream. **85** *—S.H. (5/1/2005)*

Dry Creek Vineyard 2002 Fumé Blanc (Sonoma County) $13. 86 *—S.H. (12/15/2003)*

Dry Creek Vineyard 1999 Fumé Blanc (Sonoma County) $12. 84 *—S.H. (11/15/2000)*

Dry Creek Vineyard 2002 DCV3 Fumé Blanc (Dry Creek Valley) $18. 86 *(12/31/2003)*

Dry Creek Vineyard 1998 Limited Edition DCV3 Fumé Blanc (Dry Creek Valley) $16. 90 *(2/1/2000)*

Dry Creek Vineyard 2001 Reserve Fumé Blanc (Dry Creek Valley) $18. 88 *(12/31/2003)*

Dry Creek Vineyard 1999 Reserve Fumé Blanc (Dry Creek Valley) $18. 82 *(8/1/2002)*

Dry Creek Vineyard 1997 Reserve Fumé Blanc (Dry Creek Valley) $16. 90 *—L.W. (2/1/2000)*

Dry Creek Vineyard 1999 Meritage (Sonoma County) $28. 90 *—S.H. (11/15/2002)*

Dry Creek Vineyard 2002 Merlot (Sonoma County) $19. Showing the balance and elegance this winery is known for, this Merlot is earthy, with coffee, herb, blackberry, and cherry flavors that finish in a swirl of dry, rather sticky tannins. It's not an ager, but will be fine now with richly marbled meats and hard cheeses. **87** *—S.H. (12/15/2005)*

Dry Creek Vineyard 1998 Merlot (Sonoma County) $21. 85 *—S.H. (2/1/2001)*

Dry Creek Vineyard 1998 Reserve Cuvée Merlot (Dry Creek Valley) $35. 84 *— (11/15/2002)*

Dry Creek Vineyard 1999 Pinot Noir (California) $20. 86 *—S.H. (5/1/2001)*

Dry Creek Vineyard 2000 Soleil Limited Edition Sauvignon Blanc (Sonoma County) $20. 86 *—S.H. (9/1/2002)*

Dry Creek Vineyard 1998 Vintner's Selection Syrah (Dry Creek Valley) $25. 86 *(11/1/2001)*

Dry Creek Vineyard 2001 Beeson Ranch Zinfandel (Dry Creek Valley) $30. 89 *(12/31/2003)*

Dry Creek Vineyard 2001 Heritage Clone Zinfandel (Sonoma County) $15. 88 *(11/1/2003)*

Dry Creek Vineyard 1999 Heritage Clone Zinfandel (Sonoma County) $15. 86 *—S.H. (11/15/2001)*

Dry Creek Vineyard 1997 Heritage Clone Zinfandel (Sonoma County) $15. 90 *—P.G. (11/15/1999)*

Dry Creek Vineyard 2002 Old Vine Zinfandel (Sonoma County) $25. From century-old vines, mainly in Dry Creek Valley, this is a big Zin, jam-packed with purple- and black-skinned stone fruits and berries. The wine is certainly tannic now, and extremely dry. It will be okay now with rich meats and cheeses, but probably better by 2006. **90** *—S.H. (11/15/2005)*

Dry Creek Vineyard 2000 Old Vines Zinfandel (Sonoma County) $21. 87 *—S.H. (2/1/2003)*

Dry Creek Vineyard 1998 Old Vines Zinfandel (Sonoma County) $19. 86 *—S.H. (12/1/2000)*

Dry Creek Vineyard 1999 Reserve Zinfandel (Dry Creek Valley) $30. Here's a Zin that makes you think. What is Zin? Does it have an upper price limit? This wine is very dry and ripe, although the fruity, berry flavors are deeply buried under the tannins. It's as velvety smooth as a cult Cabernet, without offering the immediate pleasure and depth. Will it age? This is new style Zin at its best, an experiment in the making . **90** *—S.H. (3/1/2004)*

Dry Creek Vineyard 1997 Reserve Zinfandel (Dry Creek Valley) $30. 90 *—P.G. (3/1/2001)*

Dry Creek Vineyard 2001 Somers Ranch Zinfandel (Dry Creek Valley) $30. 90 *(12/31/2003)*

DUCK POND

Duck Pond 1997 Cabernet Franc (Columbia Valley (WA)) $95. 90 *—S.H. (12/31/2003)*

Duck Pond 2000 Cabernet Sauvignon (Columbia Valley (Oregon)) $12. 83 *—P.G. (12/1/2003)*

Duck Pond 1998 Chardonnay (Oregon) $10. 87 Best Buy *—S.H. (9/1/2000)*

Duck Pond 1997 Merlot (Columbia Valley (WA)) $12. 82 *—P.G. (6/1/2000)*

Duck Pond 1997 Pinot Grigio (Oregon) $9. 85 *(8/1/1999)*

Duck Pond 2002 Pinot Gris (Oregon) $12. 86 *—P.G. (12/1/2003)*

Duck Pond 2003 Pinot Noir (Oregon) $12. Earthy scents of wet stem and soil lead into light flavors of rhubarb and wild strawberry. Very light and simple. **83** *—P.G. (10/1/2004)*

Duck Pond 1998 Pinot Noir (Willamette Valley) $9. 83 *—J.C. (12/1/2000)*

Duck Pond 2002 Syrah (Columbia Valley (WA)) $12. Great color, dense purple/garnet, and thick scents of blackberries tell you this is a heckuva good $12 wine. Hits the palate with a solid grip, the dense blackberry fruit perked up with white pepper and toast, and finishes big and smoky, with tarry tannins. **88 Best Buy** *—P.G. (11/15/2004)*

Duck Pond 1999 Fries' Desert Wind Vineyard Syrah (Columbia Valley (WA)) $35. 85 *(11/1/2001)*

DUCK WALK

Duck Walk 1997 Cabernet Sauvignon (North Fork of Long Island) $19. 85 *—J.C. (4/1/2001)*

Duck Walk 1997 Reserve Chardonnay (Long Island) $13. 87 Best Buy *—J.C. (4/1/2001)*

Duck Walk 1997 Reserve Merlot (North Fork of Long Island) $19. 86 *—J.C. (4/1/2001)*

Duck Walk 1997 Pinot Meunier (The Hamptons, Long Island) $9. 87 Best Buy *—J.C. (4/1/2001)*

DUCKHORN

Duckhorn 2000 Cabernet Sauvignon (Napa Valley) $55. Polished and supple, with good currant and cherry flavors backed up by smooth tannins. A very nice Cabernet, although not in the same league as Duckhorn's single-vineyard or estate Cabs. **87** *—S.H. (8/1/2004)*

Duckhorn 2001 Estate Cabernet Sauvignon (Napa Valley) $85. The most immediately drinkable of Duckhorn's '01s. It's soft and juicy, with smooth tannins and accessible flavors of cassis-infused cocoa and spices, with good lift from acidity. Dramatic now, and should age well through 2010. **92** *—S.H. (5/1/2005)*

Duckhorn 1998 Estate Grown Cabernet Sauvignon (Napa Valley) $80. 89 *(6/1/2002)*

Duckhorn 2000 Monitor Ledge Vineyard Cabernet Sauvignon (Napa Valley) $90. Rich, nervy, and intense yet generous. Slowly unfolds well-oaked flavors of blackberries, cassis, and chocolate across the palate. There's also a minerality that adds tang and firmness. Gorgeous extract, amazingly long finish, with near-perfect balance and harmony. **92** *—S.H. (8/1/2004)*

Duckhorn 2001 Patzimaro Vineyard Cabernet Sauvignon (Napa Valley) $90. Similar to the Stout bottling, a rather dry, tannic wine, filled with dark stone fruit flavors. Grips the palate with dusty astringency now, but aging should soften and release the underlying sweetness and fruit. Nice overall balance and concentration. Hold beyond 2010. **92** *—S.H. (5/1/2005)*

Duckhorn 1999 Patzimaro Vineyard Est Grown St. Helena Cabernet Sauvignon (Napa Valley) $90. 90 *(2/1/2003)*

Duckhorn 1997 Merlot (Napa Valley) $36. 90 *(3/1/2000)*

Duckhorn 2001 Merlot (Howell Mountain) $70. Wow, what a wine. Tremendous, focused, and intense. This Merlot is massive in cassis and black currant flavors, and very well-oaked. Most notable are the tannins. They're powerful and insistent, yet so smooth, so finely knit that they're totally drinkable now, although you may want to give the wine until 2006 to settle down. **93 Editors' Choice** *—S.H. (12/1/2005)*

Duckhorn 2000 Merlot (Napa Valley) $46. 90 *—K.F. (4/1/2003)*

Duckhorn 2001 Estate Merlot (Napa Valley) $82. Graceful, delicious, complex, and drinkable. Super-oaky, with vanilla, toast, and wood spice, but the massive cherry and blackberry fruit easily absorbs it. The tannins are rich and ripe, forming a dusty coating that carries sweetness through the finish. Beautiful, extraordinary Napa Merlot. **94** *—S.H. (8/1/2004)*

Duckhorn 2000 Estate Grown Merlot (Napa Valley) $80. Concentrated and muscular, showing more structure than many Cabernets from this challenging vintage. Black cherries, toast, and mocha sweep across the palate in slightly monolithic waves; this wine needs some time in the bottle to develop additional complexity and soften the firm finish. Try after 2008. **90 Cellar Selection** *(5/1/2004)*

Duckhorn 1997 Estate Grown Merlot (Napa Valley) $65. **89** *—J.C. (6/1/2001)*

Duckhorn 1998 Howell Mountain Merlot (Napa Valley) $50. **89** *—K.F. (4/1/2003)*

Duckhorn 1999 Three Palms Merlot (Napa Valley) $70. **92** *—K.F. (4/1/2003)*

Duckhorn 2001 Three Palms Vineyard Merlot (Napa Valley) $77. Tannic as usual from this single vineyard near Calistoga, but with a great heart of cherry and blackberry fruit and wonderful suggestions of herbs and nettles. Bone dry, but ripe in sweet fruit, the quintessence of cherry. An obvious cellar candidate that will hold through the decade. **93** *—S.H. (8/1/2004)*

Duckhorn 1997 Three Palms Vineyard Merlot (Napa Valley) $60. **88** *—J.C. (6/1/2001)*

Duckhorn 2001 Decoy Red Blend (Napa Valley) $26. A dry and distinguished Bordeaux blend, with smooth, rich tannins and good character. Black currants and cherries, herbs and cocoa, and toasted oak mingle on the palate, leading to a fine finish. **88** *—S.H. (5/1/2005)*

Duckhorn 2002 Sauvignon Blanc (Napa Valley) $22. Supple and harmonious with refreshing acidity. Handles the juicy citrus, fig and melon flavors with finesse, showing a real mastery of the variety. **88** *—S.H. (8/1/2004)*

USA

DUKE

DUKE 2001 Merlot (California) $9. **85 Best Buy** *—S.H. (12/31/2003)*

DUNCAN PEAK

Duncan Peak 1998 Cabernet Sauvignon (Mendocino County) $35. **90** *—S.H. (6/1/2002)*

DUNDEE SPRINGS

Dundee Springs 1999 Pinot Gris (Oregon) $12. **85** *—P.G. (8/1/2002)*

DUNHAM

Dunham 1999 Cabernet Sauvignon (Columbia Valley (WA)) $45. **88** *—C.S. (12/31/2002)*

Dunham 2003 Shirley Mays Sémillon (Walla Walla (WA)) $35. Sémillon may well be the best white wine made in Washington, and Dunham's is right at the top of the list. Barrel-fermented, estate grown, and showing plenty of toasty new wood, it's deliciously ripe and sweetly fruity, like succulent peaches and fresh citrus. **91** *—P.G. (11/15/2004)*

Dunham 2002 Syrah (Columbia Valley (WA)) $45. The first thing you notice, apart from the density and magnificent color of this wine, is the perfume. Floral, complex, and inviting with spicy citrus scents, it sets up the wine with an elegant, inviting entry that brings nuance and subtlety to a variety that can sometimes behave like an overblown Zinfandel. Here it is world class. **92** *—P.G. (11/15/2004)*

Dunham 2000 Syrah (Columbia Valley (WA)) $45. **92** *—P.G. (9/1/2002)*

Dunham 1999 Lewis Vineyard Syrah (Columbia Valley (WA)) $45. **92 Cellar Selection** *(11/1/2001)*

DUNNEWOOD

Dunnewood 1998 Cabernet Sauvignon (North Coast) $8. **83** *—S.H. (5/1/2001)*

Dunnewood 1996 Dry Silk Seven Arches Vyd Rese Cabernet Sauvignon (Sonoma County) $13. **86** *(7/1/2000)*

Dunnewood 1997 Signature Clara's Vineyards Cabernet Sauvignon (Mendocino) $13. **89 Best Buy** *—S.H. (5/1/2001)*

Dunnewood 2001 Chardonnay (Mendocino County) $9. **84** *—S.H. (6/1/2003)*

Dunnewood 1998 Chardonnay (North Coast) $8. **83 Best Buy** *—S.H. (7/1/2000)*

Dunnewood 2000 Signature Chardonnay (Carneros) $13. **84** *—S.H. (6/1/2003)*

Dunnewood 1999 Merlot (Mendocino County) $9. **84** *—S.H. (5/1/2002)*

Dunnewood 1997 Reserve Merlot (Napa Valley) $13. **84** *(7/1/2000)*

Dunnewood 1999 Pinot Noir (North Coast) $9. **80** *(10/1/2002)*

Dunnewood 1997 Barrel Select Coastal Series Pinot Noir (North Coast) $9. **84 Best Buy** *(7/1/2000)*

Dunnewood 1997 Reserve Sangiovese (Mendocino County) $14. **84** *(7/1/2000)*

Dunnewood 2000 Sauvignon Blanc (Mendocino County) $7. **84** *—S.H. (5/1/2002)*

Dunnewood 1998 Vintner's Select Coastal Serie Sauvignon Blanc (Mendocino County) $8. **83** *(7/1/2000)*

Dunnewood 2002 Zinfandel (Mendocino County) $9. This is the kind of Zin that goes well with just about anything, from salmon to burgers. It's dry and balanced, with good flavors of berries, coffee, and spices. **85 Best Buy** *—S.H. (2/1/2005)*

Dunnewood 1998 Zinfandel (Mendocino County) $9. **85** *—S.H. (5/1/2002)*

DUNNING VINEYARDS

Dunning Vineyards 2002 Westside Syrah (Paso Robles) $24. A big, ripe, exuberant Syrah, quite high in alcohol and long on jammy cherry-blackberry fruit, dusted with mocha. Finishes dry and long in fruity concentration. **87** *—S.H. (12/1/2004)*

DURNEY

Durney 1993 Estate Bottled Cabernet Sauvignon (Carmel Valley) $25. **85** *—S.H. (7/1/1999)*

Durney 1998 Heller Estate Merlot (Carmel Valley) $26. **86** *—J.C. (6/1/2001)*

DUSTED VALLEY

Dusted Valley 2003 Viognier (Columbia Valley (WA)) $20. Starts with a piercing nose of citrus and pineapple, that leads into a welcome burst of fresh, round, pretty fruit flavors of peach and apricot. No rough edges here, and no heat, just a plump, smooth, pleasing wine. **88** *—P.G. (11/15/2004)*

DUTCH HENRY WINERY

Dutch Henry Winery 2001 Argos Meritage (Napa Valley) $38. Light and a bit herbal, with easy tannins and a streak of red cherries and spice. Finishes very dry and somewhat astringent. Good with steak. **85** *—S.H. (10/3/2004)*

DUTCHER CROSSING

Dutcher Crossing 2003 Chardonnay (Russian River Valley) $22. Here's a good, all-purpose Chard when you want one that's oaky, ripe, dryish-sweetish, and creamy. It has pretty peach, apple, and vanilla flavors, and a slight roughness to the finish. **85** *—S.H. (8/1/2005)*

DUTTON ESTATE WINERY

Dutton Estate Winery 2002 Dutton Palms Vineyard Chardonnay (Russian River Valley) $40. Smooth and supple, a rich Chard with forward flavors of ripe white peaches, pears, and tropical fruits. Picks up buttered toast and smoky vanilla notes midway. Finishes firm with crisp acidity. **91** *—S.H. (12/31/2004)*

Dutton Estate Winery 2003 Cherry Ridge Vineyard Syrah (Russian River Valley) $34. Displays a vaguely Rhônish quality in its herbal, near-rhubarb and white pepper aromatics. Placed alongside flavors of tart berries and a relatively light mouthfeel, you might mistake this wine for a modest Crozes-Hermitage. **86** *(9/1/2005)*

DUTTON-GOLDFIELD

Dutton-Goldfield 2003 Dutton Ranch Chardonnay (Russian River Valley) $30. Shows great class and finesse with its well-ripened fruit that's controlled with a clean minerality and high acidity. Oak and lees are both there, in supporting roles. The finish is ultra-clean and citrusy, in this complex, dry white wine. **91 Editors' Choice** *—S.H. (10/1/2005)*

Dutton-Goldfield 2001 Dutton Ranch Chardonnay (Russian River Valley) $30. **86** *—S.H. (12/15/2003)*

Dutton-Goldfield 1998 Dutton Ranch Chardonnay (Russian River Valley) $28. **87** *(3/1/2000)*

Dutton-Goldfield 2000 Rued Vineyard Chardonnay (Russian River Valley) $45. **90** *—S.H. (12/15/2002)*

Dutton-Goldfield 2001 Rued Vineyard Dutton Ranch Chardonnay (Russian River Valley) $40. **91** *—S.H. (12/15/2003)*

Dutton-Goldfield 2002 Devil's Gulch Ranch Pinot Noir (Marin County) $48. This wine's cool-climate origins show in the intense, lemony acidity that undergirds the cherry, blueberry, and spicy-clove flavors. Drinks smooth and elegant, a dry, powerful wine with some tannins to shed. Drink now through 2006. **90** *(11/1/2004)*

Dutton-Goldfield 2003 Dutton Ranch Pinot Noir (Russian River Valley) $35. With a tomato-skin bitterness that considerable oak treatment can't quite diminish, this Pinot is saved by a finish of sweet, ripe cherries. Still, it's a study in contrasts. It shows elegance and harmony one minute, then that rustic note emerges. **86** *—S.H. (12/15/2005)*

Dutton-Goldfield 2001 Dutton Ranch Pinot Noir (Russian River Valley) $35. Equal parts cherry-berry fruit and earthier notes of tobacco, cola, and rhubarb comprise this dry, complex wine. It's young, with dusty tannins and firm acids, and possesses a balanced elegance that make it an ideal partner to lamb or beef. **91** *—S.H. (4/1/2004)*

Dutton-Goldfield 1999 Dutton Ranch Pinot Noir (Russian River Valley) $40. **93** *—S.H. (7/1/2002)*

Dutton-Goldfield 2000 Dutton Ranch Maurice Galante Vineyard Pinot Noir (Russian River Valley) $55. **90** *(10/1/2002)*

Dutton-Goldfield 1999 Freestone Hill Vineyard Pinot Noir (Russian River Valley) $55. **92** *—S.H. (7/1/2002)*

Dutton-Goldfield 2002 Sanchietti Vineyard Pinot Noir (Russian River Valley) $52. A real beauty. Shows complex notes of black cherry, tree bark, cocoa, chocolate, and smoky oak throughout, with a supple, delicate mouthfeel. Crisp acidity and a long, spicy finish make it extra attractive. **90** *(11/1/2004)*

Dutton-Goldfield 2001 Dutton Ranch Cherry Ridge Vineyard Syrah (Russian River Valley) $35. Wickedly, sinfully good. This is fruit detonation in the mouth, a blast of pure, sweet cassis, currant, plum, and chocolate. The tannins are a velvety wonder, the oak lavish and thick, but perfectly in balance to the size. Opulent and hedonistic, it's best in its sensual, seductive youth. **93 Editors' Choice** *—S.H. (6/1/2004)*

Dutton-Goldfield 2002 Dutton Ranch Morelli Lane Vineyard Zinfandel (Russian River Valley) $35. A well-structured, elegant Zinfandel that's framed in silky tannins and marked by focused acidity. Flavors are layered to reveal black cherry, licorice, tar, herbs, spice, chocolate, and a hint of coffee as well. Long and fairly lush at the end. **91** *—J.M. (12/31/2004)*

Dutton-Goldfield 2000 Morelli Lane Vineyard Zinfandel (Russian River Valley) $35. 94 Cellar Selection *—S.H. (12/1/2002)*

DYNAMITE VINEYARDS

Dynamite Vineyards 2002 Cabernet Sauvignon (North Coast) $17. Ripe and juicy in currant and chocolate flavors, with a good backbone of tannins and acids. Turns a bit raw on the finish, but will be nice now with rich meats. **85** *—S.H. (2/1/2005)*

Dynamite Vineyards 2000 Red Hills Cabernet Sauvignon (Lake County) $25. 87 *—S.H. (12/31/2003)*

USA

Dynamite Vineyards 2001 Merlot (North Coast) $17. This wine is big and rich, and feels plush and smooth in the mouth. You'll find flavors of cherries, plums, herbs and coffee, and thick but ripe tannins. It's nuanced in its appeal. **87** *—S.H. (5/1/2004)*

Dynamite Vineyards 2002 Sauvignon Blanc (Lake County) $11. A pleasant quaffer, with mild melon and citrus flavors, finishing with moderate length. **84** *—J.M. (4/1/2004)*

Dynamite Vineyards 2003 Zinfandel (Mendocino County) $17. This is a bone-dry, slightly overripe Zin, with dusty, briary aromas and flavors of raisins, bitter dark chocolate, and ripe plums. It's a serious Zin, a little hot but with plenty of sophistication. **88** *—S.H. (10/1/2005)*

E & J GALLO

E & J Gallo 1998 Estate Chardonnay (Northern Sonoma) $50. 92 *(7/1/2001)*

E B FOOTE

E B Foote 1999 Cabernet Sauvignon (Columbia Valley (WA)) $16. 84 *—D.T. (12/31/2002)*

E B Foote 1998 Chardonnay (Columbia Valley (WA)) $12. 85 *—P.G. (6/1/2000)*

E B Foote 1999 Chardonnay (Columbia Valley (WA)) $12. 82 *—P.G. (7/1/2002)*

E B Foote 1998 Merlot (Columbia Valley (WA)) $16. 87 *—P.G. (6/1/2001)*

E B Foote 2001 Syrah (Columbia Valley (WA)) $18. 82 *—M.S. (6/1/2003)*

E. B. Foote 2003 Syrah (Columbia Valley (WA)) $16. A step up from the last time we reviewed an E.B. Foote Syrah, this version combines bright berry flavors with peppery notes in a plump, mouthfilling wine that turns tart on the finish. **86** *(9/1/2005)*

EAGLE & ROSE ESTATE

Eagle & Rose Estate 1998 Cabernet Sauvignon (Napa Valley) $NA. 84 *—S.H. (12/1/2001)*

Eagle & Rose Estate 1999 Merlot (Napa Valley) $24. 87 *—S.H. (11/15/2002)*

Eagle & Rose Estate 1999 Sangiovese (Napa Valley) $24. 81 *—S.H. (11/15/2002)*

Eagle & Rose Estate 2000 Sauvignon Blanc (Napa Valley) $16. 84 *—S.H. (9/1/2003)*

Eagle & Rose Estate 1998 Sauvignon Blanc (Napa Valley) $16. 88 *—S.H. (11/15/2000)*

EAGLEPOINT RANCH

Eaglepoint Ranch 2004 Grenache (Mendocino County) $18. The ranch is way up in the Mayacamas range, and its red wines are always concentrated. This Grenache is surprisingly light in structure, almost like a Beaujolais, but rich in sweet cherry pie fruit, dry, and elegant. **87** *—S.H. (12/31/2005)*

Eaglepoint Ranch 2001 Grenache (Mendocino County) $14. On the light-bodied side, with silky tannins. It's structured like a Pinot Noir, with cola, raspberry, cranberry, and rhubarb tea flavors that are a little thin, but nice and different. **86** *—S.H. (5/1/2004)*

Eaglepoint Ranch 2002 Petite Sirah (Mendocino County) $24. After all the soft red wines lately, it's almost a relief to gag on some real tannins. Dry and spicy, with big-time black cherry pie flavors, complete with the baked, buttery crust. **87** *—S.H. (3/1/2005)*

Eaglepoint Ranch 2001 Coro Mendocino Red Blend (Mendocino) $35. Firm and focused on the palate, the wine shows off a blend of black cherry, coffee, spice, toast, and herb notes that are neatly framed in ripe tannins. The finish is moderate in length, ending with a clean edge. **89** *—J.M. (9/1/2004)*

Eaglepoint Ranch 2000 Syrah (Mendocino) $22. 88 *—S.H. (12/1/2003)*

EARTHQUAKE

Earthquake 2003 Syrah (Lodi) $25. West Coast Editor Steve Heimoff liked this wine a lot more than the two other tasters, so if you normally follow his suggestions, you may want to give this wine a try. He found it very ripe and extracted, with rich, sweet tannins. Our other reviewers found it less appealing, even a little unrefined and alcoholic. **87** *(9/1/2005)*

EASTON

Easton 2001 Barbera (Shenandoah Valley (CA)) $20. Fruity, tannic, and full-bodied, a workhorse grape and wine that strives for elegance and finesse, and comes close. Cherries, leather, lots of herbs, and a finish of slightly sweetened coffee suggest robust foods. The high acidity will cut right through fats **86** *—S.H. (6/1/2004)*

Easton 2000 Cabernet Sauvignon (California) $15. 90 Best Buy *—S.H. (6/1/2003)*

Easton 2003 Sauvignon Blanc (Sierra Foothills) $16. This is a fairly dry wine, tart in acids and citrus fruits, but enriched with highlights of figs and melons that give it some sweetness in the finish. It seems to have a little smoky oak in there, too. Easy to like, and the slight sweetness will pay well against fruits or sole sautéed in butter sauce. **85** *—S.H. (8/1/2005)*

Easton 2002 Zinfandel (Amador County) $13. Blackberries and cherries coexist side by side with Porty, raisiny flavors in this rough-and-ready mountain Zin. There seems to be a little residual sugar, to judge by the sweetness. It'll be fine with a pizza pie. **85** *—S.H. (6/1/2004)*

Easton 2001 Zinfandel (Fiddletown) $25. So rich in flavor, it's like liquid candy, a purée of raspberries, cherries, and blueberries, with a little brown sugar thrown in for good measure. But it's technically dry, with lush, smooth tannins. Distinctive, concentrated, and intense. **90** *—S.H. (6/1/2004)*

Easton 2001 Zinfandel (Amador County) $13. 84 *—S.H. (9/1/2003)*

Easton 2000 Zinfandel (Shenandoah Valley (CA)) $30. 93 Editors' Choice *—S.H. (9/1/2003)*

Easton 2000 Zinfandel (Shenandoah Valley (CA)) $22. 88 *—S.H. (9/1/2003)*

Easton 1999 Zinfandel (Fiddletown) $25. 91 *—S.H. (3/1/2002)*

Easton 2002 Estate Bottled Zinfandel (Shenandoah Valley (CA)) $30. This is a delicious Zin, easy to drink, but it's far from simple. With the elegant mouthfeel of a soft Merlot, it offers rich, almost decadent flavors of black raspberries and cherry mocha, candied ginger, creme de cassis, and white pepper. **90** *—S.H. (8/1/2005)*

Easton House NV Lot No. 0102 Red Blend (California) $10. Rustic, thickly textured and fruity, but soft and easy, this honest country wine is clean and satisfying. It has strong berry flavors that most people will appreciate. **84** *—S.H. (8/1/2005)*

EBERLE

Eberle 2001 Sauret Vineyard Barbera (Paso Robles) $18. 86 *—S.H. (12/1/2003)*

Eberle 2000 Cabernet Sauvignon (Paso Robles) $23. 85 *—S.H. (11/15/2003)*

Eberle 2002 Estate Cabernet Sauvignon (Paso Robles) $27. Eberle's estate Cab is a seriously attractive wine, due mainly to its soft, velvety tannins and delicious blackberry and cherry flavors. A hint of raisins is there, but adds seasoning to the finish. **91** *—S.H. (11/15/2005)*

Eberle 1997 Estate Bottled Cabernet Sauvignon (Paso Robles) $30. 86 *(11/1/2000)*

Eberle 2002 Vineyard Selection Cabernet Sauvignon (Paso Robles) $17. Showing good Cabernet character, this pleasant wine has blackberry, currant, and cocoa flavors, wrapped in soft, gentle tannins. It's nicely dry, and finishes with a bite of pepper. **86** *—S.H. (11/15/2005)*

Eberle 2002 Cabernet Sauvignon-Syrah (Paso Robles) $24. Fancy, plush fare from this veteran South Coast producer. Floods the palate with ripe blackberry, cherry, mocha, and peppery spice flavors wrapped in soft, luxuriously sweet tannins. The finish is long and reprises the cherry-and-spice theme. **91** *—S.H. (12/15/2004)*

Eberle 2004 Chardonnay (Paso Robles) $16. The heat of Paso hasn't given this Chard much acidity, but in its place you'll find beautifully ripened fruit. It tastes like peaches floating in natural cream, drizzled with honey and vanilla and just a dash of créme de cassis. It's really quite an impressive wine. **90** *—S.H. (11/15/2005)*

Eberle 2003 Estate Chardonnay (Paso Robles) $16. Lots of toasty oak, plenty of ripe tropical fruit in this polished, friendly wine. The creamy texture and long, spicy finish bring it all together. **87** *—S.H. (12/15/2004)*

Eberle 2004 Muscat Canelli (Paso Robles) $12. The first time I ever had Eberle's Muscat, I thought it was the perfect garden sipper. It still is. Redolent with aromas of flowers and orchard fruits, it's semisweet and clean, with a long, spicy finish. **87 Best Buy** *—S.H. (11/15/2005)*

Eberle 2003 Cabernet Sauvignon-Syrah Red Blend (Paso Robles) $24. As rich as Eberle's Cabernets are, Syrah seems to bring an added dimension of decadent cherry-berry liqueur to the blend. The wine is velvety soft in tannins, and so fruity, it finishes with a honeyed sweetness. **88** *—S.H. (11/15/2005)*

Eberle 2003 Roussanne (Paso Robles) $22. Deliciously drinkable for its soft, creamy texture and juicy flavors of peaches and cream, exotic tropical fruits, vanilla, and honey. This dry wine is great all by itself. **87** *—S.H. (12/15/2004)*

Eberle 2003 Sangiovese (Paso Robles) $16. With 15% alcohol, this wine's hot, with a prickly, peppery finish. But that's part of its personality, which also includes plummy, black cherry, and coffee flavors. It's very dry, and should be good with beef grilled as the sun goes down. **85** *—S.H. (11/15/2005)*

Eberle 2001 Filipponi & Thompson Vineyard Sangiovese (Paso Robles) $16. 84 *—S.H. (12/1/2003)*

Eberle 2001 Reid Vineyard Syrah (Paso Robles) $20. Like Eberle's Steinbeck Syrah, the flavors here are excellent, suggesting spicy plums and blackberries, with a rich edge of ground coffee and a mélange of spices and dried herbs. The tannins also are good and rich. Once again, the problem is excessive softness. The mouthfeel is weak and lacks grip. **85** *—S.H. (2/1/2004)*

Eberle 1997 Reid Vineyard Syrah (Paso Robles) $18. 88 *—S.H. (6/1/1999)*

Eberle 2002 Rosé Syrah (Paso Robles) $14. Eberle has a way with rosé wines, and this one is very pleasant. It has flavors of strawberries and raspberries and spices that are richly ripe, but the wine is dry. It has a good boost of acidity and will be refreshingly cool on a hot afternoon. **85** *—S.H. (3/1/2004)*

Eberle 2003 Steinbeck Vineyard Syrah (Paso Robles) $24. What great aromas start things off here. It's all about chocolate and cassis, roasted coffeebeans and smoky vanilla.Then things fall off. The wine turns overly flabby, almost flat in the mouth. But it is dry. **84** *—S.H. (11/15/2005)*

USA

Eberle 2001 Steinbeck Vineyard Syrah (Paso Robles) $20. A little chewy, with big tannins framing the charry, smoky-edged plum, blackberry, and black cherry flavors. Toasty oak and vanilla notes add a framework that finishes with moderate length. **87** *(2/1/2004)*

Eberle 2002 Steinbeck Vineyard Reserve Syrah (Paso Robles) $45. Eberle has built more tannic structure into this reserve wine than into their regular Steinbeck Syrah. That seems to have come at the cost of some fruity ripeness, however. At the same time, there's a curious sweetness. It adds up to an awkwardness that's unlikely to change with age. **84** *—S.H. (11/15/2005)*

Eberle 1998 Glenrose Vineyard Viognier (Paso Robles) $20. 87 *—S.H (10/1/1999)*

Eberle 2003 Mill Road Vineyard Viognier (Paso Robles) $18. Filled with fruity flavors ranging from ripe white peaches to papayas, this pleasantly crisp wine also has a spicy, floral finish that lasts for a long time, and leaves behind a taste of honey. **85** *—S.H. (12/15/2004)*

Eberle 2001 Mill Road Vineyard Viognier (Paso Robles) $18. 90 *—J.M. (12/15/2002)*

Eberle 2003 Remo Belli Vineyard Zinfandel (Paso Robles) $22. There seems to be too much residual sugar in this soft Zin. Too bad, because it's smooth, with yummy blackberry, cherry, and chocolate flavors. **84** *—S.H. (11/15/2005)*

Eberle 2001 Remo Belli Vineyard Zinfandel (Paso Robles) $18. 88 *(11/1/2003)*

Eberle 2002 Steinbeck Vineyard Zinfandel (Paso Robles) $16. You can taste the sun in every chocolaty, wild berry, and cassis-infused sip, and thankfully the wine is fully dry. Perfect with barbecue, and delicious all by its lonesome. **90** *—S.H. (12/15/2004)*

ECHELON

Echelon 2002 Cabernet Sauvignon (Hames Valley) $12. This is a good everyday red wine, clean, and with some richness. It's full-bodied, with blackberry-cherry and earth flavors, and a pretty finish of currants. **84** *—S.H. (8/1/2005)*

Echelon 2000 Cabernet Sauvignon (California) $13. 83 *—J.M. (12/31/2002)*

Echelon 2003 Chardonnay (Central Coast) $12. Soupy-soft, simple, and cloying, with the flavor of sweetened apricot and peach syrup. **81** *—S.H. (12/1/2005)*

Echelon 1997 Merlot (Central Coast) $15. 84 *—S.H. (7/1/2000)*

Echelon 2001 Merlot (Central Coast) $12. Here's a decent, everyday sipper in a full-bodied red wine. It's dry enough to accompany a steak or roast, with modest berry flavors that turn astringent on the finish. Perfect for backyard gatherings where barbecue is the theme. **84** *—S.H. (2/1/2004)*

Echelon 2001 Pinot Grigio (Central Coast) $11. 84 *—J.M. (9/1/2003)*

Echelon 2003 Pinot Noir (Central Coast) $10. The Chalone Wine Group created the Echelon brand in 1997 to offer a range of inexpensive wines to complement Chalone's single-vineyard bottlings. This Pinot Noir certainly tastes much better than its price would have you believe. With fruit coming mainly from growers in the cool-climate Santa Lucia Highlands above California's Salinas Valley, the wine is packed with sweet strawberry and cherry flavors, layers of wood, and soft tannins. **86 Best Buy** *—R.V. (11/15/2004)*

Echelon 2001 Pinot Noir (Central Coast) $12. 84 *—M.S. (12/1/2003)*

Echelon 1997 Pinot Noir (Central Coast) $NA. 83 *— (10/1/1999)*

Echelon 2002 Esperanza Vineyard Syrah (Clarksburg) $10. This lovely Syrah could be one of your basic house reds. It's dry and smooth, with pure flavors of blackberries, pepper, cocoa, and oak. Firm and acidic enough to stand up to rich meats. **85 Best Buy** *—S.H. (4/1/2005)*

Echelon 2000 Esperanza Vineyard Syrah (Clarksburg) $10. 84 Best Buy *—J.M. (11/15/2002)*

Echelon 2003 Driving Range Vineyard Zinfandel (Contra Costa County) $13. Hits all the wrong buttons for me, with its porty, cooked berry aroma and dry, harsh tannins. **82** *—S.H. (8/1/2005)*

ECKERT

Eckert 2000 Petite Sirah (Lodi) $18. A heavy wine, and Porty too, with aromas of caramelized wood, sweet raisins, and pie crust. It's fruity-rich in very ripe blackberry flavors that are carried in a syrupy texture. **83** —*S.H. (3/1/2004)*

EDGEFIELD

Edgefield 1998 Chukar Ridge Vineyard Syrah (Columbia Valley (WA)) $11. 88 Best Buy *(10/1/2001)*

Edgewood 1995 Tradition Bordeaux Blend (Napa Valley) $30. 88 *(3/1/2000)*

Edgewood 2000 Cabernet Sauvignon (Napa Valley) $24. This is a delicious regional Cabernet. It has ripe, gentle tannins, supportive acidity, a pedigreed mouthfeel, and succulent oak. The black currant and cassis flavors are a little thin in the middle. **88** —*S.H. (2/1/2004)*

Edgewood 2000 Frediani Vineyard Cabernet Sauvignon (Napa Valley) $40. This single-vineyard Cab from Edgewood is quite different from their other wines. This is the mintiest of the current releases, with a scent of menthol and eucalyptus that may come from nearby trees. It's also minty in the mouth, but that doesn't stop the blackberry flavors a bit. It's ready to drink now, with sturdy tannins. **90** —*S.H. (2/1/2004)*

Edgewood 2000 Reserve Cabernet Sauvignon (Napa Valley) $50. Lots to admire in this fancy Napa Cab, with its focused currant and cassis flavors, elaborate but balanced overlay of toasty oak and sweet, rich tannins. There's also a scour of acidity that prickles on the finish. Doesn't overwhelm, but is easily able to stand up to fine cuisine. **91** —*S.H. (5/1/2004)*

Edgewood 2002 Chardonnay (Napa-Sonoma) $20. This fun wine is loaded with spicy pear, tangerine, tropical fruit, and citrus flavors that have been lavished with smoky oak. It's long and deep in the mouth, with a crisp burst of acidity. **89** —*S.H. (2/1/2004)*

Edgewood 2001 Malbec (Napa Valley) $20. One of the few varietal Malbecs in California, this wine is inky black in color, and very heavy and dense in the mouth. It has flavors of the darkest stone fruits veering into chocolate and peat, and is absolutely dry. A curiosity, it may develop with longterm cellaring. **86** —*S.H. (9/1/2004)*

Edgewood 2000 Emmolo Vineyard Malbec (Napa Valley) $40. As good as Edgewood's regular Malbec is, this almost black wine is better. The gooey cherry-pie flavors are riper and sweeter, the tannins are thicker and softer, and the oak is more notable. This is one of those wines whose flavors are so powerful they startle. It's a killer with babyback ribs. **91** —*S.H. (3/1/2004)*

Edgewood 1999 Reserve Malbec (Napa Valley) $50. Not as likeable as the winery's other two Malbecs, with thick, astringent tannins and a very dry, puckery finish. The theory seems to be ageability, but there isn't enough fruit for the long haul. **86** —*S.H. (3/1/2004)*

Edgewood 1996 Merlot (Napa Valley) $20. 88 —*M.S. (3/1/2000)*

Edgewood 2000 Merlot (Napa Valley) $24. Hits all the right notes, with its splendid flavors of black currants, cassis, chocolate, ripe plums, herbs, and smoky vanilla. Glides across the palate with the softest imaginable tannins, like butter, but the structure is firm. Close your eyes and enjoy the long finish. **91** *(2/1/2004)*

Edgewood 2000 Nepenthes Vineyard Merlot (Napa Valley) $40. Only 182 cases were produced of this spectacularly ripe, juicy Merlot, which floods the palate with enormous flavors of blackberries, cherries, chocolate fudge, caramel, and vanilla. The soft tannins are a wonder, the smoky oak perfectly applied. **93** —*S.H. (2/1/2004)*

Edgewood 1999 Tradition Red Blend (Napa Valley) $35. 92 —*S.H. (12/31/2003)*

Edgewood 2002 Sauvignon Blanc (Napa Valley) $15. 86 —*S.H. (12/15/2003)*

Edgewood 2000 Sauvignon Blanc (Napa Valley) $20. 81 *(8/1/2002)*

Edgewood 1996 Zinfandel (Napa Valley) $14. 87 Best Buy —*J.C. (5/1/2000)*

Edgewood 2000 Zinfandel (Napa Valley) $20. 82 —*S.H. (9/1/2003)*

EDMEADES

Edmeades 2000 Chardonnay (Anderson Valley) $18. 91 —*S.H. (5/1/2002)*

Edmeades 1996 Eaglepoint Vineyard Petite Sirah (Mendocino) $20. 89 —*S.H. (5/1/2000)*

Edmeades 2000 Pinot Noir (Anderson Valley) $20. Let this wine breathe for a little while because there's a dustiness that hides the underlying cherry and blueberry aromas. Once in the mouth, it's fruity and delicate, with cherry-berry flavors enhanced by mocha, vanilla, and cinnamon. Feels silky on the palate, with a very crisp streak of acidity. **87** —*S.H. (3/1/2004)*

Edmeades 1998 Pinot Noir (Anderson Valley) $16. 83 —*S.H. (2/1/2001)*

Edmeades 2003 Zinfandel (Mendocino) $19. A big, brawny, high-alcohol Zin, dry and fairly tannic, and balanced in cherry, tobacco, herb, and cocoa flavors. There's nothing subtle about this exuberant wine, which will be great with a big piece of red meat. **88** —*S.H. (8/1/2005)*

Edmeades 2000 Zinfandel (Mendocino) $19. Here's a big, super-ripe Zin, with explosive flavors of cherries and raspberries and a full-throated mouthfeel. It's filled with ripe, sweet fruit, but is dry. It's also quite high in alcohol, and finishes hot. **86** —*S.H. (3/1/2004)*

Edmeades 1998 Zinfandel (Mendocino Ridge) $25. 90 —*P.G. (3/1/2001)*

Edmeades 2002 Alden Vineyard Late Harvest Zinfandel (Mendocino) $16. With their Zin grapes approaching Port levels anyway, Edmeades is a natural for a dessert wine. But this one should be richer and sweeter. It's as if the decision were made to keep it off-dry, blurring the line between it and the regular Zins. **85** *—S.H. (11/15/2004)*

Edmeades 1999 Ciapusci Zinfandel (Mendocino Ridge) $25. 92 *—S.H. (11/1/2002)*

Edmeades 2001 Ciapusci Vineyard Zinfandel (Mendocino Ridge) $25. 84 *(11/1/2003)*

Edmeades 1997 Ciapusci Vineyard Zinfandel (Mendocino Ridge) $36. 88 *—S.H. (5/1/2000)*

Edmeades 1999 Eaglepoint Ranch Zinfandel (Mendocino) $25. 86 *—S.H. (11/1/2002)*

Edmeades 2001 Piffero Vineyard Zinfandel (Mendocino) $25. 84 *(11/1/2003)*

Edmeades 2002 Zeni Vineyard Zinfandel (Mendocino Ridge) $29. Would you believe 17.5% alcohol, and there's still residual sugar? That's what these old mountain vines did in 2001's heat waves. Berry, chocolate, and Porty flavors and firm tannins. **86** *—S.H. (11/15/2004)*

Edmeades 1999 Zeni Vineyard Zinfandel (Mendocino Ridge) $25. 93 Editors' Choice *—S.H. (11/1/2002)*

USA

EDMUNDS ST JOHN

Edmunds St John 2000 Los Robles Viejos Rozet Red Blend (Paso Robles) $28. 87 *—S.H. (11/15/2002)*

Edmunds St John 1996 Durell Vineyard Syrah (Sonoma Valley) $25. 91 *—S.H. (6/1/1999)*

Edmunds St John 1999 Wylie-Fenaughty Syrah (El Dorado) $32. 84 *(11/1/2001)*

Edmunds St John 1998 Alban/Durell Vineyards Viognier (California) $20. 93 *—S.H. (10/1/1999)*

EDNA VALLEY VINEYARD

Edna Valley Vineyard 2004 Paragon Chardonnay (Edna Valley) $15. This wine shows those crisp, bright, mouthwatering Central Coast acids. They perk up the lime and tropical fruit flavors enhanced with a touch of vanilla and smoke from barrels. Finishes spicy and dry. **85** *—S.H. (12/1/2005)*

Edna Valley Vineyard 2002 Paragon Chardonnay (Edna Valley) $14. Sure, it's super-oaky. But it's good, delicious oak, and all that smoky vanilla and buttercream blend in just fine with the tropical fruit. The buttery, creamy texture seems soft, because it could have more acidity, but it sure tastes good, and is a value in a big, sweet Chard. **89 Best Buy** *—S.H. (6/1/2004)*

Edna Valley Vineyard 2000 Paragon Chardonnay (Edna Valley) $17. 86 *—S.H. (6/1/2003)*

Edna Valley Vineyard 1997 Paragon Vineyard Chardonnay (Edna Valley) $17. 92 *—L.W. (7/1/1999)*

Edna Valley Vineyard 2003 Paragon Pinot Noir (Edna Valley) $20. This is the kind of Pinot that you can drink everyday without flinching at the price. It's representative of the coast, a light-bodied but full-flavored wine with tremendous cherry fruit, cola, spice, and oak, and a dry finish. **87** *—S.H. (10/1/2005)*

Edna Valley Vineyard 2000 Paragon Pinot Noir (Edna Valley) $23. 89 *—J.M. (5/1/2002)*

Edna Valley Vineyard 1997 Paragon Pinot Noir (Central Coast) $20. 86 *(11/15/1999)*

Edna Valley Vineyard 2002 Paragon Sauvignon Blanc (Edna Valley) $14. A bright, refreshing style that's packed with grapefruit, gooseberry, and lemon flavors. It's quite grassy, fairly complex and really delicious. Long and fresh at the end. **89** *—J.M. (9/1/2004)*

Edna Valley Vineyard 2001 Paragon Syrah (Central Coast) $14. Strikes the palate with a certain fierceness of tannins and rough, briary texture, then calms down to offer modest fruit. **84** *—S.H. (6/1/2004)*

Edna Valley Vineyard 1998 Fralich Vineyard Viognier (Paso Robles) $18. 88 *—S.H. (10/1/1999)*

EHLERS ESTATE

Ehlers Estate 2000 Cabernet Sauvignon (Napa Valley) $28. Chock full of smoky, toasty, licorice, and herb flavors. The wine also shows hints of cassis and blackberry, all couched in modest tannins, finishing with moderate length. **87** *—J.M. (4/1/2004)*

EHLERS GROVE

Ehlers Grove 1998 Chardonnay (Carneros) $30. 88 *(6/1/2000)*

EL ALACRAN

El Alacran 2002 Mourvèdre (Amador County) $34. Dry, simple, and berryish, with rustic tannins. **83** *—S.H. (4/1/2005)*

EL MOLINO

El Molino 2003 Chardonnay (Rutherford) $40. Chardonnay in Rutherford? Yes, and a very good one. It has polished peach and apple flavors as well as a sweet, rich coat of oak, and is balanced, crisp and dry. **89** *—S.H. (12/15/2005)*

El Molino 1999 Chardonnay (Rutherford) $40. 90 *(7/1/2001)*

El Molino 1999 Pinot Noir (Napa Valley) $51. 87 *(10/1/2002)*

ELAINE MARIA

Elaine Maria 2002 Reserve Merlot (Alexander Valley) $28. Riper than the regular Merlot, with a good core of red and black cherry fruit, and finishes dry and herbal. Full-bodied and fairly tannic, but balanced and complex. A new winery started by a member of the Foppiano family. **88** *—S.H. (5/1/2005)*

ELAN

Elan 1997 Cabernet Sauvignon (Atlas Peak) $45. **88** *(11/1/2000)*

Elan 2000 Cabernet Sauvignon (Atlas Peak) $42. A very dense, chocolaty wine, with jammy currant and blackberry fruit. The new oak hasn't yet been fully integrated. Below all that are firm but polished tannins and fine acidity. A few years of aging should lighten it. **88** *—S.H. (11/15/2004)*

ELARA

Elara 2000 Tollini Vineyard Petite Sirah (Mendocino County) $27. **89** *—S.H. (12/31/2003)*

Elara 2000 Syrah (McDowell Valley) $32. **87** *—S.H. (12/15/2003)*

ELIZABETH

Elizabeth 1998 Sauvignon Blanc (Redwood Valley) $14. **87** *—S.H. (5/1/2000)*

Elizabeth 1997 Zinfandel (Redwood Valley) $18. **81** *—P.G. (11/15/1999)*

ELK COVE

Elk Cove 2004 Pinot Gris (Willamette Valley) $17. Hits with a bit of sharpness and a high-toned edge. The fruit is ripe but the wine seems a bit disjointed. Some breathing time, maybe even decanting, is a good idea. **86** *—P.G. (8/1/2005)*

Elk Cove 2001 Pinot Gris (Willamette Valley) $15. **91 Editors' Choice** *—P.G. (8/1/2003)*

Elk Cove 1998 Pinot Gris (Willamette Valley) $15. **88 Editors' Choice** *(8/1/1999)*

Elk Cove 2002 Pinot Noir (Willamette Valley) $24. It takes a moment for the SO2 to burn off, but there is nice black cherry fruit waiting underneath, and hints of leather. Tannic and a bit rough through the finish. **86** *(11/1/2004)*

Elk Cove 2000 Pinot Noir (Willamette Valley) $20. **89** *—P.G. (4/1/2003)*

Elk Cove 1998 Pinot Noir (Willamette Valley) $18. **90 Best Buy** *—M.S. (12/1/2000)*

Elk Cove 2000 La Bohéme Pinot Noir (Oregon) $34. **88** *—P.G. (4/1/2003)*

Elk Cove 2002 La Bohéme Pinot Noir (Willamette Valley) $36. Though this is Elk Cove's premier vineyard, its appeal is not for all. If you like smoke, leather, and tannin, this is your style. Chocolate, burnt coffee, and smoked meat are here in abundance, but where's the fruit? **86** *(11/1/2004)*

Elk Cove 2002 Reserve Pinot Noir (Willamette Valley) $60. Highly enjoyable and distinctive, with a soft, supple palate that smoothes together rich plum, blackberry, and black cherry fruit. It's lean but not sour, subtle and lingering, with good grip and a hint of underbrush. **90** *(11/1/2004)*

Elk Cove 2001 Roosevelt Pinot Noir (Willamette Valley) $32. **90** *—P.G. (12/1/2003)*

Elk Cove 1999 Roosevelt Pinot Noir (Oregon) $48. **89** *—P.G. (4/1/2002)*

Elk Cove 2003 Shea Pinot Noir (Willamette Valley) $36. The blackberry and blueberry fruit flavors are a Shea Vineyard signature. In this hot year the juice is sweet and the wine soft and tannic, broadly flavorful, but the awkward acids suggest that some acidification was necessary. Needs a little time. **88** *—P.G. (8/1/2005)*

Elk Cove 2002 Windhill Pinot Noir (Willamette Valley) $30. This pleasant, fruity effort falls squarely in the middle of the Elk Cove lineup, showing fresh, clean red fruits and a broad, accessible palate. **88** *—P.G. (2/1/2005)*

Elk Cove 2000 Windhill Pinot Noir (Oregon) $34. **89** *—P.G. (4/1/2003)*

Elk Cove 1997 Windhill Pinot Noir (Willamette Valley) $28. **86** *(11/15/1999)*

Elk Cove 2001 Riesling (Willamette Valley) $12. **86** *—J.C. (8/1/2003)*

Elk Cove 1999 Brut Sparkling Blend (Oregon) $22. **89** *—M.S. (6/1/2003)*

Elk Cove 2001 Del Rio Viognier (Rogue Valley) $22. **88** *—M.S. (8/1/2003)*

ELKE

Elke 1997 Donnelly Creek Vyd Pinot Noir (Anderson Valley) $24. **89** *(10/1/2000)*

ELKHORN PEAK

Elkhorn Peak 2000 Fagan Creek Merlot (Napa Valley) $18. A nice, easy-drinking Merlot, with herb, blackberry, and coffee flavors a a full-bodied mouthfeel. A little rough around the edges, but a pretty good value for a Napa Merlot. **85** *—S.H. (11/15/2004)*

Elkhorn Peak 1999 Fagan Creek Vineyard Pinot Noir (Napa Valley) $30. Rather heavy for a Pinot Noir, and soft, too. The flavors veer toward coffee, cherry, and cola. Finishes simple and dry. **83** *—S.H. (8/1/2005)*

ELLISTON

Elliston 1997 Sunol Valley Vineyard Pinot Grigio (Central Coast) $10. 87 Best Buy *(8/1/1999)*

ELYSE

Elyse 1999 Morisoli Vineyard Cabernet Sauvignon (Napa Valley) $57. 89 *—J.M. (2/1/2003)*

Elyse 2001 Tietjen Vineyard Cabernet Sauvignon (Napa Valley) $65. Shows some good black cherry and blackberry flavors, with an earthier, herbal, and leathery side, and the tannins stand out. Should soften in a few years. Drink now through 2008. **86** *—S.H. (5/1/2005)*

Elyse 2003 Petite Sirah (Rutherford) $36. About as fancy as Petite Sirah gets. Has the bones and authority of a great Cab. Lush, smooth tannins and full-bodied, with powerful, intense flavors of blackberries, plums, espresso, peppery spices, and subtle notes from oak barrels. **92** *—S.H. (10/1/2005)*

Elyse 2002 D'Adventure Rhône Red Blend (California) $25. Smells closed and alcoholic, and turns tough and gritty in acids and tannins in the mouth. The flavors veer toward cherries, coffee, and tobacco. Rhône blend. **85** *—S.H. (5/1/2005)*

Elyse 1999 Syrah (Napa Valley) $35. 87 *—J.M. (2/1/2003)*

Elyse 2002 Morisoli Vineyard Zinfandel (Napa Valley) $35. From a Rutherford vineyard, a smooth Zin with an excellent mouthfeel: velvety yet firm. It's fully dry but very high in alcohol. Flavor-wise, the berries are compromised by stalky, green notes.by stalky, green notes. **85** *—S.H. (5/1/2005)*

EMERALD BAY

Emerald Bay 1997 Cabernet Sauvignon (California) $7. 83 *(2/1/2000)*

Emerald Bay 1997 Merlot (California) $7. 85 *(2/1/2000)*

EMILIO'S TERRACE

Emilio's Terrace 1999 Estate Cabernet Sauvignon (Napa Valley) $45. 93 Editors' Choice *—J.M. (2/1/2003)*

EMMOLO

Emmolo 2000 Rutherford Sauvignon Blanc (Napa Valley) $16. 85 *(8/1/2002)*

ENCORE

Encore 2002 San Bernabe Vineyard White Medley White Blend (Monterey) $18. From Monterra, a delicious blend of Sauvignon Blanc, Pinot Blanc, Muscat Canelli, and Viognier. Each variety contributes a different fruity flavor. Smooth and a little sweet, with a nice cut of acidity. **87** *—S.H. (12/15/2004)*

ENGELMANN

Engelmann 2000 Sangiovese (California) $12. 81 *—S.H. (12/1/2002)*

ENOTRIA

Enotria 1999 Arneis (Mendocino) $14. 84 *—S.H. (8/1/2001)*

Enotria 1999 Barbera (Mendocino) $13. 81 *—S.H. (5/1/2002)*

Enotria 1999 Dolcetto (Mendocino) $16. 84 *—S.H. (5/1/2002)*

EOLA HILLS

Eola Hills 1998 LBV Port Style Cabernet Sauvignon (Oregon) $18. 86 *—J.M. (12/1/2002)*

Eola Hills 1998 Merlot (Oregon) $12. 85 *—C.S. (12/31/2002)*

Eola Hills 1999 Pinot Noir (Oregon) $12. 84 Best Buy *(10/1/2002)*

Eola Hills 1999 La Creole Reserve Pinot Noir (Oregon) $25. 81 *(10/1/2002)*

Eola Hills 2002 La Creole Vineyard Pinot Noir (Eola Hills) $20. Notes of cabbage, plum tomato, and green bean give this a somewhat medicinal, pungent character. Tannic, thin, and difficult. **84** *(11/1/2004)*

Eola Hills 2001 Wolf Hill Vineyard Pinot Noir (Oregon) $40. This is a tangy, food-friendly style, with tart fruit that suggests cranberries and pomegranate. There is also a distinctive minty quality that's almost eucalyptus (but I don't know that eucalyptus grows in Oregon). Right at the finish line some sweet cherry slips in. **87** *—P.G. (10/1/2004)*

Eola Hills 1999 Wolf Hill Vineyard Reserve Pinot Noir (Oregon) $40. 88 *(10/1/2002)*

Eola Hills 2000 Syrah (Oregon) $12. 85 *—R.V. (12/31/2002)*

Eola Hills 2000 Reserve Syrah (Columbia Valley (OR)) $20. Unusual but compelling to some reviewers, but one thing is for sure: This wine is no fruit bomb. The nose has red fruit doused in tons of fragrant spice (cinnamon, clove, curry). Dry on the palate, with red berry and cherry fruit, unsweetened chocolate and cedar flavors. Toast and menthol on the finish. **85** *(9/1/2005)*

Eola Hills 1999 Old Vines Zinfandel (Lodi) $25. 86 *—D.T. (3/1/2002)*

USA

EOS

EOS 2000 French Connection Cabernet Blend (Paso Robles) $20. 86 *—S.H. (5/1/2003)*

EOS 2001 Cabernet Sauvignon (Paso Robles) $18. Rich, soft, and juicy in blackberry, cherry, raisin, and chocolate fruit, with such a sweetly luscious feeling in the mouth. There's a firm structure of dusty tannins that suggests pairing with a barbecued lamb chop. **89** *—S.H. (2/1/2004)*

EOS 1999 Cabernet Sauvignon (Paso Robles) $15. 88 *—M.M. (4/1/2002)*

EOS 1999 Reserve Cabernet Sauvignon (Paso Robles) $24. 89 *—M.M. (4/1/2002)*

EOS 1997 Chardonnay (Paso Robles) $15. 88 *(11/15/1999)*

EOS 2002 Chardonnay (Paso Robles) $15. Opens with the aromas of baked apples and tapioca, and has apple custard flavors in a heavy texture, although it's dry. Very full-bodied, and a little bitter on the finish. **84** *—S.H. (6/1/2004)*

EOS 2000 Chardonnay (Paso Robles) $14. 85 *—M.M. (4/1/2002)*

EOS 2003 Cupa Grandis Grand Barrel Reserve Chardonnay (Paso Robles) $40. This flavorful Chard puts its fruit up front. The flavors include apples, pears, and dusty brown Asian spices. It's been fairly heavily worked, and is a bit soft in acids, and very creamy. Will be nice with lobster bisque. **89** *—S.H. (11/1/2005)*

EOS 1999 Reserve Chardonnay (Paso Robles) $24. 87 *—M.M. (4/1/2002)*

EOS 2003 Brothers Ranch Vineyard 4, Block 8 Fumé Blanc (Paso Robles) $20. Dusty sawdust aromas run heavy on the nose, with peach and nectarine aromas sitting in reserve. Fairly reserved in terms of flavors, with light fruit duking it out with the more aggressive wood notes. Where it does its best is in the area of balance: citric acids even out any wood and weight. **86** *(7/1/2005)*

EOS 2000 Reserve Fumé Blanc (Paso Robles) $19. 88 *(8/1/2002)*

EOS 2000 Merlot (Paso Robles) $18. 87 *—S.H. (11/15/2002)*

EOS 2000 Tears of Dew Late Harvest Moscato (Paso Robles) $20. 90 *—S.H. (12/1/2002)*

EOS 2001 Tears of Dew Late Harvest Moscato (Paso Robles) $20. 93 *—S.H. (12/1/2003)*

EOS 2003 Tears of Dew Late Harvest Moscato Muscat Canelli (Paso Robles) $20. It's time to admit this wine into the elite of California dessert sippers. It's always dependably rewarding in apricot, wild honey, and vanilla flavors, unctuously sweet, and well-balanced in acids. This year's offering is true to form. **93 Editors' Choice** *—S.H. (11/1/2005)*

EOS 2001 Cupa Grandis, Peck Ranch Vineyard Block P7 Petite Sirah (Paso Robles) $40. With this thick, dark wine, the folks from EOS have pumped up the volume. It's super soft and supple, with velvety tannins and lots of black cherry, coffee, chocolate, herb, spice, vanilla, toast, and earth flavors. The wine also has some high-toned qualities that bright up on the finish. **92** *—J.M. (6/1/2004)*

EOS 2000 Reserve Petite Sirah (Paso Robles) $25. 85 *(4/1/2003)*

EOS 1996 Zephyrus Vineyard Petite Sirah (Paso Robles) $17. 88 *(11/15/1999)*

EOS 1999 Torre del Gobbo Red Blend (Paso Robles) $22. 86 *—M.M. (4/1/2002)*

EOS 2002 Sauvignon Blanc (Paso Robles) $15. Fresh and lively, with pretty herb, spice, lemon, grapefruit, pepper, grass, and mineral notes. The wine is light textured, yet hangs in there with a clean finish. **88** *—J.M. (6/1/2004)*

EOS 2000 Estate Bottled Sauvignon Blanc (Paso Robles) $14. 87 *—M.M. (4/1/2002)*

EOS 2002 Zinfandel (Paso Robles) $15. An awkward wine that keeps its alcohol moderate at the cost of residual sugar. Some will like this old-fashioned, jug-wine style. **82** *—S.H. (11/1/2005)*

EOS 2000 Zinfandel (Paso Robles) $16. 86 *—S.H. (12/1/2002)*

EOS 1999 Estate Bottled Zinfandel (Paso Robles) $15. 87 *—D.T. (3/1/2002)*

EOS 1999 Port Zinfandel (Paso Robles) $27. 88 *—M.M. (4/1/2002)*

EPIPHANY

Epiphany 2002 Rodney's Vineyard Petite Sirah (Santa Barbara County) $25. One of the blacker wines of the year, and also one of the more alcoholic, with 15.9%. Massively fruited, just explodes with blackberry and cherry marmalade, dusted with chocolate and cinnamon. It sure is tasty, but is it a dry table wine? **87** *—S.H. (11/1/2005)*

Epiphany 1999 Pinot Gris (Santa Barbara County) $18. 87 *—S.H. (9/1/2003)*

Epiphany 1999 Rodney's Rhône Red Blend (Santa Barbara County) $36. 85 *—S.H. (9/1/2003)*

Epiphany 1999 Stonewall Vineyard Syrah (California) $45. 89 *(11/1/2001)*

EPONYMOUS

Eponymous 2000 Red Wine Cabernet Sauvignon-Merlot (Napa Valley) $50. A new wine from Robert Pepi, and an ambitious one. The veteran winemaker has crafted an aromatic, rather tannic wine of great structure and potential. Shows ripe blackberry and cherry flavors that are elaborately oaked, with fresh acidity. Drink after 2006. Mostly Cabernet with a splash of Merlot. **90** *—S.H. (10/1/2004)*

EQUUS

Equus 1999 James Berry Vineyard Grenache (Paso Robles) $18. 86 *—S.H. (2/1/2003)*

Equus 2000 Roussanne (Paso Robles) $16. 85 *—S.H. (3/1/2003)*

Equus 1998 Syrah (Paso Robles) $22. 86 *(11/1/2001)*

ERATH

Erath 1997 Niederberger Vyd Reserve Chardonnay (Willamette Valley) $35. 91 *—S.H. (12/31/1999)*

Erath 2003 Pinot Blanc (Willamette Valley) $13. Pretty, pale straw, with nuanced scents and flavors straddling the pear/melon axis. The alcohol is a sensible 13%, and the wine has a lovely balance without sacrificing complexity. **88 Best Buy** *—P.G. (2/1/2005)*

Erath 2003 Pinot Gris (Oregon) $13. Erath's pinot gris is a tart, lemony wine, with a slightly waxy, muted flavor, and a hint of sweatiness to the nose. It takes a distant second to the winery's excellent pinot blanc. **85** *—P.G. (2/1/2005)*

Erath 2002 Pinot Noir (Oregon) $16. Concentrated and ripe, perhaps just a bit stewed, but textured and lively, with plenty of front-loaded flavor. Though slightly raisiny, the flavors are inviting and fruit-driven. Ready to drink right now. **87** *(11/1/2004)*

USA

Erath 2000 Pinot Noir (Oregon) $15. 86 Best Buy *(10/1/2002)*

Erath 1998 Pinot Noir (Willamette Valley) $16. 87 Best Buy *—M.S. (12/1/2000)*

Erath 2002 Estate Selection Pinot Noir (Willamette Valley) $30. Elegant, classy, in a lighter style, but nuanced with subtle suggestions of meat, mixed fruits, and cinnamon. This is not a big wine, nor does it overreach itself. Balanced and clean, with the sort of supple tang that suggests it will improve in the cellar. **87** *(11/1/2004)*

Erath 1999 Leland Pinot Noir (Willamette Valley) $45. 89 *(10/1/2002)*

Erath 1996 Prince Hill Pinot Noir (Willamette Valley) $35. 85 *(10/1/1999)*

Erath 1998 Reserve Pinot Noir (Willamette Valley) $34. 89 *—J.C. (12/1/2000)*

ERIC ROSS

Eric Ross 1999 Klapp Pinot Noir (Russian River Valley) $40. 85 *(10/1/2002)*

ESHCOL RANCH

Eshcol Ranch 2001 Cabernet Sauvignon (California) $10. Everything's right about this nice Cab, from the ripe blackberry and mocha flavors to the smooth tannins, dry balance and fruity finish. It could use a little more concentration, though. **84** *—S.H. (12/15/2005)*

ESSER CELLARS

Esser Cellars 2001 Cabernet Sauvignon (California) $8. 87 Best Buy *—S.H. (6/1/2003)*

Esser Cellars 2002 Chardonnay (California) $9. 82 *—S.H. (12/31/2003)*

Esser Cellars 2001 Merlot (California) $8. This dry wine has a clean, swift mouthfeel, dominated by fresh acidity and firm young tannins. There's just enough berry-cherry flavor to stand on its own or accompany a good steak. **85** *—S.H. (4/1/2004)*

ESTANCIA

Estancia 1997 Cabernet Sauvignon (California) $15. 84 *—S.H. (7/1/2000)*

Estancia 2002 Keyes Canyon Ranches Cabernet Sauvignon (Paso Robles) $16. This is a young, taut red wine. It's quite dry, and the tannins shut it down a bit. But you'll find intense flavors of blackberries and cherries, and a tasty coating of oak. Drink over the next year. **86** *—S.H. (8/1/2005)*

Estancia 2002 Pinnacles Chardonnay (Monterey) $12. A bit lean in fruity flavor, but not bad for the price. You get some polished peach and apple flavors, oaky, vanilla notes and that crisp Central Coast acidity. **84** *—S.H. (11/15/2004)*

Estancia 1998 Pinnacles Chardonnay (Monterey County) $12. 89 *—S.H. (5/1/2000)*

Estancia 1998 Single Vineyard Reserve Chardonnay (Monterey County) $20. 87 *(6/1/2000)*

Estancia 2000 Red Meritage (Alexander Valley) $35. Well-charred oak dominates now, with its toasty vanillins, but underneath lurks a very pretty wine. The black currant and cherry flavors are sweetly delicious, and the tannins are soft and lush. This appealing wine is easy to fall in love with. Give it a few years to knit together. **90** *—S.H. (1/1/2005)*

Estancia 2004 Pinot Grigio (California) $15. This off-dry wine brings gardens to mind. It is one of those perfectly adaptable, all-purpose white wines that goes with just about anything. It tastes of tree-ripe peaches, gardenias, and honeysuckle, and has pleasant acidity to offset the sweetness. **84** *—S.H. (7/1/2005)*

Estancia 2002 Pinot Grigio (California) $15. This crisp, delicate charmer is a perfect wine to end the workday with. It's got light flavors of citrus and melon, and is high in acidity and very clean. It's also bone dry. **87** *—S.H. (2/1/2004)*

Estancia 2000 Pinnacles Pinot Noir (Monterey) $16. 87 *—J.M. (5/1/2002)*

Estancia 2003 Pinnacles Ranches Pinot Noir (Monterey) $15. It's awfully hard to make a really good Pinot Noir for less than, say, $30. This wine tries hard. It shows true Pinot character in the dry, silky mouthfeel, crisp acids and pleasant fruit flavors, which finish with coffee and cocoa. **86** *—S.H. (12/1/2005)*

Estancia 2000 Proprietor's Selection Pinot Noir (Monterey) $10. Bargain hunters have long known Estancia as a haven for values, and this lovely wine continues the tradition. It shows true Monterey terroir in the translucent color, delicately silky structure, bright, citrusy acids and flavors of cherries, cola, sassafras, and sweet tea. You'll also find an overlay of smoky oak. This classic cool-climate Pinot Noir is the perfect food wine, and a terrific everyday one for Pinotphiles. **87 Best Buy** *—S.H. (11/15/2004)*

Estancia 2003 Stonewall Vineyard Pinot Noir (Santa Lucia Highlands) $25. This vineyard is in the tenderloin of the appellation, where most Pinots cost far more. This is a pretty good wine that needs tinkering; it could be far better. It's rich in fruit, but is heavy, and could use more finesse. **85** *—S.H. (12/1/2005)*

Estancia 2002 Stonewall Vineyard Reserve Pinot Noir (Santa Lucia Highlands) $22. A very good wine, at a fair price for a single-vineyard Pinot of this caliber from this appellation. It shows the well-ripened cherry fruit and good acidity that characterize the Highlands, with a nice overlay of toasty oak and vanilla, and is dry and balanced. Lacks the complexity of its famous neighbors, but is worthy of praise on price alone. **88 Editors' Choice** *—S.H. (8/1/2005)*

Estancia 1996 Duo Tuscan Blend (Sonoma County) $22. 90 *—S.H. (11/1/1999)*

ESTATE RAFFAELE

Estate Raffaele 2002 Clareta Red Blend (California) $22. This blend of Cabernet Sauvignon, Tempranillo, and Grenache is forward in ripe berry flavors, and is soft in acids and tannins. Smacks of the warm sunshine and is dry. **84** *—S.H. (10/1/2005)*

ESTERLINA

Esterlina 1999 Chardonnay (Anderson Valley) $20. 87 *—S.H. (5/1/2002)*

Esterlina 2001 Merlot (Cole Ranch) $18. From one of the tiniest AVAs in California, a Mendocino wine that straddles the balance between cherry-infused ripeness and earthier, more tannic dryness. Those tannins reprise on the finish, leaving behind a dusty astringency. **85** *—S.H. (10/1/2004)*

Esterlina 1998 Pinot Noir (Anderson Valley) $35. 85 *—S.H. (5/1/2002)*

Esterlina 2004 Riesling (Cole Ranch) $16. Frankly off-dry to semi-sweet, but with pronounced acidity to balance, this is a Spätlese-style Riesling. It's rich in garden fruit and flower flavors, with a savory spiciness and a long, clean aftertaste. **86** *—S.H. (12/1/2005)*

Esterlina 1999 Ferrington Vineyards Sauvignon Blanc (Anderson Valley) $18. 84 *—S.H. (5/1/2002)*

Esterlina 1999 White Riesling (Mendocino) $13. 90 *—S.H. (5/1/2002)*

ETUDE

Etude 2002 Cabernet Sauvignon (Napa Valley) $90. The backbone of this wine is from Oakville and Rutherford. It's a classic Napa Cab from what has turned out to be a fine vintage. There's the velvety cassis and chocolate fruit ripeness you expect, and the lavish oak, but good tannins and acids prevent the decadent flavors from turning flabby. Still, the wine's approachability argues for early consumption. **93** *—S.H. (12/1/2005)*

Etude 2000 Cabernet Sauvignon (Napa Valley) $80. Not really at its best now, a subdued, shy wine offering little beyond serious tannins and an earthiness infused with cassis. The finish is very astringent and sticky, yet the intense, lingering taste of cherries and currants suggests cellaring through 2008, if not longer. **90** *—S.H. (6/1/2004)*

Etude 1998 Pinot Blanc (Carneros) $25. 91 *—S.H. (2/1/2001)*

Etude 2002 Pinot Noir (Carneros) $40. Rather herbal and spicy, bursting with anise, Asian spicebox aromas. Cherries and sweet herbs in the mouth, with a spicy finish. The soft tannins make it instantly drinkable. **89** *(11/1/2004)*

Etude 2000 Pinot Noir (Carneros) $40. 90 *—M.S. (12/1/2003)*

Etude 2001 Heirloom Pinot Noir (Carneros) $80. This tiny-production wine (only 480 cases were made) is luscious and opulent. It compels for the sheer intensity of the red and black cherry, rosehip tea, cola, and spicy flavors. Goes beyond mere flavor in its balance and harmony, and defines a light-bodied, silky style of great refinement and finesse. **92** *—S.H. (12/1/2004)*

EUGENE WINE CELLARS

Eugene Wine Cellars 1999 Melon (Oregon) $14. 85 *—P.G. (11/1/2001)*

Eugene Wine Cellars 1999 Pinot Noir (Oregon) $15. 82 *—P.G. (11/1/2001)*

Eugene Wine Cellars 1999 Viognier (Oregon) $18. 84 *—P.G. (11/1/2001)*

EVERETT RIDGE

Everett Ridge 1999 Cabernet Sauvignon (Dry Creek Valley) $28. 84 *—S.H. (12/15/2003)*

Everett Ridge 2003 Powerhouse Vineyard Sauvignon Blanc (Mendocino County) $15. Very dry and tart with acids, but with a rich sweetness from well-ripened citrus fruits, figs, and honeydew melon. Shows real flair and style. 86 *—S.H. (12/15/2004)*

Everett Ridge 2000 Powerhouse Vineyard Sauvignon Blanc (Mendocino) $13. 85 *(9/1/2003)*

Everett Ridge 2001 Nuns Canyon Vineyard Syrah (Sonoma Valley) $28. Big, thick, and heavy in plummy, chocolate and white pepper flavors, with sturdy tannins. You can taste the heat in the finish, where the wine turns prickly, with a note of raisins. Drink with barbecue seasoned with garlic. 85 *—S.H. (12/15/2004)*

Everett Ridge 1999 Nuns Canyon Vineyard Syrah (Sonoma Valley) $26. 89 *(11/1/2001)*

Everett Ridge 2000 Zinfandel (Dry Creek Valley) $28. 83 *—S.H. (9/1/2003)*

Everett Ridge 1997 Old Vines Zinfandel (Dry Creek Valley) $20. 89 *—S.H. (2/1/2000)*

USA

EVESHAM WOOD

Evesham Wood 1997 Estate Vineyard Pinot Noir (Willamette Valley) $21. 84 *(10/1/1999)*

Evesham Wood 1997 Shea Vineyard Cuvée 'J' Pinot Noir (Willamette Valley) $27.5. 86 *(10/1/1999)*

EXP

EXP 2000 Syrah (Dunnigan Hills) $14. 83 *—S.H. (12/1/2002)*

EXP 1999 Tempranillo (Dunnigan Hills) $25. 88 *—S.H. (12/1/2002)*

EXP 2001 Viognier (Dunnigan Hills) $14. 82 *—S.H. (12/15/2002)*

FAGAN CREEK

Fagan Creek 2002 Horsley Vineyards Syrah (Dunnigan Hills) $16. While one taster found this wine "delicately herbal," another pegged that element of the aromatics as "rhubarb." Strawberry and cherry flavors flesh out this full-bodied wine that finishes spicy and tannic but fruit-filled. 88 *(9/1/2005)*

FAILLA

Failla 2003 Phoenix Ranch Syrah (Napa Valley) $38. Tastes like the real Rhône thing, from its meaty and coffee-tinged aromas to its peppery, blackberry flavors. But the structure is more Californian, soft and full, if a tiny bit lacking in texture. Peppery notes reprise on the long finish. Drink now–2012. 90 *(9/1/2005)*

Failla Jordan 2001 Hirsch Vineyard Pinot Noir (Sonoma Coast) $48. 91 *—S.H. (7/1/2003)*

Failla Jordan 2000 Estate Syrah (Sonoma Coast) $48. 92 Editors' Choice *—J.M. (12/1/2002)*

FALCONE

Falcone 2002 Mia's Vineyard Syrah (Paso Robles) $28. This Syrah shows Paso's warm climate in the soft texture and ripe blackberry, cherry, and spice flavors, but it has a hint of green beans and roasted coffee that either add complexity or detract from the jammy fruit, depending on your viewpoint. 85 *(9/1/2005)*

FALCOR

Falcor 2001 Chardonnay (Napa Valley) $35. Oak stars in this wine, with its toasty, wood, and vanilla aromas and flavors. It's a good wine, but could use greater freshness and intensity, especially at this price.. 85 *—S.H. (5/1/2005)*

FALKNER

Falkner 2000 Chardonnay (South Coast) $8. 80 *—S.H. (10/1/2003)*

Falkner 2002 Meritage (Temecula) $30. This wine is kind of lean, with an astringent dryness framing thin fruit flavors. It's surprising, because Falkner's '02 Merlot is really a very good wine. 83 *—S.H. (12/15/2005)*

Falkner 2000 Muscat Canelli (South Coast) $12. 85 *—S.H. (12/15/2003)*

Falkner 2001 Riesling (Temecula) $13. 84 *—S.H. (12/31/2003)*

Falkner 2000 Sauvignon Blanc (South Coast) $10. 86 *—S.H. (4/1/2002)*

Falkner 2001 Viognier (Temecula) $13. 82 *—S.H. (12/1/2003)*

FALLBROOK

Fallbrook 2001 Reserve Cabernet Sauvignon (California) $16. Simple and soft to the point of flatness. Despite the pretty blackberry and cocoa flavors, the wine lacks life. 83 *—S.H. (10/1/2005)*

Fallbrook 2000 Special Selection Cabernet Sauvignon (California) $25. There are some good blackberry and currant flavors here, as well as sturdy, supportive tannins, but the wine is a little on the sweet side. There's also a sharpness in the finish. Drink now. 84 *—S.H. (10/1/2005)*

Fallbrook 2002 Sleepy Hollow Vineyard Chardonnay (Monterey) $20. A little bitter in acidity, but that's by itself. A nice buttery lobster will certainly complement it. Otherwise, it has rich tropical fruit and a zesty minerality, and a long finish. **87** *—S.H. (10/1/2005)*

Fallbrook 2000 Special Selection Merlot (California) $25. You'll find some tannins and herbaceous aromas and flavors in this Cab, which actually give it good grip, and makes it easier to pair with complex foods. It's very dry, with plummy, blackberry flavors. **86** *—S.H. (10/1/2005)*

FANTESCA

Fantesca 2002 Cabernet Sauvignon (Spring Mountain) $60. This new brand, from veteran winemaker Nils Venge and friends, is excellent despite the awful name. It achieves that elusive goal of joining big-time, ripe fruit with subtlety and charm to produce a wine of complexity. The cassis, cherry, and oak flavors hit strong, then settle down and let the balance take over. **92 Editors' Choice** *—S.H. (12/15/2005)*

FANUCCHI

Fanucchi 2001 Old Vine Zinfandel (Russian River Valley) $29. **87** *(11/1/2003)*

Fanucchi 1998 Old Vine Zinfandel (Russian River Valley) $29. **88** *—S.H. (12/1/2002)*

Fanucchi 1996 Old Vine Zinfandel (Russian River Valley) $35. **91** *—S.H. (9/1/1999)*

FAR NIENTE

Far Niente 1997 Cabernet Sauvignon (Napa Valley) $100. **93** *(11/1/2000)*

Far Niente 1998 Chardonnay (Napa Valley) $44. **91** *—S.H. (2/1/2000)*

Far Niente 2002 Chardonnay (Napa Valley) $52. The winemaker notes that this wine has undergone no malolactic fermentation, which is rare in an expensive Chard because you don't get that big, fat, rich buttery softness. What you do get is pure pear and tropical fruit that is elaborately oaked in really good barrels. It is fancy and detailed but not blowsy. **91** *—S.H. (11/15/2004)*

Far Niente 1999 Estate Bottled Chardonnay (Napa Valley) $52. **90** *(7/1/2001)*

FARELLA-PARK

Farella-Park 1997 Cabernet Sauvignon (Napa Valley) $32. **91** *(11/1/2000)*

Farella-Park 1996 Merlot (Napa Valley) $24. **90** *—S.H. (7/1/2000)*

FENESTRA

Fenestra 2001 Chardonnay (Livermore Valley) $16. Like a drink of cold water with a squirt of lemon juice. Dry and acidic. **81** *—S.H. (4/1/2004)*

Fenestra 2000 Merlot (Livermore Valley) $19. Smells a little baked, with raisiny, pruny aromas, and this impression is confirmed on tasting. The flavor is rather like raisins that have been soaked in espresso, with a splash of blackberry liqueur. Give it a little chill to offset the heat. **84** *—S.H. (6/1/2004)*

Fenestra 1999 Petite Sirah (Lodi) $17. **86** *(4/1/2003)*

Fenestra 2002 Dry Rose Rosé Blend (California) $8. A Rhône-style blend. It's one of the darker rosés, and rather heavy-bodied too, with extracted, jammy flavors of fresh black raspberries and cherries. It's dry, with enough power to stand up to a big, juicy cheesburger. **83** *—S.H. (6/1/2004)*

Fenestra 2002 Sauvignon Blanc (Livermore Valley) $16. This wine has barely more flavor than tap water. Impossible to recommend, except that it is clean and without technical flaws. **81** *—S.H. (3/1/2004)*

Fenestra 2002 Semonnay Sémillon-Chardonnay (Livermore Valley) $13. Blend of Sémillon and Chardonnay, and if anything, even more watery than this winery's varietals. A drag and ripoff. **81** *—S.H. (3/1/2004)*

Fenestra 2000 Estate Syrah (Livermore Valley) $15. Intensely peppery, enough to turn off some tasters but turn on others, depending on your individual stylistic preferences. Besides pepper, there's some lavender-like floral notes and a decent helping of red berry fruit along with a supple, easygoing mouthfeel. **88 Editors' Choice** *(9/1/2005)*

Fenestra 2002 Viognier (Contra Costa County) $17. A little rough in texture, with some well-integrated peach, kiwi, and vanillas that are accompanied by good acidity. Despite the ripe flavors, this is a fully dry wine. **85** *—S.H. (6/1/2004)*

FERNWOOD

Fernwood 2002 Zinfandel (El Dorado) $27. Porty and notably sweet, with lots of fruit. **82** *—S.H. (2/1/2005)*

FERRARI-CARANO

Ferrari-Carano 2000 Eldorado Noir Black Muscat (Russian River Valley) $25. **86** *(11/1/2002)*

Ferrari-Carano 1999 Trésor Red Table Wine Bordeaux Blend (Sonoma County) $32. All 5 Bordeaux varieties comprise this complex but young wine. It's sharp in fresh tannins, with a rich core of sweet black cherry fruit. Needs some big, greasy steak to match it, but should develop gracefully for some time. **92** *—S.H. (12/1/2004)*

Ferrari-Carano 2001 Trésor Cabernet Blend (Alexander Valley) $45. With fruit sourced from everywhere from Dry Creek to Carneros, this Cabernet-based wine is a good, blended effort, with true varietal character if no particular complexity. It's balanced, fruity and tannic, but too expensive for what you get. **86** *—S.H. (12/1/2005)*

Ferrari-Carano 2001 Cabernet Sauvignon (Sonoma County) $28. Very oaky. The enormity of char, vanilla, and toast, has not yet integrated with the wine it frames. The underlying flavors are ripe and opulent, spreading over the palate with cherry pie, crème de cassis, and chocolate. Give this beautiful wine until 2005 or beyond. **91** *—S.H. (8/1/2004)*

Ferrari-Carano 1998 Tremonte Cabernet Sauvignon (Alexander Valley) $38. 86 *(11/1/2002)*

Ferrari-Carano 1997 Chardonnay (Sonoma County) $22. 92 *—M.S. (7/1/1999)*

Ferrari-Carano 2001 Chardonnay (Alexander Valley) $23. Soft, ripe, and oaky, with leesy flavors and notes of apples and tropical fruits. The creamy texture fans out over the palate, finishing with a honeyed smoothness. **86** *—S.H. (8/1/2004)*

Ferrari-Carano 2003 Reserve Chardonnay (Napa-Sonoma) $42. The Reserve has always been oaky, but this may be the oakiest yet. That toasty, caramelly vanilla thing hits hard. Fortunately, the underlying tropical fruit stands up to all the wood. I like this wine, but this is about as far as a winemaker should push oak. **89** *—S.H. (12/1/2005)*

USA

Ferrari-Carano 2001 Reserve Chardonnay (Carneros) $32. All the bells and whistles are here, from the malolactic fermentation that makes the wine soft and buttery to the heavy lees contact to barrel fermentation with lots of new oak. The result is creamy and complex, framing modest flavors of apples, tangerines, and peaches. **89** *—S.H. (8/1/2004)*

Ferrari-Carano 1999 Reserve Chardonnay (Napa County) $32. 89 *(7/1/2001)*

Ferrari-Carano 1998 Fumé Blanc (Sonoma County) $12. 89 Best Buy *—S.H. (3/1/2000)*

Ferrari-Carano 2004 Fumé Blanc (Sonoma County) $16. A fruit-forward, slightly sweet and zesty-clean Sauvignon Blanc. The lemon, lime, fig, and melon flavors are tasty. **84** *—S.H. (12/1/2005)*

Ferrari-Carano 2002 Fumé Blanc (Sonoma County) $15. 85 *—S.H. (7/1/2003)*

Ferrari-Carano 2000 Fumé Blanc (Sonoma County) $15. 87 *—J.M. (11/15/2001)*

Ferrari-Carano 2002 Merlot (Sonoma County) $25. Merlot has not been the winery's strong suit over the years, but with this vintage, something has changed. The wine is lush and complex. There are enormously deep cherry, mocha, and oak flavors, with the rich tannic structure Ferrari-Carano's reds always have the classic finish. **91** *—S.H. (12/1/2005)*

Ferrari-Carano 1999 Merlot (Sonoma County) $23. 87 *(11/1/2002)*

Ferrari-Carano 1997 Vineyards of Tremonte Merlot (Sonoma County) $28. 86 *—J.C. (6/1/2001)*

Ferrari-Carano 1999 Siena Red Blend (Sonoma County) $28. 91 *(11/1/2002)*

Ferrari-Carano 1997 Vineyards of Tremonte Sangiovese (Alexander Valley) $28. 88 *—S.H. (12/1/2001)*

Ferrari-Carano 1998 Storey Creek Vineyard Sauvignon Blanc (Russian River Valley) $15. 90 *—S.H. (3/1/2000)*

Ferrari-Carano 1996 Siena Tuscan Blend (Sonoma County) $28. 90 *(10/1/1999)*

FESS PARKER

Fess Parker 1998 Chardonnay (Santa Barbara County) $16. 87 *(6/1/2000)*

Fess Parker 1996 American Tradition Reserve Chardonnay (Santa Barbara County) $22. 91 *—S.H. (7/1/1999)*

Fess Parker 1997 Santa Barbara County Chardonnay (Santa Barbara County) $15. 89 *—S.H. (7/1/1999)*

Fess Parker 2000 Pinot Noir (Santa Barbara County) $20. 86 *—S.H. (2/1/2003)*

Fess Parker 2000 American Tradition Reserve Pinot Noir (Santa Barbara) $45. 85 *(10/1/2002)*

Fess Parker 2003 Ashley's Vineyard Pinot Noir (Santa Rita Hills) $45. If you had to take one red wine to that proverbial desert island, this might be it. It's simply delicious. The cherry, black raspberry, cocoa, coffee, cola, and spice flavors are enormously deep and long, yet such is the acidity that the wine is filled with life and zest. Just marvelous, and probably best now and over the next year or two. **94 Editors' Choice** *—S.H. (11/1/2005)*

Fess Parker 2001 Ashley's Vineyard Pinot Noir (Santa Barbara County) $45. A monumental Pinot that showcases the potential of the Santa Rita Hills area. This wine impresses with the depth and complexity of its raspberry, cherry, spicebox, tobacco, and vanilla flavors that coat the palate with delicious intensity. For all its size, the acids and tannins are fine and balanced, keeping the mouthfeel silky and refined. **93** *—S.H. (3/1/2004)*

Fess Parker 2000 Bien Nacido Vineyard Pinot Noir (Santa Barbara County) $45. 85 *(10/1/2002)*

Fess Parker 2000 Dierberg Vineyard Pinot Noir (Santa Barbara) $45. 85 *(10/1/2002)*

Fess Parker 2000 Marcella's Vineyard Pinot Noir (Santa Barbara County) $45. **88** *(10/1/2002)*

Fess Parker 1997 Santa Barbara County Pinot Noir (Santa Maria Valley) $18. **90** *(10/1/1999)*

Fess Parker 1997 Syrah (Santa Barbara County) $18. **89** *—S.H. (10/1/1999)*

Fess Parker 2002 Syrah (Santa Barbara County) $18. Two of our reviewers found this wine overly tannic and rough on the finish, while the other praised its supple tannins and creamy texture. All agreed on the ample blackberry fruit and heavyhanded oak, which make the wine somewhat obvious. We just couldn't agree on where this wine is headed in the future. **84** *(9/1/2005)*

Fess Parker 1999 Syrah (Santa Barbara County) $20. **87** *—S.H. (7/1/2002)*

Fess Parker 2000 American Tradition Reserve Syrah (Santa Barbara County) $32. **88** *—S.H. (10/1/2003)*

Fess Parker 2002 Rodney's Vineyard Syrah (Santa Barbara County) $36. Clearly astringent, but this wine may have a good future. The flavors of ripe, sweet blackberries, and smoky espresso are dramatic, and so is the vibrant, lemony acidity. Hold until 2007 while you wait for the components to come together. **86** *(9/1/2005)*

Fess Parker 1999 Rodney's Vineyard Syrah (Santa Barbara County) $30. **89** *(11/1/2001)*

Fess Parker 1997 Viognier (Santa Barbara) $18. **91** *—S.H. (6/1/1999)*

Fess Parker 2000 Viognier (Santa Barbara County) $20. **90 Editors' Choice** *—S.H. (11/15/2001)*

Fess Parker 2001 White Riesling (Santa Barbara County) $12. **85** *—S.H. (9/1/2003)*

FEZER

Fetzer 1997 Barrel Select Cabernet Sauvignon (North Coast) $15. **88 Best Buy** *—P.G. (12/15/2000)*

Fetzer 1999 Five Rivers Ranch Cabernet Sauvignon (Central Coast) $13. **87** *(11/15/2001)*

Fetzer 1998 Reserve Cabernet Sauvignon (Napa Valley) $40. **87** *— (11/15/2002)*

Fetzer 2003 Valley Oaks Cabernet Sauvignon (California) $9. From this consistent value producer, a nice everyday Cab, with good flavors of blackberries and herbs, and fine, dusty tannins. It turns even richer on the finish, with a lingering taste of oak. **85 Best Buy** *—S.H. (12/15/2005)*

Fetzer 1998 Valley Oaks Cabernet Sauvignon (California) $13. **83** *(5/1/2001)*

Fetzer 2000 Barrel Select Chardonnay (Mendocino County) $13. **84** *—S.H. (5/1/2002)*

Fetzer 2003 Five Rivers Ranch Chardonnay (Monterey County) $13. Has some fruity flavors and a smattering of oak. Finishes with cloying sweetness. **82** *—S.H. (5/1/2005)*

Fetzer 1999 Sundial Chardonnay (California) $9. **81** *—S.H. (10/1/2000)*

Fetzer 2004 Valley Oaks Chardonnay (California) $9. Has the most delectable fragrance of white peaches and vanilla. In the mouth, the peach flavors are joined by powerful kiwi and pineapple. For all the fruit, the wine is dry, crisp and balanced. **87 Best Buy** *—S.H. (12/1/2005)*

Fetzer 2001 Echo Ridge Gewürztraminer (California) $8. **87** *—S.H. (9/1/2003)*

Fetzer 2004 Valley Oaks Gewürztraminer (California) $9. Take an explosion in a fruit store, sprinkle it with dusted cinnamon and nutmeg, then add some white sugar. That's this semisweet wine, which fortunately has good balancing acidity. **83** *—S.H. (12/1/2005)*

Fetzer 2002 Echo Ridge Johannisberg Riesling (California) $6. **87 Best Buy** *—S.H. (11/15/2003)*

Fetzer 1999 Echo Ridge Johannisberg Riesling (California) $10. **82** *(5/1/2001)*

Fetzer 2001 Barrel Select Merlot (Sonoma County) $14. Another nice, inexpensive value from this winery. The plum and currant flavors are joined with sage to make a dry wine with character and charm. There's a weightiness in the midpalate that's like more expensive Merlots. **85** *—S.H. (4/1/2004)*

Fetzer 1998 Barrel Select Merlot (Sonoma County) $13. **85** *—J.C. (6/1/2001)*

Fetzer 2000 Eagle Peak Merlot (California) $9. **86 Best Buy** *—S.H. (6/1/2002)*

Fetzer 1998 Eagle Peak Merlot (California) $9. **82** *—S.H. (7/1/2000)*

Fetzer 2003 Valley Oaks Merlot (California) $9. Fetzer as much as anyone in America is responsible for quaffable, inexpensive vin ordinaire, and this fine Merlot is the latest example. It's dry and balanced, with a polished richness that belies the everyday price. **85 Best Buy** *—S.H. (12/31/2005)*

Fetzer 2000 Barrel Select Pinot Noir (Sonoma County) $15. **81** *(10/1/2002)*

Fetzer 1998 Barrel Select Pinot Noir (California) $15. **87** *—P.G. (12/15/2000)*

Fetzer 1999 Bien Nacido Reserve Pinot Noir (Santa Barbara County) $28. **91** *—S.H. (12/15/2001)*

Fetzer 2000 Bien Nacido Vineyard Blocks G + Q Winemaker's Reserve Pinot Noir (Santa Maria Valley) $40. **89** *(10/1/2002)*

Fetzer 2001 Five Rivers Ranch Pinot Noir (Santa Barbara County) $7. You get some real Pinot character in this light and delicately fruity wine. It's very dry, with flavors of raspberries, cherries, and blueberries, and is smooth on the palate. **85 Best Buy** *—S.H. (2/1/2004)*

Fetzer 2000 Five Rivers Ranch Pinot Noir (Central Coast) $14. **84** *(10/1/2002)*

Fetzer 2004 Valley Oaks Riesling (California) $9. There's enough residual sugar here to qualify it as a dessert wine, although it's not labeled as such. The flavors are of peaches and vanilla, with good acidity. **82** *—S.H. (12/1/2005)*

Fetzer 1999 Echo Ridge Sauvignon Blanc (California) $10. **85** *(5/1/2001)*

Fetzer 2004 Valley Oaks Sauvignon Blanc (California) $9. Here's a nice wine that's easy and clean, but has some real nuances that make it a repeat sipper. It's dryish, with just a hint of sweetness to the citrus, peach, and apple flavors, and balanced with fine acids. **85 Best Buy** *—S.H. (12/1/2005)*

Fetzer 2001 Valley Oaks Shiraz (California) $9. Light, fruity, and simple, here's a Shiraz to match up against similar versions from Australia. Minty notes accent crisp red berry flavors, finishing tart and supple. **85 Best Buy** *(9/1/2005)*

USA

Fetzer 1999 Valley Oaks Syrah (California) $9. **86 Best Buy** *—S.H. (9/1/2002)*

Fetzer 2004 Valley Oaks Rosé Syrah (California) $9. Dark for a rosé, and full-bodied, this blush Syrah is long and strong in raspberry flavors that finish with a touch of vanilla and white pepper. It's a tasty sipper, nice and dry, almost as robust as Pinot Noir. **86 Best Buy** *—S.H. (12/1/2005)*

Fetzer 2001 Barrel Select Zinfandel (Mendocino County) $14. **87** *—J.M. (11/1/2003)*

Fetzer 1998 Barrel Select Zinfandel (Mendocino County) $12. **90** *—S.H. (5/1/2002)*

Fetzer 1999 Echo Ridge Zinfandel (California) $7. **82** *(5/1/2001)*

Fetzer 1996 Home Ranch Zinfandel (California) $8. **83** *—S.H. (9/1/1999)*

Fetzer 2002 Valley Oaks Zinfandel (California) $9. Shows Zin's briary, brambly side, and is intensely dry and a little thin, with moderate alcohol. Ultimately simple, this is a decent simple for pizza or BBQ. **83** *—S.H. (10/1/2005)*

Fetzer 1998 Valley Oaks Zinfandel (California) $11. **81** *(5/1/2001)*

FIDDLEHEAD

Fiddlehead 1998 Pinot Noir (Willamette Valley) $36. **87** *—S.H. (12/31/2002)*

Fiddlehead 2001 Lollapalooza Fiddlestix Pinot Noir (Santa Ynez Valley) $50. Pinot that dramatically illlustrates the potential of the Santa Rita Hills. Succulent, intense flavors of black cherries and blueberries, sweet and ripe, are complexed with mocha and dusted with pepper and other spices. All this is encased in a dry silky mouthfeel. **92** *—S.H. (3/1/2004)*

Fiddlehead 2000 Sauvignon Blanc (Santa Ynez Valley) $22. **88** *—S.H. (9/1/2003)*

Fiddlehead Cellars 2002 Happy Canyon Sauvignon Blanc (Santa Ynez Valley) $22. Buttery and lactic, without much verve. Maybe it's over the hill, or maybe it just isn't as good as what we expected from this label. A flabby wine with sweet, mealy flavors. **81** *(7/1/2005)*

FIDELITAS

Fidelitas 2003 Cabernet Sauvignon (Columbia Valley (WA)) $30. Great vineyard sources (Gamache, Klipsun) start things right, and this pureblooded, 100% Cab, though pushed to the point of showing some volatile high tones, compensates with saturated flavors of ripe berries, complemented with buttery oak. The silky finish can't help but win your heart. **90** *—P.G. (12/15/2005)*

Fidelitas 2001 Meritage (Columbia Valley (WA)) $35. A 61% Cab, 25% Merlot, 7% Cab Franc, 7% Malbec blend, it opens with a lovely, inviting nose and shows layered fruits buttressed with chocolate and baking spices. A soft entry and a silky, chocolaty mouthfeel; not a blockbuster, but delicious and beautifully balanced. **89** *—P.G. (12/15/2004)*

Fidelitas 2003 Merlot (Columbia Valley (WA)) $25. Sweet and tangy, with clean, pretty cherry and blackberry fruit. This is nicely balanced, with the oak pulled back a bit and the fruit taking the spotlight. A young, supple, silky and well-crafted 100% varietal Merlot. **88** *—P.G. (12/15/2005)*

Fidelitas 2004 Sémillon (Columbia Valley (WA)) $18. Rich straw-gold, it already is showing signs of oxidation, with scents of wheat, clover, lemon, and apple. Rich, round, and full-bodied, this drink-now wine offers citrus fruits, figs, and melon, with a lovely ripeness. **89** *—P.G. (12/15/2005)*

Fidelitas 2003 Syrah (Columbia Valley (WA)) $35. The are hints of volatility and oxidation, but it makes for a more immediately drinkable Syrah, with plenty of berries and preserves, light touches of toast, and a nice finish of butter and caramel. Drink soon. **89** *—P.G. (12/15/2005)*

Fidelitas 2001 Syrah (Yakima Valley) $35. **91** *—P.G. (11/20/2003)*

FIELD STONE

Field Stone 2000 Cabernet Sauvignon (Alexander Valley) $22. Lean and awkward, with thin, cherry-berry flavors and a bit of residual sugar that makes it cloying. That sweetness emphasizes the tough, hard tannins. **82** *—S.H. (5/1/2004)*

Field Stone 1998 Chardonnay (Sonoma County) $16. **86** *(6/1/2000)*

Field Stone 1999 Staten Family Reserve Petite Sirah (Alexander Valley) $30. **84** *(4/1/2003)*

Field Stone 2003 Syrah (Alexander Valley) $22. Cedary and savory on the nose, then delivers cherry-berry fruit accented by leather and more cedar. It's relatively structured for a California Syrah despite not being a heavyweight, so hold it 2–3 years, then drink it over the next five. **86** *(9/1/2005)*

FIELDING HILLS

Fielding Hills 2003 Cabernet Sauvignon (Columbia Valley (WA)) $30. Dark, tannic, and saturated, this deeply colored Cabernet shows ripe tannins and dense fruits, dominated by cassis, berry, and plum. The oak regimen adds layers of smoke, tar, licorice, and it's all wrapped up in a long, chewy, earthy finish. **93 Editors' Choice** *—P.G. (12/15/2005)*

Fielding Hills 2002 Cabernet Sauvignon-Syrah (Columbia Valley (WA)) $28. Fairly light, with simple fruit flavors that are a bit overshadowed by the new oak. Perhaps a pullback from 100% new barrels would be worth considering. Nonetheless, this is a very pleasant and good-tasting effort. **88** *—P.G. (11/1/2005)*

Fielding Hills 2002 Merlot (Columbia Valley (WA)) $28. A new winery, in Washington's emerging Columbia Cascade wine region, whose early releases have been superb. This well-handled Merlot mixes pleasing oak with bright, black cherry fruit, and hints of stone. **91** *—P.G. (6/1/2005)*

Fielding Hills 2002 Riverbend Red (Columbia Valley (WA)) $28. An emerging trend in Washington is to spice up the standard Bordeaux Cab-Merlot mix with a splash of Syrah; in this instance, 6%. The wine is dark and smoky, yet taut and nervy rather than jammy. Clean fruit and well-managed oak contribute to a lovely, balanced, lively, and textured red blend. **90** *—P.G. (6/1/2005)*

FIFE

Fife 1997 Cabernet Sauvignon (Napa Valley) $30. **88** *(11/1/2000)*

Fife 1999 Reserve Cabernet Sauvignon (Spring Mountain) $45. Re-released at nearly six years of age. One sniff is all you need to know there's a lot of new, toasted oak here. It's a big, dark, extracted wine, and also a very tannic one, with a deep core of ripe blackberry and blueberry flavors. Despite its age, it still needs time. Best to let it come around by, say, 2008. **91** *—S.H. (10/1/2005)*

Fife 1997 Redhead Vyd Carignane (Redwood Valley) $19. **90** *—S.H. (3/1/2000)*

Fife 1997 Redhead Petite Sirah (Redwood Valley) $24. **89** *—S.H. (10/1/1999)*

Fife 2000 L'Attitude Rhône Red Blend (Mendocino) $20. **86** *—S.H. (12/1/2003)*

Fife 1997 L'Attitude Rhône Red Blend (Mendocino) $18. **93** *—S.H. (3/1/2000)*

Fife 2002 Syrah (Mendocino) $20. Seems a bit thinly fruited, but still boasts enough raspberry and cherry flavors to get the job done. It's a lean, focused style, and it finishes with a dry astringency that may or may not improve with age. **83** *(9/1/2005)*

Fife 1999 Max Vineyard Syrah (Napa Valley) $35. Starts off smelling oaky and spicy, then reveals rich waft of spicy gingerbread and blackberry marmalade aromas and flavors. At nearly five years, the tannins are turning gentle and soft, although there's still some good acidity. **89** *—S.H. (12/1/2004)*

Fife 2000 Old Yokayo Rancho Vineyard Syrah (Mendocino) $30. Has a bit of a reductive character that blows off to reveal sweet cherry and black raspberry fruit. Finishes very dry, with some firmly gritty tannins. **86** *—S.H. (12/1/2004)*

Fife 2001 Mendocino Uplands Zinfandel (Mendocino) $17. **89** *(11/1/2003)*

Fife 1997 Redhead Vineyard Zinfandel (Redwood Valley) $24. **91** *—S.H. (5/1/2000)*

Fife 2000 Whaler Vineyard Zinfandel (Mendocino County) $20. **92** *—S.H. (5/1/2002)*

FILSINGER

Filsinger 1999 Fumé Blanc (Temecula) $7. **83** *—S.H. (4/1/2002)*

FIREFALL

Firefall 1999 Lone Meadow Vineyard Syrah (El Dorado) $20. **90** *—S.H. (12/1/2002)*

FIRESTEED

Firesteed 2003 Pinot Gris (Oregon) $10. Firesteed goes from strength to strength; this is their best Gris to date, enhanced perhaps by the unusually warm vintage. Its ripe fruit tastes like biting into a juicy pear picked right off the tree. Succulent, round, and sweetly spicy, with noticeable residual sugar but very appealing semi-tropical flavors. **88 Best Buy** *—P.G. (11/15/2005)*

Firesteed 2003 Pinot Noir (Oregon) $10. A fine alternative to simple, sweet blush wines is this value Oregon Pinot. The color suggests it is older than an '03, but that just makes it more approachable. Yes

USA

it's light, but it's not generic. It offers round varietal flavors of sweet strawberries, hints of herbs, and a dash of vanilla. **87 Best Buy** *—P.G. (8/1/2005)*

Firesteed 2001 Pinot Noir (Willamette Valley) $19. Firesteed's mid-tier Pinot benefits from an extra couple of years of bottle age, delivering mature flavors of red fruits, textured with pine resin, herb, lemon oil, and a hint of tomato leaf. Elegant and balanced, it's a great choice for those who prefer some age on their Pinot. **88** *—P.G. (8/1/2005)*

Firesteed 1999 Pinot Noir (Oregon) $10. **84** *—S.H. (8/1/2002)*

FIRESTONE

Firestone 2002 Vintage Reserve Bordeaux Blend (Santa Ynez Valley) $32. Raw in acids and tannins, with thin fruit that lets the alcohol poke through, this dry, austere wine just manages to suggest cherries. **82** *—S.H. (12/31/2005)*

Firestone 2002 Cabernet Sauvignon (Santa Ynez Valley) $18. Simple, dry, and fruity, with blackberry, plum, olive, thyme, and oak flavors backed up by firm but smooth tannins. Drink now. **84** *—S.H. (11/1/2005)*

Firestone 2000 Cabernet Sauvignon (Santa Ynez Valley) $18. **83** *—S.H. (8/1/2003)*

Firestone 2000 Chardonnay (Santa Barbara) $16. **87** *—J.M. (12/15/2002)*

Firestone 2002 Santa Barbara Chardonnay (Santa Barbara County) $16. Citrusy and acidic, with background flavors of peaches and tropical fruits. This is a varietally correct Chard, clean and balanced. It will go fine with scallops or shrimp. **85** *—S.H. (8/1/2004)*

Firestone 2004 Gewürztraminer (Santa Barbara County) $11. Here's a Gewürz that should be easy to identify blind. It's richly aromatic in honeysuckle, lime, cinnamon, and spice flavors, with a smoky edge, and drinks fruity and slightly sweet. Good acidity keeps it clean and sharp. **85** *—S.H. (11/1/2005)*

Firestone 2001 Gewürztraminer (Santa Barbara) $9. **87 Best Buy** *—J.M. (11/15/2002)*

Firestone 2002 Estate Bottled Gewürztraminer (Santa Ynez Valley) $9. Pretty thin sledding here, a watery wine with faint traces of citrus fruits that finish sugary. Hard to find much to praise about it. **82** *—S.H. (3/1/2004)*

Firestone 2000 Merlot (Santa Ynez Valley) $18. **85** *—S.H. (8/1/2003)*

Firestone 1997 Winemaker's Reserve Merlot (Santa Ynez Valley) $25. **84** *—J.C. (7/1/2000)*

Firestone 2002 Riesling (Central Coast) $8. **86 Best Buy** *—J.M. (8/1/2003)*

Firestone 2004 Vineyard Select Riesling (Central Coast) $10. This is a nice interpretation of an Alsatian-style Riesling. It's off dry, with ripe peach and wildflower flavors and crisp acids and minerals. Thoroughly clean and vibrant through the finish. **84** *—S.H. (10/1/2005)*

Firestone 2004 Sauvignon Blanc (Santa Ynez Valley) $12. Here's a nice summer white that offers up plenty of fruity flavor, and won't break the bank. Shows spearmint, lemon and lime, peach, and vanilla fruit that drinks pretty dry, with a good backbone of acidity. **84** *—S.H. (11/1/2005)*

Firestone 2002 Sauvignon Blanc (Santa Ynez Valley) $12. **83** *—S.H. (12/15/2003)*

Firestone 2000 Sauvignon Blanc (Santa Barbara County) $10. **85** *—S.H. (11/15/2001)*

Firestone 2002 Syrah (Santa Ynez Valley) $18. Briary, herbal notes accent sweetly ripe notes of black cherries in this bouncy, medium-weight quaffer. Bright acids provide zest, making the wine finish crisp and clean. **85** *(9/1/2005)*

Firestone 2000 Syrah (Santa Ynez Valley) $18. **88 Best Buy** *—J.M. (11/15/2002)*

FISHER

Fisher 2001 Coach Insignia Cabernet Sauvignon (Napa Valley) $65. Opens with complex aromas of cassis and new smoky oak, and turns lush and smooth when it hits the palate, yet at times seems almost too ripe. Gorgeous now, and should improve through 2015. **90** *—S.H. (5/1/2005)*

Fisher 2001 Coach Insignia Chardonnay (Sonoma County) $32. This very complex wine is a blend of grapes from various parts of the county. It shows a myriad of flavors ranging from tropical tree fruits to limes and crisp, green apples, and has been well-oaked. The texture is creamy and opulent. Don't chill it too much, because you'll lose some of the high-end nuances. **93** *—S.H. (4/1/2004)*

Fisher 1997 Coach Insignia Chardonnay (Sonoma County) $25. **89** *—S.H. (11/15/1999)*

Fisher 1999 Paladini Vineyards Chardonnay (Carneros) $45. **92** *(7/1/2001)*

Fisher 1997 RCF Merlot (Napa Valley) $28. **89** *—S.H. (12/31/1999)*

FITZPATRICK

Fitzpatrick 1999 Grenache (El Dorado County) $17. **85** *—S.H. (12/15/2001)*

Fitzpatrick 2000 Syrah (Fair Play) $20. **85** *—S.H. (6/1/2003)*

FIVE RIVERS

Five Rivers 2002 Cabernet Sauvignon (Paso Robles) $10. This textbook Paso Cabernet is soft, although fairly tannic, with very ripe flavors of blackberries, chocolate, and coffee. It's simple, but so balanced and clean, it's just yummy. **85 Best Buy** *—S.H. (12/1/2005)*

Five Rivers 2004 Chardonnay (Monterey County) $10. Lots of oak flavoring on this modestly fruity wine. It's dryish, with the flavor of canned peaches and vanilla. **82** *—S.H. (12/1/2005)*

Five Rivers 2002 Merlot (Central Coast) $10. This simple wine opens with plum sauce and oak aromas, then turns soft, dry and heavy in the mouth. It's fully dry. Not bad for less demanding occasions. **83** *—S.H. (12/1/2005)*

Five Rivers 2003 Pinot Noir (Santa Barbara County) $10. A little hot and rubbery, with earthy, coffee flavors that turn cherryish on the finish. Dry and silky texture. **83** *—S.H. (10/1/2005)*

FLOODGATE

Floodgate 2000 Pinot Noir (Anderson Valley) $30. 87 *(10/1/2002)*

FLORA SPRINGS

Flora Springs 2002 Trilogy Cabernet Blend (Napa Valley) $60. No longer made from just three varieties, this Trilogy has all five Bordeaux grapes. It's complex but young in cassis and oak, with a dry, dusty spread of tannins. Those tannins will play well now with well-marbled smoky, grilled beef, but the wine should hold through 2010. **91** *—S.H. (12/1/2005)*

Flora Springs 2001 Cabernet Sauvignon (Napa Valley) $30. Nice and easy Cabernet, with a real touch of class. This wine is dry and balanced and a little tannic, and the herb and currant flavors are splashed with a sweet perfume of oak. **86** *—S.H. (10/1/2004)*

Flora Springs 2002 25th Anniversary Cabernet Sauvignon (Napa Valley) $150. This is certainly a good wine, ripe and delicious in cherry, black currant, and chocolate flavors, with rich, intricate tannins and a long, rich finish. It's luscious, but very soft, and doesn't seem likely to age. **87** *—S.H. (12/31/2005)*

Flora Springs 2002 Holy Smoke Vineyard Cabernet Sauvignon (Napa Valley) $85. Marches to a different beat. Something about the aroma brings to mind dry, hot summer days when the hills smell of dust and eucalyptus. Turns a lot fruitier in the mouth, with cherries and blackberries and firm, sturdy tannins. Elegant now, and should develop beyond 2010. **91** *—S.H. (10/1/2005)*

Flora Springs 2002 Out-of-Sight Vineyard Cabernet Sauvignon (Napa Valley) $85. The least of Flora Springs' impressive single-vineyard '02s, a tannic, rather herbacous wine suggesting blackberries, but still a very good wine. It's bone dry, showing an austerity now that might soften after five or six years. **88** *—S.H. (10/1/2005)*

Flora Springs 2002 Rutherford Hillside Reserve Cabernet Sauvignon (Napa Valley) $100. Showing the best structure of Flora Springs' impressive quartet of '04 vineyard desigated Cabs, this is a firm, well-sculpted wine whose pedigree stands out, but it needs time. It's a big, tannic, closed wine, dry and astringent. But there's a gigantic heart of blackberry fruit, and I would be surprised if this wine doesn't turn into a real beauty by 2010. **94** *—S.H. (10/1/2005)*

Flora Springs 1999 Rutherford Hillside Reserve Cabernet Sauvignon (Napa Valley) $100. 87 *—S.H. (12/31/2002)*

Flora Springs 1996 Trilogy Cabernet Sauvignon (Napa Valley) $45. 94 *(11/15/1999)*

Flora Springs 1999 Wild Boar Vineyard Cabernet Sauvignon (Napa Valley) $60. 87 *—S.H. (11/15/2002)*

Flora Springs 1996 Wild Boar Vyd Cabernet Sauvignon (Napa Valley) $40. 89 *(9/1/2000)*

Flora Springs 2000 Poggio del Papa Cabernet Sauvignon-Sangiovese (Napa Valley) $35. 88 *—S.H. (5/1/2003)*

Flora Springs 2003 Barrel-Fermented Chardonnay (Napa Valley) $22. A nice Chard, with lively acidity and a modest coating of oak that frames peach and apple flavors. Easy to drink, and fine by itself or as a backup to fresh-cracked crab. **85** *—S.H. (10/1/2005)*

Flora Springs 2000 Barrel-Fermented Reserve Chardonnay (Napa Valley) $25. 92 *—S.H. (5/1/2002)*

Flora Springs 1998 Lavender Hill Vineyard Chardonnay (Napa Valley) $30. 85 *(6/1/2000)*

Flora Springs 2003 Select Cuvée Chardonnay (Napa Valley) $35. From the pretty golden color, to the powerful aromas of tropical fruits and toasty oak, to the full-throttle flavors and creamy texture, this is a wonderful Chard. It has complexities that unravel as the wine warms in the glass. **91** *—S.H. (10/1/2005)*

Flora Springs 2003 Merlot (Napa Valley) $25. Dry and balanced, this Merlot has blackberry, mocha and anise flavors and well-developed tannins, with a bite of acidity in the finish. Drink now and for the next two years. **86** *—S.H. (12/1/2005)*

Flora Springs 2001 Merlot (Napa Valley) $22. 86 *—S.H. (12/1/2003)*

Flora Springs 1999 Windfall Vineyard Merlot (Napa Valley) $50. 91 *—S.H. (6/1/2002)*

Flora Springs 2000 Pinot Grigio (Napa Valley) $12. 85 *—S.H. (11/15/2001)*

Flora Springs 1998 Lavender Hill Pinot Noir (Napa Valley) $33. 87 *(10/1/2000)*

Flora Springs 2001 Trilogy Red Blend (Napa Valley) $60. Comes down on the tough side, with tannins that bury the fruit. Clearly a young, rather aggressive wine, but one whose deep core of black cherry and blackberry fruit has good potential. Cellar for a good six years. **90** *—S.H. (9/1/2004)*

Flora Springs 1998 Sangiovese (Napa Valley) $17. 90 *—S.H. (12/15/1999)*

Flora Springs 1998 Sauvignon Blanc (Napa Valley) $12. 89 *—S.H. (3/1/2000)*

Flora Springs 2002 Soliloquy Sauvignon Blanc (Napa Valley) $25. A bright textured, medium-bodied wine that serves up a pleasing blend of lemon, melon, herb, and grapefruit flavors. A bit steely edged, it's clean and fresh on the finish. **88** *—J.M. (9/1/2004)*

Flora Springs 2000 Soliloquy Sauvignon Blanc (Napa Valley) $22. 90 *—S.H. (9/1/2003)*

Flora Springs 1999 Poggio del Papa Tuscan Blend (Napa Valley) $35. 91 *—S.H. (7/1/2002)*

FLOWERS

Flowers 2001 Andreen-Gale Cuvée Chardonnay (Sonoma Coast) $44. This is an intense, brilliantly focused wine that displays near perfect balance. The flavors are of fresh, savory lemondrop veering into spicy mango and are well oaked, while the acidity is superb, lending a steely tang to the richness. The finish lasts a full minute. This classic coast Chardonnay will hold and slowly become nutty and complex through the decade. **94** *—S.H. (8/1/2004)*

Flowers 2001 Andreen-Gale Cuvée Pinot Noir (Sonoma Coast) $48. Big, extremely ripe, a bit hot in alcohol, definitely full-bodied for a Pinot, with humungous fruit and a scour of tough tannins. It was very hot in the coastal hills this vintage and the wines were bigger than usual. If you can get past the size, this wine is luscious. **92** *—S.H. (8/1/2004)*

Flowers 2000 Keefer Ranch Pinot Noir (Green Valley) $44. 92 Cellar Selection *(10/1/2002)*

FLYING GOAT CELLARS

Flying Goat Cellars 2003 Dierberg Vineyard Pinot Noir (Santa Maria Valley) $34. Tannic, heavy, and a bit hot, and not offering much pleasure now, although it's properly dry, and there's a solid core of black cherry fruit. Finishes with a grapeskin bitterness. **84** *—S.H. (8/1/2005)*

Flying Goat Cellars 2003 Rio Vista Vineyard Pinot Noir (Santa Rita Hills) $38. Very dark, and rather heavy in texture, this is an earthy wine. The flavors suggest coffee and black cherries. **84** *—S.H. (8/1/2005)*

FLYNN

Flynn 1998 Cellar Select Clos d'Or Pinot Noir (Oregon) $10. 81 *—M.S. (12/1/2000)*

FOLEY

Foley 2001 Chardonnay (Santa Maria Valley) $35. A smooth textured wine, with pretty caramel, apricot, peach, melon, butterscotch, herb, and citrus flavors. Fairly rich, yet clean on the finish. **88** *—J.M. (2/1/2004)*

Foley 2000 Barrel Select Bien Nacido Vineyard Chardonnay (Santa Barbara County) $27. 89 *—S.H. (12/1/2003)*

Foley 1999 Dierberg Vineyard Chardonnay (Santa Maria Valley) $35. 87 *(7/1/2001)*

Foley 2002 Rancho Santa Rosa Chardonnay (Santa Rita Hills) $30. There's an earthy tightness to this wine (as well as high acidity and a mineral-laden stoniness) that will not appeal to fans of big, ripe Chards. Consumers need to know that before buying. That said, it is elegant. **88** *—S.H. (5/1/2005)*

Foley 2003 Rancho Santa Rosa Pinot Noir (Santa Rita Hills) $38. Sort of a junior version of Foley's block designations, this wine nonetheless is complex and delicious. It's broad and ripe in cherry, cola, spice, and oak flavors, with a nice, silky mouthfeel and brisk acidity. **87** *—S.H. (12/15/2005)*

Foley 2003 Rancho Santa Rosa Barrel Select Pinot Noir (Santa Rita Hills) $50. If you want to know why Santa Rita Hills Pinot is so celebrated, just take a sip. Dry, elegant, complex, and totally satisfying, the wine has a myriad of cherry, black raspberry, cola, rhubarb, coffee, and spice flavors and the silkiest, most satiny texture imaginable, with crisp acids. Beautiful now and through 2007. **93** *—S.H. (12/15/2005)*

Foley 2003 Rancho Santa Rosa Block 4A Clone 2A Pinot Noir (Santa Rita Hills) $45. Co-released with the '03 Barrel Select, this Pinot is more fruit-forward, more immediately accessible and a little sweeter in cherries and vanilla. It is, in a word, fabulous. If you're looking for a Pinot that's flashy right now, this is the one. Defines the world-class status of Santa Rita Pinot. **93** *—S.H. (12/15/2005)*

Foley 2002 Rancho Santa Rosa Block 4D Pommard Clone Pinot Noir (Santa Rita Hills) $45. Among the brilliant expressions of this terroir-based appellation is this old-clone Pinot. It's complex and deep in earthy, mushroomy essence, with a dry grip, and needs time to express its sweet cherry-cocoa core. This compelling wine will improve through 2010. **94** *—S.H. (5/1/2005)*

Foley 2002 Rancho Santa Rosa Block 5C Dijon Clone 667 Pinot Noir (Santa Rita Hills) $45. I like this wine for its delicate texture and silky mouthfeel, and the interplay of complex earth, mushroom, coffee, rhubarb, and bitter tea flavors. It's not a fruit bomb, and that's the whole point. It's unrelievedly dry except for a finish of sweetness from fruit and oak. **92** *—S.H. (5/1/2005)*

Foley 2003 Sauvignon Blanc (Santa Barbara County) $16. A raw, juicy, brisk and utterly delightful wine. Acids hit big-time, and the lemon and gooseberry flavors wake the taste buds up. **90 Editors' Choice** *—S.H. (5/1/2005)*

Foley 2003 Rancho Santa Rosa Syrah (Santa Rita Hills) $30. Mixed berries, sprinkled with white and black pepper, are carried along on a smooth, creamy texture and linger delicately on the finish. Delicious, but it almost seems too clean. **88** *(9/1/2005)*

FOLIE À DEUX

Folie à Deux 1999 Harvey Vineyard Barbera (Amador County) $8. **88** *—S.H. (12/15/2001)*

Folie à Deux 2000 Cabernet Sauvignon (Napa Valley) $26. **90** *—S.H. (11/15/2003)*

Folie à Deux 1999 Cabernet Sauvignon (Napa Valley) $26. **91** *—S.H. (11/15/2002)*

Folie à Deux 2000 Private Reserve Cabernet Sauvignon (Napa Valley) $45. Tough, herbal, and hard in the mouth, this tannic wine offers modest blackberry flavors and a dose of oak. It turns syrupy-sweet on the finish. **84** *—S.H. (2/1/2005)*

Folie à Deux 1998 Reserve Cabernet Sauvignon (Napa Valley) $36. **84** *—S.H. (12/15/2000)*

Folie à Deux 1997 (Napa Valley) $18. **88** *—S.H. (9/1/2000)*

Folie à Deux 1997 Chardonnay (Napa Valley) $18. **84** *(6/1/2000)*

Folie à Deux 2001 Chenin Blanc (Napa County) $18. **86** *—S.H. (9/1/2003)*

Folie à Deux 1997 Merlot (Napa Valley) $24. **88** *—S.H. (7/1/2000)*

Folie à Deux 1999 Sangiovese (Napa Valley) $18. **86** *—S.H. (12/15/2001)*

Folie à Deux 1999 Lani's Vineyard Syrah (Amador County) $26. **88** *(11/1/2001)*

Folie à Deux 1997 Zinfandel (Amador County) $18. **87** *(9/1/1999)*

Folie à Deux 2000 Zinfandel (Amador County) $18. **88** *—S.H. (9/1/2003)*

Folie à Deux 1999 Bowman Vineyard Zinfandel (Amador County) $26. A beautiful Zin, among the best ever, with its near perfect balance of fruit, alcohol, and tannins. Gorgeous flavors burst on the palate, black cherries, blackberries, cassis, white chocolate, espresso, and cinnamon, to name a few. The wine is totally dry, but so ripe, it tastes sweet. Completely addictive, a joy for lovers of dry, balanced Zins, and a triumph for the winemaking team. **94** *—S.H. (3/1/2004)*

Folie à Deux 1998 D'Agostini Vineyard Old Vine Zinfandel (Amador County) $22. **90** *—P.G. (3/1/2001)*

Folie à Deux 1999 DeMille Vineyard Old Vine Zinfandel (Amador County) $24. **90** *—S.H. (12/15/2001)*

Folie à Deux 1997 Eschen Vineyard Old Vine Zinfandel (Fiddletown) $22. **88** *(9/1/1999)*

Folie à Deux 1998 La Grande Folie Old Vine Zinfandel (Amador County) $44. **87** *—P.G. (3/1/2001)*

Folie à Deux 2004 Ménage à Trois Rosé Blend (California) $12. This rosé is an easy-drinking bottling that has enough fruity complexity and bright acidity to recommend it. A blend of Merlot, Syrah, and Gewürztraminer, it's a creamy mélange of raspberries, cinnamon, rose petal, and tobacco, and very dry. **85** *—S.H. (11/1/2005)*

FOPPIANO

Foppiano 2001 Cabernet Sauvignon (Russian River Valley) $17. Nice, ripe, and balanced, a Cab that's easy to drink for its delicious blackberry and cherry flavors and smooth tannins, yet holds extra layers of nuance and interest. **86** *—S.H. (5/1/2005)*

Foppiano 2001 Riverside Collection Cabernet Sauvignon (California) $7. Over-ripe and pruny, with a burnt, Porty smell. Harsh and astringent. **82** *—S.H. (10/1/2004)*

Foppiano 2001 Merlot (Russian River Valley) $15. There's some good cherry fruit here, and the tannins are soft and intricate, but the wine has an overtly unripe green stemminess that detracts. **84** *—S.H. (5/1/2005)*

Foppiano 1997 Petite Sirah (Sonoma County) $17. **91** *—M.S (5/1/2000)*

Foppiano 2000 Petite Sirah (Sonoma County) $23. **90** *—S.H. (12/1/2002)*

Foppiano 2002 Bacigalupi Vineyard Petite Sirah (Russian River Valley) $17. This vineyard is in the warmest part of Russian River Valley, and that extra heat shows in the flavors of dark stone fruits, such as plums and pomegranates. The wine also is very tough in tannins, numbing the palate through the bone-dry finish. It will take a dozen years to soften this bruiser, but it's a fine example of its genre. **87** *—S.H. (8/1/2004)*

Foppiano 2002 Estate Petite Sirah (Russian River Valley) $23. Nobody in California tries harder than Foppiano, and it's dry, robust, tannic and well-made, with a core of sweet blackberry fruit that should hold it well for a long time. Could be great with a rich sirloin steak in a dark reduction sauce. **90** *—S.H. (8/1/2005)*

Foppiano 2002 Pinot Noir (Russian River Valley) $23. A dry, medium-bodied Pinot that shows very ripe fruit, easy tannins, and a crisp bite of acidity. The flavors are delicious, all black cherries, sweet rhubarb tea, cola, vanilla, and cinnamon. It's a wine you'll find yourself reaching for a second and a third time. **90** *—S.H. (12/15/2005)*

Foppiano 2002 Sangiovese (Alexander Valley) $17. Here's a wine that will even please those who say they don't like red wine. It's nice and light but with delicious flavors of ripe red stone fruits and spicy red berries and a touch of vanilla. Feels silky and clean through the spicy finish. **86** *—S.H. (8/1/2005)*

Foppiano 2002 Zinfandel (Dry Creek Valley) $15. Absolutely easy to drink, a soft, silky wine with pleasantly ripe berry and cherry flavors. Has a rich Asian spiciness throughout, and is dry and balanced. **84** *—S.H. (8/1/2005)*

Foppiano 2000 Zinfandel (Dry Creek Valley) $15. **86** *—S.H. (12/1/2002)*

FORCHINI

Forchini 2000 Proprietor's Reserve Pinot Noir (Russian River Valley) $24. **86** *(10/1/2002)*

Forchini 2001 Proprietor's Reserve Zinfandel (Dry Creek Valley) $24. **82** *(11/1/2003)*

FOREFATHERS

Forefathers 2000 Cabernet Sauvignon (Alexander Valley) $32. **92 Editors' Choice** *—S.H. (11/15/2003)*

FOREST GLEN

Forest Glen 2002 Oak Barrel Selection Cabernet Sauvignon (California) $10. A well-behaved, rustic Cab, with pleasant blackberry, cherry, and oak flavors. Very dry, with good varietal character, and a country-style personality. **85 Best Buy** *—S.H. (6/1/2005)*

Forest Glen 2001 Reserve Cabernet Sauvignon (Sonoma County) $34. Forest Glen's first ever reserve bottling is very dark, very dry, and very tannic, to the point of palate-searing astringency. It also seems to have high acids, creating a sour taste and burn on the finish. **82** *—S.H. (11/15/2005)*

Forest Glen 2000 Chardonnay (California) $10. **84** *—S.H. (12/15/2002)*

Forest Glen 1999 Forest Fire Chardonnay (California) $8. **84** *—S.H. (2/1/2001)*

Forest Glen 2002 Oak Barrel-Fermented Chardonnay (California) $10. There is indeed some barrel-fermented character here, including vanilla, smoky aromas, and a creamy texture. It's modestly flavored with apples and peaches. **84** *—S.H. (6/1/2004)*

Forest Glen 1999 Oak Barrel-Fermented Chardonnay (California) $10. **82** *—S.H. (5/1/2001)*

Forest Glen 2000 Merlot (California) $10. **84** *—S.H. (8/1/2003)*

Forest Glen 1998 Merlot (California) $10. **83** *—S.H. (11/15/2000)*

Forest Glen 2002 Oak Barrel Selection Merlot (California) $10. You get lots of bang for your buck in this modest wine. It's fully dry, with smooth tannins, a refreshing bite of acidity, and flavorful notes of blackberries and dark chocolate. All that fruit persists through the long finish. **85** *—S.H. (6/1/2004)*

Forest Glen 2004 White Merlot (California) $10. There's a rich cherry and vanilla flavor to this wine, with enough residual sugar to make it off-dry. Fortunately, there's also a nice, clean backbone of acidity to make it balanced. **84** *—S.H. (11/15/2005)*

Forest Glen 2001 Pinot Grigio (Sonoma) $10. **84** *—S.H. (9/1/2003)*

Forest Glen 1999 Pinot Grigio (California) $11. **84** *—S.H. (8/1/2001)*

Forest Glen 2002 Oak Barrel Selection Shiraz (California) $10. A decent quaff, featuring modest cherry-berry fruit and an earthy, herbal undercurrent. Smooth in the mouth, then thins out a bit on the finish. **84** *(9/1/2005)*

FORESTVILLE

ForestVille 1999 Cabernet Sauvignon (California) $6. **84** *—S.H. (11/15/2002)*

ForestVille 2002 Chardonnay (Sonoma County) $6. Nothing going on in this deficient wine except alcohol. Not a trace of fruit. **81** *—S.H. (11/15/2004)*

ForestVille 1997 Chardonnay (California) $6. **81** *—J.C. (10/1/1999)*

ForestVille 2003 Gewürztraminer (California) $6. Lots of true varietal character in this versatile, tasty wine, with ripe fruit, crisp acids and loads of tingly cinnamon and nutmeg spice. Technically dry, but sweet in peaches and wildflowers. A nice value. **85 Best Buy** *—S.H. (10/1/2005)*

ForestVille 2000 Merlot (California) $6. **84** *—S.H. (11/15/2002)*

ForestVille 2003 Reserve Pinot Noir (Sonoma County) $16. Shows restraint in the reined-in cherry and herb flavors and modest oak, but it's not a simple wine. It has layers of interest that drink dry and balanced. **85** *—S.H. (5/1/2005)*

ForestVille 1997 Sauvignon Blanc (California) $8. **82** *(3/1/2000)*

ForestVille 2002 Shiraz (Sonoma County) $6. Kind of sharp and acidic at first, but then the ripe, jammy black cherry flavors spread over the mouth and last through the finish. A nice, simple wine for everyday occasions—and look at the bargain price. **84 Best Buy** *—S.H. (12/1/2004)*

ForestVille 1999 Shiraz (California) $6. **83** *(10/1/2001)*

ForestVille 2002 Zinfandel (California) $6. Fresh, jammy, and sharp in acids, this good-value Zin features berry flavors with an earthy edge. It's very dry. Good for pizza. **83** *—S.H. (10/1/2004)*

FORGERON

Forgeron 2002 Cabernet Sauvignon (Columbia Valley (WA)) $30. Reductive, closed down, and musty. Possibly slightly corked, but a second bottle showed the same musty, closed down flavors. The wine simply falls off a cliff in the midpalate. **84** —*P.G. (12/15/2005)*

Forgeron 2003 Chardonnay (Columbia Valley (WA)) $19. This tasty effort, sourced mostly from the outstanding DuBrul Vineyard, brightly combines crisp, lime-edged acidity with moderate tropical fruit flavors of pineapple, green apple, and pear. Plenty of barrel spice gives it a fresh-baked apple-pie finish. **88** —*P.G. (6/1/2005)*

Forgeron 2001 Syrah (Columbia Valley (WA)) $29. Dense, dark color, scented with meaty fruit, smoke, toast, and tar, this is quintessential Washington Syrah. It simply delivers, in spades, everything you want: sweet berries, spicy, toasty oak, and highlights of cinnamon and pepper. **91** —*P.G. (9/1/2004)*

FORIS

Foris 2000 Chardonnay (Rogue Valley) $11. **86** —*P.G. (8/1/2002)*

Foris 2000 Gewürztraminer (Rogue Valley) $11. **91 Best Buy** —*P.G. (4/1/2002)*

Foris 1998 Merlot (Rogue Valley) $18. **85** —*P.G. (4/1/2002)*

Foris 2000 Pinot Blanc (Rogue Valley) $13. **87** —*P.G. (4/1/2002)*

Foris 1999 Pinot Noir (Rogue Valley) $16. **87** —*P.G. (4/1/2002)*

FORT ROSS VINEYARD

Fort Ross Vineyard 2002 Chardonnay (Sonoma Coast) $32. Made in the same style as the Reserve. Shows a cool-climate profile of stones, minerals, cold metal, and high acidity, and is dry, elegant, and ageworthy. Softening notes from oak provide sweetness. Distinct. **91** —*S.H. (5/1/2005)*

Fort Ross Vineyard 2001 Pinot Noir (Sonoma Coast) $34. Aromas offer less than ripe rhubarb, mint, and cola alongside riper cherries and cocoa, but in the mouth, it explodes in sweet fruit and smoke. Light in body, delicately acidic, yet incredibly complex. A beautiful Pinot. **92** —*S.H. (5/1/2005)*

FORTH

Forth 2001 Cabernet Sauvignon (Dry Creek Valley) $30. Actually a single-vineyard Cab. Doesn't merit as good a score as Forth's less expensive '02 All Boys Cab because of the astringent tannins, which rob it of instant appeal. Might age, but it's a gamble. **87** —*S.H. (10/1/2005)*

Forth 2002 All Boys Cabernet Sauvignon (Dry Creek Valley) $18. Here's a nice Cab that's easy to like for its ripe berry, chocolate, olive, and herb flavors and rich, smooth texture, yet it has a fancy complexity that will translate to a fine dinner. Drink now for the sheer exuberance of youth. **90** —*S.H. (10/1/2005)*

Forth 2002 Syrah (Dry Creek Valley) $25. With the extra heat it gets in warm Dry Creek, this Syrah is very ripe in blackberry, black cherry and even blackstrap molasses flavors, although it's totally dry. The fine structure gives it balance and finesse. **87** —*S.H. (9/1/2005)*

FORTRESS

Fortress 2004 Musqué Clone Sauvignon Blanc (Lake County) $21. These Lake County Sauvignons sure are getting interesting. This one is an amazing wine, bone dry, tingly-tart, and filled with gooseberry, grapefruit, and minerals. It stimulates some feral instinct in the mouth, living up to its savage, wild name. **90** —*S.H. (11/1/2005)*

FOUNTAIN GROVE

Fountain Grove 1998 Chardonnay (California) $10. **83** —*L.W. (12/31/1999)*

Fountain Grove 1998 Sauvignon Blanc (North Coast) $10. **86** —*L.W. (5/1/2000)*

FOUR SONS

Four Sons 2002 Merlot (Carneros) $25. Drinks a bit simple and rustic, with chewy tannins and dried herbs, but there's no denying the plethora of ripe blackberry, plum, cherry, and mocha flavors. **84** —*S.H. (12/15/2005)*

FOUR VINES

Four Vines 2002 Old Vine Cuvée Zinfandel (California) $10. Here's a country-style wine with nice Zinny flavors of berries and mocha and smooth, ripe tannins. Loses a point or two for a sharp, weird sweet-and-sour note on the finish. **83** —*S.H. (12/15/2005)*

FOX CREEK

Fox Creek 1997 Ceago Vinegarden Chardonnay (Santa Ynez Valley) $35. **88** —*M.M. (10/1/1999)*

FOX RUN

Fox Run 1999 Cabernet Franc (Finger Lakes) $20. If you like wood, you'll like this wine. There's a slight acrid note, but mostly it's very toasty and oaky, with sweet caramel flavors and a tangy finish. **83** —*J.C. (1/1/2004)*

Fox Run 1999 Chardonnay (Finger Lakes) $9. **87 Best Buy** —*J.C. (7/1/2002)*

Fox Run 2002 Pinot Noir (Finger Lakes) $15. A nice, light-bodied wine with some pretty flavors of cherries, vanilla, and leather. Has a smooth, creamy texture and an elegant mouthfeel that's almost Burgundian. **86** *(11/1/2004)*

Fox Run 1997 Estate-grown Reserve Pinot Noir (Finger Lakes) $20. 85 *(10/1/1999)*

Fox Run 2000 Sable Seneca Lake Estate Grown Red Blend (Finger Lakes) $13. 85 *—J.M. (3/1/2003)*

Fox Run 1999 Riesling (Finger Lakes) $9. 86 *(11/15/2001)*

FOXEN

Foxen 1998 Chardonnay (Santa Maria Valley) $20. 92 *(6/1/2000)*

Foxen 2003 Tinaquaic Vineyard Chardonnay (Santa Maria Valley) $24. They put the words "dry farmed" on the label to indicate, I suppose, extra concentration, and indeed, this is an intense Chard. It's bone dry, well-oaked, high in acidity, and intricately layered in tropical fruit and orange custard flavors. Combines elegance, style, and power in the glass. **93 Editors' Choice** *—S.H. (12/15/2005)*

Foxen 1997 Tinaquaic Vineyard Chardonnay (Santa Maria Valley) $30. 90 *(6/1/2000)*

Foxen 1999 Chenin Blanc (Santa Barbara County) $14. 86 *—S.H. (5/1/2001)*

Foxen 2000 Pinot Noir (Santa Maria Valley) $24. 90 *(10/1/2002)*

Foxen 1997 Bien Nacido Vineyard Pinot Noir (Santa Maria Valley) $30. 89 *(10/1/1999)*

Foxen 2003 Julia's Vineyard Pinot Noir (Santa Maria Valley) $42. This is a very fruity Pinot, and also a tannic one. It's youthful now, with those sharp, fermenty acids and primary cherry fruit flavors that signal the need for time to knit together. **90** *—S.H. (12/15/2005)*

Foxen 1997 Julia's Vineyard Pinot Noir (Santa Maria Valley) $30. 91 *(10/1/1999)*

Foxen 1994 Sanford & Benedict Vineyard Pinot Noir (Santa Ynez Valley) $NA. Alcohol 13.6%. Brilliantly clear. Darker that the '93. Blast of dusty spices, sweet char, vanilla, oodles of red cherries. Terrifically sweet cherry and raspberry fruit, enormous middle palate. Flamboyant, hedonistic. Medium-bodied, with good acidity and firm tannins. Beautiful now–2012. **94 Editors' Choice** *—S.H. (6/1/2005)*

Foxen 2003 Sea Smoke Vineyard Pinot Noir (Santa Rita Hills) $60. Foxen has co-released three single-vineyard Pinots, and to my mind this is the best. It's the most closed, tannic, and complex, a dark, brooding wine whose depths have swirls of black stone fruits, sweet leather, mocha, spice, and oak. It drinks rich and satisfying now, and should develop well over the next five years. **92** *—S.H. (12/15/2005)*

Foxen 2000 Carhartt Vineyard Syrah (Santa Ynez Valley) $30. A richly fruity wine that offers up plush blackberry, cherry, bitter chocolate, and herb flavors that are dry and crisp, plus a smooth, velvety mouthfeel. The tannins are kind of tough, though. **88** *—S.H. (3/1/2004)*

Foxen 1999 Morehouse Vineyard Syrah (Santa Ynez Valley) $35. 81 *(11/1/2001)*

Foxen 2002 Tianquaic Vineyard Syrah (Santa Maria Valley) $30. If anything, even more serious and complex than Foxen's Santa Ynez bottling. Shows a distinctive cool-climate character with its aromas and flavors of white pepper, raw meat, cola, and cassis, and the wonderfully rich, thick, sweet tannins. The blockbuster is of awesome quality, and will age through the decade if you can keep your hands off of it. **84** *—S.H. (12/1/2004)*

Foxen 2000 Williamson-Dore Vineyard Syrah (Santa Ynez Valley) $30. Dinstinctly peppery, although there are underpinnings of blackberry, smoke, and oak. Feels quite posh and suave in the mouth, with smooth, rich tannins and crisp acids that spread blackberry and cherry flavors across the palate. Could use some depth, but otherwise a tasty wine. **89** *—S.H. (3/1/2004)*

FOXGLOVE

Foxglove 2001 Chardonnay (Edna Valley) $13. 84 *—S.H. (6/1/2003)*

FOXRIDGE

FoxRidge 1997 Merlot (Northern Sonoma) $11. 84 *—J.C. (7/1/2000)*

FRALICH

Fralich 2002 Harry's Patio Red Blend (Paso Robles) $15. Just barely good. Raspingly dry, with a sharp cut of acid and some green flavors, but it'll be fine with a cheeseburger. **83** *—S.H. (8/1/2005)*

Fralich 2003 Fralich Vineyard Viognier (Paso Robles) $22. Strong flavors in this easy-drinking wine. Lots of white peaches, bananas, butter, and honey, in a creamy texture that's soft on the finish. **85** *—S.H. (8/1/2005)*

FRANCIS COPPOLA

Francis Coppola 1998 Black Label Bordeaux Blend (California) $17. 82 *—S.H. (7/1/2000)*

Francis Coppola 2000 Director's Reserve Cabernet Sauvignon (Napa Valley) $30. 86 *—S.H. (12/31/2002)*

Francis Coppola 1998 Diamond Series Chardonnay (California) $15. 88 *(6/1/2000)*

Francis Coppola 2001 Rosso Red Blend (California) $9. 89 Best Buy *—S.H. (11/15/2003)*

Francis Coppola 2001 Director's Reserve Sauvignon Blanc (Napa Valley) $18. 88 *—S.H. (10/1/2003)*

Francis Coppola 2003 Diamond Collection Green Label Syrah-Shiraz Syrah (California) $16. Bright cherry-berry flavors tinged with a healthy dollop of vanilla and a soft, creamy mouthfeel give this wine easy accessibility and mass appeal. No, it's not profound, but

USA

it's a nice mouthful of red wine at an affordable price. **85** *(9/1/2005)*

Francis Coppola 1997 Diamond Series Zinfandel (California) $14. 82 *—J.C. (2/1/2000)*

FRANCISCAN

Franciscan 1998 Cabernet Sauvignon (Napa Valley) $25. 86 *—J.M. (12/31/2001)*

Franciscan 2002 Oakville Estate Cabernet Sauvignon (Napa Valley) $25. Exemplifies its terroir and vintage with its impeccable balance, and the way the ripe, sophisticated tannins wrap around the fleshy black currant, olive, chocolate, and herb flavors. Finishes with some sweetness from charry oak. **91** *—S.H. (8/1/2005)*

Franciscan 2001 Cuvée Sauvage Chardonnay (Carneros) $35. 88 *—S.H. (12/15/2003)*

Franciscan 2003 Oakville Estate Chardonnay (Napa Valley) $17. This pleasant quaffer offers up good Chard character. The apple, peach, and pear flavors have a creamy texture, and just a touch of smoky oak. Turns a bit tart on the finish. **84** *—S.H. (12/1/2005)*

Franciscan 1999 Oakville Estate Chardonnay (Napa Valley) $18. 87 *—J.M. (5/1/2002)*

Franciscan 1997 Oakville Estate Chardonnay (Napa Valley) $17. 91 *—L.W. (6/1/2003)*

Franciscan 2000 Oakville Estate Cuvée Sauvage Chardonnay (Carneros) $35. 92 *—S.H. (2/1/2003)*

Franciscan 2001 Merlot (Napa Valley) $22. So filled with sweet cocoa, it's almost like liquid milk chocolate, poured over ripe black cherries and sprinkled with vanilla. Oak adds a toasty edge. This dry wine is as luscious as the California sun could make it. **87** *—S.H. (12/15/2004)*

Franciscan 2002 Oakville Estate Merlot (Napa Valley) $22. Fruity and very easy to drink for its soft, rich texture and polished finish. Offers flavors of black cherries and cassis, with a chocolaty undertow. Like velvet, and finishes with a kick of tannin. **88** *—S.H. (8/1/2005)*

Franciscan 1999 Oakville Estate Merlot (Napa Valley) $22. 92 *—J.M. (5/1/2002)*

FRANK FAMILY

Frank Family 2001 Cabernet Sauvignon (Rutherford) $65. Polished, supple, and well-balanced. The cherry, herb, and oak flavors are held by sturdy but pliant tannins and a good volume of acidity. Epitomizes a classic Rutherford interpretation. **90** *—S.H. (10/1/2004)*

Frank Family 1999 Reserve Cabernet Sauvignon (Rutherford) $65. 94 Cellar Selection *—S.H. (12/31/2002)*

Frank Family 2000 Chardonnay (Napa Valley) $29. 90 *—S.H. (9/1/2002)*

FRANUS

Franus 1999 Rancho Chimiles Cabernet Sauvignon (Napa Valley) $40. Here's a generous Cab that offers ripe black currant, plum, herb, and mocha flavors, and a good amount of toasty oak. It's very dry, with smooth, dusty tannins. Finishes with a bit of astringency, but may soften up in a few years. **89** *—S.H. (5/1/2004)*

Franus 2001 Brandlin Vineyard Zinfandel (Mount Veeder) $22. Starts off with bright raspberry notes in the nose. On the palate, it's fruity and spicy, with a blend of cherry, plum, cinnamon, toast, and vanilla flavors. **88** *—J.M. (4/1/2004)*

FRAZIER

Frazier 1999 Lupine Hill Vineyard Cabernet Sauvignon (Napa Valley) $45. 86 *—S.H. (11/15/2002)*

Frazier 1996 Lupine Hill Vineyard Cabernet Sauvignon (Napa Valley) $36. 86 *—M.S. (12/31/1999)*

Frazier 1999 Lupine Hill Merlot (Napa Valley) $35. 93 *—S.H. (11/15/2002)*

FREEMARK ABBEY

Freemark Abbey 1996 Cabernet Sauvignon (Napa Valley) $27. 85 *—S.H. (7/1/2000)*

Freemark Abbey 2001 Cabernet Sauvignon (Napa Valley) $35. Dry and tannic in youth. It's not a particularly ripe wine, but subtle in meshing blackberry fruit flavors with sweet dried herbs and bitter coffee. They strove for balance and harmony, and succeeded. Now through 2010. **89** *—S.H. (3/1/2005)*

Freemark Abbey 1997 Bosché Cabernet Sauvignon (Napa Valley) $68. 90 *(6/1/2003)*

Freemark Abbey 2001 Bosché Vineyard Cabernet Sauvignon (Rutherford) $65. One of the best Cabs of the vintage. It's still a young wine, all primary black currant and plum fruit flavors and toasted oak, with complex notes of coffee and mocha. This wine is extraordinarily rich and finely balanced, displaying power, elegance, finesse, and an unreal depth of fruit along with great length. Drink now through 2015. **96 Editors' Choice** *—S.H. (12/15/2005)*

Freemark Abbey 2000 Sycamore Cabernet Sauvignon (Napa Valley) $60. This wine is tough and thin in fruit, and very dry. There's a suggestion of cherries, but this is a lot of money to pay for something that isn't a sure thing. **84** *—S.H. (8/1/2005)*

Freemark Abbey 1994 Sycamore Vineyards Cabernet Sauvignon (Napa Valley) $39. 93 *(11/15/1999)*

Freemark Abbey 1993 Sycamore Vineyards Cabernet Sauvignon (Napa Valley) $35. 94 *—S.H. (6/1/1999)*

Freemark Abbey 1998 Chardonnay (Napa Valley) $19. 84 *(6/1/2000)*

Freemark Abbey 1997 Carpy Ranch Chardonnay (Napa Valley) $26. 85 *(6/1/2000)*

Freemark Abbey 1997 Napa Valley Chardonnay (Napa Valley) $18. 87 *—S.H. (6/1/1999)*

Freemark Abbey 1996 Merlot (Napa Valley) $23. 89 *—S.H. (6/1/1999)*

Freemark Abbey 2001 Merlot (Rutherford) $27. A distinctive Merlot that shows true terroir. The aromatics include white pepper, raw meat, and exotic herbs such as tarragon, as well as oak. That sounds strange, but familiar cherry and blackberry flavors rule the mouth. Firm in tannins, and totally dry. Earns extra points for its uniqueness. **91** *—S.H. (3/1/2005)*

Freemark Abbey 1999 Merlot (Rutherford) $25. 85 *(6/1/2003)*

Freemark Abbey 2003 Viognier (Rutherford) $24. Dry white wines don't get much riper or more exotic than this. This full-bodied wine is jammed with tropical fruit, honeysuckle, meringue, crème brulée and spice flavors that last through a long finish. It's as rich as cream, yet dry and crisp. Compelling and delicious. **92** *—S.H. (12/15/2004)*

Freemark Abbey 2000 Carpy Ranch Viognier (Napa Valley) $25. 87 *—J.M. (12/15/2002)*

USA

FREESTONE

Freestone 1997 Merlot (Napa Valley) $18. 87 *—J.C. (7/1/2000)*

FREI BROTHERS

Frei Brothers 2000 Redwood Creek Cabernet Sauvignon (California) $8. 87 *—S.H. (3/1/2003)*

Frei Brothers 1999 Reserve Cabernet Sauvignon (Alexander Valley) $24. 86 *—S.H. (12/31/2002)*

Frei Brothers 2003 Reserve Chardonnay (Russian River Valley) $20. Rich in well-ripened fruit flavors and with a sweet coat of smoky oak and vanilla, this Chard also has a structural integrity based on crispness and vitality. It's not a soft, creamy Chard, but a firm one, with exotic fruit. **89** *—S.H. (12/1/2005)*

Frei Brothers 2001 Redwood Creek Merlot (California) $7. Smells a bit briary and minty, but once you take a sip, it delivers plenty of ripe, sophisticated cherry-berry fruit. The tannins are smooth and polished. There's lots to like in this dry, full-bodied dinner wine at a giveaway price. **86** *—S.H. (4/1/2004)*

Frei Brothers 2001 Reserve Merlot (Dry Creek Valley) $20. 85 *—S.H. (12/1/2003)*

Frei Brothers 2003 Reserve Pinot Noir (Russian River Valley) $24. Raw in acids, juicy in briary wild berry flavors with a chocolatey finish, this dry wine is a little jagged around the edges. May soften in a year or so. **84** *—S.H. (10/1/2005)*

Frei Brothers 2001 Redwood Creek Sauvignon Blanc (California) $8. 85 *—S.H. (3/1/2003)*

FRENCH HILL

French Hill 2002 Barbera (Sierra Foothills) $39. Expensive, but worth it for the exciting coffee, smoky new oak, cigar box, black cherry, and tar aromas and flavors that are very complex. Drinks smooth and clean, rich in tannins, really top rate. One of the best Barberas of recent memory. **92** *—S.H. (3/1/2005)*

French Hill 2001 Grand Reserve Barbera (El Dorado) $39. 85 *—S.H. (12/1/2003)*

French Hill 2002 Grand Reserve Pinotage (Amador County) $32. Full-bodied and dry, and softly tannic, with a mélange of blackberry, leather, herb, and tobacco flavors and a touch of oak. This complex wine is food-friendly. **87** *—S.H. (3/1/2005)*

FREY

Frey 2000 Petite Sirah (Mendocino) $12. 82 *—S.H. (5/1/2002)*

Frey 1999 Butow Vineyards Syrah (Redwood Valley) $11. 88 Best Buy *(10/1/2001)*

FRIAS

Frias 2002 Cabernet Sauvignon (Spring Mountain) $65. Not as powerful as the '01, this Cab is still an impressive wine. It's dry, with ripe cherry and cassis flavors, smooth, complex tannins and an elaborate overlay of oak. Very dry, and best now and through 2008. **89** *—S.H. (10/1/2005)*

Frias 1998 Private Reserve Cabernet Sauvignon (Napa Valley) $50. 83 *—S.H. (11/15/2002)*

FRICK

Frick 1995 Cinsault (Dry Creek Valley) $15. 85 *—M.S. (6/1/1999)*

Frick 1998 Syrah (Dry Creek Valley) $21. 88 *(11/1/2001)*

FRITZ

Fritz 2000 Cabernet Sauvignon (Sonoma County) $29. Tough, dry, and tannic, with herbal flavors. The wine is a blend from Dry Creek Valley and Rockpile AVAs, regions that need a good vintage to make good Cab. They didn't get one in 2000. **84** —*S.H. (11/15/2004)*

Fritz 2001 Dutton Ranch Chardonnay (Russian River Valley) $20. The acidity is bright and juicy, lending a citrus edge to the green apple and spiced pear flavors. Oak adds softness and cream, but the acids really star. **89** —*S.H. (6/1/2004)*

Fritz 1997 Dutton Ranch Chardonnay (Russian River Valley) $20. 92 —*S.H. (11/1/1999)*

Fritz 1998 Dutton Vineyard Chardonnay (Russian River Valley) $22. 87 —*S.H. (2/1/2001)*

Fritz 1998 Ruxton Vineyard Chardonnay (Russian River Valley) $27. 89 —*S.H. (2/1/2001)*

Fritz 2000 Shop Block Dutton Ranch Chardonnay (Russian River Valley) $22. 90 —*S.H. (12/31/2003)*

Fritz 1997 Merlot (Dry Creek Valley) $18. 85 —*L.W. (12/31/1999)*

Fritz 2000 Dutton Ranch Pinot Noir (Russian River Valley) $29. 85 *(10/1/2002)*

Fritz 1998 Jenner Vineyard Sauvignon Blanc (Dry Creek Valley) $12. 87 —*S.H. (3/1/2000)*

Fritz 2002 Zinfandel (Dry Creek Valley) $23. This fine wine exemplifies Zin's wild and woolly character in this appellation, one of its natural homes. The flavors are of briary berries, dusty herbs, and bitter chocolate, and while the tannins are firm, they allow the fruit through. Its astringency calls for rich pasta dishes or hard cheeses. **87** —*S.H. (10/1/2004)*

Fritz 1999 Old Vine Zinfandel (Dry Creek Valley) $25. 87 —*J.M. (3/1/2002)*

Fritz 1997 Roger's Reserve Zinfandel (Dry Creek Valley) $30. 88 3 —*L.W. (2/1/2000)*

FROG'S LEAP

Frog's Leap 2000 Rutherford Cabernet Blend (Napa Valley) $65. 93 —*S.H. (11/15/2003)*

Frog's Leap 1997 Cabernet Sauvignon (Napa Valley) $30. 91 *(11/1/2000)*

Frog's Leap 2002 Cabernet Sauvignon (Rutherford) $65. Seems a bit light for this vintage and appellation. There are minty, wintergreen aromas along with riper cherries and chocolate, and a bitterness or sharpness to the finish. **85** —*S.H. (12/15/2005)*

Frog's Leap 1999 Cabernet Sauvignon (Napa Valley) $35. 90 —*M.S. (11/15/2002)*

Frog's Leap 2003 Chardonnay (Napa Valley) $24. Lots of pleasantly ripe pear, peach, and apple fruit, with crisp acids and good wood. Easy to drink, with a slight roughness of texture. **85** —*S.H. (5/1/2005)*

Frog's Leap 2000 Chardonnay (Napa Valley) $22. 88 —*J.M. (5/1/2002)*

Frog's Leap 1998 Merlot (Napa Valley) $28. 86 —*J.C. (6/1/2001)*

Frog's Leap 2004 Sauvignon Blanc (Rutherford) $16. Grabs your interest for its intense varietal character and overall balance and harmony. Zesty lemondrop, gooseberry, fig, and vanilla flavors dominate, leading to a dry finish that's rich in acids. Has the weight of a Chardonnay. **90 Editors' Choice** —*S.H. (11/1/2005)*

Frog's Leap 2001 Sauvignon Blanc (Napa Valley) $16. 88 *(8/1/2002)*

Frog's Leap 2004 Leapfrogmilch White Blend (Napa Valley) $14. Very tart in acids, and dry as dust. The main problem with this amusingly-named wine is its thinness. It's watery throughout. **82** —*S.H. (10/1/2005)*

Frog's Leap 2003 Zinfandel (Napa Valley) $25. What a good job Frog's Leap has done in crafting a Zin with all the balance and harmony of a fine Cabernet, yet with Zin's distinctive personality. Wild, briary flavors of blueberries and black raspberries drink spicy and rich in this dry, addictive wine. **91 Editors' Choice** —*S.H. (11/1/2005)*

Frog's Leap 2001 Zinfandel (Rutherford) $22. 86 *(11/1/2003)*

Frog's Leap 1999 Zinfandel (Napa Valley) $22. 85 —*D.T. (3/1/2002)*

FULL CIRCLE

Full Circle 2003 Chardonnay (California) $8. Lots to admire here, and not just the price. This is a dry, smooth wine, with good varietal character. The apple and peach flavors are lightly oaked. Best Buy **85 Best Buy** —*S.H. (3/1/2005)*

FUSÉE

Fusée 2003 Cabernet Sauvignon (California) $6. At six bucks a pop, you can't go wrong with this rich, smooth, dry Cabernet. It shows appealing flavors of blackberries, blueberries, cherries, and chocolate fudge, and although it's a little light, that richly satisfying fruit carries the day. **85 Best Buy** —*S.H. (11/15/2005)*

Fusée 2003 Chardonnay (California) $6. If you like ripe, fruity Chards with a creamy texture and a touch of smoky oak, this is a super value. It has flavors of peaches, vanilla, buttered toast, and honey. Best Buy **84 Best Buy** —*S.H. (4/1/2005)*

Fusée 2002 Merlot (California) $6. How do they do it at this price? This great value is chockfull of delicious cherry, blackberry, and mocha flavors. It's dry and smooth, with a long finish. Buy it by the case. **86 Best Buy** —*S.H. (4/1/2005)*

Fusée 2002 Syrah (California) $6. Dark, young, and jammy, and so fresh in grapy flavors and acids, it tastes like it came straight from the fermenting tank. Clean, dry, and filled with blackberry, cocoa, and coffee flavors. Good value in a fun wine. **85 Best Buy** —*S.H. (12/31/2004)*

Fusée 2000 Syrah (California) $5. 90 Best Buy —*S.H. (11/15/2003)*

GABRIELLI

Gabrielli 2001 Coro Mednocino Red Blend (Mendocino) $35. A smoky edged wine with a strong licorice center. Coffee and toast are also at the fore, though primary fruit flavors take a back seat. Tannins are moderate—a bit rustic on the palate. **85** —*J.M. (9/1/2004)*

Gabrielli 2000 Rosato Sangiovese (Redwood Valley) $28. 85 —*S.H. (5/1/2002)*

Gabrielli 1999 Zinfandel (Redwood Valley) $18. 84 —*S.H. (11/1/2002)*

Gabrielli 1997 Goforth Vineyard Zinfandel (Redwood Valley) $20. 87 —*S.H. (5/1/2000)*

GAINEY

Gainey 2002 Chardonnay (Santa Barbara County) $18. Polished and tasty, a nice Chard notable for its bright burst of citrusy acids. The fruit is tangerines, pineapples, and mangoes. **86** —*S.H. (11/15/2004)*

Gainey 2000 Chardonnay (Santa Barbara County) $18. 90 —*S.H. (12/15/2002)*

Gainey 1999 Limited Selection Chardonnay (Santa Barbara County) $28. 92 —*S.H. (12/15/2002)*

Gainey 1997 Triada Grenache (Santa Ynez Valley) $16. 90 —*S.H. (10/1/1999)*

Gainey 2001 Merlot (Santa Ynez Valley) $19. Gainey was one of the first Santa Barbara wineries to nail Merlot, and while the Limited Selection is richer, their regular release is no slouch. Deeply extracted in black currant fruit, well-oaked, and balanced in tannins and acids, it has that sumptuous mouthfeel you associate with upscale red wines. **90** —*S.H. (3/1/2005)*

Gainey 2002 Limited Selection Merlot (Santa Ynez Valley) $34. Richer, firmer and more distinguished than Gainey's regular '02 Merlot, this wine shows black cherry flavors and firm, dusty tannins. It's very dry and elegant. Doesn't seem like an ager, so drink up. **90** —*S.H. (10/1/2005)*

Gainey 1998 Limited Selection Merlot (Santa Ynez Valley) $35. 88 —*J.M. (7/1/2002)*

Gainey 2001 Limited Selection Pinot Noir (Santa Barbara County) $35. 93 Editors' Choice —*S.H. (7/1/2003)*

Gainey 2000 Riesling (Santa Ynez Valley) $12. 84 —*S.H. (11/15/2001)*

Gainey 2003 Sauvignon Blanc (Santa Ynez Valley) $14. This wine is fierce in that sauvage character of citrus rind, gooseberry, tart green kiwi, and white pepper flavors, but it's very balanced, with a crisp spine of zesty acidity, and the finish turns ripely sweet in fruit. It's a pleasant sipper with some real elegance. **86** —*S.H. (12/15/2005)*

Gainey 2002 Limited Sauvignon Blanc (Santa Ynez Valley) $30. Well oaked. You pick up on the charry smoke and vanilla right away. But then the fruit hits, all ripe figs and sweet green grasses and lemons and limes and even hints of pineapple. With the fresh acidity, it all combines to a big, lush wine, with a clean, food-friendly scour. **91** —*S.H. (2/1/2005)*

Gainey 2001 Limited Selection Sauvignon Blanc (Santa Ynez Valley) $21. 87 —*S.H. (10/1/2003)*

Gainey 1998 Limited Selection Sauvignon Blanc (Santa Ynez Valley) $20. 90 —*S.H. (11/15/2000)*

Gainey 2002 Limited Selection Syrah (Santa Barbara County) $35. I wish this Syrah were a bit riper, or more concentrated, because it's got a very pretty structure. You'll find cherry, pepper, leather, and plum flavors, but they're diluted, and snap to a quick finish. **85** —*S.H. (9/1/2005)*

GALANTE

Galante 2001 Blackjack Pasture Cabernet Sauvignon (Carmel Valley) $60. This is not one of your out-of-the-gate lush Napa treats. It's young and tightly wound, a wine whose tannins and new oak are wrapped around the cherry and cassis fruit like the bandages on a mummy. Balanced and harmonious, this is one of the more solid cellar candidates of this splendid vintage. **92 Cellar Selection** —*S.H. (10/1/2004)*

Galante 1997 Blackjack Pasture Cabernet Sauvignon (Carmel Valley) $40. 93 —*S.H. (2/1/2000)*

Galante 2000 Rancho Galante Cabernet Sauvignon (Carmel Valley) $20. 90 Editors' Choice —*S.H. (11/15/2003)*

Galante 2001 Red Rose Hill Cabernet Sauvignon (Carmel Valley) $30. It took a while for this wine to open up, because it's closed and brooding at first. Opens with a cigarette ash aroma you sometimes find in terroir-driven wines. Tannic; airing reveals lush cherry and cassis flavors and a rich overlay of fine smoky oak. Seems a natural for the cellar, and could age to greatness by 2010. **90** —*S.H. (10/1/2004)*

Galante 1997 Red Rose Hill Cabernet Sauvignon (Carmel Valley) $28. 91 —*S.H. (2/1/2000)*

GALLEANO

Galleano 1999 Dos Rancheros Zinfandel (Cucamonga Valley) $18. 87 *—S.H. (4/1/2002)*

Galleano NV Old Vines Zinfandel (Cucamonga Valley) $6. Tastes like a Central Valley Port, with over-ripe berry flavors and thick, numbing tannins, although it's not as sweet as Galleano's more expensive Zins. **81** *—S.H. (3/1/2004)*

Galleano 2001 Pioneers Legendary Old Vines Zinfandel (Cucamonga Valley) $16. Pretty much identical with this winery's Dos Rancheros bottling, a sweet wine. If anything, even more tannic, and numbs the palate so that sugar is just about the only thing you can taste. **80** *—S.H. (3/1/2004)*

GALLERON

Galleron 2001 Morisoli Vineyard Cabernet Sauvignon (Rutherford) $100. Very ripe and classic in the sweet black currant, red cherry, cassis, and fine smoky oak flavors and rich, gentle tannins. Very generous in flavor and mouthfeel. A little soft, and drinking well right now. Defines elegance and richness. **90** *—S.H. (10/1/2004)*

Galleron 1999 Morisoli Vineyard Cabernet Sauvignon (Napa Valley) $100. 95 *—S.H. (12/31/2002)*

Galleron 2000 Jaeger Vineyard Merlot (Napa Valley) $32. Soft and gentle, with herb, coffee, and cherry flavors. Oak adds vanilla and smoky notes. The flavors are marvelous, yet you wish the wine had a firmer structure. Finishes dry. **85** *—S.H. (2/1/2005)*

GALLERON LAINE

Galleron Laine 1998 Lo Vecchio Estate Vineyard Chardonnay (Napa Valley) $35. 88 *(7/1/2001)*

GALLO OF SONOMA

Gallo of Sonoma 2000 Barrelli Creek Vineyard Barbera (Alexander Valley) $24. 88 *—S.H. (2/1/2003)*

Gallo of Sonoma 1999 Barelli Creek Cabernet Sauvignon (Alexander Valley) $32. 88 *—S.H. (8/1/2003)*

Gallo of Sonoma 1994 Barrelli Creek Cabernet Sauvignon (Sonoma County) $18. 88 *—S.H. (11/1/1999)*

Gallo of Sonoma 1998 Frei Ranch Vineyard Cabernet Sauvignon (Dry Creek Valley) $30. 90 *—S.H. (8/1/2003)*

Gallo of Sonoma 2000 Reserve Cabernet Sauvignon (Sonoma County) $13. 89 *—S.H. (3/1/2003)*

Gallo of Sonoma 1998 Stefani Vineyard Cabernet Sauvignon (Dry Creek Valley) $30. 91 Editors' Choice *—S.H. (5/1/2003)*

Gallo of Sonoma 2001 Chardonnay (Sonoma County) $11. 86 Best Buy *—S.H. (6/1/2003)*

Gallo of Sonoma 2000 Laguna Vineyard Chardonnay (Russian River Valley) $24. 90 *—S.H. (12/15/2002)*

Gallo of Sonoma 2000 Reserve Chardonnay (Sonoma County) $11. 87 Best Buy *—S.H. (12/15/2002)*

Gallo of Sonoma 1999 Stefani Vineyard Chardonnay (Dry Creek Valley) $23. 91 *—S.H. (2/1/2003)*

Gallo of Sonoma 2001 Two Rock Vineyard Chardonnay (Sonoma Coast) $28. 88 *—J.M. (6/1/2003)*

Gallo of Sonoma 2000 Merlot (Sonoma County) $11. 86 *—S.H. (11/15/2002)*

Gallo of Sonoma 2001 Reserve Merlot (Sonoma County) $11. What a fine wine this is. The plummy, cherry flavors are layered with an edge of sage and other dried herbs, and the tannins are rich but easy. There's real elegance and finesse here. **89** *—S.H. (4/1/2004)*

Gallo of Sonoma 1997 Pinot Noir (Russian River Valley) $12. 87 *(11/15/1999)*

Gallo of Sonoma 1999 Pinot Noir (Sonoma County) $13. 85 *(10/1/2002)*

Gallo of Sonoma 2003 Reserve Pinot Noir (Sonoma Coast) $13. A terrific wine at a giveaway price, this coastal bottling shows a rich, complex texture and is very dry. The flavors unfold one by one on the palate: cherries, cocoa, cola, plums, blackberries, and spices are highlighted by a burst of crisp acids. **89 Best Buy** *—S.H. (10/1/2005)*

Gallo of Sonoma 2000 Reserve Pinot Noir (Sonoma County) $13. 81 *—M.S. (12/1/2003)*

Gallo of Sonoma 1997 Sangiovese (Sonoma County) $11. 87 *—S.H. (12/15/1999)*

Gallo of Sonoma 1999 Barrel Aged Sangiovese (Alexander Valley) $13. 87 *—S.H. (12/1/2002)*

Gallo of Sonoma 1996 Zinfandel (Dry Creek Valley) $11. 86 Best Buy *—M.S. (9/1/1999)*

Gallo of Sonoma 1999 Barrelli Creek Vineyard Zinfandel (Alexander Valley) $22. 88 *—S.H. (2/1/2003)*

Gallo of Sonoma 1999 Frei Ranch Vineyard Zinfandel (Dry Creek Valley) $22. 91 *—S.H. (2/1/2003)*

Gallo of Sonoma 1997 Frei Vineyard Zinfandel (Dry Creek Valley) $19. 84 *(3/1/2001)*

GALLUCIO FAMILY WINERIES

Gallucio Family Wineries 2002 Barile Dolce Chardonnay (North Fork of Long Island) $35. 82 *—J.C. (10/2/2004)*

GAMACHE

Gamache 2003 Syrah (Columbia Valley (WA)) $28. Peppery and a bit meaty or leathery on the nose, this wine then moves into briary, berry fruit on the palate. Pleasant enough, but has a rather light, textureless mouthfeel, making it seem a touch dilute. **84** *(9/1/2005)*

GAN EDEN

Gan Eden 1994 Chardonnay (Sonoma County) $13. 82 *(4/1/2001)*

GARGIULO

Gargiulo 2002 Money Road Ranch Merlot (Oakville) $35. Drinking very dry and pretty tannic now, this Merlot is not at its best. But there's lots of rich, ripe blackberry and cherry fruit. Try cellaring for a few years to let it all come together. **88** *—S.H. (11/1/2005)*

Gargiulo 2000 Aprile Sangiovese (Napa Valley) $25. 88 *—J.M. (9/1/2003)*

GARRETSON

Garretson 2003 The Spainnéach Grenache (Paso Robles) $28. Very good on its own, this wine will challenge chefs due to its unique qualities. It's light-bodied, with an array of candied fruit flavors ranging from raspberries and red cherries to white chocolate powder and vanilla. It's probably technically dry, but seems sweet. **88** *—S.H. (10/1/2005)*

Garretson 2003 The Graosta Mourvèdre (Paso Robles) $28. Tasted along with Garretson's other reds, this one's considerably crisper and livelier in the mouth. It's also drier, with a tobacco and roasted coffee bean edge to the cherries and red plums. The finish is long on cherry fruit. **89** *—S.H. (10/1/2005)*

Garretson 2003 G Red (Central Coast) $20. This is Garretson's least expensive, regional wine, but it's quite good. Based on Mourvèdre, it's creamy smooth, with cherry and cocoa flavors and a streak of earthiness. It's not fruit-driven, and is companionable with a wide range of foods. **87** *—S.H. (10/1/2005)*

Garretson 2004 G White (Central Coast) $18. This Rhône white, which contains Viognier and Roussanne, is flavorful and refreshing. It has flavors of white peach, honeysuckle, and tropical fruits, and is basically dry, although the fruitiness and glycerine give it a honeyed finish. **87** *—S.H. (10/1/2005)*

Garretson 2003 The Celeidh Rosé Blend (Paso Robles) $18. Very robust and full-bodied, jammy, and rich in fresh young cherry, berry, vanilla, and spice flavors. Drinks almost sweet, but it's a dry wine, and a lot of fun. Syrah, Mourvèdre, Grenache, Roussanne. **86** *—S.H. (12/31/2004)*

Garretson 2001 The Aisling Syrah (Paso Robles) $30. A distinctive, eccentric Syrah, due mainly to the aromatics, which are unusually powerful in dried leather, porcini mushroom, and cocoa. You'll find blackberries and black cherries in the mouth, and oak. Bottom line is a soft, dry wine, balanced and complex, showing real terroir. **91** *—S.H. (12/31/2004)*

Garretson 1999 Alban Vineyard The Finné Syrah (Edna Valley) $60. 91 *(11/1/2001)*

Garretson 2003 Mon Amie Bassetti Vineyard Syrah (San Luis Obispo County) $50. Thick and syrupy, with a suggestion of sweetness, this Syrah is jammy and simple, finishing with noticeable alcohol (it's labeled at 16.8%). **82** *(9/1/2005)*

Garretson 2003 The Aisling Syrah (Paso Robles) $30. Combines slightly sweet-tasting cherry fruit with notes of burnt sugar, coffee, and chocolate in an angular wine that's firmly tannic. Picks up a hint of pepper on the finish. **83** *(9/1/2005)*

Garretson 2003 The Bulladoir Syrah (Paso Robles) $65. Too sweet-tasting for our tasters, whether from residual sugar or just the combination of high alcohol and super-ripe fruit. **80** *(9/1/2005)*

Garretson 2003 The Craic Syrah (Central Coast) $30. A bit hot according to some tasters, a bit sweet according to others, this Syrah boasts moderately intense aromas of coffee and berries, flavors of caramel and marshmallow and a tart finish. **83** *(9/1/2005)*

Garretson 2001 Viognier (Santa Ynez Valley) $30. 91 *—J.M. (12/15/2002)*

GARY FARRELL

Gary Farrell 1998 Encounter Bordeaux Blend (Sonoma County) $60. 90 *—D.T. (6/1/2002)*

Gary Farrell 1996 Encounter Pine Mountain Bordeaux Blend (Pine Mountain) $42. 89 *—J.C. (11/1/1999)*

Gary Farrell 2000 Cabernet Sauvignon (Sonoma County) $34. Right now, it shows its tannins and acids strongly, and is relieved only by hints of cherries, plums, and currants. Yet the finish turns ripely sweet. Best after 2010. **88** *—S.H. (11/15/2004)*

Gary Farrell 1999 Hillside Vineyard Selection Cabernet Sauvignon (Sonoma County) $34. 92 *—M.S. (11/15/2002)*

Gary Farrell 1999 Chardonnay (Russian River Valley) $30. 88 *(7/1/2001)*

Gary Farrell 1999 Bien Nacido Vineyard Chardonnay (Santa Barbara County) $30. 85 *(7/1/2001)*

Gary Farrell 2003 Cresta Ridge Vineyard Chardonnay (Russian River Valley) $38. California Chardonnay doesn't get much leaner or tarter than this acid-filled bottling by a vintner known for picking early. The idea is to streamline the wine, so instead of peaches and pineapples, you get minerals, dried herbs, and citrus. It's a good food wine. **88** *—S.H. (11/1/2005)*

Gary Farrell 2002 Rochioli-Allen Vineyards Chardonnay (Russian River Valley) $38. Farrell likes to pick early, and thus trades opulence for acidity, elegance, and possible ageworthiness. Here you'll find a tight, lemony wine, very crisp. The wine is marked by oak and lees, which add flavor and textural nuances, but it remains flinty and austere. **90** *—S.H. (11/15/2004)*

Gary Farrell 2003 Starr Ridge Vineyard Chardonnay (Russian River Valley) $38. This interesting Chard strikes Chablisian notes in the mineral flavors that veer into apples, peaches, and pineapples, and the high natural acidity. The wine trades opulence for a steely, structural elegance, and a complexity in the finish that fascinates. **91** *—S.H. (12/1/2005)*

Gary Farrell 2002 Westside Farms Chardonnay (Russian River Valley) $34. Intense in lemon drop, buttercream, and smoky, buttered toast, with very high acidity, this is a Chard of elegance and power rather than flamboyance. It finishes with a clean note of minerals and gunmetal. **91** *—S.H. (5/1/2005)*

Gary Farrell 1997 Calypso Vineyard Merlot (Russian River Valley) $32. **88** *—J.C. (7/1/2000)*

Gary Farrell 1998 Pinot Noir (Russian River Valley) $30. **89** *(10/1/2000)*

Gary Farrell 2002 Pinot Noir (Russian River Valley) $32. Straddles the line between ripeness and its opposite, with beet, tomato, mint, and cherry flavors. Lean and tart in acids, and light in body, but harmonious. **86** *(11/1/2004)*

Gary Farrell 1999 Pinot Noir (Russian River Valley) $34. **89** *(10/1/2002)*

Gary Farrell 1999 Allen Vineyard Pinot Noir (Russian River Valley) $50. **89** *(10/1/2002)*

Gary Farrell 1997 Allen Vineyard Pinot Noir (Russian River Valley) $NA. Turning brown and orange, and picking up old Pinot notes of dried cherries, potpourri, mocha, and spice, in a very dry, silky, elegantly structured wine. Acids are bright. Pleasant, but not profound. Drink up. **88** *—S.H. (6/1/2005)*

Gary Farrell 2002 Allen Vineyard Hillside Blocks Pinot Noir (Russian River Valley) $50. Monumental, magnificent. Russian River Pinot hardly gets much better. Huge flavors of blackberries, tart red cherries, coffee, cola, cherry tomato, and generous Asian spices, all of it well-oaked, and the acidity is crisp and cleansing. Layered and never stops changing in the glass. This is beautiful now, and should hold and improve through 2008. **94** *—S.H. (5/1/2005)*

Gary Farrell 2000 Olivet Lane Vineyards Pinot Noir (Russian River Valley) $38. **87** *(10/1/2002)*

Gary Farrell 2002 Rochioli Vineyard Pinot Noir (Russian River Valley) $50. There's a masculinity to this Pinot, with its crisp acids, firm body and stony minerality. It possesses a youthful austerity, but with hidden depths. There's a rich core of ripe blackberry and cherry fruit, and oak plays a supporting role. It will not really show well without cellaring. Best after 2008. **91** *—S.H. (11/1/2004)*

Gary Farrell 1997 Rochioli Vineyard Pinot Noir (Russian River Valley) $50. **91** *(10/1/1999)*

Gary Farrell 2002 Rochioli-Allen Vineyards Pinot Noir (Russian River Valley) $60. Paler in color, lighter in body than most of his Russian River neighbors, and higher in acidity, this cherry-infused wine, with its voluptuous coating of oak, is more Pinot-like than the Syrah-like Pinots that are currently critics' darlings. In its youth, it seems awkward, even simple, but could be a keeper. **92** *—S.H. (6/1/2005)*

Gary Farrell 2003 Russian River Selection Pinot Noir (Russian River Valley) $34. Although it's a bit one-dimensional, this is textbook Pinot Noir. It's lightly silky and delicate in the mouth, and dry, with crisp acids carrying flavors of cherries, cola, and spice. **85** *—S.H. (11/1/2005)*

Gary Farrell 2003 Starr Ridge Vineyard Pinot Noir (Russian River Valley) $45. This is the kind of Pinot Noir that is styled in a leaner, tauter, more acidic way meant to complement food and be cellarworthy. Nonetheless the impressive cherry and blackberry flavors are flattering. **90** *—S.H. (11/1/2005)*

Gary Farrell 2000 Encounter Red Blend (Sonoma County) $60. True to the house style, this young, dark wine will not wow you immediately. It's tight now, weighed under by tannins and acidity. Yet there's a succulence in the middle palate that suggests just-ripe black cherries and spicy blackberries. It seems balanced and harmonious enough for extended aging. **90** *—S.H. (9/1/2004)*

Gary Farrell 2004 Redwood Ranch Sauvignon Blanc (Sonoma County) $24. This Sauvignon Blanc certainly is grassy. It's also intensely feline. Acidity, as you might expect, is high, and the finish is dry. This stylish wine will have its fans. **85** *—S.H. (11/1/2005)*

Gary Farrell 2001 Redwood Ranch Sauvignon Blanc (Sonoma County) $20. **87** *(8/1/2002)*

Gary Farrell 2002 Zinfandel (Dry Creek Valley) $24. Here's a Zin that teases with sweet wild berry tart and rhubarb pie flavors, then pulls back at the last minute, leaving behind a peppery scour and acids. Finishes a bit herbal and tannic. **86** *—S.H. (10/1/2004)*

Gary Farrell 2000 Bradford Mountain Vineyard Zinfandel (Dry Creek Valley) $36. **89** *—M.S. (11/1/2002)*

Gary Farrell 1999 Maple Vineyard Zinfandel (Dry Creek Valley) $30. **88** *—D.T. (3/1/2002)*

Gary Farrell 2002 Maple Vineyard Tina's Block Zinfandel (Dry Creek Valley) $36. A most interesting Zin for the exciting line it straddles. Just when you think it's one of those over-the-top residual sweeties, it pulls back. There are a few raisiny notes intermingled with ripe blackberries, but the wine is fully dry, with rich tannins and an earthy finish. **89** *—S.H. (10/1/2004)*

Gary Farrell 2000 Rice Vineyard Zinfandel (Russian River Valley) $27. 87 *—M.S. (11/1/2002)*

GEORIS WINERY

Georis Winery 2000 Cabernet Sauvignon (Carmel Valley) $34. Not quite ripe, with blackberry flavors side by side with earthy tobacco and mushroom. The tannins are firm and a bit hard. A good wine, but pricey for the quality. **85** *—S.H. (5/1/2004)*

GEYSER PEAK

Geyser Peak 1998 Reserve Alexandre Cabernet Blend (Alexander Valley) $45. 90 *—S.H. (9/1/2002)*

Geyser Peak 1997 Cabernet Franc (Sonoma County) $20. 92 *—S.H. (7/1/2000)*

Geyser Peak 2001 Cabernet Sauvignon (Alexander Valley) $18. Plush and sleek, with black currant, cherry, herb, and coffee flavors that are wrapped in gentle but complex tannins. Oak adds smoke and vanilla accents. **89** *—S.H. (11/15/2004)*

Geyser Peak 1999 Cabernet Sauvignon (Sonoma County) $17. 90 *—S.H. (6/1/2002)*

Geyser Peak 2001 Block Collection Kuimelis Vineyard Cabernet Sauvignon (Alexander Valley) $32. This mountain Cab has a very dark color, and the tannins are intense and scouring. Will the core of black cherry and blackberry fruit outlive the tannins? The jury's out, but it merits this score by virtue of its overall class and distinction. If you open it now, decant for as long as you can. **90** *—S.H. (11/15/2004)*

Geyser Peak 1999 Block Collection Kuimelis Vineyard Cabernet Sauvignon (Alexander Valley) $26. 91 *—S.H. (11/15/2002)*

Geyser Peak 1998 Kuimelis Vineyard Cabernet Sauvignon (Alexander Valley) $28. 88 *—S.H. (7/1/2002)*

Geyser Peak 2002 Kumelis Vineyard Cabernet Sauvignon (Alexander Valley) $42. I've been impressed by this wine for years. Made from a high mountain vineyard in the Mayacamas range, it's dense in black currant, cherry, and herb flavors, and well-structured, with a pretty coat of oak. Firm but pliant tannins and good, crisp acids frame the fruit, lending this Cab elegance and subtlety. Should develop well for 10 years. **92 Cellar Selection** *—S.H. (11/1/2005)*

Geyser Peak 2000 Reserve Cabernet Sauvignon (Sonoma County) $40. 91 *(11/1/2003)*

Geyser Peak 1997 Reserve Cabernet Sauvignon (Sonoma County) $40. 91 *—S.H. (12/15/2000)*

Geyser Peak 1998 Vallerga Vineyard Cabernet Sauvignon (Napa Valley) $35. 86 *—S.H. (6/1/2002)*

Geyser Peak 1998 Chardonnay (Sonoma County) $12. 86 *—L.W. (3/1/2000)*

Geyser Peak 2003 Chardonnay (Russian River Valley) $19. Soft and a little thin, with lemondrop flavors and generous oak. This wine is fully dry, and has a pleasant, creamy texture. **85** *—S.H. (10/1/2005)*

Geyser Peak 2002 Chardonnay (Sonoma County) $12. Ripe pear and tropical fruits, a spicy mouthfeel, polished oak and a touch of lees, a creamy texture, a slightly sweet, fruity finish—it's all here. Designed to appeal to popular tastes at an everyday price. **85** *—S.H. (10/1/2004)*

Geyser Peak 2000 Chardonnay (Sonoma County) $12. 84 *—S.H. (5/1/2002)*

Geyser Peak 1998 Chardonnay (Russian River Valley) $20. 88 *(1/1/2000)*

Geyser Peak 2001 Block Collection Ricci Vineyard Chardonnay (Carneros) $21. 89 *—S.H. (6/1/2003)*

Geyser Peak 2003 Reserve Chardonnay (Alexander Valley) $25. Bright, perky fruit stars in this lovely wine. It's ripe in pineapple and tangerine, with a rich, custard and meringue finish, but it's dry and complex. Easy to like. **90 Editors' Choice** *—S.H. (10/1/2005)*

Geyser Peak 2001 Reserve Chardonnay (Alexander Valley) $23. 87 *(11/1/2003)*

Geyser Peak 1997 Reserve Chardonnay (Sonoma County) $23. 87 *(1/1/2000)*

Geyser Peak 2003 Ricci Vineyard Chardonnay (Carneros) $23. A very distinct single-vineyard Chard marked by an array of toasted spice notes. Chinese five-spice flavors frame citrus, fig, lime peel, and apricot flavors that finish with a sweet-and-sour aftertaste. It's soft, dry and balanced. **91 Editors' Choice** *—S.H. (11/1/2005)*

Geyser Peak 1997 Sonoma Valley Chardonnay (Sonoma Valley) $14. 87 Best Buy *—S.H. (7/1/1999)*

Geyser Peak 1998 Johannisberg Riesling (California) $8. 85 Best Buy *—S.H. (9/1/1999)*

Geyser Peak 2001 Reserve Alexandre Meritage (Alexander Valley) $49. The '01 Cabs keep rolling out. This Cabernet blend has some tight tannins that make it dry and astringent right now. It's nowhere near ready. But it should reveal its hearty blackberry and coffee flavors by 2007, and for quite a long time after. **90** *—S.H. (11/1/2005)*

Geyser Peak 2002 Merlot (Alexander Valley) $19. Hot, raw and unbalanced, this is not a successful wine despite good fruity flavor. **81** —*S.H. (11/1/2005)*

Geyser Peak 2000 Merlot (Sonoma County) $17. 85 —*S.H. (8/1/2003)*

Geyser Peak 1997 Merlot (Sonoma County) $16. 86 —*L.W. (12/31/1999)*

Geyser Peak 1999 Block Collection Shorenstein Vineyard Merlot (Sonoma Valley) $26. 87 —*S.H. (11/15/2002)*

Geyser Peak 2001 Block Collection Shorenstein Vineyard Merlot (Sonoma Valley) $26. The winery seems to have held back this Merlot as long as they dared, for it is still a very dry, tannic wine. That said, there's some rich cherry and black currant fruit. It will play off a good steak, or you can try aging it through this decade. **87** —*S.H. (11/1/2005)*

Geyser Peak 2001 Reserve Merlot (Knights Valley) $40. Dry and raspingly tannic, this wine offers little now in the way of fruit. **82** —*S.H. (11/1/2005)*

Geyser Peak 1999 Reserve Merlot (Sonoma County) $40. 93 —*S.H. (11/15/2002)*

Geyser Peak 1997 Reserve Merlot (Sonoma County) $32. 88 —*S.H. (7/1/2000)*

Geyser Peak 2000 Late Harvest Reserve Riesling (Mendocino) $19. 88 —*J.M. (12/1/2002)*

Geyser Peak 2004 Sauvignon Blanc (California) $12. When I was a kid I worked on a farm and baled hay, and this wine brought back memories. Fresh, green grass, sweet dried grass, and lemon and lime aromas lead to intensely fruity flavors that finish too sweet. **84** —*S.H. (12/31/2005)*

Geyser Peak 2002 Sauvignon Blanc (Russian River Valley) $20. 90 Editors' Choice *(11/1/2003)*

Geyser Peak 2001 Sauvignon Blanc (California) $10. 86 —*S.H. (9/1/2002)*

Geyser Peak 1999 Sauvignon Blanc (Sonoma County) $9. 84 —*S.H. (5/1/2000)*

Geyser Peak 2004 Block Collection River Road Ranch Sauvignon Blanc (Russian River Valley) $21. Interesting and aromatic. Notes of honey, apricot, and clover aromas. Quite tight and lean in the mouth, but with mouthwatering flavors of crisp green apple, lime, and mineral. Finishes sharp and wet, with piercing acidity. An individual wine. **90 Editors' Choice** *(7/1/2005)*

Geyser Peak 1997 Shiraz (Sonoma County) $16. 88 —*S.H. (5/1/2000)*

Geyser Peak 2001 Shiraz (Sonoma County) $18. Blackberry, herb, and tobacco flavors drink very dry, and are framed in big, dusty tannins. Might develop with a bit of age. Fine now with short ribs, barbecue. **85** —*S.H. (12/1/2004)*

Geyser Peak 1999 Shiraz (Sonoma County) $17. 82 *(10/1/2001)*

Geyser Peak 2000 Reserve Shiraz (Sonoma County) $46. Soft and supple in tannins, with just a bit of a sandpapery grip, this dry red has sweetly ripe black currant flavors with a coating of spicy oak and hints of soy sauce. Doesn't appear to have the stuff to age, so drink now. **86** *(9/1/2005)*

Geyser Peak 1998 Reserve Shiraz (Sonoma County) $40. 86 *(11/1/2001)*

Geyser Peak 2003 Block Collection Preston Vineyard Viognier (Dry Creek Valley) $19. Takes a controlled approach to a variety that is often over the top. You'll find the usual exotic tropical fruit and ripe peach notes, but they're trimmed with sour citrus, and the acidity helps maintain balance. Dry and elegant, this wine defines the possibilities of upscale Viognier. **90** —*S.H. (11/15/2004)*

Geyser Peak 2000 Block Collection Sonoma Moment Viognier (Alexander Valley) $19. 90 —*J.M. (12/15/2002)*

Geyser Peak 1997 Zinfandel (Sonoma County) $16. 84 *(5/1/2000)*

Geyser Peak 1996 Zinfandel (Sonoma County) $20. 86 *(1/1/2000)*

Geyser Peak 2002 Block Collection Lopez Vineyard Zinfandel (Cucamonga Valley) $30. An old-style Zin from this old growing region near L.A. It's rustic, with intense mocha and berry flavors that drink a little sweet. Soft in acids, it's an interesting wine to pair with food. **86** —*S.H. (12/15/2004)*

Geyser Peak 2001 Block Collection, Sandy Lane Vineyard Zinfandel (Contra Costa County) $30. 88 *(11/1/2003)*

Geyser Peak 1997 Winemaker's Selection Zinfandel (Cucamonga Valley) $30. 89 *(1/1/2000)*

GIACINTO

Giacinto 1999 Red Blend (Sonoma County) $30. 86 —*S.H. (12/1/2002)*

GIRARD

Girard 1999 Bordeaux Blend (Napa Valley) $40. 92 Editors' Choice —*S.H. (11/15/2002)*

Girard 2002 Cabernet Franc (Napa Valley) $40. Dry and firm and well-structured, this Cab Franc offers a complex array of fruit, herb, earth, and oak notes, and that elusive drink-me-again quality. **91** —*S.H. (7/1/2005)*

Girard 1997 Chardonnay (Napa Valley) $28. 86 *(6/1/2000)*

Girard 2000 Chardonnay (Russian River Valley) $24. 89 *—J.M. (5/1/2002)*

Girard 2003 Petite Sirah (Napa Valley) $24. Classic Petite Sirah, full-bodied, rich, totally dry, very tannic and fruity. So good now with something big, like short ribs, that it will be difficult to cellar, but this is a wine that will soften and sweeten over many years. And what a finish, long in ripe, wild blackberries, cherries, and coffee. **92 Cellar Selection** *—S.H. (12/1/2005)*

Girard 2000 Petite Sirah (Napa Valley) $24. 87 *—S.H. (12/1/2002)*

Girard 2002 Napa Valley Red Wine Red Blend (Napa Valley) $40. A blend of all five Bordeaux varieties, this is a balanced, harmonious wine, although it's light in flavor and soft texture for a Napa Cabernet-based claret. Because it's not all that rich, it will do best against simpler fare, such as a standing rib roast or beef carpaccio. **86** *—S.H. (12/31/2005)*

Girard 2003 Sauvignon Blanc (Napa Valley) $15. This refreshingly crisp, clean wine comes from one of California's most consistent Sauvignon Blanc producers. It's rich in ripe citrus, juicy green apple and spicy fig flavors, with a smooth, honeyed finish. **88** *—S.H. (12/1/2004)*

Girard 2000 Sauvignon Blanc (Napa Valley) $15. 90 *—J.C. (5/1/2002)*

Girard 2001 Zinfandel (Napa Valley) $24. **91 Editors' Choice** *(11/1/2003)*

USA

GIRARDET

Girardet 1999 Reserve Baco Noir (Umpqua Valley) $32. 85 *—P.G. (4/1/2002)*

Girardet 2000 Pinot Gris (Umpqua Valley) $12. 85 *—P.G. (8/1/2002)*

Girardet 1998 Barrel Select Pinot Noir (Umpqua Valley) $16. 82 *—M.S. (12/1/2000)*

Girardet 1999 Premiere Cuvée Pinot Noir (Umpqua Valley) $59. 87 *—P.G. (8/1/2002)*

Girardet 1998 Reserve Pinot Noir (Umpqua Valley) $35. 88 *—J.C. (12/1/2000)*

Girardet 2001 Estate Riesling (Umpqua Valley) $8. **87 Best Buy** *—P.G. (8/1/2002)*

GLACIER'S END

Glacier's End NV Merlot (North Fork of Long Island) $10. **85 Best Buy** *—J.C. (3/1/2002)*

GLASS MOUNTAIN

Glass Mountain 1999 Cabernet Sauvignon (California) $10. **87 Best Buy** *—C.S. (11/15/2002)*

Glass Mountain 1999 Syrah (California) $10. 87 *—J.C. (9/1/2002)*

GLEN ELLEN

Glen Ellen 1998 Reserve Cabernet Sauvignon (California) $7. 83 *—S.H. (12/15/2000)*

Glen Ellen 2000 Proprietor's Reserve Gamay (Sonoma) $NA. 82 *—S.H. (9/1/2002)*

Glen Ellen 1998 Reserve Merlot (California) $7. 83 *(6/1/2001)*

Glen Ellen 1998 Reserve White Zinfandel (California) $7. 83 *—S.H. (2/1/2001)*

GLEN FIONA

Glen Fiona 1998 Syrah (Walla Walla (WA)) $40. 88 *—P.G. (9/1/2000)*

Glen Fiona 2000 Bacchus Vineyard Syrah (Columbia Valley (WA)) $20. 84 *(10/1/2001)*

Glen Fiona 1997 Basket Press Reserve Syrah (Walla Walla (WA)) $55. 93 *—P.G. (11/15/2000)*

Glen Fiona 1999 Puncheon Aged Syrah (Walla Walla (WA)) $40. 86 *(11/1/2001)*

GLENORA

Glenora 1998 Brut Champagne Blend (Finger Lakes) $15. 86 *—J.M. (12/1/2002)*

Glenora 2002 Riesling (Finger Lakes) $21. 85 *—J.C. (8/1/2003)*

Glenora 2002 Dry Riesling (Finger Lakes) $10. 86 *—J.C. (8/1/2003)*

Glenora 2000 Dry Riesling (Finger Lakes) $9. 84 *—J.C. (6/19/2003)*

Glenora 2000 Vintner's Select Riesling (Finger Lakes) $15. Made from handpicked fruit from a single vineyard, this wine is a huge step up from Glenora's regular bottling. The bright green-apple aromas and flavors feature delicate touches of diesel and lime and finish crisp and tart. Just off-dry, with a light, lively feel in the mouth that would work well with Asian cuisine. **87** *—J.C. (1/1/2004)*

GLORIA FERRER

Gloria Ferrer 1990 Carneros Cuvée Brut LD (Carneros) $32. 88 *—S.H. (12/15/1999)*

Gloria Ferrer 1992 Royal Cuvée Brut (Carneros) $22. 88 *—S.H. (12/1/2000)*

Gloria Ferrer 1991 Royal Cuvée Brut (Carneros) $20. 89 *—J.C. (12/1/1999)*

Gloria Ferrer 1998 Chardonnay (Carneros) $20. 88 *(6/1/2000)*

Gloria Ferrer 2001 Chardonnay (Carneros) $18. **89** *—S.H. (12/1/2003)*

Gloria Ferrer 1998 Merlot (Carneros) $23. **81** *—J.M. (12/1/2001)*

Gloria Ferrer 2002 Pinot Noir (Carneros) $26. Weak and tart, with cola, herb, and mocha flavors. Finishes watery and diluted. **84** *(11/1/2004)*

Gloria Ferrer 1999 Pinot Noir (Carneros) $24. **84** *(10/1/2002)*

Gloria Ferrer 2002 Etesian Pinot Noir (Sonoma County) $12. Light color, almost orange at the rim, and delicate and simple, this wine shows spicy cola and cherry soda flavors, with good acidity. **85** *(11/1/2004)*

Gloria Ferrer 2000 Rust Rock Terrace Vineyard Pinot Noir (Carneros) $40. Great Carneros Pinot. Fabulously ripe fruity flavors range from raspberries through cherries and currants, sprinkled with cinnamon and nutmeg. Sweet and earthy, like espresso with brown sugar. Totally dry, and silky all the way down. **93** *—S.H. (3/1/2004)*

Gloria Ferrer 2000 Blanc de Blancs (Carneros) $22. **90** *—S.H. (12/1/2003)*

Gloria Ferrer NV Blanc de Noirs (Sonoma County) $18. **87** *—S.H. (12/1/2003)*

Gloria Ferrer NV Brut Rosé (Carneros) $35. **90** *—S.H. (12/1/2003)*

Gloria Ferrer 1995 Carneros Cuvée (Carneros) $50. Very dry, apparently with a low dosage, which makes those bony acids stick out ever more. Pretty austere now, showing little beyond intense citrus, yeast, and char. Such is the balance that it's likely to age well. Hold through 2006, then try again. **91** *—S.H. (12/31/2004)*

Gloria Ferrer 1996 Royal Cuvée Brut (Carneros) $24. Beginning to show its age as the fruit drops. Picking up crushed mineral, dried lime, vanilla, and hints of dusty herbs, but still vibrant and fresh. Should continue to do interesting things over the years. **89** *—S.H. (12/31/2004)*

Gloria Ferrer NV Brut (Sonoma County) $18. Tasty bubbly here, a smooth, polished wine with pronounced lime, raspberry, and vanilla flavors complexed with yeast and smoke. Dry and vibrant, this is easy to drink. **86** *—S.H. (12/31/2004)*

Gloria Ferrer 2001 Syrah (Carneros) $22. With its green and herbal notes on the nose that pick up hints of mint and spice, this is not a fruit-driven Syrah. Rather, it relies on spice and herb, buoyed along by cherry fruit. Turns a bit hard on the finish. Age and risk the fruit drying out, or drink young and deal with the tannins? **85** *(9/1/2005)*

GNEISS

Gneiss 2000 Reserve Cabernet Sauvignon (Napa Valley) $39. **87** *—S.H. (11/15/2003)*

GODSPEED

Godspeed 1999 Cabernet Sauvignon (Mount Veeder) $31. Good fruit and oak on this black currant-scented Cab, but the tannins are rough and numbing, even at five-plus years. Doesn't seem likely to soften before the fruit falls out, so drink up. **85** *—S.H. (5/1/2005)*

GODWIN

Godwin 2000 Moss Oak Vineyard Merlot (Alexander Valley) $35. A Merlot-based blend that's extraordinarily soft and charming. It has lush flavors of chocolate, blackberry pie, coffee, and spicy oak, and smooth, gentle tannins. As sweetly fruity as it is, it could use more structure. **86** *—S.H. (12/31/2004)*

GOLD DIGGER CELLARS

Gold Digger Cellars 2000 Chardonnay (Washington) $15. **82** *—P.G. (2/1/2002)*

GOLD HILL

Gold Hill 1999 Cabernet Sauvignon (El Dorado) $25. **86** *—S.H. (9/1/2002)*

GOLDEN VALLEY

Golden Valley 1997 St. Herman's Vineyard Chardonnay (Willamette Valley) $15. **88** *—P.G. (9/1/2000)*

GOLDENEYE

Goldeneye 2001 Pinot Noir (Anderson Valley) $48. What perfume! Delicate but insistent oaky char and vanilla hit first, followed by raspberry, cherry, cola, and cotton candy. The beautifully silky, light texture reveals sweet raspberry and cherry flavors, tinged with vanilla and cinnamon. Uncommonly beguiling and delicious. **92** *—S.H. (8/1/2004)*

Goldeneye 1999 Pinot Noir (Anderson Valley) $45. **93** *—S.H. (5/1/2002)*

GOLDSCHMIDT

Goldschmidt 2001 Game Ranch Cabernet Sauvignon (Oakville) $65. Dark, oaky, very dry, and tannic in youth, this well-structured Cab needs time. Those tannins sting and shut down the middle palate, but the bright blackberry and cherry fruit shines through. Should hold and improve for five years in a cool cellar. **91** *—S.H. (12/15/2005)*

Goldschmidt 2000 Vyborny Vineyard Cabernet Sauvignon (Alexander Valley) $65. This tough vintage presented the difficulty of achieving ripeness with balance. This wine struggles, but does pretty well. It's a wine to drink now, with its edge of black currant, enhanced with oak, that fades fairly quickly. **90** *—S.H. (2/1/2004)*

GOOSE RIDGE

Goose Ridge 1999 Cabernet Sauvignon-Merlot (Columbia Valley (WA)) $39. **86** *—C.S. (12/31/2002)*

Goose Ridge 2002 Chardonnay (Columbia Valley (WA)) $21. This is really heavy on the vanilla-flavored oak. Buttered nuts and popcorn, it's all here, but the fruit gets buried. **85** *—P.G. (11/15/2004)*

Goose Ridge 2001 Chardonnay (Columbia Valley (WA)) $18. Big, buttery aromas fly out of the glass, but behind them you'll find sweet, ripe fruit, with mixed flavors of apple, banana, and peach. Smooth stuff. **88** *—P.G. (9/1/2004)*

Goose Ridge 2001 Vireo Red Wine Red Blend (Columbia Valley (WA)) $30. A third each of Cabernet, Merlot, and Syrah, this challenging wine just fails to shed its tough, chewy, tannic wrapping. There are some pleasant herbal accents, but the rough tannins and unintegrated, slightly bitter barrel flavors don't offer much pleasure. **85** *—P.G. (11/15/2004)*

Goose Ridge 2002 Syrah (Columbia Valley (WA)) $25. Coffee, cola, and cedar upfront, followed by hints of game and white pepper. Vanilla and caramel notes surge forward on the finish. Dominated by oak, but with just enough savory fruit character to keep it afloat. **88** *(9/1/2005)*

Goose Ridge 2000 Syrah (Columbia Valley (WA)) $26. A silky, satiny Syrah that seduces with its vivid, powerful fruit and pleasing oak. The entry is soft and sweet, and the wine opens up to fill the palate with juicy ripe fruit leading into flavors of toasted coconut and milk chocolate. **91 Editors' Choice** *—P.G. (1/1/2004)*

USA

GOOSECROSS

Goosecross 1998 Chardonnay (Napa Valley) $22. **88** *(6/1/2000)*

Goosecross 1999 Syrah (California) $25. **85** *(11/1/2001)*

GORDON BROTHERS

Gordon Brothers 1999 Cabernet Sauvignon (Columbia Valley (WA)) $22. **87** *—P.G. (9/1/2002)*

Gordon Brothers 1999 Estate Grown Chardonnay (Columbia Valley (WA)) $20. **88** *—P.G. (7/1/2002)*

Gordon Brothers 1998 Tradition Red Wine Red Blend (Columbia Valley (WA)) $50. **88** *—P.G. (12/31/2001)*

Gordon Brothers 2002 Syrah (Columbia Valley (WA)) $18. Schizophrenic juice, which starts off herbal and green—bordering on asparagus—before settling down and delivering coffee, dill, blackberry, and vanilla flavors on a creamy-textured mouthfeel. Then it thins out on the finish, fading to lemony acids. **84** *(9/1/2005)*

Gordon Brothers 1999 Estate Syrah (Columbia Valley (WA)) $30. **82** *(11/1/2001)*

GRAND CRU

Grand Cru 2002 Sauvignon Blanc (California) $8. **84 Best Buy** *—S.H. (12/15/2003)*

GRANDE RONDE

Grande Ronde 2000 Seven Hills Vineyard Cabernet Sauvignon (Walla Walla (WA)) $40. **86** *—P.G. (12/31/2003)*

Grande Ronde 1999 Seven Hills Vineyard Merlot (Walla Walla (WA)) $40. **85** *—P.G. (12/31/2003)*

GRANITE SPRINGS

Granite Springs 1999 Petite Sirah (El Dorado) $20. **88** *—S.H. (9/1/2002)*

Granite Springs 2000 Syrah (Fair Play) $18. **87** *—S.H. (2/1/2003)*

Granite Springs 2001 Zinfandel (El Dorado) $30. **84** *(11/1/2003)*

GRANVILLE

Granville 2000 Holstein Vineyard Pinot Gris (Oregon) $16. **80** *—P.G. (2/1/2002)*

GRAVITY HILLS

Gravity Hills 2002 Killer Climb Syrah (Paso Robles) $45. This big, solidly built wine's flavors revolve around darker notes of coffee, game, and tar, There's enough dark fruit to flesh out the midpalate with blackberry and plum before the finish turns tannic and drying. Drink young with a rare hunk of steak. **87** *(9/1/2005)*

GRAYSON

Grayson 2003 Cabernet Sauvignon (Paso Robles) $10. Soft in both tannins and acids, this Cab has upfront juicy flavors of black cherries and mocha, and is fully dry. It's a nice, easy-drinking red wine. **84** *—S.H. (12/1/2005)*

Grayson 2004 Chardonnay (North Coast) $10. Soft and simple, with decent peach and banana flavors, this Chard has a creamy texture and a dry, spicy finish. **83** *—S.H. (12/1/2005)*

GRAZIANO

Graziano 2001 Coro Mendocino Red Blend (Mendocino) $35. Bright and fresh tasting, with moderate tannins that surround a core of blackberry, cherry, coffee, and spice flavors. The finish is moderate in length, with a slightly drying edge. **87** *—J.M. (9/1/2004)*

GREAT WESTERN

Great Western NV Brut (New York) $10. **81** *—S.H. (12/31/2000)*

Great Western NV Extra Dry (New York) $10. 80 *—S.H. (6/1/2001)*

GREEN & RED

Green & Red 1998 Chiles Mill Vineyard Zinfandel (Napa Valley) $22. 89 *—P.G. (2/1/2001)*

GREENWOOD RIDGE

Greenwood Ridge 1999 Cabernet Sauvignon (Mendocino Ridge) $30. 92 *—S.H. (5/1/2002)*

Greenwood Ridge 1999 Du Pratt Vineyard Chardonnay (Mendocino Ridge) $24. 90 *—S.H. (5/1/2002)*

Greenwood Ridge 1997 Merlot (Mendocino Ridge) $24. 90 *—S.H. (3/1/2000)*

Greenwood Ridge 2001 Merlot (Mendocino Ridge) $25. From a winery that shows a deft hand at everything it tackles, a concentrated, young Merlot. Distinctive for its rich acids as well as the deep core of blackberry and coffee flavors and firm tannins. **88** *—S.H. (10/1/2004)*

Greenwood Ridge 2003 Pinot Grigio (Anderson Valley) $16. Very dry to the point of tartness, with a lemony, citrusy flavor, but it's enriched with a touch of spicy fig and apricot. After you swallow, the palate feels fresh, with a clean, spicy finish. This is a great cocktail or food wine. **87** *—S.H. (10/1/2004)*

Greenwood Ridge 2003 Pinot Noir (Mendocino Ridge) $25. You'll find crisp, bright acids framing very dry flavors of cherries, coffee, cola, and rhubarb in this cool-climate wine. It's not a lush, fleshy Pinot, but one that celebrates its rather austere, elegant structure. **87** *—S.H. (12/31/2005)*

Greenwood Ridge 2000 Pinot Noir (Mendocino Ridge) $30. 86 *—S.H. (5/1/2002)*

Greenwood Ridge 2002 Estate Pinot Noir (Mendocino Ridge) $25. This is a dark, fairly tannic Pinot, with flavors of blue and black stone fruits and berries, and neutral oak. It's acidic and very dry. Not showing much finesse, but a good wine. **85** *—S.H. (3/1/2005)*

Greenwood Ridge 2000 Riesling (Mendocino Ridge) $12. 91 Best Buy *—S.H. (5/1/2002)*

Greenwood Ridge 1998 Sauvignon Blanc (Anderson Valley) $12. 89 *—L.W. (11/1/1999)*

Greenwood Ridge 2002 Sauvignon Blanc (Anderson Valley) $16. 90 *—S.H. (12/15/2003)*

Greenwood Ridge 2004 Sémillon (Anderson Valley) $16. This variety doesn't have much of an identity in California, and this wine doesn't clarify things. It's very dry and clean and austere in citrus fruits, with a wash of fig, sort of like a Sauvignon Blanc. **86** *—S.H. (12/31/2005)*

Greenwood Ridge 2002 White Riesling (Mendocino Ridge) $15. 89 *—S.H. (12/31/2003)*

Greenwood Ridge 1998 Estate Bottled White Riesling (Mendocino County) $NA. 88 *(8/1/2000)*

Greenwood Ridge 1998 Zinfandel (Sonoma County) $21. 90 *—S.H. (2/1/2000)*

GREY FOX

Grey Fox NV Butte County Cabernet Sauvignon (California) $10. 83 *—S.H. (2/1/2000)*

Grey Fox NV Merlot (Napa Valley) $20. 84 *—S.H. (3/1/2000)*

GRGICH HILLS

Grgich Hills 2001 Cabernet Sauvignon (Napa Valley) $55. You could drink this classic Cab now, tannic as it is, because any wine this balanced and fine can be appreciated. Better to leave it be for five or ten years. It's a dramatic wine, dense in black currants and black cherries, with a crème de cassis-like unctuousness. Oak has been judiciously applied. After all the new kids on the block have come and gone, Grgich Hills still stands. **93** *—S.H. (11/15/2005)*

Grgich Hills 1999 Cabernet Sauvignon (Napa Valley) $50. 92 *—S.H. (5/1/2003)*

Grgich Hills 1997 Yountville Selection Cabernet Sauvignon (Napa Valley) $95. Despite its age, this wine still is pretty tannic, but the worse problem is a vegetal character. There's a suggestion of canned asparagus despite scads of oak. Not going anywhere. **84** *—S.H. (2/1/2005)*

Grgich Hills 2002 Chardonnay (Napa Valley) $35. Crisp and dry, a minerally wine with earthy, citrus flavors and a firm structure. For a little richness, there's a streak of peach on the finish. **85** *—S.H. (6/1/2005)*

Grgich Hills 2000 Chardonnay (Napa Valley) $33. 91 *—S.H. (12/15/2002)*

Grgich Hills 2001 Carneros Selection Chardonnay (Napa Valley) $58. Really spectacular for its concentration and the sheer intensity of the way the fruit, oak and lees flood the palate, yet crisp, balanced and elegant. Mango, papaya, peach, pineapple, vanilla, buttered toast, the works. All comes together in the long, spicy finish. **93** *—S.H. (12/31/2004)*

Grgich Hills 2003 Estate Dry Fumé Blanc (Napa Valley) $26. After the sulfur blows off, you'll find a clean, crisp wine of great structure and balance. Firmly acidic, with well-ripened flavors of lime, fig, and spicy melon. Picks up rich subtleties through the finish. **88** *—S.H. (12/15/2004)*

Grgich Hills 2001 Private Reserve Style Fumé Blanc (Napa Valley) $18. 85 *—S.H. (7/1/2003)*

Grgich Hills 2001 Merlot (Napa Valley) $46. Ripe, with rich black cherry and mocha flavors, but achieves real complexity and finesse in the structure. Rich acids and lush, sweet tannins provide the underlying architecture. Dry and flamboyant, and drinking well now. **91** *—S.H. (12/15/2004)*

Grgich Hills 1999 Merlot (Napa Valley) $38. **89** *—S.H. (8/1/2003)*

Grgich Hills 2000 Violetta Late Harvest White Blend (Napa Valley) $50. **93 Editors' Choice** *—S.H. (12/1/2002)*

Grgich Hills 1996 Zinfandel (Sonoma) $20. **92** *—M.S. (11/1/1999)*

Grgich Hills 2001 Zinfandel (Napa Valley) $29. Brings a Cabernet-like balance to this often over-the-top variety, with lush tannins framing fully ripened wild berry, pepper and coffee flavors. Fully dry, with adequate tannins, and soft in acidity, it will make a fine complement to barbecue. **87** *—S.H. (2/1/2005)*

Grgich Hills 1998 Zinfandel (Sonoma County) $28. **88** *—P.G. (3/1/2001)*

Grgich Hills 1997 Zinfandel (Sonoma County) $20. **89** *—S.H. (5/1/2000)*

USA

GRIFFIN CREEK

Griffin Creek 1999 Cabernet Sauvignon (Rogue Valley) $35. **87** *—P.G. (4/1/2002)*

Griffin Creek 2000 Merlot (Rogue Valley) $30. Dark and tannic, with a sappy streak of cherry surrounded by strong flavors of herb, tar, licorice, and smoke. A big and strongly flavorful wine in a distinctive style peculiar to southern Oregon. **86** *—P.G. (8/1/2005)*

Griffin Creek 1998 Merlot (Rogue Valley) $40. **85** *—P.G. (11/1/2001)*

Griffin Creek 2001 Pinot Gris (Rogue Valley) $18. **81** *—M.S. (12/31/2002)*

Griffin Creek 1999 Pinot Noir (Rogue Valley) $35. **88** *—P.G. (4/1/2002)*

Griffin Creek 2000 Syrah (Rogue Valley) $33. **86** *—M.S. (9/1/2003)*

Griffin Creek 1998 Syrah (Rogue Valley) $35. **87** *(11/1/2001)*

Griffin Creek 2002 Viognier (Rogue Valley) $25. This wine opens with a very appealing bouquet of tropical and citrus scents, highlighted by tangerine and orange peel. The citrus circus continues in the mouth, mixing lemon and lime, orange and mango, with enough acid to keep it lively and the right note of a tannic edge at the borderline. **88** *—P.G. (2/1/2005)*

GRISTINA

Gristina 1998 Cabernet Franc (North Fork of Long Island) $22. **85** *—J.C. (4/1/2001)*

Gristina 1999 Chardonnay (North Fork of Long Island) $20. **85** *—J.C. (4/1/2001)*

Gristina 2000 Apaucuck Chardonnay (Long Island) $10. **87 Best Buy** *—J.M. (7/1/2002)*

Gristina 1998 Andy's Field Merlot (North Fork of Long Island) $27. **89** *—J.C. (4/1/2001)*

GROTH

Groth 1996 Cabernet Sauvignon (Napa Valley) $40. **92** *—L.W. (11/1/1999)*

Groth 2001 Cabernet Sauvignon (Oakville) $50. Tighter and earthier than many '01 Napa Cabs, and not offering as much decadent enjoyment, although its still a pretty good wine. Full-bodied and oaky, with a touch of raisins. **86** *—S.H. (2/1/2005)*

Groth 1998 Sauvignon Blanc (Napa Valley) $14. **90** *—L.W. (11/1/1999)*

GROVE STREET

Grove Street 2001 Cabernet Sauvignon (Alexander Valley) $12. There's real finesse and flavor in this soft, supple wine. It shows plush blackberry, cherry, and herb flavors wrapped in rich but easy tannins. This is a decent price for a wine of this quality. **86** *—S.H. (10/1/2004)*

Grove Street 2001 Chardonnay (Sonoma County) $7. Why break the bank for everyday occasions? This fruity, oaky Chard will do just fine. It's clean, with the taste of peaches. **84** *—S.H. (6/1/2004)*

Grove Street 2001 Pinot Noir (Russian River Valley) $13. The aroma is a bit musty, but fortunately, there are prettier scents of cherries and spicy vanilla. Tastes a lot richer and cleaner than it smells. **84** *—S.H. (6/1/2004)*

GRUET

Gruet 1996 Blanc de Blancs Champagne Blend (New Mexico) $22. **88 Editors' Choice** *—M.M. (12/1/2001)*

Gruet 2000 Cuvée Gilbert Gruet Pinot Noir (New Mexico) $24. **81** *(10/1/2002)*

GRYPHON

Gryphon 2000 Reserve Pinot Noir (Anderson Valley) $65. Quite delicate in structure, a pale wine with light, silky tannins and adequate acidity. The flavors are modulated, suggesting strawberries, cherry cola, rhubarb, root beer, and coffee. It's rather one-sided now, but may surprise with age. **88** *—S.H. (8/1/2004)*

GUENOC

Guenoc 2002 Cabernet Sauvignon (California) $11. Green and stemmy, with a sharp cut of acidity, and a cherry medicine finish. **82** *—S.H. (8/1/2005)*

Guenoc 1999 Beckstoffer IV Cabernet Sauvignon (Napa Valley) $55. **84** *—S.H. (11/15/2003)*

Guenoc 1997 Reserve Beckstoffer IV Vineyar Cabernet Sauvignon (Napa Valley) $41. **90** *(11/1/2000)*

Guenoc 1998 Chardonnay (North Coast) $16. **87** *(6/1/2000)*

Guenoc 1998 Genevieve Magoon Reserve Chardonnay (Guenoc Valley) $30. **86** *(6/1/2000)*

Guenoc 1999 Genevieve Magoon Vineyard Reserve Tutu Chardonnay (Guenoc Valley) $40. **91** *(7/1/2001)*

Guenoc 2001 Petite Sirah (North Coast) $18. This Petite Sirah isn't showing well now, unless you're a fan of big, dark, inky, tannic, dry, heavy red wines. It does have deep cherry and blackberry flavors. **83** *—S.H. (12/1/2005)*

Guenoc 2000 Serpentine Meadow Petite Sirah (Guenoc Valley) $35. A huge wine, yet balanced and even elegant. Filled with ripe cherries, blackberries, grilled meat, white chocolate, and smoky oak, and sturdy in tannins, although they're soft and sweet. Delicious now, and should age effortlessly through this decade. **92** *—S.H. (3/1/2005)*

Guenoc 2000 Vintage Port (Guenoc Valley) $30. A delicious dessert wine, dark ruby in color, and super-aromatic with caramelized wood, black currant, chocolate, and vanilla notes. The chocolate fudge, blackberry tart, and spicy gingerbread flavors are intense. Very sweet, yet balanced with acidity. Makes you think of winter fireplaces, chocolate truffles, and someone special. **94** *—S.H. (2/1/2005)*

Guenoc 1997 Sauvignon Blanc (North Coast) $13. **85** *—L.W. (9/1/1999)*

Guenoc 2000 Estate Selection Sauvignon Blanc (North Coast) $15. **90 Editors' Choice** *(8/1/2002)*

Guenoc 2001 Zinfandel (California) $12. **87 Best Buy** *(11/1/2003)*

GUILLIAMS

Guilliams 2004 *Barrel Sample* Cabernet Sauvignon (Napa Valley) $NA. Starts out intense, nervous, and taut with acidity and tannins, but is very concentrated in fresh blackberry-cherry fruit. Should age well. **92** *—S.H. (8/1/2004)*

GUNDLACH BUNDSCHU

Gundlach Bundschu 2002 Rhinefarm Vineyard Cabernet Sauvignon (Sonoma Valley) $32. The vineyard is on the border of Sonoma Valley and Carneros, and this complex Cab shows signs of warm and cool influences. The fruit is rich in cassis, currant, and cocoa, but there's a firm tannin and acid structure that gives balance. It's not an ager, so drink now. **89** *—S.H. (12/1/2005)*

Gundlach Bundschu 1998 Rhinefarm Vyds Chardonnay (Sonoma Valley) $18. **85** *(6/1/2000)*

Gundlach Bundschu 1998 Rhinefarm Vineyard Merlot (Sonoma Valley) $26. **85** *—J.M. (12/1/2001)*

Gundlach Bundschu 1999 Rhinefarm Vineyard Pinot Noir (Sonoma Valley) $26. **87** *—S.H. (7/1/2002)*

Gundlach Bundschu 2001 Rhinefarm Vineyard Zinfandel (Sonoma Valley) $32. **90** *(11/1/2003)*

GYPSY DANCER

Gypsy Dancer 2002 Gary & Christine's Vineyard Pinot Noir (Oregon) $34. Not much fruit to be found here, just lots of dried herbs and pungent spices. There are barrel flavors of vanilla and cocoa, and a lean, tannic finish. **83** *(11/1/2004)*

H. GRAY

H. Gray 1999 Cabernet Sauvignon (Yountville) $25. **92 Editors' Choice** *—S.H. (8/1/2003)*

H. Gray 2001 Bad Boy Zinfandel (Amador County) $20. If you call your wine "Bad Boy," you'd better back it up with some bad-ass flavor. This is a nice enough wine, but hardly "bad." Somewhat candy-like, with cherry cough syrup and spice up front and hints of smoke and licorice on the finish. A bit cloying at the end. **82** *—J.M. (4/1/2004)*

HACIENDA

Hacienda 1999 Clair de Lune Cabernet Sauvignon (California) $7. **83** *—S.H. (11/15/2002)*

Hacienda 2002 Clair de Lune Merlot (California) $7. Lots of juicy, tutti-fruity flavor in this dry, easy wine. Blackberries, cherries, cocoa, and even a little dab of smoky oak. **84 Best Buy** *—S.H. (12/31/2004)*

Hacienda 2002 Clair de Lune Sauvignon Blanc (California) $7. Clean and zesty, an easy wine with lemon and lime flavors spiced up with an edge of pepper. There's a tad of sugary ripeness that makes it mellow. **83** *—S.H. (12/1/2004)*

HAGAFEN

Hagafen 1999 Cabernet Sauvignon (Napa Valley) $36. **84** *—J.M. (7/1/2002)*

Hagafen 2001 Estate Bottled Cabernet Sauvignon (Napa Valley) $40. A nice, user-friendly California Cabernet, with bold cassis, blackberry, and vanilla aromas and similar flavors, underscored by a dose of tobacco. Supple tannins shine on the finish, which features a heavy dose of vanilla. **88** *—J.C. (4/1/2005)*

Hagafen 2000 Chardonnay (Napa Valley) $18. **86** *—S.H. (9/1/2002)*

Hagafen 2002 Estate Bottled Merlot (Napa Valley) $27. Intensely oaky, with powerful vanilla aromas and flavors that come close to swamping the modest black cherry fruit. Creamy-textured on the palate, with a touch of dried spices on the finish. **84** *—J.C. (4/1/2005)*

Hagafen 2004 Sauvignon Blanc (Napa Valley) $15. Opens with a great big burst of freshly sliced grapefruit sprinkled with cinnamon and nutmeg, and tastes just as crisply refreshing. The citrusy fruit and bright acidity clean the palate, preparing it for food. **88** *—S.H. (10/1/2005)*

Hagafen 2001 Brut Cuvée Sparkling Blend (Napa Valley) $30. Robust and elegant, this bubbly has Chardonnay flavors of peaches, while Pinot Noir gives it a cherry tinge and a fuller body. It's crisp in acids, and finishes with a fine bread dough taste and pronounced sweetness that's almost off-dry. **86** *—S.H. (12/31/2005)*

Hagafen 2001 Syrah (Napa Valley) $27. Lots of smoky, toasty oak here, with just barely enough cherry-scented fruit to support it. Nice velvety texture on the finish, though. **85** *—J.C. (4/1/2005)*

Hagafen 1999 Syrah (Napa Valley) $NA. **90** *(11/1/2001)*

HAHN

Hahn 2002 Meritage Bordeaux Blend (Central Coast) $20. A pretty good blend of all five Bordeaux grapes, dominated by Merlot, and marked by effusively fruity aromas and flavors. The fruit is conjoined with well-toasted oak that adds caramel and smoky, spicy notes. Very satisfying, with enough tannins to warrant a few years of aging. **88** *—S.H. (6/1/2004)*

Hahn 2003 Cabernet Sauvignon (Central Coast) $14. Extremely ripe in cherry, blackberry, currant, and cocoa fruit, this wine is excessively soft, and has a baked cherry sweetness on the finish. Yet it's easy to drink and enjoyable. **83** *—S.H. (11/1/2005)*

Hahn 2001 Cabernet Sauvignon (Central Coast) $12. **84** *—S.H. (6/1/2003)*

Hahn 2003 Chardonnay (Monterey) $14. Flamboyant tropical fruit flavors star in this polished, likeable wine. Pineapples, mangos, melons, peaches, and spicy pears, with a dollop of vanilla and buttered toast, all in a creamy texture. **86** *—S.H. (6/1/2005)*

Hahn 2001 Chardonnay (Monterey) $12. **86** *—S.H. (6/1/2003)*

Hahn 1999 Meritage (Santa Lucia Highlands) $18. **87** *(9/1/2002)*

Hahn 2003 Merlot (Monterey) $14. Rich and oaky, this Merlot features flavors of blackberries, cherries, and chocolate, although it's fully dry and not too powerful in alcohol. This is a good price for a full-bodied red of this class. **88** *—S.H. (11/1/2005)*

Hahn 2001 Merlot (Monterey) $12. **86** *—S.H. (8/1/2003)*

Hahn 2002 Syrah (Central Coast) $14. The rough edges are smoothed and softened by the ripeness of the cherry and blackberry fruit and a nice touch of smoky oak. Finishes dry and clean, a good food wine. **84** *—S.H. (10/1/2004)*

HALL

Hall 2002 Cabernet Sauvignon (Napa Valley) $35. This is certainly a big wine, almost brawny in blackberry and currant fruit. It's probably laboratory dry, although the ripeness creates the impression of jam. A bit rough in tannins, it may benefit from a few years of cellaring. **86** *—S.H. (10/1/2005)*

Hall 2002 Merlot (Napa Valley) $28. This Merlot is a little over-ripe, to judge by the raisiny note that shows up in the finish, but the main core of black cherries and cocoa is delicious. The tannins are thick, soft, sweet, ripe and easy. **86** *—S.H. (11/15/2005)*

Hall 2004 Sauvignon Blanc (Napa Valley) $20. You might mistake this for one of those Marlboroughs, so rich is it in gooseberry, green hay and lemon-and-lime flavors. The acidity isn't at New Zealand levels, but it's fine for this dry, likeable, and super-versatile wine. **86** *—S.H. (11/15/2005)*

HALLAUER

Hallauer 2002 Syrah (Santa Ynez Valley) $21. Roasted fruit aromas are joined by notes of tar on the nose. The palate deals creamy blueberry and vanilla flavors. One taster found it a little sweet; another indicates the unlikelihood of it lasting too long in the cellar. 350 cases produced. **87** *(9/1/2005)*

HALO

Halo 1997 Cabernet Sauvignon (Napa Valley) $125. **93** *—S.H. (12/1/2001)*

HAMACHER

Hamacher 1999 Cuvée Forets Diverses Chardonnay (Oregon) $25. **89** *—P.G. (8/1/2002)*

Hamacher 1997 Willamette Valley Pinot Noir (Willamette Valley) $30. **91** *(10/1/1999)*

USA

HAMES VALLEY VINEYARDS

Hames Valley Vineyards 2001 Cabernet Sauvignon (Monterey) $19. There are some good black currant and blackberry flavors here, although the tannins are quite tough and dry. They leave a puckery, hard feeling through the finish. **84** *—S.H. (10/1/2004)*

Hames Valley Vineyards 2003 Sauvignon Blanc (Monterey) $15. Heavy and full-bodied, with citrus, currant, and herb flavors. Finishes very dry, with a scour of acidity. **84** *—S.H. (10/1/2004)*

HANDLEY

Handley 1995 Blanc de Blancs (Anderson Valley) $30. **86** *—S.H. (12/15/2000)*

Handley 1998 Brut (Anderson Valley) $29. **89** *—S.H. (12/1/2003)*

Handley 1997 Brut (Anderson Valley) $29. **88** *—S.H. (12/1/2002)*

Handley 1995 Brut (Anderson Valley) $25. **88** *—S.H. (12/1/2000)*

Handley 1997 Brut Rosé (Anderson Valley) $28. **89** *(6/1/2001)*

Handley 1998 Chardonnay (Dry Creek Valley) $20. **85** *(6/1/2000)*

Handley 2001 Chardonnay (Anderson Valley) $16. **88** *—S.H. (8/1/2003)*

Handley 1999 Chardonnay (Anderson Valley) $17. **85** *—S.H. (11/15/2001)*

Handley 2003 Handley Vineyard Chardonnay (Dry Creek Valley) $18. Polished and elegant, this Chard has real complexity. Works beautifully to integrate its dry apple, peach, and pineapple flavors, oak-driven cream and crisp acids into a coherent whole. **91** *—S.H. (10/1/2005)*

Handley 1999 Handley Vineyard Chardonnay (Dry Creek Valley) $19. **86** *—S.H. (11/15/2001)*

Handley 2002 Gewürztraminer (Anderson Valley) $15. **85** *—S.H. (12/31/2003)*

Handley 2000 Gewürztraminer (Anderson Valley) $14. **85** *—S.H. (11/15/2001)*

Handley 2001 Pinot Gris (Anderson Valley) $16. **86** *—S.H. (9/1/2003)*

Handley 1999 Pinot Gris (Anderson Valley) $16. **87** *—S.H. (8/1/2001)*

Handley 1999 Pinot Mystére Pinot Meunier (Anderson Valley) $20. **83** *—S.H. (11/15/2001)*

Handley 2002 Pinot Noir (Mendocino County) $18. A nice little commune-style Pinot, with a bit of polish and complexity. The cherry and spice flavors are dry, with an edge of tannins. **85** *—S.H. (11/1/2004)*

Handley 2001 Pinot Noir (Anderson Valley) $25. This vintage the grapes got nice and ripe, and it shows in the lush cherry and black raspberry flavors. They're enriched with oak, and the bright acids and easy tannins add a firm structural component to this drinkable wine. **87** *—S.H. (4/1/2004)*

Handley 1999 Pinot Noir (Anderson Valley) $26. **88** *—S.H. (7/1/2002)*

Handley 2001 Estate Reserve Pinot Noir (Anderson Valley) $23. Sharp in acids, with dusty tannins and a silky texture, the fruit in this pretty wine reminds you of raspberries and red cherries, along with herbs and pepper. While not particularly complex, it's elegant and food-friendly. **89** *—S.H. (12/1/2004)*

Handley 1998 Reserve Pinot Noir (Anderson Valley) $48. **88** *—S.H. (12/15/2001)*

Handley 2003 Rosé Pinot Noir (Mendocino County) $NA. Shows its Pinot origins in the body, which is fat and firmly flavored with raspberries and tobacco. Dry and attractive, this blush wine is robust enough to enjoy with lamb chops. **85** *—S.H. (12/1/2004)*

Handley 2002 Riesling (Mendocino) $12. **87** *—J.M. (8/1/2003)*

Handley 2001 Ferrington Vineyard Sauvignon Blanc (Anderson Valley) $14. **90** *—S.H. (3/1/2003)*

Handley 1999 Ferrington Vineyard Sauvignon Blanc (Anderson Valley) $14. **88** *—S.H. (11/15/2001)*

Handley 2002 Handley Vineyard Sauvignon Blanc (Dry Creek Valley) $15. Hews to the profile of previous vintages with its citrus, fig, herb, and green apple flavors, with hints of dried straw. The crisp acids and slight note of honey balance each other out, making it tasty and balanced as well as food-friendly. **86** *—S.H. (2/1/2004)*

Handley 2002 Zinfandel (Redwood Valley) $20. This easy, soft Zin gives lots of pleasure. It features berry, candied Lifesaver and spicy flavors, with gentle tannins lasting into a long finish. **86** *—S.H. (2/1/2005)*

Handley 2000 Williams Vineyard Zinfandel (Anderson Valley) $26. **86** *—S.H. (5/1/2002)*

HANNA

Hanna 1996 Cabernet Sauvignon (Sonoma County) $21. **90** *(11/15/1999)*

Hanna 1999 Cabernet Sauvignon (Alexander Valley) $25. **86** *—S.H. (6/1/2002)*

Hanna 2001 Bismark Mountain Vineyard Cabernet Sauvignon (Sonoma Valley) $61. From one of the highest vineyards in Sonoma County, this is a tannic wine, although the tannins, in the modern style, are soft and intricate. It's oaky, soft, and quite extracted, with a black currant syrup mouthfeel. **85** *—S.H. (11/1/2005)*

Hanna 2001 Estate Grown Cabernet Sauvignon (Sonoma County) $27. A bit soft and herbal, with hints of tobacco, dried herbs, cherries, and leather, and dry, easy tannins. That makes it sound like a classic Cab from this Sonoma County appellation. It's easy to drink, but that doesn't mean it doesn't possess some interesting complexities. **88** *—S.H. (6/1/2004)*

Hanna 2001 Chardonnay (Russian River Valley) $18. 87 *—S.H. (12/1/2003)*

Hanna 2002 Estate Grown Chardonnay (Russian River Valley) $18. Here's a crowd pleaser, with its ripe, almost tropical fruit flavors that burst beyond peaches and pears into papaya and an overlay of smoky oak,. Mouthfeel is creamy; it's a complex sipper, and clean as a whistle. **89** *—S.H. (6/1/2004)*

Hanna 1999 Merlot (Alexander Valley) $25. 88 *—S.H. (9/1/2002)*

Hanna 1997 Proprietor Grown Merlot (Sonoma County) $22. 84 *—J.C. (6/1/2001)*

Hanna 2002 Estate Grown Pinot Noir (Russian River Valley) $27. Starts off very oaky, with underlying notes of strawberries, cherries, and earthy mushrooms. Tasters liked its delicate body, creamy texture, and elegant finish. **85** *(11/1/2004)*

Hanna 1998 Sauvignon Blanc (Russian River Valley) $12. 85 *—S.H. (11/1/1999)*

Hanna 1999 Reserve Sauvignon Blanc (Russian River Valley) $24. 88 *—S.H. (9/1/2002)*

Hanna 2001 Slusser Road Vineyard Sauvignon Blanc (Russian River Valley) $16. 85 *—S.H. (9/1/2003)*

Hanna 1999 Bismark Ranch Syrah (Sonoma Valley) $48. A disappointing wine that opens with starkly unripe, vegetal aromas and never quite overcomes its tough herbaceousness. It's very dry, with rasping tannins and an astringent finish. Tasted twice. **82** *—S.H. (8/1/2005)*

Hanna 1997 Bismark Ranch Zinfandel (Sonoma Valley) $45. 88 *—P.G. (3/1/2001)*

Hanna 2001 Proprietor Grown Zinfandel (Alexander Valley) $46. 89 *—J.M. (11/1/2003)*

HANZELL

Hanzell 2001 Chardonnay (Sonoma Valley) $55. A fabulous and exciting Chard. It's a big wine, with powerful pear, tropical fruit, and oriental spice flavors, and well oaked. But it's balanced with clean acidity, and feels elegant all the way through. This is a wine with a history of aging well. Drink now, but will hold and improve for at least ten years. **94** *—S.H. (12/31/2004)*

Hanzell 1997 Chardonnay (Sonoma Valley) $42. 92 *—S.H. (11/15/2000)*

Hanzell 2000 Pinot Noir (Sonoma Valley) $75. The acids hit you first. They perk up a creamy wine with pleasant flavors of cherries, cola, mocha and spice. It's dry and balanced. The impression is of a lovely Pinot that combines delicacy and elegance with power. Drink now and over the next four years. **90** *—S.H. (2/1/2005)*

Hanzell 1997 Pinot Noir (Sonoma Valley) $50. 94 Cellar Selection *—S.H. (12/15/2001)*

HARBINGER

Harbinger 2001 Merlot (Napa Valley) $14. There's lots of plummy richness in this dry, smooth red wine. It also has inviting flavors of cassis, mocha, and cherry, and is finished with oak-barrel notes of spicy vanilla and toast. Acids and tannins show up on the finish. **86** *—S.H. (5/1/2004)*

HARGRAVE

Hargrave 1999 Chardonnay (North Fork of Long Island) $14. Despite the winery's rechristening as Castello di Borghese, this is the Hargrave label, which was used for the 1999 vintage. Pear-nectar and clove aromas and flavors turn slightly appley, then lemony on the abbreviated finish. **83** *—J.C. (1/1/2004)*

Hargrave NV Chardonette (North Fork of Long Island) $7. 83 *—J.C. (4/1/2001)*

Hargrave 1999 Merlot (North Fork of Long Island) $18. Starts off okay, with black cherries and caramel, but with air, a sour pine-resin note takes over the aromas and flavors. Finishes with more caramel and some dusty cranberries. **81** *—J.C. (1/1/2004)*

Hargrave 1998 Pinot Noir (North Fork of Long Island) $35. 84 *—J.C. (4/1/2001)*

Hargrave 1999 Sauvignon Blanc (North Fork of Long Island) $11. 85 *—J.C. (4/1/2001)*

HARLAN ESTATE

Harlan Estate 1999 Red Blend (Napa Valley) $200. 96 *—J.M. (7/1/2003)*

HARLEQUIN

Harlequin 2003 Sundance Vineyard Syrah (Columbia Valley (WA)) $28. A north-facing vineyard gives grapes extended hang time and moderates the high Wahluke heat. It's 100% Syrah, 30% whole cluster fermented in 20% new French oak. Good, juicy, with very tart, snappy cranberry/raspberry flavors. Lovely nuances of wet earth, black tea and soy. A substantial, ageworthy effort. **91** *—P.G. (12/15/2005)*

Harmonique 2002 Delicacé Pinot Noir (Anderson Valley) $48. Of Harmonique's two Pinots, this is the more "Burgundian." It's paler in color and ineffably silky, with a mélange of cherry, cola, beetroot, and tobacco flavors, and a nice mushroomy earthiness. Could develop for a few more years. **90** —*S.H. (11/1/2005)*

HARMONY CELLARS

Harmony Cellars 2002 Zinfandel (Paso Robles) $18. Tough, bone dry, and gritty in tannins, with astringent berry skin flavors and a hint of leather and raisins on the finish. Drink now. **84** —*S.H. (8/1/2005)*

HARRINGTON

Harrington 2002 Hirsch Vineyard Pinot Noir (Sonoma Coast) $54. A lovely wine, pale in color and delicate as silk. It's dry and crisp in acids, with a wonderful array of red cherry, cola, candied ginger, rosehip tea, vanilla, spice, and smoky oak flavors. Feels light as a feather on the palate, yet lingers long and rich on the finish. **93** —*S.H. (8/1/2005)*

HARRISON

Harrison 1999 Reserve Cabernet Sauvignon (Napa Valley) $100. **91** —*S.H. (11/15/2003)*

Harrison 2000 Reserve Chardonnay (Napa Valley) $45. Harrison seems to have put as much oak on their Chard as they do on their Cabernets. Opens with the powerful perfume of toasted wood, wood sap, caramel, and vanilla cookie. Far below is a good wine with citrusy, appley fruit and good acidity. **85** —*S.H. (8/1/2004)*

Harrison 2001 Merlot (Napa Valley) $40. A brilliant Merlot that excites for the way it straddles the line between ultra-ripe fruit and more subtle, earthy tones. The taste of perfectly ripened cherries is sweet and pure, and mingles with plums, peppery spice, and green olives. The oak is heavy, but this wine loves it. Finally, the tannins are fabulously sweet and rich. **93** —*S.H. (8/1/2004)*

Harrison 2001 Claret Red Blend (Napa Valley) $37. Olives, oak, cassis, and cocoa star in the aroma. Turns a bit tough in the mouth, with cherry, blackberry, and earthy flavors. The tannins and sweet fruit in the finish suggest age worthiness. Important to decant well in advance if you drink it now. **89** —*S.H. (3/1/2005)*

Harrison 2001 Syrah (Napa Valley) $33. The Northern Rhône is the model here. Opens with a burst of white pepper and blackberry flavors, well oaked, and turns rich, big and long in the mouth, with powerful blackberry, cherry, and oak flavors. The tannins are pronounced and negotiable. Probably best now. **91** —*S.H. (3/1/2005)*

HART WINERY

Hart Winery 2002 Syrah (South Coast) $24. One of the most pleasant surprises of this tasting was how well the wines from Hart, a small winery located in Temecula, performed. This effort boasts wonderfully complex aromas of cedar, bacon fat, and cherries, round, mouthfilling flavors and a long, crisp finish. **89** *(9/1/2005)*

Hart Winery 1998 Syrah (Temecula) $24. **85** *(11/1/2001)*

HARTFORD

Hartford 2000 Chardonnay (Sonoma Coast) $22. **90** *(7/1/2002)*

Hartford 1999 Laura's Chardonnay (Sonoma Coast) $54. **93** *(7/1/2001)*

Hartford 1999 Seascape Vineyard Chardonnay (Sonoma County) $46. **87** *(7/1/2001)*

Hartford 1999 Stone Côte Vineyard Chardonnay (Sonoma County) $33. **91** *(7/1/2001)*

Hartford 2000 Pinot Noir (Sonoma Coast) $25. **89** *(8/1/2003)*

Hartford 1999 Arrendell Vineyard Pinot Noir (Russian River Valley) $65. **92** *(7/1/2002)*

Hartford 2000 Dutton-Sanchietti Pinot Noir (Russian River Valley) $50. **93** *(8/1/2003)*

Hartford 1999 Marin Pinot Noir (Marin County) $50. **92 Cellar Selection** *(7/1/2002)*

Hartford 2000 Sevens Bench Vineyard Pinot Noir (Carneros) $50. **92 Cellar Selection** *(8/1/2003)*

Hartford 2000 Velvet Sisters Vineyard Pinot Noir (Anderson Valley) $50. **91** *(8/1/2003)*

Hartford 1999 Zinfandel (Russian River Valley) $34. **91** *(7/1/2002)*

Hartford 2001 Fanucchi-Wood Road Vineyard Zinfandel (Russian River Valley) $34. **92** *(11/1/2003)*

Hartford 1999 Hartford Vineyard Zinfandel (Russian River Valley) $34. **93 Editors' Choice** *(7/1/2002)*

Hartford 1999 Highwire Vineyard Zinfandel (Russian River Valley) $34. **93** *(7/1/2002)*

HARTWELL

Hartwell 2000 Cabernet Sauvignon (Stags Leap District) $100. **93** —*S.H. (11/15/2003)*

Hartwell 2001 Estate Grown Cabernet Sauvignon (Stags Leap District) $115. Rich, creamy, and lush on the palate, with loads of cassis that just roll on and on through the velvety finish. But is no simple fruit bomb—it also delivers plenty of dried herb and tobacco complexity wrapped in toast and vanilla. Drink now—2015. **93** —*J.C. (10/1/2004)*

Hartwell 1997 Sunshine Vyd Cabernet Sauvignon (Stags Leap District) $95. **93** *(11/1/2000)*

Hartwell 2000 Merlot (Stags Leap District) $60. **91** —*J.M. (11/15/2002)*

HARVEST MOON

Harvest Moon 2002 Pitts Home Ranch Zinfandel (Russian River Valley) $28. What a beauty. Soft and lush, yet firm in the mouth, with a lovely mélange of wild black cherry, cocoa, pepper, and leather flavors. Finishes with a ripe note of sweet raisiny cassis. For all the sweetness, it's dry and balanced. **93** *—S.H. (8/1/2005)*

HATCHER

Hatcher 2002 Estate Zinfandel (Calaveras County) $18. Nice Zin, balanced and dry, with an easy, sillky mouth feel. Shows upfront spice, berry, cherry and coffee flavors. Notable for its harmony. **88** *—S.H. (3/1/2005)*

HAUER OF THE DAUEN

Hauer of the Dauen 1998 Estate Bottled Pinot Noir (Willamette Valley) $14. **81** *—J.C. (12/1/2000)*

HAVENS

Havens 2003 Albariño (Carneros) $24. Sort of Pinot Grigio-like, with its tart, lemon and apple flavors and crisp acidity. Seems a bit simple at first blush, but that zesty acidity makes the mouth water and long for food, like chevre or grilled veggies. **85** *—S.H. (10/1/2004)*

Havens 2001 Merlot (Napa Valley) $24. This is a full-bodied Merlot, dark and fairly tannic, with young acids undergirding flavors of currants, black cherries, and dark bitter chocolate. It's hard now, and will wake up with a good piece of meat, but should soften with a few years of age. **87** *—S.H. (6/1/2005)*

Havens 2000 Reserve Merlot (Carneros) $32. This fine Merlot has many interesting features. The flavors are very complex, mingling fruits, berries, spices, herbs, and oak. It's a tannic, dry wine, but balanced and harmonious. It lacks the stuffing for aging, and will be best over the next few years. **88** *—S.H. (10/1/2004)*

Havens 2002 Syrah (Napa Valley) $24. Creamy and full-bodied, with lush coffee notes accented by blackberries and pepper, finishing on a wiry, herbal note. One reviewer found some rubbery, meaty notes that detracted from the overall experience. Drink now. **87** *(9/1/2005)*

Havens 2000 Syrah (Napa Valley) $24. **90** *—S.H. (12/1/2003)*

Havens 1999 Hudson T Reserve Syrah (Napa Valley) $45. **93** *—S.H. (7/1/2002)*

Havens 2000 Hudson Vineyard Syrah (Carneros) $45. This is a good wine from a less-than-successful vintage. The blackberry flavors have a raw, unfinished edge that liberal oak cannot sweeten. There's also a streak of tart acidity that leads to a dry, puckery finish. **86** *—S.H. (5/1/2004)*

HAWK CREST

Hawk Crest 1996 Cabernet Sauvignon (California) $9. **83** *—S.H. (11/1/1999)*

Hawk Crest 2000 Cabernet Sauvignon (California) $14. **82** *—S.H. (8/1/2003)*

Hawk Crest 2002 Chardonnay (California) $11. Okay Chard for everyday purposes, with decent fruit flavors. It's dry, clean, and tart on the finish. **83** *—S.H. (6/1/2004)*

Hawk Crest 1998 Chardonnay (California) $10. **83** *—S.H. (2/1/2001)*

Hawk Crest 1998 Vineyard Selection Chardonnay (California) $15. **88** *(6/1/2000)*

Hawk Crest 2001 Merlot (California) $14. You get a lot for your bucks with this dry, full-bodied red wine. It has pleasant flavors of plums, cherries, and herbs, with rich, supportive tannins and a fruity, oaky finish. **85** *—S.H. (6/1/2004)*

Hawk Crest 1996 Vineyard Select Reserve Merlot (California) $16. **82** *—L.W. (9/1/1999)*

HAWLEY

Hawley 2001 Cabernet Sauvignon (Dry Creek Valley) $28. Opens with a sulfury smell that's slow to blow off, masking the underlying blackberry aroma. In the mouth, it's quite extracted and jammy in berry fruit, yet the tannins are tough and astringent. Drinks like a simple country wine. **84** *—S.H. (5/1/2004)*

Hawley 2004 Chardonnay (Russian River Valley) $21. There's plenty of ripe fruit in this wine, but it tastes kind of aggressive in oak, with scads of toast and vanilla-woodsap flavors that aren't really needed, since the pineapple, pear, and peach flavors are delicious by themselves. It would be interesting to try this unoaked. **84** *—S.H. (12/31/2005)*

Hawley 2001 Bradford Mountain Merlot (Dry Creek Valley) $26. This interesting wine takes your basic berry-cherry Merlot flavors and boosts them with more complex notes of sweet sweaty leather, olives, and violets. There's also an elaborate layering of smoky oak. I wish the wine were a little firmer in acidity, but it's very nice. **86** *—S.H. (11/1/2005)*

Hawley 1999 Bradford Mountain Merlot (Dry Creek Valley) $24. **88** *—S.H. (11/15/2002)*

Hawley 2002 Oehlman Vineyard Pinot Noir (Russian River Valley) $32. Rather earthy and wanting fruit. Lots of leather and cedar, a tough, chewy wine that reveals cherries on the finish. **84** *(11/1/2004)*

Hawley 2004 Viognier (Placer County) $20. This Sierra Foothills wine is fruity enough, even semisweet, in flowery peach and vanilla flavors, but there's a rough-hewn edge that tells you it's a rustic wine. **83** *—S.H. (11/1/2005)*

Hawley 2001 Viognier (Placer County) $21. 85 *—S.H. (12/15/2002)*

HAYMAN & HILL

Hayman & Hill 2004 Reserve Selection Chardonnay (Russian River Valley) $14. Lots of toasty oak on this very dry wine, and a big burst of citrusy acids. In fact the fruit veers toward lemons, limes, and grapefruits, just nudging into riper green apples and peaches. 85 *—S.H. (12/15/2005)*

Hayman & Hill 2003 Reserve Pinot Noir (Edna Valley) $14. This Pinot is a good value. It shows lots of panache in the elegantly silky mouthfeel, dryness, crisp acids and subtle flavors of cherries, spices, and oak. Feels classy in the mouth, and is a good ambassador of its cool-climate appellation. 86 *—S.H. (7/1/2005)*

Hayman & Hill 2002 Reserve Selection Shiraz-Viognier (Monterey County) $14. The 7% Viognier goes a long way. The big, bright boost of citrus and acidity dominates. The Syrah itself is soft and plummy-chocolaty, with a smear of tannins. 84 *—S.H. (12/15/2005)*

Hayman & Hill 2001 Reserve Selection Zinfandel (Dry Creek Valley) $15. 88 *(11/1/2003)*

HAYWOOD

Haywood 1999 Vintner's Select Chardonnay (California) $10. 82 *—S.H. (8/1/2001)*

Haywood 1998 Vintner's Select Merlot (California) $10. 82 *—M.S. (7/1/2000)*

Haywood 1996 Los Chamizal Estate Rocky Terr Zinfandel (Sonoma Valley) $23. 92 *—S.H. (11/1/1999)*

Haywood 1998 Los Chamizal Vineyard Zinfandel (Sonoma County) $20. 88 *—S.H. (8/1/2001)*

Haywood 1998 Rocky Terrace Zinfandel (Sonoma County) $35. 86 *—S.H. (8/1/2001)*

HDV

HdV 2002 Chardonnay (Carneros) $55. This is an elegant, minerally Chard, whose primary features are lime, green grapes, and steel flavors, and brisk, tangy acids. Its leanness is partially alleviated by oak, which brings cream and smoke. The finish is elegant and penetrating. 89 *—S.H. (5/1/2005)*

HdV 2001 Red Blend (Carneros) $65. They pulled out all the stops, starting with fully ripened grapes that give huge blackberry, cassis, cherry, and plum flavors. Elaborate oak adds even more sweet notes, and modern tannin management results in a very soft, elaborate mouthfeel. This stylish Merlot-Cabernet blend has lots of appeal. 91 *—S.H. (5/1/2004)*

HdV 2002 Syrah (Carneros) $48. This is a dark, dense wine that smells better than it tastes. Aromas are of dusty black pepper, pure cassis, wild blackberry, smoky oak, and a hint of smoked meat or leather. The opulent flavors are of intense cassis and cherry, and the tannins are beautifully soft and complex. My gripe, and it's a big one, is a sugary sweetness that makes the wine almost cloying. 86 *—S.H. (9/1/2004)*

HEALDSBURG

Healdsburg 2001 Cabernet Sauvignon (California) $8. 84 *—S.H. (11/15/2003)*

Healdsburg 2001 Merlot (California) $8. 84 *—S.H. (12/1/2003)*

HEALDSBURG VITICULTURAL SOCIETY

Healdsburg Viticultural Society 2002 Reserve Cabernet Sauvignon (Dry Creek Valley) $13. Defines a style entirely separate from Napa's. Has those rustic Dry Creek tannins and even a briary edge to the blackberries and cherries, and is totally dry. Well-made and elegant. 88 *—S.H. (11/15/2004)*

HEDGES

Hedges 1997 Three Vineyards Bordeaux Blend (Columbia Valley (WA)) $21. 90 *—S.H. (4/1/2000)*

Hedges 1999 Red Mountain Reserve Cabernet Sauvignon (Columbia Valley (WA)) $42. 94 Editors' Choice *—P.G. (6/1/2002)*

Hedges 2001 Three Vineyards Red Wine Cabernet Sauvignon-Merlot (Red Mountain) $18. An estate grown cabernet (56%) merlot (44%) blend, from the winery whose efforts spearheaded the successful campaign to certify Red Mountain as an AVA. Big, dark, and toasty, with roasted flavors, like black cherries soaked in bourbon, augmented with pepper and barrel spice. Flavorful and balanced, with pretty scents of orange peel. 90 Best Buy *—P.G. (12/1/2004)*

Hedges 1998 Fumé Chardonnay (Columbia Valley (WA)) $9. 88 *—S.H. (2/1/2000)*

Hedges 2001 CMS Red Blend (Columbia Valley (WA)) $10. 89 Best Buy *—P.G. (11/15/2003)*

Hedges 2002 CMS Red Wine Red Blend (Columbia Valley (WA)) $12. Cabernet, merlot, syrah, and cab franc are the C, M and S in the name. Strong roasted coffee scents set off the brisk entry; the syrah seems to juice up the fruit while the cabs punch up the tannins. There are a lot of smoky, roasted flavors, and the wine has a good solid grip. Very tasty and appealing. 89 Best Buy *—P.G. (12/1/2004)*

Hedges 1998 Red Mountain Reserve Red Blend (Columbia Valley (WA)) $45. 92 *(10/1/2001)*

Hedges 1998 Three Vineyards Red Blend (Columbia Valley (WA)) $22. 91 Editors' Choice *(10/1/2001)*

Hedges 2002 Bel Villa Estate North Block Syrah (Red Mountain) $75. On the leaner, more structured side of things, which might have penalized it in our tasting format, but which also may bode well for future development. Smoke, vanilla, and toast accent bright raspberry and mineral shadings, finishing with some dry, astringent tannins. **86** *(9/1/2005)*

Hedges 2000 White Blend (Columbia Valley (WA)) $9. 90 Best Buy *—P.G. (10/1/2001)*

HEITZ

Heitz 2000 Cabernet Sauvignon (Napa Valley) $35. Big and rugged, with blackberry and herb flavors that finish very dry and tannic. A blend from various parts of Napa Valley. **84** *—S.H. (11/15/2004)*

Heitz 1994 Trailside Cabernet Sauvignon (Napa Valley) $49. 89 *(3/1/2000)*

HELLER ESTATE

Heller Estate 2003 Estate Chardonnay (Carmel Valley) $22. From a warmish Monterey County appellation comes this soft, creamy Chard. It has pretty flavors of very ripe white peaches and apricots, drizzled with vanilla, and seems a little sweet. **85** *—S.H. (11/1/2005)*

Heller Estate 2002 Toby's Vintage Merlot Port (Carmel Valley) $35. Drinks very sweet, with caramel, fudge, cherry marmalade, and vanilla flavors. The balance is a little off, but with a wedge of double chocolate cake, no one will care. **87** *—S.H. (11/1/2005)*

HENDRY

Hendry 2001 Red Wine Bordeaux Blend (Napa Valley) $30. A delicious and balanced wine that suggests the greatness of this vintage. It hits the mouth with firm, dusty tannins, and then the flavors explode. You'll find blackberries, cherries, and currants, intensely sweet and concentrated, and lavish but appropriate new oak. Finishes with an acidic verve that suggests aging. A blend of all five classic Bordeaux varieties. **93** *—S.H. (5/1/2004)*

Hendry 1999 Block 8 Cabernet Sauvignon (Napa Valley) $40. 90 *—S.H. (11/15/2003)*

Hendry 2002 Blocks 19 & 20 Chardonnay (Napa Valley) $25. This soft wine has an earthiness to it, with nuances of yellow stone fruits, but it's more about herbs. Finishes quick. **85** *—S.H. (12/15/2004)*

Hendry 2000 Blocks 19 and 20 Chardonnay (Napa Valley) $25. 92 *—S.H. (12/15/2002)*

Hendry 2000 Blocks 9 and 21 Chardonnay (Napa Valley) $25. 91 *—S.H. (12/15/2002)*

Hendry 2001 Blocks 4 & 5 Pinot Noir (Napa Valley) $27. This is a big, rich wine, with substantial tannins and quite a bit of body. It feels like it was grown in a warmer climate, with its plummy, black and blue fruit flavors. But it has a velvety softness that makes it enjoyable now. **86** *—S.H. (4/1/2004)*

Hendry 1999 Hendry Vineyard Pinot Noir (Napa Valley) $27. 92 *—S.H. (9/1/2003)*

Hendry 2002 Hendry Ranch Red Blend (Napa Valley) $30. This Bordeaux blend is firm in the mouth, exhibiting rich tannins, and a full-bodied dryness. However the flavors are spectacularly up front, featuring ripe cassis and black currant, milk chocolate, vanilla, and a toasted smokiness from oak. Addictively good wine. **91** *—S.H. (8/1/2005)*

Hendry 2000 Block 28 Zinfandel (Napa Valley) $28. 91 *—S.H. (9/1/2003)*

Hendry 2002 Block 7 Zinfandel (Napa Valley) $27. A rich, lush, round wine that's quite fruit forward, showing plenty of black cherry, plum, strawberry, chocolate, herb, spice, and blueberry flavors. Extremely soft textured, yet structured. A sexy, plush style that's long on the finish. **90** *—J.M. (12/31/2004)*

Hendry 2000 Block 7 Zinfandel (Napa Valley) $20. 91 *—S.H. (9/1/2003)*

Hendry 1997 Block 7 Zinfandel (Napa Valley) $20. 83 *—P.G. (11/15/1999)*

HENEHAN HILLS

Henehan Hills 2001 Zinfandel (Dry Creek Valley) $19. Solidy rustic, the kind of country wine you fall in love with at that B&B, then discover it's not as good as when you drank it gazing over the vineyard. Dry, earthy-fruity, and acidic. **84** *—S.H. (8/1/2005)*

HENRY ESTATE

Henry Estate 1999 Gewürztraminer (Umpqua Valley) $10. 82 *—P.G. (11/1/2001)*

Henry Estate 2001 Müller-Thurgau (Umpqua Valley) $9. 88 Best Buy *—P.G. (8/1/2002)*

Henry Estate 2002 Pinot Noir (Umpqua Valley) $18. Smoky, beet, and bark, with some vanilla. Light, dry, thin. **83** *(11/1/2004)*

Henry Estate 1999 Pinot Noir (Oregon) $51. 87 *(10/1/2002)*

Henry Estate 1998 Barrel Select Pinot Noir (Umpqua Valley) $25. 87 *—P.G. (8/1/2002)*

Henry Estate 2001 Umpqua Cuvee Pinot Noir (Umpqua Valley) $39. 82 *—M.S. (8/1/2003)*

Henry Estate 1999 Henry the V Red Blend (Umpqua Valley) $23. 86 *—P.G. (8/1/2002)*

HERMANN J. WIEMER

Hermann J. Wiemer 1997 Cuvée Brut 2000 (Finger Lakes) $23. **84** *(12/31/2000)*

HERON

Heron 2002 Cabernet Sauvignon (California) $11. Smells pleasantly interesting and complex, with a delicate interplay of blackberry, oak, and white pepper, but there's a letdown in the mouth. There, the wine turns sharp and acidic, although dry. Drink now. **83** *—S.H. (12/15/2005)*

Heron 2003 Chardonnay (California) $11. A great value in Chard at this price for its ripe, up front flavors of pineapples and pears, creamy smooth texture and spicy finish. There's a lot of oak, too. **85 Best Buy** *—S.H. (8/1/2005)*

Heron 2003 Merlot (California) $11. This Merlot is simple and a little thin, but it satisfies because it's so clean and dry. The tannins are rich and dusty, while the cherry-berry flavors pick up steam on the finish. **84** *—S.H. (12/15/2005)*

Heron 1999 Merlot (California) $13. **83** *—D.T. (2/1/2002)*

Heron 2002 Pinot Noir (California) $12. Many of the grapes from this statewide appellation wine must have come from cool coastal regions: it's crisp, delicate, and well-flavored, with cola, cherry, and spice notes. **85** *—S.H. (8/1/2005)*

Heron 2002 Syrah (California) $12. Kind of heavy and rough in texture, but decently dry, with a range of blackberry, cassis, coffee, and earth flavors. A red wine to drink with food, not ponder over. **84** *—S.H. (8/1/2005)*

HERON HILL

Heron Hill 2002 Semi-Dry Riesling (New York) $11. **81** *—J.C. (8/1/2003)*

HERZOG

Herzog 2000 Special Edition Warnecke Vineyard Cabernet Sauvignon (Chalk Hill) $52. **93** *—S.H. (11/15/2003)*

Herzog 2002 Special Reserve Cabernet Sauvignon (Napa Valley) $34. There's a dry bitterness and a green unripeness that make this Cab disappointing. Tannic and acidic, with a bare suggestion of cherry fruit. **82** *—S.H. (12/31/2005)*

Herzog 1997 Special Reserve Cabernet Sauvignon (Sonoma County) $32. **86** *(11/1/2000)*

Herzog 2000 Special Reserve Chardonnay (Russian River Valley) $27. **92 Editors' Choice** *—S.H. (12/15/2003)*

Herzog 2002 Special Reserve Merlot (Alexander Valley) $30. The fruit is way too thin in this wine, which is a major disappointment as Herzog has been on such a roll with reds. You get alcohol and oak and not much else. **82** *—S.H. (12/31/2005)*

Herzog 2003 Special Reserve Syrah (Edna Valley) $30. From one of California's coolest appellations, this Syrah is inky dark and fairly acidic. It's tannic, but the tannins are rich and fine and drinkable now. The wealth of flavors include blackberries, mocha, the sweet, caramelly vanilla of oak, and peppery spices. **92** *—S.H. (12/31/2005)*

Herzog 2001 Special Reserve Syrah (Edna Valley) $30. **94** *—S.H. (1/1/2002)*

HESS

Hess 2002 Small Block Series Syrah (Napa Valley) $32. Despite a warm, inviting nose of brandied cherries and blackberries, the mouthfeel doesn't display much richness or texture and the finish shows a touch of alcoholic heat. **83** *(9/1/2005)*

HESS COLLECTION

Hess Collection 2001 Cabernet Sauvignon (Mount Veeder) $40. Very, very tannic and closed now, which isn't surprising given its mountain appellation, this young Cab needs time in the cellar. But it should develop well. It's balanced, and there's a core of sweet blackberry and cherry fruit that should emerge by 2010. **90 Cellar Selection** *—S.H. (11/1/2005)*

Hess Collection 1995 Cabernet Sauvignon (Napa Valley) $25. **91** *(10/1/1999)*

Hess Collection 1999 Estate Cabernet Sauvignon (Napa Valley) $20. **90 Editors' Choice** *—S.H. (11/15/2003)*

Hess Collection 2000 Select Cabernet Sauvignon (California-Washington) $15. **85** *—S.H. (2/4/2003)*

Hess Collection 2003 Chardonnay (Napa Valley) $19. This is a fairly simple wine that has been rather heavily oaked.It has pleasant flavors of peaches, mangoes, cinnamon, and cream, with lots of vanilla and char. **86** *—S.H. (11/1/2005)*

Hess Collection 2001 Chardonnay (Napa Valley) $19. **90** *—S.H. (12/1/2003)*

Hess Collection 2002 Mountain Cuvée Red Blend (Mount Veeder) $35. A successful wine that shows its mountain origins in the density and concentration of tannins and flavors, yet it's so soft, in the modern way, it's immediately drinkable. Dry, robust flavors of black cherries, chocolate, and wild herbs. **90** *—S.H. (10/1/2005)*

Hess Collection 1998 Select Syrah (California) $13. **84** *(10/1/2001)*

HESS ESTATE

Hess Estate 2002 Cabernet Sauvignon (Napa Valley) $20. Hess almost always nails the vintage, and this is a nice example of a good, not great, Cab. It tastes mountainy, to judge from the tannins and fruit concentration. Will be good now with rich, well-marbled beef, but should develop for a few years. **87** *—S.H. (11/1/2005)*

HESS SELECT

Hess Select 2002 Cabernet Sauvignon (California) $15. Polished and ripe, this softly tannic wine shows ripe black currant, cherry, and smoky oak flavors. It has just enough acidity to make it lively. **85** *—S.H. (6/1/2005)*

Hess Select 2003 Syrah (California) $14. A decent value, the 2003 Hess Select Syrah starts off with scents of black cherries and blackberries, then turns earthier on the palate, finishing with flavors of coffee and some rustic tannins. **86** *(9/1/2005)*

HEWITT

Hewitt 2002 Cabernet Sauvignon (Rutherford) $75. Sumptuously intense fruit, fine toasted oak, and lush, smooth tannins all come together in this dramatic wine. It's a wonder of modern Napa Valley, offering delicious cassis, chocolate, and cherry flavors, with enough acidity for balance. Doesn't seem like an ager, but it sure is good now. **92** *—S.H. (12/15/2005)*

HIDDEN CELLARS

Hidden Cellars 1996 Cabernet Sauvignon (Mendocino) $15. **87** *—S.H. (3/1/2000)*

Hidden Cellars 2002 Alchemy Sauvignon Blanc (Mendocino) $13. Really too lean and watery to recommend, although it's clean and dry. **82** *—S.H. (12/1/2004)*

Hidden Cellars 1998 Syrah (Mendocino) $15. **86** *(10/1/2001)*

Hidden Cellars 1997 Medocino Heritage Zania-Hitzma Zinfandel (Mendocino County) $28. **90** *—S.H. (9/1/1999)*

Hidden Cellars 1997 Mendocino Heritage Pacini Vine Zinfandel (Mendocino County) $28. **89** *—S.H. (9/1/1999)*

Hidden Cellars 1998 Old Vines Zinfandel (Mendocino) $13. **86** *—S.H. (5/1/2002)*

Hidden Cellars 1996 Sorcery Zinfandel (Mendocino County) $28. **90** *—S.H. (11/1/1999)*

HIDDEN MOUNTAIN RANCH

Hidden Mountain Ranch 1997 Zinfandel (California) $16. **83** *—S.H. (2/1/2000)*

HIGH PASS

High Pass 1998 Pinot Noir (Willamette Valley) $16. **83** *—J.C. (12/1/2000)*

HIGH VALLEY

High Valley 2003 Cabernet Sauvignon (Lake County) $25. This Cab tastes like it comes from a hot climate. It's soft in acids and tannins, with slightly sweet flavors of cherry liqueur. **83** *—S.H. (11/1/2005)*

High Valley 2003 Sauvignon Blanc (Lake County) $18. A bit thin in lemony flavor, with crisp acids and an edge of vanilla and sweet clover on the finish. Very dry and clean. Fine with picnic fare. **84** *—S.H. (12/15/2004)*

HIGHTOWER CELLARS

Hightower Cellars 2000 Cabernet Sauvignon (Columbia Valley (WA)) $31. This is an interesting mix of fruit from Walla Walla, Red Mountain and Columbia Valley vineyards. Scents of alfalfa and spice lead into a loose-knit, engaging wine with a chalky, tannic finish. Another year or two will help smooth it out. **88** *—P.G. (9/1/2004)*

Hightower Cellars 2000 Merlot (Columbia Valley (WA)) $28. Good vineyard sources and adept handling make for a tight, muscular Merlot that succeeds in a lackluster vintage. This shows some muscle, with firm, plump fruit and solid underpinnings of smooth tannin. Black olive/herbal notes add complexity. **89** *—P.G. (9/1/2004)*

HILL FAMILY ESTATE

Hill Family Estate 2001 Origin Cabernet Sauvignon-Merlot (Napa Valley) $38. Kicks off with a velvety texture of ripe smooth tannins. They support a fine-tuned blend of cocoa, black cherry, herb, toast, plum, and chocolate flavors. Quite elegant, with a smooth, silky finish. Great price for this kind of quality. **91 Editors' Choice** *—J.M. (10/1/2004)*

Hill Family Estate 2001 Beau Terre Vineyard Merlot (Napa Valley) $32. Smooth textured and framed in rich, ripe tannins, this classy Merlot serves up a lush, complex blend of black cherry, cassis, blackberry, sage, thyme, and coffee flavors. Silky sleek on the long finish. **91** *—J.M. (9/1/2004)*

HINMAN

Hinman 1999 Chardonnay (Oregon) $10. **82** *—P.G. (4/1/2002)*

Hinman 1999 Pinot Noir (Oregon) $13. **86** *—P.G. (4/1/2002)*

Hinman 2002 Riesling (Oregon) $8. **87** *—P.G. (12/1/2003)*

HITCHING POST

Hitching Post 1988 Benedict Vineyard Pinot Noir (Santa Ynez Valley) $NA. Note the "Benedict Vineyard" label, from a time when Sanford had lost control. Alcohol 13.5%. Good color, cloudy with sediment. Rich red cherry aroma, anise, sweet beet, smoky char, spice. Dry, full-bodied, rich in dark cherry fruit. Still tannic, should develop. Now-2010. **90** *—S.H. (6/1/2005)*

Hitching Post 2001 Santa Rita's Earth Pinot Noir (Santa Rita Hills) $30. Defines Pinot from this AVA, with its succulent cherry, raspberry, and blackberry flavors and clean acidity. For all the deliciousness it's a tad obvious, as if all the beauty were a veneer of sweet fruit. The challenge is to develop depth and substance. **89** *—S.H. (3/1/2004)*

HOGUE

Hogue 1998 Bordeaux Blend (Columbia Valley (WA)) $10. 88 *—P.G. (6/1/2000)*

Hogue 2002 Cabernet Sauvignon (Columbia Valley (WA)) $9. This is a fine effort in this price range. It has some real muscle, firm, stiff tannins and tight, herbal fruit. Nicely rounded at the end, with toasty, smoky oak filling in for the finish. **87 Best Buy** *—P.G. (7/1/2004)*

Hogue 2001 Genesis Cabernet Sauvignon (Columbia Valley (WA)) $17. Hogue has a light touch with this accessible, well-blended cab, which includes 9% cab franc, 7% merlot, and splashes of syrah and lemberger. For all that, it shows simple, strawberry-flavored fruit, with more tannin than power, and an earthy finish. **84** *—P.G. (11/15/2004)*

Hogue 1999 Genesis Cabernet Sauvignon (Columbia Valley (WA)) $17. 85 *—S.H. (12/31/2002)*

Hogue 2000 Reserve Cabernet Sauvignon (Columbia Valley (WA)) $30. 93 *—S.H. (1/1/2002)*

Hogue 1999 Vineyard Selection Cabernet Sauvignon (Columbia Valley (WA)) $17. 87 *—P.G. (6/1/2002)*

Hogue 1997 Cabernet Sauvignon-Merlot (Columbia Valley (WA)) $9. 88 Best Buy *—S.H. (7/1/1999)*

Hogue 1999 Cabernet Sauvignon-Merlot (Columbia Valley (WA)) $10. 85 *—P.G. (6/1/2001)*

Hogue 2002 Chardonnay (Columbia Valley (WA)) $10. Nothing flashy here, just straightforward, tart fruit flavors leaning to apple, white peach and other cool-climate fruit. **86** *—P.G. (9/1/2004)*

Hogue 1999 Chardonnay (Columbia Valley (WA)) $10. 88 Best Buy *—P.G. (6/1/2001)*

Hogue 2002 Genesis Chardonnay (Columbia Valley (WA)) $16. This is mainstream Chardonnay. Light pineapple fruit is smothered in the buttered popcorn scents and flavors of French oak and malolactic fermentation. **87** *—P.G. (11/15/2004)*

Hogue 2002 Reserve Chardonnay (Columbia Valley (WA)) $22. This is for fans of the big, oaky style. It has plenty of sweet oak, wrapped around pineapple/tropical fruit. What Washington adds to the equation is acid, which gives the wine a solid underpinning that lifts it on the palate, and keeps it food friendly. **88** *—P.G. (9/1/2004)*

Hogue 1999 Vineyard Selection Chardonnay (Columbia Valley (WA)) $14. 89 *—P.G. (6/1/2001)*

Hogue 1998 Fumé Blanc (Columbia Valley (WA)) $8. 88 *—L.W. (11/1/1999)*

Hogue 2001 Fumé Blanc (Columbia Valley (WA)) $10. 86 *—S.H. (12/31/2002)*

Hogue 1999 Gewürztraminer (Columbia Valley (WA)) $7. 85 *—P.G. (6/1/2000)*

Hogue 2003 Gewürztraminer (Columbia Valley (WA)) $10. Neat new red label for Hogue, and a further extension of their fruit-forward style. A lush, broad, accessible wine with tropical fruits displayed against a sweet, lightly spicy backdrop. **86** *—P.G. (7/1/2004)*

Hogue 2000 Gewürztraminer (Columbia Valley (WA)) $8. 87 Best Buy *—P.G. (6/1/2001)*

Hogue 1998 Johannisberg Riesling (Columbia Valley (WA)) $NA. 86 *—L.W. (9/1/1999)*

Hogue 2000 Johannisberg Riesling (Columbia Valley (WA)) $8. 86 *—P.G. (6/1/2001)*

Hogue 2001 Terroir Lemberger (Columbia Valley (WA)) $20. Hogue has always done well with this oddball, Austrian grape, and this ramps it up a flavor notch or two, with the addition of 20% Syrah. Spicy, grapey and loaded with black cherry flavors, it finishes with broad, smooth tannins. **88** *—P.G. (1/1/2004)*

Hogue 2002 Merlot (Columbia Valley (WA)) $9. Hogue's striking new label and comfortable $9 price point seem to be aimed at bringing in loyal, long term customers. This is the right sort of wine for that; simple, pleasant, fairly generic but soundly made and, one suspects, reliably consistent year in and year out. **85** *—P.G. (7/1/2004)*

Hogue 2000 Merlot (Columbia Valley (WA)) $10. 85 *—P.G. (6/1/2002)*

Hogue 2001 Genesis Merlot (Columbia Valley (WA)) $17. A cool climate style of merlot, with firm, herbal fruit dominating, despite the inclusion of some juice from warmer Wahluke Slope vineyards. Hints of volatile acidity and some hard, rough tannins make this a wine that can benefit from extended aeration. **84** *—P.P. (11/15/2004)*

Hogue 2001 Reserve Merlot (Columbia Valley (WA)) $30. Smooth and silky, it shows plenty of black cherry fruit, with a pleasing roundness and a very soft, plush landing. Very drinkable. **87** *—P.G. (9/1/2004)*

Hogue 1999 Vineyard Selection Merlot (Columbia Valley (WA)) $17. 87 *—P.G. (6/1/2002)*

Hogue 2003 Pinot Grigio (Columbia Valley (WA)) $10. Friendly, fruity, likeable wines such as this may steal some of Oregon's thunder when it comes to affordable Pinot Gris. Fresh flavors of pear and apple are softly cushioned in a spicy wine with hints of citrus rind adding interest to the finish. **87** *—P.G. (7/1/2004)*

Hogue 2001 Pinot Gris (Columbia Valley (WA)) $10. 86 Best Buy —*S.H. (12/31/2002)*

Hogue 1998 Genesis Pinot Gris (Yakima Valley) $13. 89 —*L.W. (2/1/2000)*

Hogue 1997 Genesis Schwartzman Vineyard Riesling (Yakima Valley) $13. 90 —*L.W. (8/19/2003)*

Hogue 2002 Terroir Riesling (Columbia Valley (WA)) $13. Very ripe, even hot for Riesling, this wine can only be described as unctuous. Packed with fat, tropical fruit, it tastes like a big fruit salad. Mango, papaya, and other flavors contribute plenty of big pleasure. **88 Best Buy** —*P.G. (11/15/2004)*

Hogue 2001 Terroir Sangiovese (Columbia Valley (WA)) $25. This limited-production (137 cases) wine is made primarily of Walla Walla Seven Hills Vineyard fruit, which lends a soft, pleasantly fruity cherry pie character. Four other red grapes are blended in, which gives it a generic red, rather than varietal, palate. **87** —*P.G. (9/1/2004)*

Hogue 1998 Sémillon (Columbia Valley (WA)) $7. 86 *(2/1/2000)*

Hogue 1999 Genesis Sémillon (Columbia Valley (WA)) $13. 85 —*P.G. (12/31/2001)*

Hogue 1997 Barrel Select Syrah (Columbia Valley (WA)) $15. 87 —*S.H. (11/1/1999)*

Hogue 2001 Genesis Syrah (Columbia Valley (WA)) $16. Complex and inviting on the nose, with aromas of ripe blackberries, toasty oak and pepper. Loses a little steam on the palate, where it shows less fruit and more herbal, rhubarby notes. Still, very good in a somewhat herbal idiom. **87** *(9/1/2005)*

Hogue 1997 Genesis Syrah (Columbia Valley (WA)) $25. 88 —*P.G. (9/1/2000)*

Hogue 2001 Terroir Syrah (Columbia Valley (WA)) $25. The opening scents are of black cherry with a bit of nail polish, and the wine hits the palate in a disjointed way. Perhaps the addition of Lemberger should be re-thought; it makes the finish tart and grapy, and devalues the Syrah. And how can a wine from three completely different growing regions be called "terroir"? **85** —*P.G. (9/1/2004)*

Hogue 2003 Genesis Viognier (Columbia Valley (WA)) $16. Crisp and citric, this steely style of viognier tastes of green apples, lime, and gooseberry. Some slightly bitter citrus skin flavors add interest to the finish, which is lively and hints at oak. But what's the story on the weird little cartoon character on the label? **87** —*P.G. (4/1/2005)*

Hogue 2000 Vineyard Selection Viognier (Columbia Valley (WA)) $16. 88 Best Buy —*P.G. (10/1/2001)*

HOLDREDGE

Holdredge 2002 Pinot Noir (Russian River Valley) $30. An easy, one-dimensional Pinot, with simple flavors of cola, coffee, and cherries, in a dry, very light wine. **84** —*S.H. (11/1/2004)*

HOLLY'S HILL

Holly's Hill 2000 Chardonnay (El Dorado) $15. 85 —*S.H. (12/15/2002)*

Holly's Hill 2003 Rosé Traditionnel Grenache (El Dorado) $12. Quite full-bodied for a blush, and strong in fruity, spicy flavors. The tastes of strawberries, raspberries, and cinnamonny pepper flood the mouth, perked up by good acids. Fully dry, it's a great food wine, and a great value. **87 Best Buy** —*S.H. (12/15/2004)*

Holly's Hill 2003 Tranquille Blanc Rhône White Blend (El Dorado) $16. Easy drinking, with peach and vanilla flavors and a creamy texture. Finishes dry. A white Rhône blend of Viognier and Roussanne. **84** —*S.H. (12/15/2004)*

Holly's Hill 2000 Syrah (El Dorado) $22. 84 —*S.H. (6/1/2003)*

Holly's Hill 2002 Wylie-Fenaughty Syrah (El Dorado) $22. A little sharp in acids, and a bit rough around the edges. This country-style wine has good fruit and a little residual sweetness. **83** —*S.H. (12/15/2004)*

Holly's Hill 2000 Vin Doux Viognier (California) $18. 82 —*S.H. (12/31/2001)*

Holly's Hill 1999 Zinfandel (Amador County) $17. 87 —*S.H. (7/1/2002)*

HOLLYWOOD & VINE

Hollywood & Vine 1999 Cabernet Sauvignon (Napa Valley) $75. 92 —*J.M. (6/1/2002)*

HOME HILL

Home Hill 2002 Pinot Noir (Carneros) $30. Smells white peppery and hits the palate with a raw quality of acidic espresso, cola, and oak, although sweet black cherry flavors emerge after a while. Drink now. **84** —*S.H. (4/1/2004)*

HOMEWOOD

Homewood 1997 Kunde Vineyard Zinfandel (Sonoma Valley) $16. 82 —*S.H. (11/15/2001)*

HONIG

Honig 2001 Cabernet Sauvignon (Napa Valley) $30. Ripe in blackberry fruit, with chocolate, root beer, and currant notes, and well-oaked, this dry wine shows plenty of polish and flair. It drinks well now, and has soft, velvety tannins. **87** —*S.H. (12/15/2004)*

Honig 2001 Sauvignon Blanc (Napa Valley) $14. 90 Best Buy —*J.M. (11/15/2002)*

HOODSPORT

Hoodsport 1998 Cabernet Franc (Yakima Valley) $20. 82 *—S.H. (9/1/2000)*

Hoodsport 1998 Reserve Chardonnay (Yakima Valley) $17. 88 *—S.H. (11/15/2000)*

Hoodsport 1998 Gewürztraminer (Yakima Valley) $9. 83 *—S.H. (11/15/2000)*

Hoodsport 2002 Pinot Noir (Oregon) $27. Simple, with a soft, creamy, mint and vanilla aroma. Tart rhubarb flavors, or perhaps strawberries and cream, fill up the middle. **85** *(11/1/2004)*

Hoodsport 2002 Syrah (Yakima Valley) $27. Ultra-ripe blackberries carry a suggestion of briary-brambly stemminess in addition to the jammy fruit flavors. Creamy and supple in the mouth, ending on a soft, easy note. **88** *(9/1/2005)*

HOOK & LADDER

Hook & Ladder 2003 Third Alarm Reserve Chardonnay (Russian River Valley) $25. Harsh and unrewarding, this thin Chard has a bitter, tobaccoey quality, and a medicinal finish. **81** *—S.H. (12/31/2005)*

Hook & Ladder 2003 White Zinfandel (Russian River Valley) $8. A typical white Zin, pale pink in color, with strawberry and vanilla aromas that drink off-dry. It's clean and crisp in acids. **83** *—S.H. (10/1/2005)*

HOP KILN

Hop Kiln 1997 Chardonnay (Russian River Valley) $18. 88 *—S.H. (11/1/1999)*

Hop Kiln NV Rushin' River Red (California) $15. Rich, ripe and lush, this wine could only be from a warm climate in the New World. It's super-fruity but dry, with smooth, intricate tannins. The flavors range from red cherries and succulent forest blackberries to mocha and cinnamon spice. **87** *—S.H. (12/31/2005)*

Hop Kiln 2001 Turtle Creek Vineyard Zinfandel (Russian River Valley) $16. 84 *(11/1/2003)*

HOPKINS VINEYARD

Hopkins Vineyard 1999 Estate Bottled Chardonnay (Western Connecticut Highlands) $15. 84 *—J.M. (7/1/2002)*

HOURGLASS

Hourglass 2000 Cabernet Sauvignon (Napa Valley) $85. 95 Editors' Choice *—J.M. (12/15/2003)*

Hourglass 1997 Cabernet Sauvignon (Napa Valley) $125. 95 *—J.M. (12/31/2001)*

HOWELL MOUNTAIN VINEYARDS

Howell Mountain Vineyards 2000 Cabernet Sauvignon (Napa Valley) $36. 84 *—S.H. (12/15/2003)*

Howell Mountain Vineyards 2001 Black Sears Vineyard Cabernet Sauvignon (Howell Mountain) $75. Black as midnight and tough in tannins. Don't touch this baby for a long time! Dry, balanced, and oaky, it shows tremendous blackberry and currant fruit that should begin to reveal itself by 2010. **93** *—S.H. (6/1/2005)*

Howell Mountain Vineyards 2002 Beatty Ranch Zinfandel (Howell Mountain) $38. How big this wine is, but how drinkable now. It's not just the fruit, which ranges from blackberries to cherries and cocoa, it's the tannic structure. Somehow it's soft and intense at once. Totally dry, and not overly alcoholic, this Zin picks up even more power on the finish. **93** *—S.H. (10/1/2005)*

Howell Mountain Vineyards 1997 Beatty Ranch Zinfandel (Howell Mountain) $NA. 90 Best Buy *—S.H. (6/1/1999)*

Howell Mountain Vineyards 2001 Black Sears Vineyard Zinfandel (Napa Valley) $34. 92 *(11/1/2003)*

Howell Mountain Vineyards 2001 Old Vine Zinfandel (Howell Mountain) $24. 87 *(11/1/2003)*

Howell Mountain Vineyards 2002 Old Vines Zinfandel (Howell Mountain) $26. Kind of tough in the mouth at this time, with aggressive tannins that effectively bury the blackberry flavors. There's also a streak of hung meat or smoky leather that adds dimension. Best to let it soften for a few years. **87** *—S.H. (10/1/2005)*

HRM REX GOLIATH

HRM Rex Goliath NV Cabernet Sauvignon (Central Coast) $8. 80 *—J.M. (6/1/2003)*

HRM Rex Goliath 2004 Chardonnay (Central Coast) $9. This Chard is kind of thin in fruit and top heavy in oak. It tastes of alcohol mildly flavored with peach essence and slathered in toast and vanilla. **82** *—S.H. (12/15/2005)*

HRM Rex Goliath 2001 Free Range Chardonnay (Central Coast) $8. 84 *—S.H. (12/31/2003)*

HRM Rex Goliath NV Merlot (Central Coast) $8. 82 *—J.M. (9/1/2003)*

HRM Rex Goliath 2004 Pinot Grigio (California) $9. This deliciously gulpable PG shows why the varietal is so popular in America. Beautifully dry and crisp, full flavored in lemon, lime, peach and pepper notes, and clean through the finish, and you can't beat that everyday price. **85 Best Buy** *—S.H. (12/15/2005)*

HRM Rex Goliath 2001 Free Range Pinot Noir (Central Coast) $8. 84 *—S.H. (7/1/2003)*

HUG

Hug 2003 Bassetti Vineyard Syrah (San Luis Obispo County) $40. This crisp, medium-weight wine starts off with scents of rubber and smoke that give way to bright berry fruit. Very vibrant and tart on the finish, where it picks up hints of coffee and plum. **86** *(9/1/2005)*

HUNDRED ACRE

Hundred Acre 2000 Cabernet Sauvignon (Napa Valley) $100. 95 Cellar Selection *—J.M. (11/15/2002)*

HUNNICUTT

Hunnicutt 2002 Zinfandel (Napa Valley) $28. This Zin has the classic structure of a fine Cabernet, with firm, dusty tannins, a full-bodied mouthfeel and flavors of dark stone fruits and blackberries. What makes it altogether Zinny is the brambly, peppery fruit. Should be great with a grilled steak. **91** *—S.H. (12/31/2004)*

HUNT CELLARS

Hunt Cellars 1998 Cabernet Sauvignon (Paso Robles) $40. 84 *—S.H. (5/1/2003)*

Hunt Cellars 2000 Destiny Vineyards Mt. Christo Block Cab-Ovation Cabernet Sauvignon (Paso Robles) $60. Pungently dry, this earthy wine has tobacco and herb flavors that finish with a suggestion of cherries. It's not a fruity wine, although it is a fairly tannic one. **86** *—S.H. (10/1/2005)*

Hunt Cellars 2000 Moonlight Sonata Chardonnay (Central Coast) $24. 84 *—S.H. (12/15/2002)*

Hunt Cellars 1997 Petite Sirah (Central Coast) $35. 90 *—S.H. (12/1/2002)*

Hunt Cellars 2001 Destiny Vineyards Duet Red Blend (Paso Robles) $32. This Cab-Syrah blend, from a winery that's worked very hard on its reds over the years, is rewarding for its big, up front surge of blackberry, cherry, and cocoa flavors that last through a long, spicy finish. It's balanced in alcohol, and dry. **89** *—S.H. (12/1/2005)*

Hunt Cellars 2000 Destiny Vineyards Rhapsody Sangiovese (Paso Robles) $20. 84 *—S.H. (9/1/2003)*

Hunt Cellars 1997 Calif Syrah (California) $25. 84 *(11/1/2001)*

Hunt Cellars 1999 Serenade Syrah (California) $22. 87 *—S.H. (12/1/2002)*

Hunt Cellars 2001 Old Vines Zinfandel (Paso Robles) $28. 85 *(11/1/2003)*

Hunt Cellars 2001 Outlaw Ridge Vineyard, Lower Bench Zinfandel (Paso Robles) $30. 87 *—J.M. (11/1/2003)*

Hunt Cellars 1999 Zinphony Zinfandel (Paso Robles) $20. 84 *—S.H. (11/1/2002)*

Hunt Cellars 1999 Zinphony #2 Reserve Zinfandel (Paso Robles) $24. 91 *—S.H. (9/1/2002)*

HUNT COUNTRY VINEYARDS

Hunt Country Vineyards 2001 Late Harvest Riesling (Finger Lakes) $15. 83 *—J.C. (8/1/2003)*

HUNTER HILL VINEYARD & WINERY

Hunter Hill Vineyard & Winery 2001 Old Vine Schulenburg Vineyard Zinfandel (Lodi) $17. 81 *(11/1/2003)*

HUNTINGTON

Huntington 2003 Cabernet Sauvignon (California) $12. A full-throttle Cab, rich and ripe in intense cherry, plum, blackberry, and coffee flavors, although fully dry. A little on the soft, simple side, though. **84** *—S.H. (11/15/2005)*

Huntington 2001 Cabernet Sauvignon (Napa Valley) $18. 89 *—S.H. (11/15/2003)*

Huntington 2002 Chardonnay (Russian River Valley) $15. Simple, with fruity flavors and oak shadings that finish dry. **83** *—S.H. (12/31/2004)*

Huntington 2000 Chardonnay (Russian River Valley) $15. 88 *—S.H. (5/1/2003)*

Huntington 2004 Earthquake Sauvignon Blanc (Sonoma County) $12. Here's a pleasant SB, unchallenging with its up front fig, gooseberry, citrus, and melon flavors and crisp acids. Has some pretty levels of spicy complexity in the finish. **85** *—S.H. (11/15/2005)*

Huntington 2002 Earthquake Sauvignon Blanc (Napa County) $12. 86 *—S.H. (12/15/2003)*

HUSCH

Husch 2000 La Ribera Vineyards Cabernet Sauvignon (Mendocino) $18. Here's a good, enjoyable wine not without minor deficiencies. You'll find some hearty flavors of cherries, blackberries, and toast, as well as notable tannins. There's an astringent coarseness throughout that may soften in time. **86** *—S.H. (8/1/2004)*

Husch 2003 Chardonnay (Mendocino) $14. When I think of Husch wines I think of acidity, and this wine has lots of it. It's perfectly dry and tart, with ripe green-apple flavors and a pleasant spiciness. **87** *—S.H. (11/1/2005)*

Husch 1998 Estate Bottled Chardonnay (Mendocino County) $13. 87 *—S.H. (5/1/2000)*

USA

Husch 2000 Special Reserve Chardonnay (Anderson Valley) $25. 85 *—S.H. (12/1/2003)*

Husch 1998 Special Reserve Chardonnay (Anderson Valley) $25. 85 *—S.H. (5/1/2002)*

Husch 2002 Gewürztraminer (Anderson Valley) $12. 85 *—S.H. (12/31/2003)*

Husch 2000 Gewürztraminer (Anderson Valley) $11. 85 *—S.H. (5/1/2002)*

Husch 2001 La Ribera Vineyards Merlot (Mendocino) $25. Thin, astringent, and mouth-puckeringly dry, this wine offers little relief in the way of fruit. The palate searches for cherries and berries and encounters alcohol and harshness. Strange, considering the ripe vintage. **83** *—S.H. (8/1/2004)*

Husch 2003 Pinot Noir (Anderson Valley) $21. This is a very pure, clear Pinot Noir. It doesn't have a lot of alcohol, extract or oak. It's ripe in cherries and blueberries, but not over-ripe. The acidity is bright and the mouthfeel is silky. In other words, it's super-drinkable. **90 Editors' Choice** *—S.H. (11/1/2005)*

Husch 2000 Pinot Noir (Anderson Valley) $18. 85 *—S.H. (12/1/2003)*

Husch 2000 Apple Hill Vineyard Pinot Noir (Anderson Valley) $35. 90 *(10/1/2002)*

Husch 2003 Sauvignon Blanc (Mendocino) $12. Nicely drinkable for its firm acids, steely backbone, and fig and grapefruit flavors sweetened with a touch ofoak. Try with seared halibut with a fruity salsa topping. **85** *—S.H. (11/1/2005)*

Husch 2001 La Ribera Vineyards Sauvignon Blanc (Mendocino) $12. 86 *—S.H. (3/1/2003)*

Husch 2003 Renegade Sauvignon Blanc (Mendocino) $18. Made from wild yeasts, hence the name, this wine is twice the size of Husch's regular '03 Sauvignon Blanc. It's rich and intense in fig, apple, grapefruit, honeydew, and spice flavors, with a creamy texture brightened by firm acids and sweetened with considerable oak. One of the more rewarding Sauvignon Blancs I've had in a while. **91 Editors' Choice** *—S.H. (11/1/2005)*

HYATT

Hyatt 1997 Bordeaux Blend (Yakima Valley) $11. 84 *—P.G. (6/1/2000)*

Hyatt 1997 Reserve Cabernet Sauvignon (Yakima Valley) $25. 88 *—P.G. (6/1/2000)*

Hyatt 1998 Chardonnay (Yakima Valley) $11. 89 *—P.G. (6/1/2000)*

Hyatt 1999 Chardonnay (Yakima Valley) $10. 86 *—P.G. (9/1/2002)*

Hyatt 1998 Fumé Blanc (Yakima Valley) $11. 87 *—P.G. (6/1/2000)*

Hyatt 1999 Merlot (Yakima Valley) $12. 84 *—P.G. (9/1/2002)*

Hyatt 1997 Reserve Merlot (Yakima Valley) $25. 86 *—P.G. (6/1/2000)*

Hyatt 2001 Syrah (Yakima Valley) $13. While one taster found this wine disturbingly close to vegetal, others were more enthusiastic, calling it soft and expansive. There's some red fruit on the nose, but the flavors are darker, more akin to blackberry according to this wine's proponents. **86** *(9/1/2005)*

Hyatt 2000 Reserve Syrah (Yakima Valley) $18. 83 *—P.G. (9/1/2002)*

HYDE VINEYARD

Hyde Vineyard 2001 Merlot-Cabernet Sauvignon (Carneros) $65. They pulled out all the stops, starting with fully ripened grapes that give huge blackberry, cassis, cherry, and plum flavors. Elaborate oak adds even more sweet notes, and modern tannin management results in a very soft, elaborate mouthfeel. This stylish Merlot-Cabernet blend has lots of appeal. **91** *—S.H. (5/1/2004)*

ICARIA CREEK

Icaria Creek 1997 Cabernet Sauvignon (Alexander Valley) $45. 87 *(8/1/2003)*

Icaria Creek 2001 Estate Hillside Cabernet Sauvignon (Alexander Valley) $38. Soft and surprisingly herbaceous for the vintage, with blackberry and cherry flavors edged with dill. Feels rather flat, too. Would benefit from greater concentration and acidity. **84** *—S.H. (10/1/2004)*

ICI/LA-BAS

Ici/La-Bas 1998 Philippine Chardonnay (Mendocino County) $35. 89 *(7/1/2001)*

Ici/La-Bas 1997 Les Revelles-OR/CA Vineyard Se Pinot Noir (Willamette Valley & Anderson Valley) $35. 88 *— (10/1/1999)*

IDYLWOOD

Idylwood 1999 Corral Creek Vyd Pinot Noir (Willamette Valley) $25. 87 *—P.G. (4/1/2002)*

IL CUORE

Il Cuore 1996 Rosso Classico Red Blend (California) $11. 85 *—J.C. (10/1/1999)*

IL PODERE DELL'OLIVOS

Il Podere Dell'Olivos 1998 Tocai (Central Coast) $12. 88 *—S.H. (12/1/2001)*

ILONA

Ilona 1999 Meritage (Napa Valley) $70. 92 *—M.M. (11/15/2002)*

IMAGERY

Imagery 2000 Artist Collection Barbera (Sonoma Valley) $31. **89** *—S.H. (12/1/2003)*

Imagery 1997 Rancho Salina Vyd Bordeaux Blend (Sonoma Valley) $35. **87** *(11/1/2000)*

Imagery 2002 Artist Collection Cabernet Franc (Sonoma County) $34. The main problem with this wine is that it's excessively soft. Despite the delicious flavors of cherries, cocoa, and mint, and the rich, thick, sweet tannins, it falls flat in the mouth, and lacks vibrancy. **84** *—S.H. (12/15/2005)*

Imagery 1998 Artist Collection Cabernet Franc (Sonoma Valley) $27. **85** *—S.H. (12/1/2001)*

Imagery 1999 Ash Creek Vineyard Cabernet Sauvignon (Alexander Valley) $35. **85** *—S.H. (8/1/2003)*

Imagery 1999 Sunny Slope Vineyard Cabernet Sauvignon (Sonoma Valley) $35. **86** *—S.H. (8/1/2003)*

Imagery 2000 Vineyard Collection Ash Creek Vineyard Cabernet Sauvignon (Alexander Valley) $35. After struggling with this vineyard for a number of years, Joe Benziger seems to have gotten a handle on this finicky mountain fruit. Even in this so-so vintage, the wine is complex and pleasurable, although tannic. Hold until 2008. **92** *—S.H. (4/1/2005)*

Imagery 1999 Ricci Vineyard Chardonnay (Carneros) $25. **87** *—S.H. (12/1/2001)*

Imagery 2001 Malbec (North Coast) $33. This dark, heavy wine is fully dry, but has ripe flavors of blackberries, blueberries, and black cherries that are so sweet, they verge on chocolate. It's a big wine that calls for roasts and similar fare. **86** *—S.H. (10/1/2004)*

Imagery 2000 Artist Collection Malbec (North Coast) $33. A disappointment, given winemaker Joe Benziger's success with individual Bordeaux varieties. Smacks of under-ripe grapes, with stalky, green, vegetal aromas and flavors, although there's a streak of blackberry. The tannins kick in mid-palate and turn astringent through the dry finish. **84** *—S.H. (4/1/2004)*

Imagery 2002 Sunny Slope Vineyard Merlot (Sonoma Valley) $35. Good as it is, this wine is having acidity problems, meaning it's overly soft and melted. Yes, it has delicious flavors of black cherries, chocolate, and oak, and the tannins are smooth and luxurious, but what about balance? **85** *—S.H. (12/15/2005)*

Imagery 1999 Sunny Slope Vineyard Merlot (Sonoma Valley) $29. **85** *—S.H. (8/1/2003)*

Imagery 2001 Petite Sirah (Paso Robles) $35. Bigtime Pet here, an enormously ripe and extracted wine. It's huge in chocolate and cassis flavors that are almost sweet, although the wine is totally dry and balanced. The tannins are smooth enough to drink tonight with appropriately sized chow. **89** *—S.H. (10/1/2004)*

Imagery 2000 Artist Collection Petite Sirah (Paso Robles) $35. **86** *—S.H. (8/1/2003)*

Imagery 1999 Shell Creek Petite Sirah (Paso Robles) $35. **90** *—S.H. (12/1/2001)*

Imagery 2000 Artist Collection Petite Verdot (Sonoma County) $33. A big, darkly colored wine, Hulk-sized in its mouthfilling flavors. They range from very ripe, jammy summer blackberries, plums, and blueberries to dark chocolate and coffee, and are very dry. There's a dusty sprinkling of tannins in the mouth that demands rich foods, such as duck, steak or lamb. **90** *—S.H. (4/1/2004)*

Imagery 1999 Bien Nacido Vineyard Pinot Blanc (Santa Maria Valley) $21. **86** *—S.H. (12/1/2001)*

Imagery 1999 Rancho Salina Vineyard Red Blend (Sonoma Valley) $29. **85** *—S.H. (12/1/2001)*

Imagery 2002 Artist Collection Sangiovese (Dry Creek Valley) $24. Not Imagery's most successful wine. This red is very soft, with a lifeless mouthfeel and uninteresting flavors of berries and too much oak. **82** *—S.H. (10/1/2005)*

Imagery 1999 Artist Collection Sangiovese (Sonoma County) $22. **90 Editors' Choice** *—S.H. (9/1/2003)*

Imagery 1999 Polesky Vineyard-Red Hill Vineyard Sangiovese (Sonoma County) $21. **85** *—S.H. (12/1/2001)*

Imagery 2004 Artist Collection Viognier (Sonoma County) $24. I love this wine for the way the winemaker has reined in Viognier's tendency toward over-the-topness, yet not sacrificed its exotic character. It's characterized by vibrant acids and a clean, cool mouthfeel, with complex notes of white peach, honeysuckle, mango, vanilla, and spice that finish thoroughly dry. **90 Editors' Choice** *—S.H. (12/15/2005)*

Imagery 1999 Creek Vineyard Viognier (Alexander Valley) $25. **87** *—S.H. (12/1/2001)*

Imagery 2000 Artist Collection White Burgundy White Blend (California) $25. **86** *—S.H. (7/1/2003)*

Imagery 2002 White Burgundy White Blend (North Coast) $25. Chardonnay, Pinot Blanc, and Pinot Meunier comprise this smooth, suave white wine. It's got Chard-like features modulated with a nutty, flowery streak, and is very dry, with an overlay of smoky oak. **86** *—S.H. (10/1/2004)*

Imagery 2004 Wow Oui White Burgundy White Blend (Sonoma County) $24. I've never had a blend of Sauvignon Blanc and Muscat Canelli, but this delicious wine argues for more. It has Sauvignon's dry, acidic citrusy character, while the Muscat adds a rich orange blossom note. Simply wonderful and refreshingly different. **90** *—S.H. (12/15/2005)*

Imagery 2002 Taylor Vineyard Zinfandel (Dry Creek Valley) $40. Imagery continues to bring a full-blown, baroque interpretation to its interesting single-vineyard wines. This Zin is ultra-ripe, exhibiting chocolate, cherry, and coffee flavors, and is soft in tannins. Yet there's a grip and dryness that make it complex. **90** *—S.H. (10/1/2005)*

INDIAN SPRINGS

Indian Springs 1997 Cabernet Franc (Nevada County) $15. **90** *—S.H. (2/1/2000)*

Indian Springs 1997 Cabernet Sauvignon (Nevada County) $13. **84** *—S.H. (12/31/1999)*

Indian Springs 2000 Chardonnay (Nevada County) $14. **86** *—S.H. (12/31/2001)*

Indian Springs 1999 Sangiovese (Nevada County) $16. **85** *—S.H. (9/12/2002)*

Indian Springs 2000 Sémillon (Nevada County) $10. **83** *—S.H. (9/12/2002)*

Indian Springs 2001 Syrah (Nevada County) $18. This is a richly fruity, full-bodied wine with lots of sweet blackberry, plum, and cherry-chocolate flavors. It's dry and clean, with soft, complex tannins. There's real distinction here, from a part of California you don't hear much about. **87** *—S.H. (5/1/2004)*

Indian Springs 1997 Viognier (Nevada County) $14. **83** *—S.H. (6/1/1999)*

INDIGO HILLS

Indigo Hills NV Sparkling Wine (North Coast) $12. **86** *—S.H. (12/15/1999)*

Indigo Hills 2000 Chardonnay (Central Coast) $12. **83** *—S.H. (5/1/2002)*

Indigo Hills 1999 Pinot Noir (Central Coast) $14. **83** *(10/1/2002)*

IO

Io 2001 Rhône Red Blend (Santa Barbara County) $30. With a good track record, this Santa Barbara Rhône blend continues to delight as a full-bodied and dry red wine. As in previous years, the fruit is ripe and up front, all blackberries accented with white pepper and grilled meat notes. It's fairly tannic and calls for rich, marbled meats. **90** *—S.H. (12/15/2005)*

Io 2000 Rhône Red Blend (Santa Barbara County) $30. Savory and meaty to some, impossibly brett-ridden to others; this is admittedly gamy—even barnyardy—but if you like funk in your Syrah, bring in dis one. Does have a velvety mouthfeel and some blackberry fruit, so it's not one-dimensional. **85** *(9/1/2005)*

Io 1998 Syrah (Santa Barbara County) $60. **90** *(11/1/2001)*

Io 2001 Ryan Road Vineyard Syrah (San Luis Obispo County) $35. **93 Editors' Choice** *—S.H. (10/1/2003)*

Io 2001 Upper Bench Syrah (Santa Maria Valley) $35. **92 Editors' Choice** *—S.H. (10/1/2003)*

IRISH

Irish 2003 Chenin Blanc (Clarksburg) $16. Apples, spearmint, and ripe white peaches, with refreshing acidity. Very clean, and a bit sweet on the finish. **85** *—S.H. (3/1/2005)*

Irish 2003 Late Harvest Petite Sirah (Lodi) $22. Oozes chocolate fudge, gooey cherry pie, and vanilla sprinkle flavors, and drinks pretty sweet, with a soft, velvety mouth feel and crisp, balancing acidity. Delicious, decadent dessert wine. **88** *—S.H. (2/1/2005)*

IRON HORSE

Iron Horse 1997 Benchmark T-bar-T Bordeaux Blend (Sonoma County) $50. **94** *(11/1/2000)*

Iron Horse 1999 T-bar-T Benchmark Cabernet Blend (Alexander Valley) $56. **92** *—S.H. (7/1/2002)*

Iron Horse 1999 T-bar-T Cabernet Franc (Alexander Valley) $26. **86** *—S.H. (9/1/2002)*

Iron Horse 1996 Cabernet Sauvignon (Sonoma County) $23. **91** *(11/1/1999)*

Iron Horse 2001 T-bar-T Proprietor Grown Cabernet Sauvignon (Alexander Valley) $35. Right up there with the best of Iron Horse's recent Cabs. This one's dry and balanced, with a complex array of blackberry, cherry, herb, and spice flavors that finish long and ripe. There's a scour of tannins that suggests midterm ageability. Now through 2008. **92** *—S.H. (10/1/2004)*

Iron Horse 1991 Brut (Sonoma County-Green Valley) $28. **86** *(12/15/1999)*

Iron Horse 1993 Blanc de Blancs (Sonoma County-Green Valley) $34. **88** *—S.H. (12/1/2001)*

Iron Horse 1994 Classic Vintage Brut (Sonoma County-Green Valley) $25. **85** *(12/15/1999)*

Iron Horse 1992 Brut LD (Sonoma County-Green Valley) $50. **91** *(12/1/2001)*

Iron Horse 2000 Brut Rosé (Sonoma County-Green Valley) $30. Strong and full-bodied, with raspberry-cherry, dough and vanilla flavors and a rich, creamy texture. A little sharp in acids, with irregular mousse, and with a lovely, rich finish. **89** *—S.H. (12/31/2004)*

Iron Horse 1996 Brut Rosé (Sonoma County-Green Valley) $30. 84 *(12/1/2001)*

Iron Horse 1995 Brut Rosé (Sonoma County) $30. 90 *(12/1/2000)*

Iron Horse 1994 Brut Vrais Amis (Sonoma County-Green Valley) $29. 90 *—L.W. (12/1/1999)*

Iron Horse 1999 Classic Vintage Brut (Sonoma County-Green Valley) $28. Similar to the Wedding Cuvée but finer, a smooth wine with suggestions of lime, vanilla, lees, and dough, that's dry, with just a hint of sweet dosage. There's a rich creaminess and elegance to the structure that showcase the wine's pedigree. **90** *—S.H. (12/31/2004)*

Iron Horse 1996 Classic Vintage Brut (Sonoma County-Green Valley) $28. 87 *—S.H. (12/1/2001)*

Iron Horse 1998 Good Luck Cuvée (Sonoma County) $24. 86 *—J.M. (12/1/2002)*

Iron Horse 1996 Russian Cuvée (Sonoma County-Green Valley) $26. 86 *—S.H. (12/1/2001)*

Iron Horse 1995 Vrais Amis (Sonoma County) $26. 90 *(12/1/2000)*

Iron Horse 1999 Wedding Cuvée (Sonoma County) $28. 87 *—P.G. (12/1/2002)*

Iron Horse 1997 Wedding Cuvée Brut (Sonoma County-Green Valley) $28. 90 *—S.H. (12/1/2000)*

Iron Horse 2000 Chardonnay (Green Valley) $26. 92 *—S.H. (12/15/2002)*

Iron Horse 1993 Blanc De Blancs Chardonnay (Green Valley) $34. 88 *—S.H. (12/1/2001)*

Iron Horse 2001 Corral Vineyard Chardonnay (Green Valley) $37. 91 *—S.H. (12/1/2003)*

Iron Horse 1997 Cuvée Joy Chardonnay (Sonoma County-Green Valley) $30. 92 *—L.W. (3/1/2000)*

Iron Horse 2001 Estate Bottled Chardonnay (Green Valley) $26. First rate, a winemaker's wine made from grapes with a real smack of terroir. High, citrusy acidity marks the well-ripened mango, tangerine, and smoky-vanilla and leesy flavors that are wrapped in a richly creamy texture. Bold and complex. **90** *—S.H. (6/1/2004)*

Iron Horse 2001 Thomas Road Chardonnay (Green Valley) $37. 91 *—S.H. (12/1/2003)*

Iron Horse 2002 T-bar-T Vineyard Merlot (Alexander Valley) $30. After all the Sideways kicks Merlot took, this wine shows there's a real future for the variety, if vintners will take it seriously. It has the classic structure of a Cabernet, yet is softer and gentler, although no less complex and rewarding. The cherry compote, cocoa, and vanilla flavors are reminiscent of the candies and desserts we grew up with, with sophistication and flair. **92** *—S.H. (11/15/2005)*

Iron Horse 1997 Pinot Noir (Sonoma County-Green Valley) $24. 90 *(10/1/1999)*

Iron Horse 2000 Pinot Noir (Green Valley) $30. 91 Editors' Choice *(10/1/2002)*

Iron Horse 2000 Corral Vineyard Pinot Noir (Green Valley) $60. 90 *(10/1/2002)*

Iron Horse 2001 Estate Bottled Pinot Noir (Green Valley) $30. This pale-colored Pinot is somewhat lean rather than fleshy, due probably to its cool location, but it is a wonderful example of how terroir can be exploited by great grapegrowing and winemaking. Crisp and steely in acidity, it is elaborately oaked, with succulent flavors of raspberries, tangerine zest, vanilla custard, and sugared coffee. **90** *—S.H. (6/1/2004)*

Iron Horse 2001 Thomas Road Pinot Noir (Green Valley) $60. In this vintage the grapes became very ripe, and the flavors burst on the palate. Raspberry and cherry star, with supporting roles from espresso, earthy mushrooms, and peppery spices. Yet there is some heat from alcohol, and the acidity could be brighter. **89** *—S.H. (2/1/2004)*

Iron Horse 1998 Thomas Road Vineyard Pinot Noir (Sonoma County) $50. 90 *—S.H. (2/1/2001)*

Iron Horse 2004 Rosé de Pinot Noir Rosé Blend (Green Valley) $15. My oh my, is this pink wine tasty. It's pure essence of strawberries, ripe, clean, and dry, backed up by firm, cool climate acidity. Try this juicy blush with salmon sautéed in butter and garlic, with a sprinkle of black pepper. **88** *—S.H. (11/15/2005)*

Iron Horse 1996 Sangiovese (Sonoma County) $22. 91 *—S.H. (10/1/1999)*

Iron Horse 2003 Rosato di Sangiovese (Alexander Valley) $10. My one non-Oz wine is this rosé; it falls more into the "light red" than "pink-colored white" category, in terms of weight and flavor. Berry aromas have cream-nutty accents, while on the palate the berries take on earthy nuances. From Iron Horse, who are as adept at big reds as they are at sparklers, and continues to surprise us. **86 Best Buy** *—D.T. (11/15/2004)*

Iron Horse 1999 T bar T Proprietor Grown Sangiovese (Alexander Valley) $24. 87 *—S.H. (9/1/2003)*

Iron Horse 1997 Cuvée Joy Sauvignon Blanc (Sonoma County) $24. 89 *—S.H. (9/1/2000)*

Iron Horse 1997 Blanc de Blancs (Green Valley) $34. Interesting that Iron Horse has released this at eight years of age. It's still a young, acidic wine, but is mellowing, with a tantalizingly sweet core of peaches and cream just edging into crème brulée. This complex bubbly should develop well throughout the decade. **90 Editors' Choice** *—S.H. (12/31/2005)*

Iron Horse 1996 Blanc de Blancs LD (Green Valley) $60. There's more going on in this wine than in a New York minute. It's rich and young, brimming with acid, yeast and citrus fruit, and with a finish of toast and char. But it has a depth and nobility that make it complex and ageworthy. Should hold easily through 2010. **93 Cellar Selection** *—S.H. (12/31/2005)*

Iron Horse 1996 Brut LD (Sonoma County-Green Valley) $50. 91 *—S.H. (12/1/2003)*

Iron Horse 1997 Brut Rosé (Green Valley) $30. 89 *—J.M. (12/1/2003)*

Iron Horse 1998 Classic Vintage Brut (Sonoma County-Green Valley) $28. 87 *—S.H. (12/1/2003)*

Iron Horse 1999 Russian Cuvée (Sonoma County-Green Valley) $28. A bit sweeter than Iron Horse's drier bruts, and very polished, with subtle raspberry, lime, yeast, and smoky-vanilla flavors and good acidity. Easy and delicious to drink, but complex and nuanced in all the right ways. **88** *—S.H. (12/31/2004)*

Iron Horse 2002 Wedding Cuvée (Green Valley) $34. Maybe it's all marketing, but this does seem to be an ideal wedding-toast bubbly. There's something for everyone. Despite being almost all Pinot Noir, it's light and delicate, with a crisp elegance and a fine mousse, and that effervescent pleasure that only a fine bubbly provides. **91 Editors' Choice** *—S.H. (12/31/2005)*

Iron Horse 2000 Viognier (Alexander Valley) $17. 90 Editors' Choice *—S.H. (11/15/2001)*

Iron Horse 2002 T-bar-T Viognier (Alexander Valley) $24. 90 *—S.H. (12/1/2003)*

Iron Horse 2000 Cuvée R White Blend (Alexander Valley) $17. 88 *—S.H. (11/15/2001)*

Iron Horse 2002 T-bar-T Cuvée R White Blend (Alexander Valley) $19. 90 *—S.H. (12/1/2003)*

IRONSTONE

Ironstone 1999 Cabernet Franc (California) $10. 83 *—S.H. (12/1/2002)*

Ironstone 1999 Reserve Cabernet Franc (Sierra Foothills) $18. 89 *—S.H. (12/1/2002)*

Ironstone 1998 Cabernet Sauvignon (California) $9. 86 Best Buy *(8/1/2001)*

Ironstone 1997 Reserve Cabernet Sauvignon (Sierra Foothills) $24. 88 *(8/1/2001)*

Ironstone 1999 Chardonnay (California) $9. 85 *(8/1/2001)*

Ironstone 1998 Reserve Chardonnay (California) $16. 87 *(8/1/2001)*

Ironstone 2000 Merlot (California) $10. 87 Best Buy *—S.H. (11/15/2002)*

Ironstone 1997 Merlot (California) $11. 85 *(11/15/1999)*

Ironstone 2003 Xpression Red Blend (California) $8. A little sweet, silky, and light in body, with raspberry-cherry flavors. Darker than a rose. Try chilling before you drink. **85 Best Buy** *—S.H. (2/1/2005)*

Ironstone 2002 Shiraz (California) $10. A good wine at a good price. Though the mouthfeel is a bit flat, with baked-fruit flavors and powdery feel, its starts and ends nicely. It smells like black cherry preserves, and finishes with cinnamon and spice. **85 Best Buy** *(9/1/2005)*

Ironstone 1999 Shiraz (California) $9. 86 Best Buy *(8/1/2001)*

Ironstone 2000 Obsession Symphony White Blend (California) $7. 84 *(8/1/2001)*

Ironstone 2000 Zinfandel (California) $10. 85 *—D.T. (3/1/2002)*

Ironstone 2000 Reserve Old Vines Zinfandel (Lodi) $18. 87 *—S.H. (11/1/2002)*

ISENHOWER CELLARS

Isenhower Cellars 2001 Red Paintbrush Merlot (Columbia Valley (WA)) $25. This could be labeled Merlot, but the winery has apparently elected to go with flower names for its wines. By any name it's delicious, with sweet cherry fruit framed in big, dark toasted flavors from new American and French barrels. It's a big wine that keeps the alcohol under 14% and consequently does not fatigue the palate. **89** *—P.G. (9/1/2004)*

Isenhower Cellars 2003 Looking Glass Syrah (Columbia Valley (WA)) $22. Ripe and soft, with a creamy mouthfeel and a finish that slides away rather quickly, this Syrah is almost too facile, too easy to drink; it doesn't require any thought, the coffee and berry flavors just slip down effortlessly. **85** *(9/1/2005)*

Isenhower Cellars 2001 Wild Alfalfa Syrah (Columbia Valley (WA)) $25. Beautiful fruit is the star here, showing complex flavors of blackberry, brambleberry, and loganberry, nicely set off against sweet oak. Just a perfect balance, with some life ahead, but why wait. It's really a treasure right now. **90 Editors' Choice** *—P.G. (9/1/2004)*

J VINEYARDS & WINERY

J Vineyards & Winery 1997 Brut Champagne Blend (Russian River Valley) $28. 88 *—M.M. (12/1/2001)*

J Vineyards & Winery 1998 Pinot Gris (Russian River Valley) $16. 90 *—S.H. (11/1/1999)*

J Vineyards & Winery 2002 Pinot Gris (Russian River Valley) $18. 87 *—S.H. (7/1/2003)*

J Vineyards & Winery 2000 Pinot Gris (Sonoma County) $NA. **88** *—J.M. (9/1/2003)*

J Vineyards & Winery 2000 Pinot Noir (Russian River Valley) $24. A blend from throughout the valley, this is a lighter-style wine made in a delicious, accessible manner. It offers flavors of raspberries, strawberries, spices, smoke, and vanilla, and is silky on the palate. Finishes with a graceful elegance. **87** *—S.H. (2/1/2004)*

J Vineyards & Winery 1999 Estate Bottled Pinot Noir (Russian River Valley) $20. **84** *(10/1/2002)*

J Vineyards & Winery 2000 Robert Thomas Vineyard Pinot Noir (Russian River Valley) $40. A single-vineyard wine from a warmer part of the appellation. The extra heat and sunshine show in the ripe, fleshy flavors of cherries and raspberries, full-bodied mouthfeel, and soft acids. Finishes with a smoky edge of wood and spice. **89** *—S.H. (4/1/2004)*

J Vineyards & Winery 1999 Vintage Brut Sparkling Blend (Russian River Valley) $30. Very refined and smooth in the mouth, with an ultra-creamy texture that carries subtle flavors of lemongrass, vanilla, and yeast. Very dry, with crisp acids. This is a bubbly that feels rich and elegant all the way down. **90** *—S.H. (12/31/2004)*

J Vineyards & Winery 2002 Hoot Owl Vineyards Viognier (Russian River Valley) $28. **90** *—S.H. (12/31/2003)*

USA

J. BOOKWALTER

J. Bookwalter 2002 Cabernet Sauvignon (Columbia Valley (WA)) $38. It's 100% Cab, and perfectly captures the uniqueness of great Washington Cabernet Sauvignon. There's power and structure without the jammy thickness of California Cabs; it's sleeker, more tart, more vertically structured than they are. Still quite youthful and compact, with tangy red fruits and a spicy frame; good length finishing with licorice, cedar, tar, and leaf. **91 Cellar Selection** *—P.G. (12/15/2005)*

J. Bookwalter 2003 Johannisberg Riesling (Columbia Valley (WA)) $12. This may well be the best Riesling being made in Washington at the moment. Off-dry and very lightly carbonated, it explodes with a bouquet of flower flavors that hit you with lilac, citrus blossom, talcum powder, and more. Lively and tight, the flavors gather strength and concentration as they move through a myriad of pretty fruits, finally resolving in a long, slightly honeyed finish. A masterful effort. **93 Best Buy** *—P.G. (11/15/2004)*

J. Bookwalter 2003 Merlot (Columbia Valley (WA)) $36. Predominantly Merlot, the blend also includes Cabernet Sauvignon, Malbec, and Petit Verdot (7% each). Smooth, supple, and silky, it's dense and deeply saturated—inky to the eye and thick against the glass. The flavors show plenty of char and chocolate, with mocha, coffee bean, cherry, and cassis thickly applied. Lip-smacking flavor bolstered with natural acids, sweet tannins, and a long finish. **89** *—P.G. (12/15/2005)*

J. Bookwalter 2004 Riesling (Columbia Valley (WA)) $16. Despite its 1.9% residual sugar, this is succulent, not sweet. An exceptionally fragrant wine, lush with blossoms, sweet peach, mango, and pear. Beautifully ripened and concentrated; vibrant so that it seems to shimmer in the mouth, like a wave breaking over the palate. Poised, racy, fruity, and sensuous, it just goes on and on. **92 Editors' Choice** *—P.G. (12/15/2005)*

J. DAVIES

J. Davies 2001 Cabernet Sauvignon (Diamond Mountain) $65. From this longtime bubbly producer (Schramsberg), a Cab that shows its mountain origins in the noticeable tannins. That doesn't mean it's not drinkable now. It is, because the tannins are ripe and sweet. It does mean that this is a wine to age. Finishes long and harmonious. Now through 2010 and beyond. **92** *—S.H. (12/31/2004)*

J. GARCIA

J. Garcia 2001 Merlot (Sonoma County) $15. Drinks rather harsh and jagged, although there's a core of blackberry fruit that hits midway and lasts through the finish. In fact the fruit saves it, but unless you're a hardcore Deadhead, you can do better for the dough. **84** *—S.H. (12/15/2004)*

J. JACAMAN

J. Jacaman 2003 Pinot Noir (Russian River Valley) $35. This winery's '02 Pinot was very good. The '03 is even better. It's richer and more nuanced, offering savory flavors of cherries, coffee, sweet rhubarb pie, cola, cocoa, and spice flavors that unfold in waves in the mouth. Dry and crisp, with some dusty tannins, this wine will be best in its tasty youth. **90** *—S.H. (12/1/2005)*

J. LOHR

J. Lohr 2000 POM Bordeaux Blend (Paso Robles) $50. Here's what warmish Paso Robles does so well, in the right hands. This Merlot-based blend is fabulously gooey in cassis, chocolate fudge, red currant, and vanilla flavors. The terroir keeps acidity low, so the wine is very soft, but it's so decadently rich, you'll like it anyway. **88** *—S.H. (11/15/2005)*

J. Lohr 2000 St. E Cabernet Blend (Paso Robles) $50. How ripe the grapes got this vintage. This wine is bursting with fudgy chocolate, cassis, raspberry, and coffee flavors. But it's too soft, with almost no structure, and too sweet. The finish tastes like melted brown sugar and butter. **83** *—S.H. (11/15/2005)*

J. Lohr 1999 Hilltop Cabernet Sauvignon (Paso Robles) $32. **90** *—S.H. (11/15/2003)*

J. Lohr 1997 Hilltop Vyd Cabernet Sauvignon (Paso Robles) $33. **91** *(11/1/2000)*

J. Lohr 2001 Seven Oaks Cabernet Sauvignon (Paso Robles) $15. **87** *(12/1/2003)*

J. Lohr 1999 Arroyo Vista Chardonnay (Arroyo Seco) $25. **89** *—S.H. (12/31/2001)*

J. Lohr 2001 Arroyo Vista Vineyard Chardonnay (Arroyo Seco) $25. 89 *(12/1/2003)*

J. Lohr 2003 Riverstone Chardonnay (Arroyo Seco) $14. One of the best Chards in this price category, this Monterey example is rich in tropical fruit, peach, and spice flavors, and crisp in acidity. It has smoky oak, buttercream, a bit of lees—in other words, the works. **90 Best Buy** *—S.H. (11/15/2005)*

J. Lohr 1998 Riverstone Chardonnay (Monterey County) $15. 88 *(6/1/2000)*

J. Lohr 2001 Los Osos Merlot (Paso Robles) $15. 86 *(12/1/2003)*

J. Lohr 1999 Cuvée Pom Red Wine Red Blend (Paso Robles) $50. 90 *(12/1/2003)*

J. Lohr 2003 Wildflower Valdeguie Red Blend (Monterey) $7. What is California Valdeguie? Darned if I know. This one's fresh and jammy in cherry fruit, with a piercing cut of acidity, almost like a Beaujolais Nouveau. It's dry and fun. **84 Best Buy** *—S.H. (5/1/2005)*

J. Lohr 2003 Carol's Vineyard Sauvignon Blanc (Napa Valley) $18. This is a crisp, refreshing sipper that's long on fruity flavor. Bright acidity under girds the lemon and lime, grapefruit, peach, and slightly grassy flavors, and the finish is spicy and clean. **87** *—S.H. (2/1/2005)*

J. Lohr 2001 Carol's Vineyard Sauvignon Blanc (Napa Valley) $18. 84 *(8/1/2002)*

J. Lohr 2001 South Ridge Syrah (Paso Robles) $15. This enjoyable wine is soft and tasty, with black currant, cherry, Indian pudding, and herb flavors. It's round and supple in the mouth, with sweet, easy tannins. Finishes with just a bit of acidity, and will be a perfect match for roast beef. **86** *—S.H. (4/1/2004)*

J. Lohr 1997 South Ridge Syrah (Paso Robles) $14. 90 *—S.H. (2/1/2000)*

J. Lohr 2001 Bramblewood Zinfandel (Lodi) $15. 86 *(11/1/2003)*

J. LYNNE

J. Lynne 2002 Chardonnay (Russian River Valley) $18. A very nice Russian River Chardonnay, with those pretty apple, pear, and pineapple flavors, crisp, cool-climate acids, and spicy finish. There's a lot of toasty oak, too. **87** *—S.H. (8/1/2005)*

J. Lynne 2002 Cameron Ranch Vineyard Pinot Noir (Russian River Valley) $22. Simple and easy, with some nice attributes. Starts with smoky, oaky aromas leading to cherry flavors and an elegant texture. This is a good regional-style wine. **84** *(11/1/2004)*

J. WILKES

J. Wilkes 2003 Bien Nacido Vineyard Block Q Pinot Noir (Santa Barbara County) $50. This Pinot is deep, full-bodied, and rich, with a succulent core of black cherry, mocha, and spice flavors, and is dry despite the ripe fruitiness. **91** *—S.H. (12/15/2005)*

J.C. CELLARS

J.C. Cellars 1997 St. George Vineyard Petite Sirah (Napa Valley) $35. 84 *—S.H. (6/1/1999)*

J.C. Cellars 1997 Mesa Vineyard Syrah (Santa Barbara County) $20. 89 *—S.H. (6/1/1999)*

J.C. Cellars 1998 Alegria Vineyard Zinfandel (Russian River Valley) $30. 90 *—S.H. (5/1/2000)*

J.C. Cellars 1998 Rhodes Vineyard Zinfandel (Redwood Valley) $26. 87 *—S.H. (5/1/2000)*

J.J. MCHALE

J.J. McHale 2000 Lolonis Vineyard Chardonnay (Redwood Valley) $33. 84 *—S.H. (12/15/2002)*

J.J. McHale 2000 Pinot Noir (Anderson Valley) $33. 86 *(10/1/2002)*

J.J. McHale 1999 Syrah (Clear Lake) $29. 86 *—S.H. (12/1/2002)*

J.K. CARRIÈRE

J.K. Carrière 2002 Provocateur Pinot Noir (Willamette Valley) $18. Sweet, candied apple fruit. The mouthfeel is light, the flavors simple. There's a pleasant, slightly peppery edge to the finish. **85** *(11/1/2004)*

JADE MOUNTAIN

Jade Mountain 1997 Caldwell Vineyard Merlot (Napa Valley) $34. 88 *—L.W. (12/31/1999)*

Jade Mountain 2003 Mourvèdre (Contra Costa County) $18. Mourvèdre is a difficult wine to make. The grapes need heat, which they obviously got in this soft, rich bottling, with grapey, chocolaty flavors. But there's a rough-edged quality the wine-maker believes will evolve with age. I'm not so sure. **87** *—S.H. (11/1/2005)*

Jade Mountain 2001 Mourvèdre (Contra Costa County) $18. 88 *—J.M. (12/1/2003)*

Jade Mountain 2002 La Provençale Red Blend (California) $16. This blend of Mourvèdre, Syrah, Grenache, and Viognier is medium-bodied, dry and rich. It has a Merlot-like mouthfeel, with its soft, lush tannins, but the flavors are all about the Rhône. Spices and chocolate frame intense blackberries, cherry liqueur, coffee, and sweet lavender. **88** *—S.H. (10/1/2004)*

Jade Mountain 2003 La Provencale Rhône Red Blend (California) $16. I love this 4-variety Rhône blend of Contra Costa, Monterey, and Mount Veeder fruit. It combines warm region jammy fruit with cool climate acids. Just delicious in cherries, raspberries, and milk chocolate, with a silky, crisp, balanced structure. Great price for a wine of this complexity. **89 Editors' Choice** *—S.H. (11/1/2005)*

Jade Mountain 2003 Syrah (Monterey County) $15. Jammy and a bit bulky, this attempt at a Monterey Syrah from a brand that made its reputation in Napa is a bit of a disappointment. The big currant, plum, and vanilla flavors are tasty, but lack depth and richness. **83** *(9/1/2005)*

Jade Mountain 2002 Syrah (Napa Valley) $27. Super Syrah, just fabulous in blackberry, cherry, milk chocolate, sweet leather, herb, and oak flavors, and with such a lush, smooth mouthfeel. Just oozes quality, from the dramatic first taste to the ultralong finish. **92** *—S.H. (10/1/2004)*

Jade Mountain 1999 Syrah (Napa Valley) $25. 89 *—J.M. (7/1/2002)*

Jade Mountain 1997 Hudson Vineyard Syrah (Napa Valley) $32. 90 *(2/1/2000)*

Jade Mountain 2000 Paras Vineyard Syrah (Mount Veeder) $50. This is a richly textured, lush, complex wine brimming with a well integrated blend of earth tones, black cherry, raspberry, anise, tea, coffee, chocolate, herb, spice, and toast flavors. Long and seductive to the end, it's hard hold to back and just sip this hedonistic blend. **93** *—J.M. (4/1/2004)*

Jade Mountain 2000 Paras Vineyard P-10 Syrah (Mount Veeder) $75. Still plenty of grippy tannins in this wine, which has some Grenache and Viognier. But the astringency doesn't mask the huge flavors of black cherries and sweet oak. Displays pure mountain character of intensity and power. Drink now through 2010. **93** *—S.H. (5/1/2005)*

Jade Mountain 2001 Paras Vineyard Viognier (Mount Veeder) $30. 88 *—J.M. (5/1/2003)*

JAFFURS

Jaffurs 1997 Mourvèdre (Santa Barbara County) $20. 89 *—S.H. (6/1/1999)*

Jaffurs 1997 Roussanne (Santa Barbara) $19. 87 *—S.H. (6/1/1999)*

Jaffurs 2003 Syrah (Santa Barbara County) $23. Soft and velvety in the mouth, with striking aromas of mint, pepper, and blackberries, this blended Syrah from Craig Jaffurs represents a solid value. It even firms up a bit on the finish, suggesting that while it is delicious now, it should drink well for at least 4–5 years. **88** *(9/1/2005)*

Jaffurs 2001 Syrah (Santa Barbara County) $23. Craig Jaffurs's most basic Syrah is pretty good stuff. It is rich and dense, with deep flavors of currants, plums, molasses, pepper, and tobacco. The texture is smooth as velvet. This voluptuous wine is a pleasure to sip. **89** *—S.H. (2/1/2004)*

Jaffurs 2002 Bien Nacido Vineyard Syrah (Santa Barbara County) $30. There's not much difference between Jaffurs' three cool-climate, single-vineyard Syrahs (Bien Nacido, Thompson, and Melville). This one's firm, taut and rich in chocolaty-blackberry, roasted coffeebean and spice flavors, with a sweet finish. **90** *—S.H. (5/1/2005)*

Jaffurs 1999 Bien Nacido Vineyard Syrah (Santa Barbara County) $30. 86 *—S.H. (7/1/2002)*

Jaffurs 2003 Melville Vineyard Syrah (Santa Barbara County) $38. Our favorite of Craig Jaffurs' 2003 lineup was this coffee-scented offering from the young Melville Vineyard. Blackberry and pepper add varietal spice and California lushness to the mix. This is a big, full-bodied wine, with velvety tannins on the long finish. **91 Editors' Choice** *(9/1/2005)*

Jaffurs 2001 Melville Vineyard Syrah (Santa Barbara County) $32. So tannic and astringent, you can barely feel anything else in the mouth. Blackberry? Cherry? Hard to tell. Dry, tough, and puckery; not likely to go anywhere. **85** *—S.H. (3/1/2004)*

Jaffurs 2001 Stolpman Vineyard Syrah (Santa Barbara County) $32. 90 *—S.H. (10/1/2003)*

Jaffurs 2003 Thompson Vineyard Syrah (Santa Barbara County) $34. The nature of this wine's tannins divided the panel, with one taster finding it too tannic, while another felt it would age well. On balance, it's a well-made wine, with ample blackberry fruit and peppery spice, tinged with hints of coffee and cinnamon. **89** *(9/1/2005)*

Jaffurs 2001 Thompson Vineyard Syrah (Santa Barbara County) $34. This is a young wine, fairly tannic, acidic, and peppery now. It is very clean and well made, and possesses a deep core of cherry-berry fruit. It will improve with a few years in the cellar, but if you drink it now, pair it with roast duck. **91** *—S.H. (2/1/2004)*

Jaffurs 1997 Viognier (Santa Barbara) $22. 87 *—S.H. (6/1/1999)*

Jaffurs 2002 Viognier (Santa Barbara County) $23. 91 Editors' Choice *—S.H. (12/1/2003)*

JAMIESON CANYON

Jamieson Canyon 1999 Cabernet Sauvignon (Napa Valley) $20. 91 Editors' Choice *—S.H. (8/1/2003)*

Jamieson Canyon 1999 Merlot (Napa Valley) $17. 90 Editors' Choice *—S.H. (8/1/2003)*

JANKRIS

JanKris 2003 Riatta Red Blend (Paso Robles) $9. A nice, easy drinking, everyday sort of red. It's dry and clean, with berry and tobacco flavors. Sangiovese, Zinfandel, Cabernet Sauvignon. **84** *—S.H. (4/1/2005)*

JanKris 2002 Tres Ranchos Zinfandel (Paso Robles) $9. Ripe and chocolaty, with soft tannins. There's a nice hit of black cherries and pepper mid-palate. **84** *—S.H. (4/1/2005)*

JANUIK WINERY

Januik Winery 2000 Cold Creek Vineyard Chardonnay (Columbia Valley (WA)) $NA. Cold Creek is arguable Château Ste. Michelle's premiere vineyard; Januik was their winemaker until recently, and they generously offered him fruit for his new winery. He's taken the crisp, ripe, perfectly defined fruit of the vineyard and ramped it up; new oak adds layers of toast and the grapes seem extra ripe, with a honeyed richness. Exceptional. **91** *—P.G. (9/1/2004)*

Januik Winery 2002 Syrah (Columbia Valley (WA)) $30. Former Château Ste. Michelle winemaker Mike Januik has crafted a very approachable, inviting Syrah. Scents of coffee and blackberry jam waft from the glass and are echoed in the flavors, wich also pick up a bit of vanilla. Soft and creamy-textured, the tannins are supremely soft on the finish. Drink now. **87** *(9/1/2005)*

JARVIS

Jarvis 1999 Reserve Chardonnay (Napa Valley) $58. **87** *(7/1/2001)*

JEFFERSON VIENYARDS

Jefferson Vienyards 2002 Signature Meritage (Monticello) $24. Nicely structured, but where's the fruit? Despite a rich, dark color, the flavors are of tobacco, earth, and menthol. Drying tannins on the finish. **82** *—J.C. (9/1/2005)*

JEKEL

Jekel 2001 Sanctuary Bordeaux Blend (Arroyo Seco) $NA. This wine's blackberry fruit wears a hearty overlay of chocolate and coffee. The nose follows the same profile, with a dash of anise or eucalyptus. Acids on the finish are firm and crisp. A food-friendly wine; a blend of 59% Merlot, 39% Cabernet Sauvignon, with small parts Petit Verdot, Malbec, and Cabernet Franc. **89** *(9/2/2004)*

Jekel 1995 Sanctuary Estate Reserve Bordeaux Blend (Monterey) $26. **86** *—S.H. (7/1/1999)*

Jekel 1997 Sanctuary Cabernet Blend (Arroyo Seco) $28. **91 Editors' Choice** *—S.H. (12/1/2001)*

Jekel 1998 F.O.S. Reserve Chardonnay (Monterey) $22. **87** *—S.H. (11/15/2000)*

Jekel 1999 FOS Reserve Gravelstone Vineyard Est. Res. Collection Chardonnay (Monterey) $18. **90 Editors' Choice** *—S.H. (8/1/2003)*

Jekel 2002 Gravelstone Chardonnay (Monterey) $14. Butter, pear, and cinnamon aromas preface tropical fruit on the palate. Feels round and medium-weight, with oak not so obvious until the finish. Even so, Winemaker Cara Morrison says that future vintages will show even less wood. **86** *(9/2/2004)*

Jekel 1999 Gravelstone Chardonnay (Monterey) $11. **87 Best Buy** *—S.H. (11/15/2001)*

Jekel 1997 Gravelstone Chardonnay (Monterey) $15. **88** *—S.H. (10/1/1999)*

Jekel 2000 Sanctuary Reserve Malbec (Arroyo Seco) $NA. It's not often that you find an American Malbec that's so easy to drink. Aromas are of coffee and nut, and maybe some dust or wheat. On the palate it's understated but sturdy, with soft tannins and a wheaty-dusty overlay to its plum plum fruit. A straightforward wine, of solid quality. Drink now–2009. **88** *(9/2/2004)*

Jekel 2002 Winemaker's Collection Merlot (Monterey) $15. There's a disagreeable sharpness and bitterness to this wine. Even for a vin de table, it's tough going. **82** *—S.H. (12/31/2005)*

Jekel 1999 Winemaker's Collection Merlot (Monterey) $15. **84** *—S.H. (6/1/2002)*

Jekel 1999 Pinot Noir (Arroyo Seco) $15. **86** *—S.H. (12/15/2001)*

Jekel 1999 Winemaker's Collection Pinot Noir (Monterey) $15. **87** *—S.H. (5/1/2002)*

Jekel 2002 Riesling (Monterey) $11. Aromas are of light, fresh pineapple and a little petrol, and pineapple flavors persist on the palate. It's crisp and minerally in the mouth, and finishes with a gooseberry-green brightness. **86** *(9/2/2004)*

Jekel 1999 Riesling (Monterey) $10. **87** *(8/1/2001)*

Jekel 2002 Winemaker's Collection Riesling (Monterey) $9. Another fine JR from this respected Salinas Valley winery. It's strongly flavored, with extracted peach, honeysuckle, gingerbread, and citrus flavors, and a minerally streak suggesting flint. The acids are bright and firm. This dry wine finishes with a ton of spices. **86** *—S.H. (4/1/2004)*

Jekel 2003 Winemaker's Selection Riesling (Monterey) $9. Fancy name for a simple wine. It's dryish and crisp, and light in flavor, with traces of peaches and wildflowers. **83** *—S.H. (5/1/2005)*

Jekel 2000 Syrah (Monterey) $15. **88 Best Buy** *—S.H. (10/1/2003)*

Jekel 1998 Winemaker's Collection Syrah (Monterey) $16. **88 Editors' Choice** *(10/1/2001)*

JEPSON

Jepson NV Blanc de Blanc Brut (Mendocino County) $20. **84** *—J.C. (12/1/2001)*

Jepson 1989 Late Disgorged (Mendocino County) $35. **90** *—L.W. (12/1/1999)*

Jepson 1999 Estate Select Chardonnay (Mendocino) $16. **91** *—S.H. (5/1/2002)*

Jepson 1997 Estate Select Chardonnay (Mendocino) $15. **89** *—L.W. (11/15/1999)*

Jepson 2000 Sauvignon Blanc (Mendocino County) $11. **87** *—S.H. (5/1/2002)*

Jepson 2002 Syrah (Mendocino) $20. Here's an elegant, full-bodied Syrah that tastes good on the first sip, then gets better as you go along. It has wonderful balance, with firm, dusty tannins and fine acidity framing well-ripened cherry, mocha, and white pepper flavors. **90** *—S.H. (12/15/2005)*

Jepson 2000 Viognier (Mendocino County) $16. **86** *—S.H. (5/1/2002)*

Jepson 2000 Feliz Creek Cuvée Estate Select White Blend (Mendocino County) $9. **86** *—S.H. (5/1/2002)*

JERIKO

Jeriko 2000 Chardonnay (Mendocino) $19. **85** *—S.H. (6/1/2003)*

JESSIE'S GROVE

Jessie's Grove 2001 Westwind, Old Vine Zinfandel (Lodi) $20. **84** *(11/1/2003)*

JESSUP CELLARS

Jessup Cellars 1997 Lauer Vineyard Cabernet Sauvignon (Napa Valley) $39. **91** *(11/1/2000)*

Jessup Cellars 1999 Port (Napa Valley) $25. Richly textured with plump, ripe, silky tannins. The wine kicks off with a burst of chocolate, then settles down to reveal black cherry, cassis, blackberry, and spice flavors. Long and lush to the end. **90** *—J.M. (3/1/2004)*

USA

Jessup Cellars 2001 Zinfandel (Napa Valley) $28. Starts off with an unattractive smell suggesting sulfur or dirty socks. In the mouth, there's a fine wine, but the odor is impossible. **82** *—S.H. (10/1/2004)*

JEWEL

Jewel 2002 Cabernet Sauvignon (Lodi) $10. Lots of almost sweet blackberry and cherry fruit in this dryish wine. It's a bit too soft in tannins and acids, and collapses on the finish, except for the intense fruit, which lingers. **84** *—S.H. (11/1/2005)*

Jewel 2000 Firma Cabernet Sauvignon-Sangiovese (California) $NA. Country-style Super-Tuscan wine here, with berry and herb flavors wrapped in rough tannins, crisp acids, and a bitter, peppery finish. For all that, it has a nice rusticity that will go well with hearty foods like pasta with tomato sauce. A Sangiovese-Cabernet Sauvignon blend, with a dash of Merlot. **86** *—S.H. (3/1/2004)*

Jewel 2003 Un-Oaked Chardonnay (Monterey) $10. With no wood, what you get are the pure fruit flavors of sweetly ripe peaches, pineapples, and mangoes in this delightful wine, which has enough brisk acidity to balance. A very good value. **87 Best Buy** *—S.H. (11/1/2005)*

Jewel 2002 Petite Sirah (California) $10. Here's a big, dark, peppery wine, rich in plummy blackberry fruit and completely dry. It's modest in alcohol, with a long, rich finish. Hard to imagine anything better with BBQ ribs slathered in sauce. What a great value. **87 Best Buy** *—S.H. (12/15/2004)*

Jewel 2000 Petite Sirah (California) $10. **81** *(4/1/2003)*

Jewel 2002 Pinot Noir (California) $10. Good value for the pretty flavors of sour cherry, tomato, and toasty oak, and the spicy finish. Feels clean and varietally correct, and turns sweet in oak and spice on the finish. **85** *(11/1/2004)*

Jewel 2004 Dry Rosé Blend (Lodi) $10. This tasty blush wine tastes like it comes from France. It's filled with the aromas of lavender, wild thyme, and chamomile, with fruity nuances of strawberries. Surprisingly rich and complex, with a full body and a dry finish. Great value. **87 Best Buy** *—S.H. (11/1/2005)*

Jewel 2001 Shiraz (California) $10. You'll find stewed fruit flavors in this everyday wine, but it's nicely dry, with smooth tannins and a rich, plummy finish. **84** *—S.H. (12/15/2004)*

Jewel 2004 Viognier (California) $10. Offers lots of juicy flavors, with a creamy texture and a clean spine of acidity. Peaches, apricots, sweet lime, honeysuckle, and honey, with a dry finish. Very nice. **85 Best Buy** *—S.H. (11/1/2005)*

Jewel 2002 Viognier (California) $10. **86 Best Buy** *—S.H. (6/1/2003)*

Jewel 2001 Old Vine Zinfandel (Lodi) $10. **82** *—J.M. (11/1/2003)*

JEZEBEL

Jezebel 2003 Pinot Noir (Willamette Valley) $18. This is a lighter, grapey style of pinot noir but nonetheless delicious. Moderately ripe, with no vegetal notes, it features mixed blue and red fruits that lead smoothly into a textured, lightly tannic finish. **88** *—P.G. (2/1/2005)*

Jezebel 2003 Blanc White Blend (Willamette Valley) $12. Sineann's Peter Rosback and Rex Hill's Aron Hess have teamed up to make this wonderful blend of Gewürztraminer, Riesling, Pinot gris, Pinot blanc, and Chardonnay. Usually such "mutt" wines are a disjointed mess, but this one keeps its focus. There is a great fruit forward attack that leads into mixed flavors of stone fruits with sweet hints of honey and butterscotch. **89 Best Buy** *—P.G. (2/1/2005)*

JM CELLARS

JM Cellars 2000 Cabernet Sauvignon (Red Mountain) $30. **87** *—P.G. (9/1/2003)*

JM Cellars 2003 Klipsun Vineyard Sauvignon Blanc (Red Mountain) $18. Crisp and pungent with ripe aromas and flavors of peach, apricot, pear, and anise. Barrel-fermented and aged sur lie for six months in 50% new French oak; it retains enough firm acid to keep it lively and balanced, and the fruit shines. **89** *—P.G. (12/1/2004)*

JODAR

Jodar 1999 Cabernet Sauvignon (El Dorado County) $18. **82** *—S.H. (11/15/2003)*

JOE DOBBES

Joe Dobbes 1997 Signature Cuvée Pinot Noir (Willamette Valley) $54. **85** *(10/1/1999)*

JOLIESSE

Joliesse 2003 Chardonnay (California) $8. A pleasant, easy Chard that's light on fruit but balanced and dry. You'll find modest peach and oak flavors and crisp acids. **84 Best Buy** *—S.H. (12/15/2004)*

Joliesse 2002 Lot 57 Limited Edition Shiraz (California) $9. **85** *—J.C. (7/1/2003)*

Joliesse 2001 Limited Edition Zinfandel (California) $10. **86** *(11/1/2003)*

JONES FAMILY

Jones Family 1999 Cabernet Sauvignon (Napa Valley) $85. **94** *— (11/15/2002)*

JORDAN

Jordan 1995 Cabernet Sauvignon (Sonoma County) $38. **91** *—S.H. (11/1/1999)*

Jordan 1998 Cabernet Sauvignon (Sonoma County) $45. **85** *— (11/15/2002)*

Jordan 2000 Chardonnay (Russian River Valley) $26. **91** *—S.H. (2/1/2003)*

JORY

Jory 1997 Lion Oaks Ranch Sangre De Dono Syrah (Santa Clara Valley) $50. **85** *—J.C. (2/1/2000)*

JOSEPH FILIPPI

Joseph Filippi 2001 Zinfandel (Cucamonga Valley) $18. **84** *(11/1/2003)*

JOSEPH PHELPS

Joseph Phelps 1997 Insignia Bordeaux Blend (Napa Valley) $120. **95** *(11/1/2000)*

Joseph Phelps 1997 Cabernet Sauvignon (Napa Valley) $35. **90** *(11/1/2000)*

Joseph Phelps 2001 Cabernet Sauvignon (Napa Valley) $65. This is the sort of Cab you sip and immediately like. It's not only rich in currant and oak, with elaborate tannins, but possesses that extra dimension of pedigree due to the balance and harmony. Not for the cellar, but great now for your best foods. **89** *—S.H. (10/1/2004)*

Joseph Phelps 1999 Cabernet Sauvignon (Napa Valley) $42. **88** *—S.H. (6/1/2002)*

Joseph Phelps 2001 Backus Cabernet Sauvignon (Oakville) $150. Tasted alongside a bevy of Oakville Cabs, this beauty was the star of the show. It's a huge, masculine wine, authoritative, and ageable. Pours dark and drinks tannic and oaky, with a massive core of cassis, cherry, and chocolate fruit encased in perfect tannins. What grace and power, what balance. Drink now through 2016, at least. **97 Cellar Selection** *—S.H. (11/1/2005)*

Joseph Phelps 1999 Backus Vineyard Cabernet Sauvignon (Oakville) $150. **96 Cellar Selection** *—J.M. (2/1/2003)*

Joseph Phelps 1998 Chardonnay (Carneros) $22. **90** *(6/1/2000)*

Joseph Phelps 2002 Ovation Chardonnay (Napa Valley) $48. A controlled explosion best describes this year's Ovation. Always intense and concentrated, it exhibits well-ripened apple, pear, and pineapple flavors with plenty of lees and smoky oak, and finishes with clean acidity. Yet it maintains a steely minerality throughout. **92** *—S.H. (3/1/2005)*

Joseph Phelps 2001 Ovation Chardonnay (Napa Valley) $44. **92** *—S.H. (12/15/2003)*

Joseph Phelps 1999 Ovation Chardonnay (Napa Valley) $45. **91** *(7/1/2001)*

Joseph Phelps 1997 Ovation Chardonnay (Napa Valley) $40. **92** *—L.W. (10/1/1999)*

Joseph Phelps 2002 Merlot (Napa Valley) $40. Take a sip, and you think, Wow, that's good. Dark, deeply aromatic in black currants, mocha java coffee, subtle herbs, green olives, and fine oak. Turns sweet but dry in blackberry and cherry flavors wrapped in beautifully ripe, soft, expressive tannins. **92** *—S.H. (10/1/2005)*

Joseph Phelps 1999 Le Mistral Red Blend (California) $25. **88** *—S.H. (12/15/2001)*

Joseph Phelps 2002 Le Mistral Rhône Red Blend (Monterey County) $30. Combines Syrah's blackberries and Grenache's raspberries to produce an intensely fruity wine. It's dry and smoothly textured, with soft tannins and acids. Delicious with spicy broiled chicken. **90 Editors' Choice** *—S.H. (10/1/2005)*

Joseph Phelps 2000 Le Mistral Rhône Red Blend (California) $25. **91 Editors' Choice** *—S.H. (12/1/2003)*

Joseph Phelps 1998 Sauvignon Blanc (Napa Valley) $15. **81** *(3/1/2000)*

Joseph Phelps 2002 Syrah (Napa Valley) $35. This offering from one of California's Syrah pioneers seems a touch tannic and earthy, but also features sturdy blackberry fruit and a creamy mouthfeel. **85** *(9/1/2005)*

Joseph Phelps 1999 Syrah (Napa Valley) $NA. **90** *—S.H. (6/1/2003)*

Joseph Phelps 1996 Vin du Mistral Syrah (California) $30. **87** *—L.W (10/1/1999)*

Joseph Phelps 2001 Viognier (Napa Valley) $35. 90 —*S.H. (3/1/2003)*

JOSEPH SWAN VINEYARDS

Joseph Swan Vineyards 2000 Cuvée de Trois Pinot Noir (Russian River Valley) $20. 89 *(10/1/2002)*

Joseph Swan Vineyards 1999 Steiner Vineyard Pinot Noir (Sonoma Mountain) $25. 83 *(10/1/2002)*

JOULLIAN

Joullian 2001 Chardonnay (Monterey) $15. Oak and lees add extra layers of complex interest to this smooth wine. It has pretty flavors of apples, peaches, and honeydew, and those Monterey acids are firm and bright. The finish is notable for its rich spices and length. **88** —*S.H. (2/1/2004)*

Joullian 1999 Chardonnay (Monterey) $15. 85 —*S.H. (12/15/2002)*

Joullian 2000 Roger Rose Vineyard Chardonnay (Monterey) $23. 87 —*S.H. (12/1/2003)*

Joullian 1999 Sleepy Hollow Vineyard Chardonnay (Monterey) $27. 90 —*S.H. (5/1/2002)*

Joullian 2000 Sauvignon Blanc (Carmel Valley) $14. 88 —*S.H. (9/1/2003)*

USA

Joullian 2002 Syrah (Carmel Valley) $30. Quite a lush Syrah. It's perfectly ripened and brimming with black cherry, blackberry, and chocolate flavors, but has complexity in the smooth tannins and polished overlay of oak. Finishes dry and long. Try with short ribs. **88** —*S.H. (6/1/2005)*

Joullian 2002 Sias Cuvée Zinfandel (Carmel Valley) $20. Dry and medium-bodied, a different type of Zin. It's more restrained than most, offering berry, leather, and coffee flavors, and while it's smooth in the mouth, the acid-tannin balance is quite complex. Turns increasingly interesting on the finish. **90** —*S.H. (8/1/2005)*

JUDD

Judd 2001 Cranston Vineyard Petite Sirah (California) $26. A ripe, bigboned red wine that's dry and fruity enough to stand up to barbecue or a nice pot roast. It's got chocolaty, blackberry flavors and sturdy tannins. **85** —*S.H. (6/1/2005)*

JUDD'S HILL

Judd's Hill 1999 Estate Cabernet Blend (Napa Valley) $75. 90 —*S.H. (11/15/2003)*

Judd's Hill 2001 Cabernet Sauvignon (Napa Valley) $40. Classic '01 in the perfectly ripened fruit, which shows a balance of cassis, chocolate, and olive flavors, lush, firm tannins, and the overall impeccability. There's great oak here, and it meshes perfectly. Drink now through 2014. **93** —*S.H. (6/1/2005)*

Judd's Hill 1999 Merlot (Napa Valley) $26. 89 —*S.H. (12/1/2003)*

Judd's Hill 1999 Summers Ranch Merlot (Knights Valley) $30. 86 —*S.H. (12/1/2003)*

JUSLYN VINEYARDS

Juslyn Vineyards 2001 Cabernet Sauvignon (Napa Valley) $55. Ripe and juicy, with black currant, blackberry jam, and cherry flavors and smooth tannins. Lacks a bit of depth, but the richness works. **86** —*S.H. (5/1/2005)*

Juslyn Vineyards 2000 Cabernet Sauvignon (Napa Valley) $50. This understated wine doesn't overwhelm with fruit, but creeps up on you subtlely. The cherry and herb flavors are delicate, and judiciously balanced with tannins and oak. It's a feminine wine that will marry well with roasts, poultry, and soft cheeses. **89** —*S.H. (4/1/2004)*

Juslyn Vineyards 2000 Estate Cabernet Sauvignon (Spring Mountain) $85. A big, dense, sturdy wine, rich in tannins and with the structure to age. It's rather muted now, but buried deep is a solid core of blackberry, cassis, herb, and olive flavors that turn up on the finish. Best after 2006. **91** —*S.H. (4/1/2004)*

Juslyn Vineyards 2000 Vineyard Select Cabernet Sauvignon (Napa Valley) $75. A lighter style of Cab, with pretty black cherry, blackberry, and herb flavors and softly sweet tannins. Notable for its balance and harmony, this elegant wine will support, not overwhelm, fine food. **90** —*S.H. (4/1/2004)*

Juslyn Vineyards 1998 Vineyard Select Cabernet Sauvignon (Napa Valley) $75. 86 —*C.S. (6/1/2002)*

Juslyn Vineyards 2002 Sauvignon Blanc (Napa Valley) $NA. Takes this varietal's citrusy, grassy flavors and lifts them into riper fig, melon, and peach. The bright acidity is balanced by rich, sweet tannins and a creamy texture from barrel fermentation. The result is a charming wine, dry, and satisfying. **87** —*S.H. (2/1/2004)*

JUSTIN

Justin 1999 Isosceles Cabernet Blend (Paso Robles) $48. 92 —*J.M. (11/15/2002)*

Justin 1999 Cabernet Sauvignon (Paso Robles) $23. 89 —*J.M. (11/15/2002)*

Justin 2000 Chardonnay (Paso Robles) $19. 87 —*J.M. (12/15/2002)*

Justin 2003 Reserve Chardonnay (Paso Robles) $22. Comes across as rather soft and a bit simple, with earth, peach, and apple flavors that have been generously oaked. Could use more liveliness and crispness. **84** —*S.H. (7/1/2005)*

Justin 2002 Justification Merlot-Cabernet Franc (Paso Robles) $40. This Cab Franc and Merlot blend is elegant and refined. Notable for the subtle interplay of dried earth, blueberry, and oak flavors with the rich tannins. It's a wine of enormous charm and finesse. Bone dry, and packing a long, fruity finish. **92** *—S.H. (12/31/2004)*

Justin 2003 Sauvignon Blanc (Edna Valley) $13. Yes, it's dry and clean, but bitter in lean citrus flavors, and cuttingly acidic. Citrus and acidity are good, but not to this extent. Oysters, however, will pair well. **84** *—S.H. (8/1/2005)*

Justin 2000 Syrah (Paso Robles) $22. **89** *—S.H. (12/15/2003)*

Justin 1998 Mac Gillivray Vineyard Syrah (Paso Robles) $23. **84** *(11/1/2001)*

Justin 2002 Reserve Tempranillo (Paso Robles) $30. An unpleasant wine. Not really flawed, just thin, with vaguely bitter cherry flavors, and acidic, offering little pleasure **83** *—S.H. (8/1/2005)*

Justin 1999 Zinfandel (Paso Robles) $23. **85** *—M.S. (11/1/2002)*

KATHRYN KENNEDY

Kathryn Kennedy 2001 Syrah (Santa Cruz County) $36. **87** *—S.H. (12/15/2003)*

KAUTZ

Kautz 1997 Library Collection Chardonnay (California) $15. **85** *(6/1/2000)*

KAZMER & BLAISE

Kazmer & Blaise 2001 Primo's Hill Pinot Noir (Carneros) $42. From Acacia winemaker Michael Terrien, a personal project and a very fine wine. It possesses its appellation's character of silky tannins, crisp acids, and up front, jammy fruit. Cherries, coffee, tobacco, and herbs flood the palate, with enough body to suggest roast duck or lamb chops. **90** *—S.H. (4/1/2004)*

KEEGAN

Keegan 1997 Chardonnay (Knights Valley) $28. **90** *(6/1/2000)*

Keegan 2002 Buena Tierra Vineyard Chardonnay (Russian River Valley) $38. Richer up front pineapple and savory white peach flavors than Keegan's Ritchie bottling, and with similar oak, it's a more forward, palate-flattering wine, and a softer one, as well. Made in the popular style, this is a real crowd-pleaser. **90** *—S.H. (5/1/2005)*

Keegan 2002 Pinot Noir (Russian River Valley) $34. Nicely captures Pinot's delicacy and silkiness, with easy tannins that carry spicy cherry and oak flavors. This is an elegant wine, although you find yourself wishing it had more stuffing in the middle. **87** *—S.H. (5/1/2005)*

Keegan 2002 E Block Pinot Noir (Russian River Valley) $48. The palate impression is of cherries and raspberries baked into pie, with a buttery, flaky, smoky crust and a dusting of cinnamon and brown sugar, all wrapped in silk and satin. Would get a higher score if it had greater intensity and depth of flavor. **89** *—S.H. (5/1/2005)*

Keenan 1995 Cabernet Sauvignon (Napa Valley) $27. **91** *—S.H. (2/1/2000)*

Keenan 1998 Cabernet Sauvignon (Napa Valley) $40. **88** *—J.M. (6/1/2002)*

Keenan 1996 Cabernet Sauvignon (Napa Valley) $36. **87** *—J.M. (12/1/2001)*

Keenan 1998 Chardonnay (Napa Valley) $18. **84** *(6/1/2000)*

Keenan 2003 Chardonnay (Spring Mountain) $24. Simple and earthy, with peach, pear and sweet oak flavors, and a slightly rough mouthfeel. Finishes with an awkward sweetness. **84** *—S.H. (6/1/2005)*

Keenan 1999 Chardonnay (Napa Valley) $22. **87** *—J.M. (11/15/2001)*

Keenan 1999 Merlot (Napa Valley) $30. **89** *—J.M. (12/31/2003)*

Keenan 2000 Reserve Merlot (Spring Mountain) $48. One of the best Merlots of the vintage, a rich, sumptuous wine that excites due to its impressive components. Complex black currant, cassis, mocha, herb, and smoky oak flavors flood the palate, while tannins and acidity rein it all in. An exciting experience, and gets even better with a few hours of air. **93** *—S.H. (6/1/2004)*

Keenan 1999 Mernet Merlot-Cabernet Sauvignon (Napa Valley) $75. **91** *—J.M. (11/15/2003)*

Keenan 2001 Mernet Reserve Red Blend (Napa Valley) $75. Easy to drink for its soft richness, yet complex in structure, this well-oaked wine has ripe flavors of cherry liqueur, black raspberries, and white chocolate, with a peppery, spicy finish. The acidity is refreshing. Merlot and the two Cabernets, in case you couldn't figure it out from the proprietary name. **92** *—S.H. (2/1/2005)*

USA

KELHAM

Kelham 1999 Cabernet Sauvignon (Oakville) $45. **90** *—S.H. (2/1/2003)*

Kelham 1999 Reserve Cabernet Sauvignon (Oakville) $75. **93** *—S.H. (2/1/2003)*

Kelham 1999 Merlot (Oakville) $45. **93 Editors' Choice** *—S.H. (2/1/2003)*

KELTIE BROOK

Keltie Brook 1998 Merlot (California) $13. **87** *—J.C. (7/1/2000)*

KEMPTON CLARK

Kempton Clark 1997 Lopez Ranch Zinfandel (Cucamonga Valley) $18. **83** *—P.G. (11/15/1999)*

Kempton Clark 1997 Mad Zin Zinfandel (California) $12. **81** *—P.G. (11/15/1999)*

KEN BROWN

Ken Brown 2003 Syrah (Santa Barbara County) $28. Veteran winemaker Ken Brown, lately of Mondavi-owned Io, has his own new brand. This Syrah is clearly cool-climate, with peppery aromas, thick tannins and bone-dry flavors of dark stone fruits. It's not an undisputed success, but is a wine worth following. **87** *—S.H. (12/31/2005)*

KENDALL-JACKSON

Kendall-Jackson 2001 Cabernet Sauvignon (California) $15. Rich and fruity, a textbook North Coast Cab. The flavors of black cherry, coffee, herbs, and a smattering of smoky oak are well-balanced with firm tannins and good acidity. **86** *—S.H. (10/1/2004)*

Kendall-Jackson 1997 Elite Cabernet Sauvignon (Napa Valley) $100. 91 *(11/1/2000)*

Kendall-Jackson 1997 Grand Reserve Cabernet Sauvignon (California) $60. 93 *(11/1/2000)*

Kendall-Jackson 2002 Grand Reserve Sonoma-Napa-Mendocino Counties Cabernet Sauvignon (California) $26. Very tannic now, and dusty dry, so you might want to hang onto it for a while, or try with something rich and fatty. The fruit is good, suggesting blackberries and coffee. **85** *—S.H. (10/1/2005)*

Kendall-Jackson 1999 Great Estates Cabernet Sauvignon (Napa Valley) $40. 92 *—S.H. (11/15/2003)*

Kendall-Jackson 1998 Great Estates Cabernet Sauvignon (Napa Valley) $49. 90 *—S.H. (12/31/2002)*

Kendall-Jackson 2002 Hawkeye Mountain Estate Cabernet Sauvignon (Sonoma County) $45. From a high mountain vineyard over the Alexander Valley, a wine of extraordinarily tough tannins. The wine is clearly built for the cellar. Deep down you'll find a solid core of well-ripened cherry fruit, but it's basically undrinkable now. It could blossom into greatness, however, after 2010. **91** *—S.H. (8/1/2004)*

Kendall-Jackson 2002 Vintner's Reserve Cabernet Sauvignon (Napa-Mendocino-Sonoma) $16. This is a pretty nice, average Cabernet, dry and balanced, with good fruit flavors. It's a little pricy for what you get, though, and is marred by a bitterness in the finish. **84** *—S.H. (12/31/2005)*

Kendall-Jackson 2000 Vintner's Reserve Cabernet Sauvignon (California) $16. This is a pretty good Cab, with polished flavors of blackberries, cherries, dried herbs, and coffee. The tannins are smooth and chunky, leading to a slightly astringent finish. **86** *—S.H. (6/1/2004)*

Kendall-Jackson 1996 Vintner's Reserve Cabernet Sauvignon (California) $21. 86 *— (2/1/2000)*

Kendall-Jackson 2000 Collage Cabernet Sauvignon-Merlot (California) $9. 84 *—S.H. (6/1/2002)*

Kendall-Jackson 1999 Collage Cabernet Sauvignon-Shiraz (California) $9. 86 Best Buy *—S.H. (5/1/2001)*

Kendall-Jackson 2001 Camelot Bench Chardonnay (Santa Maria Valley) $17. 89 *—S.H. (12/1/2003)*

Kendall-Jackson 1999 Camelot Vineyard Chardonnay (Santa Maria Valley) $17. 85 *—S.H. (5/1/2001)*

Kendall-Jackson 2003 Grand Reserve Chardonnay (California) $20. There are some apple and peach flavors in this wine, and also a strong citrusy note that lends acidic brilliance to the mouthfeel. There's also an earthy, tobaccoey flavor throughout that might play well off grilled winter root vegetables. **85** *—S.H. (10/1/2005)*

Kendall-Jackson 2001 Grand Reserve Chardonnay (California) $20. 91 Editors' Choice *—S.H. (12/1/2003)*

Kendall-Jackson 1998 Grand Reserve Chardonnay (California) $25. 89 *(6/1/2000)*

Kendall-Jackson 2000 Great Estates Chardonnay (Santa Barbara County) $25. 88 *—S.H. (5/1/2003)*

Kendall-Jackson 2000 Great Estates Chardonnay (Arroyo Seco) $25. 88 *—S.H. (5/1/2003)*

Kendall-Jackson 1999 Great Estates Chardonnay (Sonoma Coast) $22. 88 *—S.H. (8/1/2003)*

Kendall-Jackson 1997 Paradise Vineyard Chardonnay (Arroyo Seco) $17. 87 *(6/1/2000)*

Kendall-Jackson 1998 Stature Chardonnay (Santa Maria Valley) $60. 90 *(7/1/2001)*

Kendall-Jackson 2001 Vintner's Reserve Chardonnay (California) $12. 84 *—S.H. (6/1/2003)*

Kendall-Jackson 1998 Vintner's Reserve Chardonnay (California) $12. 85 *—S.H. (11/15/2000)*

Kendall-Jackson 2001 Stature Meritage (Napa Valley) $120. Already bottled, this wine isn't scheduled to be released until March 2005. If you like your Cabs big, rich, and chewy (and who doesn't?) it's never to early to start badgering your retailer or wholesaler to try to get you some of the 613 cases produced. Toasty notes accent dark chocolate and plum scents, while intense cassis flavors fill the mouth. Sturdy; try after 2006. **93 Cellar Selection** *(3/1/2004)*

Kendall-Jackson 1996 Buckeye Vineyard Merlot (Sonoma County) $33. 86 *—J.C. (7/1/2000)*

Kendall-Jackson 1995 Grand Reserve Merlot (California) $47. 89 *—S.H. (3/1/2000)*

Kendall-Jackson 1999 Great Estates Merlot (Sonoma County) $35. 91 *—S.H. (12/31/2002)*

USA

Kendall-Jackson 1998 Great Estates Merlot (Alexander Valley) $40. 89 *—S.H. (12/1/2001)*

Kendall-Jackson 2000 Stature Merlot (Sonoma County) $60. Everything that money can buy has gone into this wine, but it cannot rise above its vintage. It's rich in oak, with firm, rich tannins, and the winemaker squeezed black currant, plum, and tobacco flavors from the grapes. But there's a thinness that leads to a short, astringent finish. **86** *—S.H. (12/15/2004)*

Kendall-Jackson 2001 Vintner's Reserve Merlot (California) $15. A nice, plummy wine with some real richness. Round, full-bodied, and firm, with a coffee-earthy finish that sets off the fruit. Fairly tannic and very dry. **86** *—S.H. (10/1/2004)*

Kendall-Jackson 2000 Vintner's Reserve Merlot (California) $16. 86 *—S.H. (8/1/2003)*

Kendall-Jackson 1999 Great Estates Pinot Noir (Monterey County) $32. 89 *(10/1/2002)*

Kendall-Jackson 2002 Seco Highlands Estate Pinot Noir (Monterey County) $35. A new wine from K-J. It's high in cool-weather acidity that tingles the mouth, while the flavors are modest, ranging from raspberries, cola, coffee, and vanilla to various dusty herbs and rose-hip tea. Could use more fatness and charm, but it's an interesting wine, and one to watch. **88** *—S.H. (11/1/2004)*

Kendall-Jackson 2003 Vintner's Reserve Pinot Noir (California) $14. This Pinot is very dry, and it fulfills the basic varietal requirements of a silky texture with crisp acids. You'll find modest flavors of cherries and leather. **84** *—S.H. (6/1/2005)*

Kendall-Jackson 2001 Vintner's Reserve Pinot Noir (California) $14. 85 *—S.H. (7/1/2003)*

Kendall-Jackson 1999 Vintner's Reserve Pinot Noir (California) $12. 86 *—S.H. (11/15/2001)*

Kendall-Jackson 1998 Collage Red Blend (California) $9. 84 *—S.H. (5/1/2001)*

Kendall-Jackson 2002 Collage Zinfandel-Shiraz Red Blend (California) $10. Simple, rather sweet and candied, with raspberry and cocoa butter flavors and a soft, fruity finish. Nice with mushroom pizza. **83** *—S.H. (6/1/2005)*

Kendall-Jackson 2004 Vintner's Reserve Riesling (California) $10. Slightly sweet, especially on the finish, where the citrus and fig flavors turn decidely honeyed. This is a soft, slightly common wine. **83** *—S.H. (10/1/2005)*

Kendall-Jackson 1999 Sauvignon Blanc (California) $10. 84 *—S.H. (5/1/2001)*

Kendall-Jackson 2002 Vintner's Reserve Sauvignon Blanc (California) $10. Nice and drinkable, a simple wine with slightly sweet flavors of citrus fruits and the acidity you expect from this varietal. It will go with almost anything, so don't be too fussy. **84** *—S.H. (2/1/2004)*

Kendall-Jackson 2000 Vintner's Reserve Sauvignon Blanc (California) $9. 83 *—S.H. (9/12/2002)*

Kendall-Jackson 1997 Vintner's Reserve Sauvignon Blanc (California) $9. 86 *— (9/1/1999)*

Kendall-Jackson 1999 Grand Reserve Syrah (California) $22. 87 *(11/1/2001)*

Kendall-Jackson 2001 Vintner's Reserve Syrah (California) $14. Smells and tastes just like what it is, a young, fresh and jammy wine, sharp in acidity and vibrant with blackberry and cherry flavors. Extremely dry, but with a nice ripe sheen. **84** *—S.H. (12/1/2004)*

Kendall-Jackson 1997 Vintner's Reserve Syrah (California) $17. 88 *—S.H. (2/1/2000)*

Kendall-Jackson 2000 Great Estates Zinfandel (Mendocino) $25. 91 *—S.H. (12/1/2002)*

Kendall-Jackson 2002 Vintner's Reserve Zinfandel (California) $12. Made in a popular style, this jammy wine has cherry, blackberry and spiced rum flavors that are ripe and pure, with a pleasantly tannic texture. Easy to like. **86** *—S.H. (6/1/2005)*

Kendall-Jackson 1997 Vintner's Reserve Zinfandel (California) $17. 83 *—J.C. (2/1/2000)*

KENT RASMUSSEN

Kent Rasmussen 1996 Reserve Chardonnay (Napa Valley) $45. 92 *(7/1/2001)*

Kent Rasmussen 1996 Pinot Noir (Carneros) $27. 88 *—M.S. (6/1/1999)*

KENWOOD

Kenwood 2002 Cabernet Sauvignon (Sonoma County) $18. Showing some rough, inelegant edges, this Cab doesn't seem fully ripened. The blackberry and cherry flavors finish with a green note, and the wine is fully dry. **83** *—S.H. (12/15/2005)*

Kenwood 2000 Cabernet Sauvignon (Sonoma County) $16. 86 *—S.H. (11/15/2003)*

Kenwood 1998 Cabernet Sauvignon (Sonoma County) $22. 86 *—S.H. (12/1/2001)*

Kenwood 1999 Artist Series Cabernet Sauvignon (Sonoma County) $70. The grapes come from high mountain vineyards that yield small berries. This wine is young, tough, and tannic. It's not one of your softly opulent '99s that immediately seduces. There is a deep core of blackberry, cherry, and cassis fruit and a lush overlay of oak. This

25th vintage of Artist Series is a serious cellar candidate. Best after 2008. **91** *—S.H. (4/1/2004)*

Kenwood 1997 Artist Series Cabernet Sauvignon (Sonoma County) $75. 93 *(4/1/2002)*

Kenwood 1995 Artist Series Cabernet Sauvignon (Sonoma Valley) $65. 92 *(4/1/2002)*

Kenwood 1993 Artist Series Cabernet Sauvignon (Sonoma County) $75. 91 *(4/1/2002)*

Kenwood 1991 Artist Series Cabernet Sauvignon (Sonoma County) $75. 90 *(4/1/2002)*

Kenwood 1989 Artist Series Cabernet Sauvignon (Sonoma County) $75. 87 *(4/1/2002)*

Kenwood 1987 Artist Series Cabernet Sauvignon (Sonoma County) $75. 88 *(4/1/2002)*

Kenwood 1999 Jack London Cabernet Sauvignon (Sonoma Valley) $35. 88 *—S.H. (11/15/2002)*

Kenwood 2001 Jack London Vineyard Cabernet Sauvignon (Sonoma Valley) $30. A big, softly tannic wine that can be consumed with pleasure now or held up to 10 years, this shows classic aromas and flavors of smoke, cassis, and vanilla and a long, fruit-driven finish. **90** *(12/15/2005)*

Kenwood 2000 Jack London Vineyard Cabernet Sauvignon (Sonoma Valley) $30. On the leaner, more herbal side of the spectrum, with cherry flavors spiced with a piny or resinous green note. Finishes a bit hard and astringent, but not likely to improve with age, so enjoy it now with rare steak. **85** *(12/15/2005)*

Kenwood 1998 Jack London Vineyard Cabernet Sauvignon (Sonoma Valley) $NA. A difficult vintage that should have been drunk in its youth, the '98 shows a strong herbal component, lacks fruit and features a clipped, high-acid finish. **83** *(12/15/2005)*

Kenwood 1997 Jack London Vineyard Cabernet Sauvignon (Sonoma Valley) $NA. This Cab, from a vintage that has been criticized for a perceived lack of longevity, is still chugging right along. Smoky and toasty on the nose, it adds flavors of superripe fruit on the palate: dates, figs and prunes. Richly textured, with a long, still-chewy finish. Drink now–2010. **89** *(12/15/2005)*

Kenwood 1995 Jack London Vineyard Cabernet Sauvignon (Sonoma Valley) $NA. Just beginning to drop its fruit, making the focus now on earth and tobacco flavors. This doesn't seem as ripe as the '94, but shows a bit more structure, ending on a slightly astringent note. Drink up. **88** *(12/15/2005)*

Kenwood 1993 Jack London Vineyard Cabernet Sauvignon (Sonoma Valley) $NA. On the downhill slide, this still packs in enough tobacco, earth, molasses, and prune flavor to remain pleasurable. **84** *(12/15/2005)*

USA

Kenwood 1997 Jack London Vyd Cabernet Sauvignon (Sonoma Valley) $35. 91 *(11/1/2000)*

Kenwood 2003 Chardonnay (Sonoma County) $15. Easy to like for its tropical fruit and pear flavors that are well oaked, and the rich, creamy texture. Fine, crisp acids follow on the long finish, leading to a clean, spicy mouth feel. **87** *—S.H. (12/31/2004)*

Kenwood 2000 Chardonnay (Sonoma County) $15. 85 *—S.H. (12/31/2001)*

Kenwood 1998 Chardonnay (Sonoma County) $15. 84 *(6/1/2000)*

Kenwood 2003 Reserve Chardonnay (Russian River Valley) $20. Shows proper Chard character in the peach flavors, oaky overtones and creamy texture. Could use more concentration, though, as it's rather weak on the finish. **84** *—S.H. (6/1/2005)*

Kenwood 2001 Reserve Chardonnay (Russian River Valley) $20. 87 *bS.H. (12/15/2002)*

Kenwood 1999 Reserve Chardonnay (Sonoma County) $20. 88 *—J.M. (11/15/2001)*

Kenwood 2002 Shows Vineyard Pedigree Chardonnay (Sonoma County) $15. 85 *—S.H. (12/1/2003)*

Kenwood 2000 Gewürztraminer (Sonoma County) $11. 84 *—S.H. (11/15/2001)*

Kenwood 2000 Merlot (Sonoma County) $17. 87 *—S.H. (9/1/2003)*

Kenwood 1998 Merlot (Sonoma County) $17. 87 *—S.H. (2/1/2001)*

Kenwood 2001 Jack London Vineyard Merlot (Sonoma Valley) $24. Oak dominates this 100% Merlot. The barrels lend vanilla and smoke notes and an oaky sharpness that covers the underlying cherry fruit. Youthful tannins also cover it up. Drink now through 2006. **85** *—S.H. (12/15/2004)*

Kenwood 1999 Jack London Vineyard Merlot (Sonoma Valley) $30. 88 *—J.M. (9/1/2002)*

Kenwood 1998 Massara Merlot (Sonoma Valley) $25. 85 *—S.H. (9/1/2002)*

Kenwood 2001 Reserve Merlot (Sonoma Valley) $25. Smooth and polished, and very dry, with blackberry flavors and a touch of herbaceousness. Just as good as Kenwood's less expensive '02 Merlot. **86** *—S.H. (10/1/2005)*

Kenwood 1999 Reserve-Massara Merlot (Sonoma Valley) $25. 89 *—S.H. (10/1/2003)*

Kenwood 2002 Pinot Noir (Russian River Valley) $17. Picture-postcard cool-climate Pinot, with young, fresh cherry, strawberry, and mint aromas, a modest overlay of smoky oak, and refreshing acidity. Delicate and feminine, this silky wine is elegant and crisp through the finish. **88** *(11/1/2004)*

Kenwood 2000 Pinot Noir (Russian River Valley) $17. 85 — *(7/1/2003)*

Kenwood 2000 Jack London Pinot Noir (Sonoma Valley) $20. 80 *(10/1/2002)*

Kenwood 1999 Reserve-Olivet Pinot Noir (Russian River Valley) $30. 89 *(10/1/2002)*

Kenwood 2003 Sauvignon Blanc (Sonoma County) $11. Lovers of grassy, citrusy, and bone-dry white wines will go gaga over this one. It has those hay and gooseberry notes, only lightly touched by oak, that drink so fresh and vibrant, accompanied by crisp acidity. Good value. **86 Best Buy** *—S.H. (12/31/2004)*

Kenwood 2001 Sauvignon Blanc (Sonoma County) $12. 85 *—S.H. (9/1/2003)*

Kenwood 1999 Sauvignon Blanc (Sonoma County) $12. 85 *—S.H. (11/15/2000)*

Kenwood 2004 Reserve Sauvignon Blanc (Sonoma County) $15. Kenwood's regular Sauvignon Blanc was a hard act to top. This one costs two bucks more, and while it's richer in creamy oak and lees, it's really not better, just different. It's a yummy, complex wine, and this is a great price for this quality. **90 Best Buy** *—S.H. (12/1/2005)*

Kenwood 2001 Reserve Sauvignon Blanc (Sonoma County) $15. 86 *—S.H. (9/1/2003)*

Kenwood 1997 Reserve Sauvignon Blanc (Sonoma County) $16. 87 *—L.W. (9/1/1999)*

Kenwood 2001 Zinfandel (Sonoma County) $16. 87 *(11/1/2003)*

Kenwood 1999 Zinfandel (Sonoma County) $16. 84 *—J.M. (3/1/2002)*

Kenwood 1997 Zinfandel (Sonoma Valley) $15. 89 *—P.G. (11/15/1999)*

Kenwood 2002 Jack London Vineyard Zinfandel (Sonoma Valley) $20. A solid Zin, rich in blackberry, cassis, cherry, coffee, and spice flavors, and dry. It shows a nice balance of fruit, acidity, and tannins, with a smooth mouthfeel. **88** *—S.H. (4/1/2005)*

Kenwood 2000 Jack London Vineyard Zinfandel (Sonoma Valley) $20. 86 *—S.H. (3/1/2003)*

Kenwood 1998 Jack London Vineyard Zinfandel (Sonoma Valley) $20. 86 *(3/1/2001)*

Kenwood 1999 Mazzoni Zinfandel (Sonoma County) $20. 88 *—J.M. (3/1/2002)*

Kenwood 1999 Nuns Canyon Zinfandel (Sonoma Valley) $20. 86 *—J.M. (3/1/2002)*

Kenwood 1997 Old Vine Zinfandel (California) $16. 85 *—P.G. (11/15/1999)*

Kenwood 2002 Reserve Zinfandel (Sonoma County) $20. Shows real Zinny character with its brambly berry fruit, which tastes of the sun in every ripe taste. Lots of spicy notes, with an edge of espresso. This dry wine is soft in acids and tannins. **85** *—S.H. (2/1/2005)*

Kenwood 2000 Reserve Mazzoni Vineyard Zinfandel (Sonoma County) $20. 86 *—S.H. (3/1/2003)*

Kenwood 1997 Upper Weise Vineyard Zinfandel (Sonoma Valley) $15. 86 *(3/1/2001)*

KESTREL

Kestrel 1997 Cabernet Sauvignon (Columbia Valley (WA)) $21. 85 *—P.G. (9/1/2002)*

Kestrel 2002 Old Vine Estate Cabernet Sauvignon (Yakima Valley) $50. Hard and tannic with scents of old leather. Very slowly the black cherry fruit emerges, along with moist earth, coconut, and vanilla. Barrel flavors overpower the lightweight fruit, which is simply plowed under with oak. The hot, bitter tannins add a jarring note to the finish. **85** *—P.G. (12/15/2005)*

Kestrel 1999 Merlot (Yakima Valley) $20. Juicy and delicious, this is from the best vintage of the past decade, and it's just now opening up and showing its stuff. Ripe flavors of bright berries give it a Zin-like attack, but the back end is all Washington, with fleshy, chewy fruit and smoky tannins. **88** *—P.G. (12/15/2004)*

Kestrel 1998 Old Vine Merlot (Yakima Valley) $50. 93 Editors' Choice *—P.G. (9/1/2002)*

Kestrel 2000 Syrah (Yakima Valley) $28. 88 *—P.G. (9/1/2002)*

Kestrel 2002 Estate Syrah (Yakima Valley) $20. There's some nice mixed berry fruit and hints of toast and lavender and a soft, supple mouthfeel, but despite a label showing only 13.8% alcohol, this wine seemed slightly hot to all three of our tasters. **83** *(9/1/2005)*

Kestrel 2002 Signature Edition Co-Ferment Syrah (Yakima Valley) $38. Shows some pretty red berry and violet notes, but they're slathered in vanilla, caramel, and cinnamon toast. The lavish oaking gives it a smooth, attractive mouthfeel, but two of our reviewers found this wine too alcoholic. **85** *(9/1/2005)*

KING ESTATE

King Estate 1999 Chardonnay (Oregon) $10. 84 *—S.H. (12/1/2003)*

King Estate 1996 Chardonnay (Oregon) $14. 88 *—M.M. (12/31/1999)*

King Estate 1997 Reserve Chardonnay (Oregon) $15. 89 *—P.G. (8/1/2003)*

King Estate 2001 Pinot Gris (Oregon) $15. 84 *—S.H. (12/1/2003)*

King Estate 1998 Pinot Gris (Oregon) $14. 88 — *(3/1/2002)*

King Estate 2003 Domaine Pinot Gris (Oregon) $25. King Estate's new high-end Domaine wines, organically grown and certified, are off to a great start with this exceptional pinot gris. Stone fruits and citrus peel flavors dominate, layered, and textural. The fruit is fleshy but not fat, with pear, papaya, and mixed tropical highlights, and a crisp, snappy, clean finish. **91** *—P.G. (2/1/2005)*

King Estate 2000 Reserve Pinot Gris (Oregon) $20. 90 Editors' Choice *(3/1/2002)*

King Estate 2001 Vin Glace Pinot Gris (Oregon) $18. 86 *—S.H. (12/1/2003)*

King Estate 2001 Pinot Noir (Oregon) $22. Herbal and sharp in acids, with austere, tobacco, and herb flavors that just manage to break into cherries. Finishes dry and tannic. **84** *—S.H. (12/15/2004)*

King Estate 1999 Pinot Noir (Oregon) $22. 88 *(10/1/2002)*

King Estate 1996 Pinot Noir (Oregon) $18. 84 *(10/1/1999)*

King Estate 2002 Domaine Pinot Noir (Oregon) $50. This latest release of King Estate's top-of-the-line Domaine bottling shows that the 2001 was no fluke. A serious effort, juicy and concentrated, it opens with lovely scents of Pinot cherry-berry and plum fruit, layered with earth, wood, leaf, spice, and plenty of tart fruit. The new oak is there but restrained, and the structure suggests that putting this one away for a few years will be very rewarding. **91 Cellar Selection** *—P.G. (11/15/2005)*

King Estate 1999 Domaine Pinot Noir (Oregon) $50. 91 Editors' Choice *(10/1/2002)*

King Estate 1999 Pfeiffer Vineyards Pinot Noir (Willamette Valley) $40. 89 *—P.G. (8/1/2002)*

King Estate 1999 Reserve Pinot Noir (Oregon) $35. 90 *—P.G. (8/1/2002)*

King Estate 1998 Late Harvest Riesling (Oregon) $18. 87 *—J.C. (12/31/1999)*

KINGS RIDGE

Kings Ridge 2000 Pinot Noir (Oregon) $15. 87 Best Buy *—P.G. (4/1/2002)*

KIONA

Kiona 2001 Cabernet Sauvignon (Washington) $20. A tight, spicy cab, with a gamy streak running through peppery, sweet black-cherry fruit. Plenty of firm tannins, and some early suggestions of lead pencil and tobacco, along with anise and smoke. **88** *—P.G. (5/1/2004)*

Kiona 2001 Estate Bottled Reserve Cabernet Sauvignon (Red Mountain) $32. Their reserve Cab, from their own Red Mountain vineyard, is this winery's finest effort. The 2001 is not quite as penetrating and powerful as the magnificent 1999, but it is a stylish, polished, almost steely wine with medium-term aging potential, perfectly ripened fruit, a fine focus and highlights of Red Mountain minerals. **90** *—P.G. (5/1/2004)*

Kiona 1998 Cabernet Sauvignon-Merlot (Washington) $10. 85 *—P.G. (11/15/2000)*

Kiona 1998 Chardonnay (Washington) $10. 85 *—P.G. (11/15/2000)*

Kiona 1998 Reserve Chardonnay (Columbia Valley (WA)) $18. 86 *—P.G. (11/15/2000)*

Kiona 1998 Chenin Blanc (Columbia Valley (WA)) $6. 87 *—P.G. (8/19/2003)*

Kiona 2001 Lemberger (Columbia Valley (WA)) $10. At one time, Lemberger (also known as Blaufrankisch) was touted as the Zinfandel of Washington. Now that Washington actually makes Zinfandel, not to mention Syrah, poor old Lem has lost a bit of lustre. Nonetheless Kiona's was, and is, one of the best. Soft, grapy, fruity, simple, and scrumptious. **87 Best Buy** *—P.G. (5/1/2004)*

Kiona 1998 Merlot (Columbia Valley (WA)) $20. 87 *—P.G. (9/1/2002)*

Kiona 2001 Estate Bottled Reserve Merlot (Red Mountain) $30. Soft, plummy, and lightly spiced, this seems a bit thin and green, given the premier vineyard and an exceptional vintage. Somehow the fruit didn't go the extra mile, and the wine doesn't have the weight and complexity of past Kiona reserves. **87** *—P.G. (5/1/2004)*

Kiona 2003 Dry Riesling (Columbia Valley (WA)) $8. A whiff of bottling sulfur blows off quickly, leading into a bold, vivacious, crisply defined, dry, and fruit-driven wine. Nicely mixes honeysuckle, Meyer lemon, and hints of pink grapefruit with a textured, mineral finish. **89 Best Buy** *—P.G. (5/1/2004)*

Kiona 2003 White Riesling (Columbia Valley (WA)) $8. This off-dry version is a perfect wine for Thai food. The fruit nicely combines tropical flavors with citrus; there is a hint of sweetness, and the elegant, stylish finish continues indefinitely. Graceful and seductive. **89 Best Buy** *—P.G. (5/1/2004)*

Kiona 1998 Sémillon (Columbia Valley (WA)) $9. 87 Best Buy *—P.G. (11/15/2000)*

Kiona 1998 Syrah (Yakima Valley) $30. 85 *(11/1/2001)*

Kiona 1998 White Riesling (Columbia Valley (WA)) $6. 85 *—P.G. (11/15/2000)*

Kiona 1998 Late Harvest White Riesling (Yakima Valley) $7. 88 Best Buy *—P.G. (11/15/2000)*

KIRKLAND RANCH

Kirkland Ranch 1998 Estate Cabernet Sauvignon (Napa Valley) $36. 91 Cellar Selection *(9/1/2001)*

Kirkland Ranch 1999 Chardonnay (Napa Valley) $20. 88 *(9/1/2001)*

Kirkland Ranch 1998 Merlot (Napa Valley) $24. 87 *(9/1/2001)*

Kirkland Ranch 2000 Pinot Noir (Napa Valley) $32. 81 *(10/1/2002)*

KIT FOX

Kit Fox 2002 Sunflower Vineyard Cabernet Sauvignon (California) $14. Hot and awkward, with earthy flavors and a harsh finish. **82** *—S.H. (5/1/2005)*

Kit Fox 2001 Cabernet Sauvignon-Syrah (California) $14. 83 *—S.H. (11/15/2003)*

Kit Fox 2002 Syrah (California) $15. Lots of stubborn sulfur. Earthy, tough flavors, with a dry, rasping finish. **83** *—S.H. (5/1/2005)*

Kit Fox 2001 Viognier (California) $12. 84 *—S.H. (7/1/2003)*

KLUGE ESTATE

Kluge Estate 2002 Brut Chardonnay (Albemarle County) $38. Despite its relative youth, this Virgina-made sparkler is pungently toasty on the nose, then moves into green apple and lime flavors. It does show its dosage a little, but finishes with decent flourishes of smoke, toast, and citrus. **86** *—J.C. (6/1/2005)*

KNAPP

Knapp 2000 Chardonnay (Cayuga Lake) $11. 86 *—J.M. (1/1/2003)*

Knapp 2002 Dry Riesling (Cayuga Lake) $11. 85 *—J.C. (8/1/2003)*

KOEHLER

Koehler 2003 Sauvignon Blanc (Santa Ynez Valley) $12. Not a bad price for this modest wine, which satisfies for its upfront citrus and fig flavors and bone dry finish. Really cleans out the old palate. **84** *—S.H. (10/1/2005)*

KORBEL

Korbel NV Brut Kosher Champagne (California) $18. 84 *(12/15/1999)*

Korbel 1996 Le Premier Reserve (Russian River Valley) $25. 90 *—S.H. (12/1/2002)*

Korbel 1997 Master's Reserve Blanc de Noir (Russian River Valley) $14. 82 *—P.G. (12/31/2000)*

Korbel 1999 Natural (Sonoma County) $13. 87 *(12/1/2002)*

Korbel NV Natural (Sonoma County) $13. 85 Best Buy *—M.M. (12/1/2001)*

Korbel NV Rouge (Sonoma County) $13. **86 Best Buy** *—M.M. (12/1/2001)*

Korbel NV Blanc de Noirs (California) $11. A rich, full-bodied wine with lush flavors of cherries, raspberries, vanilla, smoke, and yeast. It's dry and creamy, with bright acids and a long, satisfying finish. Best Buy **87 Best Buy** *—S.H. (12/31/2004)*

Korbel NV Brut (California) $11. One of Korbel's most consistent wines, this brut shows a rich elegance and balance, with doughy flavors of peaches and a hint of smoke, vanilla, and cherry. **87 Best Buy** *—S.H. (12/31/2005)*

Korbel NV Brut Rosé (California) $11. With lots of Pinot Noir and Gamay, this salmon-colored wine is full-bodied. It shows cherry and raspberry flavors alongside the yeast, smoke and vanilla. Dry, round, and creamy, and easy to inhale. **87 Best Buy** *—S.H. (12/31/2004)*

Korbel NV Chardonnay Champagne (California) $11. Tastes like a country-style Chardonnay with bubbles. The flavors of peaches and green apples have a doughy edge, and the wine is elegant and dry. **85** *—S.H. (12/31/2005)*

Korbel 1997 Le Premier (Russian River Valley) $25. 89 *—J.M. (12/1/2003)*

Korbel 2002 Natural (Russian River Valley) $14. With minimum dosage, this is drier than Korbel's other brut styles, and also rougher in texture. It showcases citrus, bread dough, and spicy flavors. **85** *—S.H. (12/31/2004)*

USA

KOSTA BROWNE

Kosta Browne 2002 Pinot Noir (Russian River Valley) $34. Most tasters found the aroma dominated by oak, cocoa, and herbs, but there's a deep core of tart cherry and rhubarb fruit that, laced with youthful acidity, is clean and refreshing. **86** *(11/1/2004)*

Kosta Browne 2000 Cohn Vineyard Pinot Noir (Russian River Valley) $48. **92** *—J.M. (7/1/2003)*

KOVES-NEWLAN

Koves-Newlan 2002 Cabernet Franc (Napa Valley) $30. Rather aggressive now in acids and tannins, with lots of oak and cherry and earth flavors. Simple now, but might knit together and improve in a year or two. **84** *—S.H. (7/1/2005)*

Koves-Newlan 2002 Estate Cabernet Sauvignon (Oak Knoll) $35. Oak Knoll is a southern Napa Valley appellation, cooler than Oakville or Rutherford or even the mountains, which is maybe why this young wine is so tannicly dry and acidic. **84** *—S.H. (12/31/2005)*

Koves-Newlan 2002 Napa Valley Chardonnay (Napa Valley) $25. Oaky and leesy, from the first whiff to the finish. You pick up on the toast and char and the sweet-sour lees. The problem is the fruit, which is watery. The diluted apple flavors let the acidity dominate the mouthfeel. **84** *—S.H. (9/1/2004)*

Koves-Newlan 2003 Estate Pinot Noir (Napa Valley) $26. Shows proper varietal character in the light, silky texture, dryness and acidity, but the flavors are really thin. **83** *—S.H. (11/15/2005)*

Koves-Newlan 2001 Estate Pinot Noir (Napa Valley) $26. Rather soft in texture and a little one-dimensional, but you'll find pleasant cherry, cola and oak flavors and a rich tannin-oak complex. Finishes dry and elegant. **85** *—S.H. (4/1/2005)*

Koves-Newlan 1997 Reserve Pinot Noir (Napa Valley) $26. 89 *—S.H. (9/1/2002)*

KRAMER

Kramer 2002 Estate Pinot Noir (Willamette Valley) $20. Similar to the Rebecca's, with dead leaf/silage aromas. The fruit shows tart cranberry and a bit of bitter chocolate at the end. **84** *(11/1/2004)*

Kramer 2002 Reserve Pinot Noir (Yamhill County) $30. There's a grassy herbal note on top, but the wine is fresh and forward, with mixed, ripe fruits and some root beerish spice in the finish. **86** *(11/1/2004)*

USA

KULETO ESTATE

Kuleto Estate 2001 Cabernet Sauvignon (Napa Valley) $50. Like a rich dessert, cherry-centered, drizzled with crème de cassis, vanilla, and oaky caramel, with a cherry-coffee finish. Almost sweet, but not too much. Stylish and tasty. **87** *—S.H. (4/1/2005)*

Kuleto Estate 2002 Sangiovese (Napa Valley) $25. What a match for dinner: This wine's high acidity will cut through cheese or meat easily, and its bigtime cherry and blackberry flavors would complement garlicky, tomato sauce nicely. Finishes dry, with a dusting of tannin. **88** *—S.H. (12/15/2005)*

Kuleto Estate 2002 Estate Syrah (Napa Valley) $40. Features a roasted, smoky nose reminiscent of campfire or toasted marshmallows: a compelling feature. That's followed by meaty flavors, some coffee and earth notes and a plump mouthfeel. Everything is going along smoothly until the finish, which turns excessively tart, adding a discordant note to an otherwise very good wine. **86** *(9/1/2005)*

Kuleto Estate 2002 Zinfandel (Napa Valley) $28. Quite successful, with its complex array of pepper, cherry, mocha, and vanilla aromas and flavors and rich, sweet tannins. Has the finesse of a Cabernet, with Zin's wild, spicy edge. The elaborate finish is sweet and very long. **90** *—S.H. (12/15/2004)*

Kuleto Estate Family Vineyards 2001 Syrah (Napa Valley) $36. Soft, ripely sweet, filled with fruity flavors, draped with smoky oak, and frankly delicious. It's made in the international style, with long, fat flavors that coat the palate and linger into the finish. It will go with a wide range of foods. **90** *—S.H. (5/1/2004)*

Kuleto Villa 1998 Native Son Sangiovese (Napa Valley) $32. 88 *—S.H. (12/1/2001)*

KUNDE

Kunde 2001 Cabernet Sauvignon (Sonoma Valley) $21. Rich and long in flavor, and wonderfully smooth, this is a gentle Cab that possesses some real complexity. Combines ripe blackberries, cherries, and oak with sweet tannins, and finishes soft, with a rich vanilla flourish. **90** *—S.H. (12/31/2004)*

Kunde 1998 Cabernet Sauvignon (Sonoma Valley) $20. 87 *—S.H. (11/15/2001)*

Kunde 1999 Drummond Vineyard Cabernet Sauvignon (Sonoma Valley) $30. Smells earthy and mushroomy, with modest flavors of blackberries. Feels flat in acidity in the mouth. A disappointment, especially considering the vintage. Tasted twice, with consistent results. **84** *—S.H. (5/1/2004)*

Kunde 1996 Drummond Vineyard Cabernet Sauvignon (Sonoma Valley) $24. 87 *—S.H. (12/15/2000)*

Kunde 2001 Reserve Cabernet Sauvignon (Sonoma Valley) $60. Really too young to drink now—it's tannic and acidic, with that primary fruit jamminess of an immature wine. Yet it's an excellent Cabernet. Should only improve over the next two or three years. **91** *—S.H. (8/1/2005)*

Kunde 1997 Chardonnay (Sonoma Valley) $15. 88 *(11/1/1999)*

Kunde 2003 Chardonnay (Sonoma Valley) $16. Here's a big, ripe, creamy, oaky Chardonnay. The oak stars, contributing flamboyant vanilla, char, and woody spices, but there's plenty of fruit flavor ranging from apples and peaches all the way to papayas. **86** *—S.H. (8/1/2005)*

Kunde 2000 Chardonnay (Sonoma Valley) $16. 87 *—S.H. (9/1/2002)*

Kunde 1997 C.S. Ridge Chardonnay (Sonoma Valley) $20. 92 *(11/1/1999)*

Kunde 1999 C.S. Ridge Vineyard Chardonnay (Sonoma Valley) $22. 90 *—S.H. (5/1/2002)*

Kunde 2001 Estate Grown, C.S. Ridge Vineyard Chardonnay (Sonoma Valley) $22. Bright and pure in tangerine and tropical fruit flavors, with a delicious spiciness and oaky vanilla creaminess. Wish it had a tad more concentration in the middle, but it's still a very good wine. **89** *—S.H. (12/15/2004)*

Kunde 1997 Kinneybrook Vineyard Chardonnay (Sonoma Valley) $20. 92 *(11/1/1999)*

Kunde 2001 Reserve Chardonnay (Sonoma Valley) $35. This outstanding Chard is polished and absolutely delicious. The pineapple, peach, pear, and nectarine flavors have been enhanced with charry oak and a dose of lees. Creamy smooth in texture, this flavorful wine is sprinkled with a sweet tang of spice that lasts through the long finish. **91** *—S.H. (2/1/2004)*

Kunde 1999 Reserve Chardonnay (Sonoma Valley) $35. **91** *—S.H. (12/31/2001)*

Kunde 1999 Wildwood Vineyard Chardonnay (Sonoma Valley) $22. **93** *—S.H. (5/1/2002)*

Kunde 2000 Wildwood Vineyard Estate Bottled Chardonnay (Sonoma Valley) $22. **87** *—S.H. (12/15/2002)*

Kunde 1998 Magnolia Lane Vineyard Fumé Blanc (Sonoma Valley) $12. **87** *—L.W. (5/1/2000)*

Kunde 2000 Merlot (Sonoma Valley) $18. **87** *— (11/15/2002)*

Kunde 2003 Block 4SB20 Sauvignon Blanc (Sonoma Valley) $19. A bit pricy, but a good wine for its crisp, minerally mouthfeel and bone-dry, palate-cleansing finish. Has intense flavors of lemons and grapefruits. **87** *—S.H. (10/1/2005)*

Kunde 2003 Magnolia Lane Sauvignon Blanc (Sonoma Valley) $15. The best Magnolia in recent memory. Rich and sophisticated in gooseberry, fig, and vanilla flavors, totally dry, and with crisp acidity, this wine is clean and refreshing. Cries out for oysters, or just about anything. **88** *—S.H. (12/31/2004)*

Kunde 2001 Magnolia Lane Sauvignon Blanc (Sonoma Valley) $14. **86** *—S.H. (9/1/2003)*

Kunde 1999 Magnolia Lane Sauvignon Blanc (Sonoma Valley) $13. **87 Editors' Choice** *—S.H. (8/1/2001)*

Kunde 1999 Syrah (Sonoma Valley) $23. **87** *(11/1/2001)*

Kunde 1997 Estate Bottled Syrah (Sonoma Valley) $20. **90** *(2/1/2000)*

Kunde 2004 Viognier (Sonoma Valley) $24. Wow, is this wine ever unripe. It has the skunky, cat pee smell of the greenest Sauvignon Blanc, and is raspingly dry and acidic. Weird for a variety famed for its exotic fruitiness. **83** *—S.H. (12/31/2005)*

Kunde 2002 Viognier (Sonoma Valley) $23. Few wineries have a more consistent track record with this rare Rhône white than Kunde. This year, as usual, the wine is brilliant in tropical fruit, apple, peach, honeysuckle, and buttery-vanilla flavors. It's well-balanced with acids and just a touch of oak. **90** *—S.H. (2/1/2004)*

Kunde 2000 Viognier (Sonoma Valley) $23. **87** *—J.M. (12/15/2002)*

Kunde 1999 Zinfandel (Sonoma Valley) $15. **82** *—S.H. (11/15/2001)*

Kunde 2001 Century Vines Zinfandel (Sonoma Valley) $25. **85** *(11/1/2003)*

Kunde 2000 Estate Bottled Zinfandel (Sonoma Valley) $16. **85** *—S.H. (11/1/2002)*

Kunde 1997 Robusto Zinfandel (Sonoma Valley) $30. **89** *—S.H. (5/1/2000)*

Kunde 1999 Shaw Vineyard Century Vines Zinfandel (Sonoma Valley) $25. **86** *—S.H. (7/1/2002)*

Kunde 1997 Shaw Vineyard Century Vines Zinfandel (Sonoma Valley) $24. **87** *—P.G. (11/15/1999)*

KUNIN

Kunin 2003 Syrah (Santa Barbara County) $28. This SBC Syrah's flavors are very ripe, with accents of coffee and meat. Full and soft in the mouth, it's an all-purpose, enjoyable wine. **87** *(9/1/2005)*

Kunin 2000 Syrah (Santa Maria Valley) $35. **85** *—S.H. (12/1/2002)*

Kunin 2002 Alisos Vineyard Syrah (Santa Barbara County) $35. A good, though overdone, wine. Intense in the mouth, but it is heavy on the earth, prune, and coffee flavors. A smooth feel segues into a mocha-laden finish; 300 cases produced. **86** *(9/1/2005)*

Kunin 2000 French Camp Syrah (Paso Robles) $28. **85** *—S.H. (12/1/2002)*

Kunin 2000 Stolpman Vineyard Viognier (Santa Ynez Valley) $28. **91** *—J.M. (12/15/2002)*

KYNSI

Kynsi 2002 Pinot Noir (Edna Valley) $28. Opens with lots of toasty oak, but as nice as those charry, vanilla accents are, this wine can't quite overcome a certain rustic character, despite scads of well-ripened black cherry and raspberry flavors. **85** *—S.H. (10/1/2005)*

Kynsi 1999 Paragon Vineyard Pinot Noir (Edna Valley) $25. **88** *—R.V. (7/1/2003)*

Kynsi 2002 Edna Ranch Vineyard Syrah (Edna Valley) $28. Edna Valley is one of the coolest prime coastal areas in California, and this wine is fresh in acidity. It starts with a burst of white pepper and black currants, then turns long and juicy in the mouth, showing just how ripe the grapes got. This is beautiful Syrah, balanced, rich, and nuanced. **92 Editors' Choice** *(9/1/2005)*

Kynsi 1998 South Ridge Vineyard Syrah (Paso Robles) $25. **83** *—S.H. (7/1/2002)*

L'AVENTURE

L'Aventure 2002 Cuvée Côte a Côte Red Blend (Paso Robles) $70. Quite delicious, and despite the full-bodiedness, it's balanced and elegant. Offers a generous mouthful of black cherries, blackberries, chocolate, and sweet meats, wrapped in rich, thick, sweet tannins. Might be a little tricky to pair with foods due to high alcohol. Try something enormously rich. Grenache-Syrah blend. **92** *—S.H. (6/1/2005)*

L'Aventure 2002 Optimus Red Blend (Paso Robles) $50. This complex Syrah and (with a little Zin) showcases both varieties at their western Paso Robles best. The Syrah is rich in dark berry-cherry and mocha flavors, while the Cabernet adds cassis and a nice tannic structure. I'm not sure what the 4 % of Zin brings, maybe a wild, peppery note. The final impression is of real class and distinction. Drink now and for the next few years. **94 Editors' Choice** *—S.H. (10/1/2005)*

L'Aventure 2000 Optimus Red Blend (Paso Robles) $45. 93 *—S.H. (11/15/2003)*

L'Aventure 2001 Syrah (Paso Robles) $NA. There is certainly some warm weather influence in the sinfully ripe blackberry pie and cherry tart flavors. On the other hand, cooler winds from the Pacific have left intact the citrusy acidity and edgy tannins. The result is elegance and charm, a showcase for this emerging appellation. **91** *—S.H. (6/1/2004)*

L'Aventure 1999 Syrah (Paso Robles) $36. 90 *(11/1/2001)*

USA

L'ECOLE NO 41

L'Ecole No 41 1999 Apogee Pepper Bridge Vineyard Bordeaux Blend (Walla Walla (WA)) $42. 90 *—P.G. (6/1/2002)*

L'Ecole No 41 2002 Pepper Bridge Vineyard Apogee Bordeaux Blend (Walla Walla (WA)) $45. L'Ecole's Bordeaux blend is divided equally between Merlot (48%) and Cab Sauvignon (48%), with Cab Franc (4%) filling out the rest. Forward and open, it carries scents and flavors of light cherry, blackberry, and hints of herb. Very smooth and supple, flavorful and easy to drink, but just a bit light for a Meritage-style wine. **88** *—P.G. (4/1/2005)*

L'Ecole No 41 1998 Pepper Bridge Vineyard Apogee Bordeaux Blend (Walla Walla (WA)) $42. 90 *—P.G. (6/1/2001)*

L'Ecole No 41 2002 Cabernet Sauvignon (Columbia Valley (WA)) $30. L'Ecole does a really nice job with this 100% pure varietal wine, which smells of sweet black cherry fruit, cinnamon, spice, and smoke. Very satisfying on the palate, it is smooth and supple, seems to expand and layer itself seamlessly as it cascades through the mouth, and lasts a good long while. Sweet, ripe fruit and nicely managed tannins, with some potential to age for 8–10 years. **90 Cellar Selection** *—P.G. (4/1/2005)*

L'Ecole No 41 2000 Cabernet Sauvignon (Columbia Valley (WA)) $30. L'Ecole does a really nice job with this friendly wine, which is forward, accessible, and unchallenging. Perfect with pizza, burgers, or Friday night poker games, it captures sweet, ripe fruit and nicely managed tannins. **87** *—P.G. (9/1/2004)*

L'Ecole No 41 1999 Cabernet Sauvignon (Walla Walla (WA)) $36. 87 *—P.G. (12/31/2002)*

L'Ecole No 41 1998 Cabernet Sauvignon (Walla Walla (WA)) $36. 91 *—P.G. (12/31/2001)*

L'Ecole No 41 1997 Cabernet Sauvignon (Walla Walla (WA)) $33. 89 *—J.C. (6/1/2001)*

L'Ecole No 41 2003 Chardonnay (Columbia Valley (WA)) $20. A young, soft, and very pleasant wine, with flavors of red delicious apples and suggestions of pear. Broad and smooth, forward and easy-drinking. Nice hints of toast and cinnamon add interest. **87** *—P.G. (4/1/2005)*

L'Ecole No 41 2000 Chardonnay (Columbia Valley (WA)) $19. 88 *—P.G. (2/1/2002)*

L'Ecole No 41 2001 Walla Voila Chenin Blanc (Washington) $12. 89 *—P.G. (9/1/2002)*

L'Ecole No 41 2000 Merlot (Columbia Valley (WA)) $29. 87 *—P.G. (9/1/2002)*

L'Ecole No 41 1999 Merlot (Columbia Valley (WA)) $30. 86 *—P.G. (12/31/2001)*

L'Ecole No 41 1998 Merlot (Columbia Valley (WA)) $36. 87 *—P.G. (6/1/2001)*

L'Ecole No 41 1999 Seven Hills Vineyard Merlot (Walla Walla (WA)) $40. 91 *—P.G. (12/31/2001)*

L'Ecole No 41 2003 Barrel-Fermented Sémillon (Columbia Valley (WA)) $15. L'Ecole's other two Sémillons are 100%, but this budget bottling smartly blends in just the right amount (13%) of Sauvignon Blanc, filling in the tart kiwi-flavored fruit and light herbs with hints of creamy, spicy oak. **90 Best Buy** *—P.G. (4/1/2005)*

L'Ecole No 41 1999 Barrel-Fermented Sémillon (Columbia Valley (WA)) $15. 89 *—P.G. (6/1/2001)*

L'Ecole No 41 2000 Barrel-Fermented Sémillon (Columbia Valley (WA)) $15. 88 Best Buy *—P.G. (12/31/2001)*

L'Ecole No 41 2001 Fries Vineyard Sémillon (Washington) $20. From an excellent source that has traditionally provided L'Ecole's best Sémillon. The wine is so big, so bursting with ripe and delicious fruit, yet perfectly balanced and complex, that it makes you wonder: why doesn't anyone else do this with Sémillon? It's flat out stunning, revelatory. **93 Editors' Choice** *—P.G. (9/1/2004)*

L'Ecole No 41 1999 Fries Vineyard Sémillon (Wahluke Slope) $22. 92 *—P.G. (6/1/2001)*

L'Ecole No 41 2002 Fries Vineyard-Wahluke Slope Sémillon (Washington) $20. From a source that has traditionally provided L'Ecole's best Sémillon. Consistent year after year, this is a big, bold wine, bursting with ripe and delicious fruit. It's not quite up to the winery's extraordinary 2001, but this vintage tilts slightly towards the hot end of the flavor spectrum, while remaining lush, toasty, and satisfying. **90** *—P.G. (7/1/2004)*

L'Ecole No 41 2001 Seven Hills Vineyard Sémillon (Walla Walla (WA)) $20. Pure sémillon, with a ripe, honeyed richness to it. This is a soft, luscious wine, round and slightly oxidized, ready to drink and quite flavorful with distinctive streaks of Asian spice, herb, and honey. The flavors last and last. **90** *—P.G. (9/1/2004)*

L'Ecole No 41 1999 Seven Hills Vineyard Sémillon (Walla Walla (WA)) $22. 93 Editors' Choice *—P.G. (6/1/2001)*

L'Ecole No 41 2003 Seven Hills Vineyard Syrah (Walla Walla (WA)) $37. A corpulent Syrah, with lots of dark plum and sweet oak flavors and just enough pepper to keep things interesting. Finishes with a powerful blast of coffee and caramel. **87** *(9/1/2005)*

L'Ecole No 41 1999 Seven Hills Vineyard Syrah (Walla Walla (WA)) $34. 92 Editors' Choice *(11/1/2001)*

L'UVAGGIO DI GIACOMO

L'Uvaggio di Giacomo 2000 Il Gufo Barbera (California) $16. 84 *—S.H. (2/1/2003)*

L'Uvaggio di Giacomo 1999 Il Leopardo Nebbiolo (California) $18. 85 *—S.H. (2/1/2003)*

L. PRESTON

L. Preston 2000 Red Blend (Dry Creek Valley) $24. 84 *—S.H. (12/1/2002)*

LA BETE

La Bete 1998 Knight's Gambit Vyd Pinot Noir (Willamette Valley) $40. 92 *—M.M. (12/1/2000)*

La Bete 2002 Sélection du Cave Pinot Noir (Oregon) $20. Fairly simple, this is quite tart, citric, and on the edge of unripe. Orange peel and rhubarb are the dominant notes, and it's refreshing, though possibly too tart for some tasters. **86** *(11/1/2004)*

LA CREMA

La Crema 2001 Chardonnay (Sonoma Coast) $16. 87 *—S.H. (8/1/2003)*

La Crema 2000 Chardonnay (Russian River Valley) $24. 85 *—S.H. (7/1/2003)*

La Crema 1999 Chardonnay (Russian River Valley) $30. 90 *(7/1/2001)*

La Crema 1997 Cold Coast Vineyards Chardonnay (Sonoma Coast) $16. 90 *—S.H. (11/1/1999)*

La Crema 1997 Reserve Chardonnay (Russian River Valley) $27. 90 *(6/1/2000)*

La Crema 2000 Pinot Noir (Sonoma Coast) $25. 85 *(10/1/2002)*

La Crema 2000 Pinot Noir (Carneros) $26. 90 Editors' Choice *(10/1/2002)*

La Crema 1999 Pinot Noir (Carneros) $35. 87 *—S.H. (12/15/2001)*

La Crema 2002 Syrah (Sonoma County) $24. A very supple, easy-to-drink version of Syrah that showcases cherry-berry fruit carried along on a plush bed of cedary oak. A bit simple. **83** *(9/1/2005)*

La Crema 2000 Viognier (Sonoma Valley) $24. 84 *—S.H. (12/15/2001)*

LA FAMIGLIA DI ROBERT MONDAVI

La Famiglia di Robert Mondavi 1999 Barbera (California) $19. 86 *—S.H. (12/1/2002)*

La Famiglia di Robert Mondavi 1997 Barbera (California) $20. 87 *—S.H. (9/1/2000)*

La Famiglia di Robert Mondavi 1999 Moscato Bianco Moscato (California) $11. 90 *—S.H. (12/31/2000)*

La Famiglia di Robert Mondavi 1997 Pinot Grigio (California) $16. 88 *—M.S. (11/15/1999)*

La Famiglia di Robert Mondavi 2002 Pinot Grigio (California) $15. Tastes like the production on this wine was really stretched. The flavors are thin, tasting of lemon and grapefruit juices dissolved in water. There's lots of acidity, too. But it's pleasantly clean. **84** *—S.H. (8/1/2004)*

La Famiglia di Robert Mondavi 1999 Pinot Gris (Anderson Valley) $16. 86 *—S.H. (8/1/2001)*

La Famiglia di Robert Mondavi 1997 Sangiovese (California) $19. 89 *—S.H. (9/1/2000)*

La Famiglia di Robert Mondavi 2000 Sangiovese (California) $20. 87 *—S.H. (9/1/2003)*

La Famiglia di Robert Mondavi 1999 Colmera Tuscan Blend (Napa Valley) $45. This blend of Sangiovese, Syrah and Teroldego is very soft, and glides over the palate like a silk sheet. It is very dry, and has berry and herb flavors. It seems designed by Tim Mondavi for the table, for it is an understated, subtle wine, not an authoritative one. **86** *—S.H. (3/1/2004)*

LA FERME MARTIN

La Ferme Martin 1998 Merlot (Long Island) $14. 85 *—J.C. (4/1/2001)*

LA GARZA

La Garza 1999 Reserve Cabernet Sauvignon (Oregon) $27. 84 *—C.S. (12/31/2002)*

LA JOTA VINEYARD

La Jota Vineyard 2001 Cabernet Franc (Howell Mountain) $62. I know of no Cab Franc that costs more than this, but this is a very good wine. Be forewarned, it's high in alcohol and thick in tannins, so forget about drinking it now. Deep down inside is a teasing core of ripe, sweetly decadent cherry fruit that's yearning to be free. Hold until 2010. **91** *—S.H. (11/15/2004)*

La Jota Vineyard 2004 *Barrel Sample* Cabernet Sauvignon (Napa Valley) $NA. Gorgeous aromas of blackberry tart, vanilla, and oak lead to strong, rich fruity flavors of cherries and blackberries. So ripe, it finishes almost sweet. Rich in tannins, and compelling for its depth and harmony. **93** *—S.H. (8/1/2004)*

La Jota Vineyard 2001 Petite Sirah (Howell Mountain) $46. Big, rich in fruit, astringent in tannins, crisp in acids, high in alcohol, and well-oaked. The flavors are the darkest stone fruits. Drink now with short ribs or lamb, or age as long as you want. It will outlive you. **88** *—S.H. (11/15/2004)*

LA ROCHELLE

La Rochelle 2001 Pinot Noir (Monterey) $18. Good example of cool Central Coast Pinot, with its polished, jammy flavors of cherry and raspberry and dusty spices, complexed with smoky oak. Bright acidity and gentle tannins make for an easy drink. A little light, but a pretty good value. **86** *—S.H. (3/1/2004)*

USA

LA SIRENA

La Sirena 2001 Cabernet Sauvignon (Napa Valley) $125. Very distinctive, opening with pencil lead and cedar-cigar box aromas. Very fine and pure. Airing coaxes out the deep blackberry, red and black cherry, and blueberry flavors. Finishes with a sweep of sweet fennel. Well-structured and delicious now, and should age beyond 2010. **93** *—S.H. (11/1/2005)*

La Sirena 2002 Syrah (Santa Ynez Valley) $45. Nice nose on this wine, blending graham cracker, marshmallow, and chocolate notes into a veritable smoregasbord of aromas. Doesn't quite have the same richness on the palate, however, and turns a bit tart on the finish. **86** *(9/1/2005)*

LA STORIA

La Storia 2002 Zinfandel (Alexander Valley) $28. A ton of smoky, charry oak has been slathered on this wine, lending it caramel and butterscotch aromas, but it's also terrifically fruity. Bursting with ripe cherry and black raspberry flavors that drink dry and balanced. From Trentadue. **88** *—S.H. (3/1/2005)*

LA TOUR

La Tour 2002 Chardonnay (Napa Valley) $18. This deliciously lush and richly textured wine is blessed with a fine blend of ripe, tropical flavors redolent of papaya and mango. It's got good acidity for balance and also shows subtle hints of citrus and melon flavors. In fact, it tastes like it costs twice as much as the suggested retail price. A first release from Tom LaTour, better known as the head of the San Francisco-based Kimpton Hotel Group. The grapes were grown on his Mt. Veeder vineyard. **91** *—J.M. (10/1/2004)*

LACHINI

Lachini 2002 Pinot Noir (Willamette Valley) $30. Smoky and aggressive, this is a wham-bam style with enough saddle leather to call in the cavalry. Toast, coffee, smoke, and caramel pile on oaky flavors. It's big, rough-hewn, and tannic, but tasty. **88** *(11/1/2004)*

Lachini 2002 Lachini Family Estate Pinot Noir (Willamette Valley) $35. Seductive floral accents make a nice entry, and the wine, tart and juicy, carries aromas and flavors of orange peel, sour cherry, and bitter chocolate. **87** *(11/1/2004)*

LADERA

Ladera 2002 Cabernet Sauvignon (Howell Mountain) $65. Tasted alongside Ladera's '01 Lone Canyon Cab, this is better structured. The acid and tannin ballet is an exciting one, joined by rich smoky oak and a ripe Cabernet expression of black currants and cassis that's delicious. This is a major-league wine that should develop through 2010. **92 Cellar Selection** *—S.H. (12/1/2005)*

Ladera 2001 Lone Canyon Vineyard Cabernet Sauvignon (Napa Valley) $65. A lovely Cab. Although it's got some richly dry tannins, it's soft and melted enough to drink now. The flavors of black currants, cassis, and cocoa harmonize perfectly with finely toasted oak. **89** *—S.H. (12/1/2005)*

LAETITIA

Laetitia 1997 Cuvée M (Arroyo Grande Valley) $28. **88** *—J.M. (12/1/2001)*

Laetitia 2004 Chardonnay (Arroyo Grande Valley) $16. This Chard shows the boldly ripe flavors of tropical fruits, roasted hazelnuts, buttercream, Asian spices, and toast that many California Chards have, but also a distinctively high acidity that pushes those flavors out and makes them sing. **92 Editors' Choice** *—S.H. (12/31/2005)*

Laetitia 2001 Estate Chardonnay (Arroyo Grande Valley) $18. **90 Editors' Choice** *—S.H. (5/1/2003)*

Laetitia 1997 Estate Reserve Chardonnay (Arroyo Grande Valley) $26. **92** *—L.W. (11/15/1999)*

Laetitia 1998 Reserve Chardonnay (Arroyo Grande Valley) $33. **89** *(7/1/2001)*

Laetitia 2004 Pinot Blanc (Arroyo Grande Valley) $16. Well-structured and totally dry, with very high acidity and intense flavors of citrus fruits, figs, green apples, and slightly unripe peaches. This polished, elegant wine is a natural with a wide variety of food. **88** *—S.H. (12/31/2005)*

Laetitia 1999 Estate Pinot Blanc (Arroyo Grande Valley) $16. 90 Editors' Choice *—S.H. (11/15/2001)*

Laetitia 2000 Pinot Noir (Arroyo Grande Valley) $25. 87 *(10/1/2002)*

Laetitia 1999 Pinot Noir (Santa Barbara County) $25. 91 *—J.M. (7/1/2002)*

Laetitia 2002 Estate Pinot Noir (Arroyo Grande Valley) $25. Shows rich charcoal, roast coffee, cherry, anise, vanilla, and cola flavors, in a medium-bodied wine that's balanced and dry. There's some real complexity in the flavors and crisp acidity. Powerful tannins suggest aging. Drink now through 2007. **88** *—S.H. (11/1/2004)*

Laetitia 2000 Estate Reserve Pinot Noir (Arroyo Grande Valley) $35. 88 *—S.H. (7/1/2003)*

Laetitia 1997 Estate Reserve Pinot Noir (Arroyo Grande Valley) $33. 91 *(10/1/1999)*

Laetitia 2002 La Colline Pinot Noir (Arroyo Grande Valley) $60. This is a masculine Pinot, deep in color and muscular, but elegant. Think Armani. The flavors veer toward dark fruits and berries, such as blackberries, spicy blue plums, coffee bean, and even bitter dark chocolate, yet the wine possesses an airy, lilting quality, thanks to soft tannins and brisk acidity. **92** *—S.H. (2/1/2005)*

Laetitia 1999 La Colline Pinot Noir (Arroyo Grande Valley) $60. 92 Cellar Selection *(10/1/2002)*

Laetitia 2003 Les Galets Pinot Noir (Arroyo Grande Valley) $60. This block designate from Laetitia's estate vineyard comes from a warmer, eastern site. It is high in acidity and extremely dry. The flavors and mouthfeel are so complex that it takes several sips to grasp what's going on, by which time the wine has climbed to even higher levels. This is truly great California Pinot Noir. **95** *—S.H. (12/1/2005)*

Laetitia 2001 Les Galets Pinot Noir (Arroyo Grande Valley) $60. Les Galets, from Laetitia's estate vineyard, is a brilliant wine. It's fuller and denser than the companion La Colline bottling, with plum and spicy blackberry flavors and a molasses, Indian pudding note. Tannins are evident but not intrusive. This serious Pinot Noir is built to improve in the cellar through 2007. **92** *—S.H. (6/1/2004)*

Laetitia 2002 Reserve Pinot Noir (Arroyo Grande Valley) $40. A beautiful Pinot of considerable power and subtlety. Shows ripe flavors of blackberries, blueberries, and cocoa, with minerals and hard spices. There's a firmness to the mouth feel but also a lusciousness, and the silky finish is polished. **90** *—S.H. (2/1/2005)*

Laetitia 2000 Brut Cocquard (Arroyo Grande Valley) $25. 87 *—J.M. (12/1/2003)*

Laetitia NV Brut Cuvée (Arroyo Grande Valley) $18. Bone dry and elegantly clean in acidity, this doughy, austere wine is less fruity than most California bruts, with accents of lime peel and vanilla. **86** *—S.H. (12/31/2005)*

Laetitia 2001 Brut de Noir (Arroyo Grande Valley) $25. This is the fullest-bodied of Laetitia's crop of bubblies. It has a tinge of raspberries and strawberries, but is still an elegantly structured, silky wine, a nice interpretation of Central Coast sparkling wine. **88** *—S.H. (12/31/2005)*

Laetitia 2003 Syrah (Arroyo Grande Valley) $25. There aren't many Arroyo Grande Syrahs, this being Burgundian terroir, but this one aspires to Côte Rôtie standards. It's a fine and interesting wine. Shows white pepper and blackberry flavors, quite dry and well-oaked, with intricate tannins. Best now and through 2006. **92** *—S.H. (12/31/2005)*

LAFOND

Lafond 1998 Lafond Vineyard Chardonnay (Santa Ynez Valley) $30. 87 *(7/1/2001)*

Lafond 1997 Sweeney Canyon Chardonnay (Santa Ynez Valley) $28. 87 *(6/1/2000)*

Lafond 2000 Lafond Vineyard Pinot Noir (Santa Ynez Valley) $35. A good wine but just a tad simple. The aromas are on the weedy, hay side, with suggestions of forest floor and oak, and in the mouth, coffee and bitter cherry flavors fight their way up through thick tannins. Possibly a victim of its vintage. **86** *—S.H. (2/1/2004)*

Lafond 1997 Lafond Vineyard Pinot Noir (Santa Ynez Valley) $35. 82 *—S.H. (2/1/2001)*

Lafond 2000 Joughin Vineyard Syrah (Santa Ynez Valley) $30. From a warmer, inland vineyard, a well-structured Syrah with lush tannins, good acids, and a fancy overall mouthfeel that nevertheless is thin in fruit. The hay, straw, and herb flavors just manage to suggest blackberries. Still, the wine's bones are good. **86** *—S.H. (3/1/2004)*

Lafond 1998 Lafond Vineyard Syrah (Santa Ynez Valley) $28. 90 *(11/1/2001)*

Lafond 2000 SRH Syrah (Santa Ynez Valley) $18. 89 *—S.H. (12/1/2002)*

LAGIER

Lagier Meredith 2000 Syrah (Mount Veeder) $50. A fine mountain wine, tough and tannic in youth, with a gritty tightness and bite of fresh acidity in the finish. But there's a dense core of cherry-berry fruit and an earth, mushroomy concentration that suggests ageability. **88** *—S.H. (2/1/2004)*

LAGO DI MERLO

Lago di Merlo 2001 Sangiovese (Dry Creek Valley) $19. This wine is delicate and crisply silky. It has cherry and kirsch flavors that turn a bit hot and burnt in the finish. **84** *—S.H. (11/1/2005)*

LAIL

Lail 2001 J. Daniel Cuvée Cabernet Sauvignon (Napa Valley) $80. Made from Howell Mountain grapes, yet rich and approachable in youth. There are huge, chewy tannins, but they're sweet, and frame black currant and cherry-chocolate fudge flavors. This makes it sound like a dessert wine, but it's dry and balanced and entirely satisfying. **92** *—S.H. (10/1/2004)*

Lail 1999 J. Daniel Cuvée Cabernet Sauvignon (Napa Valley) $80. 95 Editors' Choice *—S.H. (11/15/2002)*

Lail 2002 Blueprint Merlot-Cabernet Sauvignon (Napa Valley) $45. Dominated by Merlot, this is a soft wine with cherry, blueberry, and blackberry flavors. There's an earthiness that keeps it from being a fruit bomb, as well as a sweetness from oak, that will delight chefs figuring out how to prepare duck or lamb. Very dry and complex, with a lingering finish, it is delicious now, and should hold for five years. **93 Editors' Choice** *—S.H. (11/1/2005)*

LAIRD

Laird 2000 Cabernet Sauvignon (Napa Valley) $60. Four-plus years have not helped this unripe wine. It remains herbal and even vegetal, with a tough, astringent finish, despite some nice oak. **82** *—S.H. (8/1/2005)*

Laird 1999 Rutherford Ranch Cabernet Sauvignon (Rutherford) $75. 91 *—D.T. (6/1/2002)*

Laird 1999 Chardonnay (Napa Valley) $40. 88 *(7/1/2001)*

LAKE SONOMA

Lake Sonoma 2001 Cabernet Sauvignon (Alexander Valley) $22. Still pretty tannic after all these years, and with a sharp bitterness in the finish, this wine is at its peak. It has cherry and cassis flavors and is a little sweet. **82** *—S.H. (12/15/2005)*

Lake Sonoma 1999 Cabernet Sauvignon (Alexander Valley) $22. 86 *—S.H. (10/1/2003)*

Lake Sonoma 2004 Chardonnay (Russian River Valley) $16. Too oaky for my tastes, this wine brims with spicy, smoky new-woody flavors and woodsap sweetness that overshadow the fruit. Aren't we past the toothpick stage? **83** *—S.H. (12/15/2005)*

Lake Sonoma 2002 Chardonnay (Russian River Valley) $15. For the past few years, Lake Sonoma has been crafting intensely oaky, well-ripened Chards that offer lots of drinking pleasure. This wine is redolent of peaches and tropical fruits, and is spicy and smooth. **86** *—S.H. (6/1/2004)*

Lake Sonoma 2000 Chardonnay (Russian River Valley) $15. 84 *—J.M. (12/15/2002)*

Lake Sonoma 1998 Chardonnay (Russian River Valley) $17. 88 *(6/1/2000)*

Lake Sonoma 2003 Fumé Blanc (Dry Creek Valley) $14. A really beautiful white wine, really distinctive for its flavors of grassy hay and citrus fruits with richer notes of sweet figs, spicy melons, and smoky oak. Quite complex, with a creamy texture, and not overly sweet. **88 Best Buy** *—S.H. (3/1/2005)*

Lake Sonoma 2002 Zinfandel (Dry Creek Valley) $16. Soft and dry, this is a generic, medium-bodied red wine that could be anything. It has berry and chocolate flavors, and a gentle scour of tannins. **84** *—S.H. (10/1/2005)*

Lake Sonoma 2000 Zinfandel (Dry Creek Valley) $17. 86 *—S.H. (3/1/2003)*

Lake Sonoma 1999 Zinfandel (Dry Creek Valley) $15. 85 *—J.M. (3/1/2002)*

Lake Sonoma 1997 Old Vine Zinfandel (Sonoma County) $17. 91 Editors' Choice *—P.G. (3/1/2001)*

Lake Sonoma 1999 Old Vine Saini Farms Zinfandel (Dry Creek Valley) $20. 89 *—J.M. (11/1/2002)*

Lake Sonoma 1998 Saini Farms Old Vine Zinfandel (Dry Creek Valley) $24. 86 *—J.M. (11/15/2001)*

LAMBERT BRIDGE

Lambert Bridge 1998 Crane Creek Cuvée Bordeaux Blend (Dry Creek Valley) $50. 92 *—S.H. (6/1/2002)*

Lambert Bridge 1999 Crane Creek Cuvée Cabernet Blend (Dry Creek Valley) $50. 88 *—S.H. (5/1/2003)*

Lambert Bridge 2001 Chardonnay (Sonoma County) $20. 85 *—S.H. (12/1/2003)*

Lambert Bridge 1999 Chardonnay (Sonoma County) $20. 89 *—J.M. (11/15/2001)*

Lambert Bridge 1997 Chardonnay (Dry Creek Valley) $24. 90 *—L.W. (10/1/1999)*

Lambert Bridge 2002 Merlot (Sonoma County) $26. Made from about 90% Dry Creek fruit, Lambert Bridge's Merlot is very dry and softly scented with red cherry, sweet pipe tobacco, and coffee flavors nudging into cocoa. It has a delicate, refined mouthfeel, showing less power than sheer finesse. **90** *—S.H. (11/1/2005)*

Lambert Bridge 1999 Merlot (Sonoma County) $24. 92 Editors' Choice *—S.H. (7/1/2002)*

Lambert Bridge 2000 Old Vine Cuvée, Bacchi Vineyards Red Blend (Russian River Valley) $32. 87 *—J.M. (11/15/2002)*

Lambert Bridge 2001 Sauvignon Blanc (Dry Creek Valley) $16. 85 *—J.M. (9/1/2003)*

Lambert Bridge 2000 Dry Creek Sauvignon Blanc (Dry Creek Valley) $16. 85 *(9/1/2003)*

Lambert Bridge 2000 Viognier (Placer County) $20. 88 *—J.M. (11/15/2001)*

Lambert Bridge 2003 Damiano Vineyards Viognier (Placer County) $20. Has all the flamboyant tropical fruit, wildflower, spice, white chocolate, and buttery vanilla flavors you could want. This is the type of Viognier that grabs your attention and demands equally exotic fare. Try with duck with a fruity, gingery sauce. 88 *—S.H. (2/1/2005)*

Lambert Bridge 2000 Zinfandel (Dry Creek Valley) $24. 84 *—S.H. (11/1/2002)*

Lambert Bridge 1997 Dry Creek Valley Zinfandel (Dry Creek Valley) $22. 91 *—L.W. (9/1/1999)*

LAMOREAUX LANDING

Lamoreaux Landing NV Pinot Noir (Finger Lakes) $12. 87 *(11/15/1999)*

LANCASTER

Lancaster 1999 Estate Bottled Bordeaux Blend (Alexander Valley) $65. 89 *(10/1/2003)*

Lancaster 2002 Estate Red Wine Cabernet Blend (Alexander Valley) $70. There's a classic Alexander Valley softness and herbaceousness to the cherry, cassis, blueberry, and oak flavors of this Cab, and while it's rich and balanced enough to drink with the best steak you can find, it should age for a while. Best now through 2009. 90 *—S.H. (12/15/2005)*

LANDMARK

Landmark 2001 Damaris Reserve Chardonnay (Sonoma) $30. Lush, creamy, and soft, featuring bold flavors of mango, pineapple, and ripe pear framed in plenty of oak. The finish is long and spicy. This opulent Chard is a real crowd-pleaser. 92 Editors' Choice *—S.H. (2/1/2004)*

Landmark 1998 Damaris Reserve Chardonnay (Sonoma County) $32. 86 *(10/1/2000)*

Landmark 2002 Lorenzo Chardonnay (Russian River Valley) $45. This is a nice, rich Chard, with good peach and pineapple flavors and pronounced oak shadings. It's dry, with good acidity and a creamy mouthfeel. 87 *—S.H. (8/1/2005)*

Landmark 2001 Overlook Chardonnay (Sonoma) $25. 87 *—S.H. (12/15/2003)*

Landmark 1998 Overlook Chardonnay (Sonoma County) $22. 85 *(6/1/2000)*

Landmark 1999 Grand Detour Van Der Kamp Pinot Noir (Sonoma Mountain) $45. 86 *(10/1/2002)*

Landmark 2001 Grand Detour Van der Kamp Vineyards Pinot Noir (Sonoma Mountain) $30. Shows classic cool coastal Pinot Noir characteristics of light-bodied, silky smooth tannins, crisp acidity and delightful flavors of ripe raspberries, red cherries, cola, and spices. A little one-dimensional, but totally drinkable. 88 *—S.H. (10/1/2005)*

Landmark 1999 Kastania Vineyard Pinot Noir (Sonoma Coast) $45. 89 *(10/1/2002)*

LANE TANNER

Lane Tanner 2000 Pinot Noir (Santa Maria Valley) $22. 87 *—S.H. (7/1/2003)*

Lane Tanner 2000 Bien Nacido Vineyard Pinot Noir (Santa Maria Valley) $28. 91 Editors' Choice *—S.H. (7/1/2003)*

Lane Tanner 2003 Julia's Vineyard Pinot Noir (Santa Maria Valley) $30. Hard and resistant, both in acids and in fruit. Suggestions of cherries are offset by green, stalky notes. Finishes very dry. Not going anywhere, so drink up. 86 *—S.H. (10/1/2005)*

Lane Tanner 2002 Melville Vineyard Pinot Noir (Santa Rita Hills) $25. Long and rich in ripe black cherry, blueberry, and blackberry flavors, with an exquisite edge of dusty spice, this fully dry wine excites for its balance and seductiveness. It's silky and airy, but a serious Pinot Noir. So good now it's hard to resist, but could actually improve over the next 5 years. 93 Editors' Choice *—S.H. (10/1/2005)*

Lane Tanner 1997 Syrah (San Luis Obispo County) $20. 88 *—S.H. (10/1/1999)*

Lane Tanner 2000 French Camp Vineyard Syrah (San Luis Obispo County) $20. 89 *—S.H. (9/1/2002)*

Lane Tanner 2001 Reserve Syrah (Santa Barbara County) $22. Delicately fruited and tart, with some minty-wintergreen notes and cherry-berry flavors. Built on acidity rather than tannin, as you might expect from a winemaker known for her Pinot Noirs. 84 *(9/1/2005)*

LANG & REED

Lang & Reed 2000 Cabernet Franc (Napa Valley) $21. 87 *—M.S. (12/1/2002)*

Lang & Reed 2000 Wild Hare Cabernet Franc (Rutherford) $15. 84 *—J.M. (11/15/2001)*

LANGTRY

Langtry 1998 Bordeaux Blend (Guenoc Valley) $23. 84 *—L.W. (3/1/2000)*

Langtry 1997 Meritage Bordeaux Blend (North Coast) $50. 91 *(11/1/2000)*

Langtry 2002 Meritage White Blend (Guenoc Valley) $20. Easy drinking, dry white wine, crisp in acids and clean of finish, with earthy, citrus, and peach flavors. It's the kind of wine that seems to go with everything. **85** *—S.H. (12/31/2004)*

LAPIS LUNA

Lapis Luna 2000 Merlot (California) $10. A dry, fairly tannic wine that intrigues with an array of plums, herbs, coffee, and tobacco. Don't turn away because it's not fruity. There's some real complexity and elegance here. **86 Best Buy** *—S.H. (12/15/2004)*

LARAINE

Laraine 2002 Gerber Vineyards Syrah (Sierra Foothills) $22. Plummy and chocolaty and a little sweet. Finishes oaky, with some raisiny notes, and very soft. **84** *—S.H. (2/1/2005)*

LARKMEAD

Larkmead 2001 Merlot (Napa Valley) $35. Smooth and supple, with pretty cherry, smoke, and vanilla flavors and a hint of smoked meat or bacon fat. Drinks easy in tannins, with a dry finish. **85** *—S.H. (12/15/2004)*

USA

LATAH CREEK

Latah Creek 2002 Chardonnay (Washington) $11. 88 Best Buy *—P.G. (12/31/2003)*

Latah Creek 2002 Moscato d'Latah Moscato (Washington) $14. 86 *—P.G. (12/31/2003)*

LATCHAM

Latcham 2000 Sauvignon Blanc (El Dorado) $12. 89 Best Buy *—S.H. (9/1/2002)*

Latcham 2001 Special Reserve Zinfandel (El Dorado) $25. 86 *(11/1/2003)*

LATITUDE 46° N

Latitude 46° N 2004 Clifton Cuvée Red Wine Syrah (Columbia Valley (WA)) $18. At 76% Syrah, this red blend (the balance is Grenache) just squeaked past our tasting censors. It's a bit soft and jammy, also high in alcohol, but boasts loads of ripe cherry-berry fruit backed by a hint of chocolate. **83** *(9/1/2005)*

LATOUR

LaTour 2003 Chardonnay (Napa Valley) $39. A little too sweet, both in oak and in fruit, for a dry table wine. But the flavors, of white peaches and lime custard, are tasty. **84** *—S.H. (10/1/2005)*

LAUREL GLEN

Laurel Glen 2000 Cabernet Sauvignon (Sonoma Mountain) $50. In vintages like this, Laurel Glen can be a tough love. This version is extremely dry and raspingly tannic and herbal, with black cherry and sweet oak shadings. Will it soften and sweeten with age? Roll the dice until 2008. **87** *—S.H. (10/1/2004)*

Laurel Glen 1999 Cabernet Sauvignon (Sonoma Mountain) $50. 92 *—S.H. (11/15/2002)*

Laurel Glen 2001 Counterpoint Cabernet Sauvignon (Sonoma Mountain) $25. What a great junior sibling to the real Laurel Glen. Super-ripe in black currant and cassis fruit, this dry wine has firm, ripe tannins, and is well-oaked. Polished and supple. Drink now. **87** *—S.H. (12/15/2004)*

Laurel Glen 1999 Counterpoint Cabernet Sauvignon (Sonoma Mountain) $25. 91 *—S.H. (9/12/2002)*

Laurel Glen 1999 Red Blend (California) $9. 86 Best Buy *—S.H. (7/1/2002)*

Laurel Glen 2001 Reds (California) $8. This wine has become quite popular with the public, mainly due to its price, but I have often found it stemmy and crude. In its favor it has bigtime fruit and easy tannins, and sloshes around the mouth quite well. Zin, Petite Sirah, and Carignane. **84** *—S.H. (9/1/2004)*

Laurel Glen 1999 Old Vine Za Zin Zinfandel (California) $18. 90 *—S.H. (7/1/2002)*

Laurel Glen 2000 Za Zin Zinfandel (Lodi) $15. 85 *—S.H. (11/1/2002)*

LAUREL LAKE

Laurel Lake 1998 Reserve Cabernet Sauvignon (North Fork of Long Island) $18. 82 *—J.C. (4/1/2001)*

Laurel Lake 1999 Reserve Chardonnay (North Fork of Long Island) $15. A lean style, with unripe pear notes married to a pencilly cedar-graphite combination. Very lemony and tart on the finish, this Chard will probably be at its best with shellfish. **87** *—J.C. (1/1/2004)*

Laurel Lake 2000 Merlot (North Fork of Long Island) $14. 82 *—J.C. (10/2/2004)*

LAURIER

Laurier 2000 Chardonnay (Carneros) $15. 86 *—S.H. (6/1/2003)*

Laurier 2000 Merlot (Dry Creek Valley) $15. Here's a wine with charm and elegance. Very dry, with cherry-berry flavors and a streak of sweet dill and tobacco. Has a rich, creamy texture and a sweet hit of oak. **85** *—S.H. (10/1/2004)*

LAUTERBACH

Lauterbach 2001 Pinot Noir (Russian River Valley) $32. A nice Russian River Pinot, with its pretty flavors of sweet cherries, root beer, and spice, and the crisp acidity that cool nights bring. Glides across the palate like silk, but has some over-ripe raisiny flavors that detract. **87** *—S.H. (12/1/2004)*

LAVA CAP

Lava Cap 2000 Granite Hill Reserve Petite Sirah (El Dorado) $30. **83** *(4/1/2003)*

Lava Cap 2001 Reserve Syrah (El Dorado) $20. Starts promising, with delicate scents of herbs, cherries, menthol, and a hint of citrus peel, but quickly accelerates into jammy, cooked raspberries and lashings of vanilla that turn inexplicably tart and aggressive on the finish. Perplexing. **84** *(9/1/2005)*

Lava Cap 1998 Reserve Syrah (El Dorado) $20. **89** *(10/1/2001)*

LAWRENCE J. BARGETTO

Lawrence J. Bargetto 1998 Chardonnay (Santa Cruz Mountains) $20. **89** *(6/1/2000)*

LAWSON RANCH

Lawson Ranch 2002 Lockwood Vineyard Chardonnay (Monterey County) $8. This likeable wine gets the basic Chard job done with its creamy texture, veneer of sweet, toasty oak, and flavors of peaches, pineapples, and pears. Nice spices on the finish. **84 Best Buy** *—S.H. (7/1/2005)*

LAZY CREEK

Lazy Creek 2000 Gewürztraminer (Anderson Valley) $16. **89** *—S.H. (5/1/2002)*

Lazy Creek 1999 Barrel #9 Gewürztraminer (Anderson Valley) $27. **87** *—S.H. (5/1/2002)*

Lazy Creek 1999 Pinot Noir (Anderson Valley) $26. **94** *—S.H. (5/1/2002)*

LE BON VIN DE LA NAPA VALLEY

Le Bon Vin de la Napa Valley 2003 Cabernet Sauvignon (Napa Valley) $10. This new wine from Don Sebastiani & Sons is a value worth seeking out. It shows real Napa finesse, in the smooth, rich tannins and classic Cabernet black currant and cherry flavors, with a sweet coating of oak. **85 Best Buy** *—S.H. (12/31/2005)*

LE CUVIER

Le Cuvier 1999 Zinfandel (San Luis Obispo County) $30. **88** *—J.M. (2/1/2003)*

LE VIN

Le Vin 2000 Chardonnay (Russian River Valley) $19. **88** *—S.H. (8/1/2003)*

LEAL VINEYARDS

Leal Vineyards 2001 Cabernet Sauvignon (San Benito County) $24. Here's a full-bodied, fruity Cab, rich in blackberries and cherries and all sorts of other berries and fruits. It's a little hot, but easy to drink. **84** *—S.H. (10/1/2005)*

Leal Vineyards 2001 Carnivàl Meritage (San Benito County) $24. Fruity, but overly soft and sweet, with a sugary finish. **81** *—S.H. (11/15/2005)*

Leal Vineyards 2003 Estate Grown Threesome Rhône Style Blend Rhône Red Blend (San Benito County) $24. This Rhône blend is rustic and super-fruity, with an astringent, tannic mouthfeel and a semisweet finish. It seems overpriced for what you get. **83** *—S.H. (12/31/2005)*

Leal Vineyards 2002 Estate Grown Syrah (San Benito County) $24. Lush and creamy, according to one taster, undefined and flabby says another. Both agree on the wine's super-ripe fruit—akin to blackberry brandy—and ultrasoft tannins. It's just a question of personal preference. **86** *(9/1/2005)*

LEAPING HORSE

Leaping Horse 2001 Chardonnay (Lodi) $5. **84** *—S.H. (2/1/2003)*

Leaping Horse 2003 Shiraz (Lodi) $5. A little too soft in acids, and gooey in cassis and oak flavors, but this wine has good, rich tannins and a chocolaty taste on the finish. **84 Best Buy** *—S.H. (8/1/2005)*

LEAPING LIZARD

Leaping Lizard 2003 Chardonnay (Napa Valley) $10. One of the better values out there right now, this Chard features flavors of juicy yellow peach, green apple, and pineapple, with a touch of spicy, vanilla-tinged oak, housed in a soft, creamy texture. **85 Best Buy** *—S.H. (11/15/2005)*

LEDGEWOOD CREEK

Ledgewood Creek 2002 Limited Reserve Suisun Valley Chardonnay (North Coast) $18. Ultra-ripe in all sorts of fruity flavors, notably pear, and with a rich application of smoky oak, this wine will appeal to fans of big, unctuous Chards. It's spicy and long on the finish, too. **85** *—S.H. (6/1/2004)*

Ledgewood Creek 2001 Suisun Valley Chardonnay (North Coast) $13. **83** *—S.H. (10/1/2003)*

LEDSON

Ledson 2002 Cabernet Franc (Alexander Valley) $48. Here's a very ripe Cabernet Franc whose plummy flavors veer into dried prunes. It's dry, and a little hot, but there's something nice about it. It's honest and forthright, and will support food without overwhelming it. **86** *—S.H. (7/1/2005)*

Ledson 2002 Reserve Cabernet Sauvignon (Alexander Valley) $110. Semisweet and rustic, this cherry and cassis-flavored wine is also soft and flabby. A ton of oak doesn't really help to make it any better than it is. **82** *—S.H. (12/31/2005)*

Ledson 2002 Chardonnay (Russian River Valley) $24. Quite a smooth and polished Chard. It impresses for its up front apple and pear flavors, and is balanced, dry and crisp. Fills the mouth with spice through the finish. **87** *—S.H. (8/1/2004)*

Ledson 2000 Chardonnay (Arroyo Seco) $20. 86 *—S.H. (5/1/2003)*

Ledson 1999 Reserve Chardonnay (Russian River Valley) $32. 88 *(7/1/2001)*

Ledson 2000 Johannisberg Riesling (Monterey) $16. 87 *—S.H. (6/1/2002)*

Ledson 1998 Merlot (Sonoma Valley) $34. 93 *—S.H. (7/1/2002)*

Ledson 2002 Pinot Noir (Russian River Valley) $36. Starts off a little minty and green, although you'll find an undercurrent of racy red cherry. It's not the most opulent Pinot, but the crisp acids and silky smooth tannins offer lots to like. **85** *—S.H. (11/1/2004)*

Ledson 2000 Rosé Blend (California) $14. 87 *—S.H. (9/10/2002)*

Ledson 2003 Sauvignon Blanc (Russian River Valley) $20. Polished and clean, a wine whose grassy, citrus flavors are enhanced with notes of melon and smoky oak. Turns thin in the middle, with an oaky, spicy finish. **85** *—S.H. (12/15/2004)*

Ledson 2000 Sauvignon Blanc (Napa Valley) $18. 87 *(8/1/2002)*

Ledson 2002 Century Vine Zinfandel (Russian River Valley) $46. Lots of perky acidity here, to offset and balance the super-ripe black currant and cocoa flavors. There's a spicy note of licorice or anise that adds to the profile. Fancy stuff. Search out the perfect recipe for this one. **90** *—S.H. (10/1/2005)*

Ledson 2001 Old Vine Zinfandel (Russian River Valley) $30. How close a good Zin gets to great Cab is well-illustrated with this complex, plush wine. It's dry, soft and clean, and brimming with ripe, chocolatey fruit. What makes it uniquely varietal is the brambly pepperiness. **89** *—S.H. (12/31/2004)*

Ledson 1999 Old Vine Zinfandel (Dry Creek Valley) $28. 87 *—S.H. (7/1/2002)*

Ledson 1999 Old Vines Zinfandel (Russian River Valley) $36. 88 *—S.H. (7/1/2002)*

LEEWARD

Leeward 1998 Reserve Chardonnay (Edna Valley) $16. 85 *(6/1/2000)*

Leeward 1997 Bien Nacido Vineyard Pinot Noir (Santa Barbara County) $20. 86 *(11/15/1999)*

LEHRER

Lehrer 2002 Syrah (Contra Costa County) $34. Supple and creamy, with roasted fruit and coffee flavors joined by vanilla and caramel notes. Some meat and molasses flavors chime in on the finish, which features a burst of citrusy acidity. **84** *(9/1/2005)*

LEMELSON

Lemelson 2000 Wascher Vineyard Chardonnay (Willamette Valley) $26. 90 *—P.G. (9/1/2003)*

Lemelson 1999 Pinot Gris (Oregon) $18. 88 *—P.G. (2/1/2002)*

Lemelson 2001 Pinot Noir (Oregon) $13. 88 *—P.G. (4/1/2003)*

Lemelson 2002 Jerome Reserve Pinot Noir (Willamette Valley) $44. The top of the Lemelson line, this tart, clean, refreshing wine is saturated with the flavors of just-picked berries. An excellent food wine, with bracing acid and a firm grip. **90** *(11/1/2004)*

Lemelson 1999 Jerome Reserve Pinot Noir (Willamette Valley) $44. 91 *—P.G. (12/31/2001)*

Lemelson 2002 Resonance Vineyard Pinot Noir (Willamette Valley) $38. Pretty cherry and plum scents open into richer, sweeter sensations of blackberry pie. Medium weight, soft, and accessible, it finishes with sweet, chocolaty oak. **88** *(11/1/2004)*

Lemelson 2000 Stermer Vineyard Pinot Noir (Willamette Valley) $38. 89 *—P.G. (4/1/2003)*

Lemelson 2000 Thea's Selection Pinot Noir (Willamette Valley) $29. 88 *—P.G. (4/1/2003)*

Lemelson 2002 Thea's Selection Pinot Noir (Willamette Valley) $29. Very pretty, satiny, creamy, and delicious. Flavors of black cherry and cream are mixed with sassafras and spice, a very winning combination. **88** *(11/1/2004)*

LENZ

Lenz 1997 Cabernet Sauvignon (North Fork of Long Island) $30. 88 *—J.C. (4/1/2001)*

Lenz 1998 Gold Label Chardonnay (North Fork of Long Island) $25. 87 *—J.C. (4/1/2001)*

Lenz 1998 Gewürztraminer (North Fork of Long Island) $12. 87 Best Buy *—J.C. (4/1/2001)*

Lenz 1997 Estate Bottled Merlot (North Fork of Long Island) $55. 91 Cellar Selection *—J.C. (4/1/2001)*

LEONARDO FAMILY VINEYARDS

Leonardo Family Vineyards 2001 Cabernet Sauvignon (Lodi) $12. 85 *—S.H. (8/1/2003)*

Leonardo Family Vineyards 2002 Pinot Grigio (California) $10. 85 *—S.H. (12/1/2003)*

LEONETTI CELLAR

Leonetti Cellar 2001 Reserve Bordeaux Blend (Walla Walla (WA)) $95. Reserve is their version of a classic Bordeaux blend; this vintage pencils out as 48% Cabernet Sauvignon, 37% Merlot, the rest split evenly between Cab Franc and Petit Verdot. Sweet black cherry fruit is married seamlessly to layers of different flavored chocolates; long, silky, seamless, and seductive. Styled for near-term enjoyment. **94** *—P.G. (11/15/2004)*

Leonetti Cellar 2002 Cabernet Sauvignon (Walla Walla (WA)) $65. Leonetti continues to hit the high marks it sets for itself in this, its 25th vintage. The Walla Walla Cab includes 10% Merlot and small batches of Cab Franc and Carmenère. The astonishing, classic Leonetti aromas of penetrating, ripe black fruits, cedar, coffee, and chocolate are there in spades, but the overall impression is that the oak has been pulled back just a bit, or perhaps the fruit is just that much riper. Violets and lead pencil continue the stream of sensuous highlights, as the wine winds into its pungent, densely saturated finish. **94** *—P.G. (12/15/2005)*

Leonetti Cellar 2000 Cabernet Sauvignon (Walla Walla (WA)) $65. 93 *—P.G. (9/1/2003)*

Leonetti Cellar 1998 Cabernet Sauvignon (Columbia Valley (WA)) $60. 95 *—P.G. (10/1/2001)*

Leonetti Cellar 1998 Reserve Cabernet Sauvignon (Walla Walla (WA)) $95. 96 *—P.G. (10/1/2001)*

Leonetti Cellar 2002 Merlot (Columbia Valley (WA)) $55. Firm and muscular, this delivers powerful, concentrated red currant, cherry and berry fruit, tightly wrapped and resonant. Young and compact, the wine just begins to hint at the complexity it contains, with notes of herb, leaf, and barrel spice. Good weight and concentration, plus exceptional length and precision. **92 Editors' Choice** *—P.G. (11/15/2004)*

Leonetti Cellar 2000 Merlot (Columbia Valley (WA)) $55. 91 *—P.G. (9/1/2002)*

Leonetti Cellar 1998 Merlot (Columbia Valley (WA)) $50. 94 *—P.G. (11/15/2000)*

Leonetti Cellar 2002 Sangiovese (Walla Walla (WA)) $50. Don't let the apparent lightness of this stylish Sangio fool you; its elegant demeanor does not in any way mean it is wimpy. Here is fresh, lively fruit, spiced with citrus rind, showing clean, varietal fruit and a perfect kiss of oak. **91** *—P.G. (11/15/2004)*

Leonetti Cellar 2000 Sangiovese (Walla Walla (WA)) $50. 91 *—P.G. (9/1/2002)*

Leonetti Cellar 1998 Sangiovese (Walla Walla (WA)) $50. 91 *—P.G. (11/15/2000)*

LEVERONI

Leveroni 2003 Chardonnay (Carneros) $16. A nice example of a Carneros Chard, balanced in tree fruit flavors, with crisp acidity and a hint of pear liqueur on the finish. It's clean and refreshing. **85** *—S.H. (4/1/2005)*

Leveroni 2002 Merlot (Sonoma Valley) $18. What a nice wine this is. It's dry and balanced, and although there's a complex structure of tannins, it's drinkable now. The flavors veer between blackberries, plums, coffee, leather and dusty spices. **90** *—S.H. (4/1/2005)*

Leveroni 2004 Pinot Noir (Sonoma Valley) $18. One sniff and you know the grapes were baked. Smells like that gummy filling that burbles over the edge of a cherry pie in the oven. In the mouth, it's a little more forgiving, but still finishes with the taste of raisins. **83** *—S.H. (12/15/2005)*

Leveroni 2003 Syrah (Sonoma Valley) $18. The texture is smooth and fine, the tannins just right, but the fruitiness is too up front, in your face. There's just unrestrained gobs of cherries and jammy berries. Whatever happened to balance? **83** *—S.H. (12/15/2005)*

LEWIS

Lewis 1997 Reserve Cabernet Sauvignon (Napa Valley) $60. 96 Cellar Selection *(11/1/2000)*

Lewis 2002 Syrah (Napa Valley) $60. In the lush, richly textured and oaky style that seems to becoming typical of Napa Syrah, this wine stands out as an exemplar of the type. Vanilla-infused berries finish long, with a hint of alcohol and a touch of coconut. A touch lacking in typical Syrah-like complexity, but an excellent wine. **90** *(9/1/2005)*

LIBERTY SCHOOL

Liberty School 2003 Cabernet Sauvignon (California) $12. This is a good price for a Cab that's dry, balanced, and elegant. It's obviously not a blockbuster, but the way the cherry, and blackberry flavors interact with oak and dried herbs makes the wine charming and even complex. **87 Best Buy** *—S.H. (12/15/2005)*

Liberty School 2003 Chardonnay (Central Coast) $12. This Chard has some decent citrus and peach fruit, but it's really too tart and sour to offer much pleasure. **82** *—S.H. (12/15/2005)*

Liberty School 2000 Chardonnay (Central Coast) $14. 82 *—S.H. (9/1/2003)*

LIEB

Lieb 1993 Champagne Blend (North Fork of Long Island) $20. 86 *—J.C. (4/1/2001)*

Lieb 1997 Reserve Merlot (North Fork of Long Island) $20. 88 *—J.C. (4/1/2001)*

LIGHTHOUSE

Lighthouse 2002 Crescendo Chardonnay (Central Coast) $15. Offers lime, pineapple, and mango flavors—even a hint of banana—with bright acidity and hints of vanilla and buttered toast. There's nothing subtle about this Chard. **87** *—S.H. (7/1/2005)*

LILY

Lily 2002 Chardonnay (Sonoma County) $16. Not showing much beyond a huge, unbalanced plaster of charred oak. Smells and tastes like toothpicks. **83** *—S.H. (8/1/2005)*

LIMERICK LANE

Limerick Lane 2003 Collins Vineyard Syrah (Russian River Valley) $28. While this Syrah may not quite reach the heights of the old-vine Zinfandel from this vineyard, the vines are several decades younger. Even now, the results are impressive: bold raspberry fruit is couched in ultra-ripe tannins and framed by hints of vanilla. It even picks up some spice and game notes on the finish. **89** *(9/1/2005)*

Limerick Lane 1999 Collins Vineyard Syrah (Russian River Valley) $36. 90 *(11/1/2001)*

Limerick Lane 2001 Collins Vineyard Zinfandel (Russian River Valley) $26. 86 *(11/1/2003)*

Limerick Lane 1998 Collins Vineyard Zinfandel (Russian River Valley) $26. 90 *(3/1/2001)*

LINCOURT

Lincourt 2002 Chardonnay (Santa Barbara County) $18. Cool-climate Chard, with crisp, outspoken acidity and flinty flavors. A scour of fresh lime and mineral hits in the middle, leading to sweet oak on the aftertaste. **87** *—S.H. (5/1/2005)*

Lincourt 2001 Pinot Noir (Santa Barbara County) $22. Released along with the '02, this wine still tastes young and fresh. It has cool Southland acids and is delicate in structure, with a mélange of herb, rhubarb, and cherry flavors. **87** *—S.H. (5/1/2005)*

Lincourt 2003 Syrah (Santa Barbara County) $20. Squeaky clean, richly fruity and perfectly inviting, this ripe, elegant Syrah starts with modest blackberry notes, then opens up to show more raspberry and vanilla shadings. Not a blockbuster, just ripe, creamy, and well crafted. Good value, too. **89** *(9/1/2005)*

LINDEN

Linden 2001 Glen Manor Bordeaux Blend (Virginia) $29. Black cherry, tobacco, and brown sugar scents start this wine down the right track, and the mouthfeel is supple and creamy, but things come a bit unglued on the short-lived finish, where the flavors turn tart. **83** *—J.C. (9/1/2005)*

Linden 1997 Reserve Red Bordeaux Blend (Virginia) $28. The barrels seem expensive: the copious flamboyant smoky, toasty oak is soft, forward, and tasty. But the fruit doesn't quite measure up, leaving a bit of a hollow in the midpalate. A blend of 65% Cabernet Sauvignon, 27% Cabernet Franc, 5% Petit Verdot, and 3% Merlot. **83** *—J.C. (1/1/2004)*

Linden 1999 Glen Manor Red Blend (Virginia) $23. 84 *—M.S. (3/1/2003)*

Linden 2000 Vidal Blanc (Virginia) $22. 89 *—J.M. (1/1/2003)*

LINNE CALODO

Linne Calodo 2003 Nemesis Rhône Red Blend (Paso Robles) $60. Nemesis contains almost 90% Syrah, the highest percentage of Linne Calodo's three current red releases. It's a big, dark wine, saturated with cassis and dark chocolate flavors, with delicious notes of cherries, raspberries, and oak. It has an interesting and complex tannin-acid structure. This compelling, authoritative Rhône blend showcases the brilliance of its terroir. **94 Editors' Choice** *—S.H. (10/1/2005)*

Linne Calodo 2003 Sticks and Stones Rhône Red Blend (Paso Robles) $60. With a majority of Grenache, this wine flatters with pure, sweet red and black cherry flavors. Syrah seems to bring color and depth, while Mourvèdre contributes a delicious chocolate note. The wine is fully dry, high in alcohol, soft in acidity and utterly delicious. **92 Editors' Choice** *—S.H. (10/1/2005)*

LION VALLEY

Lion Valley 1999 Reserve Chardonnay (Willamette Valley) $16. 83 *—S.H. (4/1/2002)*

LIPARITA

Liparita 2001 Cabernet Sauvignon (Napa Valley) $38. Assembled from various parts of the valley, this classic Napa Cab showcases well-ripened black currant, French roast coffee, and oak flavors, and a smooth, rich, and complex texture. It's bold enough in firm tannins to age through this decade. **92** *—S.H. (5/1/2005)*

Liparita 1997 Cabernet Sauvignon (Napa Valley) $45. 92 *(11/1/2000)*

Liparita 1997 Vineyard Reserve Cabernet Sauvignon (Napa Valley) $65. 88 *(11/1/2000)*

Liparita 1998 Chardonnay (Carneros) $33. 88 *(7/1/2001)*

Liparita 1999 Sauvignon Blanc (Napa Valley) $18. 91 Editors' Choice *—S.H. (5/1/2001)*

LITTLE VALLEY

Little Valley 1999 White Rabbit Cabernet Sauvignon (San Francisco Bay) $18. 83 *—S.H. (11/15/2003)*

LIVINGSTON

Livingston 1996 Moffett Vineyard Cabernet Sauvignon (Napa Valley) $50. 88 *(3/1/2000)*

LIVINGSTON MOFFETT

Livingston Moffett 2002 Mitchell Vineyard Syrah (Napa Valley) $27. This Syrah receives a split vote from the panel, its fans lauding the rich, jammy aromas and flavors of blackberry and spice, and its soft tealike tannins on the finish. Its detractors found a stalky note on the palate, but could still applaud the wine's mouthfeel. **87** *(9/1/2005)*

Livingston-Moffett 1997 Gemstone Vineyard Bordeaux Blend (Napa Valley) $75. 90 *(11/1/2000)*

Livingston-Moffett 1999 Mitchell Vineyard Syrah (Napa Valley) $35. 89 *(11/1/2001)*

LLANO ESTACADO

Llano Estacado 1998 Celler Select Cabernet Sauvignon (Texas) $18. 90 *—S.H. (5/1/2001)*

Llano Estacado 2000 Cellar Select Chardonnay (Texas) $18. 90 *—S.H. (5/1/2001)*

Llano Estacado 1999 Passionelle Rhône Red Blend (Texas) $9. 84 *—S.H. (5/1/2001)*

LOCKWOOD

Lockwood 2001 Estate Cabernet Sauvignon (Monterey County) $12. This easy Cab gets the job done with its dry, smooth flavors of blackberries and cherries and a gentle touch of oak. It has enough tannins to cut through a big steak or chop, and finishes clean. **85** *—S.H. (7/1/2005)*

Lockwood 1999 Estate Grown & Estate Bottled Cabernet Sauvignon (Monterey) $15. 86 *— (11/15/2002)*

Lockwood 2000 Estate Grown & Bottled Chardonnay (Monterey) $15. 86 *—S.H. (2/1/2003)*

Lockwood 1998 VSR Chardonnay (Monterey) $35. 90 *(7/1/2001)*

Lockwood 1997 VSR Meritage (Monterey County) $45. 92 Editors' Choice *(6/1/2001)*

Lockwood 1997 Merlot (Monterey County) $18. 88 Best Buy *(6/1/2001)*

Lockwood 1999 Estate Grown & Estate Bottled Merlot (Monterey) $15. 86 *— (11/15/2002)*

Lockwood 1998 Pinot Blanc (Monterey) $12. 85 *(6/1/2001)*

Lockwood 1999 Sauvignon Blanc (Monterey County) $12. 87 Best Buy *(6/1/2001)*

Lockwood 1998 Estate Grown Sauvignon Blanc (Monterey) $11. 87 *—L.W. (5/1/2000)*

Lockwood 1996 Syrah (Monterey County) $15. 87 *—L.W. (2/1/2000)*

Lockwood 1999 Syrah (Monterey) $16. 85 *—S.H. (12/1/2002)*

Lockwood 2002 Shale Ridge Syrah (Monterey) $8. You'll like this fresh, young wine for its jammy blackberry and cherry flavors and rich, full-bodied texture. It's dry and spicy, with a long, fruity finish. **84** *—S.H. (4/1/2004)*

LOGAN

Logan 2001 Sleepy Hollow Vineyard Chardonnay (Monterey County) $18. From vintner Rob Talbott, a less expensive version of his single-vineyard Chard. It's crisp and oaky, with a suggestive leesy mouthfeel, and very dry. The flavors are complex, but highlighted by fresh pineapple and gingery spices. **87** *—S.H. (2/1/2004)*

Logan 2000 Pinot Noir (Monterey County) $18. From Robert Talbott, an easy "Intro to Monterey Pinot Noir" kind of wine. It has earthy cherry, cola, and rhubarb flavors, is very dry, and shows the crisp acidity and silky tannins you expect from the variety. **85** *—S.H. (10/1/2004)*

Logan 1999 Sleepy Hollow Vineyard Pinot Noir (Monterey County) $20. From Robert Talbott. This isn't a bad Pinot, although it's pretty tannic and also has some minty, tomatoey notes, in addition to the riper blackberries. Will satisfy Pinotphiles for its soft, silky tannins, crisp acids and complexity. **86** *—S.H. (2/1/2004)*

LOKOYA

Lokoya 2002 Cabernet Sauvignon (Mount Veeder) $120. There's something almost Zinny about this wine, with its brambly, briary notes of wild blueberries and blackberries and sun-warmed summer bark and dust. It possesses fabulous intensity, but those mountain tannins are palate-numbing, and they shut down the finish. Demands time beyond 2010. **94 Cellar Selection** *—S.H. (5/1/2005)*

LOLONIS

Lolonis 2001 Cabernet Sauvignon (Redwood Valley) $22. Long and rich in sun-ripened fruit, just brimming with blackberry jam and sweet chocolate flavors, spiced up with oak. Dry and balanced, an easy-to-drink wine with real complexity and flair. **87** *—S.H. (10/1/2004)*

Lolonis 1999 Private Reserve Cabernet Sauvignon (Redwood Valley) $35. Soft and delicate in structure, a gentle wine that has some pretty flavors of cherries and blackberries. It's a bit tart in acidity, and will be good with a rich steak. **85** *—S.H. (3/1/2004)*

Lolonis 2001 Winegrower Selection Cabernet Sauvignon (Redwood Valley) $32. A bit over-ripe, with chocolate-covered raisin flavors beside the fresher ones of blackberries. It's dry and clean, though, with a long, sweet finish. **84** *—S.H. (10/1/2004)*

Lolonis NV Carignane (Redwood Valley) $14. **86** *—S.H. (5/1/2002)*

Lolonis 1997 Chardonnay (Redwood Valley) $21. **86** *—S.H. (3/1/2000)*

Lolonis 1997 Late Harvest Chardonnay (Redwood Valley) $35. **88** *—S.H. (6/1/2003)*

Lolonis 2003 Fumé Blanc (Redwood Valley) $13. Very dry and crisp, with dusty, palate-stimulating acidity that frames citrus and fig. A good choice for goat cheese and grilled veggies on toast. **85** *—S.H. (12/1/2004)*

Lolonis 2000 Fumé Blanc (Redwood Valley) $14. **87** *—S.H. (5/1/2002)*

USA

Lolonis 2001 Merlot (Redwood Valley) $22. They say the 24-hour temperature shift in this Mendocino appellation swings by a huge amount. In this case, the hot daytime has yielded raisiny flavors, while the cool nighttimes provide the crisp acidity needed for balance. The result is interesting. **85** *—S.H. (6/1/2004)*

Lolonis 1999 Private Reserve Merlot (Redwood Valley) $28. **88** *—S.H. (8/1/2003)*

Lolonis 1997 Private Reserve Merlot (Redwood Valley) $28. **88** *(6/1/2001)*

Lolonis 2000 Petros Merlot-Syrah (Redwood Valley) $70. Pours dark and has closed, earthy aromas with a suggestion of blackberries and toast. This is a very dry, young wine, filled with acids and tannins, with a core of berry fruit. A blend of Merlot and Syrah. **84** *—S.H. (5/1/2004)*

Lolonis 1999 Orpheus-Private Reserve Petite Sirah (Redwood Valley) $35. **84** *(4/1/2003)*

Lolonis 2001 Ladybug Red Old Vines Red Wine Red Blend (Redwood Valley) $13. An enjoyable country wine. It's fruity, dry, and full-bodied, with the simple pleasures a well-made wine brings. **85** *—S.H. (6/1/2004)*

Lolonis 1998 Petros Red Blend (Redwood Valley) $70. **90** *—S.H. (5/1/2002)*

Lolonis 2002 Winegrower Selection Syrah (Redwood Valley) $32. I like the underlying wine here. It's rich in cassis and mocha fruit, and has excellently firm tannins and balancing acidity. On the downside, I find the wine overoaked. **86** *—S.H. (12/1/2005)*

Lolonis 2003 Zinfandel (Redwood Valley) $20. This Zin wine is so ripe, the fruit tastes cooked, like the goo that oozes out from an oven-baked cherry or raspberry pie. There are also chocolate fudge notes, with a cassis finish. It's pretty exotic, but dry. **85** *—S.H. (12/1/2005)*

Lolonis 2001 Zinfandel (Redwood Valley) $18. **90 Editors' Choice** *(11/1/2003)*

Lolonis 1999 Zinfandel (Redwood Valley) $20. **84** *—S.H. (5/1/2002)*

Lolonis 1999 Beaucage Vineyard Zinfandel (Redwood Valley) $30. **83** *—S.H. (5/1/2002)*

Lolonis 1996 Private Reserve Zinfandel (Redwood Valley) $25. **88** *—J.C. (9/1/1999)*

Lolonis 1998 Tollini Vineyard Zinfandel (Redwood Valley) $28. **87** *—P.G. (3/1/2001)*

Lolonis 2002 Winegrowers Selection Tollini Vineyard Zinfandel (Redwood Valley) $32. Clearly huge in fruit, this big wine startles with blackberry, cherry, raspberry, and cocoa flavors. If it was any riper it would have residual sugar, but it's dry. It's also rather rustic in the way the tannins and briary texture stick out, but it's a classic California Zin. **86** *—S.H. (8/1/2005)*

LONDER

Londer 2002 Kent Ritchie Vineyard Chardonnay (Sonoma Coast) $35. Fascinating wine, with a cool edge of minerally acidity that teases the palate with intense green apple and ripe peach flavors, and a lavish overlay of what tastes like new French oak. It all comes together in this fine, plush Chardonnay. **90** *—S.H. (6/1/2004)*

Londer 2002 Dry Gewürztraminer (Anderson Valley) $20. Has aromas and flavors of a wide array of fruits, spices, and wildflowers. It has very svelte acidity and is fully dry, but could use more concentration. **85** *—S.H. (6/1/2004)*

Londer 2001 Pinot Noir (Anderson Valley) $28. A rather lean wine that tries to find charm, but can't quite overcome the acidity and tannins. There's not a whole lot of fruit, but the cola and coffee flavors should perk up against a rich, marbled steak. **85** *—S.H. (6/1/2004)*

Londer 2001 Paraboll Pinot Noir (Anderson Valley) $42. Lean and herbal, with an Heirloom tomato edge, although there are hints of black cherry. The spareness only accentuates the acidity and tannins. A generous dollop of oak adds notes of smoke and vanilla. There's an angular elegance, though, and the wine may develop complexities in the bottle. **86** *—S.H. (6/1/2004)*

LONE CANARY

Lone Canary NV Red Bordeaux Blend (Yakima Valley) $13. A blend of Cab, Merlot, and Syrah, this forward, tasty effort charms with cherries and grapes, then surprises with a solid center core of plump cassis and raspberries, gently leading into a fruit-driven finish. A lot of bang for the buck. **88 Best Buy** *—P.G. (9/1/2004)*

Lone Canary NV Red Red Blend (Yakima Valley) $13. **85** *—P.G. (12/31/2003)*

Lone Canary 2003 Sauvignon Blanc (Yakima Valley) $10. The second vintage from Lone Canary follows right in the footsteps of the '02, with juicy, plump, tangy fruit front and center. Ripe with sweet grapefruit, pineapple, and citrus, it retains enough acid to keep it lively through the finish. **88 Best Buy** *—P.G. (9/1/2004)*

LONETREE

Lonetree 1997 Sangiovese (Mendocino) $17. **89** *—S.H. (9/1/2000)*

Lonetree 1998 Eaglepoint Ranch Syrah (Mendocino) $20. **87** *(10/1/2001)*

Lonetree 1996 Zinfandel (Mendocino) $16. **88** *—S.H. (5/1/2000)*

LONG MEADOW RANCH

Long Meadow Ranch 1997 Cabernet Sauvignon (Napa Valley) $50. **90** *(11/1/2000)*

Long Meadow Ranch 2001 Cabernet Sauvignon (Napa Valley) $55. A very fine wine that showcases Napa's rich, ripe tannins and perfectly ripened cassis fruit flavors. Oak, of course, brings vanilla, smoke, and additional sweetness. Not for the long haul, so best now for a few years. **90** *—S.H. (5/1/2005)*

Long Meadow Ranch 1998 Cabernet Sauvignon (Napa Valley) $57. **87** *—S.H. (11/15/2002)*

LONG RIDGE GROVE VINEYARDS

Long Ridge Grove Vineyards 2002 Chardonnay (California) $10. From the vast sea of statewide Chardonnay out there comes this perfectly acceptable wine. It has peach and apple flavors and some oak, and is creamy and dry. **84** *—S.H. (6/1/2004)*

LONG VINEYARDS

Long Vineyards 1998 Cabernet Sauvignon (Napa Valley) $60. **92** *—J.M. (12/1/2001)*

Long Vineyards 2002 Laird Family Vineyard Pinot Grigio (Carneros) $18. A tasty, easy wine that brims with spearmint chewing gum and sweet grapefruit flavors that veer into riper tropical fruits. It's crisp in acidity, with a good structure. Versatile at the table, and a great aperitif drink. **86** *—S.H. (2/1/2004)*

Long Vineyards 1999 Seghesio Vineyards Sangiovese (Sonoma County) $25. **85** *—J.M. (12/1/2001)*

LONGBOARD

Longboard 1999 Rochioli Vineyard Cabernet Sauvignon (Russian River Valley) $50. **93 Editors' Choice** *—S.H. (11/15/2002)*

Longboard 2002 Syrah (Russian River Valley) $33. Dark, big, and rich, and very fine. Starts off with elaborate and inviting aromas of smoky oak, blackberries, cocoa, coffee, and spice, and turns super-rich in the mouth, offering oodles of ripe, berry fruit and oak. Dry, with soft, lush tannins and complex, it's a beauty. **91** *—S.H. (12/31/2004)*

Longboard 2000 Syrah (Russian River Valley) $29. **91** *—S.H. (12/1/2002)*

Longboard 2002 Dakine Syrah (Russian River Valley) $47. Interesting to contrast this to Longboard's regular Syrah. This single-vineyard bottling is darker and considerably more tannic, although the aromatics and flavors are similar. It's elaborately oaked, and too astringent to enjoy now. The regular is the wine to drink in the next few years. Try after 2008. **90** *—S.H. (12/31/2004)*

LONGFELLOW

Longfellow 2001 Cabernet Sauvignon (Napa Valley) $50. A bit funky in smell and rough in texture, with herbal and berry flavors. Lots of tannins, not much fruit. **83** *—S.H. (5/1/2005)*

Longfellow 2001 Pinot Noir (Los Carneros) $36. A spicy rich wine, packed with bing cherry, raspberry, toast, menthol, and herb flavors. It's got good, but moderate length on the finish, backed by supple tannins and a bit of a licorice edge at the end. **89** *—J.C. (3/1/2004)*

Longfellow 2001 Syrah (Dry Creek Valley) $29. Opens with pretty strong notes of freshly ground white pepper, but turns lusciously fruity in the mouth, with cherry-berry flavors. The tannins are gritty and firm, leaving a dry, slightly scouring finish. A rack of lamb would be the perfect accompaniment. **87** *—S.H. (2/1/2004)*

LONGORIA

Longoria 2000 Blues Cuvée Cabernet Franc (Santa Ynez Valley) $25. **87** *—S.H. (6/1/2003)*

Longoria 2000 Clos Pepe Vineyard Chardonnay (Santa Barbara) $32. **90** *—S.H. (12/15/2002)*

Longoria 1999 Huber Vineyard Chardonnay (Santa Ynez Valley) $32. **86** *(7/1/2001)*

Longoria 1999 Mt. Carmel Vineyard Chardonnay (Santa Ynez Valley) $60. **88** *(7/1/2001)*

Longoria 1998 Santa Rita Cuvée Chardonnay (Santa Ynez Valley) $25. 87 *(6/1/2000)*

Longoria 2000 Santa Rita Hills Chardonnay (Santa Barbara County) $25. 92 *—S.H. (9/1/2002)*

Longoria 1999 Merlot (Santa Barbara County) $28. 87 *—S.H. (4/1/2003)*

Longoria 2002 Pinot Grigio (Santa Barbara County) $18. 88 *—S.H. (12/1/2003)*

Longoria 2001 Bien Nacido Vineyard Pinot Noir (Santa Maria Valley) $36. 85 *—S.H. (7/1/2003)*

Longoria 2002 Fe Ciega Vineyard Pinot Noir (Santa Rita Hills) $40. Similar to Longoria's Mt. Carmel bottling, but trades a shade of opulence for greater tannins and an earthy, tobaccoey note beside the cherries, mocha, and oak. Rich and complex, with firm acids and a silky texture. Serious Pinot Noir. **91 Editors' Choice** *—S.H. (11/1/2004)*

Longoria 2001 Mt. Carmel Pinot Noir (Santa Rita Hills) $50. 92 *—S.H. (10/1/2003)*

Longoria 2000 Mt. Carmel Vineyard Pinot Noir (Santa Barbara County) $50. 88 *(10/1/2002)*

Longoria 2001 Syrah (Santa Barbara County) $22. An excellent red wine, with nice body and structure. The flavors range from plums and black cherries to white pepper, and the tannins are voluptuously soft and complex. It's totally dry, a beautiful wine to pair with your finest foods. **92 Editors' Choice** *—S.H. (2/1/2004)*

Longoria 2001 Alisos Vineyard Syrah (Santa Barbara County) $22. A brilliant and impressive wine whose rich fruit, lush tannins, and structure recommend it. A mélange of blackberries and plums, with notes of mushrooms, herbs, and peppery spices. It's fully dry, but the fruit flavors are so ripe, they finish with a delicious sweetness. Drinkable now, but also cellarworthy. **93** *—S.H. (2/1/2004)*

LOOKOUT RIDGE

Lookout Ridge 2001 Keefer Ranch Pinot Noir (Sonoma Coast) $45. Fans of sheer volume will exult, but this wine, good as it is, is a bit overblown. It overwhelms with oak as well as berry flavor so ripe, it approaches chocolate-coated raisins. It is an interesting, well-made Pinot, yet would benefit from greater elegance and a lighter, defter touch. **88** *—S.H. (6/1/2005)*

LORANE VALLEY

Lorane Valley 1996 Chardonnay (Oregon) $10. 86 *—M.M. (12/31/1999)*

LORING WINE COMPANY

Loring Wine Company 2000 Clos Pepe Pinot Noir (Santa Lucia Highlands) $40. 91 Editors' Choice *(10/1/2002)*

Loring Wine Company 2003 Garys' Vineyard Pinot Noir (Santa Lucia Highlands) $46. As delicious as this wine is, it still treads the dangerous line of oversize. It's dark, full-bodied and dense in sweet blackberry, chocolate, and cherry flavors. It was easily ripened to its considerable size but there's something to be said for restraint and subtlety, especially with Pinot Noir. **90** *—S.H. (7/1/2005)*

Loring Wine Company 2000 Garys' Vineyard Pinot Noir (Santa Lucia Highlands) $40. 92 Editors' Choice *(10/1/2002)*

Loring Wine Company 2002 Rosella's Vineyard Pinot Noir (Santa Lucia Highlands) $46. Dark, heavy, and chocolatey. You might think you were drinking Syrah, it's so dense. It's a good, in fact a delicious wine, but where is the delicacy and elegance of Pinot Noir? Might age, but who knows? **85** *—S.H. (11/1/2004)*

LOST CANYON

Lost Canyon 2003 Dutton Ranch Morelli Lane Vineyard Pinot Noir (Russian River Valley) $38. Opens with peppermint, pepper, and oak aromas, and while there are richer cherry and spice flavors, this is still a sharp, eccentric wine. **84** *—S.H. (10/1/2005)*

Lost Canyon 2003 Las Brisas Vineyard Pinot Noir (Carneros) $38. While technically good, this is not a satisfying wine. It's lean and tart, and not quite ripe, with green flavors partially relieved by red cherries. **83** *—S.H. (10/1/2005)*

Lost Canyon 2003 Saralee's Vineyard Pinot Noir (Russian River Valley) $38. Smells funky, vegetal and even a little unclean, although some will call it barnyardy. Acidly sharp and austere in the mouth, and dry. **82** *—S.H. (10/1/2005)*

Lost Canyon 2003 Alegria Vineyard Syrah (Russian River Valley) $33. Quite high in acidity, but also pumped full of blackberry fruit, this Syrah comes across as a bit monolithic and tight at this stage of its evolution. Masses of soft tannins give promise for the future, so hold 2–3 years and see what develops. **87** *(9/1/2005)*

Lost Canyon 2003 Stage Gulch Vineyard Syrah (Sonoma Coast) $33. This bottling is similar to Lost Canyon's Trenton Station Russian River Syrah, in the cherry flavors, firm acids, and tannins and long finish. It may be a little tarter, but it's in the same ballpark. Drink it now, to best appreciate the fresh, savory fruit. **88** *(9/1/2005)*

Lost Canyon 2001 Stage Gulch Vineyard Syrah (Sonoma Coast) $33. 87 *—S.H. (12/15/2003)*

LOST RIVER

Lost River 2002 Cabernet Sauvignon (Columbia Valley (WA)) $23. Good fruit to start, with solid black cherry and berry notes well-matched to the new oak. But it seems to hit a wall mid-palate and fall off; perhaps it's just a bit of bottle shock. Score could improve with more time in bottle. **88** *—P.G. (4/1/2005)*

Lost River 2003 Sémillon (Columbia Valley (WA)) $14. What a score! This is sexy sémillon, kissed with honey and flowers, and supple with a round core of delicious, intriguing, complex fruits. Pear, apple, blood orange, and more are wrapped in a thoroughly delicious, well-rounded mid-palate, and the wine extends itself effortlessly into a lingering, delicious finish. Light enough to be food friendly, yet complex and wonderfully concentrated. **92 Best Buy** *—P.G. (12/1/2004)*

LOUIS M. MARTINI

Louis M. Martini 1995 Barbera (Lake County) $12. 87 Best Buy *—M.S. (9/1/2000)*

Louis M. Martini 2002 Cabernet Sauvignon (Napa Valley) $24. Here's a Cab made in Martini's old style, which was a dry, fairly tannic wine low in alcohol compared to today, and consequently less ripe, although there are some raisiny notes indicating unbalanced bunches. Drink now. **85** *—S.H. (12/1/2005)*

Louis M. Martini 2000 Cabernet Sauvignon (Napa Valley) $24. Earthy and herbal, with sage, dill, and mushroom flavors, and a streak of red cherry that only partly relieves the austerity. The tannins are tough and gritty, and lead to a dry, puckery finish. **84** *—S.H. (2/1/2004)*

Louis M. Martini 1999 Ghost Pines Vineyard Family Vineyard Selection Cabernet Sauvignon (Chiles Valley) $30. 84 *—S.H. (11/15/2003)*

Louis M. Martini 2000 Monte Rosso Vineyard Cabernet Sauvignon (Sonoma Valley) $55. Despite the difficulty of the vintage, this is a very good effort. It's bigger, fuller, and more-extracted than the '99, with muscular cedar, cassis, and graphite aromas and flavors. Drink, 2008–2012. **88** *(9/1/2005)*

Louis M. Martini 1999 Monte Rosso Vineyard Cabernet Sauvignon (Sonoma Valley) $50. 88 *—J.M. (11/15/2002)*

Louis M. Martini 1998 Monte Rosso Vineyard Cabernet Sauvignon (Sonoma Valley) $65. Already bricking a little bit at the rim, wines like this gave the '98 vintage a bad rep. The wine is still good, but nowhere what it can be, with fading fruit, green herbs, and sharp acidity on the finish. **85** *(9/1/2005)*

Louis M. Martini 1997 Monte Rosso Vyd Cabernet Sauvignon (Sonoma Valley) $40. 93 *(11/1/2000)*

Louis M. Martini 2001 Reserve Cabernet Sauvignon (Alexander Valley) $35. Has a flashy, showy nose of toasty, smoky oak, and vanilla, but also plenty of blackberry and cassis fruit. Ripe, lush, and oak-laden, but with enough chewy tannins to suggest cellaring a couple of years. **89** *(9/1/2005)*

Louis M. Martini 2000 Reserve Cabernet Sauvignon (Alexander Valley) $35. A beautifully balanced wine that shows how to make the best of a lesser vintage. The cherry, blackberry, and blueberry flavors are delicately framed in smoky oak, with a lush, smooth texture. **91** *—S.H. (2/1/2004)*

Louis M. Martini NV Family Vineyard Selection Del Rio Vineyard Chardonnay (Russian River Valley) $21. 84 *—S.H. (8/1/2001)*

Louis M. Martini 2001 Monte Rosso Vineyard Folle Blanche (Sonoma Valley) $18. 87 *—J.M. (9/1/2003)*

Louis M. Martini 2000 Del Rio Vineyard Gewürztraminer (Russian River Valley) $18. 88 *—S.H. (6/1/2002)*

Louis M. Martini 1997 Merlot (Chiles Valley) $25. 90 *—S.H. (11/15/2000)*

Louis M. Martini 1999 Ghost Pines Vineyard-Family Vineyard Selection Merlot (Chiles Valley) $27. 83 *—S.H. (12/1/2003)*

Louis M. Martini 2001 Monte Rosso Vineyard Sémillon (Sonoma Valley) $18. 87 *—S.H. (12/15/2002)*

Louis M. Martini 1999 Gnarly Vine Monte Rosso Vineyard Zinfandel (Sonoma Valley) $40. 87 *—J.M. (12/1/2002)*

Louis M. Martini 2001 Monte Rosso Vineyard Zinfandel (Sonoma Valley) $20. 84 *(11/1/2003)*

Louis M. Martini 1999 Monte Rosso Vineyard Zinfandel (Sonoma Valley) $30. 90 *—S.H. (12/15/2001)*

Louis M. Martini 1998 Monte Rosso Vineyard Gnarly Vine Zinfandel (Sonoma Valley) $40. 91 *—S.H. (12/15/2001)*

LOXTON

Loxton 2002 Sonoma Hillside Vineyards Syrah (Sonoma County) $24. Grilled meat and ripe berries combine in this medium-weight Syrah blended from five hillside vineyards. Australian winemaker Chris Loxton has crafted an admirably balanced wine that finishes with driving acidity and good length. **86** *(9/1/2005)*

LUCAS & LEWELLEN

Lucas & Lewellen 2001 Cabernet Franc (Santa Barbara County) $22. The cherry fruity sure ripened up, yet there's a sharpness and rusticity to this wine that detract. No obvious faults, though. **83** *—S.H. (7/1/2005)*

Lucas & Lewellen 2001 Côte del Sol Cabernet Sauvignon (Santa Barbara County) $32. Vegetal, unripe, with gluey-sweet flavors. **80** *—S.H. (8/1/2005)*

Lucas & Lewellen 2001 Valley View Vineyard Cabernet Sauvignon (Santa Barbara County) $25. Smells moldy, with berry flavors and a flat texture. **81** *—S.H. (8/1/2005)*

Lucas & Lewellen 2003 Chardonnay (Santa Barbara County) $15. Rustic, despite some ripe peach and other stone fruit flavors and what tastes vaguely like oak. **83** *—S.H. (8/1/2005)*

Lucas & Lewellen 2000 Goodchild Vineyard Chardonnay (Santa Barbara County) $20. 89 *—S.H. (12/15/2003)*

Lucas & Lewellen 2001 Merlot (Santa Barbara County) $21. Raw, with an unclean smell and sweet, medicinal flavors. **81** *—S.H. (8/1/2005)*

Lucas & Lewellen 2002 Petite Sirah (Santa Barbara County) $26. Dark and very tannic, and as dry as dust, this wine shows the deep core of plummy blackberries that the variety is known for, but could use finesse. **84** *—S.H. (8/1/2005)*

Lucas & Lewellen 2001 Vin Gris Pinot Noir (Santa Barbara County) $12. 87 *—S.H. (10/1/2003)*

Lucas & Lewellen 2001 Sauvignon Blanc (Santa Barbara County) $12. 86 *—S.H. (12/31/2003)*

LUCAS VINEYARDS

Lucas Vineyards NV Lucas Blanc de Blancs Chardonnay (Finger Lakes) $15. 82 *—J.C. (12/1/2003)*

Lucas Vineyards 2002 Semi-Dry Riesling (Finger Lakes) $10. 86 *—J.C. (8/1/2003)*

USA

LUCCA

Lucca NV Vino Rosso di Santa Barbara Red Wine Sangiovese (California) $10. A simple but very likeable blend that shows nice berry, plum, and earth flavors wrapped in sturdy, smooth tannins. It's very dry and balanced, with a tasty finish. Just about the perfect spaghetti wine. **86 Best Buy** *—S.H. (3/1/2005)*

LUNA

Luna 1999 Merlot (Napa Valley) $32. 88 *—S.H. (9/12/2002)*

Luna 2002 Sangiovese (Napa Valley) $18. Some will like the extracted, ripely sweet blackberry and cherry flavors, but not me. There's also that stinging Sangiovese acidity. **82** *—S.H. (12/15/2005)*

Luna 1999 Reserve Sangiovese (Napa Valley) $50. 88 *—S.H. (5/1/2002)*

LYETH

Lyeth 2002 L de Lyeth Cabernet Sauvignon (Sonoma County) $11. Bone dry, fairly astringent in tannins and with berry, coffee, and herb flavors, this wine is clean and correct. Fine for most everyday purposes. **83** *—S.H. (10/1/2004)*

Lyeth 2002 Meritage (Sonoma County) $15. Elegant rather than powerful, this Bordeaux blend shows earth, cherry, blackberry, and herb flavors wrapped in gentle oak. It's a bit tannic, just enough to bite into a nice piece of beef. **86** *—S.H. (2/1/2005)*

Lyeth 2002 L de Lyeth Merlot (Sonoma County) $11. A nice, balanced wine, with some good plummy, berry-cherry flavors. It's soft, easy, and very dry, and has an extra edge of complexity that makes it a good value. **85** *—S.H. (10/1/2004)*

LYNCH

Lynch 2002 Cabernet Sauvignon (Napa Valley) $60. A tightly wound, good cellar candidate. Balanced in rich tannins and acids, with solid cassis and cherry fruit and a sweet veneer of oak, it's splendid tonight with a steak, but should really hit its stride in a few years. **92** *—S.H. (7/1/2005)*

Lynch 2002 Lynch Knoll Vineyard Syrah (Spring Mountain) $65. This Syrah aims high. It's dry, rich, and full-bodied, with rich tannins and oak, and is fruity enough for the core of cassis to develop for several years. On the other hand, it has a sharp finish that may crack this wine up before the tannins fall out. **90** *—S.H. (7/1/2005)*

LYNMAR

Lynmar 2003 Chardonnay (Russian River Valley) $22. Too leesy and oaky for my taste, with tough, earthy-lemony flavors underneath. Acidity is tart. **84** *—S.H. (5/1/2005)*

Lynmar 2002 Quail Cuvée Chardonnay (Russian River Valley) $30. There's a ton of winemaker bells and whistles here, notably oak and lees, but they can't overcome the wine's lean earthiness. The result is unbalanced, although not unpleasurable. **85** *—S.H. (5/1/2005)*

Lynmar 1999 Pinot Noir (Russian River Valley) $28. 86 *—S.H. (2/1/2003)*

Lynmar 2001 Quail Hill Vineyard Quail Cuvée Pinot Noir (Russian River Valley) $35. Gorgeous. The grapes ripened perfectly, yielding lushly sweet cherry, raspberry, and sweet coffee flavors that have been enhanced with smoky, spicy oak. Completely dry, this seductively delicious wine is wonderfully silky, and finishes long. **93** *—S.H. (12/15/2004)*

Lynmar 1999 Reserve Pinot Noir (Russian River Valley) $50. 88 *—S.H. (2/1/2003)*

M. COSENTINO

M. Cosentino 1997 M. Coz Bordeaux Blend (Napa Valley) $100. 88 *(11/1/2000)*

M. Cosentino 1998 The Poet Bordeaux Blend (Napa Valley) $65. 88 *—J.M. (6/1/2002)*

M. Cosentino 1996 The Poet Bordeaux Blend (Napa Valley) $40. 87 *(2/1/2000)*

M. Cosentino 2001 Cabernet Franc (St. Helena) $34. This sure is a pretty wine. It's lighter in body than a mid-valley Cab Sauvignon, and veers more toward cherry than blackberry fruit. It's also gussied up with toasty oak. Finishes dry, rich and harmonious. **90** *—S.H. (3/1/2005)*

M. Cosentino 1999 Cabernet Franc (Napa Valley) $34. 84 *—S.H. (9/1/2002)*

M. Cosentino 2002 Cabernet Sauvignon (Napa Valley) $45. This isn't a wine to cellar. But it's a beautiful young wine now, one of the most attractive '02s around to accompany a fine meal. It's intricate in cassis and oak flavors, with flamboyantly ripe, complex tannins, and crisper acidity than Napa usually offers. Seems to improve with every sip. **90** *—S.H. (11/1/2005)*

M. Cosentino 2000 Cabernet Sauvignon (Napa Valley) $34. 85 *—S.H. (12/31/2003)*

M. Cosentino 2002 Hoopes Ranch Cabernet Sauvignon (Oakville) $75. What a great job Mitch Cosentino does with Bordeaux varieties. This one continues the tradition. Rich and dramatic in cassis, cherry, and toast, this balanced wine has smooth, polished tannins and a long finish. Remarkably good now, it should develop for many years. **94 Cellar Selection** *—S.H. (11/1/2005)*

M. Cosentino 2001 Reserve Cabernet Sauvignon (Napa Valley) $80. Exceptionally ripe in black cherries, blackberries, cassis, and chocolate, and sweet in fruit juice essence, although it's technically dry. Polished and smooth, with a nice edge of acids and tannins for grip. Almost too flamboyant in sweet opulence. Anything more in this direction will be excessive. **90** *—S.H. (4/1/2005)*

M. Cosentino 1999 Reserve Cabernet Sauvignon (Yountville) $80. 87 *—S.H. (11/15/2002)*

M. Cosentino 2000 Charbono (Napa Valley) $25. Drink this robust wine with barbecued pork ribs and don't be too fussy. It's dry and tannic enough to slice through grease. **84** *—S.H. (10/1/2005)*

M. Cosentino 2002 Chardonnay (Napa Valley) $25. From the cooler Oak Knoll district, a spicy, ripe Chard that's big in everything. Super tropical fruit flavors, lavishly toasted new oak, lots of lees, and all the other bells and whistles. **88** *—S.H. (12/1/2004)*

M. Cosentino 2001 Chardonnay (Napa Valley) $22. 84 *—S.H. (12/31/2003)*

M. Cosentino 1999 Chardonnay (California) $18. 86 *—S.H. (8/1/2001)*

M. Cosentino 1998 Barrel-Fermented Chardonnay (California) $20. 86 *(6/1/2000)*

M. Cosentino 2002 CE2V Chardonnay (Napa Valley) $28. Almost overripe, almost too alcoholic, almost overextracted, and flirts with being too oaky, but not quite, all of which makes this a big, fat Chardonnay that tests the limits. Nothing subtle about the blast of flavors and huge mouthfeel. As rich as it is, try with lobster and drawn butter. **90** *—S.H. (8/1/2004)*

M. Cosentino 2001 The Sculptor Reserve Chardonnay (Napa Valley) $30. This wine wins you over by the sheer force of its exuberant personality. It has a range of citrus, peach, and tropical fruit flavors that are tightly wound together by high acidity, while new oak adds aromatic and textural elements. **89** *—S.H. (2/1/2004)*

M. Cosentino 1999 The Sculptor Reserve Chardonnay (Napa Valley) $34. 85 *(7/1/2001)*

M. Cosentino 2002 Dolcetto (Lodi) $18. This inky black, very tannic and dry wine is tough going. There are deeply buried dark stone fruit and herb flavors that may emerge with many years of aging. Meanwhile, it's best with something like short ribs. **84** *—S.H. (11/15/2004)*

M. Cosentino 2002 Gewürztraminer (Yountville) $22. Fruity, flowery, intense and enormously spicy. Cinnamon, nutmeg, coriander, cardamom, and white pepper dance on the palate. Finishes nicely dry; a complex table wine. **88** *—S.H. (10/1/2005)*

M. Cosentino 2000 Gewürztraminer (Yountville) $22. 86 *—S.H. (6/1/2002)*

M. Cosentino 1998 Estate Yountville Gewürztraminer (Napa Valley) $22. 87 *—L.W. (9/1/1999)*

M. Cosentino 2002 M. Coz Meritage (Napa Valley) $125. Most of the grapes come from Yountville, a coolish Napa region. Buried below the tannins are enormously ripe blackberries, cherries, and red currants. The wine is impeccably balanced. The tannins will cut through a good steak now, but you can age this Cab through the decade. **92 Cellar Selection** *—S.H. (12/31/2005)*

M. Cosentino 1999 M. Coz Meritage (Napa Valley) $100. 92 *—S.H. (11/15/2002)*

M. Cosentino 2000 The Poet Meritage (Napa Valley) $65. There are black currant and cassis flavors and very strong tannins, the kind that make your tongue stick to the gums. It's a big wine but not a concentrated one, and is unlikely to age. Drink now. **87** *—S.H. (5/1/2004)*

M. Cosentino 1997 Merlot (California) $20. 86 *(3/1/2000)*

M. Cosentino 2002 Merlot (Oakville) $90. This 100% Merlot is so voluptuous, it reminds you of a great Pomerol. It's big and rich in black cherry, vanilla, and smoky char, with a nice, peppery finish. Shows great weight and volume, and lots of elegance. **92** *—S.H. (11/1/2005)*

M. Cosentino 2001 Merlot (Napa Valley) $38. This Merlot contains massive flavors of cherries, with a spicy, figgy streak. The oversized tannins add to the impression of heft, but they're very ripe, sweet, and easy. Of course, lots of new oak is in keeping with the fruit. Delicious and succulent, and perfect with a very rich cut of beef. **92** *—S.H. (9/1/2004)*

M. Cosentino 1999 Estate Merlot (Oakville) $90. 93 *—S.H. (9/12/2002)*

M. Cosentino 2000 Reserve Merlot (Napa Valley) $38. Tons of smoky, vanilla-tinged oak has been plastered over a wine whose underlying flavors are of black currants and cassis. The result is pleasing to the palate, with a level of complexity enhanced by rich tannins. This supple wine is best consumed early. **90** *—S.H. (4/1/2004)*

M. Cosentino 2001 Sonoma Valley Nebbiolo (Sonoma Valley) $28. Not much Nebbiolo out there in California, but this is a good and interesting one. It's dark, dense, and mouthfilling, oozing sweet plum, black currant, chocolate, tobacco, and pepper flavors that are wrapped in luscious tannins. Finishes dry and firm. **90** *—S.H. (9/1/2004)*

M. Cosentino 2001 Knoll Family Vineyard Petite Sirah (Lodi) $24. 80 *(4/1/2003)*

M. Cosentino 2001 Pinot Grigio (California) $18. 84 *—S.H. (9/1/2003)*

M. Cosentino 2002 Pinot Noir (Russian River Valley) $35. In making a lateral move to Pinot Noir, Mitch Cosentino brings a Napa Cabernet sensibility to this variety. This is a big, dark, extracted Pinot, an attractive wine with its chocolate and blueberry flavors, but rather heavy-handed for a wine that should be elegant and crisp. **85** *—S.H. (11/1/2005)*

M. Cosentino 2001 Pinot Noir (Yountville) $34. A fascinating, rich, and complex wine. Starts with jazzy Lifesaver flavors and combines them with warmer notes of baked cherry tart and sweet tobacco. It's all well-oaked. Silky smooth in the mouth, dry in sugar but ripe in fruity flavor, and finishes with a wonderful edge of Oriental spice and mocha. **92 Editors' Choice** *—S.H. (5/1/2004)*

M. Cosentino 2000 Pinot Noir (Yountville) $30. 87 *(10/1/2002)*

M. Cosentino 1999 Il Chiaretto Red Blend (Yountville) $20. 88 *—S.H. (11/15/2001)*

M. Cosentino 2002 Med Red (Lodi) $12. This blend of five obscure varieties has generic red and blackberry flavors. It's very tannic and dry, a wine that leaves your palate puckering. Okay for pizza. **84** *—S.H. (6/1/2004)*

M. Cosentino 2001 CE2V Sangiovese (Napa Valley) $30. Big wine, full bodied, but with gentle tannins and crisp acids, and very dry. There's a suggestion of cherries and tobacco. Would go well with rich cheeses or your best tomato sauce. **90** *—S.H. (8/1/2005)*

M. Cosentino 2003 Il Chiaretto Sangiovese (California) $18. Unbalanced and rustic, with a sugary, soda-pop taste to the cola flavors. As far from Chianti as you can get. **82** *—S.H. (12/15/2005)*

M. Cosentino 2000 Il Chiaretto Sangiovese (California) $20. 90 Editors' Choice *—S.H. (9/1/2003)*

M. Cosentino 2000 The Sem Sémillon (Napa Valley) $18. 90 Editors' Choice *—S.H. (12/1/2003)*

M. Cosentino 2000 The Novelist Meritage Sémillon-Sauvignon Blanc (California) $16. 89 *—S.H. (7/1/2003)*

M. Cosentino 1997 Il Chiaretto Tuscan Blend (California) $18. 88 *—J.C. (10/1/1999)*

M. Cosentino 2000 Vin Doux Viognier Kay Viognier (California) $30. 88 *—S.H. (9/1/2002)*

M. Cosentino 2001 Avant et Apres White Blend (California) $16. Slightly sweet, with a bit of botrytis in the aroma. Beyond the sweetness are modest flavors of apples and pears. **84** *—S.H. (6/1/2004)*

M. Cosentino 2002 Cigar Zinfandel (Lodi) $27. Pushes the table wine envelope with nearly 16% alcohol, and while it's fully dry, it strikes the palate as ponderous. Heavy tannins and a tobaccoey herbaceousness smother whatever fruit is in there. **84** *—S.H. (10/1/2004)*

M. Cosentino 1998 Cigar Zin Zinfandel (California) $22. 92 *—P.G. (11/15/1999)*

M. Cosentino 2003 The Zin Zinfandel (California) $30. Drinks almost sweet in cassis and sugared espresso flavors, and seems to have some residual sugar despite 15.2 percent alcohol. Fans of this genre will love it. **84** *—S.H. (10/1/2005)*

M. Cosentino 2001 The ZIN Zinfandel (Lodi) $30. 87 *(11/1/2003)*

M. Cosentino 1997 The Zin Zinfandel (California) $22. 93 *—P.G. (11/15/1999)*

M. TRINCHERO

M. Trinchero 1997 Family Selection Cabernet Sauvignon (Santa Barbara County) $13. 86 Best Buy *—S.H. (12/15/2000)*

M. Trinchero 1998 Coastal Selection Chardonnay (California) $12. 86 *—S.H. (12/31/1999)*

M. Trinchero 1999 Marios Reserve Chardonnay (Napa Valley) $30. 92 *(7/1/2001)*

M. Trinchero 1998 Family Selection Merlot (California) $12. 87 Best Buy *—S.H. (5/1/2001)*

M.G. VALLEJO

M.G. Vallejo 2000 Pinot Noir (Sonoma) $11. 83 *(10/1/2002)*

MACARI

Macari 2000 Alexandra Bordeaux Blend (North Fork of Long Island) $65. Starts with some scents of asphalt and tree bark, then clears up to reveal ripe black cherry aromas. This Merlot-dominated blend (69%) is firmly built but not hard, with notes of tobacco and earth that add welcome complexity. Finishes with good length and crisp acidity. **87** *—J.C. (10/2/2004)*

Macari 1997 Bergen Road Bordeaux Blend (North Fork of Long Island) $32. 87 *—J.C. (4/1/2001)*

USA

Macari NV Brut (North Fork of Long Island) $21. 84 —*D.T. (12/1/2001)*

Macari 2003 Early Wine Chardonnay (North Fork of Long Island) $12. Bottled just over a month after harvest, this light, crisp Chardonnay would make a decent shellfish white. Lime, peach, and mineral notes finish clean and fresh, with a zesty, citrusy aftertaste. **84** —*J.C. (10/2/2004)*

Macari 1998 Reserve Chardonnay (North Fork of Long Island) $22. 85 —*J.C. (4/1/2001)*

Macari 2001 Reserve Merlot (North Fork of Long Island) $NA. A toasty, vanilla-scented Merlot that boasts a plump, appealing mouthfeel, but seems to lack sufficient fruit to carry the weight of all the oak. Finishes with a hint of mocha. **83** —*J.C. (10/2/2004)*

Macari 2002 Block E White Blend (North Fork of Long Island) $36. This blend of Chardonnay (70%) and Sauvignon Blanc (30%) seems to have seen better days. It smells of roasted corn and butter, and comes across almost sweet and fat in the mouth. **82** —*J.C. (10/2/2004)*

MACCALLUM

MacCallum 2002 DJ Red Cabernet Sauvignon-Syrah (Yakima Valley) $28. Syrah makes up almost three quarters of the blend; the rest is Cabernet, and the results are spectacular. This tiny winery (50 cases of this were produced) has come up with a meaty, substantial, poised and polished effort that offers both heft and elegance—a rare combo. Dense, deep blueberry in color, it sends up evocative scents of violets and berries, then smoothes into a silky middle with cedar, sandalwood, lead pencil, and licorice. Soft, substantial tannins keep it gliding through a long, satisfying finish. **93** —*P.G. (12/15/2004)*

MACCHIA

Macchia 2001 Barbero Vineyard Voluptuous Zinfandel (Lodi) $18. 87 *(11/1/2003)*

Macchia 2001 Generous Zinfandel (Lodi) $16. 86 *(11/1/2003)*

MACLEAN

Maclean 2002 Cabernet Sauvignon (Napa Valley) $45. This is a better wine than Maclean's '01, riper and richer. It shows blackberry, cassis, and oak flavors, and a good structure. Still, it could use greater concentration. **85** —*S.H. (12/1/2005)*

Maclean 2003 Sauvignon Blanc (Napa Valley) $18. On the sweet side, as if the grapefruit, fig, and apple flavors had some sugar put in, but that's mostly offset by good acidity. Still, it's not a completely dry wine, so be forewarned. **84** —*S.H. (11/1/2005)*

MACMURRAY RANCH

MacMurray Ranch 2003 Pinot Gris (Russian River Valley) $20. This is an elegant white wine, dry, crisp, and sophisticated. Shows flashy flavors of citrus fruits, roasted almond, and vanilla. Try as an alternative to Sauvignon Blanc. **87** —*S.H. (5/1/2005)*

MacMurray Ranch 2001 Pinot Gris (Russian River Valley) $23. 86 —*S.H. (9/1/2003)*

MacMurray Ranch 2003 Pinot Noir (Russian River Valley) $35. A big, full-bodied Pinot, with flavors of cola, black cherry, earth, and mushroom. A heat spike led to high sugars, says winemaker Susan Doyle, but the flavors lagged behind, requiring longer hang time. Slightly tough on the finish, this is a ruggedly masculine wine. **87** *(11/1/2005)*

MacMurray Ranch 2001 Pinot Noir (Sonoma Coast) $15. 83 —*S.H. (7/1/2003)*

MacMurray Ranch 2003 River Cuvée Pinot Noir (Russian River Valley) $60. Mainly Dijon clones off Martini's Del Rio property cropped at a measly 1.5 tons per acre, this wine shows good concentration and a full, soft mouthfeel. Cherry and vanilla flavors predominate, with a hint of mint adding some herbal complexity. Ends on dark chocolate and coffee notes; could use a little more length and fruit on the finish. Only 400 cases produced. **89** *(11/1/2005)*

MACPHAIL

MacPhail 2002 Pinot Noir (Russian River Valley) $40. Delicate and light, showing smoky, hay and herb, coffee, and floral aromas. The flavors of sassafras and citrus peel lead to a spicy finish. Not showing much fruit, though. **86** *(11/1/2004)*

MacPhail 2003 Toulouse Vineyard Pinot Noir (Anderson Valley) $35. Pale in color, light in body, this Pinot is elegant. It's dry and acidic, with cola, red cherry, coffee, and vanilla flavors that finish in a swirl of spice. **87** —*S.H. (12/15/2005)*

MACROSTIE

MacRostie 2003 Chardonnay (Carneros) $20. Firm in acids and minerals, and with well-oaked apple, citrus, and peach flavors, this streamlined Chardonnay is clean and balanced. It's a good accompaniment to cracked crab. **90 Editors' Choice** —*S.H. (10/1/2005)*

MacRostie 1998 Chardonnay (Carneros) $19. 86 *(6/1/2000)*

MacRostie 1998 Reserve Chardonnay (Carneros) $33. 88 *(7/1/2001)*

MacRostie 2001 Wildcat Mountain Vineyard Chardonnay (Carneros) $30. Impressive for its taut, tightly knit flavors of apples, peaches, and pears, held together by firm acids and a smattering of dusty tannins. A high percentage of oak also contributes tannins, as well as sweet vanilla and toast. **89** —*S.H. (11/15/2004)*

MacRostie 1996 Merlot (Carneros) $26. 87 —*M.S. (6/1/1999)*

MacRostie 2001 Pinot Noir (Carneros) $24. Light in color and in body, marked by delicate cola, rhubarb, and cranberry flavors. Drinks dry and crisp in acids. Picks up a bit of sweet oaky complexity on the finish. **85** *—S.H. (5/1/2004)*

MacRostie 2001 Beresini Vineyard Reserve Pinot Noir (Carneros) $27. Here's a Pinot Noir that's light, silky, and elegant. You can taste the cool climate in the crisp acidity that undergirds the cherry, cola, and rosehip tea flavors, and the finish is dry and clean. Not too much oak stands between the fruit and the palate. **87** *—S.H. (12/1/2004)*

MacRostie 2001 Wildcat Mountain Vineyard Syrah (Carneros) $39. Here is cool-climate Syrah. There is a white pepper aroma that leaps from the glass, and the acids and tannins are much more pronounced. Yet there are also underlying blackberry and plum flavors that are rich, ripe, and dense. The wonderful structure and finesse is easily worth the price. **93 Editors' Choice** *—S.H. (5/1/2004)*

MADDALENA

Maddalena 1999 Cabernet Sauvignon (Central Coast) $13. **84** *—S.H. (5/1/2003)*

Maddalena 2002 Chardonnay (Monterey) $10. A great value for its great big burst of juicy peach, pear, and tropical fruit flavors and the crisp acidic flair of its mouthfeel. Totally dry and balanced, it shows little oak, but the flavors stand on their own. **86 Best Buy** *—S.H. (11/15/2004)*

Maddalena 2000 Chardonnay (Monterey) $10. **85** *—S.H. (6/1/2003)*

Maddalena 2003 Muscat Canelli (Paso Robles) $10. Overtly sweet, with orange and vanilla flavors, and lively acidity. This would be a lovely wine to sip on a summer day, or with fresh fruit. **85 Best Buy** *—S.H. (5/1/2005)*

Maddalena 2002 Pinot Grigio (Monterey) $11. **85** *—S.H. (12/1/2003)*

Maddalena 1998 Loma Vista Vineyard Pinot Grigio (Arroyo Seco) $9. **86 Best Buy** *(8/1/1999)*

Maddalena 2003 Riesling (Monterey) $10. Not really dry, more off-dry, with clean aromas and flavors of petrol, peaches, wildflowers, and vanilla. Enjoy this crisp, pleasant wine with fresh fruit or sautéed trout, or as an apéritif. **85 Best Buy** *—S.H. (12/1/2004)*

Maddalena 2004 Sauvignon Blanc (Paso Robles) $12. Simple and rich in spearmint, peach, fig, and vanilla flavors, this white wine has a semisweet taste, and just enough tartness to keep it from cloying. **83** *—S.H. (12/1/2005)*

Maddalena 2002 Syrah (Central Coast) $13. This is a dry, fruity wine that shows good Syrah character. It's smooth and balanced, with cherry and blackberry flavors and a tannic finish. A blend of Monterey and Paso Robles fruit. **84** *—S.H. (12/31/2005)*

MADONNA

Madonna 2001 Due Ragazzi Reserve Pinot Noir (Carneros) $55. Dijon clones seem to give a purity of fruit that leaps out of the glass, and here you'll find focused cherry and cola flavors, with intriguingly complex notes of mint and smoky oak. The wine drinks young, acidic and tannic now, but should soften and sweeten in a few years. **86** *—S.H. (12/1/2004)*

MADONNA ESTATE MONT ST. JOHN

Madonna Estate Mont St. John 2000 Chardonnay (Carneros) $16. **85** *—S.H. (6/1/2003)*

MADRIGAL

Madrigal 1996 Petite Sirah (Napa Valley) $24. **84** *—M.S. (6/1/1999)*

Madrigal 2000 Petite Sirah (Napa Valley) $33. **88** *(4/1/2003)*

Madrigal 2001 Zinfandel (Napa Valley) $26. Sleek and smooth textured, this fleshy, velvety wine is packed with lovely plum, black cherry, cedar, herb, spice, and chocolate flavors. It's lush, long, and rich, yet offers a good measure of finesse and elegance. Not over the top, just terrific. **91** *—J.M. (8/1/2004)*

MADRONA

Madrona 2002 Malbec (El Dorado) $27. Here's an understated claret-style wine that doesn't overwhelm with any one thing, just satisfies with overall balance and style. It's dry and complex, with a seamless integration of blackberry fruit and oak, and supportive tannins. **90** *—S.H. (7/1/2005)*

Madrona 2002 New-World Port (El Dorado) $24. Not quite off-dry, but with a little sweetness, an earthy, chocolatey wine that's neither here nor there. **84** *—S.H. (7/1/2005)*

Madrona 2001 Riesling (El Dorado) $10. **82** *—J.M. (8/1/2003)*

Madrona 1999 Dry Riesling (El Dorado) $14. **85** *—S.H. (8/1/2001)*

Madrona 1999 Reserve Syrah (El Dorado) $20. **87** *—S.H. (2/1/2003)*

Madrona 2003 Zinfandel (El Dorado) $15. An interesting and likeable wine. It's dry, but packed with ripe cherry pie flavors and a dusting of powdered sugar and cocoa, and a tiny taste of currants. Would benefit from greater acidity or tannins. **87** *—S.H. (10/1/2005)*

Madrona 1997 Late Harvest Zinfandel (El Dorado) $16. **84** *—S.H. (5/1/2000)*

Madrona 1997 Reserve Zinfandel (Paso Robles) $18. **89** *—S.H. (5/1/2000)*

MAHONEY

Mahoney 2002 Mahoney Vineyard Pinot Noir (Carneros) $36. Fairly tannic fare from Carneros Creek's Francis Mahoney, and not showing much now, but it may be a keeper. You'll find a rich and interesting mélange of tobacco, earth, and herbs, with a tease of black cherry and spice. Very dry and crisp on the finish. **86** *—S.H. (11/1/2004)*

MAKOR

Makor 2001 Zinfandel (Arroyo Grande Valley) $12. **87** *(11/1/2003)*

MALVOLIO

Malvolio 2001 Laetitia Vineyard Block A Pinot Noir (Arroyo Grande Valley) $48. This wonderful wine trades a bit of Block I's seductive immediacy for a richer, darker structure you may want to cellar for a few years. The flavors suggest plums, blackberries, and black cherries complexed with chocolate and coffee, but that silky Pinot texture remains alluring. **92** *—S.H. (10/1/2004)*

Malvolio 2001 Laetitia Vineyard Block I Pinot Noir (Arroyo Grande Valley) $48. Wow, what a delicious Pinot. It's lusciously silky in the mouth, with great acids framing a complex array of flavors ranging from red cherries, black raspberries, and oaky vanilla to Asian spices and sweet tobacco. Absolutely addictive and compelling, and shows what this vineyard is capable of. **93** *—S.H. (10/1/2004)*

Malvolio 2002 Laetitia Vineyard Clone 667 Pinot Noir (Arroyo Grande Valley) $48. A big, rich, and complex wine. It's almost Syrah-like, dark and bold in smoky, meaty, plum, and chocolate flavors, but is saved by crisp acidity and a smooth silkiness. Really good, and will get better for a year or two. **89** *(11/1/2004)*

MANDOLINA

Mandolina 2002 Rosato Rosé Blend (Santa Barbara County) $12. An uncomplicated and zippy little wine that pours a pretty coppery-red color and smells like freshly picked strawberries. The strawberry and raspberry flavors are peppery-spicy, and there's a tiny amount of sweetness to offset the acidity. **85** *—S.H. (3/1/2004)*

MANNING ESTATES

Manning Estates 2002 Chardonnay (Central Coast) $8. **84** *—S.H. (12/31/2003)*

MARCELINA

Marcelina 1995 Cabernet Sauvignon (Napa Valley) $25. **87** *—L.W. (11/1/1999)*

Marcelina 2003 Chardonnay (Carneros) $24. Pretty acidic now, and dry, with the flavor of grapefruit and lime juice and a squeeze of peach syrup. There's a mineral thing going on in the finish. **86** *—S.H. (10/1/2005)*

Marcelina 1997 Chardonnay (Napa Valley) $22. **88** *(6/1/2000)*

MARGUERITE-RYAN

Marguerite-Ryan 2000 Pisoni Vineyards Pinot Noir (Santa Lucia Highlands) $48. **92** *—J.M. (7/1/2003)*

MARIAH

Mariah 1999 Merlot (Mendocino Ridge) $30. **93** *—S.H. (5/1/2002)*

Mariah 1999 Syrah (Mendocino Ridge) $30. **85** *—S.H. (5/1/2002)*

Mariah 2001 Zinfandel (Mendocino Ridge) $30. Say hello to this marvelously ripe, cheerful Zin. It totally turns you on. The marvelously ripe flavors range from sweet cherries to a baked blackberry tart dusted with cinnamon and cocoa, and finished with a bite of fig. Soft, unctuous tannins, rich acids, total balance. Released simultaneously with the '00, but so much better at the same price. **93 Editors' Choice** *—S.H. (2/1/2005)*

Mariah 1999 Zinfandel (Mendocino Ridge) $31. **90** *—S.H. (5/1/2002)*

MARICOPA

Maricopa 1999 Shiraz (California) $8. **87 Best Buy** *(10/1/2001)*

MARILYN REMARK

Marilyn Remark 2002 Wild Horse Road Vineyard Grenache (Monterey County) $45. From a warmer part of Monterey, but you can taste the herbs and fresh acids that the last of the chilly winds bring. They join tart red cherries, rhubarb, and touches of oak to frame this dry, delicate wine. It possesses subtleties that keep you coming back for more **88** *—S.H. (12/31/2004)*

Marilyn Remark 2004 Loma Pacific Vineyard Marsanne (Monterey County) $30. This is a fun wine. It has a rich, creamy texture, and is very flavorful, with white peach, apricot, spice, and sweet oak flavors. The finish is oaky and bright with acidity. **86** *—S.H. (12/1/2005)*

Marilyn Remark 2002 Loma Pacific Vineyard Marsanne (Monterey County) $28. A dramatically good wine from a new winery that bears watching. It has the rich, creamy flair of a top Chardonnay, but with more exotic flavors. They include white peach, guava, wildflowers and spicy lemon zest. Bone dry, with a sleek, minerally spine of acid. **91** *—S.H. (2/1/2004)*

Marilyn Remark 2004 Rosé de Saignee Rosé Blend (Monterey County) $22. You can smell the cherries in this Syrah and Grenache blend as soon as you pop the cork. Vibrant in red cherry, strawberry, raspberry, rose petal, and vanilla flavors, it's bone dry and crisp. This blush wine shows real class. **87** *—S.H. (12/1/2005)*

Marilyn Remark 2003 Arroyo Loma Vineyard Syrah (Monterey County) $35. Seems a bit thin on fruit and dominated by toasty oak, picking up a caramelly, toasted marshmallow flavor on the finish. **82** *(9/1/2005)*

MARIMAR ESTATE

Marimar Estate 2002 Don Miguel Vineyard Chardonnay (Russian River Valley) $28. I loved Marimar Torres's Dobles Lias Chard, released earlier, for many of the reasons I like this one. First is the brilliant acidity, brisk, bold, and palate-stimulating. Then there's the complex palate, full of sweet green apple, pineapple, mango, mineral, vanilla, and buttered toast flavors. **93 Editors' Choice** *—S.H. (11/15/2005)*

Marimar Estate 2002 Don Miguel Vineyard Pinot Noir (Russian River Valley) $35. Pours dark, smells strong and clean, showing cherries, vanilla, oak, spices, and herbs. Full-bodied, crisp in acids and with sturdy tannins, but lacks the stuffing for a higher score. **86** *(11/1/2004)*

Marimar Estate 2003 Don Miguel Vineyard Earthquake Block Pinot Noir (Russian River Valley) $42. Structure defines this superb Pinot Noir. It's dramatic in fruit, with tantalizingly ripe black cherry and cola flavors, and has been generously oaked, but it's the classic acid-tannin balance elevates it. Like all great Pinots, it teases the palate, now one thing, now another. Drink now through 2007. **93** *—S.H. (11/15/2005)*

MARIMAR TORRES

Marimar Torres 2000 Don Miguel Dobles Lias Chardonnay (Russian River Valley) $40. **92** *—S.H. (12/15/2002)*

Marimar Torres 2000 Don Miguel Vineyard Chardonnay (Russian River Valley) $26. **92** *—S.H. (5/1/2003)*

Marimar Torres 1997 Don Miguel Vineyard Chardonnay (Russian River Valley) $25. **85** *(6/1/2000)*

Marimar Torres 2001 Don Miguel Vineyard Pinot Noir (Russian River Valley) $35. The wine is dark and big, as you might expect given the vintage. Feels heavy and earthy, with a mélange of beet, cherry tomato, coffee, cola, and oak flavors, and rich tannins on the finish. Not showing much delicacy or refinement now. Try after 2006. **88** *—S.H. (12/1/2004)*

Marimar Torres 1999 Don Miguel Vineyard Pinot Noir (Russian River Valley) $32. **89** *(10/1/2002)*

MARIO PERELLI-MINETTI

Mario Perelli-Minetti 2001 Cabernet Sauvignon (Napa Valley) $21. A little ordinary, but an okay Cab, although at this price you'll do better elsewhere. Berries and herbs, with dry tannins on the finish. **84** *—S.H. (10/1/2005)*

USA

MARK RIDGE

Mark Ridge 2000 Merlot (California) $9. **86 Best Buy** *—S.H. (11/15/2002)*

MARK RYAN

Mark Ryan 2003 Gun Metal Red Bordeaux Blend (Columbia Valley (WA)) $35. This Bordeaux blend is 64% Cabernet Sauvignon, 21% Merlot, and 15% Cab Franc. The cooler region allows the fruit to ripen while keeping its grip and muscle. It's lush but not jammy; showing herb and wood (20 months in French oak), bacon, and smoke. The finish is layered with cedar, leaf, and resonant, plummy fruits. Beautifully long and balanced. 350 cases made. **90** *—P.G. (12/15/2005)*

Mark Ryan 2003 Bad Lands Red (Red Mountain) $45. An intriguing blend of two-thirds Kiona Syrah, one-third Ciel du Cheval Petit Verdot, this textural wine retains its Syrah aromatics but bulks up tannicly from the PV, which contributes green herb and eucalyptus spice notes also. Winemaker Mark McNeilly is on to something special here, though a small hole remains right in the midpalate. The finish resonates with an herbal/minty spice note. Just 97 cases made. **89** *—P.G. (12/15/2005)*

Mark Ryan 2003 Long Haul Red (Red Mountain) $37. The Long Haul is the winery's "Right Bank" blend, it's 48% Merlot, 45% Cab Franc, and 7% Petit Verdot. All Ciel du Cheval fruit, it's big but structured, melding buoyant cherry fruit to a gravelly mineral base. It's a meaty, tannic wine, but the minerality keeps it lively and rich without being too heavy. Has some green-tea flavors in the tannins; the whole package is a jump forward in polish and grace from previous vintages. Just 225 cases produced. **92** *—P.G. (12/15/2005)*

MARK WEST

Mark West 1999 Gewürztraminer (Sonoma County) $12. **87** *—S.H. (5/1/2001)*

Mark West 2004 Pinot Noir (Central Coast) $9. Lots to like in this simple, varietally proper Pinot. It's light bodied and silky, with a very soft texture and pretty flavors of cola, cherries, blackberries, and toast. Finishes dry and spicy. **84** *—S.H. (12/15/2005)*

MARKHAM

Markham 1996 Cabernet Sauvignon (Napa Valley) $22. **89** *—S.H. (2/1/2000)*

Markham 2002 Chardonnay (Napa Valley) $19. A bells and whistles Chard that pulls out all the stops for richness. Ripe tropical fruit and peach flavors swim in smoky oak with vanilla and spice overtones. The texture is creamy, with crisp acidity. **86** *—S.H. (12/1/2004)*

Markham 1999 Chardonnay (Napa Valley) $17. **82** *—J.M. (12/15/2002)*

Markham 1997 Reserve Chardonnay (Napa Valley) $28. 91 *—L.W. (11/15/1999)*

Markham 2002 Merlot (Napa Valley) $22. Definitely on the ripe, intense side, with strong flavors of currants and anise-infused chocolate, but keeps its balance and integrity, mainly through the fine acid-tannin balance. Not too oaky, either, and what a great, long finish. 88 *—S.H. (8/1/2005)*

Markham 1998 Reserve Merlot (Napa Valley) $38. 85 *—J.M. (11/15/2002)*

Markham 1996 Reserve Merlot (Napa Valley) $35. 92 *—M.S. (3/1/2000)*

Markham 1998 Petite Sirah (Napa Valley) $24. 88 *—J.C. (9/1/2002)*

Markham 2004 Sauvignon Blanc (Napa Valley) $14. Classic coastal-style Sauvignon, bright and crisp in acids, yet very ripe and rich in fruit. The figs, melons, sweet white peaches and pink grapefruit flavors are easy and delicious. 85 *—S.H. (11/15/2005)*

Markham 2001 Sauvignon Blanc (Napa Valley) $13. 88 *(9/1/2003)*

Markham 2002 Zinfandel (Napa Valley) $20. Easy and gentle, with well-ripened cherry-berry flavors mingled with green peppercorn and dill, this Zin offers pleasure for its soft tannins and long finish. It has a dry, fruity, spicy finish. 85 *—S.H. (12/1/2005)*

Markham 1999 Zinfandel (Napa Valley) $17. 85 *—P.G. (3/1/2002)*

MARR

Marr 1999 Vine Hill Syrah (Russian River Valley) $25. 85 *—S.H. (12/1/2002)*

MARSHALL

Marshall 2001 Cabernet Franc (Napa Valley) $28. Starts with an unpleasant asparagus smell. It's dry, tannic and simple on the palate. 81 *—S.H. (11/1/2005)*

MARSHALL FAMILY WINES

Marshall Family Wines 2003 Syrah (Napa Valley) $26. Has some dense blackberry and plum flavors but they're buried deep under a blanket of road tar and rubber that never truly dissipates. Oaky, too. 83 *(9/1/2005)*

MARSTON FAMILY

Marston Family 2000 Cabernet Sauvignon (Spring Mountain) $60. Somewhat lean and firm textured, with powdery tannins that frame a core of blackberry, cassis, anise, herbs, and spice. The finish is moderate in length, with a hint of astringency. With time, the wine should age quite gracefully. Best after 2006. 88 *—J.M. (2/1/2004)*

Marston Family 2002 Proprietor Grown Cabernet Sauvignon (Spring Mountain) $80. This Cab flirts with over-ripeness, and just manages to avoid it. Another day or two on the vine, and those currant and chocolate flavors would have been raisins. Winemaker Philippe Melka has lavished considerable oak on it, and it shows in the raw, cedar and ash aroma. Drink now. 86 *—S.H. (11/15/2005)*

MARTELLA

Martella 2003 Fairbairn Ranch Syrah (Mendocino) $45. From the long-time winemaker at Thomas Fogarty in the Santa Cruz Mountains comes this lush fruit bomb from Mendocino. Cedar and vanilla mark the nose, but the palate couches ripe plummy fruit in a cradle of vanilla. Finishes with a touch of heat. The bad news? Only 76 cases made. 88 *(9/1/2005)*

Martella 2000 Hammer Syrah (California) $23. 87 *—S.H. (12/1/2002)*

MARTHA CLARA

Martha Clara 2000 6025 Bordeaux Blend (North Fork of Long Island) $NA. 84 *—J.C. (10/2/2004)*

Martha Clara 1999 Chardonnay (North Fork of Long Island) $10. 83 *—J.C. (4/1/2001)*

Martha Clara 1999 Estate Reserve Chardonnay (North Fork of Long Island) $17. 87 *—J.M. (7/1/2002)*

Martha Clara 2000 Gewürztraminer (North Fork of Long Island) $15. 85 *—J.C. (3/1/2002)*

Martha Clara 2000 Riesling (North Fork of Long Island) $15. This medium-weight Riesling has distinctive oil-shale aromas that meld well with the melon, apple, pear, and lime flavors. The tart finish lingers, bringing in a note of slightly bitter citrus rind. 87 *—J.C. (1/1/2004)*

Martha Clara 1999 Sémillon-Chardonnay (North Fork of Long Island) $15. 84 *—J.C. (4/1/2001)*

Martha Clara 1999 Viognier (North Fork of Long Island) $15. 81 *—J.C. (4/1/2001)*

MARTIN & WEYRICH

Martin & Weyrich 2001 Cabernet Sauvignon (Paso Robles) $40. A fine effort. It was so easy to get ripeness in this long, warm vintage, which shows in the sunburst of blackberry, cherry, and spicy black plum flavors that mark this Cab. It's soft and supple in the mouth, with a pleasingly sweet finish. 86 *—S.H. (10/1/2004)*

Martin & Weyrich 2000 Etrusco Cabernet Sauvignon (Paso Robles) $22. A fruity, dry wine that combines Cabernet's structure and blackberry and herb flavors with Sangiovese's cherries and acidity. Full-bodied and tasty, with easy, complex tannins. 86 *—S.H. (10/1/2004)*

Martin & Weyrich 1998 Chardonnay (Edna Valley) $18. 86 *(6/1/2000)*

Martin & Weyrich 1998 Hidden Valley Chardonnay (Paso Robles) $13. 88 Best Buy *—S.H. (5/1/2000)*

Martin & Weyrich 1998 Reserve Chardonnay (Edna Valley) $28. 88 *(6/1/2000)*

Martin & Weyrich 1999 Nebbiolo (Paso Robles) $15. 86 *—S.H. (12/1/2001)*

Martin & Weyrich 1999 Insieme Red Blend (Paso Robles) $16. 86 *—S.H. (11/15/2002)*

Martin & Weyrich 2001 Syrah (York Mountain) $25. Quite firm and tannic, with good acids too. Opens with strong white pepper aromas that air out to reveal luscious cassis and cherry liqueur aromas and flavors. Likely to develop further for a few years. **88** *—S.H. (12/1/2004)*

Martin & Weyrich 1997 Ueberroth Vineyard Zinfandel (Paso Robles) $22. 87 *—P.G. (3/1/2001)*

MARTIN BROTHERS

Martin Brothers 1997 Pinot Grigio (Paso Robles) $12. 82 *(8/1/1999)*

MARTIN FAMILY VINEYARDS

Martin Family Vineyards 1999 Cabernet Sauvignon (Napa Valley) $44. 87 *—J.M. (12/15/2003)*

Martin Family Vineyards 1999 Syrah (Alexander Valley) $32. 85 *—J.M. (12/15/2003)*

Martin Family Vineyards 2001 Rattlesnake Rock Zinfandel (Russian River Valley) $32. Cola and cherry notes are at the core of this burly Zin. Tannins are soft, and the flavors are framed by mild spice and toast with hints of black cherry and herbs. It seems a little sweet on the finish. **87** *—J.M. (3/1/2004)*

Martin Family Vineyards 2001 The Rooster Zinfandel (Dry Creek Valley) $32. Quite rich and cherry-like. The wine also serves up chocolate, plum, jammy strawberry and anise flavors. It's got a touch of sweetness too—plus plenty of body and smooth, supple tannins. **87** *—J.M. (3/1/2004)*

MARTIN RAY

Martin Ray 2001 Cabernet Sauvignon (Santa Cruz Mountains) $50. This concentrated and intense mountain Cabernet is an obvious cellar candidate. Its huge tannins fan out across the palate, leaving behind a dusty astringency. Yet it's so sweet in chocolate and black currant fruit that it's drinkable right away. Should easily make it to the 20-year mark. **93** *—S.H. (5/1/2005)*

Martin Ray 2001 Napa, Sonoma & Mendocino Counties Cabernet Sauvignon (California) $16. This is a good, rich Cabernet, rather generic in style, which is to say it's dry and ripe in black currant fruit, well-oaked, and with fine, dusty tannins. Drink now. **87** *—S.H. (10/1/2005)*

Martin Ray 2004 Chardonnay (Russian River Valley) $16. Simple but drinkable, this Chard has fruit and oak flavors, a creamy texture and crisp acids. It's fully dry. **83** *—S.H. (12/31/2005)*

Martin Ray 2004 Angeline Chardonnay (Russian River Valley) $10. A little raw and green, but there are some Chardy flavors of peaches, cream and spices, and the wine is dry and creamy. **83** *—S.H. (12/31/2005)*

Martin Ray 2000 Mariage Chardonnay (Russian River Valley) $16. 86 *—S.H. (5/1/2003)*

Martin Ray 1998 Mariage Chardonnay (California) $18. 86 *(6/1/2000)*

Martin Ray 2002 Merlot (Napa Valley) $16. You won't notice this wine's over-ripe, raisiny flavors, and alcoholic warmth if you just quaff it. **83** *—S.H. (11/1/2005)*

Martin Ray 2001 Diamond Mountain Merlot (Napa Valley) $40. A beautiful Merlot that lives up to the promise of "the soft Cabernet." It does have a velvety, cushiony mouthfeel, with blackberry and cocoa flavors, and achieves a harmony and balance rare in this varietal. Absolutely first-rate. **92** *—S.H. (5/1/2005)*

Martin Ray 1997 Pinot Noir (Russian River Valley) $40. 88 *—M.S. (5/1/2000)*

Martin Ray 2003 Angeline Pinot Noir (Russian River Valley) $10. A nice wine with real varietal character, a smooth mouthfeel, crisp acids and ripe flavors of raspberries, cherries, and mocha. Try this as a first course leading up to the expensive stuff. **86 Best Buy** *—S.H. (6/1/2005)*

MARTINE'S

Martine's 2000 Syrah (California) $17. 86 *(10/1/2003)*

MARTINI & PRATI

Martini & Prati 1999 Tower Hill Pinot Noir (California) $14. 80 *(10/1/2002)*

MARYHILL

Maryhill 2003 Pinot Gris (Willamette Valley) $13. The fruit is from Oregon, and lacks the crisp authority of the Washington style. Ripe, loose-knit, and tasting of sweet cracker in the finish, it closes out with a bit of candy-sweet sugar. **85** *—P.G. (10/1/2004)*

Maryhill 2002 Sangiovese (Columbia Valley (WA)) $16. Light and pleasantly fruity, but showing little of the varietal character of the grape. The fruit is tart, with rhubarb and pie cherry, and the finish is notable for some distinctive smoke and charcoal spice. **86** *—P.G. (9/1/2004)*

Maryhill 2003 Syrah (Columbia Valley (WA)) $16. Smooth, flavorful and fairly priced—what else could one want? It's starts off a bit toasty and smoky, then delivers waves of caramel, smoked meat, and berry flavor, supple tannins, and an elegant finish. **89 Editors' Choice** *(9/1/2005)*

Maryhill 2001 Reserve Syrah (Columbia Valley (WA)) $28. A substantial effort, with supple, grapy, black cherry fruit suffused with smoke, pepper, and meaty tannins. Young and relatively hard, it needs a little breathing time to soften up, but it's a delicious, well-made wine. **90 Editors' Choice** *—P.G. (9/1/2004)*

Maryhill 2002 Zinfandel (Columbia Valley (WA)) $22. Maryhill is making more Zin than anyone in Washington, and has proven that there is a place for it there. The fruit is ripe but not jammy, and the acids stay up there despite the high 15% alcohol. Bright berries and a kiss of oak set the style; there's a touch of Mendocino-style incense in the finish. **87** *—P.G. (9/1/2004)*

MASSET WINERY

Masset Winery 2000 Cabernet Sauvignon (Yakima Valley) $20. Good color, plenty of very astringent tannins, and hints of some black cherry, fruit, but it's buried in earthy tannins. **83** *—P.G. (1/1/2004)*

MASUT

Masut 2003 Pinot Noir (Redwood Valley) $30. This is a dry, charming wine, a junior partner to Masut's Block Seven bottling. It has ripe, pure cherry flavors and a chocolaty finish. It's very gentle, with low acids and tannins. **86** *—S.H. (10/1/2005)*

Masut 2001 Pinot Noir (Redwood Valley) $30. **88** *—S.H. (7/1/2003)*

MATANZAS CREEK

Matanzas Creek 2000 Cabernet Sauvignon (Sonoma County) $35. **86** *—M.S. (11/15/2003)*

Matanzas Creek 1998 Chardonnay (Sonoma County) $33. **87** *(7/1/2001)*

Matanzas Creek 2000 Merlot (Sonoma County) $30. A bit muddled and herbaceous, with roasted black cherries joined by notes of toast and barrel char. **85** *(1/21/2004)*

Matanzas Creek 2000 Sauvignon Blanc (Sonoma County) $22. **89** *(8/1/2002)*

MATTHEWS

Matthews 2001 Bordeaux Blend (Columbia Valley (WA)) $50. A full-bore Bordeaux blend with all five varieties. Two-thirds Cabernet Sauvignon sets the backbone, and the wine unfolds with plenty of power, dark, plummy fruit and full, roasted espresso-like barrel flavors. If there's a down spot it's the acidic tang to the finish, which seems a bit jagged. **90** *—P.G. (6/1/2005)*

Matthews 2002 Red Blend (Columbia Valley (WA)) $50. This young, dense, saturated, complex, and extremely tight wine is sappy and packed with myriad berries and red/blue fruits. It is wrapped in stiff, hard, thick, dark tannins that add tight layers of moist earth, black tea, roots, and bitter chocolate. This baby needs time. **94** *—P.G. (12/15/2005)*

Matthews 2003 Hedges Estate Vineyard Syrah (Red Mountain) $50. Ripe and thick is the name of the game here: Aromas are one step away from Porty, and flavors are of very ripe mulberries and blueberries. It's thick and syrupy on the palate, and chewy on the finish, with enough fresh acidity to keep it in good balance. 175 cases produced. **89** *(9/1/2005)*

MAURITSON WINES

Mauritson Wines 2002 Zinfandel (Dry Creek Valley) $24. Made by sixth generation growers, this Zin is rich and extracted, with plum, berry, spice, and tobacco flavors. It's built with strong acids and tannins that should pull it through the next ten years, but it's a lovely wine now. **90 Editors' Choice** *—S.H. (11/1/2005)*

Mauritson Wines 2001 Growers Reserve Zinfandel (Dry Creek Valley) $33. Mainly from hillside grapes, this Zin is far more tannic and concentrated than Mauritson's regular Zin. But it's by no means undrinkable, because the blackberry, blueberry, and pepper flavors are just delicious. Still, it should benefit from a few years of aging. **91** *—S.H. (11/1/2005)*

MAYACAMAS

Mayacamas 2002 Sauvignon Blanc (Napa Valley) $20. One of the best Sauvignons of this or any vintage, a brilliant and evocative wine of great style and flair. Powerfully dry, with citrus, fig, apple, and peppery spice flavors and a lush overlay of oak. Compelling for its intensity and complexity. **93** *—S.H. (12/15/2004)*

MAYO

Mayo 2000 Los Chamizal Vineyard Cabernet Sauvignon (Sonoma Valley) $35. **87** *—S.H. (4/1/2003)*

Mayo 2001 Napa River Ranch Vineyard Cabernet Sauvignon (Napa Valley) $35. Very ripe and extracted, verging on black currant marmalade, although it's technically dry, but lavish oak lends a wood-sap sweetness. The tannins are ripe and gentle, providing a plush mouthfeel. Glamorous and balanced. **90** *—S.H. (6/1/2004)*

Mayo 2002 Laurel Hill Vineyard Chardonnay (Sonoma Valley) $20. Extraordinarily ripe from a hot vintage, this Chard takes spiced apple flavors and bakes them into a tart, sprinkled with toasted cinnamon and nutmeg. It's also really oaky. Too big for cracked crab, but try with poached salmon in a creamy aioli. **87** *—S.H. (6/1/2004)*

Mayo 2002 Piner Ranch Vineyard Pinot Noir (Russian River Valley) $30. Very nice, a rich, juicy Pinot that unfolds layers of flavor on the palate. Enters dry, then releases a sunburst of spicy cherry and blackberry fruit with overtones of mocha and white pepper. Quite full bodied, but keeps its silky lightness throughout. **89** *—S.H. (11/1/2004)*

Mayo 1998 Piner Ranch Vineyard Pinot Noir (Russian River Valley) $35. 91 *—J.C. (12/15/2000)*

Mayo 1998 Sangiacomo Vineyards Pinot Noir (Carneros) $35. 87 *—J.C. (12/15/2000)*

Mayo 2001 Unwooded Emma's Vineyard Sauvignon Blanc (Napa Valley) $20. 86 *—S.H. (9/1/2003)*

Mayo 2001 Page Nord Vineyard Syrah (Napa Valley) $30. 85 *—S.H. (12/15/2003)*

Mayo 2000 Ricci Vineyard Old Vines Zinfandel (Russian River Valley) $25. 83 *—S.H. (11/1/2002)*

Mayo 2001 Ricci Vineyard Old Vines Zinfandel (Russian River Valley) $25. 91 Editors' Choice *(11/1/2003)*

Mayo 2001 Ricci Vineyard Reserve Old Vines Zinfandel (Russian River Valley) $38. 89 *(11/1/2003)*

MAYO FAMILY

Mayo Family 2003 Laurel Hill Vineyard Unwooded Chardonnay (Sonoma Valley) $15. Strong in ripe apple flavors, with an herbal, earthy character and some tannins, this is a tough wine that finishes with some almond-skin bitterness. It's bone dry. **85** *—S.H. (4/1/2005)*

MAYSARA

Maysara 2003 Pinot Gris (Willamette Valley) $15. This is very nice, crisp and fresh, with pure fresh cut pear fruit flavors, and hints of pear skin and citrus rind. There's good texture, mouthfeel, and body, with crisp minerality setting off the ripe fruit. A nice, smooth, unwooded finish. **88** *—P.G. (2/1/2005)*

Maysara 2002 Delara Pinot Noir (Willamette Valley) $45. A proprietary name for a barrel select reserve. Round and sweetly fruity, it's easy to see why these 12 barrels stood out from the pack. Yet this forward, ripe wine may be at its best sooner than the more layered estate cuvée. Two thirds new oak lends a tasty vanilla element to the finish. **89** *—P.G. (2/1/2005)*

Maysara 2002 Estate Cuvée Pinot Noir (Willamette Valley) $32. Pleasing, well-integrated scents show herb, leaf, bacon, and much more. There's a delicate balance to the way the dried herbs and pretty fruit flavors mix, and a velvety mouth feel that finishes off with a dab of cocoa. **89** *(11/1/2004)*

Maysara 2001 Estate Cuvée Pinot Noir (Willamette Valley) $32. 89 Cellar Selection *—P.G. (12/1/2003)*

Maysara 2001 Reserve Pinot Noir (Willamette Valley) $22. 89 Editors' Choice *—P.G. (12/1/2003)*

MAZZOCCO

Mazzocco 1999 Matrix Bordeaux Blend (Dry Creek Valley) $40. This charming wine is probably drinking at its peak now. It's a little light in body, but nearly five years of bottle age has mellowed the tannins. You'll find pleasant cherry-berry flavors leading to a gently sweet finish. **87** *—S.H. (12/1/2004)*

Mazzocco 1995 Cabernet Sauvignon (Sonoma County) $18. 88 *—L.W. (12/31/1999)*

Mazzocco 1999 Reserve Cabernet Sauvignon (Dry Creek Valley) $50. Still bruising in tannins. Will this wine ever mellow out? The answer is yes, to judge by the still-fresh blackberry and cherry fruit that doesn't seem to have aged at all. Hold for another five years. **87** *—S.H. (12/31/2004)*

Mazzocco 1998 River Lane Chardonnay (Sonoma County) $15. 87 *(12/31/1999)*

Mazzocco 2000 River Lane Vineyards Chardonnay (Sonoma County) $18. 86 *—S.H. (6/1/2003)*

Mazzocco 1996 Merlot (Dry Creek Valley) $20. 83 *(12/31/1999)*

Mazzocco 2002 Sauvignon Blanc (Russian River Valley) $14. You'll find a dry, crisp white wine, with modest citrus and figgy-melon flavors. But there are intriguing notes of fresh herbs sprinkled throughout, like lavender, thyme, anise, and dill, which make this ideal for food pairing. **87** *—S.H. (2/1/2005)*

Mazzocco 2001 Bevill Vineyards Viognier (Dry Creek Valley) $24. Nice spicy fruit in this clean, crisp wine. It has flavors of peach, mango, pineapple, and citrus fruits, and an almost Gewürz-like spiciness. A touch of oak brings smoky vanilla. **86** *—S.H. (2/1/2005)*

Mazzocco 1996 Zinfandel (Dry Creek Valley) $18. 88 *—L.W. (9/1/1999)*

Mazzocco 2001 Zinfandel (Dry Creek Valley) $16. 86 *(11/1/2003)*

Mazzocco 2001 Cuneo & Saini Zinfandel (Dry Creek Valley) $22. 87 *(11/1/2003)*

Mazzocco 1997 Cuneo & Saini Vineyard Zinfandel (Dry Creek Valley) $22. 89 *—D.T. (3/1/2002)*

Mazzocco 2001 Quinn Vineyard Zinfandel (Dry Creek Valley) $22. Light and earthy, this wine seems overcropped, given the vintage and the single vineyard sourcing. It's thin in black cherry and coffee flavors, and very dry. **84** *—S.H. (10/1/2005)*

Mazzocco 1997 Quinn Vineyard Zinfandel (Dry Creek Valley) $22. 91 *—D.T. (3/1/2002)*

Mazzocco 2001 Stone Ranch Zinfandel (Alexander Valley) $22. A polished, Merlot-style Zin, soft and velvety in body. The cherry and earth flavors are dry, and dusty tannins show up in the finish. **85** *—S.H. (10/1/2005)*

MCCRAY RIDGE

McCray Ridge 2000 Two Moon Vineyard Merlot (Dry Creek Valley) $30. There are some gritty tannins to this wine that make it chewy, almost like a food. It has pretty cherry and blackberry flavors and good acidity that balance the tannins out. Has extra layers of complexity that add interest. **89** *—S.H. (9/1/2004)*

McCray Ridge 2000 Two Moon Vineyard Luna Miel Merlot-Cabernet Sauvignon (Dry Creek Valley) $32. There's some good cherry-berry fruit here, with a solid overlay of oak, and the wine is completely dry. Feels rough and sharp, though, with acidity and tannins. Merlot-Cabernet blend. **84** *—S.H. (11/15/2004)*

MCCREA

McCrea 2000 Elerding Vineyard Chardonnay (Yakima Valley) $30. 90 *—P.G. (7/1/2002)*

McCrea 2000 Syrah (Yakima Valley) $35. 88 *—P.G. (9/1/2002)*

McCrea 1998 Syrah (Yakima Valley) $28. 90 *—P.G. (6/1/2000)*

McCrea 2000 Amerique Syrah (Yakima Valley) $40. 90 *—P.G. (9/1/2002)*

McCrea 1999 Boushey Grande Côte Vineyard Syrah (Yakima Valley) $42. 91 *—S.H. (6/1/2002)*

McCrea 1998 Boushley Vineyards Syrah (Yakima Valley) $35. 90 *—P.G. (9/1/2000)*

McCrea 2002 Ciel du Cheval Vineyard Syrah (Red Mountain) $55. One of Washington's Rhône pioneers, McCrea is still one of the best. The Ciel du Cheval bottling boasts a smoky, hickory-like note alongside hints of game and a supersized dollop of blackberry fruit. The texture is rich and velvety, the flavors satisfying. **89** *(9/1/2005)*

McCrea 1999 Cile du Cheval Vineyard Syrah (Yakima Valley) $45. 86 *(11/1/2001)*

McCrea 2002 Cuvée Orleans Syrah (Yakima Valley) $60. Normally winemaker Doug McCrea's top wine, this year we gave the nod to his Ciel du Cheval bottling, which seemed to have a bit more tannin. The Cuvée Orleans boasts lush blackberry and cassis flavors, hints of meat and pepper, but falls off just a bit on the finish. **87** *(9/1/2005)*

McCrea 2001 Yakima Valley Syrah (Yakima Valley) $38. 88 *—P.G. (12/31/2003)*

McCrea 2000 Viognier (Yakima Valley) $23. 91 *—P.G. (9/1/2002)*

McCrea 2000 La Mer White Blend (Yakima Valley) $18. 89 *—P.G. (9/1/2002)*

MCDOWELL

McDowell 1997 Grenache Rosé Grenache (Mendocino) $9. 88 Best Buy *—S.H. (6/1/1999)*

McDowell 2001 Marsanne (Mendocino) $16. 85 *—S.H. (6/1/2003)*

McDowell 2000 Reserve Petite Sirah (Mendocino) $20. 83 *(4/1/2003)*

McDowell 2000 Syrah (Mendocino County) $12. 85 *—S.H. (12/1/2002)*

McDowell 1997 Syrah (Mendocino) $12. 88 *—M.G. (11/15/1999)*

McDowell 1999 Reserve McDowell Valley Syrah (Mendocino) $24. 90 *(11/1/2001)*

McDowell 2000 Viognier (Mendocino) $16. 87 *—S.H. (5/1/2002)*

MCILROY

McIlroy 1999 Salzgeber Vineyard Cabernet Franc (Russian River Valley) $24. 83 *—S.H. (9/1/2002)*

McIlroy 2000 Aquarius Ranch Late Harvest Gewürztraminer (Russian River Valley) $13. 89 Best Buy *—S.H. (9/1/2002)*

McIlroy 1999 Aquarius Ranch Pinot Noir (Russian River Valley) $24. 86 *—S.H. (9/1/2002)*

MCINTYRE VINEYARDS

McIntyre Vineyards 2003 Chardonnay (Monterey County) $13. Drinks rather rough and syrupy, with the flavor of canned peaches and an oaky veneer. **82** *—S.H. (12/1/2005)*

McIntyre Vineyards 1998 L'Homme Qui Ris Sparkling Blend (Monterey County) $22. 84 *—J.C. (12/1/2003)*

MCKENZIE-MUELLER

McKenzie-Mueller 2001 Cabernet Sauvignon (Napa Valley) $40. Harsh and difficult, with dry tannins and a gluey mouthfeel that makes the blackberry flavors taste medicinal. **83** *—S.H. (7/1/2005)*

McKenzie-Mueller 2001 Merlot (Carneros) $28. Comes down on the rustic side, but offers pleasant flavors of cherries, roast coffee, and cocoa, in a dry wine. **84** *—S.H. (7/1/2005)*

McKenzie-Mueller 2001 Pinot Noir (Carneros) $28. Harsh, with burnt cherry notes that make the tannins and acids stick out. No major flaws, but it's hard to like. **82** *—S.H. (7/1/2005)*

MCKINLEY SPRINGS

McKinley Springs 2002 Syrah (Columbia Valley (WA)) $24. This new winery has a first release that is tough to peg. It is so incredibly dense and Port-like in color and aroma that you expect it to slam into the palate like a tropical storm, but it doesn't hit quite that hard. Oxidized and showing more baking spices than fruit, it nonetheless is a flavorful effort that will bring some enjoyment in the near term. **86** *—P.G. (12/15/2004)*

MCMANIS

McManis 2003 Cabernet Sauvignon (California) $10. A little sweet in residual sugar, but otherwise a nice wine, with soft tannins and ripe flavors of cherries and chocolate. **84** *—S.H. (12/31/2004)*

McManis 2001 Cabernet Sauvignon (California) $9. **82** *—S.H. (12/31/2002)*

McManis 2004 Chardonnay (River Junction) $10. With its easy flavors of apples and peaches and touch of spicy oak, this everyday Chard is a pretty good buy. It's soft, but that fruit is ripe and pretty. **84** *—S.H. (11/15/2005)*

McManis 2000 Chardonnay (California) $9. **84** *—S.H. (5/1/2002)*

McManis 2003 Merlot (California) $10. Earthy, with cherry cough medicine flavors and a sharp finish. **82** *—S.H. (12/15/2004)*

McManis 2001 Merlot (California) $9. **85** *—S.H. (12/31/2002)*

McManis 2004 Petite Sirah (California) $11. Ultra-dry, tannic, full-bodied, strong, and red, this country-style wine is something you'd drink with barbecued ribs. The flavors of blackberries and coffee are enriched by some oak. **83** *—S.H. (12/31/2005)*

McManis 2004 Pinot Grigio (California) $10. Plenty of ripe, semisweet fig, citrus, and cantaloupe flavors in this crisp wine. It has a fizziness that's not unpleasant. **84** *—S.H. (7/1/2005)*

McManis 2003 Syrah (California) $10. Rather soft and thick in texture, a low tannin, low acid wine with flavors of sweetened coffee, cherry compote and rhubarb pie. Easy and gentle. **84** *—S.H. (12/31/2004)*

McManis 2001 Syrah (California) $9. **84** *—S.H. (12/1/2002)*

McManis 2003 Viognier (California) $10. Run, don't walk, to stock up on this by the case. If you have a hankering for a fruity, spicy dry white wine, balanced with crisp acidity and with plenty of finesse, this is it. Tropical fruits, wildflowers, peaches, vanilla, you name it. **88 Best Buy** *—S.H. (12/15/2004)*

MCNAB RIDGE

McNab Ridge 2000 Meritage (Mendocino County) $20. What's likeable about this Bordeaux blend is its dryness. It doesn't slam you with over-the-top, extracted fruit, but is controlled in its herb and blackberry flavors and smooth but firm tannins. **90** *—S.H. (11/15/2004)*

McNab Ridge 1998 Merlot (Mendocino County) $15. **84** *—S.H. (5/1/2002)*

McNab Ridge 2000 Petite Sirah (Mendocino County) $18. **81** *(4/1/2003)*

McNab Ridge 2003 Sauvignon Blanc (Mendocino) $12. Sweet, fresh grass, lemon and lime, fig, and vanilla mark this dry wine. It has a pleasantly clean streak of acidity to offset the fruity flavors. **85** *—S.H. (12/15/2004)*

MCPRICE MYERS

McPrice Myers 2002 Larner Vineyard Syrah (Santa Ynez Valley) $25. Here's a beautiful, lush aromatic mélange of pepper, smoky vanilla, cassis, gingerbread, and bacon. Really complex and compelling, and it drinks as fine as it smells. Just delicious, with soft, rich tannins and a long, mellow finish. **92** *—S.H. (12/1/2004)*

MEADOR

Meador 1998 Maverick Syrah (Arroyo Seco) $50. **83** *(11/1/2001)*

MEANDER

Meander 2003 Cabernet Sauvignon (Napa Valley) $65. This ambitious effort doesn't succeed due to a sharpness throughout, a tart, wintergreen note that detracts. Everything else, the oak, the tannins, is fine. **84** *—S.H. (12/31/2005)*

MEEKER

Meeker 1997 Gold Leaf Cuvée Zinfandel (Dry Creek Valley) $18. **82** *—P.G. (3/1/2001)*

MELROSE

Melrose 2002 Reserve Pinot Noir (Umpqua Valley) $26. Very spicy, with a tart entry and some sour cherry fruit. Elegant, feminine and plush through the middle. **88** *(11/1/2004)*

MELVILLE

Melville 2002 Clone 76 Inox Chardonnay (Santa Rita Hills) $28. **86** *—S.H. (12/15/2003)*

Melville 2001 Carrie's Pinot Noir (Santa Rita Hills) $40. **90** *—S.H. (10/1/2003)*

Melville 2000 Syrah (Santa Rita Hills) $24. **86** *—S.H. (12/1/2002)*

MENDELSON

Mendelson 1999 Dessert Wine Pinot Gris (Napa Valley) $35. **85** *—J.M. (12/1/2002)*

Mendelson 2001 Pinot Noir (Santa Lucia Highlands) $38. Redolent of black cherries and cola in the nose. On the palate, it fans out to reveal spice, more cherry, strawberries, bacon, cedar, tea, and spice flavors. Tannins are powdery but ripe, while the finish is bright. **89** *—J.M. (2/1/2004)*

MENDOCINO COLLECTION

Mendocino Collection 1997 SketchBook Collection Merlot (Mendocino) $23. **84** *(11/1/1999)*

MENDOCINO GOLD

Mendocino Gold 2001 Chardonnay (Mendocino County) $10. **86 Best Buy** *—S.H. (6/1/2003)*

MENDOCINO HILL

Mendocino Hill 1999 Syrah (Mendocino County) $20. **88** *—S.H. (5/1/2002)*

MEOLA VINEYARDS

Meola Vineyards 2002 Venezia Cabernet Sauvignon (Alexander Valley) $60. Very ripe and extracted, with bigtime blackberry, cherry, blueberry, cassis, and vanilla-oaky flavors, this Cab has a slightly rustic mouthfeel. It's so fruity, it tastes almost semisweet, although it's technically dry. **85** *—S.H. (12/15/2005)*

MER SOLEIL

Mer Soleil 2001 Chardonnay (Central Coast) $42. Hard to figure why the Wagners of Caymus don't put the fine Santa Lucia Highlands AVA on the front label, but there's no questioning the quality of this wine. It's brilliant in tropical fruit and pear flavors, with a lavish overlay of smoky oak and a very long, sweet finish. Has those citrusy, minerally Monterey acids that perk up the flavors, making them even richer. **92** *—S.H. (2/1/2004)*

Mer Soleil 1999 Chardonnay (Central Coast) $40. **93** *—J.M. (12/15/2002)*

Mer Soleil 2000 Late Harvest White Wine White Blend (Santa Lucia Highlands) $36. **92** *—J.M. (9/1/2003)*

MERIDIAN

Meridian 2004 Chardonnay (Santa Barbara County) $10. It's rich in Chardonnay character, with tropical fruit, peach, pear, and oak flavors set in a richly creamy, honeyed texture that's highlighted by brisk, South Coast acidity. **87 Best Buy** *—S.H. (12/31/2005)*

Meridian 2002 Chardonnay (Santa Barbara) $10. The price is right, but this wine is rather skimpy in fruit, over-oaked and too sweet. **83** *—S.H. (2/1/2005)*

Meridian 2000 Chardonnay (Santa Barbara County) $11. **87 Best Buy** *—S.H. (12/31/2001)*

Meridian 1999 Limited Release Chardonnay (Santa Barbara County) $22. **89** *—S.H. (12/15/2002)*

Meridian 1999 Reserve Chardonnay (Edna Valley) $14. **88 Best Buy** *—S.H. (12/15/2002)*

Meridian 2002 Gewürztraminer (Santa Barbara County) $8. **85** *—S.H. (12/31/2003)*

Meridian 2003 Pinot Grigio (California) $11. A very refreshing wine, clean and zesty, with fig, peach, lime, pineapple, and buttercream flavors. Pretty complex for this price. **85** *—S.H. (7/1/2005)*

Meridian 2003 Pinot Noir (Central Coast) $11. Decent, with cherry and cocoa flavors, and dry through the finish. There's a burnt element that makes it harsh, though. **83** *—S.H. (7/1/2005)*

Meridian 1999 Pinot Noir (Santa Barbara County) $11. **86 Best Buy** *—S.H. (12/15/2001)*

Meridian 1996 Coastal Reserve Pinot Noir (Santa Barbara County) $22. **90** *(10/1/1999)*

Meridian 1998 Reserve Pinot Noir (Santa Barbara County) $22. **88** *—S.H. (12/15/2000)*

Meridian 2000 Sauvignon Blanc (California) $8. **86** *—S.H. (9/12/2002)*

Meridian 2002 Reserve Syrah (Santa Barbara County) $16. Pretty tannic in its adolescence, and would probably have benefited from additional time before release. Underneath the bitter astringency are blackberry and coffee flavors. As tough as it is on its own, it will greatly benefit from a big, greasy leg of roasted lamb. **86** *—S.H. (12/1/2004)*

MERRIAM VINEYARDS

Merriam Vineyards 2000 Cabernet Sauvignon (Dry Creek Valley) $35. How dark this wine is. It opens with a brambly, dusty aroma, like wild berries on a hot summer day, as well as hints of dried leather and toast. In the mouth, there's a burst of black currant that quickly disappears into the tannins. Best after 2006. **86** *—S.H. (6/1/2004)*

Merriam Vineyards 2001 Windacre Merlot (Russian River Valley) $35. A great Merlot that completely satisfies for its dryness, its firm, ripe tannins, and its lush interplay of blackberry, cherry, tobacco, and dark chocolate flavors. The finish goes on forever. As tannic as it is, it will be fine with a nice steak, or you can stick it in the cellar for a few years and let it soften. **93** *—S.H. (12/15/2004)*

MERRY EDWARDS

Merry Edwards 2003 Pinot Noir (Sonoma Coast) $29. Displays classic cool climate character in the stimulating acids and brisk tannins. Is it a cellarworthy wine? Probably not. There's blackberry and cherry fruit, but this dry, elegant wine isn't built for the long haul. **87** *—S.H. (12/1/2005)*

Merry Edwards 2002 Pinot Noir (Russian River Valley) $32. This is an easy, all-purpose Pinot despite some fairly hefty tannins. It glides over the tongue carrying cola, cherry, rhubarb, heirloom tomato, and smoky flavors, and finishes dry. **86** *—S.H. (4/1/2005)*

Merry Edwards 2001 Pinot Noir (Russian River Valley) $32. A lovely Pinot that rises above everyday status to achieve real depth and complexity, although it's not on a par with Merry's single-vineyard releases. It's light and silky, with spicy flavors of cherries, rhubarb, tea, vanilla, and toast. **87** *—S.H. (6/1/2004)*

Merry Edwards 2002 Klopp Ranch Pinot Noir (Russian River Valley) $48. Dark, super-extracted in fruit, and rather hot and heavy, with some complexity. It has a rich mélange of blackberry, black cherry, cola, espresso, briar, sweet leather, and spicy flavors, and is fairly tannic and bone dry. A cellar candidate, it will pair well with lamb or beef. **89** *—S.H. (4/1/2005)*

Merry Edwards 2000 Klopp Ranch Pinot Noir (Russian River Valley) $48. 92 *—S.H. (2/1/2003)*

Merry Edwards 2000 Meredith Estate Pinot Noir (Sonoma Coast) $45. 91 *—S.H. (2/1/2003)*

Merry Edwards 2000 Olivet Lane Pinot Noir (Russian River Valley) $48. 94 *—S.H. (2/1/2003)*

Merry Edwards 2002 Olivet Lane Methode a la Ancienne Pinot Noir (Russian River Valley) $51. A somewhat controversial wine for its earthy complexities of rhubarb, tomatoes, beets and oak, and cinnamon and clove overlay. Delicate in structure, with strong acids and tannins, some will find it Burgundian while others will find it thin. **86** *(11/1/2004)*

Merry Edwards 2000 Windsor Gardens Pinot Noir (Russian River Valley) $54. 92 *—S.H. (2/1/2003)*

USA

MERRYVALE

Merryvale 1997 Beckstoffer Vyd Bordeaux Blend (Napa Valley) $45. 93 *(11/1/2000)*

Merryvale 1998 Profile Bordeaux Blend (Napa Valley) $90. 96 Cellar Selection *—J.M. (12/1/2001)*

Merryvale 1996 Profile Bordeaux Blend (Napa Valley) $75. 86 *(7/1/2000)*

Merryvale 1999 Cabernet Sauvignon (Napa Valley) $26. 88 *—S.H. (6/1/2002)*

Merryvale 2002 Beckstoffer Clone Six Cabernet Sauvignon (Rutherford) $88. Exceptionally ripe and expressive even among the flamboyant 2002 Rutherfords, with a pleasing note of vanilla and char from oak, this Cab is rich in cherry fruit flavors. The tannins are sweet and fine, and sturdy enough to carry it through 2010. **90** *—S.H. (12/15/2005)*

Merryvale 2001 Beckstoffer Vineyard X Cabernet Sauvignon (Oakville) $75. From a vineyard just behind Brix restaurant, this is a soft-textured, full-bodied Cab with dark plum and earth flavors. Picks up hints of tobacco and chocolate on the finish. **90** *(7/1/2005)*

Merryvale 2000 Beckstoffer Vineyard Clone Six Cabernet Sauvignon (Rutherford) $75. 91 *—S.H. (11/15/2003)*

Merryvale 2000 Beckstoffer Vineyard X Cabernet Sauvignon (Oakville) $75. 92 *—J.M. (12/15/2003)*

Merryvale 2000 Reserve Cabernet Sauvignon (Napa Valley) $35. 86 *—S.H. (12/31/2003)*

Merryvale 1998 Reserve Cabernet Sauvignon (Napa Valley) $39. 88 *—J.M. (12/1/2001)*

Merryvale 2001 Starmont Cabernet Sauvignon (Napa Valley) $24. I love this wine for the effortless way it charms. Everything's restrained, from the currant and cherry flavors to the oak, while the softly sweet tannins create a smooth, mellow mouthfeel. It's a feminine Cab that will support, not compete with, the best foods. **91 Editors' Choice** *—S.H. (6/1/2004)*

Merryvale 2001 Dutton Ranch Chardonnay (Russian River Valley) $29. Solidly in the Merryvale style, featuring exuberantly ripe fruit and lavish oak balanced with acidity. The intense flavors veer toward spicy pears, pineapple, and white peach, and last through a long finish. **91** *—S.H. (2/1/2004)*

Merryvale 1999 Dutton Ranch Chardonnay (Russian River Valley) $35. 91 *—J.M. (12/15/2002)*

Merryvale 2002 Reserve Chardonnay (Carneros) $30. Bigger and richer than the Starmont bottling, with correspondingly heavier oak. Lots of toast and grilled pineapple and peach notes on the nose, followed by a mouthfilling wine laced with smoky accents. Echoes of butter and dark toast on the finish. **90** *(7/1/2005)*

Merryvale 2000 Reserve Chardonnay (Carneros) $29. 86 *—S.H. (6/1/2003)*

Merryvale 2001 Silhouette Chardonnay (Napa Valley) $45. Lots of new oak and lees lend this wine toasty, yeasty, creamy notes, with vanilla on the finish. The fruit? It's green apples and papayas, with liberal acids. Feels a bit tight now, and could develop for a few years. **92** *—S.H. (12/31/2004)*

Merryvale 1999 Silhouette Chardonnay (Napa Valley) $49. 93 *—S.H. (5/1/2002)*

Merryvale 2002 Starmont Chardonnay (Napa Valley) $19. A bit over-oaked, with those buttery, caramelly aromas and flavors dominating the underlying apple tart fruit. But it's rich and complicated, offering up an array of oriental spices that pack a real punch on the finish. **87** *—S.H. (6/1/2004)*

Merryvale 2000 Starmont Chardonnay (Napa Valley) $20. 86 *—S.H. (5/1/2002)*

Merryvale 1998 Starmont Chardonnay (Napa Valley) $20. **89** *(6/1/2000)*

Merryvale 2001 Beckstoffer Vineyard Las Amigas Vineyard Merlot (Carneros) $39. The tannins and acids hit the palate broadside, leaving it dry and rasping. There are some cherry flavors deep inside, and of course oak. Not likely to age. **85** *—S.H. (12/15/2004)*

Merryvale 2001 Reserve Merlot (Napa Valley) $32. An easy to like Merlot, with the weight of Cabernet. Smooth, ripely soft tannins, lots of smoky new oak, and true varietal flavors of ripe cherries, black raspberries, cocoa, and vanilla. Finishes soft and fruity. **88** *—S.H. (2/1/2005)*

Merryvale 1999 Reserve Merlot (Napa Valley) $39. **92** *—S.H. (11/15/2002)*

Merryvale 2001 Starmont Merlot (Napa Valley) $22. Another winning red wine from Merryvale. It goes beyond the ripe berry-cherry, herb and oak-infused flavors to achieve real class and distinction. Those rich, sweet tannins are really classy. **90** *—S.H. (6/1/2004)*

Merryvale 1998 Beckstoffer Vineyard Merlot-Cabernet Sauvignon (Napa Valley) $60. **92** *—J.M. (12/1/2001)*

Merryvale 2003 Pinot Noir (Carneros) $40. This is a plump, corpulent Pinot with soft tannins and loads of plum, black cherry, and cola flavors. Has some cinnamon and clove notes as well, and a warm, velvety finish. **89** *(7/1/2005)*

Merryvale 2000 Pinot Noir (Sonoma Coast) $44. **92** *—S.H. (2/1/2003)*

Merryvale 1999 Profile Red Blend (Napa Valley) $90. **90** *—S.H. (12/31/2002)*

Merryvale 1999 Juliana Vineyard Sauvignon Blanc (Napa Valley) $22. **87** *—S.H. (11/15/2000)*

Merryvale 1998 Reserve Sauvignon Blanc (Napa Valley) $22. **86** *(3/1/2000)*

Merryvale 2002 Starmont Sauvignon Blanc (Napa Valley) $16. Fresh and lively on the palate, the wine is redolent of lemon, lime, grapefruit, and herbs. It's got good structure, leaving a clean, fresh taste on the palate and finishes with moderate length. **87** *—J.M. (2/1/2004)*

Merryvale 2002 Syrah (Napa Valley) $30. A bit peppery and herbal, but with plenty of crisp, tangy fruit at its core. The overall impression is of a wine that's a bit rustic and rough but solid and well made. **85** *(9/1/2005)*

METTLER FAMILY VINEYARDS

Mettler Family Vineyards 2002 Cabernet Sauvignon (Lodi) $25. There's a stewed quality to the fruit, and heat in the finish. that make this Cab not worth the price. Will work with simple fare. **83** *—S.H. (11/1/2005)*

Mettler Family Vineyards 2000 Cabernet Sauvignon (Lodi) $24. **87** *—M.S. (11/15/2003)*

Mettler Family Vineyards 2001 Petite Sirah (Lodi) $26. Pretty nice wine, a full-bodied, dry red with pleasant berry-cherry flavors and dusty tannins. Pricey for what you get. May age well. **85** *—S.H. (6/1/2004)*

MIA'S PLAYGROUND

Mia's Playground 2002 Cabernet Sauvignon (Alexander Valley) $16. A simple, kind of rough and earthy Cab, thin in fruit, which accentuates the tannins. It's dry and spicy on the finish. **83** *—S.H. (5/1/2005)*

Mia's Playground 2002 Merlot (Dry Creek Valley) $16. Simple, fruity and soft, with an easy tannic structure, this Merlot is at its best now for the rich berry and cherry flavors, with a hint of chocolate. **83** *—S.H. (12/1/2005)*

Mia's Playground 2003 Zinfandel (Dry Creek Valley) $16. Super-tasty in blackberry, cherry, and chocolate flavors, this Zin couldn't possibly be riper or fruitier. On the other hand, it could be crisper. Those flavors, while delicious, feel a bit syrupy, due to insufficient acidity. **85** *—S.H. (12/1/2005)*

MICHAEL CHIARELLO

Michael Chiarello 2000 Eileen Cabernet Sauvignon (Napa Valley) $45. One of the darker Cabs of the year, and dominated by tough, numbing tannins. Will it age? There are deliciously sweet blackberry and cherry flavors that emerge after you swallow. Not really ready, but with a big T-bone, will be enjoyable. **87** *—S.H. (5/1/2004)*

Michael Chiarello 2001 Roux Old Vine Petite Sirah (Napa Valley) $45. This is an old-style Pet, black as night, and the mouthfeel is dominated by massive tannins that sting with toughness. A deep core of cherry fruit is buried now; by 2011, this wine will soften and sweeten. **88** *—S.H. (5/1/2004)*

Michael Chiarello 2001 Felicia Old Vine Zinfandel (Napa Valley) $45. The pretty cherry and blackberry flavors have a peppery, spicy edge, in this very dry wine. It's rather rough in structure, with jagged tannins that are accentuated by acidity. **85** *—S.H. (2/1/2004)*

Michael Chiarello 2000 Giana Young Vines Zinfandel (Napa Valley) $28. **89** *—J.M. (9/1/2003)*

Michael Chiarello 2001 Gianna Zinfandel (Napa Valley) $30. This wine carries its zippy acidity well. The bright edge highlights a dense core of cherry, raspberry, and cola flavors, all framed in toasty oak with hints of vanilla. Spice and herb notes add interest, while the finish is long and lush. **90** *—J.M. (9/1/2004)*

MICHAEL POZZAN

Michael Pozzan 2003 Annabella Special Selection Chardonnay (Napa Valley) $12. Super-oaky, just oozing high char and sweet caramel. Underneath is ripe tropical fruit, with a sweet finish. If you like this style, it's a good value. **84** *—S.H. (3/1/2005)*

Michael Pozzan 1997 Reserve Red Blend (Napa Valley) $13. 88 *(11/15/1999)*

MICHAEL SULLBERG

Michael Sullberg 2001 Cabernet Sauvignon (California) $9. 85 *—S.H. (11/15/2003)*

MICHAEL-SCOTT

Michael-Scott 2001 Balliet Vineyard Cabernet Sauvignon (Napa Valley) $35. Black currant, herb, and chocolate flavors are wrapped in dry tannins with elbows. They scour the mouth, giving a rustic mouthfeel. The finish is fruity, very dry, and puckery. **85** *—S.H. (6/1/2004)*

Michael-Scott 2001 Stagnaro Vineyard Zinfandel (Napa Valley) $22. 87 *(11/1/2003)*

MICHAUD

Michaud 2000 Pinot Noir (Chalone) $45. 85 *—S.H. (7/1/2003)*

Michaud 2000 Syrah (Chalone) $35. 92 Cellar Selection *—S.H. (10/1/2003)*

MICHEL-SCHLUMBERGER

Michel-Schlumberger 2001 Cabernet Sauvignon (Dry Creek Valley) $32. Cabs from this appellation, no matter how ripe they are, always seem to have a brawny, briary edge to them, and this wine is no exception. The blackberries might have been picked in a dusty, thorny patch. Something about the acidy, tannic structure is appealing. **91** *—S.H. (12/31/2004)*

Michel-Schlumberger 1997 Benchland Cabernet Sauvignon (Dry Creek Valley) $27. 87 *—S.H. (9/1/2000)*

Michel-Schlumberger 1997 Chardonnay (Dry Creek Valley) $20. 92 *—S.H. (11/1/1999)*

Michel-Schlumberger 1999 Chardonnay (Dry Creek Valley) $20. 86 *—S.H. (11/15/2001)*

Michel-Schlumberger 1998 Merlot (Dry Creek Valley) $21. 89 *—S.H. (12/1/2001)*

Michel-Schlumberger 2003 Pinot Blanc (Dry Creek Valley) $21. An interesting wine with an array of citrus, peach, and tart pineapple flavors, very high acidity, and a super-long finish. It tingles on the palate, and is refreshing and ultra-clean. Has some complexity, and is a natural for food. **87** *—S.H. (12/1/2004)*

MIDNIGHT CELLARS

Midnight Cellars 2000 Mare Nectaris Reserve Bordeaux Blend (Paso Robles) $35. Quintessential Paso Cab blend, rich, dry, and soft. You'll find cherry and coffee flavors, with an herbal edge, wrapped in gentle but richly textured tannins and low acidity. **88** *—S.H. (2/1/2005)*

Midnight Cellars 1999 Mare Nectaris Cabernet Blend (Paso Robles) $35. 88 *—M.S. (5/1/2003)*

Midnight Cellars 2001 Moonlight Cabernet Franc (Paso Robles) $22. Heavy, soft, and dry, with some sharp tannins framing the cherry and coffee flavors, but it'll do with a juicy cheeseburger. **83** *—S.H. (5/1/2005)*

Midnight Cellars 2001 Nebula Cabernet Sauvignon (Paso Robles) $19. Tannic, soft, dry, and uninteresting, with a caramelly, Porty smell. **81** *—S.H. (5/1/2005)*

Midnight Cellars 1997 Nebula Cabernet Sauvignon (Paso Robles) $22. 88 *—S.H. (8/1/2001)*

Midnight Cellars 1997 Chardonnay (Paso Robles) $18. 84 *(6/1/2000)*

Midnight Cellars 1999 Equinox Chardonnay (Paso Robles) $18. 86 *—S.H. (11/15/2001)*

Midnight Cellars 1999 Eclipse Merlot (Paso Robles) $22. 86 *—S.H. (12/1/2001)*

Midnight Cellars 1999 Estate Merlot (Paso Robles) $23. 84 *—S.H. (12/1/2001)*

Midnight Cellars 2000 Full Moon Red Blend (Paso Robles) $10. 83 *—S.H. (11/15/2002)*

Midnight Cellars 2002 Gemini Red Blend (Paso Robles) $32. This blend of Syrah and Zinfandel is soft and pleasant. It has flavors of cherries, cocoa, and vanilla cream. **84** *—S.H. (4/1/2005)*

Midnight Cellars 1999 Starlight Sangiovese (Paso Robles) $22. 85 *—S.H. (9/1/2002)*

Midnight Cellars 2002 Nocturne Syrah (Paso Robles) $19. There's plenty of fruit in this country-style wine. The fruit consists of all sorts of black and red berries and stone fruits, with an edge of espresso and oaky caramel. The country is in the rugged texture, which calls for a good steak. **85** *—S.H. (12/1/2005)*

Midnight Cellars 2000 Nocturne Syrah (Paso Robles) $26. 85 *—S.H. (12/1/2002)*

Midnight Cellars 2001 Vineyard Select Syrah (Paso Robles) $48. Heavy, with a raw mouthfeel to the black cherry flavors. Finishes dry and astringent, but clean. **83** *—S.H. (3/1/2005)*

Midnight Cellars 2000 Zinfandel (Paso Robles) $18. 83 —*M.S. (9/1/2003)*

Midnight Cellars 1999 Crescent Zinfandel (Paso Robles) $22. 87 —*D.T. (3/1/2002)*

Midnight Cellars 1999 Estate Zinfandel (Paso Robles) $26. 88 —*D.T. (3/1/2002)*

MIDSUMMER CELLARS

Midsummer Cellars 2001 Hickok Traulsen Zinfandel (Napa Valley) $22. 85 *(11/1/2003)*

MIGRATION

Migration 2002 Pinot Noir (Anderson Valley) $26. Pretty dark and rich, a big, full-bodied wine with complex flavors of cherry, tobacco, earth, coffee, mint, and cola, and some sweet chocolate in the finish. This is a muscular, fruit-driven wine, but could use more subtlety and elegance. **87** *(11/1/2004)*

MILL CREEK

Mill Creek 2001 Zinfandel (Russian River Valley) $22. 89 —*J.M. (11/1/2003)*

MILLBROOK

Millbrook 2000 Cabernet Franc (New York) $18. 83 —*M.S. (2/27/2003)*

Millbrook 1999 Proprietor's Special Reserve Chardonnay (Hudson River Region) $16. 85 —*J.M. (2/27/2003)*

Millbrook 2001 Tocai Friulano Estate Bottled Tocai (Hudson River Region) $12. 88 Best Buy —*J.M. (2/27/2003)*

MILLIAIRE

Milliaire 2002 Eagle's Nest Petite Sirah (Lodi) $18. Very peppery and fruity, a big, dark wine loaded with blackberries. Soft, and finishes a little sweet. **84** —*S.H. (2/1/2005)*

Milliaire 2001 Clock Spring Zinfandel (Sierra Foothills) $18. Dramatic in the power and intensity of its ripe brambly, briary berry flavors, with touches of earth, tobacco, and sweet ground spices. Despite the flamboyance, remains balanced and controlled. Defines these ancient Foothills Zins. **91 Editors' Choice** —*S.H. (2/1/2005)*

Milliaire 2001 Ghirardelli Zinfandel (Sierra Foothills) $18. From old head-pruned vines, a big, kick-butt Zin crammed with jammy wild berry and spicy flavors. Dry and balanced, very long in the finish, rich and bold. **90** —*S.H. (2/1/2005)*

MILONE

Milone 1996 Bells Echo Vineyard Echo Bordeaux Blend (Mendocino) $25. 91 —*S.H. (3/1/2000)*

Milone 1997 Hopland Cuvée Chardonnay (Mendocino) $10. 88 —*S.H. (3/1/2000)*

Milone 1997 Bells Echo Vineyards Echo Red Blend (Mendocino County) $30. 83 —*S.H. (5/1/2002)*

Milone 1997 Sanel Valley Vineyard Zinfandel (Mendocino County) $15. 88 *(5/1/2000)*

MINER

Miner 2002 Cabernet Sauvignon (Oakville) $50. A little earthy and rustic, this Cab has a tobacco-and-herb edge to the blackberry and coffee flavors. It's very dry and fairly tannic, with pronounced oak. Has some elegance, but doesn't seem to be an ager, so drink now. **85** —*S.H. (12/15/2005)*

Miner 2000 Cabernet Sauvignon (Oakville) $50. 87 —*S.H. (11/15/2003)*

Miner 1997 Cabernet Sauvignon (Oakville) $60. 86 *(11/1/2000)*

Miner 2003 Chardonnay (Napa Valley) $28. I actually like this wine more than Miner's more expensive '02 Wild Yeast Chard, with which it was simultaneously released. It's not as overwrought. Here, the tasty fruit takes over, with good results. **87** —*S.H. (7/1/2005)*

Miner 2000 Chardonnay (Napa Valley) $30. 85 —*S.H. (6/1/2003)*

Miner 2002 Wild Yeast Chardonnay (Napa Valley) $50. There's certainly a lot of flashy oak and lees here, contributing pretty vanilla and caramel flavors. But there's something disjointed about the underlying wine, which lacks vibrancy. **86** —*S.H. (7/1/2005)*

Miner 2001 Stagecoach Vineyard Merlot (Napa Valley) $28. From a famed vineyard, a strong and pedigreed wine. The structure immediately alerts you that it's an excellent wine, with its firm, sweet tannins, ripe fruit and crisp acids, not to mention the fine oak. Rather astringent now, but the flood of cherry and blackberry flavor suggests cellaring until 2006. **92** —*S.H. (12/15/2004)*

Miner 2000 Stagecoach Vineyard Merlot (Napa Valley) $35. 93 Editors' Choice —*S.H. (12/1/2003)*

Miner 2002 Garys' Vineyard Pinot Noir (Santa Lucia Highlands) $50. Paler in color than Miner's Rosella's bottling, and more delicately structured, but there's nothing shy about the flavors. They're richly intricate, a tapestry of red cherry, cola, rosehip tea, cinnamon, mocha, vanilla, and smoky oak. Simply delicious, and so smooth, so fine in the mouth. **93** —*S.H. (11/1/2004)*

Miner 2002 Rosella's Vineyard Pinot Noir (Santa Lucia Highlands) $50. This classic cool-climate Pinot Noir shows the crisp acids, silky texture and lush, intricate flavors induced by nighttime fog and daily sunshine. Those flavors run to cherries, with nuances of cola, rhubarb, oaky vanilla and peppery spice. Not only a fun wine, but a complex one that distinguishes the appellation. **92** *—S.H. (11/1/2004)*

Miner 2000 Rosato Rosé Blend (Mendocino) $13. 87 *—J.M. (11/15/2001)*

Miner 2002 Syrah (Napa Valley) $28. A soft-textured, easy-drinking Syrah that one reviewer called a nice everyday, by-the-glass wine. Slightly candied cherry-berry fruit is accented by dried spices that seem to fade rapidly on the finish. **84** *(9/1/2005)*

Miner 2004 Simpson Vineyard Viognier (California) $20. Viognier's fruity, floral aspects are toned down with an herbal, earthy note. There's some good, firm acidity. From Madera County, in the Central Valley. **84** *—S.H. (12/1/2005)*

Miner 2002 Simpson Vineyard Viognier (California) $20. 84 *—S.H. (12/1/2003)*

MIRABELLE

Mirabelle NV Brut Champagne Blend (North Coast) $16. 87 *—J.M. (12/1/2002)*

MIRASSOU

Mirassou 2002 Cabernet Sauvignon (California) $10. Rather unripe, with green mint and cherry flavors and a sharpness through the finish. **82** *—S.H. (11/1/2005)*

Mirassou 1999 Coastal Selection Cabernet Sauvignon (Central Coast) $11. 87 Best Buy *—S.H. (11/15/2002)*

Mirassou 2002 Chardonnay (California) $10. Shows its cool coastal origins (according to Mirassou, it could be labeled Monterey County) in its tight, citrusy fruit and crisp acids. There's hint of butter to go with notes of sweet corn and custard. **84** *(11/15/2004)*

Mirassou 1999 Coastal Selection Chardonnay (Monterey County) $13. 85 *—S.H. (11/15/2001)*

Mirassou 1998 Harvest Reserve Chardonnay (Monterey County) $16. 88 *(6/1/2000)*

Mirassou 1998 Mission Vineyard Chardonnay (Monterey County) $24. 91 *—S.H. (2/1/2000)*

Mirassou 1999 Showcase Selection Chardonnay (Monterey County) $30. 89 *(7/1/2001)*

Mirassou 2002 Merlot (California) $10. Pretty basic fare, raw, and harsh, but with some redeeming berry flavors that finish dry. **82** *—S.H. (11/1/2005)*

Mirassou 1999 Coastal Selection Merlot (Monterey) $11. 84 *— (11/15/2002)*

Mirassou 1998 Harvest Reserve Merlot (Monterey County) $18. 85 *—S.H. (7/1/2002)*

Mirassou 1999 Mirassou Harvest Reserve Merlot (Monterey County) $18. 85 *—S.H. (11/15/2002)*

Mirassou 2000 Coastal Selection Pinot Blanc (Monterey County) $12. 88 *—S.H. (9/1/2003)*

Mirassou 1997 Limited Bottling Fifth Generat Pinot Blanc (Monterey County) $16. 87 *—S.H. (9/1/1999)*

Mirassou 1999 Mission Vineyard Pinot Blanc (Arroyo Seco) $24. 85 *—S.H. (12/15/2001)*

Mirassou 1997 Pinot Noir (Monterey County) $11. 84 *(11/15/1999)*

Mirassou 1999 Coastal Selection Pinot Noir (Central Coast) $13. 82 *—S.H. (12/15/2001)*

Mirassou 1998 Coastal Selection Pinot Noir (Monterey County) $14. 83 *—S.H. (11/15/2001)*

Mirassou 1997 Harvest Reserve Pinot Noir (Monterey County) $16. 86 *(12/15/1999)*

Mirassou 1999 Showcase Selection Pinot Noir (Monterey County) $30. 89 *(10/1/2002)*

Mirassou 2004 Riesling (Monterey) $10. Frankly sweet, with sugary citrus, peach, and wintergreen flavors, this wine fortunately has decent acidity to make it crisp and clean. **83** *—S.H. (12/1/2005)*

Mirassou 2000 Coastal Selection Riesling (Monterey County) $8. 85 *—S.H. (6/1/2002)*

Mirassou 2003 Sauvignon Blanc (Calaveras County) $10. Plump, yet crisp, this fruit-forward Sauvignon has something for everyone: a hint of grassiness, ripe stone fruit, and fig flavors and decent freshness on the finish. **85 Best Buy** *(11/15/2004)*

MIRO

Miro 2001 Coyote Ridge Vineyard Petite Sirah (Dry Creek Valley) $35. Stone cold classic Sonoma Petite Sirah, black in color, brooding, dense in body, and brilliantly fruity. The sweet, smooth tannins hold massive flavors ranging from black currants and coffee to grilled meat and plenty of smoky oak. Easy to drink now, but should age well for many years. From a branch of the Trentadue winery. **92** *—S.H. (3/1/2005)*

MITCHELL

Mitchell 1999 Reserve Malbec (El Dorado) $21. 82 *—S.H. (5/1/2002)*

MITCHELL KATZ WINERY

Mitchell Katz Winery 2001 Crackerbox Vineyards Sangiovese (Livermore Valley) $22. 82 —*S.H. (12/1/2003)*

MIXED BAG

Mixed Bag 2002 White Wine White Blend (California) $10. Dry and rustic, with crisp acids, this earthy wine has some fruity flavors. 83 —*S.H. (5/1/2005)*

MOKELUMNE GLEN

Mokelumne Glen 2001 Zinfandel (Lodi) $12. 88 Best Buy *(11/1/2003)*

MONT PELLIER

Mont Pellier 2000 Viognier (California) $7. 85 Best Buy —*S.H. (12/15/2002)*

MONTE LAGO

Monte Lago 2000 Single Vineyard Sauvignon Blanc (Clear Lake) $20. 86 *(8/1/2002)*

MONTE VOLPE

Monte Volpe 1999 Montepulciano (Mendocino) $14. 84 —*S.H. (5/1/2002)*

Monte Volpe 2000 Pinot Grigio (Mendocino) $13. 85 —*S.H. (5/1/2002)*

Monte Volpe 1997 Sangiovese (Mendocino) $16. 88 —*M.S. (9/1/2000)*

MONTEMAGGIORE

Montemaggiore 2002 Paolo's Vineyard Syrah (Dry Creek Valley) $32. A bit tough in tannins, but it seduces with tart plum and ripe cherry flavors, and hints of leather and coffee. It's a full-bodied, thickly textured wine that could use a year or two to come together. 88 *(9/1/2005)*

MONTEREY PENINSULA

Monterey Peninsula 1997 SleepyHollow Vyd-Doctor's Rese Pinot Noir (Monterey County) $22. 90 *(10/1/1999)*

MONTEREY VINEYARD

Monterey Vineyard 1998 Chardonnay (Monterey County) $7. 83 —*S.H. (5/1/2000)*

Monterey Vineyard 1997 Merlot (California) $7. 82 —*J.C. (7/1/2000)*

Monterey Vineyard 1999 Pinot Noir (Central Coast) $7. 81 —*S.H. (12/15/2000)*

MONTERRA

Monterra 2000 Cabernet Sauvignon (Monterey County) $13. 84 *(12/1/2002)*

Monterra 1998 Chardonnay (Monterey) $9. 87 *(9/1/2000)*

Monterra 2000 Merlot (Monterey County) $13. 86 *(12/1/2002)*

Monterra 1996 Promise Merlot (Monterey) $10. 87 *(11/15/1999)*

Monterra 2001 Encore Rosé Blend (Monterey County) $18. 85 *(12/1/2002)*

Monterra 1998 Sangiovese (Monterey) $9. 83 *(9/1/2000)*

Monterra 2001 Syrah (Monterey County) $10. Fruity, rough, and dry. The blackberry-cherry flavors are very ripe, and have a chocolaty finish. 83 —*S.H. (12/15/2004)*

Monterra 1998 Syrah (Monterey) $13. 84 *(10/1/2001)*

Monterra 2000 Encore White Blend (Monterey County) $18. 85 *(12/1/2002)*

Monterra 1998 Zinfandel (Monterey) $9. 82 *(9/1/2000)*

MONTEVINA

Montevina 2003 Barbera (Amador County) $10. Pasta with tomato sauce comes to mind when drinking this dry wine, with its berry flavors and thick tannins. It's rustic and easy, a carafe sipper that's clean and easy in price. 83 —*S.H. (12/1/2005)*

Montevina 1998 Barbera (Amador County) $12. 87 —*S.H. (11/15/2001)*

Montevina 1996 Terra d'Oro Barbera (Amador County) $18. 84 —*S.H. (10/1/1999)*

Montevina 2000 Fumé Blanc (California) $7. 85 Best Buy *(8/1/2001)*

Montevina 2000 Rosato Nebbiolo (Sierra Foothills) $8. 84 —*S.H. (11/15/2001)*

Montevina 2002 Pinot Grigio (California) $10. 85 —*M.S. (12/1/2003)*

Montevina 2000 Pinot Grigio (California) $10. 86 *(8/1/2001)*

Montevina 1998 Sangiovese (Amador County) $12. 85 —*S.H. (9/1/2003)*

Montevina 1998 Terra d'Oro Sangiovese (Amador County) $18. 83 —*S.H. (11/15/2001)*

Montevina 2001 Sauvignon Blanc (California) $10. 85 Best Buy *—S.H. (3/1/2003)*

Montevina 2000 Syrah (Amador County) $10. 84 *—S.H. (6/1/2003)*

Montevina 2002 Terra d'Oro Syrah (Amador County) $20. Combines clean berry and vanilla flavors in an easy-to-drink, somewhat light-bodied wine. A bit simple, with a dash of heat on the finish. **83** *(9/1/2005)*

Montevina 2001 Terra d'Oro Syrah (Amador County) $15. This Syrah might strike you at first as austere, because the first impression is of moderated plums, herbs, and tobacco. But that doesn't take into account the balance, integrity and harmony that make it an ideal food wine. **89** *—S.H. (6/1/2004)*

Montevina 2002 Zinfandel (Sierra Foothills) $10. Simple, with berry-cherry and cocoa flavors and an undertow of pepper, this Zin is soft and smooth. It has a long, fruity finish and isn't too alcoholic or hot. **84 Best Buy** *—S.H. (12/1/2005)*

Montevina 1999 Zinfandel (Amador County) $12. 88 Best Buy *—S.H. (11/15/2001)*

Montevina 1997 Zinfandel (Amador County) $10. 86 *—P.G. (11/15/1999)*

Montevina 1998 SHR Field Blend Zinfandel (Sierra Foothills) $14. 87 *(8/1/2001)*

Montevina 1999 Terra d'Oro Zinfandel (Amador County) $18. 89 *—S.H. (2/1/2003)*

Montevina 1996 Terra d'Oro Zinfandel (Amador County) $16. 86 *—S.H. (9/1/1999)*

Montevina 2002 Terra d'Oro Home Vineyard Zinfandel (Amador County) $24. Smells and tastes overripe, with suggestions of raisins and stewed prunes. The flavors veer toward chocolate fudge, although it's not an especially sweet wine. It's certainly distinctive, and will have its fans. **85** *—S.H. (4/1/2005)*

Montevina 2001 Terra d'Oro Deaver Vineyard Old Vine Zinfandel (Amador County) $21. Delicous and rich, with gobs of sweet ripe cherry and blackberry flavor. The tannins are lovely, too, very ripe and soft but intricate as velvet. There's a note throughout of sweetened coffee that adds interest. **89** *—S.H. (6/1/2004)*

Montevina 2000 Terra d'Oro SHR Field Blend Zinfandel (Amador County) $24. A very successful Zin, big and brawny and authoritative in its berry and cherry flavors with layers of leather, grilled meat, and herbs. A hint of raisins adds nuance but doesn't detract. Big and lush, a fireplace wine for mid-winter. **90** *—S.H. (3/1/2005)*

MONTHAVEN

Monthaven 2001 Cabernet Sauvignon (Central Coast) $12. Riper than last year, and $2 more expensive, too, but gets the same score because it's too sweet. Nice aromas of smoky currants, and some good, ripe blackberry flavors, but why did they keep so much sugar in? **84** *—S.H. (3/1/2004)*

Monthaven 2000 Pinot Noir (California) $10. 84 *—S.H. (7/1/2003)*

Monthaven 2000 Zinfandel (California) $10. 83 *—S.H. (9/1/2003)*

MONTICELLO VINEYARDS

Monticello Vineyards 2000 Proprietary Bordeaux Blend (Napa Valley) $50. 91 *—S.H. (8/1/2003)*

Monticello Vineyards 1997 Corley Reserve Cabernet Sauvignon (Napa Valley) $65. 91 *(11/1/2000)*

Monticello Vineyards 1999 Jefferson Cuvée Cabernet Sauvignon (Napa Valley) $34. 90 *—S.H. (2/1/2003)*

Monticello Vineyards 2001 Reserve Cabernet Sauvignon (Napa Valley) $75. A very fine wine, rich, full-bodied, and sensationally ripe. Floods the mouth with cassis and oak flavors, and the tannins are sweet and intricate. Feels great just to slosh it around the palate. **92** *—S.H. (2/1/2005)*

Monticello Vineyards 2001 Tietjen Vineyard Cabernet Sauvignon (Rutherford) $45. Dark, almost black. An interesting note of pine tar floats over the classic blackberry, cherry, and plum aromas, and also lots of sweet, charry oak. Rather hard with tannins now, but what a long, fruity finish. Best after 2008. **91** *—S.H. (10/1/2004)*

Monticello Vineyards 1999 Tietjen Vineyard Cabernet Sauvignon (Napa Valley) $55. 89 *—S.H. (12/31/2002)*

Monticello Vineyards 1999 Corley Reserve Chardonnay (Napa Valley) $40. 89 *(7/1/2001)*

Monticello Vineyards 2003 Estate Chardonnay (Napa Valley) $26. A medium-weight Chard with mainstream attributes: toasty oak, ripe pears and a plump, custardy mouthfeel. Finishes with a bit of alcoholic warmth. **85** *(5/1/2005)*

Monticello Vineyards 1999 Merlot (Napa Valley) $30. 93 Editors' Choice *—S.H. (2/1/2003)*

Monticello Vineyards 1997 Corley Family Vyds Pinot Noir (Napa Valley) $24. 87 *(12/15/1999)*

Monticello Vineyards 2003 Estate Grown Pinot Noir (Oak Knoll) $34. With a deep, mulchy taste of the earth that's reminiscent of cured tobacco, mushrooms, and roasted coffeebean, this full-bodied Pinot also shows plum and blackberry notes that are slightly baked. It's a hearty, soft wine, but not a rustic one. **86** *—S.H. (12/15/2005)*

MONTINORE

Montinore 1999 Winemaker's Reserve Chardonnay (Willamette Valley) $18. 83 *—P.G. (2/1/2002)*

Montinore 2003 Gewürztraminer (Willamette Valley) $9. A mouthful of fresh grapefruit and lime. The bracing, citrus fruit is backed with some wet stone mineral and enough tannin to give the finish some muscle. Nothing delicate here, but plenty of flavor. **87 Best Buy** *—P.G. (10/1/2004)*

Montinore 2001 Late Harvest Estate Bottled Gewürztraminer (Willamette Valley) $9. 87 Best Buy *—M.S. (8/1/2003)*

Montinore 2000 Müller-Thurgau (Willamette Valley) $7. 80 *—M.S. (8/1/2003)*

Montinore 2004 Pinot Gris (Willamette Valley) $10. This winery's Pinot Gris always has a fair amount of color, but sometimes it drifts over from straw to tawny gold, right on the edge of oxidation. Here there is a vegetal/grassy tone that dominates; missing is the fresh pear fruit. **82** *—P.G. (11/15/2005)*

Montinore 2002 Pinot Gris (Willamette Valley) $10. 88 Best Buy *—P.G. (12/1/2003)*

Montinore 2000 Pinot Gris (Willamette Valley) $10. 84 *—P.G. (4/1/2002)*

Montinore 2003 Pinot Noir (Willamette Valley) $14. Tastes like black cherry cola. The ripe, lush style flirts with oxidation, loads in the vanilla flavors, and finishes with a burst of heat. Needs the mellowing influence of food to show its best. **84** *—P.G. (11/15/2005)*

Montinore 2001 Pinot Noir (Willamette Valley) $13. 86 *—P.G. (12/1/2003)*

Montinore 1999 Pinot Noir (Willamette Valley) $13. 83 *—P.G. (4/1/2002)*

Montinore 1999 Graham's Block 7 Pinot Noir (Willamette Valley) $30. 90 Cellar Selection *—P.G. (12/31/2001)*

Montinore 1999 Parson's Ridge Vineyard Pinot Noir (Willamette Valley) $30. 89 *—P.G. (12/31/2001)*

Montinore 2000 Pierce's Elbow Vineyard Pinot Noir (Willamette Valley) $30. 87 *—P.G. (12/31/2002)*

Montinore 2000 Winemaker's Reserve Pinot Noir (Willamette Valley) $19. 88 *—P.G. (12/31/2002)*

Montinore 2002 Winemaker's Reserve Pinot Noir (Willamette Valley) $19. The reserve is a bigger version of the regular Pinot, with more heat, more tannin, more bite. Sharp, hot, and acidic, with green tannins that seem to thin out the finish. **83** *—P.G. (11/15/2005)*

Montinore 2004 Semi-Dry Riesling (Willamette Valley) $9. Off-dry and light, this looks to be well on its way to oxidation. Brown apples, slightly baked and flat tasting. **83** *—P.G. (11/15/2005)*

Montinore 2001 Semi-Dry Estate Bottled Riesling (Willamette Valley) $9. 85 *—K.F. (12/31/2002)*

MONTONA

Montona 2000 Reserve Cabernet Sauvignon (Napa Valley) $50. Re-released after an additional two years in bottle, this wine, which was very good in 2003, is on a downhill slide. It's losing fruit, cracking up as the Brits say. From Andretti. **83** *—S.H. (12/1/2005)*

Montona 2002 Chardonnay (Napa Valley) $30. Winemaker bells and whistles, such as smoky oak and creamy lees, star in this earthy wine, which has been re-released after two years. It doesn't seem at all old. There's enough peach and apple flavor to make it balanced. **88** *—S.H. (12/1/2005)*

Montona 2001 Merlot (Napa Valley) $40. Like Montona's 2000 Cab, this wine also has been re-released since its debut in 2003, and it, too, has gone downhill. The wine is losing fruit and picking up harsh acidity, although it's still drinkable. **83** *—S.H. (12/1/2005)*

MONTPELLIER

Montpellier 2001 Merlot (California) $7. You'll be surprised how much richness there is here. Oodles of sweet black cherry fruit, with a hint of oak, and it's all dry and crisp. Thank the grape glut for this incredible value. **86** *—S.H. (9/1/2004)*

Montpellier 1999 Pinot Noir (California) $8. 83 *(10/1/2002)*

Montpellier 1999 Syrah (California) $7. 86 Best Buy *— (10/1/2001)*

MOON MOUNTAIN VINEYARD

Moon Mountain Vineyard 2000 Cabernet Franc (Sonoma Valley) $30. The essence of black cherries is the taste that floods the palate, with rich overlays of oak. There are sturdy tannins yet they are gentle, making the wine immediately enjoyable. This is a firm, full-bodied red wine that will be delicious with lamb or steak. **90** *—S.H. (5/1/2004)*

Moon Mountain Vineyard 2000 Reserve Cabernet Sauvignon (Sonoma Valley) $40. Starts off with pretty black currant and black cherry flavors, and a lush overlay of oak. Fills the mouth with fruit, and then it suddenly turns tough and dry from those stubborn, hard mountain tannins. May age out. **86** *—S.H. (5/1/2004)*

Moon Mountain Vineyard 2002 Vadasz Vineyard Sauvignon Blanc (Sonoma Valley) $20. This single-vineyard release is richer than the winery's Reserve, but it stays true to the house style, which is a citrusy grassiness and extreme dryness. The flavors veer toward grapefruit juice, fig and melon, with creamier notes from oak barrels. Has sharp acidity. **87** *—S.H. (5/1/2004)*

Moon Mountain Vineyard 2002 Monte Rosso Zinfandel (Sonoma Valley) $30. From this famous old mountain vineyard, a dense and concentrated Zin that blows you away with deliciousness. It's very dark and young, with a flair of acidity and sweet tannins, and blackberry, cassis, and mocha flavors that finish with a super-ripe raisiny note. But that slight Portiness is a seasoning element, and does not distract. **92** *—S.H. (6/1/2004)*

MORGAN

Morgan 1998 Chardonnay (Monterey County) $20. 87 *(6/1/2000)*

Morgan 2003 Chardonnay (Monterey) $20. Displays all the flair of Monterey's terroir, with tropical fruit flavors and crisp, bright acidity that makes even this rich wine finish clean. Oak adds just the right touch of charry vanilla. **90** *—S.H. (11/15/2005)*

Morgan 2000 Chardonnay (Monterey) $20. 88 *—J.M. (5/1/2002)*

Morgan 2001 Barrel-Fermented Chardonnay (Monterey) $20. High acidity adds a metallic, mineral firmness to the peach and pear flavors, while oak and lees contribute softer, creamy notes. This sleek wine is vibrant and perky through the spicy finish. **90 Editors' Choice** *—S.H. (2/1/2004)*

Morgan 2002 Double L Vineyard Chardonnay (Santa Lucia Highlands) $34. A wonderful Chard. Don't chill it too much or you'll miss the interplay of ripe tropical fruits, oak, creamy lees, butterscotch, and oriental spices. Bright in citrusy acids and elegant, it will be great alone, or try with something hedonistic, like broiled lobster with melted butter. **92 Editors' Choice** *—S.H. (3/1/2005)*

Morgan 2000 Double L Vineyard Chardonnay (Santa Lucia Highlands) $36. 88 *—J.M. (12/15/2002)*

USA

Morgan 2002 Hat Trick Double L Vineyard Chardonnay (Santa Lucia Highlands) $50. This low production barrel selection from Morgan's Double L Vineyard is one of the best Chards of the vintage. Has everything Double L has, but more. Fabulous weight and density, and tiers of flavors ranging from pineapples through peaches, crème brulée and butterscotch. Fat, almost meaty, yet dry, elegant, and refined. **96 Editors' Choice** *—S.H. (5/1/2005)*

Morgan 2003 Metallico Chardonnay (Santa Lucia Highlands) $20. This will be an education for those who have never tried a totally unoaked Chardonnay made from really good grapes. You get to taste the pure flavors of pineapple, peach, and spice that mark this appellation, as well as the zesty cut of acidity. **86** *—S.H. (12/1/2004)*

Morgan 2001 Metallico Chardonnay (Santa Lucia Highlands) $20. 87 *—S.H. (12/15/2002)*

Morgan 1998 Reserve Chardonnay (Monterey) $30. 90 *(6/1/2000)*

Morgan 2001 Rosella's Vineyard Chardonnay (Santa Lucia Highlands) $34. Tropical fruit flavors explode in honeyed richness, thrilling the palate with sweet mango and nectarine, but beautiful acidity makes it crisp and clean. Loads of oak, too. Defines this cool-climate appellation for Chardonnay in its pinpoint balance of acid to fruit. **91** *—S.H. (2/1/2004)*

Morgan 2002 Rosella's Vineyard Chardonnay (Santa Lucia Highlands) $34. So ripe, yet so crisp in acids, a Chard that showcases the Burgundian climate of its appellation. Oozes bright, pure, spicy tropical fruit and mineral flavors that are totally dry. Oak and lees contribute buttered toast, vanilla, and a chewy creaminess. **91** *—S.H. (3/1/2005)*

Morgan 2004 R&D Franscioni Vineyard Pinot Gris (Santa Lucia Highlands) $16. I find most California Pinot Gris, or Grigio, simple, soft, and semisweet. This commendable wine by contrast is brilliantly structured, with keen acids boosting key lime, sweet thyme, and vanilla flavors. It's easily among the best of its genre. **88** *—S.H. (11/15/2005)*

Morgan 2002 R&D Franscioni Vineyard Pinot Gris (Santa Lucia Highlands) $16. 84 *—S.H. (12/1/2003)*

Morgan 1997 Pinot Noir (Monterey County) $20. 84 *(11/15/1999)*

Morgan 2000 Pinot Noir (Santa Lucia Highlands) $22. 90 *—S.H. (2/1/2003)*

Morgan 1999 Pinot Noir (Monterey) $24. 88 *—S.H. (12/15/2001)*

Morgan 2003 Double L Vineyard Pinot Noir (Santa Lucia Highlands) $50. Morgan has released three single-vineyard '03 Pinots, and it's hard, fun work choosing the best. For me, it's the Double L. It's a firm, fairly tannic and dry wine, rich, balanced, and intricately structured. Combines the taste of cherries, blackberries, and coffee with smoky oak to offer intensely complex pleasure now. Should develop well over several years. **94 Editors' Choice** *—S.H. (12/15/2005)*

Morgan 2001 Double L Vineyard Pinot Noir (Santa Lucia Highlands) $42. There's a wealth of extracted fruit here that astonishes for its sweet ripeness, strength, and complexity. Cherries and raspberries star, along with coffee, mocha, and all sorts of Asian spices. All this flavor is wrapped in a silky, crisp wine with a lilting, airy texture. **92** *—S.H. (8/1/2004)*

Morgan 2003 Garys' Vineyard Pinot Noir (Santa Lucia Highlands) $45. Compared to Double L, Garys' is a shade more obvious, but that's a royal comparison. This is a terrific wine in its own right, rich and fruity, wonderfully oaked, complex, and totally satisfying in a Pinotesque way. It's a firm, masculine, elegant wine, with beautiful acidity, and should hold well for a number of years. **93 Editors' Choice** *—S.H. (12/15/2005)*

Morgan 2001 Garys' Vineyard Pinot Noir (Santa Lucia Highlands) $35. Everybody wants grapes from this vineyard for its fabulous terroir, which usually yields wines of impeccable balance and lushness. This wine is light and delicate in structure, with beautifully firm acids and sweetly complex flavors of cherry pie, mocha, and vanilla. It's a pleasure to sip. **93** *—S.H. (8/1/2004)*

Morgan 1999 Reserve Pinot Noir (Santa Lucia Highlands) $38. 89 *—S.H. (12/15/2001)*

Morgan 2002 Rosella's Vineyard Pinot Noir (Santa Lucia Highlands) $38. Totally aromatic, with cherry, vanilla, spice, cola, gingerbread and smoky scents leaping out of the glass. It's no less flavorful.

Deliciously sippible and dry, with a polished, silky mouthfeel and a crisp finish. **91** *—S.H. (3/1/2005)*

Morgan 2000 Rosella's Vineyard Pinot Noir (Santa Lucia Highlands) $38. **91** *—S.H. (7/1/2003)*

Morgan 2002 Twelve Clones Pinot Noir (Santa Lucia Highlands) $22. Very ripe and intense in cherry and blackberry fruit, with nuances of beet and tomato and a lavish overlay of smoky oak and vanilla. Drinks fully dry, with some astringent tannins that provide good grip. Finishes with a velvety, fruit-driven aftertaste. **87** *(11/1/2004)*

Morgan 2003 Côtes du Crow's Rhône Red Blend (Monterey) $22. Some Rhône blends burst with fruit. This one has cherries, but it's an understated, elegant wine, dry and earthy-herbal, with dusty tannins. This blend of Grenache and Syrah has complexity and style. **89 Best Buy** *—S.H. (11/15/2005)*

Morgan 1998 Sauvignon Blanc (California) $12. **88** *—M.S. (11/15/1999)*

Morgan 2003 Sauvignon Blanc (Monterey) $14. I don't know if this is the Musque clone, but it's all about gooseberries and bright Meyer lemon and lime flavors with mouth-searing acidity. Powerful finish, intensely clean, and a natural for food. Try with a salad of endive, pink grapefruit, and sautéed scallops. **89 Best Buy** *—S.H. (11/15/2005)*

Morgan 2001 Sauvignon Blanc (Monterey) $14. **88** *—S.H. (3/1/2003)*

Morgan 1997 Syrah (Monterey) $15. **87** *—S.H. (6/1/1999)*

Morgan 2001 Syrah (Monterey) $22. Grapes from warmer parts of the county lend blackberries and chocolate, while those from cooler ones contribute herbs and acidity. It's a pretty good wine, but there are harsh, twiggy elements and some fierce tannins that are unlikely to wilt with age. **85** *—S.H. (12/1/2004)*

Morgan 2002 Tierra Mar Syrah (Monterey County) $35. Toasty and cedary on the nose, but the oak is more integrated on the palate, where ripe blackberries, plums, and coffee take charge. Nicely balanced, with crisp acids balancing the fruity concentration and supple tannins. **89** *(9/1/2005)*

Morgan 2000 Tierra Mar Syrah (Santa Lucia Highlands) $35. **94 Editors' Choice** *—S.H. (12/1/2003)*

MORRISON LANE

Morrison Lane 2002 Syrah (Walla Walla (WA)) $NA. Jammy and almost sweet-tasting, with masses of basic blackberry fruit laced with vanilla. Broad and mouthfilling, with a trace of heat on the finish. **86** *(9/1/2005)*

MOSBY

Mosby 1997 Santa Barbara County Chardonnay (Santa Barbara County) $10. **85** *—S.H. (7/1/1999)*

Mosby 2002 Cortese (Santa Barbara County) $14. A simple white wine that opens with flavors of lemon, peach, avocado, and vanilla. The flavors are citrusy, with a soft texture, low in acidity. The finish is very dry and citrusy. **85** *—S.H. (3/1/2004)*

Mosby 2002 La Seduzione Lagrein (California) $26. Very dry, very tannic, not offering much on its own now, but there's a muscle of black cherry fruit that a a long-cooked pork or beef stew could release. Might also age, if you feel like rolling the dice. **86** *—S.H. (10/1/2005)*

Mosby 1998 Pinot Grigio (Santa Barbara County) $14. **83** *—S.H. (3/1/2000)*

Mosby 2003 Pinot Grigio (Santa Barbara County) $14. Fresh and succulent, with ripe flavors of apples, citrus fruits, figs and spices. Fundamentally dry, with good acids, this is an easy wine to like. **84** *—S.H. (11/15/2004)*

Mosby 2003 Primitivo (Monterey County) $20. Smells a little funky, and tastes harsh and angular, with gritty tannins and slightly sweet cherry flavors. **82** *—S.H. (12/1/2005)*

Mosby 2000 Roc Michel Fremir Rhône Red Blend (Monterey County) $18. A Rhône blend marked by baked, earthy aromas of blackberry tart and coffee, and dry flavors of blackberries. There is a very distinctive taste of chocolatey cassis that persists through the finish, and is very strong, although it is dry. Acids are soft, but the tannins are strong and persistant. A blend of Syrah and Mourvèdre. **87** *—S.H. (3/1/2004)*

Mosby 2003 Sangiovese (Santa Barbara County) $22. Hot and harsh in texture, this rustic wine shows espresso and blackberry flavors, and is dry, with gritty tannins. **82** *—S.H. (12/1/2005)*

Mosby 1996 Vigna della Casa Vecchia Sangiovese (Santa Barbara County) $18. **88** *—S.H. (12/15/1999)*

Mosby 2002 Teroldego (Santa Barbara County) $24. Thick and cloying, with the texture and flavor of cherry cough syrup. **82** *—S.H. (3/1/2005)*

Mosby 2003 Traminer (Santa Barbara County) $16. Very Gewürzty with its spice-accented flavors of lush fruits and wildflowers. It's a dry wine, but almost sweet with ripe honey. Finishes bracing and clean. **85** *—S.H. (12/1/2004)*

MOTIF

Motif NV Classic Champagne Blend (California) $8. **83** *—S.H. (6/1/2001)*

MOUNT AUKUM

Mount Aukum 2003 Syrah (El Dorado) $16. Dried herbs make for a tea-like, leafy bouquet, while the palate is crowded with syrupy blackberries. It's a bit of a disconnect that may work for some tasters but not for others. **85** *(9/1/2005)*

MOUNT EDEN

Mount Eden 2001 Estate Cabernet Sauvignon (Santa Cruz Mountains) $35. This ageable wine is young and tannic now, with an astringent finish. Cherry and blackberry stuffing is down there for the long haul. Best after 2010 and beyond. **90** *—S.H. (6/1/2005)*

Mount Eden 1999 Old Vine Reserve Cabernet Sauvignon (Santa Cruz Mountains) $55. 92 Cellar Selection *—S.H. (8/1/2003)*

Mount Eden 1999 Chardonnay (Santa Cruz Mountains) $45. 94 Editors' Choice *—S.H. (2/1/2003)*

Mount Eden 1998 MacGregor Vyd Chardonnay (Edna Valley) $18. 87 *(6/1/2000)*

Mount Eden 2000 MacGregor Vineyard Chardonnay (Edna Valley) $18. 91 *—S.H. (2/1/2003)*

Mount Eden 2002 Wolff Vineyard Chardonnay (Edna Valley) $17. An odd wine, with aromas and lean flavors ranging from vegetal to tart citrus fruits, and austerely dry. Clean, but hard to like. **82** *—S.H. (6/1/2005)*

Mount Eden 1999 Pinot Noir (Santa Cruz Mountains) $45. 92 Editors' Choice *(10/1/2002)*

MOUNT PALOMAR

Mount Palomar 1999 Meritage (Temecula) $18. 89 *—S.H. (11/15/2002)*

Mount Palomar NV Limited Reserve Port (California) $28. 90 *—S.H. (9/12/2002)*

Mount Palomar 2001 Riesling (Temecula) $9. 83 *—S.H. (12/31/2003)*

MOUNT PLEASANT WINERY

Mount Pleasant Winery 2003 Brut Imperial Sparkling Blend (Augusta) $16. A bit on the heavy side, with faint scents of watermelon and cotton candy, but will have its fans for its attractive light coppery-pink color and amiable, off-dry nature. **83** *—J.C. (6/1/2005)*

MOUNT ST. HELENA

Mount St. Helena 2003 Rosé of Charbono (Napa Valley) $16. Sulfury and awkward, with a strawberry-banana taste and a mawkish finish. **81** *—S.H. (11/1/2005)*

Mount St. Helena 2003 Sauvignon Blanc (Napa Valley) $16. Another enormously fruity Sauvignon Blanc, jam-packed with ripe fig, peach, melon, and citrus flavors, with a spicy finish. Simple and likeable. **84** *—S.H. (11/1/2005)*

MOUNT VEEDER

Mount Veeder 1995 Reserve Bordeaux Blend (Mount Veeder) $50. 92 *(11/1/1999)*

Mount Veeder 2001 Cabernet Sauvignon (Napa Valley) $40. Oaky and ripe; full of blackberry, cherry, and chocolaty fruit, with complex nuances of green olives and sweet, fresh herbs. You can feel the dusty tannins in your gums on the finish, but they're ripe and fine. Showy now, and should age effortlessly through the decade. **91** *—S.H. (10/1/2004)*

MOUNTAIN DOME

Mountain Dome NV Brut (Columbia Valley (OR)) $15. Mountain Dome has won a faithful following in the Northwest by making accessible, broadly flavorful bubbly that comes as close to a fruit bomb as fizz ever does. This is a clean, fresh and quite tasty effort, two thirds Pinot Noir and one third Chardonnay. **86** *—P.G. (12/31/2004)*

Mountain Dome NV Brut Rosé (Washington) $26. 86 *—P.G. (12/1/2003)*

MOUNTAIN VIEW

Mountain View 1997 Pinot Noir (California) $8. 83 *(11/15/1999)*

MT. VERNON

Mt. Vernon 2000 Cabernet Sauvignon (Sierra Foothills) $28. 84 *—S.H. (8/1/2003)*

MUMM CUVÉE NAPA

Mumm Cuvée Napa 1997 Blanc de Blancs (Napa Valley) $22. 88 *—S.H. (12/1/2002)*

Mumm Cuvée Napa 1997 DVX (Napa Valley) $45. 87 *—P.G. (12/1/2002)*

Mumm Cuvée Napa NV XXV Anniversary Reserve Brut (Napa Valley) $25. A brut-style, very dry blend that's mainly Chardonnay and Pinot Noir. Offers lots to like with its suggestion of lime and raspberry encased in smoky vanilla and doughy yeast flavors. Crisp acidity makes it clean. **87** *—S.H. (12/31/2004)*

Mumm Cuvée Napa NV Blanc de Noirs (Napa Valley) $18. With a pretty copper color and a delicate, complex aroma of dough, yeast, fresh strawberries and vanilla, this rosé bubbly is a delight. It's bone dry, with a full body and a long, clean finish. **87** *—S.H. (12/31/2005)*

Mumm Cuvée Napa NV Brut Prestige (Napa Valley) $18. 86 *—S.H. (12/1/2003)*

Mumm Cuvée Napa NV Cuvée M (Napa Valley) $18. With a slightly sweet finish that accentuates the fruit but doesn't cloy, this bubbly is crisp and clean, and despite that edge of sugar, it holds its own in dry country. Primarily Pinot Noir and Chardonnay, it has good acidity. **87** *—S.H. (12/31/2005)*

Mumm Cuvée Napa NV Reserve Brut (Napa Valley) $25. The smoothest and suavest of Mumm's current offerings, this fruit-forward bubbly has a slightly sweet dosage. Fortunately, it's crisp in acidity. The peach, bread dough, vanilla, and cherry flavors are delicious, with a long aftertaste. **89** *—S.H. (12/31/2005)*

MURPHY-GOODE

Murphy-Goode 2001 Wild Card Claret Bordeaux Blend (Alexander Valley) $19. Tastes like the grapes were picked relatively early, for the tannins are strong, acidity is high, and you don't find lush fruit. There are hints of blackberries, but this is a streamlined wine, perhaps designed for food. **86** *—S.H. (8/1/2004)*

Murphy-Goode 2001 Cabernet Sauvignon (Alexander Valley) $22. Full-bodied and robust even for a Cabernet, with strong tannins that frame blackberry, currant, dill, and earthy flavors. Finishes very dry and prickly with tannic astringency. May soften in a year or two but it's not an ager. **85** *—S.H. (8/1/2004)*

Murphy-Goode 1999 Cabernet Sauvignon (Alexander Valley) $22. 90 Editors' Choice *—S.H. (12/1/2001)*

Murphy-Goode 1999 Goode-Ready Cabernet Sauvignon (Alexander Valley) $18. 85 *—S.H. (11/15/2001)*

Murphy-Goode 1997 Sarah Block Swan Song Reserve Cabernet Sauvignon (Sonoma County) $39. 90 *(11/1/2000)*

Murphy-Goode 2001 Chardonnay (Sonoma County) $15. This fine Chard has the steely structure and citrusy acids of a cool climate wine. It's not a lush or hedonistic, but controlled, with its apple and pear flavors and touch of oak and lees. **87** *—S.H. (5/1/2004)*

Murphy-Goode 1999 Chardonnay (Sonoma County) $15. 88 Best Buy *—J.M. (11/15/2001)*

Murphy-Goode 2002 Island Block Chardonnay (Alexander Valley) $19. Very well-oaked, this full-throttle Chard features smoky, vanilla-tinged buttered toast aromas leading to a fruity, spicy finish. The flavors suggest golden-skinned tree fruits and honey. **87** *—S.H. (11/1/2005)*

Murphy-Goode 1999 Island Block Reserve Chardonnay (Alexander Valley) $21. 87 *—J.M. (12/1/2001)*

Murphy-Goode 2001 Fumé Blanc (Sonoma County) $13. 86 *—S.H. (7/1/2003)*

Murphy-Goode 1997 Reserve Fumé Blanc (Sonoma County) $24. 91 *—S.H. (9/1/1999)*

Murphy-Goode 2001 Merlot (Alexander Valley) $19. Defines its appellation with soft, lusciously sweet tannins, a gentle mouthfeel and well-ripened cherry and blackberry fruit. As drinkable as it is, it's also a complex wine, with many different nuances. If only it had a bit more concentration. **88** *—S.H. (5/1/2004)*

Murphy-Goode 1999 Merlot (Alexander Valley) $19. 89 *—J.M. (7/1/2002)*

Murphy-Goode 1999 Reserve Robert Young Vineyards Merlot (Alexander Valley) $45. 92 *—S.H. (2/1/2003)*

Murphy-Goode 2000 Robert Young Vineyards Reserve Merlot (Alexander Valley) $45. This concentrated wine almost startles with the richness of its black cherry, currant, olive, chocolate, and spicebox flavors. They flood the mouth, but are well-balanced by smooth, polished tannins that have been burnished to a sheen, good acidity and a lush overlay of oak. As extracted as it is, it's balanced and harmonious. **93** *—S.H. (8/1/2004)*

Murphy-Goode 2001 Murphy Ranch Petite Verdot (Alexander Valley) $35. Rather hard in tannins now, a tough young wine that will rise up to something like short ribs. Best to leave it alone for 3 or 4 years. Blackberries, rich and intense, form its heart. **90** *—S.H. (10/1/2005)*

Murphy-Goode 1999 Pinot Noir (Russian River Valley) $35. 87 *(12/15/2001)*

Murphy-Goode 2000 J&K Vineyard Pinot Noir (Russian River Valley) $35. 87 *(10/1/2002)*

Murphy-Goode 1999 Fumé II The Deuce Sauvignon Blanc (Sonoma County) $24. 86 *(8/1/2002)*

Murphy-Goode 1999 Reserve Fumé Sauvignon Blanc (Sonoma County) $17. 88 *—J.M. (11/15/2001)*

Murphy-Goode 2000 The Deuce Sauvignon Blanc (Alexander Valley) $24. 87 *—S.H. (10/1/2003)*

Murphy-Goode 2000 Liar's Dice Zinfandel (Sonoma County) $20. 87 *—J.M. (11/1/2002)*

Murphy-Goode 1998 Liar's Dice Zinfandel (Sonoma County) $17. 91 Editors' Choice *—P.G. (3/1/2001)*

Murphy-Goode 2001 Liar's Dice, TJM Zinfandel (Sonoma County) $20. 88 *(11/1/2003)*

Murphy-Goode 2000 Snake Eyes Zinfandel (Alexander Valley) $35. 90 *—S.H. (2/1/2003)*

Murphy-Goode 2002 Snake Eyes, Ellis Ranch Reserve Zinfandel (Alexander Valley) $35. A wonderful Zin that combines lushly ripe fruit with a smooth, velvety mouth feel. Blackberries, cherries, spicy blueberries, and cocoa flavors drink sweet in fruity essence, yet the wine is dry. Has the balance and elegance of a fine Cabernet, with Zin's distinct personality. **92** *—S.H. (3/1/2005)*

MURRIETA'S WELL

Murrieta's Well 1999 Vendimia Red Wine Bordeaux Blend (Livermore Valley) $35. Lots to like in this soft and earthy Bordeaux blend, with the tobacco and herb flavors teased by hints of blackberries and cherries. Oak doesn't overwhelm, but adds graceful touches. Has the balance to age. **87** *—S.H. (3/1/2004)*

Murrieta's Well 1998 Vendimia Sémillon-Sauvignon Blanc (Livermore Valley) $20. **86** *—S.H. (11/15/2001)*

Murrieta's Well 1997 Zinfandel (Livermore Valley) $29. **88** *—S.H. (12/15/2001)*

MUTT LYNCH

Mutt Lynch 1999 Merlot Over and Play Dead Merlot (Livermore Valley) $20. **90** *—J.M. (12/31/2001)*

Mutt Lynch 1999 Domaine du Bone Zinfandel (Dry Creek Valley) $20. **88** *—J.M. (12/15/2001)*

Mutt Lynch 2001 Portrait of a Mutt Zinfandel (Sonoma County) $15. **88** *(11/1/2003)*

MYSTIC CLIFFS

Mystic Cliffs 1999 Chardonnay (California) $7. **84 Best Buy** *—S.H. (5/1/2001)*

Mystic Cliffs 1997 Winemaker's Select Merlot (Monterey County) $11. **83** *(3/1/2000)*

Mystic Wines 1999 Hillside Vineyard Merlot (Columbia Valley (OR)) $24. Very earthy and stemmy in the nose, the fruit buried in scents of bark and soil. The wine is a bit rough and tumble in the mouth, more powerful than many Merlots, but less smooth and sweet than the truly ripe ones. This is tannic, herbal, and quite astringent. **83** *—P.G. (2/1/2004)*

Mystic Wines 2001 Syrah (Columbia Valley (OR)) $20. Spicy, supple, and silky fruit lights up the front of this excellent wine. Black pepper spice highlights the midpalate, and the wine glides to a smooth, modestly long finish. **87** *—P.G. (2/1/2004)*

NADEAU FAMILY VINTNERS

Nadeau Family Vintners 2002 Critical Mass Zinfandel (Paso Robles) $28. This is the softest, richest, and fruitiest of Nadeau's three new Zins. It's dense in cherry and chocolate fudge flavors, with a cherry liqueur finish. Has practically no tannins, and just enough acidity to prevent cloying. **88** *—S.H. (11/1/2005)*

Nadeau Family Vintners 2001 Mooney Homestead Zinfandel (Paso Robles) $28. **88** *(11/1/2003)*

NALLE

Nalle 2003 Hopkins Vineyard Pinot Noir (Russian River Valley) $38. This wine is less alcoholic, leaner, and higher in acidity than many others. As a result, it's a chiseled wine, showing cola, cherry, clove, and cinnamon flavors, with a lean herbaceousness. It should develop well over the next 6–8 years. **90 Cellar Selection** *—S.H. (11/1/2005)*

Nalle 1999 Zinfandel (Sonoma County) $28. **88** *—J.M. (3/1/2002)*

NAPA CREEK

Napa Creek 2000 Cabernet Sauvignon (Napa Valley) $12. Nice Cab you can enjoy on ordinary occasions, and a pretty good value, especially for the upscale appellation. It has pleasant flavors of ripe blackberries and cherries, and round, sweet tannins. **85** *—S.H. (6/1/2004)*

Napa Creek 2002 Chardonnay (Napa Valley) $12. Here's a smooth, creamy Chard with flavors of apples, peaches, buttered toast, vanilla, and plenty of oriental spices. The rich flavors last through a long finish. Has enough complexity to stand up to cracked crab, with a sourdough baguette. **87** *—S.H. (6/1/2004)*

NAPA DAN

Napa Dan 2003 Cabernet Sauvignon (Napa Valley) $30. A fine, full-bodied Cab, fleshy and fat in blackberry and cassis flavors and a grilled-meat chewiness. This fully dry wine has rich, sweet tannins and a good finish. It should hold and improve a bit with several years in the bottle. **87** *—S.H. (7/1/2005)*

NAPA REDWOODS ESTATE

Napa Redwoods Estate 2000 Alden Perry Reserve Castle Rock Vineyard Red Wine Bordeaux Blend (Mount Veeder) $48. Smooth and velvety drinking, and a very good food wine for its modulated berry and herb flavors and firm acids. This is a wine that does not overwhelm with size, but it is elegant and balanced and shows its pedigree well. **89** *—S.H. (5/1/2004)*

Napa Redwoods Estate 2001 Castle Rock Vineyard Merlot (Mount Veeder) $38. This well-crafted Merlot has pleasant flavors of plums, blackberries and coffee that are wrapped in smooth tannins. It is very dry, and feels round and supple in the mouth. There are some less ripe herbal flavors that limit ageability, but it's a good table wine. **90** *—S.H. (5/1/2004)*

Napa Redwoods Estate 2001 Alden Perry Reserve Red Blend (Mount Veeder) $48. Cherry, berry, and herb flavors are buried inside big-time tannins that numb the palate, in this dry, smoothly textured wine. It's questionable whether the wine has enough stuffing for the cellar. **87** *—S.H. (11/15/2004)*

NAPA RIDGE

Napa Ridge 2000 Cabernet Sauvignon (Napa Valley) $12. Pretty darned good Cab, a softly fruity wine with some real class. The cherry flavors have a nice edge of smoky oak, and the velvety texture is easy. **85** *—S.H. (11/15/2004)*

Napa Ridge 1997 Coastal Vines Cabernet Sauvignon (Central Coast) $11. 87 *(11/15/1999)*

Napa Ridge 2003 Chardonnay (Napa Valley) $12. This Chardonnay is showing plenty of well-toasted oak, vanilla, and caramel flavors and some very ripe tropical-fruit flavors. The creamy texture leads to a slightly rough finish. **84** *—S.H. (7/1/2005)*

Napa Ridge 1998 Chardonnay (North Coast) $10. 83 *—S.H. (8/1/2001)*

Napa Ridge 1996 Reserve Chardonnay (North Coast) $17. 87 *—J.C. (10/1/1999)*

Napa Ridge 2003 Coastal Ridge Merlot (California) $7. The fruit here is so pretty—it's all black cherries and black raspberries. It's a little rustic, but perfectly drinkable, and you can't beat the price. **84 Best Buy** *—S.H. (11/1/2005)*

Napa Ridge 1998 Coastal Vines Merlot (California) $10. 81 *—S.H. (8/1/2001)*

Napa Ridge 1999 Pinot Grigio (California) $10. 84 *—S.H. (8/1/2001)*

Napa Ridge 2001 Pinot Noir (North Coast) $10. 84 *—S.H. (7/1/2003)*

Napa Ridge 1998 Shiraz (Stanislaus County) $10. 85 *—S.H. (10/1/2001)*

Napa Ridge 1998 Triad White Blend (North Coast) $9. 85 *—S.H. (8/1/2001)*

NAPA VALLEY VINEYARDS

Napa Valley Vineyards 2003 Chardonnay (Napa Valley) $15. Pretty nasty, with vegetal aromas and medicinal flavors. **81** *—S.H. (10/1/2005)*

NAPA WINE CO.

Napa Wine Co. 2001 Cabernet Sauvignon (Napa Valley) $32. Smooth and supple, with ripe black currant and oak flavors framed by polished tannins. There's a good, sandpapery grip to the mouth feel that suggests pairing with rich meats, or you can age this wine through the decade. **91** *—S.H. (3/1/2005)*

Napa Wine Co. 1999 Cabernet Sauvignon (Napa Valley) $32. 92 *—J.M. (2/1/2003)*

Napa Wine Co. 1999 Pinot Blanc (Napa Valley) $18. 88 *—J.M. (11/15/2001)*

Napa Wine Co. 1998 Sauvignon Blanc (Napa Valley) $18. 89 *—L.W. (3/1/2000)*

Napa Wine Co. 2001 Sauvignon Blanc (Oakville) $18. 85 *(8/1/2002)*

Napa Wine Co. 2001 Zinfandel (Napa Valley) $20. 89 *(11/1/2003)*

NAVARRO

Navarro 1997 Cabernet Sauvignon (Mendocino) $25. 91 *—S.H. (5/1/2002)*

Navarro 2001 Chardonnay (Anderson Valley) $18. 92 Editors' Choice *—S.H. (12/1/2003)*

Navarro 1999 Chardonnay (Mendocino) $13. 86 *—S.H. (12/31/2001)*

Navarro 1999 Premiere Reserve Chardonnay (Anderson Valley) $18. 87 *—S.H. (12/31/2001)*

Navarro 2002 Gewürztraminer (Anderson Valley) $16. This perennial fave is spicier than usual this year. It brims with fresh gingersnap and vanilla aromas, with big, big flavors of spiced apples, nutmeg, and ripe white peach. Versatile and fun. **87** *—S.H. (6/1/2004)*

Navarro 2002 Cluster Select Late Harvest Gewürztraminer (Anderson Valley) $25. Outrageously sweet and delicious, a wine that blows your mind with the first sip. It's powerful in apricot, banana flambé and vanilla cream flavors, with a viscous texture that stains the glass with glycerine. Dessert in a glass. **93** *—S.H. (6/1/2004)*

Navarro 1997 Late Harvest Gewürztraminer (Anderson Valley) $45. 92 *—L.W. (9/1/1999)*

Navarro 1999 Mourvèdre (Mendocino) $19. 89 *—S.H. (5/1/2002)*

Navarro 1999 Dry Muscat Blanc Muscat (Anderson Valley) $18. 86 *—S.H. (12/15/2001)*

Navarro 2002 Pinot Gris (Anderson Valley) $16. A fresh, zesty and incredibly aromatic wine that satisfies at every level. The crisp acidity supports bright flavors of extremely ripe peaches, mangoes, figs, vanilla, and smoke. **88** *—S.H. (6/1/2004)*

Navarro 2001 Pinot Noir (Mendocino) $14. Navarro has held the line on prices, and this Pinot Noir is possibly the best Pinot value on the market. It is not a blockbuster. It is a pleasant wine, with a truly varietal character that includes flavors of ripe cherries, orange zest and dusty spices and a fine, silky mouthfeel. **88** *—S.H. (2/1/2004)*

Navarro 1999 Methode a l'Ancienne Pinot Noir (Anderson Valley) $19. 87 *—S.H. (12/15/2001)*

Navarro 2000 Navarrouge Red Blend (Mendocino) $9. 86 Best Buy *—S.H. (5/1/2002)*

Navarro 2002 Rosé Blend (Mendocino) $13. This great wine kind of sneaks up on you. First you think it's just a modest little blush wine, but it's awfully hard not to take another sip. Then you realize how good it is. Raspberries, vanilla, and cinnamon, and bone dry. Made from Grenache and Syrah. Another super value from Navarro. **88** *—S.H. (3/1/2004)*

Navarro 2002 Cuvée 128 Sauvignon Blanc (Mendocino) $14. Fresh, young, tart and tasty with fig, melon, citrus, and straw flavors. Bracing acidity makes it clean. Although this wine is very dry, it feels quite rich in the mouth, and finishes long in fruit. **87** —*S.H. (6/1/2004)*

Navarro 1998 Cuvée 128 Sauvignon Blanc (Mendocino) $13. **91 Best Buy** —*S.H. (9/1/2000)*

Navarro 2000 White Riesling (Anderson Valley) $14. **88** —*S.H. (5/1/2002)*

Navarro 2001 Zinfandel (Mendocino) $19. A very ripe, almost overblown style that emphasizes berry-cherry fruit, cola, and milk chocolate flavors that are almost flamboyant. Totally dry; a bit hot in alcohol. **87** —*S.H. (6/1/2004)*

NEESE

Neese 2000 Nonno Guiseppe Zinfandel (Redwood Valley) $17. **87** —*S.H. (9/12/2002)*

NELMS ROAD

Nelms Road 2000 Cabernet Sauvignon (Columbia Valley (WA)) $25. **87** —*P.G. (6/1/2002)*

Nelms Road 2000 Merlot (Columbia Valley (WA)) $20. **87** —*P.G. (6/1/2002)*

NELSON

Nelson 1997 Cabernet Franc (Sonoma Valley) $24. **84** —*S.H. (2/1/2001)*

NEVADA CITY

Nevada City 2001 Vin Cinq Bordeaux Blend (Sierra Foothills) $16. A Bordeaux blend, it's dry and balanced, with some nice cherry-berry flavors and a touch of oak. Could use a little more ripeness and finesse. **84** —*S.H. (6/1/2004)*

Nevada City 2000 Cabernet Sauvignon (Sierra Foothills) $16. Rustic and dry, with puckery tannins, this earthy wine blends coffee and herb flavors with a touch of berry. **83** —*S.H. (6/1/2004)*

Nevada City 2000 Petite Sirah (Sierra Foothills) $28. **85** *(4/1/2003)*

Nevada City 2001 Syrah (Sierra Foothills) $20. Well-ripened cherry-blackberry fruit is floating in sturdy, rough tannins that make the mouthfeel rugged. It's an honest country-style wine, but seems expensive. **85** —*S.H. (6/1/2004)*

Nevada City 2000 Zinfandel (Sierra Foothills) $15. A distinctive, old fashioned California mountain Zin. It's strong in alcohol, very ripe in blackberry flavor, and tannic and rustic in texture, with just a touch of Porty raisins. **85** —*S.H. (6/1/2004)*

NEVEU

Neveu 2003 Pinot Gris (Siskiyou County) $13. Rustic and thin-flavored, with odd citrus and medicinal flavors. **82** —*S.H. (5/1/2005)*

NEW LAND

New Land 1997 Pinot Noir (Finger Lakes) $13. **83** *(10/1/1999)*

NEWLAN

Newlan 1998 Chardonnay (Napa Valley) $16. **88** *(6/1/2000)*

Newlan 1999 Chardonnay (Napa Valley) $18. **86** —*S.H. (11/15/2001)*

Newlan 1998 Merlot (Napa Valley) $20. **85** —*S.H. (2/1/2001)*

Newlan 1999 Pinot Noir (Napa Valley) $20. **87** —*S.H. (9/1/2002)*

Newlan 1997 Reseve Pinot Noir (Napa Valley) $26. **89** —*S.H. (9/1/2002)*

Newlan 1997 Zinfandel (Sonoma County) $20. **86** —*S.H. (5/1/2000)*

Newlan 1998 Zinfandel (Napa Valley) $22. **87** —*P.G. (3/1/2001)*

Newlan 1997 Wallstrum Family Zinfandel (Sonoma County) $20. **83** —*P.G. (3/1/2001)*

NEWSOME-HARLOW

Newsome-Harlow 2003 Big John's Vineyard Zinfandel (Calaveras County) $24. This is one of those juicily extracted Zins that blasts a hole in the palate. It has big flavors of black, blue, and red wild berries, with a stimulating peppery finish. A dry wine with dusty tannins that will cut through meats and cheeses. **89** —*S.H. (10/1/2005)*

Newsome-Harlow 2002 Big John's Vineyard Zinfandel (Calaveras County) $24. Clean, balanced, and smooth despite the tannins, because the acidity is low. The wine features berry flavors with an earthy, dill finish. **84** —*S.H. (5/1/2005)*

NEWTON

Newton 2000 Unfiltered Cabernet Sauvignon (Napa Valley) $41. **88** —*S.H. (11/15/2003)*

Newton 1998 Naturally Fermented Chardonnay (Sonoma County) $23. **86** *(6/1/2000)*

Newton 2000 Unfiltered Chardonnay (Napa Valley) $42. **90** —*S.H. (12/1/2003)*

Newton 2000 Unfiltered Merlot (Spring Mountain) $NA. **91** —*S.H. (12/31/2003)*

NEYERS

Neyers 2001 Cuvée d'Honeur Syrah (Napa Valley) $45. 94 Editors' Choice *—S.H. (11/1/2003)*

Neyers 2001 Tofanelli Vineyard Zinfandel (Napa Valley) $35. 91 *(11/1/2003)*

NICHOLAS COLE CELLARS

Nicholas Cole Cellars 2001 Claret Bordeaux Blend (Columbia Valley (WA)) $46. Half Cab Sauvignon, half Cab Franc, from two top vineyards (Champoux and Klipsun), this wine has improved dramatically since its initial release. Truly Bordeaux-like, it has fascinating streaks of lead pencil, tar, and leather, layered and textured, behind supple, substantial cassis and berry fruit. Balanced and deep. 93 *—P.G. (4/1/2005)*

NICHOLS

Nichols 1997 Central Coast Blend Pinot Noir (Central Coast) $38. 84 *(10/1/1999)*

Nichols 1997 Paragon Vineyard Pinot Noir (Edna Valley) $33. 88 *(10/1/1999)*

Nichols 1997 Sharon's Vineyard Pinot Noir (Santa Barbara County) $36. 88 *(10/1/1999)*

NICKEL & NICKEL

Nickel & Nickel 1997 Carpenter Vyd Cabernet Sauvignon (Napa Valley) $75. 92 *(11/1/2000)*

Nickel & Nickel 1999 Dragonfly Vineyard Cabernet Sauvignon (Napa Valley) $90. 92 Cellar Selection *—M.S. (5/1/2003)*

Nickel & Nickel 2001 John C. Sullenger Vineyard Cabernet Sauvignon (Oakville) $75. A stunning Cabernet, rich, pure and powerful. Blackberries, currants, oak, and sweet fresh herbs flood the palate. It's a tannic wine, with a hard-edged mouthfeel, but the tannins are so sweet, it's tempting to uncork now. Drink right away, or age for 10 years and let it develop magic. 94 *—S.H. (10/1/2004)*

Nickel & Nickel 1998 John C. Sullenger Vineyard Cabernet Sauvignon (Oakville) $75. 87 *—J.M. (12/31/2001)*

Nickel & Nickel 1997 Rock Cairn Cabernet Sauvignon (Oakville) $75. 90 *(11/1/2000)*

Nickel & Nickel 2002 Stelling Vineyard Cabernet Sauvignon (Oakville) $130. This is the most expensive of N&N's current Cab lineup and also a remarkably good wine. It combines flamboyantly ripe fruit with a fine, rich structure and balance, although it's a little soft. The complex flavors of blackberries, blueberries, and cherries are well-oaked, and the finish is long and spicy. 92 *—S.H. (12/1/2005)*

Nickel & Nickel 1999 Stelling Vineyard Cabernet Sauvignon (Oakville) $125. 91 *—J.C. (6/1/2003)*

Nickel & Nickel 1997 Stelling Vineyard Cabernet Sauvignon (Oakville) $95. 93 *(11/1/2000)*

Nickel & Nickel 2002 Vogt Vineyard Cabernet Sauvignon (Howell Mountain) $75. Dark, dry, and firmly tannic, this seems to be one for the cellar, although for how long is a challenge. The fruit is terrifically ripe in black currants and cassis, and the tannins are gorgeously thick, but there's a softness that makes me wonder if the balance is there for very long. 85 *—S.H. (12/1/2005)*

Nickel & Nickel 2000 John's Creek Chardonnay (Napa Valley) $50. 87 *—J.M. (12/15/2002)*

Nickel & Nickel 1999 John's Creek Vineyard Chardonnay (Napa Valley) $50. 89 *(7/1/2001)*

Nickel & Nickel 2002 Searby Vineyard Chardonnay (Russian River Valley) $35. This great wine manages to be delicate and assertive at the same time. The delicacy lies in the tart citrus, apple, and herb flavors and crisp acidity that make the wine almost weightless. The power is in its tightly coiled intensity. 92 *—S.H. (9/1/2004)*

Nickel & Nickel 2002 Truchard Vineyard Chardonnay (Carneros) $35. Crafted along leanly tailored, elegant lines, this wine has high acidity and a citrusy, mineral character. It's a wine of great structural integrity, focused, and pristine, although it's also oaky. The right foods will coax out the inherent sweetness and Oriental spice. 90 *—S.H. (9/1/2004)*

Nickel & Nickel 2000 Truchard Vineyard Chardonnay (Carneros) $35. 89 *—J.M. (12/15/2002)*

Nickel & Nickel 2001 Harris Vineyard Merlot (Oakville) $40. This intense and concentrated wine shows a youthful precocity, but it also has the balance and stuffing to age gracefully. The cassis, cherry, smoky oak, mocha, and mint flavors are generous, and the tannins are notable but negotiable. Drink now through the decade. 91 *—S.H. (12/15/2004)*

Nickel & Nickel 2002 Sori Bricco Vineyard Merlot (Diamond Mountain) $40. This dry, tannic Merlot has simple flavors that are a bit unripe. There's a green-bean streak that just barely breaks into coffeebean and plum. It's not going anywhere. 82 *—S.H. (12/1/2005)*

Nickel & Nickel 2002 Suscol Ranch Merlot (Napa Valley) $50. A fabulous Merlot that impresses with its instant deliciousness and complexity, yet is likely to hang in there and improve. Dark and full-bodied, with black currant, plum, grilled meat, olive, dark chocolate, and spice flavors. The tannic structure is intricate, soft, and complex. Drink now through 2010. 93 *—S.H. (10/1/2005)*

Nickel & Nickel 2002 Darien Vineyard Syrah (Russian River Valley) $40. Starts off on the savory side of Syrah, with coffee and meat aromas and flavors taking the lead over the black cherry fruit. But then it picks up brighter berry notes on the long, textured finish. Tannic enough to want rare beef. 87 *(9/1/2005)*

Nickel & Nickel 2001 Dyer Vineyard Syrah (Carneros) $35. Young, dark and brooding, and pretty oaky and tannic now, but all the signs point to an ageable wine. Chew on it and find a rich core of black cherry pie flavors, edged with mocha and white pepper. Best after 2005. **91** *—S.H. (12/1/2004)*

Nickel & Nickel 1998 Ponzo Vineyard Zinfandel (Russian River Valley) $45. 88 *—D.T. (3/1/2002)*

NIEBAUM-COPPOLA

Niebaum-Coppola 2001 Rubicon Cabernet Blend (Rutherford) $100. An excellent wine, and clearly an ager, but I don't think it's in the league of the magnificent '99. It's too young to enjoy now, to judge from the closed, astringent, oaky, tannic mouthfeel. But there's certainly some powerful cassis fruit. Hold until at least 2008. Eventually, it could stun. **90** *—S.H. (10/1/2005)*

Niebaum-Coppola 2001 Cabernet Franc (Rutherford) $44. Impressive for its sheer size, a dark, muscular wine jammed with juicy cherry and currant flavors. Drinks dry, with firm but sculpted tannins. It's on the tough side. At its youthful best now with a juicy steak. **86** *—S.H. (5/1/2004)*

Niebaum-Coppola 2002 Cask Cabernet Sauvignon (Rutherford) $65. Shows quite oaky now, with powerful notes of vanilla, char, and wood sap, but it's also rich in cherry fruit, with a touch of grilled meat. Texturally, this Cab is dense, smooth, fine, and very dry, with substantial tannins. It's too young now, but should be a beauty by 2008 and beyond. **93 Cellar Selection** *—S.H. (12/15/2005)*

USA

Niebaum-Coppola 1999 Cask Cabernet Cabernet Sauvignon (Rutherford) $65. 93 *—S.H. (2/1/2003)*

Niebaum-Coppola 2001 Estate Cask Cabernet Sauvignon (Rutherford) $110. Dramatic from the get-go, an amazing wine that oozes well-ripened black currant, cassis, mocha, and oak aromas and flavors. Exuberantly, decadently rich, with a chocolate fudge sweetness, although it's totally dry. The tannins are ripe, sweet, smooth, and unctuous. Would score even higher were it not for a softness that could limit its ageworthiness. **93** *—S.H. (10/1/2004)*

Niebaum-Coppola 1997 Merlot (Napa Valley) $40. 89 *—S.H. (7/1/2000)*

Niebaum-Coppola 1999 Merlot (Rutherford) $44. 90 *—S.H. (6/1/2002)*

Niebaum-Coppola 2000 Rubicon Red Blend (Rutherford) $100. 90 *—S.H. (11/15/2003)*

Niebaum-Coppola 2002 Blancaneax Rhône White Blend (Rutherford) $30. Pale in color, and with elusive aromas that suggest wildflowers, peaches, and apricots, this is an exotic blend of Marsanne, Roussanne, Chardonnay, and Viognier. It turns full-bodied in the mouth, and complex in fruity, spicy flavors. **89** *—S.H. (9/1/2004)*

Niebaum-Coppola 2000 RC Reserve Syrah (Rutherford) $56. 94 Editors' Choice *—S.H. (12/1/2003)*

Niebaum-Coppola 2000 Edizione Pennino Zinfandel (Rutherford) $44. 88 *—S.H. (2/1/2003)*

Niebaum-Coppola 1998 Edizione Pennino Zinfandel (Napa Valley) $40. 89 *—D.T. (3/1/2002)*

NIGHT OWL

Night Owl 2003 San Bernabe Vineyard Pinot Noir (Monterey County) $14. This vineyard in the southern Salinas Valley has been getting really interesting in recent years. This is the first Bernabe Pinot Noir that's captured my attention. It's dry and nicely varietal, scoring well on the deliciousness scale. **86** *—S.H. (12/15/2005)*

NINE GABLES

Nine Gables 2001 Pifari Cedar Vista Vineyard Zinfandel (Shenandoah Valley (CA)) $20. Tasted like sweetened coffee with an astringent finish. **81** *—S.H. (3/1/2005)*

NOCETO

Noceto 1997 Sangiovese (Shenandoah Valley (CA)) $13. 90 *—S.H. (12/15/1999)*

Noceto 1998 Riserva Sangiovese (Shenandoah Valley (CA)) $22. 87 *—S.H. (12/1/2001)*

NONNE GIUSEPPE

Nonne Giuseppe 2001 Neese Vineyards Zinfandel (Redwood Valley) $15. Extremely high in alcohol, this wine starts with raisiny, stewed prune aromas, but it's totally dry, and actually has some nice berry and coffee flavors. Made in the old style, it will have its aficionados. **84** *—S.H. (12/31/2004)*

NORMAN

Norman 2003 Vino Rosado Dry Rosé (Paso Robles) $15. There are a lot of blush wines on the market these days, and this is a nice one. It's completely dry, with intriguing flavors of raspberries, spices, and herbs. Very delicate and rich, with real complexity. Grenache and Syrah. **86** *—S.H. (12/1/2004)*

Norman 2002 Syrah (Paso Robles) $20. Strives for class and finesse with its moderate alcohol, dry finish, and delicate balance of plummy, coffee, tobacco, and earth flavors. The tannins are still kind of edgy and rough, but there's a nice fruity sweetness. **85** *—S.H. (12/15/2004)*

Norman 1998 Monster Zinfandel (Paso Robles) $18. 85 *—P.G. (3/1/2001)*

Norman 2000 Old Vine Zinfandel Port Zinfandel (Cucamonga Valley) $20. Sure is sweet, with a super-sugary blast of late-harvest blackberry, caramel, and toffee-coffee flavors. Yet there's a good cut of acidity to balance. Try with vanilla ice cream. **86** *—S.H. (12/15/2004)*

Norman 2002 The Monster Zinfandel (Paso Robles) $20. Don't look for finesse in a wine called "the monster." It's truly Hulkian in wild, brambly berry and pepper fruit and high in alcohol. It's also mercifully dry. **85** *—S.H. (11/15/2004)*

NORTHSTAR

Northstar 2002 Merlot (Walla Walla (WA)) $60. The winery's Walla Walla bottling, though it accounts for less than a tenth of the 9,000- case production, is far more substantial and varietal than the Columbia Valley Merlot. Thick, chalky tannins, chewy blueberry/cherry fruit, good weight and length bring some power to what is otherwise a straightforward, rather tannic wine. **88** *—P.G. (12/15/2005)*

Northstar 2001 Merlot (Walla Walla (WA)) $60. This is the second vintage for Northstar's Walla Walla bottling, and the vintage is slightly better, with more substantial weight and tannin. Walla Walla strawberry fruit flavors are here in abundance, with nicely managed oak and a long, smooth mid-palate. **90** *—P.G. (7/1/2004)*

Northstar 1999 Merlot (Columbia Valley (WA)) $50. 94 Editors' Choice *—P.G. (9/1/2002)*

NOTA BENE CELLARS

Nota Bene Cellars 2002 Syrah (Washington) $22. Smells of baked berries, cinnamon, and pie crust. In the mouth, it has meat, leather, soy, and briar flavors and a long, drying finish. **84** *(9/1/2005)*

NOVELLA

Novella 2001 Chardonnay (Paso Robles) $11. Smells nice, with apple, smoke, and vanilla flavors. Turns modestly flavorful in the mouth, with some pleasant fruit and a spicy finish. **84** *—S.H. (6/1/2004)*

Novella 2000 Merlot (California) $11. Smells aggressively green and stalky, then turns bizarrely sweet and Port-like. **80** *—S.H. (6/1/2004)*

Novella 2003 Muscat Canelli (Paso Robles) $10. Paso Robles is making a play for the most congenial home in California to sweet Muscat, under any name, and this wine shows why. It's crisp and acidic, sweet but not cloying, and offers wonderful flavors of mangoes, papayas, and honey-sweetened peach pie. Addictively good, and the alcohol is only 11.5%. **94 Best Buy** *—S.H. (11/1/2005)*

Novella 2002 Brothers Ranch Vineyard Pinot Grigio (Paso Robles) $13. Fresh and fruity, with sweetish flavors of apples, cotton candy, and peaches. Seems like it has a little sugar, but it's nice and crisp with acidity. **84** *—S.H. (6/1/2004)*

Novella 1999 Synergy Red Blend (Paso Robles) $11. 90 Best Buy *—M.M. (4/1/2002)*

NOVELTY HILL

Novelty Hill 2001 Cabernet Sauvignon (Columbia Valley (WA)) $20. The Cab is a bit heavier than Novelty's Merlot, but tastes much the same, with young, primary, light cherry fruit flavors that show little concentration or depth. One dimensional and light. **86** *—P.G. (12/15/2004)*

Novelty Hill 2001 Conner Lee Vineyard Chardonnay (Columbia Valley (WA)) $22. The second vintage for this new winery, whose wines are made by the talented Mike Januik. Outstanding fruit anchors this terrific Chardonnay, which is layered with citrus and tropical fruits, streaks of vanilla and mint, and leads into a long, taut finish. **91 Editors' Choice** *—P.G. (9/1/2004)*

Novelty Hill 2000 Merlot (Columbia Valley (WA)) $25. This is a good benchmark Merlot, with open, complex flavors of red berries and currants. The fruit is nicely balanced against medium acids and modest hints of oak, making this a restrained, complete, and classy wine for discriminating palates. **89** *—P.G. (9/1/2004)*

Novelty Hill 2000 Klipsun Vineyard Sauvignon Blanc (Red Mountain) $19. 92 *—P.G. (9/1/2002)*

Novelty Hill 2002 Stillwater Creek Vineyard Syrah (Columbia Valley (WA)) $28. Following some grassy, hay-like scents, the fruit comes across as a bit raisiny and Port-like in flavor. Turns tart, almost citrusy on the finish, with drying tannins. **83** *(9/1/2005)*

NOVY CELLARS

Novy Cellars 2000 Syrah (Napa Valley) $22. 92 *—S.H. (12/1/2002)*

Novy Cellars 2000 Gary's Syrah (Santa Lucia Highlands) $35. 90 *—S.H. (12/1/2002)*

Novy Cellars 2003 Judge Family Vineyard Syrah (Bennett Valley) $32. Seems almost over-ripe and under-ripe at the same time, with jammy blackberry notes vying with herbal, green ones. Touches of caramel give it a sweetish tinge on the finish. **84** *(9/1/2005)*

Novy Cellars 2002 Page-Nord Vineyard Syrah (Napa Valley) $30. Interesting to contrast this with Novy's Rosella's bottling. It's much firmer in structure, with sturdier tannins, although they're sweet. It also seems oakier and sweeter all around. Blackberries, coffee, and cocoa are the flavors. **90** *—S.H. (3/1/2005)*

Novy Cellars 2002 Rosella's Vineyard Syrah (Santa Lucia Highlands) $30. This AVA is best known for Pinots that can be Syrah-like in weight. Here's a real Syrah, and it's outstanding. Dark and dense, but fresh in acids, with ripely sweet tannins, it shows an intense peppery note accompanied by flamboyant blackberry and coffee flavors. Finishes dry and smooth. **92** *—S.H. (3/1/2005)*

O'BRIEN

O'Brien 2001 Estate Merlot (Napa Valley) $36. Sturdy and firm in tannins, dry and fairly oaky, with plummy, herb flavors, this wine is pretty closed down now, although a good piece of meat will wake it up. Might soften and improve in a year or so. **86** *—S.H. (5/1/2005)*

O'SHAUGHNESSY

O'Shaughnessy 2001 Cabernet Sauvignon (Howell Mountain) $54. Dark, full-bodied, and rich, with well-detailed black currant and cocoa flavors and a flamboyant but balanced coating of new oak. Impresses not only for its power, but for the soft luxury of its mouthfeel. Beautiful now, and perhaps best over the next 5 years to capture in its youth. **94 Editors' Choice** *—S.H. (10/1/2005)*

OAK KNOLL

Oak Knoll 1997 Pinot Gris (Willamette Valley) $13. 85 *— (8/1/1999)*

Oak Knoll 2000 Pinot Gris (Willamette Valley) $13. 87 *—P.G. (8/1/2002)*

Oak Knoll 1999 Pinot Noir (Willamette Valley) $15. 82 *(10/1/2002)*

Oak Knoll 1999 Five Mountains Vineyard Pinot Noir (Willamette Valley) $30. 83 *(10/1/2002)*

Oak Knoll 1998 Vintage Reserve Pinot Noir (Willamette Valley) $38. 83 *—J.C. (12/1/2000)*

Oak Knoll 2000 Willamette Valley Pinot Noir (Willamette Valley) $NA. Simple and one-dimensional, a wine that has easy flavors of tea, cola, and cherries, and is very dry. Tart acidity makes it prickly, and the finish is swift and clean. **84** *—S.H. (8/1/2004)*

OAKFORD

Oakford 1996 Cabernet Sauvignon (Oakville) $75. 92 *(12/31/1999)*

Oakford 2001 Cabernet Sauvignon (Oakville) $85. This Cab is so good, you'll want to drink it now, but it should age well for a decade. Rich and delicious in ripe black cherry, blackberry, cassis, and chocolate, and well-oaked, it's aided by firm tannins and good acidity. **93 Cellar Selection** *—S.H. (11/1/2005)*

Oakford 1997 Estate Grown Cabernet Sauvignon (Oakville) $85. 90 *(11/1/2000)*

OAKVILLE RANCH

Oakville Ranch 2001 Estate Robert's Blend Bordeaux Blend (Oakville) $75. Shows true Cabernet character in the dry, smooth tannins, rich, full-bodied mouthfeel and harmonious flavors of black currants, coffee, and oak. It all comes together to make a polished, soft wine. Drink now through 2008. **88** *—S.H. (12/15/2005)*

Oakville Ranch 2000 Cabernet Sauvignon (Oakville) $42. Still quite firm in dry tannins, with bell pepper, herb, and coffee flavors, although there's a core of cherry fruit. Doesn't seem like it's going anywhere. **85** *—S.H. (3/1/2005)*

Oakville Ranch 2000 Robert's Blend Cabernet Sauvignon-Cabernet Franc (Oakville) $75. Pretty tough and tannic now, with a bone-dry, mouth-numbingly austere feeling throughout, and doesn't seem to have the fruity stuffing to develop. You'll find traces of blackberries in the gritty finish. **84** *—S.H. (8/1/2005)*

Oakville Ranch 2001 Vista Vineyard Chardonnay (Oakville) $30. Rather sharp and tart in green apple bitterness, and pretty acidic through the finish, although the oak and cream make up for it. But that structure works in favor of food. **85** *—S.H. (3/1/2005)*

Oakville Ranch 2002 Field Blend Red Blend (Oakville) $30. The blend is Zinfandel, Petite Sirah, and Carignane on this enjoyable mélange. It could be anything, but is awfully good, with its rich, ripe tannins and smooth flavors of berries, cherries, and coffee. Drink whenever you need something dry and full bodied. **88** *—S.H. (12/15/2005)*

OASIS

Oasis 1998 Dry Gewürztraminer (Virginia) $18. 81 *—J.C. (8/1/1999)*

OBSIDIAN

Obsidian 2002 Obsidian Ridge Vineyard Cabernet Sauvignon (Lake County) $25. It is no insult to Lake County to say this is the best Cabernet I have ever had from there. It smells importantly ripe and finely oaked, and possesses succulent cassis, cherry, and chocolate flavors, with an earthy edge of fine herbs. From Acacia's Michael Terrien. **90** *—S.H. (11/15/2004)*

OLD BROOKVILLE

Old Brookville 2000 Gold Coast Reserve Chardonnay (Long Island) $14. 81 *—J.M. (9/10/2002)*

OLSON OGDEN

Olson Ogden 2003 Syrah (Sonoma County) $22. Grape is the dominant fruit flavor here, jazzed up by spice, graham cracker, and vanilla notes on both the nose and the palate. Has decent grip on the palate, and fades into a grape jelly/lollipop finish. **87** *(9/1/2005)*

Olson Ogden 2002 Unti Vineyard Syrah (Dry Creek Valley) $29. There's lots to admire in this dry, complex wine. It starts with a burst of white pepper, grilled meat, and blackberry aromas, then turns ripe in the mouth, with blackberry and Kahlúa flavors. There are some sturdy tannins throughout. **89** *—S.H. (5/1/2005)*

OPOLO

Opolo 2001 Estate Cabernet Sauvignon (Paso Robles) $30. Rather vegetal on the opening, and turns only modestly fruity in the mouth. **82** *—S.H. (5/1/2005)*

Opolo 2002 Merlot (Paso Robles) $26. A solid effort, soft and clean, with likeable cherry and blackberry fruit. Finishes with a dusting of fine tannins. **84** *—S.H. (5/1/2005)*

Opolo 2002 Pinot Noir (Paso Robles) $24. A little heavy and rough, but the flavorful cherries, cocoa, and spices are tasty, and the wine is clean and balanced. **84** *—S.H. (5/1/2005)*

Opolo 2003 Roussanne (Central Coast) $20. Okay wine, dry and with good acidity, but kind of generic. Features peach and cashew flavors, and a smoky finish. **84** *—S.H. (5/1/2005)*

Opolo 2001 Estate Syrah (Paso Robles) $24. This gentle wine does what Paso so effortlessly accomplishes. It's soft, juicy, and filled with forward fruit flavor, but is by no means one-dimensional. Cherries, blackberries, mocha, and peppery spices unfold in waves, and the finish is clean and dry. **90** *—S.H. (5/1/2005)*

Opolo 2003 Mountain Zinfandel (Paso Robles) $24. You don't have to peek at the label to know this is a high-alcohol wine. The 16.6% burns the palate. It's also deficient in acidity, so while the cassis and chocolate flavors are fine, it's unbalanced. **83** *—S.H. (5/1/2005)*

Opolo 2003 Summit Creek Zinfandel (Paso Robles) $18. Ripe in blackberry and cocoa flavors, smooth in sweet tannins, this very nice Zin showcases Paso's ability to produce soft, immediately drinkable red wines. **85** *—S.H. (5/1/2005)*

OPTIMA

Optima 2003 Rosé of Cabernet Sauvignon (Alexander Valley) $13. Seems like there's a lot of blush wines from major varieties and good appellations out there these days. This dry wine is fairly fruity and simple, with good acidity. **83** *—S.H. (10/1/2004)*

OPUS ONE

Opus One 2000 Bordeaux Blend (Napa Valley) $125. Made in the Opus style, which is graceful, limpid, and elegant, but with hidden depths of authority and power. The blackberry, cherry, and oak flavors are pretty, but the wine is most notable for its harmony and grace. Tannins play only a supportive role, but they will let this wine age effortlessly for many years. **92** *—S.H. (12/1/2004)*

ORBIS

Orbis 2000 Chardonnay (Carneros) $19. **91 Editors' Choice** *—S.H. (12/15/2002)*

ORFILA

Orfila 1997 Ambassador's Reserve Limited B Merlot (San Diego County) $25. **81** *—J.C. (7/1/2000)*

Orfila 1999 Pinot Noir (Edna Valley) $35. **84** *—S.H. (2/1/2003)*

Orfila NV Lotus Cuvée Lot #123 Rhône White Blend (San Pasqual) $28. This Rhône blend is ripe to the point of off-dry, with flamboyant flavors of ripe white peaches, lime pie, vanilla custard, and smoke. With a creamy texture, it has a long aftertaste. **86** *—S.H. (5/1/2005)*

Orfila 2001 Di Collina Sangiovese (San Pasqual) $20. Very dry, and deficient in acids, this wine has cherry flavors and is rustic. **83** *—S.H. (5/1/2005)*

Orfila 1999 Limited Bottling Val de la Mer Syrah (San Pasqual) $25. **85** *—S.H. (12/15/2003)*

Orfila 1998 Lotus Cuvée Viognier (San Pasqual) $28. **89** *—S.H. (4/1/2002)*

Orfila 2002 Gold Rush Old Vines Zinfandel (California) $24. You'd expect a smaller appellation than "California" given the words on the label. Too sweet. **82** *—S.H. (5/1/2005)*

ORGANIC VINTNERS

Organic Vintners 2003 California Collection Vegan Cabernet Sauvignon (Mendocino) $15. This clean, dry wine has forward varietal flavors of blackberries and cherries, and a firm backbone of tannins that will cut through a good piece of beef. **85** *—S.H. (8/1/2005)*

ORIEL

Oriel 2002 Midnight Rambler Cabernet Sauvignon (Rutherford) $30. This ripe, forward Cab is extracted in fruit, and made soft in the modern style. It displays flavors of black cherries and cassis, with vanilla and char from oak, and a sweet herb note. Almost sweet, but fundamentally dry, it's a nice steak wine. **87** *—S.H. (11/1/2005)*

Oriel 2003 Jasper Pinot Noir (Russian River Valley) $25. Straightforward, cool-climate Pinot, extracted and jammy in black cherries, cola, and mocha, and fairly heavy on the wood. Also has good acidity and a silky, though fairly full-bodied, texture. **85** *—S.H. (11/1/2005)*

ORIGIN

Origin 2002 Family Home Cabernet Sauvignon (Napa Valley) $55. Marginally richer and riper than Origin's Heritage Sites Red Wine, but, costing considerably more, it's a lesser value. This is a somewhat tannic wine with herb and cherry flavors, and a sharpness throughout. **88** *—S.H. (10/1/2005)*

ORIGIN NAPA

Origin Napa 2003 Gamble Vineyard Sauvignon Blanc (Napa Valley) $27. Pungent and ripe, with aggressive citrus and stone-fruit aromas. Tastes a bit like a powder-based fruit drink, with grapefruit and gritty, acid-driven lemon characteristics. Quite zippy and tangy on the finish. **86** *(7/1/2005)*

Origin Napa 2002 Heart Block Sauvignon Blanc (Napa Valley) $50. No, the price isn't a typo. This dry wine brims with lime peel, fig, vanilla and peppery spice flavors, and possesses a polished elegance in its tart acids and dusting of tannins. It has the creamy texture of a nice Chard, plus a very long finish. **90** *—S.H. (12/15/2004)*

OROGENY

Orogeny 2002 Pinot Noir (Sonoma County-Green Valley) $25. Ripe and oaky in vanilla and toast, with a layer of cola and cherries emerging after airing. Tastes very ripe and full, and a bit heavy, with a chocolatey finish. Could benefit from a few years in bottle. **85** *(11/1/2004)*

ORTMAN FAMILY

Ortman Family 2000 Cabernet Sauvignon (Napa Valley) $50. First you notice the gentleness and soothing softness, the way the tannins spread like a Persian carpet across the tongue. Then the purity of the flavors strikes, as the black currants, olives, smoky oak, and dried herbs unfold in waves. This is a classy glass of wine. Drink now, though. **91** *—S.H. (5/1/2004)*

Ortman Family 2002 Chardonnay (Edna Valley) $25. This cool Central Coast wine has tropical fruit and lemondrop flavors as well as zesty acidity. Veteran winemaker Chuck Ortman has added a substantial amount of toasted oak. The result is a clean, flavorful wine. **87** *—S.H. (6/1/2005)*

Ortman Family 2003 Pinot Noir (Willamette Valley) $30. The thick tannins, up front acids and deeply buried core of cherry, tobacco, and plum fruit suggest cellaring. Certainly the wine isn't showing a lot now. **84** *—S.H. (12/1/2005)*

Ortman Family 2002 Pinot Noir (Santa Barbara County) $34. A lovely Pinot, supple and velvety in the mouth, and loaded with personality. Big, juicy flavors of cherries, black raspberries, and coffee, with toast and vanilla overtones. As rich as it is, this dry wine is elegant and complex. **90** *—S.H. (11/1/2004)*

Ortman Family 2003 Fiddlestix Vineyard Pinot Noir (Santa Rita Hills) $40. Bone dry, acidic, and tannic, and seemingly early picked, because there's not a whole lot of fruit, this is a lean Pinot Noir. Finishes with a scour of bitter coffee and cherryskin. **85** *—S.H. (12/1/2005)*

Ortman Family 2003 Syrah (San Luis Obispo County) $25. Veteran winemaker Chuck Ortman (formerly of Meridian) and his family are behind this wine, which boasts intriguing scents of white pepper, raw meat, dried herbs and mixed berries. On the palate, it's true to the Ortman style of favoring elegance over weight, turning a little tart and lemony on the finish. **86** *(9/1/2005)*

Ortman Family 2001 Syrah (San Luis Obispo County) $25. Veteran Chuck Ortman took some tough as nails, tannic Edna Valley fruit and tried his best to soften and fatten it with Paso Robles grapes. The cool climate won out. This wine is hard and firm, dry, and astringent. If you have the patience, it may reward cellaring for at least 10 years. **86** *—S.H. (5/1/2004)*

OS WINERY

OS Winery 2003 Red Blend (Columbia Valley (WA)) $20. This high-toned wine is packed with supple, juicy fruit, big and round and ripe. It's almost half Lemberger, Washington's answer to Zinfandel, and it has been vinified in neutral oak for full fruit impact. The vineyard sources—Klipsun, Champoux, and Sheridan—are exceptional for a "mutt" wine. **88** *—P.G. (12/15/2005)*

OSPREY'S DOMINION

Osprey's Dominion 2000 Merlot (North Fork of Long Island) $18. **84** *—J.C. (10/2/2004)*

OUTPOST

Outpost 2000 Pringle Family Vineyard Zinfandel (Howell Mountain) $45. **94** *—C.S. (11/1/2002)*

OWEN-SULLIVAN

Owen-Sullivan 2000 Champoux Vineyard Cabernet Franc (Columbia Valley (WA)) $25. **88** *—P.G. (6/1/2002)*

Owen-Sullivan 2002 Ulysses Merlot-Cabernet Sauvignon (Yakima Valley) $50. This vintage is vineyard designated (Sheridan Vineyard) and 80% merlot; the rest cabernet sauvignon. A ripe, plumy wine, showing a lifted nose bordering on volatility. Despite the pretty fruit, the finish is somewhat bitter, almost scorched. **87** *—P.G. (6/1/2005)*

PACIFIC ECHO

Pacific Echo 1995 Blanc de Blancs Champagne Blend (Anderson Valley) $27. **89** *(12/31/2000)*

Pacific Echo NV Brut Champagne Blend (Mendocino County) $22. **87** *—P.G. (12/31/2000)*

Pacific Echo 1997 Brut Rosé Champagne Blend (Mendocino County) $27. **90** *—S.H. (6/1/2001)*

Pacific Echo 1995 Private Reserve Brut Champagne Blend (Anderson Valley) $31. **88** *—M.M. (12/31/2000)*

Pacific Echo 1996 Blanc de Blancs Sparkling Blend (Anderson Valley) $27. **91** *—J.M. (12/1/2003)*

Pacific Echo 1998 Brut Rosé Sparkling Blend (Anderson Valley) $24. **91** **Editors' Choice** *—J.M. (12/1/2003)*

PACIFIC STAR

Pacific Star 1996 Venturi Vineyard Charbono (Mendocino County) $32. **89** *—S.H. (12/1/2001)*

Pacific Star 1999 Liebelt Vineyards Merlot (Lodi) $20. **83** *—S.H. (7/1/2002)*

Pacific Star 1999 Meadows Vineyard Mourvèdre (Contra Costa County) $20. **84** *—S.H. (11/15/2001)*

Pacific Star 1999 Reserve Petite Sirah (Mendocino County) $26. 86 *—S.H. (9/1/2003)*

Pacific Star 1999 Dad's Daily Red (California) $12. 83 *—S.H. (11/15/2002)*

Pacific Star 1999 Zinfandel (Mendocino County) $14. 82 *—S.H. (12/15/2001)*

PAGE

Page 1999 Bordeaux Blend (Napa Valley) $58. 93 Cellar Selection *—J.M. (5/1/2003)*

PAGE CELLARS

Page Cellars 2002 Syrah (Columbia Valley (WA)) $37. Very fruity, with sweet, grapy flavors verging on Port. The super-ripe fruit catches your immediate attention, then hits an odd spot with a gluey back palate that is entirely disconnected from the front. 85 *—P.G. (11/15/2004)*

PAIGE

Paige 23 2000 Syrah (Santa Barbara County) $21. 93 Editors' Choice *—S.H. (12/1/2002)*

PAINTER BRIDGE

Painter Bridge 2001 Chardonnay (California) $7. 87 Best Buy *—S.H. (2/1/2003)*

PALMAZ

Palmaz 2001 Cabernet Sauvignon (Napa Valley) $100. An inaugural wine from the Palmaz family and winemaker Randy Dunn. Massive, huge, all currant, cassis, and cherry fruit, with an elaborate overlay of smoky oak. The bigtime tannins are thick but softly sweet. Drink now through 2008. 90 *—S.H. (5/1/2005)*

PALMER

Palmer 1995 Select Reserve Bordeaux Blend (North Fork of Long Island) $25. 84 *—J.C. (12/1/1999)*

Palmer 1997 Proprietor's Reserve Cabernet Franc (North Fork of Long Island) $18. 88 *—J.C. (12/1/1999)*

Palmer 1995 Barrel-Fermented Chardonnay (North Fork of Long Island) $17. 81 *—J.C. (8/1/2000)*

Palmer 1997 Estate Chardonnay (North Fork of Long Island) $12. 84 *—J.C. (8/1/1999)*

Palmer 1999 Gewürztraminer (North Fork of Long Island) $15. 84 *—J.C. (4/1/2001)*

Palmer 1997 Merlot (North Fork of Long Island) $18. 83 *—J.C. (4/1/2001)*

Palmer 1998 Vintner's Cuvée Merlot (North Fork of Long Island) $10. Looks prematurely mature, already browning at the rim. Smells it, too. Slightly acrid tobacco and dried parsley aromas turn into cedary cigar-box flavors in the mouth, and the finish seems to be thinning out. Lean and over-mature, but still has a sense of elegance. 83 *—J.C. (1/1/2004)*

Palmer 1997 Lieb Vineyards Pinot Blanc (North Fork of Long Island) $13. 86 *—J.C. (8/1/1999)*

Palmer 1998 Select Reserve White Blend (North Fork of Long Island) $14. 86 *—J.C. (4/1/2001)*

Palmeri 2002 Stagecoach Vineyard Syrah (Napa Valley) $47. Fruit seems easy to achieve in Syrah, but balance and elegance are more difficult goals. This fine wine is exuberantly fruity—red and black cherries—and adds notes of pecan pie, chocolate, and spice. Full and soft in the mouth, yet tangy and fresh on the finish. 89 *(9/1/2005)*

PALOMA

Paloma 1999 Syrah (Spring Mountain) $36. 90 *(11/1/2001)*

PALUMBO FAMILY VINEYARDS

Palumbo Family Vineyards 2000 Tre Fratelli Bordeaux Blend (Temecula) $28. A Bordeaux blend from this warmish appellation east of L.A. It's a bit musty on opening, with Porty aromas of cooked raisins and caramel. Drinks rich in sweet berry fruit, with some residual sugar on the finish. 82 *—S.H. (4/1/2004)*

PANTHER CREEK

Panther Creek 2000 Arcus Pinot Noir (Willamette Valley) $60. 91 Cellar Selection *(10/1/2002)*

Panther Creek 2000 Bednarik Vineyard Pinot Noir (Willamette Valley) $48. 86 *(10/1/2002)*

Panther Creek 2000 Freedom Hill Pinot Noir (Willamette Valley) $48. 86 *(10/1/2002)*

Panther Creek 1998 Freedom Hill Vineyard Pinot Noir (Willamette Valley) $48. 91 *—J.C. (12/1/2000)*

Panther Creek 2002 Nysa Vineyard Pinot Noir (Willamette Valley) $40. Tight, hard young fruit is overshadowed with big, butterscotch barrel flavors. Pleasant and unexpressive. 85 *(11/1/2004)*

Panther Creek 1999 Nysa Vineyard Pinot Noir (Willamette Valley) $49. 88 *—J.C. (11/1/2001)*

Panther Creek 2000 Red Hills Pinot Noir (Willamette Valley) $60. 87 *(10/1/2002)*

Panther Creek 1999 Reserve Pinot Noir (Willamette Valley) $40. 87 *(11/1/2001)*

Panther Creek 2002 Shea Vineyard Pinot Noir (Willamette Valley) $40. Mingled red fruits, including cranberry, red currant, and raspberry, are swathed in new oak. Tough, with dry tannins and plenty of vanilla, it needs more time to knit together, but all the right pieces are here. **88** *(11/1/2004)*

Panther Creek 1999 Shea Vineyard Pinot Noir (Willamette Valley) $49. 89 *(11/1/2001)*

Panther Creek 2000 Winemaker's Cuvée Pinot Noir (Oregon) $35. 87 *(10/1/2002)*

Panther Creek 2002 Winemaker's Cuvée Pinot Noir (Oregon) $25. Balanced and light, showing a hint of leathery mustiness. Cherry and plum flavors are sweet and simple, and there's a light touch of chocolate rounding out the tangy finish. **86** *(11/1/2004)*

PANZA

Panza 2000 Stag's Leap Ranch Petite Sirah (Napa Valley) $NA. 88 *(4/1/2003)*

PAOLETTI

Paoletti 1997 Non Plus Ultra Cabernet Sauvignon (Napa Valley) $110. 90 *(11/1/2000)*

PAPAPIETRO PERRY

Papapietro Perry 2002 Peters Vineyard Pinot Noir (Sonoma Coast) $42. There's a silky, crisp quality that makes this wine vibrant. It carries flavors of raspberries and red cherries dusted with brown sugar and smoky oak, and reveals cinnamon, nutmeg, and other spices on the finish. There's a definite sweetness throughout, which chefs will note. **90** *—S.H. (3/1/2005)*

PAPIO

Papio 2004 Chardonnay (California) $6. So tart and citrusy, it's more like Sauvignon Blanc. It's an easy sipper with enough lemon and lime fruit and creaminess to make it a value. **84 Best Buy** *—S.H. (12/31/2005)*

PARADIGM

Paradigm 2001 Cabernet Sauvignon (Oakville) $53. Made by Heidi Barrett, a gracefully soft, impressively balanced wine, with ripe, almost sweet cassis, cherry, and cocoa flavors. Sure is easy to drink, but also has the structural harmony to hang in there for up to 10 years. **91** *—S.H. (11/1/2005)*

PARADIS

Paradis 1997 Woodbridge Ranch Cabernet Sauvignon (California) $12. 80 *—S.H. (11/15/2001)*

Paradis 1997 Woodbridge Ranch Merlot (California) $10. 85 Best Buy *—J.C. (6/1/2001)*

PARADISE RIDGE

Paradise Ridge 2000 Cabernet Sauvignon (Sonoma County) $28. 85 *—S.H. (10/1/2003)*

Paradise Ridge 1998 Cabernet Sauvignon (Sonoma County) $22. 82 *—S.H. (12/1/2001)*

Paradise Ridge 2001 Ladi's Vineyard Cabernet Sauvignon (Sonoma County) $29. You get a combo of ripe blackberry and cherry alongside sharp green tea notes in this wine. It's dry, with smooth tannins and an astringent finish. **85** *—S.H. (2/1/2005)*

Paradise Ridge 2002 Nagasawa Vineyard Chardonnay (Sonoma County) $22. Lots of winemaker influence here in the leesy quality and oaky notes that have been added to an underlying wine tasting of apples and pears. The result is a dry, complex Chard that finishes with a bite of green apple acidity. **87** *—S.H. (2/1/2005)*

Paradise Ridge 2000 Nagasawa Vineyard Chardonnay (Sonoma County) $18. 87 *—S.H. (12/31/2001)*

Paradise Ridge 2001 Merlot (Sonoma County) $28. This wine is clean, good and tasty. It's not especially complex, but shows berry, cherry, spice and oak flavors that are wrapped in a soft, balanced package. **86** *—S.H. (12/1/2005)*

Paradise Ridge 1999 Ladi's Vineyard Merlot (Sonoma County) $23. 84 *—S.H. (7/1/2002)*

Paradise Ridge 2002 Pinot Noir (Russian River Valley) $29. Opens with jammy cherry fruit, cocoa, roasted meat, and smoky oak, and has plenty of cherry, coffee, and cola flavors, but needs just a little more grace and finesse. Still, this dry wine could soften and come together by 2005. **86** *(11/1/2004)*

Paradise Ridge 2002 Elizabeth and Henry's Vineyard Pinot Noir (Russian River Valley) $29. Dark and glyceriney, a big, extracted wine that's a bit clumsy now, but has potential. Notable for the big cherry and plum flavors and super-sized tannins, and high alcohol. Should benefit from a year or two of bottle age. **87** *(11/1/2004)*

Paradise Ridge 2001 Grandview Vineyard Sauvignon Blanc (Sonoma County) $14. 87 *—S.H. (9/1/2003)*

Paradise Ridge 1999 Grandview Vineyard Sauvignon Blanc (Sonoma County) $14. 82 *—S.H. (11/15/2001)*

Paradise Ridge 2001 Hoenselaars Vineyard Upper Block Syrah (Sonoma County) $32. 90 *—S.H. (12/15/2003)*

Paradise Ridge 2001 Ladi's Vineyard Syrah (Sonoma County) $28. This is a clean and well-made Syrah with notes of white pepper and blackberry. It's generous in the mouth, although the tannins are quite pronounced. Very dry and balanced, it will be great with lamb, filet mignon, or roast pork. **87** *—S.H. (12/1/2004)*

Paradise Ridge 1999 Ladi's Vineyard Syrah (Sonoma County) $25. 84 *—S.H. (7/1/2002)*

Paradise Ridge 2001 Hoenselaars Vineyard Lower Block Zinfandel (Sonoma County) $25. A tasty Zin that flatters the mouth with deliciously ripe, gooey flavors of blackberry and mulberry jam, with a long, spicy finish. The texture is smooth and velvety and the tannins are thick but friendly. You'd never believe it has nearly 16 percent alcohol, it's so balanced. **90** *—S.H. (3/1/2004)*

PARADUXX

Paraduxx 2002 Red Blend (Napa Valley) $43. Tasty in blackberry jam and sugared espresso flavors, although technically dry, this wine is pretty tannic, with a slightly rustic edge. It's full-bodied enough to go with big, sturdy roasts and strongly-flavored cheeses. **87** *—S.H. (8/1/2005)*

Paraduxx 2002 Paraduxx Red Blend (Napa Valley) $43. This is a blend of Zinfandel, Cabernet Sauvignon, and Merlot from Duckhorn. It shows its Napa origins in the ripeness of fruit and smooth, rich tannins. The blackberry, cherry, and chocolate flavors turn a bit soft and sweet on the finish. **84** *—S.H. (12/1/2005)*

PARAISO VINEYARDS

Paraiso Vineyards 2003 Chardonnay (Santa Lucia Highlands) $18. I like this smooth, dry wine, although it's rather overworked. The oak and lees are a bit obvious, yet the papaya and peach fruit flavors, and the acidity, are powerful enough to make it all work. **86** *—S.H. (12/1/2005)*

Paraiso Vineyards 2001 Chardonnay (Santa Lucia Highlands) $16. 86 *(10/1/2003)*

Paraiso Vineyards 1999 Chardonnay (Monterey County) $16. 89 *—S.H. (5/1/2001)*

Paraiso Vineyards 1997 Chardonnay (Santa Lucia Highlands) $16. 85 *—L.W. (7/1/1999)*

Paraiso Vineyards 1998 Pinot Blanc (Santa Lucia Highlands) $13. 86 *(3/1/2000)*

Paraiso Vineyards 1997 Reserve Pinot Blanc (Santa Lucia Highlands) $23. 87 *—J.C. (11/1/1999)*

Paraiso Vineyards 2002 Pinot Noir (Monterey County) $20. Tough and earthy, not showing much in the way of fruit. The mouthfeel is sandpapery. **83** *—S.H. (5/1/2005)*

Paraiso Vineyards 2000 Pinot Noir (Santa Lucia Highlands) $16. 83 *(10/1/2002)*

Paraiso Vineyards 2002 West Terrace Pinot Noir (Santa Lucia Highlands) $40. This Pinot may develop additional bottle complexities, but right now it's extremely dry and rather thin in fruit, with a tobacco and herb streak that makes the acids and tannins stick out. It doesn't possess the lushness of the '01, but rather has a lean elegance. **86** *—S.H. (12/1/2005)*

Paraiso Vineyards 2000 West Terrace Pinot Noir (Santa Lucia Highlands) $32. 88 *(10/1/2003)*

Paraiso Vineyards 2001 Riesling (Monterey County) $14. 85 *—S.H. (9/1/2003)*

Paraiso Vineyards 1999 Riesling (Monterey County) $10. 88 Best Buy *—S.H. (5/1/2001)*

Paraiso Vineyards 2002 Syrah (Santa Lucia Highlands) $20. Slightly herbal and peppery, backed by tart cherry-berry flavors and hints of vanilla and chocolate. Supple, without much apparent tannin, but built instead around crisp acids. Turns slightly cranberryish on the finish, simultaneously picking up a luscious hint of hickory smoke. **87** *(9/1/2005)*

Paraiso Vineyards 2000 Syrah (Santa Lucia Highlands) $24. 86 *—S.H. (6/1/2003)*

Paraiso Vineyards 1997 Syrah (Santa Lucia Highlands) $23. 91 *(11/1/1999)*

Paraiso Vineyards 2000 Wedding Hill Syrah (Santa Lucia Highlands) $40. 89 *(10/1/2003)*

PARDUCCI

Parducci 2001 Cabernet Sauvignon (California) $10. Young and grapy, a baby of a wine brimming with juicy flavors of blackberries, cherries and toast. It has a spine of crisp, citrusy acidity. Exuberant and fresh. **85** *—S.H. (5/1/2004)*

Parducci 1999 Cabernet Sauvignon (Mendocino) $9. 88 *—S.H. (5/1/2002)*

Parducci 2002 Chardonnay (Mendocino County) $10. Watery and dry, with the barest suggestion of melons. **82** *—S.H. (10/1/2004)*

Parducci 2000 Chardonnay (Mendocino) $9. 87 *—S.H. (5/1/2002)*

Parducci 1998 Reserve Chardonnay (Mendocino County) $16. 81 *(6/1/2000)*

Parducci 2001 Merlot (California) $9. 85 *—S.H. (12/1/2003)*

Parducci 2000 Petite Sirah (California) $10. 85 *—S.H. (12/31/2003)*

Parducci 2002 Pinot Noir (Mendocino County) $10. Smells a bit musty and earthy, with some pleasant cherry-berry flavors and silky tannins. Not a bad little wine. **83** *—S.H. (11/1/2004)*

Parducci 2001 Pinot Noir (Mendocino) $9. **83** *—S.H. (12/1/2003)*

Parducci 1999 Red Blend (Mendocino) $5. **83** *—S.H. (11/15/2003)*

Parducci 1997 Sangiovese (Mendocino County) $10. **87** *—S.H. (12/15/1999)*

Parducci 2002 Sauvignon Blanc (Lake County) $8. **84 Best Buy** *—S.H. (10/1/2003)*

Parducci 2001 White Blend (North Coast) $5. **83** *—S.H. (7/1/2003)*

Parducci 1997 Vineyard Select Zinfandel (Mendocino) $10. **83** *—P.G. (11/15/1999)*

Parducci 2002 White Zinfandel (California) $5. A pleasantly fruity, copper-colored wine, with raspberry and peach flavors. Straddles the line between dry and slightly sweet, and finishes with a trace of almond-skin bitterness. **84** *—S.H. (3/1/2004)*

PARRY CELLARS

Parry Cellars 2001 Cabernet Sauvignon (Napa Valley) $46. Opens with a powerful and appealing scent of cherry and black currant fruit that's dressed up with smoky oak. Impressive for its balance and elegance despite the ripe flavors, and accessible now for its gentle tannins. Will surely age well. **90** *—S.H. (10/3/2004)*

USA

PARSONAGE VILLAGE

Parsonage Village 2001 Cabernet Sauvignon (Carmel Valley) $42. Starts off with a disturbing aroma of pickled dill and canned asparagus that makes it hard to enjoy the wine once you taste. There are some polished cherry and berry flavors. **82** *—S.H. (8/1/2004)*

Parsonage Village 2001 Chardonnay (Carmel Valley) $36. Dark, somewhat heavy and quite ripe, a wine with a multitude of intense flavors that range from sweet cherries to blackberry pie and Kahlúa. There's even a note of blueberries floating in the firm tannins. Finishes dry, with astringency, suggesting aging for a year or so. **86** *—S.H. (9/1/2004)*

Parsonage Village 2001 Carmelstone Reserve Syrah (Carmel Valley) $54. The model was the Northern Rhône, with its opening blast of white pepper and complex mélange of plummy currants and smoky leather. In the mouth, this wine is dense and full-bodied, dry, fairly tannic, and very rich. On the finish, the currants powerfully return, coating the palate for a long time. A very good and interesting wine. **91** *—S.H. (8/1/2004)*

PASCHAL

Paschal 1998 Cabernet Sauvignon (Applegate Valley) $28. **87** *—P.G. (4/1/2002)*

Paschal 1999 Chardonnay (Rogue Valley) $16. **88** *—P.G. (8/1/2002)*

Paschal 2001 Estate Grown Chardonnay (Rogue Valley) $18. **85** *—M.S. (9/1/2003)*

Paschal 2000 Pinot Blanc (Rogue Valley) $16. **90 Editors' Choice** *—P.G. (8/1/2002)*

Paschal 1999 Pinot Gris (Rogue Valley) $18. **82** *—P.G. (2/1/2002)*

Paschal 2001 Syrah (Rogue Valley) $26. **85** *—M.S. (9/1/2003)*

PATIANNA ORGANIC VINEYARDS

Patianna Organic Vineyards 2004 Sauvignon Blanc (Mendocino County) $16. Very New Zealandy in the bone-dry flavors of gooseberries, lime peel, and honeysuckle, and the zingy edge of acidity, this fine white wine was grown biodynamically by a member of the Fetzer family. It has a long, rich, spicy finish. **87** *—S.H. (12/15/2005)*

Patianna Organic Vineyards 2003 Fairbairn Ranch Syrah (Mendocino County) $30. From a winery practicing biodynamic grapegrowing, this is a big, sturdy Syrah, very dry, and pretty tannic. It's also very clean, with strong flavors of roasted coffee and blackberries. The size calls for sturdy, rich, barbecued meats. **90** *—S.H. (11/15/2005)*

PATIT CREEK CELLARS

Patit Creek Cellars 2000 Merlot (Walla Walla (WA)) $32. **88** *—P.G. (9/1/2003)*

PATTON VALLEY VINEYARD

Patton Valley Vineyard 2002 Pinot Noir (Willamette Valley) $30. Estate-grown fruit is done here in a fresh, bright, citrusy style. Vivid and delicious, with snap and precision, this aromatic Pinot Noir has orange peel highlights and a pungent, tartly fruity palate. Food-friendly and nuanced, and a nice break from the jammy style. **91** *—P.G. (8/1/2005)*

Patton Valley Vineyard 2000 Pinot Noir (Oregon) $28. **88** *—P.G. (12/31/2002)*

PATZ & HALL

Patz & Hall 2002 Durell Vineyard Chardonnay (Sonoma Valley) $38. Smells and tastes like oak, with opulent vanillins, smoke, and buttered toast. Yet it's thin on fruit. There are suggestions of tart green apples and hints of white peach. Turns a bit watery on the finish, except for the oak. **86** *—S.H. (4/1/2004)*

Patz & Hall 1999 Woolsey Road Vineyard Chardonnay (Russian River Valley) $37. **92 Cellar Selection** *(7/1/2001)*

Patz & Hall 2002 Alder Springs Vineyard Pinot Noir (Mendocino County) $50. Closed at first, requires decanting to bring out the rich core of black cherry and dried spice aromas, and their template of smoky oak. Thick in youthful tannins now, and oaky, but a very good wine, rich and intense. Best after 2007. **90** *(11/1/2004)*

Patz & Hall 2002 Hyde Vineyard Pinot Noir (Carneros) $50. Starts off a bit sulfury. A full-bodied wine, balanced and harmonious. Exhibits ripe, big fruit and intriguing herbal notes, and isn't overly alcoholic. Solid, middle-of-the-road Pinot. **86** *(11/1/2004)*

Patz & Hall 2001 Pisoni Vineyard Pinot Noir (Santa Lucia Highlands) $70. What a price, but what a wine. For starters, it's huge in cherry compote flavors, drizzled with sweet mocha, vanilla, and powdered sugar. That makes it sound like a dessert wine, but it's dry, with rich, ripe tannins and firm acids. What it lacks in subtlety it more than makes up for in sheer decadence. **93** *—S.H. (4/1/2004)*

PAUL HOBBS

Paul Hobbs 2000 Beckstoffer Tokalon Vineyard Cabernet Sauvignon (Napa Valley) $NA. Minty, oaky, coffee, and blackberry aroma, gingersnap cookie. Tastes big, ripe, boldly tannic. Very dry. Not showing well, could improve after 2008. **85** *—S.H. (6/1/2005)*

Paul Hobbs 1999 Chardonnay (Russian River Valley) $38. **91** *(7/1/2001)*

PAUL MATTHEW

Paul Matthew 2002 Pinot Noir (Russian River Valley) $25. Forward in jammy red fruit, cranberry, and watermelon flavors, with a light, delicate mouthfeel, this flavorful wine turns milk chocolatey on the finish. **85** *(11/1/2004)*

PAUL THOMAS

Paul Thomas 1999 Cabernet Sauvignon (Washington) $8. **84** *—P.G. (6/1/2002)*

Paul Thomas 1997 Chardonnay (Washington) $7. **83** *—J.C. (11/1/1999)*

Paul Thomas 1997 Reserve Chardonnay (Columbia Valley (WA)) $11. **91** **Best Buy** *—M.M. (11/1/1999)*

PAUMANOK

Paumanok 2000 Assemblage Bordeaux Blend (North Fork of Long Island) $36. **86** *—J.C. (10/2/2004)*

Paumanok 1998 Cabernet Sauvignon (North Fork of Long Island) $18. **84** *—J.C. (4/1/2001)*

Paumanok 1999 Barrel-Fermented Chardonnay (North Fork of Long Island) $17. **85** *—J.C. (4/1/2001)*

Paumanok NV Festival Chardonnay (North Fork of Long Island) $10. **84** *—J.C. (4/1/2001)*

Paumanok 2000 Grand Vintage Merlot (North Fork of Long Island) $36. **83** *—J.C. (10/2/2004)*

Paumanok 2000 Dry Riesling (North Fork of Long Island) $15. **87** *—J.C. (4/1/2001)*

Paumanok 1998 Late Harvest Riesling (North Fork of Long Island) $27. **87** *—J.C. (4/1/2001)*

Paumanok 2000 Semi Dry Riesling (North Fork of Long Island) $15. **83** *—J.C. (4/1/2001)*

PAVILION

Pavilion 2002 Cabernet Sauvignon (Napa Valley) $12. Not a bad wine at all. Has cherry-berry fruit, with gritty, sweet tannins. Totally dry. **84** *—S.H. (5/1/2005)*

Pavilion 2003 Chardonnay (Napa Valley) $11. A very well-behaved Chard and a good value from this appellation. It's pretty rich in appley flavors, with bright acids and a smoky veneer of sweet oak. **86** *—S.H. (10/1/2004)*

PAVIN & RILEY

Pavin & Riley 2001 Merlot (Columbia Valley (WA)) $12. **86** *—P.G. (12/31/2003)*

PAVONA

Pavona 1997 Paraiso Springs Pinot Blanc (Santa Lucia Highlands) $13. **90** *—L.W. (3/1/2000)*

Pavona 1999 Pinot Noir (Monterey County) $18. **88** *—S.H. (11/15/2001)*

Pavona 1999 Peacock Blue Ltd. Release Syrah (California) $21. **85** *(11/1/2001)*

Pavona 1999 Purple Peacock Syrah (Lodi) $18. A full-bodied wine that rides a bit rough in the mouth, with ripe flavors of cherries, blackberries, and coffee and a bit of raisining. The finish also turns hot. Try with a pepper-rubbed pork tenderloin. **85** *—S.H. (9/1/2004)*

PEACHY CANYON

Peachy Canyon 2001 Para Siempre Cabernet Blend (Paso Robles) $38. This is a good, dry wine, with some punchy tannins. It's quite soft in the mouth, with flavors of cherries, herbs, and earth. **86** *—S.H. (7/1/2005)*

Peachy Canyon 2000 DeVine Cabernet Sauvignon (Paso Robles) $30. **85** *—S.H. (11/15/2003)*

Peachy Canyon 2000 DeVine Cabernet Sauvignon (Paso Robles) $50. Seems off all down the line, from the dull smell to the overly soft texture. On the other hand there's some pretty cherry-berry fruit. **83** —*S.H. (12/31/2004)*

Peachy Canyon 2001 Merlot (Paso Robles) $23. Soft, dry, and earthy, this is a wine that will benefit from a little decanting, which should bring out the underlying cherry and plum fruit. Has a bitter chocolate note that's appealing. **86** —*S.H. (7/1/2005)*

Peachy Canyon 1999 Merlot (Paso Robles) $23. 86 —*S.H. (6/1/2002)*

Peachy Canyon 2001 Petite Sirah (Paso Robles) $22. You have the right to elegance and finesse in a Petite Sirah, and you get it here. Dry, soft and balanced, it retains Pet's big-boned exuberance, while corralling the flavors and tannins to claret levels. **90** —*S.H. (11/15/2004)*

Peachy Canyon 2000 Para Siempre Red Blend (Paso Robles) $38. Simple, drinkable, but with noticeable flaws, especially the funky smell. Merlot-based blend. **82** —*S.H. (12/31/2004)*

Peachy Canyon 1999 Zinfandel (Paso Robles) $15. 89 Best Buy —*S.H. (12/15/2001)*

Peachy Canyon 1999 Benito Dusi Ranch Zinfandel (Paso Robles) $26. 91 Editors' Choice —*S.H. (12/15/2001)*

Peachy Canyon 1997 Dusi Ranch Zinfandel (Paso Robles) $26. 89 —*P.G. (11/15/1999)*

USA

Peachy Canyon 1997 Eastside Zinfandel (Paso Robles) $15. 85 —*P.G. (11/15/1999)*

Peachy Canyon 2001 Especial Zinfandel (Paso Robles) $30. 91 *(11/1/2003)*

Peachy Canyon 1997 Especial Zinfandel (Paso Robles) $28. 86 —*P.G. (11/15/1999)*

Peachy Canyon 1998 Estate Bottled Zinfandel (Paso Robles) $30. 89 —*P.G. (3/1/2001)*

Peachy Canyon 2002 Incredible Red Bin 114 Zinfandel (Paso Robles) $12. Balanced and dry, here's a Zin you can have with elegant food. It's dry, and the alcohol is below 14%. The berry and spice flavors are juicy. Good value in a Zin. **86** —*S.H. (11/15/2004)*

Peachy Canyon 2001 Incredible Red, Bin 113 Zinfandel (Paso Robles) $12. 80 *(11/1/2003)*

Peachy Canyon 2001 Mr. Wilson's Vineyard Zinfandel (Paso Robles) $26. 88 *(11/1/2003)*

Peachy Canyon 1999 Mustang Springs Zinfandel (Paso Robles) $26. 90 —*S.H. (12/15/2001)*

Peachy Canyon NV Mustang Springs Port Zinfandel (Paso Robles) $NA. 86 —*S.H. (11/15/2001)*

Peachy Canyon NV Mustang Springs Ranch Port Zinfandel (Paso Robles) $40. 85 —*S.H. (9/1/2002)*

Peachy Canyon 2001 Old School House Zinfandel (Paso Robles) $26. 90 *(11/1/2003)*

Peachy Canyon 2003 Snow Vineyard Zinfandel (Paso Robles) $26. This is a hot wine, with 15.5% of alcohol, and that heat dominates the pleasant berry, cherry, and mocha flavors. The wine is fully dry, but it's hard to get around the prickly, peppery burn on the palate. **83** —*S.H. (12/1/2005)*

Peachy Canyon 2001 Westside Zinfandel (Paso Robles) $19. 90 Editors' Choice *(11/1/2003)*

Peachy Canyon 1999 Westside Zinfandel (Paso Robles) $19. 87 —*S.H. (12/15/2001)*

PEACOCK FAMILY VINEYARD

Peacock Family Vineyard 2001 Cabernet Sauvignon (Spring Mountain) $60. Some of the grapes got over-ripe during this remarkably long, dry, warm vintage, to judge from the raisiny aromas. Then, too, the wine has a hot mouthfeel and finish. **84** —*S.H. (12/1/2005)*

PECONIC BAY WINERY

Peconic Bay Winery 2002 Steel-Fermented Chardonnay (North Fork of Long Island) $13. 84 —*J.C. (10/2/2004)*

Peconic Bay Winery 2003 Riesling (North Fork of Long Island) $13. 83 —*J.C. (10/2/2004)*

Peconic Bay Winery 2003 Polaris Ice Wine Riesling (North Fork of Long Island) $35. 85 —*J.C. (10/2/2004)*

PEDRONCELLI

Pedroncelli 2000 Petite Sirah (Dry Creek Valley) $15. 85 *(4/1/2003)*

Pedroncelli 2000 F. Johnson Vineyard Pinot Noir (Russian River Valley) $NA. 88 *(10/1/2002)*

Pedroncelli 2001 Mother Clone Zinfandel (Dry Creek Valley) $14. 80 —*J.M. (11/1/2003)*

Pedroncelli 1996 Pedroni-Bushnell Zinfandel (Dry Creek Valley) $14. 84 —*P.G. (11/15/1999)*

PEIRANO

Peirano 2002 Cabernet Sauvignon (Lodi) $10. There are some good Cab qualities in the blackberry fruit and full-bodied firmness, but there's also a rustic edginess to the mouthfeel. Still, it's a good-value Cabernet. **84** —*S.H. (11/15/2004)*

Peirano 2001 Autumn's Blush Cabernet Sauvignon (Lodi) $9. A rosé made from Cabernet Sauvignon, but not showing much varietal character. Delicate peach and apricot flavors drink rather sweet and flabby. **82** —*S.H. (2/1/2004)*

Peirano 1999 Chardonnay (Lodi) $11. 86 —*S.H. (12/15/2002)*

Peirano 2001 The Heritage Collection Chardonnay (Lodi) $15. Dry and tart, a sleek wine that offers a prickly mouthfeel without a whole lot of fruit. The modest flavors are of grapefruit juice with a squeeze of peach. **83** —*S.H. (4/1/2004)*

Peirano 1998 Six Clones Merlot (Lodi) $10. 86 Best Buy —*S.H. (6/1/2002)*

Peirano 2002 The Heritage Collection Petite Sirah (Lodi) $18. A little thin for my tastes, in the sense that it teases with the suggestion of black cherries but then withholds. In place of the anticipated fruit you get a flush of tannins and acids. **84** —*S.H. (11/15/2004)*

Peirano 2002 The Heritage Collection Sauvignon Blanc (Lodi) $12. This is quite a fine Sauvignon Blanc, easily as good as many coastal versions costing more. The flavors range from sweet citrus fruits through figs and melons, while a splash of Viognier adds a rich, exotic note. Brilliant too for its crisp acidity, making it clean and refreshing. **87 Best Buy** —*S.H. (12/1/2004)*

Peirano 1999 The Heritage Collection Shiraz (Lodi) $17. With a little bottle age, this soft wine is picking up bottle bouquet of dried violets and Kahlúa, in addition to the plum, blackberry, and olive tapenade notes. Drinks very rich, dry and spicy, scattering an array of dusty brown allspice and Chinese spice around the mouth. **89** —*S.H. (3/1/2004)*

Peirano 2001 The Heritage Collection Viognier (Lodi) $15. 83 —*S.H. (12/31/2003)*

Peirano 1997 Old Vine Zinfandel (Lodi) $10. 91 —*S.H. (9/1/2002)*

PEJU

Peju 2001 Cabernet Franc (Rutherford) $65. This is among the best Cab Francs ever bottled in California. Normally in need of toning up with other Bordeaux grapes, this 100% varietal wine needs no help. It is profoundly good, with the weight and tannins of Cabernet Sauvignon but a silky, feminine quality all its own. Subtle and nuanced; it doesn't hit you over the head with extraction and oak, but is complex, layered, measured. **93** —*S.H. (8/1/2004)*

Peju 1999 Cabernet Franc (Napa Valley) $30. 85 —*S.H. (12/1/2002)*

Peju 2002 Reserve Cabernet Franc (Rutherford) $90. Nobody is trying harder to master Cab Franc, and this noble wine continues Peju's streak. It's voluptuously soft, but not too soft, with enough acidity and tannins for structure. Meanwhile, the flavors are a wonder. Black currants, red and black cherries, white chocolate, sweet vanilla, and an edge of smoky char, to name a few. Drink now. **90** —*S.H. (11/1/2005)*

Peju 1999 Cabernet Sauvignon (Napa Valley) $48. 92 —*S.H. (11/15/2002)*

Peju 2001 Estate Cabernet Sauvignon (Napa Valley) $38. Released a full year after the excellent Rutherford Cab, with which it has much in common. It's ample in berry, cherry, and currant fruit, and oak has been applied judiciously. What's harder to convey is its balance and wonderful structure. Has an elegance and sweet harmony throughout. **91** —*S.H. (11/1/2005)*

Peju 1997 Estate Bottled Reserve Cabernet Sauvignon (Rutherford) $95. 90 *(11/1/2000)*

Peju 2000 Reserve Cabernet Sauvignon (Rutherford) $85. I think the philosophy here was to harvest the grapes at lower sugars and higher acids, then plaster the juice with oak, and create an ageable wine. It may well develop later in the decade, but now this is a tough, tannic, astringent wine. There's no guarantee, but try around 2010. **85** —*S.H. (8/1/2004)*

Peju 1998 Reserve Cabernet Sauvignon (Rutherford) $85. 87 —*S.H. (6/1/2002)*

Peju 2001 Chardonnay (Napa Valley) $22. 84 —*S.H. (6/1/2003)*

Peju 2002 Lianna Late Harvest Chardonnay (Napa Valley) $45. Delicious and savory, an intensely sweet wine, brimming with wild honey and cane sugar, that smacks of ripe apricots and peach sorbet sprinkled with the zest of tangerines. There's an intense vanilla flavor throughout. **90** —*S.H. (8/1/2004)*

Peju 2001 Merlot (Napa Valley) $35. The polished tannins, creamy oak, and blackberry flavors are all satisfying, yet this wine is marred by an edge of raisins and stewed prunes caused by over-ripe grapes. The cooked flavor will not age away. **84** —*S.H. (8/1/2004)*

Peju 2002 Estate Merlot (Napa Valley) $35. A satisfyingly rich Merlot, soft and feminine, yet showing real character in the fine tannins and gentle acids that frame the fruit. The flavors, of cherries and sweet oak, are flattering to the palate. **87** —*S.H. (11/1/2005)*

Peju NV Provence Rosé Blend (California) $18. The reds give the cherry-berry fruit, the dusty tannins and, obviously, the darkish color. Colombard contributes a fresh, grapy tartness. A simple, dry, easy-drinking rosé. **84** —*S.H. (12/31/2005)*

Peju 2000 Sauvignon Blanc (Napa Valley) $22. 82 —*S.H. (9/1/2002)*

Peju 1999 Syrah (Napa Valley) $65. 84 —*S.H. (12/1/2002)*

Peju Province 2001 Reserve Cabernet Sauvignon (Rutherford) $85. Ripe, soft, and hedonistic, an instantly likeable wine for its sheer opulence. Just bursting with sweet cherry, blackberry, milk chocolate, and smoky oak flavors wrapped in sweet, smooth tannins. Drinking absolutely beautiful now and throughout the next ten years. **92** —*S.H. (10/1/2004)*

Peju Province 2001 Estate Syrah (Napa Valley) $32. Pretty tannic at this point, but you'll find ripe black cherry and sweet oak flavors poking through. There's also a cocoa note that adds richness. Calls for a good steak, preferably barbecued. **88** —*S.H. (3/1/2005)*

Peju Province 2002 Reserve Zinfandel (Napa Valley) $45. It's tempting to score this wine even higher, because it's so decadently delicious. Just oozes chocolate, cassis, pecan pie, French roast coffee, and vanilla flavors, wrapped in ripe, soft tannins. The quibble is that it finishes as sweet as a dessert wine, although it's probably technically dry. **92** *—S.H. (3/1/2005)*

PELLEGRINI

Pellegrini 1997 Vintner's Pride Encore Bordeaux Blend (North Fork of Long Island) $29. 88 *—J.C. (4/1/2001)*

Pellegrini 1995 Cabernet Sauvignon (North Fork of Long Island) $35. 87 *—J.C. (4/1/2001)*

Pellegrini 2003 Old Vine Carignane (Redwood Valley) $16. Soft and easy, with flavors of ripe red cherries and earthiness, this wine is very dry. Finishes a bit sharp, but will be fine with cheeses and meats. **84** *—S.H. (3/1/2005)*

Pellegrini 2001 Chardonnay (North Fork of Long Island) $13. 82 *—J.C. (10/2/2004)*

Pellegrini 1998 Chardonnay (North Fork of Long Island) $13. 86 *—J.C. (4/1/2001)*

Pellegrini 1997 Merlot (North Fork of Long Island) $17. 87 *—J.C. (4/1/2001)*

Pellegrini 1999 Eastend Select Merlot (North Fork of Long Island) $12. 84 *—J.C. (4/1/2001)*

Pellegrini 1997 Olivet Lane Estate Pinot Noir (Russian River Valley) $20. 87 *(10/1/1999)*

Pellegrini 1998 Vintner's Pride Encore Unfiltered Estate Grown Red Blend (North Fork of Long Island) $29. 86 *—J.M. (3/1/2003)*

Pellegrini 2003 Eight Cousins Vineyard Zinfandel (Sonoma County) $24. A nice, easy Zin with some special features. It's dry and balanced in alcohol, acids, and tannins, with ripe flavors and a smooth mouth feel. The touch of rusticity should play well against ribs and barbecued chicken. **85** *—S.H. (2/1/2005)*

PEND D'OREILLE

Pend d'Oreille 2001 Cabernet Sauvignon (Columbia Valley (WA)) $16. This comes on like a fairly simple cherry and chocolate Cab, until some herbal (some might say stemmy) flavors kick in midpalate. The finish is oaky, mixing chocolate and coffee streaks. **87** *—P.G. (6/1/2005)*

Pend d'Oreille 1998 Cabernet Sauvignon (Columbia Valley (WA)) $16. 85 *—D.T. (12/31/2002)*

Pend d'Oreille 2000 Bistro Blanc Chardonnay (Washington) $11. 86 *—M.S. (6/1/2003)*

Pend d'Oreille 2001 Merlot (Columbia Valley (WA)) $20. There is a distinctly herbal scent, green olive, thyme, and bark, that is often found in cool climate Washington grapes. Some sour cherry and rough tannins suggest that it would be best with spicy, smoky grilled meats. **84** *—P.G. (9/1/2004)*

Pend d'Oreille 2002 Sauvignon Blanc (Washington) $8. This Idaho winery uses Washington fruit to deliver this light, crisp, pleasant wine. This wine offers pale green berry flavors, lemon zest, and the barest hint of spice on the refreshing finish. **86** *—P.G. (9/1/2004)*

PENDULUM

Pendulum 2003 Red Blend (Columbia Valley (WA)) $25. Pendulum is a collaboration with Allen Shoup (Long Shadows), and that, plus the fact that this 1,500-case red wine is a mix of eight different varieties, suggests that it is crafted from barrels that did not make the final blend for Long Shadows. There is plenty of expensive, toasty new oak in the nose, cedar and smoke and black olive also, but the wine doesn't really have any focus. Pleasant, especially for the new oak. **87** *—P.G. (12/15/2005)*

PENNER-ASH

Penner-Ash 1999 Pinot Noir (Willamette Valley) $49. 88 *(10/1/2002)*

PEPI

Pepi 2004 Chardonnay (California) $9. Shows plenty of Chard character in the creamy, buttery texture, with its pleasant flavors of peaches, vanilla and toast. This is a nice by-the-glass wine for restaurants. **84** *—S.H. (11/15/2005)*

Pepi 2002 Chardonnay (Napa Valley) $14. This is a classic New World Chardonnay, ripe with apple, peach, and tropical fruit flavors, and lavishly oaked with smoky vanillins. It has a creamy texture, a bite of acidity and a spicy finish. **85** *—S.H. (2/1/2004)*

Pepi 2002 Merlot (California) $8. I always think of wines like this as pizza wines. This one has succulent, jammy cherry-berry fruit. It's dry, and has a good grip of tannin. There's a young, fresh sharpness that will cut right through mozzarella. **84** *—S.H. (10/1/2004)*

Pepi 2004 Pinot Grigio (California) $11. This is not only a great price, it's a nice wine. It's dry and smooth and crisp, with juicy apple, lemondrop, cinnamon and vanilla flavors that don't stop coming. Great as an apéritif. **86 Best Buy** *—S.H. (11/15/2005)*

Pepi 2001 Pinot Grigio (Willamette Valley) $11. 85 *—M.S. (8/1/2003)*

Pepi 1998 Colline di Sassi Red Blend (Alexander Valley) $25. 92 Editors' Choice *—S.H. (12/15/2001)*

Pepi 1999 Sangiovese (California) $14. 90 Best Buy *—S.H. (12/1/2002)*

Pepi 1997 Two-Heart Canopy Sangiovese (California) $17. 87 *—S.H. (12/15/1999)*

USA

Pepi 2003 Sauvignon Blanc (California) $8. A bit aggressive in lemony, gooseberry flavor, but it's clean and tart, and wakes your palate right up. Perfect for seaside snacks, picnics, cocktails. **84 Best Buy** *—S.H. (12/1/2004)*

Pepi 1999 Two Heart Canopy Sauvignon Blanc (California) $12. 84 *—S.H. (12/15/2001)*

Pepi 2002 Shiraz (California) $8. I was shocked on seeing the price, because this wine is really good. It's far from a blockbuster, but is rich in fruit and spice, with a fine, dry mouthfeel, and minus the grating feeling an inexpensive young Shiraz can have. **86 Best Buy** *—S.H. (12/1/2004)*

PEPPER BRIDGE

Pepper Bridge 1999 Cabernet Sauvignon (Walla Walla (WA)) $50. 90 *—P.G. (6/1/2002)*

Pepper Bridge 2001 Merlot (Walla Walla (WA)) $45. The warm, broad, strawberry/cherry flavors of Pepper Bridge fruit are in evidence here. There are also hints of dill and bell pepper, leather, and saddle, and some well-managed herbal notes that add interest and balance. **88** *—P.G. (7/1/2004)*

Pepper Bridge 2002 Seven Hills Vineyard Reserve Red Blend (Walla Walla (WA)) $50. It's about 80% Cabernet, 20% Merlot, all from the Seven Hills vineyard. Classy, polished and nicely balanced, it has plenty of pretty oak, but also some interesting streaks of green coffee and green tea, tobacco, light smoke and pretty berry fruit, with just a hint of citrus. **90** *—P.G. (12/15/2005)*

PEPPERWOOD GROVE

Pepperwood Grove 2003 Cabernet Sauvignon (California) $8. This is ripe enough, but tastes too sugary sweet, and has a raw, unfinished edge. **82** *—S.H. (11/15/2005)*

Pepperwood Grove 1998 Chardonnay (California) $7. 84 *—S.H. (5/1/2000)*

Pepperwood Grove 2003 Merlot (California) $9. Shows the class of a more expensive Merlot in the rich, smooth structure, pure flavors and overlay of good oak. Finishes sweet with cherries and mocha. **85 Best Buy** *—S.H. (6/1/2005)*

Pepperwood Grove 2004 Pinot Grigio (California) $8. This offering from Don Sebastiani & Sons shows why Pinot Grigio is so popular. It shows citrus, peach, and white pepper flavors, accompanied by crisp acids, and finishes a little sweet. Instantly appealing to the palate, it's got a giveaway price. **85 Best Buy** *—S.H. (11/15/2005)*

Pepperwood Grove 2003 Pinot Noir (California) $9. Easy and enjoyable Pinot, with real varietal character in the soft, silky texture, crispness and cherry, cola, cinnamon and vanilla flavors. **85** *—S.H. (3/1/2005)*

Pepperwood Grove 2000 Pinot Noir (California) $9. 84 Best Buy *(10/1/2002)*

Pepperwood Grove 2002 Syrah (California) $9. Well-ripened, with an almost candied flavor of cherries, raspberries, and peppermint, but it feels dry and crisp. Finishes with a rich, smooth tannic structure. **86 Best Buy** *—S.H. (6/1/2005)*

Pepperwood Grove 2004 Viognier (California) $8. If you like super-fruity Viogniers, you'll love this blast of peaches, papayas, passion fruit, white pepper, and vanilla. It's clean, simple and refreshing. **84 Best Buy** *—S.H. (11/15/2005)*

Pepperwood Grove 2002 Viognier (California) $9. 84 *—S.H. (12/31/2003)*

Pepperwood Grove 1997 Zinfandel (California) $7. 83 *—S.H. (5/1/2000)*

Pepperwood Grove 1999 California Cuvée Zinfandel (California) $7. 83 *—D.T. (3/1/2002)*

PER SEMPRE

Per Sempre 1999 The Lisa Shiraz (Napa Valley) $60. 85 *(11/1/2001)*

PERALTA

Peralta 2001 Cabernet Sauvignon (Central Coast) $10. A nice, juicy Cab with pretty berry-cherry flavors and sweet tannins. It's dry and balanced and a good value. Primarily Paso Robles. **84** *—S.H. (10/1/2004)*

Peralta 2003 Sauvignon Blanc (Paso Robles) $8. Thin and bizarre, with vegetal flavors. Avoid. **81** *—S.H. (12/1/2004)*

PERBACCO CELLARS

Perbacco Cellars 2001 Chardonnay (Edna Valley) $20. Unripe, with vegetal aromas and weak fruity flavors. Also overoaked. **82** *—S.H. (6/1/2005)*

Perbacco Cellars 2002 Pinot Noir (Arroyo Grande Valley) $25. Very soft, smooth, and rather thick, this is one of those Pinots that flatters with scads of ripe fruit and toasty oak. It's certainly delicious in cherry, cocoa, and spice, but has a certain one dimensionality. **87** *—S.H. (6/1/2005)*

PERFECT 10

Perfect 10 2003 Blonde Chardonnay (Monterey) $10. Good melon, apple and vanilla aromas precede honey, vanilla, and spice flavors. It's sweet, ripe and easy to drink, with touches of wood and marshmallow. Where this concept wine scores best is on the tongue: It has generous acidity and enough body to ensure balance. **85 Best Buy** *—M.S. (11/1/2005)*

PERRY CREEK

Perry Creek 1999 Estate Bottled Cabernet Sauvignon (El Dorado) $14. **82** *—S.H. (11/15/2002)*

Perry Creek 2002 Chardonnay (El Dorado) $14. An everyday Chard, with pleasant peach and apple flavors and a bit of oak. Dry and crisp in acids, and easy to drink. **84** *—S.H. (10/1/2004)*

Perry Creek 2000 Estate Bottled Merlot (El Dorado) $12. **85** *—S.H. (11/15/2002)*

Perry Creek 2003 Estate Bottled Muscat Canelli (El Dorado) $10. A slightly sweet wine with pleasant peach and apricot flavors and refreshing acidity. Low in alcohol, too. **84** *—S.H. (10/1/2004)*

Perry Creek 1996 Syrah (El Dorado) $15. **90** *—S.H. (10/1/1999)*

Perry Creek 1999 Syrah (El Dorado) $16. **85** *—S.H. (6/1/2003)*

Perry Creek 1998 Estate Bottled Syrah (El Dorado) $16. **85** *(10/1/2001)*

Perry Creek 2002 Wild Turkey Ridge Cellar Select Syrah (El Dorado) $28. Another love-it-or-hate-it wine that ended up with a mid-80s score. Supporters touted the wine's blackberry and blueberry fruit and richly textured tannins that should allow the wine to improve with age, while detractors focused on candied fruit and a finish they found short. **85** *(9/1/2005)*

USA

Perry Creek 2000 Viognier (El Dorado) $16. **86** *—S.H. (12/15/2002)*

Perry Creek 2001 Estate Bottled Viognier (El Dorado) $16. **83** *—S.H. (12/15/2002)*

Perry Creek 2001 Zinfandel (El Dorado) $12. **87** *(11/1/2003)*

Perry Creek 2000 Cellar Select Spanish Creek Ranch Zinfandel (El Dorado) $24. **84** *—S.H. (11/1/2002)*

Perry Creek 2001 Zin Man Zinfandel (Sierra Foothills) $12. **84** *(11/1/2003)*

Perry Creek 1998 Zin Man Zinfandel (Sierra Foothills) $12. **83** *—P.G. (3/1/2001)*

PESSAGNO

Pessagno 2001 Sleepy Hollow Vineyard Chardonnay (Santa Lucia Highlands) $25. Fresh honey, peach, toast, mineral, cinnamon, spice, and herb notes give pleasing complexity to this elegant wine. It's packed with flavor, richly textured, yet bright and firm on the finish, which ends with a refreshing citrus note. Great price for a wine of this quality. **93 Editors' Choice** *—J.M. (6/1/2004)*

Pessagno 1999 Sleepy Hollow Vineyard Chardonnay (Santa Lucia Highlands) $35. **92** *—J.M. (12/1/2001)*

Pessagno 2000 Central Avenue Vineyard Pinot Noir (Monterey) $25. **85** *(10/1/2002)*

Pessagno 2001 Gary's Vineyard Pinot Noir (Santa Lucia Highlands) $50. Smooth textured, yet with a pleasing bright, spicy edge. The wine shows a complex blend of bing cherry, plum, pepper, spice, coffee, earth, and anise flavors. Soft tannins give it a round mouthfeel. The finish is long and bright. **92** *—J.M. (6/1/2004)*

Pessagno 1999 Gary's Vineyard Pinot Noir (Santa Lucia Highlands) $50. **92** *—J.M. (12/15/2001)*

Pessagno 2001 Spring Grove Vineyards Pinot Noir (San Benito County) $25. Fresh and refined, with a fine-tuned core of cherry, spice, cola, leather, herb, and earth flavors. The wine is smooth textured and elegant, serving up a long, silky finish. Classy Pinot from the Central Coast. **90** *—J.M. (6/1/2004)*

Pessagno 2001 Idyll Times Vineyard Zinfandel (San Benito County) $21. **89** *—J.M. (11/1/2003)*

PETER MCCOY

Peter McCoy 1997 Clos des Pierres Reserve Chardonnay (Knights Valley) $45. **85** *(7/1/2001)*

PETER MICHAEL WINERY

Peter Michael Winery 2001 Belle Côte Chardonnay (Sonoma County) $60. This opulent, all-too-drinkable wine offers powerful aromas and flavors of ripe Bosc pears that are liberally oaked. It is a big, muscular wine, with a rich texture of buttery cream and fine lees, and a tight spine of acidity. Will hold in your cellar for many years, but it's superb now. **92** *—S.H. (2/1/2004)*

Peter Michael Winery 1999 Cuvée Indigene Chardonnay (Sonoma County) $85. **92 Cellar Selection** *(7/1/2001)*

Peter Michael Winery 1999 La Carriere Chardonnay (Sonoma County) $60. **90** *(7/1/2001)*

Peter Michael Winery 2001 Mon Plaisir Chardonnay (Sonoma County) $60. Rich and tart, a spice-packed wine brimming with flavors of pears and tropical fruits that are tightly wound around a core of fresh young acids. The oak has been lavishly applied. Fine now, but will benefit from a few years of age. **91** *—S.H. (2/1/2004)*

Peter Michael Winery 2001 L'Apres Midi Sauvignon Blanc (Sonoma County) $38. Apple, citrus, and peach flavors co-mingle in this dry, pretty wine. It has crisp acidity and a nice overlay of oak that adds buttery, smoky, vanilla notes. Best now through 2004. **86** *—S.H. (2/1/2004)*

PETER PAUL WINES

Peter Paul Wines 2001 Merlot (Napa Valley) $39. Rich, semisweet and heavy, this wine opens with a swampy undertow that competes with the blackberries. Tastes pretty good, though, with ripe berries, cherries, and spices. **84** *—S.H. (10/1/2005)*

PETERS FAMILY

Peters Family 2002 Gardner Vineyard Cabernet Sauvignon (Sierra Foothills) $34. It's bizarre that this Cab is so much more expensive than Peters' '02 Meritage, which was released at the same time. This isn't nearly as fine. It's rustic and soft, with an edgy mouthfeel. **84** —*S.H. (12/1/2005)*

Peters Family 2003 Sangiacomo Vineyard Chardonnay (Carneros) $30. Richer than the '02, this single-vineyard Chard is crisp and bright in acidic structure, with oak and lees to add complexity. The underlying flavors suggest citrus fruits, peaches, pears, apricots, and mangoes. **90** —*S.H. (12/1/2005)*

Peters Family 2001 Meritage (California) $25. Lots of class and distinction in this dry Bordeaux blend. It has aromas of cassis and smoky oak, with currant, cherry, and herb flavors. The tannins are soft and complex. **88** —*S.H. (10/1/2004)*

PETERSON

Peterson 1998 Agraria Big Barn Red Cabernet Blend (Dry Creek Valley) $52. **86** —*S.H. (5/1/2003)*

Peterson 2000 Bradford Mountain Vineyard Cabernet Sauvignon (Dry Creek Valley) $29. Very tannic; puckers the palate and leaves it dry and brisk. There is a stream of plummy blackberry fruit but it doesn't seem rich enough to warrant aging. Drink soon. **85** —*S.H. (10/1/2004)*

Peterson 1999 Floodgate Vineyard Pinot Noir (Anderson Valley) $28. **88** —*S.H. (7/1/2002)*

Peterson 1998 Zinfandel (Dry Creek Valley) $18. **87** —*P.G. (3/1/2001)*

Peterson 1997 Bradford Mountain Zinfandel (Dry Creek Valley) $21. **91** **Editors' Choice** —*P.G. (3/1/2001)*

PETRONI

Petroni 2000 Poggio Alla Pietra Sangiovese (Sonoma Valley) $55. Extremely dry, rather rugged in tannins, and with unresolved acids, this is a tough wine softened just a bit with a streak of ripe cherry fruit. Will be fine with cheese and tomato sauce. **84** —*S.H. (12/31/2004)*

PEZZI KING

Pezzi King 1998 Chardonnay (Sonoma County) $17. **86** *(6/1/2000)*

Pezzi King 2000 Pinot Noir (Russian River Valley) $30. **88** *(10/1/2002)*

Pezzi King 2003 Jane's Reserve Sauvignon Blanc (Mendocino County) $27. Lemon is the dominant character of the nose. Flavors of buttery vanilla, likely derived from oak, soften the citrus flavors. On the finish, it's long and citrusy, and here a swath of oak comes on adding cinnamon and spice flavors. **87** *(7/1/2005)*

Pezzi King 1997 Estate Zinfandel (Dry Creek Valley) $26. **87** —*P.G. (11/15/1999)*

Pezzi King 2000 Old Vines Zinfandel (Dry Creek Valley) $25. Bright and effusive, with lots of ripe cherry, raspberry, plum, and blackberry flavors. Spice and herbs and interest to the blend, which is framed in ripe, firm tannins and shows a hint of vanilla and toast. Finishes with moderate length. **88** —*J.M. (6/11/2004)*

PHEASANT VALLEY

Pheasant Valley 2003 Celilo Vineyard Chardonnay (Washington) $15. Fruit from one of the top two or three Chardonnay vineyards in Washington shows its crisp green-apple spine with plenty of toasty oak to add spice. Somehow manages to be both firm and fleshy at once. **90** —*P.G. (6/1/2005)*

PHILIP STALEY

Philip Staley 1999 Chardonnay (Russian River Valley) $15. **87** —*S.H. (5/1/2001)*

Philip Staley 1999 Staley Vineyard Grenache (Russian River Valley) $18. **89** —*S.H. (7/1/2002)*

Philip Staley 1998 Mourvèdre (Russian River Valley) $16. **87** —*S.H. (7/1/2002)*

Philip Staley 2000 Somers Vineyard Petite Sirah (Dry Creek Valley) $24. **86** *(4/1/2003)*

Philip Staley NV The Coat of the Roan Foal 1 Rhône Red Blend (California) $12. A Rhône-style blend of Syrah, Grenache, Carignan, Mourvèdre, and Petite Sirah, and it's really quite stylish and even complex, despite the modest price. Exceedingly dry, with flavors of dried cherries and all sorts of herbs, and a peppery edge. **89** —*S.H. (8/1/2004)*

Philip Staley 1998 Syrah (Russian River Valley) $18. **86** —*S.H. (7/1/2002)*

Philip Staley 2002 Staley Vineyard Viognier (Russian River Valley) $22. Here's a full-throttle, well-structured wine whose streamlined flavors of lemons and limes, nettles, chamomile, gun metal, and vanilla skirt around the tendency of Viognier to be overly exotic. A great sunburst of acidity backs the flavors up, accentuating the wine's dryness. **89** —*S.H. (8/1/2004)*

Philip Staley 2000 Staley Vineyard Viognier (Russian River Valley) $21. **83** —*S.H. (9/1/2003)*

Philip Staley 2001 Duet White Blend (Sonoma County) $17. **90** —*S.H. (12/15/2002)*

PHILIPPE-LORRAINE

Philippe-Lorraine 1998 Chardonnay (Napa Valley) $18. **87** *(6/1/2000)*

Philippe-Lorraine 1998 Merlot (Napa Valley) $23. 88 —*S.H. (12/1/2001)*

PHILLIPS

Phillips 1997 Reserve Merlot (California) $15. 87 —*J.C. (3/1/2000)*

Phillips 1999 Old Vine Zinfandel (Lodi) $20. 83 —*D.T. (3/1/2002)*

PHOENIX

Phoenix 2000 Cabernet Sauvignon (Napa Valley) $28. 92 Editors' Choice —*S.H. (11/15/2003)*

Phoenix 2000 Reserve Pinot Noir (Napa Valley) $23. 87 —*S.H. (12/1/2003)*

Phoenix 1999 Blood of Jupitor Sangiovese (Napa Valley) $20. 84 —*S.H. (9/12/2002)*

PIETRA SANTA

Pietra Santa 2002 Chardonnay (California) $14. Ripe and rich in tropical fruit flavors, and well-oaked, this polished wine offers lots of pleasure. Finishes long and spicy. **86** —*S.H. (12/15/2004)*

Pietra Santa 2000 Dolcetto (Cienega Valley) $25. Dry, raw, and tannic, with a cherry skin bitterness, but there are no obvious flaws. It's just a simple country wine. **83** —*S.H. (6/1/2005)*

Pietra Santa 2000 Merlot (Cienega Valley) $18. Oak stars, with its toasty, caramelly notes, but underneath there's not a lot going on. The flavors veer toward blackberries, and the texture is very soft. **84** —*S.H. (12/15/2004)*

Pietra Santa 2002 Pinot Grigio (California) $14. This is a good white wine that satisfies for its total dryness, refreshing acidity, and flavors of Meyer lemons, just-ripened figs and straw. A dollop of Chardonnay adds distinction. **86** —*S.H. (12/15/2004)*

Pietra Santa 2000 Sasso Rosso Red Blend (California) $14. A rustic, country-style wine meant for easy drinking with pasta and beef stew. It's dry and a little tannic. **84** —*S.H. (12/15/2004)*

Pietra Santa 1998 Sasso Rosso Red Blend (California) $13. 87 —*J.C. (12/1/2001)*

Pietra Santa 2000 Sangiovese (Cienega Valley) $24. Super-dry, acidic, and herbaceous, a rasping wine that makes your gums pucker with astringency. Still, it good for its style. Those acids should cut through a rich pasta primavera. **84** —*S.H. (12/31/2004)*

Pietra Santa 2000 Zinfandel (Cienega Valley) $20. Hot with alcohol, and cloying with residual sugar. Unbalanced. **82** —*S.H. (12/31/2004)*

PIÑA

Piña 2001 Estate Cabernet Sauvignon (Howell Mountain) $54. This is a wine that will change your perception of Howell Mountain Cabs as wines that you have to cellar to enjoy. Yes, it's tannic enough for the long haul, but so good now, it's hard not to drink it. Packed with ripe, rich currant, cherry, and sweet tobacco fruit, with vanilla and cocoa seasonings, it's absolutely delicious. Drink now through 2012. **94 Editors' Choice** —*S.H. (11/1/2005)*

PINDAR VINEYARDS

Pindar Vineyards 1995 Cuvée Rare Chardonnay (Long Island) $28. 86 —*J.C. (4/1/2001)*

Pindar Vineyards 1998 Reserve Chardonnay (Long Island) $13. 86 —*J.C. (4/1/2001)*

Pindar Vineyards 1999 Ice Wine Johannisberg Riesling (Long Island) $35. 90 —*J.C. (4/1/2001)*

Pindar Vineyards 1997 Port (Long Island) $25. 86 —*J.C. (4/1/2001)*

Pindar Vineyards 1997 Syrah (Long Island) $25. 87 —*J.C. (4/1/2001)*

PINE RIDGE

Pine Ridge 1999 Andrus Reserve Bordeaux Blend (Napa Valley) $135. 90 —*J.C. (6/1/2003)*

Pine Ridge 1997 Cabernet Sauvignon (Stags Leap District) $50. 95 *(11/1/2000)*

Pine Ridge 1997 Cabernet Sauvignon (Howell Mountain) $50. 89 *(11/1/2000)*

Pine Ridge 2001 Cabernet Sauvignon (Rutherford) $37. Young and tight, with hard tannins and some citrusy acids that obscure the fruit. Yet there's a dense nucleus of sweet red and black cherry and cassis, and all the elements are balanced and harmonious. Nice now, but if you can, allow it to age for at least seven years. **91** —*S.H. (10/1/2004)*

Pine Ridge 2001 Cabernet Sauvignon (Oakville) $55. A big, exuberant wine, filled with power but a bit wanting in grace at this stage of its life. The fruit is ripe and explosive, the oak similarly sized, and so are the tannins. All the parts aren't working in harmony, but should pull together just fine by 2010. **89** —*S.H. (10/1/2004)*

Pine Ridge 2000 Cabernet Sauvignon (Rutherford) $37. 87 —*J.M. (8/1/2003)*

Pine Ridge 1999 Chardonnay (Stags Leap District) $40. 87 *(7/1/2001)*

Pine Ridge 2001 Dijon Clones Chardonnay (Carneros) $25. 89 —*J.M. (8/1/2003)*

USA

Pine Ridge 1998 Dijon Clones Chardonnay (Carneros) $25. 88 *(6/1/2000)*

Pine Ridge 2001 Onyx Malbec (Napa Valley) $50. A Malbec-based blend, and wouldn't you know it from the black color. Smells young and hung-meaty, with overtones of herbs and oak, but the suggestion of black currants is irresistable. Turns massive in the mouth, flooded with fruity flavor, and tannic, with a dry, hard finish. Certainly cellar-worthy. Try after 2006. **91** *—S.H. (12/31/2004)*

Pine Ridge 1998 White Blend (California) $11. 89 *—M.S. (11/1/1999)*

PIPER SONOMA

Piper Sonoma NV Brut Champagne Blend (Sonoma County) $19. 85 *(12/1/2001)*

Piper Sonoma NV Blanc de Noir Sparkling Blend (California) $18. 85 *—J.C. (12/1/2003)*

Piper Sonoma NV Brut Sparkling Blend (Sonoma County) $20. A bit rough in texture, but polished in sweet vanilla, smoke, dough, and subtle peach and citrus flavors. Has just enough dosage to make it finish round. **87** *—S.H. (12/31/2004)*

PISONI

Pisoni 2002 Pinot Noir (Santa Lucia Highlands) $60. Dark and dramatic. This is an enormous wine, super-extracted in cherry, blackberry, and mocha flavors, but totally dry. Almost Syrah-like, except for the silky tannins. Not particularly nuanced now, but the gamble is on ageability. Drink now and through the decade. **92** *—S.H. (11/1/2004)*

Pisoni 2000 Estate Pinot Noir (Santa Lucia Highlands) $NA. Dark. Lovely aromatics of red and black cherry, char, oak. Drinks full-bodied and rich, with some tannins to shed, but not quite the distinction of the '99. **90** *—S.H. (6/1/2005)*

Pisoni 1998 Estate Pinot Noir (Santa Lucia Highlands) $NA. First commercial bottling from Pisoni. Just as fresh as a new wine, really fruity, with ripe cherry, cocoa, cigar box, anise, cinnamon, and pepper notes. Drinks rich and intense. This dry, silky, harmonious wine is just beautiful. **93** *—S.H. (6/1/2005)*

Pisoni 1996 Pinot Noir (Santa Lucia Highlands) $NA. Another non-commercial bottling. Dark. Opens with lavish layers of cherries, cocoa, brown spices, charcoal. Drinks enormously rich and full-bodied, very forward in cherry and blackberry fruit. Tannins still sturdy. Still young and dramatic, with a sweet Heirloom tomato and balsamic finish. **92** *—S.H. (6/1/2005)*

PLUMPJACK

Plumpjack 1997 Cabernet Sauvignon (Oakville) $44. 94 *—S.H. (2/1/2000)*

Plumpjack 2002 Estate Cabernet Sauvignon (Oakville) $62. Not in the same ripeness league as the '01, but still an enormously attractive wine. It's just a bit leaner, but perhaps more structured. Shows blackberry, currant, coffee, oak, and herb flavors and some fairly big tannins. Nice now, but should hold and improve through 2010. **90** *—S.H. (10/1/2005)*

Plumpjack 1999 Reserve Chardonnay (Napa Valley) $40. 86 *(7/1/2001)*

PONTIN DEL ROZA

Pontin del Roza 1999 Cabernet Sauvignon (Yakima Valley) $18. 87 *—P.G. (9/1/2002)*

Pontin del Roza 2000 Pinot Grigio (Yakima Valley) $12. 85 *—P.G. (9/1/2002)*

Pontin del Roza 2000 Sangiovese (Yakima Valley) $23. 84 *—P.G. (9/1/2002)*

PONZI

Ponzi 2004 Arneis (Willamette Valley) $20. It's too bad Ponzi doesn't make more of this gorgeous wine, or inspire someone else in Oregon to plant it. Penetrating scents and flavors show pineapple, citrus, peach, and tropical fruits, and the piercing aromatics blossom on the tongue into a long, seductive, marmalade of a wine. Unique and flavorful. **88** *—P.G. (11/15/2005)*

Ponzi 1997 Clonal Chardonnay (Willamette Valley) $22. 89 *—S.H. (12/31/1999)*

Ponzi 1999 Reserve Chardonnay (Willamette Valley) $25. 92 Editors' Choice *—P.G. (8/1/2002)*

Ponzi 2001 Pinot Blanc (Willamette Valley) $15. 89 Best Buy *—M.S. (12/31/2002)*

Ponzi 2004 Pinot Gris (Willamette Valley) $17. This excellent Gris enters the mouth full-on with soft, appealing flavors of cantaloupe, pear, and pineapple. Then it rather quickly slips away. **87** *—P.G. (11/15/2005)*

Ponzi 2003 Pinot Noir (Willamette Valley) $30. Softer in 2003 than in more normal vintages, this shows ripe red fruit flavors, chewy tannins and spicy tobacco notes. Despite the heat and ripeness, it retains an herbal undertone, and the tannins have a bit of a green edge to them. **88** *—P.G. (11/15/2005)*

Ponzi 1998 Pinot Noir (Willamette Valley) $25. 92 *—M.S. (12/1/2000)*

Ponzi 1996 Reserve Pinot Noir (Willamette Valley) $48. 88 *(10/1/1999)*

POPE VALLEY WINERY

Pope Valley Winery 2001 Chenin Blanc (Napa Valley) $16. 88 *—J.M. (12/15/2003)*

Pope Valley Winery 2001 Zinfandel Port Zinfandel (Napa Valley) $35. Smells caramelly and rich in blackberries, and then turns semi-sweet in the mouth, with cassis, chocolate, and coffee flavors. The tannins show up on the finish. **84** *—S.H. (6/1/2005)*

POWERS

Powers 1999 Chardonnay (Columbia Valley (WA)) $10. 85 *—P.G. (2/1/2002)*

Powers 1998 Parallel 46 Red Blend (Columbia Valley (WA)) $30. 88 *—P.G. (12/31/2001)*

PRAGER

Prager NV Noble Companion Tawny Port Cabernet Sauvignon (Napa Valley) $45. 93 *—S.H. (12/1/2003)*

Prager 1999 Port Petite Sirah (California) $32. 93 Editors' Choice *—S.H. (12/1/2003)*

Prager NV Noble Companion Tawny Port (Napa Valley) $45. Turning a delicate tea-brown in color, this lovely wine explodes with aromas of toffee, milk chocolate, dark honey, butterscotch, and coffee. It's very sweet, with an ultra-smooth texture and a wonderful grip of acidity that makes it clean and compelling. Drink now. Made from Cabernet Sauvignon. **92** *—S.H. (12/15/2004)*

Prager 2001 Sweet Clair Late Harvest Riesling (Napa Valley) $27. 85 *—S.H. (12/1/2003)*

PRAXIS

Praxis 2003 Pinot Noir (Monterey) $15. Silky and light in texture, with good cool-climate acidity, and earthy, cherry-cola flavors that finish thin. **84** *—S.H. (12/15/2004)*

Praxis 2002 Viognier (Lodi) $15. A fruity quaff that features flavors redolent of apricots, peaches, lemons, and grapefruit. Acidity is bright, giving the finish some balance and freshness. **86** *—J.M. (4/1/2004)*

PREJEAN

Prejean 2001 Semi-Dry Riesling (Finger Lakes) $9. 84 *—J.C. (8/1/2003)*

PRESIDIO

Presidio 1999 Merlot (Santa Barbara County) $18. With some Cabernet Franc, and from the east end of Santa Ynez Valley, the two best Bordeaux reds in the appellation combine to make a soft, juicy wine, with ripe berry flavors and some herbal notes, and a smooth finish. **87** *—S.H. (3/1/2004)*

PRESTON

Preston 1995 Platinum Red Bordeaux Blend (Columbia Valley (WA)) $17. 81 *—S.H. (9/1/2000)*

Preston 1997 Cabernet Sauvignon (Columbia Valley (WA)) $12. 85 *—P.G. (6/1/2001)*

Preston 1998 Chardonnay (Columbia Valley (WA)) $10. 81 *—P.G. (6/1/2000)*

Preston 1998 Beaujolais Rosé Gamay (Columbia Valley (WA)) $10. 82 *—P.G. (6/1/2000)*

Preston 1998 Merlot (Columbia Valley (WA)) $12. 82 *—P.G. (6/1/2002)*

Preston 1999 Reserve Merlot (Columbia Valley (WA)) $22. 89 *—C.S. (12/31/2002)*

Preston 1997 Mourvèdre (Dry Creek Valley) $16. 90 *—S.H. (2/1/2000)*

Preston 1996 Vineyard Select Mourvèdre (Dry Creek Valley) $20. 86 *—S.H. (6/1/1999)*

Preston 2002 L. Preston Red Blend (Dry Creek Valley) $25. Here's a big, dark, rustic red. It's effusive in red stone fruit and berry flavors, framed in vigorous tannins that lend the wine grip and structure. Despite the volume, it's easy to quaff. Syrah, Cinsault, and Mourvèdre. **88** *—S.H. (11/1/2005)*

Preston 1997 Cuvée de Fumé Sauvignon Blanc (Dry Creek Valley) $12. 89 *—S.H. (9/1/1999)*

Preston 1998 Syrah (Dry Creek Valley) $18. 90 *—S.H. (2/1/2000)*

Preston 1997 Estate Grown Syrah (Dry Creek Valley) $18. 86 *(6/1/1999)*

Preston 2002 Preston Vineyard Syrah (Columbia Valley (WA)) $23. The big question for this wine is: Will it ever come into balance? It's got broad, mouthfilling flavors of coffee, caramel, prune, and vanilla, all cut short on the finish by masses of tough, chewy tannins. **84** *(9/1/2005)*

Preston 2000 Old Vine/Old Clone Zinfandel (Dry Creek Valley) $20. 93 *—S.H. (12/1/2002)*

Preston 1997 Old Vines/Old Clones Zinfandel (Dry Creek Valley) $15. 89 *—P.G. (11/15/1999)*

PRESTON OF DRY CREEK

Preston of Dry Creek 2002 Cinsault (Dry Creek Valley) $20. A simple, country-style wine, with cherry flavors. It's dry and tannic. It's not Cinsault's fault that by itself it can only make an innocent little wine. **83** *—S.H. (10/1/2004)*

Preston of Dry Creek 2002 Vogensen Bench Syrah-Sirah Red Blend (Dry Creek Valley) $20. Dark and vigorous, with blueberry and plum fla-

USA

vors and a soft, easygoing mouthfeel. A bit light and simply fruity, but a decent quaff. **86** *(9/1/2005)*

Preston of Dry Creek 2000 Vin Gris Rosé Blend (Dry Creek Valley) $11. 87 Best Buy *—S.H. (11/15/2001)*

Preston of Dry Creek 2000 Hartsock Estate Reserve Sauvignon Blanc (Dry Creek Valley) $16. 87 *—S.H. (11/15/2001)*

Preston of Dry Creek 1999 Estate Syrah (Dry Creek Valley) $20. 89 *(10/1/2001)*

Preston of Dry Creek 2000 Vogensen Bench Syrah (Dry Creek Valley) $22. 87 *—S.H. (12/15/2003)*

Preston of Dry Creek 2002 Viognier (Dry Creek Valley) $25. 87 *—S.H. (6/1/2003)*

Preston of Dry Creek 2002 Old Vines/Old Clones Zinfandel (Dry Creek Valley) $24. Fairly full bodied and thick on the palate. The wine shows off some nice spice and cherry flavors, but it also has a bit of an herbal edge to it. Tannins are firm but mild, while the finish is a bit short. **85** *—J.M. (10/1/2004)*

PRETTY-SMITH

Pretty-Smith 1999 Cabernet Franc (Paso Robles) $18. 85 *—S.H. (9/1/2002)*

Pretty-Smith 1999 Chardonnay (Paso Robles) $16. 81 *—S.H. (9/12/2002)*

Pretty-Smith 1999 Merlot (California) $18. 87 *—S.H. (9/12/2002)*

PRIDE MOUNTAIN

Pride Mountain 2000 Cabernet Franc (Sonoma County) $52. 95 Cellar Selection *—S.H. (12/1/2002)*

Pride Mountain 1997 Cabernet Sauvignon (Napa Valley) $36. 92 *(11/1/2000)*

Pride Mountain 2000 Cabernet Sauvignon (Napa Valley) $56. 93 Editors' Choice *—S.H. (2/1/2003)*

Pride Mountain 1996 Napa Valley Cabernet Sauvignon (Napa Valley) $30. 91 Cellar Selection *—L.W. (7/1/1999)*

Pride Mountain 2000 Chardonnay (Napa Valley) $35. 90 *—S.H. (5/1/2002)*

Pride Mountain 2002 Merlot (Napa-Sonoma) $52. What a fabulous Merlot. Yes, it's dense in texture, like molten metal, with melted tannins, but it's kept lively with clean acids. Meanwhile, the flavors are sheer mountain fruit: concentrated blackberries and cherries and decadent mocha. Complex, elegant, and addictively good. **93 Editors' Choice** *—S.H. (6/1/2005)*

Pride Mountain 1999 Merlot (Napa-Sonoma) $48. 94 Editors' Choice *—S.H. (6/1/2002)*

Pride Mountain 2000 Vintner's Select Wind Whistle Vineyard Merlot (Napa County) $65. 91 Cellar Selection *—S.H. (8/1/2003)*

Pride Mountain 2003 Syrah (Sonoma County) $55. Winemaker Bob Foley prefers older barrels for his Syrah, which lets the massive mountain fruit shine through. The result has a savory, meaty quality to the blackberry fruit, and picks up complex notes of coffee and pepper as well. A bit firm on the finish for current consumption; this is one of the rare California Syrahs that needs 2–3 years of cellaring. **91 Cellar Selection** *(9/1/2005)*

Pride Mountain 2001 Viognier (Sonoma County) $40. 90 *—S.H. (6/1/2003)*

PRIMOS

Primos 2003 Sangiovese (Redwood Valley) $25. Vintage #1 smells very new-oaky. The wine itself is ripe in cherries, but has the flaw of excessive residual sugar, making it cloying. Let's hope Vintage #2 is dry. **82** *—S.H. (11/1/2005)*

PRINCE MICHEL DE VIRGINIA

Prince Michel de Virginia 1997 Barrel Select Chardonnay (Virginia) $19. 84 *—J.C. (8/1/1999)*

PROSPERO

Prospero 2001 Chardonnay (Russian River Valley) $18. Simple and fruity, with syrupy flavors of canned peaches and pears and an overlay of oak-like notes. Finishes watery and sweet. **83** *—S.H. (4/1/2004)*

Prospero 1997 Reserve Merlot (Mendocino) $14. An acidic, tannic wine that overwhelms the mouth with tough astringency. It's certainly clean and dry, and is firm enough to stand up to, say, spaghetti with marinara sauce. On its own, it's pretty thin. **83** *—S.H. (2/1/2004)*

PROVENANCE VINEYARDS

Provenance Vineyards 2002 Cabernet Sauvignon (Oakville) $40. Very dark and young now—this wine needs to be cellared. It's powerfully tannic, with a burst of acidity; the mouthfeel is dusty and astringent. Has enough fruit to last beyond 2008. **89** *—S.H. (6/1/2005)*

Provenance Vineyards 2001 Cabernet Sauvignon (Rutherford) $35. Strives for balance and harmony and achieves both in the way the black cherry and herb flavors play off the tannins, acids, and oak. Bone dry, this impeccable wine will develop further complexities for many years. **91 Editors' Choice** *—S.H. (10/1/2004)*

Provenance Vineyards 2000 Cabernet Sauvignon (Rutherford) $35. 87 *—J.M. (6/1/2003)*

Provenance Vineyards 2002 Merlot (Carneros) $27. Lots to like in this full-bodied, dry wine. It's showing good flavors of blackberries and currants, chocolate, and red cherries, and sweet oak. It finishes with a bit of fiery tannins and acids, though, suggesting very rich fare. **88** *—S.H. (6/1/2005)*

Provenance Vineyards 2000 Merlot (Carneros) $28. 92 *—J.M. (8/1/2003)*

Provenance Vineyards 2003 Sauvignon Blanc (Rutherford) $19. Another Rutherford Sauvignon Blanc. What's going on? This one's crisp in acids and mouthwatering in citrus fruits, enriched with a touch of fig. Completely dry, it's a great food wine, but delicious on its own. **88** *—S.H. (12/1/2004)*

PROVISOR

Provisor 2002 Syrah (Dry Creek Valley) $30. Dark as a moonless midnight, dry as a desert, and chockful of thick, dusty tannins, but saved by overall balance and complexity and a deep core of black cherry fruit. Almost impossible to drink now except with something huge, like lamb. Should develop nicely through 2010. **90** *—S.H. (3/1/2005)*

QMS GROUP

QMS Group 2002 Writer's Block Syrah (Lake County) $14. Reduced and sulfury on the nose to one reviewer, while the others, who liked it more, found stewed fruit and a bristly, tart mouthfeel. **81** *(9/1/2005)*

QUADY

Quady 1998 Electra Orange Muscat (California) $NA. 87 *(12/31/1999)*

QUAIL CREEK

Quail Creek 1999 Cabernet Sauvignon (California) $10. 87 Best Buy *—S.H. (8/1/2001)*

Quail Creek 1999 Chardonnay (California) $10. 84 *—S.H. (5/1/2001)*

QUAIL RIDGE

Quail Ridge 2001 Cabernet Sauvignon (Napa Valley) $16. Rough in texture, sharp in vinegary acids, this is a hard wine to like. It's not going anywhere, but the fruity flavors wlll be fine with simple fare. **83** *—S.H. (11/1/2005)*

Quail Ridge 1997 Volker Eisele Vineyard Reserve Cabernet Sauvignon (Napa Valley) $45. 92 *—S.H. (8/1/2001)*

Quail Ridge 2000 Reserve Chardonnay (Mendocino) $24. 86 *—S.H. (10/1/2003)*

Quail Ridge 1998 Volker Eisele Vineyard Merlot (Napa Valley) $40. 91 Cellar Selection *—S.H. (8/1/2001)*

Quail Ridge 1997 Reserve Barrel-Fermented Sauvignon Blanc (Rutherford) $15. 85 *—M.M. (3/1/2000)*

QUATRO

Quatro 1997 Cabernet Sauvignon (Sonoma County) $16. 86 *—S.H. (2/1/2000)*

Quatro 1997 Merlot (Sonoma County) $16. 84 *(3/1/1999)*

QUILCEDA CREEK

Quilceda Creek 2001 Cabernet Sauvignon (Washington) $80. This is an almost-pure, Champoux Vineyard Cabernet, the best of the best. It's extremely aromatic, rich, and textured, tight and dense. As it slowly opens it reveals layer upon layer of black fruits, mineral, salt, and lovely, evanescent hints of herb. It does not show its 14.9% alcohol except for a slight bit of heat in the finish. Very, very young; Quilceda Creek Cabs may be the longest lived in Washington. **95 Cellar Selection** *—P.G. (9/1/2004)*

Quilceda Creek 1998 Cabernet Sauvignon (Washington) $60. 95 Editors' Choice *—P.G. (6/1/2002)*

Quilceda Creek 1999 Merlot (Washington) $60. 94 *—P.G. (6/1/2002)*

Quilceda Creek 2002 Red Blend (Columbia Valley (WA)) $35. Fragrant and inviting with sweet aromas of raspberries and ripe cherries. Not a hint of anything vegetal or off in any way; this is the finest declassified wine I've ever tasted. "If it's not a 95 right out of the barrel," says Alex Golitzun, "it's declassified." The blend is 70% Cabernet Sauvignon, 20% Merlot, and 10% Cab Franc. Medium-light in the mouth, with pretty cinnamon and baking spices, and a clean, crisp palate impression. Reasonably concentrated, it finishes lightly smoky and thoroughly delicious. **93** *—P.G. (12/15/2005)*

Quilceda Creek 2001 Red Wine Red Blend (Columbia Valley (WA)) $35. Quilceda's second wine is gorgeous, supple, and sweet with lovely Cabernet cassis and smooth hints of licorice and chocolate. Though not as concentrated as the Cabernet, it is immediately delicious, and would put to shame most wines in its price category. **92 Editors' Choice** *—P.G. (9/1/2004)*

QUINTANA

Quintana 2000 Cabernet Sauvignon (North Coast) $18. 87 *—S.H. (4/1/2003)*

QUINTESSA

Quintessa 1996 Bordeaux Blend (Rutherford) $90. 90 *(9/1/2000)*

Quintessa 1999 Bordeaux Blend (Rutherford) $100. 93 *—S.H. (12/31/2002)*

Quintessa 2000 Red Wine Red Blend (Rutherford) $100. 92 Cellar Selection *—S.H. (12/31/2003)*

QUIVIRA

Quivira 2001 Wine Creek Ranch Mourvèdre (Dry Creek Valley) $15. 85 *—S.H. (9/1/2003)*

Quivira 1997 Cuvée Red Blend (Dry Creek Valley) $13. 85 *—L.W. (6/1/1999)*

Quivira 2003 Steelhead Red Blend (Dry Creek Valley) $18. Tasted beside the 2002, which is soft and flamboyant, this younger wine is tighter and fresher. Both wines are dominated by Grenache, which should release its time-bomb cherriness by the end of 2005. This Châteauneuf-style blend also contains Mourvèdre, Syrah, and Zinfandel. **88** *—S.H. (11/1/2005)*

Quivira 2003 Fig Tree Vineyard Sauvignon Blanc (Dry Creek Valley) $16. From estate grapes, this intensely flavored wine shows citron, lemongrass, and fig flavors, brightened by acid. Sémillon, barrel fermentation and sur lie aging all bring a rich, nutty creaminess, and a slight sweetness, to the finish. **87** *—S.H. (8/1/2005)*

Quivira 1999 Fig Tree Vineyard Sauvignon Blanc (Dry Creek Valley) $18. 87 *(8/1/2002)*

Quivira 2002 Wine Creek Ranch Syrah (Dry Creek Valley) $24. Funky on the nose, with sulfury notes that not all tasters will find attractive or have the patience to deal with. But beyond the funk there's a big, full-bodied, impressive wine, loaded with blackberries, vanilla, and pepper. **86** *(9/1/2005)*

Quivira 2003 Zinfandel (Dry Creek Valley) $20. Shows real Dry Creek character, which is a dry, claret-like balance, modest alcohol, well-ripened fruit, and smooth, grippy tannins, with an herbal undertow. The raspberry, cherry, and blackberry fruit marries well with sweet oak. **90 Editors' Choice** *—S.H. (11/1/2005)*

Quivira 2000 Zinfandel (Dry Creek Valley) $20. 85 *—S.H. (11/1/2002)*

Quivira 2000 Anderson Ranch Zinfandel (Dry Creek Valley) $35. 90 *—S.H. (11/1/2002)*

Quivira 1997 Reserve Zinfandel (Dry Creek Valley) $25. 91 *—L.W. (2/1/2000)*

QUPÉ

Qupé 1997 Bien Nacido Cuvée Chardonnay (Santa Barbara County) $16. 87 *—S.H. (9/1/1999)*

Qupé 1998 Bien Nacido Reserve Chardonnay (Santa Barbara County) $25. 89 *(6/1/2000)*

Qupé 2001 Bien Nacido Vineyard Block Eleven Reserve Chardonnay (Santa Maria Valley) $25. Dessert in a dry white wine. Tastes like ripe green apple compote, gingersnap cookies, vanilla ice cream, and smoky maple syrup all mixed together, with bright acidity to make it come alive. How good and rich this cool-coast, southland wine is. **89** *—S.H. (6/1/2004)*

Qupé 2002 Bien Nacido Vineyard Y-Block Chardonnay (Santa Maria Valley) $18. Instantly appealing for its well-oaked flavors of ripe tropical fruits, intense spices, and clean, zesty acidity. There's a streak of sweet-and-sour lees throughout. A relative value considering its pedigree. **86** *—S.H. (6/1/2004)*

Qupé 1997 Los Olivos Cuvée Red Blend (Santa Barbara County) $18. 90 *—S.H. (10/1/1999)*

Qupé 2001 Alban Vineyard Roussanne (Edna Valley) $25. Super-fruity. Peaches, nectarines, limes, wildflowers, and lots of honey, vanilla, and spice all mingle together, brightened with crisp, citrusy acids. It's intricately balanced and totally dry. **88** *—S.H. (6/1/2004)*

Qupé 1996 Alban Vineyard Roussanne (Edna Valley) $25. 91 *—S.H. (6/1/1999)*

Qupé 2002 Bien Nacido Hillside Estate Syrah (Santa Maria Valley) $40. Built for the long haul, right now this wine isn't showing its full potential. Instead it's a mass of promise—of dense coffee, spice, and black olive flavors waiting for some day in the future when they will blossom. They're reined in tight right now, but the long finish of this wine plainly identifies its ultimate high quality. Try in 2010. **88** *(9/1/2005)*

Qupé 1999 Bien Nacido Reserve Syrah (Santa Barbara County) $25. 86 *(11/1/2001)*

Qupé 2001 Bien Nacido Vineyard Syrah (Santa Maria Valley) $25. Always a wine that needs a good six years in a good vintage to mature, this release is marked by plummy, blackberry, and chocolate flavors that are framed in stiff tannins. It's not a blockbuster, but should gain complexity by 2007. **87** *—S.H. (6/1/2004)*

Qupé 1997 Bien Nacido Vineyard Reserve Syrah (Santa Barbara County) $25. 91 *—S.H. (6/1/1999)*

R.H. PHILLIPS

R.H. Phillips 2002 Cabernet Sauvignon (Dunnigan Hills) $9. Very dry, rich in sturdy tannins, and pleasant in berry, earth, and coffee flavors, this is an easy-drinking wine at a fair price. **84** *—S.H. (6/1/2005)*

R.H. Phillips 1996 Toasted Head Cabernet Sauvignon (Mendocino) $18. 91 *—S.H. (5/1/2002)*

R.H. Phillips 2000 Chardonnay (Dunnigan Hills) $9. 84 *—S.H. (9/12/2002)*

R.H. Phillips 2001 Toasted Head Chardonnay (Dunnigan Hills) $16. 86 *—S.H. (12/15/2002)*

R.H. Phillips 1999 Toasted Head Chardonnay (Dunnigan Hills) $14. 83 *—S.H. (11/15/2000)*

R.H. Phillips 1999 Toasted Head Giguiere Ranch Chardonnay (Dunnigan Hills) $25. 87 *—S.H. (12/15/2002)*

R.H. Phillips 1998 Merlot (Dunnigan Hills) $9. **82** —*S.H. (11/15/2000)*

R.H. Phillips 1997 Toasted Head Merlot (Dunnigan Hills) $17. **86** —*M.S. (3/1/2000)*

R.H. Phillips 2001 Sauvignon Blanc (Dunnigan Hills) $10. **86** —*S.H. (9/1/2003)*

R.H. Phillips 1998 Night Harvest Sauvignon Blanc (Dunnigan Hills) $7. **87 Best Buy** —*M.M. (9/1/1999)*

R.H. Phillips 2002 EXP Syrah (Dunnigan Hills) $14. Slightly marred by a hint of nail polish on the nose, but otherwise notable mostly for its lack of defining features. There's some modest red berry and chocolate fruit and a short finish. **82** *(9/1/2005)*

R.H. Phillips 1999 Toasted Head EXP Syrah (Dunnigan Hills) $25. **85** —*S.H. (12/1/2002)*

RABBIT RIDGE

Rabbit Ridge 2003 Chardonnay (Paso Robles) $14. Soft in acids, fat and lush in fruit, and enjoyable. The tropical fruit, vanilla, and smoky oak flavors are explosive but dry, and very spicy. **85** —*S.H. (12/15/2004)*

Rabbit Ridge 2001 Avventura Reserve Red Blend (California) $25. This Sangiovese, Cabernet Sauvignon, and Merlot blend is ripe in fruit, with chocolate cherry flavors. It's quite soft in both acidity and tannins. Provides plenty of flavor, and a good cut of meat should make it even sweeter. **85** —*S.H. (12/15/2004)*

Rabbit Ridge 2001 Brunello Clone Sangiovese (Paso Robles) $14. Tannic and a bit herbal, but saved by decent cherry flavors in the finish. Perfectly dry, and not too hot. Pasta with lots of cheese and hearty short ribs will be good companions. **84** —*S.H. (12/31/2004)*

Rabbit Ridge 2002 Syrah (Paso Robles) $18. A lovely drinking wine, with nicely modulated plummy, chocolate flavors wrapped in rich, sweet tannins. Dry and balanced, with not too much alcohol, it has style and class. **87** —*S.H. (12/15/2004)*

Rabbit Ridge 2003 Westside Viognier (Paso Robles) $18. What a treat, with its gobs of juicy fruit, spicy mango, and papaya flavors and the excellent spine of acidity that makes it drink crisp and clean. Exotically flamboyant, but manages to be dry and balanced. **88** —*S.H. (12/15/2004)*

RACCHUS

Racchus 2003 Chardonnay (Sonoma County) $10. This screwtopped Chard is perfectly nice for everyday drinking. It's fruity, dry, and clean, with white peach and sweet melon flavors and a smooth, spicy finish. **84** —*S.H. (12/1/2005)*

RADIO-COTEAU

Radio-Coteau 2003 Timbervine Syrah (Russian River Valley) $55. This is a lush, heady, plummy wine, complete with spice, black pepper, and a fair amount of oak. The elements work together as a harmonious, velvety whole, and come to a long close. **91** *(9/1/2005)*

RAFANELLI

Rafanelli 2001 Merlot (Dry Creek Valley) $26. Even for 2001, this is a tremendous Merlot, huge in flavor, and stunning for its volume. Atypically, it has an almost Rhône-like quality of violets and lavender, sweet anise, and cherries, and the woody, charry new oak really stands out. This beautiful wine is very long in the middle and finish, and should improve for several years. **92 Editors' Choice** —*S.H. (11/1/2005)*

RAINBOW RIDGE

Rainbow Ridge 2003 Chardonnay (California) $13. Earthy, with an herbal, tobaccoey edge to the peach, pineapple, and oaky flavors. Drinks dry and soft, with a finish of almond skin bitterness. **84** —*S.H. (3/1/2005)*

Rainbow Ridge 2003 Avid White Chardonnay (California) $10. With no oak, this is a clean, fruity wine, and dry, with peach and apricot flavors and balancing acids. It feels nice and richly spicy in the mouth. **85 Best Buy** —*S.H. (12/31/2005)*

Rainbow Ridge 2003 Flaming Red (California) $10. This blend of Cabernet, Merlot, Syrah, and Sangiovese is a country-style wine, rustic and a little sweet on the finish. But it's a clean, easy sipper, especially at this price. **83** —*S.H. (12/31/2005)*

RAMEY

Ramey 1996 Chardonnay (Carneros) $65. **96** *(11/15/1999)*

Ramey 1997 Hudson Vineyard Chardonnay (Carneros) $48. **93** *(5/1/2000)*

Ramey 1997 Hyde Vineyard Chardonnay (Carneros) $46. **95** *(5/1/2000)*

RAMSAY

Ramsay 1996 Reserve Merlot (Carneros) $26. **86** —*J.C. (7/1/2000)*

RAMSPECK

Ramspeck 2001 Cabernet Sauvignon (North Coast) $18. **85** —*S.H. (12/15/2003)*

Ramspeck 2001 Pinot Noir (North Coast) $18. **82** —*S.H. (7/1/2003)*

RANCHO ARROYO GRANDE

Rancho Arroyo Grande 2002 Private Reserve Chardonnay (Arroyo Grande Valley) $15. Here's an everyday Chard with interesting features. It has citrusy, lime zest flavors and high acidity, and the absolute dryness serves to accentuate the tartness. That makes it very clean, with a razorsharp edge that will be nice with fresh cracked crab. **86** *—S.H. (9/1/2004)*

Rancho Arroyo Grande 2002 Thereza Cuvée Rhône Red Blend (Arroyo Grande Valley) $20. With Syrah, Mourvèdre, Grenache, and Counoise, this is a California Provençal-style wine. It's rich in berry, spice, and herb flavors, with finely ground tannins, and is soft, dry and enjoyable. **85** *—S.H. (12/1/2005)*

Rancho Arroyo Grande 2001 Syrah (Arroyo Grande Valley) $28. 86 *—S.H. (12/15/2003)*

Rancho Arroyo Grande 2001 Zinfandel (Arroyo Grande Valley) $18. 87 *(11/1/2003)*

Rancho Arroyo Grande 2003 Estate Zinfandel (Arroyo Grande Valley) $15. From a warmer, inland part of this appellation, which probably should have its own AVA, comes this slightly raisined Zin, which is reminiscent of many inland valley reds. It's rather hot, soft, and Porty. **84** *—S.H. (12/1/2005)*

RANCHO SISQUOC

Rancho Sisquoc 1997 Cabernet Sauvignon (Santa Maria Valley) $22. 81 *—S.H. (9/1/2000)*

Rancho Sisquoc 1998 Chardonnay (Santa Maria Valley) $18. 84 *—S.H. (10/1/2000)*

Rancho Sisquoc 2002 Flood Family Vineyards Chardonnay (Santa Barbara County) $18. Oaky and leesy, with a range of fruits from apples through peaches and pineapples, and tingly with dusty spices and acidity. This is a clean, food-friendly Chard, not too sweet **87** *—S.H. (3/1/2005)*

Rancho Sisquoc 1999 Flood Family Vineyard Pinot Noir (Santa Maria Valley) $40. 84 *(10/1/2002)*

Rancho Sisquoc 1998 Sauvignon Blanc (Santa Maria Valley) $14. 83 *—S.H. (9/1/2000)*

RANCHO ZABACO

Rancho Zabaco 2002 Pinot Gris (Sonoma Coast) $20. 88 *—S.H. (12/1/2003)*

Rancho Zabaco 2001 Reserve Pinot Gris (Sonoma County) $18. 87 *(8/1/2002)*

Rancho Zabaco 2001 Sauvignon Blanc (Russian River Valley) $18. 89 *—J.M. (9/1/2003)*

Rancho Zabaco 2004 Dancing Bull Sauvignon Blanc (California) $10. This is a good price for this New Zealand-style wine. It's dry and crisp in gooseberry, lime, and fig flavors, and bursts with cinnamon and white pepper spice on the finish. **85 Best Buy** *—S.H. (12/15/2005)*

Rancho Zabaco 2002 Dancing Bull Sauvignon Blanc (California) $10. 84 *—S.H. (12/31/2003)*

Rancho Zabaco 2001 Reserve Sauvignon Blanc (Sonoma County) $18. 86 *(8/1/2002)*

Rancho Zabaco 2002 Zinfandel (Dry Creek Valley) $18. You'll find a chewiness to this wine from tannins, but sweet fruit, low acidity, and oak soften it to gentility. Has the feel of a fine Cabernet, with Zin's distinctive spicy, feral quality. If it were more intense, it would be an excellent wine. **86** *—S.H. (11/15/2005)*

Rancho Zabaco 1998 Zinfandel (Dry Creek Valley) $17. 87 *—D.T. (3/1/2002)*

Rancho Zabaco 2001 Chiotti Vineyard Zinfandel (Dry Creek Valley) $28. 91 *(11/1/2003)*

Rancho Zabaco 1999 Chiotti Vineyard Zinfandel (Dry Creek Valley) $22. 88 *(7/1/2001)*

Rancho Zabaco 2001 Dancing Bull Zinfandel (California) $12. 89 Best Buy *—S.H. (11/15/2002)*

Rancho Zabaco 2000 Reserve Zinfandel (Dry Creek Valley) $20. 90 *—S.H. (9/1/2003)*

Rancho Zabaco 2001 Sonoma Heritage Vines Zinfandel (Sonoma County) $18. 86 *(11/1/2003)*

Rancho Zabaco 1999 Stefani Vineyard Zinfandel (Dry Creek Valley) $28. 92 *—P.G. (3/1/2002)*

RAPHAEL

Raphael 1999 Merlot (North Fork of Long Island) $38. This one of New York's full-priced wines, an attempt at the big time. But it's light and herbal, with oregano and tomato aromas and heavy barrel notes of rubber and char. The palate is dry, lean and leathery, with only a modicum of strawberry fruit. And the finish is bitter and long. **84** *—M.S. (1/1/2004)*

RAPTOR RIDGE

Raptor Ridge 2003 Coeur de Terre Vineyard Pinot Noir (Willamette Valley) $29. More of the big, brawny, super-ripe house style, this one a tad over the top at 15.8% alcohol. Jammy, forward, strawberry/cherry preserves drive this broad, flavorful, drink-now wine. **88** *—P.G. (8/1/2005)*

Raptor Ridge 2003 Meredith Mitchell Vineyard Pinot Noir (Willamette Valley) $29. Extremely intense, ripe, almost (yet not) hot at 15.1%

alcohol. Juicy and fruit-driven, this full-tilt, jammy wine packs lots of punch with its overflowing bowl of cherries and berries, but keeps itself on track with a zippy spine and dense, concentrated finish. **93 Editors' Choice** *—P.G. (8/1/2005)*

Raptor Ridge 2003 Reserve Pinot Noir (Willamette Valley) $29. Big and flat out delicious, this clean, appealing wine sports sweet raspberry and bing cherry fruit, high-toned aromatics and a lively, crisp mouthfeel. Well-made and high octane (15.3%). **90** *—P.G. (8/1/2005)*

Raptor Ridge 2000 Shea Vineyard Pinot Noir (Willamette Valley) $35. 86 *—M.S. (7/1/2003)*

Raptor Ridge 2003 Yamhill County Cuvée Pinot Noir (Willamette Valley) $18. Pretty cherry candy color, with flavors to follow. This is a fruit basket of a wine, friendly, light, and flavorful. A multi-vineyard, barrel-aged blend. **88** *—P.G. (8/1/2005)*

RAVENSWOOD

Ravenswood 2003 Vintners Blend Cabernet Sauvignon (California) $10. A little rough, but this is a pretty good price for a varietally correct wine with some distinction. It shows real Cab character in the blackberry, coffee, and herb flavors that finish dry. **84** *—S.H. (12/1/2005)*

USA

Ravenswood 2003 Vintners Blend Chardonnay (California) $10. Fruity, semisweet and heavily oaked, this bland Chardonnay has too much unnatural wood. **82** *—S.H. (8/1/2005)*

Ravenswood 1997 Vintners Blend Merlot (California) $11. 85 *(11/15/1999)*

Ravenswood 2002 Vintners Blend Merlot (California) $10. You get a big bang for your buck here. It's a terrifically fruity wine, packed with black cherry and blackberry flavors that are long and persistent through the finish. Soft in tannins, and so ripely sweet you could pour it over vanilla ice cream, but it's a dry wine. **86** *—S.H. (9/1/2004)*

Ravenswood 1999 Icon Rhône Red Blend (Sonoma County) $20. 84 *—S.H. (7/1/2002)*

Ravenswood 2000 Zinfandel (Lodi) $15. 85 *—S.H. (5/1/2003)*

Ravenswood 2000 Zinfandel (Napa Valley) $17. 87 *(5/1/2003)*

Ravenswood 1999 Zinfandel (Mendocino) $14. 87 *—D.T. (3/1/2002)*

Ravenswood 1999 Zinfandel (Napa Valley) $15. 88 *—D.T. (3/1/2002)*

Ravenswood 1999 Zinfandel (Sonoma County) $15. 86 *—S.H. (12/15/2001)*

Ravenswood 2001 Barricia Zinfandel (Sonoma Valley) $35. 87 *(11/1/2003)*

Ravenswood 1999 Barricia Zinfandel (Sonoma Valley) $30. 89 *—D.T. (3/1/2002)*

Ravenswood 2001 Belloni Zinfandel (Russian River Valley) $35. 88 *(11/1/2003)*

Ravenswood 2002 Big River Zinfandel (Alexander Valley) $30. Less ripe than Ravenswood's other Sonoma Zins, with an herbal edge to the cherry and cocoa flavors, and not as balanced. The tannins are more pronounced, too. **86** *—S.H. (3/1/2005)*

Ravenswood 2000 Big River Zinfandel (Alexander Valley) $35. 85 *—S.H. (5/1/2003)*

Ravenswood 2002 Cooke Zinfandel (Sonoma County) $50. Compared to Ravenswood's Monte Rossa, a shade less intense and concentrated, but more elegant. Dark and aromatic, with briary herb and tobacco flavors and, under the tannins, blackberries and coffee. Should develop further by 2006. **89** *—S.H. (3/1/2005)*

Ravenswood 1997 Cooke Zinfandel (Sonoma Valley) $28. 89 *—S.H. (5/1/2000)*

Ravenswood 2001 Dickerson Zinfandel (Napa Valley) $35. 88 *(11/1/2003)*

Ravenswood 1999 Dickerson Zinfandel (Napa Valley) $30. 90 *—D.T. (3/1/2002)*

Ravenswood 1997 Lodi Zinfandel (Sonoma County) $14. 88 *—P.G. (11/15/1999)*

Ravenswood 2001 Monte Rosso Zinfandel (Sonoma Valley) $35. 86 *(11/1/2003)*

Ravenswood 1999 Monte Rosso Zinfandel (Sonoma Valley) $30. 89 *—D.T. (3/1/2002)*

Ravenswood 2001 Old Hill Zinfandel (Sonoma Valley) $46. 89 *(11/1/2003)*

Ravenswood 1999 Old Hill Zinfandel (Sonoma Valley) $36. 92 *—D.T. (3/1/2002)*

Ravenswood 2001 Teldeschi Zinfandel (Dry Creek Valley) $35. 87 *(11/1/2003)*

Ravenswood 1999 Teldeschi Zinfandel (Dry Creek Valley) $30. 90 *—D.T. (3/1/2002)*

Ravenswood 2003 Vintners Blend Zinfandel (California) $10. Textbook rural, rustic California Zin, meaning it's dry, peppery, and herbal-fruity, with firm tannins and modest alcohol. Shows Ravenswood's deft hand at blending statewide grapes. **84** *—S.H. (12/1/2005)*

RAYE'S HILL

Raye's Hill 2000 Merlot (Anderson Valley) $26. Lots of smoky oak has been lavished on this wine, which can't quite overcome a certain leanness. Beneath the wood is a tannic, basic-cherry-flavored Merlot, with an edge of coffee and sage. But it's elegant and clean. **85** *—S.H. (6/1/2004)*

Raye's Hill 2003 Hein Vineyard Pinot Blanc (Anderson Valley) $18. There are lush and ripe peach and mango flavors in this spicy wine, and it's dry, with a thick, heavy texture. Finishes with a massive fruitiness. **84** *—S.H. (12/15/2004)*

Raye's Hill 2001 Pinot Noir (Anderson Valley) $15. Earthy and simple, with some berry and spice flavors. Dry and tart. **83** *—S.H. (12/15/2004)*

Raye's Hill 1999 Pinot Noir (Russian River Valley) $20. 84 *(10/1/2002)*

Raye's Hill 1998 Pinot Noir (Anderson Valley) $24. 88 *—S.H. (5/1/2002)*

Raye's Hill 2002 Wightman House Vineyard Pinot Noir (Anderson Valley) $22. Easy drinking, and showing some interest in the cola, dried spice, mocha, hay, and menthol aromas. Turns rather sharp in acidity in the mouth, and lacks the stuffing to age. Drink up. **85** *(11/1/2004)*

RAYMOND

Raymond 2001 Amberhill Cabernet Sauvignon (California) $10. Shows real attributes of a fine Cab, with a slightly fierce edge tugging it down a bit. Still, the black currant flavors, oak, and fine tannins are very nice. **84** *—S.H. (10/1/2004)*

Raymond 2002 Estates Cabernet Sauvignon (Napa Valley) $20. Marked by strong, drying tannins, this wine has blackberry, herb, and tobacco flavors and citrusy acids. Between the tannins and the acids, it's a tough, astringent Cab. Might benefit from a year or two of aging. **85** *—S.H. (11/1/2005)*

Raymond 1999 Generations Cabernet Sauvignon (Napa Valley) $65. One of the final releases of the '99 vintage, this wine is just beginning to show its age. It's quite soft and delicate, although there remains a scour of tough tannin. The flavors were once of blackberries but they're starting to break up into dried herbs and coffee. An interesting wine at an awkward age that will appeal to connoisseurs. **89** *—S.H. (8/1/2004)*

Raymond 1998 Generations Cabernet Sauvignon (Napa Valley) $80. 86 *—S.H. (6/1/2002)*

Raymond 1996 Generations Cabernet Sauvignon (Napa Valley) $50. 92 *—S.H. (7/1/2000)*

Raymond 2001 Reserve Cabernet Sauvignon (St. Helena) $50. Classic Napa in balance, classic Raymond in user-friendliness, and classic '01 in overall quality. This is a well-structured Cab, infused with cassis and oak, and possesses the tannins and acids for the long haul. Drinking well now, and will easily last through 2010. **90** *—S.H. (6/1/2005)*

Raymond 2000 Reserve Cabernet Sauvignon (Napa Valley) $40. 92 Editors' Choice *—S.H. (11/15/2003)*

Raymond 1997 Reserve Cabernet Sauvignon (Napa Valley) $23. 90 *—S.H. (3/1/2000)*

Raymond 2003 Chardonnay (Monterey) $13. Here's a super-drinkable Chard. It's rich in jazzy lime custard, mango, peach, and vanilla honey flavors, accompanied by bright acidity, all of it wrapped in a creamy texture. This is a great price for such a good wine. **88 Best Buy** *—S.H. (11/1/2005)*

Raymond 2002 Estate Chardonnay (Monterey) $10. Three cheers to Raymond for producing a Chard this nice at such a great price. It's rich in tropical fruit, peach, and oak flavors, with opulent spices, and is very dry. What a super value! **87 Best Buy** *—S.H. (12/1/2004)*

Raymond 2000 Estates Chardonnay (Monterey) $12. 86 *—S.H. (9/1/2002)*

Raymond 1998 Generations Chardonnay (Napa Valley) $30. 83 *(7/1/2001)*

Raymond 1996 Generations Chardonnay (Napa Valley) $28. 89 *(10/1/1999)*

Raymond 2001 Reserve Chardonnay (Napa Valley) $19. 90 *—S.H. (12/1/2003)*

Raymond 1998 Reserve Chardonnay (Napa Valley) $15. 85 *(6/1/2000)*

Raymond 2001 Merlot (California) $10. A serviceable red wine with some nice features for the price. It's dry and balanced, with blackberry and herb flavors. **84** *—S.H. (12/15/2004)*

Raymond 2000 Amberhill Merlot (California) $9. 85 *—S.H. (12/1/2003)*

Raymond 2000 Reserve Merlot (Napa Valley) $22. 91 *—S.H. (12/31/2003)*

Raymond 1997 Reserve Merlot (Napa Valley) $22. 89 *—S.H. (7/1/2000)*

Raymond 2003 Reserve Sauvignon Blanc (Napa Valley) $12. Simple and thin, with slightly sweet peach and lemonade flavors. Finishes with a clean scour of acidity. **83** *—S.H. (11/1/2005)*

Raymond 2001 Reserve Sauvignon Blanc (Napa Valley) $11. 87 Best Buy *—S.H. (10/1/2003)*

Raymond 1998 Reserve Sauvignon Blanc (Napa Valley) $11. 86 *—S.H. (9/1/2000)*

Raymond 1998 Reserve Zinfandel (Napa Valley) $16. 81 *—D.T. (3/1/2002)*

Raymond Burr 2000 Cabernet Sauvignon (Dry Creek Valley) $38. 84 *—S.H. (11/15/2003)*

Raymond Burr 1998 Cabernet Sauvignon (Dry Creek Valley) $38. 86 *—J.M. (6/1/2002)*

RDLR

RDLR 2002 Syrah (Mendocino County) $24. Super-dark and extracted, and soft in acids, this is a Syrah that seems to come from a hot climate. The flavors are of blackberries, coffee, and tobacco, with a tarry element, and finish very dry. **86** *—S.H. (9/1/2005)*

RED NEWT CELLARS

Red Newt Cellars 2002 Riesling (Finger Lakes) $13. 88 Best Buy *—J.C. (8/1/2003)*

RED SKY

Red Sky 2002 Syrah (Washington) $25. Although at first glance this wine doesn't impress, it seems to get better every time you go back to it, fleshing out with air and slowly revealing more and more nuance. In fact, this rating may seem conservative in a couple of years. Toasty and constructed by oak, gradually showing spice and blackberry flavors that linger delicately on the finish. **87** *(9/1/2005)*

RED ZEPPELIN

Red Zeppelin 2003 Syrah (Central Coast) $14. Rustic, edgy, and rather sharp, this Syrah has some dark fruit flavors right next to green, minty ones. It's dry. **83** *—S.H. (12/1/2005)*

REDWOOD

Redwood 2000 Cabernet Sauvignon (California) $9. 85 Best Buy *—S.H. (6/1/2003)*

Redwood 2000 Merlot (California) $9. 85 Best Buy *—S.H. (8/1/2003)*

REED

Reed 2000 Fralich Vineyard Syrah (Paso Robles) $29. 89 *—S.H. (12/1/2002)*

REFLECTIONS

Reflections 2000 Meritage (Alexander Valley) $55. Opens with herbal, earthy aromas, and drinks tannic and a bit thin in fruit, although oak adds softening and sweetening notes. Drink now. **84** *—S.H. (6/1/2005)*

REGUSCI

Regusci 2002 Merlot (Napa Valley) $40. There's something warm-hearted about this wine. Maybe it's the velvety softness, or the touch of toasted wood, or the flavors that suggest sun-ripened blackberries. Whatever it is, it's easy and delicious, but quite complex. **91** *—S.H. (10/1/2005)*

REININGER

Reininger 2002 Carmenère (Walla Walla (WA)) $35. This is 100% Carmenère; a delicious, chewy, tart, racy wine with strong herbal elements and lots of black pepper. Woody and herbal, with powerful tannins, it needs some breathing time; then it opens out and lengthens through a rich, silky finish. **90** *—P.G. (12/15/2005)*

Reininger 1999 Red Table Wine Red Blend (Walla Walla (WA)) $20. 88 *—P.G. (12/31/2001)*

Reininger 1999 Syrah (Walla Walla (WA)) $29. 86 *(11/1/2001)*

RENAISSANCE

Renaissance 1998 Estate Bottled Chardonnay (North Yuba) $17. 82 *(6/1/2000)*

Renaissance 1997 Première Cuvée Chardonnay (North Yuba) $35. 85 *(7/1/2001)*

Renaissance 1999 Mediterranean Red (North Yuba) $21. 81 *—S.H. (12/1/2001)*

Renaissance 1999 Zinfandel (North Yuba) $19. 81 *—S.H. (11/15/2001)*

RENARD

Renard 2000 Arroyo Vineyards Syrah (Napa Valley) $28. Nowhere near as lush or complex as the Santa Rita Hills bottling, but still a good wine. Grown in Calistoga, it is ultra-ripe, brimming with plum pudding and blackberry flavors. The alcohol is high, and the wine finishes soft, with a touch of Porty raisins. **86** *—S.H. (2/1/2004)*

Renwood 2002 Sierra Series Barbera (Sierra Foothills) $10. Fairly light in color and body for a Barbera, just a little fleshier than a good Pinot Noir, although the flavors are much different. Plums, tobacco, and mocha describe them nicely. A nice sipper for Italian fare. **85** *—S.H. (6/1/2004)*

RENWOOD

Renwood 2001 Orange Muscat (Shenandoah Valley (CA)) $12. 87 *—S.H. (12/1/2002)*

Renwood NV Port (Sierra Foothills) $15. Made from traditional Port, this wine is rather like a good tawny. It's very sweet, with compellingly delicious dark chocolate, coffee, cherry pie, and spicy flavors, and a smooth, mellow texture. Not an ager, so enjoy now. **88** *—S.H. (6/1/2004)*

Renwood 2000 Syrah (Amador County) $25. 87 *—S.H. (2/1/2003)*

USA

Renwood 2003 Select Series Rosé Syrah (California) $9. Thin in flavor, with watered-down strawberry and raspberry, but dry and clean, and zesty in acidity. Nice for a casual lunch. **83** —*S.H. (10/1/2004)*

Renwood 2001 Sierra Series Syrah (Sierra Foothills) $12. 86 —*S.H. (2/1/2003)*

Renwood 1999 Sierra Series Syrah (California) $12. 84 *(10/1/2001)*

Renwood 2001 Viognier (Shenandoah Valley (CA)) $25. 88 —*S.H. (12/15/2002)*

Renwood 2002 Select Series Viognier (Lodi) $NA. Simple and a little spritzy with effervescence, a pleasant wine with bubblegummy, spicy flavors and good acidity. Easy to drink, with a quick finish. **83** —*S.H. (6/1/2004)*

Renwood 2001 Sierra Series Viognier (California) $12. 85 —*S.H. (5/1/2003)*

Renwood 2001 Zinfandel (Fiddletown) $25. As big as Zin gets, displaying massive flavors of all sorts of wild forest berries, mocha, coffee, and an array of oriental spices. The lush tannins are the perfect frame for all that flavor. Rather hot with alcohol on the finish. **90** —*S.H. (6/1/2004)*

Renwood 1997 D'Agostini Bros Zinfandel (Shenandoah Valley (CA)) $30. 87 —*P.G. (11/15/1999)*

Renwood 1999 D'Agostini Bros Zinfandel (Amador County) $30. 88 —*D.T. (3/1/2002)*

Renwood 2001 Grandmére Zinfandel (Amador County) $25. The tannins are so ripe and sweet, so soft and intricate, in this decadently fruity, feminine wine. It has flavors of ripe blackberries, dusted with cocoa and sprinkled with tangerine zest. This is seriously good stuff, and impossible to resist. **92** —*S.H. (6/1/2004)*

Renwood 1999 Grandmére Zinfandel (Amador County) $25. 87 —*D.T. (3/1/2002)*

Renwood 1997 Grandmére Zinfandel (Amador County) $25. 81 *(3/1/2001)*

Renwood 2000 Grandpére Zinfandel (Shenandoah Valley (CA)) $32. 86 —*S.H. (2/1/2003)*

Renwood 2001 Jack Rabbit Flat Zinfandel (Amador County) $30. The 2000 Jack Rabbit was very good. This one, from a better vintage, is much better. It's the perfect example of a mountain Zin that's big and bold, with its pure flavors of cherry, mocha, raspberry tart, coffee, vanilla, and dusty spices that flood the mouth, and finish with a tannic bite. **91** —*S.H. (6/1/2004)*

Renwood 1999 Jack Rabbit Flat Zinfandel (Amador County) $30. 86 —*D.T. (3/1/2002)*

Renwood 2000 Old Vine Zinfandel (Amador County) $20. 87 —*S.H. (12/1/2002)*

Renwood 2002 Sierra Series Zinfandel (Sierra Foothills) $10. From a producer that's shown a deft hand at this variety, a good interpretation at an everyday price. It's balanced and even, with earthy, bitter cherry, and herb flavors, and completely dry. **85** —*S.H. (12/15/2004)*

RETZLAFF

Retzlaff 2000 Cabernet Sauvignon-Merlot (Livermore Valley) $38. 83 —*S.H. (11/15/2003)*

Retzlaff 1998 Estate Bottled Chardonnay (Livermore Valley) $16. 85 *(6/1/2000)*

REVERIE

Reverie 2000 Special Reserve Estate Cabernet Blend (Diamond Mountain) $55. Compelling for its ripeness, balance, harmony, and the way those tannins work to pull it all together. This Cab-based wine has it all, blackberries, cherries, cocoa, great acidity, wonderful oak. Ultimately, it's the soft, intricate tannic structure that makes it complex. **91** —*S.H. (10/1/2005)*

REX HILL

Rex Hill 1993 Champagne Blend (Oregon) $24. 86 —*P.G. (12/1/2000)*

Rex Hill 1999 Chardonnay (Willamette Valley) $17. 88 —*S.H. (8/1/2002)*

Rex Hill 2003 Unwooded Chardonnay (Willamette Valley) $16. It's all about the fruit here, with a mix of tropical flavors across a broad, friendly palate. Not a California-style fruit-bomb, but fresh and plenty ripe. **86** —*P.G. (8/1/2005)*

Rex Hill 2001 Unwooded Chardonnay (Willamette Valley) $17. Following the Aussie lead, this unwooded wine is straightforward and oak-free. The fruit is simple and dry, like a crisp bite of an apple, and the finish has a little bit of spice to it. **87** —*P.G. (2/1/2004)*

Rex Hill 1997 Pinot Gris (Willamette Valley) $12.5. 84 — *(8/1/1999)*

Rex Hill 2001 Pinot Gris (Willamette Valley) $14. Clean, varietal, and almost steely in its concentration. Hinting at citrus and mineral, it is subtly persistent. **88 Best Buy** —*P.G. (2/1/2004)*

Rex Hill 1999 Pinot Gris (Willamette Valley) $14. 84 —*S.H. (8/1/2002)*

Rex Hill 2002 Carabella Vineyard Pinot Gris (Oregon) $28. This is the best of the new Rex Hill lineup, a perfectly ripened, beautifully balanced wine with an appealing mix of tart fruit, mineral, and spice. **90** —*P.G. (2/1/2004)*

Rex Hill 2003 Jacob-Hart Vineyard Pinot Gris (Willamette Valley) $24. Medium-bodied with spice, citrus, and melon flavors, this vineyard designate keeps its focus and finishes with a nice lift of savory spice. **88** *—P.G. (8/1/2005)*

Rex Hill 1999 Jacob-Hart Vineyard Reserve Pinot Gris (Oregon) $18. 88 *—S.H. (8/1/2002)*

Rex Hill 2002 Reserve Pinot Gris (Oregon) $21. New label, new winemaker and new lineup of vineyard-designated Pinot Gris in 2002, beginning with this very ripe, round, and flavorful reserve. There is more fleshy fruit than in previous vintages, but the wine retains its balance, elegance and varietal character. **89** *—P.G. (2/1/2004)*

Rex Hill 2000 Reserve Pinot Gris (Oregon) $18. 90 *—S.H. (8/1/2002)*

Rex Hill 2002 Pinot Noir (Willamette Valley) $24. Light and tight, showing some vanilla/cocoa scents and feeble flavors of tea leaf and sour cherry. **84** *(11/1/2004)*

Rex Hill 1999 Pinot Noir (Willamette Valley) $24. 85 *—S.H. (8/1/2002)*

Rex Hill 2002 Carabella Vineyard Pinot Noir (Oregon) $52. A terrific vineyard that expresses itself here with a complex bouquet of floral, citrus, and sweet red fruits. There's a distinct citrus peel scent and follow-through flavors, leading into a ripe, succulent, sweet core of cranberry and cherry. Plenty of snap, shape, and definition in this classy effort. **90** *(11/1/2004)*

Rex Hill 2001 Dundee Hills Cuvée Pinot Noir (Oregon) $30. This is all forward, sweet fruit that tastes like strawberry preserves. Behind it is some milk chocolate and cream, but the flavors have not yet knit together. **86** *—P.G. (2/1/2004)*

Rex Hill 2002 Jacob-Hart Vineyard Pinot Noir (Oregon) $52. For whatever reasons, this did not show nearly as well as the rest of the strong lineup from Rex Hill in 2002. Perhaps just a bad bottle, but there were off, sweaty aromas, burnt and sour, and the flavors never came together; it felt awkward and incomplete. **84** *(11/1/2004)*

Rex Hill 2001 Jacob-Hart Vineyard Pinot Noir (Oregon) $52. Nice effort, a chewy mix of tangy red fruits, nicely complemented with spice and chocolatey oak. There is a milk chocolate smoothness in the mouth, which turns a bit flat at the end. **88** *—P.G. (2/1/2005)*

Rex Hill 2001 Kings Ridge Pinot Noir (Oregon) $17. This is simple and plain, but surprisingly sweet and extracted, with a fruity core of pretty cherries. Forward and fruit-driven, it's very well made for its price. **87** *—P.G. (2/1/2005)*

Rex Hill 2001 Maresh Vineyard Pinot Noir (Oregon) $52. This is a great vineyard, that delivers fruit that deserves to be showcased on its own. Precisely defined, tart fruit braced against sharp acids bring out the cranberry wild raspberry flavors; there is a sharp, spicy herbal streak as well, hinting at licorice or anise. Good concentration through a long finish. **91** *—P.G. (2/1/2005)*

Rex Hill 2001 Maresh Vineyard Loie's Block Pinot Noir (Oregon) $75. From the winery's oldest block of vines, this punches up the blue and black fruits a notch above the regular Maresh (pronounced marsh). There is a strong (perhaps a bit too strong) vanilla note, along with the vineyard's characteristic herbal/anise flavor. **90** *—P.G. (2/1/2005)*

Rex Hill 2001 Melrose Vineyard Pinot Noir (Oregon) $49. A rich, deeply colored wine that shows intense scents of spicy cranberry and cherry. Despite the sharp attack, in the mouth it tastes of young, grapey fruit; pleasant but light. **88** *—P.G. (2/1/2005)*

Rex Hill 2002 Reserve Pinot Noir (Oregon) $45. Tightly wound, it opens slowly into a solid, full-flavored, rather chunky style of Pinot laced with the flavors of cola, root beer, and vanilla. Plump and juicy, it's enjoyable rather than profound. **89** *(11/1/2004)*

Rex Hill 2000 Reserve Pinot Noir (Oregon) $48. A big wine, with forward, tough, chewy flavors of cherry cola and tea. Pleasant, but very light and simple in the finish. **87** *—P.G. (2/1/2004)*

Rex Hill 1997 Reserve Pinot Noir (Willamette Valley) $45. 83 *(11/15/1999)*

Rex Hill 2001 Seven Springs Vineyard Pinot Noir (Oregon) $49. This wine definitely hits the leafy, herbal notes hard. Tomato scents carry through on the palate, with a bit of peppery spice. **87** *—P.G. (2/1/2005)*

Rex Hill 2002 Southern Oregon Cuvée Pinot Noir (Oregon) $29. A light but very lively wine, with plums and herbs. Supple and elegant, it gives a lot of complex pleasure despite its modest weight. **88** *(11/1/2004)*

Rex Hill 2001 Weber Vineyards Pinot Noir (Oregon) $49. Supple, light, cherry-scented with some typical tomato leaf notes. The rough tannins are beginning to smooth out as the wine turns the corner from raw youth. Pleasant hints of mushroom in the finish. **88** *—P.G. (2/1/2005)*

Rex Hill 2002 Sauvignon Blanc (Oregon) $15. Sauv blanc has never quite taken hold in Oregon, but wines such as this make you wonder why not. Pretty and packed with honeydew, kiwi, gooseberry and beeswax, it brings lifted, high acid precision and a hint of minerality to the juicy, tangy bedrock citrus. **89** *—P.G. (2/1/2005)*

Rex Hill 2000 Sauvignon Blanc (Willamette Valley) $12. 88 *—S.H. (12/31/2002)*

REY SOL

Rey Sol 1999 Syrah (South Coast) $18. 86 *—S.H. (4/1/2002)*

REYNOLDS

Reynolds 2002 Reserve Cabernet Sauvignon (Stags Leap District) $89. Much better than Reynold's Napa bottling. Maybe it's Stags Leap, maybe block selection, but it's a true reserve, richer, denser, and more concentrated, complex, and rewarding. Deep in cassis and plum fruit, it's quite a tannic wine. Hold until 2007 and beyond. **91 Cellar Selection** *—S.H. (11/15/2005)*

USA

Reynolds 2003 Pinot Noir (Russian River Valley) $45. A year or two might benefit this very dry wine. It's crisply acidic and earthy, with flavors of sweet tobacco, espresso, bitter cherry, and fresh sage. Made in a lighter-bodied style, it's a versatile, elegant food wine. **86** *—S.H. (11/15/2005)*

Reynolds Family Winery 2001 Reserve Cabernet Sauvignon (Stags Leap District) $85. Beautifully combines layers of silky-smooth fruit—cassis and cherries—with spice notes of cinnamon and vanilla. A creamy texture and a long, richly tannic finish wrap up this impressive package. Drink now–2015. **91** *—J.C. (10/1/2004)*

Reynolds Family Winery 2002 Pinot Noir (Russian River Valley) $45. A hard wine to like. Smells like menthol and raisins, and drinks too sweet for a dry table wine. **82** *(11/1/2004)*

Reynolds Family Winery 2002 Persistence Red Blend (Napa Valley) $50. With Syrah blended into Bordeaux varieties, this wine has a dry mouthfeel that carries complexity from entry to finish. It's fruity, but young, and true to its southerly Oak Knoll terroir, which is harder, more tannic and acidic, than further north. Try holding for a year or two to soften and sweeten. **87** *—S.H. (11/15/2005)*

RIBOLI

Riboli 1997 Cabernet Sauvignon (Rutherford) $45. **81** *—J.M. (12/1/2001)*

RIDEAU

Rideau 2003 Reserve Chardonnay (Santa Barbara County) $48. A combination of intensely ripe fruit and lavish oak has created explosive mango, pineapple custard, and smoky vanilla flavors. This huge, New World Chard is almost over the top, but good acidity helps balance it. **87** *—S.H. (12/31/2005)*

Rideau 2004 In-Circle Cellar Club Le Fleur de Lis Rosé Pinot Noir (Santa Barbara County) $22. One of the fuller-bodied rosés you'll have this year, this copper-colored wine is fat, juicy and fruity. The tangerine and peach flavors are a little sweet and cloying. **83** *—S.H. (12/31/2005)*

Rideau 2004 Riesling (Santa Barbara County) $22. The winery probably intended this to be a kabinett-style, dryish wine, but it's sweet enough to be considered a dessert wine. It has apple, peach and wildflower flavors, with good acids. **85** *—S.H. (12/31/2005)*

Rideau 2003 Sangiovese (Central Coast) $28. With nearly 16% alcohol, this is a heady wine, but it's dry and balanced, and doesn't taste hot. There are very deep and attractive flavors of blackberries, set in a softly tannic, oak-tinged texture. A great barbecue wine. **88** *—S.H. (12/31/2005)*

Rideau 2003 Iris Estate Bon Temps Vineyard Syrah (Santa Ynez Valley) $55. Combines an intensely pepery note with dense plum-cake fruit and elevated (16.4%) alcohol, yet remains appealing thanks to a full, rich mouthfeel and supple tannins. The plum, dried spice, and pepper flavors mostly obscure the high alcohol, leading to a long, spicy finish. **87** *(9/1/2005)*

Rideau 2004 Iris Estate Viognier (Santa Ynez Valley) $48. White pepper sprinkled over guava and apricot fruit, drizzled with vanilla and a splash of citrusy lime juice— these are some of the flavors in this crisp, fresh, and tangy wine. It's delicious, elegant, and lush to the point of decadence. **90** *—S.H. (12/31/2005)*

RIDGE

Ridge 2001 Home Ranch Cabernet Sauvignon-Merlot (Santa Cruz Mountains) $60. Almost evenly divided between Cabernet Sauvignon and Merlot, this is a big mountain wine, filled with the flavors of ripe blackberries, blueberries, and oak. It's young in tannins and acids. It possesses an extraordinary sense of balance and intensity, but is probably best left to age until 2008. **93 Cellar Selection** *—S.H. (2/1/2005)*

Ridge 1997 Chardonnay (Santa Cruz Mountains) $28. **89** *(6/1/2000)*

Ridge 1997 Chardonnay (California) $17. **93** *—M.S. (10/1/1999)*

Ridge 1996 York Creek Petite Sirah (Spring Mountain) $20. **88** *—J.C. (11/1/1999)*

Ridge 1999 Geyserville Red Blend (Sonoma County) $30. **90** *—D.T. (3/1/2002)*

Ridge 2001 Monte Bello Red Blend (Santa Cruz Mountains) $120. Without doubt this is a wine to cellar. It's massive in flavor, with the purist black currant and cassis fruit you can imagine, and the huge plaster of sweet oak is perfectly balanced. Then there are the tannins. They're fine and complex, but gritty. There's an astringency throughout that a great steak will cut through, but it would be infanticide to open this before, say, 2010. Should improve through 2020 and beyond. **97 Cellar Selection** *—S.H. (4/1/2005)*

Ridge 1997 Lytton Estate Syrah (Dry Creek Valley) $28. **89** *—S.H. (10/1/1999)*

Ridge 2001 Zinfandel (Paso Robles) $25. **88** *(11/1/2003)*

Ridge 1997 Dusi Ranch-Late Picked Zinfandel (Paso Robles) $22. **91** *—J.C. (9/1/1999)*

Ridge 1998 Geyserville Zinfandel (Sonoma County) $30. **90** *—P.G. (3/1/2001)*

Ridge 2001 Llewelyn Zinfandel (Sonoma County) $22. **90 Editors' Choice** *(11/1/2003)*

Ridge 2000 Lytton Springs Zinfandel (California) $30. **93** *—S.H. (9/1/2002)*

Ridge 1997 Lytton Springs Zinfandel (Dry Creek Valley) $28. **93** *—J.C. (9/1/1999)*

USA

Ridge 2001 Sonoma Station Zinfandel (Sonoma County) $18. 88 *(11/1/2003)*

Ridge 2002 Spring Mountain District Zinfandel (Napa Valley) $24. With a little Petite Sirah, this is a firm, fairly tannic wine. It has a deep core of black cherry and cocoa, with hints of sage. The size suggests aging through 2008, but it will be delicious now with roast tenderloin of pork in a sauce made from the wine. 89 *—S.H. (4/1/2005)*

RIDGEFIELD

Ridgefield 2002 Pinot Gris (Red Mountain) $9. This is a distinctive style of Pinot Gris, harder and more herbaceous than either the soft, tropical California bottlings or the fleshy, pear-flavored wines of Oregon. This is closer to a sémillon, with tart citrus fruit and citrus rind flavors, a spicy middle, and some firm tannins. **88 Best Buy** *—P.G. (9/1/2004)*

RIO DULCE

Rio Dulce NV White Red Wine (California) $4. Not red, but more of a rosé, with intriguing aromas of raspberry sorbet and vanilla. Soda-poppy, with crisp acids, raspberry flavors, and a semi-sweet finish. **84 Best Buy** *—S.H. (12/31/2004)*

RIO SECO

Rio Seco 1999 Rio Seco Vineyard Syrah (Paso Robles) $16. 83 *—S.H. (12/1/2002)*

Rio Seco 1999 Rio Seco Vineyard Zinfandel (Paso Robles) $24. 82 *—S.H. (11/1/2002)*

RIOS-LOVELL ESTATE WINERY

Rios-Lovell Estate Winery 2000 Petite Sirah (Livermore Valley) $22. Smells funky and herbal, with sweet cough medicine flavors and a gluey texture. 82 *—S.H. (3/1/2004)*

RISTOW ESTATE

Ristow Estate 2001 Quinta de Pedras Vineyard Cabernet Sauvignon (Napa Valley) $64. How a Cab can be completely soft yet filled with power is a wonder of modern winemaking technique. This is such a wine. It's dry and dustily grippy in tannins, with a finely astringent finish, and will easily hold for a decade. Now, a good steak will cut through the density and coax out the cassis and cherry fruit. 93 *—S.H. (12/31/2005)*

RITCHIE CREEK

Ritchie Creek 1999 Cabernet Sauvignon (Spring Mountain) $58. 87 *—S.H. (11/15/2002)*

RIVER ROAD VINEYARDS

River Road Vineyards 2001 Proprietors Reserve Chardonnay (Russian River Valley) $14. 85 *—S.H. (6/1/2003)*

RIVER'S EDGE

River's Edge 2002 Pinot Noir (Umpqua Valley) $16. This earthy, oaky wine carries middle of the road flavors into a short, hot, astringent finish. 85 *(11/1/2004)*

River's Edge 2002 Barrel Select Pinot Noir (Umpqua Valley) $21. There's plenty of barrel all right, and the spicy, vanilla, and toasted coconut flavors to prove it. The fruit is a bit dilute and slightly baked, with hints of clove. 85 *(11/1/2004)*

River's Edge 2002 Bradley Vineyard Pinot Noir (Umpqua Valley) $18. Mint and wintergreen notes are evident, and a bit of rubbery Band-Aid. But the wine has better fruit than its siblings, showing more ripeness, a solid mid palate, and good spicy highlights. 86 *(11/1/2004)*

River's Edge 2000 Elkton Vineyard Pinot Noir (Umpqua Valley) $19. 87 *—P.G. (12/31/2002)*

RIVERSIDE

Riverside 2002 Cabernet Sauvignon (California) $8. Heavy and gluey, with an odd medicinal flavor and a cherry cough drop finish. 81 *—S.H. (12/15/2005)*

Riverside 1997 Syrah (California) $8. 83 *(10/1/2001)*

Riverside NV White Zinfandel (California) $6. Frankly sweet, this simple wine is ripe in strawberry and raspberry flavors, and has decent acidity. 82 *—S.H. (12/15/2005)*

ROAR

Roar 2002 Pinot Noir (Santa Lucia Highlands) $31. Starts off with minty, cherry, and cinnamon aromas, then reveals rich flavors of roasted coffee, cherry, and oak. Creamy and lush on the palate, and dry. 86 *(11/1/2004)*

Roar 2002 Pisoni Vineyard Pinot Noir (Santa Lucia Highlands) $48. Dark as a Syrah, and with the weight of a big red, this wine shows massively ripe aromas and flavors of meat, blackberries, coffee, and oak, and rich, gentle tannins. It's a very good wine but it doesn't really have the delicacy you expect in a Pinot Noir. 87 *—S.H. (11/1/2004)*

Roar 2002 Rosella's Vineyard Pinot Noir (Santa Lucia Highlands) $44. Lots of charm. Once the sulfur blows off, you get ripe red and black cherry, vanilla, oak, and spice notes, wrapped in a silky texture with bright, crisp acids. Notable for its balanced and long finish. 88 *(11/1/2004)*

Roar 2003 Syrah (Santa Lucia Highlands) $32. Big and ripe on the nose, with scents of caramel, vanilla, and red berries, but above all, alcohol. If you are less sensitive to high alcohol levels than we are, you may like this flashy Syrah more than we did. **83** *(9/1/2005)*

ROBERT CRAIG

Robert Craig 1997 Affinity Bordeaux Blend (Napa Valley) $44. **92** *(11/1/2000)*

Robert Craig 1997 Cabernet Sauvignon (Mount Veeder) $44. **91** *(11/1/2000)*

Robert Craig 2002 Cabernet Sauvignon (Mount Veeder) $55. Drinkable now despite lush, firm tannins, this Cab lets its fruit star. The black currant, black cherry pie, mocha, and vanilla spice flavors are delicious and compelling, and the finish is dry, elegant, and upscale. **91** *—S.H. (12/1/2005)*

Robert Craig 2001 Cabernet Sauvignon (Mount Veeder) $50. Tighter and more tannic than this winery's Howell Mountain bottling, and more concentrated in blackberry and cherry essence. This is an extraordinarily young wine that defines the vintage's potential. It requires patience, but the balance is such that it's a lock for the long haul. Cellar until 2010 and beyond. **93 Cellar Selection** *—S.H. (10/1/2004)*

Robert Craig 1997 Chardonnay (Carneros) $24. **93** *—M.S. (10/1/1999)*

Robert Craig 2000 Chardonnay (Russian River Valley) $24. **86** *—S.H. (2/1/2003)*

Robert Craig 1997 Syrah (Paso Robles) $24. **86** *(3/1/2000)*

Robert Craig 1999 Syrah (Paso Robles) $28. **86** *(11/1/2001)*

ROBERT HALL

Robert Hall 2003 Cabernet Sauvignon (Paso Robles) $18. Simple, soft, and intensely fruity, this Cab is bursting with the ripest red cherry, tobacco, cocoa, spice, and smoke flavors. It's easy to imagine sipping this with grilled meats and poultry. **84** *—S.H. (11/1/2005)*

Robert Hall 2004 Chardonnay (Paso Robles) $16. You'll find good flavors of apples and peaches in this soft, dryish wine, as well as an earthiness. It has some oaky notes, and finishes with a touch of citrus. **84** *—S.H. (11/1/2005)*

Robert Hall 2003 Hall Ranch Meritage (Paso Robles) $34. Here's a wine that's very soft in acids, with melted tannins. It's a little flabby, but nicely dry, with ripe flavors of blackberries, green olives, coffee, and spices. Will go well with a grilled steak. **84** *—S.H. (12/31/2005)*

Robert Hall 2002 Merlot (Paso Robles) $18. A little hot and flabby, but with some lively cherry-berry flavors, this innocuous Merlot will back up most anything that needs a dry red. **84** *—S.H. (11/1/2005)*

Robert Hall 2003 Rhône de Robles Rhône Red Blend (Paso Robles) $18. This dark, awkward wine is a little sharp around the edges, with a rough earthiness framing herb and berry flavors. **82** *—S.H. (11/1/2005)*

Robert Hall 2004 Sauvignon Blanc (Paso Robles) $14. Although this dry, Musque-clone wine will go with just about anything, try it with a smoky, honey-baked ham sandwich on a lightly toasted sourdough baguette, slathered with Dijon mustard and garlicky mayo, and layered with sliced fresh tomato, butter lettuce, roasted red pepper, and crumbly chevre. My goodness, pure heaven. **85** *—S.H. (11/1/2005)*

Robert Hall 2002 Syrah (Paso Robles) $18. An easy to like Syrah with good character. It's fruity in cherry and chocolate flavors, and very dry, with a pepper and spice aftertaste. **85** *—S.H. (12/1/2004)*

Robert Hall 2001 Hall Ranch Syrah (Paso Robles) $30. From the east side of the appellation, a polished, supple wine, with easy tannins and the flavors of red and black cherries. Has interesting nuances of coffee, plums, and spices, too. **87** *—S.H. (12/1/2004)*

Robert Hall 1999 Huerhuero Creek Syrah (Paso Robles) $26. **84** *—S.H. (12/1/2002)*

Robert Hall 2000 Zinfandel (Paso Robles) $22. **87** *—S.H. (11/1/2002)*

ROBERT HUNTER

Robert Hunter 1997 Brut de Noirs (Sonoma Valley) $35. This is a sharp, awkward wine, in which the lees stick out. It's fruity and doughy, but lacks elegance. **82** *—S.H. (12/31/2005)*

Robert Hunter 1994 Brut de Noirs (Sonoma Valley) $30. **88** *—S.H. (12/1/2000)*

ROBERT KARL

Robert Karl 2000 Cabernet Sauvignon (Columbia Valley (WA)) $20. **87** *—P.G. (12/31/2003)*

Robert Karl 2002 Sauvignon Blanc (Columbia Valley (WA)) $10. **86** *—P.G. (12/31/2003)*

ROBERT MONDAVI

Robert Mondavi 1996 Cabernet Sauvignon (Napa Valley) $26. **91** *—L.W. (10/1/1999)*

Robert Mondavi 2001 Cabernet Sauvignon (Stags Leap District) $40. There's a leathery edge to the blackberry, blueberry, and oak flavors, and a bigger, more full-bodied texture. The tannins also are thicker. This is the least accessible of Mondavi's new Cabs, but such is the concentration that aging should be no problem at all. Drink now through 2015. **92** *—S.H. (10/1/2004)*

Robert Mondavi 2001 Cabernet Sauvignon (Napa Valley) $25. Showcases the restraint in fruit that characterizes Mondavi, and so different from many of his neighbors' lavishly ripe Cabs. The hallmark is elegance and drinkability, with its moderated berry flavors, earthiness and robust tannins. Should age well through the decade. **89** *—S.H. (10/1/2004)*

Robert Mondavi 2000 Cabernet Sauvignon (Napa Valley) $30. 92 Editors' Choice *—S.H. (11/15/2003)*

Robert Mondavi 1999 Cabernet Sauvignon (Oakville) $50. 90 *—S.H. (2/1/2003)*

Robert Mondavi 1998 Cabernet Sauvignon (Stags Leap District) $50. 91 *—S.H. (12/1/2001)*

Robert Mondavi 1996 Cabernet Sauvignon (Stags Leap District) $45. 86 *—S.H. (9/1/1999)*

Robert Mondavi 1996 30th Anniversary To Kalon Cabernet Sauvignon (Napa Valley) $NA. 100 percent To Kalon [including Detert and Horton]. Similar to the '91. Rather stubborn at first. The fruit is there, the balance, acidity, oak, but hasn't knitted together. Disjointed but distinguished. Could really surprise later on. 2010 and beyond. **89 Cellar Selection** *—S.H. (6/1/2005)*

Robert Mondavi 1997 Coastal Cabernet Sauvignon (North Coast) $13. 86 *—S.H. (2/1/2000)*

Robert Mondavi 1998 Equilibrium Cabernet Sauvignon (Stags Leap District) $85. 92 *—S.H. (12/1/2001)*

Robert Mondavi 1998 Marjorie's Sunrise Cabernet Sauvignon (Oakville) $85. 95 *—S.H. (12/1/2001)*

USA

Robert Mondavi 2003 Private Selection Cabernet Sauvignon (California) $11. Very soft and a little sweet, this Cab shows forward flavors of black cherries and blackberries, and some sharp, edgy tannins. **83** *—S.H. (12/15/2005)*

Robert Mondavi 2001 Reserve Cabernet Sauvignon (Napa Valley) $125. Contains 67% To Kalon Vineyard fruit. Still a baby. Closed, brooding, very deep, very dry. Fabulous cassis fruit, a huge wine. Lots of delicious, sweet new oak. Superbly balanced, impressive. Drinkable now, but best 2010–2020. **94 Cellar Selection** *—S.H. (6/1/2005)*

Robert Mondavi 1999 Reserve Cabernet Sauvignon (Napa Valley) $125. 96 Cellar Selection *—S.H. (11/15/2002)*

Robert Mondavi 1998 Reserve Cabernet Sauvignon (Napa Valley) $125. 92 *—S.H. (12/1/2001)*

Robert Mondavi 1991 Reserve Cabernet Sauvignon (Napa Valley) $NA. 54% To Kalon. Showing good varietal character. Fresh, attractive. One of Genevieve Janssen's favorites. To me, on the first pour it was unyielding, tight, closed. After lots of time in the glass, became more forthcoming. Needs lots of decanting. Now-2016. **90 Cellar Selection** *—S.H. (6/1/2005)*

Robert Mondavi 1978 Reserve Cabernet Sauvignon (Napa Valley) $NA. Unknown % of To Kalon; the winemaker thinks "a big chunk, maybe most." Still good color, getting a pretty bouquet of old cabernet. Delicate, inviting, refined, not at all morbid. Very dry, lots of week cassis. Soft, distinguished, still lots of life ahead. Sweet vanilla, butter. Old claret. Now–2010. **94 Editors' Choice** *—S.H. (6/1/2005)*

Robert Mondavi 1999 To Kalon Reserve Cabernet Sauvignon (Oakville) $150. 94 Cellar Selection *—S.H. (2/1/2003)*

Robert Mondavi 1999 To Kalon Vineyard Reserve Cabernet Sauvignon (Napa Valley) $NA. Oaky. A bit backward, closed. Lots of primary fruit varietal character in the aroma. Coffee, smoke, ash, cedar. In the mouth, potent black currants, cassis, massive middle. Wonderful tannins, rich, ripe, sweet. The finish is long and intense. 2006–2020. **97 Editors' Choice** *—S.H. (6/1/2005)*

Robert Mondavi 1997 To Kalon Vineyard Reserve Cabernet Sauvignon (Napa Valley) $NA. Younger, bigger, tighter than the '96. Lots of currants up front; chocolate layer cake. Fairly tannic. A bit sharp in acids and lacks the elegance of '96. Should develop well after 2010. **92 Cellar Selection** *—S.H. (6/1/2005)*

Robert Mondavi 1997 Chardonnay (Napa Valley) $20. 87 *(6/1/2000)*

Robert Mondavi 2002 Chardonnay (Carneros) $25. It's all about ripe apples and oak in this crisp, elegant wine. Like biting into a fresh Granny Smith, that burst of acidic flavor startles, but is quickly softened by sweet oak. **90** *—S.H. (12/15/2004)*

Robert Mondavi 2001 Chardonnay (Carneros) $25. 87 *—S.H. (12/1/2003)*

Robert Mondavi 1999 Chardonnay (Carneros) $23. 86 *—S.H. (12/1/2001)*

Robert Mondavi 1997 Carneros District Chardonnay (Carneros) $23. 88 *(6/1/2000)*

Robert Mondavi 1999 Coastal Chardonnay (Central Coast) $NA. 87 Best Buy *—S.H. (5/1/2001)*

Robert Mondavi 2000 Huichica Hills Chardonnay (Carneros) $50. 92 *—S.H. (10/1/2003)*

Robert Mondavi 2003 Private Selection Chardonnay (Central Coast) $11. There's Monterey fruit in here, to judge by the rich lime zest flavor and crisp acidity. There's also a great deal of oak flavor in this easy, likeable Chardonnay. It finishes dry and clean. **84** *—S.H. (12/15/2005)*

Robert Mondavi 2001 Private Selection Chardonnay (Central Coast) $11. 83 *—S.H. (8/1/2003)*

Robert Mondavi 2000 Reserve Chardonnay (Napa Valley) $38. 91 *—S.H. (8/1/2003)*

Robert Mondavi 1997 Reserve Chardonnay (Napa Valley) $36. 90 *—S.H. (12/31/1999)*

Robert Mondavi 2001 Fumé Blanc (North Coast) $11. 83 *—S.H. (7/1/2003)*

Robert Mondavi 1997 Fumé Blanc (Napa Valley) $13. 83 *—M.S. (6/1/1999)*

Robert Mondavi 2003 Private Selection Fumé Blanc (North Coast) $11. Here's a wine of sophistication for those who like their whites ultra-dry and with some prickly acidity. The flavors are light but pleasant, suggesting grapefruit, melon, and fig. Mondavi's Fumé is especially notable for its balance. **86 Best Buy** *—S.H. (12/15/2005)*

Robert Mondavi 1997 Reserve To Kalon Fumé Blanc (Napa Valley) $NA. Breaking down. Somewhat vegetal. Some good citrus and passion-flower fruit remains. Interesting, but its prime is past. **84** *—S.H. (6/1/2005)*

Robert Mondavi 2002 To Kalon Vineyard I Block Fumé Blanc (Napa Valley) $65. Explosive. Like the Reserve Fumé on steroids. Tons of tropical fruit, persimmon, passion fruit, lime, and fig, with rich, bright acidity, all seamlessly married to oak. Showy, flashy, and flamboyant. **94 Editors' Choice** *—S.H. (6/1/2005)*

Robert Mondavi 2001 To Kalon Vineyard Reserve Fumé Blanc (Napa Valley) $35. You have to give Mondavi credit for sticking to the dry, acidic theme in this wine over the years. It's classic in its own way. Tart to the point of lemony astringency, almost raw, with a richer overlay of fine oak and lees. Really gets the juices flowing. **90** *—S.H. (12/15/2004)*

Robert Mondavi 1998 To Kalon Vineyard Reserve Fumé Blanc (Napa Valley) $28. 88 *—S.H. (11/15/2000)*

Robert Mondavi 2000 Unfiltered Fumé Blanc (Napa Valley) $19. 89 *(8/1/2002)*

Robert Mondavi 2001 Coastal Private Selection Johannisberg Riesling (Central Coast) $9. 84 *—S.H. (9/1/2003)*

Robert Mondavi 2003 Private Selection Johannisberg Riesling (Central Coast) $11. Slightly sweet, with honeyed flavors of flowers and white peach, this wine gets the job done with crisp acidity. **83** *—S.H. (9/1/2004)*

Robert Mondavi 1998 Malbec (Stags Leap District) $45. 89 *—S.H. (12/1/2001)*

Robert Mondavi 2000 Merlot (Napa Valley) $21. Opens with scents of green olives, sweaty leather, currants, and spice, in addition to smoky oak. On the palate, there is plenty of rich, polished blackberry flavor. The tannins poke up and are a bit hard, but they're nothing a good steak can't handle. Drink now. **87** *—S.H. (6/1/2004)*

Robert Mondavi 1998 Merlot (Napa Valley) $28. 87 *—S.H. (12/1/2001)*

Robert Mondavi 1997 Merlot (Carneros) $35. 87 *—S.H. (11/15/2000)*

Robert Mondavi 1999 Coastal Merlot (Central Coast) $11. 83 *—S.H. (5/1/2001)*

Robert Mondavi 2003 Private Selection Merlot (California) $11. Intensely jammy in blueberry and black cherry flavors, and sharp in young, juicy grape acidity, this basically dry wine has a lot of fruity ripeness in the finish, with a touch of cocoa and vanilla. **83** *—S.H. (12/15/2005)*

Robert Mondavi 2001 Moscato d'Oro Moscato (Napa Valley) $18. 88 *—S.H. (12/1/2003)*

Robert Mondavi 2004 Private Selection Pinot Grigio (California) $11. Definitely on the ripely sweet side, but nicely crisp in acids, this cocktail-style wine has rich and juicy flavors of pineapples, pears, figs, apples, and dusty spices. **85** *—S.H. (12/15/2005)*

Robert Mondavi 1997 Pinot Noir (Napa Valley) $19. 86 *(10/1/1999)*

Robert Mondavi 2002 Pinot Noir (Carneros) $35. Tasters found an off-smell that quickly blew off to reveal oaky, minty, cherry notes. The flavors suggest cherries, root beer, and Hawaiian punch. Very dry, silky, and crisp in acids. **86** *(11/1/2004)*

Robert Mondavi 2001 Pinot Noir (Carneros) $40. 88 *—S.H. (12/1/2003)*

Robert Mondavi 2000 Pinot Noir (Carneros) $40. 89 *(10/1/2002)*

Robert Mondavi 1999 Coastal Pinot Noir (Central Coast) $12. 83 *—S.H. (12/15/2000)*

Robert Mondavi 2000 Coastal Private Selection Pinot Noir (Central Coast) $13. 84 *(10/1/2002)*

Robert Mondavi 1999 PNX Pinot Noir (Carneros) $45. 91 *—S.H. (12/15/2001)*

Robert Mondavi 2002 Private Selection Pinot Noir (Central Coast) $11. Strawberries, cherries, smoke, and coffee flavors in this delicately structured, somewhat lean wine. It has good acidity and a pleasant mouthfeel. **85** *(11/1/2004)*

Robert Mondavi 2002 Reserve Pinot Noir (Napa Valley) $50. Everyone agreed on how nice this wine is, without being great. It's delicate and crisp in acids, offering pleasant sour cherry, tea, and charry flavors. Achieves elegance in the silky and racy finish. **87** *(11/1/2004)*

Robert Mondavi 2000 Reserve Pinot Noir (Napa Valley) $50. 87 *(10/1/2002)*

Robert Mondavi 1997 Reserve Pinot Noir (Napa Valley) $50. 89 *(10/1/1999)*

Robert Mondavi 1997 Sauvignon Blanc (Stags Leap District) $18. 89 *—S.H. (9/1/1999)*

Robert Mondavi 2002 Sauvignon Blanc (Stags Leap District) $23. If tart acidity and grassy Sauvignons are your thing, you'll love this. It's dry as dust, mouthwatering in acids and the flavors are solidly hay-like and gooseberry. The finish of sweet lemon and lime and sweet oak provide richness. **86** *—S.H. (12/15/2004)*

Robert Mondavi 1999 Sauvignon Blanc (Stags Leap District) $23. 86 *—S.H. (12/1/2001)*

Robert Mondavi 1999 Botrytis Sauvignon Blanc (Napa Valley) $50. 90 *—S.H. (12/1/2003)*

Robert Mondavi 1998 Coastal Sauvignon Blanc (Central Coast) $9. 85 *(3/1/2000)*

Robert Mondavi 2003 Private Selection Sauvignon Blanc (Central Coast) $9. Tastes too sweet for a variety that should be dry and crisp. Almost desserty with the sugary finish to the apple, pear, and fig flavors. **84** *—S.H. (12/15/2004)*

Robert Mondavi 2001 Private Selection Sauvignon Blanc (Central Coast) $9. 83 *—S.H. (10/1/2003)*

Robert Mondavi 1999 Coastal Syrah (Central Coast) $14. 83 *(10/1/2001)*

Robert Mondavi 2000 Coastal Private Selection Syrah (Central Coast) $11. 83 *—S.H. (12/1/2002)*

Robert Mondavi 2001 Zinfandel (Napa Valley) $21. 88 *—J.M. (11/1/2003)*

Robert Mondavi 1997 Coastal Zinfandel (North Coast) $12. 84 *—S.H. (2/1/2000)*

Robert Mondavi 2003 Private Selection Zinfandel (California) $11. A nice Zin and while it's a little light, this is a decent price for a wine of this character. It's dry and full-bodied, with ripe cherry, blackberry, raisin, and chocolate flavors and a spicy finish. **86 Best Buy** *—S.H. (12/15/2005)*

Robert Mondavi 2001 Private Selection Zinfandel (North Coast) $11. 81 *(11/1/2003)*

USA

ROBERT PECOTA

Robert Pecota 1997 Steven Andre Vineyard Merlot (Napa Valley) $30. 92 *—S.H. (3/1/2000)*

Robert Pecota 1999 Syrah (Monterey County) $24. 84 *(11/1/2001)*

ROBERT RUE VINEYARD

Robert Rue Vineyard 2001 Wood Road Century Old Vines Zinfandel (Russian River Valley) $30. 90 *(11/1/2003)*

ROBERT SINSKEY

Robert Sinskey 1997 Chardonnay (Carneros) $25. 92 *—S.H. (2/1/2000)*

Robert Sinskey 1995 Reserve Merlot (Carneros) $33. 89 *—S.H. (3/1/2000)*

Robert Sinskey 2001 Four Vineyards Pinot Noir (Carneros) $46. A fruit-driven Pinot Noir that still manages to evoke so many of the undergrowth, damp leaf aromas associated with this elusive grape variety. It has elegance, subtlety, mineral flavors, and spicy, smoky, toasty wood. From vines that were first planted in 1982, this is a wine that should evolve well over five to ten years. **91** *—R.V. (4/1/2005)*

Robert Sinskey 2001 Three Amigos Vineyard Pinot Noir (Carneros) $46. A soft, seductive style of Pinot Noir, full of ripe, strawberry flavors and very pure fruit tastes. There are firm tannins, but they do not dominate the smoky fruit along with flavors of dark plums, and beautiful acidity. A lovely, understated wine. **89** *—R.V. (4/1/2005)*

ROBERT STEMMLER

Robert Stemmler 2002 Three Clone Chardonnay (Carneros) $26. Very bright and zingy, with that brilliant shine of citrusy acidity you find in a good Carneros Chard. The apple, peach, and spice flavors finish in a rich, creamy swirl of fruit and oak. **90** *—S.H. (12/15/2005)*

Robert Stemmler 2000 Pinot Noir (Carneros) $38. 90 *(10/1/2002)*

Robert Stemmler 2002 Ferguson Block Pinot Noir (Carneros) $40. The flavors are rich, spanning cherry pie and raspberry tart, vanilla, and cinnamon-sprinkled cappuccino, and a hint of ripe, sweet Heirloom tomato. For all the richness, the wine is dry, silky, and balanced. **91 Editors' Choice** *—S.H. (12/15/2005)*

Robert Stemmler 2002 Nugent Vineyard Pinot Noir (Russian River Valley) $32. Tasted beside Stemmler's estate Pinot, this one's richer and more concentrated, but very similar, even though it's from a different appellation, suggesting a consistent winemaker approach. It's medium-bodied and silky, with ripe rhubarb, cola, and cherry-pie flavors finished with oak and vanilla. Drink this elegant and complex wine now. **88** *—S.H. (12/15/2005)*

ROBERT YOUNG

Robert Young 2000 Scion Bordeaux Blend (Alexander Valley) $60. After a trio of stunning successes, this year's Scion, well made as it is, just can't outrun the vintage.The berry-cherry flavors are less forceful than in the '99, with a touch of dill. Still, it's a soothing wine, with soft, gentle tannins and powerful oak. **88** *—S.H. (12/1/2004)*

Robert Young 1999 Scion Cabernet Blend (Alexander Valley) $50. 96 Editors' Choice *—S.H. (11/15/2003)*

Robert Young 2002 Chardonnay (Alexander Valley) $37. Another winning Chard, consistent with past vintages. Oozes flamboyant tropical fruit flavors, complex Asian spices and plenty of buttered toast and caramel char from good oak. All this in a rich, soft, vanilla-custardy texture that fills the mouth with pleasure. Drink now. **93 Editors' Choice** *—S.H. (8/1/2005)*

Robert Young 1999 Chardonnay (Alexander Valley) $35. 96 Editors' Choice *—S.H. (12/1/2001)*

ROBLEDO

Robledo 2000 Pinot Noir (Carneros) $27. **86** *—J.M. (7/1/2003)*

ROCCA

Rocca 2001 Cabernet Sauvignon (Yountville) $50. A fine Cab that shows off its pedigree in the ripe, exuberant cherry and blackberry flavors and the smooth, sweet tannins. Oak plays a large part in this wine's creamy sweetness. Some dusty tannins show up in the finish. Drinkable now. **90** *—S.H. (6/1/2005)*

Rocca 2001 Syrah (Yountville) $38. Quite firm and tannic in its youth, but shows promise in the overall balance, and the core of rich, ripe cherry and blackberry fruit. There's a meaty, leathery edge that meshes well with oak on the finish. Should develop through 2008. **90** *—S.H. (6/1/2005)*

Rocca 1999 Syrah (Yountville) $38. **90** *—S.H. (10/1/2003)*

ROCHE

Roche 1998 Barrel Select Reserve Chardonnay (Carneros) $30. **86** *(6/1/2000)*

ROCHIOLI

Rochioli 1998 Estate Chardonnay (Russian River Valley) $29. **89** *(6/1/2000)*

Rochioli 2001 Estate Grown Chardonnay (Russian River Valley) $37. **93** *—S.H. (7/1/2003)*

Rochioli 2002 Pinot Noir (Russian River Valley) $40. Simple, dry, and friendly, with modest black cherry and vanilla flavors. Easy to drink, with a soft mouthfeel. **84** *(11/1/2004)*

Rochioli 1999 Pinot Noir (Russian River Valley) $37. **88** *(10/1/2002)*

Rochioli 1999 East Block Pinot Noir (Russian River Valley) $NA. 14.2%. Pretty. Char-toast, allspice, 5 spice, cola, tea, cocoa, dried cherry skin, pepper. In the mouth, a blast of sweet oak and cherry, but very dry. Rich, full-bodied, dry, sour cherry. Intricate. Fairly tannic. Sweet, cocoa-ey finish. Now–2010. **93** *—S.H. (6/1/2005)*

Rochioli 1994 East Block Reserve Pinot Noir (Russian River Valley) $NA. Only 13 percent alcohol. Smells ripe and oaky. Red cherries, spices, root beer, cola. Touch of sweet beet. Nice balance of cherries and more herbal notes. Beautiful tannins, acids. **90** *—S.H. (6/1/2005)*

Rochioli 2000 River Block Pinot Noir (Russian River Valley) $55. **89** *—S.H. (2/1/2003)*

Rochioli 1999 Three Corner Vineyard Pinot Noir (Russian River Valley) $NA. 13.5%. Very dry. Dusty. Tomato, cola, rhubarb, spice rub. Young. Sour cherry. Bone dry. Fairly big, tight, awkward now. Huge, angular. Needs a few years to soften and settle down. **92** *—S.H. (6/1/2005)*

Rochioli 1994 Three Corner Vineyard Reserve Pinot Noir (Russian River Valley) $NA. Turning leafy-foresty, very delicate. Subtle tea, clove, cinnamon, cherry, dusty, cedar, cocoa. Fresh. Lots of sweet fruit, cherries, balanced, silky, so supple and clean. Lots of rich dusty tannins. Bone dry. Complex, interesting. Now–2010. **94** *—S.H. (6/1/2005)*

Rochioli 2000 West Block Pinot Noir (Russian River Valley) $65. **94 Editors' Choice** *—S.H. (2/1/2003)*

Rochioli 1997 West Block Pinot Noir (Russian River Valley) $NA. Fairly tannic, herbal, pale. Very thin, transparent in flavor. Used to be "delicious" (Tom Rochioli) but past its prime. **84** *—S.H. (6/1/2005)*

Rochioli 1994 West Block Reserve Pinot Noir (Russian River Valley) $NA. More herbal than Three Corner. Tomatoes, rhubarb, cola, not quite ripe. Anise, cocoa powder. Dry, brittle. Showing its age, but interesting and layered. **87** *—S.H. (6/1/2005)*

Rochioli 1998 Sauvignon Blanc (Russian River Valley) $22. **90** *(11/1/1999)*

Rochioli 2003 Sauvignon Blanc (Russian River Valley) $29. Another wonderful Rochioli Sauvignon, which always seems to have that extra something most other ones don't. You'll find the usual ripe citrus, fig, and melon, but it's extra deep, with the most wonderful balance of acidity. **90** *—S.H. (12/1/2004)*

Rochioli 2001 Sauvignon Blanc (Russian River Valley) $24. **90 Editors' Choice** *(8/1/2002)*

ROCK RABBIT

Rock Rabbit 2003 Syrah (Central Coast) $10. For ten bucks this is pretty good. Kind of simple and soft, but you'll find plenty of blackberry, blueberry, and cherry flavors, with a creamy, milk chocolaty taste. **84** *—S.H. (12/1/2005)*

ROCKBLOCK

Rockblock 2002 Carpenter Hill Vineyard Syrah (Rogue Valley) $40. One of several microproduction wines (50 cases of this bottling) from Rockblock, the Carpenter Hill Syrah offers up a lovely combination of dried spices and fresh blackberries couched in a silky texture. Velvety and extremely supple on the finish, giving a great sense of elegance. **90** *(9/1/2005)*

Rockblock 2000 Del Rio Vineyard Syrah (Rogue Valley) $40. Rockblock is a new brand launched by Domaine Serene to showcase Syrah. Full, lush, satiny fruit explodes across the palate, wrapped in stiff, smoky, but well-managed tannins. **90** *—P.G. (2/1/2004)*

Rockblock 2000 Seven Hills Vineyard Syrah (Walla Walla (OR)) $40. Though technically in Oregon, this well-known vineyard is most closely associated with the many Walla Walla (Washington) wineries that purchase its fruit. This is great juice, ripe and vibrant, with pretty, luscious blackberry and black cherry fruit, sweetly wrapped in cinnamon-spiced oak. **91** *—P.G. (2/1/2004)*

ROCKING HORSE

Rocking Horse 2001 Garvey Family Vineyard Cabernet Sauvignon (Rutherford) $30. An average Cabernet made in an average way, with very ripe blackberry and chocolate flavors, melted tannins, and obvious oak. Finishes like a cup of cocoa. **84** —*S.H. (10/1/2005)*

Rocking Horse 2000 Merlot (Napa Valley) $20. Soft and simple, with blackberry and cocoa flavors and an oakiness that brings vanilla and char to the aftertaste. Finishes too sweet. **83** —*S.H. (10/1/2005)*

Rocking Horse 2001 Zinfandel (Napa Valley) $18. Very dry, high enough in acids to create a tart mouthfeel, this is a balanced wine with earthy, berry flavors. It's not a show-stopper, but has subtle sophistication that won't overshadow carefully prepared foods. **87** —*S.H. (10/1/2005)*

Rocking Horse 1998 Zinfandel (Napa Valley) $18. 87 *(3/1/2001)*

ROCKLAND

Rockland 2000 Petite Sirah (Napa Valley) $30. 90 *(4/1/2003)*

ROCKLEDGE VINEYARDS

Rockledge Vineyards 2001 Cabernet Sauvignon (St. Helena) $45. Quite sleek and elegant, with a fine-tuned core of richly textured flavors, redolent of cassis, blackberry, coffee, tar, herbs, anise, and toast. The tannins are firm but ripe, giving good structure to the wine, which tastes like Bordeaux in a great vintage. Long and lush on the finish. A good price for this kind of quality. **91** —*J.M. (8/1/2004)*

Rockledge Vineyards 2002 The Rocks Cabernet Sauvignon (St. Helena) $49. This first wine of Rockledge has much more integrity than the regular '02. It shows the same forward cherry and blackberry flavors, but firmer tannins, resulting in a greater structure. It's not going anywhere, so drink now. **88** —*S.H. (11/1/2005)*

Rockledge Vineyards 2001 Primitivo (Napa Valley) $24. Somewhat floral up front, with a sleek, elegant mouthfeel. Silky smooth tannins frame a core of black cherry, coffee, herb, spice, anise, herb, and clove flavors. It's made in a classy style from Zinfandel's alter ego, Primitivo, which is just a clone of the quintessential California variety. **90** —*J.M. (8/1/2004)*

Rockledge Vineyards 2002 Zinfandel (Napa Valley) $22. My oh my, this Zin is ripe. It's fully dry, but tastes as sweet as a cherry pie, drizzled with cassis and dusted with cocoa. Too soft, though. **84** —*S.H. (11/1/2005)*

Rockledge Vineyards 2000 Zinfandel (Napa Valley) $22. 88 —*J.M. (11/1/2002)*

RODNEY STRONG

Rodney Strong 2000 Symmetry Meritage Cabernet Blend (Alexander Valley) $55. Smooth and polished, with a great, velvety mouthfeel, this balanced wine shows intense cassis flavors modulated with sweet herbs and toasty oak. It's really quite elegant now, and should hold through the decade. **91** —*S.H. (10/1/2005)*

Rodney Strong 2002 Cabernet Sauvignon (Sonoma County) $19. Juicy, flavorful and just a bit raw, this dry wine offers up black currants, smoke, and vanilla, the classic recipe for California Cab. It has a wonderfully long, rich finish. **87** —*S.H. (11/1/2005)*

Rodney Strong 2000 Cabernet Sauvignon (Sonoma County) $18. 90 —*S.H. (3/1/2003)*

Rodney Strong 1998 Cabernet Sauvignon (Sonoma County) $16. 88 —*S.H. (5/1/2001)*

Rodney Strong 2001 Alden Vineyards Cabernet Sauvignon (Alexander Valley) $30. From a vineyard way high in the Mayacamas Mountains above Alexander Valley, this Cab has massive, palate-numbing tannins. But it's also humongous in blackberries and cherries, and is balanced. There's no reason it shouldn't do fabulous things in the cellar. Drink after 2008. **91 Cellar Selection** —*S.H. (11/1/2005)*

Rodney Strong 1998 Alden Vineyards Cabernet Sauvignon (Alexander Valley) $30. 84 —*S.H. (11/15/2002)*

Rodney Strong 2000 Alexander's Crown Cabernet Sauvignon (Alexander Valley) $28. 90 —*S.H. (11/15/2003)*

Rodney Strong 1998 Alexander's Crown Vineyard Cabernet Sauvignon (Alexander Valley) $28. 86 —*S.H. (8/1/2003)*

Rodney Strong 1996 Alexander's Crown Vyd Cabernet Sauvignon (Northern Sonoma) $25. 86 *(12/31/1999)*

Rodney Strong 1999 Reserve Cabernet Sauvignon (Sonoma County) $40. 86 —*S.H. (11/15/2003)*

Rodney Strong 1996 Reserve Cabernet Sauvignon (Northern Sonoma) $40. 92 — *(9/1/2000)*

Rodney Strong 1999 Symmetry Cabernet Sauvignon (Alexander Valley) $55. From Rodney Strong, an oaky, ripe wine made in the international Cabernet style. It's strong and extracted in fruit, and drenched with woody char and vanilla. Some tough tannins lurk throughout. **85** —*S.H. (11/15/2004)*

Rodney Strong 2003 Chardonnay (Sonoma County) $15. Here's a fine, flavorful Chard. It's got jazzy flavors of white peaches, pineapples, vanilla custard, buttered toast, and Asian spices, wrapped in a rich, creamy texture. **89** —*S.H. (11/1/2005)*

Rodney Strong 2002 Chardonnay (Sonoma County) $18. Just what the doctor ordered in a rich Chard. It's lavish in ripe peach, tropical fruit, and vanilla flavors, with the sweetness of a fresh-baked buttery biscuit. The creamy texture carries spice flavors through a long finish. **90 Editors' Choice** —*S.H. (6/1/2004)*

Rodney Strong 1999 Chardonnay (Sonoma County) $14. 86 —*S.H. (11/15/2000)*

Rodney Strong 2000 Chalk Hill Chardonnay (Sonoma County) $18. 85 *—S.H. (5/1/2002)*

Rodney Strong 1997 Chalk Hill Chardonnay (Sonoma County) $14. 88 *(11/15/1999)*

Rodney Strong 1999 Chalk Hill Vineyard Reseve Chardonnay (Sonoma County) $30. 87 *—S.H. (12/15/2002)*

Rodney Strong 1997 Reserve Chalk Hill Vyd Chardonnay (Northern Sonoma) $30. 92 *—S.H. (11/1/1999)*

Rodney Strong 2001 Merlot (Sonoma County) $18. Smooth, sophisticated, and fancy tasting with its balance of plummy, blackberry fruit, rich tannins, and alcohol. Drinks fully dry, with good acidity. **87** *—S.H. (5/1/2005)*

Rodney Strong 1999 Merlot (Sonoma County) $18. 89 *—S.H. (7/1/2002)*

Rodney Strong 1997 Merlot (Sonoma County) $16. 88 *—S.H. (11/15/2000)*

Rodney Strong 2002 Pinot Noir (Russian River Valley) $19. There's a dividing line between Pinots that are good and simple and those that are fabulously complex. This delightfully drinkable wine is right in the middle. As easy as it is, it possesses layers of fruit and minerals, and is thoroughly dry and balanced. **89** *—S.H. (8/1/2005)*

Rodney Strong 1997 Estate Bottled Pinot Noir (Russian River Valley) $16. **86** *(12/15/1999)*

Rodney Strong 2002 Jane's Vineyard Reserve Pinot Noir (Russian River Valley) $35. Simple and fruity, with one-dimensional cherry, cola, and coffee flavors that drink dry and silky, with crisp acidity. The finish turns tart in dusty tannins. **84** *—S.H. (12/31/2005)*

Rodney Strong 1998 Reserve Pinot Noir (Northern Sonoma) $30. 87 *—S.H. (12/15/2001)*

Rodney Strong 2002 Charlotte's Home Sauvignon Blanc (Sonoma Valley) $12. 87 *—S.H. (12/31/2003)*

Rodney Strong 2001 Charlotte's Home Vineyard Sauvignon Blanc (Sonoma County) $12. 86 *—S.H. (9/1/2003)*

Rodney Strong 1999 Knotty Vines Zinfandel (Northern Sonoma) $18. 86 *—S.H. (9/1/2002)*

Rodney Strong 1997 Old Vines Zinfandel (Sonoma County) $18. 87 *—P.G. (3/1/2001)*

ROEDERER ESTATE

Roederer Estate NV Brut Champagne Blend (Anderson Valley) $20. 88 *—S.H. (12/1/2000)*

Roederer Estate NV Brut Rosé Champagne Blend (Anderson Valley) $26. 88 *—S.H. (12/1/2002)*

Roederer Estate NV Brut Rosé Champagne Blend (Anderson Valley) $30. 90 *—S.H. (12/1/2000)*

Roederer Estate NV Brut Rosé Champagne Blend (Anderson Valley) $24. 89 *(12/1/2001)*

Roederer Estate 1996 L'Ermitage Champagne Blend (Anderson Valley) $42. 93 *—S.H. (12/15/2001)*

Roederer Estate 1993 L'Ermitage Champagne Blend (Mendocino) $38. 92 *—E.M. (11/15/1999)*

Roederer Estate NV Brut Sparkling Blend (Anderson Valley) $22. Starts with wonderfully complex scents of dough, char, butterscotchy smoke, lemon chiffon pie, and vanilla. The flavors are equally complex. Would score higher if not for a certain roughness of texture. **88** *—S.H. (12/31/2004)*

Roederer Estate 1999 L'Ermitage Sparkling Blend (Anderson Valley) $45. Extraordinarily fine for its smoothness and finesse, and the way the wine glides over the palate with a yeasty creaminess that turns smoky and spicy on the finish. The dosage stands out, yet this bubbly is also very acidic now. It should age well for at least 10 years. **94** *—S.H. (6/1/2005)*

Roederer Estate 1998 L'Ermitage Sparkling Blend (Anderson Valley) $45. Among the top sparklers in California, the wine this year is even more smooth and polished. It's positively French in its classic structure and elegance. Feels ultra-refined in the mouth, with subtle flavors of dough, smoke, and fruit. **93** *—S.H. (12/31/2004)*

RONAN

Ronan 2003 Lakeview Vineyards Reserve Cabernet Franc (Monterey County) $24. Clumsy, with a harsh mouthfeel and a sugary edge to the cherry flavors. **81** *—S.H. (12/31/2005)*

Ronan 2003 Lakeview Vineyards Petite Sirah (Monterey County) $26. Tannic and acidic, this wine tastes like it could have used a couple extra days of hang time in order to develop more fruitiness and sugar. The blackberry and coffee flavors have a green, peppery edge. Drink now. **83** *—S.H. (12/31/2005)*

ROSA D'ORO

Rosa d'Oro 2001 Barbera (Lake County) $17. Still a tough, bitter wine at 4 years, with a slightly sweet finish. Not going anywhere. **82** *—S.H. (5/1/2005)*

Rosa d'Oro 2002 Syrah (Lake County) $16. A little too sweet, too rustic, and too soft for a higher score. There are also notes of over-ripeness. **82** *—S.H. (5/1/2005)*

ROSENBLUM

Rosenblum 2001 Holbrook Mitchell Trio Bordeaux Blend (Napa Valley) $36. A Bordeaux blend and a very good one, with plush black currant, cherry, and smoky flavors grounded in earthier tobacco and herbs. The tannins are rich and firm. This classy wine exudes pleasure and is best in its youth. **92 Editors' Choice** *—S.H. (10/3/2004)*

Rosenblum 2002 Yates Ranch Cabernet Franc (Napa Valley) $28. Super ripe in cassis and chocolate, almost decadently soft and gooey, and fully dry, without too much alcohol. Good but ultimately simple, like a sauce you'd pour over ice cream or cake. **86** *—S.H. (12/31/2004)*

Rosenblum 2000 CRS Yates Ranch Reserve Cabernet Sauvignon (Mount Veeder) $25. This flagship Rosenblum wine does not disappoint, with its expressive black currant and cassis aromas and flavors. The overlay of toasted oak adds a sweet vanilla edge. Softly textured, with a bright spine of acidity that keeps it fresh. **92** *—S.H. (2/1/2004)*

Rosenblum 1997 Reserve Cabernet Sauvignon (Napa Valley) $45. 91 *(11/1/2000)*

Rosenblum 1998 Chardonnay (Edna Valley) $19. 87 *(6/1/2000)*

Rosenblum 2000 Lone Oak Vineyard Chardonnay (Russian River Valley) $35. 86 *—S.H. (5/1/2003)*

Rosenblum 1998 Lone Oak Vyd Reserve Chardonnay (Russian River Valley) $24. 88 *(6/1/2000)*

Rosenblum 2001 Napa Valley Select Chardonnay (Napa Valley) $14. 85 *—S.H. (6/1/2003)*

Rosenblum 2000 RustRidge Vineyard Chardonnay (Napa Valley) $30. 87 *—S.H. (9/1/2003)*

Rosenblum 2001 Marsanne (Dry Creek Valley) $15. An unusual and distinctive Rhône white. It has the weight and texture of a good Chardonnay, with flavors that ping-pong between flamboyant mango and guava, and crisper notes of ripe green apples. The creamy texture is rich and unctuous. **89** *—S.H. (2/1/2004)*

Rosenblum 2002 Lone Oak Vineyard Merlot (Russian River Valley) $30. Ripe, juicy, and balanced, with satisfying blackberry, black cherry, coffee, and oaky vanilla flavors wrapped in smooth tannins. This polished wine is supple and elegant through the finish. **89** *—S.H. (12/31/2004)*

Rosenblum 1998 Lone Oak Vineyard Merlot (Russian River Valley) $18. 87 *—J.C. (6/1/2001)*

Rosenblum 1997 Oakville Merlot (Napa Valley) $14. 85 *(11/15/1999)*

Rosenblum 2000 Muscat de Glacier Muscat (California) $22. 90 *—S.H. (9/1/2003)*

Rosenblum 2002 Pickett Road Petite Sirah (Napa Valley) $24. As balanced and impressive as a fine Napa Cabernet, with its sweet tannins, velvety texture, and overall quality. The only difference is in the flavors. Here, you get cassis, cherries, chocolate, and that distinctive brambly pepperiness that Zin owns. **92** *—S.H. (12/15/2004)*

Rosenblum 2000 Pickett Road Petite Sirah (Napa Valley) $28. 90 *—S.H. (9/1/2003)*

Rosenblum 2001 Rockpile Road Vineyard Petite Sirah (Dry Creek Valley) $34. This is a very rich wine with blackberry, cassis, chocolate, and spice flavors, and this richness is framed in lavishly fine, thick tannins and lots of smoky oak. It's very dry, with a long finish. Easily one of the best of the current crop of Petite Sirahs. It will age, if you can keep your hands off it. **91** *—S.H. (4/1/2004)*

Rosenblum 1999 Rockpile Road Vineyards Petite Sirah (Dry Creek Valley) $25. 89 Cellar Selection *—S.H. (12/1/2001)*

Rosenblum 2002 Château La Paws Côte du Bone Blanc Rhône White Blend (California) $13. From Rosenblum, a blend of Viognier and Roussanne, with fruit and honey flavors. But don't expect a dry wine. It tastes almost as sweet as a late harvest dessert wine. **83** *—S.H. (10/1/2005)*

Rosenblum 2003 Fess Parker Vineyard Roussanne (Santa Barbara County) $18. Honeysuckle, buttercup blossom, sweet buttered biscuit, peach custard, vanilla. Sound sweet? Tastes sweet. A challenging wine to review. Undeniably delicious, but brings the word "dry" into new territory. **87** *—S.H. (10/1/2005)*

Rosenblum 1997 Syrah (Solano County) $18. 83 *—S.H. (6/1/1999)*

Rosenblum 2002 Abba Vineyard Syrah (Lodi) $18. A big, ripe, galumphing Syrah that's almost Port-like in its chocolatey, stewed blackberry flavors, although it is dry. Not for the faint of heart at 15-plus alcohol. **84** *—S.H. (12/1/2004)*

Rosenblum 2000 England-Shaw Vineyard Syrah (Solano County) $37. 87 *—S.H. (6/1/2003)*

Rosenblum 2001 England-Shaw Vineyard Syrah (Solano County) $30. 84 *—S.H. (12/15/2003)*

Rosenblum 1999 England-Shaw Vyd Syrah (Solano County) $21. 89 *(11/1/2001)*

Rosenblum 2003 Hillside Vineyards Syrah (Sonoma County) $28. A blend of fruit from several Sonoma vineyards, this wine features Rosenblum's hallmark lavish oak and concentrated fruit. Caramel, coffee, and vanilla notes complement full, soft notes of blackberry and plum. Long and a bit tannic on the finish, this wine is approachable now, yet promises to be even better in another year or two. **88** *(9/1/2005)*

Rosenblum 2001 Hillside Vineyards Syrah (Sonoma County) $26. Rich and fruity, a hugely flavorful wine stuffed with black currant, cherry, plum, coffee, and herb flavors. It's pretty tannic now, with lots of acidity, but the fruit is big enough to pair with beef or cheese. **86** *—S.H. (4/1/2004)*

Rosenblum 2003 Rominger Vineyard Syrah (Yolo County) $26. Intense and tannic, yet well-managed and ageworthy. White pepper and plum on the nose, with masses of well-ripened tannins and rich fruit alongside. From a hillside vineyard planted to French clones that yielded only 1.5 tons per acre, we can only hope wines like this represent the future of California Syrah. **91 Editors' Choice** *(9/1/2005)*

Rosenblum 2002 Kathy's Cuvée Viognier (Lodi) $14. An exotic Viognier, packed with wild flavors, everything from mangoes and papayas through bananas to honeysuckle and ripe white peach. Finishes with a honeyed sweetness, yet it's basically dry. **87** *—S.H. (11/15/2004)*

Rosenblum 2000 Late Harvest Ripkin Ranch Viognier (Lodi) $22. 86 *—S.H. (5/1/2003)*

Rosenblum 2000 Ripkin Vineyard Viognier (Lodi) $14. 88 Best Buy *S.H. (11/15/2001)*

Rosenblum 2001 Rodney's Vineyard Viognier (Santa Barbara County) $25. 86 *—S.H. (3/1/2003)*

Rosenblum 1998 Alegria Zinfandel (Russian River Valley) $26. 91 *—P.G. (3/1/2001)*

Rosenblum 2001 Alegria Vineyard Zinfandel (Russian River Valley) $22. 87 *(11/1/2003)*

Rosenblum 1997 Alegria Vyd Zinfandel (Russian River Valley) $30. 83 *—J.C. (2/1/2000)*

Rosenblum 1997 Annette's Reserve Rhodes Vineyard Zinfandel (Redwood Valley) $26. 89 *—P.G. (11/15/1999)*

Rosenblum 2001 Annette's Reserve Rhodes Vineyard Zinfandel (Redwood Valley) $28. 84 *(11/1/2003)*

Rosenblum 1999 Annette's Reserve Rhodes Vineyard Zinfandel (Redwood Valley) $27. 91 Editors' Choice *—S.H. (9/1/2002)*

Rosenblum 2000 Carla's Vineyards Zinfandel (San Francisco Bay) $29. 85 *—S.H. (5/1/2003)*

Rosenblum 2001 Castanho Vineyard Zinfandel Port Zinfandel (San Francisco Bay) $17. 83 *—S.H. (12/15/2003)*

Rosenblum 2002 Continente Vineyard Zinfandel (San Francisco Bay) $18. From Contra Costa, a thick, rather syrupy Zin, soft in acids, with gooey chocolate and cassis flavors. Seems more like something you'd pour over ice cream than a dinner wine, but lots of people like this style. **85** *—S.H. (12/31/2004)*

Rosenblum 2000 Continente Vineyard Zinfandel (San Francisco Bay) $20. 88 *—S.H. (5/1/2003)*

Rosenblum 1997 Continente Vineyard Zinfandel (Contra Costa County) $19. 90 *—J.C. (9/1/1999)*

Rosenblum 2001 Cullinane Vineyard Zinfandel (Sonoma County) $45. 89 *(11/1/2003)*

Rosenblum 2002 Eagle Point Vineyard Zinfandel (Mendocino County) $27. A solid effort in a big Zin that could have been unbalanced but isn't. Dark and dry, with lush tannins and a full-bodied mouth feel, and long, rich flavors of berries, spices, and coffee. Has that brawny, briary Zin character that does so well with barbecue. **89** *—S.H. (12/31/2004)*

Rosenblum 2002 Harris Kratka Vineyard Zinfandel (Alexander Valley) $30. An earthy, rustic Zin with the robust wild fruit and robust tannins that often mark the variety. Completely dry and moderate in alcohol, the wine shows blackberry, coffee, and spice flavors, with a streak of orange rind. **85** *—S.H. (11/15/2004)*

Rosenblum 2002 Hendry Vineyard Zinfandel (Napa Valley) $40. A fabulously complex Zin, decadent in the elaboration of ripe cassis and chocolate fruit, lush oak trappings, and texture like a mink coat. Lots of alcohol here, but so dry and balanced, you hardly notice. **92** *—S.H. (3/1/2005)*

Rosenblum 2000 Hendry Vineyard Reserve Zinfandel (Napa Valley) $47. 92 *—S.H. (3/1/2003)*

Rosenblum 1997 Hendry Vineyard Reserve Zinfandel (Napa Valley) $30. 86 *—J.C. (2/1/2000)*

Rosenblum 2001 Lyons Vineyard 25th Anniversary Zinfandel (Napa Valley) $38. 90 *(11/1/2003)*

Rosenblum 2001 Monte Rosso Vineyard Zinfandel (Sonoma County) $38. 89 *(11/1/2003)*

Rosenblum 2001 Oakley Vineyards Zinfandel (San Francisco Bay) $12. Nowhere near the class and style of Rosenblum's more expensive Zins. Smells tobaccoey and earthy, and drinks rough in texture, with pronounced sweetness. **83** *—S.H. (3/1/2004)*

Rosenblum 2000 Old Vines Zinfandel (Russian River Valley) $18. 89 Editors' Choice *—S.H. (5/1/2003)*

Rosenblum 2003 Planchon Vineyard Zinfandel (San Francisco Bay) $22. From Contra Costa County, a dark, dry wine with very high alcohol (15.6%) that flirts with Portiness but avoids it. Still the blackberry and chocolate flavors have a hint of raisins. Really an only-in-California Zin. **87** *—S.H. (10/1/2005)*

Rosenblum 2001 Planchon Vineyard Zinfandel (San Francisco Bay) $19. 91 Editors' Choice *(11/1/2003)*

Rosenblum 2002 Richard Sauret Vineyard Zinfandel (Paso Robles) $18. My favorite Rosenblum Zin of the vintage. Delicious for its rich blackberry, raspberry, chocolate, and toffee flavors, with easy, sweet but complex tannins, and completely dry. The fruit flatters the palate like a fur coat on a bare thigh. Irresistibly good. **90** *—S.H. (12/31/2004)*

Rosenblum 2000 Richard Sauret Vineyard Zinfandel (Paso Robles) $24. **87** *—S.H. (2/1/2003)*

Rosenblum 2001 Rockpile Road Zinfandel (Dry Creek Valley) $26. **86** *(11/1/2003)*

Rosenblum 2002 Rockpile Road Vineyard Zinfandel (Dry Creek Valley) $26. Big in flavor, high in alcohol, this is an only-in-California Zin. The ripe flavors are explosive, delighting the mouth with cassis, cherry, milk chocolate, and vanilla fudge flavors, but as sweet as this sounds, the wine is totally dry. Lip-smackingly good. **92** *—S.H. (12/15/2004)*

Rosenblum 1997 RustRidge Vineyard Zinfandel (Napa Valley) $22. **88** *—P.G. (11/15/1999)*

Rosenblum 1998 RustRidge Vineyard Zinfandel (Napa Valley) $18. **87** *(3/1/2001)*

Rosenblum 2001 Samsel Vineyard/Maggie's Reserve Zinfandel (Sonoma Valley) $42. **90** *(11/1/2000)*

Rosenblum 1998 St. Peter's Church Vineyard Zinfandel (Sonoma County) $40. **88** *(3/1/2001)*

Rosenblum 2002 Vintners Cuvée XXVI Zinfandel (California) $9. This is a good price for a wine of this caliber. Rich and thick in jammy cherry, mocha, and spice flavors, dry, and with ripe, sweet tannins. It's rather hot in alcohol, but that's what Zin lovers like with ribs slathered in sauce. **86 Best Buy** *—S.H. (12/31/2004)*

USA

Rosenblum NV Vintners Cuvée XXIV Zinfandel (California) $11. Super-basic Zin, with brambly flavors of assorted wild berries and a strong herbal tobacco note. Bone dry, with pretty fierce tannins that coat the palate. Best with simple, rich fare, like pizza. **84** *—S.H. (3/1/2004)*

Rosenblum NV Vintner's Cuvée XXI Zinfandel (California) $10. **88 Best Buy** *—P.G. (3/1/2001)*

ROSENTHAL

Rosenthal 2000 The Malibu Estate Chardonnay (Malibu-Newton Canyon) $22. **87** *—J.M. (5/1/2002)*

ROSENTHAL-MALIBU ESTATE

Rosenthal-Malibu Estate 2001 Cabernet Sauvignon (Malibu-Newton Canyon) $35. Smells like asparagus, tastes sweet and flat, with cherry cough medicine flavors. **81** *—S.H. (12/1/2005)*

Rosenthal-Malibu Estate 1999 Founder's Reserve Cabernet Sauvignon (Malibu-Newton Canyon) $70. Certainly richer and more balanced in every way than this winery's regular '99 Cabernet. It has well-ripened blackberry and spicy plum flavors that are generously oaked, and is dry. **90** *—S.H. (11/15/2004)*

Rosenthal-Malibu Estate 2001 The Devon Vineyard Merlot (Malibu-Newton Canyon) $25. A schizophrenic wine. It smells vegetal, like canned asparagus, but tastes better, with berry-cherry flavors and a polished texture. **83** *—S.H. (12/1/2005)*

ROSHAMBO

Roshambo 2003 Chardonnay (California) $10. Pretty nice for this price, with lots of oak framing tropical fruit and spice flavors and a creamy texture. Bright, crisp acidity helps to maintain balance. **85 Best Buy** *—S.H. (10/1/2005)*

Roshambo 2003 Rock Paper Scissors Merlot (California) $10. Smooth and ripe, this good value wine is loaded with cherry, blackberry, and chocolate flavors. It's soft, with a nice backbone of tannins. **85 Best Buy** *—S.H. (10/1/2005)*

Roshambo 2002 Justice Syrah (Dry Creek Valley) $21. Young, fresh, and jammy, this Syrah might benefit from a year or two in the cellar. It's dry and filled with blueberry, blackberry, and cherry flavors, with a cut of dusty tannins. Good now with steak, or hold through 2007. **87** *—S.H. (12/15/2005)*

Roshambo 2004 Think Rosé of Syrah (Sonoma County) $15. Unusually dark and full-bodied for a rosé, this wine could almost be served at room temperature. It's dry, with ripe, jammy cherry and black raspberry flavors, and a spicy, peppery finish. **86** *—S.H. (12/15/2005)*

Roshambo 2001 Zinfandel (Dry Creek Valley) $21. Rich in berry and herb flavors, this Zin has the crisp tannins and dry, brambly taste associated with the appellation. There's a peppery edge to the sweet, wild blackberries and blueberries that really perks up the palate. **90** *—S.H. (10/1/2004)*

Roshambo 2002 The Reverend Zinfandel (Dry Creek Valley) $21. Clean, balanced, and very drinkable, this Zin shows well-ripened cherry-berry flavors and smooth, rich tannins, and finishes dry. It's an easy, assured wine that shows real Dry Creek character. **86** *—S.H. (12/15/2005)*

ROTH

Roth 2002 Cabernet Sauvignon (Alexander Valley) $40. A very nice and smooth Cab, with a texture like velvet and an elegant overall feeling. It shows cassis, green olive, smoke, and cedar flavors and is bone dry. **88** *—S.H. (5/1/2005)*

ROUND HILL

Round Hill 2000 Cabernet Sauvignon (California) $8. **84** *—S.H. (11/15/2003)*

Round Hill 2003 Chardonnay (California) $9. Drinks like what it is, a country-style wine, rustic and clean. Provides enough fruit, cream and oak to satisfy. **83** *—S.H. (10/1/2005)*

Round Hill 2002 White Zinfandel (California) $4. Of course it's possible to make a good white Zin, but this isn't it. It's a thinly flavored, slightly sweet plonk, with a trace of raspberries. You get what you pay for. **82** *—S.H. (3/1/2004)*

ROW ELEVEN

Row Eleven 2002 Pinot Noir (Santa Maria Valley) $29. This is a big Pinot, dark and full-bodied, Rhône-like. It is not typical Santa Maria, although the acidity is cool-climate. It's very dry and fairly tannic, and calls for a slow-cooked meat dish, like short ribs, to play off its smoky, cherry flavors. **88** *—S.H. (10/1/2005)*

ROWLAND

Rowland 2001 Mountainside Cabernet Sauvignon (Napa Valley) $27. Seems to possess that mountain character of a tightly wound wine, tannic and firm, with a rich and solid core of black cherry and currant fruit. Those tannins are pretty fierce now, but should develop nicely. Best after 2008. **90** *—S.H. (10/1/2004)*

Rowland 1999 Red Triangle Cabernet Sauvignon (Napa Valley) $28. **92** *—S.H. (6/1/2002)*

Rowland 1999 Red Triangle Syrah (Napa Valley) $24. **88** *(11/1/2001)*

ROYAL OAKS

Royal Oaks 1999 Aristocrat Bordeaux Blend (Santa Ynez Valley) $18. **89** *—S.H. (4/1/2002)*

Royal Oaks 2000 Chardonnay (Santa Ynez Valley) $16. **85** *—S.H. (4/1/2002)*

Royal Oaks 1999 Los Alamos Vineyard Reserve Chardonnay (Santa Barbara) $20. **88** *—S.H. (5/1/2001)*

Royal Oaks 1998 Whitegate Vineyard Chardonnay (Santa Ynez Valley) $20. **86** *(6/1/2000)*

Royal Oaks 1998 Merlot (Santa Ynez Valley) $20. **86** *—S.H. (5/1/2001)*

Royal Oaks 2000 Westerly Vineyard Merlot (Santa Ynez Valley) $30. From the warmest part of the appellation, this is a well-ripened, juicy wine whose cherry, berry, and tobacco flavors are easy to like. Soft and silky on the palate, a gentle sipper with some spicy complexities. **86** *—S.H. (3/1/2004)*

Royal Oaks 2000 Pinot Noir (Santa Maria Valley) $22. **88** *—S.H. (4/1/2002)*

Royal Oaks 2000 Sauvignon Blanc (Santa Barbara County) $15. **85** *—S.H. (4/1/2002)*

Royal Oaks 2000 Reserve Sauvignon Blanc (Santa Ynez Valley) $19. **86** *—S.H. (4/1/2002)*

Royal Oaks 2001 Westerly Vineyard Sauvignon Blanc (Santa Ynez Valley) $22. **85** *—S.H. (12/31/2003)*

Royal Oaks 2001 Westerly Vineyard Viognier (Santa Ynez Valley) $28. **87** *—S.H. (12/31/2003)*

RUBICON ESTATE

Rubicon Estate 2002 Cask Cabernet Sauvignon (Rutherford) $65. This is not the same wine as Niebaum-Coppola's Cask Cabernet, although it sells for the same price. It's made in a different style, more tannic and not as apparently oaky. To judge from the depth of flavor, it's extremely cellarworthy. Should unfold by 2008 and develop for years beyond. **90 Cellar Selection** *—S.H. (12/15/2005)*

RUBISSOW-SARGENT

Rubissow-Sargent 2000 Reserve Cabernet Sauvignon (Mount Veeder) $75. Smells beautiful, with a nuanced perfume of rich cassis, black cherry, and new smoky oak and vanilla. But be warned, the tannins are potent. They grip the palate and fundamentally close it down. Absolutely requires further cellaring. Drink 2010-2020. **89 Cellar Selection** *—S.H. (5/1/2005)*

RUDD

Rudd 2001 Cabernet Sauvignon (Oakville) $75. Classic Oakville, detailed and refined, powerful in fruit and tannins; assertive and authoritative, yet manages to be graceful and elegant. A fulfilling wine, balanced and harmonious. Clearly has the stuffing to enjoy a ripe old age. Drink now through 2015. **94 Cellar Selection** *—S.H. (10/1/2004)*

Rudd 1998 Chardonnay (Russian River Valley) $35. **87** *(7/1/2001)*

Rudd 2000 Estate Red Wine Red Blend (Oakville) $100. A notable success for the vintage, Rudd's Estate offering does display slightly herbal characteristics, but amply compensates for that with plenty of lush, rich fruit. Oak-imparted toast and supple tannins frame ripe berry flavors that extend through the finish. Drink now–2010. **92** *—J.C. (5/1/2004)*

RULO WINERY

Rulo Winery 2002 Cabernet Sauvignon (Columbia Valley (WA)) $30. Pure, classic Cabernet. Young, tight, tannic and tart, yet it is already drinking well and built for aging. Great balance and structure. **92** *—P.G. (9/1/2004)*

Rulo Winery 2003 Vanessa Vineyard Chardonnay (Walla Walla (WA)) $20. From a two acre plot in Walla Walla, this lush, elegant wine shows Kurt Schlicker's deft, complex approach to winemaking. 100% barrel-fermented, it clocks in at 14% alcohol and tastes of clean fruit, with light hints of buttered toast and toasted nuts. Elegant and sophisticated, it shows a deft touch with the wood. **91** *—P.G. (12/15/2005)*

Rulo Winery 2001 Syrah (Columbia Valley (WA)) $18. **89** *—P.G. (9/1/2003)*

Rulo Winery 2003 Viognier (Walla Walla (WA)) $18. A full, intense wine, with concentrated scents of perfumed citrus. The flavors are big but balanced, and the wine captures the elegance and power of the grape with perfect symmetry. **90** *—P.G. (9/1/2004)*

RUSACK

Rusack 2001 Anacapa Bordeaux Blend (Santa Ynez Valley) $38. 90 *—S.H. (10/1/2003)*

Rusack 2002 Anacapa Cabernet Blend (Santa Ynez Valley) $36. This wine is okay, but rather sour and green. It offers little palate pleasure, and is the victim, not of winemaking, but of terroir. Santa Ynez is not Cabernet country! **84** *—S.H. (10/1/2005)*

Rusack 2002 Chardonnay (Santa Barbara County) $18. Well-oaked, this likeable wine features perky, citrusy acids that frame an array of peach, pineapple, sweet lime, and other tropical fruits flavors. The texture is really pretty, like buttercream. Finishes with a touch of lees. **90 Editors' Choice** *—S.H. (6/1/2004)*

Rusack 2003 Reserve Chardonnay (Santa Maria Valley) $32. Very similar in terroir-driven flavors to Rusack's less expensive Chardonnay, with citrus and orange blossom flavors, a steely, minerally note and modest oak. The structure is more angular, with very high acidity leading to a long finish. **91** *—S.H. (10/1/2005)*

Rusack 1997 Reserve Chardonnay (Santa Maria Valley) $30. 90 *(6/1/2000)*

Rusack 1997 Silver Moon Merlot (Santa Ynez Valley) $15. 85 *—J.C. (7/1/2000)*

Rusack 2001 Pinot Noir (Santa Maria Valley) $25. 85 *—S.H. (7/1/2003)*

Rusack 2000 Pinot Noir (Santa Maria Valley) $28. 84 *(10/1/2002)*

Rusack 2001 Reserve Pinot Noir (Santa Rita Hills) $32. 86 *—S.H. (7/1/2003)*

Rusack 2002 Sauvignon Blanc (Santa Ynez Valley) $15. 87 *—S.H. (12/31/2003)*

Rusack 2001 Syrah (Santa Ynez Valley) $25. A blend from around the appellation, and a charming wine that lacks a bit of fruity richness, but makes up for it with its intricate tannin-acid structure and overall finesse. Flavors of blackberry, herbs, and black tea are detailed; the wine's exceeding dryness invites contemplation. **90** *—S.H. (3/1/2004)*

Rusack 1999 Estate Vineyard Syrah (Santa Barbara County) $25. 88 *(11/1/2001)*

RUSSELL CREEK

Russell Creek 2002 Walla Walla Valley & Columbia Valley Cabernet Sauvignon (Washington) $28. This 100% Cab is thick and chewy, with lots of chocolatey tannin, and a solid core of cherry/berry fruit. Substantial and tasty, if a bit one-dimensional. **88** *—P.G. (4/1/2005)*

Russell Creek 2002 Merlot (Walla Walla (WA)) $26. Very smooth, succulent style which marries fresh berry flavor to lots of milk chocolatey oak. It's appealing, broadly accessible, fairly simplistic, but certainly delicious. **87** *—P.G. (4/1/2005)*

Russell Creek 2002 Winemakers Select Merlot (Walla Walla (WA)) $36. The winemakers select is bigger than the regular bottling, with high-toned fruit, bigger and rougher tannins, and more obvious oak. The extra extraction makes it less, not more accessible for near-term drinking. **87** *—P.G. (4/1/2005)*

RUSSIAN HILL

Russian Hill 2003 Gail Ann's Vineyard Chardonnay (Russian River Valley) $28. If you like your Chards citrusy, tart, and on the mineral side, this is for you. Some will find it thin, others will call it elegant and food friendly. For me, at this price, it's a disappointment, although it's certainly oaky. **84** *—S.H. (12/15/2005)*

Russian Hill 2001 Gail Ann's Vineyard Chardonnay (Russian River Valley) $26. Lots of toasty, vanilliny oak has been sprinkled on the pear, cinnamon apple and tropical fruit flavors of this rich but dry wine. It has good structure, with crisp acids and sweet tannins. It's lush, but elegant through a very long, fruity finish. **91** *—S.H. (5/1/2004)*

Russian Hill 2002 Pinot Noir (Sonoma Coast) $42. A fascinating Pinot that showcases the evolution of the varietal in this cool-climate growing region. The fruit isn't quite ripe, with tomato, cola, and rhubarb flavors, although oak does its best to fatten and sweeten. The wine is totally dry and rather tart. It's also dense and full-bodied, with the weight of Merlot. **89** *—S.H. (3/1/2005)*

Russian Hill 2000 Pinot Noir (Russian River Valley) $28. 89 *(10/1/2002)*

Russian Hill 2002 Estate Pinot Noir (Russian River Valley) $33. Rather heavy in texture, with the weight of a Rhône wine, and thick, fruity flavors of plums, heirloom tomatoes, cola, espresso, and oak. Very dry, with smooth tannins. This is a big Pinot, clean and complex, although not particularly delicate. **87** *—S.H. (3/1/2005)*

Russian Hill 1999 Leras Vineyard Pinot Noir (Russian River Valley) $44. 89 *(10/1/2002)*

Russian Hill 2002 Syrah (Russian River Valley) $22. Creamy and soft-textured, Russian Hill's blended Syrah is an easy-to-drink Syrah made for immediate appeal. Caramel, coffee, and vanilla notes envelop ripe red berries in a cocoon of accessibility. Drink now. **88** *(9/1/2005)*

Russian Hill 2002 Ellen's Block Syrah (Russian River Valley) $30. All three tasters preferred Russian Hill's blended Syrah, but the Ellen's Block bottling is no slouch. Green herb and peppery notes dominate the nose, but add meat and violet notes with airing. Tart red berries play a supporting role, couched in firm tannins. **86** *(9/1/2005)*

Russian Hill 2002 Top Block Syrah (Russian River Valley) $30. Thickly textured and low in acidity, this Syrah also boasts plenty of mixed berry fruit and dried spices. A hint of white chocolate gives a rich, fatty note, while pepper and cloves linger on the finish. **85** *(9/1/2005)*

Russian Hill 2001 Windsor Oaks Summit Syrah (Russian River Valley) $40. Marked by rich oak and massive flavors of blackberry jam, Indian pudding and cocoa, with a sprinkling of white pepper through the long finish. The tannins are pretty strong now, suggesting midterm aging, but it will be great with roast lamb. **90** *(5/1/2004)*

RUSTRIDGE

RustRidge 1998 Cabernet Sauvignon (Napa Valley) $28. 83 *—S.H. (12/1/2001)*

RustRidge 1999 Chardonnay (Napa Valley) $22. 86 *—S.H. (12/1/2001)*

RustRidge 1999 Sauvignon Blanc (Napa Valley) $20. 84 *—S.H. (11/15/2001)*

RustRidge 1997 Zinfandel (Napa Valley) $18. 87 *—P.G. (11/15/1999)*

RUTHERFORD GROVE

Rutherford Grove 2001 Cabernet Sauvignon (Napa Valley) $40. Very ripe and forward in cherry and blackberry fruit flavors, while the oak adds toast and vanilla notes. Finishes dry, with sturdy, dusty tannins leading to a sharp finish. **87** *—S.H. (10/1/2005)*

Rutherford Grove 2001 Merlot (Napa Valley) $28. Very dry and rather tart, this simple wine has easy flavors of berries, herbs, and oak. It's a little astringent, and at its best now. **84** *—S.H. (10/1/2005)*

Rutherford Grove 2003 Sauvignon Blanc (Rutherford) $14. It's rich in appley, citrus fruit flavors, with spicy fig notes, and the acidity and balance are really good. Has that sweet edge you get in many California Sauvignons. **86** *—S.H. (9/1/2004)*

RUTHERFORD HILL

Rutherford Hill 1999 25th Anniversary Cabernet Sauvignon (Napa Valley) $30. 90 *—C.S. (11/15/2002)*

Rutherford Hill 1998 Chardonnay (Napa Valley) $17. 88 *(11/1/2001)*

Rutherford Hill 1997 Reserve Chardonnay (Carneros) $28. 88 *(11/1/2001)*

Rutherford Hill 2002 Merlot (Napa Valley) $25. Pretty smooth and supple, this is a very soft, high thread-count wine that glides across the palate. It carries very ripe flavors of cherries and cocoa, with a finish that's almost sweet. **84** *—S.H. (11/1/2005)*

Rutherford Hill 1999 Merlot (Napa Valley) $24. 87 *(11/1/2001)*

Rutherford Hill 1997 Merlot (Napa Valley) $21. 90 *(11/1/2001)*

Rutherford Hill 1995 Merlot (Napa Valley) $20. 86 *(11/1/2001)*

Rutherford Hill 2002 Reserve Merlot (Napa Valley) $76. What a beautiful wine. It has Merlot's fleshy softness, but with a firm structure of finely ground tannins. Flavorwise, it packs cherry, blackberry, plum, coffee, and cocoa flavors, with oak contributing a rich overlay of sweet vanilla and char. Drink now in its exuberant youth. **92 Editors' Choice** *—S.H. (11/1/2005)*

Rutherford Hill 1999 Reserve Merlot (Napa Valley) $70. 90 *—K.F. (4/1/2003)*

Rutherford Hill 1996 Reserve Merlot (Napa Valley) $50. 88 *(11/1/2001)*

Rutherford Hill 2003 Rosé of Merlot (Napa Valley) $19. Seems pricey for a rather thin, inert wine. A flavorful blush Merlot from Napa would be a good thing, but this one is just too diluted. **83** *—S.H. (12/15/2004)*

Rutherford Hill 1996 22nd Anniversary Sangiovese (Napa Valley) $30. 88 *—M.S. (9/1/2000)*

RUTHERFORD OAKS

Rutherford Oaks 2000 Hozhoni Vineyard Syrah (Rutherford) $30. 88 *—J.M. (6/1/2003)*

Rutherford Ranch 2001 Cabernet Sauvignon (Napa Valley) $15. Okay drinking from a great vintage, but it's a tough, acidic young wine. Satisfies with cherry and oak flavors in the finish. **83** *—S.H. (10/1/2005)*

Rutherford Ranch 1999 Silverado Trail Vineyard Limited Release Reserve Cabernet Sauvignon (Napa Valley) $35. A very good Cab with polished blackberry, plum, and herb flavors, and some gritty tannins that turn astringent on the finish, although they're accompanied by ripe, sweet fruit. It's very dry, with a great structure that calls for fine foods. **89** *—S.H. (5/1/2004)*

Rutherford Ranch 2003 Chardonnay (Napa Valley) $13. Dry, earthy, and a little green and herbal, this wine shows modest apple and peach flavors. It's the kind of Chard you can gulp easily without worrying about the price. **84** *—S.H. (10/1/2005)*

Rutherford Ranch 2000 Chardonnay (Napa Valley) $12. 84 *—S.H. (6/1/2003)*

Rutherford Ranch 2000 Merlot (Napa Valley) $12. 84 *—S.H. (12/31/2002)*

Rutherford Ranch 2000 Zinfandel (Napa Valley) $14. Good, rich, and ripe, a feisty little Zin with all kinds of tasty flavors. Blackberries, blueberries, pecan pie, sweet dried herbs, orange zest, vanilla, and smoke, to name a few. Completely dry, with soft, easy tannins and a firm mouthfeel. Really fine, although it turns just a bit thin on the finish, but that's nitpicking. **87** *—S.H. (3/1/2004)*

RUTHERFORD VINTNERS

Rutherford Vintners 1999 Barrel Select Syrah (Stanislaus County) $9. 83 *(10/1/2001)*

RUTZ

Rutz 1998 Chardonnay (Russian River Valley) $20. 87 *—S.H. (5/1/2001)*

Rutz 2000 Dutton Ranch Chardonnay (Russian River Valley) $35. 92 *—S.H. (12/1/2003)*

Rutz 2001 Maison Grand Cru Chardonnay (Russian River Valley) $30. This is a high-acid Chardonnay that's not one of those buttery fruit bombs. It hits with a mouthful of minerals and stones, as well as lees and oak, but there is a tantalizing hint of lemon curd and peach yogurt. Will benefit from a little airing. **91** *—S.H. (8/1/2005)*

Rutz 1999 Maison Grand Cru Chardonnay (Russian River Valley) $25. 92 Editors' Choice *(9/1/2002)*

Rutz 2001 Pinot Noir (Sonoma Coast) $18. 91 Editors' Choice *—S.H. (12/1/2003)*

Rutz 1998 Pinot Noir (Russian River Valley) $20. 87 *—S.H. (5/1/2001)*

Rutz 2001 Dutton Ranch Pinot Noir (Russian River Valley) $38. An exquisite jewel of a Pinot, crisp, dry, delicate, and light-bodied, with a satin and silk texture, yet complex in flavor. Layers of raspberry, cherry, mocha, cola, rhubarb, and peppery spice unfold in waves, through a long, richly sweet finish. **91** *—S.H. (8/1/2005)*

Rutz 2001 Maison Grand Cru Pinot Noir (Russian River Valley) $30. The fabulous wine showcases the best that Russian River can give Pinot, and wisely avoids the overripe tendency now common in the appellation. Elegant, light-bodied, silky and crisp, with elaborately complex flavors that range from sweet raspberries, cocoa, cherries, and cola to bitter cranberries and coffee. Simply irresistable, and it doesn't aspire to be an ager. Drink now for its exuberant, flashy beauty. **92 Editors' Choice** *—S.H. (8/1/2005)*

Rutz 1999 Maison Grand Cru Pinot Noir (Russian River Valley) $25. 87 *—S.H. (9/1/2002)*

Rutz 1999 Martinelli Vineyard Pinot Noir (Russian River Valley) $30. 87 *—S.H. (9/1/2002)*

Rutz 2002 Windsor Gardens Pinot Noir (Russian River Valley) $60. Rather heavy and thick for a Pinot, with cherry, coffee, and cocoa flavors that finish dry. Fans of fuller-bodied Pinots will like this style, but it really could use more delicacy. **85** *—S.H. (12/15/2005)*

RYAN PATRICK

Ryan Patrick 2002 Rock Island Red Bordeaux Blend (Columbia Valley (WA)) $18. Named not for a railroad line, but the winery's home town, this blend remains essentially the same as 2001 — 56% Merlot, 39% Cabernet Sauvignon, and 5% Cab Franc. Shows a rougher profile, with big flavors of raw meat, plum, grape, and earth. The core of pure, sweet cherry fruit ramps up the quality, which is excellent for the price. **88** *—P.G. (12/1/2004)*

Ryan Patrick 2003 Estate Chardonnay (Columbia Valley (WA)) $18. Consistent with the stylish '02, this young, spicy wine hits the palate with bright, snappy flavors of pineapple, lime, and green berries. Some buttery toast nicely fills in the back end. **89** *—P.G. (12/1/2004)*

Ryan Patrick 2001 Red Blend (Columbia Valley (WA)) $29. Tasty, though rough, it comes on with chocolatey fruit, green coffee bean tannins, sweet toast, and ultimately, a very pleasing set of flavors. The cherry fruit, nuanced with tobacco leaf and herb, prevails over the somewhat rustic structure. **89** *—P.G. (12/1/2004)*

Ryan Patrick 2003 Vin d'Été White Blend (Columbia Valley (WA)) $20. This "summer wine" blend is mostly Sauvignon Blanc, with about 16% Sémillon adding lemongrass and lanolin. Soft, lightly nutty, almost Italian in style, it is smooth and rich across the palate, with a pleasing nuttiness to the lingering finish. **88** *—P.G. (12/1/2004)*

S. ANDERSON

S. Anderson 1994 Blanc de Blanc (Napa Valley) $46. 90 *—S.H. (12/1/2000)*

S. Anderson 1996 Blanc de Noirs (Napa Valley) $28. 90 *—S.H. (12/1/2000)*

S. Anderson 1996 Brut (Napa Valley) $28. 86 *—S.H. (12/1/2000)*

S. P. DRUMMER

S. P. Drummer 1999 Blair Vineyard Cabernet Blend (Napa Valley) $45. 93 *—J.M. (11/15/2002)*

S.E. CHASE FAMILY CELLARS

S.E. Chase Family Cellars 2000 Zinfandel (Napa Valley) $36. 91 *—J.M. (9/1/2003)*

SABLE RIDGE

Sable Ridge 1999 Petite Sirah (Russian River Valley) $28. 92 *—S.H. (9/1/2002)*

Sable Ridge 1998 Old Vine Zinfandel (Lodi) $18. 85 *—S.H. (11/15/2001)*

SADDLEBACK

Saddleback 2000 Cabernet Sauvignon (Napa Valley) $48. 92 *—J.M. (12/31/2003)*

Saddleback 2001 Merlot (Napa Valley) $36. 87 *—J.M. (12/31/2003)*

Saddleback 2001 Pinot Grigio (Napa Valley) $18. 87 *—J.M. (12/1/2003)*

Saddleback 1997 Zinfandel (Napa Valley) $26. 85 *—S.H. (5/1/2000)*

Saddleback Cellars 2003 Sauvignon Blanc (Napa Valley) $20. Fully oaked, thus you get aromas of butter, vanilla, and ultra-ripe melon. Plenty of smoke and butter carries onto the palate, where green apple and citrus come into the picture. Solidly structured, with more than enough wood to satisfy a hungry beaver. **86** *(7/1/2005)*

SAGELANDS

Sagelands 2001 Four Corners Cabernet Sauvignon (Columbia Valley (WA)) $12. This is a really nice Cabernet. It's very oaky, but the acidy structure and sappy, fresh young blackberry fruit provide more than enough counterpoint to all that sweet wood. The tannins are just beautiful. An incredible value in New World Cabernet. **88** *—S.H. (1/1/2004)*

Sagelands 2002 Four Corners Merlot (Washington) $12. A very pretty wine, smooth and supple, with more finesse than ever before. It displays clean plum and strawberry fruit flavors and well-managed tannins. A light touch with the American oak gives it a bit of extra flavor. **87 Best Buy** *—P.G. (4/1/2005)*

Sagelands 2000 Four Corners Merlot (Columbia Valley (WA)) $15. 86 *—P.G. (9/1/2002)*

SAINT GREGORY

Saint Gregory 1998 Pinot Blanc (Mendocino) $14. 83 *—S.H. (8/1/2001)*

SAINT LAURENT

Saint Laurent 2001 Solé Riché Red Bordeaux Blend (Columbia Valley (WA)) $22. This oddly named blend of Merlot, Cabernet, and Cab Franc is a well-made effort, with moderately ripe fruit flavors of plum and black cherry, green tea tannins, and spicy oak. Still hard and a showing some stemmy tannins, but should smooth out with a little more bottle time. **86** *—P.G. (4/1/2005)*

Saint Laurent 2003 Chardonnay (Columbia Valley (WA)) $15. Soft and smooth, with flavors of peach, banana, and papaya. Broadly fruity and accessible, but lacks focus and definition. **85** *—P.G. (4/1/2005)*

SAINTSBURY

Saintsbury 2001 Chardonnay (Carneros) $20. 88 *—S.H. (8/1/2003)*

Saintsbury 1999 Reserve Chardonnay (Carneros) $35. 87 *(7/1/2001)*

Saintsbury 2002 Pinot Noir (Carneros) $26. Rather simple and thin, and not quite ripe, with stemmy, grassy flavors, but saved by the cherry finish and supple texture. **84** *(11/1/2004)*

Saintsbury 2000 Pinot Noir (Carneros) $24. 86 *(10/1/2002)*

Saintsbury 1999 Brown Ranch-Estate Bottled Pinot Noir (Carneros) $75. 87 *(10/1/2002)*

Saintsbury 1998 Garnet Pinot Noir (Carneros) $15. 81 *(10/1/1999)*

Saintsbury 1999 Reserve Pinot Noir (Carneros) $50. 86 *—S.H. (7/1/2003)*

SAKONNET

Sakonnet 1996 Brut Champagne Blend (Southeastern New England) $30. 87 *—K.F. (12/1/2002)*

Sakonnet 1999 Chardonnay (Finger Lakes) $15. 89 *—J.C. (7/1/2002)*

SALMON CREEK

Salmon Creek 1999 Cabernet Sauvignon (California) $NA. 85 **Best Buy** *—S.H. (7/1/2002)*

SALMON HARBOR

Salmon Harbor 2000 Chardonnay (Washington) $8. 85 *—P.G. (2/1/2002)*

Salmon Harbor 2000 Merlot (Washington) $9. 87 *—P.G. (12/31/2001)*

SALMON RUN

Salmon Run 2001 Chardonnay (New York) $10. 82 *—J.M. (1/1/2003)*

SALVESTRIN

Salvestrin 1999 Cabernet Sauvignon (Napa Valley) $45. 88 *—S.H. (8/1/2003)*

Salvestrin 2001 Salvestrin Estate Vineyard Cabernet Sauvignon (Napa Valley) $45. Classic Napa Valley '01 Cab. Ripe, soft, complex, juicy, and delicious, showing up front black currant, cassis, chocolate, and smoky oak, with a caramel richness from well-charred wood. The tannins are deft, lush, and sweet. Gets more interesting as it warms up on the table. Try decanting for a few hours. **90** *—S.H. (8/1/2005)*

SAN JUAN VINEYARDS

San Juan Vineyards 2001 Reserve Chardonnay (Columbia Valley (WA)) $17. Has a strong core of pear and ripe apple, buttressed with some spicy oak. The wood tannins are now showing a hard, slightly bitter edge, but if the finish smooths out the wine could rate higher. **86** *—P.G. (5/1/2004)*

San Juan Vineyards 2001 Merlot (Yakima Valley) $23. 100% Merlot, with Yakima Valley black olive/black cherry flavors, nicely ripened, and set against milk chocolaty oak. The barrel flavors of mocha and Bourbon overtake the modest fruit, but it's a very tasty quaff. **86** *—P.G. (5/1/2004)*

San Juan Vineyards 2002 Syrah (Columbia Valley (WA)) $23. Almost tropically fruity, this wine's ultra-ripe berries nevertheless turn tart and balanced on the finish. Pepper and herb notes add complexity. It's not the richest, most textured wine, but it's crisp, clean and—most of all—delivers pleasure. **86** *(9/1/2005)*

SAN SABA

San Saba 1997 Chardonnay (Monterey County) $20. **81** *(6/1/2000)*

San Saba 1998 Chardonnay (Central Coast) $20. **88** *(6/1/2000)*

San Saba 2003 Merlot (Monterey) $22. Soft and cloying, this wine has medicinal cherry and chocolate flavors. **81** *—S.H. (12/15/2005)*

San Saba 1999 Pinot Noir (Central Coast) $19. **86** *—S.H. (2/1/2003)*

SAN SIMEON

San Simeon 2002 Chardonnay (Monterey) $19. Tight and lemony, with firm acids that make the tastebuds whistle. This is a dry Chard well suited to crab dishes. **85** *—S.H. (6/1/2005)*

San Simeon 2002 Merlot (Paso Robles) $22. Drinks very soft, almost collapsed, in the mouth, but the flavors are pretty enough, suggesting a red cherry tart drizzled with vanilla and sprinkled with cocoa. The wine is fully dry, with dusty tannins on the finish. **85** *—S.H. (12/1/2005)*

San Simeon 2002 Petite Sirah (Paso Robles) $22. Harsh in texture and cloying, with cherry cough medicine flavors. **81** *—S.H. (12/1/2005)*

San Simeon 2000 100% Petite Sirah (Paso Robles) $22. **85** *—S.H. (9/1/2003)*

San Simeon 2002 Pinot Noir (Monterey County) $18. Fruity and simple, with bright cherry and vanilla flavors. Rather oaky-sweet throughout. **84** *(11/1/2004)*

San Simeon 1999 Pinot Noir (Monterey) $18. **87** *—J.M. (11/15/2001)*

San Simeon 2001 Syrah (Monterey) $20. Rich and smooth, with finely-grained tannins framing ripe plum, blackberry, cocoa, and sweet-coffee flavors. There's a lot going on in this elegant, sophisticated wine. **89** *—S.H. (6/1/2005)*

San Simeon 1999 Syrah (Arroyo Seco) $16. **85** *—S.H. (7/1/2002)*

SANDHILL

Sandhill 2000 Cabernet Sauvignon (Red Mountain) $25. Forward, medium-style Cabernet with clean cassis and cherry flavors, some light herb and a firm mineral streak in the tight, chalky finish. **85** *—P.G. (1/1/2004)*

Sandhill 2000 Merlot (Red Mountain) $20. Another excellent Merlot from Sandhill, though not as big as the previous vintage. This is more loose, more open, with flavors of cherry and raspberry out front. Firm acids and the stiff, mineral finish that characterizes Red Mountain grapes. **88** *—P.G. (9/1/2004)*

SANFORD

Sanford 1998 Chardonnay (Santa Barbara County) $19. **83** *(6/1/2000)*

Sanford 2002 Chardonnay (Santa Rita Hills) $21. A lovely Chard, filled with crisp acids and steely, stony minerals. The fruit flavors suggest powerfully ripened tropical fruits, and there's a bracing overlay of oak. Notable for its balance and integrity. **90** *—S.H. (4/1/2005)*

Sanford 2000 Chardonnay (Santa Barbara) $19. **89** *—J.M. (5/1/2002)*

Sanford 1998 Barrel Select Chardonnay (Santa Barbara County) $30. **85** *(6/1/2000)*

Sanford 1997 Santa Barbara County Chardonnay (Santa Barbara County) $18. **89** *—S.H. (7/1/1999)*

Sanford 2001 Pinot Noir (Santa Rita Hills) $30. Silky and fine in the mouth, with cherry, raspberry, vanilla, and oak flavors. Finishes oaky and dry. This is a fun, easy wine that will be a good with many different foods. **86** *—S.H. (4/1/2005)*

Sanford 2000 La Rinconada Pinot Noir (Santa Barbara County) $50. **90** *(10/1/2002)*

Sanford 2002 Sanford & Benedict Vineyard Pinot Noir (Santa Barbara County) $43. This is a big, ripe, juicy Pinot, with powerful cherry and blueberry flavors accented with nuances of cola, coffee, cocoa, and oak. It's rich and intricately detailed, and very young, even impertinent. Give it a few years to soften and sweeten. Should improve for five years or more. **93 Cellar Selection** *—S.H. (6/1/2005)*

Sanford 2000 Sanford & Benedict Vineyard Pinot Noir (Santa Barbara County) $NA. Spicy, oaky, rhubarb, beet, lots of sweet cherries, and raspberries. Jammier, fruitier than the ABC 2000, though less delicate and elegant, and rather more accessible. Perhaps less acidic; certainly higher alcohol. **91** *—S.H. (6/1/2005)*

Sanford 1999 Sanford & Benedict Vineyard Pinot Noir (Santa Barbara County) $NA. Good, rich pure garnet color. Excitingly clean, spicy cherry, beet, oak aromas seamlessly meshing into pure Pinot. Lively in bright, zingy acidity. Long, rich, intense in cherry fruit, rosehip tea, cola, root beer, smoky oak. Vibrant, distinguished, delicious. **94 Editors' Choice** *—S.H. (6/1/2005)*

Sanford 1997 Sanford & Benedict Vineyard Pinot Noir (Santa Barbara County) $23. 87 *(12/15/1999)*

Sanford 2000 Sanford and Benedict Vineyard Pinot Noir (Santa Barbara County) $43. 89 *(10/1/2002)*

Sanford 2004 Pinot Noir Vin Gris Rosé Blend (Santa Rita Hills) $14. Light in color, even for a rosé, but there's nothing shy about the flavors. This wine is powerful and complex in red cherries, tobacco, vanilla, and sweet Provençal herbs, and is totally dry, with a fine acidic structure. 87 *—S.H. (12/1/2005)*

Sanford 1997 Sauvignon Blanc (Central Coast) $14. 88 *—S.H. (9/1/1999)*

SANFORD & BENEDICT

Sanford & Benedict 1980 Pinot Noir (Santa Ynez Valley) $NA. Pale, browning. Sediment. Potpourri bouquet, cedar, cigar box, raspberry-cherry crème brulée. Delicate, dry, refined. Rosehip tea, spice flavors. Elegant, silky, still some sweet fruit. Finishes vibrant, crisp, very fine. Alcohol only 12 percent! 92 *—S.H. (6/1/2005)*

SANTA BARBARA WINERY

Santa Barbara Winery 1997 Reserve Chardonnay (Santa Ynez Valley) $24. 84 *(6/1/2000)*

Santa Barbara Winery 2000 Pinot Noir (Santa Barbara County) $13. 86 Best Buy *(10/1/2002)*

Santa Barbara Winery 2001 ZCS Red Blend (California) $13. 85 *—J.M. (12/31/2003)*

Santa Barbara Winery 1998 Late Harvest Sauvignon Blanc (Santa Ynez Valley) $30. 92 *—J.M. (12/1/2002)*

Santa Barbara Winery 2003 Rosé Syrah (Santa Rita Hills) $14. Fairly dark and full-bodied for a rosé, and you'll find cherry-plummy flavors with a finish of white pepper. 84 *—S.H. (10/1/2004)*

SANTO STEFANO

Santo Stefano 1997 Cabernet Sauvignon (Sonoma County) $30. 86 *(11/1/2000)*

SAPPHIRE HILL

Sapphire Hill 1998 Chardonnay (Russian River Valley) $22. 84 *(6/1/2000)*

Sapphire Hill 2000 Winberrie Old Vine Zinfandel (Russian River Valley) $30. 87 *—S.H. (9/1/2002)*

SARIAH CELLARS

Sariah Cellars 2000 Syrah (Red Mountain) $25. 87 *—P.G. (9/1/2002)*

SATURDAY RED

Saturday Red NV 1 Liter Red Blend (California) $9. All this wine wants to be is a useful, friendly, everyday red, and it succeeds quite well. Made from Lodi area grapes, it's dry, full-bodied, and fruity, with a good dusting of tannin. 84 *—S.H. (12/15/2005)*

SAUCELITO CANYON

Saucelito Canyon 2003 Estate Zinfandel (Arroyo Grande Valley) $18. This is the sort of Zin that turns me off. It's not only hot in alcohol, it's definitely sweet in residual sugar, with the flavors of rum-soaked raisins. 82 *—S.H. (10/1/2005)*

Saucelito Canyon 2001 Late Harvest Zinfandel (Arroyo Grande Valley) $20. Decadance in a glass, a brutally delicious wine with flavors of cassis, sweet cherry pie, kirsch, and melted white chocolate sweetened with sugar. It's all framed in a texture of pure velvet. This heady dessert wine wears its high alcohol well. 91 *—S.H. (3/1/2004)*

SAUSAL

Sausal 2002 Cabernet Sauvignon (Alexander Valley) $30. Soft in acids and gentle in tannins, and a little sweet on the finish, this Cab has cherry marmalade and spice flavors. 84 *—S.H. (11/1/2005)*

Sausal 2000 Cabernet Sauvignon (Alexander Valley) $26. 90 *—S.H. (3/1/2003)*

Sausal 2001 Zinfandel (Alexander Valley) $14. 81 *(11/1/2003)*

Sausal 2002 Century Vines Zinfandel (Alexander Valley) $28. Wonderful Zin. Showcases just what these old vines are capable of. Intense, focused flavors of cherries, raspberries, and ripe pomegranates, wrapped in a rich, creamy texture that finishes with a scour of spice. Totally dry, and best of all, it's not too high in alcohol. 92 Editors' Choice *—S.H. (11/1/2005)*

Sausal 2000 Century Vines Zinfandel (Alexander Valley) $26. 89 *—S.H. (9/1/2003)*

Sausal 2002 Old Vine Zinfandel (Alexander Valley) $18. Here's an old-timey Zin, dry, fruity, robust, and spicy. Don't be too fussy, just grill the sausages and enjoy. 86 *—S.H. (8/1/2005)*

Sausal 2002 Private Reserve Zinfandel (Alexander Valley) $22. Here's a big, bold, brawny Zin, rustic and earthy, the kind that will go down easily with barbecue. It's powerful in briary wild blueberries, with a cocoa finish and lots of peppery spice. 88 *—S.H. (11/1/2005)*

Sausal 2000 Private Reserve Zinfandel (Alexander Valley) $20. 88 *—S.H. (9/1/2003)*

Sausal 1996 Sogno della Famiglia Zinfandel (Sonoma County) $25. 90 *(9/1/1999)*

SAUVIGNON REPUBLIC

Sauvignon Republic 2003 Sauvignon Blanc (Russian River Valley) $16. This new label isn't off to a good start, to judge by the watery flavors here. Doesn't taste like much of anything, except alcohol and a drop of lime. **82** *—S.H. (5/1/2005)*

SAVANNAH-CHANELLE

Savannah-Chanelle 1998 Laetitia Vineyard Pinot Blanc (Arroyo Grande Valley) $16. 88 *—S.H. (3/1/2000)*

Savannah-Chanelle 2002 Pinot Noir (Russian River Valley) $22. Minty, oaky, and herbal, a simple, dry wine with modest black cherry and toast flavors. Clean and decent, if not very complex. **85** *(11/1/2004)*

Savannah-Chanelle 2000 Pinot Noir (Central Coast) $20. 85 *—S.H. (5/1/2002)*

Savannah-Chanelle 2002 Armagh Vineyard Pinot Noir (Sonoma Coast) $30. Attractive for the aromatics and the pretty flavors of tart cherries, vanilla, and herbs, Crisp, supple, and elegant in the mouth, this polished wine has a long, oaky-sweet finish. **86** *(11/1/2004)*

Savannah-Chanelle 2002 Garys' Vineyard Pinot Noir (Santa Lucia Highlands) $35. One of this winery's best single-vineyard offerings, showing plenty of cherry, plum, cola, and vanilla flavors despite a light, delicate structure. Complex, spicy, and dry through the finish. **88** *(11/1/2004)*

Savannah-Chanelle 2002 Sleepy Hollow Vineyard Pinot Noir (Santa Lucia Highlands) $25. Very fruity and ripe. Hits strong with forward, jammy cherry, rhubarb, fresh herb, and sweet oak, and tastes racy and savory. Ultimately, though, it's a bit simple in structure. **85** *(11/1/2004)*

Savannah-Chanelle 2002 Coast View Vineyard Syrah (Monterey County) $18. Smoky and tarry on the nose, followed by blueberry, blackberry, coffee, and caramel flavors. Round and velvety in the mouth, lush, with a soft, easygoing finish. **87** *(9/1/2005)*

Savannah-Chanelle 1998 Zinfandel (Paso Robles) $22. 87 *—P.G. (3/1/2001)*

Savannah-Chanelle 1997 Westside Zinfandel (Paso Robles) $18. 88 *—S.H. (5/1/2000)*

SAVIAH CELLARS

Saviah Cellars 2000 Uné Vallee Bordeaux Blend (Columbia Valley (WA)) $28. 86 *—P.G. (9/1/2003)*

Saviah Cellars 2003 Syrah (Walla Walla (WA)) $28. This fleshy sexpot of a Syrah doesn't show a lot of structure, so drink it up over the next year or two for its lush fudge, spicecake and dried fruit flavors. **88** *(9/1/2005)*

Saviah Cellars 2002 Syrah (Red Mountain) $26. Young, grapy, and seductively laden with primary red and blue fruits; a big step forward from their 2001. The grapes come from a young vineyard high on the mountain called "The Ranch at the End of the Road" and show why Syrah is as important to the region's future as Cabernet or Merlot. **90** *—P.G. (11/15/2004)*

Saviah Cellars 2000 Syrah (Red Mountain) $30. 87 *—P.G. (9/1/2003)*

SAWTOOTH

Sawtooth 1999 Merlot (Idaho) $14. 86 *—M.S. (4/1/2003)*

SAWYER

Sawyer 1999 Bradford Meritage Bordeaux Blend (Napa Valley) $42. 92 *—S.H. (11/15/2002)*

Sawyer 2001 Cabernet Sauvignon (Rutherford) $46. Here's a Cab without the sweet flamboyance of some, but it possesses a balance and elegance that make it versatile at the table. The blackberry and herb flavors are framed in rich tannins. **89** *—S.H. (10/1/2004)*

Sawyer 2000 Bradford Meritage (Rutherford) $42. This blend of four varieties, topped by Cabernet Sauvignon and Merlot, shows off its terroir in the richly smooth, soft, complex tannins. There are pleasant flavors of blackberries and cassis, as well as an earthy streak that brings to mind mushrooms sautéed in soy sauce. It will probably age, but is terrific now with a grilled ribeye steak. **91** *—S.H. (6/1/2004)*

Sawyer 1999 Merlot (Rutherford) $34. 93 *—S.H. (11/15/2002)*

Sawyer 2002 Sauvignon Blanc (Rutherford) $15. It's rare to find a Sauvignon Blanc from this appellation, and rarer still to get one this good. It's full-bodied, dry and tart, with a mélange of flavors including citrus fruits, grilled figs, ripe melons, and currants. As it sits on the table, the better and more complex it gets. **91 Best Buy** *—S.H. (12/1/2004)*

Sawyer 2004 Estate Sauvignon Blanc (Rutherford) $17. Very soft and gentle in the mouth, this fruity wine seems to lack the vivacity you want in a Sauvignon Blanc. But the flavors of white currants, fig, vanilla, lemon, and lime are very nice. **84** *—S.H. (12/15/2005)*

SAWYER CELLARS

Sawyer Cellars 2000 Merlot (Rutherford) $34. 93 *—S.H. (12/31/2003)*

SAXON BROWN

Saxon Brown 1999 Pinot Noir (Russian River Valley) $35. 90 *—S.H. (2/1/2003)*

Saxon Brown 2002 Syrah (Napa Valley) $40. The panel's scores for this wine ranged from 80 to 88, so you know it was somewhat controversial. One reviewer found it slightly volatile and raisiny, while at the other extreme, another found it dense, chocolaty, and complex. One you'll definitely want to taste for yourself. **84** *(9/1/2005)*

Saxon Brown 2000 Casa Santinamaria Old Vine Zinfandel (Sonoma Valley) $35. Marches to the beat of good Cabernet with its cassis and chocolate aromas and flavors, lush, complex tannins and overlay of finely smoked French oak. But the persistant undertow of wild, brambly berry and the peppery finish finger it as Zin. **90** *—S.H. (3/1/2004)*

Saxon Brown 1999 Fighting Brothers Cuvée Zinfandel (Sonoma Valley) $30. **86** *—S.H. (2/1/2003)*

SAXUM

Saxum 2003 Bone Rock Syrah (Paso Robles) $56. Here's a young wine that opens with a blast of white pepper, then airs slowly to reveal layers of cassis, grilled meat, chocolate, anise, tar, and toasty oak. In the mouth, it's flamboyant and full-bodied, a little soft, but decadent. This wine is so rich in fruit, you could pour it over vanilla ice cream. It will be fabulous with a charbroiled steak. **94 Editors' Choice** *—S.H. (10/1/2005)*

Saxum 2002 Bone Rock James Berry Vineyard Syrah (Paso Robles) $52. This is awesome Syrah. It starts with wonderfully rich and inviting aromas of Provencal herbs, such as thyme, bay leaf, and rosemary, and a note of lavender. The fruit is all cherries and blackberries, sweet and pure, seasoned with smoky oak. Fresh in acids, backed with firm but soft and complex tannins, this is a dramatic and beautiful wine. What a long, rich finish. **95** *—S.H. (12/31/2004)*

Saxum 2002 Broken Stones Syrah (Paso Robles) $35. Sweet, refined, and pure, a wine that feels delicate despite massive fruit and a considerable overlay of oak. Cherry, smoke, oriental spice, and hung meat flavors are wrapped in smooth, polished tannins. The finish is clean and long. **91** *—S.H. (12/1/2004)*

SBRAGIA

Sbragia 2001 Rancho Del Oso Cabernet Sauvignon (Howell Mountain) $75. Beringer's longtime executive winemaker Ed Sbragia finally has own brand, and this is his first, eagerly anticipated Cabernet. Like Beringer's Private Reserve, it's a gigantic wine. Concentrated and intense in currant, cherries, and cocoa, solidly oaked, and those Howell Mountain tannins are sweet and ripe. Delicious now. Soft, so it's hard to predict how long it will age. Through 2010? **94** *—S.H. (5/1/2005)*

SCHARFFENBERGER

Scharffenberger NV Brut Sparkling Blend (Mendocino County) $15. Here's a dry, classic-style brut, balanced, and elegant. It has subtle flavors of wheat straw, smoke, and bread dough, and clean acids. A little rough, with a rich finish. **87** *—S.H. (12/31/2004)*

SCHEID VINEYARDS

Scheid Vineyards 2001 Riverview Vineyard Pinot Noir (Monterey) $20. Simple and light, with cola, coffee, and cherry flavors, and a slight dusting of smoky oak. Silky in texture, with good, crisp acids. **84** *—S.H. (12/15/2004)*

SCHERRER

Scherrer 2001 Scherrer Vineyard Cabernet Sauvignon (Alexander Valley) $42. Both of Scherrer's '01 Cabs are quite distinctive, but this vineyard designate is superior both in terms of flavor and structure. It's a big wine that rewards in cassis, black currants, and cocoa, and even though it's very soft, it's layered and complex. **93** *—S.H. (11/15/2005)*

Scherrer 2002 Fort Ross Vineyard Reserve Chardonnay (Sonoma Coast) $28. Released at the same price as Scherrer's regular Chard from this vineyard, this one's more intense and focused in tropical fruit. It may have more oak, too, to judge from the flamboyant spice and vanilla. Either way, it's a darned good wine. **92** *—S.H. (11/15/2005)*

Scherrer 2002 Scherrer Vineyard Chardonnay (Alexander Valley) $25. By far the softest of Scherrer's Chards, this one's slightly earthy, like sautéed peach slices wrapped in grape leaves. It also shows its oak treatment in the char and vanilla notes, and tons of spice. **88** *—S.H. (11/15/2005)*

Scherrer 2002 Pinot Noir (Sonoma Coast) $30. Shows real coastal character in the bright, crisp acids that tingle the palate, and the cola, rhubarb and cherry flavors that end with peppery spices. The silky, airy texture is pure Pinot. **87** *—S.H. (11/15/2005)*

Scherrer 2000 Pinot Noir (Russian River Valley) $35. **87** *(10/1/2002)*

Scherrer 2000 Helfer Pinot Noir (Russian River Valley) $35. **86** *(10/1/2002)*

Scherrer 2002 Laguna Pinot Noir (Russian River Valley) $35. I don't know why Scherrer's Laguna bottling costs the same as their regular Russian River Pinot, because it's a better wine. Firmly structured in acids and tannins, it shows waves of cherries, black raspberries, cola, sweet leather, rhubarb, and spices that are endlessly complex and rewarding. **93** *—S.H. (11/15/2005)*

Scherrer 1999 Old Mature Vines Zinfandel (Alexander Valley) $28. **92** *—J.M. (3/1/2002)*

Scherrer 2001 Scherrer Old & Mature Vines Zinfandel (Alexander Valley) $28. **91** *(11/1/2003)*

SCHNEIDER

Schneider 1998 Cabernet Franc (North Fork of Long Island) $24. **87** *—J.C. (4/1/2001)*

SCHRADER

Schrader 2002 Beckstoffer Tokalon Vineyard Cabernet Sauvignon (Oakville) $75. Smells young, closed and dusty, with toast accenting cocoa and cherries. Very dry, tannic, and earthy. Finishes astringent in tannins. Needs lots of time but should be a very good bottle by 2008. **89** *—S.H. (6/1/2005)*

Schrader 2000 Beckstoffer Tokalon Vineyard Cabernet Sauvignon (Napa Valley) $75. Minty, green aroma. Herbal, with oak and modest blackberries. Well-made, elegant, but thin. Drink now. **85** *—S.H. (6/1/2005)*

SCHRAMSBERG

Schramsberg 1998 Blanc de Blancs (California) $30. 86 *—D.T. (12/1/2001)*

Schramsberg 1999 Blanc de Noirs (California) $31. Smooth, yet still has crisp acidity and bubbles. The flavors are subtle: not-yet-ripe strawberries, vanilla, a squeeze of lime, smoke, yeasty bread dough. **91** *—S.H. (6/1/2004)*

Schramsberg 1996 Blanc de Noirs (Napa Valley) $29. 87 *—P.G. (12/31/2000)*

Schramsberg 1995 Blanc de Noirs (Napa Valley) $27. 87 *—J.C. (12/1/1999)*

Schramsberg 1996 Cuvée de Pinot Brut Rosé (Napa Valley) $27. 86 *—J.C. (12/1/1999)*

Schramsberg 1996 J. Schram (Napa County) $80. 93 Editors' Choice *—S.H. (12/1/2002)*

Schramsberg 1993 J. Schram (Napa Valley) $65. 93 *(12/31/2000)*

Schramsberg 1994 Reserve (Napa Valley) $47. 90 *—S.H. (12/31/2000)*

Schramsberg 1998 Blanc de Noirs (California) $30. 92 Editors' Choice *—S.H. (12/1/2002)*

Schramsberg 2000 Blanc de Blancs (Napa-Sonoma) $30. This is really a beautiful bubbly. It's dry, balanced, and elegantly structured, with fine acidity and a deft suggestion of bread dough and yeast on top of subtle citrus and smoke notes. Easy to drink, clean as a whistle, a real beauty. **90** *—S.H. (12/31/2004)*

Schramsberg 1994 Blanc de Blancs Late Disgorged (Napa County) $60. This is a highly pedigreed wine. You can judge that by the exceptionally smooth texture, and the fine quality of all the parts. It's elegant and complex, and despite being 11 years old, the wine is still scoury and pert in acids, guaranteeing it a long future. The dosage gives it a honeyed finish. **92** *—S.H. (12/31/2005)*

Schramsberg 2001 Blanc de Noirs Brut (North Coast) $30. A pale copper color, Schramsberg's Blanc de Noirs is richer than the Blanc de Blancs, with a fuller body. It's also a little more coarse, with pretty flavors of cherry cream and yeast. Try this powerful bubbly with curried lamb. **89** *—S.H. (12/31/2005)*

Schramsberg 2002 Brut Rosé (North Coast) $36. This is the fullest, biggest of Schramsberg's current lineup of bruts, a powerfully fruity but dry wine that never loses sight of elegance, delicacy, and finesse. There's something joyfully effervescent about the way the cherry, cream, yeast, and spice flavors come together and play on the palate. **92** *—S.H. (12/31/2005)*

Schramsberg 2000 Brut Rosé (California) $33. 92 *—S.H. (12/1/2003)*

Schramsberg 2002 Cremant Demi-Sec (North Coast) $36. If you like your bubbly a little sweet but balanced and elegant, with a high-class touch, this is a good choice. Believe it or not, it's based on the grape Flora, supported by Gewürztraminer. It's fruity, with a honeyed finish and wonderful acidity. **85** *—S.H. (12/31/2005)*

Schramsberg 1999 J. Schram (North Coast) $80. Compared to the winery's '99 Reserve, with which it was co-released, this bubbly is slightly sweeter, softer, and smoother. It's a fancy wine, drinkable now with crab cakes or smoked salmon or on its own, of course. Chardonnay-based, the wine possesses a light elegance and very great finesse. But it should age well over the next ten years. **93 Cellar Selection** *—S.H. (12/31/2005)*

Schramsberg 1997 J. Schram (California) $80. 93 *—S.H. (12/1/2003)*

Schramsberg NV Mirabelle (California) $17. 84 *—S.H. (12/1/2003)*

Schramsberg 1999 Reserve (North Coast) $70. For starters, this is a very fine wine, architecturally clean, bone dry, and strong in acids. It's too young to fully enjoy now, though, all raw elbows and yeast. If you don't mind that edgy sharpness, try it as an apéritif, but it will benefit from five years or longer in the cellar. **90 Cellar Selection** *—S.H. (12/31/2005)*

Schramsberg 1997 Reserve (California) $60. If you read the review of Schramsberg's J. Schram, you'll get a sense of this wine. It's nearly identical, but less refined, a bit rougher by comparison. Still, it's a very fine wine, youthful and sharp in acids, but balanced and controlled. Very tight, and clearly needs time. 2006 and beyond. **91** *—S.H. (12/31/2004)*

Schramsberg 1994 Reserve Late Disgorged (Napa Valley) $200. This is a gigantic wine, but it's so well-structured and refined, so beautiful, you can drink it now and fall in love with it. It's perfectly balanced, enormously complex, and not too sweet; the highest-scoring California sparkler we've ever tasted, blending rich toasty notes with well-ripened fruit. This fabulous wine should come together, mellow, and gain complexity for a decade. Only available in magnums or larger bottles. **97 Editors' Choice** *(12/31/2005)*

SCHUG

Schug 2001 Cabernet Sauvignon (Sonoma Valley) $20. Fairly soft in the mouth with a smooth, chalky texture; the mixed plum fruit on the palate is juicy, yet not jammy or over-ripe. Aromas are of plums and black soil. A nice Cabernet, at an agreeable price. **88** *(5/1/2004)*

Schug 1997 Cabernet Sauvignon (Sonoma Valley) $20. **84** *—S.H. (12/15/2000)*

Schug 2000 Heritage Reserve Cabernet Sauvignon (Sonoma Valley) $50. This Cab's black fruit is sturdy, rather than fleshy and ripe—not surprising, since the fruit comes from a cool part of the valley. In the mouth, tannins are chewy, and fairly soft; finishes with chalk, char, and a little herb. Contains 24% Merlot. **89** *(5/1/2004)*

Schug 1997 Heritage Reserve Cabernet Sauvignon (Sonoma Valley) $40. **94** *(11/1/2000)*

Schug 1998 Chardonnay (Sonoma Valley) $14. **87** *—S.H. (5/1/2000)*

Schug 2004 Chardonnay (Carneros) $20. Ripe enough in fruit, with massive, explosive peach custard, key lime pie, and vanilla flavors and a solid overlay of smoky oak. The finish is quick and somewhat simple. **85** *—S.H. (12/31/2005)*

Schug 2001 Chardonnay (Sonoma Valley) $15. **86** *—S.H. (12/1/2003)*

Schug 2000 Chardonnay (Sonoma Valley) $15. **85** *—S.H. (5/1/2002)*

Schug 1998 Chardonnay (Carneros) $18. **93** *—S.H. (11/15/2000)*

Schug 1996 Carneros Reserve Chardonnay (Carneros) $25. **91** *—S.H. (6/1/1999)*

Schug 2002 Heritage Reserve Chardonnay (Carneros) $30. An elegant Chardonnay, with a smooth mouthfeel. Has a yellow-fruit core that's not at all tropical. Finishes with nuances of nut, ginger, and spice. A good food wine, more complementary than showy. **89** *(5/1/2004)*

Schug 2000 Heritage Reserve Chardonnay (Carneros) $30. **87** *—S.H. (5/1/2002)*

Schug 1998 Heritage Reserve Chardonnay (Carneros) $25. **88** *(6/1/2000)*

Schug 2000 Merlot (Sonoma Valley) $20. **90** *—S.H. (12/31/2003)*

Schug 2001 Heritage Reserve Merlot (Carneros) $30. Soft and gentle, with olive, black cherry, and coffee flavors, this wine also shows heat in the midpalate through the finish. **85** *—S.H. (5/1/2005)*

Schug 1997 Heritage Reserve Merlot (Carneros) $35. **89** *—S.H. (11/15/2000)*

Schug 1997 Pinot Noir (Carneros) $18. **83** *(10/1/1999)*

Schug 2002 Pinot Noir (Carneros) $20. A good entry-level Pinot, with flavors of seeped tea, earth. and bright cherries. Similar flavors show on the finish, where there's also some dried spice and herb notes. On the lean side in terms of body, but still a very good wine. **87** *(5/1/2004)*

Schug 2001 Pinot Noir (Carneros) $20. **88** *—S.H. (12/1/2003)*

Schug 2000 Pinot Noir (Carneros) $20. **88** *—S.H. (4/1/2003)*

Schug 1999 Pinot Noir (Carneros) $20. **83** *(10/1/2002)*

Schug 2003 Heritage Reserve Pinot Noir (Carneros) $30. This veteran winery continues to produce a Pinot Noir that's less mind-blowingly opulent than some, hewing stubbornly to European traditions of balance. Acidity and tannins co-star with oak. Schug's flavors get riper every vintage, this year cornering sweet black cherries and spicy cola. **89** *—S.H. (12/31/2005)*

Schug 2001 Heritage Reserve Pinot Noir (Carneros) $30. Classic Schug, a very dry young wine with concentrated black stone fruit flavors, tobacco and lots of herbs. It is well-structured. The tannins are easy and fine, and the acids are firm and crisp. This wine has proven its ability to improve with age. Best after 2007. **91** *—S.H. (4/1/2004)*

Schug 1999 Heritage Reserve Pinot Noir (Carneros) $30. **92** *—S.H. (2/1/2003)*

Schug 1997 Heritage Reserve Pinot Noir (Carneros) $30. **86** *(11/15/1999)*

Schug 1998 Sauvignon Blanc (North Coast) $12. **90 Best Buy** *(3/1/2000)*

Schug 2003 Sauvignon Blanc (Sonoma County) $15. Sweet in fig, honeydew, apple, and spice flavors, this wine has enough acidity to balance out the richness. Has a creamy mouthfeel that adds to the pleasure. **86** *—S.H. (5/1/2005)*

Schug 2001 Sauvignon Blanc (Sonoma County) $15. **84** *—S.H. (9/1/2003)*

Schug 2001 Rouge de Noirs Sparkling Blend (Carneros) $25. From Pinot Noir grapes. It's rare to find a California bubbly this red in color. Opens with bright and expressive cherry, vanilla, and yeast aromas, and turns rich in cherry fruit in the mouth. Unusually full-bodied for a sparkling wine, but very fine. **90** *—S.H. (6/1/2005)*

SCHWEIGER

Schweiger 1999 Cabernet Sauvignon (Spring Mountain) $48. **86** *—S.H. (12/15/2003)*

Schweiger 1999 Merlot (Spring Mountain) $45. **89** *—S.H. (10/1/2003)*

Schweiger 2000 Dedication Red Blend (Spring Mountain) $65. **88** *—S.H. (12/31/2003)*

SCOTT AARON

Scott Aaron 2003 Integrity Cabernet Blend (Paso Robles) $60. If you can open the faux wax capsule on this pompously packaged bottle, you'll find a vin ordinaire Bordeaux blend. It's lifelessly soft, with herb and berry flavors, and a dry finish. **82** *—S.H. (12/15/2005)*

SCOTT PAUL

Scott Paul 1999 Kent Ritchie Vineyard Chardonnay (Sonoma County) $35. **89** *(7/1/2001)*

Scott Paul 2002 Cuvée Martha Pirrie Pinot Noir (Willamette Valley) $20. Sour and sweaty to start, this wine never quite opened up. Slightly sweet, moderately spicy, and lacking in charm, it retained a sweaty, horsey undertone through the finish. **84** *(11/1/2004)*

Scott Paul 2002 La Paulée Pinot Noir (Willamette Valley) $30. Pretty black cherry and cranberry fruit, hints of mushroom, and a good, lingering finish that leads into roasted coffee, nutmeg, and other spices. Ageworthy, but delicious now. **88** *(11/1/2004)*

Scott Paul 1999 Pisoni Vineyard Pinot Noir (Santa Lucia Highlands) $38. **89** *(10/1/2002)*

SCREAMING EAGLE

Screaming Eagle 2001 Cabernet Sauvignon (Oakville) $250. The oak certainly screams out, and it's good oak, freshly hewn and smokily charred. Underneath is super-ripe fruit, plummy to the point of milk chocolate pudding. This big, heavily extracted Cab is classic Eagle in style. **91** *—S.H. (10/1/2004)*

SCREW KAPPA NAPA

Screw Kappa Napa 2002 Cabernet Sauvignon (Napa Valley) $12. A soft, supple, user-friendly Cab, with cassis, dried spices, and hints of brown sugar or caramel. Smooth and easy to drink. **85** *(12/1/2004)*

Screw Kappa Napa 2004 Chardonnay (Napa Valley) $14. There's lots of richness in this well-ripened wine, with tropical fruit and peach flavors, a creamy texture and a notable overlay of spicy, vanilla-tinged charred oak. **84** *—S.H. (12/15/2005)*

Screw Kappa Napa 2002 Chardonnay (Napa Valley) $12. Lighter and fruitier than the Aquinas Chard, this one features similar toast and nut nuances but also bright pineapple and pear flavors. **84** *(12/1/2004)*

Screw Kappa Napa 2002 Merlot (Napa Valley) $12. Some minty notes add nuance to this wine's black cherry, plum, and spice aromas and flavors. Brown sugar and allspice notes on the finish balance the wine's assertive tannins. **85** *(12/1/2004)*

Screw Kappa Napa 2003 Sauvignon Blanc (Napa Valley) $14. Another successful bottling from this brand that nails the style of ripe, slightly sweet fruit, offset by crisp acidity, and delicious flavors of figs, peach custard, and vanilla. Easy to like. **85** *—S.H. (12/15/2005)*

SEA SMOKE

Sea Smoke 2002 Botella Pinot Noir (Santa Rita Hills) $25. Another fine wine from this interesting producer. It's dark, ripe, and extracted, with blackberry, chocolate, cherry, and caramel flavors. It is similar to Sea Smoke's Ten bottling in its huge, Rhône-like flavors and texture. Almost guaranteed to age well through 2010. **89** *(11/1/2004)*

Sea Smoke 2002 Southing Pinot Noir (Santa Rita Hills) $45. Everyone found this wine muscular and full-bodied, and noted it's ripe flavors of blackberries that veer into chocolate and high alcohol. As rich as the flavors are, tasters felt the wine could use more elegance and finesse. **87** *(11/1/2004)*

Sea Smoke 2002 Ten Pinot Noir (Santa Rita Hills) $65. Everybody liked the complexity and balance of this big wine. Opens with a blast of blackberry, cherry pie, smoky vanilla, and molasses, leading to a very rich, full-bodied mouthfeel. Superextracted and tannic, but balanced and elegant nonetheless. Now through 2007. **90** *(11/1/2004)*

SEASIDE

Seaside 2003 Chardonnay (California) $11. Here's your basic, average Chard, clean and proper. It's got a malted mouthfeel with peach and cream flavors. **83** *—S.H. (12/31/2005)*

SEAVEY

Seavey 1997 Cabernet Sauvignon (Napa Valley) $64. **92** *(11/1/2000)*

SEBASTIANI

Sebastiani 2000 Appellation Selection Barbera (Sonoma Valley) $18. **89** *—S.H. (12/1/2002)*

Sebastiani 2001 Appellation Selection Barbera (Sonoma Valley) $15. You don't expect much elegance or breed from a Barbera, but this Cabernet-like wine has both. It's rich in plum, blackberry, and chocolate flavors, and has very gentle but complex tannins. Feels smooth on the palate, with a firm finish. Nice now, and will age for a decade or two. **90 Best Buy** *—S.H. (11/15/2004)*

Sebastiani 2001 Cabernet Sauvignon (Sonoma County) $17. What you get in this pretty wine is the character of a much more expensive Cab, just a little thinned down. Black currant and cherry flavors, a nice veneer of oak, rich, intricate tannins and good acidity combine to make this balanced. **87** *—S.H. (2/1/2005)*

Sebastiani 1998 Cabernet Sauvignon (Sonoma Valley) $24. **90** *—S.H. (11/15/2002)*

Sebastiani 2002 Appellation Selection Cabernet Sauvignon (Alexander Valley) $28. This is a dark, tannic wine that's slightly unbalanced. It

USA

seems to have some residual sugar, making any sort of aging iffy. If not, it still seems sweet. **84** *—S.H. (10/1/2005)*

Sebastiani 1999 Appellation Selection Cabernet Sauvignon (Alexander Valley) $24. 90 *—S.H. (11/15/2002)*

Sebastiani 1999 Cherryblock Cabernet Sauvignon (Sonoma Valley) $70. 90 *(7/1/2003)*

Sebastiani 1996 Cherryblock Cabernet Sauvignon (Sonoma Valley) $95. 87 *(7/1/2003)*

Sebastiani 1992 Cherryblock Cabernet Sauvignon (Sonoma Valley) $120. 87 *(7/1/2003)*

Sebastiani 1986 Cherryblock Cabernet Sauvignon (Sonoma Valley) $170. 86 *(7/1/2003)*

Sebastiani 1991 Cherryblock Vineyard Cabernet Sauvignon (Sonoma Valley) $160. 88 *(7/1/2003)*

Sebastiani 1999 Sonoma County Selection Cabernet Sauvignon (Sonoma County) $17. 90 Editors' Choice *—S.H. (3/1/2003)*

Sebastiani 1997 Chardonnay (Sonoma County) $13. 87 *—M.S. (10/1/1999)*

Sebastiani 2000 Chardonnay (Sonoma County) $12. 82 *—S.H. (12/15/2002)*

Sebastiani 2001 Dutton Ranch Chardonnay (Russian River Valley) $25. 85 *—S.H. (12/1/2003)*

Sebastiani 1998 Dutton Ranch Chardonnay (Russian River Valley) $33. 87 *(10/1/2000)*

Sebastiani 1996 Merlot (Sonoma County) $16. 90 *(3/1/2000)*

Sebastiani 2001 Merlot (Alexander Valley) $24. A wine that excites, not only for its deliciously gooey flavors, but for the restraint and subtlety of its structure. Those flavors are rich and extracted, ranging from black currants, fine coffee, and the ripest black cherries to the sweet vanillins and toast contributed by oak. The tannins are a wonder, sweet and lush, and the finish grows even sweeter. **92 Editors' Choice** *—S.H. (5/1/2004)*

Sebastiani 2000 Merlot (Sonoma County) $17. Here's a soft, gentle wine that's gooey-rich in cherry, cocoa-puff, and ripe, sweet black raspberry flavors. Lightly oaked, it has a cleansing, espresso bitterness on the finish. **87** *—S.H. (2/1/2005)*

Sebastiani 1998 Merlot (Sonoma County) $22. 88 *—S.H. (7/1/2002)*

Sebastiani 1998 Madrone Ranch Merlot (Sonoma Valley) $40. 91 *—S.H. (7/1/2002)*

Sebastiani 2002 Pinot Noir (Sonoma Coast) $15. Rather light in fruit, with sour cherry, tomato, and rhubarb flavors. One taster found the polished texture and spicy finish is pleasing. **85** *(11/1/2004)*

Sebastiani 2000 Pinot Noir (Sonoma Coast) $15. 89 Best Buy *(10/1/2002)*

Sebastiani 1999 Pinot Noir (Russian River Valley) $22. 87 *(10/1/2002)*

Sebastiani 2002 Sonoma County Selection Pinot Noir (Sonoma Coast) $15. Pinots in this price range can be risky, but this one represents a good investment. It's got real Sonoma personality in the silky texture, crisp coastal acids, and raspberry, cherry, vanilla, and cola flavors. **86** *—S.H. (6/1/2004)*

Sebastiani 2002 Secolo Red Blend (Sonoma County) $30. This is a blend of Cabernet Sauvignon, Merlot, and Zinfandel. The Bordeaux varieties make for a balanced claret, rich in black currant flavors. The Zin is way in the background, but seems to add spice and a brambly edge. Oak brings cigar box and cedar complexities. Drink now. **92 Editors' Choice** *—S.H. (11/1/2005)*

Sebastiani 2000 Cohen Vineyard Sauvignon Blanc (Russian River Valley) $18. 86 *(7/1/2003)*

Sebastiani 1999 Domenici Vineyards Zinfandel (Sonoma Valley) $25. 86 *—S.H. (9/1/2002)*

Sebastiani 2000 Old Vines Zinfandel (Sonoma Valley) $20. Here's a good, easy-drinking Zin with some pleasant black cherry, tobacco, and spice flavors that are wrapped in firm, dusty tannins. It's very dry and balanced in acidity and wood, and will be versatile with everything from pizza to pork. **86** *—S.H. (9/1/2004)*

Sebastiani 1998 Old Vines Zinfandel (Sonoma County) $22. 87 *—P.G. (3/1/2001)*

SEBASTOPOL

Sebastopol 2001 Dutton Ranch Chardonnay (Russian River Valley) $24. Shares much in common with the winery's Morelli bottling, except it's a shade less rich. Spicy tropical fruit flavors, smoky oak, a creamy texture and bright acidity make it wonderful to drink now. **90** *—S.H. (12/15/2004)*

Sebastopol 1998 Dutton Ranch Chardonnay (Russian River Valley) $22. 91 *—S.H. (11/1/1999)*

Sebastopol 2001 Dutton Ranch Morelli Lane Vineyard Chardonnay (Russian River Valley) $40. Absolutely delicious, a Chard to ponder, or just to enjoy. Voluptuous flavors of tropical fruits, figs, and spiced plums flood the mouth to the edge of sweetness. This wine is well-oaked, with a rich, creamy texture and an enormously long, spicy finish. **92** *—S.H. (12/15/2004)*

Sebastopol 2002 Dutton Estate Thomas Road Vineyard Pinot Noir (Russian River Valley) $40. Perfect varietal notes of strawberry and tart cherry fruit wrapped in well-charred oak and vanilla. Cool-climate acidity gives the wine a citrusy bite. The silky mouthfeel continues through the long, spicy finish. Easy to like this one. **87** *(11/1/2004)*

Sebastopol 1999 Dutton Ranch Pinot Noir (Green Valley) $30. 93 *—S.H. (7/1/2002)*

Sebastopol 2001 Dutton Ranch Morelli Lane Vineyard Pinot Noir (Russian River Valley) $40. Despite its translucency, this is a big wine in flavor. Fills the mouth with lush cherry, leather, smoke, cola, rhubarb, spicy pepper, and sweet rosehip tea flavors accented with fine smoky oak. What a lovely texture, delicate and silky, yet firm. **91** *—S.H. (12/15/2004)*

Sebastopol 2000 Dutton Ranch Morelli Lane Vineyard Pinot Noir (Russian River Valley) $46. 87 *(10/1/2002)*

Sebastopol 1999 Dutton Estate Gail Ann's Vineyard Syrah (Russian River Valley) $24. 84 *(11/1/2001)*

Sebastopol 2000 Dutton Ranch Gail Ann's Vineyard Syrah (Russian River Valley) $32. 94 Editors' Choice *—S.H. (6/24/2003)*

SECRET HOUSE

Secret House 1998 Pinot Noir (Willamette Valley) $22. 84 *—M.S. (12/1/2000)*

SEGHESIO

Seghesio 2000 Arneis (Russian River Valley) $15. 84 *—S.H. (11/15/2001)*

Seghesio 2001 San Lorenzo Petite Sirah (Alexander Valley) $30. Somewhat astringent, the wine nonetheless harbors a fine blend of black plum, licorice, coffee, chocolate, spice, and herb flavors. It's a big wine that might actually benefit from cellaring. Meanwhile, try it with a big, juicy steak. **89** *(3/1/2004)*

Seghesio 1999 Pinot Noir (Russian River Valley) $25. 88 *—S.H. (12/15/2001)*

Seghesio 1998 Sangiovese (Sonoma County) $20. 87 *—S.H. (12/15/1999)*

Seghesio 1999 Chianti Station Sangiovese (Alexander Valley) $32. This delicate wine has flavors of cherries, Chinese tea, and tobacco. It is dry and acidic; the tannins assert themselves immediately, especially on the finish where they turn tough and sticky. It is not an opulent wine but it's a complex, layered one, dry and tart. Will probably be at its best with food such as roast duck with a cherry sauce, or Chinese barbecued pork. **89** *—S.H. (4/1/2004)*

Seghesio 1998 Zinfandel (Sonoma County) $15. 88 *—S.H. (2/1/2000)*

Seghesio 2000 Zinfandel (Sonoma County) $19. 85 *—S.H. (11/1/2002)*

Seghesio 2000 Cortina Zinfandel (Dry Creek Valley) $30. 87 *—S.H. (11/1/2002)*

Seghesio 2001 Home Ranch Zinfandel (Alexander Valley) $30. 87 *(11/1/2003)*

USA

Seghesio 1998 Home Ranch Zinfandel (Sonoma County) $26. 89 *—P.G. (3/1/2001)*

Seghesio 1998 Old Vine Zinfandel (Sonoma County) $18. 87 *—P.G. (3/1/2001)*

Seghesio 1998 San Lorenzo Zinfandel (Sonoma County) $28. 91 *—P.G. (3/1/2001)*

SELBY

Selby 1999 Dave Selby Reserve Chardonnay (Sonoma County) $40. 93 *—J.M. (12/1/2001)*

Selby 2002 Merlot (Sonoma County) $24. Ripe in cherry and chocolate fruit, with a slightly rustic mouthfeel of edgy tannins and an earthy, mushroomy quality, this Merlot has enough fanciness to accompany a nice leg of lamb or roast pork. **87** *—S.H. (12/15/2005)*

Selby 1999 Syrah (Sonoma County) $24. 84 *(11/1/2001)*

SELENE

Selene 2000 Hyde Vineyards Sauvignon Blanc (Carneros) $29. 86 *(8/1/2002)*

SEQUOIA GROVE

Sequoia Grove 1999 Cabernet Sauvignon (Napa Valley) $29. 86 *—S.H. (11/15/2002)*

Sequoia Grove 2001 Reserve Cabernet Sauvignon (Rutherford) $55. This is one California Cab that hasn't gone over the top, beautifully balancing dried spices and vanilla with bold berry and cassis fruit. It's medium-bodied, its tannins and alcohol in check, finishing long and soft. Drink now–2012. **93 Editors' Choice** *(12/1/2005)*

Sequoia Grove 1999 Reserve Cabernet Sauvignon (Rutherford) $55. 94 Editors' Choice *—S.H. (12/31/2002)*

Sequoia Grove 1997 Chardonnay (Carneros) $16. 84 *(6/1/2000)*

SEVEN DEADLY ZINS

Seven Deadly Zins 2001 Zinfandel (Lodi) $16. 89 *—J.M. (11/1/2003)*

SEVEN HILLS

Seven Hills 2002 Cabernet Sauvignon (Columbia Valley (WA)) $30. This Klipsun vineyard/Red Mountain Cab is thickly tannic and showing fairly strong herbal/black olive flavors, along with wild berry. Big and a bit rugged, but great for steaks. **88** *—P.G. (12/15/2005)*

Seven Hills 1998 Cabernet Sauvignon (Columbia Valley (WA)) $20. 90 Editors' Choice *—P.G. (6/1/2001)*

Seven Hills 1998 Klipsun Vineyard Cabernet Sauvignon (Columbia Valley (WA)) $25. 92 Editors' Choice *—P.G. (6/1/2001)*

Seven Hills 1999 Seven Hills Vineyard Cabernet Sauvignon (Walla Walla (WA)) $30. 91 Editors' Choice *—P.G. (6/1/2002)*

Seven Hills 1997 Seven Hills Vineyard Cabernet Sauvignon (Walla Walla (WA)) $25. 89 *—P.G. (11/15/2000)*

Seven Hills 1998 Walla Walla Valley Reserve Cabernet Sauvignon (Walla Walla (WA)) $32. 93 *—P.G. (6/1/2001)*

Seven Hills 1999 Kilpsun Vineyard Merlot (Columbia Valley (WA)) $28. 91 Cellar Selection *—P.G. (6/1/2002)*

Seven Hills 1999 Reserve Merlot (Columbia Valley (WA)) $40. 89 *—P.G. (6/1/2002)*

Seven Hills 2000 Seven Hills Vineyard Merlot (Walla Walla (WA)) $28. 89 *—P.G. (9/1/2002)*

Seven Hills 1998 Seven Hills Vineyard Merlot (Columbia Valley (WA)) $25. 89 *—P.G. (6/1/2001)*

Seven Hills 1998 Seven Hills Vineyard Reserve Merlot (Walla Walla (WA)) $32. 91 *—P.G. (6/1/2001)*

Seven Hills 1999 Pinot Gris (Willamette Valley) $12. 87 *—P.G. (11/15/2000)*

Seven Hills 2003 Ciel du Cheval Red Blend (Red Mountain) $30. Many wineries work with the spectacular grapes grown at Ciel on Red Mountain, but Seven Hills uses it to craft a deceptively light and airy wine, that promotes elegance and grace over sheer power. Let this wine breathe—decanting would be a good idea—and it fills out into a classic show of tart black cherry, plum, and cranberry fruit, along with gravelly stone. Deceptively concentrated, supple, and tart with finishing whiffs of sandalwood and cinnamon. A fine display of sensitive, detailed winemaking. **91** *—P.G. (12/15/2005)*

Seven Hills 2001 Riesling (Columbia Valley (WA)) $10. 88 *—P.G. (9/1/2002)*

Seven Hills 1999 Syrah (Walla Walla (WA)) $32. 87 *(11/1/2001)*

Seven Hills 1998 Syrah (Walla Walla (WA)) $30. 84 *—P.G. (9/1/2000)*

SEVEN LIONS WINERY

Seven Lions Winery 2000 Blakeman Vineyard Chardonnay (Anderson Valley) $NA. 88 *—S.H. (2/1/2003)*

Seven Lions Winery 2000 Wes Cameron Vineyard 60 Year Old Wente Clone Chardonnay (Russian River Valley) $35. 90 *—J.M. (12/15/2002)*

Seven Lions Winery 1999 Butch & David's Knoll Pinot Noir (Russian River Valley) $65. 84 *(10/1/2002)*

Seven Lions Winery 1999 Joe and Emily's Vineyard Zinfandel (Russian River Valley) $65. 88 *—D.T. (3/1/2002)*

Seven Lions Winery 2000 Poor Man's Flat Vineyards 100 Year Old Vines Zinfandel (Russian River Valley) $30. 86 *—S.H. (9/1/2002)*

SEVEN PEAKS

Seven Peaks 2002 Cabernet Sauvignon (Central Coast) $15. This is quite a good Cab for the ripe currant and black cherry flavors, firm tannins, and smooth mouthfeel. It has that fancy complexity you want from a good red wine, and is priced fairly for the quality. **87** *—S.H. (11/15/2004)*

Seven Peaks 2000 Chardonnay (Central Coast) $12. 82 *—S.H. (6/1/2003)*

Seven Peaks 2002 Merlot (Paso Robles) $15. Soft, juicy, and easy, this wine has excellently ripe berry-cherry flavors and a nice grip of tannins. It's very dry, and picks up interest with the long, pepper-spice finish. **85** *—S.H. (12/15/2004)*

Seven Peaks 2002 Shiraz (Paso Robles) $17. Here's a nice, easy drinking dry red wine from a region that produces them so easily. It's clean and friendly, with juicy fruit and spice flavors and soft acids and tannins. **84** *—S.H. (12/1/2004)*

SEVENTH MOON

Seventh Moon 2001 Merlot (California) $10. If you can overlook the green, minty aspects of less-than-ripe grapes, you'll find a very dry wine, sharp in acids, with a streak of black cherry. **83** *—S.H. (8/1/2004)*

SHADOW CANYON

Shadow Canyon 2001 Shadow Canyon Vineyard Cabernet Sauvignon (Yorkville Highlands) $30. 87 *—S.H. (2/4/2003)*

Shadow Canyon 2002 Paeonia Bien Nacido Vineyard Late Harvest Pinot Blanc (Santa Maria Valley) $45. This sweetie is totally decadent. It's not only the residual sugar, which is a mind-blowing 28 percent, it's the wealth of apricot jam, vanilla, wild honey, and cinnamon spice flavors that blast the palate to ecstasy. Has a syrupy, liqueur-like texture that would be cloying were it not for the excellent acidity. This is one of the best dessert wines of the year. **94** *—S.H. (12/1/2004)*

Shadow Canyon 2003 Shadow Canyon Vineyard Syrah (York Mountain) $38. From this old appellation west of Paso Robles, a big, rich wine with extremely ripe blackberry, cherry, and blueberry flavors and a long, spicy finish. It's pretty tannic now, but that astringency will cut right through a juicy steak or even Chinese-style duck. **90** *—S.H. (12/1/2004)*

Shadow Canyon 2001 Shadow Canyon Vineyard Syrah (Yorkville Highlands) $40. From a coolish appellation west of Paso Robles, a very good interpretation of a cool-climate Syrah. It is fruity, with cherry and blackberry flavors that have an edge of leather and white pepper, and the tannins are firm, but they are smooth, ripe, and thoroughly enjoyable. A winery to watch. **92** *—S.H. (3/1/2004)*

SHADOW HILL

Shadow Hill 1998 Cabernet Sauvignon (Washington) $11. **85** *—P.G. (6/1/2001)*

SHAFER

Shafer 1997 Cabernet Sauvignon (Napa Valley) $45. **89** *(11/1/2000)*

Shafer 1999 Cabernet Sauvignon (Napa Valley) $48. **93** *—S.H. (6/1/2002)*

Shafer 2000 Hillside Select Cabernet Sauvignon (Stags Leap District) $150. Extremely well-oaked, with lovely tannins that are soft and gentle, and subtle flavors of black currants and herbs that finish a little thin. It's a very good wine but certainly not on a par with the magnificent '99. Drink now. **89** *—S.H. (12/31/2004)*

Shafer 1997 Hillside Select Cabernet Sauvignon (Stags Leap District) $150. **96** *—S.H. (12/31/2001)*

Shafer 2001 Napa Valley Cabernet Sauvignon (Napa Valley) $52. Shafer makes it look so easy to produce these lush, massively textured Cabs. This baby has polished flavors of cassis and cherry so rich that they practically overwhelm the powerful tannins. It will certainly be succulent now with a juicy T-bone but is clearly a cellar candidate. However, age will rob it of the robust, juicy fruit of youth. **94** *—S.H. (10/1/2004)*

USA

Shafer 2002 Red Shoulder Ranch Chardonnay (Carneros) $38. This Chardonnay has a long life ahead of it. Strikes the palate as extraordinarily rich with steely, mineral notes and underlying tropical fruit flavors. As good as it is now, it would be a shame to consume it too early. Best after 2006. **92** *—S.H. (9/1/2004)*

Shafer 2000 Red Shoulder Ranch Chardonnay (Carneros) $37. **93 Editors' Choice** *—S.H. (12/15/2002)*

Shafer 1998 Red Shoulder Ranch Chardonnay (Carneros) $35. **91** *(10/1/2000)*

Shafer 1997 Merlot (Napa Valley) $35. **91** *—L.W. (12/31/1999)*

Shafer 2002 Merlot (Napa Valley) $41. A Merlot that showcases ripe blackberry, cherry, and cocoa flavors with lush, sweet tannins. A little soft, but who cares. The oaky overlay merges well. Gentle and drinkable, yet complex and layered. **89** *—S.H. (12/31/2004)*

Shafer 2000 Merlot (Napa Valley) $39. **93** *—S.H. (12/31/2002)*

Shafer 1998 Merlot (Napa Valley) $36. **90** *—J.C. (6/1/2001)*

Shafer 2002 Firebreak Sangiovese (Napa Valley) $36. Continues the tradition of ripe, intricate Firebreaks of recent years, although not quite in the same class as the '99, '00, or '01. Still, it shares the intense cherry and cassis fruit, smooth, complex tannins and delicious veneer of oak. Drink now. **91** *—S.H. (10/1/2005)*

Shafer 2000 Firebreak Sangiovese (Napa Valley) $33. **93 Editors' Choice** *—S.H. (9/1/2003)*

Shafer 2002 Relentless Syrah (Napa Valley) $62. Epitomizes the rich, extracted style of Napa Syrah, cramming jammy blackberries onto a large, sturdy structure, framed by considerable toasty oak. Yet despite the concentration, it doesn't lack for complexity; there are hints of coffee, chocolate, meat, and leather to be sniffed out, and these should become even more notable after cellaring. Drink 2008–2015, maybe beyond. **91 Cellar Selection** *(9/1/2005)*

Shafer 1999 Relentless Syrah (Napa Valley) $46. **94 Cellar Selection** *—J.M. (5/1/2002)*

SHALE RIDGE VINEYARD

Shale Ridge Vineyard 2001 Estate Grown & Bottled Cabernet Sauvignon (Monterey County) $8. **85 Best Buy** *—S.H. (11/15/2003)*

Shale Ridge Vineyard 2002 Lockwood Vineyard Chardonnay (Monterey County) $8. A real value at this price, considering its rich array of tropical fruit and creamy texture. Finishes with a swirl of spicy vanilla. **85 Best Buy** *—S.H. (7/1/2005)*

Shale Ridge Vineyard 2001 Estate Grown & Estate Bottled Sauvignon Blanc (Monterey County) $8. **86 Best Buy** *—S.H. (10/1/2003)*

Shale Ridge Vineyard 2001 Estate Grown & Bottled Syrah (Monterey County) $8. **87 Best Buy** *—S.H. (12/1/2003)*

SHANNON RIDGE

Shannon Ridge 2002 Petite Sirah (Lake County) $27. This is a big wine, but it shows considerable finesse. Pours inky black, and explodes in mulberry, cassis, coffee, and herb flavors that are very dry. The tannins are chewy, suggesting either aging through the decade, or something rib-sticking, like short ribs. **88** *—S.H. (6/1/2005)*

Shannon Ridge 2003 Syrah (Lake County) $30. This full-bodied Syrah skirts the boundary of over-ripe, with some reviewers calling it dense, smooth, and supple, while Tasting Director Joe Czerwinski found it thick and Port-like. At nearly 16% alcohol, maybe he has a point. But for lovers of the style, this chocolaty Syrah will hit the mark. **85** *(9/1/2005)*

SHARP CELLARS

Sharp Cellars 2003 Tyla's Point Vineyards Pinot Blanc (Sonoma Valley) $19. For a variety with little identity in California, this one has plenty of personality. It's nutty and creamy, with detailed flavors of citrus rind and peach and a rich, but balancing, overlay of oak. It's also very dry with good acidity. **90 Editors' Choice** *—S.H. (6/1/2005)*

SHEA

Shea 2000 Shea Vineyard Chardonnay (Willamette Valley) $25. 90 —*P.G. (12/31/2002)*

Shea 2002 Block 32 Pinot Noir (Willamette Valley) $48. Leathery and ripe, with the vineyard's classic blackberry and cassis fruit. Plenty of smoky oak gives it a tannic heaviness that is a bit unbalanced. 86 *(11/1/2004)*

Shea 2002 Shea Vineyard Estate Pinot Noir (Willamette Valley) $35. Pungent, austere, and awkward with distracting scents of sulfur and cracker. There's light cherry fruit here, quite tart and tannic, unyielding. 84 *(11/1/2004)*

Shea 2002 Shea Vineyard Pommard Clone Pinot Noir (Willamette Valley) $38. This has a funky nose, with barnyard scents of leather and manure. The wine seems to fall off in the mid-palate, then comes back to finish with some thick flavors of blackberry, black cherry, and spicy oak. Somewhat controversial. 87 *(11/1/2004)*

SHELDRAKE POINT

Sheldrake Point 2002 Dry Riesling (Finger Lakes) $13. 86 —*J.C. (8/1/2003)*

SHELTON VINEYARDS

Shelton Vineyards 2002 Riesling (North Carolina) $10. 86 —*J.C. (8/1/2003)*

SHENANDOAH

Shenandoah 2000 Reserve Barbera (Shenandoah Valley (CA)) $24. 87 —*S.H. (12/1/2002)*

Shenandoah 2002 Rezerve Barbera (Shenandoah Valley (CA)) $24. Mountain red wine, big, bold, brawny, hot, and packed with ripe red and black stone fruit flavors. Completely dry, with outsized but velvety tannins, this wine defines a long-lived style of Barbera, and is really quite wonderful. 91 —*S.H. (9/1/2004)*

Shenandoah 2000 Rezerve Cabernet Sauvignon (Shenandoah Valley (CA)) $24. 85 —*S.H. (11/15/2003)*

Shenandoah 2002 Rezerve Primitivo Red Blend (Shenandoah Valley (CA)) $24. Porty in its inky black color, caramelized aroma, raisiny flavors and burn from high alcohol, although there's no residual sweetness. Has plummy, chocolaty notes all the way through, and is quite tannic. 86 —*S.H. (9/1/2004)*

Shenandoah 1999 Sangiovese (Amador County) $13. 82 —*S.H. (12/1/2002)*

Shenandoah 2004 Sauvignon Blanc (Amador County) $11. Opens with a minty, eucalyptus-like aroma, and taste dry and bitter, with herbal, spicy flavors. Unusual, even exotic for Sauvignon Blanc, but not unattractive. 85 —*S.H. (10/1/2005)*

Shenandoah 2002 Sauvignon Blanc (Amador County) $10. 84 —*S.H. (7/1/2003)*

Shenandoah 2002 Rezerve White Port (Shenandoah Valley (CA)) $11. Made from the Viognier grape, this is a very sweet wine that oozes flavors of orange custard, honeysuckle, vanilla, caramel, and white fudge. It's tremendously spicy, with a firm acidity that creates a clean zestiness despite the sugar. 90 —*S.H. (9/1/2004)*

Shenandoah 2002 Rezerve Zinfandel (Shenandoah Valley (CA)) $24. From Sobon Estate, and certainly richer and meatier than the regular Sobon Zins, yet marked by similar characteristics. It's hot in alcohol, over-ripe in raisiny flavors, and thick and heavy in the mouth, although it's nicely dry. 86 —*S.H. (9/1/2004)*

Shenandoah 2003 Special Reserve Zinfandel (Amador County) $10. Good price for a lusty Zin filled with ripe cherry, blackberry, and chocolate flavors. It has that briary nettle quality that marks the variety, and is soft. 85 Best Buy —*S.H. (10/1/2005)*

Shenandoah 2001 Special Reserve Zinfandel (Amador County) $10. 87 Best Buy *(11/1/2003)*

Shenandoah 1997 Special Reserve Zinfandel (Amador County) $9. 87 Best Buy —*L.W. (9/1/1999)*

Shenandoah 2003 White Zinfandel (Shenandoah Valley (CA)) $6. There's not much color to this pale wine, and not much flavor either, except for sugar and weak, diluted strawberries. But it's acceptable. 83 —*S.H. (9/1/2004)*

Shenandoah VA 1997 Founder's Reserve Chambourcin (Shenandoah Valley) $17. 86 —*J.C (8/1/1999)*

Shenandoah VA 1997 Founder's Reserve Chardonnay (Virginia) $16. 82 —*J.C. (8/1/1999)*

SHERIDAN VINEYARD

Sheridan Vineyard 2000 Red Blend (Yakima Valley) $30. 86 —*P.G. (9/1/2003)*

Sheridan Vineyard 2002 Syrah (Yakima Valley) $36. Smells just like blackberry preserves at first, but reveals additional complexity with a little time in the glass, developing hints of pepper and herbs. Ultrasmooth in the mouth—almost a little syrupy in consistency—leading elegantly into a full, creamy-textured finish. 88 *(9/1/2005)*

SHERWIN FAMILY

Sherwin Family 1996 Cabernet Sauvignon (Spring Mountain) $52. 92 —*J.C. (7/1/2000)*

SHERWOOD HOUSE VINEYARDS

Sherwood House Vineyards 2001 Merlot (North Fork of Long Island) $27. 83 —*J.C. (10/2/2004)*

SHOOTING STAR

Shooting Star 2000 Aligoté (Washington) $13. 85 *—P.G. (6/1/2002)*

Shooting Star 2001 Blue Franc Lemberger (Washington) $12. 88 Best Buy *—C.S. (12/31/2002)*

Shooting Star 2000 Pinot Noir (Carneros) $14. 81 *(10/1/2002)*

Shooting Star 1999 Syrah (Lake County) $12. 84 *(10/1/2001)*

Shooting Star 1998 Zinfandel (Lake County) $12. 87 *—P.G. (3/1/2001)*

SHOWKET

Showket 2001 Cabernet Sauvignon (Oakville) $75. How sweet the fruit got during this ripe vintage. There's a crème de cassis flavor and a liqueury texture, drizzled with a sprinkle of vanilla dust and cinnamon. That makes it sound like a dessert wine, but it's dry. The balanced structure suggests midterm aging. **92** *—S.H. (10/1/2004)*

Showket 1997 Sangiovese (Napa Valley) $35. 88 *—S.H. (12/15/1999)*

Showket 2001 Sangiovese (Oakville) $30. A dark wine, impressive for its brooding color, oak, and tremendous black currant and cherry fruit. Don't expect anything Tuscan; this is chocolaty and soft, but quite delicious. In the top ranks of current Sangioveses. **89** *—S.H. (10/1/2005)*

SIDURI

Siduri 2002 Pinot Noir (Central Coast) $25. This Pinot, a blend from a large, cool region, shows modest aromas and flavors of cherries, herbs, and tobacco. It's very dry, with some sharp acids and earthy tannins. Try this versatile table wine with barbecued sausages, and pasta with olive oil and herbs. **85** *—S.H. (5/1/2004)*

Siduri 2001 Pinot Noir (Sonoma Coast) $28. 91 Editors' Choice *—S.H. (7/1/2003)*

Siduri 1999 Pinot Noir (Santa Lucia Highlands) $34. 88 *(10/1/2002)*

Siduri 2001 Garys' Vineyard Pinot Noir (Santa Lucia Highlands) $50. From this well-regarded vineyard, a big, juicy wine that is very ripe and jammy. It offers up an array of blackberry, cherry, boysenberry, espresso, and tobacco flavors, emphasized with Asian spice. Very dry, with silky tannins and crisp acidity. **88** *—S.H. (3/1/2004)*

Siduri 1999 Garys' Vineyard Pinot Noir (Santa Lucia Highlands) $49. 90 *(10/1/2002)*

Siduri 1999 Hirsch Vineyard Pinot Noir (Sonoma County) $49. 90 *(10/1/2002)*

Siduri 1997 Hirsch Vineyard Pinot Noir (Sonoma Coast) $42. 92 *(10/1/1999)*

Siduri 2000 Pisoni Pinot Noir (Santa Lucia Highlands) $50. 93 Editors' Choice *(10/1/2002)*

Siduri 2000 Van der Kamp Pinot Noir (Sonoma Mountain) $48. 83 *(10/1/2002)*

Siduri 1999 Van Der Kamp Vineyard Pinot Noir (Sonoma Mountain) $49. 87 *(10/1/2002)*

SIERRA CLUB

Sierra Club 2000 Atira Vineyards Cabernet Sauvignon (Napa Valley) $19. Decently drinkable, with some sweetness to the cherry-berry flavors, and a rough mouthfeel that turns gritty with tannins in the finish. **83** *—S.H. (8/1/2005)*

SIERRA VISTA

Sierra Vista 2001 Belle Rose Rhône Red Blend (El Dorado) $9. 86 *—S.H. (9/1/2003)*

Sierra Vista 2000 Fleur de Montagne Rhône Red Blend (El Dorado) $21. 85 *—S.H. (5/1/2003)*

Sierra Vista 1997 Five Star Reserve Syrah (El Dorado County) $60. 90 *(11/1/2001)*

Sierra Vista 1997 Red Rock Ridge Syrah (El Dorado County) $19. 89 *—S.H. (10/1/1999)*

Sierra Vista 1998 Viognier (El Dorado County) $20. 89 *—S.H. (10/1/1999)*

Sierra Vista 1999 Reeves Zinfandel (El Dorado) $16. 85 *—S.H. (11/1/2002)*

SIGNORELLO

Signorello 1997 Padrone Bordeaux Blend (Napa Valley) $125. 92 *(11/1/2000)*

Signorello 1997 Cabernet Sauvignon (Napa Valley) $48. 91 *—S.H. (2/1/2000)*

Signorello 1999 Cabernet Sauvignon (Napa Valley) $48. 91 *—S.H. (6/1/2002)*

Signorello 2000 Estate Unfiltered Cabernet Sauvignon (Napa Valley) $48. 89 *—S.H. (6/1/2003)*

Signorello 1998 Estate Chardonnay (Napa Valley) $38. 89 *—S.H. (5/1/2000)*

Signorello 2002 Hope's Cuvée Chardonnay (Napa Valley) $60. The acids are high, the oak is powerful and this densely structured wine is

USA

wrapped in a cloak of steel and mineral. It hasn't all come together yet. But the flavors are ripe and pure, straddling the line between tropical fruits and juicy apples, and this is one of those rare Chards that needs age. Best toward 2005, and will hold for several years afterward. **93** *—S.H. (8/1/2004)*

Signorello 1999 Hope's Cuvée Chardonnay (Napa Valley) $60. 89 *(7/1/2001)*

Signorello 2001 Vieilles Vignes Chardonnay (Napa Valley) $38. 90 *—S.H. (6/1/2003)*

Signorello 1999 Estate Merlot (Napa Valley) $45. 89 *—S.H. (2/1/2003)*

Signorello 2001 Las Amigas Vineyard Pinot Noir (Carneros) $32. There's an amazing density to this wine, which has a molten quality to the mouthfeel. It's as if the cherry, raspberry, mocha, and cinnamon flavors were dissolved in mercury. On the other hand, the tannin-acid structure is a wonder. Intricate and dry, this single-vineyard beauty feels easy and silky. **93** *—S.H. (4/1/2004)*

Signorello 1999 Las Amigas Vineyard Pinot Noir (Carneros) $50. 89 *—S.H. (9/1/2003)*

Signorello 1997 Las Amigas Vineyard Pinot Noir (Carneros) $45. 90 *(10/1/1999)*

Signorello 1998 Barrel-Fermented Sémillon (Napa Valley) $22. 91 Editors' Choice *—S.H. (8/1/2001)*

Signorello 2000 Seta Semillon-Sauvignon Blanc (Napa Valley) $25. 90 *—S.H. (9/12/2002)*

Signorello 2002 Seta White Wine Sémillon-Sauvignon Blanc (Napa Valley) $25. This fabulous blend of Sémillon and Sauvignon Blanc approaches a great white Bordeaux in complexity and sheer deliciousness. There's a lushness and intricacy to the texture beyond the ripe peach, lemongrass, fig, and buttercream flavors. The result is balanced, elegant, and harmonious, with great finesse. One of the best wines of its type in recent vintages. **92** *—S.H. (8/1/2004)*

Signorello 2002 Estate Syrah (Napa Valley) $32. Straddles a fine line between ripe, plummy-blackberry flavors and a leathery, peppery side. You'll also like the plush, rich tannic structure. Best now. **91** *—S.H. (6/1/2005)*

Signorello 2002 Luvisi Vineyard Zinfandel (Napa Valley) $34. Oaky and jammy and a little sweet in cherry flavors, this Zin also finishes hot. It lacks overall finesse, especially at this price. **84** *—S.H. (6/1/2005)*

Signorello 2000 Luvisi Vineyard Zinfandel (Napa Valley) $34. 85 *—S.H. (3/1/2003)*

SILK OAK

Silk Oak 1999 Chardonnay (Lodi) $16. 80 *—S.H. (11/15/2001)*

SILVAN RIDGE

Silvan Ridge 1999 Cabernet Sauvignon (Rogue Valley) $26. 84 *—C.S. (12/31/2002)*

Silvan Ridge 1999 Bing Vineyard Ice Wine Gewürztraminer (Umpqua Valley) $20. 92 *—J.M. (12/1/2002)*

Silvan Ridge 2002 Early Muscat-Semi Sparkling Muscat (Oregon) $14. 85 *—M.S. (8/1/2003)*

Silvan Ridge 2001 Pinot Gris (Oregon) $14. 83 *—M.S. (8/1/2003)*

Silvan Ridge 2000 Pinot Noir (Willamette Valley) $23. 86 *—M.S. (9/1/2003)*

Silvan Ridge 1998 Pinot Noir (Willamette Valley) $22. 87 *—S.H. (8/1/2002)*

Silvan Ridge 1996 Eola Springs Vineyard Pinot Noir (Willamette Valley) $26. 85 *(10/1/1999)*

Silvan Ridge 2001 Del Rio Vineyard Syrah (Rogue Valley) $20. Southern Oregon is working hard on growing Syrah, and this is a promising effort. Thick, hard tannins are characteristic of this vineyard's fruit, which has a tight, concentrated core of cherry liqueur. It's young, hard, and tart, but promising. Give it time. **87** *—P.G. (10/1/2004)*

Silvan Ridge 2002 Del Rio Vineyard Viognier (Rogue Valley) $18. 86 *—P.G. (12/1/2003)*

SILVER

Silver 2000 Cabernet Sauvignon (Santa Barbara County) $30. 88 *—J.M. (12/31/2003)*

Silver 2000 Nebbiolo (Santa Barbara County) $22. 88 *—J.M. (12/1/2003)*

Silver 2001 Lake Marie Vineyard Pinot Noir (Santa Barbara County) $40. A smooth, complex wine brimming with pretty cherry, anise, spice, and herb flavors. A hint of sage and thyme adds finesses to the finish, which is long. Well-balanced and fine-crafted. **90** *—J.M. (12/31/2004)*

Silver 2000 Sangiovese (Santa Barbara County) $28. 89 *—J.M. (2/1/2003)*

Silver 2001 Vogelzang Vineyard Viognier (Santa Barbara County) $22. 89 *—J.M. (6/1/2003)*

SILVER LAKE

Silver Lake 1998 Reserve Cabernet Sauvignon (Columbia Valley (WA)) $25. 84 *—C.S. (12/31/2002)*

Silver Lake 2000 Chardonnay (Columbia Valley (WA)) $12. 85 *—M.S. (6/1/2003)*

Silver Lake 2000 Reserve Chardonnay (Columbia Valley (WA)) $14. 88 *—M.S. (6/1/2003)*

Silver Lake 2001 Fumé Blanc (Columbia Valley (WA)) $9. 84 *—M.S. (6/1/2003)*

Silver Lake 1999 Reserve Merlot (Columbia Valley (WA)) $25. 89 *—C.S. (12/31/2002)*

SILVER MOUNTAIN

Silver Mountain 1997 Chardonnay (Santa Cruz Mountains) $18. 85 *(6/1/2000)*

SILVER PINES

Silver Pines 2003 Sauvignon Blanc (Sonoma Mountain) $35. An extraordinary Sauvignon Blanc, and so clean. If you like your Marlboroughs, you'll love the dry gooseberry, hay, and lime zest flavors, with their edges of white pepper and smoke. Possesses real complexity in the penetratingly crisp acids and long finish. **90** *—S.H. (12/31/2004)*

SILVER RIDGE

Silver Ridge 2003 Chardonnay (California) $10. Lots of peach, pear, and pineapple fruit here, with a tasty layer of vanilla and smoke. A good value. **84** *—S.H. (8/1/2005)*

Silver Ridge 1999 Barrel Select Syrah (California) $10. 86 *(10/1/2001)*

SILVER RIDGE VINEYARDS

Silver Ridge Vineyards 2000 Barrel Select Syrah (California) $10. 86 Best Buy *—S.H. (10/1/2003)*

SILVER ROSE CELLARS

Silver Rose Cellars 1999 Chardonnay (Napa Valley) $23. 86 *—J.M. (12/31/2001)*

SILVER SPUR

Silver Spur 2003 Sangiacomo Vineyards Chardonnay (Carneros) $18. Properly varietal, with peach, pear, and spice flavors and a woody, creamy texture, but can't quite rise above average. **83** *—S.H. (10/1/2005)*

SILVER STONE WINERY

Silver Stone Winery 2001 Cabernet Sauvignon (California) $9. You'll get real Cab character in this wine, with its black currant and oak flavors. It's dry and balanced and has some real richness. **85 Best Buy** *—S.H. (10/1/2004)*

Silver Stone Winery 2003 Chardonnay (California) $9. A pretty good everyday Chard, with peach and oak flavors and a creamy texture. Finishes a little syrupy. **83** *—S.H. (10/1/2005)*

Silver Stone Winery 2003 Bien Nacido Vineyard Chardonnay (Santa Maria Valley) $25. A decent Chardonnay with some interest, although it's a little thin on the finish. Smells of toasty oak, vanilla, butterscotch, and tangerines, and while that sounds good, the intensity isn't so great. **85** *—S.H. (10/1/2005)*

Silver Stone Winery 1999 Merlot (California) $9. The fruity flavors are beginning to dry out, yet there's still some cherry-berry stuff going on. Tannins turn tough and gritty on the finish. **83** *—S.H. (5/1/2004)*

Silver Stone Winery 2001 Shiraz (California) $9. A bit sharp in youthful acidity, but the jammy berry and cherry flavors are tasty, and the wine is serviceable. **83** *—S.H. (6/1/2004)*

Silver Stone Winery 2002 Hall Ranch Syrah (Paso Robles) $33. Table wines hardly get bigger in fruit than this soft, luscious wine. It's explosive in red cherry, chocolate fudge, pecan pie, and spice flavors, but seems totally dry. It would have scored higher had one taster not been bothered by some nail polish and vinegar notes. **85** *(9/1/2005)*

SILVER THREAD

Silver Thread 1999 Reserve Chardonnay (Finger Lakes) $17. A breakthrough Chardonnay from upstate New York. Aromas of toasted nuts and buttered spiced pears are classic, with flavors of cinnamon, pears, and cashews that feel custardy in the mouth. Finishes long, with tangy acids and nutty overtones. Editors' Choice. **90 Editors' Choice** *—J.C. (1/1/2004)*

Silver Thread 2002 Riesling (Finger Lakes) $13. 90 Best Buy *—J.C. (8/1/2003)*

SILVERADO

Silverado 2000 Cabernet Sauvignon (Napa Valley) $35. This is a wine of pedigree. It shows in the exquisite acids and tannins and overall balance of its parts, including oak. The flavors are classic black currants and cassis, with a nice edge of dried herbs. Not a blockbuster, it's probably at its best now. **90** *—S.H. (5/1/2004)*

Silverado 1999 Cabernet Sauvignon (Stags Leap District) $65. 95 Editors' Choice *—S.H. (11/15/2002)*

Silverado 2001 Limited Reserve Cabernet Sauvignon (Napa Valley) $100. Another fabulous Cab from this supernatural vintage. It stuns for the ripeness of the black currant, cherry, and chocolate fruit, and the richness of the soft, sweet tannins. So easy to drink, yet never loses its sense of balance, harmony, and complexity. **94** *—S.H. (12/31/2004)*

Silverado 2000 Single-Vineyard Selection Cabernet Sauvignon (Stags Leap District) $65. A very fine wine that is soft and voluptuous in

USA

the mouth. Its power is in the deep core of blackberry fruit and the tightly wound tannins. Not a long-term ager, but should gain complexity through 2008. **90** *—S.H. (11/15/2004)*

Silverado 1997 Chardonnay (Napa Valley) $21. 90 *—S.H. (11/15/1999)*

Silverado 2001 Chardonnay (Napa Valley) $20. 87 *—S.H. (6/1/2003)*

Silverado 1999 Chardonnay (Napa Valley) $20. 86 *—J.M. (5/1/2002)*

Silverado 2000 Merlot (Napa Valley) $25. Soft and supple in the mouth, with ripe blackberries and spiced plums joined by smoky oak. Firms up on the finish, showing some rough edges, but still an excellent effort from a challenging vintage. **90** *(5/1/2004)*

Silverado 1997 Sangiovese (Napa Valley) $20. 88 *—S.H. (12/15/1999)*

Silverado 1998 Sangiovese (Napa Valley) $18. 88 *—S.H. (5/1/2002)*

Silverado 2002 Sauvignon Blanc (Napa Valley) $16. Quite lovely in the nose, with a vivid passionfruit quality. On the palate, it's fairly lean, though refreshing, with a core of lemon and grapefruit, finishing with a grassy edge. Perfect for shellfish. **88** *—J.M. (9/1/2004)*

Silverado 2001 Sauvignon Blanc (Napa Valley) $14. 86 *—S.H. (3/1/2003)*

SILVERSMITH

Silversmith 2000 Petite Sirah (Redwood Valley) $30. 80 *(4/1/2003)*

SIMI

Simi 2002 Cabernet Sauvignon (Alexander Valley) $25. Tough and raw in texture, with dried herb and coffee flavors. **83** *—S.H. (3/1/2005)*

Simi 1996 Cabernet Sauvignon (Sonoma County) $24. 86 *—L.W. (12/31/1999)*

Simi 2000 Landslide Vineyard Cabernet Sauvignon (Alexander Valley) $40. Dense and tannic, with lots of black currant and cherry flavors and elaborate oak. Acids and tannins help it to achieve a certain complexity. Notable for its smooth structure. It's best consumed soon, with a good steak. **90** *—S.H. (4/1/2004)*

Simi 1999 Reserve Cabernet Sauvignon (Alexander Valley) $75. 94 Cellar Selection *—S.H. (12/31/2003)*

Simi 1995 Reserve Cabernet Sauvignon (Sonoma County) $45. 93 *—L.W. (12/31/1999)*

Simi 2003 Chardonnay (Sonoma County) $17. Fruity, oaky, creamy, and slightly sweet, this Chard is solidly in the international style. It offers flavors of peaches, pears, vanilla, and buttered toast. **85** *—S.H. (3/1/2005)*

Simi 1999 Chardonnay (Sonoma County) $21. 88 *—J.M. (12/1/2001)*

Simi 1997 Chardonnay (Sonoma County) $19. 89 *—S.H. (10/1/1999)*

Simi 1999 Goldfields Vineyard Reserve Chardonnay (Russian River Valley) $30. 87 *—S.H. (2/1/2003)*

Simi 2002 Reserve Chardonnay (Russian River Valley) $25. Textbook RRV Chard, with its bright, clean acids and savory flavors of ripe apples, pears, and minerals, and dusty spices. All of this is well oaked, but the vanilla and char fit in just fine. The creamy texture adds allure. **90** *—S.H. (3/1/2005)*

Simi 1996 Reserve Chardonnay (Russian River Valley) $29. 89 *—S.H. (10/1/1999)*

Simi 2002 Merlot (Sonoma County) $20. A middle of the road Merlot, dry and fairly tannic, with berry and earth flavors. **83** *—S.H. (3/1/2005)*

Simi 2003 Sauvignon Blanc (Sonoma County) $14. Pleasant and clean, a zesty wine of bright acidity boosting slightly sweet flavors of peaches, figs, spices, and smoky oak. This is a pretty, cocktail-style wine. **85** *—S.H. (12/15/2004)*

Simi 2001 Sauvignon Blanc (Sonoma County) $14. 86 *—S.H. (3/1/2003)*

Simi 1999 Sauvignon Blanc (Sonoma County) $15. 87 *—J.M. (11/15/2001)*

Simi 1999 Reserve Sendal Sauvignon Blanc (Sonoma County) $20. 91 *—S.H. (9/1/2002)*

Simi 1996 Sendal Sauvignon Blanc (Sonoma County) $20. 89 *—S.H. (9/1/1999)*

Simi 1999 Reserve-Sendal White Blend (Sonoma County) $20. 91 Editors' Choice *—S.H. (9/1/2002)*

SINE QUA NON

Sine Qua Non 2002 Whisperin' E Rhône White Blend (California) $72. This is a very fine dry white wine. It's intense in ripe fruit, but is hardly a bomb, the flavors reined in by superb acids, judicious oak, and a minerality and earthiness that ground the power. A blend of Roussane, Viognier, and Chardonnay. **93** *—S.H. (6/1/2005)*

Sine Qua Non 1998 E-Raised Syrah (California) $75. 93 *(11/1/2001)*

Sine Qua Non 1999 The Marauder Syrah (California) $75. 91 *(7/1/2002)*

SINEANN

Sineann 2001 Baby Poux Vineyard Cabernet Sauvignon (Columbia Valley (WA)) $27. 90 *—P.G. (12/31/2003)*

Sineann 2001 McDuffee Vineyard Cabernet Sauvignon (Columbia Valley (OR)) $30. 89 *—P.G. (12/1/2003)*

Sineann 2002 Celilo Vineyard Gewürztraminer (Columbia Valley (WA)) $18. 90 *—P.G. (12/31/2003)*

Sineann 2002 Reed & Reynolds Gewürztraminer (Willamette Valley) $18. 91 Editors' Choice *—P.G. (12/1/2003)*

Sineann 2003 Hillside Merlot (Columbia Valley (OR)) $30. Very tight, still pulling itself together. Give this one lots of breathing time! There is plenty of concentrated black cherry and plum fruit, and hints of clove and Asian spice. Not your typical Merlot; this has real muscle and concentration. 91 *—P.G. (4/1/2005)*

Sineann 2002 Pinot Gris (Oregon) $15. 89 *—P.G. (12/1/2003)*

Sineann 2003 Pinot Noir (Oregon) $30. The best Oregon bottling ever from this exceptional producer. Spectacular, ripe, plush aromatics open into plummy, jammy, purely varietal fruit. But there is more, a textural complexity that incorporates light herb, leaf, and vanilla notes. This has it all, and offers every bit as much pleasure as any of the single-vineyard bottlings. 92 *—P.G. (12/15/2004)*

Sineann 2001 Covey Ridge Pinot Noir (Oregon) $42. 88 *—P.G. (12/1/2003)*

Sineann 2003 Phelps Creek Vineyard Pinot Noir (Columbia Gorge) $42. Sporting the brand-new Columbia Gorge AVA designation, this terroir-driven Pinot, from the Oregon side of the Columbia River, is a world apart from the Willamette Valley Pinots commonly associated with the state. Here the purity of sweet Bing cherry fruit is buttressed with clear mineral notes, and wrapped in very pleasing, caramel and cocoa barrel flavors. It shows a tart, tangy spine that keeps it balanced and extends the fruit flavors well into the long, crisp finish. 93 Editors' Choice *—P.G. (12/15/2004)*

Sineann 2000 Reed & Reynolds Vineyard Pinot Noir (Oregon) $54. 88 *—P.G. (12/31/2002)*

Sineann 2003 Whistling Ridge Vineyard Pinot Noir (Columbia Valley (OR)) $36. The cherry flavors are so concentrated here that it is almost like a liqueur, with some pretty raspberry highlights as well. Compact and wrapped in toast and cracker, this is stylish and elegant despite the density and concentration. Firmly tannic, it seems destined to age along classic Burgundian lines. Cellar 8–10 years. 91 Cellar Selection *—P.G. (12/15/2004)*

Sineann 2003 Red Table Wine Red Blend (Oregon) $12. In case you miss the hard to read Red Table Wine print, there's a cartoon drawing of a red table with wine on it on the label. An unidentified blend, it tastes of strawberries, raspberries, and milk chocolate, in a light (for Sineann) and very pleasant blend. Just a hint of stem in the tannins. 87 Best Buy *—P.G. (4/1/2005)*

Sineann 2002 Medici Vineyard Riesling (Willamette Valley) $15. 92 Best Buy *—P.G. (12/1/2003)*

Sineann 2000 Old Vine Zinfandel (Columbia Valley (OR)) $36. 92 *—P.G. (12/31/2002)*

SINGLE LEAF

Single Leaf 1999 Cabernet Franc (El Dorado) $16. 82 *—S.H. (9/1/2002)*

Single Leaf NV Pammie's Cuvée Zinfandel (El Dorado County) $10. This Zin-based blend is Exhibit A in what can go wrong if you're not careful up under the fierce, thin-air summer sun of the Sierra Foothills. It is filled with the hot, bitter taste of raisins that have been drained of all their sweetness. That leaves tannins and alcohol and not much else. 82 *—S.H. (3/1/2004)*

SISKIYOU VINEYARDS

Siskiyou Vineyards 2000 La Cave Rouge Bordeaux Blend (Oregon) $15. 86 *—P.G. (8/1/2002)*

Siskiyou Vineyards 1999 La Cave Blanche White Blend (Oregon) $10. 86 *—P.G. (8/1/2002)*

SIX PRONG

Six Prong 2003 Red Wine Red Blend (Columbia Valley (WA)) $13. Very dark, plum-colored wine with a super ripe nose of raisins and ripe red fruits. The mongrel blend (30% Cabernet Sauvignon, 23% Sangiovese, 13% Merlot, 12% Malbec, 11% Grenache, 11% Syrah) delivers strong scents and flavors of toast and coffee, surprising in a wine at this price. Round, mature flavors give the impression that some older wine has been blended in, though it has not. The soft, fruit-driven center leads into a toasty finish with substantial, medium-grained tannins. 88 Best Buy *—P.G. (11/15/2005)*

SKETCHBOOK

Sketchbook 2000 Mendocino Collection Cabernet Sauvignon (Mendocino) $22. 87 *—S.H. (10/1/2003)*

Sketchbook 2001 Estate Syrah (Mendocino) $23. Smells a little funky, with a raw meat note floating on top of the blackberry and cherry aromas. Turns extremely dry and tannic in the mouth; it may mellow out in a year or two. 84 *—S.H. (6/1/2004)*

SKEWIS

Skewis 2001 Demuth Vineyard Pinot Noir (Anderson Valley) $35. Pretty aromas of cherries, cola, tea, smoke, and vanilla, and very delicate in the mouth. Not especially concentrated, but elegant in tea and cola flavors and an overlay of oak. 86 *—S.H. (12/15/2004)*

Skewis 2001 Salzgeber Vineyard Pinot Noir (Russian River Valley) $40. Fleshy and opulent, with forward cherry, raspberry, and earthy-rhubarb flavors and a lush mouthfeel. Bone dry, with orange peel acidity and a sprinkling of dusty tannins, this is a great food wine. **90** *—S.H. (12/15/2004)*

SMITH & HOOK

Smith & Hook 1996 Baroness Reserve Cabernet Sauvignon (Santa Lucia Highlands) $40. **84** *—L.W. (12/31/1999)*

Smith & Hook 2001 Grande Reserve Cabernet Sauvignon (Santa Lucia Highlands) $20. There will never be a lushly ripe Cab from this cool appellation, but no one has worked harder to craft interesting ones than Smith & Hook. This release is rich in earthy flavors and tannins. It has tantalizing hints of black cherries, and is very dry. It's a fine food wine with considerable finesse. **89** *—S.H. (10/3/2004)*

SMITH WOOTON

Smith Wooton 1999 Cabernet Franc (Napa Valley) $40. **84** *—S.H. (12/1/2002)*

Smith Wooton 2001 Gallagher's Vineyard Cabernet Franc (Napa Valley) $32. A bit sharp in acids, with a raw mouthfeel and the fresh taste of just-picked berries, this dry, young wine is best paired with rich fare, like barbecue. **84** *—S.H. (7/1/2005)*

SMITH-MADRONE

Smith-Madrone 2001 Cabernet Sauvignon (Napa Valley) $35. Power is the name of the game here. It starts with the intense currant and oak aromas, then really shows up in the mouth, which is very tannic and closed. But there's a tantalizing hint of blackberries that bodes well for the future. Hold for a few years. **89** *—S.H. (8/1/2005)*

Smith-Madrone 2002 Chardonnay (Napa Valley) $25. Nice and crisp in acids, with a sleek oak coat that adds smoke and vanilla notes, this Chard sure tastes good by itself. But it's balanced and food-friendly, with flavors of perfectly ripened white peaches. **88** *—S.H. (8/1/2005)*

Smith-Madrone 2001 Riesling (Napa Valley) $17. **90** *—S.H. (8/1/2003)*

SMOKING LOON

Smoking Loon 2003 Cabernet Sauvignon (California) $9. Richness and depth, at a giveaway price. This dry, full-bodied wine features cherries, blackberries, and good, smoky oak. **85 Best Buy** *—S.H. (7/1/2005)*

Smoking Loon 2003 Chardonnay (California) $9. Starts with spicy oak and smoky vanilla flavors, and offers modest peach and tropical fruit flavors suggesting pineapple grilled on a skewer. Clean and tasty. **86 Best Buy** *—S.H. (3/1/2005)*

Smoking Loon 2002 Merlot (California) $9. Dry and a little tannic, with deep flavors of blue and black stone fruits, such as plums. Turns a bit thin after you swallow. **84** *—S.H. (5/1/2005)*

Smoking Loon 2004 Pinot Noir (California) $9. This tastes like it came from premium cool growing areas. It's crisp in acids, light-bodied and dry. The flavors are all on the surface, but totally delicious. They include raspberries, red cherries, cola, cocoa, vanilla, toast, and Asian spices. **86 Best Buy** *—S.H. (12/1/2005)*

Smoking Loon 2002 Pinot Noir (California) $9. Straightforward, with modest cherry and floral aromas and flavors and a delicate structure. Good, clean, and simple. **84 Best Buy** *(11/1/2004)*

Smoking Loon 2003 Syrah (California) $9. This Syrah deals plenty of sweet fruit flavors (blackberry preserves, ripe plums) on the palate, and much the same (plus some herb) on the nose. A simple, easy wine at a good price. **86 Best Buy** *(9/1/2005)*

Smoking Loon 2004 Viognier (California) $9. Provides all the flowery, exotic fruits you expect from a Viognier, in a dry, crisp wine. Has a minerally backbone that adds structure. **84 Best Buy** *—S.H. (10/1/2005)*

Smoking Loon 2000 Viognier (California) $10. **82** *—J.M. (12/15/2002)*

SNOB HILL WINERY

Snob Hill Winery 2002 Le Snoot Chardonnay (North Coast) $11. This is your basic everyday oaky Chard, and if it's not the world's greatest, it gets the job done. Lots of ripe pears and tropical fruits. **84** *—S.H. (12/31/2004)*

SNOQUALMIE

Snoqualmie 2002 Reserve Cabernet Sauvignon (Columbia Valley (WA)) $23. A compact wine, with more than a trace of sweaty saddle, along with red currant, herbs, and spice. Depending upon your liking for barnyard notes, this could warrant a higher score. **87** *—P.G. (6/1/2005)*

Snoqualmie 1997 Reserve Cabernet Sauvignon (Columbia Valley (WA)) $21. **86** *—P.G. (9/1/2000)*

Snoqualmie 2001 Rosebud Vineyard Cabernet Sauvignon (Columbia Valley (WA)) $15. Fragrant with pleasant whiffs of barnyard, leather, and spice over firm cassis and pomegranate fruit, this shows lots of penetrating flavor as well. Tart cranberries and clean, nose-tickling scents of fresh roasted coffee suggest a much pricier Cab. There's just a hint of green to the tannins, but overall a very nice effort. **88 Best Buy** *—P.G. (12/15/2004)*

Snoqualmie 1998 Chardonnay (Columbia Valley (WA)) $11. **85** *—P.G. (6/1/2000)*

Snoqualmie 2000 Chardonnay (Columbia Valley (WA)) $11. **87 Best Buy** *—P.G. (7/1/2002)*

Snoqualmie 2000 Chenin Blanc (Columbia Valley (WA)) $7. **84** *—S.H. (6/1/2002)*

Snoqualmie 2001 Reserve Merlot (Columbia Valley (WA)) $23. Smooth and chocolaty, with lots of supple fruit and layers of sweet oak. This is a wine to gulp down by the glass, with foods such as pizza and burgers. There's plenty of creamy vanilla to soften the finish. **89** —*P.G. (5/1/2004)*

Snoqualmie 1999 Reserve Merlot (Columbia Valley (WA)) $23. 86 —*P.G. (6/1/2002)*

Snoqualmie 2004 Winemaker's Select Riesling (Columbia Valley (WA)) $7. Here's another delicious Riesling, this one sweet and penetrating, with surprisingly deep and protracted flavors of candied orange peel, lemon peel, and grapefruit. Drink this lovely wine with fruit-driven desserts, or chill it and sip it all by itself. **88 Best Buy** —*P.G. (11/15/2005)*

Snoqualmie 2001 Sauvignon Blanc (Columbia Valley (WA)) $7. 81 —*M.S. (6/1/2003)*

Snoqualmie 2001 Syrah (Columbia Valley (WA)) $11. There is no better entry-level Syrah made in Washington than Snoqualmie, which captures the forward, juicy, tart, and mixed berry flavors of the grape without drowning them in new oak. Tannins are soft and lightly toasty, and the sappy tang of the fruit sails through a smooth finish. **88 Best Buy** —*P.G. (7/1/2004)*

Snoqualmie 1999 Syrah (Columbia Valley (WA)) $11. 87 Best Buy —*P.G. (10/1/2001)*

Snoqualmie 2001 Reserve Syrah (Columbia Valley (WA)) $23. Young and ripe, this has the juicy, spicy red fruits that distinguish Washington Syrah, outlined with tart acids and set against a splashy background of new French and American oak. **90 Editors' Choice** —*P.G. (5/1/2004)*

USA

SNOWDEN

Snowden 2001 Cabernet Sauvignon (Napa Valley) $60. Kicks off with heady aromas of blackberry, tar, licorice, spice, and modest earth tones. On the palate it fans out to reveal complex layers of more black fruit, cinnamon, anise, cardamom, and herbs. It's framed in firm tannins, finishing long. **91** —*J.M. (12/31/2004)*

Snowden 1997 Lost Vineyard Cabernet Sauvignon (Napa Valley) $30. 88 *(11/1/2000)*

SOBON ESTATE

Sobon Estate 2002 Reserve Carignane (Amador County) $24. It's hard to make an elegant wine from this workhorse variety, but this one tries. Very dry, with earth, coffee, sweet tobacco, and red stone fruit flavors, it has smooth tannins and crisp acidity. Extra credit for the sweetly fruity finish. **86** —*S.H. (10/1/2004)*

Sobon Estate 1999 Primitivo (Shenandoah Valley (CA)) $16. 83 —*S.H. (12/1/2002)*

Sobon Estate 1998 Primitivo (Shenandoah Valley (CA)) $19. 84 —*S.H. (8/1/2001)*

Sobon Estate 2004 Rezerve Rosé Blend (Amador County) $10. Delicious in cherries, raspberries, and vanilla, with subtle herb flavors, this blush is dry, crisp, and balanced. It's really a lovely rosé that will be versatile at the table. **86 Best Buy** —*S.H. (12/15/2005)*

Sobon Estate 2000 Roussanne (Shenandoah Valley (CA)) $15. 86 —*S.H. (12/15/2002)*

Sobon Estate 1998 Sangiovese (Amador County) $13. 87 —*L.W. (10/1/1999)*

Sobon Estate 1999 Syrah (Shenandoah Valley (CA)) $15. 86 *(10/1/2001)*

Sobon Estate 2001 Rezerve Syrah (Shenandoah Valley (CA)) $24. Rich in jammy currant, blackberry, and cherry flavors, this very dry wine also has a peppery, molasses edge that adds complexity. The tannins are sizable, thick, and dusty, so this wine calls for a juicy steak. **86** —*S.H. (12/1/2004)*

Sobon Estate 2000 Viognier (Shenandoah Valley (CA)) $15. 83 —*S.H. (12/15/2002)*

Sobon Estate 2001 Zinfandel (Fiddletown) $20. Right off the bat, starts with a disturbingly Porty note of raisins, pie crust, and chocolate, suggesting overly ripe grapes. The winemaker kept the alcohol under 15 percent, but the wine tastes sweet and hot. Fans of this Sierra style will appreciate it. **84** —*S.H. (3/1/2004)*

Sobon Estate 2002 Cougar Hill Zinfandel (Shenandoah Valley (CA)) $17. Smells sugary and caramelly, like Port, although it's basically dry in the mouth, with flavors of ripe blackberries and cocoa. Nice with barbecue, burgers, sausage. **84** —*S.H. (4/1/2005)*

Sobon Estate 2000 Cougar Hill Zinfandel (Shenandoah Valley (CA)) $17. 88 —*S.H. (11/1/2002)*

Sobon Estate 2000 Fiddletown Zinfandel (Shenandoah Valley (CA)) $18. 86 —*S.H. (11/1/2002)*

Sobon Estate 2002 Old Vines Zinfandel (Shenandoah Valley (CA)) $12. Shows why this part of the Foothills has achieved such a stellar reputation for Zin. It's a big wine, packed with sweet cherry, black raspberry, pepper, and smoky vanilla flavors, but drinks balanced and gentle. **91 Best Buy** —*S.H. (11/15/2004)*

Sobon Estate 2000 Reserve Zinfandel (Shenandoah Valley (CA)) $24. 84 —*S.H. (11/1/2002)*

Sobon Estate 2002 ReZerve Zinfandel (Shenandoah Valley (CA)) $24. Well-ripened in black cherry and blueberry flavors, this Zin is also ripe and sweet in tannins. It's softly textured, with highlights of cocoa, dried herbs, coffee, and white pepper. Has the elegant structure of a fine Cabernet Sauvignon. **90** —*S.H. (10/1/2005)*

Sobon Estate 2003 Rocky Top Zinfandel (Amador County) $18. A style of Zin not to my liking. Dry and hot, with tobacco and berry flavors and raw elbows of tannin. Turns raisiny and pruny on the finish. **83** —*S.H. (10/1/2005)*

Sobon Estate 2001 Rocky Top Zinfandel (Shenandoah Valley (CA)) $16. **87** *(11/1/2003)*

Sobon Estate 1998 Rocky Top Zinfandel (Shenandoah Valley (CA)) $15. **85** —*P.G. (3/1/2001)*

Sobon Estate 1997 Rocky Top Vineyards Zinfandel (Shenandoah Valley (CA)) $15. **90** —*L.W. (11/1/1999)*

SOCKEYE

Sockeye 2002 Cabernet Sauvignon (Washington) $11. This is a firmly fruity, tart, steak-friendly wine with some good 'grip' and a solid core of peppery black cherry fruit. Light notes of licorice and roasted coffee finish up quickly; the blend includes six percent Merlot. 2500 cases were made. **87 Best Buy** —*P.G. (11/15/2005)*

SOFIA

Sofia 2000 Blanc de Blancs Champagne Blend (California) $20. **83** *(12/1/2001)*

SOGNO

Sogno 2000 Giocchino Red Blend (El Dorado) $16. **82** —*S.H. (5/1/2002)*

Sogno 2001 Zinfandel (El Dorado County) $14. **81** *(11/1/2003)*

SOKOL BLOSSER

Sokol Blosser 1998 Pinot Gris (Willamette Valley) $16. **82** *(8/1/1999)*

Sokol Blosser 2001 Pinot Gris (Willamette Valley) $18. **85** —*M.S. (8/1/2003)*

Sokol Blosser 1997 Pinot Noir (Willamette Valley) $20. **86** *(10/1/1999)*

Sokol Blosser 2000 Pinot Noir (Willamette Valley) $25. **87** —*P.G. (4/1/2003)*

Sokol Blosser 1998 Pinot Noir (Willamette Valley) $28. **87** —*P.G. (4/1/2002)*

Sokol Blosser 1998 Old Vineyard Block Pinot Noir (Willamette Valley) $65. **89** —*P.G. (4/1/2002)*

Sokol Blosser 2001 Twelve Row Block Pinot Noir (Willamette Valley) $66. The name refers to a small section of vineyard planted in 1975, in the heart of a mini-banana belt in the area. It's a gorgeous looking wine, that breathes class and elegance. Well-defined cranberry, raspberry, and cherry fruit flavors come to a focused middle; it's a high-wire style, still young and fresh, but certainly ageworthy. Cellar Candidate (6–10 years). **92 Cellar Selection** —*P.G. (2/1/2005)*

Sokol Blosser 1999 Twelve Row Block Limited Production Pinot Noir (Willamette Valley) $65. **86** —*P.G. (4/1/2003)*

Sokol Blosser 1998 Watershed Block Pinot Noir (Willamette Valley) $65. **90** —*P.G. (4/1/2002)*

Sokol Blosser NV Evolution 5th Edition White Blend (Oregon) $15. **86** —*P.G. (4/1/2002)*

SOLARIS

Solaris 2002 Reserve Cabernet Sauvignon (Napa Valley) $25. Soft and luxurious as an aged tapestry, this wine shows intricate layers of blackberries and black currants, cherries, cocoa, anise, and smoky oak. Although it's fully dry, the fruit is so lush, it feels sweet. Drink now and through 2006. **87** —*S.H. (12/15/2005)*

Solaris 2003 Chardonnay (North Coast) $13. Fruity and simple, with peach and citrus flavors that weaken on the finish. **83** —*S.H. (6/1/2005)*

Solaris 2003 Pinot Noir (Carneros) $13. Raw and tough, with overly sweet, cherry cough medicine flavors. **81** —*S.H. (6/1/2005)*

SOLEIL & TERROIR

Soleil & Terroir 1997 Edna Ranch Vineyard Reserve Pinot Noir (Edna Valley) $30. **86** *(10/1/1999)*

SOLÉNA

Soléna 2003 Pinot Gris (Oregon) $18. Laurent Montalieu, who made so many memorable Pinot Gris during his years at WillaKenzie, shows a masterful touch here again. The pure expression of pear-flavored Pinot Gris fruit anchors the wine from the core out, enhanced with natural, varietal spice. No malolactic fermentation, no oak. Just a lovely expression of great fruit. **90** —*P.G. (8/1/2005)*

SONNET

Sonnet 2003 Kruse Vineyard Pinot Noir (York Mountain) $40. From a new winery in this coolish Central Coast appellation, this is a pretty good early effort. It has rich, gooey blackberry and chocolate flavors, but is a little soft in acids, although the silky mouthfeel is a delight. Advice: go for better structure and complexity, less ripeness. **86** —*S.H. (8/1/2005)*

SONOMA CREEK

Sonoma Creek 2000 Pinot Noir (Sonoma County) $9. **84 Best Buy** *(10/1/2002)*

Sonoma Creek 1998 Duarte Old Vine Zinfandel (Contra Costa County) $15. 89 *—P.G. (3/1/2001)*

SONOMA HILL

Sonoma Hill 2002 Chardonnay (Sonoma County) $13. Starts with modest aromas of fruits and oak that turn tart and earthy in the mouth, with suggestions of peaches and apples. Finishes short and dry. 83 *—S.H. (4/1/2004)*

Sonoma Hill 2002 Pinot Noir (Sonoma County) $12. Oaky and weak in flavor, with modest cherry and spice tastes and a chocolaty finish. Crisp and tart in acids. 84 *(11/1/2004)*

SONOMA-CUTRER

Sonoma-Cutrer 1997 Les Pierres Chardonnay (Sonoma Valley) $30. 86 *(6/1/2000)*

Sonoma-Cutrer 1997 The Cutrer Chardonnay (Russian River Valley) $30. 89 *—W.E (6/1/2000)*

SONORA

Sonora 1997 Story Vyd Zinfandel (Shenandoah Valley (CA)) $19. 86 *—P.G. (11/15/1999)*

Sonora 1997 TC Vineyard Old Vine Zinfandel (Amador County) $19. 86 *—P.G. (11/15/1999)*

SOOS CREEK

Soos Creek 1999 Cabernet Sauvignon (Columbia Valley (WA)) $30. 92 *—P.G. (6/1/2002)*

Soos Creek 1998 Champoux Vineyard Cabernet Sauvignon (Columbia Valley (WA)) $30. 89 *—P.G. (10/1/2001)*

Soos Creek NV Sundance Red Blend (Columbia Valley (WA)) $20. 90 *—P.G. (6/1/2002)*

SPANN VINEYARDS

Spann Vineyards 2001 Mayacamas Range Five Barrels Cabernet Sauvignon (Sonoma Valley) $30. Balanced, with good acidity and easy tannins framing a nice mix of cherry-berry flavors and a tobacco, coffee, and herb edge. Aims for elegance and detail rather than power. 87 *—S.H. (12/15/2004)*

Spann Vineyards 2001 Red Blend (Sonoma County) $18. Balanced, complex, and elegant, a lovely dry wine with cherry, herb, cola, and oak flavors. Has extra qualities of harmony and grace that make it excellent. Zin, Mourvèdre, and Alicante Bouschet. 90 *—S.H. (12/15/2004)*

Spann Vineyards 2002 Syrah (Sonoma County) $20. Showing rich, fruity concentration and good balance, this is an appealing Syrah. It's full-bodied and very soft, with cascades of red and black cherry flavors and a mocha mousse finish. 86 *(9/1/2005)*

Spann Vineyards 2002 Mo Zin Zinfandel (Sonoma County) $18. This delightful wine allows Zin to express its wild and woolly, feral side, but keeps it balanced. The briary, brambly berry flavors drink bone dry, with firm tannins. 86 *—S.H. (10/1/2005)*

SPELLETICH CELLARS

Spelletich Cellars 1998 Bodog Red Bordeaux Blend (Napa Valley) $25. 86 *(8/1/2001)*

Spelletich Cellars 1998 Cabernet Sauvignon (Napa Valley) $80. 90 *—S.H. (8/1/2001)*

Spelletich Cellars 2000 Ochoa Chardonnay (Carneros) $29. 89 *—S.H. (12/15/2002)*

Spelletich Cellars 1999 Spotted Owl Chardonnay (Mount Veeder) $25. 90 *(8/1/2001)*

Spelletich Cellars 2001 Alviso Vineyard Zinfandel (Amador County) $24. 84 *(11/1/2003)*

SPENCER ROLOSON

Spencer Roloson 2001 Palaterra Red Blend (California) $16. This big, brawling bruiser of a red wine is a blend of Carignan, Syrah, and Valdigue. It has outsized tannins, a rugged texture, and enormously extracted fruit. Cherries, blackberries, black raspberries, chocolate, and coffee cascade across the palate, and finish dry and spicy. 87 *—S.H. (11/15/2004)*

Spencer Roloson 2002 Palaterra Red Wine Red Blend (California) $16. Straddles the line between an innocent little country wine and a pedigreed red. It is dry, and has forward-fruit flavors of cherries, blackberries, and cocoa, and sturdy tannins. Might improve for a year or two. One-third each Carignane, Syrah, Valdiguie. 86 *—S.H. (6/1/2005)*

Spencer Roloson 2002 Balyeat Vineyard Sauvignon Blanc (Chiles Valley) $24. For a nice, light, and delicate Sauvignon Blanc, this one's hard to beat. It's got great fruity flavors of lemon and lime and peach, with refreshing acidity. Smooth and polished, this is a great cocktail wine. 87 *—S.H. (12/1/2004)*

Spencer Roloson 1999 Sueno Syrah (Lodi) $28. 89 *—S.H. (12/1/2002)*

Spencer Roloson 2001 Tempranillo (Clear Lake) $26. You could almost mistake it for a warm-climate Syrah, with its rich but dry blackberry, chocolate, and herb flavors and full-bodied tannins, yet there's a dustiness that makes it unique. 87 *—S.H. (3/1/2004)*

Spencer Roloson 2000 Viognier (Rutherford) $19. 86 *—S.H. (9/1/2002)*

USA

Spencer Roloson 2003 Sueno Vineyard Viognier (Lodi) $26. Not over the top like so many others, but keeps its lively menagerie of tropical fruit, vanilla, wildflower, and oak flavors controlled by crisp acidity. A pretty lime-and-honeysuckle flavor lasts forever on the finish. **90** *—S.H. (6/1/2005)*

Spencer Roloson 1999 Zinfandel (Sonoma County) $25. **84** *—S.H. (11/1/2002)*

Spencer Roloson 1999 Zinfandel (Chiles Valley) $30. **84** *—S.H. (11/1/2002)*

SPOTTSWOODE

Spottswoode 2001 Estate Cabernet Sauvignon (Napa Valley) $90. Another fabulous '01 Napa Cab. This beauty maintains a pleasing balance between the sheer power of its well-ripened cherry and blackberry fruit flavors, and an earthy quality grounded in firm tannins and good acidity. Totally balanced, dry, and harmonious, this Cab exudes elegance and style. Drink now through 2015. **94** *—S.H. (3/1/2005)*

Spottswoode 2003 Sauvignon Blanc (Napa Valley) $32. Terrific Sauv Blanc, rich, dry, and complex. Brims with citrus, fig, and melon flavors, with riper tropical fruit notes and an oaky veneer. Perfect with shrimp in risotto and goat cheese. **90** *—S.H. (3/1/2005)*

SPRING MOUNTAIN

Spring Mountain 1997 Miravalle-La Perla-Chevalier Bordeaux Blend (Spring Mountain) $50. **89** *(11/1/2000)*

Spring Mountain 2002 Estate Cabernet Sauvignon (Spring Mountain) $50. The mountain plays its part in the intense tannins and concentrated fruit. You could drink it now against rich fare, but it's also a cellar candidate. It's a tough, dry, masculine wine, with heady currant and blackberry flavors and a lot of new French oak. Drink now and for the next 15 years. **92** *—S.H. (12/31/2005)*

Spring Mountain 2000 Estate Cabernet Sauvignon-Merlot (Spring Mountain) $50. **92** *—S.H. (11/15/2003)*

Spring Mountain 1999 Reserve Red Wine Red Blend (Napa Valley) $50. **92** *—S.H. (12/31/2003)*

Spring Mountain 2001 Sauvignon Blanc (Spring Mountain) $28. **84** *—S.H. (10/1/2003)*

Spring Mountain Vineyard 2001 Bordeaux Blend (Napa Valley) $50. This is a big, lushly textured wine that has the intensity of mountain fruit without the hard tannins. Blackberry and vanilla coat the palate, followed by lingering notes of plum, cassis, and sweet oak. **92** *(6/6/2005)*

Spring Mountain Vineyard 2001 Estate Syrah (Napa Valley) $50. Chewy and tannic, this densely packed Syrah deserves 2–3 years of cellar time before opening. Dark berry and tobacco notes mark the nose, while the flavors revolve around berries, chocolate fudge, and olive. **88** *(9/1/2005)*

ST AMANT

St. Amant 1999 Barbera (Lodi) $14. **88** *—S.H. (11/15/2001)*

St. Amant 1999 Reserve Syrah (Amador County) $18. **89** *—S.H. (11/15/2001)*

ST STALEY THOMAS

St. Staley Thomas 1997 Chardonnay (Russian River Valley) $13. **92 Best Buy** *—L.W. (7/1/1999)*

ST. AMANT WINERY

St. Amant Winery 2001 Marian's Vineyard Zinfandel (Lodi) $20. **87** *(11/1/2003)*

ST. CLEMENT

St. Clement 1999 Oroppas Bordeaux Blend (Napa Valley) $50. **88** *—J.M. (6/1/2002)*

St. Clement 1997 Cabernet Sauvignon (Howell Mountain) $65. **92** *(11/1/2000)*

St. Clement 2000 Cabernet Sauvignon (Napa Valley) $35. Firm and polished, an elegant Cab with pretty flavors of blackberries, currants, dried herbs, and dark chocolate, with hints of menthol and an oaky overlay. The fruit turns a bit thin on the finish, and picks up some astringent tannins. **87** *—S.H. (4/1/2004)*

St. Clement 1998 Cabernet Sauvignon (Napa Valley) $35. **86** *—S.H. (6/1/2002)*

St. Clement 1996 Cabernet Sauvignon (Howell Mountain) $50. **90** *—S.H. (9/1/2000)*

St. Clement 1999 Howell Mountain Cabernet Sauvignon (Napa Valley) $70. **89** *(8/1/2003)*

St. Clement 2002 Star Vineyard Cabernet Sauvignon (Rutherford) $80. This wine is very ripe in red cherry and currant fruit, with a mocha edge and a touch of prunes in the finish. It's a little inelegant now, with a sharpness that accentuates the tannins. May calm down in a year or two. **85** *—S.H. (12/31/2005)*

St. Clement 2001 Chardonnay (Napa Valley) $16. Textbook all the way. Well-ripened apples, pears, and peaches, crisp, citrusy acids, and oaky wood are what you get in this clean, well-made wine. The texture is rich and creamy. **87** *—S.H. (6/1/2004)*

St. Clement 1999 Abbotts Vineyard Chardonnay (Carneros) $23. **86** *—S.H. (5/1/2002)*

St. Clement 1997 Merlot (Napa Valley) $26. **89** *—S.H. (7/1/2000)*

St. Clement 1999 Merlot (Napa Valley) $28. 92 *—S.H. (6/1/2002)*

St. Clement 1999 Petite Sirah (Napa Valley) $32. 90 *—S.H. (9/1/2002)*

St. Clement 1998 Sauvignon Blanc (Napa Valley) $13. 88 *—S.H. (3/1/2000)*

St. Clement 1999 Sauvignon Blanc (Napa Valley) $13. 84 *—S.H. (8/1/2001)*

ST. FRANCIS

St. Francis 2000 Cabernet Sauvignon (Sonoma County) $16. 90 Editors' Choice *—S.H. (11/15/2003)*

St. Francis 1997 Kings Ridge Reserve Cabernet Sauvignon (Sonoma County) $85. 87 *—J.C. (6/1/2003)*

St. Francis 2001 Nuns Canyon Reserve Cabernet Sauvignon (Sonoma County) $28. This soft, fully-ripened Cabernet boasts aromas of cocoa, cassis, and chocolate fudge, veering dangerously close to prune and over-ripeness. Still, it maintains a precarious sense of balance and a wonderfully silky mouthfeel that suggest near-term drinking. Drink now–2010. **89** *(11/15/2005)*

St. Francis 1997 Reserve Cabernet Sauvignon (Sonoma Valley) $40. 90 *(11/1/2000)*

St. Francis 2001 Chardonnay (Sonoma County) $12. 87 Best Buy *—S.H. (9/1/2003)*

St. Francis 1999 Chardonnay (Sonoma County) $13. 87 Best Buy *—S.H. (5/1/2001)*

St. Francis 2001 Behler Reserve Chardonnay (Sonoma Valley) $24. 88 *—S.H. (12/15/2003)*

St. Francis 2000 Anthem Meritage (Sonoma Valley) $55. A blend of all five Bordeaux varieties, this wine is soft, and flatters with its polished flavors and fine veneer of oak. The flavors shift from blackberries and cherries to sweet herbs and back again, and finish with a kick of tannin. Very drinkable now, and should improve for a few years. **91** *—S.H. (10/1/2004)*

St. Francis 1998 Merlot (Sonoma County) $25. 86 *—S.H. (6/1/2001)*

St. Francis 1997 Merlot (Sonoma County) $20. 87 *—J.C. (7/1/2000)*

St. Francis 1999 Behler Reserve Merlot (Sonoma Valley) $45. 90 *—S.H. (12/31/2003)*

St. Francis 2001 Port (Sonoma County) $25. This interesting California version of a Port is rich, balanced, and inviting. It features an array of crème de cassis, chocolate fudge, vanilla, and spice flavors wrapped in a velvety texture. Refreshing acidity cuts through the sweetness. Cab Sauvignon, Merlot, Syrah, Zinfandel, and Alicante Bouschet. **91** *—S.H. (12/1/2004)*

St. Francis 2002 Syrah (Sonoma County) $20. Stewed and pruny, with a dull mouthfeel and syrupy texture. What went wrong here? **82** *(9/1/2005)*

St. Francis 2002 Old Vines Zinfandel (Sonoma Valley) $18. Briary and medium-weight, with a hint of vinyl on the nose as well. The blackberry and raisin fruit gives the impression of warmth, then thins out and turns a bit tart and cranberryish on the finish. **85** *(11/15/2005)*

St. Francis 2001 Old Vines Zinfandel (Sonoma County) $22. 88 *(11/1/2003)*

St. Francis 1999 Old Vines Zinfandel (Sonoma County) $22. 88 *—S.H. (11/1/2002)*

St. Francis 1997 Old Vines Zinfandel (Sonoma County) $24. 90 *—P.G. (11/15/1999)*

St. Francis 2002 Pagani Vineyard Reserve Zinfandel (Sonoma County) $46. According to winemaker Tom Mackey, "size counts with Zin," and his Pagani Vineyard Zin has never lacked for size. There's some smoke and vanilla-scented oak, but there's also masses of Zinberry fruit and a juicy, fresh finish, with none of the raisin notes that can sometimes creep into high-octane Zins. **90** *(11/15/2005)*

St. Francis 2001 Pagani Vineyard Reserve Zinfandel (Sonoma Valley) $45. Clearly stands above the competition for its exquisite harmony. Completely dry but totally ripe, with well-developed spicy blackberry and dark chocolate flavors, and wonderfully rich, sweet tannins. So balanced, you don't notice the 15.6 percent alcohol. Only in California, and a world class wine. **93** *—S.H. (11/15/2004)*

St. Francis 1999 Pagani Vineyard Reserve Zinfandel (Sonoma Valley) $44. 92 *—S.H. (9/1/2002)*

ST. GEORGE

St. George 2003 Chardonnay (Sonoma County) $10. Common and rustic, this is a Chard that is properly fruity, although it has some vegetal flavors. **82** *—S.H. (10/1/2005)*

St. George 2001 Barrel Reserve Chardonnay (Sonoma County) $9. Super-oaky, with what smells and tastes like heavy char that gives it a burnt, ashy note, although there are some decent peach flavors. **82** *—S.H. (11/1/2005)*

ST. INNOCENT

St. Innocent 1998 Freedom Hill Vineyard Pinot Blanc (Willamette Valley) $14. 81 *—L.W. (12/31/1999)*

ST. SUPERY

St. Supery 1998 Bordeaux Blend (Napa Valley) $20. 90 *—L.W. (2/1/2000)*

USA

St. Supery 1999 Dollarhide Ranch Cabernet Sauvignon (Napa Valley) $70. **91** *—J.M. (6/1/2003)*

St. Supery 1999 Limited Edition Cabernet Sauvignon-Merlot (Rutherford) $60. **90** *—M.S. (11/15/2002)*

St. Supery 2000 Chardonnay (Napa Valley) $19. **87** *—J.M. (2/1/2003)*

St. Supery 1999 Final Blend Meritage (Napa Valley) $50. **89** *(7/1/2002)*

St. Supery 2000 White Meritage (Napa Valley) $22. **87** *(7/1/2002)*

St. Supery 2001 Sweet White Moscato (California) $15. **89** *(7/1/2002)*

St. Supery 2001 Sauvignon Blanc (Napa Valley) $15. **88** *(7/1/2002)*

St. Supery 2002 Syrah (Napa Valley) $35. Soft and voluptuous, if a bit obvious and simple, with sweet-tasting, candied cherry fruit, and hints of black pepper. **84** *(9/1/2005)*

STAG HOLLOW

Stag Hollow 1998 Vendange Sélection Pinot Noir (Willamette Valley) $45. **83** *—M.S. (12/1/2000)*

STAG'S LEAP WINE CELLARS

Stag's Leap Wine Cellars 2000 Cabernet Sauvignon (Napa Valley) $45. **91** *—S.H. (3/1/2003)*

Stag's Leap Wine Cellars 2002 Artemis Cabernet Sauvignon (Napa Valley) $48. Elegant and refined, but rather short, this is a wine for near-term consumption. It has earth, herb, and cherry flavors and is dry in tannins. Drink while your big '01s are sleeping. **87** *—S.H. (5/1/2005)*

Stag's Leap Wine Cellars 2001 Cask 23 Cabernet Sauvignon (Napa Valley) $150. Classic Napa Cab, right up there with the greats. Somehow manages to combine monstrous power with understated elegance. The strength is obviously in the ripe fruit and elaborate oak, while the subtlety lies in the soft tannins and impeccable balance. It's a wine you return to over and over, trying to figure it out, but it's always a step ahead. Drink now, with rich fare, or age through 2020. **96 Cellar Selection** *—S.H. (2/1/2005)*

Stag's Leap Wine Cellars 1999 Cask 23 Cabernet Sauvignon (Napa Valley) $150. **92** *—S.H. (2/1/2003)*

Stag's Leap Wine Cellars 2000 Fay Cabernet Sauvignon (Napa Valley) $75. A little light, but silky smooth, with a caressing mouthfeel that pushes polished cherry and tobacco flavors softly along. Turns tart and a little peppery on the finish; drink now. **88** *(2/1/2004)*

Stag's Leap Wine Cellars 1998 Fay Vineyard Cabernet Sauvignon (Napa Valley) $75. **93** *—S.H. (6/1/2002)*

Stag's Leap Wine Cellars 1999 S.L.V. Cabernet Sauvignon (Napa Valley) $100. **91** *—S.H. (2/1/2003)*

Stag's Leap Wine Cellars 2000 SLV Cabernet Sauvignon (Napa Valley) $100. Slightly richer and earthier than the Fay this year, with black cherry and tobacco flavors that glide effortlessly across the palate thanks to a wonderfully supple texture. It does thin out a little on the finish, so it might be best consumed over the near term. **90** *(2/1/2004)*

Stag's Leap Wine Cellars 2003 Chardonnay (Napa Valley) $29. This wine is a bit tough and gritty, with an earthy, tobaccoey edge, but it has enough cream, green apple, and peach flavors to satisfy. Finishes fully dry, with spices and apples. **87** *—S.H. (7/1/2005)*

Stag's Leap Wine Cellars 1999 Chardonnay (Napa Valley) $30. **91** *(7/1/2001)*

Stag's Leap Wine Cellars 2002 Arcadia Vineyard Chardonnay (Napa Valley) $45. This is a tight, lemony Chardonnay for those who lean more toward the old Chablis style. It's a very dry, structural wine whose acids and tannins star as much as the fruit. Great elegance and pizzazz. **90** *—S.H. (12/15/2004)*

Stag's Leap Wine Cellars 1999 Arcadia Vineyard Chardonnay (Napa Valley) $45. **88** *(7/1/2001)*

Stag's Leap Wine Cellars 1997 Napa Valley Chardonnay (Napa Valley) $26. **90** *—S.H. (7/1/2000)*

Stag's Leap Wine Cellars 1998 Reserve Chardonnay (Napa Valley) $45. **92** *(7/1/2001)*

Stag's Leap Wine Cellars 2000 Merlot (Napa Valley) $40. Shows varietally correct aromas and flavors of black cherries, mocha, and dried herbs, also some smoke and toast. It's good wine, but fairly tart, lacking the expansiveness and lushness that would bring it to the next level. A victim of the vintage? **86** *(2/1/2004)*

Stag's Leap Wine Cellars 1997 Merlot (Napa Valley) $35. **93** *—S.H. (2/1/2001)*

Stag's Leap Wine Cellars 2001 Sauvignon Blanc (Napa Valley) $20. Ripe and melony, with smoke and fig notes adding complexity. It's a little creamy and pleasantly plump in the midpalate, then turns tart and grapefruity on the finish. **87** *—S.H. (2/1/2004)*

Stag's Leap Wine Cellars 2000 Rancho Chimiles Sauvignon Blanc (Napa Valley) $28. **87** *(8/1/2002)*

STAGLIN

Staglin 2001 Cabernet Sauvignon (Rutherford) $110. One of the best Rutherford wines of the vintage. Dramatically concentrated, everything's on steroids, but controlled and beautiful. Very ripe and plush, oaky and young, fabulously expressive. Flavors are of black currants, sweet cherries, vanilla, smoke. A perfect expression of youthful brilliance and ageworthiness. **96** *—S.H. (10/1/2004)*

Staglin 1999 Cabernet Sauvignon (Rutherford) $85. **92** *(12/15/2002)*

Staglin 2000 Salus Cabernet Sauvignon (Napa Valley) $50. Lots of briary, currant, and blueberry flavors in this soft, appealing wine, with feathery tannins that melt on the finish. It's oaky, too. As tasty as it is, it loses a few points for the simple structure and lack of intensity. **86** *—S.H. (4/1/2004)*

Staglin 2000 Chardonnay (Rutherford) $50. 90 *(12/15/2002)*

Staglin 2000 Salus Chardonnay (Rutherford) $35. 87 *(12/15/2002)*

STAGS' LEAP WINERY

Stags' Leap Winery 2002 Cabernet Sauvignon (Napa Valley) $45. This is a very good Cab. The wine is balanced, oaky, and tannic, with the elegant power associated with this winery and appellation. Still, it's astringent now and doesn't seem ageable. Drink now. **87** *—S.H. (12/15/2005)*

Stags' Leap Winery 1999 Cabernet Sauvignon (Napa Valley) $40. 92 *—S.H. (3/1/2003)*

Stags' Leap Winery 1997 Cabernet Sauvignon (Napa Valley) $35. 94 *(11/1/2000)*

Stags' Leap Winery 1996 Cabernet Sauvignon (Napa Valley) $32. 92 *(12/31/1999)*

Stags' Leap Winery 2000 Estate Reserve Cabernet Sauvignon (Napa Valley) $65. This is a wonderfully drinkable wine now. Even though it's not a big bruiser for the cellar, it shows impeccable pedigree in the smooth, unctuous texture and the subtle interplay of black currants and oak. Possesses undeniable elegance. **90** *—S.H. (5/1/2005)*

Stags' Leap Winery 2004 Chardonnay (Napa Valley) $24. Apple sauce, peach purée, buttercream, vanilla, and cinnamon spice flavors characterize this tasty Napa Chard. It has a scour of refreshing acidity and a long, pleasant, fairly complex finish. **88** *—S.H. (12/15/2005)*

Stags' Leap Winery 2001 Chardonnay (Napa Valley) $22. 91 Editors' Choice *—S.H. (5/1/2003)*

Stags' Leap Winery 1998 Chardonnay (Napa Valley) $21. 85 *(6/1/2000)*

Stags' Leap Winery 2001 Merlot (Napa Valley) $31. This is a seriously good Merlot. They got the fruit gorgeously ripe so that it bursts with sunny cassis and cherry flavor, and then they drenched it with high-end toasted oak. Near-perfect tannins, and just-right acidity provide the finishing touches. Elegant. **93** *—S.H. (12/15/2004)*

Stags' Leap Winery 1998 Merlot (Napa Valley) $31. 86 *—S.H. (6/1/2001)*

Stags' Leap Winery 2000 Estate Grown Reserve Merlot (Napa Valley) $50. 91 *—S.H. (12/31/2003)*

Stags' Leap Winery 2002 Petite Sirah (Napa Valley) $35. Well, this is your basic inky dark, tannic Pet wine, from a producer with a long track record. It's a wine meant to be stuck away in a cool cellar for a decade or longer, and there's no reason not to, given the astringency and the fabulously molten core of blackberry and cherry fruit. Should begin to be approachable after 2008; hold for years after. **90 Cellar Selection** *—S.H. (12/15/2005)*

Stags' Leap Winery 2000 Petite Sirah (Napa Valley) $31. A smooth-textured wine that is complex and redolent of black cherry, anise, cinnamon, herb, cassis, and coffee flavors. Tannins are firm and supple, and the finish is long and generous. **91** *—J.M. (8/1/2004)*

Stags' Leap Winery 1998 Petite Sirah (Napa Valley) $32. 90 *—J.M. (5/1/2002)*

Stags' Leap Winery 2000 Ne Cede Malis Red Blend (Napa Valley) $54. From old vines, this blend of Carignane, Grenache, and Syrah is a rich, nuanced wine. Even non-sophisticates will find this smooth, delicious, and enjoyable, although savvy tasters will appreciate the complexity. **92** *—S.H. (5/1/2005)*

Stags' Leap Winery 1997 Ne Cede Malis Rhône Red Blend (Stags Leap District) $50. 89 *—J.M. (12/1/2001)*

Stags' Leap Winery 2000 Syrah (Napa Valley) $29. 86 *—J.M. (6/1/2003)*

Stags' Leap Winery 2002 Viognier (Napa Valley) $25. This one's superdry and tight in acids and displays citrus flavors. You might think it was Sauvignon Blanc, except for the peacock's tail of white peach and mango on the finish. A great food wine. **87** *—S.H. (11/15/2004)*

Stags' Leap Winery 1999 Viognier (Napa Valley) $25. 92 Editors' Choice *—J.M. (12/1/2001)*

STANDING STONE

Standing Stone 1997 Cabernet Franc (Finger Lakes) $16. 86 *—J.C. (12/1/1999)*

Standing Stone 2000 Gewürztraminer (Finger Lakes) $NA. 91 *—J.M. (12/1/2002)*

Standing Stone 1997 Pinot Noir (Finger Lakes) $14. 84 *(10/1/1999)*

Standing Stone 2002 Estate Bottled Riesling (Finger Lakes) $12. 89 Best Buy *—J.C. (8/1/2003)*

STANGELAND

Stangeland 2000 Estate Reserve Pinot Noir (Willamette Valley) $39. 85 *(10/1/2002)*

Stangeland 1999 Martha's Vineyard II Pinot Noir (Willamette Valley) $30. 84 *(10/1/2002)*

Stangeland 2000 Winemaker's Estate Reserve Pinot Noir (Willamette Valley) $59. 90 *(10/1/2002)*

STANTON

Stanton 2002 Cabernet Sauvignon (Oakville) $65. This wine is a bit too sweet, soft, and obvious for me, although some will admire the blackberry, cassis, and chocolate flavors. Seems at its best now, although a few years of cellaring won't hurt. 86 *—S.H. (11/1/2005)*

STAR LANE VINEYARD

Star Lane Vineyard 2003 Sauvignon Blanc (Santa Ynez Valley) $25. Rather heavy on the nose, with cream of wheat, toasty wood, and white fruit. Quite straightforward with an acidic streak that brings it to attention. Good mouthfeel and elegant, if not exactly the most fruit-forward kid on the block. 87 *(7/1/2005)*

STARRY NIGHT

Starry Night 2002 Adara Rhône Red Blend (California) $14. This Rhône blend is sharp in acids and a bit green, but has some good cherry fruit. It's a solid country effort. 83 *—S.H. (12/15/2004)*

Starry Night 2003 Zinfandel (Lodi) $16. Smells great, doesn't taste that good. That's the story on this Zin. The aroma's promising in Zinny wild berries, peppery spices, and chocolate, but the wine turns sweet and too soft in the mouth. 83 *—S.H. (12/1/2005)*

Starry Night 2001 Old Vine Zinfandel (Russian River Valley) $22. 88 *(11/1/2003)*

Starry Night 2001 Tom Feeney Ranch, Old Vine Zinfandel (Russian River Valley) $26. Starts off with rich earth, coffee, and spice aromas that lead into a bright-edged, fruit-driven wine redolent of black cherry, blackberry, black pepper, herbs, coffee, and chocolate notes. Zippy acidity keeps it bright on the finish. Complex, yet still fun. 90 *—J.M. (6/1/2004)*

STATON HILLS

Staton Hills 1995 Cabernet Sauvignon (Columbia Valley (WA)) $17. 87 *—M.S. (9/1/1999)*

STE. CHAPELLE

Ste. Chapelle 2000 Winemaker's Series Cabernet Sauvignon (Idaho) $10. 88 *—P.G. (9/1/2002)*

Ste. Chapelle NV Spumante Champagne Blend (Idaho) $8. 81 *—P.G. (6/1/2001)*

Ste. Chapelle 2001 Soft Chenin Blanc (Idaho) $6. 86 *—P.G. (9/1/2002)*

Ste. Chapelle 1998 Gewürztraminer (Idaho) $7. 81 *—J.C. (9/1/1999)*

Ste. Chapelle 2001 Johannisberg Riesling (Idaho) $6. 88 *—P.G. (9/1/2002)*

Ste. Chapelle 1997 Sally's Summit Vineyard Dry Johannisberg Riesling (Idaho) $10. 87 *—J.C. (9/1/1999)*

Ste. Chapelle 2000 Value Series Merlot (Idaho) $7. 87 *—P.G. (9/1/2002)*

Ste. Chapelle 1998 Riesling (Idaho) $6. 83 *—J.C. (9/1/1999)*

Ste. Chapelle 1998 Special Harvest Riesling (Idaho) $8. 85 *—J.C. (9/1/1999)*

Ste. Chapelle 2000 Winemaker's Series Syrah (Idaho) $10. 86 *—P.G. (9/1/2002)*

STEELE

Steele 1998 Bien Nacido Vineyard Chardonnay (Santa Barbara) $30. 92 Best Buy *(7/1/2001)*

Steele 1998 Cuvée Chardonnay (California) $18. 90 *(6/1/2000)*

Steele 1997 Du Pratt Vineyard (Late Harvest) Chardonnay (Mendocino) $30. 87 *—J.M. (6/1/2003)*

Steele 1998 Durell Vineyard Chardonnay (Carneros) $28. 87 *(6/1/2000)*

Steele 1998 Goodchild Vineyard Chardonnay (Santa Barbara County) $30. 87 *(7/1/2001)*

Steele 1998 Lolonis Vineyard Chardonnay (Mendocino) $32. 89 *(7/1/2001)*

Steele 1998 Parmelee-Hill Vineyard Chardonnay (Sonoma Valley) $30. 89 *(7/1/2001)*

Steele 1997 Sangiacomo Vyd Chardonnay (Carneros) $24. 93 *—L.W. (6/1/1999)*

Steele 1999 Fumé Blanc (Lake County) $16. 88 *(8/1/2002)*

Steele 1997 Clear Lake Merlot (Lake County) $22. 86 *—J.C. (7/1/2000)*

Steele 1998 Bien Nacido Vineyard Pinot Blanc (Santa Barbara County) $16. 84 *—L.W. (3/1/2000)*

Steele 2001 Pinot Noir (Anderson Valley) $22. Cola, leather, and cherry aromas and flavors, in that order. There are tough tannins in this dry wine. 83 *—S.H. (12/1/2004)*

Steele 2000 Bien Nacido Vineyard Pinot Noir (Santa Barbara County) $30. Getting old, with the fresh fruit fading to leathery, earthy flavors. The tannins are still firm, and so are the acids. Unlikely to develop, so drink now. 84 *—S.H. (12/1/2004)*

Steele 1999 Durell Vineyard Pinot Noir (Carneros) $28. 88 *(10/1/2002)*

Steele 1999 Goodchild Vineyard Pinot Noir (Santa Barbara) $32. 88 *(10/1/2002)*

Steele 1999 Sangiacomo Vineyard Pinot Noir (Carneros) $32. 88 *(10/1/2002)*

Steele 2001 Clear Lake Syrah (Lake County) $16. A split decision from our panel, but all agreed that oak was a dominant feature, with descriptors ranging from lots of sawdust and vanilla to pie crust. On the fruit, opinions were less unanimous, ranging from cherry to raisin, hence the wishy-washy rating. 85 *(9/1/2005)*

Steele 2001 Parmelee-Hill Vineyard Syrah (Sonoma Valley) $22. Quite different from other bottlings off this vineyard, Jed Steele's version stresses meaty, savory notes and lashings of caramel-drizzled vanilla toast. Finishes with soft tannins and more oak-derived flavors. 84 *(9/1/2005)*

Steele 2001 Viognier (Lake County) $18. 85 *—M.S. (5/1/2003)*

Steele 1998 Catfish Vineyard Zinfandel (Clear Lake) $19. 91 *—P.G. (3/1/2001)*

Steele 1997 Pacini Vineyard Zinfandel (Mendocino County) $24. 85 *—J.C. (9/1/1999)*

USA

STEFAN DANIELS

Stefan Daniels 2001 Sauvignon Blanc (Redwood Valley) $15. 86 *—S.H. (12/31/2003)*

Stefan Daniels 2000 Lockeford Syrah (Lodi) $15. Not a big wine, but with some nice plum and blackberry flavors, with hints of coffee, dark chocolate, and herbs. Completely dry, and fairly tannic, too, although the fruit leaves behind a rich sweetness on the finish. 87 *—S.H. (3/1/2004)*

STELLA MARIS

Stella Maris 2002 Red Blend (Columbia Valley (WA)) $29. The Stella Maris, a Northstar second label, is a standout among a largely undistinguished crop of 2002s. Sweet fruit shows tangy flavors of red currant and berry, which carry the wine into a puckery finish. It's round and pleasing, though without much weight. 87 *—P.G. (12/15/2005)*

STELTZNER

Steltzner 1998 Cabernet Sauvignon (Napa Valley) $28. 90 *—S.H. (6/1/2002)*

STEPHAN RIDGE

Stephan Ridge 2000 L'Adventure Estate Cuvée Red Blend (Paso Robles) $75. 92 Editors' Choice *—S.H. (11/15/2003)*

STEPHEN ROSS

Stephen Ross 2000 Edna Ranch Chardonnay (Edna Valley) $20. 85 *—S.H. (6/1/2003)*

Stephen Ross 2002 Pinot Noir (Edna Valley) $28. A marvelously plush, complex wine. Earthy aromas, sautéed mushrooms, cola, smoked meat, ripe cherries, and raspberries and Oriental spices combine in a dense, lush mouthfeel. Fabulous length and harmony in the finish. This is seriously fine Pinot Noir. Drink now or through 2006. 91 Editors' Choice *(11/1/2004)*

Stephen Ross 2002 Bien Nacido Vineyard Pinot Noir (Santa Maria Valley) $35. Complex aromatics here, with cherry, cola, root beer, orange peel, and smoky oak among other notes. Drinks crisp in acidity and clean, with a polished, supple texture. Some tannins on the finish provide grip. 87 *(11/1/2004)*

Stephen Ross 2000 Chamisal Vineyard Pinot Noir (Edna Valley) $40. 90 Editors' Choice *(10/1/2002)*

Stephen Ross 2000 Edna Ranch Pinot Noir (Edna Valley) $40. 86 *(10/1/2002)*

Stephen Ross 2001 Dante Dusi Vineyard Zinfandel (Paso Robles) $22. 90 Editors' Choice *(11/1/2003)*

Stephen Ross 1999 Dusi Vineyard/Martini Vineyard Zinfandel (Paso Robles) $20. 85 *—S.H. (12/15/2001)*

Stephen Ross 1999 Monte Rosso Vineyard Zinfandel (Sonoma Valley) $28. 92 Editors' Choice *—S.H. (12/15/2001)*

STEPHEN VINCENT

Stephen Vincent 2003 Merlot (California) $10. Starts with an inviting, warm aroma of fine Bordeaux, but turns unexpectedly sweet and sharp in the mouth. A letdown. 82 *—S.H. (12/31/2005)*

Stephen Vincent 2003 Sauvignon Blanc (Lake County) $9. These Lake County Sauvignon Blancs can be really good values, and this one definitely is. With its juicy flavors of citrus, fig, white peach, and vanilla, and bright, crisp acids, it's a fine cocktail wine, and versatile with food. 85 Best Buy *—S.H. (12/31/2005)*

STERLING

Sterling 2002 Cabernet Sauvignon (Napa Valley) $24. Gentle and rich, this Cab shows smooth, sweet tannins and a nice touch of oak. The underlying fruit flavors are of blackberries and cassis, with a touch of cinnamon-dusted mocha coffee. 85 *—S.H. (12/1/2005)*

Sterling 1999 Diamond Mountain Ranch Cabernet Sauvignon (Napa Valley) $40. 92 *(6/1/2002)*

Sterling 1997 Diamond Mountain Ranch Vyd Cabernet Sauvignon (Napa Valley) $40. 93 *(11/1/2000)*

Sterling 2000 Reserve Cabernet Sauvignon (Napa Valley) $70. Starts off soft, oaky, and sweet in fruit, with cherry-berry flavors that are easy on the palate. Could use more complexity and concentration in the middle, and turns a bit astringent on the finish. **86** —*S.H. (5/1/2004)*

Sterling 1997 Reserve Cabernet Sauvignon (Napa Valley) $60. 90 *(11/1/2000)*

Sterling 2002 Vintner's Collection Cabernet Sauvignon (Central Coast) $15. Good varietal character, with blackberry and earthy flavors, a touch of oak, rich tannins, and dry. It's all slimmed down, though, in this rustic, country-style Cab. **84** —*S.H. (7/1/2005)*

Sterling 2000 Vintner's Collection Cabernet Sauvignon (Central Coast) $13. 86 —*S.H. (4/1/2003)*

Sterling 2003 Chardonnay (Napa County) $17. Lots of smoky, vanilla-scented and caramelized oak has been put on this wine, but the flavors themselves are thin and watery **84** —*S.H. (3/1/2005)*

Sterling 2001 Chardonnay (North Coast) $17. 86 —*S.H. (12/15/2002)*

Sterling 2001 Reserve Chardonnay (Napa Valley) $40. 91 —*S.H. (12/1/2003)*

Sterling 2004 Vintner's Collection Chardonnay (Central Coast) $14. Nice and sweet in oak and ripe, forward peaches, pears, apricots, and spices, with a touch of tropical fruit, this everyday Chard also pleases for its creamy texture and smooth finish. **84** —*S.H. (12/1/2005)*

Sterling 2003 Vintners' Collection Chardonnay (Central Coast) $11. A workhorse Chard that fulfills the basic requirements, with peach, buttered toast, and vanilla flavors and a creamy texture. The finish is clean and spicy. **84** —*S.H. (10/1/2004)*

Sterling 2000 Winery Lake Chardonnay (Carneros) $25. 88 —*S.H. (2/1/2003)*

Sterling 1999 Winery Lake Vineyard Chardonnay (Carneros) $25. 89 *(9/1/2001)*

Sterling 2002 Merlot (Napa Valley) $22. Shows all the fine qualities you want in a Merlot, such as ripe, sweet cherry, and blackberry fruit, finely ground tannins, balancing acidity, and a touch of oak. If only it had concentration, it would be a far better wine. **85** —*S.H. (12/1/2005)*

Sterling 1998 Merlot (Napa Valley) $23. 83 —*S.H. (6/1/2001)*

Sterling 1997 Diamond Mountain Ranch Vyd Merlot (Napa Valley) $30. 86 —*J.C. (7/1/2000)*

Sterling 2000 Reserve Merlot (Napa Valley) $65. Soft enough, with a gentle mouthfeel and lots of new oak. The flavors veer toward blackberries and coffee, but there are hollow spots. Turns rough and unsteady on the finish, with unripe tannins. **86** —*S.H. (5/1/2004)*

Sterling 1998 Reserve Merlot (Napa Valley) $71. 91 Cellar Selection *(9/1/2001)*

Sterling 1998 Three Palms Vineyard Merlot (Napa Valley) $56. 89 *(9/1/2001)*

Sterling 2002 Vintner's Collection Merlot (Central Coast) $13. Drinks a bit heavy and thick, but there's no denying the juicy flavors. Plums, sweet blackberries, cherries, and herbs flood the mouth, leading to some astringency from tannins. **85** —*S.H. (10/1/2004)*

Sterling 2001 Vintner's Collection Merlot (Central Coast) $13. 85 —*S.H. (12/1/2003)*

Sterling 1996 Winery Lake Merlot (Carneros) $35. 89 —*M.S. (3/1/2000)*

Sterling 1997 Winery Lake Vineyard Merlot (Carneros) $35. 89 —*M.S. (3/1/2000)*

Sterling 2003 Vintner's Collection Pinot Noir (Central Coast) $13. A bit simple, but with nice raspberry, cherry, cocoa, and oak flavors, and a silky mouthfeel. It's dry and crisp, with a rich, fruity finish. **84** —*S.H. (7/1/2005)*

Sterling 2002 Winery Lake Pinot Noir (Carneros) $25. Delicate and refined, with candied cherry, cinnamon, and leather aromas and flavors. Drinks delicate and crisp in the mouth, with a silky texture. Finishes rather short. **85** *(11/1/2004)*

Sterling 1999 Winery Lake Pinot Noir (Carneros) $27. 88 *(9/1/2001)*

Sterling 1997 Winery Lake Vineyard Pinot Noir (Carneros) $21. 90 *(10/1/1999)*

Sterling 2004 Sauvignon Blanc (Napa Valley) $13. Although this wine is simple and has a quick finish, it's clean and fruity, with slightly sweet lemon, lime and grapefruit flavors. **83** —*S.H. (11/15/2005)*

Sterling 2002 Sauvignon Blanc (North Coast) $14. 86 —*S.H. (12/1/2003)*

Sterling 2003 Vintner's Collection Shiraz (Central Coast) $13. Dry and a bit rustic, this wine features earthy, cherry flavors and some gritty tannins. The cherries really show up on the finish. Try it with rich fare. **84** —*S.H. (7/1/2005)*

Sterling 2001 Vintner's Collection Shiraz (Central Coast) $13. 85 —*S.H. (12/15/2003)*

STEVEN KENT

Steven Kent 2000 Cabernet Sauvignon (Livermore Valley) $45. 92 —*S.H. (10/1/2003)*

Steven Kent 2001 Vincerre Cabernet Sauvignon-Barbera (Livermore Valley) $40. Not on a par with the 2000 release, due, I think, to the decision to include a majority of Barbera with the Sangiovese and Cabernet Sauvignon. The Barbera completely dominates the other varieties, with a rustic simplicity, heaviness and leathery chewiness. **85** —*S.H. (8/1/2004)*

Steven Kent 1999 Folkendt Vineyard Merrillie Chardonnay (Livermore Valley) $36. **93** —*S.H. (12/15/2001)*

Steven Kent 2000 Merrillie Chardonnay (Livermore Valley) $36. **92** —*S.H. (12/15/2002)*

Steven Kent 2001 Zin-Tonga Zinfandel (Livermore Valley) $32. **91** *(11/1/2003)*

STEVENOT

Stevenot 2001 Cabernet Sauvignon (Calaveras County) $12. Textbook Cabernet, with pure cassis and black currant flavors, very dry, and the tannins are smooth and polished. Oak adds smoke, toast, and a woody sweetness. A little soft in acids, but it sure is good. **89 Best Buy** —*S.H. (10/1/2005)*

Stevenot 2001 Chardonnay (Calaveras County) $28. Much oakier and more leesy than Stevenot's estate Chard. Unleashes a blast of well-toasted oak and vanilla that frames underlying flavors of pineapples and pears. Finishes soft, with an earthy, tobaccoey edge. **86** —*S.H. (9/1/2004)*

USA

Stevenot 2002 Calaveras County Chardonnay (Calaveras County) $12. Opens with candied peach and tropical fruit aromas that lead to a full-flavored wine brimming with pineapple, peach, vanilla, buttered toast, and cinnamon. The acidity is fine, the texture creamy in this easy drinking Chard. **84** —*S.H. (9/1/2004)*

Stevenot 2003 Graciano (Calaveras County) $22. Complex aromas of green olives, grilled meat, cherries, cheese, and lightly smoked oak turn light-bodied in the mouth, with pretty cherry and mocha flavors **86** —*S.H. (3/1/2005)*

Stevenot 2001 Merlot (Calaveras County) $12. This is a nice, smooth Merlot that lives up to its reputation as the soft Cabernet. It's fruity in blackberry, cherry, and coffee flavors, and spicy. On the finish, cassis, pure and true. **90 Best Buy** —*S.H. (10/1/2005)*

Stevenot 2002 Canterbury Vineyard Syrah (Calaveras County) $22. Smells and tastes a bit like herb-marinated grilled beef, with basil and oregano notes along with smoky, toasty scents from barrel-aging. A bit on the lean side, with a tart and cranberryish finish. **85** *(9/1/2005)*

Stevenot 1999 Canterbury Vineyard Syrah (Calaveras County) $16. **86** *(10/1/2001)*

Stevenot 1999 Tempranillo (Calaveras County) $18. **87** —*J.M. (5/1/2002)*

Stevenot 2003 Verdelho (California) $16. You could easily mistake this for a Sauvignon Blanc, with its lemonade-citrus aromas. It has intense lemon and lime flavors that skirt the edge of sweetness, but high acidity provides a tart edge of balance. **86** —*S.H. (9/1/2004)*

Stevenot 2001 Silverspoons Vineyard Verdelho (California) $16. Very Sauvignon Blanc-y, with bright citrusy acidity framing intense lemon, lime, fig, and honeydew melon flavors. Finishes dry, crisp, and refreshing. **87** —*S.H. (3/1/2005)*

Stevenot 2001 Costello Vineyard Zinfandel (Sierra Foothills) $32. **80** *(11/1/2003)*

STEVENSON-BARRIE

Stevenson-Barrie 1999 Shea Vineyard Pinot Noir (Willamette Valley) $35. **89** —*P.G. (11/1/2001)*

STG

STG 2003 Chardonnay (Chalk Hill) $13. If there's any fruit in this massively oaked wine, it's hard to find. Little but char, vanilla, and toast hit you, with a sweet dill finish. **82** —*S.H. (11/1/2005)*

STG 2003 Merlot (Russian River Valley) $14. Rough around the edges, with earthy tobacco and cherry flavors, this is a big, dry, pretty tannic red wine. Best with a barbecued steak if you're a little fussy, but not too demanding. **84** —*S.H. (10/1/2005)*

STOLLER

Stoller 2002 Pinot Noir (Willamette Valley) $42. This is an over-the-top, Zinfandel-style Pinot, with a pungent, roasted, alcoholic nose. Aggressive and hot, it does not achieve any sort of balance, and simply feels overwrought. **85** *(11/1/2004)*

STOLPMAN

Stolpman 2001 La Croce Red Blend (Santa Ynez Valley) $19. **91** —*S.H. (10/1/2003)*

Stolpman 2002 Rosato Rosé Blend (Santa Ynez Valley) $NA. A happy rosé wine, fairly deep in color, and the spowerful raspberry and cherry flavors attest to lots of extraction. Fully dry, with a nice bite of acidity, this full-bodied wine finishes with a long, spicy finish. **86** —*S.H. (3/1/2004)*

Stolpman 2003 Estate Grown Syrah (Santa Ynez Valley) $25. Peppery and youthful on the nose, this Syrah has good grab in the mid-palate, and black plum and berry fruit to recommend it. One taster found it a little on the lean side, with a tart finish. **87** *(9/1/2005)*

Stolpman 2001 Angeli Tuscan Blend (Santa Ynez Valley) $42. **92** —*S.H. (10/1/2003)*

STONE CREEK

Stone Creek 1998 Special Selection Chardonnay (California) $7. **80** —*J.C. (10/1/1999)*

Stone Creek 1998 Special Selection Merlot (California) $8. **84 Best Buy** *(6/1/2001)*

Stone Creek 2001 Special Selection Zinfandel (California) $8. **82** *(11/1/2003)*

STONE WOLF

Stone Wolf 2001 Chardonnay (Willamette Valley) $10. **85** —*P.G. (12/31/2002)*

STONECROFT

Stonecroft 1998 Reserve Pinot Noir (Willamette Valley) $30. **88** —*M.M. (12/1/2000)*

STONEGATE

Stonegate 2001 Cabernet Sauvignon (Napa Valley) $25. All four of Stonegate's Bordeaux single-varietal wines, including this one, share the same characteristics of dryness, rich fruitiness, and strong, dry tannins. They march against the prevailing soft, gooey style, and seem to be built for cellaring. Try holding this Cab past 2007. **87** —*S.H. (8/1/2005)*

Stonegate 1998 Cabernet Sauvignon (Napa Valley) $29. **90** —*S.H. (12/1/2001)*

Stonegate 2001 Diamond Mountain Reserve Spaulding Vineyard Cabernet Sauvignon (Napa Valley) $50. It's extraordinarily, mouth-numbingly tannic, and acidic, too, but even that can't stop the cascade of blackberries and black currants from throttling the mouth. This is an ageable wine, well able to stand and improve beyond 2010. **92 Cellar Selection** —*S.H. (8/1/2005)*

Stonegate 1998 Estate Bottled Chardonnay (Napa Valley) $18. **84** *(6/1/2000)*

Stonegate 2000 Merlot (Napa Valley) $22. **84** —*S.H. (12/15/2003)*

Stonegate 1998 Merlot (Napa Valley) $22. **88** —*S.H. (2/1/2001)*

Stonegate 2003 Sauvignon Blanc (Napa Valley) $14. I had this dry white wine with Chinese food and it was perfect. The citrus and peach fruitiness played off the inherent sweetness of soy sauce and ginger, while the wine's acidity cut through the oils. It's also pleasant on its own. **86** —*S.H. (8/1/2005)*

STONEHEDGE

Stonehedge 2000 Cabernet Sauvignon (California) $10. **83** —*S.H. (6/1/2002)*

Stonehedge 2000 Chardonnay (California) $10. **82** —*S.H. (5/1/2002)*

Stonehedge 2000 Merlot (California) $10. **85** —*S.H. (6/1/2002)*

Stonehedge 2000 Reserve Petite Sirah (Mendocino) $35. **91** —*S.H. (9/1/2003)*

Stonehedge 2003 Sauvignon Blanc (California) $10. One of the drier Sauvignons out there, bony and minerally, with tart acids that make it mouthwateringly clean. Picks up lemon and fig flavors in the finish. A nice cocktail-style wine at a good price. **84** —*S.H. (8/1/2005)*

Stonehedge 2000 Sauvignon Blanc (California) $10. **84** —*S.H. (9/1/2002)*

Stonehedge 1999 Syrah (California) $10. **86** *(10/1/2001)*

Stonehedge 2000 Zinfandel (California) $10. **86 Best Buy** —*S.H. (7/1/2002)*

Stonehedge 1997 Reserve Zinfandel (Napa Valley) $25. **88** —*P.G. (2/1/2001)*

STONESTREET

Stonestreet 1997 Cabernet Sauvignon (Sonoma County) $35. **86** *(11/1/2000)*

Stonestreet 2001 Christopher's Cabernet Sauvignon (Alexander Valley) $80. I have watched this wine for some time and know that it is an ager, especially in a great vintage like this one. Made from very high Mayacamas Mountain grapes, it's relentlessly tannic in its youth. But the core of black cherry and cassis is fabulous. Hold until 2010. **93 Cellar Selection** —*S.H. (7/1/2005)*

Stonestreet 1997 Christopher's Vineyard Cabernet Sauvignon (Sonoma County) $70. **90** *(11/1/2000)*

Stonestreet 1999 Block 66 Alexander Mountain Chardonnay (Alexander Valley) $34. **88** *(9/1/2003)*

Stonestreet 2001 Upper Barn Chardonnay (Alexander Valley) $40. I get the idea of this wine. It's to craft a mountain Chard that's lean and acidic now, but a cellar candidate. It is indeed tight and austere, not offering a lot of satisfaction beyond oak and a hint of spicy pear on the finish. If you're adventurous, hold until 2006. **89** —*S.H. (7/1/2005)*

Stonestreet 1998 Upper Barn Chardonnay (Sonoma County) $40. **87** *(7/1/2001)*

Stonestreet 2001 Upper Barn Sauvignon Blanc (Alexander Valley) $20. Ripe and intriguing, and holding onto its form after four years. Delivers some creamy lemon pudding aromas that are backed by flavors of citrus, apple, and egg yolk. Solid on the finish, and appealing. Even offers a bit of cannoli/crème brulée flavor at the end. **88** *(7/1/2005)*

Stonestreet 1999 Upper Barn Vineyard Sauvignon Blanc (Alexander Valley) $23. 87 *(8/1/2002)*

STONY HILL

Stony Hill 2001 Chardonnay (Napa Valley) $27. Stony Hill Chards are famous for their longevity, but the price of that is hardness in youth. This is a mineral-laden, acidic young wine. The fruit has barely begun clawing its way to the surface. I've had Stony Hill Chards at 20-plus years of age and they were fabulous. Best after 2010. 92 *—S.H. (5/1/2005)*

Stony Hill 1999 Chardonnay (Napa Valley) $27. 93 *—S.H. (5/1/2002)*

Stony Hill 2002 Gewürztraminer (Napa Valley) $15. Tough, light, bone dry and acidic, with pretty spice and floral notes, but rather thin on the fruit. You'll find diluted citrus flavors just veering into peach. 84 *—S.H. (2/1/2004)*

Stony Hill 2000 Gewürztraminer (Napa Valley) $15. 88 *—S.H. (6/1/2002)*

Stony Hill 2002 White Riesling (Napa Valley) $15. Disappointingly thin this vintage. The palate expects a rush of fruit, but encounters watery grapefruit and lime flavors and acidity. The rich floral and riper tree fruit notes just aren't there. 84 *—S.H. (2/1/2004)*

Stony Hill 2000 White Riesling (Napa Valley) $15. 90 *—S.H. (6/1/2002)*

STONY RIDGE WINERY

Stony Ridge Winery 2000 Reserve Johannisberg Riesling (Monterey) $10. 88 **Best Buy** *—S.H. (12/31/2003)*

STORRS

Storrs 2002 Viento Vineyard Gewürztraminer (Monterey) $14. I wish this wine were firmer and steelier, because it really has beautiful perfume and taste, but it's soft. It's showcases Gewürz's exotic side, with dusty spices, tropical fruits, and flowers. 85 *—S.H. (5/1/2005)*

Storrs 2000 Rusty Ridge Petite Sirah (Santa Clara County) $22. 83 *(4/1/2003)*

Storrs 2002 Riverview Vineyard White Riesling (Monterey) $14. Here's an Alsatian-style wine, with fairly dry but vigorously rich flavors of honeysuckle, peach, slate, and vanilla. If it had crisper acidity, it would be a great wine. 86 *—S.H. (5/1/2005)*

STORYBOOK MOUNTAIN

Storybook Mountain 2001 Eastern Exposures Zinfandel (Napa Valley) $30. 88 *(11/1/2003)*

Storybook Mountain 1997 Eastern Exposures Zinfandel (Napa Valley) $25. 95 *—P.G. (11/15/1999)*

Storybook Mountain 2001 Mayacamas Range Zinfandel (Napa Valley) $20. 87 *(11/1/2003)*

Storybook Mountain 1997 Mayacamas Range Zinfandel (Napa Valley) $20. 88 *—P.G. (11/15/1999)*

Storybook Mountain 2000 The First Hurrah Zinfandel (Atlas Peak) $25. 88 *—S.H. (11/1/2002)*

STRANGELAND

Strangeland 2002 Pinot Noir (Willamette Valley) $20. Clove stands out, above cherry and vanilla, some earthy, stemmy tannins, and a tough, unripe, tomatoey finish. 83 *(11/1/2004)*

Strangeland 2002 Winemaker's Estate Reserve Pinot Noir (Willamette Valley) $60. Pale, oaky, herbal, with very light, rhubarb fruit and roasted coconut. Way too tannic. 82 *(11/1/2004)*

STRATFORD

Stratford 1999 Syrah (California) $18. 84 *—S.H. (7/1/2002)*

STRYKER SONOMA

Stryker Sonoma 2001 Syrah (Dry Creek Valley) $22. Floral and spicy on the nose, with hints of berry zinger tea. Picks up hints of cherries and chocolate on the palate, but without adding any weight, then finishes crisp and clean. Pretty, but light. 83 *(9/1/2005)*

Stryker Sonoma 2002 Estate Syrah (Alexander Valley) $22. Much different in style from Stryker Sonoma's Dry Creek Syrah, this bottling is riper and more intense. Lush plum and blackberry flavors are broad and mouthfilling, picking up hints of vanilla on the abbreviated finish. Drink now. 85 *(9/1/2005)*

STUART CELLARS

Stuart Cellars 1998 Vintage Zinfandel (Temecula) $42. 95 *—S.H. (4/1/2002)*

STUHLMULLER VINEYARDS

Stuhlmuller Vineyards 1999 Cabernet Sauvignon (Alexander Valley) $35. 84 *—S.H. (12/15/2003)*

Stuhlmuller Vineyards 2001 Estate Cabernet Sauvignon (Alexander Valley) $32. This is a young, dynamic wine that's fancy enough to have with your best food. It shows well-ripened fruit flavors, and is very dry, with a good boost of acidity. Also has some pretty good tannins to cut through beef. I think it's at its best now and for the next three years. 90 *—S.H. (10/1/2005)*

Stuhlmuller Vineyards 1999 Chardonnay (Alexander Valley) $23. 88 *—J.M. (5/1/2002)*

Stuhlmuller Vineyards 2000 Estate Bottled Chardonnay (Alexander Valley) $23. **84** —*S.H. (8/1/2003)*

SULLIVAN

Sullivan 2000 Cabernet Sauvignon (Rutherford) $50. Tastes better than it smells. The aromas are herbal, stalky, and even raw vegetal, with an overlay of toasty oak. In the mouth, some blackberry flavors show up, but it's a thin wine and not going anywhere. Still, the rich, soft structure saves it. **85** —*S.H. (2/1/2004)*

Sullivan 2002 Estate Reserve Cabernet Sauvignon (Rutherford) $85. Forward and lush, with a beautiful structure, this dry, balanced wine has cherry, cassis, wintergreen, and oak flavors that finish in a swirl of complexity. This fine wine defines the elegance and femininity of a great Rutherford Cab, and should age well through 2012. **93 Editors' Choice** —*S.H. (12/15/2005)*

SULLIVAN BIRNEY

Sullivan Birney 2002 Sonoma Coast Chardonnay (Sonoma Coast) $30. Nobody ages Chardonnay, but maybe they should, as the profile of these coastal Chards emerges. This wine is high in acidity, metallic, and lemony in fruit. There's a toughness that the softening, sweetening qualities of oak cannot blur. It's a gamble, but try cellaring until 2005 and try again. **88** —*S.H. (8/1/2004)*

Sullivan Birney 2002 Pinot Noir (Sonoma Coast) $28. Easy and simple, rather than profound, with candied raspberry and rhubarb aromas. Rather tart in acids. **83** *(11/1/2004)*

Sullivan Birney 2001 Katherine Vineyard Pinot Noir (Sonoma Mountain) $30. This is a new winery to me, and this fabulous release displays its great promise. The wine is dark and dense, with an immature aroma of smoky wood, baked cherry tart, and vanilla. In the mouth it has complex cherry, berry, and spice flavors that are folded into rich but soft tannins. Finishes long. **93 Editors' Choice** —*S.H. (5/1/2004)*

SUMMERLAND

Summerland 2002 Chardonnay (Santa Barbara County) $14. A nice enough Chard for everyday purposes, with some nicely ripened tropical fruit flavors. Has an earthiness in the middle, but finishes fruity and spicy. **84** —*S.H. (9/1/2004)*

Summerland 2001 Merlot (Santa Barbara County) $16. Thin and rather weedy, with modest cherry flavors and smooth tannins. Fulfills the basics. **83** —*S.H. (12/15/2004)*

Summerland 2002 Bien Nacido Vineyard Block T Pinot Noir (Santa Maria Valley) $30. A Pinot that goes straight down the middle in varietal correctness but isn't very exciting. Black cherry, oak, and spice flavors drink somewhat tannic, and the acidity is quite high. **84** *(11/1/2004)*

Summerland 2002 Syrah (Paso Robles) $16. Over-ripe and too sweet, a Porty wine with raisiny, caramel and chocolate flavors, a dense texture, and a sugary finish. That's just not right for a varietal that supposed to be a dry table wine. **83** —*S.H. (12/1/2004)*

SUMMERS

Summers 2002 Cabernet Sauvignon (Napa Valley) $36. The plush blackberry, cassis, and chocolate flavors hit you on the first sip, flooding the palate, and then acids and tannins kick in to balance. There's a roughness that keeps this Cab from the front ranks, but it has charm. Drink now. **87** —*S.H. (11/1/2005)*

Summers 2000 Cabernet Sauvignon (Napa Valley) $38. **93 Editors' Choice** —*S.H. (11/15/2003)*

Summers 2000 Villa Andriano Charbono (Napa Valley) $24. **84** —*S.H. (12/1/2002)*

Summers 1999 Merlot (Knights Valley) $24. **85** —*S.H. (11/15/2002)*

Summers 2000 Viognier (Monterey) $18. **90 Editors' Choice** —*S.H. (12/15/2002)*

Summers 2003 Villa Adriana Vineyard Zinfandel (Napa Valley) $28. Summers has established a good track record with this single-vineyard Zin, and while it's not quite in the same league as the '01 or '02, it's very good. Ripe and striking in cherry and tobacco flavors, and liberally spiced, it has a fine, claret-like balance. **88** —*S.H. (8/1/2005)*

Summers 2002 Villa Andriana Vineyard Estate Zinfandel (Napa Valley) $28. This interestingly complex Zin shows lots of forward cherry, blueberry, black raspberry, and cocoa fruit, sprinkled with peppery spices, and is fully dry. Shows lots of classy balance in the way the sweet tannins, acidity, and subtle oak interplay with the fruit. **90** —*S.H. (6/1/2005)*

SUMMERWOOD

Summerwood 2001 Diosa Red Blend (Paso Robles) $50. Vibrant cherry, chocolate, olive, and woody-smoky aromas lead to a soft and accessible red wine. Feels good and supple, with generous fruit. Finishes with a dusting of fine tannins. Decant, or best after 2005. Syrah-Mourvèdre-Grenache. **89** —*S.H. (12/31/2004)*

Summerwood 2003 Diosa Rhône Red Blend (Paso Robles) $50. The fruit stars in this Rhône red blend. It's all summer-sweet raspberries, cherry compote infused with milk chocolate and a trickle of cassis, drizzled with vanilla, and smoked in oak barrels. The wine is very soft, yet with enough acidity to provide balance and freshness. **91** —*S.H. (10/1/2005)*

Summerwood 2002 Diosa Syrah (Paso Robles) $50. Dark and ripe, with soft acids and tannins and a velvety texture carrying chocolate and blackberry flavors. Fully dry, though, and balanced. Mainly Syrah, with splashes of Grenache and Roussanne. **86** —*S.H. (12/15/2004)*

Summerwood 2001 Zinfandel (Paso Robles) $18. **84** *(11/1/2003)*

SUMMIT LAKE

Summit Lake 2001 Zinfandel (Howell Mountain) $20. Fairly rugged in tannins, with an edgy mouthfeel, this wine shows earth, blackberry, and coffee flavors. It's very dry. **85** —*S.H. (5/1/2005)*

Summit Lake 1999 Zinfandel (Howell Mountain) $22. **92** —*S.H. (9/1/2002)*

Summit Lake 1996 Howell Mountain Zinfandel (Napa Valley) $23. **85** —*P.G. (11/15/1999)*

SUNCÉ VINEYARD & WINERY

Suncé Vineyard & Winery 2001 Pl. Franicevic Stryker's Vineyard Meritage Cabernet Sauvignon (Clear Lake) $40. A nice, well-crafted Cab that pleases on several levels. It's got good varietal character, from the blackberry and currant flavors accented with oak to the soft, sweet tannins. The wine needs more depth and concentration, though, and finishes thin. **86** —*S.H. (6/1/2004)*

Suncé Vineyard & Winery 2000 Pl. Franicevic Stryker's Vineyard Meritage (Clear Lake) $65. Awkward, with a mixture of blackberry and stalky flavors. The elaborate oak doesn't really help. **83** —*S.H. (6/1/2004)*

Suncé Vineyard & Winery 2001 La Rochelle Vineyard Pinot Noir (Monterey) $18. Good example of cool Central Coast Pinot, with its polished, jammy flavors of cherry and raspberry and dusty spices, complexed with smoky oak. Bright acidity and gentle tannins make for an easy drink. Light, but a pretty good value. **86** —*S.H. (12/1/2005)*

Suncé Vineyard & Winery 2001 Pl. Franicevic Piner Ranch Vineyard Pinot Noir (Russian River Valley) $32. Simple, with basic varietal identity, namely, the silky smooth tannins and crisp acidity that underlie cola and watered-down raspberry flavors. My sample bottle was a little fizzy. **83** —*S.H. (6/1/2004)*

USA

SUNSET

Sunset 1999 Zinfandel (Dry Creek Valley) $23. **85** —*S.H. (9/1/2002)*

SUNSTONE

Sunstone 2001 Chardonnay (Santa Barbara County) $18. **86** —*S.H. (12/15/2002)*

Sunstone 2000 Merlot (Santa Ynez Valley) $24. **85** —*S.H. (11/15/2002)*

Sunstone 1999 Reserve Merlot (Santa Ynez Valley) $30. **88** —*S.H. (11/15/2002)*

Sunstone 1999 Syrah (Santa Ynez Valley) $40. **90** —*S.H. (12/1/2002)*

SURH LUCHTEL

Surh Luchtel 2002 Cabernet Sauvignon (Napa Valley) $38. I would decant this wine for a few hours, because at first it's tough and herbal. Once it opens, it shows pretty cherry flavors, and the oak, while lavish, is proportional. Dry and youthful in tannins. Drink now through 2010. **88** —*S.H. (10/1/2005)*

Surh Luchtel 1999 Cabernet Sauvignon (Napa Valley) $40. **92** —*S.H. (8/1/2003)*

Surh Luchtel 1999 Mosaic Cabernet Sauvignon-Merlot (North Coast) $23. **86** —*S.H. (9/1/2002)*

Surh Luchtel 2003 Garys' Vineyard Pinot Noir (Santa Lucia Highlands) $42. Cabernet specialist Surh Luchtel turns its hand to Central Coast Pinot Noir, with some success. The quality of the grapes must be responsible for the succulent, long-finishing black cherry and blueberry fruit, as well as the good acids. **87** —*S.H. (10/1/2005)*

Surh Luchtel 1999 Zinfandel (Napa Valley) $27. **85** —*S.H. (9/1/2002)*

Sutter Home 2003 White Cabernet Sauvignon (California) $5. Holds onto some real Cabernet character with its red currant and cherry flavors and smooth tannins. Tastes just off dry and clean. **84 Best Buy** —*S.H. (11/15/2004)*

SUTTER HOME

Sutter Home 1999 Chardonnay (California) $6. **84** —*S.H. (2/1/2001)*

Sutter Home 2002 Family Vineyard Selection Chardonnay (California) $11. Juicy, ripely fruity, and oaky, with a creamy texture. Finishes with banana cream pie. **84** —*S.H. (10/1/2004)*

Sutter Home 1998 Rosé Merlot (California) $7. **80** —*J.F. (8/1/2001)*

Sutter Home 2000 Moscato (California) $5. **85 Best Buy** —*S.H. (11/15/2001)*

Sutter Home 1997 Pinot Noir (California) $6. **84** —*T.R. (11/15/1999)*

Sutter Home 1998 Shiraz (California) $6. **82** —*S.H. (2/1/2000)*

Sutter Home 1999 Zinfandel (California) $6. **83** —*S.H. (2/1/2001)*

Sutter Home 2002 White Zinfandel (California) $7. A pale, very fruity wine that gives white Zinfanatics everything they want at a good price. Raspberries, vanilla, and a sweet finish. **83** —*S.H. (9/1/2004)*

SWANSON

Swanson 1996 Alexis Bordeaux Blend (Napa Valley) $35. **91** —*S.H. (6/1/1999)*

Swanson 1999 Alexis Cabernet Sauvignon-Syrah (Napa Valley) $35. 91 *—C.S. (11/15/2002)*

Swanson 1997 Merlot (Napa Valley) $28. 88 *—J.C. (7/1/2000)*

Swanson 2001 Merlot (Oakville) $32. From a winery that seldom stumbles, a lush, sexy Merlot. Its cassis, unsweetened chocolate, and oak flavors are wrapped in chewy tannins that make your tongue stick to the gums. It's a young, dramatic wine. Drink now, with roast duck or pork tenderloin. **91** *—S.H. (5/1/2005)*

Swanson 1999 Merlot (Napa Valley) $21. 87 *—D.T. (12/31/2002)*

Swanson 1998 Pinot Grigio (Napa Valley) $18. 86 *(8/1/1999)*

Swanson 2002 Alexis Red Blend (Oakville) $55. This unconventional blend of Cabernet, Syrah, and Merlot is a classic Napa red, soft, and luxurious and decadent, yet with a firm structure. It's enormously flavorful in sweet cassis and chocolate, with a firm, dry finish. **90** *—S.H. (11/1/2005)*

Swanson 1997 Sangiovese (Napa Valley) $24. 92 *—S.H. (11/1/1999)*

Swanson 1998 Syrah (Napa Valley) $45. 89 *(11/1/2001)*

SWITCHBACK RIDGE

Switchback Ridge 2000 Peterson Family Vineyard Merlot (Napa Valley) $48. 92 *—J.M. (8/1/2003)*

Switchback Ridge 2000 Peterson Family Vineyard Petite Sirah (Napa Valley) $45. 91 *(4/1/2003)*

SYNCLINE

Syncline 2003 Late Harvest Chenin Blanc (Columbia Valley (WA)) $18. From 22-year-old vines, this is 100% barrel-fermented, and retains 20.5% residual sugar. Still, it's not cloying; it's lively with stone fruits, mown hay, and some high-toned esters. It tastes of apples, butterscotch, and candy; finishes long with plenty of acid support. **92** *—P.G. (9/1/2004)*

Syncline 2002 Celilo Vineyard Pinot Noir (Washington) $20. A sturdy style, with thick, not heavy flavors of strawberry and pomegranate and cranberry. An interesting style, neither Oregonian nor Burgundian, but big and broad, with somewhat rustic but flavorful fruit. Perfumed, clean, and lightly spicy. **88** *—P.G. (11/1/2004)*

Syncline 2002 Milbrandt Vineyards Syrah (Columbia Valley (WA)) $20. Sweet, spicy, almost pungent with meaty, bright berry scents. It shows a beautiful nose, fragrant and seductive, spiced with white pepper, blueberry, and violets. It's clean and lifted, with everything—alcohol included—in balance. **89** *—P.G. (9/1/2004)*

Syncline 2002 Reserve Syrah (Columbia Valley (WA)) $30. The blend is 94% Syrah, 5% Grenache, and 1% Viognier. New oak is apparent, displaying roasted coffee, bitter chocolate, and vanilla cream flavors. Very smooth. **90** *—P.G. (9/1/2004)*

Syncline 2004 Viognier (Columbia Valley (WA)) $20. 360 cases were made of this rich and creamy Viognier. Scents of lemon and lime and rose petals lead into flavors of Meyer lemon, with a custardy mouthfeel. The wine retains a pleasing, citrus/tangerine crispness through the finish. **89** *—P.G. (12/15/2005)*

SYZYGY

Syzygy 2003 Syrah (Walla Walla (WA)) $28. Don't ask us how to pronounce the name, we just have to spell it. Combines herbal, minty notes with bright red berries borne along a creamy mouthfeel. Shows just a touch of alcoholic heat on the finish. **87** *(9/1/2005)*

TABLAS CREEK

Tablas Creek 2000 Antithesis Chardonnay (Paso Robles) $35. 91 *—J.M. (5/1/2002)*

Tablas Creek 2003 Mourvèdre (Paso Robles) $32. Like others in California, Tablas struggles to find Mourvèdre's soul. This wine shows flavors of blackberries, plums, and chocolate, with an undercurrent of wild herbs and oak. Yet it's thick and soft. The challenge is to find life and structure. **84** *—S.H. (10/1/2005)*

Tablas Creek 2002 Esprit de Beaucastel Red Blend (Paso Robles) $40. This Mourvèdre-dominated wine doesn't have the super-hung meat, gamy aroma that plagued previous vintages. Instead, it offers complex aromas of ripe stone fruits and berries, with a suggestion of leather, herbs, and smoky oak. It's soft and creamy, but the tannins kick in on the finish. Drinkable now, and could improve dramatically through the decade. **89** *—S.H. (2/1/2005)*

Tablas Creek 2003 Côtes de Tablas Rhône Red Blend (Paso Robles) $20. A little simple, but the cherry and vanilla flavors are so tasty, you reach for another glass. There are complexities of vanilla, mocha, cinnamon, and white pepper in this blend of Grenache, Syrah, Mourvèdre, and Counoise. **86** *—S.H. (10/1/2005)*

Tablas Creek 2000 Esprit de Beaucastel Rhône Red Blend (Paso Robles) $35. 91 *—S.H. (12/1/2003)*

Tablas Creek 2000 Rose Rhône Red Blend (Paso Robles) $27. 90 *—S.H. (9/1/2003)*

Tablas Creek 2003 Vin de Paille Rhône White Blend (Paso Robles) $65. One of the few paille-style wines in California, but I must say this method of inducing sweetness doesn't threaten good old-fashioned botrytis. There's a rusticity to the sweet apricot flavors that does not justify the price. **84** *—S.H. (10/1/2005)*

Tablas Creek 2002 Rosé Blend (Paso Robles) $26. One of the darker rosés you'll ever see, rose petal in color. Opens with clean, inviting aromas of cherries and raspberries, and drinks enormously flavorful, with all sorts of wild berries and tree fruits flooding the palate. Beautiful acidity, the kind that tingles the tongue and makes the wine come alive. Finishes dry and balanced. One of the best California rosés in memory. **90** *—S.H. (3/1/2004)*

Tablas Creek 2004 Rosé (Paso Robles) $25. The purest, most powerful aromas and flavors of cherries dominate this Rhône blend, but it's not a simple wine. The cherries are joined with red raspberries, vanilla, sweet anise, white pepper, and tangerine zest, boosted by crisp acidity. This is a beautiful, dry, long-finished wine. **90** *—S.H. (10/1/2005)*

Tablas Creek 2002 Roussanne (Paso Robles) $26. Distinctive for its white chocolate flavor and rich, creamy texture. There are also flamboyant notes of guava, nectarine, peach, wildflowers, vanilla, and smoke. This opulent wine is filled with vibrant acidity, and is excellently balanced. It is a sure candidate to improve for at least five years in the cellar. **90** *—S.H. (2/1/2004)*

Tablas Creek 2000 Clos Blanc White Blend (Paso Robles) $35. **92** *—J.M. (9/1/2002)*

Tablas Creek 2003 Esprit de Beaucastel Blanc White Blend (Paso Robles) $35. A fabulous white Rhone blend of enormous complexity and charm. Fills the mouth with butterscotch, crème brulée, pineapple, stony mineral, vanilla, impossibly ripe white peach, and creamy hazelnut flavors, and as sweet as that sounds, the wine is dry and crisp. The greatest Esprit Blanc ever. Roussanne, Grenache Blanc, and Viognier. **95** *—S.H. (2/1/2005)*

Tablas Creek 2001 Esprit de Beaucastel Blanc White Blend (Paso Robles) $35. **94** *—S.H. (12/1/2003)*

Tablas Creek 1997 Tablas Blanc White Blend (Paso Robles) $30. **92** *—S.H. (10/1/1999)*

TABLE ROCK

Table Rock 1999 Pinot Noir (Rogue Valley) $16. **85** *(10/1/2002)*

TAFT STREET

Taft Street 1998 Chardonnay (Russian River Valley) $15. **88** *(6/1/2000)*

Taft Street 2003 Pinot Noir (Sonoma Coast) $15. This is a pretty nice Pinot that straddles the line between complex and simple. It's very dry and tart with acids, with an earthy, mushroomy profile that carries notes of cherries, blackberries, and oak. A good price for a wine of this quality from this appellation. **87** *—S.H. (12/15/2005)*

Taft Street 1997 Zinfandel (Sonoma County) $12. **83** *—P.G. (11/15/1999)*

Taft Street 2003 Old Vines Zinfandel (Russian River Valley) $20. Rustic and semisweet, this Zin is very fruity. It has a briary, peppery edge to the cherries and blackberries. **82** *—S.H. (12/15/2005)*

TAGARIS

Tagaris 2001 Johannisberg Riesling (Columbia Valley (WA)) $7. **88** *—P.G. (9/1/2002)*

TALBOTT

Talbott 2002 Cuvée Cynthia Chardonnay (Monterey County) $55. Anyone can get ripe flavors from Chardonnay grapes these days, and this barrel selection, from the famous Sleepy Hollow Vineyard, is bold in kiwi, pear, and nectarine fruit, with toasty oak and lees seasoning. What makes it spectacular is the acidity, which gashes the palate like a bolt of lightning. Endlessly complex, this is a Chardonnay to linger over. Let it warm up in the glass and watch it change. **95 Editors' Choice** *—S.H. (12/31/2005)*

Talbott 2001 Diamond T Estate Chardonnay (Monterey) $65. Tasted with Talbott's wickedly decadent 2002 Cuvée Cynthia. This is a more eccentric wine, showing its extra year of age, and that is its strength and its weakness. The fruit is turning autumn leafy, with hints of oregano and dill, but is bone dry and clean. **87** *—S.H. (12/31/2005)*

Talbott 1998 Diamond T Estate Chardonnay (Monterey) $55. **91** *(7/1/2001)*

Talbott 2001 Sleepy Hollow Chardonnay (Monterey County) $42. What a wonderful wine! It's juicy and zesty in fresh acidity, a wine that makes the palate come alive. At the same time, dazzlingly rich in ripe tropical fruit, spice, and oak, with a long, honeyed finish. Oozes decadence, and will hang in there for 3 to 5 years. **93** *—S.H. (12/1/2004)*

Talbott 2000 Sleepy Hollow Vineyard Chardonnay (Monterey County) $42. **93** *—S.H. (12/1/2003)*

Talbott 1998 Sleepy Hollow Vineyard Chardonnay (Monterey) $35. **88** *(7/1/2001)*

Talbott 2001 Logan Pinot Noir (Monterey) $18. A pretty dreadful wine from an otherwise esteemed producer. Clearly vegetal, with asparagus aromas and a syrupy texture. **81** *—S.H. (10/1/2005)*

TALISMAN

Talisman 2001 Pinot Noir (Russian River Valley) $36. A smooth-textured wine, with pretty cherry notes at its core. It fans out to reveal hints of licorice, smoke, and herbs, all framed in elegant tannins. The finish is moderate in length. **89** *—J.M. (10/1/2004)*

Talisman 2002 Truchard Vineyard Pinot Noir (Carneros) $38. This is a delicious and complex wine that expresses the essence of Carneros Pinot Noir: balance, elegance, and harmony. Not a blockbuster in the Santa Lucia sense, it's a silky, feminine wine, with a great depth of cherry, cola, and mocha flavor, and a racy, sensual mouthfeel. **92** *—S.H. (12/15/2005)*

TALLEY

Talley 1999 Chardonnay (Arroyo Grande Valley) $24. **93** *(12/31/2001)*

Talley 1999 Oliver's Vineyard Chardonnay (Edna Valley) $20. **88** *—S.H. (2/1/2001)*

USA

Talley 2002 Oliver's Vineyard Chardonnay (Edna Valley) $20. Oak hits you first, bringing vanilla, buttered toast, and wood spice. Beyond that, the tropical fruit flavors are strong. This is an interesting, rich wine, and while it is not great, it represents the seductive power of well-grown Chards from this area. **89** *—S.H. (6/1/2004)*

Talley 2003 Rincon Vineyard Chardonnay (Arroyo Grande Valley) $36. This is a young, tight wine. It stuns with strong acidity and a bitter lime zest, almost gooseberry tartness. But it's nobly structured, and badly in need of a year or two in the cellar, or extended decanting. Oxygen and warming up bring out exciting notes of tropical fruits, buttercream and oak. **92** *—S.H. (12/1/2005)*

Talley 1997 Rincon Vineyard Chardonnay (Arroyo Grande Valley) $20. **88** *—S.H. (10/1/1999)*

Talley 1999 Rosemary's Vineyard Chardonnay (Arroyo Seco) $40. **89** *(7/1/2001)*

Talley 2002 Pinot Noir (Arroyo Grande Valley) $30. Oaky, with a blast of smoky char and caramel riding over cherry vanilla. Wonderful mouthfeel, rich, full-bodied, and dry, and lush in tannins and acidity. Near-perfect balance. **88** *(11/1/2004)*

Talley 1998 Pinot Noir (Arroyo Grande Valley) $28. **86** *—S.H. (2/1/2001)*

Talley 1997 Estate Pinot Noir (Arroyo Grande Valley) $28. **91** *(10/1/1999)*

Talley 2002 Rincon Vineyard Pinot Noir (Arroyo Grande Valley) $48. Just beautiful. Smoky oak, chocolate, cherry, vanilla, sweet herbs, lavender, thyme, oriental spice, just goes on and on. Huge, rich, balanced, and so smooth, bursting with ripe, sweet fruit. Gorgeous tannin-acid balance, and such a delicate mouthfeel. **94** *(11/1/2004)*

Talley 2000 Rincon Vineyard Pinot Noir (Arroyo Grande Valley) $45. **92** *—S.H. (2/1/2003)*

Talley 1997 Rincon Vineyard Pinot Noir (Arroyo Grande Valley) $40. **89** *(10/1/1999)*

Talley 2002 Rosemary's Vineyard Pinot Noir (Arroyo Grande Valley) $62. An amazing Pinot Noir, very serious stuff. Big, bold, dark, and decadently rich. Oozing with cherry pie, mocha, and oak, with gorgeously firm acids and a smooth, complex texture. Just outstanding. A bit high in alcohol, though. **93** *(11/1/2004)*

Talley 1999 Rosemary's Vineyard Pinot Noir (Arroyo Grande Valley) $60. **86** *—S.H. (7/1/2002)*

TALOMAS

Talomas 2000 Cabernet Sauvignon-Merlot (California) $14. **85** *—S.H. (8/1/2003)*

Talomas 2001 Basket Press Reserve Syrah (Central Coast) $50. This massive Syrah blows your mind with cassis, roasted coffeebean, spiced plum, chocolate, and sweet oak aromas and flavors, and a and lush texture. Every sip explodes with taste sensations. The score would be higher if the wine had a firmer structure. It spreads all over the place, and needs reining in. **91** *—S.H. (12/15/2004)*

TALUS

Talus 2003 Chardonnay (California) $8. Thin and simple, but clean. You get modest peach flavors with oak shadings. **83** *—S.H. (2/1/2005)*

Talus 2003 Merlot (Lodi) $8. This affordable Merlot shows lots of up front fruit. It's packed with ripe cherries and blackberries, with chocolaty notes, but it's dry and balanced. The finish is soft and polished. **85 Best Buy** *—S.H. (11/15/2005)*

Talus 2000 Merlot (California) $9. **84** *—S.H. (9/1/2003)*

Talus 2003 Pinot Grigio (California) $8. Far too sweet for a Pinot Grigio. Tastes more like a simple Riesling. **83** *—S.H. (3/1/2005)*

Talus 2002 Pinot Noir (California) $8. Stewed fruits and alcohol, with a dollop of oak. Yet it's dry, clean, and drinkable. **83** *—S.H. (2/1/2005)*

Talus 1997 Red Blend (California) $9. **86** *(11/15/1999)*

Talus 2002 Shiraz (Lodi) $8. Soft, clean, and dry, with simple cherry and berry flavors and peppery spice. Easy to drink with Italian fare, burgers, or a ham sandwich. **84** *—S.H. (2/1/2005)*

Talus 1999 Shiraz (California) $8. **83** *(10/1/2001)*

Talus 2002 Zinfandel (Lodi) $8. Lots of ripe berry and spice flavors in this dry, friendly wine. It's very soft, but has good acidity. Try with BBQ salmon or ribs. **84** *—S.H. (2/1/2005)*

Talus 2000 Zinfandel (California) $9. **83** *—S.H. (3/1/2003)*

TAMARACK CELLARS

Tamarack Cellars 2001 Cabernet Sauvignon (Columbia Valley (WA)) $32. This is a nice blend of top vineyards from Walla Walla, Red Mountain, and the Columbia Valley. The winery has tamed down the tough tannins and intrusive oak of past vintages, and created a much more approachable, yet still complex and ageworthy wine. **88** *—P.G. (5/1/2004)*

Tamarack Cellars 2002 Chardonnay (Columbia Valley (WA)) $18. This under-sung Walla Walla winery improves with each new vintage. This is seductive, ripe, and buttery, with citrus and tropical fruit flavors and smooth, buttery oak. It's delicious and balanced for consumption with food. **88** *—P.G. (5/1/2004)*

Tamarack Cellars 2000 Merlot (Columbia Valley (WA)) $28. **89** *—P.G. (9/1/2002)*

Tamarack Cellars 2001 Du Brul Vineyard Reserve Red Blend (Yakima Valley) $NA. Grapes from one of the valley's top vineyards create this Bordeaux blend of 62% Cabernet Sauvignon, 31% Merlot, and 7% Cab Franc. Fragrant with scents of sandalwood, rose petals, toast, and lead pencil, the wine grudgingly opens out into a beautifully balanced, elegant palate of sweet cherry, cranberry, and pomegranate. Modest in size, but complex and delicious. **90** *—P.G. (5/1/2004)*

TAMÁS ESTATES

Tamás Estates 1999 Pinot Grigio (Monterey County) $11. **84** *—S.H. (11/15/2001)*

Tamás Estates 2001 Sangiovese (Livermore Valley) $18. **90 Editors' Choice** *—S.H. (12/1/2003)*

TAMBER BEY

Tamber Bey 2002 Cabernet Sauvignon (Oakville) $50. Made in a less ripe style than many of its neighbors, which makes it something of an outlier in Oakville, this Cab is a bit herbal and tightly wound in acids and tannins. It could be an ager. Try holding until 2007. **87** *—S.H. (11/1/2005)*

TANDEM

Tandem 2002 Ritchie Vineyard Chardonnay (Sonoma Coast) $42. Tasted alongside Tandem's Sangiacomo bottling, this wine shares many of the same characteristics, including crisp acidity, minerality, and a seamless integration of oak. However, it's richer and fatter, although far from fat. It's a wine of intense structure and finesse. **90** *—S.H. (12/31/2004)*

Tandem 2002 Auction Block Pinot Noir (Sonoma Coast) $60. Proceeds for this priciest of Tandem's '02s go to charity, but it's not the winery's best. It's dark, extracted, and jammy, and rather heavy and flat. **86** *—S.H. (11/1/2004)*

Tandem 2002 Keefer Ranch Pinot Noir (Green Valley) $38. A wine with silky, gentle tannins and cherry-berry, coffee, and herb flavors, touched with smoky oak, that finish dry and smooth. My only quibble is with a certain syrupy thickness and heaviness in the texture. **88** *—S.H. (11/1/2004)*

Tandem 2003 Van der Kamp Vineyard Pinot Noir (Sonoma Mountain) $48. This is a very soft, sensuous Pinot, low in tannins, with a smooth, creamy mouthfeel. The flavors are rich and exuberant in smoky red cherries, raspberries, and cola. The softness suggests against extended cellaring, but why wouldn't you want this silky, complex wine now? **91** *—S.H. (11/1/2005)*

Tandem 2001 Gabrielli Vineyard Sangiovese (Redwood Valley) $32. Under the hot sun the grapes got ripe, and the wine offers loads of blackberry, cherry, coffee, and dried herb flavors. Beyond that, it's dry, with gentle tannins and quite a powerful punch of alcohol. Makes you realize what a difficult grape Sangiovese is. **87** *—S.H. (12/31/2004)*

TANTALUS

Tantalus 1999 Sémillon (Russian River Valley) $14. **88 Best Buy** *—S.H. (11/15/2001)*

TANTARA

Tantara 2000 Talley Vineyard Chardonnay (Arroyo Grande Valley) $30. **92** *—S.H. (12/15/2002)*

Tantara 2000 Dierberg Vineyard Pinot Noir (Santa Maria Valley) $40. **89** *—S.H. (2/1/2003)*

Tantara 2000 La Colline Vineyard Pinot Noir (Arroyo Grande Valley) $40. **89** *—S.H. (2/1/2003)*

TARA BELLA

Tara Bella 1999 Cabernet Sauvignon (Napa Valley) $60. **90** *—S.H. (11/15/2003)*

TARARA

Tarara 1997 Vidal Blanc (Virginia) $13. **80** *—J.C. (8/1/1999)*

TARIUS

Tarius 1999 Pinot Noir (Santa Lucia Highlands) $36. **86** *(10/1/2002)*

Tarius 1997 Pisoni Vineyard Pinot Noir (Santa Lucia Highlands) $39. **88** *(11/15/1999)*

Tarius 1999 Aldine Vineyard Zinfandel (Mendocino) $29. **84** *—D.T. (3/1/2002)*

Tarius 1999 Korte Ranch Zinfandel (Napa Valley) $29. **88** *—D.T. (3/1/2002)*

TATE CREEK

Tate Creek 1999 Cabernet Sauvignon (California) $6. **82** *—S.H. (6/1/2002)*

Tate Creek 1999 Syrah (California) $6. **84** *—S.H. (9/1/2002)*

TAYLOR

Taylor 2002 Hillside Chardonnay (Stags Leap District) $34. You'll find a wine that's tight and shut down right now. It has strong acids and even some tannins, with citrusy flavors that have a hint of pear. Could use more generosity. **88** *—S.H. (8/1/2004)*

TAZ

Taz 2001 Merlot (Santa Barbara County) $20. Crisp and herbal, this is Taz's least successful offering, but it's still solid. Toast, sour cherries, mint, and other green herbs mark the palate. Finishes long, but tart. **86** *(12/15/2004)*

Taz 2003 Pinot Noir (Santa Barbara County) $25. This countywide blend is properly dry and silky, but the fruit is thin, leaving the alcohol sticking out like a sore thumb. **84** *—S.H. (12/31/2005)*

Taz 2003 Cuyama River Pinot Noir (Santa Maria Valley) $28. You immediately pick up on the cool-climate origins of this wine. It's all rhubarb and cola, an impression confirmed with the first taste. Acidity stars here, but there are riper flavors of black cherries. Rich tannins, too. The wine is totally dry. It hasn't come together yet. Try aging until 2007. **88** *—S.H. (12/1/2005)*

Taz 2002 Fiddlestix Vineyard Pinot Noir (Santa Rita Hills) $35. This rich, full-bodied Pinot is no simple fruit bomb, featuring complex aromas of smoke, mineral, and rockdust that blend seamlessly into flavors of black cherries, anise, and dried spices. Finishes with supple tannins and juicy acidity. **92 Editors' Choice** *(11/1/2004)*

Taz 2003 Goat Rock Syrah (Santa Maria Valley) $28. This cool-climate Syrah has Hermitage in its sights, and is well worth the price. Bone dry, full-bodied, and distinguished, the wine opens with white pepper and cassis aromas, and turns deliciously complex in the mouth, offering waves of black currants, grilled meat, and oak that finish tannic. Drink now through 2010. **92 Cellar Selection** *—S.H. (12/1/2005)*

TEATOWN CELLARS

Teatown Cellars 2000 Chardonnay (Napa Valley) $30. **83** *—J.M. (5/1/2002)*

TEFFT CELLARS

Tefft Cellars 1999 Merlot (Yakima Valley) $15. **86** *—P.G. (9/1/2002)*

TENSLEY

Tensley 2001 Colson Canyon Vineyard Syrah (Santa Barbara County) $30. Different in profile from Tensley's other two bottlings. From northern Santa Barbara County, it opens with aromas of jammy currants, grilled meat, anise, and smoke and vanilla from oak. It is rich in juicy fruit flavors, notably blackberries and cherries, and the tannins are not as tough as those in the other offerings. **89** *—S.H. (3/1/2004)*

Tensley 2001 Thompson Vineyard Syrah (Santa Barbara County) $30. Vibrant and fruity, with blackberry, cherry, black raspberry, leather, smoke, and herb flavors that erupt from the glass. The flavors are deliciously rich and ripe, in a smoothly textured body, but the tannins are tough and astringent, as they are in the Purisima Mountain bottling. **87** *—S.H. (3/1/2004)*

TERRA BLANCA

Terra Blanca 1999 Syrah (Red Mountain) $20. **87** *(10/1/2001)*

Terra Blanca 1999 Block 8 Syrah (Washington) $28. **85** *(11/1/2001)*

TERRA D'ORO

Terra d'Oro 1997 Barbera (Amador County) $22. **88** *—S.H. (8/1/2001)*

Terra d'Oro 2000 Deaver Vineyard Old Vine Zinfandel (Amador County) $24. **90** *—S.H. (9/1/2003)*

Terra d'Oro 2000 Home Vineyard Zinfandel (Amador County) $24. **90** *—S.H. (9/1/2003)*

Terra d'Oro 1999 SHR Field Blend Zinfandel (Amador County) $12. **89** *—P.G. (3/1/2002)*

TERRA VALENTINE

Terra Valentine 1999 Cabernet Sauvignon (Spring Mountain) $35. **90** *—S.H. (2/1/2003)*

Terra Valentine 1999 Wurtele Vineyard Cabernet Sauvignon (Spring Mountain) $50. **93 Editors' Choice** *—S.H. (2/1/2003)*

TERRE ROUGE

Terre Rouge 1999 Mourvèdre (Amador County) $20. **90** *—S.H. (7/1/2002)*

Terre Rouge 1997 Rhône Red Blend (Sierra Foothills) $20. **84** *—S.H. (7/1/2002)*

Terre Rouge 1999 Syrah (Sierra Foothills) $22. **93** *—S.H. (7/1/2002)*

Terre Rouge 1998 Sentinel Oak Vineyard Pyramid Bloc Syrah (Shenandoah Valley (CA)) $30. **89** *—S.H. (8/1/2001)*

Terre Rouge 1999 Enigma White Blend (Sierra Foothills) $18. **93 Editors' Choice** *—S.H. (8/1/2001)*

TESTAROSSA

Testarossa 1998 Chardonnay (Santa Maria Valley) $26. **88** *—S.H. (10/1/2000)*

Testarossa 2001 Bien Nacido Vineyard Chardonnay (Santa Lucia Highlands) $35. **87** *—S.H. (12/15/2003)*

Testarossa 1999 Bien Nacido Vineyard Chardonnay (Santa Maria Valley) $32. **87** *(7/1/2001)*

Testarossa 2003 Castello Chardonnay (Central Coast) $26. Crisp acidity marks this cool-climate wine. The acids balance out the sweet vanilla and oak, and the fruity flavors, which veer toward pineapple, mango, and peach. There's a rich swirl of Asian spice throughout. **88** *—S.H. (7/1/2005)*

Testarossa 2001 Castello Chardonnay (Santa Barbara) $26. **83** *—S.H. (10/1/2003)*

USA

Testarossa 2003 Diana's Reserve Chardonnay (California) $50. Super-rich, oaky, and ripe in the Testarossa style, this flamboyant wine bursts with tropical fruit, spice, buttered toast, and vanilla aromas and flavors. The texture is creamy, and the acidity high in this crowd pleaser. **90** *—S.H. (11/15/2005)*

Testarossa 2003 Michaud Vineyard Chardonnay (Chalone) $36. There are earthy, leesy, and oaky-woody aromas and flavors to this wine. It's surprisingly unfruity, although there are notes of peaches and tropical fruits in the finish. Dry and crisp in acids. **87** *—S.H. (10/1/2005)*

Testarossa 2000 Michaud Vineyard Chardonnay (Chalone) $36. 93 *—S.H. (12/15/2002)*

Testarossa 2003 Rosella's Vineyard Chardonnay (Santa Lucia Highlands) $36. This is a big, ripe Chard, well-oaked and brimming with spice and tropical fruit flavors. Plays to the popular taste for rich, creamy Chards that flood the mouth and last through a long finish. Try with lobster bisque. **90** *—S.H. (7/1/2005)*

Testarossa 2002 Signature Reserve Chardonnay (California) $44. A statewide appellation is usually a lesser wine, but this gigantic beauty is the product of the best lots from select vineyards. It's super-intense in pineapple, mango, vanilla, caramel, coconut, and toasted meringue flavors, with a smooth texture. Finishes with a trace of leesy bitterness, which adds complexity. **93** *—S.H. (6/1/2004)*

Testarossa 1998 Signature Reserve Chardonnay (California) $42. 91 *(7/1/2001)*

Testarossa 2003 Sleepy Hollow Vineyard Chardonnay (Santa Lucia Highlands) $36. Rather earthy and herbal, despite plenty of sweet oak. As it airs and warms, pear and citrus flavors emerge. Made in a leaner, acidic, perhaps more food-friendly fashion. **86** *—S.H. (10/1/2005)*

Testarossa 2000 Sleepy Hollow Vineyard Chardonnay (Santa Lucia Highlands) $34. 92 *—S.H. (12/15/2002)*

Testarossa 2002 Bien Nacido Vineyard Pinot Noir (Santa Maria Valley) $49. Very attractive aroma, with raspberries, cherries, vanilla, cocoa, pepper, clove, and smoke all screaming, "Drink me!" Silky smooth; seductive on the palate, lush, and long. The finish lasts for a good minute. **89** *(11/1/2004)*

Testarossa 1999 Bien Nacido Vineyard Pinot Noir (Santa Maria Valley) $40. 91 *—S.H. (12/15/2001)*

Testarossa 2003 Cuvée Niclaire Pinot Noir (California) $75. The California appellation is because the wine is made from three Santa Lucia Highlands vineyards and Bien Nacido. It's a really good wine. The cool vineyards give it brisk acidity, while the ripe grapes lend deep flavors of cherries and black raspberries. Oak does its spicy, complexing thing. Shows Pinot's translucent, elegant, silky texture. **93** *—S.H. (11/15/2005)*

Testarossa 2000 Cuvée Niclaire Pinot Noir (Santa Lucia Highlands) $68. 91 *—S.H. (2/1/2003)*

Testarossa 1998 Cuvée Niclaire Reserve Pinot Noir (Santa Lucia Highlands) $60. 94 Cellar Selection *—S.H. (12/15/2001)*

Testarossa 2003 Elder Series Bien Nacido Vineyard Pinot Noir (Santa Lucia Highlands) $54. This well-crafted single-vineyard wine, offers immediate pleasure. We're talking about intense cherry liqueur, raspberry, cola, and root beer flavors that are opulently ripe, although the wine itself is correctly dry. Light and silky, with crisp acidity and a lingering aftertaste. Drink now. **90** *—S.H. (7/1/2005)*

Testarossa 1999 Garys' Vineyard Pinot Noir (Santa Maria Valley) $40. 91 *—S.H. (12/15/2001)*

Testarossa 2002 Garys' Vineyard Pinot Noir (Santa Lucia Highlands) $55. Ripe, dry, and well made, with complex aromas of cherries, sweet herbs, coffee, menthol, and smoky oak. Full-bodied and big, with a voluptuous mouthfeel. Delicious on its own, and a versatile food wine. **88** *(11/1/2004)*

Testarossa 2000 Garys' Vineyard Pinot Noir (Santa Lucia Highlands) $45. 91 *(10/1/2002)*

Testarossa 2003 Palazzio Pinot Noir (Central Coast) $32. Lots of richness and sophistication here, packed with black cherry, mulberry, cola, coffee, and spice flavors. It's dry, with an elegantly silky texture firmed up by crisp acidity. What you see is what you get. Drink now with a good, charbroiled steak. **88** *—S.H. (7/1/2005)*

Testarossa 2001 Palazzio Pinot Noir (Monterey) $32. 85 *—S.H. (7/1/2003)*

Testarossa 2000 Pisoni Pinot Noir (Santa Lucia Highlands) $55. 92 *(10/1/2002)*

Testarossa 2003 Pisoni Vineyard Pinot Noir (Santa Lucia Highlands) $54. This is, shall we say, a voluminous Pinot, the kind this vineyard produces regularly. It's dark, full-bodied, and rich in black and red berry fruit, with fresh acidity. We now know that a Pisoni Pinot like this will improve in the cellar. Best to let it be until 2008. **92 Cellar Selection** *—S.H. (11/15/2005)*

Testarossa 2003 Rosella's Vineyard Pinot Noir (Santa Lucia Highlands) $54. Luscious. Right now it's youthfully perky in acids, with a slightly thick mouthfeel, but it's a heck of a Pinot that should soften by 2006. Then, those massive cherry flavors will be delicious. **90** *—S.H. (10/1/2005)*

Testarossa 2001 Rosella's Vineyard Pinot Noir (Santa Lucia Highlands) $50. 88 *—S.H. (7/1/2003)*

Testarossa 2003 Sleepy Hollow Vineyard Pinot Noir (Santa Lucia Highlands) $54. A lighter-bodied Pinot, fairly pale in color and delicately structured. The fruit struggled to ripen, and straddles the line between cherries and tomatoes. Finishes rich in smoky oak. **89** *—S.H. (10/1/2005)*

Testarossa 2001 Sleepy Hollow Vineyard Pinot Noir (Santa Lucia Highlands) $50. 89 —*S.H. (7/1/2003)*

Testarossa 2002 Gary's Vineyard Syrah (Santa Lucia Highlands) $42. This is a complex Syrah whose cool-climate origins show in the peppery, leathery profile and crisp acids. It's absolutely dry, and the tannins, while pronounced, are easily negotiated. As good as it is, it could use more fruity concentration. 89 —*S.H. (7/1/2005)*

THE ACADEMY

The Academy 2000 Merlot (Applegate Valley) $20. 85 —*P.G. (8/1/2002)*

THE EYRIE VINEYARDS

The Eyrie Vineyards 1999 Estate Grown Chardonnay (Willamette Valley) $18. 87 —*P.G. (9/1/2003)*

The Eyrie Vineyards 2000 Pinot Gris (Willamette Valley) $15. 91 Best Buy —*P.G. (8/1/2003)*

The Eyrie Vineyards 1999 Reserve Pinot Noir (Willamette Valley) $35. 91 —*P.G. (4/1/2003)*

THE MATRIARCH

The Matriarch 2001 Cabernet Blend (Napa Valley) $75. This second label of Bond is right up there with the named wines. It is virtually undistinguishable from Vecina, although perhaps a shade less profound and more obvious. A terrific Cabernet-based wine, rich, powerful, and ageable. At less than half the price of Bond, it's a comparative value. **94 Editors' Choice** —*S.H. (6/1/2005)*

THE ORGANIC WINE WORKS

The Organic Wine Works 2001 Proprietors Reserve Merlot (Mendocino County) $19. Drinks a bit hot and harsh. The blackberry, plum, and chocolate flavors veer on the edge of raisins, and the tannins feel rough and jagged. Finishes very dry, with good fruity length and a trace of bitterness. 85 —*S.H. (2/1/2004)*

THE PRISONER

The Prisoner 2000 Red Blend (Napa Valley) $28. 90 —*J.M. (4/1/2003)*

THE SEVEN BROTHERS

The Seven Brothers 2001 Sauvignon Blanc (Clear Lake) $10. Fairly lightweight, without any of the distinguishing marks of this normally somewhat assertive varietal. It shows hints of melon and citrus, however, and will not offend. 80 —*J.M. (9/1/2004)*

THE TERRACES

The Terraces 1999 Cabernet Sauvignon (Napa Valley) $60. 90 *(8/1/2003)*

THE WILLIAMSBURG WINERY

The Williamsburg Winery 2003 Acte 12 of Sixteen Nineteen Chardonnay (Virginia) $16. A solid effort, this wine, named after a law requiring colonists to plant vineyards, boasts aromas of tropical fruit and grilled nuts, toasty, citrusy flavors and a lemon-pineapple finish. 86 —*J.C. (9/1/2005)*

THOMAS COYNE

Thomas Coyne 1996 Merlot (Sonoma County) $21. 91 *(11/15/1999)*

Thomas Coyne 2000 Petite Sirah (California) $16. 82 *(4/1/2003)*

Thomas Coyne 1996 Quest Red Blend (California) $10. 86 —*S.H. (6/1/1999)*

Thomas Coyne 1998 Syrah (California) $12. 83 —*S.H. (7/1/2002)*

Thomas Coyne 2000 Viognier (California) $15. 85 —*S.H. (11/15/2001)*

THOMAS FOGARTY

Thomas Fogarty 2001 Cabernet Sauvignon (Santa Cruz Mountains) $55. These mountains seem to give Cab that extra nudge of ripeness and balance that makes the best of them supreme. It's incredibly rich in black currant and sweet cassis, and the smoky edge of oak is perfect. You can hardly keep your hands off it, but try aging until its 10th birthday and beyond. 93 —*S.H. (10/1/2004)*

Thomas Fogarty 2000 Cabernet Sauvignon (Napa Valley) $50. Quite full-bodied and rich in cassis and black currant fruit, this Cabernet feels weighty in the mouth. Partly that's due to the ripe fruit, and partly to the oak. It has an astringent scour of tannins, suggesting at least a few years of ageability. 88 —*S.H. (11/15/2004)*

Thomas Fogarty 1998 Chardonnay (Monterey County) $19. 88 *(6/1/2000)*

Thomas Fogarty 2002 Chardonnay (Santa Cruz Mountains) $24. Comes down firmly on the steely, cool-climate side, with high acidity and flavors of apples and citrus fruits. Sur lies aging adds richer, creamy and yeasty notes, while oak does its smoky, vanilla thing. An interesting, complex food wine. 88 —*S.H. (2/1/2005)*

Thomas Fogarty 1997 Estate Reserve Chardonnay (Santa Cruz Mountains) $30. 91 *(6/1/2000)*

Thomas Fogarty 2002 Gewürztraminer (Monterey) $15. 86 —*S.H. (12/31/2003)*

Thomas Fogarty 2001 Gewürztraminer (Monterey) $14. 87 —*S.H. (9/1/2003)*

Thomas Fogarty 2001 Merlot (Santa Cruz Mountains) $32. Although there is a mountain intensity to the intense blackberry and cherry flavors and rich tannins, this wine is probably at its best now. It's very dry and rich, with evident oak, and a distinguished finish. **91** *—S.H. (10/1/2005)*

Thomas Fogarty 1999 Merlot (Santa Cruz Mountains) $28. **91** *—S.H. (10/1/2003)*

Thomas Fogarty 2001 Pinot Noir (Santa Cruz Mountains) $25. A very nice Pinot. If it shows no particular complexity, it's has a textbook silky texture, dryness, and flavors of cherries, coffee, and oak. **87** *—S.H. (2/1/2005)*

Thomas Fogarty 1999 Pinot Noir (Santa Cruz Mountains) $23. **88** *(10/1/2002)*

Thomas Fogarty 2001 Estate Reserve Pinot Noir (Santa Cruz Mountains) $45. This very good wine may improve with a few years of cellaring. It's fairly tannic and bright with citrusy acids, and there's a wonderful complex core of flavor that includes black cherry, bitter chocolate, coffee, sweet dried herbs, and pepper. Silky smooth. Now through 2008. **89** *—S.H. (12/1/2004)*

Thomas Fogarty 2002 Rapley Trail Vineyard Block M Pinot Noir (Santa Cruz Mountains) $65. Richer by a hair than the Block B bottling, with black cherry and vanilla flavors leading to a chocolatey finish. Nice supple mouthfeel. **86** *(11/1/2004)*

THORNTON

Thornton 1999 Cabernet Sauvignon-Merlot (South Coast) $13. **82** *—S.H. (9/1/2002)*

Thornton NV Brut (California) $11. **86** *—S.H. (12/15/2000)*

Thornton 1995 Brut Reserve (California) $21. **90** *—S.H. (12/15/2000)*

Thornton 1995 Brut Reserve Natural (California) $35. **87** *—S.H. (12/15/2000)*

Thornton NV Cuvée de Frontignan (California) $22. **85** *—S.H. (12/1/2002)*

Thornton NV Limited Release Blanc de Noir (Temecula) $22. **86** *—S.H. (12/1/2002)*

Thornton 2000 Dos Vinedos Cuvée Coastal Reserve Chardonnay (South Coast) $10. **87** *—S.H. (5/1/2002)*

Thornton 2000 Miramonte Vineyards Pinot Blanc (South Coast) $10. **86** *—S.H. (9/1/2002)*

Thornton 1999 Temecula Valley Sangiovese (South Coast) $12. **82** *—S.H. (5/1/2002)*

Thornton 1999 Miramonte Vineyards Limited Bottling Syrah (South Coast) $15. **84** *(10/1/2001)*

THREE RIVERS

Three Rivers 2003 Meritage White Wine Bordeaux White Blend (Columbia Valley (WA)) $19. Great price for this sophisticated white Bordeaux blend, which melds supple fruit with light toast and refreshing acids. Thirty percent Sémillon seems just the perfect counterbalance to the vivid citrus flavors of the Sauvignon Blanc. **92 Editors' Choice** *—P.G. (6/1/2005)*

Three Rivers 2001 Cabernet Sauvignon (Columbia Valley (WA)) $19. Tough and chewy, this somewhat inaccessible wine consists of hard, tart red fruits and chalky tannins that are right on the edge of being green and stemmy. Decanting would be a good idea. **85** *—P.G. (12/15/2004)*

Three Rivers 2001 Champoux Vineyard Cabernet Sauvignon (Columbia Valley (WA)) $39. This premier vineyard grows some of the state's best Cabernet: naturally dense, dark, licorice, and mineral-infused black cherry fruit. Tannins are stiff, but well-managed within the framework of ripe, tangy fruit. This is a wine that can take plenty of oak without showing it. Very nice effort. **91** *—P.G. (7/1/2004)*

Three Rivers 2003 Chardonnay (Columbia Valley (WA)) $17. Consistent from vintage to vintage, Three Rivers makes their Chardonnay in a soft, buttery, palate-pleasing style, showing round fruit flavors spiced up with citrus highlights. A very good value. **89** *—P.G. (6/1/2005)*

Three Rivers 2001 Chardonnay (Columbia Valley (WA)) $17. Nice and smooth, with a palate-pleasing mix of round stone fruits and sweet toasty oak. Nothing overblown or too buttery about this wine, just smooth, supple, flavorful fruit. **88** *—P.G. (7/1/2004)*

Three Rivers 1999 Chardonnay (Columbia Valley (WA)) $22. **87** *—P.G. (7/1/2002)*

Three Rivers 1999 Meritage (Columbia Valley (WA)) $45. **89** *—P.G. (2/1/2002)*

Three Rivers 2001 Merlot (Columbia Valley (WA)) $19. A very good representation of mid-priced Washington Merlot, this boasts chunky black cherry fruit wrapped in smoky tannins and some chalky earth. Full, dense and still a bit austere, but built to age well for another 6–8 years. **87** *—P.G. (7/1/2004)*

Three Rivers 1999 Merlot (Columbia Valley (WA)) $28. **86** *—P.G. (6/1/2002)*

Three Rivers 2000 Reserve Merlot (Columbia Valley (WA)) $37. **91** *—P.G. (9/1/2002)*

Three Rivers 2001 River's Red Table Wine Red Blend (Columbia Valley (WA)) $15. A good junkyard blend of Syrah, Cabernet Sauvignon, and Cab Franc, this has plenty of rough tannin but there is also sweet cherry fruit out in front. A great quaffing wine, perfect for swilling with summer grilling. **86** *—P.G. (7/1/2004)*

Three Rivers 2003 Pepper Bridge Vineyard Sangiovese (Walla Walla (WA)) $39. There isn't much Sangio in Washington, but the Pepper Bridge fruit is the pick of the litter. Ripe and nicely colored, this is 100% Sangiovese and actually shows some hints of pepper, tobacco, and tea leaf. Still, the vineyard is in Walla Walla, not Tuscany, and the wine tastes more like a lightweight Syrah than a Chianti. **87** *—P.G. (6/1/2005)*

Three Rivers 2002 Pepper Bridge Vineyards Sangiovese (Walla Walla (WA)) $39. This is a firm, taut, even steely Sangio, with tart fruit flavors of strawberry and currant. Tannins are firm and slightly green, and there is an earthy, mineral undercurrent. Still quite young and tightly wound. **87** *—P.G. (7/1/2004)*

Three Rivers 2002 Syrah (Columbia Valley (WA)) $24. Dark, sappy, peppery, and super-saturated, this is not a shy style. There is luscious blueberry/blackberry fruit aplenty, adorned with new oak accents of toast and coffee. The tannins are powerful, firm, and spicy, but well balanced, and the young wine, still battened down tight, has a supple elegance. **89** *—P.G. (6/1/2005)*

Three Rivers 2000 Syrah (Columbia Valley (WA)) $32. **88** *—P.G. (9/1/2002)*

Three Rivers 2003 Ahler Vineyard Syrah (Walla Walla (WA)) $39. Seems slightly confected, starting from its aromas of Nilla Wafers and jelly and persisting through the jammy red-berry flavors outlined in vanilla. Turns chewy on the finish. **85** *(9/1/2005)*

Three Rivers 2003 Boushey Vineyards Syrah (Yakima Valley) $39. Made in a big, lush style, this Syrah comes across as a little Port-like, thanks to rich, chocolaty fruit and spicecake notes, but retains a sense of balance and elegance. For fans of soft, mouthfilling wines, not those looking for laser-beam focus. **87** *(9/1/2005)*

Three Rivers 2000 Boushey Vineyard Syrah (Yakima Valley) $42. **91** *—P.G. (9/1/2002)*

Three Rivers 2002 Meritage White Wine White Blend (Columbia Valley (WA)) $19. The classic blend is 76% Sauvignon Blanc and 24% Sémillon, a grape that does particularly well in Washington state. Smooth and round, with sweet flavors of ripe peaches and hints of mango. Clean and supple; ready to drink. **89** *—P.G. (7/1/2004)*

THREE SAINTS

Three Saints 2002 Chardonnay (Santa Maria Valley) $20. Earns its stripes with ripe flavors of passion fruit, guava, mango, and other tropical fruits whose sweetness is balanced by crisp acidity. They really jammed the oak on, so there's a ton of toast, spice and vanilla. **88** *—S.H. (9/1/2004)*

Three Saints 2002 Estate Grown Pinot Noir (Santa Maria Valley) $20. Dark and earthy in its youth, showing tomato and dried spice aromas, and pretty closed and tannic. But there's a big core of cherry and mocha fruit deep down inside, and the wine feels rich and balanced. Decant, or age for a few years. **88** *(11/1/2004)*

THREE THIEVES

Three Thieves 2004 Circle K Ranch Pinot Noir (California) $10. What do you get at this price in a 1-liter jug? Plenty of pleasure. Sure, this isn't a dazzlingly rich Pinot, but it's clean, varietally true, and super-drinkable. **84 Best Buy** *—S.H. (12/31/2005)*

THUMBPRINT CELLARS

Thumbprint Cellars 2002 Schneider Vineyard Cabernet Sauvignon (Alexander Valley) $35. Starts off oaky and strong in char and toasty vanilla, and while the wood overpowers the underlying wine, which is quite delicate, it adds a sweet touch to this otherwise earthy, soft, cherry-tinged Cab. **87** *—S.H. (11/1/2005)*

Thumbprint Cellars 2002 Schneider Vineyard Pinot Noir (Russian River Valley) $36. Light in color, but robust, this Pinot has pure aromas that invite you right in. Rhubarb, red cherry, cola, tangerine zest, and peppery spice flavors come together in a silky-smooth wine that's rich in sweet, toasty oak. Very fine. **92 Editors' Choice** *—S.H. (11/1/2005)*

Thumbprint Cellars 2001 C. Teldeschi Vineyard Zinfandel (Dry Creek Valley) $30. **87** *(11/1/2003)*

THUNDER MOUNTAIN

Thunder Mountain 1996 Bate's Ranch Cabernet Sauvignon (Santa Cruz County) $39. **92** *—M.S. (7/1/1999)*

Thunder Mountain 1997 Miller Vineyards 'Doc's' Cabernet Sauvignon (Cienega Valley) $48. **84** *(11/1/2000)*

Thunder Mountain 1999 Beauregard Ranch Chardonnay (Santa Cruz Mountains) $43. **90** *—J.M. (12/15/2002)*

Thunder Mountain 1997 Ciardella Vineyard Chardonnay (Santa Cruz Mountains) $29. **92** *—J.C. (7/1/1999)*

Thunder Mountain 1998 DeRose Vineyard Chardonnay (Cienega Valley) $34. **90** *(10/1/2000)*

Thunder Mountain 1999 Veranda Vineyards Pinot Noir (Santa Cruz Mountains) $48. **83** *(10/1/2002)*

THURSTON WOLFE

Thurston Wolfe 2001 Blue Franc Lemberger (Yakima Valley) $14. **86** *—P.G. (12/31/2003)*

Thurston Wolfe 1998 Blue Franc Lemberger-Cabernet (Columbia Valley (WA)) $14. **86** *—P.G. (11/15/2000)*

Thurston Wolfe 2002 Zephyr Ridge Vineyard Petite Sirah (Columbia Valley (WA)) $18. Very little Petite Sirah is planted in Washington, and this may well be the first 100% varietal bottling ever made. It's a big, brawny wine as you would expect, done in a take-no-prisoners style. Inky and dense, with concentrated black cherry and blackberry flavors, along with some black pepper and bark. **88** —*P.G. (12/15/2004)*

Thurston Wolfe 2003 JTW's Port (Washington) $20. This is truly a tour de force; a domestic Port that is not either sticky, too sweet, too hot or unidentifiable as being in any way related to true Port. Credit the use of Touriga Nacional for two thirds of the blend; the rest is Petite Sirah. Intense, extraordinary power in the mixed fruits, enlivened with spicy citrus, clove, orange peel and pungent blossoms. **94 Editors' Choice** —*P.G. (6/1/2005)*

Thurston Wolfe 2002 Sangiovese (Columbia Valley (WA)) $20. Strong scents of tar, funk, meat, leather, and silage jump from the glass. This is a take-no-prisoners wine, rustic, flavorful, and distinctive. Though the tannins are tough and chewy, the fruit has plenty of acid to lift it back off the ground. **86** —*P.G. (12/1/2004)*

Thurston Wolfe 1998 Syrah (Columbia Valley (WA)) $20. **90** —*P.G. (9/1/2000)*

Thurston Wolfe 2000 Syrah (Columbia Valley (WA)) $18. **90** —*P.G. (9/1/2002)*

Thurston Wolfe 2002 PGV White Blend (Columbia Valley (WA)) $12. **87** —*P.G. (12/31/2003)*

Thurston Wolfe 2001 Pinot Gris-Viognier White Blend (Columbia Valley (WA)) $13. **86** —*P.G. (9/1/2002)*

Thurston Wolfe 2001 Zinfandel (Columbia Valley (WA)) $17. **88** —*P.G. (12/31/2003)*

Thurston Wolfe 1998 Burgess Vineyard Zinfandel (Columbia Valley (WA)) $20. **87** —*P.G. (11/15/2000)*

USA

TIN BARN

Tin Barn 2001 Coryelle Fields Syrah (Sonoma Coast) $32. From a region typically thought of as being too cool for the variety, this Syrah possesses that characteristic cracked-pepper scent along with strands of dried herbs that add immense appeal to the solid core of blackberry fruit. Long and tart on the finish, with tannins that are so soft, they glide across the palate. **90** —*J.C. (5/1/2004)*

Tin Barn 2001 Zinfandel (Russian River Valley) $25. Quite bright on the palate, with firm tannins and pretty, zippy cherry, spice, tar, raspberry, and herb flavors. The texture is a bit powdery but should calm down nicely with a little more bottle age. **88** —*J.M. (3/1/2004)*

Tin Barn 2001 Jensen Lane Vineyard Zinfandel (Russian River Valley) $27. **87** *(11/1/2003)*

TIN ROOF

Tin Roof 2002 Chardonnay (Sonoma County) $9. Serviceable Chard, with modest apple and peach flavors. Finishes dry and tart. A screwtop wine from Murphy-Goode. **83** —*S.H. (6/1/2004)*

Tin Roof 2003 Sauvignon Blanc (North Coast) $9. As fragrant as fresh-picked lemons, limes, and oranges, sliced and slightly squeezed, with a drizzle of vanilla and honey. Finishes with acidity and stony minerals. Second label from Murphy-Goode. **86 Best Buy** —*S.H. (3/1/2005)*

Tin Roof 2002 Syrah-Cabernet (California) $9. There's an abundance of ripe berry-cherry and spice fruit in this dry, full-bodied wine, which also has silky tannins and a liberal dose of smoky oak. It's robust and satisfying, in a rustic way. **84** —*S.H. (12/15/2004)*

TITUS

Titus 2002 Cabernet Sauvignon (Napa Valley) $39. A fine Cab that showcases the ripe fruit and soft, intricate tannins the valley specializes in. It's a little bit soft, but those flavors are just delicious. Lots of oak, too. **87** —*S.H. (10/1/2005)*

Titus 1999 Cabernet Sauvignon (Napa Valley) $36. **88** —*K.F. (8/1/2003)*

Titus 2000 Zinfandel (Mendocino County) $24. **90** —*J.M. (9/1/2003)*

TOAD HALL

Toad Hall 2002 Bodacious Cabernet Blend (Napa Valley) $30. Kind of harsh and raw, this wine shows herbal flavors and dry tannins. It's not going anywhere, so drink up. **82** —*S.H. (10/1/2005)*

Toad Hall 2002 Lavender Hill Pinot Noir (Carneros) $22. A very nice, easy-drinking Pinot marked by cola, cherry, coffee, and spice flavors that's fancy without being particularly complex. It possesses a silkiness and dryness that make it a versatile companion to a wide range of foods. From Flora Springs. **88** —*S.H. (11/1/2004)*

Toad Hall 2002 Lavender Hill Vineyards Pinot Noir (Carneros) $22. Middle of the road Pinot, dry, silky and balanced, with cherry, cola, and rhubarb flavors. There's a hit of tannins in the finish. **84** —*S.H. (2/1/2005)*

Toad Hall 1999 Bodacious Red Blend (Napa Valley) $30. At 5 years, this wine remains tannic, with modest blackberry and oak flavors. Turns dry and astringent on the finish, and not likely to go anywhere, but it's okay. **84** —*S.H. (2/1/2005)*

TOASTED HEAD

Toasted Head 1999 Meritage Bordeaux Blend (Dunnigan Hills) $25. **87** —*S.H. (11/15/2002)*

Toasted Head 2002 Cabernet Sauvignon (Alexander Valley) $18. Soft, thin, and simple. Just barely gets across a few scrawny berry flavors before it melts into a hot finish. **82** —*S.H. (10/1/2005)*

Toasted Head 1999 Merlot (Dunnigan Hills) $18. **87** —*S.H. (6/1/2002)*

TOBIN JAMES

Tobin James 1997 Notorious Cabernet Franc (Paso Robles) $18. 90 Editors' Choice *—S.H. (5/1/2001)*

Tobin James 1999 Radiance Chardonnay (Paso Robles) $16. 84 *—S.H. (5/1/2001)*

Tobin James 2000 James Gang Reserve Late Harvest Muscat (Paso Robles) $20. 90 *—S.H. (12/31/2001)*

Tobin James 1997 Ranchito Canyon Vineyard Petite Sirah (Paso Robles) $18. 88 *—S.H. (5/1/2001)*

Tobin James 1999 James Gang Reserve Refosco Red Blend (Paso Robles) $38. 87 *—S.H. (12/15/2001)*

Tobin James 1999 Rock-N-Roll Syrah (Paso Robles) $16. 83 *(10/1/2001)*

Tobin James 2001 Ballistic Zinfandel (Paso Robles) $15. 85 *(11/1/2003)*

Tobin James 1997 Blue Moon Reserve Zinfandel (Paso Robles) $35. 90 *—S.H. (5/1/2000)*

Tobin James 2001 Dusi Vineyard Zinfandel (Paso Robles) $28. 88 *(11/1/2003)*

Tobin James 2001 James Gang Reserve Zinfandel (Paso Robles) $28. 88 *(11/1/2003)*

Tobin James 1998 James Gang Reserve Zinfandel (Paso Robles) $26. 87 *(3/1/2001)*

TOLOSA

Tolosa 2003 Edna Ranch Chardonnay (Edna Valley) $20. There's something about certain Central Coast Chards that's delicious, bright, pure in tangerine, papaya, and honey, brilliant in acidity, and just so drinkable. This is one. It's quite a wine, andat this price, a comparative value. **92 Editors' Choice** *—S.H. (11/1/2005)*

Tolosa 2004 Edna Ranch No Oak Chardonnay (Edna Valley) $16. If you don't put oak on a Chardonnay, you better have some powerful fruit. It's hard to imagine any Chard being fruitier than this. Absolutely delicious in apples, limes, peaches, and pineapples, with wonderfully bright acidity. **90 Editors' Choice** *—S.H. (11/1/2005)*

Tolosa 2000 Edna Ranch Pinot Noir (Edna Valley) $30. 88 *(10/1/2002)*

Tolosa 2002 Edna Ranch 1772 Pinot Noir (Edna Valley) $52. Showcases its coastal origins with high acids, intense fruit, and purity of varietal character. This isn't one of those dark, alcoholic Pinots, but a silky, elegant one. But there's nothing shy about the powerful cherry, Raspberry, coffee, and cinnamon flavors. Has a raisiny over-ripeness that adds seasoning. **90** *—S.H. (11/1/2005)*

Tolosa 2002 Edna Ranch Syrah (Edna Valley) $20. They got real ripeness in this superb vintage, resulting in a big wine that's long on jammy cherries, blackberries, and dusty Chinese spices. Drinks dry and full-bodied, with a firm finish. **89** *—S.H. (12/1/2004)*

Tolosa 2003 Edna Ranch 1772 Syrah (Edna Valley) $46. Starts with lovely peppery-spicy notes that include meaty elements and hints of cardamon and cinnamon, all backed up by lush blackberry fruit. Nicely rich and complex, with a hint of warmth showing through on the finish. **90** *(9/1/2005)*

TOPANGA

Topanga 2003 Celadon Esperanza Vineyard Grenache (Clarksburg) $20. A lovely, fresh, and focused white wine that offers a classy blend of melon, peach, apple, apricot, herb, and mineral flavors. These are layered in a complex, yet easy-to-drink manner. Smooth yet firm, it's got great balance and a good finish. **90** *—J.M. (10/1/2005)*

TOPEL

Topel 1999 Cabernet Sauvignon (Mendocino) $45. 90 *—C.S. (5/1/2002)*

Topel 2002 Cuvée Donnis Syrah (Monterey) $25. Smells a bit green—mint or dill perhaps—as well as fruity. Big, vibrant blackberry and black currant flavors follow up on the palate, finishing crisp and clean. **85** *(9/1/2005)*

TOPOLOS

Topolos 1997 Muscat L'Orange Orange Muscat (California) $9. 81 *—J.C. (12/31/1999)*

Topolos 1997 Pagani Ranch Zinfandel (Sonoma Valley) $30. 88 *—J.C. (5/1/2000)*

Topolos 1997 Rossi Ranch Zinfandel (Sonoma Valley) $25. 86 *—J.C. (5/1/2000)*

TORII MOR

Torii Mor 2000 Pinot Blanc (Rogue Valley) $18. 87 *—P.G. (8/1/2002)*

Torii Mor 2002 Pinot Gris (Oregon) $13. A pleasing, bone dry style that mixes stone fruits (peach, apricot, pear) with lovely hints of cinnamon candy. Nice balance throughout, and a good, long, clean resolution. **88** *—P.G. (10/1/2004)*

Torii Mor 2002 Reserve Pinot Gris (Oregon) $18. It sometimes seems as if winemakers, in pursuit of that something extra, overdo their reserve wines. Here the fresh, balanced flavors of the regular bottle have been sacrificed to a wine with more concentration, but less finesse. The fruit seems a bit oxidized, and the mouthfeel flat. **86** *—P.G. (10/1/2004)*

Torii Mor 2001 Pinot Noir (Oregon) $17. There is definitely an herbal, resiny character here, with up front scents of pine needles and beetroot. But the wine is balanced, the tannins are restrained, and the flavors nicely melded together. It is structured to improve over the next 4–6 years. **87** *—P.G. (10/1/2004)*

Torii Mor 1997 Pinot Noir (Oregon) $20. **87** *(11/15/1999)*

Torii Mor 1999 Amelia Rosé Cuvée Pinot Noir (Yamhill County) $45. **89** *—J.C. (11/1/2001)*

Torii Mor 1998 Balcombe Vineyard Pinot Noir (Willamette Valley) $38. **89** *—J.C. (12/1/2000)*

Torii Mor 2001 Deux Verres Pinot Noir (Willamette Valley) $40. The name means "two glasses"—the suggestion being that you'll want more than one. Fair enough. It's a substantial, well-managed wine, with some chewy cherry fruit wrapped in herbal flavors of stem and skin. Good fruit in the middle, with the alcohol and oak in check. **88** *—P.G. (10/1/2004)*

Torii Mor 2002 Olson Vineyard Pinot Noir (Yamhill County) $42. Expressively fruity, bright, polished and nicely delineated. Pretty, but it lacks concentration. **85** *(11/1/2004)*

Torii Mor 1999 Olson Vineyard Pinot Noir (Yamhill County) $50. **90** *—J.C. (11/1/2001)*

Torii Mor 2002 Reserve Deux Verres Pinot Noir (Willamette Valley) $35. Firm and authoritative upon entry, with a hard core of spicy cherry fruit. This wine gives the impression that it will expand with more time, but at the moment is tightly wrapped and tannic. **85** *(11/1/2004)*

Torii Mor 2002 Seven Springs Vineyard Pinot Noir (Polk County) $40. Some definite off-notes suggesting garlic, skunk cabbage, and unripe, earthy grapes. Something is amiss here. **83** *(11/1/2004)*

Torii Mor 2002 Temperance Hill Vineyard Pinot Noir (Polk County) $40. Cherries and herbs to start, with a distinctive, spicy edge to the nose. The bright cherry fruit comes open with some breathing time, and this knits beautifully together into a soft, lush, harmonious wine with just the right accents of bark and root to add interest. **90** *(11/1/2004)*

Torii Mor 1998 Temperance Hill Vineyard Pinot Noir (Polk County) $40. **87** *—M.S. (12/1/2000)*

TOTT'S

Tott's NV Blanc de Noir (California) $7. **80** *—S.H. (12/15/1999)*

Tott's 2000 Reserve Cuvée Brut (California) $7. **82** *—S.H. (12/15/1999)*

Tott's NV Extra Dry (California) $7. A little sweet, rough, and sandpapery, but with good fruit and dough, this gets the bubbly job done at a fair price. **83** *—S.H. (12/31/2005)*

TREANA

Treana 2000 Red Blend (Central Coast) $35. This appealing wine from Paso Robles has well-ripened plum, blackberry, cassis, and herb flavors, and a smoothly elegant texture. It is very dry, and those warm southland tannins are sweet and smooth. Finishes with some astringency. A blend of Cabernet Sauvignon, Merlot, and Syrah. **88** *—S.H. (5/1/2004)*

Treana 1999 Red Table Wine Red Blend (Central Coast) $35. **89** *—J.M. (9/1/2003)*

Treana 2001 Mer Soleil Vineyard Rhône White Blend (Central Coast) $25. **93** *—S.H. (7/1/2003)*

Treana 1999 Mer Soleil Vineyard Rhône White Blend (Central Coast) $25. **91** *—J.M. (9/1/2002)*

Treana 2002 Austin Hope Syrah (Paso Robles) $42. The vineyard is in the cooler, western part of the AVA, and the wine opens with a promising blast of white pepper. Turns rich, full-bodied and complex, with an array of blackberry, plum, coffee, cigar tobacco, spice, and oak notes. The tannins are fairly thick and astringent, suggesting lamb, pork tenderloin or similar fare. **92** *—S.H. (4/1/2005)*

Treana 2000 Austin Hope Syrah (Paso Robles) $48. **89** *—S.H. (12/1/2003)*

Treana 1997 Mer Soleil Vineyard White Blend (Central Coast) $25. **86** *(10/1/1999)*

TREFETHEN

Trefethen 1995 Reserve Cabernet Sauvignon (Napa Valley) $60. **90** *(3/1/2000)*

Trefethen 2000 Chardonnay (Napa Valley) $22. **87** *—S.H. (2/1/2003)*

Trefethen 1995 Library Selection Chardonnay (Napa Valley) $37. **89** *(7/1/2001)*

Trefethen 1999 Dry Riesling (Napa Valley) $15. **83** *(9/1/2000)*

Trefethen 2001 Late Harvest Riesling (Napa Valley) $40. **92** *—J.M. (12/31/2003)*

TRELLIS

Trellis 1999 Cabernet Sauvignon (Sonoma County) $19. **86** *—S.H. (6/1/2003)*

Trellis 1997 Reserve Cabernet Sauvignon (Sonoma County) $39. **88** *—S.H. (12/15/2000)*

Trellis 2000 Chardonnay (Russian River Valley) $15. **85** *—S.H. (6/1/2003)*

Trellis 2001 Clone #15 Chardonnay (Russian River Valley) $25. 89 *—S.H. (5/1/2003)*

Trellis 2000 Merlot (Alexander Valley) $17. Quite ripe and seductive, with heady aromas of black currant, cassis, and well-charred oak, and soft, lovely tannins. Glides across the tongue like velvet, carrying complex, pretty flavors. Try cellaring for a year to let the flavors knit together. 90 *—S.H. (9/1/2004)*

Trellis 1997 Sauvignon Blanc (Sonoma County) $13. 88 *—S.H. (11/1/1999)*

Trellis 1998 Special Selection Sauvignon Blanc (Sonoma County) $11. 84 *(9/1/2000)*

TRENTADUE

Trentadue 2000 La Storia Red Meritage (Alexander Valley) $45. A lovely wine, solidly in the classic North Coast style of elaborate fruit and lush, soft tannins. Floods the mouth with delicious blackberry and currant flavors, well-framed with smoky vanillins from oak barrels. Straddles a nice line between sweetness and toughness. Best now. 90 *—S.H. (5/1/2004)*

Trentadue 2002 Petite Sirah (Alexander Valley) $28. From a "Pet" pioneer, a big, dark, thick red wine. It's soft but rich in tannins, and very ripe in blackberry, chocolate, and coffee flavors. It's also very oaky. Easy to drink, and earns extra points for nuance. 89 *—S.H. (3/1/2005)*

Trentadue 2002 Old Patch Red (North Coast) $16. Tastes like an old-style red wine, very dry and rugged in texture, yet able to stand up to tomato sauce and animal fat. The berry flavors are encased in firm tannins and crisp acids. 84 *—S.H. (5/1/2004)*

Trentadue 2000 La Storia Cuvée 32 Sangiovese (Alexander Valley) $32. Although this wine is mainly Sangiovese, the 18% of Cabernet Sauvignon rules, with its intense black currant and cassis flavors. New French oak also stars, contributing smoky vanillins. It's a lush wine that highlights its appellation's soft but complex tannins. As drinkable as it is, it will probably develop through the decade. 92 *—S.H. (5/1/2004)*

Trentadue 2000 Viognier (Dry Creek Valley) $18. 89 *—J.M. (12/15/2002)*

Trentadue 2001 Zinfandel (Dry Creek Valley) $14. 89 Best Buy *(11/1/2003)*

TRES SABORES

Tres Sabores 2001 Perspective Cabernet Sauvignon (Rutherford) $45. Oaky, with a meaty, leathery edge to the blackberry and cherry flavors, and very dry. The tannins are rich and firm but sweet and fine, and don't get in the way. Long in the finish, this balanced wine should hold well for 10 years. 89 *—S.H. (10/1/2004)*

Tres Sabores 2001 Ken Bernards Zinfandel (Rutherford) $38. 90 *(11/1/2003)*

Tres Sabores 2001 Rudy Zuidema Zinfandel (Rutherford) $38. 90 *(11/1/2003)*

TREY MARIE

Trey Marie 1999 Trutina Cabernet Sauvignon-Merlot (Columbia Valley (WA)) $29. 87 *—D.T. (12/31/2002)*

TRIA

Tria 1998 Pinot Noir (Carneros) $21. 86 *—S.H. (12/15/2001)*

Tria 1997 Syrah (Monterey) $19. 86 *—S.H. (11/15/2001)*

Tria 1998 Zinfandel (Dry Creek Valley) $18. 87 *—S.H. (11/15/2001)*

TRINCHERO

Trinchero 2001 Chicken Ranch Reserve Cabernet Sauvignon (Rutherford) $24. Lovely balance and finesse. Shows deft restraint in the blackberry and coffee flavors that finish with an herbal streak of green olive, and in the subtle oak nuances. Good price for the appellation and ageworthiness. 89 *—S.H. (10/1/2004)*

Trinchero 1999 Family Selection Cabernet Sauvignon (California) $12. 85 *—S.H. (2/1/2003)*

Trinchero 2001 Lewelling Vineyard Cabernet Sauvignon (Napa Valley) $45. Here's an easy Cab. It's soft and smooth, and dryish, although the blackberry and coffee flavors are very ripe and sweet, with a chocolaty finish that contains a touch of raisins. 85 *—S.H. (10/1/2005)*

Trinchero 2001 Main Street Vineyard Cabernet Sauvignon (St. Helena) $40. Good black currant and coffee flavors, but a little soft in acidity, which makes the sticky tannins more evident than they ought to be. Turns truly tough and astringent on the finish. 84 *—S.H. (10/1/2005)*

Trinchero 1998 Mario's Reserve Cabernet Sauvignon (Napa Valley) $40. 90 *—S.H. (6/1/2002)*

Trinchero 2003 Reserve Chicken Ranch Vineyard Cabernet Sauvignon (Rutherford) $30. Seems to have been picked earlier than most Napa Cabs, to judge by the acids, firm tannins, and the fruit that was snapped off before it developed voluptuous flavors. This is not a hedonistic wine nor is it an ager, but a dry red that won't compete with food. 86 *—S.H. (12/31/2005)*

Trinchero 1999 Family Selection Chardonnay (California) $12. 85 *(8/1/2001)*

Trinchero 2000 Trinity Oaks Vineyard Chardonnay (California) $10. 85 *—S.H. (6/1/2003)*

USA

Trinchero 2002 Chicken Ranch Vineyard Merlot (Rutherford) $25. Smooth, oaky, and flavorful in cocoa, black cherry and cassis flavors, this crowd-pleasing wine is solidly in the international style. It's ripe, extracted, and soft, with a nice edge of tannins. **87** *—S.H. (10/1/2005)*

Trinchero 2002 Family Selection Merlot (Monterey County) $10. This is a great value in a dry red dinner wine. Sourced from three counties, it's fairly rich in cherry and black raspberries, with sweet, thick tannins and a dry finish. Balanced and harmonious. **86** *—S.H. (10/1/2004)*

Trinchero 1999 Family Selection Merlot (California) $12. 87 Best Buy *—J.M. (6/1/2002)*

Trinchero 1998 Family Selection Merlot (California) $12. 88 *(8/1/2001)*

Trinchero 1998 Proprietor's Series Moscato (California) $12. 89 *—S.H. (5/1/2001)*

Trinchero 2003 Family Selection Pinot Noir (Napa Valley) $10. A good entry-level Pinot. It has all the correct textbook characteristics, including a silky texture, cherry and spice flavors and a clean finish. **84** *—S.H. (10/1/2004)*

Trinchero 2000 Sauvignon Blanc (California) $12. 85 *—J.M. (9/1/2002)*

Trinchero 2001 Family Selection Sauvignon Blanc (California) $12. 84 *—S.H. (3/1/2003)*

Trinchero 1998 Proprietor's Series Sauvignon Blanc (Monterey County) $14. 85 *—S.H. (5/1/2001)*

TRINITAS

Trinitas 2002 Petite Sirah (Russian River Valley) $32. Be prepared to cellar this wine because it's very tannic. It should age well, with its crisp acids and lush core of black cherry, blackberry pie, and milk chocolate flavors. However, it will be great now with a juicy steak. **88** *—S.H. (12/15/2004)*

Trinitas 2004 Pinot Blanc (Russian River Valley) $20. If you thought Pinot Blanc was a Chardonnay wannabe, think again. This one's more like a Sauvignon Blanc, with its dry, tart citrus flavors and high acidity, although that touch of peaches and cream on the finish gives it away. **87** *—S.H. (11/15/2005)*

Trinitas 2003 Old Vine Cuvée Red Blend (Contra Costa County) $18. A field blend from an old vineyard, this food-friendly mixture of who knows how many varieties is dry, rustic, and attractive for its full-bodied richness. It's not a particularly fruity wine, but has earthy flavors, like coffee and tobacco, with a dried cherry finish. **86** *—S.H. (11/15/2005)*

Trinitas 2002 Bigalow Vineyard Zinfandel (Contra Costa County) $28. Porty, tannic, and high in alcohol, with raisiny flavors. **82** *—S.H. (12/15/2004)*

TRINITY OAKS

Trinity Oaks 1998 Cabernet Sauvignon (California) $10. 86 *(8/1/2001)*

Trinity Oaks 1998 Merlot (California) $10. 83 *(8/1/2001)*

Trinity Oaks 1999 Zinfandel (California) $10. 87 Best Buy *(8/1/2001)*

TROON VINEYARDS

Troon Vineyards 1999 Reserve Cabernet Sauvignon (Applegate Valley) $19. 85 *—P.G. (8/1/2002)*

TRUCHARD

Truchard 1997 Cabernet Sauvignon (Carneros) $35. 94 *(11/1/2000)*

Truchard 1998 Cabernet Sauvignon (Carneros) $38. 85 *—J.M. (6/1/2002)*

Truchard 1995 Reserve Cabernet Sauvignon (Carneros) $55. 88 *—L.W. (12/31/1999)*

Truchard 2000 Chardonnay (Carneros) $30. 90 *—S.H. (5/1/2003)*

Truchard 1998 Chardonnay (Carneros) $28. 90 *(6/1/2000)*

Truchard 1998 Merlot (Carneros) $32. 88 *—J.M. (6/1/2002)*

Truchard 2000 Pinot Noir (Carneros) $32. 89 *(10/1/2002)*

Truchard 2002 Roussanne (Carneros) $25. Has a rich, buttery creaminess and very forward tropical fruit flavors that are like a great Chard, but there's a broad, nutty taste and texture, and a distinctly floral note, that make it distinct. Try this soft, flavorful wine as an alternative to Chardonnay. **90** *—S.H. (8/1/2005)*

Truchard 1997 Syrah (Carneros) $30. 89 *—S.H. (6/1/1999)*

Truchard 1999 Estate/Carneros Syrah (Carneros) $35. 88 *(11/1/2001)*

Truchard 2000 AVA's: Carneros/Napa Valley Zinfandel (California) $28. 88 *—S.H. (9/1/2002)*

TUALATIN ESTATE

Tualatin Estate 1999 Estate Grown Chardonnay (Willamette Valley) $18. 86 *—M.S. (9/1/2003)*

Tualatin Estate 1999 Pinot Blanc (Oregon) $15. 88 Best Buy *—M.M. (11/1/2001)*

Tualatin Estate 2001 Estate Grown Pinot Blanc (Willamette Valley) $11. 87 Best Buy *—P.G. (12/1/2003)*

Tualatin Estate 1999 Pinot Noir (Willamette Valley) $24. 88 *—P.G. (4/1/2002)*

TUCKER

Tucker 2001 Gewürztraminer (Yakima Valley) $7. **86** —*P.G. (9/1/2002)*

TUDOR WINES

Tudor Wines 2003 Pinot Noir (Santa Lucia Highlands) $35. Size marks this wine. It's huge in flavor, swamping the palate with black and red cherries, pomegranates, sweet rhubarb pie, coffee, and vanilla. At the same time, it's fairly light in color, and certainly light and silky in body, with crisp acids. Shows enough complexity to serve with your finest entrées. **90** —*S.H. (12/1/2005)*

Tudor Wines 2000 Tondre Vineyard Pinot Noir (Santa Lucia Highlands) $25. **87** —*S.H. (12/1/2003)*

TULE BAY

Tule Bay 2000 Merlot (Mendocino County) $15. A modest red wine with plummy flavors that have a strong edge of herbs. It's fully dry, with some dusty tannins that turn astringent on the finish. **84** —*S.H. (2/1/2004)*

TULIP HILL

Tulip Hill 2001 Mount Oso Vineyard Cabernet Sauvignon (California) $22. Acidity and tannins burn the mouth in this thin, rustic wine, which has faint cherry and berry flavors. **82** —*S.H. (11/15/2004)*

Tulip Hill 2001 Mount Oso Vineyard Chardonnay (California) $22. There's something sharp and vegetal to this wine despite a generous helping of sweet oak. **82** —*S.H. (11/15/2004)*

Tulip Hill 2002 Mount Oso Vineyard Mirage Merlot-Syrah (California) $24. This unusual Merlot-Syrah blend is fresh and tasty. It has soft tannins, a gentle mouthfeel, and ripe flavors of cherries and chocolate cream pie, although it's fully dry. **87** —*S.H. (10/1/2004)*

Tulip Hill 2001 Mt. Oso Vineyard Syrah (California) $16. A little heavy in body, with berry-cherry flavors and nice tannins. This dry wine has an earthy, herbal edge to it, but the solid core of fruit is enjoyable. **85** —*S.H. (5/1/2004)*

TURLEY

Turley 2000 Estate Petite Sirah (Napa Valley) $60. **83** *(4/1/2003)*

Turley 2000 Tofanelli Vineyard Zinfandel (Napa Valley) $32. **92** —*J.M. (9/1/2003)*

TURNBULL

Turnbull 2001 Petite Sirah (Oakville) $35. **87** *(4/1/2003)*

Turnbull 2004 Sauvignon Blanc (Oakville) $16. Oakville is beginning to come out with some pretty interesting Sauvignon Blancs, and this is one of them. Good as it is, I wish it were more concentrated, because it would be fabulous. It's crisp, clean, bone dry, and complex, with a swirl of citrus, peach, green herb, tobacco, mineral, and oak flavors leading to a satisfying finish. **88** —*S.H. (12/15/2005)*

Turnbull 1998 Syrah (Oakville) $25. **86** *(11/1/2001)*

TURNER ROAD

Turner Road 2003 Cabernet Sauvignon (Paso Robles) $11. Kind of hot and peppery, and a little over-ripe, but shows a polished texture and lots of tasty currant, blackberry, and bitter chocolate flavors. **84** —*S.H. (6/1/2005)*

Turner Road 2003 Chardonnay (Central Coast) $11. Has real Monterey character in the ripe tropical fruits and zesty acidity, only the flavors are a bit thin. If you can find this wine for a few bucks less, it's a real value. **84** —*S.H. (6/1/2005)*

Turner Road 2002 Shiraz (Lodi) $11. Soft, dry, and easy, with ripe blackberry, cherry, and cocoa flavors that finish with a dusting of pepper and spice. **84** —*S.H. (6/1/2005)*

TURNING LEAF

Turning Leaf 2003 Sonoma Reserve Chardonnay (Sonoma County) $12. This is obviously a cool climate Chard, to judge from the brisk acids, citrusy flavors, and hint of minerality that makes the wine bracing and strong. Yet oak and lees lend softening, complexing notes. **87 Best Buy** —*S.H. (12/15/2005)*

Turning Leaf 2002 Coastal Reserve Pinot Noir (North Coast) $10. Smells and tastes a bit herbal and peppery, with plummy flavors. Very dry, with gentle, soft tannins. **83** —*S.H. (11/1/2004)*

Turning Leaf 2003 Sonoma Reserve Pinot Noir (Sonoma County) $11. Pretty thin despite the price. You get alcohol and oak, with thinned-down cherry cola flavors. **83** —*S.H. (10/1/2005)*

Turning Leaf 2002 Vineyards Riesling (Monterey County) $9. Here's a refreshing summer quaffer with off-dry flavors of apricots and peaches and good acidity. Enjoy with watermelon, fried chicken, and similar fare. **84** —*S.H. (12/1/2004)*

Turning Leaf 1999 Shiraz (California) $8. **83** *(10/1/2001)*

TUSK 'N RED

Tusk 'n Red 2003 Red Wine Red Blend (Mendocino County) $15. This old-style field blend leaves little to the imagination. It's full-bodied, dry, and astringently tannic, with fruity, earthy flavors. **83** —*S.H. (12/31/2005)*

TWIN FIN

Twin Fin 2002 Cabernet Sauvignon (California) $10. This is a gently structured, full-bodied wine with pizazz and flair. It's rich in cherry, currant, and coffee flavors, in a dry, elegant package. **85 Best Buy** *—S.H. (10/1/2005)*

Twin Fin 2003 Merlot (California) $10. This is a good value Merlot because there's a lot going on in the bottle, at a fair price. The wine is fully dry and balanced. Flavorwise, it offers a subtle blend of cherries, herbs, sweet tobacco, and smoky oak. Nothing stands out, but the end result is a gentle wine that you don't get tired of sipping. **85 Best Buy** *—S.H. (12/15/2005)*

Twin Fin 2004 Pinot Grigio (California) $10. This is a crisp, dry wine with citrus and apple flavors, and a pleasing scour of spice. It will go well with a wide variety of food. Finishes with lively acids. **85 Best Buy** *—S.H. (7/1/2005)*

Twin Fin 2003 Pinot Noir (California) $10. A nice, rich red wine, dry and soft, with black cherry flavors veering into chocolate and a silky mouthfeel. Shows real complexity in the balanced interplay of tannins, fruit, and acids. **85 Best Buy** *—S.H. (10/1/2005)*

Twin Fin 2002 Shiraz (California) $10. Jammy and sweet-tasting, with the emphasis on cherry and cranberry flavors. The texture is soft, the finish a bit rough, but this is a serviceable sipper. **82** *(9/1/2005)*

USA

TWISTED OAK

Twisted Oak 2002 The Spaniard Red Blend (Calaveras County) $35. Compared to Twisted Oak's *%#&@! Rhône blend, this is more full-bodied and tannic, no doubt due to the Cabernet Sauvignon and Petit Verdot in the blend, which also includes Tempranillo. It's rich in black currants and spices and a touch of smoky oak. Very sophisticated, it represents a tremendous advancement in Calaveras County winemaking. **92** *—S.H. (11/15/2005)*

Twisted Oak 2002 *%#&@! Rhône Red Blend (Sierra Foothills) $28. A Rhône blend with a really weird name. Extremely dry and tannic, with a rasping bite on the tongue, although there are some pretty flavors of cherries, chocolate, and peppery spices. You can taste the sunny ripeness of the grapes. **86** *—S.H. (12/1/2004)*

Twisted Oak 2003 Tanner Syrah (Calaveras County) $28. Rustic, with big, drying tannins on the finish, this wine divided the panel. All enjoyed it for its bold, gutsy dried-fruit flavors and sense of Sierra Foothills individuality, but two reviewers felt the tannins were a bit overpowering in the long run and the wine should be enjoyed young. One felt the wine would age well. Our advice? Buy two, try one and decide when to drink the other one yourself. **87** *(9/1/2005)*

Twisted Oak 2002 Tempranillo (Calaveras County) $22. Very Cabernet-like, with its full-bodied flavors of blackberries and cherries and big tannins. The difference is a subtle floweriness. Finishes dry and oaky. **85** *—S.H. (9/1/2004)*

Twisted Oak 2003 Viognier (Calaveras County) $18. Here's a beautiful Viognier, filled with ripe tropical fruit and flavor notes, spices, minerals, and smoky oak. It's crisp in acids, balanced, and elegant, with a fabulously long, spicy finish. Just first rate. **91** *—S.H. (2/1/2005)*

TWO ANGELS

Two Angels 2004 Shannon Ridge Sauvignon Blanc (Lake County) $15. Lake County is making a play as the best place in California for inexpensive Sauvignon Blanc, and this wine shows why. It's dry and very crisp, with pure, intense flavors of figs and pineapples, and is simply irresistible. **86** *—S.H. (10/1/2005)*

TWO TONE FARM

Two Tone Farm 2002 Chardonnay (Napa Valley) $13. Toasty and ripe in tropical fruit, vanilla, and buttered toast, this is a fancy Chard at an everyday price. Stays clean with fresh acidity. **88 Best Buy** *—S.H. (3/1/2005)*

TY CATON

Ty Caton 2001 Cabernet Sauvignon (Sonoma Valley) $24. A soft, easy Cab, with gentle tannins, low acidity, and blackberry fruit that seems just a little baked. Goes down gently, with a fruity finish. **86** *—S.H. (12/31/2004)*

Ty Caton 2002 Ty Caton Vineyards Syrah (Sonoma Valley) $19. A well-ripened Syrah with lots of plump fruit. Although it's dry, the plummy coffee and chocolate flavors are sweet in fruity essence. Feels plush and soft in the mouth, with a long, berry-and-spice finish. **88** *—S.H. (12/15/2004)*

TYEE

Tyee 1997 Pinot Blanc (Willamette Valley) $12. **83** *—D.T. (11/1/2001)*

UNITED WE STAND

United We Stand 2003 Reserve Merlot (California) $10. Not even the most patriotic American will drink this harsh, vegetal wine. **80** *—S.H. (3/1/2005)*

UNTI

Unti 2003 Barbera (Dry Creek Valley) $24. Drink this dark, chewy wine with full-flavored Italian beef or veal dishes. It's packed with dry, strong tannins and is high in acids. By itself it's austere, but rich meats will coax out the blackberry and roasted coffee flavors **87** *—S.H. (11/1/2005)*

Unti 2004 Rosé Grenache (Dry Creek Valley) $16. From a warmer part of Dry Creek Valley, Rhône specialist Unti has crafted a pale, but rich, blush wine with such an inviting aroma of raspberry sorbet and vanilla, you can't wait to dive in. It doesn't disappoint, being delicately silky and drily delicious. Try with grilled sausage and raw veggies with a spicy hummus dip. **88** *—S.H. (8/1/2005)*

Unti 2003 Sangiovese (Dry Creek Valley) $30. Unti has succeeded in overcoming Sangiovese's tendency to dull herbaceousness in favor of a cherried, blackberry richness. Tannins and acids, however, are hefty, suggesting rich cheeses, olive oil, and fatty meats. Drink now through 2011. 89 *—S.H. (11/1/2005)*

Unti 2002 Benchland Syrah (Dry Creek Valley) $30. Hits the palate with the force of a sledgehammer: Very tannic and dry, but with enough blackberry flavor to (mostly) balance things out. West Coast Editor Steve Heimoff was a huge proponent of this wine, calling it likely to age gracefully for a decade, while Tasting Director Joe Czerwinski was less enthusiastic, finding the tannins hard. 88 *(9/1/2005)*

URSA

Ursa 2002 Merlot (Santa Clara Valley) $16. Smells sharp and minty, like toothpaste, with green, stalky overtones. In the mouth, you'll find modest cherry and berry flavors and some sweet oak. 84 *—S.H. (8/1/2004)*

Ursa 2002 Petite Sirah (Lodi) $16. Full-bodied and dense on the palate, this wine is very dry, carrying plummy, herbal flavors and thick tannins. At first it came across as simple and dull. But then a certain taste of the earth perked it up. Spicy barbecued pork or beef will nicely set it off. 86 *—S.H. (8/1/2004)*

V. SATTUI

V. Sattui 2002 Cabernet Sauvignon (Napa Valley) $29. An interesting, enjoyable wine that straddles the line between age-me and drink-me-now. It's ripe and forward in sunny blackberry and cherry fruit, dry and balanced, with a tasteful edge of oak. But it's so balanced, it should hang in there for a decade. 90 *—S.H. (12/1/2005)*

V. Sattui 2000 Cabernet Sauvignon (Napa Valley) $21. 84 *—S.H. (12/15/2003)*

V. Sattui 1999 Morisoli Cabernet Sauvignon (Napa Valley) $32. 87 *—S.H. (11/15/2002)*

V. Sattui 1999 Preston Cabernet Sauvignon (Napa Valley) $32. 87 *—S.H. (11/15/2002)*

V. Sattui 1999 Suzanne's Cabernet Sauvignon (Napa Valley) $25. 87 *—S.H. (11/15/2002)*

V. Sattui 2000 Carsi Chardonnay (Napa Valley) $21. 84 *—S.H. (12/15/2002)*

V. Sattui 2001 Carsi Vineyard Old Vine Chardonnay (Napa Valley) $25. 89 *—S.H. (8/1/2003)*

V. Sattui 2001 Rouge Gamay (California) $15. 83 *—S.H. (12/1/2002)*

V. Sattui 2001 Off-Dry Johannisberg Riesling (Napa Valley) $15. 85 *—S.H. (9/1/2003)*

V. Sattui 1999 Merlot (Napa Valley) $24. 90 *—S.H. (11/15/2002)*

V. Sattui NV Angelica Muscat (California) $22. 88 *—S.H. (12/1/2002)*

V. Sattui 2003 Henry Ranch Pinot Noir (Carneros) $NA. This is a Pinot that's too soft, almost flabby in texture. The softness accentuates the ripeness of the raspberry and coffee flavors, making them a little cloying. 82 *—S.H. (12/1/2005)*

V. Sattui 1999 Sattui Family Red (California) $13. 86 *—S.H. (5/1/2002)*

V. Sattui 2000 Duarte Vineyard Ancient Vine Zinfandel (Contra Costa County) $35. 86 *—S.H. (12/1/2002)*

V. Sattui NV Madeira Zinfandel (California) $29. 90 *—S.H. (12/1/2002)*

V. Sattui 2000 Suzanne's Vineyard Zinfandel (Napa Valley) $20. 86 *—S.H. (9/1/2003)*

VACHE

Vache 2000 Cabernet Sauvignon (Cienega Valley) $37. Dry and smooth, and a bit coarse, this wine shows berry, oak, and leather flavors. Short finish. 84 *—S.H. (5/1/2005)*

Vache 2001 Chardonnay (Cienega Valley) $37. Smells vegetal and oaky, but tastes a little better. Finishes sweet. 83 *—S.H. (4/1/2005)*

Vache 2001 Pinot Noir (Cienega Valley) $37. Smells rubbery, and drinks dry and harsh. 82 *—S.H. (4/1/2005)*

VALLEY OF THE MOON

Valley of the Moon 2001 Cuvée de la Luna Cabernet Blend (Sonoma County) $30. Combining ripe fruit with substantial oak, this Bordeaux blend is another example of how great the '01 vintage continues to be. The flavors, of cassis, black currants, cocoa, and licorice, are impressively deep and long-lasting. Drink now and over the next few years. 91 *—S.H. (11/15/2005)*

Valley of the Moon 2001 Cabernet Sauvignon (Sonoma County) $20. At four-plus years, this wine has mellowed to extreme softness, although it retains balancing acidity. It's on the light side, flavor-wise, with suggestions of cola and cherries, and is totally dry. 84 *—S.H. (11/15/2005)*

Valley of the Moon 1998 Cabernet Sauvignon (Sonoma Valley) $20. 86 *—J.M. (6/1/2002)*

Valley of the Moon 2004 Chardonnay (Sonoma County) $16. This is a full-bodied, heavy Chard, a bit on the soft side, with a balance of apple, dried herb, and peach flavors that taste well-oaked. It's fully dry. 84 *—S.H. (12/31/2005)*

Valley of the Moon 2002 Chardonnay (Sonoma County) $15. 90 Editors' Choice *—S.H. (12/15/2003)*

Valley of the Moon 2000 Chardonnay (Sonoma County) $14. 87 *—J.M. (5/1/2002)*

Valley of the Moon 1998 Chardonnay (Sonoma County) $17. 86 *(6/1/2000)*

Valley of the Moon 2000 Cuvée de la Luna Meritage (Sonoma County) $25. This Bordeaux blend is rich, complex, and satisfying. Everything's reined in, and in balance. The fruity flavor is quite ripe, the tannins smooth and intricate, the oak shadings just right to accompany fine food without competing with it. **90** *—S.H. (6/1/2004)*

Valley of the Moon 2003 Pinot Blanc (Sonoma County) $15. Young, fresh, and jammy in lime, peach, and nectarine flavors, this wine has crisp acids and a clean, fruity finish. Will go well with fruit. **85** *—S.H. (5/1/2005)*

Valley of the Moon 2001 Pinot Blanc (Sonoma County) $15. 87 *—J.M. (12/15/2002)*

Valley of the Moon 1999 Pinot Blanc (Sonoma County) $15. 88 *—S.H. (2/1/2001)*

Valley of the Moon 2003 Pinot Noir (Carneros) $20. A bit earthy, with herb, cherry, and spice flavors, this Pinot is dry, with gentle tannins and crisp acids. The fruity finish is very pretty. **85** *—S.H. (11/15/2005)*

USA

Valley of the Moon 2001 Pinot Noir (Carneros) $20. 90 Editors' Choice *—S.H. (12/1/2003)*

Valley of the Moon 2002 Sangiovese (Sonoma County) $16. Chianti-like, a dry, acidic wine with pronounced cherry flavors and easy tannins. Of course, it's riper than anything you're likely to get from Tuscany, and those cherries veer into cocoa. **86** *—S.H. (10/1/2005)*

Valley of the Moon 2000 Sangiovese (Sonoma County) $15. 89 *—S.H. (12/1/2003)*

Valley of the Moon 1998 Sangiovese (Sonoma County) $16. 90 *—S.H. (7/1/2002)*

Valley of the Moon 2001 Syrah (Sonoma County) $15. A winning wine. It's polished enough to enjoy with almost anything that calls for a dry red wine, but Syrah aficionados will appreciate the intricate interplay of cherry, leather, pepper, and oak flavors and soft tannins. **88** *—S.H. (12/15/2004)*

Valley of the Moon 1999 Syrah (Sonoma County) $15. 85 *—J.M. (12/1/2002)*

Valley of the Moon 2002 Zinfandel (Sonoma County) $15. Nowhere near as good as the 2001, with thinner flavors, but it's still a good Zin. Blackberries, coffee, and herbs, in thick but gentle tannins. **85** *—S.H. (5/1/2005)*

Valley of the Moon 1998 Zinfandel (Sonoma County) $15. 88 Best Buy *—S.H. (11/15/2001)*

VALLEY VIEW VINEYARD

Valley View Vineyard 2000 Anna Maria Chardonnay (Oregon) $15. 87 *—P.G. (8/1/2002)*

Valley View Vineyard 1999 Meritage (Rogue Valley) $40. 88 *—P.G. (4/1/2002)*

Valley View Vineyard 1999 Anna Maria Old Stage Vineyard Merlot (Rogue Valley) $22. 87 *—P.G. (8/1/2002)*

Valley View Vineyard 1999 Anna Maria Pinot Gris (Rogue Valley) $12. 86 *—P.G. (8/1/2002)*

VAN ASPEREN

Van Asperen 1995 Cabernet Sauvignon (Napa Valley) $18. 88 *—L.W. (7/1/1999)*

Van Asperen 1997 Zinfandel (Napa Valley) $18. 90 *(5/1/2000)*

VAN DER HEYDEN

Van Der Heyden 2000 Chardonnay (Napa Valley) $18. 85 *—S.H. (12/1/2003)*

VAN DUZER

Van Duzer 2002 Pinot Gris (Willamette Valley) $13. 87 *—P.G. (12/1/2003)*

Van Duzer 2001 Pinot Noir (Willamette Valley) $19. 84 *—P.G. (12/1/2003)*

Van Duzer 2002 Estate Pinot Noir (Willamette Valley) $22. Cherry fruit and plenty of chocolaty, mocha barrel flavors. Mainstream, clean, and simple. The twin parts—fruit and oak—are like two halves of a sandwich, separate, equal, but unintegrated. **86** *(11/1/2004)*

Van Duzer 2002 Homestead Block Pinot Noir (Willamette Valley) $33. Plum, citrus, and some brambly red fruits are mixed together, creating a forward, fruity wine with plenty of toasty oak up front. **86** *(11/1/2004)*

VAN RUITEN-TAYLOR

Van Ruiten-Taylor 1999 Chardonnay (Lodi) $10. 84 *—S.H. (11/15/2001)*

VARNER

Varner 2001 Bee Block Chardonnay (Santa Cruz Mountains) $32. 92 *—S.H. (5/1/2003)*

Varner 2000 Spring Ridge Vineyard Amphitheater Block Chardonnay (Santa Cruz County) $30. 87 *—S.H. (5/1/2002)*

VELOCITY

Velocity 2002 Red Wine Red Blend (Rogue Valley) $30. A new project from Gus Janeway, showcasing his careful and detailed touch with Rogue valley grapes. The blend is 30% Malbec, 30% Cabernet Sauvignon, 21% Merlot, 12% Cab Franc, and 7% Syrah, but rather than being a smorgasbord it is a focused, complex and layered wine that all knits together. Most telling, Janeway has successfully tamed to tough, rugged tannins that are the biggest challenge for southern Oregon reds. **88** *—P.G. (2/1/2005)*

VENEZIA

Venezia 1997 Regusci Vineyard Chardonnay (Napa Valley) $20. 83 *—J.C. (10/1/1999)*

Venezia 1996 Alegria Vineyard Sangiovese (Russian River Valley) $23. 83 *—J.C. (10/1/1999)*

Venezia 1996 Van Noy Vineyard Sangiovese (Russian River Valley) $22. 86 *—J.C. (10/1/1999)*

VENGE

Venge 2000 Family Reserve Cabernet Sauvignon (Oakville) $95. This is a young wine marked by intense tannins, intense cassis fruit, and intense oak. All three elements stand out. You'll want to cellar for a good six years to allow it all to mature and come together. **90** *—S.H. (11/1/2005)*

Venge 2001 Family Reserve Merlot (Oakville) $46. This wine sure is oaky now, although it's sweet, high-class oak. But there's a broad swath of ripe blackberry and cherry fruit, and enough tannins to hold this pretty wine for at least ten years. **91 Cellar Selection** *—S.H. (11/1/2005)*

Venge 2000 Scout's Honor Red Blend (Napa Valley) $30. 89 *—J.M. (11/15/2003)*

Venge 2003 Syrah (Napa Valley) $32. A wood-dominated wine at the moment, this Syrah from Nils Venge showcases modest blackberry fruit buried under an avalanche of oak-derived toast and cinnamon. Drying on the finish, but might improve with short-term cellaring. **84** *(9/1/2005)*

VENTANA

Ventana 2001 Cabernet Sauvignon (Arroyo Seco) $18. Dark and dense, a full-bodied Cab with herbal, even vegetal aromas and flavors accompanying riper notes of blackberries. The tannins are on the fierce side. **84** *—S.H. (10/1/2004)*

Ventana 2000 Due Amici Cabernet Sauvignon-Sangiovese (Arroyo Seco) $18. 87 *—S.H. (2/1/2003)*

Ventana 1999 Chardonnay (Arroyo Seco) $14. 86 *—S.H. (12/31/2001)*

Ventana 2000 Gold Stripe Chardonnay (Arroyo Seco) $14. 86 *—S.H. (9/1/2002)*

Ventana 2000 Dry Chenin Blanc (Monterey) $12. 85 *—S.H. (9/1/2002)*

Ventana 2001 Gewürztraminer (Arroyo Seco) $12. 88 *—S.H. (9/1/2003)*

Ventana 2000 Merlot (Arroyo Seco) $18. 85 *—S.H. (4/1/2003)*

Ventana 1999 Muscat d'Orange Muscat (Monterey) $12. 87 *—S.H. (9/1/2002)*

Ventana 1999 Pinot Blanc (Monterey) $14. 87 *—S.H. (2/1/2001)*

Ventana 2001 Riesling (Arroyo Seco) $12. 87 *—S.H. (9/1/2003)*

Ventana 1997 Sauvignon Blanc (Monterey County) $9. 88 Best Buy *—S.H. (2/1/2000)*

Ventana 2001 Syrah (Arroyo Seco) $18. This junior version of Ventana's Maverick Syrah is quite good, with its polished blackberry, plum, and coffee flavors and stylish tannins. It's dry, with a firm tannic grip that will prove an ample match to a leg of lamb. Finishes long and fruity, suggesting midterm ageability. **90** *—S.H. (9/1/2004)*

Ventana 1999 Syrah (Arroyo Seco) $20. 85 *—S.H. (9/1/2002)*

VENUS

Venus 1999 Eve Zinfandel (Sonoma County) $22. 87 *—D.T. (3/1/2002)*

VERITÉ

Verité 2000 Le Desir Meritage (Sonoma County) $100. 86 *—S.H. (11/15/2003)*

Verité 1999 La Joie Red Blend (Sonoma County) $100. 90 *—S.H. (11/15/2003)*

VERSANT VINEYARDS

Versant Vineyards 2001 Cabernet Sauvignon (Napa Valley) $70. Richly textured and plush on the palate, with a broad array of raspberry, black cherry, plum, spice, coffee, herb, and cocoa flavors, all couched in firm, ripe tannins and sweet oak. Only 200 cases made from this relatively new producer high in the hills of Napa. **92** *—J.M. (6/1/2004)*

VIA FIRENZE

Via Firenze 1995 Dolcetto (Napa Valley) $15. 85 *—M.S. (6/1/1999)*

VIADER

Viader 2002 Cabernet Blend (Napa Valley) $85. This wine has delicious flavors of cherries, blackberries, and oak, and is complex enough to return to glass after glass. At the same time, it's overly soft and simple in structure, and will not age. **87** *—S.H. (11/1/2005)*

Viader 1999 Red Blend (Napa Valley) $75. **92** *—J.M. (6/1/2002)*

Viader 2001 Syrah (Napa Valley) $65. Dense and taut in acids and fresh tannins, a young, chewy wine with a good future, to judge from the muscularity. Black cherry, pepper, and herbs are framed in plenty of new oak. Immature, but should age well. Try after 2008. **92** *—S.H. (12/15/2004)*

VIANO

Viano 2001 Reserve Selection Old Vines Zinfandel Port (Contra Costa County) $11. Simple, soft, and not even that sweet, this is a thin wine with modest chocolate and cherry flavors. The thinness makes the alcohol stand out. **82** *—S.H. (12/15/2005)*

VIANSA

Viansa 2002 Athena Dolcetto (California) $19. Almost a late-harvest wine, with its sweetish flavors of currants and raisins with their edge of chocolatey hazelnut. Dusty tannins kick in on the finish. This is an old-style wine that still has aficionados. **84** *—S.H. (9/1/2004)*

USA

VICTOR HUGO

Victor Hugo 2000 Petite Sirah (Paso Robles) $18. **86** *(4/1/2003)*

Victor Hugo 2001 Zinfandel (Paso Robles) $16. **81** *(11/1/2003)*

VIERRA VINEYARDS

Vierra Vineyards 2002 Claret Bordeaux Blend (Walla Walla (WA)) $20. Very nice fruit, polished and bright, with big berry/cherry flavors standing out against firm acids. Nicely made, forward and accessible, with plump, juicy fruit. 50% Cab Sauvignon, 10% Cab Franc, and 40% Merlot. **88** *—P.G. (7/1/2004)*

VIEUX

Vieux-Os 2002 Ira Carter Vineyard Zinfandel (Napa Valley) $36. A bright, zippy style that still shows depth, with complex layers of black cherry, black currant, ginger, coffee, herb, and cinnamon flavors. The wine is framed in firm tannins that give good structure and finishes long. From Fred Schrader, best known for his Cabernet. **90** *—J.M. (10/1/2004)*

VIGIL

Vigil 1997 Terra Vin Reserve Red Blend (Napa Valley) $22. **92** *—L.W. (11/1/1999)*

Vigil 1998 Marissa Vineyard Zinfandel (California) $16. **85** *—P.G. (3/1/2001)*

Vigil 1998 Tres Condados Zinfandel (California) $14. **87** *—P.G. (3/1/2001)*

VILLA CREEK

Villa Creek 2002 James Berry Vineyard Garnacha (Paso Robles) $24. 100 percent Grenache, with lovely French herb, cherry, raspberry, and vanilla-oaky aromas and flavors. Lush, soft, and rich in the mouth, with a good grip of acids and tannins. Easy and delightful, with real complexity. **90** *—S.H. (12/31/2004)*

Villa Creek 2002 James Berry Vineyard High Road Red Blend (Paso Robles) $40. You'll find tons of bacon, meat, leather, ripe blackberry, and cassis aromas and flavors in this Chateauneuf-style blend of Grenache, Syrah, and Mourvèdre. It's sweet, gently soft, and harmonious, with lively acids and a good, clean mouthfeel. **92** *—S.H. (12/31/2004)*

Villa Creek 2001 Avenger Rhône Red Blend (Paso Robles) $20. The first-ever wine from this West Side property, and a very great wine it is. A beautifully balanced Rhône blend with aromas of raspberry, cherry, sweet wood smoke, and vanilla, it is extracted and jammy, but complex. Layers of oak, chocolate, cherry, cream, and spices cascade across the palate. The finish is long and spicy-sweet. **94** *—S.H. (3/1/2004)*

VILLA MT. EDEN

Villa Mt. Eden 1997 Coastal Cabernet Sauvignon (California) $10. **80** *—S.H. (7/1/2000)*

Villa Mt. Eden 1998 Grand Reserve Cabernet Sauvignon (Napa Valley) $20. **84** *—S.H. (11/15/2001)*

Villa Mt. Eden 2001 Grande Reserve Tall Trees Vineyard Cabernet Sauvignon (Napa Valley) $15. From Yountville, a nice, dry wine, with polished cherry and blackberry flavors and enough oak to satisfy. Medium-bodied, with a soft, easy mouthfeel. **85** *—S.H. (10/1/2004)*

Villa Mt. Eden 1997 Chardonnay (California) $10. **87** *—S.H. (2/1/2000)*

Villa Mt. Eden 2004 Bien Nacido Vineyard Grand Reserve Chardonnay (Santa Maria Valley) $15. From this famous vineyard comes a pretty good Chardonnay. It's a bit thin in fruit, with a green peppercorn edge to the peaches, but the creamy texture and oaky veneer offer pleasure. **84** *—S.H. (12/31/2005)*

Villa Mt. Eden 2002 Bien Nacido Vineyard Grand Reserve Chardonnay (Santa Maria Valley) $15. This is not a bad price for such a good wine, from such a pedigreed vineyard. It's classic cool South Coast, with a crisp spine of citrusy acids that brighten the tropical fruit flavors. This is a generous, fat wine that offers lots of pleasure. **90** **Best Buy** *—S.H. (6/1/2004)*

Villa Mt. Eden 2001 Bien Nacido Vineyard Signature Chardonnay (Santa Maria Valley) $32. Santa Barbara seems to produce these exquisitely layered Chardonnays so effortlessly. The cool coastal climate has preserved vital acids, while a long growing season allowed the most extraordinary tropical fruit flavors to develop. Finally, there are the rich, creamy influences from oak and lees. This four-year-old wine shows no sign at all of age. **92** *—S.H. (12/1/2005)*

Villa Mt. Eden 1999 Coastal Chardonnay (Monterey County) $10. **84** *—S.H. (11/15/2001)*

Villa Mt. Eden 1999 Grand Reserve Chardonnay (Santa Maria Valley) $17. **88** *—S.H. (11/15/2001)*

Villa Mt. Eden 1997 Coastal Merlot (California) $10. **88 Best Buy** *—J.C. (3/1/2000)*

Villa Mt. Eden 1997 Bien Nacido Vineyard Grand Res Pinot Noir (Santa Maria Valley) $20. **86** *(10/1/1999)*

Villa Mt. Eden 1998 Bien Nacido Vineyard Grand Reserve Pinot Noir (Santa Maria Valley) $20. **89** *—S.H. (12/15/2000)*

Villa Mt. Eden 1999 Coastal Pinot Noir (California) $10. **85** *—J.C. (11/15/2001)*

Villa Mt. Eden 2000 Grand Reserve Pinot Noir (Sonoma County) $22. **89** *(10/1/2002)*

Villa Mt. Eden 1999 Coastal Sauvignon Blanc (Central Coast) $10. **85** *—S.H. (11/15/2000)*

Villa Mt. Eden 1999 Coastal Syrah (California) $10. **84** *(10/1/2001)*

Villa Mt. Eden 1999 Fox Creek Vyd Grand Reserve Zinfandel (Sierra Foothills) $21. **91** *—S.H. (12/15/2001)*

Villa Mt. Eden 2002 Grand Reserve Mead Ranch Vineyard Zinfandel (Napa Valley) $22. When they talk about claret-like Zins, they have this one in mind. It has the effortlessly controlled balance, the smooth tannins of a fine Napa Cab, but never loses Zin's peppery, wild, fresh-from-the-forest personality, or zesty acidity. This is Zin at a very high level of expression. **92 Editors' Choice** *—S.H. (12/1/2005)*

Villa Mt. Eden 1995 Grand Reserve Monte Rosso Vine Zinfandel (Sonoma Valley) $20. **92** *—S.H> (9/1/1999)*

Villa Mt. Eden 1999 Mead Ranch Vyd Grand Reserve Zinfandel (Napa Valley) $21. **90** *—S.H. (12/15/2001)*

Villa Mt. Eden 1998 Monte Rosso Vineyard Grand Reserve Zinfandel (Sonoma Valley) $21. **90 Editors' Choice** *—P.G. (3/1/2001)*

Villa Mt. Eden 1999 Old Vines Zinfandel (Napa Valley) $10. **87** *—S.H. (12/9/2002)*

VILLICANA

Villicana 2000 Cabernet Sauvignon (Paso Robles) $25. Framed in smoky, toasty oak, the wine serves up moderate char, blackberry, and plum flavors. Tannins are a bit rustic, and the finish is somewhat powdery. **84** *—J.M. (4/1/2004)*

VINA ROBLES

Vina Robles 2002 Cabernet Sauvignon (Paso Robles) $19. Despite a roughness around the edges, this Cab appeals with its ripe flavors of cherry jam, blackberries, and espresso coffee. It's very dry, with a soft complexity that makes it easy to drink. **84** *—S.H. (12/31/2005)*

Vina Robles 2002 Jardine Petite Sirah (Paso Robles) $26. Dark, tannic, dry and way too thin. Tastes like it was watered down. **82** *—S.H. (10/1/2005)*

Vina Robles 2003 Signature Red Blend (Paso Robles) $29. This Petit Verdot, Syrah, and Petite Sirah blend has absolutely delicious flavors, stunning in fact. Blackberry jam, blueberries, cassis, chocolate, coffee, toasty oak, spices, the list goes on and on. Plus, it's dry. The only critique is that it's overly soft, in the manner of Paso Robles. **87** *—S.H. (12/31/2005)*

Vina Robles 2001 Jardine Vineyard Sauvignon Blanc (Paso Robles) $14. Tart and crisp, this pleasant sipper offers lots to like in a dry, stylish white wine. The citrus, peach, and fig flavors are in harmonious balance with the acids, and are not overly sweet. **86** *—S.H. (8/1/2004)*

Vina Robles 2000 Estate Syrah (Paso Robles) $19. The tannins have sharp elbows in this wine, with its modest cherry and blackberry flavors. It's very dry, and there's quite a hefty dose of citrusy acids. The result is rather angular and austere. **84** *—S.H. (8/1/2004)*

Vina Robles 2004 Roseum Syrah (Paso Robles) $13. This blush wine has Viognier blended in with Syrah. It's a pretty salmon color, and has flavors of raspberries, peaches, and vanilla. Fully dry, it will be nice with grilled salmon. **84** *—S.H. (11/15/2005)*

Vina Robles 2002 Westside Zinfandel (Paso Robles) $24. So ripe, so sweet, so soft, it's almost like chocolate-infused cherry juice. High alcohol, though, gives it a kick. **87** *—S.H. (10/1/2005)*

VINE CLIFF

Vine Cliff 2002 Cabernet Sauvignon (Napa Valley) $45. This blend of Oakville and Calistoga is marked by intensely ripe cherry, cassis, cocoa, and oak flavors and fabulous balance. Superbly rich and massive, with rich, smooth tannins, this lovely Cab maintains elegance and structural integrity through the long, polished finish. It's better than most Napa Cabs that cost far more, making it a fantastic value. **95 Editors' Choice** *—S.H. (11/1/2005)*

Vine Cliff 2001 Cabernet Sauvignon (Oakville) $75. This is a difficult wine to drink now, due to its palate-numbing tannins. Yet there's something big and flashy going on. The finish is long in black currant fruit, so stunningly rich it can only survive as the tannins fall out. Try after 2008, but it could go long beyond that. **91** *—S.H. (10/1/2004)*

Vine Cliff 1998 Cabernet Sauvignon (Oakville) $75. **83** *—D.T. (6/1/2002)*

Vine Cliff 1996 Oakville Estate Cabernet Sauvignon (Napa Valley) $45. **91** *(3/1/2000)*

Vine Cliff 1997 Chardonnay (Napa Valley) $34. **87** *(10/1/2000)*

Vine Cliff 2002 Chardonnay (Napa Valley) $25. A fine wine, with enough oaky richness to please Chard lovers. The flavors suggest cool peach custard sprinkled with vanilla and a drizzle of butterscotch sauce, while the acids keep this gooey quality crisp and fresh. **90** *—S.H. (11/15/2004)*

Vine Cliff 2003 Bien Nacido Vineyard Chardonnay (Santa Maria Valley) $34. From down Santa Maria way comes this high-acid wine, with yummy flavors of pineapple custard, key lime pie, and vanilla spice, all of it pepped up with lots of rich, toasty oak. **90** *—S.H. (12/31/2005)*

Vine Cliff 2000 Bien Nacido Vineyard Chardonnay (Santa Maria Valley) $39. **94 Editors' Choice** *—S.H. (2/1/2003)*

Vine Cliff 1997 Merlot (Napa Valley) $35. **87** *—J.C. (7/1/2000)*

VINEYARD 29

Vineyard 29 1999 Cabernet Sauvignon (Napa Valley) $160. **95 Cellar Selection** *—C.S. (12/31/2002)*

VINEYARD 7&8

Vineyard 7&8 2001 Vineyard 8 Reserve Chardonnay (Spring Mountain) $45. Fresh and racy, with big, tight acidity and a stony minerality that brings the Central Coast to mind. There are underlying fruit complexities of lime zest and pineapple, with a buttercream texture and a sweet layering of toasty oak. Distinguished Chardonnay. **92** *—S.H. (8/1/2005)*

VINO CON BRIO

Vino Con Brio 2001 Pinotage (Lodi) $20. Soft, flat, and dry, with light flavors and a hot finish. **81** *—S.H. (5/1/2005)*

Vino Con Brio 2001 Goehring Vineyard Sangiovese (Lodi) $16. Smells old, tired, and vegetal, and doesn't taste much better. **81** *—S.H. (5/1/2005)*

Vino Con Brio 2001 Ripken Vineyard Viognier (Lodi) $17. **85** *—S.H. (6/1/2003)*

Vino Con Brio 1999 Matzin Old Vines Zinfandel (Lodi) $21. Clearly from a hot appellation, with raisiny flavors veering into Swiss chocolate, and a texture so rich and unctuous, it coats the palate like honey. But this wine is dry and has flair and interest. It's California's own, unlike any other in the world. **85** *—S.H. (3/1/2004)*

VINOCE

Vinoce 1999 Bordeaux Blend (Mount Veeder) $60. **92** *—J.M. (2/1/2003)*

VINUM CELLARS

Vinum Cellars 2000 CNW-Wilson Vineyards Chenin Blanc (Clarksburg) $10. **86** *(11/15/2001)*

Vinum Cellars 2000 Vista Verde Vineyard Late Harvest Gewürztraminer (San Benito County) $20. **91** *—J.M. (12/1/2002)*

Vinum Cellars 2002 Vista Verde Vineyard Syrah (San Benito County) $22. Reviewers came up with very different reads on this wine, but rated it unanimously: One found aromas of chocolate and herb, with sour plum flavors; another taster commented on the thick, syrupy aromas and flavors. All found it lean in the mouth, with soft tannins. **84** *(9/1/2005)*

Vinum Cellars 2003 Vista Verde Vineyard Viognier (San Benito County) $22. Shows Viognier's exotic side in the wildly lush tropical fruit, white peach, vanilla, and honeysuckle flavors, but stays nicely dry and balanced in acids. Nothing subtle here, just plenty of fruity flavor to set off against slightly sweet Asian-inspired fare. **85** *—S.H. (8/1/2005)*

Vinum Cellars 2002 Elephantus Blanc White Blend (California) $15. Rustic and dry, this wine has tart acids and an earthy, herbal taste with highlights of lemons. Based on Chenin Blanc, it has a touch of Viognier that adds a peach note to the finish. **84** *—S.H. (8/1/2005)*

VIRGIN

Virgin 2001 Sauvignon Blanc (Central Coast) $11. **85** *—S.H. (12/31/2003)*

VITA LUCE

Vita Luce 2002 Syrah (Paso Robles) $36. Full and intense, packed with all of the sun-warmed flavors Paso Robles can offer, ranging from savory, meaty flavors to jammy raspberry fruit. Firmly tannic on the finish; a bit rustic but flavorful and bold. **87** *(9/1/2005)*

VJB

VJB 2002 Dante Cabernet Sauvignon (Sonoma County) $36. With a bit of Sangiovese blended in, this wine is earthier, drier and tarter than VJB's "V" Cabernet, with which it was released. It has flavors of herbs and cherries, and is very dry. The extra acidity and firmer structure make it a more interesting wine, perfect for a barbecued steak. **91** *—S.H. (11/15/2005)*

VJB 1999 Dante Cabernet Sauvignon (Sonoma County) $23. 89 —*S.H. (11/15/2002)*

VJB 2001 V Private Reserve Cabernet Sauvignon (Sonoma County) $40. This smooth, dry wine shows all the hallmarks of this warm, balanced vintage. It has up front black currant, cherry marmalade, chocolate, and spicy flavors, with very soft, gentle tannins, balancing acids and a deft touch of smoky oak. **89** —*S.H. (11/15/2005)*

VJB 2002 Syrah (Alexander Valley) $28. Huge jammy fruit is the hallmark of this wine, with blackberries cascading over the palate in a mouthfilling rush. Some coffee, meaty, and hay-like notes add complexity. Tastes almost sweet, yet clamps down on the finish with drying tannins. **87** *(9/1/2005)*

VOLKER EISELE

Volker Eisele 2002 Terzetto Bordeaux Blend (Napa Valley) $75. With one-third each of Cabernet Sauvignon, Cab Franc, and Merlot, this wine hits many high notes, including the delicate, elegant fruity-oaky balance, soft, rich tannins and just-right oak. On the minus side, it's too soft. It lacks that vivacity and structure that a great wine requires. **87** —*S.H. (12/1/2005)*

Volker Eisele 2002 Cabernet Sauvignon (Napa Valley) $38. From highlands vineyards in Napa's Chiles Valley, this is a young, tough Cab. It has some dry, numbing tannins. Still, there's a heart of blackberry and currant fruit, and good acidity. Try cellaring for a couple years to soften. **88** —*S.H. (12/1/2005)*

Volker Eisele 1999 Cabernet Sauvignon (Napa Valley) $40. 92 —*J.M. (2/1/2003)*

Volker Eisele 2004 Gemini White Blend (Napa Valley) $25. The winery seems to have put more Sémillon in this year, possibly to ameliorate the feline aspects of the Sauvignon Blanc. The result is a richer, more complex wine which barrel fermentation in partially new French oak helps. The flavors include honeydew melon, figs, and pink grapefruit. **90** —*S.H. (12/1/2005)*

VON STRASSER

Von Strasser 2001 Sori Bricco Vineyard Bordeaux Blend (Diamond Mountain) $60. A luscious wine that merges Cabernet's tough, mountain personality with softer, more chocolaty notes to produce a smooth, polished wine. Complex in flavor, young in acids and tannins, it should age well through this decade, but is nice now with sturdy fare. **91** —*S.H. (2/1/2005)*

Von Strasser 2001 Cabernet Sauvignon (Diamond Mountain) $50. Fine and complex. The streamlined texture hits you first, with its balance and harmony. There's a subtle interplay of ripe black currant and cassis fruit with herbs. Dry and elegant. **88** —*S.H. (2/1/2005)*

Von Strasser 1999 Diamond Mountain Cabernet Sauvignon (Napa Valley) $50. **91** —*J.M. (6/1/2002)*

Von Strasser 2000 Estate Vineyards Cabernet Sauvignon (Diamond Mountain) $70. 91 *(8/1/2003)*

Von Strasser 1997 Chardonnay (Diamond Mountain) $36. 89 —*M.S. (10/1/1999)*

Von Strasser 2000 Rainin Vineyard Chardonnay (Diamond Mountain) $40. Almost as tight as the Aurora bottling, maybe a shade richer in pear fruit flavors. Still, it's a lean wine, a structural drink dominated by acids, alcohol, and dusty tannins. Oak provides vanilla. The finish turns tart and earthy. **87** —*S.H. (2/1/2004)*

Von Strasser 2001 Reserve Red Blend (Diamond Mountain) $100. This is a big wine for folks who like to age their Cabs. It's huge in mountain tannins now, but the underlying structure is so fine, and the cassis and cherry fruit so pure, that it's guaranteed to improve through this decade and beyond. **93** —*S.H. (2/1/2005)*

Von Strasser 1999 Sori Bricco Vineyards Red Blend (Diamond Mountain) $60. **90** —*S.H. (11/15/2002)*

Von Strasser 2000 Monhoff Vineyard Zinfandel (Diamond Mountain) $40. **88** *(8/1/2003)*

VOSS

Voss 2001 Sauvignon Blanc (Napa Valley) $18. 88 —*S.H. (9/1/2003)*

Voss 1998 Sauvignon Blanc (Napa Valley) $15. 86 *(3/1/2000)*

Voss 1997 Botrytis Sauvignon Blanc (Napa Valley) $NA. 86 —*J.C. (12/31/1999)*

Voss 1999 Shiraz (Napa Valley) $25. 90 *(11/1/2001)*

Voss 2001 Ocala Syrah (Napa Valley) $45. Compared to Voss's regular Syrah, this one is more concentrated and packed with fruit, blending mixed berries with shadings of cinnamon and black pepper. Lingers elegantly on the finish. **88** *(9/1/2005)*

Voss 2000 Botrytis White Blend (Napa Valley) $25. 95 —*S.H. (12/1/2002)*

W.H. SMITH

W.H. Smith 2002 Maritime Ridge Pinot Noir (Sonoma Coast) $45. I would have held this wine back for at least an additional year to let the grapey, cherry, raspberry, and chocolate flavors and sweet oak knit together, but cellaring it will do that. It is a very fine wine, silky and potentially complex. All the parts are there. Hold until 2005. **92** —*S.H. (11/1/2004)*

WAGNER

Wagner 2002 Fermented Dry Riesling (Finger Lakes) $10. 84 —*J.C. (8/1/2003)*

Wagner 1998 Ice Wine Vidal Blanc (Finger Lakes) $18. 81 *—J.C. (3/1/2001)*

Wagner 1999 Late Harvest Vignoles (Finger Lakes) $15. 86 *—J.C. (3/1/2001)*

WALLA WALLA

Walla Walla 2002 Cabernet Sauvignon (Columbia Valley (WA)) $35. Classy from the get-go, with an appealing mix of strawberry preserves, anise, licorice candy, smoke, and cedar. The fruit and oak are beautifully matched and laced together, and the flavors unfold with a slightly salty, mineral edge. Long, persistent and consistently interesting, right through the finishing notes of dried herb and toasted nuts. 92 *—P.G. (12/15/2005)*

Walla Walla 1997 Windrow Vineyard Cabernet Sauvignon (Washington) $32. 90 *—M.S. (4/1/2000)*

Walla Walla 2000 Merlot (Walla Walla (WA)) $25. 91 *—P.G. (9/1/2002)*

WALTER DACON

Walter Dacon 2003 C'est Syrah Beaux Syrah (Columbia Valley (WA)) $35. Spicy, smoky, toasty notes, courtesy of American oak aging, accent this wine, nose to close. It's supple and soft on the palate, with mixed berry flavors. Grows tart toward the finish, when lively acids emerge. 88 *(9/1/2005)*

Walter Dacon 2003 C'est Syrah Magnifique Syrah (Yakima Valley) $38. Spicy on the nose. The smooth, supple palate offers baked blackberry flavors that fade into a medium-long finish. One reviewer found the finish a little hard and metallic, and another lauded it for its meaty, brown-sugary flavors. 87 *(9/1/2005)*

WASHINGTON HILLS

Washington Hills 2000 Fumé Blanc (Yakima Valley) $7. 86 Best Buy *—P.G. (6/1/2002)*

Washington Hills 2001 Dry Riesling (Columbia Valley (WA)) $7. 88 *—P.G. (12/31/2002)*

Washington Hills 2002 Shiraz (Columbia Valley (WA)) $9. Another well-priced offering out of Washington's Columbia Valley, this one offering pretty caramel and coffee scents and raspberry and herb flavors. It's light in body, but creamy-textured, with a decent finish that echoes with coffee, vanilla, and ground pepper. 85 Best Buy *(9/1/2005)*

Washington Hills 1999 Syrah (Columbia Valley (WA)) $14. 83 *(10/1/2001)*

WATERBROOK

Waterbrook 1997 Cabernet Sauvignon (Columbia Valley (WA)) $22. 90 *— (6/1/2000)*

Waterbrook 1998 Chardonnay (Columbia Valley (WA)) $9. 85 *—P.G. (6/1/2000)*

Waterbrook 1997 Merlot (Columbia Valley (WA)) $20. 89 *—P.G. (6/1/2000)*

Waterbrook 1999 Mélange Red Blend (Columbia Valley (WA)) $15. 86 *—P.G. (6/1/2001)*

Waterbrook 2001 Sauvignon Blanc (Columbia Valley (WA)) $14. 88 *—P.G. (9/1/2002)*

Waterbrook 2000 Klipsun Vineyard Sauvignon Blanc (Red Mountain) $9. 88 *—P.G. (11/15/2001)*

Waterbrook 2002 Syrah (Columbia Valley (WA)) $20. There's plenty of color here, and scents of citrus and toast, but the fruit is quite tart and light, lacking any of the flesh that makes Syrah such a crowd-pleaser. This hits the palate with a crisp, clean, thin seam of flavor, balanced but quite light. 86 *—P.G. (11/15/2004)*

WATERSTONE

Waterstone 2002 Cabernet Sauvignon (Napa Valley) $20. Shows an herbaceous, earthy element that dilutes the fruity flavors, and this is compounded by tough tannins that lock in on the finish. Beef, lamb, or similar fare will coax out the underlying sweetness. 85 *—S.H. (6/1/2005)*

Waterstone 2002 Chardonnay (Carneros) $18. Citrusy, oaky, and leesy, with high acidity. This is a sleek, streamlined Chard whose lemon and green apple flavors are enriched with smoke and vanilla. 86 *—S.H. (12/31/2004)*

Waterstone 2001 Pinot Noir (Carneros) $18. Marked by the cherry, cola, and peppery spice flavors and silky tannins that characterize the Carneros, this light-bodied wine is also a good value. It's not a blockbuster, but has plenty of charm and some complexity. 86 *—S.H. (10/1/2004)*

WATTLE CREEK

Wattle Creek 1997 Cabernet Sauvignon (Sonoma County) $50. 90 *(11/1/2000)*

Wattle Creek 2000 Alexander Valley Cabernet Sauvignon (Alexander Valley) $47. Notable for the soft, velvety texture that glides over the palate and leaves behind a pleasant scour of tannin. The flavors are restrained but elegant, suggesting black currant, cherry, and sage. This balanced wine is feminine in its charm. 89 *—S.H. (8/1/2004)*

Wattle Creek 1999 Chardonnay (Sonoma County) $30. 87 *(6/1/2001)*

Wattle Creek 2004 Sauvignon Blanc (Mendocino) $15. Strong, distinctive, and powerful, this Sauvignon Blanc explodes with gooseberry, lime zest, grapefruit, vanilla, and wildflower flavors. It's light-bod-

USA

ied and very dry, with super acidity that makes it clean and vibrant. **86** *—S.H. (12/1/2005)*

Wattle Creek 2001 Sauvignon Blanc (Mendocino County) $18. **89** *(8/1/2002)*

Wattle Creek 2001 Shiraz (Alexander Valley) $25. Has some pretty dried spice notes, particularly on the finish, but also a whole lot of drying, oaky flavors backed by tart berries. Rather lean and ungenerous. **84** *(9/1/2005)*

Wattle Creek 2000 Alexander Valley Shiraz (Alexander Valley) $35. They called it Shiraz instead of Syrah, I guess, because it's a young, jammy wine with lots of forward fruit. Those blackberry and plum flavors are accompanied by some pretty fierce tannins, although the acids are soft and low. At this price, you expect more breed and finesse. **85** *—S.H. (8/1/2004)*

Wattle Creek 1999 Viognier (Sonoma County) $24. **88** *(6/1/2001)*

WATTS

Watts 1999 Old Vine Zinfandel (Lodi) $14. **90 Best Buy** *—S.H. (9/1/2002)*

WAUGH CELLARS

Waugh Cellars 2002 Indindoli Vineyard Chardonnay (Russian River Valley) $28. **86** *—S.H. (12/1/2003)*

Waugh Cellars 2002 Susy's Cuvée Sauvignon Blanc (Napa Valley) $24. **86** *—S.H. (12/15/2003)*

Waugh Cellars 2002 Zinfandel (Dry Creek Valley) $35. Overtly sweet, with Porty flavors, but clean. If this is your style, enjoy. **82** *—S.H. (2/1/2005)*

WEDELL CELLARS

Wedell Cellars 1999 Chardonnay (Edna Valley) $24. **86** *—S.H. (6/1/2003)*

Wedell Cellars 2000 Hillside Vineyard Pinot Noir (Edna Valley) $90. **92** *—S.H. (7/1/2003)*

WEDGE MOUNTAIN

Wedge Mountain 2003 Dry White Riesling (Columbia Valley (WA)) $14. Nice effort in a bone-dry style; it's immaculate, crisply fruity, with spice and citrus peel lingering through the extended finish. **88** *—P.G. (12/15/2004)*

WEINSTOCK CELLARS

Weinstock Cellars 1997 Chardonnay (California) $11. **86** *(4/1/2001)*

Weinstock Cellars 2002 Cellar Select Zinfandel (Lodi) $18. Distinctly Zinny in the wild blackberry and raspberry flavors and that briary, brambly mouthfeel, with its overtones of pepper. This is a medium-bodied wine with very soft tannins. It's dry, but there's a creamy cocoa taste on the finish. **85** *—S.H. (8/1/2005)*

WEISINGER'S OF ASHLAND

Weisinger's of Ashland 1999 Petite Pompadour Bordeaux Blend (Rogue Valley) $25. **85** *—P.G. (4/1/2002)*

Weisinger's of Ashland 1999 Chardonnay (Rogue Valley) $15. **87** *—P.G. (2/1/2002)*

Weisinger's of Ashland 1997 Merlot (Rogue Valley) $19. **83** *—P.G. (6/1/2000)*

Weisinger's of Ashland NV Mescolare-Lot 12 Red Blend (Rogue Valley) $19. **83** *—M.S. (8/1/2003)*

Weisinger's of Ashland 1999 Sémillon-Chardonnay (Rogue Valley) $15. **84** *—P.G. (8/1/2002)*

WELLINGTON

Wellington 2001 Cabernet Sauvignon (Sonoma Valley) $20. A good wine, with honest varietal flavors and easy tannins. Turns dry and rich, with up front black currant fruit flavors lightly seasoned with oak. **85** *—S.H. (5/1/2005)*

Wellington 2001 Hulen Vineyard Cabernet Sauvignon (Dry Creek Valley) $28. A very nice, well-structured Cab. It has blackberry flavors with a rich earthiness, and a unique note of blueberries; the oak is light and subtle. Finishes with a scour of rustic tannins. At its best now. **88** *—S.H. (6/1/2005)*

Wellington 2001 Mohrhardt Ridge Cabernet Sauvignon (Sonoma County) $22. Here's a plush, well-ripened Cab with forward flavors of black currants, cocoa, and oak. It has velvety tannins and finishes with an overall impression of sweetness. Best in its youth. **90** *—S.H. (5/1/2005)*

Wellington 1997 Mohrhardt Ridge Vineyard Cabernet Sauvignon (Sonoma County) $18. **88** *— (9/1/2000)*

Wellington 2002 Chardonnay (Sonoma County) $16. A good, common wine, with fruity flavors and an earthiness to it. Finishes sweet and soft. **84** *—S.H. (5/1/2005)*

Wellington 2000 Chardonnay (Sonoma Valley) $17. **86** *—S.H. (6/1/2003)*

Wellington 2000 Estate Grown Marsanne (Sonoma County) $20. **83** *—S.H. (6/1/2003)*

Wellington 2001 Estate Merlot (Sonoma Valley) $18. Lots to like here, with a chocolaty, creamy smooth mouthfeel that carries rich, ripe flavors of black cherries and cocoa. **86** *—S.H. (5/1/2005)*

Wellington 1997 Côtes de Sonoma Old Vines Red Blend (Sonoma Valley) $18. 88 *—S.H. (6/1/1999)*

Wellington 2002 Roussanne (Sonoma County) $18. As white wines go, this is tasty enough, with semisweet fruity flavors and a good balance of cream and acidity. 84 *—S.H. (5/1/2005)*

Wellington 1998 Sauvignon Blanc (Sonoma Mountain) $14. 87 *—L.W. (3/1/2000)*

Wellington 2001 Sauvignon Blanc (Sonoma Mountain) $14. 84 *—S.H. (7/1/2003)*

Wellington 2000 Syrah (Sonoma County) $20. 85 *—S.H. (12/15/2003)*

Wellington 2001 Timbervine Ranch Viognier (Russian River Valley) $20. 82 *—S.H. (6/1/2003)*

Wellington 1997 Zinfandel (Russian River Valley) $16. 87 *—L.W. (2/1/2000)*

Wellington 2000 Zinfandel (Sonoma Valley) $22. 84 *—S.H. (9/1/2003)*

WENTE

USA

Wente 2000 Cabernet Sauvignon (Livermore Valley) $13. 83 *—S.H. (12/31/2003)*

Wente 2000 Charles Wetmore Reserve Cabernet Sauvignon (Livermore Valley) $27. Wente's top offering is rather thin and herbal, and the oak overlay does little to help. There are some modest blackberry and cherry flavors, but the absence of fruit leaves the astringent tannins and alcohol front and center. 84 *—S.H. (3/1/2004)*

Wente 1998 Charles Wetmore Reserve Cabernet Sauvignon (Livermore Valley) $24. 91 Editors' Choice *—S.H. (12/1/2001)*

Wente 1996 Charles Wetmore Reserve Cabernet Sauvignon (Livermore Valley) $20. 89 *(1/1/2000)*

Wente 2001 Wetmore Reserve Cabernet Sauvignon (Livermore Valley) $25. Wente's Reserve got real ripe and sweet under its hot sun. The grapes fattened and oozed black currants and chocolate, and the winemaker put on sweet, spicy oak. This is a good, generous wine with sweetly smooth tannins, and it's soft. Drink now. 89 *—S.H. (12/31/2004)*

Wente 2001 Chardonnay (San Francisco Bay) $8. 86 *—S.H. (12/15/2003)*

Wente 2000 Riva Ranch Reserve Chardonnay (Arroyo Seco) $15. 92 Best Buy *—S.H. (12/15/2002)*

Wente 1998 Riva Ranch Reserve Chardonnay (Arroyo Seco) $15. 85 *(6/1/2000)*

Wente 2003 The Nth Degree Chardonnay (Livermore Valley) $35. Despite the best efforts of a new generation of Wentes to make Chardonnay succeed in Livermore, they can't subdue Mother Nature. It's just too hot out there. This is a decent wine, with good fruit and lots of attention to detail, but it lacks freshness and acidity. 86 *—S.H. (11/1/2005)*

Wente 2001 Merlot (Central Coast) $12. There are plenty of plummy, blackberry and black cherry flavors and it's quite dry, with soft, east tannins and a pinch of tight acidity. Turns a bit thin on the finish. A nice quaffer. 85 *—S.H. (2/1/2004)*

Wente 1997 Crane Ridge Reserve Merlot (Livermore Valley) $16. 87 *(1/1/2000)*

Wente 2000 Reliz Creek Reserve Pinot Noir (Arroyo Seco) $17. 88 *—S.H. (2/1/2003)*

Wente 1999 Sauvignon Blanc (Central Coast) $8. 86 Best Buy *—S.H. (11/15/2001)*

Wente 2002 Vineyard Selection Sauvignon Blanc (Livermore Valley) $9. One of the drier whites recently, as tart as biting into a fresh grapefruit. Cleanses the palate and is refreshing in its own right. 85 Best Buy *—S.H. (10/1/2005)*

Wente 2002 Syrah (Livermore Valley) $12. Seemed a bit confected to our tasters, with watermelon and strawberry flavors that lacked varietal typicity yet didn't lack some charm. A rather simple, fruity wine that maintains a certain appeal. 84 *(9/1/2005)*

WESTOVER VINEYARDS

Westover Vineyards 2002 Palomares Vineyards Reserve Chardonnay (San Francisco Bay) $15. Dominated by char and the dilly, sharp scent of new American oak, although beneath that is some rich apple and pear fruit. The texture is creamy, acidity high in this otherwise nice wine, except for that opening aroma. 84 *—S.H. (3/1/2004)*

WESTPORT RIVERS

Westport Rivers 1999 Estate Classic Chardonnay (Southeastern New England) $18. Connecticut does Chardonnay, combining buttered popcorn aromas with anise and toast. Lithe and lean on the palate, loaded with green apple and lemon flavors that finish tart. Another good shellfish Chard. 86 *—J.C. (1/1/2004)*

WESTREY

Westrey 2002 Pinot Noir (Willamette Valley) $19. Lots of almost tropical fruit flavors here, forward and braced with citrusy acidity. Very drinkable, but definitely a lightweight. 86 *(11/1/2004)*

Westrey 1999 Croft-Bailey Pinot Noir (Willamette Valley) $22. 86 *—S.H. (8/1/2002)*

Westrey 1997 Reserve Pinot Noir (Willamette Valley) $27. 88 *(10/1/1999)*

Westrey 1999 Temperance Hill Pinot Noir (Willamette Valley) $22. 87 *—S.H. (8/1/2002)*

WHALER

Whaler 1999 Flagship Zinfandel (Mendocino) $NA. 84 *—S.H. (11/1/2002)*

WHETSTONE

Whetstone 2002 Savoy Vineyard Pinot Noir (Anderson Valley) $46. Simple and enjoyable for its supple texture, tangy spices, and cherry and herb flavors that finish a little sweet. Decant to let some sulfur blow off. 84 *(11/1/2004)*

WHIDBEY ISLAND WINERY

Whidbey Island Winery 1999 Merlot (Yakima Valley) $15. 85 *—P.G. (2/1/2002)*

Whidbey Island Winery 2002 Syrah (Yakima Valley) $19. Worth buying by the case if you can find it (only 270 cases were produced), as this wine is underpriced relative to its quality. Blackberry fruit is accented by hints of dried spices, pepper, licorice, mineral, and smoke. Picks up vanilla notes on the lush, captivating palate, then finishes long. 90 Editors' Choice *(9/1/2005)*

WHITCRAFT

Whitcraft 2000 French Camp Vineyard Lagrein (San Luis Obispo County) $20. 89 Editors' Choice *—S.H. (8/1/2003)*

WHITE CRANE WINERY

White Crane Winery 2001 Folkendt Vineyard Cabernet Sauvignon (Livermore Valley) $48. 83 *—S.H. (11/15/2003)*

WHITE HAWK

White Hawk 2000 Syrah (Santa Maria Valley) $30. A dark-hued wine, brimming with black cherry, cola, and spice aromas. On the palate, it's richly textured, with bitter herb and charry smoke tones followed by chocolate, blackberry, and sage flavors. Tannins are a little rustic, but on the whole, this wine serves up plenty of hedonistic pleasure. A first release. 90 *—J.M. (4/1/2004)*

WHITE HERON

White Heron 2002 Roussanne (Columbia Valley (WA)) $15. Bigger and more robust than Viognier, Roussanne is the "other" white Rhône grape. A fragrant, flavorful, lush, plush, soft, and seductive wine that's ready to rock right now. 88 *—P.G. (11/15/2004)*

WHITE OAK

White Oak 1999 Maripose Cabernet Sauvignon (Napa Valley) $22. 83 *—S.H. (9/12/2002)*

White Oak 2001 Chardonnay (Russian River Valley) $20. 86 *—S.H. (12/31/2003)*

White Oak 1999 Chardonnay (Russian River Valley) $17. 90 *—S.H. (5/1/2002)*

White Oak 2001 Merlot (Napa Valley) $24. Balanced, soft, and feminine, with generous black currant, cassis, and olive flavors. Feels plush on the palate, with an easy but complex structure. Tannins kick in on the finish. Best now through 2006. 90 *—S.H. (6/1/2004)*

White Oak 2000 Merlot (Napa Valley) $24. 82 *—S.H. (11/15/2002)*

White Oak 2004 Sauvignon Blanc (Russian River Valley) $15. This Sauvignon is very New Zealandy in gooseberry, green grass, alfalfa, and citrus fruit. It's also totally dry, with good, crisp acids. It has a complex, layered creaminess that lifts it above the ordinary. 88 *—S.H. (12/1/2005)*

White Oak 2002 Sauvignon Blanc (Napa Valley) $13. 87 *—S.H. (12/1/2003)*

White Oak 2001 20th Vintage Sauvignon Blanc (North Coast) $12. 83 *—S.H. (9/1/2003)*

White Oak 2002 Syrah (Napa Valley) $25. A lovely wine that reveals everything in the first sip. Black currant s, smoked meat, milk chocolate and vanilla mingle together in soft tannins and easy acids. Finishes long and sweet. 87 *—S.H. (12/31/2004)*

White Oak 2000 Zinfandel (Alexander Valley) $24. 88 *—S.H. (11/1/2002)*

WHITE ROSE

White Rose 2002 Pinot Noir (Yamhill County) $65. This is bright and clear in the glass; it shines like a ruby. Light, with sweet/tart candy cherry fruit flavors, it tastes of cherry Lifesavers and tart cranberry. Fun, pretty, and solidly fruity, it is very appealing. But it seems a bit insubstantial for the price. 87 *—P.G. (2/1/2005)*

WHITE TRUCK

White Truck 2004 White Blend (California) $9. Here's an easy-drinking, dry, fruity white wine made from Sauvignon Blanc, Pinot Grigio, Viognier, and Chardonnay. From Cline Cellars. 85 Best Buy *—S.H. (12/31/2005)*

WHITEHALL LANE

Whitehall Lane 2001 Cabernet Sauvignon (Napa Valley) $40. So ripe in black currant and mocha fruit, so rich in sweet tannins, so well-structured. It's an impeccable Cabernet that's beautiful now, but should hold through the decade. **93 Editors' Choice** *—S.H. (10/1/2004)*

Whitehall Lane 1997 Leonardini Vyd Cabernet Sauvignon (Napa Valley) $75. 90 *(11/1/2000)*

Whitehall Lane 2001 Reserve Cabernet Sauvignon (Napa Valley) $70. A sensational Cab that exhibits power and opulence in the ripe black currant , cherry, cocoa, and new oak flavors, yet is subtlely balanced and harmonious. Showcases preternaturally gorgeous tannins, soft and sweet. The more you sip, the greater the impression. **95 Cellar Selection** *—S.H. (4/1/2005)*

Whitehall Lane 1998 Chardonnay (Carneros) $20. 89 *(6/1/2000)*

Whitehall Lane 1997 Merlot (Napa Valley) $24. 87 *—L.W. (12/31/1999)*

Whitehall Lane 1998 Sauvignon Blanc (Rutherford) $15. 90 *—S.H. (2/1/2000)*

Whitehall Lane 2003 Sauvignon Blanc (Napa Valley) $15. Displays intensity in the citrus, melon, and fig flavors that are so rich and concentrated, they're almost sweet. This is a crisp, dry wine, with a spicy finish. **87** *—S.H. (12/15/2004)*

WHITFORD

Whitford 2001 Haynes Vineyard Chardonnay (Napa Valley) $19. 91 Editors' Choice *—S.H. (12/1/2003)*

Whitford 2001 Pinot Noir (Napa Valley) $22. From the theoretically cooler southern part of the valley, but still a region too warm to preserve Pinot's delicacy. Not a bad wine at all, with its pretty flavors of cherry pie, rich overlay of oak, and silky mouthfeel. But from a varietal point of view, rather hot and baked, with a stewed note throughout. **85** *—S.H. (2/1/2004)*

WHITFORD CELLARS

Whitford Cellars 2002 Haynes Vineyard Chardonnay (Napa Valley) $20. Clean and sleek, a rather austere Chard whose flavors veer toward green apples and figs, with good acidity. Finishes with some earthiness. **85** *—S.H. (10/1/2005)*

WHITMAN CELLARS

Whitman Cellars 2002 Cabernet Sauvignon (Walla Walla (WA)) $36. It's not always easy making a pure varietal, as this is. Without the addition of Merlot and Cab Franc, as in Whitman's other 2002 reds, this has a tighter, sleeker profile, with tart flavors of plum, rhubarb, and sour cherry. **85** *—P.G. (12/15/2005)*

Whitman Cellars 1999 Seven Hills Cabernet Sauvignon (Walla Walla (WA)) $40. 86 *—P.G. (6/1/2002)*

Whitman Cellars 2001 Merlot (Walla Walla (WA)) $32. Scents of new oak jump out, with pretty, plummy fruit behind. Right now the wine seems a bit oaky, but time may smooth it out. The finish is tight and chewy. **86** *—P.G. (5/1/2004)*

Whitman Cellars 2002 Narcissa Red Blend (Walla Walla (WA)) $24. There's plenty of toast for lovers of new oak, with cinnamon and mocha giving it an assertive come-on like a vinous Frappucino. The core fruit is soft and round, mixing cherries and plums in with all that toast and chocolate. Pleasant and smooth; best for near-term drinking. **86** *—P.G. (12/15/2005)*

Whitman Cellars 2002 Syrah (Walla Walla (WA)) $28. Tight and slightly rubbery when first opened, but soon the spicy notes of chocolate, coffee, and cinnamon come through over tasty cherry fruit. Styled more like a Merlot than a Syrah, it's a smooth, nicely balanced, and really tasty effort. **88** *—P.G. (12/15/2004)*

WIDGEON HILLS

Widgeon Hills 2002 HRP Ranch Area 51 Syrah (Yakima Valley) $22. Despite the name, there's nothing alien about this wine—it just delivers briary, herbal notes layered over more classic blackberry and plum flavors. Broad and soft, so drink now. **86** *(9/1/2005)*

WILD BUNCH

Wild Bunch 2003 Red Wine Red Blend (California) $10. An inexpensive house wine to buy by the case. A blend of Zin, Syrah, and Barbera, it showcases the richness of each variety, and is dry and interesting. A great vin ordinaire from Montevina, which is owned by the Trinchero family. **86 Best Buy** *—S.H. (12/31/2005)*

WILD COYOTE

Wild Coyote 2001 Li-senshes Zinfandel (Paso Robles) $14. 84 *(11/1/2003)*

WILD HORSE

Wild Horse 1997 Cabernet Sauvignon (Paso Robles) $19. 85 *—S.H. (2/1/2000)*

Wild Horse 1999 Cabernet Sauvignon (Paso Robles) $20. 83 *—S.H. (11/15/2002)*

Wild Horse 2004 Chardonnay (Central Coast) $18. Ripe, user-friendly Chardonnay. Vanilla, toast, and pear aromas and flavors delivered with a plump, easy to swallow mouthfeel enlivened by just a touch of citrusy zip on the finish. **86** *(10/1/2005)*

Wild Horse 2002 Chardonnay (Central Coast) $16. A bit on the thin side, but you'll find some decent peach and apple flavors, and the requisite dollop of smoky oak. Turns watery on the finish. Seems pricy for what you get. **84** *—S.H. (4/1/2004)*

Wild Horse 1997 Merlot (Paso Robles) $18. 83 *—S.H. (12/31/1999)*

USA

Wild Horse 2002 Merlot (Paso Robles) $20. Soft in acidity and light in color, with briary, coffee, and plum flavors. Gritty tannins on the finish. **83** *—S.H. (5/1/2005)*

Wild Horse 1999 Merlot (Paso Robles) $18. 87 *—S.H. (9/1/2003)*

Wild Horse 1997 Pinot Noir (Central Coast) $20. 87 *—J.C. (5/1/2000)*

Wild Horse 2000 Pinot Noir (Central Coast) $20. 86 *(10/1/2002)*

Wild Horse 2002 Syrah (Paso Robles) $18. Smells like good Syrah should, with complex scents of espresso, meat, and even a gamy edge layered over fresh blackberries. It's medium-bodied, crisper than the Cabernet, with just a hint of black pepper on the finish. Drink now. **88** *(10/1/2005)*

Wild Horse 2002 James Berry Vineyard Syrah (Paso Robles) $38. Big and firmly structured, this inky Syrah comes from a series of terraces at this justly renowned vineyard. Cinnamon, toast, and coffee notes from new oak complement bold blackberry fruit. Hold 3–5 years. **90** *(10/1/2005)*

Wild Horse 2004 Viognier (Central Coast) $18. This plump, medium-bodied wine is made in a fruit-forward, easily accessible style. On the nose you get hints of sweet corn, white pepper, and nasturtium blossoms, while the palate rounds out with flavors of pear, apricot, and a bit of dusty minerality. **87** *(10/1/2005)*

Wild Horse 2002 Viognier (Central Coast) $16. Easy drinking and tasty with flavors of peaches, oranges, and vanilla. Balances the richness out with crisp acidity and a light touch of oak. This is a nice cocktail-style wine. **85** *—S.H. (11/15/2004)*

Wild Horse 2001 Zinfandel (Paso Robles) $16. 85 *(11/1/2003)*

WILDHURST

Wildhurst 1997 Chardonnay (Clear Lake) $11. 85 *—M.S. (10/1/1999)*

Wildhurst 1997 Private Reserve Chardonnay (Sonoma County) $18. 80 *(6/1/2000)*

Wildhurst 2002 Reserve Merlot (Lake County) $16. Here's a Merlot that lives up to the moniker of the soft Cab. It's gentle in the mouth, with polished flavors of cherries and chocolate. Easy to drink, with some real complexity. **87** *—S.H. (12/15/2004)*

Wildhurst 2001 Sauvignon Blanc (Clear Lake) $11. 86 *—S.H. (7/1/2003)*

Wildhurst 2004 Reserve Sauvignon Blanc (Lake County) $11. I love the aroma on this wine, all figgy-citrusy and so clean. It leads you to expect a bone-dry, intense wine, and that's pretty much what you get. Clean and acidic, with focused lemon and lime flavors. **86 Best Buy** *—S.H. (10/1/2005)*

Wildhurst 1998 Catfish Vineyard Zinfandel (Clear Lake) $14. 88 *—P.G. (3/1/2001)*

WILLAKENZIE

WillaKenzie 1999 Estelle Chardonnay (Willamette Valley) $25. 89 *—P.G. (8/1/2002)*

WillaKenzie 2004 Pinot Blanc (Willamette Valley) $18. The Pinot Blanc from this property is one of the best in Oregon, though not as big and brawny overall as their Pinot Gris. Stone fruits and green apple flavors mix nicely in a tart but not sour wine that shows a bit of cinnamon/baking spice also. **87** *—P.G. (11/15/2005)*

WillaKenzie 1997 Pinot Grigio (Willamette Valley) $15. 87 *(8/1/1999)*

WillaKenzie 2001 Pinot Gris (Oregon) $20. 92 Editors' Choice *—P.G. (8/1/2002)*

WillaKenzie 1999 Pinot Gris (Oregon) $16. 90 *—P.G. (9/1/2000)*

WillaKenzie 1998 Pinot Meunier (Oregon) $20. 88 *— (9/1/2000)*

WillaKenzie 2002 Aliette Pinot Noir (Willamette Valley) $36. This is very fruity, with a sweet, grapy, Kool-Aid character. Candied and sweet up front, it shows substantial, dry, tea-like tannins as it resolves. **86** *(11/1/2004)*

WillaKenzie 2000 Kiana Pinot Noir (Willamette Valley) $35. 88 *(10/1/2002)*

WillaKenzie 1997 Pierre Leon Pinot Noir (Willamette Valley) $30. 87 *(10/1/1999)*

WILLAMETTE VALLEY VINEYARDS

Willamette Valley Vineyards 2000 Chardonnay (Willamette Valley) $10. 88 Best Buy *—P.G. (12/1/2003)*

Willamette Valley Vineyards 2000 Late Harvest Ehrenfelser (Willamette Valley) $20. 88 *—J.M. (12/1/2002)*

Willamette Valley Vineyards 2004 Pinot Gris (Oregon) $15. Pinot Gris has never been more popular, and this user-friendly, soft, and spicy style is bursting with varietal flavors of fresh cut pears. The splash of acid keeps the flavors on their toes (and dancing on your tongue) through a smooth, lingering finish. Great with sandwiches, salmon, salads, and savory dips. **89** *—P.G. (8/1/2005)*

Willamette Valley Vineyards 2001 Pinot Gris (Willamette Valley) $13. 82 *—M.S. (8/1/2003)*

Willamette Valley Vineyards 2000 Founder's Reserve Pinot Gris (Willamette Valley) $18. 88 *—P.G. (4/1/2002)*

Willamette Valley Vineyards 1999 Pinot Noir (Oregon) $17. 84 *(10/1/2002)*

Willamette Valley Vineyards 2002 Estate Pinot Noir (Willamette Valley) $30. More than a hint of green bean in the nose. This wine has a vegetal streak, but recovers long enough to show some pleasant flavors of pomegranate and light red cherry. **84** *(11/1/2004)*

Willamette Valley Vineyards 1999 Estate Vyd Pinot Noir (Willamette Valley) $45. 85 *—P.G. (4/1/2002)*

Willamette Valley Vineyards 2002 Freedom Hill Vineyard Pinot Noir (Willamette Valley) $45. Controversial, some tasters found it elegant and classical; others thought it was reductive and bitter. The fruit is clean and varietal, and the wine is crisp and acidic, though the finish is tough and tannic. 85 *(11/1/2004)*

Willamette Valley Vineyards 1998 Freedom Hill Vineyard Pinot Noir (Willamette Valley) $44. 91 *—M.M. (11/1/2001)*

Willamette Valley Vineyards 1999 Hoodview Vineyard Pinot Noir (Oregon) $45. 86 *—P.G. (4/1/2002)*

Willamette Valley Vineyards 2000 Joe Dobbes Signature Cuvée Pinot Noir (Willamette Valley) $42. 88 *(10/1/2002)*

Willamette Valley Vineyards 2000 Karina Vineyard Pinot Noir (Willamette Valley) $31. 83 *(10/1/2002)*

Willamette Valley Vineyards 1999 Karina Vyd Pinot Noir (Willamette Valley) $45. 90 *—P.G. (4/1/2002)*

Willamette Valley Vineyards 1998 O'Connor Vineyard Pinot Noir (Willamette Valley) $39. 88 *—M.S. (9/1/2003)*

Willamette Valley Vineyards 2000 Whole Cluster Pinot Noir (Oregon) $12. 86 Best Buy *(10/1/2002)*

Willamette Valley Vineyards 2001 Riesling (Oregon) $8. 88 *—P.G. (8/1/2003)*

Willamette Valley Vineyards 2001 Viognier (Rogue Valley) $28. 87 *—P.G. (12/1/2003)*

USA

WILLIAM HILL

William Hill 1997 Cabernet Sauvignon (Napa Valley) $20. 86 *(3/1/2000)*

William Hill 1996 Cabernet Sauvignon (Napa Valley) $16. 88 *(11/1/1999)*

William Hill 2001 Cabernet Sauvignon (Napa Valley) $22. This lovely Cab is soft and lush in blackberry and cherry fruit, with a pretty veneer of smoky oak. It has enough structure and finesse to accompany good food. Really satisfies for its sheer drinkability. 89 *—S.H. (10/1/2004)*

William Hill 1999 Cabernet Sauvignon (Napa Valley) $22. 86 *—S.H. (9/12/2002)*

William Hill 2001 Reserve Cabernet Sauvignon (Napa Valley) $36. Released about a year later than the regular '01, this is still a pretty tannic Cab. But it's rich enough now to have with a good steak, and in fact a beef dish with a wine reduction sauce could be perfect. The oak is smoky-sweet and filled with vanilla, the overall impression high-class. 92 *—S.H. (11/15/2005)*

William Hill 1998 Reserve Cabernet Sauvignon (Napa Valley) $38. 85 *—S.H. (11/15/2002)*

William Hill 1995 Reserve Cabernet Sauvignon (Napa Valley) $27. 91 *(11/1/1999)*

William Hill 1998 Chardonnay (Napa Valley) $15. 86 *(6/1/2000)*

William Hill 1997 Chardonnay (Napa Valley) $14. 88 *(11/1/1999)*

William Hill 2002 Chardonnay (Napa Valley) $15. What a perfect cocktail wine. It's so refreshing in tropical fruit, buttercream, and sweet oak. But the spicy complexity also calls for very rich fare, such as broiled lobster. 89 *—S.H. (10/1/2004)*

William Hill 2000 Chardonnay (Napa Valley) $15. 88 *—J.M. (5/1/2002)*

William Hill 2003 Reserve Chardonnay (Napa Valley) $20. The regular Chard was released last spring. The Reserve, out now, is quite a better wine. It's rich, oaky, and creamy, with a great big burst of tropical fruit and peach flavors and scads of sweet cinnamon and vanilla on the finish. 88 *—S.H. (12/31/2005)*

William Hill 2000 Reserve Chardonnay (Napa Valley) $23. 90 *—S.H. (12/15/2002)*

William Hill 1997 Reserve Chardonnay (Napa Valley) $20. 90 *(11/1/1999)*

William Hill 1996 Merlot (Napa Valley) $18. 89 *(11/1/1999)*

William Hill 2000 Merlot (Napa Valley) $21. Rich and balanced, an easy-drinking Merlot that packs in plenty of plum, blackberry, and dried herb flavors. Goes down smooth due to the soft tannins, but there's decent structure and a spicy finish. 87 *—S.H. (2/1/2004)*

William Hill 1998 Merlot (Napa Valley) $22. 83 *—S.H. (8/1/2001)*

WILLIAMS SELYEM

Williams Selyem 2001 Allen Vineyard Chardonnay (Russian River Valley) $48. The aroma changes with every sniff, ranging from ripe apple to sweet pear, smoky, clove-accented oak, butterscotch, Asian spice, Juicy Fruit gum, the works. It's enormous, a long hangtime wine of high alcohol and massive extraction. Hard to describe the nuance and complexity. 94 *—S.H. (2/1/2004)*

Williams Selyem 2000 Hawk Hill Vineyard Chardonnay (Russian River Valley) $44. 92 *—J.M. (2/1/2003)*

Williams Selyem 2000 Heintz Vineyard Chardonnay (Russian River Valley) $40. 93 *—J.M. (2/1/2003)*

Williams Selyem 2003 Vista Verde Vineyard Late Harvest Gewürztraminer (San Benito County) $35. Winemaster Bob Cabral has crafted a dessert wine that's sweet, balanced, and refined, in no small part due to excellent acidity, which keeps you coming back. The flavors of apricots, honey and spices are delicious, and finish long and clean. 91 *—S.H. (11/1/2005)*

Williams Selyem 2000 Vista Verde Vineyard Late Harvest Gewürztraminer (San Benito County) $32. **93** *—J.M. (9/1/2003)*

Williams Selyem 2003 Pinot Noir (Sonoma County) $32. Although the immediate impact of this wine is obvious in the soft silk and satin mouthfeel and cherry, cola, mocha, and spice flavors, it's not a simple wine. The palate understands the complexity, and wants more...and more...and more. **90** *—S.H. (11/1/2005)*

Williams Selyem 2003 Pinot Noir (Central Coast) $29. This textbook regional Pinot Noir displays a deft touch in the delicacy and silky finesse of the body, while holding nothing back in the way of flavor. Cherries, cola, sweet leather, and dusty spices come together in a dry, smooth finish. **88** *—S.H. (11/1/2005)*

Williams Selyem 2002 Pinot Noir (Sonoma Coast) $35. Fruity and simple aromas of orange popsicle, cherry Lifesaver, and mocha lead to a thick, rather soft wine, with ripe, heavy flavors. Might turn into something more interesting in a few years. **86** *(11/1/2004)*

Williams Selyem 2002 Pinot Noir (Russian River Valley) $39. Smoky, cedary oak stars here, and the wine is closed at first. After airing, it shows chocolate, leather, and raisiny notes, with some complexity. Needs short-term cellaring to show its best. **87** *(11/1/2004)*

Williams Selyem 2000 Pinot Noir (Sonoma Coast) $34. **88** *—J.M. (2/1/2003)*

Williams Selyem 2000 Pinot Noir (Russian River Valley) $39. **87** *—S.H. (2/1/2003)*

Williams Selyem 2002 Allen Vineyard Pinot Noir (Russian River Valley) $72. Somewhat of a disappointment for all tasters. Opens with smoky, new oak aromas and a young, grapy mèlange of blackberries and chocolate. Rich in tannins, with a chunky mouthfeel. Hard to really find nuance in it now, but try aging and see what develops. **85** *(11/1/2004)*

Williams Selyem 2000 Allen Vineyard Pinot Noir (Russian River Valley) $NA. Alcohol 14.2%. Still pretty tannic and youthful, with perky acids, and not showing at all its age. Big in fruit, with cherries and blueberries. Oak adds its thing, and there's a cocoa finish. No sign at all of raisins or over-ripeness. Beautiful now, and should hold throughout the decade. **92** *—S.H. (6/1/2005)*

Williams Selyem 1995 Allen Vineyard Pinot Noir (Russian River Valley) $NA. 13.7% alcohol. Really past its prime. Showing its age in the dull, cherry, vanilla, and oak aromas and flat, tart mouthfeel. Lovers of old Pinot will find it exciting. **84** *—S.H. (6/1/2005)*

Williams Selyem 2001 Coastlands Vineyard Pinot Noir (Sonoma Coast) $59. From a chillier part of the appellation, a wine that struggled to get ripe. Smells of mint and menthol, with cedar, Asian spice, and coffee nuances. In the mouth, it's bone dry. Not a fruit-driven Pinot, but interesting for the interplay of acids and tannins. **87** *—S.H. (5/1/2004)*

Williams Selyem 2002 Ferrington Vineyard Pinot Noir (Anderson Valley) $59. Tasters found consensus that this wine, while ripe, failed to inspire, beyond offering pleasant cherry, mocha, spice, and oak flavors. It's heavy, alcoholic, and tannic, but might soften with a few years of age. **84** *(11/1/2004)*

Williams Selyem 2002 Flax Vineyard Pinot Noir (Russian River Valley) $49. Another Williams Selyem wine that tasters had differing opinions about. Several liked its rich array of black cherry, spicy plum, and smoky oak, and overall balance and lushness. But one reviewer found it flabby and soft, with some residual sugar. You decide. **90** *(11/1/2004)*

Williams Selyem 2001 Hirsch Vineyard Pinot Noir (Sonoma Coast) $59. From a very warm vintage, an enormously ripe, fruity wine. The dramatic aromas include smoky oak, dried autumn leaves, and herbs, cherry, cranberry, and dried porcini, with similar flavors. Fabulously interesting and complex, a rich, sweetly earthy wine whose tannins and weight promise even better things to come. **92** *—S.H. (5/1/2004)*

Williams Selyem 1997 Olivet Lane Pinot Noir (Russian River Valley) $45. **90** *(10/1/1999)*

Williams Selyem 2002 Precious Mountain Vineyard Pinot Noir (Sonoma Coast) $80. A controversial wine among the tasters. Some found it seriously rich and deep in fruit, while others called it simple and hot in alcohol. It's certainly dark and brooding now. Berry-cherry flavors and lots of oak, with a lush, soft mouthfeel. Aging is a gamble. **87** *(11/1/2004)*

Williams Selyem 1999 Rochioli Riverblock Pinot Noir (Russian River Valley) $60. **88** *(10/1/2002)*

Williams Selyem 2001 Rochioli Riverblock Vineyard Pinot Noir (Russian River Valley) $64. The '99 was a joy and so is this stunning wine. It has a perfume of violets, blackberries, dried autumn leaves, succulent raspberry tart, licorice, coffee, and all sorts of other wholesome scents. The flavors, which are similar, drink complete and complex, at once subtle and compelling. Absolutely addictive in its interesting complexities, and undoubtedly will improve with a few years in the bottle. **93** *—S.H. (5/1/2004)*

Williams Selyem 2002 Vista Verde Vineyard Pinot Noir (San Benito County) $49. A big, fruity wine, bursting with chocolate fudge, black cherry, and vanilla flavors, and made vibrant with keen acidity. Feels plush and warming in the mouth, and could develop for a few more years. **90** *(11/1/2004)*

Williams Selyem 2000 Vista Verde Vineyard Pinot Noir (San Benito County) $32. **90** *—J.M. (7/1/2003)*

Williams Selyem 2001 Weir Vineyard Pinot Noir (Yorkville Highlands) $48. Some will like the distinctive coffee, cola, menthol, cherry candy, and mineral flavors, and the rather heavy, thick mouthfeel of this tannic wine. It should soften up with a few years in the bottle. **86** *—S.H. (5/1/2004)*

Williams Selyem 2003 Westside Road Neighbors Pinot Noir (Russian River Valley) $62. Compared to the winery's regular Russian River bottling, this is considerably more tannic. Yet it doesn't take long for the spiced plum pudding, cherry compote, black raspberry, cola, and smoky oak flavors to kick in. Fantastic now, and should hold for the remainder of this decade. 93 *—S.H. (11/1/2005)*

Williams Selyem 2001 Zinfandel (Russian River Valley) $25. 90 *(11/1/2003)*

Williams Selyem 2003 Bacigalupi Vineyard Zinfandel (Russian River Valley) $42. I criticized Williams Selyem's Feeney Vineyard Zin for overly high alcohol, at 15.8 percent. This one is an inexcusable 16.3 percent. I wish someone would explain to me why it's necessary to harvest at these levels, unless you're making Port. 80 *—S.H. (11/1/2005)*

Williams Selyem 2002 Feeney Vineyard Zinfandel (Russian River Valley) $38. The downside of this wine is its enormous alcohol, nearly 16 percent. That's the price you pay for a dry wine with gargantuan flavors. Black currants, cherry pie, tobacco, pepper, bitter chocolate, and dill only begin to describe the palate. Yet the wine is balanced and even elegant. Truly an only-in-California experience. 91 *—S.H. (10/1/2004)*

WILLIAMSON

Williamson 2003 Amourette Chardonnay (Dry Creek Valley) $28. A touch of dust, dried sage, clover, and dried tobacco accompanies the peach and apricot flavors in this wine. The finish is semisweet, and a bit soft. 84 *—S.H. (12/1/2005)*

WILLIS HALL

Willis Hall 2003 Stone Tree Reserve Syrah (Columbia Valley (WA)) $35. Divergent opinions on this wine, but it's mostly academic, as only 25 cases were produced. One taster found it smooth and creamy in the mouth, with building layers of berry and spice flavors; the other found it weedy, stewy, and watery. If you try a bottle, let us know what you think. 86 *(9/1/2005)*

WILLOW CREST

Willow Crest 1999 Cabernet Franc (Yakima Valley) $15. 88 *—P.G. (6/1/2002)*

Willow Crest 2000 Pinot Gris (Yakima Valley) $8. 87 Best Buy *—P.G. (6/1/2002)*

Willow Crest 1998 Sparkling Syrah (Yakima Valley) $15. 84 *—M.M. (12/1/2001)*

WILLOWBROOK CELLARS

WillowBrook Cellars 2001 Owl Ridge Vineyards Chardonnay (Russian River Valley) $28. 88 *—S.H. (7/1/2003)*

WILRIDGE

Wilridge 1998 Klipsun Vineyards Cabernet Sauvignon (Yakima Valley) $29. 90 *—P.G. (6/1/2001)*

Wilridge 2000 Klipsun Vineyards Merlot (Red Mountain) $NA. Hard and tough, this wine shows a core of black cherry with streaks of mineral and metal, but the tannins are in the way. Some additional bottle time will be a big help. 86 *—P.G. (9/1/2004)*

Wilridge 1998 Spring Valley Vineyards Merlot (Walla Walla (WA)) $29. 90 *—P.G. (6/1/2002)*

WILSON

Wilson 1999 Sydney Vineyard Cabernet Sauvignon (Dry Creek Valley) $28. 87 *—S.H. (11/15/2003)*

Wilson 2001 Isabella Late Harvest Chenin Blanc (Clarksburg) $16. 86 *—J.M. (12/1/2002)*

Wilson 2001 Petite Sirah (Clarksburg) $10. 82 *(4/1/2003)*

Wilson 2000 Carl's Vineyard Zinfandel (Dry Creek Valley) $25. 84 *—S.H. (9/1/2003)*

WINCHESTER

Winchester 2000 Syrah (Paso Robles) $30. 91 *—S.H. (12/1/2002)*

WINDMILL

Windmill 2003 Syrah (Lodi) $12. Jammy and soft, with cherry and vanilla flavors that hang just this side of flabby. Picks up attractive brown sugar and caramel notes on the tangy finish. 84 *(9/1/2005)*

WINDSOR

Windsor 1999 Private Reserve Cabernet Sauvignon (Mendocino) $17. 86 *—S.H. (11/15/2002)*

Windsor 1997 Barrel-Fermented Private Reser Chardonnay (Russian River Valley) $17. 83 *(6/1/2000)*

Windsor 2000 Middle Ridge Vineyard Private Reserve Fumé Blanc (Mendocino County) $13. 86 *—S.H. (12/15/2001)*

Windsor 1999 40th Anniversary Reserve Merlot (Dry Creek Valley) $40. 84 *(11/15/2002)*

Windsor 1998 Signature Series Merlot (Sonoma County) $25. 86 *—S.H. (6/1/2001)*

Windsor 1998 Toni Stockhausen Signature Series Merlot (Sonoma County) $25. 87 *—S.H. (12/1/2001)*

Windsor 1999 Petite Sirah (Mendocino County) $13. 83 *(4/1/2003)*

USA

Windsor 1999 Private Reserve Pinot Noir (Sonoma County) $17. 85 *(10/1/2002)*

Windsor 2000 Private Reserve Sémillon (Mendocino) $15. 86 *—S.H. (12/15/2001)*

Windsor 1997 Zinfandel (Sonoma County) $18. 86 *—P.G. (3/1/2001)*

Windsor 1997 Private Reserve Zinfandel (Mendocino) $15. 85 *—P.G. (3/1/2001)*

Windsor 1999 Toni Stockhausen Signature Series Zinfandel (Mendocino County) $17. 90 Best Buy *—S.H. (12/15/2001)*

WINDWARD VINEYARD

Windward Vineyard 2000 Monopole Pinot Noir (Paso Robles) $30. 85 *(10/1/2002)*

WINDY OAKS

Windy Oaks 1999 Pinot Noir (Santa Cruz County) $39. 86 *—S.H. (12/1/2003)*

Windy Oaks 2001 Schultze Family Vineyard Estate Reserve Pinot Noir (Santa Cruz Mountains) $36. A deft and suave Pinot, racy and elegant, all silk and satin on the palate. Yet there's nothing shy about the assertive flavors. Cherries and black raspberries flood the mouth, encased in rich acids and a vivid coat of oak. 91 Editors' Choice *—S.H. (11/1/2005)*

WINE BLOCK

Wine Block 2002 Cabernet Sauvignon (California) $10. At the equivalent of five bucks a bottle, this is a super value in Cabernet. You'll find real richness in the ripe black currant, chocolate, and sweet oak flavors, and in the smooth texture. It's also wonderfully dry and balanced. 86 Best Buy *—S.H. (12/1/2005)*

Wine Block 2002 Merlot (California) $10. I like this wine a lot for the great fruit. It's just jam-packed with ripe cherries, black raspberries, sweet blackberries, coffee, and cocoa flavors that are rich in fruity essence, yet dry, soft, and balanced. This is a good value in a red table wine. 86 Best Buy *—S.H. (12/1/2005)*

WINEGLASS CELLARS

Wineglass Cellars 2000 Cabernet Sauvignon (Yakima Valley) $20. Tangy and pleasantly herbal, this has light red berry and tomato leaf scents, set against firm Washington fruit. Good feel to the midpalate; it's made in a drink-now style, but strong enough to hang tough with grilled meats. 87 *—P.G. (9/1/2004)*

Wineglass Cellars 1999 Cabernet Sauvignon (Yakima Valley) $21. A late release '99, this displays the tough, chewy tannins of that excellent vintage, and has the dry, tight, concentrated flavors of a good unclassified Bordeaux. Air it out and some nice spice starts to emerge. This is a fine effort in a good year. 88 *—P.G. (9/1/2004)*

Wineglass Cellars 2000 Elerding Vineyard Cabernet Sauvignon (Yakima Valley) $45. This wine shows thinnish flavors of pomegranate, cranberry, and rhubarb, despite the hefty 14.5% alcohol. The fruit has not quite met the oak on an even playing field, and the whole seems less than the sum of its parts. 87 *—P.G. (9/1/2004)*

Wineglass Cellars 1999 Elerding Vineyard Cabernet Sauvignon (Yakima Valley) $45. 92 *—P.G. (6/1/2002)*

Wineglass Cellars 2000 Reserve Cabernet Sauvignon (Yakima Valley) $28. This is a very well-made, sleekly styled wine, with classy mixed red fruits leading into a sweet, sculpted midpalate. The fruit is perfectly ripe, and the oak is a seasoning, not a lumber yard. A textbook example of Washington Cabernet. 90 *—P.G. (9/1/2004)*

Wineglass Cellars 2003 Chardonnay (Yakima Valley) $13. Macintosh apple, whiskey barrel, and some volatile high notes set this wine in motion. The midpalate fruit is crisp and tangy, with a citrusy snap to the finish. 85 *—P.G. (9/1/2004)*

Wineglass Cellars 1999 Chardonnay (Yakima Valley) $13. 88 Best Buy *—P.G. (6/1/2001)*

Wineglass Cellars 2001 Merlot (Yakima Valley) $22. Dark, ripe, and vinous, this is a flavorful wine with plump, pruney fruit above oak-driven flavors of roasted nuts and milk chocolate. Tasty, near-term drinking. 88 *—P.G. (9/1/2004)*

Wineglass Cellars 1999 Merlot (Yakima Valley) $22. 90 *—P.G. (2/1/2002)*

Wineglass Cellars 1998 DuBrul Vineyard Merlot (Yakima Valley) $30. 91 *—P.G. (6/1/2001)*

Wineglass Cellars 1999 Reserve Merlot (Yakima Valley) $35. 88 *—P.G. (6/1/2002)*

Wineglass Cellars 2000 Rich Harvest Red Blend (Yakima Valley) $50. Tannic and firm, this has some pretty cherry fruit lurking behind the stiff tannins. It's still tight, despite the bottle time, but it's well made. Nice oak flavors of hazelnut, spice, and sandalwood liven up the finish. 89 *—P.G. (9/1/2004)*

Wineglass Cellars NV Batch 00 Zinfandel (America) $19. From Lodi grapes, this hi-test (15.5% alcohol) Zin has plenty of sweet grapey, cherry fruit. There's a liquorous flavor from the alcohol and possibly the barrels, and some green tannins. This one will appeal to those who like Amador Zins; it's built to drink now rather than later. 86 *—P.G. (1/1/2004)*

WINESMITH

WineSmith 2002 Student Vineyard Faux Chablis Chardonnay (Napa Valley) $30. What they seem to mean by "faux Chablis" is searingly high acidity, little or no oak, rasping dryness and early-picked, green fruit that's supposed to be minerally. Not a generous wine. 84 *—S.H. (11/1/2005)*

WINTER'S HILL

Winter's Hill 2000 Pinot Gris (Willamette Valley) $12. 87 —*P.G. (2/1/2002)*

Winter's Hill 2000 Pinot Noir (Willamette Valley) $25. 88 —*P.G. (12/1/2003)*

Winter's Hill 2002 Reserve Pinot Noir (Willamette Valley) $29. Tight and resiny, it hints at pine needles and mint, along with plenty of vanilla-laced oak. The toasted, oaky component seems over-matched to the thin fruit. **85** *(11/1/2004)*

WITNESS TREE

Witness Tree 1997 Estate Pinot Noir (Willamette Valley) $34. 85 *(11/15/1999)*

Witness Tree 1997 Vintage Select Pinot Noir (Willamette Valley) $18. 90 *(11/15/1999)*

WOLFF

Wolff 2002 Old Vines Chardonnay (Edna Valley) $19. Balanced and harmonious, and has extra clarity due to its lovely acidity. There's an array of fruity flavor ranging from ripe green apples to candied grapefruit and mango, while oak adds vanilla and toast. Finishes long and spicy. **90** —*S.H. (9/1/2004)*

Wolff 2001 Dijon Clones Selection Pinot Noir (Edna Valley) $25. 87 —*S.H. (7/1/2003)*

Wolff 2001 Syrah (Edna Valley) $18. 88 —*S.H. (6/1/2003)*

WÖLFFER

Wölffer 1998 Cabernet Franc (The Hamptons, Long Island) $25. 88 —*J.C. (4/1/2001)*

Wölffer 1995 Brut Champagne Blend (The Hamptons, Long Island) $30. 87 —*J.C. (4/1/2001)*

Wölffer 2000 Estate Selection Chardonnay (The Hamptons, Long Island) $27. 84 —*J.C. (10/2/2004)*

Wölffer 2003 Late Harvest Chardonnay (Long Island) $35. 87 —*J.C. (10/2/2004)*

Wölffer 1999 Reserve Chardonnay (The Hamptons, Long Island) $19. A disappointing effort from this normally reliable producer. The tropical fruit is dominated by buttered popcorn, caramel, and charred oak. Feels almost oily in the mouth but without the substance to sustain it. **83** —*J.C. (1/1/2004)*

Wölffer 1998 Merlot (The Hamptons, Long Island) $20. 87 —*J.C. (4/1/2001)*

Wölffer 1999 Estate Selection Merlot (The Hamptons, Long Island) $33. 88 —*J.M. (1/1/2003)*

Wölffer 2000 La Ferme Martin Merlot (The Hamptons, Long Island) $14. 83 —*J.C. (10/2/2004)*

Wölffer 2002 Pinot Noir (The Hamptons, Long Island) $50. Light in color, and turning orange at the rim, this soft, gentle wine has pretty flavors of cherries, mocha, and cola. It's very delicate, with a good balance of tannins to acids. **88** *(11/1/2004)*

Wölffer 1999 Rosé Blend (Long Island) $11. 84 —*J.C. (4/1/2001)*

Wölffer 1998 Cuvée Christian Brut Sparkling Blend (The Hamptons, Long Island) $27. 86 —*M.S. (6/1/2003)*

WOODBRIDGE

Woodbridge 1997 Barbera (Lodi) $12. 88 Best Buy —*S.H. (11/15/2001)*

Woodbridge 2002 Cabernet Sauvignon (California) $8. Lean, although clean, with earthy flavors and dry, smooth tannins. Fine for those big block parties where value counts. **83** —*S.H. (7/1/2005)*

Woodbridge 1998 Cabernet Sauvignon (California) $8. 82 —*S.H. (5/1/2001)*

Woodbridge 2001 Red Dirt Ridge Cabernet Sauvignon (Lodi) $11. Clean, country-style and not bad for a Cabernet of this price. Marked by good flavors of blackberries and herbs and dry tannins. This full-bodied wine has real quality and is a very good value. **84** —*S.H. (10/1/2004)*

Woodbridge 1999 Twin Oaks Cabernet Sauvignon (California) $12. 85 —*S.H. (12/31/2002)*

Woodbridge 2003 Chardonnay (California) $8. A workhorse Chard, fruity and simple, with an artificially oaky, slightly sweet taste. **83** —*S.H. (7/1/2005)*

Woodbridge 1999 Chardonnay (California) $9. 83 —*S.H. (5/1/2001)*

Woodbridge 2002 California Chardonnay (California) $8. You'll find modest apple and peach flavors in this easy-drinking wine. It has a nice creamy texture, although it's a bit watery on the finish. **83** —*S.H. (9/1/2004)*

Woodbridge 2001 Select Vineyard Series Ghost Oak Chardonnay (California) $11. 84 *(11/15/2003)*

Woodbridge 2003 Johannisberg Riesling (California) $7. Fruity and clean, with flowery, peach, and apple flavors and good acidity. This is a wine that will appeal to people seeking something white that's comfortable and affordable. **84 Best Buy** —*S.H. (12/1/2004)*

Woodbridge 1997 Merlot (California) $8. 80 —*L.W. (12/31/1999)*

Woodbridge 2000 Merlot (California) $9. 83 —*S.H. (12/31/2002)*

Woodbridge 1998 Merlot (California) $8. 83 *—S.H. (9/1/2003)*

Woodbridge 2000 Clay Hollow (PT) Merlot (California) $11. 84 *(11/15/2003)*

Woodbridge 1998 Winemaker's Selection Muscat (California) $12. 89 Best Buy *—S.H. (12/1/2003)*

Woodbridge 2002 Pinot Grigio (California) $8. 83 *—S.H. (12/1/2003)*

Woodbridge 1997 Portacinco Port (Lodi) $20. Made from traditional Port varieties, Woodbridge's Portacinco is always a rich, sweet dessert wine, satisfying in fruit and body. You'll find dark chocolate, white chocolate, cassis, and cherry flavors, with good balancing acidity. **88 Editors' Choice** *—S.H. (7/1/2005)*

Woodbridge 1994 Portacinco Port (California) $20. 90 *—S.H. (12/31/2000)*

Woodbridge 2001 Sauvignon Blanc (California) $6. 84 Best Buy *—S.H. (7/1/2003)*

Woodbridge 1999 Sauvignon Blanc (California) $7. 83 *—S.H. (11/15/2000)*

Woodbridge 2000 Syrah (California) $9. 88 Best Buy *—S.H. (12/1/2002)*

Woodbridge 1997 Zinfandel (California) $7. 82 *—S.H. (2/1/2000)*

Woodbridge 2001 Zinfandel (California) $7. 82 *(11/1/2003)*

Woodbridge 1999 Zinfandel (California) $6. 84 *—S.H. (9/12/2002)*

Woodbridge 2000 Select Vineyard Series-Old Vine-Fish Net Creek Zinfandel (Lodi) $11. 86 *(11/15/2003)*

Woodbridge 2002 White Zinfandel (California) $5. Simple and crisp, with decent flavors of raspberries and a peppery tinge. Fundamentally a dry wine, but there's a honeyed richness that will make it ideal for a hot summer day at the beach. Stock up the cooler! **84** *—S.H. (3/1/2004)*

WOODEN VALLEY

Wooden Valley 1999 Suisun Valley Cabernet Sauvignon (Solano County) $12. 86 *—S.H. (11/15/2003)*

WOODENHEAD

Woodenhead 2000 Elk Prairie Pinot Noir (California) $42. 85 *(10/1/2002)*

Woodenhead 2001 Martinelli Road Vineyard Old Vine Zinfandel (Russian River Valley) $30. 87 *(11/1/2003)*

WOODINVILLE

Woodinville Wine Company 2002 Syrah (Washington) $28. Very juicy, fruity, and showing a lot of tangy citrus flavors. This is a fruit-loaded wine, pleasing and forward, but lacking much stuffing or follow-through. **87** *—P.G. (11/15/2004)*

WOODWARD CANYON

Woodward Canyon 2000 Estate Red Bordeaux Blend (Walla Walla (WA)) $55. 91 *—P.G. (9/1/2003)*

Woodward Canyon 2001 Artist Series Cabernet Sauvignon (Columbia Valley (WA)) $42. A big, tannic Cabernet that flexes its cassis and blackberry muscles and cloaks itself in layers of tar and smoky oak. Hints of leaf and earth emerge with time, but this is very young and compact. A serious wine that needs substantial decanting and/or cellar time. **91** *—P.G. (7/1/2004)*

Woodward Canyon 1998 Artist Series #7 Cabernet Sauvignon (Washington) $37. 93 *—P.G. (11/15/2000)*

Woodward Canyon 1999 Klipsun Vineyard Cabernet Sauvignon (Columbia Valley (WA)) $45. 89 *—P.G. (6/1/2002)*

Woodward Canyon 2000 Old Vines Cabernet Sauvignon (Columbia Valley (WA)) $67. 92 *—P.G. (9/1/2003)*

Woodward Canyon 1998 Old Vines Cabernet Sauvignon (Columbia Valley (WA)) $60. 94 Cellar Selection *—P.G. (6/1/2001)*

Woodward Canyon 2002 Chardonnay (Columbia Valley (WA)) $33. Mixed, roasted nuts set up the layered aromas. Following are layers of stone fruits, spicy and textured, and fresh, ballpark roasted peanut flavors. Good penetration and a nice balance that captures the flavors of oak without making the wine oaky. **91** *—P.G. (7/1/2004)*

Woodward Canyon 2000 Chardonnay (Columbia Valley (WA)) $33. 88 *—P.G. (7/1/2002)*

Woodward Canyon 1998 Unfined/Unfiltered Estate Chardonnay (Walla Walla (WA)) $40. 93 *—P.G. (6/1/2001)*

Woodward Canyon 2000 Merlot (Columbia Valley (WA)) $38. 88 *—P.G. (9/1/2002)*

Woodward Canyon 1999 Charbonneau Merlot-Cabernet Sauvignon (Walla Walla (WA)) $50. 87 *—P.G. (6/1/2002)*

Woodward Canyon 2002 Dry White Riesling (Columbia Valley (WA)) $22. This limited-production Riesling is a tasting room favorite, with ripe but not heavy flavors of fresh-cut pear and apple extending into a long, textured, and thoroughly delicious finish. Clearly one of the top Rieslings in a state known for them. **89** *—P.G. (5/1/2004)*

Woodward Canyon 2003 Estate Sauvignon Blanc (Walla Walla (WA)) $24. Edgeless and hard to quantify. The nose smells like peach juice and aged cheese, while the palate offers very little heft or zest. A flat wine without much pulse. **81** *(7/1/2005)*

Woodward Canyon 2002 Syrah (Columbia Valley (WA)) $34. Lusciously creamy and supple for Syrah—although it could be criticized on precisely those grounds. Caramel and toffee from oak, but there's also plenty of meaty, blackberry fruit and a long finish. **86** *(9/1/2005)*

Woodward Canyon 1999 Charbonneau Blanc White Blend (Walla Walla (WA)) $28. **90** *—P.G. (6/1/2001)*

WOOLDRIDGE CREEK

Wooldridge Creek 1999 Merlot (Applegate Valley) $16. **85** *—P.G. (8/1/2002)*

Wooldridge Creek 1999 Syrah (Applegate Valley) $16. **84** *—P.G. (8/1/2002)*

Wooldridge Creek 1999 Viognier (Rogue Valley) $20. **83** *—P.G. (4/1/2002)*

WORK

Work 2002 Sauvignon Blanc (Napa Valley) $23. **89** *—S.H. (12/1/2003)*

WORKHORSE

Workhorse 2000 Syrah (Dry Creek Valley) $15. A rather earthy and closed wine, and pretty tannic, too. There are some blackberry flavors but the mouthfeel is tough, and the finish turns astringent. May benefit from five years of aging. **82** *—S.H. (3/1/2004)*

WORTHY

Worthy 2002 Sophia's Cuvée Red Blend (Napa Valley) $29. This Bordeaux blend, made with all five red grapes, is fruity in cherry, cocoa, blackberry, and oak flavors, with smooth, sophisticated tannins. Made solidly in the new style of softness, ultra-ripeness, and highish alcohol. **88** *—S.H. (10/1/2005)*

WYVERN

Wyvern 1998 Cabernet Sauvignon (Yakima Valley) $25. **90** *—S.H. (6/1/2002)*

X

X 2002 Cabernet Sauvignon (Napa Valley) $22. A perfectly fine Napa Cab that makes all the right moves, without necessarily inspiring. It's dry and ripe in currant fruit, with firm, sweet tannins and good oak. **85** *—S.H. (10/1/2005)*

X 2000 Cabernet Sauvignon (Napa Valley) $20. **81** *—S.H. (11/15/2002)*

X 2002 Chardonnay (Carneros) $19. This oaky wine has vanilla and buttered toast aromas, but it's pretty watery in the mouth. There are some peach and apple flavors. **84** *—S.H. (10/1/2004)*

X 2000 Chardonnay (Russian River Valley) $15. **90 Best Buy** *—S.H. (12/31/2003)*

X 2002 Merlot (Napa Valley) $25. Oaky and full-bodied, with earthy-cherry flavors, this is a dry wine that has lots of hard-edged tannins. It's rustic in its impact, and could soften and sweeten with a few years of age. **86** *—S.H. (8/1/2005)*

X 2003 Truchard Vineyard Pinot Noir (Carneros) $22. Dark, full-bodied, and rich in black currants and oak, this is more like a Syrah than Pinot, except for the silky tannins. Exemplifies the ripe, high-alcohol style so prevalent in the North Coast. It's a good wine, but atypical for a Pinot. **88** *—S.H. (10/1/2005)*

X 2002 Red X Red Blend (California) $13. Rustic and country-style, with rugged tannins and a harsh mouth feel, but saved by rich berry flavors. Fine with pizza, burgers. Syrah, Merlot, Cab Franc, Cab Sauvignon. **84** *—S.H. (4/1/2005)*

X 2002 Sauvignon Blanc (Lake County) $15. **89** *—S.H. (12/15/2003)*

X 2003 Eutenier Sylar Vineyard Sauvignon Blanc (Lake County) $17. There are some good lime, fig, and melon flavors here, but they're really watered down. Definitely needs more concentration, especially at this price. **84** *—S.H. (3/1/2005)*

YAKIMA CELLARS

Yakima Cellars 2002 Elephant Mountain Vineyard Syrah (Yakima Valley) $20. This wine caused a big rift among our panelists. One appreciated the wine's meaty, blackberry, coffee-like flavors. A dissenter, however, found roasted-fruit aromas and charred flavors that were detractions. Could age 3–5 years. **87** *(9/1/2005)*

YAMHILL VALLEY

Yamhill Valley 1998 Pinot Blanc (Oregon) $14. **85** *—L.W. (12/31/1999)*

Yamhill Valley 1999 Reserve Pinot Noir (Willamette Valley) $30. **87** *(10/1/2002)*

Yamhill Valley 1997 Reserve Pinot Noir (Willamette Valley) $29. **83** *(10/1/1999)*

YN

YN 2000 White Blend (California) $4. **83** *—S.H. (6/1/2002)*

YOAKIM BRIDGE

Yoakim Bridge 2002 Zinfandel (Dry Creek Valley) $30. This richly textured Zin comes from old vines off the estate, in the warmer, upper part of the valley. It's ripe, with suggestions of raisins, but it's not over-ripe or hot. In fact, it's a chewy wine long in cherries and pepper. **88** —*S.H. (11/1/2005)*

Yoakim Bridge 1999 Zinfandel (Dry Creek Valley) $25. **90** —*S.H. (12/15/2001)*

YORK MOUNTAIN WINERY

York Mountain Winery 2002 Pinot Noir (Paso Robles) $25. Here's a nice, easy Pinot made in an accessible style. It's soft and fruity, with cherry and herb flavors that finish with a touch of oak. **84** —*S.H. (2/1/2005)*

York Mountain Winery 2001 Pinot Noir (San Luis Obispo County) $15. Pale in color and tart with acids, this user-friendly wine has flavors of cola, rhubarb, and cherries and a dollop of oak. It's dry and silky in the mouth. **84** —*S.H. (2/1/2005)*

YORKVILLE CELLARS

Yorkville Cellars 1997 Richard the Lion-Heart Bordeaux Blend (Mendocino County) $25. **90** —*S.H. (6/1/2002)*

Yorkville Cellars 1998 Cabernet Franc (Mendocino) $17. **84** —*S.H. (5/1/2002)*

Yorkville Cellars 1999 Cabernet Sauvignon (Yorkville Highlands) $19. **85** —*S.H. (5/1/2003)*

Yorkville Cellars 2001 Rennie Vineyard Cabernet Sauvignon (Yorkville Highlands) $22. From a Mendocino winery that makes steady but sure progress in Bordeaux varieties, a rich, ripe wine, with big flavors of blackberries and chocolate. **88** —*S.H. (10/1/2004)*

Yorkville Cellars 1997 Malbec (Yorkville Highlands) $17. **89** —*S.H. (9/1/2002)*

Yorkville Cellars 1997 Merlot (Mendocino) $18. **85** —*S.H. (6/1/2002)*

Yorkville Cellars 1998 Petite Verdot (Mendocino County) $17. **84** —*S.H. (5/1/2002)*

Yorkville Cellars 2001 Sauvignon Blanc (Yorkville Highlands) $13. **88** —*S.H. (9/1/2003)*

Yorkville Cellars 1999 Eleanor of Aquitaine Sauvignon Blanc (Mendocino) $17. **84** —*S.H. (5/1/2002)*

Z-52

Z-52 2002 Agnes' Vineyard Old Vines Zinfandel (Lodi) $16. Drink this country-style Zin with grilled meats or poultry. It's dry and fruity, with blackberry and spice flavors. Finishes a bit sweet, which suggests a rich, tomato-based BBQ sauce with a little brown sugar or molasses. **84** —*S.H. (12/1/2005)*

Z-52 2003 Clockspring Vineyard Old Vines Zinfandel (Amador County) $20. This single-vineyard wine showcases the ripeness and smoothness of Amador Zin at its best. It has briary, wild berry flavors, with a roasted coffee and chocolate finish. It's a rustic wine, which is a huge part of its appeal. **88** —*S.H. (12/1/2005)*

ZACA MESA

Zaca Mesa 1998 Chardonnay (Santa Barbara County) $15. **88** *(6/1/2000)*

Zaca Mesa 1997 Zaca Vineyards Chardonnay (Santa Barbara County) $13. **85** —*S.H. (7/1/1999)*

Zaca Mesa 2001 Z-Gris Red Blend (Santa Ynez Valley) $9. **85** —*S.H. (9/1/2003)*

Zaca Mesa 2000 Z Cuvée Rhône Red Blend (Santa Barbara County) $16. **87** —*S.H. (11/15/2002)*

Zaca Mesa 2000 Z Gris Rhône Red Blend (Santa Barbara County) $9. **82** —*J.F. (8/1/2001)*

Zaca Mesa 1997 Z-Gris Rosé Rhône Red Blend (Santa Barbara County) $8. **89 Best Buy** —*S.H. (6/1/1999)*

Zaca Mesa 2003 Estate Roussanne (Santa Ynez Valley) $25. There were some unripe, even vegetal notes in the bottle I opened, and the wine smacked mainly of oak, although the taste of canned peaches turned up on the finish. **82** —*S.H. (10/1/2005)*

Zaca Mesa 2002 Syrah (Santa Ynez Valley) $20. A bit lean and constricted on the midpalate, but there is some lovely blackberry fruit, so maybe it just needs a little time to blossom. Hints of black pepper and coffee add complexity, while the finish turns tart. **86** *(9/1/2005)*

Zaca Mesa 2002 Black Bear Block Syrah (Santa Ynez Valley) $50. Densely packed and tightly wound, this richly tannic and thickly textured Syrah needs plenty of time to come around. Scents of flavors of blackberry, hickory smoke, and cured meats are enticing, but hard to get at right now. See if cellaring this bear several years will tame it. **87** *(9/1/2005)*

Zaca Mesa 1999 Black Bear Block Syrah (Santa Ynez Valley) $45. **92** —*S.H. (2/1/2003)*

Zaca Mesa 2002 Eight Barrel Syrah (Santa Ynez Valley) $35. Mint-garnished raspberries and blackberries mingle with dusty earth on the nose of this attractive Syrah. Delivers more red fruit on the palate, where it feels smooth and silky. A lighter style, but pretty. **85** *(9/1/2005)*

Zaca Mesa 2001 The Mesa O & N Syrah (Santa Ynez Valley) $40. It's fascinating to taste this side by side with Zaca Mesa's Black Bear Block bottling. This one is certainly drier and a lot more tannic, and requires more patience. From entry to finish it's a bit numbing, but those cassis, blackberry, cherry, and coffee flavors, plus the overall balance, bode well. Hold until 2007. **92** —*S.H. (8/1/2005)*

Zaca Mesa 2004 Viognier (Santa Ynez Valley) $15. There's not much oak on this wine, but there is quite a bit of lees, which gives it a rich, creamy mouthfeel. The flavors are ripe and juicy, suggesting pineapples and lime zest, peaches, and tangy tangerines. The wine is nicely dry. **87** *—S.H. (12/31/2005)*

Zaca Mesa 2003 Estate Viognier (Santa Ynez Valley) $15. Very dry, and a little tart in acids, with spice, peach, and pear flavors. There's a creamy texture that makes it a pleasant sipper. **85** *—S.H. (10/1/2005)*

ZAHTILA

Zahtila 2002 Cabernet Sauvignon (Napa Valley) $33. There's an orchard of fruit in this dry, smooth wine. The flavors range from blackberries and plums to cherries, with slightly bitter coffee notes. The tannins and acids stick out a bit now. Try holding until mid-2006. **86** *—S.H. (12/1/2005)*

Zahtila 2000 Beckstoffer Georges III Cabernet Sauvignon (Rutherford) $40. The blackberry, currant, and sweet plum flavors are saturated with an overlay of oak that adds vanilla and smoke to an already overweight wine. Tannins are soft, and the wine feels like velvet gliding across the palate. Hold until 2006. **86** *—S.H. (2/1/2004)*

Zahtila 2001 Beckstoffer Vineyard Georges III Cabernet Sauvignon (Rutherford) $48. Too young now, but there's every indication of longterm potential, from the balance and harmony to the dense, chewy nucleus of potent cherry, cassis, and mocha flavors. This brilliant young wine should begin to be drinkable in a few years, and will age through 2020. **93** *—S.H. (10/1/2004)*

ZD

ZD 2002 Cabernet Sauvignon (Napa Valley) $42. Shows good varietal character in the full-bodied mouthfeel and well-ripened cherry and blackberry fruit. The oak is subtle, even a little rustic. Thoroughly dry, with some gritty tannins to negotiate. Drink now. **86** *—S.H. (8/1/2005)*

ZD 1999 Cabernet Sauvignon (Napa Valley) $42. **88** *(3/1/2003)*

ZD 1999 Reserve Cabernet Sauvignon (Napa Valley) $100. **91** *(3/1/2003)*

ZD 2002 Reserve Chardonnay (Napa Valley) $48. This is quite a dry Chard, rustic and earthy and even a bit austere, although the dryness is relieved both by pronounced oak and an underlying current of pear and peach fruit that shows up in the finish. **87** *—S.H. (8/1/2005)*

ZD 1998 Reserve Chardonnay (Napa Valley) $48. **92** *(7/1/2001)*

ZD 2002 Pinot Noir (Carneros) $30. Ripe cherry, chocolate, vanilla, and herb flavors swarm out of the glass, leading to a medium-bodied mouthfeel with cherry and herb flavors. Feels soft and gentle in the mouth, balanced and smooth. **88** *(11/1/2004)*

ZD 2002 Reserve Pinot Noir (Carneros) $48. Smoke, herb, cherry, and tomato notes intermingle in the aroma of this tasty wine. It's a bit one-dimensional, but creamy and ripe in fruit, with firm tannins on the finish. **87** *(11/1/2004)*

ZD NV Abacus IV Red Blend (Napa Valley) $300. **93** *(3/1/2003)*

ZEALEAR

Zealear 2002 Bolero Syrah (California) $20. This is a black, velvety soft, dense wine. It is dry, with interesting plum, blackberry, leather, and cocoa flavors. It's not very concentrated, but offers pleasure. **85** *—S.H. (5/1/2005)*

ZEFINA

Zefina 2001 Serience Red Wine Red Blend (Columbia Valley (WA)) $35. Unusual mix includes Grenache, Syrah, Mourvèdre, and Counoise. Forward, ripe aromas of berries, cherries, and plums atop layers of tobacco and malted chocolate. Soft and accessible, but somewhat shapeless. **87** *—P.G. (1/1/2004)*

Zefina 2001 Zinfandel (Columbia Valley (WA)) $25. Homegrown Zin is catching on in Washington, and this captures the style nicely. Claret-like, with bright berries and juniper spice highlight a taut, fresh, tangy wine. **88** *—P.G. (1/1/2004)*

ZENAIDA

Zenaida Cellars 2001 Sangiovese (Paso Robles) $21. **81** *—S.H. (9/1/2003)*

Zenaida Cellars 1999 Syrah (Paso Robles) $20. **91** *—S.H. (11/15/2001)*

ZINGARO

Zingaro 2000 Zinfandel (Mendocino) $13. **84** *—S.H. (9/1/2003)*

ZUCCA

Zucca 2003 Tesoro Red Wine Red Blend (Sierra Foothills) $15. This Zin-Syrah blend is a bit raisiny and Porty. Finishes sweet. **83** *—S.H. (2/1/2005)*

USA

Glossary

Acidity: A naturally occurring component of every wine; the level of perceived sharpness; a key element to a wine's longevity; a leading determinant of balance.

Ageworthy: Wines whose general characteristics make it likely that they will improve with age.

Alcohol: The end product of fermentation; technically ethyl alcohol resulting from the interaction of natural grape sugars and yeast; generally above 12.5 percent in dry table wines.

Alsace: A highly regarded wine region in eastern France renowned for dry and sweet wines made from Riesling, Gewürztraminer, Pinot Blanc, Pinot Gris, and others.

Amarone: A succulent higher-alcohol red wine hailing from the Veneto region in northern Italy; made primarily from Corvina grapes dried on racks before pressing.

AOC: *Appellation d'Origine Contrôlée*, a French term for a denominated, governed wine region, such as Margaux or Nuits-St.-Georges.

Aroma: A scent that's a component of the bouquet or nose; i.e. cherry is an aromatic component of a fruity bouquet.

AVA: American Viticultural Area; a denominated American wine region approved by the Bureau of Alcohol, Tobacco, and Firearms.

Bacchus: The Roman god of wine, known as Dionysus in ancient Greece; a hybrid white grape from Germany.

Balance: The level of harmony between acidity, tannins, fruit, oak, and other elements in a wine; a perceived quality that is more individual than scientific.

Barrel Fermented: A process by which wine (usually white) is fermented in oak barrels rather than in stainless steel tanks; a richer, creamier, oakier style of wine.

Barrique: French for "barrel," generally a barrel of 225 liters.

Beaujolais: A juicy, flavorful red wine made from Gamay grapes grown in the region of the same name.

Beaujolais Nouveau: The first Beaujolais wine of the harvest; its annual release date is the third Thursday in November.

Blanc de Blancs: The name for Champagne made entirely from Chardonnay grapes.

Blanc de Noirs: The name for Champagne made entirely from red grapes, either Pinot Noir or Pinot Meunier, or both.

Blend: The process whereby two or more grape varieties are combined after separate fermentation; common blends include Côtes de Rhône and red and white Bordeaux.

Blush: A wine made from red grapes but which appears pink or salmon in color because the grape skins were removed from the fermenting juice before more color could be imparted; more commonly referred to as Rosé.

Bodega: Spanish for winery; literally "room where barrels are stored."

Body: The impression of weight on one's palate; "light," "medium," and "full" are common body qualifiers.

Bordeaux: A city on the Garonne River in southwest France; a large wine-producing region with more than a dozen subregions; a red wine made mostly from Cabernet Sauvignon, Merlot, and Cabernet Franc; a white wine made from Sauvignon Blanc and Sémillon.

Botrytis Cinerea: (also Noble Rot) A beneficial mold that causes grapes to shrivel and sugars to concentrate, resulting in sweet, unctuous wines; common botrytis wines include Sauternes, Tokay, and German Beerenauslese.

Bouquet: The sum of a wine's aromas; how a wine smells as a whole; a key determinant of quality.

Breathe: The process of letting a wine open up via the introduction of air.

Brettanomyces: An undesirable yeast that reeks of sweaty saddle scents.

Brix: A scale used to measure the level of sugar in unfermented grapes. Multiplying brix by 0.55 will yield a wine's future alcohol level.

Brut: A French term used to describe the driest Champagnes.

Burgundy: A prominent French wine region stretching from Chablis in the north to Lyons in the south; Pinot Noir is the grape for red Burgundy, Chardonnay for white.

Cabernet Franc: A red grape common to Bordeaux; characteristics include an herbal, leafy flavor and a soft, fleshy texture.

Cabernet Sauvignon: A powerful, tannic red grape of noble heritage; the base grape for many red Bordeaux and most of the best red wines from California, Washington, Chile, and South Africa; capable of aging for decades.

Cap: Grape solids like pits, skins, and stems that rise to the top of a tank during fermentation; what gives red wines color, tannins, and weight.

Carbonic Maceration: A wine-making process in which whole grapes are sealed in a fermenter with carbon dioxide and left to ferment without yeast and grape crushing.

Cava: Spanish for "cellar," but also a Spanish sparkling wine made in the traditional Champagne style from Xarello, Macabeo, and Parellada grapes.

Chablis: A town and wine region east of Paris known for steely, minerally Chardonnay.

Champagne: A denominated region northeast of Paris in which Chardonnay, Pinot Noir, and Pinot Meunier grapes are made into sparkling wine.

Chaptalization: The process of adding sugar to fermenting grapes in order to increase alcohol.

Chardonnay: Arguably the best and most widely planted white wine grape in the world.

Château: French for "castle;" an estate with its own vineyards.

Chenin Blanc: A white grape common in the Loire Valley of France.

Chianti: A scenic, hilly section of Tuscany known for fruity red wines made mostly from Sangiovese grapes.

Claret: An English name for red Bordeaux.

Clos: Pronounced "Cloh," this French word once applied only to vineyards surrounded by walls.

Color: A key determinant of a wine's age and quality; white wines grow darker in color as they age while red wines turn brownish orange.

Cooperative: A winery owned jointly by multiple grape growers.

Corked: A wine with musty, mushroomy aromas and flavors resulting from a cork tainted by TCA (trichloroanisol).

Crianza: A Spanish term for a red wine that has been aged in oak barrels for at least one year.

Cru: A French term for ranking a wine's inherent quality, i.e. Cru Bourgeois, Cru Classé, Premier Cru, and Grand Cru.

Decant: The process of transferring wine from a bottle to another holding vessel. The purpose is generally to aerate a young wine or to separate an older wine from any sediment.

Denominación de Origen: Spanish for appellation of origin; like the French AOC or Italian DOC.

Denominazione di Origine Controllata: Italian for a controlled wine region; similar to the French AOC or Spanish DO.

Disgorge: The process by which final sediments are removed from traditionally made sparkling wines prior to the adding of the dosage.

Dosage: A sweetened spirit added at the very end to Champagne and other traditionally made sparkling wines. It determines whether a wine is brut, extra dry, dry, or semisweet.

Douro: A river in Portugal as well as the wine region famous for producing Port wines.

Dry: A wine containing no more than 0.2 percent unfermented sugar.

Earthy: A term used to describe aromas and flavors that have a certain soil-like quality.

Enology: The science of wine production; an enologist is a professional winemaker; an enophile is someone who enjoys wine.

Fermentation: The process by which sugar is transformed into alcohol; how grape juice interacts with yeast to become wine.

Filtration: The process by which wine is clarified before bottling.

Fining: Part of the clarification process whereby elements are added to the wine, i.e. egg whites, in order to capture solids prior to filtration.

Fortified Wine: A wine in which brandy is introduced during fermentation; sugars and sweetness are high due to the suspended fermentation.

Fumé Blanc: A name created by Robert Mondavi to describe dry Sauvignon Blanc.

Gamay: A red grape exceedingly popular in the Beaujolais region of France.

Gewürztraminer: A sweet and spicy white grape popular in eastern France, Germany, Austria, northern Italy, and California.

Graft: A vineyard technique in which the bud-producing part of a grapevine is attached to an existing root.

Gran Reserva: A Spanish term used for wines that are aged in wood and bottles for at least five years prior to release.

Grand Cru: French for "great growth;" the very best vineyards.

Green: A term used to describe underripe, vegetal flavors in a wine.

Grenache: A hearty, productive red grape popular in southern France as well as in Spain, where it is called Garnacha.

Grüner Veltliner: A white grape popular in Austria that makes lean, fruity, racy wines.

Haut: A French word meaning "high." It applies to quality as well as altitude.

Hectare: A metric measure equal to 10,000 square meters or 2.47 acres.

Hectoliter: A metric measure equal to 100 liters or 26.4 gallons.

Herbaceous: An aroma or flavor similar to green; often an indication of underripe grapes or fruit grown in a cool climate.

Hollow: A term used to describe a wine that doesn't have depth or body.

Hybrid: The genetic crossing of two or more grape types; common hybrids include Müller-Thurgau and Bacchus.

Ice Wine: From the German *eiswein*, this is a wine made from frozen grapes; Germany, Austria, and Canada are leading ice wine producers.

Jeroboam: An oversized bottle equal to six regular 750 ml bottles.

Kabinett: A German term for a wine of quality; usually the driest of Germany's best Rieslings.

Kosher: A wine made according to strict Jewish rules under rabbinical supervision.

Labrusca: Grape types native to North America, such as Concord and

Catawba.

Late Harvest: A term used to describe dessert wines made from grapes left on the vines for an extra long period, often until botrytis has set in.

Lees: Heavy sediment left in the barrel by fermenting wines; a combination of spent yeast cells and grape solids.

Legs: A term used to describe how wine sticks to the inside of a wineglass after drinking or swirling.

Library Wines: Wines kept by the bottler as a reference of previous wines bottled.

Loire: A river in central France as well as a wine region famous for Chenin Blanc, Sauvignon Blanc, and Cabernet Franc.

Maceration: The process of allowing grape juice and skins to ferment together, thereby imparting color, tannins, and aromas.

Madeira: A fortified wine that has been made on a Portuguese island off the coast of Morocco since the fifteenth century.

Maderized: Stemming from the word Madeira, this term means oxidization in a hot environment.

Magnum: A bottle equal to two regular 750 ml bottles.

Malbec: A hearty red grape of French origin now exceedingly popular in Argentina.

Malolactic Fermentation: A secondary fermentation, often occurring in barrels, whereby harsher malic acid is converted into creamier lactic acid.

Médoc: A section of Bordeaux on the west bank of the Gironde Estuary known for great red wines; Margaux, St. Estèphe, and Pauillac are three leading AOCs in the Médoc.

Merlot: A lauded red grape popular in Bordeaux and throughout the world; large amounts of Merlot exist in Italy, the United States, South America, and elsewhere.

Must: Crushed grapes about to go or going through fermentation.

Nebbiolo: A red grape popular in the Piedmont region of northwest Italy; the grape that yields both Barolo and Barbaresco.

Négociant: A French term for a person or company that buys wines from others and then labels it under his or her own name; stems from the French word for "shipper."

Noble Rot: *see* Botrytis Cinerea.

Nose: Synonymous with "bouquet;" the sum of a wine's aromas.

Oaky: A term used to describe woody aromas and flavors; butter, popcorn, and toast notes are found in "oaky" wines.

Organic: Grapes grown without the aid of chemical-based fertilizers, pesticides, or herbicides.

Oxidized: A wine that is no longer fresh because it was exposed to too much air.

pH: An indication of a wine's acidity expressed by how much hydrogen is in it.

Phylloxera: A voracious vine louse that over time has destroyed vineyards in Europe and California.

Piedmont: An area in northwest Italy known for Barolo, Barbaresco, Barbera, Dolcetto, and Moscato.

Pinot Blanc: A white grape popular in Alsace, Germany, and elsewhere.

Pinot Gris: Also called Pinot Grigio, this is a grayish-purple grape that yields a white wine with a refreshing character.

Pinot Noir: The prime red grape of Burgundy, Champagne, and Oregon.

Pinotage: A hybrid between Pinot Noir and Cinsault that's grown almost exclusively in South Africa.

Plonk: A derogatory name for cheap, poor-tasting wine.

Pomace: The mass of skins, pits, and stems left over after fermentation; used to make grappa in Italy and marc in France.

Port: A sweet, fortified wine made in the Douro Valley of Portugal and aged in the coastal town of Vila Nova de Gaia; variations include Vintage, Tawny, Late Bottled Vintage, Ruby, White, and others.

Premier Cru: French for "first growth;" a high-quality vineyard but one not as good as Grand Cru.

Press: The process by which grape juice is extracted prior to fermentation; a machine that extracts juice from grapes.

Primeur (en): A French term for wine sold while it is sill in the barrels; known as "futures" in English-speaking countries.

Pruning: The annual vineyard chore of trimming back plants from the previous harvest.

Racking: The process of moving wine from barrel to barrel, while leaving sediment behind.

Reserva: A Spanish term for a red wine that has spent at least three years in barrels and bottles before release.

Reserve: A largely American term indicating a wine of higher quality; it has no legal meaning.

Rhône: A river in southwest France surrounded by villages producing wines mostly from Syrah; the name of the wine-producing valley in France.

Riddling: The process of rotating Champagne bottles in order to shift sediment toward the cork.

Riesling: Along with Chardonnay, one of the top white grapes in the world; most popular in Germany, Alsace, and Austria.

Rioja: A well-known region in Spain known for traditional red wines made from the Tempranillo grape.

Rosé: French for "pink," used to describe a category of refreshing wines that are pink in color but are made from red grapes.

Sancerre: An area in the Loire Valley known mostly for wines made from Sauvignon Blanc.

Sangiovese: A red grape native to Tuscany; the base grape for Chianti, Brunello di Montalcino, Morellino di Scansano, and others.

Sauternes: A sweet Bordeaux white wine made from botrytized Sémillon and Sauvignon Blanc.

Sauvignon Blanc: A white grape planted throughout the world; increasingly the signature wine of New Zealand.

Sémillon: A plump white grape popular in Bordeaux and Australia; the base for Sauternes.

Sherry: A fortified wine from a denominated region in southwest Spain; styles include fino, manzanilla, oloroso, and amontillado.

Shiraz: The Australian name for Syrah; also used in South Africa and sparingly in the United States.

Silky: A term used to describe a wine with an especially smooth mouthfeel.

Solera: The Spanish system of blending wines of different ages to create a harmonious end product; a stack of barrels holding wines of various ages.

Sommelier: Technically a wine steward, but one potentially with a great degree of wine knowledge as well as a diploma of sorts in wine studies.

Spicy: A term used to describe certain aromas and flavors that may be sharp, woody, or sweet.

Split: A quarter-bottle of wine; a single-serving bottle equal to 175 milliliters.

Steely: A term used to describe an extremely crisp, acidic wine that was not aged in barrels.

Stemmy: A term used to describe harsh, green characteristics in a wine.

Super Tuscan: A red wine from Tuscany that is not made in accordance with established DOC rules; often a blended wine of superior quality containing Cabernet Sauvignon and/or Merlot.

Supple: A term used to describe smooth, balanced wines.

Syrah: A red grape planted extensively in the Rhône Valley of France, Australia, and elsewhere; a spicy, full, and tannic wine that usually requires aging before it can be enjoyed.

Table Wine: A term used to describe wines of between 10 and 14 percent alcohol; in Europe, table wines are those that are made outside of regulated regions or by unapproved methods.

Tannins: Phenolic compounds that exist in most plants; in grapes, tannins are found primarily in the skins and pits; tannins are astringent and provide structure to a wine; over time, tannins die off, making wines less harsh.

Tempranillo: The most popular red grape in Spain; common in Rioja and Ribera del Duero.

Terroir: A French term for the combination of soil, climate, and all other factors that influence the ultimate character of a wine.

Tokay: A dessert wine made in Hungary from dried Furmint grapes.

Trichloroanisole (TCA): A natural compound that at higher levels can impart "musty" flavors and aromas to wines, other beverages and foods. Wines that contain TCA at a detectable level are described as either being "corked" or having "corkiness," a damp, musty smell from a tainted cork.

Trocken: German for "dry."

Varietal: A wine made from just one grape type and named after that grape; the opposite of a blend.

Varietal Character: The distinct flavors, aromas, and other characteristics of each type of grape used to make wine.

Veneto: A large wine-producing region in northern Italy.

Vin Santo: Sweet wine from Tuscany made from late-harvest Trebbiano and Malvasia grapes.

Viticulture: The science and business of growing wine grapes.

Vintage: A particular year in the wine business; a specific harvest.

Viognier: A fragrant, powerful white grape grown in the Rhône Valley of France and elsewhere.

Volatile Acidity (VA): The development or presence of naturally occurring organic acids (acetic acid) in wine.

Yeast: Organisms that issue enzymes that trigger the fermentation process; yeasts can be natural or commercial.

Yield: The amount of grapes harvested in a particular year.

Zinfandel: A popular grape in California of disputed origin; scientists say it is related to grapes in Croatia and southern Italy.

Index

C

D

F

G

H

M

N

Q

T

U

V